MICROSOFT OFFICE 95

INTRODUCTORY CONCEPTS AND TECHNIQUES

Gary B. Shelly
Thomas J. Cashman
Misty E. Vermaat

Contributing Authors
Marvin M. Boetcher
Steven G. Forsythe
Sherry L. Green
Philip J. Pratt
James S. Quasney
Tim J. Walker

A DIVISION OF COURSE TECHNOLOGY
ONE CORPORATE PLACE • 55 FERNCROFT ROAD
DANVERS MA 01923

an International Thomson Publishing company 

SHELLY CASHMAN SERIES®

DANVERS • ALBANY • BONN • CAMBRIDGE • CINCINNATI • LONDON • MADRID • MELBOURNE
MEXICO CITY • NEW YORK • PARIS • SAN FRANCISCO • TOKYO • TORONTO • WASHINGTON

© 1996 boyd & fraser publishing company
A Division of Course Technology
One Corporate Place • 55 Ferncroft Road
Danvers, Massachusetts 01923-4016

International Thomson Publishing
boyd & fraser publishing company is an ITP company.
The ITP trademark is used under license.

Printed in the United States of America

For more information, contact boyd & fraser publishing company:

boyd & fraser publishing company
A Division of Course Technology
One Corporate Place • 55 Ferncroft Road
Danvers, Massachusetts 01923-4016, USA

International Thomson Editores
Campos Eliseos 385, Piso 7
Colonia Polanco
11560 Mexico D.F. Mexico

International Thomson Publishing Europe
Berkshire House
168-173 High Holborn
London, WC1V 7AA, United Kingdom

International Thomson Publishing GmbH
Konigswinterer Strasse 418
53227 Bonn, Germany

Thomas Nelson Australia
102 Dodds Street
South Melbourne
Victoria 3205 Australia

International Thomson Publishing Asia
Block 211, Henderson Road #08-03
Henderson Industrial Park
Singapore 0315

Nelson Canada
1120 Birchmont Road
Scarborough, Ontario
Canada M1K 5G4

International Thomson Publishing Japan
Hirakawa-cho Kyowa Building, 3F
2-2-1 Hirakawa-cho, Chiyoda-ku
Tokyo 102, Japan

ISBN 0-7895-0742-0 (perfect bound)
ISBN 0-7895-1229-7 (spiral bound)

PHOTO CREDITS: Introduction to Computers *Figure 1*, C-1 Photography; (A) Tony Stone Images-John Riley; (B) The Gamma Liason Network-James P. Wilson; (C) The National Institute of Industrial Ownership, Frederic Pitchal-Sygma; (D) Tony Stone-Images-Kevin Horan; (E) Gamma Liason, Shahn Kermani-Tot-Tech Computers; (F) Comshare; (G) Steve Reneker; (H) International Business Machines Corp.; (I) Sygma; *Figure 2*, Scott R. Goodwin Inc.; *Figure 3*, Tony Stone Images-Mitch Kezar; *Figure 4*, Scott R. Goodwin, Inc.; Figure 5, Epson (Manning, Selvege & Lee); *Figure 6*, Comshare; *Figure 7*, Comshare; *Figure 8*, Scott R. Goodwin Inc.; *Figure 9*, Hewlett Packard; *Figure 11*, Hewlett Packard; *Figure 12*, NEC Technology, Multisync; *Figure 13*, International Business Machines Corp.; *Figure 15*, Jerry Spagnoli; Figure 16, Greg Hadel; *Figure 19*, Jerry Spagnoli; *Figure 20*, Microscience International Corp.; *Figure 21*, 3M Corp.; Illustrations, Greg Herrington, Stephanie Nance. **Microsoft Windows 95** *Project 1, page WIN 1.4* Bill Gates, © Matthew McVay, Stock Boston; Seattle Skyline, © Paul Conklin, PhotoEdit; *page WIN 1.5* International Business Machines Corp.; *Project 2, page WIN 2.3* Quantum Corp. **Microsoft Excel 7 for Windows 95** *Project 1, page E 1.4* Dan Bricklin and Bob Frankston, VisiCalc Corporation; *Project 2, page E 2.3* Ferrari F50, John Lamm, *Road & Track*; **Microsoft Access 7 for Windows 95** *Project 1, page A 1.4* ESPNET TO GO, Motorola Inc.; *page A 1.5* Satellite Dish, Jim Zuckerman/Westlight; *Project 2, page A 2.2* PeaPod, PeaPod LP; *Project 3, page A 3.2* Motorola Mobile Workstation 9100-386, Motorola Inc.; *page A 3.3*, Employee Using a Mobile Workstation, Northern Illinois Gas Company; **Microsoft Schedule+ 7 for Windows 95** *Project 1, page S 1.2* Timex Data Link Watch, Timex Corporation; **Office 95 Integration** *Project 1, page I 1.2* Kodak DC50, Eastman Kodak, Inc.; *page I 1.3* The Agency Manager® (TAM) Proposal, Applied Systems, Inc.; *Additional Photographs*, SoftKey International, Inc.

3 4 5 6 7 8 9 10 BC 0 9 8 7 6

MICROSOFT OFFICE 95
INTRODUCTORY CONCEPTS AND TECHNIQUES

CONTENTS

Introduction to Computers COM1

Microsoft Windows 95 WIN1

PROJECT ONE
FUNDAMENTALS OF USING WINDOWS 95

PROJECT TWO

Using Word's Wizards and Templates to Create a Cover Letter and Resume

PROJECT THREE

Creating a Research Paper with a Table

INTEGRATION FEATURE

Embedding WordArt to Add Special Text Effects to a Word Document

Microsoft Excel 7 E 1.1

PROJECT ONE

Creating a Worksheet and Embedded Chart

PROJECT TWO

QUERYING A DATABASE USING THE SELECT QUERY WINDOW

PROJECT THREE

MAINTAINING A DATABASE USING THE DESIGN AND UPDATE FEATURES OF ACCESS

INTEGRATION FEATURE

Integrating Excel Worksheet Data into an Access Database

Microsoft PowerPoint 7 — PP 1.1

PROJECT ONE

Using a Design Template and Style Checker to Create a Presentation

PROJECT TWO

USING OUTLINE VIEW AND CLIP ART TO CREATE AN ELECTRONIC SLIDE SHOW

INTEGRATION FEATURE

LINKING AN EXCEL CHART TO A POWERPOINT PRESENTATION

Preface

Shelly Cashman Series® Microsoft Windows 95 Books

The Shelly Cashman Series Microsoft Windows 95 books reinforce the fact that you made the right choice when you use a Shelly Cashman Series book. The Shelly Cashman Series Microsoft Windows 3.1 books were used by more schools and more students than any other series in textbook publishing. Yet the Shelly Cashman Series team wanted to produce even better books for Windows 95, so the books were thoroughly redesigned to present material in an even easier to understand format and with more project-ending activities. Features such as Other Ways and More Abouts were added to give in-depth knowledge to the student. The opening of each project provides a fascinating perspective of the subject covered in the project. Completely redesigned student assignments include the unique Cases and Places. This book provides the finest educational experience for a student learning about computer software.

Objectives of This Textbook

Microsoft Office 95: Introductory Concepts and Techniques is intended for a three-unit course that presents the Microsoft Office 95 products: Microsoft Word 7, Microsoft Excel 7, Microsoft Access 7, Microsoft PowerPoint 7, Microsoft Schedule+ 7, and an Office 95 Integration project incorporating Object Linking and Embedding (OLE). No experience is assumed. The objectives of this book are:

More *About* **a Cover Letter**

You should always send a personalized cover letter with every resume. A cover letter should highlight aspects of your background relevant to the position. Because it is often difficult to recall past achievements and activities, you should keep a personal personnel file containing documents that outline your accomplishments.

- To teach the fundamentals of Microsoft Windows 95
- To give students an in-depth understanding of word processing, spreadsheets, databases, presentations, personal information management, and OLE
- To provide a knowledge base of the Microsoft Office 95 products on which students can build
- To expose students to examples of the computer as a useful tool
- To help students who are working on their own

When students complete the course using this textbook, they will have a firm knowledge and understanding of Windows 95 and Office 95.

The Shelly Cashman Approach

Features of the Shelly Cashman Series Windows 95 books include:

- **Project Orientation:** Each project in the book uses the unique Shelly Cashman Series screen-by-screen, step-by-step approach.
- **Screen-by-Screen, Step-by-Step Instructions:** Each of the tasks required to complete a project is identified throughout the development of the project. Then, steps to

accomplish the task are specified. The steps are accompanied by screens. The student is not told to perform a step without seeing the result of the step on a color screen. Hence, students learn from this book the same as if they were using a computer.

- **Thoroughly Tested Projects:** The computer screens in the Shelly Cashman Series Windows 95 books are shot directly from the author's computer. The screen is shot immediately after the author performs the step specified in the text. Therefore, every screen in the book is correct because it is produced only after performing a specific step, resulting in unprecedented quality in a computer textbook.
- **Multiple Ways to Use the Book:** The book can be used in a variety of ways, including: (a) Lecture and textbook approach – The instructor lectures on the material in the book. The student reads and studies the material and then applies the knowledge to an application on the computer; (b) Tutorial approach – The student performs each specified step on a computer. At the end of the project, the student has solved the problem and is ready to solve comparable student assignments; (c) Other approaches – Many teachers lecture on the material and then require their students to perform each step in the project, reinforcing the material lectured. The students then complete one or more of the In the Lab exercises; and (d) Reference – Each task in a project is clearly identified. Therefore, the material serves as a complete reference.
- **Windows/Graphical User Interface Approach:** Windows 95 provides a graphical user interface and all the examples in this book use this interface. Thus, the mouse is the preferred user communication tool. The secondary, or right, mouse button is used extensively.
- **Other Ways Boxes for Reference:** Windows 95 provides a wide variety of ways to carry out a given task. The Other Ways boxes displayed at the end of most of the step-by-step sequences specify the other ways to do the task completed in the steps. Thus, the steps and the Other Ways box make a comprehensive reference unit. You no longer have to reference tables at the end of a chapter or the end of a book.

OtherWays

1. Click Cut button on Standard toolbar, position insertion point at location where text is to be pasted, click Paste button on Standard toolbar
2. On Edit menu click Cut, position insertion point at location where text is to be pasted, on Edit menu click Paste
3. Press CTRL+X, position insertion point at location where text is to be pasted, press CTRL+V

Organization of This Textbook

Microsoft Office 95: Introductory Concepts and Techniques consists of a brief introduction to computers, two projects on Microsoft Windows 95, an introduction to Microsoft Office 95, three projects each on Microsoft Word 7, Microsoft Excel 7, and Microsoft Access 7, two projects on Microsoft PowerPoint 7, one project on Microsoft Schedule+ 7, four short Integration features following each application, and one project on integrating all the Office 95 applications. A short description of each follows.

Introduction to Computers

Many students taking a course in the use of Microsoft Office 95 will have little previous experience with computers. For this reason, this textbook begins with a section titled *Introduction to Computers* that covers essential computer hardware and software concepts and information on how to purchase, install, and maintain a personal computer.

Microsoft Windows 95

To effectively use the Microsoft Office application software products, students need a practical knowledge of Windows 95. Thus, two Windows 95 projects are included as an introduction to the graphical user interface.

Project 1 – Fundamentals of Using Windows 95 In Project 1, students learn about user interfaces and Windows 95. Topics include using the Windows 95 desktop as a work area; using the mouse; the keyboard and keyboard shortcuts; using context-sensitive menus; sizing and scrolling windows; creating a document by starting an application program; saving a document to disk; printing a document; closing a program; modifying a document; using Windows 95 Help; and shutting down Windows 95.

Project 2 – Using Windows Explorer In Project 2, students are introduced to Windows Explorer. Topics include displaying the contents of a folder; expanding and collapsing a folder; creating a folder; changing the view; selecting and copying a group of files; creating, renaming, and deleting a folder; and renaming and deleting a file.

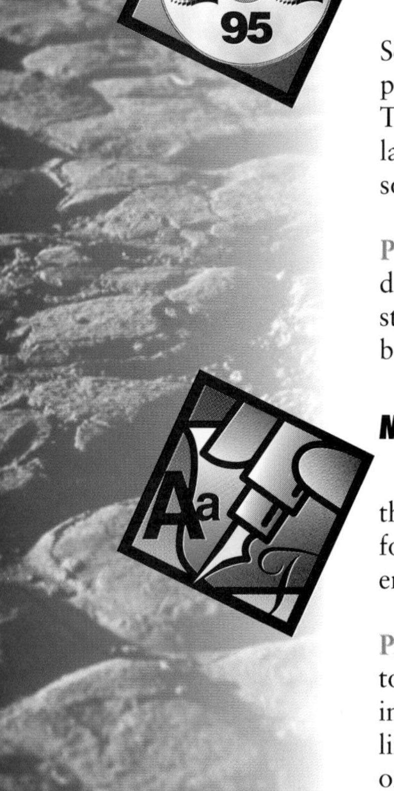

Microsoft Office 95

The Office 95 applications include Word 7, Excel 7, Access 7, PowerPoint 7, and Schedule+ 7. These applications have a similar look and feel to them. Any one of these products can be started via the Start button on the Microsoft Office Shortcut Bar. Therefore, a project introducing the Office 95 applications and how to use and manipulate the Office Shortcut Bar immediately precedes the presentation of the individual software products.

Project 1 – An Introduction to Microsoft Office 95 In this project, students are introduced to the Office 95 product line and to the Office Shortcut Bar. Topics include how to start an application, switch to an application, and quit an application; and how to add a button and remove a button from the Office Shortcut Bar.

Microsoft Word 7 for Windows 95

After presenting the basic computer concepts, Windows 95, and an introduction to the Office 95 products, this textbook provides detailed instruction on how to use Word 7 for Windows 95. The material is divided into three projects followed by a section on embedding.

Project 1 – Creating and Editing a Word Document In Project 1, students are introduced to Word terminology and the Word window by preparing an announcement. Topics include starting and quitting Word; entering text; saving a document; selecting characters, lines, and paragraphs; centering, bolding, italicizing, and changing the font and font size of selected text; adding bullets to paragraphs; importing and scaling a graphic; checking spelling; printing a document; opening a document; correcting errors; and using Word's online Help.

Project 2 – Using Word's Wizards and Templates to Create a Cover Letter and Resume In Project 2, students create a resume using Word's Resume Wizard. While personalizing the resume, students add borders and shading; align text vertically with the TAB key; use Word's AutoFormat feature; drag and drop selected text; and use print preview. Then, students create a cover letter using a letter template in Word. While personalizing the cover letter, students create and insert an AutoText entry and modify formatting applied by a style. Finally, students copy text from one open Word document to another and then close all open Word documents.

Project 3 – Creating a Research Paper with a Table In Project 3, students use the MLA style of documentation to create a research paper. Topics include changing margins; adjusting line spacing; using a header to number pages; first-line indenting paragraphs; using Word's AutoCorrect and spell check features as they type; creating a table using Word's table Wizard; entering data into a Word table; adding a footnote; inserting a hard page break; creating a hanging indent; sorting paragraphs; using the thesaurus; and counting words in a document.

Table 3-1

YOU TYPE	*TO DISPLAY*
(c)	©
(r)	®
(tm)	™
:)	☺
:|	😐
:(	☹
-->	→
<--	←
==>	→
<==	←
<=>	↔

Integration Feature – Embedding WordArt to Add Special Text Effects to a Word Document In this section, students are introduced to WordArt, an application included with Word. Using the announcement built in Project 1, students create a new headline in WordArt and then embed the new headline into the Word document. The following WordArt special effects are introduced: changing the shape of the text, stretching the text, bolding the text, and adding a shadow to the text.

Microsoft Excel 7 for Windows 95

Following the three projects on Word 7 for Windows 95, this textbook presents three projects on Excel 7 for Windows 95, followed by a section on linking a worksheet to a Word document.

Project 1 – Creating a Worksheet and Embedded Chart In Project 1, students are introduced to Excel terminology, the Excel window, and the basic characteristics of a worksheet and workbook. Topics include starting and exiting Excel; entering text and numbers; selecting a range; using the AutoSum button; copying using the fill handle; changing font size; bolding; centering across columns; using the AutoFormat command; charting using the ChartWizard; saving and opening a workbook; editing a worksheet; using the AutoCalculate area; and obtaining online Help.

Project 2 – Formulas, Formatting, and Creating Charts In Project 2, students use formulas and functions to build a worksheet and learn more about formatting and printing a worksheet. Topics include entering formulas; using functions; formatting text; formatting numbers; drawing borders and adding colors; changing the widths of columns and rows; spell checking; creating a 3-D pie chart on a separate sheet; previewing a worksheet; printing a section of a worksheet; and displaying and printing the formulas in a worksheet.

Project 3 – What-If-Analysis and Working with Large Worksheets In Project 3, students learn how to work with larger worksheets, how to create a worksheet based on assumptions, how to use the IF function and absolute cell references, and how to perform what-if-analysis. Topics include assigning global formats; using the fill handle to create a series; deleting, inserting, copying, and moving data on a worksheet; displaying and docking toolbars; adding drop shadows to ranges; freezing titles; changing the magnification of worksheets; displaying different parts of the worksheet using panes; and simple what-if-analysis and goal seeking.

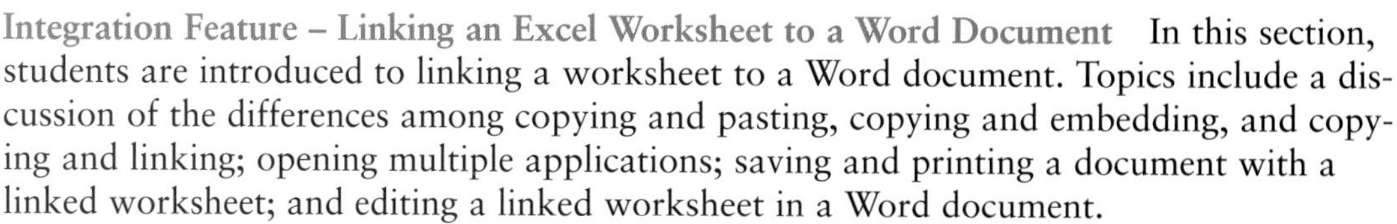

Integration Feature – Linking an Excel Worksheet to a Word Document In this section, students are introduced to linking a worksheet to a Word document. Topics include a discussion of the differences among copying and pasting, copying and embedding, and copying and linking; opening multiple applications; saving and printing a document with a linked worksheet; and editing a linked worksheet in a Word document.

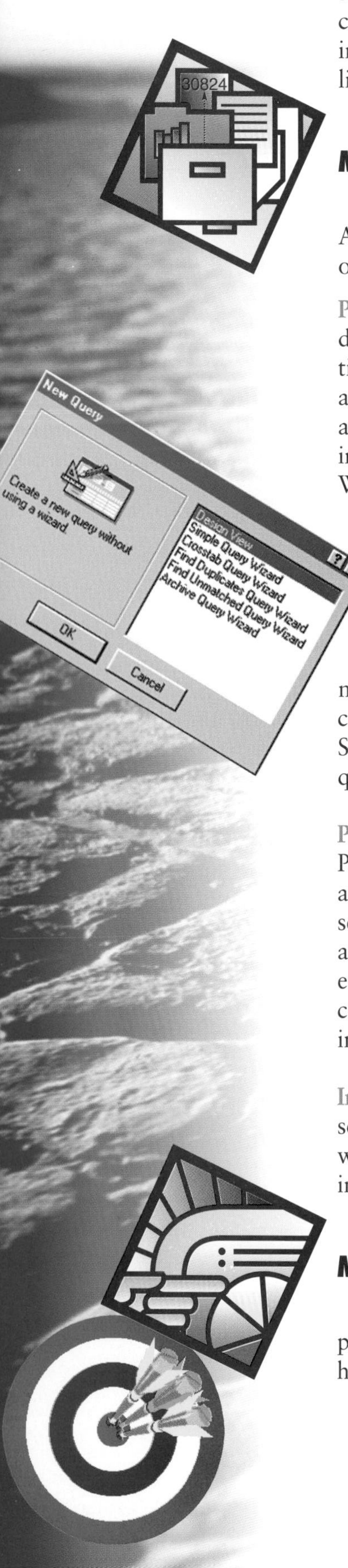

Microsoft Access 7 for Windows 95

Following Excel 7 for Windows 95, this textbook provides detailed instruction on Access 7 for Windows 95. The topics are divided into three projects followed by a section on integrating a worksheet into a database.

Project 1 – Creating a Database Using Design and Datasheet Views In Project 1, students are introduced to Access terminology, the Access window, and the basic characteristics of databases. Topics include starting and exiting Access; creating a database; creating a table; defining fields; opening a table; adding records to a table; closing a table; opening and closing a database; and previewing and printing the contents of a table. Other topics in this project include using a form to view data; creating a report using the Report Wizard; and using online Help. Students also learn how to design a database to eliminate redundancy.

Project 2 – Querying a Database Using the Select Query Window In Project 2, students learn how to ask questions concerning the data in their databases by using queries. Topics include creating and running queries; printing the results of queries; displaying only selected fields; using character data in criteria; using wildcards; using numeric data in criteria; using various comparison operators; and creating compound criteria. Other topics include sorting; joining tables; and restricting records in a join. Students learn to use computed fields, statistics, and grouping and also how to save a query.

Project 3 – Maintaining a Database Using the Design and Update Features of Access In Project 3, students learn how to maintain a database. Topics include using Datasheet view and Form view to add new records, to change existing records, and to delete records and searching for a record. Students also learn how to change the structure of a table; how to add additional fields and to change characteristics of existing fields; how to create a variety of validation rules; and how to specify referential integrity. Students perform mass changes and deletions using queries. They also create single-field and multiple-field indexes.

Integration Feature – Integrating Excel Worksheet Data into an Access Database In this section, students learn how to use the Import Spreadsheet Wizard to integrate an Excel worksheet into an Access database. Topics include opening an Excel workbook; converting an Excel worksheet to an Access database; and using the Access table.

Microsoft PowerPoint 7 for Windows 95

Following Access 7 for Windows 95, this textbook includes two projects on creating presentation graphics using PowerPoint 7 for Windows 95 followed by a section showing how to link a chart to a presentation.

Project 1 – Using a Design Template and Style Checker to Create a Presentation In Project 1, students are introduced to PowerPoint terminology, the PowerPoint window, and the basics of creating a multiple-level bulleted list presentation. Topics include starting PowerPoint; establishing the design of the presentation by selecting a Design Template; displaying information on every slide; changing text style; decreasing font size; saving a presentation; displaying slides in an electronic slide show; closing a presentation; opening an existing presentation; checking a presentation for spelling errors; identifying design inconsistencies using Style Checker, editing a presentation to correct errors; adjusting line spacing; displaying and printing a presentation in black and white; and obtaining online Help.

Project 2 – Using Outline View and Clip Art to Create an Electronic Slide Show In Project 2, students create a presentation in Outline view and learn how to insert clip art. Topics include creating a slide presentation by promoting and demoting text in Outline view; changing slide layouts; inserting clip art; adding slide transition effects and text build effects; running an animated electronic slide show; printing a presentation outline; printing presentation slides in Outline view; rearranging slide order; copying and pasting slides; and using the Undo button to reverse the last edit.

Integration Feature – Linking an Excel Chart to a PowerPoint Presentation In this section, students are introduced to the linking feature of OLE by showing them how to link an Excel pie chart to a PowerPoint slide using the insert object method. Topics include linking a chart object to a slide; scaling a linked object; and saving a linked presentation.

Microsoft Schedule+ 7 for Windows 95

Following PowerPoint 7 for Windows 95, students are introduced to Schedule+ 7 for Windows 95, a useful personal information management system.

Project 1 – Personal Information Management Using Schedule+ for Windows 95 In this project, students explore the benefits of personal information management systems by using Schedule+ to create a schedule. Topics include starting and exiting Schedule+; generating and managing daily, weekly, and monthly schedules; editing existing schedule entries; printing and saving a schedule; creating a To Do List; adding events to the calendar; and compiling an address book.

Office 95 Integration

Following Schedule+ 7 for Windows 95, the book concludes with a project on Office 95 Integration.

Project 1 – Introduction to Integrating Office 95 Applications In this project, students are introduced to the seamless partnership of the Microsoft Office 95 applications, which allows the sharing of information among Word, Excel, Access, PowerPoint, Schedule+, and Binder. Topics include creating and editing an embedded chart in an Excel workbook; creating a letterhead using WordArt; inserting clip art into a letterhead; linking an Excel worksheet and chart to a Word document; querying an Access table; inserting merge fields in a Word document to create a Mail Merge main document; merging a Word document with an Access query to create form letters and labels; creating and printing a report based on an Access query; creating a

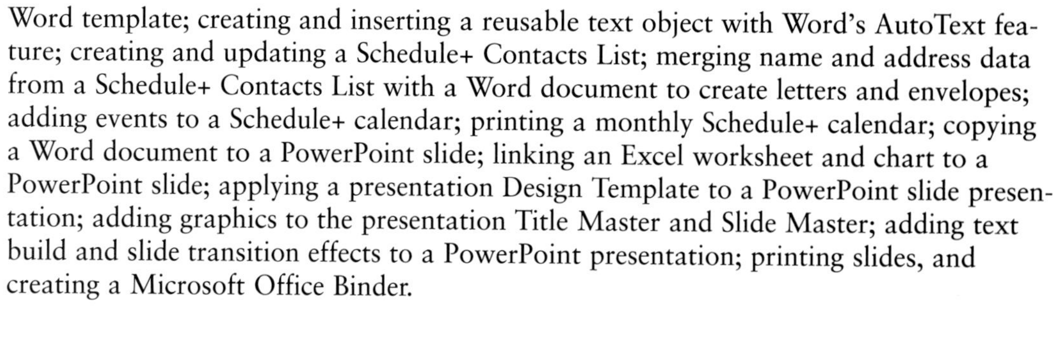

Word template; creating and inserting a reusable text object with Word's AutoText feature; creating and updating a Schedule+ Contacts List; merging name and address data from a Schedule+ Contacts List with a Word document to create letters and envelopes; adding events to a Schedule+ calendar; printing a monthly Schedule+ calendar; copying a Word document to a PowerPoint slide; linking an Excel worksheet and chart to a PowerPoint slide; applying a presentation Design Template to a PowerPoint slide presentation; adding graphics to the presentation Title Master and Slide Master; adding text build and slide transition effects to a PowerPoint presentation; printing slides, and creating a Microsoft Office Binder.

End-of-Project Student Activities

A notable strength of the Shelly Cashman Series Windows 95 books is the extensive student activities at the end of each project. Well-structured student activities can make the difference between students merely participating in a class and students retaining the information they learn. These activities include all of the following sections.

- What You Should Know   A listing of the tasks completed within a project together with the pages where the step-by-step, screen-by-screen explanations appear. This section provides a perfect study review for the student.
- Test Your Knowledge   Four pencil-and-paper activities designed to determine the student's understanding of the material in the project. Included are true/false questions, multiple-choice questions, and two short-answer exercises.
- Use Help   Any user of Windows 95 must know how to use Help. Therefore, this book contains two Help exercises per project. These exercises alone distinguish the Shelly Cashman Series from any other set of Windows 95 instructional materials.
- Apply Your Knowledge   This exercise requires the student to open and manipulate a file from the Student Floppy Disk that accompanies the book.
- In the Lab   Three in-depth assignments per project that require the student to apply the knowledge gained in the project to solve problems on a computer.
- Cases and Places   Seven unique case studies allow students to apply their knowledge to real-world situations.

Instructor's Support Package

A comprehensive Instructor's Support Package accompanies this textbook in the form of an electronic Instructor's Manual and teaching and testing aids on CD-ROM. The Instructor's Manual and most of the aids also are available to registered instructors on the Shelly Cashman home page (http://www.bf.com/scseries.html). The CD-ROM (ISBN 0-7895-0720-X) is available through your Course Technology representative or by calling 1-800-648-7450. The contents of the Instructor's Manual and additional support materials on the CD-ROM are listed below.

- Instructor's Manual   The Instructor's Manual includes the following for each project: project objectives; project overview; detailed lesson plans with page number references; teacher notes and activities; answers to the end-of-project exercises;

test bank of 110 questions for every project (50 true/false, 25 multiple-choice, and 35 fill-in-the blanks); and transparency references.

- **CD-ROM** The CD-ROM includes the following:
  - **Figures on CD-ROM** Illustrations for every screen in the textbook are available. Use this ancillary to create a slide show from the illustrations for lecture or to print transparencies for use in lecture with an overhead.
  - **ElecMan** ElecMan stands for *Elec*tronic *Man*ual. ElecMan is a Microsoft Word version of the Instructor's Manual, including all lecture notes and the test bank. The files allow you to modify the lecture notes or generate quizzes and exams from the test bank using your word processor.
  - **Course Test Manager** Designed by Course Technology, this cutting edge Windows-based testing software helps instructors design and administer tests and pre-tests. The full-featured online program permits students to take tests at the computer where their grades are computed immediately following completion of the exam. Automatic statistics collection, student guides customized to the student's performance, and printed tests are only a few of the features.
  - **Lecture Success System** Lecture Success System files are for use with the application software, a personal computer, and projection device to explain and illustrate the step-by-step, screen-by-screen development of a project in the textbook without entering large amounts of data.
  - **Lab Tests** Tests that parallel the In the Lab assignments are supplied for the purpose of testing students in the laboratory on the material covered in the project.
  - **Instructor's Lab Solutions** Solutions and required files for all the In the Lab assignments at the end of each project are available.
  - **Student Files** All the files that are required by the student to complete the Apply Your Knowledge exercises or advanced projects are included.

Shelly Cashman Online

Shelly Cashman Online is a World Wide Web service available to instructors and students of computer education. Visit Shelly Cashman Online at http://www.bf.com/scseries.html. Shelly Cashman Online is divided into four areas:

- **Series Information** Information on the Shelly Cashman Series products.
- **The Community** Opportunities to discuss your course and your ideas with instructors in your field and with the Shelly Cashman Series team.
- **Teaching Resources** This area includes password-protected data from Instructor's Floppy Disks that can be downloaded, course outlines, teaching tips, and ancillaries such as ElecMan.
- **Student Center** Dedicated to students learning about computers with Shelly Cashman Series textbooks and software. This area includes cool links, data from Student Floppy Disks that can be downloaded, and much more.

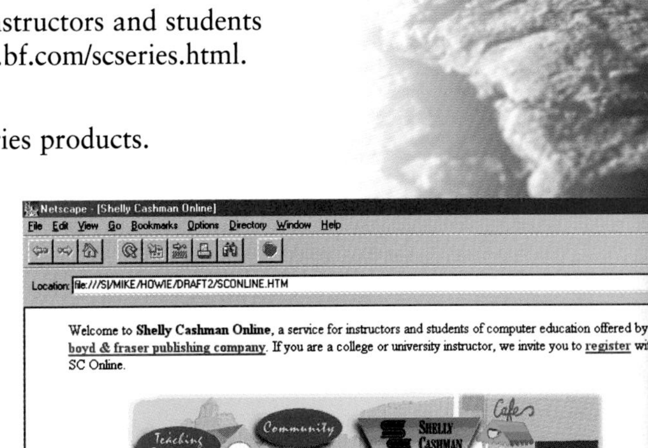

Acknowledgments

The Shelly Cashman Series would not be the leading computer education series without the contributions of outstanding publishing professionals. First, and foremost, among them is Becky Herrington, director of production and designer. She is the heart and soul of the Shelly Cashman Series, and it is only through her leadership, dedication, and tireless efforts that superior products are made possible. Becky created and produced the award-winning Windows 95 series of books.

Under Becky's direction, the following individuals made significant contributions to these books: Peter Schiller, production manager; Ginny Harvey, series administrator and manuscript editor; Ken Russo, senior illustrator and cover artist; Mike Bodnar, Stephanie Nance, Greg Herrington, and Dave Bonnewitz, Quark artists and illustrators; Patti Garbarino, editorial assistant; Jeanne Black, Quark expert; Cristina Haley, indexer; Debora Chisty, Cherilyn King, Marilyn Markowicz, Marilyn Martin, and Nancy Lamm, proofreaders; Sarah Evertson of Image Quest, photo researcher; Henry Blackham, cover photographer; and Kent Lauer, cover glass work. Special mention must go to Suzanne Biron, Becky Herrington, and Michael Gregson for the outstanding book design, and to Ken Russo for the cover design.

Special recognition also must go to Tracy Murphy, series associate editor and Mike Campbell, World Wide Web and multimedia guru. The efforts of Jim Quasney, series editor, are unmatched in publishing. Without Jim, none of this happens. Particular thanks go to Tom Walker, president of boyd & fraser publishing company. His creativity, support, and understanding are vital ingredients to the success of the Shelly Cashman Series.

Gary B. Shelly
Thomas J. Cashman
Misty E. Vermaat

http://www.bf.com/scseries.html

Shelly Cashman Series – Traditionally Bound Textbooks

The Shelly Cashman Series presents computer textbooks across the entire spectrum including both Windows- and DOS-based personal computer applications in a variety of traditionally bound textbooks, as shown in the table below. For more information, see your Course Technology representative or call 1-800-648-7450.

	COMPUTERS
Computers	Using Computers: A Gateway to Information, World Wide Web Edition Using Computers: A Gateway to Information, World Wide Web Brief Edition Using Computers: A Gateway to Information, World Wide Web Edition and Exploring Computers: A Record of Discovery with CD-ROM Using Computers: A Gateway to Information Using Computers: A Gateway to Information, Brief Edition Exploring Computers: A Record of Discovery with CD-ROM A Record of Discovery for Exploring Computers Study Guide for Using Computers: A Gateway to Information, World Wide Web Edition Study Guide for Using Computers: A Gateway to Information
and Windows Apps	Using Computers: A Gateway to Information and Microsoft Office (also in spiral bound) Using Computers: A Gateway to Information and Microsoft Works 3.0 (also in spiral bound)
and Programming	Using Computers: A Gateway to Information and Programming in QBasic
	WINDOWS APPLICATIONS
Integrated Packages	Microsoft Office 95: Introductory Concepts and Techniques (also in spiral bound) Microsoft Office 4.3 running under Windows 95: Introductory Concepts and Techniques (also in spiral bound) Microsoft Office: Introductory Concepts and Techniques (also in spiral bound) Microsoft Office: Advanced Concepts and Techniques (also in spiral bound) Microsoft Works 4.0 for Windows 95* • Microsoft Works 4.0 for Windows 95—Short Course Microsoft Works 3.0 (also in spiral bound)* • Microsoft Works 2.0 (also in spiral bound) Microsoft Works 3.0—Short Course
Windows	Microsoft Windows 95: Introductory Concepts and Techniques (96-page) Introduction to Microsoft Windows 95 (224-page) Microsoft Windows 95: Complete Concepts and Techniques Microsoft Windows 3.1 Introductory Concepts and Techniques Microsoft Windows 3.1 Complete Concepts and Techniques
Windows Applications	Microsoft Word 2.0, Microsoft Excel 4, and Paradox 1.0 (also in spiral bound)
Word Processing	Microsoft Word 7 • Microsoft Word 6* • Microsoft Word 2.0 WordPerfect 6.1* • WordPerfect 6* • WordPerfect 5.2
Spreadsheets	Microsoft Excel 7 • Microsoft Excel 5* • Microsoft Excel 4 Lotus 1-2-3 Release 5* • Lotus 1-2-3 Release 4* Quattro Pro 6 • Quattro Pro 5
Database Management	Microsoft Access 7 • Microsoft Access 2* Paradox 7 • Paradox 5 • Paradox 4.5 • Paradox 1.0 • Visual dBASE 5/5.5
Presentation Graphics	Microsoft PowerPoint 7 • Microsoft PowerPoint 4*
	DOS APPLICATIONS
Operating Systems	DOS 6 Introductory Concepts and Techniques DOS 6 and Microsoft Windows 3.1 Introductory Concepts and Techniques
Integrated Package	Microsoft Works 3.0 (also in spiral bound)
Word Processing	WordPerfect 6.1 • WordPerfect 6.0 WordPerfect 5.1 Step-by-Step Function Key Edition • WordPerfect 5.1 Function Key Edition
Spreadsheets	Lotus 1-2-3 Release 4 • Lotus 1-2-3 Release 2.4 • Lotus 1-2-3 Release 2.3 Lotus 1-2-3 Release 2.2 • Lotus 1-2-3 Release 2.01 Quattro Pro 3.0 • Quattro with 1-2-3 Menus (with Educational Software)
Database Management	dBASE 5 • dBASE IV Version 1.1 • dBASE III PLUS (with Educational Software) Paradox 4.5 • Paradox 3.5 (with Educational Software)
	PROGRAMMING AND NETWORKING
Programming	Microsoft Visual Basic 3.0 for Windows* Microsoft BASIC QBasic • QBasic: An Introduction to Programming Structured COBOL Programming
Networking	Novell NetWare for Users Business Data Communications: Introductory Concepts and Techniques
Internet	The Internet: Introductory Concepts and Techniques (UNIX) Netscape Navigator 2 running under Windows 95 • Netscape Navigator 2 running under Windows 3.1 Netscape Navigator: An Introduction (Version 1.1)
	SYSTEMS ANALYSIS
Systems Analysis	Systems Analysis and Design, Second Edition

*Also available as a Double Diamond Edition, which is a shortened version of the complete book

Shelly Cashman Series – **Custom Edition**® Program

If you do not find a Shelly Cashman Series traditionally bound textbook to fit your needs, the Shelly Cashman Series' unique **Custom Edition** program allows you to choose from a number of options and create a textbook perfectly suited to your course. Features of the **Custom Edition** program are:

- Textbooks that match the content of your course
- Windows- and DOS-based materials for the latest versions of personal computer applications software
- Shelly Cashman Series quality, with the same full-color materials and Shelly Cashman Series pedagogy found in the traditionally bound books
- Affordable pricing so your students receive the **Custom Edition** at a cost similar to that of traditionally bound books

The table on the right summarizes the available materials.

For more information, see your Course Technology representative or call 1-800-648-7450.

For Shelly Cashman Series information, visit Shelly Cashman Series Online at **http://www. bf.com/scseries.html**

COMPUTERS	
Computers	Using Computers: A Gateway to Information, World Wide Web Edition Using Computers: A Gateway to Information, World Wide Web Brief Edition Using Computers: A Gateway to Information Using Computers: A Gateway to Information, Brief Edition A Record of Discovery for Exploring Computers (available with CD-ROM) Study Guide for Using Computers: A Gateway to Information, World Wide Web Edition Study Guide for Using Computers: A Gateway to Information Introduction to Computers (32-page)
OPERATING SYSTEMS	
Windows	Microsoft Windows 95: Introductory Concepts and Techniques (96-page) Introduction to Microsoft Windows 95 (224-page) Microsoft Windows 95: Complete Concepts and Techniques Microsoft Windows 3.1 Introductory Concepts and Techniques Microsoft Windows 3.1 Complete Concepts and Techniques
DOS	Introduction to DOS 6 (using DOS prompt) Introduction to DOS 5.0 (using DOS shell) Introduction to DOS 5.0 or earlier (using DOS prompt)
WINDOWS APPLICATIONS	
Integrated Packages	Microsoft Works 4.0 for Windows 95* Microsoft Works 4.0 for Windows 95—Short Course Microsoft Works 3.0* Microsoft Works 3.0—Short Course Microsoft Works 2.0
Microsoft Office	Using Microsoft Office (16-page) Object Linking and Embedding (OLE) (32-page) Schedule+ 7
Word Processing	Microsoft Word 7 • Microsoft Word 6* • Microsoft Word 2.0 WordPerfect 6.1* • WordPerfect 6* • WordPerfect 5.2
Spreadsheets	Microsoft Excel 7 • Microsoft Excel 5* • Microsoft Excel 4 Lotus 1-2-3 Release 5* • Lotus 1-2-3 Release 4* Quattro Pro 6 • Quattro Pro 5
Database Management	Microsoft Access 7 • Microsoft Access 2* Paradox 7 • Paradox 5 • Paradox 4.5 • Paradox 1.0 Visual dBASE 5/5.5
Presentation Graphics	Microsoft PowerPoint 7 • Microsoft PowerPoint 4*
DOS APPLICATIONS	
Integrated Package	Microsoft Works 3.0
Word Processing	WordPerfect 6.1 • WordPerfect 6.0 WordPerfect 5.1 Step-by-Step Function Key Edition WordPerfect 5.1 Function Key Edition Microsoft Word 5.0
Spreadsheets	Lotus 1-2-3 Release 4 • Lotus 1-2-3 Release 2.4 • Lotus 1-2-3 Release 2.3 Lotus 1-2-3 Release 2.2 • Lotus 1-2-3 Release 2.01 Quattro Pro 3.0 Quattro with 1-2-3 Menus
Database Management	dBASE 5 • dBASE IV Version 1.1 • dBASE III PLUS Paradox 4.5 • Paradox 3.5
PROGRAMMING AND NETWORKING	
Programming	Microsoft Visual Basic 3.0 for Windows* Microsoft BASIC QBasic
Networking	Novell NetWare for Users
Internet	The Internet: Introductory Concepts and Techniques (UNIX) Netscape Navigator 2 running under Windows 95 Netscape Navigator 2 running under Windows 3.1 Netscape Navigator: An Introduction (Version 1.1)

*Also available as a mini-module

INTRODUCTION TO COMPUTERS

Objectives

After completing this chapter, you will be able to:

- Define the term computer and discuss the four basic computer operations: input, processing, output, and storage
- Define data and information
- Explain the principal components of the computer and their use
- Describe the use and handling of floppy disks and hard disks
- Discuss computer software and explain the difference between system software and application software
- Describe several types of personal computer application software
- Discuss computer communications channels and equipment and LAN and WAN computer networks
- Explain how to purchase, install, and maintain a personal computer system

Every day, computers impact how individuals work and how they live. The use of personal computers continues to increase and has made computing available to almost anyone. In addition, advances in communication technology allow people to use personal computer systems to easily and quickly access and send information to other computers and computer users.At home, at work, and in the field, computers are helping people to do their work faster, more accurately, and in some cases, in ways that previously would not have been possible.

WHY STUDY COMPUTERS AND APPLICATION SOFTWARE?

Today, many people believe that knowing how to use a computer, is a basic skill necessary to succeed in business or to function effectively in society. As you can see in Figure 1, the use of computer technology is widespread in the world. It is important to understand that while computers are used in many different ways, there are certain types of common applications computer users need to know. It is this type of software that you will learn as you use this book. Given the widespread use and availability of computer systems, knowing how to use common application software on a computer system is an essential skill for practically everyone.

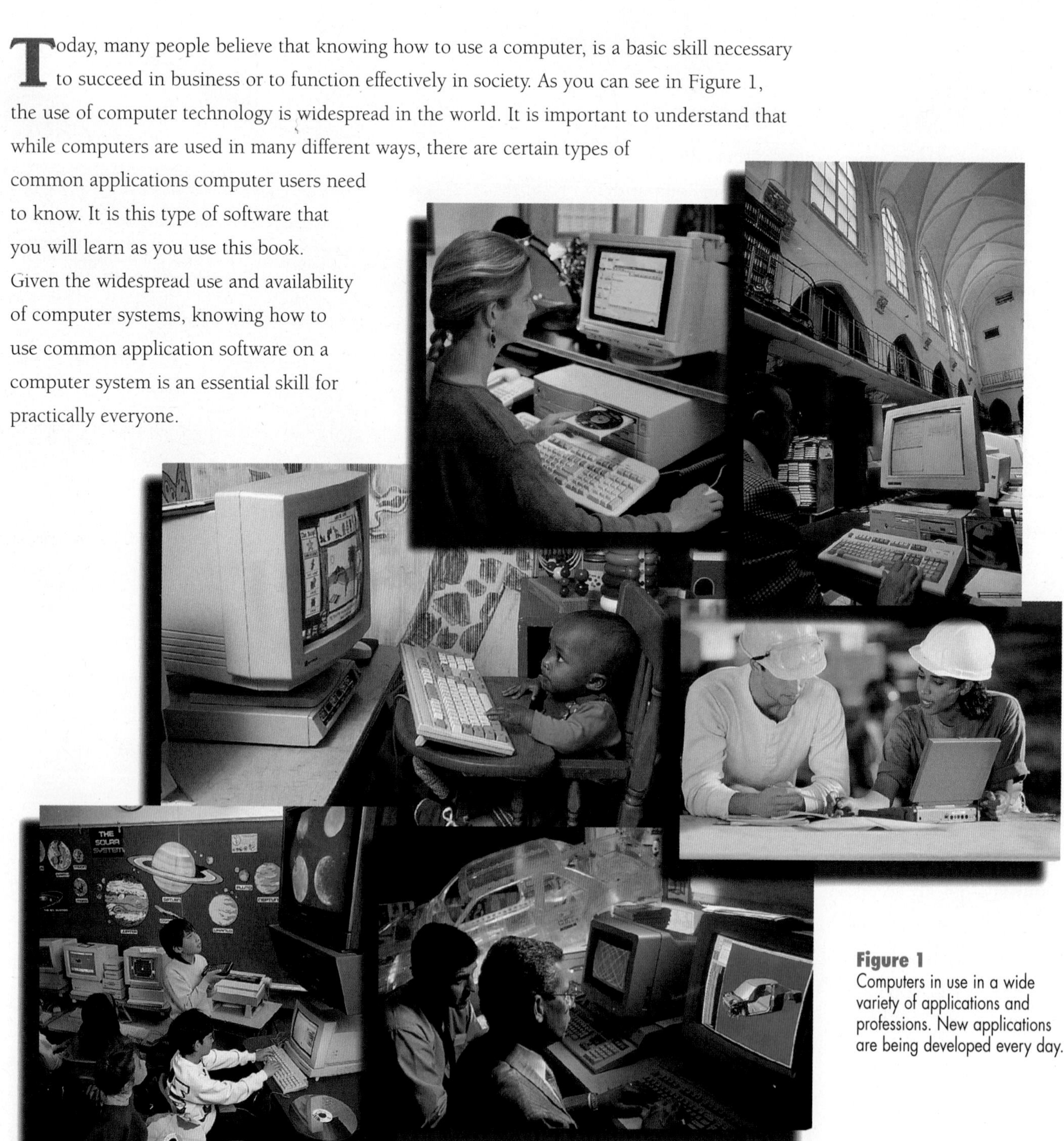

Figure 1
Computers in use in a wide variety of applications and professions. New applications are being developed every day.

Before you learn about application software, however, it will help if you understand what a computer is, the components of a computer, and the types of software used on computers. These topics are explained in this chapter. Also included is information that describes computer networks and a list of guidelines for purchasing, installing, and maintaining a personal computer.

WHAT IS A COMPUTER?

The most obvious question related to understanding computers is, "What is a computer?" A **computer** is an electronic device, operating under the control of instructions stored in its own memory unit, that can accept data (input), process data arithmetically and logically, produce output from the processing, and store the results for future use. Generally the term is used to describe a collection of devices that function together as a system. An example of the devices that make up a personal computer, or microcomputer, is shown in Figure 2.

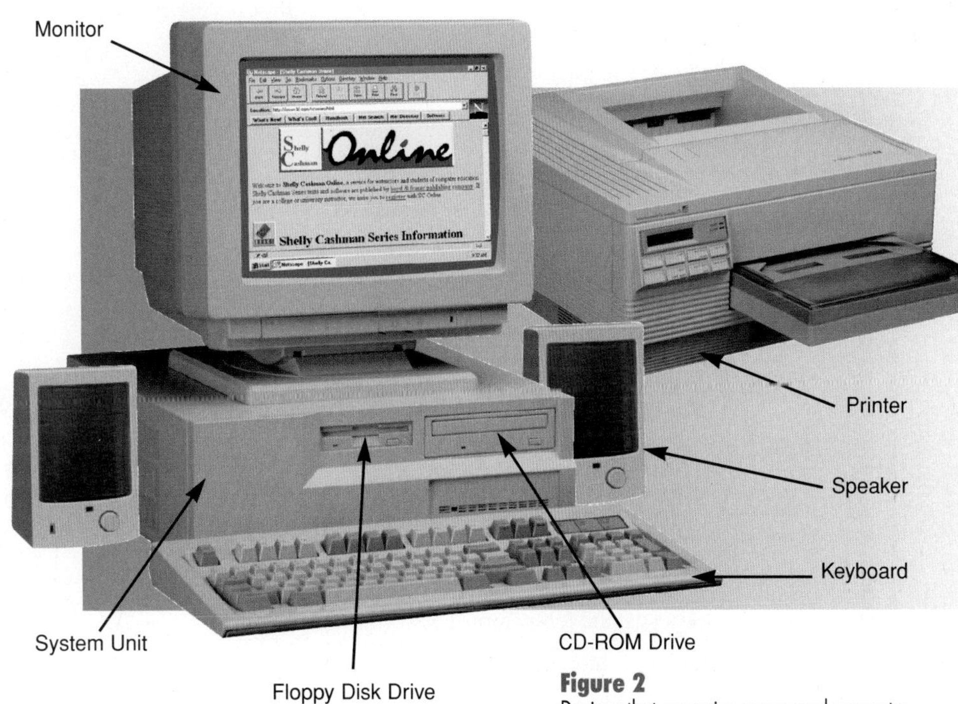

Figure 2
Devices that comprise a personal computer.

WHAT DOES A COMPUTER DO?

Whether small or large, computers can perform four general operations. These operations comprise the **information processing cycle** and are: input, process, output, and storage. Collectively, these operations describe the procedures a computer performs to process data into information and store it for future use.

All computer processing requires data. **Data** refers to the raw facts, including numbers, words, images, and sounds, given to a computer during the input operation. In the processing phase, the computer manipulates the data to create information. **Information** refers to data processed into a form that has meaning and is useful. During the output operation, the information that has been created is put into some form, such as a printed report, an invoice, or a paycheck. The information can also be placed in computer storage for future use.

These operations occur through the use of electronic circuits contained on small silicon chips inside the computer (Figure 3). Because these electronic circuits rarely fail and the data flows along these circuits at close to the speed of light, processing can be accomplished in billionths of a second. Thus, the computer is a powerful tool because it can perform these four operations reliably and quickly.

The people who either use the computer directly or use the information it provides are called **computer users**, **end users**, or sometimes, just **users**.

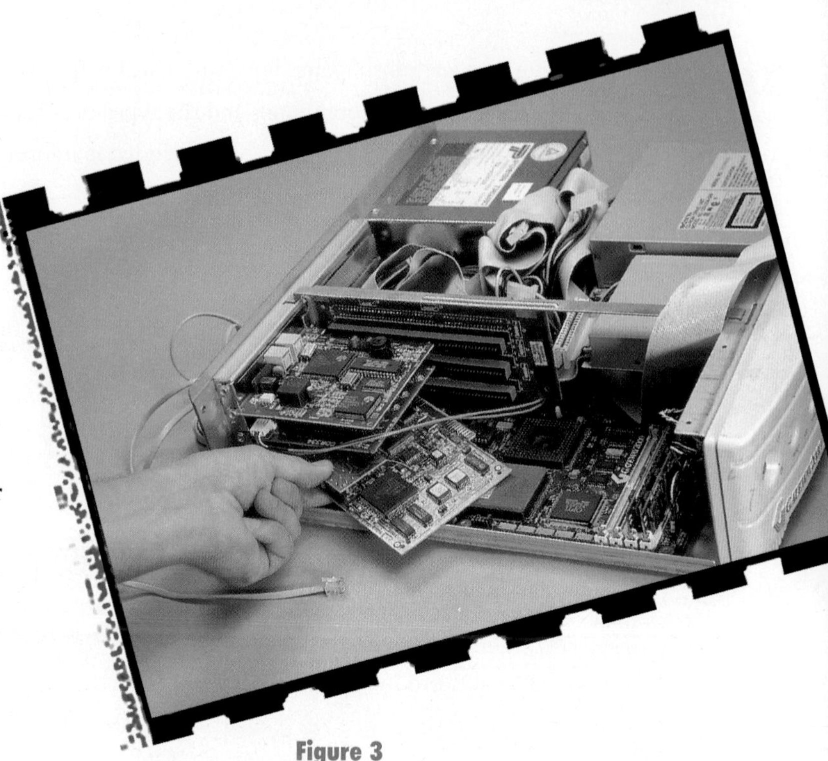

Figure 3
Inside a computer are chips and other electronic components that process data in billionths of a second.

HOW DOES A COMPUTER KNOW WHAT TO DO?

For a computer to perform the operations in the information processing cycle, it must be given a detailed set of instructions that tell it exactly what to do. These instructions are called a **computer program**, or **software**. Before processing for a specific job begins, the computer program corresponding to that job is stored in the computer. Once the program is stored, the computer can begin to operate by executing the program's first instruction. The computer executes one program instruction after another until the job is complete.

WHAT ARE THE COMPONENTS OF A COMPUTER?

To understand how computers process data into information, you need to examine the primary components of the computer. The four primary components of a computer are: input devices, the processor unit, output devices, and auxiliary storage units (Figure 4).

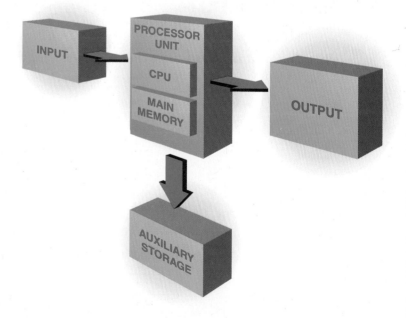

Figure 4
A computer is composed of input devices through which data is entered into the computer; the processor that processes data stored in main memory; output devices on which the results of the processing are made available; and auxiliary storage units that store data for future processing.

Input Devices

Input devices allow you to enter data into main memory. The two primary input devices used are the keyboard and the mouse.

The Keyboard

The most commonly used input device is the **keyboard**, on which data is entered by manually keying in or typing. The keyboard on most computers is laid out in much the same manner as the one shown in Figure 5. The alphabetic keys are arranged like those on a typewriter.

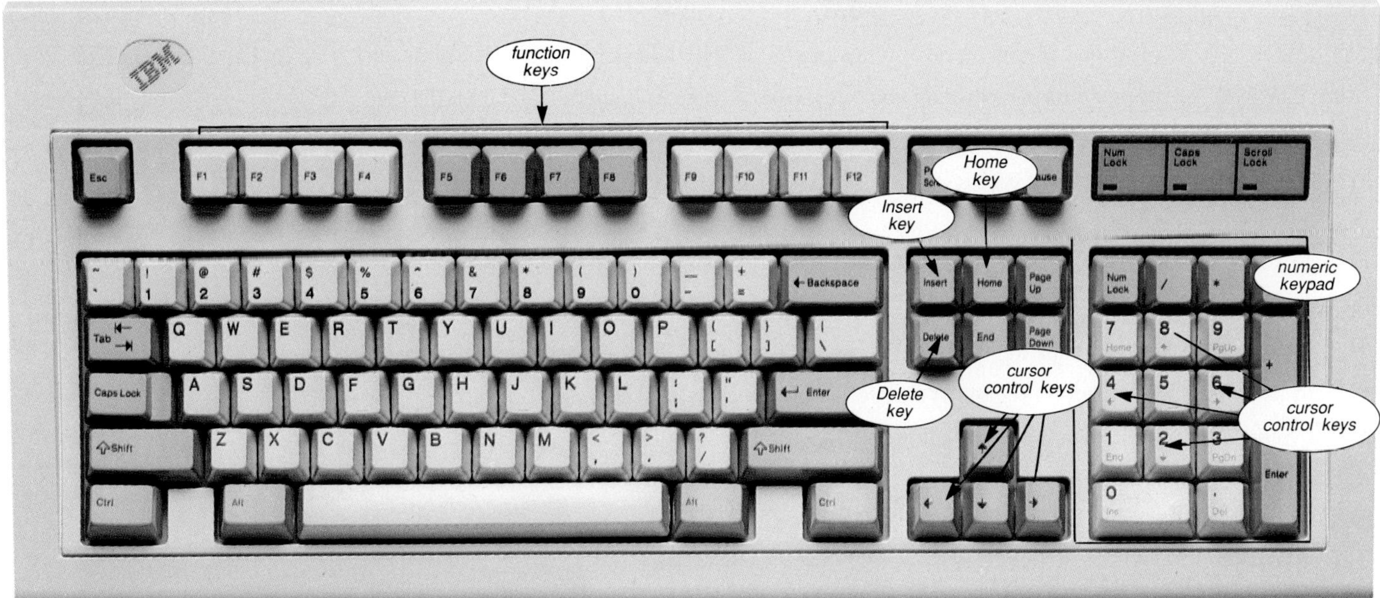

Figure 5
This keyboard represents most personal computer keyboards.

A **numeric keypad** or t is located on the right side of most keyboards. This arrangement of keys allows you to enter numeric data rapidly. To activate the numeric keypad you press and engage the NUMLOCK key located above the numeric keypad. The NUMLOCK key activates the numeric keypad so when the keys are pressed, numeric characters are entered into the computer memory and appear on the screen. A light turns on at the top right of the keyboard to indicate that the numeric keys are in use.

The **cursor** or **insertion point** is a symbol, such as a small vertical line, which indicates where you are working on the screen. The cursor **control keys**, or **arrow key**s, allow you to move the cursor around the screen. Pressing the **UP ARROW** (↑) key causes the cursor to move upward on the screen. The **DOWN ARROW** (↓) key causes the cursor to move down; the **LEFT ARROW** (←) and **RIGHT ARROW** (→) keys cause the cursor to move left and right on the screen. On the keyboard in Figure 5, there are two sets of cursor control keys. One set is included as part of the numeric keypad. The second set of cursor control keys is located between the typewriter keys and the numeric keypad. To use the numeric keypad for cursor control, the NUMLOCK key must be disengaged. If the NUMLOCK key is engaged (indicated by the fact that as you press any numeric keypad key, a number appears on the screen), you can return to the cursor mode by pressing the NUMLOCK key. On most keyboards, a NUMLOCK light will indicate when the numeric keypad is in the numeric mode or the cursor mode.

The other keys on the keypad-PAGE UP, PAGE DOWN, HOME, and END—have various functions depending on the software you use. Some programs make no use of these keys; others use the **PAGE UP** and **PAGE DOWN** keys, for example, to display previous or following pages of data on the screen. Some software uses the **HOME** key to move the cursor to the upper left corner of the screen. Likewise, the **END** key may be used to move the cursor to the end of a line of text or to the bottom of the screen, depending on the software.

Function keys on many keyboards can be programmed to accomplish specific tasks. For example, a function key might be used as a help key. Whenever that key is pressed, messages display that give instructions to help the user. The keyboard in Figure 5 has twelve function keys located across the top of the keyboard.

Other keys have special uses in some applications. The SHIFT keys have several functions. They work as they do on a typewriter, allowing you to type capital letters. The SHIFT key is always used to type the symbol on the upper portion of any key on the keyboard.

The keyboard has a **BACKSPACE** key, a **TAB** key, an **INSERT** key and a **DELETE** key that perform the functions their names indicate.

The **ESC** (**ESCAPE**) key is generally used by computer software to cancel an instruction or exit from a situation. The use of the ESC key varies between software packages.

As with the ESC key, many keys are assigned special meaning by the computer software. Certain keys may be used more frequently than others by one piece of software but rarely used by another. It is this flexibility that allows you to use the computer in so many different applications.

The Mouse

A **mouse** (Figure 6) is a pointing device you can use instead of the cursor control keys. You lay the palm of your hand over the mouse and move it across the surface of a pad that provides traction for a rolling ball on the bottom of the mouse. The mouse detects the direction of the ball movement and sends this information to the screen to move the cursor. You press buttons on top of the mouse to indicate your choices of actions from lists or icons displayed on the screen.

Figure 6
The mouse input device is used to move the cursor and choose selections on the computer screen.

The Processor Unit

The **processor unit** is composed of the central processing unit and main memory. The **central processing unit** (**CPU**) contains the electronic circuits that cause processing to occur. The CPU interprets instructions to the computer, performs the logical and arithmetic processing operations, and causes the input and output operations to occur. On personal computers, the CPU is designed into a chip called a **microprocessor** (Figure 7). The Pentium Pro microprocessor shown in Figure 7 can fit in the palm of your hand. It contains 5.5 million transistors and is able to perform 250 million instructions per second.

Figure 7
A Pentium Pro microprocessor from Intel Corporation. The microprocessor circuits are located in the center. Small gold wires lead from the circuits to the pins that fit in the microprocessor socket on the main circuit board of the computer.The pins provide an electronic connection to different parts of the computer.

Main memory, also called **random access memory**, or **RAM**, consists of electronic components that store data including numbers, letters of the alphabet, graphics, and sound. Any data to be processed must be stored in main memory. The amount of main memory in computers is typically measured in kilobytes or megabytes. One **kilobyte** (**K** or **KB**) equals approximately 1,000 memory locations and one **megabyte** (**M** or **MB**) equals approximately 1 million memory locations. A memory location, or **byte**, usually stores one character. Therefore, a computer with 8MB of main memory can store approximately 8 million characters. One megabyte can hold approximately 500 pages of text information.

Output Devices

Output devices make the information resulting from processing available for use. The output from computers can be presented in many forms, such as a printed report or color graphics. When a computer is used for processing tasks, such as word processing, spreadsheets, or database management, the two output devices most commonly used are the printer and the television-like display device.

Printers

Printers used with computers can be either impact printers or nonimpact printers. An **impact printer** prints by striking an inked ribbon against the paper. One type of impact printer used with personal computers is the dot matrix printer (Figure 8).

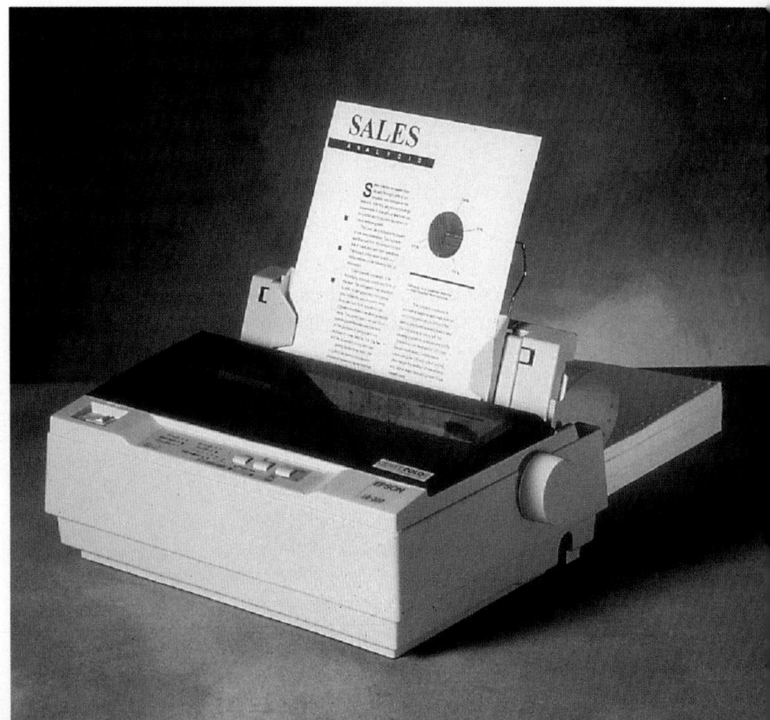

Figure 8
Dot matrix are the least expensive of the personal computer printers. Some can be purchased for less than $200. Advantages of dot matrix printers include the capability to handle wide paper and to print multipart forms.

Nonimpact printers, such as inkjet printers and laser printers (Figure 9), form characters by means other than striking a ribbon against paper. One advantage of using a nonimpact printer is that it can print higher quality text and graphics than an impact printer, such as the dot matrix. Nonimpact printers also do a better job printing different font styles (Figure 10) and they are quiet.

The popular and affordable **inkjet printer** forms a character by using a nozzle that sprays drops of ink onto the page. Ink jet printers produce excellent images. They can print on average 3 pages (black) per minute and 1 page (color) per minute. Color inkjet printers are quite popular among personal computer users today.

Laser printers work similar to a copying machine by converting data from the computer into a beam of light that is focused on a photoconductor drum, forming the images to be printed (Figure 11). The photoconductor attracts particles of toner that are fused by heat and pressure onto paper to produce an image. Laser printers produce high-quality black or color output and are used for applications that combine text and graphics such as **desktop publishing** (Figure 12). Laser printers for personal computers can cost from $500 to more than $10,000. They can print four to sixteen pages of text and graphics per minute.

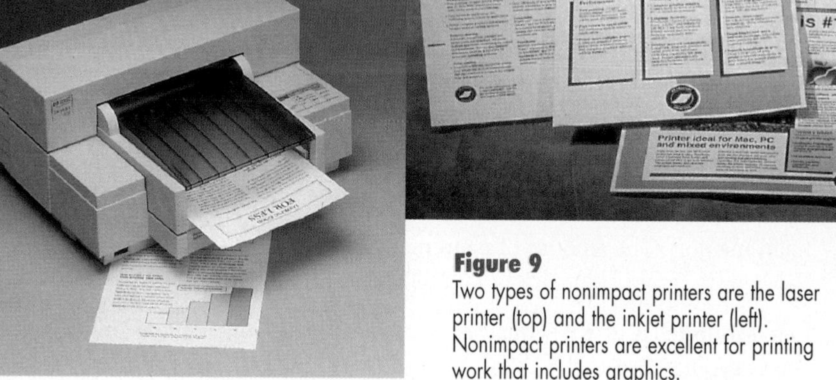

Figure 9
Two types of nonimpact printers are the laser printer (top) and the inkjet printer (left). Nonimpact printers are excellent for printing work that includes graphics.

Figure 10
Nonimpact printers do an excellent job of printing text in different typefaces, referred to as fonts. Technically, a font is a typeface in a particular size. It is common, however, to refer to the different typefaces as fonts. Dot matrix printers can print some fonts but usually at a slower rate and poorer quality than nonimpact printers. The names of four different typefaces (fonts) are shown.

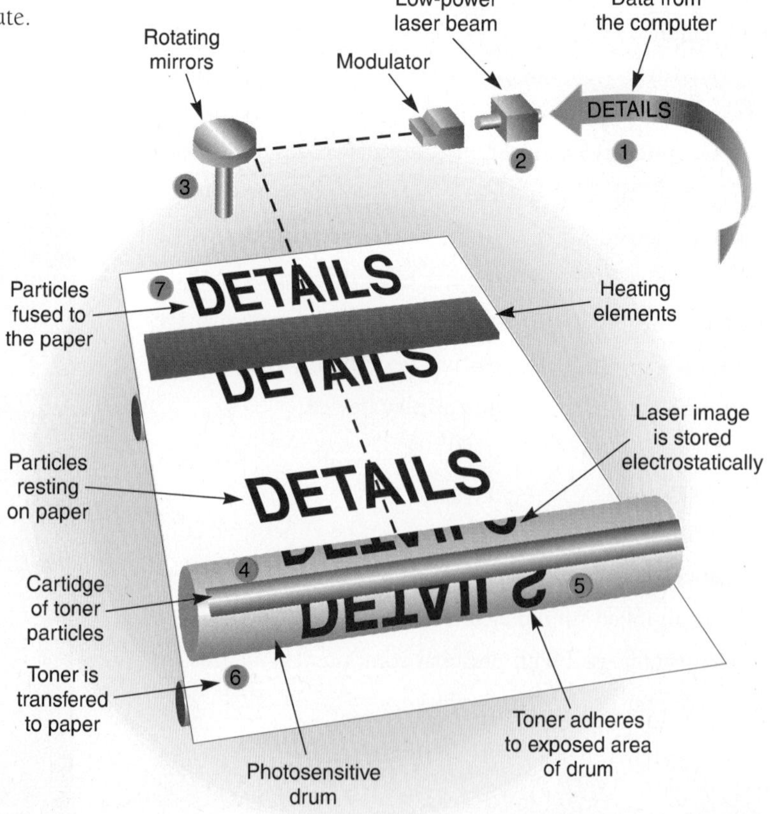

Figure 11 ▶
Laser printers use a process similar to a copying machine. Data from the computer, such as the word DETAILS (1), is converted into a laser beam (2) that is directed by a mirror (3) to a photosensitive drum (4). The areas on the drum touched by the laser attract toner particles (5) that transferred to the paper (6). The toner is fused to the paper with feat and pressure(7).

Computer Screens

Most full-size personal computers use a TV-like display device called a **screen**, **monitor**, or **CRT** (cathode ray tube) (Figure 13). Portable computers use a flat panel **liquid crystal display (LCD)** technology similar to a digital watch. The surface of the screen is made up of individual picture elements called **pixels**. Each pixel can be illuminated to form characters and graphic shapes (Figure 14). Color screens have three colored dots (red, green, and blue) for each pixel.These dots can be turned on to display different colors. Most color monitors today use super **VGA** (video graphics array) technology that improves the display significantly over older technology.

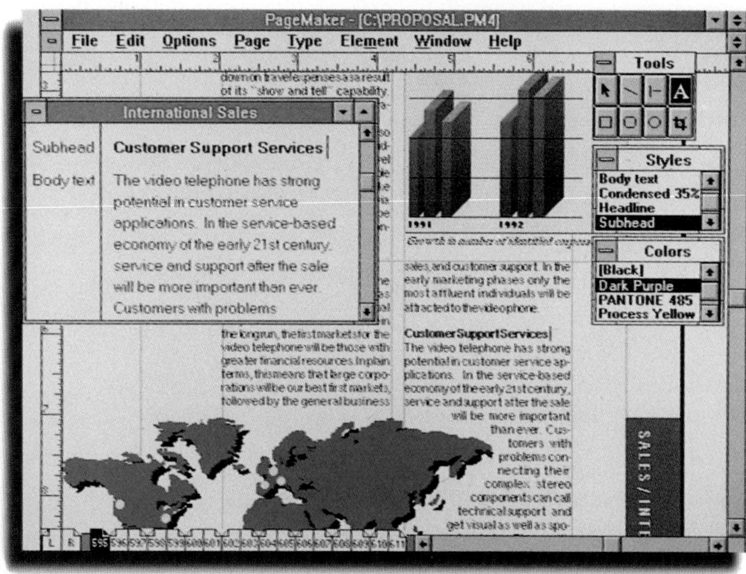

Figure 12
Desktop publishing software, such as PageMaker shown above, is used to produce high-quality documents that combine text and graphics. Such documents are often printed on laser printers.

Figure 13
Almost all personal computer systems now come with color screens. Color can be used to enhance the information displayed so the user can understand it more quickly.

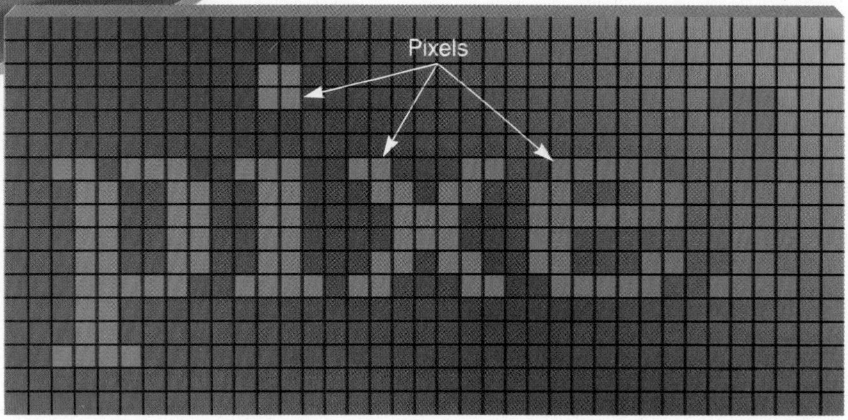

Pixels

Figure 14
Pixel is an abbreviation of the words picture element, one of thousands of spots on a computer screen that can be turned on and off to form text and graphics

Auxiliary Storage

Auxiliary storage devices are used to store instructions and data when they are not being used in main memory. Two types of auxiliary storage most often used on personal computers are floppy disks and hard disks. CD-ROM disk drives are also becoming common.

Floppy Disks

A **floppy disk** is a circular piece of oxide-coated plastic that stores data as magnetic spots. Floppy disks are available in various sizes and storage capacities. Personal computers most commonly use floppy disks that are 3½-inches in diameter (Figure 15). The once dominant 5¼-inch floppy disk (Figure 15) is seldom used today.

To read data stored on a floppy disk or to store data on a floppy disk, you insert the floppy disk in a disk drive (Figure 16). You can tell that the computer is reading data on the floppy disk or writing data on it because a light on the floppy disk drive will come on while read/write operations are taking place. Do not try to insert or remove a floppy disk when the light is on as you could cause permanent damage to the data stored on it.

The storage capacities of floppy disk drives and the related floppy disks can vary widely (Figure 17). The number of characters that can be stored on a floppy disk depends on two factors: (1) the recording density of the bits on a track; and (2) the number of tracks on the floppy disk.

Figure 15
The most commonly used floppy disk for personal computers is the 3½-inch size on the right. The once-dominant 5¼ -inch floppy disk on the left is seldom used today. Although they are smaller in size—the 3½-inch floppy disk can store more data.

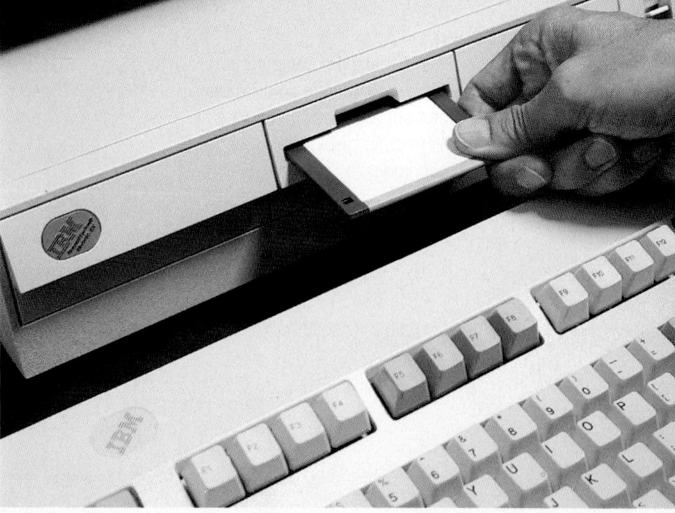

Figure 16
A user inserts a 3½-inch floppy disk into the disk drive of a personal computer.

DIAMETER (INCHES)	DESCRIPTION	CAPACITY (BYTES)
5.25	Double-sided, double-density	360KB
5.25	Double-sided, high-density	1.25MB
3.5	Double-sided, double-density	720KB
3.5	Double-sided, high-density	1.44MB

Figure 17
Storage capacities of different size and type floppy disk

Disk drives found on most personal computers use 3½-inch floppy disks that can store 720,000 bytes or 1.44 million bytes of data. 3½-inch floppy disks have a rigid plastic housing that protects the magnetic surface of the floppy disk. Another type of disk drive often found on older computers uses 5¼-inch floppy disks. The 5¼-inch floppy disks can store from 360,000 bytes or 1.2 million bytes of data.

The recording density is stated in **bits per inch** (**bpi**)—the number of magnetic spots that can be recorded on a floppy disk in a one-inch circumference of the innermost track on the floppy disk. Floppy disks and disk drives used today are identified as being double-density or high-density. You need to be aware of the density of floppy disks used by your system because data stored on high-density floppy disks, for example, can not be processed by a computer that has only double-density disk drives.

The second factor that influences the number of characters that can be stored is the number of tracks on the floppy disk. A **track** is a very narrow recording band forming a full circle around the floppy disk (Figure 18).

The tracks are separated from each other by a very narrow blank gap. Each track on a floppy disk is divided into sectors. The term **sector** is used to refer to a pie-shaped section of the disk. It is also used to refer to a section of track. Sectors are the basic units for floppy disk storage. When data is read from a floppy disk, it reads a minimum of one full sector from a track. When data is stored on a floppy disk, it writes one full sector on a track at a time. The tracks and sectors on the floppy disk and the number of characters that can be stored in each sector are defined by a special formatting program that is used with the computer.

Data stored in sectors on a floppy disk must be retrieved and placed into main memory to be processed. The time required to access and retrieve data, called the **access time**, can be important in some applications. The access time for floppy disks varies from about 175 milliseconds (one millisecond equals 1/1000 of a second) to approximately 300 milliseconds. On average, data stored in a single sector on a floppy disk can be retrieved in approximately 1/15 to 1/3 of a second.

Floppy disk care is important to preserve stored data. Properly handled, floppy disks can store data indefinitely. However, the surface of the floppy disk can be damaged and the data stored can be lost if the floppy disk is handled improperly.

Figure 18
Each track on a floppy disk is a narrow, circular band. On a diskette containing 80 tracks, the outside track is called track 0 and the inside track is called track 79. The disk surface is divided into sectors.

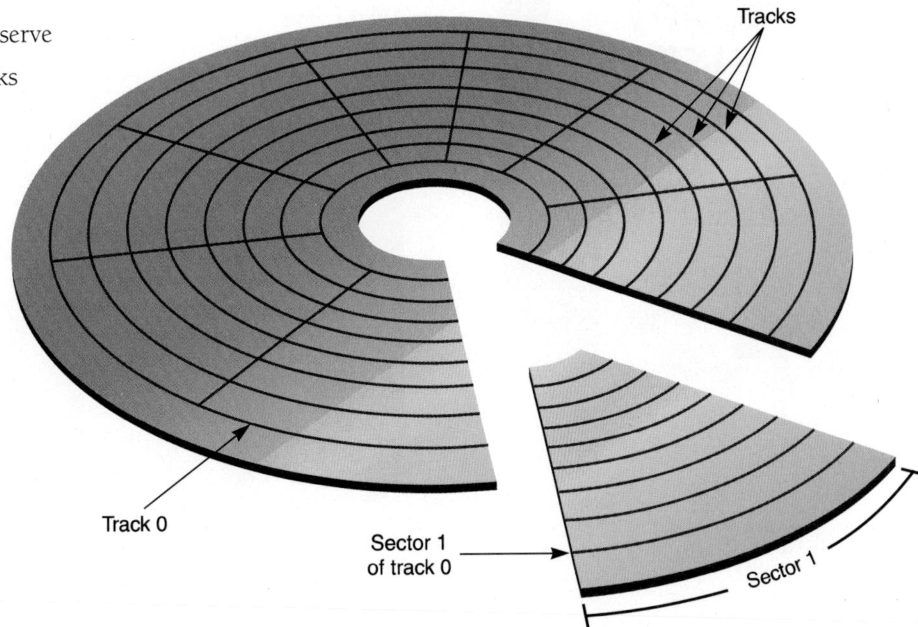

A floppy disk will give you very good service if you follow a few simple procedures:

Keep floppy disks in their original box or in a special floppy disk storage box to protect them from dirt and dust and prevent them from being accidentally bent. Store floppy disks in their protective containers. Store the container away from heat and direct sunlight. Magnetic and electrical equipment, including telephones, radios, and televisions, can erase the data on a floppy disk, so do not place floppy disks near such devices. Do not place heavy objects on a floppy disk, because the weight can pinch the covering, causing damage when the disk drive attempts to rotate.

To affix one of the self-adhesive labels supplied with most floppy disks, it is best to write or type the information on the label before you place the label on the floppy disk. If the label is already on the floppy disk, use only a felt-tip pen to write on the label, and press lightly. Do not use ball point pens, pencils, or erasers on labels that are already on floppy disks.

To use the floppy disk, grasp the floppy disk on the side away from the side to be inserted into the disk drive. Slide the floppy disk carefully into the slot on the disk drive.

The floppy disk write-protect feature (Figure 19) prevents the accidental erasure of the data stored on a floppy disk by preventing the disk drive from writing new data or erasing existing data.

On the 3½-inch floppy disk, a small switch can slide to cover and uncover the write-protection window. On a 3½-inch floppy disk, when the window is uncovered the data is protected.

Figure 19
Data cannot be written on the 3½-inch floppy disk on the left because the window in the corner of the floppy disk is open. A small piece of plastic covers the window of the 3½-inch floppy disk on the right, so data can be written on this floppy disk.

Hard Disk

Another form of auxiliary storage is a hard disk. A **hard disk** consists of one or more rigid metal platters coated with a metal oxide material that allows data to be magnetically recorded on the surface of the platters (Figure 20). Although hard disks are available in removable cartridge form, most disks cannot be removed from the computer. As with floppy disks, the data is recorded on hard disks on a series of tracks. The tracks are divided into sectors when the disk is formatted.

Figure 20
The protective cover of this hard disk drive has been removed. A read/write head is at the end of the access arm that extends over the recording surface, called a platter.

The hard disk platters spin at a high rate of speed, typically 3,600 revolutions per minute. When reading data from the disk, the read head senses the magnetic spots that are recorded on the disk along the various tracks and transfers that data to main memory. When writing, the data is transferred from main memory and is stored as magnetic spots on the tracks on the recording surface of one or more of the disk platters. When reading or writing, the read/write heads on a hard disk drive do not actually touch the surface of the disk.

The number of platters permanently mounted on the spindle of a hard disk varies. On most drives, each surface of the platter can be used to store data. Thus, if a hard disk drive uses one platter, two surfaces are available for data. If the drive uses two platters, four sets of read/write heads read and record data from the four surfaces. Storage capacities of internally mounted fixed disks for personal computers range from 240 million characters to more than one billion characters. Larger capacity, stand-alone hard disk units are also available that can store several billion bytes of information. One billion bytes is called a **gigabyte** (**GB**).

The amount of effective storage on both hard disks and floppy disks can be increased by the use of compression programs. **Compression programs** use sophisticated formulas to replace spaces and repeated text and graphics patterns with codes that can later be used to recreate the compressed data. Text files can be compressed the most; as much as an eighth of their original volume. Graphics files can be compressed the least. Overall, a 5-to-1 compression ratio is average.

Figure 21
CD-ROM disk drives allow the user to access tremendous amounts of prerecorded information—more than 600MB of data can be stored on one CD-ROM disk.

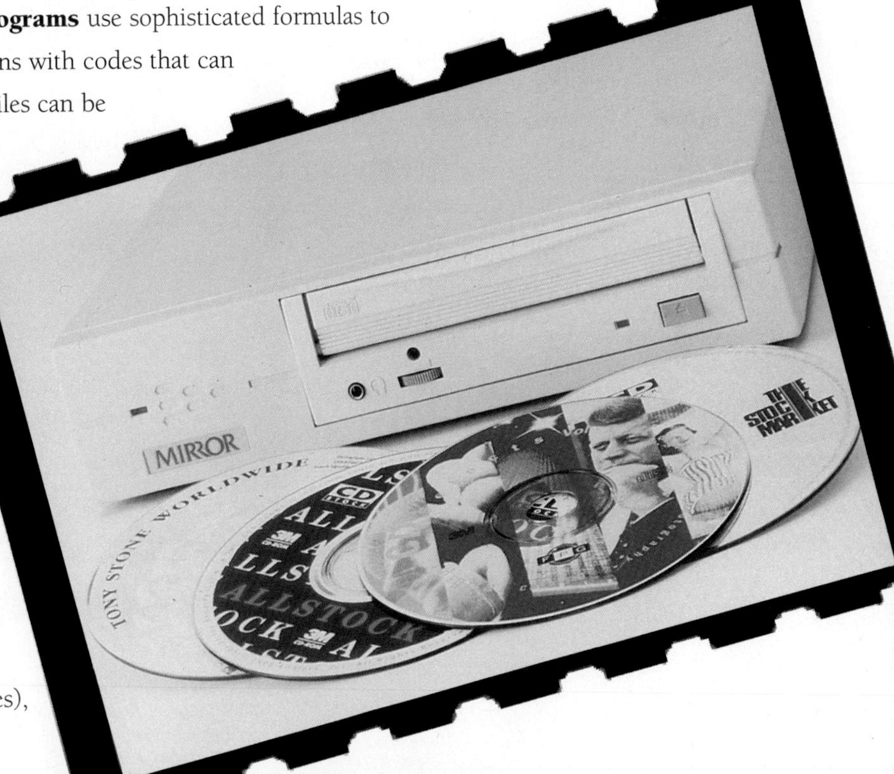

CD-ROM

Compact disk read-only memory (**CD-ROM**) disks are increasingly used to store large amounts of prerecorded information (Figure 21). Each CD-ROM disk can store more than 600 million bytes of data-the equivalent of 300,000 pages of text. Because of their large storage capacity, CD-ROM is often used for multimedia material. **Multimedia** combines text, graphics, video (pictures), and audio (sound) (Figure 22 on the next page).

COMPUTER SOFTWARE

Computer software is the key to productive use of computers. With the correct software, a computer can become a valuable tool. Software can be categorized into two types: system software and application software.

System Software

System software consists of programs to control the operations of computer equipment. An important part of system software is a set of programs called the **operating system**. Instructions in the operating system tell the computer how to perform the functions of loading, storing, and executing an application and how to transfer data. For a computer to operate, an operating system must be stored in the computer's main memory. When a computer is started, the operating system is loaded into the computer and stored in main memory. This process is called **booting**.

Today, many computers use an operating system that has a **graphical user interface** (**GUI**) that provides visual clues such as icon symbols to help the user. Each **icon** represents an application, such as word processing, or a file or document where data is stored. Microsoft **Windows 95** (Figure 23) is a widely used graphical operating system. Apple Macintosh computers also have a graphical user interface operating system. **DOS** (**Disk Operating System**) is an older but still widely used operating system.

Application Software

Application software consists of programs that tell a computer how to produce information. The different ways people use computers in their careers or in their personal lives, are examples of types of application software. Business, scientific, and educational programs are all examples of application software.

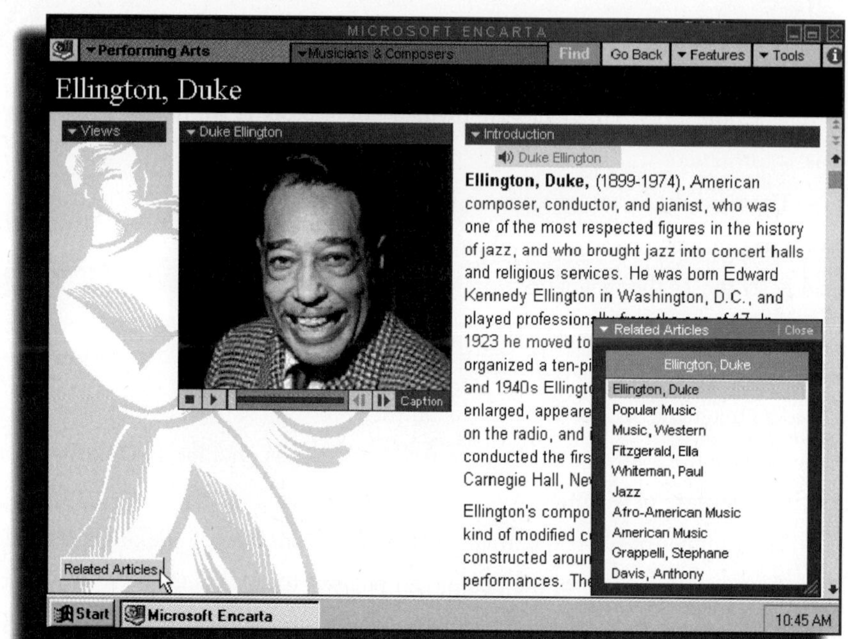

Figure 22
Microsoft Encarta is a multimedia encyclopedia available on a CD-ROM disk. Text, graphics, sound, video, and animation are all available. The speaker-shaped icon at the top of the text indicates that a sound item is available. In this topic, if the user clicks the speaker icon, a portion of Duke Ellington's music plays.

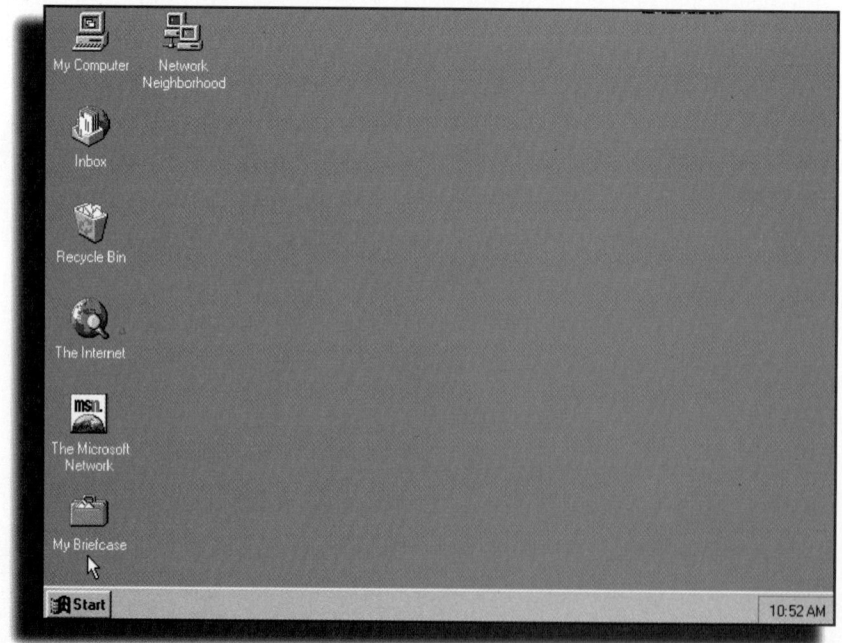

Figure 23
A graphical user interface such as Microsoft Windows 95 makes the computer easier to use. The small pictures, or symbols, on the screen are called icons. The icons represent different processing options that the user can choose.

PERSONAL COMPUTER APPLICATION SOFTWARE PACKAGES

Personal computer users often use application software packages. Some of the most commonly used packages are: word processing, electronic spreadsheet, presentation graphics, database, communications, and electronic mail software.

Word processing software (Figure 24) is used to create and print documents. A key advantage of word processing software is its capability to make changes easily in documents, such as correcting spelling, changing margins, and adding, deleting, or relocating entire paragraphs. These changes would be difficult and time consuming to make using manual methods such as a typewriter. With a word processor, documents can be printed quickly and accurately and easily stored on a disk for future use. Word processing software is oriented toward working with text, but most word processing packages can also include numeric and graphic information.

Electronic spreadsheet software (Figure 25) allows the user to add, subtract, and perform user-defined calculations on rows and columns of numbers. These numbers can be changed and the spreadsheet quickly recalculates the new results. Electronic spreadsheet software eliminates the tedious recalculations required with manual methods. Spreadsheet information is frequently converted into a graphic form. Graphics capabilities are now included in most spreadsheet packages.

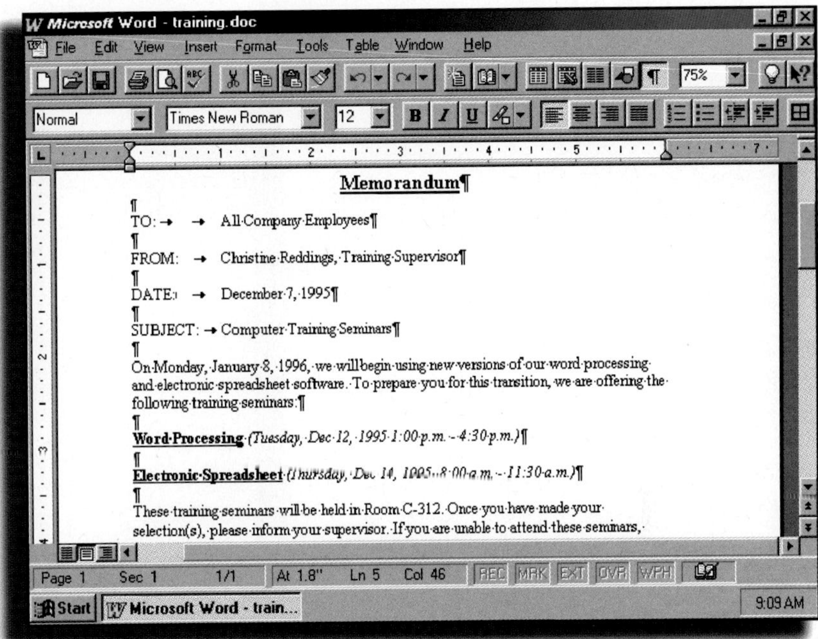

Figure 24
Word processing software is used to write letters, memos, and other documents. As the user types words and letters, they display on the screen. The user can easily add, delete, and change any text entered until the document looks exactly as desired. The user can then save the document on auxiliary storage and can also print it on a printer.

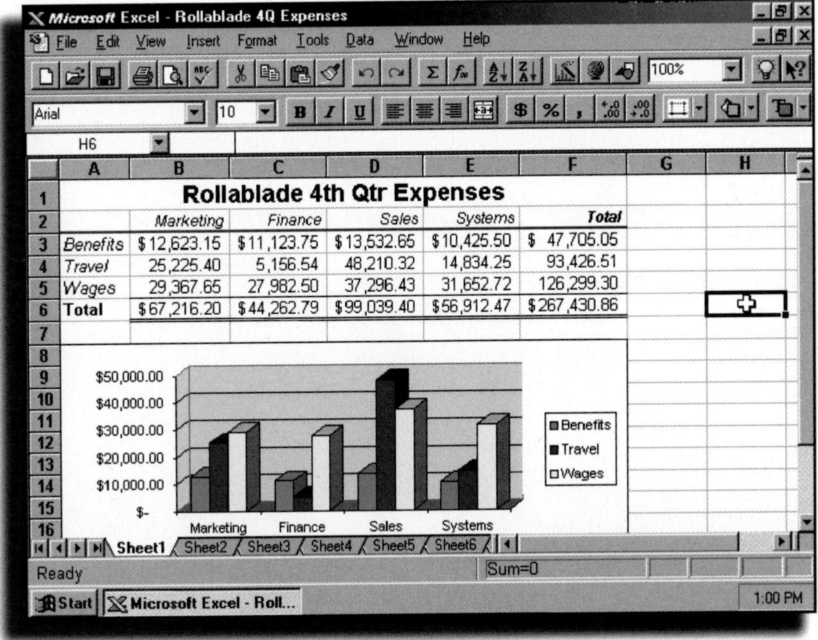

Figure 25
Electronic spreadsheet software is frequently used by people who work with numbers. The user enters the data and the formulas to be used on the data and the computer calculates the results. Most spreadsheet programs have the capability to use numeric data to generate charts, such as the above bar chart.

Database software (Figure 26) allows the user to enter, retrieve, and update data in an organized and efficient manner. These software packages have flexible inquiry and reporting capabilities that allow users to access the data in different ways and create custom reports that include some or all of the information in the database.

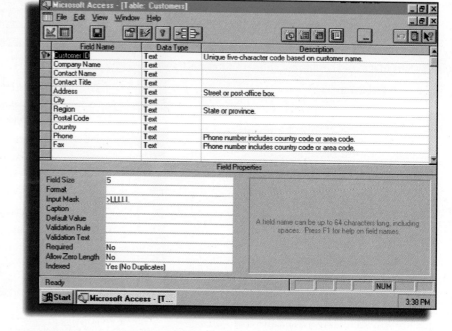

Microsoft Access - [Table: Customers]

File Edit View Window Help

Field Name	Data Type	Description
Customer ID	Text	Unique five-character code based on customer name.
Company Name	Text	
Contact Name	Text	
Contact Title	Text	
Address	Text	Street or post-office box.
City	Text	
Region	Text	State or province.
Postal Code	Text	
Country	Text	
Phone	Text	Phone number includes country code or area code.
Fax	Text	Phone number includes country code or area code.

Field Properties

Field Size	5
Format	
Input Mask	>LLLLL
Caption	
Default Value	
Validation Rule	
Validation Text	
Required	No
Allow Zero Length	No
Indexed	Yes (No Duplicates)

A field name can be up to 64 characters long, including spaces. Press F1 for help on field names.

Ready NUM

Start Microsoft Access - [T... 3:38 PM

Figure 26
Database software allows the user to enter retrieve and update data in an organiszed and efficient manner. This database table illustrates how a business organized customer information. Once the table is defined, the user can add, delete, change, display, print, or reorganize the database records.

Presentation graphics software (Figure 27) allows the user to create documents called slides to be used in making presentations. Using special projection devices, the slides are projected directly from the computer. In addition, the slides can be printed and used as handouts, or converted into transparencies and displayed on overhead projectors. Presentation graphics software includes many special effects, color, and art that enhance information presented on a slide. Because slides frequently include numeric data, presentation graphics software includes the capability to convert the numeric data into many forms of charts.

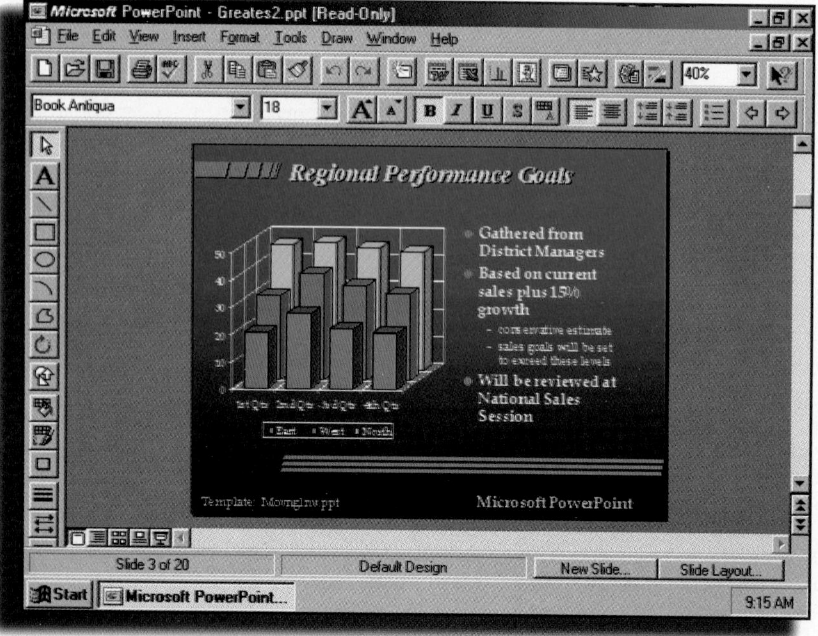

Figure 27
Presentation graphics software allows the user to create documents called slides for use in presentations. Using special projection devices, the slides display as they appear on the computer screen. The slides can also be printed and used as handouts or converted into transparencies to be used with overhead projectors.

Communications software (Figure 28) is used to transmit data and information from one computer to another. For the transfer to take place, each computer must have communications software. Organizations use communications software to transfer information from one location to another. Many individuals use communications software to access on-line databases that provide iinformation on current events, airline schedules, finances, weather, and hundreds of other subjects.

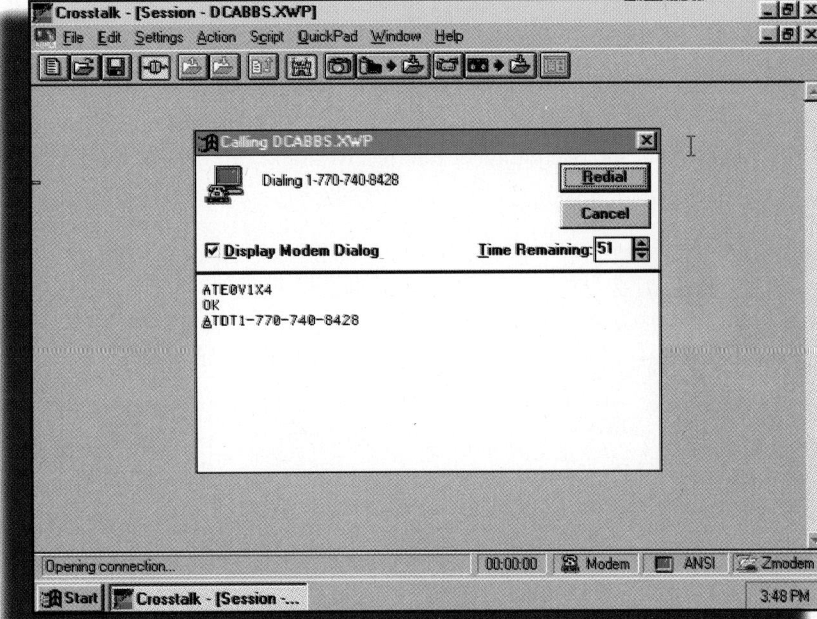

Figure 28
Communications software allows users to transmit data from one computer to another. This software enables the user to choose a previously entered phone number of another computer. Once the number is chosen, the communications software dials the number and establishes a communication link. The user can then transfer data or run programs on the remote computer.

Electronic mail software, also called **e-mail** (Figure 29), allows users to send messages to and receive messages from other computer users. The other users may be on the same computer network or on a separate computer system reached through the use of communications equipment and software.

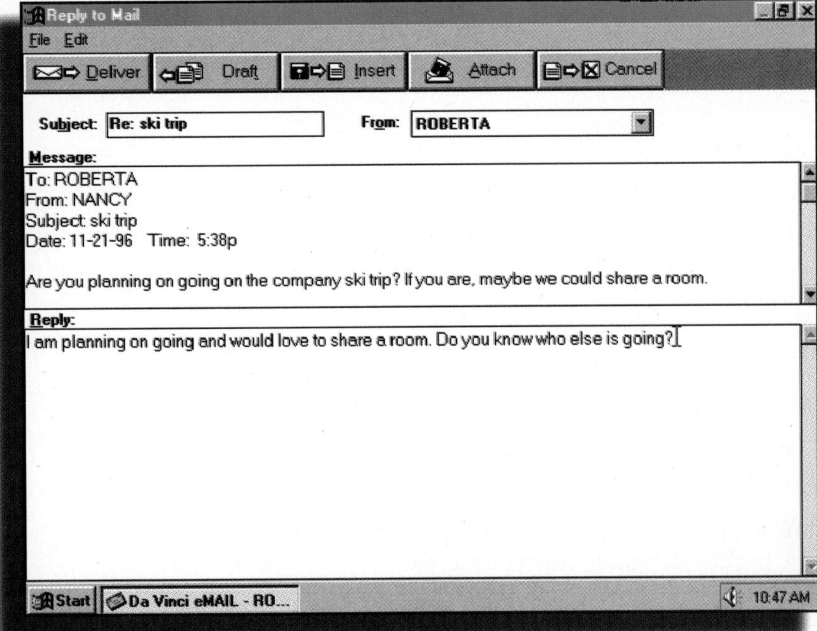

Figure 29
Electronic mail software allows users to send and receive messages with other computer users. Each user has an electronic mail box to which messages are sent. This software enables a user to add a reply to a received message and then send the reply back to the person who sent the original message.

WHAT IS COMMUNICATIONS?

Communications refers to the transmission of data and information over a communications channel, such as a standard telephone line, between one computer and another computer. Figure 30 shows the basic model for a communications system. This model consists of the following equipment:

- A computer
- Communications equipment that sends (and can usually receive) data
- The communications channel over which the data is sent
- Communications equipment that receives (and can usually send) data
- Another computer

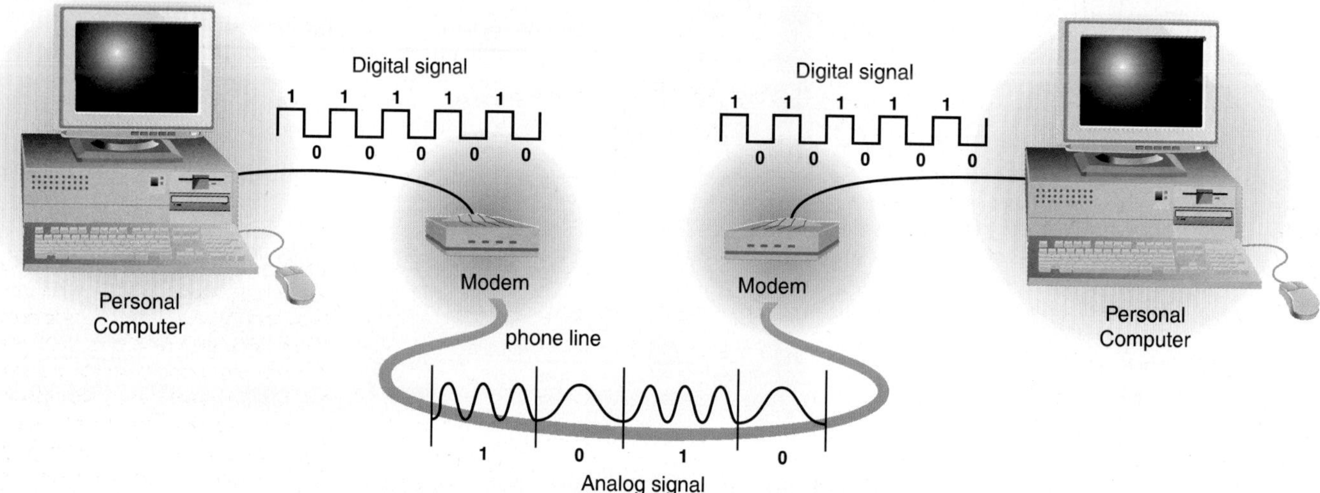

Figure 30
The basic model of a communications system. Individual electrical pulses of the digital signal from the computer are converted into analog (electrical wave) signals for transmission over voice telephone lines. At the computer receiving end, another modem converts the analog signals back into digital signals that can be processed by the computer.

The basic model also includes communications software. When two computers are communicating with each other, compatible communications software is required on each system.

Communications is important to understand because of online services and the trend to network computers. With communications equipment and software, access is available to an increasing amount and variety of information and services. **Online information services** such as Prodigy and America On-Line offer the latest news, weather, sports, and financial information along with shopping, entertainment, and electronic mail.

Browsers such as Netscape Navigator (Figure 31) allow users to access information easily from thousands of computers around the world. The network of worldwide computers is called the **Internet**. A subset of the Internet is called the World Wide Web. The **World Wide Web (WWW)** allows users to visit sites that have text, graphics, video, and sound and have hypertext links to other information and Web sites. Electronic **bulletin boards** can be found in most cities with hundreds available in large metropolitan areas. An **electronic bulletin board system (BBS)** is a computer and at least one phone line that allows users to *chat* with the computer operator, called the **system operator (sys op)** or, if more than one phone line is available, with other BBS users. BBS users can also leave messages for other users. BBSs are often devoted to a specific subject area such as games, hobbies, or a specific type of computer or software. Many computer hardware and software companies operate BBSs so users of their products can share information.

Communications Channels

A **communications channel** is the path the data follows as it is transmitted from the sending equipment to the receiving equipment in a communications system. These channels are made up of one or more **transmission media**, including twisted pair wire, coaxial cable, fiber optics, microwave transmission, satellite transmission, and wireless transmission.

Communications Equipment

If a personal computer is within approximately 1,000 feet of another computer, the two devices can usually be directly connected by a cable. If the devices are more than 1,000 feet, however, the electrical signal weakens to the point that some type of special communications equipment is required to increase or change the signal to transmit it farther. A variety of communications equipment exists to perform this task, but the equipment most often used is a modem.

Computers are designed to process data as **digital signals**, individual electrical pulses grouped together to represent characters. Telephone equipment was originally designed to carry only voice transmission, which is comprised of a continuous electrical wave called an **analog signal** (see Figure 30). Thus, a special piece of equipment called a modem converts between the digital signals and analog signals so telephone lines can carry data. A **modem** converts the digital signals of a computer to analog signals that are transmitted over a communications channel. A modem also converts analog signals it receives into digital signals used by a computer. The word modem comes from a combination of the words *mo*dulate, which means to change into a sound or analog signal, and *dem*odulate, which means to convert an analog signal into a digital signal. A modem is needed at both the sending and receiving ends of a communications channel. A modem may be an external stand-alone device that is connected to the computer and phone line or an internal circuit board that is installed inside the computer.

Modems can transmit data at rates from 1,200 to 28,800 bits per second (bps). Most personal computers use a 9,600 bps or higher modem. Business or heavier volume users would use faster and more expensive modems.

Figure 31
Use of the Internet has been made easier with browser programs such as Netscape Navigator. Browsers allow users to access World Wide Web (WWW or Web) sites that have text, graphics, video, and sound and have hypertext links to other information and Web sites. This screen shows haw Netscape Navigator displays the first page of information (called a home page) located at the Web site of Netscape Communications Corporation, the developer of Netscape Navigatior.

COMMUNICATION NETWORKS

A communication **network** is a collection of computers and other equipment using communications channels to share hardware, software, data, and information. Networks are classified as either local area networks or wide area networks.

Local Area Networks (LANs)

A **local area network**, or **LAN**, is a privately owned communications network and covers a limited geographic area, such as a school computer laboratory, an office, a building, or a group of buildings.

The LAN consists of a communications channel connecting a group of personal computers to one another. Very sophisticated LANs are capable of connecting a variety of office devices, such as word processing equipment, computer terminals, video equipment, and personal computers.

Three common applications of local area networks are hardware, software, and information resource sharing. **Hardware resource sharing** allows each personal computer in the network to access and use devices that would be too expensive to provide for each user or would not be justified for each user because of only occasional use. For example, when a number of personal computers are used on the network, each may need to use a laser printer. Using a LAN, the purchase of one laser printer serves the entire network. Whenever a personal computer user on the network needs the laser printer, it is accessed over the network. Figure 32 depicts a simple local area network consisting of four personal computers linked together by a cable. Three of the personal computers (computer 1 in the sales and marketing department, computer 2 in the accounting department, and computer 3 in the personnel department) are available for use at all times. Computer 4 is used as a server, which is dedicated to handling the communications needs of the other computers in the network. The users of this LAN have connected the laser printer to the server. Using the LAN, all computers and the server can use the printer.

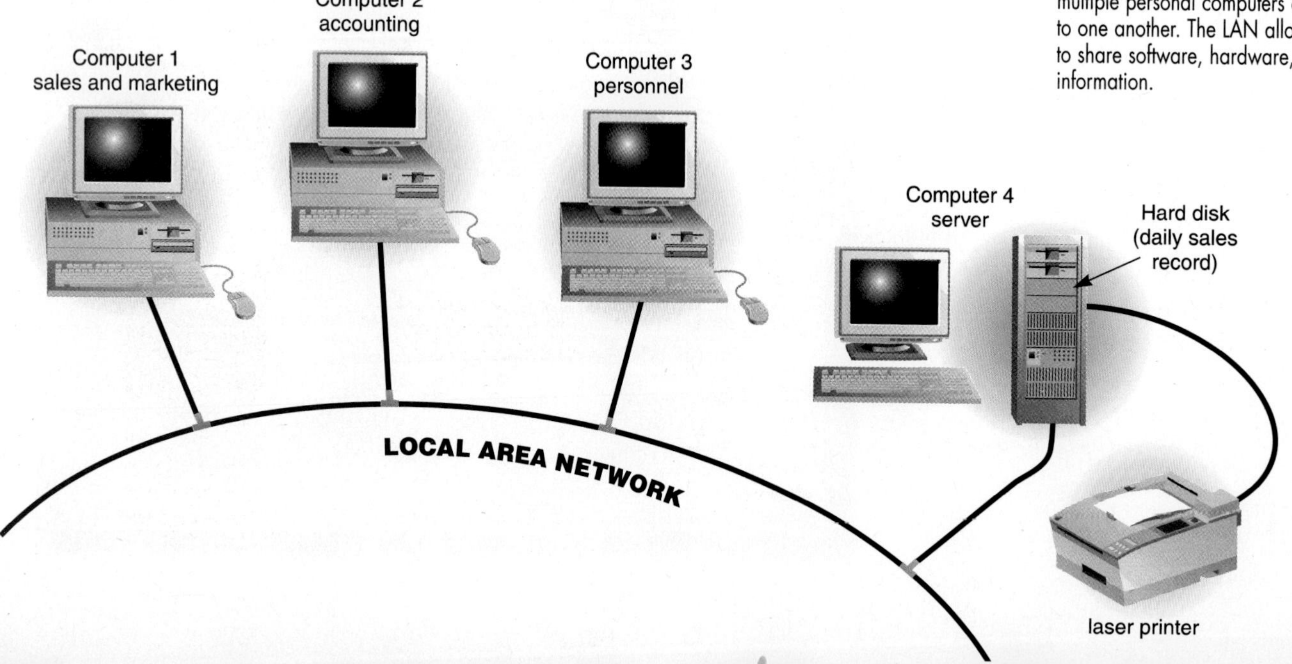

Figure 32
A local area network (LAN) consists of multiple personal computers connected to one another. The LAN allows users to share software, hardware, and information.

Frequently used software is another type of resource sharing that often occurs on a local area network. For example, if all users need access to word processing software, the software can be stored on the hard disk of the server and accessed by all users as needed. This is more convenient and faster than having the software stored on a floppy disk and available at each computer.

Information resource sharing allows anyone using a personal computer on the local area network to access data stored on any other computer in the network. In actual practice, hardware resource sharing and information resource sharing are often combined. The capability to access and store data on common auxiliary storage is an important feature of many local area networks.

Information resource sharing is usually provided by using either the file server or client-server method. Using the **file server** method, the server sends an entire file at a time. The requesting computer then performs the processing. With the **client-server** method, processing tasks are divided between the server computer and the client computer requesting the information. Figure 33 illustrates how the two methods would process a request for information stored on the server system for customers with balances over $1,000. With the file server method, all customer records would be transferred to the requesting computer. The requesting computer would then process the records to identify the customers with balances over $1,000. With the client-server method, the server system would review the customers' records and only transfer records of customers meeting the criteria. The client-server method greatly reduces the amount of data sent over a network but requires a more powerful server system.

Figure 33
A request for information about customers with balances over $1,000 would be processed differently by the file server and client-server networks.

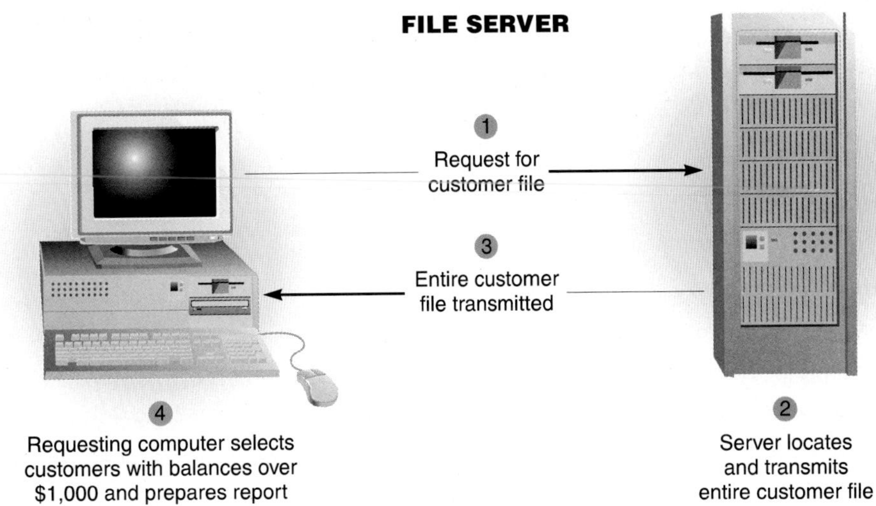
FILE SERVER
1 Request for customer file
3 Entire customer file transmitted
4 Requesting computer selects customers with balances over $1,000 and prepares report
2 Server locates and transmits entire customer file

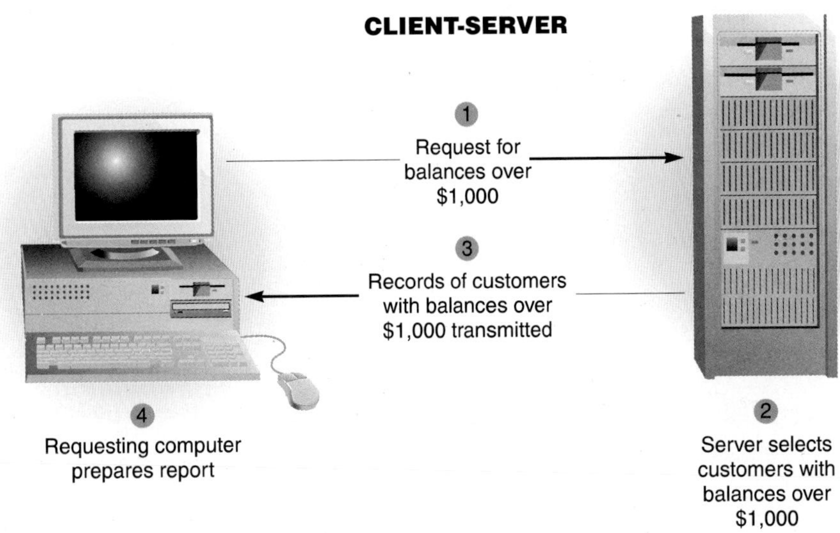
CLIENT-SERVER
1 Request for balances over $1,000
3 Records of customers with balances over $1,000 transmitted
4 Requesting computer prepares report
2 Server selects customers with balances over $1,000

Wide Area Networks (WANs)

A **wide area network**, or **WAN**, is geographic in scope (as opposed to local) and uses telephone lines, microwaves, satellites, or a combination of communications channels (Figure 34). Public wide area network companies include common carriers such as the telephone companies.

Telephone company deregulation has encouraged a number of companies to build their own wide area networks. Communications companies, such as MCI, have built WANs to compete with other communications companies.

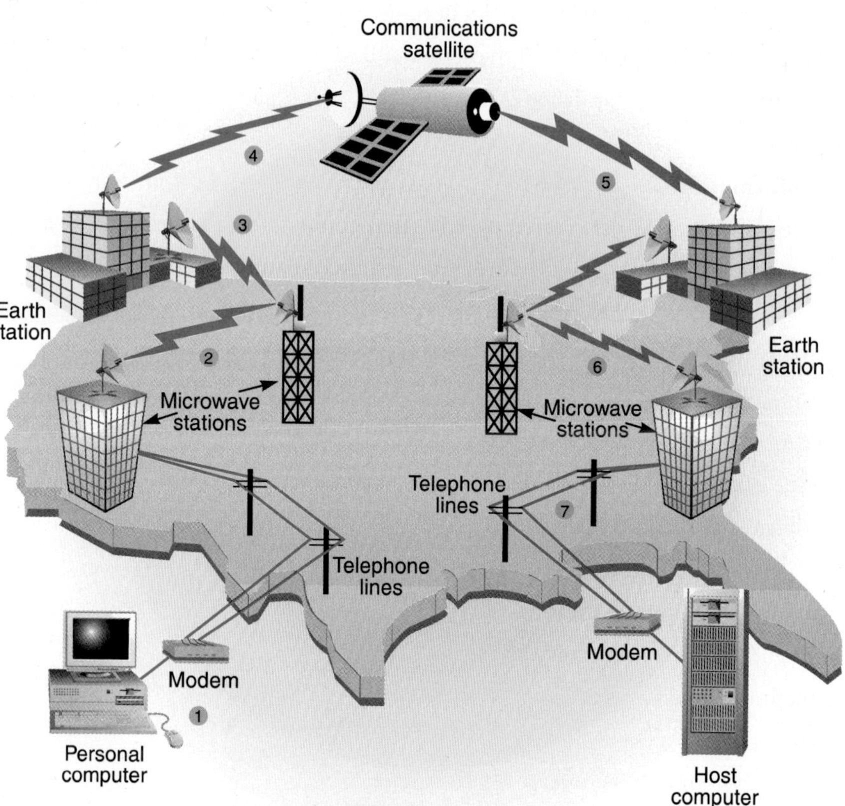

Figure 34
A wide area network (WAN) may use a number of different communications channels such as telephone lines, microwaves, and satellites.

HOW TO PURCHASE A COMPUTER SYSTEM

The personal computer (PC) is the most widely purchased type of system. The following guidelines assume you are purchasing an IBM compatible PC, to be used for home or light business use. That is not meant to imply that Macintosh or other types of computer systems are not worth considering. Software requirements and the need to be compatible with other systems you may work with should determine the type of system you purchase. Most businesses use IBM compatible PCs. A laptop (portable) computer would be an appropriate choice if your situation requires that you have a computer with you when you travel.

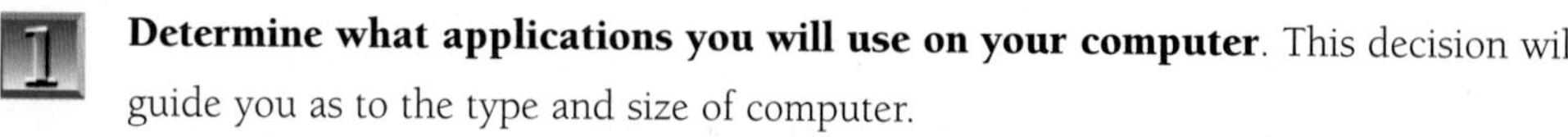

1 **Determine what applications you will use on your computer**. This decision will guide you as to the type and size of computer.

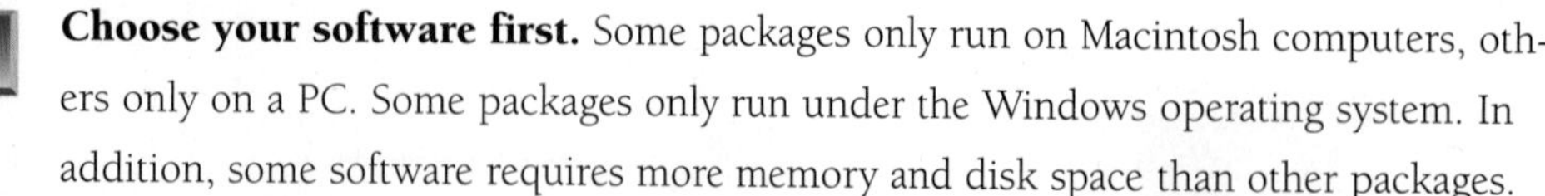

2 **Choose your software first.** Some packages only run on Macintosh computers, others only on a PC. Some packages only run under the Windows operating system. In addition, some software requires more memory and disk space than other packages.

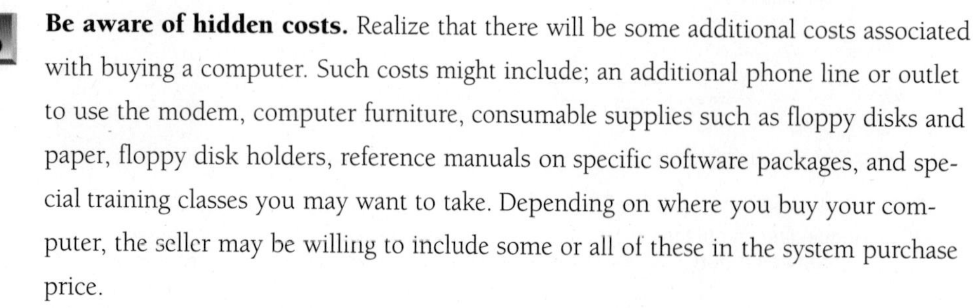

3 **Be aware of hidden costs.** Realize that there will be some additional costs associated with buying a computer. Such costs might include; an additional phone line or outlet to use the modem, computer furniture, consumable supplies such as floppy disks and paper, floppy disk holders, reference manuals on specific software packages, and special training classes you may want to take. Depending on where you buy your computer, the seller may be willing to include some or all of these in the system purchase price.

Buy equipment that meets the *Energy Star* power consumption guidelines. These guidelines require that computer systems, monitors, and printers, reduce electrical consumption if they have not been used for some period of time, usually several minutes. Equipment meeting the guidelines can display the *Energy Star* logo.

Use a spreadsheet like the one shown in Figure 35 to compare purchase alternatives. Use a separate sheet of paper to take notes on each vendor's system and then summarize the information on the spreadsheet.

Figure 35
A spreadsheet is an effective way to summarize and compare the prices and equipment offered by different system vendors.

Consider buying from local computer dealers and direct mail companies. Each has certain advantages. The local dealer can more easily provide hands-on support, if necessary. With a mail order company, you are usually limited to speaking to someone over the phone. Mail order companies usually, but not always, offer the lowest prices. The important thing to do when shopping for a system is to make sure you are comparing identical or similar configurations.

7

Consider more than just price. Don't necessarily buy the lowest cost system. Consider intangibles such as how long the vendor has been in business, its reputation for quality, and reputation for support.

Look for free software. Many system vendors now include free software with their systems. Some even let you choose which software you want. Such software only has value, however, if you would have purchased it if it had not come with the computer.

System Cost Comparison Worksheet

		Desired	#1	#2	#3	#4
Base System	Mfr	--				
	Model					
	Processor	Pentium				
	Speed	100MHz				
	Power supply	150watts				
	Expansion slots	5				
	Local bus video	yes				
	Operating System	Windows				
	Price					
Memory	RAM	16MB				
	L2 Cache	256K				
	Price					
Disk	Mfr					
	Size	1.0GB				
	Price					
Video Graphics	Mfr/Model					
	Memory	2MB				
	Price					
Floppy Disk Drive	3.5 inch	3.5 inch				
	Combo 3.5/5.25					
Color Monitor	Mfr/Model					
	Size	15 inch				
	Dot Pitch	0.28mm				
	Price					
Sound Card	Mfr/Model					
	Price					
Speakers	Mfr/Model					
	Watts					
	Size	2 inch				
	Price					
CD-ROM	Mfr/Model					
	Speed	Quad				
	Price					
Mouse	Mfr					
	Price					
Fax Modem	Mfr/Model					
	Speed	28.8kbps				
	Price					
Printer	Mfr/Model					
	Type	ink jet				
	Speed	6ppm				
	Price					
Surge Protector	Mfr/Model					
	Price					
Tape Backup	Mfr/Model					
	Price					
UPS	Mfr/Model					
	Price					
Other	Sales Tax					
	Shipping					
	1 YR Warranty	standard				
	1 YR On-Site Svc					
	3 YR On-Site Svc					
	TOTAL					
Software	List free software					

Buy a system compatible with the one you use elsewhere. If you use a personal computer at work or at some other organization, make sure the computer you buy is compatible. That way, if you need or want to, you can work on projects at home.

Consider purchasing an on-site service agreement. If you use your system for business or otherwise can't afford to be without your computer,consider purchasing an on-site service agreement. Many of the mail order vendors offer such support through third-party companies. Such agreements usually state that a technician will be on-site within 24 hours. Some systems include on-site service for only the first year. It is usually less expensive to extend the service for two or three years when you buy the computer rather than waiting to buy the service agreement later.

Use a credit card to purchase your system. Many credit cards now have purchase protection benefits that cover you in case of loss or damage to purchased goods. Some also extend the warranty of any products purchased with the card. Paying by credit card also gives you time to install and use the system before you have to pay for it. Finally, if you're dissatisfied with the system and can't reach an agreement with the seller, paying by credit card gives you certain rights regarding withholding payment until the dispute is resolved. Check your credit card agreement for specific details.

Buy a system that will last you for at least three years. Studies show that many users become dissatisfied because they didn't buy a powerful enough system. Consider the following system configuration guidelines. Each of the components will be discussed separately:

Base System Components:

Pentium Processor, 100 megahertz,
150 watt power supply
1.0 GB hard disk drive
16 MB of RAM
3 open expansion slots
1 open expansion bay
local bus video card with 2 MB of memory
1 parallel and 2 serial ports
3½-inch floppy disk drive
15- or 17-inch SVGA color monitor
mouse or other pointing device
enhanced keyboard
ink-jet or personal laser printer
surge protector
latest version of operating system
FCC Class B approved

Optional Equipment

28.8 Kbps fax modem
sound card and speakers
4X CD-ROM drive
color ink jet printer
tape backup
uninterruptable power supply

Processor: A Pentium processor with a speed rating of 100 megahertz is needed for today's more sophisticated software, even word processing software. Buy a system that can be upgraded to the next generation processor.

Power Supply: 150 watts. If the power supply is too small, it will not be capable of supporting additional expansion cards you may want to add in the future. The power supply should be **UL** (Underwriters Laboratory) approved.

Hard Disk: 1 gigabyte (GB). Each new release of software requires more hard disk space. Even with disk compression programs, disk space is used up fast. Start with more space on your disk than you ever think you will need.

Memory (RAM): 16 megabytes (MB) Like disk space, the new applications are demanding more memory. It is easier and less expensive to obtain the memory when you buy the system than if you wait until later.

Expansion Slots: At least three open slots. Expansion slots are needed for a modem sound card, scanners, tape drives, video capture boards, and other equipment you may want to add in the future as your needs change and the price of this equipment becomes lower.

Expansion Bay: At least one open bay. An expansion (drive) bay will let you add another disk or floppy disk drive, a tape drive, or a CD-ROM drive.

Local Bus Video Card: Local bus video cards provide faster video performance than video cards that use the slower expansion bus. Make sure the video card has at least 2 MB of memory.

Ports: At least one parallel and two serial ports. The parallel port will be used for your printer. The serial ports can be used for additional printers, external modems, joysticks, a mouse, and some network connections.

Floppy Disk Drives: Most software is now distributed on 3½-inch floppy disks or CD-ROMs. If you need to read the older 5¼-inch floppy disks, consider buying a combination floppy disk drive, which is only slightly more expensive than a single 3½-inch floppy disk drive. The combination device has both 3½-inch and 5¼-inch floppy disk drives in a single unit.

Color Monitor: 15- or 17-inch. This is one device where it pays to spend a little more money. A 17-inch super VGA (SVGA) monitor with a dot pitch of 0.28mm or less will display graphics better than a 15-inch model. For health reasons, make sure you pick a low radiation model. Also, look for a monitor with an antiglare coating on the screen or consider buying an antiglare filter that mounts on the front of the screen.

Pointing Device: Most systems include a mouse as part of the base package. Some people prefer to use a trackball.

Enhanced Keyboard: Almost always included with the system. Check to make sure the keyboard is the *enhanced* and not the older *standard* model. The enhanced keyboard also is sometimes called the *101* keyboard because it has 101 keys (some enhanced keyboards have even more keys). If you are concerned about possible wrist injuries, get one of the ergonomically designed keyboards.

Printer: Inkjet and laser printers produce excellent graphic output and now are only slightly more expensive than dot matrix printers, which now are used primarily for multipart form printing applications. Inexpensive color inkjet printers also are available.

Surge Protecter: A voltage spike can literally destroy your system. It is low cost insurance to protect yourself with a surge protector. Do not merely buy a fused multiple plug outlet from the local hardware store. Buy a surge protector designed for computers with a separate protected jack for your phone (modem) line.

Operating System: Almost all new systems come with an operating system, but it is not always the most current version. Make sure the operating system is the one you want and is the latest version.

FFC Class B Approved: The Federal Communications Commission (FCC) provides radio frequency emission standards that computer manufacturers must meet. If a computer does not meet the FCC standards, it could cause interference with radio and television reception. Class B standards apply to computers used in a home. Class A standards apply to a business installation.

Fax Modem: 28.8 Kbps (Kilobytes per second) speed for both the modem and fax. Volumes of information are available via the Internet. In addition, many software vendors provide assistance and free software upgrades via bulletin boards. For the speed they provide, 28.8 Kbps modems are worth the extra money. Facsimile (fax) capability costs only a few dollars more and gives you additional communication options.

Sound Card and Speakers: More and more software and support materials are incorporating sound. For the best quality sound, buy amplified speakers with their own powered amplifier and a separate subwoofer.

CD-ROM Drive: Multimedia requires a CD-ROM drive. Also, many large software programs are now available on CD-ROM, which greatly reduces installation time. Get at least a quad speed model (transfer rate of 600 Kbps).

Tape Backup: Larger hard disks make backing up data on floppy disks impractical. Internal or external tape backup systems are the most common solution. Some portable units, great if you have more than one system, are designed to connect to your printer port. The small tapes can store the equivalent of hundreds of floppy disks.

Uninterruptable Power Supply (UPS): A UPS uses batteries to start or keep your system running if the main electrical power is turned off. The length of time they provide depends on the size of the batteries and the electrical requirements of your system but usually is at least 10 minutes. The idea of a UPS is to give you enough time to save your work. Get a UPS that is rated for your size system.

HOW TO INSTALL A COMPUTER SYSTEM

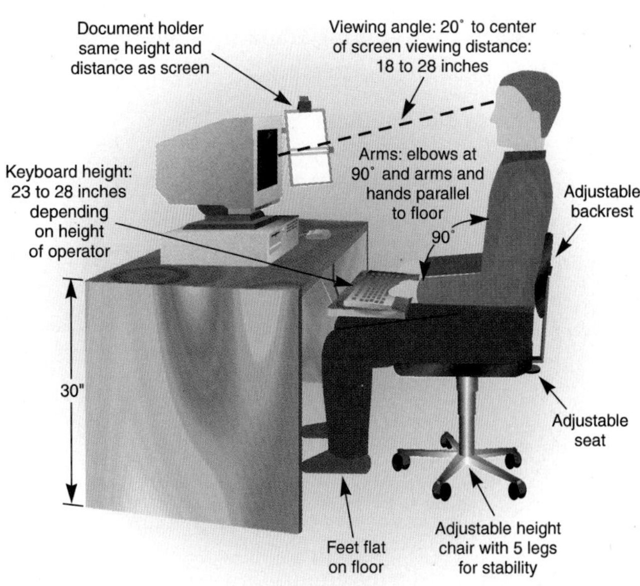

Figure 36
More than anything else, a well-designed work area should be flexible to allow adjustment to the height and build of different individuals. Good lighting and air quality should also be considered.

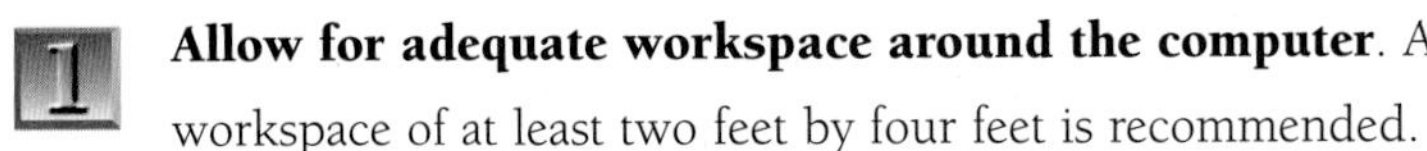

1. **Allow for adequate workspace around the computer.** A workspace of at least two feet by four feet is recommended.
2. **Install bookshelves.** Bookshelves above and/or to the side of the computer area are useful for keeping manuals and other reference materials handy.
3. **Install your computer in a well-designed work area.** The height of your chair, keyboard, monitor, and work surface is important and can affect your health. See Figure 36 for specific guidelines.
4. **Use a document holder.** To minimize neck and eye strain, obtain a document holder that holds documents at the same height and distance as your computer screen.

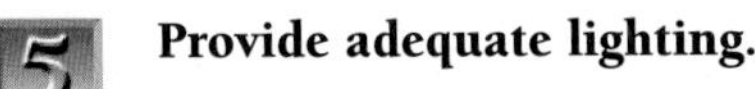

5. **Provide adequate lighting.**
6. **While working at your computer, be aware of health issues.** See Figure 37 for a list of computer user health guidelines.
7. **Install or move a phone near the computer.** Having a phone near the computer really helps if you need to call a vendor about a hardware or software problem. Oftentimes the vendor support person can talk you through the correction while you're on the phone. To avoid data loss, however, don't place floppy disks on the phone or any other electrical or electronic equipment.
8. **Obtain a computer tool set.** Computer tool sets are available from computer dealers, office supply stores, and mail order companies. These sets will have the right-sized screwdrivers and other tools to work on your system. Get one that comes in a zippered carrying case to keep all the tools together.
9. **Save all the paperwork that comes with your system.** Keep it in an accessible place with the paperwork from your other computer-related purchases. To keep different-sized documents together, consider putting them in a plastic zip-lock bag.
10. **Record the serial numbers of all your equipment and software.** Write the serial numbers on the outside of the manuals that came with the equipment as well as in a single list that contains the serial numbers of all your equipment and software.

Figure 37
All computer users should follow the Computer User Health Guidelines to maintain their health.

COMPUTER USER HEALTH GUIDELINES
1. Work in a well-designed work area. Figure 36 illustrates the guidelines
2. Alternate work activites to prevent physical and mental fatique. If possible, change the order of your work to provide some variety.
3. Take frequent breaks. At least once per hour, get out of your chair and move around. Every two hours, take at least a 15 minute break.
4. Incorporate hand, arm, and body stretching exercises into your breaks. At lunch, try to get outside and walk.
5. Make sure your computer monitor is designed to minimize electromagnetic radiation.
6. Try to eliminate or minimize surrounding noise. Noisy environments contribute to stress and tension.
7. If you frequently have to use the phone and the computer at the same time, consider using a telephone headset. Cradling the phone between your head and shoulder can cause muscle strain.
8. Be aware of symptoms of repetitive strain injuries; soreness, pain, numbness, or weakness in neck, shoulders, arms, wrists, and hands. Don't ignore early signs; seek medical advice.

Keep the shipping containers and packing materials for all your equipment. This material will come in handy if you have to return your equipment for servicing or have to move it to another location.

Look at the inside of your computer. Before you connect power to your system, remove the computer case cover and visually inspect the internal components. The user manual usually identifies what each component does. Look for any disconnected wires, loose screws or washers, or any other obvious signs of trouble. Be careful not to touch anything inside the case unless you are grounded. Static electricity can permanently damage the microprocessor chips on the circuit boards. Before you replace the cover, take several photographs of the computer showing the location of the circuit boards. These photos may save you from taking the cover off in the future if you or a vendor has a question about what equipment controller card is installed in what expansion slot.

Identify device connectors. At the back of your system there are a number of connectors for the printer, the monitor, the mouse, a phone line, etc. If they aren't already identified by the manufacturer, use a marking pen to write the purpose of each connector on the back of the computer case.

Complete and send in your equipment and software registration cards right away. If you're already entered in the vendors user database, it can save you time when you call in with a support question. Being a registered user also makes you eligible for special pricing on software upgrades.

Install your system in an area where the temperature and humidity can be maintained. Try to maintain a constant temperature between 60 and 80 degrees fahrenheit when the computer is operating. High temperatures and humidity can damage electronic components. Be careful when using space heaters; their hot, dry air has been known to cause disk problems.

Keep your computer area clean. Avoid eating and drinking around the computer. Smoking should be avoided also. Cigarette smoke can quickly cause damage to the floppy disk drives and floppy disk surfaces.

Check your insurance. Some policies have limits on the amount of computer equipment they cover. Other policies don't cover computer equipment at all if it is used for a business (a separate policy is required).

HOW TO MAINTAIN YOUR COMPUTER SYSTEM

Learn to use system diagnostic programs. If a set didn't come with your system, obtain one. These programs help you identify and possibly solve problems before you call for technical assistance. Some system manufacturers now include diagnostic programs with their systems and ask that you run the programs before you call for help.

2 **Start a notebook that includes information on your system.** This notebook should be a single source of information about your entire system, both hardware and software. Each time you make a change to your system, adding or removing hardware or software, or when you change system parameters, you should record the change in the notebook. Items to include in the notebook are the following:

- ✔Serial numbers of all equipment and software.
- ✔Vendor support phone numbers. These numbers are often buried in user manuals. Look up these numbers once and record all of them on a single sheet of paper at the front of your notebook.
- ✔Dates when software was installed or uninstalled.
- ✔Date and vendor for each equipment and software purchase.
- ✔Notes on discussions with vendor support personnel.
- ✔A chronological history of any equipment or software problems. This history can be helpful if the problem persists and you have to call several times.

3 **Periodically review disk directories and delete unneeded files**. Files have a way of building up and can quickly use up your disk space. If you think you may need a file in the future, back it up to a floppy disk.

4 **Any time you work inside your computer turn the power off and disconnect the equipment from the power source.** In addition, before you touch anything inside the computer, touch an unpainted metal surface such as the power supply. This will discharge any static electricity that could damage internal components.

5 **Reduce the need to clean the inside of your system by keeping the surrounding area dirt and dust free.** Floppy disk cleaners are available but should be used sparingly (some owners never use them unless they experience floppy disk problems). If dust builds up inside the computer it should be carefully removed with compressed air and a small vacuum. Don't touch the components with the vacuum.

6 **Backup key files and data.** Use the operating system or a utility program to create an emergency disk to help restart the computer if it crashes. Important data files should be copied regularly to floppy disks, tape, or another computer.

Figure 38
How a virus program can be transmitted from one computer to another.

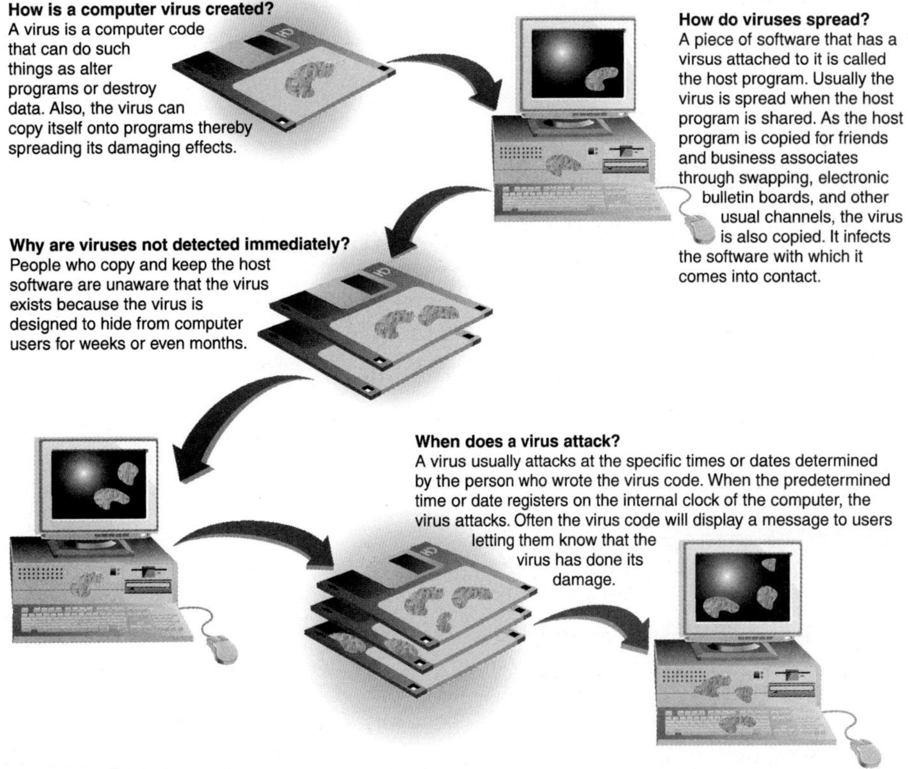

A COMPUTER VIRUS: WHAT IT IS AND HOW IT SPREADS
How is a computer virus created?
A virus is a computer code that can do such things as alter programs or destroy data. Also, the virus can copy itself onto programs thereby spreading its damaging effects.
How do viruses spread?
A piece of software that has a virsus attached to it is called the host program. Usually the virus is spread when the host program is shared. As the host program is copied for friends and business associates through swapping, electronic bulletin boards, and other usual channels, the virus is also copied. It infects the software with which it comes into contact.
Why are viruses not detected immediately?
People who copy and keep the host software are unaware that the virus exists because the virus is designed to hide from computer users for weeks or even months.
When does a virus attack?
A virus usually attacks at the specific times or dates determined by the person who wrote the virus code. When the predetermined time or date registers on the internal clock of the computer, the virus attacks. Often the virus code will display a message to users letting them know that the virus has done its damage.

Protect your system from computer viruses. Computer viruses are programs designed to *infect* computer systems by copying themselves into other computer files (Figure 38). The virus program spreads when the infected files are used by or copied to another system. On the previous page virus programs are dangerous because they are often designed to damage the files of the infected system. Protect yourself from viruses by installing an anti-virus program on your computer.

SUMMARY OF INTRODUCTION TO COMPUTERS

As you learn to use the software taught in this book, you will also become familiar with the components and operation of your computer system. When you need help understanding how the components of your system function, refer to this introduction. You can also refer to this section for information on computer communications and for guidelines when you decide to purchase a computer system of your own.

STUDENT ASSIGNMENTS

Student Assignment 1: True/False

Instructions: Circle T if the statement is true or F if the statement is false.

T F 1. A computer is an electronic device, operating under the control of instructions stored in its own memory unit, that can accept data (input), process data arithmetically and logically, produce output from the processing, and store the results for future use.

T F 2. Information refers to data processed into a form that has meaning and is useful.

T F 3. A computer program is a detailed set of instructions that tells a computer exactly what to do.

T F 4. A mouse is a communications device used to convert between digital and analog signals so telephone lines can carry data.

T F 5. The central processing unit contains the processor unit and main memory.

T F 6. A laser printer is an impact printer that provides high-quality output.

T F 7. Auxiliary storage is used to store instructions and data when they are not being used in main memory.

T F 8. A floppy disk is considered to be a form of main memory.

T F 9. CD-ROM is often used for multimedia material that combines text, graphics, video, and sound.

T F 10. The operating system tells the computer how to perform functions such as how to load, store, and execute an application program and how to transfer data between the input/output devices and main memory.

T F 11. Programs such as database management, spreadsheet, and word processing software are called system software.

T F 12. For data to be transferred from one computer to another over communications lines, communications software is required only on the sending computer.

T F 13. A communications network is a collection of computers and other equipment that use communications channels to share hardware, software, data, and information.

T F 14. Determining what applications you will use on your computer will help you to purchase a computer that is the type and size that meets your needs.

T F 15. The path the data follows as it is transmitted from the sending equipment to the receiving equipment in a communications system is called a modem.

T F 16. Computer equipment that meets the power consumption guidelines can display the *Energy Star* logo

T F 17. An on-site maintenance agreement is important if you cannot be without the use of your computer.

T F 18. An anti-virus program is used to protect your computer equipment and software.

T F 19. When purchasing a computer, consider only the price because one computer is no different from another.

T F 20. A LAN allows you to share software but not hardware.

Student Assignments 2: Multiple Choice

Instructions: Circle the correct response.

1 The four operations performed by a computer include _________.
a. input, control, output, and storage
b. interface, processing, output, and memory
c. input, output, processing, and storage
d. input, logical/rational, arithmetic, and output

2. A hand-held input device that controls the cursor location is _________.
a. the cursor control keyboard
b. a mouse
c. a modem
d. the CRT

3. A printer that forms images without striking the paper is _________.
a. an impact printer
b. a nonimpact printer.
c. an inkjet printer
d. both b and c

4. The amount of storage provided by a floppy disk is a function of _________.
a. the thickness of the floppy disk
b. the recording density of bits on the track
c. the number of recording tracks on the floppy disk
d. both b and c

5. Portable computers use a flat panel screen called _________.
a. a multichrome monitor
b. a cathode ray tube
c. a liquid crystal display
d. a monochrome monitor

6. When not in use, floppy disks should be _________.
a. stored away from magnetic fields
b. stored away from heat and direct sunlight
c. stored in a floppy disk box or cabinet
d. all of the above

7. CD-ROM is a type of _________.
a. main memory
b. auxiliary storage
c. communications equipment
d. system software

8. An operating system is considered part of _________.
a. word processing software
b. database software
c. system software
d. spreadsheet software

9. The type of application software most commonly used to create and print documents is _________.
a. word processing b. electronic spreadsheet c. database d. none of the above

10. The type of application software most commonly used to send messages to and receive messages from other computer users is _________.
a. electronic mail b. database c. presentation graphics d. none of the above

Student Assignment 3: Comparing Personal Computer Advertisements

Instructions: Obtain a copy of a recent computer magazine and review the advertisements for desktop personal computer systems. Compare ads for the least and most expensive desktop systems you can find. Discuss the differences.

Student Assignment 4: Evaluating On-Line Information Services

Instructions: Prodigy and America On-Line both offer consumer oriented on-line information services. Contact each company and request each to send you information on the specific services it offers. Try to talk to someone who actually uses one or both of the services. Discuss how each service is priced and the differences between the two on-line services.

Student Assignment 5: Visiting Local Computer Retail Stores

Instructions: Visit local computer retail stores and compare the various types of computers and support equipment available. Ask about warranties, repair services, hardware setup, training, and related issues. Report on the knowledge of the sales staff assisting you and their willingness to answer your questions. Does the store have standard hardware packages, or are they willing to configure a system to your specific needs? Would you feel confident buying a computer from this store?

INDEX

PHOTO CREDITS

Figure 1, C-1 Photography; (A) Tony Stone Images-John Riley; (B) The Gamma Liason Network-James P. Wilson; (C) The National Institute of Industrial Ownership, Frederic Pitchal-Sygma; (D) Tony Stone-Images-Kevin Horan; (E) Gamma Liason, Shahn Kermani-Tot-Tech Computers; (F) Comshare; (G) Steve Reneker; (H) International Business Machines Corp.; (I) Sygma; Figure 2, Scott R. Goodwin Inc.; Figure 3, Tony Stone Images-Mitch Kezar; Figure 4, Scott R. Goodwin,Inc.; Figure; 5, Epson (Manning, Selvege & Lee); Figure 6, Comshare; Figure 7, Comshare; Figure 8, Scott R. Goodwin Inc.; Figure 10, Hewlett Packard; Figure 11, Hewlett Packard; Figure 12, NEC Technology, Multisync; Figure 13, International Business Machines Corp.; Figure 15, Jerry Spagnoli; Figure 16, Greg Hadel; Figure 19, Jerry Spagnoli; Figure 20, Microscience International Corp.; Figure 21, 3M Corp.; Illustrations, Greg Herrington, Stephanie Nance.

PROJECT ONE

Fundamentals of Using Windows 95

Objectives:

You will have mastered the material in this project when you can:

- Describe Microsoft Windows 95
- Describe a user interface
- Identify the objects on the Microsoft Windows 95 desktop
- Perform the basic mouse operations: point, click, right-click, double-click, drag, and right-drag
- Open a Windows 95 window
- Maximize, minimize, and restore a Windows 95 window
- Close a Windows 95 window
- Resize a window
- Scroll in a window
- Move a window on the Windows 95 desktop
- Understand keyboard shortcut notation
- Start an application program
- Create a written document
- Save a document on disk
- Print a document
- Close an application program
- Modify a document stored on disk
- Use Windows 95 Help
- Shut down Windows 95

PROJECT TWO

Using Windows Explorer

Objectives:

You will have mastered the material in this project when you can:

- Start Windows Explorer
- Understand the elements of the Exploring – My Computer window
- Display the contents of a folder
- Expand and collapse a folder
- Change the view
- Select and copy one file or a group of files
- Create, rename, and delete a folder
- Rename and delete a file

A $14 Billion Mistake

Digital Research officials would not yield to IBM's demands

Have you ever missed a meeting you should have attended but something else was more important? Did you lose $14 billion dollars because you were absent? Gary Kildall might have.

In the 1970s, Kildall's company, Digital Research, had developed an operating system called CP/M that was used on most microcomputers except the Apple II. Kildall was a leader in the microcomputer software business. Then, in 1980, IBM came calling.

Having decided to build a personal computer, IBM approached Bill Gates, president of a small company called Microsoft, in Redmond, Washington, to create the operating system. Gates demurred, suggesting IBM contact Kildall.

MICROSOFT

MS-DOS

Bill Gates

SEATTLE COMPUTER PRODUCTS

When IBM arrived for the meeting in Pacific Grove, California, Kildall was off flying his airplane. The reasons are not entirely clear. Some say Kildall was a free spirit and not inclined to do business with the monolithic IBM. Kildall claimed he was flying to another important meeting.

Without Kildall at the meeting, IBM insisted on knowing everything about CP/M while disclosing nothing about its new computer. Fearing IBM would steal their secrets, Digital Research officials would not yield to IBM's demands. Rebuffed, IBM scurried back to Gates.

Sensing an opportunity, Gates agreed to provide an operating system to IBM even though he had no idea how. It just so happened, however, that a small company named Seattle Computer Products, almost next door to Microsoft, was writing an operating system called QDOS v0.110 (QDOS stood for Quick and Dirty Operating System).

Gates learned of QDOS and approached Seattle Computer Products to ask if the operating system was for sale. For a few favors and a little money, Microsoft, in December 1980, acquired non-exclusive rights to QDOS. Later, Microsoft acquired all rights and renamed the operating system MS-DOS. Seattle Computer Products received about $1 million.

Microsoft made substantial changes to MS-DOS and when IBM announced its personal computer in August 1981, MS-DOS was the operating system. The IBM machine was an instant hit. Microsoft sold millions of copies of MS-DOS and grew to be the largest software company in the world. Bill Gates became the world's richest man, with assets in excess of $14 billion dollars.

And Gary Kildall? He continued to develop software at Digital Research. Eventually, Digital Research was sold to Novell, Inc. In the summer of 1994, Kildall died. He left a legacy as an early pioneer who made a significant contribution to microcomputing, but perhaps his most memorable act was missing a meeting.

QDOS

```
Enter today's date (m-d-y): 8-4-1981

The IBM Personal Computer DOS
Version 1.00 (C)Copyright IBM Corp 1981

A>
```

Courtesy of Tim Paterson, reprinted by permission of Microsoft Corporation.

The Microsoft Disk Operating System, or MS-DOS, was shipped as PC-DOS on the original IBM Personal Computer and later with many IBM compatible machines. Like other operating systems, MS-DOS oversees all the functions of a computer. Various upgrades to MS-DOS and further product refinements led to the release of Windows, an operating system that uses a graphical user interface. Microsoft's current version of Windows, released in August of 1995, is called Windows 95.

CP/M

Gary Kildall

Digital Research

Microsoft sold millions of copies of MS-DOS and grew to be the largest software company in the world

Microsoft
Windows 95

Fundamentals of Using Windows 95

Case Perspective

Need: Each day millions of Windows 95 users turn on their computers, whether at home, in the office, at school, on an airplane, or at the beach. When the computer starts, the first image on the monitor is the Windows 95 desktop. If these users did not know how to start application programs from the desktop, manipulate files and images on the desktop, and preserve the work accomplished, their computers would be useless. You have just acquired a computer containing Windows 95. Your task is to learn the basics of Windows 95 so your computer will be useful to you.

Introduction

An **operating system** is the set of computer instructions, called a computer program, that controls the allocation of computer hardware such as memory, disk devices, printers, and CD-ROM drives, and provides the capability for you to communicate with your computer. The most popular and widely used operating system for personal computers is **Microsoft Windows. Microsoft Windows 95** (called Windows 95 for the rest of this book), the newest version of Microsoft Windows, allows you to easily communicate with and control your computer. Windows 95 is easier to use and more efficient than previous versions of Windows and can be customized to fit individual needs. Windows 95 simplifies the process of working with documents and applications, transferring data between documents, and organizing the manner in which you interact with your computer.

In Project 1, you will learn about Windows 95 and how to use the Windows 95 user interface.

Microsoft Windows 95

Microsoft Windows 95 is an operating system that performs every function necessary for you to communicate with and use your computer. Unlike previous versions of Windows, no associated operating system is required. Windows 95 is called a **32-bit operating system** because it uses 32 bits for addressing and other purposes, which means the operating system can address more than four gigabytes of RAM and perform tasks faster than older operating systems.

Windows 95 is designed to be compatible with all existing **application programs**, which are programs that perform an application-related function such as word processing. To use the application programs that can be executed under Windows 95, you must know about the Windows 95 user interface.

What Is a User Interface?

A **user interface** is the combination of hardware and software that you use to communicate with and control your computer. Through the user interface, you are able to make selections on your computer, request information from your computer, and respond to messages displayed by your computer. Thus, a user interface provides the means for dialogue between you and your computer.

Hardware and software together form the user interface. Among the hardware devices associated with a user interface are the monitor, keyboard, and mouse (Figure 1-1) The monitor displays messages and provides information. You respond by entering data in the form of a command or other response using the keyboard or mouse. Among the responses available to you are responses that specify what application program to run, what document to open, when to print, and where to store data for future use.

The computer software associated with the user interface consists of the programs that engage you in dialogue (Figure 1-1). The computer software determines the messages you receive, the manner in which you should respond, and the actions that occur based on your responses.

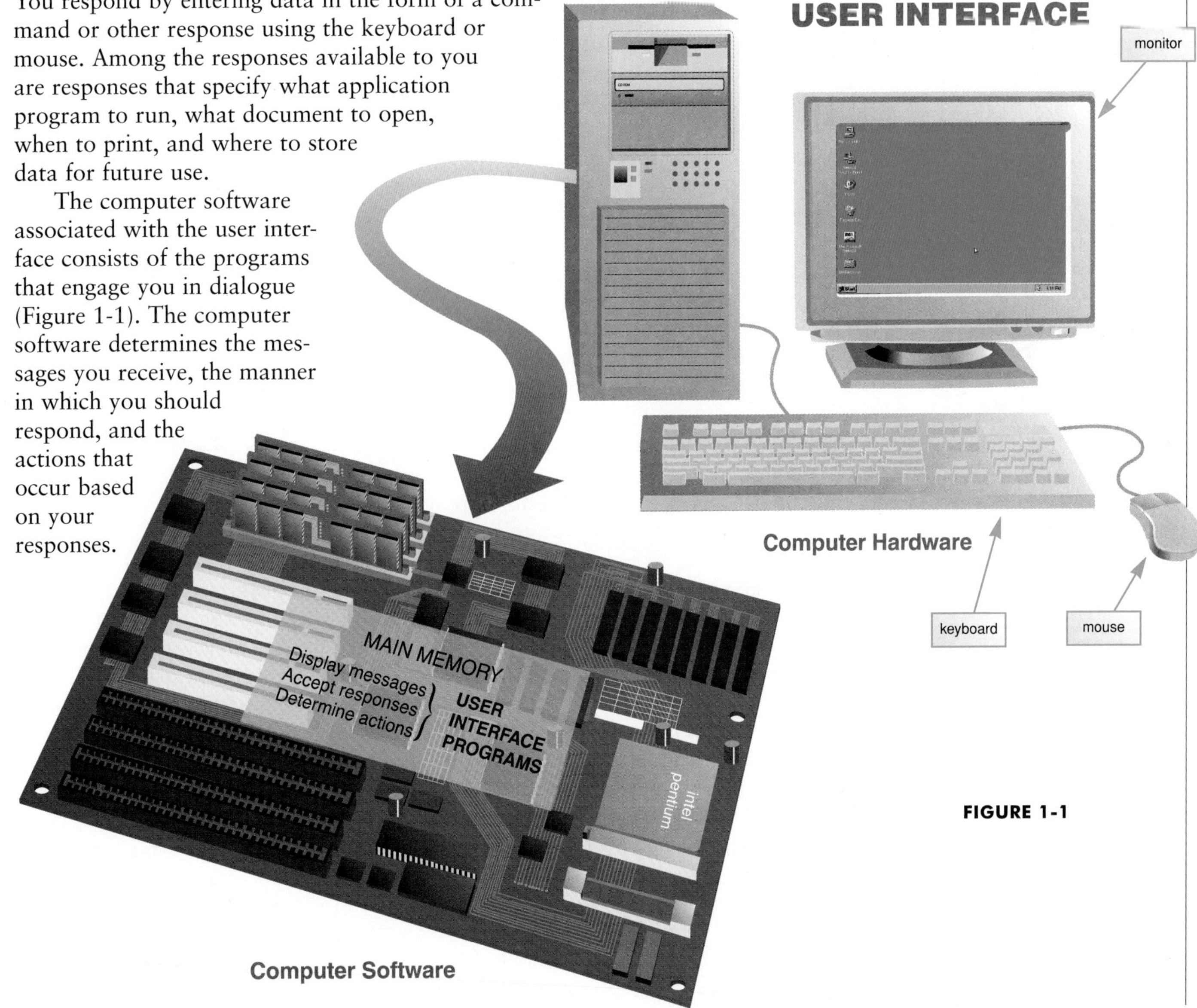

FIGURE 1-1

The goal of an effective user interface is to be **user friendly**, meaning that the software can be used easily by individuals with limited training. Research studies have indicated that the use of graphics can play an important role in aiding users to interact effectively with a computer. A **graphical user interface**, or **GUI** (pronounced gooey), is a user interface that displays graphics in addition to text when it communicates with the user.

FIGURE 1-2

The Windows 95 graphical user interface was carefully designed to be easier to set up, simpler to learn, and faster and more powerful than previous versions of Microsoft Windows.

Starting Microsoft Windows 95

When you turn on your computer, an introductory screen consisting of the Windows 95 logo and the Microsoft Windows 95 name displays on a blue sky and clouds background (Figure 1-2).

The screen clears and several items display on a background called the **desktop**. The default color of the desktop background is green, but your computer may display a different color. Your screen might display as shown in Figure 1-3. It also might display without the Welcome screen shown in Figure 1-3.

The items on the desktop in Figure 1-3 include six icons and their names on the left of the desktop, the Welcome screen in the center of the desktop, and the taskbar at the bottom of the desktop. Through the use of the six **icons**, you can view the contents of your computer (**My Computer**), work with other computers connected to your computer (**Network Neighborhood**), receive and send electronic faxes and mail (e-mail) from or to other computers (**Inbox**), discard unneeded objects (**Recycle Bin**), connect to the Microsoft online service (**The Microsoft Network**), and transfer data to and from a portable computer (**My Briefcase**). Your computer's desktop might contain more, fewer, or some different icons because the desktop of your computer can be customized.

The Welcome screen that might display on your desktop is shown in Figure 1-3. The **title bar**, which is dark blue in color at the top of the screen, identifies the name of the screen (Welcome) and contains the Close button, which can be used to close the Welcome screen. In the Welcome screen, a welcome message (Welcome to Windows 95) displays together with a helpful tip for using Windows 95, a check box containing a check mark, and several command buttons. The **check box** represents an option to display the Welcome screen each time Windows 95 starts that you can turn on or turn off. The **command buttons** allow you to perform different operations such as displaying the next tip or closing the screen.

Below the screen is the mouse pointer. On the desktop, the **mouse pointer** is the shape of a block arrow. The mouse pointer allows you to point to items on the desktop.

More *About* the Windows 95 Interface

Thousands of hours were spent developing the Windows 95 graphical user interface. Of tremendous importance in the development were Microsoft's usability labs, where everyone from raw beginners to experts interacted with many different versions of the interface. The taskbar and other significant features of the interface emerged from the experiences in these labs.

The **taskbar** at the bottom of the screen in Figure 1-3 contains the Start button, the Welcome button, and the Tray status area. The **Start button** provides an entry point to begin using the features of Windows 95, the Welcome button indicates the Welcome screen is open on the desktop, and the current time (6:06 PM) displays in the Tray status area.

Nearly every item on the Windows 95 desktop is considered an object. Even the desktop itself is an object. Every **object** has properties. The **properties** of an object are unique to that specific object and may affect what can be done to the object or what the object does. For example, the properties of an object may be the color of the object, such as the color of the desktop.

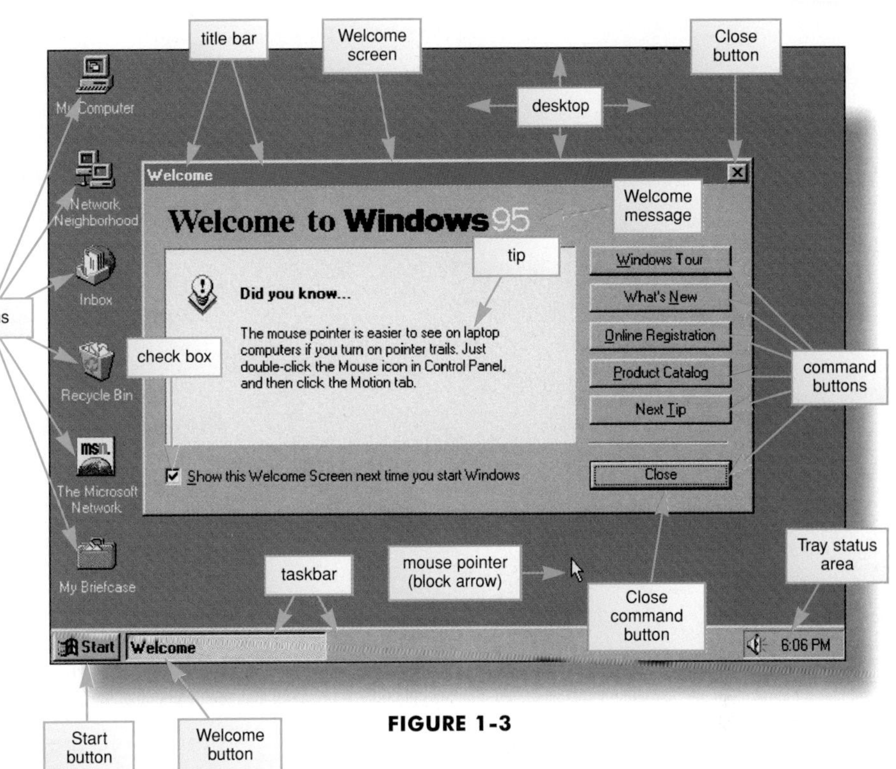

FIGURE 1-3

Closing the Welcome Screen

As noted, the Welcome screen might display when you start Windows 95. If the Welcome screen does display on the desktop, normally you should close it prior to beginning any other operations using Windows 95. To close the Welcome screen, complete the following step.

TO CLOSE THE WELCOME SCREEN

Step 1: Press the ESC key on the keyboard as shown in Figure 1-4.

The Welcome screen closes.

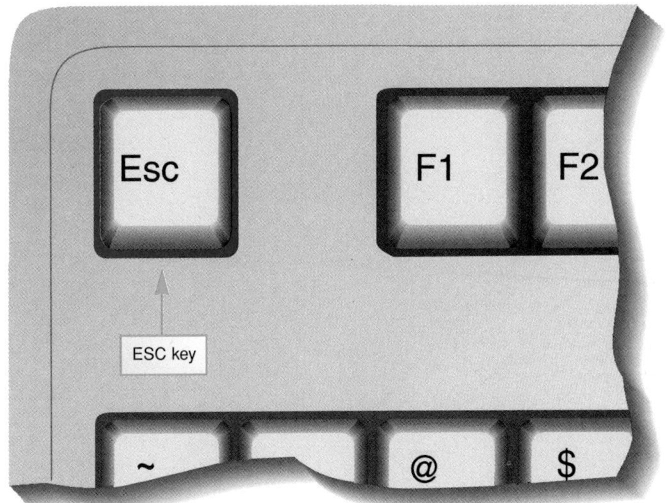

FIGURE 1-4

The Desktop as a Work Area

The Windows 95 desktop and the objects on the desktop were designed to emulate a work area in an office or at home. The Windows desktop may be thought of as an electronic version of the top of your desk. You can move objects around on the desktop, look at them and then put them aside, and so on. In Project 1, you will learn how to interact with and communicate with the Windows 95 desktop.

More *About* the Mouse

The mouse, though invented in the 1960's, was not widely used until the Apple Macintosh computer became available in 1984. Even then, some high-brows called mouse users "wimps." Today, the mouse is an indispensable tool for every computer user.

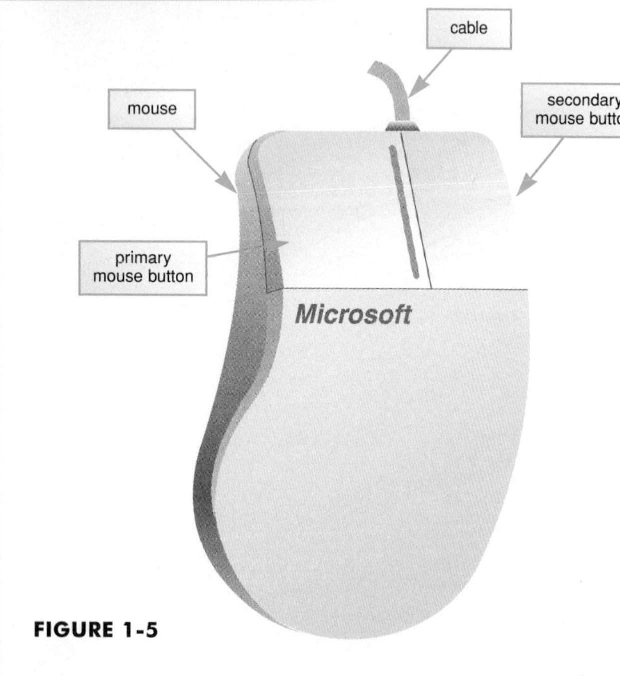

FIGURE 1-5

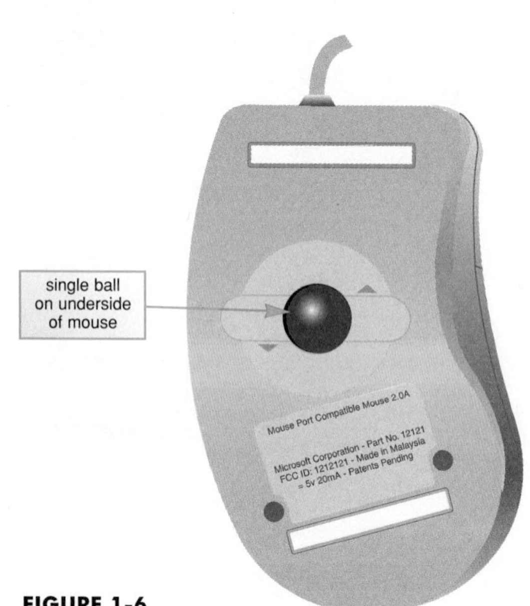

FIGURE 1-6

Communicating with Microsoft Windows 95

The Windows 95 interface provides the means for dialogue between you and your computer. Part of this dialogue involves your requesting information from your computer and responding to messages displayed by your computer. You can request information and respond to messages using either a mouse or a keyboard.

Mouse Operations

A **mouse** is a pointing device used with Windows 95 that is attached to the computer by a cable. It contains two buttons — the primary mouse button and the secondary mouse button (Figure 1-5). The **primary mouse button** is typically the left mouse button and the **secondary mouse button** is typically the right mouse button although Windows 95 allows you to switch them. In this book, the left mouse button is the primary mouse button and the right mouse button is the secondary mouse button.

Using the mouse, you can perform the following operations: (1) point; (2) click; (3) right-click; (4) double-click; (5) drag; and (6) right-drag. These operations are demonstrated on the following pages.

Point and Click

Point means you move the mouse across a flat surface until the mouse pointer rests on the item of choice on the desktop. As you move the mouse across a flat surface, the movement of a ball on the underside of the mouse (Figure 1-6) is electronically sensed, and the mouse pointer moves across the desktop in the same direction.

Click means you press and release the primary mouse button, which in this book is the left mouse button. In most cases, you must point to an item before you click. To become acquainted with the use of a mouse, perform the following steps to point to and click various objects on the desktop.

Steps To Point and Click

1 Point to the Start button on the taskbar by moving the mouse across a flat surface until the mouse pointer rests on the Start button.

The mouse pointer points to the Start button and a ***ToolTip*** *(Click here to begin) displays (Figure 1-7). The ToolTip, which provides instructions, displays on the desktop for approximately five seconds.*

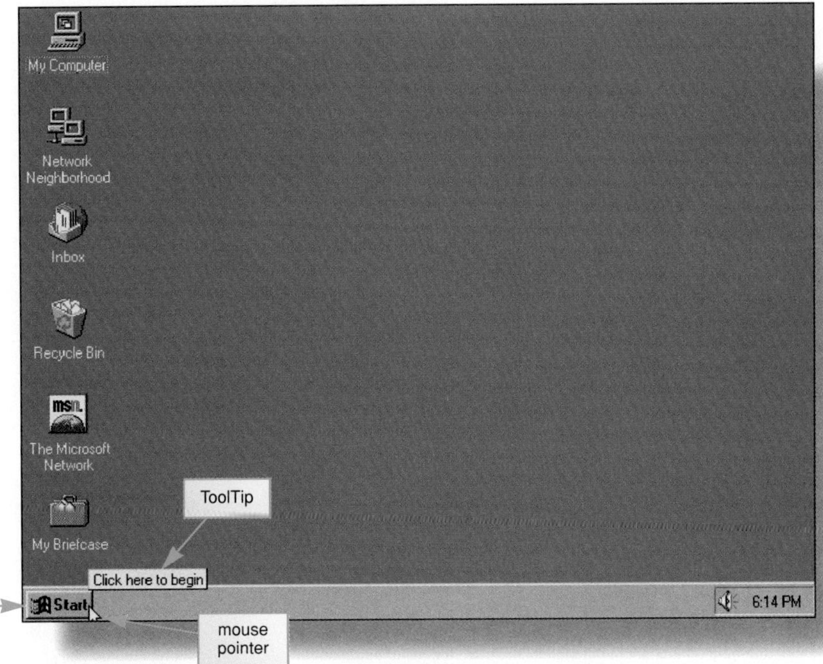

FIGURE 1-7

2 Click the Start button on the taskbar by pressing and releasing the left mouse button.

Windows 95 opens the ***Start menu*** *and indents the Start button (Figure 1-8). A* ***menu*** *is a list of related commands. Nine commands display on the Start menu. A* ***command*** *directs Windows 95 to perform a specific action such as opening another menu or shutting down the operating system. Each command consists of an icon and a command name. Some commands (Run and Shut Down) are followed by an* ***ellipsis*** *(...) to indicate Windows 95 requires more information before executing the command. Other commands (Programs, Documents, Settings, and Find) are followed by a* ***right arrow****. A right arrow indicates that pointing to the command will open a submenu containing more commands.*

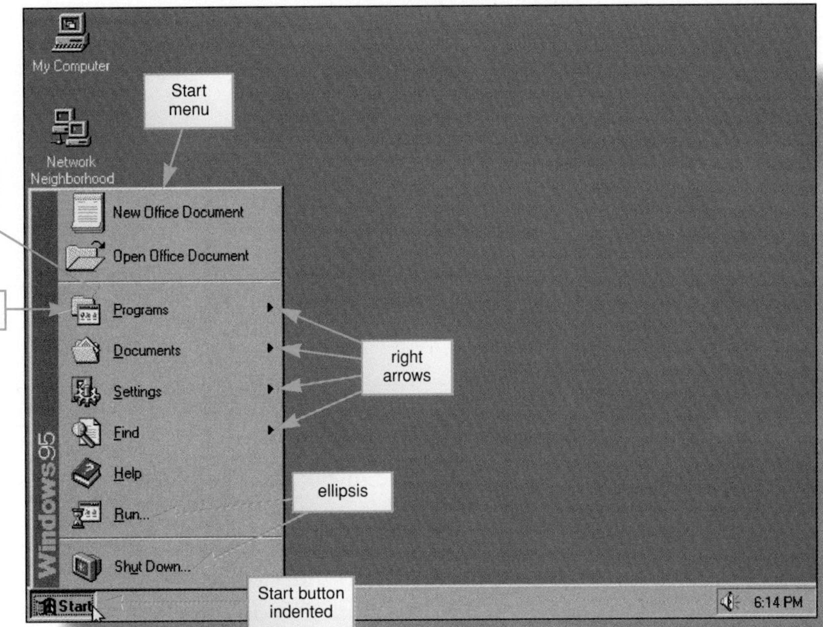

FIGURE 1-8

3 **Point to Programs on the Start menu.**

*When you point to Programs, Windows 95 highlights the Programs command on the Start menu and opens the **Programs submenu** (Figure 1-9). A **submenu** is a menu that displays when you point to a command that is followed by a right arrow.*

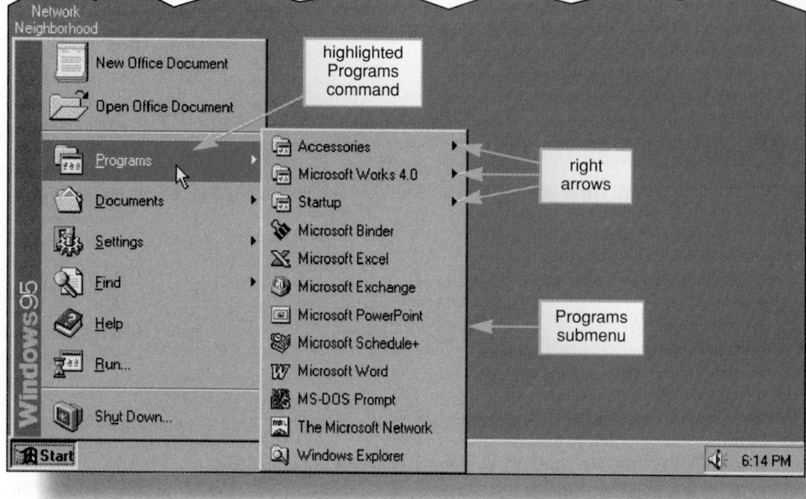

FIGURE 1-9

4 **Point to an open area of the desktop and then click the open area of the desktop.**

Windows 95 closes the Start menu and the Programs submenu (Figure 1-10). The mouse pointer points to the desktop. To close a menu anytime, click anywhere on the desktop except the menu itself. The Start button is not indented.

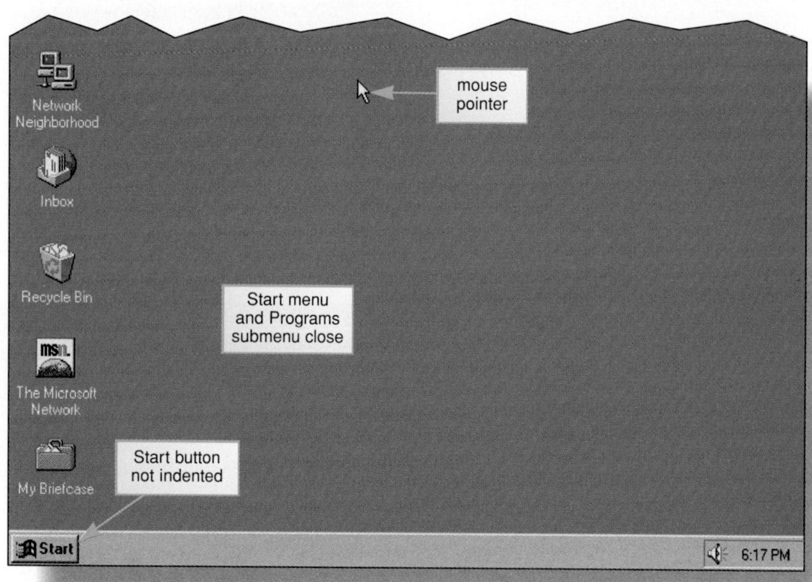

FIGURE 1-10

More *About* Buttons

Buttons on the desktop and in programs are in integral part of Windows 95. When you point to them, their function displays in a ToolTip. When you click them, they appear to indent on the screen to mimic what would happen if you pushed an actual button. All buttons in Windows 95 behave in the same manner.

Notice in Figure 1-9 that whenever you point to a command on a menu, the command is highlighted.

When you click an object such as the Start button in Figure 1-8 on the previous page, you must point to the object before you click. In the steps that follow, the instruction that directs you to point to a particular item and then click is, Click the particular item. For example, Click the Start button, means point to the Start button and then click.

Right-Click

Right-click means you press and release the secondary mouse button, which in this book is the right mouse button. As when you use the primary mouse button, normally you will point to an object on the screen prior to right-clicking. Perform the following steps to right-click the desktop.

Steps To Right-Click

1 Point to an open area on the desktop and press and release the right mouse button.

Windows 95 displays a context-sensitive menu containing six commands (Figure 1-11). Right-clicking an object, such as the desktop, opens a ***context-sensitive menu*** *(also referred to as a* ***shortcut menu*** *or an* ***object menu****) that contains a set of commands specifically for use with that object. The Paste command in Figure 1-11 is dimmed, meaning that command cannot be used at the current time.*

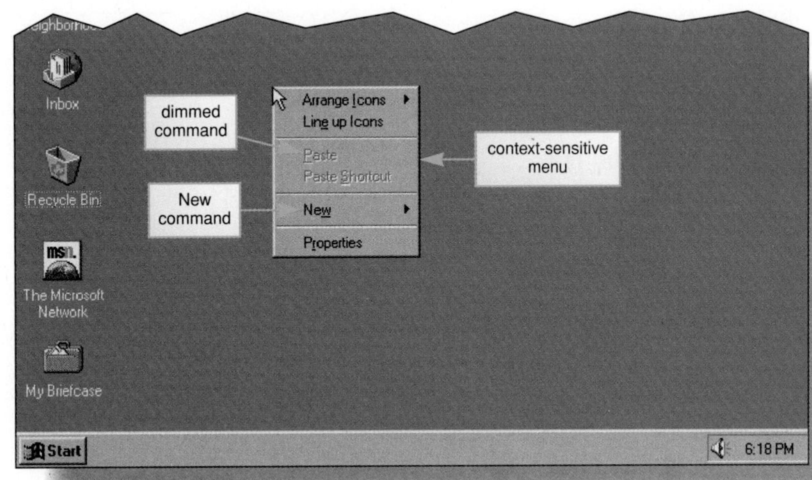

FIGURE 1-11

2 Point to New on the context-sensitive menu.

When you move the mouse pointer to the New command, Windows 95 highlights the New command and opens the ***New submenu*** *(Figure 1-12). The New submenu contains a variety of commands. The number of commands and the actual commands that display on your computer might be different.*

3 Point to an open area of the desktop and click the open area to remove the context-sensitive menu and the New submenu.

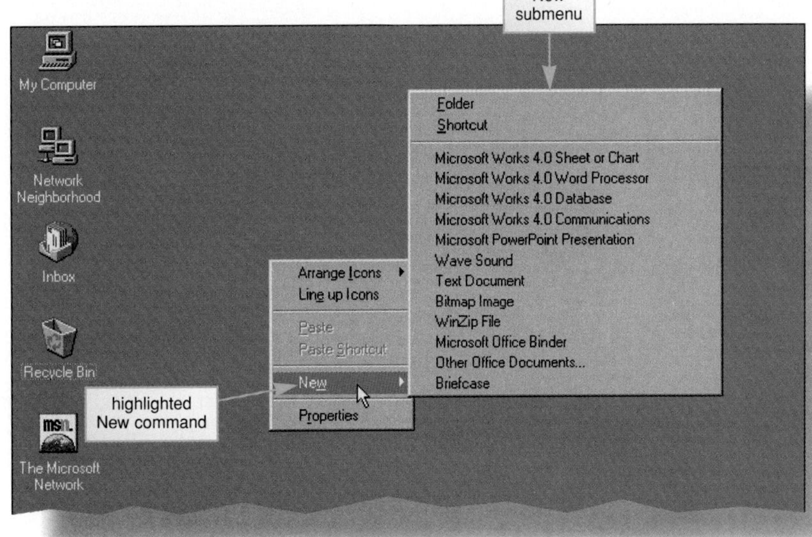

FIGURE 1-12

Whenever you right-click an object, a context-sensitive, or shortcut, menu will display. As you will see, the use of shortcut menus speeds up your work and adds flexibility to your interface with the computer.

Double-Click

Double-click means you quickly press and release the left mouse button twice without moving the mouse. In most cases, you must point to an item before you double-click. Perform the step on the next page to open the My Computer window on the desktop by double-clicking the My Computer icon.

Steps To Open a Window by Double-Clicking

1 Point to the My Computer icon on the desktop and double-click by quickly pressing and releasing the left mouse button twice without moving the mouse.

Windows 95 opens the My Computer window and adds the My Computer button to the taskbar (Figure 1-13). The My Computer window is the active window. The ***active window*** *is the window currently being used. Whenever you double-click an object that can be opened, Windows 95 will open the object; and the open object will be identified by a button on the taskbar. The active window is identified by the indented button.*

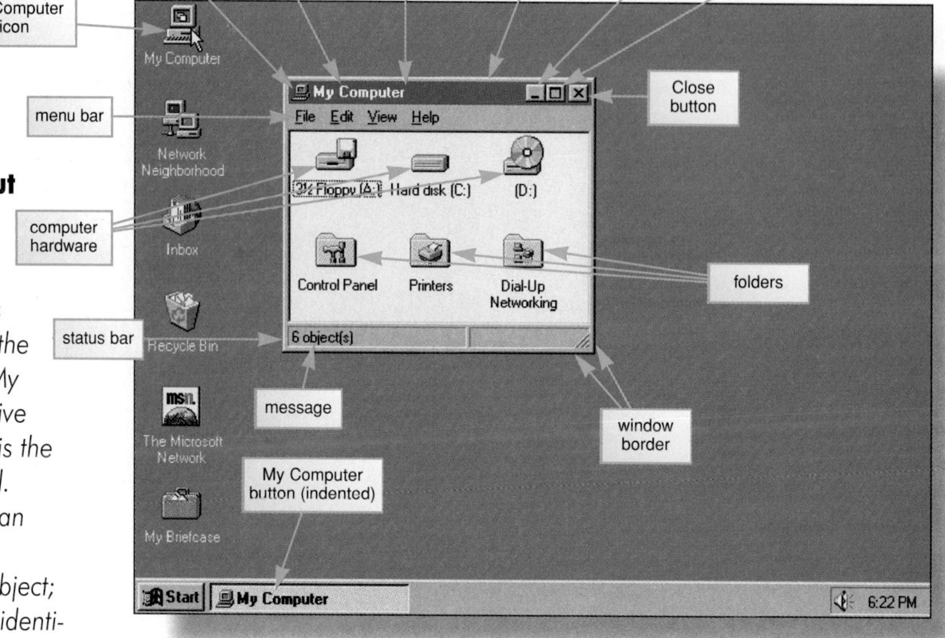

FIGURE 1-13

More About Double-Clicking

Double-clicking is the most difficult mouse skill to learn. Many people have a tendency to move the mouse before they click a second time, even when they do not want to move the mouse. You should find, however, that with a little practice double-clicking becomes quite natural.

More About My Computer

The trade press and media have poked fun at the icon name, My Computer. One wag said no one should use Windows 95 for more than five minutes without changing the name (which is easily done). Microsoft responds that in its usability labs, My Computer was the most easily understood name by beginning computer users.

My Computer Window

The thin line, or **window border**, surrounding the My Computer window in Figure 1-13 determines its shape and size. The **title bar** at the top of the window contains a small icon that is the same as the icon on the desktop and the **window title** (My Computer) that identifies the window. The color of the title bar (dark blue) and the indented My Computer button on the taskbar indicate the My Computer window is the active window. The color of the active window on your computer might be different from the dark blue color.

Clicking the icon at the left on the title bar will open the Control menu, which contains commands to carry out actions associated with the My Computer window. At the right on the title bar are three buttons, the Minimize button, the Maximize button, and the Close button, that can be used to specify the size of the window and can close the window.

The **menu bar**, a horizontal bar below the title bar of a window (see Figure 1-13), contains a list of menu names for the My Computer window: File, Edit, View, and Help. One letter in each menu name is underlined. You can open a menu by clicking the menu name on the menu bar.

Six icons display in the My Computer window. A name below each icon identifies the icon. The three icons in the top row represent a 3½ floppy disk drive (3½ Floppy [A:]), a hard disk drive (Hard disk [C:]), and a CD-ROM drive ([D:]). The contents of the My Computer window on your computer might be different than shown in Figure 1-13.

The icons in the second row are folders. A **folder** is an object created to contain related documents, applications, and other folders. A folder in Windows 95 contains items in much the same way a folder on your desk contains items. If you double-click a folder, the items within the folder display in a window. A message at the left of the **status bar** located at the bottom of the window indicates the window contains six objects (see Figure 1-13).

Minimize Button

Two buttons on the title bar of a window, the Minimize button and the Maximize button, allow you to control the way a window displays or does not display on the desktop. When you click the **Minimize button** (see Figure 1-13), the My Computer window no longer displays on the desktop and the indented My Computer button on the taskbar changes to a non-indented button. A minimized window or application program is still open but it does not display on the screen. To minimize and then redisplay the My Computer window, complete the following steps.

More About Minimizing Windows

Window management on the Windows 95 desktop is important in order to keep the desktop uncluttered. You will find yourself frequently minimizing windows, and then later reopening them with a click of a button on the taskbar.

Steps To Minimize and Redisplay a Window

1 Point to the Minimize button on the title bar of the My Computer window.

The mouse pointer points to the Minimize button on the My Computer window title bar (Figure 1-14). The My Computer button on the taskbar is indented.

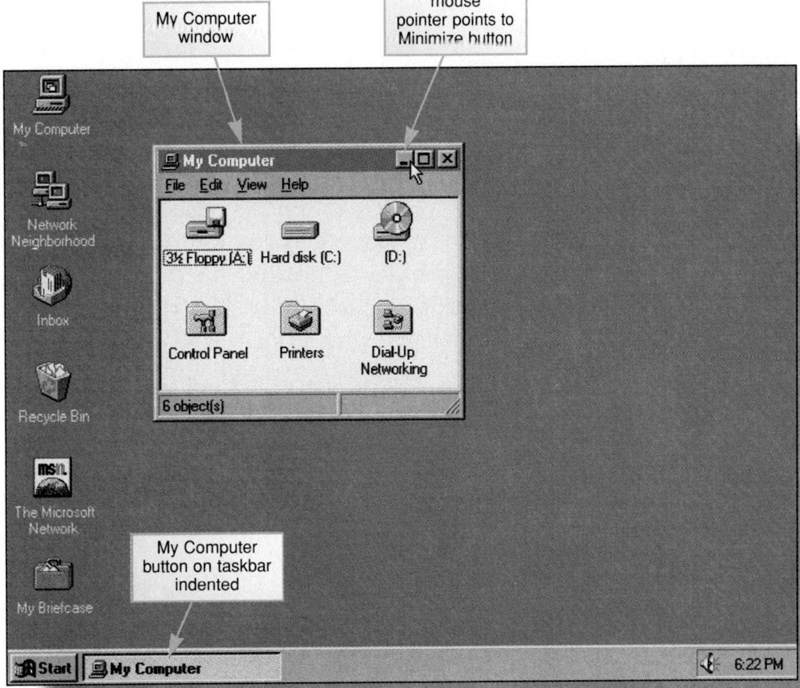

FIGURE 1-14

2 Click the Minimize button.

The My Computer window disappears from the desktop and the My Computer button on the taskbar changes to a non-indented button (Figure 1-15).

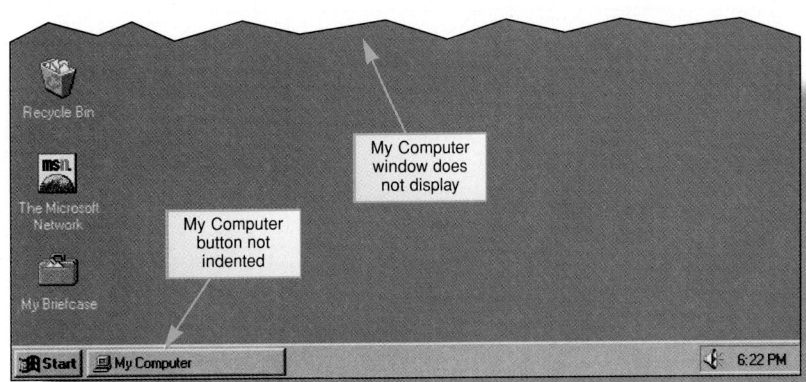

FIGURE 1-15

3 **Click the My Computer button on the taskbar.**

The My Computer window displays on the desktop in the same place and size as before it was minimized (Figure 1-16). In addition, the My Computer window is the active window because it contains the dark blue title bar and the My Computer button on the taskbar is indented.

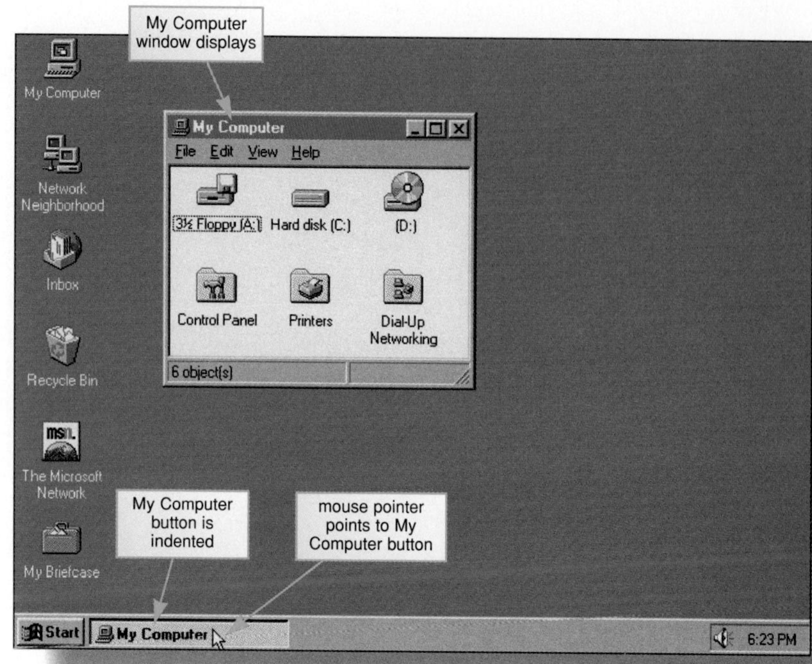

FIGURE 1-16

More *About* Maximizing Windows

Many application programs run in a maximized window by default. Often you will find that you want to work with maximized windows.

Whenever a window is minimized, it does not display on the desktop but a non-indented button for the window does display on the taskbar. Whenever you want a window that has been minimized to display and be the active window, click the window's button on the taskbar.

Maximize and Restore Buttons

The **Maximize button** maximizes a window so the window fills the entire screen, making it easier to see the contents of the window. When a window is maximized, the **Restore button** replaces the Maximize button on the title bar. Clicking the Restore button will return the window to its size before maximizing. To maximize and restore the My Computer window, complete the following steps.

Steps To Maximize and Restore a Window

1 **Point to the Maximize button on the title bar of the My Computer window.**

The mouse pointer points to the Maximize button on the title bar of the My Computer window (Figure 1-17).

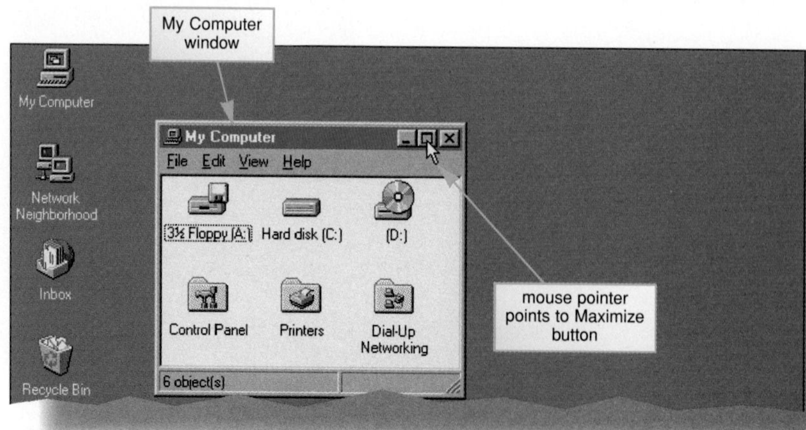

FIGURE 1-17

2 **Click the Maximize button.**

The My Computer window expands so it and the taskbar fill the entire screen (Figure 1-18). The Restore button replaces the Maximize button. The My Computer button on the taskbar does not change. The My Computer window is still the active window.

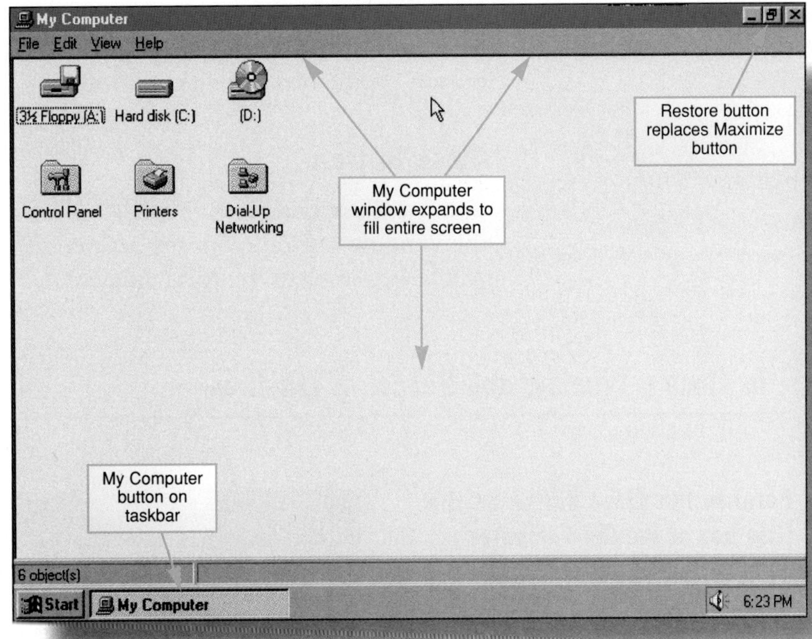

FIGURE 1-18

3 **Point to the Restore button on the title bar of the My Computer window.**

The mouse pointer points to the Restore button on the title bar of the My Computer window (Figure 1-19).

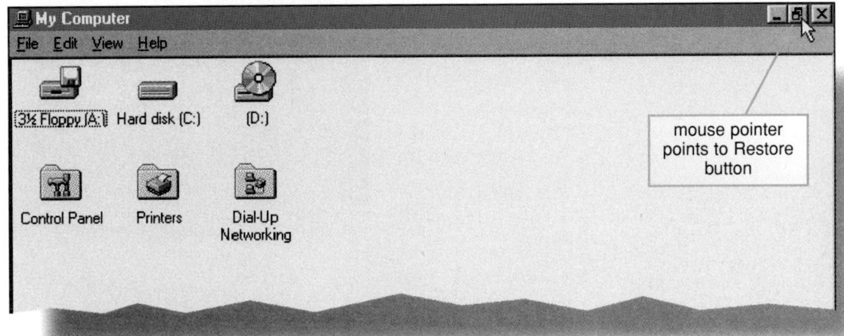

FIGURE 1-19

4 **Click the Restore button.**

The My Computer window returns to the size and position it occupied before being maximized (Figure 1-20). The My Computer button on the taskbar does not change. The Maximize button replaces the Restore button.

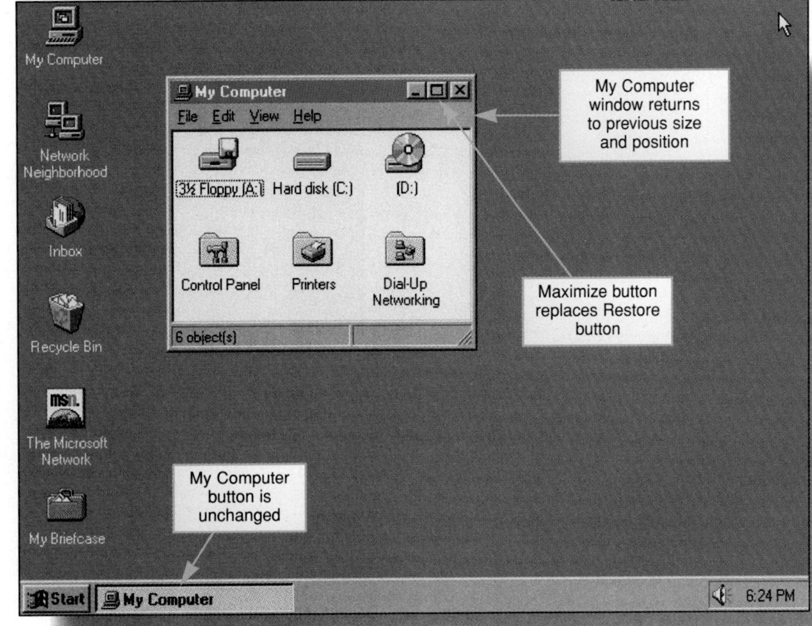

FIGURE 1-20

More About the Close Button

The Close button is a new innovation for Windows 95. In previous versions of Windows, the user had to either double-click a button or click a command from a menu to close the window.

When a window is maximized, you can also minimize the window by clicking the Minimize button. If, after minimizing the window, you click the window button on the taskbar, the window will return to its maximized size.

Close Button

The **Close button** on the title bar of a window closes the window and removes the window button from the taskbar. To close and then reopen the My Computer window, complete the following steps.

Steps To Close a Window and Reopen a Window

1. **Point to the Close button on the title bar of the My Computer window.**

   The mouse pointer points to the Close button on the title bar of the My Computer window (Figure 1-21).

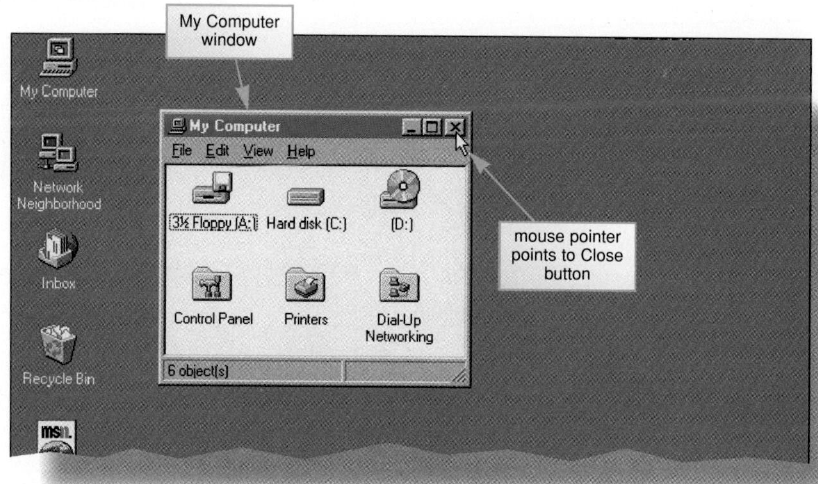

FIGURE 1-21

2. **Click the Close button.**

   The My Computer window closes and the My Computer button no longer displays on the taskbar (Figure 1-22).

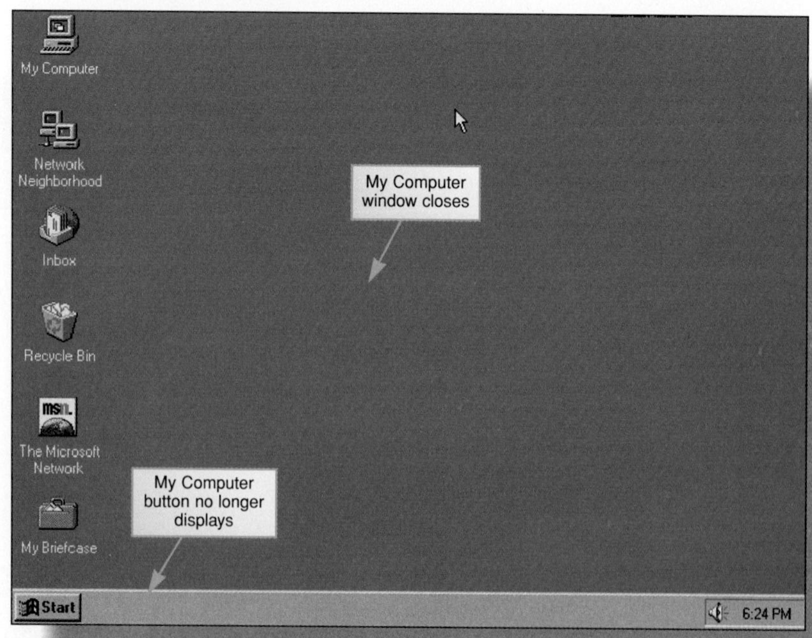

FIGURE 1-22

3 Point to and double-click the My Computer icon on the desktop.

The My Computer window opens and displays on the screen (Figure 1-23). The My Computer button displays on the taskbar.

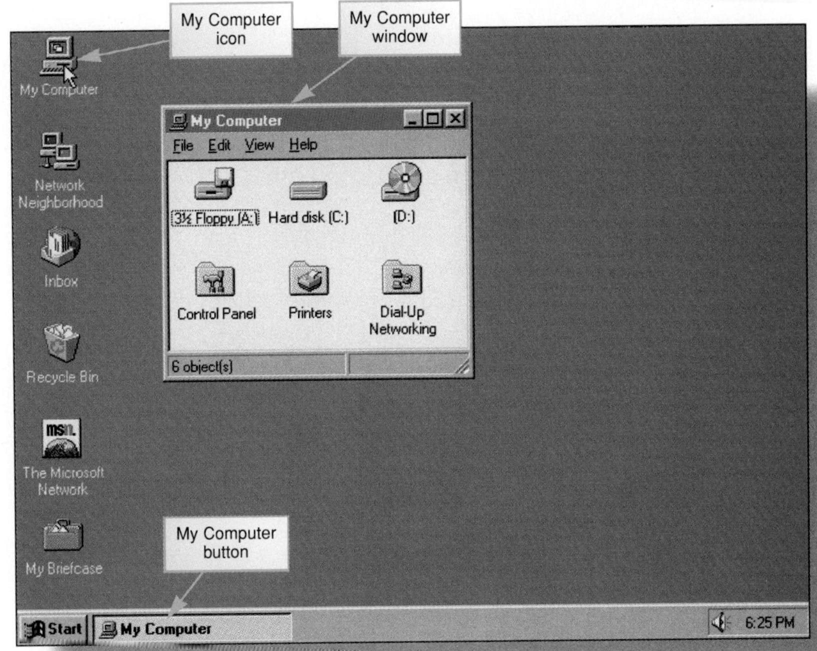

FIGURE 1-23

Drag

Drag means you point to an item, hold down the left mouse button, move the item to the desired location on the screen, and then release the left mouse button. You can move any open window to another location on the desktop by pointing to the title bar of the window and dragging the window. To drag the My Computer window, perform the following steps.

More About Dragging

Dragging is the second-most difficult skill to learn with a mouse. You may want to practice dragging a few times so you are comfortable with it.

To Move an Object by Dragging

1 Point to the My Computer window title bar.

The mouse pointer points to the My Computer window title bar (Figure 1-24).

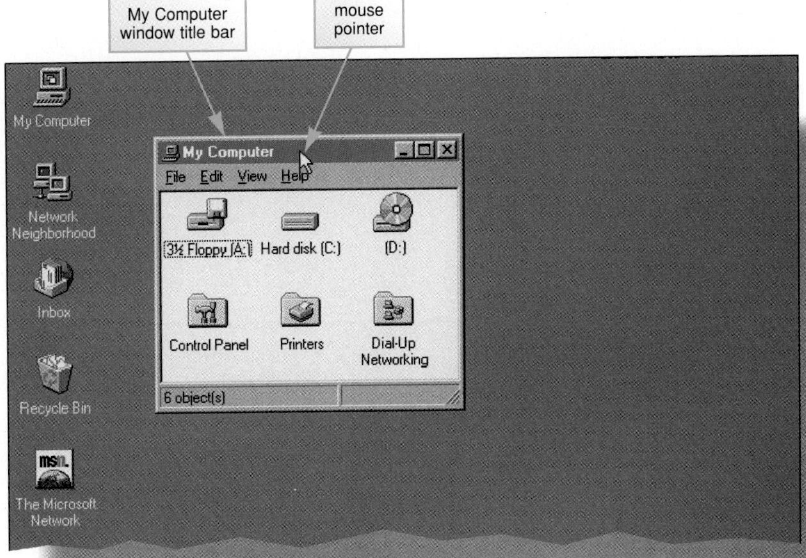

FIGURE 1-24

2 **Hold down the left mouse button and then move the mouse so the window outline moves to the center of the desktop (do not release the left mouse button).**

As you drag the My Computer window, Windows 95 displays an outline of the window (Figure 1-25). The outline, which can be positioned anywhere on the desktop, specifies where the window will display when you release the left mouse button.

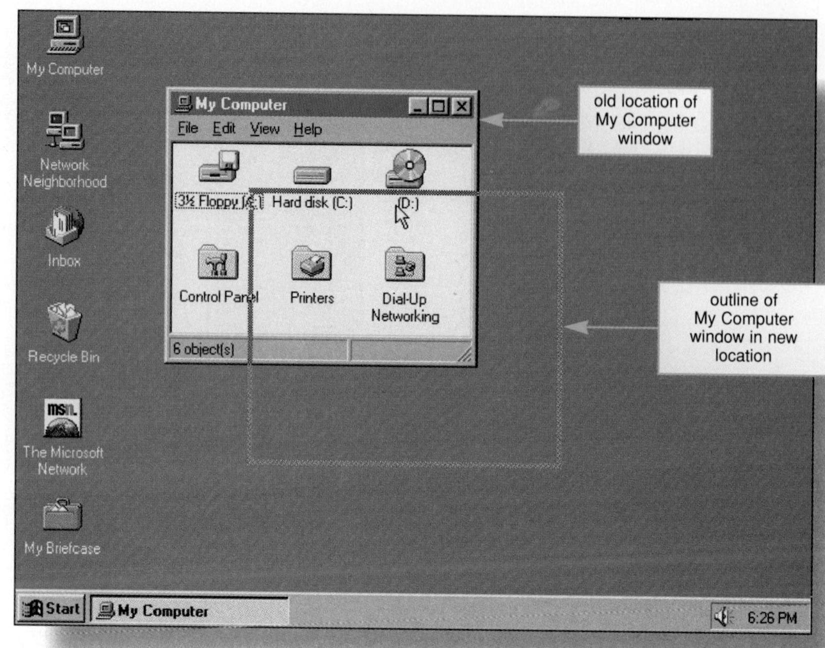

FIGURE 1-25

3 **Release the left mouse button.**

Windows 95 moves the My Computer window to the location the outline occupied prior to releasing the left mouse button (Figure 1-26).

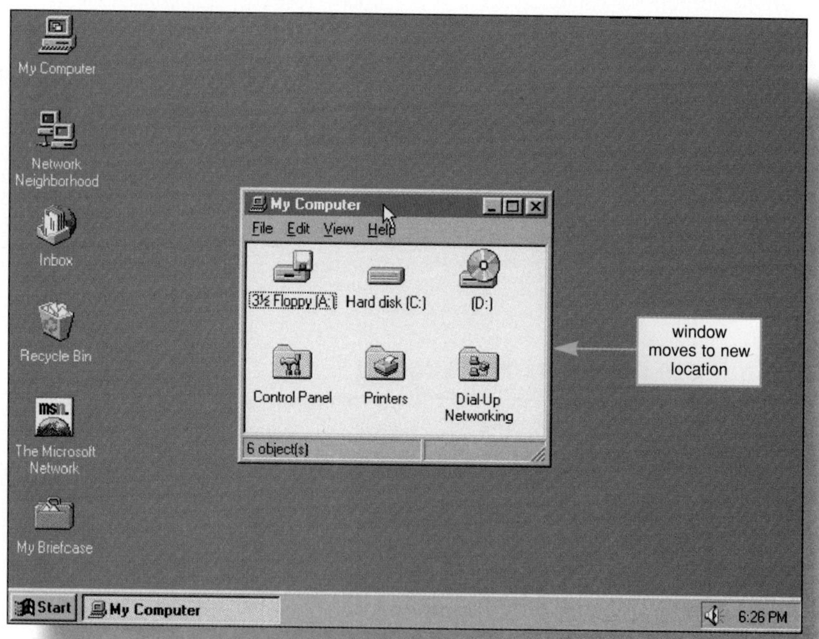

FIGURE 1-26

Sizing a Window by Dragging

You can use dragging for more than just moving an item or object. For example, you can drag the border of a window to change the size of the window. To change the size of the My Computer window, complete the following step.

More About Window Sizing

Windows 95 remembers the size of a window when you close the window. When you reopen the window, it will display in the same size as when you closed it.

Steps To Size a Window by Dragging

1 Position the mouse pointer over the lower right corner of the My Computer window until the mouse pointer changes to a two-headed arrow. Drag the lower right corner upward and to the left until the window on your desktop resembles the window in Figure 1-27.

As you drag the lower right corner, the My Computer window changes size and a vertical scroll bar displays (Figure 1-27). A ***scroll bar*** *is a bar that displays at the right edge and/or bottom edge of a window when the window contents are not completely visible. A vertical scroll bar contains an* ***up scroll arrow****, a* ***down scroll arrow****, and a* ***scroll box****.*

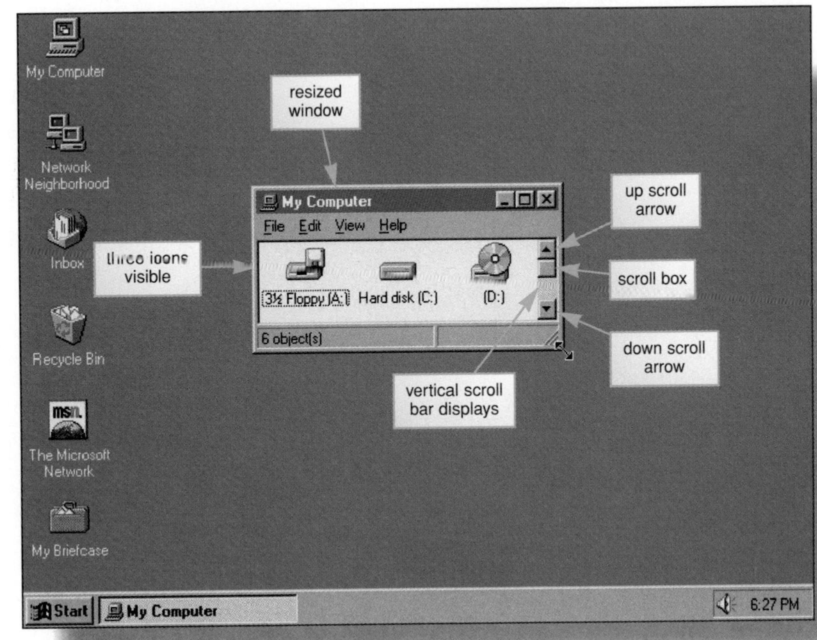

FIGURE 1-27

The size of the scroll box in any window is dependent on the amount of the window that is not visible. The smaller the scroll box, the more of the window that is not visible. In addition to dragging a corner of a window, you can also drag any of the borders of a window.

Scrolling in a Window

You can use the scroll bar to view the contents of a window that are not visible. Scrolling can be accomplished in three ways: click the scroll arrows; click the scroll bar; and drag the scroll box.

To display the contents of the My Computer window by scrolling using scroll arrows, complete the steps on the next page.

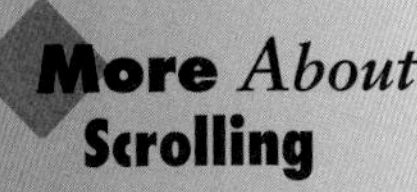

More About Scrolling

Most people will either maximize a window or size it so all the objects in the window are visible to avoid scrolling because scrolling takes time. It is more efficient not to have to scroll in a window.

To Scroll a Window Using Scroll Arrows

1 Point to the down scroll arrow on the vertical scroll bar.

The mouse pointer points to the down scroll arrow on the scroll bar (Figure 1-28).

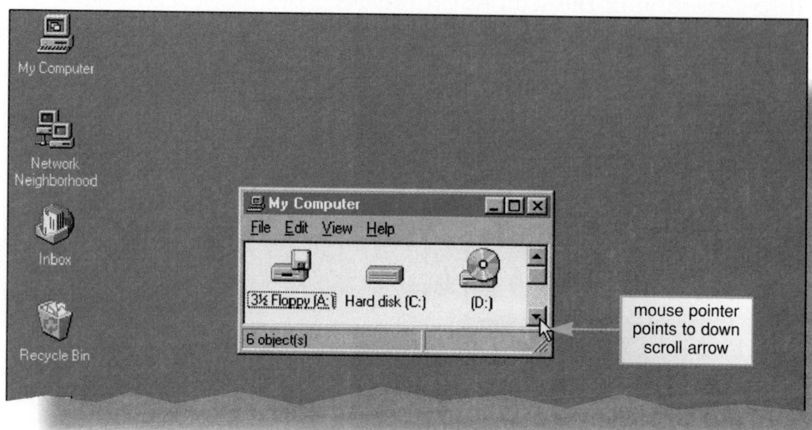

FIGURE 1-28

2 Click the down scroll arrow one time.

The window scrolls down (the icons move up in the window) and displays the tops of icons not previously visible (Figure 1-29). Because the window size does not change when you scroll, the contents of the window will change, as seen in the difference between Figure 1-28 and Figure 1-29.

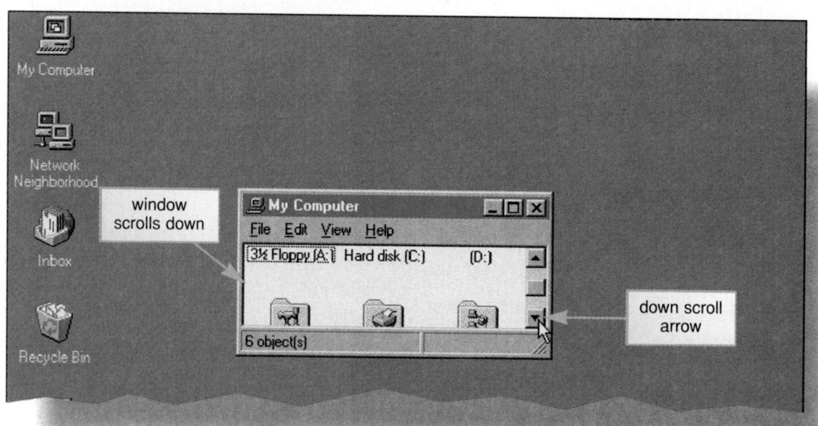

FIGURE 1-29

3 Click the down scroll arrow two more times.

The scroll box moves to the bottom of the scroll bar and the icons in the last row of the window display (Figure 1-30).

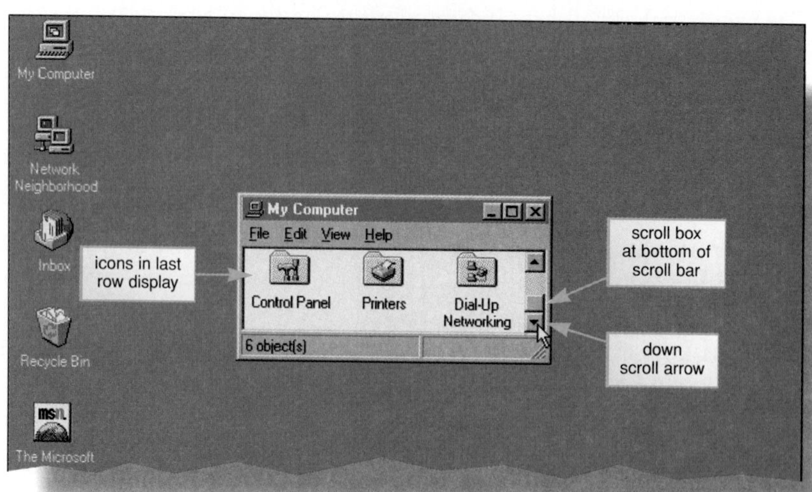

FIGURE 1-30

You can continuously scroll through a window using scroll arrows by clicking the up or down scroll arrow and holding down the left mouse button. The window continues to scroll until you release the left mouse button or you reach the top or bottom of the window.

You can also scroll by clicking the scroll bar itself. When you click the scroll bar, the window moves up or down a greater distance than when you click the scroll arrows.

A third way in which you can scroll through a window to view the window's contents is by dragging the scroll box. When you drag the scroll box, the window moves up or down as you drag.

Being able to view the contents of a window by scrolling is an important Windows 95 skill because the entire contents of a window may not be visible.

Resizing a Window

You might want to return a window to its original size. To return the My Computer window to about its original size, complete the following steps.

TO RESIZE A WINDOW

Step 1: Position the mouse pointer over the lower right corner of the My Computer window border until the mouse pointer changes to a two-headed arrow.

Step 2: Drag the lower right corner of the My Computer window until the window is the same size as shown in Figure 1-26 on page WIN 1.18, and then release the mouse button.

The My Computer window is about the same size as before you changed it.

Closing a Window

After you have completed your work in a window, normally you will close the window. To close the My Computer window, complete the following steps.

TO CLOSE A WINDOW

Step 1: Point to the Close button on the right of the title bar in the My Computer window.

Step 2: Click the Close button.

The My Computer window closes and the desktop contains no open windows.

Right-Drag

Right-drag means you point to an item, hold down the right mouse button, move the item to the desired location, and then release the right mouse button. When you right-drag an object, a context-sensitive menu displays. The context-sensitive menu contains commands specifically for use with the object being dragged. To right-drag the My Briefcase icon to the center of the desktop, perform the steps on the next page. If the My Briefcase icon does not display on your desktop, you will be unable to perform Step 1 through Step 3 on the next page.

More *About* **the Scroll Bar**

In many application programs, clicking the scroll bar will move the window a full screen's worth of information up or down. You can step through a word processing document screen by screen, for example, by clicking the scroll bar.

More *About* **the Scroll Box**

Dragging the scroll box is the most efficient technique to scroll long distances. In many application programs, such as Microsoft Word 7, as you scroll using the scroll box, the page number of the document displays next to the scroll box.

More *About* **Scrolling Guidelines**

General scrolling guidelines: (1) To scroll short distances (line by line), click the scroll arrows; (2) To scroll one screen at a time, click the scroll bar; (3) To scroll long distances, drag the scroll box.

To Right-Drag

1. Point to the My Briefcase icon on the desktop, hold down the right mouse button, drag the icon diagonally toward the center of the desktop, and then release the right mouse button.

The dragged My Briefcase ghosted icon and a context-sensitive menu display in the center of the desktop (Figure 1-31). The My Briefcase icon remains at its original location on the left of the screen. The context-sensitive menu contains four commands: Move Here, Copy Here, Create Shortcut(s) Here, and Cancel. The Move Here command in bold (dark) type identifies what happens if you were to drag the My Briefcase icon with the left mouse button.

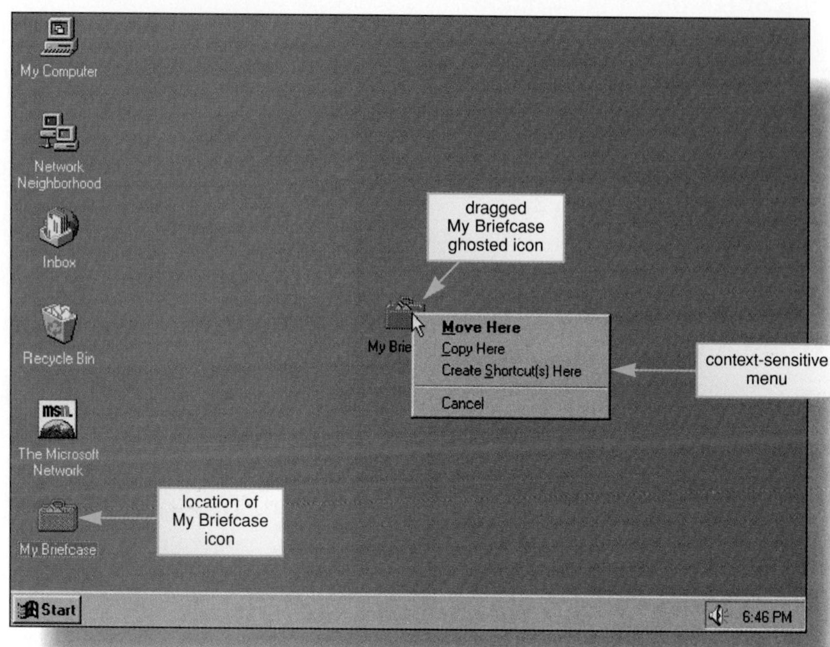

FIGURE 1-31

2. Point to Cancel on the context-sensitive menu.

The mouse pointer points to Cancel on the context-sensitive menu (Figure 1-32). The Cancel command is highlighted.

3. Click Cancel on the context-sensitive menu.

The context-sensitive menu and the dragged My Briefcase icon disappear from the screen.

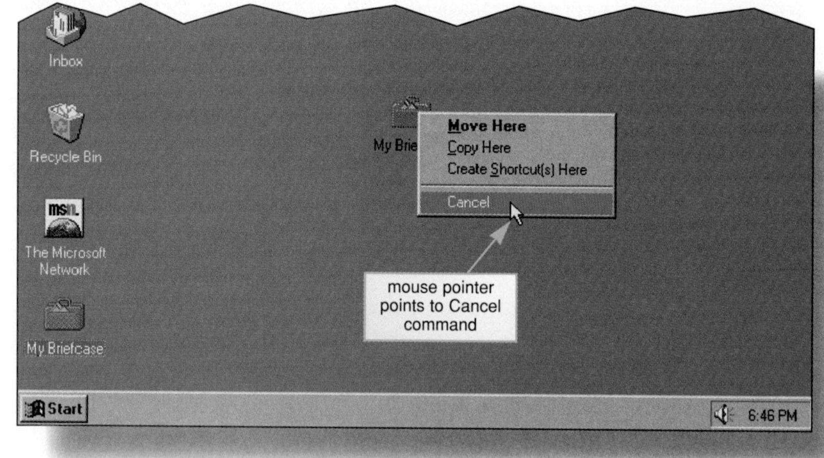

FIGURE 1-32

More *About* Right-Dragging

Right-dragging was not even available on earlier versions of Windows, so you might find people familiar with Windows not even considering right-dragging. Because it always produces a context-sensitive menu, however, right-dragging is the safest way to drag.

Whenever you begin an operation but do not want to complete the operation, click Cancel on a context-sensitive menu or click the Cancel button in a dialog box. The Cancel command will reset anything you have done.

If you click Move Here on the context-sensitive menu shown in Figure 1-31, Windows 95 will move the icon from its current location to the new location. If you click the Copy Here command, the icon will be copied to the new location and two icons will display on the desktop. Windows 95 automatically will give the second icon and the associated file a different name. If you click the Create Shortcut(s) Here command, a special object called a shortcut will be created.

Although you can move icons by dragging with the primary (left) mouse button and by right-dragging with the secondary (right) mouse button, it is strongly suggested you right-drag because a menu displays and you can specify the exact operation you want to occur. When you drag using the left mouse button, a default operation takes place and the operation may not do what you want.

The Keyboard and Keyboard Shortcuts

FIGURE 1-33a

The **keyboard** is an input device on which you manually key, or type, data. Figure 1-33a shows the enhanced IBM 101-key keyboard and Figure 1-33b shows a Microsoft keyboard designed specifically for use with Windows 95. Many tasks you accomplish with a mouse also can be accomplished using a keyboard.

To perform tasks using the keyboard, you must understand the notation used to identify which keys to press. This notation is used throughout Windows 95 to identify **keyboard shortcuts.**

Keyboard shortcuts consist of: (1) pressing a single key (example: press F1); or, (2) holding down one key and pressing a second key, as shown by two key names separated with a plus sign (example: press CTRL+ESC). For example, to obtain Help about Windows 95, you can press the F1 key. To open the Start menu, hold down the CTRL key and press the ESC key (press CTRL+ESC).

FIGURE 1-33b

Often, computer users will use keyboard shortcuts for operations they perform frequently. For example, many users find pressing the F1 key to start Windows 95 Help easier than using the Start menu as shown later in this project. As a user, you will likely find your own combination of keyboard and mouse operations that particularly suit you, but it is strongly recommended that generally you use the mouse.

More *About* **the Microsoft Keyboard**

The Microsoft keyboard in Figure 1-33(b) not only has special keys for Windows 95, but also is designed ergonomically so you type with your hands apart. It takes a little time to get used to, but several authors on the Shelly Cashman Series writing team report they type faster with more accuracy and less fatigue when using the keyboard.

Creating a Document by Starting an Application Program

A **program** is a set of computer instructions that carries out a task on your computer. An **application program** is a program that allows you to accomplish a specific task for which that program is designed. For example, a word processing program is an application program that allows you to create written documents, a spreadsheet program is an application program that allows you to create spreadsheets and charts, and a presentation graphics application program allows you to create graphic presentations for display on a computer or as slides.

More About Application Programs

Some application programs, such as Notepad, are part of Windows 95. Most application programs, however, such as Microsoft Office 95, Lotus SmartSuite 96, and others must be purchased separately from Windows 95.

The most common activity on a computer is to run an application program to accomplish tasks using the computer. You can start an application program by using the Start button on the taskbar.

To illustrate the use of an application program to create a written document, assume each morning you create a daily reminders list so you will remember the tasks you must accomplish throughout the day. You print the document containing the reminders for your use. On occasion, you must update the daily reminders list as events occur during the day. You have decided to use **Notepad**, a popular application program available with Windows 95, to create your list.

To create the list, one method you can use with Windows 95 is to start the Notepad application program using the Start button on the taskbar. After the Notepad program is started, you can enter your daily reminders.

To start the Notepad program, perform the following steps.

Steps To Start a Program

1 **Click the Start button on the taskbar. Point to Programs on the Start menu. Point to Accessories on the Programs submenu. If you happen to point to another command on one of the menus or submenus, a different submenu might display. Merely move the mouse so it points to Programs and then Accessories to display the correct menu and submenus.**

Windows 95 opens the Start menu, the Programs submenu, and the Accessories submenu (Figure 1-34). The mouse pointer points to Accessories on the Programs submenu. The Accessories submenu contains the Notepad command to start the Notepad program. Notice that whenever you point to a menu name that has a right arrow following it, a submenu displays. You might find more, fewer, or different commands on the submenus on your computer.

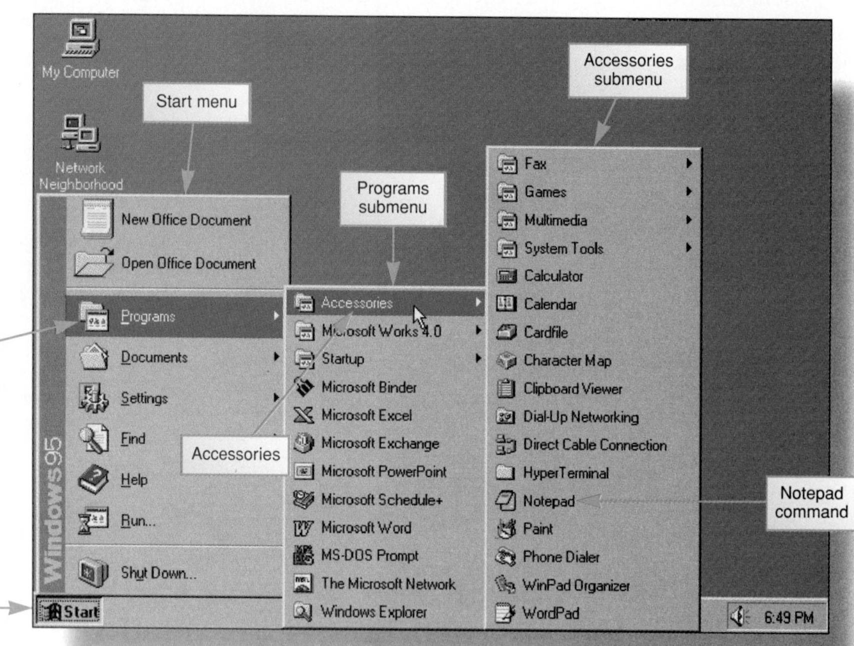

FIGURE 1-34

2 Point to Notepad on the Accessories submenu.

When the mouse pointer points to Notepad on the Accessories submenu, the Notepad command is highlighted (Figure 1-35).

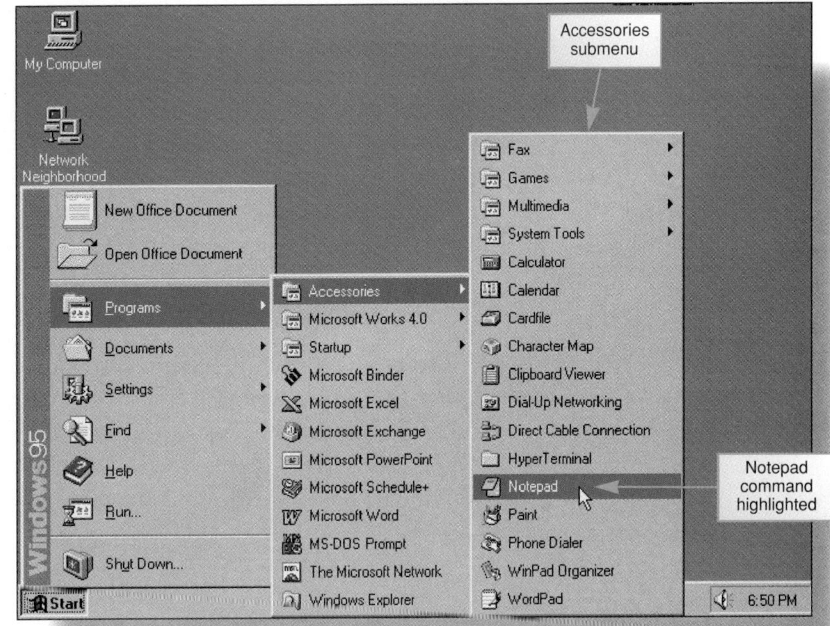

FIGURE 1-35

3 Click Notepad.

Windows 95 starts the Notepad program by opening the Notepad window on the desktop and adding an indented Notepad button to the taskbar (Figure 1-36). Notepad is the active window (dark blue title bar). The word Untitled in the window title (Untitled - Notepad) and on the Notepad button indicates the document has not been saved on disk. The menu bar contains the following menu names: File, Edit, Search, and Help. The area below the menu bar contains an insertion point and two scroll bars. The **insertion point** *is a flashing vertical line that indicates the point at which text typed on the keyboard will be displayed. The scroll bars do not contain scroll boxes, indicating the document is not large enough to allow scrolling.*

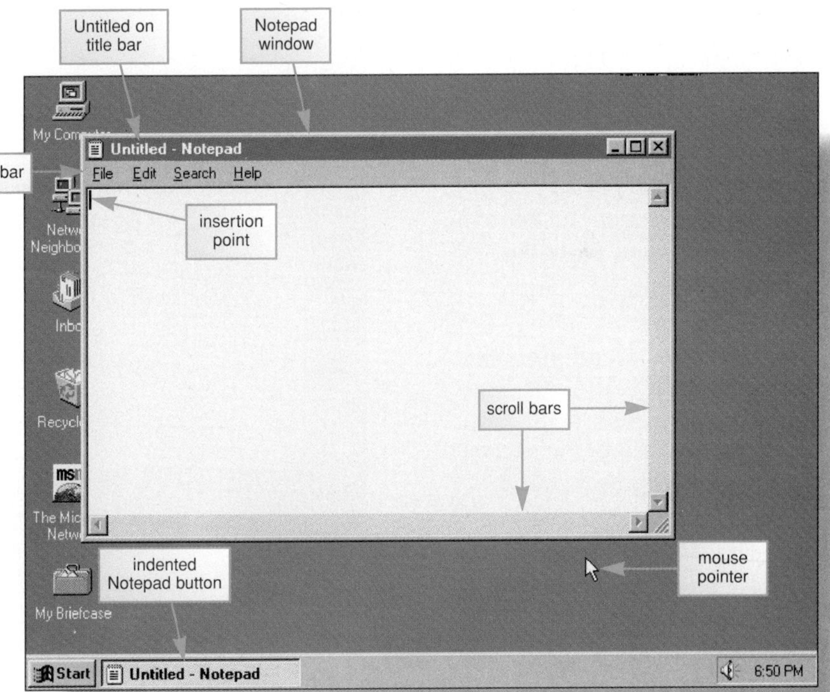

FIGURE 1-36

OtherWays

1. Right-click desktop, point to New, click Text Document, double-click the New Text Document icon
2. Click Start button, click Run, type `Notepad`, click OK button
3. Press CTRL+ESC, press R, type `Notepad`, press ENTER key

After you have started an application program such as Notepad, you can use the program to prepare your document.

Windows 95 provides a number of ways in which to accomplish a particular task. When a task is illustrated by a series of steps in this book, those steps may not be the only way in which the task can be done. If you can accomplish the same task using other methods, the Other Ways box specifies the other methods. In each case, the method shown in the steps is the preferred method, but it is important you are aware of all the techniques you can use.

Creating a Document

To create a document in Notepad, you must type the text you want in the document. After typing a line of text, press the ENTER key to indicate the end of the line. If you press the ENTER key when the insertion point is on a line by itself, Notepad inserts a blank line in the document. To create the Daily Reminders document, perform the following step.

Steps To Create a Document

1 **Type** `Daily Reminders - Wednesday` **and press the ENTER key twice. Type** `1. Call Tim Hoyle - Photoshop retouch due` **and press the ENTER key. Type** `2. Memo to Linda Tomms - Meeting next week` **and press the ENTER key. Type** `3. Lunch with Harris - Noon, Remmington's` **and press the ENTER key.**

The first five lines of the document are entered (Figure 1-37). A blank line is inserted following the first line. The insertion point is positioned on the sixth line of the document.

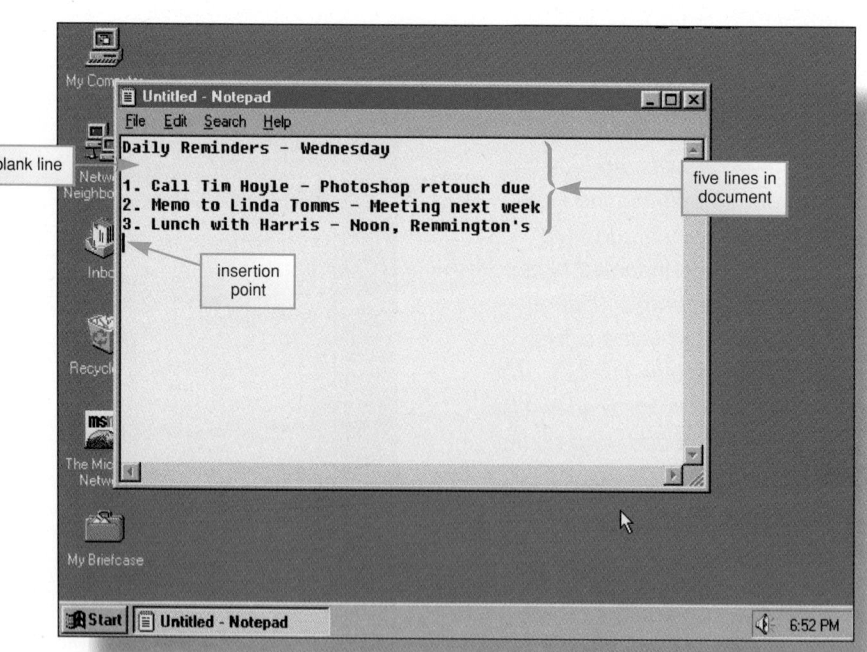

FIGURE 1-37

More About Saving a Document

Most people who have used a computer can tell at least one horror story of working on their computer for a long stretch of time and then losing the work because of some malfunction with the computer or even with the operating system or application program. Be Warned: Save and save often to protect the work you have completed on your computer.

Saving a Document on Disk

When you create a document using a program such as Notepad, the document is stored in the main memory (RAM) of your computer. If you close the program without saving the document or if your computer accidentally loses electrical power, the document will be lost. To protect against the accidental loss of a document and to allow you to easily modify the document in the future, you can save the document on disk.

When you save a document, you must assign a filename to the document. All documents are identified by a filename. Typical filenames are Daily Reminders - Wednesday, Mileage Log, and Automobile Maintenance. A filename can contain up to 255 characters, including spaces. Any uppercase or lowercase character is valid when creating a filename, except a backslash (\), slash (/), colon (:), asterisk (*), question mark (?), quotation mark ("), less than symbol (<), greater than symbol (>), or vertical bar (|). Filenames cannot be CON, AUX, COM1, COM2, COM3, COM4, LPT1, LPT2, LPT3, PRN, or NUL.

To associate a document with an application, Windows 95 assigns an extension of a period and up to three characters to each document. All documents created using the Notepad program, which are text documents, are saved with the .TXT extension. To save the document you created using Notepad on a floppy disk in drive A of your computer using the filename, Daily Reminders - Wednesday, perform the following steps.

More About Filenames

Because of restrictions with Microsoft DOS, previous versions of Windows allowed filenames of only eight or fewer characters. F56QPSLA, and similar indecipherable names, were common. Microsoft touts the long filename capability of Windows 95 as a significant breakthrough. Apple Macintosh users, however, shrug and ask what's the big deal. They have used long filenames for years.

Steps To Save a Document on Disk

1 Insert a formatted floppy disk into drive A on your computer. Click File on the menu bar.

Windows 95 highlights the File menu name on the menu bar and opens the File menu in the Notepad window (Figure 1-38). The mouse pointer points to File on the menu bar.

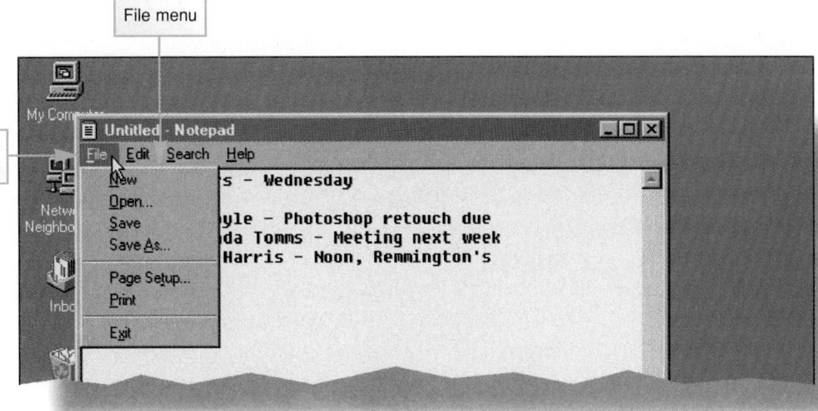

FIGURE 1-38

2 Point to Save As on the File menu.

*The mouse pointer points to the Save As command on the File menu (Figure 1-39). The ellipsis (...) following the Save As command indicates Windows 95 requires more information to carry out the Save As command and will open a dialog box when you click Save As. A **dialog box** displays whenever Windows 95 needs to supply information to you or wants you to enter information or select among several options.*

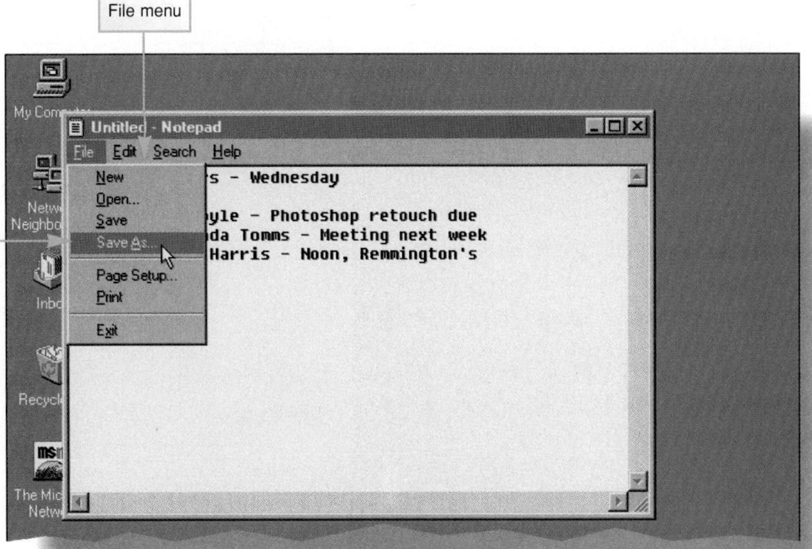

FIGURE 1-39

3 **Click Save As.**

Windows 95 displays the Save As dialog box (Figure 1-40). The Save As dialog box becomes the active window (dark blue title bar) and the Notepad window becomes the **inactive window** *(light blue title bar). The Save As dialog box contains the Save in drop-down list box. A* **drop-down list box** *is a rectangular box containing text and a down arrow on the right. The Save in drop-down list box displays the Desktop icon and Desktop name. The entry in the Save in drop-down list box indicates where the file will be stored. At the bottom of the dialog box is the File name text box. A* **text box** *is a rectangular area in which you can enter text. The File name text box contains the highlighted entry, Untitled. When you type the filename from the keyboard, the filename will replace the highlighted entry in the File name text box.*

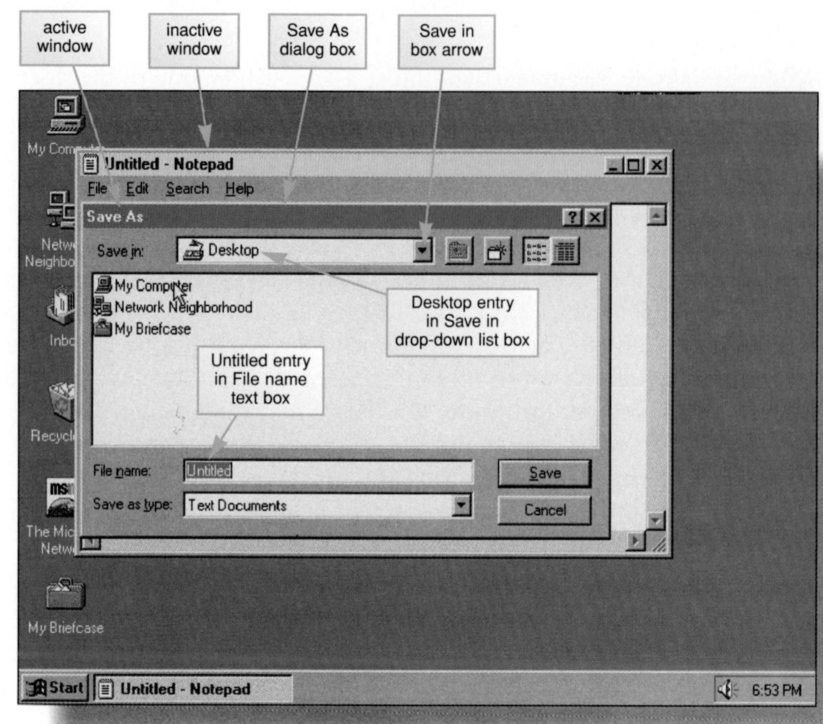

FIGURE 1-40

4 **Type** `Daily Reminders - Wednesday` **in the File name text box. Point to the Save in box arrow.**

The filename, Daily Reminders – Wednesday, and an insertion point display in the File name text box (Figure 1-41). When you save this document, Notepad will automatically add the .TXT extension. The mouse pointer points to the Save in box arrow.

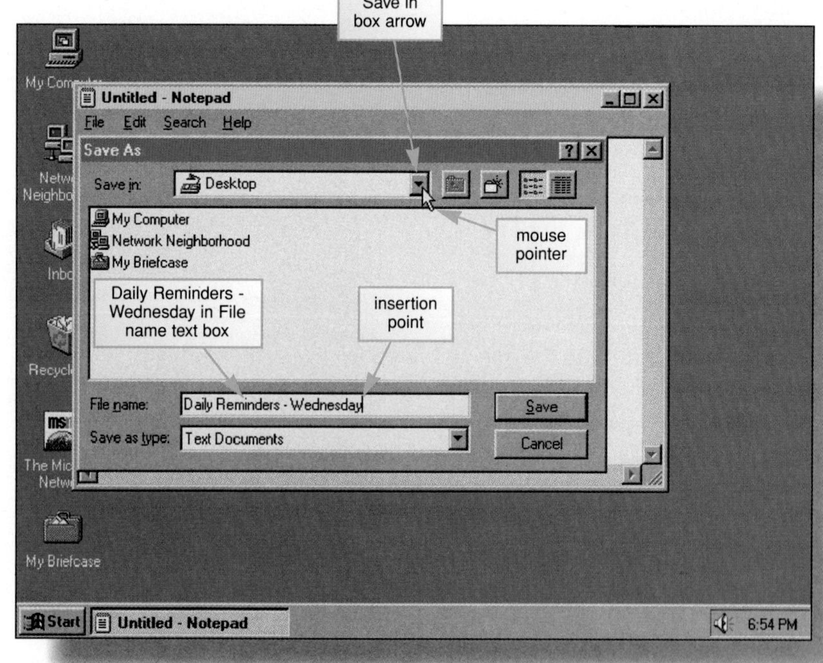

FIGURE 1-41

5 **Click the Save in box arrow and then point to the 3½ Floppy [A:] icon.**

Windows 95 displays the Save in drop-down list (Figure 1-42). The list contains various elements of your computer, including the Desktop, My Computer, Network Neighborhood, and My Briefcase. Within My Computer are 3½ Floppy [A:], Hard disk [C:], and [D:]. When you point to the 3½ Floppy [A:] icon, the entry in the list is highlighted.

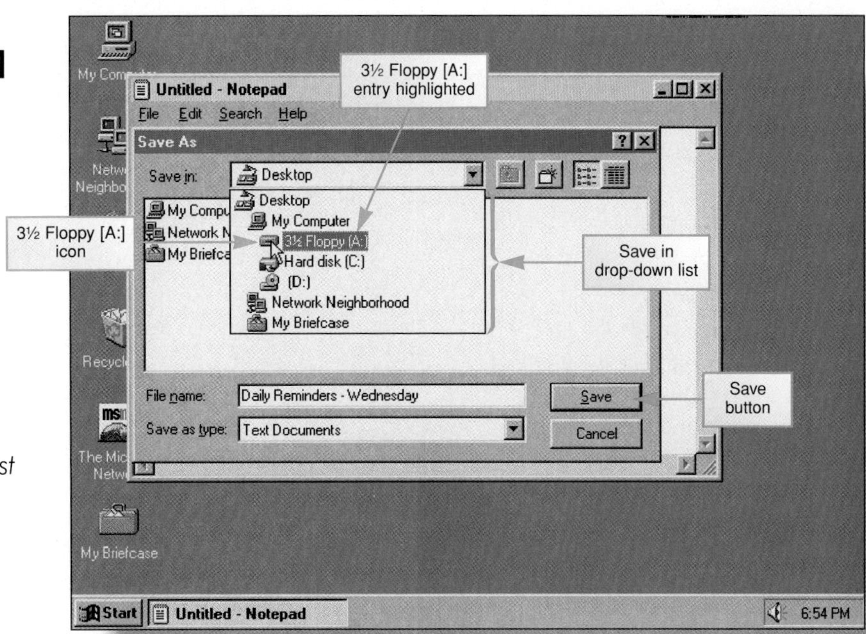

FIGURE 1-42

6 **Click the 3½ Floppy [A:] icon and then point to the Save button.**

The 3½ Floppy [A:] entry displays in the Save in drop-down list box (Figure 1-43). This specifies that the file will be saved on the floppy disk in drive A using the filename specified in the File name text box. The mouse pointer points to the Save button.

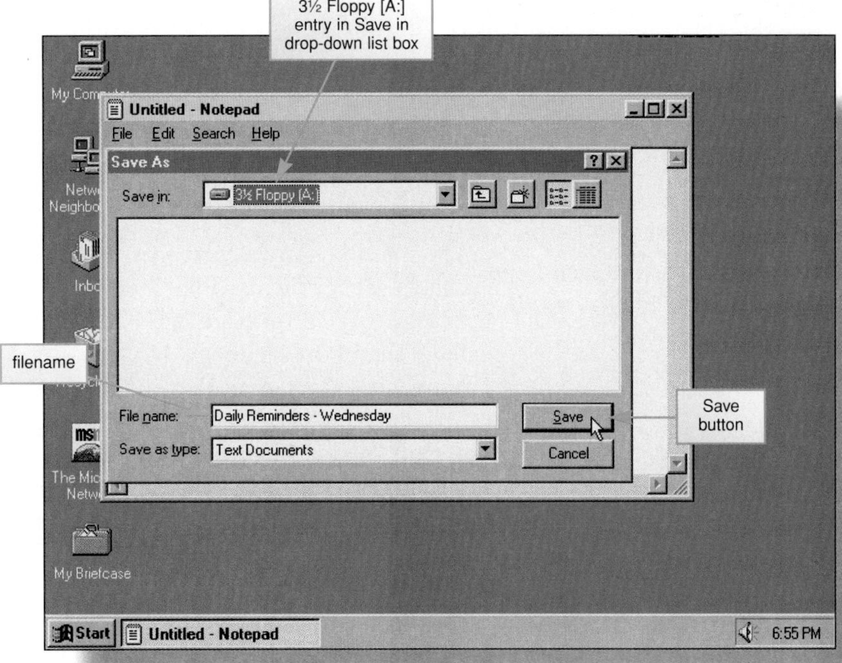

FIGURE 1-43

Click the Save button.

Windows 95 displays an ***hourglass icon*** *while saving the Daily Reminders - Wednesday document on the floppy disk in drive A, closes the Save As dialog box, makes the Notepad window the active window, and inserts the filename on the Notepad window title bar and on the button on the taskbar (Figure 1-44). The filename on the title bar may or may not display the .TXT extension, depending on the setting on your computer. The hourglass icon indicates Windows 95 requires a brief interval of time to save the document. The filename on the button on the taskbar (Daily Reminders - We...) contains an ellipsis to indicate the entire button name does not fit on the button. To display the entire button name for a button on the taskbar, point to the button.*

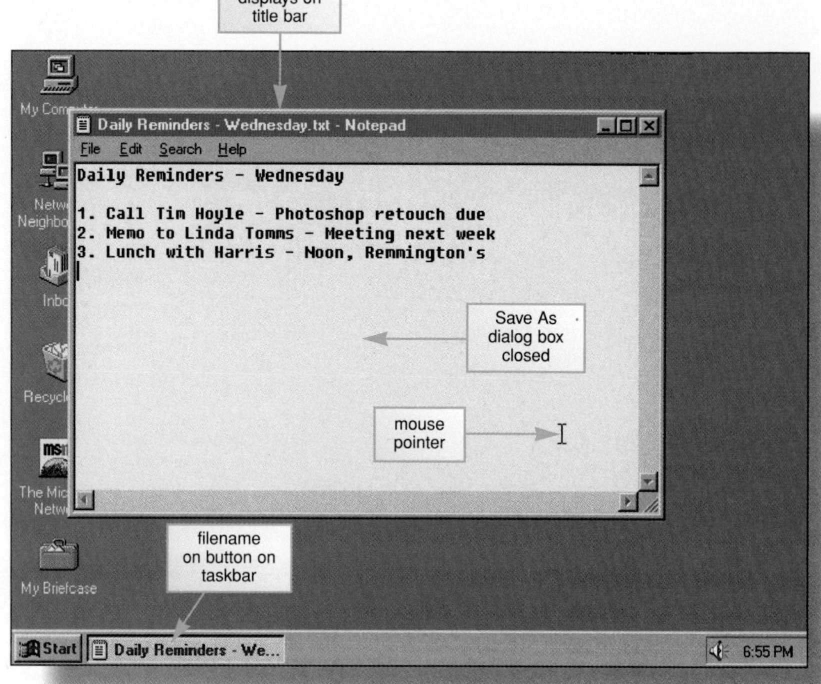

FIGURE 1-44

OtherWays

1. On File menu click Save, type filename, select drive and folder, click Save button
2. Press ALT+F, press A, type filename, select drive and folder, press S

The method shown in the previous steps for saving a file on a floppy disk can be used to save a file on a hard disk, such as drive C, or even on the desktop.

In Figure 1-38 on page WIN 1.27, the File menu displays. Once you have opened a menu on the menu bar, you need merely point to another menu name on the menu bar to open that menu. Thus, in Figure 1-38, if you point to Edit on the menu bar, the Edit menu will display. If you accidentally move the mouse pointer off the menu you want to display, point back to the menu name to display the desired menu. To close a menu without carrying out a command, click anywhere on the desktop except on the menu.

Printing a Document

More About Printing

Printing is and will remain important for documents. Many sophisticated application programs, however, are extending the printing capability to include transmitting faxes, sending e-mail, and even posting documents on Web pages of the World Wide Web.

Quite often, after creating a document and saving it, you will want to print it. Printing can be accomplished directly from an application program. To print the Daily Reminders – Wednesday document, perform the following steps.

Steps To Print a Document

1 Click File on the menu bar and then point to Print on the File menu.

The File menu displays and the mouse pointer points to the Print command (Figure 1-45). As with all menu commands when you point to them, the Print command is highlighted.

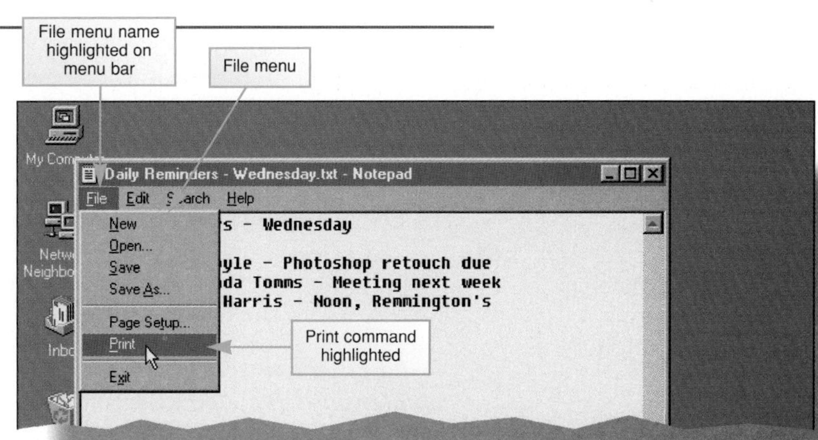

FIGURE 1-45

2 Click Print.

A Notepad dialog box briefly displays with a message that indicates the Daily Reminders document is being printed (Figure 1-46). The dialog box disappears after the report has been printed. To cancel printing, you can click the Cancel button. The printed report is shown in Figure 1-47. Notepad automatically places the filename at the top of the page and a page number at the bottom of the page.

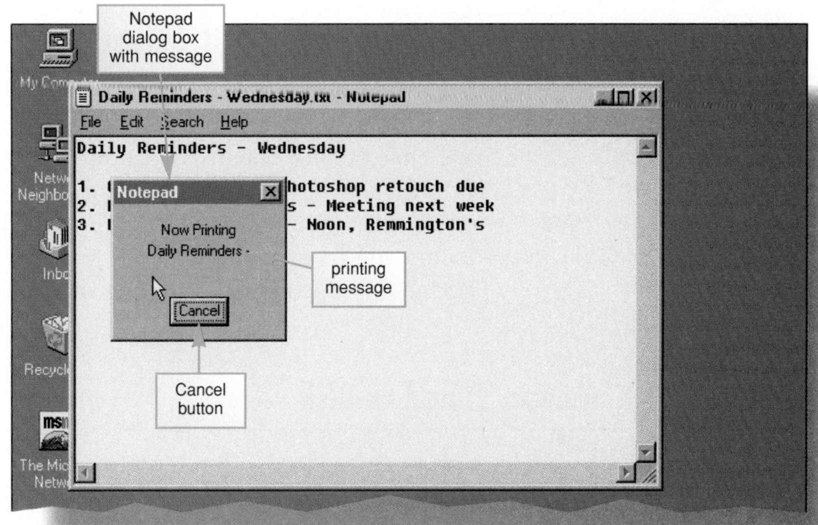

FIGURE 1-46

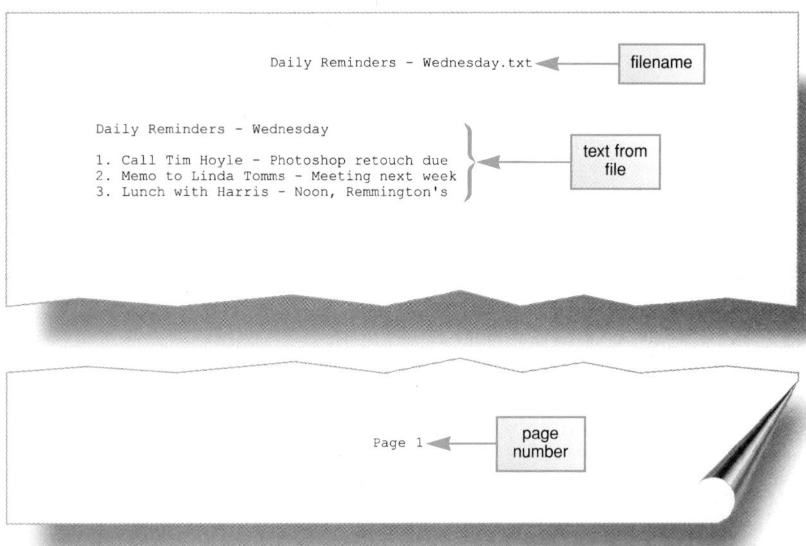

FIGURE 1-47

OtherWays

1. Press ALT+F, press P

Closing a Program

After creating the Daily Reminders – Wednesday document, saving the document on the floppy disk in drive A, and printing it, your use of the Notepad program is complete. Therefore, the Notepad program should be closed by performing the following steps.

TO CLOSE A PROGRAM

Step 1: Point to the Close button on the Notepad title bar.
Step 2: Click the Close button.

Windows 95 closes the Daily Reminders – Wednesday.txt – Notepad window and removes the Daily Reminders – Wednesday.txt – Notepad button from the taskbar.

OtherWays

1. Double-click Notepad logo on title bar
2. On File menu click Exit
3. Press ALT+F4

Modifying a Document Stored on Disk

Many documents you create will need to be modified at some point in time after you have created them. For example, the Daily Reminders - Wednesday document should be modified each time you determine another task to be done. To modify an existing document, you can start the application program and open the document. To start the Notepad program and open the Daily Reminders – Wednesday document, complete the following steps.

Steps To Open a Document Stored on Disk

1 Click the Start button on the taskbar. Point to Programs. Point to Accessories. Point to Notepad.

The Start menu, Programs submenu, and Accessories submenu display (Figure 1-48). The mouse pointer points to the Notepad command.

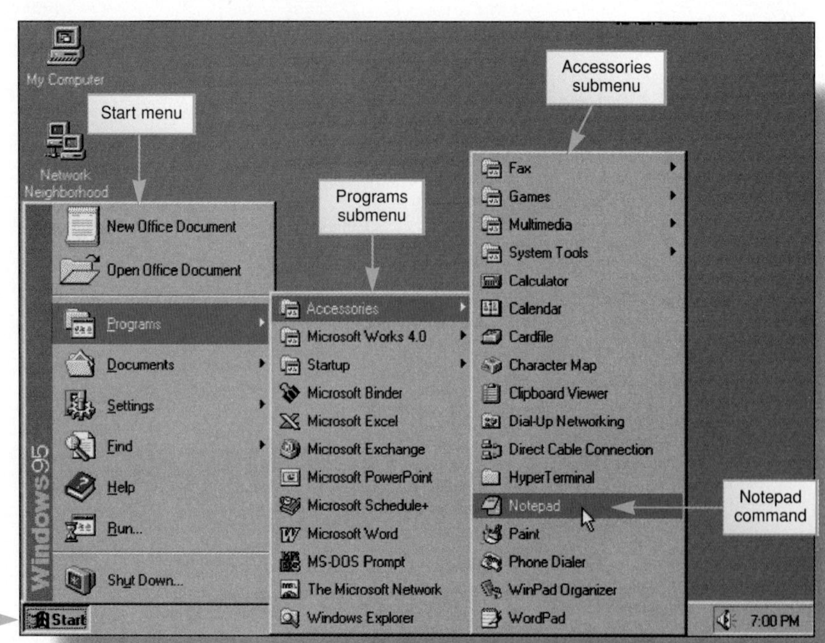

FIGURE 1-48

2 **Click Notepad. When the Notepad window opens, click File on the menu bar and then point to Open on the File menu.**

Windows 95 starts the Notepad program (Figure 1-49). The Untitled – Notepad button on the taskbar indicates no document has been opened. The File menu displays and the mouse pointer points to the Open command.

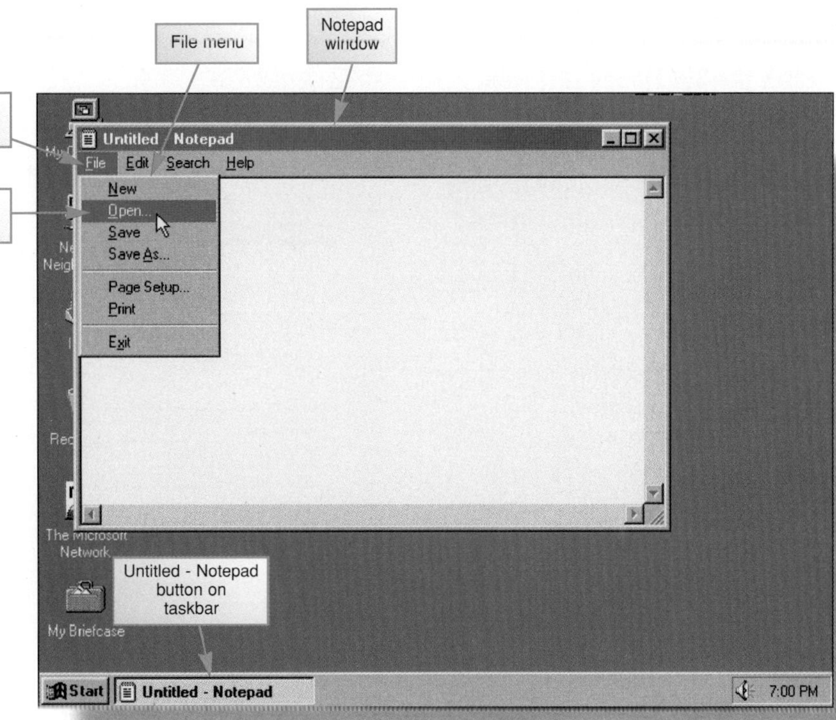

FIGURE 1-49

3 **Click Open. Click the Look in box arrow. Point to the 3½ Floppy [A:] icon.**

Windows 95 displays the Open dialog box (Figure 1-50). When you click the Look in box arrow, the Look in drop-down list displays. The mouse pointer points to the 3½ Floppy [A:] icon. The 3½ Floppy [A:] entry is highlighted.

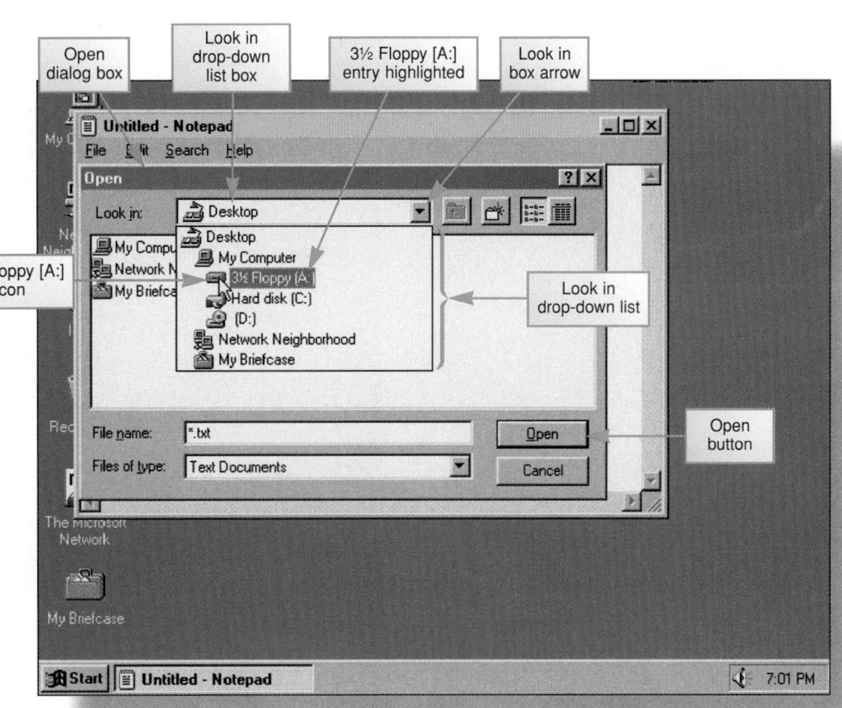

FIGURE 1-50

4 **Click the 3½ Floppy [A:] icon. When the filenames display in the window, click Daily Reminders – Wednesday.txt and then point to the Open button.**

Windows 95 places the 3½ Floppy [A:] icon and entry in the Look in drop-down list box, indicating that the file to be opened is found on the floppy disk in drive A (Figure 1-51). The names of folders and/or text document files stored on the floppy disk in drive A are displayed in the window below the Look in drop-down list box. The Daily Reminders - Wednesday.txt file is selected, as indicated by the highlight, and the mouse pointer points to the Open button. Notice that the Daily Reminders – Wednesday.txt filename displays in the File name text box, indicating this is the file that will be opened.

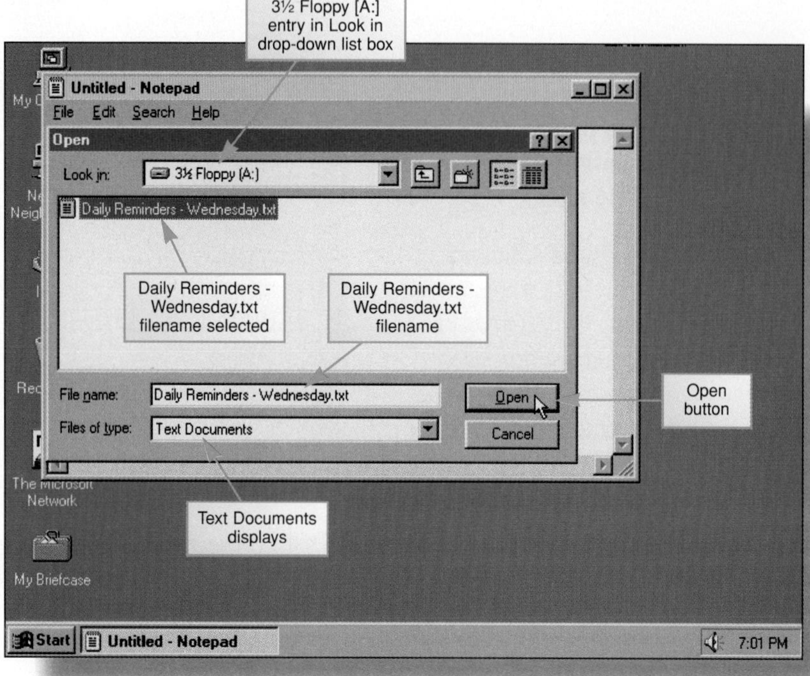

FIGURE 1-51

5 **Click the Open button.**

Windows 95 opens the Daily Reminders – Wednesday.txt file and displays it in the Notepad window (Figure 1-52). The filename displays on the title bar of the Notepad window and on the button on the taskbar.

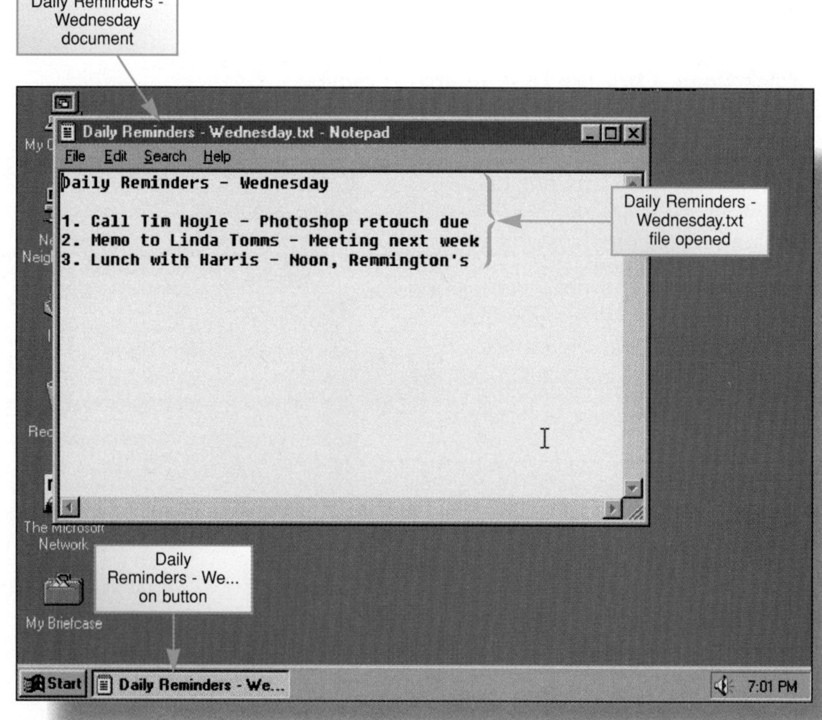

FIGURE 1-52

OtherWays

1. Double-click My Computer icon, double-click drive A icon, double-click file icon
2. Press ALT+F, press O, select drive and folder, type filename, press O

After opening the Daily Reminders – Wednesday document, perform the following step to modify the document by adding another line.

TO MODIFY A DOCUMENT

Step 1: Press the DOWN ARROW key five times, type `4. E-Mail Sue Wells - Adobe Illustrator drawing` as the new line, and then press the ENTER key.

After modifying the Daily Reminders – Wednesday document, you should save the modified document on the floppy disk in drive A using the same filename. To save the modified document on the disk, complete the following steps.

To Save a Modified Document on Disk

1 Click File on the menu bar and then point to Save.

The File menu opens and the mouse pointer points to the Save command (Figure 1-53). The Save command is used to save a file that has already been created.

2 Click Save.

The modified document is stored on the floppy disk in drive A and the Notepad window remains open. Whenever you use the Save command, the document is stored using the same filename in the same location from which it was opened.

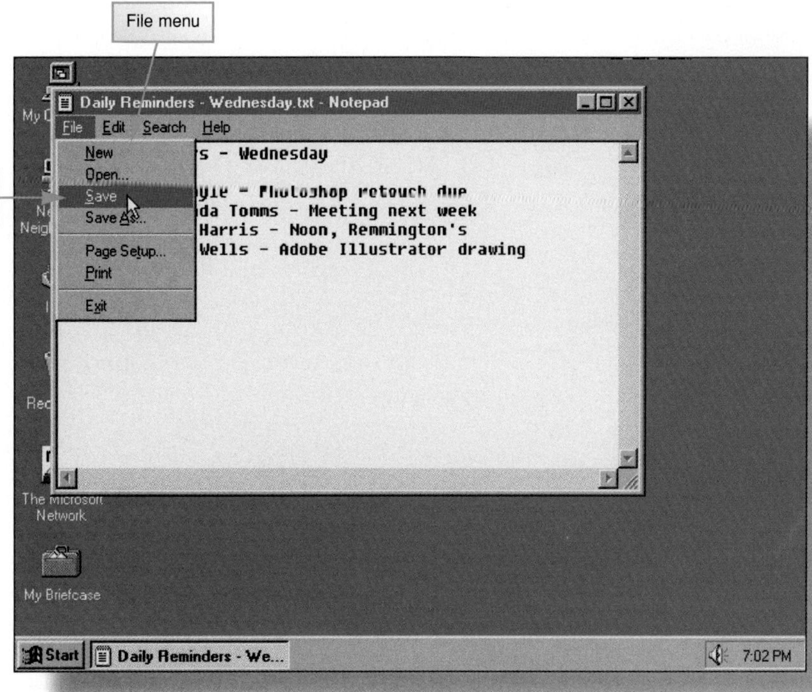

FIGURE 1-53

Other Ways

1. Press ALT+F, press S

If you want to print the modified document, click File on the menu bar and then click Print on the File menu in the same manner as shown in Figure 1-45 and Figure 1-46 on page WIN 1.31.

Closing the Notepad Program

After modifying the document and storing the modified document on the floppy disk in drive A, normally you will close the Notepad program. To close the Notepad program, complete the step on the next page.

WINDOWS 95 TIPS
■ You can close the Notepad program by double-clicking the icon to the left of the window title on the title bar.

LECTURE NOTES
■ Emphasize that Windows Help is available for Windows 95 and all applications running under Windows 95.

TO CLOSE A PROGRAM

Step 1: Click the Close button on the right of the Notepad title bar.

The Notepad window closes and the Notepad button on the taskbar disappears.

Modifying an existing document is a common occurrence and should be well understood when using Windows 95.

Using Windows Help

More *About* **Windows 95 Help**

If you purchased an operating system or application program five years ago, you received at least one, and more often several, thick and heavy technical manuals that explained the software. With Windows 95, you receive a skinny manual less than 100 pages in length. The online Help feature of Windows 95 replaces reams and reams of printed pages in hard-to-understand technical manuals.

One of the more powerful application programs for use in Windows 95 is Windows Help. Windows Help is available when using Windows 95, or when using any application program running under Windows 95, to assist you in using Windows 95 and the various application programs. It contains answers to virtually any question you can ask with respect to Windows 95.

Contents Sheet

Windows 95 Help provides a variety of ways in which to obtain information. One method to find a Help topic involves using the Contents sheet to browse through Help topics by category. To illustrate this method, you will use Windows 95 Help to determine how to find a topic in Help. To start Help, complete the following steps.

ILLUSTRATIONS
Figures 1-54 and 1-55

Steps To Start Help

1 **Click the Start button on the taskbar. Point to Help on the Start menu.**

Windows 95 opens the Start menu (Figure 1-54). Because the mouse pointer points to the Help command, the Help command is highlighted.

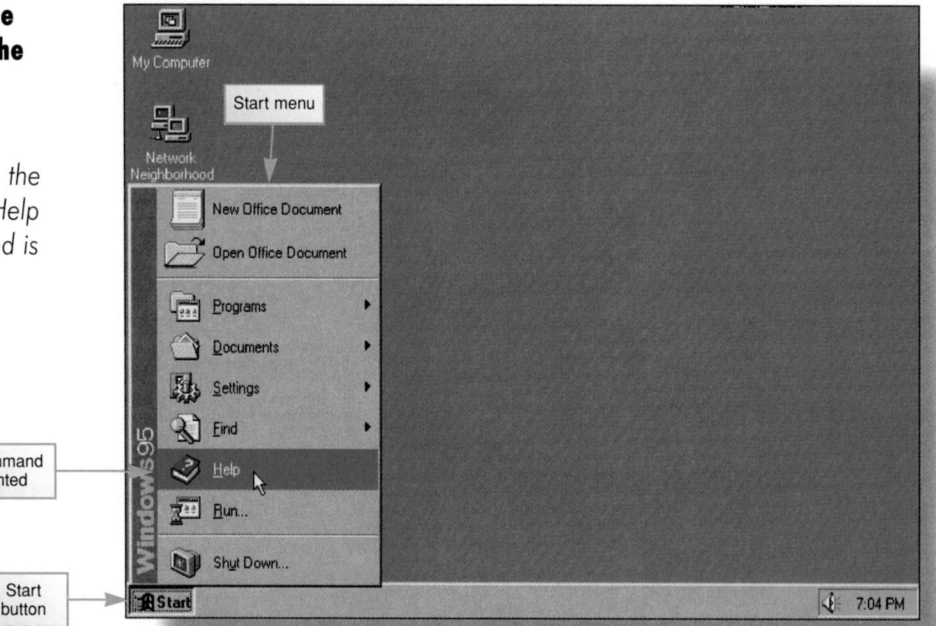

FIGURE 1-54

2 Click Help on the Start menu. If the Contents sheet does not display, click the Contents tab.

Windows 95 opens the Help Topics: Windows Help window (Figure 1-55). The window contains three ***tabs*** *(Contents, Index, and Find). The* ***Contents sheet*** *is visible in the window. Clicking either the Index tab or the Find tab opens the Index or Find sheet, respectively. The Contents sheet contains two* ***Help topics*** *preceded by a question mark icon and five books. Each book consists of a closed book icon followed by a book name. The first Help topic, Tour: Ten minutes to using Windows, is highlighted. Three command buttons (Display, Print, and Cancel) display at the bottom of the window.*

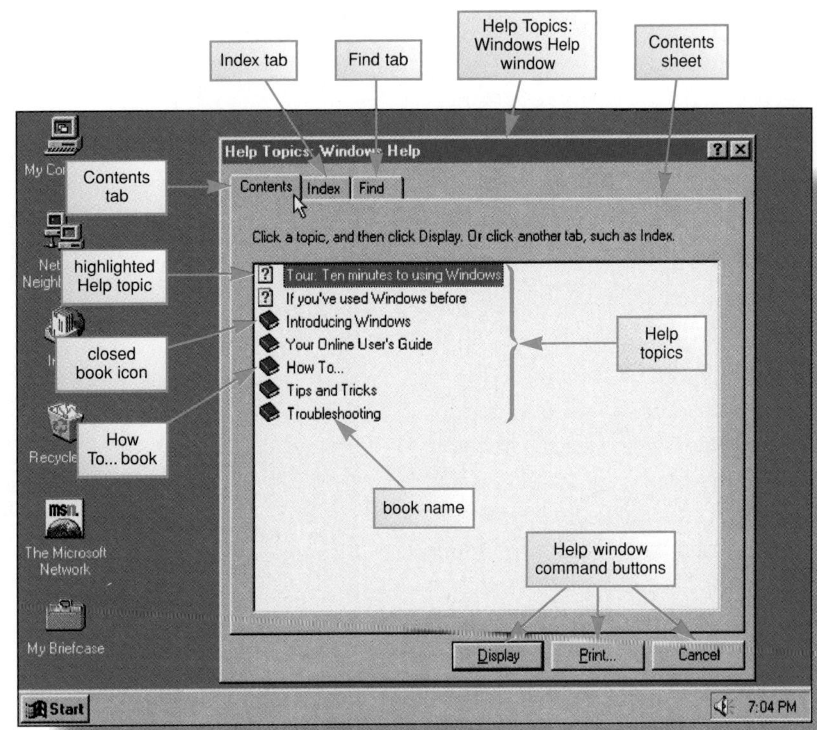

FIGURE 1-55

OtherWays

1. Press F1, press CTRL+TAB or CTRL+SHIFT+TAB to highlight desired sheet

In the Help window shown in Figure 1-55, the closed book icon indicates Help topics or more books are contained within the book. The question mark icon indicates a Help topic without any further subdivisions.

In addition to starting Help by using the Start button, you can also start Help by pressing the F1 key.

After starting Help, the next step is to find the topic in which you are interested. To find the topic that describes how to find a topic in Help, complete the steps on the next two pages.

To Use Help to Find a Topic in Help

1 **Double-click How To... in the Help Topics: Windows Help window. Point to the Use Help closed book.**

Windows 95 highlights the How To book and opens the How To book (Figure 1-56). The ellipsis following the How To book indicates additional books will display when you open the book. The list of closed book icons indicates more Help information is available. The mouse pointer points to the Use Help closed book icon. The Close button in Figure 1-56 replaces the Display button in Figure 1-55. If you click the Close button, the How To book will close and the list of books below the How To book disappears.

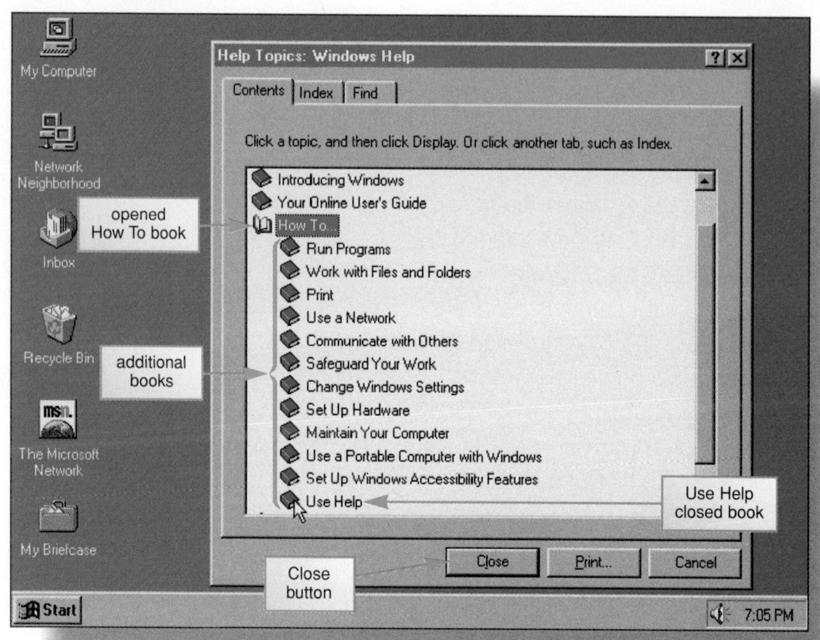

FIGURE 1-56

2 **Double-click the Use Help closed book icon and then point to Finding a topic in Help in the opened Use Help book.**

Windows 95 opens the Use Help book and displays several Help topics in the book (Figure 1-57). The mouse pointer points to Finding a topic in Help.

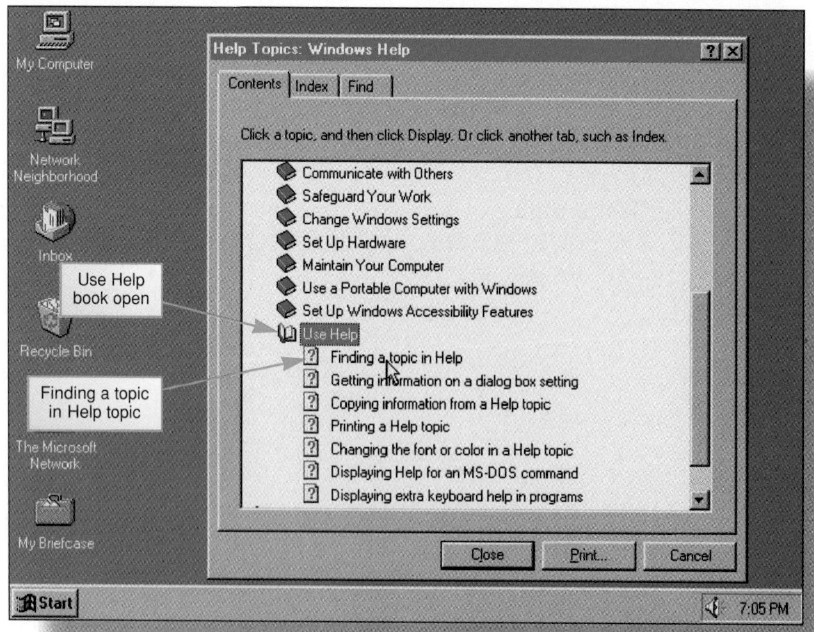

FIGURE 1-57

3 Double-click Finding a topic in Help.

Windows 95 closes the Help Topics: Windows Help window and opens the Windows Help window (Figure 1-58). The window contains three buttons (Help Topics, Back, and Options), steps to find a topic in Help, and a Tip. The Windows Help button displays on the taskbar.

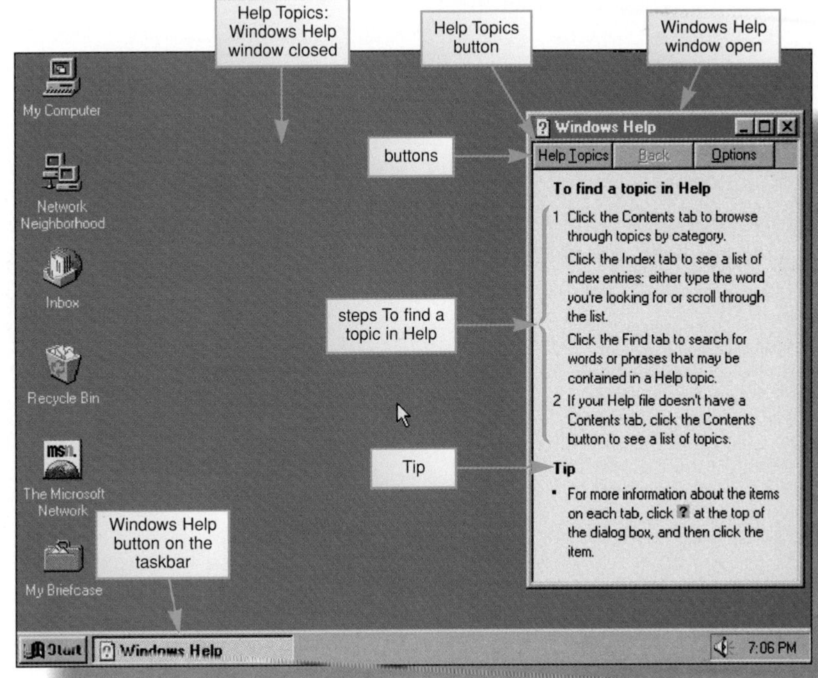

FIGURE 1-58

4 After reading the information in the Windows Help window, click the Help Topics button in the Windows Help window.

The Help Topics: Windows Help window displays together with the Windows Help window (Figure 1-59).

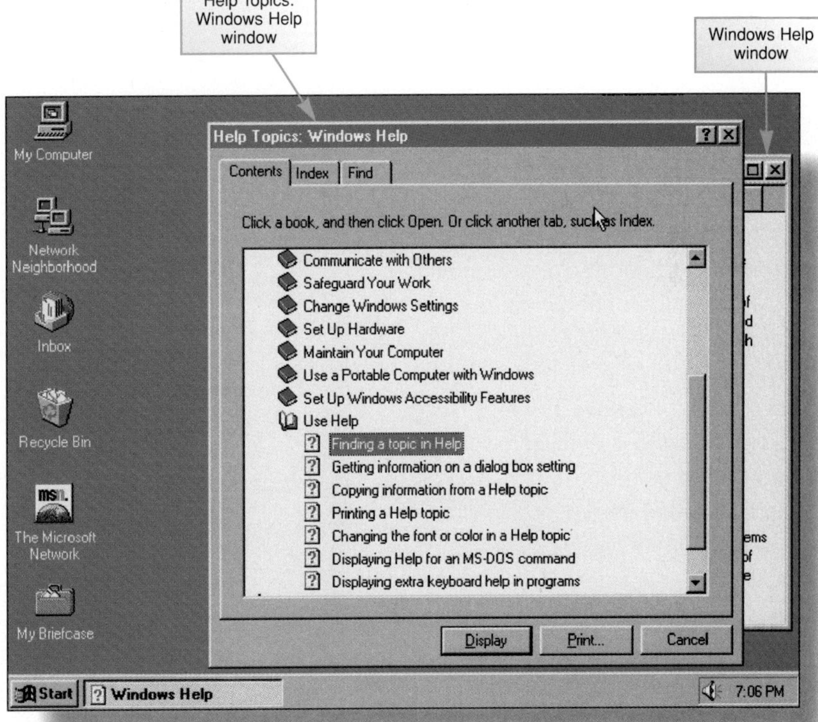

FIGURE 1-59

*Other*Ways

1. Press DOWN ARROW until book or topic highlighted, press ENTER, continue until Help topic displays, read Help topic, press T

More *About* **the Index Sheet**

The Index sheet is probably the best source of information in Windows Help because you can enter the subject you are interested in. Sometimes, however, you will have to be creative to discover the index entry that answers your question because the most obvious entry will not always lead to your answer.

Clicking the Help Topics button in the Windows Help window will always display the Help Topics: Windows Help window.

In Figure 1-58 on the previous page, if you click the Back button in the Windows Help window (when the button is not dimmed), Windows 95 will display the previously displayed Help topic. Clicking the Options button in the Windows Help window allows you to annotate a Help topic, copy or print a Help topic, change the font and color scheme of Help windows, and control how Help windows display in relation to other windows on the desktop.

Notice also in Figure 1-58 that the Windows Help title bar contains a Minimize button, a Maximize button, and a Close button. You can minimize and maximize the Windows Help window, and you can also close the Windows Help window without returning to the Help Topics: Windows Help window.

Index Sheet

A second method to find answers to your questions about Windows 95 or application programs is the Index sheet. The **Index sheet** lists a large number of index entries, each of which references one or more Help screens. To learn more about Windows 95 basic skills by using the Index sheet, and to see an example of animation available with Help, complete the following steps.

To Use the Help Index Sheet

1. **Click the Index tab. Type** `basic skills` **(the flashing insertion point is positioned in the text box). Point to the Display button.**

The Index sheet displays, including a list of entries that can be referenced (Figure 1-60). When you type an entry, the list automatically scrolls and the entry you type, such as basic skills, is highlighted. To see additional entries, use the scroll bar at the right of the list. To highlight an entry in the list, click the entry. On some computers, the basic skills entry may not be present. On those machines, select another topic of interest to you.

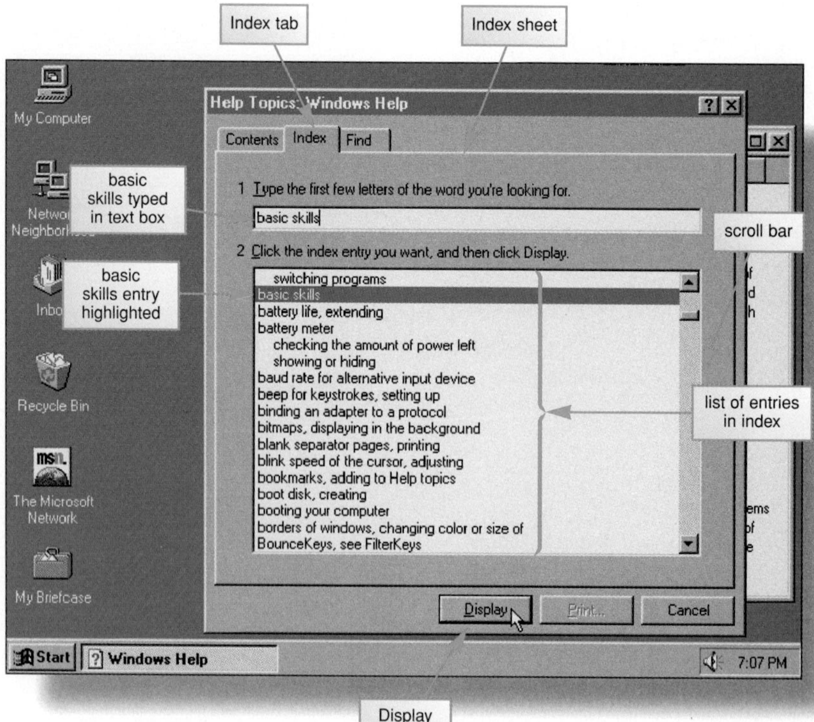

FIGURE 1-60

2 **Click the Display button. Click the Maximize button in the Windows Help title bar. Point to the Sizing windows button.**

The Windows Help window opens and a screen titled, The Basics, displays (Figure 1-61). The window is maximized and the Restore button displays in place of the Maximize button. The screen includes six buttons to learn Windows essentials and a picture of the Windows 95 desktop. When the mouse pointer is positioned on one of the buttons, it changes to a hand with a pointing finger. The Windows Help button displays on the taskbar.

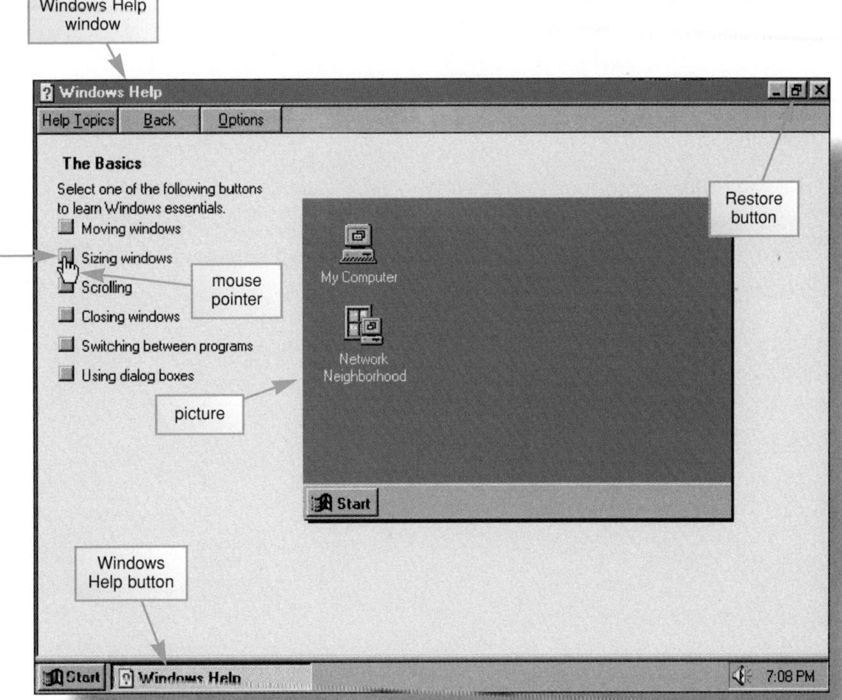

FIGURE 1-61

3 **Click the Sizing windows button. Point to the Play button (the button with the right arrow) below the picture on the right.**

The words, Sizing windows, display in bold, the My Computer window is added to the picture on the right, and the controls to play the animation display (Figure 1-62). The Play button will play the animation, the Option button displays a series of options regarding the animation, and the slide indicates progress when the animation plays. Text that explains how to accomplish the task, such as sizing windows, displays above the picture. On some computers, the animation might not be available. On those computers, instead of displaying the animation picture, the message, Unable to display graphic, will display on the screen. The text above the picture that explains how to perform the task still displays.

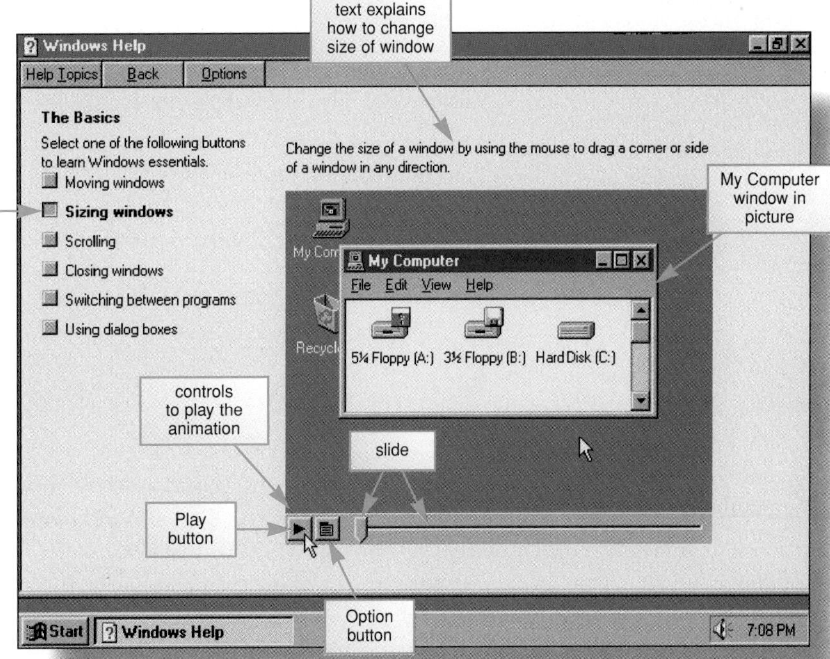

FIGURE 1-62

4 Click the Play button if it displays on the screen.

The Play button changes to a Stop button and the animation plays (Figure 1-63). The slide indicates the progress of the animation.

5 When the animation is complete, click any buttons you wish to view other animations.

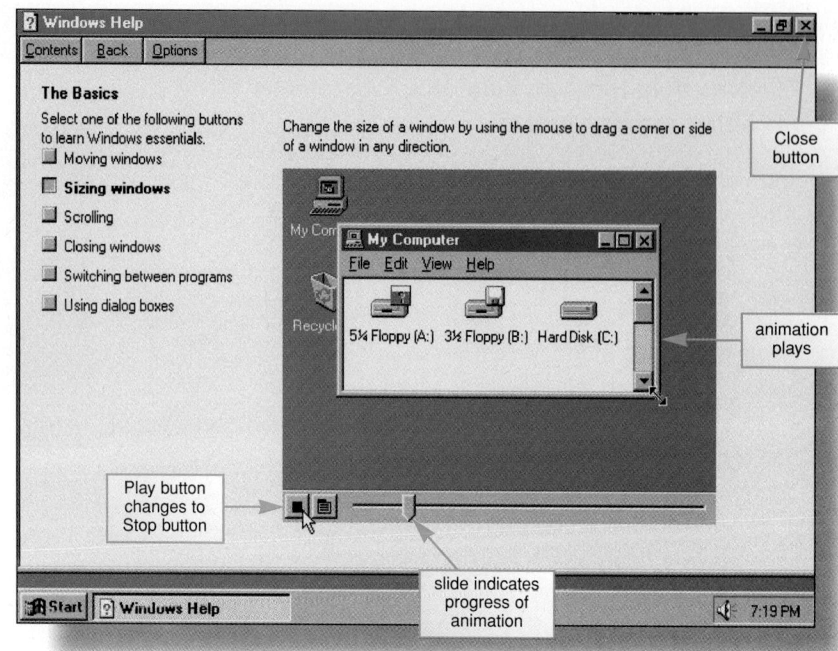

FIGURE 1-63

*Other*Ways

1. Press CTRL+TAB, type topic name, press ENTER, press ALT+SPACEBAR, press X, press TAB until topic highlighted, press ENTER, click Play button

After viewing Help topics, normally you will close Windows Help. To close Windows Help, complete the following step.

TO CLOSE WINDOWS HELP

Step 1: Click the Close button on the title bar of the Windows Help window.

Windows 95 closes the Windows Help window.

Shutting Down Windows 95

After completing your work with Windows 95, you might want to shut down Windows 95 using the **Shut Down command** on the Start menu. If you are sure you want to shut down Windows 95, perform the steps on the next page. If you are not sure about shutting down Windows 95, read the following steps without actually performing them.

More *About* Shut Down Procedures

Some users of Windows 95 have turned off their computer without following the shut down procedure only to find data they thought they had stored on disk was lost. Because of the way Windows 95 writes data on the disk, it is important you shut down windows properly so you do not lose your work.

To Shut Down Windows 95

1 **Click the Start button on the taskbar and then point to Shut Down on the Start menu.**

Windows 95 displays the Start menu (Figure 1-64). The Shut Down command is highlighted because the mouse pointer points to it.

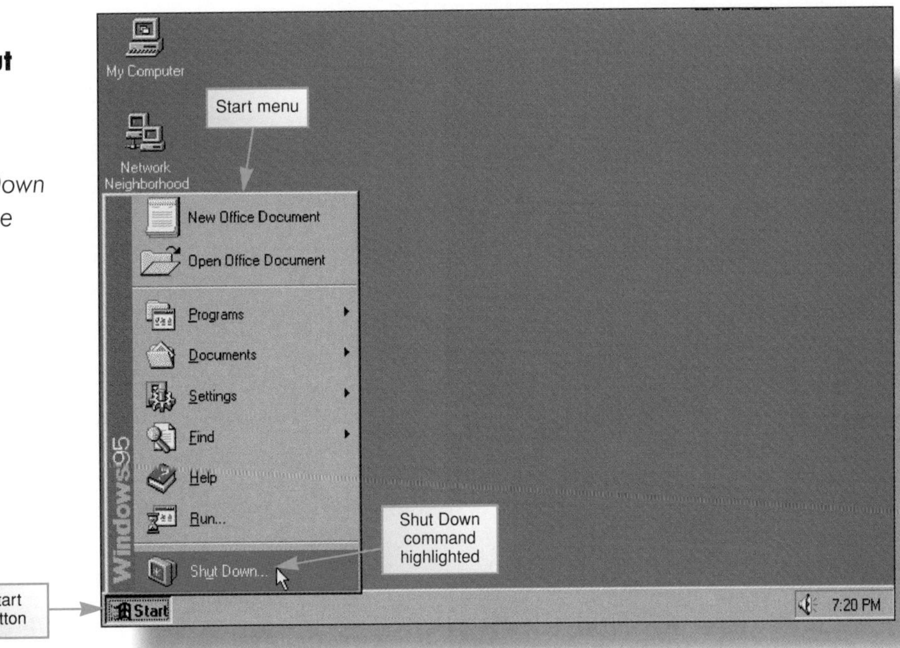

FIGURE 1-64

2 **Click Shut Down. Point to the Yes button in the Shut Down Windows dialog box.**

Windows 95 darkens the entire desktop and opens the Shut Down Windows dialog box (Figure 1-65). The dialog box contains four option buttons. The selected option button, Shut down the computer?, indicates that clicking the Yes button will shut down Windows 95.

3 **Click the Yes button.**

Two screens display while Windows 95 is shutting down. The first screen containing the text, Shutting down Windows, displays momentarily while Windows 95 is being shut down. Then, a second screen containing the text, It is okay to turn off your computer, displays. At this point you can to turn off your computer. When shutting down Windows 95, you should never turn off your computer before this last screen displays.

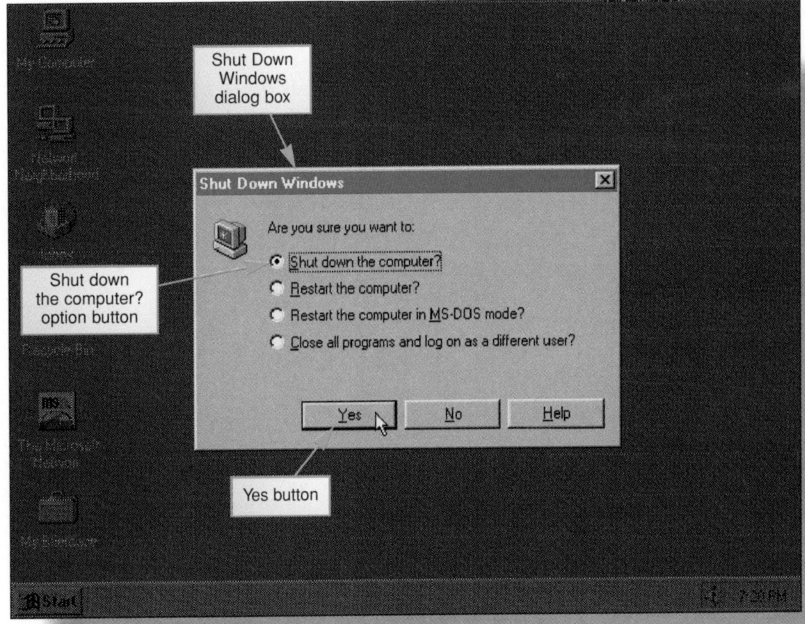

FIGURE 1-65

*Other*Ways

1. Press CTRL+ESC, press U, press UP ARROW or DOWN ARROW until option button selected, press ENTER
2. Press ALT+F4, press UP ARROW or DOWN ARROW until option button selected, press ENTER

If you accidentally click Shut Down on the Start menu and you do not want to shut down Windows 95, click the No button in the Shut Down Windows dialog box to return to normal Windows 95 operation.

Project Summary

Project 1 illustrated the Microsoft Windows 95 graphical user interface. You started Windows 95, learned the parts of the desktop, and learned to point, click, right-click, double-click, drag, and right-drag. You created a document by starting Notepad, entering text, saving the document on a floppy disk, and printing the document. You then modified the Notepad document and saved the modified document. Using both the Help Content and the Help Index sheets you obtained Help about Microsoft Windows 95. You shut down Windows 95 using the Shut Down command on the Start menu.

What You Should Know

Having completed this project, you should now be able to perform the following tasks:

- Close a Program *(WIN 1.32, WIN 1.36)*
- Close the Welcome Screen *(WIN 1.7)*
- Close a Window *(WIN 1.20)*
- Close a Window and Reopen a Window *(WIN 1.16)*
- Close Windows Help *(WIN 1.42)*
- Create a Document *(WIN 1.26)*
- Maximize and Restore a Window *(WIN 1.14)*
- Minimize and Redisplay a Window *(WIN 1.13)*
- Modify a Document *(WIN 1.35)*
- Move an Object by Dragging *(WIN 1.17)*
- Open a Document Stored on Disk *(WIN 1.32)*
- Open a Window by Double-Clicking *(WIN 1.12)*
- Point and Click *(WIN 1.9)*
- Print a Document *(WIN 1.31)*
- Resize a Window *(WIN 1.21)*
- Right-Click *(WIN 1.11)*
- Right-Drag *(WIN 1.22)*
- Save a Document on Disk *(WIN 1.27)*
- Save a Modified Document on Disk *(WIN 1.35)*
- Scroll a Window Using Scroll Arrows *(WIN 1.20)*
- Shut Down Windows 95 *(WIN 1.43)*
- Size a Window by Dragging *(WIN 1.19)*
- Start a Program *(WIN 1.24)*
- Start Help *(WIN 1.36)*
- Use Help to Find a Topic in Help *(WIN 1.38)*
- Use the Help Index Sheet *(WIN 1.40)*

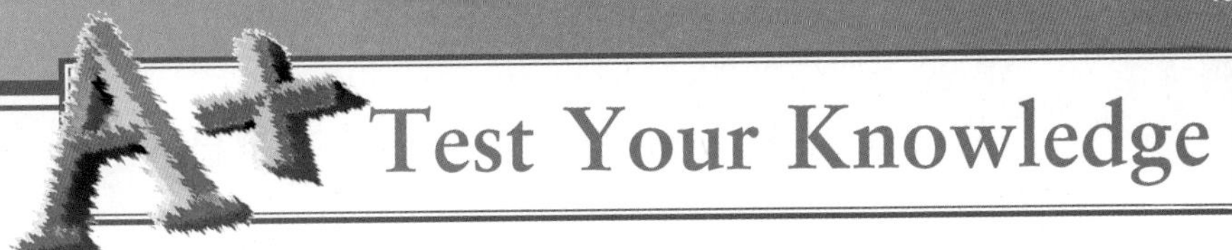

Test Your Knowledge

1 True/False

Instructions: Circle T if the statement is true or F if the statement is false.

T F 1. A user interface is a combination of computer hardware and computer software.
T F 2. Click means press the right mouse button.
T F 3. When you drag an object on the desktop, Windows 95 displays a context-sensitive menu.
T F 4. You can resize a window by dragging the title bar of the window.
T F 5. Daily Reminders - Friday and Mileage Log are valid filenames.
T F 6. To save a new document created using Notepad, click Save As on the File menu.
T F 7. To print a document, click Print on the File menu.
T F 8. To open a document stored on a floppy disk, click Open on the Start menu.
T F 9. You can start Help by clicking the Start button and then clicking Help on the Start menu.
T F 10. To find an item in the Windows Help Index, type the first few characters of the item in the text box on the Contents sheet.

2 Multiple Choice

Instructions: Circle the correct response.

1. Through a user interface, the user is able to __________.
   a. control the computer
   b. request information from the computer
   c. respond to messages displayed by the computer
   d. all of the above
2. A context-sensitive menu opens when you __________ a(n) __________.
   a. right-click, object
   b. click, menu name on the menu bar
   c. click, submenu
   d. double-click, indented button on the taskbar
3. In this book, a dark blue title bar and an indented button on the taskbar indicate a window is __________.
   a. inactive
   b. minimized
   c. closed
   d. active
4. To view contents of a window that are not currently visible in the window, use the __________.
   a. title bar
   b. scroll bar
   c. menu bar
   d. Restore button

(continued)

Test Your Knowledge

Multiple Choice *(continued)*

5. __________ is holding down the right mouse button, moving an item to the desired location, and then releasing the right mouse button.
   a. Double-clicking
   b. Right-clicking
   c. Right-dragging
   d. Pointing
6. The Notepad command used to start the Notepad application program is located on the __________ (sub)menu.
   a. Start
   b. Accessories
   c. Programs
   d. Help
7. To quit the Notepad application and close its window, __________.
   a. click the Close button on the Notepad title bar
   b. click File on the menu bar
   c. double-click the Notepad title bar
   d. click the Minimize button on the Notepad title bar
8. To save a Notepad document after modifying the document, __________.
   a. click the Close button on the Notepad title bar
   b. click the Minimize button on the Notepad title bar
   c. click Save on the File menu
   d. click Exit on the File menu
9. For information about an item on the Index sheet of the Help Topics: Windows Help window, __________.
   a. press the F1 key
   b. click the Question Mark button in the top right corner of the dialog box and then click the item
   c. click the Find tab in the Help Topics: Windows Help window
   d. press CTRL+F3
10. To shut down Windows 95, __________.
    a. click the Start button, click Shut Down on the Start menu, click the Shut down the computer? option button, and then click the Yes button
    b. click the Shut Down button on the Windows 95 File menu
    c. click the taskbar, click Close down Windows 95, and then click the Yes button
    d. press the F10 key and then click the Yes button

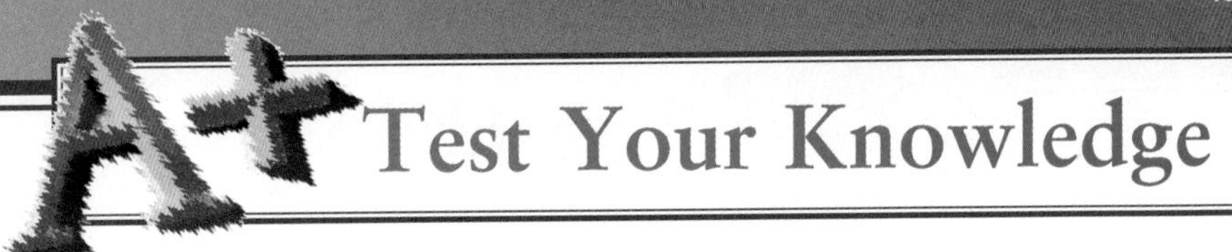

3 Identifying Objects on the Desktop

Instructions: On the desktop in Figure 1-66, arrows point to several items or objects on the desktop. Identify the items or objects in the spaces provided.

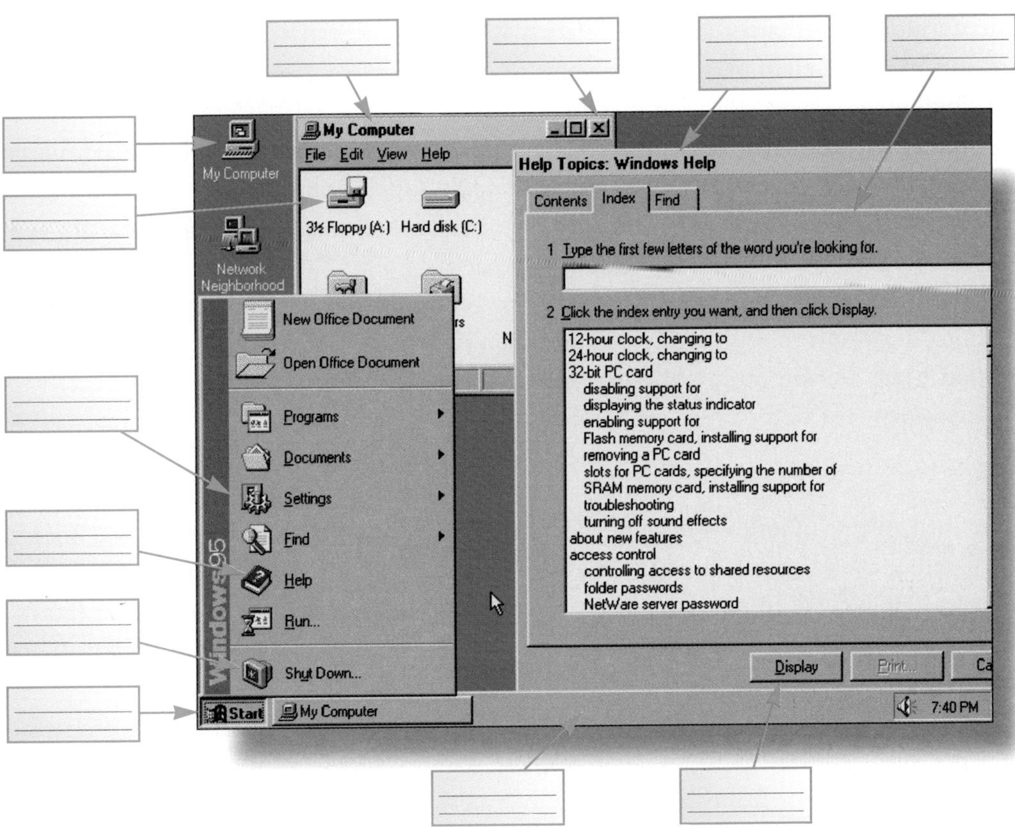

FIGURE 1-66

4 Saving a Document

Instructions: List the steps in the spaces provided to save a new Notepad file on a floppy disk in drive A using the filename, This is my file.

Step 1: ______________________________

Step 2: ______________________________

Step 3: ______________________________

Step 4: ______________________________

Step 5: ______________________________

Step 6: ______________________________

Step 7: ______________________________

Use Help

1 Using Windows Help

Instructions: Use Windows Help and a computer to perform the following tasks.

Part 1: *Using the Question Mark Button*

1. Start Microsoft Windows 95 if necessary.
2. Click the Start button. Click Help on the Start menu to open the Help Topics: Windows Help window. If the Contents tab sheet does not display, click the Contents tab.
3. Click the Question Mark button on the title bar. The mouse pointer changes to a block arrow with question mark pointer. Click the list box containing the Help topics and Help books. A pop-up window explaining the list box displays. Click an open area of the list box to remove the pop-up window.
4. Click the Question Mark button on the title bar and then click the Display button.
5. Click the Question Mark button on the title bar and then click the Print button.
6. Click the Question Mark button on the title bar and then click the Cancel button.
7. Click an open area of the list box to remove the pop-up window.

Part 2: *Finding What's New with Windows 95*

1. Double-click the Introducing Windows book to open the book. Double-click the Welcome book to open the book. Double-click the A List of What's New book to open the book. Double-click the A new look and feel Help topic to open the Windows Help window. Click the first button (Start button and taskbar) and read the contents of the What's New window.
2. Click the Close button in the What's New window.
3. Click the Help Topics button in the Windows Help window to open the Help Topics: Windows Help window. Click the Print button in the Help Topics: Windows Help window. Click the OK button in the Print dialog box to print the Help topic (A new look and feel).
4. Click the Help Topics button in the Windows Help window.
5. Double-click the Welcome book to close the book.

Part 3: *Learning About Getting Your Work Done*

1. Double-click the Getting Your Work Done book to open the book. Double-click the Saving your work Help topic. Click the Save button and read the pop-up window.
2. Click other items in the Save As dialog box and read the pop-up windows.
3. Click the Help Topics button in the Windows Help window to open the Help Topics: Windows Help window. Click the Print button in the Help Topics: Windows Help window. Click the OK button in the Print dialog box to print the Saving your work Help topic.
4. Click the Close buttons in the Windows Help windows to close the windows.

Use Help

2 Using Windows Help to Obtain Help

Instructions: Use Windows Help and a computer to perform the following tasks.

1. Find Help about viewing the Welcome screen that displays when you start Windows 95 by looking in the Tips of the Day book within the Tips and Tricks book in the Help Topics: Windows Help window. Answer the following questions in the spaces provided.
   a. How can you open the Welcome screen? ______________________________
   b. How can you see the list of tips in the Welcome screen? ______________________
   c. Open the Welcome screen. Cycle through the tips in the Welcome screen. How can you set your computer's clock? ______________________________
   d. Click the What's New button in the Welcome screen. According to Help, how do you start a program? ______________________________
   e. Close the Welcome screen. Click the Help Topics button in the Windows Help window.
2. Find Help about keyboard shortcuts by looking in the Keyboard Shortcuts book. Answer the following questions in the spaces provided.
   a. What keyboard shortcut is used to quit a program? ______________________
   b. What keyboard shortcut is used to display the Start menu? ______________________
   c. What keyboard shortcut is used to view the shortcut menu for a selected item? __________
   d. What keyboard shortcut is used to rename an item? ______________________
   e. What keyboard shortcut is used to open the Save in list box (drop-down list box)? __________
   f. Click the Help Topics button in the Windows Help window.
3. Find Help about Notepad by looking in the For Writing and Drawing book. Answer the following questions in the spaces provided.
   a. Can you create or edit a text file that requires formatting using Notepad? __________
   b. What size file can you create using Notepad? ______________________
   c. Which program can you use to create a larger file? ______________________
   d. What is the only format used by Notepad to store a file? ______________________
4. Find Help about the Internet by looking in the Welcome to the Information Highway book. Answer the following questions in the spaces provided.
   a. List one source of online information available on the Internet. ______________________
   b. How do you use The Microsoft Network to sign up for the Internet?
   c. Where else can you find information about connecting to the Internet? __________
5. Find Help about what to do if you have a problem starting Windows 95. The process of solving such a problem is called troubleshooting. Answer the following questions in the spaces provided.
   a. What size floppy disk do you need to create a startup disk? ______________________
   b. To start Windows in safe mode, what do you do when you see the message "Starting Windows 95?" ______________________
6. Answer the following questions in the spaces provided.
   a. List two ways you can get Help in a dialog box: ______________________; __________.
   b. How can you print information displayed in a Help pop-up window?
   ____

(continued)

Use Help

Use Help *(continued)*

7. You have been assigned to obtain information on software licensing. Answer the following questions, and find and print information from Windows Help that supports your answers.
   a. How is computer software protected by law?
   b. What is software piracy? Why should you be concerned?
   c. Can you use your own software on both your desktop and your laptop computers?
   d. How can you identify illegal software?
8. Close all open Windows Help windows.

In the Lab

1 Improving Your Mouse Skills

Instructions: Use a computer to perform the following tasks:

1. Start Microsoft Windows 95 if necessary.
2. Click the Start button on the taskbar, point to Programs on the Start menu, point to Accessories on the Programs submenu, point to Games on the Accessories submenu, and click Solitaire on the Games submenu.
3. Click the Maximize button in the Solitaire window.
4. Click Help on the Solitaire menu bar.
5. Click Help Topics on the Help menu.
6. If the Contents sheet does not display, click the Contents tab.
7. Review the How to play Solitaire and Scoring information Help topics on the Contents sheet.
8. After reviewing the topics, close all Help windows.
9. Play the game of Solitaire.
10. Click the Close button on the Solitaire title bar to close the game.

2 Starting an Application, Creating a Document, and Modifying a Document

Instructions: Perform the following steps to start the Notepad application and create and modify a document.

***Part 1:** Creating a Document*

1. Start Microsoft Windows 95 if necessary.
2. Click the Start button. Point to Programs on the Start menu. Point to Accessories on the Programs submenu. Click Notepad on the Accessories submenu.

In the Lab

3. Enter the document shown in Figure 1-67 in the Notepad document.
4. Insert a formatted floppy disk in drive A of your computer.
5. Click File on the menu bar. Click Save As on the File menu.
6. Type `Office Supplies Shopping List - Tuesday` in the File name text box.
7. Click the Save in box arrow. Click the 3½ Floppy [A:] icon. Click the Save button.
8. Click File on the menu bar. Click Print on the File menu.
9. Click the Close button on the Notepad title bar.
10. If you are not completing Part 2 of this assignment, remove your floppy disk from drive A.

```
Office Supplies Shopping List - Tuesday

1. Staples
2. 2 boxes of copier paper
3. Toner for computer printer
4. Box of formatted floppy disks
```

FIGURE 1-67

Part 2: ***Modifying a Document***

1. Click the Start button, point to Programs on the Start menu, point to Accessories on the Programs submenu, and then click Notepad on the Accessories submenu.
2. Click File on the menu bar and then click Open on the File menu. Click the Look in box arrow and then click the 3½ Floppy [A:] icon. Click Office Supplies Shopping List - Tuesday. Click the Open button.
3. Press the DOWN ARROW key six times. Type `5. Two boxes of black ink pens` and then press the ENTER key.
4. Click File on the menu bar and then click Save on the File menu.
5. Click File on the menu bar and then click Print on the File menu.
6. Click the Close button on the Notepad title bar.
7. Remove the floppy disk from drive A of your computer.

3 Creating a Document

Instructions: As a student, you would like to give a copy of your daily schedule to your parents and friends so you can be contacted in an emergency. To do this, you want to create a document for each weekday (Monday through Friday). Each document will have an appropriate title and contain your daily school and personal schedule. Each course in the document will contain the start and finish time for the course, course number, course title, room number, and instructor name. Other entries for extracurricular activities, sporting events, or personal events also will be included in the documents. Print the five documents on the printer and follow directions from your instructor for turning in this assignment. Store the five documents on a floppy disk.

Cases and Places

The difficulty of these case studies varies:

◗ Case studies preceded by a single half moon are the least difficult. You can complete these case studies using your own computer or a computer in the lab.
◗◗ Case studies preceded by two half moons are more difficult. You must research the topic presented using the Internet, a library, or another resource, and then prepare a brief written report.
◗◗◗ Case studies preceded by three half moons are the most difficult. You must visit a store or business to obtain the necessary information, and then use it to create a brief written report.

1 ◗ Your employer is concerned that some people in the company are not putting enough thought into software purchases. She has prepared a list of steps she would like everyone to follow when acquiring software (Figure 1-68).

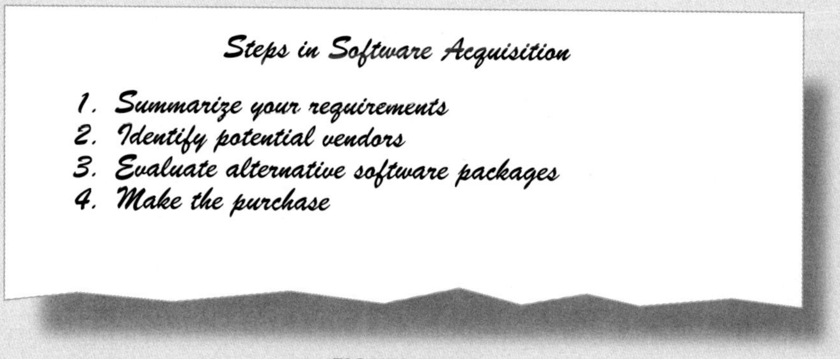

Steps in Software Acquisition

1. *Summarize your requirements*
2. *Identify potential vendors*
3. *Evaluate alternative software packages*
4. *Make the purchase*

FIGURE 1-68

You have been asked to use WordPad to prepare a copy of this list that can be posted in every department. Use the concepts and techniques presented in this project to start WordPad and create, save, and print the document. After you have printed one copy of the document, try experimenting with different WordPad features to make the list more eye-catching. If you like your changes, save and print a revised copy of the document. If WordPad is not available on your machine, use Notepad.

2 ◗ The local community center has asked you to teach an introductory class on Windows 95 to a group of adults with little previous computer experience. The center director has sent you a note about one of his concerns (Figure 1-69).

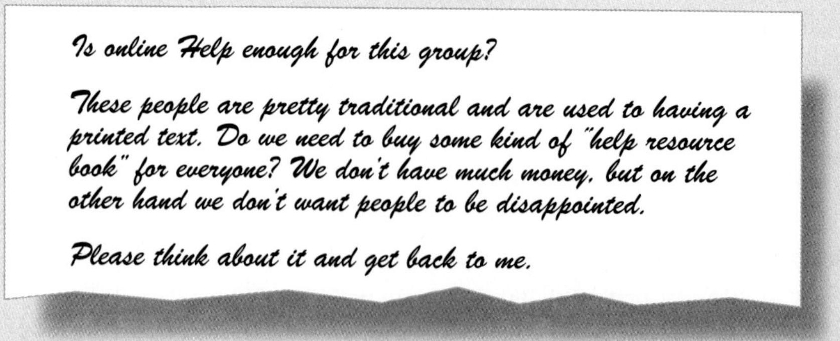

Is online Help enough for this group?

These people are pretty traditional and are used to having a printed text. Do we need to buy some kind of "help resource book" for everyone? We don't have much money, but on the other hand we don't want people to be disappointed.

Please think about it and get back to me.

FIGURE 1-69

Think of two topics about which people in the class may have questions. Use online Help to find answers to the questions. Consider how you would find answers to the same questions using a book. Write a response to the center director describing the advantages and disadvantages of using online Help instead of a book. Explain why you feel the class does or does not need a resource book. To make the director aware of online Help's limitations, tell how you think Microsoft could improve Help in Windows 95.

Cases and Places

3 ▸▸ Early personal computer operating systems were adequate, but they were not user-friendly and had few advanced features. Over the past several years, however, personal computer operating systems have become increasingly easy to use, and some now offer features once available only on mainframe computers. Using the Internet, a library, or other research facility, write a brief report on four personal computer operating systems. Describe the systems, pointing out their similarities and differences. Discuss the advantages and disadvantages of each. Finally, tell which operating system you would purchase for your personal computer and explain why.

4 ▸▸ Many feel that Windows 95 was one of the most heavily promoted products ever released. Using the Internet, current computer magazines, or other resources, prepare a brief report on the background of Windows 95. Explain why Windows 95 was two years behind schedule and how it was promoted. Discuss the ways in which Windows 95 is different from earlier versions of Windows (such as Windows 3.1). Based on reviews of the new operating system, describe what people like and do not like about Windows 95. Finally, from what you have learned and your own experience, explain how you think Windows 95 could be improved.

5 ▸▸▸ Software must be compatible with (able to work with) the operating system of the computer on which it will be used. Visit a software vendor and find the five application packages (word processing programs, spreadsheet programs, games, and so on) you would most like to have. List the names of the packages and the operating system used by each. Make a second list of five similar packages that are compatible (meaning they use the same operating system). Using your two lists, write a brief report on how the need to purchase compatible software can affect buying application packages and even the choice of an operating system.

6 ▸▸▸ Because of the many important tasks it performs, most businesses put a great deal of thought into choosing an operating system for their personal computers. Interview people at a local business on the operating system they use with their personal computers. Based on your interviews, write a brief report on why the business chose that operating system, how satisfied they are with it, and under what circumstances they might consider switching to a different operating system.

7 ▸▸▸ In a recent television commercial from Apple Computers, a frustrated father tries to use Windows 95 to display pictures of dinosaurs for his young son. After waiting impatiently, the boy tells his father he is going next door to the neighbor's because they have a Mac. Visit a computer vendor and try an operating system with a graphical user interface other than Windows 95, such as Macintosh System 7.5 or OS/2. Write a brief report comparing the operating system to Windows 95, and explain which operating system you would prefer to have on your personal computer.

Putting the Squeeze on DATA

In 1994, a federal district court ruled that Microsoft violated the rights of Stac Electronics in the data compression software component of MS-DOS 6.2, Microsoft's operating system. In response, Microsoft paid Stac a royalty of $43 million and replaced MS-DOS 6.2 with version 6.21, which did not contain the offending code.

Why the lawsuit? Data compression software, which allows you to store more data on your hard disk, is an important component of your computer's software and is so valuable to its developers that they will sue to protect their rights.

Disk storage capacity has not always been critical. Indeed, the first personal computers did not have disk storage. Instead, they used slow, unreliable tape cassettes. Then, in 1978, Apple demonstrated its first working prototype of the Apple

1978

320K

floppy disk drive. The drive could store 320,000 bytes, or characters, on a floppy disk 5.25 inches in diameter. It was a marvel and, by the end of 1978, Apple had sold more than 270,000 floppy disk drives.

It was not long, however, before computer users craved more disk storage. Apple announced its first hard disk drive in 1981. The drive could store five megabytes, but cost $3,500 ($700 per megabyte). By 1983, a hard disk drive could store 44 megabytes. Clearly the race was on to build drives that, today, store upwards of one gigabyte (one billion characters) at a price of about 25 cents per megabyte.

The hardware manufacturers were not the only ones trying to squeeze more data onto disks. Software companies developed data compression schemes that increased the apparent capacity of hard disks by storing the contents in a compressed form. Compressing data occurs in two ways. First, the software restructures the files on your hard disk so the data is stored more efficiently. Second, data is coded so redundancies in the data are reduced.

Some personal computer applications could not occur without data compression. For example, an uncompressed ten-second video requires nearly 200 megabytes of storage. This means an entire gigabyte drive would be consumed by a one-minute video if the video data was not compressed.

Compression, using hardware, software, or a combination of the two, is big business, and millions of dollars are being spent to develop new compression schemes. In the future, whether you are retrieving a word processing file from your hard disk or conducting a video conference over your network, it is likely the data will be stored and transmitted as compressed data.

1996 ONE GIGABYTE

Microsoft
Windows 95

Using Windows Explorer

Case Perspective

Need: Your organization has finally made the decision to switch to Windows 95 from Windows 3.1. Although most everyone is excited about the change, many are apprehensive about file management. Few of them ever felt comfortable with Windows 3.1 File Manager and, as a result, hardly ever used it. Your boss has read in computer magazines that in order to effectively use Windows 95, people must learn Windows Explorer. She has asked you to teach a class with an emphasis on file management to all employees who will be using Windows 95. Your goal in Project 2 is to become competent using Windows Explorer so you can teach the class.

Introduction

Windows Explorer is an application program included with Windows 95 that allows you to view the contents of the computer, the hierarchy of folders on the computer, and the files and folders in each folder.

Windows Explorer also allows you to organize the files and folders on the computer by copying and moving the files and folders. In this project, you will use Windows Explorer to (1) work with the files and folders on your computer; (2) select and copy a group of files between the hard drive and a floppy disk; (3) create, rename, and delete a folder on floppy disk; and (4) rename and delete a file on floppy disk. These are common operations that you should understand how to perform.

Starting Windows 95

As explained in Project 1, when you turn on the computer, an introductory screen consisting of the Windows 95 logo and the Microsoft Windows 95 name displays on a blue sky and clouds background. The screen clears and Windows 95 displays several items on the desktop.

If the Welcome to Windows screen displays on your desktop, click the Close button on the title bar to close the screen. Six icons (My Computer, Network Neighborhood, Inbox, Recycle Bin, The Microsoft Network, and My Briefcase) display along the left edge of the desktop, the Microsoft Office Manager toolbar displays in the upper right corner of the desktop, and the taskbar displays along the bottom of the desktop (Figure 2-1).

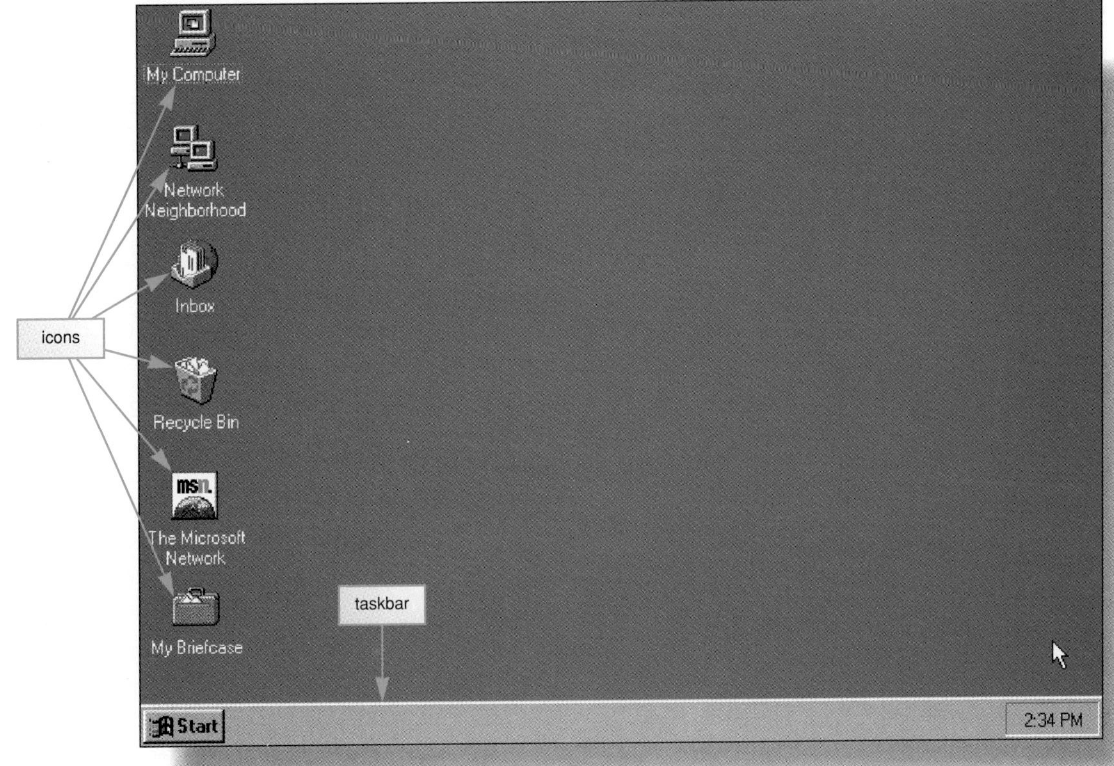

FIGURE 2-1

Starting Windows Explorer and Maximizing Its Window

To start Windows Explorer and explore the files and folders on the computer, right-click the My Computer icon on the desktop, which opens a context-sensitive menu, and then click the Explore command on the menu to open the Exploring – My Computer window. To maximize the Exploring – My Computer window, click the Maximize button on the title bar.

Steps To Start Windows Explorer and Maximize Its Window

1. **Right-click the My Computer icon to open a context-sensitive menu, and then point to the Explore command on the menu.**

Windows 95 highlights the My Computer icon, opens a context-sensitive menu, and highlights the Explore command on the menu (Figure 2-2). The mouse pointer points to the Explore command on the menu.

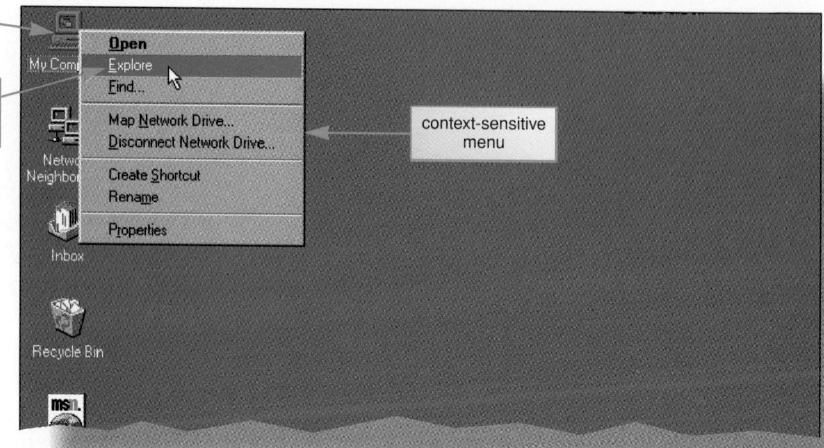

FIGURE 2-2

2. **Click Explore on the context-sensitive menu, and then click the Maximize button on the Exploring – My Computer title bar.**

Windows 95 opens and maximizes the Exploring – My Computer window and adds the indented Exploring – My Compu... button to the taskbar (Figure 2-3).

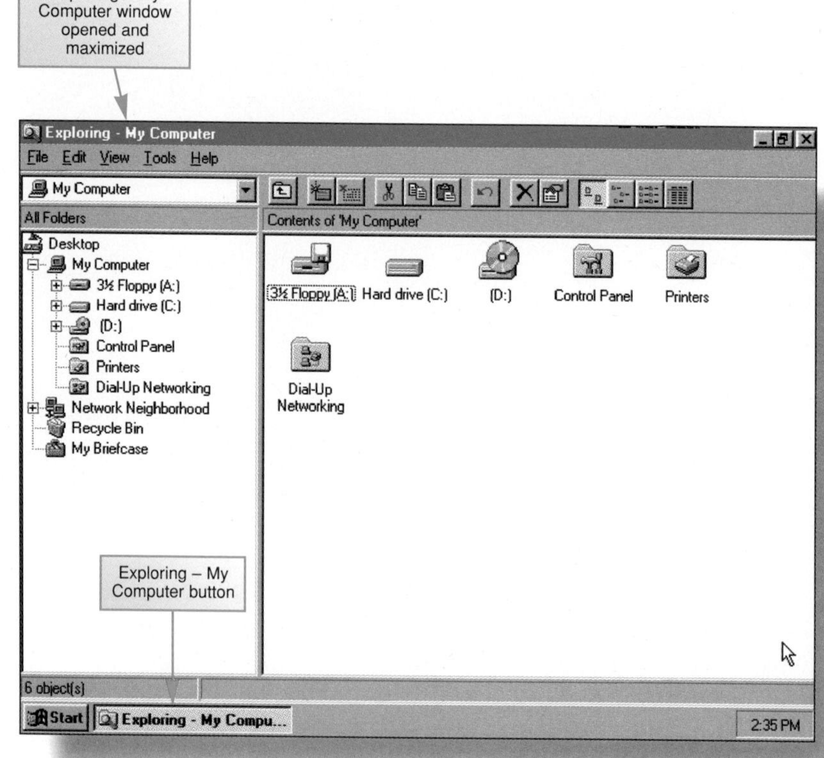

FIGURE 2-3

OtherWays

1. Right-click Start button, click Explore on context-sensitive menu
2. Click Start button, point to Programs, click Windows Explorer on the Programs submenu
3. Right-click Network Neighborhood icon, or Inbox icon, or Recycle Bin icon, or The Microsoft Network icon, or My Briefcase icon, click Explore on context-sensitive menu
4. Right-click Start button or any icons in 3 above, press E

Windows Explorer

When you start Windows Explorer by right-clicking the My Computer icon, Windows 95 opens the Exploring – My Computer window (Figure 2-4). The menu bar contains the File, Edit, View, Tools, and Help menu names.

These menus contain commands to organize and work with the drives on the computer and the files and folders on those drives.

Below the menu bar is a toolbar. The **toolbar** contains a drop-down list box and thirteen buttons. The drop-down list box contains an icon and the My Computer folder name. The entry in the drop-down list box, called the **current folder**, indicates Windows Explorer was started by right-clicking the My Computer icon. The buttons on the toolbar provide a quick way to perform commonly used tasks in Windows Explorer. Many of the buttons correspond to the commands available from the menu bar. Pointing to a button on the toolbar displays a ToolTip identifying the button. If the toolbar does not display in the Exploring – My Computer window on your computer, click View on the menu bar and then click Toolbar on the View menu.

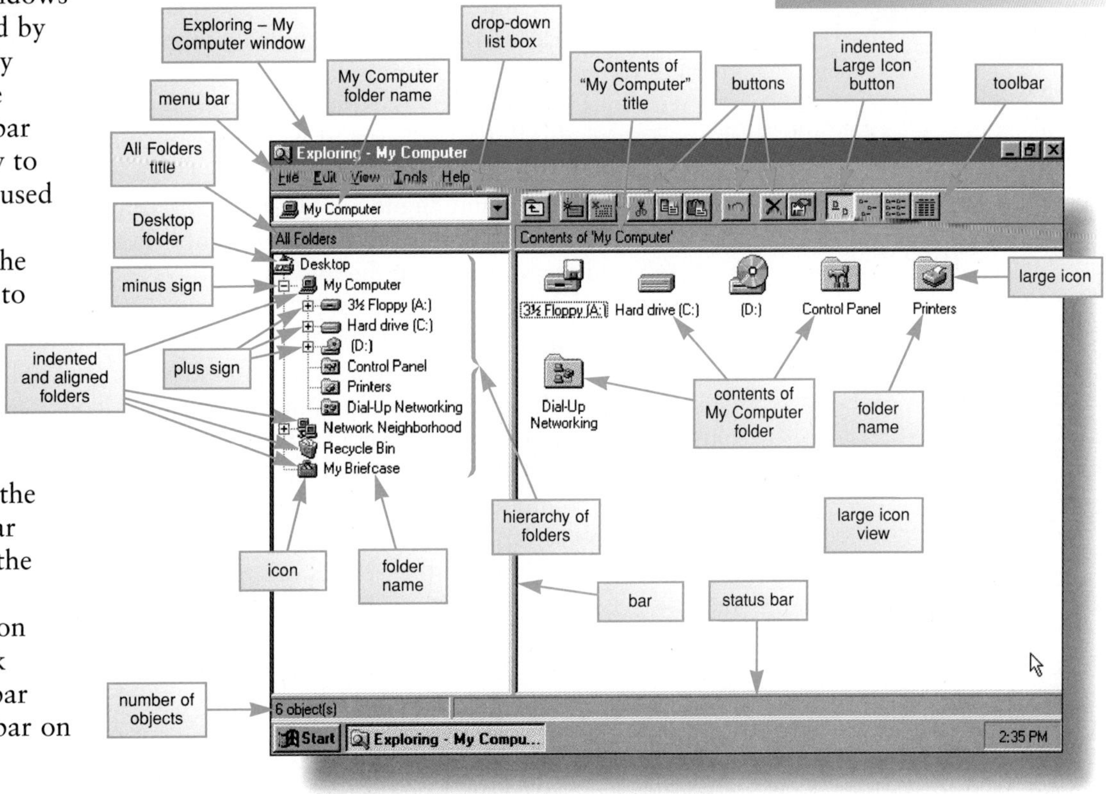

FIGURE 2-4

The window is divided into two areas separated by a bar. The left side of the window, identified by the All Folders title, contains a **hierarchy** of folders on the computer. The right side of the window, identified by the Contents of 'My Computer' title, displays the contents of the current folder (My Computer). In Figure 2-4, the Contents side contains the icons and folder names of six folders (3½ Floppy [A:], Hard drive [C:], and [D:], Control Panel, Printers, and Dial-Up Networking). These folders may be different on your computer. You change the size of the All Folders and Contents sides of the window by dragging the bar that separates the two sides.

Each folder in the All Folders side of the window is represented by an icon and folder name. The first folder, consisting of an icon and the Desktop folder name, represents the desktop of the computer. The four folders indented and aligned below the Desktop folder name (My Computer, Network Neighborhood,

More About Explorer

For those familiar with Windows 3.1, Windows 95 Explorer bears some resemblance to File Manager. Microsoft, however, made significant improvements and changed the basic way the program works. Those who passionately disliked File Manager might find Explorer a better way to perform file maintenance.

More About a Hierarchy

One definition of hierarchy in Webster's Ninth New Collegiate Dictionary is, "a division of angels." While no one would argue angels have anything to do with Windows 95, some preach that working with a hierarchical structure as presented by Explorer is less secular ("of or relating to the worldly") and more spiritual ("of or relating to supernatural phenomena") than the straight-forward showing of files in windows. What do you think?

Recycle Bin, and My Briefcase) are connected to the vertical line below the Desktop icon. These folders correspond to four of the six icons displayed on the left edge of the desktop (see Figure 2-1 on page WIN 2.5). These folders may be different on your computer.

Windows 95 displays a minus sign (–) in a box to the left of any icon in the All Folders side to indicate the corresponding folder contains one or more folders that are visible in the All Folders side. These folders, called **subfolders**, are indented and aligned below the folder name.

In Figure 2-4 on the previous page, a minus sign precedes the My Computer icon, and six subfolders are indented and display below the My Computer folder name. The six subfolders (3½ Floppy [A:], Hard drive [C:], [D:], Control Panel, Printers, and Dial-Up Networking) correspond to the six folders in the Contents side. Clicking the minus sign, referred to as **collapsing the folder**, removes the indented subfolders from the hierarchy of folders in the All Folders side and changes the minus sign to a plus sign.

Windows 95 displays a plus sign (+) in a box to the left of an icon to indicate the corresponding folder consists of one or more subfolders that arc not visible in the All Folders side of the window. In Figure 2-4, a plus sign precedes the first three icons indented and aligned below the My Computer name (3½ Floppy [A:], Hard drive [C:], [D:]) and the Network Neighborhood icon. Clicking the plus sign, referred to as **expanding the folders**, displays a list of indented subfolders and changes the plus sign to a minus sign.

If neither a plus sign nor a minus sign displays to the left of an icon, the folder does not contain subfolders. In Figure 2-4, the Control Panel, Printers, Dial-Up Networking, Recycle Bin, and My Briefcase icons are not preceded by a plus or minus sign and do not contain subfolders.

The status bar at the bottom of the Exploring – My Computer window indicates the number of folders, or objects, displayed in the Contents side of the window (6 object(s)). Depending upon the objects displayed in the Contents side, the amount of disk space the objects occupy and the amount of unused disk space may also display on the status bar. If the status bar does not display in the Exploring – My Computer window on your computer, click View on the menu bar and then click Status Bar on the View menu.

In addition to using Windows Explorer to explore your computer by right-clicking the My Computer icon, you can also use Windows Explorer to explore different aspects of your computer by right-clicking the Start button on the taskbar and the Network Neighborhood, Inbox, Recycle Bin, The Microsoft Network, and My Briefcase icons on the desktop.

Displaying the Contents of a Folder

In Figure 2-4 on the previous page, the current folder (My Computer) displays in the drop-down list box on the toolbar and the Contents side of the window contains the subfolders in the My Computer folder. In addition to displaying the contents of the My Computer folder, the contents of any folder in the All Folders side can be displayed in the Contents side. Perform the following steps to display the contents of the Hard drive [C:] folder.

Steps To Display the Contents of a Folder

1 Point to the Hard drive [C:] folder name in the All Folders side of the Exploring – My Computer window (Figure 2-5).

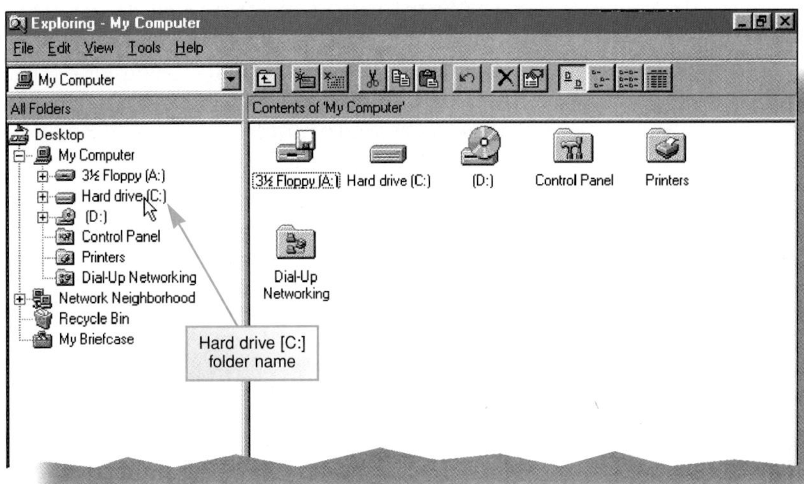

FIGURE 2-5

2 Click the Hard drive [C:] folder name.

Windows 95 highlights the Hard drive [C:] folder name in the All Folders side, changes the current folder in the drop-down list box to the Hard drive [C:] folder, displays the contents of the Hard drive [C:] folder in the Contents side, changes the window title to contain the current folder name (Exploring – Hard drive [C:]), changes the button on the taskbar to contain the current folder name, and changes the messages on the status bar (Figure 2-6). The status bar messages indicate there are 82 objects and 19 hidden objects in the Hard drive [C:] folder, the objects occupy 25.9MB of disk space, and the amount of unused disk space is 12.5MB. The contents of the Hard drive [C:] folder may be different on your computer.

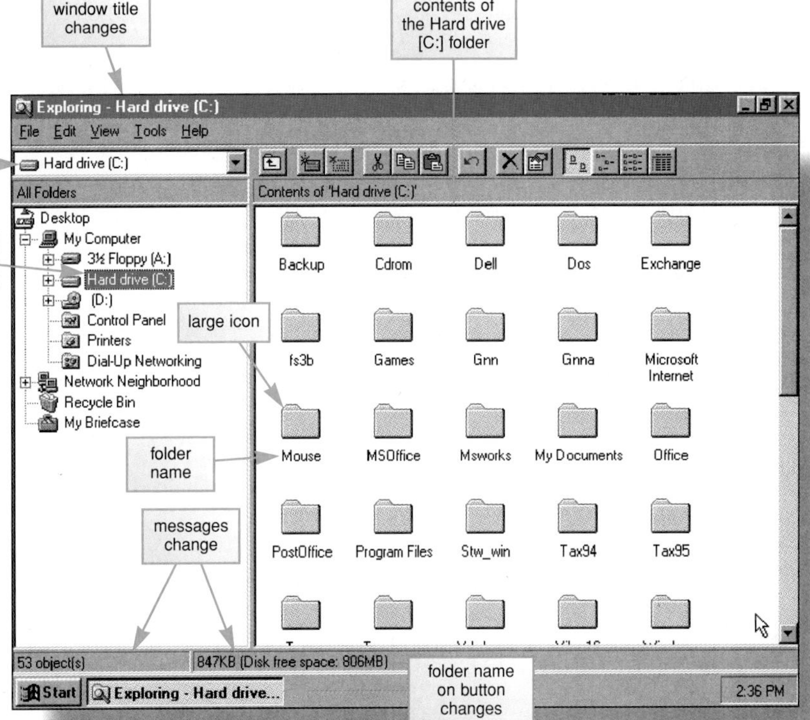

FIGURE 2-6

OtherWays

1. Double-click Hard disk [C:] icon in Contents side
2. Press TAB until any icon in All Folders side highlighted, press DOWN ARROW or UP ARROW until Hard disk [C:] highlighted in Contents side

In addition to displaying the contents of the Hard drive [C:] folder, you can display the contents of the other folders by clicking the corresponding icon or folder name in the All Folders side. The contents of the folder you click will then display in the Contents side of the window.

Expanding a Folder

Currently, the Hard drive [C:] folder is highlighted in the All Folders side of the Exploring – Hard drive [C:] window and the contents of the Hard drive [C:] folder display in the Contents side of the window. Windows 95 displays a plus sign (+) to the left of the Hard drive [C:] icon to indicate the folder contains subfolders that are not visible in the hierarchy of folders in the All Folders side of the window. To expand the Hard drive [C:] folder and display its subfolders, click the plus sign to the left of the Hard drive [C:] icon. Perform the following steps to expand the Hard drive [C:] folder.

To Expand a Folder

1 Point to the plus sign to the left of the Hard drive [C:] icon in the All Folders side of the Exploring – Hard drive [C:] window (Figure 2-7).

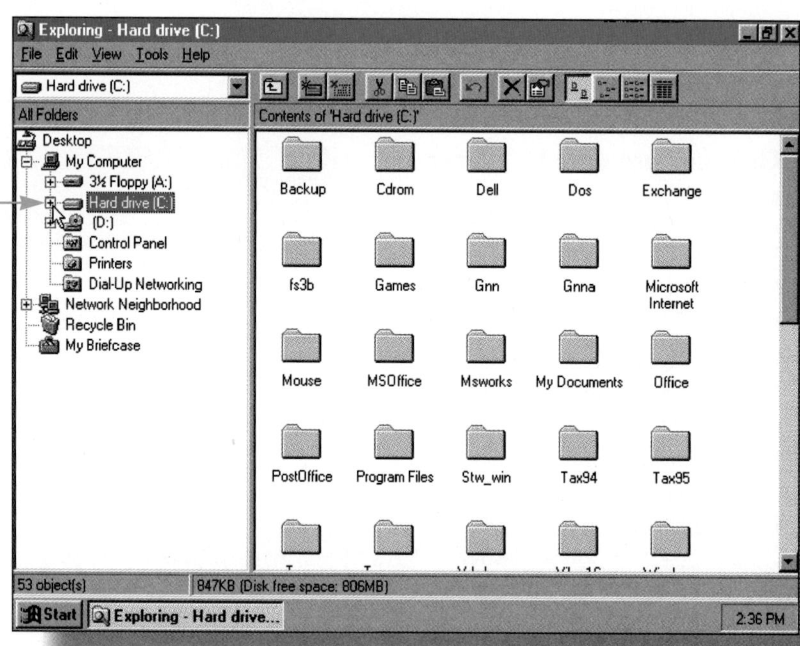

FIGURE 2-7

2 **Click the plus sign to display the subfolders in the Hard drive [C:] folder.**

Windows 95 replaces the plus sign preceding the Hard drive [C:] icon with a minus sign, displays a vertical scroll bar, and expands the Hard drive [C:] folder to include its subfolders, indented and aligned below the Hard drive [C:] folder name, (Figure 2-8). Each subfolder in the Hard drive [C:] folder is identified by a closed folder icon and folder name. The window title, current folder in the drop-down list box on the toolbar, and the files and folders in the Contents side of the window remain unchanged.

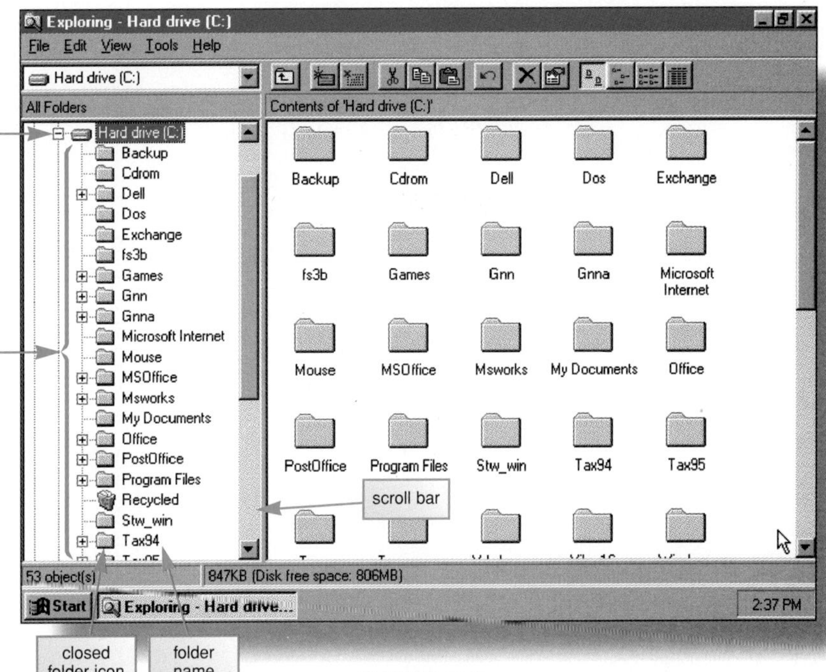

FIGURE 2-8

*Other*Ways

1. Double-click the folder icon
2. Select folder to expand, press PLUS on numeric keypad
3. Select folder to expand, press RIGHT ARROW

Collapsing a Folder

Currently, the subfolders in the Hard drive [C:] folder display indented and aligned below the Hard drive [C:] folder name (see Figure 2-8). Windows 95 displays a minus sign (–) to the left of the Hard drive [C:] icon to indicate the folder is expanded. To collapse the Hard drive [C:] folder and then remove its subfolders from the hierarchy of folders in the All Folders side, click the minus sign preceding the Hard drive [C:] icon. Perform the following steps to collapse the Hard drive [C:] folder.

To Collapse a Folder

1 **Point to the minus sign preceding the Hard drive [C:] icon in the All Folders side of the Exploring – Hard drive [C:] window (Figure 2-9).**

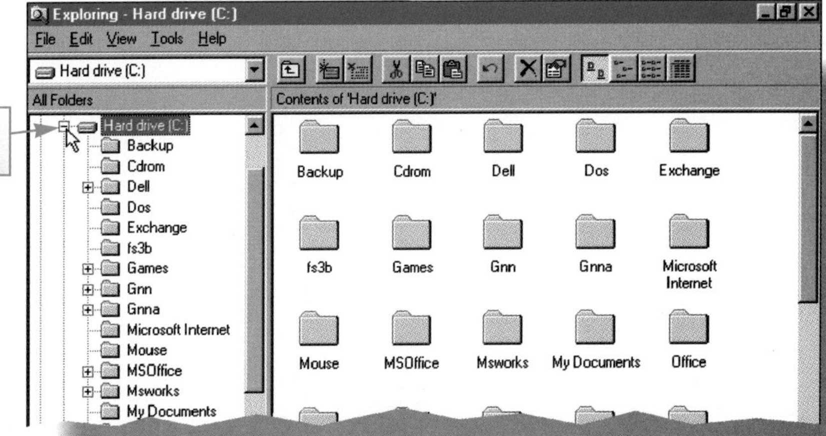

FIGURE 2-9

2 **Click the minus sign to display the Hard drive [C:] folder without its subfolders.**

Windows 95 replaces the minus sign preceding the Hard drive [C:] icon with a plus sign and removes the subfolders in the Hard drive [C:] folder from the hierarchy of folders (Figure 2-10).

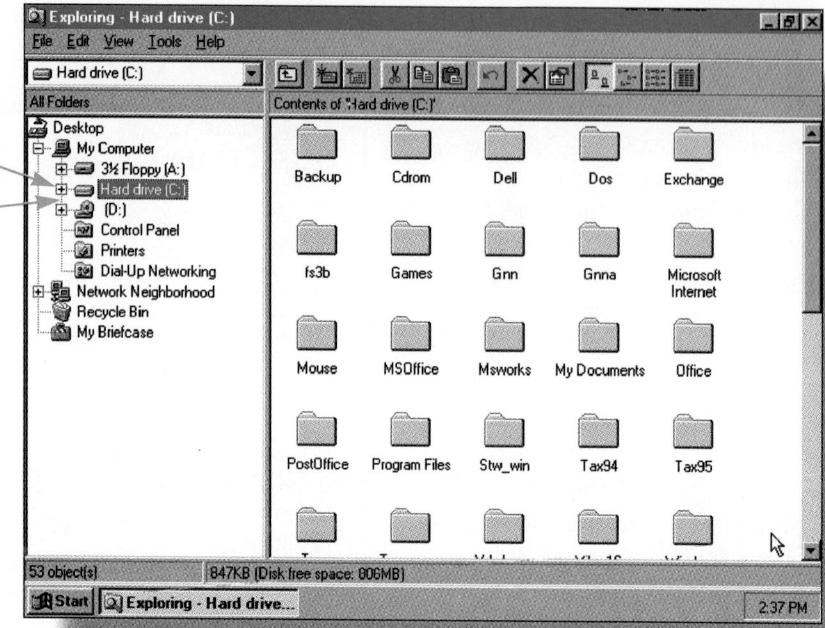

FIGURE 2-10

OtherWays

1. Highlight folder icon, press MINUS SIGN on numeric keypad
2. Double-click the folder icon
3. Select folder to collapse, press LEFT ARROW

Copying Files to a Folder on a Floppy Disk

One common operation that every student should understand how to perform is copying a file or group of files from one disk to another disk or from one folder to another folder. On the following pages, you will create a new folder, named My Files, on the floppy disk in drive A, select a group of files in the Windows folder on drive C, and copy the files from the Windows folder on drive C to the My Files folder on drive A.

When copying files, the drive and folder containing the files to be copied are called the **source drive** and **source folder**, respectively. The drive and folder to which the files are copied are called the **destination drive** and **destination folder**, respectively. Thus, the Windows folder is the source folder, drive C is the source drive, the My Files folder is the destination folder, and drive A is the destination drive.

Creating a New Folder

In preparation for selecting and copying files from a folder on the hard drive to a folder on the floppy disk in drive A, a new folder with the name of My Files will be created on the floppy disk. Perform the following steps to create the new folder.

Steps To Create a New Folder

1 **Insert a formatted floppy disk into drive A on your computer.**

2 **Click the 3½ Floppy [A:] folder name in the All Folders side of the Exploring – Hard drive [C:] window and then point to an open area of the Contents side of the window.**

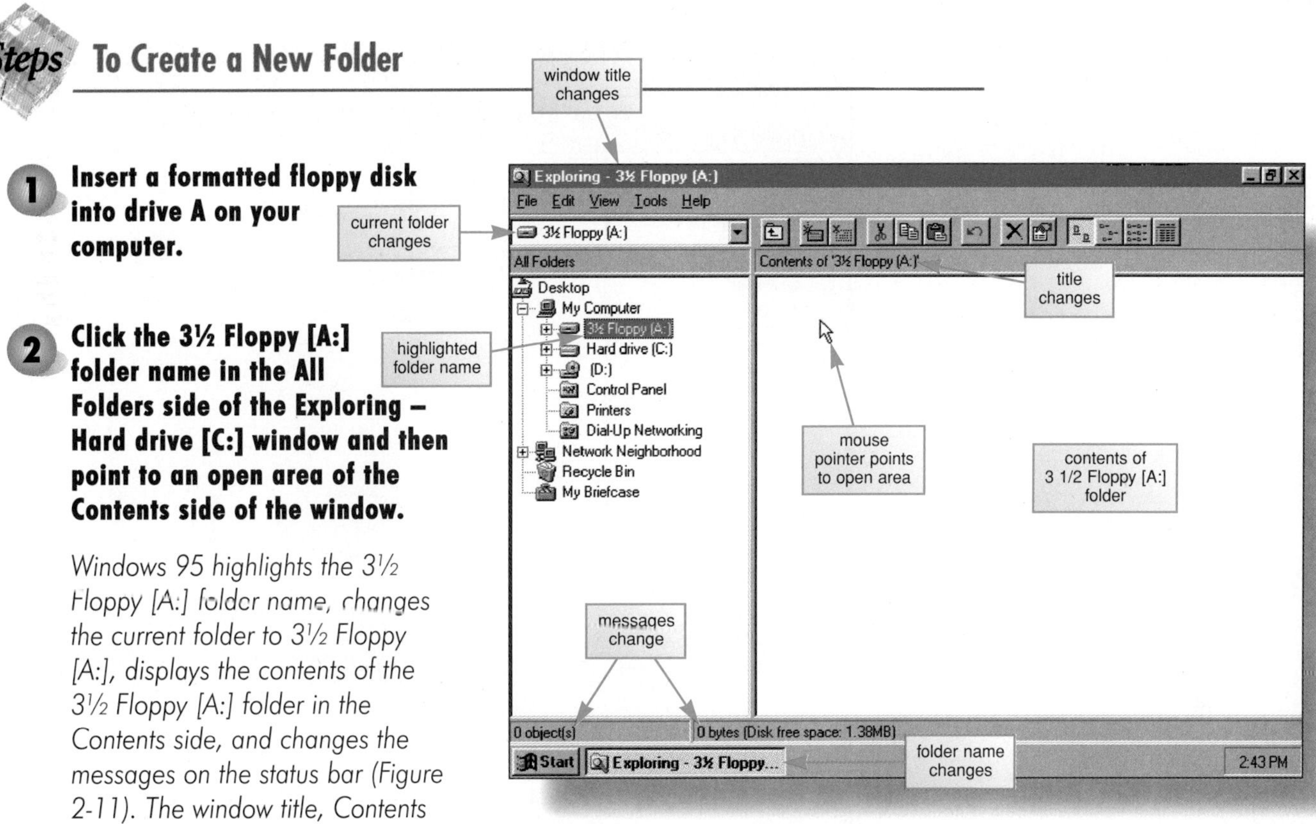

FIGURE 2-11

Windows 95 highlights the 3½ Floppy [A:] folder name, changes the current folder to 3½ Floppy [A:], displays the contents of the 3½ Floppy [A:] folder in the Contents side, and changes the messages on the status bar (Figure 2-11). The window title, Contents side title, and button on the taskbar change to include the 3½ Floppy [A:] folder name. Currently, no files or folders display in the Contents side. The files and folders may be different on your computer. The mouse pointer points to an open area of the Contents side.

3 **Right-click the open area of the Contents side of the window to open a context-sensitive menu and then point to New on the menu.**

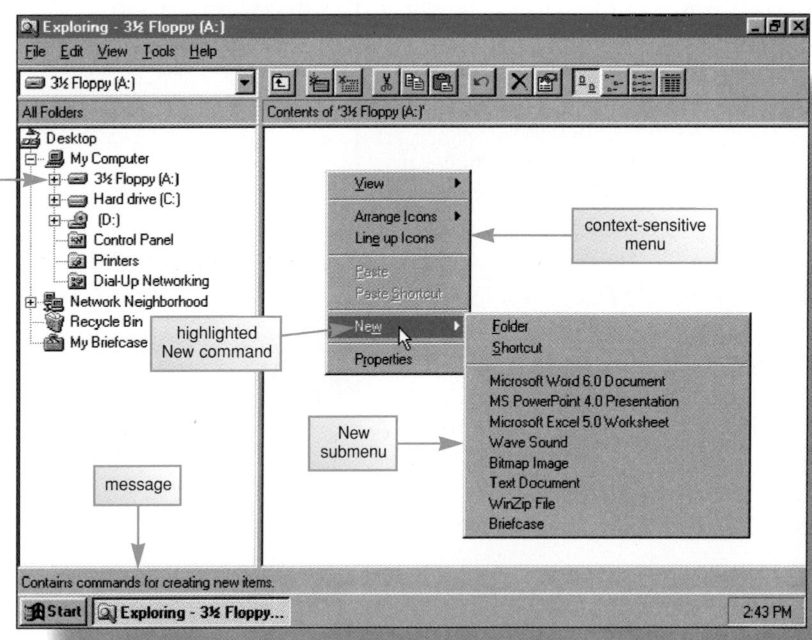

FIGURE 2-12

Windows 95 opens a context-sensitive menu and the New submenu, highlights the New command in the context-sensitive menu, and displays a message on the status bar (Figure 2-12). The message, Contains commands for creating new items., indicates the New submenu contains commands that allow you to create new items in the Contents side. The mouse pointer points to the New command. Although no subfolders display in the Contents side and no plus sign should precede the 3½ Floppy [A:] icon in the All Folders area, a plus sign precedes the icon.

4 **Point to Folder on the New submenu.**

Windows 95 highlights the Folder command on the New submenu and displays the message, Creates a new, empty folder., on the status bar (Figure 2-13). The mouse pointer points to the Folder command. Clicking the Folder command will create a folder in the Contents side of the window using the default folder name, New Folder.

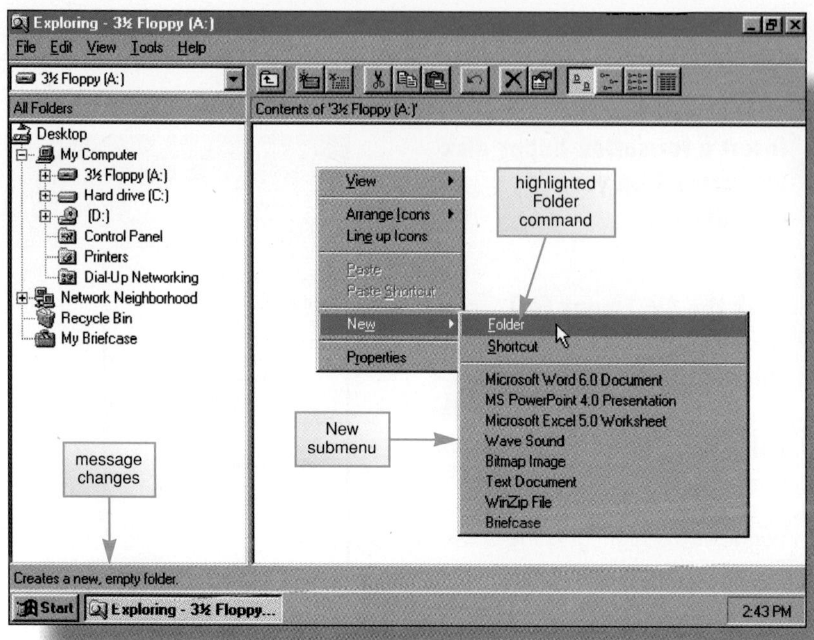

FIGURE 2-13

5 **Click Folder on the New submenu.**

Windows 95 closes the context-sensitive menu and New submenu, displays the highlighted New Folder icon in the Contents side, and changes the message on the status bar (Figure 2-14). The text box below the icon contains the highlighted default folder name, New Folder, followed by the insertion point. A plus sign continues to display to the left of the 3½ Floppy [A:] icon to indicate the 3½ Floppy [A:] folder contains the New Folder subfolder. The message on the status bar indicates one object is selected in the Contents side.

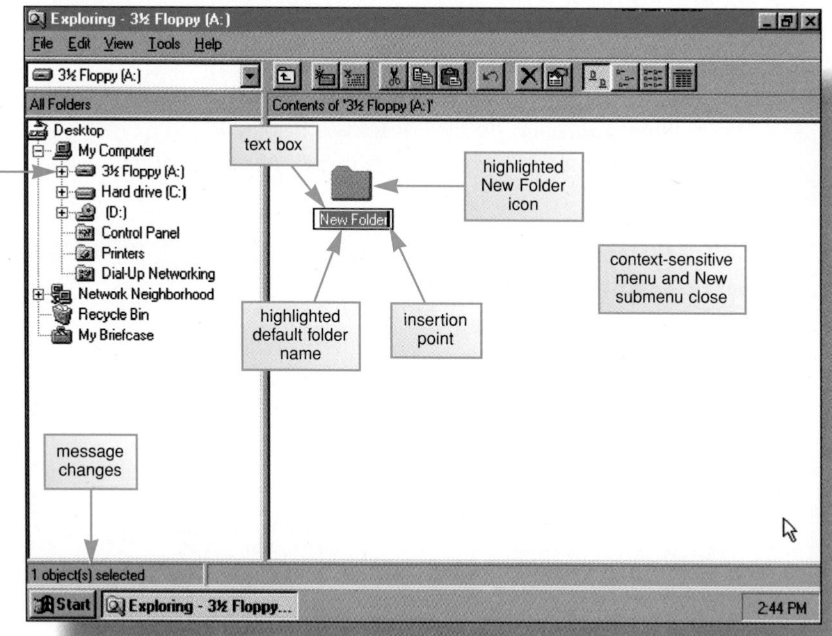

FIGURE 2-14

6 Type `My Files` **in the text box and then press the ENTER key.**

The new folder name, My Files, is entered and Windows 95 removes the text box (Figure 2-15).

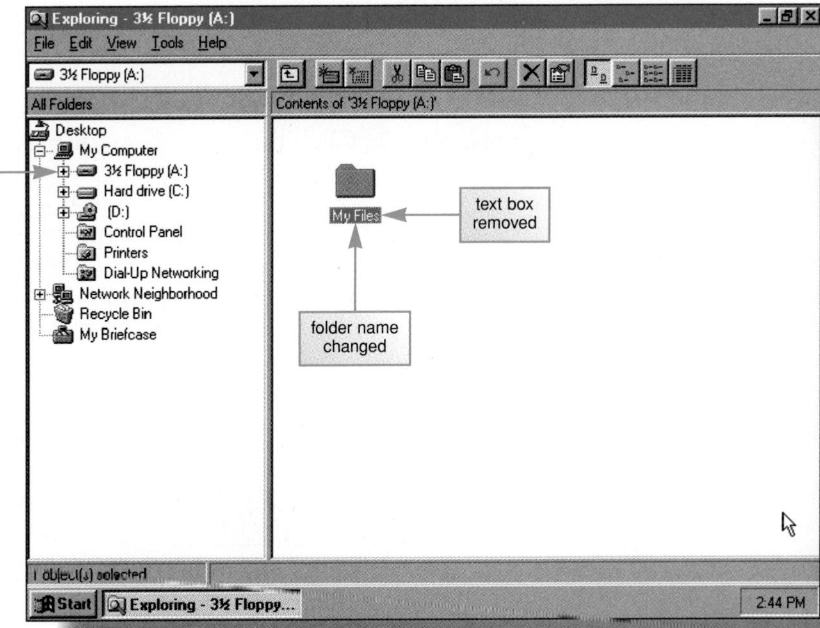

FIGURE 2-15

OtherWays

1. Select drive, click File on the menu bar, on File menu click New, click Folder on New submenu

After creating the My Files folder on the floppy disk in drive A, you can save files in the folder or copy files from other folders to the folder. On the following pages, you will copy a group of files consisting of the Black Thatch, Bubbles, and Circles files from the Windows folder on drive C to the My Files folder on drive A.

Displaying the Destination Folder

To copy the three files from the Windows folder on drive C to the My Files folder on drive A, the files to be copied will be selected in the Contents side and right-dragged to the My Files folder in the All Folders side. Prior to selecting or right-dragging the files, the destination folder (My Files folder on drive A) must be visible in the All Folders side and the three files to be copied must be visible in the Contents side.

Currently, the plus sign (+) to the left of the 3½ Floppy [A:] icon indicates the folder contains one or more subfolders that are not visible in the All Folders side (see Figure 2-15). Perform the steps on the next page to expand the 3½ Floppy [A:] folder to display the My Files subfolder.

TO EXPAND THE 3½ FLOPPY [A:] FOLDER

Step 1: Point to the plus sign to the left of the 3½ Floppy [A:] icon in the All Folders side of the Exploring – 3½ Floppy [A:] window.
Step 2: Click the plus sign to display the subfolders in the 3½ Floppy [A:] folder.

Windows 95 replaces the plus sign preceding the 3½ Floppy [A:] folder with a minus sign, highlights the 3½ Floppy [A:] folder name, and displays the subfolders in the 3½ Floppy [A:] folder, indented and aligned below the 3½ Floppy [A:] folder name (Figure 2-16). Currently, only one subfolder (My Files) displays.

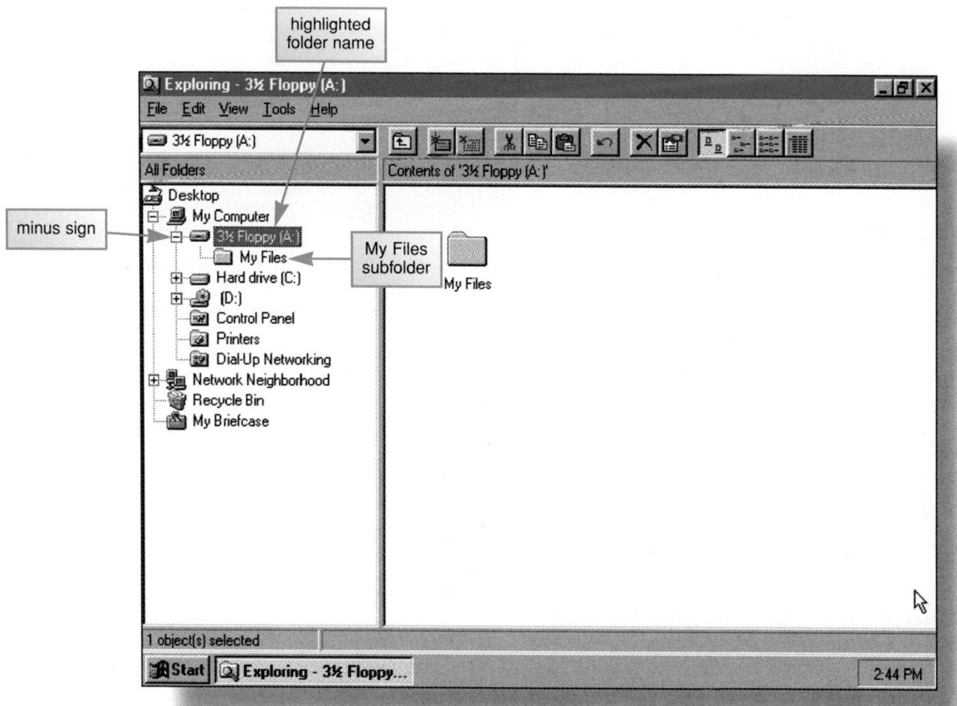

FIGURE 2-16

OtherWays

1. Right-click 3½ Floppy [A:] icon, click Explore

Displaying the Contents of the Windows Folder

Currently, the My Files folder displays in the Contents side of the Exploring – 3½ Floppy [A:] window. To copy files from the source folder (Windows folder on drive C) to the My Files folder, the Windows folder must be visible in the All Folders side. To make the Windows folder visible, you must expand the Hard drive [C:] folder, scroll the All Folders side to make the Windows folder name visible, and then click the Windows folder name to display the contents of the Windows folder in the Contents side. Perform the following steps to display the contents of the Windows folder.

Steps To Display the Contents of a Folder

1 **Click the plus sign to the left of the Hard drive [C:] icon in the All Folders side of the Exploring – 3½ Floppy [A:] window, scroll the All Folders side to make the Windows folder name visible, and then point to the Windows folder name.**

*Windows 95 replaces the plus sign to the left of the Hard drive [C:] icon with a minus sign, displays the subfolders in the Hard drive [C:] folder, and scrolls the hierarchy of folders in the All Folders side to make the Windows folder visible (Figure 2-17). In addition to folders and other files, the Windows folder contains a series of predefined graphics, called **clip art files**, that can be used with application programs. The mouse pointer points to the Windows folder name. The plus sign to the left of the Hard drive [C:] icon is not visible in Figure 2-17.*

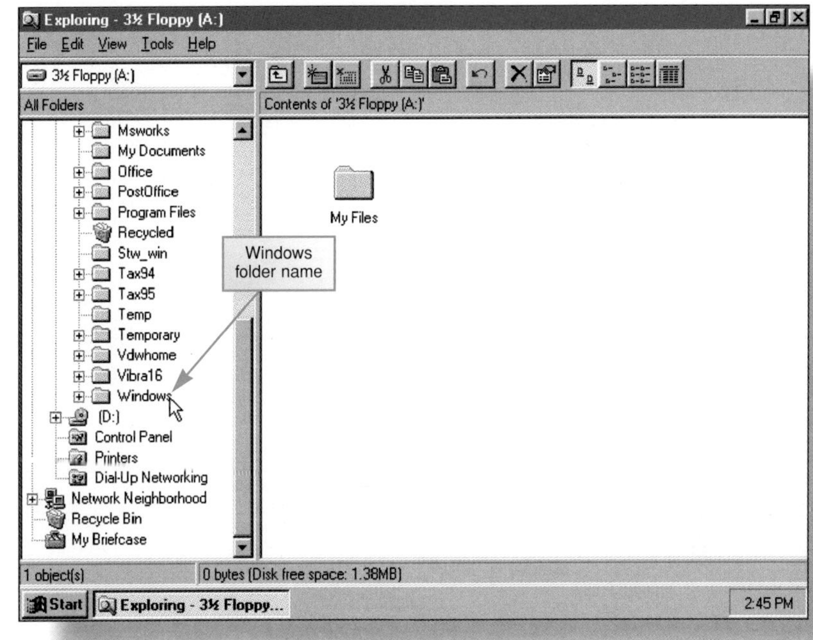

FIGURE 2-17

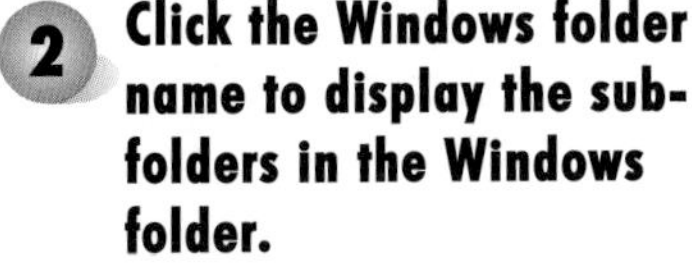

2 **Click the Windows folder name to display the subfolders in the Windows folder.**

Windows 95 highlights the Windows folder name in the All Folders side of the window, changes the closed folder icon to the left of the Windows folder name to an open folder icon, and displays the contents of the Windows folder in the Contents side (Figure 2-18).

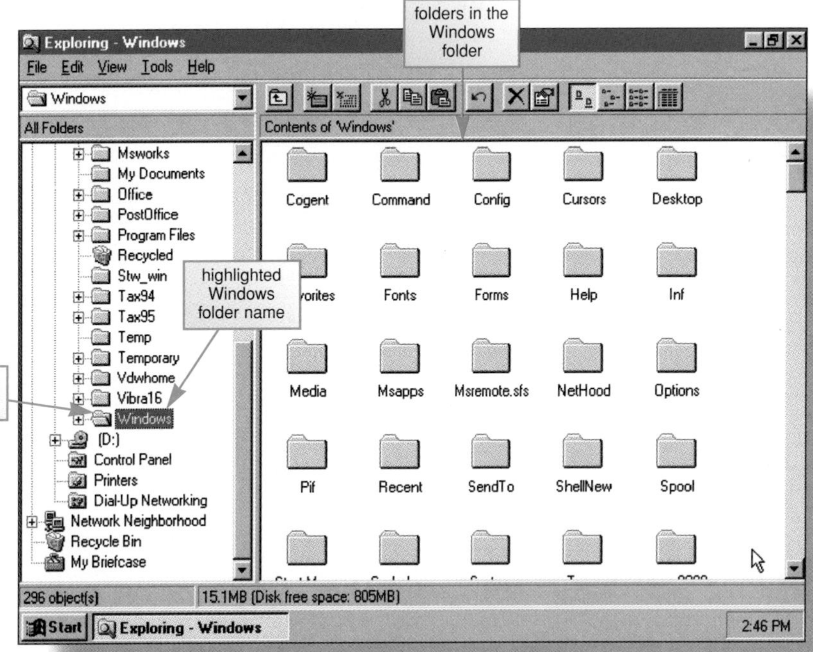

FIGURE 2-18

3 Scroll the Contents side to make the files in the Windows folder visible.

One folder (Wordview folder) and several files display in the Contents side of the window (Figure 2-19). Each file is identified by a large icon and a filename. The files and folders in the Windows folder may be different and the file extensions may not display on your computer.

FIGURE 2-19

Changing the View

In Figure 2-19, the files and folder in the Contents side of the Exploring – Windows window display in large icons view. In **large icons view**, each file and folder is represented by a large icon and a filename or folder name. Other views include the small icons, list, and details views. The list view is often useful when copying or moving files from one location to another location. In **list view**, each file or folder is represented by a smaller icon and name, and the files and folders are arranged in columns. Perform the following steps to change from large icons view to list view.

Steps To Change to List View

1 **Right-click any open area in the Contents side of the Exploring – Windows window to open a context-sensitive menu, point to View on the context-sensitive menu, and then point to List on the View submenu.**

Windows 95 opens a context-sensitive menu, highlights the View command on the context-sensitive menu, opens the View submenu, and highlights the List command on the View submenu (Figure 2-20). A large dot to the left of the Large Icons command on the View submenu indicates files and folders in the Contents side display in large icons view. The mouse pointer points to the List command. Clicking the List command will display the files and folders in the Contents side in list view.

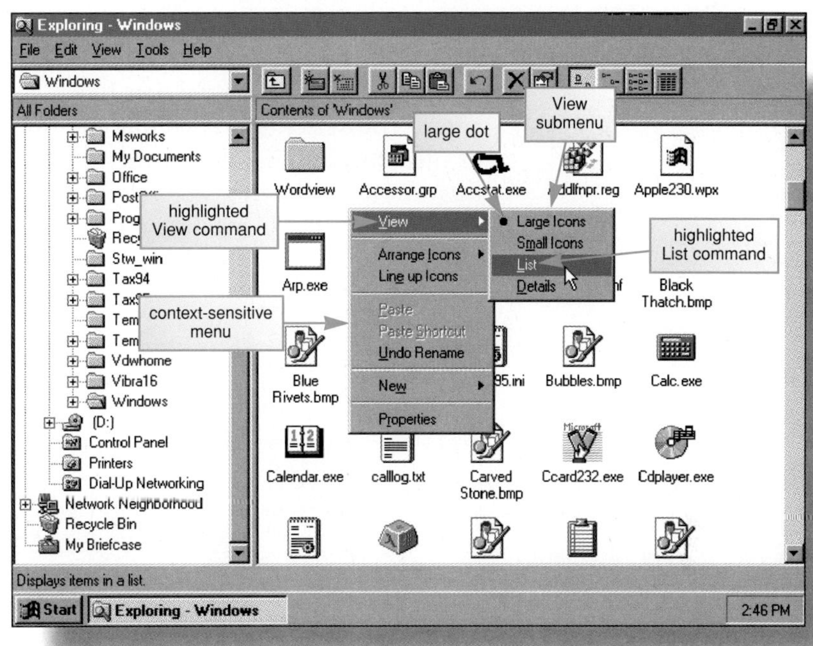

FIGURE 2-20

2 **Click List on the View submenu.**

Windows 95 displays the files and folders in the Contents side of the window in list view, indents the List button on the toolbar, and returns the Large Icons button to normal (Figure 2-21).

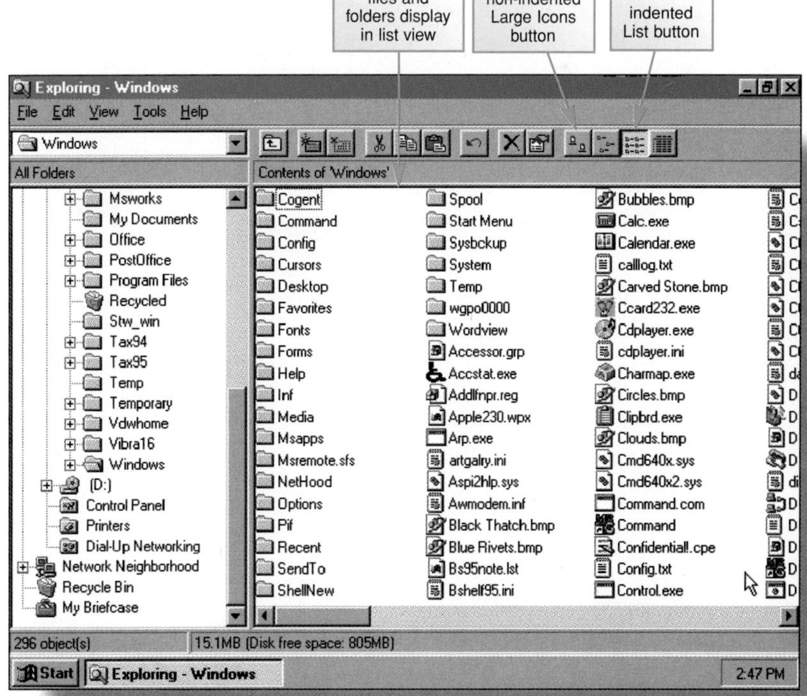

FIGURE 2-21

*Other*Ways

1. On View menu click List
2. Click List button on toolbar
3. Press ALT+V, press L

Selecting a Group of Files

You can easily copy a single file or group of files from one folder to another folder using Windows Explorer. To copy a single file, select the file in the Contents side of the window and right-drag the highlighted file to the folder in the All Folders side where the file is to be copied. Group files are copied in a similar fashion. Select the first file in a group of files by clicking its icon or filename. You select the remaining files in the group by pointing to each file icon or filename, holding down the CTRL key, and clicking the file icon or filename. Perform the following steps to select the group of files consisting of the Black Thatch.bmp, Bubbles.bmp, and Circles.bmp files.

Steps To Select a Group of Files

1 Select the Black Thatch.bmp file by clicking the Black Thatch.bmp filename, and then point to the Bubbles.bmp filename.

Windows highlights the Black Thatch.bmp file in the Contents side and displays two messages on the status bar (Figure 2-22). The messages indicate that one file is selected (1 object(s) selected) and the size of the file (182 bytes). The mouse pointer points to the Bubbles.bmp filename.

FIGURE 2-22

2 **Hold down the CTRL key, click the Bubbles.bmp filename, release the CTRL key, and then point to the Circles.bmp filename.**

The Black Thatch.bmp and Bubbles.bmp files are highlighted, and the two messages on the status bar change to reflect the additional file selected (Figure 2-23). The messages indicate that two files are selected (2 object(s) selected) and the size of the two files (2.24KB). The mouse pointer points to the Circles.bmp filename.

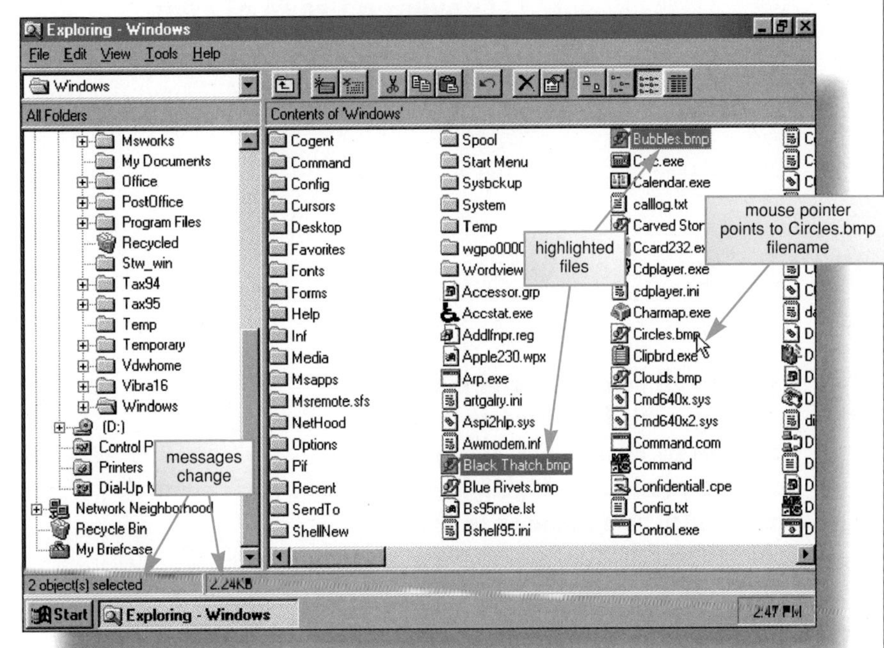

FIGURE 2-23

3 **Hold down the CTRL key, click the Circles.bmp filename, and then release the CTRL key.**

The group of files consisting of the Black Thatch.bmp, Bubbles.bmp, and Circles.bmp files is highlighted, and the messages on the status bar change to reflect the selection of a third file (Figure 2-24). The messages indicate that three files are selected (3 object(s) selected) and the size of the three files (2.43KB).

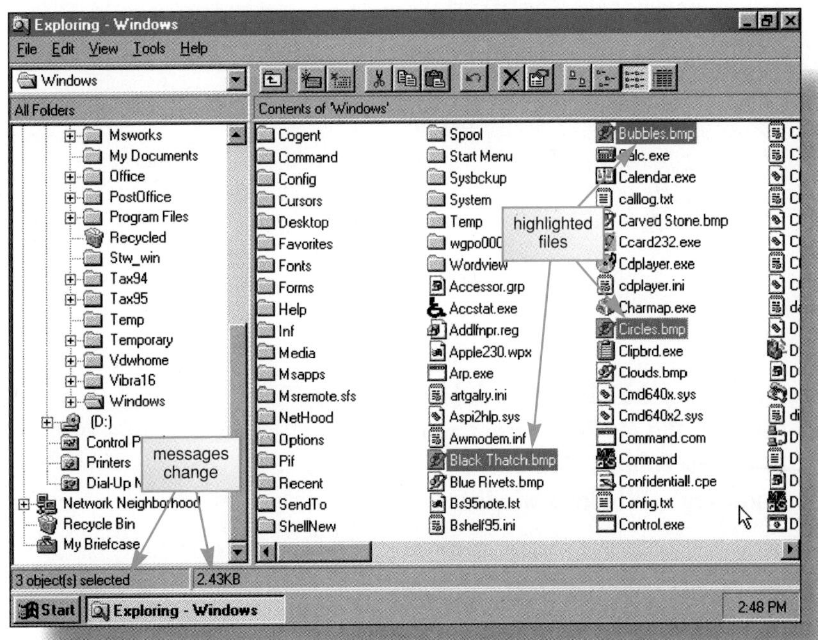

FIGURE 2-24

*Other*Ways

1. Use arrow keys to select first file, hold down SHIFT key to move to next file, press SPACEBAR
2. To select contiguous files, select first filename, hold down SHIFT key, click last filename
3. To select all files, click Edit on menu bar, click Select All

Copying a Group of Files

After selecting a group of files, copy the files to the My Files folder on drive A by pointing to any highlighted filename in the Contents side, and right-dragging the filename to the My Files folder in the All Folders side. Perform the following steps to copy a group of files.

To Copy a Group of Files

1 **Scroll the All Folders side of the Exploring – Windows window to make the My Files folder visible and then point to the highlighted Black Thatch.bmp filename in the Contents side.**

Windows 95 scrolls the All Folders side to make the My Files folder visible (Figure 2-25). The mouse pointer points to the highlighted Black Thatch.bmp filename in the Contents side.

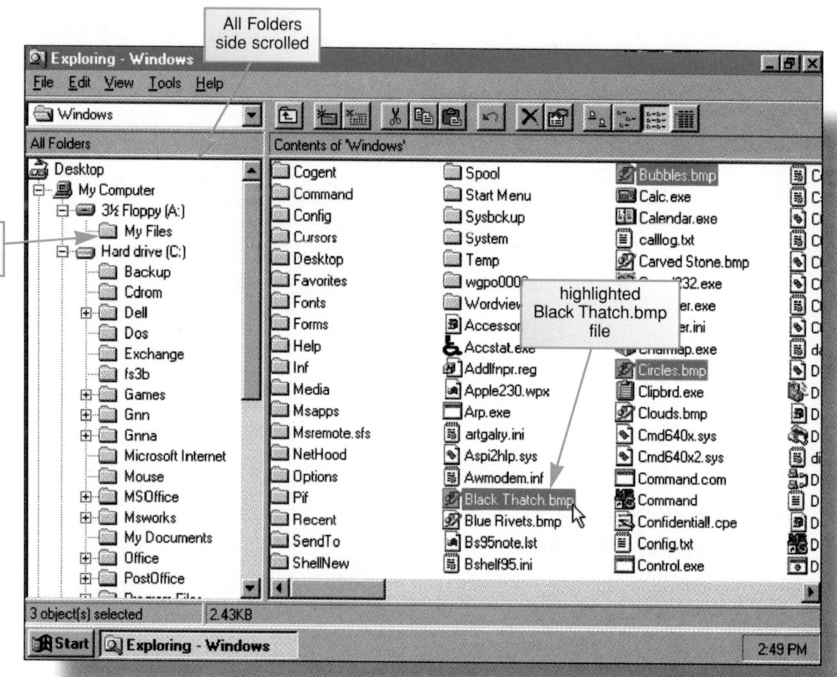

FIGURE 2-25

2 **Right-drag the Black Thatch.bmp file over the My Files folder name in the All Folders side of the Exploring – Windows window.**

As you drag the file, Windows 95 displays an outline of an icon and a horizontal line of one or more of the three files being copied and highlights the My Files folder name (Figure 2-26). The mouse pointer contains a plus sign to indicate the group of files is being copied, not moved.

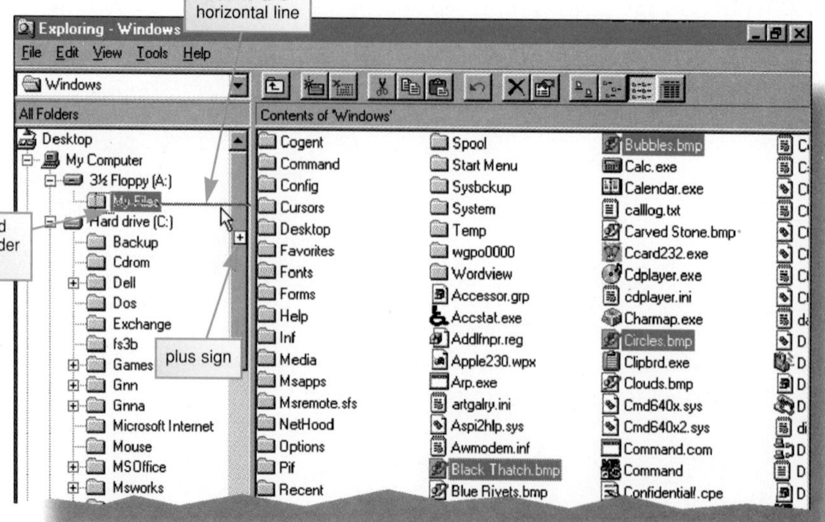

3 **Release the right mouse button to open a context-sensitive menu, and then point to the Copy Here command on the menu.**

Windows 95 opens a context-sensitive menu and highlights the Copy Here command on the menu (Figure 2-27). The mouse pointer points to the Copy Here command. Clicking the Copy Here command will copy the three files to the My Files folder.

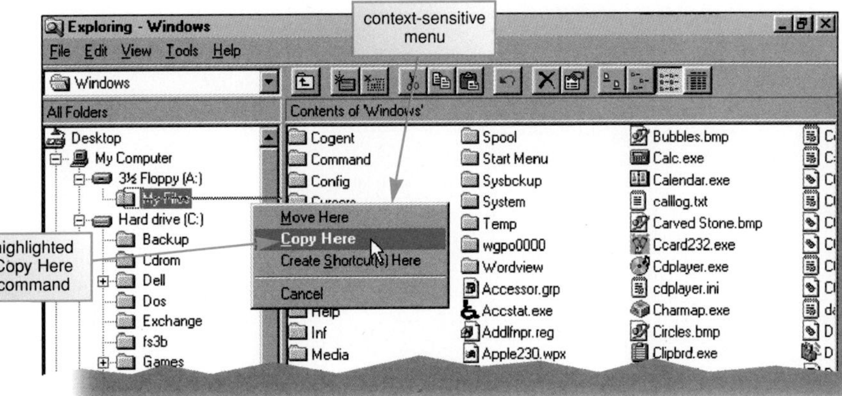

FIGURE 2-27

4 **Click Copy Here on the context-sensitive menu.**

Windows 95 opens the Copying dialog box, and the dialog box remains on the screen while Windows 95 copies each file to the My Files folder (Figure 2-28). The Copying dialog box shown in Figure 2-28 indicates the Black Thatch.bmp file is currently being copied.

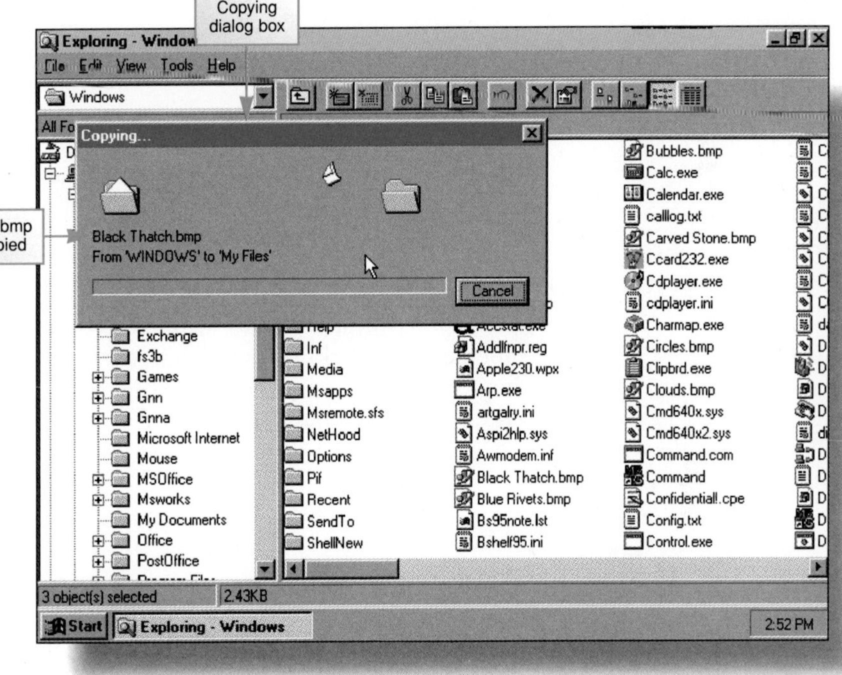

FIGURE 2-28

Other Ways

1. Right-drag file to copy from Contents side to folder icon in All Folders side, click Copy on context-sensitive menu
2. Select file to copy in Contents side, click Edit on menu bar, click Copy on Edit menu, select folder icon to receive copy, click Edit on menu bar, click Paste on Edit menu

Displaying the Contents of the My Files Folder

After copying a group of files, you should verify that the files were copied into the correct folder. To view the files that were copied to the My Files folder, click the My Files folder name in the All Folders side.

More *About* Copying and Moving

"Copying, moving, it's all the same to me," you might be tempted to say. They're not the same at all! When you copy a file, it will be located at two different places - the place it was copied to and the place it was copied from. When a file is moved, it will be located at only one place - where it was moved to. Many users have been sorry they did not distinguish the difference when a file they thought they had copied was moved instead.

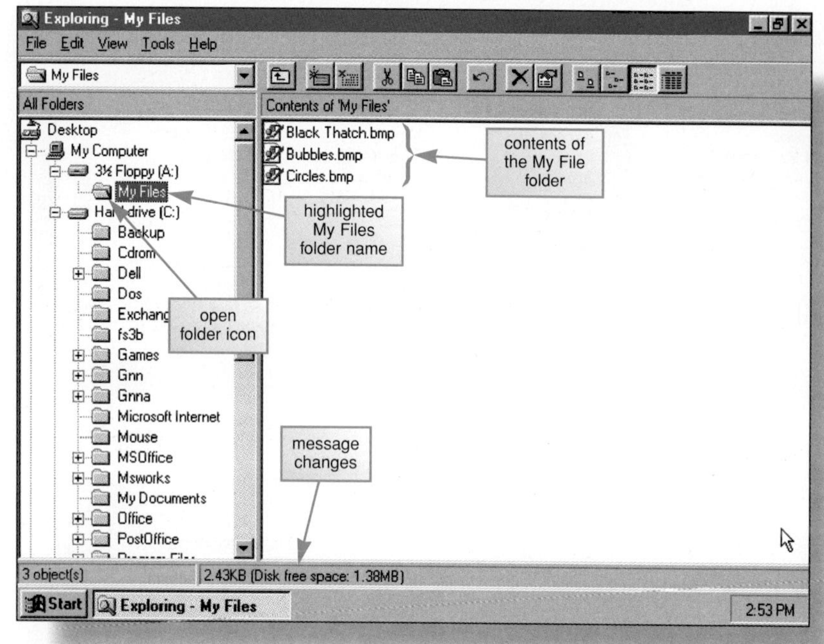

FIGURE 2-29

TO DISPLAY THE CONTENTS OF A FOLDER

Step 1: Point to the My Files folder name in the All Folders side of the Exploring – Windows window.

Step 2: Click the My Files folder name in the All Folders side.

Windows 95 highlights the My Files folder name in the All Folders side, replaces the closed folder icon to the left of the My Files folder name with an open folder icon, displays the contents of the My Files folder in the Contents side, and changes the message on the status bar (Figure 2-29). The status bar message indicates 1.38MB of free disk space on the disk in drive A.

More *About* **Renaming a File or Folder**

A file or folder name can contain up to 255 characters, including spaces. But, they cannot contain any of the following characters: \ /:*?"<>|.

Renaming a File or Folder

Sometimes, you may want to rename a file or folder on disk. You change the filename by clicking the filename twice, typing the new filename, and pressing the ENTER key. Perform the following steps to change the name of the Circles.bmp file on drive A to Blue Circles.bmp.

To Rename a File

1 **Point to the Circles.bmp filename in the Contents side.**

The mouse pointer points to the Circles.bmp filename (Figure 2-30).

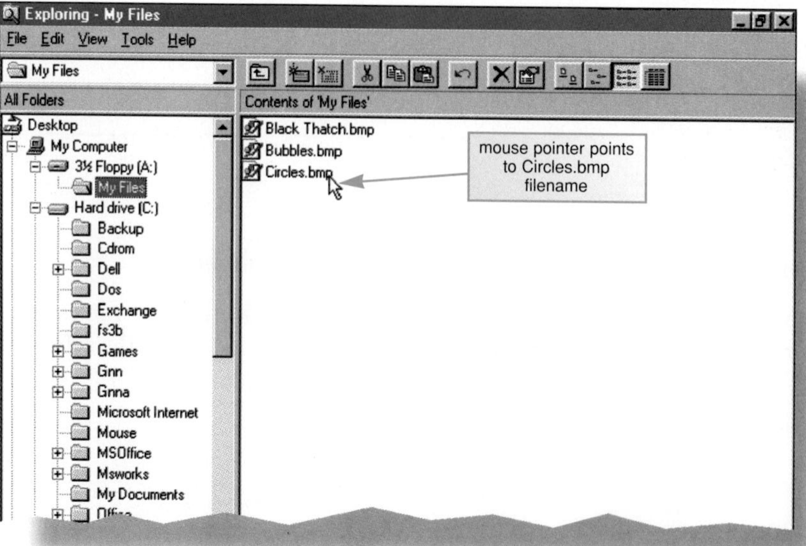

FIGURE 2-30

2 Click the Circles.bmp filename twice (do not double-click the filename).

Windows 95 displays a text box containing the highlighted Circles.bmp filename and insertion point (Figure 2-31).

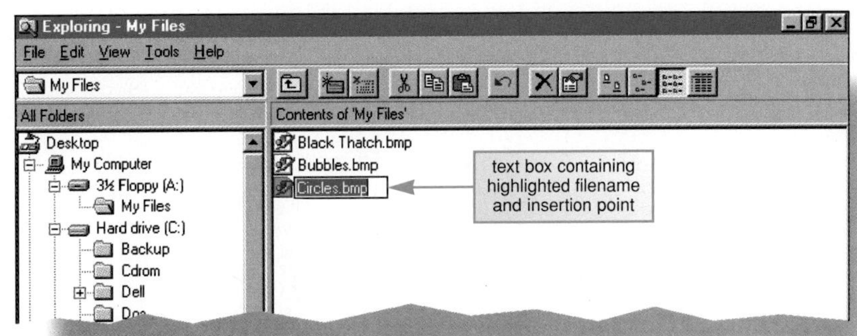

FIGURE 2-31

3 Type `Blue Circles.bmp` **and then press the ENTER key.**

Windows 95 changes the filename to Blue Circles.bmp and removes the box surrounding the filename (Figure 2-32).

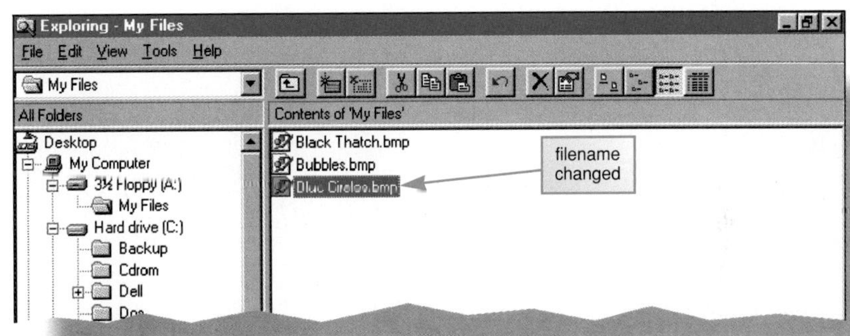

FIGURE 2-32

*Other*Ways

1. Right-click filename in Contents side, click Rename on context-sensitive menu, type name, press ENTER
2. Select filename in Contents side, click File on menu bar, click Rename on File menu, type name, press ENTER

To change a folder name, click the folder name twice, type the new folder name, and press the ENTER key. Perform the steps below and on the next page to change the name of the My Files folder to Clip Art Files.

Steps To Rename a Folder

1 Point to the My Files folder name in the All Folders side of the Exploring – My Files window.

The mouse pointer points to the My Files folder name (Figure 2-33).

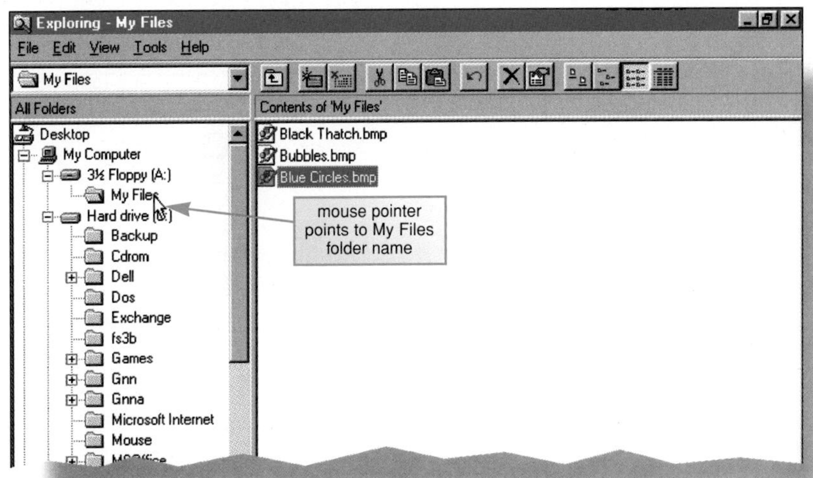

FIGURE 2-33

2 **Click the My Files folder name twice (do not double-click the folder name).**

Windows 95 displays a text box containing the highlighted My Files name and insertion point (Figure 2-34).

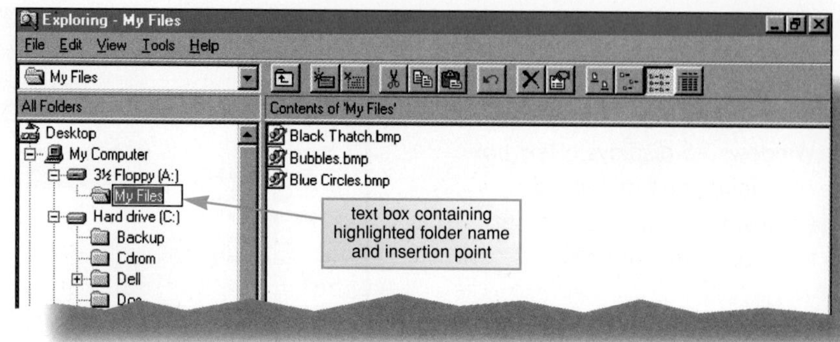

FIGURE 2-34

3 **Type** `Clip Art Files` **and then press the ENTER key.**

Windows 95 changes the folder name to Clip Art Files and removes the box surrounding the folder name (Figure 2-35). The new folder name replaces the old folder name in the window title, drop-down list box, Contents side title, and button on the taskbar.

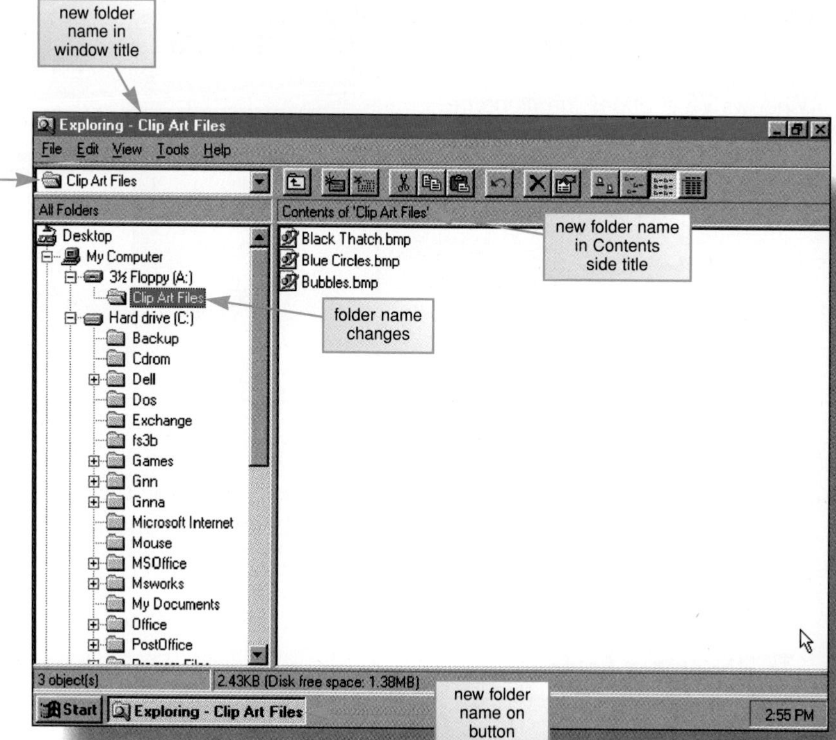

FIGURE 2-35

Other Ways

1. Click folder name, press F2, type new name, press ENTER
2. Click folder name, click File on menu bar, click Rename, type new name, press ENTER

Deleting a File or Folder

When you no longer need a file or folder, you can delete it. Two methods are commonly used to delete a file or folder. One method uses the Delete command on the context-sensitive menu that opens when you right-click the filename or folder name. Another method involves right-dragging the unneeded file or folder to the **Recycle Bin**. The Recycle Bin icon is located at the left edge of the desktop (see Figure 2-1 on page WIN 2.5).

When you delete a file or folder on the hard drive using the Recycle Bin, Windows 95 stores the deleted file or folder temporarily in the Recycle Bin until you permanently discard the contents of the Recycle Bin by emptying the Recycle Bin. Until the Recycle Bin is emptied, you can retrieve the files and folders you deleted in error. Unlike deleting files or folders on the hard drive, when you delete a file or folder located on a floppy disk, the file or folder is deleted immediately and not stored in the Recycle Bin.

On the following pages, you will delete the Bubbles.bmp and Black Thatch.bmp files. The Bubbles.bmp file will be deleted by right-clicking the Bubbles.bmp filename and then clicking the Delete command on a context-sensitive menu. Next, the Black Thatch.bmp file will be deleted by dragging the Black Thatch.bmp file to the Recycle Bin.

More *About* **Deleting Files**

A few years ago, someone proposed that the Delete command be removed from operating systems. It seems an entire database was deleted by an employee who thought he knew what he was doing, resulting in a company that could not function for more than a week while the database was rebuilt. Millions of dollars in revenue were lost. The Delete command is still around, but it should be considered a dangerous weapon.

Deleting a File by Right-Clicking Its Filename

To delete a file using the Delete command on a context-sensitive menu, right-click the filename in the Contents side to open a context-sensitive menu and then click the Delete command on the menu. To illustrate how to delete a file by right-clicking, perform the steps below and on the next page to delete the Bubbles.bmp file.

Steps To Delete a File by Right-Clicking

1 **Right-click the Bubbles.bmp filename in the Contents side of the Exploring – Clip Art Files window and then point to the Delete command on the context-sensitive menu.**

Windows 95 opens a context-sensitive menu and highlights the Bubbles.bmp filename (Figure 2-36). The mouse pointer points to the Delete command on the menu.

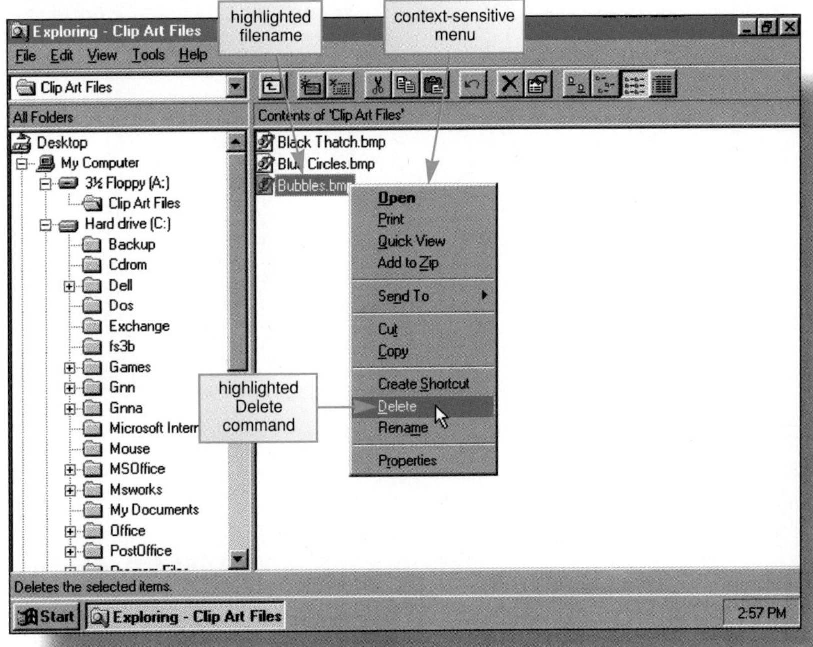

FIGURE 2-36

2 **Click Delete on the context-sensitive menu. When the Confirm File Delete dialog box opens, point to the Yes button.**

Windows 95 opens the Deleting dialog box and then opens a Confirm File Delete dialog box on top of the Deleting dialog box (Figure 2-37). The Confirm File Delete dialog box contains the message, Are you sure you want to delete 'Bubbles.bmp'?, and the Yes and No command buttons. The mouse pointer points to the Yes button. Clicking the Yes button confirms the deletion of the Bubbles.bmp file and causes the file to be deleted.

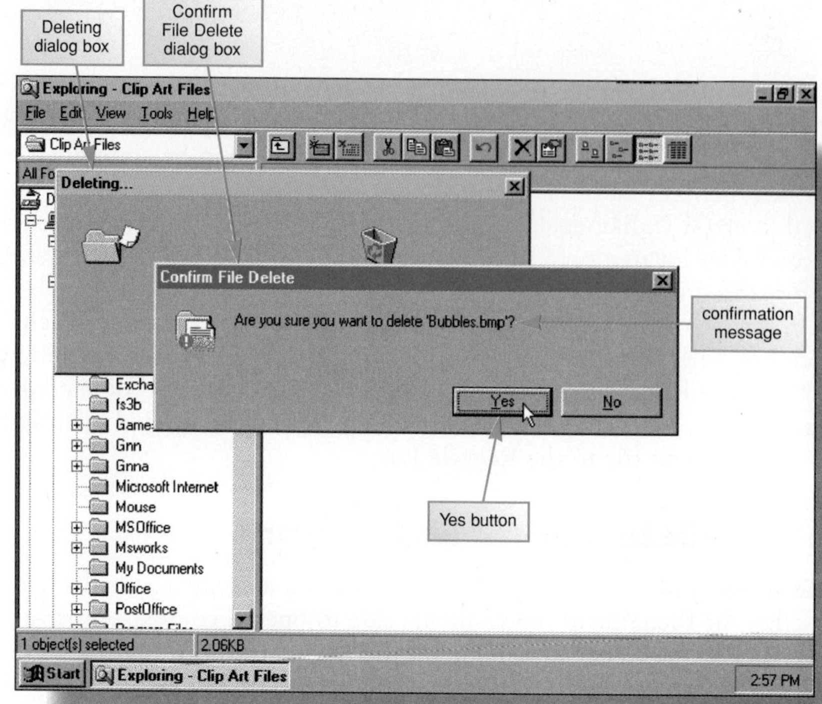

FIGURE 2-37

3 **Click the Yes button in the Confirm File Delete dialog box.**

Windows 95 closes the Confirm File Delete dialog box, displays the Deleting dialog box while the file is being deleted, and then removes the Bubbles.bmp file from the Contents side (Figure 2-38).

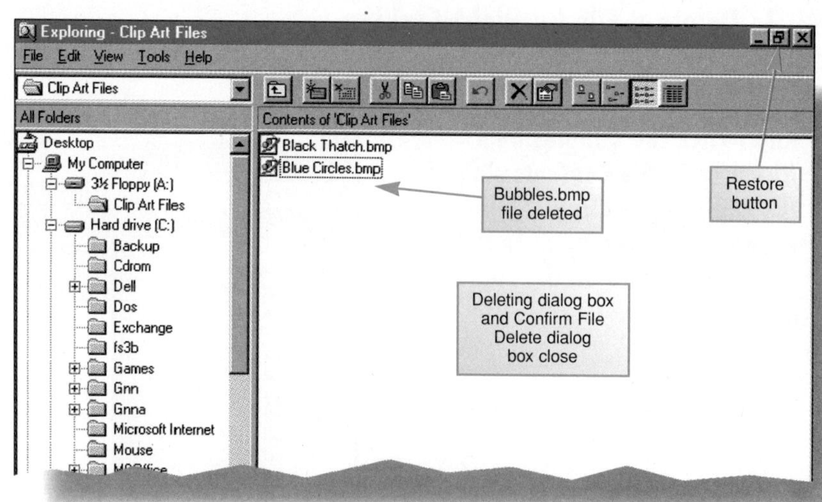

FIGURE 2-38

***Other* Ways**

1. Click filename, press DELETE

More About Deleting Files

Warning! This is your last warning! Be EXTREMELY careful when deleting files. Hours and weeks of hard work can be lost with one click of a button. If you are going to delete files or folders from your hard disk, consider making a backup of those files so that if you inadvertently delete something you need, you will be able to recover.

Deleting a File by Right-Dragging Its Filename

Another method to delete a file is to right-drag the filename from the Contents side of the window to the Recycle Bin icon on the desktop to open a context-sensitive menu, and then click the Move Here command on the context-sensitive menu. Currently, the Exploring – Clip Art Files window is maximized and occupies the entire desktop. With a maximized window, you cannot right-drag a file to the Recycle Bin. To allow you to right-drag a file, restore the Exploring – Clip Art Files window to its original size by clicking the Restore button on the title bar. Perform the following steps to delete the Black Thatch.bmp file by right-dragging its filename.

To Delete a File by Right-Dragging

1 Click the Restore button on the Exploring – Clip Art Files window title bar and then point to the Black Thatch.bmp filename in the Contents side of the window.

Windows 95 restores the Exploring – Clip Art Files window to its original size before maximizing the window and replaces the Restore button on the title bar with the Maximize button (Figure 2-39). The mouse pointer points to the Black Thatch.bmp filename in the Contents side of the window.

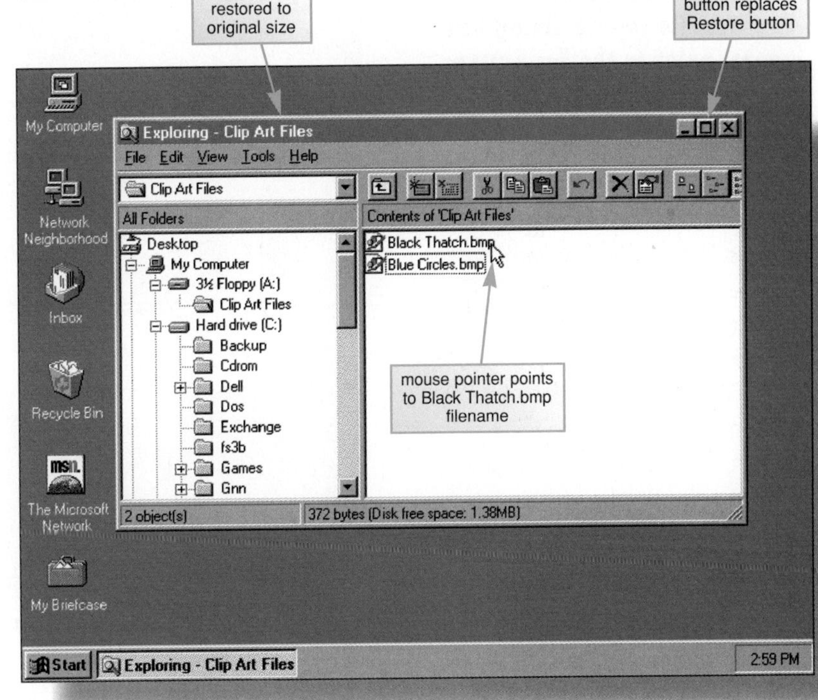

FIGURE 2-39

2 Right-drag the Black Thatch.bmp filename over the Recycle Bin icon, and then point to the Move Here command on the context-sensitive menu.

Windows 95 opens a context-sensitive menu and highlights the Move Here command on the menu (Figure 2-40). The Black Thatch.bmp filename displays on top of the Recycle Bin icon on the desktop and the mouse pointer points to the Move Here command on the menu.

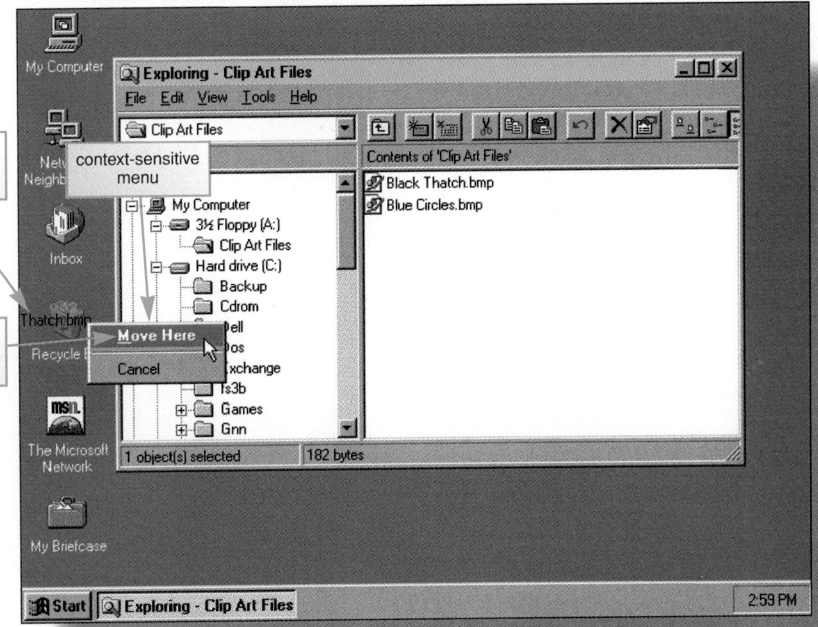

FIGURE 2-40

3 Click Move Here on the context-sensitive menu. When the Confirm File Delete dialog box opens, point to the Yes button.

Windows 95 opens the Deleting dialog box and then opens the Confirm File Delete dialog box on top of the Deleting dialog box (Figure 2-41). The Confirm File Delete dialog box contains the message, Are you sure you want to delete 'Black Thatch.bmp'?, and the Yes and No command buttons. The mouse pointer points to the Yes button. Clicking the Yes button confirms the deletion of the Black Thatch.bmp file and causes the file to be deleted.

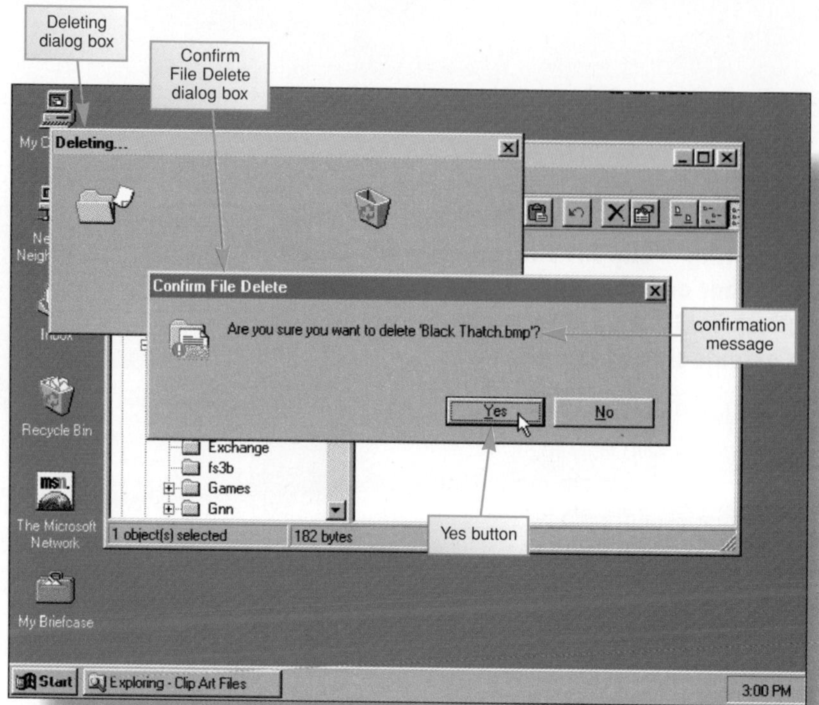

FIGURE 2-41

4 Click the Yes button in the Confirm File Delete dialog box.

Windows 95 closes the Confirm File Delete dialog box, displays the Deleting dialog box while the file is being deleted, and then removes the Black Thatch.bmp file from the Contents side (Figure 2-42).

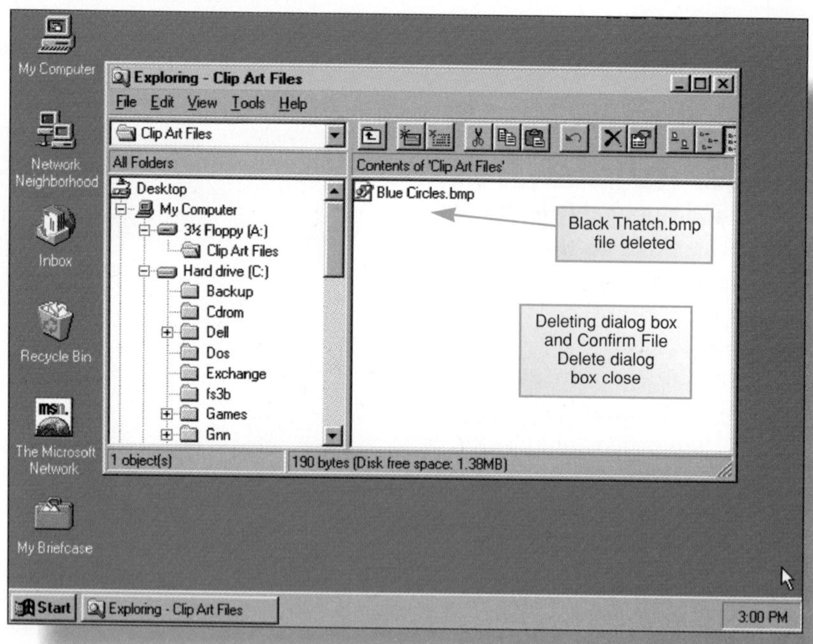

FIGURE 2-42

More About the Recycle Bin

Once you delete a file or folder, it's gone forever – True or False? Windows stores deleted files and folders in the Recycle Bin. You can recover files or folders you delete in error using the Recycle Bin.

Whether you delete a file by right-clicking or right-dragging, you can use the file selection techniques illustrated earlier in this project to delete a group of files. When deleting a group of files, click the Yes button in the Confirm Multiple File Delete dialog box to confirm the deletion of the group of files.

Deleting a Folder

When you delete a folder, Windows 95 deletes any files or subfolders in the folder. You can delete a folder using the two methods shown earlier to delete files (right-clicking or right-dragging). Perform the steps below and on the next page to delete the Clip Art Files folder on drive A by right-dragging the folder to the Recycle Bin.

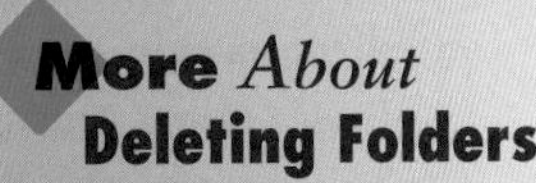

More About Deleting Folders

If you drag a folder to the Recycle Bin, only the files in that folder appear in the Recycle Bin. If you restore a file that was originally located in a deleted folder, Windows recreates the folder, and then restores the file to it.

Steps To Delete a Folder

1 **Point to the Clip Art Files folder name in the All Folders side of the Exploring – Clip Art Files window (Figure 2-43).**

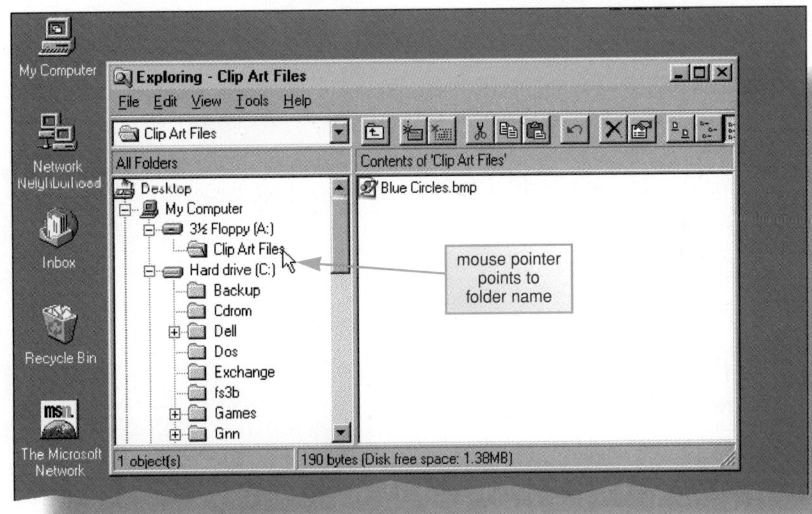

FIGURE 2-43

2 **Right-drag the Clip Art Files icon in the All Folders side to the Recycle Bin icon, and then point to the Move Here command on the context-sensitive menu.**

Windows 95 opens a context-sensitive menu (Figure 2-44). The mouse pointer points to the highlighted Move Here command on the menu.

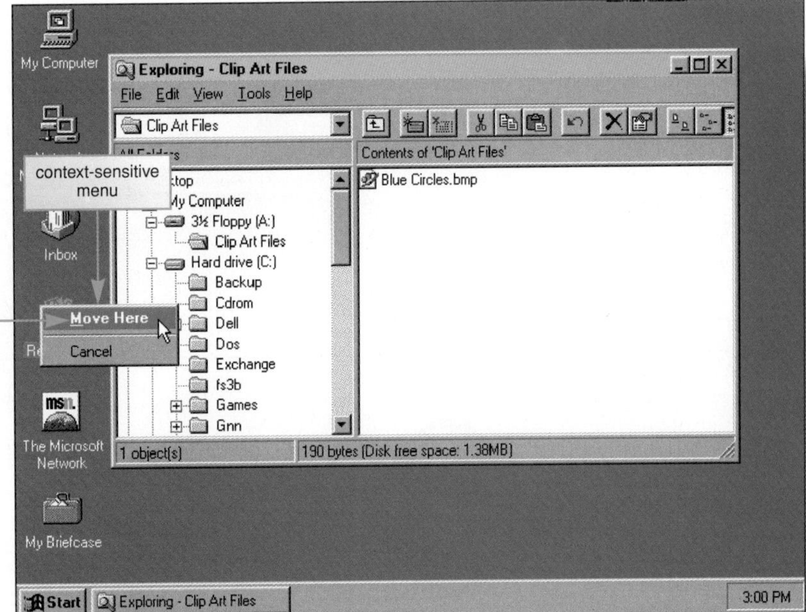

FIGURE 2-44

3 **Click Move Here on the context-sensitive menu. When the Confirm Folder Delete dialog box opens, point to the Yes button.**

Windows 95 opens the Deleting dialog box and then opens the Confirm Folder Delete dialog box on top of the Deleting dialog box (Figure 2-45). The Confirm Folder Delete dialog box contains the message, Are you sure you want to remove the folder 'Clip Art Files' and all its contents?, and the Yes and No command buttons. The mouse pointer points to the Yes button. Clicking the Yes button confirms the deletion of the Clip Art Files folder and causes the folder and its contents to be deleted.

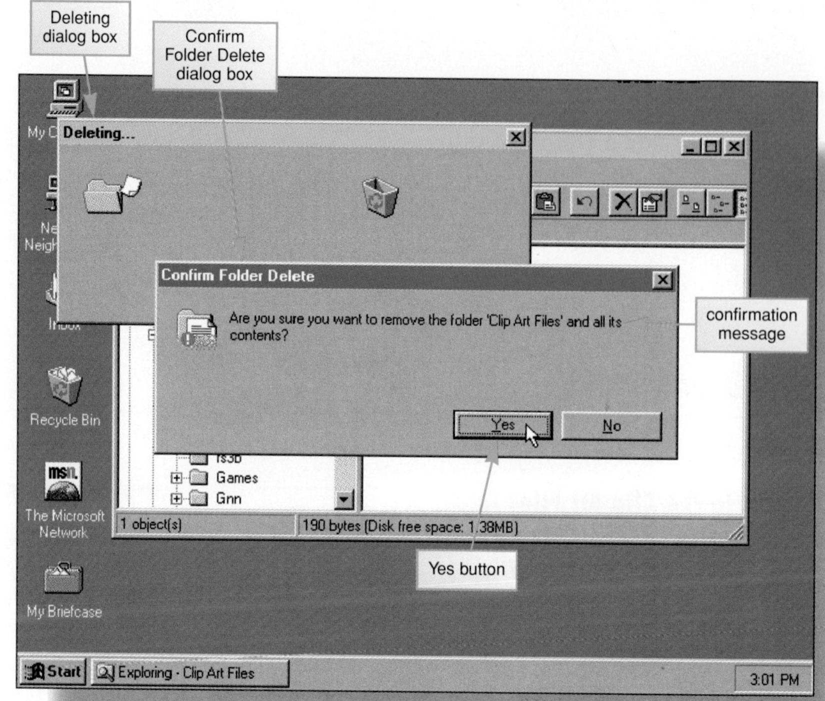

FIGURE 2-45

4 **Click the Yes button in the Confirm Folder Delete dialog box.**

Windows 95 closes the Confirm Folder Delete dialog box, displays the Deleting dialog box while the folder is being deleted, removes the Clip Art Files folder from the All Folders side, and replaces the minus sign preceding the 3½ Floppy [A:] icon with a plus sign (Figure 2-46).

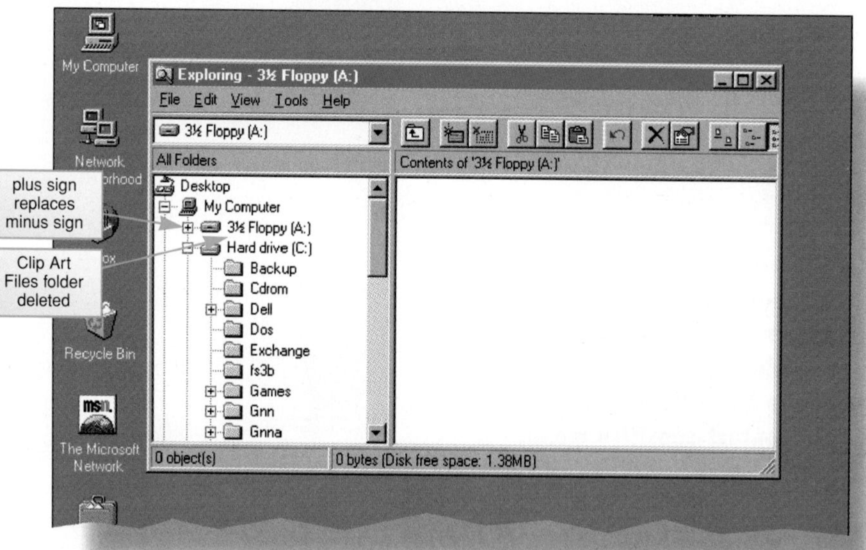

FIGURE 2-46

5 **Remove the floppy disk from drive A.**

***Other* Ways**

1. Click folder name, press DELETE

Quitting Windows Explorer and Shutting Down Windows 95

After completing work with Windows Explorer, quit Windows Explorer using the Close button on the Windows Explorer title bar, and then shut down Windows using the Shut Down command on the Start menu.

Perform the following steps to quit Windows Explorer.

TO QUIT AN APPLICATION

Step 1: Point to the Close button in the Exploring window.
Step 2: Click the Close button.

Windows 95 closes the Windows Explorer window and quits Windows Explorer.

Perform the following steps to shut down Windows 95.

TO SHUT DOWN WINDOWS 95

Step 1: Click the Start button on the taskbar.
Step 2: Click Shut Down on the Start menu.
Step 3: Click the Yes button in the Shut Down Windows dialog box.
Step 4: Turn off the computer.

Project Summary

In this project, you used Windows Explorer to select and copy a group of files, change views, display the contents of a folder, create a folder, expand and collapse a folder and rename and delete a file and a folder.

What You Should Know

Having completed this project, you should now be able to perform the following tasks:

- Change to List View *(WIN 2.19)*
- Collapse a Folder *(WIN 2.11)*
- Copy a Group of Files *(WIN 2.22)*
- Create a New Folder *(WIN 2.13)*
- Delete a File by Right-Clicking *(WIN 2.27)*
- Delete a File by Right-Dragging *(WIN 2.29)*
- Delete a Folder *(WIN 2.31)*
- Display the Contents of a Folder *(WIN 2.9, WIN 2.17, WIN 2.24)*
- Expand a Folder *(WIN 2.10)*
- Expand the 3½ Floppy [A:] Folder *(WIN 2.16)*
- Quit an Application *(WIN 2.33)*
- Rename a File *(WIN 2.24)*
- Rename a Folder *(WIN 2.25)*
- Select a Group of Files *(WIN 2.20)*
- Shut Down Windows 95 *(WIN 2.33)*
- Start Windows Explorer and Maximize Its Window *(WIN 2.6)*

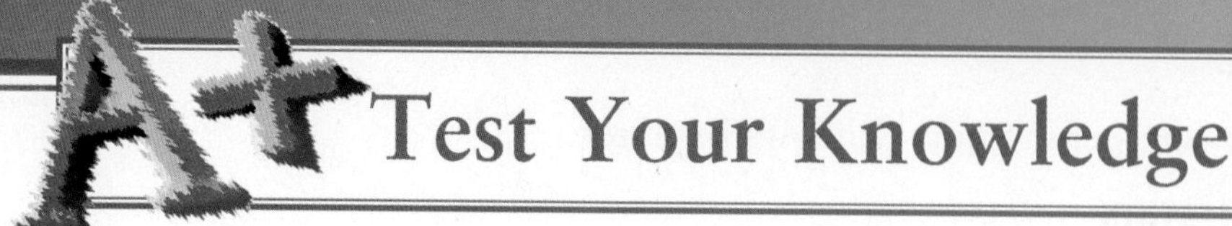

Test Your Knowledge

1 True/False

Instructions: Circle T if the statement is true or F if the statement is false.

T F 1. Windows Explorer is an application you can use to organize and work with the files and folders on the computer.
T F 2. Double-clicking the My Computer icon is the best way to open Windows Explorer.
T F 3. The contents of the current folder are displayed in the All Folders side.
T F 4. To display the contents of drive C on your computer in the Contents side, click the plus sign in the small box next to the drive C icon.
T F 5. A folder that is contained within another folder is called a subfolder.
T F 6. To display the contents of a folder, right-click its folder name.
T F 7. Collapsing a folder removes the subfolders from the hierarchy of folders in the All Folders side.
T F 8. After you expand a drive or folder, the information in the Contents side is always the same as the information displayed below the drive or folder icon in the All Folders side.
T F 9. The source folder is the folder containing the files to be copied.
T F 10. You select a group of files in the Contents side by pointing to each icon or filename and clicking the left mouse button.

2 Multiple Choice

Instructions: Circle the correct response.

1. The drop-down list box in the Exploring - My Computer window contains the ____________________.
   a. hierarchy of folders
   b. source folder
   c. files in the current folder
   d. current folder
2. The ____________________ contains the hierarchy of folders on the computer.
   a. Contents side
   b. status bar
   c. All Folders side
   d. toolbar

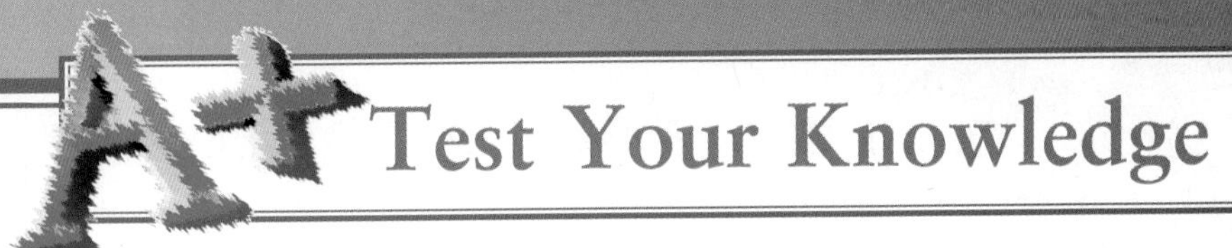

Test Your Knowledge

3. To display the contents of a folder in the Contents side, ______________________.
   a. double-click the plus sign next to the folder icon
   b. right-click the folder icon in the All Folders side
   c. click the folder icon in the Contents side
   d. click the folder icon in the All Folders side
4. You ______________________ the minus sign preceding a folder icon to expand a folder.
   a. click
   b. drag
   c. double-click
   d. point to
5. When an expanded file is collapsed in the All Folders side, ______________________.
   a. the expansion closes and the contents of the folder display in the Contents side
   b. the entire Exploring - My Computer window closes
   c. the computer beeps at you because you cannot perform this activity
   d. the My Computer window opens
6. To select multiple files in the Contents side, ______________________.
   a. right-click each file icon
   b. hold down the SHIFT key and then click each file icon you want to select
   c. hold down the CTRL key and then click each file icon you want to select
   d. hold down the CTRL key and then double-click each file icon you want to select
7. After selecting a group of files, you ______________________ the group to copy the files to a new folder.
   a. click
   b. right-drag
   c. double-click
   d. none of the above
8. In ______________________ view, each file or folder in the Contents side is represented by a smaller icon, and the files or folders are arranged in columns.
   a. large icons
   b. small icons
   c. list
   d. details
9. A file or folder can be renamed by ______________________.
   a. right-dragging its filename
   b. double-clicking its filename
   c. dragging its filename
   d. clicking its filename twice

(continued)

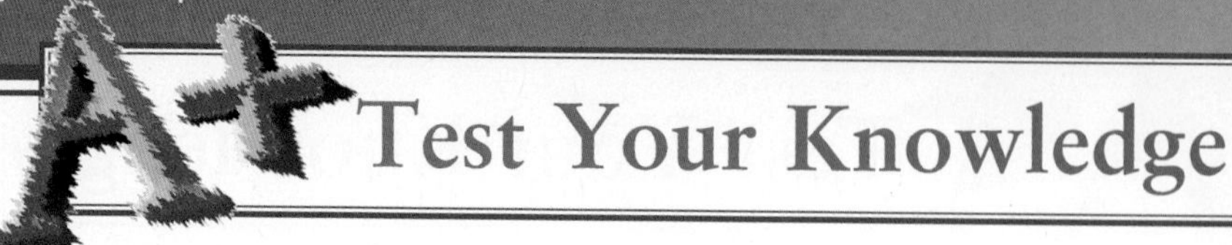

Multiple Choice *(continued)*

10. A file can be deleted by right-dragging the filename from the Contents side of the window to the ________________________ icon on the desktop.
    a. My Computer
    b. Network Neighborhood
    c. Recycle Bin
    d. My Briefcase

3 Understanding the Exploring - My Computer Window

Instructions: In Figure 2-47 arrows point to several items in the Exploring - My Computer window. Identify the items or objects in the spaces provided.

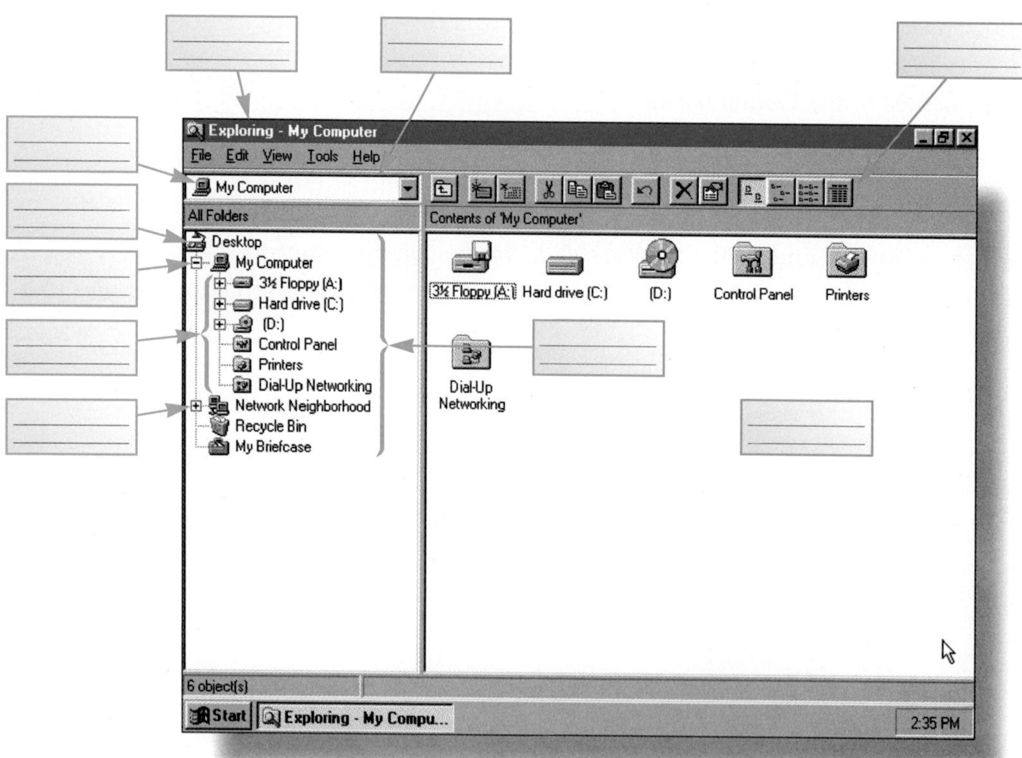

FIGURE 2-47

Use Help

1 Using Windows Help

Instructions: Use Windows Help and a computer to perform the following tasks.

1. Start Microsoft Windows 95 if necessary.
2. Answer the following questions about paths.
   a. What is a path? ______________________________
   b. What does a path include? ______________________________
   c. How do you specify a path? ______________________________
   d. What do you do if your filename contains more than eight characters? ____________________
3. Open the Help Topics: Windows Help window. Click the Index tab if necessary and then type `windows explorer` in the text box. Click demo in the Windows Explorer list and then click the Display button. In the Windows Help window, play the demonstration.
   a. How does the demonstration open Windows Explorer? ______________________________
   b. What folders are contained on drive C in the demonstration? ______________________________
4. How can you cause Explorer to start each time you start Windows 95? ____________________
5. You have recently written a business letter to a manager named Lori Hill. You explained CD-ROM drives to her. You want to see what else you said in the letter, but you can neither remember the name of the file nor where you stored the file on your computer. You read something in your Windows 95 manual that the Find command could be used to find lost files. Using Help, determine what you must do to find your letter. Write those steps in the spaces provided.

   ____

   ____

   ____
6. You and a friend both recently bought computers. She was lucky and received a color printer as her birthday gift. You would like to print some of your more colorful documents on her color printer. You have heard that for not too much money you can buy a network card and some cable and hook up your computers on a network. Then, you can print documents stored on your computer on her color printer. Using Windows Help, determine if you can share her printer. If so, what must you do in Windows 95 to make this become a reality. Print the Help pages that document your answer.
7. You can hardly believe that last week you won a laptop computer at a charity dance. The application programs on the laptop are the same as those on your desktop computer. The only trouble is that when you use your laptop computer to modify a file, you would like the same file on your desktop also to be modified. In that way, you can work on the file either on your desktop computer or on your laptop computer. A friend mentioned that the My Briefcase feature of Windows 95 allows you to do what you want to do. Using Windows Help, find out all you can about My Briefcase. Print the Help pages that specify how to keep files on both your desktop and laptop computers synchronized with each other.

In the Lab

1 File and Program Properties

Instructions: Use a computer to perform the following tasks and answer the questions.

1. Start Microsoft Windows 95 if necessary.
2. Open the My Computer window.
3. Open the drive C window on your computer.
4. Scroll until the Windows icon is visible in the drive C window.
5. Right-click the Windows icon.
6. Click Open on the context-sensitive menu.
7. Scroll until the Black Thatch icon is visible. If the Black Thatch icon does not display on your computer, find another Paint icon.
8. Right-click the Black Thatch icon.
9. Click Properties on the context-sensitive menu.
10. Answer the following questions about the Black Thatch file:
    a. What type of file is Black Thatch? ____________________
    b. What is the path for the location of the Black Thatch file? (Hint: Point to the location of the file) ____
    c. What is the size (in bytes) of the Black Thatch file? ____________________
    d. What is the MS-DOS name of the Black Thatch file? __________________ The tilde (~) character is placed in the MS-DOS filename when the Windows 95 filename is greater than 8 characters. Windows 95 uses the first six characters of the long filename, the tilde character, and a number to distinguish the file from other files that might have the same first six characters.
    e. When was the file created? ________________________
    f. When was the file last modified? ______________________
    g. When was the file last accessed ? ________________________
11. Click the Cancel button in the Black Thatch Properties dialog box.
12. Scroll in the Windows window until the Notepad icon displays.
13. Right-click the Notepad icon.
14. Click Properties on the context-sensitive menu.
15. Answer the following questions:
    a. What type of file is Notepad? ______________________________
    b. What is the path of the Notepad file? ________________________
    c. How big is the Notepad file? _______________________________
    d. What is the file extension of the Notepad file? What does it stand for? ________________________
    e. What is the file version of the Notepad file? ________________________
    f. What is the file's description? ________________________
    g. Who is the copyright owner of Notepad? ________________________
    h. What language is Notepad written for? ________________________
16. Click the Cancel button in the Notepad Properties dialog box.
17. Close all open windows.

In the Lab

2 Windows Explorer

Instructions: Use a computer to perform the following tasks:

1. Start Microsoft Windows 95.
2. Right-click the My Computer icon.
3. Click Explore on the context-sensitive menu.
4. Maximize the Exploring window.
5. Drag the bar between the All Folders side and the Contents side to the center of the Exploring window. What difference do you see in the Window? ____________________

   ____
6. Return the bar to its previous location.
7. Click Tools on the menu bar.
8. Click Go to on the Tools menu.
9. Type `c:\windows` and then click the OK button in the Go To Folder dialog box. What happened in the Exploring window? ____________________
10. Click View on the menu bar and then click Small Icons on the View menu.
11. Click View on the menu bar and then click Options on the View menu.
12. Drag the Options dialog box so you can see the Contents side of the Exploring window. Click Show all files. Click the Apply button. Do any more folders display? If so, what new folders display? Did more files display?

    ____

    ____
13. Click Hide files of these types. Click Hide MS-DOS file extensions for file types that are registered. Click the Apply button. Did the filenames displayed in the Contents area change? If so, what are the changes? Give three examples of filenames that are different:

    ____

    ____
14. Click Hide MS-DOS file extensions for file types that are registered. Click Hide files of these types. Click the OK button.
15. Click View on the menu bar and then click Details on the View menu.
    a. In the Contents side, scroll until you see only file icons and then click the Name button below the Contents of 'Windows' bar. Did the sequence of file icons change? How?

       ____
    b. Click the Size button. How did the sequence of file icons change? ____________________
    c. Click the Type button. How did the sequence of file icons change? ____________________
    d. Click the Modified button. How did the sequence of folder and file icons change?

       ____
    e. Click the Name button.

(continued)

In the Lab

Windows Explorer *(continued)*

16. Click Edit on the menu bar. Click Select All on the Edit menu. If the Select All dialog box displays, click the OK button. What happened? ____________________
17. Click Edit on the menu bar. Click Invert Selection on the Edit menu. Was there any change? ____________________
18. Click File on the menu bar. Point to New on the File menu and then click Bitmap Image on the New submenu. What happened? ____________________
19. Type `In the Lab Image` and then press the ENTER key. What is the name of the bitmap image? ____________________
20. Right-click the In the Lab Image icon. Click Delete on the context-sensitive menu. Click the Yes button in the Confirm File Delete dialog box.
21. Close the Exploring window.

3 Window Toolbars

Instructions: Use a computer to perform the following tasks:

1. Open the My Computer window.
2. Maximize the My Computer window.
3. Click View on the menu bar. Click Large icons on the View menu.
4. Click View on the menu bar. If a check does not display to the left of the Toolbar command, click Toolbar on the View menu. A toolbar displays in the My Computer window (Figure 2-48).
5. Click the down arrow next to the drop-down list box containing the My Computer icon and name.
6. Click the drive C icon in the drop-down list. How did the window change? ____________________
7. Double-click the Windows icon. What happened? ____________________
8. In the Windows window, if the toolbar does not display, click View on the menu bar and then click Toolbar on the View menu.
9. Scroll down if necessary until the Argyle icon displays in the window. If the Argyle icon does not display on your computer, find another Paint icon. Click the Argyle icon and then point to the Copy button on the toolbar (Hint: To determine the function of each button on the toolbar, point to the button).
10. Click the Copy button. Do you see any change? If so, what? ____________________

In the Lab

11. Insert a formatted floppy disk in drive A of your computer.
12. Click the down arrow next to the drop-down list box containing the Windows icon and name.
13. Click the 3½ Floppy [A:] icon in the drop-down list. What happened? ____________________
14. If the toolbar does not display in the 3½ Floppy [A:] window, click View on the menu bar and then click Toolbar on the View menu.
15. In the 3½ Floppy [A:] window, click the Paste button on the toolbar. The Argyle icon displays in the 3½ Floppy [A:] window.
16. With the Argyle icon highlighted in the 3½ Floppy [A:] window, click the Delete button on the toolbar and then click the Yes button in the Confirm File Delete dialog box.
17. In the 3½ Floppy [A:] window, return the toolbar status to what it was prior to step 8. Close the 3½ Floppy [A:] window.
18. In the drive C window, click the Small Icons button and then describe the screen. ____________________
____
19 Click the List button and then describe the screen. ____________________
20. Click the Details button and then describe the screen. ____________________
21. Click the Large Icons button on the toolbar
22. Click the Up One Level button on the toolbar. What is the difference between clicking the Up One Level button and clicking My Computer in the drop-down list box? ____________________
23. Return the toolbar status to what it was prior to step 4. Close the My Computer and drive C windows.

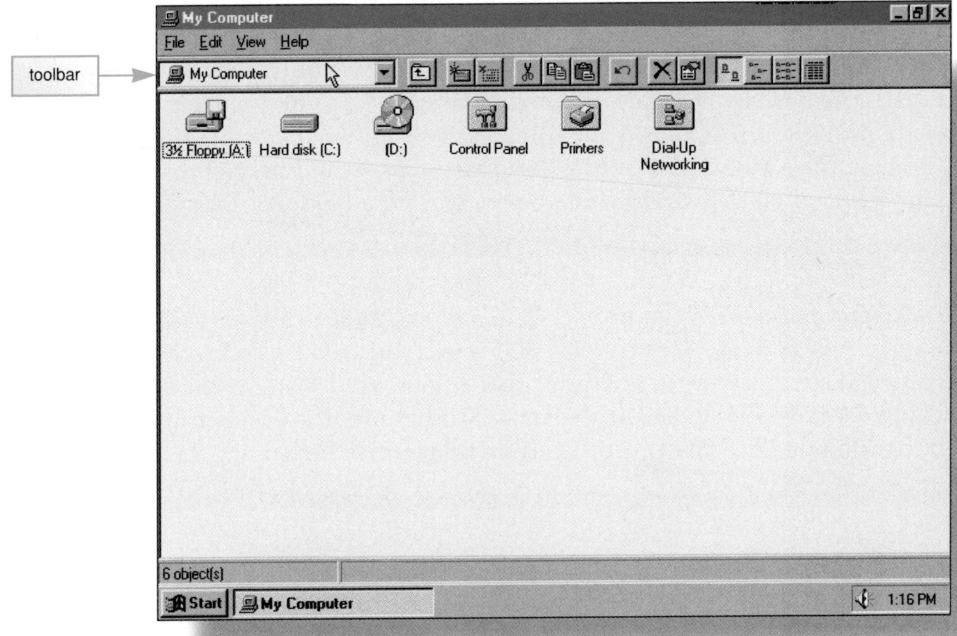

FIGURE 2-48

200 MHz

Cases and Places

The difficulty of these case studies varies:

◗ Case studies preceded by a single half moon are the least difficult. You can complete these case studies using your own computer in the lab.
◗◗ Case studies preceded by two half moons are more difficult. You must research the topic presented using the Internet, a library, or another resource, and then prepare a brief written report.
◗◗◗ Case studies preceded by three half moons are the most difficult. You must visit a store or business to obtain the necessary information, and then use it to create a brief written report.

1 ◗ A key feature of Windows 95 is the capability to modify the view of a window to suit individual preferences and needs. Using Windows Explorer, display the Hard drive [C:] folder in the Contents side and then experiment with the different commands on the View menu. Describe the effects of the Large Icons, Small Icons, List, and Details commands on the icons in the Contents side. When using details view, explain how clicking one of the buttons at the top of the Contents side (such as Name or Type) changes the window. Try out diverse arrangements of icons on the Contents side by pointing to the Arrange Icons command on the View menu and then clicking various commands on the Arrange Icons submenu. Finally, specify situations in which you think some of the views you have seen would be most appropriate.

2 ◗ When the Hard disk [C:] folder is displayed in the Contents side of the Exploring window, it is clear that an enormous number of folders and files are stored on your computer's hard disk. Imagine how hard it would be to manually search through all the folders and files to locate a specific file! Fortunately, Windows 95 provides the Find command to perform the search for you. Click Tools on the Exploring window menu bar, point to Find, and then click Files or Folders on the Find submenu. Learn about each sheet in the Find: All Files dialog box by clicking a tab (Name & Location, Date Modified, or Advanced), clicking the Help menu, clicking What's This? on the Help menu, and then clicking an item on a sheet. Try finding a file using each sheet. Finally, explain how the Find command is used and describe a circumstance in which each sheet would be useful. When you are finished, click the Close button on the window title bar to close the Find: All Files dialog box.

3 ◗◗ Backing up files is an important way to protect data and ensure it is not inadvertently lost or destroyed. File backup on a personal computer can use a variety of devices and techniques. Using the Internet, a library, personal computer magazines, or other resources, determine the types of devices used to store backed up data, the schedules, methods, and techniques for backing up data, and the consequences of not backing up data. Write a brief report of your findings.

Cases and Places

4 ▸▸ A hard disk must be maintained in order to be used most efficiently. This maintenance includes deleting old files, defragmenting a disk so it is not wasteful of space, and from time to time finding and attempting to correct disk failures. Using the Internet, a library, Windows 95 Help, or other research facilities, determine the maintenance that should be performed on hard disks, including the type of maintenance, when it should be performed, how long it takes to perform the maintenance, and the risks, if any, of not performing the maintenance. Write a brief report on the information you obtain.

5 ▸▸▸ The quest for more and faster disk storage continues as application programs grow larger and create sound and graphic files. One technique for increasing the amount of data that can be stored on a disk is disk compression. Disk compression programs, using a variety of mathematical algorithms, store data in less space on a hard disk. Many companies sell software you can load on your computer to perform the task. Windows 95 has disk compression capabilities as part of the operating system. Visit a computer store and find two disk compression programs you can buy. Write a brief report comparing the two packages to the disk compression capabilities of Windows 95. Discuss the similarities and differences between the programs and identify the program that claims to be the most efficient in compressing data.

6 ▸▸▸ Some individuals in the computer industry think both the Windows 3.1 and the Windows 95 operating systems are deficient when it comes to ease of file management. Therefore, they have developed and marketed software that augments the operating systems to provide different and, they claim, improved services for file management. Visit a computer store and inquire about products such as Symantec's Norton Navigator for Windows 95. Write a brief report comparing the products you tested with Windows 95. Explain which you prefer and why.

7 ▸▸▸ Data stored on disk is one of a company's more valuable assets. If that data were to be stolen, lost, or compromised so it could not be accessed, the company could literally go out of business. Therefore, companies go to great lengths to protect their data. Visit a company or business in your area. Find out how it protects its data against viruses, unauthorized access, and even against such natural disasters as fire and tornadoes. Prepare a brief report that describes the procedures. In your report, point out any areas where you see the company has not adequately protected its data.

Index

Microsoft Office 95

An Introduction to Microsoft Office 95

Objectives:

You will have mastered the material in this project when you can:

- Add a button to a toolbar
- Add a toolbar to the Shortcut Bar
- Create a new Microsoft Office document
- Open a Microsoft Office document
- Position the Shortcut Bar
- Remove a button from a toolbar
- Remove a toolbar from the Shortcut Bar

Microsoft Office for Windows 95

What's it all about?

Microsoft Office for Windows 95 is a collection of popular Microsoft application software products that work alike and work together as if they were a single product. Microsoft Office for Windows 95 includes Microsoft Word, Microsoft Excel, Microsoft Access, Microsoft PowerPoint, and Microsoft Schedule+.

Microsoft Word for Windows 95 is a powerful application software program that allows you to create word processing documents. You use Microsoft Word to prepare all types of personal and business communications including announcements, letters, memos, resumes, business and academic reports, and other forms of documents that can be printed or transmitted electronically. Microsoft Word can check a document for grammar and incorrectly spelled words as well as automatically correct typing errors and expand abbreviations as you type. You also can use Microsoft Word's desktop publishing features to create professional-looking brochures, advertisements, and newsletters; and use its Internet Assistant to create pages for the World Wide Web.

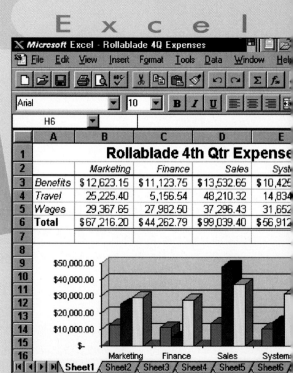

ZIMBA HAS ARRIVED!

SAND RIDGE ZOO

• Free admission, 7 days a week, dawn to dusk, year-round

WORD

Excel

Microsoft Excel - Rollablade 4Q Expenses

File Edit View Insert Format Tools Data Window Help

Arial 10

H6

	A	B	C	D	E
1		Rollablade 4th Qtr Expense			
2		Marketing	Finance	Sales	Syst
3	Benefits	$12,623.15	$11,123.75	$13,532.65	$10,425
4	Travel	25,225.40	5,156.54	48,210.32	14,834
5	Wages	29,367.65	27,982.50	37,296.43	31,652
6	Total	$67,216.20	$44,262.79	$99,039.40	$56,912

$50,000.00
$40,000.00
$30,000.00
$20,000.00
$10,000.00
$-

Marketing Finance Sales Systems

Sheet1 Sheet2 Sheet3 Sheet4 Sheet5 Sheet6

Microsoft Excel for Windows 95 is a spreadsheet program that allows you to organize data, perform calculations on the data, make decisions, create graphs and charts based upon the data, and develop professional-looking reports.

A database is a collection of data organized in a manner that allows access, retrieval, and use of that data. Microsoft Access for Windows 95 is a database management system. Microsoft Access allows you to create a database; add, change, and delete data in the database; sort data in the database; retrieve data from the database; and create forms and reports using the data in the database.

Microsoft PowerPoint for Windows 95 is a complete presentation graphics program that allows you to produce professional-looking presentations. Microsoft PowerPoint gives you the flexibility to make an informal presentation in a small conference room using overhead transparencies, make an electronic presentation using a projection device attached to a personal computer, or make a formal presentation using 35mm slides.

Microsoft Schedule+ for Windows 95 is an easy-to-use time-management tool that allows you to keep track of appointments, meetings, tasks, contacts, and events.

Two versions of Microsoft Office for Windows 95 are currently available: Standard and Professional. Microsoft Office for Windows 95 Standard contains Microsoft Word for Windows Version 7, Microsoft Excel for Windows Version 7, Microsoft PowerPoint for Windows Version 7, and Microsoft Schedule+ for Windows Version 7. Microsoft Office for Windows 95 Professional contains Microsoft Access for Windows Version 7 in addition to Microsoft Word for Windows Version 7, Excel for Windows Version 7, Microsoft PowerPoint for Windows Version 7, and Microsoft Schedule+ for Windows Version 7. The CD-ROM version of Microsoft Office for Windows 95 also contains *Getting Results with Microsoft Office for Windows 95* (an electronic version of the manual that accompanies Microsoft Office) and Microsoft Bookshelf '95 (a collection of encyclopedias and reference books). The Microsoft Office for Windows 95 Professional version was used in writing this book.

PowerPoint

SCHEDULE+

ACCESS

Therapist Table

THER NUMBER	LAST NAME	FIRST NAME	ADDRESS	CITY	STATE	ZIP CODE	BILLING	PAID
05	Hughes	Mary	4613 Essex	Burnips	MI	49277	$62,277.00	$46,245.25
08	Foster	Richard	6621 Eastern	Stockton	IN	47962	$71,245.00	$65,121.33
14	Galvez	Juanita	684 Valley	Leland	MI	47205	$34,252.50	$22,645.90

Microsoft
Office 95

An Introduction to Microsoft Office 95

Case Perspective

Your organization has recently installed Microsoft Office for Windows 95 on all computers. As the computer trainer, you realize you should know more about Microsoft Office but have not had the time to learn more about it. Since installing Microsoft Office, many employees have come to you with questions about Microsoft Office and the Microsoft Office Shortcut Bar. You have taken the time to answer their questions by sitting down with them in front of their computers and searching for the answers. From their questions, you have determined that a good starting place to learn about Microsoft Office would be to learn about the Shortcut Bar. Few employees knew that they could use the Shortcut Bar to create a new document or open an existing document. In addition, few employees knew that the Shortcut Bar could be positioned in different locations on their desktop, or the Shortcut Bar could be customized to their individual needs. With these ideas in mind, you decide to give a short seminar on how to use the Shortcut Bar. Your goal in this project is to become competent using the Shortcut Bar so you can teach the seminar.

The Microsoft Office Shortcut Bar

Turning on the computer starts Microsoft Windows 95 and Microsoft Office for Windows 95 and displays the Microsoft Office Shortcut Bar on the desktop (Figure 1-1). The **Microsoft Office Shortcut Bar** is docked, or anchored, along the top edge of the desktop and contains the Office toolbar. The **Office toolbar** contains buttons that allow you to open an existing Microsoft Office document, create a new Microsoft Office document, and perform everyday tasks, such as scheduling an appointment, tracking a task to its completion, and adding a business contact to a list of business contacts. This toolbar may appear with different buttons on your computer.

The Shortcut Bar shown in Figure 1-1 contains the Office icon displayed on a blue background and the Office toolbar. The Office toolbar consists of three groups of buttons displayed on a black background. The two buttons in the first group of buttons allow you to start a new Microsoft Office document and open an existing Microsoft Office document. The four buttons in the second group allow you to send a message using Microsoft Explorer, and make an appointment, add a task, and add a contact using Microsoft Schedule+. The four buttons in the third group of buttons allow you to access a collection of encyclopedias and reference books called Microsoft Bookshelf '95, the electronic version of the *Getting Results with Microsoft Office for Windows 95* book, short demonstrations of applications developed for use with Microsoft called Office Compatible, and the Answer Wizard help feature.

If the Microsoft Office Shortcut Bar does not display on your desktop, click the Start button, point to Programs on the Start menu, point to StartUp on the Programs submenu, and click the Microsoft Office Shortcut Bar on the StartUp submenu. If the Office toolbar does not display on the Microsoft Office Shortcut Bar, right-click the background (black area) of the Office toolbar and click Office on the context-sensitive menu.

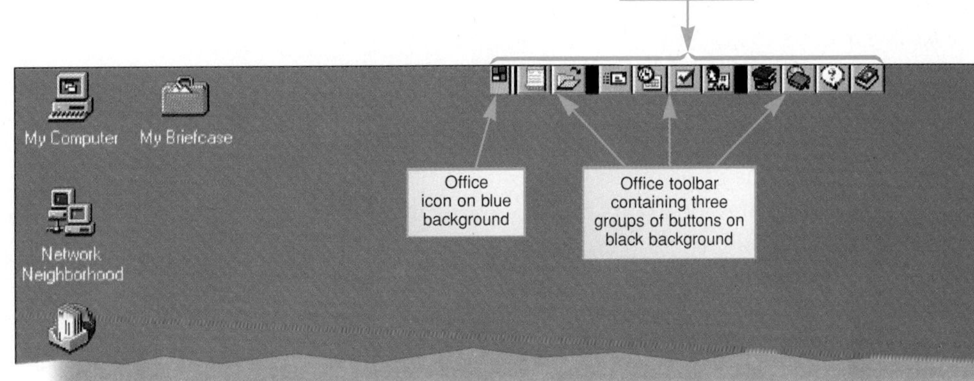

FIGURE 1-1

More *About* the Microsoft Office Shortcut Bar

To remove the Shortcut Bar, double-click the Office icon; click (or right-click) the Office icon and click Exit on the context-sensitive menu; or press ALT+F4. To display the Shortcut Bar, click the Start button, point to Programs, point to Startup, and click the Microsoft Office Shortcut Bar command.

Creating a New Microsoft Office Document

In Project 1 of *Introduction to Microsoft Windows 95*, one method of creating a new document by first starting an application was explained. In Project 2, a method of creating a document on the desktop was explained. Microsoft Office 95 makes it easy to create a new Microsoft Office document or database using a special type of a document called a template. A **template** is a predesigned, ready-to-use document into which you type information specific to the document to be created. In addition, you can also create a new document by using a blank template. To create a new document using a blank template, click the Start a New Document button on the Shortcut Bar to open the New dialog box, and then double-click one of the blank template icons in the New dialog box. Perform the following steps to create a new Microsoft Word document.

Steps To Create a New Microsoft Office Document

1 Point to the Start a New Document button on the Office toolbar.

The mouse pointer points to the Start a New Document button on the Office toolbar (Figure 1-2). The ToolTip, Start a New Document, displays below the mouse pointer.

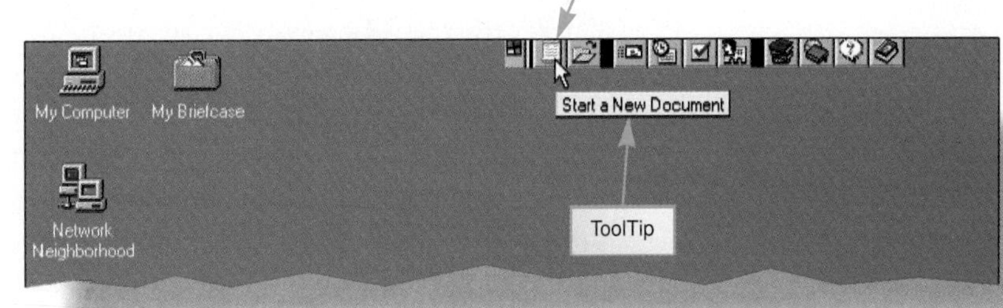

FIGURE 1-2

2 Click the Start a New Document button on the Office toolbar. Click the General tab if necessary. Point to the Blank Document icon in the New dialog box.

Windows 95 displays the New dialog box (Figure 1-3). The dialog box contains eleven tabs organized into two rows. The ***General sheet*** *displays on top of the other sheets and contains templates for several Microsoft Office applications, three buttons to change the view, and the Preview area. The mouse pointer points to the Blank Document icon.*

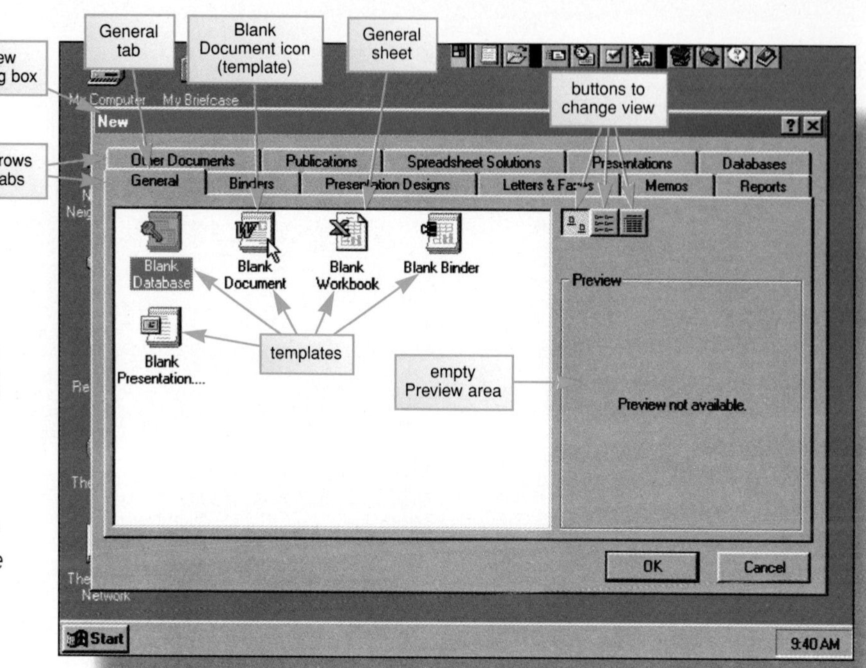

FIGURE 1-3

3 Double-click the Blank Document icon.

Windows 95 starts Microsoft Word and opens the maximized Microsoft Word application window (Figure 1-4). Once the Microsoft Word window is open, you can enter text to create a new Microsoft Word document. This process is illustrated in Project 1 of the Microsoft Word 7 section of this book.

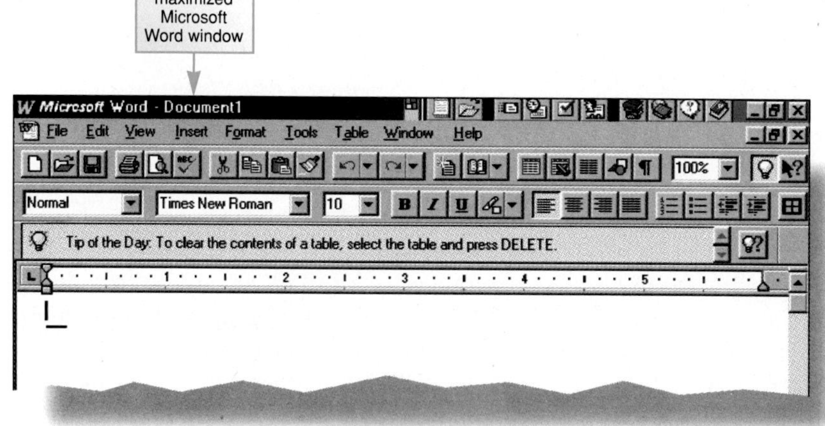

FIGURE 1-4

OtherWays

1. On Start menu, click New Office Document
2. Right-click desktop, click New, click Other Office Documents

Opening a Microsoft Office Document

Currently, the Microsoft Word application window is open on the desktop (see Figure 1-4). Windows 95 allows you to open more than one document and application program at the same time. You then can work on whichever document you wish. The concept of multiple application programs running at the same time is called **multitasking**. To illustrate two documents and two application programs running at the same time, you will open the Kevin's Lawn Care document stored in the Excel folder on the Student Floppy Disk that accompanies this book. Perform the following steps to open the Kevin's Lawn Care document.

Steps To Open a Microsoft Office Document

1. **Insert the Student Floppy Disk into Drive A on your computer.**

2. **Point to the Open a Document button on the Office toolbar.**

The mouse pointer points to the Open a Document button on the Office toolbar (Figure 1-5). The ToolTip, Open a Document, displays below the mouse pointer.

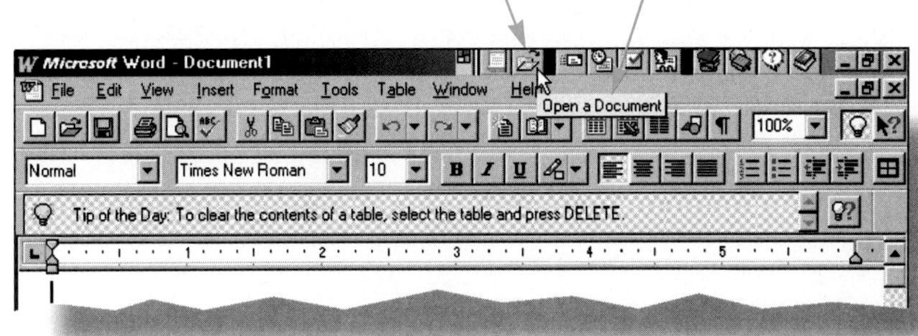

FIGURE 1-5

3. **Click the Open a Document button on the Office toolbar. Click the Look in box arrow. Point to the 3½ Floppy [A:] folder name.**

Windows 95 displays the Open dialog box (Figure 1-6). The Look in drop-down list box contains the My Documents entry. The entry in the Look in drop-down list box indicates the folder from which the document will be opened. When you click the Look in box arrow, the Look in drop-down list displays. The mouse pointer points to the highlighted 3½ Floppy [A:] folder name.

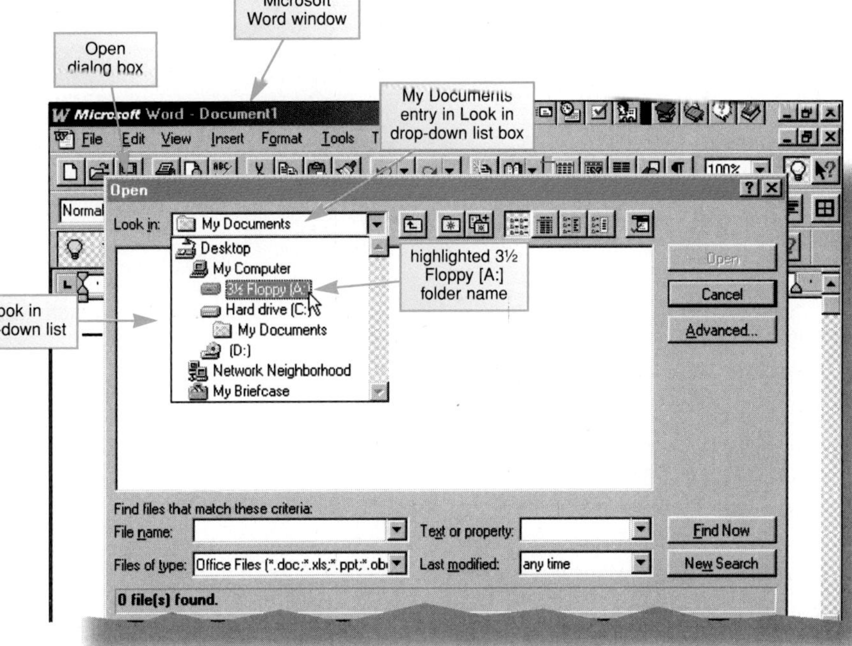

FIGURE 1-6

4. **Click the 3½ Floppy [A:] folder name. When the folders display in the window, point to the Excel folder name.**

Windows 95 displays the 3½ Floppy [A:] folder name in the Look in drop-down list box (Figure 1-7). The names of the folders on the Student Floppy Disk in drive A are displayed in the window below the drop-down list box. The mouse pointer points to the Excel folder name.

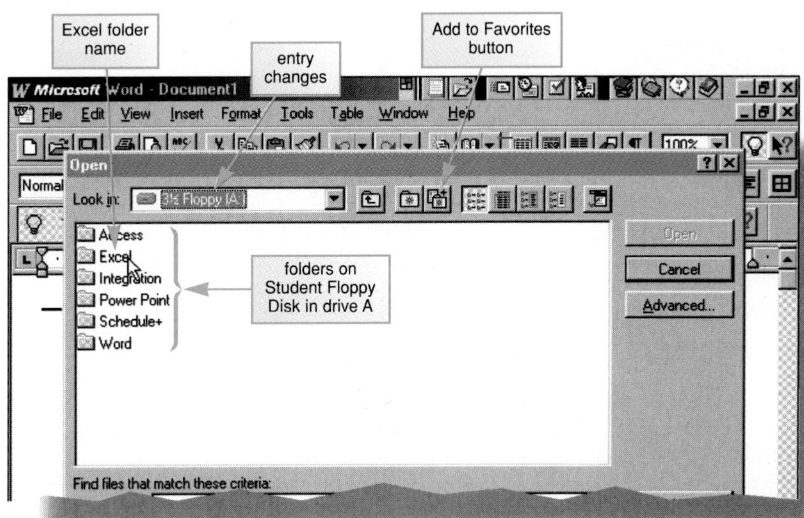

FIGURE 1-7

5 **Double-click the Excel folder name. When the filenames display, click Kevin's Lawn Care.xls, and then point to the Open button.**

Windows 95 displays the Excel entry in the Look in drop-down list box (Figure 1-8). The contents of the Excel folder display in the window. The Kevin's Lawn Care.xls filename is selected, and the mouse pointer points to the Open button.

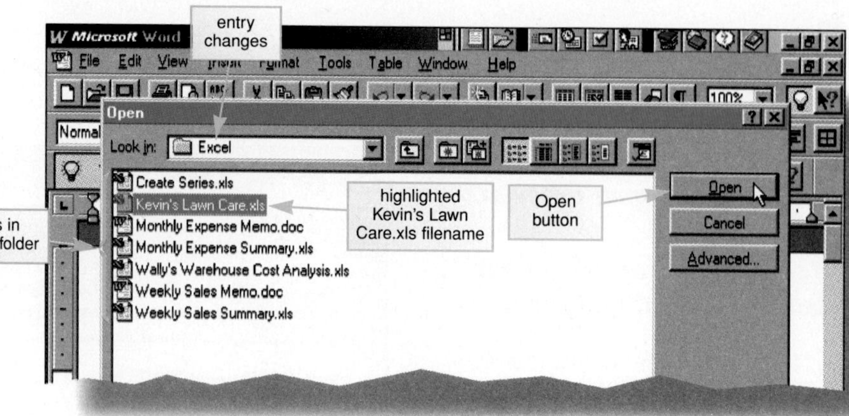

FIGURE 1-8

6 **Click the Open button.**

Windows 95 starts Microsoft Excel, opens the maximized Microsoft Excel application window, displays the Kevin's Lawn Care.xls document in the Microsoft Excel window, and adds an indented Microsoft Excel button to the taskbar (Figure 1-9). The Microsoft Word button, added to the taskbar when Microsoft Word was started, is no longer indented on the taskbar. To view the Microsoft Word window, click the Microsoft Word button on the taskbar.

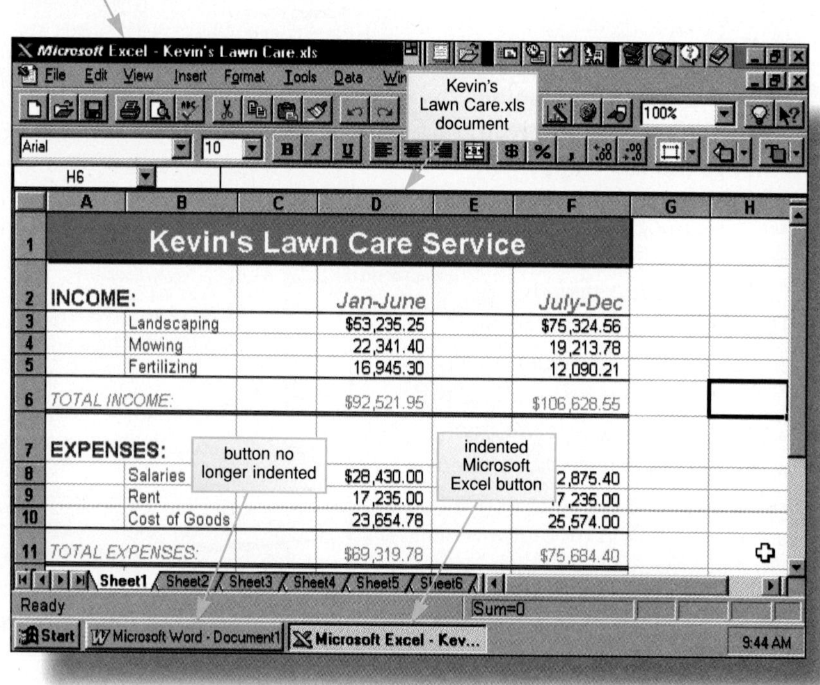

FIGURE 1-9

OtherWays

1. On Start menu, click Open Office Document

Starting and Opening Documents Using the Start Menu

More About Starting and Opening a Document

In addition to starting a new document and opening a document using the Shortcut Bar, you also can start and open documents using the New Office Document and Open Office Document commands on the Start menu.

In the previous examples, Office toolbar buttons were used to start a new document and open a document. Documents also can be started and opened using commands on the Start menu. In Microsoft Office 95, you are given a variety of ways to accomplish a task to satisfy the preferences of Microsoft Office 95's many users. The method you use is purely a matter of personal preference.

In addition, you can start each Microsoft Office application using commands on the Programs submenu. Perform the following steps to view the New Office Document and Open Office Document commands on the Start menu and the commands to start the Microsoft Office applications on the Programs submenu.

To Display the Start Menu and Programs Submenu

1 Click the Start button and point to the Programs command.

Windows 95 opens the Start menu, highlights the Programs command and displays the Programs submenu (Figure 1-10). The top portion of the Start menu contains the New Office Document and Open Office Document commands. Clicking the New Office Document command opens the New dialog box (see Figure 1-3 on page MO 1.6). Clicking the Open Office Document command opens the Open dialog box (see Figure 1-6 on page MO 1.7). The Programs submenu contains the commands to start Access, Excel, PowerPoint, Schedule+, and Word.

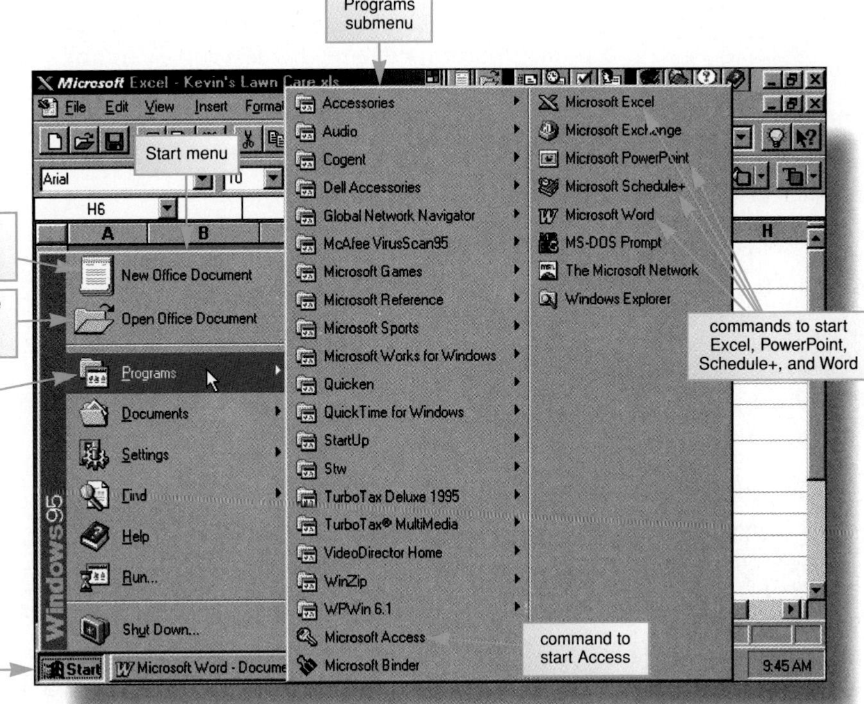

FIGURE 1-10

2 Click an area off the Start menu and Programs submenu to close the Start menu and Programs submenu.

Windows 95 closes the Start menu and Programs submenu.

OtherWays

1. Press CTRL+ESC, P

Customizing the Shortcut Bar

When Microsoft Office starts, the Shortcut Bar is docked along the top edge of the desktop and the Office toolbar displays on the Shortcut Bar (see Figure 1-1 on page MO 1.5). You can customize the Shortcut Bar by changing the position of the Shortcut Bar on the desktop, and adding or deleting a toolbar. In addition, you can customize a toolbar by adding a button to the toolbar, deleting a button from the toolbar, rearranging the order of the buttons on the toolbar, and changing the color of the toolbar.

More About Customizing the Shortcut Bar

You can automatically hide the Shortcut Bar when the bar is docked on the left, right, or bottom edge of the desktop by right-clicking the background of the toolbar and clicking the Auto Hide command. When not in use, the Shortcut Bar remains off the edge of the desktop and is replaced with a small border. Pointing to the border returns the Shortcut Bar to the desktop.

More About Positioning the Shortcut Bar

After dragging the Shortcut Bar onto the desktop, you can change the shape of the Shortcut Bar by dragging its borders or corners.

Positioning the Shortcut Bar

One way to customize the Shortcut Bar is to change the position of the Shortcut Bar on the desktop by dragging the Shortcut Bar to the left, right, or bottom edge of the desktop or to any position on the desktop. Perform the following steps to float the Shortcut Bar on the desktop, dock the Shortcut Bar along the right edge of the desktop, and then return the Shortcut Bar to its original position along the top edge of the desktop.

Steps To Position the Shortcut Bar

1 Point to the background (black area) of the Office toolbar.

The mouse pointer points to the background between the first and second group of buttons (Figure 1-11).

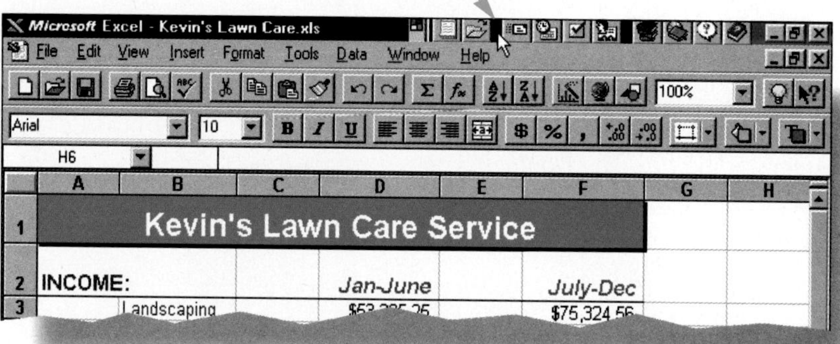

FIGURE 1-11

2 Hold down the left mouse button and drag the Shortcut Bar until it occupies the position shown in Figure 1-12.

As you drag the Shortcut Bar, Windows 95 displays an outline of the Shortcut Bar (Figure 1-12).

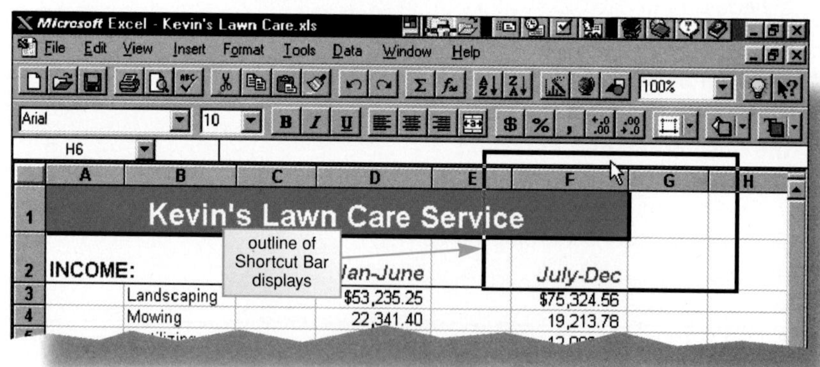

FIGURE 1-12

3 Release the left mouse button.

Windows 95 moves the Shortcut Bar to the location the outline occupied prior to releasing the left mouse button (Figure 1-13). The title bar contains the Office icon, Office Shortcut Bar title, and a Minimize button. Below the title bar, is the Office toolbar consisting of the indented Office button and title, and three groups of buttons on a graduated black background.

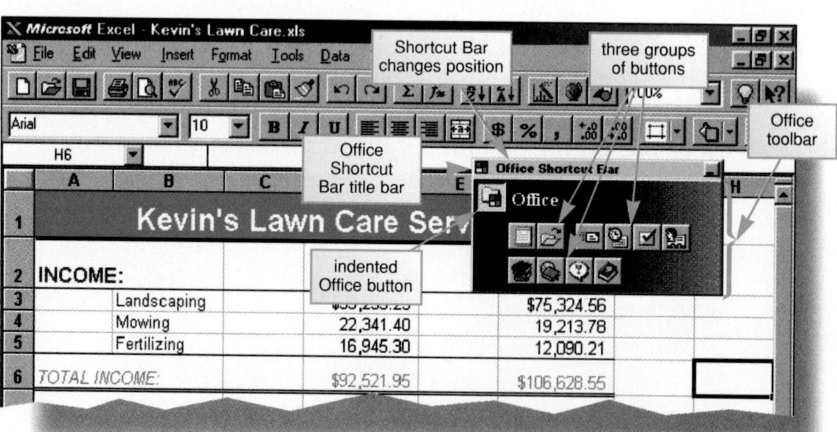

FIGURE 1-13

4 **Point to the background of the Office toolbar and drag the outline of the Shortcut Bar to the right edge of the desktop.**

Windows 95 displays the Shortcut Bar along the right edge of the desktop (Figure 1-14). The Shortcut Bar consists of the Office icon on a blue background and the Office toolbar. The Office toolbar consists of the indented Office button, the word Office, three groups of buttons, and the word Microsoft on a graduated black background.

5 **Drag the Shortcut Bar to the top edge of the desktop.**

Windows 95 returns the Shortcut Bar to its original position along the top edge of the desktop.

FIGURE 1-14

OtherWays

1. Drag the Office Shortcut Bar title bar
2. Double-click blue background below the Office icon
3. Double-click the Office Shortcut Bar title bar

Customizing the Office Toolbar

You can customize the toolbar on the Shortcut Bar by adding a button to the toolbar, deleting a button from the toolbar, rearranging the order of the buttons on the toolbar, and changing the color of the toolbar. To customize a toolbar, right-click the background of the toolbar to display a context-sensitive menu and click Customize on the menu. Perform the following steps to add the Printers button to the Office toolbar.

Steps To Add a Button to a Toolbar

1 **Right-click the background (black area) of the Office toolbar. Point to Customize on the menu.**

Windows 95 displays a context-sensitive menu (Figure 1-15). The check mark preceding the Office toolbar name indicates the Office toolbar currently displays on the Shortcut Bar. The mouse pointer points to the highlighted Customize command.

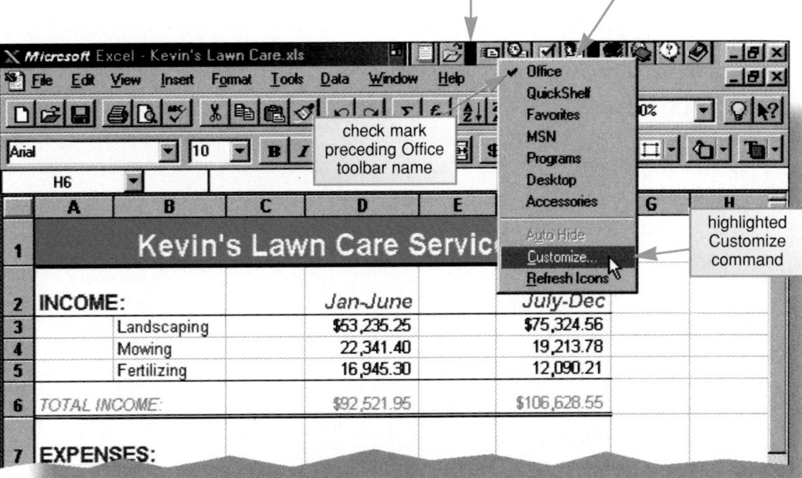

FIGURE 1-15

2 **Click Customize on the context-sensitive menu. When the Customize dialog box displays, point to the Buttons tab.**

Windows 95 displays the Customize dialog box (Figure 1-16). The **View sheet** *allows you to change the color settings for the toolbar, enlarge the size of the buttons on the toolbar, and set other options associated with the toolbar. The mouse pointer points to the Buttons tab.*

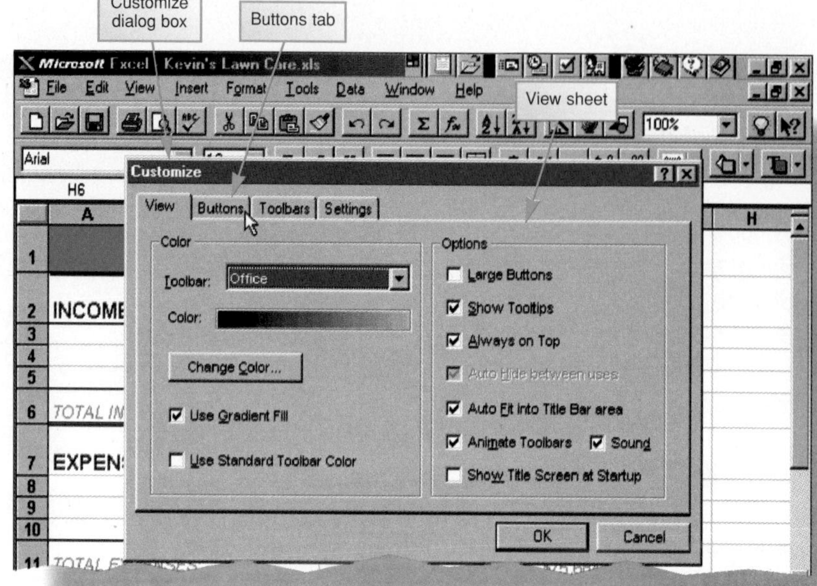

FIGURE 1-16

3 **Click the Buttons tab.**

Windows 95 displays the Buttons sheet (Figure 1-17). The Office toolbar name displays in the Toolbar drop-down list box and the Show these Files as Buttons list box contains a partial list of the tasks and applications for which buttons can be added to the toolbar. A check box containing an X displays to the left of each entry in the list box to indicate a button displays on the Office toolbar.

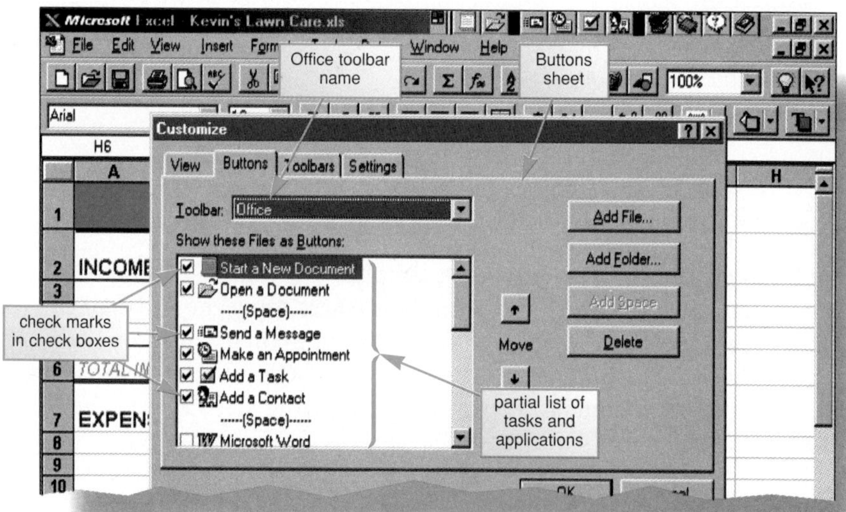

FIGURE 1-17

4 **Scroll the Show these Files as Buttons list box until the Printers entry is visible. Point to the check box to the left of the Printers entry.**

Windows 95 scrolls the list box to make the Printers entry visible (Figure 1-18). Check marks display in the check box preceding the last four entries. The mouse pointer points to the check box to the left of the Printers entry.

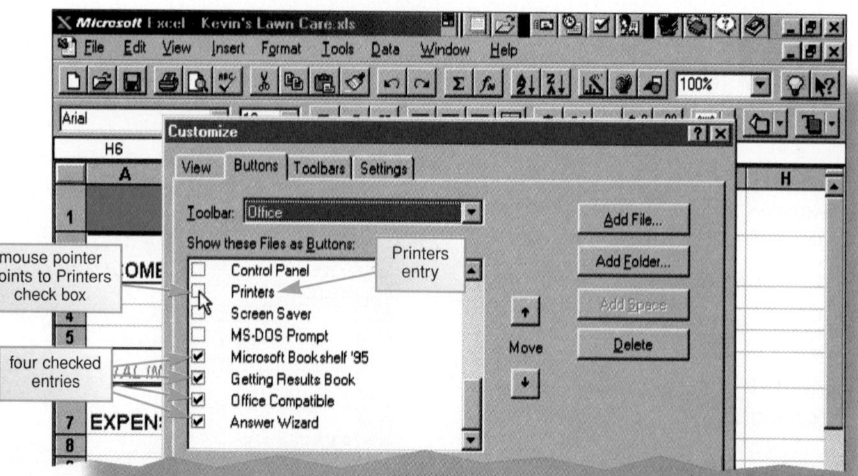

FIGURE 1-18

Click the check box to the left of the Printers entry to place an X in the check box. Point to the OK button.

Windows 95 places a check mark in the check box to the left of the Printers entry and adds the Printers button to the Office toolbar (Figure 1-19). The position the Printers button occupies on the toolbar is determined by the position the Printers entry occupies in the list box.

6 Click the OK button.

Windows 95 closes the Customize dialog box.

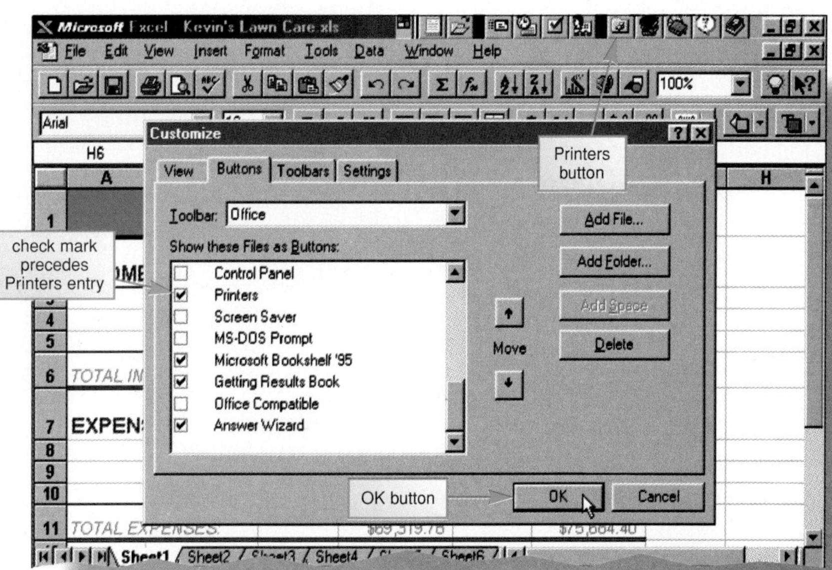

FIGURE 1-19

OtherWays

1. From Buttons tab in Customize dialog box, click Add File or Add Folder
2. Drag file or folder from My Computer or Windows Explorer to toolbar

Adding and Removing a Toolbar

In the previous example, you customized the Shortcut Bar by changing the position of the Shortcut Bar on the desktop and adding a button to the Office toolbar. Another method of customizing the Shortcut Bar is to add or remove a toolbar. Seven toolbars are available to display on the Shortcut Bar. The **Favorites toolbar** allows you to keep frequently used documents and folders in one location. To add a document or folder to the Favorites toolbar, use the Add to Favorites button in the Open dialog box shown in Figure 1-7 on page MO 1.7. Perform the following steps to add the Favorites toolbar to the Shortcut Bar.

To Add a Toolbar to the Shortcut Bar

1 Right-click the background (black area) of the Office toolbar. Point to Favorites on the context-sensitive menu.

Windows 95 displays a context-sensitive menu and highlights the Favorites toolbar name (Figure 1-20). Seven toolbar names display at the top of the menu. A check mark preceding the Office toolbar name indicates the Office toolbar currently displays on the Shortcut Bar. The mouse pointer points to the Favorites toolbar name.

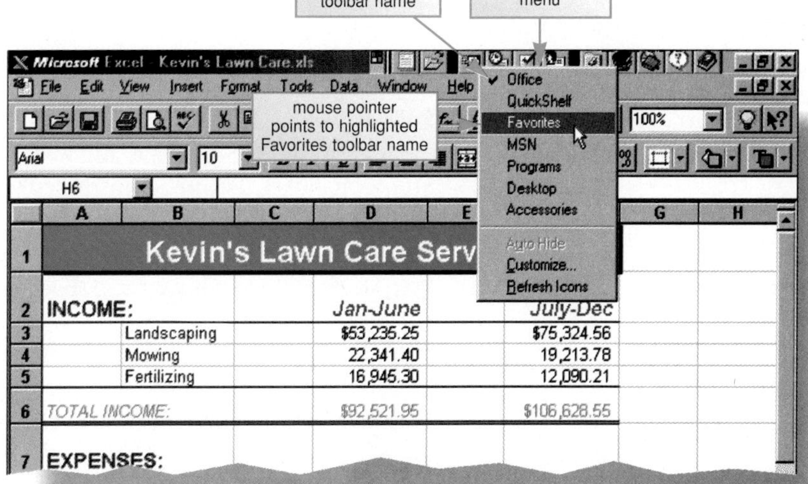

FIGURE 1-20

2 Click Favorites on the context-sensitive menu.

Windows 95 replaces the Office toolbar with the Office button and the Favorites toolbar (Figure 1-21). The Favorites toolbar consists of the Favorites button and My Documents button displayed on a brown background. The button or buttons on the Favorites toolbar on your computer may be different. Clicking the Office button replaces the Office button and Favorites toolbar with the Favorites button and Office toolbar.

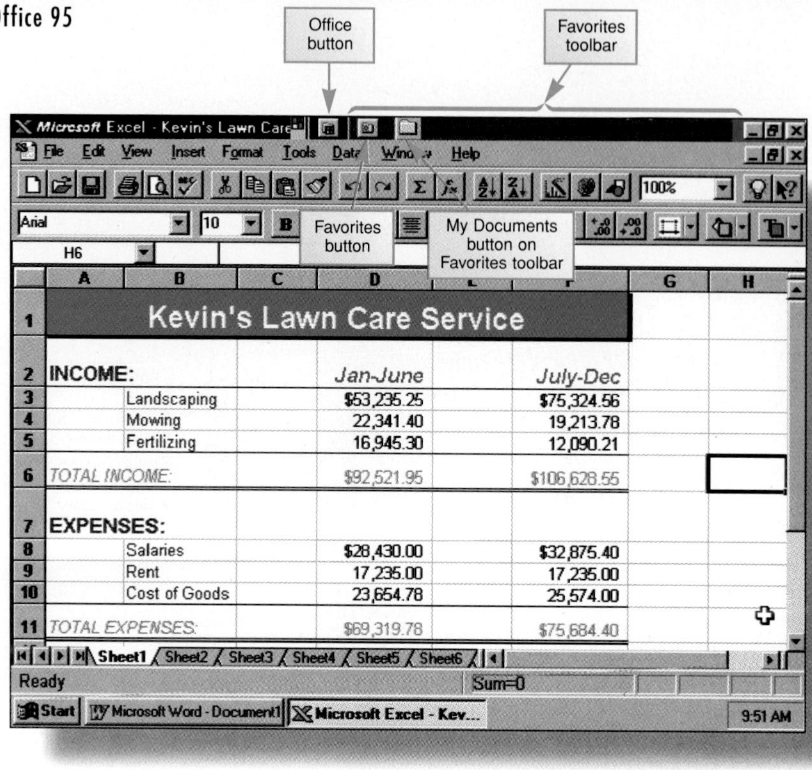

FIGURE 1-21

OtherWays

1. Right-click the background of a toolbar, click Customize, click Toolbars tab, click check box preceding toolbar name, click OK

Restoring the Shortcut Bar

Next, return the Shortcut Bar to its original appearance by removing the Favorites toolbar, removing the Printers button from the Office toolbar, and closing the Microsoft Word and Microsoft Excel programs. Then, remove the Student Floppy Disk from drive A. The steps to accomplish these tasks are summarized below.

TO REMOVE A TOOLBAR FROM THE SHORTCUT BAR

Step 1: Right-click the background (brown area) of the Favorites toolbar to display a context-sensitive menu.
Step 2: Click Favorites on the context-sensitive menu to remove the toolbar.

TO REMOVE A BUTTON FROM THE TOOLBAR

Step 1: Right-click the background (black area) of the Office toolbar to open a context-sensitive menu.
Step 2: Click Customize on the context-sensitive menu to open the Customize dialog box.
Step 3: Click the Buttons tab in the Customize dialog box.
Step 4: Scroll the Show these Files as Buttons list box until the Printers entry is visible.
Step 5: Click the check box to the left of the Printers entry to remove the X in the check box.
Step 6: Click the OK button in the Customize dialog box.

More *About* Adding and Removing Toolbars

In addition to adding a toolbar to the Shortcut Bar, you can also create your own toolbars. For information about creating a toolbar, click the Answer Wizard button on the Office toolbar, click the Index tab, and click the toolbars, adding and removing subject in the index.

TO CLOSE THE MICROSOFT WORD AND MICROSOFT EXCEL APPLICATIONS

Step 1: Click the Close button on the Microsoft Excel title bar.
Step 2: Click the Close button on the Microsoft Word title bar.

TO REMOVE THE STUDENT FLOPPY DISK

Step 1: Remove the Student Floppy Disk from drive A.

The Favorites toolbar is removed from the Shortcut Bar, the Printers button is removed from the Office toolbar, the Microsoft Word and Microsoft Excel programs are closed, and the Student Floppy Disk has been removed from drive A.

Project Summary

The purpose of this project was to introduce you to the Microsoft Office Shortcut Bar. Important topics included using the Shortcut Bar to start a new document, open an existing document, and customizing the Shortcut Bar. Customizing the Shortcut Bar consisted of positioning the Shortcut Bar in different positions on the desktop, adding a toolbar to and removing a toolbar from the Shortcut Bar, and adding buttons to and removing buttons from a toolbar. With understanding of this introduction, you are ready to begin the study of the Microsoft Office applications explained later in this book.

What You Should Know

Having completed this project, you should now be able to perform the following tasks.

- Add a Button to a Toolbar *(MO 1.11)*
- Add a Toolbar to the Shortcut Bar *(MO 1.13)*
- Create a New Microsoft Office document *(MO 1.5)*
- Open a Microsoft Office Document *(MO 1.7)*
- Position the Shortcut Bar *(MO 1.10)*
- Remove a Button from a Toolbar *(MO 1.14)*
- Remove a Toolbar from the Shortcut Bar *(MO 1.14)*

In the Lab

1 Customizing the Microsoft Office Shortcut Bar

Instructions: After using Microsoft Office 95 for several weeks, you find that you use Microsoft Word and Microsoft PowerPoint frequently and would like to add their buttons to the Office toolbar. In addition, you have recently begun to use several of the Windows Accessories included with Windows 95 and would like to add the Accessories toolbar to the Shortcut Bar. However, you do not like the color of the Accessories toolbar background and wish to change it to green. Complete the following steps to accomplish these tasks.

Part 1: *Adding Microsoft Word and Microsoft PowerPoint buttons to the Office toolbar*

1. Start Microsoft Windows 95 if necessary.
2. Display the Office toolbar on the Shortcut Bar if necessary.
3. Right-click the background (black area) of the Office toolbar.
4. Click Customize on the context-sensitive menu.
5. Click the Buttons tab in the Customize dialog box if necessary.
6. Scroll the Show these Files as Buttons list box to make the Microsoft Word and Microsoft PowerPoint entries visible.
7. Click the check box preceding the Microsoft Word entry.
8. Click the check box preceding the Microsoft PowerPoint entry.
9. Click the OK button.

Part 2: *Adding the Accessories toolbar to the Shortcut Bar*

1. Right-click the background (black area) of the Office toolbar.
2. Click Accessories on the context-sensitive menu.
3. Right-click the background of the Accessories toolbar.
4. Click Customize on the context-sensitive menu.
5. Click the View tab in the Customize dialog box if necessary.
6. Click the Change Color button to open the Color dialog box.
7. Click the green color box at the intersection of the third row and fifth column in the Basic colors palette.
8. Click the OK button in the Color dialog box.
9. Click the OK button in the Customize dialog box.

Part 3: *Restoring the Shortcut Bar*

1. Change the background color of the Accessories toolbar to blue. Use the blue color box at the intersection of the fifth row and fifth column in the Basic colors palette.
2. Remove the Accessories toolbar from the Shortcut Bar.
3. Remove the Microsoft Word and Microsoft PowerPoint buttons from the Office toolbar.

PROJECT ONE

Creating and Editing a Word Document

PROJECT TWO

Using Word's Wizards and Templates to Create a Cover Letter and Resume

PROJECT THREE

Creating a Research Paper with a Table

INTEGRATION FEATURE

Embedding WordArt to Add Special Text Effects to a Word Document

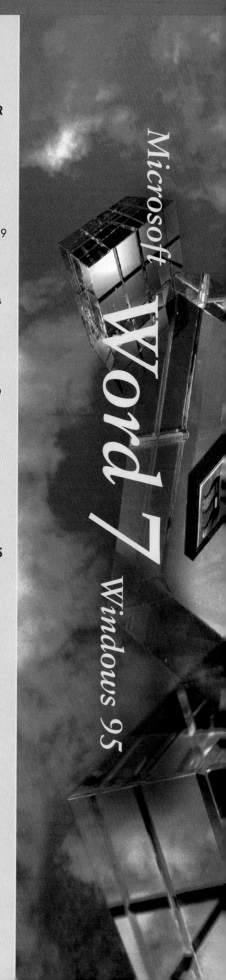

Microsoft *Word 7*

Creating and Editing a Word Document

Objectives:

You will have mastered the material in this project when you can:

- Start Word
- Describe the Word screen
- Change the default font size of all text
- Enter text into a document
- Import a graphic
- Scale an imported graphic
- Save a document
- Select text
- Center a paragraph
- Change the font size of selected text
- Bold selected text
- Change the font of selected text
- Underline selected text
- Italicize selected text
- Check a document for spelling errors
- Print a document
- Correct errors in a document
- Use Word online Help
- Quit Word

Computers CURE Writer's Cramp

Monks' Prayers Answered 2,000 Years Late

Almost 2,000 years ago, monks at St. Catherine's monastery in Mount Sinai, Greece, spent years in the scriptorium laboriously copying manuscripts, letter by letter. At the time, every book, or codex, was written by hand with pen and ink on vellum. Codex Sinaiticus, the oldest complete manuscript text of the New Testament in Greek, dates to the year 517. A copy of the scroll, used until A.D. fifth century, still survives, complete with corrections inserted by the scribe's editor.

Although they probably did not use the term, the monks were performing word processing. Word processing is the means by which words or information is transformed into a document. Today, word processing involves the use of computers, software, and printers to transform information into printed form.

The first true word processor was the Magnetic Tape/Selectric Typewriter manufactured by IBM in 1964. Its capabilities included a magnetic-tape data storage unit and retrieval device.

It was not until the 1970s, however, with the introduction of microprocessors, that computerized word processing really facilitated the production, documentation, storage, and relay of information. The publication of word processing software (the instructions or programs used by a computer to do its work) started in December 1976. Michael Shrayer wrote Electric Pencil, the first popular word processing program for microcomputers, which took the computer out of the hands of programmers and allowed "regular people to do something." Also in that year, Wang word processing was introduced and became the standard for corporate America. One challenge to overcome was the negative reputation computers had in the secretarial field. The term "word processing" was coined by Wang, IBM (Displaywriter) and other manufacturers who tried to market their products to secretaries as ". . . not computers; they're just souped-up typewriters . . . and cute little machines."

The true value of word processing is the capability to change text without redoing an entire page or numerous pages. Word processing software has basic features such as wordwrap, file insertion, move, copy, dictionary, formatting, screen orientation, and fonts. What distinguished the early programs from one another were the extra features included. MicroPro's WordStar software became the early industry standard in 1979. WordStar was a screen-oriented program that used a standard keyboard to communicate 97 commands.

In 1981, EasyWriter was written by the infamous Captain Crunch while in jail for making free long-distance phone calls. (He discovered that by blowing the toy whistle found in the Captain Crunch cereal box, a tone was emitted that released a trunk line enabling free calls.) The EasyWriter screen-oriented program memorized up to eight preset margins. MultiMate followed in 1982 as a personal computer word processing program mimicking the Wang word processor.

Microsoft Word (also known as Project Cashmere after the sweaters that Microsoft founder, Bill Gates, favored) was introduced in 1983. It featured a mouse, the capability to view and edit eight documents at the same time, multiple fonts, italics, and a graphical user interface (GUI). The next year, Satellite Software International introduced WordPerfect, available on several platforms, and Lotus began work on Symphony — an integrated word processing and spreadsheet application. Microsoft Works multimedia edition on CD-ROM became available in 1991. Many other programs and versions have been developed, but today, Microsoft Word 7 for Windows 95 is at the forefront.

Word processing software continues to be enhanced, improving accuracy, productivity, turnaround time, and costs while emulating desktop publishing capabilities. Becoming more user-friendly, some word processing programs even learn their user's writing style and offer suggestions. Future programs are being developed to adapt to their user's personality and work habits, taking the term personal computing to an entirely different level. The scriptoriums of yesterday have been replaced by the word processing capabilities of today.

Microsoft
Word 7
Windows 95

Creating and Editing a Word Document

Case Perspective

Sand Ridge Zoo, known for its huge collection of animals, is one of the largest zoological gardens in the world. Hardy animals roam freely over spacious, open-air terrain; and dangerous animals are restrained by ditches and moats – not steel bars. Heated buildings house tropical animals in cool weather. Exotic fish swim in a 15-acre aquarium, and birds fly in a 24-acre aviary.

When new exotic or rare animals join Sand Ridge Zoo, flyers announcing the new arrival are distributed to the general public. Just this week, a very rare Siberian tiger named Zimba arrived at the zoo. You have been asked to prepare an announcement that informs the public of Zimba's arrival. To add pizzazz to the announcement, you are asked to include a picture of Zimba in the announcement. The announcement also should include a description of the zoo, directions to the zoo, hours of operation, cost, and the zoo's telephone number.

You must take a picture of Zimba and scan it into a file so it can be used in the announcement. Details for the announcement, such as zoo description and directions, are available from the Marketing department of Sand Ridge Zoo. You may use prior announcements as a guide.

What Is Microsoft Word?

Microsoft Word is a full-featured word processing program that allows you to efficiently and economically create professional looking documents such as announcements, letters, resumes, and reports; and revise them easily. Word has many features designed to simplify the production of documents. For example, you can instruct Word to create a prewritten document for you, and then you can modify the document to meet your needs. Using its expanded **IntelliSense**™ technology, Word can perform tasks such as correcting text, checking spelling, and formatting text – *all while you are typing*. To improve the accuracy of your writing, Word also can check your grammar. Using Word's thesaurus, you can add variety and precision to your writing. With Word, you can easily include tables and graphics in your documents. In addition, you can use Word's desktop publishing features to create professional looking brochures, advertisements, and newsletters.

Project One – Zimba Announcement

To illustrate the features of Word, this book presents a series of projects that use Word to create documents similar to those you will encounter in the academic and business environments. Project 1 uses Word to produce the announcement shown in Figure 1-1. The announcement informs the public of the arrival of Zimba, a new Siberian tiger at Sand Ridge Zoo. Beneath the headline,

ZIMBA HAS ARRIVED!, a picture of Zimba displays to catch the attention of the reader. Beneath Zimba's picture is the zoo name, followed by a bulleted list identifying important features of Sand Ridge Zoo. Next, a brief paragraph gives the reader some background on Sand Ridge Zoo. The last line of the announcement lists the telephone number of the zoo.

Document Preparation Steps

Document preparation steps give you an overview of how the document in Figure 1-1 will be developed. The following tasks will be completed in this project:

1. Start Word.
2. Change the size of the displayed and printed characters.
3. Enter the document text.
4. Save the document on a floppy disk.
5. Format the document text (center, enlarge, bold, underline, and italicize).
6. Add bullets to the list.
7. Insert the picture.
8. Resize the picture.
9. Check the spelling of the document.
10. Save the document again.
11. Print the document.
12. Quit Word.

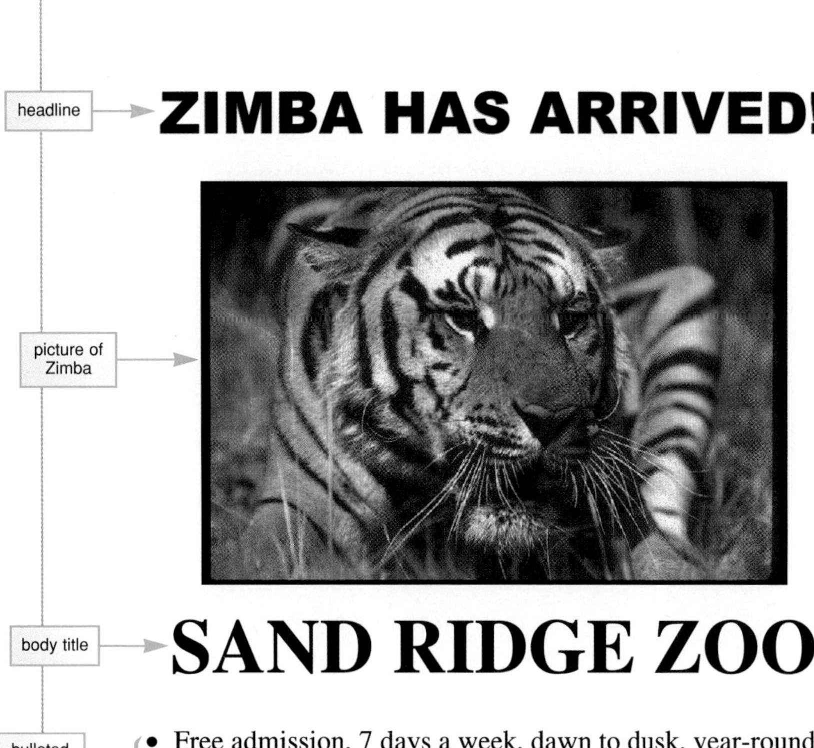

- Free admission, 7 days a week, dawn to dusk, year-round
- Easy access off Florida Turnpike at Yee-Haw Junction

Known worldwide for its ***huge collection of animals***, the Sand Ridge Zoo is a modern zoological garden that treats animals with dignity and kindness. Many animals roam freely over spacious, open-air terrain. Exotic fish swim in a 15-acre aquarium, and birds fly in a 24-acre aviary.

Call (941) 555-7456 for more information.

FIGURE 1-1

The following pages contain a detailed explanation of each of these tasks.

More About the Mouse

Some mouse users bend their wrists frequently while moving the mouse. To help prevent wrist injuries, place the mouse at least six inches from the edge of a workstation. In this location, the wrist is forced to be flat, which causes bending to occur at the elbow when the mouse is moved.

Mouse Usage

In this book, the mouse is the primary way to communicate with Word. You can perform six operations with a mouse: point, click, right-click, double-click, drag, and right-drag.

Point means you move the mouse across a flat surface until the mouse pointer rests on the item of choice on the screen. As you move the mouse, the mouse pointer moves across the screen in the same direction. **Click** means you press and release the left mouse button. The terminology used in this book to direct you to point to a particular item and then click is, Click the particular item. For example, *Click the Bold button*, means point to the Bold button and then click.

Right-click means you press and release the right mouse button. As with the left mouse button, you normally will point to an item on the screen prior to right-clicking.

In many cases, when you right-click, Word displays a **shortcut menu** that contains the commands most often used for the current activity. Thus, when these projects instruct you to display a shortcut menu, point to the item being discussed and right-click.

Double-click means you quickly press and release the left mouse button twice without moving the mouse. In most cases, you must point to an item before double-clicking. **Drag** means you point to an item, hold down the left mouse button, move the item to the desired location on the screen, and then release the left mouse button. **Right-drag** means you point to an item, hold down the right mouse button, move the item to the desired location, and then release the right mouse button.

The use of the mouse is an important skill when working with Microsoft Word for Windows 95.

Starting Word

Follow these steps to start Word, or ask your instructor how to start Word for your system.

Steps To Start Word

1 Click the Start button on the taskbar and then point to New Office Document.

The programs in the Start menu display above the Start button (Figure 1-2). The New Office Document command is highlighted on the Start menu.

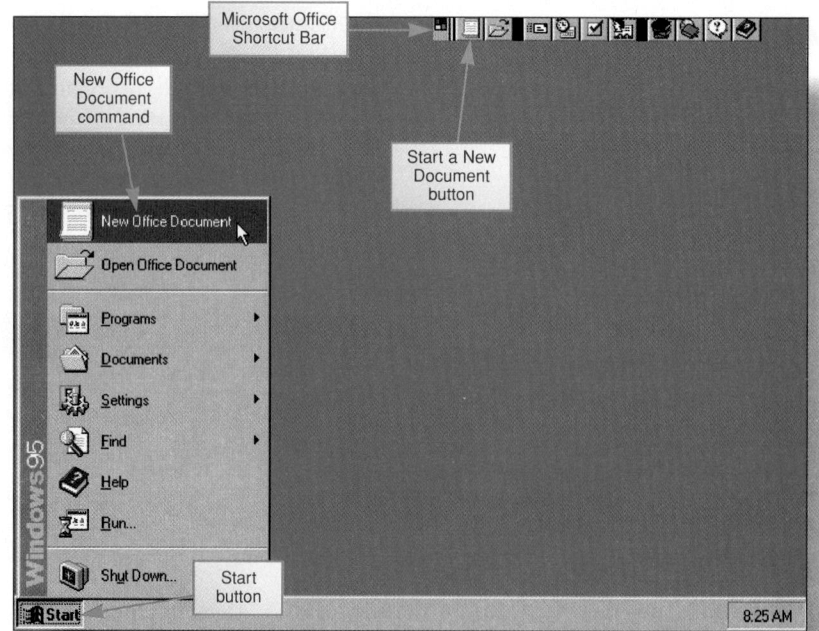

FIGURE 1-2

2 Click New Office Document. When the New dialog box displays, click the General tab to display the General sheet, if necessary.

Office displays several document icons in the General sheet in the New dialog box (Figure 1-3). Each icon represents a different type of document that you can create in Microsoft Office. In this project, you are to create a new document using Microsoft Word 7 for Windows 95.

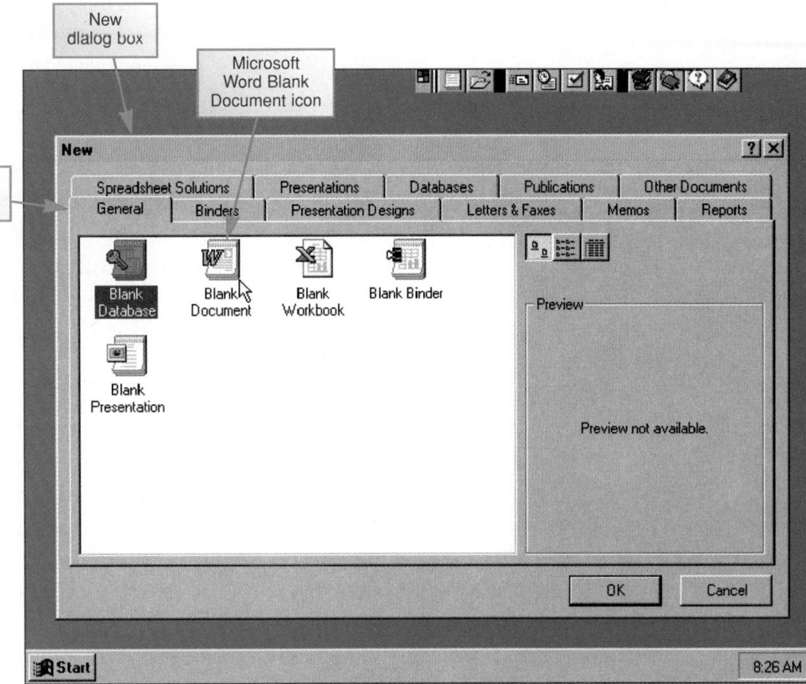

FIGURE 1-3

3 Double-click the Blank Document icon.

Office starts Word. While Word is starting, the mouse pointer changes to the shape of an ***hourglass****. After a few moments, an empty document titled Document1 displays on the Word screen (Figure 1-4).*

4 If the Word screen is not maximized, click its Maximize button.

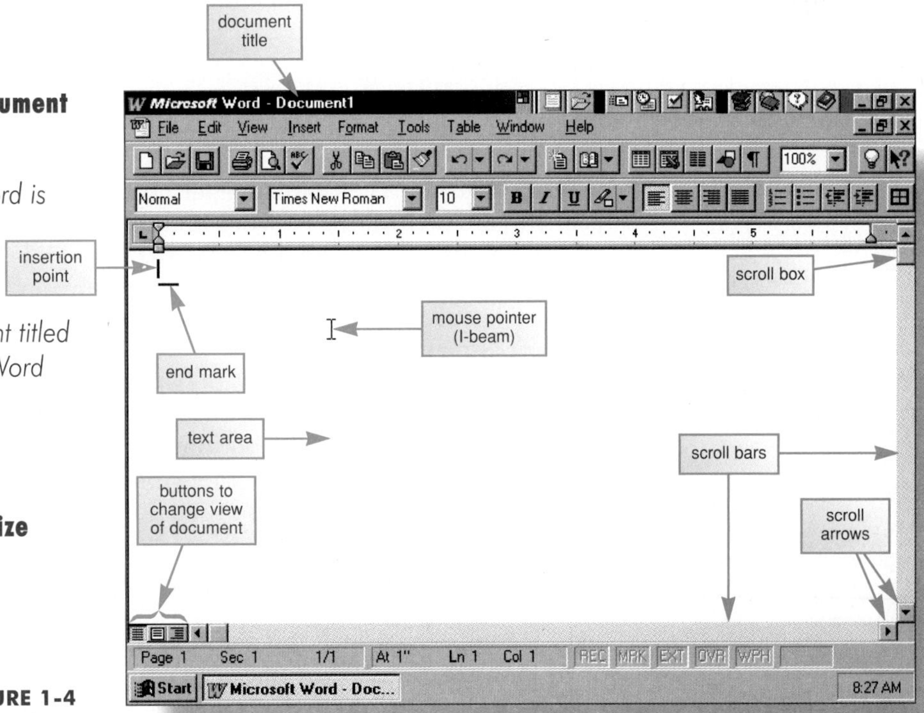

FIGURE 1-4

OtherWays

1. Right-click Start button, click Open, double-click New Office Document, double-click Blank Document icon
2. On Microsoft Office Shortcut Bar, click Start a New Document button, double-click Blank Document icon
3. On Start menu point to Programs, click Microsoft Word

The Word Screen

The **Word screen** (Figure 1-4 on the previous page) consists of a variety of features to make your work more efficient and the results more professional. If you are following along on a personal computer and your screen differs from Figure 1-4, click View on the menu bar and then click Normal.

Word Document Window

The Word document window contains several elements similar to the document windows in other applications, as well as some elements unique to Word. The main elements of the Word document window are the text area, insertion point, end mark, mouse pointer, and scroll bars (Figure 1-4 on the previous page).

TEXT AREA As you type or insert pictures, your text and graphics display in the **text area.**

INSERTION POINT The **insertion point** is a blinking vertical bar that indicates where text will be inserted as you type. As you type, the insertion point moves to the right and, when you reach the end of a line, it moves downward to the next line. You also insert graphics at the location of the insertion point.

END MARK The **end mark** indicates the end of your document. Each time you begin a new line as you type, the end mark moves downward.

MOUSE POINTER The **mouse pointer** becomes different shapes, depending on the task you are performing in Word and the pointer's location on the screen. The mouse pointer in Figure 1-4 has the shape of an I-beam. The mouse pointer displays as an I-beam when it is in the text area. Other mouse pointer shapes are described as they appear on the screen during this and subsequent projects.

SCROLL BARS You use the **scroll bars** to display different portions of your document in the document window. At the right edge of the document window is a vertical scroll bar, and at the bottom of the document window is a horizontal scroll bar. On both scroll bars, the **scroll box** indicates your current location in the document. At the left edge of the horizontal scroll bar, Word provides three buttons you can use to change the view of your document. These buttons are discussed as they are used in a later project.

Word is preset to use standard 8.5-by-11-inch paper, with 1.25-inch left and right margins and 1-inch top and bottom margins. Only a portion of your document, however, displays on the screen at one time. You view the portion of the document displayed on the screen through the **document window** (Figure 1-5).

More *About* Scroll Bars

You can use the vertical scroll bar to scroll through multi-page documents. As you drag the scroll box up or down the scroll bar, Word displays a page indicator to the left of the scroll box. The page indicator indicates the current page, if you were to release the mouse at that moment.

FIGURE 1-5

Menu Bar, Toolbars, Rulers, and Status Bar

The menu bar, toolbars, and horizontal ruler appear at the top of the screen just below the title bar (Figure 1-6 on the next page). The status bar appears at the bottom of the screen.

MENU BAR The **menu bar** displays the Word menu names. Each menu name represents a menu of commands you can use to retrieve, store, print, and format data in your document and perform other tasks. To display a menu, such as the File menu, click the menu name on the menu bar.

More About Toolbars and Ruler

If your screen does not display the toolbars or the ruler, they have been hidden. To display a toolbar, click View on the menu bar, click Toolbars, click the appropriate check box(es), and then click the OK button. To display the horizontal ruler, click View on the menu bar and then click Ruler.

TOOLBARS Just below the menu bar is the **Standard toolbar**. Immediately below the Standard toolbar is the **Formatting toolbar**.

Toolbars contain buttons and boxes that allow you to perform tasks more quickly than using the menu bar. For example, to print, click the Print button on the Standard toolbar. Each button has a picture on the face that helps you remember its function. Figure 1-7 illustrates the Standard toolbar and identifies its buttons and boxes; Figure 1-8 illustrates the Formatting toolbar. Each button and box is explained in detail as it is used in the projects.

The Standard and Formatting toolbars initially display **anchored**, or locked, below the menu bar. Additional toolbars may display automatically on the Word screen, depending on the task you are performing. These additional toolbars display either stacked beneath the Formatting toolbar or floating on the Word screen. You can rearrange the order of **stacked toolbars** and move **floating toolbars** anywhere on the Word screen. Later in the book, steps are presented that show you how to float an anchored toolbar or anchor a floating toolbar.

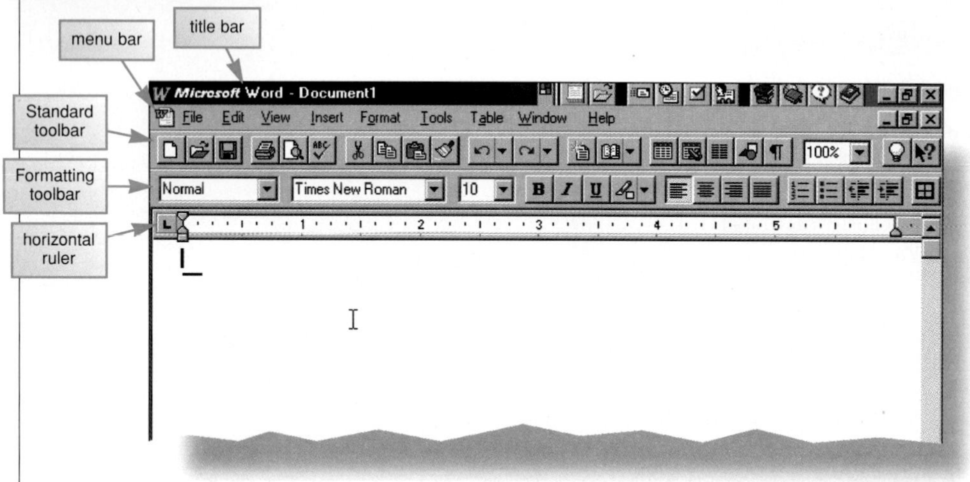

FIGURE 1-6

RULERS Below the Formatting toolbar is the **horizontal ruler** (Figure 1-9). You use the horizontal ruler, sometimes simply called the **ruler**, to set tab stops, indent paragraphs, adjust column widths, and change page margins. An additional ruler, called the **vertical ruler**, displays when you are performing certain tasks. The vertical ruler is discussed as it displays on the screen in a later project.

STATUS BAR The **status bar** is located at the bottom of the screen. From left to right the following information displays about the page shown in Figure 1-9: the page number, the section number, the page visible in the document window followed by the total number of pages in the document, the position of the insertion point in inches from the top of the page, the line number and

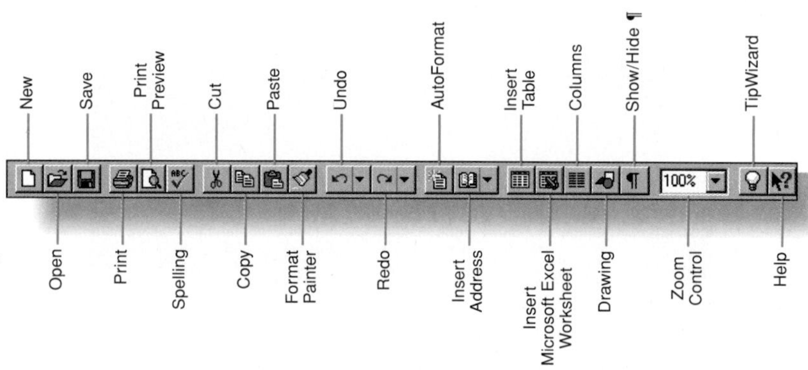

FIGURE 1-7

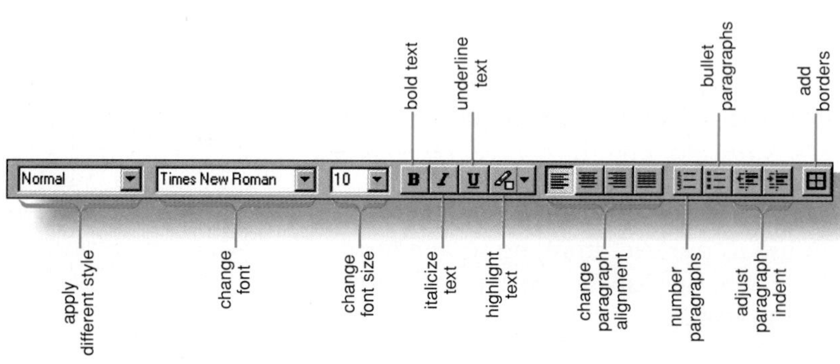

FIGURE 1-8

column number where the insertion point is located, and several **mode indicators**. If a mode indicator is darkened, it is on. For example, the dimmed OVR indicates overtype mode is off. To turn most modes on or off, double-click the mode indicator. Mode indicators are discussed as they are used in the projects.

When you begin typing on the Word screen, a spelling icon also appears at the right edge of the status bar. The spelling icon will be discussed later in this project.

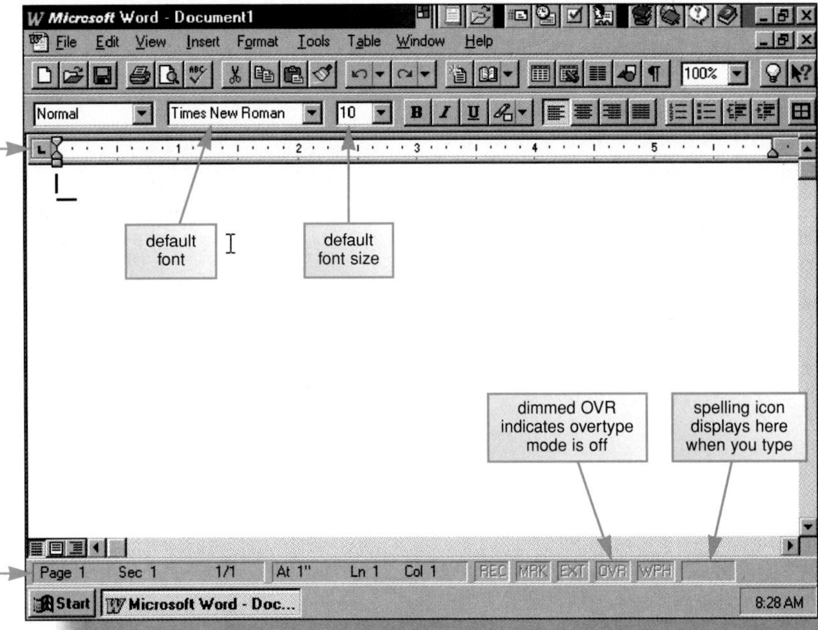

FIGURE 1-9

Depending on how you installed Word and the status of certain keys on your keyboard, your status bar may have different mode indicators on or off. For example, the dimmed WPH on the status bar indicates WordPerfect Help is off. If your WordPerfect Help mode indicator is darkened, WordPerfect Help is active and you need to deactivate it. When WordPerfect Help is on, the keys you press on the keyboard work according to WordPerfect defaults instead of Word. To deactivate the WordPerfect Help, ask for assistance from your instructor or do the following: Click Tools on the menu bar and then click Options; click the General tab; click Help for WordPerfect Users and click Navigation Keys for WordPerfect Users to deselect these check boxes; and then click the OK button in the Options dialog box.

When you point to a menu command or a toolbar button, the status bar displays a brief description of the command or button. If a task you select requires several seconds, the status bar displays a message informing you of the progress of the task.

Changing the Default Font Size

Characters that display on the screen are a specific shape and size. The **font**, or typeface, defines the appearance and shape of the letters, numbers, and special characters. The preset, or default, font is Times New Roman (Figure 1-9). The **font size** specifies the size of the characters on the screen. Font size is gauged by a measurement system called **points**. A single point is about 1/72 of one inch in height. Thus, a character with a font size of ten is about 10/72 of one inch in height. The default font size in most versions of Word is 10. If more of the characters in your document require a larger font size, you can easily change the default font size before you type. In Project 1, many of the characters in the announcement are a font size of 18. Follow the steps on the next page to change the font size before you begin entering text.

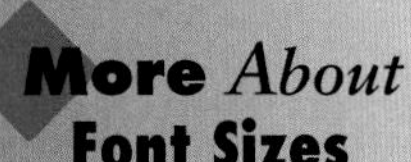

More About Font Sizes

Because many people need to wear reading glasses, you should increase the font size of characters in a document to at least 12 point. Because an announcement is usually posted on a bulletin board, its font size should be as large as possible so that the announcement attracts all potential readers.

To Change the Default Font Size Before Typing

1 Point to the Font Size box arrow on the Formatting toolbar.

The mouse pointer changes to a left-pointing block arrow when positioned on a toolbar (Figure 1-10). When you point to a toolbar button, Word displays a ***ToolTip****, which is Font Size in this case, immediately beneath the button and also displays a brief description of the button at the bottom left edge of the status bar.*

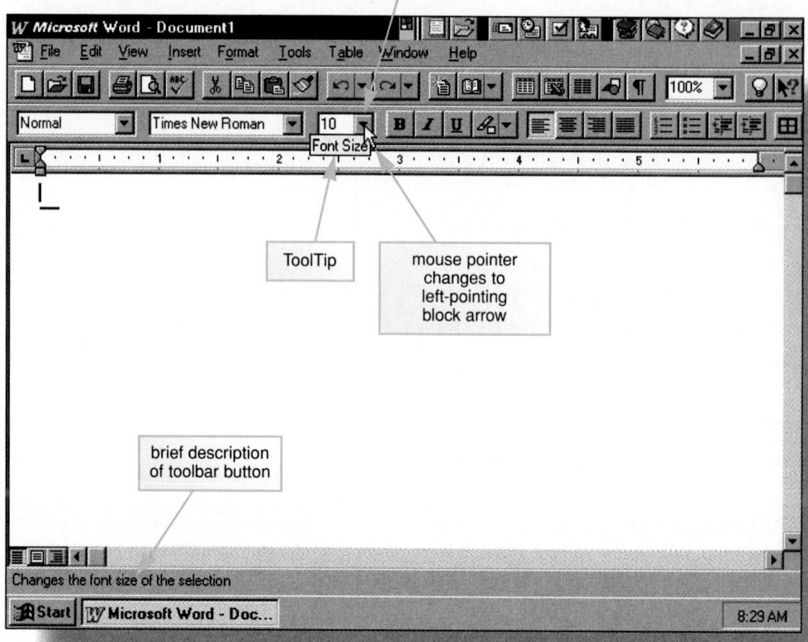

FIGURE 1-10

2 Click the Font Size box arrow on the Formatting toolbar.

A list of available font sizes displays in the Font Size drop-down list box (Figure 1-11).

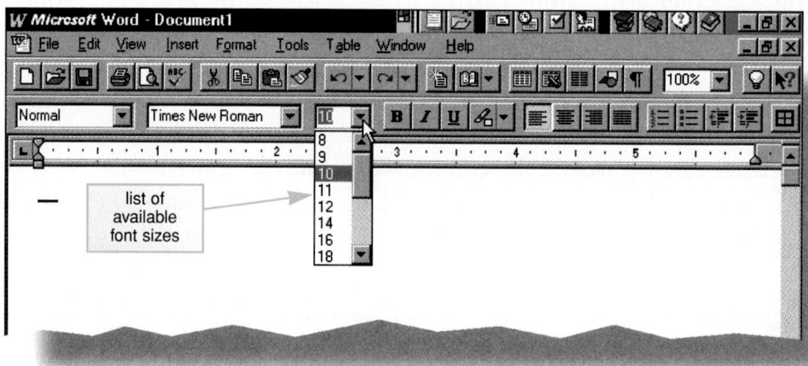

FIGURE 1-11

3 Point to font size 18.

Word highlights font size 18 in the list (Figure 1-12).

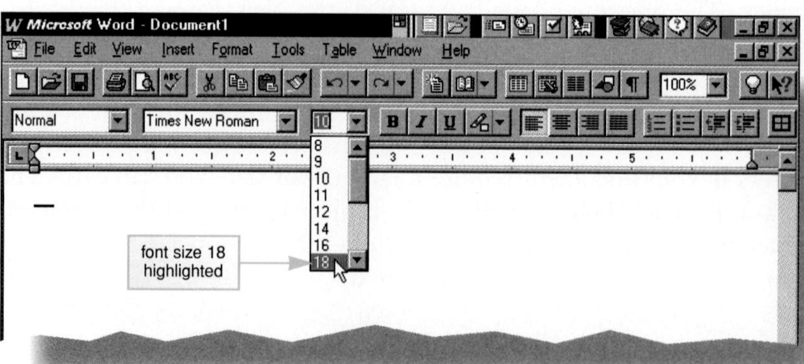

FIGURE 1-12

Click font size 18.

The font size for this document changes to 18 (Figure 1-13).

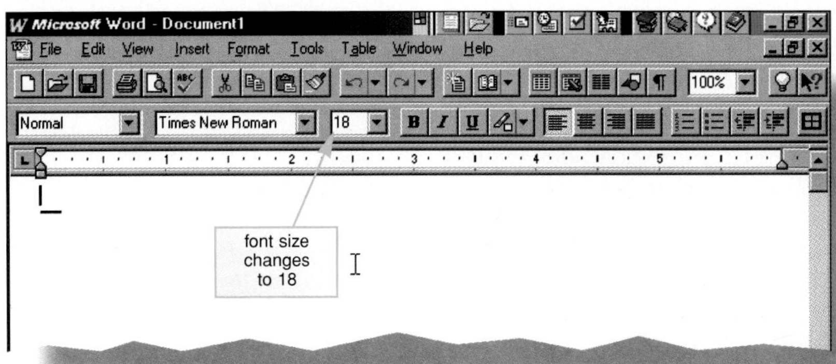

FIGURE 1-13

Other Ways

1. Right-click paragraph mark above end mark, click Font on shortcut menu, click Font tab, select desired point size in Size list, click OK button
2. On Format menu click Font, click Font tab, select desired point size in Size list, click OK button
3. Press CTRL+SHIFT+P, type desired point size, press ENTER

The new default font size takes effect immediately in your document. Word uses this font size for the remainder of this announcement.

Entering Text

To prepare a document in Word, you enter text by typing on the keyboard. In Project 1, the headline (ZIMBA HAS ARRIVED!) is capitalized. The following example explains the steps to enter the headline in all capital letters at the left margin. Later in the project, this headline will be centered across the top of the document, formatted in bold, and enlarged.

Steps To Enter Text

1. **If the CAPS LOCK indicator is not lit on your keyboard, press the CAPS LOCK key. Type** ZIMBA HAS ARRIVED! **as the headline. If at any time during typing you make an error, press the BACKSPACE key until you have deleted the text in error, and then retype the text correctly.**

   Word places the Z in ZIMBA at the location of the insertion point. As you continue typing this headline, the insertion point moves to the right (Figure 1-14).

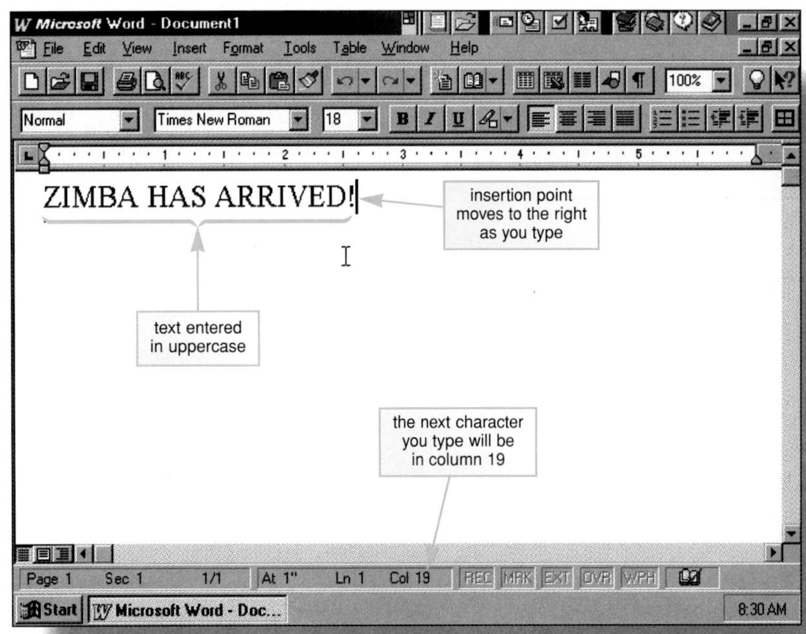

FIGURE 1-14

Press the CAPS LOCK key and then press the ENTER key.

Word creates a new paragraph by moving the insertion point to the beginning of the next line (Figure 1-15). Whenever you press the ENTER key, Word considers the previous line and the next line to be different paragraphs. Notice the status bar indicates the current position of the insertion point.

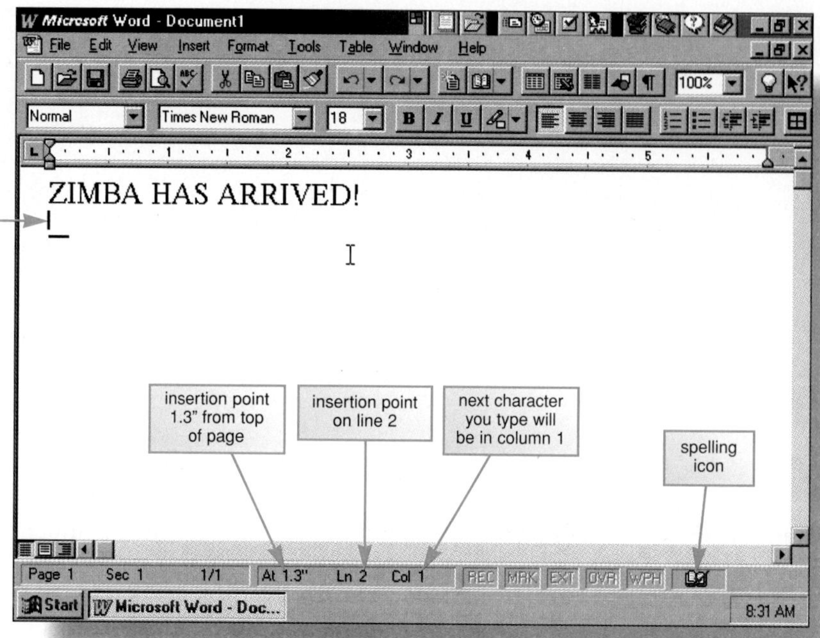

FIGURE 1-15

When you begin entering text into a document, the **spelling icon** displays at the right edge of the status bar (Figure 1-15). As you type, the spelling icon shows a pencil writing on paper. When you stop typing, the pencil changes to either a red check mark or a red X. In Figure 1-15, the spelling icon displays a red check mark. In general, if all of the words you have typed are in Word's dictionary, a red check mark appears on the spelling icon. If you type a word not in the dictionary (because it is a proper name or misspelled), a red wavy underline appears beneath the word and a red X appears on the spelling icon. As you enter text into the announcement, your spelling icon may show a red X, instead of a red check mark. Later in this project, you check spelling of the words in the announcement. At that time, the red X on the spelling icon returns to a red check mark.

Entering Blank Lines into a Document

To enter a blank line into a document, press the ENTER key without typing anything on the line. The following example explains how to enter three blank lines after the headline, ZIMBA HAS ARRIVED!

More About Headlines

Because the headline is the first item a reader notices, it should be effective. Headlines of less than four words are often typed in all-capital letters. Adding punctuation, like an exclamation point, to the end of a headline forces the reader to pause on the headline before moving into the body of the announcement.

To Enter Blank Lines into a Document

1 Press the ENTER key three times.

Word inserts three blank lines into your document beneath the headline (Figure 1-16).

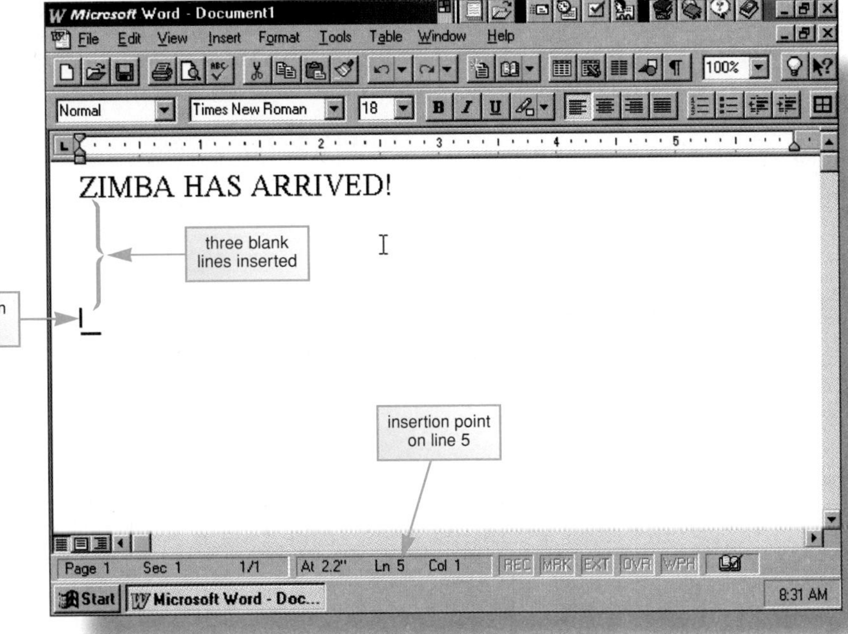

FIGURE 1-16

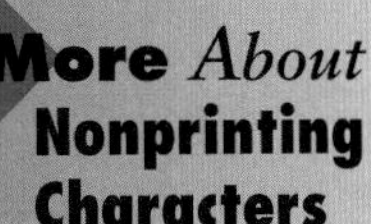

More About Nonprinting Characters

If you do not want all of the nonprinting characters to display on the screen when you click the Show/Hide ¶ button, you can selectively display them by clicking Tools on the menu bar, clicking Options, clicking the View tab, clicking the desired check boxes in the Nonprinting Characters area, and then clicking the OK button.

Displaying Nonprinting Characters

To indicate where in the document you pressed the ENTER key or SPACEBAR, you may find it helpful to display **nonprinting characters**. The paragraph mark (¶) is a nonprinting character that indicates where you pressed the ENTER key. A raised dot (•) shows where you pressed the SPACEBAR. Nonprinting characters display only on the screen. They do not appear in printed documents. Other nonprinting characters are discussed as they display on the screen in subsequent projects. The following steps illustrate how to display nonprinting characters, if they are not already displaying on your screen.

To Display Nonprinting Characters

1 Point to the Show/Hide ¶ button on the Standard toolbar.

Word displays the ToolTip for the button (Figure 1-17).

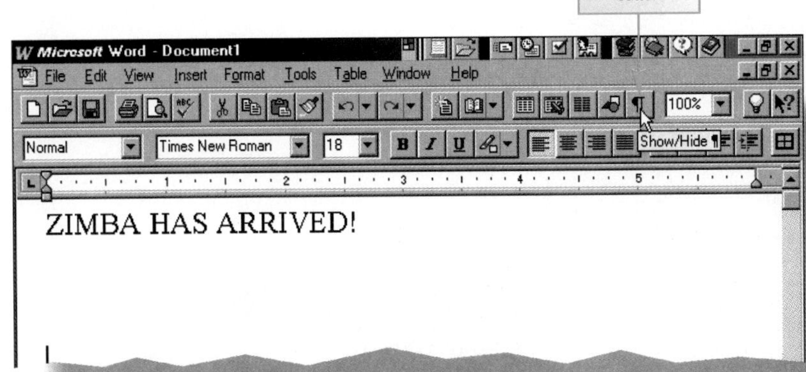

FIGURE 1-17

If it is not already recessed, click the the Show/Hide ¶ button on the Standard toolbar.

Word displays nonprinting characters on the screen, and the Show/Hide ¶ button on the Standard toolbar is recessed (Figure 1-18).

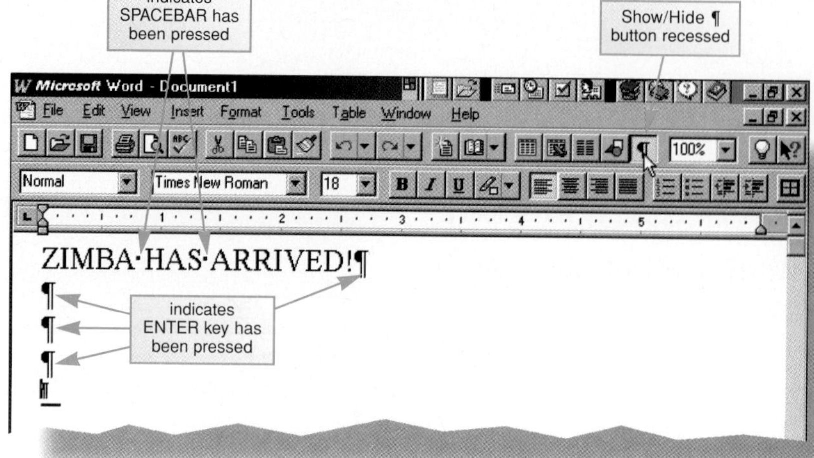

FIGURE 1-18

OtherWays

1. On Tools menu click Options, click View tab, click All, click OK button
2. Press CTRL+SHIFT+*

Notice several changes to your screen display (Figure 1-18). A paragraph mark appears at the end of each line to indicate you pressed the ENTER key. Recall that each time you press the ENTER key, Word creates a new paragraph. Because you changed the font size, the first two paragraph marks are 18 point and the one above the end mark is 10 point, the default. You cannot delete the paragraph mark above the end mark. Between each word, a raised dot appears, indicating you pressed the SPACEBAR. Finally, the Show/Hide ¶ button is recessed, or ghosted, to indicate it is selected.

If you feel the nonprinting characters clutter your screen, you can hide them by clicking the Show/Hide ¶ button again. It is recommended that you display nonprinting characters; therefore, the screens presented in this book show the nonprinting characters.

More About Entering Text

In the days of typewriters, the letter l was used for both the letter l and the number one. Keyboards, however, have both a number one and the letter l. Keyboards also have both a number zero and the letter o. Be careful to press the correct keyboard character when creating a word processing document.

Entering More Text

The next step is to enter the body title, SAND RIDGE ZOO, into the document window as explained in the steps below.

TO ENTER MORE TEXT

Step 1: Press the CAPS LOCK key. Type `SAND RIDGE ZOO` and then press the CAPS LOCK key.
Step 2: Press the ENTER key twice.

The name of the zoo displays on line 5 as shown in Figure 1-19.

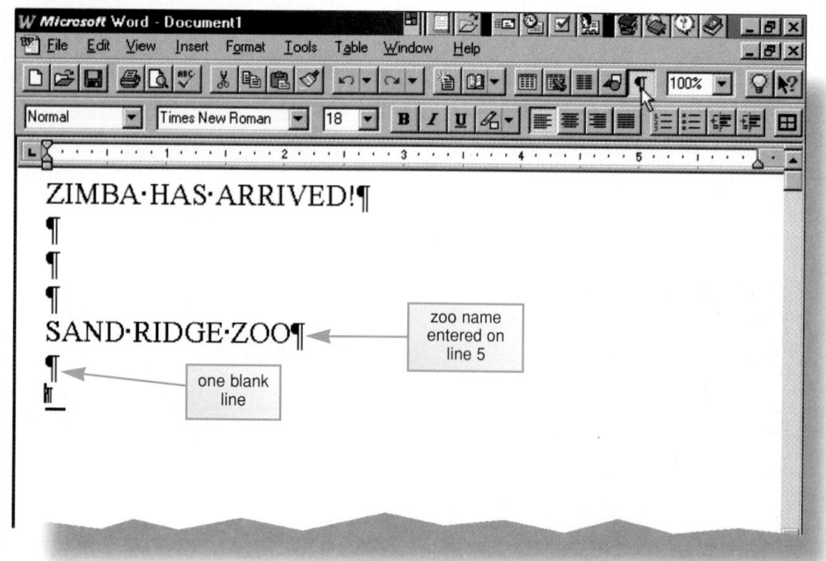

FIGURE 1-19

The next step is to enter the list beneath the zoo name. In Word, a list is a series of paragraphs. In the steps below, you enter the text of the list. Later in this project, you will format the list so bullets display in front of each item in the list as shown in Figure 1-1 on page WD 1.7.

TO ENTER A LIST OF PARAGRAPHS

Step 1: Type `Free admission, 7 days a week, dawn to dusk, year-round` and then press the ENTER key.

Step 2: Type `Easy access off Florida Turnpike at Yee-Haw Junction` as the last paragraph in the list.

The list is entered as shown in Figure 1-20.

Notice in Figure 1-20 that the word Yee has a red wavy underline beneath it. Whenever a word has been flagged with a red wavy underline, it is not in Word's dictionary. That is, the flagged word is either misspelled or a proper name that is not in the dictionary. Also notice that the spelling icon no longer displays a red check mark; instead, it now shows a red X to indicate that a word in the document is not in Word's dictionary because it either is misspelled or a proper name.

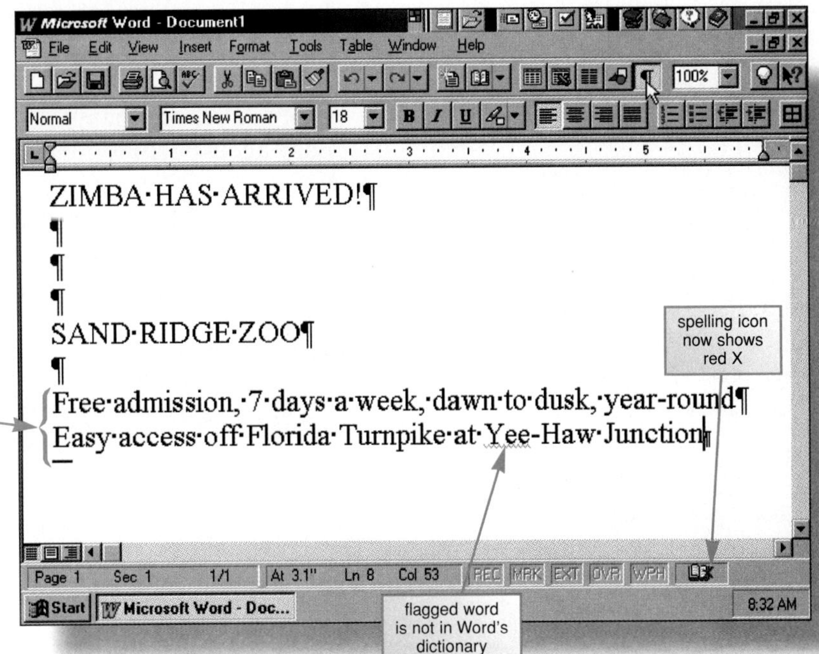

FIGURE 1-20

Depending on your typing abilities, you may have additional flagged words in your document. For this reason, it is recommended that you correct the spelling of the entire document at once later in this project, rather than correcting the flagged words as they display.

Using the Wordwrap Feature

Wordwrap allows you to type words in a paragraph continually without pressing the ENTER key at the end of each line. When the insertion point moves beyond the right margin, Word positions it automatically at the beginning of the next line. As you type, if a word extends beyond the right margin, Word also positions the word automatically on the next line with the insertion point. Thus, as you enter text using Word, do not press the ENTER key when the insertion point reaches the right margin. Because Word creates a new paragraph each time you press the ENTER key, press the ENTER key only in these circumstances:

1. To insert blank lines into a document
2. To begin a new paragraph
3. To terminate a short line of text and advance to the next line
4. In response to certain Word commands

Perform the following step to become familiar with the wordwrap feature.

Steps To Use the Wordwrap Feature

1. **Press the ENTER key twice. Type the first sentence in the paragraph beneath the list in the body of the announcement:** `Known worldwide for its huge collection of animals, the Sand Ridge Zoo is a modern zoological garden that treats animals with dignity and kindness.`

Word automatically wraps the word, Sand, to the beginning of line 11 because it is too long to fit on line 10; Word also wraps the word, animals, to line 12 because it is too long to fit on line 11 (Figure 1-21). Your document may wordwrap on a different word depending on the type of printer you are using.

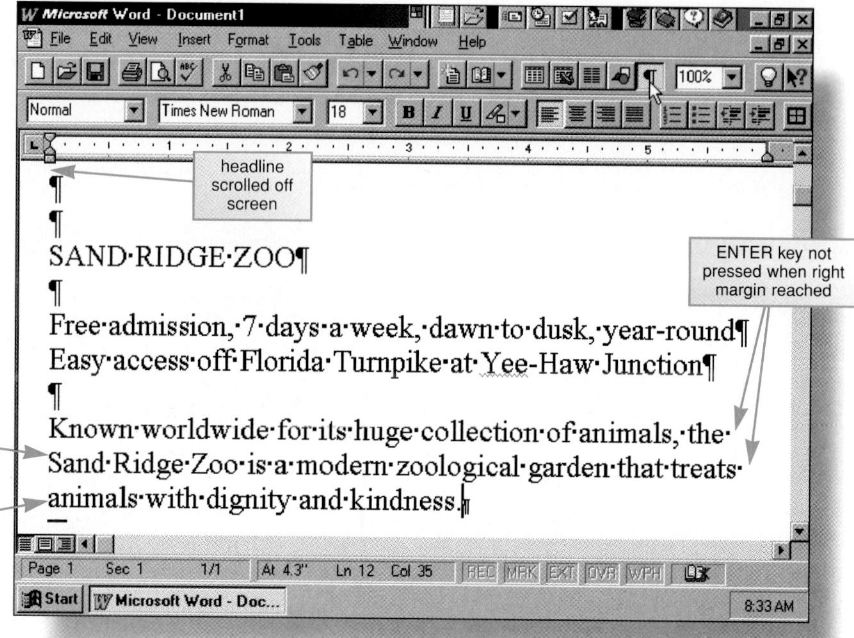

FIGURE 1-21

Notice in Figure 1-21 that the headline no longer displays in the document window. As you type more lines of text than Word can display in the text area, Word scrolls the top portion of the document upward off the screen. Although you cannot see the text once it scrolls off the screen, it still remains in the document. Recall that the document window allows you to view only a portion of your document at one time (Figure 1-5 on page WD 1.11). Your screen may scroll differently depending on the type of monitor you are using.

The next step is to enter the remainder of the paragraph and the last line into the body of the announcement as described in the steps below.

TO ENTER THE REMAINDER OF THE TEXT

Step 1: Press the SPACEBAR once. Type the next sentence in the paragraph in the body of the announcement: `Many animals roam freely over spacious, open-air terrain.`

Step 2: Press the SPACEBAR once. Type the last sentence in the paragraph in the body of the announcement: `Exotic fish swim in a 15-acre aquarium, and birds fly in a 24-acre aviary.`

Step 3: Press the ENTER key twice. Type `Call (941) 555-7456 for more information.`

The remainder of the body of the announcement is entered (Figure 1-22). Notice that Word scrolls much of the announcement off the screen.

More About Entering Sentences

Word processing documents use variable character fonts; for example, the letter w takes up more space that the letter i. Thus, it is often difficult to count the number of spaces between sentences. For this reason, the two space after a period rule is not followed when using variable character fonts.

Moving Around a Document

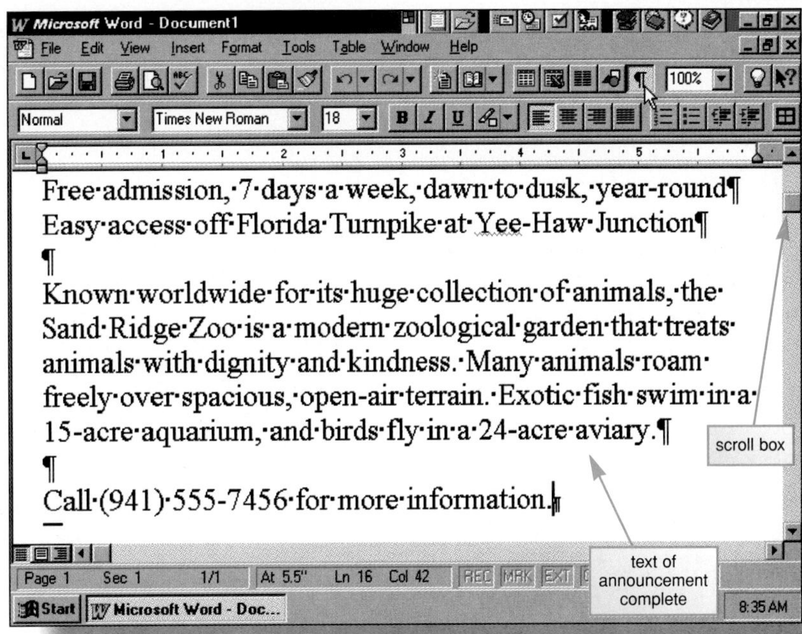

FIGURE 1-22

When Word scrolls text off the top of the screen, the scroll box on the scroll bar at the right edge of the document window moves downward (Figure 1-22). The scroll box indicates the current relative location of the insertion point in the document. You may use either the mouse or the keyboard to move the insertion point to a different location in a document. With the mouse, you use the scroll bars to bring a different portion of the document into the document window, and then click the mouse to move the insertion point to that location. When you use the keyboard, the insertion point moves automatically when you press the appropriate keys.

To move the insertion point to a portion of the document that has scrolled off the screen, drag the scroll box upward or downward. To move the document up or down one entire screenful at a time, click anywhere above or below the scroll box on the scroll bar or press the PAGE UP or PAGE DOWN key on the keyboard. To move the document up or down one line at a time in the window, click the scroll arrow at the top or bottom of the scroll bar. To move the insertion point to the top of the document using the keyboard, press CTRL+HOME; to move to the end of the document, press CTRL+END.

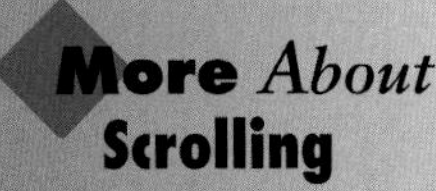

More *About* Scrolling

Computer users frequently switch between the keyboard and the mouse during a word processing session, which places strain on the wrist. To help prevent wrist injury, minimize switching. If your fingers are already on the keyboard, use keyboard keys to scroll; if your hand is already on the mouse, use the mouse to scroll.

Saving a Document

When you are creating a document in Word, the computer stores it in main memory. If the computer is turned off or if you lose electrical power, the document is lost. Hence, it is mandatory to save on disk any document that you will use later. The following steps illustrate how to save a document on a floppy disk inserted in drive A using the Save button on the Standard toolbar.

Steps To Save a New Document

1 Insert a formatted floppy disk into drive A. Point to the Save button on the Standard toolbar (Figure 1-23).

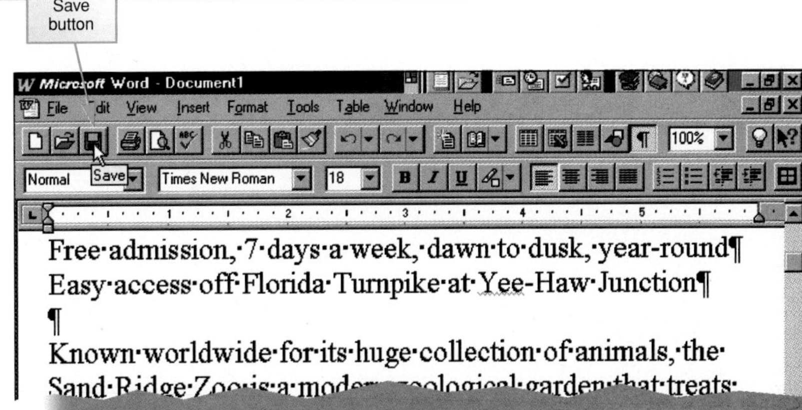

FIGURE 1-23

2 Click the Save button on the Standard toolbar.

Word displays the Save As dialog box with the insertion point blinking after the default filename, ZIMBA HAS ARRIVED, in the File name text box (Figure 1-24). Notice that Word chooses the first line of the document as the default filename. Because the filename is initially selected when the Save As dialog box displays, you can change the filename by immediately typing the new name. If you do not enter a new filename, the document will be saved with the default filename, ZIMBA HAS ARRIVED.

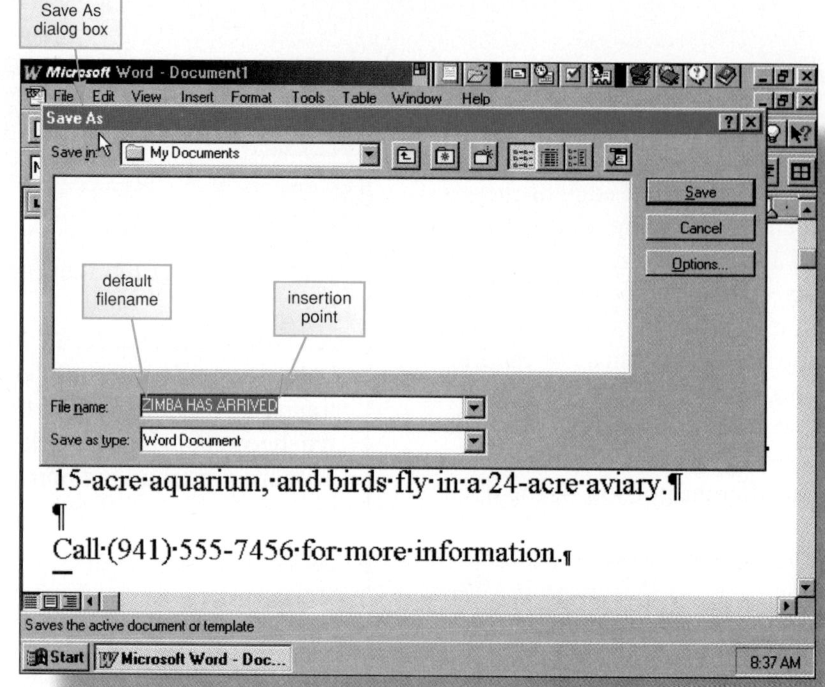

FIGURE 1-24

3 Type the filename `Zimba Announcement` **in the File name text box. Do not press the ENTER key after typing the filename.**

The filename, Zimba Announcement, displays in the File name text box (Figure 1-25). When creating filenames, you should be as meaningful as possible. Thus, the first word in this filename (Zimba) relates to the nature of this document, and the second word (Announcement) relates to the category of this document. Using this technique, all files relating to Zimba, whether it be a letter, memo, or announcement, will be grouped together in a folder. A **folder** *is a specific location on a disk. Notice that the current folder is My Documents. To change to a different drive or folder, use the Save in box.*

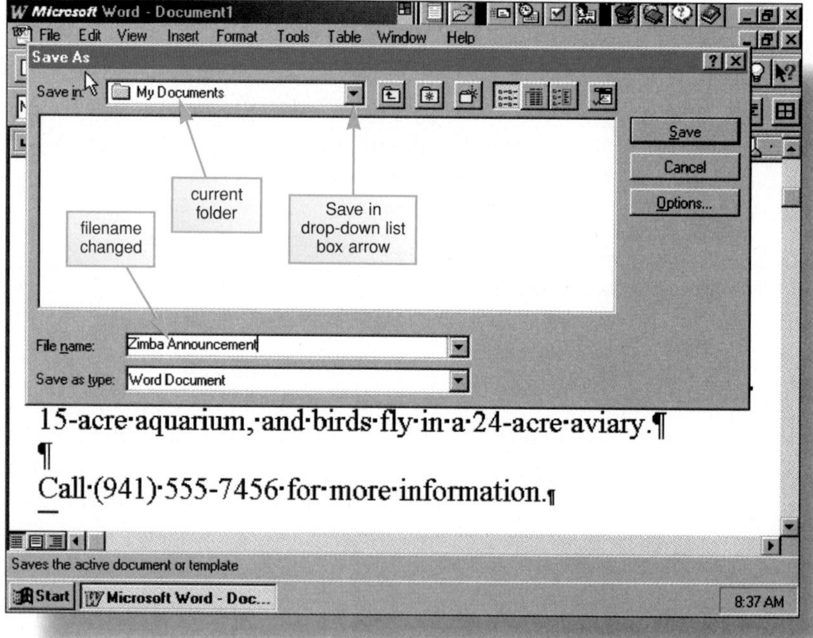

FIGURE 1-25

4 **Click the Save in box arrow and then point to 3½ Floppy [A:].**

A list of the available drives displays with 3½ floppy [A:] highlighted (Figure 1-26). Your list may differ depending on your system configuration.

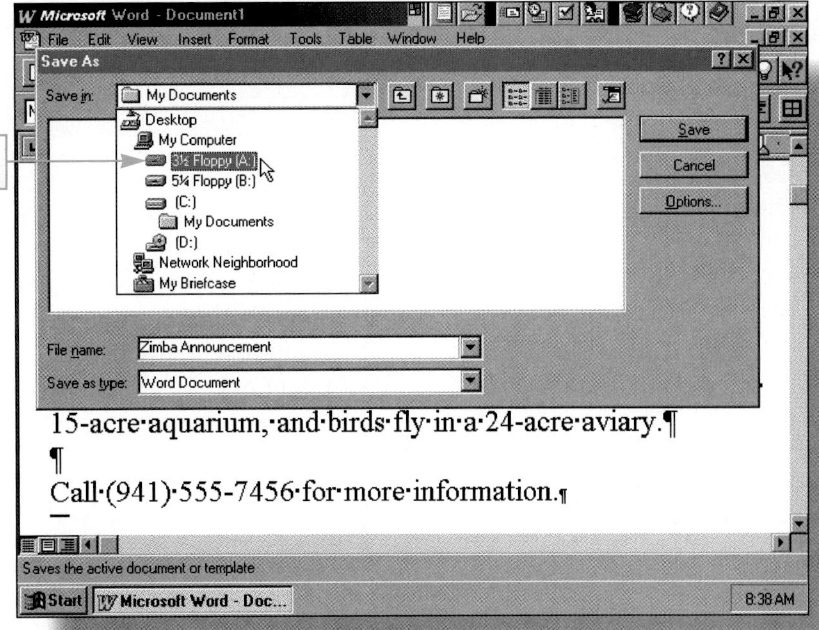

FIGURE 1-26

5 **Click 3½ Floppy [A:] and then point to the Save button in the Save As dialog box.**

Drive A becomes the selected drive (Figure 1-27). The names of existing files stored on the floppy disk in drive A display. In Figure 1-27, no files are currently stored on the floppy disk in drive A.

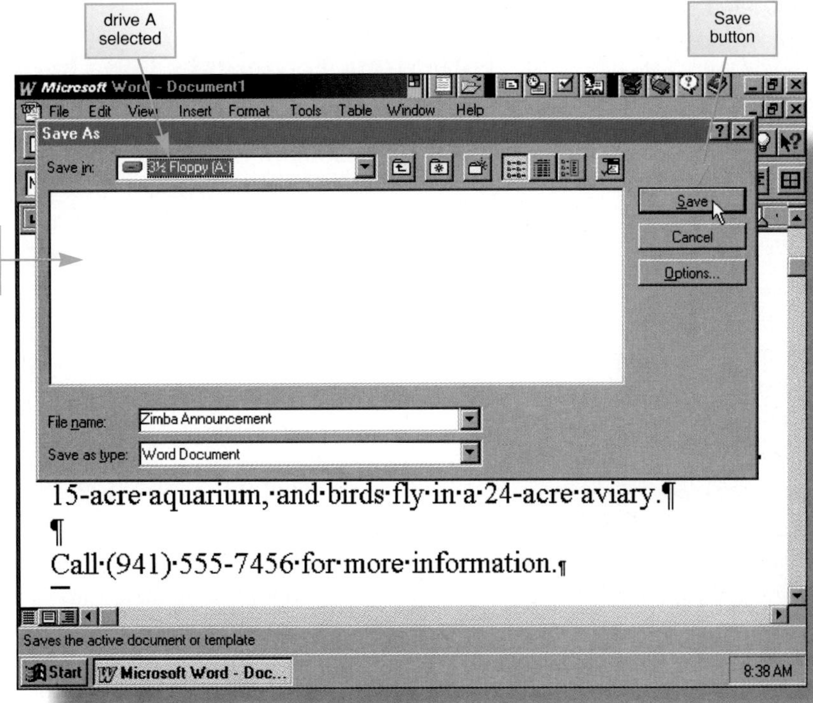

FIGURE 1-27

Click the Save button in the Save As dialog box.

Word saves the document on the floppy disk in drive A with the filename Zimba Announcement (Figure 1-28). Although the announcement is saved on a floppy disk, it also remains in main memory and displays on the screen.

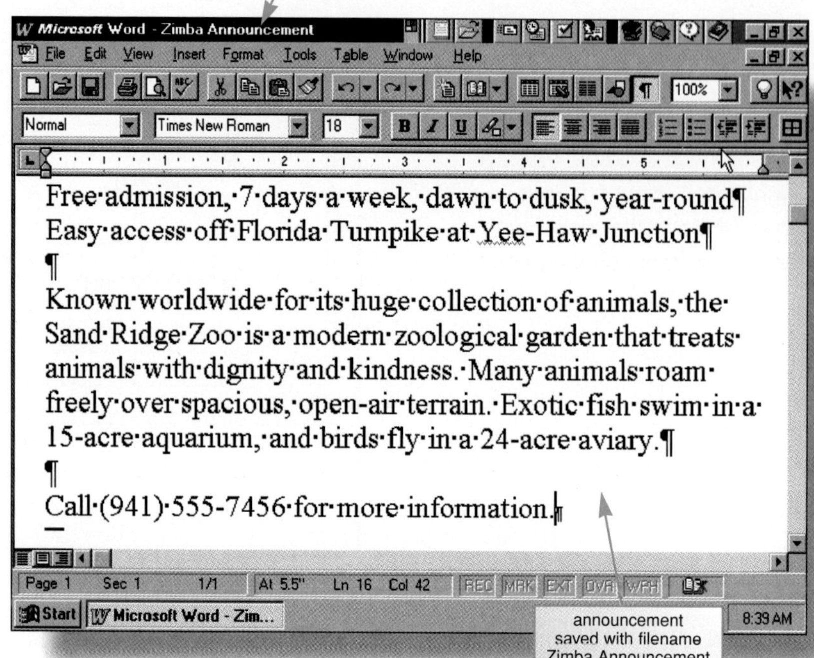

FIGURE 1-28

Other Ways

1. On File menu click Save, type filename, select location in Save in box, click Save button in dialog box
2. Press CTRL+S, type filename, select location in Save in box, click Save button in dialog box

More About Saving

When you save a document, you should create readable and meaningful filenames. A filename can be up to 255 characters, including spaces. The only invalid characters are backslash (\), slash (/), colon (:), asterisk (*), question mark (?), quotation mark ("), less than symbol (<), greather than symbol (>), and vertical bar (|).

Formatting Paragraphs and Characters in a Document

The text for Project 1 is now complete. The next step is to format the characters and paragraphs within the announcement. Paragraphs encompass the text up to and including the paragraph mark (¶). **Paragraph formatting** is the process of changing the appearance of a paragraph. For example, you can center or indent a paragraph.

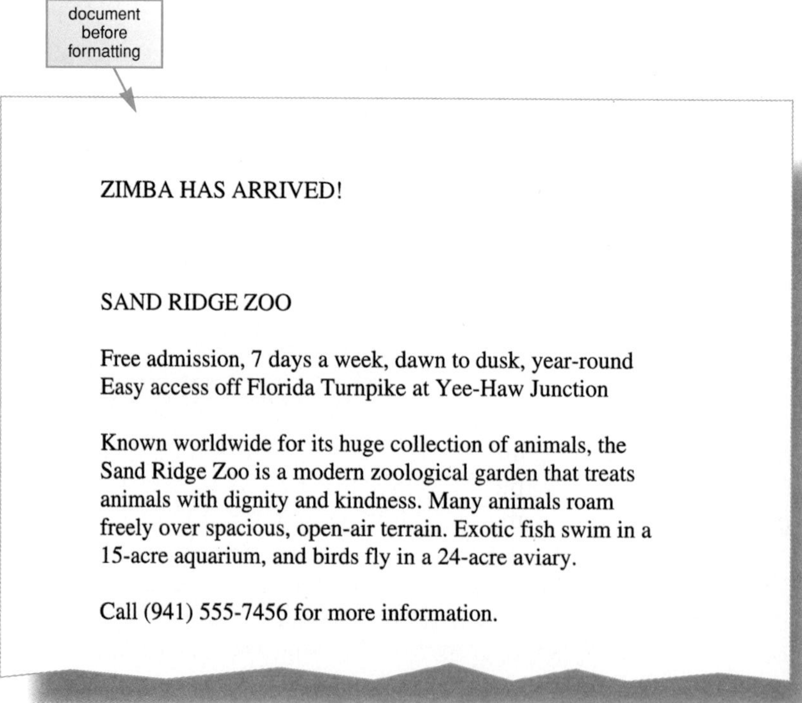

FIGURE 1-29

Characters include letters, numbers, punctuation marks, and symbols. **Character formatting** is the process of changing the way characters appear on the screen and in print. You use character formatting to emphasize certain words and improve readability of a document.

With Word, you can format before you type or apply new formats after you type. Earlier, you changed the font size before you typed any text, and then you entered the text. In this section, you format existing text.

Figure 1-29 shows the announcement before formatting the paragraphs and characters in it. Figure 1-30 shows the announcement after formatting it. As you can see from the two figures, a document that is formatted not only is easier to read, but it also looks more professional.

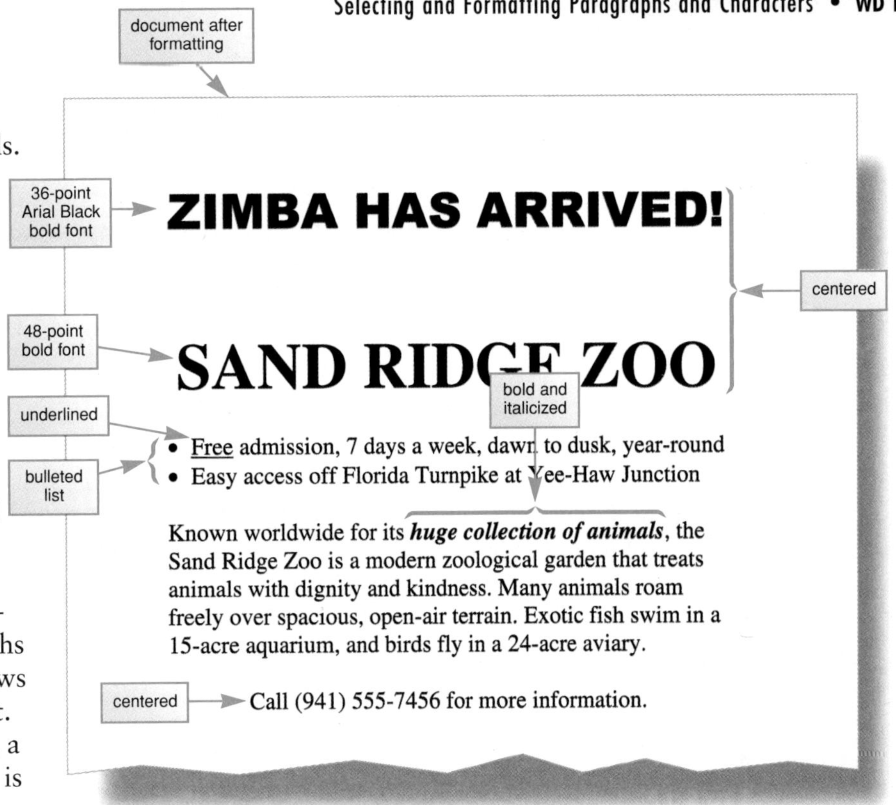

FIGURE 1-30

In the pages that follow, you will change the unformatted announcement in Figure 1-29 to the formatted announcement in Figure 1-30 using these steps:

1. Center the headline and body title across the page.
2. Bold and enlarge the headline.
3. Change the font of the headline.
4. Bold and enlarge the body title.
5. Underline a word in the list in the body of the announcement.
6. Add bullets to the list.
7. Bold and italicize a series of words in the paragraph of the announcement.
8. Center the last line of the announcement.

The process required to format the announcement is explained on the following pages. The first formatting step is to center the first two lines between the margins. Recall that each line is considered a separate paragraph because each line ends with a paragraph mark.

More About Formatting

Make a headline as large as possible without detracting from the body of the announcement. To attract attention, change the font of the headline. To pack a lot of information into a small area, use a list. Keep items in a list close together; that is, do not put blank lines between each item in the list.

Selecting and Formatting Paragraphs and Characters

To format a single paragraph, move the insertion point into the paragraph and then format it. To format multiple paragraphs in a document, however, the paragraphs you want to format first must be selected and then they can be formatted. In the same manner, to format characters, first you must select the characters to be formatted and then format your selection. Selected text is highlighted. For example, if your screen normally displays dark letters on a light background, then selected text appears as light letters on a dark background.

Selecting Multiple Paragraphs

The headline (ZIMBA HAS ARRIVED!) and the body title (SAND RIDGE ZOO) are separated by three paragraph marks. Thus, the headline and the body title are actually five separate paragraphs. Recall that each time you press the ENTER key, Word creates a new paragraph.To center the headline and body title in Project 1, first you must **select** all five paragraphs as shown in the following steps.

To Select Multiple Paragraphs

1 **Press CTRL+HOME to position the insertion point at the top of the document; that is, press and hold the CTRL key, then press the HOME key, and then release both keys. Move the mouse pointer to the left of the first paragraph to be centered (the headline) until the mouse pointer changes direction.**

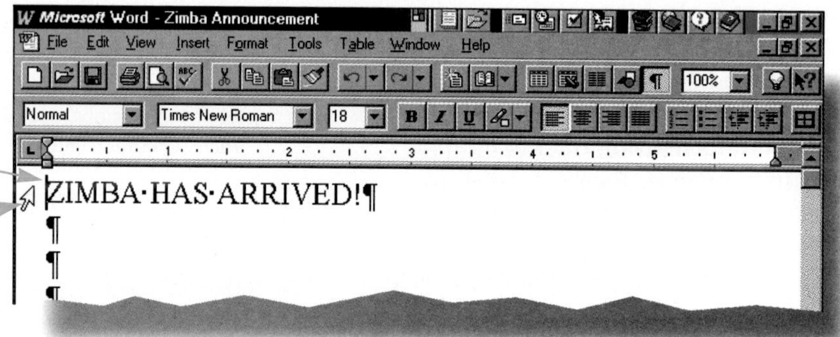

FIGURE 1-31

The mouse pointer changes to a right-pointing block arrow when positioned to the left of a paragraph (Figure 1-31).

2 **Press and hold down the left mouse button. Move the mouse pointer downward to the last line of the last paragraph to be centered (the body title) and then release the mouse button.**

All of the paragraphs to be centered are selected; that is, light letters on a dark background (Figure 1-32). Recall that the process of holding down the mouse button while moving the mouse, and then finally releasing the mouse button is called dragging the mouse.

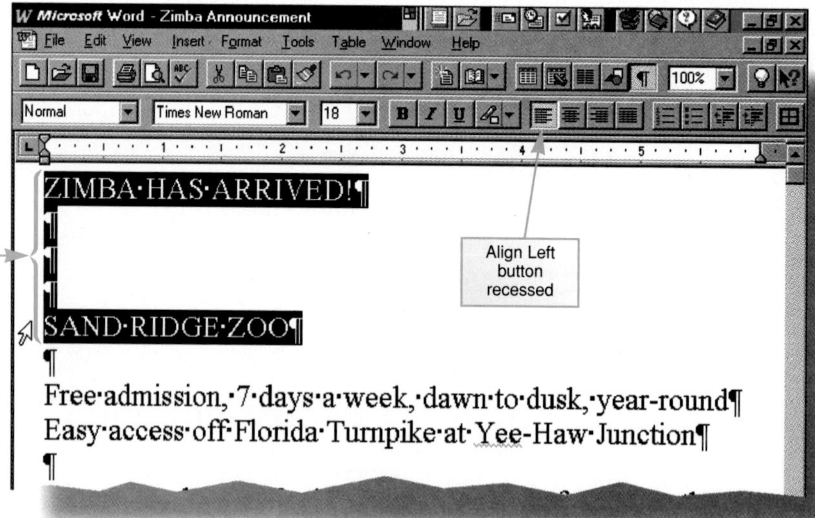

FIGURE 1-32

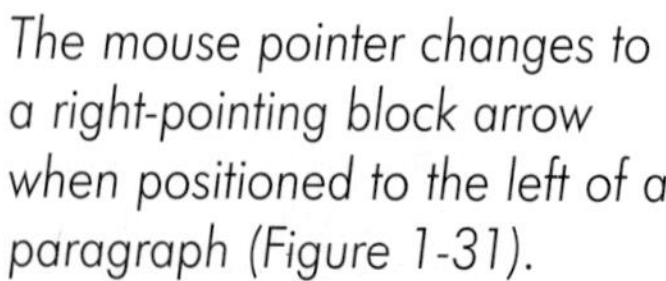

OtherWays

1. With insertion point at beginning of desired paragraph, press CTRL+SHIFT+DOWN ARROW

Centering Selected Paragraphs

The default alignment for paragraphs is **left-aligned**; that is, flush margins at the left edge, and jagged edges at the right edge. In Figure 1-32, the **Align Left button** is recessed to indicate the selected paragraphs currently are left-aligned. To center selected paragraphs, click the Center button as shown in the following steps.

To Center Selected Paragraphs

1 **With the paragraphs still selected, point to the Center button on the Formatting toolbar (Figure 1-33).**

FIGURE 1-33

2 **Click the Center button on the Formatting toolbar.**

Word centers the headline and body title between the left and right margins (Figure 1-34). The Center button on the Formatting toolbar is recessed, which indicates the highlighted paragraphs are centered.

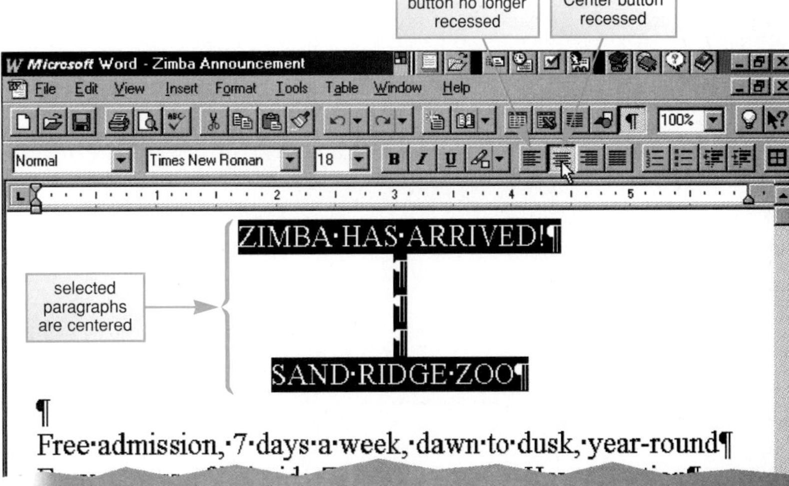

FIGURE 1-34

OtherWays

1. Right-click selected paragraph, click Paragraph on shortcut menu, click Indents and Spacing tab, click Alignment box arrow, click Centered, click OK button
2. On Format menu click Paragraph, click Indents and Spacing tab, click Alignment box arrow, click Centered, click OK button
3. Press CTRL+E

When a selected paragraph(s) is centered, the Center button on the Formatting toolbar is recessed. If, for some reason, you wanted to return the selected paragraphs to left-aligned, you would click the Align Left button on the Formatting toolbar.

The next series of steps selects the headline and formats the characters in it. In the pages that follow, you select the headline, increase the font size of the selected characters to 36, bold the selected characters, and then change the font of the selected characters to Arial Black.

Selecting a Single Line

To select the headline, the first line of the announcement, perform the following step.

To Select a Single Line

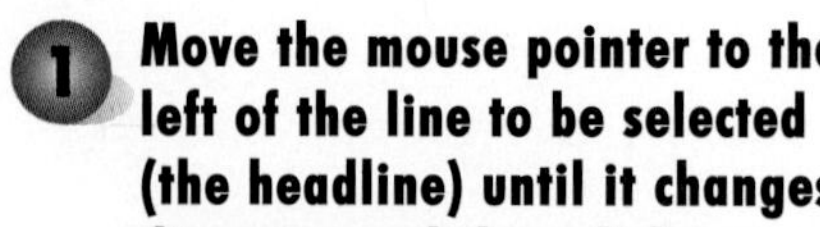

1 Move the mouse pointer to the left of the line to be selected (the headline) until it changes direction and then click.

The mouse pointer changes to a right-pointing block arrow, and the entire line to the right of the mouse pointer is selected (Figure 1-35).

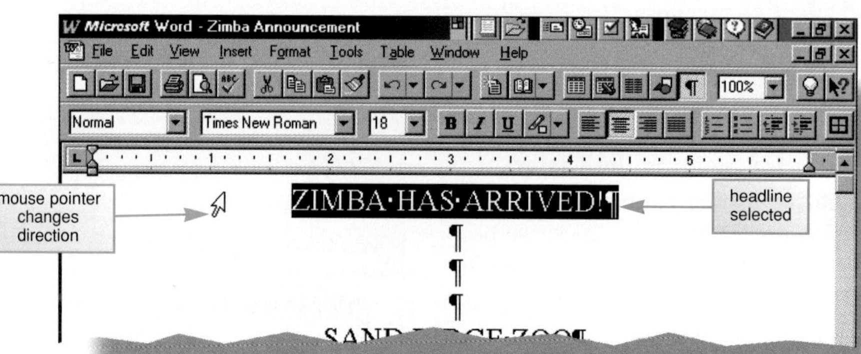

FIGURE 1-35

Other Ways

1. With insertion point at beginning of desired line, press SHIFT+DOWN ARROW

Changing the Font Size of Selected Text

The next step in formatting the headline is to increase its font size. Recall that the font size specifies the size of the characters on the screen. Earlier in this project, you changed the font size for the entire announcement from 10 to 18. The headline, however, requires a larger font size than the rest of the document. Follow these steps to increase the font size of the headline from 18 to 36 points.

To Change the Font Size of Selected Text

1 While the text is selected, click the Font Size box arrow on the Formatting toolbar, and then point to the down arrow on the Font Size scroll bar.

Word displays a list of the available font sizes (Figure 1-36). Available font sizes vary depending on the font and printer driver.

FIGURE 1-36

2 **Click the down arrow on the scroll bar until font size 36 displays in the list and then point to 36.**

Font size 36 is highlighted (Figure 1-37).

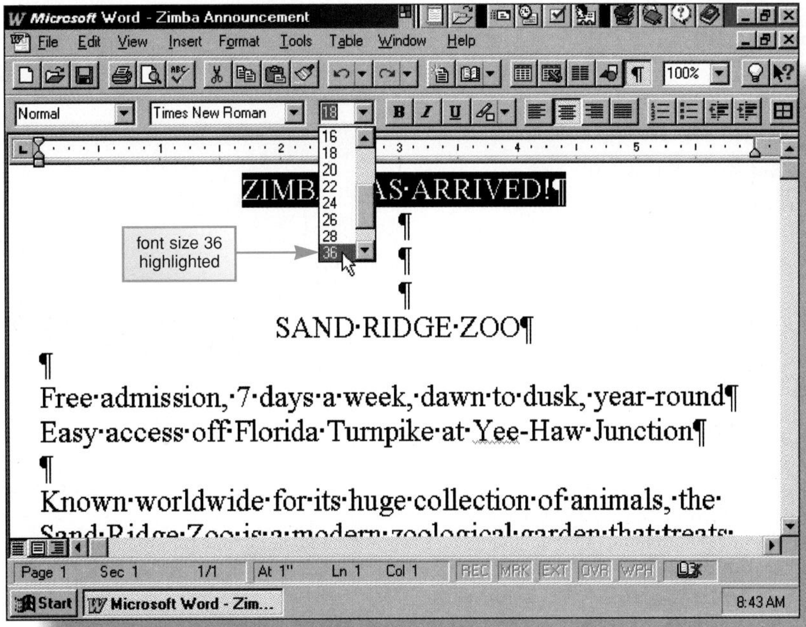

FIGURE 1-37

3 **Click font size 36.**

Word increases the font size of the headline from 18 to 36 (Figure 1-38). The Font Size box on the Formatting toolbar displays 36, indicating the selected text has a font size of 36.

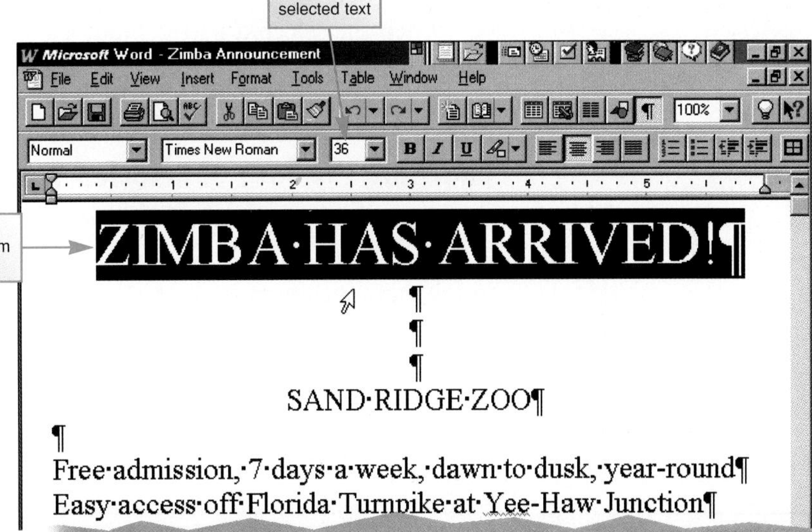

FIGURE 1-38

OtherWays

1. Right-click selected text, click Font on shortcut menu, click Font tab, select desired point size in Size list, click OK button
2. On Format menu click Font, click Font tab, select desired point size in Size list, click OK button
3. Press CTRL+SHIFT+P, type desired point size, press ENTER

Bold Selected Text

To further emphasize the headline of the announcement, perform the step on the next page to make it bold.

Steps To Bold Selected Text

1 **While the text is selected, click the Bold button on the Formatting toolbar.**

Word formats the headline in bold (Figure 1-39). The Bold button is recessed.

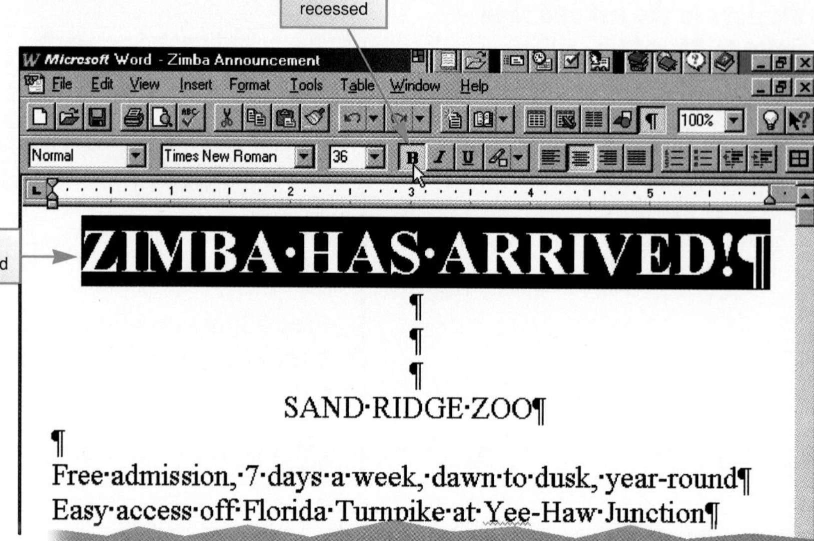

FIGURE 1-39

OtherWays

1. Right-click selected text, click Font on shortcut menu, click Font tab, click Bold in Font Style list, click OK button
2. On Format menu click Font, click Font tab, click Bold in Font Style list, click OK button
3. Press CTRL+B

When the selected text is bold, the Bold button on the Formatting toolbar is recessed. If, for some reason, you wanted to remove the bold format of the selected text, you would click the Bold button a second time.

Changing the Font of Selected Text

Recall that the default font is Times New Roman. Word, however, provides many other fonts to add variety to your documents. Thus, the font of the headline in the announcement is changed to Arial Black as shown in these steps.

Steps To Change the Font of Selected Text

1 **While the text is selected, click the Font box arrow on the Formatting toolbar, scroll through the list until Arial Black displays, and then point to Arial Black.**

Word displays a list of available fonts (Figure 1-40). Your list of available fonts may differ, depending on the type of printer you are using.

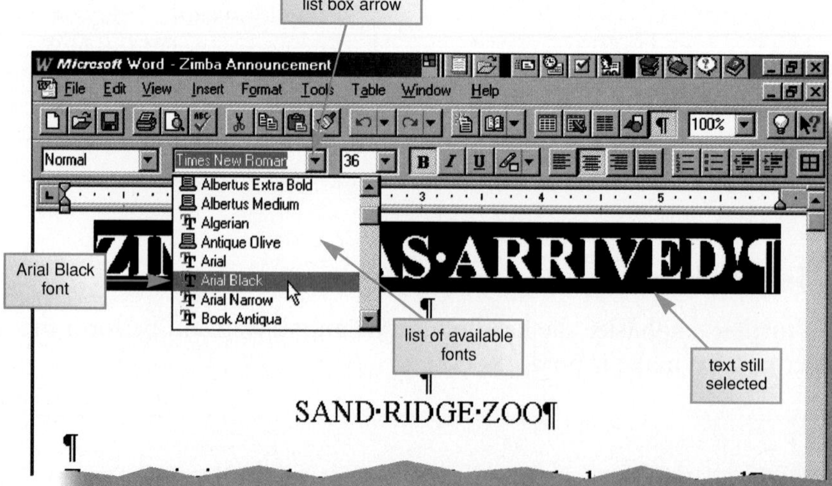

FIGURE 1-40

Click Arial Black.

Word changes the font of the selected text to Arial Black (Figure 1-41). If your headline wraps to two lines, adjust the font size so the headline fits on one line.

FIGURE 1-41

*Other*Ways

1. Right-click selected text, click Font on shortcut menu, click Font tab, select desired font in Font list, click OK button
2. On Format menu click Font, click Font tab, select desired font in Font list, click OK button
3. Press CTRL+SHIFT+F, press DOWN ARROW key, select desired Font, press ENTER

Continuing to Format Text

The next step is to select the body title (SAND RIDGE ZOO), increase its font size, and bold it.

TO INCREASE FONT SIZE AND BOLD TEXT

Step 1: Click to the left of the line to be formatted (the body title).
Step 2: Click the Font Size box arrow on the Formatting toolbar and scroll to the font size 48.
Step 3: Click font size 48.
Step 4: Click the Bold button on the Formatting toolbar.

The body title is enlarged and bold (Figure 1-42).

FIGURE 1-42

More *About* Selecting Text

Because some users are uncomfortable with dragging to select text, Word provides an alternative called the click, SHIFT+click technique. To do this, you click at the beginning of the text to select, move the mouse pointer (I-beam) to the end of the text to select, and then SHIFT+click; that is, hold down the SHIFT key while clicking the mouse.

Scrolling

Continue formatting by scrolling down one screenful so the bottom portion of the announcement displays in the document window.

To Scroll Through the Document

Position the mouse pointer beneath the scroll box on the vertical scroll bar (Figure 1-43).

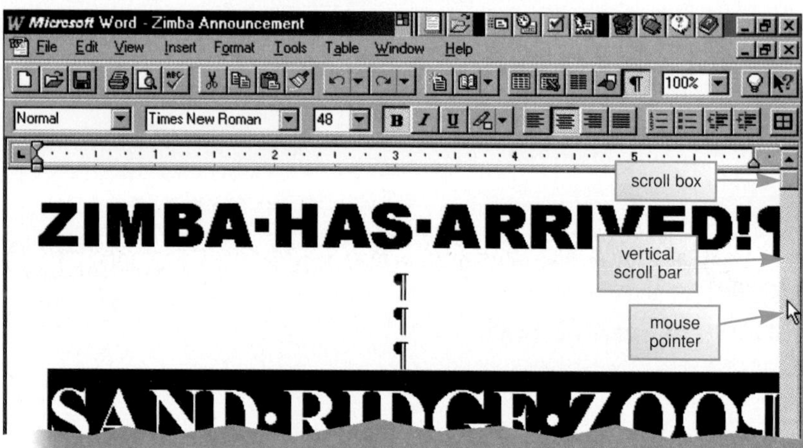

FIGURE 1-43

Click beneath the scroll box on the vertical scroll bar.

Word scrolls down one screenful in the document (Figure 1-44). Depending on your monitor type, your screen may scroll differently.

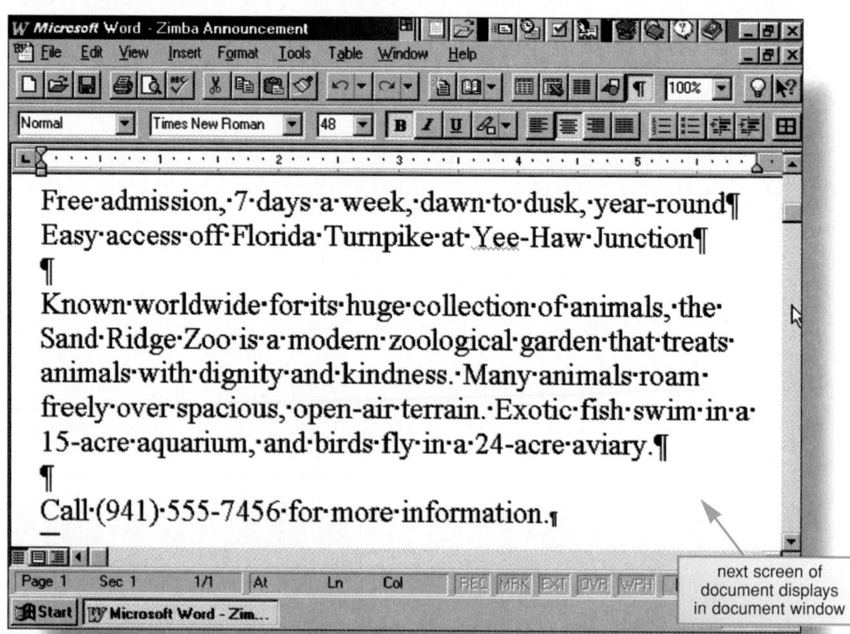

FIGURE 1-44

OtherWays

1. Drag scroll box on vertical scroll bar
2. Click above or below scroll box on vertical scroll bar
3. Press PAGE DOWN or PAGE UP

Selecting a Single Word

Follow these steps to select the word, Free, so that it can be underlined.

Steps To Select a Single Word

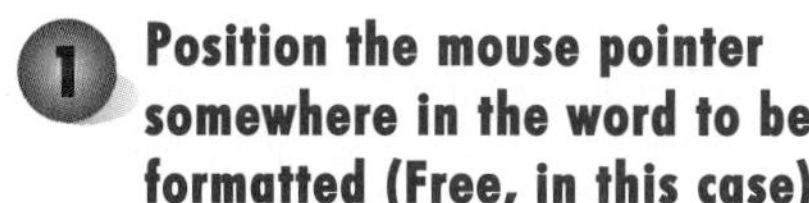

1 Position the mouse pointer somewhere in the word to be formatted (Free, in this case).

The mouse pointer's shape is an I-beam in a word that has not yet been selected (Figure 1-45).

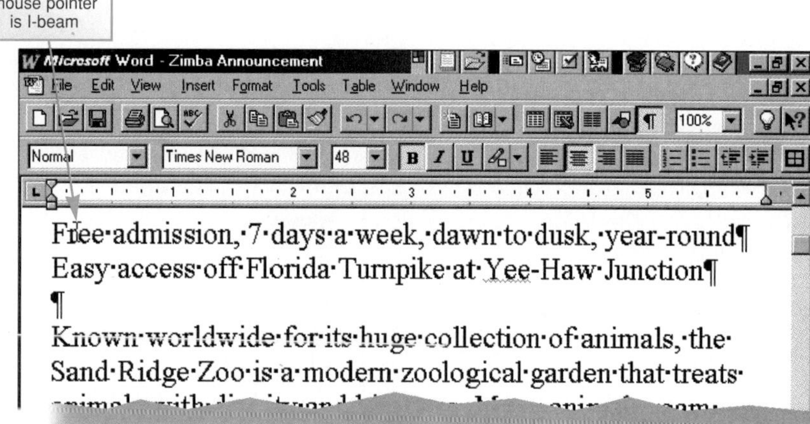

FIGURE 1-45

2 Double-click the word to be formatted.

The word, Free, is selected (Figure 1-46). Notice that when the mouse pointer is positioned in a selected word, its shape is a left-pointing block arrow.

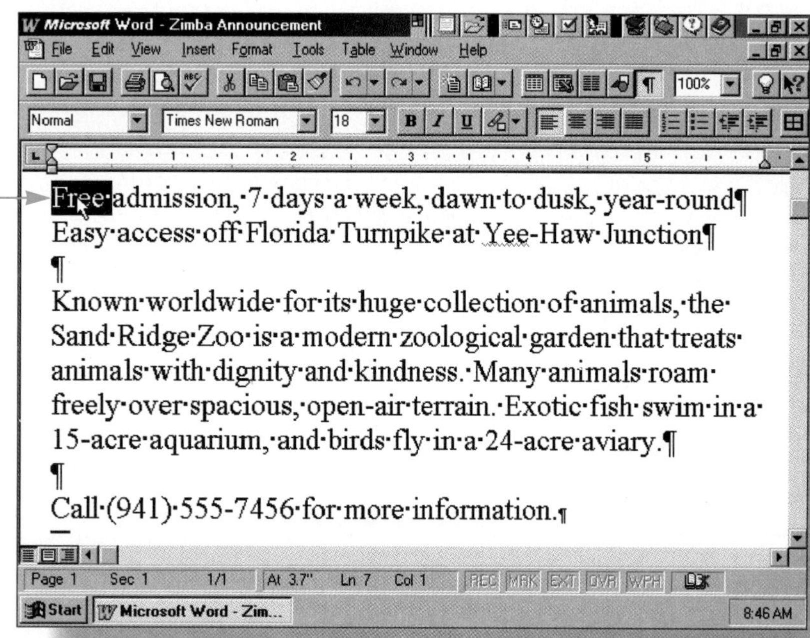

FIGURE 1-46

Other Ways

1. With insertion point at beginning of desired word, press CTRL+SHIFT+RIGHT ARROW

Underlining Selected Text

The next step is to underline the selected word, Free.

To Underline Selected Text

With the text still selected, click the Underline button on the Formatting toolbar.

The word, Free, is underlined (Figure 1-47). The Underline button is recessed.

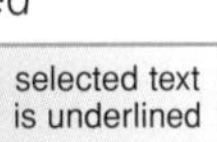

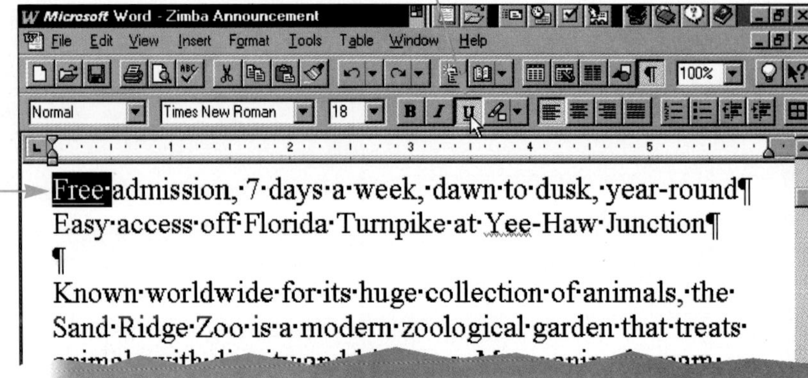

FIGURE 1-47

OtherWays

1. Right-click selected text, click Font on shortcut menu, click Font tab, click Underline box arrow, click Single, click OK button
2. On Format menu click Font, click Font tab, click Underline box arrow, click Single, click OK button
3. Press CTRL+U

When the selected text is underlined, the Underline button on the Formatting toolbar is recessed. If, for some reason, you wanted to remove the underline from the selected text, you would click the Underline button a second time.

Adding Bullets

The next formatting step is to add bullets to the list in the body of the announcement. **Bullets** are small raised dots. Bullets differ from the nonprinting character for the SPACEBAR because bullets print.

To add bullets to a list of paragraphs, select the paragraphs and add bullets to them, as shown in the following steps.

To Add Bullets to a List of Paragraphs

Point to the left of the first paragraph to be bulleted.

The mouse pointer changes direction to a right-pointing arrow (Figure 1-48).

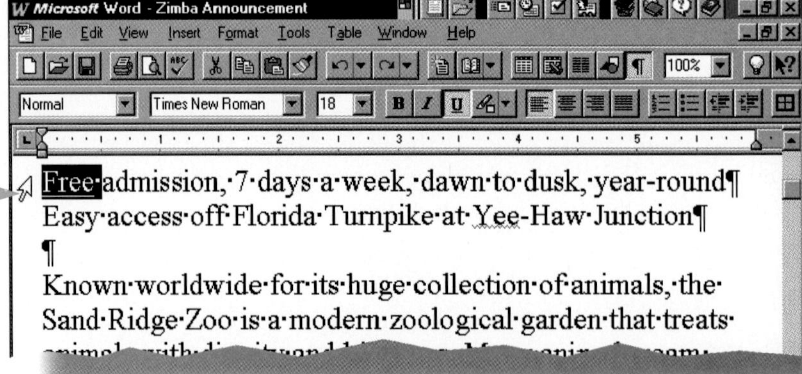

FIGURE 1-48

2 **Drag the mouse pointer downward to the last line of the last paragraph to be bulleted. Point to the Bullets button on the Formatting toolbar.**

Word selects the paragraphs to be bulleted (Figure 1-49).

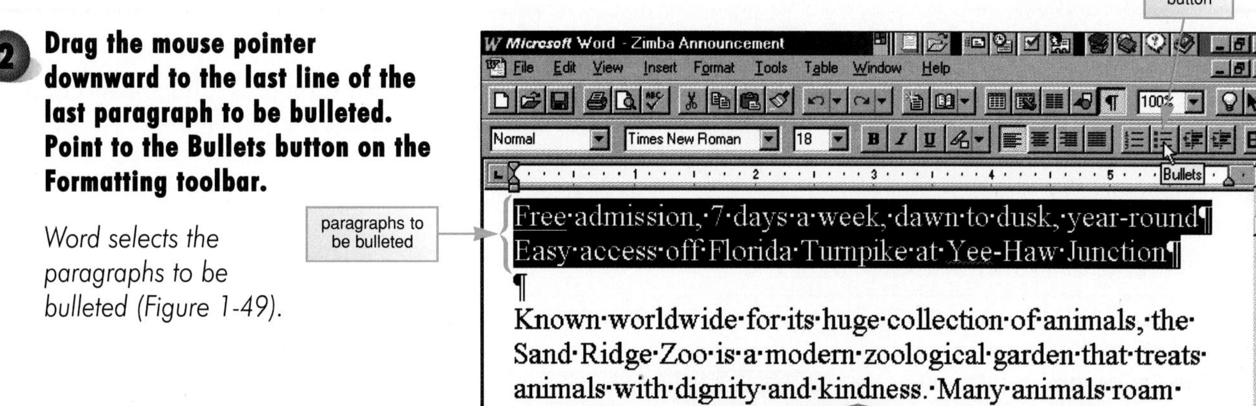

FIGURE 1-49

3 **Click the Bullets button on the Formatting toolbar.**

Word adds bullets to the paragraphs (Figure 1-50). The Bullets button is recessed.

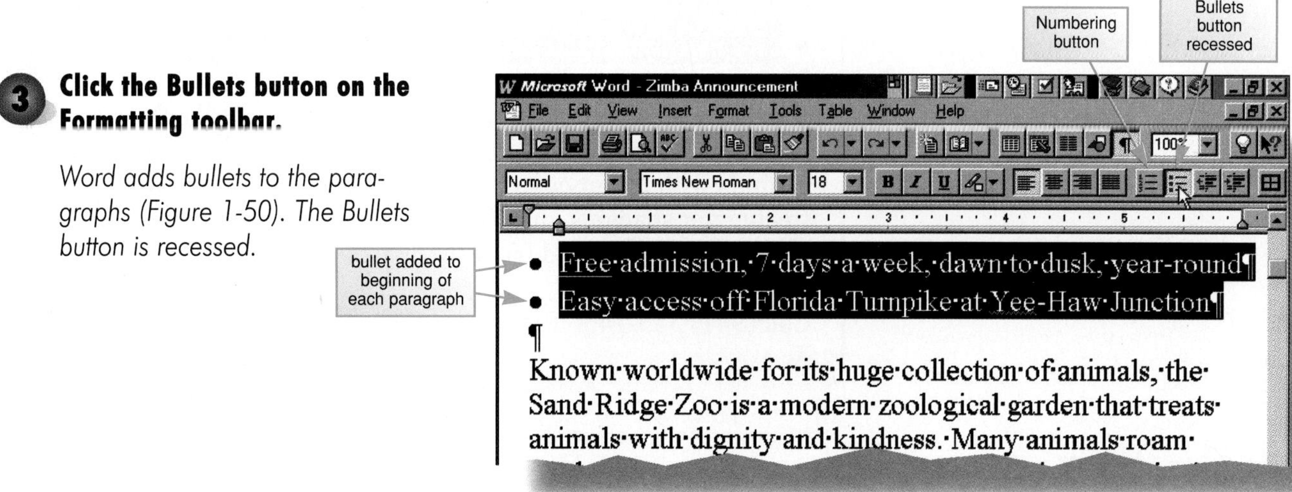

FIGURE 1-50

*Other***Ways**

1. Right-click selected paragraphs, click Bullets and Numbering on shortcut menu, click Bulleted tab, click desired bullet type, click OK button
2. On Format menu click Bullets and Numbering, click Bulleted tab, click desired bullet type, click OK button

To add numbers to the beginning of a list instead of bullets, click the Numbering button instead of the Bullets button. To remove bullets or numbers from a list, select the list and click the Bullets or Numbering button again.

If you know before you type a list that it is to be bulleted or numbered, you can add the bullets or numbers as you type, instead of formatting the list later. To add bullets, type an asterisk (*) at the beginning of the line and then type your text. When you press the ENTER key, the asterisk changes to a bullet character automatically and a bullet displays at the beginning of the next line. To add numbers, type the number one followed by a period (1.) at the beginning of the first line and then type your text. When you press the ENTER key, Word automatically places the number two (2.) at the beginning of the next line. In both cases, you need to press the ENTER key twice to stop the automatic formatting when you are finished with your list.

Selecting a Group of Words and Formatting Them

The next formatting step is to italicize and bold the phrase, huge collection of animals, in the paragraph beneath the list. First select the phrase by performing the following steps.

To Select a Group of Words

1 **Position the mouse pointer on the first character of the first word to be selected.**

The mouse pointer, an I-beam, is at the beginning of the word, huge (Figure 1-51).

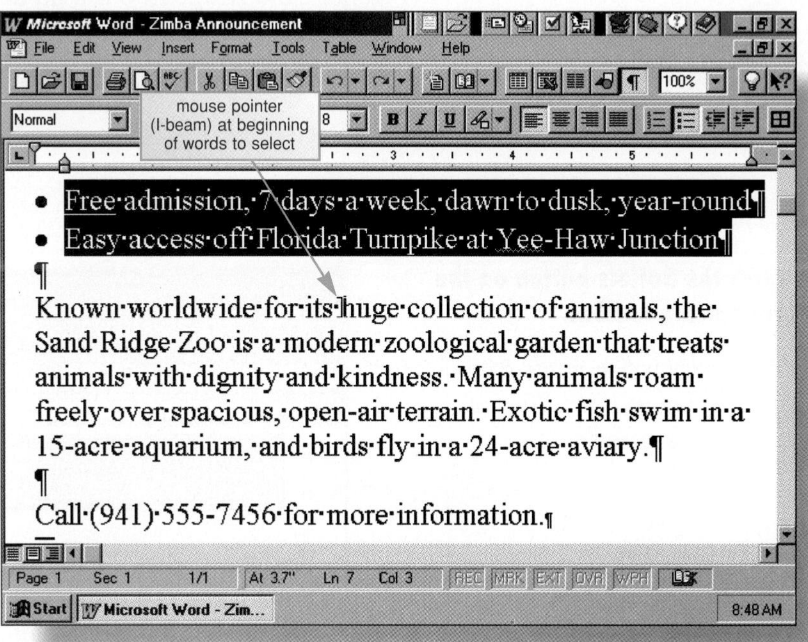

FIGURE 1-51

2 **Drag the mouse pointer through the last character of the last word to be selected.**

The phrase, huge collection of animals, is selected (Figure 1-52).

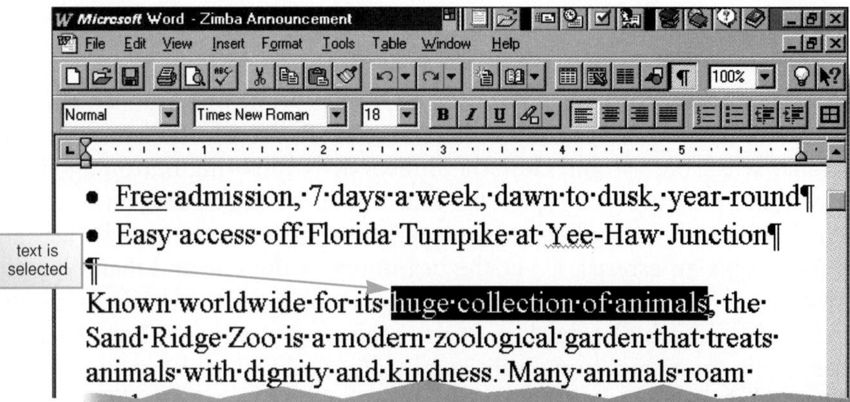

FIGURE 1-52

Other Ways

1. With insertion point at beginning of first word in the group, press F8, press CTRL+RIGHT ARROW until words are selected, press ESC

To Italicize and Bold Selected Text

1 **With the text still selected, click the Italic button on the Formatting toolbar. Click the Bold button on the Formatting toolbar. Click inside the selected text to remove the highlight.**

Word italicizes and bolds the text and positions the insertion point inside the bold and italicized text (Figure 1-53). When the insertion point is inside the bold and italicized text, the Bold and Italic buttons on the Formatting toolbar are recessed.

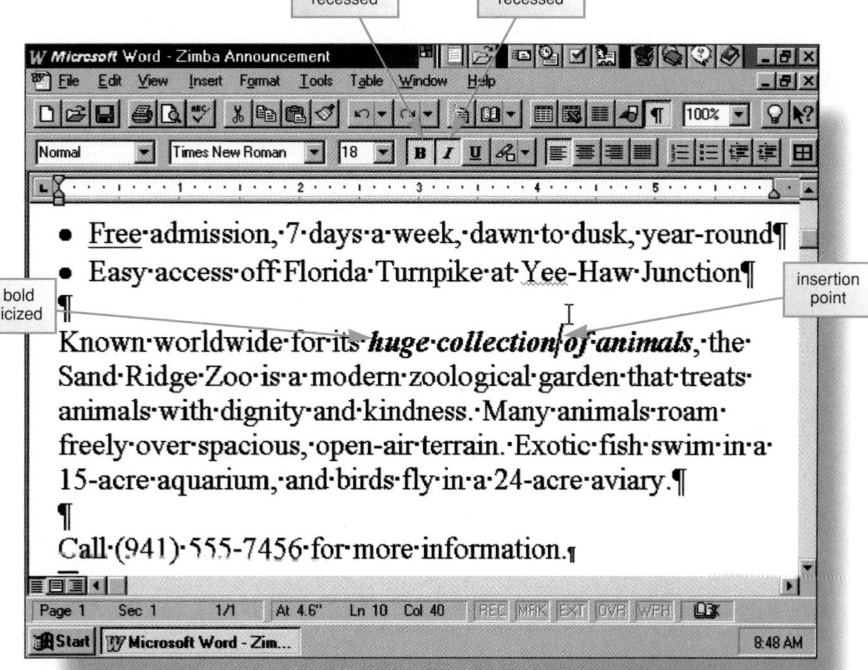

FIGURE 1-53

Other Ways

1. Right-click selected text, click Font on shortcut menu, click Font tab, click Italic in Font Style list, click OK button
2. On Format menu click Font, click Font tab, click Italic in Font Style list, click OK button
3. Press CTRL+I

To remove a highlight, click the mouse. If you click inside the highlight, the Formatting toolbar displays the formatting characteristics of the characters and paragraphs containing the insertion point.

Centering a Paragraph

The last step in formatting Project 1 is to center the last line of the announcement. Recall that paragraph formatting does not require you to select the paragraph. That is, just position the insertion point in the paragraph to be formatted and then format it accordingly.

Follow the step on the next page to center the last paragraph in the announcement.

More About Formatting Toolbar

Many of the buttons on the Formatting toolbar are toggles; that is, click them once to format the selected text; and click them again to remove the format from the selected text. For example, clicking the Italic button italicizes selected text; clicking the Italic button again de-italicizes the selected text.

To Center a Single Paragraph

1 Click somewhere in the last line of the announcement. Click the Center button on the Formatting toolbar.

The last line of the announcement is centered (Figure 1-54). Notice that you did not have to select the paragraph before centering; paragraph formatting requires only that the insertion point be somewhere in the paragraph.

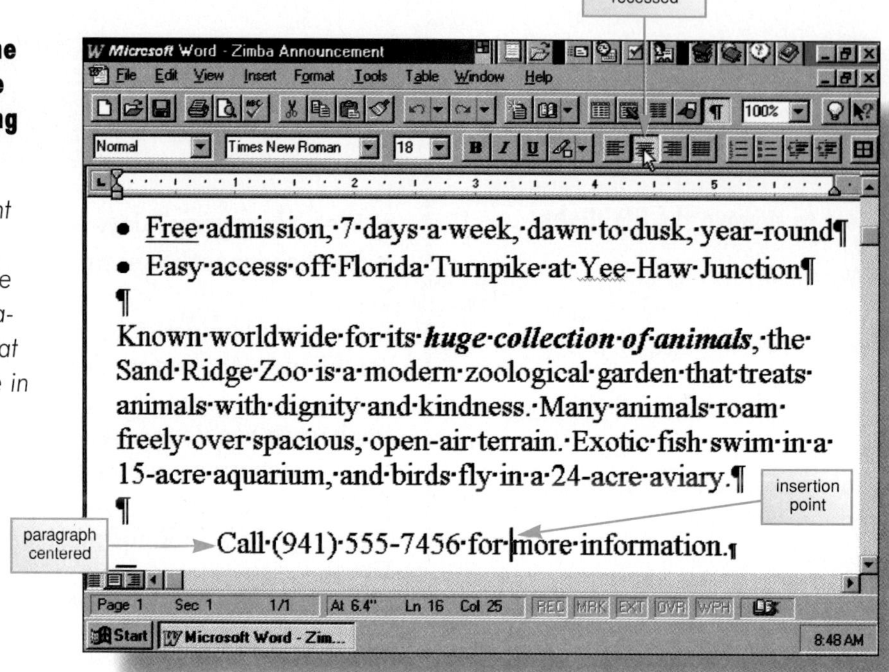

FIGURE 1-54

Other **Ways**

1. With insertion point in desired paragraph, click Paragraph on shortcut menu, click Indents and Spacing tab, click Alignment box arrow, click Centered, click OK button
2. With insertion point in desired paragraph, on Format menu click Paragraph, click Indents and Spacing tab, click Alignment box arrow, click Centered, click OK button
3. Press CTRL+E

The formatting for the announcement is now complete. The next step is to import a graphic and resize it.

Importing a Graphic File into a Word Document

Graphic files are available from a variety of sources. Microsoft Word for Windows 95 includes a series of predefined graphics called clip art files or Windows metafiles. Photographs can be scanned and saved in files or you also can purchase royalty-free photographs from a local software retailer, usually on a CD-ROM. Once you have a graphic file on disk, you can then insert, or **import**, it into a Word document by clicking the Picture command on the Insert menu. In this project, you import a photograph of a tiger as shown in the following steps.

To Import a Graphic

1. **Press CTRL+HOME. Position the insertion point where you want the graphic to be inserted. Click Insert on the menu bar.**

   The insertion point is positioned on the second paragraph mark beneath the headline of the announcement (Figure 1-55). The Insert menu and its list of commands display.

FIGURE 1-55

2. **Point to Picture (Figure 1-56).**

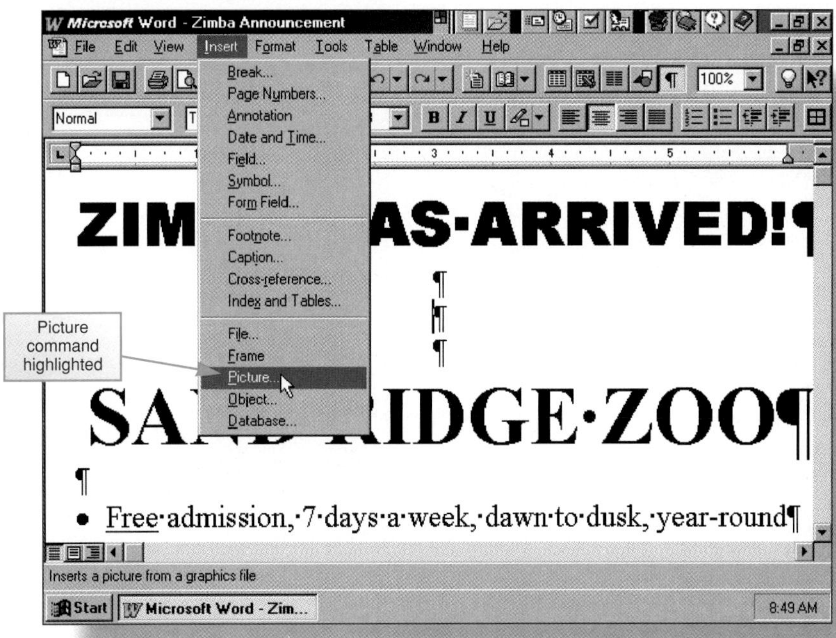

FIGURE 1-56

Click Picture. If your Preview button is not recessed in the Insert Picture dialog box, click the Preview button.

Word displays the Insert Picture dialog box (Figure 1-57). The current folder is Clipart; the graphic files supplied with Word are located in this folder. The tiger photograph is located on the Student Floppy Disk that accompanies this book.

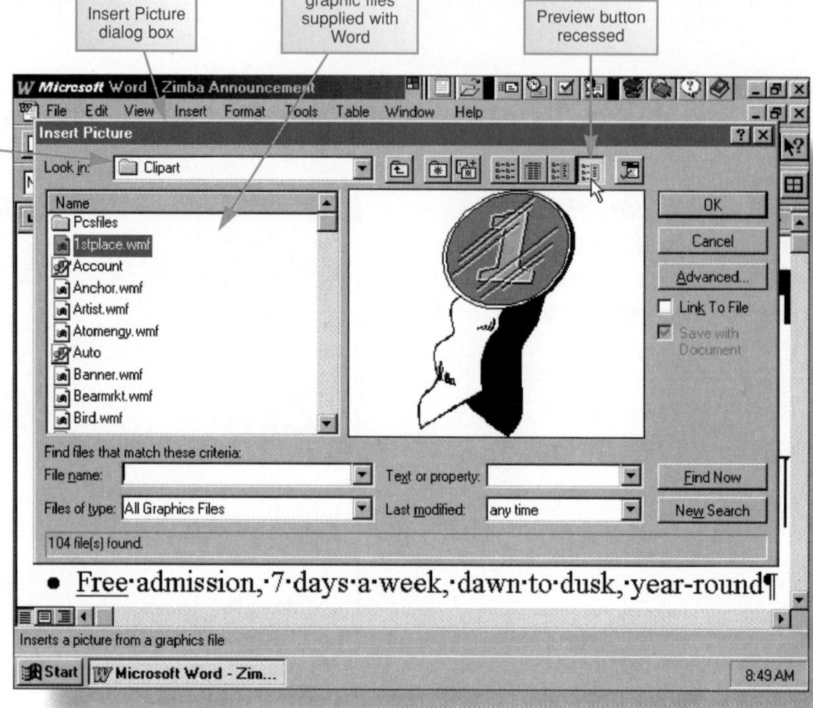

FIGURE 1-57

4 Insert the Student Floppy Disk that accompanies this book into drive A. Click the Look in box arrow. Click 3½ Floppy [A:] and then click Tiger in the Name list box.

Word highlights the filename Tiger and displays a preview of the tiger graphic (Figure 1-58).

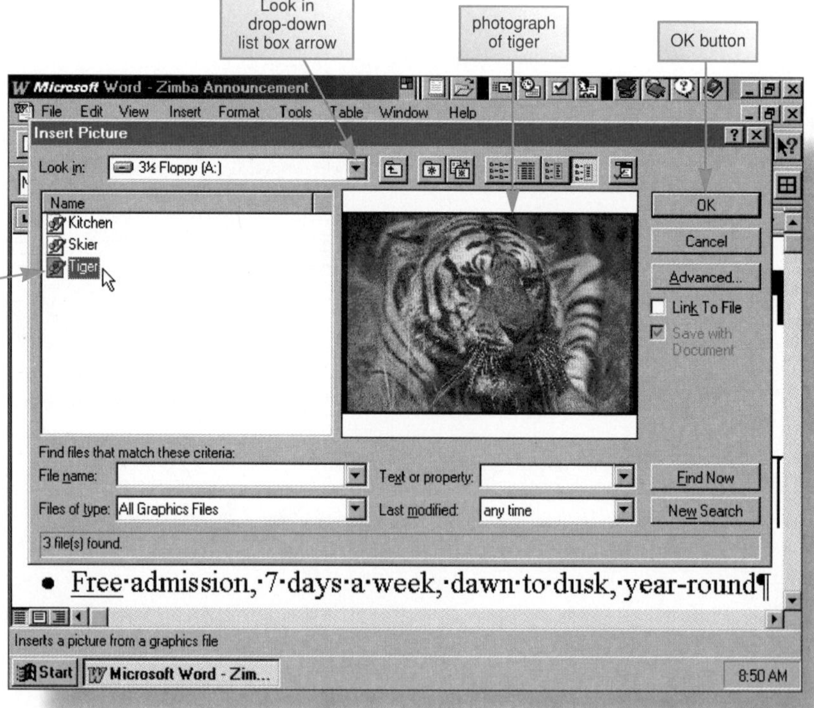

FIGURE 1-58

5 **Click the OK button.**

Word inserts the graphic into your document at the location of the insertion point (Figure 1-59).

6 **Remove the Student Floppy Disk from drive A and then reinsert your data disk into drive A to continue.**

FIGURE 1-59

The graphic in the document is part of a paragraph. Therefore, you can use any of the paragraph alignment buttons on the Formatting toolbar to reposition the graphic. Recall that earlier you formatted that paragraph mark to centered. Thus, the tiger graphic is centered across the page.

The graphic in Figure 1-59 is a little too large for this announcement. Thus, the next step is to resize the imported graphic.

Scaling an Imported Graphic

Once a graphic has been imported into a document, you can easily change its size, or **scale** it. Scaling includes both enlarging and reducing the size of a graphic. To scale a graphic, first you must select it. The steps on the next page show how to select and then scale the graphic you just imported.

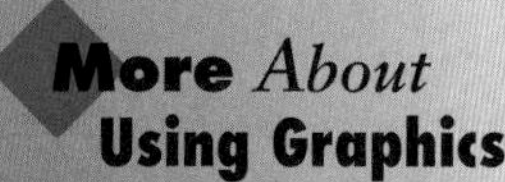

More *About* **Using Graphics**

Emphasize a graphic in an announcement by placing it at the optical center of the page. To determine optical center, divide the page in half horizontally and vertically. The optical center is located one third of the way up the vertical line from the point of intersection of the two lines.

To Scale a Graphic

1 **Click anywhere in the graphic.**

Word selects the graphic (Figure 1-60). Selected graphics display surrounded by a box with small squares, called ***sizing handles****, at each corner and middle location. You use the mouse to drag the sizing handles until the graphic is the desired size. Dragging a corner sizing handle maintains the proportions of the graphic; whereas, dragging a middle sizing handle distorts the proportions of the graphic.*

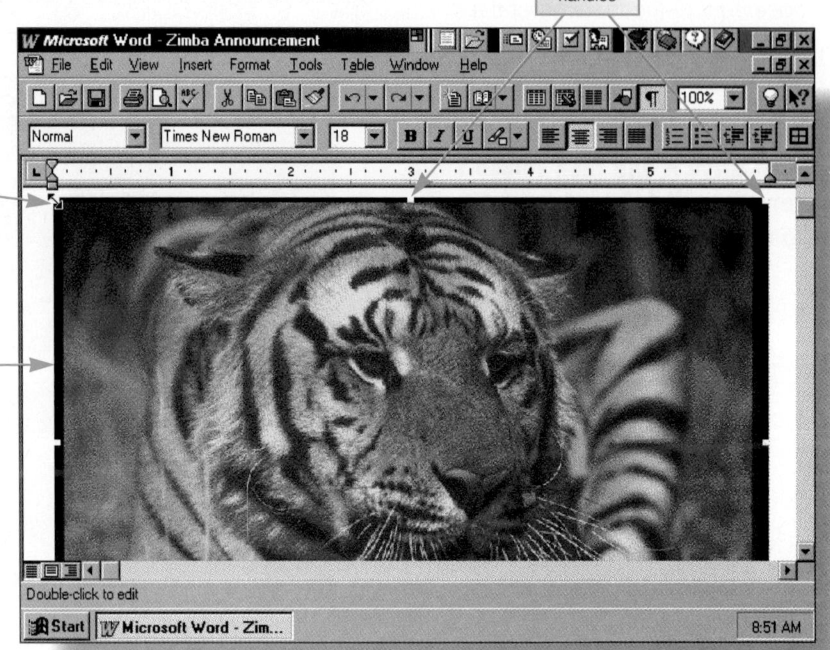

FIGURE 1-60

2 **Point to the upper left corner sizing handle.**

The mouse pointer changes to a two-headed arrow when it is on a sizing handle.

3 **Drag the sizing handle inward until the scaling percentage displayed on the status bar is 65% High 65% Wide.**

As you drag the sizing handle inward, Word displays the percentage of the imported graphic's original size on the status bar (Figure 1-61). The original percentages displayed on the status bar were 75%, which means the picture was imported at 75% of its original size; thus 100% was too large for the dimensions of the announcement.

FIGURE 1-61

Release the mouse button.

Word resizes the graphic based on the new width and height percentages (Figure 1-62).

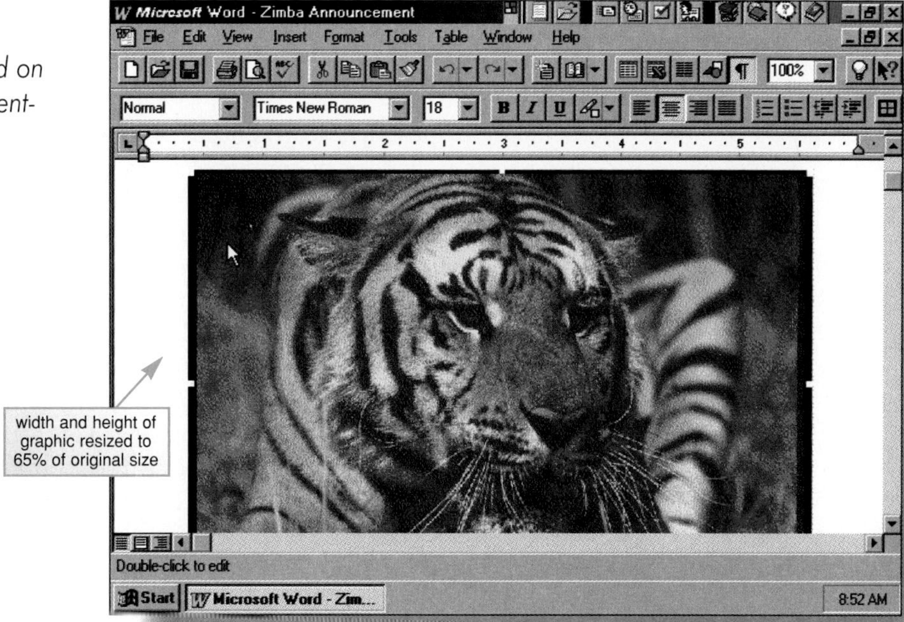

FIGURE 1-62

OtherWays

1. Click graphic, on Format menu click Picture, enter desired width and height, click OK button

Instead of scaling a selected graphic with the mouse, you also can use the Picture command on the Format menu to resize a graphic. With the Picture command, you enter exact width and height measurements. If you have a precise measurement for the graphic, use the Picture command; otherwise, drag the sizing handles to resize the graphic.

Restoring a Scaled Graphic to Its Original Size

Sometimes you might scale a graphic and realize it is the wrong size. In these cases, you may want to return the graphic to its original size and start over. To return a scaled graphic to its original size, click the graphic to select it, click Format on the menu bar and then click Picture. Then, click the Reset button in the Picture dialog box. Finally, click the OK button in the Picture dialog box.

After you have entered and formatted a document, you should ensure that no typographical errors have occurred by checking the spelling of the words in your document.

Checking Spelling

As mentioned earlier, Word checks your spelling dynamically; that is, as you type, using a main dictionary contained in the Word program. If a word you type is not in the dictionary, a red wavy underline appears beneath it and the spelling icon on the status bar displays a red X. Although you can check the spelling of the flagged word immediately, you also can check the entire document for spelling errors at once using the Spelling button on the Standard toolbar.

When you invoke Word's **spell checker** using the Spelling button, it checks the entire document. If a word is not found in the dictionary, the word is displayed in the Spelling dialog box with a message indicating the word is not in the main dictionary. From the Spelling dialog box, you may correct the word. Sometimes, however, the word is spelled correctly. For example, many names, abbreviations, and specialized terms are not in the main dictionary. In these cases, you ignore the message and continue the spelling check. The spell checker also detects duplicate words. For example, if your document contains the phrase, to the the store, the spell checker asks if you wish to delete the duplicate occurrence of the word, the.

The following steps illustrate how to spell check the Zimba Announcement. Notice in the following example that the word, spacious, has intentionally been misspelled as, spacous, to illustrate the use of Word's spell checker. If you are doing this project on a personal computer, your announcement may contain different misspelled words, depending on the accuracy of your typing.

Steps To Check the Spelling of a Document on Demand

1. **Press CTRL+HOME to position the insertion point at the top of the document. Click the Spelling button on the Standard toolbar.**

Because the insertion point is at the top of your document, Word begins the spelling check from line 1 column 1. When a word is not found in the main dictionary, Word displays the Spelling: English (US) dialog box (Figure 1-63). Word did not find Yee in its main dictionary because Yee is a road name. Yee is spelled correctly.

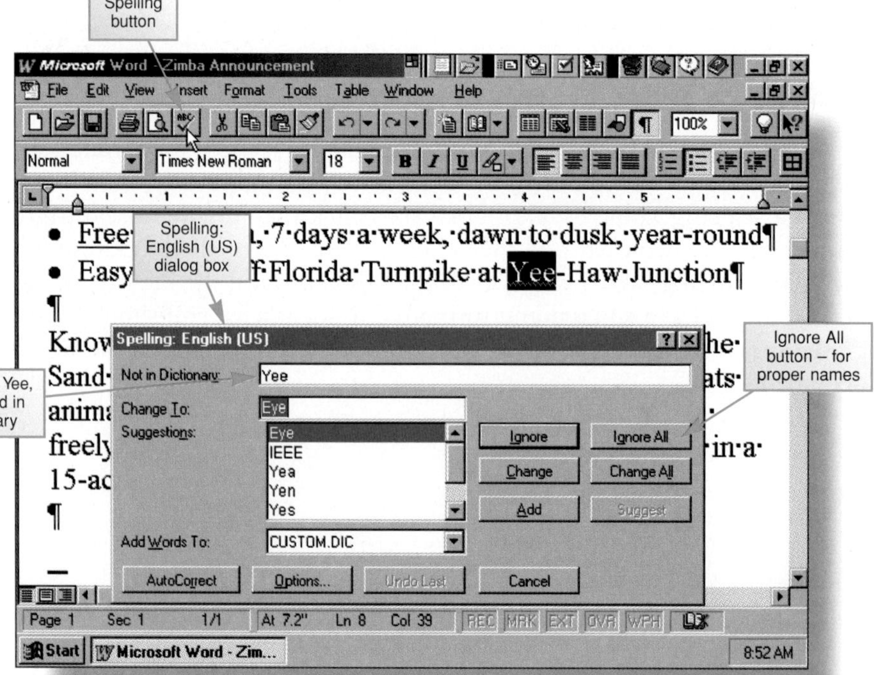

FIGURE 1-63

2 **Click the Ignore All button.**

The spelling check ignores all future occurrences of the word Yee. Word continues the spelling check until it finds the next error or reaches the end of the document. The spelling check did not find the misspelled word, spacous, in its main dictionary. The spelling check lists suggested corrections in the Suggestions list box and places its choice (spacious) in the Change To text box (Figure 1-64).

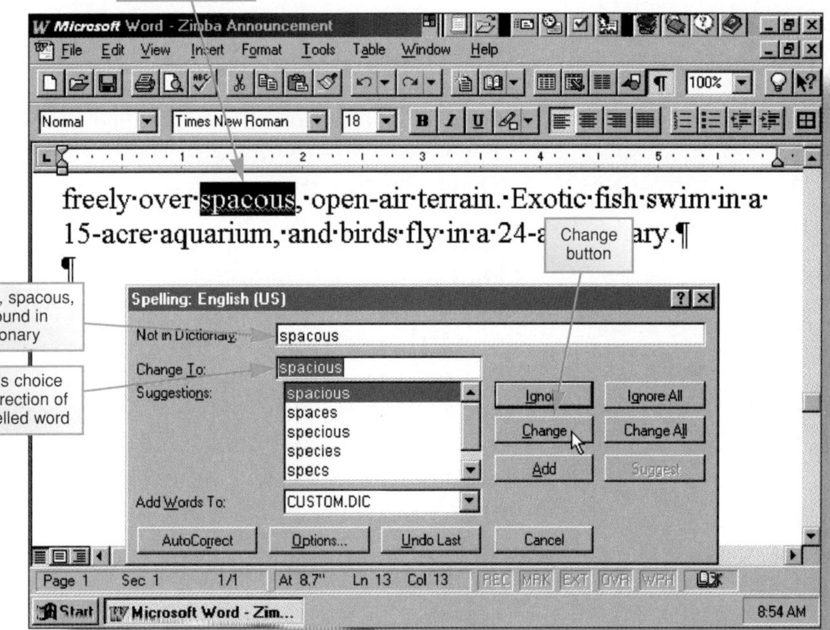

FIGURE 1-64

3 **Click the Change button.**

The spelling check changes the misspelled word (spacous) to its suggestion (spacious). Word continues to check spelling until it finds the next error or reaches the end of the document. Word displays a message that it has checked the entire document (Figure 1-65).

4 **Click the OK button.**

Word returns to your document. Your document no longer displays red wavy lines beneath words, and the red X on the spelling icon has returned to a red check mark (see Figure 1-66 on the next page).

FIGURE 1-65

OtherWays

1. On Tools menu click Spelling
2. Press F7

More About Checking Spelling

To check spelling immediately of a red wavy underlined word, right-click the word to display a list of suggested spelling corrections for the flagged word. Then, click the correct spelling on the shortcut menu. If the desired correction does not display, click Spelling on the shortcut menu to display the Spelling: English (US) dialog box.

If the suggested change made by the spelling check is not your choice (Figure 1-64 on the previous page), you can select any of the other words in the list of suggested words by clicking the desired word. The word you click displays in the Change To text box. If your choice is not in the list of suggested words, you may type your desired word directly into the Change To text box. When you click the Change button, the word in the Change To text box replaces the misspelled word.

Saving an Existing Document with the Same Filename

The announcement for Project 1 is now complete. To transfer the formatting changes, imported graphic, and spelling corrections to your floppy disk in drive A, you must save the document again. When you saved the document the first time, you assigned a filename to it (Zimba Announcement). Word automatically assigns this filename to the document each time you subsequently save it if you use the following procedure.

Steps To Save an Existing Document with the Same Filename

1 Click the Save button on the Standard toolbar.

Word saves the document on a floppy disk inserted in drive A using the currently assigned filename, Zimba Announcement. When the save is finished, the document remains in main memory and displays on the screen (Figure 1-66).

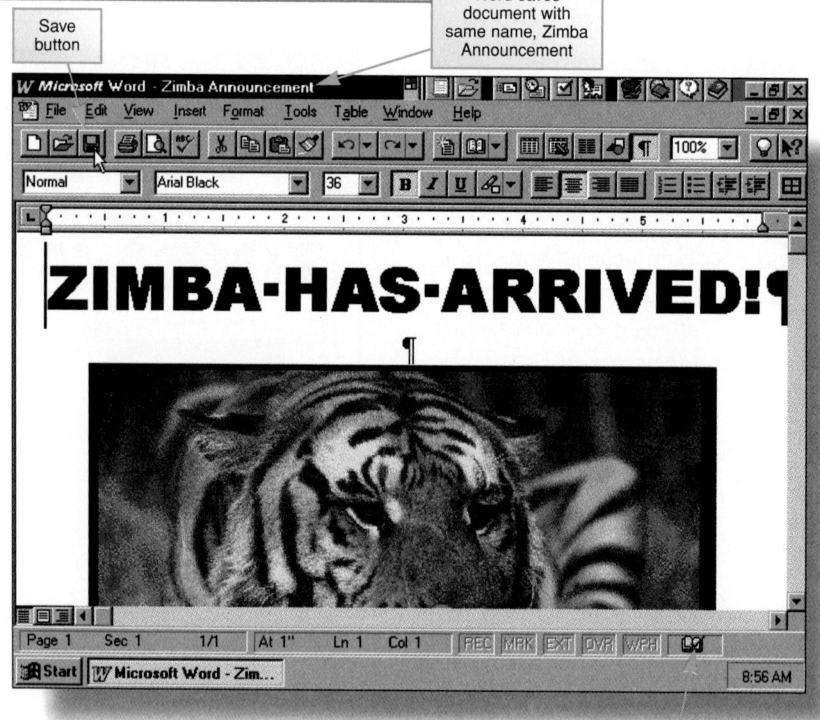

FIGURE 1-66

Other Ways

1. On File menu click Save
2. Press CTRL+S

If, for some reason, you want to save an existing document with a different filename, click Save As on the File menu to display the Save As dialog box. Then, fill in the Save As dialog box as discussed in Steps 3 through 6 on pages WD 1.22 through WD 1.24.

Printing a Document

The next step is to print the document you created. A printed version of the document is called a **hard copy** or **printout.** Perform the following steps to print the announcement created in Project 1.

Steps To Print a Document

1 Ready the printer according to the printer instructions. Click the Print button on the Standard toolbar.

The mouse pointer briefly changes to an hourglass shape, and then Word quickly displays a message on the status bar, indicating it is preparing to print the document. A few moments later, the document begins printing on the printer. The right edge of the status bar displays a printer icon while the document is printing (Figure 1-67).

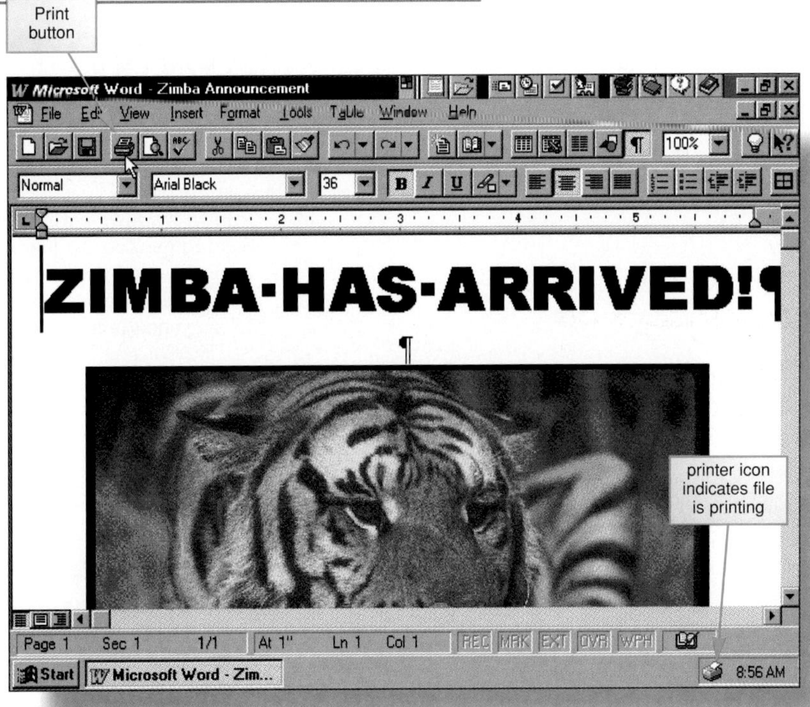

FIGURE 1-67

More About Printing

To print multiple copies of a document, click File on the menu bar, click Print, enter the number of copies in the Copies area, and then click the OK button. To print just a section of a document, select the section in the document, click File on the menu bar, click Print, click Selection in the Print Range area, and then click the OK button.

When the printer stops, retrieve the printout (Figure 1-68).

ZIMBA HAS ARRIVED!

SAND RIDGE ZOO

- <u>Free</u> admission, 7 days a week, dawn to dusk, year-round
- Easy access off Florida Turnpike at Yee-Haw Junction

Known worldwide for its ***huge collection of animals***, the Sand Ridge Zoo is a modern zoological garden that treats animals with dignity and kindness. Many animals roam freely over spacious, open-air terrain. Exotic fish swim in a 15-acre aquarium, and birds fly in a 24-acre aviary.

Call (941) 555-7456 for more information.

FIGURE 1-68

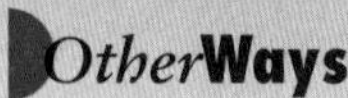

OtherWays

1. On File menu click Print, click OK button
2. Press CTRL+P, press ENTER

When you use the Print button to print a document, Word prints the entire document automatically. You may then distribute the hard copy or keep it as a permanent record of the document.

If you wanted to cancel a job that is printing or waiting to be printed, double-click the printer icon on the status bar (Figure 1-67 on the previous page). In the printer window, click the job to be canceled and then click Cancel Printing on the Document menu.

Quitting Word

After you create, save, and print the announcement, Project 1 is complete. To quit Word and return control to Windows 95, perform the following steps.

To Quit Word

1 **Point to the Close button at the right edge of the title bar (Figure 1-69).**

FIGURE 1-69

2 **Click the Close button.**

If you made changes to the document since the last save, Word displays a message asking if you want to save the changes (Figure 1-70). Click the Yes button to save changes; click the No button to ignore the changes; or click the Cancel button to return to the document. If you made no changes since saving the document, this dialog box does not display.

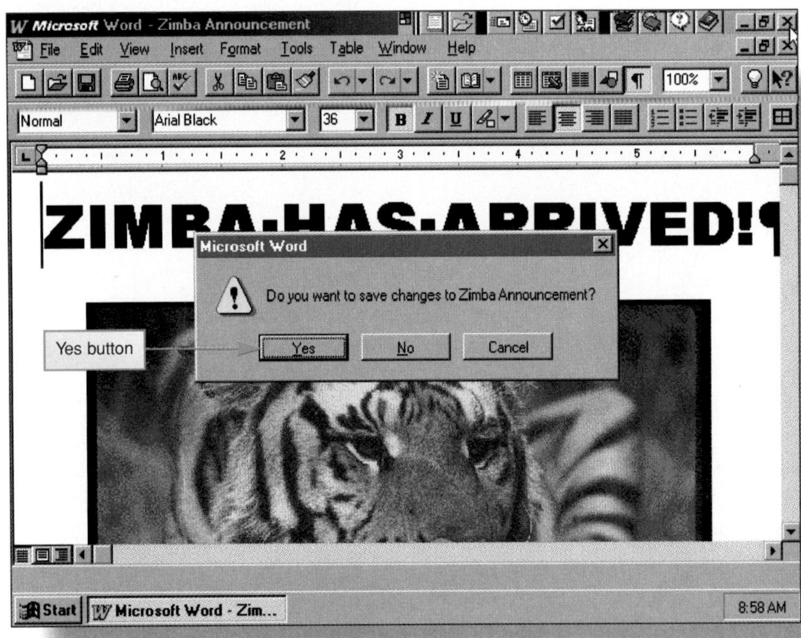

FIGURE 1-70

OtherWays

1. On File menu click Exit
2. Press ALT+F4

Project 1 is now complete. You created and formatted a document, added a graphic, checked spelling, and printed the document. You might, however, decide to change the announcement at a later date. To do this, you must start Word and then retrieve your document from the floppy disk in drive A.

Opening a Document

Earlier, you saved the document built in Project 1 on a floppy disk using the filename Zimba Announcement. Once you have created and saved a document, you will often have reason to retrieve it from the disk. For example, you might want to revise the document. The steps on the next page illustrate how to open the file, Zimba Announcement.

More About Opening a Document

You can open a recently closed document by clicking File on the menu bar and then clicking the document name on the File menu. To control the number of recent files that display on the File menu, click Tools on the menu bar, click Options, click the General tab, enter a number in Recently Used File List box, and then click the OK button.

To Open a Document

Click the Start button on the taskbar and then point to Open Office Document (Figure 1-71).

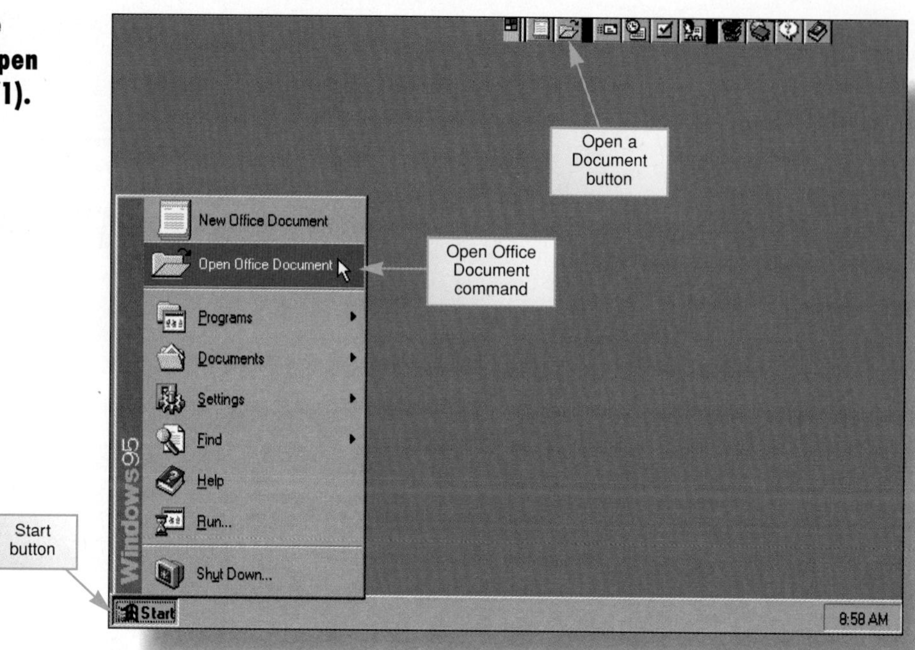

FIGURE 1-71

Click Open Office Document.

Office displays the Open dialog box (Figure 1-72). The My Documents folder displays in the Look in box. Depending on your system configuration, a different folder may display. For this project, you want to retrieve a file from a floppy disk in drive A.

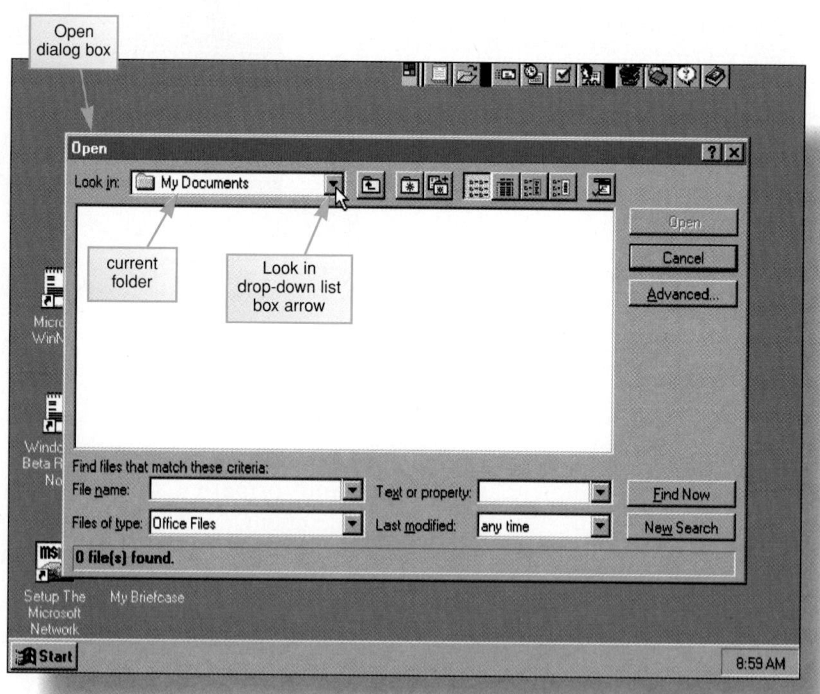

FIGURE 1-72

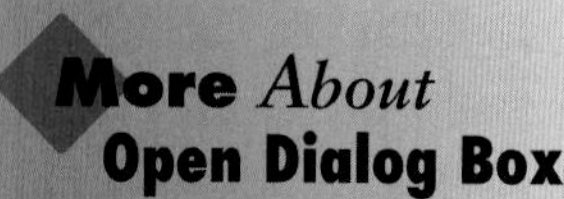

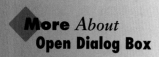

More About Open Dialog Box

You can open a file from the Open dialog box by double-clicking its filename. This is an alternative to clicking the filename and then clicking the Open button.

If necessary, click the Look in box arrow, and then click 3½ Floppy [A:]. If it is not already selected, click the filename Zimba Announcement. Point to the Open button.

Office displays the files on the floppy disk in drive A (Figure 1-73).

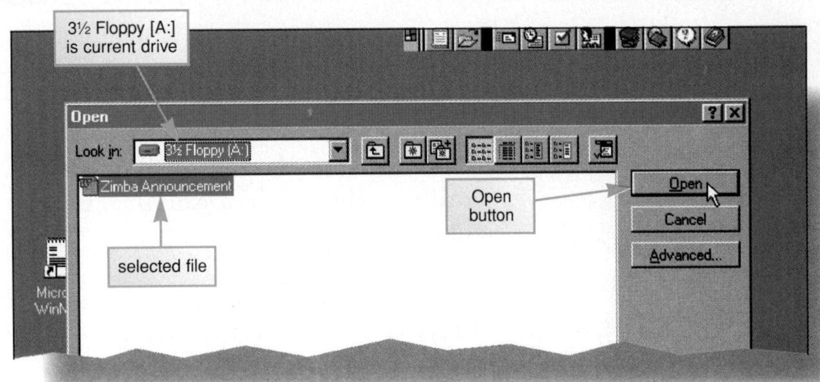

FIGURE 1-73

Click the Open button.

Office starts Word, and then Word opens the document, Zimba Announcement, from the floppy disk in drive A and displays it on the screen (Figure 1-74).

FIGURE 1-74

Correcting Errors

After creating a document, often you will find you must make changes to the document. Changes can be required because the document contains an error or because of new circumstances.

Types of Changes Made to Documents

The types of changes made to documents normally fall into one of the three following categories: additions, deletions, or modifications.

ADDITIONS Additional words, sentences, or paragraphs may be required in the document. Additions occur when you omit text from a document and are required to add it later. For example, you may accidentally forget to put the area code in front of the telephone number in the last line in Project 1.

Other Ways

1. Right-click Start button, click Open, double-click Open Office Document, select filename, click Open button
2. On Microsoft Office Shortcut Bar, click Open a Document, select filename, click Open button in dialog box
3. In Microsoft Word, on Standard toolbar click the Open button, select filename, click Open button in dialog box
4. In Microsoft Word, on File menu click Open, select filename, click Open button in dialog box
5. In Microsoft Word, press CTRL+O, select filename, press ENTER

More About
Replacing Text

If you want to replace a word or phrase with another, select the word or phrase and then immediately type the replacement text. You can toggle this feature on or off by clicking Tools on the menu bar, clicking Options, clicking the Edit tab, clicking the Typing Replaces Selection check box, and then clicking the OK button.

DELETIONS Sometimes, text in a document is incorrect or is no longer needed. For example, the zoo may close its aquarium. In this case, you would delete the sentence referring to exotic fish.

MODIFICATIONS If an error is made in a document, you might have to revise the word(s) in the text. For example, the zoo might begin charging a small fee for admission.

Word provides several methods for correcting errors in a document. For each of the error correction techniques, you first must move the insertion point to the error.

Inserting Text into an Existing Document

If you leave a word or phrase out of a sentence, you can include it in the sentence by positioning the insertion point where you intend to insert the text. Word always inserts the text to the left of the insertion point. The text to the right of the insertion point moves to the right and downward to accommodate the added text. The following steps illustrate adding the word, extreme, before the word, dignity, in the first sentence of the paragraph beneath the bulleted list in Project 1.

Steps To Insert Text into an Existing Document

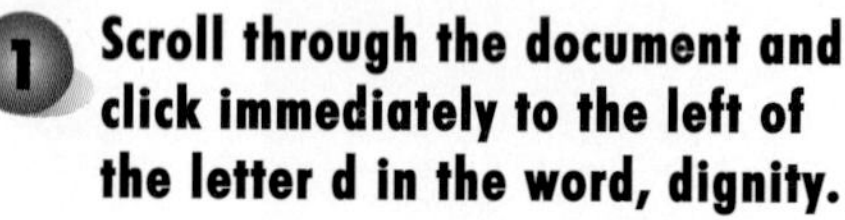

1 Scroll through the document and click immediately to the left of the letter d in the word, dignity.

The insertion point displays immediately to the left of the letter d in dignity (Figure 1-75).

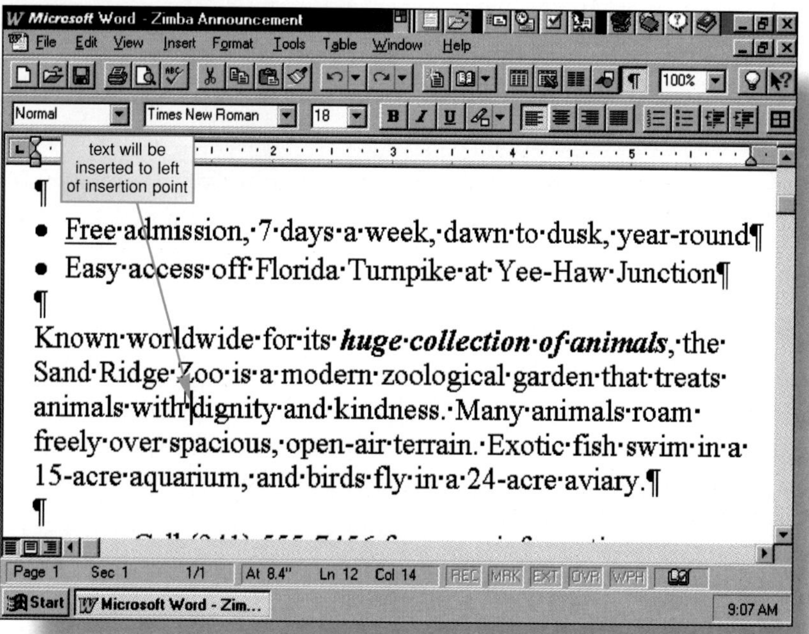

FIGURE 1-75

2 Type `extreme` **and then press the SPACEBAR.**

The word, extreme, is now inserted between the words, with and dignity, in the announcement for Project 1 (Figure 1-76).

Cut button

the word, extreme, inserted between the words, with and dignity

the word, roam, wrapped to line 13

OVR indicates overtype mode

FIGURE 1-76

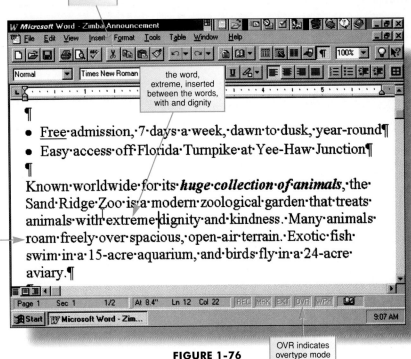

Notice in Figure 1-76 that the text to the right of the word, dignity, moved to the right and downward to accommodate the insertion of the word, extreme. That is, the word, roam, moved down to line 13.

In Word, the default typing mode is **insert mode**. In insert mode, as you type a character, Word inserts the character and moves all the characters to the right of the typed character one position to the right. In the example just given, you used insert mode to add the word, extreme. You can change to **overtype mode** by double-clicking the **OVR mode indicator** on the status bar (Figure 1-76). In overtype mode, Word replaces characters to the right of the insertion point. Clicking the OVR mode indicator a second time returns you to insert mode.

Deleting Text from an Existing Document

It is not unusual to type incorrect characters or words in a document. In such a case, to correct the error, you may want to delete certain letters or words.

TO DELETE AN INCORRECT CHARACTER IN A DOCUMENT

Step 1: Click next to the incorrect character.
Step 2: Press the BACKSPACE key to erase to the left of the insertion point; or press the DELETE key to erase to the right of the insertion point.

TO DELETE AN INCORRECT WORD OR PHRASE IN A DOCUMENT

Step 1: Select the word or phrase you want to erase.
Step 2: Right-click the selected word or phrase, and then click Cut on the shortcut menu; or click the Cut button on the Standard toolbar (Figure 1-76); or press the DELETE key.

More *About* Shortcut Menus

Right-clicking an object opens a shortcut menu (also called a context-sensitive or object menu) that contains a set of commands specifically related to the object. Depending on the object, the commands in the shortcut menu vary. A dimmed command in a shortcut menu means the command cannot be used at the current time.

Undoing Recent Actions

Word provides an Undo button on the Standard toolbar that you can use to cancel your recent command(s) or action(s). If you accidentally delete some text, you can bring it back. If you want to cancel your undo, you can use the Redo button. Some actions, such as saving or printing a document, cannot be undone or redone.

TO CANCEL YOUR MOST RECENT ACTION

Step 1: Click the Undo button on the Standard toolbar.

TO CANCEL YOUR MOST RECENT UNDO

Step 1: Click the Redo button on the Standard toolbar.

TO CANCEL A PRIOR ACTION

Step 1: Click the Undo box arrow to display the undo actions list (Figure 1-77).
Step 2: Click the action to be undone.

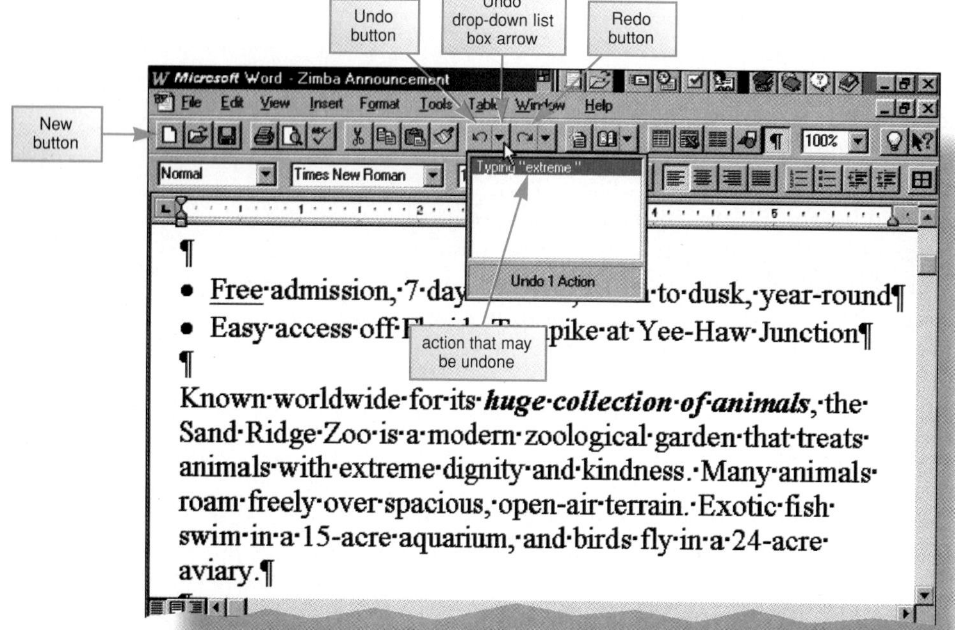

FIGURE 1-77

You also may select multiple actions by dragging the mouse through them in the undo actions list to undo a group of sequential actions.

Closing the Entire Document

Sometimes, everything goes wrong. If this happens, you may want to close the document entirely and start over. You also may want to close a document when you are finished with it so you can begin your next document. To close the document, follow these steps.

TO CLOSE THE ENTIRE DOCUMENT AND START OVER

Step 1: Click File on the menu bar.
Step 2: Click Close on the File menu.
Step 3: If Word displays the dialog box, click the No button to ignore the changes since the last time you saved the document.
Step 4: Click the New button on the Standard toolbar.

You also can close the document by clicking the Close button at the right edge of the menu bar.

Word Online Help

At any time while you are using Word, you can gain access to **online Help** through Word's Help Topics window. Used properly, this form of online assistance can increase your productivity and reduce your frustrations by minimizing the time you spend learning how to use Word.

The following sections show examples of the various types of online Help available in Word 7 for Windows 95.

More About Help

If you purchased an application program five years ago, you received one or more thick technical manuals explaining the software. With Microsoft Word for Windows 95, you receive a small manual. The online Help feature of Microsoft Word for Windows 95 replaces the reams and reams of printed pages in hard-to-understand technical manuals.

Using Word's Help Topics Dialog Box

The **Contents sheet** in the Help Topics: Microsoft Word dialog box offers you assistance when you know the general category of the topic in question, but not the specifics. Use the Contents sheet in the same manner you would use a table of contents at the beginning of a textbook. The following steps show how to use the Contents sheet to obtain information on getting assistance while you work.

Steps To Access Microsoft Word Help Topics

1 Double-click the Help button on the Standard toolbar to display the Help Topics: Microsoft Word dialog box. If your Contents sheet does not display, click the Contents tab.

The Help Topics: Microsoft Word dialog box displays (Figure 1-78). This dialog box contains four tabbed sheets: Contents, Index, Find, and Answer Wizard. In Figure 1-78, each topic in the Contents sheet is preceded by a book icon. A ***book icon*** *indicates subtopics are associated with the topic. To display a subtopic related a topic, you double-click its book icon.*

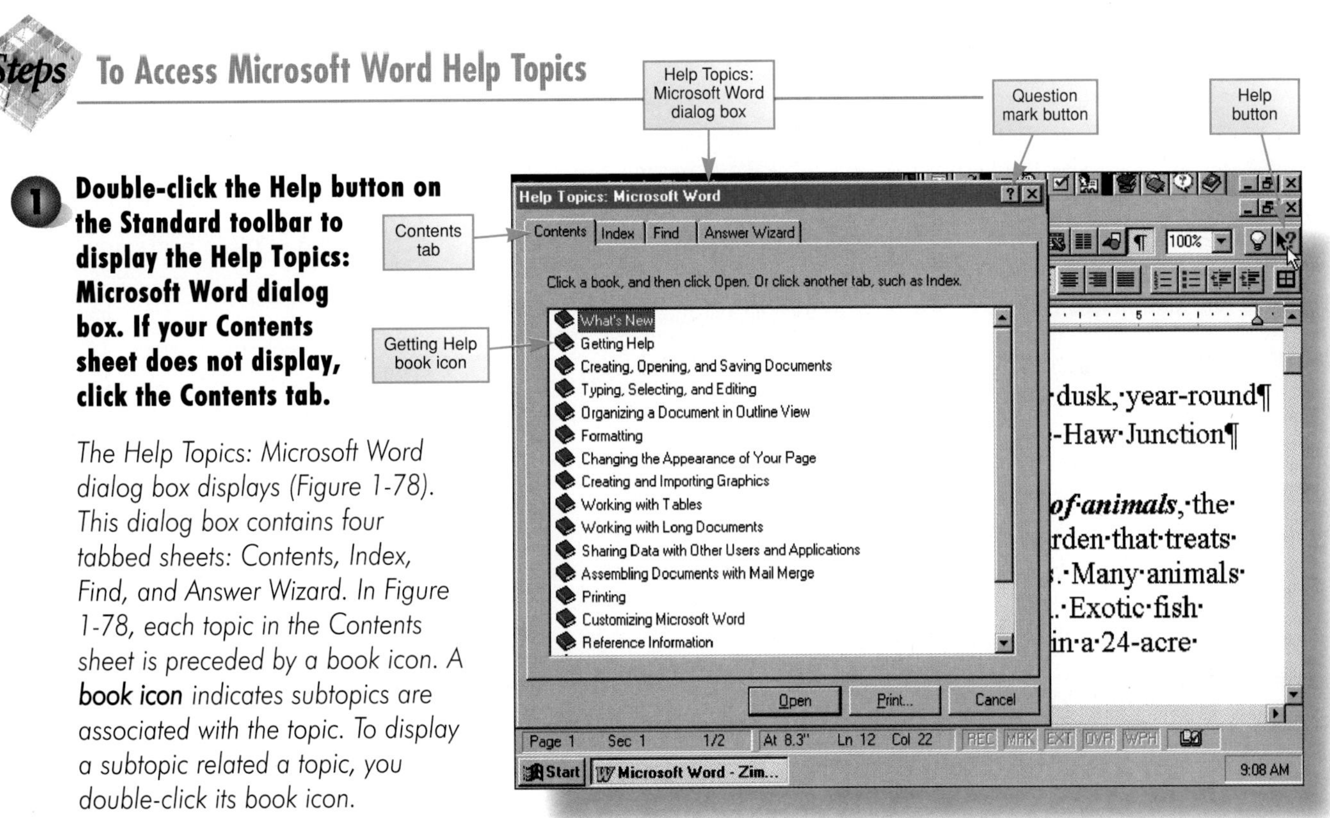

FIGURE 1-78

Double-click the Getting Help book.

Word displays a list of subtopics related to the Getting Help topic (Figure 1-79). The subtopics are preceded by a ***question mark icon****. To display information on a subtopic, you double-click its title. Notice how the Getting Help book icon opens when you double-click its book (or its title).*

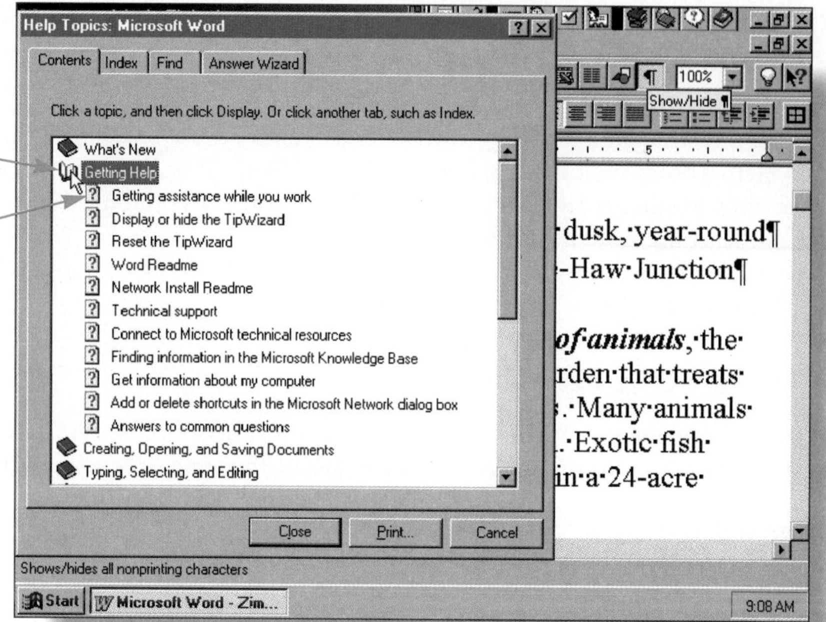

FIGURE 1-79

Double-click the Getting assistance while you work topic. Click the ScreenTips link.

Word displays a dialog box containing tips on Word's Help (Figure 1-80). As you point to a ***link*** *(a picture or phrase) on the screen, the mouse pointer's shape changes to a small hand. When you click a link, Word displays additional Help information.*

Click the Close button in the upper right corner of the Help window to close it.

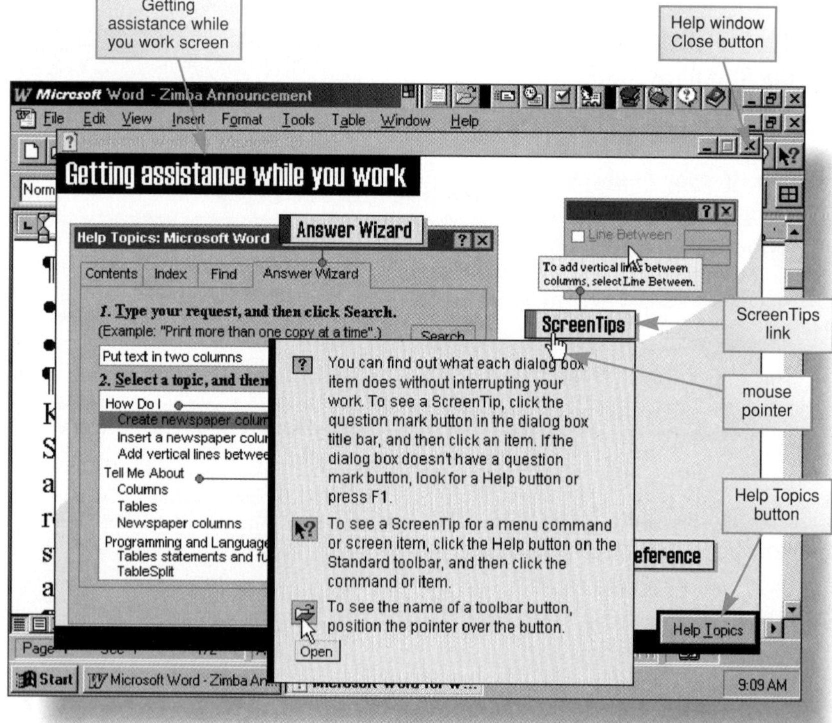

FIGURE 1-80

OtherWays

1. On Help menu click Microsoft Word Help Topics
2. Press F1

The Contents sheet in the Help Topics: Microsoft Word dialog box is much like a table of contents in the front of a book. The **Index sheet,** however, is similar to an index in the back of a book. For example, if you wanted help on removing bullets, you would display the Index sheet, type `bullets` and then double-click the removing topic to display Help on removing bullets (Figure 1-81). Then, click the Close button.

The **Find sheet** is used to locate a Help topic on a particular word or phrase. For example, if you wanted to locate the word, spelling, you would display the Find sheet, type `spelling` and then double-click the Check spelling topic to display help on spell checking (Figure 1-82). Then, click anywhere to remove the ScreenTip and click the Close button to remove the Help window.

Finally, you can use the **Answer Wizard** to obtain assistance. You access the Answer Wizard using a tabbed sheet in the Help Topics: Microsoft Word dialog box or the Help menu. For example, if you wanted to know how to assign a filename to a document, you would click Help on the menu bar and then click Answer Wizard to display the Answer Wizard sheet. Next, type `assign a filename to a document`, click the Search button, and then double-click the Naming documents topic in the Tell Me About section (Figure 1-83) to display the Microsoft Word Naming documents Help window.

In many cases, you can print the information you display through online Help. You can print the Help information by clicking the Print button if one exists or clicking the Options button and then clicking the Print Topic command. You close a Help window by clicking the Close button at the right edge of the title bar on the Help window.

The Word Help Topics has features that make it powerful and easy to use. The best way to familiarize yourself with Word Help Topics is to use it.

Help Button or Question Mark Button

To obtain Help on an item on the Word screen, click the **Help button** on the Standard toolbar. To obtain Help on an item in a Word dialog box, click the **Question mark button** that displays in the upper right corner of a dialog box.

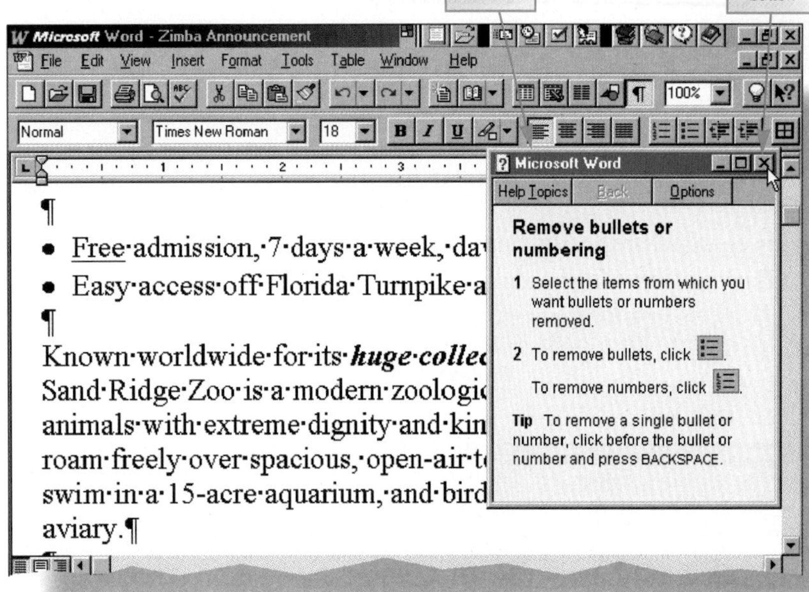

FIGURE 1-81

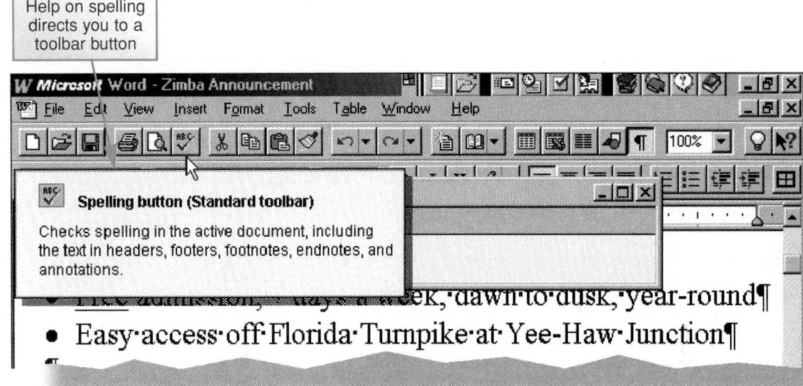

FIGURE 1-82

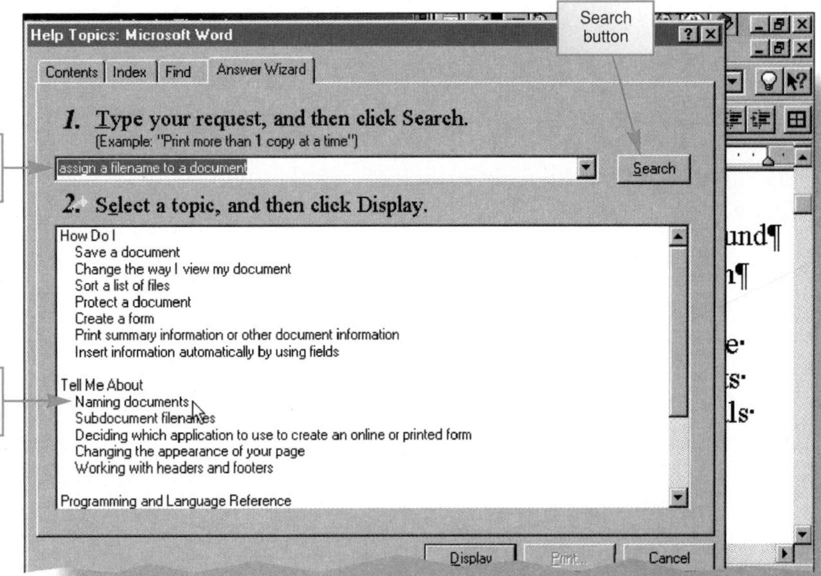

FIGURE 1-83

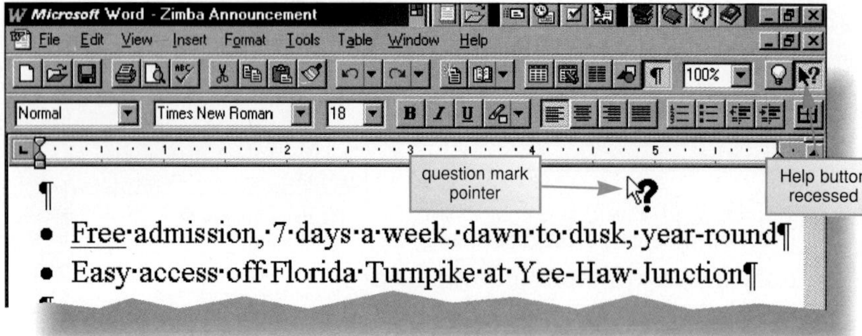

FIGURE 1-84

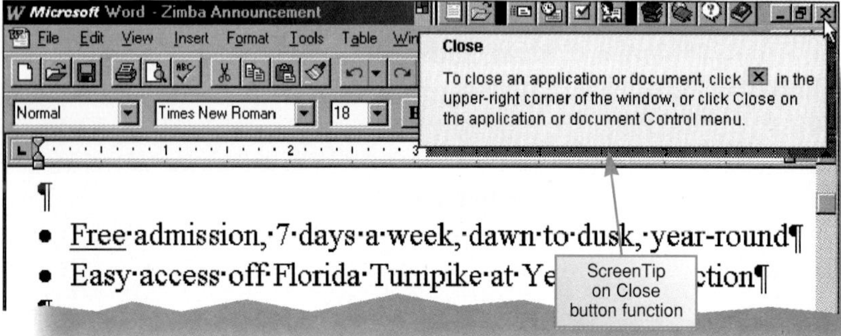

FIGURE 1-85

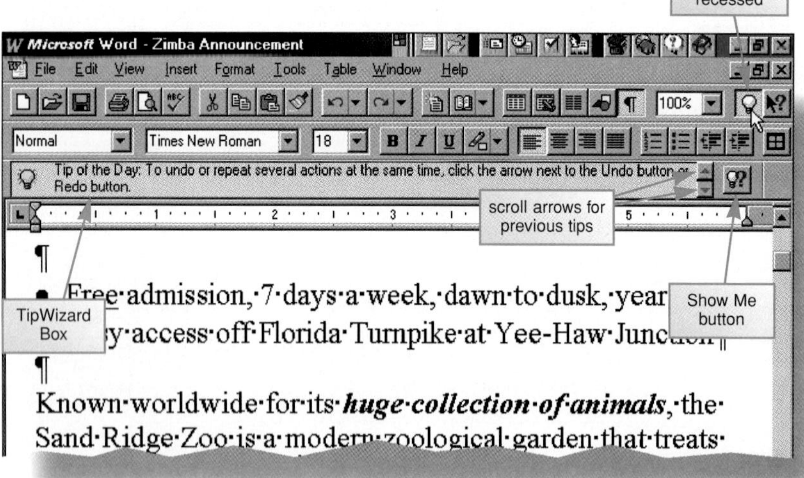

FIGURE 1-86

When you click either the Help button or the Question mark button, the mouse pointer changes to an arrow with a question mark as shown in Figure 1-84. Move the question mark pointer to any item on the Word screen or in a dialog box, and then click to display a **ScreenTip**, which offers an explanation of the item on which you clicked. For example, clicking the Close button on the title bar displays the Help message shown in Figure 1-85.

If you click text with the question mark pointer, Word displays the paragraph and character formatting of the text on which you click.

TipWizard Box

As you create a document, Word displays tips on how to work more efficiently in the **TipWizard Box.** Initially, the TipWizard Box is hidden. To display the TipWizard Box, click the **TipWizard button** on the Standard toolbar. When displayed, the TipWizard Box appears immediately below the Formatting toolbar (Figure 1-86).

Each time you start Word, a different tip, called the **Tip of the Day**, displays in the TipWizard Box. For a more detailed discussion of the displayed tip, click the Show Me button at the right edge of the TipWizard Box. As you are typing, Word may change the tip in the TipWizard Box, suggesting a more efficient way to accomplish a task or new feature related to your current task. You may click the scroll arrows on the TipWizard Box to scroll through tips that have displayed since you started Word.

To reset the TipWizard to the beginning of its tip list, hold down the CTRL key while clicking the TipWizard button. To hide the TipWizard Box, click the TipWizard button on the Standard toolbar. If the TipWizard is hidden and Word has a new tip to offer you, the bulb on the TipWizard button on the Standard toolbar lights up. To view the tip, click the TipWizard button.

Wizards

Word supplies **wizards** to assist you in creating common types of documents, such as letters, memos, resumes, and newsletters. To use a wizard, click the File on the menu bar, click New, and then select the wizard you desire. The wizard asks you a few basic questions, and then displays a formatted document on the screen for you to customize or fill in blanks. In Project 2, you will use a wizard.

Project Summary

Project 1 introduced you to starting Word and creating a document. Before entering any text in the document, you learned how to change the font size. You also learned how to save and print a document. Once you saved the document, you learned how to format paragraphs and characters in the document. Then, you imported and scaled a graphic file. Using the spelling checker, you checked the document for typographical errors. With the technologies presented, you learned to move the insertion point so you could insert, delete, and modify text. Finally, you learned to use Word online Help.

What You Should Know

Having completed this project, you now should be able to perform the following tasks:

- Access Microsoft Word Help topics *(WD 1.54)*
- Add Bullets to a List of Paragraphs *(WD 1.34)*
- Bold Selected Text *(WD 1.55, WD 1.30)*
- Cancel a Prior Action *(WD 1.54)*
- Cancel Your Most Recent Action *(WD 1.54)*
- Cancel Your Most Recent Undo *(WD 1.54)*
- Close the Entire Document and Start Over *(WD 1.54)*
- Center a Single Paragraph *(WD 1.38)*
- Center Selected Paragraphs *(WD 1.27)*
- Change a Font *(WD 1.28)*
- Change the Default Font Size Before Typing *(WD 1.14)*
- Change the Font Size of Selected Text *(WD 1.30, WD 1.28)*
- Check the Spelling of a Document on Demand *(WD 1.44)*
- Delete an Incorrect Character in a Document *(WD 1.53)*
- Delete an Incorrect Word or Phrase in a Document *(WD 1.53)*
- Display Nonprinting Characters *(WD 1.17)*
- Enter a List of Paragraphs *(WD 1.19)*
- Enter Blank Lines into a Document *(WD 1.17)*
- Enter Text *(WD 1.15)*
- Import a Graphic *(WD 1.39)*
- Insert Text into an Existing Document *(WD 1.52)*
- Italicize and Bold Selected Text *(WD 1.37)*
- Open a Document *(WD 1.50)*
- Print a Document *(WD 1.47)*
- Quit Word *(WD 1.49)*
- Save a New Document *(WD 1.21)*
- Save an Existing Document with the Same Filename *(WD 1.46)*
- Scale a Graphic *(WD 1.42)*
- Scroll Through the Document *(WD 1.32)*
- Select a Group of Words *(WD 1.36)*
- Select a Single Line *(WD 1.28)*
- Select a Single Word *(WD 1.33)*
- Select Multiple Paragraphs *(WD 1.26)*
- Start Word *(WD 1.8)*
- Underline Selected Text *(WD 1.34)*
- Use the Wordwrap Feature *(WD 1.20)*

A+ Test Your Knowledge

1 True/False

Instructions: Circle T if the statement is true or F if the statement is false.

T F 1. Microsoft Word 7 for Windows 95 is a word processing program that allows you to create and revise documents.
T F 2. The status bar is used to retrieve a document and display it in the document window.
T F 3. To create a new paragraph, press the ENTER key.
T F 4. You should always hide nonprinting characters before printing a document because nonprinting characters can make your printed document difficult to read.
T F 5. Wordwrap allows you to type continually without pressing the ENTER key at the end of each line.
T F 6. To save a document with the same filename, click the Save button on the Standard toolbar.
T F 7. When you save a document, it disappears from the screen.
T F 8. Words not in the dictionary appear with a blue dotted underline beneath them as you type.
T F 9. If you accidentally delete a word, you can bring it back by clicking the Undo button.
T F 10. To select a graphic, click anywhere inside the graphic.

2 Multiple Choice

Instructions: Circle the correct response.

1. Word is preset to use standard 8.5-by-11-inch paper, with _____-inch left and right margins and _____-inch top and bottom margins.
   a. 1.25, 1
   b. 1.5, 1.25
   c. 1, 1.5
   d. 1, 1.25
2. As you type or insert graphics, your text and graphics display in the _____.
   a. scroll bars
   b. text area
   c. insertion area
   d. TipWizard Box
3. When the mouse pointer is on a toolbar button, it has the shape of a(n) _____.
   a. I-beam
   b. hourglass
   c. left-pointing block arrow
   d. vertical bar

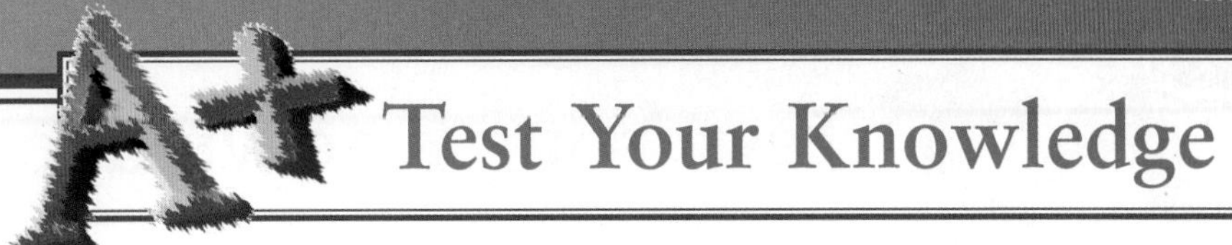

Test Your Knowledge

4. To move the document up one entire screenful at a time, _____.
   a. click the scroll box
   b. click anywhere on the scroll bar above the scroll box
   c. click the up scroll arrow at the top of the scroll bar
   d. both b and c
5. The _____ button in the TipWizard Box displays more information about a displayed tip.
   a. Help
   b. TipWizard
   c. More Help
   d. Show Me
6. To erase the character to the left of the insertion point, press the _____ key.
   a. DELETE
   b. INSERT
   c. BACKSPACE
   d. both a and c
7. Selected graphics display _____ handles at the corner and middle locations.
   a. selection
   b. sizing
   c. scaling
   d. resizing
8. When nonprinting characters display in the document window, spaces are indicated by _____.
   a. raised dots
   b. right-pointing arrows
   c. a superscripted letters
   d. question marks
9. _____ the OVR mode indicator to toggle between overtype and insert mode.
   a. Click
   b. Double-click
   c. Drag
   d. Point to
10. When you close a document, _____.
    a. it is erased from disk
    b. it is removed from the screen
    c. control is returned to Windows 95
    d. both a and c

Test Your Knowledge

3 Understanding the Word Screen

Instructions: In Figure 1-87, arrows point to major components of the Word screen. Identify the various parts of the screen in the spaces provided.

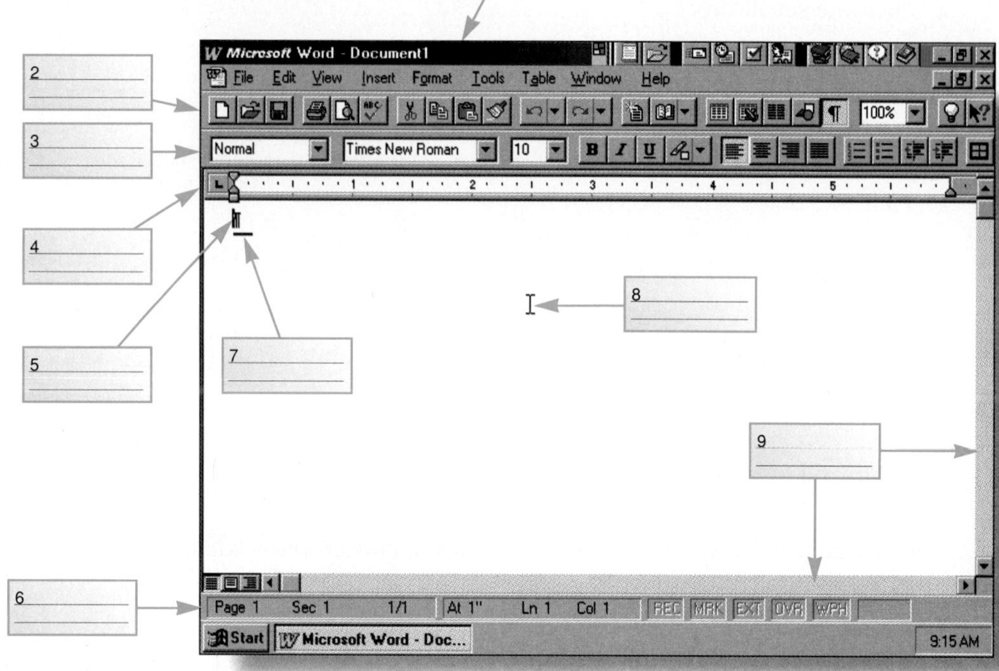

FIGURE 1-87

4 Understanding the Standard and Formatting Toolbars

Instructions: In Figure 1-88, arrows point to several of the buttons and boxes on the Standard and Formatting toolbars. In the spaces provided, briefly explain the purpose of each button and box.

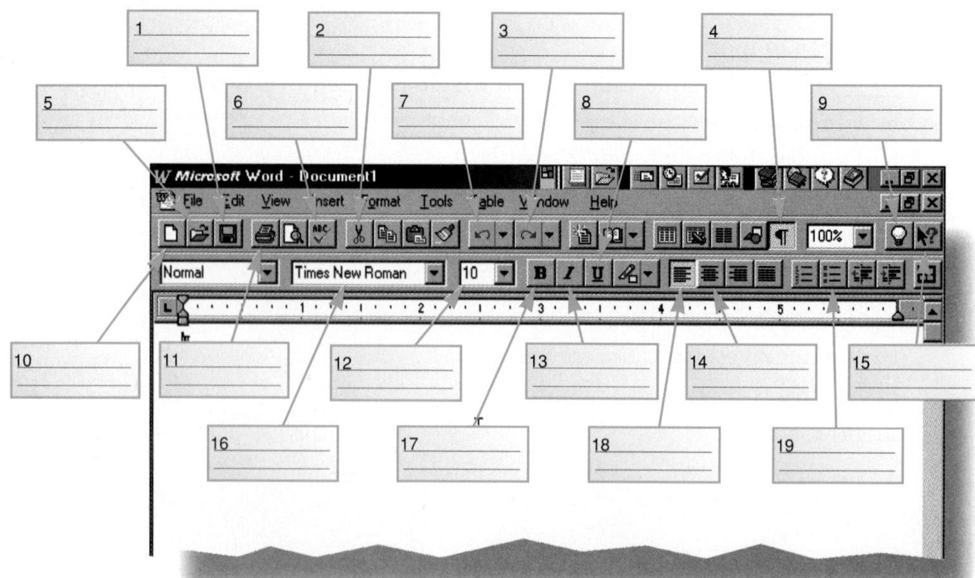

FIGURE 1-88

Use Help

1 Reviewing Project Activities

Instructions: Perform the following tasks using a computer.

1. Start Word.
2. Double-click the Help button on the Standard toolbar.
3. Click the Contents tab. Double-click the Getting Help book. Double-click the Getting assistance while you work topic (Figure 1-89).
4. Click the ScreenTips link and read the information. Click the remaining links and read their Help information. What shape is the mouse pointer as you point to links on this Help window?
5. Click the Help Topics button to return to the Help Topics: Microsoft Word display box. Click the Index tab. Type `bullets` and then click the converting numbers and bullets topic. Click the Display button to display a Help window on the selected topic.
6. Ready the printer and click the Options button. Click Print Topic and then click the OK button to produce a hard copy of the Help window.
7. Click the Help Topics button. Click the Find tab. Type `shortcut keys` and then click the Apply formatting using shortcut keys topic. Click the Display button. Click the Options button. Click Print Topic and then click the OK button.
8. Click the Help Topics button. Click the Answer Wizard tab. Type `select text` and then click the Search button. Click the select text and graphics with the mouse topic. Click the Display button. Click the Options button. Click Print Topic and then click the OK button.
9. Close any open Help window(s) by clicking its Close button in the upper right corner of the Help window title bar.
10. Click the Help button on the Standard toolbar.
11. Click the Print button on the Standard toolbar. What is the function of the Print button?

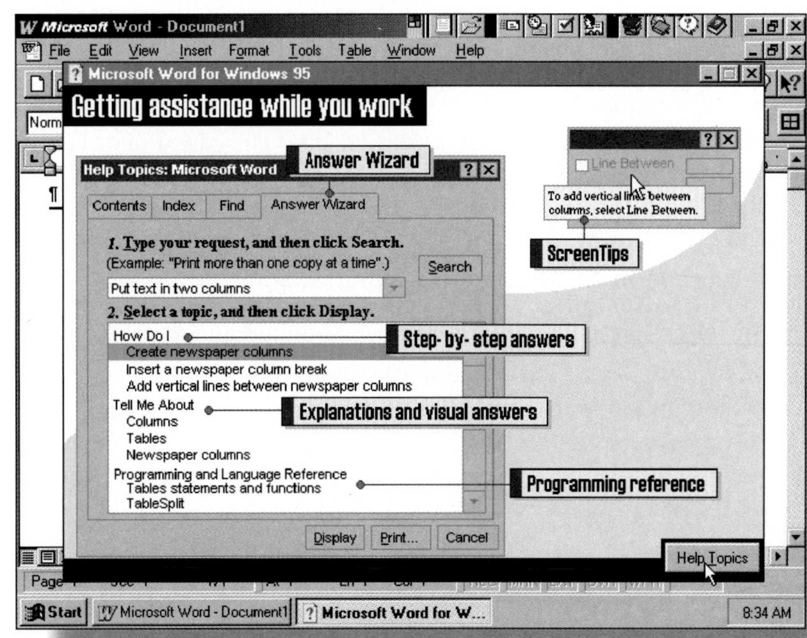

FIGURE 1-89

2 Expanding on the Basics

Instructions: Perform the following tasks using a computer and answer the questions.

Microsoft Word 7 for Windows 95 can use many graphic file types. Using the Contents tab in the Help Topics: Microsoft Word dialog box, answer the following questions:

1. What types of graphic file types do not require a special filter for Word to import?
2. What other types of graphic files can be inserted into a Word document?
3. How do you import any of these graphic files into a document?

Using the Index tab in the Help Topics: Microsoft Word dialog box, display and print the shortcut keys to edit and move text. Then, answer the questions below.

1. Which key(s) deletes one word to the left of the insertion point?
2. Which key(s) deletes one word to the right of the insertion point?
3. Which key(s) inserts an ellipsis?
4. Which key(s) selects the entire document?
5. Which key(s) moves the insertion point one paragraph down?

In Microsoft Word 7 for Windows 95, you can password-protect a document. Use the Find tab in the Help Topics: Microsoft Word dialog box to answer these questions about password-protecting documents.

1. Which dialog box is used to password-protect a document?
2. If you want to require a password to edit a document, in which text box do you type your password?
3. If you want to require a password when a document is opened or accessed, in which text box do you type your password?

Microsoft Word 7 for Windows 95 has certain file and formatting limitations. Use the Answer Wizard to obtain answers to the following questions:

1. What is the maximum number of documents that may be open at one time?
2. In megabytes, what is the maximum file size?
3. What is the maximum number of colors in a graphic?
4. In points, what is the maximum font size?

Apply Your Knowledge

CAUTION: It is recommended that you create a backup copy of the Student Floppy Disk that accompanies this book and then remove unneeded folders on the backup floppy disk to free up space. Do the following: (1) insert the Student Floppy Disk in drive A; (2) start Explorer; (3) right-click the 3½ Floppy [A:] folder in the All Folders side of the window; (4) click Copy Disk; (5) click Start and OK as required; (6) insert the backup floppy disk when requested; (7) delete folders on the backup floppy disk except the Word folder.

1 Spell Checking a Document

Instructions: Read CAUTION above. Start Word. Open the document Phantom Announcement from the Word folder on the Student Floppy Disk that accompanies this book. As shown in Figure 1-90, the document is a play announcement containing many typographical errors. You are to use Word's spelling checker to correct the errors.

Perform the following tasks:

1. Position the insertion point at the beginning of the document.
2. Start the spelling checker by clicking the Spelling button on the Standard toolbar.
3. Change the incorrect word, Opora, to Opera by pointing to Opera in the suggested list of words and then clicking. Click the Change button.
4. Change the incorrect word, Performences, to Performances by clicking the Change button.
5. Change the incorrect word, thru, to through by clicking the Change button.
6. Change the incorrect word, admision, to admission by clicking the Change button.
7. Change the incorrect word, toun, to town by pointing to town in the suggested list of words and clicking. Click the Change button.
8. Click the Ignore All button to ignore all occurrences of Willowsprings.
9. Change the incorrect word, rhe, to the by typing `the` in the Change To text box. Click the Change button.
10. Change the incorrect word, l;ve, to live by pointing to live in the suggested list of words and then clicking. Click the Change button.

misspelled words are circled to help you identify them

Phantom of the Opora

THE MASQUERADES

- Performences from July 6 thru July 19
- $10.50 for adult admision; $5.25 for children

Join the toun of Willowsprings in welcoming rhe world famous ***Masquerades*** in l;ve performances of Phantom of the the Opera. Curtain opens nitely at 7:00 p.m. at the Playhouse in Willowsprings Town Square.

For reservations, call (906) 555-2939

FIGURE 1-90

(continued)

Apply Your Knowledge

Spell Checking a Document *(continued)*

11. Click the Delete button to remove the duplicate occurrence of the word, the.
12. Change the incorrect word, nitely, to nightly by clicking the Change button.
13. Click the OK button in the Microsoft Word dialog box.
14. Click File on the menu bar, and then click Save As. Save the document using Corrected Phantom Announcement as the filename.
15. Print the revised document.

In the Lab

1 Creating an Announcement with an Imported Picture

Problem: As marketing director for Home Crafters, you create announcements outlining the specialties of your company. You have obtained a picture of a kitchen that Home Crafters remodeled recently. You have scanned it into a file called Kitchen and decide to use it in your latest announcement. The unformatted document is shown in Figure 1-91, and the formatted document is shown in Figure 1-92.

Instructions:

1. Change the font size from 10 to 20 by clicking the Font Size box arrow and then clicking 20.
2. If it is not already selected, click the Show/Hide ¶ button on the Standard toolbar to display paragraph marks and spaces.
3. Create the unformatted announcement shown in Figure 1-91. That is, enter the document without the graphic file and without any bolding, underlining, italicizing, or centering.

unformatted document

CUSTOM KITCHENS!

HOME CRAFTERS

Quality products at reasonable prices
Free in-house next day estimates

See your remodeled kitchen on our computer before making any commitments. Choose from cherry, hickory, oak, or maple cabinets. Coordinate tile and wallpaper to accent the room.

Call (708) 555-0098 for an appointment.

FIGURE 1-91

In the Lab

4. Save the document on a floppy disk with Kitchen Announcement as the filename.
5. Select the headline and body title line. Center them.
6. Select the headline. Bold it. Change its font size from 20 to 36. Change its font to Arial Black. If the headline wraps to the next line, adjust the font size so it fits on one line.
7. Select the body title line. Increase its font size from 20 to 48. Bold it.
8. Select the list beneath the title line. Add bullets to it.
9. Select the words, next day, in the bulleted list. Italicize them.
10. Select the word, before, in the paragraph. Underline it.
11. Select the last line of the announcement. Center it.
12. You will need to obtain a copy of the graphic file named Kitchen from your instructor. Import the Kitchen graphic file on the second paragraph mark beneath the headline. Scale the graphic proportionally to 65%.
13. Check the spelling of the announcement.
14. Save the announcement again with the same filename.
15. Print the announcement.

36-point Arial Black bold font

CUSTOM KITCHENS!

48-point bold

HOME CRAFTERS

- Quality products at reasonable prices
- Free in-house *next day* estimates

See your remodeled kitchen on our computer before making any commitments. Choose from cherry, hickory, oak, or maple cabinets. Coordinate tile and wallpaper to accent the room.

Call (708) 555-0098 for an appointment.

FIGURE 1-92

2 Creating an Announcement with Windows Metafiles

Problem: You are the manager of Whispery Hills, a resort known for its relaxing weekend getaways. With the spring and summer seasons approaching, you decide to prepare the document shown in Figure 1-93.

36-point Arial Black bold font → **WEEKEND GETAWAY!**

48-point bold → **WHISPERY HILLS**

- No telephones, newspapers, televisions, or radios
- No disturbances from *the real world* at Whispery Hills

Spend two nights and three days enjoying the scenic beauty and outdoor activities of our resort. ***Relax*** by the pool; ***hike*** down a nature trail; ***sail*** or ***fish*** on Breeze Lake; ***bird watch*** from Robins Peak; or read a book ***fireside*** in your cabin.

Call (906) 555-2838 for reservations.

FIGURE 1-93

Instructions:

1. Change the font size from 10 to 20 by clicking the Font Size box arrow and then clicking 20.
2. If it is not already selected, click the Show/Hide ¶ button on the Standard toolbar to display nonprinting characters.
3. Create the announcement shown in Figure 1-93. Enter the document without the graphic file and unformatted; that is, without any bolding, underlining, italicizing, or centering.
4. Save the document on a floppy disk with Weekend Announcement as the filename.
5. Select the headline and body title line. Center them.
6. Select the headline. Bold it. Change its font size from 20 to 36. Change its font to Arial Black. If the headline wraps to the next line, adjust the font size so it will fit on one line.
7. Select the body title line. Increase its font size from 20 to 48. Bold it.
8. Select the list beneath the title line. Add bullets to it.
9. Select the word, No, in each paragraph in the bulleted list and underline it.
10. Select the phrase, the real world, in the bulleted list. Italicize it.

11. Select the following words one at a time in the paragraph and bold and italicize them: relax, hike, sail, fish, bird watch, and fireside.
12. Click the last line of the announcement. Center it.
13. Windows metafiles are located in the Clipart folder. Import the graphic file called spring.wmf (in the Clipart folder) on the second paragraph mark beneath the headline. On the same line as the spring graphic, import the graphic file called summer.wmf. Scale each graphic proportionally to 132%.
14. Check the spelling of the announcement.
15. Save the announcement again with the same filename.
16. Print the announcement.

3 Composing an Announcement from a Draft

Problem: You are the activities coordinator for Pine Ridge Slopes. You want to announce the ski weekend special to the public. You have obtained a picture of a skier to use in the announcement.

Instructions: You are to create the unformatted announcement shown in Figure 1-94. The picture of the skier is in a file called Skier, which you will need to obtain from your instructor. Then, format the announcement, using the techniques presented in this project. Below are some general guidelines:

1. Center the headline and title.
2. Bullet short lists.
3. Use italics, bold, and underlining to emphasize words or phrases.
4. Change the font to emphasize text.
5. Increase the font size of the headline and title.

unformatted document

SKI THE DOOMERANG!

Pine Ridge Slopes

Package includes lodging, lift tickets, and meals
Cost is only $575 per person

Pine Ridge Slopes, known worldwide for its challenging ski runs, invites you to a weekend of exciting skiing, delicious meals, and cozy lodging. Your weekend package includes 2 breakfasts, lunches, and dinners; 2 nights' lodging; 2 day lift tickets, and 2 night lift tickets.

Call (906) 555-2939 for reservations

FIGURE 1-94

Cases and Places

The difficulty of these case studies varies:

◗ Case studies preceded by a single halfmoon are the least difficult. You are asked to create the required document based on information that has already been placed in an organized form.
◗◗ Case studies preceded by two halfmoons are more difficult. You must organize the information presented before using it to create the required document.
◗◗◗ Case studies preceded by three halfmoons are the most difficult. You must choose a specific topic, and then obtain and organize the necessary information before using it to create the required document.

1 ◗ The manager of the computer store at which you work has written a draft of an announcement promoting computer equipment that meets Energy Star guidelines (Figure 1-95). Using his text, along with his formatting suggestions, you are to produce an announcement that can be posted throughout the store. Use the concepts and techniques presented in this project to create the announcement.

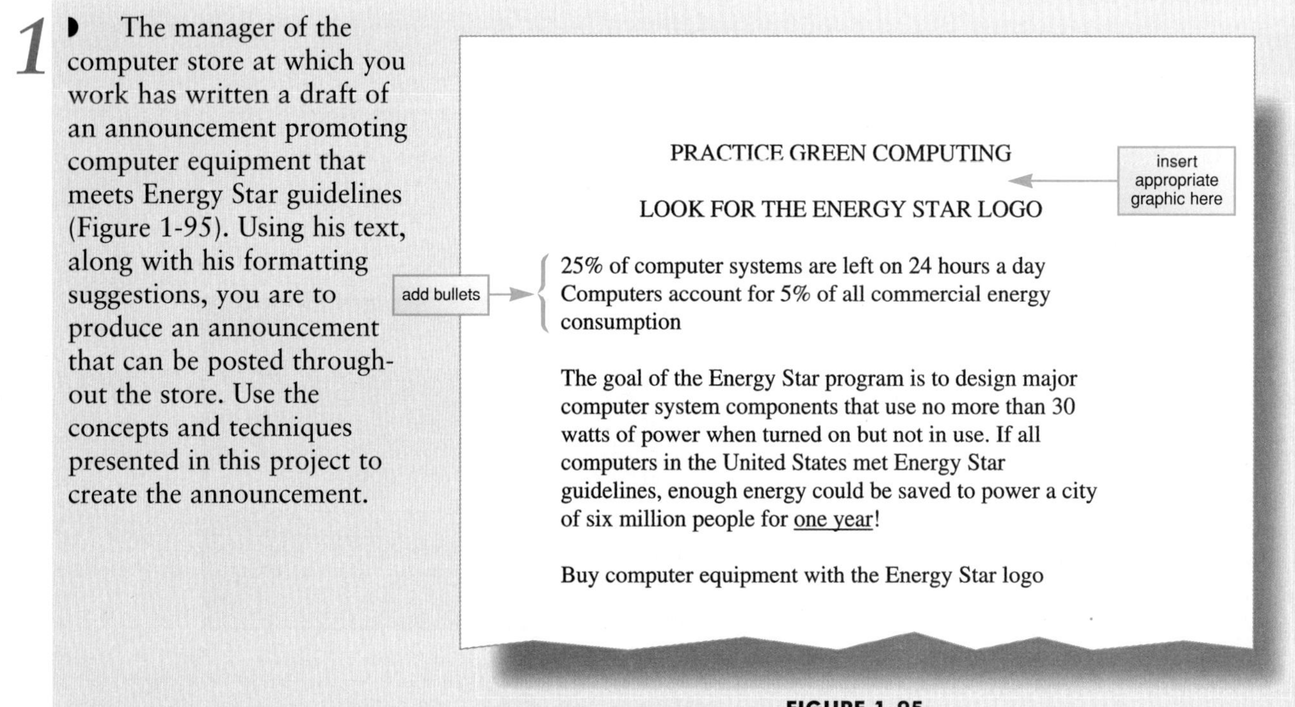
PRACTICE GREEN COMPUTING
LOOK FOR THE ENERGY STAR LOGO
insert appropriate graphic here
add bullets
25% of computer systems are left on 24 hours a day
Computers account for 5% of all commercial energy consumption
The goal of the Energy Star program is to design major computer system components that use no more than 30 watts of power when turned on but not in use. If all computers in the United States met Energy Star guidelines, enough energy could be saved to power a city of six million people for one year!
Buy computer equipment with the Energy Star logo

FIGURE 1-95

Cases and Places

2 ◗ Recognizing the anxiety that some students face before tests, your school has invited a noted expert to present a seminar on test-taking. You have been given a draft of an announcement for the seminar (Figure 1-96). Using this draft, together with the formatting suggestions indicated, you are to produce an announcement that can be displayed around school. Use the concepts and techniques presented in this project to create the announcement.

Not Happy With Your Performance on Tests?

Skinner's Test-Taking Seminar Can Help!

Some people are better test-takers than others
Test-taking is a skill that can be learned
You can improve your test scores

Do your test scores really reflect how much you know? We can help you do your best on every test. We'll give you tips on effective preparation (such as how to anticipate likely outcomes) and optimal performance (such as when it pays to guess). Modify your test-taking behavior through our proven system of reinforcement!

For more information, call B.F. at (123) 555-6677

insert appropriate graphic here

add bullets

FIGURE 1-96

3 ◗◗ Your mother, a graduate of Potter Central High School, will be celebrating her thirtieth high school reunion this year. She has asked you to prepare an announcement that can be sent to each member of the graduating class. The reunion will feature dinner at The Tailor of Gloucester, music by The Jesters, and a special guest appearance by Anne Strathers, a local celebrity. It will be held on Saturday, August 29, at 9:00 p.m. Guests will have the opportunity to reminisce about old times, catch up on current projects, and share future plans. Everyone is encouraged to take part in the fun, mischief, and hair-raising experiences. More information can be obtained by calling Mr. Jeremy Fisher at (987) 555-1234. Use the concepts and techniques presented in this project to create the announcement. Add bullets before the list of featured events and insert an appropriate graphic.

4 ◗◗ The Impressionist Vision Art Gallery is presenting an exhibition entitled Beacons to a New Age. The gallery owner has asked you to create an announcement promoting the show. Major works by Seurat, Van Gogh, Gauguin, and Cézanne will be displayed. These artists formed a bridge between 19th century Impressionism and the modern art of the 20th century. Their paintings introduced new ways of viewing and representing the world. The gallery is open Wednesday through Sunday from 1:00 p.m. to 9:00 p.m. A full-color catalog is offered with the $5.00 admission fee. More information can be obtained by calling (412) 555-6789. Add bullets before the references to the gallery hours and admission fee, and insert an appropriate graphic.

Cases and Places

5 ▶▶▶ Most schools have a place where announcements are posted. Often, so many announcements are displayed that some go unnoticed. Find a posted announcement that you think might be overlooked. Copy the text from the announcement. Using this text, together with the techniques presented in this project, create an announcement that would be more likely to catch a reader's eye. Format the announcement effectively and, if possible, include a bulleted list and suitable graphic.

6 ▶▶▶ Companies frequently advertise openings in the classified section of the newspaper. Although most of these notices are small classified ads, some are larger announcements that, in an effort to reach a greater audience, may occupy as much as a quarter of a page. Find a small classified advertisement in the help wanted section of the newspaper. Using the techniques presented in this project, rework the advertisement into an announcement suitable for a quarter of the newspaper page. Format the announcement effectively and, if possible, include a bulleted list and suitable graphic.

7 ▶▶▶ Announcements are sometimes used to promote individual products in a store. Effective marketing announcements displayed throughout a store can encourage customers to think about, and perhaps purchase, items they were not even considering when they first entered the store. Visit a computer vendor and select an item you believe could have greater sales with increased in-store advertising. Write the text for a promotional announcement and then, using the techniques presented in this project, create an announcement that could be posted around the store to enhance the sales of the item. Format the announcement effectively and, if possible, include a bulleted list and suitable graphic.

Microsoft Word 7

Windows 95

Using Word's Wizards and Templates to Create a Cover Letter and Resume

Objectives:

You will have mastered the material in this project when you can:

- Create a resume using Word's Resume Wizard
- Understand the Word screen in page layout view
- Zoom a document
- Understand styles in a document
- Add a border and shading to a paragraph
- Replace selected text with new text
- Use the TAB key to vertically align text
- Insert a line break
- AutoFormat as you type
- Select a paragraph
- Drag and drop selected text
- Use print preview to view and print a document
- Explain the components of a business letter
- Create a cover letter using a Word letter template
- Modify formatting applied by a style
- Create an AutoText entry
- Format characters using shortcut keys
- Insert an AutoText entry
- Apply a style
- Change the font size of all characters in a document
- Copy text from one open Word document to another
- Close all open Word documents

The *Ultimate* Résumé Delivery System

Developing a Sound Résumé for a Highly Competitive Marketplace

Imagine starting your job search at home, in front of your computer, cruising along the information superhighway.

Employers as prestigious as NASA Ames Research Center or as small as Nella Cutlery Inc. are searching for credible employees and subcontractors online via the various résumé banks and individual home pages. With 3-D multimedia capabilities, job candidates are creating virtual reality résumés. An interested employer could view philosophical and goal statements, selected subject research, experience the real person, and even see a video and/or audio playback. (The bearing this may have on EEO and Affirmative Action is yet to be determined.)

Most employment, recruitment, or placement specialists, however, would not have thought the age of the virtual résumé would be upon us so quickly.

Now it is not enough to look at the newspaper, set up networking appointments, and expect to get interviews that would lead to job offers. Crucial to success in today's job market is a creative approach backed by a well researched and practiced job search campaign.

Virtual Reality

This means that you should develop a sound résumé and hone the capability to market yourself as the product in a tight and highly competitive marketplace.

Prior to the advent of personal computers, candidates had one generic résumé that was reproduced and used for varied types of employment searches. Today, résumés can be personalized for a targeted employment field, company, or specific job. For example, a candidate seeking employment opportunities both in academia as well as with a manufacturing company would use two different résumés. The résumé content may be similar but the organization, format, and emphasis would be different. Perhaps a chronological résumé would be used along with a functional style. The résumé's focus always is on an error-free product, effective design, adaptation to audience expectations, and accurate descriptions.

Regardless of whether a company wishes to be run as an agile virtual enterprise or simply to utilize the World Wide Web for an online employee search function, job candidates still must begin their job search with the development of a résumé. A résumé is a summary of your background and experiences intended to interest a potential employer not only in your qualifications but also in your exact fit to the employer's needs. With the assistance of résumé wizards, such as those in Microsoft Word 7, a candidate can complete a credible document ready for reproduction whether online or printed for the more traditional job search approaches.

Whatever format you choose, remember a résumé is a screening tool used by employers to peak their interest. Ultimately, it is you and you alone that will clinch the offer.

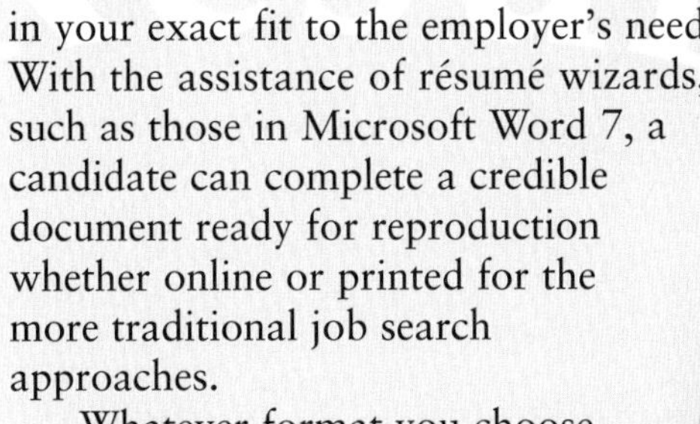

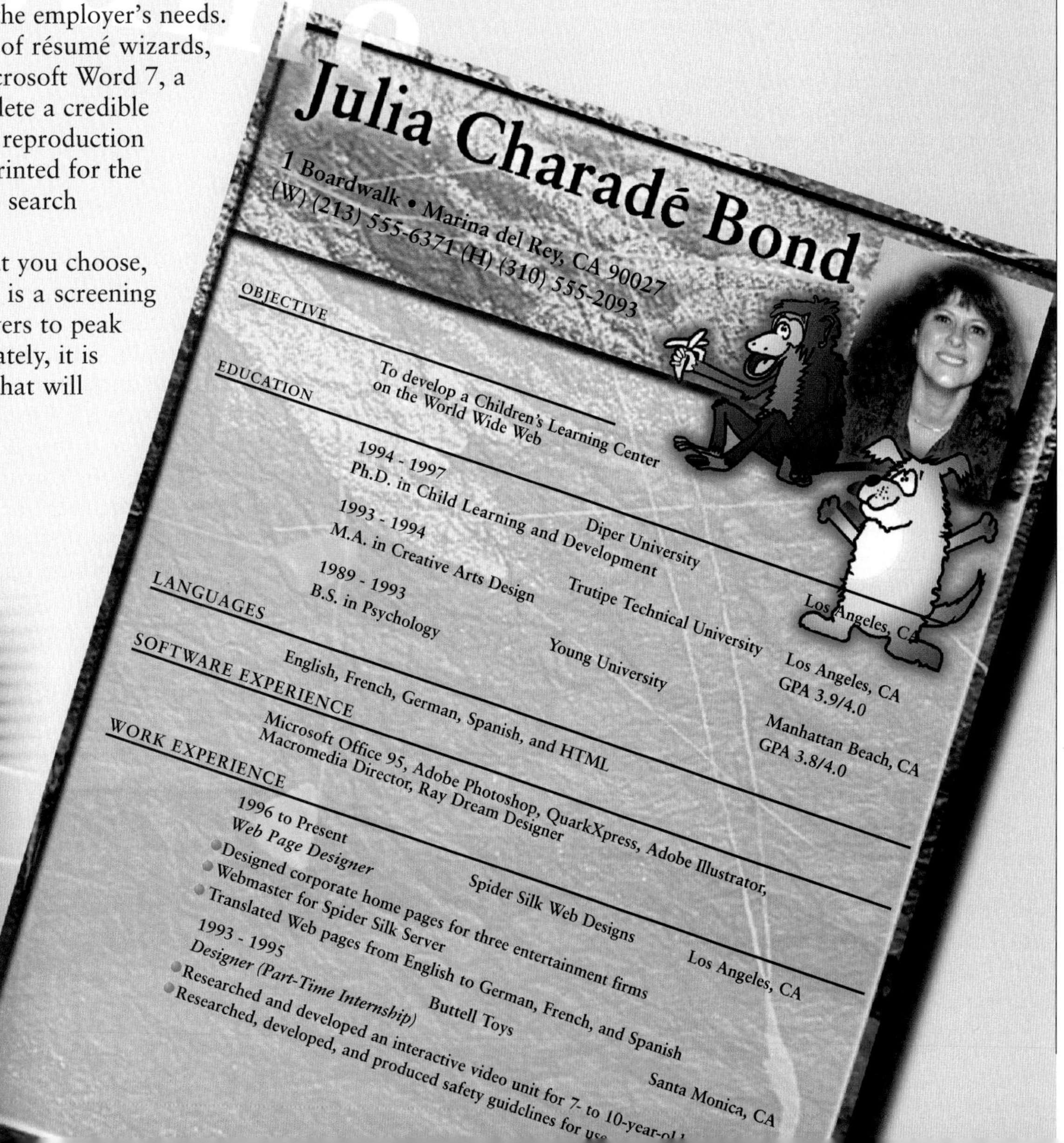

Julia Charadé Bond

1 Boardwalk • Marina del Rey, CA 90027

(W) (213) 555-6371 (H) (310) 555-2093

OBJECTIVE

To develop a Children's Learning Center on the World Wide Web

EDUCATION

1994 - 1997 Diper University Los Angeles, CA

Ph.D. in Child Learning and Development

1993 - 1994 Trutipe Technical University Los Angeles, CA

M.A. in Creative Arts Design GPA 3.9/4.0

1989 - 1993 Young University Manhattan Beach, CA

B.S. in Psychology GPA 3.8/4.0

LANGUAGES

English, French, German, Spanish, and HTML

SOFTWARE EXPERIENCE

Microsoft Office 95, Adobe Photoshop, QuarkXpress, Adobe Illustrator, Macromedia Director, Ray Dream Designer

WORK EXPERIENCE

1996 to Present

Web Page Designer Spider Silk Web Designs Los Angeles, CA

- Designed corporate home pages for three entertainment firms
- Webmaster for Spider Silk Server
- Translated Web pages from English to German, French, and Spanish

1993 - 1995

Designer (Part-Time Internship) Buttell Toys Santa Monica, CA

- Researched and developed an interactive video unit for 7- to 10-year-ol...
- Researched, developed, and produced safety guidelines for us...

Microsoft

Word 7

Windows 95

Using Word's Wizards and Templates to Create a Cover Letter and Resume

Case Perspective

Jacqueline Clare Warner will soon be graduating from Jasper University with a Bachelor of Science degree in Computer Education. Because this is her last semester at Jasper University, Jacqueline decides to prepare a resume to send to prospective employers. She wants the resume to look professional while highlighting her education and experience. Once she prepares her resume, Jacqueline's next step is to prepare a personalized cover letter to send to each prospective employer. As she reads through last Sunday's edition of the *Los Angeles Times*, she locates a classified advertisement for a multilingual user training position at L.A. Enterprises, which sounds like a position suited just for her. Jacqueline immediately begins writing a cover letter to Mr. Donald Jameson at L.A. Enterprises. In her cover letter she emphasizes her fluency in a variety of foreign languages, as well as her computer proficiency. As she places her cover letter and resume in the mail, Jacqueline dreams about a career at L.A. Enterprises.

Jacqueline creates her resume using Word's Resume Wizard, a tool designed to assist users in preparing a resume. Then, she composes her cover letter to L.A. Enterprises using a Word letter template, which creates proper business letter formatting for Jacqueline.

Introduction

At some time in your professional life, you will prepare a resume along with a personalized cover letter to send to a prospective employer(s). In addition to some personal information, a **resume** usually contains the applicant's educational background and job experience. Because employers review many resumes for each vacant position, you should carefully design your resume so it presents you as the best candidate for the job. You should attach a personalized cover letter to each resume you send. A **cover letter** enables you to elaborate on positive points in your resume; it also provides you with an opportunity to show the potential employer your written communication skills. Thus, it is important your cover letter be well written and follow proper business letter rules.

Because composing letters and resumes from scratch is a difficult process for many people, Word provides **wizards** and **templates** to assist you in these document preparations. A template is like a blueprint; that is, Word prepares the requested document with text and/or formatting common to all documents of this nature. By asking you several basic questions, Word's wizards prepare and format a document for you based on your responses. Once Word creates a document from a template or a wizard, you then either fill in the blanks or replace prewritten words in the documents.

Project Two – Cover Letter and Resume

Project 2 uses Word to produce the cover letter shown in Figure 2-1 and resume shown in Figure 2-2 on the next page. Jacqueline Clare Warner, an upcoming college graduate, is seeking a full-time position as a multilingual user trainer with a major firm in the California area. In addition to her resume, she would like to send a personalized cover letter to Mr. Donald Jameson at L.A. Enterprises detailing her work experience.

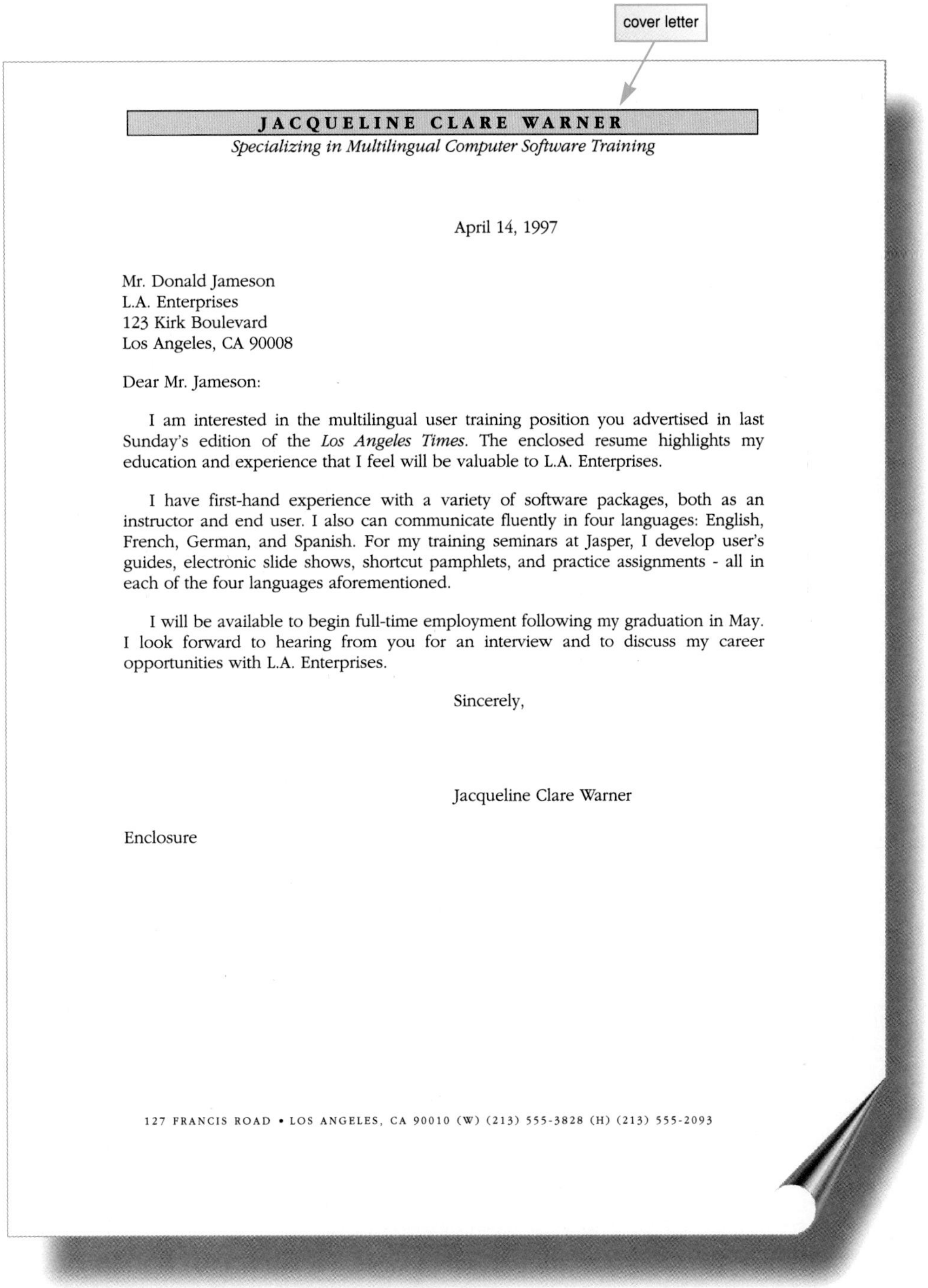

cover letter

JACQUELINE CLARE WARNER
Specializing in Multilingual Computer Software Training

April 14, 1997

Mr. Donald Jameson
L.A. Enterprises
123 Kirk Boulevard
Los Angeles, CA 90008

Dear Mr. Jameson:

I am interested in the multilingual user training position you advertised in last Sunday's edition of the *Los Angeles Times*. The enclosed resume highlights my education and experience that I feel will be valuable to L.A. Enterprises.

I have first-hand experience with a variety of software packages, both as an instructor and end user. I also can communicate fluently in four languages: English, French, German, and Spanish. For my training seminars at Jasper, I develop user's guides, electronic slide shows, shortcut pamphlets, and practice assignments - all in each of the four languages aforementioned.

I will be available to begin full-time employment following my graduation in May. I look forward to hearing from you for an interview and to discuss my career opportunities with L.A. Enterprises.

Sincerely,

Jacqueline Clare Warner

Enclosure

127 FRANCIS ROAD • LOS ANGELES, CA 90010 (W) (213) 555-3828 (H) (213) 555-2093

FIGURE 2-1

Document Preparation Steps

Document preparation steps give you an overview of how the cover letter and resume in Figures 2-1 and 2-2 on pages WD 2.5 and WD 2.6 will be developed. The following tasks will be completed in this project:

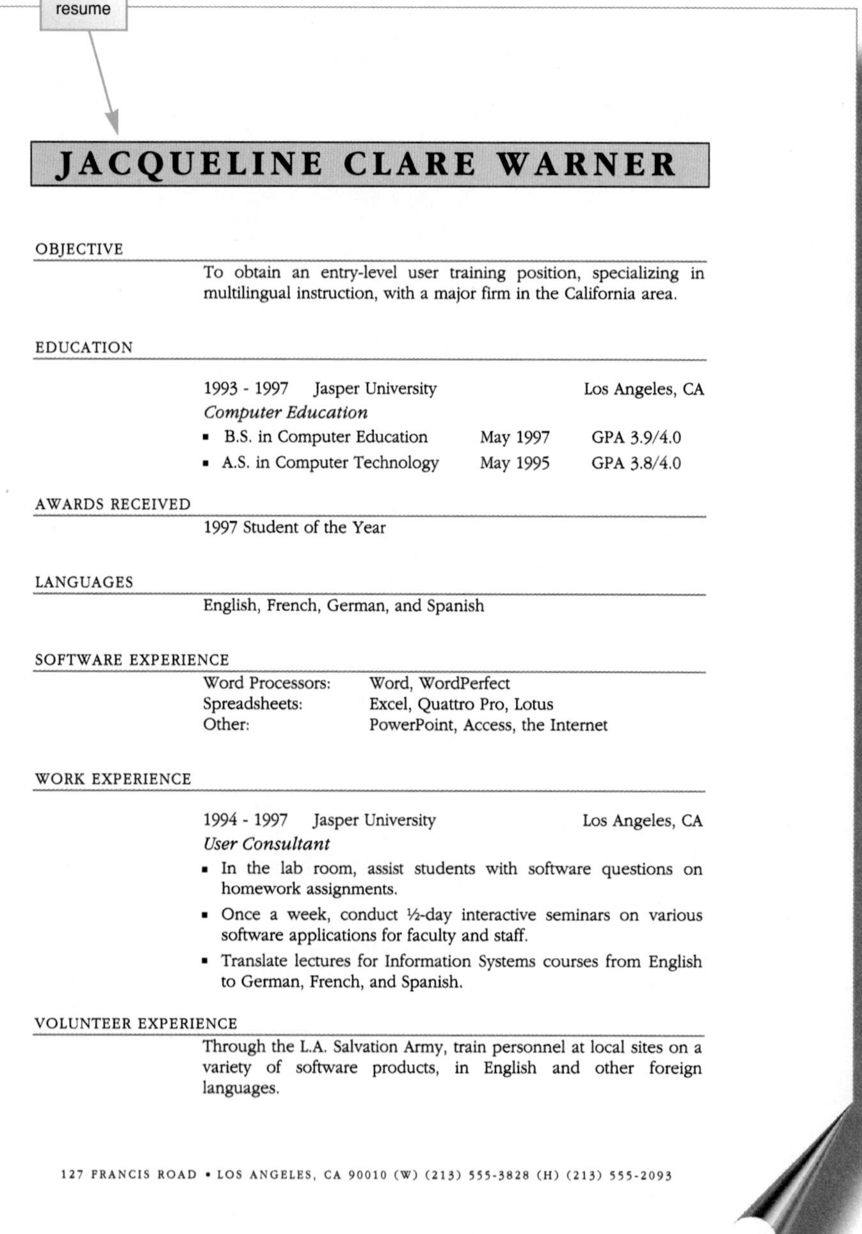

JACQUELINE CLARE WARNER

OBJECTIVE

To obtain an entry-level user training position, specializing in multilingual instruction, with a major firm in the California area.

EDUCATION

1993 - 1997 Jasper University Los Angeles, CA

Computer Education

- B.S. in Computer Education May 1997 GPA 3.9/4.0
- A.S. in Computer Technology May 1995 GPA 3.8/4.0

AWARDS RECEIVED

1997 Student of the Year

LANGUAGES

English, French, German, and Spanish

SOFTWARE EXPERIENCE

Word Processors: Word, WordPerfect
Spreadsheets: Excel, Quattro Pro, Lotus
Other: PowerPoint, Access, the Internet

WORK EXPERIENCE

1994 - 1997 Jasper University Los Angeles, CA

User Consultant

- In the lab room, assist students with software questions on homework assignments.
- Once a week, conduct ½-day interactive seminars on various software applications for faculty and staff.
- Translate lectures for Information Systems courses from English to German, French, and Spanish.

VOLUNTEER EXPERIENCE

Through the L.A. Salvation Army, train personnel at local sites on a variety of software products, in English and other foreign languages.

127 FRANCIS ROAD • LOS ANGELES, CA 90010 (W) (213) 555-3828 (H) (213) 555-2093

FIGURE 2-2

1. Start Word.
2. Use the Resume Wizard to create a resume.
3. Personalize the resume.
4. Spell check and save the resume.
5. Move a paragraph in the resume.
6. Save the resume again.
7. View and print the resume in print preview.
8. Use a letter template to create a cover letter.
9. Create an AutoText entry.
10. Type the cover letter.
11. Change the font size of the characters in the cover letter.
12. Copy the return address line from the resume to the cover letter.
13. Save the cover letter, spell check it, and print it.

The following pages contain a detailed explanation of each of these tasks.

Using Word's Resume Wizard to Create a Resume

You can either type a resume from scratch into a blank document window, or you can use a wizard and let Word format the resume with appropriate headings and spacing. Then, you can customize the resulting resume by filling in the blanks or selecting and replacing text. Follow these steps to create a resume using the Resume Wizard.

To Create a Resume Using Word's Resume Wizard

1 **Click the Start button on the taskbar and then click New Office Document. Click the Other Documents tab if necessary when the New dialog box first opens. Click the Resume Wizard icon.**

Office displays several wizard and template icons in the Other Documents sheet in the New dialog box (Figure 2-3). Icons without the word, Wizard, beneath them are templates. If you click an icon in the Other Documents sheet, a preview of the resulting document displays in the Preview area; thus, the Resume Wizard is selected and a preview of a resume displays in the Preview area.

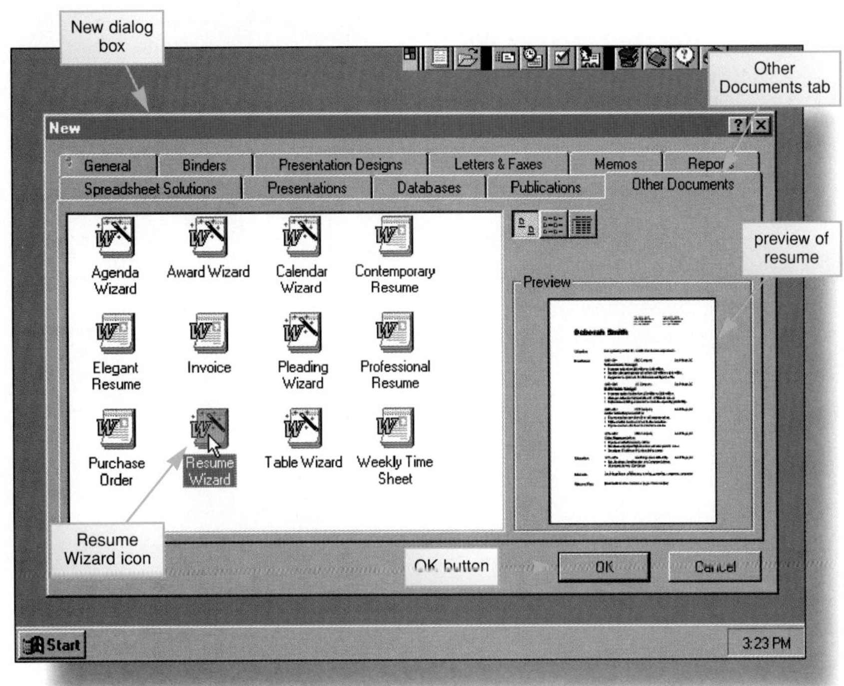

FIGURE 2-3

2 **Click the OK button.**

After a few seconds, Word displays the first of a series of Resume Wizard dialog boxes, asking for the type of resume you want to create (Figure 2-4). Your preview may be different depending on the last resume created. Be sure to read the tip in the wizard dialog boxes for helpful information.

3 **Click the Entry-level resume and then point to the Next button.**

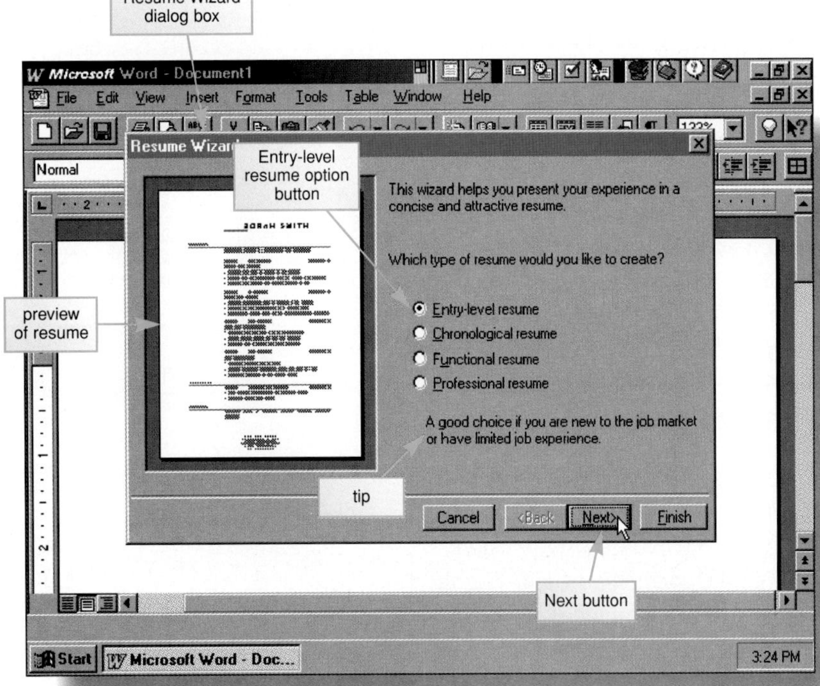

FIGURE 2-4

4 **Click the Next button. When the second Resume Wizard dialog box displays, drag the mouse pointer (I-beam) through the existing name in the Name text box.**

Word displays the next Resume Wizard dialog box (Figure 2-5). The name displayed and selected in your Name text box will be different, depending on the name of the last person using the Resume Wizard.

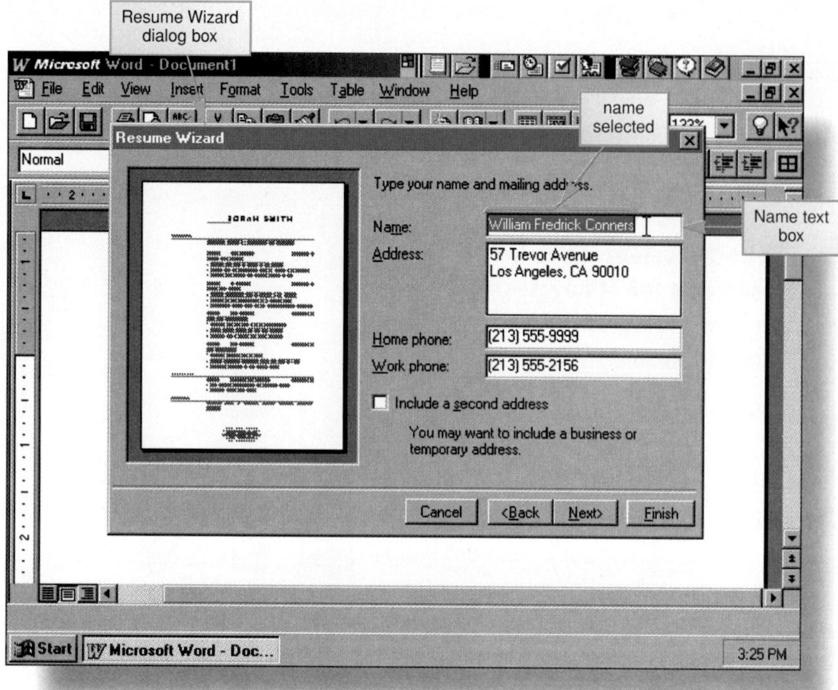

FIGURE 2-5

5 **With the name in the Name text box selected, type** `Jacqueline Clare Warner` **and then press the TAB key to advance to the Address text box. Type** `127 Francis Road` **and then press the ENTER key. Type** `Los Angeles, CA 90010` **and then press the TAB key to advance to the Home phone text box. Type** `(213) 555-2093` **and then press the TAB key to advance to the Work phone text box. Type** `(213) 555-3828` **and then point to the Next button.**

The personal information is entered in the Resume Wizard dialog box (Figure 2-6). Notice as you typed the name, Jacqueline Clare Warner, it automatically replaced the selected text in the Name text box. When you want to replace text in Word, select the text to be removed and then type the desired text.

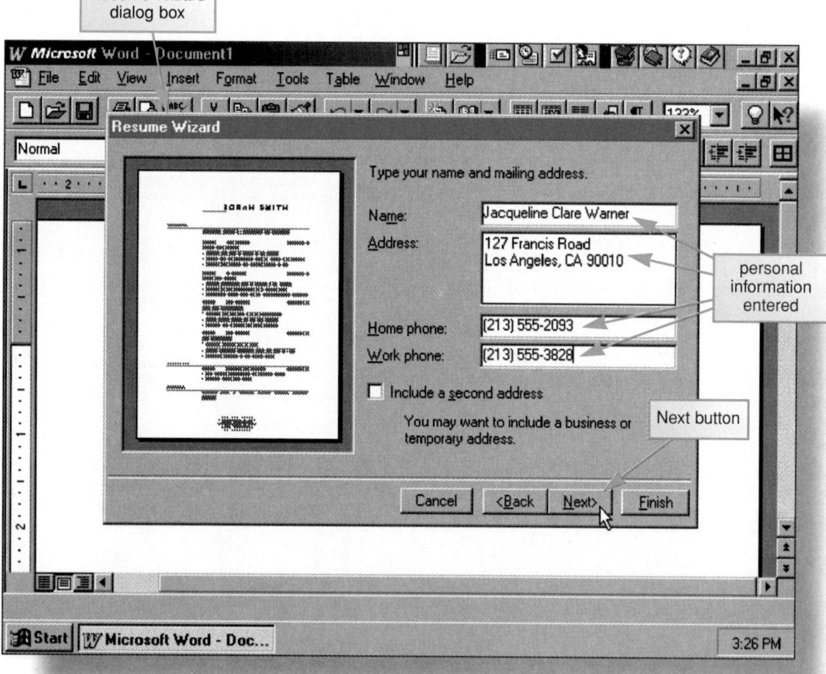

FIGURE 2-6

6 **Click the Next button. When the third Resume Wizard dialog box displays, click Interests and activities, click Hobbies, and then click References. Point to the Next button.**

Word displays the third Resume Wizard dialog box, which requests the headings you want on your resume (Figure 2-7). You want all headings to be on your resume, except for these three: Interests and activities, Hobbies, and References.

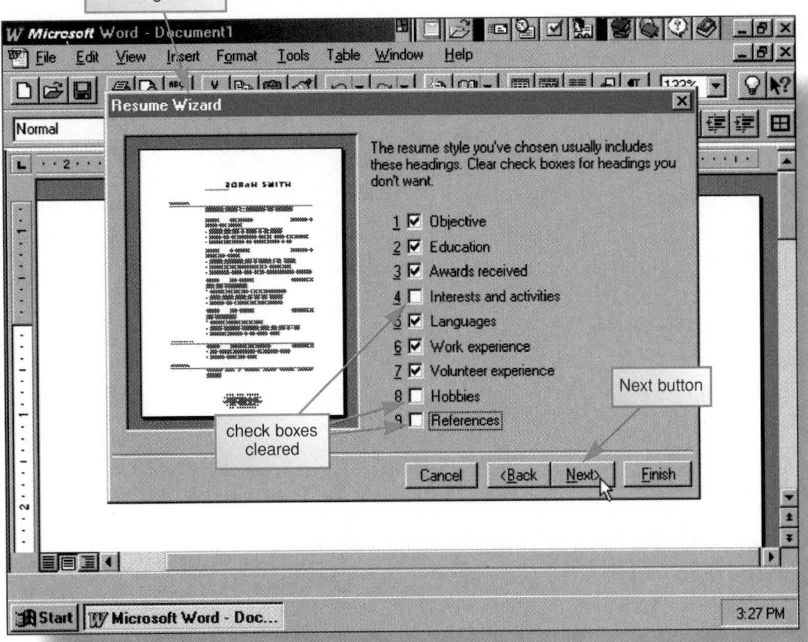

FIGURE 2-7

7 **Click the Next button. Point to the Next button in the fourth Resume Wizard dialog box.**

Word displays the next Resume Wizard dialog box, which allows you to choose additional headings for your resume (Figure 2-8). All of these check boxes should be cleared because you do not want any of these headings on your resume.

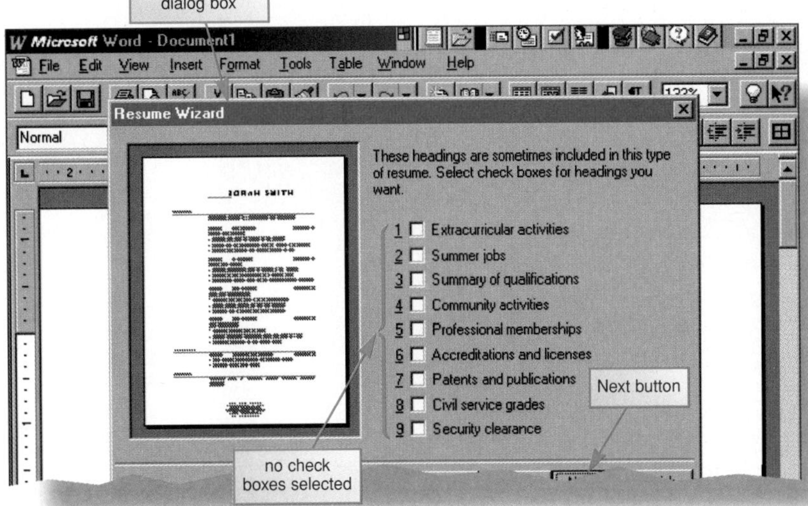

FIGURE 2-8

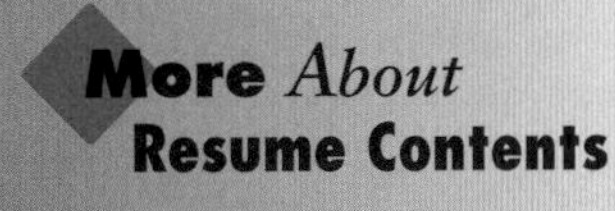

More *About* Resume Contents

Leave the following items off a resume: social security number, marital status, age, height, weight, gender, physical appearance, health, citizenship, references, reference to references, previous pay rates, reasons for leaving a prior job, current date, and high school information (if you are a college graduate).

8 **Click the Next button. When the fifth Resume Wizard dialog box displays, type** `Software experience` **in the additional headings text box. Point to the Add button.**

Word displays the fifth Resume Wizard dialog box, which allows you to enter any additional headings you want on your resume (Figure 2-9).

9 **Click the Add button.**

Word adds the heading you entered into the list of resume headings.

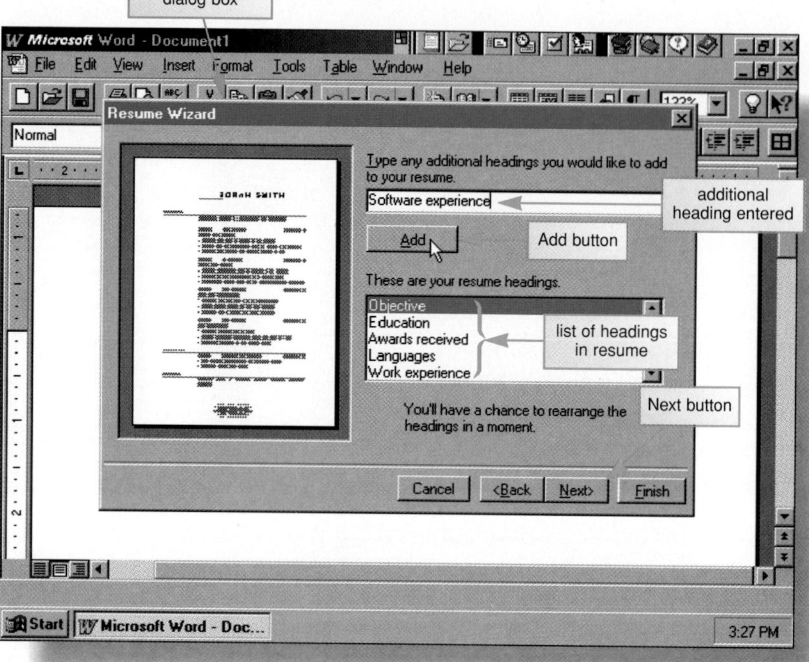

FIGURE 2-9

10 **Click the Next button. When the sixth Resume Wizard dialog box displays, click Software experience and then point to the Move Up button.**

Word displays the sixth Resume Wizard dialog box, which enables you to rearrange the order of the headings on your resume (Figure 2-10). The Software experience heading is selected. You can move any heading up or down by selecting it and clicking the appropriate button (Move Up or Move Down). The headings will display on the resume in the order the names are displayed in this dialog box.

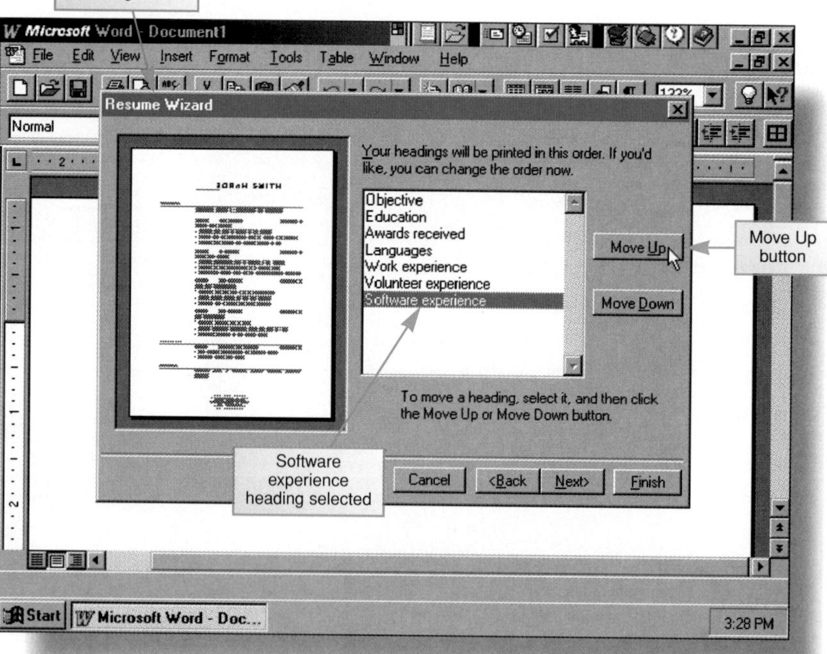

FIGURE 2-10

11 **Click the Move Up button two times and then point to the Next button.**

Word moves the heading, Software experience, up above the Work experience heading (Figure 2-11).

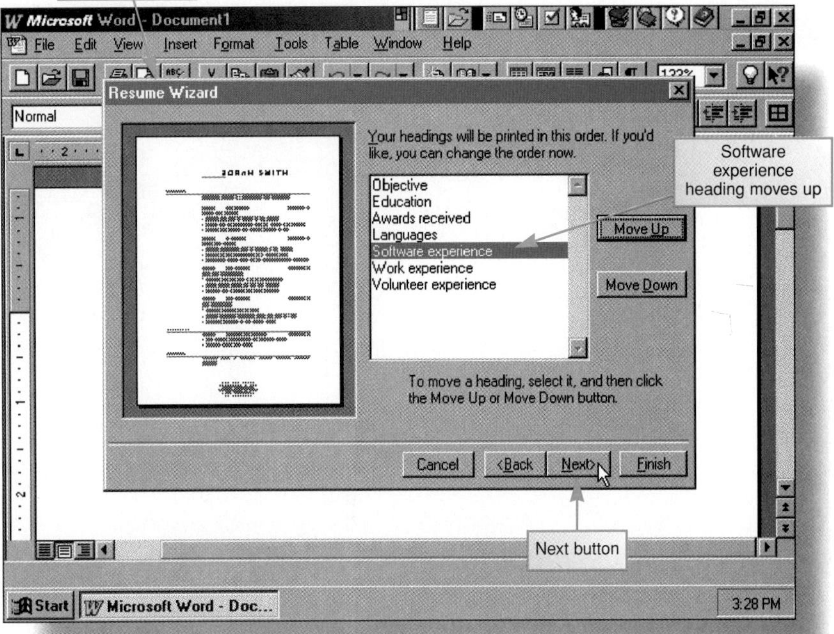

FIGURE 2-11

12 **Click the Next button. When the seventh Resume Wizard dialog box displays, click Elegant and then point to the Next button.**

Word displays the seventh Resume Wizard dialog box, requesting the style of your resume (Figure 2-12). Word provides three styles, or families, of wizards and templates: Professional, Elegant, and Contemporary.

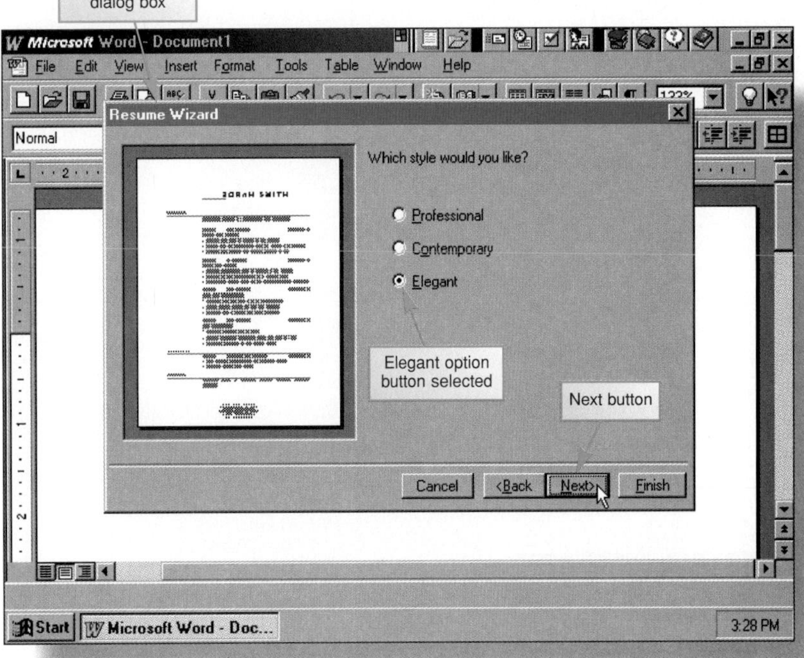

FIGURE 2-12

13 **Click the Next button. When the final Resume Wizard dialog box displays, click Just display the resume and then point to the Finish button.**

Word displays the final Resume Wizard dialog box (Figure 2-13).

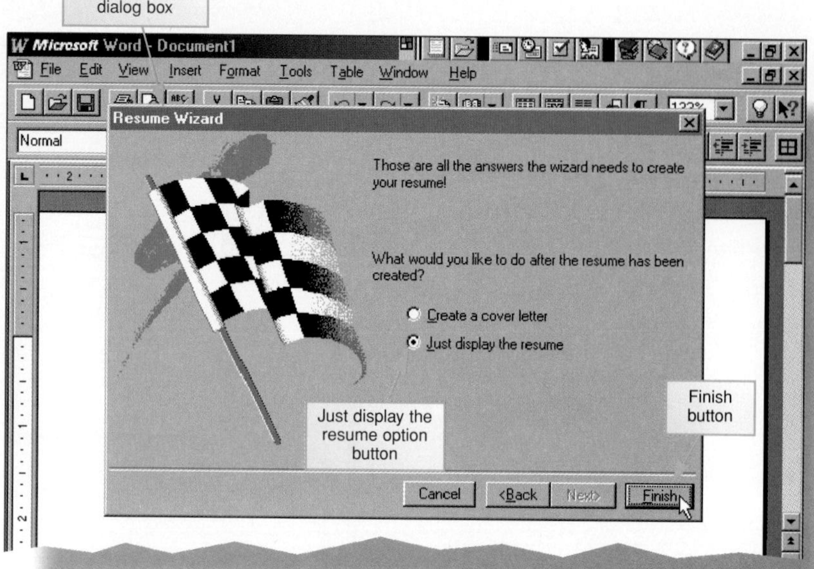

FIGURE 2-13

Click the Finish button.

Word creates an entry-level elegant style resume layout for you (Figure 2-14). You are to personalize the resume as indicated.

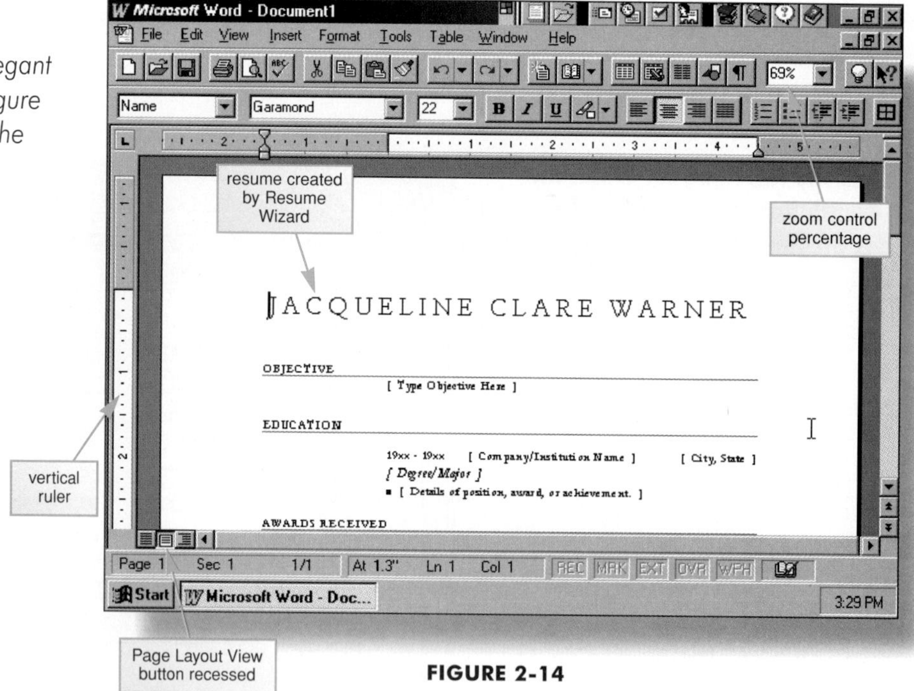

FIGURE 2-14

*Other***Ways**

1. On Microsoft Office Shortcut Bar, click Start a New Document button, click Other Documents tab, double-click Resume Wizard icon
2. On File menu click New, click Other Documents tab, double-click Resume Wizard icon

When you create a resume using the Resume Wizard, you can click the Back button in any Resume Wizard dialog box to change any previous option(s) selected. To exit from the Resume Wizard and return to the document window without creating the resume, click the Cancel button from any Resume Wizard dialog box.

In addition to the Resume Wizard, Word provides nine other wizards to assist you in creating documents: agenda, award, letter, calendar, fax, pleading, memo, table, and newsletter.

When Word displays the resume in the document window, it switches from **normal view** to **page layout view**. The announcement you created in Project 1 was in normal view. In both normal and page layout views, you can type and edit text. The difference is that page layout view shows you exactly how the printed page will look.

You can tell you are in page layout view by looking at the Word screen (Figure 2-14). Notice in page layout view, the Page Layout View button at the bottom of the Word screen is recessed. Also notice a vertical ruler now displays at the left edge of the document window in addition to the horizontal ruler at the top of the window. In page layout view, the entire piece of paper is positioned in the document window, showing precisely the positioning of the text and margins in the printed page.

To see the entire resume created by the Resume Wizard, you should print the resume.

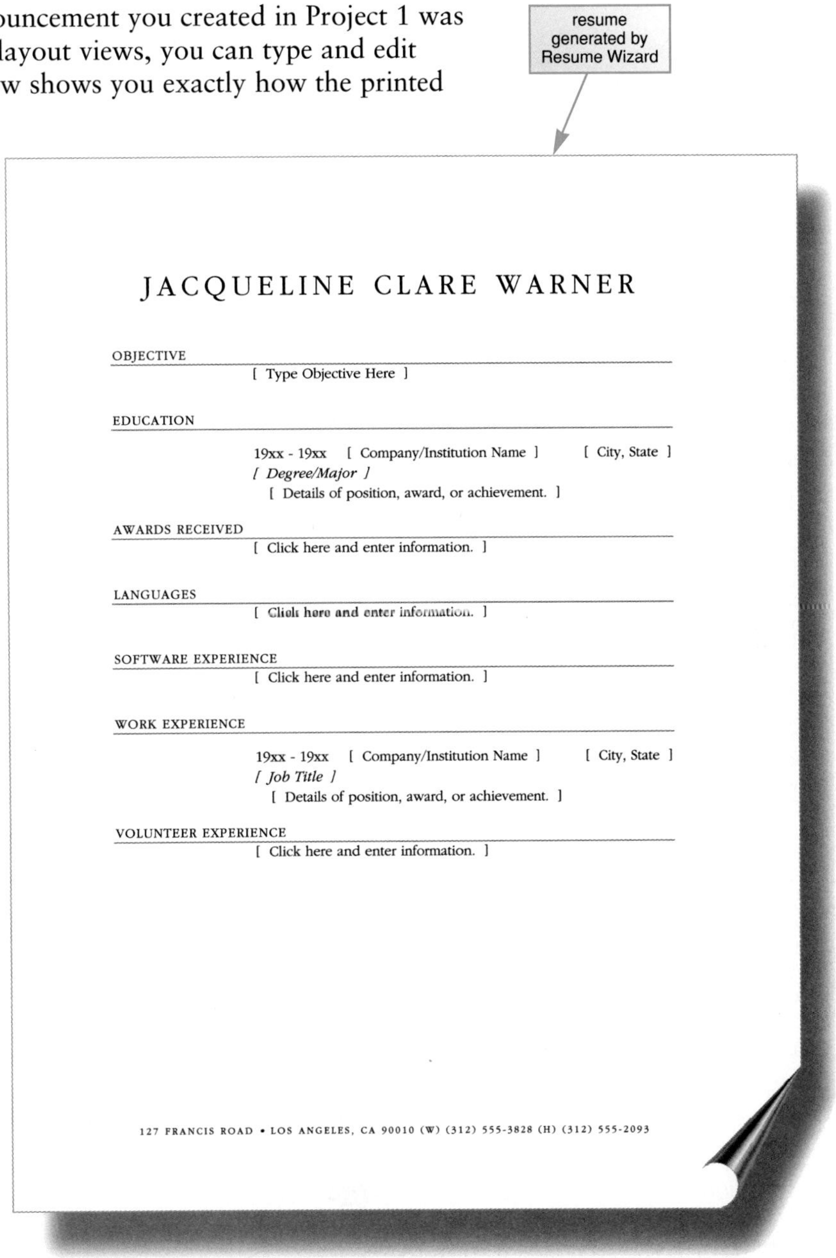

JACQUELINE CLARE WARNER

OBJECTIVE
[Type Objective Here]

EDUCATION
19xx - 19xx [Company/Institution Name] [City, State]
[Degree/Major]
[Details of position, award, or achievement.]

AWARDS RECEIVED
[Click here and enter information.]

LANGUAGES
[Click here and enter information.]

SOFTWARE EXPERIENCE
[Click here and enter information.]

WORK EXPERIENCE
19xx - 19xx [Company/Institution Name] [City, State]
[Job Title]
[Details of position, award, or achievement.]

VOLUNTEER EXPERIENCE
[Click here and enter information.]

127 FRANCIS ROAD • LOS ANGELES, CA 90010 (W) (312) 555-3828 (H) (312) 555-2093

FIGURE 2-15

TO PRINT THE RESUME CREATED BY THE RESUME WIZARD

Step 1: Ready the printer.
Step 2: Click the Print button on the Standard toolbar.
Step 3: When the printer stops, retrieve the hard copy of the resume from the printer.

The printed resume is shown in Figure 2-15.

Personalizing the Resume

The next step is to personalize the resume. First, you add emphasis and professionalism to the name at the top of the resume. Then, where Word has indicated, you type the objective, education, awards received, languages, software experience, work experience, and volunteer experience below their respective headings. In the EDUCATION and WORK EXPERIENCE sections, you select and replace text to customize these sections. The following pages show how to personalize the resume generated by the Resume Wizard.

More About a Resume

Think of your resume as an advertisement about you. A good advertisement (and resume) doesn't tout negatives; instead, it promotes positives. A resume should be accurate and truthful. It should also be up to date and customized for each job advertisement. List qualifications from most relevant to least, and be concise.

Zooming a Document on the Screen

The document displayed in Figure 2-14 on page WD 2.12 is very small, making the characters and words difficult to read. In Figure 2-14, the document displays at 69% of its normal size. Depending on your settings, your magnification percentage may be different from that shown in Figure 2-14. To make the displayed characters larger or smaller on the screen, you change the zoom control percentage as shown in the following steps.

To Zoom a Document

1. Click the Zoom Control box arrow on the Standard toolbar and then point to 75%.

A list of magnification percentages displays (Figure 2-16). Any number greater than the current percentage will increase the size of the characters on the screen, and any number smaller will decrease the size of the characters on the screen.

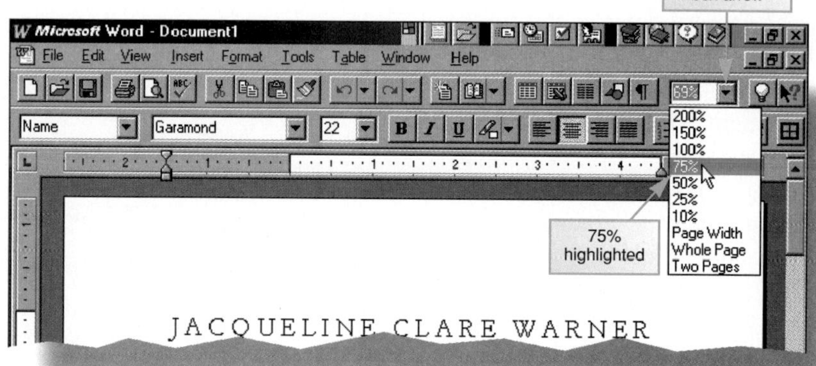

FIGURE 2-16

2. Click 75%.

The characters in the document window increase from 69% of their normal size to 75% (Figure 2-17). Notice the characters are now easier to read. The larger the magnification, the easier the characters are to read.

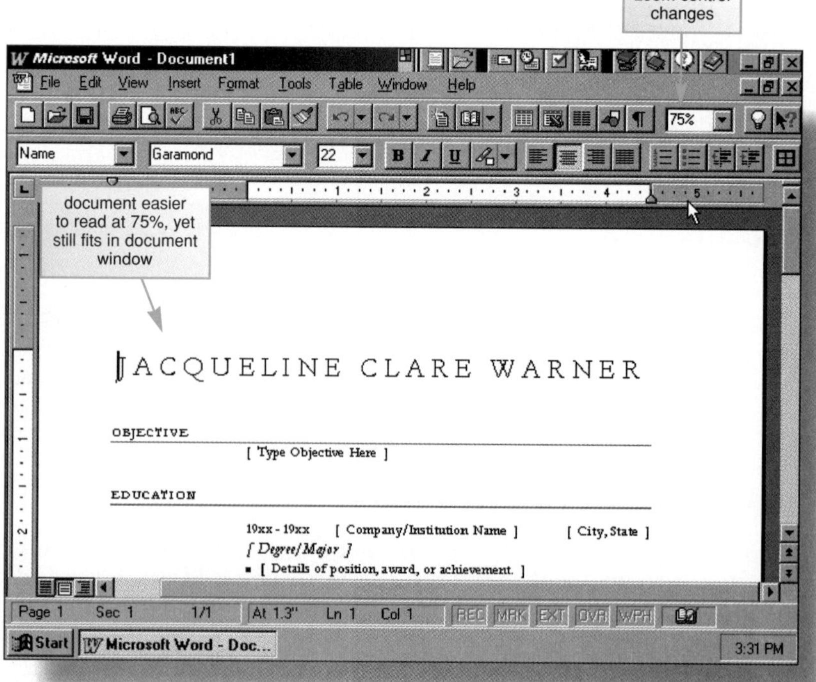

FIGURE 2-17

Other Ways

1. On View menu click Zoom, select desired zoom percentage, click OK button

Displaying Nonprinting Characters

As discussed in Project 1, it is helpful to display the nonprinting characters that indicate where in the document you press the ENTER key and SPACEBAR. Follow this step to display nonprinting characters.

TO DISPLAY NONPRINTING CHARACTERS

Step 1: Click the Show/Hide ¶ button on the Standard toolbar.

Word displays the nonprinting characters in the document window, and the Show/Hide ¶ button on the Standard toolbar is recessed (Figure 2-18 below).

Emphasizing the Name

The first line of the resume is the name. To add emphasis to the name, you want to bold it. To do this, you must select the name and then click the Bold button on the Standard toolbar as described in the following steps.

TO BOLD A LINE

Step 1: Click to the left of the name to select it.
Step 2: Click the Bold button on the Standard toolbar.
Step 3: Click inside the selection to remove the highlight.

Word bolds the characters in the name at the top of the resume (Figure 2-18).

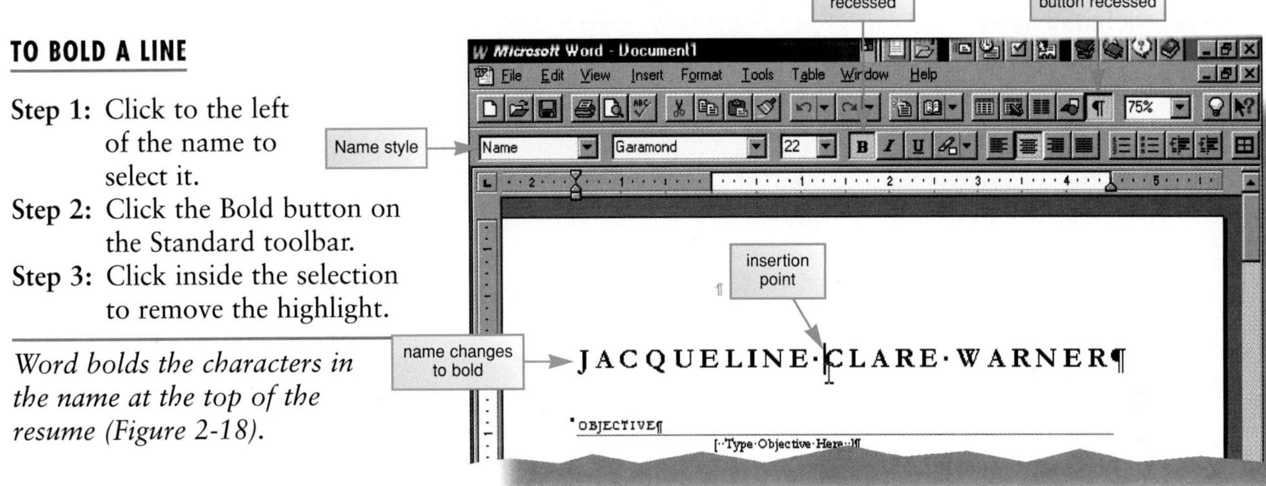

FIGURE 2-18

Styles

When you use a wizard to create a document, Word formats the document using styles. A **style** is a customized format applied to characters or paragraphs. The Style box displays the name of the style associated to the location of the insertion point. You can identify many of the characteristics assigned with a style by looking at the Formatting toolbar. In Figure 2-18, the insertion point is in a paragraph formatted with the Name style, which uses the Garamond font in 22 point for the characters and centers the paragraph.

If you click the Style box arrow on the Formatting toolbar, the list of styles associated with the current document display. Paragraph styles affect an entire paragraph; whereas, character styles affect only selected characters. In the Style list, **paragraph style** names are preceded by a document icon, which looks like a proofreader's paragraph mark (¶), and **character style** names are preceded by a document page icon, which contains the letter a.

You can change a style applied to text. You also may select the appropriate style from the Style list before entering the text so the text you type will be formatted according to the selected style. Later in this project, you will change a style.

More About Borders

If you want to add a shadowed or colored box border, you cannot use the Borders toolbar. Click Format on the menu bar and then click Borders and Shading. To add a shadow, click Shadow in the Presets area. To add color, click the Color box arrow, click the desired color and then click the OK button.

Adding a Border and Shading to a Paragraph

To add more professionalism to the name, you should draw a solid line, called a **border** in Word, around the name. You can add a border, also called a **rule** or **ruling line**, to any edge of a paragraph. That is, borders may be added above or below a paragraph, to the left or right of a paragraph, or any combination of these sides. You add borders by clicking the Borders button on the Formatting toolbar. When you click the Borders button, a **Borders toolbar** displays beneath the Formatting toolbar and the Borders button is recessed. Through the Borders toolbar, you can also shade the interior of a paragraph; the shading intensity can vary from very light to extremely dark. Add light shading inside a border surrounding the name in the resume as shown in the following steps.

Steps To Border and Shade a Paragraph

1 With the insertion point somewhere in the name paragraph, point to the Borders button on the Formatting toolbar (Figure 2-19).

Because a border is placed on the current paragraph, it is important to position the insertion point in the correct paragraph.

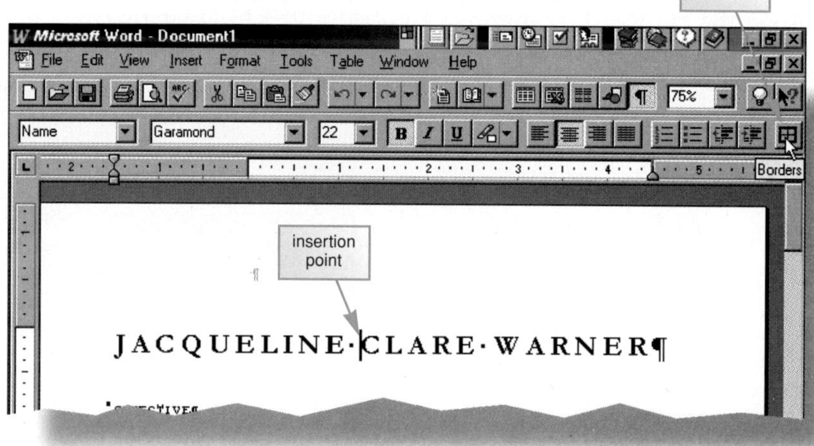

FIGURE 2-19

2 If the Borders button on your Formatting toolbar is not already recessed, click it to display the Borders toolbar.

Word displays the Borders toolbar beneath the Formatting toolbar (Figure 2-20). The Borders button on the Formatting toolbar is recessed.

3 Point to the Outside Border button on the Borders toolbar.

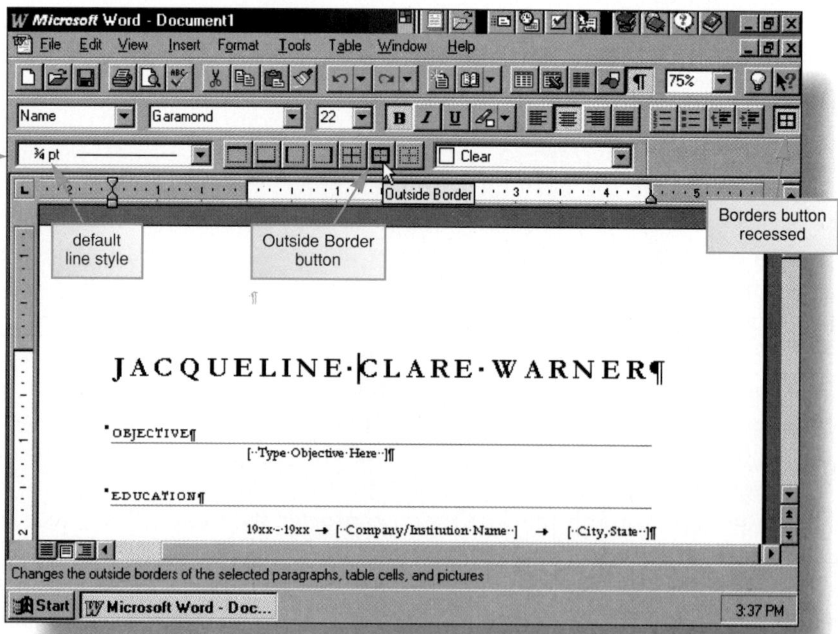

FIGURE 2-20

4 Click the Outside Border button on the Borders toolbar.

Word places a ¾ pt line style around the name paragraph (Figure 2-21). A line surrounding all edges of a paragraph is called a **box border**. *Notice that Word recesses four buttons (Top Border, Bottom Border, Left Border, and Right Border) on the Borders toolbar when you click the Outside Border button. This way, you can remove individual edges of the box border by clicking the appropriate button.*

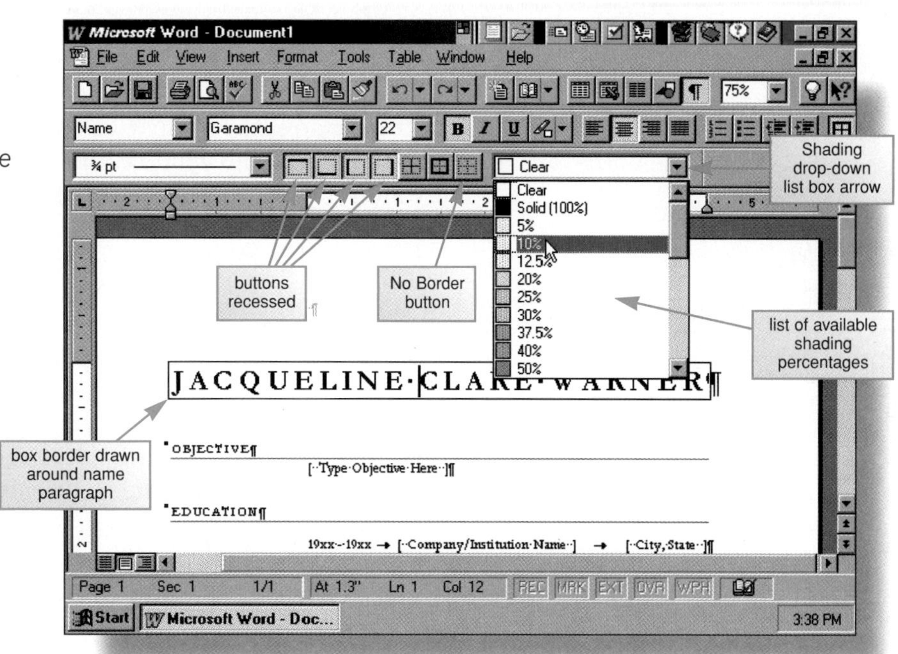

FIGURE 2-21

5 Click the Shading box arrow and then point to 10%.

Word displays a list of available shading percentages. You may choose from no shading to completely solid shading or a shading intensity somewhere between these extremes.

6 Click 10% and then click the Borders button on the Formatting toolbar.

Word darkens the inside of the box border using a shading intensity of 10% (Figure 2-22). Word removes the Borders toolbar from the Word screen, and the Borders button on the Formatting toolbar is no longer recessed.

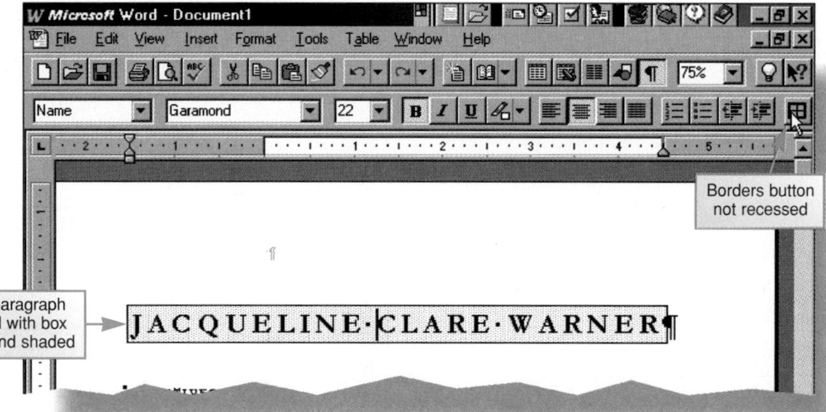

FIGURE 2-22

OtherWays

1. On Format menu click Borders and Shading, click Borders tab, select appropriate options, click Shading tab, select appropriate options, click OK button

You can add a border to any edge of a paragraph by clicking the appropriate button on the Borders toolbar. For example, to add a border to the left edge of a paragraph, position the insertion point somewhere in the paragraph and then click the Left Border button. To remove a border from a paragraph, position the insertion point somewhere in the paragraph and then click the No Border button on the Borders toolbar (Figure 2-21 above).

More *About* **Toolbars**

If you right-click any toolbar on the Word screen, a shortcut menu listing all possible Word toolbars displays. Click the desired toolbar to display it. If the buttons on a toolbar have been changed, you can restore a toolbar by clicking View on the menu bar, clicking Toolbars, clicking the toolbar name, and then clicking the Reset button.

The Borders toolbar is initially **docked**, or anchored, beneath the Formatting toolbar. You can, however, move this toolbar by pointing between two buttons or boxes on the toolbar and then dragging it to the desired location. If you drag it to an edge of the window, the toolbar will snap to the edge of the window. If you drag it to the middle of the window, the toolbar will display as a window within the Word window, called a **floating toolbar**. To dock a floating toolbar, double-click its title bar.

Selecting and Replacing Text

The next step in personalizing the resume is to select the placeholder text that the Resume Wizard placed into the resume and replace it with the personal information. The first heading on the resume is the OBJECTIVE. You enter the objective where the Resume Wizard placed the words, Type Objective Here, which is called the **placeholder text**. To do this, click the placeholder text, Type Objective Here, to select it. Then, you type the objective. As soon as you begin typing, the selected placeholder text is deleted; thus, you do not have to delete the selection before you begin typing. Follow these steps to enter the objective into the resume.

Steps To Select and Replace Resume Wizard Placeholder Text

1 Click the placeholder text, Type Objective Here.

Word highlights the placeholder text in the resume (Figure 2-23). Notice the new style is Objective in the Style box. The Objective style uses the 11-point Garamond font for characters and justified alignment for paragraphs, which explains why the Justify button on the Formatting toolbar is recessed, instead of the Align Left button. Justified paragraphs look like newspaper print; that is, they are flush on both the right and left edges.

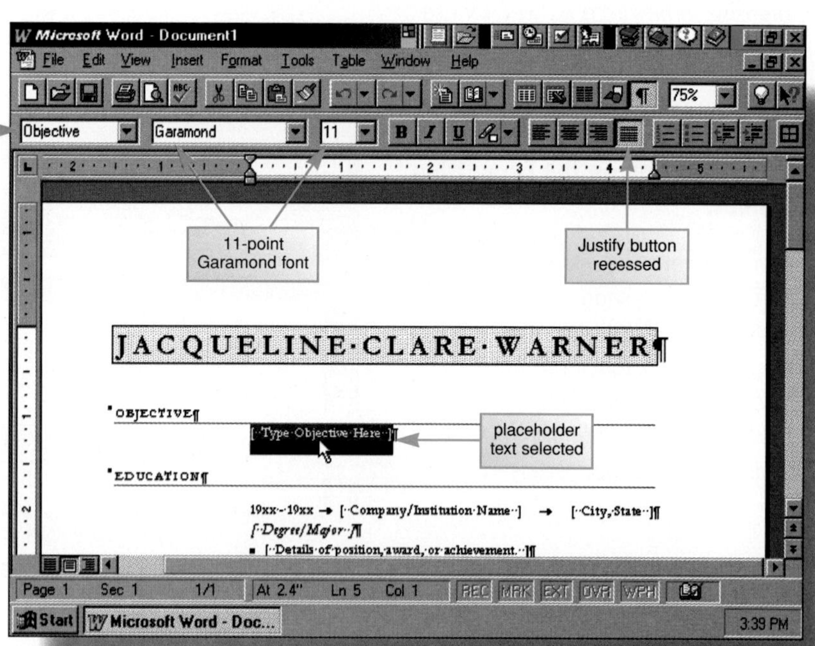

FIGURE 2-23

2 **Type** `To obtain an entry-level user training position, specializing in multilingual instruction, with a major firm in the California area.`

Word replaces the highlighted placeholder text, Type Objective Here, with the objective you type (Figure 2-24). Notice the extra white space between the words in your objective. Because justified alignment requires that the right-most character on the line ends exactly at the right margin, Word places white space between words within the line. Your document may wordwrap on a different word depending on the type of printer you are using.

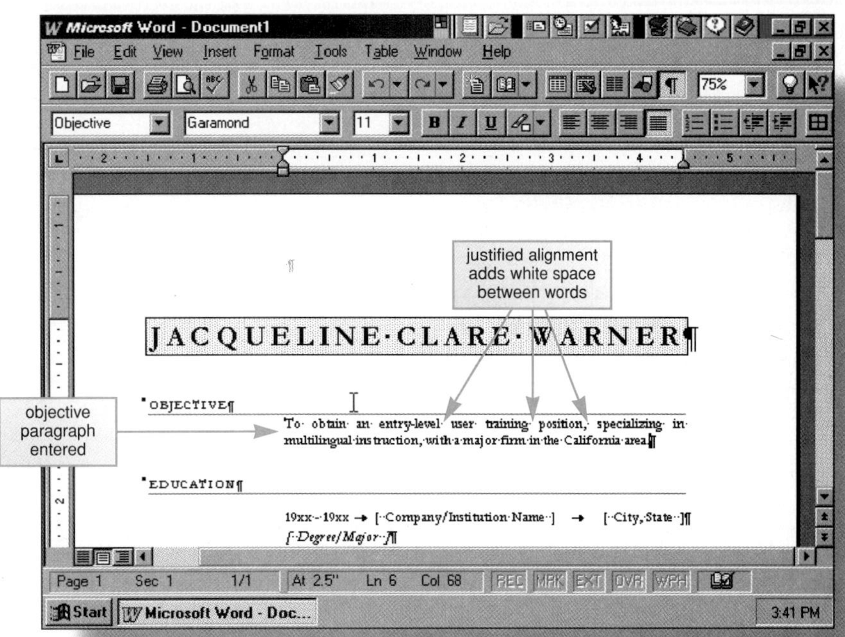

FIGURE 2-24

The next step in personalizing the resume is to replace the Wizard's words and phrases in the EDUCATION section of the resume with your own words and phrases as shown in the following steps.

Steps To Select and Replace Resume Wizard Supplied Text

1 **Scroll down, if necessary, to display the entire EDUCATION section of the resume. Drag through the xx in the first 19xx beneath the EDUCATION heading.**

Word selects the xx in the first year (Figure 2-25).

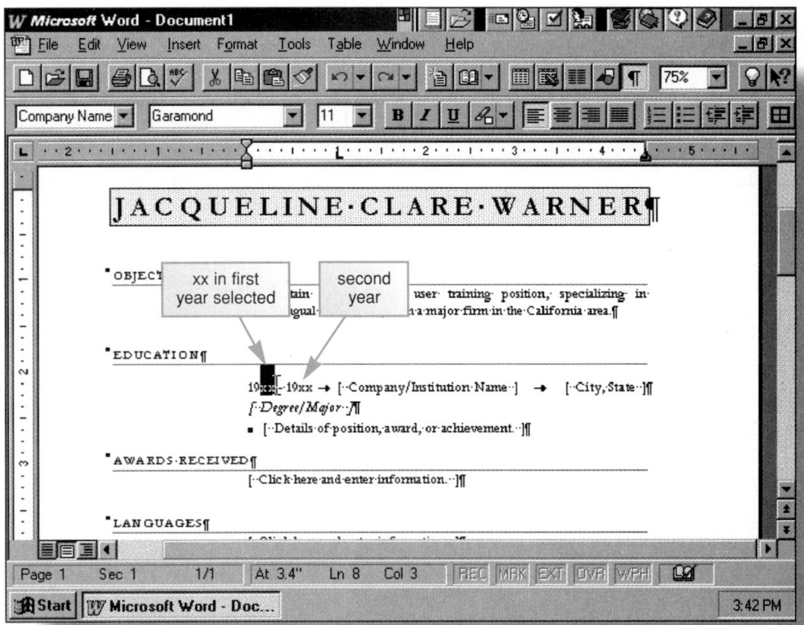

FIGURE 2-25

2 **Type** 93 **and then drag through the xx in the second year beneath the EDUCATION heading. Type** 97 **and then click the placeholder text, Company/Institution Name.**

Word highlights the placeholder text, Company/Institution Name (Figure 2-26). Notice the years now display as 1993 - 1997 below the EDUCATION heading.

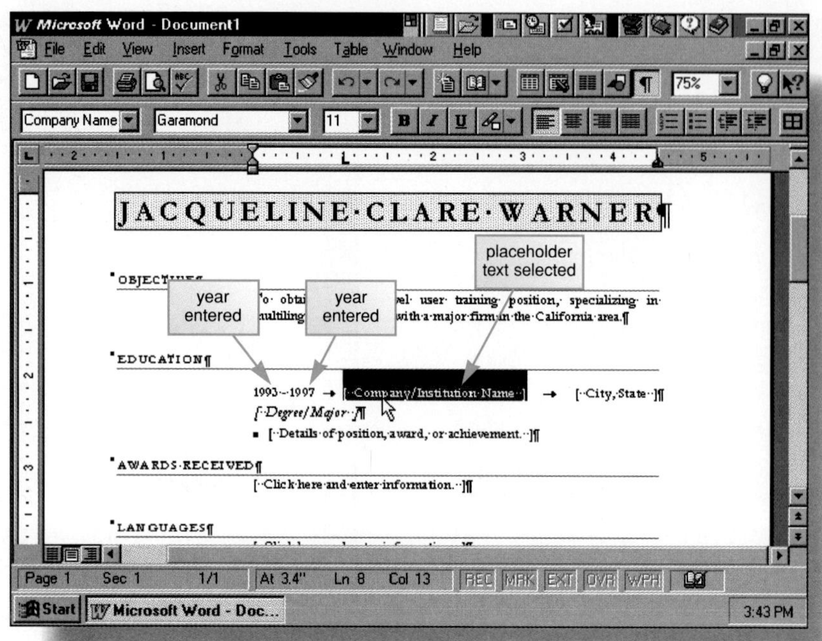

FIGURE 2-26

3 **Type** Jasper University **and then click the placeholder text, City, State. Type** Los Angeles, CA **and then click the placeholder text, *Degree/Major*. Type** Computer Education **as the degree name.**

The university name, city, state and major are entered (Figure 2-27).

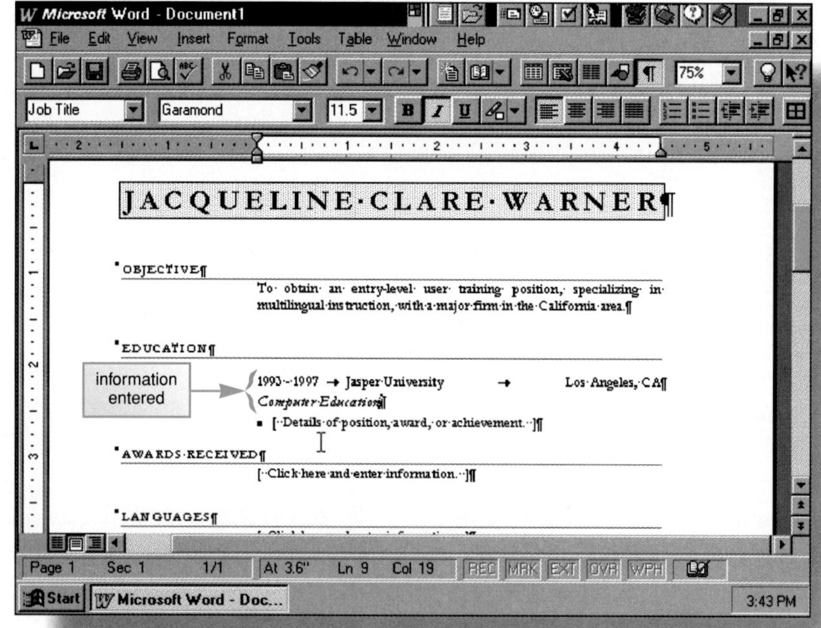

FIGURE 2-27

Using the TAB Key

The next step is to enter the degrees you obtained beneath the university name. Notice in Figure 2-28 the degree award dates and grade point averages are vertically aligned. That is, the M in May 1997 is directly above the M in May 1995, and the Gs in GPA are directly above each other. You press the TAB key to vertically align text in a document.

Word presets tab stops at every one-half inch. These preset, or **default**, tabs are indicated on the horizontal ruler by small tick marks (Figure 2-28). Perform the following steps to vertically align information with the TAB key.

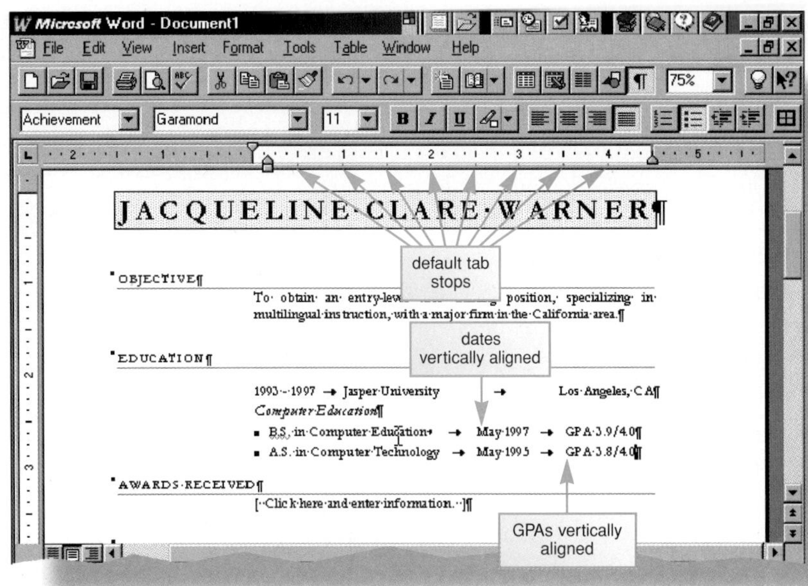

FIGURE 2-28

Steps To Vertically Align Information with the TAB Key

1. **Click the placeholder text, Details of position, award, or achievement., beneath the degree name. Type** `B.S. in Computer Education` **and then press the TAB key twice.**

   Word replaces the placeholder text beneath major and the insertion point moves two tab stops to the right (Figure 2-29). Thus, the degree date is entered at the fifth tab stop. Notice the **right-pointing arrows** *between the degree name and date. A nonprinting character, the right-pointing arrow, displays each time you press the TAB key. Recall nonprinting characters do not print; they only display in the document window. Also notice the red wavy line beneath the characters, B.S., which indicates this word is not in Word's dictionary. Recall that when you spell check the document, any red wavy lines in your document disappear.*

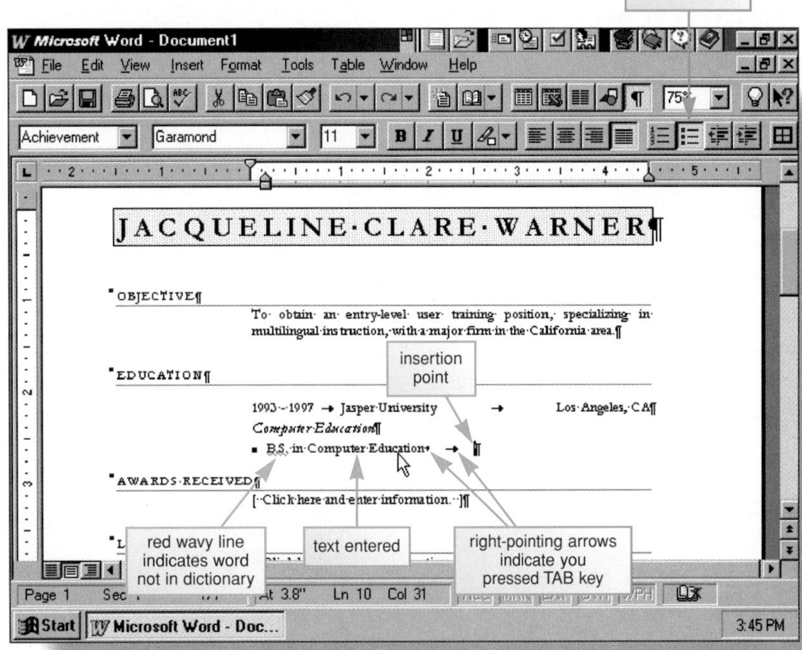

FIGURE 2-29

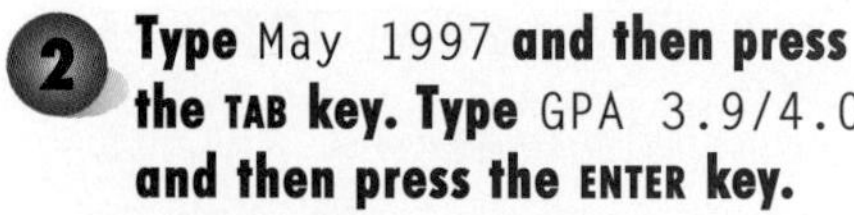

2 **Type** May 1997 **and then press the TAB key. Type** GPA 3.9/4.0 **and then press the ENTER key.**

The first degree is entered (Figure 2-30). The year is aligned slightly to the right of the 2.5-inch mark on the ruler, and the GPA is aligned slightly to the right of the 3.5-inch mark. The bullet character at the beginning of the degree line causes the text to be aligned slightly to the right of the tab stops on the ruler.

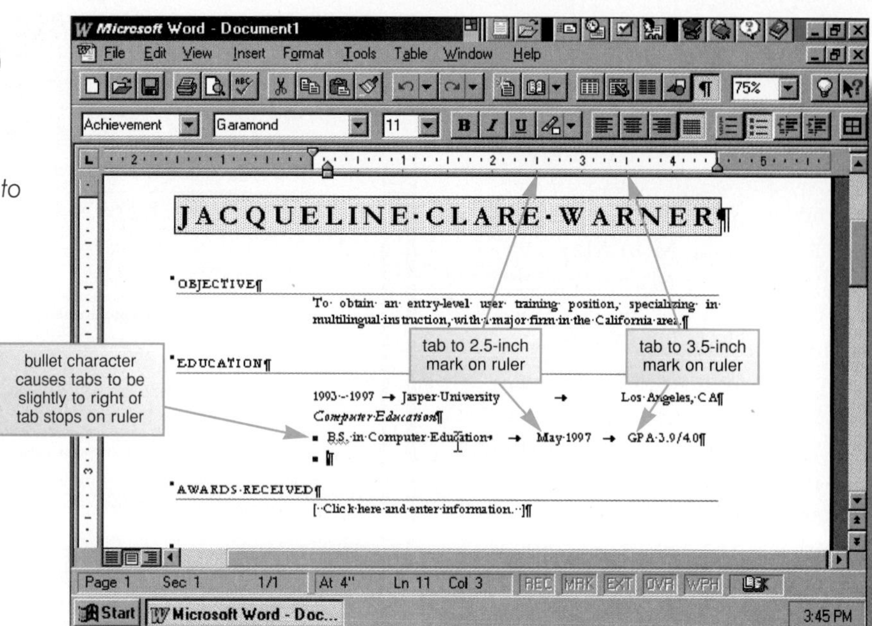

FIGURE 2-30

3 **Type** A.S. in Computer Technology **and then press the TAB key. Type** May 1995 **and then press the TAB key. Type** GPA 3.8/4.0 **as the grade point average.**

The EDUCATION section of the resume is complete (Figure 2-31). The text in the degrees awarded area is vertically aligned. Depending on your printer driver, you may need to press the TAB key additional times to vertically align the text.

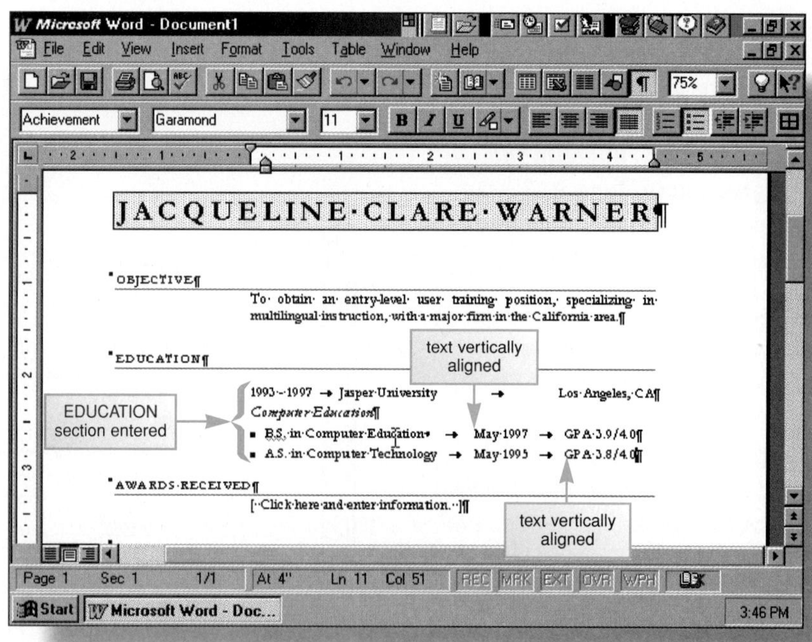

FIGURE 2-31

More *About* Aligning Text

You may be tempted to vertically align text by pressing the SPACEBAR. The problem is that word processors use variable character fonts; that is, the letter w takes up more space than the letter l. Thus, when you use the SPACEBAR to vertically align text, the column has a wavy look because each character does not begin at the same location.

The next step is to enter the details beneath the AWARDS RECEIVED and LANGUAGES headings on the resume as described on the next page.

TO ENTER THE AWARDS RECEIVED AND LANGUAGES SECTIONS

Step 1: Scroll down, if necessary, to display the AWARDS RECEIVED and LANGUAGES sections of the resume.

Step 2: Beneath the AWARDS RECEIVED heading, click the placeholder text, Click here and enter information., to select it.

Step 3: Type `1997 Student of the Year` as the award.

Step 4: Beneath the LANGUAGES heading, click the placeholder text, Click here and enter information., to select it.

Step 5: Type `English, French, German, and Spanish` as the languages.

The AWARDS RECEIVED and LANGUAGES sections are complete (Figure 2-32).

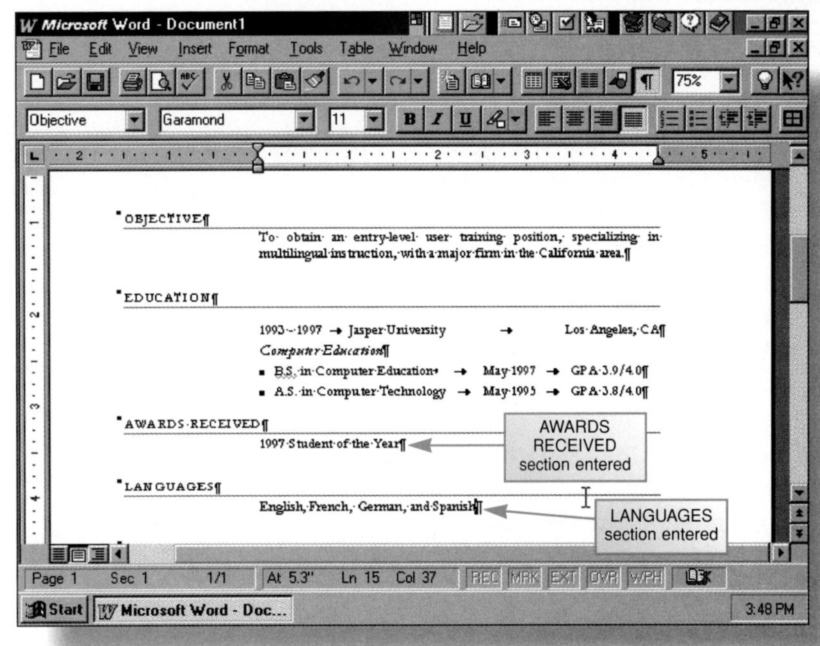

FIGURE 2-32

Entering a Line Break

The next step in personalizing the resume is to enter the SOFTWARE EXPERIENCE section. Because you want the software package names vertically aligned, you will use the TAB key to align this information vertically.

The style used for the paragraphs and characters in the SOFTWARE EXPERIENCE section is the same as for the OBJECTIVE section; that is, 11-point Garamond characters with paragraphs justified. You want the paragraphs to be left-aligned, instead of justified; thus, you change the paragraph alignment for the software experience paragraphs. The Objective style also indicates that when you press the ENTER key, the insertion point advances downward at least 11 points, which leaves nearly an entire blank line between each paragraph. Because you want the lines within the SOFTWARE EXPERIENCE section to be close to each other, you will not press the ENTER key between each type of software product. Instead, you will create a **line break**, which advances the insertion point to the beginning of the next line—ignoring any paragraph formatting instructions. Follow the steps on the next page to enter the SOFTWARE EXPERIENCE section using a line break, instead of a paragraph break.

More *About* Tab Stops

To set your own custom tab stop, position the mouse pointer in the paragraph to contain the tab and then click the ruler at the desired tab stop location. To move a custom tab stop, drag it to the left or right along the ruler. To remove a custom tab stop, drag the tab stop marker down and out of the ruler.

To Enter a Line Break

Scroll down, if necessary, to display the SOFTWARE EXPERIENCE section of the resume. Beneath the SOFTWARE EXPERIENCE heading, click the placeholder text, Click here and enter information. Click the Align Left button on the Formatting toolbar. Type `Word Processors:` **and then press the TAB key. Type** `Word, WordPerfect` **and then press SHIFT+ENTER.**

Word inserts a line break character after the software product names and moves the insertion point to the beginning of the next line (Figure 2-33). Because the ENTER key would create a new paragraph and advance the insertion point down nearly two lines due to the paragraph formatting created by the Resume Wizard, you do not want to create a new paragraph. Thus, you enter a line break to start a new line. The line break character also is a nonprinting character that displays on the screen each time you create a line break.

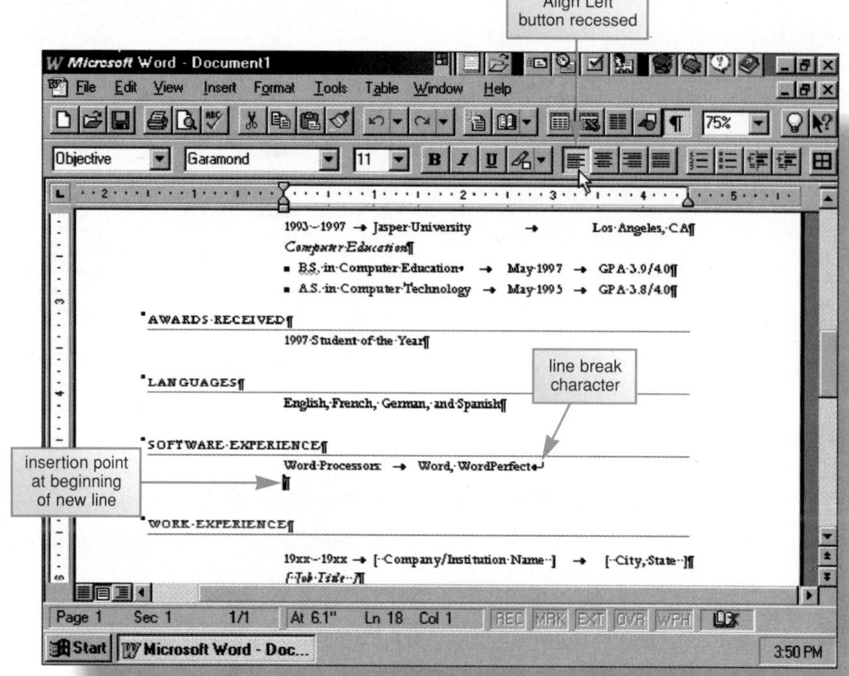

FIGURE 2-33

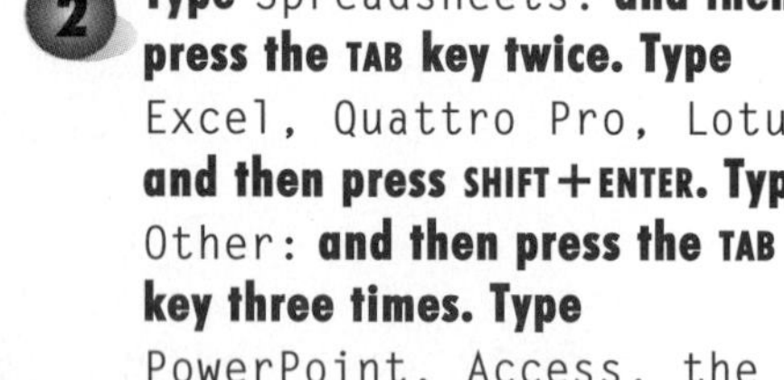

Type `Spreadsheets:` **and then press the TAB key twice. Type** `Excel, Quattro Pro, Lotus` **and then press SHIFT+ENTER. Type** `Other:` **and then press the TAB key three times. Type** `PowerPoint, Access, the Internet` **as the other software products.**

The SOFTWARE EXPERIENCE section is entered (Figure 2-34). Notice the software products are vertically aligned. Also notice the only paragraph mark in the entire section is at the end of the other software products line because you used line breaks, instead of paragraph breaks.

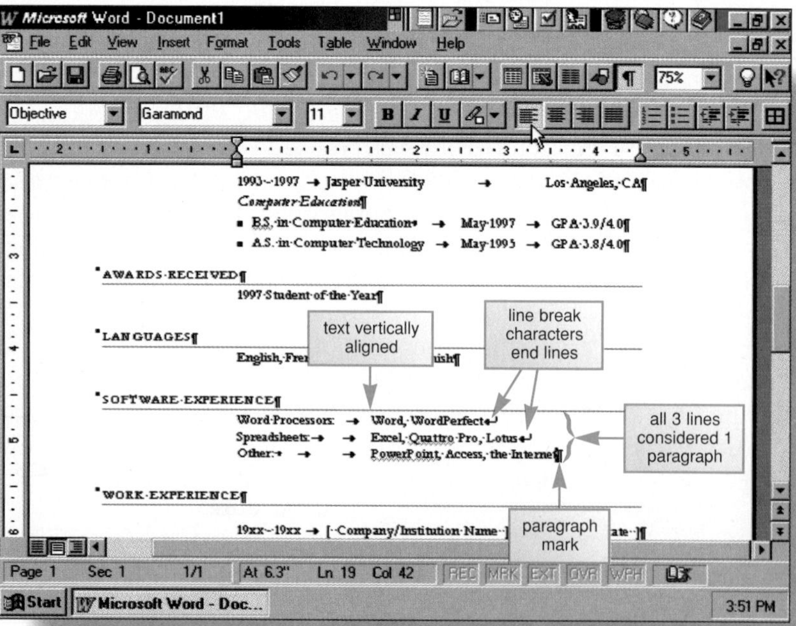

FIGURE 2-34

AutoFormatting As You Type

As you type text into a document, Word automatically formats it for you. Table 2-1 summarizes the types of AutoFormats available and their results.

In the WORK EXPERIENCE section of the resume you enter a fraction as 1/2 and then Word converts it to ½ as shown in the following steps.

Table 2-1

IF YOU TYPE ...	WORD WILL ...	EXAMPLE
a number followed by a period, hyphen, or right parenthesis and then a space or tab followed by text	create a numbered list when you press the ENTER key	1. Numbered lists 2. are easy to 3. create with Word.
an asterisk, hyphen, or dash and then a space or tab followed by text	create a bulleted list when you press the ENTER key	·Bulleted lists ·make items ·stand out.
three underscores, equal signs, or dashes and then a paragraph	create a border above the paragraph	Underscores are converted to a thick line.
a fraction and then a space or hyphen	convert the entry to fraction-like notation	½
an ordinal and then a space or hyphen	make the ordinal a superscript	2nd

Steps To Use Word's AutoFormat As You Type Feature

1 **Scroll down, if necessary, to display the WORK EXPERIENCE section of the resume. Drag through the xx in the first 19xx beneath the WORK EXPERIENCE heading, type** `94` **and then drag through the xx in the second year. Type** `97` **and then click the placeholder text, Company/Institution Name. Type** `Jasper University` **and then click the placeholder text, City, State. Type** `Los Angeles, CA` **and then click the placeholder text, *Job Title*. Type** `User Consultant` **and then click the placeholder text, Details of position, award, or achievement. Type** `In the lab room, assist students with software questions on homework assignments.` **and then press the ENTER key. Type** `Translate lectures for Information Systems courses from English to German, French, and Spanish.` **and then press the ENTER key. Type** `Once a week, conduct 1/2` **as the beginning of the third bulleted item.**

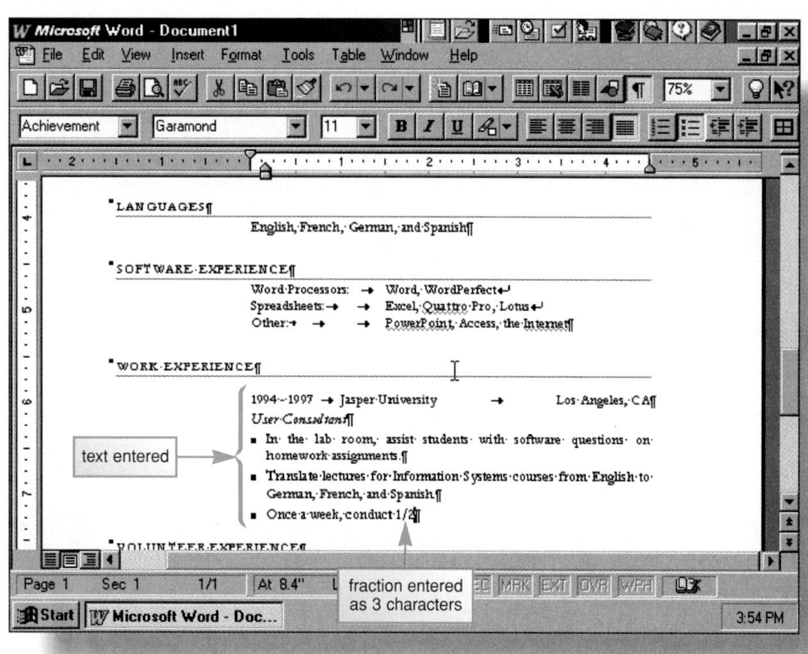

FIGURE 2-35

The fraction is entered as three separate characters: the 1, the /, and the 2 (Figure 2-35).

Type - (a hyphen). Type `day interactive seminars on various software applications for faculty and staff.`

Word AutoFormats the fraction to display as one character (½) when you type the hyphen (Figure 2-36). The WORK EXPERIENCE section in the resume is complete.

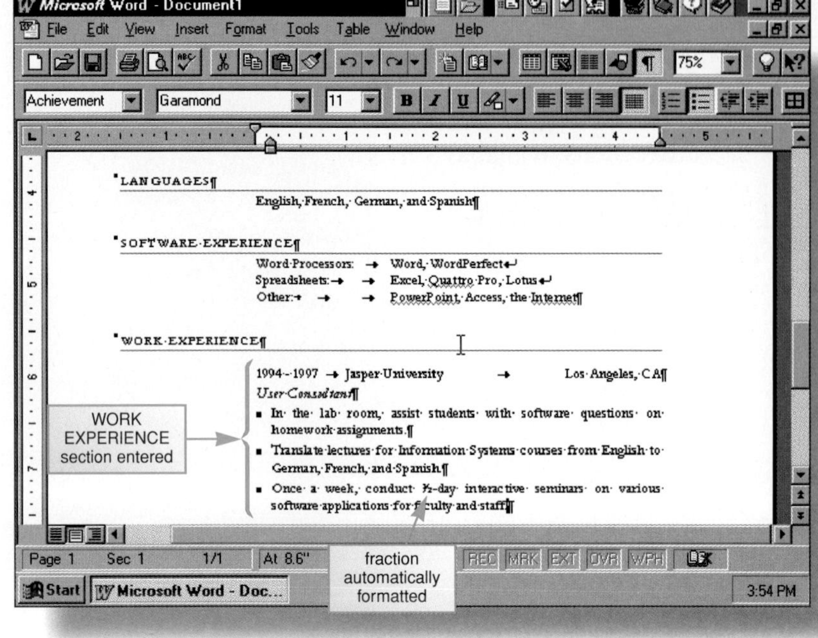

FIGURE 2-36

More *About* **As You Type**

Word has other as you type features, like correcting misspelled words. For example, teh changes to the when you press the SPACEBAR. You can also add special symbols to your writing. For example, typing :) changes to ☺ when you press the SPACEBAR. To see a complete list, click Tools on the menu bar and then click AutoCorrect.

If, for some reason, you do not want Word to AutoFormat as you type, you can turn off this feature. To do this, click Tools on the menu bar, click Options on the Tools menu, click the AutoFormat tab, turn off the check boxes, and then click the OK button.

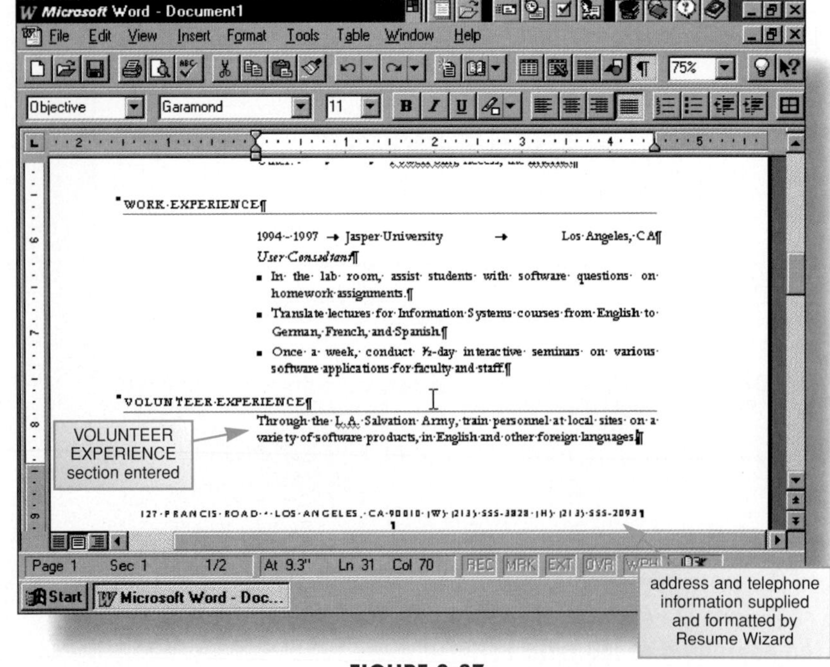

FIGURE 2-37

TO ENTER THE REMAINING SECTION OF THE RESUME

Step 1: Scroll down, if necessary, to display the VOLUNTEER EXPERIENCE section of the resume.

Step 2: Click the placeholder text, Click here and enter information.

Step 3: Type `Through the L.A. Salvation Army, train personnel at local sites on a variety of software products, in English and other foreign languages.`

The volunteer experience section of the resume is complete (Figure 2-37). Notice the Resume Wizard automatically placed your address and telephone information at the bottom of the resume.

Saving the Resume

Because you have performed several tasks thus far, you should save your resume. For a detailed example of the procedure summarized below, refer to pages WD 1.21 through WD 1.24 in Project 1.

TO SAVE A DOCUMENT

Step 1: Insert your data disk into drive A.
Step 2: Click the Save button on the Standard toolbar.
Step 3: Type `Warner Resume` in the File name text box. Do not press the ENTER key.
Step 4: Click the Save in box arrow and then click 3½ Floppy [A:].
Step 5: Click the Save button in the Save As dialog box.

Word saves the document on a floppy disk in drive A with the filename Warner Resume (Figure 2-38 on the next page).

More *About* **References**

Do not state "References Available Upon Request" on your resume; nor should you list references on the resume. Employers assume you will give references, if asked, and this information simply clutters a resume. Often you are asked to list references on your application. Be sure to give your references a copy of your resume.

Switching Two Paragraphs in the Resume

When you proofread the customized resume, you realize the second and third bulleted paragraphs in the WORK EXPERIENCE section would flow better if they were reversed. That is, you want to move the last bulleted paragraph so it is positioned as the middle bulleted paragraph.

To move paragraphs, you can either **drag and drop** one of the paragraphs or **cut and paste** one of the paragraphs. Both techniques require you to first select the paragraph to be moved. With dragging and dropping, you drag the selected paragraph to its new location and insert, or drop, it there. Cutting involves removing the selected text from the document and then placing it on the **Clipboard**, a temporary Windows storage area. Pasting is the process of copying an item from the Clipboard into the document at the location of the insertion point.

You should use the drag and drop technique to move paragraphs a short distance. When you are moving between several pages or documents, however, the cut and paste technique is more efficient. Thus, use the drag and drop technique to switch the second and third paragraphs. To do this, you first must select the paragraph to be moved as shown on the next page.

More *About* **Moving Text**

When moving text a short distance, you should use the drag-and-drop technique. To move text a longer distance, like across multiple pages, use the cut-and-paste technique or print preview. In print preview, click the Magnifier button on the Print Preview toolbar and then edit the document as you would in Normal view.

To Select a Paragraph

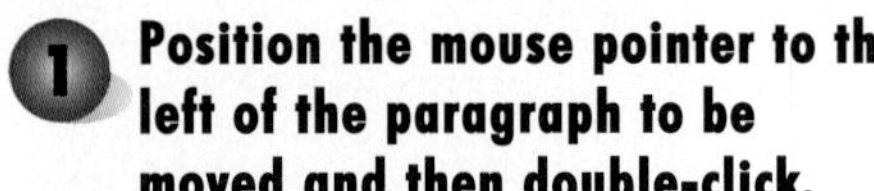

1 Position the mouse pointer to the left of the paragraph to be moved and then double-click.

Word selects the entire paragraph (Figure 2-38). Notice when you select a bulleted paragraph, the bullet character is not highlighted.

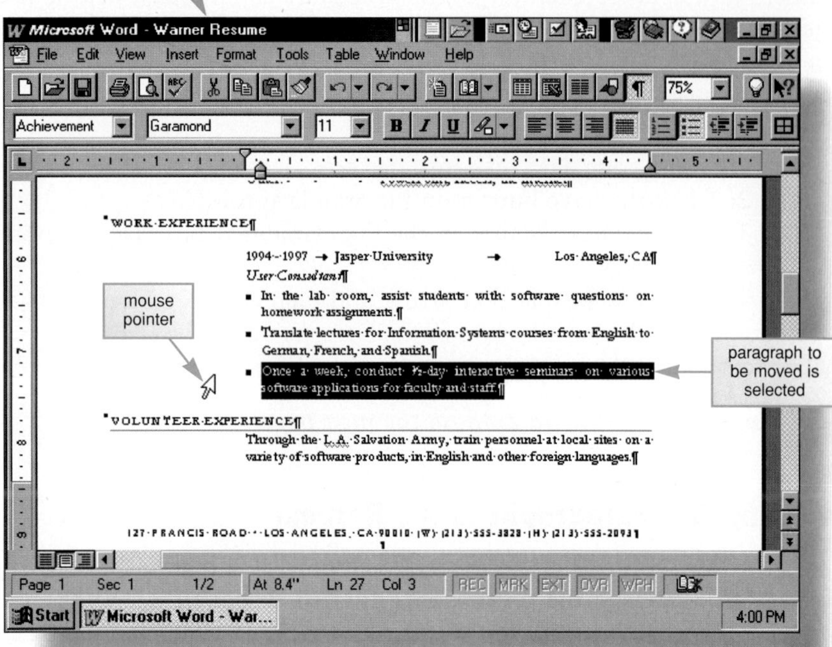

FIGURE 2-38

Other Ways

1. Triple-click the paragraph

With the paragraph to be moved selected, you can drag and drop it as shown in the following steps.

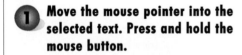

To Drag and Drop Selected Text

1 Move the mouse pointer into the selected text. Press and hold the mouse button.

When you begin to drag the selected text, the insertion point changes to a dotted insertion point and the mouse pointer has a small dotted box below it with a boxed in plus sign attached to its lower right corner (Figure 2-39).

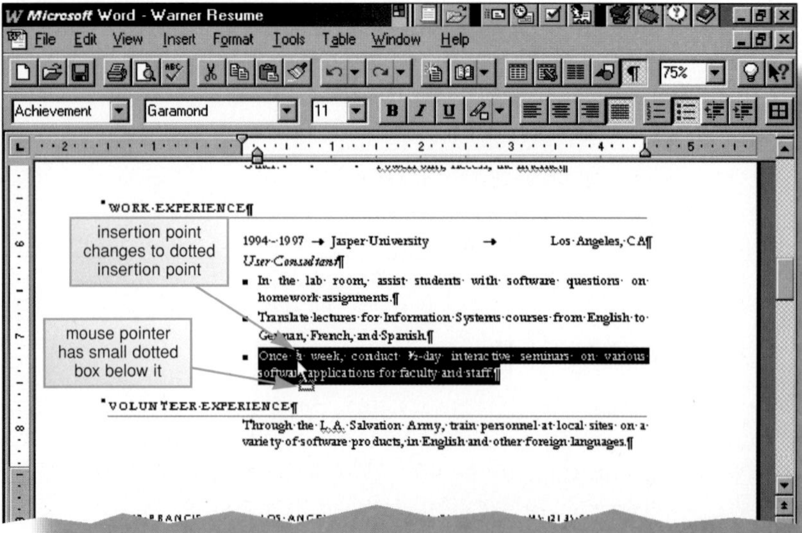

FIGURE 2-39

2 **Drag the dotted insertion point to the location where the paragraph is to be moved.**

The dotted insertion point is positioned to the left of the middle bulleted paragraph; that is, to the left of the T in Translate (Figure 2-40).

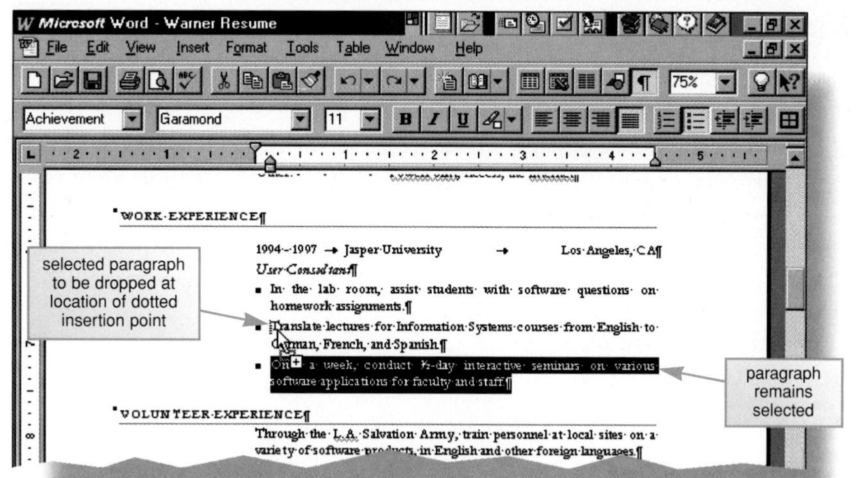

FIGURE 2-40

3 **Release the mouse button. Click outside the selection to remove the highlight.**

The selected paragraph is moved to the location of the dotted insertion point in the document (Figure 2-41). The second and third bulleted paragraphs are switched.

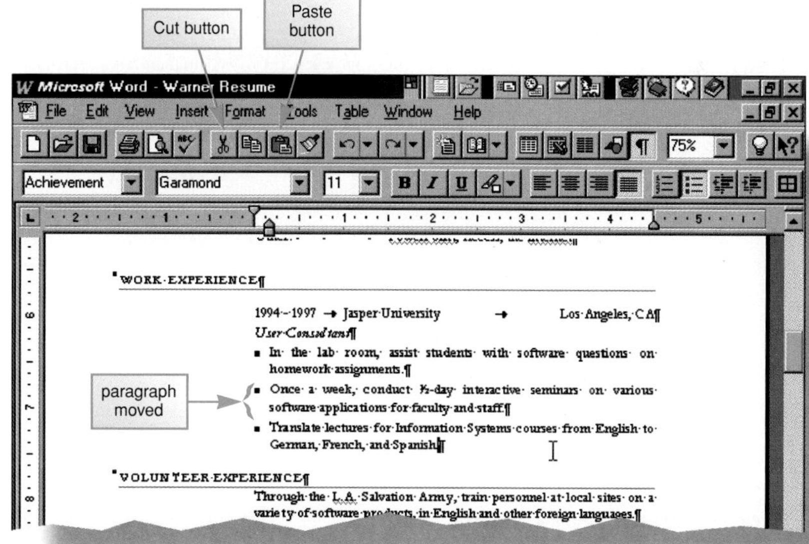

FIGURE 2-41

OtherWays

1. Click Cut button on Standard toolbar, position insertion point at location where text is to be pasted, click Paste button on Standard toolbar
2. On Edit menu click Cut, position insertion point at location where text is to be pasted, on Edit menu click Paste
3. Press CTRL+X, position insertion point at location where text is to be pasted, press CTRL+V

You can use the Undo button on the Standard toolbar if you accidentally drag and drop incorrectly or cut the wrong text.

You can use the drag and drop and cut and paste techniques to move any selected text. That is, you can move words, sentences, and phrases by selecting them and then dragging and dropping them or cutting and pasting them.

Saving Again and Spell Checking

The resume is now complete (see Figure 2-2 on page WD 2.6). After completing the resume, you should check the spelling of the document by clicking the Spelling button on the Standard toolbar. After you spell check, all the red wavy lines disappear from the document. Because you have performed tasks since the last save, you should save the resume again by clicking the Save button on the Standard toolbar.

More About Print Preview

If you want to read the contents of a page in print preview, you must magnify it. To magnify a page, be sure the Magnifier button is recessed on the Print Preview toolbar and then click in the document to zoom in or out. Magnifying a page has no effect on the printed document; it only changes the size of the characters on the screen.

Viewing and Printing the Resume in Print Preview

To see exactly how a document will look when you print it, you should display it in **print preview**. Print preview displays the entire document in reduced size on the Word screen. In print preview, you can edit and format text, adjust margins, and view multiple pages. Once you preview the document, you can print it directly from within print preview. Perform the following steps to use Print Preview.

Steps To Use Print Preview

1. **Point to the Print Preview button on the Standard toolbar (Figure 2-42).**

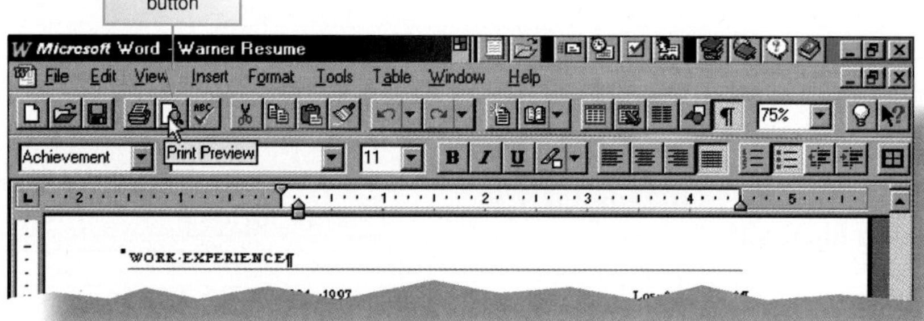

FIGURE 2-42

2. **Click the Print Preview button. If your preview displays more than one page, click the One Page button on the Print Preview toolbar.**

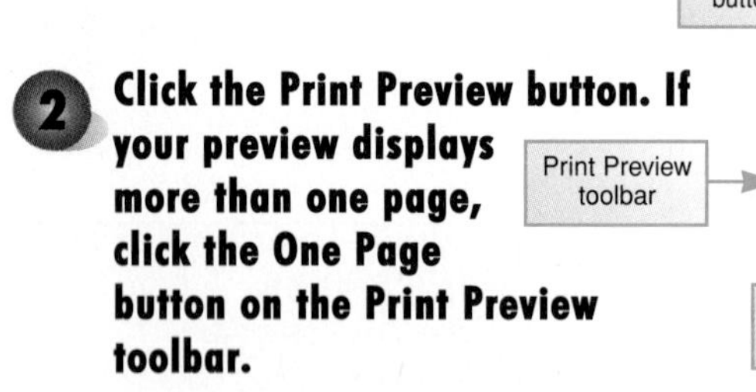

Word displays the document in print preview (Figure 2-43). The ***Print Preview toolbar*** *displays below the menu bar; the Standard and Formatting toolbars have disappeared from the screen. You use the Print Preview toolbar to zoom and print the document.*

3. **Point to the Print button on the Print Preview toolbar.**

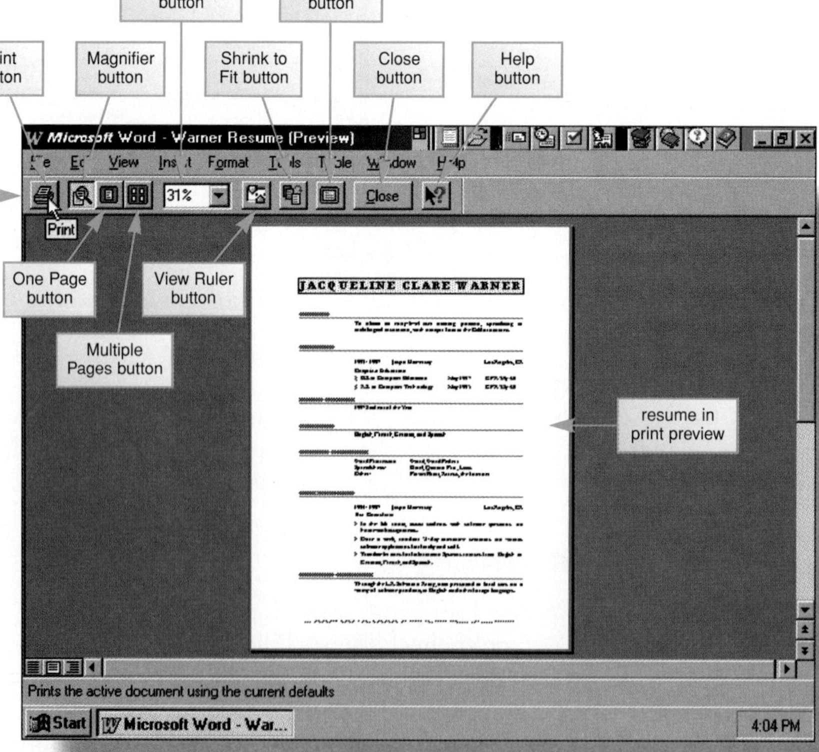

FIGURE 2-43

4 **Ready the printer. Click the Print button on the Print Preview toolbar. When the printer stops, retrieve the printout.**

Word prints the document on the printer (Figure 2-44).

5 **Click the Close button on the Print Preview toolbar.**

Word returns you to the document window (Figure 2-42).

completed resume

JACQUELINE CLARE WARNER

OBJECTIVE

To obtain an entry-level user training position, specializing in multilingual instruction, with a major firm in the California area.

EDUCATION

1993 - 1997 Jasper University Los Angeles, CA
Computer Education
- B.S. in Computer Education May 1997 GPA 3.9/4.0
- A.S. in Computer Technology May 1995 GPA 3.8/4.0

AWARDS RECEIVED

1997 Student of the Year

LANGUAGES

English, French, German, and Spanish

SOFTWARE EXPERIENCE

Word Processors: Word, WordPerfect
Spreadsheets: Excel, Quattro Pro, Lotus
Other: PowerPoint, Access, the Internet

WORK EXPERIENCE

1994 - 1997 Jasper University Los Angeles, CA
User Consultant
- In the lab room, assist students with software questions on homework assignments.
- Once a week, conduct ½-day interactive seminars on various software applications for faculty and staff.
- Translate lectures for Information Systems courses from English to German, French, and Spanish.

VOLUNTEER EXPERIENCE

Through the L.A. Salvation Army, train personnel at local sites on a variety of software products, in English and other foreign languages.

127 FRANCIS ROAD • LOS ANGELES, CA 90010 (W) (213) 555-3828 (H) (213) 555-2093

FIGURE 2-44

Other Ways

1. On File menu click Print Preview
2. Press CTRL+F2

The resume is now complete. The next step in Project 2 is to create a cover letter to send with the resume to a potential employer. Do not close the Warner Resume. You will use it again later in this project.

Creating a Cover Letter

You have created a personalized resume to send to prospective employers. The next step is to create a cover letter to attach to the resume. The following pages outline how to use Word to create and personalize a cover letter.

More About a Cover Letter

You should always send a personalized cover letter with every resume. A cover letter should highlight aspects of your background relevant to the position. Because it is often difficult to recall past achievements and activities, you should keep a personal personnel file containing documents that outline your accomplishments.

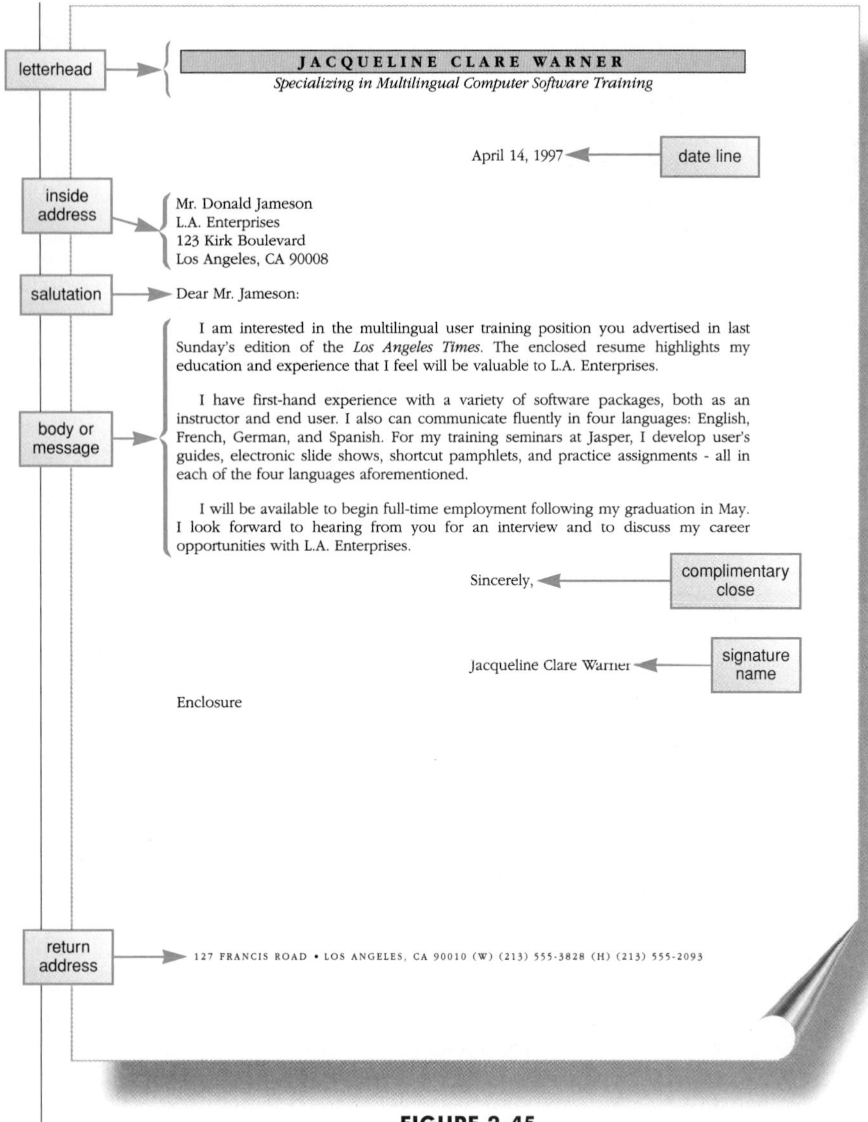
JACQUELINE CLARE WARNER
Specializing in Multilingual Computer Software Training

April 14, 1997

Mr. Donald Jameson
L.A. Enterprises
123 Kirk Boulevard
Los Angeles, CA 90008

Dear Mr. Jameson:

I am interested in the multilingual user training position you advertised in last Sunday's edition of the *Los Angeles Times*. The enclosed resume highlights my education and experience that I feel will be valuable to L.A. Enterprises.

I have first-hand experience with a variety of software packages, both as an instructor and end user. I also can communicate fluently in four languages: English, French, German, and Spanish. For my training seminars at Jasper, I develop user's guides, electronic slide shows, shortcut pamphlets, and practice assignments - all in each of the four languages aforementioned.

I will be available to begin full-time employment following my graduation in May. I look forward to hearing from you for an interview and to discuss my career opportunities with L.A. Enterprises.

Sincerely,

Jacqueline Clare Warner

Enclosure

127 FRANCIS ROAD • LOS ANGELES, CA 90010 (W) (213) 555-3828 (H) (213) 555-2093

FIGURE 2-45

Table 2-2

LETTER STYLE	FEATURES
Block	All components of the letter begin flush with the left margin.
Modified Block	The date, complimentary close, and signature block are positioned approximately five spaces to the right of center or at the right margin. All other components of the letter begin flush with the left margin.
Modified Semi-Block	The date, complimentary close, and signature block are positioned approximately five spaces to the right of center or at the right margin. The first line of each paragraph in the body of the letter is indented 5 or 10 spaces from the left margin. All other components of the letter begin flush with the left margin.

Components of a Business Letter

During your professional career, you will create many business letters. A cover letter is one type of a business letter. All business letters contain the same basic components. You should take care when preparing business letters to include all essential elements. Essential business letter elements include the date line, inside address, message, and signature block (Figure 2-45). The **date line**, which consists of the month, day, and year, is positioned two to six lines below the letterhead. The **inside address**, placed three to eight lines below the date line, usually contains the addressee's courtesy title plus full name; business affiliation; and full geographical address. The **salutation**, if present, begins two lines below the last line of the inside address. The body of the letter, the **message**, begins two lines below the salutation. Within the message, paragraphs are single-spaced internally, and double-spaced between paragraphs. Two lines below the last line of the message, the **complimentary close** displays. You capitalize only the first word in a complimentary close. The **signature block** is typed at least four lines below the complimentary close, allowing room for the author to sign his or her name.

You can follow many different styles when you create business letters. The cover letter in this project (Figure 2-45) follows the modified semi-block style. Table 2-2 outlines the differences between the common styles of business letters.

Using a Letter Template to Create a Resume Cover Letter

To create a resume cover letter, you can type a letter from scratch into a blank document window following the rules listed in the preceding paragraphs, use a wizard and let Word format the letter with appropriate spacing and layout as you did with the resume, or you can use a template. Recall that a template is like a blueprint; that is, Word prepares the requested document with text and/or formatting common to all documents of this nature. Then, you customize the letter by selecting and replacing text.

Recall that Word provides three styles, or families, of wizards and templates: Professional, Elegant, and Contemporary. If you want a related set of documents to have similar formatting, use wizards and templates from the same family — Professional, Elegant, or Contemporary. Because you used the Elegant style for the resume, you should use the Elegant style for the cover letter as shown in the following steps.

Steps To Create a Letter Using a Template in Word

1 Click File on the menu bar and then point to New (Figure 2-46).

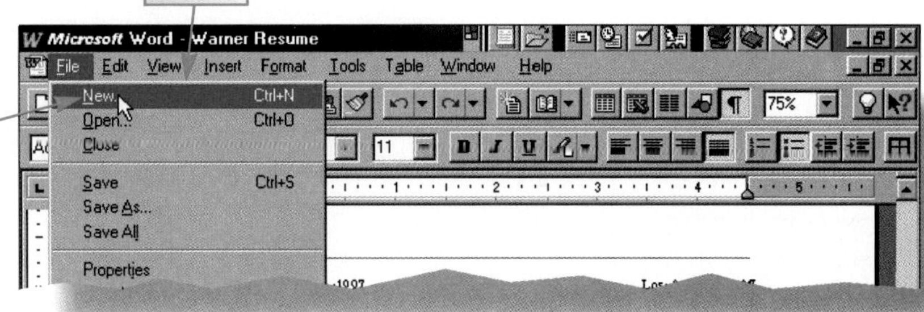

FIGURE 2-46

2 Click New. Click the Letters & Faxes tab if necessary when the New dialog box first opens. Click the Elegant Letter icon.

Word displays the New dialog box (Figure 2-47). Recall that icons without the word, wizard, beneath them are templates. The Elegant Letter icon is selected and a preview of an elegant letter displays in the Preview area. When you create a new document using the New button on the Standard toolbar, you use the ***Blank Document Template*** *located on the General tab sheet in the New dialog box. If you want to use a different template or a wizard, you must use the New dialog box.*

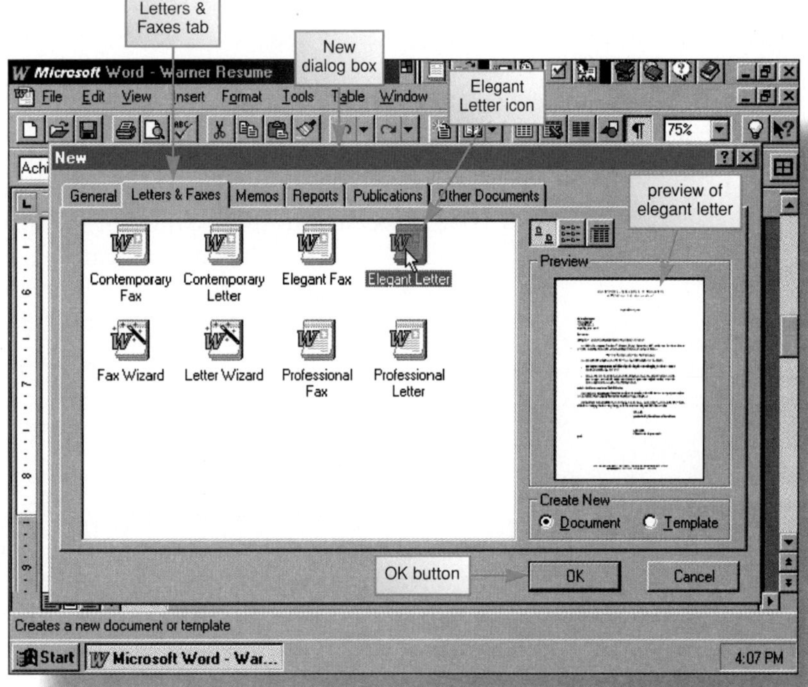

FIGURE 2-47

Click the OK button.

Word creates an Elegant style letter layout for you and displays it in a document window (Figure 2-48). Because Word displays the current date in the letter, your date line may display a different date.

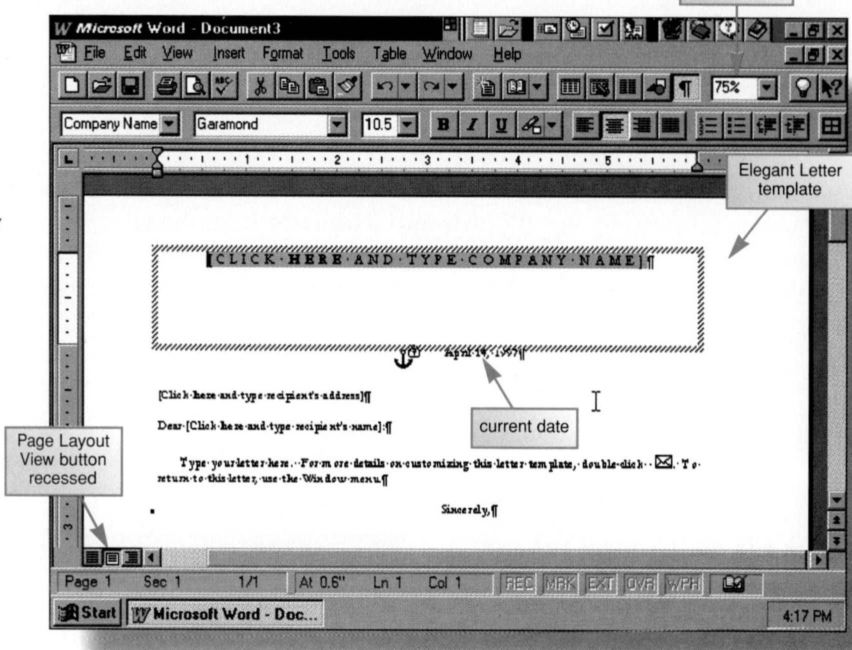

FIGURE 2-48

OtherWays

1. On Start menu click New Office Document, click Letters & Faxes tab, double-click Elegant Letter icon
2. On Microsoft Office Shortcut Bar, click Start a New Document button, click Letters & Faxes tab, double-click Elegant Letter icon

To see the entire letter created by Word, you should print it.

Printing the Cover Letter Generated Using Word's Elegant Letter Template

To print the cover letter generated by Word, click the Print button on the Standard toolbar. The resulting printout is shown in Figure 2-49.

Recall that a style is a customized format Word applies to characters or paragraphs. The Style box on the Formatting toolbar displays the name of the style associated to the location of the insertion point. The styles used in the Elegant Letter template are indicated in the printout of the cover letter in Figure 2-49. When you modify the cover letter, the style associated to the location of the insertion point will be applied to the text you type.

More About Frames

The crosshatched border surrounding the letterhead in Figure 2-48 is called a frame. A frame is an invisible container for text or graphics that can be positioned anywhere on the page. To change the contents of the frame, select the words as you would any other text and then type.

Personalizing the Cover Letter

If you compare the printout in Figure 2-49 to the cover letter in Figure 2-1 on page WD 2.5, you will notice several modifications are required. Notice how the template (Figure 2-49) creates the formatting for the business letter using the modified semi-block style. The template uses proper spacing between lines for a business letter and indicates what you should type in the respective areas of the letter via placeholder text. You can see that using a template saves you much formatting time when creating a business letter. The steps on the following pages illustrate how to personalize the cover letter.

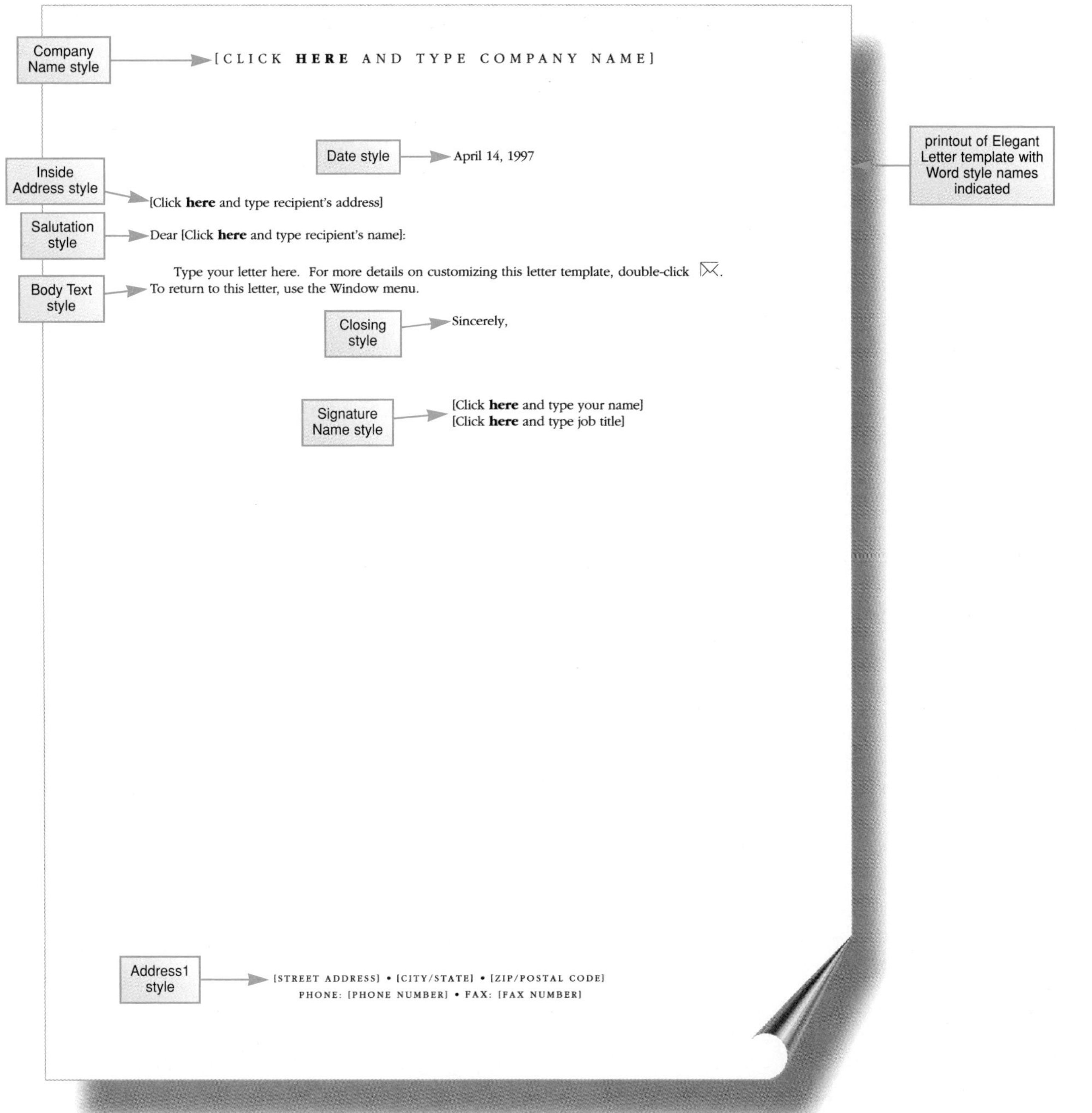

FIGURE 2-49

Zooming a Document on the Screen

As with the resume created by the Resume Wizard, the document displayed in Figure 2-48 is small, making the characters and words difficult to read. In Figure 2-48, the document displays at 75% of its normal size. Zoom the characters to 100% as described in the following steps.

TO ZOOM A DOCUMENT

Step 1: Click the Zoom Control box arrow on the Standard toolbar.
Step 2: Click 100%.

The characters in the document window increase from 75% of their normal size to 100% (Figure 2-50 on the next page).

More *About* Business Letters

A finished business letter should look like a symmetrically framed picture with even margins, all balanced below an attractive letterhead. In addition, the contents of the letter should contain proper grammar, correct spelling, logically constructed sentences, flowing paragraphs, and sound ideas.

Selecting and Replacing Template Placeholder Text

The next step in personalizing the cover letter is to select the placeholder text in the letter template and replace it with the personal information. The first placeholder text on the letter is in the letterhead, CLICK HERE AND TYPE COMPANY NAME. You want the name to display on the first line of the letterhead, outlined with a box border and shaded as described in the following steps.

TO SELECT AND REPLACE TEMPLATE PLACEHOLDER TEXT

Step 1: Click the placeholder text, CLICK HERE AND TYPE COMPANY NAME.
Step 2: Type `JACQUELINE CLARE WARNER` and then press the ENTER key.
Step 3: Click to the left of the name to select it.
Step 4: If necessary, click the Borders button on the Formatting toolbar to display the Borders toolbar.
Step 5: Click the Outside Border button on the Borders toolbar.
Step 6: Click the Shading box arrow on the Borders toolbar and then click 10%.
Step 7: Click the Borders button on the Formatting toolbar to remove the Borders toolbar from the screen.
Step 8: With the name still selected, click the Bold button on the Formatting toolbar.
Step 9: Click inside the name to remove the highlight.

The name displays on the first line of the letterhead, outlined with a box border and shaded (Figure 2-50). Notice the style of this paragraph is Company Name in the Style box. The Company Name style uses the 10.5-point Garamond font for characters with centered alignment for paragraphs, which explains why the Center button on the Formatting toolbar is recessed, instead of the Align Left button, indicating the text at the location of the insertion point is centered.

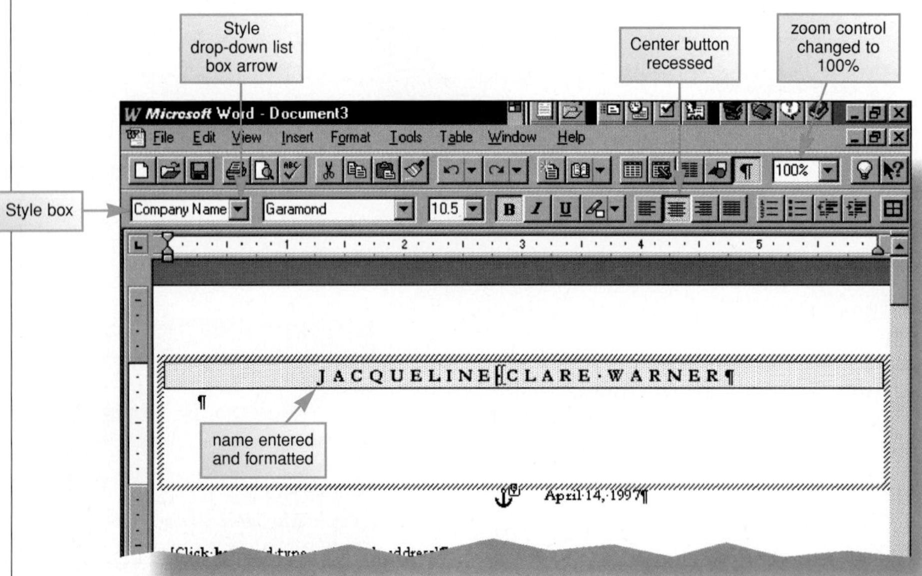

FIGURE 2-50

To add some character to your letterhead, you want to italicize your specialization on the second line of the letterhead. The first paragraph of the letterhead (the name) uses the Company Name style, and the second paragraph uses the Body Text style, which applies the 10-point Garamond font for characters with justified alignment for paragraphs. You want the specialization line to be centered with italicized characters. Thus, follow these steps to modify the formatting applied by the Body Text style.

Steps To Modify Formatting Applied by a Style

1 Click the paragraph mark below the name in the letterhead. Point to the first-line indent marker on the ruler.

Word changes the style from Company Name to Body Text (Figure 2-51). Notice the first-line indent marker on the ruler is not at the 0-inch mark on the ruler; instead it is positioned at the .25-inch mark. The first-line indent marker is used to indent the first line of each paragraph when a paragraph consists of multiple lines. In this case, the paragraph will consist of only one line. Because you want to center the line, the first-line indent marker must be at the 0-inch mark on the ruler; otherwise, the text will be off-center by one-quarter inch.

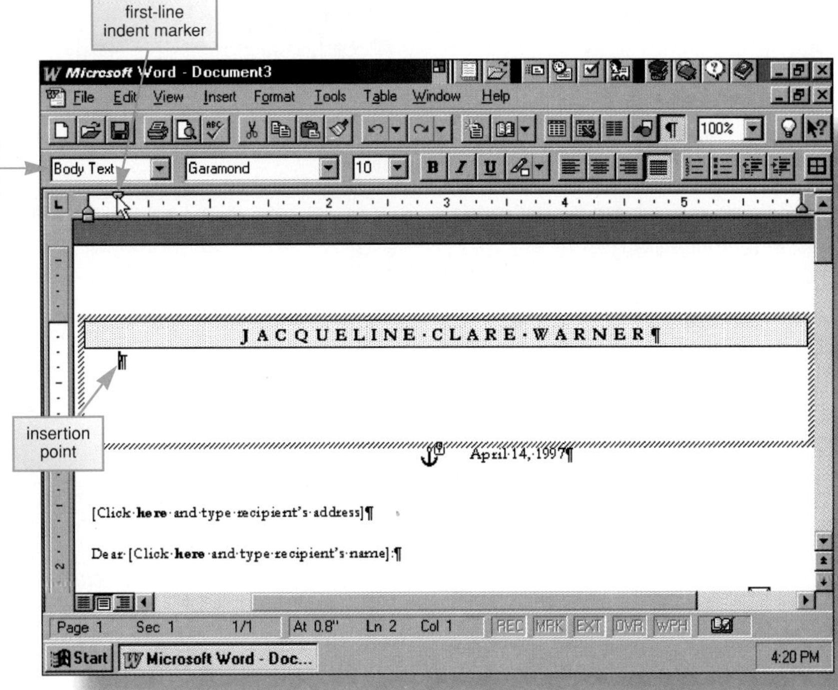

FIGURE 2-51

2 Begin dragging the first-line indent marker toward the 0-inch mark on the ruler.

As you drag the mouse, a vertical dotted line displays in the document window, indicating the location of the first-line indent marker (Figure 2-52).

0-inch mark on ruler
first-line indent marker at .25-inch mark on ruler
paragraph mark at .25-inch mark on ruler
vertical dotted line indicates position of first-line indent marker as you drag mouse

FIGURE 2-52

Release the mouse when the first-line indent marker is aligned with the 0-inch mark on the ruler.

The first-line indent marker displays at the 0-inch mark on the ruler (Figure 2-53). The paragraph mark containing the insertion point in the document window also moves to the 0-inch mark, which is positioned at the left edge of the document window. The Body Text style uses justified formatting, and you want the second line of the letterhead centered.

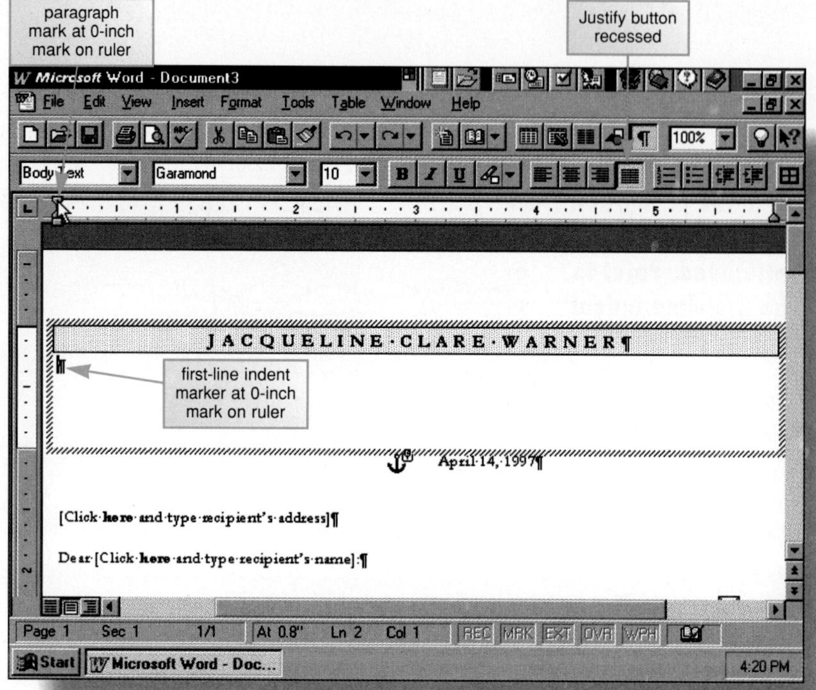

FIGURE 2-53

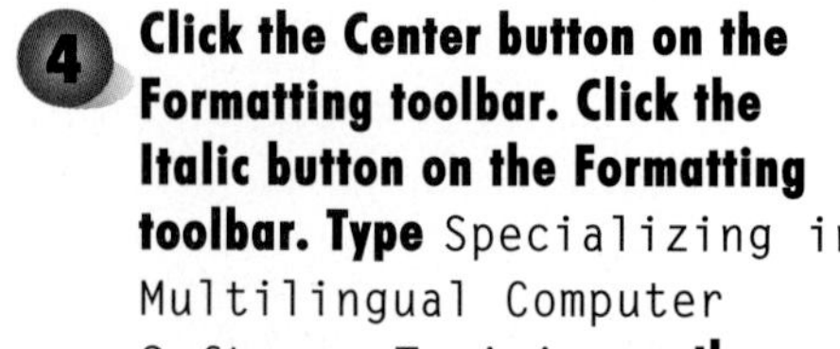

Click the Center button on the Formatting toolbar. Click the Italic button on the Formatting toolbar. Type `Specializing in Multilingual Computer Software Training` **as the specialization.**

The second line of the letterhead is entered, making the letterhead complete (Figure 2-54). The Center and Italic buttons on the Formatting toolbar are recessed, indicating the text at the insertion point is centered and italicized.

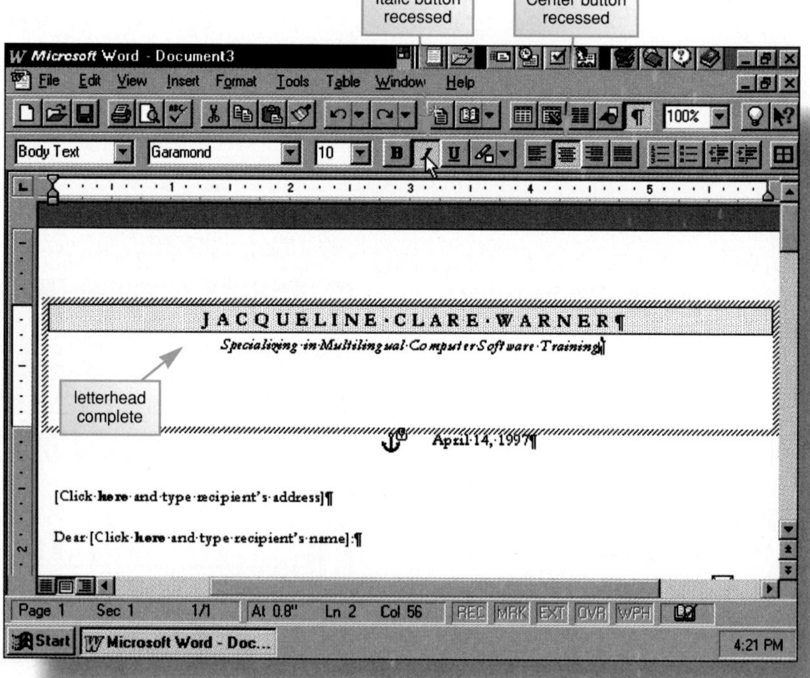

FIGURE 2-54

With the letterhead complete, the next step in personalizing the cover letter is to enter the recipient's address as described in the following steps.

TO SELECT AND REPLACE MORE INSTRUCTIONS

Step 1: Click the placeholder text beneath the date, Click here and type recipient's address, to select it.
Step 2: Type `Mr. Donald Jameson` and then press the ENTER key.
Step 3: Type `L.A. Enterprises` and then press the ENTER key.
Step 4: Type `123 Kirk Boulevard` and then press the ENTER key.
Step 5: Type `Los Angeles, CA 90008` as the city, state, and zip code.

The recipient's name, company, and address are entered (Figure 2-55). Notice the style is now Inside Address.

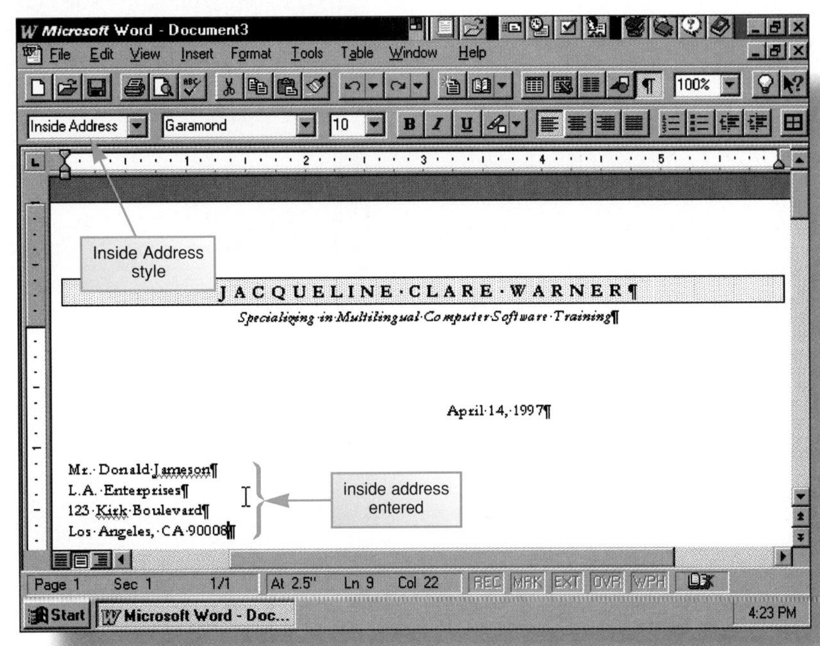

FIGURE 2-55

Creating an AutoText Entry

If you use text frequently, you can store the text in an **AutoText entry** and then use the stored entry throughout your document. That is, you only need to type the entry only once, and for all future occurrences of the text, you access the stored entry by typing its name and then pressing F3. In this way, you avoid entering the text inconsistently and incorrectly in different places in the same document. Follow these steps to create an AutoText entry for the prospective employer's company name.

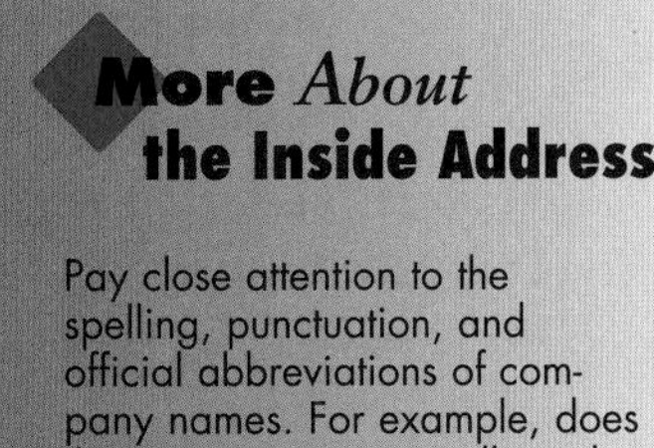

More About the Inside Address

Pay close attention to the spelling, punctuation, and official abbreviations of company names. For example, does the company name spell out the word and or use the ampersand character? Is the word Company spelled out or abbreviated? If so, how is it abbreviated?

Steps To Create an AutoText Entry

1 **Drag through the text to be stored. (Be sure not to select the paragraph mark at the end of the text.) Click Edit on the menu bar and then point to AutoText.**

Word highlights the company name, L.A. Enterprises, in the inside address (Figure 2-56). Notice the paragraph mark is not part of the selection.

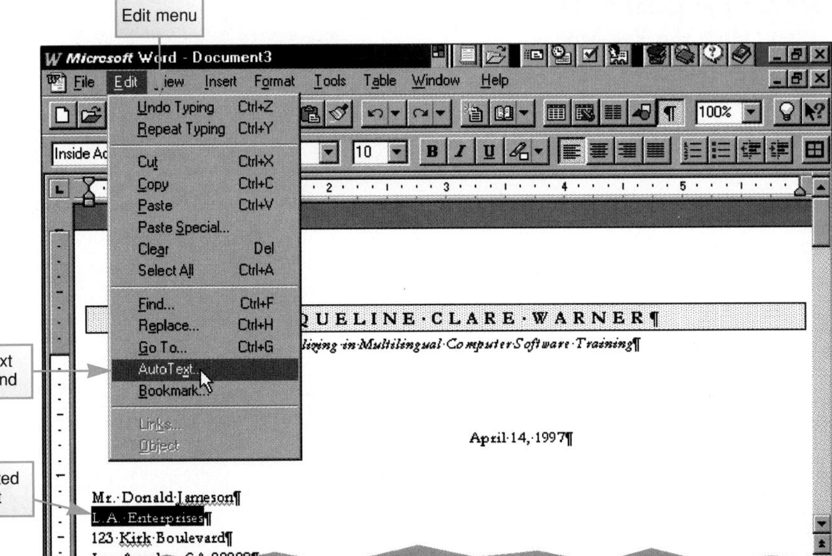

FIGURE 2-56

2 Click AutoText.

Word displays the AutoText dialog box (Figure 2-57). The selected text, L.A. Enterprises, displays in the Selection area of the AutoText dialog box. The first two words of the selected text also display in the Name text box. You want to change this name to a few characters representative of the selected text.

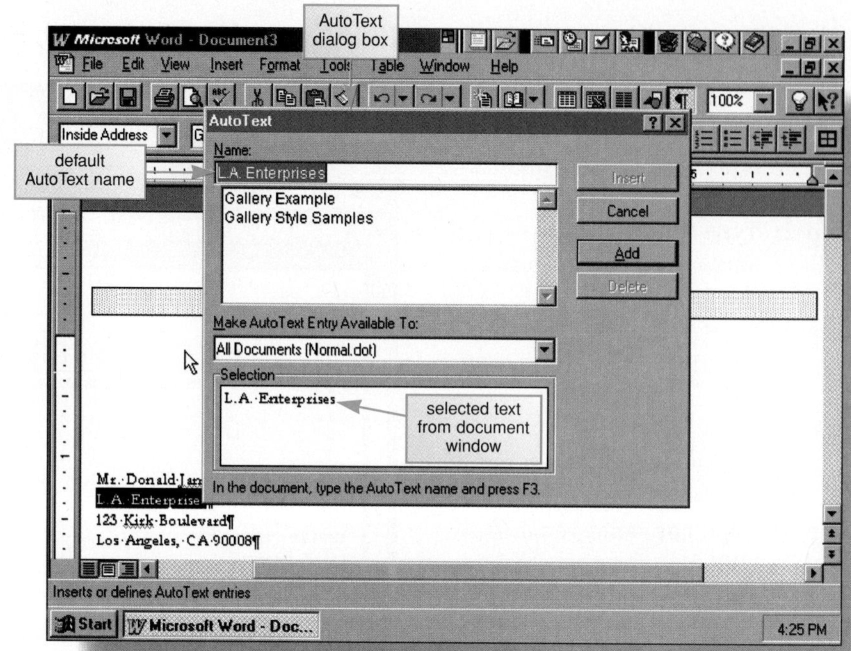

FIGURE 2-57

3 Type lae **in the Name text box and then point to the Add button.**

Word replaces the name, L.A. Enterprises, with lae in the Name text box, which in this case is the entire selection (Figure 2-58). The characters, lae, now stand for L.A. Enterprises in this document.

4 Click the Add button. If Word displays a dialog box asking if you wish to redefine the AutoText entry, click the Yes button.

Word stores the entry, removes the AutoText dialog box, and returns to the document window.

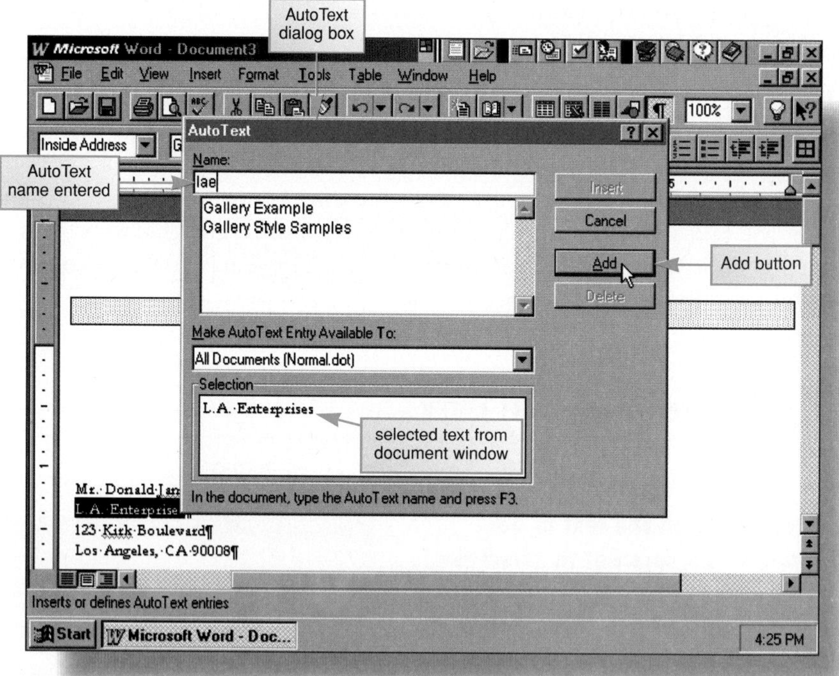

FIGURE 2-58

The name, lae, has been stored as an AutoText entry. Later in the project, you will use the AutoText entry (lae) instead of typing the company name (L.A. Enterprises) again.

The next step is to enter the salutation as described in the steps on the next page.

TO ENTER THE SALUTATION

Step 1: Scroll down, if necessary, to display the salutation.
Step 2: Click the placeholder text, Click here and type recipient's name, to select it.
Step 3: Type `Mr. Jameson` as the recipient's name.

The salutation of the cover letter now displays as shown in Figure 2-59.

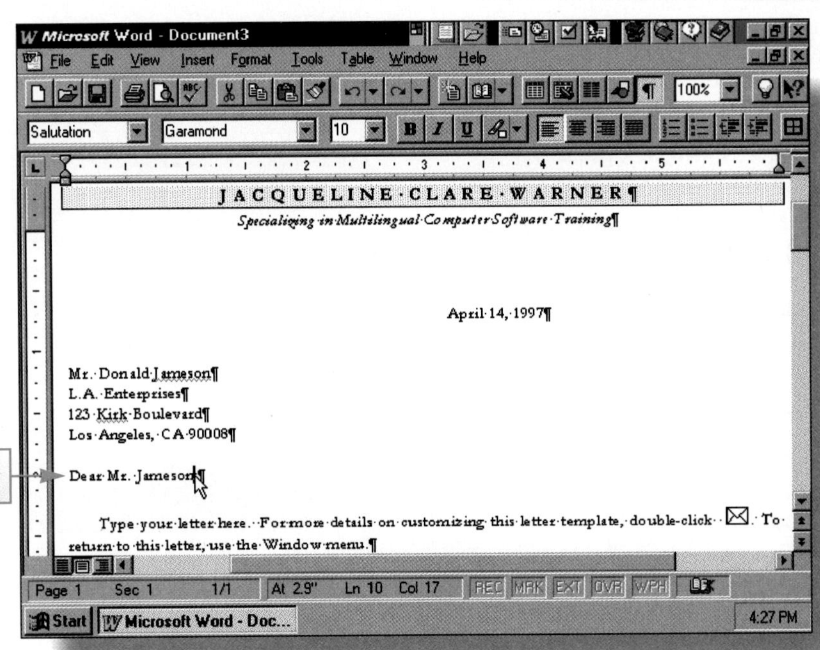

FIGURE 2-59

Saving the Cover Letter

Recall from Project 1 that it is prudent to save your work on disk at regular intervals. Because you have performed several tasks thus far, you should save your cover letter. For a detailed example of the procedure summarized below, refer to pages WD 1.21 through WD 1.24 in Project 1.

TO SAVE A DOCUMENT

Step 1: Insert your data disk into drive A.
Step 2: Click the Save button on the Standard toolbar.
Step 3: Type `Warner Cover Letter` in the File name text box. Do not press the ENTER key.
Step 4: Click the Save in box arrow and then click 3½ Floppy [A:].
Step 5: Click the Save button in the Save As dialog box.

Word saves the document on a floppy disk in drive A with the filename, Warner Cover Letter, (Figure 2-60 on the next page).

> **More About Salutations**
>
> The salutation "To whom it may concern" should be avoided – it is extremely impersonal. If you cannot obtain the name and gender of the company officer to whom you are addressing your letter, then use the recipient's title in the salutation; e.g., Dear Personnel Supervisor.

Applying Formatting Using Shortcut Keys

The next step is to type the message, or body, of the letter below the salutation. As you type paragraphs of text, you may want to format characters within the paragraph as you type them, instead of formatting them later. In Project 1, you typed all characters in the document and then selected the ones to be formatted and applied the desired formatting. In the steps on the next page, you will use **shortcut keys** to format text as you type.

To Format Characters using Shortcut Keys

Scroll down, if necessary, to display the body of the letter. Triple-click the paragraph below the salutation.

Word selects the entire paragraph, which is placeholder text (Figure 2-60). Notice the first-line indent marker on the ruler is positioned on the .25-inch mark. Recall that first-line indent is used to indent the first line of each paragraph; thus, the first line of each paragraph in the body of this letter will be indented automatically by one-quarter inch.

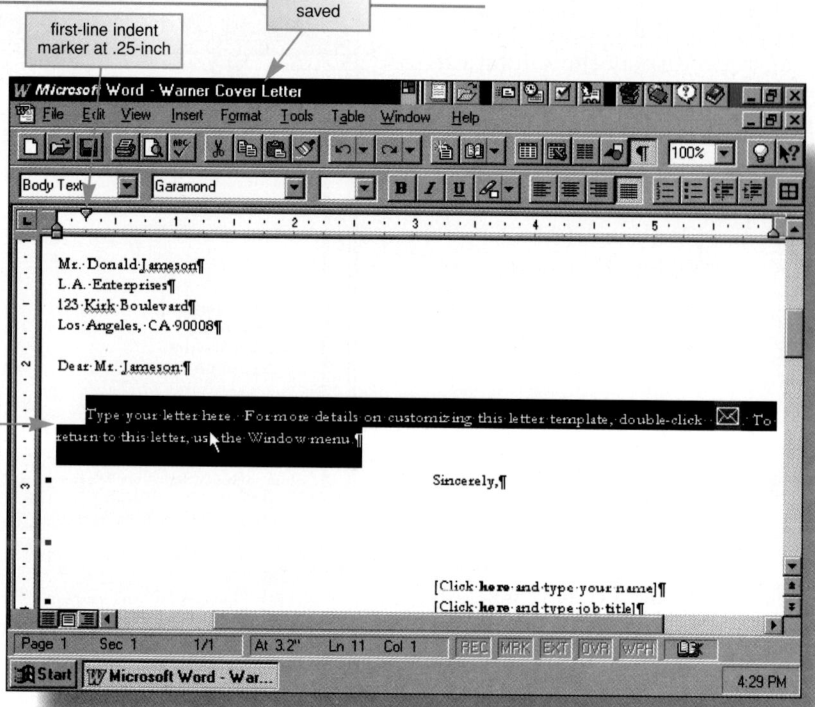

FIGURE 2-60

Type `I am interested in the multilingual user training position you advertised in last Sunday's edition of the` **and then press the SPACEBAR. Press CTRL+I.**

Word indents the first line of the paragraph by one-quarter inch (Figure 2-61). The next word to be typed is a newspaper name, which should be italicized. Because you pressed CTRL+I, the Italic button on the Formatting toolbar is recessed. When your fingers are on the keyboard, it is sometimes desirable to use a shortcut key to format text, instead of using the mouse to click a button.

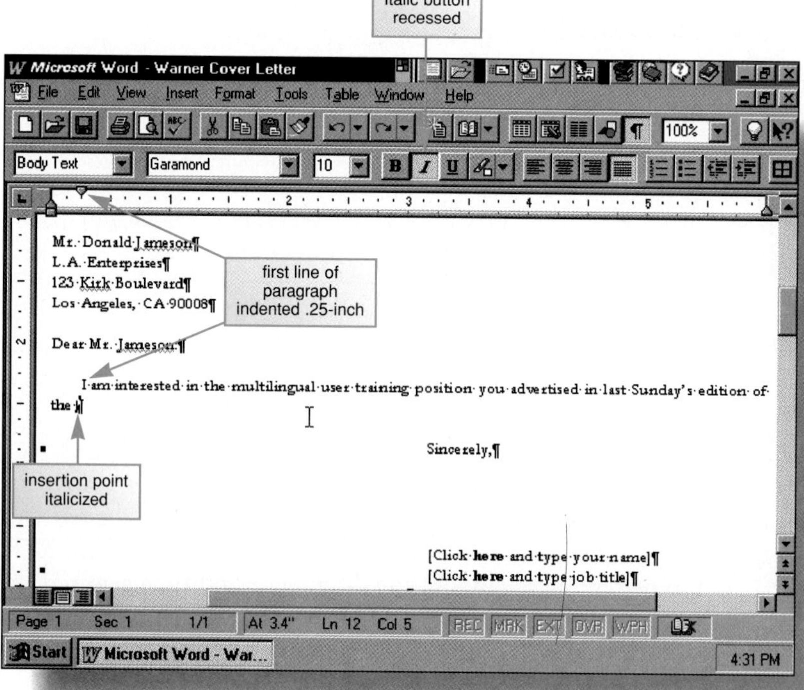

FIGURE 2-61

3 **Type** `Los Angeles Times` **and then press CTRL+I. Type** `.` **(a period) and then press the SPACEBAR once.**

The newspaper name is entered in italics (Figure 2-62). The Italic button on the Formatting toolbar is no longer recessed. CTRL+I is a ***toggle****; that is, the shortcut key is entered once to activate the button and entered again to deactivate the button.*

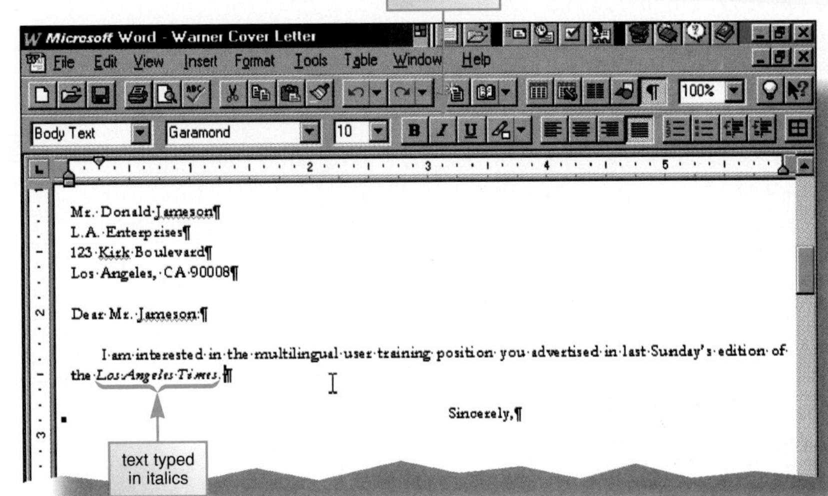

FIGURE 2-62

Many shortcut keys exist in Word for your convenience while typing. Table 2-3 lists the common shortcut keys used for formatting characters and their functions.

Table 2-3

FUNCTION	SHORTCUT KEY
Bold	CTRL+B
Capitalize letters	CTRL+SHIFT+A
Decrease font size	CTRL+SHIFT+<
Increase font size	CTRL+SHIFT+>
Italicize	CTRL+I
Remove formatting (plain text)	CTRL+SHIFT+Z
Subscript	CTRL+=
Superscript	CTRL+SHIFT+=
Underline	CTRL+U

Inserting an AutoText Entry

At the end of the next sentence in the body of the cover letter, you want to put the company name, L.A. Enterprises. Recall that earlier in this project you stored an AutoText name of lae for L.A. Enterprises. Thus, you will type lae and then press F3 to replace the characters lae with the stored AutoText entry of L.A. Enterprises as shown in these steps.

Steps To Insert an AutoText Entry

1 **Type** `The enclosed resume highlights my education and experience that I feel will be valuable to lae` **as the beginning of the sentence.**

The AutoText name of lae is entered (Figure 2-63). Pressing F3 instructs Word to locate an AutoText name of lae and replace it with the stored AutoText entry.

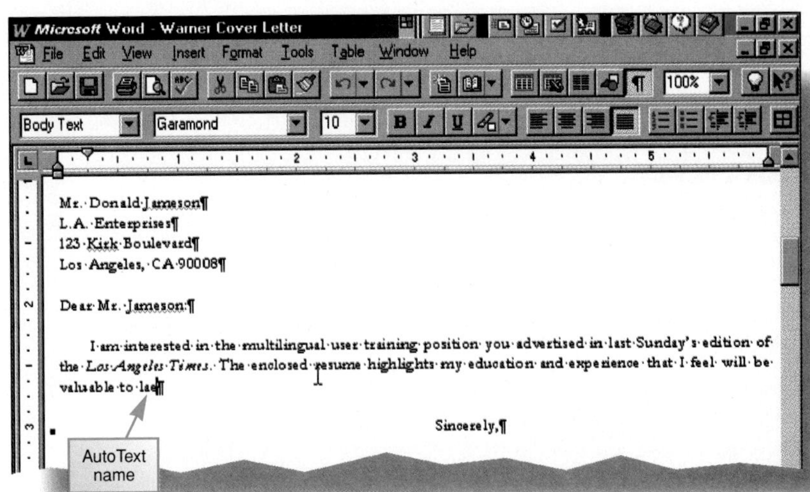

FIGURE 2-63

Press F3. Type . (a period) and then press the ENTER key.

Word replaces the characters lae in the cover letter with the stored AutoText entry, L.A. Enterprises (Figure 2-64). Notice when you press the ENTER key, Word automatically indents the first line of the next paragraph by one-quarter inch because of the setting of the first-line indent marker on the ruler.

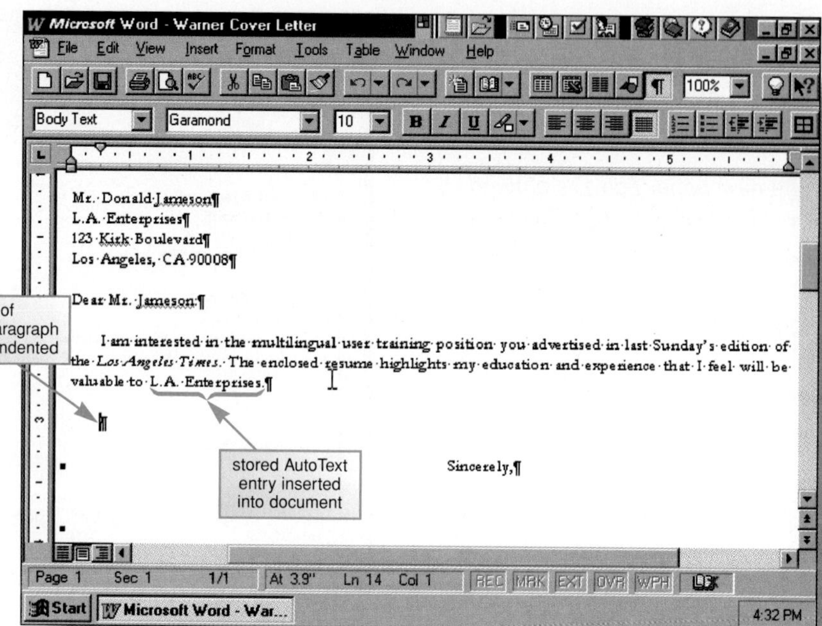

FIGURE 2-64

OtherWays

1. On Edit menu click AutoText, click desired AutoText name, click Insert

Enter the remainder of the body of the cover letter as described in the following steps.

TO FINISH THE BODY OF THE COVER LETTER

Step 1: Type `I have first-hand experience with a variety of software packages, both as an instructor and end user. I also can communicate fluently in four languages: English, French, German, and Spanish. For my training seminars at Jasper, I develop user's guides, electronic slide shows, shortcut pamphlets, and practice assignments - all in each of the four languages aforementioned.`

Step 2: Press the ENTER key. Type `I will be available to begin full-time employment following my graduation in May. I look forward to hearing from you for an interview and to discuss my career opportunities with lae` and then press F3. Type `.` (a period).

The body of the cover letter is complete (Figure 2-65). Notice the right edge of the paragraphs is aligned because the paragraph alignment for the Body Text style is justified.

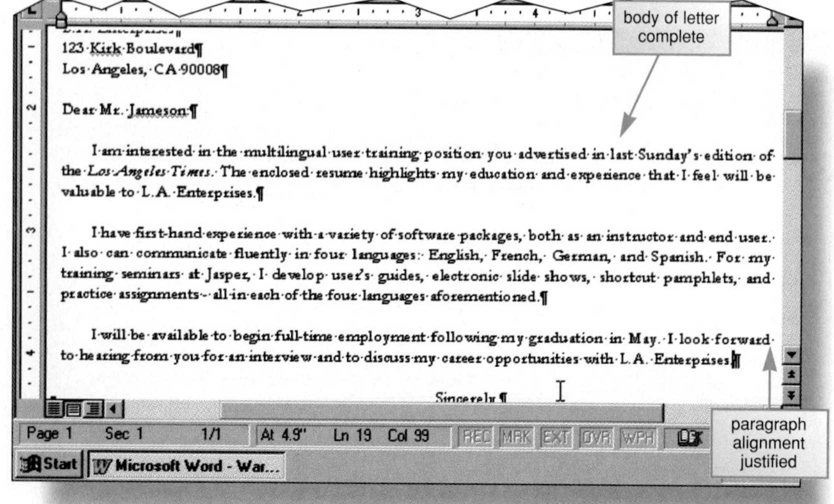

FIGURE 2-65

The next step is to enter the signature block, which in this project contains just your name. Thus, you will delete the job title line. Follow these steps to enter the signature block.

TO ENTER THE SIGNATURE BLOCK

Step 1: Scroll down, if necessary, to display the signature block.
Step 2: Click the first line of placeholder text in the signature block, Click here and type the name, to select it.
Step 3: Type `Jacqueline Clare Warner` as the name.
Step 4: Click the second line of placeholder text in the signature block, Click here and type the job title, to select it.
Step 5: Right-click the selection to display a shortcut menu and then click Cut on the shortcut menu; or press the DELETE key.

The signature block is entered (Figure 2-66).

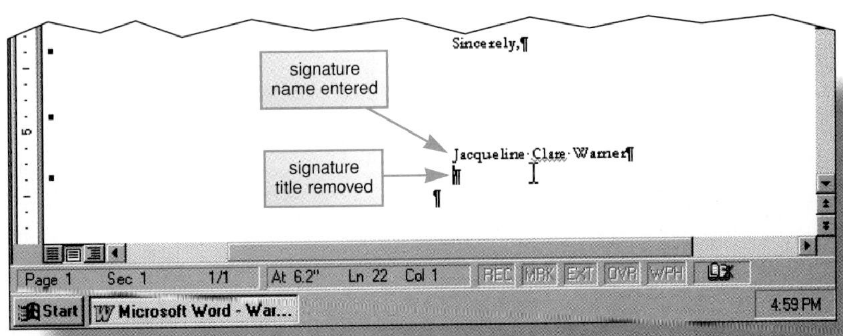

FIGURE 2-66

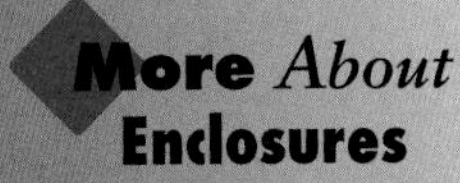

If a document contains multiple enclosures, then place the total number of enclosures in parenthesis; e.g, Enclosures (2). If the enclosures are especially important, they may be numerically listed and briefly described; e.g, Enclosures: 1. List of Top Ten Accounts. To indicate an enclosure is being mailed separately, type Separate mailing: Five-Year Plan.

Applying a Different Style

If a business letter is accompanied by an enclosure, then the word Enclosure should be positioned one to two lines below the last line of the signature block aligned flush with the left margin. Because you plan to include a copy of the resume with the cover letter, you should enter the Enclosure notation. Although the letter template did not place an enclosure notation on your Word document, the letter template does contain an Enclosure style, which you may apply to the text you type for the enclosure as shown in the following steps.

To Apply a Style

1 **Click the paragraph mark one line below the signature title line. Point to the Style box arrow on the Formatting toolbar.**

The insertion point is positioned two lines below the signature name, Jacqueline Clare Warner (Figure 2-67).

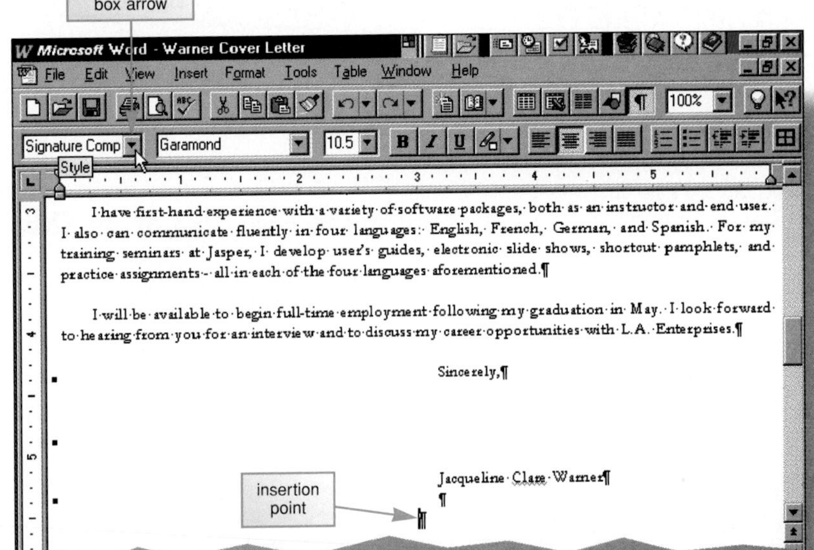

FIGURE 2-67

Click the Style box arrow. Scroll through the list of styles and then point to Enclosure.

Word highlights the Enclosure style in the Style list (Figure 2-68). Recall that style names preceded by a proofreader's paragraph mark, called a document icon, are paragraph style names and style names preceded by some form of the letter a, called a document page icon, are character styles. Thus, the Enclosure style is a paragraph style; that is, it formats a paragraph.

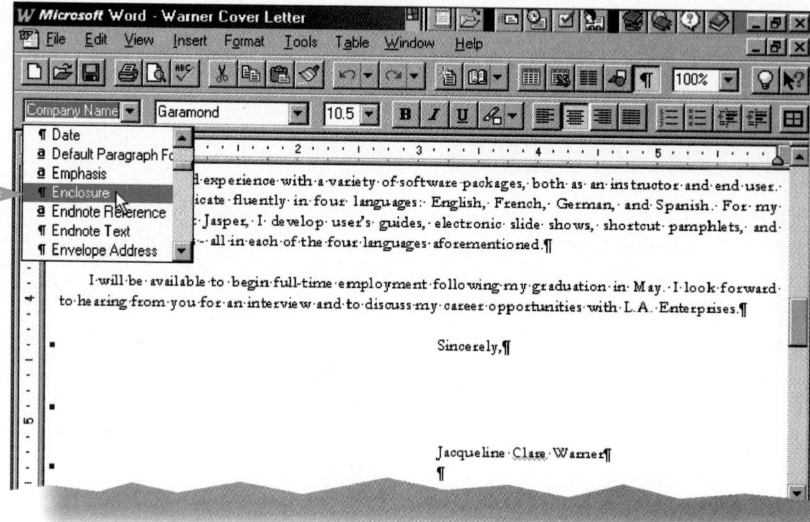

FIGURE 2-68

Click Enclosure.

Word changes the style name from Signature Company Name to Enclosure. The Enclosure style positions the insertion point at the left margin.

Type `Enclosure` **as the notation.**

Word displays the Enclosure notation left-aligned two lines below the signature block (Figure 2-69).

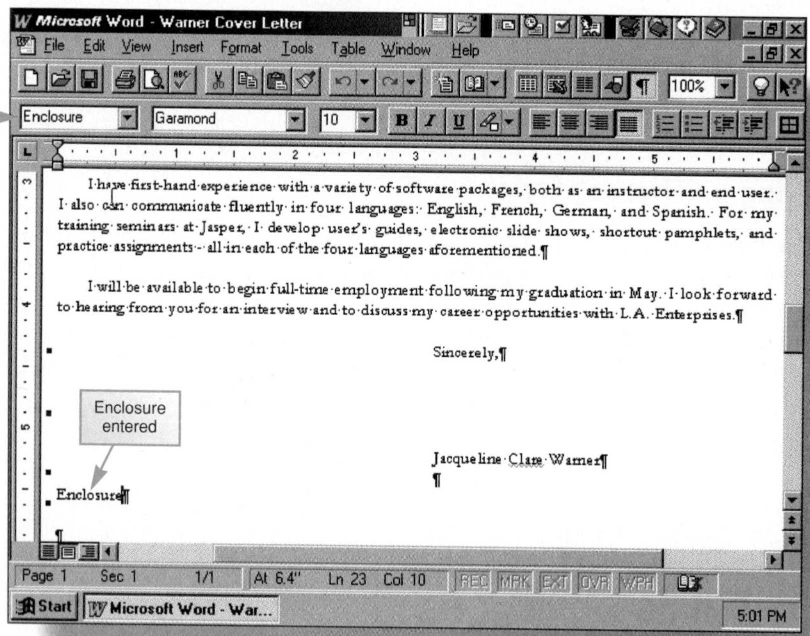

FIGURE 2-69

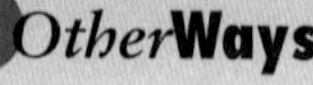

1. On Format menu click Style, select desired style in Styles list box, click OK button

Changing the Font Size of All Characters in the Cover Letter

The next process in modifying the cover letter is to change the font size of all the characters in it. Currently, the characters are 10 point, which is difficult for most people to comfortably read. Professionals recommend that business documents be written using 12 point. To change all the characters in the cover letter to 12 point, you must select the entire document first and then change the font size as shown in the following steps.

To Change the Font Size of All Characters in a Document

1 **Click Edit on the menu bar and then point to Select All (Figure 2-70).**

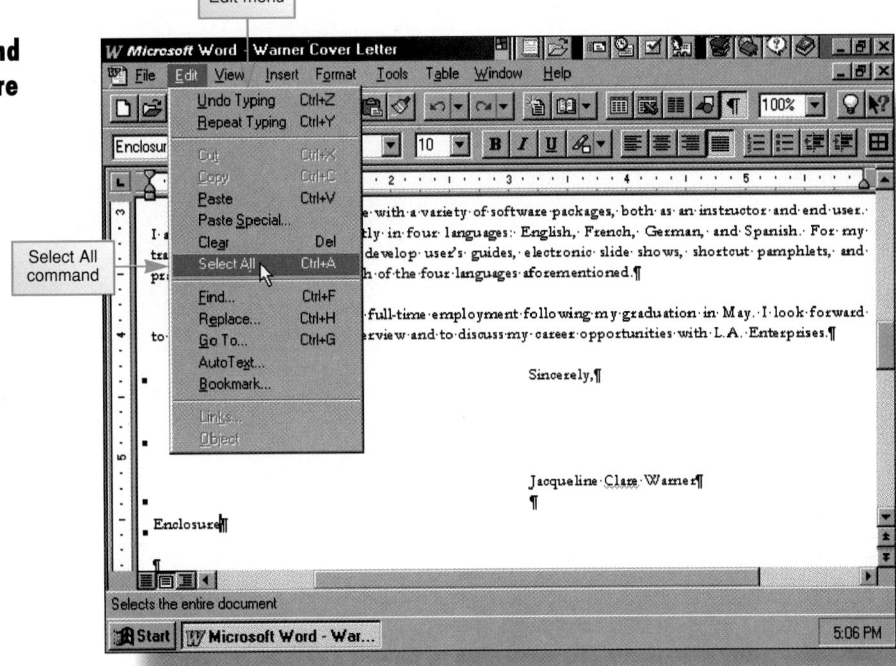

FIGURE 2-70

2 **Click Select All.**

Word highlights all the characters in the document (Figure 2-71).

3 **Click the Font Size box arrow on the Formatting toolbar and then point to 12.**

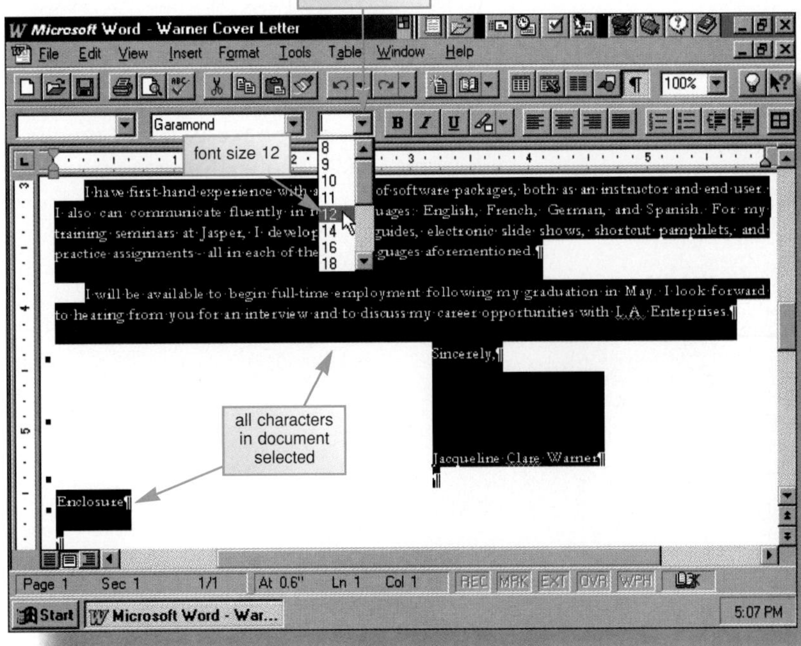

FIGURE 2-71

4. **Click 12.**

   Word changes the font size of the selected text from 10 to 12 (Figure 2-72).

5. **Click anywhere to remove the highlight.**

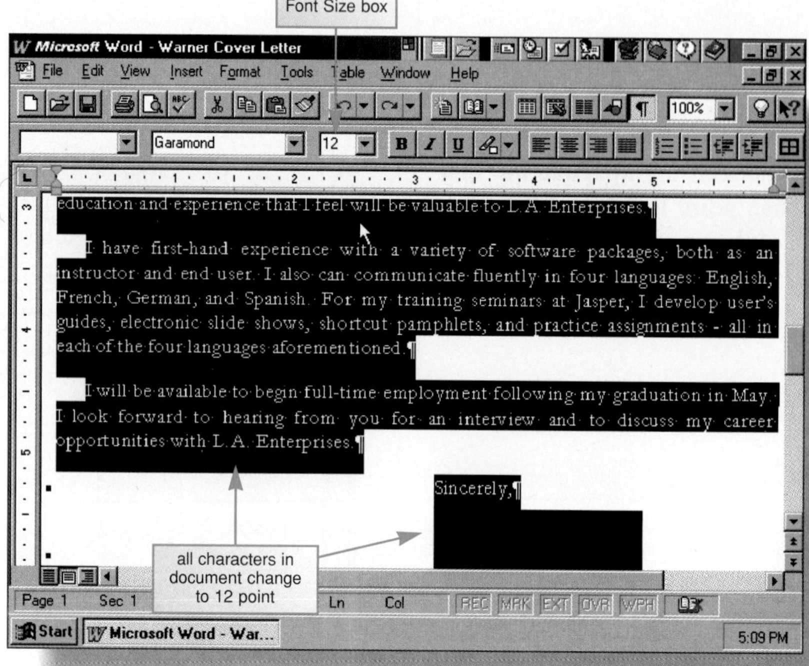

FIGURE 2-72

Other Ways

1. Press CTRL+A

Copying Text from One Open Word Document to Another

The cover letter that Word created using the letter template placed the return address information at the bottom of the letter, which you must personalize (Figure 2-49 on page WD 2.35). You either could select and enter the return address information, or you could copy it from your resume. Recall that the Resume Wizard automatically placed your return address information at the bottom of the resume (Figure 2-44 on page WD 2.31).

You currently have two documents open: Warner Cover Letter and Warner Resume. Each is in a different document window. You easily can switch back and forth between the two documents. To copy text from one open Word document to another, you select the text to be copied, click the Copy button, switch to the other open Word document, position the insertion point where you want to paste the text, and then click the Paste button as shown in these steps.

More About Selecting All Characters

You can also triple-click to the left of any paragraph in a document to select all characters in the document. However, when a document contains a frame, like the letterhead of the cover letter, this mouse technique does not work. Thus, you must use the Select All command on the Edit menu (or press CTRL+A) when a document contains a frame.

To Copy Text from One Open Word Document to Another

1 **Scroll to the bottom of the cover letter. Click Window on the menu bar and then point to 2 Warner Resume.**

Two Word documents are currently open: 1 Warner Cover Letter and 2 Warner Resume (Figure 2-73). The return address in the cover letter currently uses two lines.

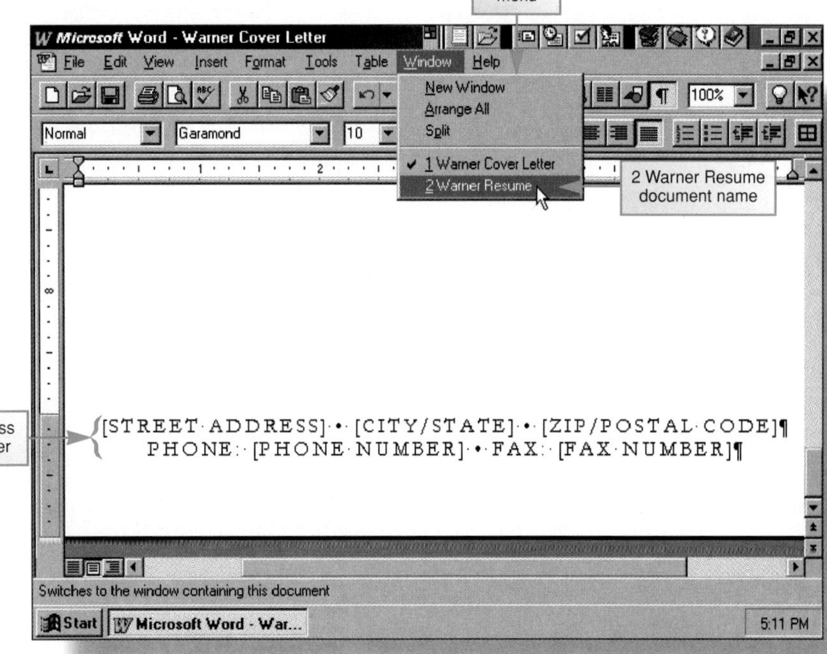

FIGURE 2-73

2 **Click 2 Warner Resume.**

Word switches from the cover letter to the resume. The document window now displays the resume you created earlier in this project.

3 **Scroll to the bottom of the resume to display the return address line. Triple-click the return address line to select it. Point to the Copy button on the Standard toolbar.**

Word selects the return address line (Figure 2-74).

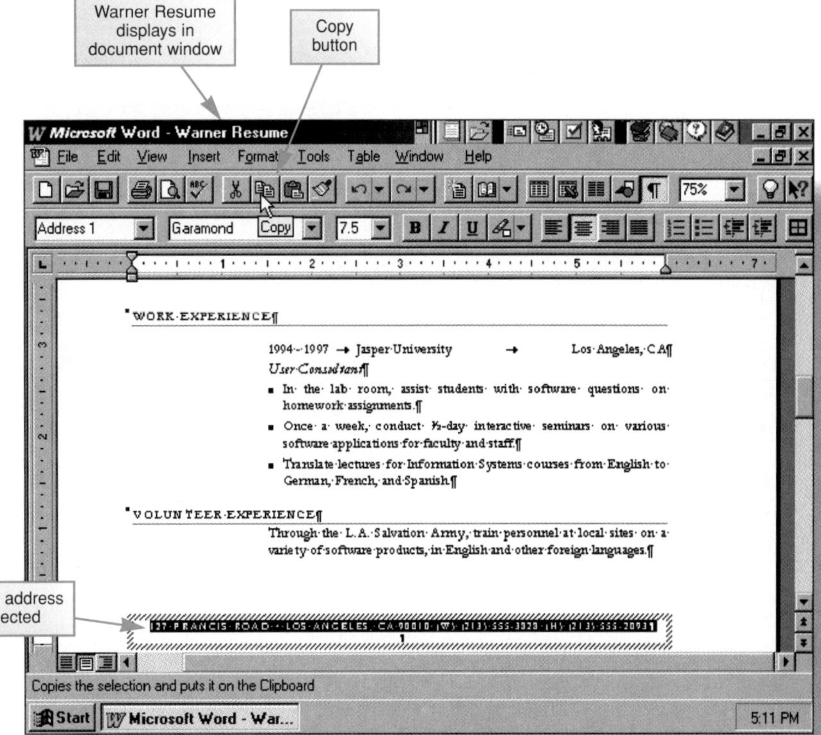

FIGURE 2-74

4 Click the Copy button on the Standard toolbar. Click Window on the menu bar and then point to 1 Warner Cover Letter (Figure 2-75).

Word copies the selection to the Clipboard.

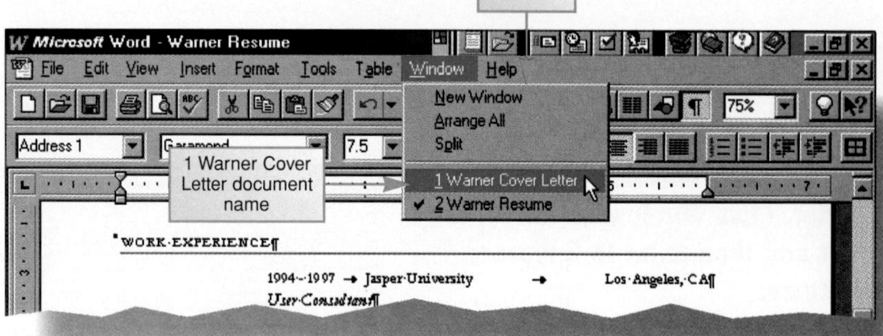

FIGURE 2-75

5 Click 1 Warner Cover Letter.

Word switches from the resume to the cover letter. The document window now displays the cover letter.

6 Point to the left of the first line in the return address and drag down to select both lines. Point to the Paste button on the Standard toolbar.

Word selects the entire return address at the bottom of the resume (Figure 2-76).

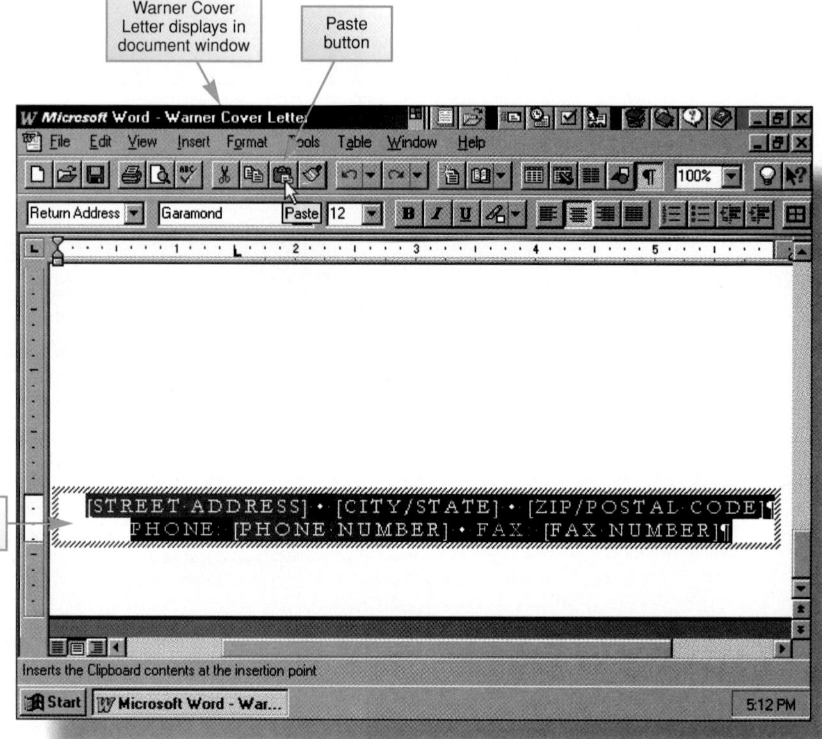

FIGURE 2-76

7 Click the Paste button on the Standard toolbar. Scroll to the bottom of the cover letter.

Word replaces the selection with the contents of the Clipboard (Figure 2-77). The return address lines in the cover letter and resume are now exact duplicates of one another.

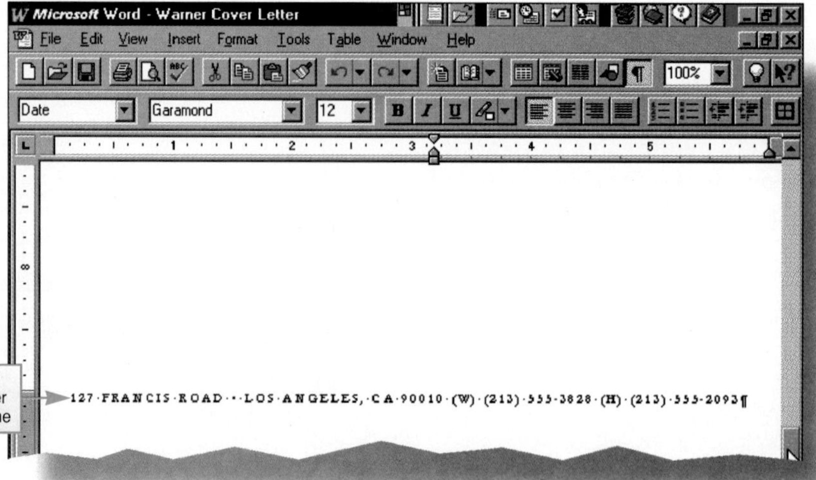

FIGURE 2-77

Other Ways

1. Select text to copy, on Edit menu click Copy, click location to paste, on Edit menu click Paste
2. Select text to copy, press CTRL+C, click location to paste, press CTRL+V

Throughout Projects 1 and 2, you have selected text and then formatted it. The text has ranged from characters to words to an entire document. Because selecting text is such a crucial function of Word, Table 2-4 summarizes the techniques used to select various forms of text with the mouse.

Saving Again, Spell Checking, and Printing the Cover Letter

The cover letter for the resume is now complete. After completing the cover letter, you should check its spelling by clicking the Spelling button on the Standard toolbar. Because you have performed several tasks since the last save, you should save the cover letter again by clicking the Save button on the Standard toolbar. Finally, you should print the cover letter by clicking the Print button on the Standard toolbar. When you remove the document from the printer, the printout displays the finished cover letter (Figure 2-78).

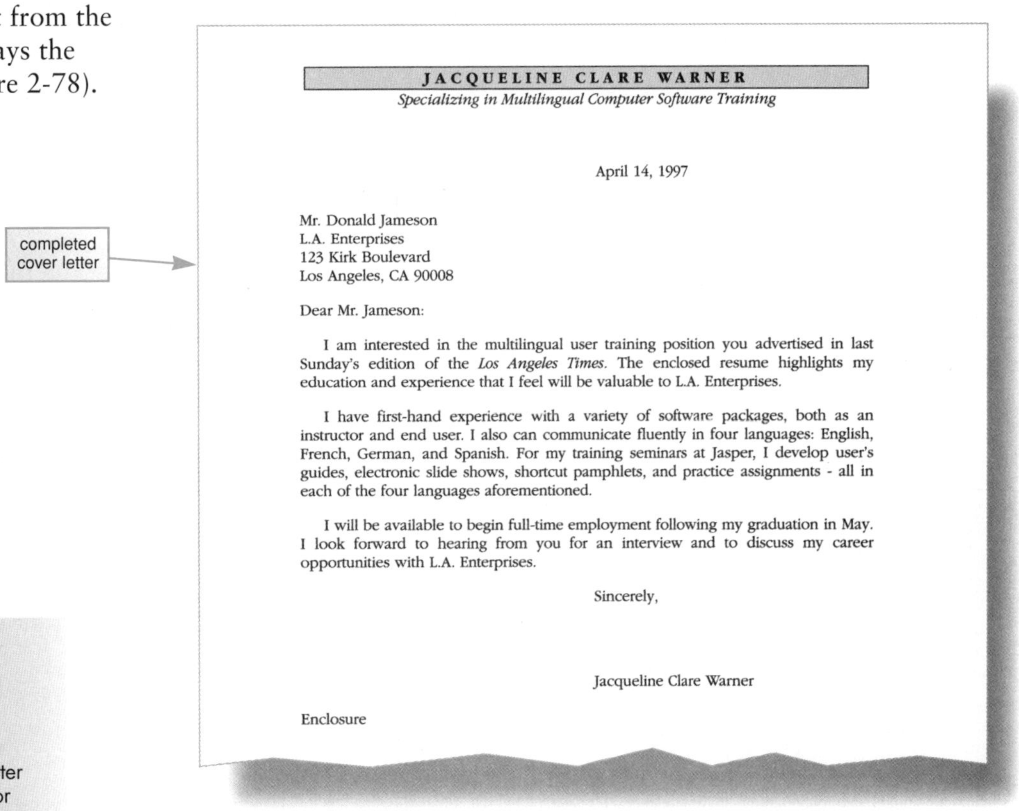

Table 2-4

ITEM TO SELECT	MOUSE ACTION
Character(s)	Drag over the character(s)
Document	Move mouse to the left of the paragraph until the mouse pointer changes direction and then triple-click
Graphic	Click the graphic
Line	Move the mouse to the left of the line until the mouse pointer changes direction and then click
Lines	Move the mouse to the left of the first line until the mouse pointer changes direction and then drag
Paragraph	Move the mouse to the left of the paragraph until the mouse pointer changes direction and then double-click; or triple-click paragraph
Paragraphs	Move the mouse to the left of pthe aragraph until the mouse pointer changes direction, double-click, and then drag
Sentence	Hold down the CTRL key and then click the sentence
Word	Double-click the word
Words	Drag over words

completed cover letter

JACQUELINE CLARE WARNER
Specializing in Multilingual Computer Software Training

April 14, 1997

Mr. Donald Jameson
L.A. Enterprises
123 Kirk Boulevard
Los Angeles, CA 90008

Dear Mr. Jameson:

I am interested in the multilingual user training position you advertised in last Sunday's edition of the *Los Angeles Times*. The enclosed resume highlights my education and experience that I feel will be valuable to L.A. Enterprises.

I have first-hand experience with a variety of software packages, both as an instructor and end user. I also can communicate fluently in four languages: English, French, German, and Spanish. For my training seminars at Jasper, I develop user's guides, electronic slide shows, shortcut pamphlets, and practice assignments - all in each of the four languages aforementioned.

I will be available to begin full-time employment following my graduation in May. I look forward to hearing from you for an interview and to discuss my career opportunities with L.A. Enterprises.

Sincerely,

Jacqueline Clare Warner

Enclosure

FIGURE 2-78

More *About* Printing

Print the resume and cover letter on standard letter-size white or ivory paper. Print a copy for yourself, and read it – especially before the interview. The interviewer is likely to have a copy, ready to ask you questions about the contents of both the resume and cover letter.

Closing All Open Files

You currently have two Word document files open: Warner Cover Letter and Warner Resume. Instead of closing each one individually, you can close all open files at once as shown in the following steps.

Steps To Close All Open Word Documents

1 Press and hold the SHIFT key and then click File on the menu bar. Release the SHIFT key. Point to Close All on the File menu.

Word displays a Close All command, instead of a Close command, in the File menu because you used the SHIFT key when clicking the menu name (Figure 2-79).

2 Click Close All.

Word closes all open documents and displays a blank document window.

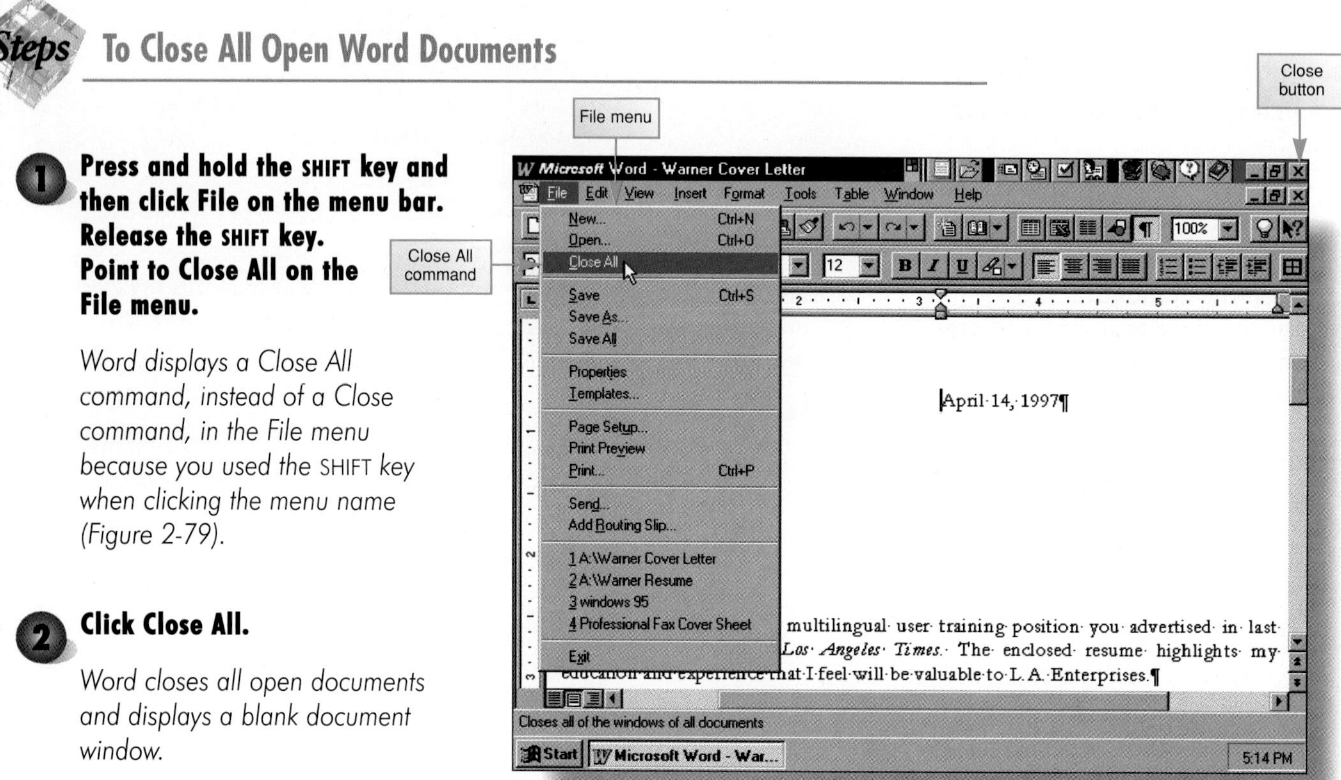

FIGURE 2-79

The final step in this project is to quit Word as described in the step below.

TO QUIT WORD

Step 1: Click the Close button at the right edge of Word's title bar.

The Word window closes.

More About Proofreading

You should be absolutely certain that your resume and accompanying cover letter are error free. Use a spell checker! Proofread for grammar errors. Set the resume and cover letter aside for a couple of days, and then proofread them again. Ask others, like a friend or teacher, to proofread them also.

Project Summary

Project 2 introduced you to creating a cover letter and a resume using Word wizards and templates. You used the Resume Wizard to create a resume. Then, you enhanced the name on the resume by adding a shaded box border. You used several formatting techniques to personalize the resume. Next, you moved a paragraph in the resume. Then, you viewed and printed the resume in print preview. You used a letter template to create a cover letter and then personalized the cover letter. You created an AutoText entry, which you used when you personalized the cover letter. Finally, you learned how to switch between and copy text from one open Word document to another and close multiple open Word documents.

What You Should Know

Having completed this project, you now should be able to perform the following tasks:

- Apply a style *(WD 2.45)*
- Bold a line *(WD 2.15)*
- Border and shade a paragraph *(WD 2.16)*
- Change the font size of all characters in a document *(WD 2.46)*
- Close all open Word documents *(WD 2.52)*
- Copy text from one open Word document to another *(WD 2.48)*
- Create a letter using a template in Word *(WD 2.33)*
- Create an AutoText entry *(WD 2.39)*
- Create a resume using Word's Resume Wizard *(WD 2.7)*
- Display nonprinting characters *(WD 2.15)*
- Drag and drop selected text *(WD 2.28)*
- Enter a line break *(WD 2.23)*
- Enter the AWARDS RECEIVED and LANGUAGES sections *(WD 2.23)*
- Enter the remaining section of the resume *(WD 2.26)*
- Enter the salutation *(WD 2.41)*
- Enter the signature block *(WD 2.45)*
- Finish the body of the cover letter *(WD 2.44)*
- Format characters using shortcut keys *(WD 2.41)*
- Insert an AutoText entry *(WD 2.43)*
- Modify formatting applied by a style *(WD 2.37)*
- Print the resume created by the Resume Wizard *(WD 2.13)*
- Quit Word *(WD 2.52)*
- Save a document *(WD 2.27* and *WD 2.41)*
- Select and replace more instructions *(WD 2.39)*
- Select and replace Resume Wizard placeholder text *(WD 2.18)*
- Select and replace Resume Wizard supplied text *(WD 2.19)*
- Select and replace template placeholder text *(WD 2.36)*
- Select a paragraph *(WD 2.28)*
- Use print preview *(WD 2.30)*
- Use Word's AutoFormat As You Type feature *(WD 2.25)*
- Vertically align information with the TAB key *(WD 2.21)*
- Zoom a document *(WD 2.14* and *WD 2.35)*

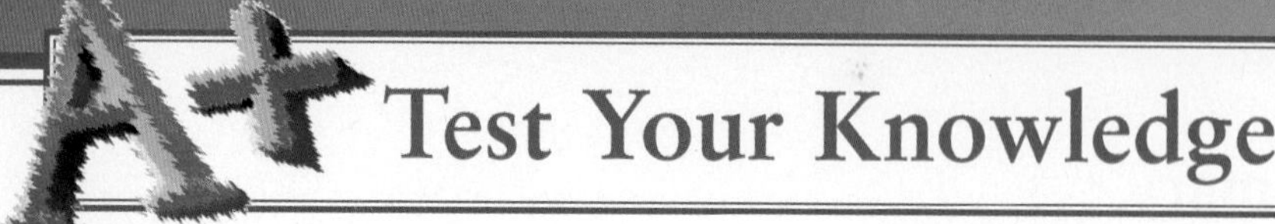

Test Your Knowledge

1 True/False

Instructions: Circle T if the statement is true or F if the statement is false.

T F 1. Word provides wizards and templates to assist you in document preparation.
T F 2. All business letters should contain a date line, inside address, message, and signature block.
T F 3. A style is a customized format that can be applied to characters or paragraphs.
T F 4. A border is a line added to the edge of a paragraph.
T F 5. When you click the Borders button, the Borders dialog box displays on the screen.
T F 6. When you paste text into a document, the Clipboard contents are erased.
T F 7. The TAB key is used to vertically align text in a document.
T F 8. You can print a document from within print preview.
T F 9. To switch from one open Word document to another, choose the Switch button on the Standard toolbar.
T F 10. In print preview, the Print Preview toolbar displays stacked below the Formatting toolbar.

2 Multiple Choice

Instructions: Circle the correct response.

1. Which of the following is optional in a business letter?
   a. signature block
   b. inside address
   c. salutation
   d. complimentary close
2. In the Style list box, style names preceded by a paragraph mark (¶) are called ______________.
   a. active styles
   b. inactive styles
   c. paragraph styles
   d. character styles
3. To align both sides of a paragraph evenly, click the ______________ button on the Formatting toolbar.
   a. Align Left
   b. Align Right
   c. Center
   d. Justify
4. You can add a border ______________.
   a. above a paragraph
   b. below a paragraph
   c. to the right edge of a paragraph
   d. all of the above

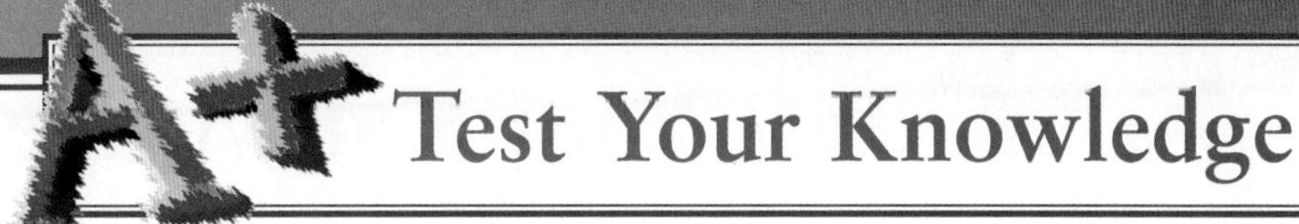

Test Your Knowledge

5. To select an entire paragraph, _______________.
   a. double-click to the left of the paragraph
   b. triple-click the paragraph
   c. both a and b
   d. neither a nor b
6. To insert an AutoText entry, type the AutoText name and then _______________.
   a. press the INSERT key
   b. click the AutoText button on the Standard toolbar
   c. double-click the AutoText name in the document
   d. press F3
7. When you press the TAB key, _______________ displays on the screen.
   a. a raised dot
   b. a paragraph mark
   c. a right-pointing arrow
   d. the letter T
8. Press _______________ to create a line break.
   a. ENTER
   b. CTRL+ENTER
   c. SHIFT+ENTER
   d. ALT+ENTER
9. To display the Close All command on the File menu, _______________.
   a. double-click File on the menu bar
   b. right-click File on the menu bar
   c. press and hold the SHIFT key and then click File on the menu bar
   d. press and hold the ALT key and then click File on the menu bar
10. In print preview, the Standard toolbar _______________.
    a. displays above the Print Preview toolbar
    b. displays below the Print Preview toolbar
    c. displays above the Formatting toolbar
    d. does not display

A+ Test Your Knowledge

3 Understanding the Components of a Business Letter

Instructions: In Figure 2-80, arrows point to components of a business letter. Identify the various elements of the letter in the spaces provided.

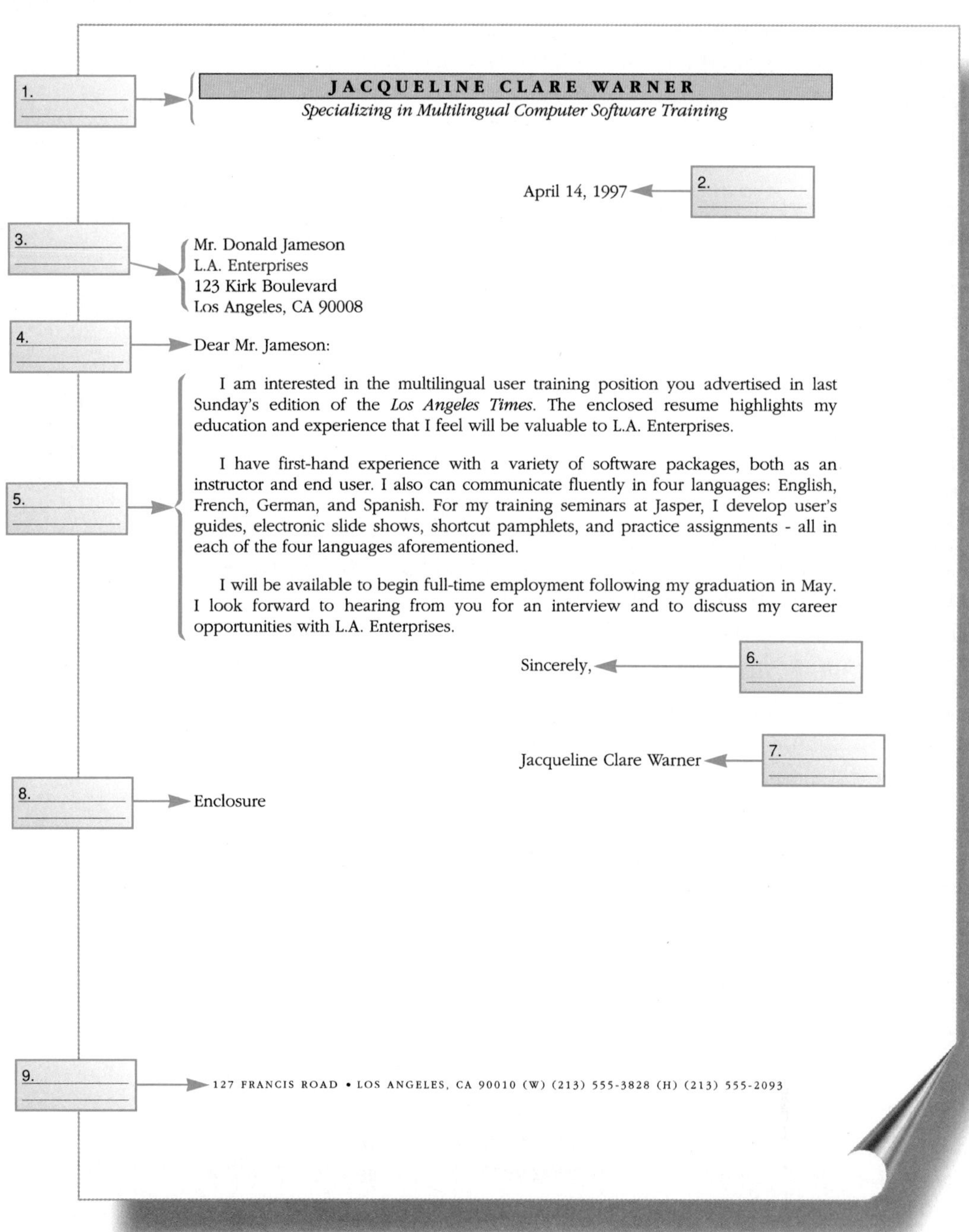

JACQUELINE CLARE WARNER
Specializing in Multilingual Computer Software Training

April 14, 1997

Mr. Donald Jameson
L.A. Enterprises
123 Kirk Boulevard
Los Angeles, CA 90008

Dear Mr. Jameson:

I am interested in the multilingual user training position you advertised in last Sunday's edition of the *Los Angeles Times*. The enclosed resume highlights my education and experience that I feel will be valuable to L.A. Enterprises.

I have first-hand experience with a variety of software packages, both as an instructor and end user. I also can communicate fluently in four languages: English, French, German, and Spanish. For my training seminars at Jasper, I develop user's guides, electronic slide shows, shortcut pamphlets, and practice assignments - all in each of the four languages aforementioned.

I will be available to begin full-time employment following my graduation in May. I look forward to hearing from you for an interview and to discuss my career opportunities with L.A. Enterprises.

Sincerely,

Jacqueline Clare Warner

Enclosure

127 FRANCIS ROAD • LOS ANGELES, CA 90010 (W) (213) 555-3828 (H) (213) 555-2093

FIGURE 2-80

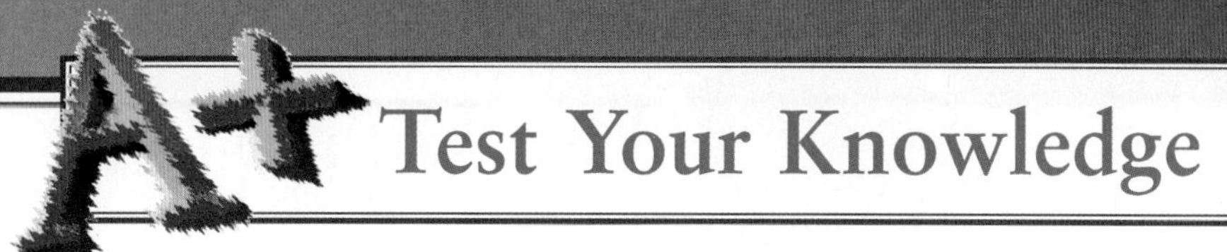

Test Your Knowledge

4 Understanding the Borders Toolbar

Instructions: In Figure 2-81, arrows point to several of the boxes and buttons on the Borders toolbar. In the spaces provided, briefly explain the purpose of each button or box.

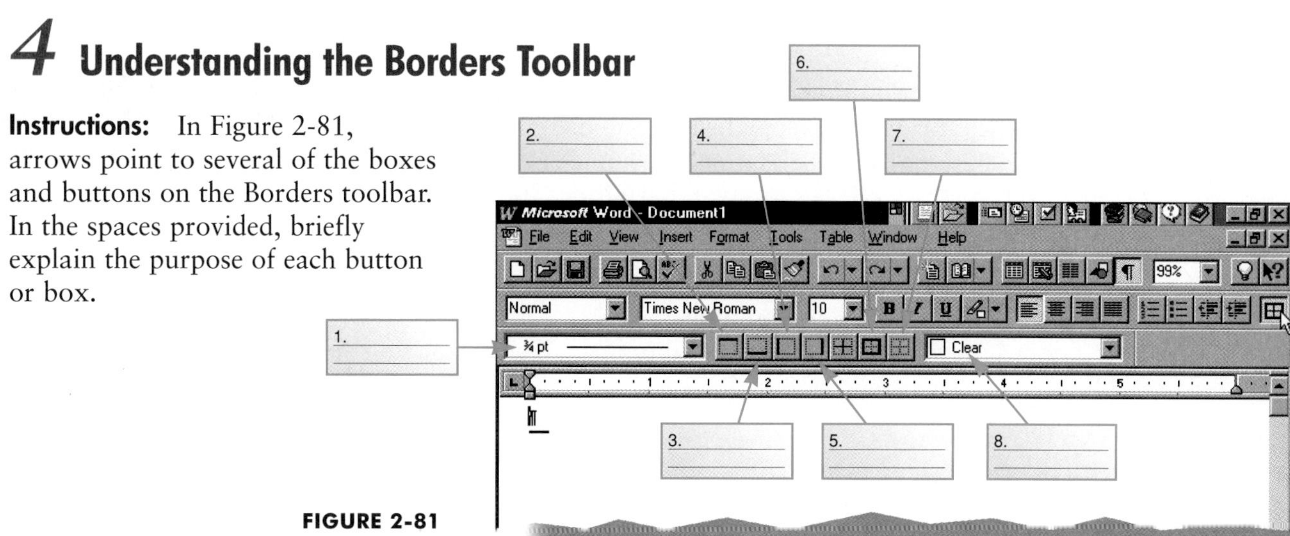

FIGURE 2-81

Use Help

1 Reviewing Project Activities

Instructions: Perform the following tasks using a computer.

1. Start Word.
2. Double-click the Help button on the Standard toolbar.
3. Click the Contents tab. Double-click the What's New book. Double-click the New Word templates topic.
4. Click Three families of templates and read the information. Click the remaining labels and read their help information. What is an example of placeholder text?
5. Click the Help Topics button to return to the Help Topics: Microsoft Word window. Click the Index tab. Type `wizards` and then click the creating documents topic. Click the Display button. Double-click Documents Word can create for me to display a Help window on the selected topic.
6. Ready the printer and click the Options button. Click Print Topic and then click the OK button to produce a hard copy of the Help window.
7. Click the Help Topics button. Click the Find tab. Type `styles` and then click the Apply a style topic. Click the Display button. Click the Options button. Click Print Topic and then click the OK button.

(continued)

Use Help

Reviewing Project Activities *(continued)*

8. Click the Help Topics button. Click the Answer Wizard tab. Type `move text` and then click the Search button. Click the Move or copy text or graphics a short distance within a window topic. Click the Display button. Click the Options button. Click Print Topic and then click the OK button.
9. Close any open Help windows by clicking their Close button in the upper right corner of the Help window's title bar.
10. Click the Help button on the Standard toolbar.
11. Click the Zoom Control box on the Standard toolbar. What is the function of the Zoom Control box?

2 Expanding on the Basics

Instructions: Perform the following tasks using a computer and answer the questions.

Print preview is an extremely valuable tool in Microsoft Word 7 for Windows 95. Using the Contents tab in the Help Topics: Microsoft Word dialog box, answer the following questions:

1. How do you edit text in print preview?
2. What is the advantage of using a TrueType font for characters in a document?
3. In print preview, how can you prevent a document from *spilling* onto a second page?

Borders and shading make paragraphs in a Word document look more professional. Using the Index tab in the Help Topics: Microsoft Word dialog box, answer the following questions:

1. Using AutoFormat As You Type, how do you place a *thin line* border, a *thick line* border, and a *double line* border above a paragraph?
2. Using the Borders toolbar, how do you add a 2 ¼ pt border below a paragraph?
3. Using the Borders toolbar, how do you remove shading from a paragraph?

In Microsoft Word 7 for Windows 95, you can view a document in many different ways, depending on your requirements. Use the Find tab in the Help Topics: Microsoft Word dialog box to answer these questions about viewing a Word document.

1. When should you use normal view?
2. What is the purpose of page layout view?
3. How do you switch to outline view? Where is the Outline View button located?
4. Using the mouse, how can you view two different parts of the same document simultaneously? How, then, do you return to a single window after splitting it?

Microsoft Word 7 for Windows 95 can be used as an electronic mail editor. Use the Answer Wizard to obtain answers to the following questions:

1. How can you set up Word as an electronic mail editor?
2. How can you create an automatic signature for electronic mail messages?
3. If you have an existing AutoText entry in a Word document, how do you modify it? How do you delete it?
4. How can you emphasize information in a message with color?

Apply Your Knowledge

1 Enhancing a Document

Instructions: Start Word. Open the document Credit Report Request from the Word folder on the Student floppy disk that accompanies this book. The document was created using the elegant style of letter in the Letter Wizard. You are to enhance the letterhead, move a paragraph, add an enclosure notation, and change the font size of all characters to 12. The completed document is shown in Figure 2-82.

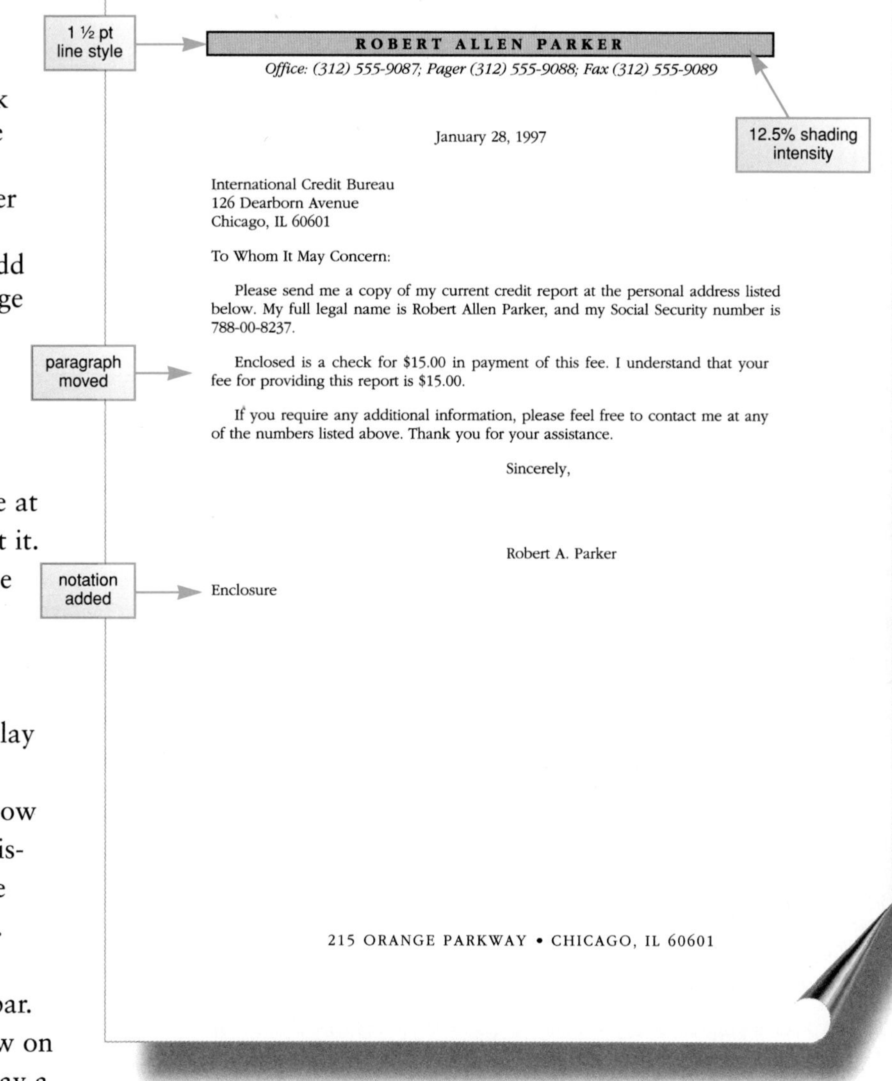

FIGURE 2-82

Perform the following tasks:

1. Click to the left of the name at the top of the letter to select it.
2. Click the Bold button on the Formatting toolbar.
3. If the Borders button on the Formatting toolbar is not recessed, click it to display the Borders toolbar.
4. Click the Line Style box arrow on the Borders toolbar to display the list of available line styles and then click 1 ½ pt.
5. Click the Outside Border button on the Borders toolbar.
6. Click the Shading box arrow on the Borders toolbar to display a list of available shading intensities and then click 12.5%.
7. Click the Borders button on the Formatting toolbar to remove the Borders toolbar.
8. Click to the left of the second line of the letterhead (the telephone numbers) to select it.
9. Click the Italic button on the Formatting toolbar.
10. Position the mouse pointer to the left of the third paragraph, which begins, Enclosed is a check for . . . . Double-click the mouse to select the paragraph. Position the mouse pointer in the selected paragraph. Press and hold down the left mouse button. Drag the insertion point to the left of the I in the paragraph beginning, If you require any additional information, . . . , and then release the mouse button.

(continued)

Apply Your Knowledge

Enhancing a Document *(continued)*

11. Position the insertion point just after the r in Parker in the signature block. Press the ENTER key twice. Click the Style box arrow on the Formatting toolbar to display a list of available styles and then scroll up to Enclosure. Click Enclosure and then type `Enclosure` as the notation.
12. Click Edit on the menu bar and then click Select All to select the entire document.
13. Click the Font Size box arrow on the Formatting toolbar and then click 12.
14. Click File on the menu bar and then click Save As. Use the filename, Revised Credit Report Request, and then save the document on your data disk.
15. Print the revised document.

In the Lab

1 Using Word's Resume Wizard to Create a Resume

Problem: You are a student at the University of North Carolina expecting to receive your Bachelor of Science degree in electrical engineering this May. As the semester's end is quickly approaching, you are beginning a search for full-time employment upon graduation. You prepare the resume shown in Figure 2-83 using Word's Resume Wizard.

Instructions:

1. Use the Resume Wizard to create a resume. Use the name and address information in Figure 2-83 when the Resume Wizard requests it.
2. Save the resume on a floppy disk with Smith Resume as the filename.
3. If necessary, click the Show/Hide ¶ button on the Standard toolbar.
4. Personalize the resume as shown in Figure 2-83. When entering multiple lines below the TECHNICAL EXPERIENCE and PROFESSIONAL MEMBERSHIPS headings, be sure to enter a line break at the end of each line, instead of a paragraph break. Use the TAB key to align EDUCATION and TECHNICAL EXPERIENCE data.
5. Check the spelling of the resume. Save the resume again with the same filename.
6. Print the resume from within print preview.

name

FREDRICK WILLIAM SMITH

OBJECTIVE

To obtain an entry-level engineering position, specializing in computers and networks, with a major electronics firm

EDUCATION

1994 - 1998 University of North Carolina Charlotte, NC
Electrical Engineering
- B.S. in Network Engineering May 1998 GPA 3.8/4.0
- A.S. in Electrical Engineering May 1996 GPA 3.8/4.0

AWARDS RECEIVED

1997 Engineering Student of the Year

TECHNICAL EXPERIENCE

Hardware: microcomputers, minicomputers, mainframes
Networks: LANs, WANs
Languages: C, C++, Visual C

WORK EXPERIENCE

1996 - 1998 Consumer Electronics Charlotte, NC
Computer Repairman
- Service microcomputers for customers, which involves fine tuning, repairing, upgrading hardware or software, and configuring.
- Offer 24-hour hot-line assistance over the telephone to customers with technical problems.
- Install computer networks for small to medium-sized businesses that purchase our hardware and software solutions.

PROFESSIONAL MEMBERSHIPS

International Association of Engineers
Engineering Management Association

HOBBIES

Classic cars and scuba diving

address information

5609 FREEMONT LANE • CHARLOTTE, NC 28208 (W) (704) 555-1583 (H) (704) 555-0932

FIGURE 2-83

2 Using the Letter Template to Create a Cover Letter

Problem: You have just prepared the resume shown in Figure 2-83 on the previous page and now are ready to create a cover letter to send to a prospective employer. In last Sunday's edition of the *North Carolina Chronicle*, you noticed an advertisement for an entry-level engineering position at Warner Electronics. You prepare the cover letter shown in Figure 2-84 to send with your resume.

Instructions:

1. If it is not already selected, click the Show/Hide ¶ button on the Standard toolbar.
2. Create an Elegant style letter by clicking the Elegant Letter icon in the Letters & Faxes sheet of the New dialog box.
3. Save the letter on a floppy disk with Smith Cover Letter as the filename.
4. Enter the letterhead so it looks like Figure 2-84.
5. Enter the inside address and then the salutation.
6. Create an AutoText entry, named we, for Warner Electronics that displays in the inside address.
7. Personalize the body of the cover letter so it matches Figure 2-84. Use the AutoText entry you created in Step 6 whenever you have to enter the company name, Warner Electronics.
8. Enter the signature block as shown in Figure 2-84.
9. Create an Enclosure paragraph.

FREDRICK WILLIAM SMITH

Engineered to Solve Computerized Electronic Problems

April 28, 1997

Ms. Anita Darby
Warner Electronics
335 Summit Boulevard
Charlotte, NC 28208

Dear Ms. Darby:

I am interested in the entry-level engineering position you advertised in last Sunday's edition of the *North Carolina Chronicle*. The enclosed resume outlines my education and experience that I feel will be valuable to Warner Electronics.

I will be receiving my Bachelor of Science degree in Electrical Engineering this May. My major focuses on computer networks. In my courses, I installed, fine tuned, and upgraded networks. I also have real-world experience with computer networks. As a part-time computer repairman at Consumer Electronics, I install and configure computer networks and assist customers. My position also includes answering technical questions on a 24-hour hot line.

Given my work and educational experience, I feel I would be a valuable asset to Warner Electronics as an electrical engineer. I will be available to begin full-time employment following my graduation in May. I look forward to hearing from you for an interview and to discuss my career opportunities with Warner Electronics.

Sincerely,

Fredrick William Smith

Enclosure

FIGURE 2-84

In the Lab

10. Change the font size of all characters in the document to 12 point.
11. Enter the return address information at the bottom of the cover letter. If you created the Smith Resume in In the Lab 1, you can open the Smith Resume and then copy the return address line from the Smith Resume to the Smith Cover Letter; otherwise refer to Figure 2-83 on page WD 2.61 for the return address information.
12. Check the spelling of the cover letter. Save the cover letter again with the same filename.
13. Print the cover letter.

3 Using the Letter Wizard to Compose a Prewritten Cover Letter

Problem: You are currently in the market for a new job and are ready to prepare a cover letter. Because you have a difficult time composing a cover letter, you would like to use Word's Letter Wizard to assist you in preparing a cover letter. In the prewritten letter, Word generates an entire sample cover letter as shown in Figure 2-85, which contains many underlined words and phrases. You must select and then replace the underlined words and phrases with your own to personalize it.

Instructions: Obtain a copy of last Sunday's newspaper. Look through the classified section and cut out a want ad in an area of interest to you. Assume you are in the market for the position being sought. Using the Letter Wizard, create a prewritten cover letter (Figure 2-85) for the want ad. When the Letter Wizard prompts you for address information, use the want ad for the inside address and your personal information for the return address. Save the cover letter with a meaningful filename. Try to be as accurate as possible when personalizing the cover letter. Follow the guidelines listed on the next page.

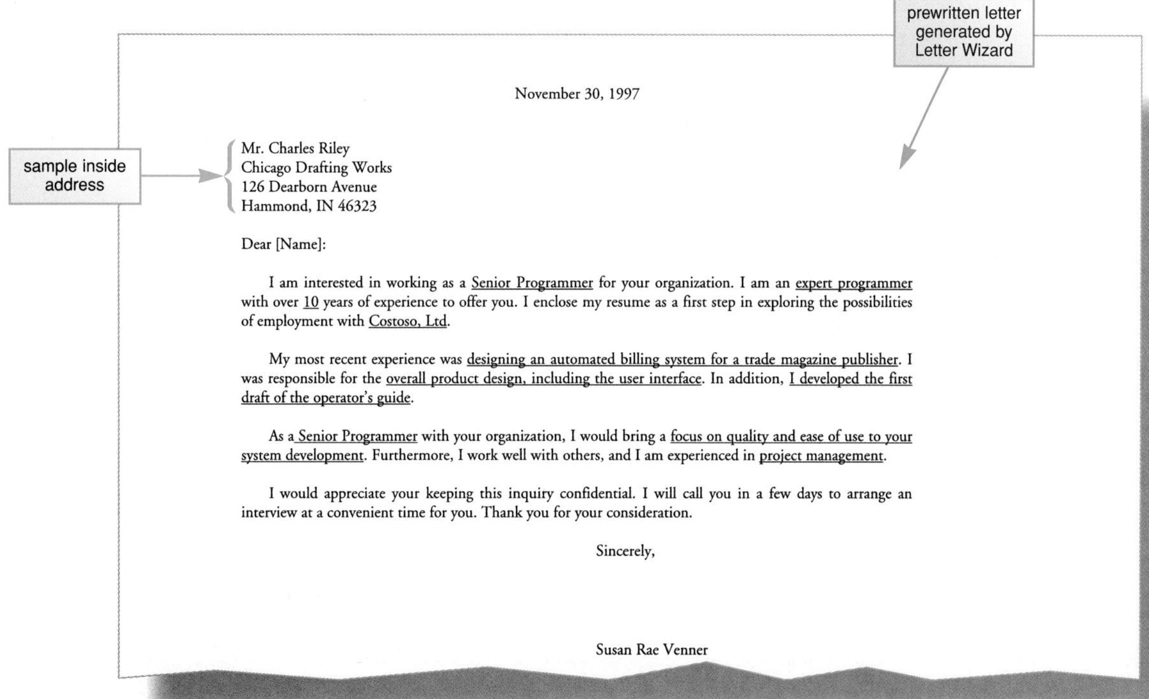

November 30, 1997

Mr. Charles Riley
Chicago Drafting Works
126 Dearborn Avenue
Hammond, IN 46323

Dear [Name]:

I am interested in working as a Senior Programmer for your organization. I am an expert programmer with over 10 years of experience to offer you. I enclose my resume as a first step in exploring the possibilities of employment with Costoso, Ltd.

My most recent experience was designing an automated billing system for a trade magazine publisher. I was responsible for the overall product design, including the user interface. In addition, I developed the first draft of the operator's guide.

As a Senior Programmer with your organization, I would bring a focus on quality and ease of use to your system development. Furthermore, I work well with others, and I am experienced in project management.

I would appreciate your keeping this inquiry confidential. I will call you in a few days to arrange an interview at a convenient time for you. Thank you for your consideration.

Sincerely,

Susan Rae Venner

FIGURE 2-85

(continued)

In the Lab

Using the Letter Wizard to Compose a Prewritten Cover Letter *(continued)*

1. Create a letterhead at the top of the prewritten cover letter.
2. Personalize the salutation.
3. In the body of the cover letter, replace all underlined words and phrases to meet your background and the advertisement. Be sure to remove the underlines once you personalize the information.
4. Read through the nonunderlined words and phrases in the body of the cover letter. Change any text as needed.
5. Change the font size of all characters in the document to 12 point.
6. Turn in the want ad with the hard copy of the cover letter.

Cases and Places

The difficulty of these case studies varies:

◗ Case studies preceded by a single half moon are the least difficult. You are asked to create the required document based on information that has already been placed in an organized form.
◗◗ Case studies preceded by two half moons are more difficult. You must organize the information presented before using it to create the required document.
◗◗◗ Case studies preceded by three half moons are the most difficult. You must decide on a specific topic, and then obtain and organize the necessary information before using it to create the required document.

1 ◗ A friend is working this summer at Mahoney Motors. She has been told to hire someone to design two awards that will be presented at an upcoming banquet. After assuring her that you can create the awards, she has given you the information in Figure 2-86.

With this information, together with the concepts and techniques presented in this project, use Word's Award Wizard to make the awards.

William Loman
Sales Achievement Award
To be presented by Thomas Henderson and Sharon Baker, co-chairpersons of the North Platt Automobile Association, on August 18.
Bill has led the region in sales for the last three months.

Thomas Packard
Top Quality Workmanship Award
To be presented by Frank Mahoney, president, and Judy Nash, service manager of Mahoney Motors, on August 18.
Tom has consistently earned the praise of customers for his care and his attention to detail.

FIGURE 2-86

Cases and Places

2 ◗ Penelope Laseré, your boss at South Shore Development, has left two contracts and the somewhat cryptic note shown in Figure 2-87 on your desk:

SOUTH SHORE DEVELOPMENT
43 Lake Avenue, Cleveland, OH 44100

Send letter to Brad Benderson (134 Tupper Street, Cleveland, OH 44100). Lease for office 156 in the Conworthy and Taylor building expires February 2. New contract renews lease for one year at a rate of $756 per month. Rate increase a result of rising utility and maintenance costs. Contracts to be signed and returned three weeks prior to expiration date.

FIGURE 2-87

With this information and Word's Letter Wizard, modify a prewritten business letter to send with the new contracts. Make whatever changes are necessary to the underlined material in the letter and then remove the underlining. Use the concepts and techniques presented in this project to format the letter.

3 ◗◗ As an editor at Equus Publishing (5625 Conway Avenue, Boston, MA 02100; Phone (617) 555-9063; Fax (617) 555-9064), you are always interested in new material. Recently you received a partial manuscript from Paul Palomino, a budding author, for a book entitled *A Horse of a Different Color*. The book seems interesting, but you are unsure about the author's slightly unorthodox approach. You have decided to ask other writers for their opinions on the book's story, characters, and style. Furthermore, you would like them to comment on the accuracy of the book's historical references. You plan to fax three pages of the manuscript to Susan Bay, a professor at Cob College (Churchill Downs, Lexington, KY 40501; Phone (606) 555-3421; Fax (606) 555-6234), and also will send copies to Harry Paint and June Gray. Use one of Word's Fax Templates or the Fax Wizard, together with the concepts and techniques presented in this project, to create and format a cover sheet for the facsimile transmission.

4 ◗◗ Mycroft Holmes, your boss at Baker Street Security, is increasingly concerned about the pilfering of office supplies. Paper clips, pens, pencils, envelopes, and so on are disappearing at an alarming rate. Holmes feels that not only does this have a negative impact on the office's cash flow, but if word of the petty theft ever leaked out, it would also seriously damage the company's reputation. Holmes has asked you to prepare a confidential memorandum regarding this matter for Arthur Watson, a department head. The memorandum should explain the problem and solicit elementary solutions. Copies of the memo should also be sent to John Moriarty and Larry Lestrade, the other department heads. Use one of Word's Memo Templates or the Memo Wizard, together with the concepts and techniques presented in this project, to create and format the interoffice memorandum.

Cases and Places

5 ▶▶▶ Major events or developments often are preceded by a press release, which provides the media with important information about the event or development, so that coverage will be thorough and accurate. Press releases can be particularly valuable to schools because they help make the local community more aware of the achievements of faculty and students. Find out about an event that will be taking place or a development that will be announced at your school in the near future. Use one of Word's Press Release Templates, together with the concepts and techniques presented in this project, to prepare a press release. When the document is completed, learn the name of a contact in the local media and send him or her a copy of the release.

6 ▶▶▶ Probably everyone has attended meetings that were chaotic affairs at which very little was accomplished. Meetings often can be made more effective with an agenda — a written plan that states when and where the meeting will take place, the subject of the meeting, the participants and their responsibilities, and the topics that will be discussed. An agenda can keep a meeting on track and help those attending prepare for the meeting. Find out about an upcoming meeting at your school, such as a club or student government meeting. Use Word's Agenda Wizard, and the concepts and techniques presented in this project, to prepare a thorough agenda for the meeting. Distribute the agenda to the relevant participants, and then attend the meeting to see if the agenda helps the meeting run more efficiently.

7 ▶▶▶ Some businesses use a brochure to promote their goods or services. These brochures present prospective clients with more information than posted advertisements, and provide written material they can take with them and review at their leisure. Visit a small company and learn as much as you can about their product. Find out how the product is unique, what features it offers, and why it would be valuable to potential buyers. Then, use Word's Brochure Template, along with the concepts and techniques presented in this project, to design a brochure advertising the product. When the brochure is complete, take it to the company and ask for their comments, suggestions, or recommendations.

Microsoft Word 7

Windows 95

Creating a Research Paper with a Table

Objectives:

You will have mastered the material in this project when you can:

- Describe the MLA documentation style for research papers
- Change the margin settings in a document
- Adjust line spacing in a document
- Use a header to number pages of a document
- Indent paragraphs
- Use Word's AutoCorrect feature
- Add a footnote to a research paper
- Spell check as you type
- Create a table using Word's Table Wizard
- Enter data into a Word table
- Insert a manual page break
- Create a hanging indent
- Sort selected paragraphs
- Use Word's thesaurus
- Display the number of words in a document

Einstein Meets the HTML *Manual of Style*

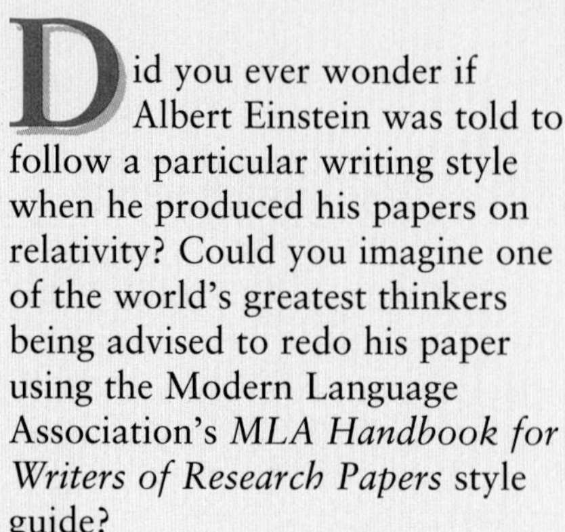

Did you ever wonder if Albert Einstein was told to follow a particular writing style when he produced his papers on relativity? Could you imagine one of the world's greatest thinkers being advised to redo his paper using the Modern Language Association's *MLA Handbook for Writers of Research Papers* style guide?

The form of a research paper often is considered as important as the content, so manuals of style have been developed to provide an orderly and consistent presentation, well documented and free of mechanical flaws. The first style rules were published in 1906, but their foundations are probably as old as the establishment of the Press itself in 1891.

As new media develop, new style guides are needed to reflect the impact of the new technology. After cruising along the WWW information superhighway with a brief stop at the Virtual Library's *HTML Manual of Style*, you might begin to question the very evolution of style manuals for writers. When Einstein wrote his General Theory of Relativity for *Annalen der*

Style Guide

E=MC²

RESEA

Physik in 1916, the accepted style for research papers was as new then as the *HTML Manual of Style* is today.

According to Sotheby's Inc., "every page of Einstein's manuscript shows extensive reworking . . . revealing the changes of thought of a great scientist who was also a notably sensitive stylist and expositor." Einstein's relativity paper was written following MLA styles that made use of only footnotes or endnotes. Although Einstein's paper initially was handwritten, imagine if after the paper was typed, some of his extensive reworkings created new footnotes. Because of the new footnotes, many of the existing notes might have to be renumbered. The entire page or even the whole document would have to be retyped to include the additional references at the bottom of the page.

Word processing software makes it easy to add, remove, or change references without having to rework the entire paper. Old style guidelines go through an evolution for easier use, just as new style guidelines are invented for new media. Today's style guidelines support parenthetical citations within the text with identified sources listed in the Works Cited page at the end of the paper. For example, instead of a lengthy footnote at the bottom of the page, Einstein's first reference simply would consist of a parenthetical citation following the sentence: "The present book is intended, . . . conversant with the mathematical apparatus of theoretical physics. (Einstein et al. [1])" The source then would be identified in the Works Cited section as:

Einstein, Albert, et al. *The Principle of Relativity: A Collection of Original Memoirs on the Special and General Theory of Relativity*. Ed. Arnold Sommerfeld. London: Metheun, 1923. Trans. of *Das Relativitatsprinzip: eine Sammlung von Abhandlungen*. Ed. Otto Blumenthal. Leipzig: Teubner, 1913.

Adapting Einstein's questioning methods, you might ponder further the evolution of writing styles based on the shift of language technology from the page to the screen. Only an Einstein, however, could predict the benefits that lie ahead.

FOOTNOTES

"every page of Einstein's manuscript shows extensive reworking . . . revealing the changes of thought of a great scientist who was also a notably sensitive stylist and expositor."

Microsoft
Word 7
Windows 95

Creating a Research Paper with a Table

Case Perspective

Caroline Rose Travis is a full-time student at Purdue University, majoring in Information Systems and Computer Programming. The professor in one of her computer classes, CIS 210, has assigned a 450- to 475-word research paper. The paper must discuss some aspect of personal computers. Because Caroline's sister recently developed tendonitis from improper mouse usage, Caroline decides to write the research paper on detecting and preventing injuries that can result from computer usage. The paper must be written according to the MLA documentation style, which specifies guidelines for report preparation. Professor Rhodes suggests students use the Internet to obtain the MLA guidelines. The paper must also contain one footnote and a table.

Caroline will interview her sister and her sister's doctor for first-hand information on tendonitis and other computer-related health injuries. Then, she plans to "surf the Internet" to obtain additional information on computer-related injuries and their prevention, as well as the guidelines for the MLA style of documentation.

Introduction

In both the academic and business environments, you will be asked to write reports. Business reports range from proposals to cost justifications to five-year plans to research findings. Academic reports focus mostly on research findings. Whether you are writing a business report or an academic report, you should follow a standard style when preparing it.

Many different styles of documentation exist for report preparation, depending on the nature of the report. Each style requires the same basic information; the differences among styles appear in the manner of presenting the information. For example, one documentation style may use the term *bibliography*; whereas, another uses *references*, and yet a third prefers *works cited*. A popular documentation style used today for research papers is presented by the **Modern Language Association (MLA)**. Thus, this project uses the **MLA style of documentation.**

Project Three — Research Paper with a Table

Project 3 illustrates the creation of a short research paper describing the health-related injuries that can afflict computer users. A table in the conclusion paragraph of the research paper outlines exercises that could prevent these types of computer-related injuries. As depicted in Figure 3-1, the paper follows the MLA style of documentation. The first two pages present the research paper and the third page lists the works cited alphabetically.

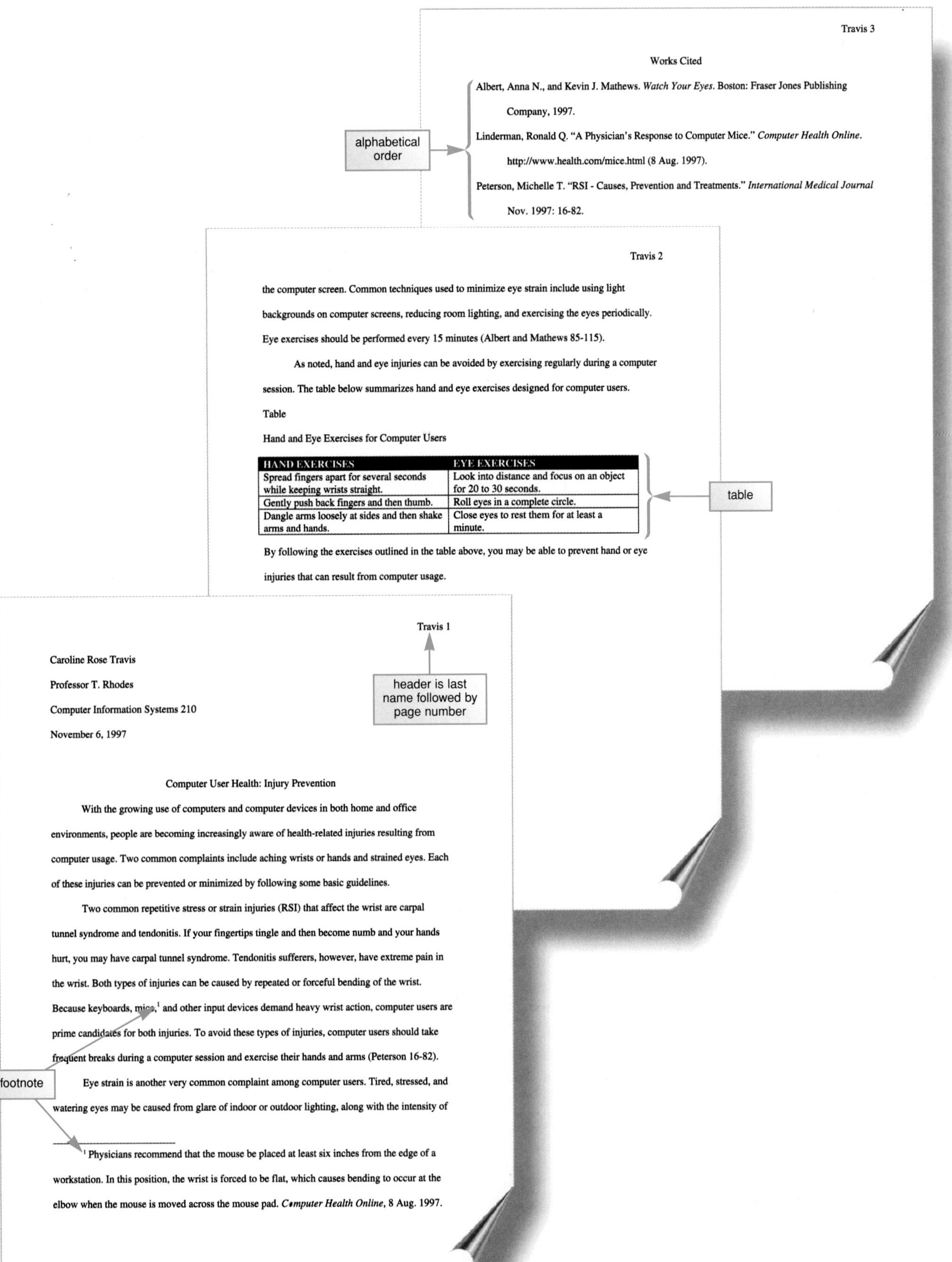
Travis 3
Works Cited
Albert, Anna N., and Kevin J. Mathews. *Watch Your Eyes.* Boston: Fraser Jones Publishing Company, 1997.
Linderman, Ronald Q. "A Physician's Response to Computer Mice." *Computer Health Online.* http://www.health.com/mice.html (8 Aug. 1997).
Peterson, Michelle T. "RSI - Causes, Prevention and Treatments." *International Medical Journal* Nov. 1997: 16-82.
alphabetical order
Travis 2
the computer screen. Common techniques used to minimize eye strain include using light backgrounds on computer screens, reducing room lighting, and exercising the eyes periodically. Eye exercises should be performed every 15 minutes (Albert and Mathews 85-115).
As noted, hand and eye injuries can be avoided by exercising regularly during a computer session. The table below summarizes hand and eye exercises designed for computer users.
Table
Hand and Eye Exercises for Computer Users
HAND EXERCISES
EYE EXERCISES
Spread fingers apart for several seconds while keeping wrists straight.
Look into distance and focus on an object for 20 to 30 seconds.
Gently push back fingers and then thumb.
Roll eyes in a complete circle.
Dangle arms loosely at sides and then shake arms and hands.
Close eyes to rest them for at least a minute.
table
By following the exercises outlined in the table above, you may be able to prevent hand or eye injuries that can result from computer usage.
Travis 1
header is last name followed by page number
Caroline Rose Travis
Professor T. Rhodes
Computer Information Systems 210
November 6, 1997
Computer User Health: Injury Prevention
With the growing use of computers and computer devices in both home and office environments, people are becoming increasingly aware of health-related injuries resulting from computer usage. Two common complaints include aching wrists or hands and strained eyes. Each of these injuries can be prevented or minimized by following some basic guidelines.
Two common repetitive stress or strain injuries (RSI) that affect the wrist are carpal tunnel syndrome and tendonitis. If your fingertips tingle and then become numb and your hands hurt, you may have carpal tunnel syndrome. Tendonitis sufferers, however, have extreme pain in the wrist. Both types of injuries can be caused by repeated or forceful bending of the wrist. Because keyboards, mice,[1] and other input devices demand heavy wrist action, computer users are prime candidates for both injuries. To avoid these types of injuries, computer users should take frequent breaks during a computer session and exercise their hands and arms (Peterson 16-82).
Eye strain is another very common complaint among computer users. Tired, stressed, and watering eyes may be caused from glare of indoor or outdoor lighting, along with the intensity of
footnote
[1] Physicians recommend that the mouse be placed at least six inches from the edge of a workstation. In this position, the wrist is forced to be flat, which causes bending to occur at the elbow when the mouse is moved across the mouse pad. *Computer Health Online*, 8 Aug. 1997.

FIGURE 3-1

More *About* Documentation Styles

Another popular documentation style is by the American Psychological Association (APA). The MLA style is the standard in the humanities; whereas, the APA style is preferred in the social sciences. Many differences exist between the two styles. For example, the APA style uses the term, References, for the bibliography.

MLA Documentation Style

When writing papers, you must be sure to adhere to some form of documentation style. The research paper in this project follows the guidelines presented by the MLA. To follow the MLA style, double-space all pages of the paper with one-inch top, bottom, left, and right margins. Indent the first word of each paragraph one-half inch from the left margin. At the right margin of each page, place a page number one-half inch above the top margin. On each page, precede the page number by your last name.

The MLA style does not require a title page; instead, it requires you to place your name and course information in a block at the left margin beginning one inch from the top of the page. Center the title two double-spaces below your name and course information. In the body of the paper, place author references in parentheses with the page number(s) where the referenced information is located. These in-text **parenthetical citations** are used instead of footnoting each source at the bottom of the page or at the end of the paper. In the MLA style, footnotes are used only for explanatory notes. In the body of the paper, use **superscripts** (raised numbers) to signal that an explanatory note exists.

According to the MLA style, explanatory notes are optional. **Explanatory notes** are used to elaborate on points discussed in the body of the paper. Explanatory notes may be placed either at the bottom of the page as footnotes or at the end of the paper as endnotes. Double-space the explanatory notes. Superscript each note's reference number, and indent it one-half inch from the left margin. Place one space following the note number before beginning the note text. At the end of the note text, you may list bibliographic information for further reference.

The MLA style uses the term **works cited** for the bibliographical references. The works cited page alphabetically lists works that are directly referenced in the paper. by each author's last name. Place the works cited on a separate numbered page. Center the title, Works Cited, one inch from the top margin. Double-space all lines. Begin the first line of each work cited at the left margin; indent subsequent lines of the same work one-half inch from the left margin.

More *About* Selecting a Topic

When you are assigned a research paper, you should be sure to select a topic that really interests you, as well as presents a thought that will appeal to your audience. To research your topic, use the following sources: library catalog, the Internet, periodical indexes, computer databases, magazines and journals, and books.

Document Preparation Steps

The following document preparation steps give you an overview of how the research paper in Figure 3-1 on the previous page will be developed in this project. The following tasks will be completed in this project:

1. Start Word.
2. Change the margin settings for the document.
3. Adjust the line spacing for the document.
4. Create a header to number pages.
5. Change the font size to 12.
6. Enter your name and course information.
7. Center the paper title.
8. Save the research paper.
9. First-line indent paragraphs in the paper.
10. Enter the research paper with footnotes and a table.
11. Insert a manual page break.
12. Enter the works cited page.
13. Sort the paragraphs on the works cited page.
14. Save the document again.
15. Use Word's thesaurus.
16. Check the number of words in the document.
17. Print the research paper.
18. Quit Word.

The following pages contain a detailed explanation of each of these tasks.

Starting Word

Follow these steps to start Word or ask your instructor how to start Word for your computer.

TO START WORD

Step 1: Click the Start button on the taskbar.
Step 2: Click New Office Document on the Start menu. When the New dialog box displays, click the General tab to display the General sheet, if necessary.
Step 3: Double-click the Blank Document icon on the General sheet.

Office starts Word. After a few moments, an empty document titled Document1 displays on the Word screen.

Displaying Nonprinting Characters

As discussed in the previous projects, it is helpful to display nonprinting characters that indicate where in the document you pressed the ENTER key, SPACEBAR, or TAB key. Follow this step to display nonprinting characters.

TO DISPLAY NONPRINTING CHARACTERS

Step 1: If the Show/Hide ¶ button on the Standard toolbar is not already recessed, click it.

Word displays nonprinting characters in the document window, and the Show/Hide ¶ button on the Standard toolbar is recessed (Figure 3-2 on the next page).

Changing the Margins

Word is preset to use standard 8.5- by 11-inch paper, with 1.25-inch left and right margins and 1-inch top and bottom margins. These margin settings affect every paragraph in the document. Often, you may want to change these default margin settings. For example, the MLA documentation style requires one-inch top, bottom, left, and right margins throughout the paper. The steps on the next page illustrate how to change the default margin settings for a document when your screen is in normal view.

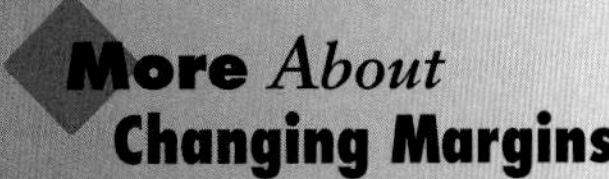

In page layout view, you can change the margins using the ruler. The current margins are shaded in gray, and the margin boundary is positioned where the gray meets the white. You drag the margin boundary to change the margin. Hold down the ALT key while dragging the margin boundary to display the margin settings.

To Change the Default Margin Settings

1 Click File on the menu bar and then point to Page Setup (Figure 3-2).

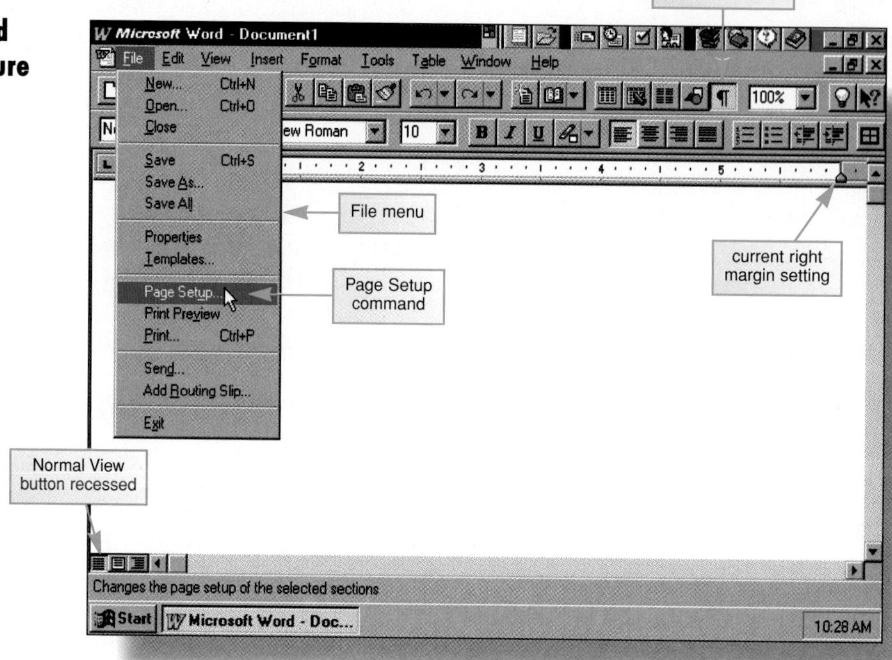

FIGURE 3-2

2 Click Page Setup. Click the Margins tab, if necessary, when the Page Setup dialog box first opens.

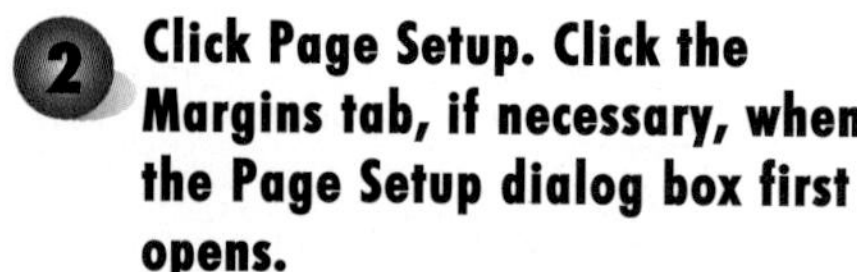

Word displays the Page Setup dialog box (Figure 3-3). Word lists the current margin settings in the respective text boxes and displays the settings graphically in the Preview area of the dialog box.

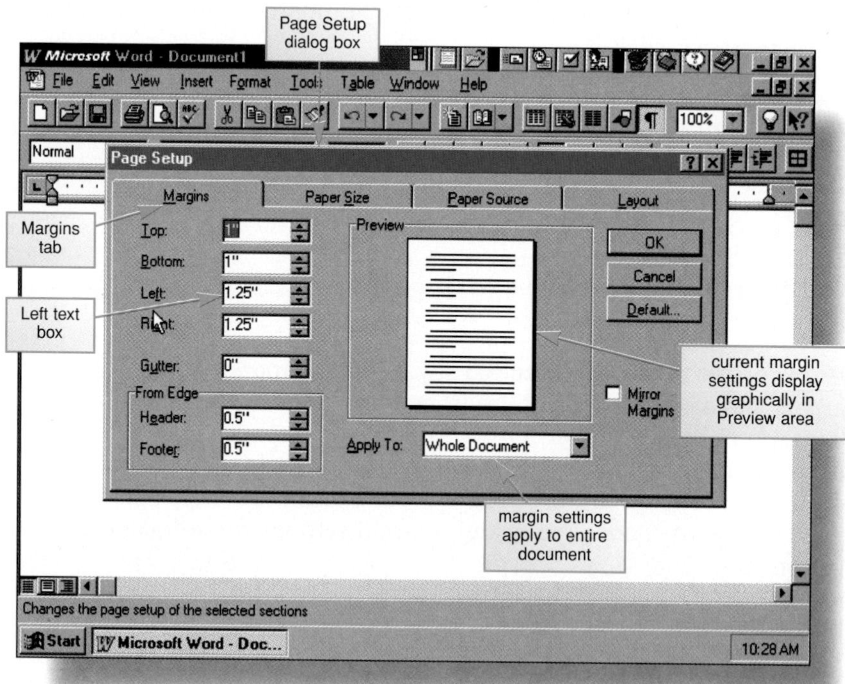

FIGURE 3-3

3 **Double-click the Left text box to highlight 1.25". Type 1 and then press the TAB key. Type 1 and then point to the OK button.**

The default left and right margin settings are changed to 1 inch (Figure 3-4). The Preview area in the Page Setup dialog box adjusts accordingly to reflect the new margin settings.

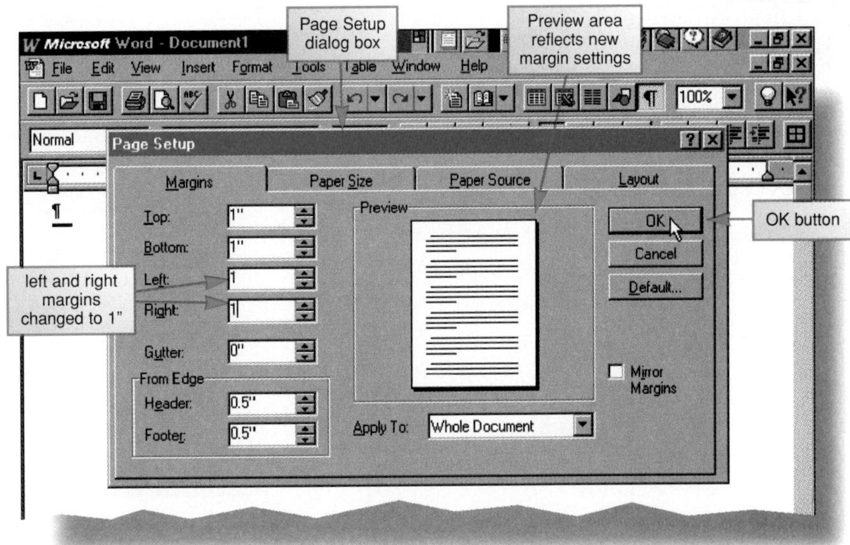

FIGURE 3-4

4 **Click the OK button.**

Word changes the left and right margins in the current document window (Figure 3-5 below).

OtherWays

1. In page layout view, drag margin boundary(s) on ruler

Compare Figure 3-2 to Figure 3-5 below. Notice that the right margin does not display in the document window in Figure 3-5, as it did in Figure 3-2, because you increased the width of your typing area when you changed the margins. The new margin settings take effect in the document immediately, and Word uses these margins for the entire document.

More About Line Spacing

Sometimes when you increase the font size of characters or import a graphic, the top of the characters or graphic is chopped off. If this happens, someone has set the line spacing in Word to exactly. To correct it, change the line spacing to At Least in the Paragraph dialog box, which accommodates the largest font or graphic.

Adjusting Line Spacing

Word, by default, single-spaces between lines of text and adjusts line height automatically to accommodate various font sizes and graphics. The MLA documentation style requires that you double-space the entire paper; that is, one blank line should display between each line of text. Thus, you must adjust the line spacing from single to double as shown in the following steps.

Steps To Double-Space a Document

1 **Right-click the paragraph mark above the end mark in the document window. Point to Paragraph on the shortcut menu.**

Word displays a shortcut menu in the document window (Figure 3-5).

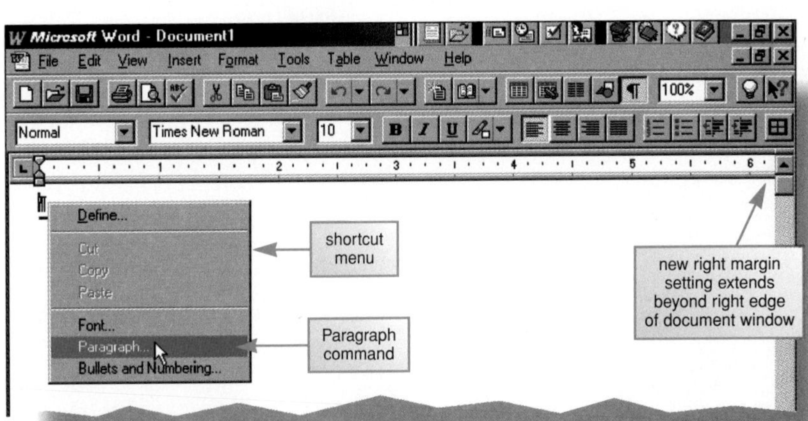

FIGURE 3-5

2 **Click Paragraph. Click the Indents and Spacing tab, if necessary, when the Paragraph dialog box first opens.**

Word displays the Paragraph dialog box, which lists the current settings in the text boxes and displays them graphically in the Preview area.

3 **Click the Line Spacing box arrow and then point to Double.**

A list of available line spacing options displays (Figure 3-6).

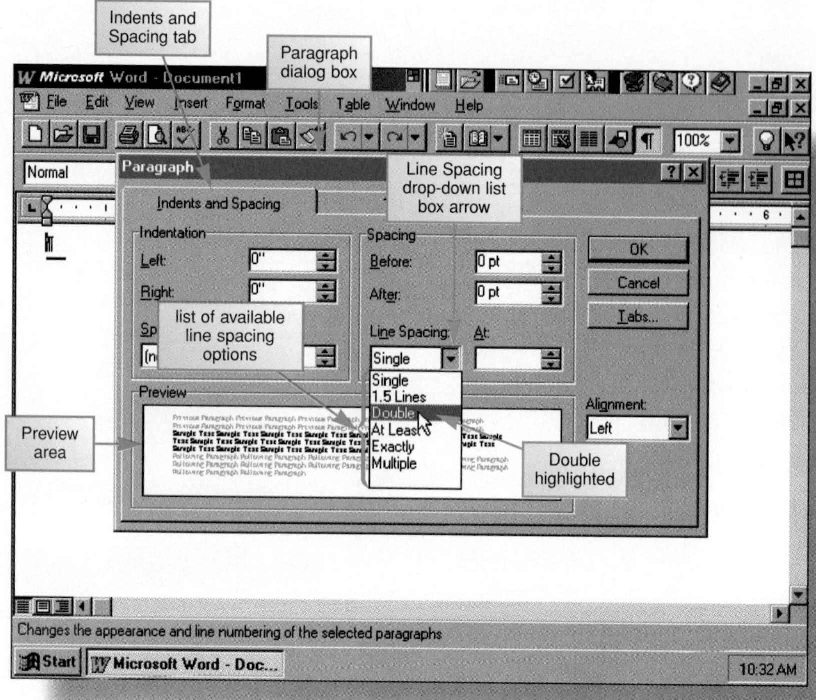

FIGURE 3-6

4 **Click Double. Point to the OK button.**

Word displays Double in the Line Spacing text box and graphically portrays the new line spacing in the Preview area (Figure 3-7).

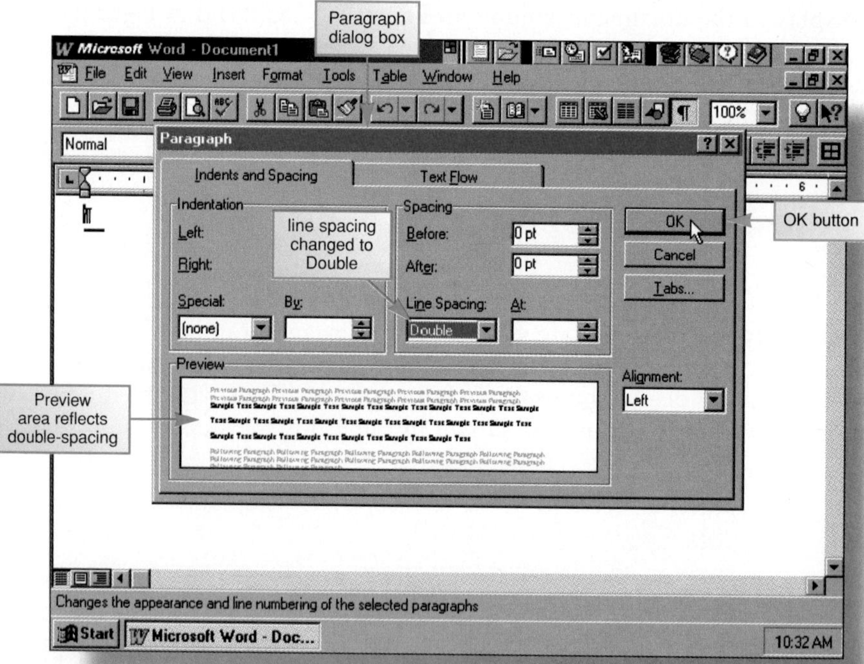

FIGURE 3-7

5 **Click the OK button.**

Word changes the line spacing to double in the current document (Figure 3-8). Notice that when line spacing is double, the end mark is positioned one blank line below the insertion point.

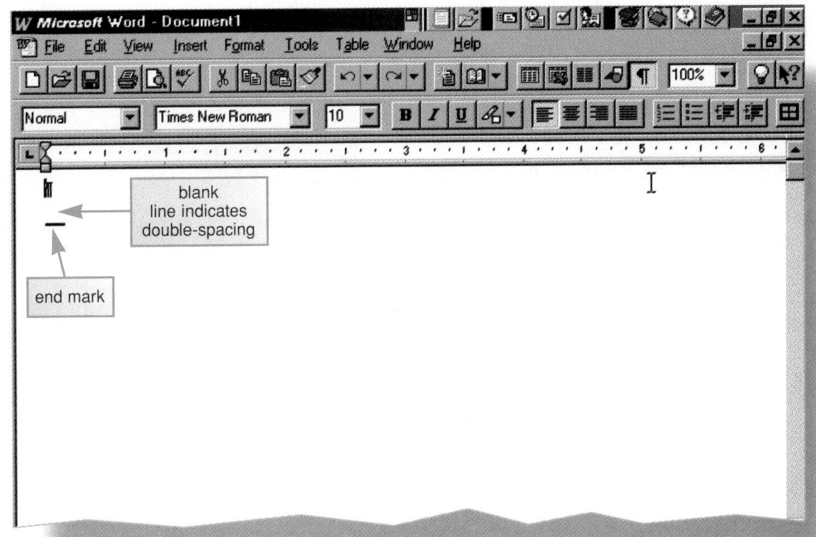

FIGURE 3-8

OtherWays

1. On Format menu, click Paragraph, click Indents and Spacing tab, click Line Spacing box arrow, and then click Double, click OK button
2. Press CTRL+2

The Line Spacing drop-down list box contains a variety of settings for the line spacing (Figure 3-6). The default, Single, and the options 1.5 Lines and Double allow Word to adjust line spacing automatically to accommodate the largest font or graphic on a line. The next two options, At Least and Exactly, enable you to specify a line spacing not provided in the first three options. The difference is that the At Least option allows Word to increase the designation if necessary; whereas, the Exactly option does not allow Word to increase the specification. With the last option, Multiple, you enter a multiple. For example, a multiple of 2 is the same as double-spacing.

Using a Header to Number Pages

In Word, you can easily number pages by clicking Insert on the menu bar and then clicking Page Numbers. Once chosen, this command places page numbers on every page after the first. You cannot, however, place your name as required by the MLA style in front of the page number with the Page Numbers command. To place your name in front of the page number, you must create a header that contains the page number.

More *About* APA Guidelines

To follow the APA style, double-space all pages of the paper with 1.5" top, bottom, left, and right margins. Indent the first word of each paragraph one-half inch from the left margin. A running head is placed in the upper right margin of each page; it consists of the page number double-spaced below a summary of the paper title.

Headers and Footers

A **header** is text you want printed at the top of each page in the document. A **footer** is text you want printed at the bottom of every page. In Word, headers are printed in the top margin one-half inch from the top of every page, and footers are printed in the bottom margin one-half inch from the bottom of each page, which meets the MLA style. Headers and footers can include both text and graphics, as well as the page number, current date, and current time.

In this project, you are to precede the page number with your last name placed one-half inch from the top of each page. Your name and the page number should print right-aligned; that is, at the right margin. Use the procedures in the steps on the next page to create the header with page numbers according to the MLA style.

Steps To Create a Header

Click View on the menu bar and then point to Header and Footer (Figure 3-9).

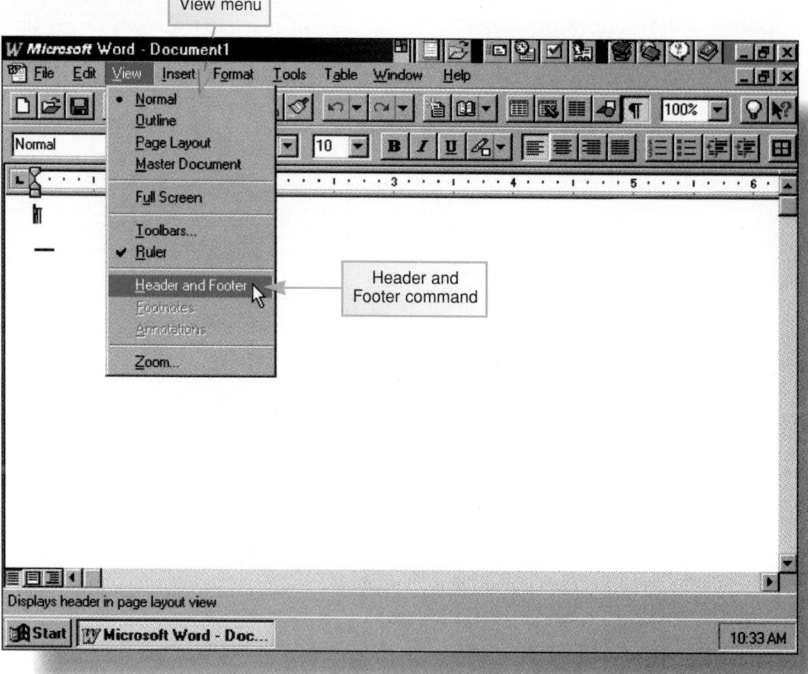

FIGURE 3-9

Click Header and Footer.

Word switches from normal to page layout view and displays the **Header and Footer toolbar** *(Figure 3-10). The Header and Footer toolbar initially floats in the middle of the document window. Recall that you can anchor a floating toolbar below the Formatting toolbar by double-clicking its title bar. You type the header text in the* **header area,** *which initially displays enclosed by a nonprinting dashed rectangle above the Header and Footer toolbar.*

Point to the Align Right button on the Formatting toolbar.

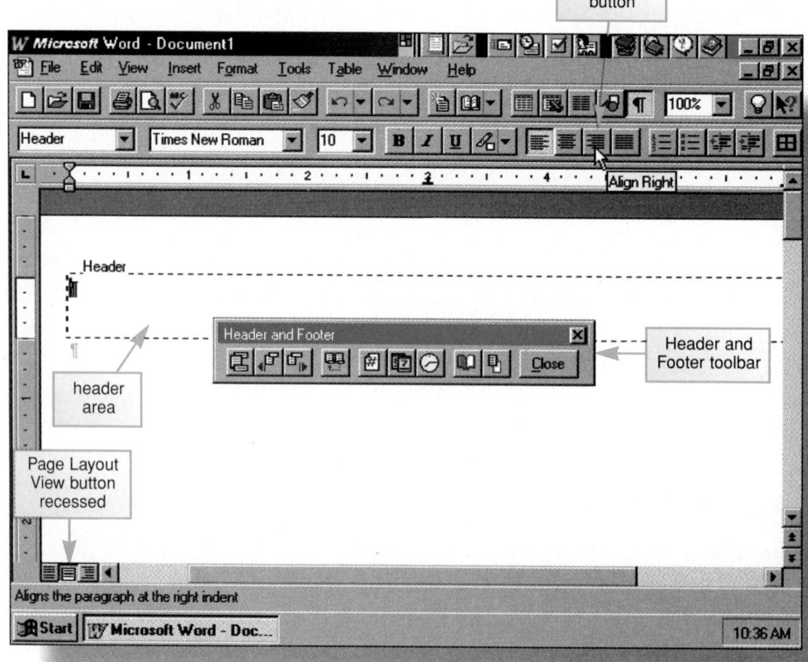

FIGURE 3-10

4 **Click the Align Right button on the Formatting toolbar. Type** Travis **and then press the SPACEBAR. Point to the Page Numbers button on the Header and Footer toolbar.**

Word displays the last name, Travis, right-aligned within the header area (Figure 3-11). The Align Right button is recessed because the paragraph containing the insertion point is right-aligned. When text is right-aligned, the right margin displays; thus, the document window and the header area have scrolled to the right so the right margin on the ruler is now visible.

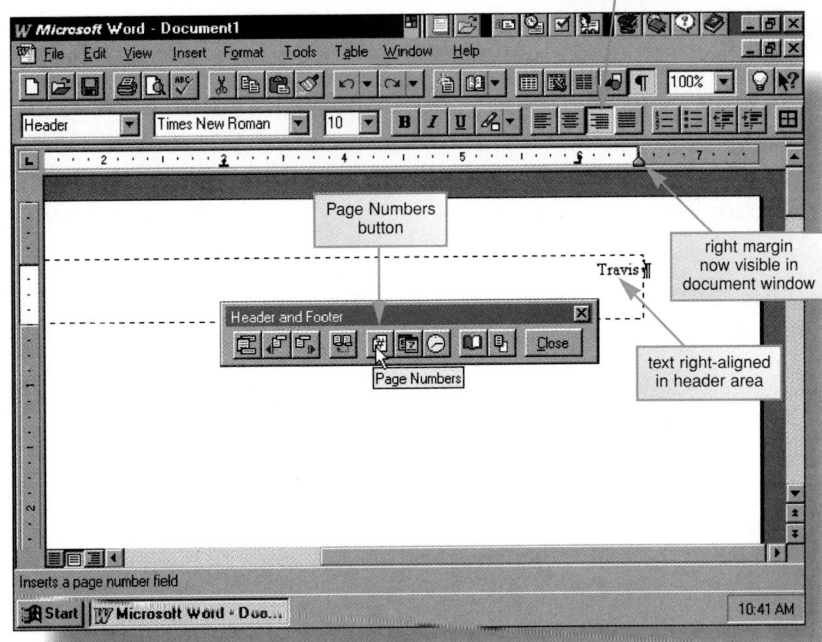

FIGURE 3-11

5 **Click the Page Numbers button.** *Word displays the page number 1 in the header area (Figure 3-12). Notice that the header text is 10 point. You want all text in your research paper to be 12 point.*

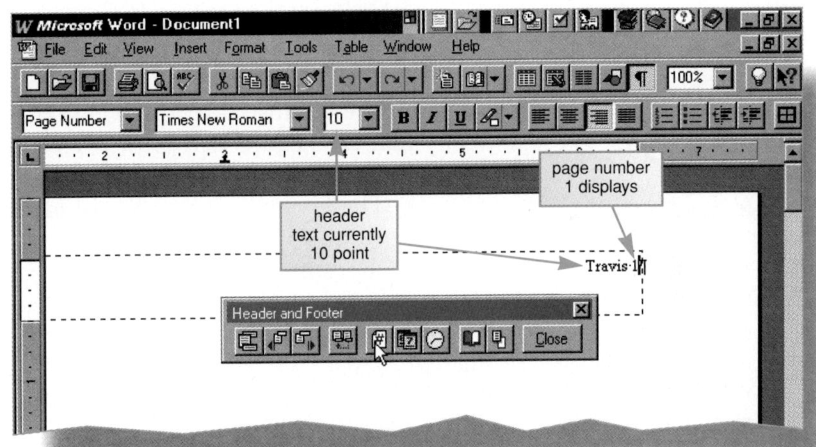

FIGURE 3-12

6 **Select the text, Travis 1, by clicking to its left. Click the Font Size box arrow on the Formatting toolbar and then point to 12.**

Word highlights the text, Travis 1, in the header area (Figure 3-13).

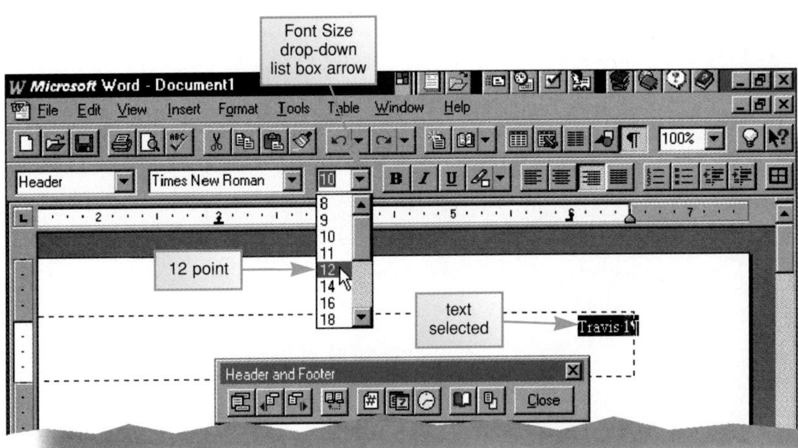

FIGURE 3-13

Click the font size 12. Point to the Close button on the Header and Footer toolbar.

Word changes the font size of the selected text from 10 to 12 (Figure 3-14).

Click the Close button on the Header and Footer toolbar.

Word closes the Header and Footer toolbar and returns to normal view (Figure 3-15).

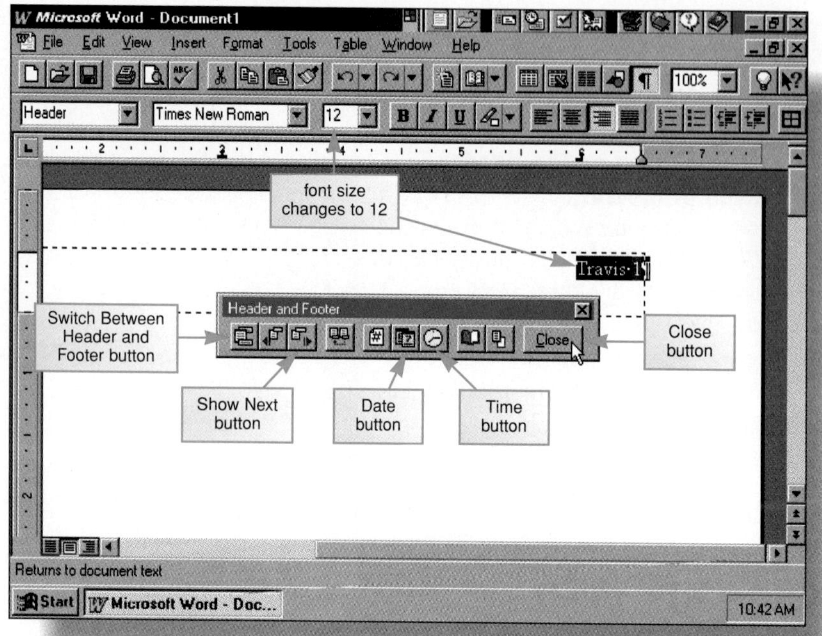

FIGURE 3-14

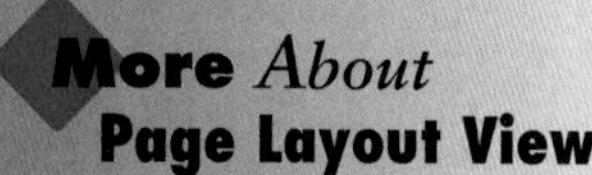

More *About* Page Layout View

To see the exact positioning of headers, footers, and notes, switch to Page Layout view. Headers and footers display dimmed in page layout view. Use the scroll bars to move around the pages of the document. To advance forward or backward an entire page, click the double arrows on the bottom of the vertical scroll bar.

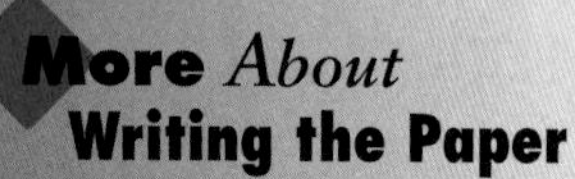

More *About* Writing the Paper

When beginning to write a paper, many students take notes to keep track of information. One method is to summarize, or condense, the information. Another is to paraphrase, or rewrite the information in your own words. And yet a third is to quote, or record the exact words of the original. Be sure to use quotation marks when directly quoting a source.

The header does not display on the screen when the document window is in normal view because it tends to clutter the screen. You will, however, want to verify that the header will print correctly. To see the header in the document window, you must switch to page layout view or display the document in print preview. These views display the header on the screen with the rest of the text.

Just as the Page Numbers button on the Header and Footer toolbar inserts the page number into the document, two other buttons on the Header and Footer toolbar (Figure 3-14 above) insert items into the document. The Date button inserts the current date into the document, and the Time button inserts the current time.

To edit an existing header, you follow the same procedure that you use to create a new header. That is, click View on the menu bar and then click Header and Footer to display the Header and Footer toolbar; or switch to Page Layout View and then double-click the dimmed header. If you have multiple headers, click the Show Next button on the Header and Footer toolbar (Figure 3-14) until the appropriate header displays in the header area. Edit the header as you would any Word text and then click the Close button on the Header and Footer toolbar.

To create a footer, click View on the menu bar, click Header and Footer, click the Switch Between Header and Footer button on the Header and Footer toolbar, and then follow the same procedure as you use to create a header.

Typing the Body of the Research Paper

The body of the research paper encompasses the first two pages in Figure 3-1 on page WD 3.5. The steps on the following pages illustrate how to enter the body of the research paper.

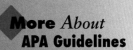

Changing the Font Size of all Characters in a Paragraph

In the prior two projects, you learned how to change the font size of characters in a document by clicking the Font Size box arrow and then selecting the desired font size. This affected the character at the location of the insertion point. When you use this method to change the font size, you may find yourself resetting the font size frequently while typing for the following reason. Often while you are typing, you notice an error and move the insertion point up to fix the error. When you position the insertion point at the end of the document to continue typing, Word returns to the Normal style, that is, 10 point. Thus, before you continue typing, you must reset the font size to 12.

An alternative that solves this problem is to select the paragraph mark above the end mark and change it to the larger font size. With this method, Word will not return to the Normal style (10 point) if you move the insertion point and then return it to the end mark to continue typing.

In this project, all characters in all paragraphs should be a font size of 12. Thus, you should select the paragraph mark before changing the font size. This way, if you move the insertion point out of the current paragraph, the font size will remain at 12 when you return to the paragraph to continue typing.

More About APA Guidelines

APA guidelines call for a title page as a separate page of a research paper, rather than entering name and course information on the first page of the paper. The running head (the brief summary of the title and the page number) should appear on the title page also, with the page number 1 on the title page.

To Change the Font Size of all Characters in a Paragraph

1 Click to the left of the paragraph mark in the upper left corner of the document window. Click the Font Size box arrow and then point to 12.

Word highlights the paragraph mark in the document window (Figure 3-15). Notice the paragraph mark currently is 10 point.

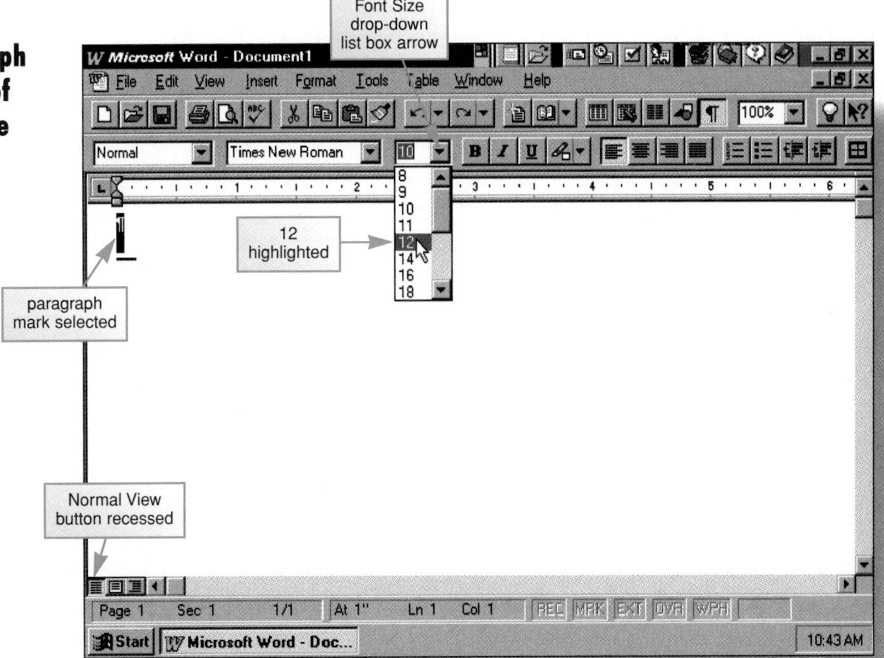

FIGURE 3-15

Click font size 12. Click in the document window to remove the selection.

Word changes the paragraph mark to 12 point and removes the selection (Figure 3-16).

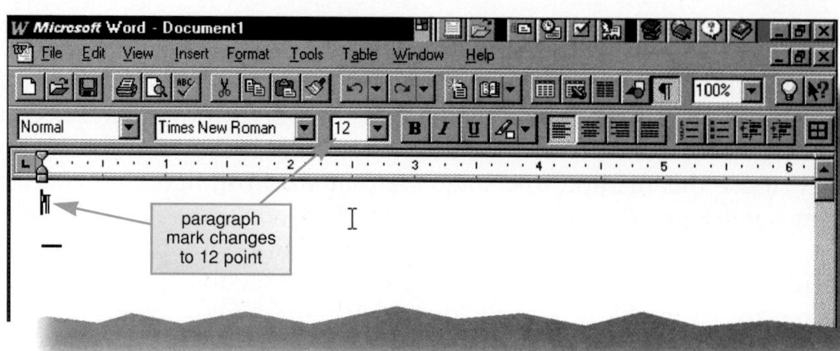

FIGURE 3-16

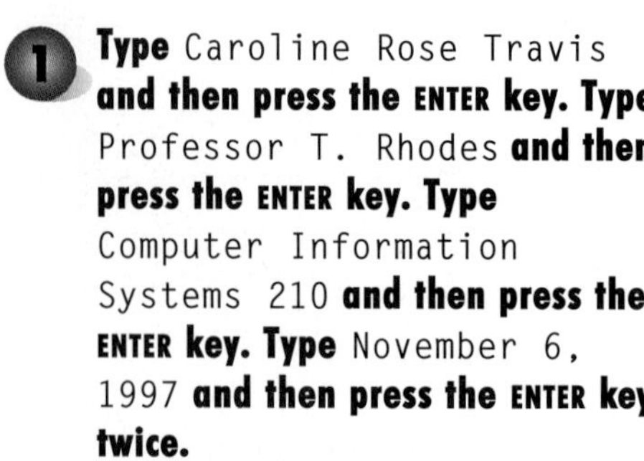

OtherWays

1. Select paragraph mark, right-click selection, click Font on shortcut menu, click Font tab, select desired point size in Size list, click OK button
2. Select paragraph mark, on Format menu click Font, click Font tab, select desired point size in Size list, click OK button
3. Select paragraph mark, press CTRL+SHIFT+P, type desired point size, press ENTER

Compare the size of the paragraph marks in Figures 3-15 on the previous page and 3-16. Notice that the paragraph mark in Figure 3-16 is larger, indicating it is now 12 point.

Entering Name and Course Information

Recall that the MLA style does not require a separate title page for research papers. Instead, you place your name and course information in a block at the top of the page at the left margin. Thus, follow the step below to begin the body of the research paper.

Steps To Enter Name and Course Information

1 Type `Caroline Rose Travis` **and then press the ENTER key. Type** `Professor T. Rhodes` **and then press the ENTER key. Type** `Computer Information Systems 210` **and then press the ENTER key. Type** `November 6, 1997` **and then press the ENTER key twice.**

The student name appears on line 1, the professor name on line 2, the course name on line 3, and the paper due date on line 4 (Figure 3-17). Each time you press the ENTER key, Word advances two lines on the screen, but increments the line counter on the status bar by only one because earlier you set line spacing to double.

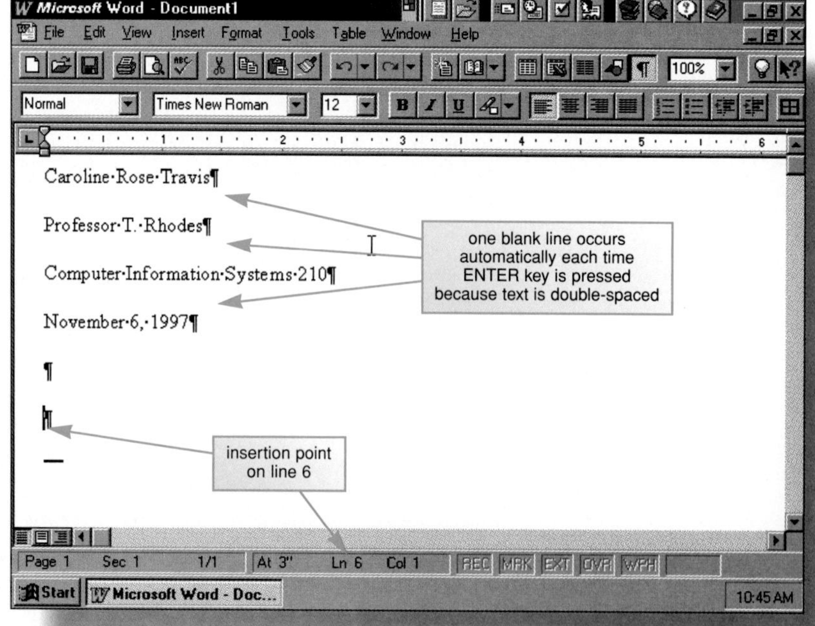

FIGURE 3-17

Centering a Paragraph Before Typing

In Project 1, you learned how to center a paragraph after you typed it. You can also center a paragraph before you type it by performing the following steps.

Steps To Center a Paragraph Before Typing

1. **Position the insertion point on the paragraph mark to be centered and then click the Center button on the Formatting toolbar. Type** `Computer User Health:Injury Prevention` **and then press the ENTER key.**

   Word centers the title between the left and right margins and the insertion point advances to line 7 (Figure 3-18). Notice that the paragraph mark and insertion point on line 7 are centered because the formatting specified in the prior paragraph (line 6) is carried forward to the next paragraph (line 7). Thus, the Center button on the Formatting toolbar remains recessed, indicating the next text you type will be centered. You do not, however, want the next line of text to be centered.

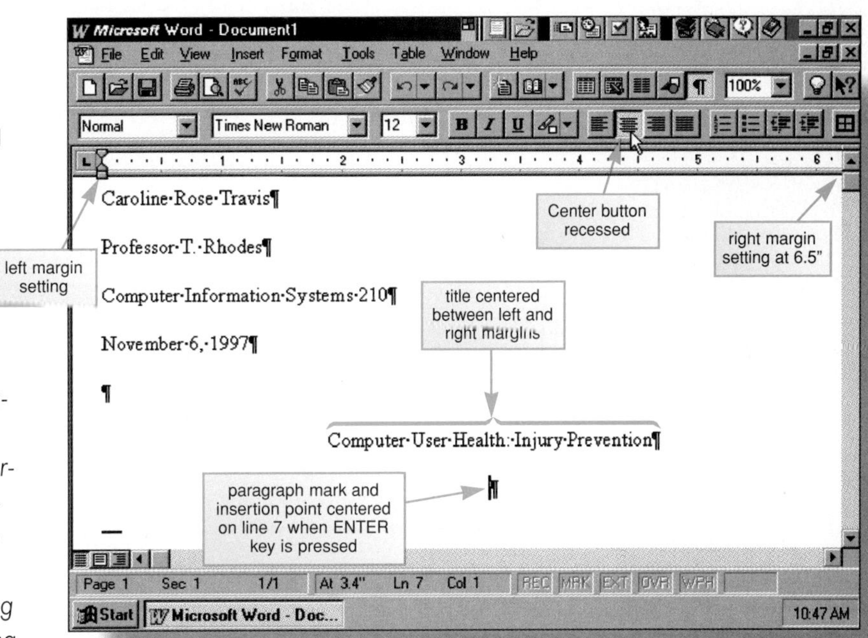

FIGURE 3-18

2. **Click the Align Left button on the Formatting toolbar.**

   Word positions the paragraph mark and the insertion point at the left margin (Figure 3-19). The next text you type will be left-aligned.

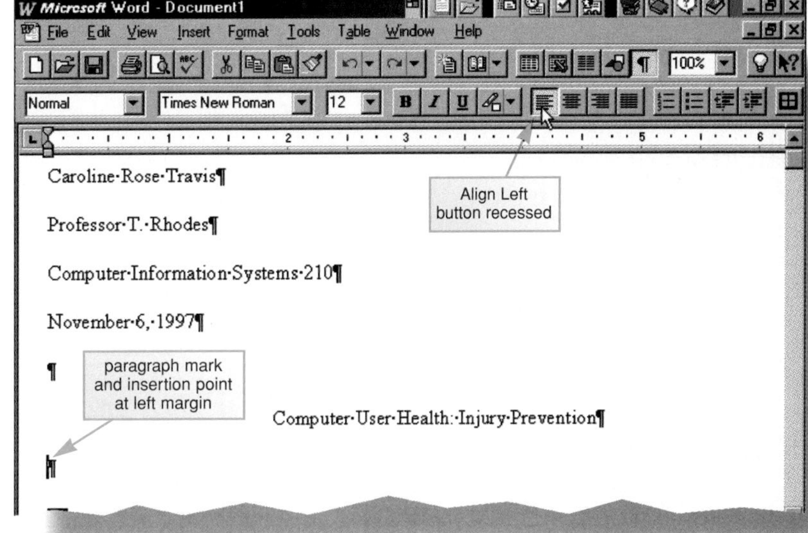

FIGURE 3-19

Other Ways

1. Right-click paragraph, click Paragraph on shortcut menu, click Indents and Spacing tab, click Alignment box arrow, click Centered, click OK button
2. On Format menu click Paragraph, click Indents and Spacing tab, click Alignment box arrow, click Centered, click OK button
3. Press CTRL+E

Saving the Research Paper

Recall that it is prudent to save your work on disk at regular intervals. Because you have performed several tasks thus far, you should save your research paper. For a detailed example of the procedure summarized below, refer to pages WD 1.21 through WD 1.24 in Project 1.

TO SAVE A DOCUMENT

Step 1: Insert your data floppy disk into drive A.
Step 2: Click the Save button on the Standard toolbar.
Step 3: Type `Travis Research Paper` in the File name text box. Do not press the ENTER key after typing the filename.
Step 4: Click the Save in box arrow and then click 3½ Floppy [A:].
Step 5: Click the Save button in the Save As dialog box.

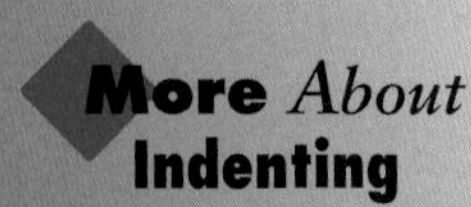

You can indent the entire left edge of a paragraph by clicking the Increase Indent button at the right edge of the Formatting toolbar. Each time you click the button, the current paragraph indents to the next tab stop. To reverse an indent, that is, decrease it by one tab stop, click the Decrease Indent button on the Formatting toolbar.

Indenting Paragraphs

According to the MLA style, the first line of each paragraph in the research paper is to be indented one-half inch from the left margin. This procedure, called **first-line indent**, can be accomplished using the horizontal ruler as shown in the following steps.

Steps To First-Line Indent Paragraphs

1 Point to the first-line indent marker on the ruler.

*The first-line indent marker is the top triangle at the 0" mark on the ruler (Figure 3-20). The bottom triangle, called the **left indent marker**, is used to change the entire left margin; whereas, the first-line indent marker affects only the first line of the paragraph.*

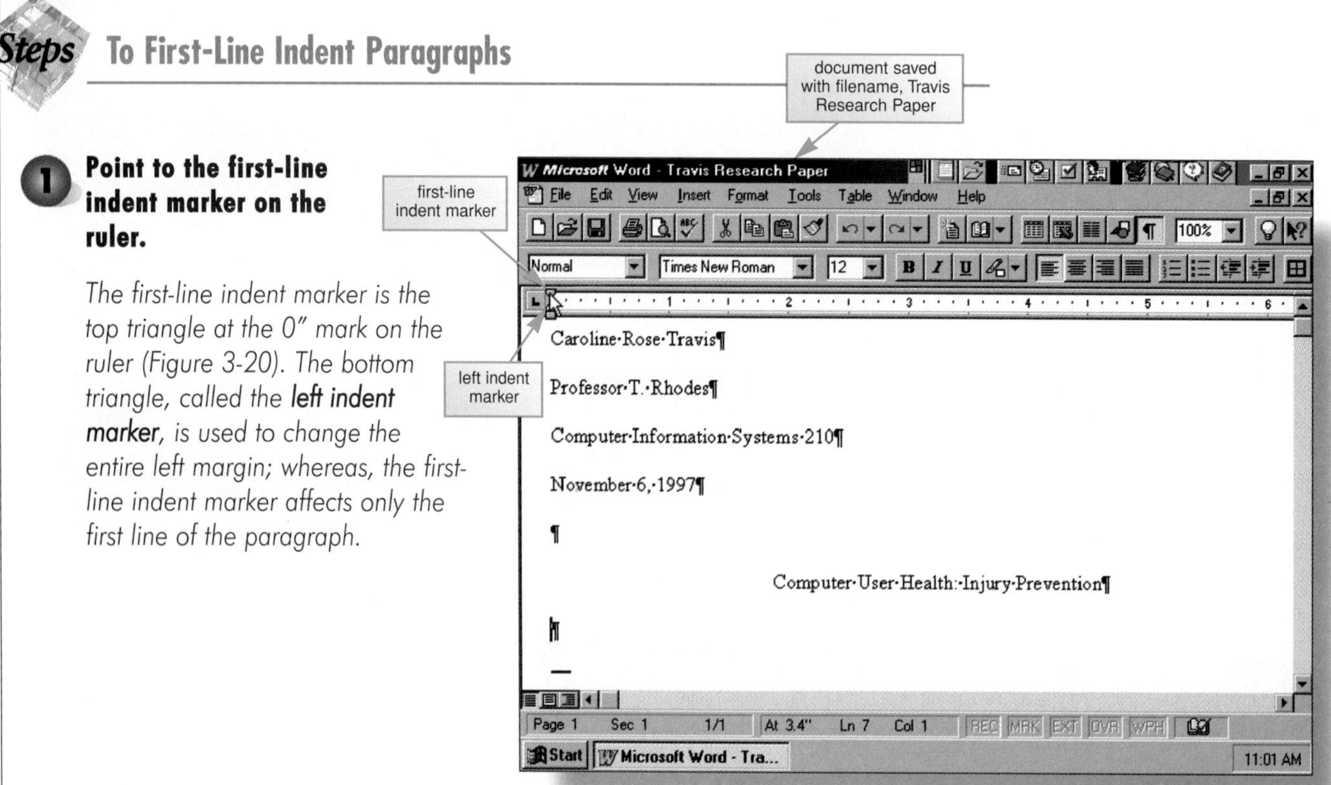

FIGURE 3-20

2 **Drag the first-line indent marker to the .5" mark on the ruler.**

As you drag the mouse, a vertical dotted line displays in the document window, indicating the proposed location of the first-line indent marker (Figure 3-21).

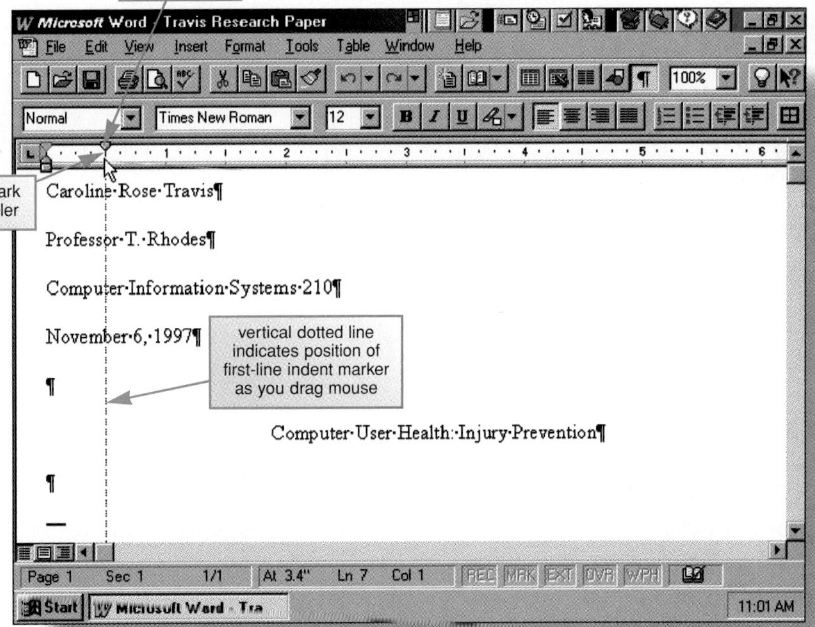

FIGURE 3-21

3 **Release the mouse button.**

The first-line indent marker displays at the location of the first tab stop, one-half inch from the left margin (Figure 3-22). The paragraph mark containing the insertion point in the document window also moves one-half inch to the right.

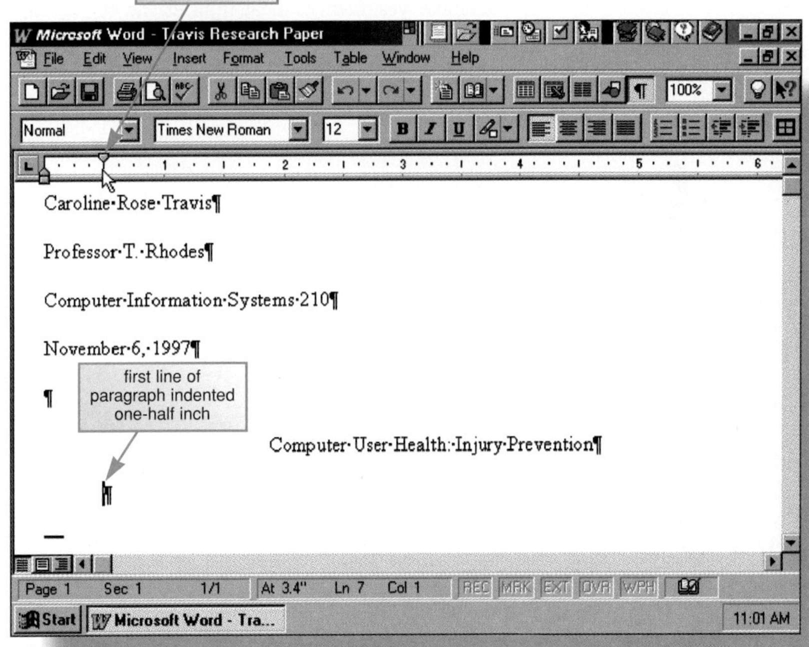

FIGURE 3-22

Type the first paragraph of the research paragraph as shown in Figure 3-24 below. Press the ENTER key. Type the first sentence of the second paragraph: `Two common repetitive stress or strain injuries (RSI) that affect the wrist are carpal tunnel syndrome and tendonitis.`

When you press the ENTER key at the end of the first paragraph of text, the insertion point automatically indents the first line of the second paragraph by one-half inch (Figure 3-23).

first line of subsequent paragraphs indented automatically when you press ENTER key

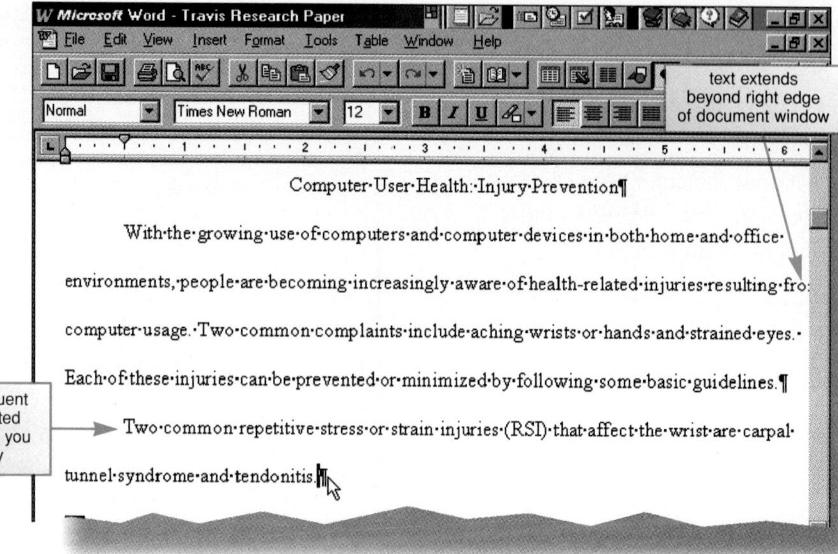

FIGURE 3-23

With the growing use of computers and computer devices in both home and office environments, people are becoming increasingly aware of health-related injuries resulting from computer usage. Two common complaints include aching wrists or hands and strained eyes. Each of these injuries can be prevented or minimized by following some basic guidelines.

FIGURE 3-24

OtherWays

1. Right-click paragraph, click Paragraph on shortcut menu, click Indents and Spacing tab, click Special box arrow, click First Line, click OK button
2. On Format menu click Paragraph, click Indents and Spacing tab, click Special box arrow, click First Line, click OK button

More About First-Line Indent

You may be tempted to use the TAB key to indent the first line of each paragraph in your research paper. Using the TAB key for this task is inefficient because you must press it each time you begin a new paragraph. Because first-line indent is a paragraph format, it is automatically carried forward when you press the ENTER key.

By setting the first-line indent with the ruler, the first-line indent format is carried automatically to each subsequent paragraph you type.

Zooming Page Width

When you changed the left and right margin settings earlier in this project, the right margin moved beyond the right edge of the document window. (Depending on your Word settings, your right margin may already appear in the document window.) Thus, some of the text at the right edge of the document does not display in the document window (Figure 3-23 above). Recall in Project 2 you zoomed the cover letter and resume to make the characters appear larger on the screen. In this project, you want to make the characters smaller.

Because you often want to see both margins in the document window at the same time, Word provides a **page width zoom**, which brings the both left and right margins into view as shown in the following steps.

Steps To Zoom Page Width

1 Click the Zoom Control box arrow on the Standard toolbar and then point to Page Width.

Word displays a list of available zoom percentages, as well as the page width zoom control option (Figure 3-25).

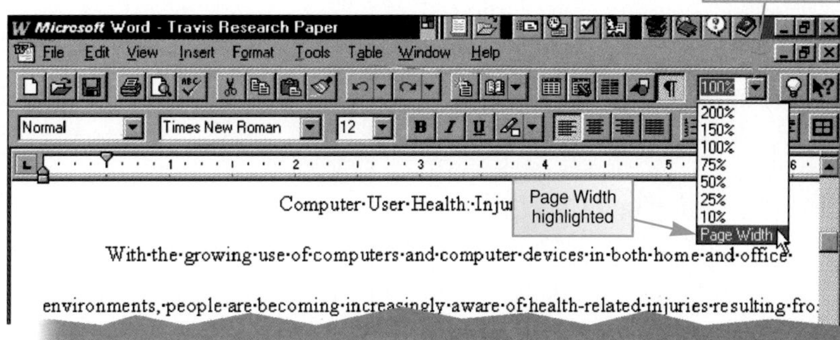

FIGURE 3-25

2 Click Page Width.

Word brings both the left and right margins into view in the document window (Figure 3-26). The Zoom Control box now displays 92%, which Word computes based on your margin settings. Your percentage may be different depending on your system configuration.

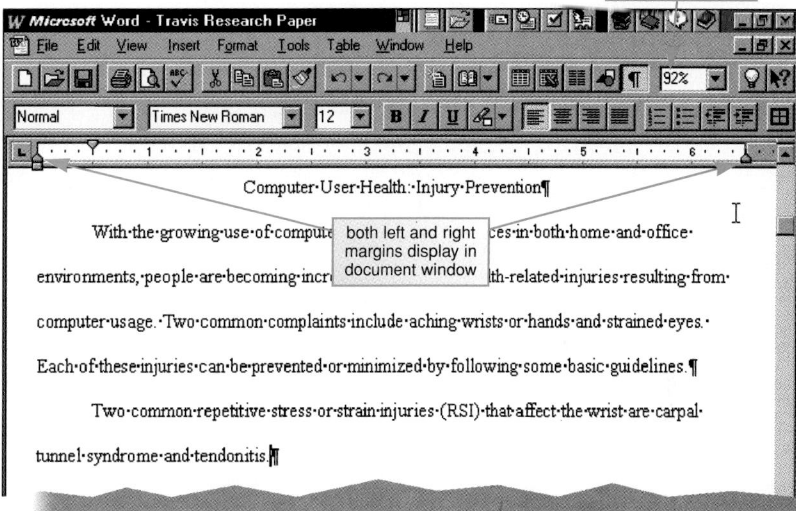

FIGURE 3-26

OtherWays

1. On View menu click Zoom, select desired zoom percentage, click OK button

If you want to zoom a percentage not displayed in the Zoom Control drop-down list box, you can click View on the menu bar, click Zoom, and then enter any zoom percentage you desire.

Using Word's AutoCorrect Feature

Because you may often misspell the same words or phrases when you type, Word provides an **AutoCorrect** feature, which automatically corrects your misspelled words as you type them into the document. For example, if you type `teh`, Word automatically changes it to `the` for you. Word has predefined many commonly misspelled words, which it automatically corrects for you as shown on the next page.

More About AutoCorrect

In addition to correcting misspelled words, the AutoCorrect feature fixes other mistakes. If you type two capital letters at the beginning of a sentence, Word makes the second letter lower case. If you forget to capitalize the first letter of a sentence, Word capitalizes it for you. Word also capitalizes names of days of the week, if you forget to.

Steps To Illustrate Word's AutoCorrect Feature

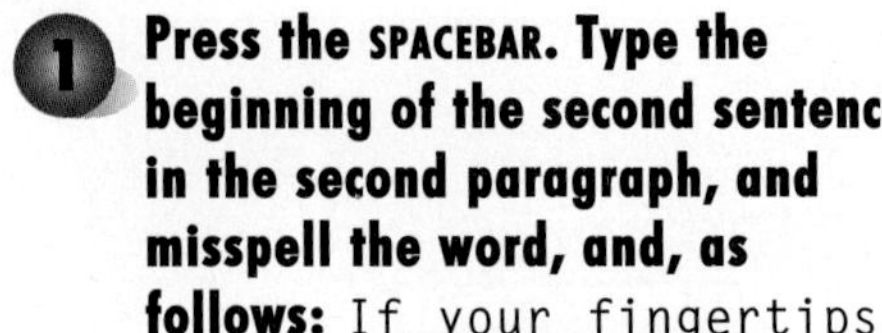

1 Press the SPACEBAR. Type the beginning of the second sentence in the second paragraph, and misspell the word, and, as follows: `If your fingertips tingle adn` **(Figure 3-27).**

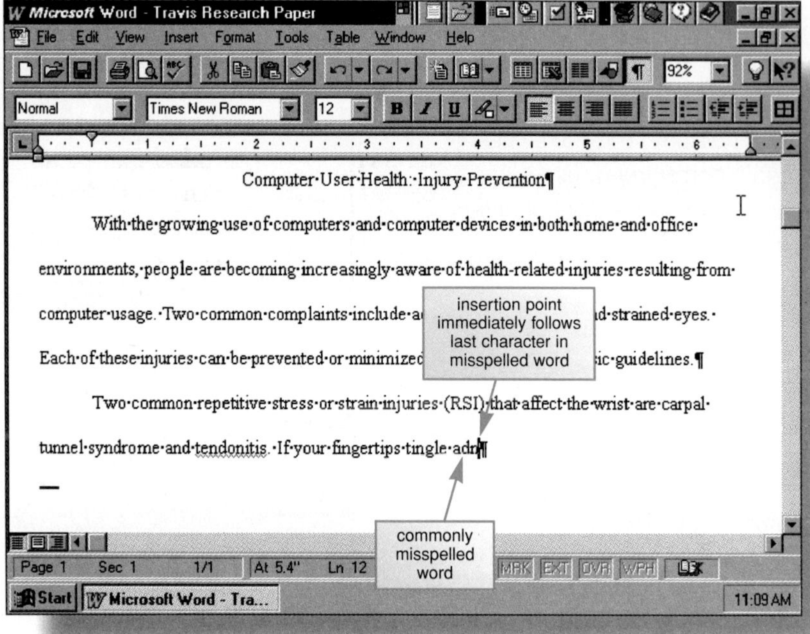

FIGURE 3-27

2 Press the SPACEBAR.

As soon as you press the SPACEBAR, Word's AutoCorrect feature detects the misspelling and corrects the word for you (Figure 3-28).

3 Type `then become numb and your hands hurt, you may have carpal tunnel syndrome.` **and then press the SPACEBAR.**

The second sentence of the second paragraph is complete (Figure 3-29).

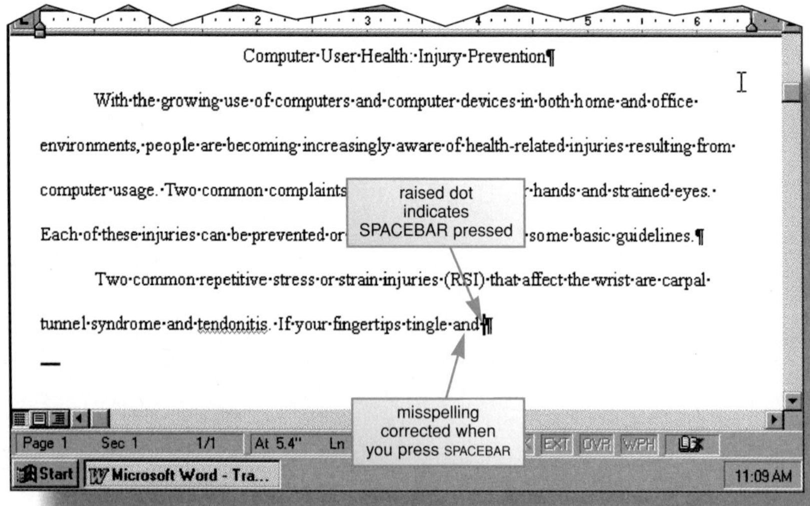

FIGURE 3-28

In addition to the commonly misspelled words predefined by the AutoCorrect feature, you can create your own AutoCorrect entries. For example, if you often misspell the word *computer* as *comptuer*, you should make an AutoCorrect entry for it as shown in these steps.

To Create an AutoCorrect Entry

1 **Click Tools on the menu bar and then point to AutoCorrect (Figure 3-29).**

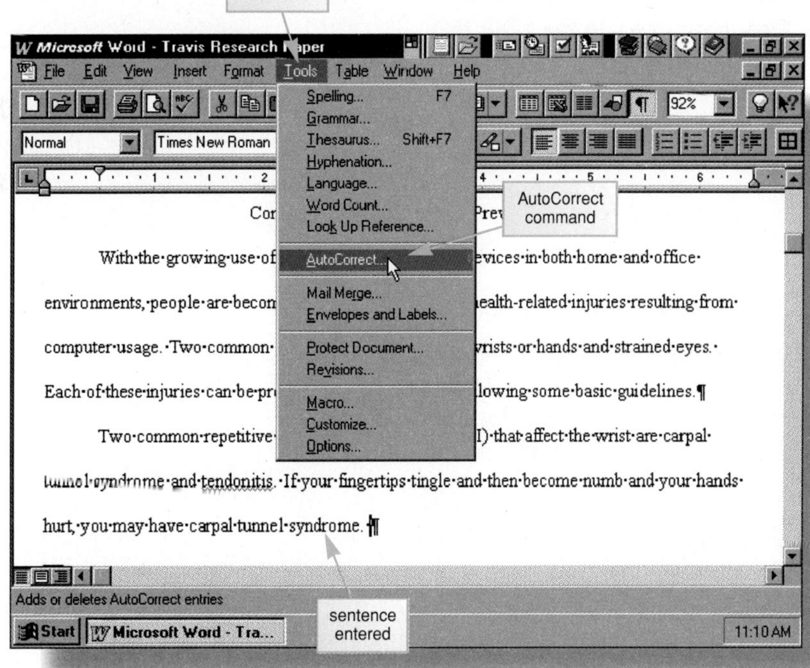

FIGURE 3-29

2 **Click AutoCorrect.**

Word displays the AutoCorrect dialog box (Figure 3-30). The insertion point is blinking in the Replace text box, ready for you to create an AutoCorrect entry.

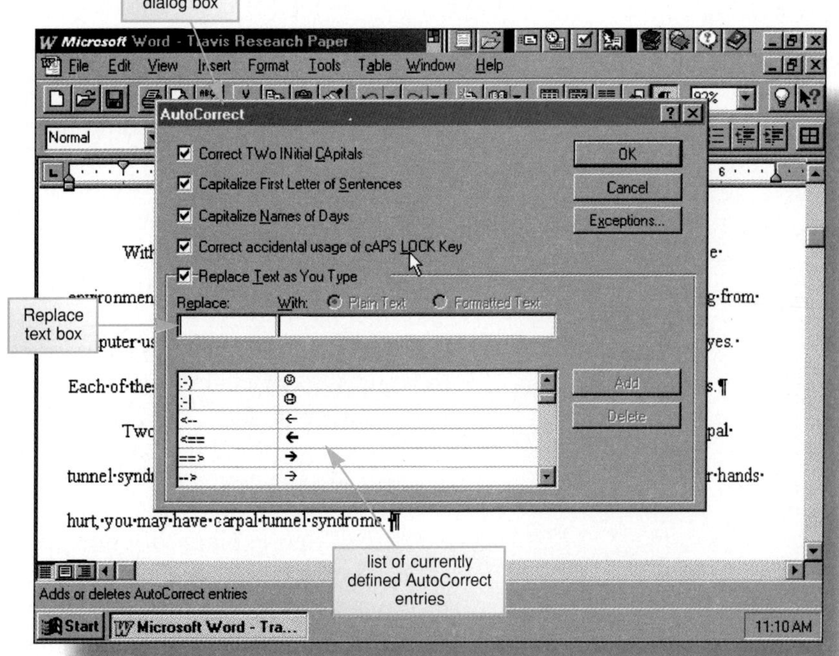

FIGURE 3-30

3 **Type** `comptuer` **in the Replace text box. Press the TAB key to advance to the With text box. Type** `computer` **in the With text box. Point to the Add button.**

The Replace text box contains the misspelled word, and the With text box contains its correct spelling (Figure 3-31).

4 **Click the Add button. (If your screen displays a Replace button, click it and then click the Yes button in the Microsoft Word dialog box.) Click the OK button.**

Word adds the entry alphabetically to the list of words to automatically correct as you type.

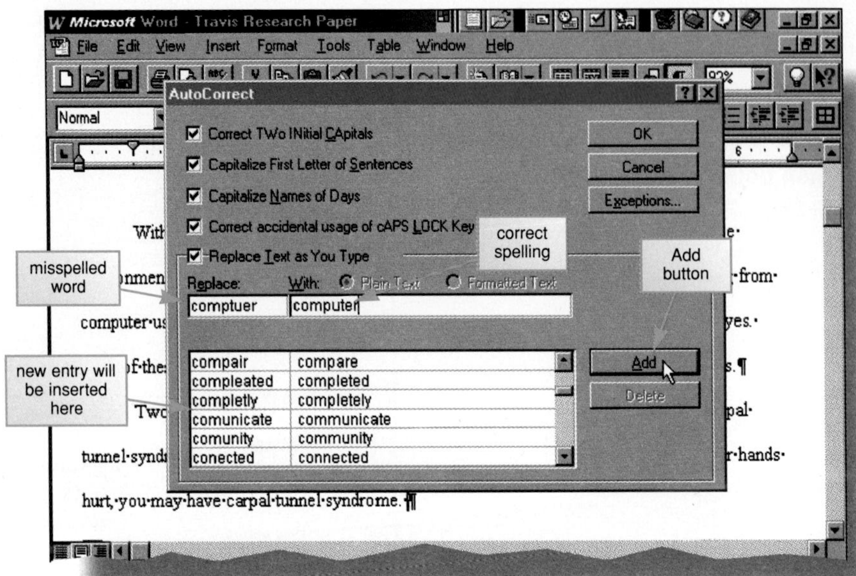

FIGURE 3-31

In addition to creating AutoCorrect entries for words you commonly misspell, you can create entries for abbreviations, codes, and so forth. For example, you can create an AutoCorrect entry for *asap*, indicating that Word should replace this text with the phrase, *as soon as possible*.

If you look at the list of AutoCorrect entries in the AutoCorrect dialog box (Figure 3-30 on the previous page), you will notice that Word also predefines commonly used symbols. For example, to add a smiling face to a document, you type :) and Word automatically changes it to ☺. Table 3-1 lists the characters you type to add arrows, faces, and symbols into a Word document.

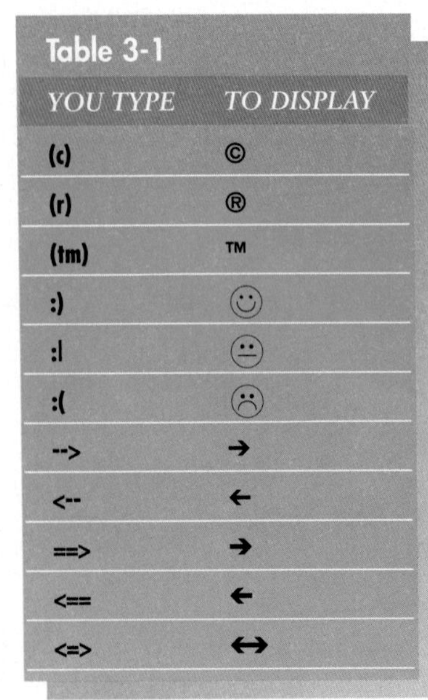

Table 3-1

YOU TYPE	TO DISPLAY
(c)	©
(r)	®
(tm)	™
:)	☺
:|	😐
:(	☹
-->	→
<--	←
==>	➔
<==	⇐
<=>	↔

If, for some reason, you do not want Word to correct automatically as you type, you can turn off the replace as you type feature by clicking Tools on the menu bar, clicking AutoCorrect, clicking the Replace Text as You Type check box to deselect it and then clicking the OK button.

In Project 2, you learned how to use the AutoText feature, which enabled you to create entries (just as you did for the AutoCorrect feature) and then insert them into the document. The difference is that the AutoCorrect feature makes the corrections for you automatically; whereas, you must press F3 or click the AutoText command before Word will make an AutoText correction.

Adding Footnotes

Recall that explanatory notes are optional in the MLA documentation style. They are used primarily to elaborate on points discussed in the body of the paper. The style specifies to use superscripts (raised numbers) to signal that an explanatory note exists either at the bottom of the page as a **footnote** or at the end of the document as an **endnote**.

Word, by default, places notes at the bottom of each page. In Word, **note text** can be any length and format. Word automatically numbers notes sequentially for you by placing a **note reference mark** in the body of the document and in front of the note text. If you rearrange, insert, or remove notes, however, the remaining note text and reference marks are renumbered according to their new sequence in the document. Follow these steps to add a footnote to the research paper.

More About Footnotes

Both the MLA and APA guidelines suggest the use of in-text parenthetical citation, as opposed to footnoting each source of material in a paper. These parenthetical acknowledgments guide the reader to the end of the paper for complete information on the source, if the reader desires it.

Steps To Add a Footnote

1 **Type the following text:** `Tendonitis sufferers, however, have extreme pain in the wrist. Both types of injuries can be caused by repeated or forceful bending of the wrist. Because keyboards, mice,` **and then click Insert on the menu bar and point to Footnote.**

The insertion point is positioned immediately after the comma following the word, mice, in the research paper (Figure 3-32).

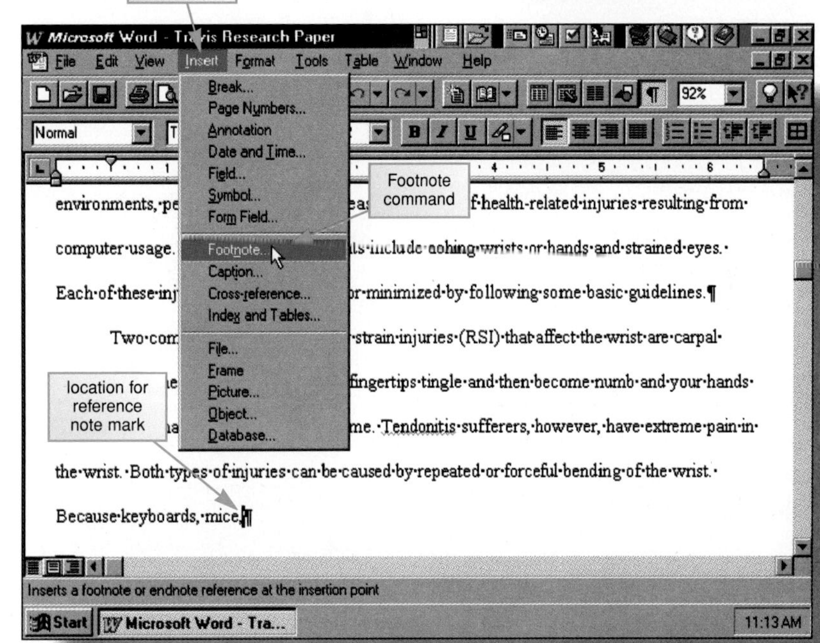

FIGURE 3-32

2 **Click Footnote. When the Footnote and Endnote dialog box displays, point to the OK button.**

Word displays the Footnote and Endnote dialog box (Figure 3-33). The bullet next to the Footnote option indicates that footnotes are the default placement for notes.

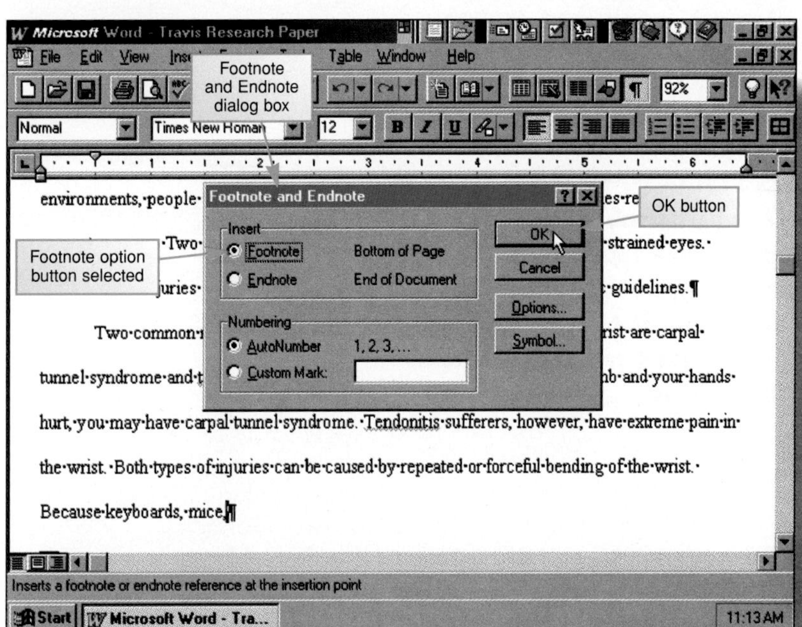

FIGURE 3-33

3 **Click the OK button.**

Word opens a note pane in the lower portion of the window with the **note reference mark** *(a superscripted 1) positioned at the left margin of the pane (Figure 3-34). A* **pane** *is an area at the bottom of the screen, which contains an option bar, a text area, and a scroll bar. The note reference mark also displays in the document window at the location of the insertion point. Note reference marks are, by default, superscripted; that is, raised above other letters. Notice that the default font size of footnote text is 10 point.*

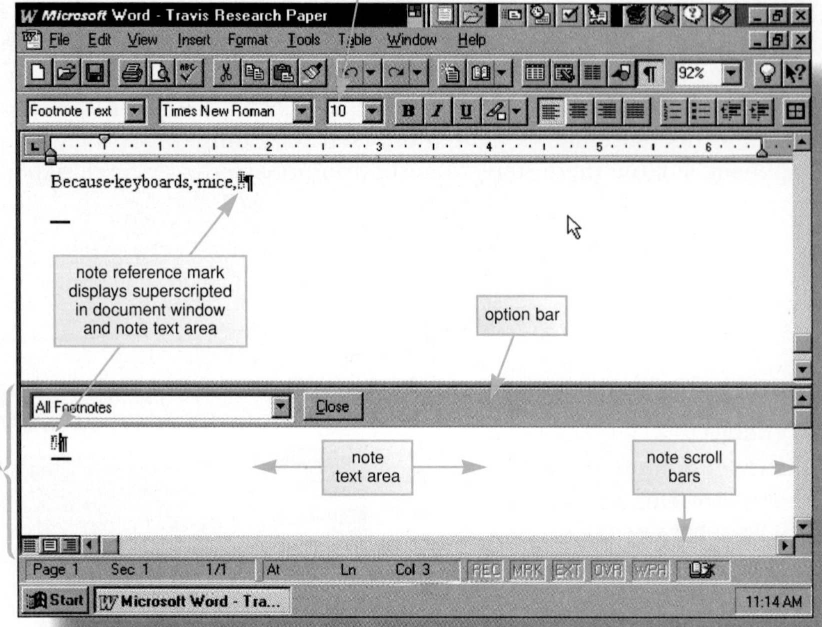

FIGURE 3-34

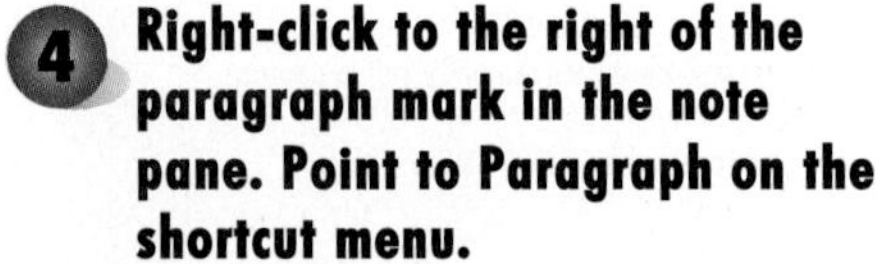

4 **Right-click to the right of the paragraph mark in the note pane. Point to Paragraph on the shortcut menu.**

Word displays a shortcut menu (Figure 3-35). Because you want to change both the first-line indent and line spacing for the notes, you will use the Paragraph dialog box to perform both changes.

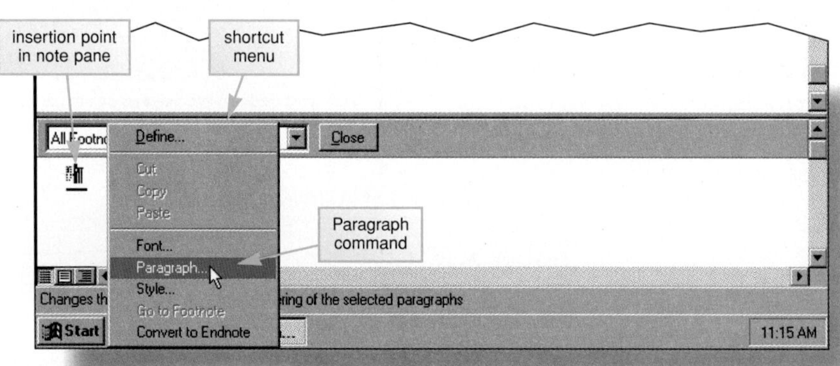

FIGURE 3-35

5 **Click Paragraph. Click the Indents and Spacing tab, if necessary, when the Paragraph dialog box first opens. Click the Special box arrow and then point to First Line.**

Word displays the Paragraph dialog box (Figure 3-36). You can change the first-line indent on the Indents and Spacing sheet in the Paragraph dialog box.

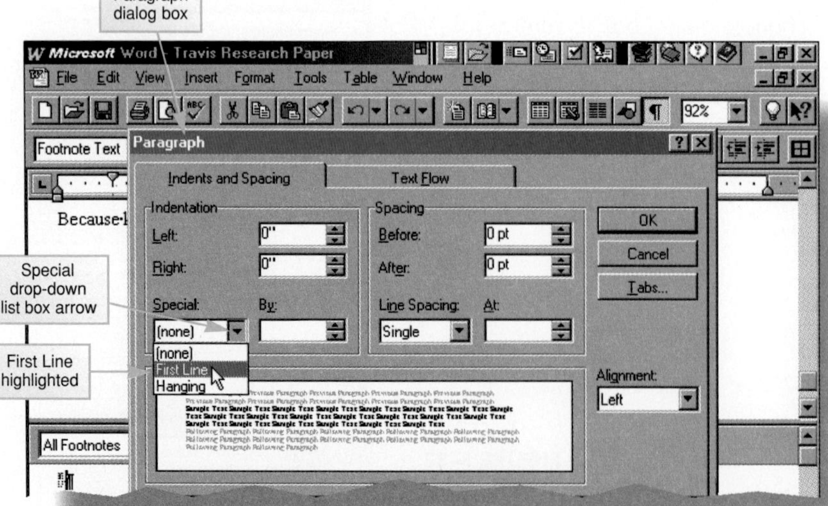

FIGURE 3-36

6 **Click First Line. Click the Line Spacing box arrow and then click Double.**

Word displays First Line in the Special box and Double in the Line Spacing box (Figure 3-37). The Preview area reflects the current settings in the Paragraph dialog box.

7 **Click the OK button.**

Word indents the first line of the note by one-half inch and sets the line spacing for the note to double.

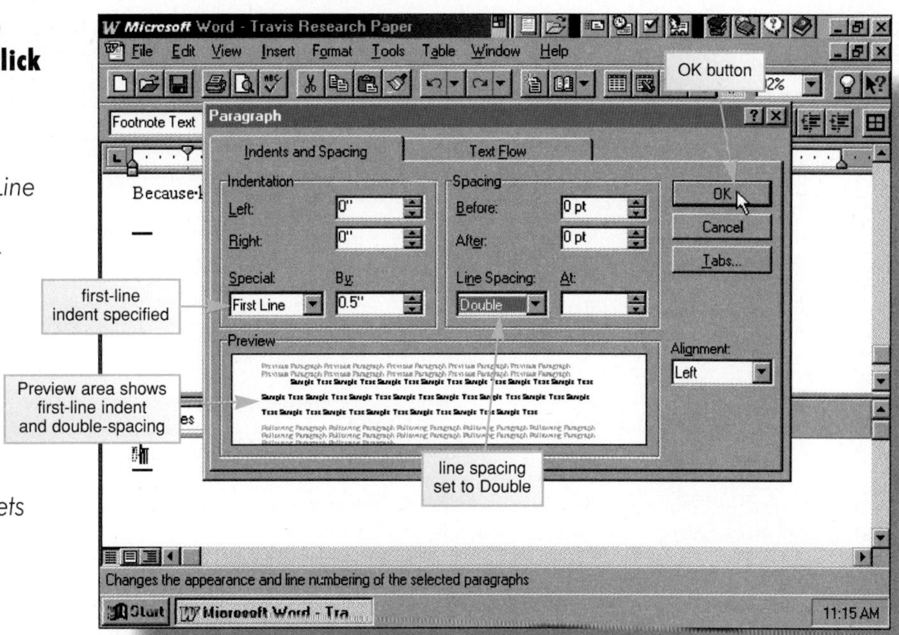

FIGURE 3-37

8 **Click the Font Size box arrow and then click 12.**

Word changes the font size of the note text from 10 to 12 (Figure 3-38).

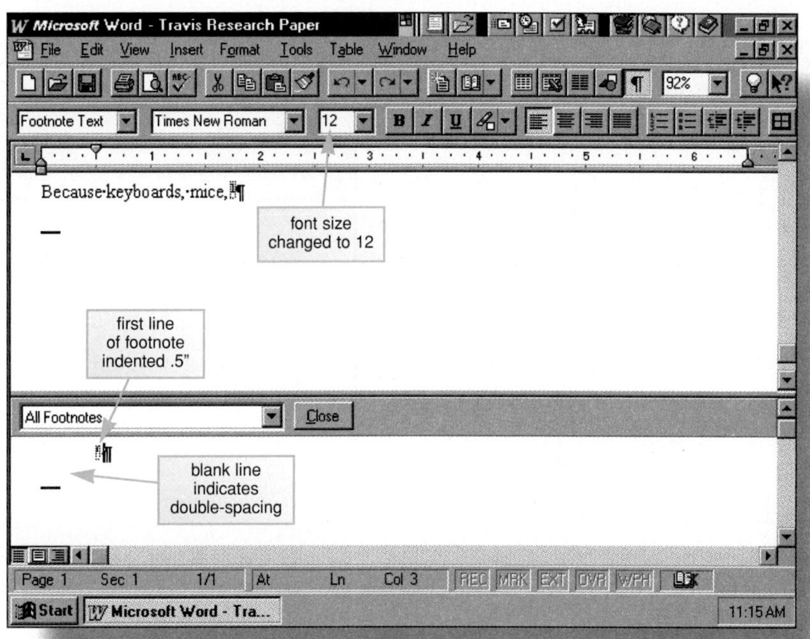

FIGURE 3-38

9 **Type the note text:** Physicians recommend that the mouse be placed at least six inches from the edge of a workstation. In this position, the wrist is forced to be flat, which causes bending to occur at the elbow when the mouse is moved across the mouse pad. *Computer Health Online*, 8 Aug. 1997.

The note is entered in the note pane (Figure 3-39).

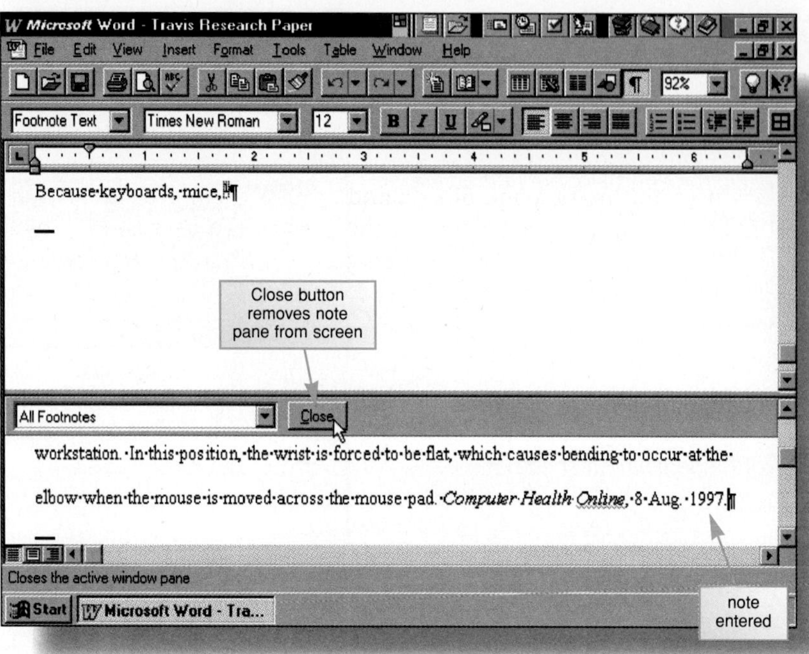

FIGURE 3-39

10 **Click the Close button on the note pane option bar.**

Word closes the note pane.

11 **Press the SPACEBAR, and then type the remainder of the paragraph:** and other input devices demand heavy wrist action, computer users are prime candidates for both injuries. To avoid these types of injuries, computer users should take frequent breaks during a computer session and exercise their hands and arms (Peterson 16-82).

The second paragraph of the research paper is entered (Figure 3-40).

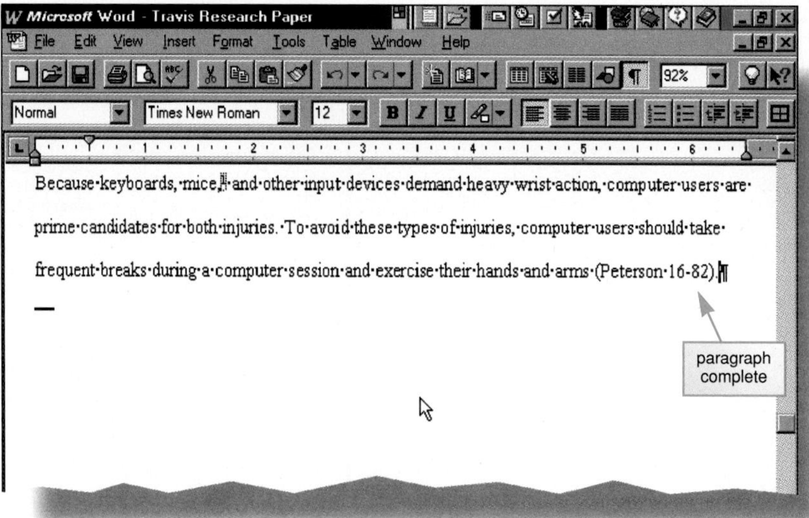

FIGURE 3-40

When Word closes the note pane and returns to the document, the note text disappears from the screen. The note text still exists, even though it is not visible in normal view. You will, however, want to verify that the footnote will print correctly. To see the footnote in the document window, you must switch to page layout view or display the document in print preview. These views display the footnote on the screen with the rest of the text.

To edit an existing footnote, click View on the menu bar and then click Footnotes to display the note pane. Edit the footnote as you would any Word text and then click the Close button on the note pane option bar.

Automatic Page Breaks

As you type documents that exceed one page, Word automatically inserts page breaks, called **automatic page breaks**, when it determines the text has filled one page according to paper size, margin settings, line spacing, and other settings. If you add text, delete text, or modify text on a page, Word recomputes the position of automatic page breaks and adjusts them accordingly. Word performs page recomputation between the keystrokes; that is, in between the pauses in your typing. Thus, Word refers to the automatic page break task as **background repagination.** In normal view, an automatic page break displays on the Word screen as a thin, dotted horizontal line. Word's automatic page break feature is illustrated in the following step.

More About Background Repagination

If background repagination has been deactivated on your system, Word stops all activities while repaginating the document. You can enable background repagination by clicking Tools on the menu bar, clicking Options, clicking the General tab, clicking the Background Repagination check box, and then clicking the OK button.

Steps To Use Automatic Page Break

1 **Press the ENTER key and then type the next paragraph of the research paper, as shown in Figure 3-42 below.**

As you begin typing the paragraph, Word places an automatic page break above the paragraph. When the paragraph extends beyond two lines, Word moves the automatic page break to the middle of the paragraph (Figure 3-41). The status bar now displays Page 2 as the current page.

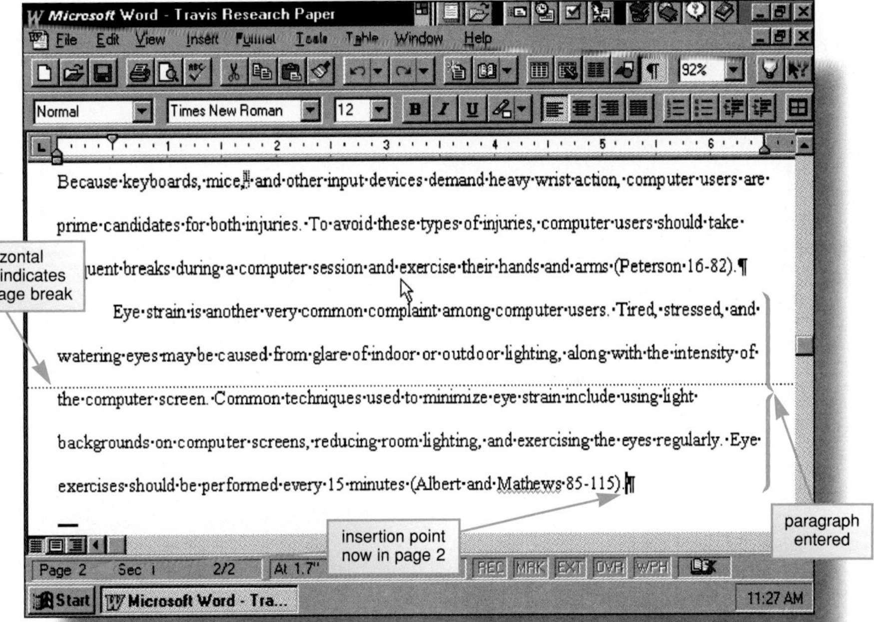

FIGURE 3-41

Eye strain is another very common complaint among computer users. Tired, stressed, and watering eyes may be caused from glare of indoor or outdoor lighting, along with the intensity of the computer screen. Common techniques used to minimize eye strain include using light backgrounds on computer screens, reducing room lighting, and exercising the eyes regularly. Eye exercises should be performed every 15 minutes (Albert and Mathews 85-115).

FIGURE 3-42

Word, by default, prevents widows and orphans from occurring in a document. A **widow** is created when the last line of a paragraph displays by itself at the top of a page, and an **orphan** occurs when the first line of a paragraph displays by itself at the bottom of a page. Thus, when you typed the first line of the third paragraph, Word placed the automatic page break above the paragraph to prevent an orphan. When you continued typing the paragraph, however, Word recognized the multiple lines in the paragraph and moved the automatic page break. If, for some reason, you wanted to allow a widow or an orphan in a document, you would right-click the paragraph in question, click Paragraph on the shortcut menu, click the Text Flow tab in the Paragraph dialog box, click Widow/Orphan Control to deselect the check box, and then click the OK button.

More *About* Flagged Words

Recall that the commands in a shortcut menu differ depending on the object on which you right-click. If you select and then right-click a word, you can cut, copy, or paste it from the shortcut menu; however, if the selected word has a red wavy underline beneath it, you can only spell check it from the shortcut menu.

Checking Spelling Automatically As You Type

In Project 1, you learned to spell check all at once; that is, check the spelling of the entire document at once by clicking the Spelling button on the Formatting toolbar. As an alternative, you can also check spelling of words as you type. Recall that Word places a red wavy underline beneath a word(s) not in its dictionary. To display a list of suggested spelling corrections for the flagged word, you right-click it. In the following example, the word, injuries, has intentionally been misspelled as injuris to illustrate Word's spell check as you type feature.

Steps To Spell Check as You Type

1. **Press the ENTER key. Type the beginning of the last paragraph:** `As noted, hand and eye injuris` **and then press the SPACEBAR.**

   Word flags the misspelled word, injuris, by placing a red wavy underline below it (Figure 3-43).

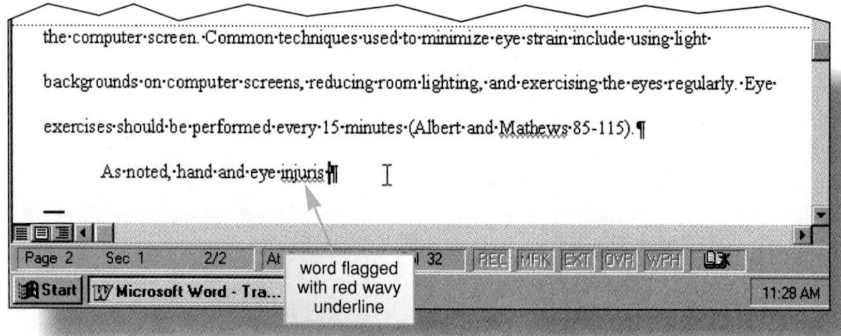

FIGURE 3-43

2. **Right-click the misspelled word, injuris. Point to injuries on the shortcut menu.**

   Word displays a shortcut menu that lists suggested spelling corrections for the flagged word (Figure 3-44).

3. **Click injuries. Press the END key and type the remainder of the sentence:** `can be avoided by exercising regularly during a computer session.`

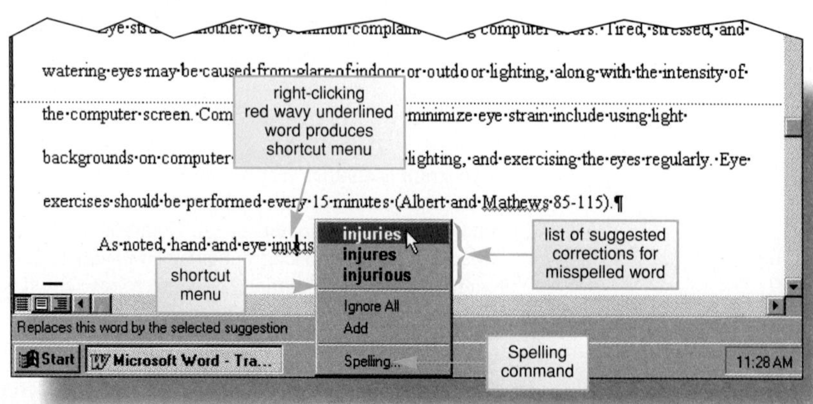

FIGURE 3-44

Word replaces the misspelled word with the selected word on the shortcut menu (Figure 3-45).

If, when you right-click the misspelled word, your desired correction is not in the list (Figure 3-44), you can display the Spelling: English (US) dialog box by clicking Spelling on the shortcut menu. For a detailed explanation of the Spelling: English (US) dialog box, see pages WD1.43 through WD1.46 in Project 1.

Creating a Table Using the Table Wizard

In the last paragraph of the research paper, you are to place a table outlining the hand and eye exercises recommended for computer users (Figure 3-1 on page WD 3.5). In Project 2, you created a table of degrees awarded in the research paper using the TAB key. In this project, you create a table using Word's table feature. A Word **table** is a collection of rows and columns. With Word, you can create a table layout from scratch or you can use a wizard. Recall that a **wizard** asks you a series of questions, and based on your responses, creates a solution for you. Because this is your first experience with Word tables, use the **Table Wizard** to create the table as shown in the following steps.

More About Word Tables

Although you can use the TAB key to create a table, many Word users prefer to use its table feature. With a Word table, you can arrange numbers in columns. For emphasis, tables can be shaded and have borders. Word tables can be sorted. And you can have Word add the contents of an entire row or column.

Steps To Create a Table Using the Table Wizard

1. **Press the SPACEBAR, and then type the text up to the location of the table:** `The table below summarizes hand and eye exercises designed for computer users.` **Press SHIFT+ENTER. Type** `Table` **and then press SHIFT+ENTER. Type** `Hand and Eye Exercises for Computer Users` **as the table title.**

Word places a line break character at the end of each line entered (Figure 3-45). Recall that a line break causes Word to ignore paragraph formatting when advancing the insertion point to the next line. Thus, Word does not first-line indent the table caption or title.

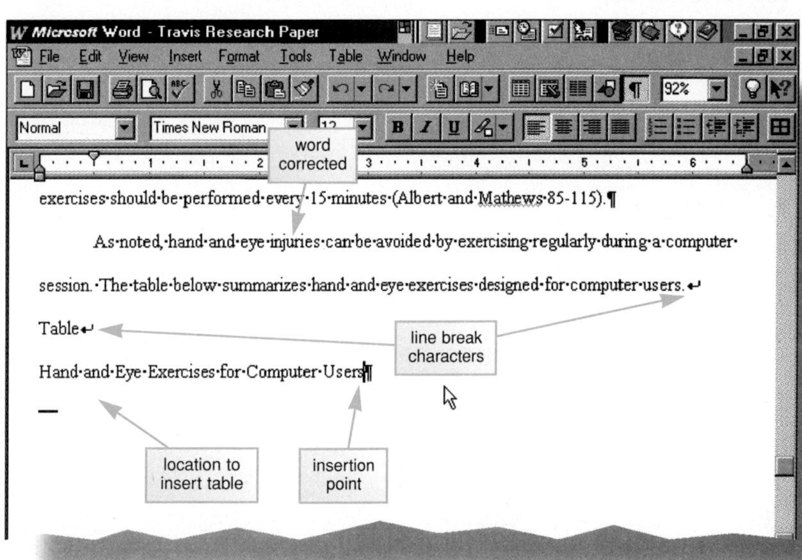

FIGURE 3-45

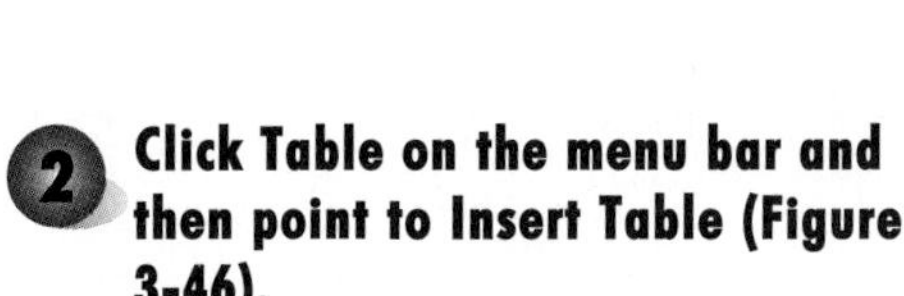

2. **Click Table on the menu bar and then point to Insert Table (Figure 3-46).**

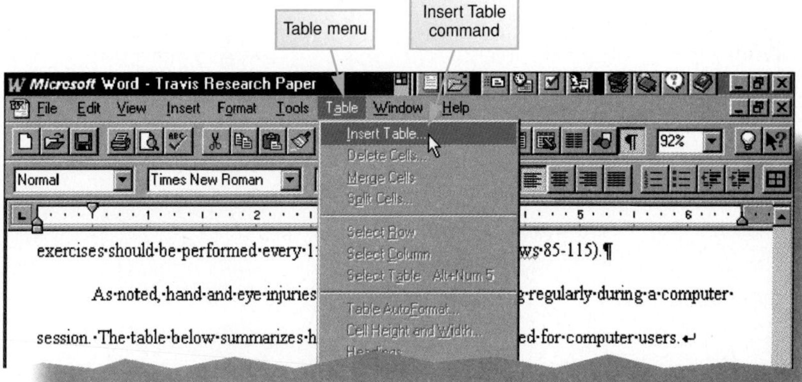

FIGURE 3-46

3 **Click Insert Table. When the Insert Table dialog box displays, point to the Wizard button.**

Word displays the Insert Table dialog box (Figure 3-47). In this dialog box, you can define your table specifications or use the Table Wizard to create the table layout.

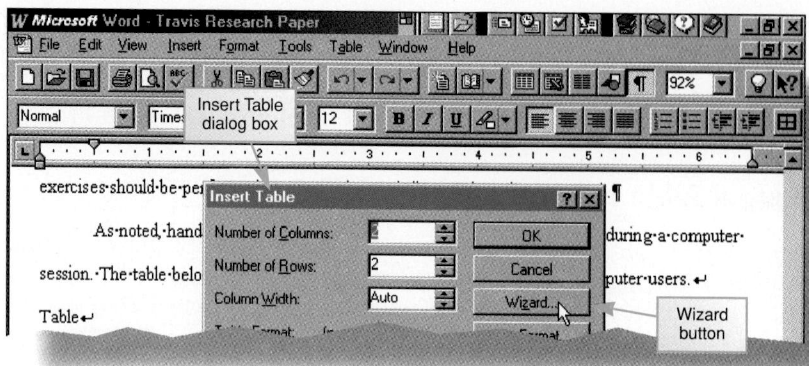

FIGURE 3-47

4 **Click the Wizard button. When the Table Wizard dialog box displays, click Style 1, if necessary, and then point to the Next button.**

Word displays the first of a series of Table Wizard dialog boxes, asking for the layout of the table you wish to create (Figure 3-48). In this project, your table will be Style 1.

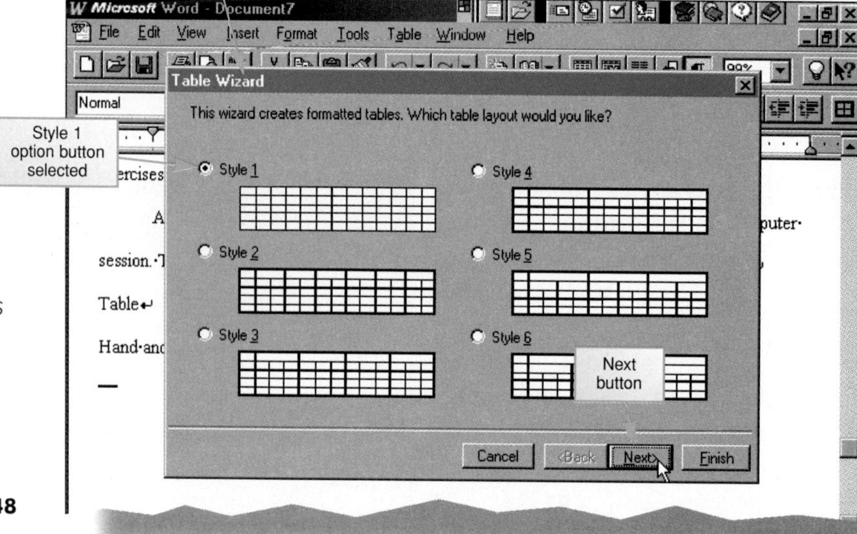

FIGURE 3-48

5 **Click the Next button. When the second Table Wizard dialog box displays, click No headings and then type** 2 **in the columns text box if necessary. Point to the Next button.**

Word displays the next Table Wizard dialog box (Figure 3-49). In this dialog box, you specify the number of columns to appear in the table and their headings, if desired. For example, you could have 12 columns, each one containing a month name.

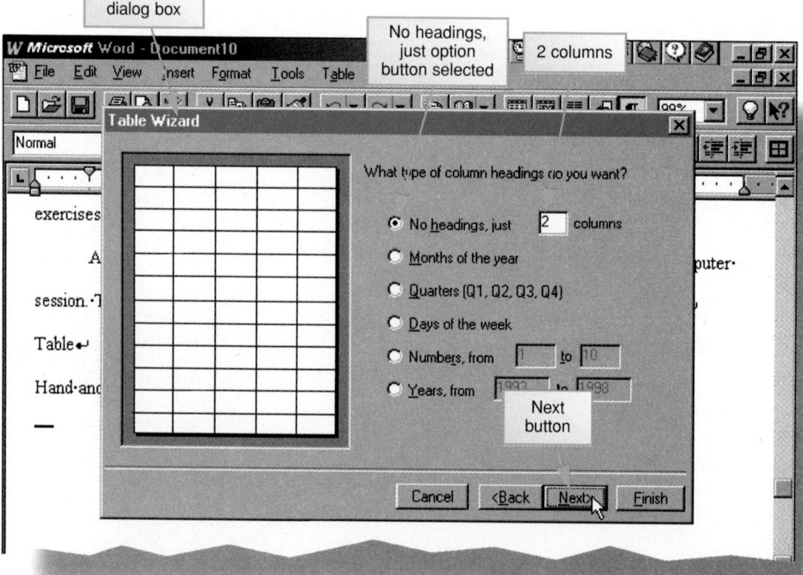

FIGURE 3-49

6 **Click the Next button. When the third Table Wizard dialog box displays, click No headings and then type** 2 **in the columns text box if necessary. Point to the Next button.**

Word displays the next Table Wizard dialog box, which requests information about the rows in your table (Figure 3-50). Like the columns, you can customize the row headings.

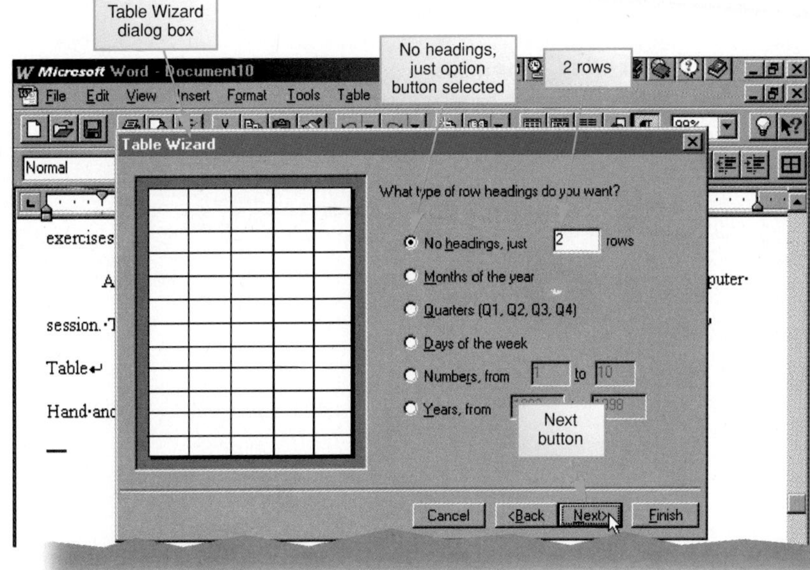

FIGURE 3-50

7 **Click the Next button. When the fourth Table Wizard dialog box displays, click Text: left-aligned, if necessary, and then point to the Next button.**

Word displays the next Table Wizard dialog box (Figure 3-51). In this dialog box, you specify how the data will be aligned within the table.

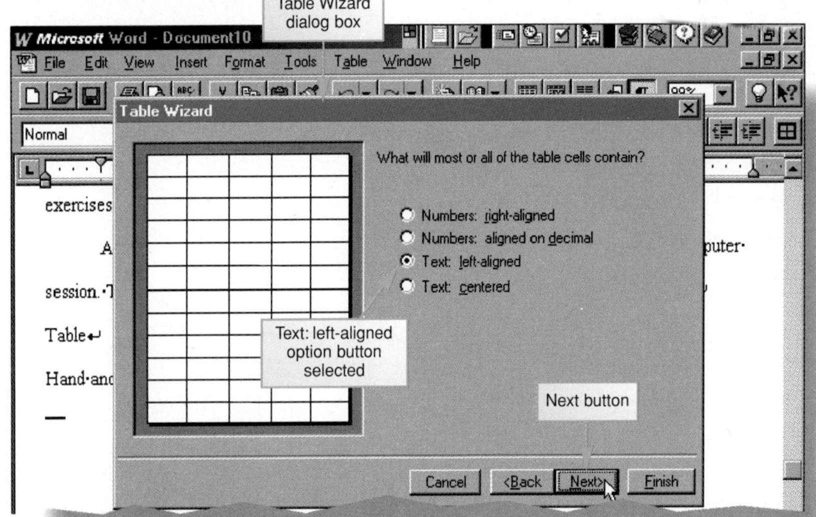

FIGURE 3-51

8 **Click the Next button. When the fifth Table Wizard dialog box displays, click Portrait, if necessary, and then point to the Next button.**

Word displays the next Table Wizard dialog box, requesting the orientation for the table (Figure 3-52). On an 8.5-by-11-inch piece of paper, portrait orientation displays the table across the 8.5-inch side; whereas, landscape displays it across the 11-inch side.

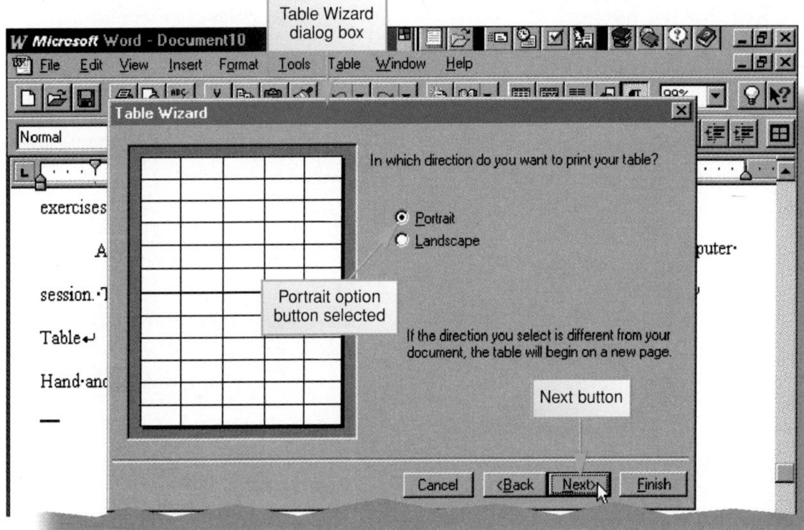

FIGURE 3-52

9 **Click the Next button. When the final Table Wizard dialog box displays, point to the Finish button.**

Word displays the final Table Wizard dialog box (Figure 3-53). Notice this dialog box informs you that you will specify shading and borders for your table in the next dialog box.

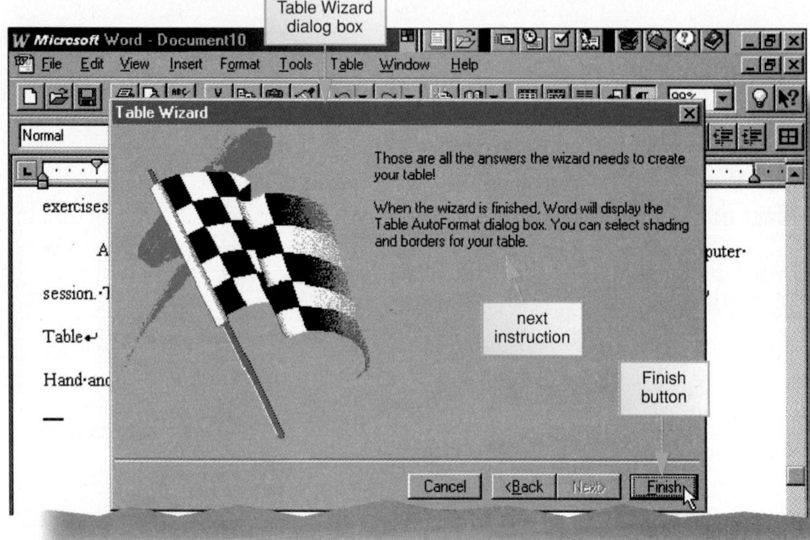

FIGURE 3-53

10 **Click the Finish button. When the Table AutoFormat dialog box displays, scroll through the list of formats and then click Grid 8. In the Formats to Apply area, click Color. In the Apply Special Formats To area, click Heading Rows. Point to the OK button.**

Word displays the Table AutoFormat dialog box (Figure 3-54). A preview of the selected options in this dialog box displays in the Preview area.

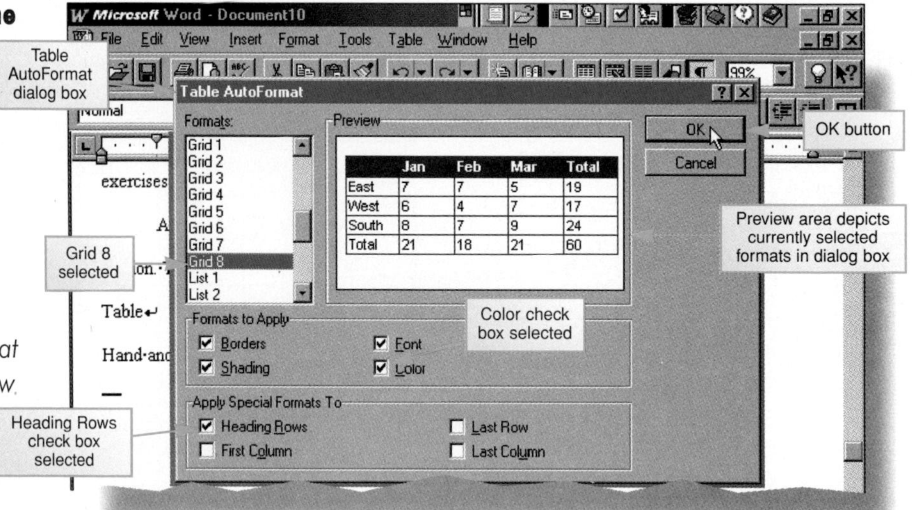

FIGURE 3-54

11 **Click the OK button.**

Word creates a table according to your specifications and places it immediately below the location of the insertion point in the document (Figure 3-55). The table has 2 rows and 2 columns, as you instructed the Table Wizard. Notice the heading row is shaded because you clicked Heading Rows in the Table AutoFormat dialog box.

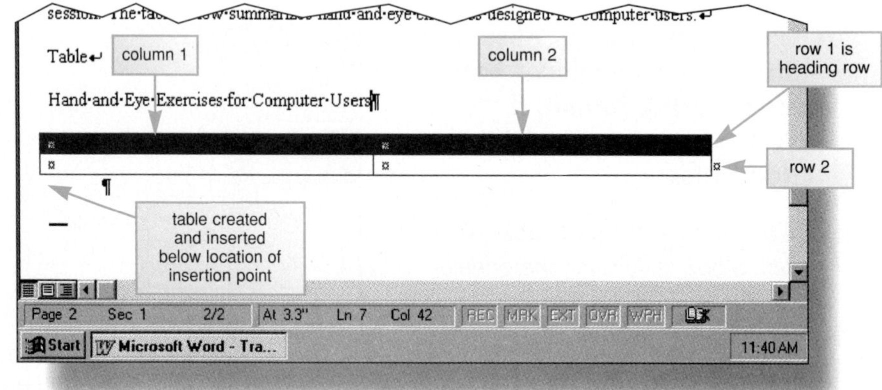

FIGURE 3-55

***Other*Ways**

1. Click Insert Table button on Standard toolbar, drag through grid
2. On Table menu click Insert Table, enter number of columns and rows, click OK button

Entering Data into the Table

The next step is to enter data into the empty table. The intersection of a row and a column is called a **cell**. Cells are filled with data. The data you enter within a cell wordwraps just as text does between the margins of a document. To place data into a cell, you click the cell and then type. To advance rightward from one cell to the next, press the TAB key. When you are at the rightmost cell in a row, also press the TAB key to move to the first cell in the next row; do not press the ENTER key. The ENTER key is used to begin a new paragraph within a cell. Perform the following steps to enter the data into the table.

More About Tables

To select a single cell in a table, click the left of the cell. To select an entire row, click to the left of the row. To select an entire column, click the column's top border. To add a row or column to the middle of a table, select the row below or column to the right; right-click the selection and then click Insert Row or Insert Column.

To Enter Data into the Table

1 Click the cell at the intersection of row 1 and column 1.

Word places the insertion point in the leftmost cell of the header row (Figure 3-56).

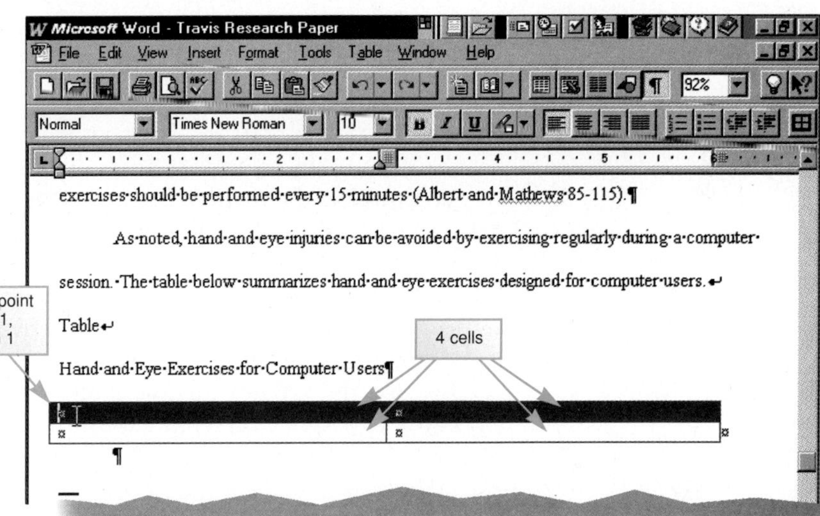

FIGURE 3-56

2 Type `HAND EXERCISES` **and then press the TAB key. Type** `EYE EXERCISES` **and then press the TAB key. Type** `Spread fingers apart for several seconds while keeping wrists straight.` **Press the TAB key. Type** `Look into distance and focus on an object for 20 to 30 seconds.`

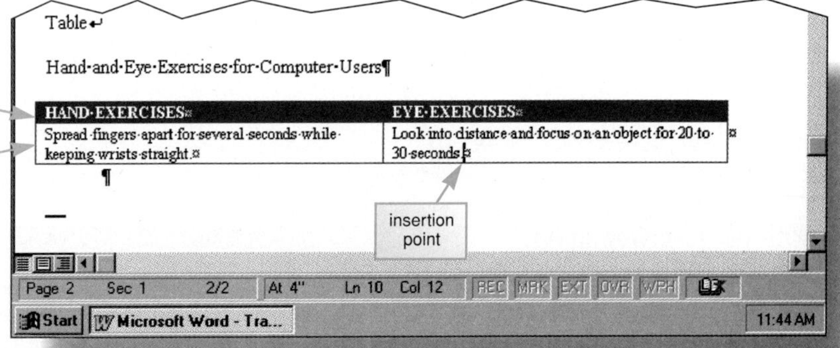

FIGURE 3-57

The table data is entered into the header row and the second row of the table (Figure 3-57). The header row is formatted automatically to bold. The insertion point is currently positioned at the cell intersecting row 2 and column 2. To create a new row at the bottom of a table, you press the TAB key while the insertion point is in the lower rightmost cell of the table.

3 **Press the TAB key. Type** Gently push back fingers and then thumb. **Press the TAB key. Type** Roll eyes in a complete circle. **Press the TAB key. Type** Dangle arms loosely at sides and then shake arms and hands. **Press the TAB key. Type** Close eyes to rest them for at least a minute.

The table data is completely entered (Figure 3-58).

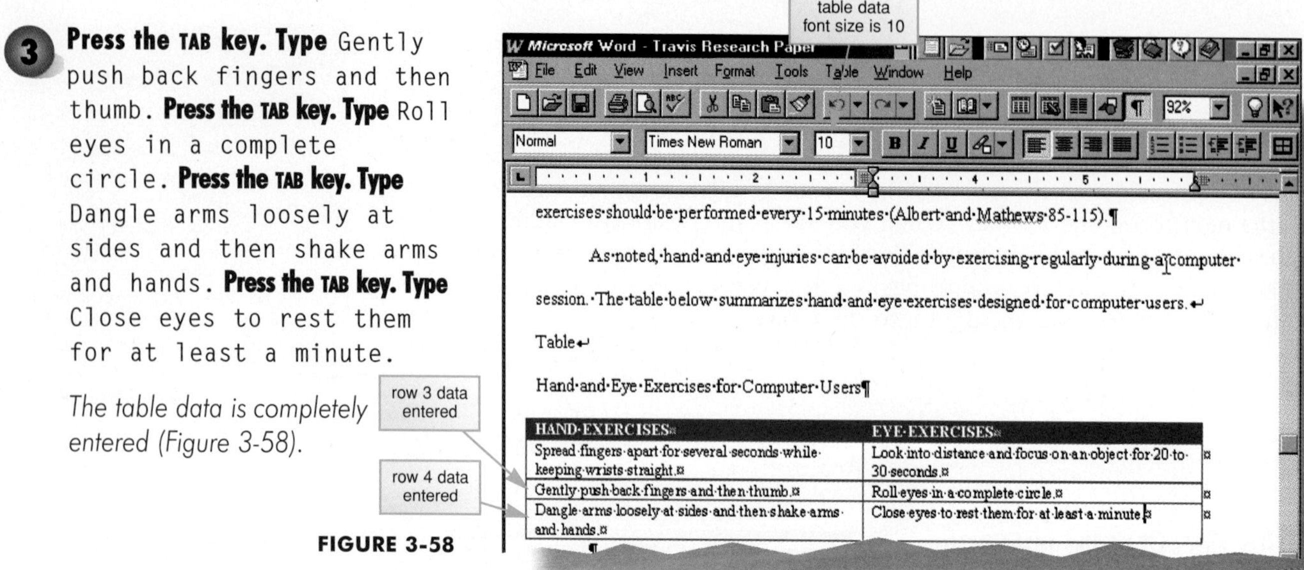

FIGURE 3-58

You modify the contents of cells just as you modify text in a document. To delete the contents of a cell, select the cell contents and then press the DELETE key. To modify text within a cell, position the insertion point in the cell by clicking the cell and then correct the entry. You can double-click the OVR indicator on the status bar to toggle between insert and overtype modes. You also may drag and drop or cut and paste the contents of cells.

Because the TAB key advances you from one cell to the next in a table, press CTRL+TAB to insert a tab character into a cell.

Changing the Font Size of All Characters in a Table

Notice in Figure 3-58 above that the font size of the characters in the table is 10 point. Thus, Word used the Normal style with the Table Wizard. To change the point size of the characters in the table, you must first select the entire table and then format as shown in these steps.

To Select an Entire Table

1 **With the insertion point somewhere in the table, click Table on the menu bar and then point to Select Table (Figure 3-59).**

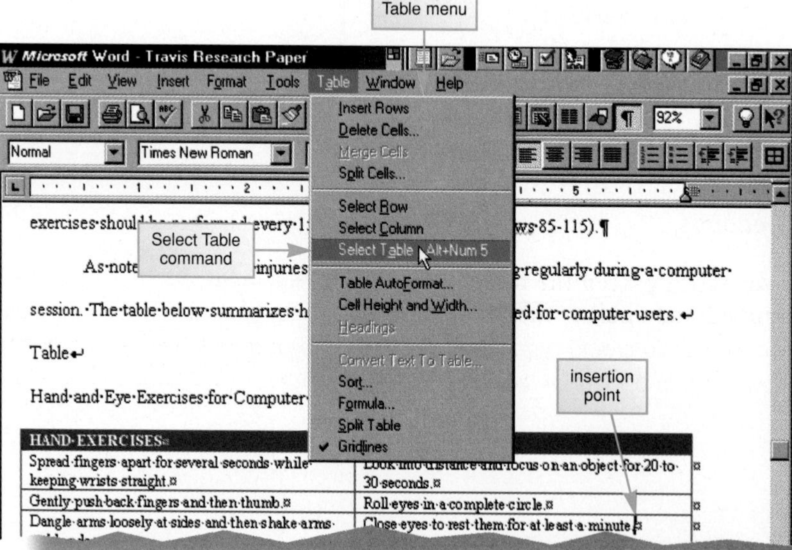

FIGURE 3-59

Click Select Table.

Word highlights the contents of the entire table (Figure 3-60).

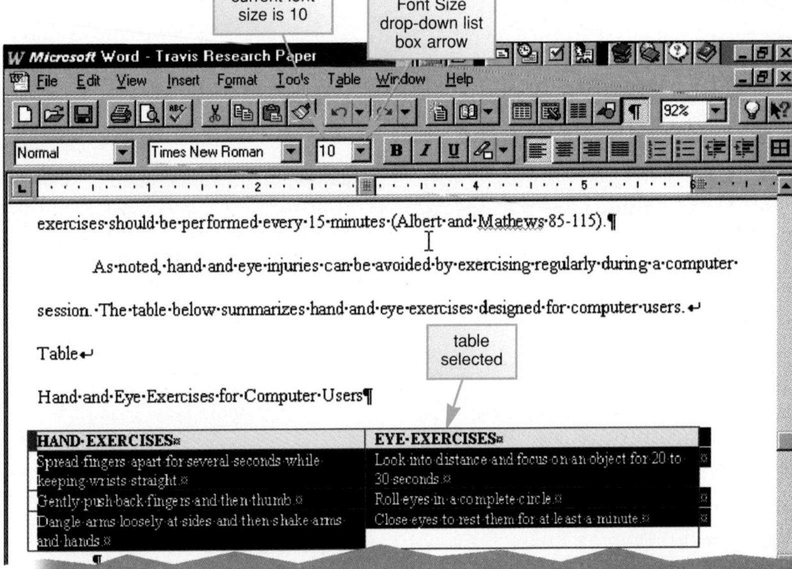

FIGURE 3-60

OtherWays

1. With the insertion point somewhere in the table, press ALT+5 (on numeric keypad)

The next step is to format the selected table as described below.

TO CHANGE THE FONT SIZE OF SELECTED CHARACTERS

Step 1: Click the Font Size box arrow.
Step 2: Click 12.
Step 3: Click outside the table to remove the highlight.

Word changes the font size of the characters in the table to 12 point (Figure 3-61).

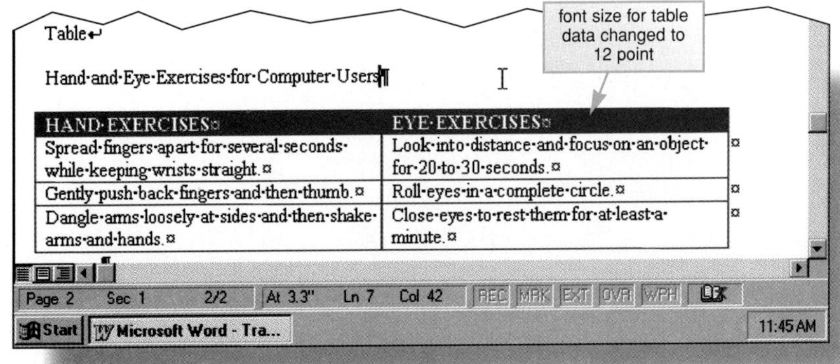

FIGURE 3-61

Changing Paragraph Formatting

When Word placed the table into the research paper, it placed a paragraph mark immediately below the table without a blank line between the paragraph mark and the table. Because the MLA style requires double-spacing of the entire document, you must change the line spacing above the paragraph mark.

Also, the text below the table is a continuation of the paragraph above the table. Thus, you do not want first-line indent to be set for this paragraph mark; you want the paragraph to continue at the left margin. Because you are performing multiple formatting changes on the paragraph mark below the table, use the Paragraph dialog box as shown in the steps on the next page.

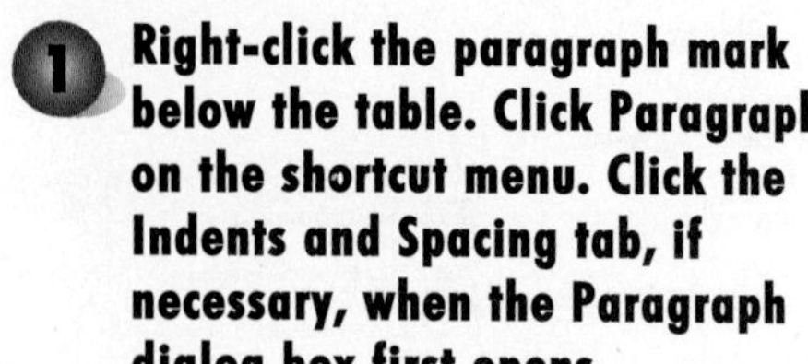

To Change Paragraph Formatting

1 Right-click the paragraph mark below the table. Click Paragraph on the shortcut menu. Click the Indents and Spacing tab, if necessary, when the Paragraph dialog box first opens.

Word displays the Paragraph dialog box. Notice that the line spacing is set to double; yet Word placed no blank lines between the table and the paragraph mark below the table.

2 Click the Special box arrow and then point to (none).

Word displays a list of Special indentation formats (Figure 3-62).

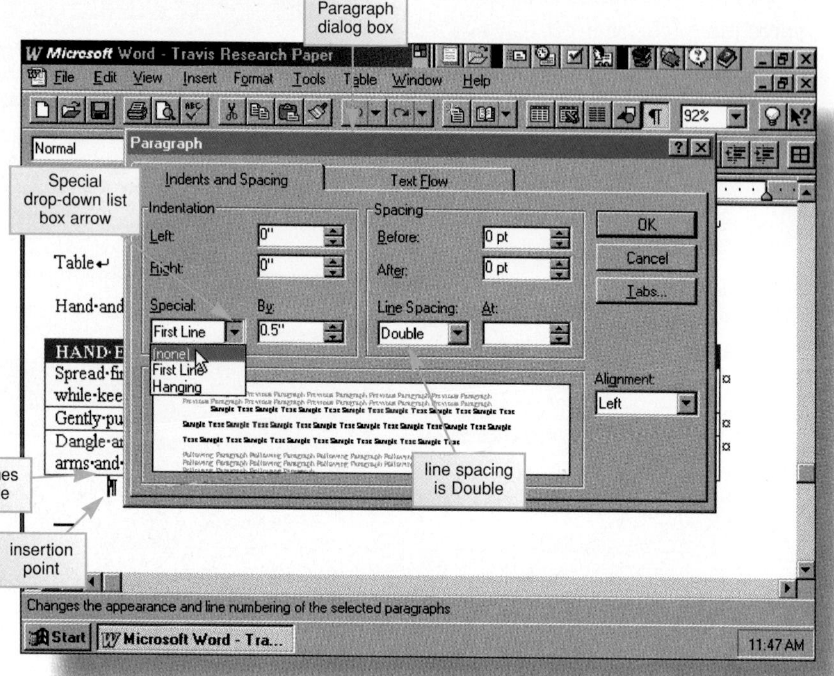

FIGURE 3-62

3 Click (none). Click the Before box up arrow twice in the Spacing area.

Word removes the first-line indent and displays 12 pt in the Before box (Figure 3-63). One blank line is equivalent to 12 points; thus, one blank line will appear before the paragraph mark containing the insertion point.

4 Click the OK button.

Word inserts a blank line between the paragraph mark and the table. The paragraph mark shifts to the left margin.

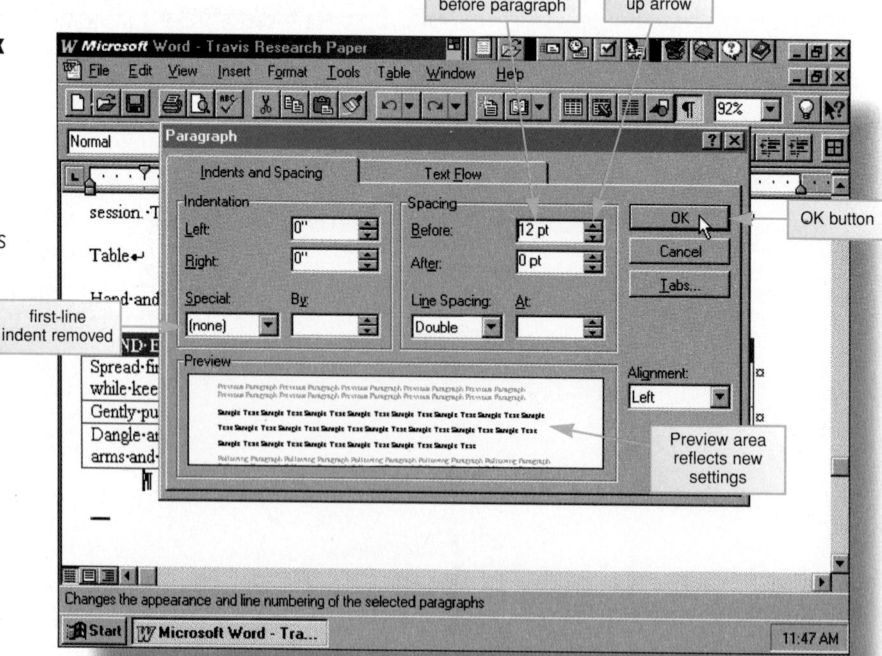

FIGURE 3-63

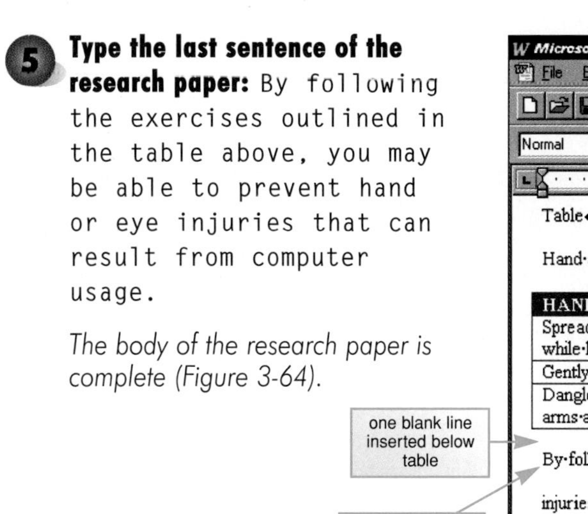

5 **Type the last sentence of the research paper:** `By following the exercises outlined in the table above, you may be able to prevent hand or eye injuries that can result from computer usage.`

The body of the research paper is complete (Figure 3-64).

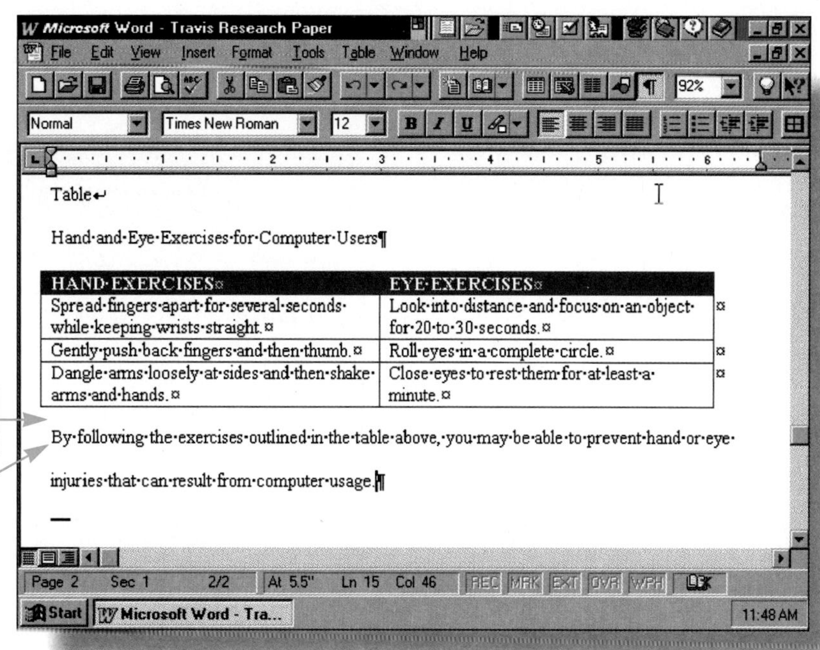

FIGURE 3-64

Creating an Alphabetical Works Cited Page

According to the MLA style, the works cited page is a bibliographical list of works you directly reference in your paper. The list is placed on a separate page with the title, Works Cited, centered one inch from the top margin. The works are to be alphabetized by author's last name. The first line of each work begins at the left margin; subsequent lines of the same work are indented one-half inch from the left margin.

The first step in creating the works cited page is to force a page break so the works display on a separate page.

More About Sources

When writing a research paper, you must acknowledge sources of information. Citing sources boils down to ethics and honesty. Caution must be used when summarizing or paraphrasing a source. Be sure to avoid plagiarism, which includes using someone else's words, as well ideas claiming their ideas as your own.

Manual Page Breaks

Because the works cited are to display on a separate numbered page, you need to insert a manual page break following the body of the research paper. A **manual page break** is one that you force into the document at a specific location. Manual page breaks display on the screen as a thin, dotted horizontal line, separated by the words, Page Break. Word never moves or adjusts manual page breaks. When you insert manual page breaks, however, Word does adjust any automatic page breaks that follow in the document. Word inserts manual page breaks just before the insertion point. Follow the steps on the next page to insert a manual page break following the body of the research paper.

More About Citing Sources

Information that is commonly known or accessible to the audience constitutes common knowledge and does not have to be listed as a parenthetical citation or in the bibliography. If, however, you question whether certain information is common knowledge, you should document it – just to be safe.

To Insert a Manual Page Break

With the insertion point at the end of the research paper, press the ENTER key. Press CTRL+0 (zero). Click Insert on the menu bar and then point to Break.

Word removes the extra blank line above the paragraph mark (Figure 3-65). Recall that you increased the spacing above the paragraph by 12 points for the paragraph beneath the table. When you pressed the ENTER key, this paragraph formatting was carried forward; thus, two blank lines displayed between these paragraphs (one for the double-spacing and one for the 12-point spacing above setting). Pressing CTRL+0 removes one blank line from above the paragraph. The insertion point is now positioned one blank line below the body of the research paper.

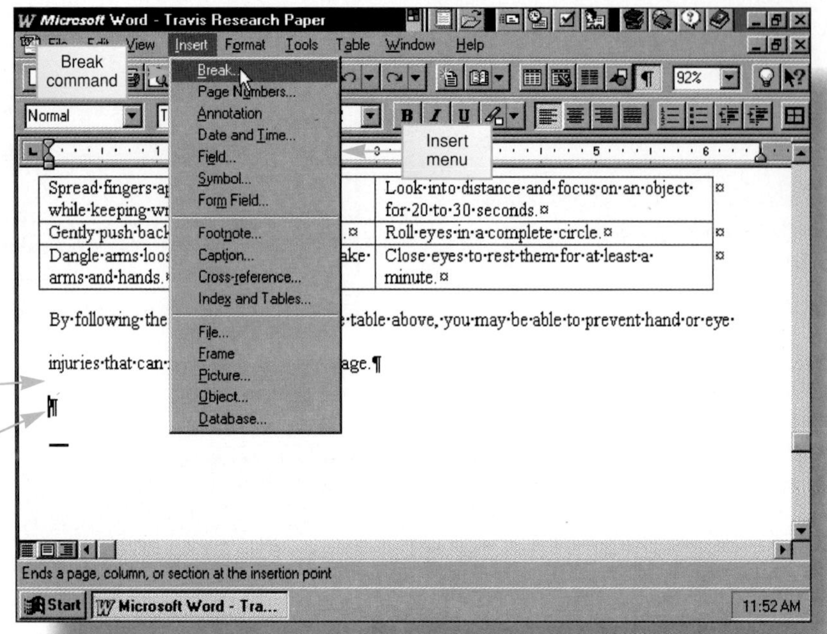

FIGURE 3-65

Click Break.

Word displays the Break dialog box (Figure 3-66). The default option is Page Break in the Break dialog box.

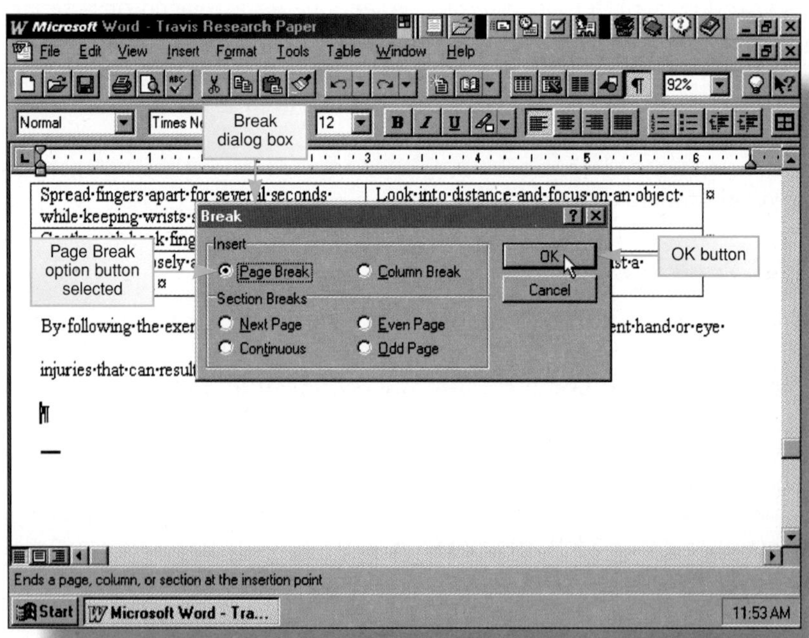

FIGURE 3-66

Click the OK button.

Word inserts a manual page break immediately above the insertion point and positions the insertion point immediately below the manual page break (Figure 3-67). The manual page break displays as a thin, dotted horizontal line with the words, Page Break, in the middle of the line. The status bar indicates the insertion point is located on page 3.

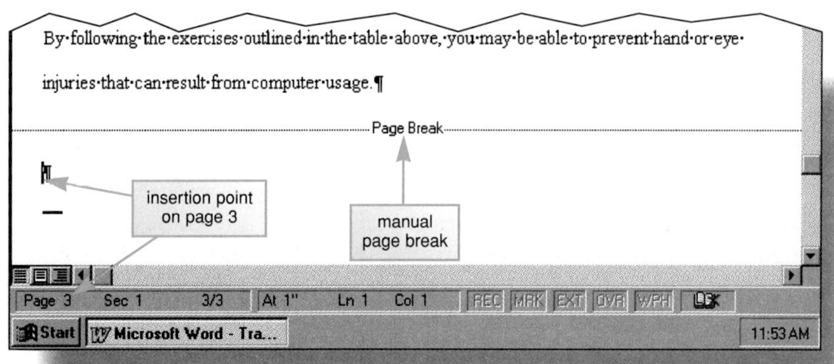

FIGURE 3-67

OtherWays

1. Press CTRL+ENTER

To remove a manual page break from your document, you must select it first by double clicking it. Then, click the Cut button on the Standard toolbar or press the DELETE key.

More About APA Style

The APA style requires the working bibliography be on a separate page, like the MLA; however, the title should be References, rather than Works Cited. The running head should appear on the References page. Guidelines for preparing reference list entries differ significantly from the MLA style. Refer to an APA handbook for specifics.

Creating a Hanging Indent

On the works cited page, the paragraphs begin at the left margin. Subsequent lines in the same paragraph are indented one-half inch from the left margin. In essence, the first line *hangs* to the left of the rest of the paragraph; thus, this type of paragraph formatting is called a **hanging indent**. Follow these steps to create a hanging indent.

Steps To Create a Hanging Indent

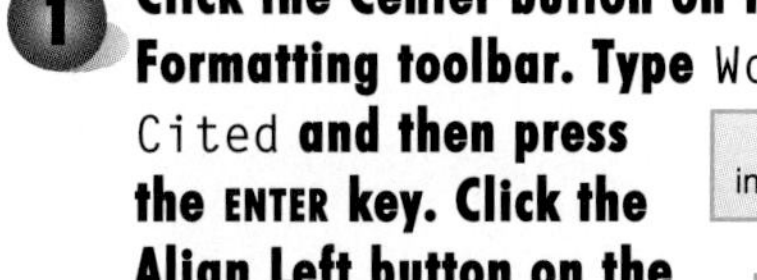

Click the Center button on the Formatting toolbar. Type `Works Cited` **and then press the ENTER key. Click the Align Left button on the Formatting toolbar. Point to the left indent marker on the ruler.**

The title, Works Cited, is entered (Figure 3-68). Recall that the bottom triangle at the left edge of the ruler is the left indent marker, and the top triangle is the first-line indent marker.

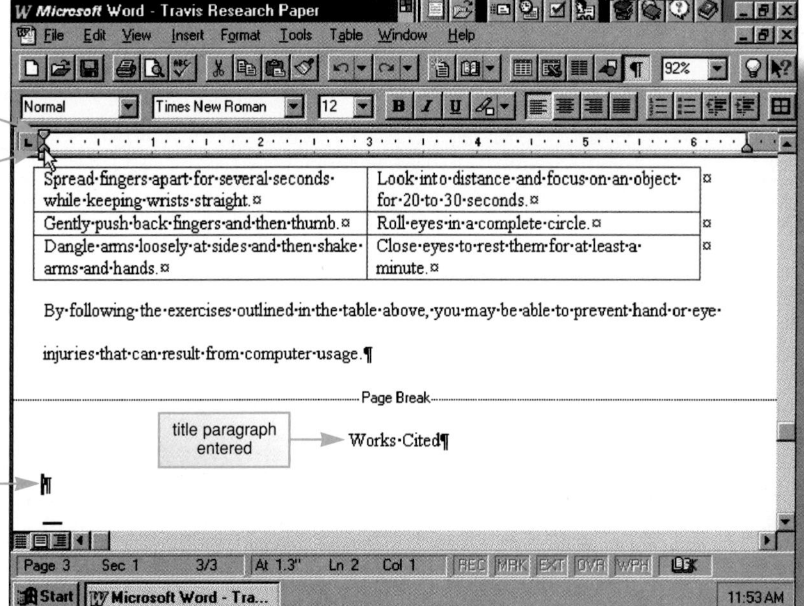

FIGURE 3-68

2 **Drag the left indent marker to the one-half inch mark on the ruler.**

The left indent marker appears at the location of the first tab stop, one-half inch from the left margin (Figure 3-69). The paragraph containing the insertion point in the document window is positioned at the left margin because only subsequent lines in the paragraph are to be indented.

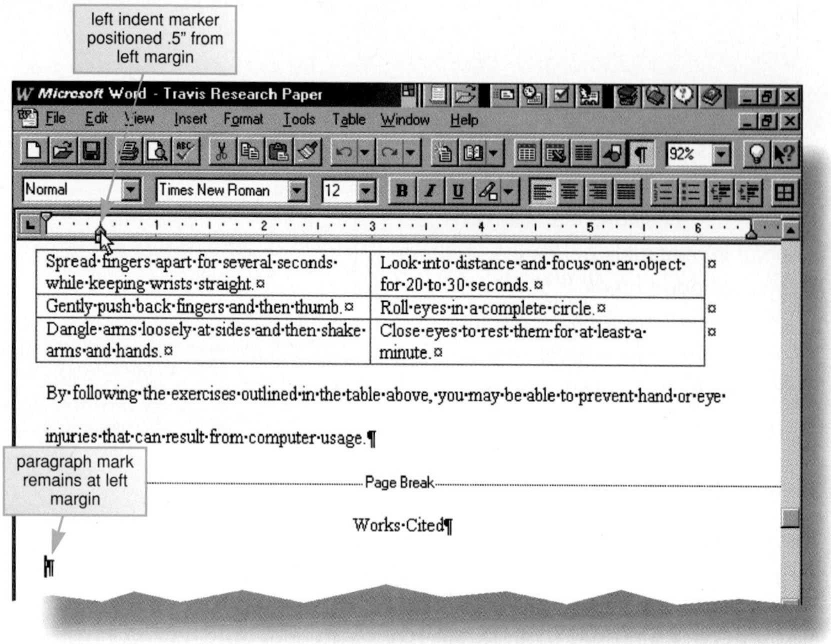

FIGURE 3-69

3 **Type the Works Cited paragraphs as shown in Figure 3-71 below.**

When Word wraps the text in each works cited paragraph, it automatically indents the second line of the paragraph by one-half inch (Figure 3-70). When you press the ENTER key at the end of the first paragraph of text, the insertion point returns automatically to the left margin for the next paragraph.

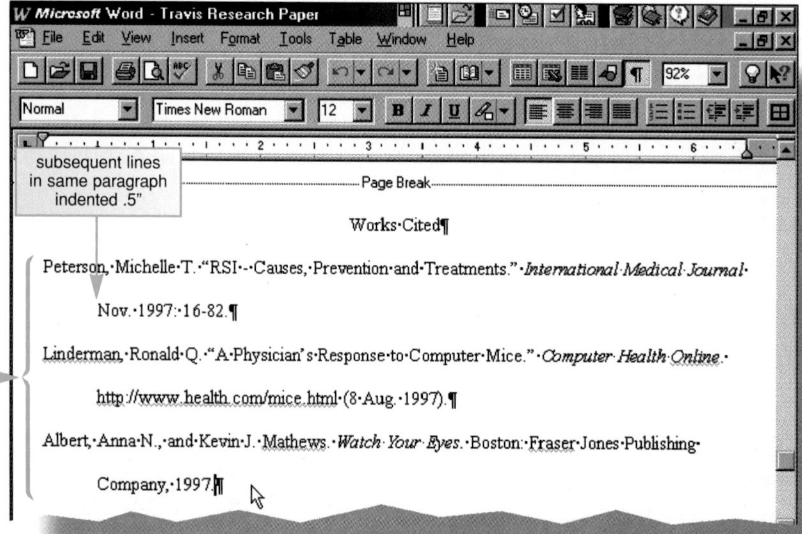

FIGURE 3-70

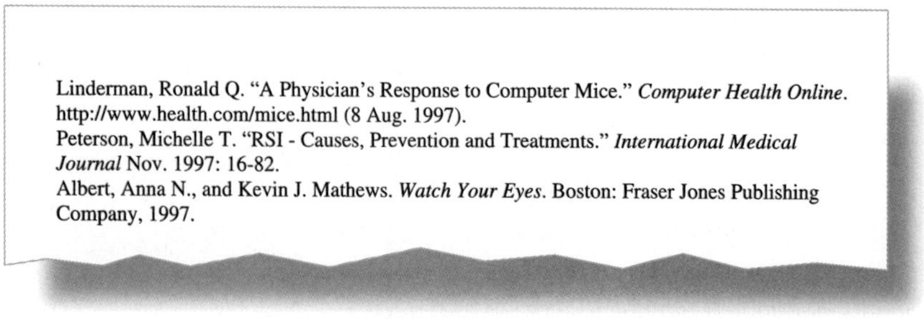

Linderman, Ronald Q. "A Physician's Response to Computer Mice." *Computer Health Online.* http://www.health.com/mice.html (8 Aug. 1997).
Peterson, Michelle T. "RSI - Causes, Prevention and Treatments." *International Medical Journal* Nov. 1997: 16-82.
Albert, Anna N., and Kevin J. Mathews. *Watch Your Eyes.* Boston: Fraser Jones Publishing Company, 1997.

FIGURE 3-71

*Other*Ways

1. Right-click paragraph, click Paragraph on shortcut menu, click Indents and Spacing tab, click Special box arrow, click Hanging, click OK button
2. On Format menu click Paragraph, click Indents and Spacing tab, click Special box arrow, click Hanging, click OK button
3. Press CTRL+T

To drag both the first-line indent and left indent markers at the same time, you drag the small box below the left indent marker.

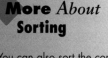

Sorting Paragraphs

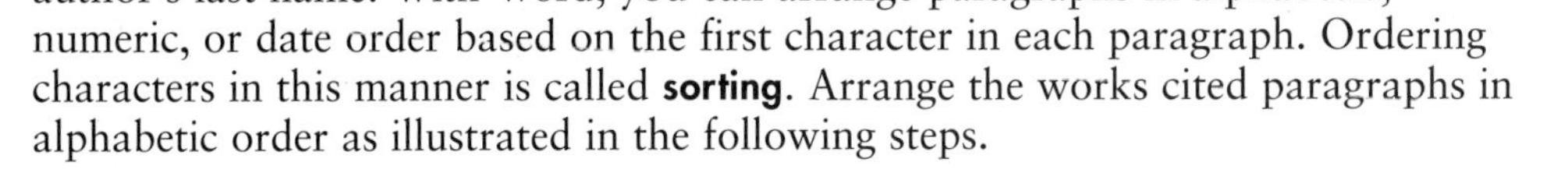

The MLA style requires that the works cited be listed in alphabetical order by author's last name. With Word, you can arrange paragraphs in alphabetic, numeric, or date order based on the first character in each paragraph. Ordering characters in this manner is called **sorting**. Arrange the works cited paragraphs in alphabetic order as illustrated in the following steps.

More About Sorting

You can also sort the contents of a table. First, select the rows in the table to be sorted. Click Table on the menu bar, click Sort Text, click Ascending or Descending, and then click the OK button. Once a document has been saved with sorted paragraphs or tables, you cannot return to original order of the paragraphs or table.

Steps To Sort Paragraphs

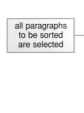

1 Select all of the works cited paragraphs by pointing to the left of the first paragraph and dragging the mouse downward. Click Table on the menu bar and then point to Sort Text.

All of the paragraphs to be sorted are selected (Figure 3-72).

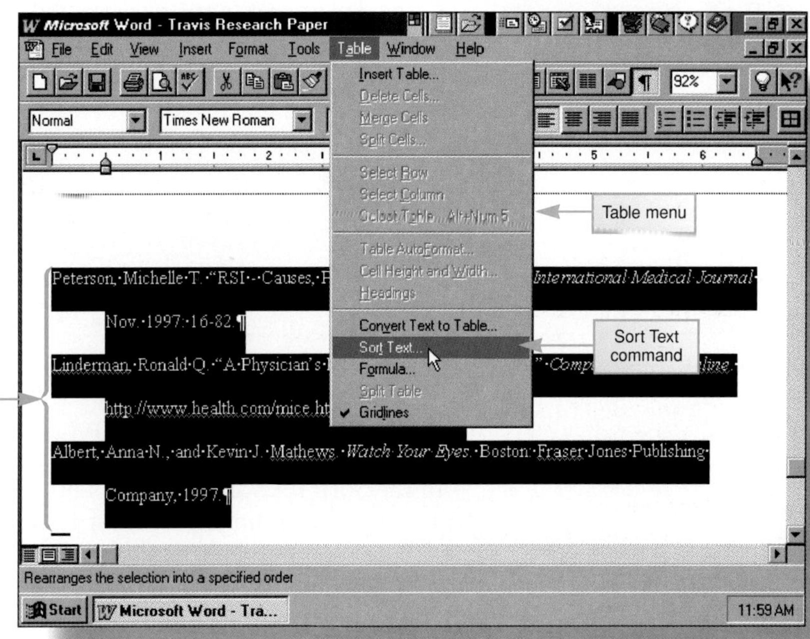

FIGURE 3-72

2 Click Sort Text.

Word displays the Sort Text dialog box (Figure 3-73). In the Sort By area, Ascending is selected. Ascending sorts in alphabetic or numeric order.

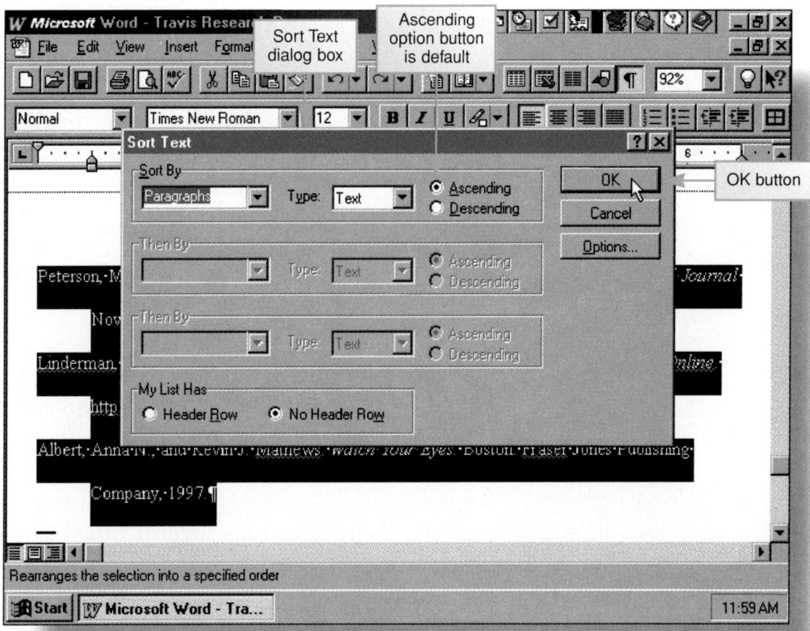

FIGURE 3-73

Click the OK button. Click outside of the selection to remove the highlight.

Word sorts the works cited paragraphs alphabetically (Figure 3-74).

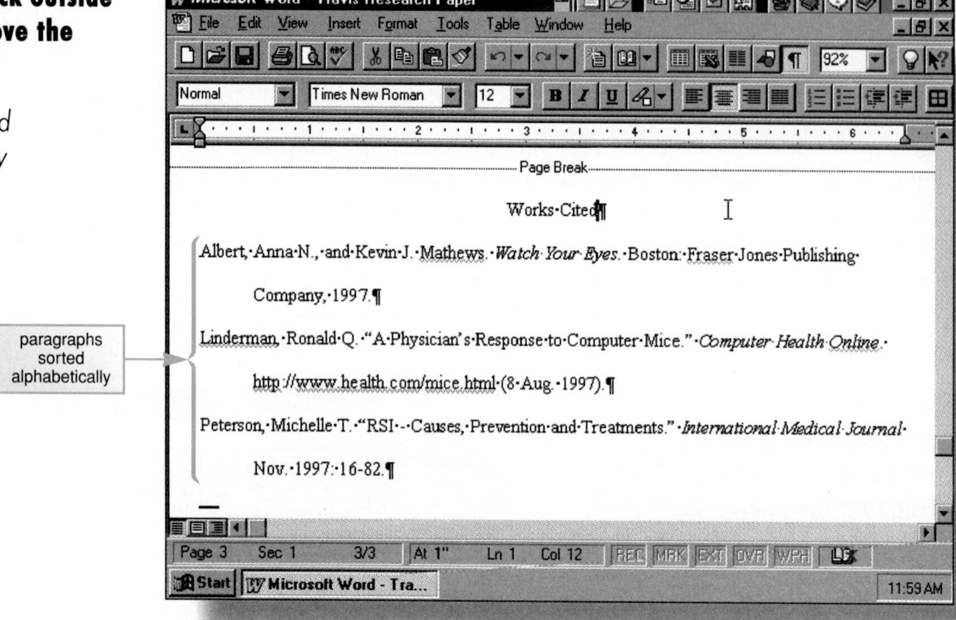

FIGURE 3-74

If you accidentally sort the wrong paragraphs, you can undo a sort by clicking the Undo button on the Standard toolbar.

In the Sort Text dialog box (Figure 3-73 on the previous page), the default sort order is Ascending. If the first character of each paragraph to be sorted is a letter, Word sorts alphabetically on the first letter of the paragraphs. If the first character of each paragraph to be sorted is a number, Word sorts numerically on the first number of the paragraphs. Word by default, orders in **ascending sort order**, which means from the beginning of the alphabet, lowest number, or earliest date. If the first character of the paragraphs to be sorted contains a mixture of letters, numbers, and dates, then the numbers appear first and letters appear last once the paragraphs are sorted. Uppercase letters appear before lowercase letters. In case of ties, Word looks to the first character with a non-identical character and sorts on that character for the paragraphs where the tie occurs.

You can also sort in descending order by clicking Descending in the Sort Text dialog box. **Descending sort order** begins sorting from the end of the alphabet, the highest number, or the most recent date.

The research paper is now complete and ready for proofreading.

More *About* **Proofreading**

When proofreading a paper, ask yourself these questions: Is the purpose clear? Does the title suggest the topic? Does the paper have an introduction, body, and conclusion? Is the thesis clear? Does each paragraph in the body relate to the thesis? Is the conclusion effective? Are all sources acknowledged?

Using Word's Proofing Tools

Before submitting a paper to be graded, you should proofread it. While proofreading, you look for grammatical errors and spelling errors. You want to be sure the transitions between sentences flow smoothly and the sentences themselves make sense. Very often, you may count the words in a paper to meet minimum word guidelines specified by an instructor. To assist you in this proofreading effort, Word provides several tools. You have already used the spell checker in this and previous projects. Two other helpful tools are the thesaurus and word count feature.

Using the Thesaurus

When writing papers, you may find that you used the same word in multiple locations or that a word you used was not quite appropriate. In these instances, you will want to look up a word similar in meaning to the duplicate or inappropriate word. These similar words are called **synonyms**. A book of synonyms is referred to as a **thesaurus**. Word provides an online thesaurus for your convenience. In this project, you used the word, regularly, at the end of the third paragraph and then again at the beginning of the fourth paragraph. To find a synonym to use in the third paragraph, perform the following steps.

Steps To Use Word's Thesaurus

1 Doublo-click the word for which you want to look up a synonym. Click Tools on the menu bar and then point to Thesaurus.

The word, regularly, is highlighted at the end of the third paragraph in the research paper (Figure 3-75).

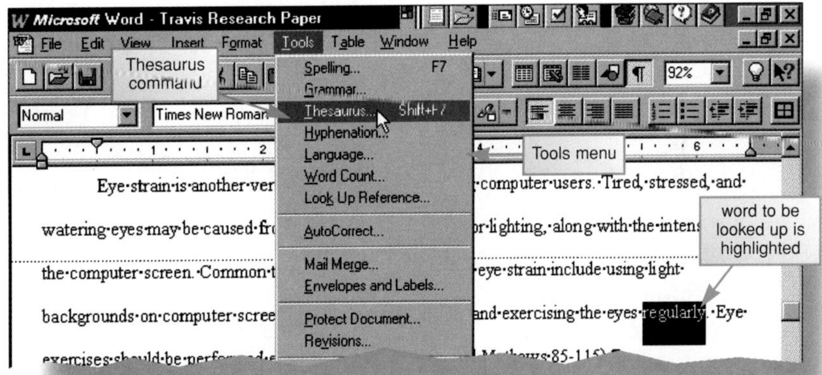

FIGURE 3-75

2 Click Thesaurus.

Word displays the Thesaurus: English (US) dialog box. The Meanings area displays the definition of the selected word, and the Replace with Synonym area displays a variety of words with similar meanings.

3 Click the synonym you want (periodically) and then point to the Replace button.

The word, periodically, is highlighted (Figure 3-76).

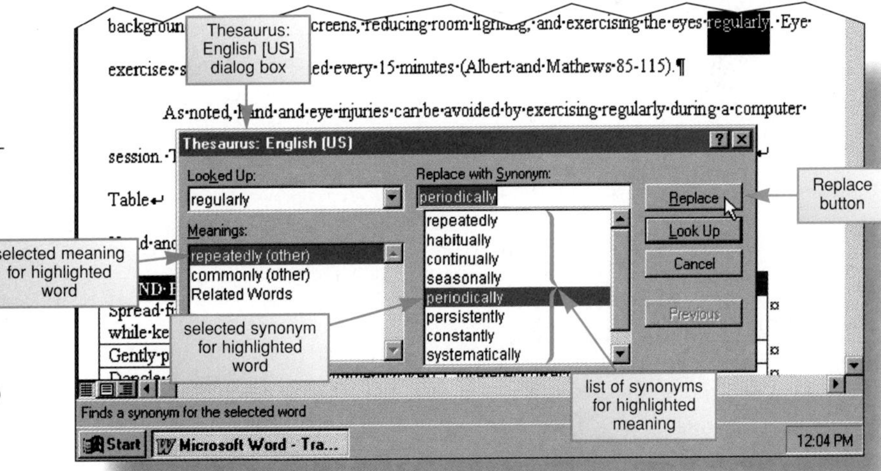

FIGURE 3-76

4 Click the Replace button.

Word replaces the word, regularly, with periodically (Figure 3-77 on the next page).

OtherWays

1. Press CTRL+F7

If multiple meanings are listed in the Meanings area, click the appropriate meaning. The Replace with Synonym area will change based on the meaning you select.

Using Word Count

Often when you write papers, you are required to compose a paper with a specified number of words. For this reason, Word provides a command that displays the number of words, as well as pages, characters, paragraphs, and lines in your document. Perform the following steps to use Word Count.

To Use Word Count

1. **Click Tools on the menu bar and then point to Word Count (Figure 3-77).**

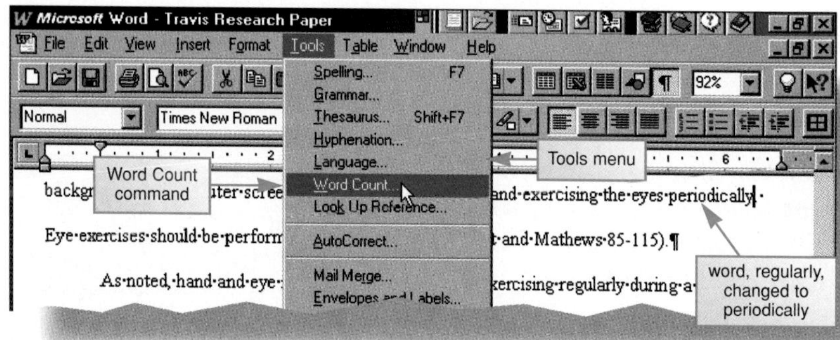

FIGURE 3-77

2. **Click Word Count. In the Word Count dialog box, click Include Footnotes and Endnotes.**

Word displays the Word Count dialog box (Figure 3-78). Word presents you with a variety of statistics on the current document, including number of pages, words, characters, paragraphs, and lines. You can choose to have note text included or not included in these statistics.

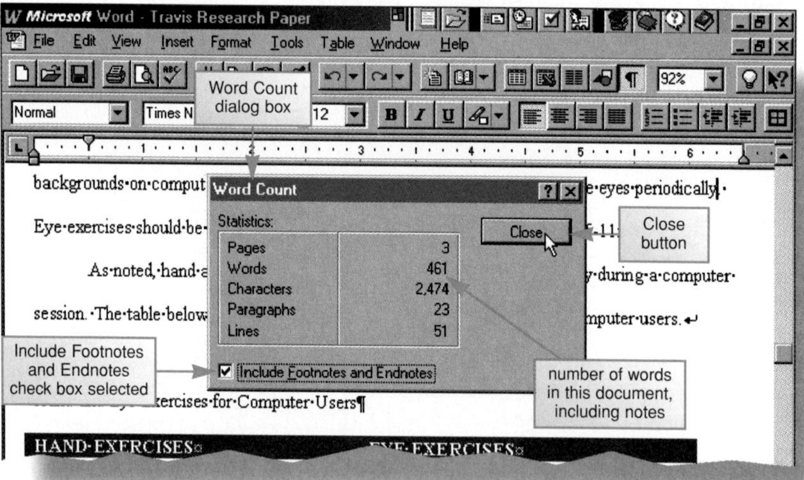

FIGURE 3-78

3. **Click Include Footnotes and Endnotes. Click the Close button in the Word Count dialog box.**

Word deselects the Include Footnotes and Endnotes check box and then returns you to the document.

If you want statistics on only a section of your document, select the section before invoking the Word Count command.

You should now change the zoom control back to 100% so the next person that uses Word will not have a reduced display.

TO RETURN ZOOM CONTROL TO 100%

Step 1: Click the Zoom Control box arrow.
Step 2: Click 100% in the list of zoom percentages.

Word displays 100% in the Zoom Control box.

Checking Spelling, Saving Again, and Printing the Document

The document is now complete. After completing the document, you should check the spelling of the document by clicking the Spelling button on the Standard toolbar. Because you have performed several tasks since the last save, you should save the research paper again by clicking the Save button on the Standard toolbar. Finally, you should print the research paper by clicking the Print button on the Standard toolbar. The document appears as shown in Figure 3-79.

Travis 3

Works Cited

Albert, Anna N., and Kevin J. Mathews. *Watch Your Eyes*. Boston: Fraser Jones Publishing Company, 1997.

Linderman, Ronald Q. "A Physician's Response to Computer Mice." *Computer Health Online*. http://www.health.com/mice.html (8 Aug. 1997).

Peterson, Michelle T. "RSI - Causes, Prevention and Treatments." *International Medical Journal* Nov. 1997: 16-82.

Travis 2

the computer screen. Common techniques used to minimize eye strain include using light backgrounds on computer screens, reducing room lighting, and exercising the eyes periodically. Eye exercises should be performed every 15 minutes (Albert and Mathews 85-115).

As noted, hand and eye injuries can be avoided by exercising regularly during a computer session. The table below summarizes hand and eye exercises designed for computer users.

Table

Hand and Eye Exercises for Computer Users

HAND EXERCISES	EYE EXERCISES
Spread fingers apart for several seconds while keeping wrists straight.	Look into distance and focus on an object for 20 to 30 seconds.
Gently push back fingers and then thumb.	Roll eyes in a complete circle.
Dangle arms loosely at sides and then shake arms and hands.	Close eyes to rest them for at least a minute.

By following the exercises outlined in the table above, you may be able to prevent hand or eye injuries that can result from computer usage.

Travis 1

Caroline Rose Travis

Professor T. Rhodes

Computer Information Systems 210

November 6, 1997

Computer User Health: Injury Prevention

With the growing use of computers and computer devices in both home and office environments, people are becoming increasingly aware of health-related injuries resulting from computer usage. Two common complaints include aching wrists or hands and strained eyes. Each of these injuries can be prevented or minimized by following some basic guidelines.

Two common repetitive stress or strain injuries (RSI) that affect the wrist are carpal tunnel syndrome and tendonitis. If your fingertips tingle and then become numb and your hands hurt, you may have carpal tunnel syndrome. Tendonitis sufferers, however, have extreme pain in the wrist. Both types of injuries can be caused by repeated or forceful bending of the wrist. Because keyboards, mice,[1] and other input devices demand heavy wrist action, computer users are prime candidates for both injuries. To avoid these types of injuries, computer users should take frequent breaks during a computer session and exercise their hands and arms (Peterson 16-82).

Eye strain is another very common complaint among computer users. Tired, stressed, and watering eyes may be caused from glare of indoor or outdoor lighting, along with the intensity of

[1] Physicians recommend that the mouse be placed at least six inches from the edge of a workstation. In this position, the wrist is forced to be flat, which causes bending to occur at the elbow when the mouse is moved across the mouse pad. *Computer Health Online*, 8 Aug. 1997.

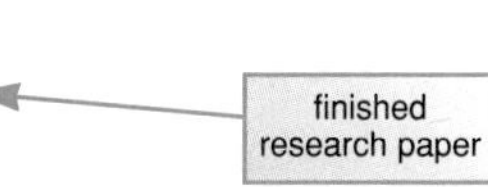

FIGURE 3-79

The final step in this project is to quit Word.

TO QUIT WORD

Step 1:Click the Close button at the right edge of Word's title bar.

The Word window closes.

Project Summary

Project 3 introduced you to creating a research paper with a table using the MLA documentation style. You learned how to change margin settings, adjust line spacing, create headers with page numbers, and indent paragraphs. You learned how to use Word's AutoCorrect and spell check as you type features. Then, you added footnotes to the research paper and a table using Word's Table Wizard. You alphabetized the works cited page by sorting its paragraphs. Finally, you used Word's thesaurus to look up synonyms and saw how to display statistics about your document.

What You Should Know

Having completed this project, you should now be able to perform the following tasks:

- Add a Footnote *(WD 3.25)*
- Center a Paragraph Before Typing *(WD 3.17)*
- Change Paragraph Formatting *(WD 3.38)*
- Change the Default Margin Settings *(WD 3.8)*
- Change the Font Size of All Characters in a Paragraph *(WD 3.15)*
- Change the Font Size of Selected Characters *(WD 3.37)*
- Create a Hanging Indent *(WD 3.41)*
- Create a Header *(WD 3.12)*
- Create an AutoCorrect Entry *(WD 3.23)*
- Create a Table Using the Table Wizard *(WD 3.31)*
- Display Nonprinting Characters *(WD 3.7)*
- Double-Space a Document *(WD 3.9)*
- Enter Data into the Table *(WD 3.35)*
- Enter Name and Course Information *(WD 3.16)*
- First-Line Indent Paragraphs *(WD 3.18)*
- Illustrate Word's AutoCorrect Feature *(WD 3.22)*
- Insert a Manual Page Break *(WD 3.40)*
- Quit Word *(WD 3.48)*
- Return Zoom Control to 100% *(WD 3.46)*
- Save a Document *(WD 3.18)*
- Select an Entire Table *(WD 3.36)*
- Sort Paragraphs *(WD 3.43)*
- Spell Check as You Type *(WD 3.30)*
- Start Word *(WD 3.7)*
- Use Automatic Page Break *(WD 3.29)*
- Use Word Count *(WD 3.46)*
- Use Word's Thesaurus *(WD 3.45)*
- Zoom Page Width *(WD 3.21)*

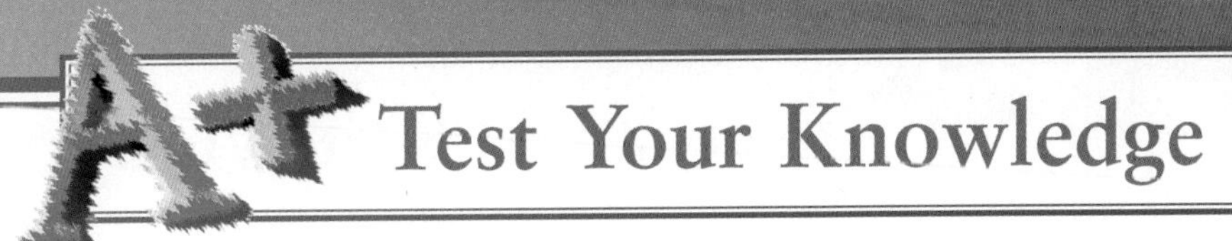

Test Your Knowledge

1 True/False

Instructions: Circle T if the statement is true or F if the statement is false.

T F 1. A popular documentation style used today for research papers is presented by the Modern Language Association (MLA).
T F 2. The MLA style uses the term references rather than bibliography.
T F 3. A header is text you want to print at the bottom of each page in a document.
T F 4. Superscripted numbers are those that appear raised above other text in a document.
T F 5. A manual page break displays on the screen as a thin, dotted horizontal line, separated by the words, Page Break.
T F 6. A Word table is a collection of rows and columns.
T F 7. A hanging indent indents the first line of each paragraph one-half inch from the left margin.
T F 8. To move from one table cell to another, press the TAB key.
T F 9. Word's thesaurus enables you to look up homonyms for a selected word.
T F 10. To obtain statistics about a document, click the Word Count button on the Standard toolbar.

2 Multiple Choice

Instructions: Circle the correct response.

1. The MLA documentation style suggests all pages of a research paper should be __________ spaced with __________-inch top, bottom, left, and right margins.
   a. single, 1 b. double, 1 c. single, 1.25 d. double, 1.25
2. Which command can you use to insert page numbers into a document?
   a. Page Numbers on the Insert menu
   b. Header and Footer on the View menu
   c. either a or b
   d. none of the above
3. The AutoCorrect feature automatically fixes misspelled words when you __________ after entering the misspelled word.
   a. press the SPACEBAR
   b. click the AutoCorrect button
   c. type a period
   d. press the ESC key
4. To efficiently indent the first line of each paragraph in a document, __________.
   a. press the TAB key at the beginning of each paragraph
   b. drag the first-line indent marker on the ruler
   c. click the First-Line button on the Standard toolbar
   d. click Indent Paragraph on the Format menu
5. A(n) __________ occurs when the last line of a paragraph prints by itself at the top of a page.
   a. twin b. orphan c. sibling d. widow

(continued)

A+ Test Your Knowledge

Multiple Choice *(continued)*

6. If the screen displays a horizontal thinly dotted line completely across the screen with the words Page Break in the middle, you have a(n) __________ in the document.
   a. footnote   b. manual page break   c. widow   d. automatic page break
7. To sort selected paragraphs in alphabetical order, click the __________ option button in the Sort Text dialog box.
   a. Alphabetical   b. Ascending   c. Descending   d. either a or b
8. Through the Word Count command, you can display the number of __________ in a document.
   a. words   b. paragraphs   c. lines   d. all of the above
9. To check spelling automatically as you type, __________ the word with the red wavy underline to display a list of suggested corrections.
   a. drag   b. click   c. right-click   d. double-click
10. Headers, footers, and footnotes appear when Word is in __________.
   a. normal view   b. page layout view   c. print preview   d. both b and c

3 Understanding the Ruler

Instructions: Answer the following questions concerning the ruler in Figure 3-80. The numbers in the figure in most cases correspond to the numbers of the questions below.

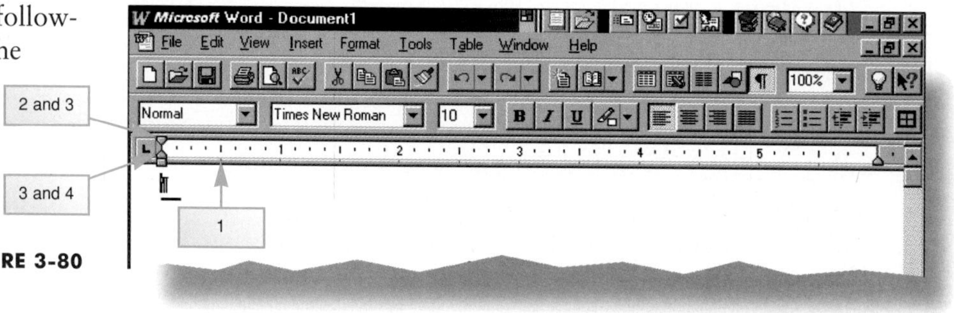

FIGURE 3-80

1. How many inches from the left margin is the first tab stop?

   ____

2. What is the name of the top triangle at the left margin?

   ____

3. What is the purpose of dragging the top triangle to the first tab stop?

   ____

4. What is the name of the bottom triangle at the left margin?

   ____

5. What is the purpose of dragging the bottom triangle to the first tab stop?

   ____

6. How do you move both triangles at the same time?

   ____

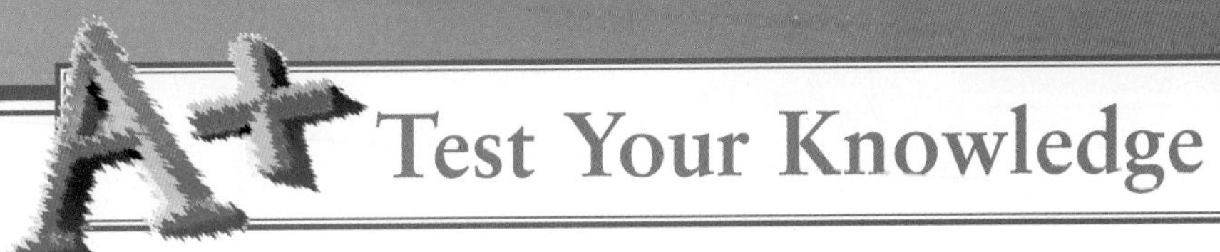

Test Your Knowledge

4 Understanding the Note Pane

Instructions: In Figure 3-81, arrows point to major components of the note pane. Identify the various parts of the note pane in the spaces provided.

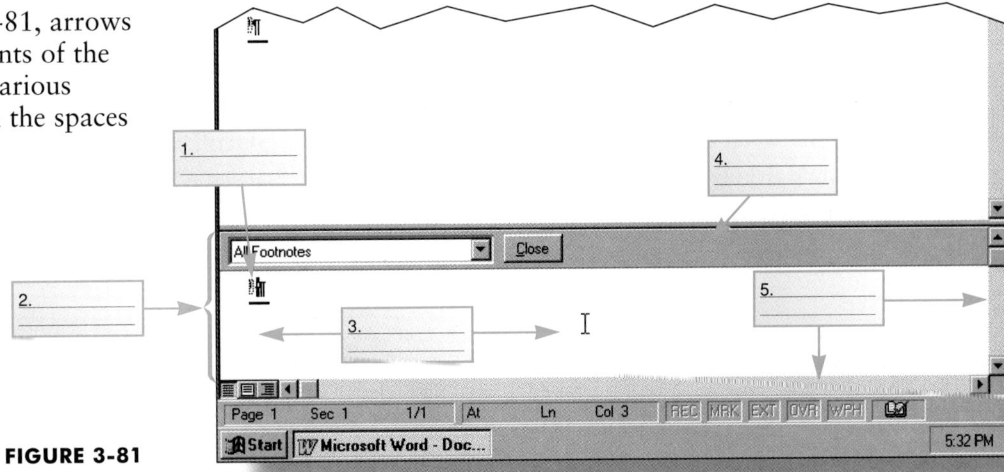

FIGURE 3-81

Use Help

1 Reviewing Project Activities

Instructions: Perform the following tasks using a computer.

1. Start Word.
2. Double-click the Help button on the Standard toolbar.
3. Click the Contents tab. Double-click the Changing the Appearance of Your Page book. Double-click the Headers and Footers book. Double-click the Working with headers and footers topic.
4. Click each of the links and read its Help information. How do you move between headers and footers using the Headers and Footers toolbar?
5. Click the Help Topics button to return to the Help Topics: Microsoft Word dialog box. Click the Index tab. Type `AutoCorrect` and then click the checking capitalization errors topic. Click the Display button. Double-click Types of changes that Word can make automatically. Then, click What happens when I use AutoCorrect? to display a Help window on the selected topic.
6. Ready the printer and click the Options button. Click Print Topic and then click the OK button to produce a hard copy of the Help window.
7. Click the Help Topics button. Click the Find tab. Type `thesaurus` in box 1 and then click the Look up words in the thesaurus topic in box 3. Click the Display button. Click the Options button. Click Print Topic and then click the OK button.

(continued)

Use Help

Reviewing Project Activities *(continued)*

8. Click the Help Topics button. Click the Answer Wizard tab. Type `indent paragraphs` in box 1 and then click the Search button. Click the Paragraph indenting vs. page margins topic. Click the Display button. Click the Options button. Click Print Topic and then click the OK button.
9. Close any open Help window(s) by clicking its Close button in the upper right corner of the Help window's title bar.
10. Click the Help button on the Standard toolbar.
11. Click the horizontal ruler. What is the function of the horizontal ruler?

2 Expanding on the Basics

Instructions: Perform the following tasks using a computer and answer the questions.

Tables are an extremely useful tool in Word 7 for Windows 95. Using the Contents tab in the Help Topics: Microsoft Word dialog box, answer the following questions about Word tables:

1. How do you select a cell? a row? a column?
2. What are the three nonprinting characters in a table?
3. How do you add a row to the end of a table? the middle of a table?
4. How can you change the width of a table column?

One proofing tool provided by Word is the grammar checker. Using the Index tab in the Help Topics: Microsoft Word dialog box, answer the following questions about the grammar checker:

1. How do you check the grammar of a document?
2. What are rule groups? Which rule groups are provided with Word?
3. How are the two following readability formulas computed: Flesch Reading Ease and Flesh-Kincaid Grade Level? What do the scores in each of these indices mean?

In Word 7 for Windows 95, you can perform many tasks while in print preview. Use the Find tab in the Help Topics: Microsoft Word dialog box to answer these questions about print preview.

1. How can you adjust the document's margins in print preview?
2. How can you edit text in a document while in print preview?
3. Which keyboard key(s) advance you forward one page in print preview? backward one page?

Use the Answer Wizard to obtain answers to the following questions about tables:

1. What is the maximum number of allowable columns in a Word table?
2. How do you sort the contents of a table?
3. How do you delete an entire table?
4. How do you clear the contents of an entire table?

Apply Your Knowledge

1 Working with a Table

Instructions: Start Word. Open the document Class Schedule from the Word folder on the Student Floppy Disk that accompanies this book. The document is a Word table created using the Table Wizard. You are to edit the table. You may need to refer to your Use Help 2 responses for information on how to select items in the table and modify them. The revised table is shown in Figure 3-82.

CLASS SCHEDULE - FALL 1997

	Mon	Tue	Wed	Thu	Fri
ACTG 200			9:30-11:00		9:30-11:00
BIOL 201		10:00-12:00		10:00-12:00	
CIS 216		2:00-4:00		2:00-4:00	
ENGL 220	11:00-12:30		11:00-12:30		
HIST 354	1:00-2:00		1:00-2:00		1:00-2:00

FIGURE 3-82

Perform the following tasks:

1. Right-click the table, click Table AutoFormat on the shortcut menu. Click Classic 2 in the Formats area of the Table AutoFormat dialog box and then click the OK button.
2. Add a new row to the table for ACTG 200, which meets on Wednesdays and Fridays from 9:30-11:00.
3. Delete the Saturday column by selecting it, right-clicking the selection, and then clicking Delete Columns on the shortcut menu. You do not have any Saturday classes scheduled.
4. Click in the table, click Table on the menu bar, and then click Select Table.
5. Right-click the selected table, click Cell Height and Width on the shortcut menu, click the Row tab if necessary, click Center in the Alignment area, and then click the OK button to center the table between the left and right margins.
6. With the table selected, click the Borders button on the Formatting toolbar to display the Borders toolbar. Click the Line Style box arrow, click ¾ pt, and then click the Inside Border button on the Borders toolbar. Click the Line Style box arrow, click 2 ¼ pt, and then click the Outside Border button on the Borders toolbar. Click the Borders button on the Formatting toolbar to remove the Borders toolbar.
7. With the table still selected, click Table on the menu bar, click Sort, and then click the OK button. Click anywhere to remove the highlight from the table.
8. Select the header row and then click the Bold button on the Formatting toolbar.
9. Select the cells containing the class times and then click the Align Right button on the Formatting toolbar.
10. Click File on the menu bar and then click Save As. Use the filename Revised Class Schedule and then save the document on your data floppy disk.
11. Print the revised table.

1 Preparing a Research Paper with a Table

Problem: You are a college student currently enrolled in an introductory computer class. Your assignment is to prepare a short research paper about the Internet (Figure 3-83).

Instructions:

1. If necessary, click the Show/Hide ¶ button on the Standard toolbar. Change all margins to 1 inch. Adjust line spacing to double. Create a header to number pages. Change the font size of all characters to 12 point. Type the name and course information at the left margin. Center and type the title. First-line indent all paragraphs.
2. Type the body of the paper as shown in Figures 3-83a through 3-83c. Format the table in the Classic 3 format with the Color and Header Rows check boxes selected. Format the characters in the table to 12 point. At the end of the body of the research paper, press the ENTER key and insert a hard page break.
3. Create the works cited page.
4. Spell check the paper. Save the document on a floppy disk with Cummins Research Paper as the filename.
5. Print the research paper.

Cummins 1

Jonathan Z. Cummins

Professor B. Eggert

Computer Information Systems 204

November 13, 1997

The Information Superhighway

The Internet is a collection of networks, each of which is composed of smaller networks. A network is one or more computer systems, terminals, and communications technologies (such as cable and telephone systems) that allow the computer systems and terminals to communicate with each other, whether they are physically located in the next building or the next continent. Two common services provided by the Internet are electronic mail and file transfer protocol.

Electronic mail, also called e-mail, is probably the most popular service on the Internet. Using e-mail, you can converse with persons across the room or on the other side of the world. Reaching a person who has an account on the Internet is simple. All you need to send mail is the person's account name and the Internet address (or domain name) of the computer on which he or she has an account. The complete e-mail address is the account name followed by the @ character, then the domain name where the account is located (Smith and Barker 35-54).

Another frequently used feature of the Internet is file transfer protocol (FTP), which allows you to send and receive files from one computer to another. As with e-mail, you need the Internet address (or domain name) of the computer containing the files in which you are interested as well as the directory where they are located. You provide the address to a program called FTP, which will then contact the remote computer where you can exchange files (Kostroman, 15 Aug. 1997).

FIGURE 3-83a

Cummins 2

With the ability to obtain thousands of programs, text, and data files comes responsibility. Software is protected by the United States copyright laws. You should be aware of the type of software you are using. The table below outlines the major types of software.

Table

Four Classifications of Software

Commercial	*Shareware*	*Freeware*	*Public Domain*
Purchase license to use software; usually copyrighted; legal to make backup copy only.	Free to evaluate with minimal fee for continued use; legal to copy and distribute to others.	Free to use; legal to copy and distribute to others; author may impose a condition on usage.	No restrictions on copying, distributing, and using.

Be aware of the type of software you are using. Respect the copyright laws and wishes of the author.

FIGURE 3-83b

Cummins 3

Works Cited

Kostroman, James L. "FTP - Exchanging Files on the Internet." *World Wide Net Group.* http://www.netgroup.com/ftp.html (15 Aug. 1997).

Smith, Karen L., and Jennifer T. Barker. *A Guide to E-mail on the Internet.* Boston: Boyd Publishing Company, 1997.

FIGURE 3-83c

2 Preparing a Research Report with Footnotes and a Table

Problem: You are a college student currently enrolled in an English class. Your assignment is to prepare a short research paper in any area of interest to you. The only requirements are that the paper be presented according to the MLA documentation style and have three references. You decide to prepare a paper discussing floppy disk storage (Figure 3-84a on the next page and Figure 3-84b on page WD 3.57).

Instructions: Perform the following tasks:

1. If it is not already recessed, click the Show/Hide ¶ button on the Standard toolbar.
2. Change all margin settings to one inch. Adjust line spacing to double. Create a header to number pages. Change the font size of all characters to 12 point. Type the name and course information at the left margin. Center and type the title. First-line indent all paragraphs in the paper.
3. Type the body of the paper as shown in Figures 3-84a and 3-84b. The table is formatted in the Colorful 1 format with the Color and special formats applied to Header Rows check boxes selected. The characters is the table are formatted to 12 point bold. At the end of the body of the research paper, press the ENTER key once and insert a hard page break.

(continued)

Preparing a Research Report with Footnotes and a Table *(continued)*

4. Create the works cited page. Enter the following works cited as separate paragraphs and alphabetize them: (1) D. Jones, Monica P., and Patricia A. Williams. "Floppy Disks." *Storage Media Online.* http://www.storage.com/floppy.html (10 Oct. 1997). (2) Adamczyk, Joann. "Personal Computer Storage Media - What You Should Know." *Microcomputer Journal* Nov. 1997: 36-74. (3) Barton, Robert. *Introductory Computer Concepts and Techniques.* Boston: International Publishing Company, 1997.
5. Check the spelling of the paper. Use Word's thesaurus to change the word, Hence, in the first paragraph to a word of your choice.
6. Save the document on a floppy disk with Jacobs Research Paper as the filename.
7. Print the research paper. Above the title of your printed research paper, hand write the number of words, including the footnote, in the research paper.

Jacobs 1

Maria R. Jacobs

Professor T. Yasmis

English 104

December 1, 1997

Disk Storage

While you create a document, the computer stores it in main memory. If the computer is turned off, or if you lose electrical power, the document is lost. Hence, it is mandatory to save on disk any document you will use later. One type of disk is the floppy disk, which is popular because it enables users to easily move or copy files from one computer to another. Floppy disks are available in a variety of sizes and densities.

A floppy disk is a thin, circular media coated with a magnetic substance that is housed in a permanent, protective jacket. With the 5¼-inch disk, the read/write head in the disk drive comes into magnetic contact with the recording surface through the slot hole in the disk's protective jacket (Jones and Williams, 10 Oct. 1997). The 2-inch and 3½-inch disks have a shutter that opens automatically to expose the recording surface when the disk is inserted in the disk drive.[1] Once inside the unit, the disk is made to spin inside its protective casing.

Floppy disks are classified into three categories: low density, high density, and very high density (Barton 22-90). A very high density disk can store twice as much data as a high-density disk. Likewise, a high-density disk can store twice as much data as a low-density disk. The

[1] The 2-inch and 3-inch disks are enclosed in a thick plastic casing. Adamczyk credits the rigidity of the casing to the durability of the disks.

FIGURE 3-84a

Jacobs 2

following table summarizes the storage capacity of the three sizes of floppy disks.

Table

Comparison of 2-, 3½-, and 5¼-Inch Disks

DISK	DENSITY	CAPACITY IN BYTES
2 inch	Low	360K
3 ½ inch	Low	720K
3 ½ inch	High	1.44M
3 ½ inch	Very High	2.88M
5 ¼ inch	Low	360K
5 ¼ inch	High	1.2M

A low-density disk drive can write to only a low-density disk. A high-density drive, however, can write to both a high-density disk or a low-density disk; and a very high density drive can write to all three types of disk densities.

Disks are delicate and should be handled and stored with care. Cold, heat, and magnetic field sources such as magnets should never come into contact with a disk. Never bend or fold disks or touch the exposed recording surface.

FIGURE 3-84b

3 Composing a Research Report with a Table and Footnotes

Problem: You have drafted the notes shown in Figure 3-85. Your assignment is to prepare a short research paper based on these notes. You are to review the notes and then rearrange and reword. Embellish the paper as you deem necessary. Add a footnote elaborating on a personal experience you have had. Create a table listing examples of peripherals. Present the paper according to the MLA documentation style.

Instructions: Perform the following tasks:

1. If it is not already recessed, click the Show/Hide ¶ button on the Standard toolbar.
2. Change all margin settings to one inch. Adjust line spacing to double. Create a header to number pages. Change the font size of all characters to 12 point. Type the name and course information at the left margin. Center and type the title. First-line indent all paragraphs in the paper.
3. Compose the body of the paper from the notes in Figure 3-85. Be sure to include footnotes and a table as specified above. At the end of the body of the research paper, press the ENTER key once and insert a hard page break.
4. Create the works cited page from the listed sources. Be sure to alphabetize the works.

(continued)

Composing a Research Report with a Table and Footnotes *(continued)*

5. Check the spelling of the paper. Save the document on a floppy disk with YourName Research Paper as the filename (where YourName is your last name).
6. Print the research paper. Above the title of your printed research paper, hand write the number of words, including the footnote, in the research paper.

Computers have four major components: input devices, a system unit, output devices, and secondary storage.

The system unit contains electrical circuits that cause processing of data to occur.
It transforms inputs into outputs (or data into information).
Types of processing include both mathematical and logical operations.
The system unit includes the central processing unit (CPU) and main memory.
Source: Computers Today, a book published by Fraser Publishing Company in Boston, 1997, pages 45-55, author Kathy L. Stinson.

Input devices are used to enter data into the computer.
Examples of input devices are a keyboard, mouse, joystick, and light pen.
Data is input into a computer.
Examples of data include employee timecards, debits and credits, and student grades.
Source: "Input Data", an article in Peripherals Today, April 1997 issue, pages 109-118, author Nancy C. Walters.

Output devices receive information from the computer.
Information is processed data. Information is output from a computer.
Printers, plotters, and monitors are examples of output devices.
Examples of information include employee paychecks, balance sheets, and report cards.
Source: "Information is Output", an article in Information Magazine, June 1997 issue, pages 80-97, author William E. Trainor.

Secondary storage devices, also called auxiliary storage devices, store instructions and data when they are not being used by the system unit.
Floppy disks, hard disks, tapes, and optical disks are examples of secondary storage devices.

Input, output, and secondary storage devices are often referred to as peripheral devices because they are attached to the system unit of the computer.

FIGURE 3-85

Cases and Places

The difficulty of these case studies varies:

◗ Case studies preceded by a single half moon are the least difficult. You are asked to create a brief research paper (about 500 words) using resources that are probably available in the classroom setting.
◗◗ Case studies preceded by two half moons are more difficult. You must write a brief research paper (about 500 words) using information acquired from resources outside the classroom, such as the school library or the Internet.
◗◗◗ Case studies preceded by three half moons are the most difficult. You must prepare a brief research paper (about 500 words) based on conventional resources, such as the school library and the Internet, and on your own experiences beyond the college environment.

For each case study, use the documentation style assigned by your instructor.

1 ◗ Studies show that people remember about 50% of what they hear, 75% of what they see, and 95% of what they teach. To reinforce your understanding of Word 7, write a brief research paper describing an undertaking that can be completed with this application (such as creating and editing a document, using templates, or preparing a research paper). Use your textbook, Word Help, and any other resources available. Tell why you think the task is important and then explain exactly how the task is performed. Include at least two footnotes and a short bibliography. Use the concepts and techniques presented in this project to format the paper.

2 ◗ Graphical user interfaces, such as Windows 95, claim to be intuitive (easy to learn), consistent (the same for various applications), and user-friendly (forgiving of mistakes). Write a brief research paper describing how well Word 7 reflects these characteristics. Use your textbook, Word Help, and any other resources available. Explain why Word 7 is (or is not) simple to master, how working with Word 7 is similar to (or different from) using Windows 95 or other applications, and in what ways Word 7 compensates for (or penalizes) user errors. Include at least two footnotes and a short bibliography. Use the concepts and techniques presented in this project to format the paper.

3 ◗ The invention of movable type is one of the most momentous achievements in history. Books, once available to only the clergy and nobility, became accessible to a broad segment of the population. Even the type of books changed, from the esoteric religious tomes of pre-printing press days to practical, "how to" texts that furthered the spread of secular knowledge. Some people believe word processing software, such as Word 7 will bring about a similar revolution in human expression by making it easier to create, edit, and format documents. Others insist, however, that word processors only help people produce just what their name implies — processed words devoid of imagination and originality. Using the school library or other resources (such as the Internet), prepare a brief research paper on the effect word processors have had, and are likely to have, on the written word. Include footnotes and a short bibliography. Use the concepts and techniques presented in this project to format the paper.

Cases and Places

4 ▸▸ The first word processing software, introduced in the late 1970s, was only slightly more sophisticated than electronic typewriters. Although documents could be created and edited, formatting and stylistic enhancements were limited. To produce truly attractive output, desktop publishing (DTP) software was used to embellish documents produced with word processing software. Today, the line between word processing software and desktop publishing software has become increasingly blurred. Modern word processing packages, such as Word 7, have many of the capabilities once found only in DTP software. Using the school library or other resources (such as the Internet), prepare a brief research paper comparing word processing and desktop publishing software. Explain how they are similar and how they are different. Discuss the future of DTP in light of the growing sophistication of word processing software. Include footnotes and a short bibliography.

5 ▸▸▸ Computers have had a tremendous impact on the entire workplace. Perhaps the position most affected by word processing software, however, is the office secretary. Once responsible for almost all of an office's written correspondence, today secretaries find that an increasing number of executives use word processing software to create and store their own documents. A secretary's duties have changed, which in some cases has resulted in a new title — administrative assistant. Using a school library or other resources (such as the Internet), learn how word processing software has transformed the office. Visit an office and talk to people about how their jobs have been changed by word processing software. Then, prepare a brief research paper on the effect word processing software has had on the modern office. Include footnotes and a short bibliography.

6 ▸▸▸ Word processing software has affected not only the appearance of documents, it has altered the writing process itself. People can adopt an almost "stream of consciousness" style when writing without fear of making mistakes. The editing capabilities of word processors, coupled with the tools available (such as a thesaurus and spell checker), make it easy to revise written work and correct errors. Because of word processing software, some educators have changed how writing is taught. Using a school library or other resources (such as the Internet), find out how word processing software has altered the way children learn to write. Visit an elementary or secondary school and talk to teachers and students about how word processing software is used. Then, prepare a brief research paper on teaching writing with word processing software. Include footnotes and a short bibliography.

7 ▸▸▸ Today, many different word processing software packages are available. Some of the more popular packages include Microsoft Word, WordPerfect, Ami Pro, and programs that are part of other packages such as Windows WordPad, Q & A Write, and the Microsoft Works Word Processor. Each word processing program has its devotees who loudly proclaim it to be the best. Using a school library or other resources (such as the Internet), compare one or more word processing software packages to Word 7. Visit a software vendor and try the alternate package, noting similarities, differences, strengths, and weaknesses. Then, prepare a brief research paper on how Word 7 stacks up against the other word processing software package you tested. Include footnotes and a short bibliography.

Embedding WordArt to Add Special Text Effects to a Word Document

Case Perspective

Recall that in Project 1 you were asked to create a flyer announcing the new arrival of Zimba, a rare Siberian tiger. Thus, you built the announcement shown in Figure 1-1 on page WD 1.7 and submitted it to the Marketing department of Sand Ridge Zoo for its approval. The department was very impressed with the design you created, especially the photograph of Zimba. Now, they have asked you to enhance the headline somehow. They want it to have a bit more pizzazz. One of the artists suggests you use the special text effects of WordArt for the characters in the headline.

You will need the announcement created in Project 1 so you can modify the headline. (If you did not create the announcement, see your instructor for a copy of it.) You will use WordArt to add special text effects to the headline. WordArt is an application included with Microsoft Word. Depending on how Word was installed on your system, you may not have WordArt. If Word was installed using the Typical setup option, then you will need to run the Setup program again to install WordArt.

Introduction

Microsoft Word includes three applications (WordArt, Equation Editor, and Graph) that allow you to create an object and then insert that object into a Word document. With WordArt, you create text with special effects; Equation Editor allows you to create mathematical equations; and Graph enables you to create charts. Thus, an **object** can be a graphic, table, chart, equation, or any other information that usually is created in an application outside of Word. The application used initially to create the object is referred to as the **source application**.

When you insert, or **embed**, an object into a Word document, the object becomes part of the Word document. Because the Word document contains the embedded object, the Word document is referred to as the **container file**. When you double-click an object embedded into a Word document, the object's source application opens inside the Microsoft Word application, allowing you to edit the object from directly within Word. Any changes you make to the object are reflected directly in the Word document. This Integration Feature illustrates the procedure to use WordArt to add special text effects to the Zimba Announcement headline. The revised announcement is shown in Figure 1 on the next page. Notice the headline is arched and has gray shading to the left of each of its characters.

title created in WordArt and embedded into Word document

ZIMBA HAS ARRIVED!

SAND RIDGE ZOO

- Free admission, 7 days a week, dawn to dusk, year-round
- Easy access off Florida Turnpike at Yee-Haw Junction

Known worldwide for its ***huge collection of animals***, the Sand Ridge Zoo is a modern zoological garden that treats animals with dignity and kindness. Many animals roam freely over spacious, open-air terrain. Exotic fish swim in a 15-acre aquarium, and birds fly in a 24-acre aviary.

Call (941) 555-7456 for more information.

FIGURE 1

Starting Word

Follow these steps to start Word and open the Zimba Announcement or ask your instructor how to start Word for your system. For a detailed explanation of these steps, refer to pages WD 1.50 and WD 1.51 in Project 1.

TO START WORD

Step 1: Insert the floppy disk containing the Zimba Announcement file into drive A.
Step 2: Click the Start button on the taskbar and then click Open Office Document on the Start menu.
Step 3: If necessary, click the Look in box arrow and then click 3½ Floppy [A:]. If it is not already selected, click the filename, Zimba Announcement.
Step 4: Click the Open button.

Office starts Word, and then Word opens the document, Zimba Announcement, from the floppy disk in drive A and displays it on the screen (see Figure 1-74 on page WD 1.51).

Because the current headline is to be replaced with a WordArt headline, the next step is to remove the existing headline as described in the following steps.

TO MODIFY A WORD DOCUMENT

Step 1: Click to the left of the headline to select it.
Step 2: Click the Cut button on the Standard toolbar or press the DELETE key.

Word removes the headline from the announcement (Figure 2). The insertion point is now on a paragraph mark centered above the picture of Zimba.

Creating a WordArt Object

As discussed earlier, WordArt is an application that enables you to add special text effects to a document. In this Integration Feature, you will use WordArt to create a new headline for the Zimba Announcement. WordArt is the source application because that is where the headline will be created. The Word document is the container file because it will contain the WordArt object, the headline. The following pages explain how to insert a WordArt object into a Word document and then use WordArt to add special effects to the text itself.

Inserting a WordArt Object

The first step in creating a WordArt object is to **insert**, or **embed**, the object into a Word document. WordArt inserts at the location of the insertion point. Follow these steps to insert a WordArt object into a Word document.

To Insert a WordArt Object into a Word Document

1 **Be sure the insertion point is on the paragraph mark above the picture of Zimba. Click Insert on the menu bar and then point to Object.**

Notice the insertion point is positioned on the paragraph mark immediately above the picture of Zimba (Figure 2). WordArt embeds the object into the document at this location.

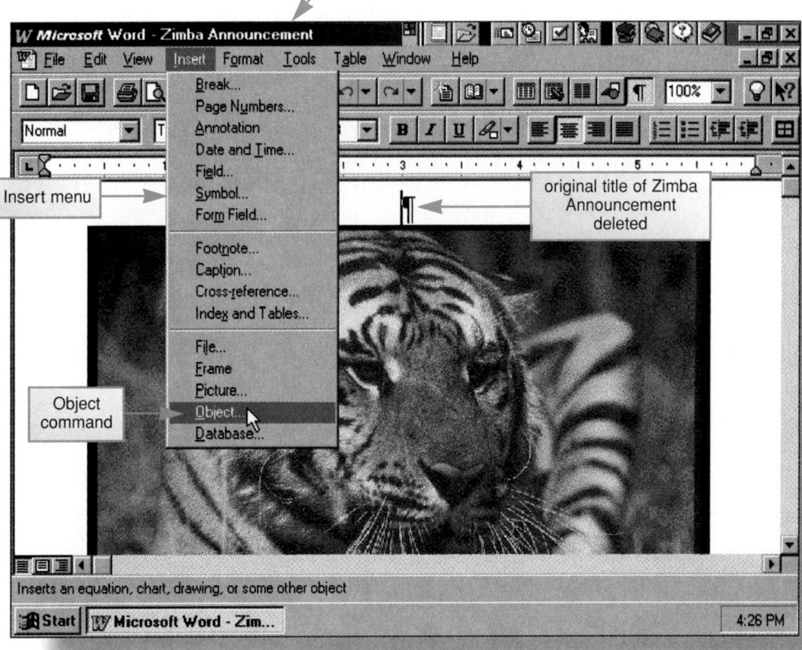

FIGURE 2

2 **Click Object. Click the Create New tab, if necessary, when the Object dialog box first opens. Scroll through the Object Type list and then click Microsoft WordArt 2.0.**

Word displays the Object dialog box (Figure 3). The Object Type list box displays the various types of objects that may be embedded into a Word document.

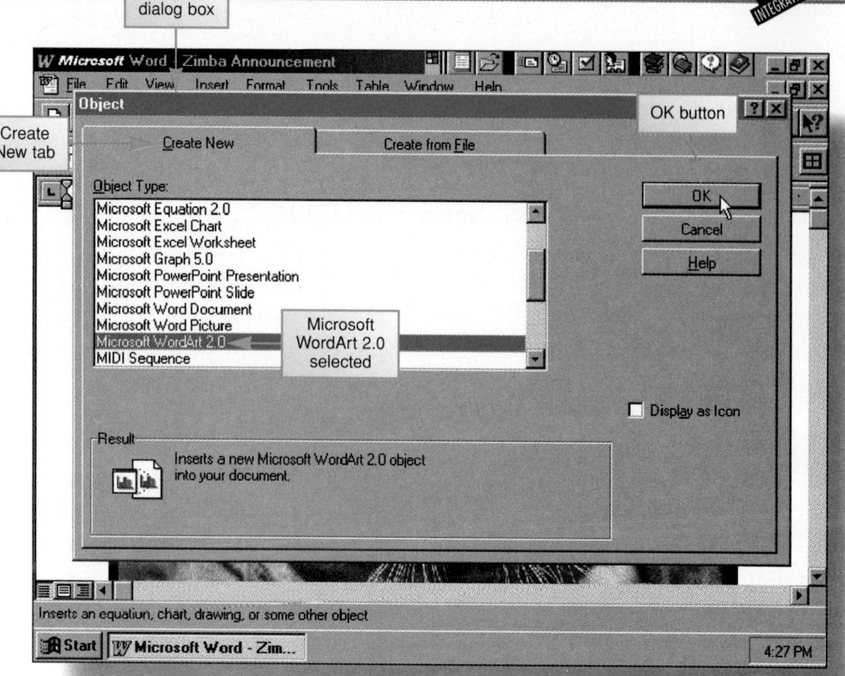

FIGURE 3

3 **Click the OK button.**

The WordArt application opens inside the Word application (Figure 4). Notice that the WordArt menu bar and toolbar display on the screen even though the taskbar indicates Word is active. In WordArt, you enter text into the text entry box, and the frame indicates the size and position of the text.

FIGURE 4

When you embed an object into an application, the source application of the object (WordArt) opens inside the container file's application (Word).

The next step is to enter the text into the text entry box as shown in the following step.

Steps To Enter Text into a Text Entry Box

1 **Type** ZIMBA HAS ARRIVED! **and then click the Update Display button in the Enter Your Text Here window.**

WordArt displays the text entered into the text entry box in the WordArt frame (Figure 5).

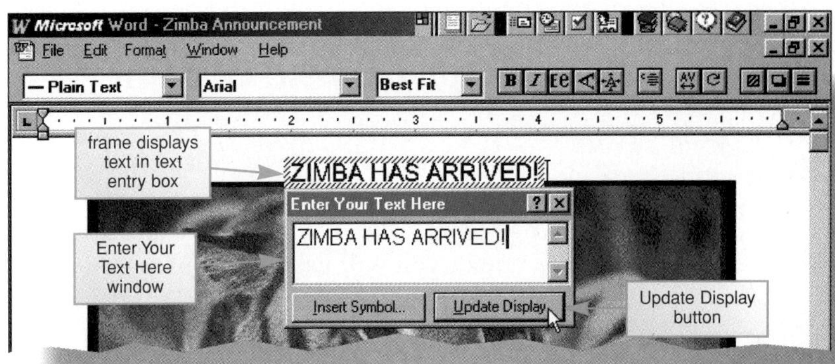

FIGURE 5

Other Ways

1. On Edit menu click Edit WordArt Text, type text

WordArt updates the text displayed in the WordArt frame whenever you click the Update Display button or whenever you complete one special effect and begin another.

Quitting WordArt

The next step is to resize the WordArt frame so it is 6 inches wide by 1 inch high; that is, it should be wider than the graphic of the tiger. You do not resize frames in WordArt; rather you resize them in Word. Thus, you must quit WordArt so the frame can be resized as shown in the following step.

More About Text Entry

To place multiple lines of text into the text entry box, press the enter key at the end of the line to begin a new line of text. To edit WordArt text, select the text to change in the text entry box, type the new text, and then click the Update Display button.

Steps To Quit WordArt

1 **Click anywhere in the document window outside the Enter Your Text Here window, WordArt toolbar, and WordArt frame.**

WordArt closes, and Word's menu bar and toolbars now display below the title bar (Figure 6). In Word, the frame no longer surrounds the WordArt; instead, sizing handles display at the corner and middle locations. Recall that you use sizing handles to scale a graphic.

FIGURE 6

After quitting WordArt, control returns to the Word program where you can scale and add other special effects to the text.

Scaling the Graphic

To change the size of WordArt text, you select the text by clicking it and then drag the sizing handles to the appropriate locations – just as you resize any other graphic. Because you know precisely the dimensions required for the WordArt text, you will use the Picture command on the Format menu to **scale**, or **resize**, the graphic. Complete the following steps to scale the WordArt graphic.

Steps To Scale a Selected WordArt Graphic

1. **With the WordArt text still selected, click Format on the menu bar and then click Picture.**

   Word displays the Picture dialog box (Figure 7).

2. **In the Size area, double-click the Width text box, type** 6 **and then press the TAB key. In the Height text box, type** 1 **and then point to the OK button.**

3. **Click the OK button.**

   Word scales the WordArt text to 6 inches by 1 inch (Figure 8). The WordArt text remains surrounded by sizing handles. The Word application is still the active application.

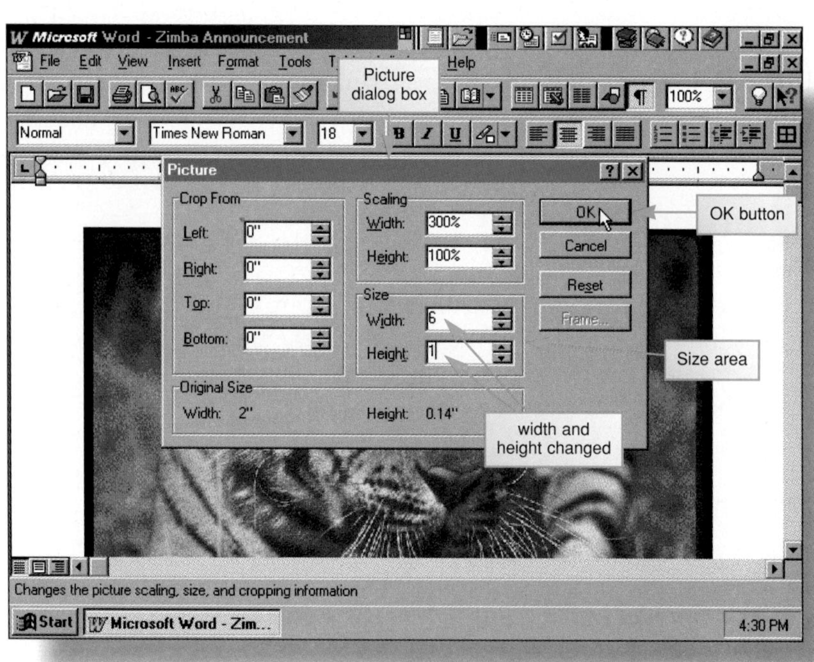

FIGURE 7

OtherWays
1. Drag sizing handles

If, for some reason, you wanted to delete WordArt text, you would click it while in Word and then click the Cut button on the Standard toolbar or press the DELETE key.

Adding Special Effects to WordArt Text

The next step is to enhance the WordArt text. Thus, you must open the WordArt text in the WordArt application. When you double-click an embedded object in its container file, the source application opens so you can edit the object in place. The next series of steps explain how to re-open WordArt and then add special text effects to the headline. First, open WordArt.

More About Special Effects

Special characters or symbols may be added to WordArt. In the text entry box, position the insertion point where you want to add the special character. Click the Insert Symbol button in the Enter Your Text Here window.

Steps To Open a Source Application

1. **Double-click the WordArt text (the headline).**

WordArt opens inside Word (Figure 8). The WordArt menu bar and toolbar display on the screen. The WordArt text is once again surrounded by a frame.

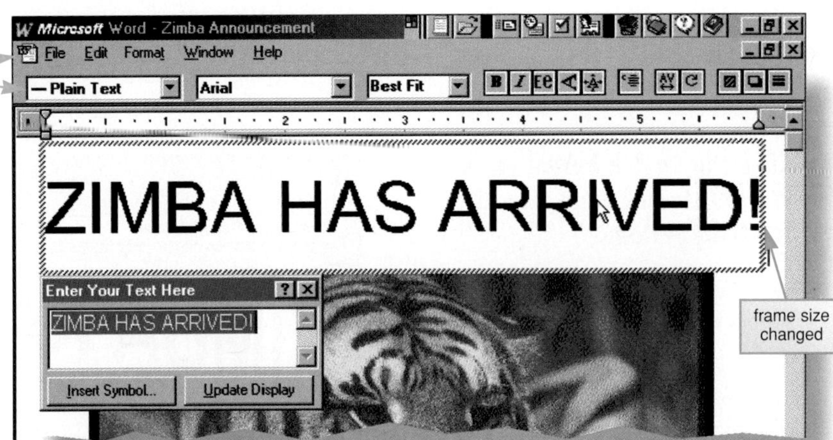

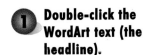

FIGURE 8

The next steps add special text effects to the WordArt headline.

Steps To Add Special Text Effects

1. **Click the Shape box arrow on the WordArt toolbar. Point to the Deflate shape (row 5, column 4 in the list).**

WordArt displays a graphic list of available shapes (Figure 9). The WordArt text forms itself into the selected shape when you click a shape.

FIGURE 9

2 Click the Deflate shape.

WordArt displays the headline in the Deflate shape (Figure 10). The selected shape name displays in the Shape text box. Notice the headline does not fill the entire frame; thus, it must be stretched to fill the entire frame.

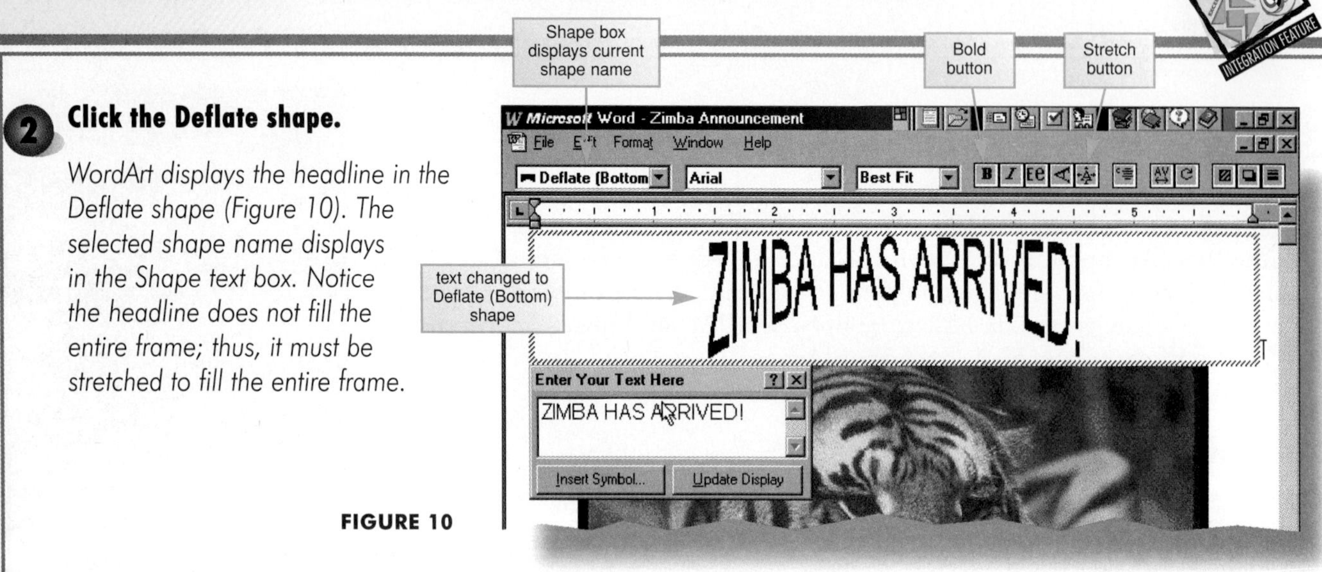

FIGURE 10

3 Click the Stretch button on the WordArt toolbar and then click the Bold button.

WordArt stretches the headline so it fills the entire frame (Figure 11). The WordArt text also displays in bold.

FIGURE 11

4 Click the Shadow button on the WordArt toolbar. When the Shadow dialog box displays, click the sixth shadow in the list and then point to the OK button.

WordArt displays the Shadow dialog box (Figure 12). The WordArt text in the background graphically shows the selected shadow. Notice the shadow displays to the left of each character in the text.

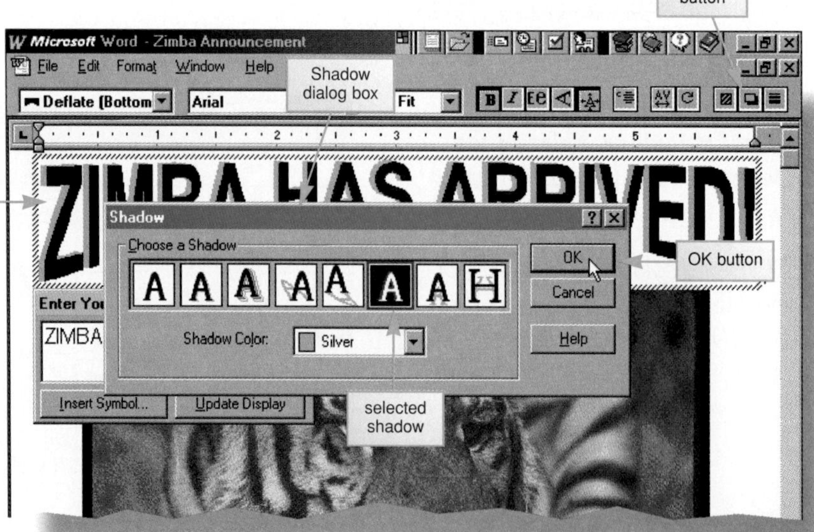

FIGURE 12

5 **Click the OK button. Click the Special Effects button on the WordArt toolbar. When the Special Effects dialog box displays, click the Slider up arrow twice.**

WordArt displays the Special Effects dialog box (Figure 13). The larger the slider percentage, the narrower the peak of the WordArt text. Thus, the S in HAS is shorter than its original height.

FIGURE 13

6 **Click the OK button to display the text in the WordArt frame.**

OtherWays

1. On Format menu click Stretch to Frame
2. On Format menu click Shadow, select desired shadow, click OK button
3. On Format menu click Rotation and Effects, enter desired values, click OK button

The next step is to quit WordArt.

TO QUIT WORDART

Step 1: Click anywhere outside the Enter Your Text Here window, WordArt toolbar, and WordArt text.

Step 2: Click outside the headline to deselect it.

WordArt closes; Word's menu bar and toolbars now display below the title bar (Figure 14).

FIGURE 14

The revision of the announcement is now complete. You should save it with a new filename, print it, and then quit Word.

Summary

This Integration Feature introduced you to the concept of embedding an object created in WordArt into a Word document. You learned how to insert a WordArt object and add WordArt special features to the WordArt text. You also learned how to quit WordArt.

In the Lab

1 Using Help

Instructions:

Start Word. Double-click the Help button on the Standard toolbar. Click the Contents tab. Double-click the Sharing Data with Other Users and Applications book. Double-click the Linking and Embedding book. Double-click the Share information between Office applications topic. Print the topic. Click the Help topics button. Double-click the Edit an embedded object topic. Print the topic. Close any open Help windows.

2 Embedding a WordArt Object into the Home Crafters Announcement

Instructions:

1. Open the file, Kitchen Announcement, from your floppy disk (see Figure 1-92 on page WD 1.67 in Project 1). Delete the current headline.
2. Insert a WordArt object at the location of the headline using the Object command on the Insert menu. Enter the title `CUSTOM KITCHENS!` into the text entry box.
3. Quit WordArt and then scale the WordArt text in Word to 6 inches by 1 inch using the Picture command on Word's Format menu.
4. Double-click the WordArt text and then add these special effects to the text in WordArt: use the Wave 1 shape; stretch the text; and bold the text.
5. Quit WordArt. Save the file using the Save As command on the File menu with Revised Kitchen Announcement as the filename. Print the revised file.

3 Embedding a WordArt Object into the Whispery Hills Announcement

Instructions:

1. Open the file, Weekend Announcement, from your floppy disk (see Figure 1-93 on page WD 1.68 in Project 1). Delete the current headline.
2. Insert a WordArt object at the location of the headline using the Object command on the Insert menu. Enter the title `WEEKEND ANNOUNCEMENT!` into the text entry box.
3. Quit WordArt and then scale the WordArt text in Word to 6 inches by 1 inch using the Picture command on Word's Format menu.
4. Double-click the WordArt text and then add these special effects to the text in WordArt: use the Triangle shape; stretch the text; bold the text; add the third shadow in the Shadow box and change its color to purple; and make the Slider 70%.
5. Quit WordArt. Save the file with Revised Weekend Announcement as the filename. Print the revised file.

PROJECT ONE

Creating a Worksheet and Embedded Chart

PROJECT TWO

Formulas, Formatting, and Creating Charts

PROJECT THREE

What-If Analysis and Working with Large Worksheets

INTEGRATION FEATURE

Linking an Excel Worksheet to a Word Document

Microsoft Excel 7

Windows 95

Creating a Worksheet and Embedded Chart

Objectives:

You will have mastered the material in this project when you can:

- Start Excel
- Describe the Excel worksheet
- Select a cell or range of cells
- Enter text and numbers
- Use the AutoSum button to sum a range of cells
- Copy a cell to a range of cells using the fill handle
- Change the size of the font in a cell
- Bold cell entries
- Center cell contents over a series of columns
- Apply the AutoFormat command to format a range
- Use the Name box to select a cell
- Create a column chart using the ChartWizard
- Save a workbook
- Print a worksheet
- Exit Excel
- Open a workbook
- Use the AutoCalculate area to determine totals
- Correct errors on a worksheet
- Use online Help to answer your questions

Electronic Spreadsheets *Launch* the Era of Personal Computers

Suppose Ebeneezer Scrooge had gone to Bob Cratchit an hour before quitting time on Christmas Eve and demanded a complete accounting of the business. Poor Cratchit, without calculator or computer, would have spent his Christmas Day laboring over his ledgers, doing the arithmetic in his head, scribing out the columns and rows of figures longhand, knowing that one math error meant he would be looking for work.

Fast-forward one hundred forty years from *A Christmas Carol* to a Harvard classroom, where graduate student Dan Bricklin watched his accounting professor laboriously erasing, re-entering, and then re-calculating tables of numbers in a worksheet. Suddenly, an idea took shape. Bricklin enlisted his friend Bob Frankston and together they designed the first electronic spreadsheet, called VisiCalc (for Visible Calculator). Many people credit VisiCalc with launching the era of the personal computer.

Since VisiCalc, designers have applied accelerating technology to produce increasingly more sophisticated versions of the computer spreadsheet. In simplest terms, an electronic spreadsheet, or worksheet, is a fast, accurate replacement for manual planning tools —

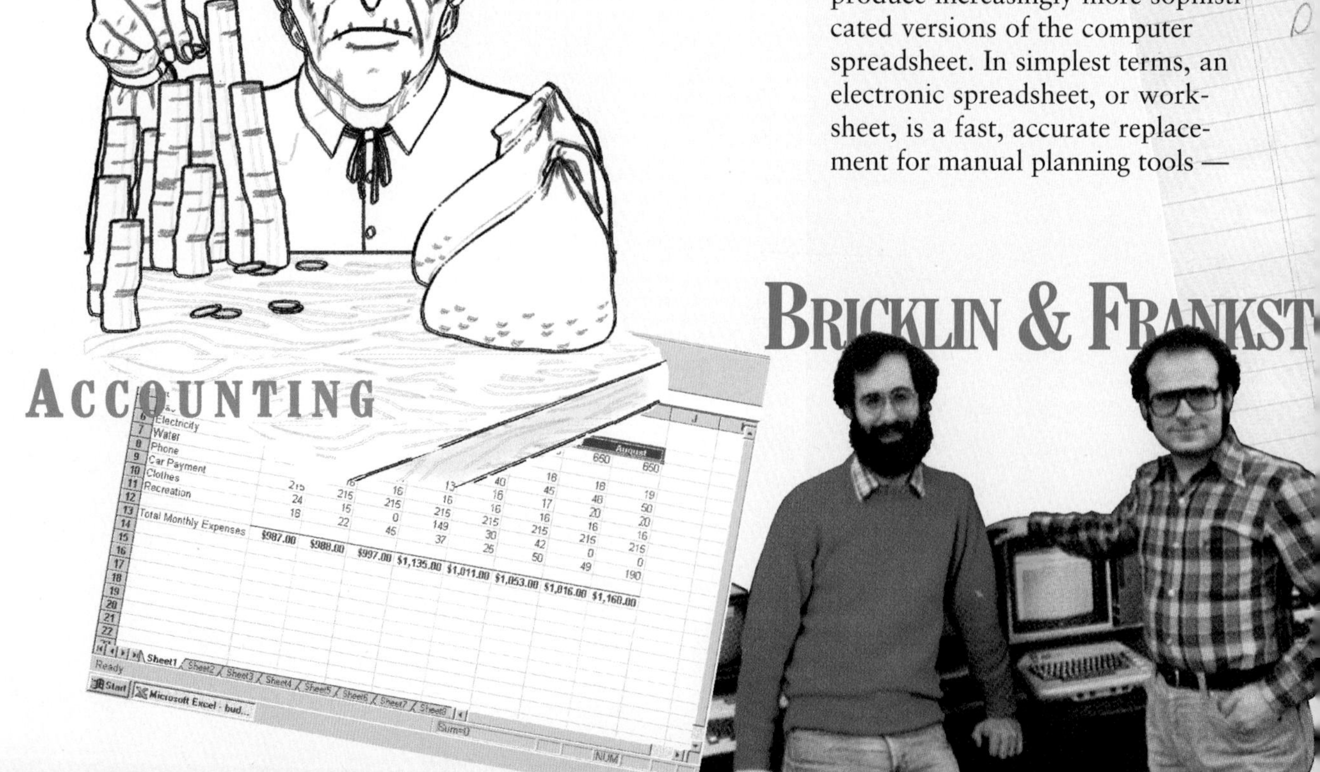

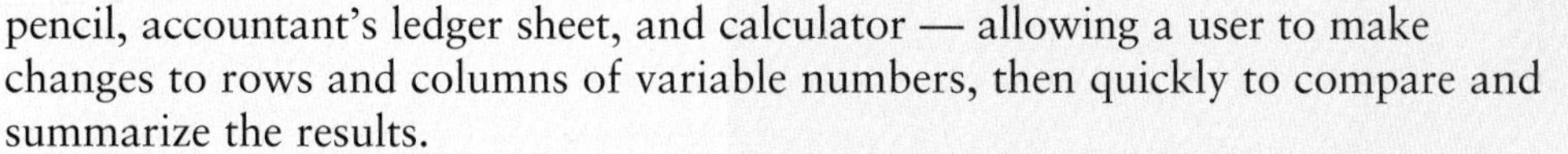

pencil, accountant's ledger sheet, and calculator — allowing a user to make changes to rows and columns of variable numbers, then quickly to compare and summarize the results.

Microsoft's Excel 7 has taken the art and science of designing worksheets to the next level, providing tools for integrating powerful worksheets with impressive graphics. Excel's intuitive graphical user interface (GUI), hundreds of user features, built-in Wizards, and online demos and examples combine power and attractiveness with ease of creation.

During college years, when most students find themselves on squeaky-tight budgets, worksheets can help in a number of ways. A budget sheet can immediately show the impact if Mom's birthday present was forgotten or a must-see concert has to be squeezed in. A worksheet can amortize student loans to project the salary one needs after graduation to handle the monthly payments. The treasury function for student clubs and organizations can also benefit from worksheet management.

Industry, science, and government routinely use worksheets to build pro forma statements for business start-ups or search for the elusive neutrino or calculate the national debt, to cite a few examples. Sometimes worksheets are of such massive scale that only supercomputers can handle the number of inputs, especially in fields such as astronomy.

Fortunately for Tiny Tim, Scrooge did not ask the impossible of Cratchit. As for Dan Bricklin and Bob Frankston, their names may not be household terms, but for millions of people today, their contribution to personal computing has saved many a midnight dark and dreary. But that is yet another story . . .

V I S I C A L C

Microsoft
Excel 7
Windows 95

Creating a Worksheet and Embedded Chart

Case Perspective

The Rollablade Company has experienced explosive growth since its inception one year ago. With the popularity of inline skates, the company has grown faster than anyone could have imagined. But therein lies the problem. The management at Rollablade feels that Personnel expenses inside the company are within tolerances, but they are not sure what all the expenses are. They have asked you to prepare a worksheet that specifies company fourth-quarter personnel expenses.

In particular, they want to know the total expenses for Benefits, Travel, and Wages in the following four departments: Marketing, Finance, Sales, and Systems. They want the totals by department and they also want the totals by type of expenses (Benefits, Travel, and Wages).

Your task is to develop a worksheet to show these expenses. In addition, Max Trealer, the president, has asked to see a graphical representation of the expenses because he has little tolerance for lists of numbers.

What Is Microsoft Excel?

Microsoft Excel is a spreadsheet program that allows you to organize data, complete calculations, make decisions, graph data, and develop professional looking reports. The three major parts of Excel are:

- ***Worksheets*** Worksheets allow you to enter, calculate, manipulate, and analyze data such as numbers and text. The term worksheet means the same as spreadsheet.
- ***Charts*** Charts pictorially represent data. Excel can draw a variety of two-dimensional and three-dimensional charts.
- ***Databases*** Databases manage data. For example, once you enter data onto a worksheet, Excel can sort the data, search for specific data, and select data that meets a criteria.

Project One – Rollablade Fourth-Quarter Expenses

From your meeting with the Rollablade management, you have determined the following needs, source of data, calculations, and graph requirements.

Need: A worksheet (Figure 1-1) that shows Rollablade's fourth-quarter expenses (Benefits, Travel, and Wages) for four departments — Marketing, Finance, Sales, and Systems. The worksheet also includes total expenses for each department, each type of expense, and total company expenses for the quarter.

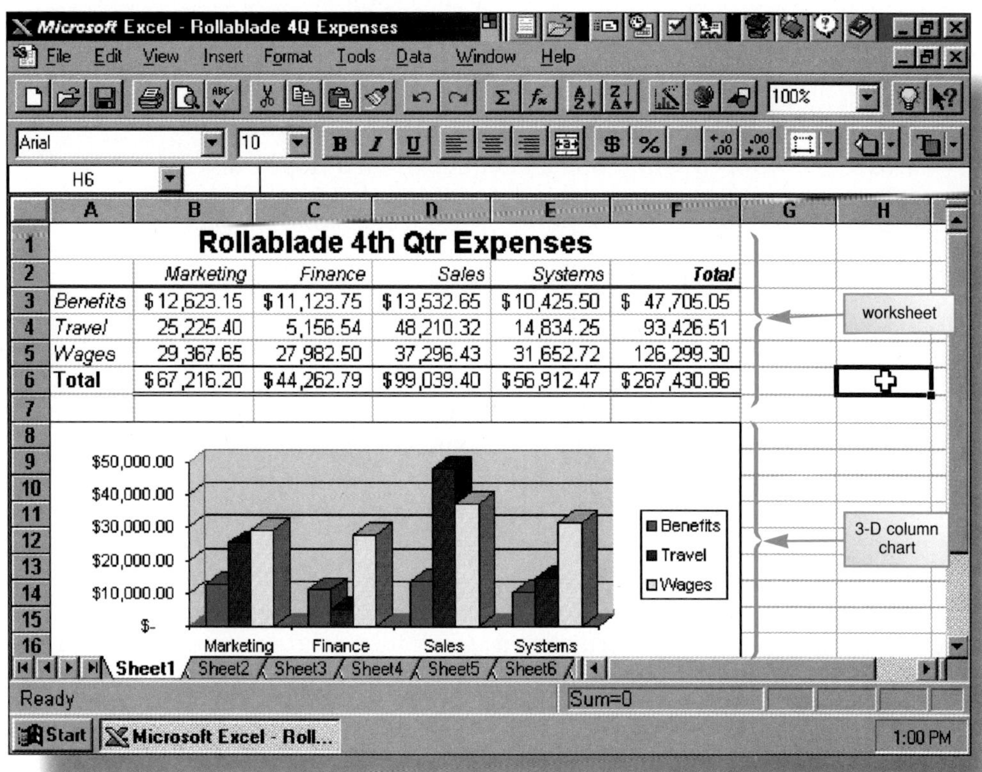

FIGURE 1-1

Source of Data: The data for the worksheet can be found in the personnel department of Rollablade. Harriet Latham, director of personnel, keeps the quarterly expense figures that are calculated by the company's accounting firm. They are typewritten on several different forms.

Calculations: You have determined that the following calculations must be made for the worksheet: (a) A sum for each of the departments (Marketing, Finance, Sales, and Systems) must be calculated; (b) A sum for each type of expense (Benefits, Travel, and Wages) must be calculated; and (c) A total for all expenses also must be calculated. In addition, management has asked that you format the worksheet so it is presentable to the board of directors at the next board meeting.

Graph Requirements: Beneath the worksheet, construct a 3-D column chart that compares the three expense categories for each of the four departments.

More *About* Excel's Ease and Power

Because of Excel's shortcut menus and toolbars, it is one of the easiest, and yet most powerful, worksheet packages available. Its easy-to-use formatting features allow you to produce professional-looking worksheets. Its powerful analytical features make it possible to answer complicated what-if questions with a few clicks of the mouse button.

More *About* Planning a Worksheet

Careful planning can significantly reduce your effort and result in a worksheet that is accurate, easy to read, flexible, and useful. In planning a worksheet, you should follow these steps: (1) define the problem, including need, source of data, calculations, and charting requirements; (2) design the worksheet; (3) enter the data and formulas; and, (4) test the worksheet.

Preparation Steps

The preparation steps below summarize how the worksheet and chart shown in Figure 1-1 will be developed in Project 1.

1. Start the Excel program.
2. Enter the worksheet title (Rollablade 4th Qtr Expenses), the column titles (Marketing, Finance, Sales, Systems, and Total), and the row titles (Benefits, Travel, Wages, and Total).
3. Enter the fourth-quarter expenses (Benefits, Travel, and Wages) for Marketing, Finance, Sales, and Systems.
4. Use the AutoSum button on the Standard toolbar to calculate the first-quarter totals for each department, for each type of expense, and the total quarterly expense for Rollablade.
5. Format the worksheet title (center it across the six columns, enlarge it, and make it bold).
6. Format the body of the worksheet (add underlines, display the numbers in dollars and cents, and add dollar signs).
7. Direct Excel to create the 3-D column chart.
8. Save the worksheet and 3-D column chart on a floppy disk.
9. Print the worksheet and 3-D column chart.
10. Exit Excel.

The following pages contain a detailed explanation of these tasks.

Mouse Usage

More *About* **the Mouse**

The mouse unit has been around as long as the personal computer itself. However, it had little use with earlier operating systems, such as MS-DOS. Few used the mouse or even attached it to their computer until recently when Windows began to dominant the market. Even with Windows 95, some former MS-DOS users prefer to use the keyboard over the mouse.

In this book, the mouse is the primary way to communicate with Excel. You can perform six operations with a mouse: point, click, right-click, double-click, drag, and right-drag.

Point means you move the mouse across a flat surface until the mouse pointer rests on the item of choice on the screen. As you move the mouse, the mouse pointer moves across the screen in the same direction. **Click** means you press and release the left mouse button. The terminology used in this book to direct you to point to a particular item and then click is, Click the particular item. For example, *Click the Bold button* means point to the Bold button and click.

Right-click means you press and release the right mouse button. As with the left mouse button, you normally will point to an item on the screen prior to right-clicking.

Double-click means you quickly press and release the left mouse button twice without moving the mouse. In most cases, you must point to an item before double-clicking. **Drag** means you point to an item, hold down the left mouse button, move the item to the desired location on the screen, and then release the left mouse button. **Right-drag** means you point to an item, hold down the right mouse button, move the item to the desired location, and then release the right mouse button.

The use of the mouse is an important skill when working with Microsoft Excel for Windows 95.

Starting Excel

To start Excel, Windows 95 must be running. Perform the following steps to start Excel.

Steps To Start Excel

1 **Click the Start button on the taskbar and then point to New Office Document (Figure 1-2).**

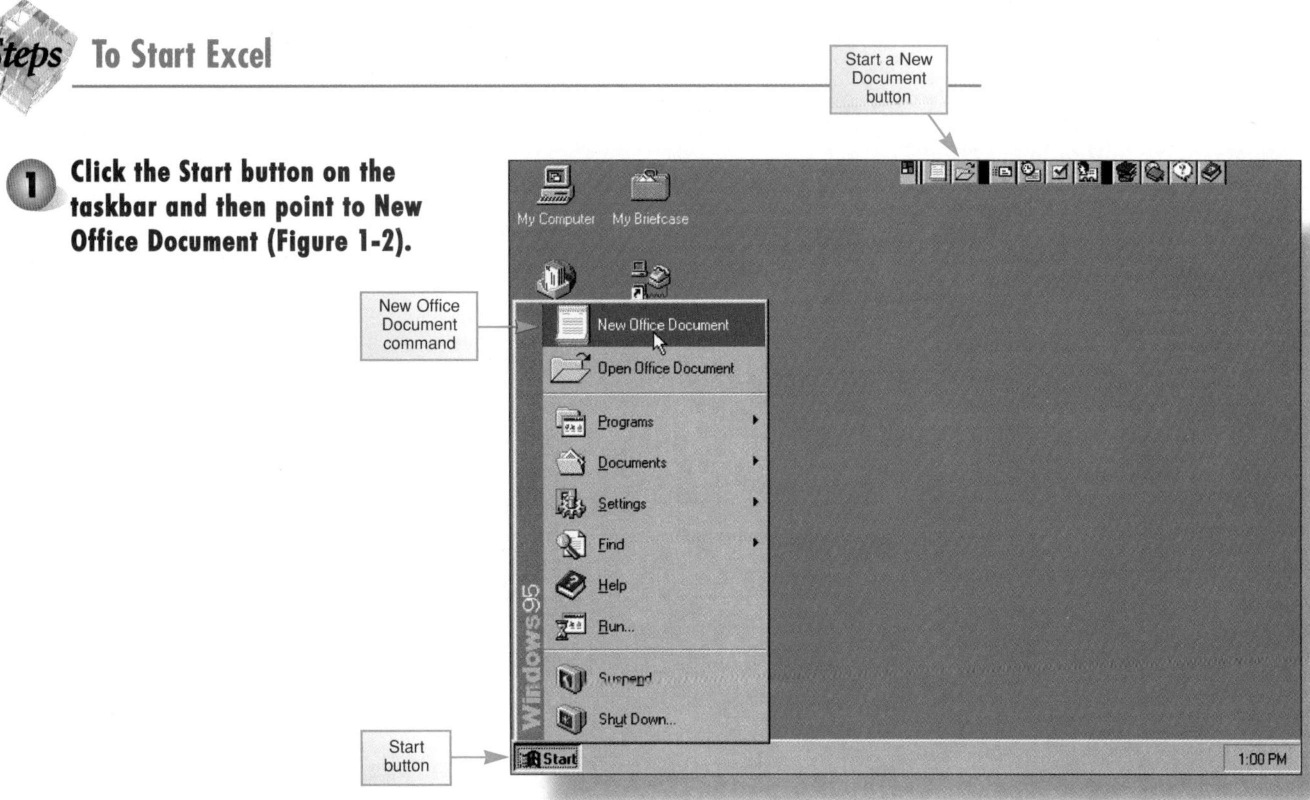

FIGURE 1-2

2 **Click New Office Document. If necessary, click the General tab in the New dialog box, and then point to the Blank Workbook icon (Figure 1-3).**

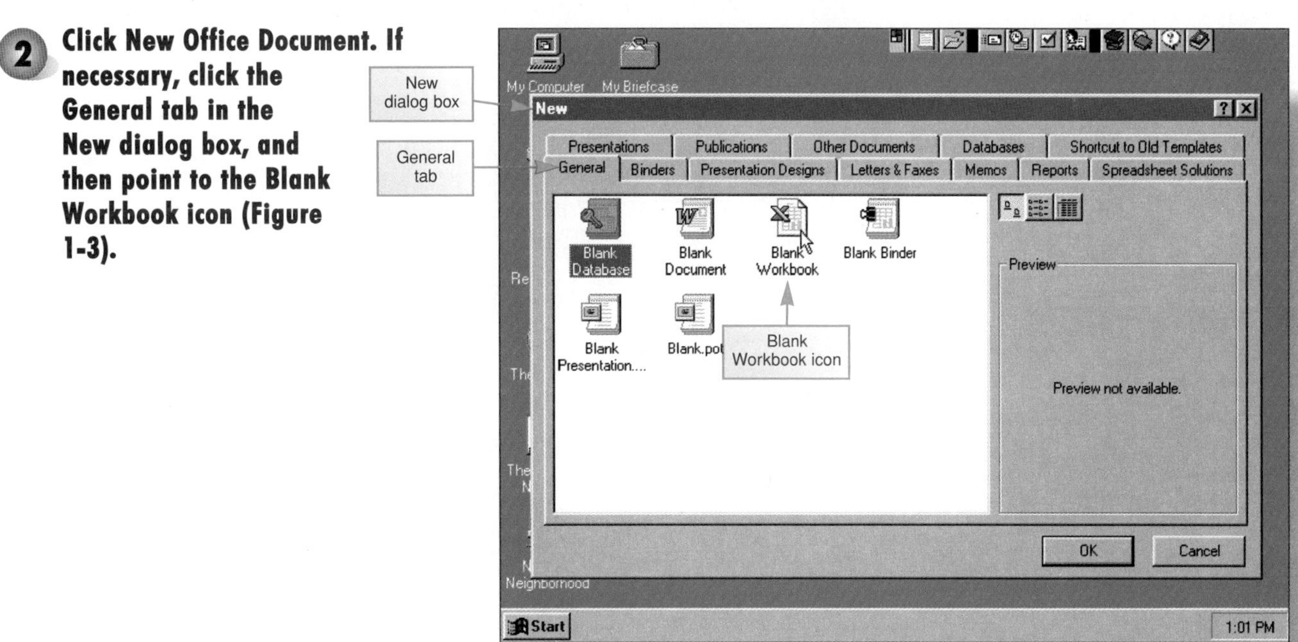

FIGURE 1-3

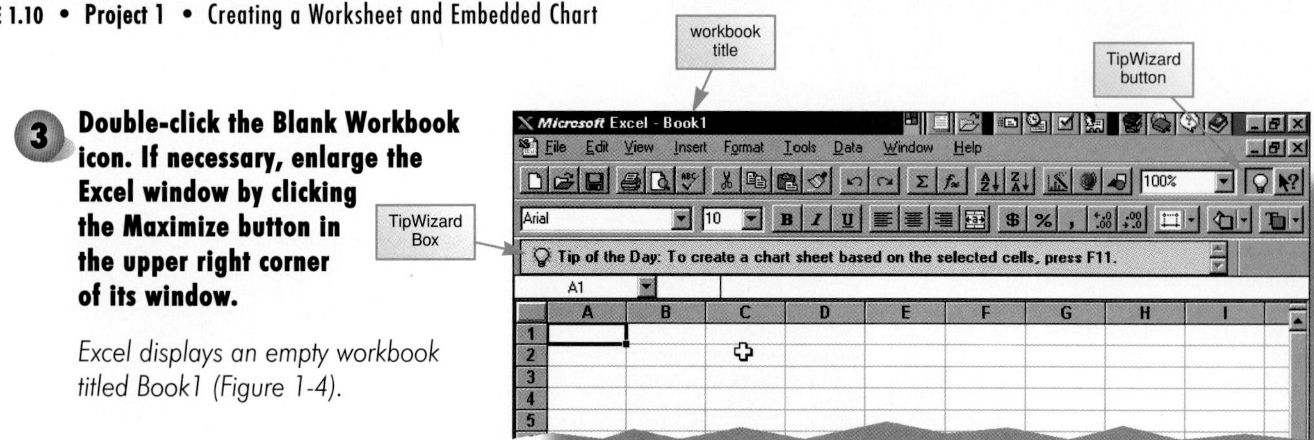

3 Double-click the Blank Workbook icon. If necessary, enlarge the Excel window by clicking the Maximize button in the upper right corner of its window.

Excel displays an empty workbook titled Book1 (Figure 1-4).

FIGURE 1-4

4 If the TipWizard Box displays (Figure 1-4), click the TipWizard button on the Standard toolbar.

Excel removes the TipWizard Box from the window and increases the display of the worksheet (Figure 1-5). The purpose of the TipWizard Box will be discussed later in this project.

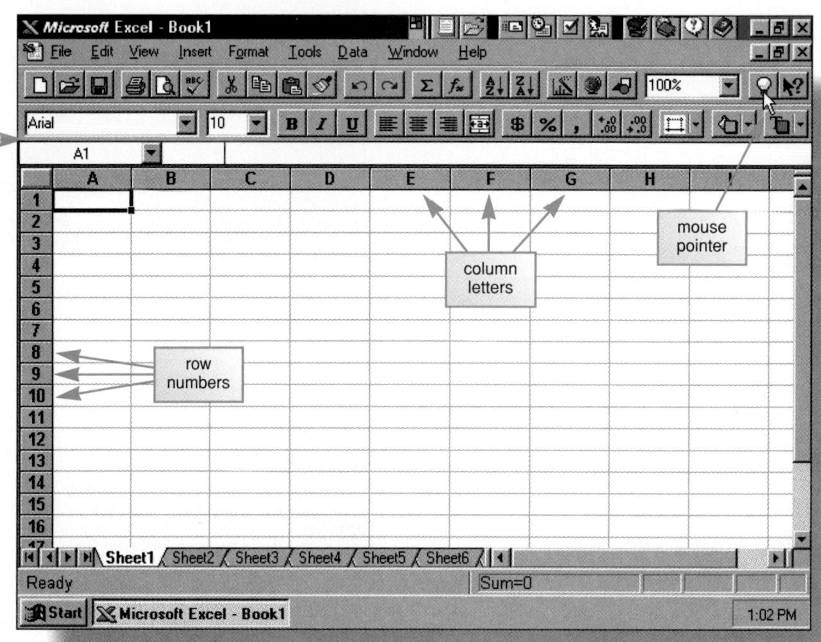

FIGURE 1-5

OtherWays

1. Right-click Start button, click Open, double-click New Office Document
2. On Microsoft Office Shortcut Bar, click Start a New Document button
3. On Start menu click Programs, click Microsoft Excel

The Excel Window

The **Excel window** consists of a variety of features to help you work more efficiently. It contains a title bar, menu bar, toolbars, formula bar, the worksheet window, sheet tabs, scroll bars, and the status bar. Each of these Excel window features and its components is described in this section.

The Workbook

When Excel starts, it creates a new empty workbook, called Book1. The **workbook** (Figure 1-6), is like a notebook. Inside the workbook are sheets, called **worksheets**. Each sheet name appears on a **sheet tab** at the bottom of the workbook. For example, Sheet1 is the name of the active worksheet displayed in the workbook called Book1. If you click on the tab labeled Sheet2, Excel displays the Sheet2 worksheet. A new workbook opens with 16 worksheets. If necessary, you can add additional worksheets to a maximum of 255. This project will use only the Sheet1 worksheet. Later projects will use multiple worksheets in a workbook.

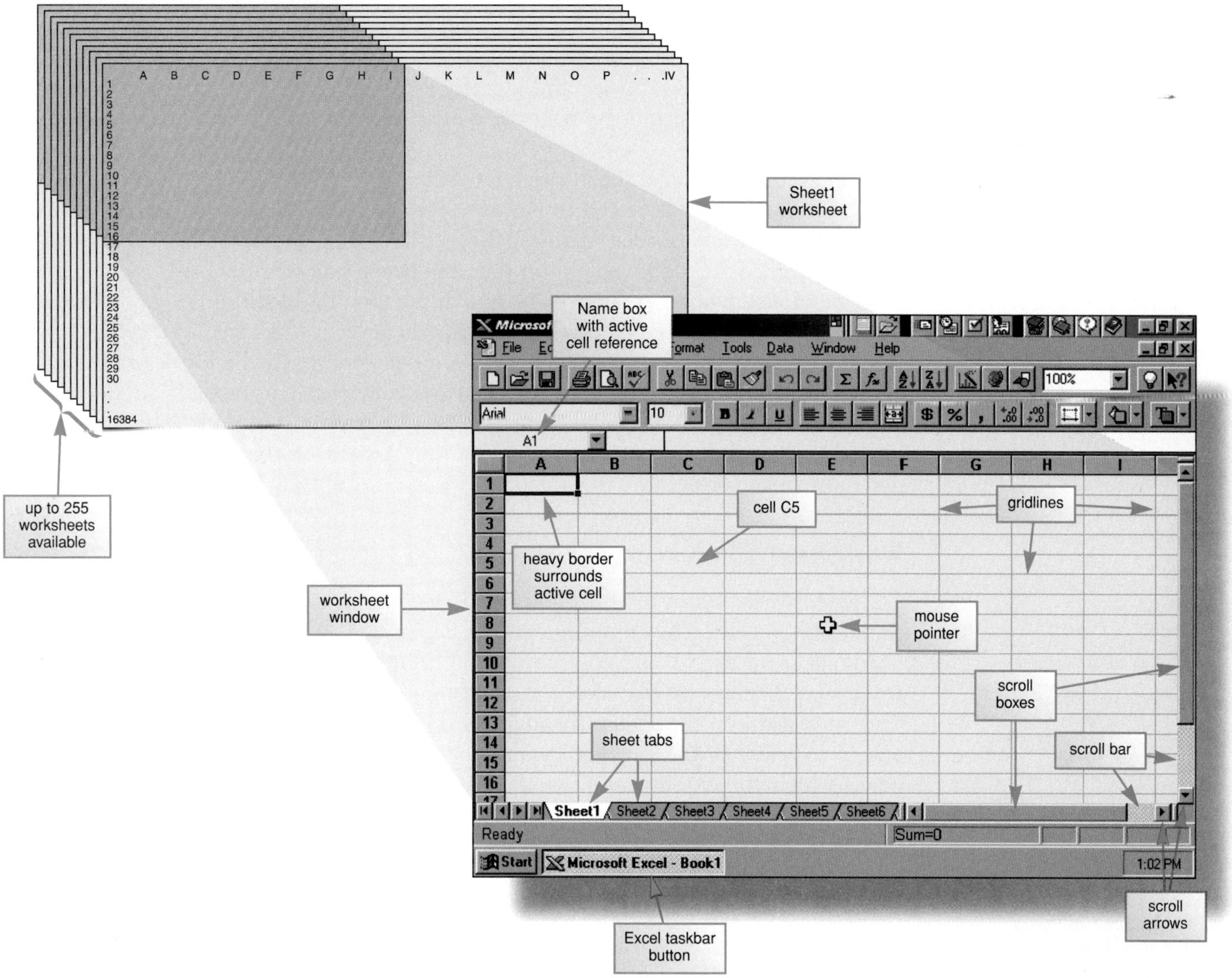

FIGURE 1-6

The Worksheet

The worksheet is organized into a rectangular grid containing columns (vertical) and rows (horizontal). A column letter above the grid, also called the column heading, identifies each **column**. A row number on the left side of the grid, also called the row heading, identifies each **row**. Nine complete columns (A through I) and sixteen complete rows (1 through 16) of the worksheet appear on the screen when the worksheet is maximized and the TipWizard Box is closed as shown earlier in Figure 1-5.

Ever feel like you're being watched? You are when you use Excel. Excel keeps an eye on the way you work. If you complete a task and Excel knows a better way to carry out the task, it will inform you in the TipWizard Box. If the TipWizard Box is hidden, the light bulb icon on the TipWizard button (Figure 1-4) will light up when Excel adds a tip to the TipWizard Box. Click the TipWizard button to display or hide the TipWizard Box.

Cell, Gridlines, Active Cell, and Mouse Pointer

The intersection of each column and row is a **cell**. A cell is the basic unit of a worksheet into which you enter data. A cell is referred to by its unique address, or **cell reference**, which is the coordinates of the intersection of a column and a row. To identify a cell, specify the column letter first, followed by the row number. For example, cell reference C5 refers to the cell located at the intersection of column C and row 5 (see Figure 1-6 on the previous page).

The horizontal and vertical lines on the worksheet itself are called **gridlines**. Gridlines make it easier to see and identify each cell in the worksheet. If desired, you can remove the gridlines from the worksheet, but it is recommended that you leave the gridlines on.

One cell on the worksheet, designated the **active cell**, is the one in which you can enter data. The active cell in Figure 1-6 is A1. Cell A1 is identified in two ways. First, a heavy border surrounds the cell. Second, the **active cell reference** displays immediately above column A in the **Name box** (Figure 1-6).

The mouse pointer in Figure 1-6 has the shape of a block plus sign. The mouse pointer displays as a **block plus sign** whenever it is located in a cell in the worksheet. Another common shape of the mouse pointer is the block arrow. The mouse pointer turns into the **block arrow** whenever you move it outside the window or when you drag cell contents between rows or columns. The other mouse pointer shapes are described when they appear on the screen during this and subsequent projects.

More *About* the Mouse Pointer

The mouse pointer can become one of fourteen different shapes, such as an arrow, cross hair, or chart symbol, depending on the task you are performing in Excel and the mouse pointer's location on the screen.

Worksheet Window

Each worksheet in a workbook has 256 columns and 16,384 rows for a total of 4,194,304 cells. The column headings begin with A and end with IV. The row headings begin with 1 and end with 16,384. Only a small fraction of the active worksheet displays on the screen at one time. You view the portion of the worksheet displayed on the screen through a **worksheet window** (Figure 1-6). Below and to the right of the worksheet window are **scroll bars**, **scroll arrows**, and **scroll boxes** which you can use to move the window around to view different parts of the active worksheet. To the right of the sheet tabs at the bottom of the screen is the tab split box. You can drag the **tab split box** (Figure 1-7) to increase or decrease the view of the sheet tabs.

More *About* the Worksheet and Window

256 columns and 16,384 rows make for a gigantic worksheet! So big in fact that you might imagine it takes up the entire wall of a large room. Go one step further and imagine you can only view a small area of the worksheet on the wall at one time through your computer screen. The bad news is you can't see the entire worksheet at any one time. The good news is that you can quickly move the computer screen over the worksheet and view any part of it.

Menu Bar, Standard Toolbar, Formatting Toolbar, Formula Bar, Sheet and Scroll Tabs, and Status Bar

The menu bar, Standard toolbar, Formatting toolbar, and formula bar appear at the top of the screen just below the title bar (Figure 1-7). The sheet tabs, tab scrolling buttons, and the status bar appear at the bottom of the screen, above the Windows 95 taskbar.

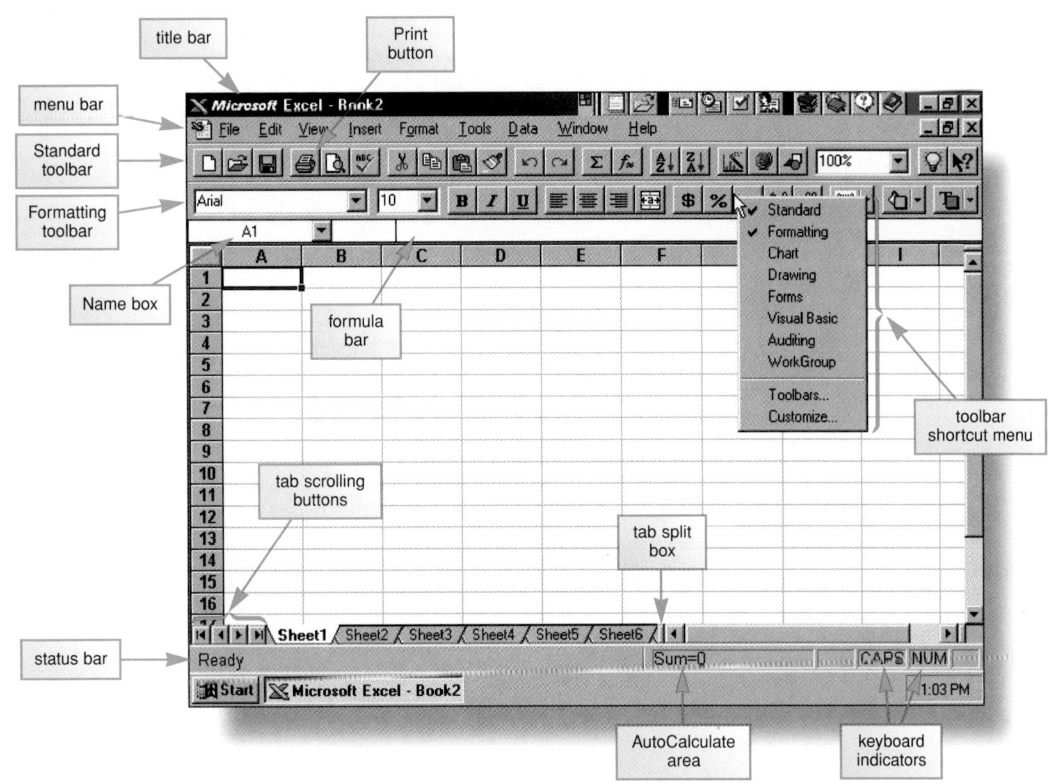

FIGURE 1-7

MENU BAR The **menu bar** displays the Excel menu names (Figure 1-7). Each menu name represents a menu of commands that you can use to retrieve, store, print, and manipulate data on the worksheet. To display a menu, such as the **File menu**, click the menu name File on the menu bar.

The menu bar can change to include other menu names depending on the type of work you are doing in Excel. For example, if you are working with a chart sheet rather than a worksheet, the menu bar names will reflect charting command options.

STANDARD TOOLBAR AND FORMATTING TOOLBAR The **Standard toolbar** and **Formatting toolbar** (Figure 1-7) contain buttons and drop-down list boxes that allow you to perform frequent tasks more quickly than when using the menu bar. For example, to print a worksheet, you click the Print button. Each button has a picture on the button face that helps you remember the button's function. Also, when you move the mouse pointer over a button or box, the name of the button or box appears below it. This is called a **ToolTip**.

Figure 1-8 on the next page illustrates the Standard and Formatting toolbars and describes the functions of the buttons. Each of the buttons and drop-down list boxes will be explained in detail when they are used in the projects.

More *About* Your Screen Display

If you're distracted by all the buttons and bars on your screen, you can increase the number of rows and columns displayed by clicking Full Screen on the View menu. Excel will immediately hide the buttons and bars, thus increasing the size of your window. Excel also displays a small toolbar with the Full Screen button on it. Click the Full Screen button to return to normal display.

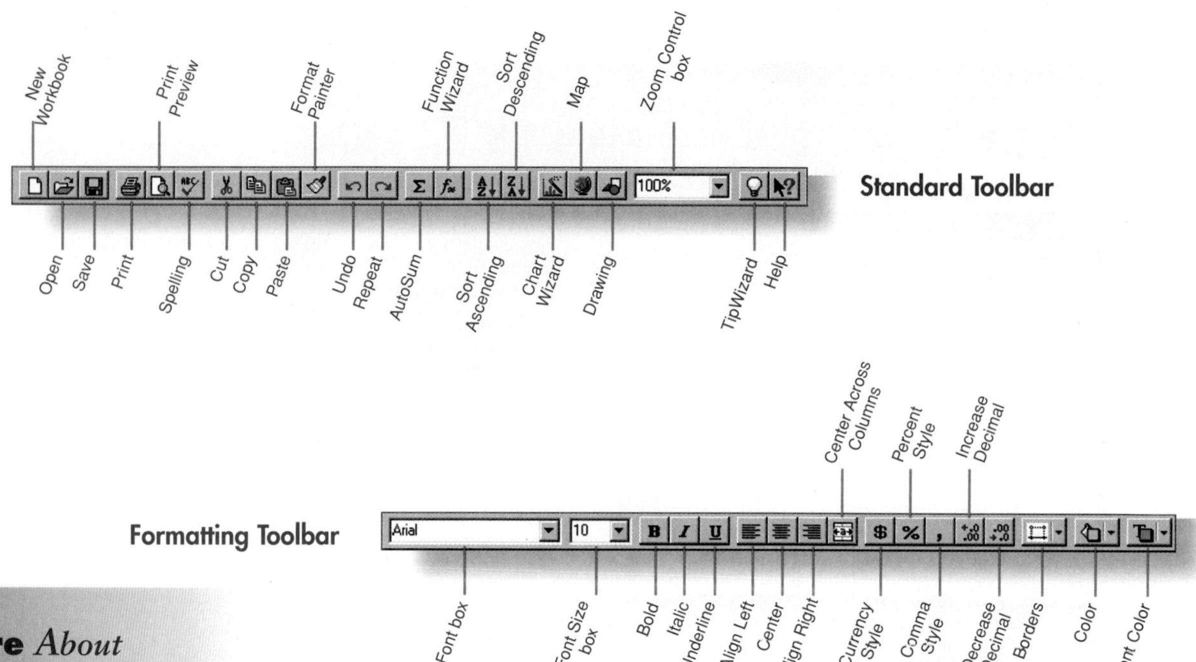

FIGURE 1-8

More *About* **Toolbars**

Do not be overly concerned if your toolbars have a different set of buttons. It probably means that a previous user changed the toolbars by using the Customize command on the shortcut menu (Figure 1-7) to add or delete buttons. To reset the Standard or Formatting toolbars so they appear as showin in Figure 1-8, right-click any toolbar, click Toolbars, click the toolbar name to reset, click the Reset button, and click the OK button.

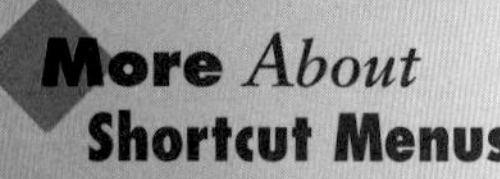

More *About* **Shortcut Menus**

Shortcut menus display the most frequently used commands that relate to the object the mouse pointer is pointing to. To display a shortcut menu, right-click the object. You can also display the shortcut menu by selecting the object and pressing SHIFT+F10. To hide a shortcut menu, click outside the shortcut menu or press ESC

Excel has several additional toolbars you can activate by clicking View on the menu bar. You can also point to a toolbar, such as the Formatting toolbar, and then right-click to display a shortcut menu, which lists the toolbars available (see Figure 1-7 on the previous page). A **shortcut menu** contains a list of commands or items to choose from that relate to the item you are pointing to when you right-click. Once a shortcut menu displays, you can click or right-click a command or item. The check mark to the left of Standard and Formatting in the shortcut menu in Figure 1-7 indicates they are displaying on the screen.

FORMULA BAR Below the Formatting toolbar is the **formula bar** (Figure 1-7). As you type, the data appears in the formula bar. Excel also displays the active cell reference on the left side of the formula bar in the Name box.

STATUS BAR Immediately above the Windows 95 taskbar is the status bar. The **status bar** displays a brief description of the command selected (highlighted) in a menu, the function of the button the mouse pointer is on (Figure 1-7), or the current activity (mode) in progress (Figure 1-7). **Mode indicators**, such as Enter and Ready, specify the current mode of Excel. When the mode is Ready, Excel is ready to accept the next command or data entry. When the mode indicator is Enter, Excel is in the process of accepting data through the keyboard for the active cell.

In the middle of the status bar is the AutoCalculate area. The **AutoCalculate area** can be used in place of a calculator to view the sum or average or other types of totals of a group of numbers on the worksheet.

Keyboard indicators, such as CAPS (Caps Lock) and NUM (Num Lock), show which keys are engaged. Keyboard indicators display on the right side of the status bar within the small rectangular boxes (Figure 1-7).

Selecting a Cell

To enter data into a cell, you must first select it. The easiest way to **select a cell** (make active) is to use the mouse to move the block plus sign to the cell and click.

An alternative method is to use the **arrow keys** that are located just to the right of the typewriter keys on the keyboard. An arrow key selects the cell adjacent to the active cell in the direction of the arrow on the key.

You know a cell is selected (active) when a heavy border surrounds the cell and the active cell reference displays in the Name box on the left side of the formula bar.

Entering Text

In Excel, any set of characters containing a letter, hyphen (as in a telephone number) or space is considered **text**. Text is used to place titles on the worksheet, such as worksheet titles, column titles, and row titles. In Project 1 (Figure 1-9), the centered worksheet title, Rollablade 4th Qtr Expenses, in row 1 identifies the worksheet. The column titles in row 2 are the names of departments (Marketing, Finance, Sales, and Systems) and Total. The row titles in column A (Benefits, Travel, Wages, and Total) identify the data in each row.

More About Entering Text

A text entry in a cell can contain from 1 to 255 characters. Text entries are primarily used to identify parts of the worksheet, such as worksheet titles, column titles, and row titles. However, there are applications in which text entries are data that you dissect, string together, and manipulate using text functions.

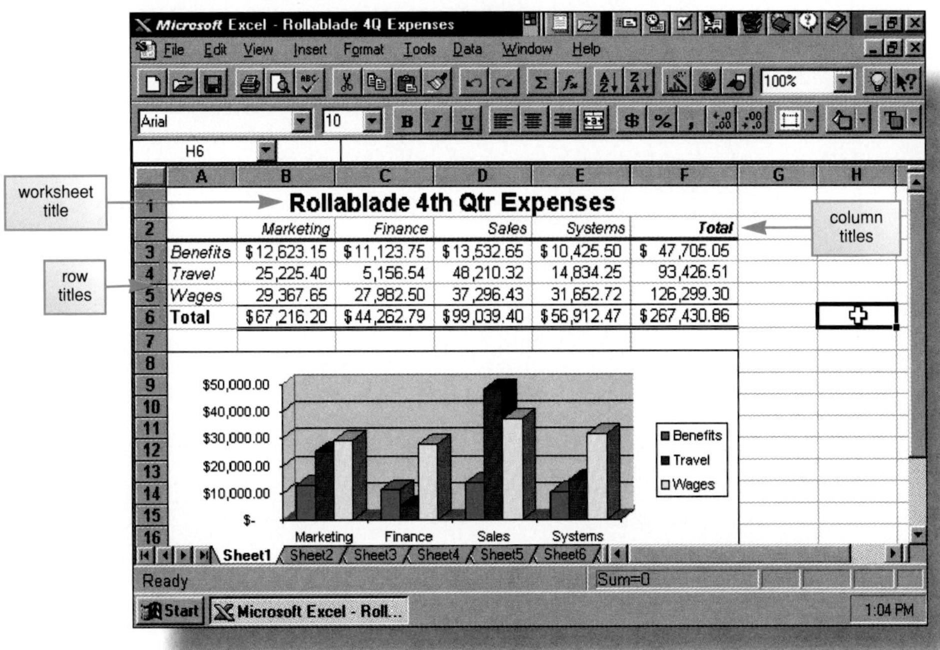

FIGURE 1-9

Entering the Worksheet Title

The following steps show how to enter the worksheet title (Rollablade 4th Qtr Expenses) into cell A1. Later in this project, the worksheet title will be centered over the column titles as shown in Figure 1-9.

Steps To Enter the Worksheet Title

1. **Click cell A1.**

   Cell A1 becomes the active cell and a heavy border surrounds it (Figure 1-10).

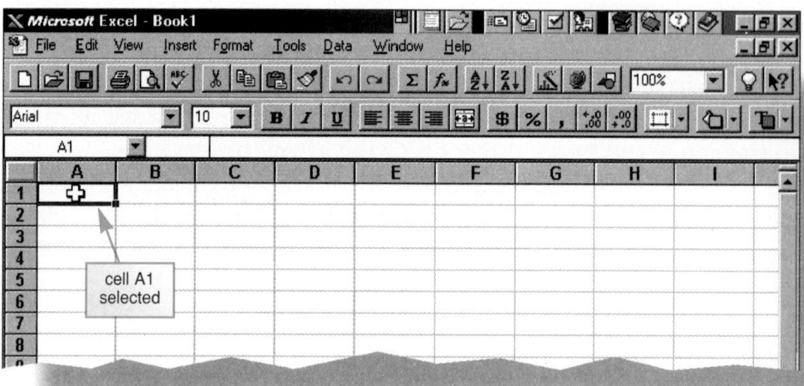

FIGURE 1-10

2. **Type** `Rollablade 4th Qtr Expenses` **in cell A1.**

   When you type the first character, the mode indicator in the status bar changes from Ready to Enter and Excel displays three boxes: the **cancel box**, *the* **enter box**, *and the* **Function Wizard box** *in the formula bar (Figure 1-11). The entire title displays in the formula bar and the text also displays in cell A1 followed immediately by the insertion point. The* **insertion point** *is a blinking vertical line that indicates where the next character typed will appear.*

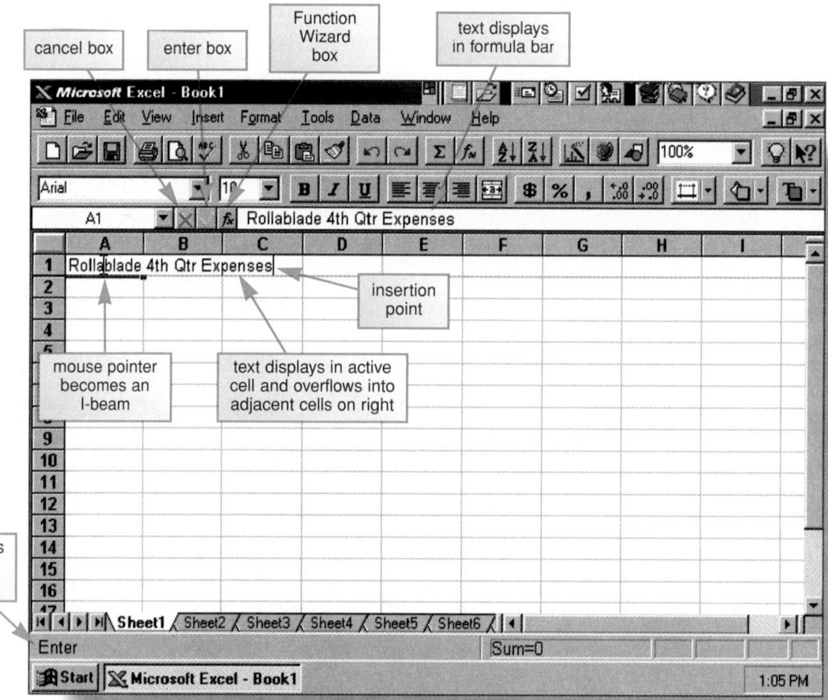

FIGURE 1-11

3. **After you type the text, point to the enter box (Figure 1-12).**

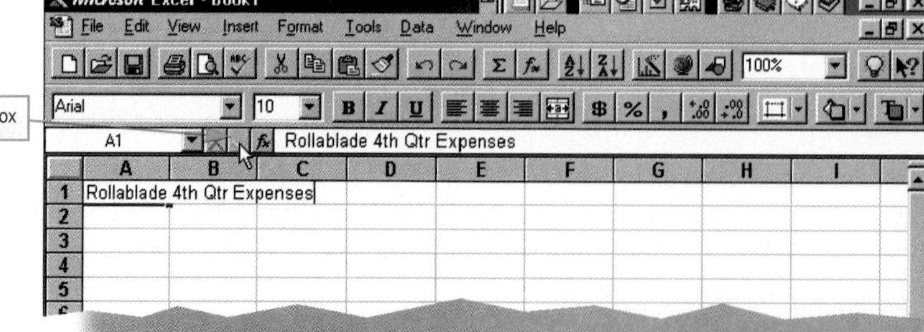

FIGURE 1-12

4 **Click the enter box to complete the entry.**

Excel enters the worksheet title in cell A1 (Figure 1-13).

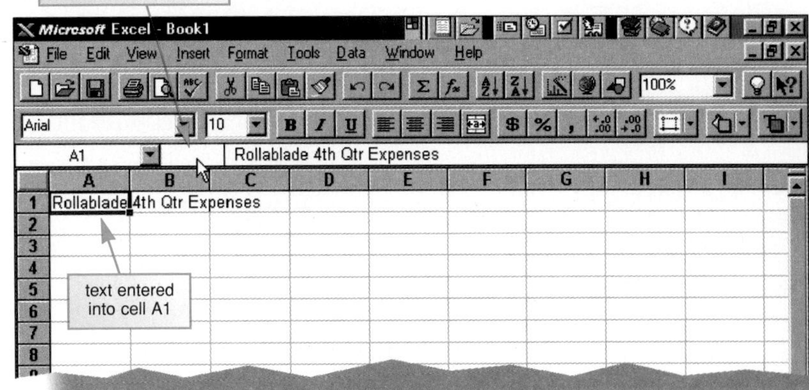

FIGURE 1-13

OtherWays

1. Click any cell other than active cell
2. Press ENTER
3. Press an arrow key
4. Press HOME, PAGE UP, PAGE DOWN, or END

When you complete a text entry into a cell, a series of events occurs. First, Excel positions the text left-justified in the active cell. **Left-justified** means the cell entry is to the far left in the cell. Therefore, the R in the company name Rollablade begins in the leftmost position of cell A1.

Second, when the text is longer than the width of a column, Excel displays the overflow characters in adjacent cells to the right as long as these adjacent cells contain no data. In Figure 1-13, the width of cell A1 is approximately nine characters. The text entered consists of 27 characters. Therefore, Excel displays the overflow characters in cells B1 and C1, because both cells are empty.

If cell B1 contained data, only the first nine characters of cell A1 would display on the worksheet. Excel would hide the overflow characters, but they would still remain stored in cell A1 and display in the formula bar whenever cell A1 was the active cell.

Third, when you complete an entry by clicking the enter box, the cell in which the text is entered remains the active cell.

More About the ENTER key

Unless you are entering large amounts of data onto a worksheet, you will probably want the ENTER key to complete an entry without changing the active cell location. If pressing the ENTER key changes the active cell location and you prefer for it to remain on the cell you entered data into, or you want it to move in another direction, click Options on the Tools menu, click the Edit tab, click the Move Selection after Enter check box to clear or select a new direction, and then click OK.

Correcting a Mistake While Typing

If you type the wrong letter and notice the error before clicking the enter box or pressing the ENTER key, use the **BACKSPACE key** to erase all the characters back to and including the one that is wrong. To cancel the entire entry before entering it into the cell, click the cancel box in the formula bar or press the **ESC key** . If you see an error in a cell, select the cell and retype the entry. Later in this project, additional error-correction techniques are covered.

AutoCorrect

The **AutoCorrect feature** of Excel works behind the scenes, correcting common mistakes when you complete text entry in a cell. AutoCorrect makes three types of corrections for you:

1. Corrects two initial capital letters by changing the second letter to lowercase.
2. Capitalizes the first letter in the names of days.

More *About* **the AutoCorrect Feature**

AutoCorrect is part of the IntelliSense™ technology that is built into Excel, which understands what you are trying to do and helps you do it.

3. Replaces commonly misspelled words with their correct spelling. For example, it will correct the misspelled word *recieve* to *receive* when you press the ENTER key, click the enter box, or press an arrow key to complete an entry. AutoCorrect will automatically correct the spelling of more than 400 words.

You can add to the list of misspelled words and their corresponding corrections or turn off any of the AutoCorrect features by clicking **AutoCorrect** on the Tools menu.

Entering Column Titles

To enter the column titles, select the appropriate cell and then enter the text, as described in the following steps.

Steps To Enter the Column Titles

1 **Click cell B2.**

Cell B2 becomes the active cell. The active cell reference in the Name box changes from A1 to B2 (Figure 1-14).

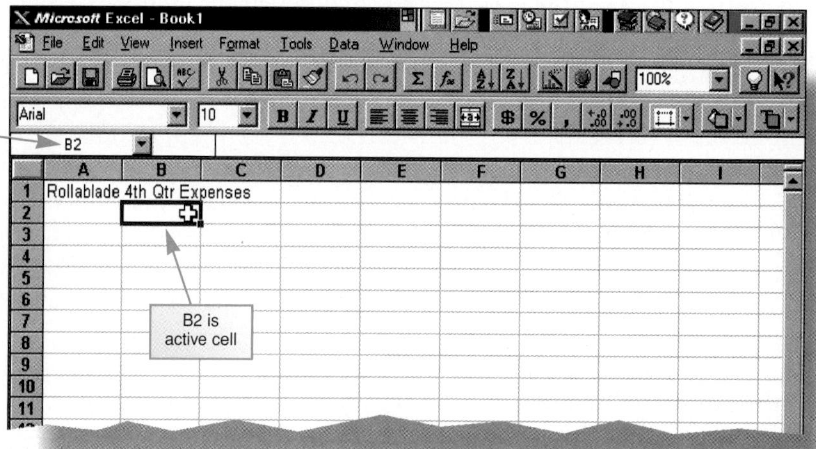

FIGURE 1-14

2 **Type** `Marketing` **in cell B2.**

Excel displays Marketing in the formula bar and in cell B2 (Figure 1-15).

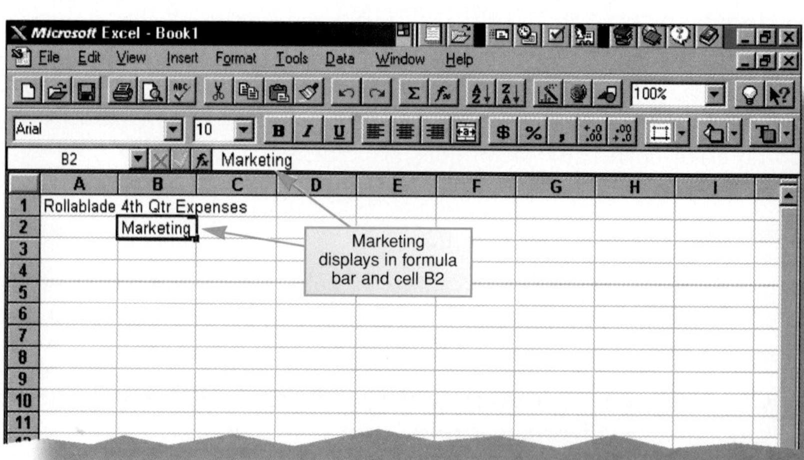

FIGURE 1-15

3 **Press the RIGHT ARROW key.**

Excel enters the column title, Marketing, in cell B2 and makes cell C2 the active cell (Figure 1-16). When you press an arrow key to complete an entry, the adjacent cell in the direction of the arrow (up, down, left, or right) becomes the active cell.

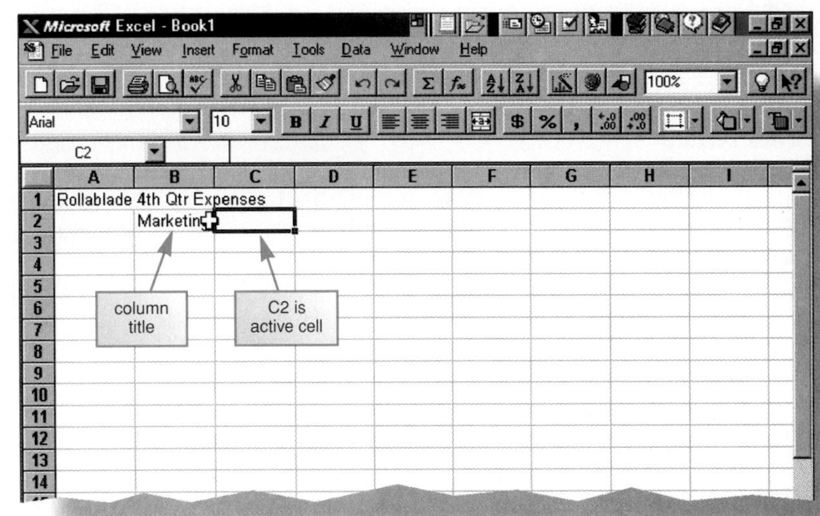

FIGURE 1-16

4 **Repeat Step 2 and Step 3 for the remaining column titles in row 2. That is, enter `Finance` in cell C2, `Sales` in cell D2, `Systems` in cell E2, and `Total` in cell F2. Complete the last column title entry in cell F2 by clicking the enter box or by pressing the ENTER key.**

The column titles display left-justified as shown in Figure 1-17.

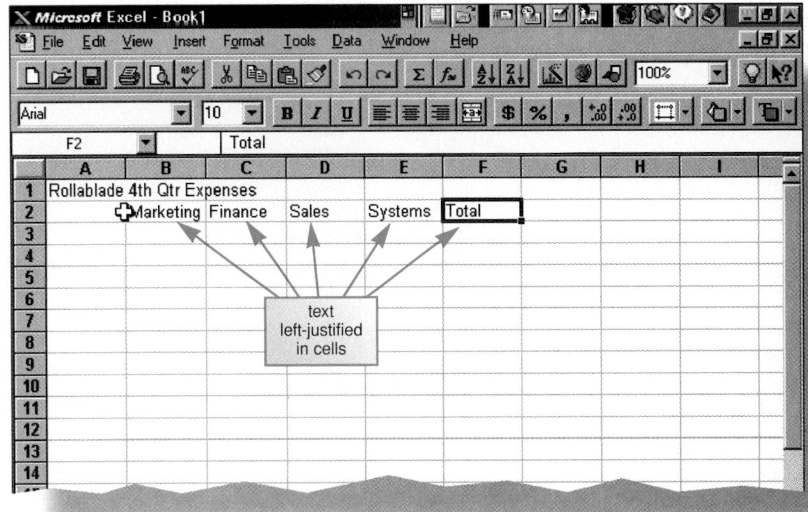

FIGURE 1-17

To complete an entry in a cell, use the arrow keys if the next entry is in an adjacent cell. If the next entry is not in an adjacent cell, click the next cell you plan to enter data in or click the enter box in the formula bar or press the ENTER key and then click the appropriate cell for the next entry.

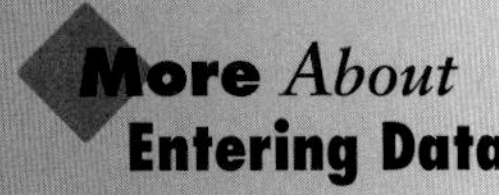

More About Entering Data

Tired of entering similar data? Excel remembers the data you have entered into consecutive cells in a column. Thus, if you enter the first few characters, Excel will handle the rest. This is called the AutoComplete feature. If you want to pick an entry from a list of column entries, right-click on a cell in the column and click Pick from List.

Entering Row Titles

The next step in developing the worksheet in Project 1 is to enter the row titles in column A. This process is similar to entering the column titles and is described in the steps on the next page.

Steps To Enter Row Titles

Click cell A3.

Cell A3 becomes the active cell (Figure 1-18). The active cell reference in the Name box changes from F2 to A3.

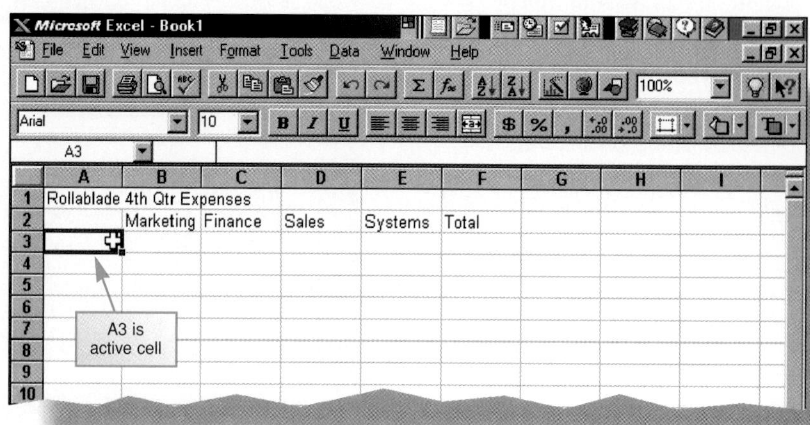

FIGURE 1-18

2 **Type** `Benefits` **and then press the DOWN ARROW key.**

Excel enters the row title Benefits in cell A3 and cell A4 becomes the active cell (Figure 1-19).

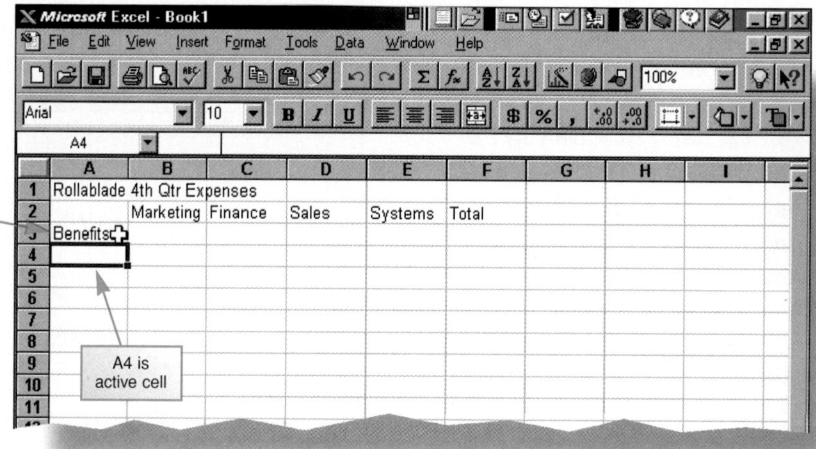

FIGURE 1-19

3 **Repeat Step 2 for the remaining row titles in column A. Enter** `Travel` **in cell A4,** `Wages` **in cell A5, and** `Total` **in cell A6. Complete the last row title in cell A6 by clicking the enter box or by pressing the ENTER key.**

The row titles display as shown in Figure 1-20.

FIGURE 1-20

Entering Numbers

In Excel, you can enter numbers into cells to represent amounts. **Numbers** can include the digits zero through nine and any one of the following special characters:

+ - ( ) , / . $ % E e

If a cell entry contains any other character (including spaces) from the keyboard, Excel interprets the entry as text and treats it accordingly. The use of the special characters is explained when they are required in a project.

In Project 1, the expenses for Benefits, Travel, and Wages for each of the four departments (Marketing, Finance, Sales, and Systems) obtained from Harriet Latham, director of personnel at Rollablade, are summarized in Table 1-1.

Table 1-1

	MARKETING	FINANCE	SALES	SYSTEMS
Benefits	$12,623.15	$11,123.75	$13,532.65	$10,425.50
Travel	25,225.40	5,156.54	48,210.32	14,834.25
Wages	29,367.65	27,982.50	37,296.43	31,652.72

These numbers must be entered in rows 3, 4, and 5. The following steps illustrate how to enter these values one row at a time.

More About Entering Numbers as Text

There are times when you will want numbers, such as zip codes, to be handled by Excel as text. To enter a number as text, start the entry with an apostrophe (').

Steps To Enter Numeric Data

1 **Click cell B3.**

Cell B3 becomes the active cell (Figure 1-21).

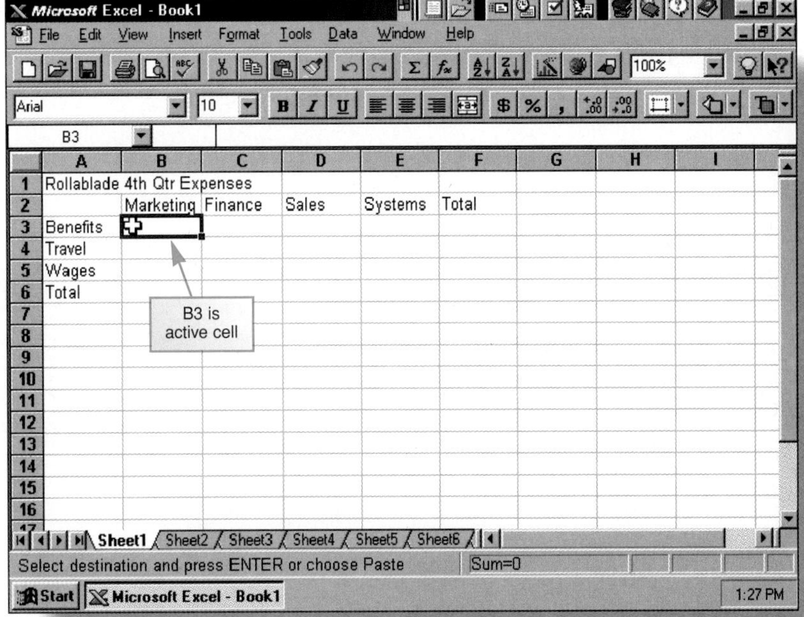

FIGURE 1-21

2 **Type** `12623.15` **and then press the RIGHT ARROW key.**

Excel enters the number 12623.15 right-justified in cell B3 and changes the active cell to cell C3 (Figure 1-22). The numbers on the worksheet are formatted with dollar signs and cents later in this project.

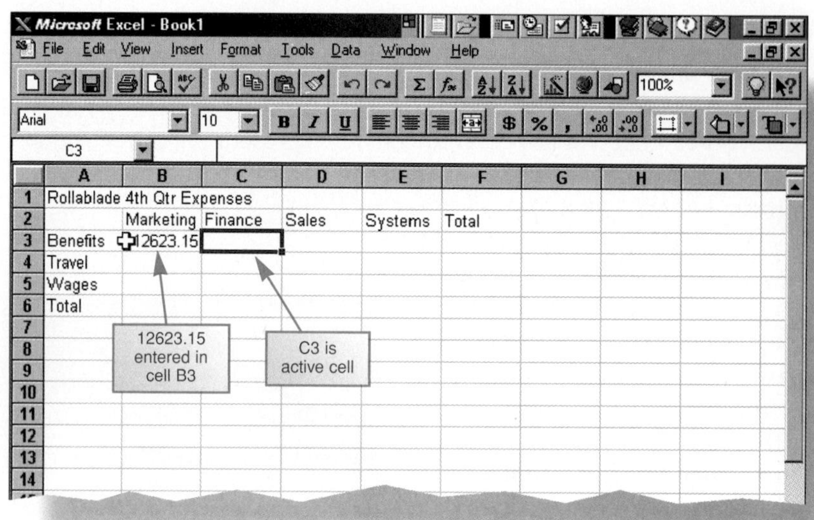

FIGURE 1-22

3 **Enter** `11123.75` **in cell C3,** `13532.65` **in cell D3, and** `10425.5` **in cell E3.**

Row 3 now contains the fourth-quarter benefit expenses all right-justified (Figure 1-23). ***Right-justified*** *means the cell entry is to the far right in the cell.*

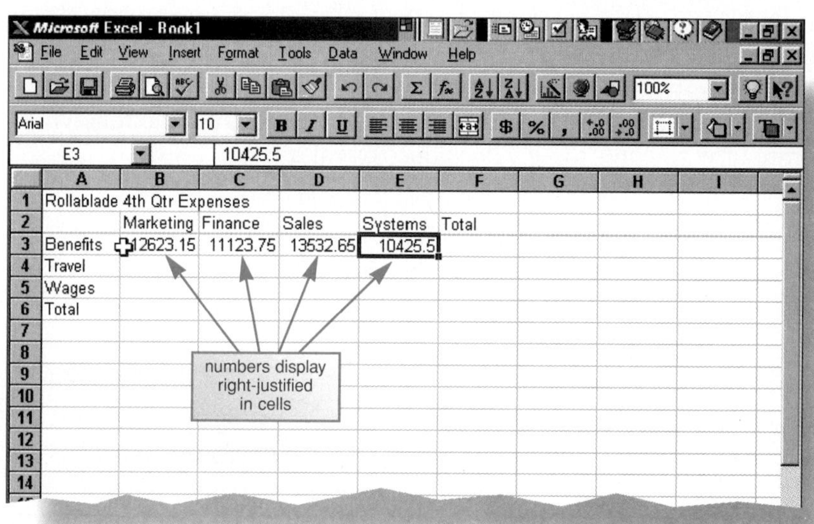

FIGURE 1-23

4 **Click cell B4 (Figure 1-24).**

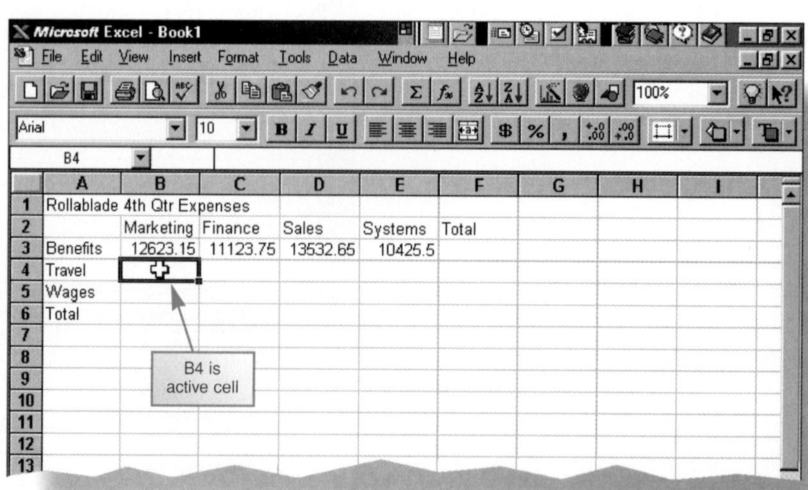

FIGURE 1-24

5 **Enter the fourth-quarter travel expenses for the four departments (**`25225.4` **for Marketing,** `5156.54` **for Finance,** `48210.32` **for Sales, and** `14834.25` **for Systems) and the 4th quarter wage expenses for the four departments (**`29367.65` **for Marketing,** `27982.5` **for Finance,** `37296.43` **for Sales, and** `31652.72` **for Systems).**

The fourth-quarter travel and wages expenses for the four departments display in row 4 and row 5 (Figure 1-25).

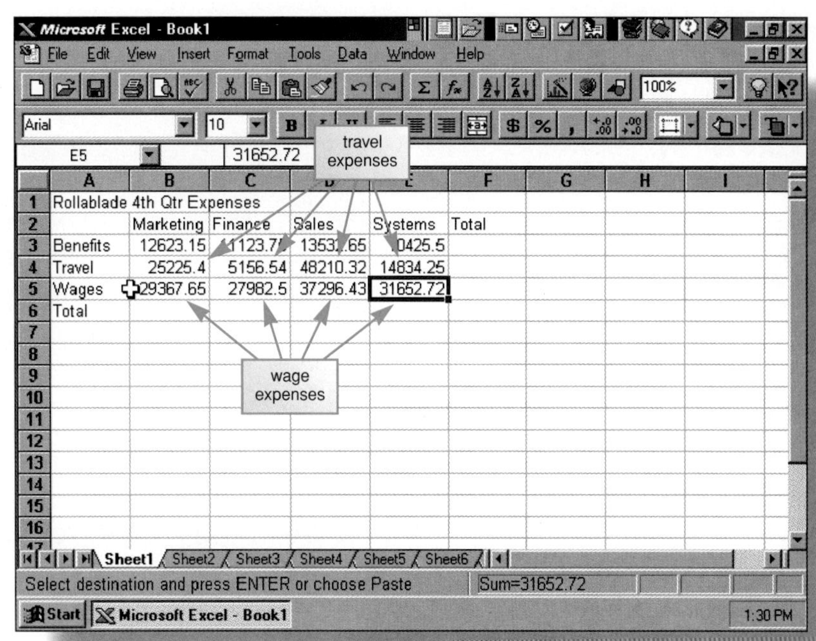

FIGURE 1-25

Steps 1 through 5 complete the numeric entries. Notice several important points. First, you are not required to type dollar signs and trailing zeros. Later, dollar signs will be added as previously described in Figure 1-1 on page E 1.7. When you enter a number that has cents, however, you must add the decimal point and the numbers representing the cents when you enter the number. You do not have to enter trailing zeros to the right of the decimal point. Second, Excel stores numbers right-justified in the cells. Third, the next section instructs Excel to calculate the totals in row 6 and in column F. Indeed, the capability of Excel to perform calculations is one of its major features.

More *About* Numbers

How big can numbers get in Excel? A number in Excel can be between approximately -1×10^{307} and 1×10^{307}. To enter a number such as 93,000,000,000 you can enter the number as it is or type 9.3E10 which stands for 9.3×10^{10}. If the cell is not wide enough to display a number, Excel will display it in Scientific format if no format has been assigned to the cell. For example, the number 12,345,678,901 displays as 1.2346E+10. If a format has been assigned to a cell with a large number, Excel displays number signs (#) in the cell to indicate the number cannot display properly, unless you widen the cell.

Calculating a Sum

The next step in creating the expense worksheet is to determine the total expenses for the Marketing department. To calculate this value in cell B6, Excel must add the numbers in cells B3, B4, and B5. Excel's **SUM function** provides a convenient means to accomplish this task.

To use the SUM function, first you must identify the cell in which the sum will be stored after it is calculated. Then, you can use the **AutoSum button** on the Standard toolbar to enter the SUM function.

Although you can enter the SUM function in cell B6 through the keyboard as =SUM(B3:B6), the following steps illustrate how to use the AutoSum button to accomplish the same task.

To Sum a Column of Numbers

1 Click cell B6.

Cell B6 becomes the active cell (Figure 1-26).

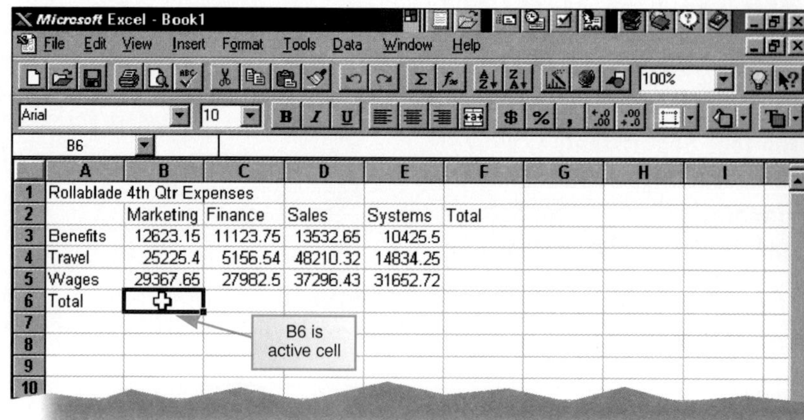

FIGURE 1-26

2 Click the AutoSum button on the Standard toolbar.

Excel responds by displaying =SUM(B3:B5) in the formula bar and in the active cell B6 (Figure 1-27). The =SUM entry identifies the SUM function. The B3:B5 within parentheses following the function name SUM is Excel's way of identifying the cells B3, B4, and B5. Excel also surrounds the proposed cells to sum with a moving border, also called a ***marquee****.*

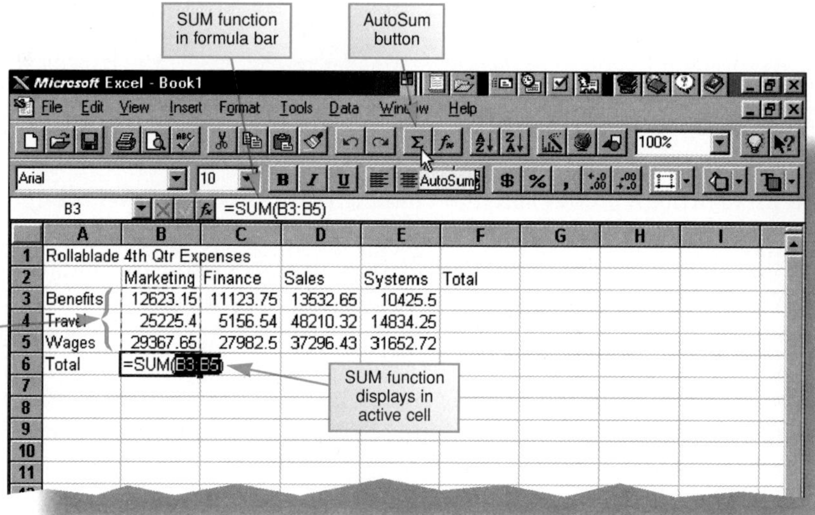

FIGURE 1-27

3 Click the AutoSum button a second time.

Excel enters the sum of the expenses for Marketing (67216.2 = 12623.15 + 25225.4+ 29367.65) in cell B6 (Figure 1-28). The SUM function assigned to cell B6 displays in the formula bar when B6 is the active cell.

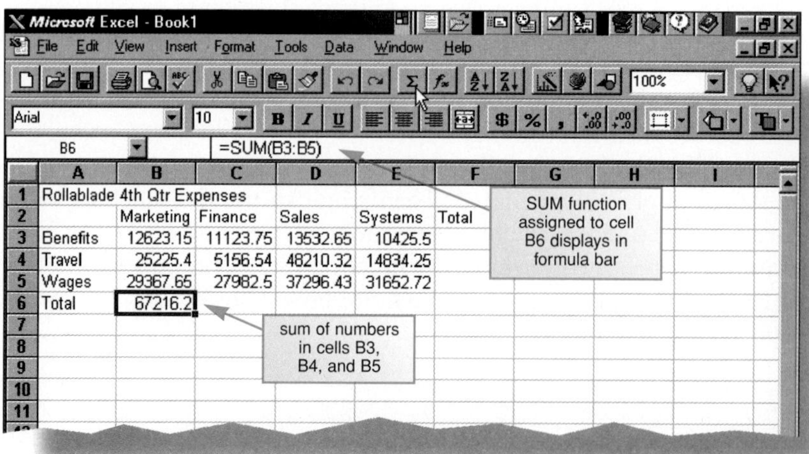

FIGURE 1-28

OtherWays

1. Press ALT+(=) for AutoSum

When you enter the SUM function using the AutoSum button, Excel automatically selects what it considers to be your choice of the group of cells to sum. The group of cells B3, B4, and B5 is called a range. A **range** is a series of two or more adjacent cells in a column or row or a rectangular group of cells. Many Excel operations, such as summing numbers, take place on cells within a range.

In proposing the range to sum, Excel first looks for a range of cells with numbers above the active cell and then to the left. If Excel proposes the wrong range, you can drag through the correct range anytime prior to clicking the AutoSum button a second time. You can also enter the correct range by typing the beginning cell reference, a colon (:), and the ending cell reference.

When using the AutoSum button, you can click it once and then click the enter box or press the ENTER key to complete the entry. Clicking the AutoSum button twice in succession, however, is the quickest way to enter the SUM function into a single cell.

Using the Fill Handle to Copy a Cell to Adjacent Cells

On the expense worksheet, Excel also must calculate the totals for Finance in cell C6, Sales in cell D6, and for Systems in cell E6. Table 1-2 illustrates the similarity between the entry in cell B6 and the entries required for the totals in cells C6, D6, and E6.

Table 1-2

CELL	SUM FUNCTION ENTRIES	REMARK
B6	=SUM(B3:B5)	Sums cells B3, B4, and B5
C6	=SUM(C3:C5)	Sums cells C3, C4, and C5
D6	=SUM(D3:D5)	Sums cells D3, D4, and D5
E6	=SUM(E3:E5)	Sums cells E3, E4, and E5

To place the SUM functions in cells C6, D6, and E6, you can follow the same steps shown in Figures 1-26 through 1-28. A second, more efficient method is to copy the SUM function from cell B6 to the range C6:E6. The cell being copied is called the **copy area**. The range of cells receiving the copy is called the **paste area**.

Notice from Table 1-2 that although the SUM function entries are similar, they are not exact copies. Each cell to the right of cell B6 has a range that is one column to the right of the previous column. When you copy cell addresses, Excel adjusts them for each new position, resulting in the SUM entries illustrated in Table 1-2. Each adjusted cell reference is called a **relative reference**.

The easiest way to copy the SUM formula from cell B6 to cells C6 and D6 is to use the fill handle. The **fill handle** is the small black square located in the lower right corner of the heavy border around the active cell (Figure 1-28). Perform the steps on the next page to use the fill handle to copy cell B6 to the adjacent cells C6:E6.

More *About* Copying and Moving Using the Mouse

Using the mouse and fill handle, you can quickly copy a cell or range of cells to an adjacent paste area as shown in the upcoming example. Another way to copy a cell or range of cells using the mouse is to select the copy area, point to the border of the copy area so the mouse pointer changes to a block arrow, and then while holding down the CTRL key, drag the copy area to the paste area. This second method requires that the paste area be the same size as the copy area. If you drag without holding down the CTRL key, Excel moves the data, rather than duplicates it.

Steps To Copy a Cell to Adjacent Cells in a Row

1 With cell B6 active, point to the fill handle.

The mouse pointer changes to a cross hair (Figure 1-29).

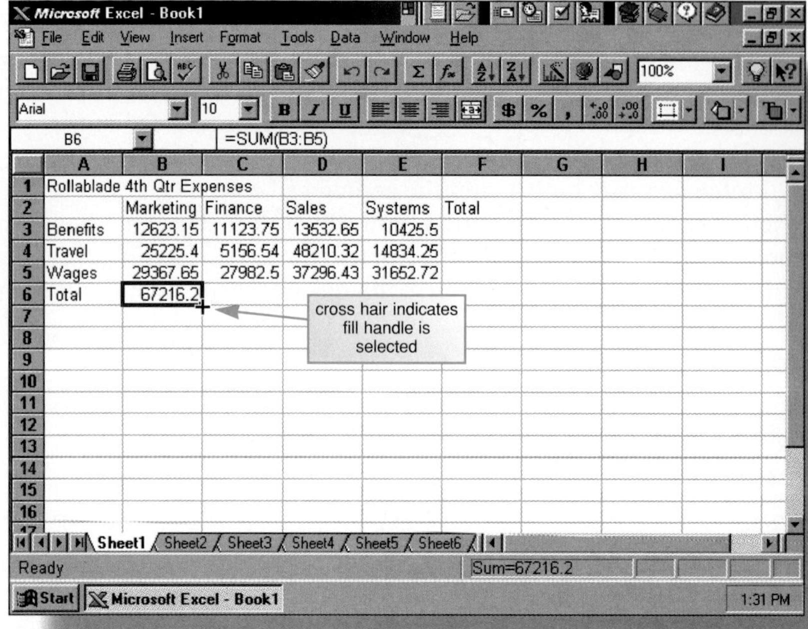

FIGURE 1-29

2 Drag the fill handle to select the paste area C6:E6.

Excel shades the border of the paste area C6:E6 (Figure 1-30).

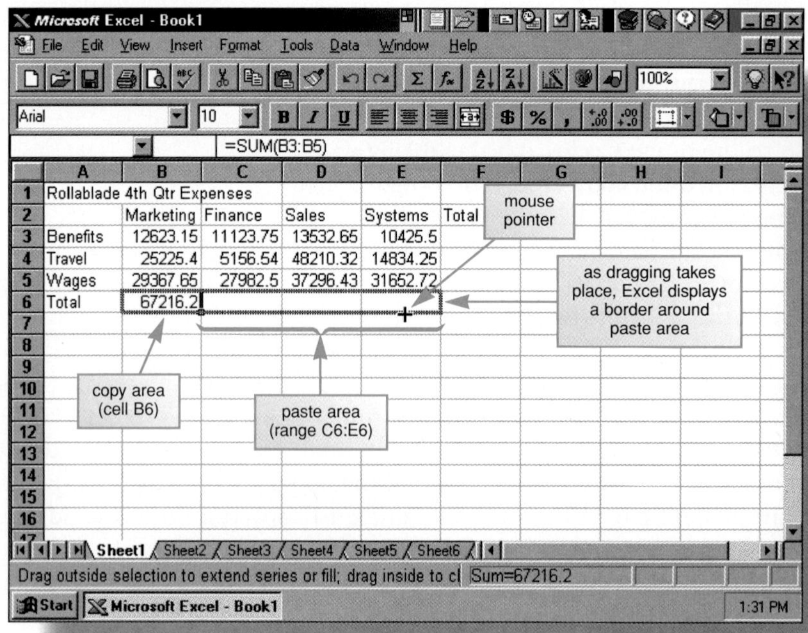

FIGURE 1-30

3 **Release the left mouse button.**

Excel copies the SUM function in cell B6 to the range C6:E6 (Figure 1-31). In addition, Excel calculates the sums and enters the results in cells C6, D6, and E6.

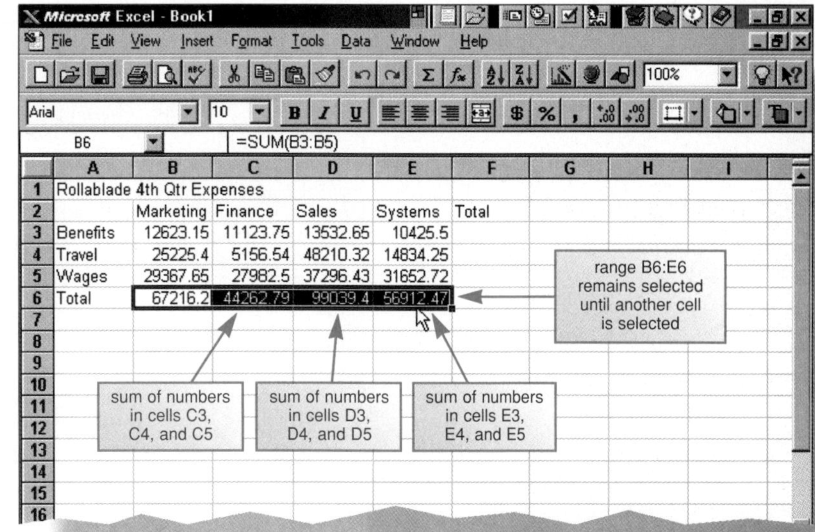

FIGURE 1-31

OtherWays

1. Right-click copy area, click Copy on shortcut menu, right-click paste area, click Paste on shortcut menu
2. Select copy area, click Copy button on Standard toolbar, select paste area, click Paste button on Standard toolbar to paste
3. Select copy area, on Edit menu click Copy, select paste area, on Edit menu click Paste
4. Select copy area, press CTRL+C, select paste area, press CTRL+V

After the copy is complete, the range remains selected. To remove the range selection, select any cell.

Determining Row Totals

The next step in building the expense worksheet is to total the individual Benefits, Travel, Wages, and company total expenses and place the sums in column F. Use the SUM function in the same manner as you did when the expenses by department were totaled in row 6. In this example, however, all the rows will be totaled at the same time. The following steps illustrate this process.

To Determine Multiple Totals at the Same Time

1 **Click cell F3.**

Cell F3 becomes the active cell (Figure 1-32).

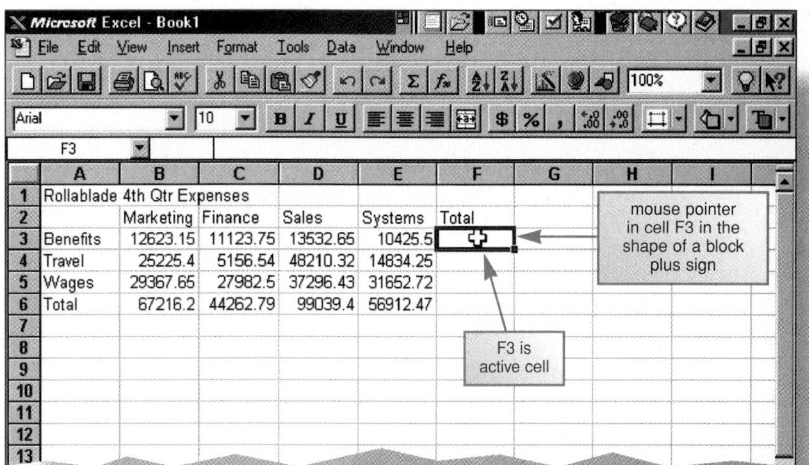

FIGURE 1-32

2 **With the mouse pointer in cell F3 and in the shape of a block plus sign, drag the mouse pointer down to cell F6.**

Excel highlights the range F3:F6 (Figure 1-33).

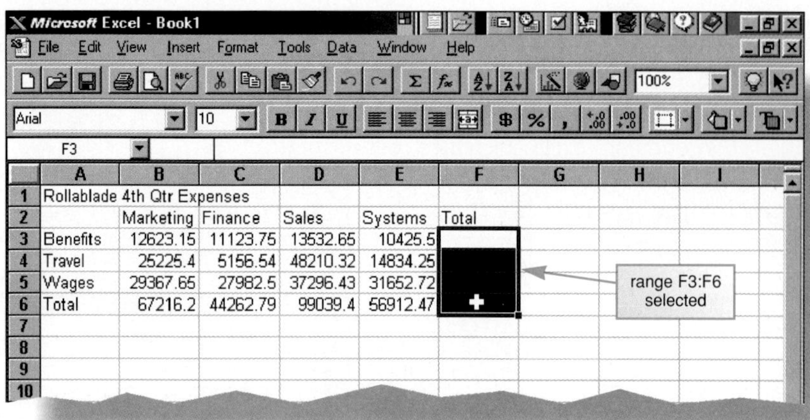

FIGURE 1-33

3 **Click the AutoSum button on the Standard toolbar.**

Excel assigns the functions =SUM(B3:E3) to cell F3, =SUM(B4:E4) to cell F4, =SUM(B5:E5) to cell F5, and =SUM(B6:E6) to cell F6, and then computes and displays the sums in the respective cells (Figure 1-34).

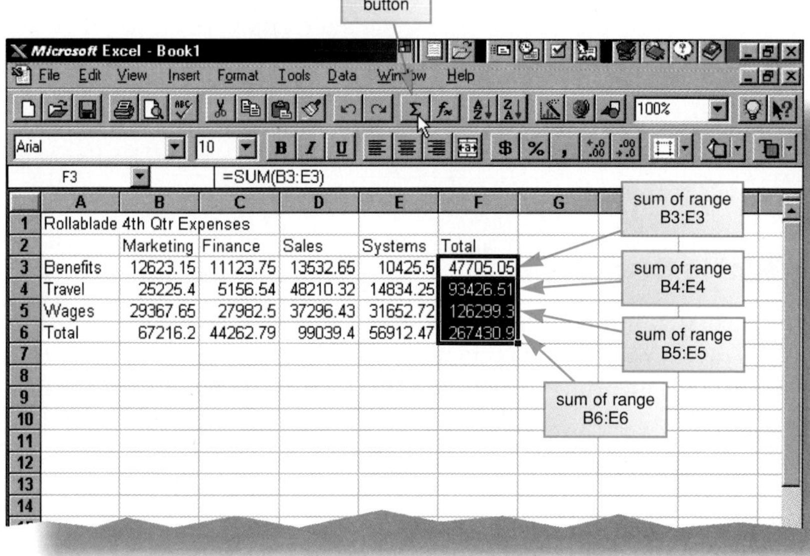

FIGURE 1-34

More *About* the AutoSum Button

In a hurry? Here's a quick way to determine all the totals in row 6 and column F in Figure 1-34 at once. Select the range (B3:F6) and click the AutoSum button. The range B3:F6 includes the numbers to sum plus an additional row (row 6) and an additional column (column F).

Because a range was selected next to rows of numbers and the AutoSum button was clicked, Excel assigned the SUM function to each cell in the selected range. Thus, four SUM functions with different ranges were assigned to the selected range, one for each row. This same procedure could have been used earlier to sum the columns. That is, rather than selecting cell B6 and clicking the AutoSum button twice and then copying the SUM function to the range C6:E6, you could have selected the range B6:E6 and then clicked the AutoSum button once.

Formatting the Worksheet

The text, numeric entries, and functions for the worksheet are now complete. The next step is to format the worksheet. You **format** a worksheet to emphasize certain entries and make the worksheet easier to read and understand.

Figure 1-35(a) shows the worksheet before formatting. Figure 1-35(b) shows the worksheet after formatting. As you can see from the two figures, a worksheet that is formatted not only is easier to read, but it also looks more professional.

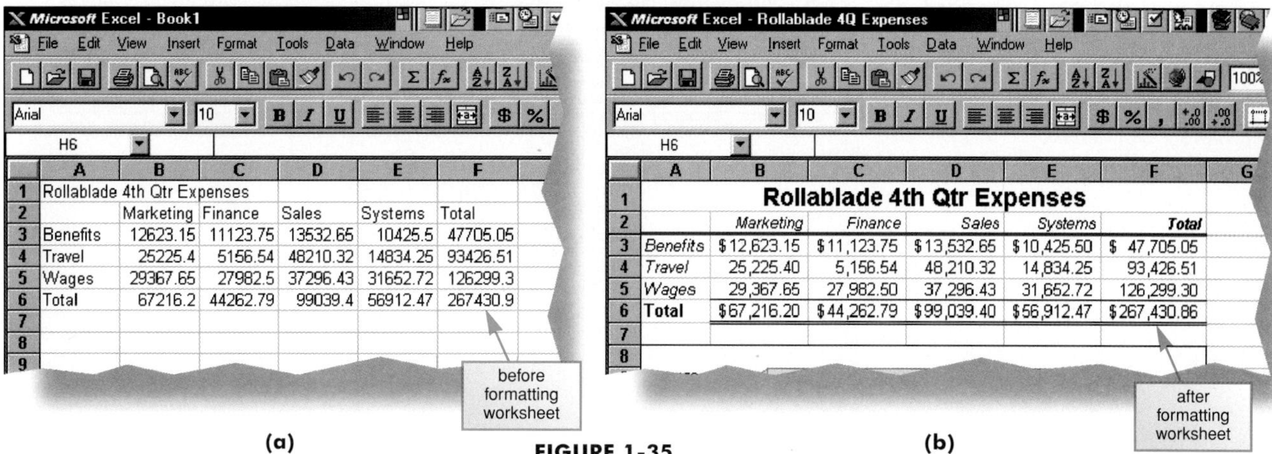

	A	B	C	D	E	F
1	Rollablade 4th Qtr Expenses					
2		Marketing	Finance	Sales	Systems	Total
3	Benefits	12623.15	11123.75	13532.65	10425.5	47705.05
4	Travel	25225.4	5156.54	48210.32	14834.25	93426.51
5	Wages	29367.65	27982.5	37296.43	31652.72	126299.3
6	Total	67216.2	44262.79	99039.4	56912.47	267430.9

	A	B	C	D	E	F
1	**Rollablade 4th Qtr Expenses**					
2		*Marketing*	*Finance*	*Sales*	*Systems*	***Total***
3	*Benefits*	$12,623.15	$11,123.75	$13,532.65	$10,425.50	$ 47,705.05
4	*Travel*	25,225.40	5,156.54	48,210.32	14,834.25	93,426.51
5	*Wages*	29,367.65	27,982.50	37,296.43	31,652.72	126,299.30
6	**Total**	$67,216.20	$44,262.79	$99,039.40	$56,912.47	$267,430.86

(a) **FIGURE 1-35** (b)

To change the unformatted worksheet in Figure 1-35a to the formatted worksheet in Figure 1-35b, the following tasks must be completed:

1. Bold the worksheet title in cell A1.
2. Enlarge the worksheet title in cell A1.
3. Center the worksheet title in cell A1 across columns A through F.
4. Format the body of the worksheet. The body of the worksheet, range A2:F6, includes the column titles, row titles, and numbers. The result is numbers represented in a dollars-and-cents format, dollar signs in the first row of numbers and the total row, and underlines that emphasize portions of the worksheet.

The process required to format the expense spreadsheet is explained on the following pages. Although the format procedures will be carried out in the order presented, you should be aware that you can make these format changes in any order.

Fonts, Font Size, and Font Style

Characters that display on the screen are a specific shape and size. The **font type** defines the appearance and shape of the letters, numbers, and special characters. The **font size** specifies the size of the characters on the screen. Character size is gauged by a measurement system called points. A single **point** is about 1/72 of one inch in height. Thus, a character with a **point size** of ten is about 10/72 of one inch in height.

Font style indicates how the characters appear. They may be normal, bold, underlined, or italicized.

When Excel begins, the default font type for the entire spreadsheet is Arial with a size of 10 point, no bold, no underline, and no italic. With Excel you have the capability to change the font characteristics in a single cell, a range of cells, the entire worksheet, or the entire workbook.

Perform the steps on the next page to bold the worksheet title in cell A1.

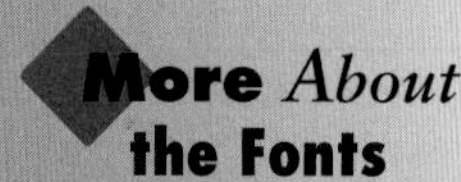

In general, use no more than two font types and font styles in a worksheet.

To Bold a Cell

1 Click cell A1 and then point to the Bold button on the Standard toolbar.

The ToolTip displays immediately below the Bold button identifying the function of the button (Figure 1-36).

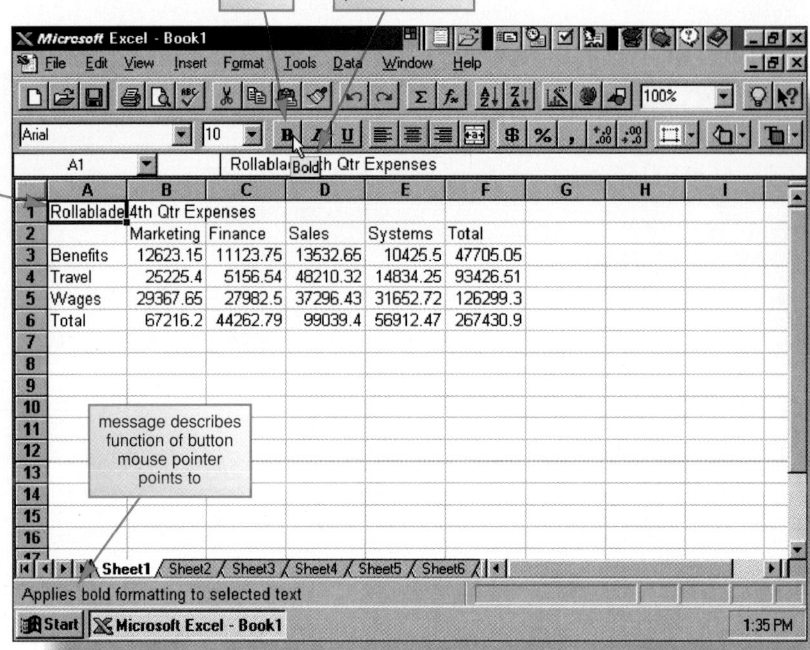

FIGURE 1-36

2 Click the Bold button.

Excel applies a bold format to the worksheet title Rollablade 4th Qtr Expenses (Figure 1-37).

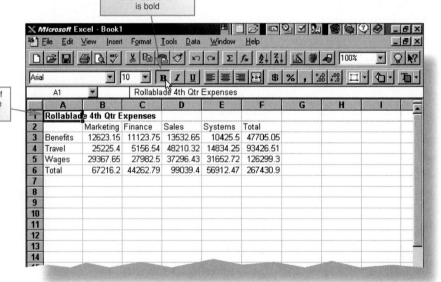

Bold button recessed (or ghosted) when active cell is bold

contents of cell A1 are bold

FIGURE 1-37

OtherWays

1. Right-click cell, click Format Cells on shortcut menu, click Font tab, click Bold, click OK button
2. On Format menu click Cells, click Font tab, click Bold, click OK button
3. Press CTRL+B

When the active cell is bold, the Bold button is recessed (Figure 1-37). Clicking the Bold button a second time removes the bold format.

Increasing the font size is the next step in formatting the worksheet title.

To Increase the Font Size of a Cell

1. **With cell A1 selected, click the Font Size box arrow on the Formatting toolbar and point to 14 in the drop-down list box (Figure 1-38).**

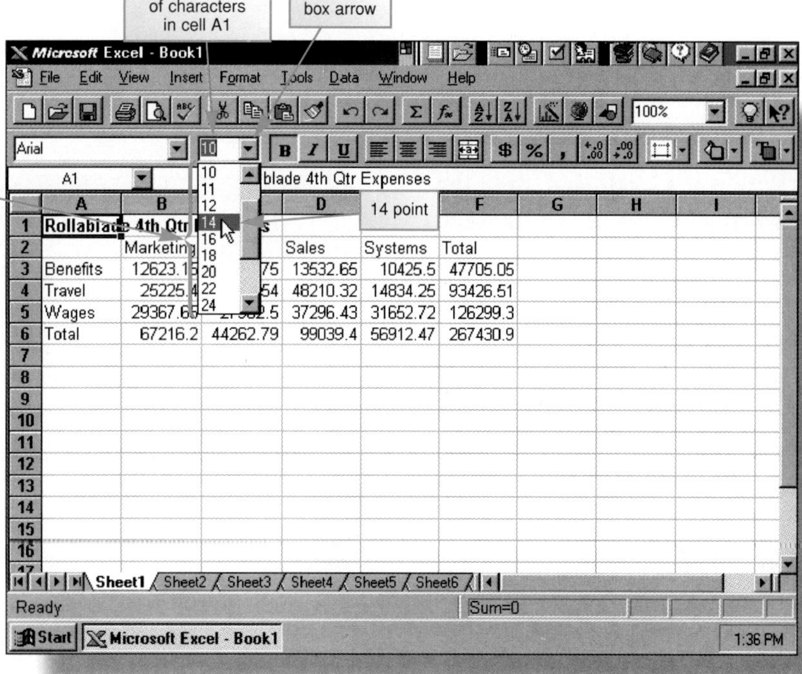

FIGURE 1-38

2. **Click 14.**

   The characters in the worksheet title in cell A1 increase from 10 point to 14 point (Figure 1-39).

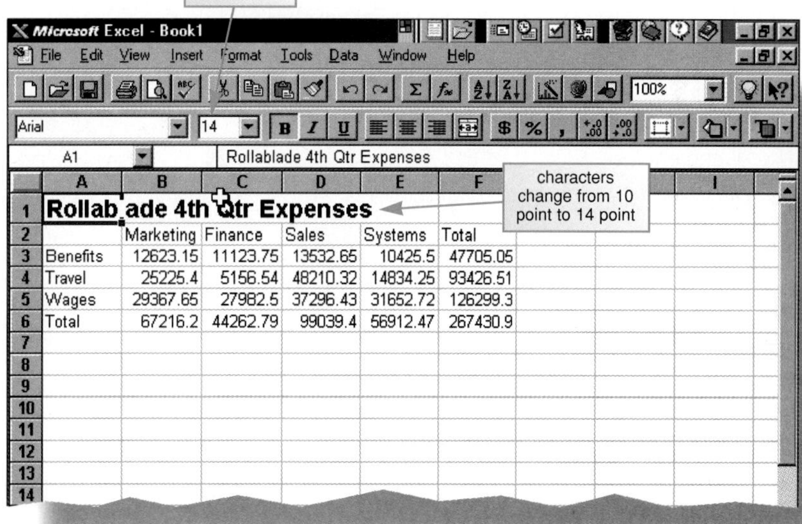

FIGURE 1-39

OtherWays

1. Right-click cell, click Format Cells on shortcut menu, click Font tab, select font size, click OK button
2. On Format menu click Cells, click Font tab, select font size, click OK button

The final step in formatting the worksheet title is to center it over columns A through F.

Steps To Center a Cell's Contents Across Columns

1 **With cell A1 selected, drag the block plus sign to the rightmost cell (F1) in the range over which to center.**

When you drag the mouse pointer over the range A1:F1, Excel highlights the cells (Figure 1-40).

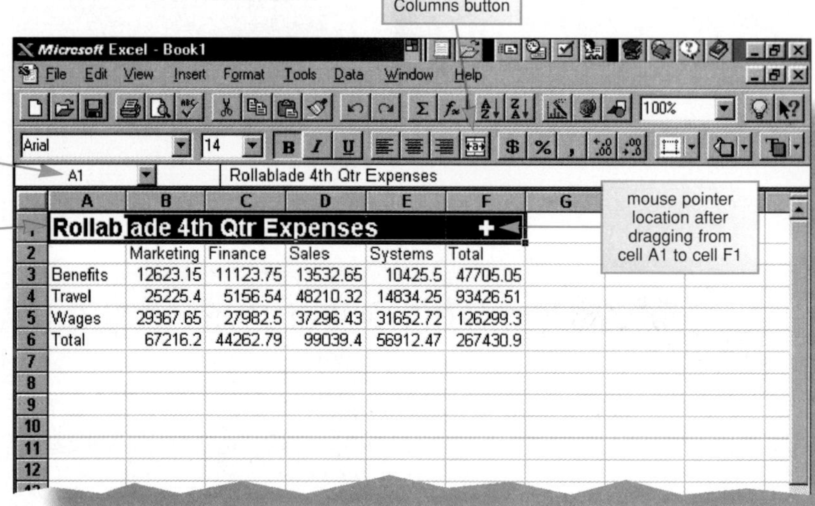

FIGURE 1-40

2 **Click the Center Across Columns button on the Formatting toolbar.**

Excel centers the contents of cell A1 across columns A through F (Figure 1-41). For the Center Across Columns button to work properly, all the cells except the leftmost cell in the range of cells must be empty.

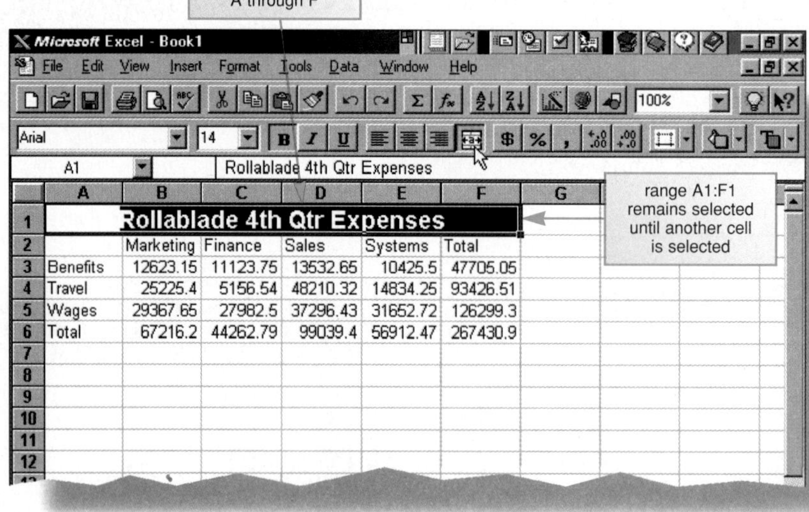

FIGURE 1-41

OtherWays

1. Right-click cell, click Format Cells on shortcut menu, click Alignment tab, click Center across selection, click OK button
2. On Format menu click Cells, click Font tab, click Alignment tab, click Center across selection, click OK button

To remove the selection from range A1:F1, select any cell in the worksheet. Most formats assigned to a cell will display on the Formatting toolbar when the cell is selected. For example, the font type and font size display in their appropriate boxes. Recessed buttons indicate an assigned format. To determine if less frequently used formats are assigned to a cell, point to the cell and right-click. Next, click **Format cells**, and then click each of the tabs in the **Format Cells dialog box**.

Using AutoFormat to Format the Body of a Worksheet

Excel has several customized format styles called **table formats** that allow you to format the body of the worksheet. The table formats can be used to give your worksheet a professional appearance. Follow these steps to automatically format the range A2:F6 in the expense worksheet using **AutoFormat** on the Format menu.

To Use AutoFormat to Format the Body of a Worksheet

1 Select cell A2, the upper left corner cell of the rectangular range to format (Figure 1-42).

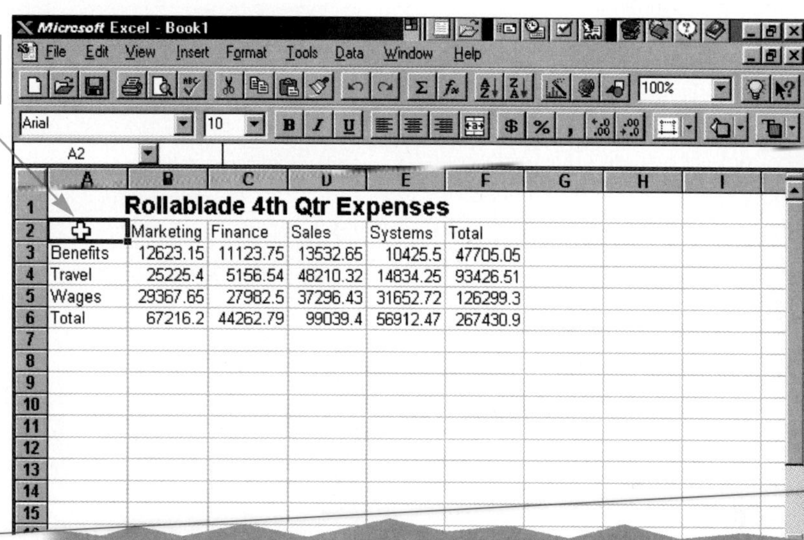

FIGURE 1-42

2 Drag the mouse pointer to cell F6, the lower right corner cell of the range to format.

Excel highlights the range to format (Figure 1-43).

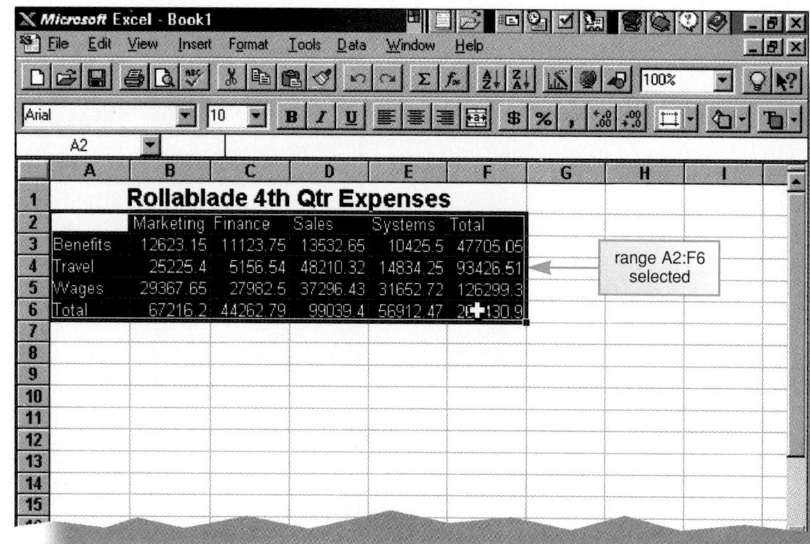

FIGURE 1-43

3 **Click Format on the menu bar and point to AutoFormat.**

The Format menu displays (Figure 1-44).

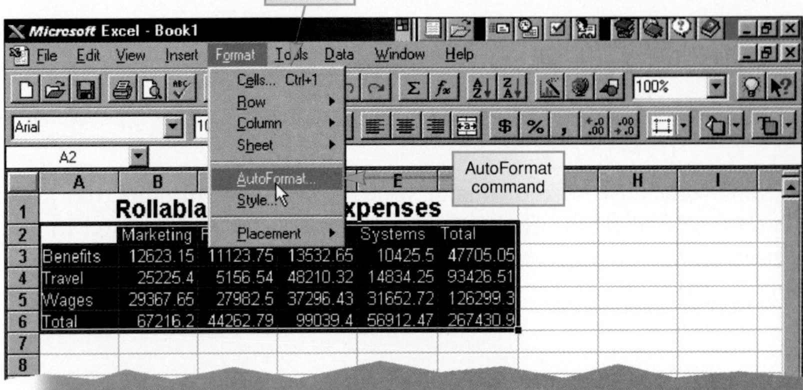

FIGURE 1-44

4 **Click AutoFormat.**

Excel displays the ***AutoFormat dialog box*** *(Figure 1-45). On the left side of the dialog box is the* ***Table Format list box*** *with the Table Format name, Simple, highlighted. In the Sample area of the dialog box is a sample of the format that corresponds to the highlighted Table Format name, Simple.*

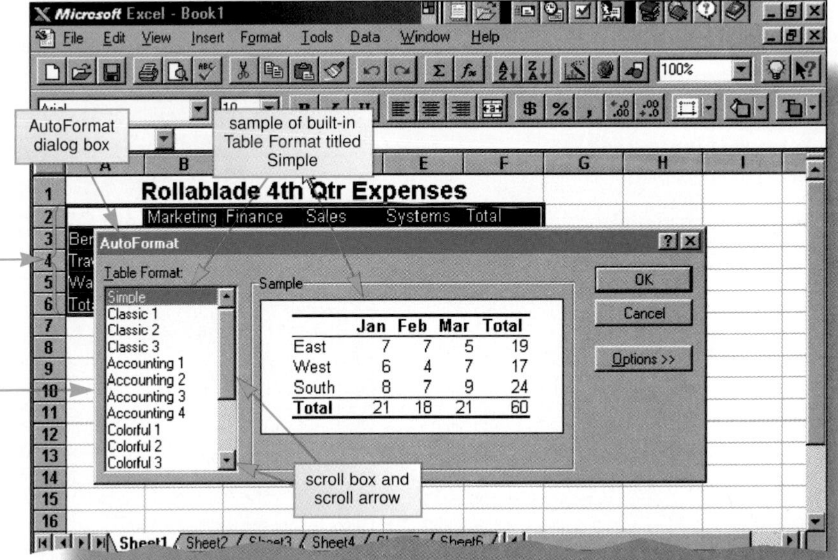

FIGURE 1-45

5 **Click Accounting 3 in the Table Format list box.**

The sample in the dialog box shows the Accounting 3 format selected (Figure 1-46).

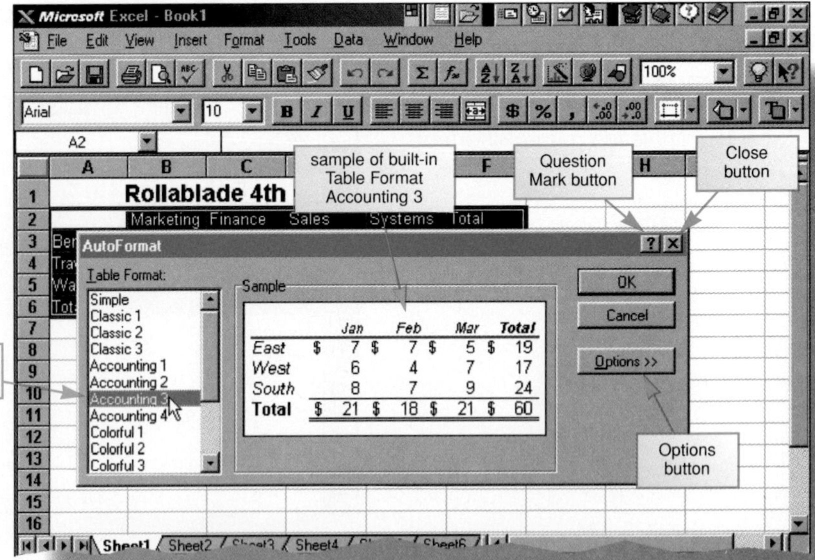

FIGURE 1-46

6 Click the OK button in the AutoFormat dialog box. Select cell H6 to deselect the range A2:F6.

Excel displays the worksheet with the range A2:F6 using the customized format, Accounting 3 (Figure 1-47).

	A	B	C	D	E	F
1		Rollablade 4th Qtr Expenses				
2		Marketing	Finance	Sales	Systems	Total
3	Benefits	$12,623.15	$11,123.75	$13,532.65	$10,425.50	$ 47,705.05
4	Travel	25,225.40	5,156.54	48,210.32	14,834.25	93,426.51
5	Wages	29,367.65	27,982.50	37,296.43	31,652.72	126,299.30
6	Total	$67,216.20	$44,262.79	$99,039.40	$56,912.47	$267,430.86

range A2:F6 formatted

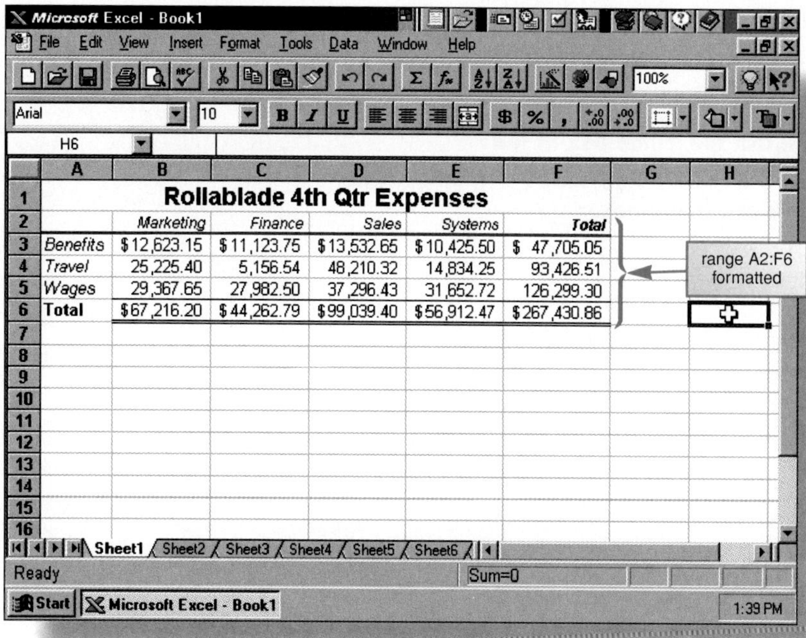

FIGURE 1-47

Excel provides seventeen customized format styles from which to choose. Each format style has different characteristics. The format characteristics associated with the customized format, Accounting 3 (Figure 1-47), include right-justification of column titles, numeric values displayed as dollars and cents, comma placement, numbers aligned on the decimal point, dollar signs in the first row of numbers and in the total row, and top and bottom borders emphasized. The width of column A has also been reduced so that the longest row title, Benefits, just fits in the column.

Notice the buttons in the AutoFormat dialog box in Figure 1-46. On the rightmost side of the title bar is the Close button. Use the **Close button** to terminate current activity without making changes. You can also use the **Cancel button** for this purpose. Use the **Question Mark button** to obtain Help on any box or button located in the dialog box. The **Options button** allows you to be selective in the formats assigned by the customized format.

The worksheet is now complete. The next step is to chart the expenses for the four departments. To create the chart, the active cell must be cell A2, the cell in the upper left corner of the range to chart. To select cell A2, you can move the mouse pointer to it and click. This is the procedure used in previous examples. You can also use the Name box to select a cell as described in the next section.

More *About* Customizing the AutoFormat

The Options button on the right side of the AutoFormat dialog box in Figure 1-46 allows you to modify the formats associated with any of the customized formats. If you assign two different customized formats to a range, Excel will add the formats of the second one to the formats of the first. Thus, if you decide to change a customized format, first select the range, then click Style on the Format menu. Then, with Normal style selected, click the OK button. This will remove all assigned formats except for the column-width changes. Next, assign the new customized format using the AutoFormat on the Format menu. Rather than using the Style command on the Format menu, you can also select the range and click Clear on the Edit menu, then click Formats on the submenu.

Using the Name Box to Select a Cell

The **Name box** is located on the left side of the formula bar. To select any cell, click the Name box and enter the cell reference of the cell you want to select. The following steps show how to select cell A2.

To Use the Name Box to Select a Cell

1 **Click the Name box in the formula bar. Type** a2 **in the Name box.**

Even though cell H6 is the active cell, the Name box displays the typed cell reference a2 (Figure 1-48).

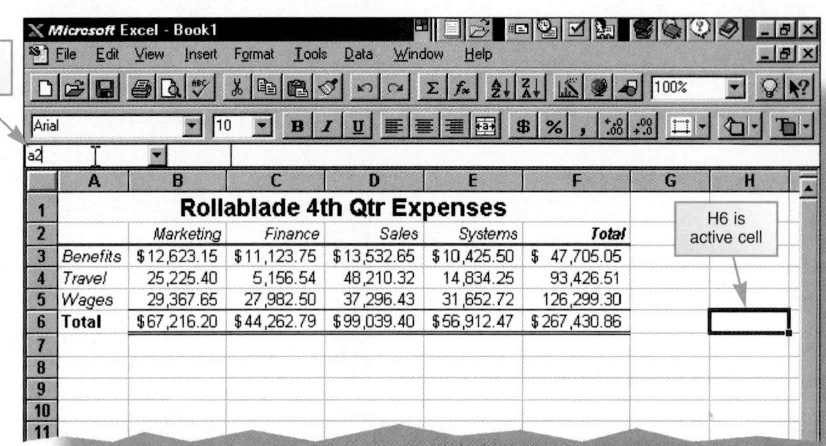

FIGURE 1-48

2 **Press the ENTER key.**

Excel changes the active cell from cell H6 to cell A2 (Figure 1-49).

A2 is active cell

	A	B	C	D	E	F	G	H
1		Rollablade 4th Qtr Expenses						
2		*Marketing*	*Finance*	*Sales*	*Systems*	***Total***		
3	*Benefits*	$12,623.15	$11,123.75	$13,532.65	$10,425.50	$ 47,705.05		
4	*Travel*	25,225.40	5,156.54	48,210.32	14,834.25	93,426.51		
5	*Wages*	29,367.65	27,982.50	37,296.43	31,652.72	126,299.30		
6	**Total**	$67,216.20	$44,262.79	$99,039.40	$56,912.47	$267,430.86		

FIGURE 1-49

More *About* **the Name Box**

If you have cells in a worksheet that you find yourself continuously selecting for one reason or another, you can select the cells one at a time and type in a name for each in the Name Box, such as Company Total for cell F6 in Figure 1-49. Then when you want to select one of the named cells, click the Name Box arrow and click the cell name in the Name Box drop-down list box.

As you will see in later projects, besides using the Name box to select any cell, you can also use it to assign names to a cell or range of cells.

Excel supports several additional ways to select a cell, as summarized in Table 1-3 at the top of the next page.

Adding a 3-D Column Chart to the Worksheet

The 3-D column chart drawn by Excel in this project is based on the data in the expense worksheet (Figure 1-50). It is called an **embedded chart** because it is drawn on the same worksheet.

Table 1-3

KEY, NAME, BOX, OR COMMAND	FUNCTION
ALT+PAGE DOWN	Selects the cell one screenful to the right and moves the window accordingly.
ALT+PAGE UP	Selects the cell one screenful to the left and moves the window accordingly.
ARROW	Selects the adjacent cell in the direction of the arrow on the key.
CTRL+ARROW	Selects the border cell of the worksheet in combination with the arrow keys and moves the window accordingly. For example, to select the rightmost cell in the row that contains the active cell, press CTRL+RIGHT ARROW. You can also press the END key, release it, and then press the arrow key to accomplish the same task.
CTRL+HOME	Selects cell A1 or the cell below and to the right of frozen titles and moves the window to the upper left corner of the worksheet.
HOME	Selects the cell at the beginning of the row that contains the active cell and moves the window accordingly.
PAGE DOWN	Selects the cell down one window from the active cell and moves the window accordingly.
PAGE UP	Selects the cell up one window from the active cell and moves the window accordingly.
Name box	Selects the cell in the worksheet that corresponds to the cell reference you enter in the Name box.
Find command on Edit menu	Finds and selects a cell in the worksheet with specific contents that you enter in the Find dialog box. If necessary, Excel moves the window to display the cell. You can press SHIFT+F5 to display the Find dialog box.
F5 or Goto command on Edit menu	Selects the cell in the worksheet that corresponds to the cell reference you enter in the Goto dialog box and moves the window accordingly.

For Marketing, the light blue column represents the quarterly Benefits expense ($12,623.15), the purple column represents the quarterly traveling expense ($25,225.40), and the light yellow column represents the quarterly wage expense ($29,367.20). For Finance, Sales, and Systems, the same color columns represent the comparable expenses. Notice in this chart that the totals from the worksheet are not represented because the totals were not in the range specified for charting.

Excel derives the scale along the vertical axis (also called **y-axis**) of the chart on the basis of the values in the worksheet. For example, no value in the range A2:F5 is less than zero or greater than $50,000.00. It also determines automatically the $10,000.00 increments along the y-axis.

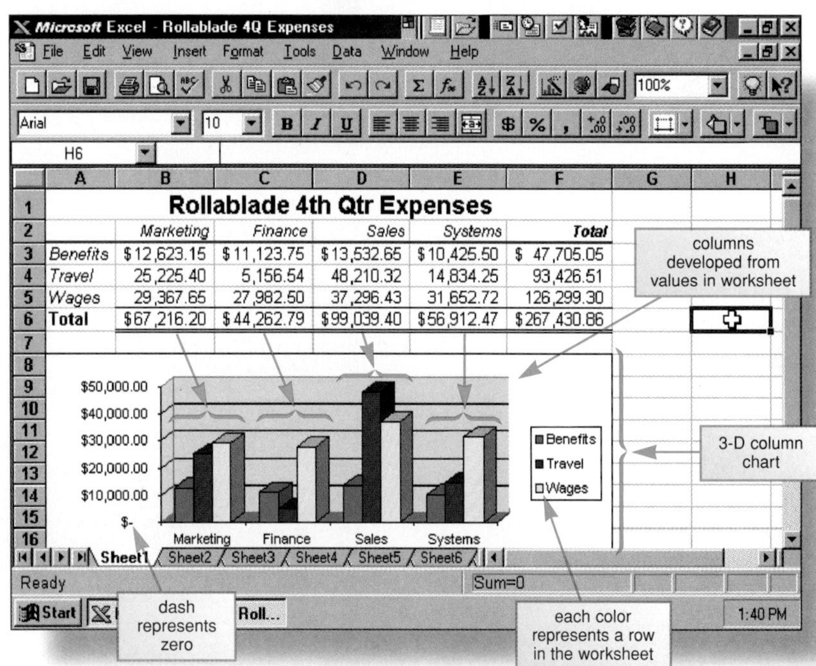

FIGURE 1-50

To draw a chart like the one in Figure 1-50 on the previous page, select the range to chart, click the **ChartWizard button** on the Standard toolbar, and select the area on the worksheet where you want the chart drawn. The area on the worksheet you select to draw the chart is called the **chart location**. In Figure 1-50, the chart is located immediately below the worksheet data. When you determine the location of the chart on the worksheet, you also determine its size by dragging the mouse pointer from the upper left corner of the chart location to the lower right corner of the chart location.

Follow these detailed steps to draw a 3-D column chart that compares the quarterly expenses for the four departments.

Steps To Add a 3-D Column Chart to the Worksheet

1 **With cell A2 selected, position the block plus sign within the cell's border (Figure 1-51).**

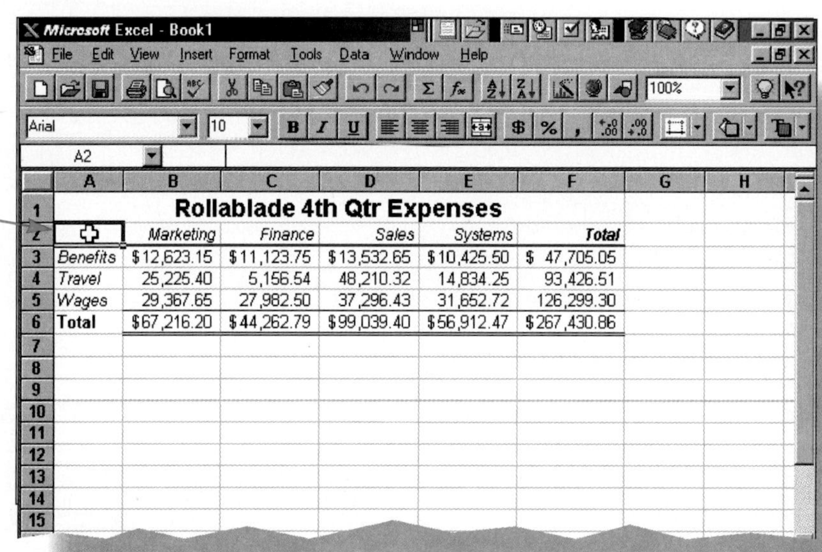

FIGURE 1-51

2 **Drag the mouse pointer to the lower right corner cell (cell E5) of the range to chart.**

Excel highlights the range to chart (Figure 1-52).

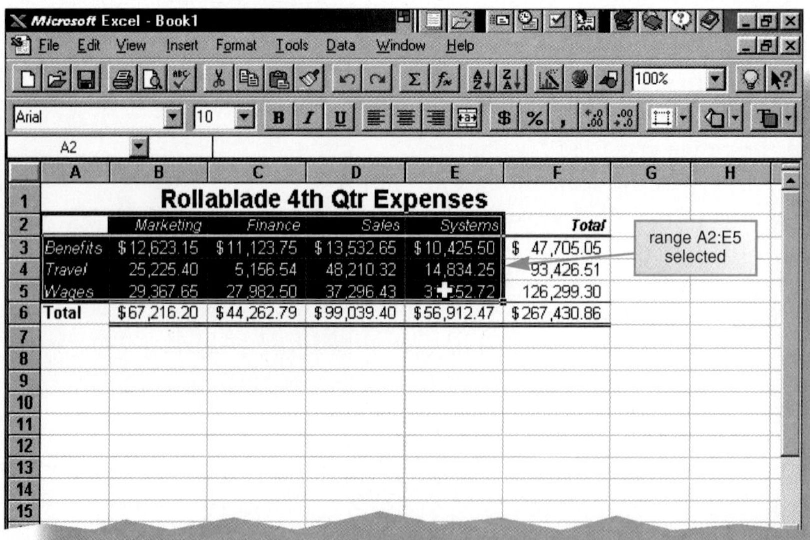

FIGURE 1-52

3 **Click the ChartWizard button on the Standard toolbar and then move the mouse pointer into the window.**

The mouse pointer changes to a cross hair with a chart symbol (Figure 1-53).

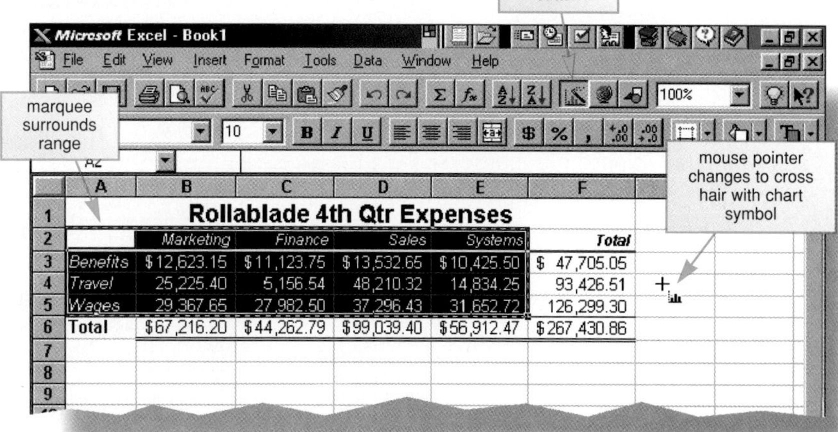

FIGURE 1-53

4 **Move the mouse pointer to the upper left corner of the desired chart location, immediately below the worksheet data (cell A8).**

A marquee surrounds the range to chart A2:E5 and the mouse pointer is in the upper left corner of cell A8. (Figure 1-54).

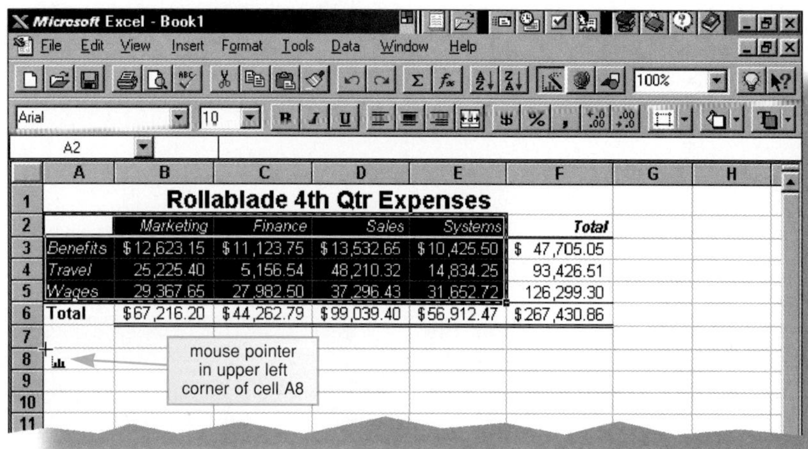

FIGURE 1-54

5 **Drag the mouse pointer to the lower right corner of the chart location (cell F17).**

The mouse pointer is positioned at the lower right corner of cell F17, and the chart location is surrounded by a solid line rectangle (Figure 1-55). You may want to hold down the ALT key while you drag so the chart location snaps to the gridlines.

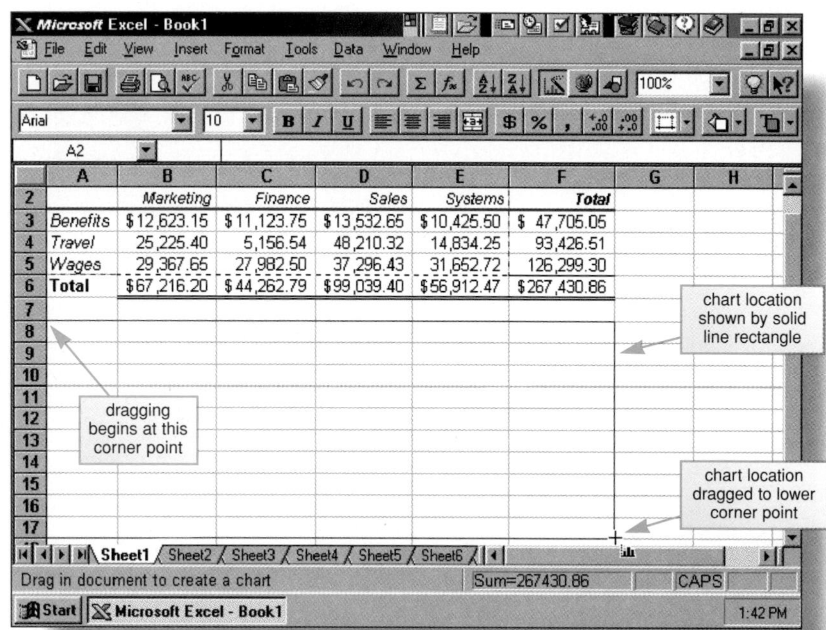

FIGURE 1-55

6 **Release the left mouse button.**

Excel responds by displaying the ***ChartWizard - Step 1 of 5 dialog box*** *when you release the mouse button after selecting the chart location (Figure 1-56).*

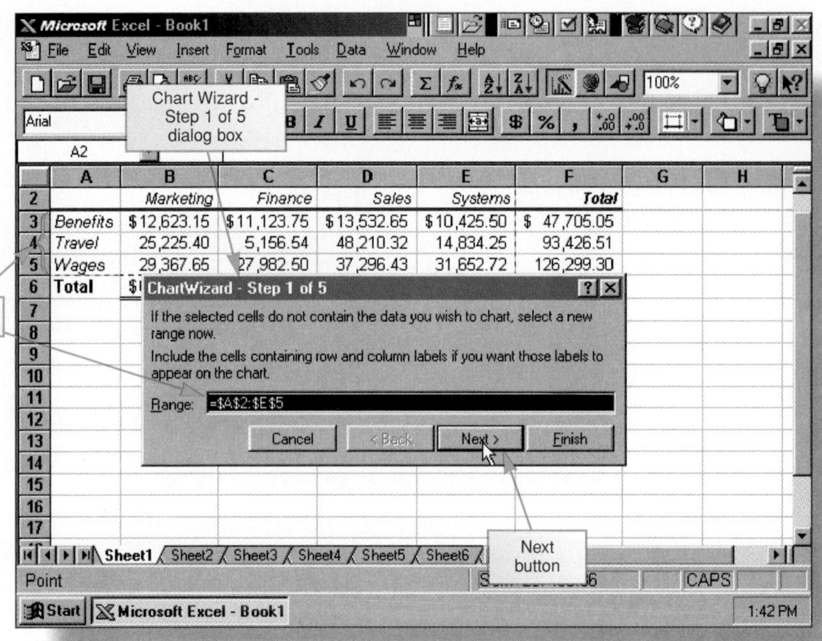

FIGURE 1-56

7 **Click the Next button. When the ChartWizard - Step 2 of 5 dialog box displays, click 3-D Column (column 2, row 3) and then point to the Finish button (Figure 1-57).**

Notice that the dialog box includes the fifteen different chart types from which you can choose.

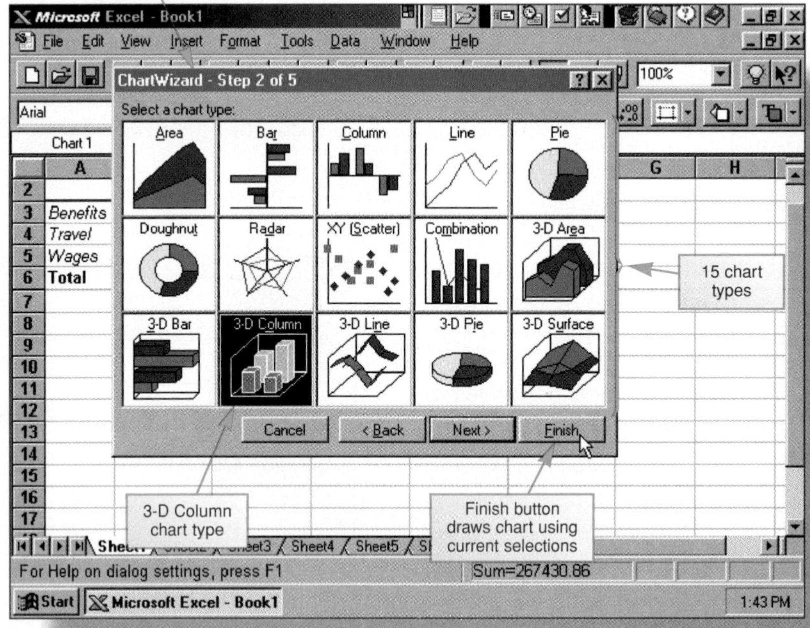

FIGURE 1-57

8 **Click the Finish button.**

Excel draws a 3-D column chart over the chart location comparing the quarterly expenses for the four departments (Figure 1-58). The small **selection squares** *(▪), or* **handles***, on the border of the chart location indicate that the chart is selected. While the chart is selected, you can drag the chart to any location on the worksheet. You can also resize the chart by dragging the handles.*

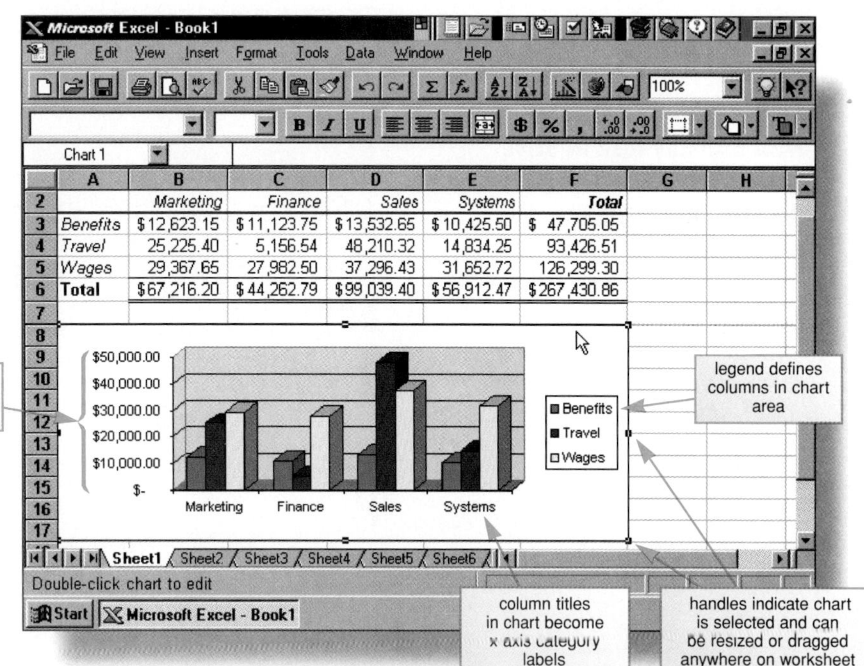

FIGURE 1-58

9 **Select a cell outside the chart location to remove the chart selection and use the vertical scroll bar to display the top of the worksheet.**

OtherWays

1. On Insert menu click Chart, click On This Sheet

The embedded 3-D column chart in Figure 1-58 compares the three quarterly expenses within each department. It also allows you to compare expenses between the departments. Notice that Excel automatically selects the entries in the row at the top of the range (row 2) as the titles for the horizontal axis (also called the **x-axis**) and draws a column for each of the twelve cells containing numbers in the range. The small box to the right of the column chart in Figure 1-58 contains the legend. The **legend** identifies each bar in the chart. Excel automatically selects the leftmost column of the range (column A) as titles within the legend. As indicated earlier, Excel also automatically scales the y-axis on the basis of the magnitude of the numbers in the graph range.

Excel offers 15 different chart types (Figure 1-57). The **default chart type** is the chart Excel draws if you click the Finish button in the first ChartWizard dialog box. When you install Excel on a computer, the default chart type is the two-dimensional column chart.

More About Changing the Chart Type

Excel has more chart types than you can imagine. You can change the embedded chart to one of the other fourteen types by double-clicking the chart location. Once a heavy gray border surrounds the chart location, right-click the chart and right-click Chart Type on the shortcut menu. You can also use the shortcut menu to format the chart to make it look more professional. Subsequent projects will discuss changing charts, sizing charts, adding text to charts, and drawing a chart on a chart sheet.

Saving a Workbook

While you are building a workbook, the computer stores it in main memory. If the computer is turned off or if you lose electrical power, the workbook is lost. Hence, it is mandatory to save on disk any workbook that you will use later. A saved workbook is referred to as a **file** or **workbook**. The steps on the next page illustrate how to save a workbook to drive A using the Save button on the Standard toolbar.

To Save a Workbook

1 **With a floppy disk in drive A, click the Save button on the Standard toolbar.**

Excel responds by displaying the ***Save As dialog box*** *(Figure 1-59). The default folder is My Documents, the default filename is Book1, and the file type is Microsoft Excel Workbook. The buttons next to the Save in drop-down list box are used to select folders and change the display of filenames in the Save As dialog box.*

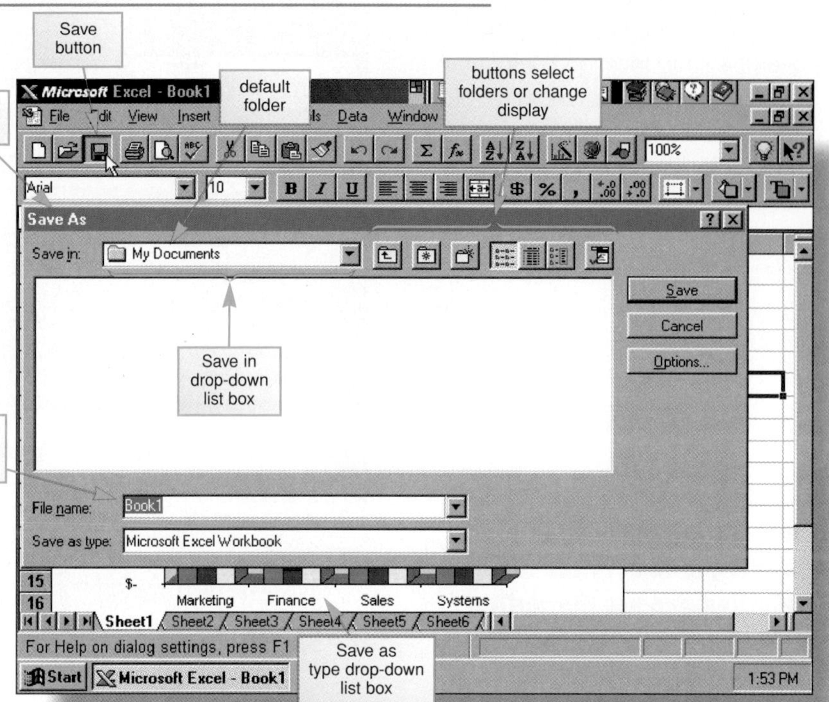

FIGURE 1-59

2 **Type** `Rollablade 4Q Expenses` **in the File name text box.**

The filename Rollablade 4Q Expenses replaces Book1 in the File name text box (Figure 1-60). A ***filename*** *can be up to 255 characters and can include spaces.*

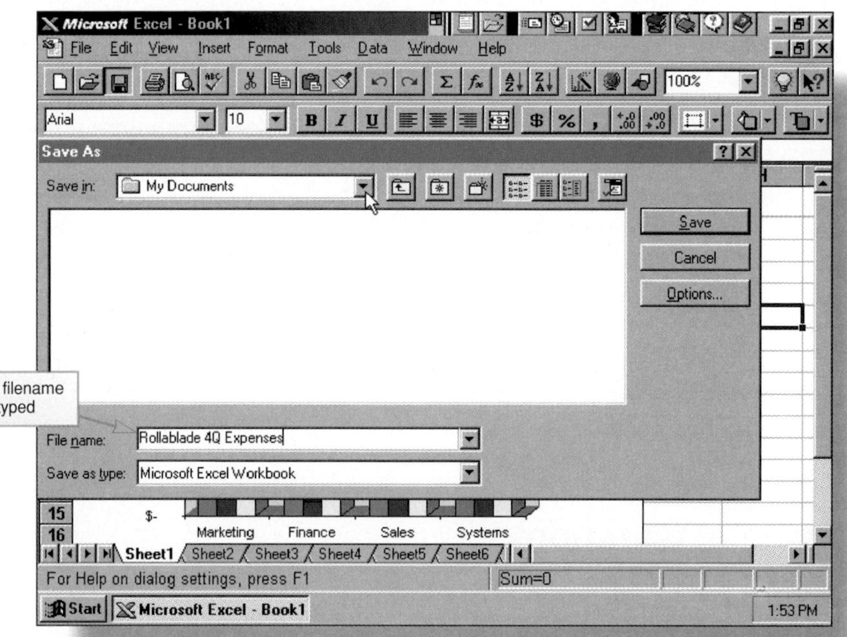

FIGURE 1-60

3 **Click the Save in box arrow and then point to the 3½ Floppy [A:] icon.**

A list of available drives and folders display (Figure 1-61).

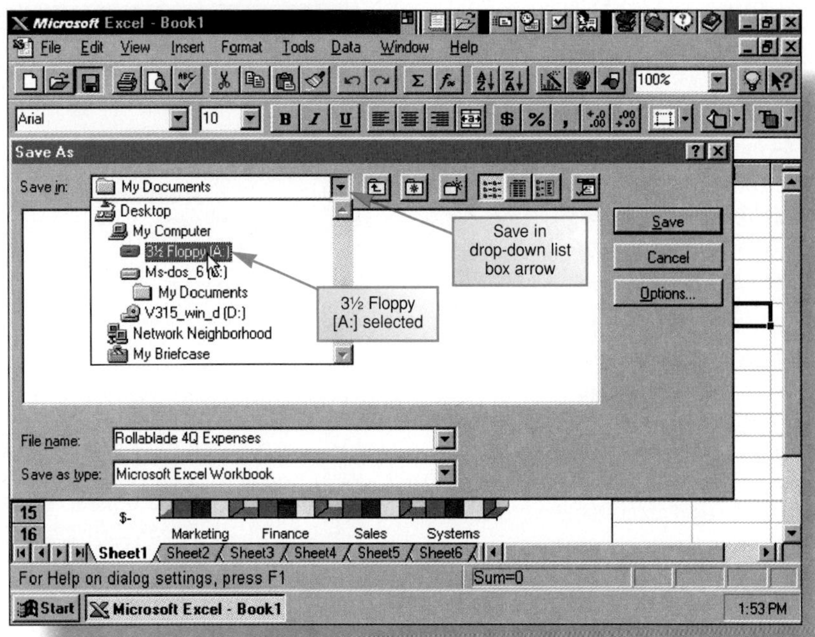

FIGURE 1-61

4 **Click 3½ Floppy [A:] icon and then point to the Save button.**

Drive A becomes the selected drive (Figure 1-62).

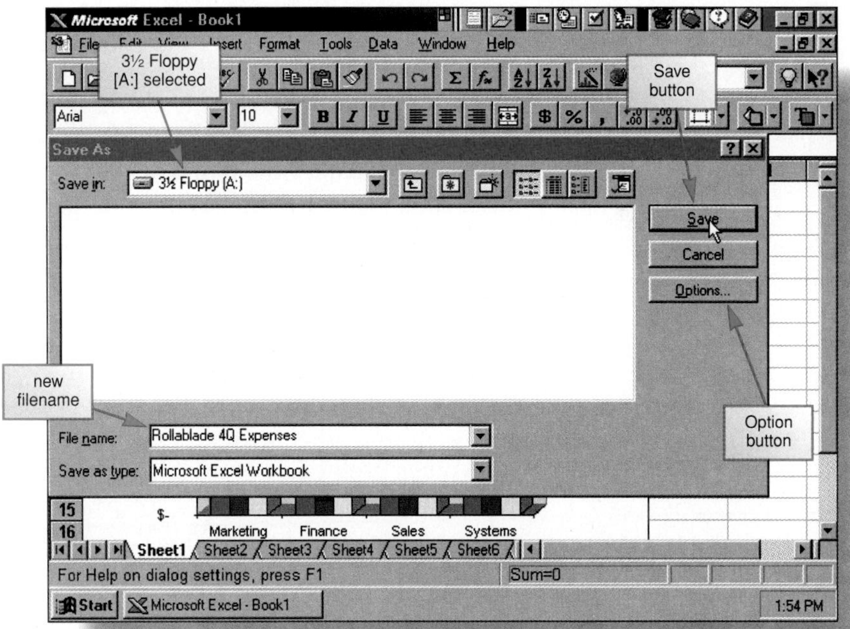

FIGURE 1-62

Click the Save button.

Excel saves the workbook on the floppy disk in drive A using the name Rollablade 4Q Expenses.xls. Excel automatically appends to the filename you entered in Step 2 the extension **.xls**, *which stands for Excel workbook. Although the Rollablade 4th Qtr Expenses workbook is saved on disk, it also remains in main memory and displays on the screen (Figure 1-63). Notice the filename in the title bar.*

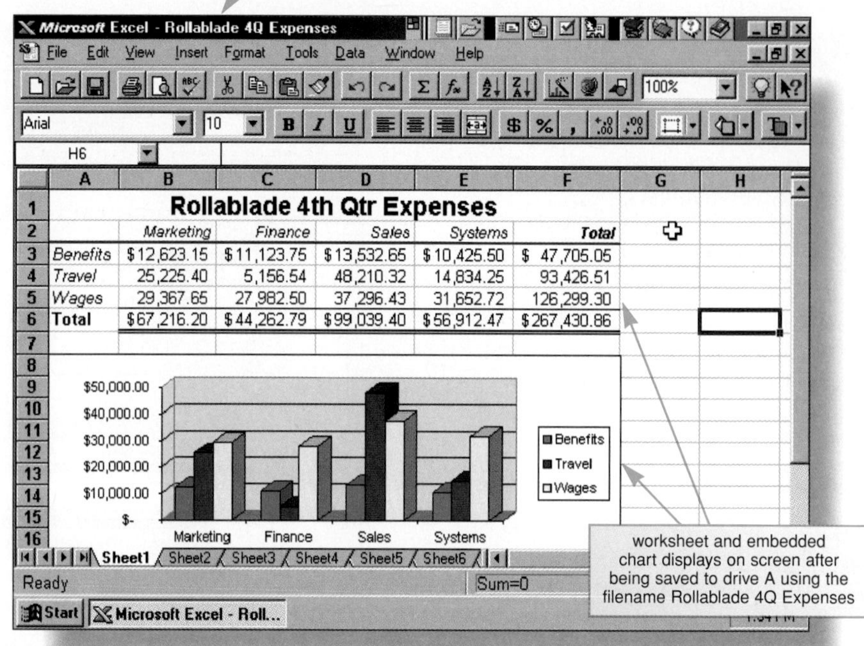

FIGURE 1-63

OtherWays

1. Right-click menu bar, click Save As, type filename, select drive or folder, click OK button
2. On File menu click Save As, type filename, select drive or folder, click OK button
3. Press CTRL+S, type filename, select drive or folder, click OK button

While Excel is saving the workbook, it momentarily changes the word Ready on the status bar to Saving. It also displays a horizontal bar on the status bar indicating the amount of the workbook saved. After the save operation is complete, Excel changes the name of the workbook in the title bar from Book1 to Rollablade 4Q Expenses (Figure 1-63).

The **Options button** in the Save As dialog box, as shown in Figure 1-62, allows you to save a backup copy of the workbook or limit access to the workbook. Saving a **backup workbook** means that each time you save a workbook, Excel copies the current version of the workbook on disk to a file with the same name with an extension of **.bak**. Thus, the second time you save a workbook, and thereafter, you will have two documents on disk with the same name, one with an extension of .xls and the other with an extension of .bak. In the case of a power failure or some other problem, use the (.bak) backup version of the document to restore your work.

You can also use the Options button to assign a password to your document. A password is case-sensitive and can be up to 15 characters long. **Case-sensitive** means Excel can differentiate between uppercase and lowercase letters If you assign a password and forget it, you cannot access the document.

The six buttons at the top of the Save As dialog box (Figure 1-62) and their functions are summarized in Table 1-4.

Table 1-4

BUTTON	FUNCTION
	Displays the contents of the next level up folder.
	Displays the contents of the Favorites folder.
	Creates a new folder.
	Displays filenames in list format with no details.
	Displays filenames in list format with details.
	Displays the properties of the highlighted file.
	Allows you to control settings, such as the sort order of filenames.

Printing the Worksheet

Once you have created the worksheet and saved it on disk, you might want to print it. A printed version of the worksheet is called a **hard copy** or **printout**.

There are several reasons why you would want a printout. First, to present the worksheet and chart to someone who does not have access to your computer, it must be in printed form. In addition, worksheets and charts are often kept for reference by persons other than those who prepare them. In many cases, the worksheets and charts are printed and kept in binders for use by others. This section describes how to print a worksheet and the embedded chart.

More About Printing

Interested in saving trees? Rather than printing a worksheet over and over until it's right, you can preview the printout on your screen, make adjustments to the worksheet, and then print only when it's exactly what you want. The Print Preview button is immediately to the right of the Print button on the Standard toolbar. Clicking it shows a perfect image on the screen of how the printout will appear on the printer. And each time you preview, rather than print, you save paper destined for the waste paper basket, which in turn saves trees.

Steps To Print a Worksheet

1. **Ready the printer according to the printer instructions.**

2. **Point to the Print button on the Standard toolbar (Figure 1-64).**

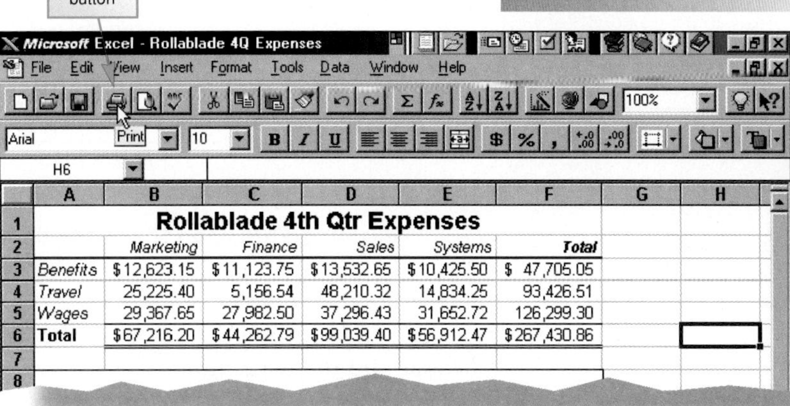

FIGURE 1-64

3. **Click the Print button.**

   Excel displays the *Printing dialog box* (Figure 1-65) that allows you to cancel the print job at any time while the system is internally creating the worksheet and chart image to send to the printer. When the Printing dialog box disappears, the printing begins. Also, notice in Figure 1-65, the vertical dotted line along the right side of the worksheet. The dotted line indicates the right border of the area being printed.

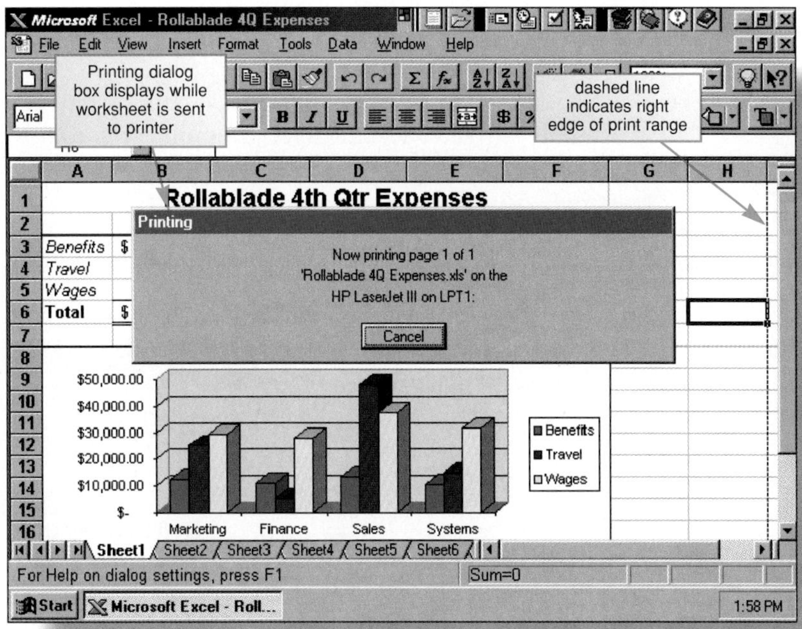

FIGURE 1-65

4 **When the printer stops, retrieve the printout (Figure 1-66).**

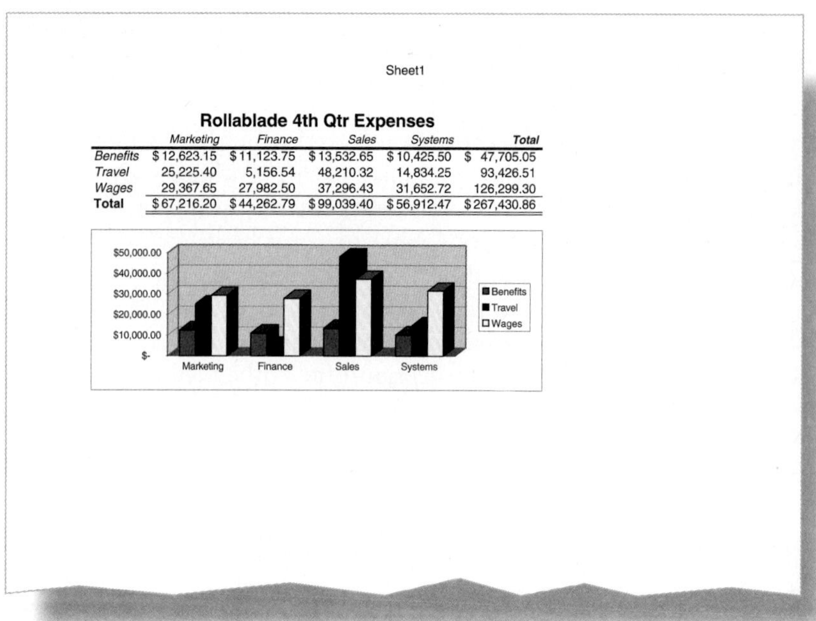

	Marketing	Finance	Sales	Systems	Total
Benefits	$ 12,623.15	$ 11,123.75	$ 13,532.65	$ 10,425.50	$ 47,705.05
Travel	25,225.40	5,156.54	48,210.32	14,834.25	93,426.51
Wages	29,367.65	27,982.50	37,296.43	31,652.72	126,299.30
Total	$ 67,216.20	$ 44,262.79	$ 99,039.40	$ 56,912.47	$ 267,430.86

FIGURE 1-66

OtherWays

1. Right-click menu bar, click Print, click OK button
2. On File menu click Print, click OK button
3. Press CTRL+P, click OK button

Notice in Figure 1-66 that Excel adds a header. A **header** is a line of text that prints at the top of each page. Although not shown in Figure 1-66, Excel also adds a footer. A **footer** is a line of text that prints at the bottom of each page. By default, Excel prints the name on the worksheet tab at the top of the screen as the header and the page number as the footer.

In Project 2, you will learn how to preview the printout on your screen before printing and how to print a selected range in a worksheet.

Exiting Excel

After you build, save, and print the worksheet and chart, Project 1 is complete. To exit Excel, complete the following steps.

Steps To Exit Excel

1 **Point to the Close button on the right side of the title bar (Figure 1-67).**

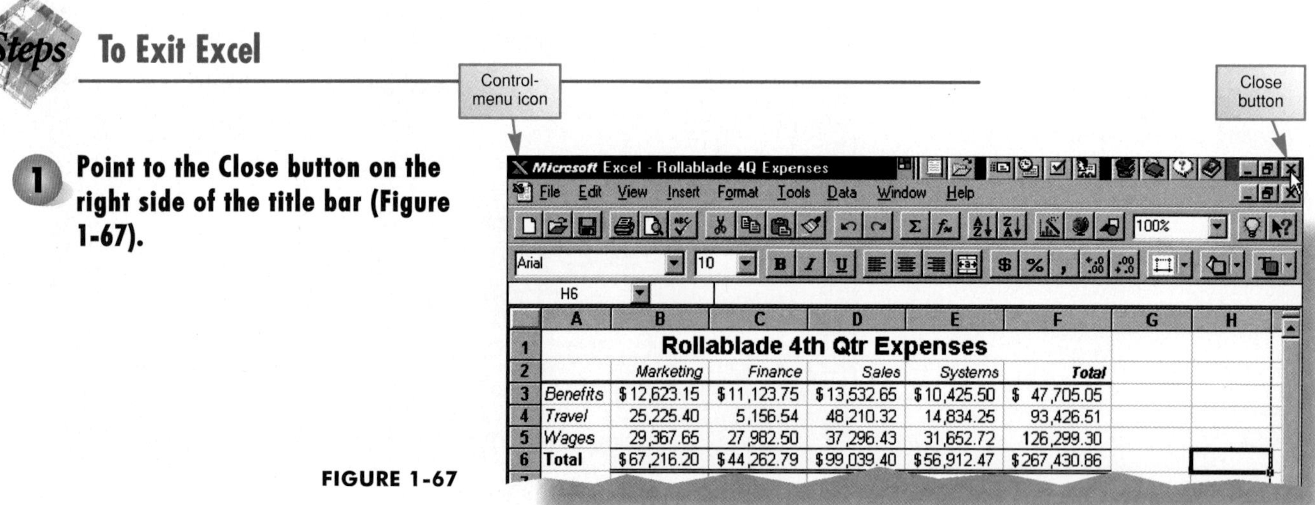

	A	B	C	D	E	F	G	H
1		Rollablade 4th Qtr Expenses						
2		Marketing	Finance	Sales	Systems	Total		
3	Benefits	$ 12,623.15	$ 11,123.75	$ 13,532.65	$ 10,425.50	$ 47,705.05		
4	Travel	25,225.40	5,156.54	48,210.32	14,834.25	93,426.51		
5	Wages	29,367.65	27,982.50	37,296.43	31,652.72	126,299.30		
6	Total	$ 67,216.20	$ 44,262.79	$ 99,039.40	$ 56,912.47	$ 267,430.86		

FIGURE 1-67

2 Click the Close button.

*If you made changes to the workbook, Excel displays the question, "Save changes in 'Rollablade 4Q Expenses.xls'?" in the **Microsoft Excel dialog box** (Figure 1-68). Click the Yes button to save the changes before exiting Excel. Click the No button to exit Excel without saving the changes. Click the Cancel button to terminate the Exit command and return to the worksheet.*

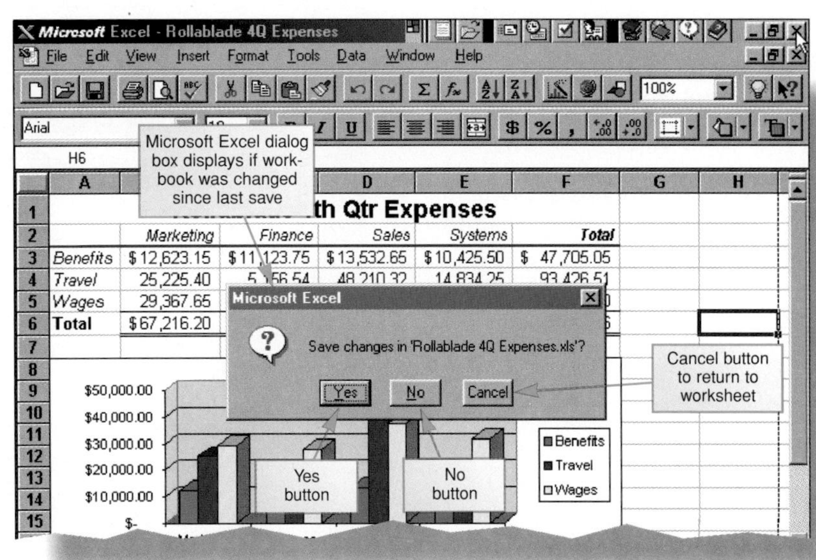

FIGURE 1-68

OtherWays

1. Double-click Control-menu icon
2. Right-click Microsoft Excel taskbar button on taskbar, click Close
3. On File menu click Exit

Starting Excel and Opening a Workbook

Once you have created and saved a workbook, often you will have reason to retrieve it from disk. For example, you might want to enter revised data, review the calculations on the worksheet, or add more data to it. The following steps assume Excel is not running.

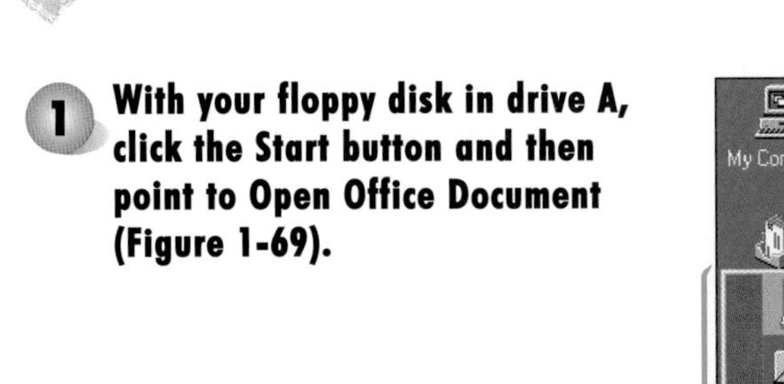

Steps To Start Excel and Open a Workbook

1 With your floppy disk in drive A, click the Start button and then point to Open Office Document (Figure 1-69).

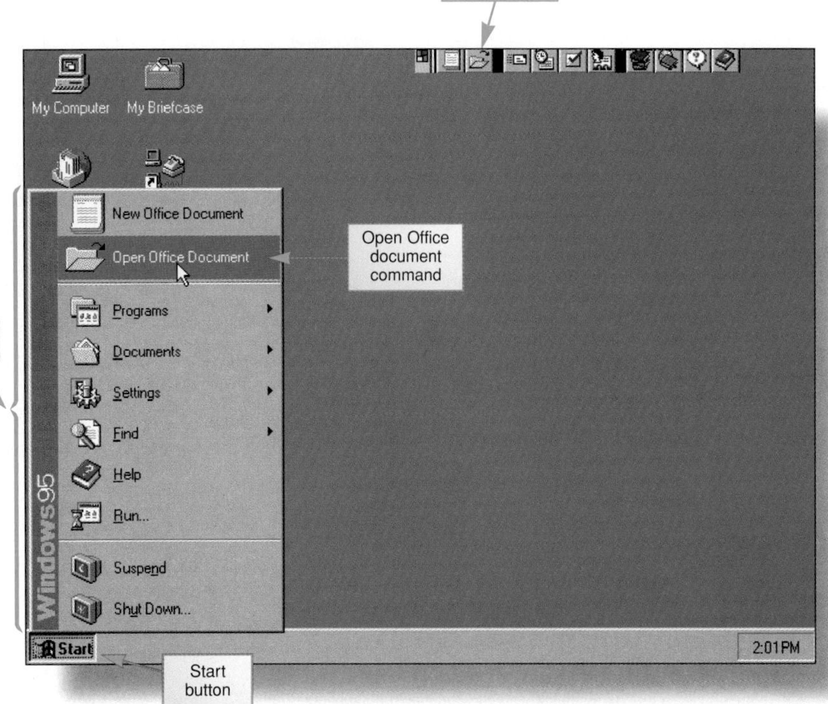

FIGURE 1-69

2 **Click Open Office Document. If necessary, click the Look in box arrow and then double-click the 3½ Floppy [A:] icon.**

The Open dialog box *displays (Figure 1-70).*

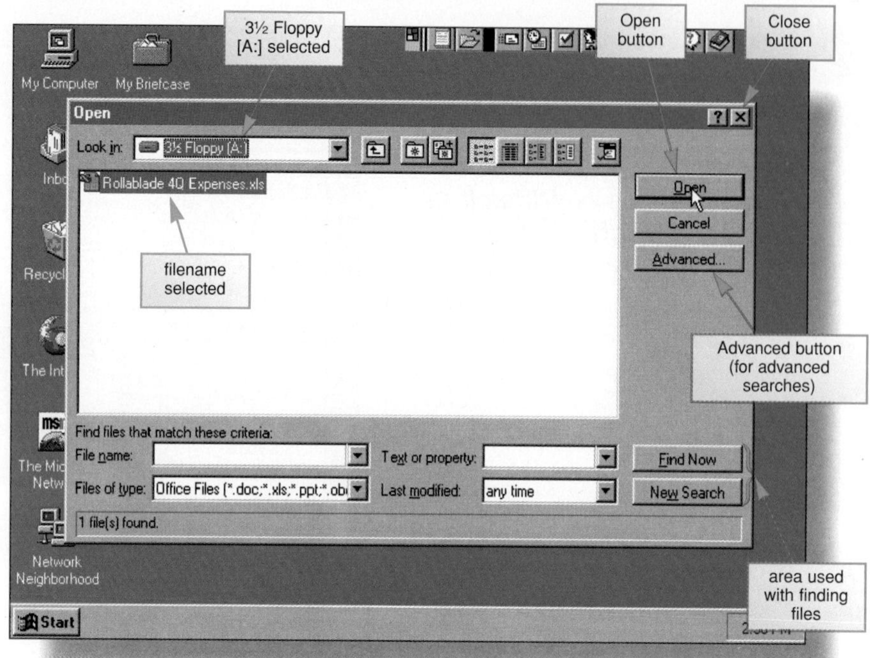

FIGURE 1-70

3 **Double-click the filename Rollablade 4Q Expenses.**

Excel starts and opens the document Rollablade 4Q Expenses.xls from drive A, and displays it on the screen (Figure 1-71). An alternative to double-clicking the filename is to click the filename and then click the Open button.

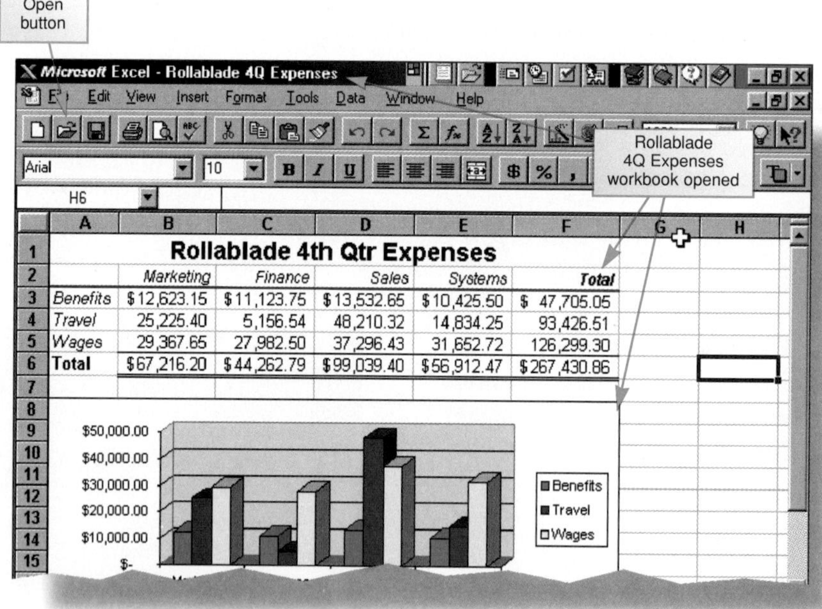

FIGURE 1-71

OtherWays

1. Double-click My Computer, click drive, click folder, double-click workbook icon
2. On Microsoft Office Shortcut Bar, click Open a Document button, select drive or folder, double-click filename
3. Click Start button, click Programs, click Microsoft Excel, click Open button on Standard toolbar, select drive or folder, double-click filename

AutoCalculate

You can easily check a total of the numbers in a range by using the AutoCalculate area on the status bar (see Figure 1-72). All you need do is select the range of cells containing the numbers you want to total. Next, point to the AutoCalculate area and right-click to display the shortcut menu. The six totals on the AutoCalculate shortcut menu (Figure 1-72) are described in Table 1-5.

More About Excel's Compatibility with Other Software Products

Do you have files that were created using another software package? Excel has the capability to save or open Lotus 1-2-3, Quattro Pro, or dBASE files. It's easy. All you have to do is select the file type on the Save As or Open dialog boxes.

Table 1-5

TOTAL	FUNCTION
Average	Displays the average of the numbers in the selected range.
Count	Displays the number of nonblank cells in the selected range.
Count Nums	Displays the number of cells containing numbers in the selected range.
Max	Displays the greatest value in the selected range.
Min	Displays the least value in the selected range.
Sum	Displays the sum of the numbers in the selected range.

The following steps show how to display the average of the Benefits expenses in the range B3:E3.

Steps To Use the AutoCalculate Area to Determine an Average

1 Select the range B3:E3. Point to the AutoCalculate area on the status bar and then right-click.

As shown in Figure 1-72, the sum of the numbers in the range B3:E3 displays ($47,705.05) because Sum is active in the AutoCalculate area (you may see a total other than the Sum on your screen). The shortcut menu listing the various types of totals displays next to the AutoCalculate area.

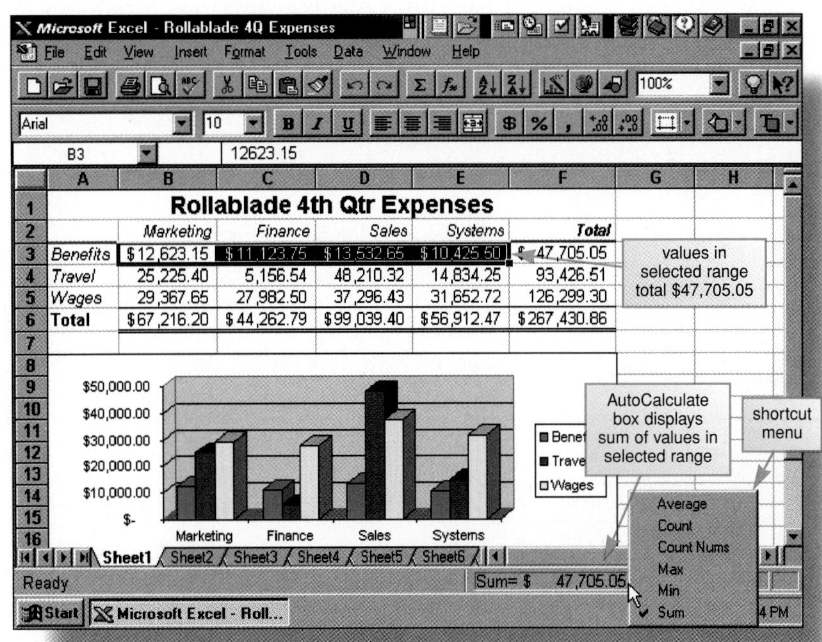

FIGURE 1-72

2 Right-click Average on the shortcut menu.

The average of the numbers in the range B3:E3 displays in the AutoCalculate area (Figure 1-73).

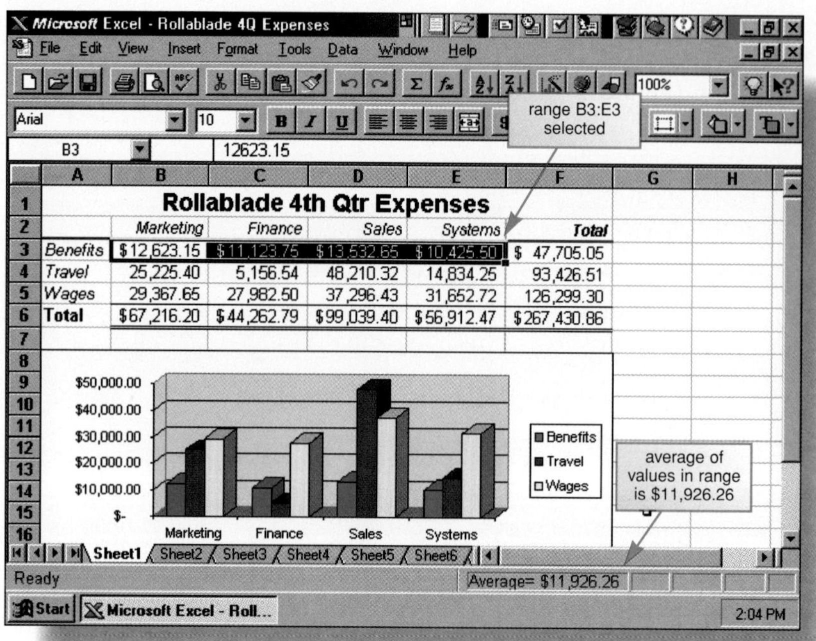

FIGURE 1-73

To change to any one of the other five totals for the range B3:E3, right-click the AutoCalculate area. Then right-click the desired total. You can see in Figure 1-72 on the previous page that a check mark to the left of the active total (Sum) indicates this total displays. Before continuing, change the total in the AutoCalculate area to Sum by pointing to it, right-clicking, and then clicking Sum on the shortcut menu.

More About Correcting Errors

Learning how to correct errors in a worksheet is critical to becoming proficient in Excel. Thus, carefully review in this section how to correct errors prior to entering data in a cell, how to do in-cell editing, how to undo the last entry, and how to clear cells.

Correcting Errors

Several methods are available for correcting errors on a worksheet. The one you choose will depend on the severity of the error and whether you notice it while typing the data in the formula bar or after you have entered the incorrect data into the cell.

Correcting Errors Prior to Entering Data into a Cell

If you notice an error prior to entering data into a cell, use one of the following:

1. Press the BACKSPACE key to erase the portion in error and then type the correct characters; or
2. If the error is too severe, click the cancel box or press the ESC key to erase the entire entry in the formula bar and then reenter the data from the beginning.

In-Cell Editing

If you find an error in the worksheet after entering the data, you can correct the error in one of two ways:

1. If the entry is short, select the cell, retype the entry correctly, and click the enter box or press the ENTER key. The new entry will replace the old entry.
2. If the entry in the cell is long and the errors are minor, the **Edit mode** may be a better choice. Use the Edit mode as described below:
   a. Double-click the cell containing the error. Excel switches to Edit mode, the active cell contents display in the formula bar, and a flashing insertion point appears in the active cell (Figure 1-74). This editing procedure is called **in-cell editing** because you can edit the contents directly in the cell. The active cell contents also display in the formula bar.
   b. Make your changes, as specified below:
      (1) To insert between two characters, place the insertion point between the two characters and begin typing. Excel inserts the new characters at the location of the insertion point.
      (2) To delete a character in the cell, move the insertion point to the left of the character you want to delete and press the **DELETE key**, or place the insertion point to the right of the character you want to delete and press the **BACKSPACE key**. You can also use the mouse to drag over the character or adjacent characters to delete and press the DELETE key or click the Cut button on the Standard toolbar.

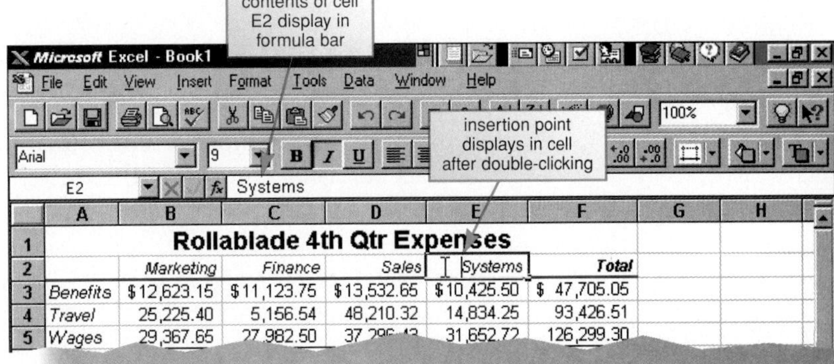

FIGURE 1-74

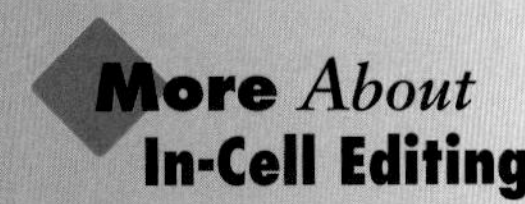

More *About* In-Cell Editing

An alternative to double-clicking the cell to edit is to select the cell and press function key F2.

More *About* Editing the Contents of a Cell

Rather than in-cell editing, you can select the cell and click in the formula bar to edit the contents.

When you are finished editing an entry, click the enter box or press the ENTER key.

When Excel enters the Edit mode, the keyboard is usually in **Insert mode**. In Insert mode, as you type a character, Excel inserts the character and moves all characters to the right of the typed character one position to the right. You can change to **Overtype mode** by pressing the **INSERT key**. In Overtype mode, Excel overtypes the character to the right of the insertion point. The INSERT key toggles the keyboard between Insert mode and Overtype mode.

While in Edit mode, you may have occasion to move the insertion point to various points in the cell, select portions of the data in the cell, or switch from inserting characters to overtyping characters. Table 1-6 summarizes the most common tasks used during in-cell editing.

Table 1-6

TASK	MOUSE	KEYBOARD
Delete selected characters	Click the Cut button on the Standard toolbar	Press DELETE
Highlight one or more adjacent characters	Drag the mouse pointer over the adjacent characters	Press SHIFT+RIGHT ARROW or SHIFT+LEFT ARROW
Move the insertion point anywhere in a cell	Click the character at the appropriate position	Press RIGHT ARROW or LEFT ARROW
Move the insertion point to the beginning of data in a cell	Point to the left of the first character and click	Press HOME
Move the insertion point to the end of data in a cell	Point to the right of the last character and click	Press END
Select all data in a cell	Double-click cell with the insertion point in the cell	
Toggle between Insert and Overtype modes		Press INSERT

Undoing the Last Entry

Excel provides an **Undo button** on the Standard toolbar (Figure 1-75) that you can use to erase the most recent cell entry. Thus, if you enter incorrect data in a cell, click the Undo button and Excel changes the cell contents to what they were prior to entering the incorrect data.

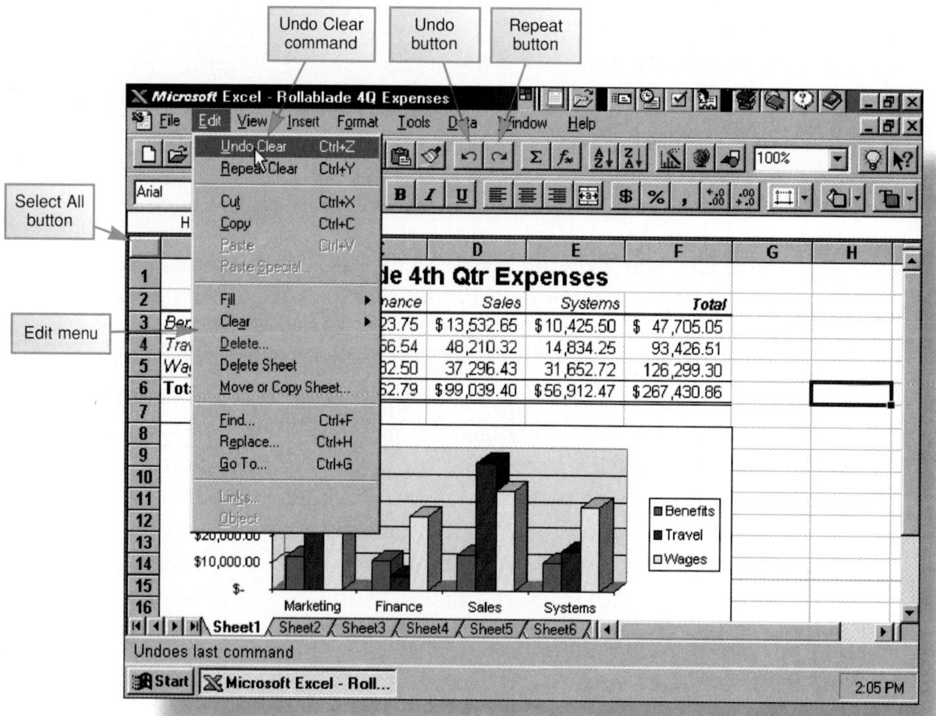

FIGURE 1-75

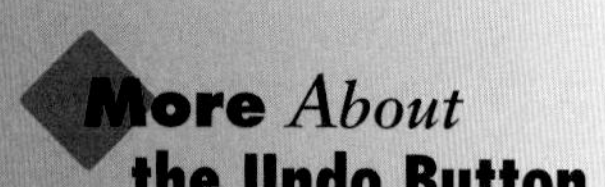

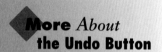

More About the Undo Button

The Undo button can undo more complicated worksheet activities than removing the latest entry from a cell. For example, most commands you issue can be undone if you click the Undo button before making another entry or issuing another command. You can't undo a save or print, but the general rule is that the Undo button can restore the worksheet data and settings to what they were the last time Excel was in Ready mode.

If Excel cannot undo an operation, then the button is inoperative. Next to the Undo button on the Standard toolbar is the Repeat button. The **Repeat button** allows you to repeat the last activity.

Finally, you can click **Undo** on the Edit menu (Figure 1-75) rather than using the Undo button. If Excel cannot undo an operation, then the words Can't Undo appear on the Edit menu in place of Undo.

Clearing a Cell or Range of Cells

It is not unusual to enter data into the wrong cell or range of cells. In such a case, to correct the error, you might want to erase or clear the data. ***Never press the SPACEBAR to enter a blank character to clear a cell.*** A blank character is text and is different from an empty cell, even though the cell may appear empty.

Excel provides three methods to clear the contents of a cell or a range of cells.

TO CLEAR CELL CONTENTS USING THE FILL HANDLE

Step 1: Select the cell or range of cells and point to the fill handle so the mouse pointer changes to a crosshair.

Step 2: Drag the fill handle back into the selected cell or range until a shadow covers the cell or cells you want to erase. Release the left mouse button.

TO CLEAR CELL CONTENTS USING THE SHORTCUT MENU

Step 1: Select the cell or range of cells to be cleared.
Step 2: Right-click the selection.
Step 3: Click Clear Contents.

TO CLEAR CELL CONTENTS USING THE DELETE KEY

Step 1: Select the cell or range of cells to be cleared.
Step 2: Press the DELETE key.

TO CLEAR CELL CONTENTS USING THE CLEAR COMMAND

Step 1: Select the cell or range of cells to be cleared.
Step 2: On the Edit menu, click Clear.
Step 3: Click All on the submenu.

You can also select a range of cells and click the Cut button on the Standard toolbar or click **Cut** on the Edit menu. Be aware, however, besides deleting the contents from the range, the Cut button or Cut command also copies the contents of the range to the clipboard.

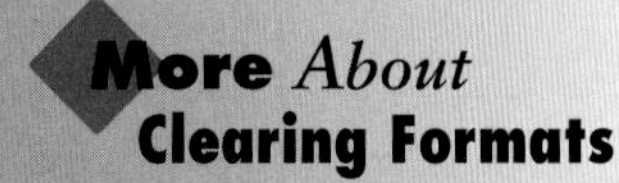

If you accidentally assign unwanted formats to a range of cells, you can use the Clear command on the Edit menu to delete the formats of a selected range. In this case, the format changes to normal. To view the characteristics of normal format, click Style on the Format menu or press ALT+' (APOSTROPHE).

Clearing the Entire Worksheet

Sometimes, everything goes wrong. If this happens, you may want to clear the worksheet entirely and start over. To clear the worksheet, follow these steps.

TO CLEAR THE ENTIRE WORKSHEET

Step 1: Click the Select All button (Figure 1-75).
Step 2: Press the DELETE key or click Clear on the Edit menu and then click All on the submenu.

An alternative to the Select All button in Step 1 is to press CTRL+A. You can also clear an entire worksheet by clicking **Close** on the File menu. If you use Close on the File menu, click the **New button** on the Standard toolbar to begin working on your next workbook.

More *About* **Global Activities**

Lotus 1-2-3 users may wonder how to carry out global activities in Excel, since there are no specific global commands. It's easy, simply click the Select All button or press CTRL+A before you issue a command, and the command will effect the entire worksheet.

TO DELETE AN EMBEDDED CHART

Step 1: Click the chart to select it.
Step 2: Press the DELETE key.

More About Online Help

Prior versions of Excel came with several thick manuals. Most beginners had difficulty figuring out which manual contained the information they were after. The online Help feature of this latest version of Excel replaces the manuals with the tools described in Table 1-7.

Excel Online Help

At any time while you are using Excel, you can answer your Excel questions by using **online Help**. Used properly, this form of online assistance can increase your productivity and reduce your frustrations by minimizing the time you spend learning how to use Excel. Table 1-7 summarizes the six categories of online Help available to you.

Table 1-7

TYPE	DESCRIPTION	ACTIVATE BY CLICKING
Contents sheet	Groups Help topics by general categories; use when you know only the general category of the topic in question	Double-click the Help button on the Standard toolbar or click Microsoft Excel Help Topics on the Help menu, and then click the Contents tab.
Index sheet	Similar to an index in a book; use when you know exactly what you want	Double-click the Help button on the Standard toolbar or click Microsoft Excel Help Topics on the Help menu, and then click the Index tab.
Find sheet	Searches the index for all phrases that include the term in question	Double-click the Help button on the Standard toolbar or click Microsoft Excel Help Topics on the Help menu, and then click the Find tab.
Answer Wizard sheet	Allows you to enter English-type questions in your own words, such as "how do i save a workbook?"	Double-click the Help button on the Standard toolbar or click Answer Wizard or Microsoft Excel Help Topics on the Help menu, and then click the Answer Wizard tab.
Question button and Help button	Used to identify unfamiliar items on the screen	In a dialog box, click the Question mark button and then click an item in the dialog box. Click the Help button on the Standard toolbar, and then click an item on the screen.
TipWizard Box	Displays ways to do your work more quickly and easily	Click the TipWizard button on the Standard toolbar to display the TipWizard.

The following sections show examples of each type of online Help described in Table 1-7.

More About the Contents Sheet

Use the Contents sheet in the same manner you would use a table of contents at the front of a textbook.

Using the Contents Sheet to Obtain Help

The **Contents sheet** in the **Help Topics dialog box** offers you assistance when you know the general category of the topic in question, but not the specifics. The following steps show how to use the Contents sheet tab to obtain information on editing the contents of cells.

Steps To Obtain Help Using the Contents Sheet

1. **Double-click the Help button on the Standard toolbar.**

   The Help Topics: Microsoft Excel dialog box displays.

2. **Click the Contents tab. In the list box, double-click the Entering, Selecting, and Editing Data book. Double-click the Editing Data book.**

   Each topic on the Contents sheet is preceded by a book or question mark icon. A ***book icon*** *indicates subtopics are available. A* ***question mark icon*** *means information will display on the topic if the title is double-clicked. Notice how the book icon opens when the book (or its title) is double-clicked. For example, two open books display in Figure 1-76.*

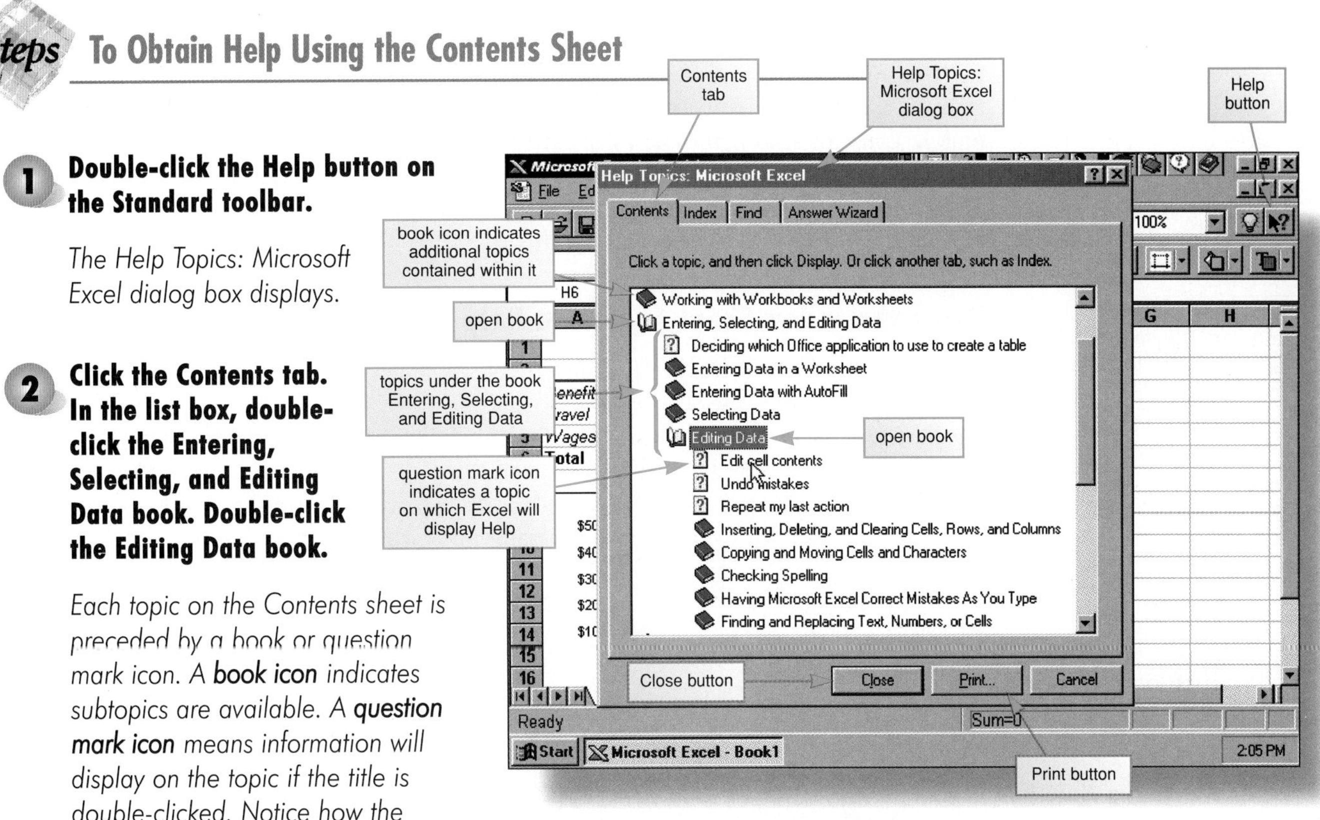

FIGURE 1-76

3. **Double-click the topic Edit cell contents listed immediately below the open book Editing Data.**

   A Microsoft Excel Help window displays describing the steps for editing a cell's contents (Figure 1-77).

4. **After reading the information, click the Close button in the Help Topics: Microsoft Excel dialog box.**

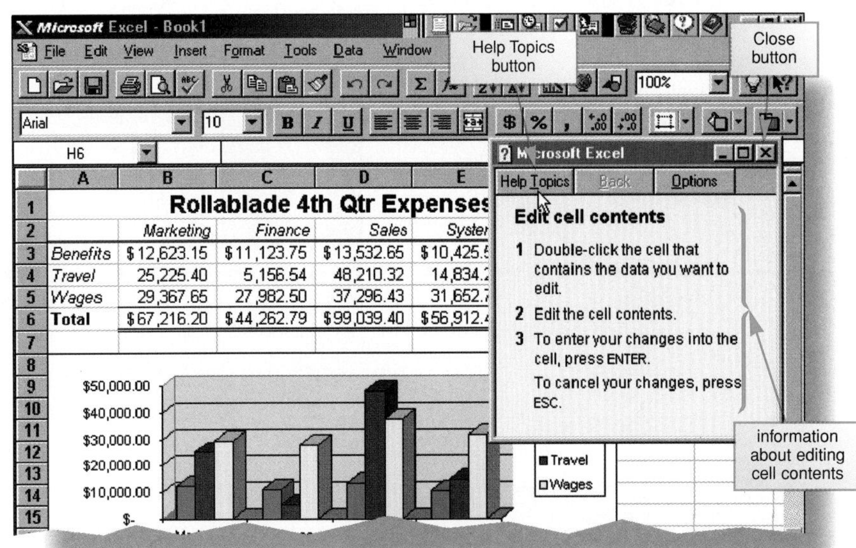

FIGURE 1-77

OtherWays

1. On Help menu click Microsoft Excel Help Topics, click Contents tab
2. Press F1, click Contents tab

Rather than double-clicking a topic in the list box, you can click it and then use the buttons at the bottom of the dialog box to open a book, display information on a topic, or print information on a topic (see Figure 1-76 on the previous page). You can also print the information by pointing to the dialog box and right-clicking (Figure 1-77) or clicking the Options button and then clicking Print Topic. To cancel the dialog box, click the Close button to return to Excel or click the Help Topics button to return to the Contents sheet.

More About the Index Sheet

If you have used the index of a book to look up terms, then you will feel comfortable with the Index sheet. It works the same way. Only you have to type the term you want information on, rather than look it up in an index.

Using the Index Sheet to Obtain Help

The next sheet in the Help Topics: Microsoft Excel dialog box is the Index sheet. Use the **Index sheet** when you know the term you want to find or at least the first few letters of the term. Use the Index sheet in the same manner you would an index at the back of a textbook.

The following steps show how to obtain information on the AutoCalculate area by using the Index sheet and entering auto, the first four letters of AutoCalculate.

Steps To Obtain Help Using the Index Sheet

1 Double-click the Help button on the Standard toolbar.

The Help Topics: Microsoft Excel dialog box displays.

2 Click the Index tab. Type `auto` **in the top box labeled 1.**

The term AutoCalculate is highlighted in the lower box labeled 2 (Figure 1-78). You may have to click AutoCalculate to highlight it.

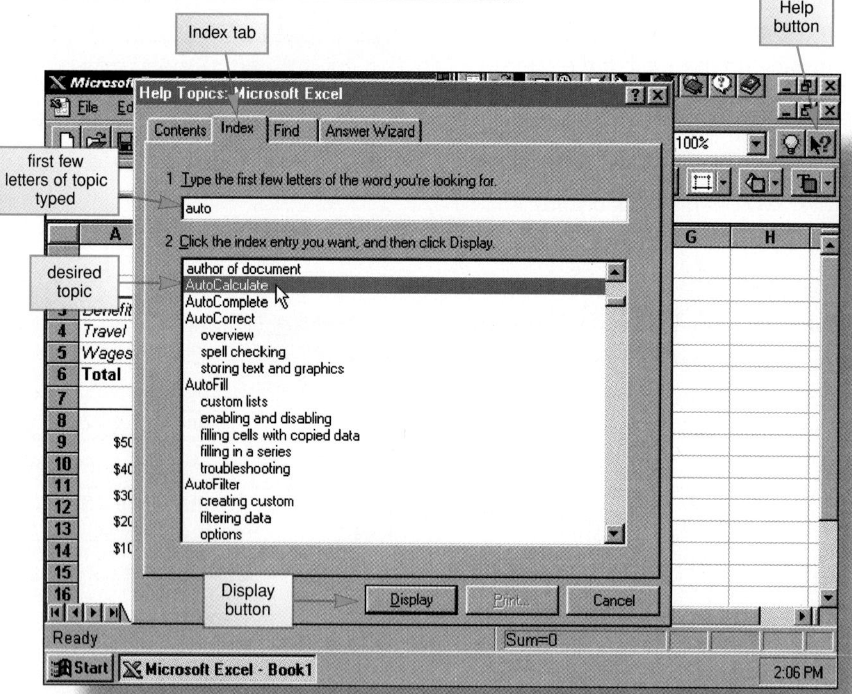

FIGURE 1-78

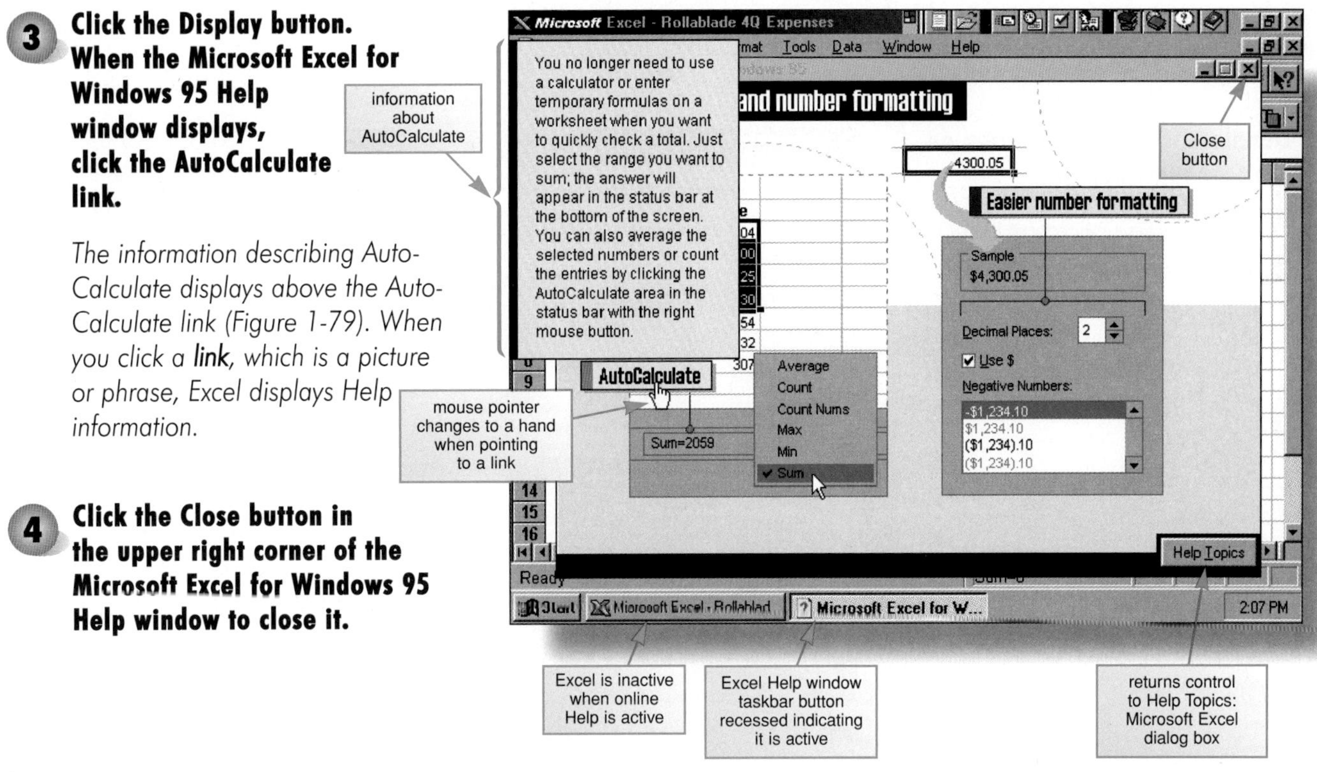

3 **Click the Display button. When the Microsoft Excel for Windows 95 Help window displays, click the AutoCalculate link.**

*The information describing AutoCalculate displays above the AutoCalculate link (Figure 1-79). When you click a **link**, which is a picture or phrase, Excel displays Help information.*

4 **Click the Close button in the upper right corner of the Microsoft Excel for Windows 95 Help window to close it.**

FIGURE 1-79

OtherWays

1. On Help menu click Microsoft Excel Help Topics, click Index tab
2. Press F1, click Index tab

Not all information you look up through online Help is printable. For example, it is not possible to print the information describing the AutoCalculate area on the status bar. Generally speaking, if the dialog box contains an Options button (see Figure 1-77 on page E 1.55), then you can print the information.

Using the Find Sheet to Obtain Help

The third sheet in the Help Topics: Microsoft Excel dialog box is the Find sheet. The **Find sheet** will return a list of all topics pertaining to the word. You can then further select words to narrow your search.

The steps on the next page show how to obtain information on using drag and drop methods to move or copy ranges in a worksheet.

More About the Find Sheet

Use the Find sheet when you know a word that is located anywhere in the term or phrase you want to look up.

To Obtain Help Using the Find Sheet

1. **Double-click the Help button on the Standard toolbar.**

   The Help Topics: Microsoft Excel dialog box displays.

2. **Click the Find tab. Type** `drag` **in the top box labeled 1.**

   Matching words display in the middle box labeled 2 and 76 topics relating to the term drag are accessible in the lower box labeled 3 (Figure 1-80). The number of topics may be different on your computer.

FIGURE 1-80

3. **Click the phrase, drag-and-drop, in the middle box labeled 2.**

   The number of topics found changes from 76 to 3 in the lower box labeled 3 (Figure 1-81).

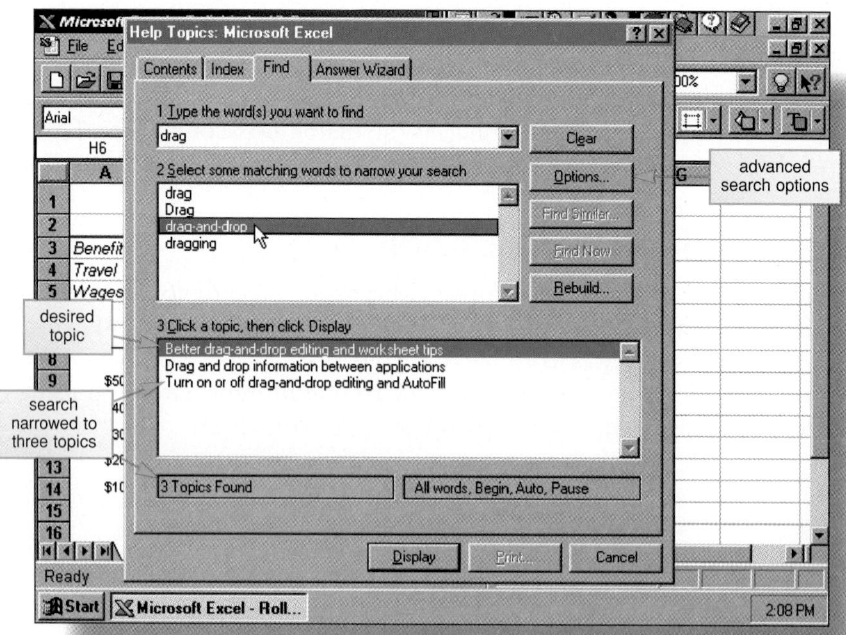

FIGURE 1-81

4 **Double-click the topic Better drag-and-drop editing and worksheet tips in the lower box labeled 3 on the Find sheet. When the Microsoft Excel for Windows 95 Help window displays, click the Drag cells between worksheets link.**

The information regarding dragging and dropping displays as shown in Figure 1-82.

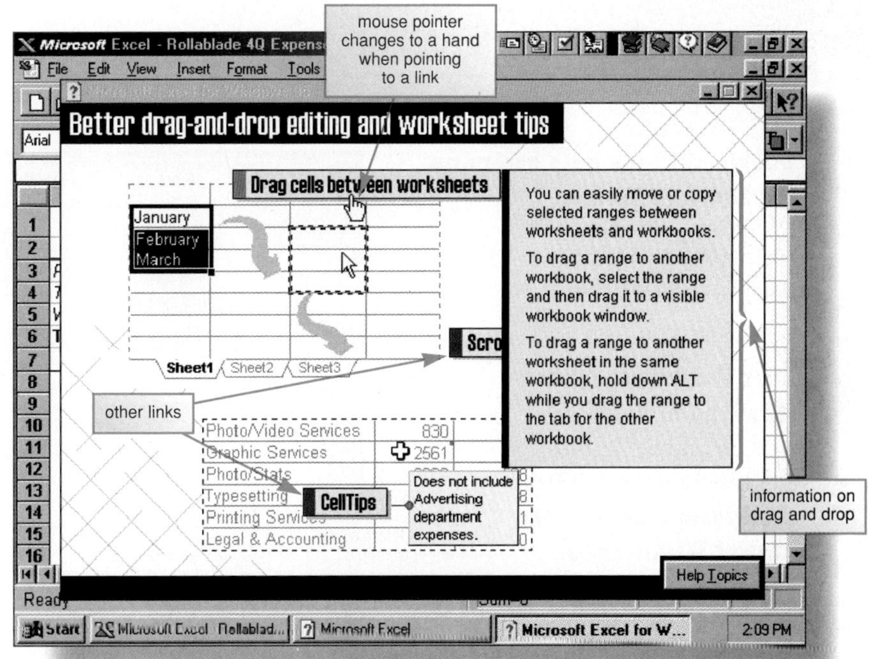

FIGURE 1-82

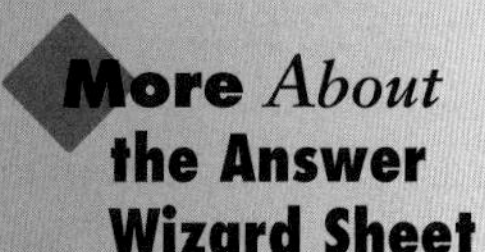

OtherWays

1. On Help menu click Microsoft Excel Help Topics, click Find tab
2. Press F1, click Find tab

You can see from the previous steps that the Find sheet allows you to enter a word similar to the Index sheet, but instead of displaying an alphabetical listing, the Find sheet lists all the phrases that include the word entered. You then can choose the appropriate phrase to narrow your search.

Using the Answer Wizard Sheet to Obtain Help

The fourth and final sheet in the Help Topics: Microsoft Excel dialog box is the Answer Wizard sheet. Simply type a question in your own words and the **Answer Wizard** will assist you. For example, when you type a question, such as "How do I sum a range?" on the Answer Wizard sheet, it responds by displaying two categories of topics – *How Do I* and *Tell Me About*. The *How Do I* topics show how to complete a task, listing a step-by-step procedure or by example. The *Tell Me About* topics give you a better understanding of the task in question.

The steps on the next page show how to obtain information on summing multiple rows and columns by entering the question, "How do I sum a range?"

More About the Answer Wizard Sheet

Use the Answer Wizard sheet when you know what you want to do, but have no idea what the task is called.

To Obtain Help Using the Answer Wizard

1. **Double-click the Help button on the Standard toolbar.**

   The Help Topics: Microsoft Excel dialog box displays.

2. **Click the Answer Wizard tab. Type** `how do i sum a range` **in the top box labeled 1. Click the Search button on the Answer Wizard sheet.**

   The Answer Wizard responds by displaying two categories (How Do I and Tell Me About) of topics in the lower box labeled 2 (Figure 1-83).

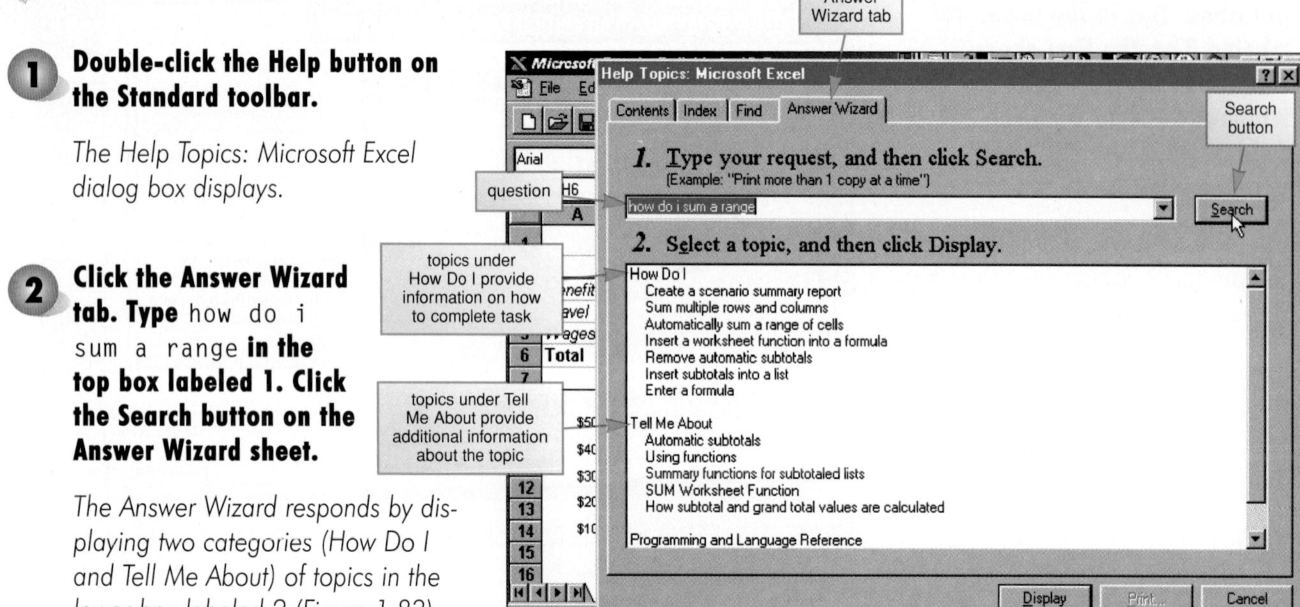

FIGURE 1-83

3. **Double-click the topic, Sum multiple rows and columns, in the lower box labeled 2.**

   A Microsoft Excel Help window displays showing the step-by-step procedures for summing multiple rows and columns (Figure 1-84).

4. **After reading the step-by-step procedures, click the Close button in the upper right corner of the dialog box to close it.**

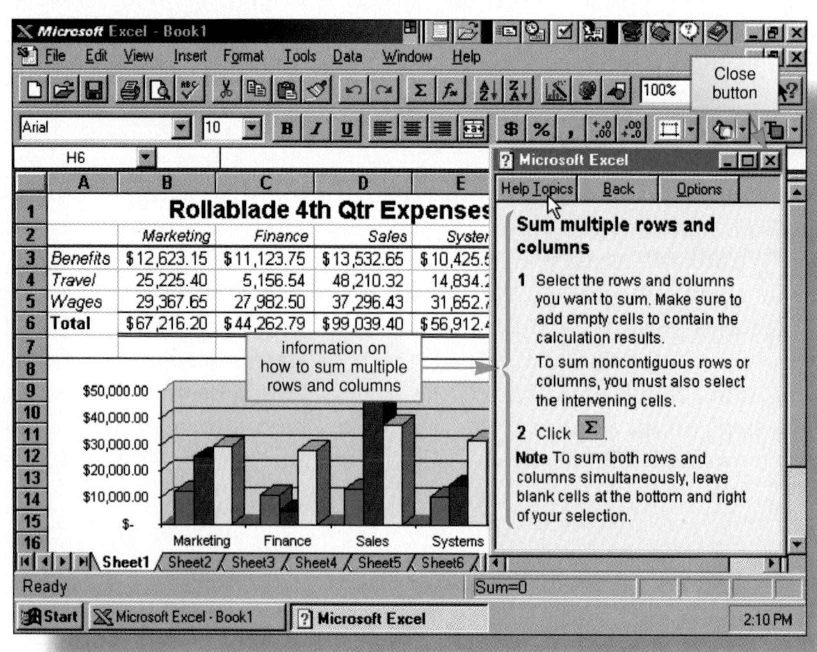

FIGURE 1-84

OtherWays

1. On Help menu click Answer Wizard
2. Press F1, click Answer Wizard tab

Here again, you can print the step-by-step procedures in Figure 1-84 by right-clicking in the Help window or by clicking the Options button. Instead of quitting online Help by clicking the Close button in Step 4, you can click the Help Topics button (Figure 1-84) to return to the Answer Wizard sheet shown in Figure 1-83.

The four online Help features (Contents, Index, Find, and Answer Wizard) of Excel presented thus far are powerful and easy to use. The best way to familiarize yourself with these Help tools is to use them. At the end of each project, there is a section titled Use Help. It is recommended that you step through these Help exercises to gain a better understanding of Excel online Help.

More *About* **Help**

The best way to familiarize yourself with the online Help features is to use them.

Using the Question Button or Help Button to Define Items on the Screen

Use the Question Mark button or Help button when you are not sure what an item on the screen is or what it does. Click either button and the mouse pointer changes to an arrow with a question mark. Next, click any item you want more information on. The **Question Mark button** displays in the upper right corner of dialog boxes, next to the Close button. For example, in Figure 1-85, the Auto-Format dialog box is on the screen. If you click the Question Mark button, and then click anywhere in the Table Format list box, an explanation of the Table Format list box displays.

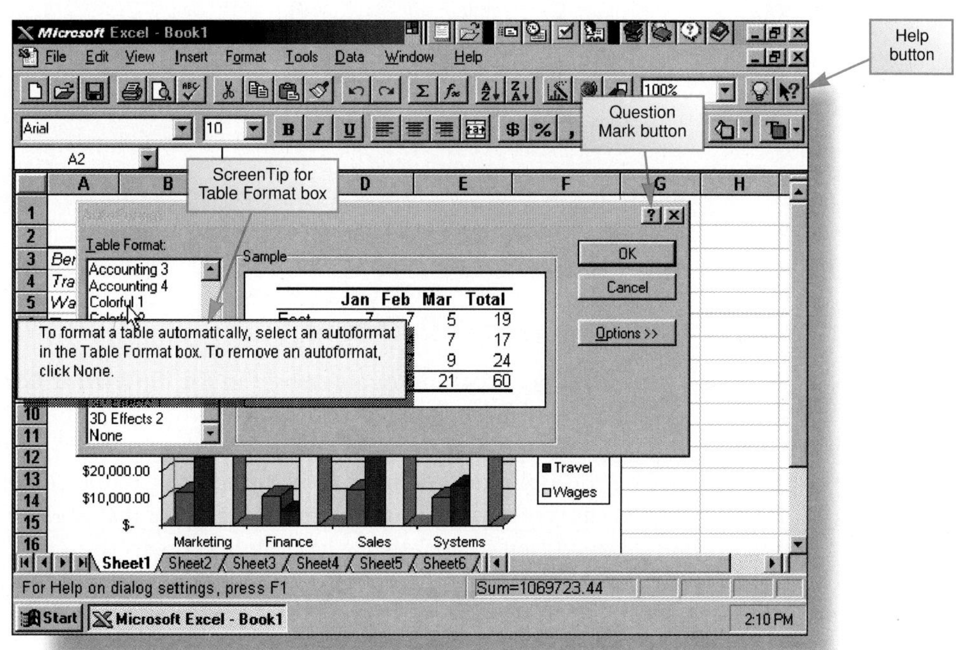

FIGURE 1-85

Whereas the Question mark button is used to display ScreenTips concerning items in a dialog box, the **Help button** on the Standard toolbar (Figure 1-85) is used to display ScreenTips concerning items on the Excel window. Once you click the Help button, you can move the arrow and question mark pointer to any menu name, button, or cell, and click to display a ScreenTip. For example, clicking the Center Across Columns button displays the ScreenTip shown in the bottom screen of Figure 1-86 on the next page. Click anywhere on the window to close the ScreenTip.

More *About* **the Question Mark Button and Help Button**

Both the Question Mark button on a dialog box and the Help button on the Standard toolbar display **ScreenTips**, which offer an explanation of the item you click when the mouse pointer changes to an arrow with a question mark.

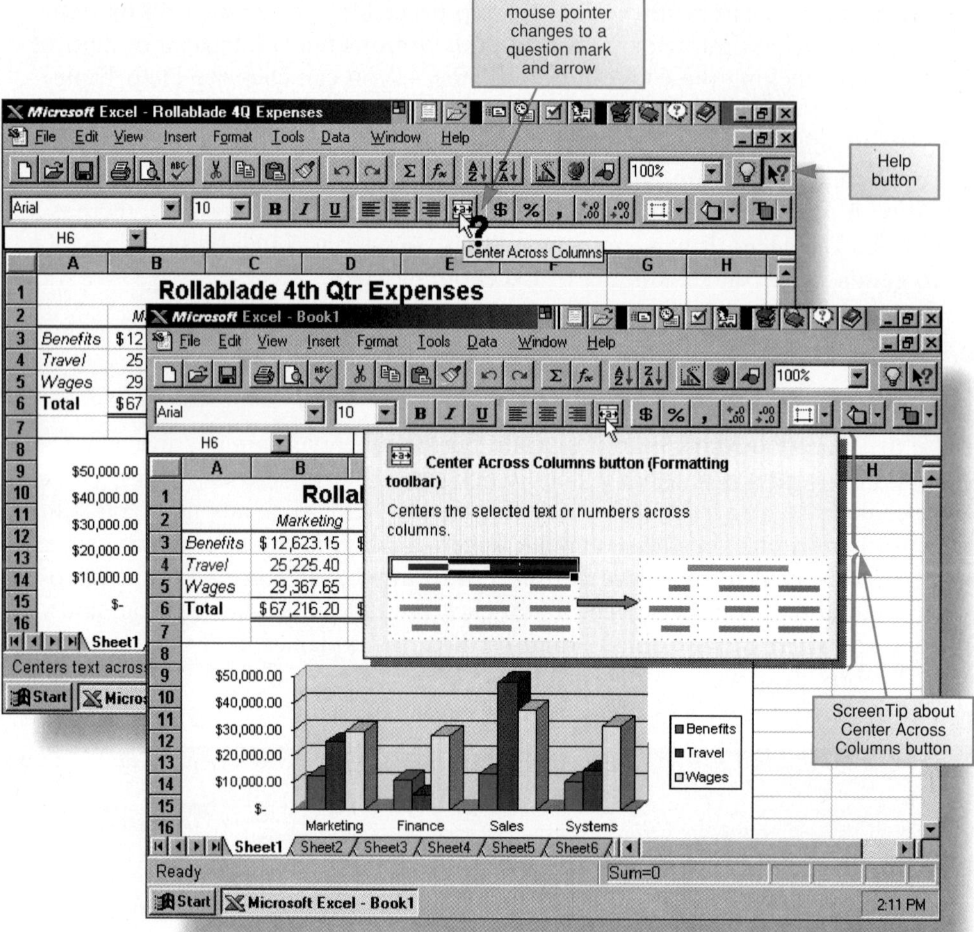

FIGURE 1-86

Information at Your Fingertips — TipWizard

Excel displays tips on how to work more efficiently in the **TipWizard Box.** When toggled on, the TipWizard Box displays at the top of the screen between the Formatting toolbar and formula bar (Figure 1-87). You toggle the TipWizard Box on or off by clicking the **TipWizard button** on the Standard toolbar. If toggled on when you start Excel, the TipWizard Box begins with a **tip of the day**. As you work through creating and editing a worksheet, Excel adds tips to the TipWizard box. The tips explain how to complete the activities you just performed more efficiently. You can scroll through these tips using the TipWizard Box.

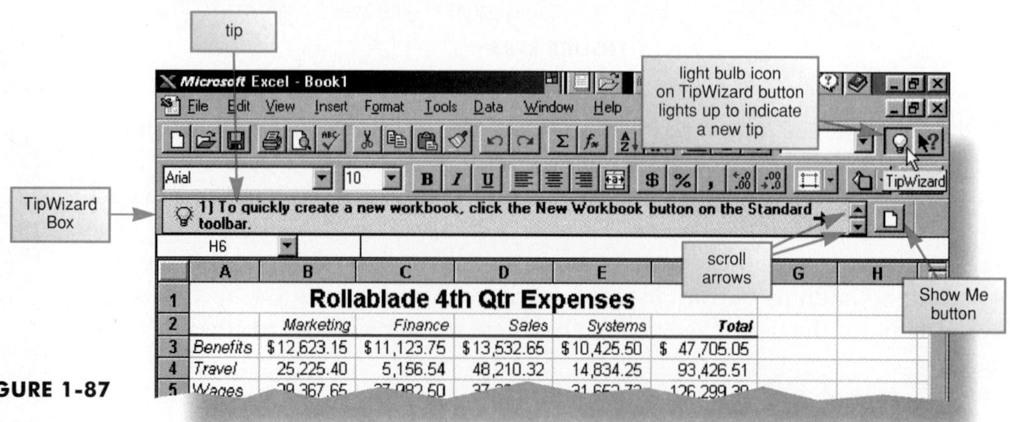

FIGURE 1-87

Exiting Excel

To exit Excel, complete the following steps.

TO EXIT EXCEL

Step 1: Click the Close button on the right side of the title bar.
Step 2: If the Microsoft Excel dialog box displays, click the No button.

More *About* Exiting Excel

Don't forget to remove your floppy disk from drive A after exiting Excel, especially if you are working in a laboratory environment. Nothing can be more frustrating than leaving all your hard work behind on a floppy disk for the next user.

Project Summary

The worksheet created in this project (Figure 1-1 on page E 1.7) allows the management of Rollablade to examine the Fourth-Quarter Expenses easily. Furthermore, the 3-D column chart should meet the needs of the president, Max Trealer, who as you recall from the Case Perspective has little tolerance for lists of numbers.

In creating the Rollablade Fourth-Quarter Expenses worksheet and chart in this project, you gained a broad knowledge about Excel. First, you were introduced to starting Excel. You learned about the Excel window and how to enter text and numbers to create a worksheet. You learned how to select a range and how to use the AutoSum button to sum numbers in a column or row. Using the fill handle, you learned how to copy a cell to adjacent cells.

Once the worksheet was built, you learned how to change the font size of the title, bold the title, and center the title over a range using buttons on the Formatting toolbar. Using the steps and techniques presented in the project, you formatted the body of the worksheet using the AutoFormat command, and you used the ChartWizard button to add a 3-D column chart. After completing the worksheet, you saved the workbook on disk and printed the worksheet. You learned how to edit data in cells. Finally, you learned how to use the six different online help tools to answer your questions.

What You Should Know

Having completed this project, you should be able to perform the following tasks:

- Add a 3-D Column Chart to the Worksheet *(E1.38)*
- Bold a Cell *(E1.30)*
- Center a Cell's Contents Across Columns *(E1.32)*
- Clear Cell Contents Using the Clear Command *(E1.53)*
- Clear Cell Contents Using the DELETE Key *(E1.53)*
- Clear Cell Contents Using the Fill Handle *(E1.52)*
- Clear Cell Contents Using the Shortcut Menu *(E1.53)*
- Clear the Entire Worksheet *(E1.53)*
- Copy a Cell to Adjacent Cells in a Row *(E1.26)*
- Delete an Embedded Chart *(E1.53)*
- Determine Multiple Totals at the Same Time *(E1.27)*
- Enter Numeric Data *(E1.21)*
- Enter Row Titles *(E1.20)*
- Enter the Column Titles *(E1.18)*
- Enter the Worksheet Title *(E1.8)*
- Exit Excel *(E1.46)*
- Increase the Font Size of a Cell *(E1.31)*
- Obtain Help Using the Answer Wizard *(E1.59)*
- Obtain Help Using the Contents Sheet *(E1.54)*
- Obtain Help Using the Find Sheet *(E1.57)*
- Obtain Help Using the Index Sheet *(E1.56)*
- Print a Worksheet *(E1.45)*
- Save a Workbook *(E1.42)*
- Start Excel *(E1.9)*
- Start Excel and Open a Workbook *(E1.47)*
- Sum a Column of Numbers *(E1.24)*
- Use AutoCalculate Area to Determine an Average *(E1.49)*
- Use AutoFormat to Format the Body of a Worksheet *(E1.33)*
- Use the Name Box to Select a Cell *(E1.36)*

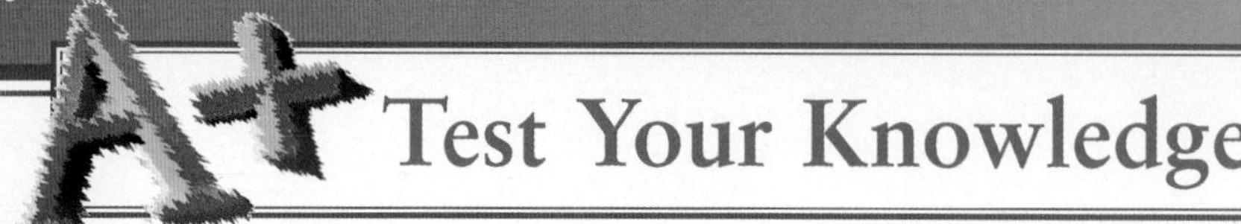

Test Your Knowledge

1 True/False

Instructions: Circle T if the statement is true or F if the statement is false.

T F 1. An Excel worksheet contains a total of 16,384 columns and 256 rows.

T F 2. Inside an Excel workbook are sheets, called worksheets.

T F 3. Each cell has a unique address made up of a row number followed by a column letter.

T F 4. The Excel taskbar button is in the title bar.

T F 5. You can use the fill handle to delete the contents of a cell.

T F 6. If you have not yet clicked the enter box or pressed the ENTER key or an arrow key to complete an entry in the formula bar, use the ESC key to erase the entry from the formula bar.

T F 7. To select the entire worksheet, click the Select All button or press CTRL+A.

T F 8. Text that contains more characters than the width of the column will always occupy two or more cells.

T F 9. The AutoCalculate area is used to enter a function, such as the SUM function, that is then assigned to the active cell when you press the ENTER key.

T F 10. Double-click the Help button on the Standard toolbar to initiate access to the Contents sheet.

2 Multiple Choice

Instructions: Circle the correct response.

1. To enlarge a reduced Excel window, click the __________ button.
   a. Maximize
   b. Undo
   c. Open
   d. Repeat
2. To enter text into a cell, the cell must be __________.
   a. defined as a text cell
   b. empty
   c. the active cell
   d. wide enough to display the entry
3. Which button do you click to display ScreenTips in a dialog box?
   a. Help button
   b. TipWizard button
   c. Question Mark button
   d. Open button

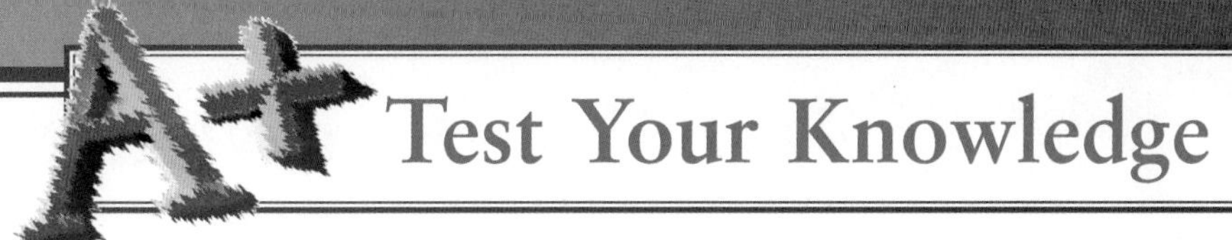

Test Your Knowledge

4. When you enter a number into the active cell, the number is __________ in the cell.
   a. right-justified
   b. left-justified
   c. centered
   d. decimal-aligned
5. When defining the chart area, hold down the __________ key to snap to the gridlines.
   a. CTRL
   b. ALT
   c. SHIFT
   d. F1
6. If a single empty cell is selected and the Sum is active in the AutoCalculate area, then Sum = __________ displays in the AutoCalculate area.
   a. 0
   b. ?
   c. ERR
   d. 1
7. To display a shortcut menu, point to the object, such as the toolbar and __________.
   a. click the Select All button
   b. double-click
   c. click and right-click simultaneously
   d. right-click
8. The fill handle is located __________.
   a. on the taskbar
   b. on the status bar
   c. on the heavy border that surrounds the active cell
   d. on the title bar
9. Which one of the following will exit Excel?
   a. Double-click the title bar.
   b. Click the Close button on the title bar.
   c. Click Close on the File menu.
   d. Click the Minimize button on the title bar.
10. To display suggestions on how to complete tasks more efficiently, click the __________ button on the Standard toolbar.
   a. TipWizard
   b. Question Mark
   c. Help
   d. Paste

Test Your Knowledge

3 Understanding the Excel Worksheet

Instructions: In Figure 1-88, arrows point to the major components of the Excel window. Identify the various parts of the windows in the spaces provided.

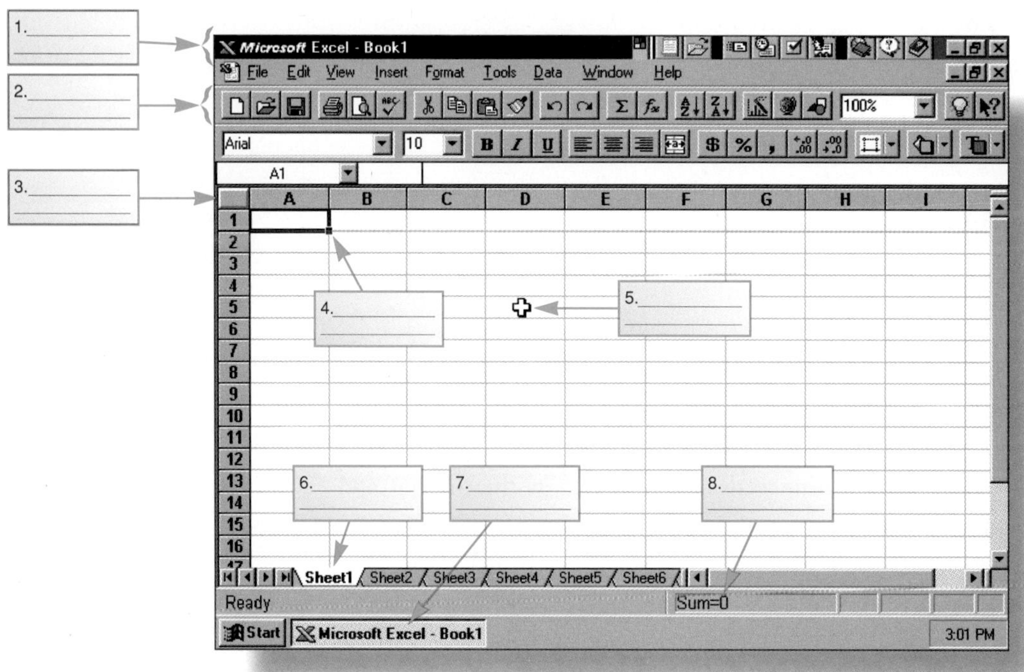

FIGURE 1-88

4 Understanding the Excel Toolbars and the Save As Dialog Box

Instructions: In the worksheet in Figure 1-89, arrows point to several of the buttons and boxes on the Standard and Formatting toolbars and in the Save As dialog box. In the spaces provided, identify each button and box.

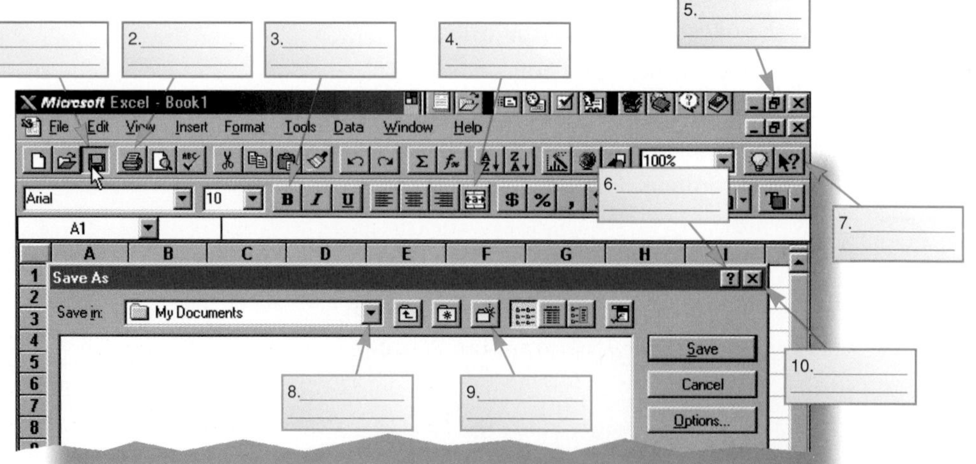

FIGURE 1-89

Use Help

1 Reviewing Project Activities

Instructions: Perform the following tasks using a computer.

1. Start Excel
2. Double-click the Help button on the Standard toolbar to display the Help Topics: Microsoft Excel dialog box.
3. Click the Contents tab. Double-click the Getting Help book. Double-click Getting assistance while you work.
4. Click the Answer Wizard link (Figure 1-90) and then read the Help information. Click the remaining four links and read their Help information. Click the Help Topics button in the lower right corner of the window to return to the Help Topics: Microsoft Excel dialog box.
5. Click the Index tab. Type `font` in the top box labeled 1 and then double-click font size under fonts in the lower box labeled 2 to display the Topics Found dialog box. Double-click Change the size of text and numbers. When the Help information displays, read it. Next, right-click within the box, and then click Print Topic. Click outside the ScreenTip. Hand in the printout to your instructor.

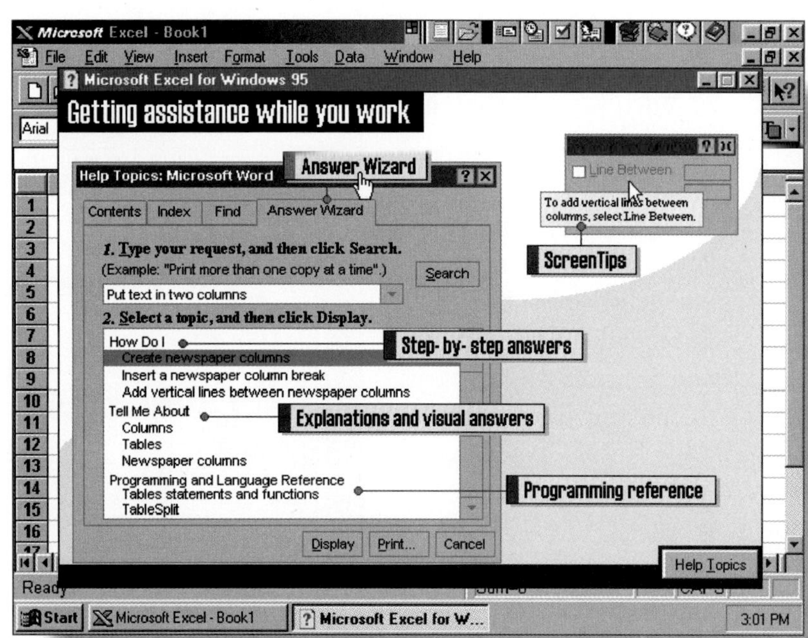

FIGURE 1-90

6. Double-click the Help button on the Standard toolbar. When the Help Topics: Microsoft Excel dialog box displays, click the Find tab. Type `chart` in the top box labeled 1. Click ChartWizard in the middle box labeled 2. Double-click create a chart in the lower box labeled 3. When the Microsoft Excel Help window displays, read it, ready the printer, right-click, and click Print Topic. Click the Insert or embed a chart on a worksheet link at the bottom of the Help window. Print the Help information. Click the Close button to close the Microsoft Excel dialog box with the Help information. Hand in the printouts to your instructor.
7. Double-click the Help button on the Standard toolbar. Click the Answer Wizard tab. Type `how do i open a workbook` in the top box labeled 1. Click the Search button. Double-click Create a new workbook in the lower box labeled 2 under How Do I. Read and print the Help information. Hand in the printout to your instructor

Use Help

2 Expanding on the Basics

Instructions: Use Excel online Help to better understand the topics listed below. Begin each of the following by double-clicking the Help button on the Standard toolbar. If you are unable to print the Help information, then answer the questions on your own paper.

1. Using the Formatting book on the Contents sheet in the Help Topics: Microsoft Excel dialog box, answer the following questions:
   a. How would you use only parts of a customized format using AutoFormat?
   b. What are the five basic formats (Figure 1-91) available in Excel?
   c. What types of fast formatting techniques does Excel have?
2. Using the key term shortcut keys and the Index tab in the Help Topics: Microsoft Excel dialog box, display and print the shortcut keys to edit and move data. Then, answer the following questions:
   a. Which key or combination keys show or hide the Standard toolbar?
   b. Which key or combination keys select an entire row?
   c. Which key or combination keys select an entire column?
   d. Which key or combination keys extend the selection to the last cell in the worksheet?
   e. Which key or combination keys extend the selection by one cell?
3. Use the Find tab in the Help Topics: Microsoft Excel dialog box to display and then print information about the function keys. Then, answer the following questions:
   a. Which key or combination keys are used to display a shortcut menu?
   b. Which key or combination keys are used to create a chart?
   c. Which key or combination keys are used to restore the size of a window?
4. Use the Answer Wizard in the Help Topics: Microsoft Excel dialog box to display and print the application workspace specifications, worksheet and workbook specifications, and the charting specifications.

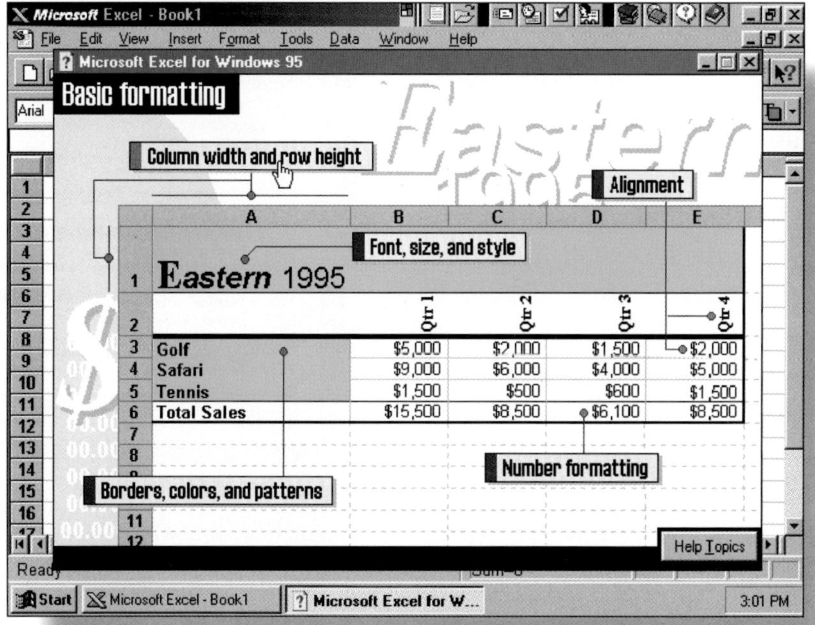

FIGURE 1-91

Apply Your Knowledge

CAUTION: It is recommended that you create a backup copy of the Student Floppy Disk that accompanies this book and then remove unneeded folders on the backup floppy disk to free up space. Do the following: (1) insert the Student Floppy Disk in drive A; (2) start Explorer; (3) right-click the 3½ Floppy [A:] folder in the All Folders side of the window; (4) click Copy Disk; (5) click Start and OK as required; (6) insert the backup floppy disk when requested; (7) delete folders on the backup floppy disk except the Excel folder.

1 Changing Data in a Worksheet

Instructions: Read the Caution box above and to the right. Start Excel. Open the workbook, Kevin's Lawn Care, from the Excel folder on the Student floppy disk that accompanies this book. As shown in Figure 1-92, the worksheet is a semiannual income and expense worksheet. Perform the following tasks:

1. Make the changes to the worksheet described in Table 1-8. As you edit the values in the cells containing numeric data, watch the total income (cells D6 and F6) and total expenses (cells D11 and F11). Each of the values in these four cells is based on the SUM function. When you enter a new value, Excel automatically recalculates the SUM functions. After you have successfully made the changes listed in the table, the total incomes in cells D6 and F6 should equal $106,077.50 and $110,420.78, respectively. The total expenses in cells D11 and F11 should equal $73,289.78 and $86,178.90, respectively.
2. Save the workbook. Use the filename Jacob's Lawn Care.
3. Print the revised worksheet.

Microsoft Excel - Kevin's Lawn Care

	A	B	C	D	E	F	G	H
1	Kevin's Lawn Care Service							
2	INCOME:			Jan-June		July-Dec		
3		Landscaping		$53,235.25		$75,324.56		
4		Mowing		22,341.40		19,213.70		
5		Fertilizing		16,945.30		12,090.21		
6	TOTAL INCOME:			$92,521.95		$106,628.55		
7	EXPENSES:							
8		Salaries		$28,430.00		$32,875.40		
9		Rent		17,235.00		17,235.00		
10		Cost of Goods		23,654.78		25,574.00		
11	TOTAL EXPENSES:			$69,319.78		$75,684.40		

FIGURE 1-92

Table 1-8

CELL	CURRENT CELL CONTENTS	CHANGE CELL CONTENTS TO
A1	Kevin's Lawn Care Service	Jacob's Lawn Care Service
D3	53235.25	58753.20
F3	75324.56	82753.25
D5	16945.30	24982.90
F5	12090.21	8453.75
D8	28430.00	32400.00
F8	32875.40	43369.90

1 Building and Modifying a Sales Analysis Worksheet

Problem: As the assistant financial manager for Hayley's Pet Shop, Inc., you have been asked by your supervisor to analyze the third-quarter sales for the company, which has stores in four cities. The third-quarter sales are shown in Table 1-9.

Table 1-9

	NEW YORK	*CHICAGO*	*LOS ANGELES*	*MIAMI*
Fish	**25,102.15**	**18,231.56**	**21,012.40**	**12,012.00**
Dogs	**42,970.50**	**37,210.00**	**29,089.12**	**39,765.23**
Cats	**21,892.70**	**18,329.34**	**26,723.15**	**22,914.50**
Birds	**9,312.45**	**12,923.21**	**9,012.56**	**8,910.32**

Instructions: Perform the following tasks:

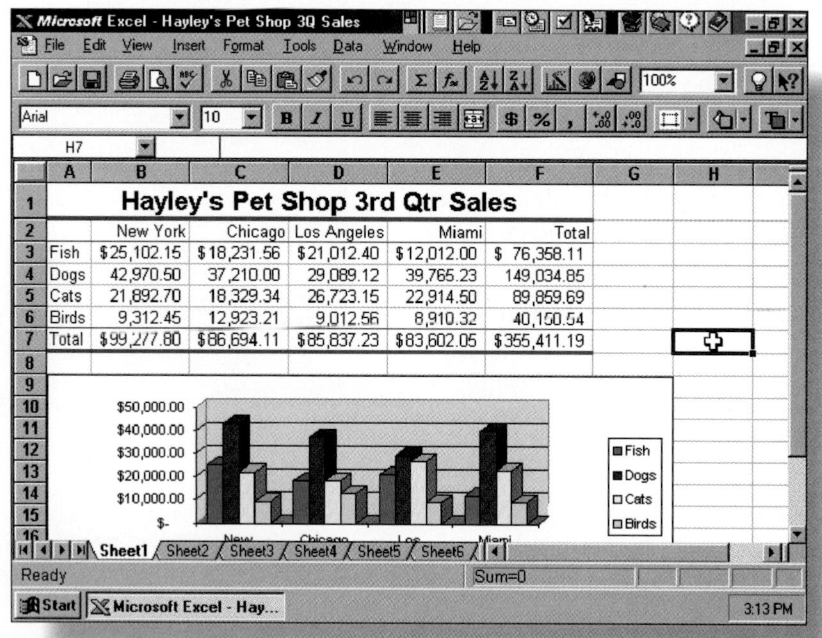

FIGURE 1-93

1. Create the worksheet shown in Figure 1-93 using the sales amounts in Table 1-9.
2. Direct Excel to determine the totals for the four store locations, the sales categories, and the company.
3. Format the worksheet title Hayley's Pet Shop 3rd Qtr Sales as 16 point, bold, and centered over columns A through F.
4. Format the range A2:F7 using the table format Accounting 2 as shown in the worksheet in Figure 1-93.
5. Use the ChartWizard button on the Standard toolbar to draw the 3-D column chart shown on the worksheet in Figure 1-93. Chart the range A2:E6.
6. Enter your name in cell A20. Enter your course, laboratory assignment number, date, and instructor name below in cells A21 through A24.
7. Save the workbook using the filename Hayley's Pet Shop 3Q Sales.
8. Print the worksheet.
9. Two corrections to the sales amounts were submitted. The correct sales amounts are: $18,567.23 for Birds in Miami and $39,598.25 for Dogs in Chicago. Enter the two corrections. After you enter the two corrections, the company total should equal $367,456.35 in cell F7. Print the worksheet containing the corrected values.

2 Creating an Annual College Expense Worksheet

Problem: You have decided to create an expense worksheet for the upcoming school year. The expenses you have determined are listed in Table 1-10.

Table 1-10

	SEMESTER 1	SEMESTER 2	SUMMER
Room & Board	1950	1950	750
Tuition	1750	1750	650
Books	350	400	125
Clothes	125	175	90
Entertainment	250	300	200
Miscellaneous	150	150	75

Instructions: Perform the following tasks:

1. Create the worksheet shown in Figure 1-94 using the expenses and category names in Table 1-10.
2. Direct Excel to determine the totals for each expense category, each semester, and the total annual expense.
3. Format the worksheet title Annual College Expenses to 18 point, bold, and centered over columns A through E.
4. Format the range A2:E9 using the table format Accounting 1 as shown in Figure 1-94.
5. Use the ChartWizard button to draw the 3-D area chart shown on the worksheet in Figure 1-94. Chart the range A2:D8 in the range A11:H24.
6. Enter your name in cell A26. Enter your course, laboratory assignment number, date, and instructor name below the chart in cells A27 through A30.
7. Save the workbook using the filename Annual College Expenses.
8. Print the worksheet.
9. Make the following changes to the Annual College Expense worksheet: Semester 1, Tuition — $3,000; Semester 2, Tuition — $3,000; and Summer, Entertainment — $1,500. The new three semester totals should be $5,825.00, $5,975.00, and $3,190.00, respectively.
10. Print the modified worksheet.

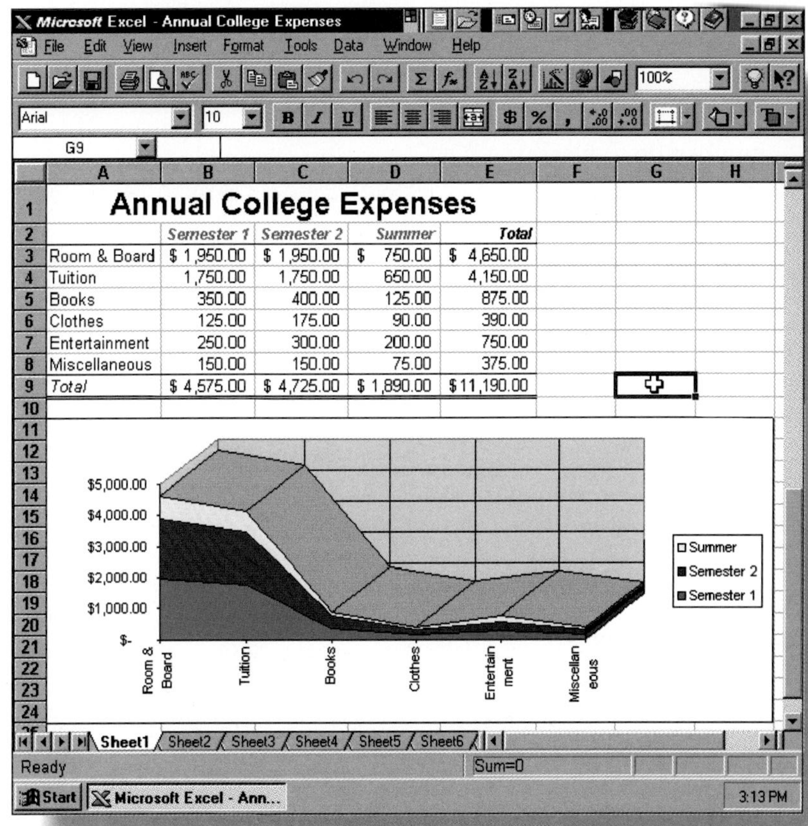

FIGURE 1-94

3 Creating a Personal Financial History Statement

Problem: For you to obtain a bank loan, the bank has requested you to supply a personal financial history statement. The statement is to include your average monthly income and all major expenses for the last seven years. The data required to prepare your financial statement is shown in Table 1-11.

Table 1-11

	1990	*1991*	*1992*	*1993*	*1994*	*1995*	*1996*
Income:							
Wages	1550	1600	1800	1850	1900	2200	2300
Tips	550	500	600	750	800	825	900
Expenses:							
Rent	850	875	900	925	975	990	1025
Utilities	160	165	175	180	180	190	210
Insurance	200	250	300	325	400	450	475
Other	290	325	375	400	425	430	435

Instructions: Using the numbers in Table 1-11, create the worksheet shown in Figure 1-95. Use the AutoSum button to calculate the total monthly income (row 7) and total monthly expenses (row 15) for each of the seven years. Make sure you begin each of the column titles with an apostrophe so the dates are not entered as numbers, or else they will be added into the totals when you apply the AutoSum button. Use the Answer Wizard and type in the question, `How do I sum`. Use the information to find all the Monthly Income totals in row 7 and column H by clicking the AutoSum button once. Apply the same techniques to find the Monthly Expenses totals in row 15 and column H.

Microsoft Excel - Personal Financial Statement

	A	B	C	D	E	F	G	H
1	Personal Financial Statement							
2								
3	Monthly Income							
4		1990	1991	1992	1993	1994	1995	1996
5	Wages	$1,550.00	$1,600.00	$1,800.00	$1,850.00	$1,900.00	$2,200.00	$2,300.00
6	Tips	550.00	500.00	600.00	750.00	800.00	825.00	900.00
7	*Total*	$2,100.00	$2,100.00	$2,400.00	$2,600.00	$2,700.00	$3,025.00	$3,200.00
8								
9	Monthly Expenses							
10		1990	1991	1992	1993	1994	1995	1996
11	Rent	$ 850.00	$ 875.00	$ 900.00	$ 925.00	$ 975.00	$ 990.00	$1,025.00
12	Utilities	160.00	165.00	175.00	180.00	180.00	190.00	210.00
13	Insurance	200.00	250.00	300.00	325.00	400.00	450.00	475.00
14	Other	290.00	325.00	375.00	400.00	425.00	430.00	435.00
15	*Total*	$1,500.00	$1,615.00	$1,750.00	$1,830.00	$1,980.00	$2,060.00	$2,145.00

FIGURE 1-95

To format the worksheet, use the table format Accounting 1 for the Monthly Income table and then again for the Monthly Expenses table. Enter your name in cell A19 and your course, laboratory assignment number, date, and instructor name in cells A20 through A23.

Save the workbook using the filename Personal Financial Statement. Print the worksheet. Use online Help to understand and then print only the selection A1:H7 of the worksheet.

Cases and Places

The difficulty of these case studies varies:

◗ Case studies preceded by a single half moon are the least difficult. You are asked to create the required document based on information that has already been placed in an organized form.
◗◗ Case studies preceded by two half moons are more difficult. You must organize the information presented before using it to create the required worksheet.
◗◗◗ Case studies preceded by three half moons are the most difficult. You must choose a specific topic, and then obtain and organize the necessary information before using it to create the required worksheet.

1 ◗ Your school's football coach has compiled the number of yards gained by this week's opponent, the Hartford Hurricanes, in each quarter over the past six games (Figure 1-96).

With this data, along with the coach's requests, you have been asked to prepare a worksheet for meetings with assistant coaches and players. Use the concepts and techniques presented in this project to create the worksheet.

Hartford Hurricanes Offensive Production in the Last Six Games

	1st Quarter	2nd Quarter	3rd Quarter	4th Quarter
Rushing	360 yd.	262 yd.	300 yd.	139 yd.
Passing	134 yd.	156 yd.	195 yd.	246 yd.

Also show:
total yards gained each quarter
total yards gained passing
total yards gained rushing
bar chart with yards gained per quarter

FIGURE 1-96

2 ◗ As a newspaper reporter, you are preparing an article on the coming election based on a recent survey of the electorate, arranged by the age of those polled (Figure 1-97).

With this data, along with your editor's suggestions, you have been asked to produce a worksheet to accompany your article. Use the concepts and techniques presented in this project to create the worksheet.

Results of Election Poll--By Age of Respondent

	18-29	30-41	42-53	54-65	66+
Wilson	345	432	124	302	645
Taft	125	532	236	279	101
Undecided	409	132	382	248	76

Include total number of people surveyed in each age group, total number for each candidate, and total number undecided. Use a bar chart to illustrate polling data.
-Ed.

FIGURE 1-97

Cases and Places

3 ▸▸ The Palace Theater is a small movie house that shows almost-current releases. Three types of tickets are sold at each presentation: general admission, senior citizen, and children's. The theater management has asked you to prepare a worksheet that can be used in reevaluating its ticket structure. During an average week, weekday evening shows generate $4,500 from general admission ticket sales, $2,500 from senior citizen ticket sales, and $1,000 from children's ticket sales. Weekend matinee shows make $3,000 from general admission ticket sales, $800 from senior citizen ticket sales, and $2,100 from children's ticket sales. Weekend evening shows earn $6,720 from general admission ticket sales, $2,400 from senior citizen ticket sales, and $1,000 from children's ticket sales. Include total revenues for each type of ticket and for each presentation time, and a bar graph illustrating ticket revenues.

4 ▸▸ The Collegiate Academy, a private school where you are a consultant, has asked you to prepare a worksheet that can be used at the next meeting of its board of directors. The worksheet is to compare the school's expenditures last year to its anticipated expenditures this year. Last year, the school spent $960,000 on staff salaries and benefits, $13,500 on books and supplies, $8,100 on equipment, and $21,000 on building and grounds maintenance. This year, the school expects to spend $1,032,000 on staff salaries and benefits, $14,850 on books and supplies, $4,700 on equipment, and $23,500 on building and grounds maintenance. Include total expenditures in each category and for each school year, and a 3-D column chart illustrating yearly expenditures. After completing the worksheet, prepare a second worksheet showing how this year's expenditures would be affected if the amount spent on staff was changed to $1,104,000 (after hiring two new teachers) and the amount spent on equipment was changed to $11,500 (after purchasing three new computers).

5 ▸▸▸ Supermarkets often boast that they have the lowest prices. Make a list of seven items that can be purchased from any supermarket. Visit at least three supermarkets and obtain a price for each of the items listed. Make sure your prices are for similar items (same size, same or similar brand name, and so on). Create a worksheet showing the price of each individual item in the store and the total price for all seven items in a particular supermarket. Include a bar graph to illustrate your data.

6 ▸▸▸ Some academic disciplines appear to attract more students of one gender than the other. Visit at least five different academic departments in your school. Find out how many males and how many females have declared majors in that department. Using this information, create a worksheet showing the number of male majors and the number of female majors in each department, the total number of majors in the department, the total number of male majors in all five departments, and the total number of female majors in all five departments. Include a bar graph to illustrate your data.

7 ▸▸▸ Car dealerships order their inventories from the manufacturer based on the car models they have sold in the previous months. Visit a local dealership and make a list of the different types of car models that are offered from one manufacturer. Find out how many of each different model was purchased during the past three months. Using this information, create a worksheet showing the number of each car model that was sold every month, the total number sold of each car model, and the total number of cars sold each month. Include a bar graph to illustrate your data.

Microsoft *Excel 7*

Windows 95

Formulas, Formatting, and Creating Charts

Objectives:

You will have mastered the material in this project when you can:

- Enter multiple lines of text in the same cell
- Enter a formula
- Use Point mode to enter formulas
- Identify the arithmetic operators +, -, *, /, %, and ^
- Apply the AVERAGE, MAX, and MIN functions
- Change the font of a cell
- Change the font of individual characters in a cell
- Color the characters and background of a cell
- Add borders to a range
- Format numbers using the Format Cells dialog box
- Align text in cells
- Change the width of a column
- Change the height of a row
- Check the spelling of a worksheet
- Create a 3-D pie chart on a separate sheet
- Format chart items
- Rename sheet tabs
- Preview how a printed copy of the worksheet will look
- Print multiple sheets
- Print a partial or complete worksheet
- Display and print the formulas version of a worksheet
- Print to fit
- Distinguish between portrait and landscape orientation

Recalculate the Formulas?

No Problem.

Imagine hugging the road in a red Formula One sports car with leather trimmed seats, triple-cool air conditioning, removable hardtop, and an aerodynamically sleek body conveying a haunting, exotic look. Imagine further that you own this street rocket. Impossible? Well, the car exists and you can figure out if you can afford it.

The car is a Ferrari F50, a Formula One racing car adapted for street use. The F50 is fast (202 MPH), incredibly expensive, and this year's ultimate fantasy machine. Only 349 of these cars will be built. Want one?

Here's the reality: Base price: $519,245. The price increases to $564,024 when you add the ten-speaker stereo system ($3,000) and sales tax ($41,779). Okay, you might say, but can I afford the monthly payments?

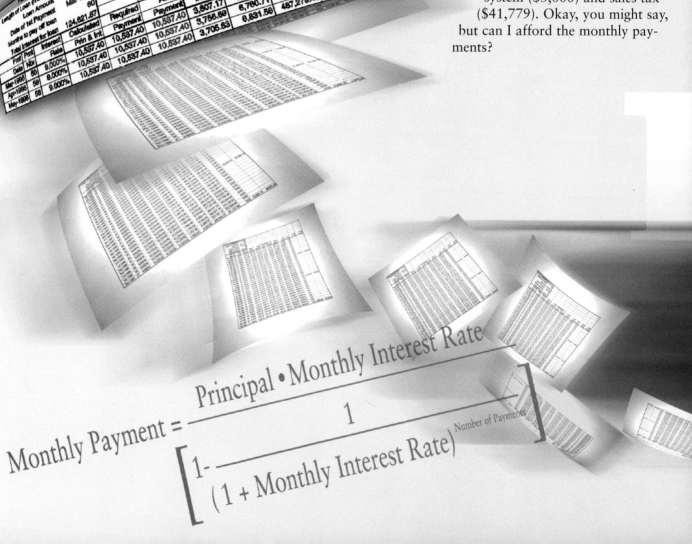

$$\text{Monthly Payment} = \frac{\text{Principal} \bullet \text{Monthly Interest Rate}}{\left[1 - \dfrac{1}{(1 + \text{Monthly Interest Rate})^{\text{Number of Payments}}}\right]}$$

After a standard down payment of 10% ($56,402), you must borrow $507,622. To determine your monthly payment, you can use the following formula:

$$\text{Monthly Payment} = \frac{\text{Principal} \bullet \text{Monthly Interest Rate}}{\left[1 - \dfrac{1}{(1 + \text{Monthly Interest Rate})^{\text{Number of Payments}}}\right]}$$

This baffling and confusing formula might cause you to throw your hands up and declare it is just not worth it. On the other hand, if you have an electronic spreadsheet program such as Excel 7, you can use it to perform the calculations quickly and easily. Assume for buying your new Ferrari you find a loan at 9% interest that you must pay off in five years (60 fixed monthly payments). When you enter this information, in less than a second Excel will provide you with your monthly payment ($10,537.40), the amount of principle and interest you pay each month, the ending balance at the end of each month, and the annual interest and annual principal you pay.

But what if you decide to save a little money by not buying the stereo, and you shop until you find a lender who will loan you the money at 8% interest? Must you go through the horror of manual calculations to determine your new monthly payment? Not if you are using Excel. Merely enter the new loan amount ($504,622) and interest rate (8%) and in a couple milliseconds, Excel will tell you your new monthly payment is only $10,231.91.

Worksheets such as Excel even enable you to work backwards. If you know how much you can afford as a monthly payment and at what interest rate, Excel can recalculate so you know the amount of money you can afford to borrow.

While it may be fantasy to own a Ferrari F50, with a few minor changes to the dollar amounts, Excel can help you decide exactly what car you can afford.

Microsoft
Excel 7
Windows 95

Formulas, Formatting, and Creating Charts

Case Perspective

Joe and Lisa Sabol own Ocean Air Art Institute, an art store that sells paintings and other art pieces. They have decided to expand their successful business by adding a second store in a neighboring town.

Joe and Lisa recently visited the loan department at the local savings and loan association and were told by Richard Leaman, the loan officer, to submit a report in the form of a worksheet that summarizes the profit potential of their current inventory. Mr. Leaman has also requested a pie chart showing the contribution of each art category to the total profit potential, so he can use it when he presents the loan request to the loan committee.

As a summer intern working for Ocean Air Art Institute, you have been assigned the task of designing and creating the worksheet and chart that satisfies the savings and loan association's requirements.

Introduction

In Project 1, you learned about entering data, summing values, how to make the worksheet easier to read, and how to draw a chart. You also learned about online Help and saving, printing, and loading a workbook from floppy disk into main memory. This project continues to emphasize these topics and presents some new ones.

The new topics include formulas, changing fonts, adding color to both characters and the background of a cell, adding borders, formatting numbers, changing the widths of columns and heights of rows, spell checking, additional charting techniques, and alternative types of worksheet displays and printouts. One alternative display and printout shows the formulas rather than the values in the worksheet. When you display the formulas in the worksheet, you see exactly what text, data, formulas, and functions you have entered into it.

Project Two – Ocean Air Art Institute

The summary notes from your meeting with Joe and Lisa, the owners of Ocean Air Art Institute, include the following: need, source of data, calculations, and graph requirements.

Need: An easy-to-read worksheet that summarizes the art pieces by category and shows the profit potential for each art category is needed. The worksheet is to include the units on hand, average unit cost, total cost, average unit selling price, total value, and profit potential for each art category. Also requested are totals and an average, maximum, and minimum for each of the calculations so the savings and loan association can, if necessary, base the loan on conditions that only certain types of art be sold in the new store.

Source of Data: The data for the inventory worksheet is available from George Kim, the part-time company controller. As part of his responsibilities as controller, Mr. Kim tracks inventory. He can supply the number of pieces of art in each art category (Oils, Watercolors, Sketches, and Acrylics) and the average unit price for each art category.

Calculations: The following calculations must be made for each of the four art categories as shown in Figure 2-1 on the next page.

1. Total Cost = Units On Hand × Average Unit Cost
   Joe and Lisa use a margin of 65%. The margin handles their overhead and profit. Thus, the Average Unit Price is calculated as follows:
   $$\text{Average Unit Price} = \text{Average Unit Cost} \times \left(\frac{1}{1 - .65}\right)$$
2. Total Value = Units On Hand × Average Unit Price
3. Profit Potential = Total Value – Total Cost
4. Compute the totals for Units On Hand, Total Cost, Total Value, and Profit Potential.
5. Use the Average, Maximum, and Minimum functions to determine the average, maximum, and minimum for the Units On Hand, Average Unit Cost, Total Cost, Average Unit Price, Total Value, and Profit Potential.

Graph Requirements: Draw a 3-D pie chart (Figure 2-1 on the next page) that shows the contribution of each of the four art categories to the total profit potential. Highlight the art category that has the greatest profit potential.

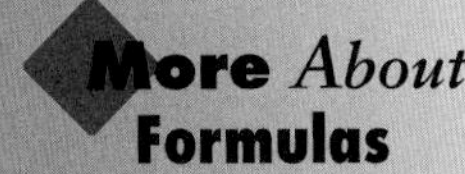

To make full use of Excel, it is important that you understand the order in which multiple operations in a formula are carried out. Excel uses the same order as in algebra. That is, first all negations (–), then all percents (%), then all exponentiations (^), then all multiplications (*) and divisions (/) from left to right, and finally all additions (+) and subtractions (–) from left to right. Parentheses can be used to override the order of operations.

Preparation Steps

The preparation steps summarize how the worksheet and chart shown in Figure 2-1 will be developed in Project 2. The following tasks will be completed in this project.

1. Start the Excel program.
2. Enter the worksheet title, column titles, row titles, and the units on hand and average unit cost for each of the four art categories.
3. Compute the Total Cost, Average Unit Price, Total Value, and Profit Potential for the first art category, Oils.
4. Copy the formulas for the remaining three art categories.
5. Use the AutoSum button to display the totals for Units On Hand, Total Cost, Total Value, and Profit Potential.
6. Determine the average, maximum, and minimum for the Units On Hand, Average Unit Cost, Total Cost, Average Unit Price, Total Value, and Profit Potential.
7. Save an intermediate copy of the workbook.

FIGURE 2-1

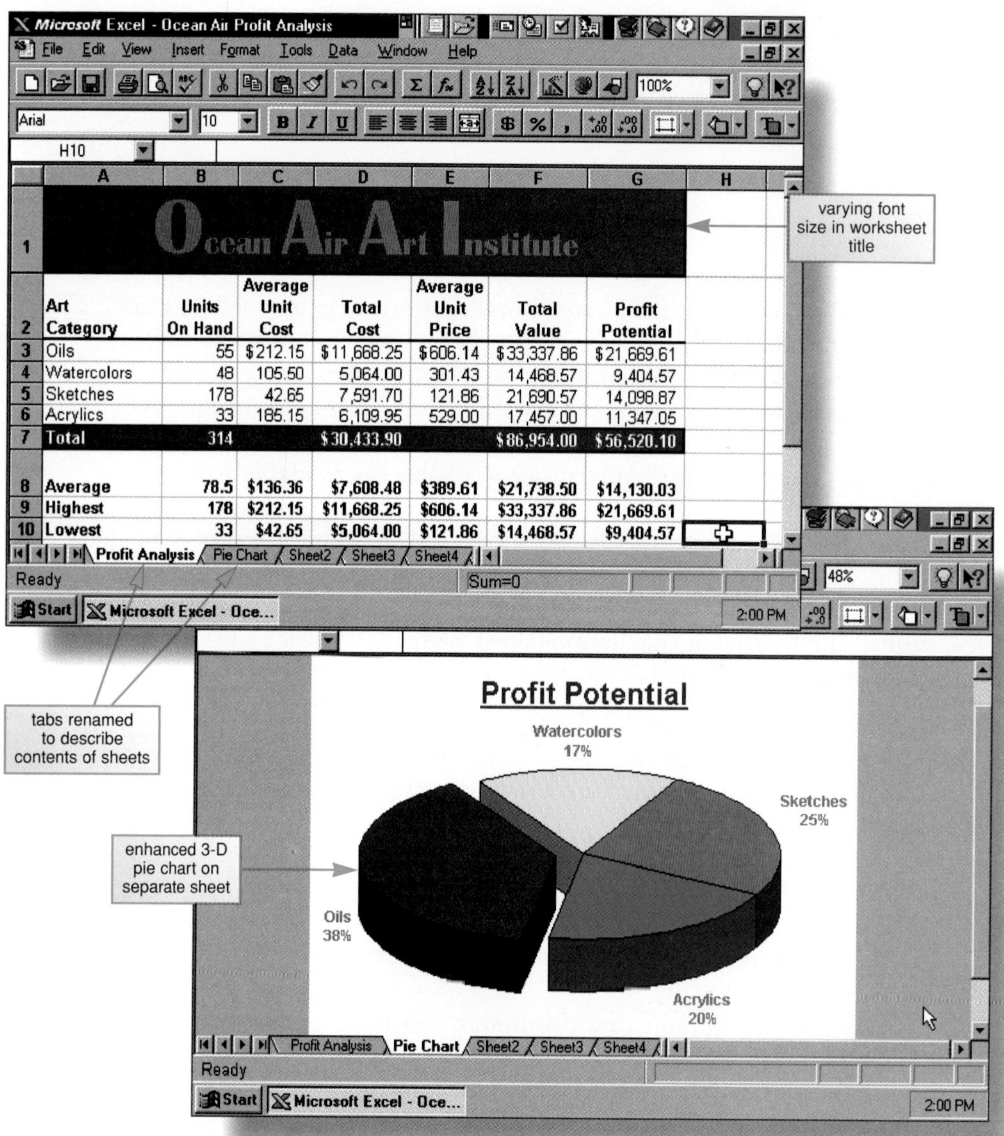

Art Category	Units On Hand	Average Unit Cost	Total Cost	Average Unit Price	Total Value	Profit Potential
Oils	55	$212.15	$11,668.25	$606.14	$33,337.86	$21,669.61
Watercolors	48	105.50	5,064.00	301.43	14,468.57	9,404.57
Sketches	178	42.65	7,591.70	121.86	21,690.57	14,098.87
Acrylics	33	185.15	6,109.95	529.00	17,457.00	11,347.05
Total	314		$30,433.90		$86,954.00	$56,520.10
Average	78.5	$136.36	$7,608.48	$389.61	$21,738.50	$14,130.03
Highest	178	$212.15	$11,668.25	$606.14	$33,337.86	$21,669.61
Lowest	33	$42.65	$5,064.00	$121.86	$14,468.57	$9,404.57

8. Format the worksheet so it has a professional appearance and is easy to read.
9. Draw the 3-D pie chart on a separate sheet. Highlight the largest slice. Improve the readability of the pie chart by using colors to emphasize the chart title and pie slice labels.
10. Rename the sheet tabs.
11. Save the workbook.
12. Preview and print the worksheet and 3-D pie chart.
13. Print the formulas version of the worksheet so the formulas can be verified.

The following pages contain a detailed explanation of these tasks.

Starting Excel

To start Excel, Windows 95 must be running. Perform the steps at the top of the next page to start Excel.

TO START EXCEL

Step 1: Click the Start button on the taskbar.
Step 2: Click New Office Document. If necessary, click the General tab in the New dialog box.
Step 3: Double-click the Blank Workbook icon.

An alternative to Steps 1 and 2 is to click the Start a New Document button on the Microsoft Office Shortcut Bar.

Entering the Titles and Numbers into the Worksheet

The worksheet title in Figure 2-1 is centered over columns A through G in row 1. Because the centered text first must be entered into the leftmost column of the area over which it is centered, it will be entered into cell A1.

The column headings in row 2 begin in cell A2 and extend through cell G2. Notice in row 2 of Figure 2-1 that multiple lines of text in each cell make up the column titles. You start a new line in a cell by pressing ALT+ENTER at the conclusion of each line, except for the last line, which is completed by clicking the enter box, pressing the ENTER key, or pressing one of the arrow keys. When you see ALT+ENTER in a step, hold down the ALT key, and while holding it down, press the ENTER key, then release both keys.

The row titles in column A begin in cell A3 and continue down to cell A10. The numbers, submitted by George Kim, the company controller, are summarized in Table 2-1. These numbers are entered into the range B3:C6. The steps required to enter the worksheet title, column titles, row titles, and numbers are outlined in the remainder of this section and are shown in Figure 2-2 on the next page.

Table 2-1

ART CATEGORY	UNITS ON HAND	AVERAGE UNIT COST
Oils	55	212.15
Watercolors	48	105.50
Sketches	178	42.65
Acrylics	33	185.15

TO ENTER THE WORKSHEET TITLE

Step 1: Select cell A1. Type `Ocean Air Art Institute` as the cell entry.
Step 2: Press the DOWN ARROW key.

The worksheet title displays as shown in cell A1 of Figure 2-2 on the next page.

More About Designing a Worksheet

With early spreadsheet packages, users often skipped rows to improve the appearance of the worksheet. With Excel it is not necessary to skip rows because you can increase the height of rows to add white space between information.

TO ENTER THE COLUMN TITLES

Step 1: With cell A2 active, type `Art`, press ALT+ENTER, type `Category`, and press the RIGHT ARROW key.
Step 2: Type `Units`, press ALT+ENTER, type `On Hand`, and press the RIGHT ARROW key.
Step 3: Type `Average`, press ALT+ENTER, type `Unit`, press ALT+ENTER, type `Cost`, and press the RIGHT ARROW key.
Step 4: Type `Total`, press ALT+ENTER, type `Cost`, and press the RIGHT ARROW key.

More About Wrapping Lengthy Text in a Cell

If you have a long text entry, such as a paragraph, you can instruct Excel to wrap the text in a cell, rather than pressing ALT+ENTER to end a line. To wrap text, click Format Cells on the shortcut menu, click the Alignment tab, and click the Wrap Text check box. Excel will automatically increase the height of the cell so the additional lines will fit. However, if you want to control the contents of a line in a cell, rather than letting Excel wrap based on the width of a cell, then you must end a line with ALT+ENTER.

Step 5: Type `Average`, press ALT+ENTER, type `Unit`, press ALT+ENTER, type `Price`, and press the RIGHT ARROW key.
Step 6: Type `Total`, press ALT+ENTER, type `Value`, and press the RIGHT ARROW key.
Step 7: Type `Profit`, press ALT+ENTER, type `Potential`, and press the RIGHT ARROW key.

The column titles display as shown in row 2 of Figure 2-2. As you add more lines to a cell through the use of the ALT+ENTER key, Excel increases the height of the entire row.

TO ENTER THE ROW TITLES

Step 1: Select cell A3. Type `Oils` and then press the DOWN ARROW key.
Step 2: Enter the row titles `Watercolors`, `Sketches`, `Acrylics`, `Total`, `Average`, `Highest`, and `Lowest` in cells A4 through A10.

The row titles display as shown in column A of Figure 2-2.

More About Entering Numbers into a Range

An efficient way to enter a set of numbers into a range of cells, such as B3:C6 in Figure 2-2, is to select the range by dragging from cell B3 to cell C6 prior to entering the numbers. After initially selecting the range, cell B3 remains the active cell. Thus, type the value for cell B3 and press the ENTER key. Excel responds by entering the number and moving the active cell selection down one cell. When you enter the last value in the first column, Excel will move the active cell selection to the top of the next column and then precede downward.

TO ENTER THE NUMBERS

Step 1: Enter `55` in cell B3 and `212.15` in cell C3.
Step 2: Enter `48` in cell B4 and `105.5` in cell C4.
Step 3: Enter `178` in cell B5 and `42.65` in cell C5.
Step 4: Enter `33` in cell B6 and `185.15` in cell C6.

The numeric entries display as shown in the range B3:C6 of Figure 2-2. Later in this project the numbers will be formatted so they are easier to read.

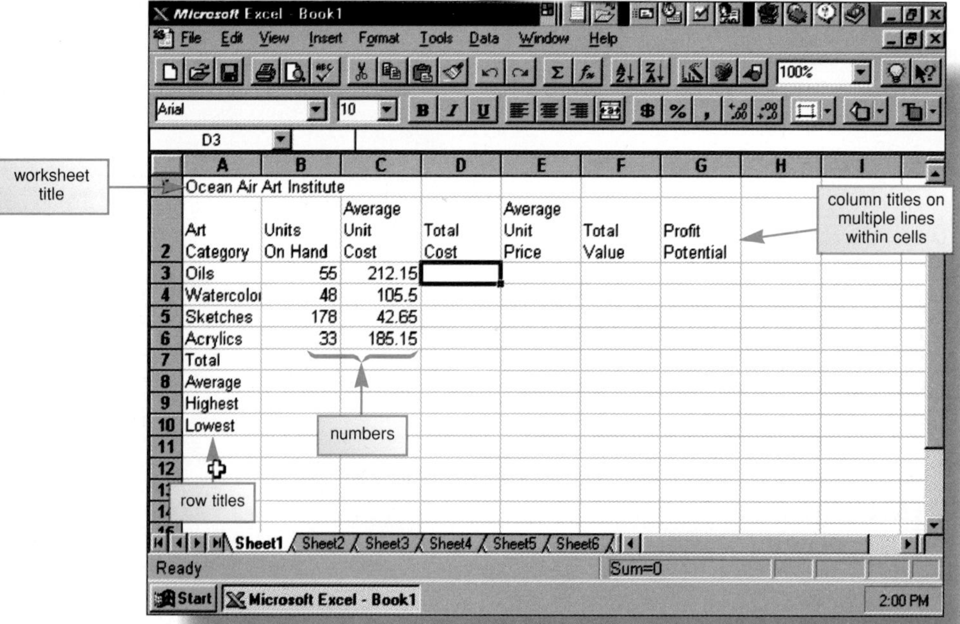

FIGURE 2-2

Entering Formulas

The total cost for each art category, which displays in column D, is equal to the corresponding units on hand in column B times the corresponding average unit cost in column C. Thus, the total cost for Oils in row 3 is obtained by multiplying 55 (cell B3) times 212.15 (cell C3).

One of the reasons Excel is such a valuable tool is because you can assign a **formula** to a cell and Excel will calculate the result. In this example, the formula in cell D3 multiplies the values in cells B3 and C3 and displays the result in cell D3.

The worksheet would be of little value if you had to manually multiply 55 x 212.15 and then enter the result, 11668.25, in cell D3, because every time the values in cells B3 and C3 change, you would have to recalculate the product and enter the new value in cell D3. By entering a formula, Excel recalculates the formula whenever a new value is entered into the worksheet. Complete the following steps to enter the formula using the keyboard.

More *About* Recalculation of Formulas

Every time you enter a value into a cell in the worksheet, Excel recalculates all formulas. It makes no difference if there is one formula or hundreds of formulas in the worksheet. Excel recalculates the formulas instantaneously. This is one of the reasons why a spreadsheet package, such as Excel, is so heavily used in business.

Steps To Enter a Simple Formula Using the Keyboard

1 **Select cell D4. Type** =b3*c3 **as the cell entry.**

The formula displays in the formula bar and in cell D3 (Figure 2-3).

formula begins with equal sign

formula displays in formula bar and in cell D3

FIGURE 2-3

2 **Press the RIGHT ARROW key.**

Instead of displaying the formula in cell D3, Excel completes the arithmetic indicated by the formula and displays the result, 11668.25 (Figure 2-4).

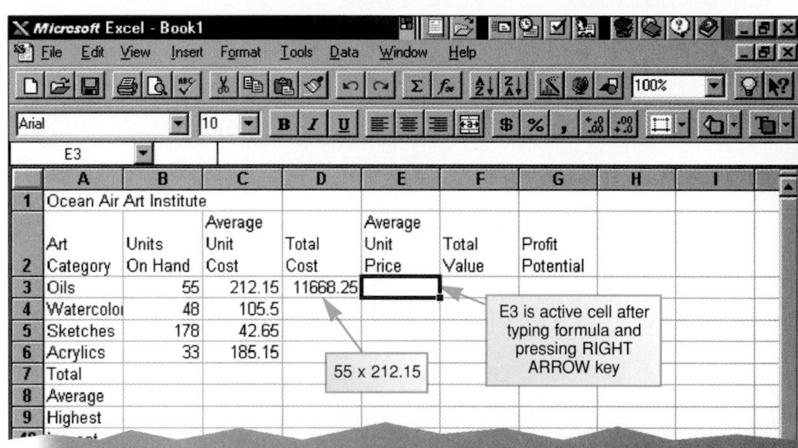

FIGURE 2-4

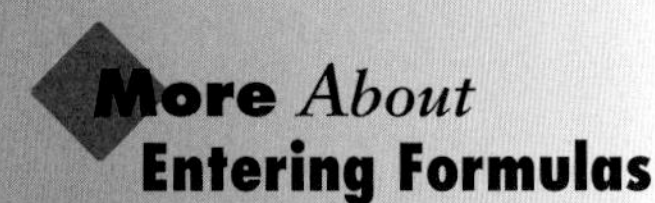

Besides the equal sign (=), you can start a formula with a plus sign (+) or a minus sign (–). However, don't forget to start with one of these three characters or the formula will be interpreted by Excel as text.

The equal sign (=) preceding b3*c3 is an important part of the formula. It alerts Excel that you are entering a formula or function and not text. The asterisk (*) following b3 is the arithmetic operator, which directs Excel to perform the **multiplication operation**. Other valid Excel arithmetic operators include + (**addition**), – (**subtraction**), / (**division**), % (**percentage**), and ^ (**exponentiation**).

You can enter formulas in uppercase or lowercase and you can add spaces between the arithmetic operators to make the formulas easier to read. That is, =b3*c3 is the same as =b3 * c3, =B3 * c3, =B3 * C3, or = b3*c3.

Order of Operations

When more than one operator is involved in a formula, Excel uses the same order of operations as in algebra. Moving from left to right in a formula, **the order of operations** is as follows: first negation (–), then all percents (%), then all exponentiations (^), then all multiplications (*) and divisions (/), and finally all additions (+) and subtractions (–). You can use **parentheses** to override the order of operations. For example, following the order of operations, 8 * 5 – 2 is equal to 38. With use of parentheses, however, 8 * (5 – 2) is equal to 24 because the parentheses instruct Excel to subtract 2 from 5 before multiplying by 8. Table 2-2 illustrates several examples of valid formulas.

Table 2-2

FORMULA	REMARK
=F6	Assigns the value in cell F6 to the active cell.
=3 + -2^2	Assigns the sum of 3 plus 4 (or 7) to the active cell.
=2 * R3 or =R3 * 2 or =(2 * R3)	Assigns two times the contents of cell R3 to the active cell.
=12 * 25%	Assigns the product of 12 times 0.25 (or 3) to the active cell.
=-A12 * A45	Assigns the negative value of the product of the values contained in cells A12 and A45 to the active cell.
=3 * (K12 - D2)	Assigns the product of three times the difference between the values contained in cells K12 and D2 to the active cell.
=A1 / C6 - A3 * A4 + A5 ^ A6	From left to right: first exponentiation (A5 ^ A6), then division (A1 / C6), then multiplication (A3 * A4), then subtraction (A1 / C6) – (A3 * A4), and finally addition (A1 / C6 – A3 * A4) + (A5 ^ A6). If cell A1 = 10, A3 = 6, A4 = 2, A5 = 5, A6 = 2, and C6 = 2, then Excel assigns the active cell the value 10 / 2 – 6 * 2 + 5 ^ 2 = 18.

Entering a Complex Formula

As indicated in the previous section, you can assign to a cell as complex a formula as required. In the Ocean Air Art Institute worksheet, the formula

$$\text{Average Unit Cost} \times \left(\frac{1}{1 - .65}\right) \qquad \text{or} \qquad \text{c3 * (1/(1 – .65))}$$

must be assigned to cell E3. The average unit cost is the value in cell C3. The formula requires that the quantity in the denominator, 1 – .65, be determined first because the difference must be divided into 1 before the multiplication takes place. Parentheses are used to control the order of operations or Excel would multiply the value in cell C3 by 1 and then divide by 1 before subtracting .65. With cell C3 equal to 212.15 (see Figure 2-4 on page E 2.9), Excel completes the operations for cell E3 as shown below:

Step 1	=c3 * (1 / (1 – .65))	=212.15 * (1 / (.35))
Step 2		=212.15 * (2.857142857)
Step 3		=606.1429

Perform the following steps to enter a complex formula using the keyboard.

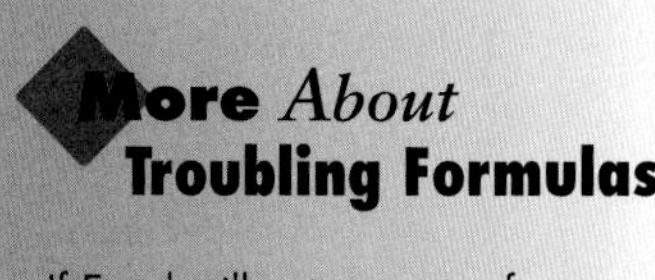

If Excel will not accept a formula, remove the equal sign from the left side and complete the entry as text. Later, after entering additional data or after you have determined the error, reinsert the equal sign.

To Enter a Complex Formula Using the Keyboard

1 **With cell E3 selected, type** `=c3*(1/(1-.65))` **as the cell entry.**

The formula displays in cell E3 as shown in Figure 2-5.

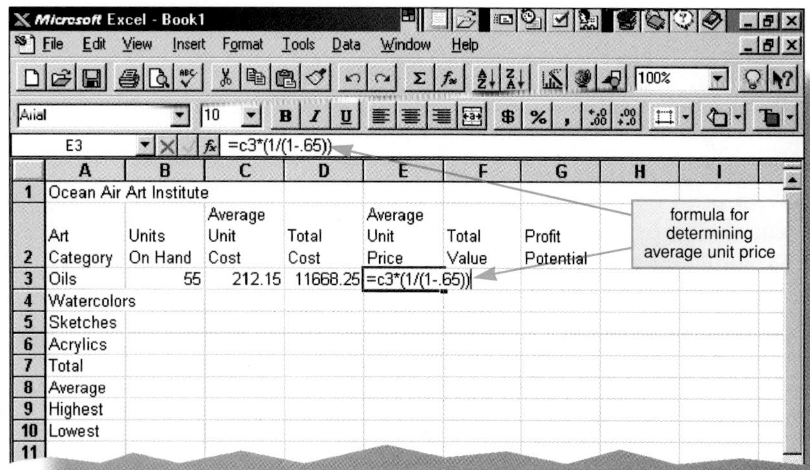

FIGURE 2-5

2 **Press the RIGHT ARROW key.**

The average unit cost for Oils displays in cell E3 (Figure 2-6).

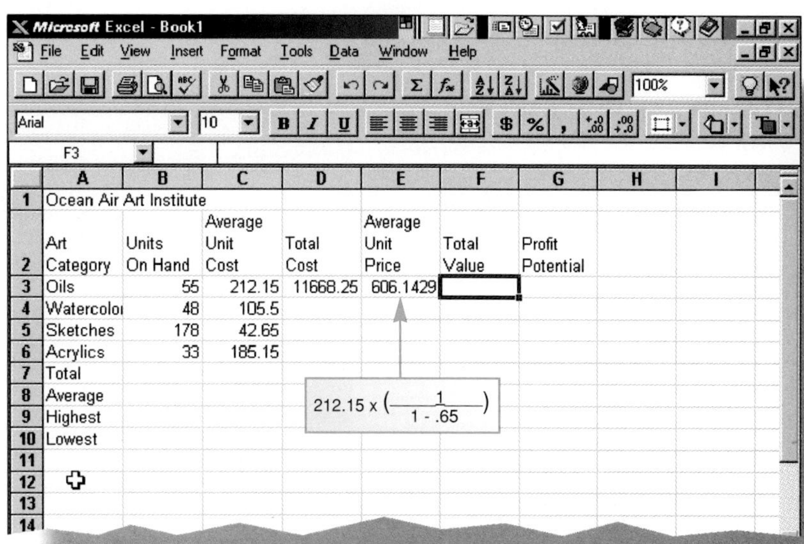

FIGURE 2-6

More About Using Point Mode

Point mode allows you to create formulas using the mouse. Instead of typing a cell reference in a formula, simply click a cell and Excel will append the corresponding cell reference at the location of the insertion point. You can also use the Customize command on the shortcut menu. It displays when you right-click a toolbar to create a new toolbar made up of buttons that represent the operators. Thus, with Excel you can enter entire formulas without ever touching the keyboard.

The first two formulas were entered into cells D3 and E3 using the keyboard. The next section shows you how to enter the formulas in cells F3 and G3 using the mouse to select cell references in a formula.

Entering Formulas Using Point Mode

In the worksheet shown in Figure 2-1 on page E 2.6, the total value of each art category displays in column F. The total value for Oils in cell F3 is equal to the units on hand (cell B3) times the average unit price (cell E3). The result in cell F3 indicates the worth of the Oil paintings inventory if all paintings were sold. The profit potential for Oils in cell G3 is equal to the total value in cell F3 minus the total cost in cell D3.

Instead of entering the formulas =b3*e3 in cell F3 and =f3 – d3 in cell G3 by using the keyboard as in the first two formulas, you can use the following steps to use the mouse and Point mode to enter the last two formulas. **Point mode** allows you to select cells for use in a formula by using the mouse.

To Enter Formulas Using Point Mode

1 **With cell F3 selected, type the equal sign (=) to begin the formula and then click cell B3.**

Excel responds by highlighting cell B3 with a marquee and by appending B3 to the equal sign in cell F3 (Figure 2-7).

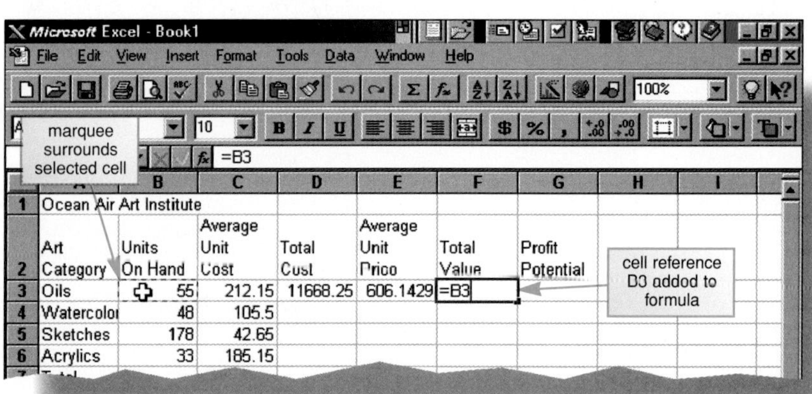

FIGURE 2-7

2 **Type the asterisk (*) and then click cell E3.**

Excel highlights cell E3 with a marquee and appends E3 to the asterisk (*) in cell F3 (Figure 2-8).

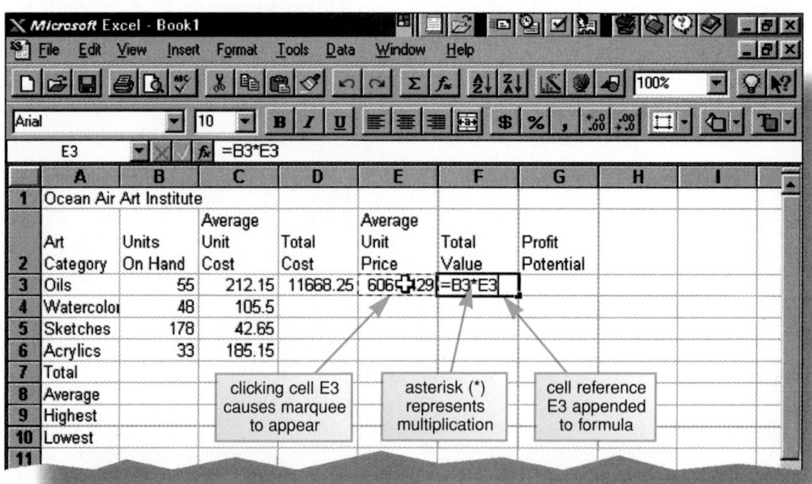

FIGURE 2-8

3 **Click the enter box or press the ENTER key. Click cell G3.**

*Excel determines the product of =B3*E3 and displays the result, 33337.86, in cell F3 (Figure 2-9).*

4 **With cell G3 selected, type = and then click cell F3. Type - and then click cell D3.**

The formula =F3 – D3 displays in cell G3 and in the formula bar (Figure 2-9).

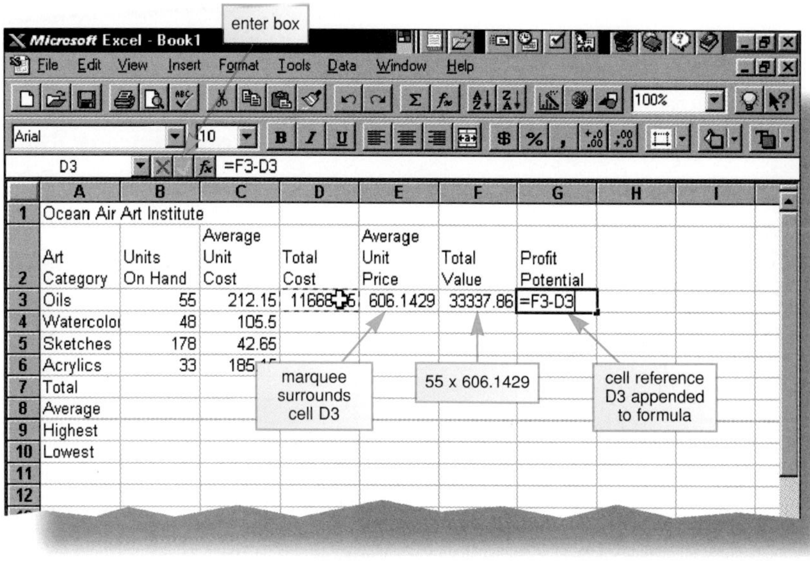

FIGURE 2-9

5 **Click the enter box or press the enter key.**

The profit potential for Oils, 21669.61, displays in cell G3 (Figure 2-10).

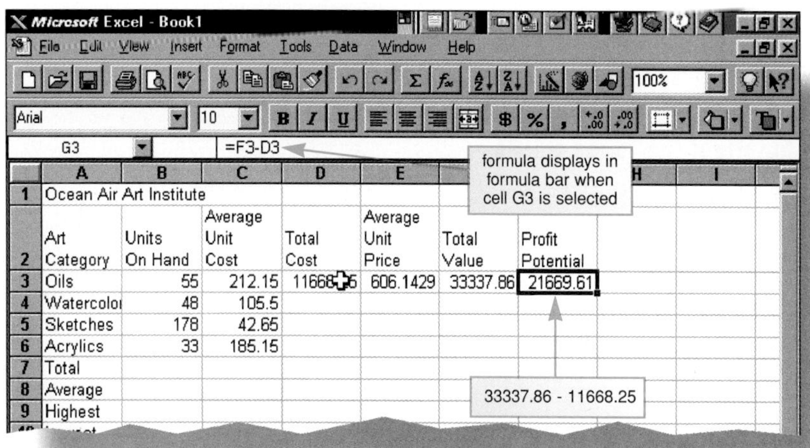

FIGURE 2-10

The four formulas for the Oils category in cells D3 through G3 are now complete. The same four formulas could be entered one at a time for Watercolors, Sketches, and Acrylics. An easier method of entering the formulas, however, is to select the four formulas in cells D3 through G3 and use the fill handle to copy them to the range D4:G6.

Copying a Range of Cells Down Rows to an Adjacent Range Using the Fill Handle

In Project 1, you learned how to copy a cell to a range of adjacent cells using the fill handle. This section shows you how to copy a range of cells to an adjacent range. Recall that when you copy a formula, Excel adjusts the cell references so the new formulas reflect computations using their respective values. Thus, if you copy downward, Excel adjusts the row portion of cell references. If you copy across, then Excel adjusts the column portion of cell references.

Perform the following steps to copy a range of cells.

To Copy a Range of Cells Down Rows to an Adjacent Range Using the Fill Handle

1. **Click cell D3 and then drag to the right to select the range D3:G3. Point to the fill handle.**

   The range D3:G3 is highlighted and the mouse pointer changes to the cross hair (Figure 2-11).

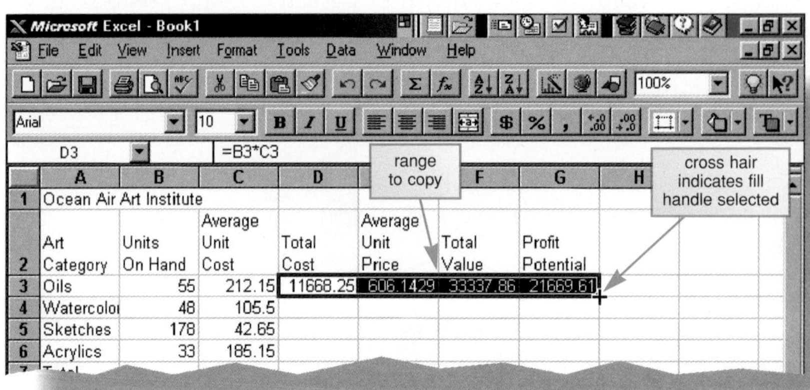

FIGURE 2-11

2. **Drag the fill handle down to highlight the range D4:G6.**

   After you release the left mouse button, Excel copies the four formulas in the range D3:G3 to the range D4:G6 and displays the total cost, average unit price, total value, and profit potential for the remaining art categories (Figure 2-12).

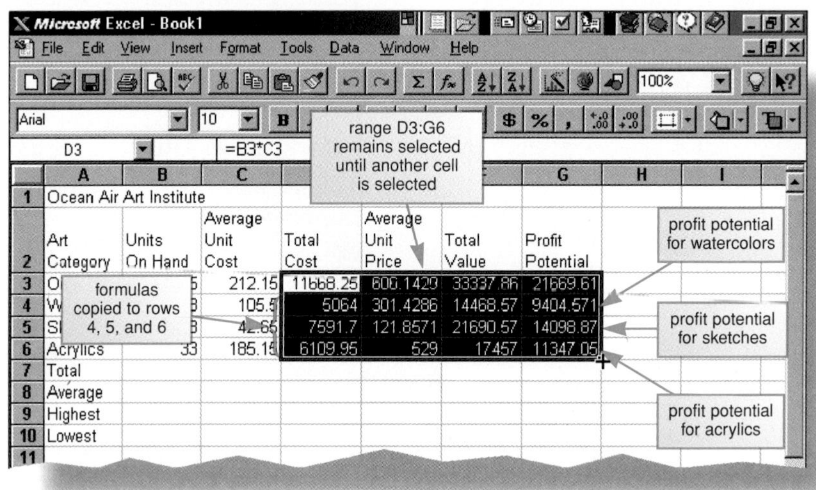

FIGURE 2-12

OtherWays

1. Select copy area, right-click copy area, click Copy on shortcut menu, right-click paste area, click Paste on shortcut menu
2. Select copy area, click Copy button on Standard toolbar, select paste area, click Paste button on Standard toolbar
3. Select copy area, on Edit menu click Copy, select paste area, on Edit menu click Paste
4. Select copy area, press CTRL+C, select paste area, press CTRL+V

Select any cell to remove the selection from the range D3:G6.

As indicated earlier, when Excel copies the four formulas in the range D3:G3 to the range D4:G6, the row references in the formula are adjusted as the formula is copied downward. For example, in column D the formula assigned to cell D4 is =B4*C4. Similarly, Excel assigns cell D5 the formula =B5*C5, and cell D6 the formula =B6*C6. When you copy downward, the row reference changes in the formula.

Calculating the Totals Using the AutoSum Button

The next step is to determine the totals in row 7 for the units on hand in column B, the total cost in column D, the total value in column F, and the profit potentialin column G. To determine the total in column B, cells B3 through B6 must be summed. You can enter the function =sum(b3:b6) in cell B7, or you can select cell B7 and then click the AutoSum button twice. Similar SUM functions or the AutoSum button can be used in cells D7, F7, and G7. The most efficient method is to use the AutoSum button as shown in the following steps.

More About Selecting a Range

If you dislike dragging to select a range, press F8 and use the arrow keys to select one corner of the range and then the cell diagonally opposite it in the proposed range. Make sure you press F8 to turn selection off after you are finished with the range or you will continue to select ranges.

TO CACULATE TOTALS USING THE AUTOSUM BUTTON

Step 1: Select cell B7. Click the AutoSum button twice. (Do not double-click.)
Step 2: Select cell D7. Click the AutoSum button twice.
Step 3: Select the range F7:G7. Click the AutoSum button once.

The four totals display in row 7 as shown in Figure 2-13.

An alternative method to calculating the totals using the AutoSum function is to select all four cells before clicking the AutoSum button. To select the nonadjacent range B7, D7, F7, and G7, select cell B7, and then hold down the CTRL key and click the remaining three cells one at a time. Next, click the AutoSum button.

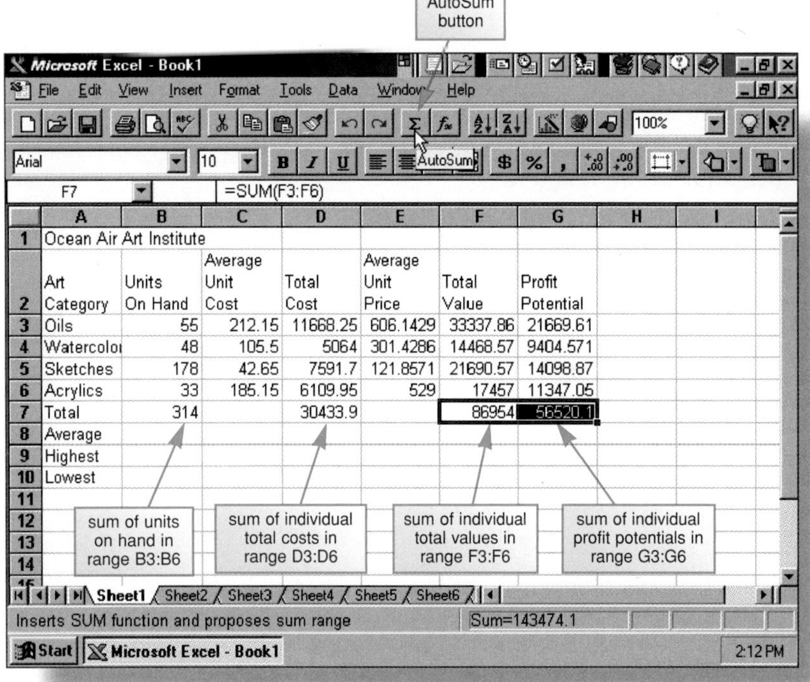

FIGURE 2-13

Using the AVERAGE, MAX, and MIN Functions

The next step in creating the Ocean Air Art Institute worksheet is to compute the average, maximum value, and minimum value for the units on hand in column B. Once the values are determined, the entries can be copied across to the other columns.

Excel includes functions to compute these statistics. A **function** is a prewritten formula that takes a value or values, performs an operation, and returns a value or values. The values that you give to a function to perform operations on are called the **arguments**. All functions begin with an equal sign and include the arguments in parentheses after the function name. For example, in the function =AVERAGE(B3:B6), the function name is AVERAGE and the argument is the range B3:B6.

Computing the Average

To determine the average of the numbers in the range B3:B6, perform the steps on the next page.

Steps To Find the Average of a Group of Numbers

1 Select cell B8. Type =average(**in the cell.**

Excel displays the beginning of the AVERAGE function in the formula bar and in cell B8 (Figure 2-14).

AVERAGE function without range displayed in formula bar and in cell B8

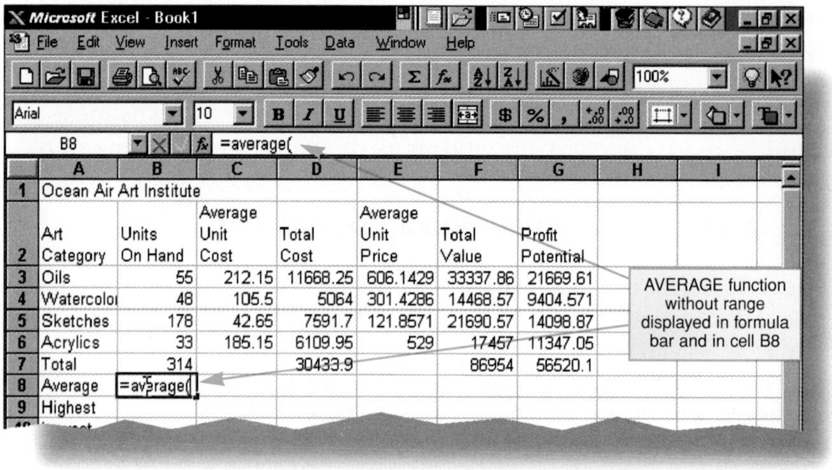

FIGURE 2-14

2 Click cell B3, the first endpoint of the range to average. Drag down to cell B6, the second endpoint of the range to average.

A marquee surrounds the range B3:B6. When you click cell B3, Excel appends cell B3 to the left parenthesis in the formula bar and highlights cell B3 with a marquee. When you begin dragging, Excel appends a colon (:) to the function and also the cell reference of the cell where the mouse pointer is located (Figure 2-15).

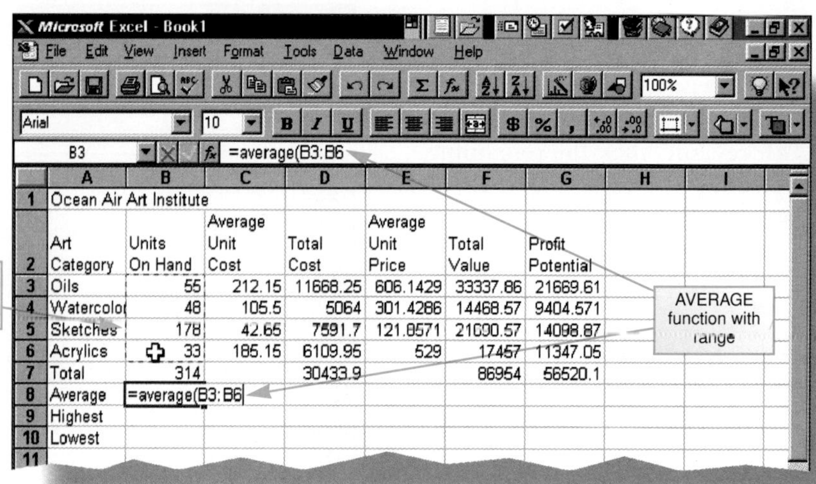

FIGURE 2-15

3 Release the left mouse button and then click the enter box or press the ENTER key.

Excel computes the average, 78.5, of the three numbers in the range B3:B6 and assigns it to cell B8 (Figure 2-16).

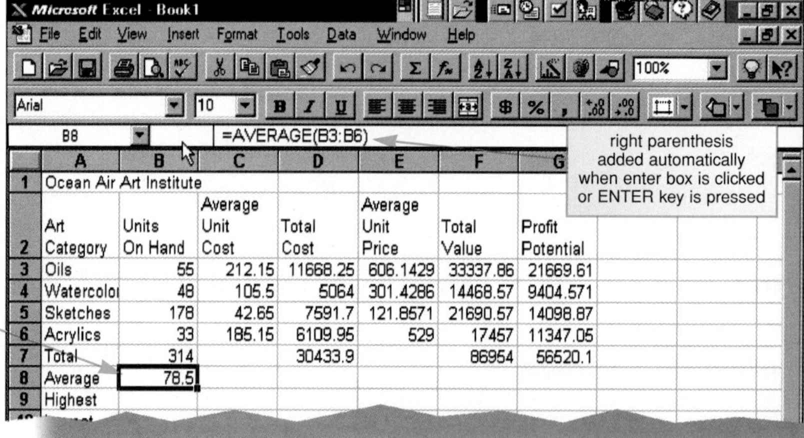

FIGURE 2-16

OtherWays

1. Click Function Wizard button on Standard toolbar, select desired function, respond in dialog boxes
2. Type =, click the function wizard box in formula bar, select desired function, respond in dialog boxes

Notice that Excel appends the right parenthesis automatically to complete the AVERAGE function when you click the enter box or press the ENTER key. The AVERAGE function requires that the range (the argument) be included within parentheses following the function name. Also, when you use the Point mode as in the previous steps, you cannot use the arrow keys to complete the entry. While in Point mode, the arrow keys change the selected cell reference in the formula being created.

In the example just illustrated, Point mode was used to select the range following the left parenthesis. Rather than use Point mode, you can type the range. If you decide to type a range, remember that the colon (:) separating the endpoints of the range is required punctuation.

More *About* Excel's Add-Ins

Excel comes with add-ins that can simplify your work. Add-ins are installed during or after the installation and activated through the Add-Ins command on the Tools menu. Some add-ins add commands to menus or controls to dialog boxes. Some of the more popular add-ins are View Manager (name and save frequently used worksheet locations), Analysis ToolPak (new function category), Engineering (engineering functions), Report Manager (additional printing capabilities), and Solver (linear and nonlinear optimization).

Calculating the Highest Value in a Range Using the MAX Function

The next step is to select cell B9 and determine the highest value in the range B3:B6. Excel has a function for displaying the highest value in a range called the **MAX function**. Enter the function name and use Point mode as described below.

TO FIND THE HIGHEST NUMBER IN A RANGE

Step 1: Select cell B9. Type `=max(` as the entry.
Step 2: Click cell B3, the first endpoint of the desired range. Drag down to cell B6, the second endpoint of the desired range.
Step 3: Release the left mouse button and then click the enter box or press the ENTER key.

Excel determines the highest value in the range B3:B6 as 178 (cell B5) and displays it in cell B9 (Figure 2-17).

Certainly it would be as easy as entering the MAX function to scan the range B3:B6 to determine the highest value in the range B4:B8 and enter the number 178 as a constant in cell B9. The display would be the same as Figure 2-17. If the values in the range B3:B6 change, however, cell B9 would continue to display 178. By using the MAX function, you are guaranteed that Excel will recalculate the highest value in the range B3:B6 each time a new value is entered into the worksheet. Scanning the range manually for the highest value also would be much more time-consuming if the worksheet contained more categories.

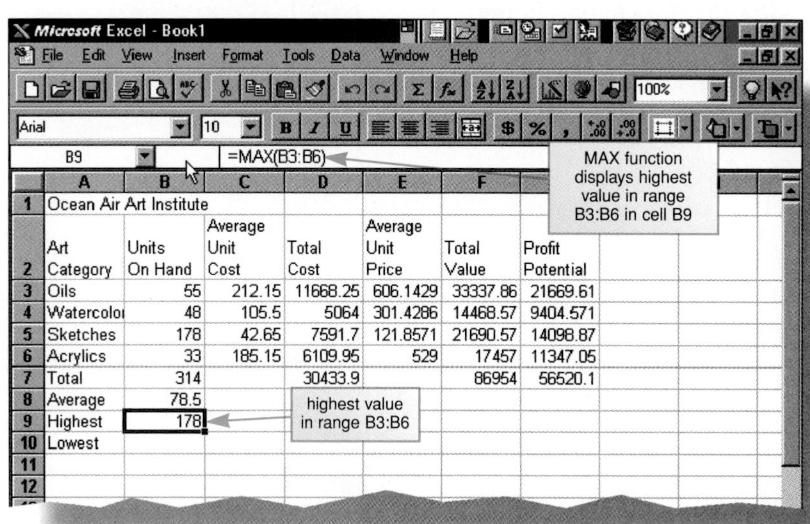

FIGURE 2-17

Entering the MIN Function Using the Function Wizard Button

The next step is to enter the **MIN function** in cell B10 to determine the lowest value in the range B3:B6. Although you could enter the MIN function in the same fashion as the MAX function, the following steps show an alternative using Excel's **Function Wizard button** on the Standard toolbar.

To Enter the MIN Function Using the Function Wizard Button

1 **Select cell B10. Click the Function Wizard button on the Standard toolbar. Click MIN in the Function Name list box in the Function Wizard - Step 1 of 2 dialog box, and then point to the Next button.**

Excel displays the **Function Wizard - Step 1 of 2 dialog box** *with Most Recently Used selected in the* **Function Category list box** *and MIN selected in the* **Function Name list box** *(Figure 2-18).*

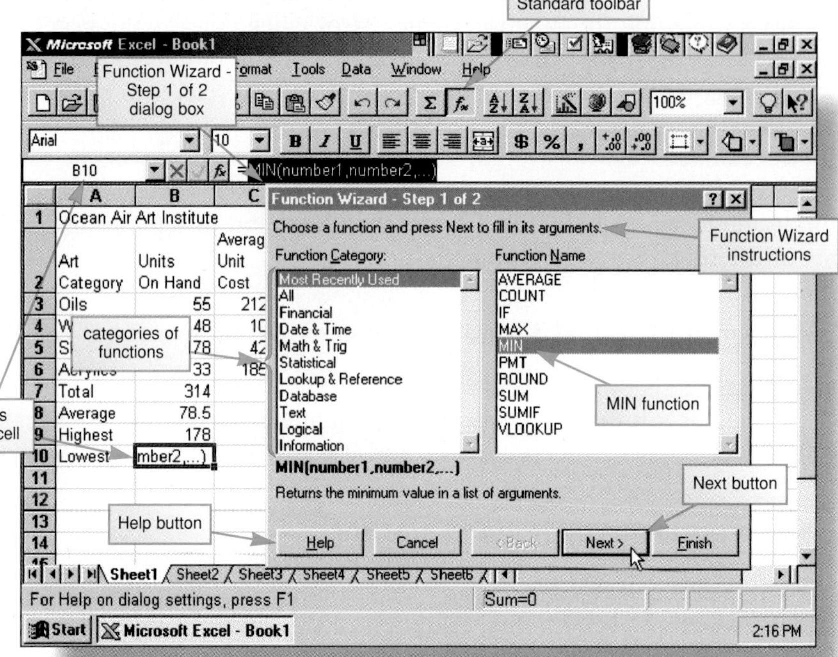

FIGURE 2-18

2 **Click the Next button in the Function Wizard - Step 1 of 2 dialog box.**

Excel displays the Function Wizard Step 2 of 2 dialog box.

3 **Use the mouse to select the range B3:B6 on the worksheet.**

Excel enters the range in the number 1 box and displays the result of =MIN(B3:B6) in the Value box (33) in the Function Wizard - Step 2 of 2 dialog box (Figure 2-19).

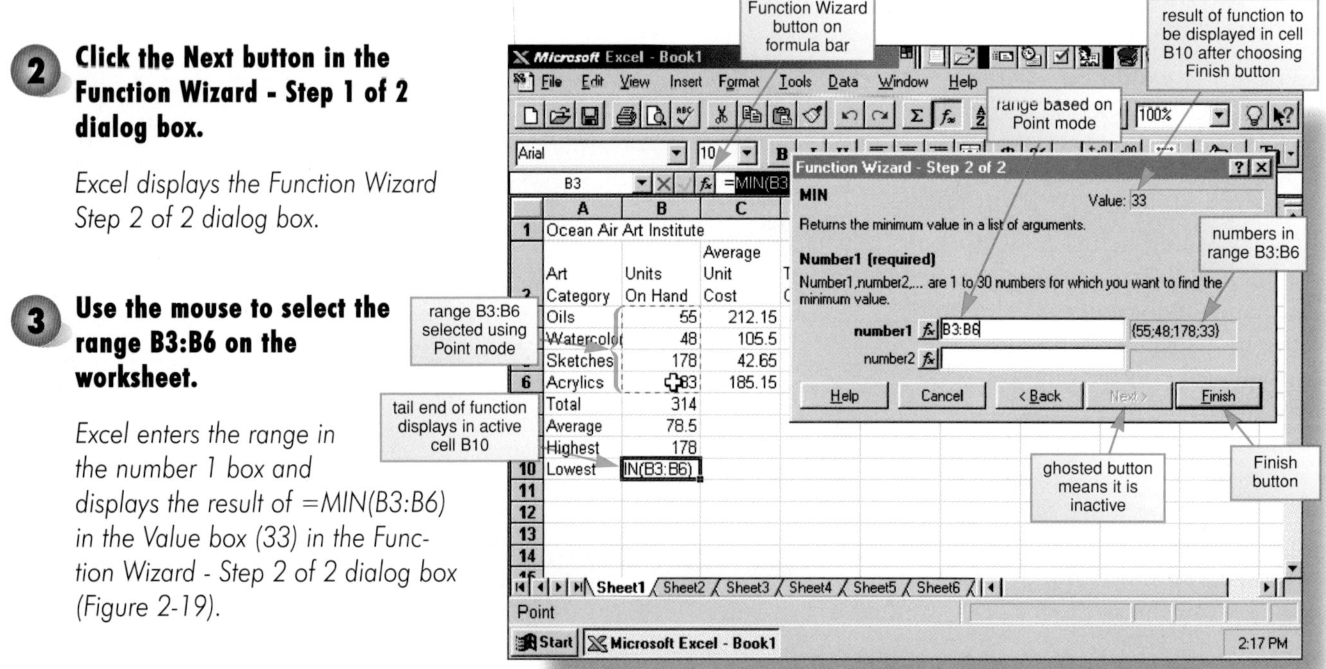

FIGURE 2-19

4 **Click the Finish button.**

Excel determines the lowest value in the range B3:B6 and displays it in cell B10 (Figure 2-20).

FIGURE 2-20

OtherWays

1. Press SHIFT+F3

You can see from the previous example that using the Function Wizard button on the Standard toolbar allows you to enter a function into a cell easily without requiring you to memorize its format. Anytime you desire to enter a function, simply click the Function Wizard button on the Standard toolbar, select the desired function, and enter the arguments.

An alternative to using the Function Wizard button on the Standard toolbar is to use the function wizard button on the formula bar, next to the enter box. This button displays only when the formula bar is active (see Figure 2-19) and is primarily used to enter a function in the middle of a formula you are entering into a cell. A third alternative for entering a function into a cell is to click Function on the Insert menu.

Thus far, you have learned to use the SUM, AVERAGE, MAX, and MIN functions. Besides these four functions, Excel has more than 400 additional functions that perform just about every type of calculation you can imagine. These functions are categorized as shown in the Function Category box in Figure 2-18. To obtain a list and description of the available functions, click Microsoft Excel Help Topics on the Help menu. When Excel displays the Help Topics: Microsoft Excel dialog box, click the Index tab, and type `functions` in the top box labeled 1. Under functions in the lower box labeled 2, scroll down and then double-click worksheet function index. One-by-one, click each category. To obtain a hard copy of any desired listing, click the Optionsbutton and then click Print Topic.

In the Function Wizard dialog box in Figure 2-19, five buttons are available. If a button is ghosted (dimmed), it means you cannot choose it. The functions of the five Function Wizard buttons are described in Table 2-3.

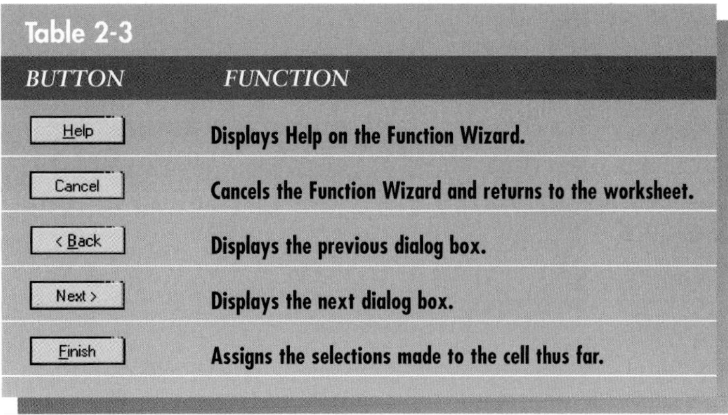

Table 2-3

BUTTON	FUNCTION
Help	Displays Help on the Function Wizard.
Cancel	Cancels the Function Wizard and returns to the worksheet.
< Back	Displays the previous dialog box.
Next >	Displays the next dialog box.
Finish	Assigns the selections made to the cell thus far.

More About Ranges

If you are an experienced Lotus 1-2-3 user and find it difficult to change your ways, you can enter a range using two periods. For example, Excel interprets B5..B10 as B5:B10.

More About Using Point Mode

In Step 3 and Figure 2-19 the range is entered in the number 1 box in the Function Wizard - Step 2 of 2 dialog box by dragging through the range on the worksheet. If part of the range is hidden by the dialog box, point to the title bar of the dialog box and drag it out of the way.

Copying the AVERAGE, MAX, and MIN Functions

The final step before formatting the worksheet is to copy the AVERAGE, MAX, and MIN functions in the range B8:B10 to the range C8:G10. Here again, the fill handle will be used to complete the copy.

Steps To Copy a Range of Cells Across Columns to an Adjacent Range Using the Fill Handle

1. **Select the range B8:B10. Drag the fill handle in the lower right corner of cell B10 and drag across to cell G10.**

   Excel highlights the copy area (range B8:B10) and displays a rectangle around the paste area (range C8:G10) (Figure 2-21).

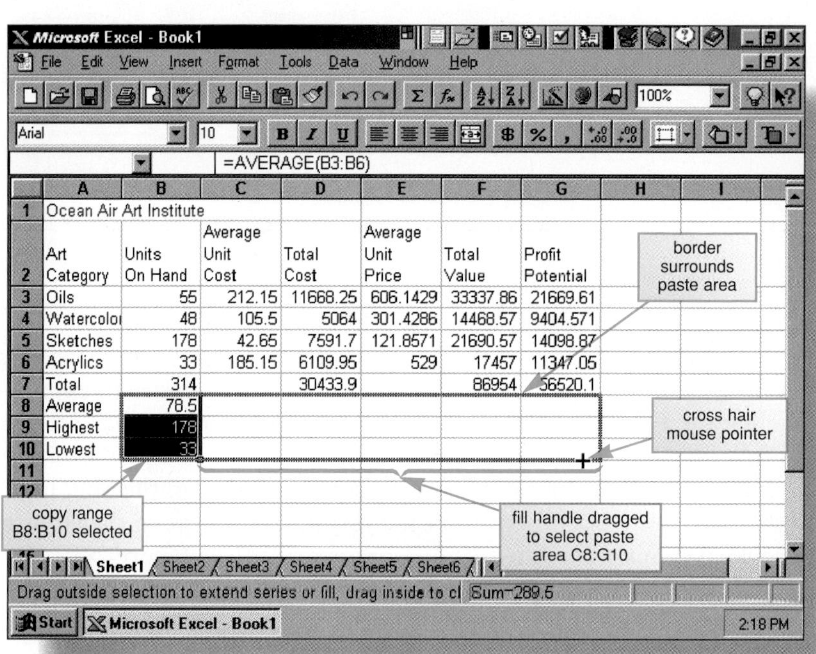

FIGURE 2-21

2. **Release the left mouse button.**

   Excel copies the three functions across the range C8:G10 (Figure 2-22).

AVERAGE, MAX, and MIN functions in range B8:B10 copied to range C8:G10

FIGURE 2-22

Here again, you must remember that Excel adjusts the ranges in the copied functions so that each function refers to the column of numbers above it. Review the numbers in rows 8 through 10 in Figure 2-22. You should see that each function is determining the appropriate value in the column above it for the numbers in rows 3 through 6.

Select any cell in the worksheet to remove the selection from the range B8:G10. This concludes entering the data and formulas into the worksheet. The next step is to format the worksheet so it is easier to read. Before proceeding, however, it is best to save an intermediate copy of the workbook.

Saving an Intermediate Copy of the Workbook

A good practice is to save intermediate copies of your work. That way, if your computer loses power or you make a serious mistake, you can always retrieve the latest copy from disk. Use the Save button on the Standard toolbar often, because you can save typing time later if the unexpected happens. For the following steps, it is assumed you have a floppy disk in drive A.

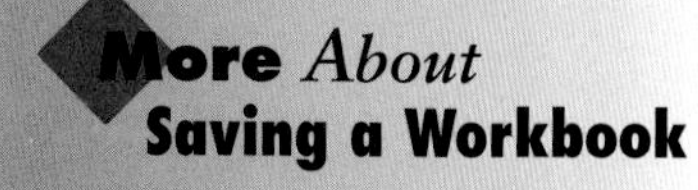

You should save your workbooks every 5 to 10 minutes so that if the system fails you can retrieve a copy without a major loss of work. You can instruct Excel to automatically save a workbook.

TO SAVE AN INTERMEDIATE COPY OF THE WORKBOOK

Step 1: Click the Save button on the Standard toolbar.
Step 2: Type `Ocean Air Profit Analysis` in the File name text box. If necessary, change to 3½ floppy [A:] in the Save in drop-down list box.

The Save As dialog box displays as shown in Figure 2-23.

Step 3: Click the Save button in the Save As dialog box.

After Excel completes the save, the worksheet remains on the screen with Ocean Air Profit Analysis in the title bar. You can immediately continue with the next activity.

Applying Formats to the Worksheet

Although the worksheet contains the data, formulas, and functions, the text and numbers need to be formatted to improve their appearance and readability.

In Project 1, you used the AutoFormat command to format the majority of the worksheet. This section describes how to change the unformatted worksheet in Figure 2-24a to the formatted worksheet in Figure 2-24b (on the next page) without using the AutoFormat command.

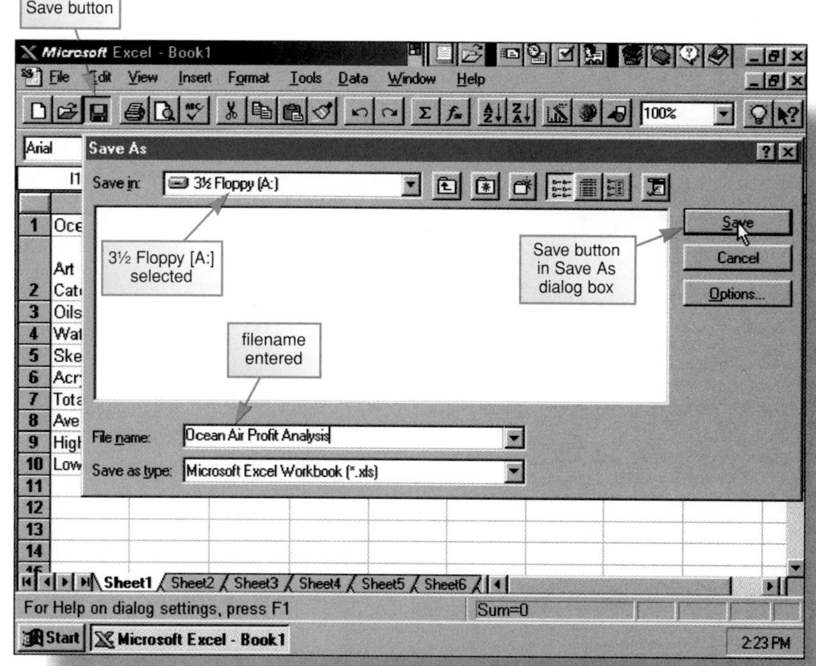

FIGURE 2-23

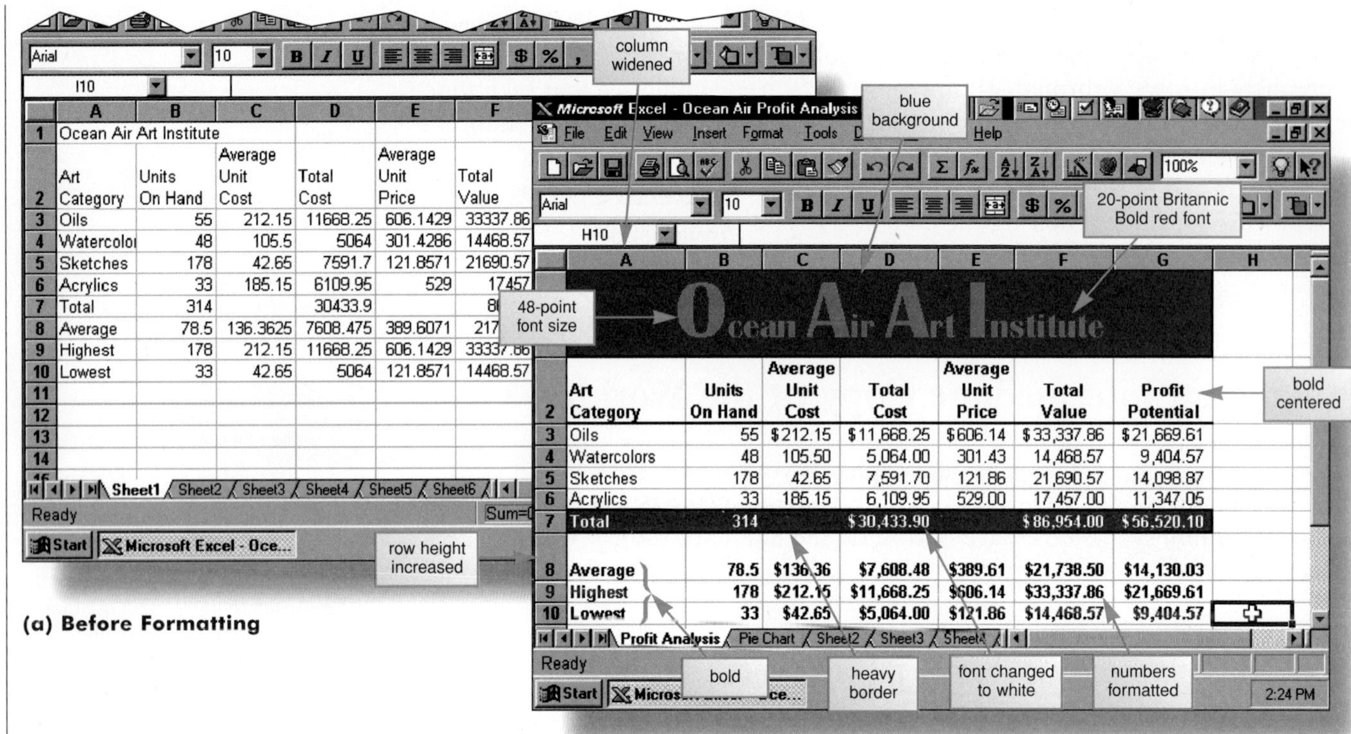

(a) Before Formatting

FIGURE 2-24

(b) After Formatting

The following outlines the type of formatting that is required in Project 2:

1. Worksheet title
   a. Font type — TrueType (TT) Britannic Bold (or TT Courier New if your system does not have TT Britannic Bold)
   b. Font size — 48 for first character in each word; 20 for subsequent characters
   c. Font color — red
   d. Background color (range A1:G1) — blue
   e. Alignment — center across columns A through G
   f. Border — outline A1:G1
2. Column titles
   a. Font style — bold
   b. Alignment — column A title left, columns B through G centered
   c. Border — underline
3. Row titles
   a. Font style — bold total titles
4. Total line
   a. Font style — bold
   b. Font color — white
   c. Background color — blue
   d. Border — outline A7:G7
5. Monetary amounts in rows 3 and 7 through 10
   a. Currency style with two decimal places
   b. Bold totals in rows 8 through 10
6. Numbers in range C4:G6
   a. Comma style with two decimal places
7. Column widths
   a. Increase column A to 13.00 characters; columns B through G to best fit

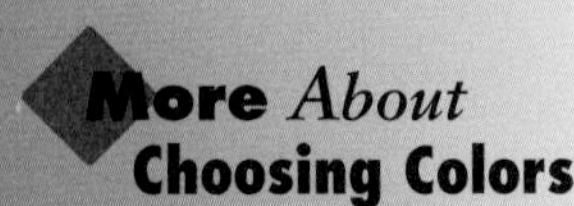

More About Choosing Colors

Knowing how people perceive colors helps you emphasize parts of your worksheet. Warmer colors (red and orange) tend to reach toward the reader. Cooler colors (blue, green, and violet) tend to pull away from the reader. Bright colors jump out of a dark background and are easiest to see. White or yellow text on a dark blue, green, purple, or black background is ideal.

8. Row heights
   a. Change row 1 to 51.00 points; row 8 to 27.75 points

Except for the Currency style assigned to the totals in rows 8 through 10, all of the above formatting can be accomplished by using the mouse and Formatting toolbar.

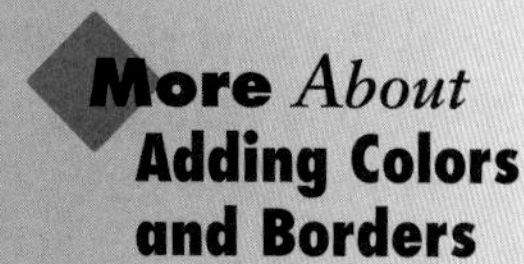

More *About* Adding Colors and Borders

Colors and borders can change a boring worksheet into an interesting and easy-to-read worksheet. Colors and borders can also be used to make important information stand out.

Applying Formats to the Worksheet Title

To emphasize the worksheet title in cell A1, the font type, size, style, and color are changed as described in the following steps. The background color blue and a border will be added later with row 7, which calls for the same background color and border.

To Format the Characters in the Worksheet Title

1 **Click cell A1.**

2 **Click the Font box arrow on the Formatting toolbar and point to TT Britannic Bold (or TT Courier New if your system does not have TT Britannic Bold).**

The Font drop-down list box displays (Figure 2-25).

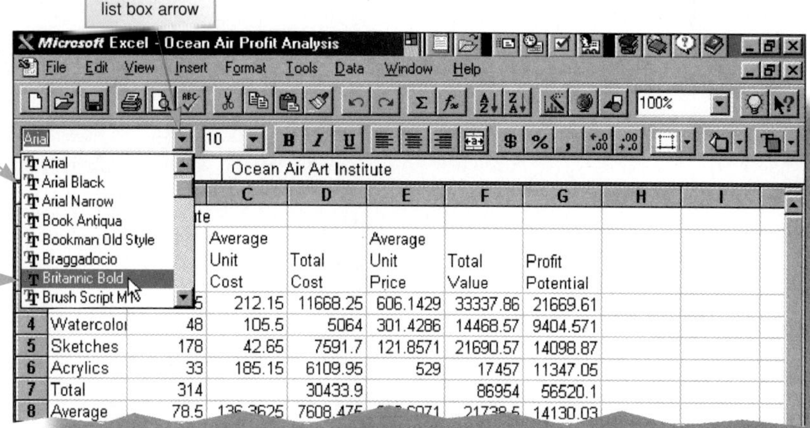

FIGURE 2-25

3 **Click TT Britannic Bold (or TT Courier New). Click the Font Size box arrow on the Formatting toolbar and point to 20.**

The characters in cell A1 display using TT Britannic Bold (or TT Courier New). The font size 20 is highlighted in the Font Size drop-down list box (Figure 2-26).

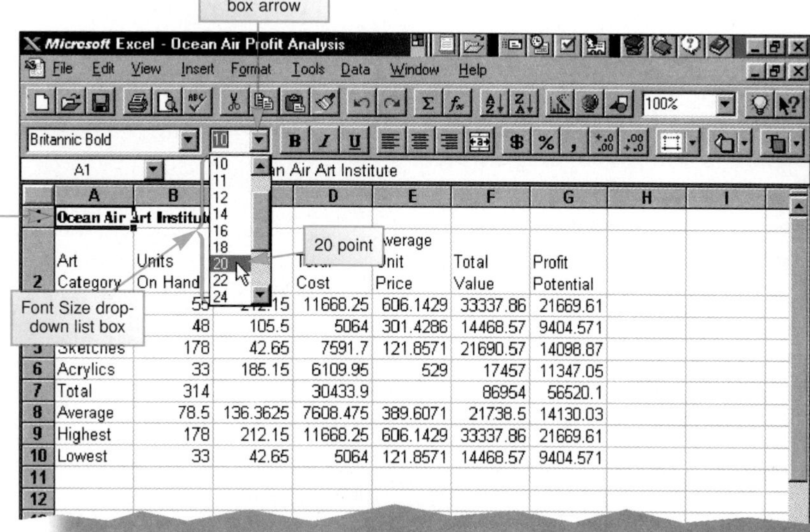

FIGURE 2-26

4 Click 20 in the Font Size drop-down list box. Double-click cell A1 to edit the cell contents. Drag across the first character O in Ocean, and then point to the Font Size box arrow.

The font in cell A1 displays in 20 point. Excel enters the Edit mode and the letter O in Ocean is selected (Figure 2-27). Excel increases the row heights of rows 1 and 2 automatically so the larger characters fit in the cells.

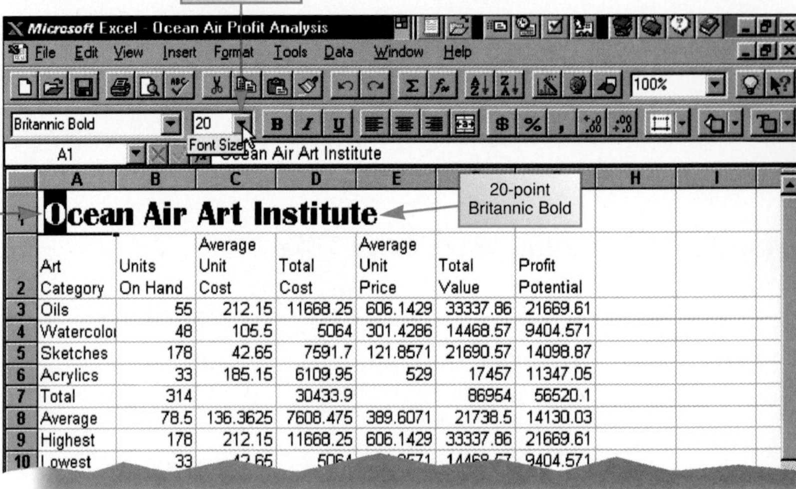

FIGURE 2-27

5 Click the Font Size box arrow and then point to 48 (Figure 2-28).

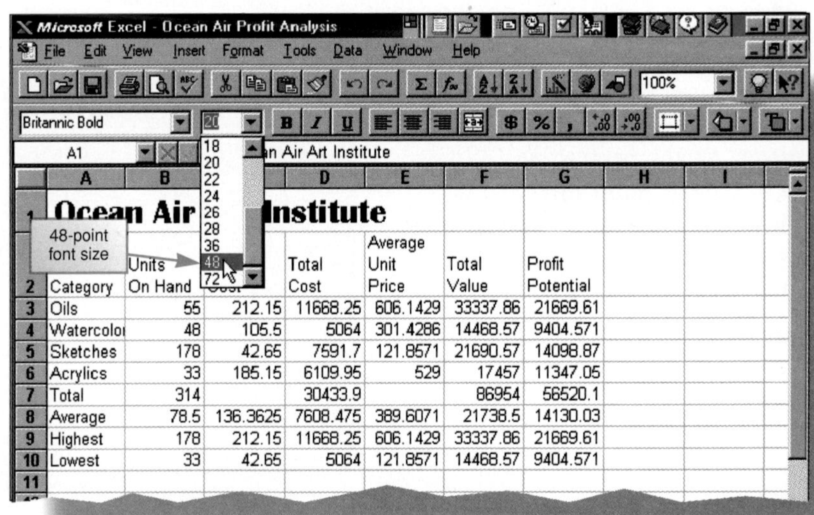

FIGURE 2-28

6 Click 48 in the Font Size box. While in Edit mode, drag across the first letter of the remaining words in the worksheet title one at a time and change their font size to 48.

The first letter of each word in the worksheet title appears larger than the other characters (Figure 2-29).

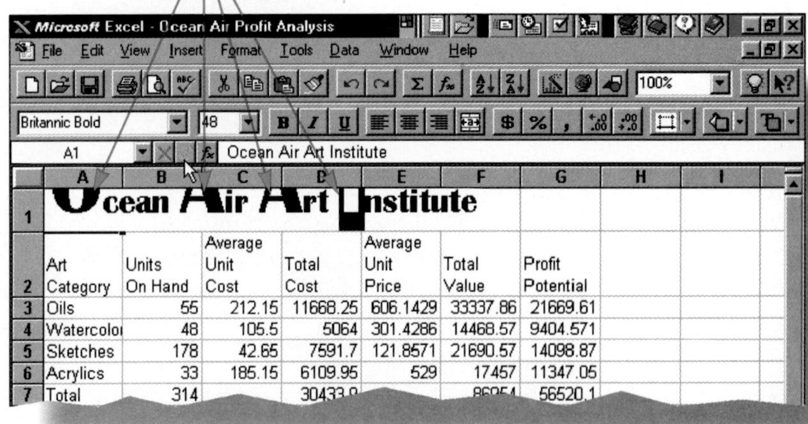

FIGURE 2-29

7 **Click the enter box or press the ENTER key to complete editing the contents of cell A1. Click the Font Color button arrow on the Formatting toolbar and point to the color red (column 3, row 1 on the Font Color palette).**

Excel displays the worksheet title with the new font sizes and increases the row height so the larger characters display in their entirety. The Font Color palette displays in the upper right corner of the screen (Figure 2-30).

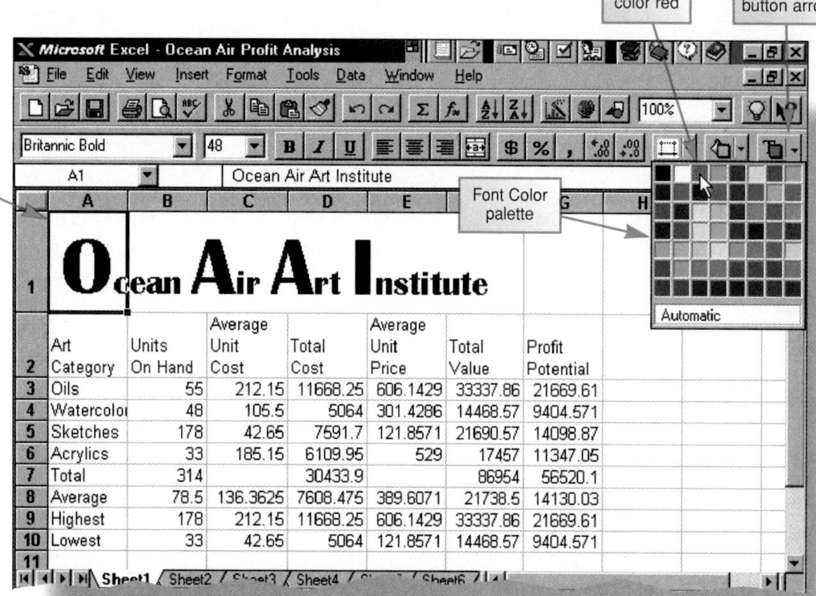

FIGURE 2-30

8 **Click the color red on the Font Color palette.**

The worksheet title is red (Figure 2-31).

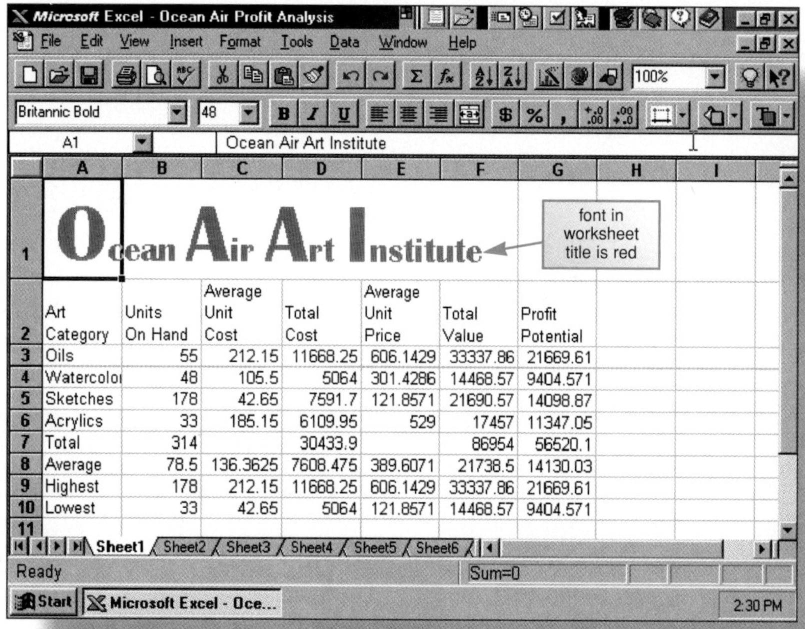

FIGURE 2-31

OtherWays

1. Right-click cell, click Format Cells, click Font tab, select font formats, click OK button
2. On the File menu click Cells, click Font tab, select font formats, click OK button
3. Press CTRL+1, click Font tab, select font formats, click OK button

When developing presentation-quality worksheets, different fonts often are used in the same worksheet. Excel allows you to change the font of individual characters in a cell or all the characters in a cell, in a range of cells, or in the entire worksheet. You can also change the font any time while the worksheet is active. For example, some Excel users prefer to change the font before they enter any data. Others change the font while they are building the worksheet or after they have entered all the data.

More About Centering Across Columns

To deselect Centering Across Columns, select the cell the title was assigned to and click the recessed Center Across Columns button on the Formatting toolbar.

The next step is to center the worksheet title across columns A through G.

TO CENTER THE WORKSHEET TITLE

Step 1: Click cell A1.
Step 2: Select the range A1:G1.
Step 3: Click the Center Across Columns button on the Formatting toolbar.

Excel centers the worksheet title in cell A1 across columns A through G (Figure 2-32).

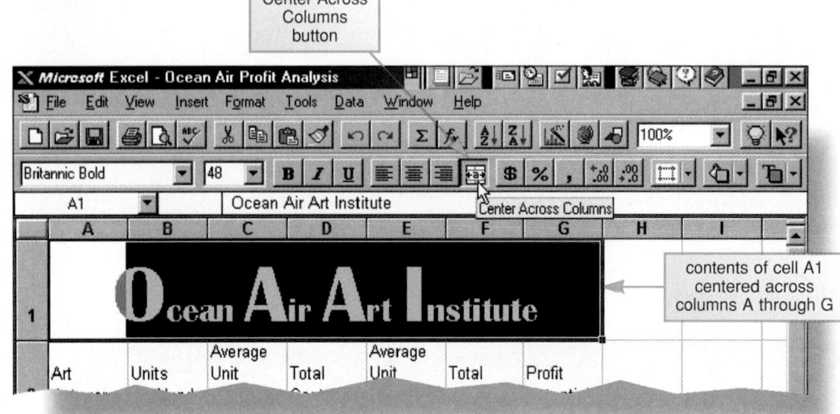

FIGURE 2-32

The final formats to be assigned to the worksheet title are the blue background color and outline border (Figure 2-24b on page E 2.22). These same formats also must be assigned to the totals in row 7. Thus, both ranges will be formatted at the same time by selecting nonadjacent ranges. You select nonadjacent ranges by selecting the first range (A1:G1) and then, while holding down the CTRL key, selecting the second range (A7:G7). Perform the following steps to change the background colors and apply an outline border.

Steps To Change the Background Colors and Apply an Outline Border

1. **Select the range A1:G1. Hold down the CTRL key and select the nonadjacent range A7:G7. Click the Color button arrow on the Formatting toolbar and then point to the color blue (column 1, row 4 on the Color palette).**

   The nonadjacent ranges A1:G1 and A7:G7 are highlighted and the Color palette displays (Figure 2-33).

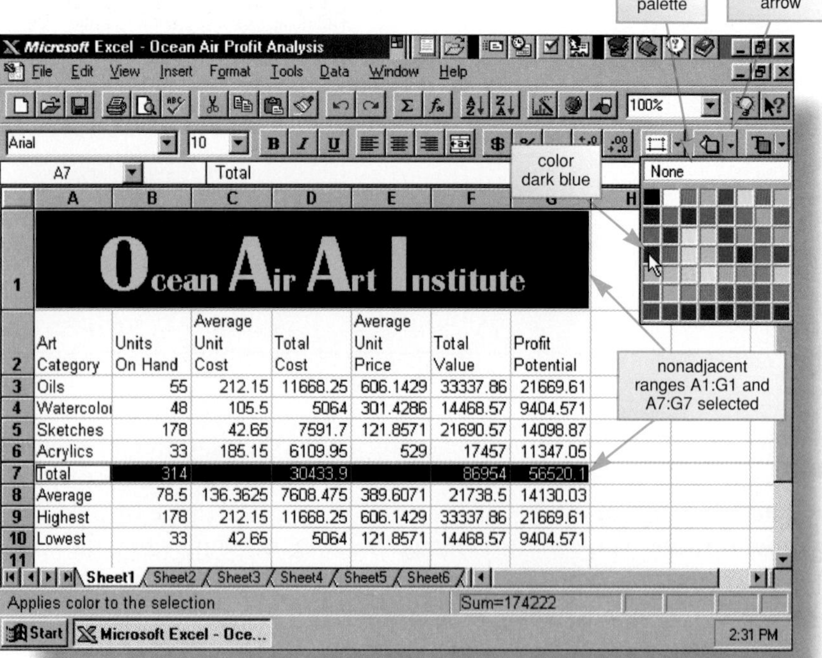

FIGURE 2-33

2 **Click the color blue on the Color palette. Click the Borders button arrow on the Formatting toolbar and then point to the heavy outline border (column 4, row 3).**

The background color of the ranges A1:G1 and A7:G7 appear yellow because they are selected and the Borders palette displays (Figure 2-34). When a cell is selected on the worksheet in the next step, the background color of the two ranges will change to blue.

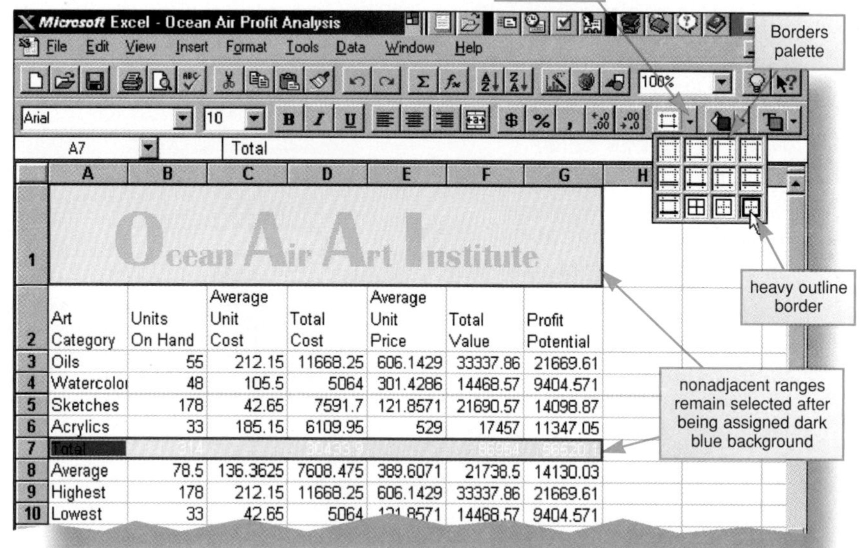

FIGURE 2-34

3 **Click the heavy outline border (column 4, row 3 on the Borders palette). Select any cell on the worksheet.**

The background color of the ranges A1:G1 and A7:G7 changes to blue and both ranges have a heavy outline border (Figure 2-35).

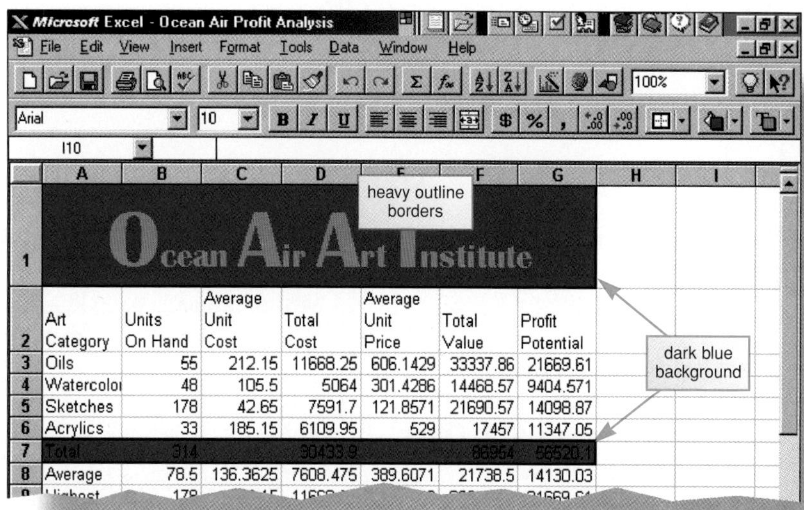

FIGURE 2-35

OtherWays

1. Right-click range, click Format Cells on shortcut menu, click Font tab, click Color arrow, click desired color, click OK button
2. On Format menu click Cells, click Font tab, click Color arrow, click desired color, click OK button
3. Right-click range, click Format Cells on shortcut menu, click Border tab, click a style, click desired border type, click OK button
4. On Format menu click Cells, click Border tab, click a style, click desired border type, click OK button

You can remove borders, such as the outline around the range A1:G1, by selecting the range and pressing CTRL+SHIFT+_. You can remove a background color by clicking the arrow on the Color button on the Formatting toolbar and clicking None on the Color palette.

Changing the Font Color and Bolding Nonadjacent Ranges

As you can see in the range A7:G7 in Figure 2-35, it is difficult to read black characters on a blue background. Complete the following steps to change the font color in the range A7:G7 to white and to bold the column titles in row 2 and totals in the range A7:G10.

To Change the Font Color and Bold Nonadjacent Ranges

1. **Select the range A7:G7.**

2. **Click the Font Color button arrow on the Formatting toolbar and then point to the color white (column 2, row 1 on the Font Color palette).**

   The Font Color palette displays as shown in Figure 2-36.

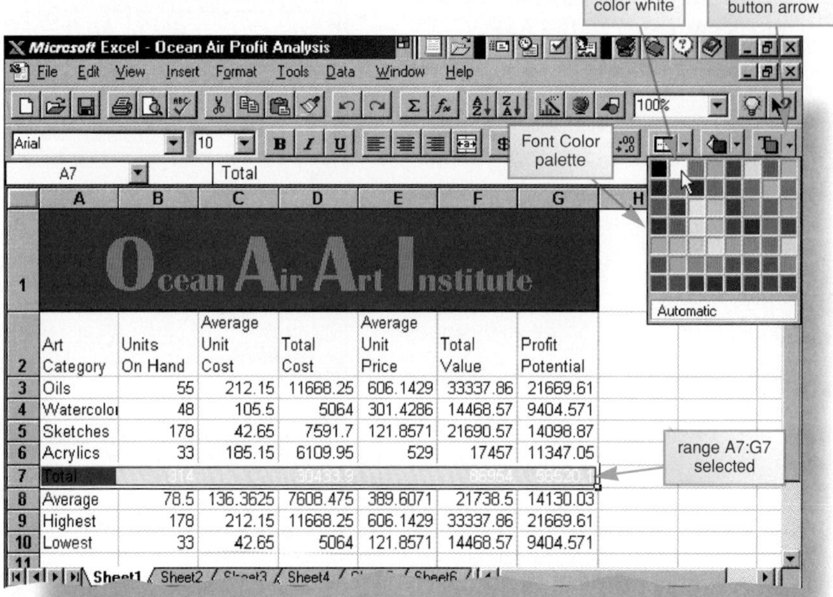

FIGURE 2-36

3. **Click the color white on the Font Color palette.**

4. **Select the range A2:G2. Hold down the CTRL key and select the nonadjacent range A7:G10. Click the Bold button on the Formatting toolbar.**

   The worksheet column titles in row 2 and the totals in the range A7:G10 display as shown in Figure 2-37.

5. **Select any cell on the worksheet to deselect the nonadjacent ranges.**

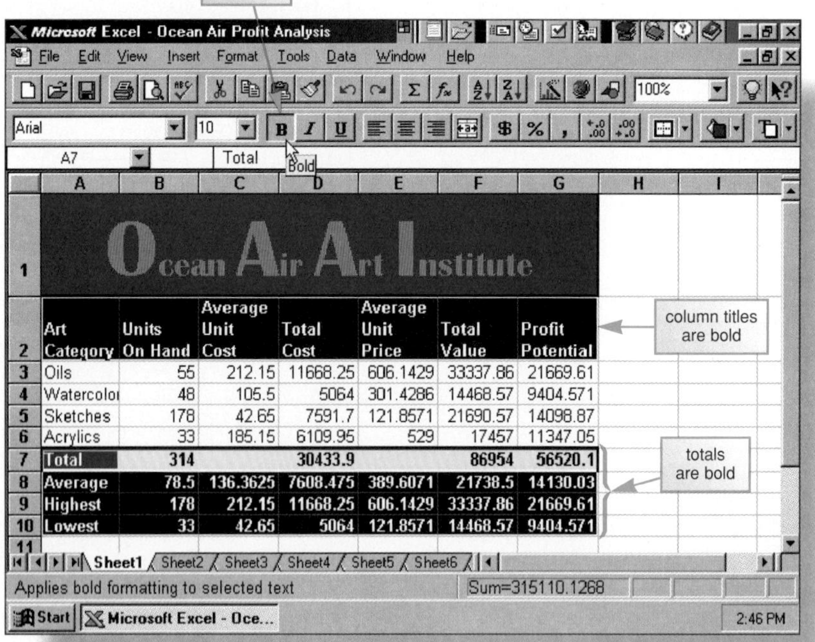

FIGURE 2-37

You can see in Figure 2-37 that the bold white characters on a blue background stand out and are much easier to read than the black characters on a blue background.

Applying Formats to the Column Titles

According to Figure 2-24b on page E 2.22, the column titles have a heavy underline. Furthermore, the title in column A is left-aligned in cell A2 and the column titles in cells B2:G2 are centered. The following steps assign these formats to the column titles.

To Underline and Center the Column Titles

1 **Select the range A2:G2. Click the Borders button arrow on the Formatting toolbar and then point to the heavy bottom border (column 2, row 2 on the Borders palette).**

The Borders palette displays (Figure 2-38).

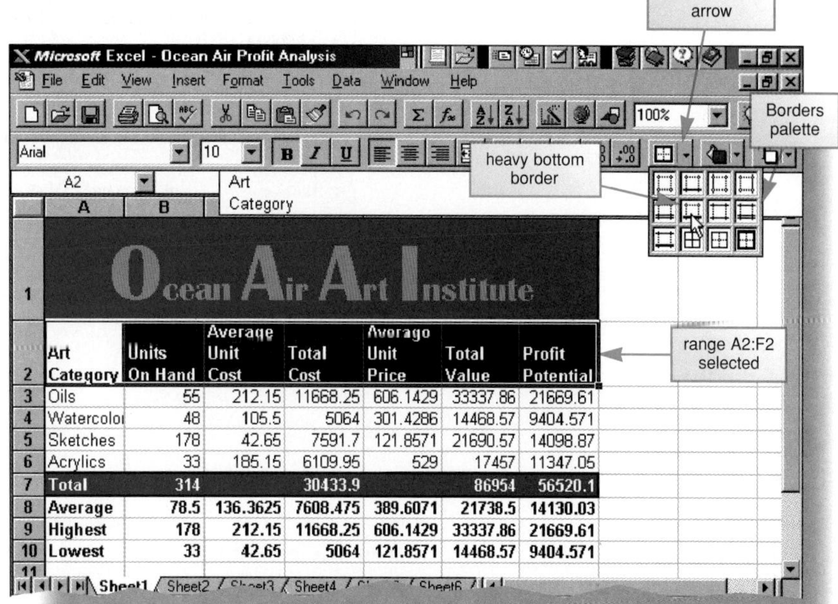

FIGURE 2-38

2 **Click the heavy bottom border. Select the range B2:G2 and then point to the Center button on the Formatting toolbar.**

The selected range B2:G2 is highlighted (Figure 2-39).

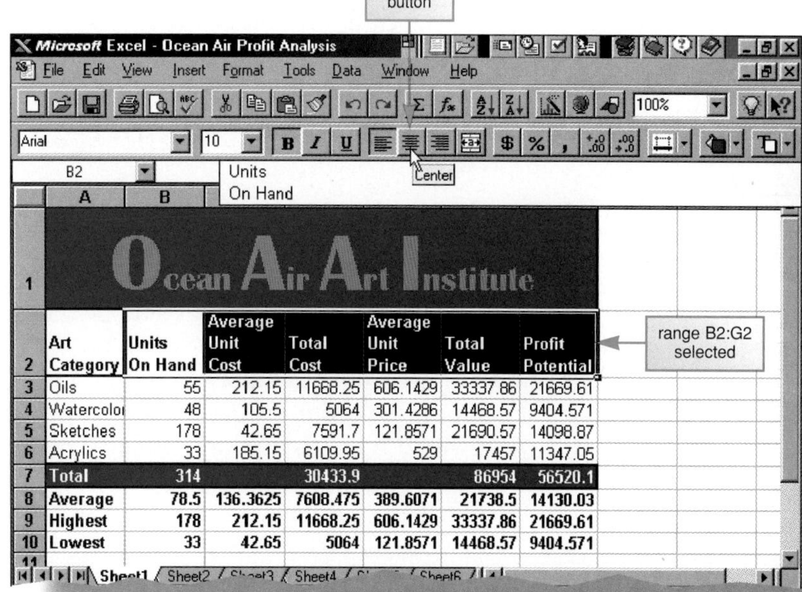

FIGURE 2-39

3 **Click the Center button and then select any cell in the worksheet.**

The column titles display as shown in Figure 2-40.

Microsoft Excel - Ocean Air Profit Analysis

Ocean Air Art Institute

Art Category	Units On Hand	Average Unit Cost	Total Cost	Average Unit Price	Total Value	Profit Potential
Oils	55	212.15	11668.25	606.1429	33337.86	21669.61
Watercolor	48	105.5	5064	301.4286	14468.57	9404.571
Sketches	178	42.65	7591.7	121.8571	21690.57	14098.87
Acrylics	33	185.15	6109.95	529	17457	11347.05
Total	314		30433.9		86954	56520.1
Average	78.5	136.3625	7608.475	389.6071	21738.5	14130.03
Highest	178	212.15	11668.25	606.1429	33337.86	21669.61
Lowest	33	42.65	5064	121.8571	14468.57	9404.571

FIGURE 2-40

OtherWays

1. Right-click range, click Format Cells on shortcut menu, click Alignment tab, click desired alignment, click OK button
2. On Format menu click Cells, click Alignment tab, click desired alignment, click OK button

You can align the contents of cells several different ways. The more common alignments are left-align, center, and right-align. These three alignments are used so often that Microsoft includes them on the Formatting toolbar. Most worksheet users left-align a column title over text as shown in column A in Figure 2-40 and center or right-align column titles over numbers. In Figure 2-40, the column titles over numbers in the range B2:G2 are centered.

You can also align text when you initially enter it into a cell by appending a special character to the front. An apostrophe (') instructs Excel to left-align the text. A caret (^) centers the text and a quotation mark (") right-aligns the text.

More *About* Aligning and Rotating Text in Cells

Besides aligning text horizontally in a cell, you can align text vertically (top, center, bottom, or justify). You can also rotate text so that the characters are below one another rather than side-by-side. To align vertically or rotate the text, click Format Cells on the shortcut menu, click the Alignment tab, and then select the type of alignment you want.

Formatting Numbers

When using Excel, you can format numbers to represent dollar amounts, whole numbers with comma placement, and percentages through the use of buttons on the Formatting toolbar. Customized format styles can be assigned using the Cells command on the Format menu or the Format Cells command on the shortcut menu.

According to Figure 2-24(b) on page E 2.22, the worksheet has an accounting report look to it in that the first row of numbers (row 3) and the monetary totals (rows 7 through 10) have dollar signs and the numbers between the first row and totals do not have dollar signs. To display a dollar sign in a number you will want to use the Currency style format.

The **Currency style** appends a dollar sign to the left of the number, inserts a comma every three positions to the left of the decimal point, and displays numbers to the nearest cent (hundredths place). The **Currency Style button** on the Formatting toolbar will assign the desired format. The dollar sign appended to the left of the number, however, is a fixed dollar sign. A **fixed dollar sign** displays to the far left in the cell, often with spaces between it and the first digit. To append a dollar sign that displays immediately to the left of the number (called a **floating dollar sign**), you need to use the Cells command on the Format menu or the Format Cells command on the shortcut menu. According to the project specifications, a fixed dollar sign is to be assigned to the numbers in rows 3 and 7. A floating dollar sign is to be assigned to the monetary totals in rows 8 through 10.

To display monetary amounts without dollar signs, you will want to use the Comma style format. The **Comma style** inserts a comma every three positions to the left of the decimal point.

The remainder of this section describes how to format the numbers in the desired fashion.

More About Formatting Numbers as You Enter Them

You can format numbers when you enter them by entering a dollar sign ($), comma (,) or percent sign (%) as part of the number. For example, if you enter 1500, Excel displays 1500. However, if you enter $1500, Excel displays $1,500.

Formatting Numbers Using Buttons on the Formatting Toolbar

The following steps show how to assign the Currency style format and Comma style format using the Currency Style button and Comma Style button on the Formatting toolbar.

To Apply a Currency Style Format and Comma Style Format Using Buttons on the Formatting Toolbar

1 Select the range C3:G3. Hold down the CTRL key and select the nonadjacent range D7:G7. Point to the Currency Style button on the Formatting toolbar.

The nonadjacent ranges display as shown in Figure 2-41.

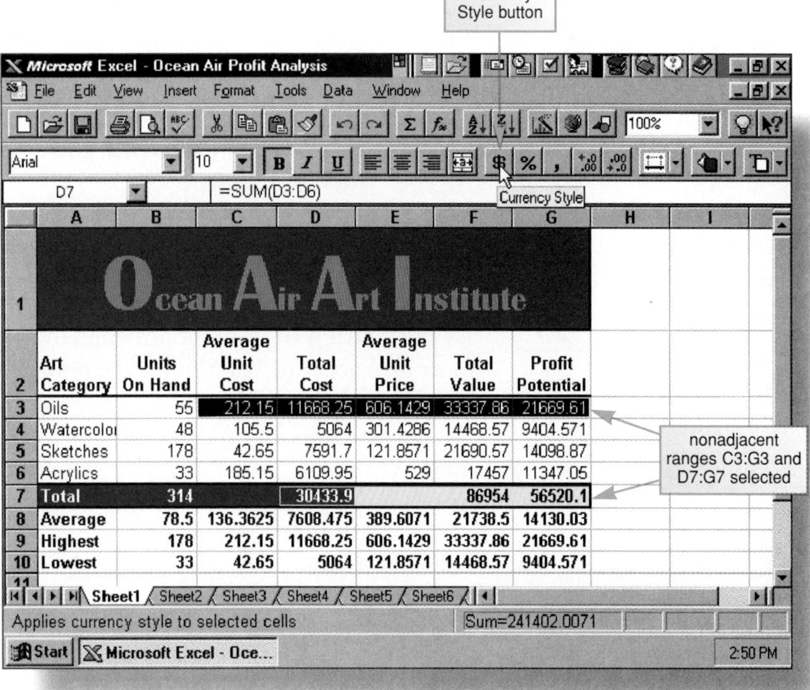

FIGURE 2-41

2 **Click the Currency Style button on the Formatting toolbar. Select the range C4:G6 and then click the Comma Style button on the Formatting toolbar.**

Several numbers in the range C3:G6 display as a sequence of number signs (#) indicating they are too large to fit in the width of the cells (Figure 2-42). Some of the smaller numbers display with the appropriate format. Later the column widths will be increased so the numbers will display in place of the number signs.

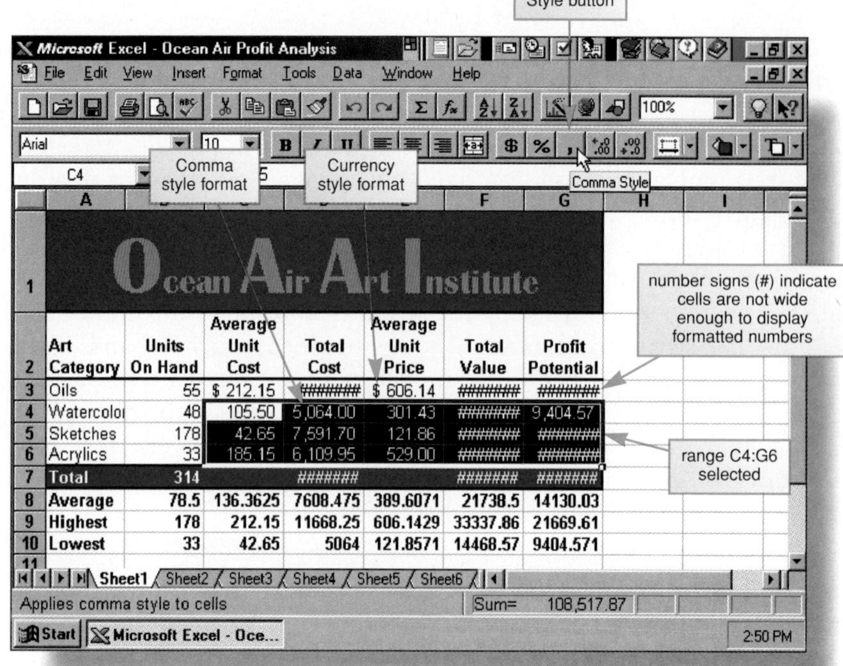

FIGURE 2-42

OtherWays

1. Right-click range, click Format Cells on shortcut menu, click Number tab, click Currency in Category list box, click OK button
2. On Format menu click Cells, click Number tab, click Currency in Category list box, click OK button

In cell C3, the dollar sign displays to the far left with spaces between it and the first digit in the cell. Thus, the Currency Style button assigns a fixed dollar sign to the number.

Excel rounds a number to fit the format selected. For example, in cell E3, Excel rounds the actual value 606.1429 down to 606.14. In cell E4, Excel rounds the actual value 301.4286 up to 301.43.

Formatting Numbers Using the Format Cells Command on the Shortcut Menu

Thus far, you have been introduced to two ways to format numbers in a worksheet. In Project 1, you formatted the numbers using the AutoFormat command on the Format menu. In the previous section, you were introduced to using the Formatting toolbar as a means of selecting a format style. A third way to format numbers is to use the Cells command on the Format menu or the Format Cells command on the shortcut menu. Using either command allows you to display numbers in any desired format you can imagine. The following steps show you how to apply the Currency style with a floating dollar sign to the totals in the range C8:G10 using the Format Cells command on the shortcut menu.

More About Formatting Numbers in Calculations

The numbers you see on your screen may not be the same ones used in calculations. When a number has more decimal places than are displayed because of your formatting, the actual number is used in the computation. For example, 32.368 is the actual number but 32.37 displays because you formatted with two decimal places.

To Apply a Currency Style with a Floating Dollar Sign Using the Format Cells Command on the Shortcut Menu

1 **Select the range C8:G10. Right-click within the selected range. Point to Format Cells.**

The shortcut menu displays as shown in Figure 2-43.

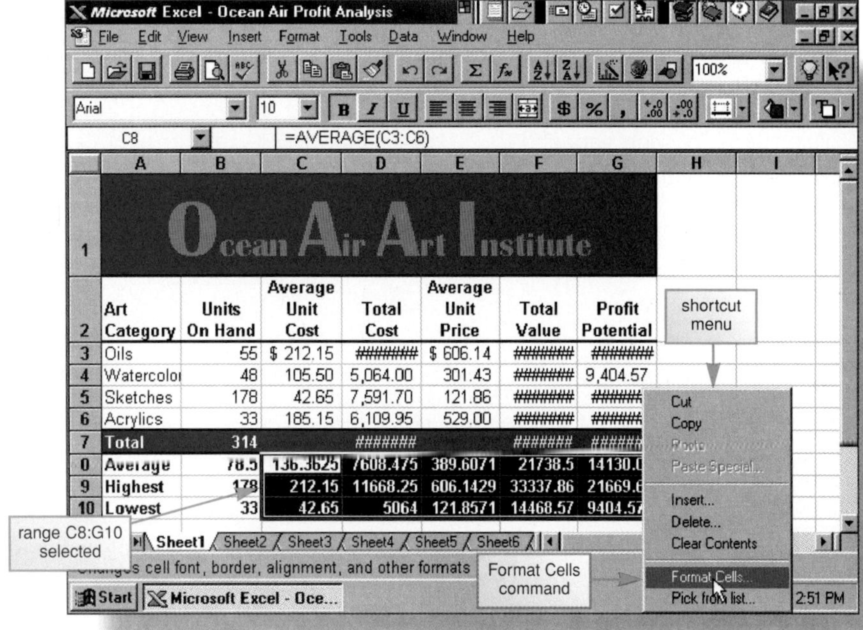

FIGURE 2-43

2 **Click Format Cells on the shortcut menu. Click the Number tab in the Format Cells dialog box.**

3 **Click Currency in the Category list box, click ($1,234.10) in the Negative Numbers list box, and then point to the OK button.**

The Format Cells dialog box *displays as shown in Figure 2-44.*

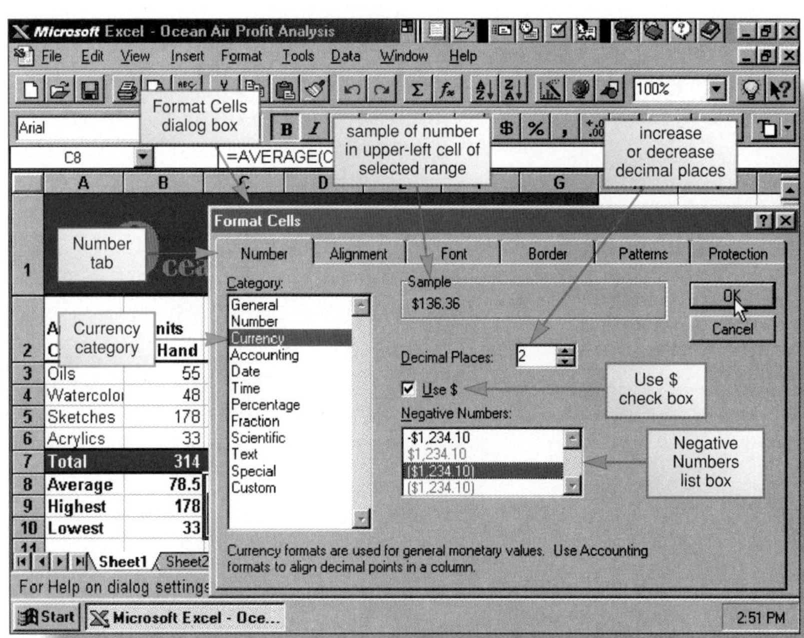

FIGURE 2-44

4 Click the OK button. click any cell outside the selected range.

The worksheet displays with the totals in rows 7 through 10 assigned the Currency style format with a floating dollar sign as shown in Figure 2-45. Here again, the number signs (#) indicate that the columns are not wide enough to display the formatted numbers.

	A	B	C	D	E	F	G
1	Ocean Air Art Institute						
2	Art Category	Units On Hand	Average Unit Cost	Total Cost	Average Unit Price	Total Value	Profit Potential
3	Oils	55	$ 212.15	#######	$ 606.14	#######	#######
4	Watercolor	48	105.50	5,064.00	301.43	#######	9,404.57
5	Sketches	178	42.65	7,591.70	121.86	#######	#######
6	Acrylics	33	185.15	6,109.95	529.00	#######	#######
7	Total	314		#######		#######	#######
8	Average	78.5	$136.36	########	$389.61	########	########
9	Highest	178	$212.15	########	$606.14	########	########
10	Lowest	33	$42.65	########	$121.86	########	########

Sheet1 / Sheet2 / Sheet3 / Sheet4 / Sheet5 / Sheet6

Ready Sum=0

Start | Microsoft Excel - Oce... 2:51 PM

Currency style format with a floating dollar sign

FIGURE 2-45

OtherWays

1. On Format menu click Cells, click Number tab, click Currency in Category list box, click OK button
2. Press CTRL+SHIFT+$

You can see the difference in the Currency style formats assigned to cells C3 and C8. The Currency style was assigned to cell C3 using the Currency Style button on the Formatting toolbar and the result is a fixed dollar sign. The Currency style was assigned to cell C8 using the Format Cells dialog box and the result is a floating dollar sign. Recall that the floating dollar sign will always display immediately to the left of the first digit and the fixed dollar sign will always display on the left side of the cell.

Figure 2-44 on the previous page shows there are 12 categories of formats from which you can choose. Once you select a category, you can select the number of decimal places, whether a dollar sign should display, and how you want negative numbers to display.

It is important to select the Negative Numbers format in Step 3 (on the previous page) because it adds a space to the right of the number as do the Currency Style and Comma Style buttons. If you do not select the proper Negative Numbers format, then the numbers will not be aligned on the decimal points in the worksheet. You can verify this by clicking one of the formatted cells and assigning the Currency category with the first Negative Numbers format (–$1,234.10) instead of ($1,234.10).

With the number formatting complete, the next step is to increase the column widths so the numbers display, rather than the number signs as is the case in Figure 2-45. The next section shows you how to increase the column widths.

More About Painting Formats

Painting is not an envious chore. But in Excel, if you know how to paint you can save yourself time and effort when formatting a worksheet. For example, if you see a cell that has the format you want to assign to another cell or range of cells, click the cell with the desired format, click the Format Painter button (the paintbrush on the Standard toolbar), and then click the cell or drag through the cells you want to paint the format with.

Changing the Widths of Columns and Heights of Rows

When Excel begins and the blank worksheet displays on the screen, all the columns have a default width of 8.43 characters and all the rows have a height of 12.75 points. A **character** is defined as TT Arial 10 point, the default font used by Excel. At any time, you can change the width of the columns or height of the rows to make the worksheet easier to read or to ensure that entries will display properly in the cells to which they are assigned.

Changing the Widths of Columns

When changing the column width, you can manually set the width or you can instruct Excel to size the column to best fit. **Best fit** means that the width of the column will be increased or decreased so the widest entry will fit in the column. The width of column A will be set manually because more space is preferred between columns A and B to improve the appearance of the report. Columns B through G will be set to best fit after widening column A. Complete the following steps to change the width of column A from 8.43 to 13.00.

Steps To Change the Width of a Column by Dragging

1. **Point to the border line between the column A and column B headings above row 1.**

   The mouse pointer becomes a split double arrow (Figure 2-46).

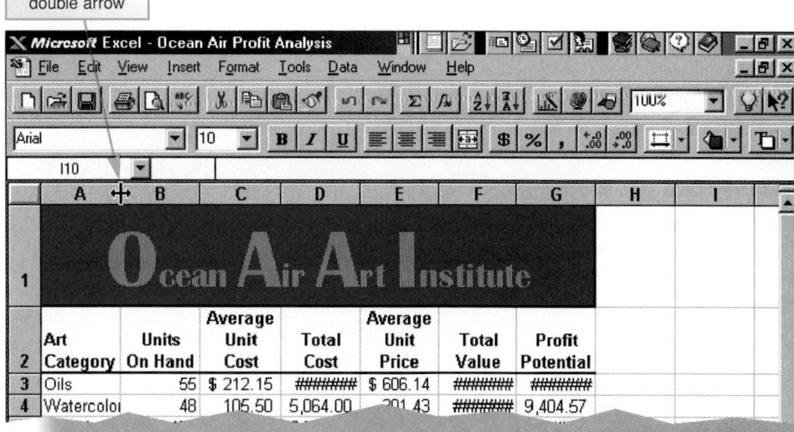

FIGURE 2-46

2. **Drag to the right until the number 13.00 displays in the Name box on the left side of the formula bar.**

   A dotted line shows the new right border of column A and the number 13.00 displays in the Name box (Figure 2-47).

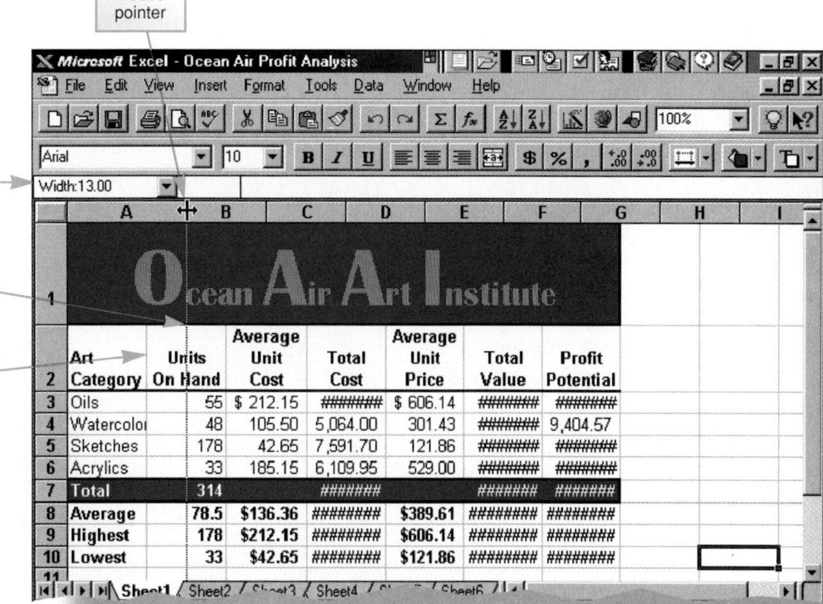

FIGURE 2-47

3 Release the left mouse button.

Excel sets the width of column A to 13.00 (Figure 2-48).

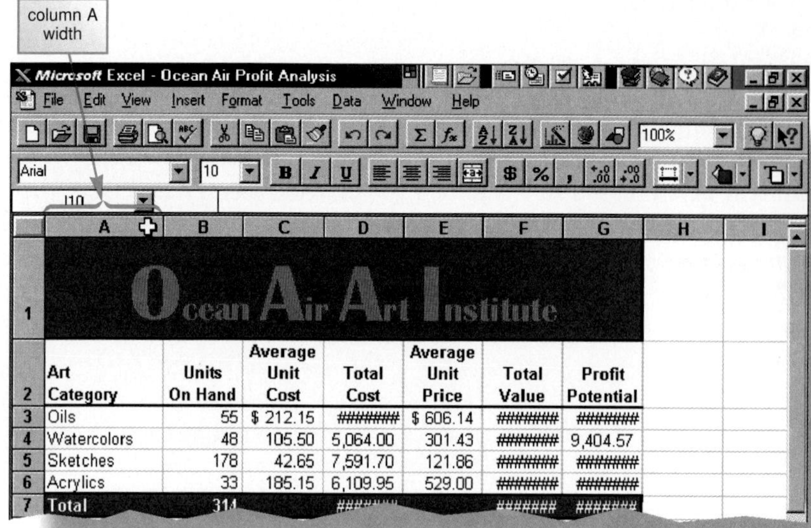

FIGURE 2-48

OtherWays

1. Right-click column heading above row 1 or drag through multiple column headings and right-click, click Column Width, enter new column width, click OK button
2. Select cell in column or select range of cells across columns, on Format menu click Column, click Width, enter new column width, click OK button

Compare the entries in column A of Figure 2-48 to Figure 2-46 on the previous page. Notice how the row title, Watercolors, displays in its entirety in Figure 2-48. Furthermore, the additional space to the right improves the worksheet's appearance.

You can also use the Column Width command on the shortcut menu. The command appears on the shortcut menu only when one or more entire columns are selected, however. You select entire columns by dragging through the column headings. Use the Column Width command instead of the mouse when you want to increase or decrease the column width significantly.

The following steps change the column widths of columns B through G to best fit.

To Change the Widths of Columns to Best Fit

1 Drag the mouse pointer from column heading B through column heading G. Move the mouse pointer to the right border of column heading G.

Columns B through G are highlighted and the mouse pointer changes to a split double arrow (Figure 2-49).

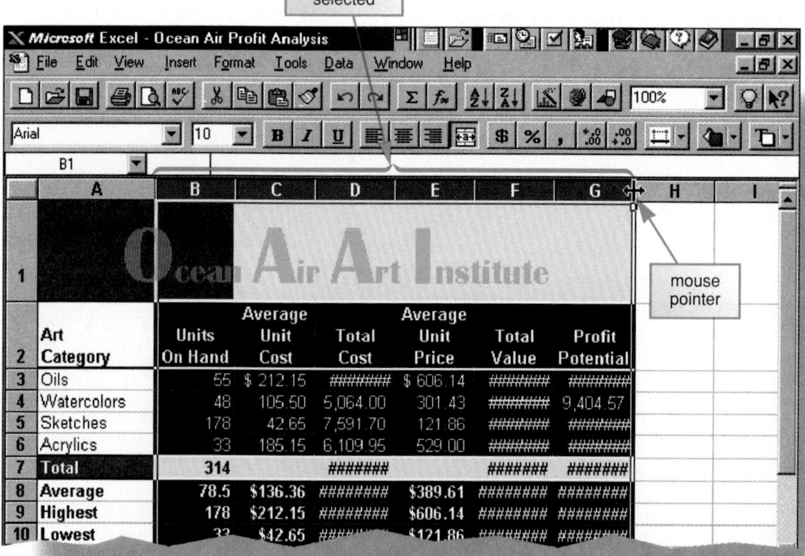

FIGURE 2-49

2 **Double-click the right border of column heading G and then click any cell in the worksheet.**

The width of columns B through G increase just enough so the widest entries in each column display completely (Figure 2-50).

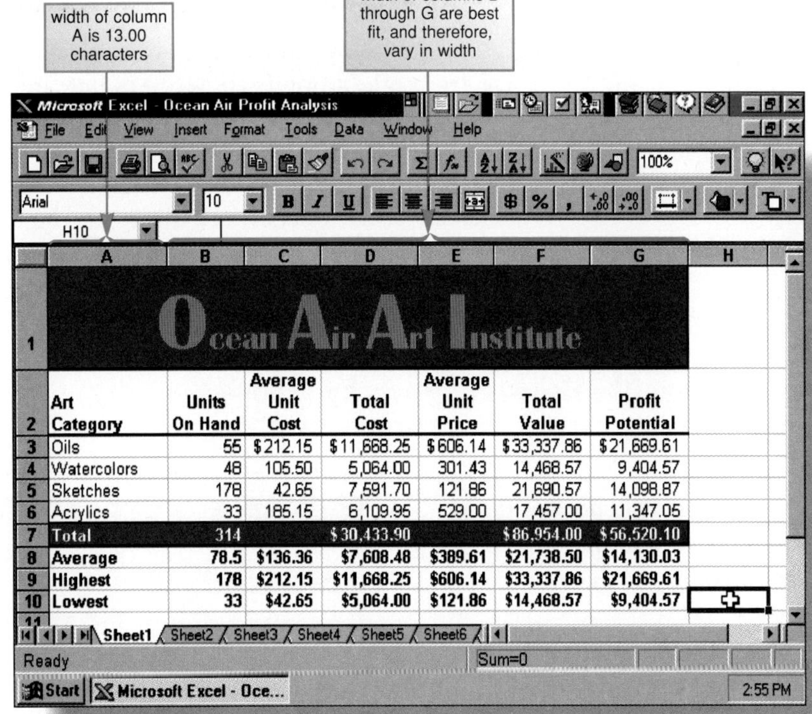

FIGURE 2-50

Compare Figure 2-50 to Figure 2-49. Columns B through G are wider in Figure 2-50 and the number signs in Figure 2-49 have been replaced with numeric values. Excel has increased the width of columns B through G just enough so all the characters in each column display. To determine the exact width of a column, move the mouse pointer to the right border line of the column heading. When the mouse pointer changes to a split double arrow, hold down the left mouse button. Excel displays the new column width in place of the cell reference in the Name box in the formula bar.

The column width can vary between zero and 255 characters. When you decrease the column width to zero, the column is hidden. **Hiding columns** is a technique you can use to hide sensitive data on the screen that you do not want others to see. When you print a worksheet, hidden columns do not print. To display a hidden column, position the mouse pointer to the left of the heading border where the hidden column is located and drag to the right.

More *About*
Best Fit

Spreadsheet specialists often use best fit twice to increase the widths of columns in a worksheet, once immediately after entering the column titles, and then again after entering and formatting the numbers in the columns.

More *About*
Hidden Columns

It often gets frustrating trying to use the mouse to unhide a range of columns. An alternative is to unhide columns using the keyboard. First select the columns to the right and left of the hidden ones and then press CTRL+SHIFT+). To use the keyboard to hide a range of columns, select the columns to hide, press CTRL+O.

Changing the Heights of Rows

When you increase the font size of a cell entry, such as Ocean Air Art Institute in cell A1, Excel increases the row height automatically so the characters display properly. You also can manually adjust the height of a row to increase or decrease space to improve the appearance of the worksheet. The row height is measured in point size. The default row height is 12.75 points. Recall from Project 1 that a point is equal to 1/72 of an inch. Thus, 12.75 points is equal to about one-sixth of an inch.

The following steps show how to use the mouse to decrease the height of row 1 from 60.75 points to 51.00 points and increase the height of row 8 from the default 12.75 points to 27.75 points. Recall that the height of row 1 was increased automatically earlier from the default 12.75 points to 60.75 points when the font size was increased. So that all rows of numbers display on the screen at one time and to allow for the increase in the height of row 8, the height of row 1 will be decreased to 51.00 points. Perform the following steps to change the heights of rows by dragging.

To Change the Heights of Rows by Dragging

1 **Move the mouse pointer to the border line between row headings 1 and 2.**

The mouse pointer changes to a split double arrow (Figure 2-51).

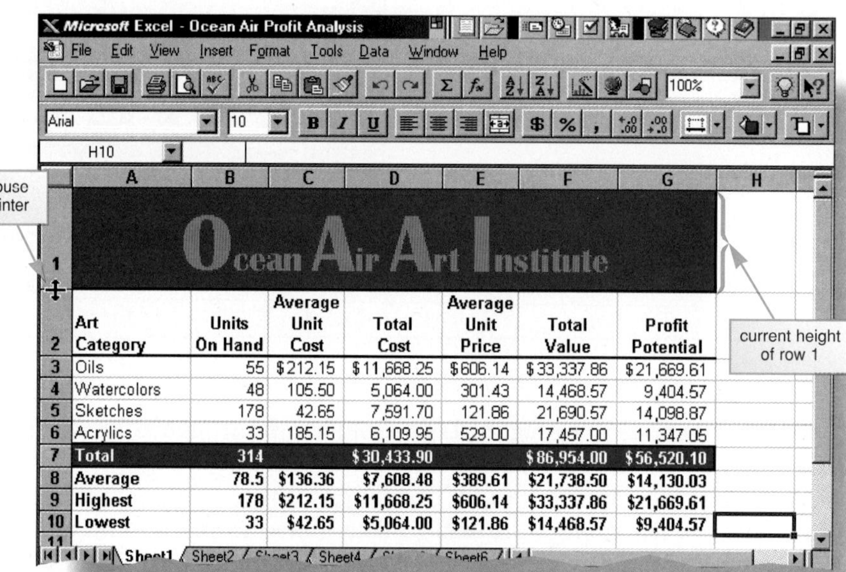

FIGURE 2-51

2 **Drag upward until 51.00 displays in the Name box on the left side of the formula bar.**

Excel displays a horizontal dotted line (Figure 2-52). The distance between the dotted line and the top of row 1 indicates the new row height for row 1.

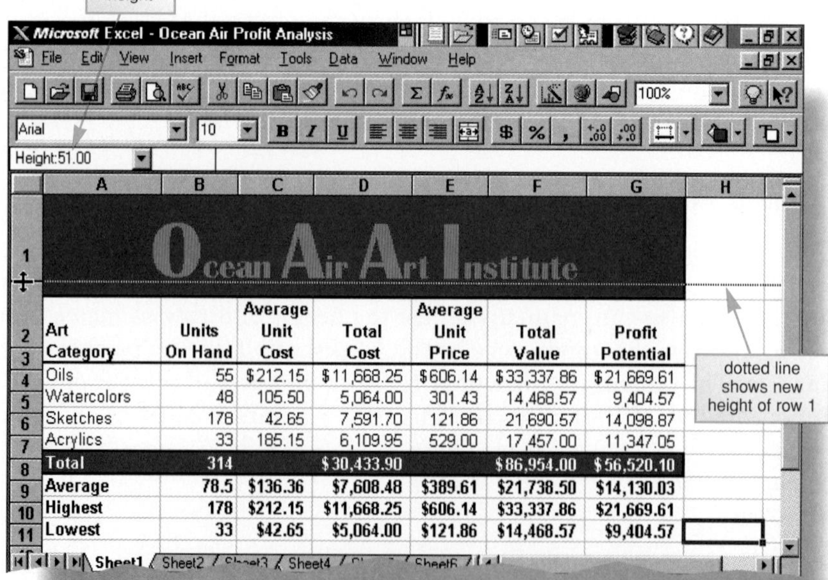

FIGURE 2-52

3 **Release the left mouse button. Move the mouse pointer to the border line between row headings 8 and 9 and then drag down until 27.75 shows in the Name box on the left side of the formula bar.**

The height of row 1 is changed to 51.00. The dotted line indicates the new height of row 8 (Figure 2-53).

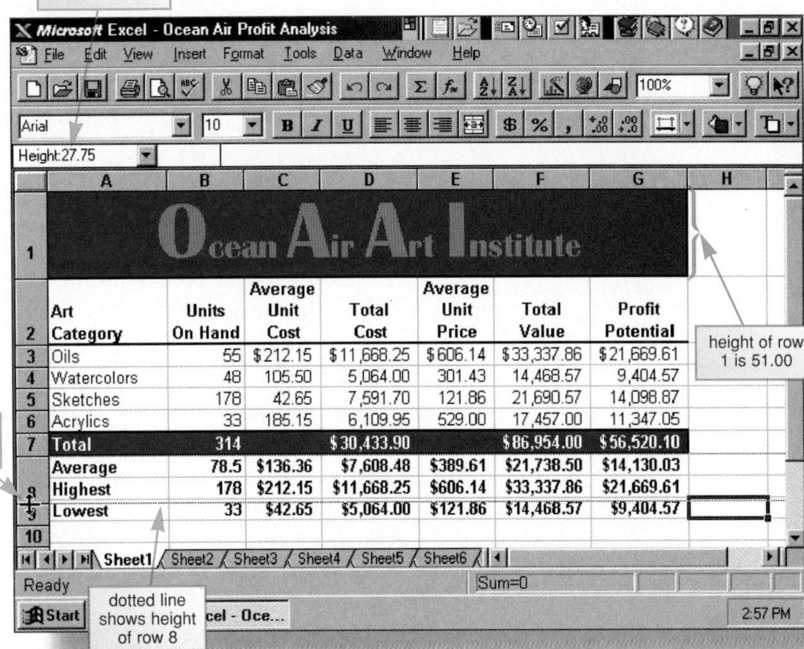

FIGURE 2-53

4 **Release the left mouse button.**

The height of row 8 changes to 27.75 points (Figure 2-54).

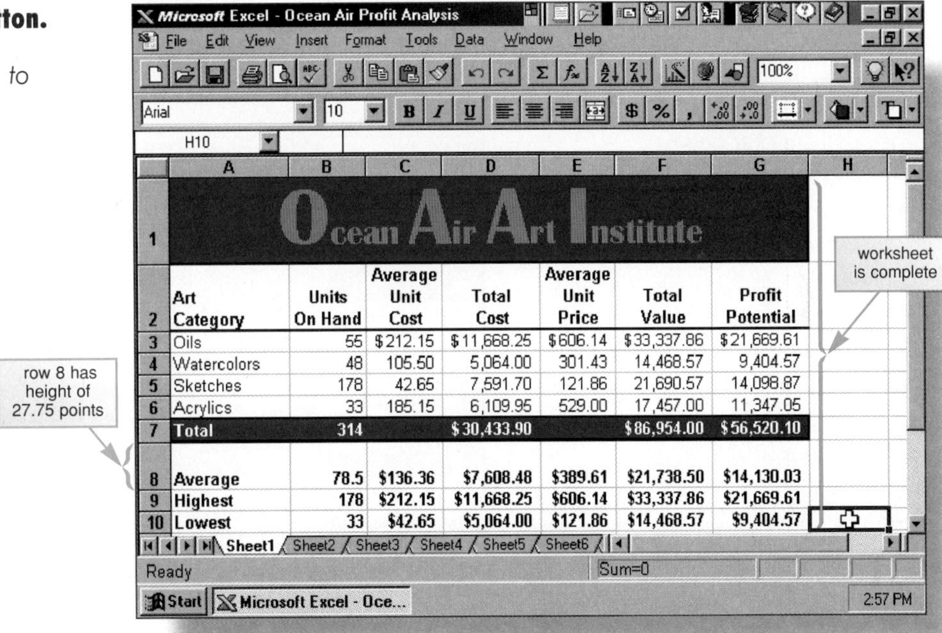

FIGURE 2-54

The row height can vary between zero and 409 points. When you decrease the row height to zero, the row is hidden. To show a hidden row, point just below the row heading border where the row is hidden and drag down.

If for some reason you want to switch back to the default row height, simply move the mouse pointer to the row border and double-click.

*Other*Ways

1. Right-click row heading to the left of column 1 or drag through multiple row headings and right-click, click Row Height, enter new row height, click OK button
2. Select cell in row or select range of cells down through rows, on Format menu click Row, click Height, enter new row height, click OK button

More About Hidden Rows

You can use the keyboard to unhide a range of rows. First select the rows immediately above and below the hidden ones and press CTRL+SHIFT+(. To use the keyboard to hide a range of rows, select the rows to hide, press CTRL+9.

The task of formatting the spreadsheet is complete. The next step is to check the spelling of the spreadsheet.

Checking Spelling

Excel has a spell checker you can use to check the worksheet for spelling errors. The spell checker looks for spelling errors by comparing words on the worksheet against words contained in its standard dictionary. If you have any specialized terms that are not in the **standard dictionary**, you can add them to a **custom dictionary** through the **Spelling dialog box.**

When the spell checker finds a word that is not in the dictionaries, it displays the word in the Spelling dialog box so you can correct it if it is misspelled.

You invoke the spell checker by clicking the **Spelling button** on the Standard toolbar. To illustrate Excel's reaction to a misspelled word, the word Highest in cell A9 is purposely misspelled as Higest, as shown in Figure 2-55.

Steps To Check Spelling in the Worksheet

1 Select cell A1. Click the Spelling button on the Standard toolbar.

The spell checker begins checking the spelling of the text in the worksheet with the active cell (cell A1) and continues checking to the right and down row by row. If the spell checker comes across a word that is not in the standard or custom dictionaries, the Spelling dialog box displays (Figure 2-55).

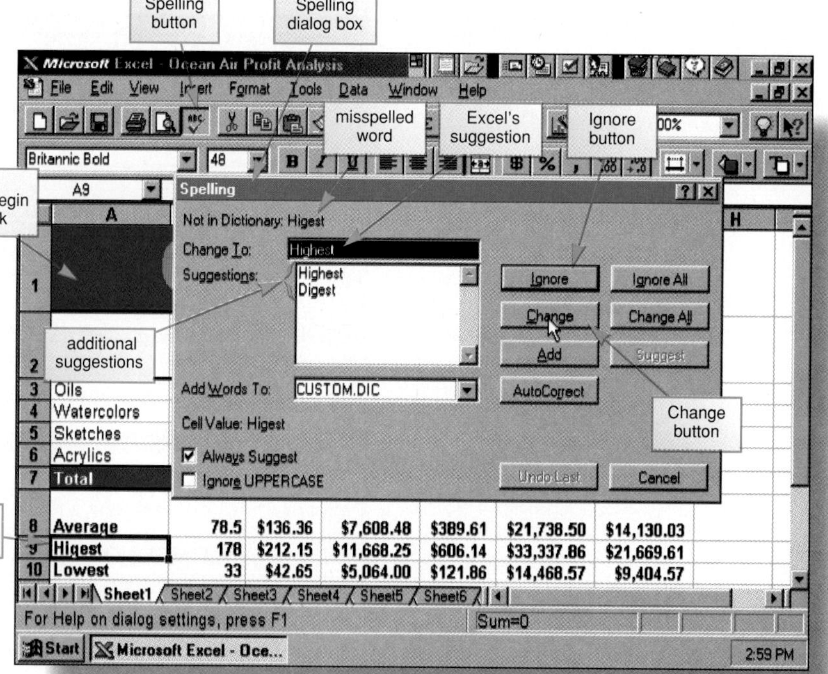

FIGURE 2-55

2 **When the spell checker displays a word in the Change To box, select one of the seven buttons to the right of the Suggestions box in the Spelling dialog box.**

In Figure 2-55 the word Highest in cell A9 is misspelled as Higest. The spell checker displays its best guess of the word you wanted (Highest) in the Change To box. Because Highest is in fact the correct spelling, click the **Change button**.

3 **Click the OK button when Excel displays the Microsoft Excel dialog box to indicate the spell checking is comploto (Figuro 2-56).**

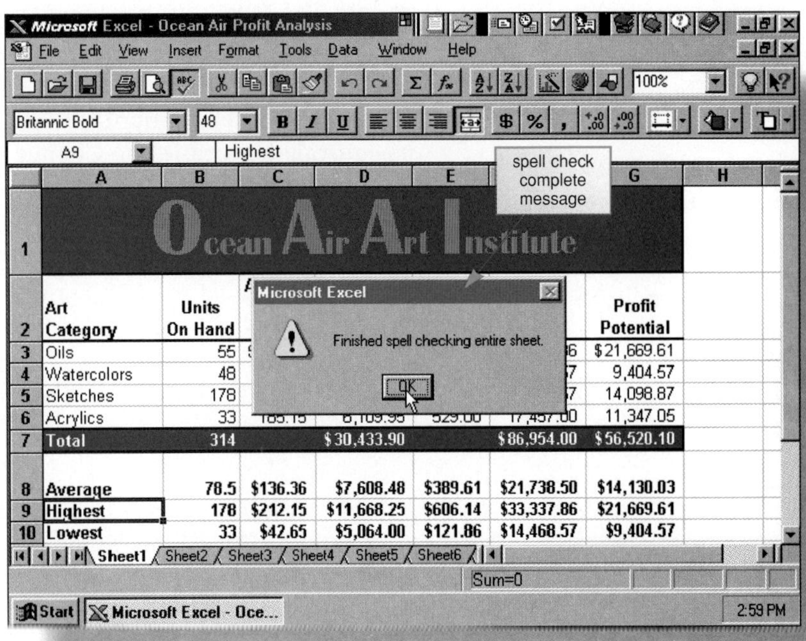

FIGURE 2-56

*Other*Ways

1. Right-click menu bar, click spelling
2. On the Tools menu click Spelling
3. Press F7

When the spell checker identifies a word not in the dictionaries, it changes the active cell to the cell containing the word not in the dictionaries. The Spelling dialog box (Figure 2-55) lists the word not in the dictionaries, a suggested correction, and a list of alternative spellings. If you agree with the suggested correction in the Change To box, click the Change button. To change the word throughout the worksheet, click the **Change All button**.

If one of the words in the Suggestions list box is correct, click the word and then click the Change button or double-click the word. If none of the listed words is correct, type the correct word and then click the Change button. To skip correcting the word, click the **Ignore button**. To have Excel ignore the word for the remainder of the worksheet, click the **Ignore All button**.

Consider these additional points regarding the spell checker:

- To check the spelling of the text in a single cell, double-click the cell and click the Spelling button on the Standard toolbar.
- When you select a single cell and the formula bar is not active before invoking the spell checker, Excel checks the entire worksheet including notes and embedded charts.
- If you select a range of cells before invoking the spell checker, Excel checks only the spelling of the words in the selected range.
- To check the spelling of a chart, select the chart before invoking the spell checker.
- To check the spelling of all the sheets in a workbook, click Select All Sheets from a sheet tab shortcut menu, and then invoke the spell checker. You display the sheet tab shortcut menu by right-clicking the sheet tab.
- If you select a cell other than cell A1 before you start the spell checker, a dialog box displays after Excel checks to the end of the worksheet asking if you want to continue checking at the beginning.

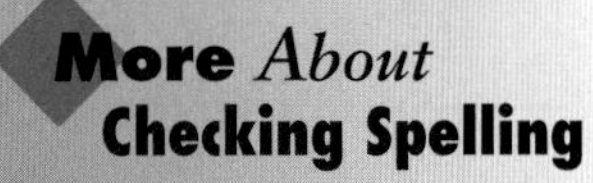

More *About* Checking Spelling

Always take the time to check the spelling of a worksheet before submitting it to your supervisor. Nothing deflates an impression more than a professional-looking report with misspelled words.

- To add words that are not in the standard dictionary to the custom dictionary, click the **Add button** in the Spelling dialog box (Figure 2-55) when Excel identifies the word.
- Click the **AutoCorrect** button (Figure 2-55) to add the misspelled word and its equivalent word in the Change To box to the AutoCorrect list. For example, if the misspelled word is *dox* and you mean *do*, then with *do* in the Change To box and *dox* the misspelled word, click the AutoCorrect button. Then, anytime in the future that you type *dox*, Excel will change it to *do*.

More *About* **Saving**

If you want to save the workbook under a new name, click the Save As command on the File menu or shortcut menu that displays when you right-click the menu. Some Excel users feel better if they save workbooks to two different drives. They use the Save button on the Standard toolbar to save the latest version of the workbook to the default drive. Then, they use the Save As command to save a second copy to another drive.

Saving the Workbook a Second Time Using the Same Filename

Earlier in this project, you saved an intermediate version of the workbook using the filename Ocean Air Profit Analysis. To save the workbook a second time using the same filename, click the Save button on the Standard toolbar. Excel automatically stores the latest version of the workbook under the same filename Ocean Air Profit Analysis without displaying the Save As dialog box as it did when you saved the workbook the first time.

If you want to save the workbook under a new name, choose the **Save As command** from the File menu or shortcut menu. For example, some Excel users use the Save button to save the latest version of the workbook to the default drive. Then, they use the Save As command to save a second copy to another drive.

You can also click Save on the File menu or shortcut menu or press SHIFT+F12 or CTRL+S to save a workbook a second time under the same filename. The shortcut menu that contains the Save command displays when you point to the menu bar.

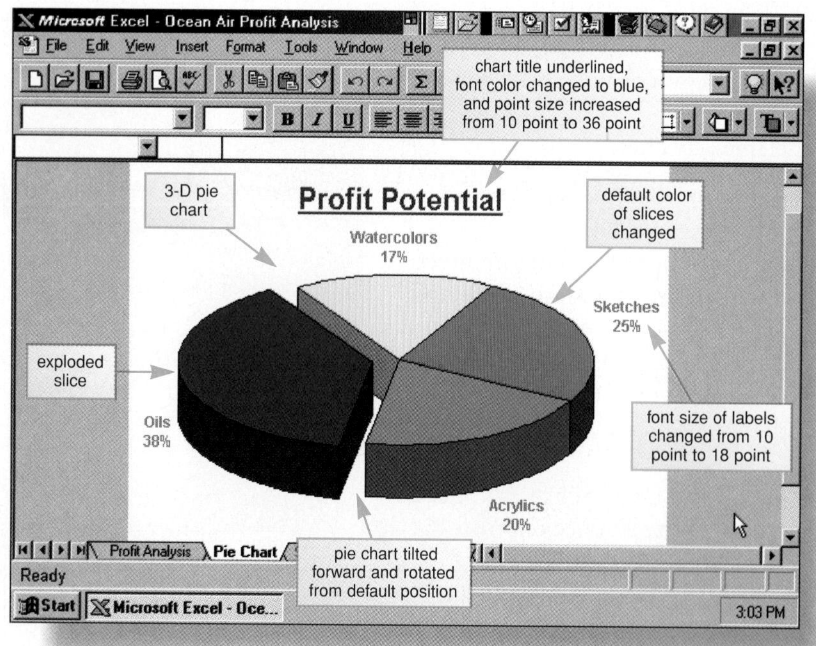

FIGURE 2-57

Adding a Pie Chart to the Workbook

The next step in this project is to draw the three-dimensional pie chart on a separate sheet as shown in Figure 2-57. A **pie chart** is used to show how 100% of an amount is divided. Each **slice** (or wedge) of the pie represents a contribution to the whole. The pie chart in Figure 2-57 shows the contribution of each art category to the company's profit potential. It is easy to see from the pie chart that Oils has the greatest profit potential and Watercolors has the least profit potential.

The pie chart in Figure 2-57 differs from the 3-D column chart in Project 1 in that it is not embedded in the worksheet. Instead, it is created on a separate sheet, called a **chart sheet**.

The range in the worksheet to graph is the nonadjacent ranges A3:A6 and G3:G6 (Figure 2-58). The art category names in the range A3:A6 will identify the slices. The entries in column A are called the **category names**. The range G3:G6 contains the data that determines the size of the slices in the pie. The entries in column G are called the **data series**. Because there are four art categories, the pie chart contains four slices.

This project also calls for emphasizing the art category with the greatest profit potential (Oils) by offsetting its slice from the main portion. A pie chart with one or more slices offset is called an **exploded pie chart.**

As described in Figure 2-57, the pie chart has also been enhanced from the default pie chart that is first drawn by rotating and tilting the pie forward, changing the colors of the slices, and modifying the chart title and labels that identify the slices.

More *About* **Charting**

Line chart, bar chart, pie chart – which chart will best describe your worksheet data? For answers, double-click the Help button on the Standard toolbar. Click the Contents tab. Double-click the following books: Working with Charts and Maps; Formatting a Chart book; and Changing the Type of Chart book. Finally, double-click the link titled, The best chart type for my data. One at a time, click the nine chart types and read the information.

Drawing the Pie Chart

To draw the pie chart on a separate sheet, you select the nonadjacent range and use the **Chart command** from the **Insert menu**. Once the chart is created, it will be formatted as shown in Figure 2-57 in the following fashion:

1. Chart title — increase the font size to 36 and change the font color to blue
2. Slice labels — increase the font size to 18 and change the font color to red
3. Explode the Oils slice
4. Rotate and tilt the pie chart so the Oils slice will display more prominently
5. Change the color of the slices of the pie chart

To Draw a Pie Chart

1 **Select the range A3:A6. Hold down the CTRL key and select the range G3:G6. On the Insert menu, click Chart and then point to As New Sheet.**

The nonadjacent ranges are selected and the Chart menu displays (Figure 2-58).

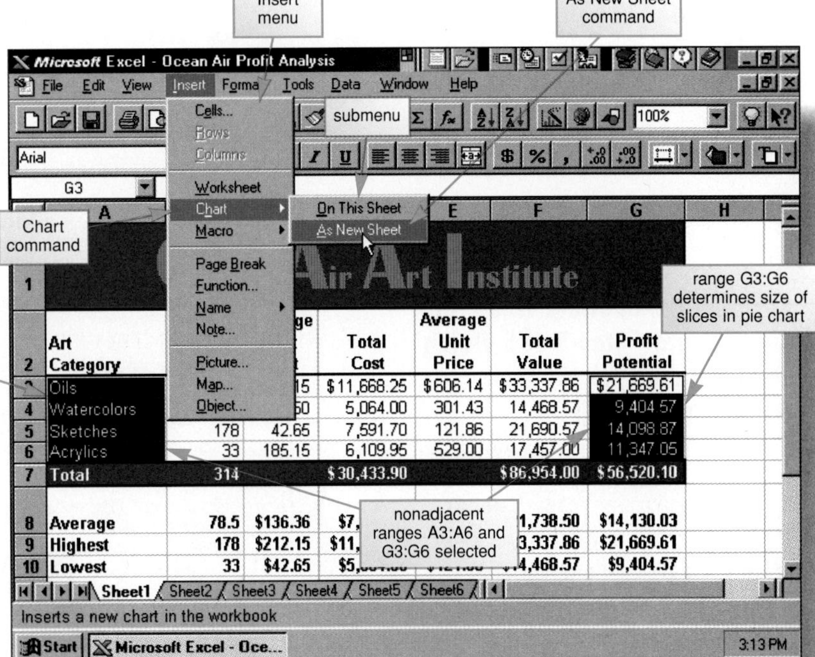

FIGURE 2-58

2 **Click As New Sheet on the Chart menu.**

Excel displays the ChartWizard – Step 1 of 5 dialog box, which shows the selected range to chart (Figure 2-59). If necessary, you can modify the range to chart in this dialog box.

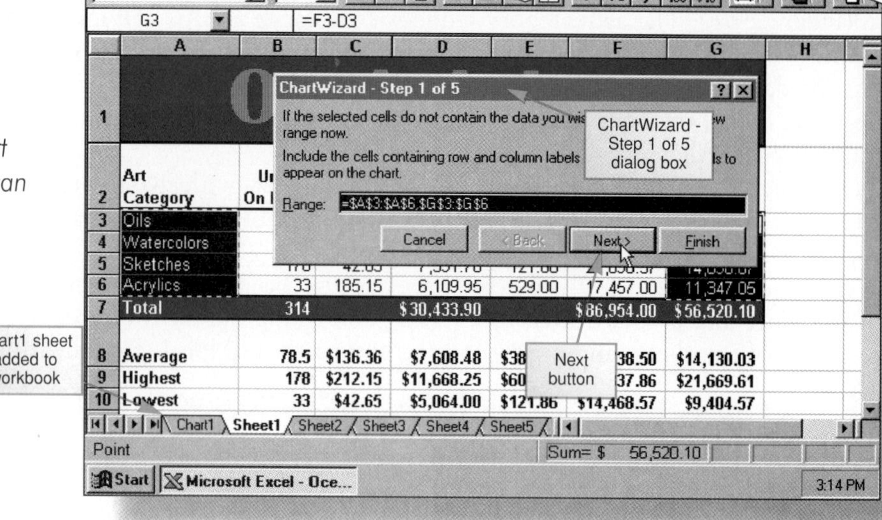

FIGURE 2-59

3 **Click the Next button. Click 3-D Pie in the ChartWizard - Step 2 of 5 dialog box.**

The ChartWizard - Step 2 of 5 dialog box displays available with 15 charts (Figure 2-60). The first nine charts in the dialog box are two-dimensional. The last six charts are three-dimensional. The 3-D Pie chart type is selected.

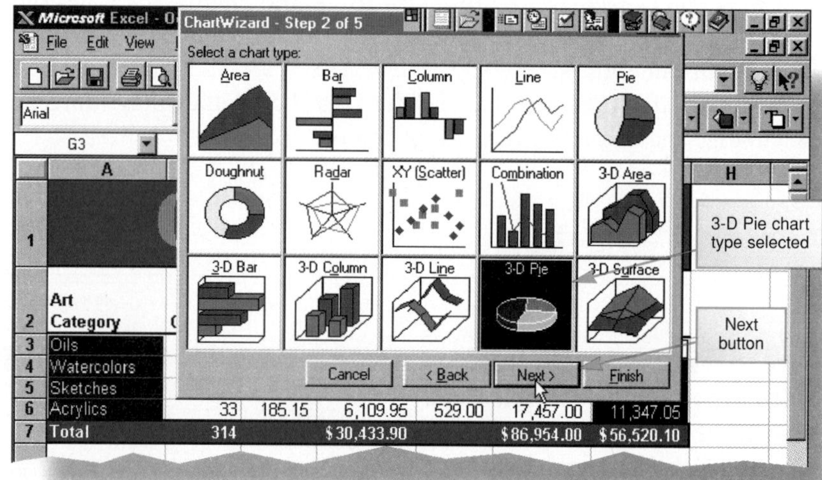

FIGURE 2-60

4 **Click the Next button. When the ChartWizard - Step 3 of 5 dialog box displays, click the last format, format 7.**

The ChartWizard - Step 3 of 5 dialog box displays with seven different 3-D pie chart formats (Figure 2-61). Format 7 with the labels and percents outside the pie chart is selected.

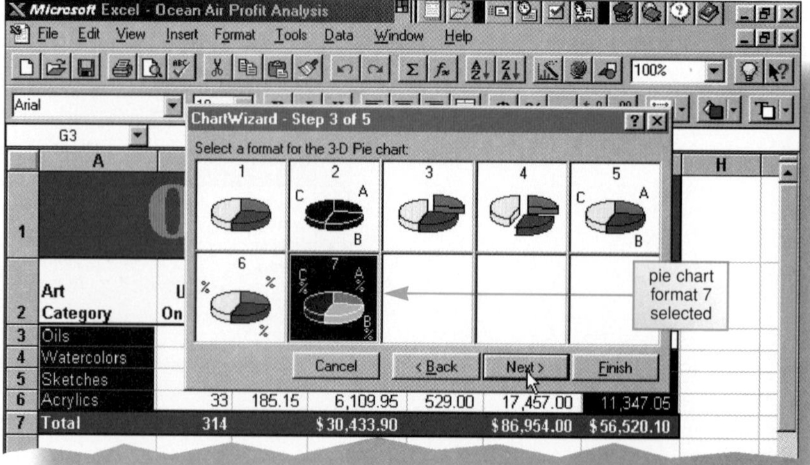

FIGURE 2-61

5 **Click the Next button. If a Microsoft Excel dialog box displays, click the OK button and then change the settings on the ChartWizard - Step 4 of 5 dialog box to agree with those shown in Figure 2-62.**

The ChartWizard - Step 4 of 5 dialog box shows a sample 3-D pie chart (Figure 2-62).

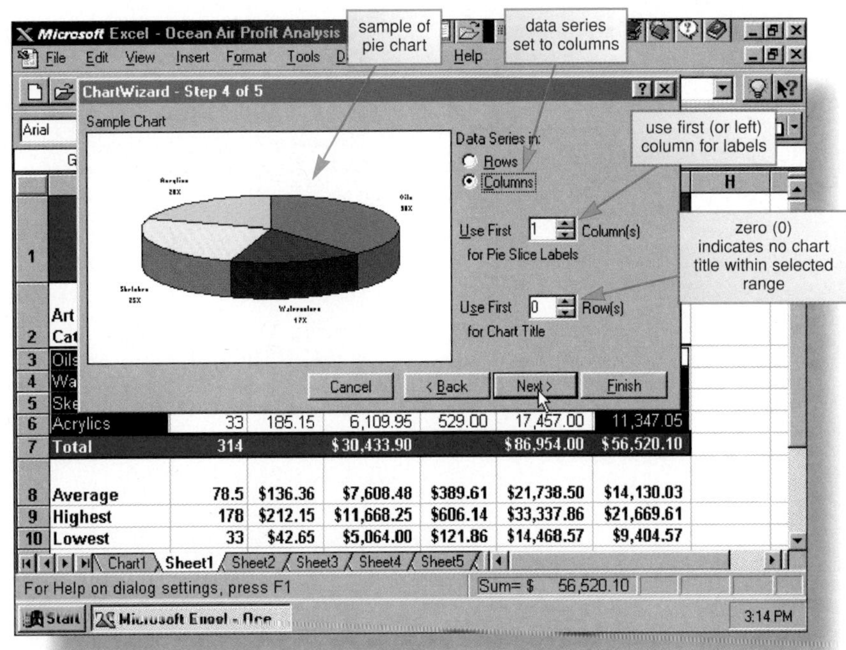

FIGURE 2-62

6 **Click the Next button. Type** `Profit Potential` **in the Chart Title box in the ChartWizard - Step 5 of 5 dialog box.**

The ChartWizard - Step 5 of 5 dialog box displays on the screen (Figure 2-63). The dialog box gives you the opportunity to add a legend and add a chart title. The chart title you enter shows in the Sample Chart area. In this case, a legend is not required to clarify the slices. Thus, the No option button is selected.

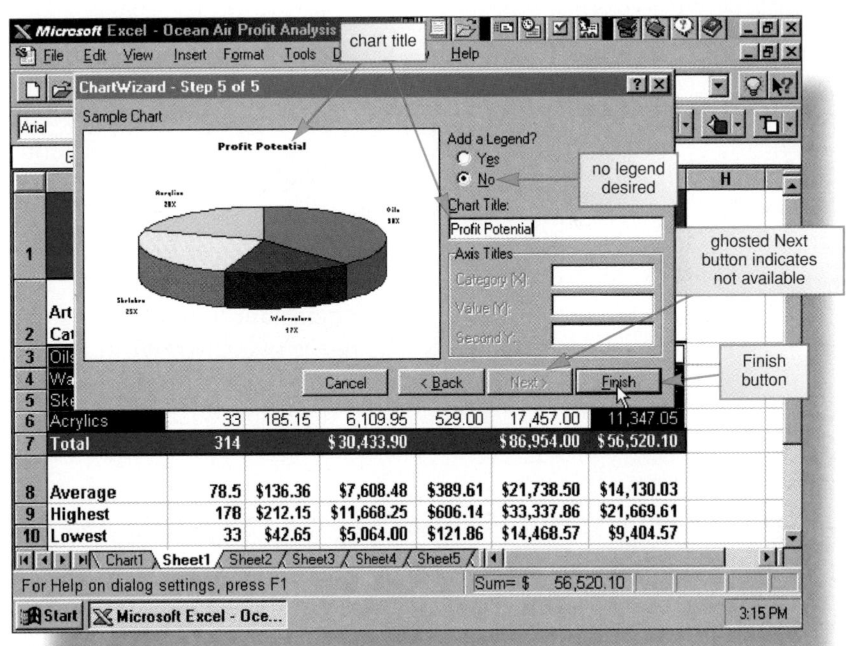

FIGURE 2-63

Click the Finish button in the ChartWizard - Step 5 of 5 dialog box.

Excel draws the three-dimensional pie chart and displays it on a sheet titled Chart1 (Figure 2-64).

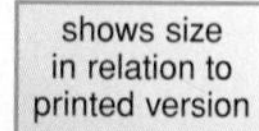

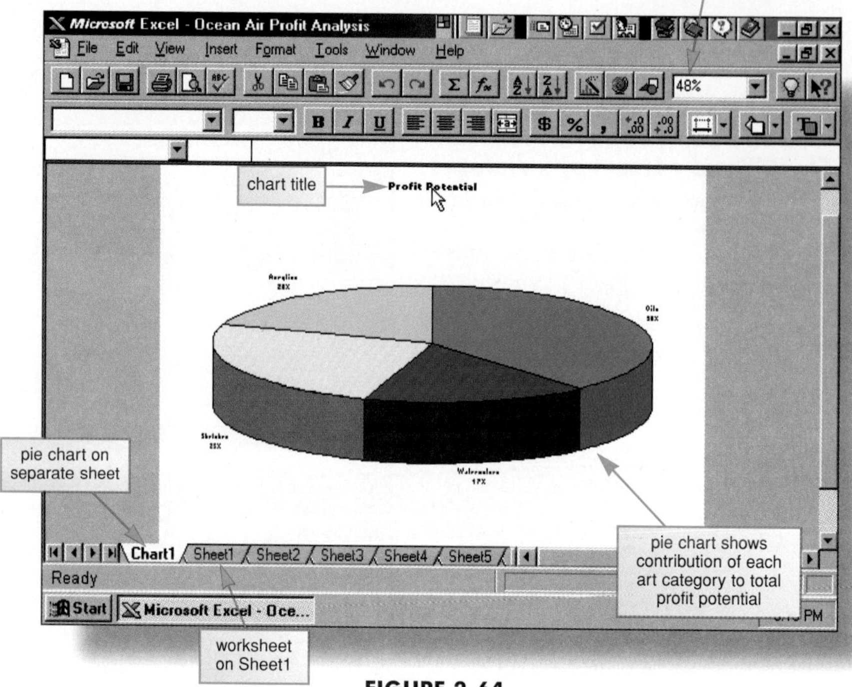

FIGURE 2-64

OtherWays

1. Select range to chart and Press F11

Each slice of the pie chart represents one of the four art categories – Oils, Watercolors, Sketches, and Acrylics. The names of the art categories and the percent contribution to the total profit potential display outside the slices. The chart title, Profit Potential, displays immediately above the pie chart.

Excel determines the direction of the data series range (down a column or across a row) on the basis of the selected range. Because the selection for the pie chart is down the worksheet (ranges A3:A7 and G3:G7), Excel sets the Data Series to Columns automatically as shown in Figure 2-62 on the previous page.

Notice in the five ChartWizard dialog boxes (Figure 2-59 through Figure 2-63) that you can return to the previous ChartWizard dialog box, return to the beginning of the ChartWizard, or create the chart with the options selected thus far while any one of the five ChartWizard dialog boxes is on the screen.

Formatting the Chart Title and Chart Labels

The next step is to format the chart title and labels that identify the slices. Before you can format a **chart item**, such as the chart title or labels, you must select it. Once a chart item is selected, you can format it using the Formatting toolbar, shortcut menu, special keys, or the Format menu. The Formatting toolbar will be used to format the chart title, similar to the way the cell entries were formatted earlier in this project. The labels will be formatted using the shortcut menu. Complete the following steps to format the chart title and labels.

Steps To Format the Chart Title and Labels

1 Click the chart title. Click the Font Size arrow on the Formatting toolbar and then click 36. Click the Underline button on the Formatting toolbar.

Excel displays a box with handles around the chart title, increases the size of the characters in the chart title, and underlines the chart title.

2 Click the Font Color button arrow on the Formatting toolbar and then point to the color blue (column 1, row 4 on the font Color palette).

The Chart1 sheet displays as shown in Figure 2-65.

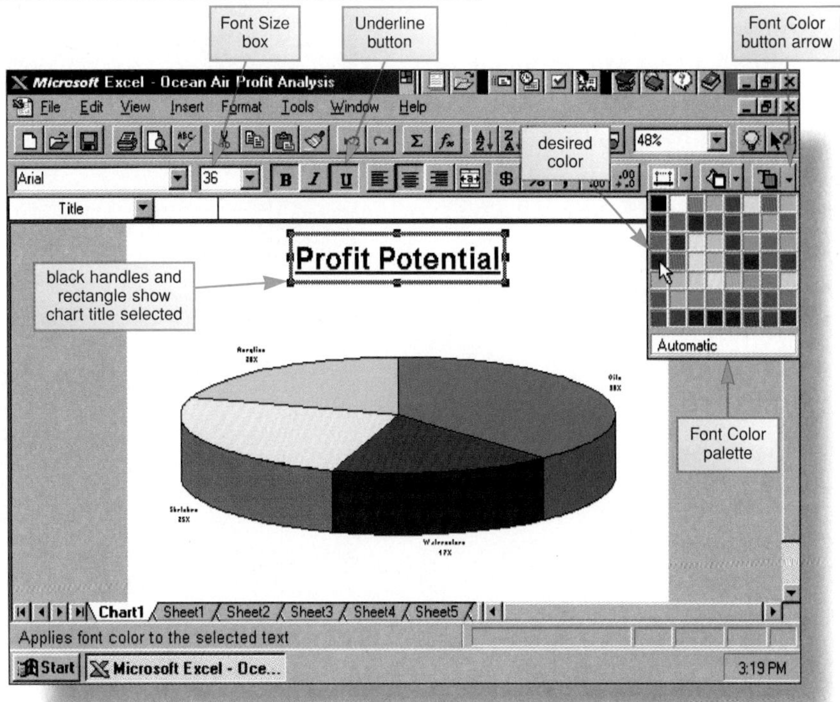

FIGURE 2-65

3 Click the color blue on the Font Color palette. Right-click one of the four labels that identify the slices. Point to Format Data Labels on the shortcut menu.

The chart title displays as shown in Figure 2-66. The labels are selected and the shortcut menu displays.

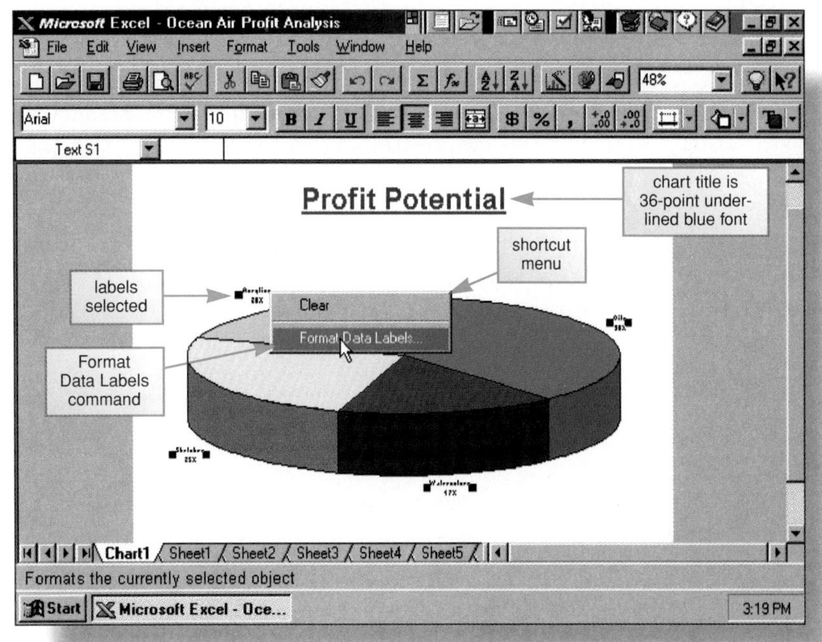

FIGURE 2-66

4 **Click Format Data Labels on the shortcut menu. When the Format Data Labels dialog box displays, click the Font tab, click Bold in the Font Style list box, click 18 in the Size list box, click the Color arrow and point to the color red (column 3, row 1 on the Color palette).**

The Format Data Labels dialog box displays as shown in Figure 2-67.

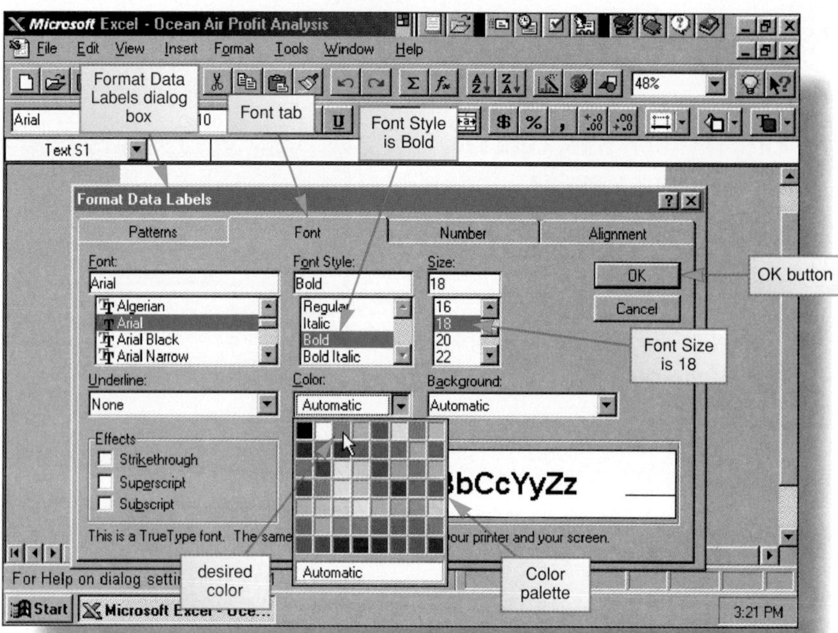

FIGURE 2-67

5 **Click the color red and then click the OK button.**

The labels that identify the slices are bold, larger, and red as shown in Figure 2-68.

OtherWays

1. Right-click title or labels, click Format Chart Title or click Format Data Labels
2. Press CTRL+B to bold, CTRL+U to underline

Compare Figure 2-68 to Figure 2-65 on the previous page. You can see in Figure 2-68 that the labels and chart title are easier to read and make the chart sheet look more professional when compared to Figure 2-65.

Notice the labels in Figure 2-66 have black handles. This means that if you want to, you can move and resize them. You can also select and format individual labels by clicking a label after all the labels have been selected. For example, to emphasize a small or large slice in a pie chart, you could make its label larger or a different color.

More About Clicking

There are a few Excel formatting activities, especially with charts, that require you to click the object twice before selecting a format. Clicking an object twice is not the same as double-clicking. For double-clicking the clicking sequence is rapid. When you are asked to click an object twice, pause before clicking a second time.

Changing the Colors of the Slices

The next step is to change the colors of the slices of the pie. The colors you see in Figure 2-68 are the default colors Excel uses when you first create a pie chart. Project 2 requires that the colors be changed to those shown earlier in Figure 2-57 on page E 2.42. To change the colors of the slices, you select them one at a time and use the Color button on the Formatting toolbar as shown in the following steps.

Steps To Change the Colors of the Pie Slices

1 **Click the Oils slice twice, once to select all the slices and once to select the individual slice. (Do not double-click.) Click the Color button arrow on the Formatting toolbar and then point to the color blue (column 1, row 4 on the color palette).**

Excel displays black handles around the Oils slice and the Color palette displays (Figure 2-68).

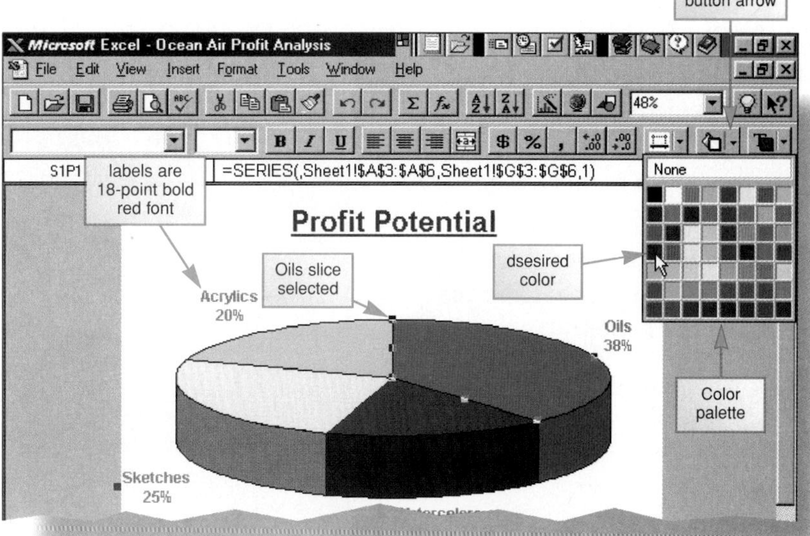

FIGURE 2-68

2 **Click the color blue.**

Excel changes the Oils slice to the color blue.

3 **One at a time, click the remaining slices and use the following colors on the Color palette for the art categories specified: Acrylics - green (column 2, row 2); Sketches - red (column 3, row 1); Watercolors - yellow (column 3, row 4). Click outside the chart area.**

The pie chart displays as shown in Figure 2-69.

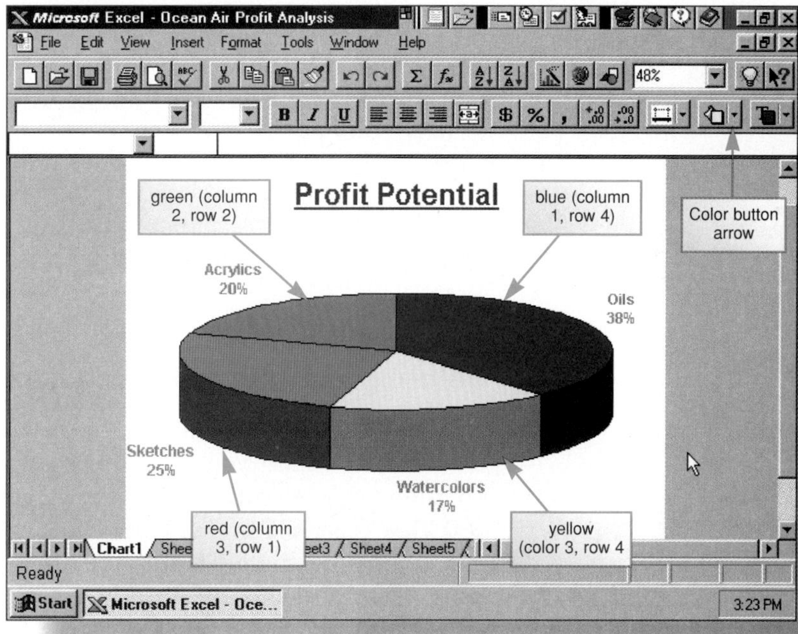

FIGURE 2-69

OtherWays

1. Right-click selected slice, click Format Data Point on shortcut menu, click Patterns tab, click color, click OK button
2. On Format menu click Selected Data Point, click Patterns tab, click color, click OK button

Exploding the Pie Chart

The next step is to emphasize the slice representing the Oils painting category by offsetting, or **exploding,** it from the rest of the slices. The reason for exploding the Oils slice is because it represents the greatest profit potential and by exploding it, the slice will be stand out. Perform the steps on the next page to offset a slice of the pie chart.

To Explode the Pie Chart

1 **Click the slice labeled Oils twice. (Do not double-click.)**

Excel surrounds the Oils slice with handles.

2 **Drag the slice to the desired position, and then release the left mouse button.**

Excel redraws the pie chart with the Oils slice offset from the rest of the pie chart (Figure 2-70).

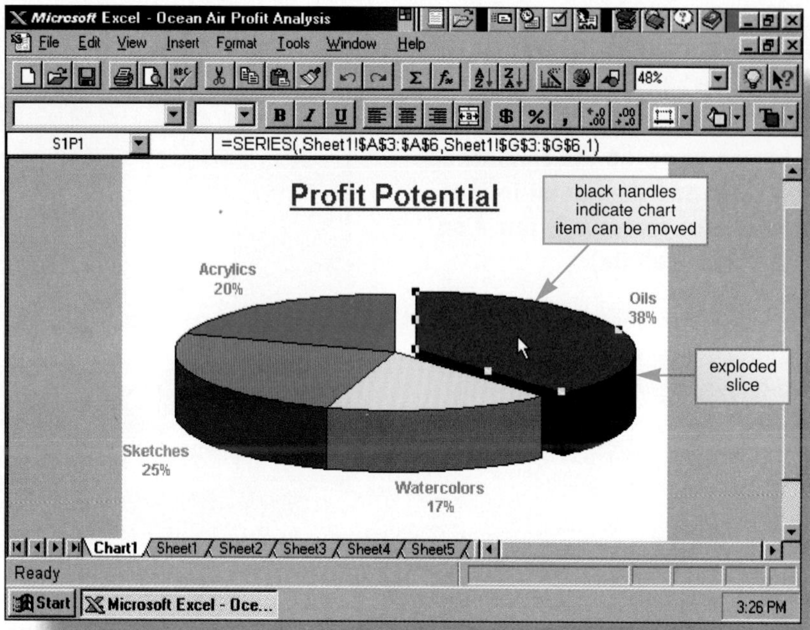

FIGURE 2-70

Although you can offset as many slices as you want, as you drag more slices away from the main portion of the pie chart, the slices become smaller. If you continue to offset slices, the pie chart becomes too small to have an impact on the reader.

Rotating and Tilting the Pie Chart

In a three-dimensional chart, you can change the view to better display the section of the chart you are trying to emphasize. Excel allows you to control the rotation angle, elevation, perspective, height, and angle of the axes by using the **3-D View command** on the Format menu or shortcut menu.

To obtain a better view of the offset for the Oils slice, you can rotate the pie chart 190 degrees to the left. The rotation angle of a pie chart is defined by the line that divides the Oils and Acrylics slices. Excel initially draws a pie chart with one of the dividing lines pointing to twelve o'clock (or zero degrees). Besides rotating the pie chart, the following steps also tilt, or change, the elevation so the pie chart is at less of an angle to the viewer.

To Rotate and Tilt the Pie Chart

1 **With the Oils slice selected, right-click the Oils slice and then point to 3-D View on the shortcut menu.**

The shortcut menu displays as shown in Figure 2-71.

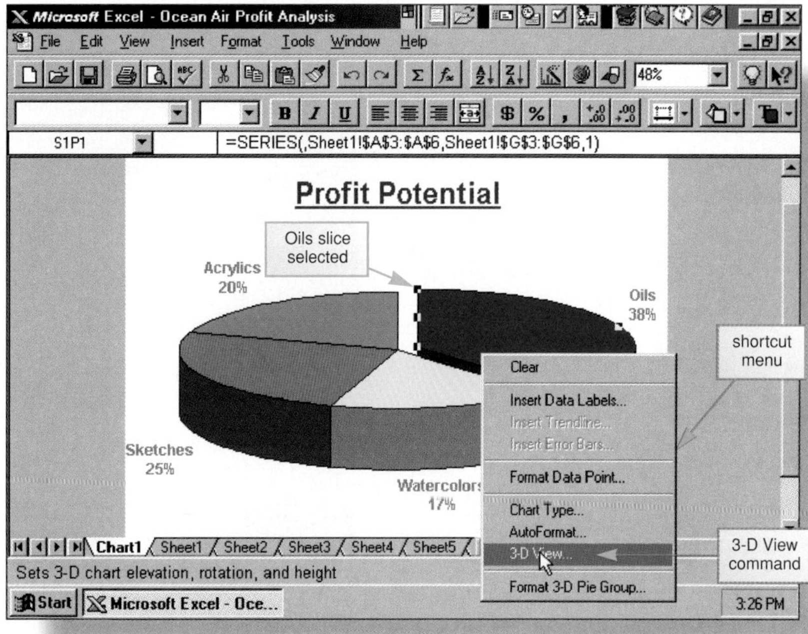

FIGURE 2-71

2 **Click 3-D View on the shortcut menu. When the Format 3-D View dialog box displays, click the up arrow button in the Format 3-D View dialog box until 25 displays in the Elevation box.**

The 3-D View dialog box displays (Figure 2-72). A sample of the pie chart displays in the dialog box. The result of increasing the elevation of the pie chart is to tilt it forward.

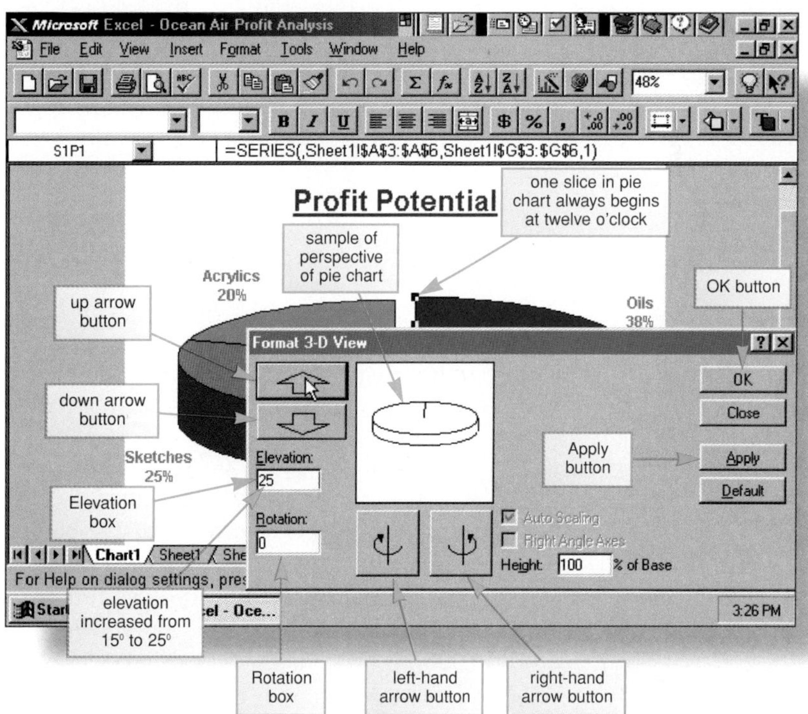

FIGURE 2-72

3 **Rotate the pie chart by clicking the right-hand arrow button until the Rotation box displays 190.**

The new rotation setting (190) displays in the Rotation box as shown in Figure 2-73. A sample of the rotated pie chart displays in the dialog box.

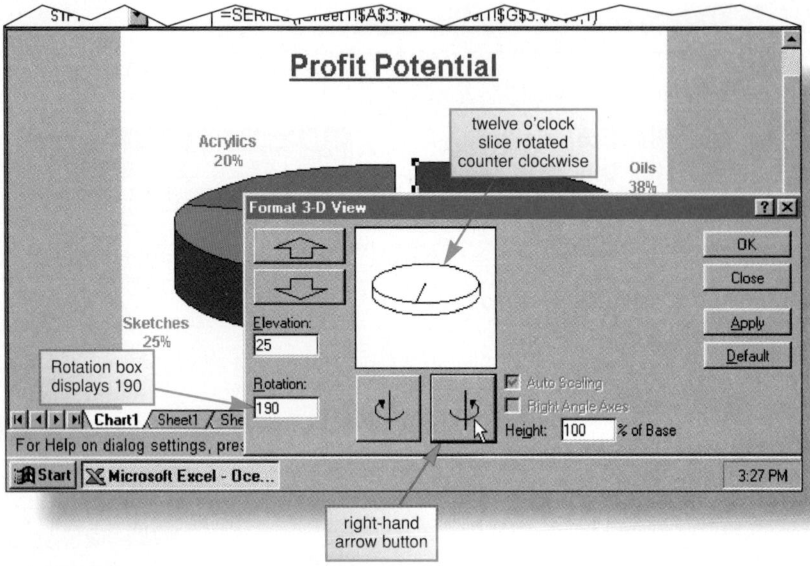

FIGURE 2-73

4 **Click the OK button on the Format 3-D View dialog box.**

Excel displays the pie chart tilted forward and rotated to the left so the space between the Oils slice and the main portion of the pie is more prominent (Figure 2-74).

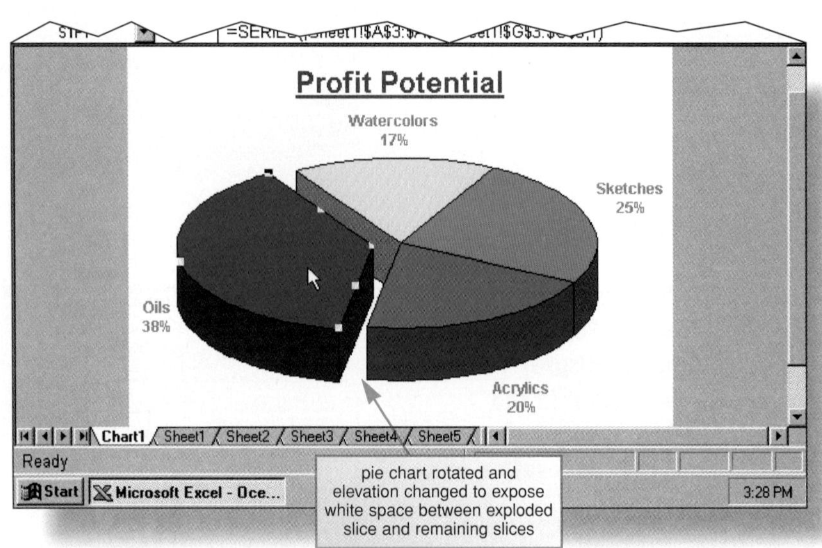

FIGURE 2-74

OtherWays

1. On the Format menu click 3-D View, select settings on Format 3-D View dialog box, click OK button

Compare Figure 2-74 to Figure 2-70 on page E 2.50. The offset of the Oils slice is more noticeable in Figure 2-74 because the pie chart has been tilted and rotated to expose the white space between the Oils slice and the main portion of the pie chart.

Besides controlling the rotation angle and elevation, you also can control the thickness of the pie chart by entering smaller or larger percents than the default 100% in the Height box (Figure 2-73).

The pie chart is complete. The next step is to change the names on the sheet tabs and rearrange the order of the sheets so the worksheet is first, followed by the chart. If you look at the sheet tabs below the pie chart in Figure 2-74, you will see that Sheet1, which contains the worksheet is behind the sheet labeled Chart1.

More About Changing a Pie Chart's Perspective

You can increase or decrease the base height (thickness) of the pie chart by changing the height to base ratio in the Format 3-D View dialog box.

Changing the Names on the Sheet Tabs and Rearranging the Order of the Sheets

At the bottom of the screen (Figure 2-75) are the tabs that allow you to display any sheet in the workbook. By default, the tab names are Sheet1, Sheet2,and so on. When you draw a chart on a separate sheet, Excel assigns the name Chart1 to the sheet tab. The following steps show you how to rename the sheet tabs and reorder the sheets so the worksheet comes before the chart sheet.

More About Sheets

To move from sheet to sheet in a workbook, you click the sheet tabs at the bottom of the window. The name of the active sheet is always bold on a white background. You can rename the sheets, add and delete sheets, and move or copy sheets within a workbook or to another workbook.

To Rename the Sheet Tabs and Rearrange the Order of the Sheets

1 Double-click the tab named Chart1 in the lower left corner of the window.

Excel displays the Rename Sheet dialog box.

2 Type `Pie Chart` **in the Name box.**

The Rename Sheet dialog box displays as shown in Figure 2-75.

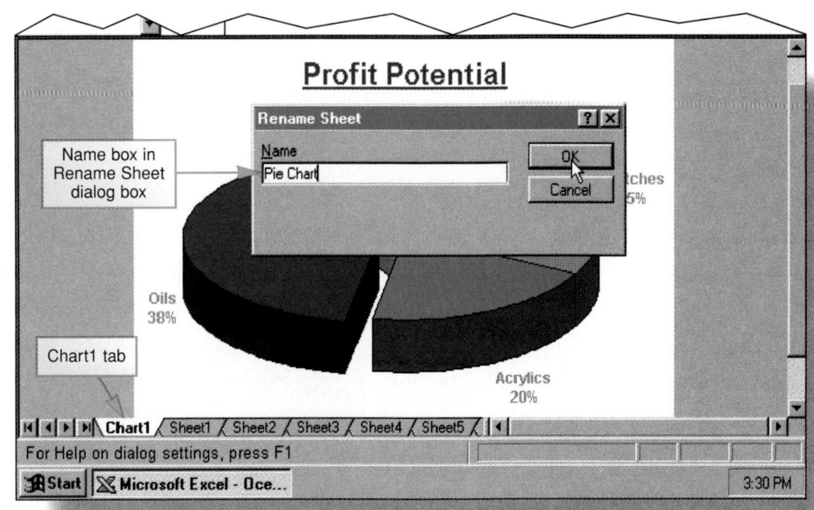

FIGURE 2-75

3 Click the OK button in the Rename Sheet dialog box. Double-click the Sheet1 tab. Type `Profit Analysis` **in the Name box.**

Excel renames the Chart1 tab Pie Chart and redisplays the Rename Sheet dialog box with the new title for the Sheet1 tab (Figure 2-76).

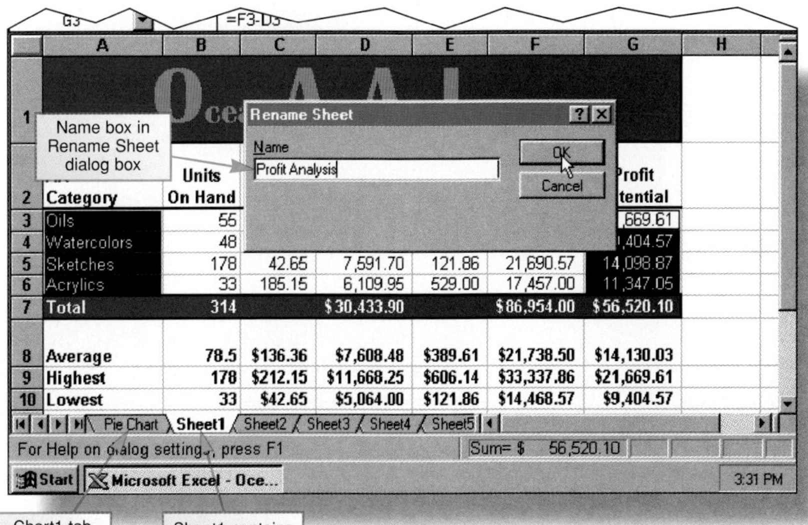

FIGURE 2-76

4 **Click the OK button in the Rename Sheet dialog box.**

Excel renames the Sheet1 tab Profit Analysis.

5 **Point to the Profit Analysis tab and drag it over the Pie Chart tab.**

The mouse pointer changes to a pointer and a document (Figure 2-77).

	A	B	C	D	E	F	G
1	Ocean Air Art Institute						
2	Art Category	Units On Hand	Average Unit Cost	Total Cost	Average Unit Price	Total Value	Profit Potential
3	Oils	55	$212.15	$11,668.25	$606.14	$33,337.86	$21,669.61
4	Watercolors	48	105.50	5,064.00	301.43	14,468.57	9,404.57
5	Sketches	178	42.65	7,591.70	121.86	21,690.57	14,098.87
6	Acrylics	33	185.15	6,109.95	529.00	17,457.00	11,347.05
7	Total	314		$30,433.90		$86,954.00	$56,520.10
8	Average	78.5	$136.36	$7,608.48	$389.61	$21,738.50	$14,130.03
9	Highest	178	$212.15	$11,668.25	$606.14	$33,337.86	$21,669.61
10	Lowest	33	$42.65	$5,064.00	$121.86	$14,468.57	$9,404.57

Pie Chart / Profit Analysis / Sheet2 / Sheet3 / Sheet4

Ready — Sum= $ 56,520.10

Profit Analysis sheet tab dragged over Pie Chart sheet tab

Sheet1 renamed Profit Analysis

FIGURE 2-77

6 **Release the left mouse button.**

Excel moves the sheet named Profit Analysis in front of the sheet named Pie Chart. The workbook for Project 2 is complete (Figure 2-78).

7 **Click the Save button on the Standard toolbar to save the workbook to disk using the filename Ocean Air Profit Analysis.**

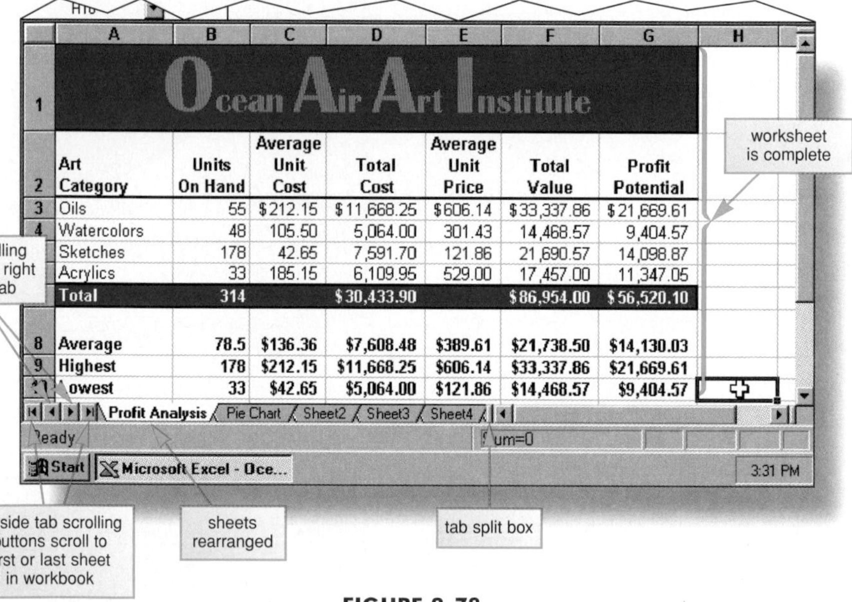

	A	B	C	D	E	F	G
1	Ocean Air Art Institute						
2	Art Category	Units On Hand	Average Unit Cost	Total Cost	Average Unit Price	Total Value	Profit Potential
3	Oils	55	$212.15	$11,668.25	$606.14	$33,337.86	$21,669.61
4	Watercolors	48	105.50	5,064.00	301.43	14,468.57	9,404.57
5	Sketches	178	42.65	7,591.70	121.86	21,690.57	14,098.87
6	Acrylics	33	185.15	6,109.95	529.00	17,457.00	11,347.05
7	Total	314		$30,433.90		$86,954.00	$56,520.10
8	Average	78.5	$136.36	$7,608.48	$389.61	$21,738.50	$14,130.03
9	Highest	178	$212.15	$11,668.25	$606.14	$33,337.86	$21,669.61
10	Lowest	33	$42.65	$5,064.00	$121.86	$14,468.57	$9,404.57

FIGURE 2-78

Other Ways

1. Right-click sheet tab, click Rename
2. Right-click sheet tab, click Move or Copy
3. On the Edit menu click Move or Copy

More About Sheet Tabs

You can use the keyboard to move from sheet to sheet in a workbook. Press CTRL+PGUP to move to the next sheet. Press CTRL+PGDN to move to the previous sheet.

The previous steps showed you how to rename the sheet tabs at the bottom of the screen and how to resequence them. Sheet names can be up to 31 characters (including spaces) in length. The longer the tab names, the fewer tabs will show. You can increase the number of tabs that show, however, by dragging the **tab split box** next to the scroll arrow (Figure 2-78) to the right. This will reduce the size of the scroll bar at the bottom of the screen. Double-click the tab split box to reset it to its normal position.

You can also use the **scroll buttons** to the left of the sheet tabs (Figure 2-78) to move between sheets. The leftmost and rightmost scroll buttons move to the first or last sheet in the workbook. The two middle scroll buttons move one sheet to the left or right.

Previewing and Printing Selected Sheets in a Workbook

In Project 1, you printed the worksheet without previewing it on the screen. By previewing the worksheet, you see exactly how it will look without generating a hard copy. Previewing a workbook can save time, paper, and the frustration of waiting for a printout only to find out it is not what you want.

The Print Preview command, as well as the Print command, will preview only selected sheets. You know a sheet is selected when the tab at the bottom of the screen is white. Thus, in Figure 2-78, the Profit Analysis sheet is selected, but the Pie Chart sheet is not. To select additional sheets, hold down the CTRL key and click any sheet tabs you want included in the preview or printout.

More About Selecting Additional Sheets

To select several consecutive sheets in a workbook, hold down the SHIFT key and click the sheet tab at the opposite end of the group to select. Thus, if Sheet1 is active and you want to select Sheet1 through Sheet5, hold down the SHIFT key and click Sheet5. Excel will select Sheet1, Sheet2, Sheet3, Sheet4, and Sheet5.

Steps To Preview Selected Sheets in a Workbook

1 Hold down the CTRL key and click the Pie Chart tab. Point to the Print Preview button on the Standard toolbar

Both sheets are selected (Figure 2-79).

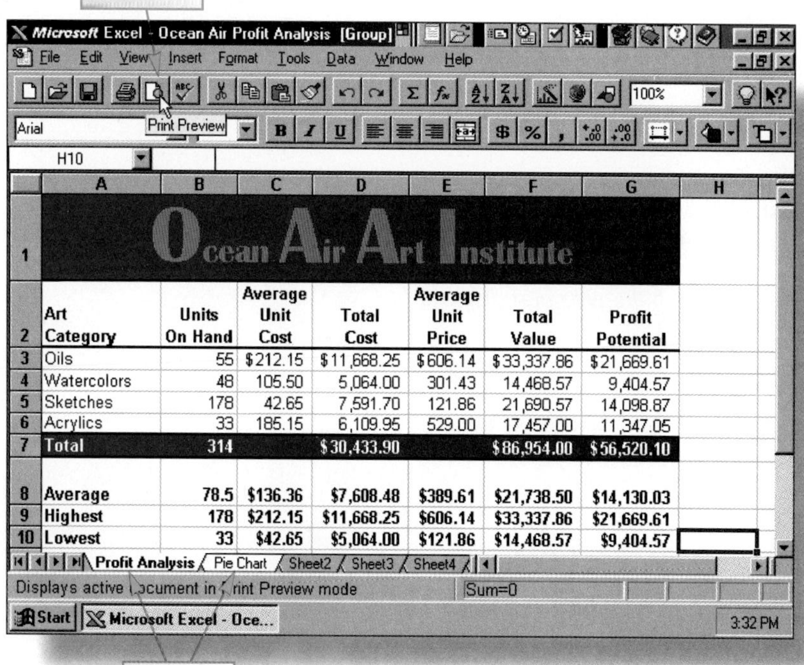

FIGURE 2-79

2 **Click the Print Preview button on the Standard toolbar.**

Excel displays a preview of the worksheet in the ***preview window*** *and the mouse pointer changes to a magnifying glass (Figure 2-80).*

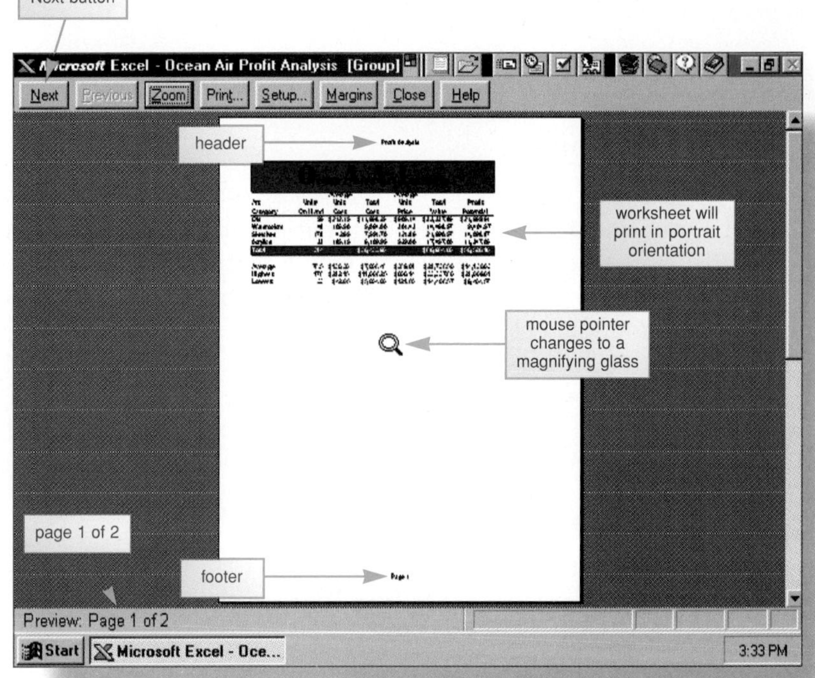

FIGURE 2-80

3 **Click the Next button to display a preview of the chart.**

A preview of the pie chart displays (Figure 2-81).

4 **Click the Close button in the preview window to return to the workbook.**

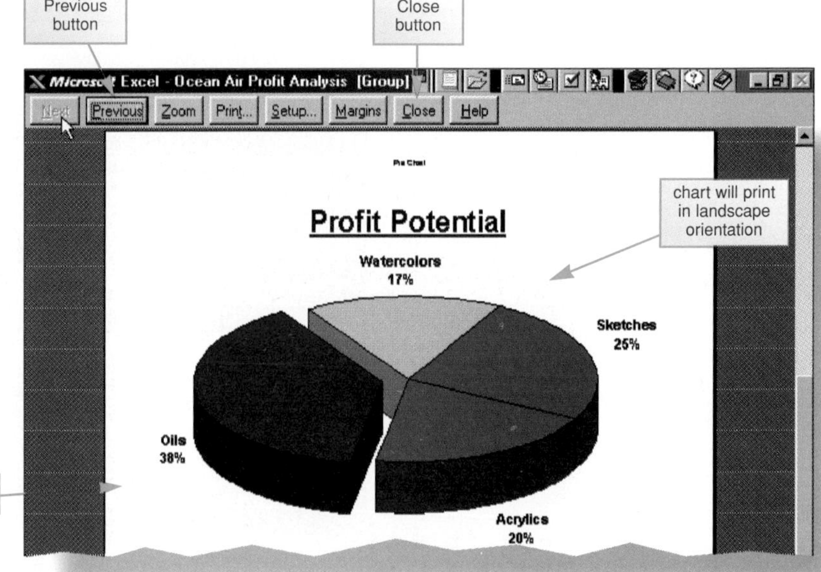

FIGURE 2-81

OtherWays

1. On File menu click Print Preview
2. On File menu click Page Setup, click Print Preview
3. Right-click menu, click Page Setup, click Print Preview

More About Print Preview

A popular button in the preview window (Figure 2-80) is the Margins button, which allows you to adjust the columns and margins. This is important, because the preview window shows the worksheet as it will print (WYSIWYG – What You See Is What You Get), whereas the screen may not.

Excel displays several buttons at the top of the preview window (Figure 2-81). The functions of these buttons are summarized in Table 2-4.

Rather than click the Next and Previous buttons to move from page to page as described in Table 2-4, you can press the PAGE UP and PAGE DOWN keys to do the same. You can also click the page in the preview window when the mouse pointer is a magnifying glass to carry out the function of the Zoom button.

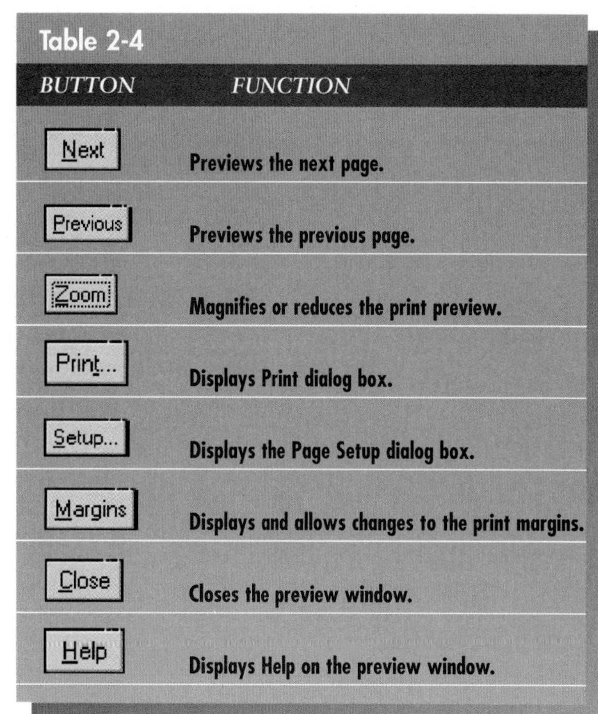

Table 2-4

BUTTON	FUNCTION
Next	Previews the next page.
Previous	Previews the previous page.
Zoom	Magnifies or reduces the print preview.
Print...	Displays Print dialog box.
Setup...	Displays the Page Setup dialog box.
Margins	Displays and allows changes to the print margins.
Close	Closes the preview window.
Help	Displays Help on the preview window.

Printing Selected Sheets in a Workbook

Although the two selected sheets could have been printed from the preview window, the following steps show how to print them using the Print button on the Standard toolbar.

To Print Selected Sheets in a Workbook

Print button

1 **If both sheets are not selected, hold down the CTRL key and click the inactive sheet tab.**

2 **Point to the Print button on the Standard toolbar (Figure 2-82).**

3 **Click the Print button.**

Excel prints the worksheet and pie chart on the printer (Figure 2-83 on the next page).

4 **Right-click the Profit Analysis tab at the bottom of the window and then click Ungroup Sheets to deselect the Pie Chart tab.**

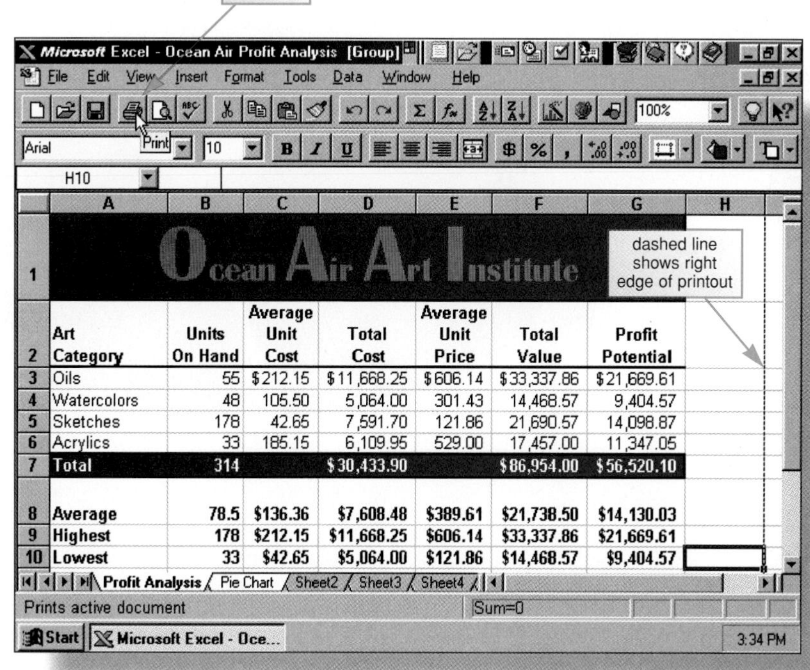

FIGURE 2-82

OtherWays

1. To print all nonblank worksheets, right-click tab, click Select All Sheets, click Print button on Standard toolbar

Notice that the worksheet is printed in portrait orientation and the chart is printed in landscape orientation (see Figure 2-83 on the next page). **Portrait orientation** means the printout is across the page width of 8.5 inches. **Landscape orientation** means the printout is across the page length of 11 inches. Excel selects landscape orientation automatically to print any chart created on a separate sheet.

Profit Analysis

Ocean Air Art Institute

Art Category	Units On Hand	Average Unit Cost	Total Cost	Average Unit Price	Total Value	Profit Potential
Oils	55	$212.15	$11,668.25	$606.14	$33,337.86	$21,669.61
Watercolors	48	105.50	5,064.00	301.43	14,468.57	9,404.57
Sketches	178	42.65	7,591.70	121.86	21,690.57	14,098.87
Acrylics	33	185.15	6,109.95	529.00	17,457.00	11,347.05
Total	314		$30,433.90		$86,954.00	$56,520.10
Average	78.5	$136.36	$7,608.48	$389.61	$21,738.50	$14,130.03
Highest	178	$212.15	$11,668.25	$606.14	$33,337.86	$21,669.61
Lowest	33	$42.65	$5,064.00	$121.86	$14,468.57	$9,404.57

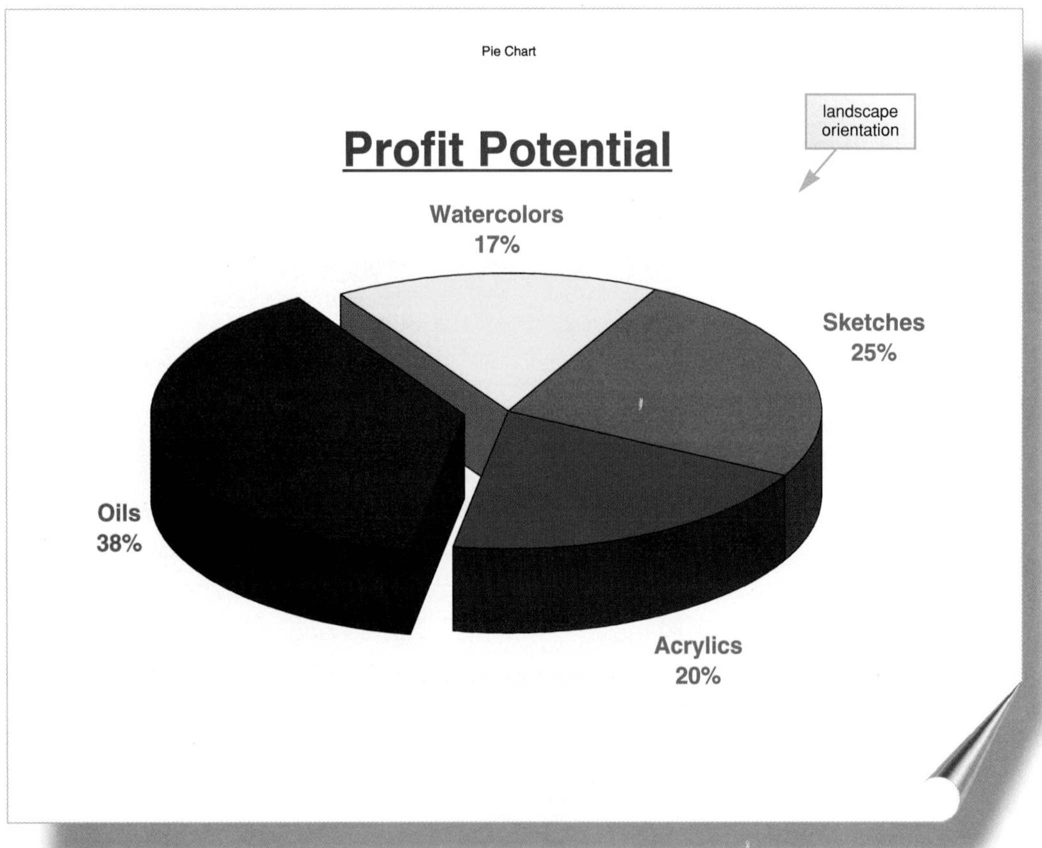

FIGURE 2-83

More About Printing

A dark font on a dark background, such as the red on blue title for Ocean Air Art Institute, will not print properly on a black and white printer. For b lack and white printing, use a light colored font for a dark background and a dark font for a light colored background.

Printing a Section of the Worksheet

You might not always want to print the entire worksheet. You can print portions of the worksheet by selecting the range of cells to print and then click Selection in the Print dialog box. The following steps show how to print the range A2:C6.

To Print a Section of the Worksheet

1 Select the range A2:C6. Right-click the menu bar.

The shortcut menu displays (Figure 2-84).

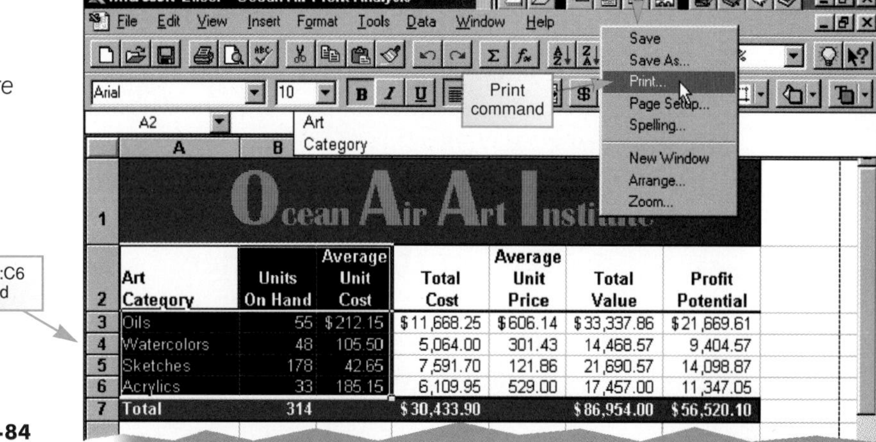

FIGURE 2-84

2 Click Print on the shortcut menu. Click Selection in the Print dialog box.

Excel displays the Print dialog box (Figure 2-85).

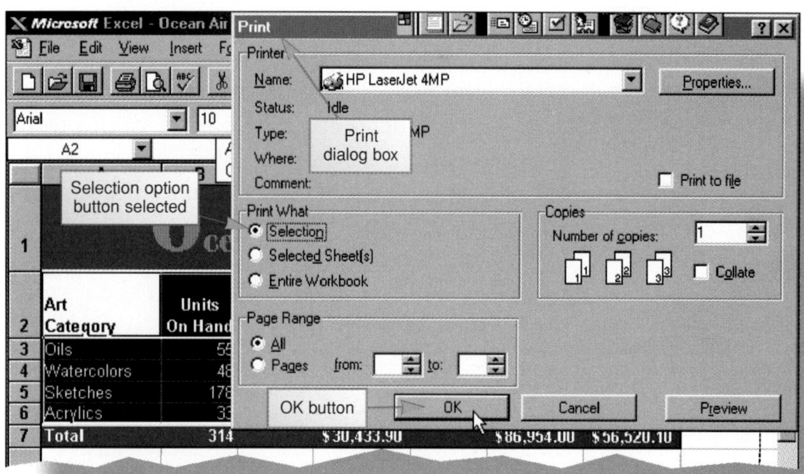

FIGURE 2-85

3 Click the OK button in the Print dialog box.

Excel prints the selected range of the worksheet on the printer (Figure 2-86).

Profit Analysis

Art Category	Units On Hand	Average Unit Cost
Oils	55	$212.15
Watercolors	48	105.50
Sketches	178	42.65
Acrylics	33	185.15

FIGURE 2-86

Other Ways

1. Select range, on File menu click Print Area, click Set Print Area, click Print button on Standard toolbar; on File menu click Print Area, click Clear Print Area

There are three option buttons in the Print What area on the Print dialog box (Figure 2-85 on the previous page). The Selection option button instructs Excel to print the selected range. The Selected Sheet(s) option button instructs Excel to print the active sheet (the one displaying on the screen) or the selected sheets. Finally, the Entire Workbook option button instructs Excel to print all the sheets in the workbook. Selecting Entire Workbook is an alternative to selecting tabs by holding down the SHIFT or CTRL keys and clicking tabs to make their sheets active. The Selected Sheet option is the default.

More About Values versus Formulas

When completing class assignments, don't enter numbers in cells that require formulas. Most instructors require their students to hand in both the values version and formulas version of the worksheet. The formulas version verifies that you entered formulas, rather than numbers in formula-based cells.

Displaying and Printing the Formulas in the Worksheet

Thus far, the worksheet has been printed exactly as it displays on the screen. This is called the **values version** of the worksheet. Another variation that you can display and print is called the formulas version. The **formulas version** displays and prints what was originally entered into the cells instead of the values in the cells. You can toggle between the values version and formulas version by pressing CTRL+` (LEFT SINGLE QUOTATION MARK to the left of the number 1 key).

The formulas version is useful for debugging a worksheet because the formulas and functions, rather than the numeric results, display and print. **Debugging** is the process of finding and correcting errors in the worksheet.

When you change from values to formulas, Excel increases the width of the columns so the formulas and text do not overflow into adjacent cells on the right. Thus, the worksheet usually becomes significantly wider when the formulas display. To fit the wide printout on one page you can use landscape orientation and the Fit to option on the Sheet sheet in the Page Setup dialog box. To change from values to formulas and print the formulas on one page, perform the following steps.

Steps To Display the Formulas in the Worksheet and Fit the Printout on One Page

1 **Press CTRL+` (LEFT SINGLE QUOTATION MARK to the left of the number 1 key).**

Excel changes the display of the worksheet from values to formulas (Figure 2-87). The formulas in the worksheet display showing unformatted numbers, formulas, and functions that were assigned to the cells. Excel increases the widths of the columns automatically.

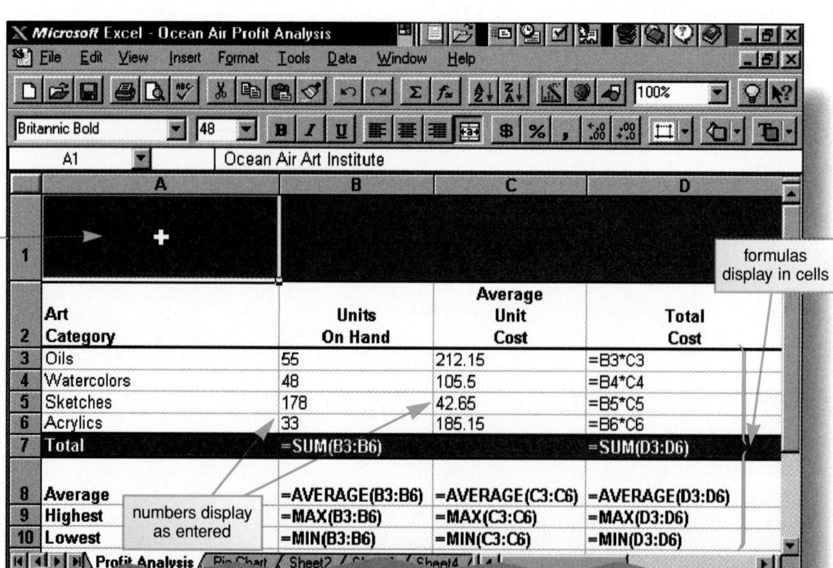

FIGURE 2-87

2 **Right-click the menu bar and then click Page Setup on the shortcut menu. When the Page Setup dialog box displays, click the Page tab, click Landscape and Fit to so the wide printout fits on one page in landscape orientation.**

Excel displays the Page Setup dialog box with the Landscape and Fit to selected (Figure 2-88).

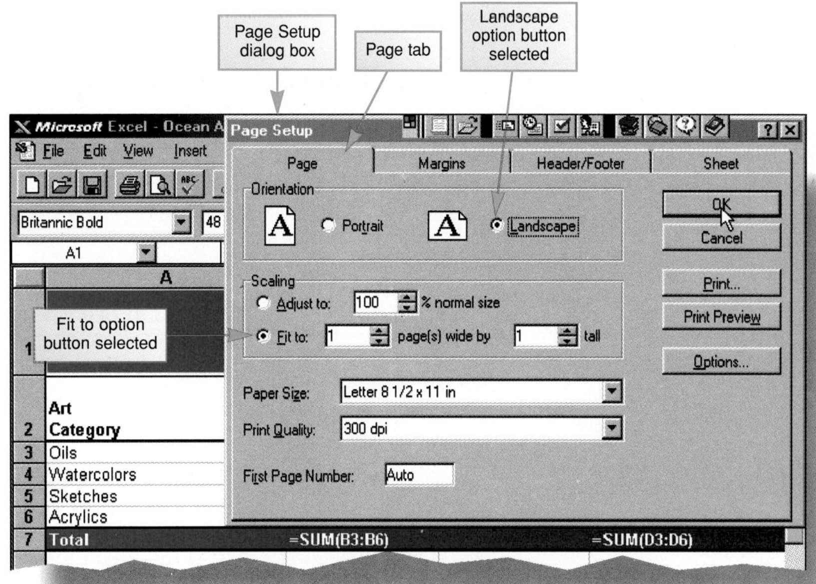

FIGURE 2-88

3 **Click the OK button in the Page Setup dialog box. Ready the printer and then click the Print button on the Standard toolbar. When you are finished with the formulas version, press CTRL+` to display the values version.**

Excel prints the formulas in the worksheet on one page in landscape orientation (Figure 2-89).

Profit Analysis

Art Category	Units On Hand	Average Unit Cost	Total Cost	Average Unit Price	Total Value	Profit Potential
Oils	55	212.15	=B3*C3	=C3*(1/(1-0.65))	=B3*E3	=F3-D3
Watercolors	48	105.5	=B4*C4	=C4*(1/(1-0.65))	=B4*E4	=F4-D4
Sketches	178	42.65	=B5*C5	=C5*(1/(1-0.65))	=B5*E5	=F5-D5
Acrylics	33	185.15	=B6*C6	=C6*(1/(1-0.65))	=B6*E6	=F6-D6
Total	=SUM(B3:B6)		=SUM(D3:D6)		=SUM(F3:F6)	=SUM(G3:G6)
Average	=AVERAGE(B3:B6)	=AVERAGE(C3:C6)	=AVERAGE(D3:D6)	=AVERAGE(E3:E6)	=AVERAGE(F3:F6)	=AVERAGE(G3:G6)
Highest	=MAX(B3:B6)	=MAX(C3:C6)	=MAX(D3:D6)	=MAX(E3:E6)	=MAX(F3:F6)	=MAX(G3:G6)
Lowest	=MIN(B3:B6)	=MIN(C3:C6)	=MIN(D3:D6)	=MIN(E3:E6)	=MIN(F3:F6)	=MIN(G3:G6)

FIGURE 2-89

OtherWays

1. On Tools menu click Options, click View tab, click Formulas check box, click OK button

Although the formulas in the worksheet were printed in the previous example, you can see from Figure 2-87 that the display on the screen can also be used for debugging errors in the worksheet.

The formulas in the worksheet were printed using the Fit to option so they would fit on one page. Anytime characters extend past the dashed line that represents the rightmost edge of the printed worksheet, the printout will be made up of multiple pages. If you prefer to print the worksheet on one page, click Fit to in the Page Setup dialog box (Figure 2-88) before you print.

More About the Fit To Option

Don't take the Fit To option lightly. Most applications involve worksheets that extend beyond the 8½-by-11-inch page. Most users want the information on one page, however, at least with respect to the width of the worksheet. Thus, the landscape orientation with the Fit To option is a common choice among Excel users.

Changing the Print Scaling Option Back to 100%

Depending on your printer driver, you may have to change the Print Scaling option back to 100% after using the Fit to option. Complete the following steps to reset the Print Scaling option so future worksheets print at 100%, instead of being squeezed on one page.

TO CHANGE THE PRINT SCALING OPTION BACK TO 100%

Step 1: Right-click the menu bar and then click the Page Setup command.
Step 2: Click the Page tab in the Page Setup dialog box. Click Adjust to in the Scaling box.
Step 3: If necessary, type 100 in the Adjust to box.
Step 4: Click the OK button in the Page Setup dialog box.

Using the Adjust to box, you can specify the percentage of reduction or enlargement in the printout of a worksheet. The default percentage is 100%. The 100% automatically changes to the percentage required whenever you click the Fit to option.

Exiting Excel

After completing the worksheet and pie chart, you can exit Excel, by performing the following steps.

TO EXIT EXCEL

Step 1: Click the Close button on the upper right side of the title bar.
Step 2: If the Microsoft Excel dialog box displays, click the Yes button.

Project Summary

The worksheet and accompanying pie chart (Figure 2-1 on page E 2.6) you created for Lisa and Joe Sabol meet the requirements set by the loan officer, Mr. Leaman, at the local savings and loan association. The report includes the units on hand, average unit cost, total cost, average unit selling price, total value, and profit potential for each art category sold by Ocean Air Art Institute, as well as the requested statistics. Finally, the pie chart dramatically shows the contribution of each art category to the total profit potential.

In creating the Ocean Air Art Institute workbook, you learned how to enter formulas, calculate an average, find the highest and lowest numbers in a range, change the font, draw borders, format numbers, and change column widths and row heights. You also learned how to create a pie chart on a separate sheet, format the pie chart, rename sheet tabs, preview a worksheet, print a workbook, print a section of a worksheet and display and print the formulas in the worksheet using the Fit to option.

What You Should Know

Having completed this project, you should be able to perform the following tasks:

- Apply Currency Style and Comma Style Formats Using the Formatting Toolbar *(E 2.31)*
- Apply a Currency Style with a Floating Dollar Sign Using the Format Cells Command on the Shortcut Menu *(E 2.33)*
- Calculate Totals Using the AutoSum Button *(E 2.14)*
- Center the Worksheet Title *(E 2.26)*
- Change the Background Colors and Apply an Outline Border *(E 2.26)*
- Change the Colors of the Pie Slices *(E 2.49)*
- Change the Font Color and Bold Nonadjacent Ranges *(E 2.28)*
- Change the Heights of Rows by Dragging *(E 2.37)*
- Change the Print Scaling Option Back to 100% *(E 2.62)*
- Change the Width of Columns by Dragging *(E 2.35)*
- Change the Widths of Columns to Best Fit *(E 2.36)*
- Check Spelling in the Worksheet *(E 2.40)*
- Copy a Range of Cells Across Columns to an Adjacent Range Using the Fill Handle *(E 2.20)*
- Copy a Range of Cells Down Rows to an Adjacent Range Using the Fill Handle *(E 2.14)*
- Display The Formulas in the Worksheet and Fit the Printout on One Page *(E 2.60)*
- Draw a Pie Chart *(E 2.43)*
- Enter a Complex Formula Using the Keyboard *(E 2.11)*
- Enter a Simple Formula Using the Keyboard *(E 2.9)*
- Enter Formulas Using Point Mode *(E 2.12)*
- Enter the Column Titles *(E 2.7)*
- Enter the MIN Function Using the Function Wizard Button *(E 2.17)*
- Enter the Numbers *(E 2.8)*
- Enter the Row Titles *(E 2.8)*
- Enter the Worksheet Title *(E 2.7)*
- Explode the Pie Chart *(E 2.50)*
- Find the Average of a Group of Numbers *(E 2.16)*
- Find the Highest Number in a Range *(E 2.17)*
- Format the Characters in the Worksheet Title *(E 2.23)*
- Format the Chart Title and Labels *(E 2.47)*
- Preview Selected Sheets in a Workbook *(E 2.55)*
- Print a Section of the Worksheet *(E 2.58)*
- Print Selected Sheets in a Workbook *(E 2.57)*
- Rename the Sheet Tabs and Rearrange the Order of the Sheets *(E 2.53)*
- Rotate and Tilt the Pie Chart *(E 2.51)*
- Save an Intermediate Copy of the Workbook *(E 2.21)*
- Start Excel *(E 2.7)*
- Underline and Center the Column Titles *(E 2.29)*

Test Your Knowledge

1 True/False

Instructions: Circle T if the statement is true or F if the statement is false.

T F 1. Use the Currency Style button on the Formatting toolbar to change the entry in a cell to different international monetary values.

T F 2. The minimum column width is zero.

T F 3. If you assign a cell the formula =12 / 3, the number 4 displays in the cell.

T F 4. In the formula =9 / 3 + 2, the addition operation (+) is completed before the division operation (/).

T F 5. The formulas =C4 * c3, =c4 * c3, and =C4*C3 result in the same value being assigned to the active cell.

T F 6. You can assign a function to a cell by typing it in the formula bar or using the Function Wizard button on the Standard toolbar.

T F 7. If you use the Point mode to enter a formula or select a range, you must click the enter box to complete the entry.

T F 8. If the function =AVERAGE(G5:G8) assigns a value of 20 to cell H10, and cell H10 is copied to cell G10, cell G10 may or may not equal 10.

T F 9. When a number is too large to fit in a cell, Excel displays at signs (@) in place of each digit in the cell.

T F 10. To increase or decrease the width of a column, use the mouse to point at the column heading right border and drag it.

2 Multiple Choice

Instructions: Circle the correct response.

1. Which one of the following arithmetic operations is completed first if they are all found in a formula with no parentheses?
   a. ^ c. /
   b. – d. *
2. The __________ preceding a formula is important because it alerts Excel that you are entering a formula and not text, such as words.
   a. exclamation point (!) c. equal sign (=)
   b. number sign (#) d. asterisk (*)
3. When you copy a formula with relative cell references across columns, __________.
   a. the row references change in the formula
   b. the column references change in the formula
   c. no references are changed in the formula
   d. the result of the formula remains the same
4. When you point to the fill handle, the mouse pointer becomes a(n) __________.
   a. cross hair c. dark plus sign with two arrowheads
   b. magnifying glass d. arrow

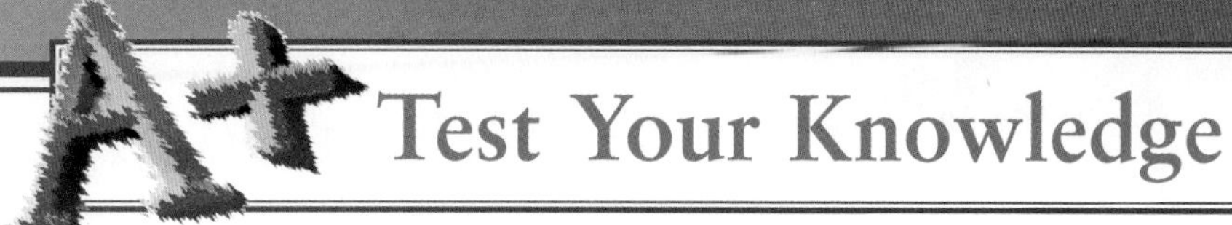

Test Your Knowledge

5. The maximum width of a column is __________ characters.
   a. 31 c. 193
   b. 63 d. 256
6. When Excel starts and the worksheet displays, all the columns have a default width of __________ and a row height of __________.
   a. 9 characters, 9.00 points
   b. 8.43 characters, 12.75 points
   c. 6 characters, 15.00 points
   d. 12.75 characters, 9.00 points
7. Which one of the following describes a column width where the user has requested that Excel determine the width to use?
   a. custom fit c. close fit
   b. usual fit d. best fit
8. When Excel displays what you actually entered into the cells, it is called the __________ version.
   a. formulas c. formatted
   b. displayed d. values
9. A sheet tab name can be up to __________ characters in length.
   a. 8 c. 31
   b. 255 d. 48
10. To rotate a selected pie chart, use the __________ command on the shortcut menu.
    a. Format Data Series c. 3-D View
    b. Chart Type d. Format 3-D Pie Group

3 Entering Formulas

Instructions: Using the values in the worksheet in Figure 2-90, write the formula that accomplishes the task for each of the following items and compute the value assigned to the specified cell.

1. Assign cell G1 the difference between cells C2 and F3.
   Formula: ____________________
   Result: ____________________
2. Assign cell A2 cell D2 divided by F5.
   Formula: ____________________
   Result: ____________________

	A	B	C	D	E	F	G	H	I
1			3	5	7	9			
2			12	10	3	4			
3			5	2	1	6			
4			21	18	30	35			
5			2	0	3	2			
6									
7									

FIGURE 2-90

(continued)

Entering Formulas *(continued)*

3. Assign cell D6 the sum of the range E1:F2, less cell C4.

   Formula: ____________________ Result ____________________

4. Assign cell H6 three times the product of cell E4 and cell E2.

   Formula: ____________________ Result: ____________________

5. Assign cell H1 the sum of the range of cells C2:C5 minus the product of cells F1 and F2.

   Formula: ____________________ Result: ____________________

6. Assign cell G2 the result of cell C5 less cell C3 raised to cell E5.

   Formula: ____________________ Result: ____________________

7. Assign cell H2 the expression (A ^ 3 - 6 * B * C) / (4 * B) where the value of A is in cell C5, the value of B is in cell D2, and the value of C is in cell F5.

   Formula: ____________________ Result: ____________________

4 Understanding Formulas

Instructions: Figure 2-91 displays the formulas version of a worksheet. In the spaces provided, indicate the numeric value assigned to the cells if the numbers display instead of the formulas.

1. D1 ____________________
2. D2 ____________________
3. D3 ____________________
4. A4 ____________________
5. B4 ____________________
6. C4 ____________________
7. D4 ____________________

Microsoft Excel - tyk2-4

	A	B	C	D	E
1	7	12	6	=A1 * (A2 + B2)	
2	5	2	8	=C3 * B2 - A3	
3	3	5	9	=4 * (C1 + A3)	
4	=A1 + B1	=10 / (B2 + C2)	=C3	=B1 ^ 2 * C3 - A2	
5					
6					
7					
8					
9					

FIGURE 2-91

? Use Help

1 Reviewing Project Activities

Instructions: Perform the following tasks using a computer.

1. Start Excel. Double-click the Help button on the Standard toolbar to display the Help Topics: Microsoft Excel dialog box. Click the Contents tab. Double-click the Creating Formulas and Auditing Workbooks book.
2. Double-click the Entering Formulas book. One at a time, double-click each of the six links in the Entering Formulas book. Read and print the information for each link. To print the information click the Print Topic command on the shortcut menu. To return to the previous dialog box, click the Help Topics button. Hand in the printouts to your instructor.
3. Repeat Step 4 for the Using Functions book.
4. If the Help Topics: Microsoft Excel dialog box is not on the screen, double-click the Help button on the Standard toolbar. Click the Find tab. Type `row height` in the top box labeled 1. Double-click Adjust row height in the lower box labeled 3, read it, and click Print Topic on the shortcut menu. Click the Close button to close the Microsoft Excel Help window. Hand in the printout.
5. Double-click the Help button on the Standard toolbar. Click the Answer Wizard tab. Type `how do i format numbers` in the top box labeled 1. Click the Search button. Double-click Number formatting in the lower box labeled 2 under Tell Me About. One at a time, click the three links.

2 Expanding on the Basics

Instructions: Use Excel online Help to better understand the topics listed below. Begin each of the following by double-clicking the Help button on the Standard toolbar. If you are unable to print the help information, then answer the questions on your own paper.

1. Double-click the Working with Charts and Maps book on the Contents sheet in the Help Topics: Microsoft Excel dialog box. Double-click the Formatting a Chart book. Double-click Changing the Type of a Chart book. Double-click the link titled, The best chart type for my data. One at a time, click each type of chart and write down when the selected chart type would be the preferred one to use. When you are finished, click the Close button and hand in your answers to your instructor.
2. Use the Find sheet in the Help Topics: Microsoft Excel dialog box to display and then print information about operator precedence. Indicate which operators are at the same level.
3. Use the Answer Wizard sheet in the Help Topics: Microsoft Excel dialog box to answer the question, *how do I use sheet tabs?* Answer the following related questions:
   a. How do I switch to another sheet?
   b. How do I select sheets in a workbook?
   c. How do I add a worksheet?
   d. How do I display more or fewer sheet tabs?
   e. How do I rename a sheet tab?

Apply Your Knowledge

1 Changing the Appearance of a Pie Chart

Instructions: Start Excel. Open the workbook Wally's Warehouse Cost Analysis from the Excel folder on the Student Floppy Disk that accompanies this book. Perform the following tasks to change the appearance of the pie chart that accompanies the worksheet to make it look like Figure 2-92.

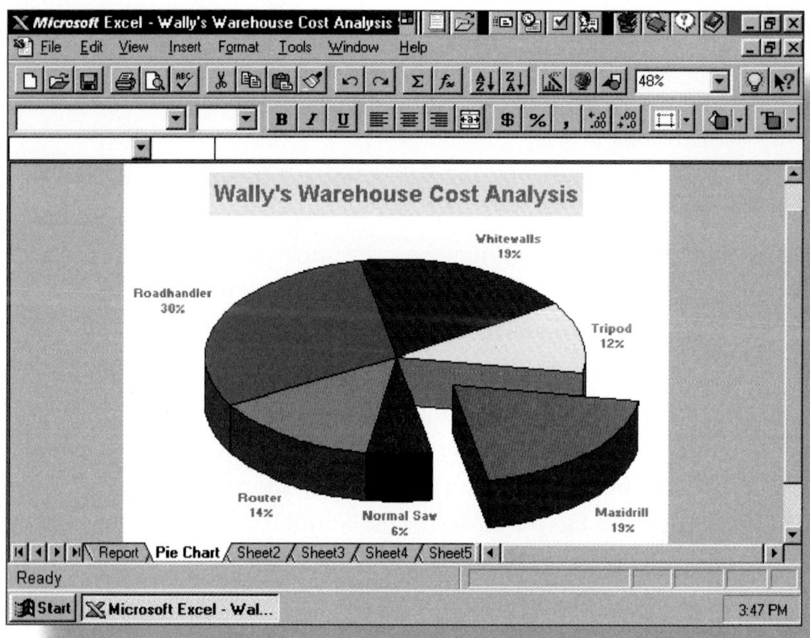

FIGURE 2-92

1. Double-click the Chart1 tab in the lower left corner of the window and rename it Pie Chart. Drag the tab titled Report to the left of the tab titled Pie Chart. Click the Pie Chart tab to display the pie chart.
2. Click the pie chart title and change the font to 28-point red (column 3, row 1). Change the title background to tan (column 4, row 5).
3. Click one of the labels that identify the slices. Change the font to 14-point bold red (column 3, row 1).
4. Click the Maxidrill slice twice. Drag it away from the other slices.
5. Right-click one of the slices. Click 3-D View. Change the elevation to 40° and the rotation to 230°.
6. If the Maxidrill slice is not selected, click it twice. (Do not double-click.) Change the color of the slice to red (column 3, row 1).
7. Print the pie chart. Save the workbook using the filename Wally's Warehouse Inventory Report 2.
8. Click the Report tab. Change the quantity on hand (column F) for Roadhandler, Tripod, and Normal Saw by incrementing each by 50 units. After the changes, the total cost in cell G9 should be $19,624.68. Click the Pie Chart tab. Notice how the slices changed size on the basis of the new entries. Hold down the CTRL key and click the Report tab. Print the selected sheets.

1 Planet Earth Sales Analysis Worksheet and 3-D Column Chart

Problem: The computer consulting firm you and a friend started recently on a part-time basis has received its first contract. The client, Planet Solutions Inc., has specified in the contract that you are to build a sales analysis worksheet that determines the sales quota and percentage of quota met for the sales representatives in Table 2-5. The desired worksheet is shown in Figure 2-93. The client has also requested a 3-D column chart (Figure 2-94 on page E2.71) that compares the net sales by sales representative.

Table 2-5

NAME	SALES AMOUNT	SALES RETURN	SALES QUOTA
Lora Wade	$692,500	$122,500	$500,000
Scott Tisooh	359,250	63,500	300,000
Max Beagle	472,099	57,100	375,000
Mandi Nice	256,350	24,950	275,000

Instructions Part 1: Perform the following tasks to build the worksheet shown in Figure 2-93.

1. Use the Select All button and the Bold button to bold the entire worksheet.
2. Increase the width of column A to 14.00 points and the width of columns B through F to 13.00 points.
3. Enter the worksheet title, Planet Solutions, in cell A1, column titles in row 2, using ALT+ENTER to start a new line in the cells, and the row titles in column A as shown in Figure 2-93.
4. Enter the sales data described in Table 2-5 in columns B, C, and E as shown in Figure 2-93. Enter the numbers without dollar signs or commas.

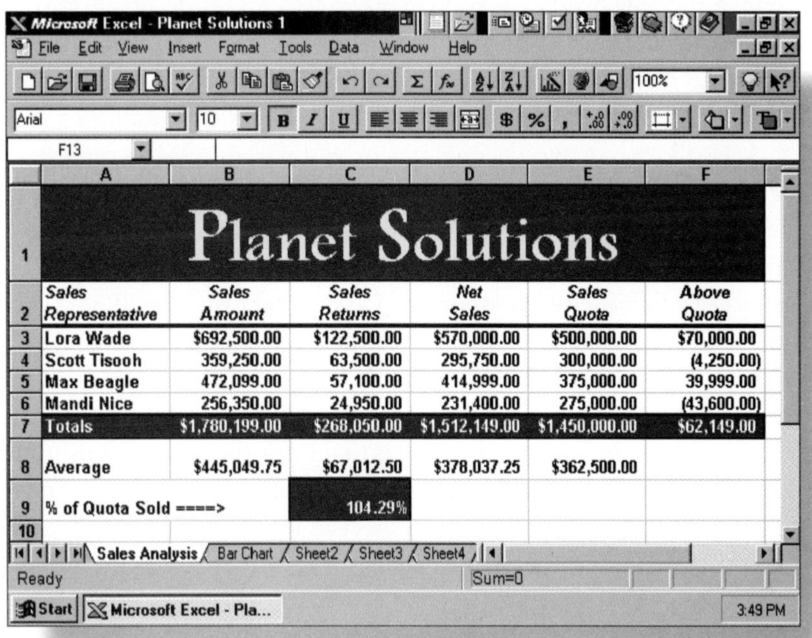

	A	B	C	D	E	F
2	Sales Representative	Sales Amount	Sales Returns	Net Sales	Sales Quota	Above Quota
3	Lora Wade	$692,500.00	$122,500.00	$570,000.00	$500,000.00	$70,000.00
4	Scott Tisooh	359,250.00	63,500.00	295,750.00	300,000.00	(4,250.00)
5	Max Beagle	472,099.00	57,100.00	414,999.00	375,000.00	39,999.00
6	Mandi Nice	256,350.00	24,950.00	231,400.00	275,000.00	(43,600.00)
7	Totals	$1,780,199.00	$268,050.00	$1,512,149.00	$1,450,000.00	$62,149.00
8	Average	$445,049.75	$67,012.50	$378,037.25	$362,500.00	
9	% of Quota Sold ====>		104.29%			

FIGURE 2-93

5. Obtain the net sales in column D by subtracting the sales returns in column C from the sales amount in column B. Enter the formula in cell D3 and copy it to the range D4:D6.
6. Obtain the above quota amounts in column F by subtracting the sales quota in column E from the net sales in column D. Enter the formula in cell F3 and copy it to the range F4:F6.

(continued)

Planet Earth Sales Analysis Worksheet and 3-D Column Chart *(continued)*

7. Obtain the totals in row 7 by adding the column values for each salesperson. In row 8, use the AVERAGE function to determine the column averages.
8. Obtain the percent of quota sold in cell C9 by dividing the total net sales amount in cell D7 by the total sales quota amount in cell E7.
9. Change the worksheet title font in cell A1 to yellow (column 6, row 1 on the Font Color palette), Footlight MT Light (or a font that is similar), and increase its size to 36 point. Edit cell A1 and increase the font size of the first letter in each word to 48 point. Center the title across columns A through F. Color the background of the ranges A1:F1, A7:F7, and C9 purple (column 1, row 2 on the Color palette). Assign a heavy outline border (column 4, row 3 on the Borders palette) to the ranges A1:F1, A7:F7, and C9.
10. Use the Italic button on the Formatting toolbar to italicize the column titles in row 2. Draw a heavy bottom border (column 2, row 2 on the Borders palette) in the range A2:F2. Center the titles in columns B through F.
11. Change the font color in the range A7:F7 and cell C9 to white (column 2, row 1 on the Font Color palette).
12. Change the row heights as follows: row 1 to 57.00 points; and rows 8 and 9 to 24.00 points.
13. Assign the Currency style with a floating dollar sign to the ranges B3:F3, B7:F7, and B8:E8. To assign the format, select a range and then right-click. Click Format Cells on the shortcut menu. Click the Number tab in the Format Cells dialog box, and then click Currency in the Category list. Click Use $. Select two decimal places and parentheses to represent negative numbers. Select the range B4:F6 and then click the Comma Style button on the Standard toolbar. Select cell C9. Click the Percent Style button on the Standard toolbar. Click the Increase Decimal button on the Standard toolbar twice to display the percent in cell C9 to hundredths.
14. Enter your name, course, laboratory assignment number (Lab 2-1), date, and instructor name below the entries in column A in separate cells.
15. Save the workbook using the filename Planet Solutions 1. Print the entire worksheet. Print only the range A2:B8.
16. Display the formulas by pressing CTRL+`. Print the formulas using Fit to in the Scaling box on the Page sheet in the Page Setup dialog box. After printing the worksheet, reset the Scaling option by clicking the Adjust to on the Page sheet in the Page Setup dialog box and then changing the percent value to 100%. Change the display from formulas to values by pressing CTRL+`.

Instructions Part 2: Increment each of the four values in the sales quota column by $5,000.00 until the percent of quota sold in cell C9 is below, yet as close as possible to, 100%. All four values in column E must be incremented the same number of times. The percent of quota sold in C9 should equal 98.83%. Save the workbook as Planet Solutions 2. Print the worksheet.

Instructions Part 3: With the percent of quota sold in cell C9 equal to 98.83% from Part 2, decrement each of the four values in the sales return column by $1,500.00 until the percent of quota sold in cell C9 is above, yet as close as possible to, 100%. Decrement all four values in column C the same number of times. Your worksheet is correct when the percent of quota sold in cell C9 is equal to 100.01%. Save the workbook as Planet Solutions 3. Print the worksheet.

In the Lab

Instructions Part 4: Open Planet Solutions 1 from Part 1. Select the range A3:A6. Use the CTRL key to select the nonadjacent range D3:D6. Click Chart on the Insert menu to create a chart as a new sheet. Draw a 3-D column chart using format number 4 (Figure 2-94). Notice the following about the chart:(a) the Data Series for this chart is in columns; (b) there is no legend on the chart; and (c) the chart does have a title of Sales by Representative.

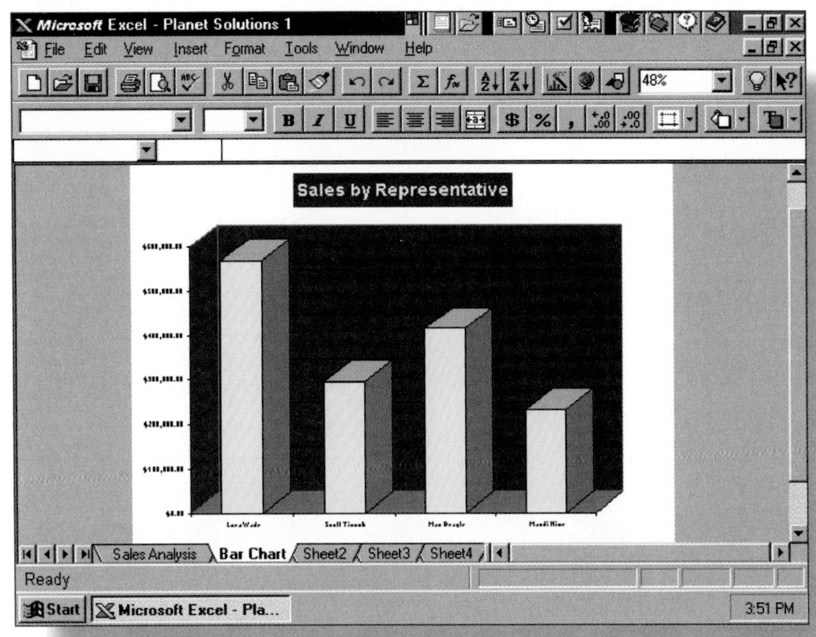

FIGURE 2-94

Once the chart displays, change the chart title as follows: font — yellow (column 6, row 1), 22 point; background purple (column 1, row 2). Change the color of the chart background to purple (column 1, row 2) and change the color of the columns to yellow (column 6, row 1). Rename the sheet tabs at the bottom of the screen to read Sales Analysis for the sheet tab corresponding to the worksheet and Bar Chart for the sheet tab corresponding to the chart. Rearrange the order of the sheet tabs so the worksheet appears first with the chart following it. Save the workbook as Planet Solutions 4. Preview and then print the entire workbook.

2 Steel Frame House Weekly Payroll Worksheet

Problem: You are enrolled in a sophomore Office Information Systems course in which the students are given projects in the local business community. You have been assigned to the Steel Frame House Company. You have been asked to prepare a weekly payroll report for the six employees in Table 2-6.

Table 2-6

EMPLOYEE	RATE PER HOUR	HOURS	DEPENDENTS
Dent, Jacob	22.50	39.5	4
Till, Kevin	28.00	64	3
Hayley, Joe	23.00	40	4
Boate, Max	14.50	46.25	1
Suzi, Jeff	13.35	12	3
Dense, Fritz	15.40	43	5

(continued)

Steel Frame House Weekly Payroll Worksheet *(continued)*

Instructions: Perform the following tasks to create a worksheet similar to the one in Figure 2-95:

1. Enter the worksheet title, Steel Frame House Weekly Payroll, in cell A1. Enter the column titles in row 2, the row titles in column A, and the data in columns B through D from Table 2-6 as shown in Figure 2-95.
2. Use the following formulas to determine the gross pay, federal tax, state tax, and net pay:
   a. Gross Pay = Rate*Hours (Hint: Assign the first employee in cell E3 the formula =B3*C3, and copy the formula in E3 to the range E4:E8 for the remaining employee).
   b. Federal Tax = 20%*(Gross Pay–Dependents*38. 46)
   c. State Tax = 3.2%*Gross Pay
   d. Net Pay = Gross Pay–(Federal Tax+State Tax)
3. Show totals for the gross pay, federal tax, state tax, and net pay in row 9.
4. Determine the average, highest, and lowest values of each column in rows 10 through 12 by using the appropriate functions.
5. Bold the worksheet title.
6. Using the buttons on the Formatting toolbar, assign the Comma style with two decimal places to the range B3:H12.
7. Bold, italicize, and draw a heavy border under the column titles in the range A2:H2. Right-align the column titles in the range B2:H2.
8. Italicize the range A9:A12. Draw a heavy top border and a light double bottom border in the range A9:H9.
9. Change the height of row 10 to 24.00 points, the width of column A to 15.00 characters, and the width of columns B through H to best fit.
10. Enter your name, course, laboratory assignment number (Lab 2-2), date, and instructor name below the entries in column A in separate but adjacent cells.
11. Save the workbook using the filename, Steel Frame House.
12. Preview and then print the worksheet.

Microsoft Excel - Steel Frame House.xls

	A	B	C	D	E	F	G	H
1	**Steel Frame House Weekly Payroll**							
2	***Employee***	***Rate***	***Hours***	***Dep.***	***Gross Pay***	***Fed. Tax***	***State Tax***	***Net Pay***
3	Dent, Jacob	22.50	39.50	4.00	888.75	146.98	28.44	713.33
4	Till, Kevin	28.00	64.00	3.00	1,792.00	335.32	57.34	1,399.33
5	Hayley, Joe	23.00	40.00	4.00	920.00	153.23	29.44	737.33
6	Boate, Max	14.50	46.25	1.00	670.63	126.43	21.46	522.73
7	Suzi, Jeff	13.35	12.00	3.00	160.20	8.96	5.13	146.11
8	Dense, Fritz	15.40	43.00	5.00	662.20	93.98	21.19	547.03
9	*Totals*		244.75		5,093.78	864.92	163.00	4,065.86
10	*Average*	19.46	40.79	3.33	848.96	144.15	27.17	677.64
11	*Highest*	28.00	64.00	5.00	1,792.00	335.32	57.34	1,399.33
12	*Lowest*	13.35	12.00	1.00	160.20	8.96	5.13	146.11

FIGURE 2-95

In the Lab

13. Press CTRL+` to change the display from values to formulas. Print the formulas version of the worksheet using the Fit to option on the Page sheet in the Page Setup dialog box. After the printer is finished, reset the worksheet to display the numbers by pressing CTRL+`. Reset the Scaling option to 100% by clicking Adjust to on the Page sheet in the Page Setup dialog box and setting the percent value to 100%.
14. Increase the number of hours worked for each employee by 8.25 hours. Total Net Pay in cell H9 should equal $4,805.59. Increase the width of column F to best fit to view the new federal tax total. Print the worksheet with the new values. Do not save the worksheet with the new values.

3 Annie's Antiques Monthly Accounts Receivable Balance Sheet

Problem: You were recently hired as a summer intern in the Accounting department of Annie's Antiques, a prosperous antique company with several outlets on the east coast. Your supervisor noticed that you had taken an Excel spreadsheet course the previous semester and approached you about an accounting project. The project she has in mind involves using Excel to generate a much-needed report that summarizes the monthly accounts receivable balance. A graphic breakdown of the data is also desired. The customer accounts receivable data in Table 2-7 is available for test purposes.

Instructions Part 1: Construct a worksheet similar to the one shown in Figure 2-96 on the next page. Include all six fields in Table 2-7 in the report plus the service charge and new balance. (Assume no negative unpaid monthly balances.)

Perform the following tasks:

1. Use the Select All button and Bold button on the Formatting toolbar to bold the entire worksheet.
2. Assign the worksheet title, Annie's Antiques, to cell A1. Assign the worksheet subtitle Monthly Accounts Receivable to cell A2.
3. Enter the column titles in the range A3:H3 as shown in Figure 2-96. Change the widths of columns A through H to best fit.
4. Enter the account numbers and row titles in column A. Enter the account numbers as text. To learn how to enter numbers as text, click the Index tab in the Help Topics: Microsoft Excel Help dialog box and look up the term, number. Select the subphrase, entering as text. Enter the remaining data in Table 2-7.

Table 2-7

ACCOUNT NUMBER	CUSTOMER NAME	BEGINNING BALANCE	PURCHASES	PAYMENTS	RETURNS
1623	Abbot, Jim	2,923.15	589.50	375.00	312.00
2245	Zell, Mary	1,298.34	237.12	125.00	0.00
3314	Hart, Ed	3,523.00	98.75	10.00	22.65
4523	Flint, Fred	2,218.75	5.50	223.00	23.10
6712	Fogs, Trina	1,625.00	89.43	10.00	0.00

(continued)

Annie's Antiques Monthly Accounts Receivable Balance Sheet *(continued)*

5. Use the following formulas to determine the service charge in column G and the new balance at the end of month in column H for each account:
   a. Service Charge = 2.25%*(Beginning Balance–Payments–Returns)
   b. New Balance = Beginning Balance+Purchases–Payments–Returns+Service Charge
6. Compute totals for the numeric columns in row 9.
7. Cell C10 should contain the appropriate function to calculate the maximum value in the range C4:C8. Copy cell C10 to the range D10:H10.

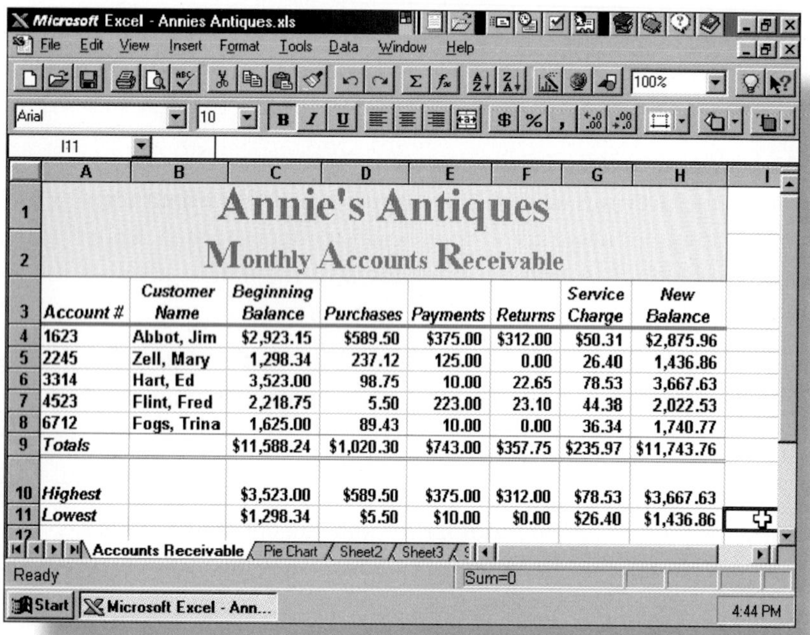

Annie's Antiques

Monthly Accounts Receivable

	Account #	Customer Name	Beginning Balance	Purchases	Payments	Returns	Service Charge	New Balance
4	1623	Abbot, Jim	$2,923.15	$589.50	$375.00	$312.00	$50.31	$2,875.96
5	2245	Zell, Mary	1,298.34	237.12	125.00	0.00	26.40	1,436.86
6	3314	Hart, Ed	3,523.00	98.75	10.00	22.65	78.53	3,667.63
7	4523	Flint, Fred	2,218.75	5.50	223.00	23.10	44.38	2,022.53
8	6712	Fogs, Trina	1,625.00	89.43	10.00	0.00	36.34	1,740.77
9	*Totals*		$11,588.24	$1,020.30	$743.00	$357.75	$235.97	$11,743.76
10	*Highest*		$3,523.00	$589.50	$375.00	$312.00	$78.53	$3,667.63
11	*Lowest*		$1,298.34	$5.50	$10.00	$0.00	$26.40	$1,436.86

FIGURE 2-96

8. Cell C11 should contain the appropriate function to calculate the minimum value in the range C4:C8. Copy cell C11 to the range D11:H11.
9. Change the worksheet title font in cell A1, to 28-point CG Times. Format the worksheet subtitle font in cell A2 to 16-point CG Times and the first letter of each word in the subtitle to 24 point. Center the worksheet titles in cells A1 and A2 across the range A1:H2. Change the heights of rows 1 through 3 and row 10 to 27.75. Add a red light border to the range A1:H2 by using the Border tab in the Format Cells dialog box.
10. Select the range A1:H2 and change the background color to light brown (column 4, row 5 of the Color palette). Change the font color in the range A1:H2 to red (column 3, row 1 of the Font Color palette).
11. Italicize the column titles and place a red heavy border below them. Center the column titles in the range A3:H3. Italicize the titles in rows 9, 10, and 11. Add a single, red light upper border and red double underline border to the range A9:H9.
12. Use the Format Cells command on the shortcut menu to format the numbers in row 4 and rows 9 through 11 to Currency style with a floating dollar sign. Use the same command to assign the Comma style (currency with no dollar sign) to the range C5:H8. The Format Cells command is preferred over the Comma Style button because the worksheet specifications call for displaying zero as 0.00 rather than as a dash (-), as shown in Figure 2-96.
13. Change the widths of columns B through H again to best fit.

In the Lab

14. Rename the sheet tab Accounts Receivable.
15. Enter your name, course, laboratory assignment number (LAB2-3), date, and instructor name below the entries in column A in separate but adjacent cells.
16. Save the workbook using the filename Annies Antiques.
17. Print the worksheet in landscape orientation. Print the range A3:C9 in portrait orientation.
18. Press CTRL+` to change the display from values to formulas, and then print to fit on one page in landscape orientation. After the printer is finished, reset the worksheet to display values by pressing CTRL+`. Reset the Scaling option to 100% by clicking Adjust to on the Page sheet in the Page Setup dialog box and setting the percent value to 100%.

Instructions Part 2: Draw the pie chart showing the contribution of each customer to the total new balance as shown in Figure 2-97. Select the nonadjacent chart ranges B4:B8 and H4:H8. The range B4:B8 will identify the slices while the range H4:H8 will determine the size of the slices. Use the Chart command on the Insert menu to create a chart on a new sheet. Draw a 3-D pie chart with a format 7 (Figure 2-97). Notice the following about the chart: (a) the Data Series for this pie chart is in columns; (b) there is no legend on the chart; and (c) the chart does have a title of Contributions to Accounts Receivable. The chart title has a light brown background and 28-point bold red font. Change the font of the data labels to 16-point bold blue, font. Change the colors of the slices to those shown in Figure 2-97. Explode the slice representing the greatest contribution. Use the 3-D View command on the short-cut menu to change the rotation to 290^0 and the elevation to 40^0. Rename the Chart1 tab Pie Chart. Rearrange the order of the sheet tabs so the worksheet appears first with the chart following it. Save the workbook using the same filename as in Part 1. Print the chart.

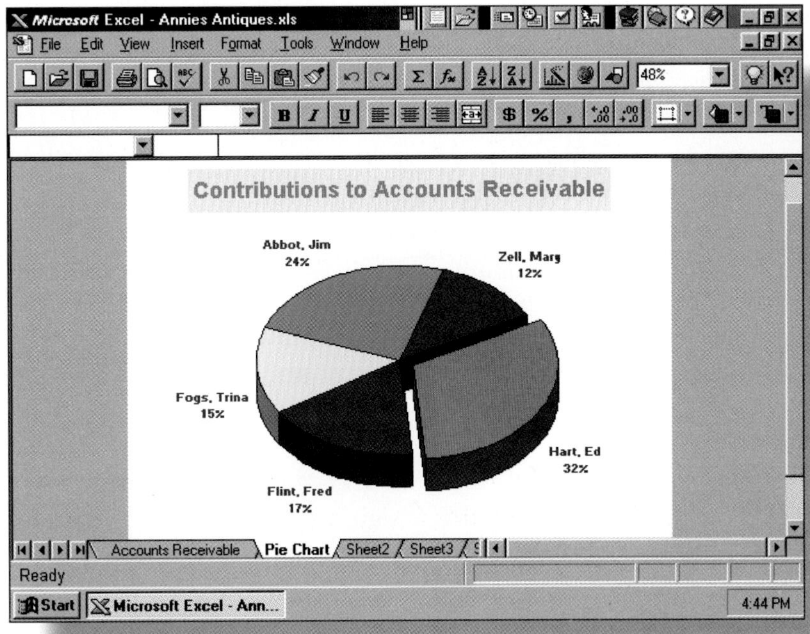

FIGURE 2-97

Cases and Places

The difficulty of these case studies varies:

◗ Case studies preceded by a single half moon are the least difficult. You are asked to create the required worksheet based on information that has already been placed in an organized form.
◗◗ Case studies preceded by two half moons are more difficult. You must organize the information presented before using it to create the desired worksheet.
◗◗◗ Case studies preceded by three half moons are the most difficult. You must choose a specific topic, and then obtain and organize the necessary information before using it to create the required worksheet.

1 ◗ Several naturalists are conducting a study of the interrelationships among five animal species on an island. The naturalists trapped animals, determined their ages, tagged the animals, and released them. Later, a second collection of animals was caught and the number of tagged animals was counted. The naturalists then tabulated their data. (Figure 2-98).

Otter Creek Island Wildlife Survey

Animal	First Catch	Animals over Median Age	Second Catch	Tagged Animals in Second Catch
Moose	32	18	25	4
Deer	326	146	95	24
Fox	148	42	114	21
Wolf	26	7	18	5
Otter	406	142	146	38

FIGURE 2-98

With these facts, you have been asked to prepare a work sheet for the naturalists that determines an estimated population for each species, the estimated number of older animals in each species, and the percentage of older animals in each species. The following formulas can be used to obtain this information:

Estimated Population = (First Catch x Second Catch) ÷ Tagged Animals

Estimated Older Animals = (Animals over Median Age ÷ First Catch) x Estimated Population

Percentage Older Animals = Estimated Older Animals ÷ Estimated Total Population

Include a total, maximum value, and minimum value for Estimated Populations and Estimated Older Animals. On a separate sheet, create an appropriate chart comparing the Estimated Populations. Use the concepts and techniques presented in this project to create and format the worksheet and chart.

Cases and Places

2 ◗ The Student Aid Committee at Hoover College offers short-term loans at simple interest. Loans are provided in five categories (tuition assistance, academic supplies, room and board, personal emergency, and travel expenses), for varying lengths of time and diverse rates of interest. At the end of the semester, the Student Aid Committee summarized their loan activity (Figure 2-99).

Hoover College Student Loans

Loan Type	Principal	Rate	Time (Years)
Tuition Assistance	$48,000.00	10%	0.33
Academic Supplies	$16,000.00	12%	0.25
Room and Board	$26,500.00	15%	0.33
Personal Emergency	$5,500.00	8%	0.17
Travel Expenses	$4,000.00	17%	0.17

FIGURE 2-99

With this data, the committee has asked you to develop a worksheet they can use at their next meeting. The worksheet should determine the interest accrued, amount due, and percentage of the total budget used for each loan type. The following formulas can be applied to obtain this information:

Interest = Principal x Rate x Time

Amount Due = Principal + Interest

Percentage of Budget = Principal ÷ Total Principal

Include a total, maximum value, and minimum value for Principal, Interest, and Amount Due. On a separate sheet, create an appropriate chart that shows the portion of the total principal each loan type uses. Use the concepts and techniques presented in this project to create and format the worksheet and chart.

3 ◗ Newton Elementary School selects students for its gifted program based on teacher recommendations and IQ (intelligence quotient) scores. The IQ scores are ascertained using the formula

$$IQ = \frac{100m}{c}$$

where m represents mental age (determined by a standardized test) and c represents chronological age. This year, eight third-graders were tested for the program. The test results were: Banks, F. (mental age 9.8, chronological age 8.2); Danko, M. (mental age 9.6, chronological age 7.8); Frieze, B. (mental age 10.0, chronological age 8.4); Hunt, N. (mental age 11.8, chronological age 8.8); Jewls, B. (mental age 11.4, chronological age 8.2); Lawson, I. (mental age 10.2, chronological age 8.6); Meyers, N. (mental age 12.4, chronological age 9.0); and Podarski, P. (mental age 11.4, chronological age 8.1). Using these figures, you have been asked to create a worksheet for the selection committee's next meeting. The worksheet should show mental age, chronological age, and IQ for each child. Include the average, maximum, and minimum for each value. On a separate sheet, make an appropriate chart illustrating every student's IQ. Use the concepts and techniques presented in this project to create and format the worksheet and chart.

200 MHz

Cases and Places

4 ▶▶ Driving the Back Roads is a small company that rents a fleet of six vintage cars: a 1906 Packard "S 24" Victoria, a 1907 S & M Simplex Limousine, a 1908 Pierce Great Arrow Touring Car, a 1908 Stanley Roadster, a 1911 Mercer Raceabout, and a 1915 Locomobile Town Coupe. The charge for renting a car is determined by the formula $c = 1000d + 8.5m$, where c is the rental charge, d is the number of days the car is rented, and m is the number of miles the car is driven. Over the past month, the Packard was rented for 13 days and driven 120.4 miles, the Simplex was rented for 16 days and driven 150.8 miles, the Pierce Arrow was rented for 14 days and driven 224.6 miles, the Stanley was rented for 15 days and driven 90.6 miles, the Mercer was rented for 24 days and driven 408.6 miles, and the Locomobile was rented for 18 days and driven 262.6 miles. Using these figures, Driving the Back Roads has asked you to create a worksheet for its monthly meeting showing the number of days each car was rented, the miles each car was driven, the net proceeds from each car, and the percentage of the company's total net proceeds each car represents. Include totals, averages, maximum, and minimum where appropriate. On a separate sheet, make a suitable chart comparing the income from each car.

5 ▶▶▶ Realtors often use a formula to determine how much money prospective buyers can afford to spend on a house. Visit a real estate office to learn how agents analyze the financial status of their clients. With their formulas and estimates of your future income, create a worksheet showing how expensive a house you could manage to buy today and five, ten, fifteen, twenty, and twenty-five years from now. Assuming you purchase a house for the amount indicated by the realtor's formula and make a down payment of 10%, ascertain the amount of money you would have to put down for each house and the amount of money you would have to borrow.

6 ▶▶▶ Veterinarians sometimes use formulas to vary the amount of medicine they prescribe based on factors such as an animal's weight or age. Visit a veterinarian's office and learn the formulas used in prescribing at least two different medications. With these formulas and the relevant information from eight animals (your pets or the pets of friends), prepare a worksheet showing how much medication each animal could be given. Where appropriate, show average, maximum, and minimum values. Include a chart illustrating how the amount of medication varies based on a relevant factor, and a formulas version of the worksheet.

7 ▶▶▶ Retailers occasionally use formulas to determine the selling price of an item based on that item's wholesale cost. Visit a store and find out any formulas that are used to price items. Ask to see a list of the wholesale costs and determine the cost of a at least six individual items that are priced on the basis of the formula you are given. With this information, prepare a worksheet showing each item's wholesale cost, retail price, and the retailer's profit. Find the retail price and retailer's profit if the items were put on sale at a 10% discount. Show totals, averages, maximums, and minimums. Include a chart illustrating what part of the profit is represented by each item when all six items are sold.

Microsoft Excel 7

Windows 95

What-If Analysis and Working with Large Worksheets

Objectives:

You will have mastered the material in this project when you can:

- Use the fill handle to create a series of month names
- Copy a cell's format to another cell using the Format Painter button
- Copy a range of cells to a nonadjacent paste area
- Freeze the column and row titles
- Insert and delete cells
- Format numbers by entering them with a format symbol
- Display the system date using the NOW function and format it
- Use the IF function to enter one value or another in a cell on the basis of a logical test
- Copy absolute cell references
- Italicize text
- Add a drop shadow to a range of cells
- Display and dock toolbars
- Create a 3-D column chart on a separate sheet
- Format the 3-D column chart
- Use the Zoom Control box to change the appearance of the worksheet
- View different parts of the worksheet through window panes
- Use Excel to answer what-if questions
- Analyze worksheet data by using the Goal Seek command

Could You Spend $1 Trillion in Your Lifetime?

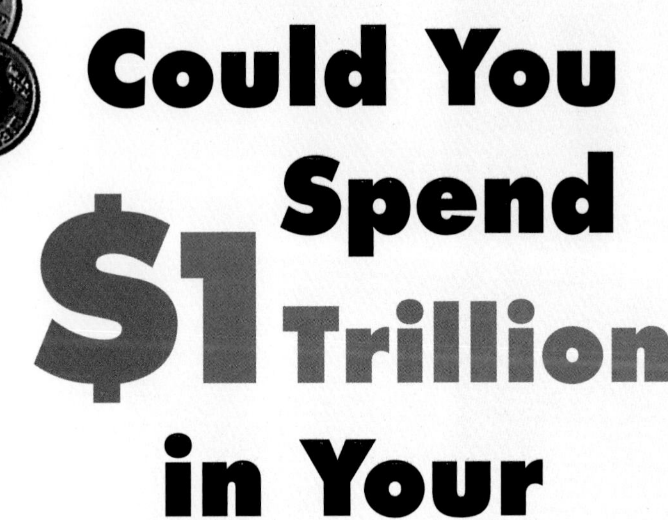

Can you imagine spending a trillion dollars; that is, ten times $100 billion? It is hard even to imagine what a trillion dollars is. If you were given a trillion $1 bills, just counting them would take you 32,000 years at a rate of one per second, twenty-four hours a day. You would break several records if you accomplished that feat.

The world is still waiting for its first trillionaire – speculated to be Asia's Richard Li, 27, or Brunei's Sultan Hassanal Bolkiah, 48. The current U.S. national debt, however, exceeds 5 trillion dollars ($5,000,000,000,000) with projected annual interest payments of $235 billion. Italy, Japan, and Australia also face debts in trillions of dollars. It is no wonder that financial counselors encourage sound fiscal control and budgeting to avoid deficit spending or debt. People who borrow are expected both to be able and willing to pay back what they owe along with an appropriate amount of interest. When working with any sum of money – whether an individual's thousands, the more than 125 American billionaires' billions, or even the nation's trillions – creating a realistic budget indeed can be difficult. Budgets provide a sense of perspective that makes it possible to

keep debt at a minimum. Although you are not responsible for preparing a national $1.64 trillion budget, knowing where your money goes is the first step in planning a sound personal budget.

Personal budgeting helps reconcile income and expenses. For instance, based on a loan calculation and budget, you could determine the Ferrari F50 you wanted to buy is out of the question. A monthly payment of $10,231.91 is just too high. The Toyota Celica, however, with a monthly payment of $570.33 is manageable. Now for the rest of your personal expenses. As a recent college graduate with a master's degree, your first job grosses $31,000 annually. Personal expenses to consider include: utilities, insurances, living expenses (such as housing, loans, transportation costs, groceries, and so on), car payments, entertainment, and credit card payments. A personal budget can help you determine if you are able to buy the condo you want on your yearly salary, and if so, how much you should borrow and realistically can afford to repay. Personal budgets track your income, expenses, net worth, and cash flow changes while organizing and analyzing your financial data in a logical format.

Electronic spreadsheet software can ease your calculations and show exactly how your money is being spent. Based on your input, a budget summary (indicating both surplus/(shortfall) and with/without contingencies) and a budget graph can be generated automatically. You can pose what-if questions to speculate on the results of budget changes or goal seek to determine what to eliminate or cut back to arrive at a month-end surplus with contingencies.

Just as the nation must examine line by line how its money is spent, personal budget calculations allow you to do the same. Initially, living within a budget may appear restrictive but it can provide a sound perspective on your fiscal management and goals. The alternative — you could easily exceed the average debt-to-asset ratio of 30 percent and end up joining the world's trillionaire debt club.

Microsoft

Excel 7

Windows 95

What-If Analysis and Working with Large Worksheets

Case Perspective

Each day millions of people connect to the World Wide Web using providers that charge a small monthly access fee. Information Mining is the premier provider in the Midwest. Each January and July, the chief financial officer (CFO), Marissa Gold, submits a report to the board of directors, titled Six-Month Projected Net Sales, Expenses, and Net Income.

In the past, Marissa manually completed the report and drew a column chart comparing projected monthly net income. When she presented her last report, several directors wanted to know the effect on the net income if the expense percent allocations were changed slightly.

While the directors waited impatiently, it took an embarrassed Marissa several minutes to calculate the answers. Marissa knew the next time she presented the semiannual projections, she would have to use a PC and an electronic worksheet to address the what-if questions. As lead worksheet specialist for Information Mining, you are to meet with Marissa, determine her needs, and create the worksheet and chart.

Introduction

This project introduces you to techniques that will enhance your capabilities to create worksheets and draw charts. You will learn about other methods for entering values in cells and formatting them. You also will learn how to use absolute cell references and how to use the IF function to assign one value or another to a cell based on a logic test.

In the previous projects, you learned how to use the Standard and Formatting toolbars. Excel has several other toolbars that can make your work easier. One such toolbar is the **Drawing toolbar**, which allows you to draw shapes, arrows, and drop shadows around cells you want to emphasize in the worksheet.

Worksheets normally are much larger than those created in the previous projects. Worksheets that extend beyond the size of the window present a viewing problem because you cannot see the entire worksheet at one time. For this reason, Excel provides several commands that allow you to rearrange the view on the screen to display critical parts of a large worksheet. These commands allow you to maintain the row and column titles on the screen at all times by freezing the titles so they always display and to view different parts of a spreadsheet through window panes.

From your work in Projects 1 and 2, you are aware of how easily charts are created. This project continues to develop new charting techniques that allow you to convey your message in a dramatic pictorial fashion.

When you set up a worksheet, you should use as many cell references in formulas as possible, rather than constant values. The cell references in a formula often are called assumptions. **Assumptions** are cells whose values you can change to determine new values for formulas. This project emphasizes the use of assumptions and introduces you to answering what-if questions such as, What if you decrease the advertising expenses assumption (cell B16 in Figure 3-1a) by 1% — how would the decrease affect the projected six-month net income (cell H13 in Figure 3-1a)? This capability of quickly analyzing the effect of changing values in a worksheet is important in making business decisions.

More *About* What-If Analysis

The ability of Excel to instantaneously answer what-if questions is the single most important reason why millions of business people use this software. Just a few short years ago, what-if questions of any complexity could only be answered by large expensive computers programmed by highly-paid computer professionals. And then you might have to wait days for the turnaround. Excel and its equivalents give the non-computer professional the capability of getting complex business-related questions answered quickly and economically.

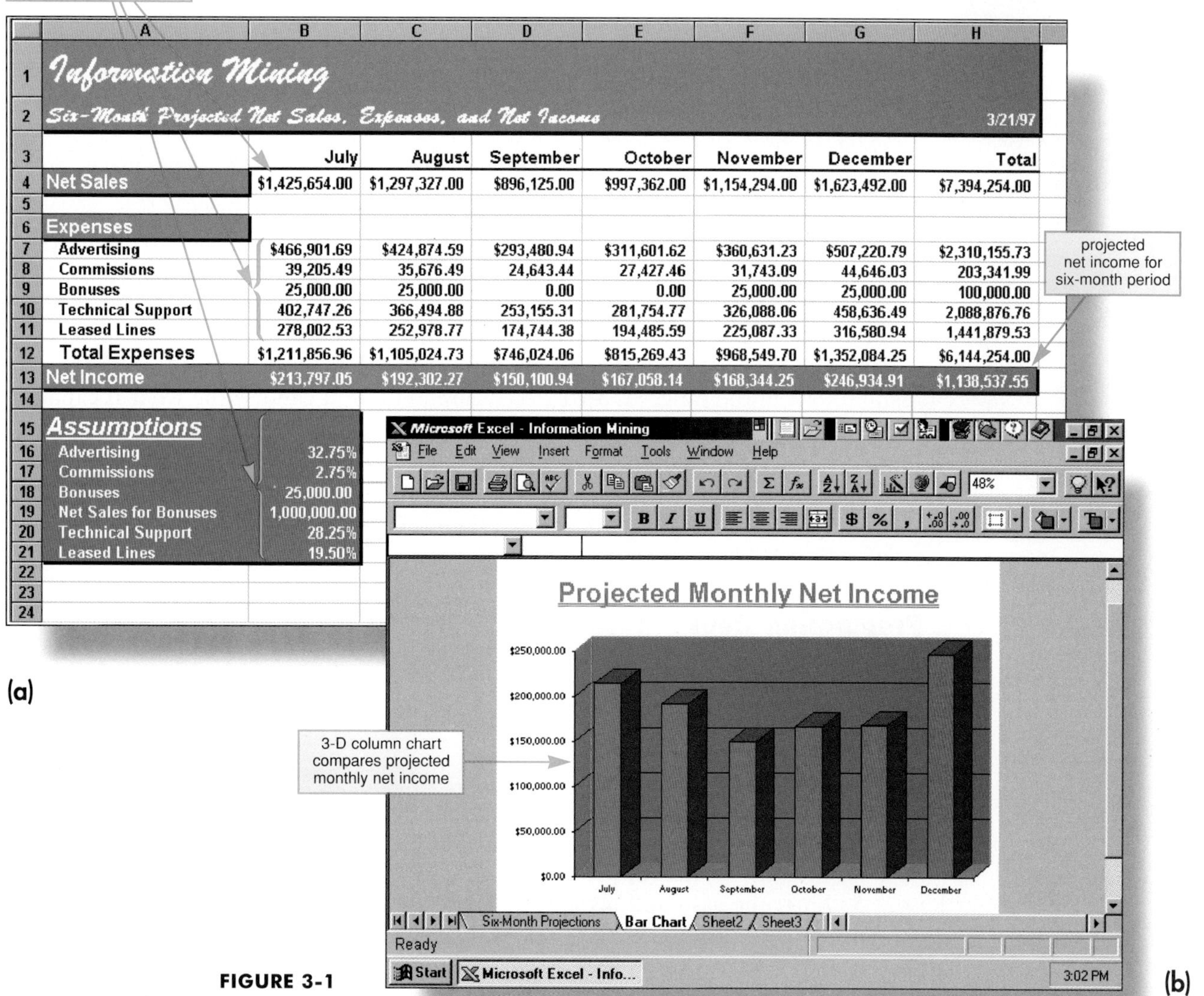

	A	B	C	D	E	F	G	H
1	Information Mining							
2	Six-Month Projected Net Sales, Expenses, and Net Income							3/21/97
3		July	August	September	October	November	December	Total
4	Net Sales	$1,425,654.00	$1,297,327.00	$896,125.00	$997,362.00	$1,154,294.00	$1,623,492.00	$7,394,254.00
5								
6	Expenses							
7	Advertising	$466,901.69	$424,874.59	$293,480.94	$311,601.62	$360,631.23	$507,220.79	$2,310,155.73
8	Commissions	39,205.49	35,676.49	24,643.44	27,427.46	31,743.09	44,646.03	203,341.99
9	Bonuses	25,000.00	25,000.00	0.00	0.00	25,000.00	25,000.00	100,000.00
10	Technical Support	402,747.26	366,494.88	253,155.31	281,754.77	326,088.06	458,636.49	2,088,876.76
11	Leased Lines	278,002.53	252,978.77	174,744.38	194,485.59	225,087.33	316,580.94	1,441,879.53
12	Total Expenses	$1,211,856.96	$1,105,024.73	$746,024.06	$815,269.43	$968,549.70	$1,352,084.25	$6,144,254.00
13	Net Income	$213,797.05	$192,302.27	$150,100.94	$167,058.14	$168,344.25	$246,934.91	$1,138,537.55
14								
15	Assumptions							
16	Advertising	32.75%						
17	Commissions	2.75%						
18	Bonuses	25,000.00						
19	Net Sales for Bonuses	1,000,000.00						
20	Technical Support	28.25%						
21	Leased Lines	19.50%						

FIGURE 3-1

Project Three – Information Mining Six-Month Projected Net Sales, Expenses, and Net Income

You took the following notes regarding the required worksheet and chart in your meeting with the CFO, Marissa Gold.

Need: A worksheet (Figure 3-1a) and 3-D column chart (Figure 3-1b) are required. The worksheet is to show Information Mining's projected monthly net sales, expenses, and net income for a six-month period. The 3-D column chart is to compare the projected monthly net incomes.

Source of Data: The projected monthly net sales (row 4 of Figure 3-1a) and the six assumptions (range A15:B21) that are used to determine the projected monthly expenses are available from the CFO.

Calculations: Each of the projected monthly expenses in the range B7:G11 of Figure 3-1a — advertising, commissions, bonuses, technical support, and leased lines — is determined by taking a percentage of the corresponding projected monthly net sales in row 4. The assumptions in the range A15:B21 are as follows:

1. The projected monthly advertising expenses are 32.75% of the projected net sales.
2. The projected monthly commissions are 2.75% of the projected net sales.
3. The projected monthly bonuses are $25,000.00 if the projected monthly net sales exceeds the net sales for bonus in cell B19 ($1,000,000.00).
4. The projected monthly technical support expenses are 28.25% of the projected sales.
5. The projected monthly leased lines expenses are 19.50% of the projected sales.

The projected total expenses for each month in row 12 of Figure 3-1a are the sum of the corresponding projected monthly expenses in rows 7 through 11. The projected monthly net income in row 13 is equal to the corresponding projected monthly net sales minus the projected monthly total expenses.

Because the projected expenses in rows 7 through 11 are dependent on the assumptions in the range A15:B21 of Figure 3-1a, you can use the what-if capability of Excel to determine the impact of changing these percent expenses on the projected monthly total expenses in row 12.

Graph Requirements: A 3-D column chart on a separate sheet (Figure 3-1b) that compares the contribution of each month to the projected net income for the six-month period.

More About Auditing a Worksheet

Studies have shown that over 25% of all business worksheets have errors. You can ensure correctness by using the Auditing command on the Tools menu. The Auditing command indicates relationships among formulas.

Preparation Steps

The following tasks will be completed in this project to create the worksheet and chart shown in Figure 3-1a and b.

1. Start the Excel program.
2. Bold all cells in the worksheet.
3. Enter the worksheet titles, column titles, and row titles. Increase the column widths.
4. Save the workbook.
5. Enter the assumptions in the range B16:B21.
6. Enter the projected net sales for each of the six months in row 4.
7. Display the system date in cell H2.

8. Enter the formulas that determine the monthly projected expenses and monthly projected net income in the range B7:G13. Determine the totals in column H.
9. Format the worksheet so it appears as shown in Figure 3-1a on page E 3.5.
10. Create the 3-D column chart that compares the monthly net incomes using the nonadjacent selection of ranges B3:G3 and B13:G13.
11. Format the 3-D column chart.
12. Check spelling, preview, print, and save the workbook.
13. Use the Zoom Control box on the Standard toolbar to change the appearance of the worksheet.
14. Divide the window into panes.
15. Analyze the data in the worksheet by changing the assumptions in the range A15:B21 and by goal seeking.

The following sections contain a detailed explanation of each of these steps.

Starting Excel

To start Excel, Windows 95 must be running. Perform the following steps to start Excel.

More About Readability

Bolding the entire worksheet makes it easier for people with less than average eyesight to read the worksheet. An alternative is to increase the font size of the entire worksheet from 10-point to 12- or 14-point.

TO START EXCEL

Step 1: Click the Start button on the taskbar.
Step 2: Click New Office Document. If necessary, click the General tab in the New dialog box.
Step 3: Double-click the Blank Workbook icon.

An alternative to Steps 1 and 2 is to click the Start a New Document button on the Microsoft Office Shortcut Bar.

Changing the Font of the Entire Worksheet to Bold

The first step is to change the font of the entire worksheet to bold so all entries are emphasized.

TO CHANGE THE FONT OF THE ENTIRE WORKSHEET TO BOLD

Step 1: Click the Select All button immediately above row heading 1 and to the left of column heading A.
Step 2: Click the Bold button on the Standard toolbar.

No immediate change takes place on the screen. As you enter text and numbers into the worksheet, however, Excel will display them in bold.

Entering the Worksheet Titles

The worksheet contains two titles, one in cell A1 and another in cell A2. In the previous projects, the titles were centered over the worksheet. With large worksheets that extend beyond the width of a window, it is best to display them in the upper left corner as shown in Figure 3-1a.

TO ENTER THE WORKSHEET TITLES

Step 1: Select cell A1 and type `Information Mining` to enter the title.
Step 2: Select cell A2 and type `Six-Month Projected Net Sales, Expenses, and Net Income` to enter the second title.
Step 3: Select cell B3.

Excel responds by displaying the worksheet titles in cells A1 and A2 in bold (Figure 3-2).

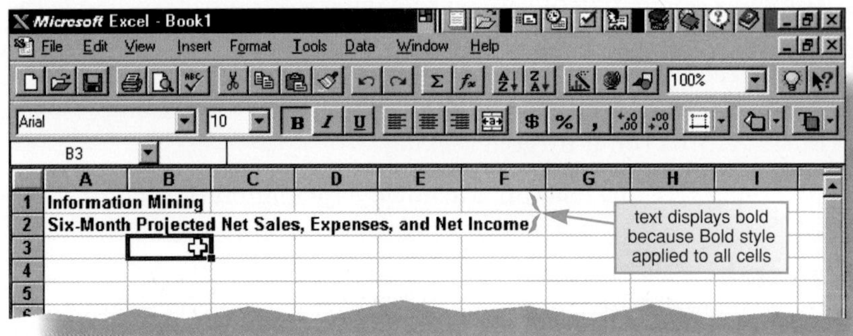

FIGURE 3-2

Using the Fill Handle to Create a Series

In Projects 1 and 2, you used the fill handle to copy a cell or a range of cells to adjacent cells. You can also use the fill handle to create a series of numbers, dates, or month names automatically. Perform the following steps to enter the month name July in cell B3, format cell B3, and then using the fill handle, create the remaining five month names August, September, October, November, and December in the range C3:G3 (see Figure 3-5).

To Use the Fill Handle to Create a Series of Month Names

1. **With cell B3 active, type `July` and then click the enter box or press the ENTER key. On the Formatting toolbar, click 11 in the Font Size drop-down list box, click the Align Right button on the Standard toolbar, and click the heavy bottom border on the Borders palette. Point to the fill handle.**

   The text, July, in cell B3 displays using the assigned formats (Figure 3-3). The mouse pointer changes to a cross hair when positioned on the fill handle.

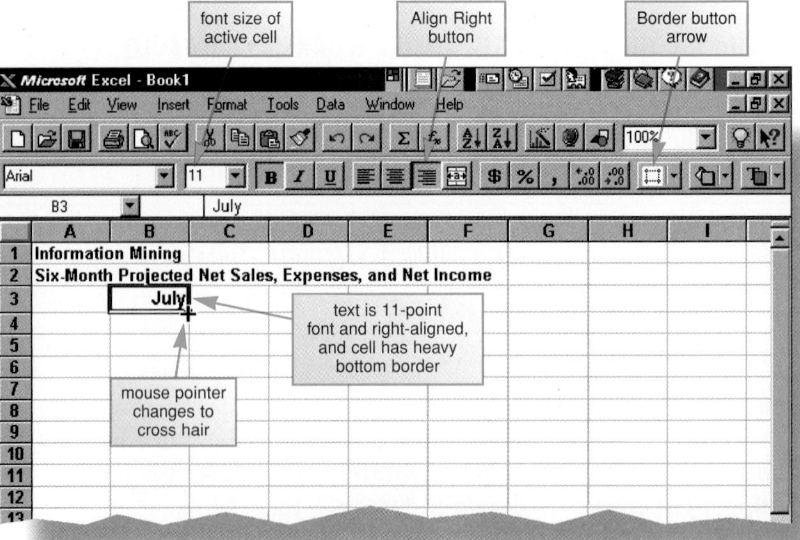

FIGURE 3-3

2 **Drag the fill handle to the right to select the range C3:G3.**

Excel displays a light border that surrounds the range selected (Figure 3-4).

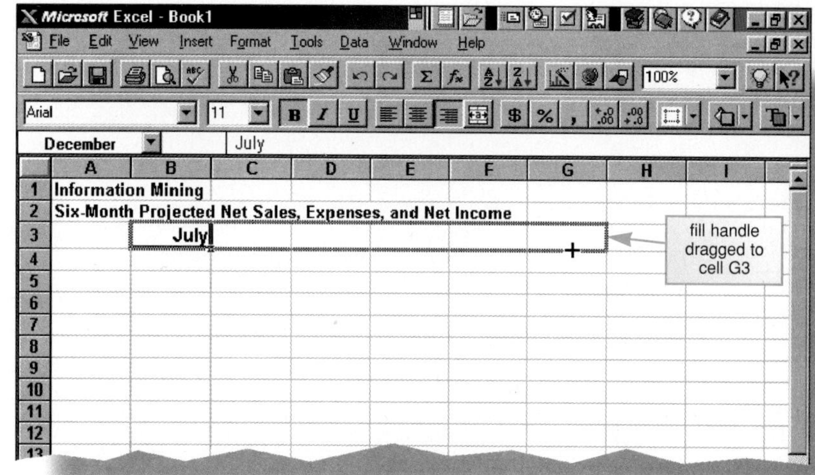

FIGURE 3-4

3 **Release the left mouse button.**

Using July in cell B3 as the basis, Excel creates the month name series August through December in the range C3:G3 (Figure 3-5). The formats assigned earlier to cell B3 (11-point font, right-aligned, and heavy bottom border) in Step 1 are copied to the range C3:G3.

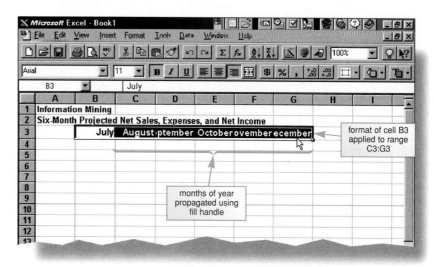

FIGURE 3-5

OtherWays

1. Enter start month in cell, right-drag fill handle in the direction you want to fill, click Fill Months on shortcut menu

Besides creating a series of values, the fill handle also copies the format of cell B3 (11-point font, right-aligned, and a heavy bottom border) to the range C3:G3. If you drag the fill handle past cell G3 in Step 2 to June, Excel continues to increment the months and will logically repeat July, August, and so on.

You can create different types of series using the fill handle. Table 3-1 on the next page illustrates several examples. Notice in Examples 4 through 7 in Table 3-1 that if you use the fill handle to create a series of numbers or non-sequential months, you are required to enter the first number in the series in one cell and the second number in the series in an adjacent cell. You then select both cells and drag the fill handle across the paste area.

More About the Fill Handle

The fill handle is one of the most popular and impressive tools available with Excel. Use it to copy or to create a data series. To use it to copy a potential series initiator, like the word January, to a paste area, hold down the CTRL key while you drag. You can also establish a custom series by dragging the fill handle with the right mouse button. If you create the wrong series, choose the Undo button on the Standard toolbar or the Undo command on the Edit menu.

Table 3-1

EXAMPLE	CONTENTS OF CELL(S) COPIED USING THE FILL HANDLE	NEXT THREE VALUES OF EXTENDED SERIES
1	6:00	7:00, 8:00, 9:00
2	Qtr3	Qtr4, Qtr1, Qtr2
3	Quarter 1	Quarter 2, Quarter 3, Quarter 4
4	Jul-97, Oct-97	Jan-98, Apr-98, Jul-98
5	1999, 2000	2001, 2002, 2003
6	1, 2	3, 4, 5
7	200, 195	190, 185, 180
8	Sun	Mon, Tue, Wed
9	Tuesday	Wednesday, Thursday, Friday
10	1st Part	2nd Part, 3rd Part, 4th Part
11	-1, -3	-5, -7, -9

Copying a Cell's Format Using the Format Painter Button

Because it is not part of the series, the last column title, Total, in cell H3 must be entered separately. Furthermore, to ensure that it appears the same as the other column titles, the same formats as the months (11-point font, right-aligned, and a heavy bottom border) must be applied to cell H3. The **Format Painter button** on the Standard toolbar allows you to copy a cell's format to another cell. The following steps enter the column title, Total, in cell H3 and format the cell using the Format Painter button.

To Copy a Cell's Format Using the Format Painter Button

1. **Select cell H3. Type** `Total` **and then press the LEFT ARROW key.**

2. **With cell G3 selected, click the Format Painter button on the Standard toolbar. Move the mouse pointer over cell H3.**

   The mouse pointer changes to a block plus sign with a paint brush (Figure 3-6).

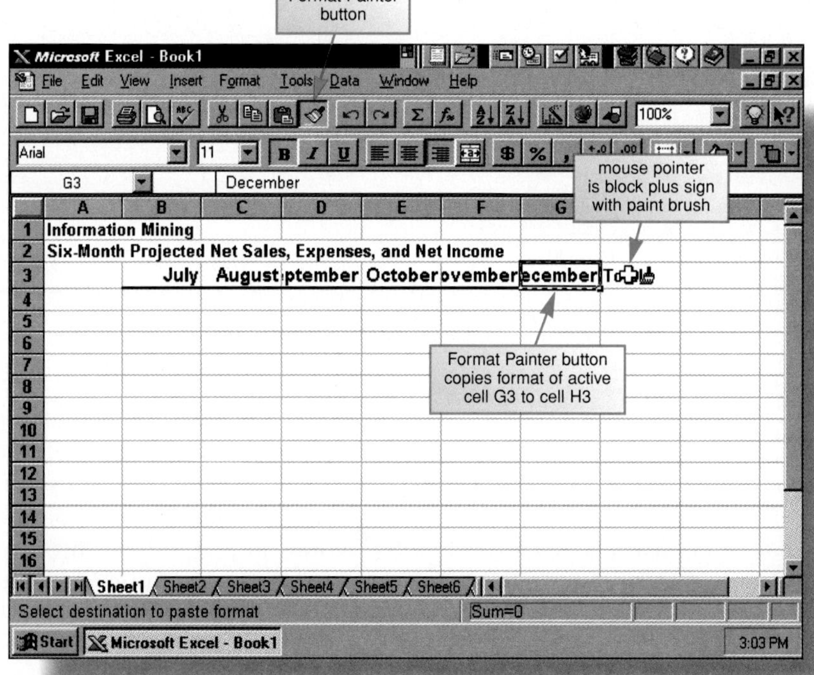

FIGURE 3-6

3 Click cell H3 to assign the format of cell G3 to cell H3. Click cell A4.

Cell H3 is assigned the same format (11-point font, right-aligned, and a heavy bottom border) as cell G3 (Figure 3-7).

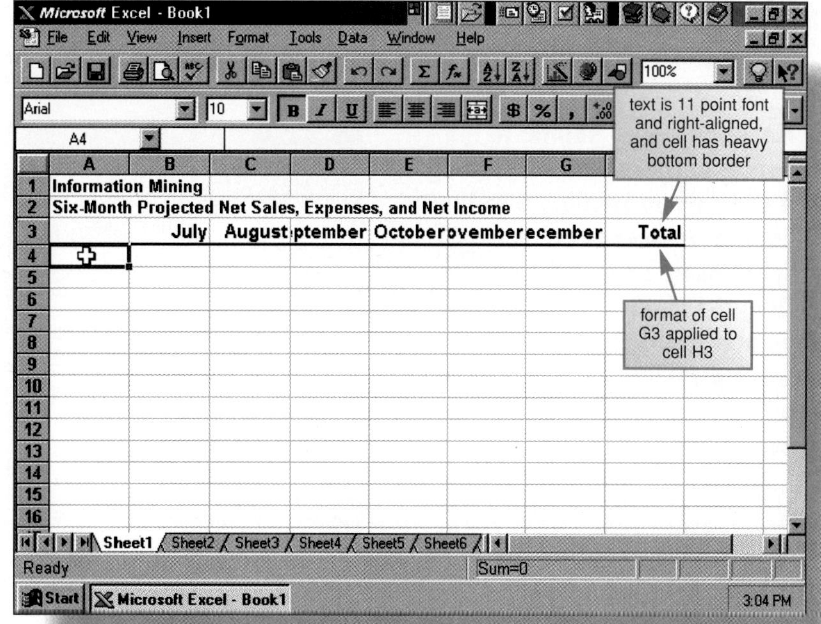

FIGURE 3-7

OtherWays

1. Click Copy button, select paste area, on Edit menu click Paste Special, click Formats, click OK button

The Format Painter button can also be used to copy the formats of a cell to a range or to copy a range to another range. To copy formats to a range of cells, select the cell or range to copy from, click the Format Painter button, and then drag through the range to which you want to paste the formats.

Increasing the Column Widths and Entering Row Titles

In Project 2, the column widths were increased after the values were entered into the worksheet. Sometimes, you may want to increase the column widths before you enter the values and then, if necessary, adjust them later. The following steps increase the column widths and add the row titles in column A down to Assumptions in cell A15.

More About the Format Painter Button

Double-click, rather than click, the Format Painter button to copy the formats to non-adjacent ranges. After double-clicking, one-by-one, drag through the ranges. Finally, click the Format Painter button to deactivate it.

More About Changing Column Widths

You can use the CTRL key to select nonadjacent columns before increasing the column width or assigning a common format.

Steps To Increase Column Widths and Enter Row Titles

1 Move the mouse pointer to the border between column heading A and column heading B so the pointer changes to a split double arrow. Drag the mouse pointer to the right until the width displayed in the Name box on the left side of the formula bar equals 25.00.

The distance between the left edge of column A and the vertical dotted line below the mouse pointer shows the proposed column width, and 25.00 displays in the Name box (Figure 3-8).

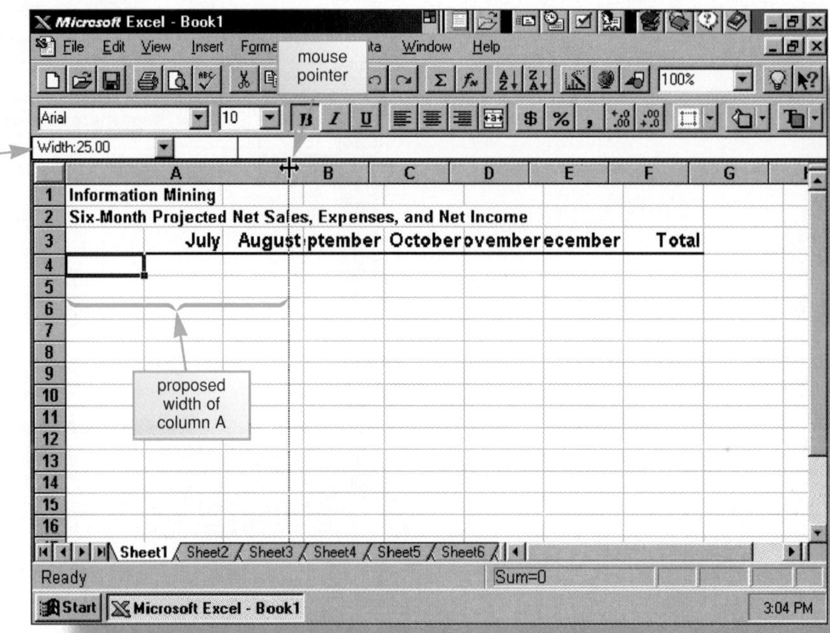

FIGURE 3-8

2 Release the left mouse button. Select columns B through G by pointing to column heading B and dragging though column heading G. Move the mouse pointer to the borderline between column headings B and C and drag the mouse to the right until the width displayed in the Name box is 13.00.

The distance between the left edge of column B and the vertical line below the mouse pointer shows the proposed column width of columns B through G, and 13.00 displays in the Name box (Figure 3-9).

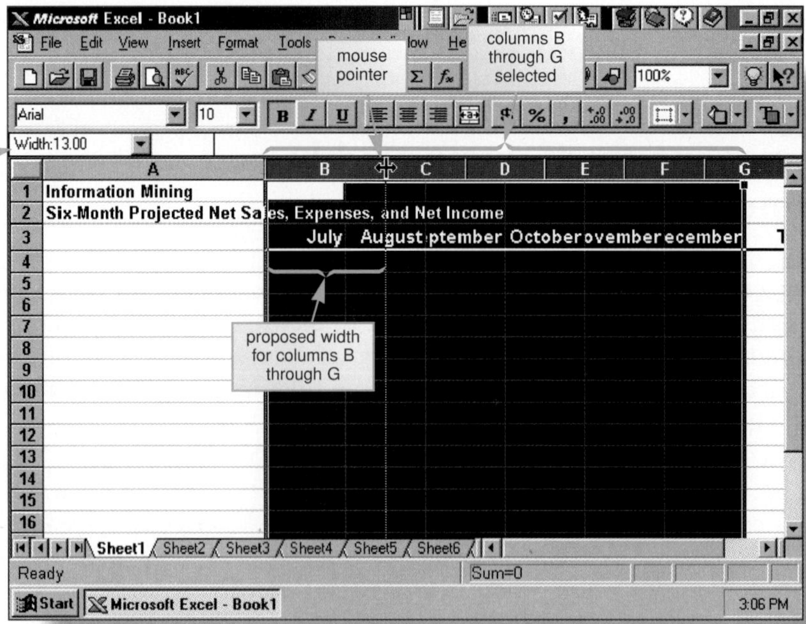

FIGURE 3-9

3 **Release the left mouse button. Use the same technique described in Step 1 to increase the width of column H to 15.00.**

4 **Enter** `Net Sales` **in cell A4,** `Expenses` **in cell A6,** ~~bbb~~`Advertising` **in cell A7 (where ~~bbb~~ represents three spaces), and** ~~bbb~~`Commissions` **in cell A8. Enter** ~~bbb~~`Bonuses` **in cell A9,** ~~bbb~~`Technical Support` **in cell A10,** ~~bbb~~`Leased Lines` **in cell A11,** ~~bbb~~`Total Expenses` **in cell A12,** `Net Income` **in cell A13, and** `Assumptions` **in cell A15 as shown in Figure 3-10.**

The row titles display as shown in Figure 3-10.

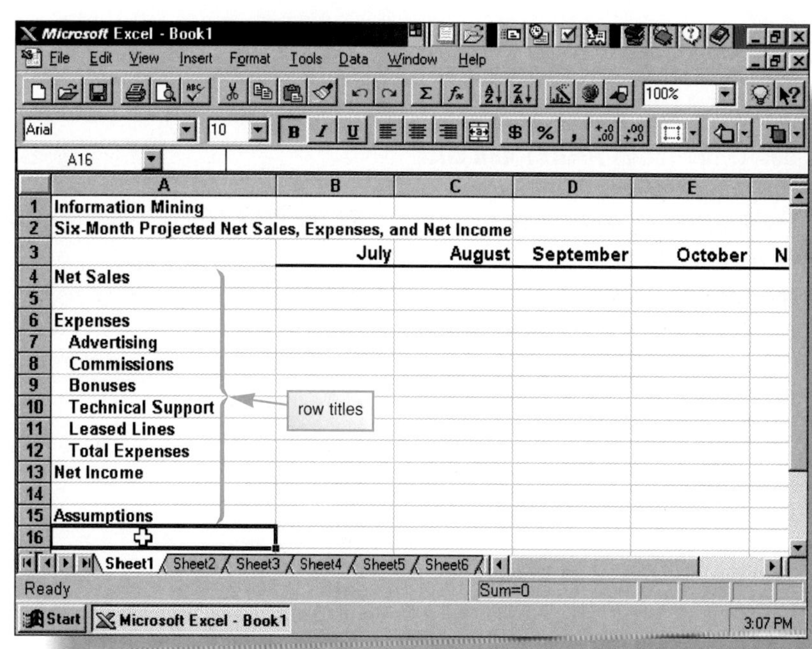

FIGURE 3-10

Copying a Range of Cells to a Nonadjacent Paste Area

According to Figure 3-1a on page E 3.5, the row titles in the Assumptions table in the range A16:A21 are the same as the row titles in the range A7:A11, except for the additional entry in cell A19. Hence, the range A7:A11 can be copied to the range A16:A20 and the additional entry in cell A19 can be inserted. Notice that the range to copy (range A7:A11) is not adjacent to the paste area (range A16:A20). In the first two projects, the fill handle worked well for copying a range of cells to an adjacent paste area, but you cannot use the fill handle to copy a range of cells to a nonadjacent paste area.

A more versatile method of copying a cell or range of cells is to use the Copy button and Paste button on the Standard toolbar. You can use these two buttons to copy a range of cells to an adjacent or nonadjacent paste area.

When you click the **Copy button**, it copies the contents and format of the selected range and places the entries on the Clipboard, replacing the Clipboard's contents. The **Copy command** on the Edit menu or shortcut menu works the same as the Copy button.

The **Paste button** copies the contents of the Clipboard to the paste area. The Paste command on the Edit menu or shortcut menu works the same as the Paste button. Use the Paste button when you are copying to more than one cell or range. Complete a single paste by pressing the ENTER key.

More *About* **Copying**

If you have a range of cells in another workbook that you want to copy into the current workbook, open the source workbook, select the range, and then click the Copy button to place the range of cells on the Clipboard. Next, activate the destination workbook by clicking its filename on the Window menu. Finally, select the paste area and press ENTER.

Steps To Copy a Range of Cells to a Nonadjacent Paste Area

1 Select the range A7:A11 and click the Copy button on the Standard toolbar. Scroll down until row 20 is visible and then click cell A16, the top cell of the paste area.

Excel surrounds the range A7:A11 with a marquee when you click the Copy button (Figure 3-11). Excel also copies the values and formats of the range A7:A11 onto the Clipboard.

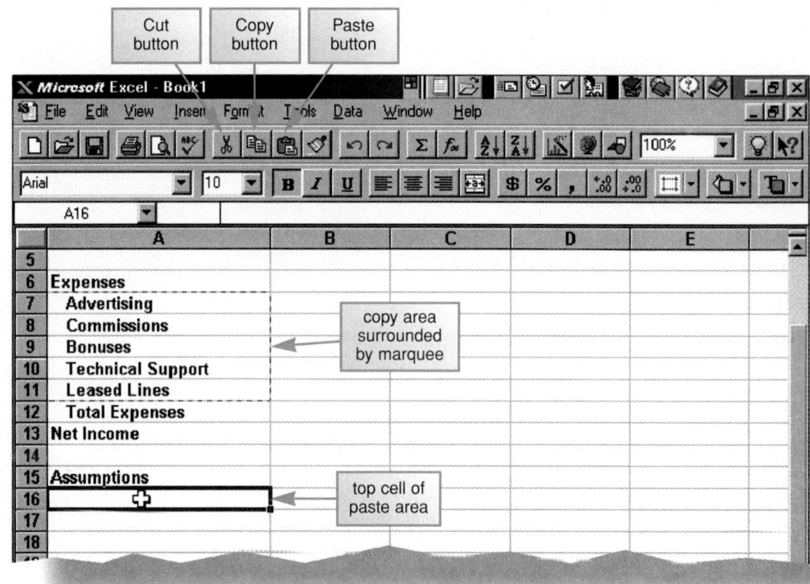

FIGURE 3-11

2 Press the ENTER key to complete the copy.

Excel copies the contents of the Clipboard (range A7:A11) to the paste area A16:A20 (Figure 3-12).

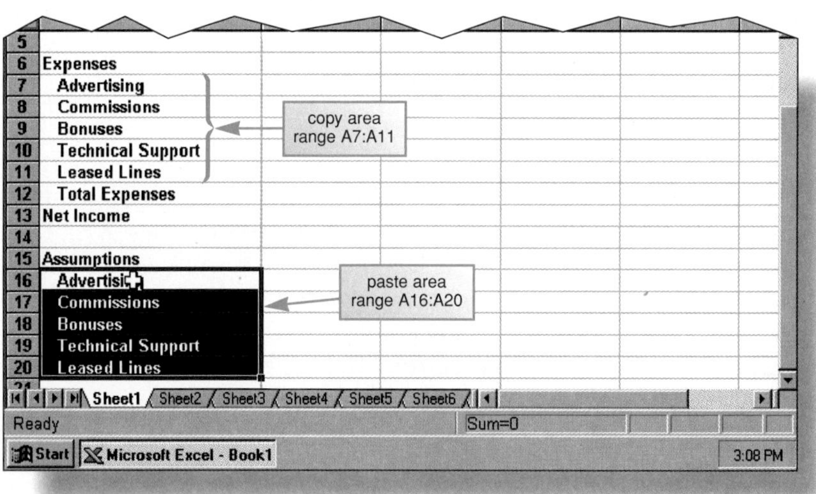

FIGURE 3-12

OtherWays

1. Select copy area, while holding down CTRL key, drag copy area to paste area
2. Right-click copy area, click Copy on shortcut menu, right-click paste area, click Paste on shortcut menu
3. Select copy area, click Copy button on Standard toolbar, select paste area, click Paste button on Standard toolbar to paste, press ESC
4. Select copy area, on Edit menu click Copy, select paste area, on Edit menu click Paste
5. Select copy area, press CTRL+C, select paste area, press CTRL+V

In Step 1 and Figure 3-11, you can see that you are not required to highlight the entire paste area (range A16:A20) before pressing the ENTER key to complete the copy. Because the paste area is exactly the same size as the range you are copying, you need only select the top left cell of the paste area. In the case of a single column range such as A16:A20, the top cell of the paste area (cell A16) is the upper left cell of the paste area.

When you complete a copy, the values and formats in the paste area are replaced with the values and formats on the Clipboard. Any data contained in the paste area prior to the copy and paste is lost. If you accidentally delete valuable data, immediately click the Undo button on the Standard toolbar or click the **Undo Paste command** on the Edit menu to undo the paste.

When you use the ENTER key to paste, the contents on the Clipboard are erased after the copy is complete. When you paste using the Paste button or Paste command on the Edit menu or shortcut menu, the contents of the Clipboard remain available for additional copying. Thus, if you plan to copy the cells to more than one paste area, click the Paste button or click Paste on the Edit menu or shortcut menu instead of pressing the ENTER key. Then, select the next paste area and invoke the Paste command again. If you paste using the Paste button or the Paste command from the Edit menu or shortcut menu, the marquee remains around the range to copy to remind you that the copied range is still on the Clipboard. To erase the marquee, press the ESC key.

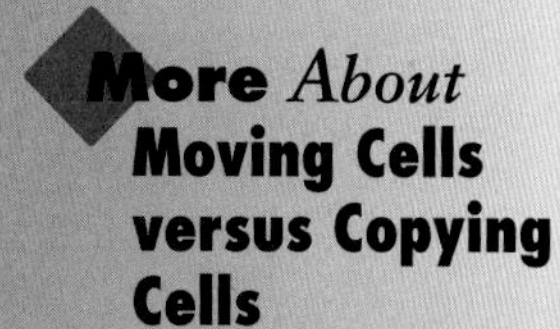

More *About* Moving Cells versus Copying Cells

You may hear someone say, "move it or copy it , its all the same." No, its not the same! When you move cells, the original location is blanked and the format is reset to the default. When you copy cells, the copy area remains intact. In short, copy cells to duplicate and move cells to rearrange.

Using Drag and Drop to Move or Copy Cells

You can use the mouse to move or copy cells. First, you select the copy area and point to the border of the range. You know you are pointing to the border of a range when the mouse pointer changes to a block arrow. To move the selected cells, drag the selection to its new location. To copy a range, hold down the CTRL key while dragging. Then release the mouse button before you release the CTRL key. Using the mouse to move or copy cells is called **drag and drop**.

Another way to move cells is to select them, click the Cut button on the Standard toolbar (Figure 3.11), select the new area, and then click the Paste button on the Standard toolbar or press the ENTER key. You can also use the **Cut command** on the Edit menu or shortcut menu.

More *About* Dragging and Dropping

If the mouse pointer does not change to an arrow when you point to the border of the range to copy, then the Drag and Drop option is turned off. To turn it on, click Options on the Tools menu, click the Edit tab, click Allow Cell Drag and Drop check box.

Inserting and Deleting Cells in a Worksheet

At any time while the worksheet is on the screen, you can add cells to insert new data or delete cells to remove unwanted data. You can insert or delete individual cells, a range of cells, entire rows, entire columns, or entire worksheets.

Inserting Rows

The **Rows command** on the Edit menu or the **Insert command** on the shortcut menu allows you to insert rows between rows that already contain values. In the Assumptions table at the bottom of the worksheet, room must be made between rows 18 and 19 to add a row for the Net Sales for Bonuses assumption (see Figure 3-1a on page E 3.5). The following steps show how to accomplish the task of inserting a new row into the worksheet.

To Insert Rows

1 Right-click row heading 19.

Row 19 is selected and the shortcut menu displays as shown in Figure 3-13.

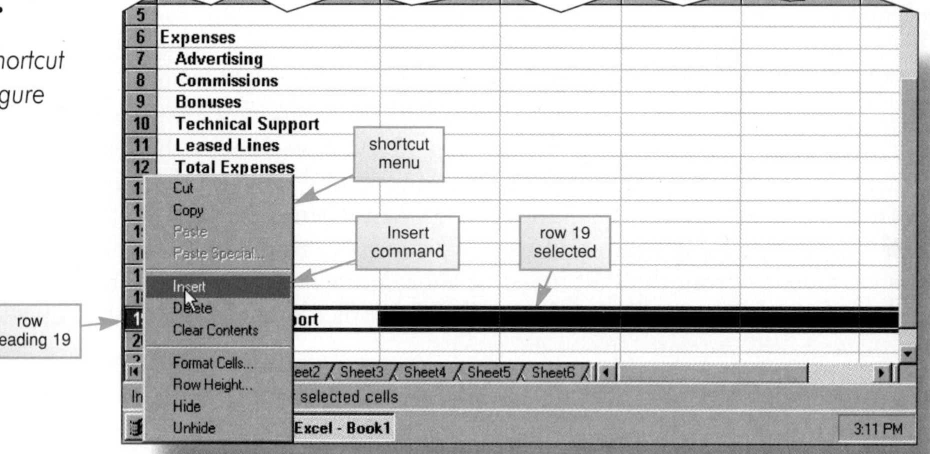

FIGURE 3-13

Click the Insert command. Click cell A19.

Excel inserts a new row by pushing down all rows below and including row 19, the one originally selected (Figure 3-14).

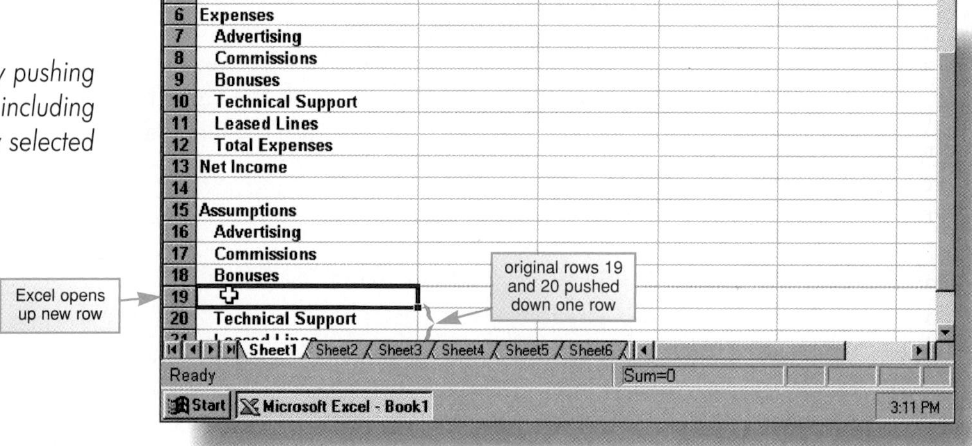

FIGURE 3-14

Other Ways

1. Select cell in row, on Insert menu click Rows
2. Select cell in row, press CTRL+SHIFT+PLUS SIGN, click Entire Row, click OK button

If the rows pushed down include any formulas, Excel adjusts the cell references to the new locations. Thus, if a formula in the worksheet references a cell in row 19 before the insert, then after the insert, the cell reference in the formula is adjusted to row 20.

The primary difference between the Insert command on the shortcut menu and the Rows command on the Insert menu is this: The Insert command on the shortcut menu requires that you select an entire row (or rows) in order to insert a row (or rows). The Rows command on the Insert menu requires that you select a single cell in a row to insert one row or a range of cells to indicate more than one row to insert. Inserted rows duplicate the format (including colors) of the row above them.

Inserting Columns

You insert columns into a worksheet in the same way you insert rows. To insert columns, begin your column selection immediately to the right of where you want Excel to insert the new blank columns. Select the number of columns you want to insert. Next, choose the Columns command from the Insert menu or the Insert command from the shortcut menu. Here again, if you use the **Columns command**, you need only select cells in the columns to push to the right, whereas you must select entire columns to use the Insert command on the shortcut menu. Inserted columns duplicate the format of the column to their left.

Inserting Individual Cells or a Range of Cells

The Insert command on the shortcut menu or the Cells command on the Insert menu allows you to insert a single cell or a range of cells. You should be aware that if you shift a single cell or a range of cells, however, they no longer may be lined up with their associated cells. To ensure that the values in the worksheet do not get out of order, it is recommended that you insert only entire rows or entire columns.

More *About* Moving and Inserting

You can move and insert between existing cells by holding down the SHIFT key while you drag the selection to the gridline where you want to insert. You can also copy and insert by holding down the CTRL and SHIFT keys while you drag the selection to the desired gridline.

Deleting Columns and Rows

The **Delete command** on the Edit menu or shortcut menu removes cells (including the data and format) from the worksheet. Deleting cells is not the same as clearing cells. The Clear command described earlier in Project 1 on page E 1.53, clears the data out of the cells, but the cells remain in the worksheet. The Delete command removes the cells from the worksheet and moves rows up when you delete rows or moves columns to the left when you delete columns.

Excel does not adjust cell references to the deleted row or column in formulas located in other cells. Excel displays the error message **#REF!** (meaning cell reference error) in those cells containing formulas that reference cells in the deleted area. For example, if cell A7 contains the formula =A4+A5 and you delete row 5, then Excel assigns the formula =A4+#REF! to cell A6 (originally cell A7) and displays the error message #REF! in cell A6, which originally was cell A7.

Deleting Individual Cells or a Range of Cells

Although Excel allows you to delete an individual cell or range of cells, you should be aware that if you shift a cell or range of cells on the worksheet, they no longer may be lined up with their associated cells. For this reason, it is recommended that you delete only entire rows or entire columns.

More *About* Undo

Inserting, copying, deleting, and moving have the potential to render a worksheet useless. Carefully review these actions before continuing on to the next task. If your not sure the action is correct, click the Undo button on the Standard toolbar.

Entering Numbers with a Format Symbol

The next step is to enter the row title, Net Sales for Bonuses, in cell A19 and enter the assumption values in the range B16:B21. The assumption numbers can be entered as decimal numbers as was done in Projects 1 and 2 and then format them later, or you can enter them with format symbols. When you enter a number with a **format symbol**, Excel immediately formats the number when it is assigned to the cell. Valid format symbols include the dollar sign ($), comma (,), and percent sign (%). If the number entered is a whole number, then it displays without any decimal places.

Table 3-2

FORMAT SYMBOL	ENTERED IN FORMULA BAR	DISPLAYS IN CELL	COMPARABLE FORMAT
$	$352	$352	Currency (0)
	$5798.62	$5,798.62	Currency (2)
	$64,123.3	$64,123.30	Currency (2)
,	9,876	9,876	Comma (0)
	7,913.3	7,913.30	Comma (2)
%	9%	9%	Percent (0)
	7.3%	7.30%	Percent (2)
	2.33%	2.33%	Percent (2)

If the number entered with a format symbol has one or more decimal places, then Excel displays the number with two decimal places. Table 3-2 illustrates several examples of numbers entered with format symbols. The number in parentheses in column 3 indicates the number of decimal places.

The following steps describe how to complete the entries in the Assumptions table and save an intermediate version of the workbook.

To Enter a Number with a Format Symbol

1. **Click cell A19 and enter the text** `bbbNet Sales for Bonuses` **(where bbb represents three spaces).**

2. **Enter** `32.75%` **in cell B16,** `2.75%` **in cell B17,** `25,000.00` **in cell B18,** `1,000,000.00` **in cell B19,** `28.25%` **in cell B20, and** `19.5%` **in cell B21.**

   The entries display in a format based on the format symbols entered with the numbers (Figure 3-15).

3. **Click the Save button on the Standard toolbar. Type the filename** `Information Mining` **in the File name text box. Click the Save in box arrow and then click the 3½ Floppy [A:] icon. Click the Save button in the Save As dialog box.**

   The workbook name in the title bar changes from Book1 to Information Mining.

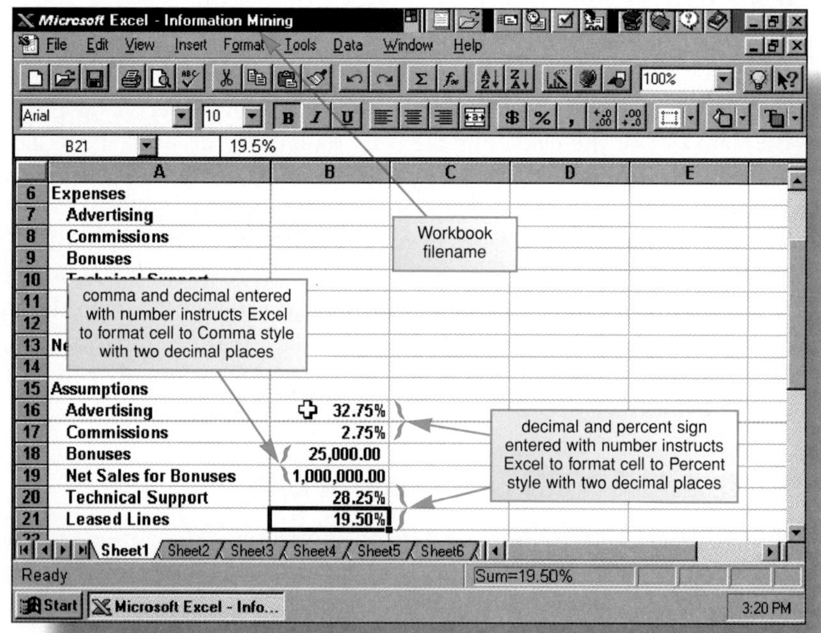

FIGURE 3-15

Freezing Worksheet Titles

Freezing worksheet titles is a useful technique for viewing large worksheets that extend beyond the window. For example, when you scroll down or to the right, the column titles in row 3 and the row titles in column A that define the numbers disappear off the screen. This makes it difficult to remember what the numbers represent. To alleviate this problem, Excel allows you to freeze the titles so they remain on the screen no matter how far down or to the right you scroll.

Complete the following steps to freeze the worksheet title and column titles in rows 1, 2, and 3, and the row titles in column A using the **Freeze Panes command** on the **Window menu**.

More *About* Freezing Titles

If you only want to freeze column headings, then select the appropriate cell in column A before you click the Freeze Panes command on the Window menu. If you only want to freeze row titles, then select the appropriate cell in row 1. To freeze both column and row titles, select the cell that is the intersection of the column and row titles.

Steps To Freeze Column and Row Titles

1 Click cell B4, the cell below the column headings you want to freeze and to the right of the row titles you want to freeze. Click Window on the menu bar and then point to Freeze Panes (Figure 3-16).

FIGURE 3-16

2 Click Freeze Panes on the Window menu.

Excel splits the window into two parts. The right border along column A changes to a thin black line indicating the split between the frozen row titles in column A and the rest of the worksheet. The bottom border in row 3 changes to a thin black line indicating the split between the frozen column titles in rows 1 through 3 and the rest of the worksheet (Figure 3-17).

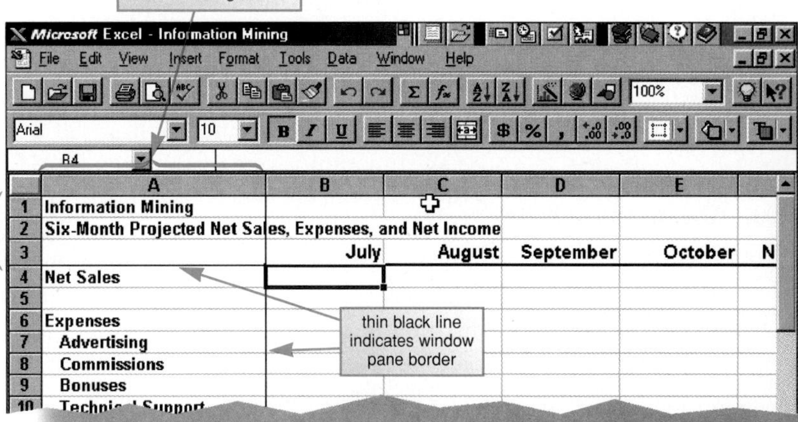

FIGURE 3-17

The row titles in column A remain on the screen even when you use the right scroll arrow to move the window to the right to display column G.

The titles are frozen until you unfreeze them. You unfreeze the titles by clicking Unfreeze Panes on the Window menu. Later steps in this project show you how to use the Unfreeze Panes command.

Entering the Projected Sales

The next step is to enter the projected sales and their total in row 4. Enter these numbers without any format symbols as shown in the following steps.

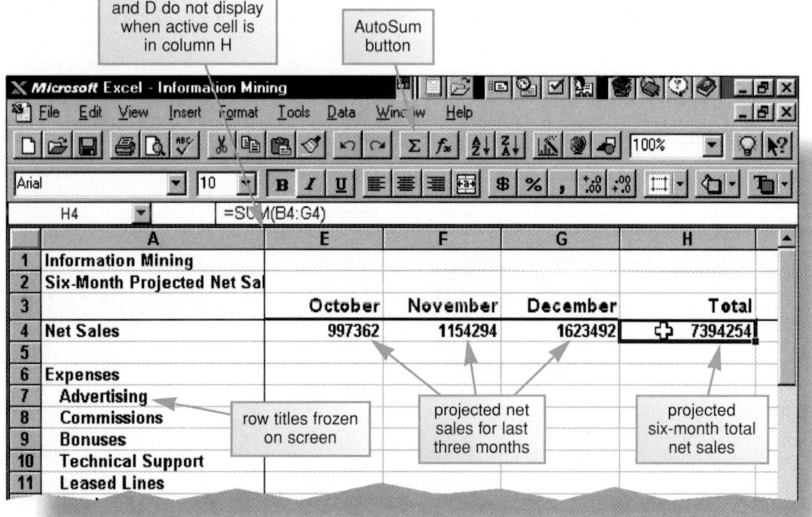

FIGURE 3-18

TO ENTER THE PROJECTED SALES

Step 1: With cell B4 selected, enter 1425654 in cell B4, 1297327 in cell C4, 896125 in cell D4, 997362 in cell E4, 1154294 in cell F4, 1623492 in cell G4.

Step 2: Click cell H4 and then click the AutoSum button on the Standard toolbar twice.

The projected six-month total net sales displays in cell H4 as shown in Figure 3-18. Notice that columns B, C, and D have scrolled off the screen, but column A remains because it was frozen earlier.

Displaying the System Date

The worksheet in Figure 3-1a on page E 3.5 includes a date stamp in cell H2. A **date stamp** is the system date of which your computer keeps track. If the computer's system date is set to the current date, which normally it is, then the date stamp is equivalent to the current date.

In information processing, a report such as a printout of the worksheet is often meaningless without a date stamp. For example, the date stamp in Project 3 is useful for showing when the six-month projections were made.

To enter the system date in a cell in the worksheet use the **NOW function**. The NOW function is one of fourteen date functions available in Excel. When assigned to a cell, the NOW function returns a decimal number in the range 1 to 65,380, corresponding to the dates January 1, 1900 through December 31, 2078 and the time of day. Excel formats the number representing the system's date and time automatically to the date and time format m/d/yy h:mm where the first m is the month, d is the day of the month, yy is the last two digits of the year, h is the hour of the day, and mm is the minutes past the hour.

The following steps show how to enter the NOW function and change the format from m/d/yy h:mm to m/d/yy where m is the month number, d is day of the month, and yy is the last two digits of the year.

More About Dates

How many days have you been alive? Enter today's date (i.e., 3/29/97) in cell A1. Next, enter your birthdate (i.e., 6/22/40) in cell A2. Finally, select cell A3 and enter the formula =A1 - A2. Cell A3 will display the number of days you have been alive.

To Enter and Format the System Date

1 **Click cell H2 and then click the Function Wizard button on the Standard toolbar.**

2 **Click Date & Time in the Function Category box and then click NOW in the Function Name box.**

The Function Wizard - Step 1 of 2 dialog box displays as shown in Figure 3-19.

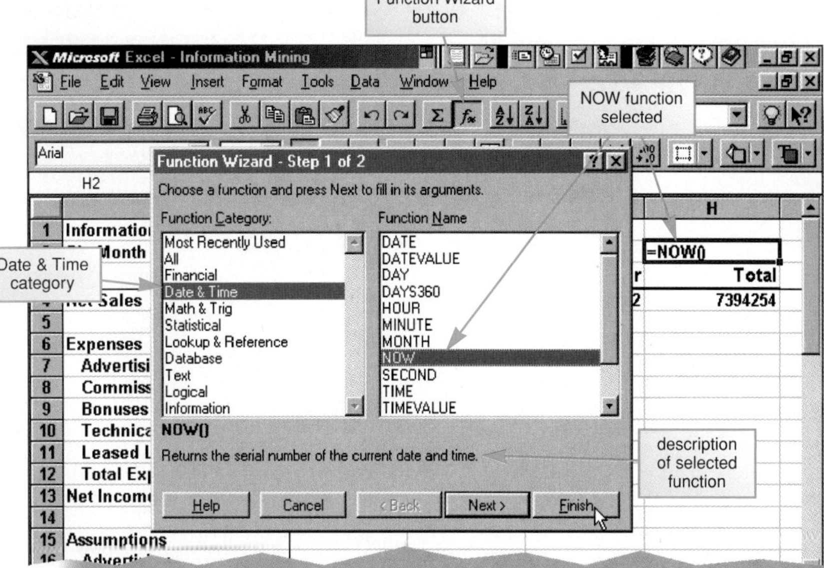

FIGURE 3-19

3 **Click the Finish button.**

Excel displays the system date and system time in cell H2 using the default date and time format m/d/yy h:mm (Figure 3-20).

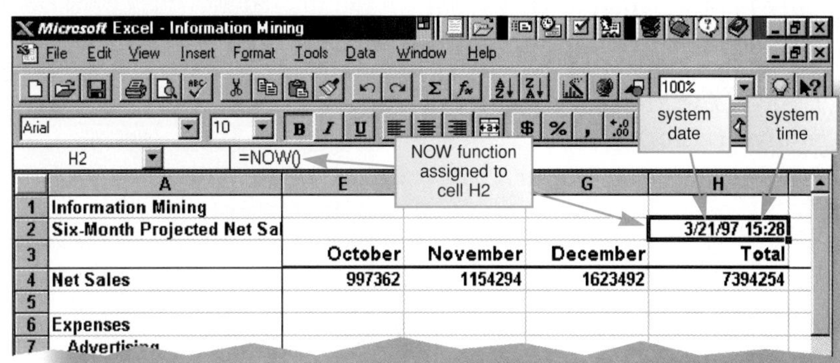

FIGURE 3-20

4 **Right-click cell H2 and then point to Format Cells.**

Excel displays the shortcut menu (Figure 3-21).

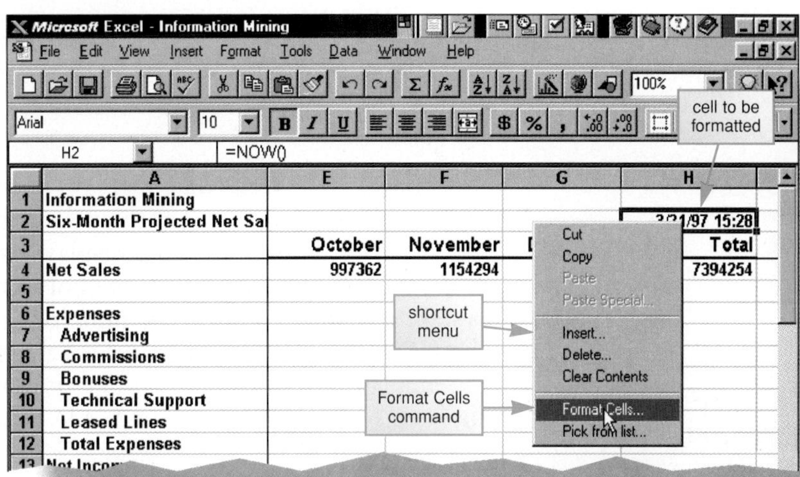

FIGURE 3-21

5 **Click the Format Cells command and then click the Number tab in the Format Cells dialog box. Click Date in the Category box and then click 3/4/95 in the Type box.**

Excel displays the Format Cells dialog box with Date and m/d/yy (3/4/95) highlighted (Figure 3-22).

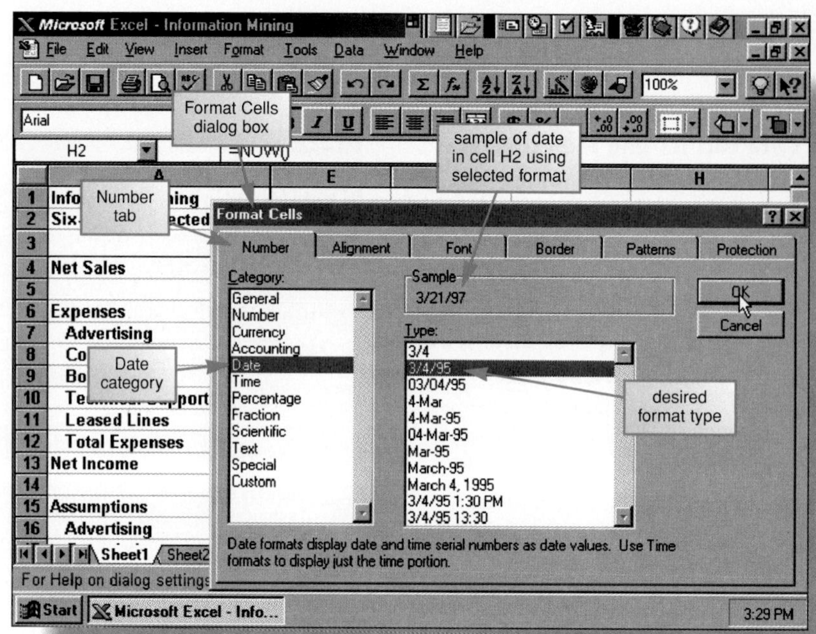

FIGURE 3-22

6 **Click the OK button in the Format Cells dialog box.**

Excel displays the date in the form m/d/yy (Figure 3-23). The date on your computer may different.

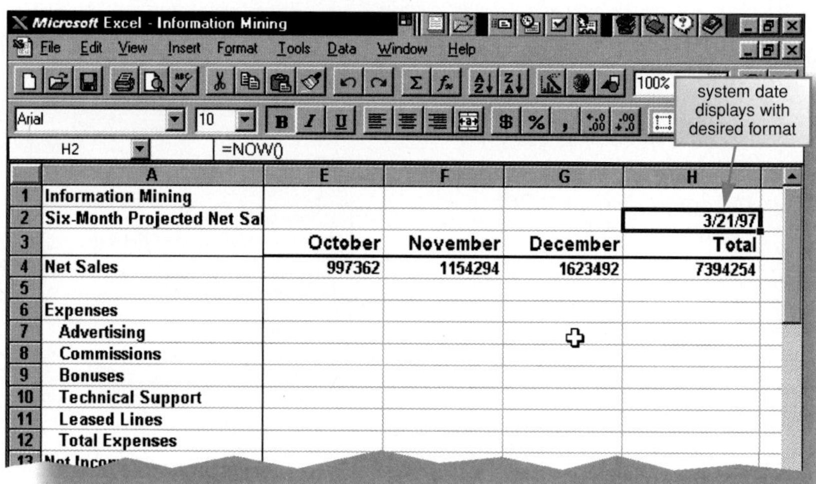

FIGURE 3-23

OtherWays

1. On Insert menu click Function, click Date & Time, click NOW, click Next button, click Finish button
2. Press CTRL+SEMICOLON (not a volatile date)

More About Date and Time

You can enter any date or time into a cell in a variety of formats such as 3/5/9, Feb-95, and 8:45 PM, and Excel will consider the entry to be a number. Excel automatically formats the entry in the same form you enter it.

In Figure 3-23, the date displays in the cell right-aligned because Excel treats a date as a number. If you format the date by applying the **General format** (Excel's default for numbers), the date displays as a number. To format a cell to General, select the General category in the Format Cells dialog box. For example, if the system time and date is 12:00 noon on January 21, 1997 and the cell containing the NOW function is assigned the General format, then Excel displays the following number in the cell:

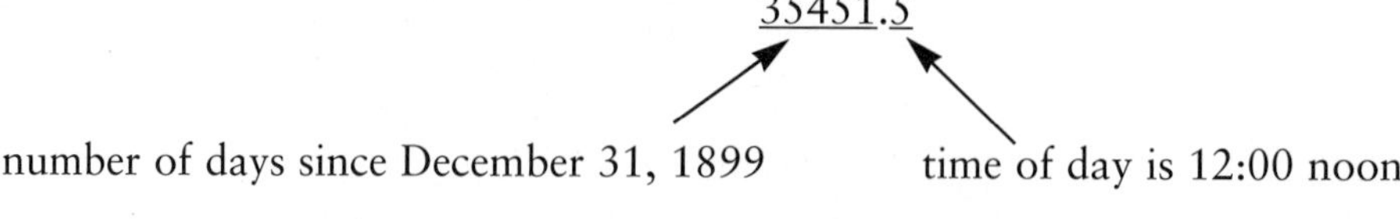

The whole number portion of the number (35451) represents the number of days since December 31, 1899. The decimal portion (.5) represents the time of day (12:00 noon).

More About Entering Fractions

How do you enter fractions? To enter a fraction, such as ½, type .5 or 0 1/2 (i.e., type zero, followed by a space, followed by the number 1, followed by a slash, followed by the number 2). If you type 1/2, Excel will store the value in the cell as the date January 2.

Absolute Versus Relative Addressing

The next step is to enter the formulas that determine the projected payroll expenses in the range B7:G13 (Figure 3-1a on page E 3.5). The projected monthly expenses are based on the projected monthly net sales in row 4 and the assumptions in the range B16:B21. The formulas for each column are the same, except for the sales in row 4. Thus, the formulas can be entered for July in column B and copied to columns C through G. The formulas for determining the July projected payroll expenses are shown in Table 3-3.

If you enter in column B the formulas as they appear in Table 3-3 and then copy them to columns C through G, Excel will adjust the cell references for each column automatically. Thus, after the copy, the August advertising in cell C7 would be =C16*C4. The cell reference C4 (August Net Sales) is correct. Cell C16 is empty, however. The need here is a way to keep a cell reference in a formula the same when it is copied. The formula for cell C7 should read =B16*C4 rather than =C16*C4.

Table 3-3

CELL	EXPENSE	FORMULA	COMMENT
B7	Advertising	=B16 * B4	Advertising % times July Net Sales
B8	Commissions	=B17 * B4	Commissions % times July Net Sales
B9	Bonuses	=IF(B4 >= B19, B18, 0)	Bonuses equals value in cell B18 or zero
B10	Technical Support	=B20 * B4	Technical Support % times July Net Sales
B11	Leased Lines	=B21 * B4	Leased Lines % times July Net Sales
B12	Total Expenses	=SUM(B7:B11)	Sum of expenses
B13	Net Income	=B4 - B12	Net Sales minus Expenses

Excel has the capability to keep a cell reference constant when it copies a formula or function by using a technique called **absolute referencing**. To specify an absolute reference in a formula, add a dollar sign ($) to the beginning of the column name, row name, or both in formulas you plan to copy. For example, $B$16 is an absolute reference and B16 is a relative reference. Both reference the same cell. The difference shows when they are copied. A formula using $B$16 instructs Excel to use the same cell (B16) as it copies the formula to a new location. A formula using B16 instructs Excel to adjust the cell reference as it copies. Table 3-4 gives some additional examples of absolute references. A cell reference with one dollar sign before either the column or the row is called a **mixed cell reference**.

Table 3-4

CELL REFERENCE	MEANING
$B$16	Both column and row references remain the same when you copy this cell reference because they are absolute.
B$16	The column reference changes when you copy this cell reference to another column because it is relative. The row reference does not change because it is absolute.
$B16	The row reference changes when you copy this cell reference to another row because it is relative. The column reference does not change because it is absolute.
B16	Both column and row references are relative. When copied to another row and column, both the row and column in the cell reference are adjusted to reflect the new location.

Entering the July Advertising and Commissions Formulas

The following steps show how to enter the advertising formula (=$B$16*B4) in cell B7 and the commissions formula (=$B$17*B4) in cell B8 for the month of January using Point mode. When you enter an absolute reference, you can type the $ or you can press F4 with the insertion point in or to the right of the cell reference you want to change to absolute.

To Enter Formulas Containing Absolute Cell References

1 Click cell B7. Type the equal sign (=) to begin a formula and then click cell B16. Press F4 to change B16 to an absolute reference in the formula. Type the asterisk (*) and then click cell B4.

The formula displays in cell B7 and in the formula bar (Figure 3-24).

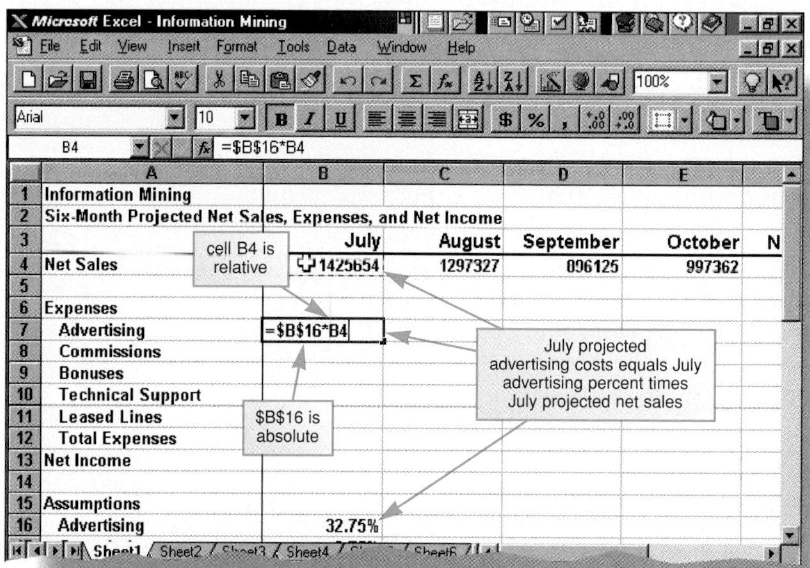

FIGURE 3-24

2 Click the enter box or press the ENTER key to complete the entry in cell B7. Click B8, type the equal sign (=) to begin a formula and then click cell B17. Press F4 to change B17 to an absolute reference in the formula. Type the asterisk (*) and click cell B4. Click the enter box or press the ENTER key.

Excel displays the results of the projected July advertising expense formula (466901.685) in cell B7 and the projected July commissions expense formula (39205.485) in cell B8 (Figure 3-25).

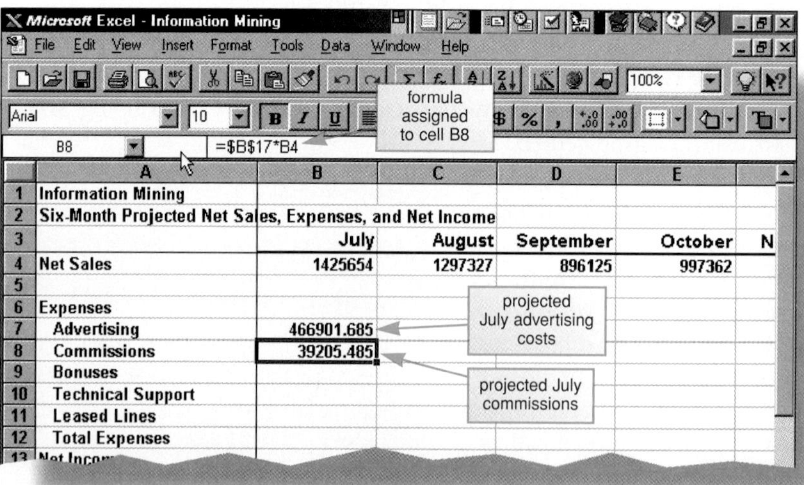

FIGURE 3-25

Making Decisions – The IF Function

If the projected July net sales in cell B4 is greater than or equal to the net sales for bonuses in cell B19, then the projected July bonuses in cell B9 is equal to the amount in cell B18 (25,000.00); otherwise, cell B9 is equal to zero. One way to assign the projected monthly bonuses in row 9 is to manually compare the projected net sales for each month in row 4 to the net sales for bonuses in cell B19 and then enter 25,000 when the corresponding projected month net sales equals or exceeds the amount in cell B19. Because the data in the worksheet changes each time you prepare the report or adjust the figures, however, you will find it preferable to have Excel assign automatically the projected monthly bonus to the entries in the appropriate cells. What you need in cell B9 is an entry that displays 25,000 or 0 (zero), depending on whether the projected July net sales in cell B4 is greater than or equal to or less than the number in cell B19.

Excel has the **IF function** that is useful when the value you want to assign to a cell is dependent on a logical test. A **logical test** is made up of two expressions and a relational operator. Each expression can be a cell reference, a number, text, a function, or a formula. A **comparison operator** is one of the following: > (greater than), < (less than), = (equal to), >= (greater than or equal to), <= (less than or equal to), <> (not equal to). For example, assume you assign cell B9 the IF function:

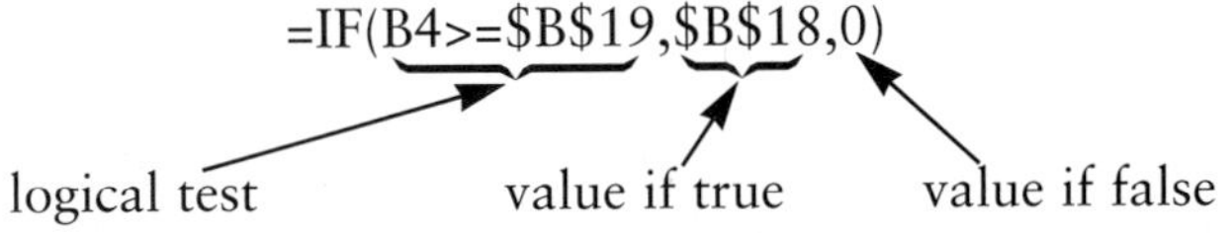

If the projected July net sales in cell B4 is greater than or equal to the value in cell B18, then 25,000 displays in cell B9. If the projected July sales in cell B4 is less than the value in cell B18, then cell B9 displays a zero.

The general form of the IF function is:

=IF(logical-test, value-if-true, value-if-false)

The argument, value-if-true, is the value you want displayed in the cell when the logical test is true. The argument, value-if-false, is the value you want displayed in the cell when the logical test is false.

Table 3-5 lists the valid relational operators and examples of their use in IF functions.

Table 3-5

RELATIONAL OPERATOR	*MEANING*	*EXAMPLE*
=	Equal to	=IF(C5 = K7, B29 - F3, K5 + S3)
<	Less than	=IF(J17 / B5 < 12, B15, B13 - 5)
>	Greater than	=IF(=SUM(T4:T9) > 300, 0, 1)
>=	Greater than or equal to	=IF(A15 >= $R$2, C4 * H5, 6)
<=	Less than or equal to	=IF(H5 + F5 <= 10, H10, 9 * B3)
<>	Not equal to	=IF(C5 <> B$5, "OK", "Not OK")

More About Absolute Referencing

Absolute referencing is one of the most difficult worksheet concepts to understand. One point to keep in mind is that there is only one command, the Copy command, that is affected by an absolute cell reference. An absolute cell reference instructs Excel to keep the same cell reference as it copies a formula from one cell to another.

More About the IF Function

Assume you want to assign the formula =F4*G6 to the active cell, but display an empty cell (blank) when the formula is equal to zero. Try this: enter =IF(F4*G6 = 0, " ", F4*G6) into the cell. This IF function assigns the blank between the quotation marks to the cell when F4*G6 is equal to zero, otherwise, it assigns the value of F4*G6 to the cell.

The following steps assign the IF function =IF(B4>=$B$19,$B$18,0) to cell B9. This function will determine whether or not the spreadsheet projects a bonus for July.

To Enter an IF Function

1 **Click cell B9, and then type** `=if(b4>=$b$19,$b$18,0` **in the cell.**

The IF function displays in cell B9 and in the formula bar (Figure 3-26).

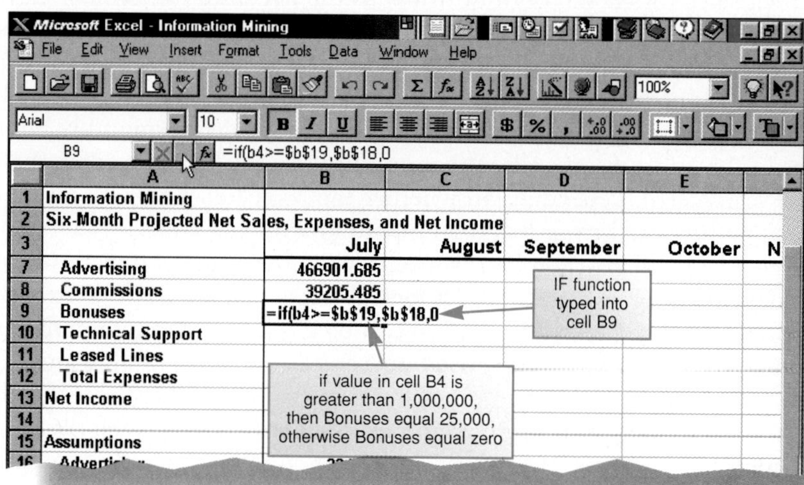

FIGURE 3-26

2 **Click the enter box or press the ENTER key.**

Excel displays 25000 in cell B9 because the value in cell B4 (1,425,654.00) is greater than or equal to the value in cell B19 (1,000,000.00) (Figure 3-27). Recall that it is not necessary to type the closing parenthesis when you enter a function.

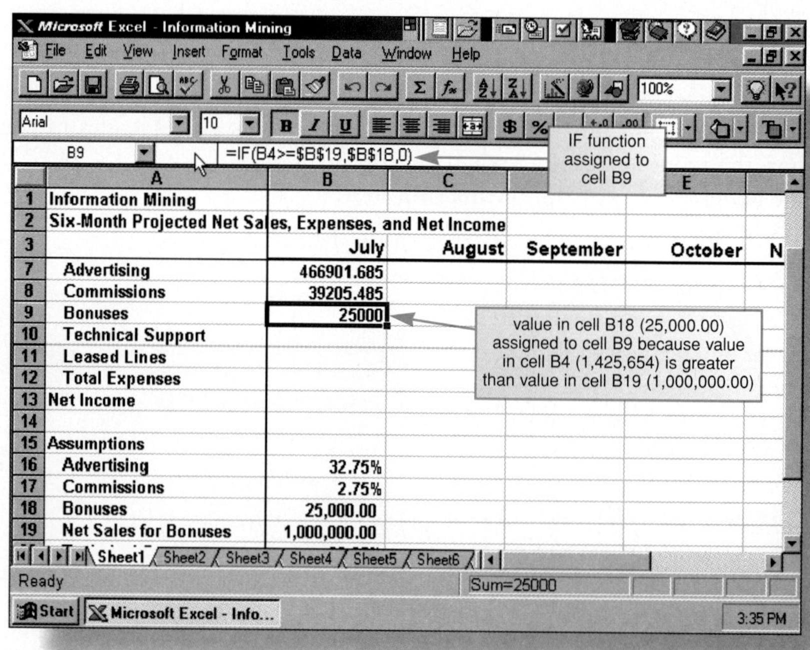

FIGURE 3-27

The value that Excel displays in cell B9 depends on the values assigned to cells B4, B18, and B19. For example, if the projected sales in cell B4 is reduced below 1,000,000.00, then the IF function in cell B9 will change the display to zero. Changing the net sales for bonuses in cell B19 to a greater amount has the same effect.

Entering the Remaining Projected Expense and Net Income Formulas for July

The projected July technical support expense in cell B10 is equal to the technical support percent in cell B20 times the projected July net sales in cell B4. Likewise, the projected July leased lines expenses in cell B11 is equal to the leased line percent in cell B21 times the projected July net sales. The projected total expenses for July in cell B12 is equal to the sum of the July expenses in the range B7:B11. The projected July net income in cell B13 is equal to the projected net sales minus the projected total expenses for July. The following steps enter the four formulas into the worksheet.

TO ENTER THE REMAINING PROJECTED EXPENSE AND NET INCOME FORMULAS FOR JULY

Step 1: Click cell B10. Type =b20*b4 and then press the DOWN ARROW key.
Step 2: Type =b21*b4 and then press the DOWN ARROW key.
Step 3: Click the AutoSum button on the Standard toolbar twice.
Step 4: Click cell B13. Type =b4-b12 and then click the enter box or press the ENTER key.

The projected January technical support, leased lines, total expenses, and net income display in cells B10, B11, B12, and B13, respectively (Figure 3-28a).

More About Freezing Formula Values

You can freeze the value of a formula by replacing the formula with the frozen value. Do the following: (1) click the cell with the formula; (2) press F2 or click in the formula bar; (3) press F9 to display the value in the formula bar; (4) click the enter box or press the ENTER key.

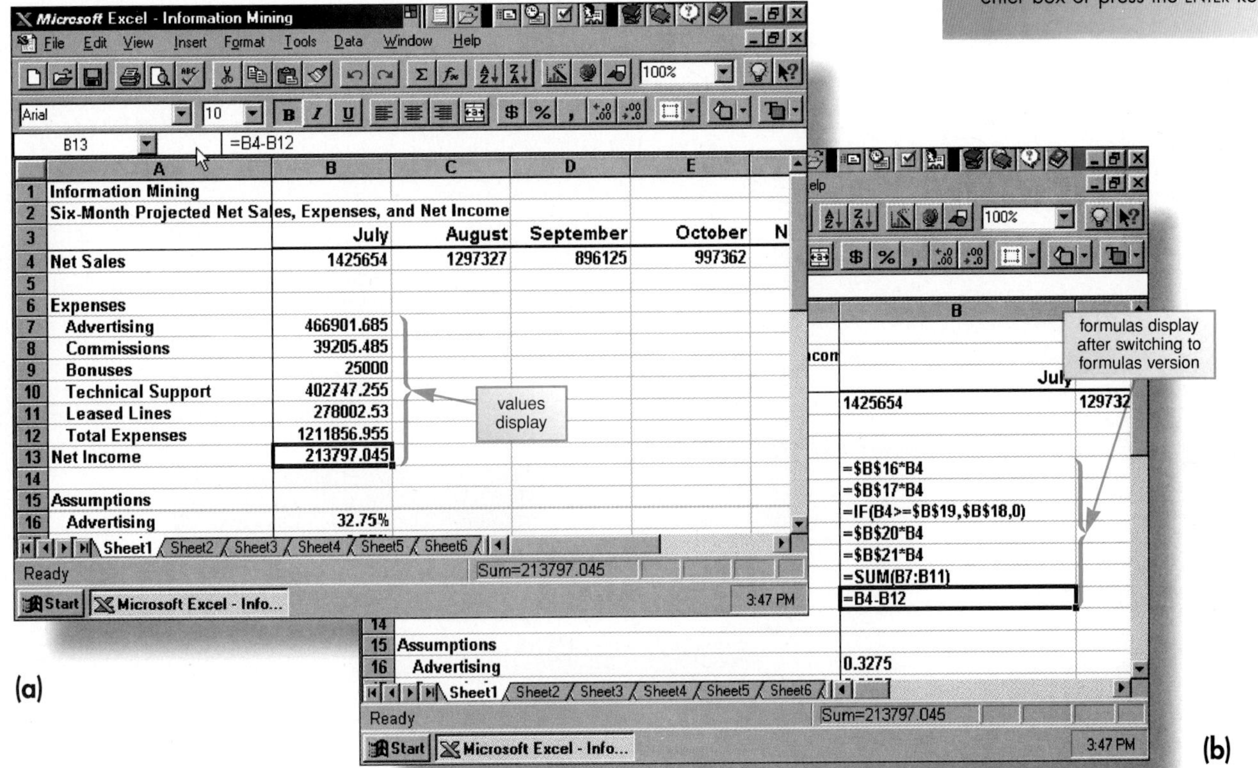

FIGURE 3-28

You can view the formulas in the worksheet by pressing CTRL+`. The display changes from Figure 3-28a to Figure 3-28b. Press CTRL+` to display the values again.

To copy the projected expenses and totals, complete the following steps using the fill handle.

To Copy the Projected Expenses and Totals Using the Fill Handle

1 Select the range B7:B13. Point to the fill handle near the lower right corner of cell B13.

The range B7:B13 is selected and the mouse pointer changes to a cross hair (Figure 3-29).

	A	B	C	D	E
1	Information Mining				
2	Six-Month Projected Net Sales, Expenses, and Net Income				
3		July	August	September	October
4	Net Sales	1425654	1297327	896125	997362
5					
6	Expenses				
7	Advertising	466901.685			
8	Commissions	39205.485			
9	Bonuses	25000			
10	Technical Support	402747.255			
11	Leased Lines	278002.53			
12	Total Expenses	1211856.955			
13	Net Income	213797.045			
14					
15	Assumptions				
16	Advertising	32.75%			

copy range is B7:B13
mouse pointer changes to a cross hair
Ready
Sum=2637510.955

FIGURE 3-29

2 Drag the fill handle to select the paste area C7:G13 and then release the left mouse button.

Excel copies the formulas in the range B7:B13 to the paste area C7:G13. The last three columns of the paste area display as shown in Figure 3-30.

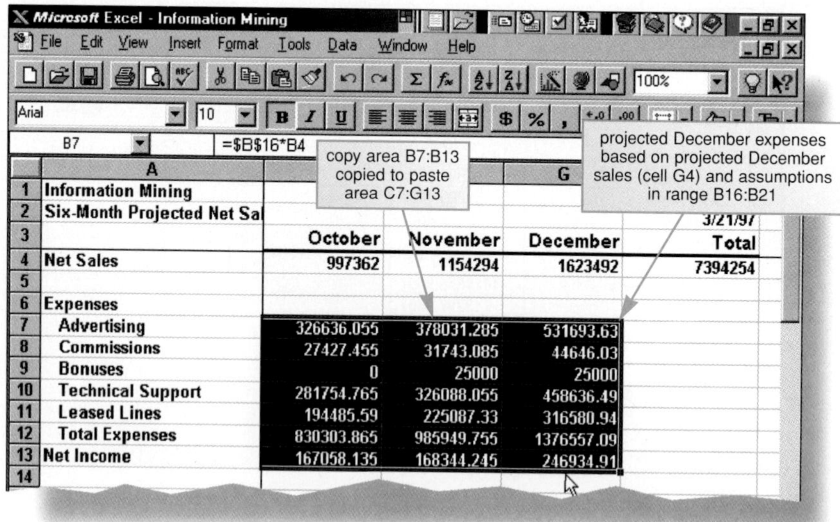

FIGURE 3-30

Determining the Projected Total Expenses by Category and Total Net Income

Follow the steps at the top of the next page to determine the total projected expenses by category and total net income in the range H7:H13.

TO DETERMINE THE PROJECTED TOTAL EXPENSES BY CATEGORY AND TOTAL NET INCOME

Step 1: Select the range H7:H13.
Step 2: Click the AutoSum button on the Standard toolbar.

The projected total payroll expenses by category and total net income display in the range H7:H13 (Figure 3-31).

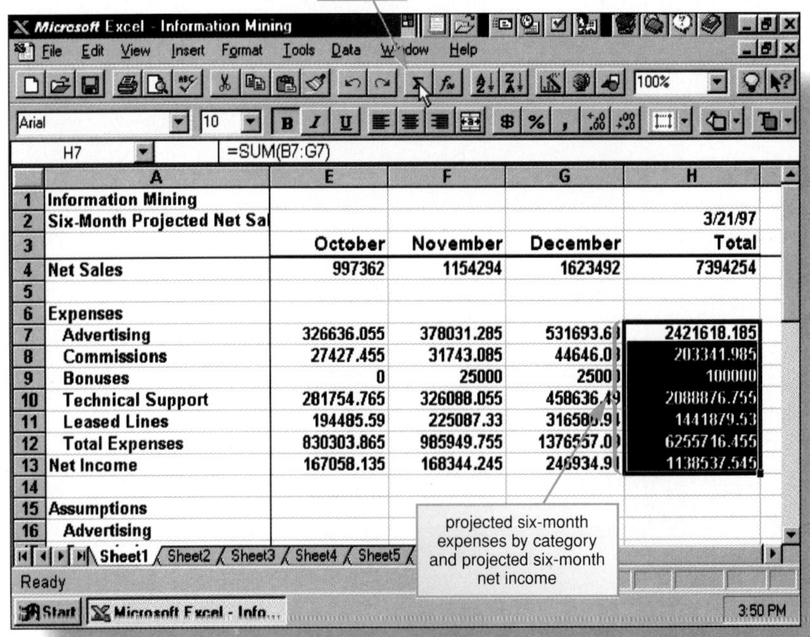

FIGURE 3-31

Unfreezing Worksheet Titles and Saving the Workbook

All the text, data, and formulas have been entered into the worksheet. The next step is to improve the appearance of the worksheet. Before modifying the worksheet's appearance, the following steps unfreeze the titles and save the workbook under its current filename Information Mining.

TO UNFREEZE THE WORKSHEET TITLES AND SAVE THE WORKBOOK

Step 1: Click cell B4 to clear the range selection from the previous steps.
Step 2: Click Window on the menu bar and then point to Unfreeze Panes (Figure 3-32).
Step 3: Click Unfreeze Panes.
Step 4: Click the Save button on the Standard toolbar.

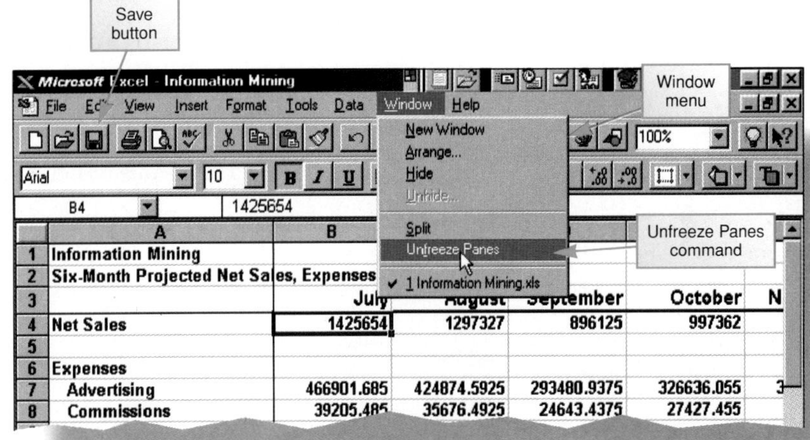

FIGURE 3-32

Excel unfreezes the titles so that column A scrolls off the screen when you scroll to the right and the first three rows scroll off the screen when you scroll down. The workbook is saved using the filename Information Mining.

Formatting the Worksheet

The worksheet in Figure 3-31 determines the projected monthly expenses and net incomes. Its appearance is uninteresting, however, even though some minimal formatting was done earlier. This section will complete the formatting of the worksheet so the numbers are easier to read and to emphasize the titles, assumptions, categories, and totals (Figure 3-33 on the next page).

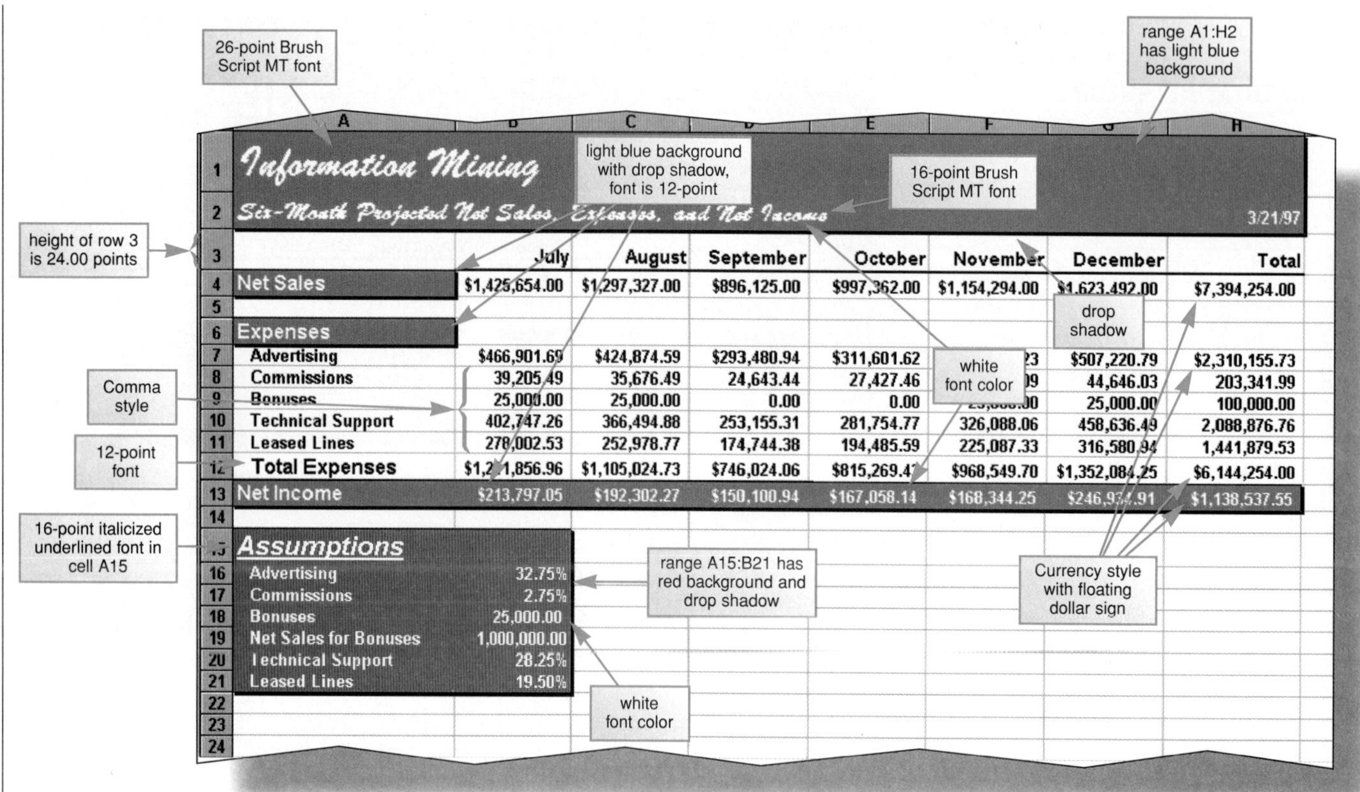

FIGURE 3-33

Formatting the Projected Sales and Payroll Expenses

Format the projected monthly net sales and expenses as follows:

1. Assign the Currency style with a floating dollar sign to rows 4, 7, 12, and 13.
2. Assign a customized Comma style to rows 8 through 11.

Assigning a Currency style with a floating dollar sign requires that you use the Format Cells command, rather than the Currency Style button on the Formatting toolbar because the button assigns a fixed dollar sign. The Comma style must also be assigned using the Format Cells command because the Comma Style button on the Formatting toolbar displays a dash (-) when a cell has a value of zero. The specifications for this worksheet call for displaying a value of zero as 0.00 (see cell D9 in Figure 3-33). The following steps format the numbers in rows 4 and 7 through 13.

To Assign Formats to the Projected Net Sales, Expenses, and Net Income

1 **Select the range B4:H4. Hold down the CTRL and select the nonadjacent ranges B7:H7 and B12:H13. Release the CTRL key. Right-click the selected range and then point to Format Cells.**

The selected range is highlighted and the shortcut menu displays as shown in Figure 3-34.

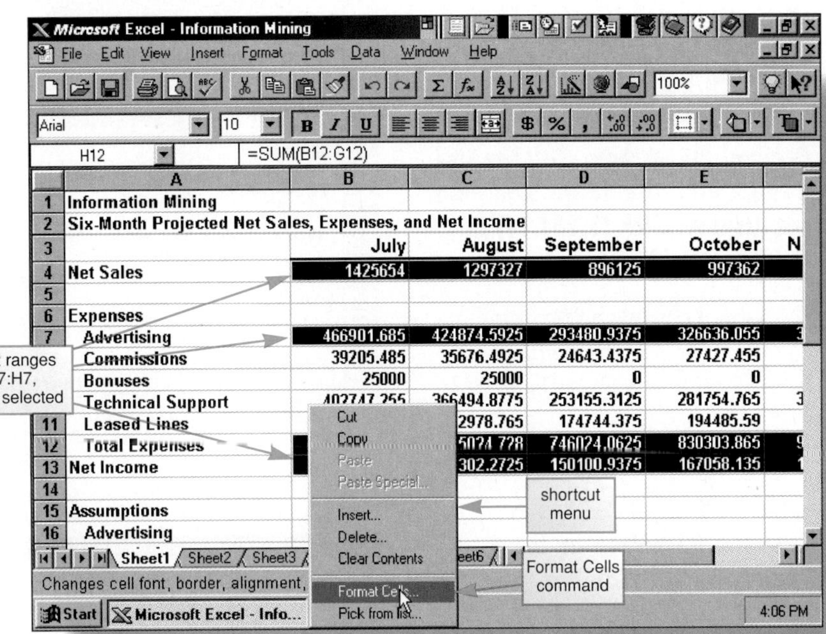

FIGURE 3-34

2 **Click Format Cells. When the Format Cells dialog box displays, click the Number tab, click Currency in the Category box, select two decimal places in the Decimal Places box, click the Use $ check box to ensure a dollar sign displays, and click ($1,234.10) in the Negative Numbers box.**

The format settings display on the Number sheet in the Format Cells dialog box as shown in Figure 3-35.

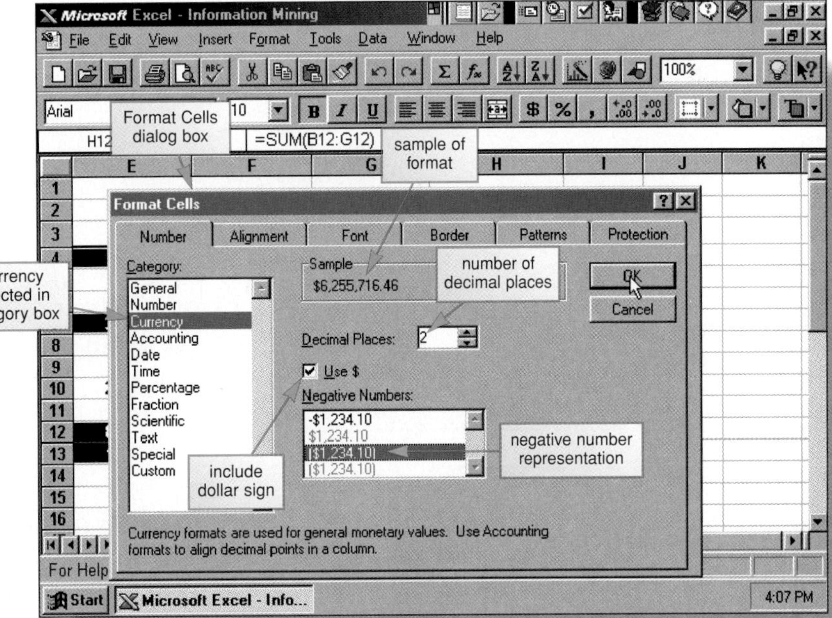

FIGURE 3-35

3 **Click the OK button on the Format Cells dialog box.**

4 **Select the range B8:H11. Right-click within the selected range. Click Format Cells on the shortcut menu. Click Currency in the Category box, select 2 in the Decimal Places box, click the Use $ check box so a dollar sign does not display, click (1,234.10) in the Negative Numbers box.**

The format settings display on the Numbers sheet in the Format Cells dialog box as shown in Figure 3-36.

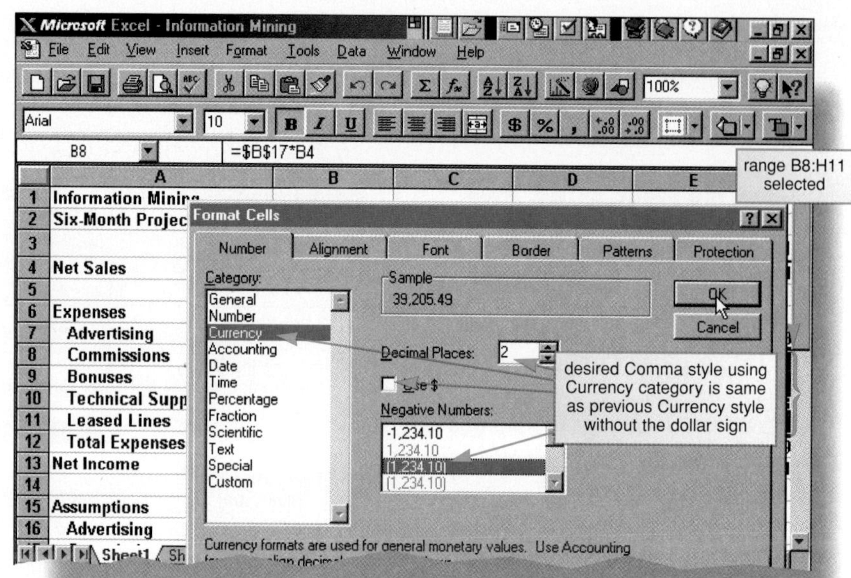

FIGURE 3-36

5 **Click the OK button on the Format Cells dialog box.**

The Currency style and Comma style formats display as shown in Figure 3-37.

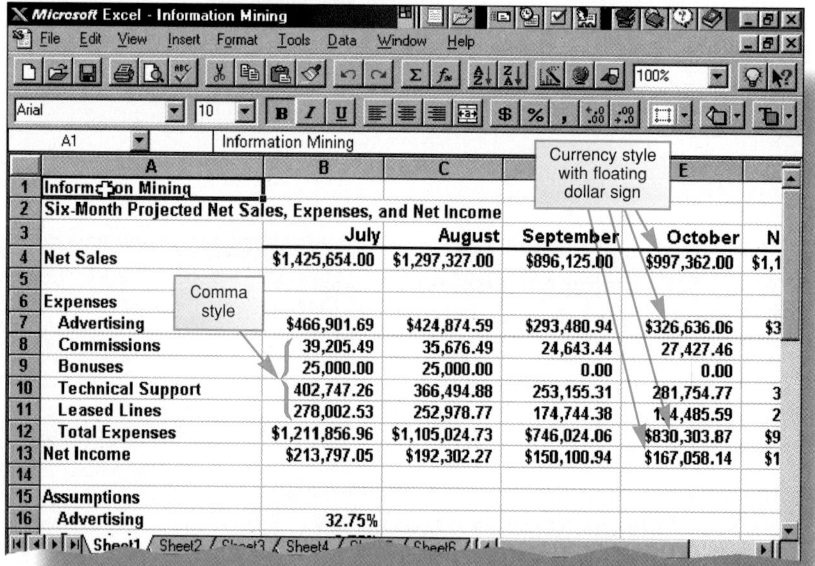

FIGURE 3-37

Instead of selecting Currency in the Category box in Step 4 (Figure 3-36), you could have selected Accounting to generate the same Comma style format. You should review the formats available under each category title. Thousands of combinations of format styles are available when you use the Format Cells dialog box to assign formats.

The next step is to format the titles at the top of the worksheet.

Formatting the Titles

To emphasize the worksheet titles in cells A1 and A2, the font type, size, and color are changed as described in the following steps.

To Format the Titles

1 **Select the range A1:A2. Click the Font box arrow. Scroll down and point to TT Brush Script MT (or a similar font).**

The Font drop-down list box displays (Figure 3-38).

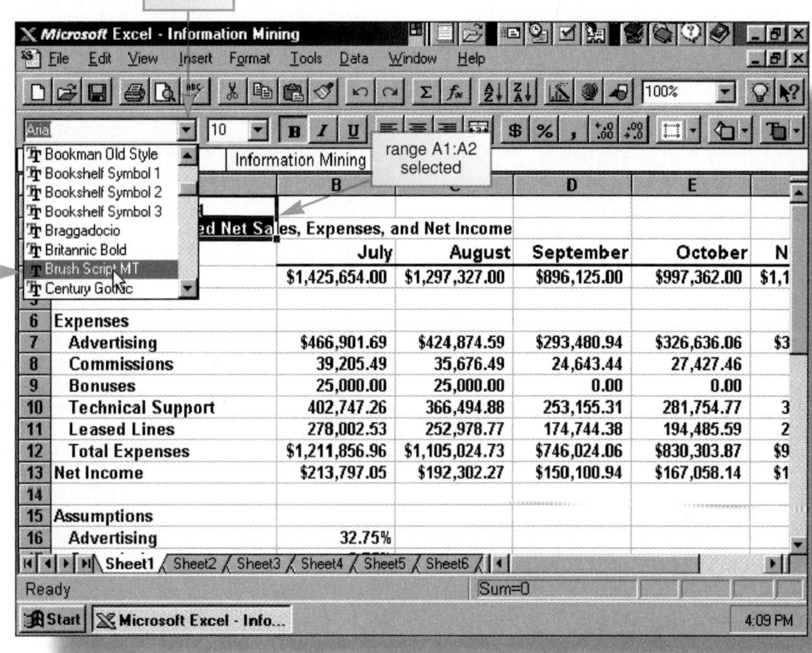

FIGURE 3-38

2 **Click TT Brush Script MT. Click cell A1. Click the Font Size box arrow and then click 26. Click cell A2. Click the Font Size box arrow and then click 16.**

The titles in the range A1:A2 display as shown in Figure 3-39.

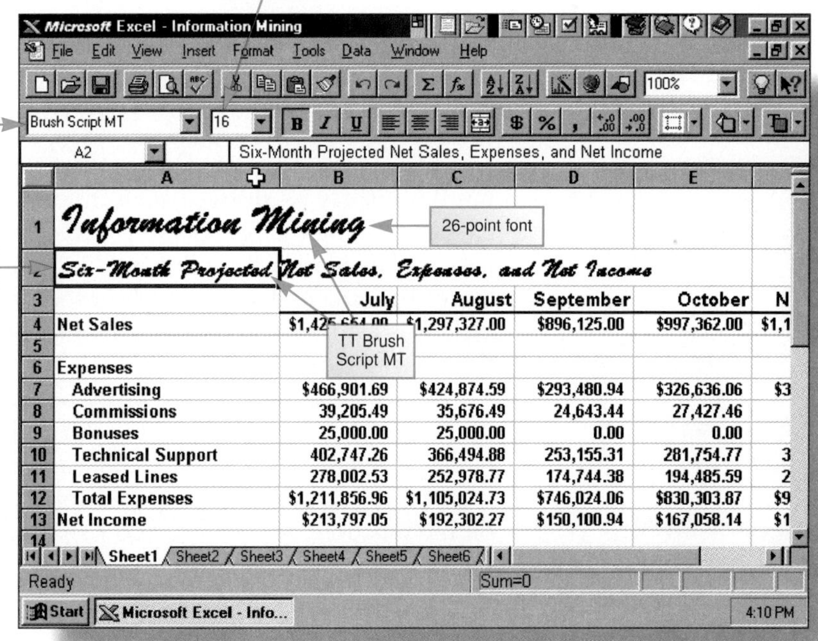

FIGURE 3-39

3 **Select the range A1:H2. Click the Color button arrow on the Formatting toolbar. Click light blue (column 1, row 3 on the Color palette). Click the Font Color button arrow on the Formatting toolbar. Point to white (column 2, row 1 on the Font Color palette).**

The selected range and Font Color palette display as shown in Figure 3-40.

4 **Click white.**

Excel changes the color of the font in the titles from black to white (see Figure 3-33 on page E 3.30).

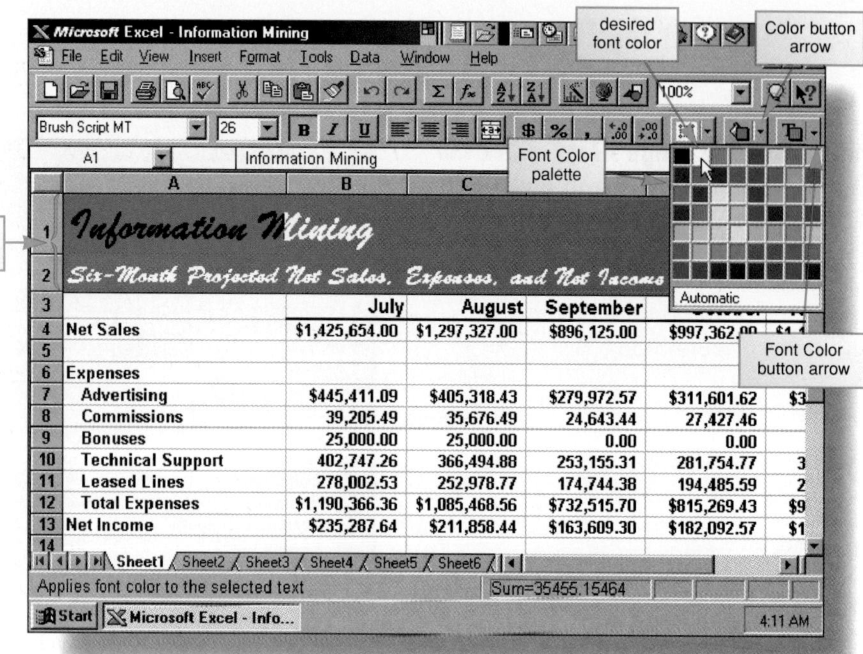

FIGURE 3-40

OtherWays

1. Right-click range, click Format Cells, click Patterns tab to color background or click Font tab to color font

With the range A1:H2 selected, the next step is to add a drop shadow. To add a drop shadow, the Drawing toolbar must display on the screen. The following section describes how to display and dock an inactive (hidden) toolbar.

Displaying the Drawing Toolbar

Excel has more than 200 buttons that you can display on toolbars. Most of the buttons display on thirteen built-in toolbars. You can also create customized toolbars containing the buttons that you often use. Two of the thirteen built-in toolbars are the Standard toolbar and Formatting toolbar that usually display at the top of the screen. Another built-in toolbar is the Drawing toolbar. The **Drawing toolbar** provides tools that can simplify adding lines, boxes, and other geometric figures to a worksheet.

You can use the shortcut menu or the Toolbars command on the View menu to display or hide any one of the thirteen toolbars. The Drawing toolbar can also be displayed or hidden by clicking the Drawing button on the Standard toolbar. Perform the steps that follow to display the Drawing toolbar, obtain information on the functions of buttons, and then dock the Drawing toolbar at the bottom of the screen.

More About Color Palettes

If your Color palette has less colors than shown on the Color palette in Figure 3-40, then your system is using a different Color palette setting. The figures in this book were created using High Color (16 bit). To check your Color palette setting, minimize all applications, right-click the desktop, click Properties, click the Settings tab, and locate the Color palette box. If you change the settings, you must restart Windows 95.

To Display the Drawing Toolbar

1 Click the Drawing button on the Standard toolbar.

The Drawing toolbar displays (Figure 3-41). Excel locates the Drawing toolbar on the screen wherever it displayed and in whatever shape it displayed the last time it was used.

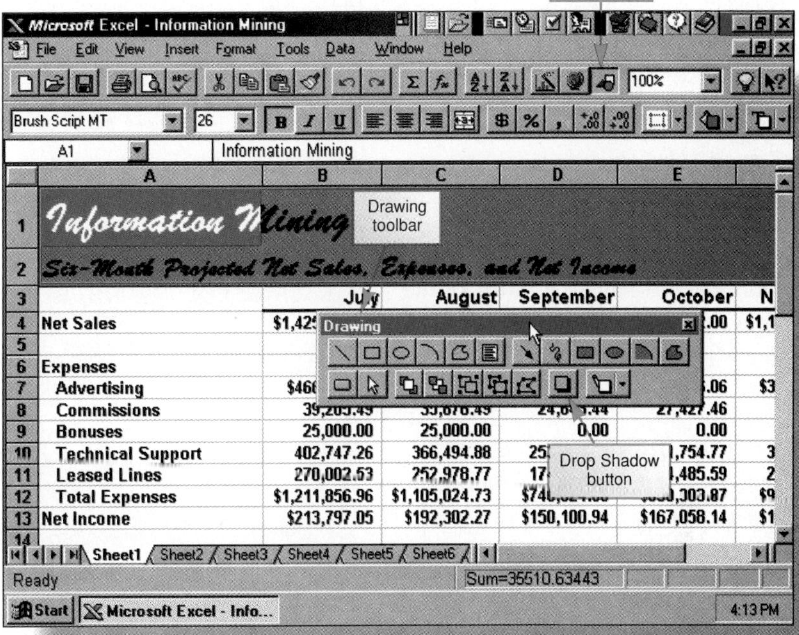

FIGURE 3-41

OtherWays

1. Right-click Standard or Formatting toolbar, click Drawing
2. On View menu click Toolbars, click Drawing check box, click OK button

In addition to moving the mouse across the textbar buttons and reading the ToolTips, you can also obtain information on any button by performing the following steps.

TO LIST THE FUNCTIONS OF BUTTONS ON A TOOLBAR

Step 1: Right-click any toolbar.
Step 2: Click Customize on the shortcut menu.
Step 3: Click a toolbar name in the Categories box.
Step 4: One at a time, click the buttons in the Buttons area and read the descriptions of the buttons at the bottom of the Customize dialog box.

Moving and Shaping a Toolbar

The Drawing toolbar in Figure 3-41 is called a **floating toolbar** because you can move it anywhere in the window. You move the toolbar by positioning the mouse pointer in a blank area within the toolbar (not on a button) and dragging it to its new location. A floating toolbar always displays in its own window with a title bar. As with any window, you can drag the toolbar window borders to resize it and you can click the Close box in the title bar to hide a floating toolbar.

Sometimes a floating toolbar gets in the way no matter where you move it. Hiding the toolbar is one solution. At times, however, you will want to keep it active as you use it. For this reason, Excel allows you to locate toolbars on the edge of its window. If you drag the toolbar close to the edge of the window, Excel positions the toolbar in a **toolbar dock**.

More About Toolbars

You can create your own toolbar and assemble the buttons you want on it by using the Customize command on the shortcut menu that displays when you right-click a toolbar.

More About Buttons

You can think of buttons as being assigned instructions that execute whenever a button is clicked.

Excel provides four toolbar docks, one on each of the four sides of the window. You can add as many toolbars to a dock as you want. However, each time you dock a toolbar, the window decreases slightly in size to compensate for the room taken up by the toolbar. The following steps show how to dock the Drawing toolbar at the bottom of the screen below the scroll bar.

Steps To Dock a Toolbar at the Bottom of the Screen

1. **Position the mouse pointer in the title bar or a blank area in the Drawing toolbar.**

2. **Drag the Drawing toolbar below the scroll bar at the bottom of the screen and release the left mouse button.**

   Excel docks the Drawing toolbar at the bottom of the screen (Figure 3-42).

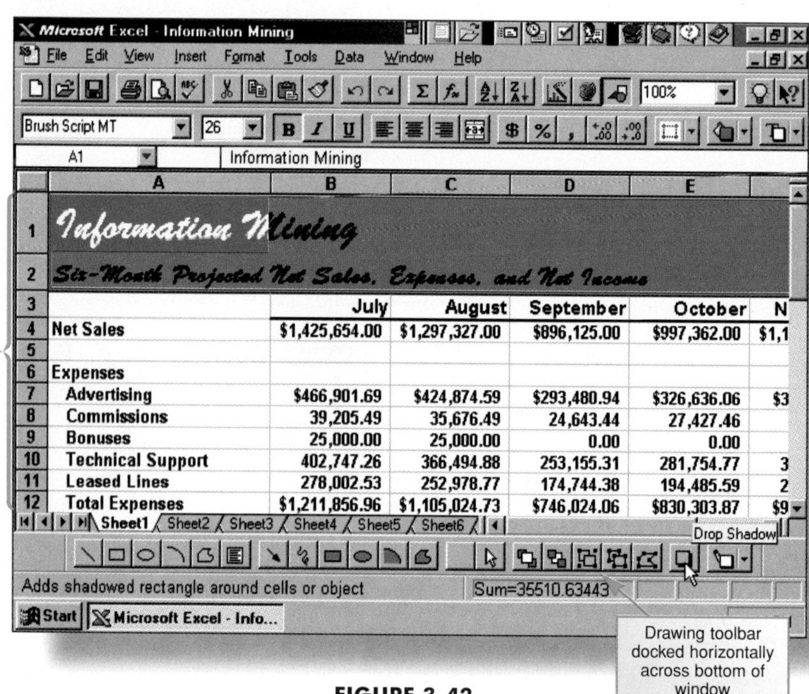

FIGURE 3-42

More About Docking Toolbars

A toolbar button that has a drop-down list box, such as the Pattern button on the far right side of the Drawing toolbar in Figure 3-42, cannot be docked on the left or right edge of the window.

Compare Figure 3-42 to Figure 3-41. Excel resizes the Drawing toolbar automatically to fit across the window and between the scroll bar and status bar. Also, the heavy window border that surrounded the floating toolbar has changed to a light border. To move a toolbar to any of the other three docks, drag the toolbar to the desired edge before releasing the left mouse button.

Adding a Drop Shadow to the Title Area

With the Drawing toolbar at the bottom of the screen, the next step is to add the drop shadow to the selected title area in the range A1:H2.

To Add a Drop Shadow

1 **With the range A1:H2 selected, click the Drop Shadow button on the Drawing toolbar. Click cell A5.**

Excel adds a drop shadow to the range A1:H2 (Figure 3-43).

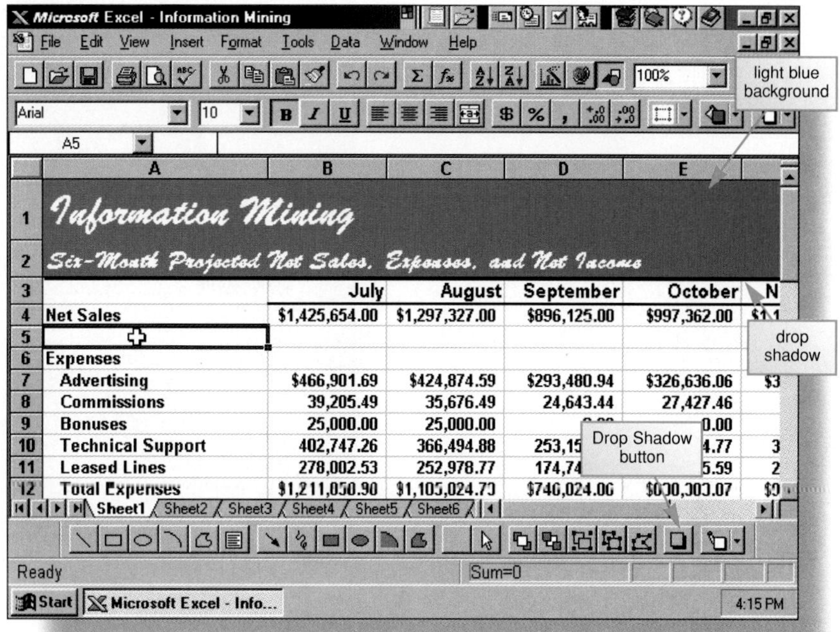

FIGURE 3-43

When you add a drop shadow to a range of cells, Excel also selects the drop shadow and surrounds it with black handles. To deselect the drop shadow, select any cell (cell A5 in Step 1 above)

More About Drop Shadows

To remove an unwanted drop shadow, click it so the handles appear on the drop shadow, and then press the DELETE key. Also, a drop shadow is a shape and not a format. Thus, if you used the Format Painter button to apply formats from a range with a drop shadow, then the drop shadow will not be copied.

Increasing the Height of the Row Containing the Column Headings

Row 3 contains the column headings. The next step is to increase the white space between the worksheet title and the column titles by increasing the height of row 3 to 24.00 points.

TO INCREASE THE HEIGHT OF A ROW

Step 1: Point to the border line between row headings 3 and 4. Drag the mouse down until a height of 24.00 displays in the Name box in the formula bar (Figure 3-44 on the next page).
Step 2: Release the left mouse button.

Excel increases the height of row 3 to 24.00 points (see Figure 3-45 on page E 3.39).

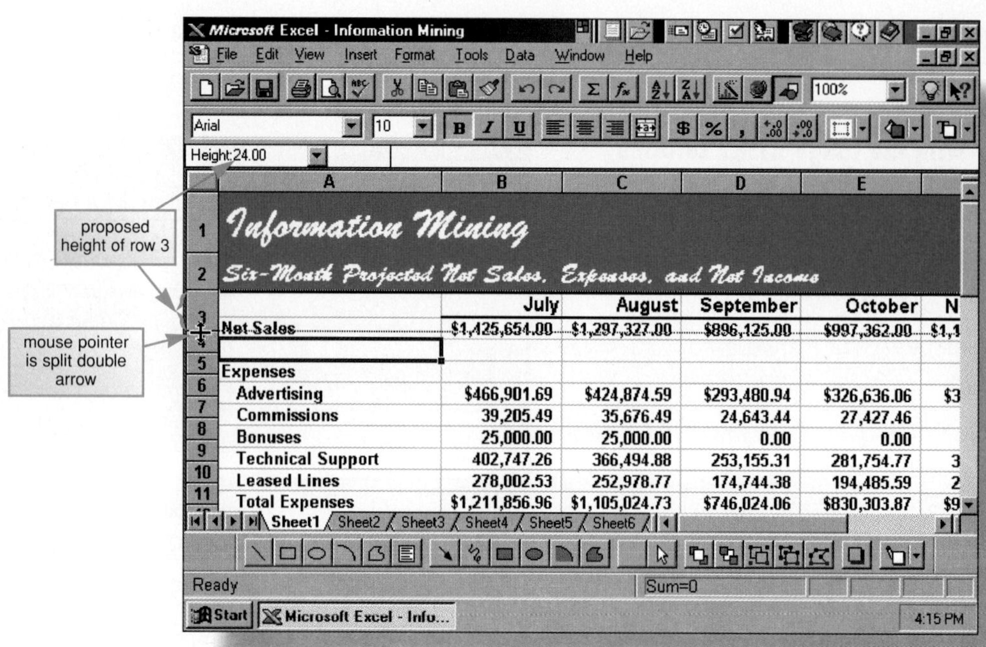

FIGURE 3-44

Formatting the Category Row Titles and Net Income Row

The specifications in Figure 3-33 on page E 3.30 requires a font size of 12 in cells A4, A6, A12, and A13. Also, cells A4, A6, and the range A13:H13 all require the same background color, font color, and drop shadows assigned earlier to the worksheet titles in the range A1:H2. If you look at the Color and Font Color buttons on the formatting toolbar in Figure 3-45 you will notice that the last colors selected and assigned to the worksheet titles are on the buttons. This means that after selecting a range to format, simply click the Color button to assign the light blue background to the range and click the Font Color button to assign the color white to the font in the range. The following steps change the font size in cells A4, A6, A12, and A13, and then add the light blue background color, white font color, and drop shadows to cells A4, A6, and the range A13:H13.

More *About* **Nonadjacent Ranges**

One of the more difficult tasks to learn is selecting nonadjacent ranges. To complete this task, do not hold down the CRTL key when you select the first range because Excel will consider the current active cell to be the first selection. Once the first range is selected, hold down the CRTL key and drag through the ranges. If a desired range is not in the window, use the scroll arrows to move the window over the range. It is not necessary to hold down the CRTL key while you move the window.

To Change Font Size, Add Background and Font Colors, and Add Drop Shadows to Nonadjacent Selections

1 **Click cell A4. Hold down the CTRL key and click cells A6, A12, and A13. Click the Font Size box arrow on the Formatting toolbar and then click 12 in the drop-down list.**

The font size in cells A4, A6, A12, and A13 changes to 12 points.

2 **Click cell A4. Hold down the CTRL key and click cell A6 and select the range A13:H13. Click the Color button to assign the nonadjacent range the light blue background color. Click the Font Color button to change the font to white.**

The nonadjacent ranges are selected and the background and font colors are changed (Figure 3-45).

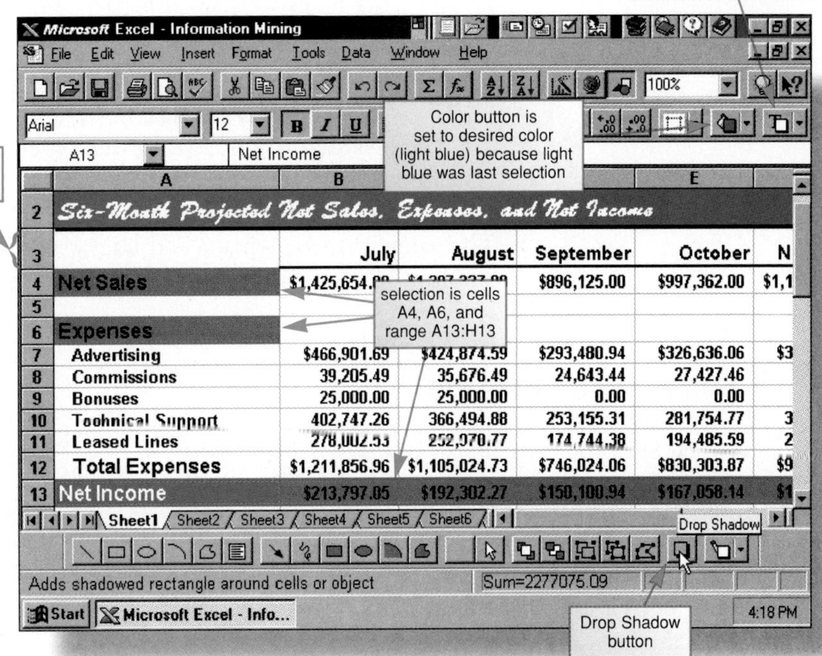

FIGURE 3-45

3 **Click the Drop Shadow button on the Drawing toolbar.**

Excel colors the nonadjacent selection and adds a drop shadow to cells A4, A6, and the range A13:H13. The drop shadow on the range A13:H13 remains selected (Figure 3-46).

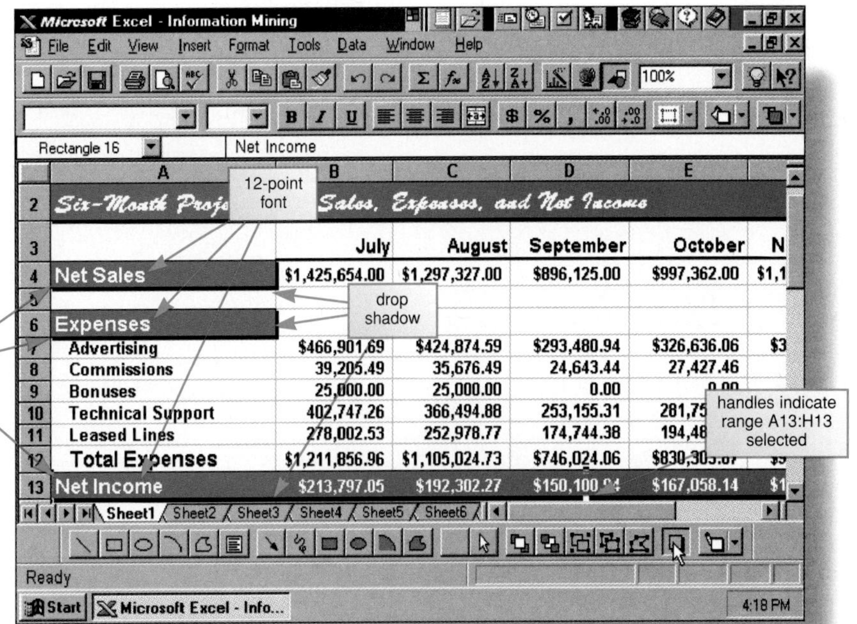

FIGURE 3-46

An alternative to formatting all three areas at once is to select each one separately and apply the formats. Although formatting cell A4 first and then using the Format Painter button on the Standard toolbar may sound like a good idea, the drop shadow is considered a shape and not a format. Thus, Excel would not paint the drop shadow on cell A6 and the range A13:H13. It would paint the background and font colors, however.

Formatting the Assumptions Table

The last step to improving the appearance of the worksheet is to format the Assumptions table in the range A15:B21. The specifications in Figure 3-33 on page E 3.30 require a 16-point italicized underlined font for the title in cell A15. The range A15:B21 has a red background color with a white font and a drop shadow surrounds it. The following steps format the Assumptions table.

To Format the Assumptions Table

1 **Click cell A15. Click the Font Size box arrow on the Formatting toolbar and click 16 point. Click the Italics button and Underline button on the Formatting toolbar.**

The table heading Assumptions displays as shown in Figure 3-47.

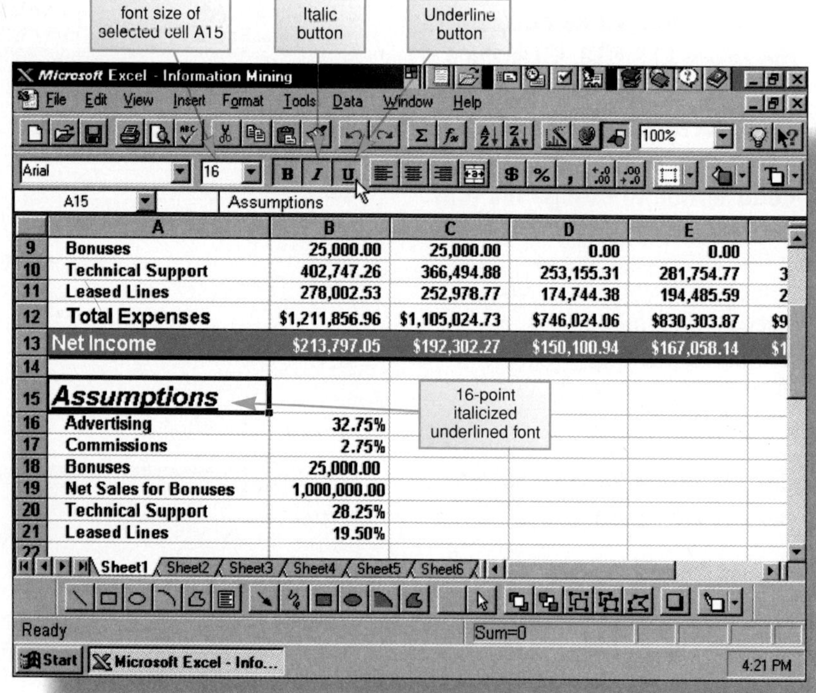

FIGURE 3-47

2 **Select the range A15:B21. Click the Color button arrow on the Formatting toolbar. Point to red (column 3, row 1 on the Color palette).**

The Color palette displays as shown in Figure 3-48.

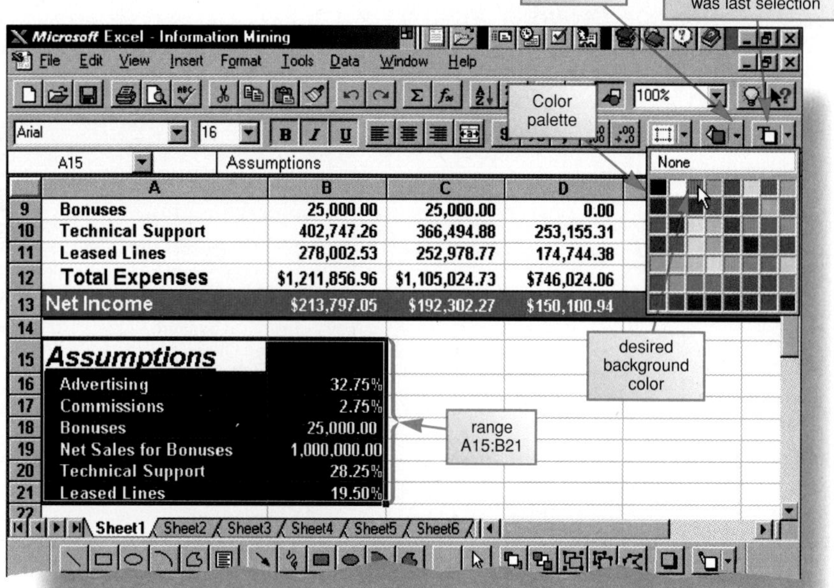

FIGURE 3-48

3 **Click red on the Color palette. Click the Font Color button on the Formatting toolbar.**

The background color of the Assumptions table is red and the font color is white.

4 **Click the Drop Shadow button on the Drawing toolbar. Select cell D21.**

The Assumptions table displays as shown in Figure 3-49.

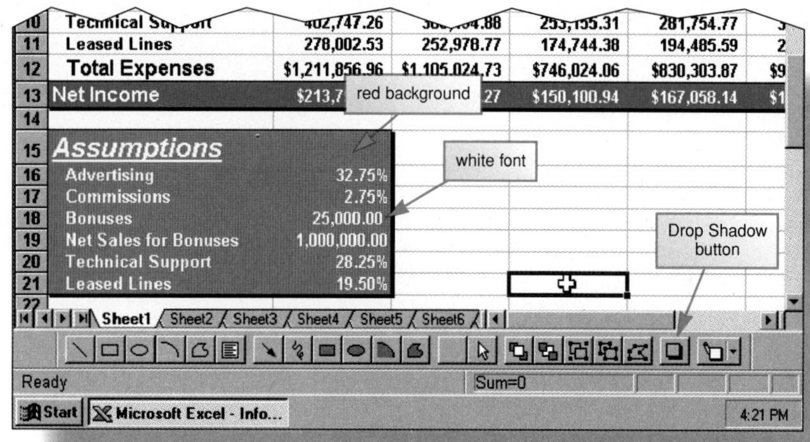

FIGURE 3-49

Notice when you assign the **italic** font style to a cell, Excel slants the characters slightly to the right as shown in cell A15 in Figure 3-49.

Hiding a Toolbar

With the formatting of the worksheet complete, the next step is to hide the Drawing toolbar docked at the bottom of the screen. As shown in the following step, you can hide the Drawing toolbar by clicking the Drawing button on the Standard toolbar.

More *About* Underlines versus Borders

An underline is different from a bottom border. An underline only underlines the characters in a cell. A bottom border encompasses the width of the entire cell and shows whether or not the cell contains characters.

To Hide the Drawing Toolbar

1 **Click the Drawing button on the Standard toolbar.**

The Drawing toolbar is removed from the screen (Figure 3-50).

Drawing button

	A	B	C	D	E
9	Bonuses	25,000.00	25,000.00	0.00	0.00
10	Technical Support	402,747.26	366,494.88	253,155.31	281,754.77
11	Leased Lines	278,002.53	252,978.77	174,744.38	194,485.59
12	Total Expenses	$1,211,856.96	$1,105,024.73	$746,024.06	$830,303.87
13	Net Income	$213,797.05	$192,302.27	$150,100.94	$167,058.14
14					
15	Assumptions				
16	Advertising	32.75%			
17	Commissions	2.75%			
18	Bonuses	25,000.00			
19	Net Sales for Bonuses	1,000,000.00			
20	Technical Support	28.25%			
21	Leased Lines	19.50%			

Drawing toolbar disappears

FIGURE 3-50

OtherWays

1. Drag docked toolbar onto screen, click its Close box
2. On View menu click Toolbars, click check box of toolbar to hide, click OK button
3. Right-click toolbar to hide, click its name on shortcut menu

The worksheet is complete. Before moving on to create the 3-D column chart, save the workbook by clicking the Save button on the Standard toolbar.

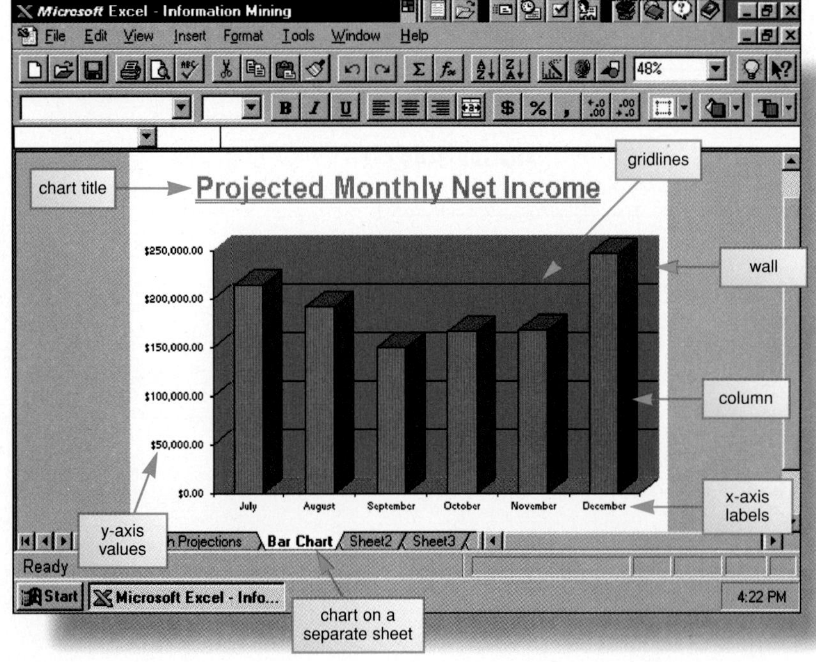

FIGURE 3-51

Creating a 3-D Column Chart on a Chart Sheet

The next step in this project is to draw the three-dimensional column chart shown in Figure 3-51. A **column chart** is used to show trends and comparisons. Each column emphasizes the magnitude of the value it represents. The column chart in Figure 3-51 compares the projected net income for each of the six months. It is easy to see from the column chart that December has the greatest projected net income.

The column chart in Figure 3-51 differs from the one in Project 1 in that it is not embedded in the worksheet. Rather, it is created on a separate chart sheet as was the pie chart in Project 2.

The ranges of the worksheet to graph are B3:G3 and B13:G13 (Figure 3-52). The month names in the range B3:G3 identify the columns and show at the bottom of the column chart. The month names in the range B3:G3 are called category names. The range B13:G13 contains the data that determines the magnitude of the columns. The values in the range are called the data series. Because six category names and six numbers are included in the data series, the column chart contains six columns.

Drawing the 3-D Column Chart

In Project 1, you used the ChartWizard button on the Standard toolbar to draw an embedded 3-D column chart. **Embedded** means the chart is on the same sheet with the worksheet. Anytime you want to create an embedded chart, the ChartWizard button is the best choice. To create a chart on a separate sheet, use the Chart command on the Insert menu as you did in Project 2 to create the pie chart. This command takes you into the ChartWizard, but first asks you if you want to create the chart on the same sheet or a separate sheet.

The following steps illustrate how to create a 3-D column chart on a separate sheet.

More About the Zoom Control Box

The chart size in Figure 3-51 is only 48% of the actual printed size. If you want to increase the size on the screen, click the Zoom Control box arrow on the Standard toolbar and click one of the larger percents. You can also type a percent in the Zoom Control box. Once you get the chart built in this project, try zooming to 75%, 100%, 200%, and Selection (default size).

To Draw a 3-D Column Chart on a Chart Sheet

1 Select the range B3:G3. Hold down the CTRL key and select the nonadjacent range B13:G13. Click Chart on the Insert menu. Point to As New Sheet on the Chart submenu.

Excel displays the Chart submenu, which allows you to choose where in the workbook you want to create the chart (Figure 3-52).

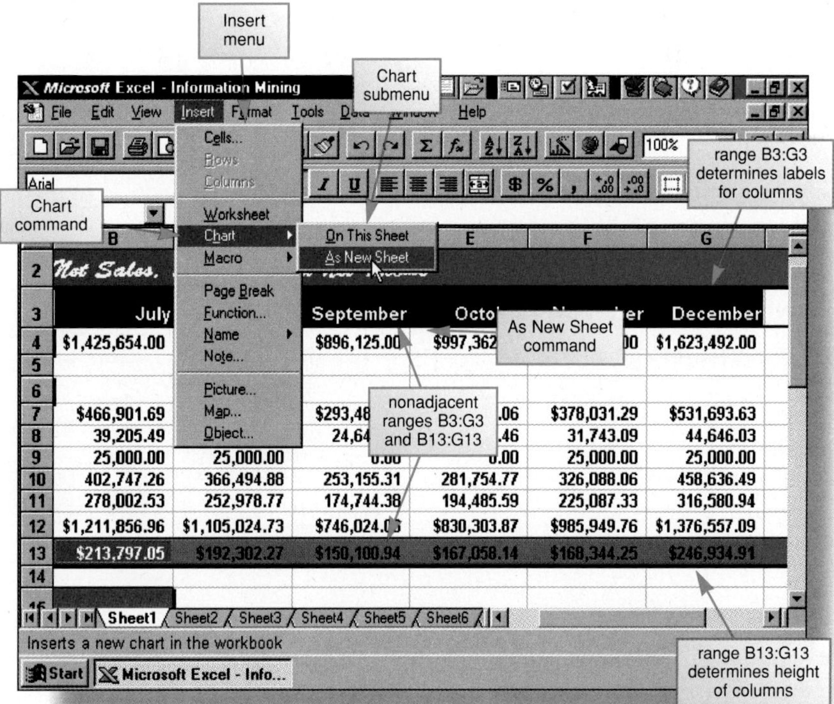

FIGURE 3-52

2 **Click As New Sheet on the Chart submenu.**

Excel displays the ChartWizard - Step 1 of 5 dialog box, which displays the selected range in the worksheet (Figure 3-53). You can type a new range or use the mouse to change the range in the worksheet if you decide you want to alter your original selection.

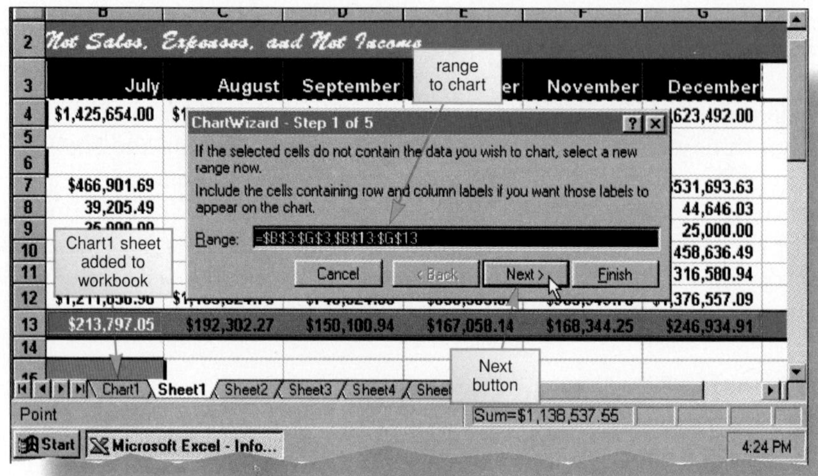

FIGURE 3-53

3 **Click the Next button. Select 3-D Column in the ChartWizard - Step 2 of 5 dialog box (Figure 3-54).**

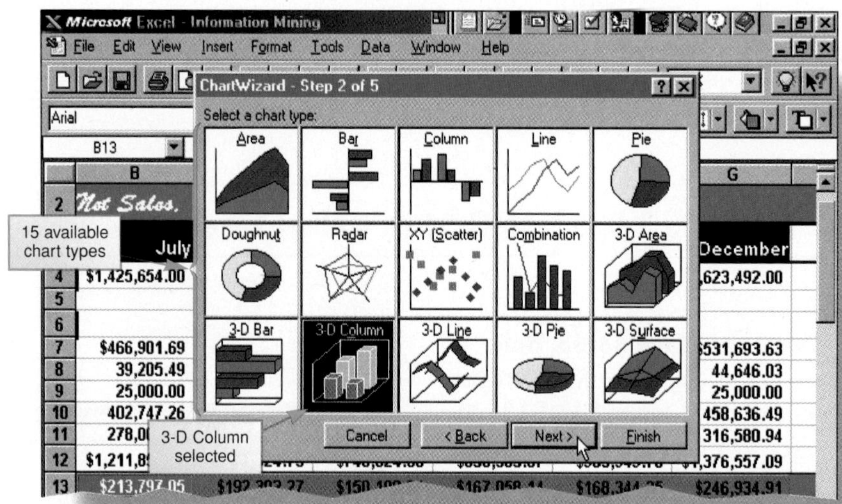

FIGURE 3-54

4 **Click the Next button. Select format 4 for the chart.**

The ChartWizard - Step 3 of 5 dialog box displays with a selection of eight different 3-D Column chart formats (Figure 3-55).

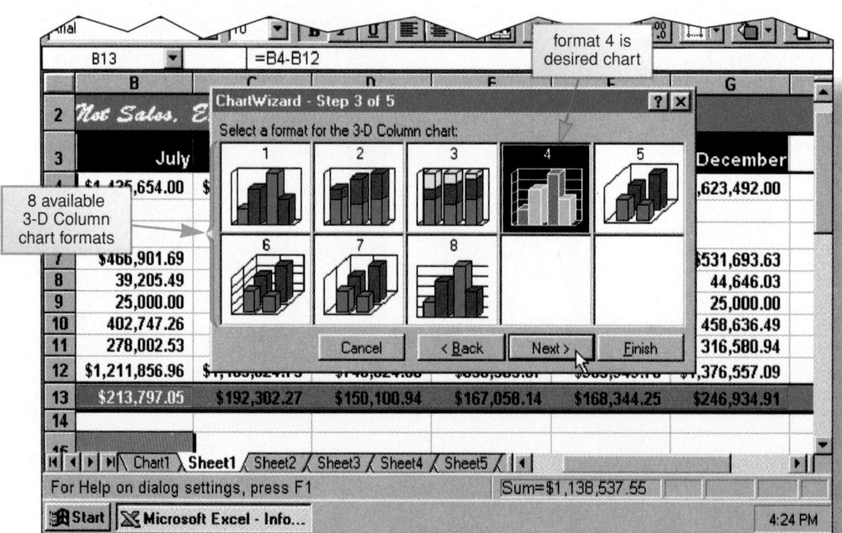

FIGURE 3-55

5 **Click the Next button.**

The ChartWizard - Step 4 of 5 dialog box displays with a sample of the 3-D column chart. (Figure 3-56).

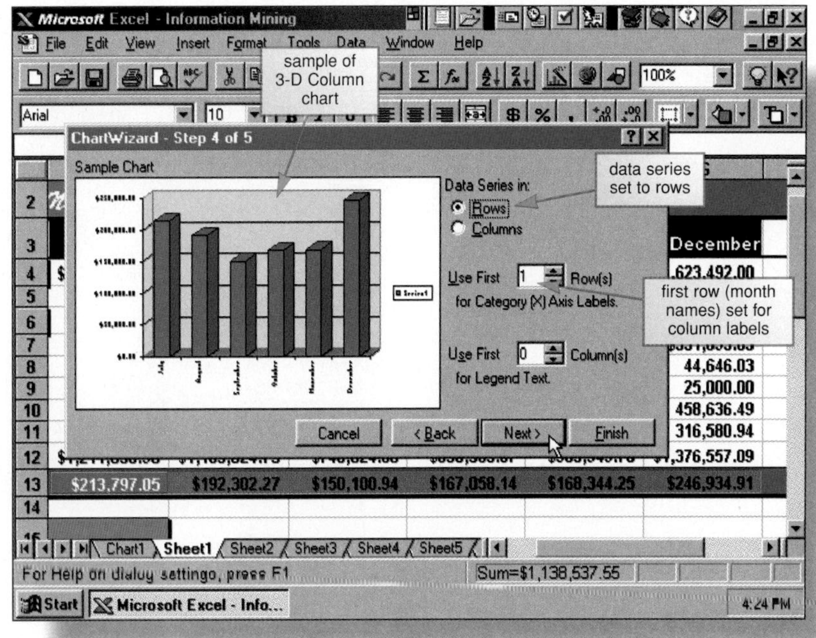

FIGURE 3-56

6 **Click the Next button. Click No under Add a Legend? Click the Chart Title box. Type** `Projected Monthly Net Income` **in the Chart Title box.**

The ChartWizard - Step 5 of 5 dialog box displays. You have the opportunity in this dialog box to add a chart title, y-axis title, x-axis title, and select whether or not you want legends to display alongside the chart. Excel changes the sample chart dynamically in the dialog box as you enter titles (Figure 3-57).

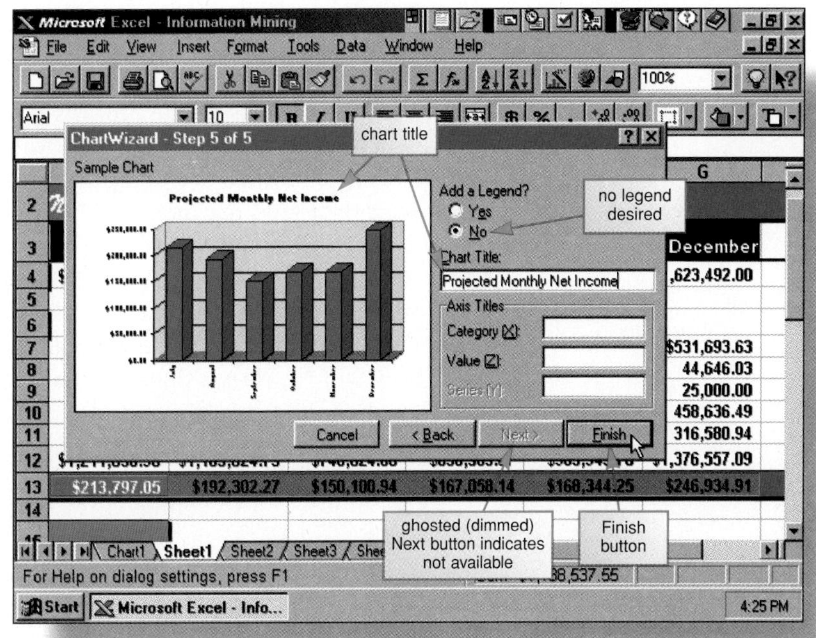

FIGURE 3-57

7 **Click the Finish button.**

Excel displays the 3-D column chart on a separate sheet (Figure 3-58).

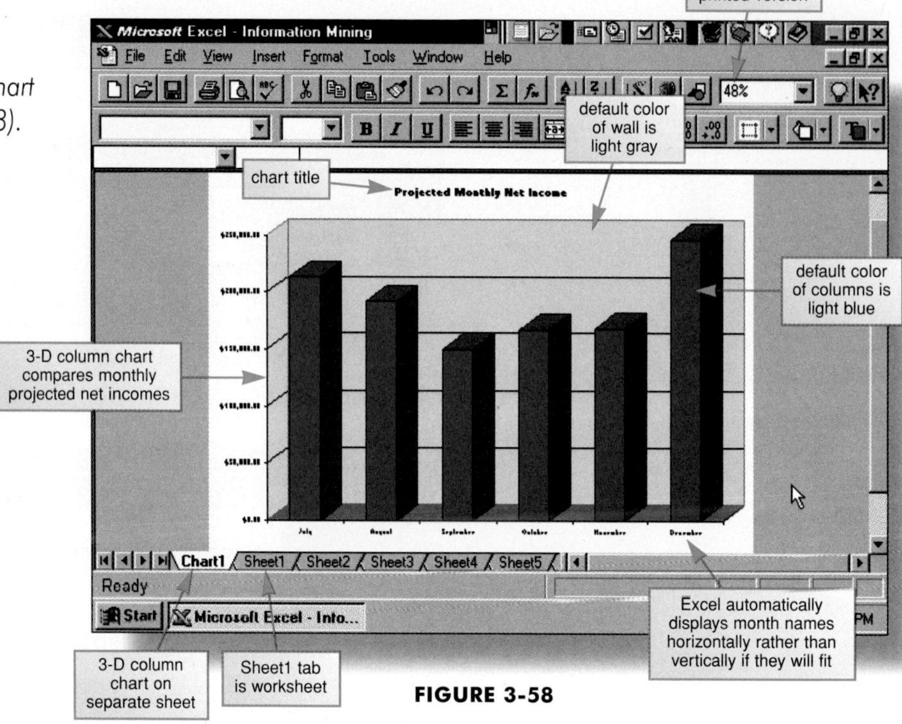

FIGURE 3-58

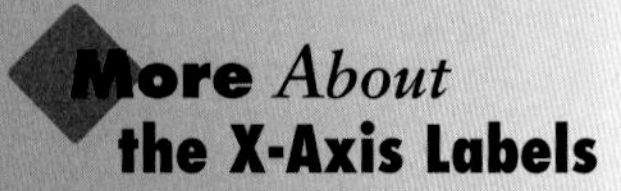

More *About* **the X-Axis Labels**

If the labels along the x-axis display vertically (see sample chart in Figure 3-57) rather than horizontally (Figure 3-58), reduce their font size by right-clicking one of the labels and clicking Format Axis. Remember, what you see on the screen is reduced by over 50% of the printed version.

Each column in the chart in Figure 3-58 represents one of the last six months of the year. The names of the months (range B3:G3) display below the corresponding columns on the x-axis. The values along the y-axis (the vertical line to the left of the columns) are determined automatically by Excel from the highest and lowest projected net incomes in the range B13:G13 of the worksheet.

In the five ChartWizard dialog boxes (Figures 3-53 through 3-57) you can return to the previous ChartWizard dialog box by clicking the Back button.

If you compare the sample chart in Figure 3-57 and the chart in Figure 3-58, you will notice that Excel automatically displays the month names horizontally when they will fit, rather than vertically as shown in Figure 3-57.

Enhancing the 3-D Column Chart

Excel allows you to change any chart item labeled in Figure 3-51 on page E 3.42. All you have to do is double-click the chart item you want to change and Excel displays a dialog box containing the changeable characteristics. To change the 3-D column chart in Figure 3-58 so it looks like the one in Figure 3-51, the following changes must be made:

1. Chart title — increase font size to 36-point, double underline, change the font color to red
2. Columns — change color to red
3. Wall — change color to light blue
4. Data labels – increase font size from 10- to 12-point

More *About* **Charting**

Press the ESC key to deselect a chart item.

Perform the following steps to enhance the 3-D column chart.

To Enhance the 3-D Column Chart

1 Right-click the chart title. Point to Format Chart Title on the shortcut menu.

Black handles and a gray rectangle surround the chart title, and Excel displays a shortcut menu (Figure 3-59).

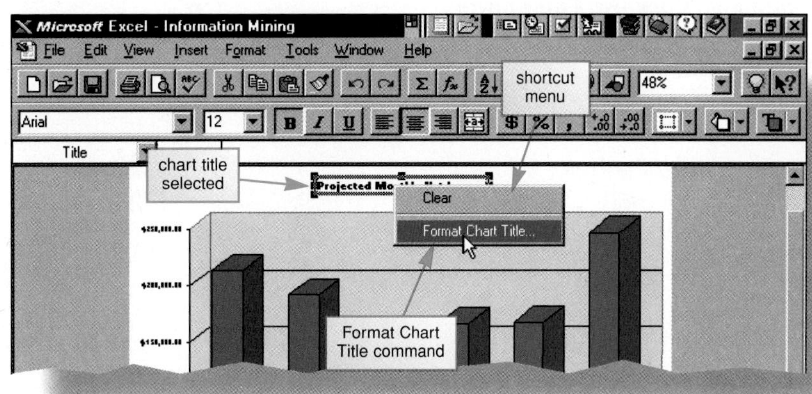

FIGURE 3-59

2 Click Format Chart Title on the shortcut menu. When the Format Chart Title dialog box displays, click the Font tab. Click 36 in the Size box, click the Underline box arrow and click Double, and click the Color box arrow and select red (column 3, row 1 on the Color palette).

The Format Chart Title dialog box displays as shown in Figure 3-60.

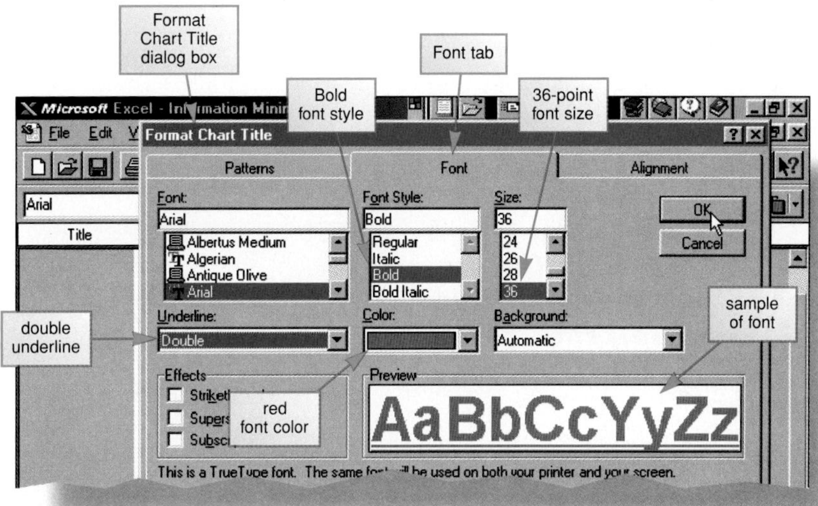

FIGURE 3-60

3 Click the OK button. Click one of the six columns in the chart. Click the Color button arrow on the Formatting toolbar.

Excel displays the formatted chart title. Handles appear at the corner points of the six columns and the Color palette displays (Figure 3-61).

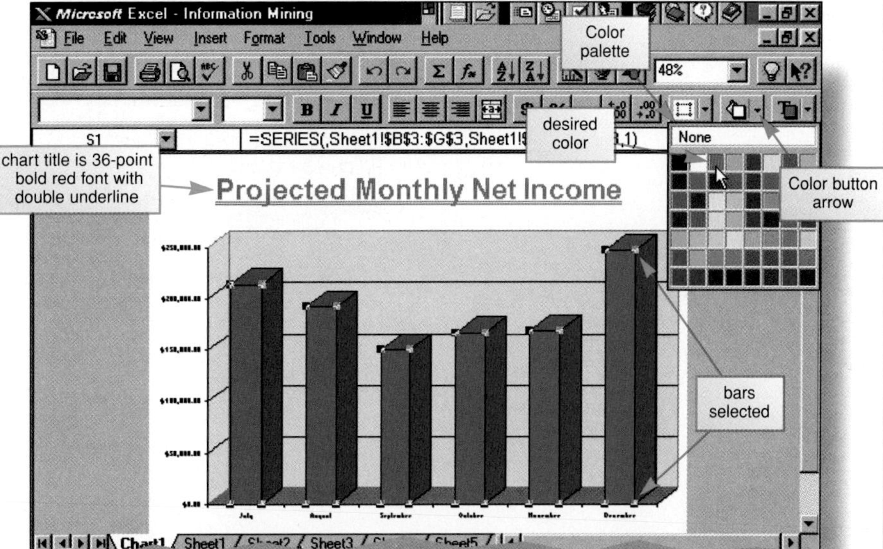

FIGURE 3-61

4 **Click red (column 3, row 1 on the Color palette). Click the wall (not the gridlines) behind the columns. Click the Color button arrow on the Formatting toolbar.**

The color of the columns are changed to red, the walls are selected, and the Color palette displays (Figure 3-62).

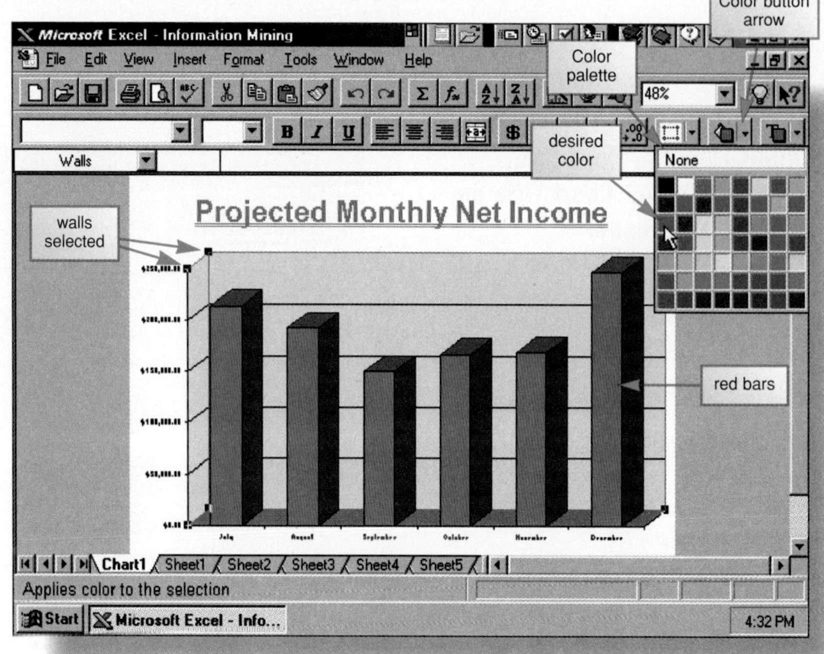

FIGURE 3-62

5 **Click light blue (column 1, row 3 on the Color palette). Click one of the labels on the y-axis. Click the Font size box arrow. Point to 12 in the Font Size drop-down list box.**

The color of the walls behind the columns changes to light blue. The vertical axis has black handles on its endpoints. The Font Size drop-down list box displays (Figure 3-63).

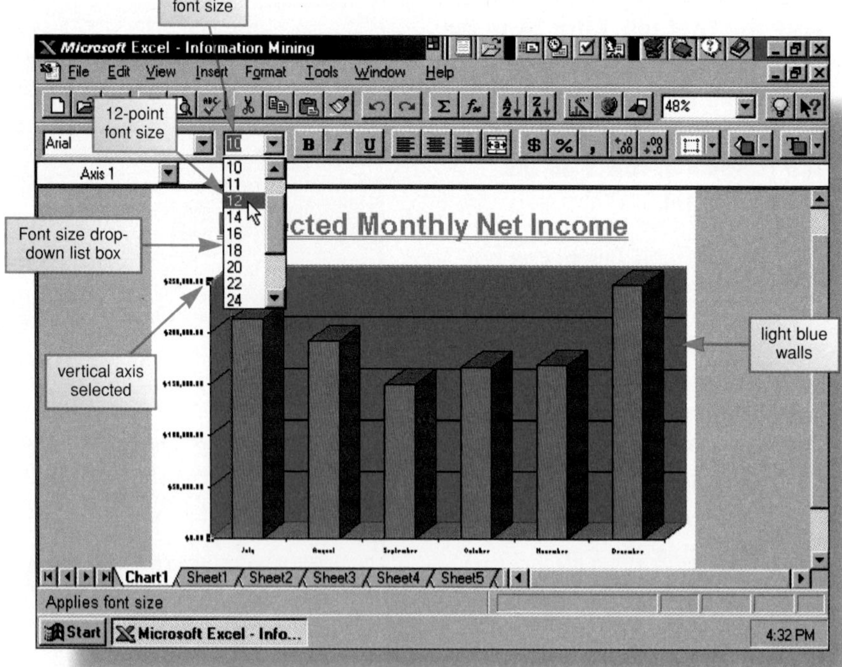

FIGURE 3-63

6 **Click 12 in the Font Size drop-down list box. Click one of the month names on the x-axis. Click the Font Size box arrow. Click 12 in the Font Size drop-down list box.**

The enhanced 3-D column chart displays as shown in Figure 3-64.

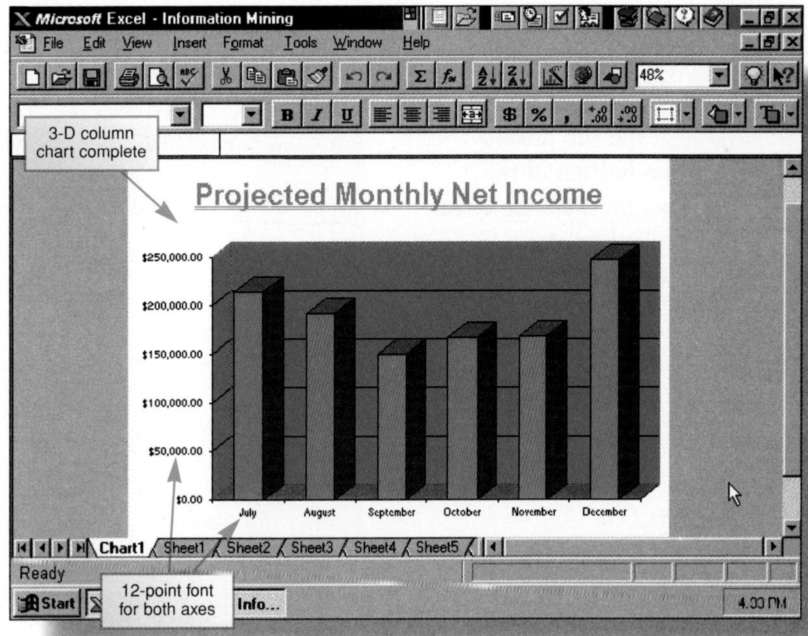

FIGURE 3-64

Other Ways

1. Double-click any chart item to display a dialog box , format item
2. Click chart item, apply formats using Formatting toolbar

Compare the chart title in Figure 3-58 on page E 3.46 to the one in Figure 3-64. You can see that the chart title stands out after being formatted. One of the drawbacks to increasing the font size of the chart title is that Excel decreases the size of the chart itself to make room for the larger font. You can select the chart, however, and increase its size if you so desire.

Changing the Name of the Sheet Tabs and Rearranging the Order of the Sheets

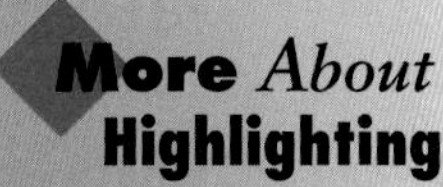

More About Highlighting

You can use the Text Box button on the Drawing toolbar to add text to highlight parts of a worksheet or chart.

The final step in creating the worksheet and 3-D column chart in Project 3 is to change the names of the tabs at the bottom of the screen. The steps on the next page show you how to rename the sheet tabs and reorder the sheets so the worksheet comes before the chart sheet.

Steps To Rename the Sheet Tabs and Rearrange the Order of the Sheets

1. **Double-click the tab named Chart1 at the bottom of the screen. When the Rename Sheet dialog box displays, type** `Bar Chart` **as shown in Figure 3-65.**

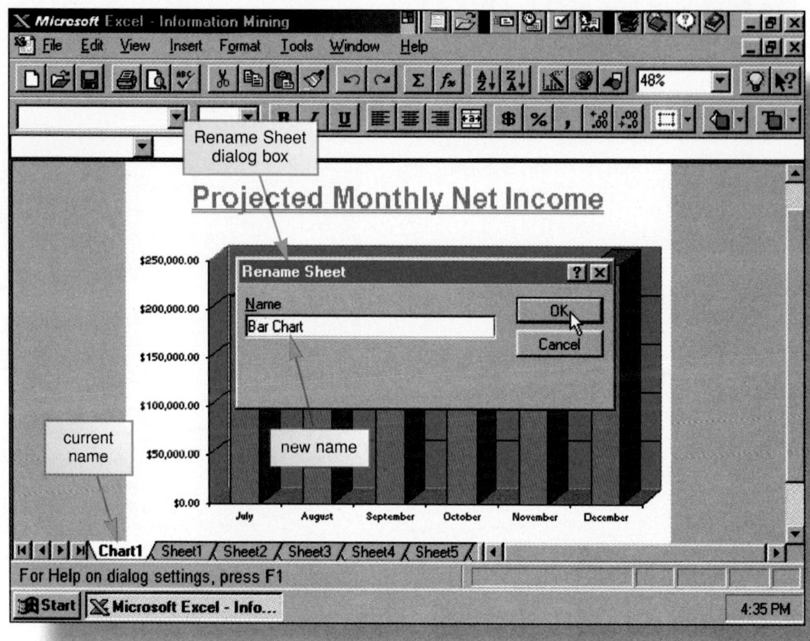

FIGURE 3-65

2. **Click the OK button in the Rename Sheet dialog box.**

3. **Repeat Steps 1 and 2 for the Sheet1 tab. Type** `Six-Month Projections` **for the tab name.**

4. **Drag the Six-Month Projections tab to the left over the Bar Chart tab.**

Excel rearranges the sequence of the sheets and displays the worksheet (Figure 3-66).

Information Mining
Six-Month Projected Net Sales, Expenses, and Net Income

		July	August	September	October	N
3		July	August	September	October	N
4	Net Sales	$1,425,654.00	$1,297,327.00	$896,125.00	$997,362.00	$1,1
7			$424,874.59	$293,480.94	$326,636.06	$3
8			35,676.49	24,643.44	27,427.46	
9			25,000.00	0.00	0.00	
10	Technical Support	402,747.26	366,494.88	253,155.31	281,754.77	3
11	Leased Lines	278,002.53	252,978.77	174,744.38	194,485.59	2
12	Total Expenses	$1,211,856.96	$1,105,024.73	$746,024.06	$830,303.87	$9

Sheet1 renamed Six-Month Projections and moved ahead of Bar Chart tab

Chart1 tab renamed Bar Chart

Six-Month Projections / Bar Chart / Sheet2 / Sheet3

Ready Sum=0

Start Microsoft Excel - Info... 4:36 PM

FIGURE 3-66

OtherWays

1. Right-click sheet tab, click Rename
2. Right-click sheet tab, click Move or Copy
3. On Edit menu click Move or Copy

Checking Spelling, Saving, Previewing, and Printing the Workbook

With the workbook complete, the next series of steps is to check spelling, save, preview, and print the workbook. Each series of steps concludes with saving the workbook to ensure the latest changes are saved to disk.

Checking Spelling of Multiple Sheets

The spell checker checks the spelling of only the selected sheets. Thus, before checking the spelling, hold down the CTRL key and click the Bar Chart tab as described in the following steps.

TO CHECK SPELLING OF MULTIPLE SHEETS

Step 1: With the Six-Month Projections sheet active, hold down the CTRL key and click the Bar Chart tab.
Step 2: Click the spelling button on the Standard toolbar. Correct any errors.
Step 3: Click the Save button on the Standard toolbar.

Previewing and Printing the Workbook

With the worksheet and chart complete, the next step is to preview and print them. Recall that Excel only previews and prints selected sheets. Because the worksheet is too wide to print in portrait, you must change the orientation to landscape.

TO PREVIEW AND PRINT THE WORKBOOK IN LANDSCAPE ORIENTATION

Step 1: If both sheets are not selected, select the inactive one by holding down the CTRL key and clicking the tab of the inactive sheet.
Step 2: Right-click the menu bar, click Page Setup, click the Page tab, click the Landscape option button, click the OK button.
Step 3: Click the Print Preview button on the Standard toolbar. When you are finished previewing, click the Close button.
Step 4: Ready the printer.
Step 5: Click the Print button on the Standard toolbar.
Step 6: Right-click the Six-Month Projections tab. Click Ungroup Sheets on the shortcut menu to deselect the Bar Chart tab.
Step 7: Click the Save button on the Standard toolbar.

The worksheet and bar chart print as shown in Figure 3-67 on the next page.

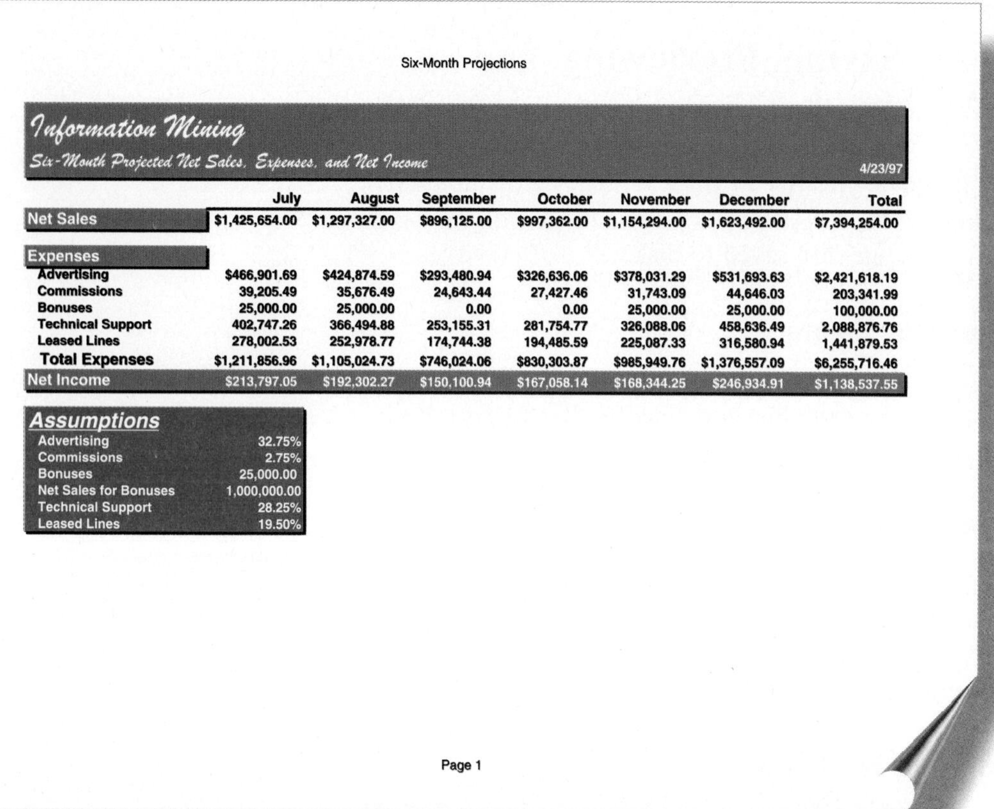

Six-Month Projections

Information Mining

Six-Month Projected Net Sales, Expenses, and Net Income

4/23/97

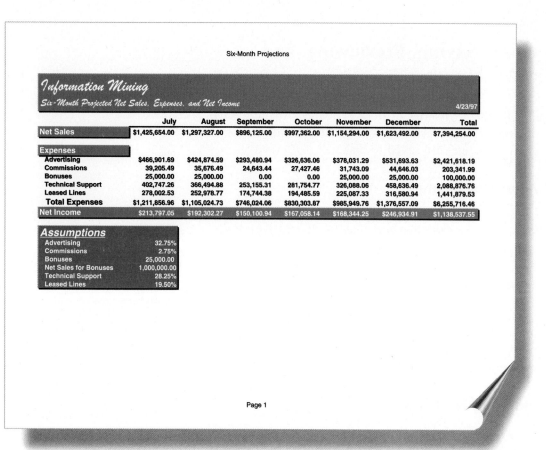

	July	August	September	October	November	December	Total
Net Sales	$1,425,654.00	$1,297,327.00	$896,125.00	$997,362.00	$1,154,294.00	$1,623,492.00	$7,394,254.00
Expenses							
Advertising	$466,901.69	$424,874.59	$293,480.94	$326,636.06	$378,031.29	$531,693.63	$2,421,618.19
Commissions	39,205.49	35,676.49	24,643.44	27,427.46	31,743.09	44,646.03	203,341.99
Bonuses	25,000.00	25,000.00	0.00	0.00	25,000.00	25,000.00	100,000.00
Technical Support	402,747.26	366,494.88	253,155.31	281,754.77	326,088.06	458,636.49	2,088,876.76
Leased Lines	278,002.53	252,978.77	174,744.38	194,485.59	225,087.33	316,580.94	1,441,879.53
Total Expenses	$1,211,856.96	$1,105,024.73	$746,024.06	$830,303.87	$985,949.76	$1,376,557.09	$6,255,716.46
Net Income	$213,797.05	$192,302.27	$150,100.94	$167,058.14	$168,344.25	$246,934.91	$1,138,537.55

Assumptions	
Advertising	32.75%
Commissions	2.75%
Bonuses	25,000.00
Net Sales for Bonuses	1,000,000.00
Technical Support	28.25%
Leased Lines	19.50%

Page 1

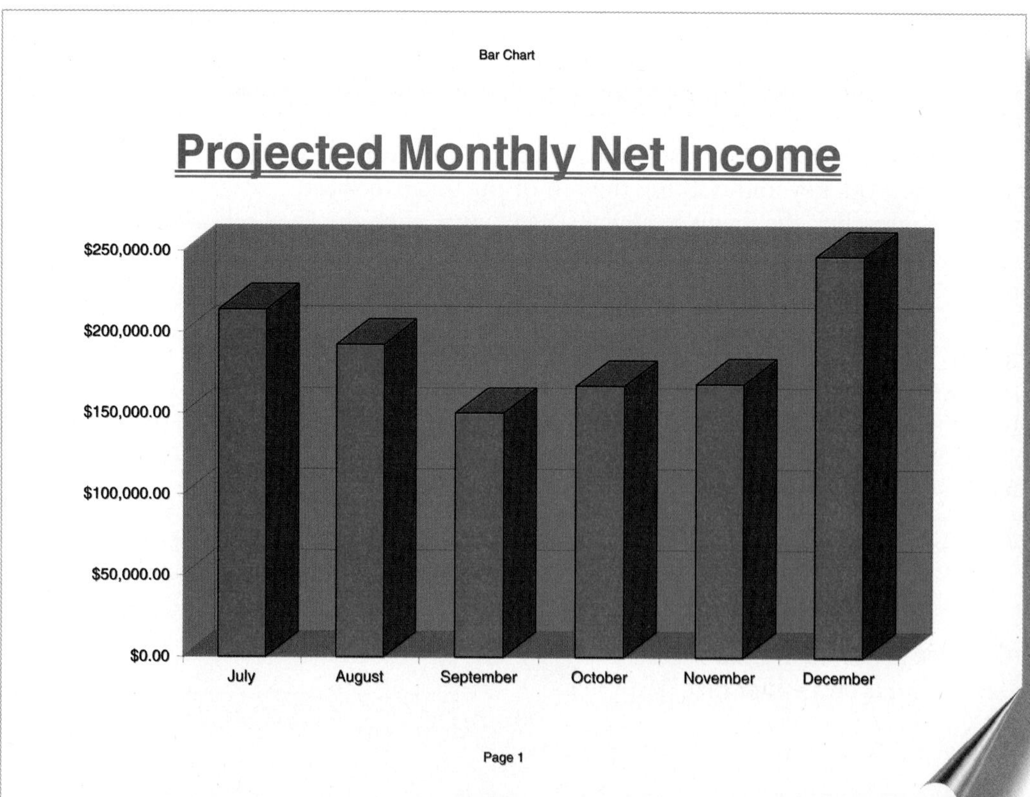

FIGURE 3-67

Changing the View of the Worksheet

With Excel, you can easily change the view of the worksheet. For example, you can magnify or shrink the worksheet on the screen. You can also view different parts of the worksheet through **window panes**.

Shrinking and Magnifying the View of a Worksheet or Chart

You can magnify (zoom in) or shrink (zoom out) the display of a worksheet or chart by using the **Zoom Control box** on the Standard toolbar. When you magnify a worksheet, the characters on the screen become large and fewer columns and rows display. Alternatively, when you shrink a worksheet, more columns and rows display. Magnifying or shrinking a worksheet affects only the view; it does not change the window size or printout of the worksheet or chart. Perform the following steps to shrink and magnify the view of the worksheet.

More About Zooming

You can type any number between 10 and 400 in the Zoom Control box on the Standard toolbar.

Steps: To Shrink and Magnify the Display of a Worksheet or Chart

1. **Click the Zoom Control box arrow on the Standard toolbar.**

   A drop-down list of percentages displays (Figure 3-68).

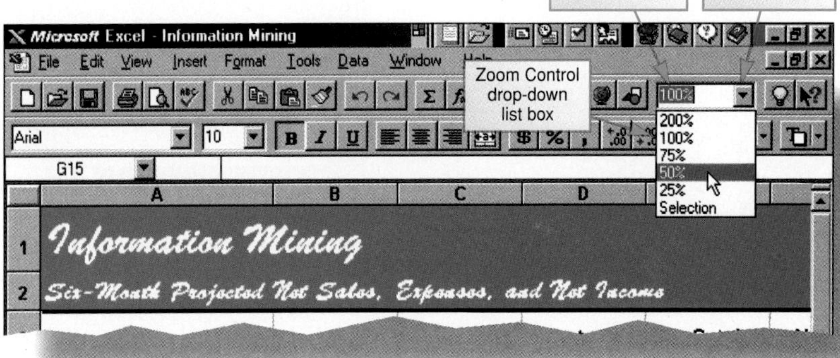

FIGURE 3-68

2. **Click 50% in the drop-down list.**

   Excel shrinks the display of the worksheet to a magnification of 50% of its normal display (Figure 3-69). With the worksheet zoomed to 50%, you can see more rows and columns than you did at 100% magnification.

3. **Click the Zoom Control box arrow on the Standard toolbar and then click 100%.**

   Excel returns to a normal display.

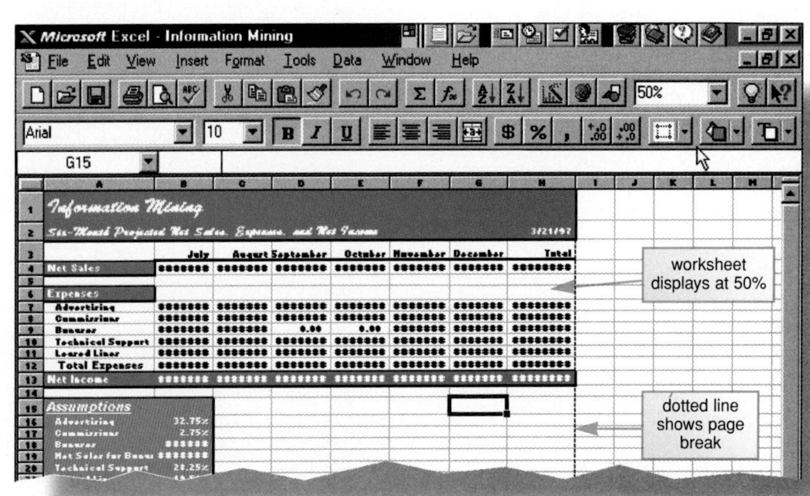

FIGURE 3-69

Other Ways

1. On View menu click Zoom, click desired magnification, click OK button

Notice in Figure 3-69 on the previous page how you get a better view of the page breaks (dotted lines) when you shrink the display of the worksheet. Depending on the type of printer you have, you can end up with the dotted lines representing the page breaks at different locations on the worksheet.

Splitting the Window into Panes

In Excel, you can split the window into two or four window panes and view different parts of a large worksheet at the same time. To split the window into four panes, select the cell where you want the four panes to intersect. Next, click the **Split command** on the Window menu. Follow the steps below to split the window into four panes.

To Split a Window into Four Panes

1. **Click cell D5, the intersection of the proposed four panes. Click Window on the menu bar and then point to Split.**

   The Window menu displays as shown in Figure 3-70.

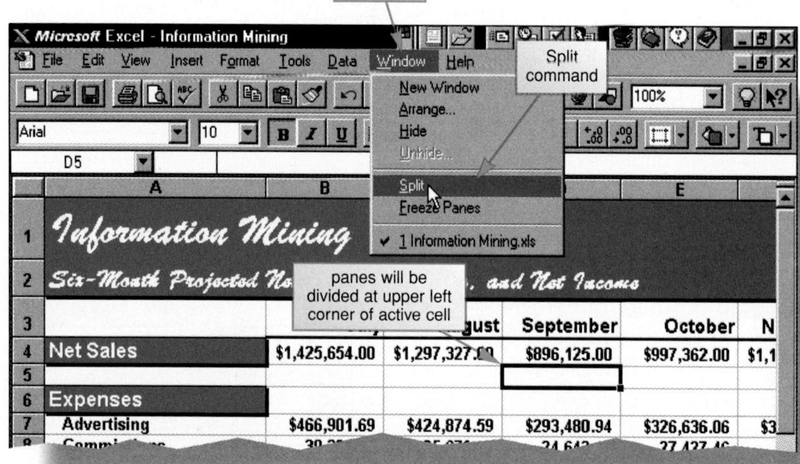

FIGURE 3-70

2. **Click Split on the Window menu. Use the scroll arrows to display the four corners of the worksheet.**

   Excel divides the window into four panes and the four corners of the worksheet display (Figure 3-71).

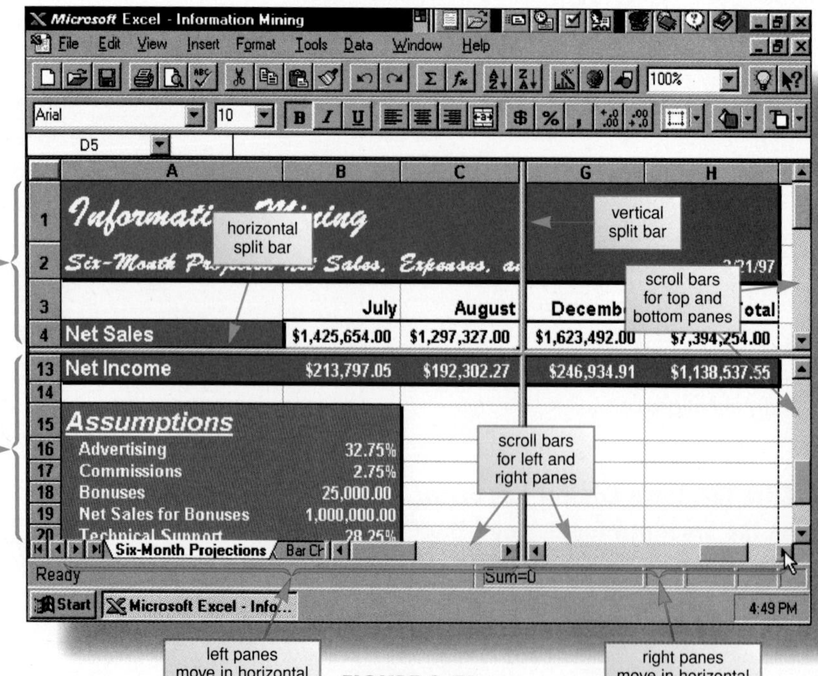

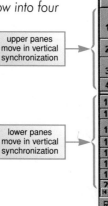

FIGURE 3-71

OtherWays

1. Drag horizontal split box and vertical split box to desired locations

The four panes in Figure 3-71 are used to display the following: (1) the upper left pane displays the range A1:C4; (2) the upper right pane displays the range G1:H4; (3) the lower left pane displays A13:C20; and (4) the lower right pane displays the range G13:H20.

The vertical bar going up and down the middle of the window is called the **vertical split bar**. The horizontal bar going across the middle of the window is called the **horizontal split bar**. If you look closely at the scroll bars below the window and to the right of the window, you will see that the panes split by the horizontal split bar scroll together vertically. The panes split by the vertical split bar scroll together horizontally. To resize the panes, drag either split bar to the desired location in the window.

You can change the values of cells in any of the four panes. Any change you make in one pane also takes effect in the other panes.

To remove one of the split bars from the window, drag the split box to the edge of the window or double-click the split bar. Follow these steps to remove both split bars.

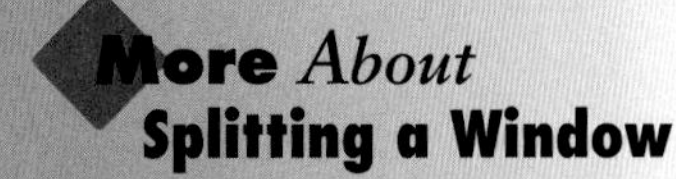

More About Splitting a Window

If you want to split the window into two panes, rather than four, drag the vertical split box or horizontal split box (Figure 3-72 on the next page) to the desired location.

TO REMOVE THE FOUR PANES FROM THE WINDOW

Step 1: Position the mouse pointer at the intersection of the horizontal and vertical split bars.

Step 2: Double-click the split four-headed arrow.

Excel removes the four panes from the window.

What-If Analysis

The automatic recalculation feature of Excel is a powerful tool that can be used to analyze worksheet data. Recall in the Case Perspective on page E 3.4 the problem Marissa Gold had when members of the board of directors suggested she change her assumptions to generate new projections. Because she had to perform this task manually, it took her several minutes. The recalculations then rendered her chart useless.

Using Excel to scrutinize the impact of changing values in cells that are referenced by a formula in another cell is called **what-if analysis** or **sensitivity analysis**. Not only does Excel recalculate all formulas in a worksheet when new data is entered, it also redraws any associated charts.

In Project 3, the projected monthly expenses and net incomes in the range A7:G13 are dependent on the **assumptions** in the range A15:B21. Thus, if you change any of the assumptions, Excel immediately recalculates the projected monthly expenses in rows 7 through 12 and the projected monthly net incomes in row 13. Finally, because the projected monthly net incomes in row 13 change, Excel redraws the 3-D column chart, which is based on these numbers.

More About What-If Analysis

Worksheets are the ultimate tool for what-if-analysis. You enter values into key cells, such as B16:B21 in the Assumptions table, and then see what happens to the dependent cells. Besides manually changing assumptions in a worksheet, Excel has additional methods for answering what-if questions, including Goal Seeking, Solver, Pivot Tables, Scenario Manager, and the Analysis ToolPak.

A what-if question for the worksheet in Project 3 might be, What if the first three assumptions in the range A15:B21 are changed as follows: Advertising 32.75% to 25.00%; Commissions 2.75% to 1.25%; Bonuses $25,000.00 to $10,000.00 — how would these changes affect the projected six-month net income in cell H13? To answer questions like this, you need only change the first three values in the assumptions table. Excel immediately answers the question regarding the projected six-month net income in cell H13 by instantaneously recalculating the worksheet and redrawing the 3-D column chart.

The following steps change the first three assumptions as indicated in the previous paragraph and determine the new projected six-month net income in cell H13. To ensure that the Assumptions table (range A15:B21) and the projected six-month net income in cell H13 show on the screen at the same time, the following steps also divide the window into two vertical panes.

Steps To Analyze Data in a Worksheet by Changing Values

1 **Use the vertical scroll bar to move the window so cell A4 is in the upper left corner of the screen.**

2 **Drag the vertical split box from the lower right corner of the screen so that the vertical split bar is positioned immediately to the right of column D. Use the right scroll arrow in the right pane to display the totals in column H.**

Excel divides the window into two vertical panes and shows the totals in column H in the pane on the right side of the window (Figure 3-72).

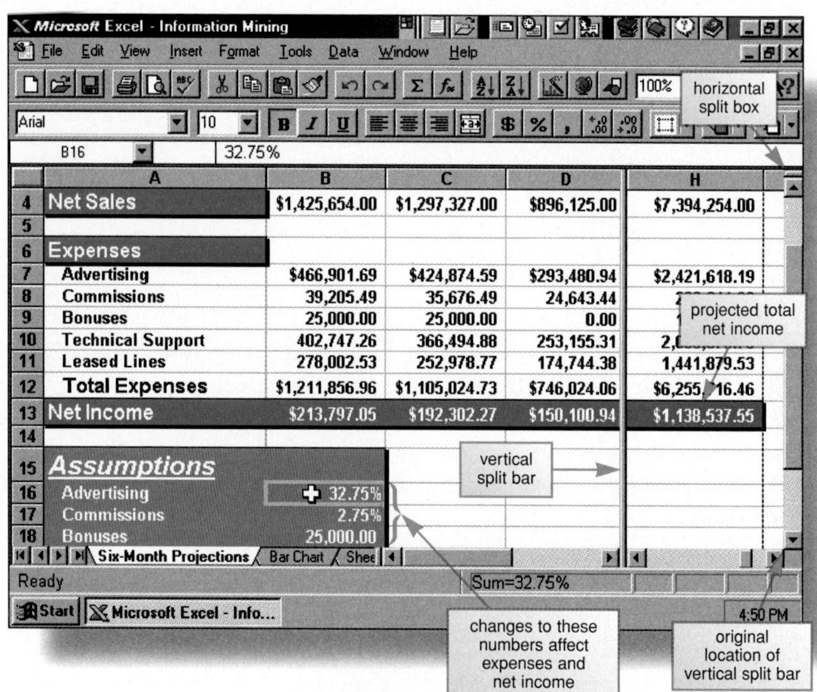

FIGURE 3-72

3 **Enter** 25.00% **in cell B16,** 1.25% **in cell B17,** 10000 **in cell B18.**

Excel immediately recalculates all the formulas in the worksheet, including the projected six-month net income in cell H13 (Figure 3-73).

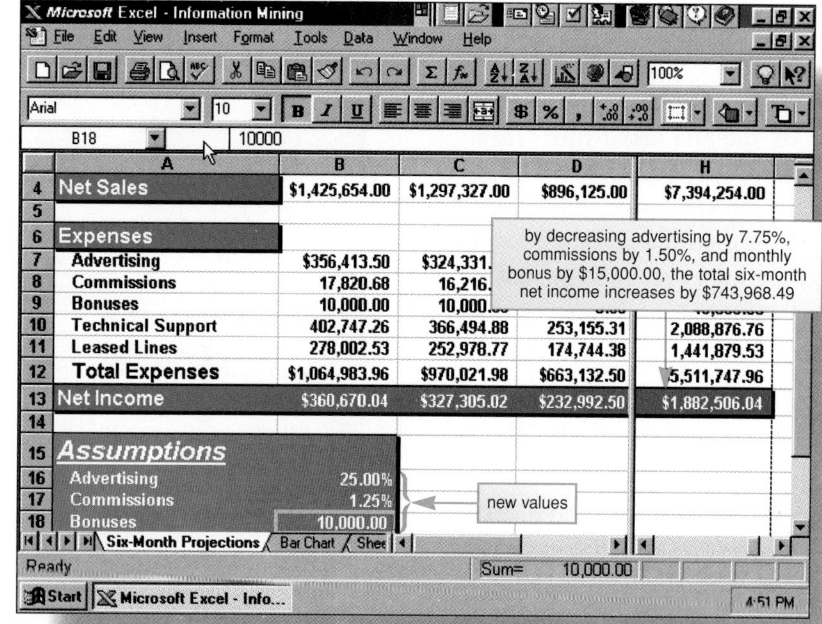
by decreasing advertising by 7.75%, commissions by 1.50%, and monthly bonus by $15,000.00, the total six-month net income increases by $743,968.49
new values

FIGURE 3-73

Each time you enter one of the new percent expenses, Excel recalculates the worksheet. This process usually takes less than one second, depending on how many calculations must be performed and the speed of your computer. Compare the projected six-month net incomes in Figures 3-73 and 3-72. By changing the values of the three assumptions (Figure 3-73), the projected six-month net income in cell H13 increases from $1,138,537.55 to $1,882,506.04. The change in the assumptions translates into an increase in the projected net income of $743,968.49 for the six-month period.

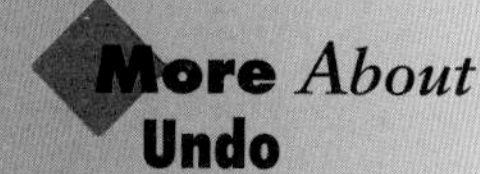

More *About* **Undo**

The Undo button is ideal for returning the worksheet to its original state after you have changed the value of a cell to answer a what-if question. Unfortunately, you can only undo the last task. Excel does not maintain a history.

Goal Seeking

If you know the result you want a formula to produce, you can use **goal seeking** to determine the value of a cell on which the formula depends. The following example reopens Information Mining and uses the **Goal Seek command** on the **Tools menu** to determine the projected advertising percentage in cell B16 that yields a projected six-month net income in cell H13 of $1,250,000.00.

To Goal Seek

1. **On the File menu click Close. Close Information Mining without saving changes. Click the Open button on the Standard toolbar and then reopen Information Mining.**

2. **Drag the vertical split box to the right of column D. Click cell H13, the cell that contains the projected six-month net income. Click Tools on the menu bar and then point to Goal Seek.**

   The vertical split bar displays to the right of column D, and the Tools menu displays (Figure 3-74).

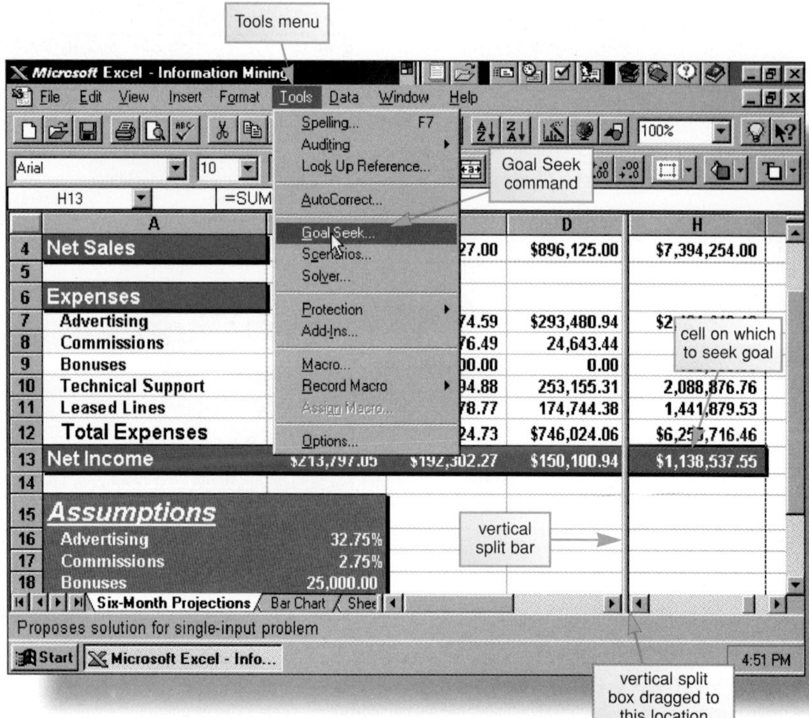

FIGURE 3-74

3. **Click Goal Seek on the Tools menu.**

   The Goal Seek dialog box displays. The Set cell box is assigned the cell reference of the active cell in the worksheet (cell H13) automatically.

4. **Type `1,250,000` in the To value box. Type `b16` in the By changing cell box.**

   The Goal Seek dialog box displays as shown in Figure 3-75.

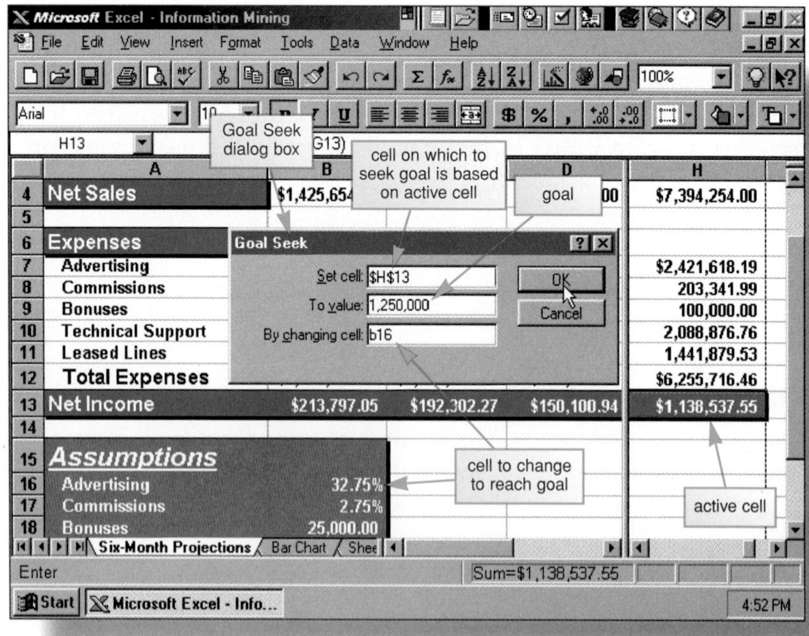

FIGURE 3-75

5 **Click the OK button in the Goal Seek dialog box. When the Goal Seeking Status dialog box displays, click the OK button.**

Excel immediately changes cell H13 from $1,138,537.55 to the desired value $1,250,000.00. More importantly, Excel changes the advertising assumption in cell B16 from 32.75% to 31.24% (Figure 3-76).

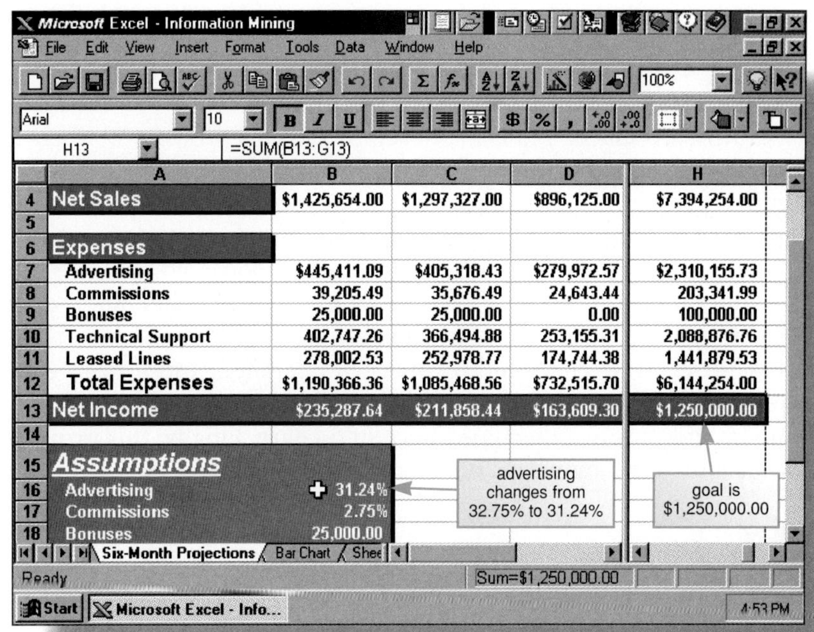

FIGURE 3-76

Goal seeking assumes you can change the value of only one cell referenced directly or indirectly. In this example, to change the projected six-month net income in cell H13 to $1,250,000.00, the advertising percentage in cell B16 must decrease by 1.51% from 32.75% to 31.24%.

You can see from this goal seeking example that it is not required that the cell to vary (cell B16) be directly referenced in the formula or function. For example, the projected six-month net income in cell H13 is determined from the function =SUM(B13:G13). Cell B16 is not mentioned (advertising assumption) in the function. The advertising assumption in cell B16, on which the projected monthly net incomes in row 13 are based, is referenced in the formulas in rows 7 through 12. Excel is able to goal seek on the projected six-month net income by varying the advertising assumption.

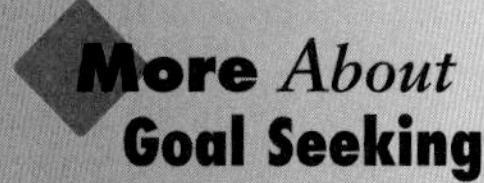

More About Goal Seeking

Goal seeking is a methodology in which you know what answer you want a cell's formula to be, but you do not know what value to place in a cell that is involved in the formula. You can goal seek by changing the value in a cell that is indirectly used in the formula as illustrated in Figure 3-76.

Exiting Excel

To exit Excel, complete the following steps.

TO EXIT EXCEL

Step 1: Click the Close button on the right side of the title bar.
Step 2: If the Microsoft Excel dialog box displays, click the No button.

Project Summary

With the worksheet and chart developed in this project, the CFO of Information Mining, Marissa Gold, can easily respond to any what-if questions asked by the board members the next time she presents her semi-annual projections. Questions that took several minutes to answer with paper and pencil can now be answered in a few seconds. Furthermore, computational errors are less likely to occur.

In creating the Information Mining workbook, you learned to work with worksheets that extend beyond the window. You learned how to use the fill handle to create a series. Using the Drawing button on the Standard toolbar, you learned to display hidden toolbars. You learned about the difference between absolute cell references and relative cell references and how to use the IF function. You also learned how to freeze titles, change the magnification of the worksheet, display different parts of the worksheets through panes, and improve the appearance of a chart. Finally, this project introduced you to using Excel to do what-if analyses by means of changing values in cells on which formulas depend and goal seeking.

What You Should Know

Having completed this project, you should be able to perform the following tasks:

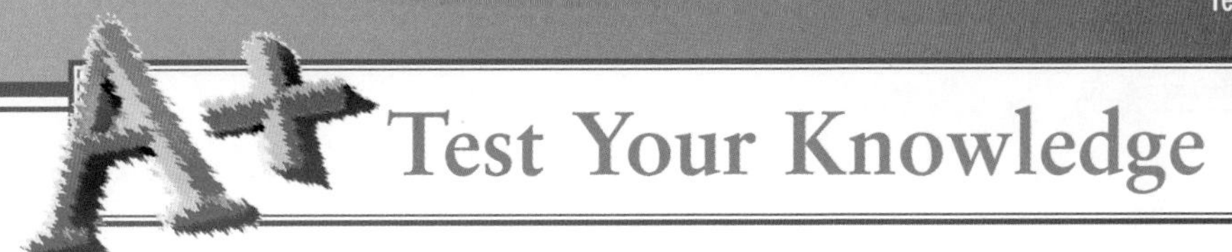

Test Your Knowledge

1 True/False

Instructions: Circle T if the statement is true or F if the statement is false.

T F 1. If you enter 1099 in cell B3, 1100 in cell B4, select the range B3:B4, and then drag the fill handle down to cell B10, Excel assigns cell B10 the value 1100.

T F 2. To copy the text July in cell C3 to all the cells in the range C4:C10, hold down the CTRL key while you drag the fill handle from cell C3 to cell C10.

T F 3. You can invoke the Paste command on the Edit menu by pressing the ENTER key.

T F 4. Excel has five toolbar docks.

T F 5. You can dock more than one toolbar at a toolbar dock.

T F 6. The $ in a cell reference affects only the Move command on the Edit menu.

T F 7. If you save a worksheet after changing the page setup characteristics, the next time you open the worksheet the page characteristics will be the same as when you saved it.

T F 8. You can split a window into, at most, four panes.

T F 9. D23 is an absolute reference, and $D$23 is a relative reference.

T F 10. If you assign cell A4 the IF function =IF(A5>A7, 1, 0) and cells A5 and A7 are equal to 7, then Excel displays the value 1 in cell A4.

2 Multiple Choice

Instructions: Circle the correct response.

1. If you assign cell C5 the value 23, cell G7 the value 6, and cell H6 the function =IF(C5>4*G7, "OK", "Not OK"), then __________ displays in cell H6.
   a. OK
   b. Not OK
   c. #REF!
   d. none of the above
2. Which one of the following buttons in the ChartWizard dialog boxes instructs Excel to draw the chart using the options selected thus far?
   a. Next
   b. Cancel
   c. Back
   d. Finish
3. Use function key __________ to change a relative reference in the formula bar to an absolute reference.
   a. F1
   b. F2
   c. F3
   d. F4

(continued)

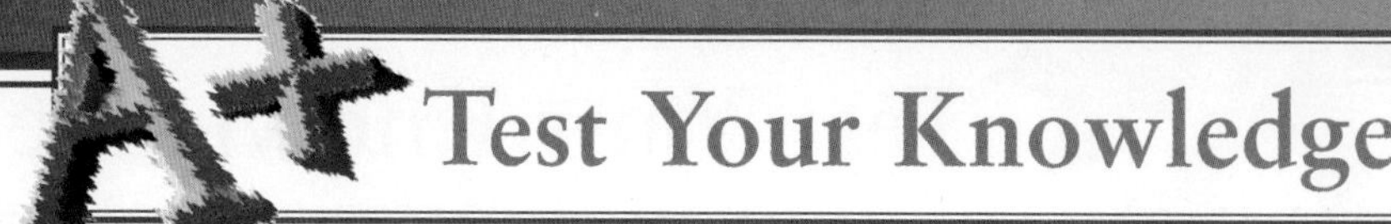

Test Your Knowledge

Multiple Choice *(continued)*

4. You can split the window into __________.
   a. two horizontal panes
   b. two vertical panes
   c. four panes
   d. all of the above
5. If you drag the fill handle to the right on cell G9, which contains December, then cell G10 will contain __________.
   a. December
   b. January
   c. November
   d. #REF!
6. To use the drag and drop method for copying a range of cells, the mouse pointer must point to the border of the range and change to the __________ shape.
   a. cross hair
   b. arrow
   c. block plus sign
   d. split double arrow
7. The horizontal and vertical split boxes are located __________.
   a. on the Standard toolbar
   b. on the Formatting toolbar
   c. next to the scroll arrows
   d. immediately to the left of the Select All button
8. When you insert rows in a worksheet, Excel __________ below the point of insertion to open up the worksheet.
   a. writes over the existing rows
   b. pushes up the rows
   c. reduces the height of the cells
   d. pushes down the rows
9. You cannot dock a toolbar if it contains a drop-down list box on the __________ of the window.
   a. bottom
   b. sides
   c. top
   d. in the middle
10. Which toolbar can be displayed or hidden by clicking a button on the Standard toolbar?
    a. Standard
    b. Drawing
    c. Formatting
    d. Chart

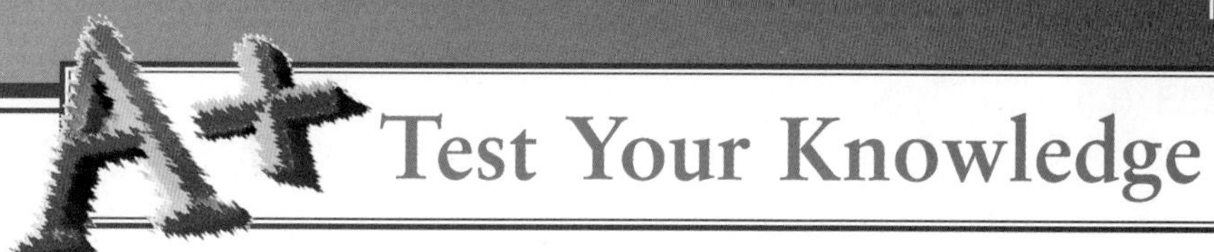

3 Understanding the Insert and Delete Commands and the IF Function

Instructions: Fill in the correct answers

1. Assume you want to insert four rows between rows 8 and 9.
   a. Select rows ____________________ through ____________________.
   b. On the shortcut menu, click ____________________.
2. You have data in rows 1 through 6. Assume you want to delete rows 2 through 4.
   a. Select rows ____________________ through ____________________.
   b. On the shortcut menu, click ____________________.
   c. In which row would the data from row 6 be located? ____________________
3. Which command on the shortcut menu results in formulas receiving the error message #REF! from cell referenced in the affected range? ____________________
4. Determine the truth value of the logical tests, given the following cell values: E1 = 500; F1 = 500; G1 = 2; H1 = 50; and I1 = 40. Enter true or false.
   a. E1 < 400 Truth value: ____________________
   b. F1 = E1 Truth value: ____________________
   c. 10 * H1 + I1 <> E1 Truth value: ____________________
   d. E1 + F1 >= 1000 Truth value: ____________________
   e. E1/H1 > G1 * 6 Truth value: ____________________
   f. 5 * G1 + I1 = H1 Truth value: ____________________
   g. 10 * I1 + 2 <= F1 + 2 Truth value: ____________________
   h. H1 -10 < I1 Truth value: ____________________
5. The active cell is cell F15. Write a function that assigns the value zero (0) or 1 to cell F15. Assign zero to cell F15 if the value in cell B3 is greater than the value in cell C12; otherwise assign 1 to cell F15.
   Function: ____
6. The active cell is cell F15. Write a function that assigns the value Credit OK or Credit Not OK to cell F15. Assign the label Credit OK if the value in cell A1 is not equal to the value in cell B1; otherwise assign the label Credit Not OK.
   Function: ____
7. Excel allows for nested IF functions. A nested IF function is one that contains another IF function in the value-if-true or value-if-false clauses. For example, =IF(A4>D3, IF(A2=4, “OK”, “NOT OK’), “MAYBE”) is a valid nested IF function. Start Excel and enter this IF function in cell B2. Enter the following sets of numbers into cells A2, A4, and D3 and write down the results in cell B2 for each: Set 1: A2=25; A4=20; D3=18; Set 2: A2=4; A4=38, Set 3= A2=4; A4=10; D3=8.

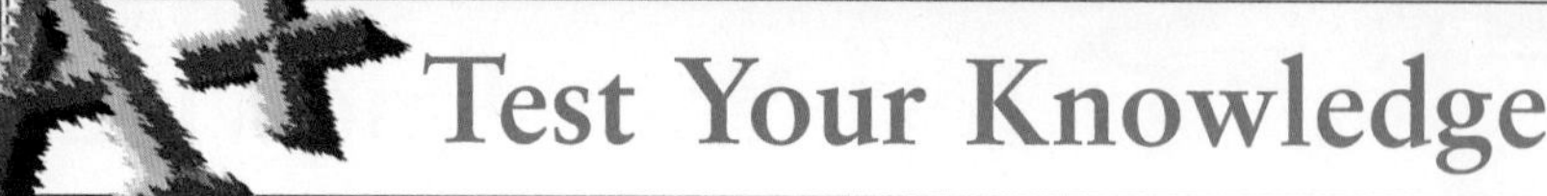

Test Your Knowledge

4 Understanding Absolute, Mixed, and Relative Referencing

Instructions: Fill in the correct answers. Use Figure 3-77 for problems 2 through 5.

1. Write cell D15 as a relative reference, absolute reference, mixed reference with the row varying, and mixed reference with the column varying.
   Relative reference: ____________________ Mixed, row varying: ____________________
   Absolute reference: ____________________ Mixed, column varying: ____________________
2. Write the formula for cell B8 that multiplies cell B1 times the sum of cells B4, B5, and B6. Write the formula so that when it is copied to cells C8 and D8, cell B1 remains absolute. Verify your formula by checking it with the values found in cells B8, C8, and D8 in Figure 3-77.
   Formula for cell B8:
   ____
   ____
3. Write the formula for cell E4 that multiplies cell A4 times the sum of cells B4, C4, and D4. Write the formula so that when it is copied to cells E5 and E6, cell A4 remains absolute. Verify your formula by checking it with the values found in cells E4, E5, and E6 in Figure 3-77.
   Formula for cell E4:
   ____
   ____

	A	B	C	D	E	F	G	H	I
1		3	5	7					
2									
3									
4	2	5	2	1	16	16			
5	3	7	3	5	30	45			
6	5	8	7	8	46	115			
7									
8		60	36	42					
9									
10		60	60	98					
11									

FIGURE 3-77

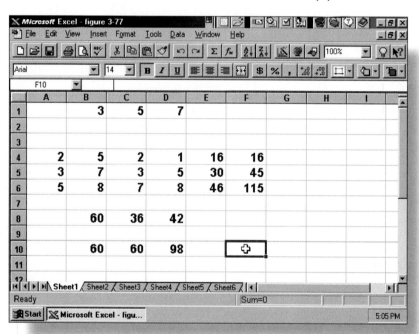

4. Write the formula for cell B10 that multiplies cell B1 times the sum of cells B4, B5, and B6. Write the formula so that when it is copied to cells C10 and D10, Excel adjusts all the cell references according to the new location. Verify your formula by checking it with the values found in cells B10, C10, and D10 in Figure 3-77.
   Formula for cell B10: ____
5. Write the formula for cell F4 that multiplies cell A4 times the sum of cells B4, C4, and D4. Write the formula so that when it is copied to cells F5 and F6, Excel adjusts all the cell addresses according to the new location. Verify your formula by checking it with the values found in cells F4, F5, and F6 in Figure 3-77.
   Formula for cell F4: ____

Use Help

1 Reviewing Project Activities

Instructions: Perform the following tasks using a computer.

1. Start Excel.
2. Double-click the Help button on the Standard toolbar to display the Help Topics dialog box.
3. Click the Contents tab. Double-click the Creating Formulas and Auditing Workbooks book.
4. Double-click the Using References book. Double-click The difference between relative and absolute references link. Read and print the information. Hand in the printout to your instructor.
5. If the Help Topics: Microsoft Excel dialog box is not on the screen, double-click the Help button on the Standard toolbar. Click the Index tab. Type `column chart` in the top box labeled 1 and then click the Display button. One at a time, click each topic in the Topics Found dialog box. Read and print the information for each topic by clicking Print Topic on the shortcut menu. To return to the Help Topics dialog box, click the Help Topic button. Hand in the printouts to your instructor.
6. If the Help Topics dialog box is not on the screen, double-click the Help button on the Standard toolbar. Click the Find tab. Type `if` in the top box labeled 1. Click IF in the middle box labeled 2, double-click IF in the bottom box labeled 3, read it, and click Print Topic on the shortcut menu. Click the Close button to close the Microsoft Excel Help window with the Help information. Hand in the printout to your instructor.
7. Double-click the Help button on the Standard toolbar. Click the Answer Wizard tab. Type `how do i goal seek` in the top box labeled 1. Click the Search button. In the bottom box labeled 2, double-click Solving problems with one or more variables under Tell Me About. One at a time, click the two links and read the Help information.

2 Expanding on the Basics

Instructions: Use Excel online Help to better understand the topics listed below. Begin each of the following by double-clicking the Help button on the Standard toolbar. If you are unable to print the Help information, then answer the questions on your own paper.

1. Double-click the Retrieving and Analyzing Data book on the Contents sheet in the Help Topics dialog box. Double-click the Solving What-If Problems book. Use the links to write a short paragraph explaining the difference between a one-variable data table and a two-variable data table. When you are finished, click the Close button and hand in your paragraph to your instructor.
2. Use the Find tab in the Help Topics: Microsoft Excel dialog box to display and then print information about the following topics and submit the printouts to your instructor: (a) freezing titles, (b) splitting a window, (c) comparison operators, (d) abramowitz.
3. Use the Answer Wizard in the Help Topics: Microsoft Excel dialog box to answer the question, *how do I fill in a series of numbers?* Answer the following related questions: (a) What types of series can Excel fill in? (b) How do I fill in a series of numbers? (c) How do I fill in a series for growth trend? (d) How do I create a custom AutoFill list?

Apply Your Knowledge

1 Creating a Series

Instructions: Start Excel. Open the workbook Create Series from the Excel folder on the Student Floppy Disk that accompanies this book. The worksheet (Figure 3-78) contains the initial values for eight different series.

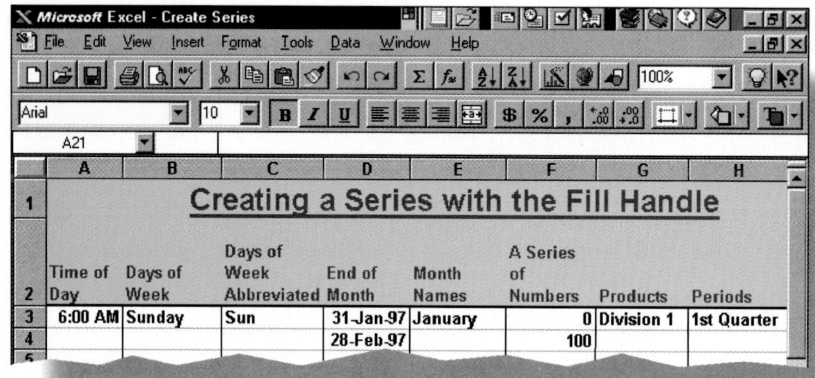

Microsoft Excel - Create Series

Creating a Series with the Fill Handle

	A	B	C	D	E	F	G	H
2	Time of Day	Days of Week	Days of Week Abbreviated	End of Month	Month Names	A Series of Numbers	Products	Periods
3	6:00 AM	Sunday	Sun	31-Jan-97	January	0	Division 1	1st Quarter
4				28-Feb-97		100		

FIGURE 3-78

Use the fill handle on one column at a time to propagate the eight different series as shown in Figure 3-79 through row 17. For example, in column A, select cell A3 and drag the fill handle down to cell A17. Your final result should be 8:00 PM in cell A17. In column D, select the range D3:D4 and drag the fill handle down to cell D17. Save the worksheet using the file name Create Series 2. Print the worksheet on one page.

Microsoft Excel - Create Series

Creating a Series with the Fill Handle

	A	B	C	D	E	F	G	H
2	Time of Day	Days of Week	Days of Week Abbreviated	End of Month	Month Names	A Series of Numbers	Products	Periods
3	6:00 AM	Sunday	Sun	31-Jan-97	January	0	Division 1	1st Quarter
4	7:00 AM	Monday	Mon	28-Feb-97	February	100	Division 2	2nd Quarter
5	8:00 AM	Tuesday	Tue	31-Mar-97	March	200	Division 3	3rd Quarter
6	9:00 AM	Wednesday	Wed	30-Apr-97	April	300	Division 4	4th Quarter
7	10:00 AM	Thursday	Thu	31-May-97	May	400	Division 5	1st Quarter
8	11:00 AM	Friday	Fri	30-Jun-97	June	500	Division 6	2nd Quarter
9	12:00 PM	Saturday	Sat	31-Jul-97	July	600	Division 7	3rd Quarter
10	1:00 PM	Sunday	Sun	31-Aug-97	August	700	Division 8	4th Quarter
11	2:00 PM	Monday	Mon	30-Sep-97	September	800	Division 9	1st Quarter
12	3:00 PM	Tuesday	Tue	31-Oct-97	October	900	Division 10	2nd Quarter
13	4:00 PM	Wednesday	Wed	30-Nov-97	November	1000	Division 11	3rd Quarter

Sheet1 / Sheet2 / Sheet3 / Sheet4 / Sheet5 / Sheet6

Ready | Sum=0

Start | Microsoft Excel - Cre... | 5:05 PM

FIGURE 3-79

1 Pointer's Pizza and Pasta Five-Year Projected Financial Statement

Problem: You are a management trainee employed by Pointer's Pizza and Pasta. Each quarter for the first year of your employment you work in a different department. This quarter you are working for the Information Systems (IS) department. Your IS supervisor noticed from your resume that you learned Microsoft Excel in college and has requested that you build a Five-Year Projected Financial Statement based on figures available from 1996 (Figure 3-80).

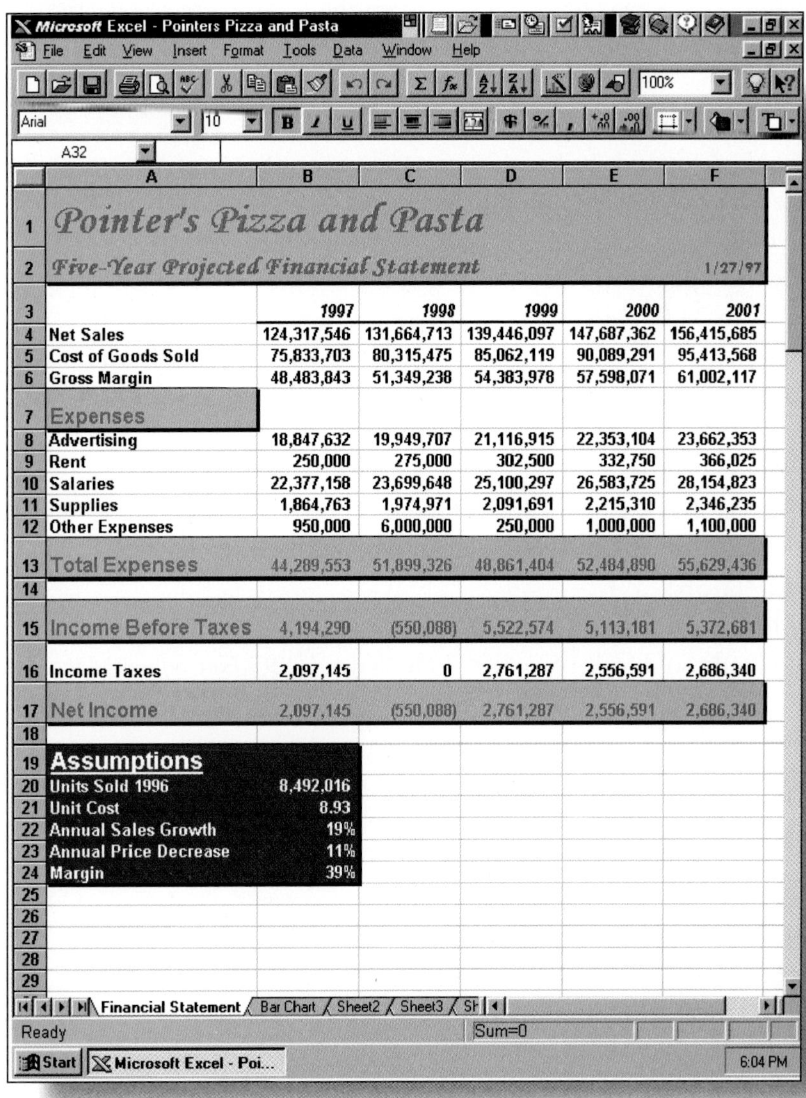

	A	B	C	D	E	F
1	*Pointer's Pizza and Pasta*					
2	*Five-Year Projected Financial Statement*					1/27/97
3		1997	1998	1999	2000	2001
4	Net Sales	124,317,546	131,664,713	139,446,097	147,687,362	156,415,685
5	Cost of Goods Sold	75,833,703	80,315,475	85,062,119	90,089,291	95,413,568
6	Gross Margin	48,483,843	51,349,238	54,383,978	57,598,071	61,002,117
7	Expenses					
8	Advertising	18,847,632	19,949,707	21,116,915	22,353,104	23,662,353
9	Rent	250,000	275,000	302,500	332,750	366,025
10	Salaries	22,377,158	23,699,648	25,100,297	26,583,725	28,154,823
11	Supplies	1,864,763	1,974,971	2,091,691	2,215,310	2,346,235
12	Other Expenses	950,000	6,000,000	250,000	1,000,000	1,100,000
13	Total Expenses	44,289,553	51,899,326	48,861,404	52,484,890	55,629,436
14						
15	Income Before Taxes	4,194,290	(550,088)	5,522,574	5,113,181	5,372,681
16	Income Taxes	2,097,145	0	2,761,287	2,556,591	2,686,340
17	Net Income	2,097,145	(550,088)	2,761,287	2,556,591	2,686,340
18						
19	Assumptions					
20	Units Sold 1996	8,492,016				
21	Unit Cost	8.93				
22	Annual Sales Growth	19%				
23	Annual Price Decrease	11%				
24	Margin	39%				
25						
26						
27						
28						
29						

FIGURE 3-80

(continued)

Pointer's Pizza and Pasta Five-Year Projected Financial Statement *(continued)*

Instructions Part 1: Do the following to create the worksheet in Figure 3-80.

Table 3-6	
ASSUMPTIONS	
Units Sold 1996	**8,492,016**
Unit Cost	**$8.93**
Annual Sales Growth	**19%**
Annual Price Decrease	**11%**
Margin	**39%**

1. Use the Select All button and Bold button to bold the entire worksheet. Enter the worksheet titles in cells A1 and A2. Enter the system date using the NOW function in cell F2. Format the date to the m/d/yy style.
2. Enter 1997 in cell B3, 1998 in cell C3, and generate the series 1997 through 2001 in the range B3:F3 using the fill handle.
3. Enter the row titles in the range A4:A24. Change the font size in cells A7, A13, A15, and A17 to 12 point. Change the font size in cell A19 to 14 point and underline the characters in the cell.
4. Change the following column widths: A = 23.43; B through F = 11.00. Change the heights of row 3, 7, 13, 15, 16, 17 to 24.00.
5. Enter the assumptions in Table 3-6 in the range B20:B24 using format symbols where appropriate.
6. Use the Format Cells dialog box to assign the Comma style with no decimal places to the range B4:F17.
7. Complete the following entries:
   a. 1997 Net Sales (cell B4) = Units Sold 1996*(Unit Cost/(1-Margin)) or =B20*(B21/(1-B24))
   b. 1998 Net Sales (cell C4) = 1997 Net Sales*(1+Annual Sales Growth)*(1-Annual Price Decrease) or =B4*(1+$B$22)*(1-$B$23)
   c. Copy cell C4 to range D4:F4.
   d. 1997 Cost of Goods Sold (cell B5) = 1997 Net Sales-(1997 Net Sales*Margin) or =B4*(1-$B$24)
   e. Copy cell B5 to range C5:F5
   f. 1997 Gross Margin (cell B6) = 1997 Net Sales-1997 Cost of Goods Sold or =B4-B5
   g. Copy cell B6 to range C6:F6
   h. 1997 Advertising (cell B8) = 200,000+15%*1997 Net Sales or =200000+15%*B4
   i. Copy cell B8 to C8:F8
   j. 1997 Rent (cell B9) = 250,000
   k. 1998 Rent (cell C9) = 1997 Rent+10%*1997 Rent or =B9*(1+10%)
   l. Copy cell C9 to range D9:F9
   m. 1997 Salaries (cell B10) = 18%*1997 Net Sales or =18%*B4
   n. Copy cell B10 to range C10:F10
   o. 1997 Supplies (cell B11) = 1.5%*1997 Net Sales or =1.5%*B4
   p. Copy cell B11 to range C11:F11
   q. Other expenses: 1997 = $950,000; 1998 = $6,000,000; 1999 = $250,000; 2000 = $1,000,000; 2001 = $1,100,000
   r. 1997 Total Expenses (cell B13) = SUM(B8:B12)

s. Copy cell B13 to range C13:F13.
t. 1997 Income Before Taxes (cell B15) = 1997 Gross Margin-1997 Total Expenses or =B6-B13
u. Copy cell B15 to range C15:F15
v. 1997 Income Taxes (cell B16): If 1997 Income Before Expenses is less than zero, then 1997 Income Taxes equal zero, otherwise 1997 Income Taxes equal 50% * 1997 Income Before Taxes or =IF(B15<0,0,50%*B15)
w. Copy cell B16 to range C16:F16
x. 1997 Net Income (cell B17) = 1997 Income Before Taxes - 1997 Income Taxes or =B15-B16
y. Copy cell B17 to range C17:F17

8. Change the font in cell A1 to 26-point Monotype Corsiva (or a similar font). Change the font in cell A2 to 16-point Monotype Corsiva (or a similar font). Change the font in cell F2 to 10-point Century Gothic (or a similar font). Change the background and font colors and add drop shadows as shown in Figure 3-80 on page E 3.68.
9. Enter your name, course, laboratory assignment (Lab 3-1), date, and instructor name in the range A27:A31. Save the workbook using the filename Pointers Pizza and Pasta.
10. Preview and print the worksheet. Preview and print the formulas (CTRL+`) in landscape orientation using Fit to in the Page Setup dialog box. After printing the formulas version, reset the print scaling to 100%. Press CTRL+` to display the values version of the worksheet. Save the workbook again.

Instructions Part 2: Draw a 3-D column chart (Figure 3-81) that compares the projected net incomes for the years 1997 through 2001. Use the nonadjacent range B3:F3 and B17:F17. Add the chart title and format it as shown in Figure 3-81. Rename and rearrange the tabs as shown in Figure 3-81. Save the workbook using the same filename as defined in Part 1. Print both sheets.

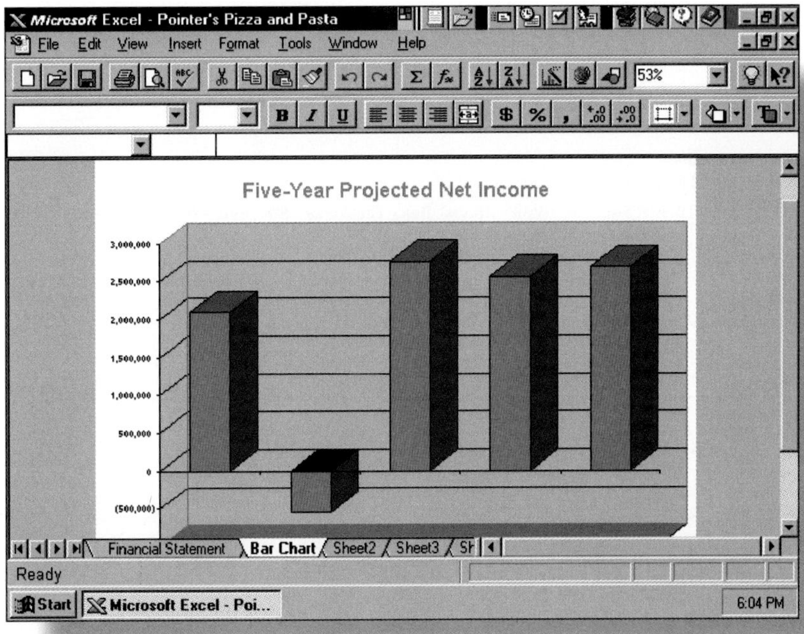

FIGURE 3-81

(continued)

Pointer's Pizza and Pasta Five-Year Projected Financial Statement *(continued)*

Instructions Part 3: If the 3-D column chart is on the screen, click the Financial Statement tab to display the worksheet. Divide the window into two panes by dragging the horizontal split bar between rows 6 and 7. Use the scroll bars to display both the top and bottom of the worksheet.

Using the numbers in columns 2 and 3 of Table 3-7, analyze the effect of changing the annual sales growth (cell B22) and annual price decrease (cell B23) on the annual net incomes in row 17. Print both the worksheet and chart for each case.

Table 3-7

CASE	ANNUAL SALES GROWTH	ANNUAL PRICE DECREASE	2001 RESULTING NET INCOME
1	5%	1%	$2,432,963
2	10%	-2%	$3,599,872
3	25%	10%	$3,647,473

Close the workbook without saving it, and then reopen it. Use the Goal Seek command to determine a margin (cell B24) that would result in a net income of $5,000,000 for 2001 in cell F17. You should end up with a margin in cell B24 of 42%. Print only the worksheet after the goal seeking is complete.

2 Modifying the Steel Frame House Weekly Payroll Worksheet

Problem: Your supervisor in the Payroll department has asked you to modify the payroll workbook developed in Exercise 2 of the In the Lab section in Project 2 on page E 2.73 so it appears as shown in Figure 3-82. If you did not complete Exercise 2, ask your instructor for a copy of the workbook Steel Frame House.

	A	B	C	D	E	F	G	H	I	J	K	L
1	Steel Frame House											
2	Weekly Payroll Report For Week Ending						12/1/97					
3	Employee	YTD Soc. Sec.	Rate	Hours	Dep.	Gross Pay	Soc. Sec.	Medicare	Fed. Tax	State Tax	Net Pay	
4	Dent, Jacob	2,395.29	22.50	39.50	2	888.75	55.10	12.89	162.37	28.44	629.95	
5	Till, Kevin	3,880.00	28.00	64.00	4	2,128.00	7.40	30.86	394.83	68.10	1,626.82	
6	Hayley, Joe	3,825.50	23.00	40.00	1	920.00	57.04	13.34	176.31	29.44	643.87	
7	Boate, Max	1,475.23	14.50	46.25	5	715.94	44.39	10.38	104.73	22.91	533.53	
8	Denise, Fritz	3,887.40	15.40	43.00	3	685.30	0.00	9.94	113.98	21.93	539.45	
9	Clozs, Lin	3,882.00	17.50	54.00	5	1,067.50	5.40	15.48	175.04	34.16	837.42	
10	Wire, Tom	2,734.12	14.95	20.00	9	299.00	18.54	4.34	0.00	9.57	266.56	
11	*Totals*	22,079.54		306.75		6,704.49	187.87	97.22	1,127.26	214.54	5,077.60	
12												
13	*Assumptions*											
14	Social Security Tax		6.20%									
15	Medicare Tax		1.45%									
16	Maximum Social Security		$3,887.40									

Payroll / Donut / Sheet2 / Sheet3 / Sheet4 / Sheet5

Ready Sum=0

FIGURE 3-82

In the Lab

The major modifications include reformatting the worksheet, time and a half for hours worked greater than 40, no federal tax if the federal tax is greater than the gross pay, and computation of the Social Security and Medicare deductions. The workbook (Steel Frame House) created earlier in Project 2 is shown in Figure 2-95 on page E 2.73.

Instructions Part 1: Open the workbook Steel Frame House created in Project 2. Perform the following tasks:

Table 3-8

NAME	YTD SOC. SEC.
Dent, Jacob	2,395.29
Till, Kevin	3,880.00
Hayley, Joe	3,825.50
Boate, Max	1,475.23
Denise, Fritz	3,887.40

1. Use the Select All button and Clear command on the Edit menu to clear all formats.
2. Bold the entire worksheet. Delete rows 10 through 12. Insert a row above row 2. Modify the worksheet title in cell A1 so it appears as shown in Figure 3-82 on the previous page. Enter the worksheet subtitle, Weekly Payroll Report For Week Ending, in cell A2.
3. Insert a new column between columns A and B. Title the new column YTD Soc. Sec. Insert two new columns between columns F and G. Title column G in cell G3 Soc. Sec. Title column H in cell H3 Medicare. Assign the NOW function to cell G2 and format it to m/d/yy. Freeze the titles in column A and rows 1 through 3.

Table 3-9

EMPLOYEE	YTD SOC. SEC.	RATE	HOURS	DEPENDENTS
Clozs, Lin	3,882.00	17. 50	54	5
Wire, Tom	2,734.12	14. 95	20	9

4. Change the column widths and row heights as follows: A = 11.00; B = 13.00; C = 9.00, D = 7.00; E = 5.00; F through K = 8.71; and row 3 = 18. Right-align the column titles in the range B3:K3.
5. Delete row 8 (Suzi, Jeff). Change Denise, Fritz's number of dependents from 5 to 3.
6. In row B, enter the YTD Social Security values listed in Table 3-8.
7. Insert two new rows immediately above the Totals row. Add the new employees listed in Table 3-9.
8. Use the Format Cells dialog box to assign a Comma style to the ranges B4:D11 and F4:K11. Center-align the range E4:E10.
9. Enter the Assumptions table in the range A13:C16 and format it as shown in Figure 3-82. Place the titles in column A and the numbers in column C.
10. Change the formulas to determine the gross pay in column F and the federal tax in column H.
    a. In cell F4, enter an IF function that applies the following logic:
    If Hours <= 40, then Gross Pay = Rate*Hours, otherwise Gross Pay = Rate*Hours+ 0. 5*Rate*(Hours–40)
    b. Copy the IF function in cell F4 to the range F5:F10.
    c. In cell I4, enter the IF function that applies the following logic:
    If (Gross Pay–Dependents*38.46) > 0, then Federal Tax = 20%*(Gross Pay–Dependents* 38.46), otherwise Federal Tax = 0
    d. Copy the IF function in cell I4 to the range I5:I10.

(continued)

Modifying the Steel Frame House Weekly Payroll Worksheet *(continued)*

11. An employee pays Social Security tax only if his or her YTD Social Security is less than the maximum Social Security in cell C16. Use the following logic to determine the Social Security tax for Jacob Dent in cell G4:
    If Soc. Sec. Tax*Gross Pay+YTD Soc. Sec.> Maximum Soc. Sec., then Maximum Soc. Sec.-YTD Soc. Sec., otherwise Soc. Sec. Tax*Gross Pay
12. Copy the IF function to the range G5:G10. Make sure references to the values in the Assumptions table are absolute.
13. In cell H4, enter the following formula and copy it to the range H5:H10:
    Medicare = Medicare Tax * Gross Pay
14. Copy the state tax in cell J4 to the range J5:J10.
15. In cell K4, enter the following formula and copy it to the range K5:K10:
    Net Pay = Gross Pay–(Soc. Sec.+Medicare+Fed. Tax+State Tax)
16. Determine any new totals as shown in row 11 of Figure 3-82 on page E 3.70.
17. Enter your name, course, laboratory assignment (Lab 3-2), date, and instructor name in the range A18:A22.
18. Unfreeze the titles. Save the workbook using the filename Steel House Frame 2.
19. Use the Zoom Control box on the Standard toolbar to change the view of the worksheet. One by one, select all the percents in the Zoom Control box. Change it back to 100%.
20. Preview the worksheet. Adjust column widths if number signs display in place of numbers. Print the worksheet in landscape orientation. Save the worksheet again.
21. Preview and print the formulas (CTRL+`) in landscape orientation using Fit to in the Page Setup dialog box. Close the worksheet without saving the latest changes.

Instructions Part 2: Open the workbook Steel Frame House 2. Using the range A4:A10 (category names) and the range K4:K10 (data series), draw a Donut chart (column 1, row 2 in the ChartWizard Step 2 of 5 dialog box) with the labels inside each piece (Figure 3-83). Add a chart title and format it appropriately. Rename the tabs as follows: Chart1 to Donut; Sheet1 to Payroll. Rearrange the tabs so the Payroll tab is to the left of the Donut tab. Save the workbook using the filename Steel Frame House 2. Preview and print both sheets.

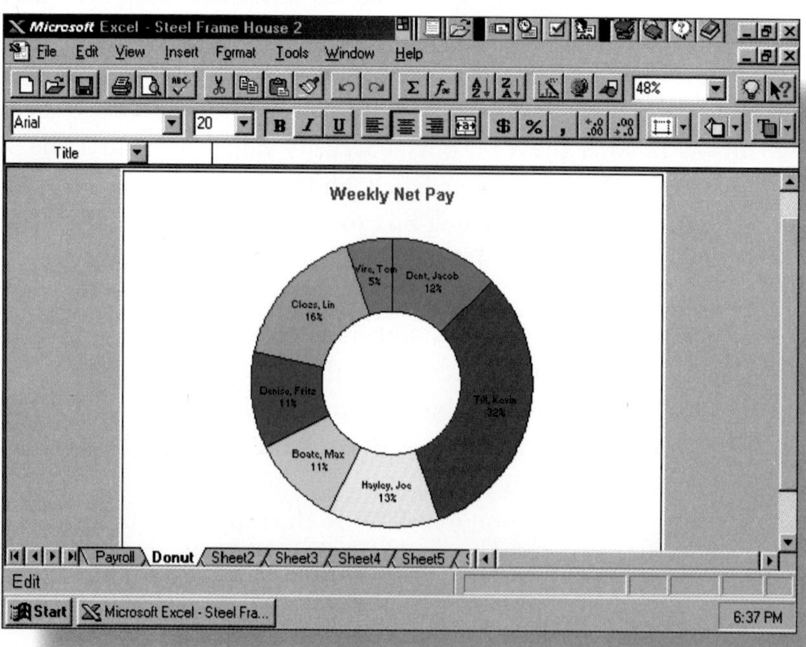

FIGURE 3-83

Instructions Part 3: If the Donut chart is on the screen, click the Payroll tab to display the worksheet. Using the numbers in the Table 3-10, analyze the effect of changing the Social Security tax in cell C14. Print the worksheet for each case. The first case should result in a total Social Security tax in cell G11 of $227.00. The second case should result in a total Social Security tax of $246.03.

Table 3-10

CASE	SOCIAL SECURITY TAX	MEDICARE TAX
1	8%	2%
2	9%	2.5%

3 Projected Quarterly Report

Problem: You are employed as a worksheet specialist by Cryptography Inc., a leader in the field of keeping secrets known only to insiders. The company utilizes assumptions, based on past business practice, to plan for the next quarter. You have been asked to create a worksheet similar to the one shown in Figure 3-84.

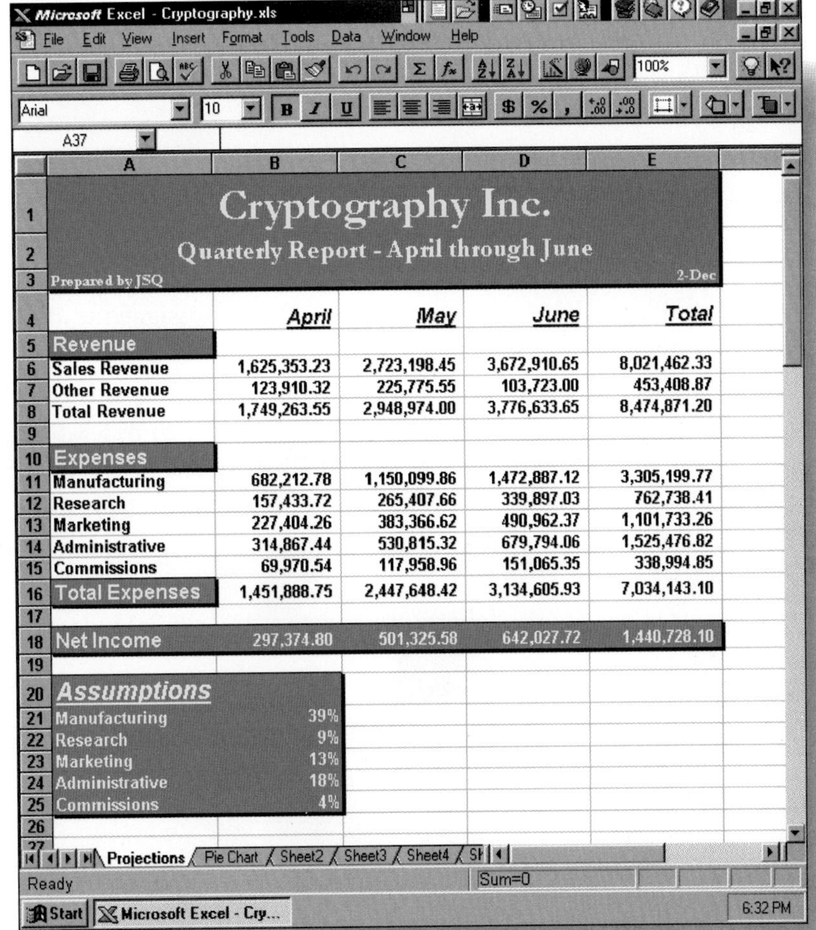

FIGURE 3-84

(continued)

In the Lab

Projected Quarterly Report *(continued)*

Instructions Part 1: Do the following to create the worksheet shown in Figure 3-84 on the previous page.

1. Bold the entire worksheet. Enter the worksheet titles in cells A1, A2, and A3. Use your own initials in cell A3. Enter the NOW function in cell E3 and format it to 4-Mar. Enter April in cell B4 and underline, italicize, and right-align it. Use the fill handle to create the month series in row 4. Enter Total in cell E4 and use the Format Painter button on the Standard toolbar to format it the same as cell D4. Enter the row titles down through Assumptions in cell A20. Copy the row titles in the range A11:A15 to the range A21:A25.
2. Use the Select All button and change the width of all the columns to 13.71. Change the widths of column A to 18.29 and column E to 14.86. Change the height of row 4 to 24.00.
3. Enter the Assumptions values in the range B21:B25.
4. Enter the sales revenue and other revenue in Table 3-11 in the range B6:D7. Determine the totals in the range E6:E7 and B8:E8.
5. Each of the expense categories in the range B11:D15 is determined by multiplying the total revenue for the month times the corresponding assumption in the Assumption table (range A20:B25). For example, the Manufacturing expense in cell B11 is equal to cell B21 times cell B8, or =B21*B8. Once the formulas are assigned to the range B11:B15, they can be copied to the range C11:D15. For the copy to work properly, however, you must make the first cell reference absolute. Thus, enter the following formulas in the designated cells: B11 = $B$21*B8; B12 = $B$22*B8; B13 = $B$23*B8; B14 = $B$24*B8; B15 = $B$25*B8.
6. Use the SUM function to determine all the totals. The net income in row 18 is equal to the total revenue for each month (row 8) minus the total expenses for each month (row 16).
7. Format the worksheet so it resembles Figure 3-84. Use Garamond font (or a similar font) in the range A1:E3.
8. Enter your name, course, laboratory assignment (Lab 3-1), date, and instructor name in the range A28:A32.
9. Save the workbook using the filename Cryptography.
10. Print the worksheet. Preview and print the formulas (CTRL+`) in landscape orientation using Fit to in the Page Setup dialog box. Press CTRL+` to display the values version of the worksheet. Save the workbook again.

Table 3-11

	APRIL	MAY	JUNE
Sales Revenue	1,625,353.23	2,723,198.45	3,672,910.65
Other Revenue	123,910.32	225,775.55	103,723.00

Instructions Part 2: Draw a 3-dimensional pie chart (Figure 3-85) that shows the monthly contribution to the quarterly net income. That is, chart the nonadjacent ranges B4:D4 (category names) and B18:D18 (data series).

Do the following to the pie chart:

1. Add the chart title and format it as shown in Figure 3-85.
2. Explode the June slice.

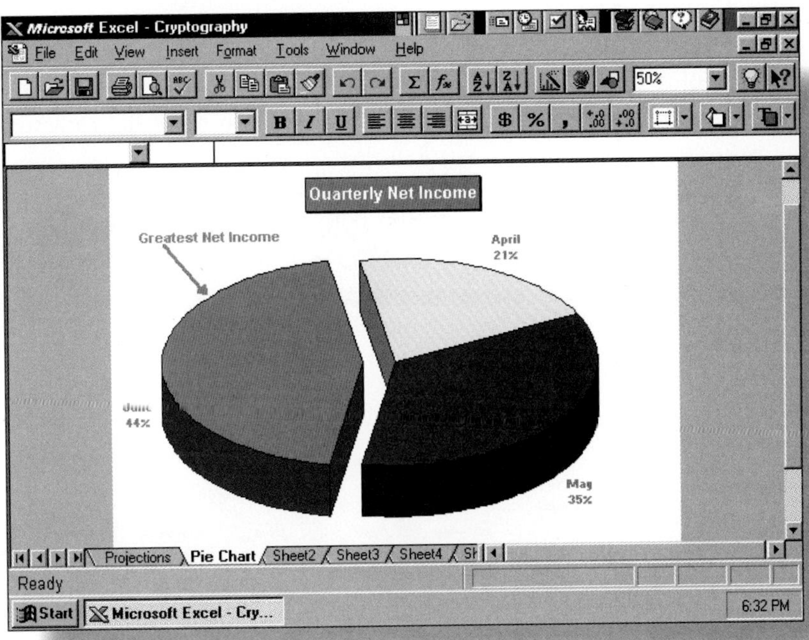

FIGURE 3-85

3. Select a slice and use the 3-D View command on the shortcut menu to change the elevation to 30° and the rotation to 350°.
4. Change the color of the slices as shown in Figure 3-85.
5. Use Help to step you through adding a text box with the phrase Greatest Net Income and an arrow pointing to the June slice. Format the text box and arrow as shown in Figure 3-85.
6. Rename the tabs as follows: Chart1 to Pie Chart; Sheet1 to Projections. Rearrange the tabs so the Projections tab is to the left of the Pie Chart tab.
7. Save the workbook using the filename Cryptography.
8. Print both sheets.

Instructions Part 3: If the 3-D pie chart is on the screen, click the Projections tab to display the worksheet shown in Figure 3-84 on page E 3.73. Using the numbers in the Table 3-12, analyze the effect of changing the assumptions in rows 21 through 25 on the quarterly net income in cell E18. Print both the worksheet and chart for each case.

You should end with the following quarterly net incomes in cell E18: Case 1 = 1,694,974.24; Case 2 = 1,271,230.68; Case 3 = 254,246.14.

Close the workbook Cryptography without saving it, and then reopen it. Use the Goal Seek command to determine the marketing percentage (cell B23) that would result in a quarterly net income of 760,000 in cell E18. You should end up with a marketing percentage of 21%. Print only the worksheet.

Table 3-12

	CASE 1	CASE 2	CASE 3
Manufacturing	35%	37%	40%
Research	10%	10%	15%
Marketing	14%	15%	17%
Administrative	16%	16%	20%
Commissions	5%	7%	5%

Cases and Places

The difficulty of these case studies varies:

◗ Case studies preceded by a single half moon are the least difficult. You are asked to create the required worksheet based on information that has already been placed in an organized form.
◗◗ Case studies preceded by two half moons are more difficult. You must organize the information presented before using it to create the required worksheet.
◗◗◗ Case studies preceded by three half moons are the most difficult. You must choose a specific topic, and then obtain and organize the necessary information before using it to create the required worksheet.

1 ◗ The Stevensville Sentinel is a small newspaper that publishes stories of local interest. Revenues are earned from subscriptions and the sale of advertising space. A fixed percentage of the proceeds is spent on marketing, payroll, commissions, production costs, and reportorial expenses. The Sentinel's editor has summarized the paper's receipts and expenditures over the past year on a bi-monthly basis as shown in Figure 3-86.

The Stevensville Sentinel
Bi-Monthly Earnings and Expenditures

Revenues:

	February	April	June	August	October	November
Subsricptions	$8,526.34	$8,526.34	$9,271.95	$12,082.14	$12,082.14	$9,721.63
Advertising	$2,500.78	$1,762.25	$2,134.56	$3,455.45	$2,987.95	$4,234.66

Expenditures:

Marketing	20.75%	
Payroll	56.50%	
Commissions	2.25%	of advertising sales
Production Costs	13.25%	
Reportorial Expenses	3.00%	

FIGURE 3-86

With this data, you have been asked to prepare a worksheet for the next shareholder's meeting showing total revenues, total expenditures, and net incomes for each bi-monthly period. Include a chart that illustrates the net incomes. One shareholder lobbied to reduce marketing expenditures 1% and payroll costs 5%. Perform a what-if analysis with another worksheet and chart reflecting the proposed changes in expenditure assumptions. Use the concepts and techniques presented in this project to create and format the worksheets and charts.

Cases and Places

2 ◗ A government agency plans to conduct experiments that will result in some radioactive waste. Although the isotopes will break apart into atoms of other elements over time, agency watchdogs are concerned about containment costs while the material is still radioactive. The agency director has asked you to prepare a worksheet showing the amount of radioactive material remaining, containment costs, estimated agency appropriations, and the percentage of appropriations that will be spent on containment every year for the next decade. The director has outlined the desired worksheet as shown in Figure 3-87.

Cost of Storing Radioactive Isotopes

	Number of Years Stored		
	1	2	3 10
Amount of Isotope X Remaining (in kg)			
Amount of Isotope Y Remaining (in kg)			
Total Remaining (in kg)			
Containment Costs			
Estimated Appropriations			
Percentage Spent on Containment			

Assumptions

Original amount of Isotope X (in kg)	700	*Original amount of Isotope Y (in kg)*	2,500
Half-life of Isotope X (in years)	1	*Half-life of Isotope Y (in years)*	0.5
Containment Cost Per Kilogram	$1,000.00	*Appropriations*	$5,000,000.00
Estimated Yearly Increase	8%		

FIGURE 3-87

These formulas have been supplied:

Amount Remaining = Original Amount x 0.5 (Number of Years Stored÷Half Life)
Containment Costs = Containment Cost Per Kilogram x Total Amount Remaining
Estimated Appropriations = Appropriations x (1+Estimated Yearly Increase) Number of Years Stored
Percentage Spent on Containment = Containment Costs÷Estimated Appropriations

The director has asked you to include a function that prints "Acceptable" below the percentage spent on containment whenever that percentage is less than 10%, and to goal seek on a second worksheet to determine how much of Isotope X can be used so the percentage spent on containment is always less than 15%. Use the concepts and techniques presented in this project to create and format the worksheets.

3 ◗◗ Geppetto, a woodcarver, is unhappy with the school his little boy attends ("They act as if his head were full of sawdust!" he grouses). Although the little boy has a tendency to stretch the truth, Geppetto believes if a school kept his "nose to the grindstone" eventually the boy's dreams would come true. Geppetto wants to save enough money to send his little boy to a private school. He has job orders for the next six months—$500 in July, $585 in August, $376 in September, $624 in October, $643 in November, and $775 in December. Each month Geppetto spends 33.75% of the money for materials, 2.5% for tools, 6.25% for his retirement account, and 40% for food and clothing. The remaining profits (orders - expenses) will be put aside for the boy's education. Geppetto's friend, JC, has agreed to provide an additional $50 whenever Geppetto's monthly profit exceeds $100. Geppetto has asked you to create a worksheet that shows orders, expenses, profits, and savings for the next six months, and totals for each category. On separate worksheets, Geppetto would like you to goal seek to determine a percentage for food and clothing if $1,000 is needed for the school, and then do a what-if analysis to determine the effect of reducing the percentage spent on materials to 25%. Use the concepts and techniques presented in this project to create and format the worksheets.

Cases and Places

4 ▸▸ Sweet Dreams is open year round, but most of the candy shop's production revolves around six holidays: Valentine's Day (2, 250 lb.), Easter (1,950 lb.), Mother's Day (1,150 lb.), Father's Day (975 lb.), Halloween (2,136 lb.), and Christmas (1,750 lb.). On these days, 28% of the store's output is fudge, 15% is taffy, 46% is boxed chocolate, and the remaining 11% is holiday-specific candy (such as chocolate hearts or candy canes). The fudge sells for $6.25 per pound, the taffy for $1.15 per pound, the boxed chocolate for $5.75 per pound, and holiday-specific candy for $1.35 per pound. Sweet Dreams is considering revising its production figures, and the management has asked you to create a worksheet it can use in making their decision. The worksheet should show the amount of each candy produced on a holiday, potential sales for each type of candy, total potential sales for each holiday, total candy produced for the six holidays, and total potential sales from each type of candy.

5 ▸▸▸ Ralph Nickleby, a wealthy uncle, has left you stock in several computer companies in his will. Your stock is in three major categories—hardware (5,000 shares in Apple, 11,500 shares in Compaq, 22,500 shares in IBM, and 7,000 shares in Intel), software (3,000 shares in Autodesk, 4,500 shares in Borland, 58,000 shares in Microsoft, and 6,500 shares in Symantec), and networking (2,500 shares in 3Com, 11,250 shares in Compaq, and 16,750 shares in Novell). Analysts assure you that on average, stock in the computer industry will return 5% per year for the next ten years. Using the latest stock prices, create a worksheet that organizes your computer stock portfolio and projects its annual worth for the next ten years. Group companies by major categories and include a total for each category.

6 ▸▸▸ Balancing budgets, a daunting task for governments at every level, also can be a significant challenge for students attending college. Whether you work part time or simply draw on a sum of money while going to school, it is necessary to equalize income and expenditures. Create and format a worksheet that reflects your monthly budget throughout the school year. Indicate the amount of money you have available each month. Hypothesize percentages for monthly expenditures (food, travel, entertainment, and so on). On the basis of these assumptions, determine expenditures for each month. Include a row for occasional, miscellaneous expenses (such as books). Ascertain the amount of money remaining at the end of each month; this amount will become part or all of the money available for the subsequent month. Perform at least one what-if analysis to examine the effect of changing one or more of the values in the worksheet.

7 ▸▸▸ Freelance workers must monitor income and business expenses carefully in order to be profitable. Painters, landscapers, consultants, and house cleaners are people who often work on a freelance basis. Interview someone who performs freelance work and build a worksheet reflecting his or her profits over the past six months. Attempt to determine the percentage of the worker's income spent on business-related expenses. Find out about any occasional expenses. With this information, and the freelance worker's income for each of the past six months, determine the worker's expenses and profits each month. Include at least one chart that illustrates an aspect of your worksheet you feel is significant—perhaps profits each month or the total money applied to every business expense.

Linking an Excel Worksheet to a Word Document

Case Perspective

Each week, the director of sales for Net Microsystems, Kevin James, sends out a memorandum to all the sales representatives in the organization showing the previous week's daily sales by office. He currently uses Word to produce the memorandum, which includes a table of the daily sales. The wording in the memorandum remains constant week to week. The table of daily sales changes each week.

Kevin recently heard of the Object Linking and Embedding (OLE) capabilities of Microsoft Office. He wants to use OLE to create the basic memorandum using Word and maintain the weekly sales in an Excel worksheet. Each week, he envisions linking the worksheet from Excel to the Word document. Once the worksheet is linked to the Word document, he can e-mail it or print it and mail it to the sales force.

As Kevin's technical assistant, you have been asked to handle the details.

Introduction

One of the more powerful features of Microsoft Office 95 is that you can incorporate parts of documents or entire documents, called **objects,** from one application into another application. For example, you can copy a worksheet created in Excel into a document created in Word (Figure 1 on the next page). In this case, the worksheet in Excel is called the **source document** (copied from) and the document in Word is called the **destination document** (copied to). Copying objects between applications can be accomplished in three ways: (1) copy and paste; (2) copy and embed; and (3) copy and link.

All of the Microsoft Office applications allow you to use these three methods to copy objects between applications. The first method uses the Copy and Paste buttons. The latter two use the Paste Special command on the Edit menu and are referred to as **Object Linking and Embedding,** or **OLE.** Table 1 on page EI 1.3 summarizes the differences among the three methods.

Copy and link is preferred over the other two methods when an object is likely to change and you want to make sure the object reflects the changes in the source document or if the object is large, such as a video clip or sound clip. Thus, if you link a worksheet to a memorandum, and update the worksheet weekly, any time you open the memorandum, the latest updates of the worksheet will display as part of the memorandum.

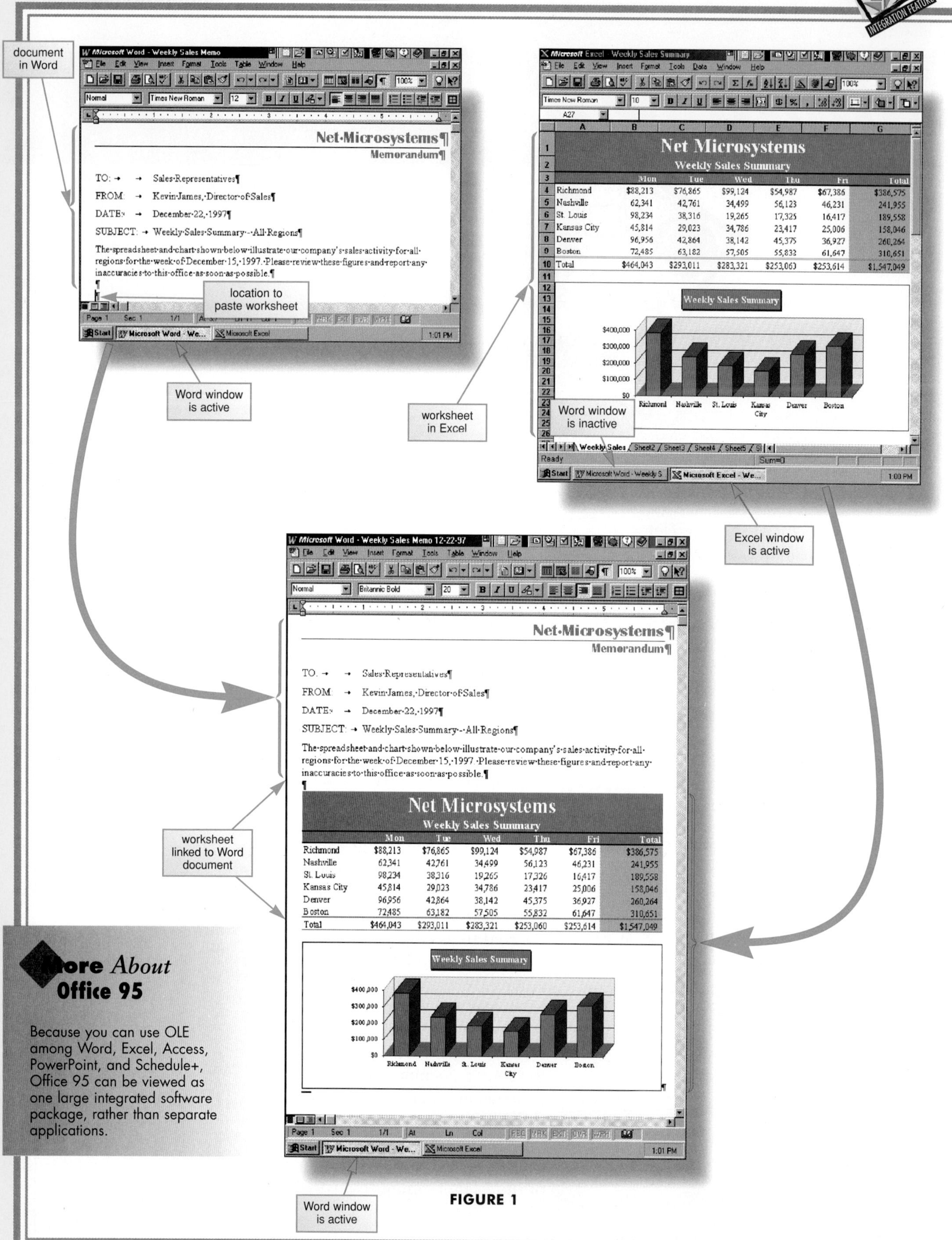

document in Word

location to paste worksheet

Word window is active

worksheet in Excel

Word window is inactive

Excel window is active

worksheet linked to Word document

Word window is active

Net·Microsystems¶
Memorandum¶

TO: → → Sales·Representatives¶

FROM: → Kevin·James,·Director·of·Sales¶

DATE: → December·22,·1997¶

SUBJECT: → Weekly·Sales·Summary·-·All·Regions¶

The·spreadsheet·and·chart·shown·below·illustrate·our·company's·sales·activity·for·all·regions·for·the·week·of·December·15,·1997.·Please·review·these·figures·and·report·any·inaccuracies·to·this·office·as·soon·as·possible.¶

Net Microsystems
Weekly Sales Summary

	Mon	Tue	Wed	Thu	Fri	Total
Richmond	$88,213	$76,865	$99,124	$54,987	$67,386	$386,575
Nashville	62,341	42,761	34,499	56,123	46,231	241,955
St. Louis	98,234	38,316	19,265	17,326	16,417	189,558
Kansas City	45,814	29,023	34,786	23,417	25,006	158,046
Denver	96,956	42,864	38,142	45,375	36,927	260,264
Boston	72,485	63,182	57,505	55,832	61,647	310,651
Total	$464,043	$293,011	$283,321	$253,060	$253,614	$1,547,049

Weekly Sales Summary

More About Office 95

Because you can use OLE among Word, Excel, Access, PowerPoint, and Schedule+, Office 95 can be viewed as one large integrated software package, rather than separate applications.

FIGURE 1

Because the weekly sales worksheet for Net Microsystems will change weekly, the copy and link method is the best method to use.

Table 1

METHOD	CHARACTERISTICS
Copy and paste	The source document becomes part of the destination document. An object may be edited, but the editing features are limited to those in the destination application. An Excel worksheet becomes a Word table. If changes are made to values in the Word table, any original Excel formulas are not recalculated.
Copy and embed	The source document becomes part of the destination document. An object may be edited in the destination application using source editing features. The Excel worksheet remains a worksheet in Word. If changes are made to values in the worksheet with Word active, Excel formulas will be recalculated. If you change the worksheet in Excel, however, changes will not show in the Word document the next time you open it.
Copy and link	The source document does not become part of the destination document even though it appears to be part of it. Instead, a link is established between the two documents so that when you open the Word document, the worksheet displays as part of it. When you attempt to edit a linked worksheet in Word, the system activates Excel. If you change the worksheet in Excel, the changes also will show in the Word document the next time you open it.

Starting Word and Excel

Both the Word document (Weekly Sales Memo) and the Excel workbook (Weekly Sales Summary) are in the Excel folder on the Student Floppy Disk that accompanies this book. The first step in linking the Excel worksheet to the Word document is both to open the document in Word and the workbook in Excel as shown in the following steps.

Steps To Open a Word Document and an Excel Workbook

1. **Click the Start button. Click Open Office Document on the Start menu. Click 3½ Floppy [A:] in the Look in box. Open the Excel folder. Double-click the filename Weekly Sales Memo.**

   Word becomes active and the Weekly Sales Memo displays (Figure 2).

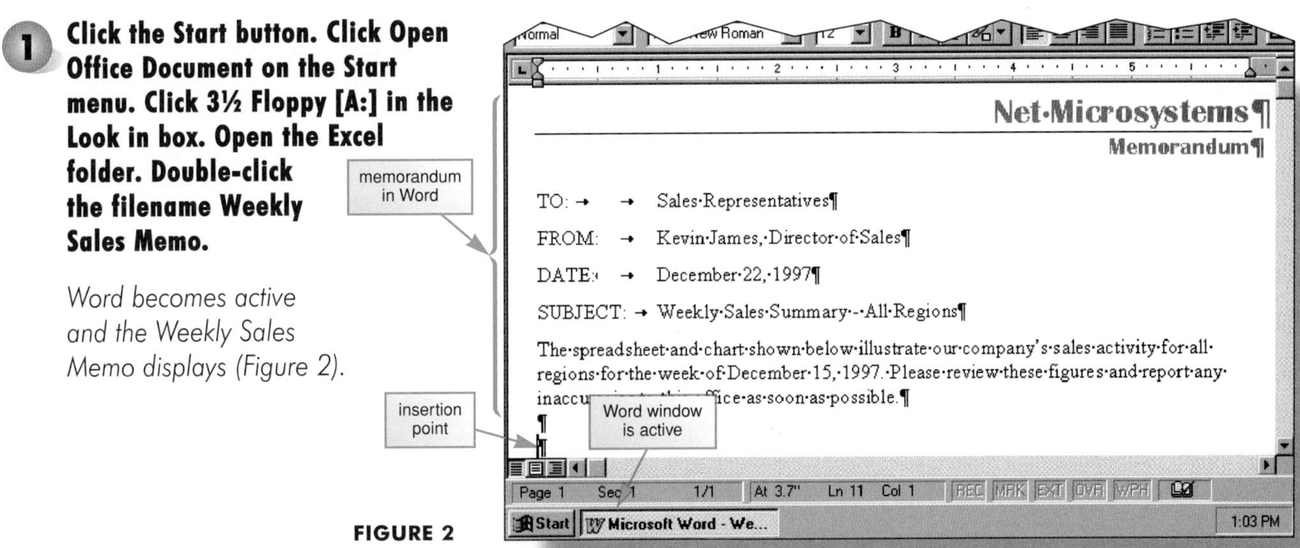

FIGURE 2

2 Click the Start button. Click Open Office Document on the Start menu. Click 3½ Floppy [A:] in the Look in box. If necessary, open the Excel folder. Double-click the filename, Weekly Sales Summary.

Excel becomes active and the Weekly Sales Summary workbook displays (Figure 3). At this point, Word is inactive, but still is in main memory. Excel is the active window as shown on the taskbar.

	Net Microsystems						
	Weekly Sales Summary						
		Mon	Tue	Wed	Thu	Fri	Total
4	Richmond	$88,213	$76,865	$99,124	$54,987	$67,386	$386,575
5	Nashville	62,341	42,761	34,499	56,123	46,231	241,955
6	St. Louis	98,234	38,316	19,265	17,326	16,417	189,558
7	Kansas City	45,814	29,023	34,786	23,417	25,006	158,046
8	Denver	96,956	42,864	38,142	45,375	36,927	260,264
9	Boston	72,485	63,182	57,505	55,832	61,647	310,651
10	Total	$464,043	$293,011	$283,321	$253,060	$253,614	$1,547,049

worksheet and chart

Weekly Sales Summary

Weekly Sales / Sheet2 / Sheet3 / Sheet4 / Sheet5

Ready — Sum=0

Start | Microsoft Word - Weekly S... | Microsoft Excel - We... | 1:03 PM

Word window is inactive

Excel window is active

FIGURE 3

OtherWays

1. On Microsoft Office Shortcut Bar, click Open a Document button

With both Word and Excel in main memory, you can switch between the applications by clicking the appropriate button on the taskbar, next to the Start button.

Linking

With both applications running, the next step is to link the Excel worksheet to the Word document as shown in the following steps.

Steps To Link the Excel Worksheet to the Word Document

1 With the Excel window active, select the range A1:G25. Click the Copy button to place the selected range on the Clipboard.

The range A1:G25 is selected (Figure 4).

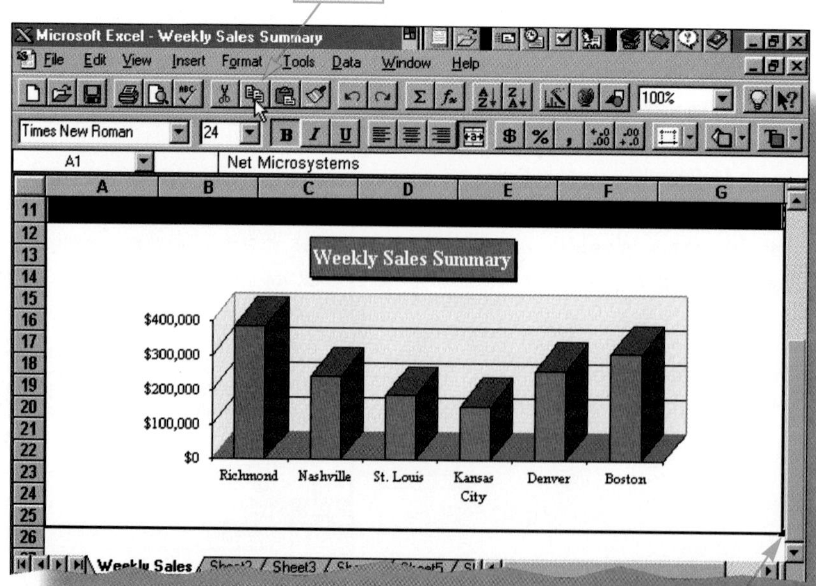

FIGURE 4

2 **Click the Microsoft Word button on the taskbar to activate the Word window. Click the last paragraph mark at the bottom of the document to position the insertion point where the worksheet will display in the document. Click Edit on the menu bar and then point to Paste Special.**

The Weekly Sales Memo document and the Edit menu display on the screen. The insertion point blinks at the bottom of the document (Figure 5).

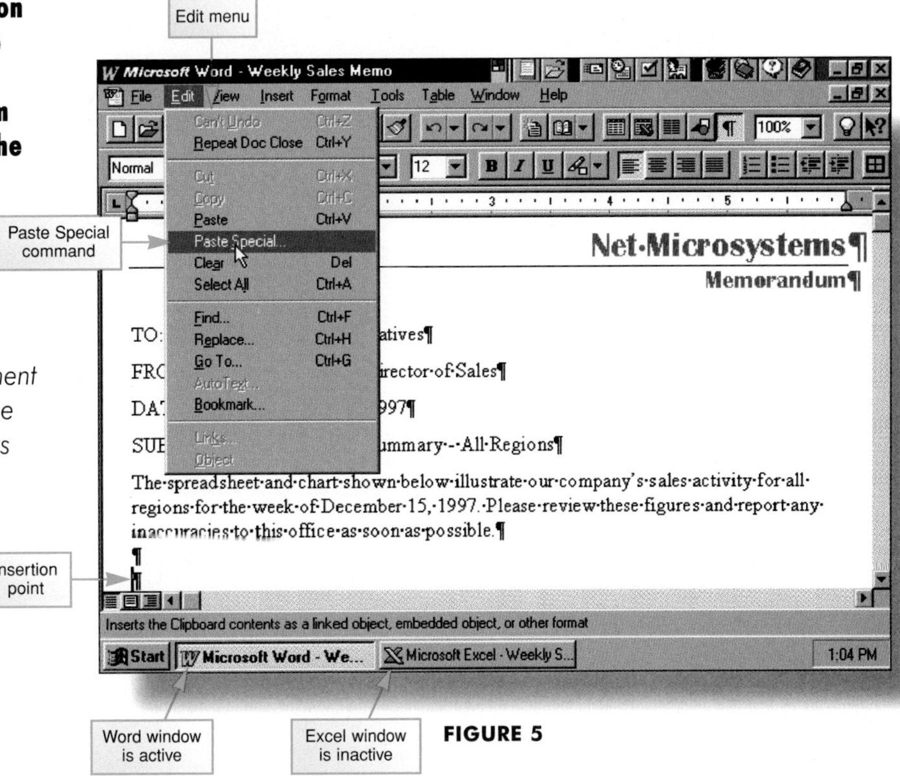

FIGURE 5

3 **Click Paste Special on the Edit menu. When the Paste Special dialog box displays, click Paste Link and then click Microsoft Excel Worksheet Object in the As box.**

The Paste Special dialog box displays as shown in Figure 6.

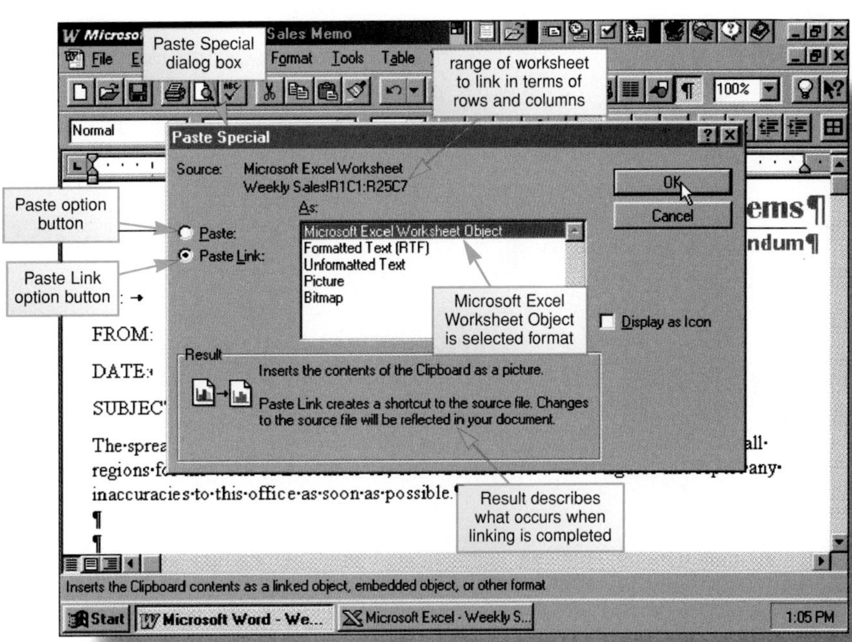

FIGURE 6

Click the OK button in the Paste Special dialog box.

The range A1:G25 of the worksheet displays in the Word document beginning at the location of the insertion point (Figure 7).

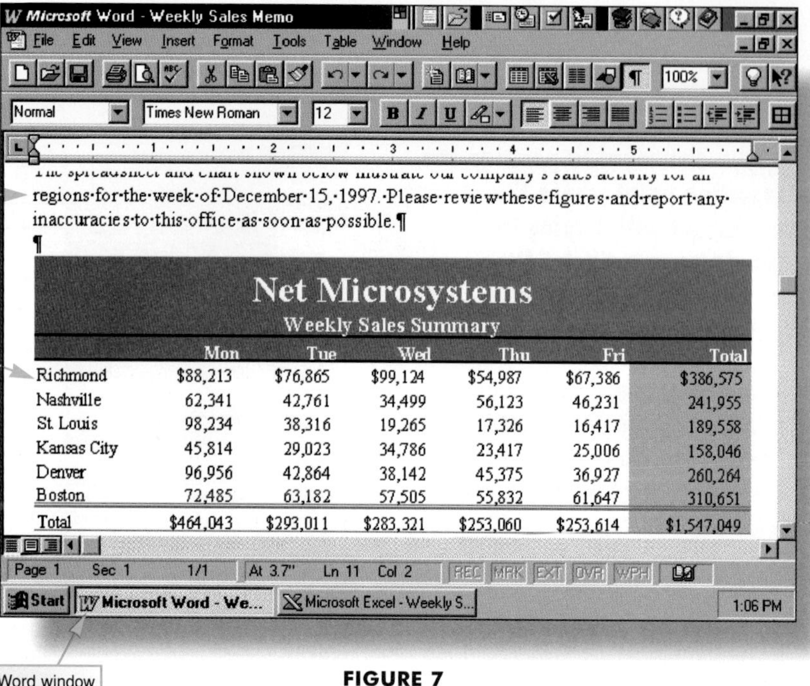

FIGURE 7

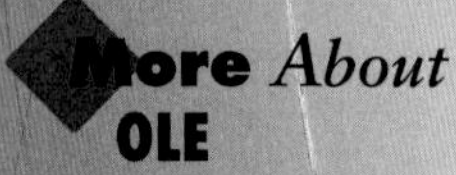

More About OLE

If you want to have more than one object at a time available for OLE, you can store objects to embed on the desktop, rather than using the Clipboard. When you use this technique, the objects are called **scrap**. To accomplish this task, part of the desktop must be visible behind the window of the source application. Next, right-drag the object onto the desktop. Once on the desktop, Windows displays the object as an icon. When the shortcut menu displays, click Create Scrap Here. Next, activate the destination document and drag the scrap from the desktop onto the destination document and drop it where you want it inserted. To delete a scrap from the desktop, right-click it and then click Delete.

The Excel workbook is now linked to the Word document. If you save the Word document and reopen it, the worksheet will display just as it does in Figure 7. If you want to delete the worksheet, simply click it and press the DELETE key. The next section shows how to print and save the memo with the link to the worksheet.

Printing and Saving the Word Document with the Link

To print the Word document and linked worksheet as a single document and then save it, complete the steps on the next page.

Steps To Print and Save the Memo with the Linked Worksheet

1 **With the Word window active, click the Print button on the Standard toolbar.**

The memo and the worksheet print as one document as shown in Figure 8.

2 **Right-click the menu bar. Click Save As. Type the filename** `Weekly Sales Memo 12-22-97` **in the File name box. Click the Save button in the Save As dialog box.**

Excel saves the Word document to your floppy disk using the filename, Weekly Sales Memo 12-22-97. The worksheet is not part of the saved file. The saved file contains a link to the workbook, Weekly Sales Memo, and information about the range to display in the Word document.

document with linked worksheet and chart printed as one entity

Net Microsystems
Memorandum

TO: Sales Representatives
FROM: Kevin James, Director of Sales
DATE: December 22, 1997
SUBJECT: Weekly Sales Summary - All Regions

The spreadsheet and chart shown below illustrate our company's sales activity for all regions for the week of December 15, 1997. Please review these figures and report any inaccuracies to this office as soon as possible.

Net Microsystems
Weekly Sales Summary

	Mon	Tue	Wed	Thu	Fri	Total
Richmond	$88,213	$76,865	$99,124	$54,987	$67,386	$386,575
Nashville	62,341	42,761	34,499	56,123	46,231	241,955
St. Louis	98,234	38,316	19,265	17,326	16,417	189,558
Kansas City	45,814	29,023	34,786	23,417	25,006	158,046
Denver	96,956	42,864	38,142	45,375	36,927	260,264
Boston	72,485	63,182	57,505	55,832	61,647	310,651
Total	$464,043	$293,011	$283,321	$253,060	$253,614	$1,547,049

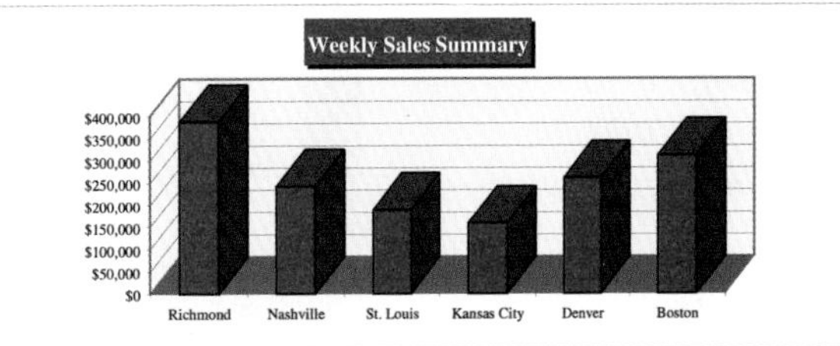

FIGURE 8

Other Ways

1. On File menu click Print, click OK button
2. Press CTRL+P, click OK button

If you exit both applications and re-open Weekly Sales Memo 12-22-97, the worksheet will display in the document even though Excel is not running. With the help of OLE, Word is able to display that portion of the linked Excel file.

The next section describes what happens when you attempt to edit the linked worksheet while Word is active.

Editing the Linked Worksheet

While the worksheet displays as part of the Word document, you can edit any of the cells in it. To edit the worksheet, double-click it. If Excel is running in main memory, the system will switch to it and display the linked workbook. If Excel is not running, the system will start it automatically and display the linked workbook. The following steps show how to change the Tuesday sales for the Boston office in cell C9 from $63,182 to $2,000.

Steps To Edit the Linked Worksheet

1. **With the Word window active and the Weekly Sales Memo 12-22-97 document active, double-click the worksheet. When the Excel window becomes active, click the Maximize button.**

   Windows switches from Word to Excel and displays the original workbook, Weekly Sales Summary.

2. **Click cell C9 and enter** 2000 **in the cell.**

   Excel recalculates all formulas in the workbook (Figure 9) and redraws the 3-D column chart.

1	Net Microsystems						
2	Weekly Sales Summary						
3		Mon	Tue	Wed	Thu	Fri	Total
4	Richmond	$88,213	$76,865	$99,124	$54,987	$67,386	$386,575
5	Nashville	62,341	42,761	34,499	56,123	46,231	241,955
6	St. Louis	98,234	38,316	19,265	17,326	16,417	189,558
7	Kansas City	45,814	29,023	34,786	23,417	25,006	158,046
8	Denver	96,956	42,864	38,142	45,375	36,927	260,264
9	Boston	72,485	2,000	57,505	55,832	61,647	249,469
10	Total	$464,043	$231,829	$283,321	$253,060	$253,614	$1,485,867

value in cell C9 changed from 63,182 to 2,000
Excel window is active
totals recalculated
Weekly Sales Summary
Weekly Sales / Sheet2 / Sheet3 / Sheet4 / Sheet5 / Sl
Ready
Sum=2,000
Start
Microsoft Word - Weekly S...
Microsoft Excel - We...
1:08 PM

FIGURE 9

3. **Click the Microsoft Word button on the taskbar.**

   The Word window becomes active. The Tuesday sales amount for the Boston office is the newly entered 2,000. New totals display for Tuesday sales, Boston sales, and the Total sales for the company (Figure 10).

4. **Exit both applications without saving the changes.**

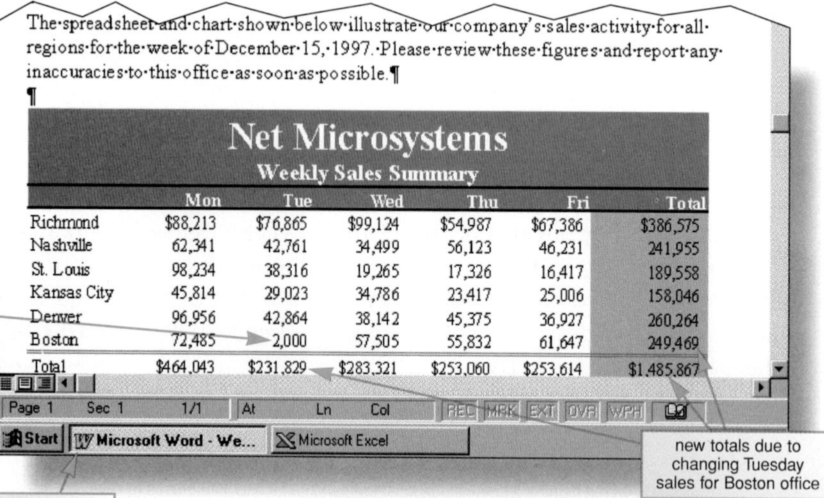

FIGURE 10

As you can see from the previous steps, when you want to edit a linked object, double-click it. Windows will activate the application and display the workbook or document from which the object came. You can then edit the object and return to the destination application. Any changes made to the object will appear in the destination document.

If you want the edited changes to the linked workbook to be permanent, you must save the workbook, Weekly Sales Summary, before exiting Excel.

Summary

With the Excel worksheet linked to the Word document, Kevin James, the director of sales, can now open the Word document each week, double-click the worksheet, and change the daily sales amounts before e-mailing the Word document or printing it and mailing it to the sales force.

This Integration Feature introduced you to linking one document to another. When you link an object to a document and save it, only a link to the object is saved with the document. You edit a linked object by double-clicking it. The system activates the application and opens the file from which the object came. If you change any part of the object and then return to the destination document, the updated object will display.

What You Should Know

Having completed this Integration Feature, you should be able to perform the following tasks:

- Edit the Linked Worksheet *(EI 1.8)*
- Link the Excel Worksheet to the Word Document *(EI 1.4)*
- Open a Word Document and an Excel Workbook *(EI 1.3)*
- Print and Save the Memo with the Linked Worksheet *(EI 1.7)*

In the Lab

1 Using Help

Instructions:

Start Excel. Double-click the Help button on the Standard toolbar to display the Help Topics: Microsoft Excel dialog box. Click the Contents tab. Double-click the Sharing Data with Other Users and Applications book. Double-click the Linking and Embedding book. Double-click and read the following links: (a) Exchanging information with other applications; (b) Share information between Office applications; and (c) Troubleshoot linking and embedding problems. Hand in one printout for each of the last two links.

2 Linking a Monthly Expense Worksheet to a Monthly Expense Memo

Problem: Your supervisor, Ms. Connie Cramer, at Dress Shoes Unlimited, sends out a monthly memo with expense figures to the regional managers. You have been asked to simplify her task by linking the monthly expense worksheet to a memo.

Instructions: Perform the following tasks.

1. One at a time, open the document Monthly Expense Memo and the workbook Monthly Expense Summary from the Excel folder on the Student Floppy Disk that accompanies this book.
2. Link the range A1:E17 to the bottom of the Monthly Expense Memo document.
3. Print and then save the document as Monthly Expense Memo 7-1-97.
4. Double-click the worksheet and increase each of the nine expense amounts by $100. Activate the Word window and print it with the new values. Close the document and workbook without saving.

3 Embedding a Monthly Expense Memo into a Monthly Expense Workbook

Problem: Your supervisor, Ms. Connie Cramer, at Dress Shoes Unlimited, has asked you to embed the Word document into the Excel workbook, rather than linking the Excel workbook to the Word document as was done in Exercise 2.

Instructions: Complete the following tasks:

1. One at a time, open the document Monthly Expense Memo and the workbook Monthly Expense Summary from the Excel folder on the Student Floppy Disk that accompanies this book.
2. Activate Excel. On the Monthly Office Expenses sheet insert 17 rows above row 1 and then select cell A1. Activate the Word document and select the entire document. Embed the Word document at the top of the worksheet on the Monthly Office Expenses sheet.
3. Print the Monthly Office Expenses sheet and then save the workbook as Monthly Expense with Memo 7-1-97.
4. With the Excel window active, double-click the embedded document and delete the first sentence. Activate the Excel window and print it with the new memo. Close the workbook and document without saving.

PROJECT ONE

Creating a Database Using Design and Datasheet Views

PROJECT TWO

Querying a Database Using the Select Query Window

PROJECT THREE

Maintaining a Database Using the Design and Update Features of Access

INTEGRATION FEATURE

Integrating Excel Worksheet Data into an Access Database

Microsoft Access 7

Windows 95

Creating a Database Using Design and Datasheet Views

You will have mastered the material in this project when you can:

- Describe databases and database management systems
- Start Access
- Describe the features of the Access screen
- Create a database
- Create a table
- Define the fields in a table
- Open a table
- Add records to an empty table
- Close a table
- Close a database
- Open a database
- Add records to a non-empty table
- Print the contents of a table
- Use a form to view data
- Create a custom report
- Use online Help
- Understand how to design a database to eliminate redundancy

THE SPORTS FAN'S *ULTIMATE* DATABASE

Sports Scores on Your Pager

BASKETBALL

FOOTBALL

BASEBALL

HOCKEY

GOLF

BOXING

AUTO RACING

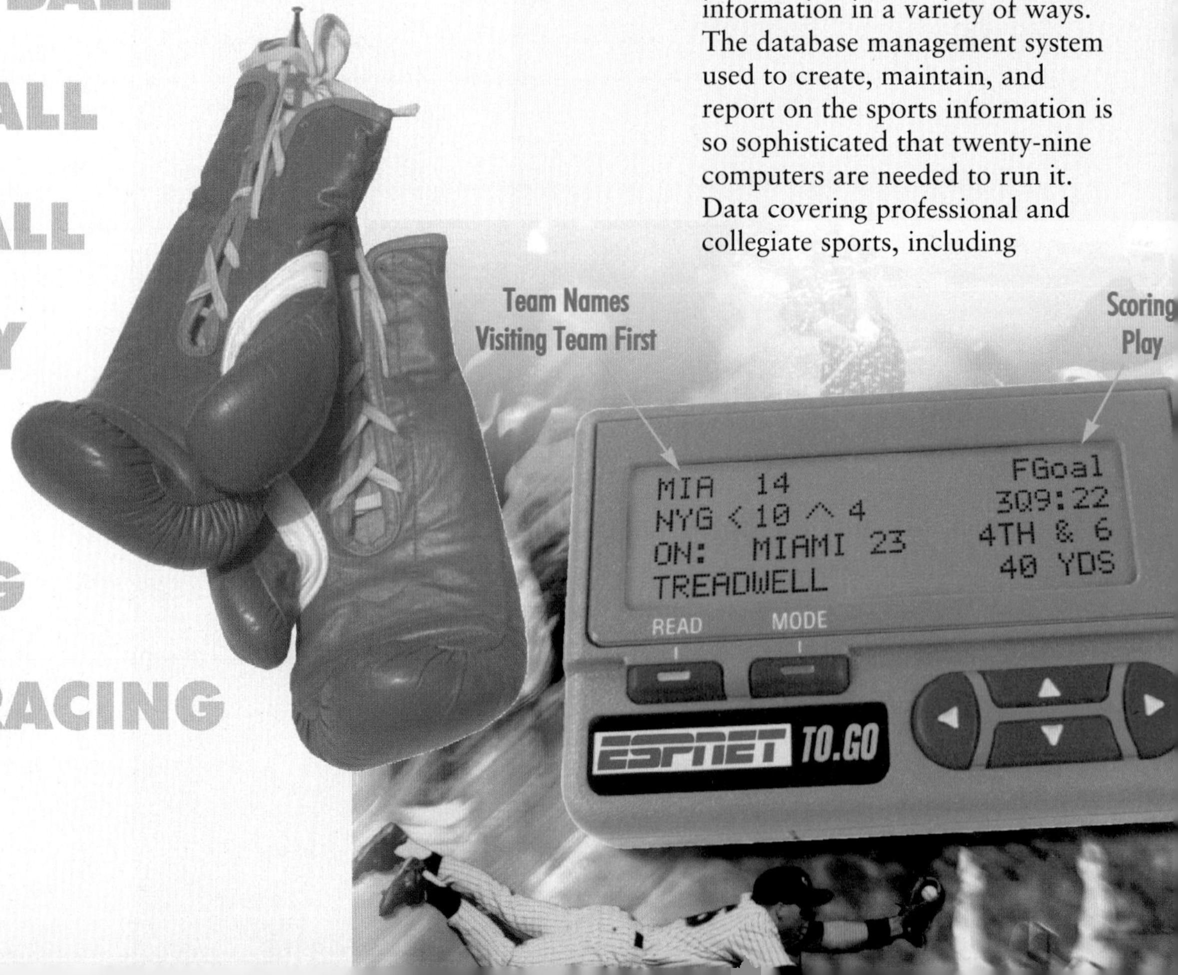

You are at your school's conference championship game. As you cheer the team to victory, your thoughts turn to professional sports. What is the score of the Lakers' game? How is Michael Jordan's injured calf muscle? Is it raining at the Western Open?

Until a few years ago, you would have had to leave the game, buy one or more newspapers, and comb the sports pages to satisfy your curiosity. Today, however, you can reach in your pocket, pull out your pager, and find the answers to these questions, along with the latest sports news, scores, game information, and trivia. It is part of ESPNET TO GO, a new wireless service on Motorola's EMBARC sports receiver.

All this information is found in a database located in Florida. A database is an organized collection of data that provides access to information in a variety of ways. The database management system used to create, maintain, and report on the sports information is so sophisticated that twenty-nine computers are needed to run it. Data covering professional and collegiate sports, including basketball, football, baseball, hockey, golf, boxing, and auto racing, is kept in more than 200 storage areas, or fields. Statistics, game schedules, injury and weather reports, and point spreads are part of the service, which also includes play situations (such as who is batting or who has the ball) for Major League Baseball and National Football League games in progress.

The data for the ESPNET database comes from many feeds, including ESPN, the largest cable network in America. Score updates, late-breaking sports news, other sports information, and commentary are transmitted to a satellite, which then relays the data to the database.

The data is checked continually for errors, sorted, and then integrated into the database. The fields in the database are updated when new information is received. For example, the field containing the halftime score of the USC-UCLA game is updated when either team scores.

Approximately every five minutes, the computer uplinks the revised database information to a satellite. This satellite then delivers the data to a network of land-based transmitters located in more than 230 metropolitan areas across the United States and Canada. These transmitters, in turn, broadcast the data to pager-like receivers or to personal computers. The wireless sports information service also is available internationally.

ESPNET TO GO was introduced in August 1995 after four years of development. The product is targeted for two groups: avid sports fans and professionals in the sports industry, such as coaches, players, and sports writers. It is used more than a million times daily by subscribers. In the future, ESPNET might be customized so users can obtain only the sports information they desire. For example, subscribers who are not interested in golf could choose to delete all information regarding that sport.

Ultimate sports fans who want to follow all the action, anywhere and anytime, find the virtual real-time information in the ESPNET database a welcome supplement to their minimum daily sports diet.

Microsoft
Access 7
Windows 95

Creating a Database Using Design and Datasheet Views

Case Perspective

The management of Mason Clinic, a physical therapy clinic, has determined that the practice has grown to the point that the maintenance of patient and therapist data can no longer be done manually. By placing the data in a database, managed by a database management system like Access, management will be able to ensure that the data is more current and more accurate than in the present manual system. They also will be able to produce a variety of useful reports. In addition, they need to be able to ask questions concerning the data in the database and obtain answers to these questions easily and rapidly.

Introduction

Creating, storing, sorting, and retrieving data are important tasks. In their personal lives, many people keep a variety of records such as names, addresses, and phone numbers of friends and business associates, records of investments, records of expenses for tax purposes, and so on. These records must be arranged for quick access. Businesses also must be able to store and access information quickly and easily. Personnel and inventory records, payroll information, patient records, order data, and accounts receivable information all are crucial and must be readily available.

The term **database** describes a collection of data organized in a manner that allows access, retrieval, and use of that data. A **database management system**, like Access, allows you to use a computer to create a database; add, change, and delete data in the database; sort the data in the database; retrieve data in the database; and create forms and reports using the data in the database.

In Access, a database consists of a collection of tables. Figure 1-1 shows a sample database for Mason Clinic. It consists of two tables. The Patient table contains information about the patients in a multiple-therapist clinic. The Therapist table contains information about the therapists in the clinic.

The rows in the tables are called records. A **record** contains information about a given person, product, or event. A row in the Patient table, for example, contains information about a specific patient.

FIGURE 1-1

Patient Table

PATIENT NUMBER	LAST NAME	FIRST NAME	ADDRESS	CITY	STATE	ZIP CODE	BALANCE	INSURANCE	THER NUMBER
AL26	Alardyce	Lisa	311 Birchwood	Lamont	MI	49160	$196.62	$180.00	05
AT73	Acton	Thomas	312 Newcastle	Homer	MI	49162	$726.42	$550.00	08
BR31	Bryce	Roger	617 College	Lamont	MI	49160	$96.00	$0.00	08
DI32	Dalton	Irene	41 Lafayette	Madison	IN	42909	$875.00	$600.00	14
GC92	Gutierez	Carlos	476 Fulton	Jackson	OH	49401	$273.00	$150.00	05
GT43	Grant	Thomas	247 Fuller	Lamont	MI	49160	$276.00	$0.00	08
JG22	Jenkins	Glen	201 Plymouth	Madison	IN	42909	$0.00	$0.00	08
LI66	Lawrence	Irving	912 Devonshire	Beulah	MI	45621	$346.50	$175.00	05
PE33	Pezato	Eduardo	346 Vernor	Homer	MI	49162	$467.12	$500.00	14
PE76	Perez	Enzo	216 Four Mile	Perry	MI	47211	$216.00	$0.00	08

Therapist Table

THER NUMBER	LAST NAME	FIRST NAME	ADDRESS	CITY	STATE	ZIP CODE	BILLING	PAID
05	Hughes	Mary	4613 Essex	Burnips	MI	49277	$62,277.00	$46,245.25
08	Foster	Richard	6621 Eastern	Stockton	IN	47962	$71,245.00	$65,121.33
14	Galvez	Juanita	684 Valley	Leland	MI	47205	$34,252.50	$22,645.90

The columns in the tables are called fields. A **field** contains a specific piece of information within a record. In the Patient table, for example, the fourth field, City, contains the city where the patient is located.

The first field in the Patient table is the Patient Number. This is a code assigned by the clinic to each patient. Like many organizations, this clinic calls it a "number" even though it actually contains letters. The patient numbers have a special format. They consist of two uppercase letters followed by a two-digit number.

These numbers are *unique*; that is, no two patients will be assigned the same number. Such a field can be used as a **unique identifier**. This simply means that a given patient number will appear only in a single record in the table. Only one record exists, for example, in which the patient number is BR31. A unique identifier also is called a **primary key**. Thus, the Patient Number field is the primary key for the Patient table.

More *About* Creating a Database

In Access, a database is stored in a single file on disk. The file has an extension of MDB. All the tables, queries, forms, reports, and programs that you create for this database are stored in this one file.

The next eight fields in the Patient table include the Last Name, First Name, Address, City, State, Zip Code, Balance, and Insurance. The Balance field contains the patient's current balance; that is, the amount the patient owes to the clinic. The Insurance field contains the portion of the balance that is expected to be covered by the patient's health insurance.

For example, patient AL26 is Lisa Alardyce. She is located at 311 Birchwood in Lamont, Michigan. The Zip Code is 49160. Her current balance (the amount she owes to the clinic) is $196.62. The portion of this amount that should be paid by her insurance company is $180.00.

Each patient is assigned to a single therapist. The last field in the Patient table, Ther Number, gives the number of the patient's therapist.

The first field in the Therapist table, Ther Number, is the number assigned by the clinic to each therapist. These numbers are unique, so Ther Number is the primary key of the Therapist table.

The other fields in the Therapist table are Last Name, First Name, Address, City, State, Zip Code, Billing, and Paid. The Billing field contains the total amount that has been billed by the therapist for the therapist's services so far this year. The Paid field contains the portion of this amount that already has been paid, either by patients or by insurance companies.

For example, therapist 05 is Mary Hughes. She lives at 4613 Essex in Burnips, Michigan. Her Zip Code is 49277. So far this year, she has billed $62,277.00, of which $46,245.25 already has been paid.

The Ther Number appears in both the Patient table and the Therapist table. It is used to relate patients and therapists. For example, in the Patient table, you see that the Ther Number for patient AL26 is 05. To find the name of this therapist, look for the row in the Therapist table that contains 05 in the Ther Number field. Once you have found it, you know the patient is assigned to Mary Hughes. To find all the patients assigned to Mary Hughes, look through the Patient table for all the patients that contain 05 in the Ther Number field. Her patients are AL26 (Lisa Alardyce), GC92 (Carlos Gutierez), and LI66 (Irving Lawrence).

Project One – Mason Clinic

Together with the management of Mason Clinic, you have determined that the data that must be maintained in the database is the data shown in Figure 1-1 on page A 1.7. You first must create the database and the tables it contains. In the process, you must define the fields contained in the two tables, including the type of data each field will contain. You then must add the appropriate records to the tables. You also must print the contents of the tables. Finally, you must create a report containing the patient number, first name, last name, balance, and insurance amount fields for each patient of Mason Clinic. Other reports and requirements for the database at Mason Clinic will be addressed with the Mason Clinic management in the future.

What Is Microsoft Access?

Microsoft Access is a powerful database management system (DBMS) that functions in the Windows environment and allows you to create and process data in a database. To illustrate the use of Access, this book presents a series of projects.

The projects use the database of patients and therapists. In Project 1, the two tables that comprise the database are created and the appropriate records are added to them. The project also uses a form to display the data in the tables. In addition, the project prepares and prints a custom report that represents the data in the database.

Overview of Project Steps

The database preparation steps give you an overview of how the database consisting of the Patient table and the Therapist table shown in Figure 1-1 will be built in this project. The following tasks will be completed in this project.

1. Start Access.
2. Create a database called Mason Clinic.
3. Create the Patient table by defining its fields.
4. Save the Patient table in the database called Mason Clinic.
5. Add data records to the Patient table.
6. Print the contents of the Patient table.
7. Create the Therapist table, save it, and add data records to it.
8. Create a form to display data in the Patient table.
9. Create and print a report that presents the data in the Patient table.

The following pages contain a detailed explanation of each of these steps.

Mouse Usage

In this book, the mouse is the primary way to communicate with Access. You can perform six operations with a mouse: point, click, right-click, double-click, drag, and right-drag.

Point means you move the mouse across a flat surface until the mouse pointer rests on the item of choice on the screen. As you move the mouse, the mouse pointer moves across the screen in the same direction. **Click** means you press and release the left mouse button. The terminology used in this book to direct you to point to a particular item and then click is, Click the particular item. For example, Click the Primary Key button on the toolbar, means point to the Primary Key button on the toolbar and then click.

Right-click means you press and release the right mouse button. As with the left mouse button, you normally will point to an item on the screen prior to right-clicking. Right-clicking produces a **shortcut menu**, which is a menu of the most frequently used commands that relate to the portion of the screen to which you are pointing. You then can select one of these commands by pointing to it and clicking the *left* mouse button.

Double-click means you quickly press and release the left mouse button twice without moving the mouse. In most cases, you must point to an item before double-clicking. **Drag** means you point to an item, hold down the left mouse button, move the item to the desired location on the screen, and then release the left mouse button. **Right-drag** means you point to an item, hold down the right mouse button, move the item to the desired location, and then release the right mouse button.

The use of the mouse is an important skill when working with Microsoft Access for Windows 95.

Starting Access and Creating a New Database

To start Access, Windows 95 must be running. Perform the following steps to start Access and create a new database.

To Start Access

1 **Place a formatted floppy disk in drive A, click the Start button, and point to New Office Document near the top of the Start menu.**

The Start menu displays (Figure 1-2).

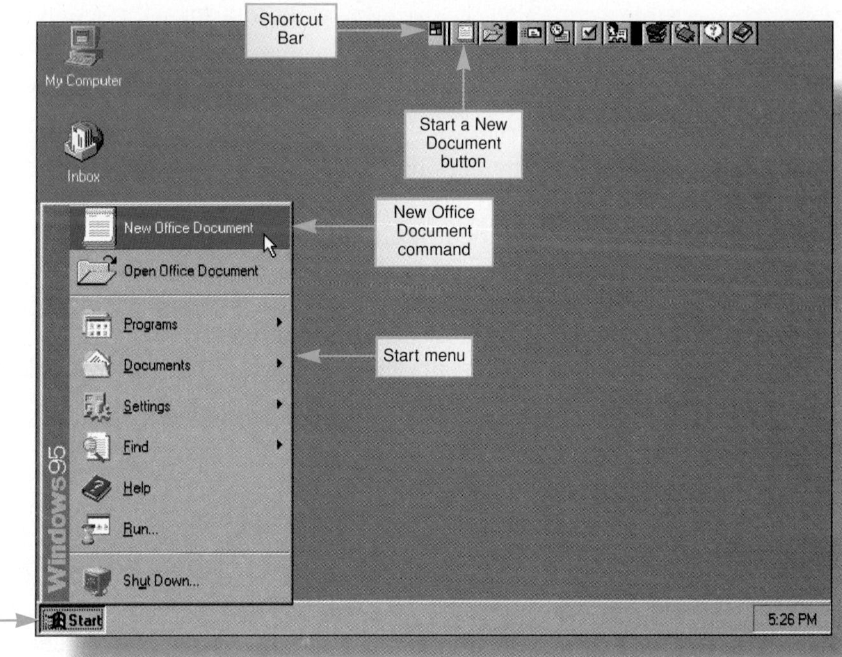

FIGURE 1-2

2 **Click New Office Document. If the General tab is not selected, that is, if it does not display in front of the other tabs, click the General tab. Make sure the Blank Database icon is selected, and then point to the OK button.**

The New dialog box displays (Figure 1-3). The Blank Database icon is selected.

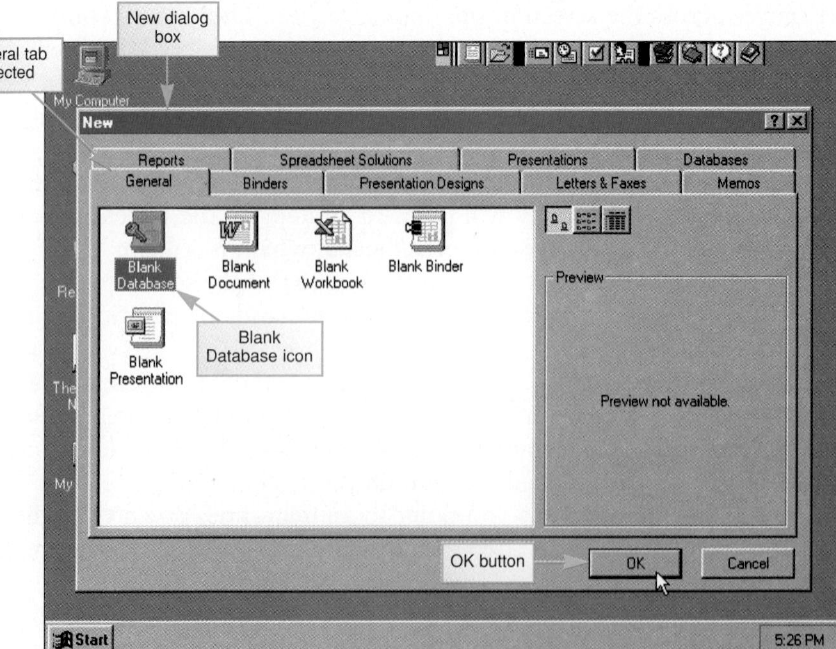

FIGURE 1-3

3 **Click the OK button, and then point to the Save in box arrow.**

The File New Database dialog box displays (Figure 1-4).

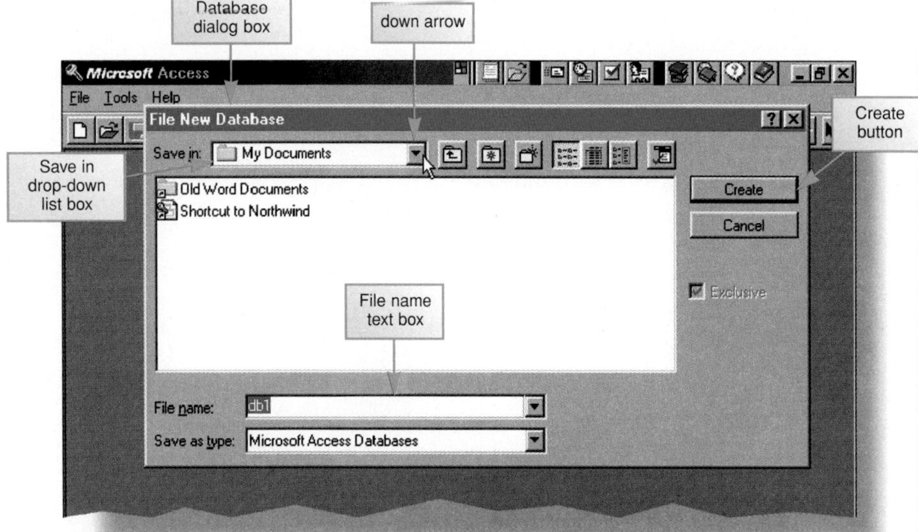

FIGURE 1-4

4 **Click the down arrow and then point to 3½ Floppy [A:].**

The Save in drop-down list displays (Figure 1-5).

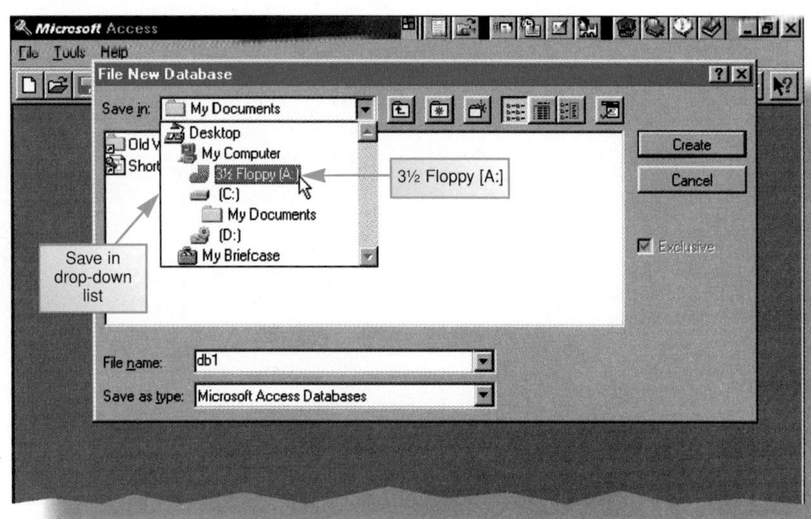

FIGURE 1-5

5 **Click 3½ Floppy [A:].**

The Save in text box contains 3½ Floppy [A:] (Figure 1-6).

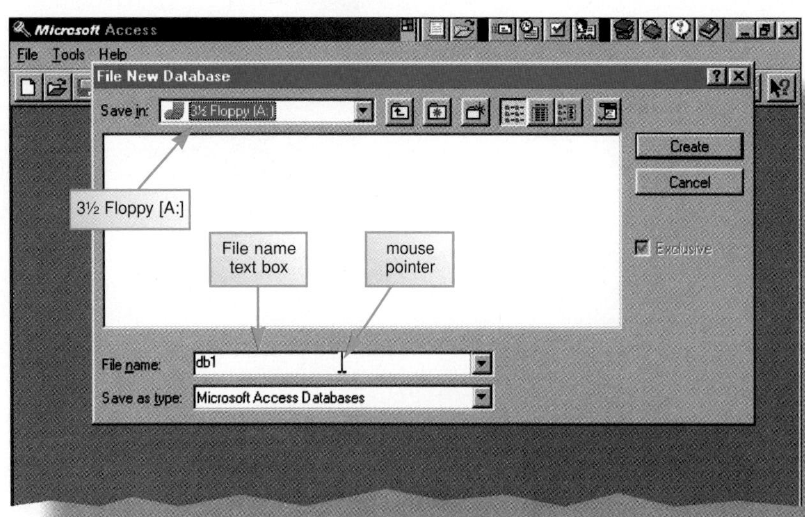

FIGURE 1-6

6 **Click in the File name text box. Repeatedly press the BACKSPACE key to delete db1, and then type** `Mason Clinic` **as the filename. Point to the Create button.**

The filename is changed to Mason Clinic (Figure 1-7).

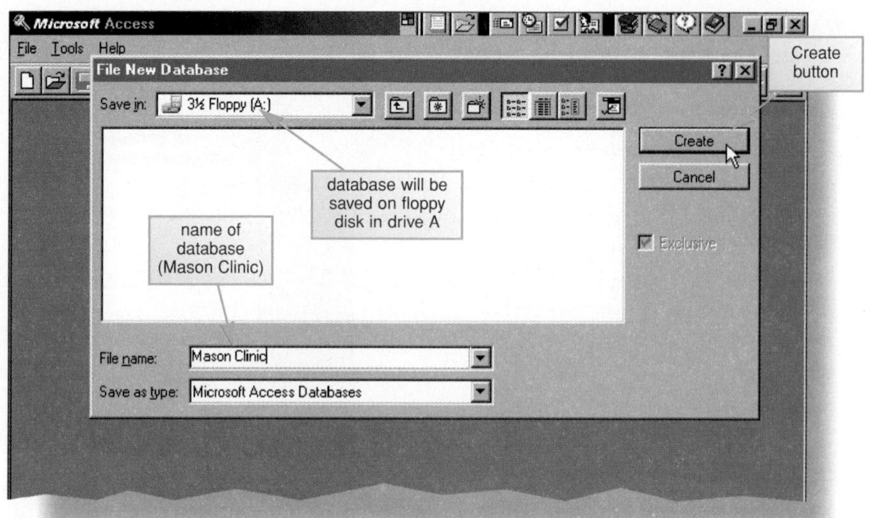

FIGURE 1-7

7 **Click the Create button to create the database.**

The Mason Clinic database is created. The Mason Clinic : Database window displays on the desktop (Figure 1-8).

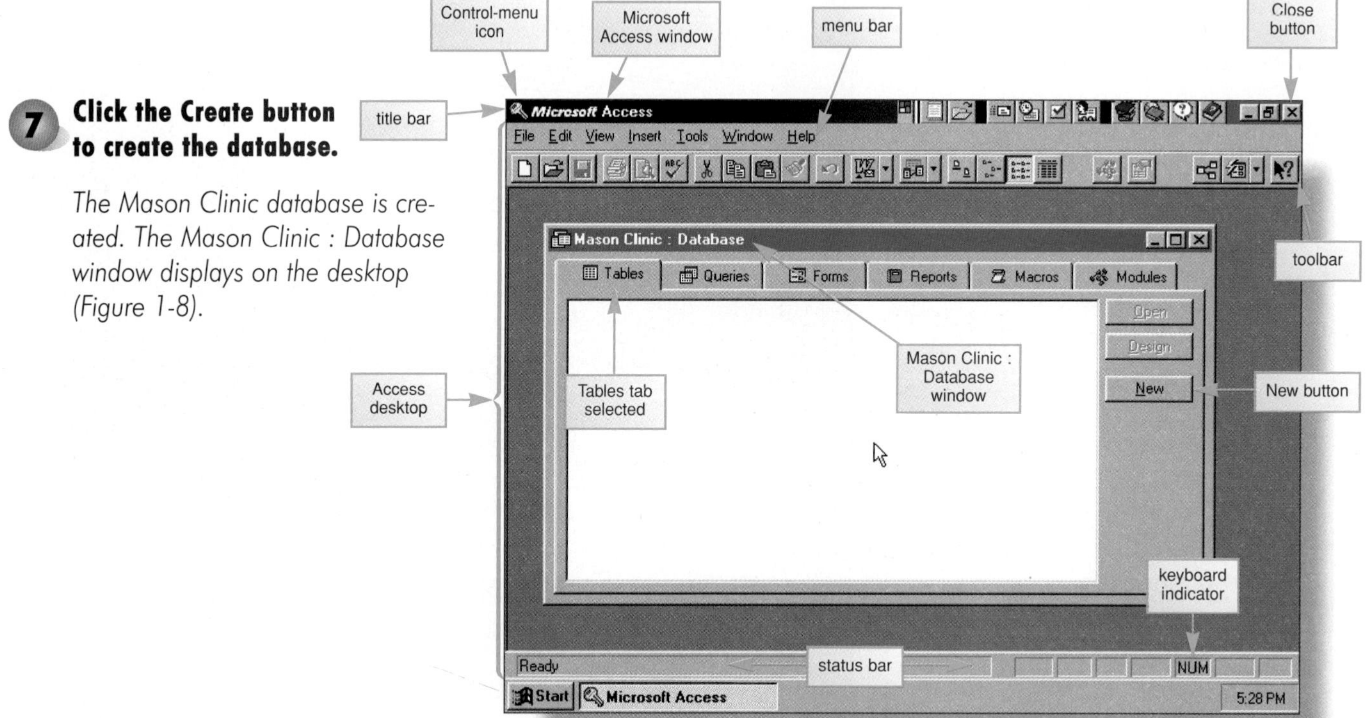

FIGURE 1-8

***Other*Ways**

1. Right-click Start button, click Open, double-click New Office Document
2. On Office Shortcut Bar, click Start a New Document button
3. On Start menu click Programs, click Microsoft Access

The Access Desktop and the Database Window

The first bar on the desktop (Figure 1-8) is the **title bar**. It displays the title of the product, Microsoft Access. The **Control-menu icon** (the key) at the left end of the title bar is used to access the **Control menu**. The button on the right is the **Close button**. Clicking a Close button closes the window.

The second bar is the **menu bar**. It contains a list of menus. You select a menu from the menu bar by clicking the menu name.

The third bar is the **toolbar**. The toolbar contains buttons that allow you to perform certain tasks more quickly than using the menu bar. Each button contains a picture, or icon, depicting its function. The specific buttons on the toolbar will vary, depending on the task on which you are working.

The **taskbar** at the bottom of the screen displays the Start button, any active windows, and the current time.

Immediately above the Windows 95 taskbar is the **status bar** (Figure 1-8). It contains special information that is appropriate for the task on which you are working. Currently, it contains the word, Ready, which means Access is ready to accept commands. Other keyboard indicators may appear such as NUM shown in Figure 1-8.

The **Database window**, referred to in Figure 1-8 as the Mason Clinic : Database window, is a special window that allows you to easily and rapidly access a variety of objects such as tables, queries, forms, and reports. To do so, you will use the various components of the window.

More *About* Toolbars

The correct toolbar will normally display. If it does not, click View on the menu bar, and then click Toolbars. Select the toolbar for the activity in which you are engaged and then click the Close button.

Creating a Table

An Access database consists of a collection of tables. Once you have created the database, you must create each of the tables within it. In this project, for example, you must create both the Patient and Therapist tables shown in Figure 1-1 on page A 1.7.

To create a table, you describe the **structure** of the table to Access by describing the fields within the table. For each field, you indicate the following:

1. **Field name** — Each field in the table must have a unique name. In the Patient table (Figure 1-9 on the next page), for example, the field names are Patient Number, Last Name, First Name, Address, City, State, Zip Code, Balance, Insurance, and Ther Number.
2. **Data type** — Data type indicates to Access the type of data the field will contain. Some fields can contain only numbers. Others, such as Balance and Insurance, can contain numbers and dollar signs. Still others, such as Last Name, First Name, and Address, can contain letters.
3. **Description** — Access allows you to enter a detailed description of the field.

More *About* Creating a Table

If you have not already determined the fields that comprise your table, you can use **Table Wizards**, which are tools that guide you through the table creation by suggesting some commonly used tables and fields. If you already know the fields you need, however, it usually is easier to just create the table yourself.

You can also assign field widths to text fields (fields whose data type is Text). This indicates the maximum number of characters that can be stored in the field. If you do not assign a width to such a field, Access assumes the width is 50.

You also must indicate which field or fields make up the **primary key**; that is, the unique identifier, for the table. In the sample database, the Patient Number field is the primary key of the Patient table and the Ther Number field is the primary key of the Therapist table.

The rules for field names are:

1. Names can be up to 64 characters in length.
2. Names can contain letters, digits, spaces, as well as most of the punctuation symbols.
3. Names cannot contain periods, exclamation points (!), or square brackets ([ ]).
4. The same name cannot be used for two different fields in the same table.

Structure of Patient Table

FIELD NAME	DATA TYPE	FIELD SIZE	PRIMARY KEY?	DESCRIPTION
Patient Number	Text	4	Yes	Patient Number (Primary Key)
Last Name	Text	10		Patient Last Name
First Name	Text	8		Patient First Name
Address	Text	15		Street Address
City	Text	15		City
State	Text	2		State (Two-Character Abbreviation)
Zip Code	Text	5		Zip Code (Five-Character Version)
Balance	Currency			Current Balance
Insurance	Currency			Expected Amount from Insurance
Ther Number	Text	2		Number of Patient's Therapist

Data for Patient Table

PATIENT NUMBER	LAST NAME	FIRST NAME	ADDRESS	CITY	STATE	ZIP CODE	BALANCE	INSURANCE	THER NUMBER
AL26	Alardyce	Lisa	311 Birchwood	Lamont	MI	49160	$196.62	$180.00	05
AT73	Acton	Thomas	312 Newcastle	Homer	MI	49162	$726.42	$550.00	08
BR31	Bryce	Roger	617 College	Lamont	MI	49160	$96.00	$0.00	08
DI32	Dalton	Irene	41 Lafayette	Madison	IN	42909	$875.00	$600.00	14
GC92	Gutierez	Carlos	476 Fulton	Jackson	OH	49401	$273.00	$150.00	05
GT43	Grant	Thomas	247 Fuller	Lamont	MI	49160	$276.00	$0.00	08
JG22	Jenkins	Glen	201 Plymouth	Madison	IN	42909	$0.00	$0.00	08
LI66	Lawrence	Irving	912 Devonshire	Beulah	MI	45621	$346.50	$175.00	05
PE33	Pezato	Eduardo	346 Vernor	Homer	MI	49162	$467.12	$500.00	14
PE76	Perez	Enzo	216 Four Mile	Perry	MI	47211	$216.00	$0.00	08

FIGURE 1-9

Each field has a data type. This indicates the type of data that can be stored in the field. The data types you will use in this project are:

1. **Text** — The field can contain any characters.
2. **Number** — The field can contain only numbers. The numbers can be either positive or negative. Fields are assigned this type so they can be used in arithmetic operations. Fields that contain numbers but will not be used for arithmetic operations are usually assigned a data type of Text. The Ther Number field, for example, is a text field because the Ther Numbers will not be involved in any arithmetic.
3. **Currency** — The field can contain only dollar amounts. The values will be displayed with dollar signs, commas, decimal points, and with two digits following the decimal point. Like numeric fields, you can use currency fields in arithmetic operations. Access automatically assigns a size to currency fields.

The list of data types that are available varies slightly from one database management system to another. In addition, the names can vary. The Access Text data type, for example, is referred to as Character in some systems.

The field names, data types, field widths, primary key information, and descriptions for the Patient table are shown in Figure 1-9. With this information, you are ready to begin creating the table. To create the table, use the following steps.

Steps To Begin Creating the Table

1 Click the New button in the Mason Clinic : Database window (see Figure 1-8 on page A 1.12). Point to Design View.

The New Table dialog box displays (Figure 1-10).

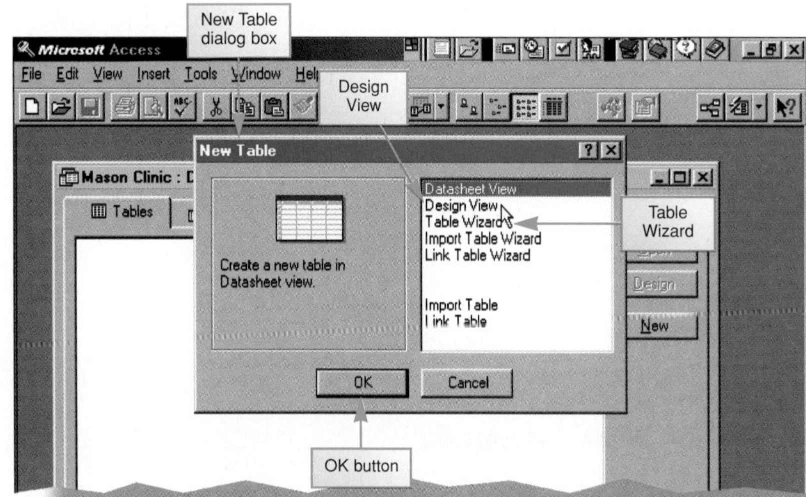

FIGURE 1-10

2 Click Design View, and then click the OK button.

The Table1 : Table window displays (Figure 1-11).

3 Click the Maximize button for the Table1 : Table window.

A maximized Table1 : Table window displays.

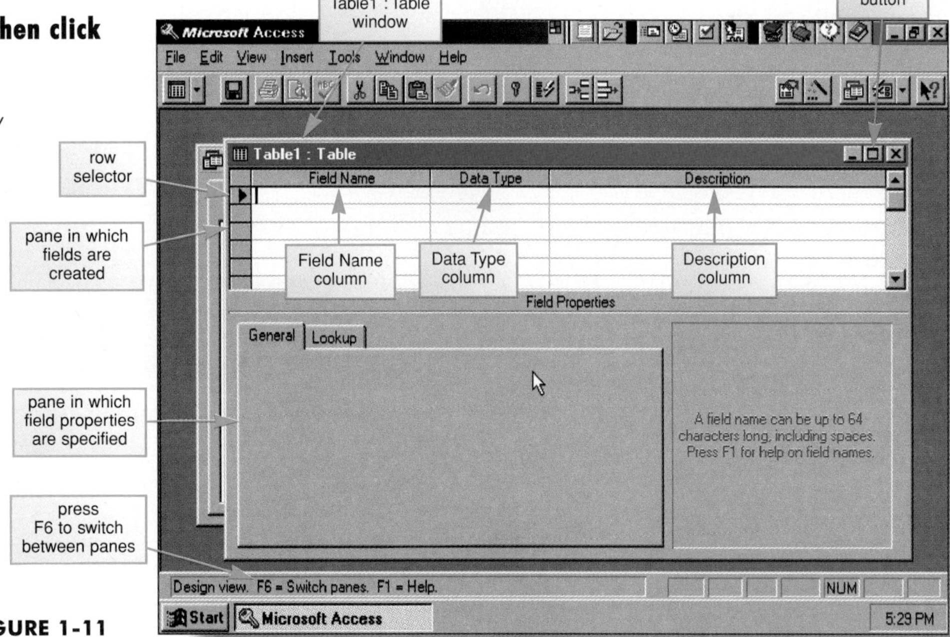

FIGURE 1-11

OtherWays

1. Click New Object button down arrow on toolbar, click New Table
2. On Insert menu click Table
3. Press ALT+N

Defining the Fields

The next step in creating the table is to define the fields by specifying the required details in the Table window. To do so, make entries in the Field Name, Data Type, and Description columns. Enter additional information in the Field Properties box in the lower portion of the Table window. To do so, press F6 to move from the upper **pane** (portion of the screen), the one where you define the fields, to the lower pane, the one where you define field properties. Enter the appropriate field size, and then press F6 to return to the upper pane. As you define the fields, the **row selector** (Figure 1-11 on page A 1.15) indicates the field you are currently describing. It currently is positioned on the first field, indicating Access is ready for you to enter the name of the first field in the Field Name column.

Perform the following steps to define the fields in the table.

To Define the Fields in the Table

1 **Type** `Patient Number` **(the name of the first field) in the Field Name column and press the TAB key.**

The words, Patient Number, display in the Field Name column and the highlight advances to the Data Type column, indicating you can enter the data type (Figure 1-12). The word, Text, one of the possible data types, currently displays. There also is an arrow you can click to display a list of available data types.

window has been maximized

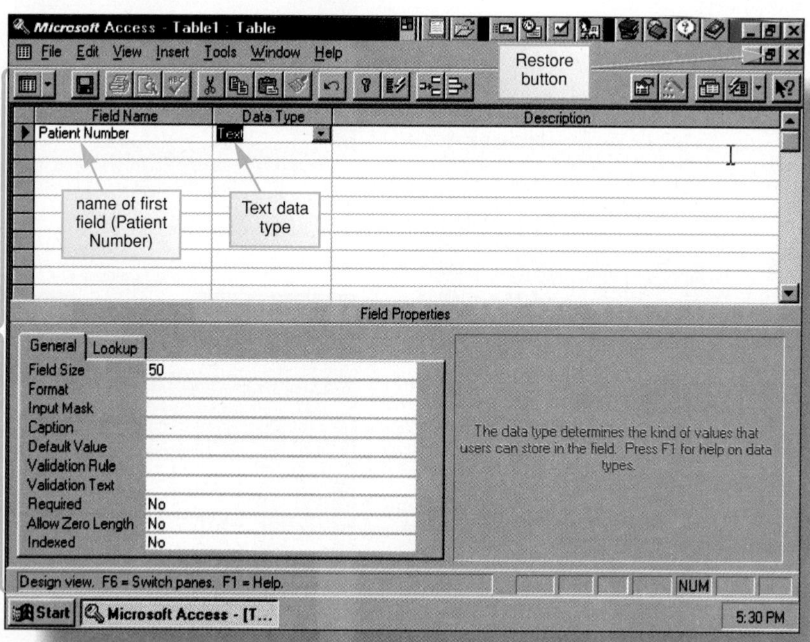

FIGURE 1-12

2 **Because Text is the correct data type, press the TAB key to move the highlight to the Description column, type** `Patient Number (Primary Key)` **as the description, and then point to the Primary Key button on the toolbar (Figure 1-13).**

A tooltip displays, which is a description of the button, partially obscuring the description of the first field.

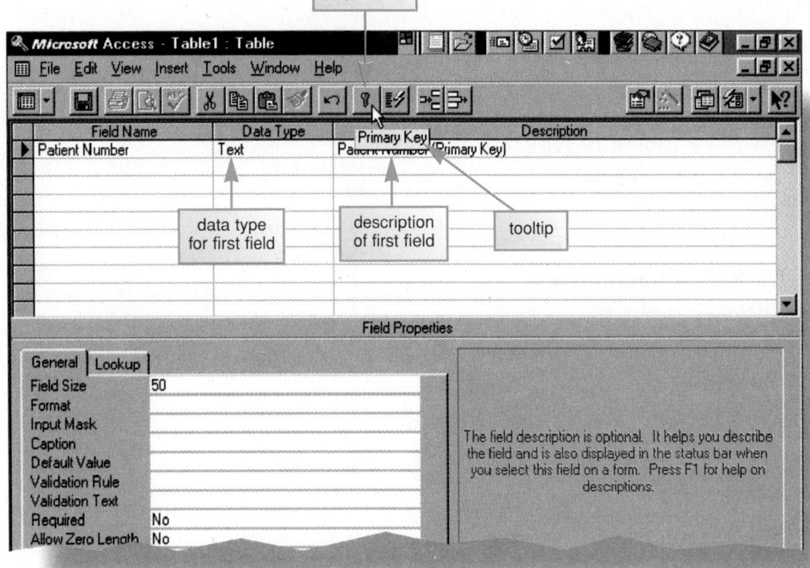

FIGURE 1-13

3 **Click the Primary Key button to make Patient Number the primary key and then press F6 to move the highlight to the Field Size text box.**

The Patient Number field is the primary key as indicated by the key symbol that appears in front of the field (Figure 1-14). The current entry in the Field Size text box (50) is highlighted.

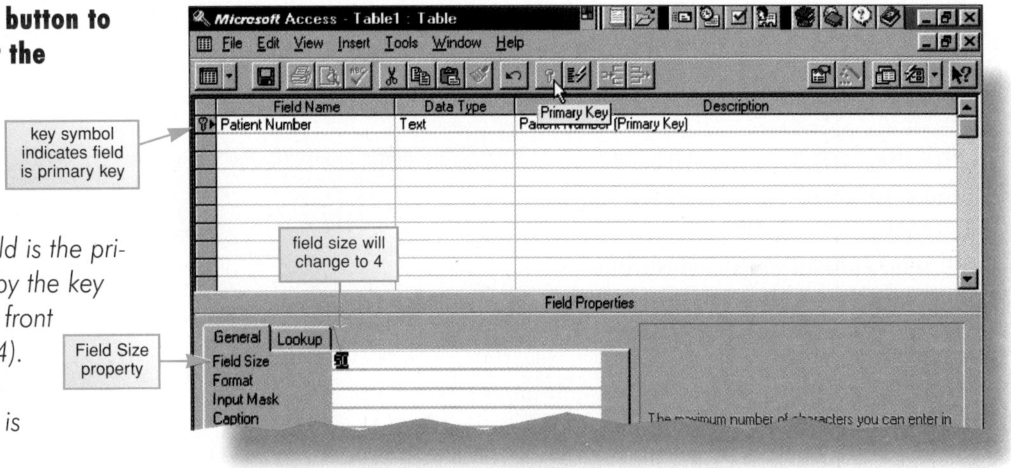

key symbol indicates field is primary key

field size will change to 4

Field Size property

FIGURE 1-14

4 **Type** 4 **as the size of the Patient Number field. Press F6 to return to the Description column for the Patient Number field, and then press the TAB key to move to the Field Name column in the second row.**

The row selector moves to the second row just below the field name Patient Number (Figure 1-15).

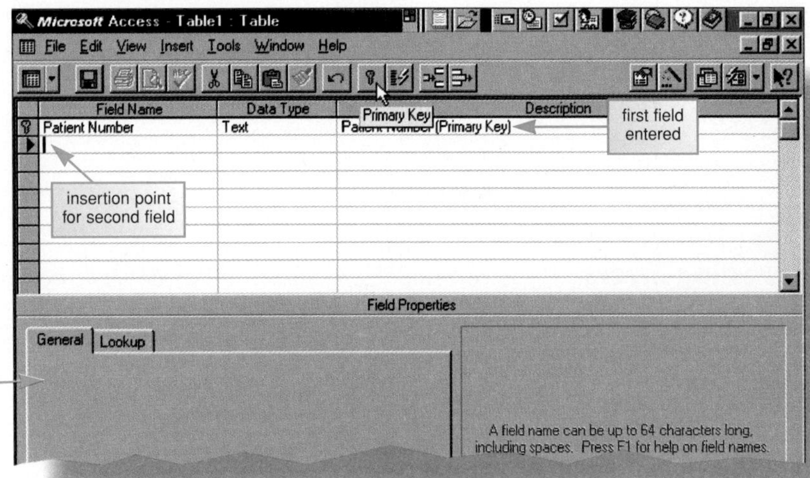

FIGURE 1-15

5 **Use the techniques illustrated in Steps 1 through 4 to make the entries from the Patient table structure shown in Figure 1-9 on page A 1.14 up through and including the name of the Balance field. You will not need to click the Primary Key button for any of these fields. Click the Data Type column down arrow and then point to the Currency data type.**

The additional fields are entered (Figure 1-16). A list of available data types displays in the Data Type column for the Balance field.

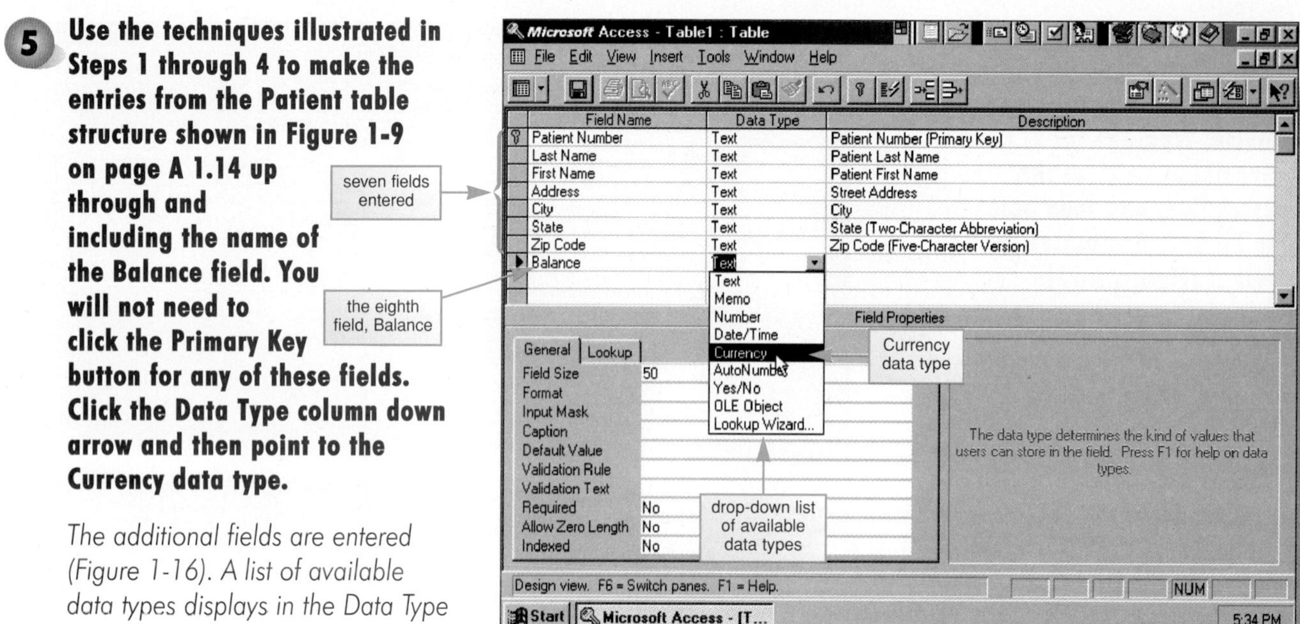

FIGURE 1-16

6 **Click the Currency data type, and then press the TAB key. Make the remaining entries from the Patient table structure shown in Figure 1-9.**

The fields are all entered (Figure 1-17)

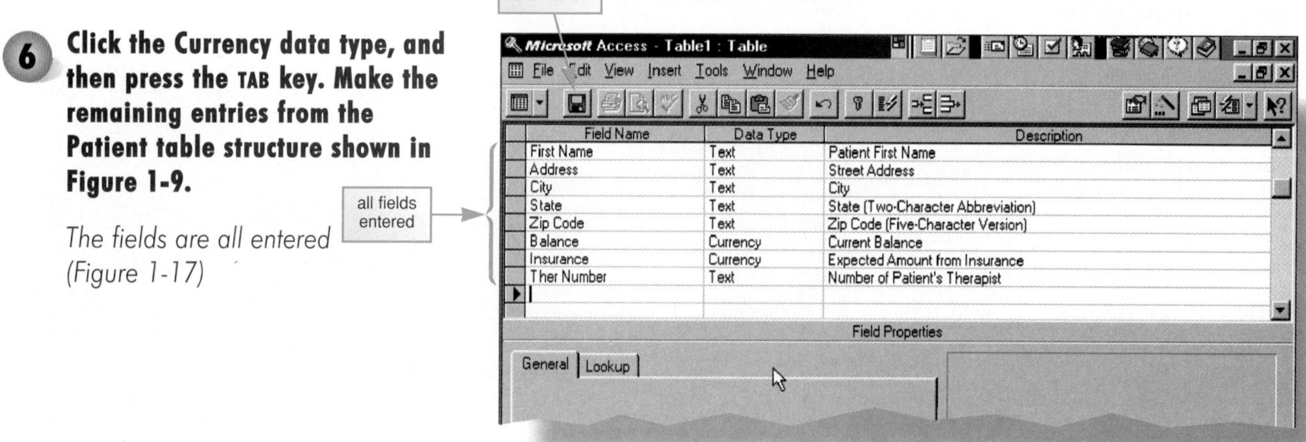

FIGURE 1-17

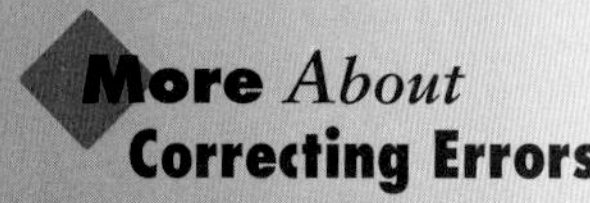

More *About* **Correcting Errors**

It is possible to correct errors in the structure even after you have entered data. Access will make all the necessary adjustments to the structure of the table as well as to the data within it. (It is simplest to make the correction, however, before any data is entered.)

Correcting Errors in the Structure

When creating a table, check the entries carefully to ensure they are correct. If you make a mistake and discover it before you press the TAB key, you can correct the error by repeatedly pressing the BACKSPACE key until the incorrect characters are removed. Then, type the correct characters. If you do not discover a mistake until later, you can click the entry with the mouse, type the correct value, and then press the ENTER key.

If you accidentally add an extra field to the structure, select the field, by clicking the leftmost column on the row that contains the field to be deleted. Once you have selected the field, press the DELETE key. This will remove the field from the structure.

If you forget a field, select the field that will follow the field you wish to add, click Edit on the menu bar, and then click Insert Row. The remaining fields move down one row, making room for the missing field. Make the entries for the new field in the usual manner.

If you made the wrong field a key field, click the correct primary key entry for the field, and then click the Primary Key button on the toolbar.

As an alternative to these steps, you may want to start over. To do so, click the Close button for the Table1 : Table window and then click No. The original desktop displays and you can repeat the process you used earlier.

Saving a Table

The Patient table structure is now complete. The final step is to **save the table** within the database. To do so, you must give the table a name.

Table names are from one to sixty-four characters in length and can contain letters, numbers, and spaces. The two table names in this project are Patient and Therapist.

To save the table, complete the following steps.

To Save the Table

1 **Click the Save button on the toolbar (see Figure 1-17). Type** `Patient` **as the name of the table in the Save As dialog box, and then point to the OK button.**

The Save As dialog box displays (Figure 1-18). The name of the table is entered in the Table Name text box.

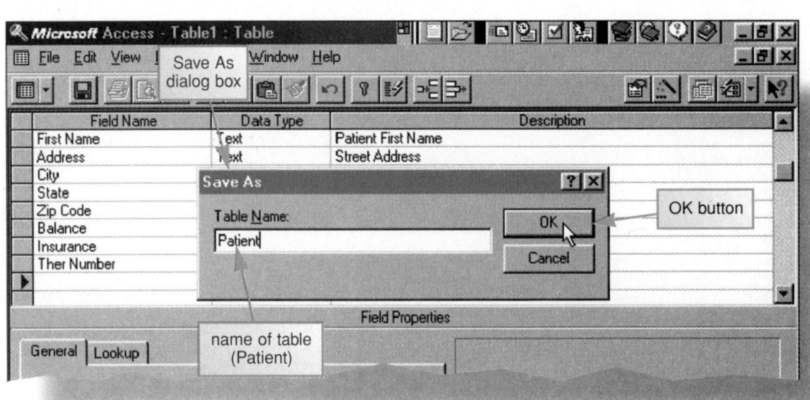

FIGURE 1-18

2 **Click the OK button, and then point to the Close button for the Patient : Table window.**

The Table is saved on the floppy disk in drive A. The name of the table is now Patient as indicated in the title bar (Figure 1-19).

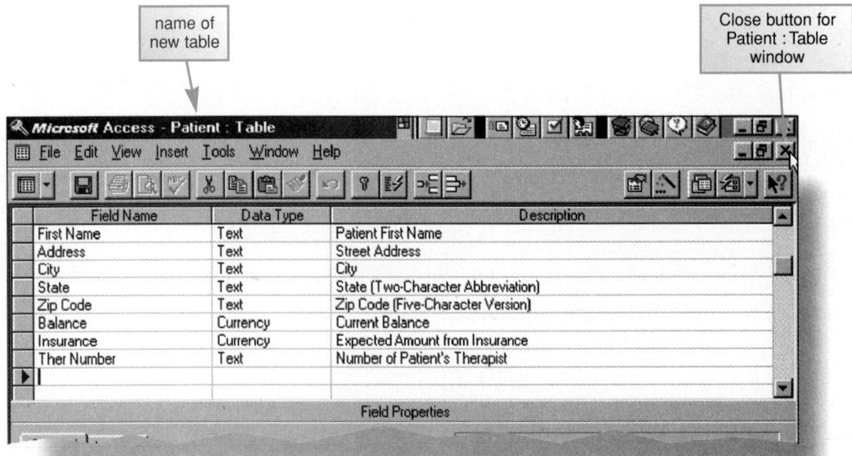

FIGURE 1-19

3 **Click the Close button for the Patient : Table window. (Be sure not to click the Close button on the first line, because this would close Microsoft Access.)**

The Patient : Table window no longer displays (Figure 1-20). The Mason Clinic : Database window displays. It is maximized because the previous window, the Patient : Table window, was maximized.

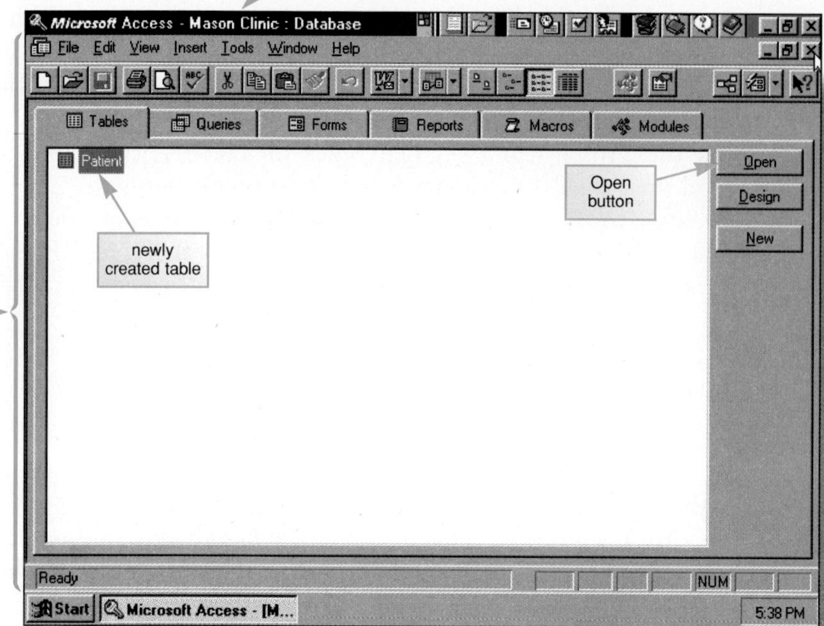

FIGURE 1-20

OtherWays

1. On File menu click Save As
2. Press CTRL+S

If you want to restore the Database window to its original size, click the window's Restore button.

More About Adding Records

When adding records to a table, each new record is saved as soon as it is entered. This is different from other tools. The rows entered in a worksheet, for example, are not saved until the entire worksheet is saved.

Adding Records to a Table

Creating a table by building the structure and saving the table is the first step in a two-step process. The second step is to **add records** to the table. To add records to a table, the table must be open. To **open a table**, select the table in the Database window and then click the Open button. The table displays in Datasheet view. In **Datasheet view**, the table is represented as a collection of rows and columns called a datasheet. It looks very much like the tables shown in Figure 1-1 on page A 1.7.

You often add records in phases. You may, for example, not have enough time to add all the records in one session. To illustrate this process, this project begins by adding the first two records in the Patient table (Figure 1-21). The remaining records are added later.

Patient Table (first 2 records)

PATIENT NUMBER	LAST NAME	FIRST NAME	ADDRESS	CITY	STATE	ZIP CODE	BALANCE	INSURANCE	THER NUMBER
AL26	Alardyce	Lisa	311 Birchwood	Lamont	MI	49160	$196.62	$180.00	05
AT73	Acton	Thomas	312 Newcastle	Homer	MI	49162	$726.42	$550.00	08

FIGURE 1-21

To open the Patient table and then add records, use the following steps.

Steps To Add Records to the Table

1 Click the Open button in the Mason Clinic : Database window (see Figure 1-20).

The Patient : Table window displays (Figure 1-22). The window contains the Datasheet view for the Patient table. The current record indicator is positioned on the first record. The status bar at the bottom of the window also indicates that the indicator is positioned on record 1.

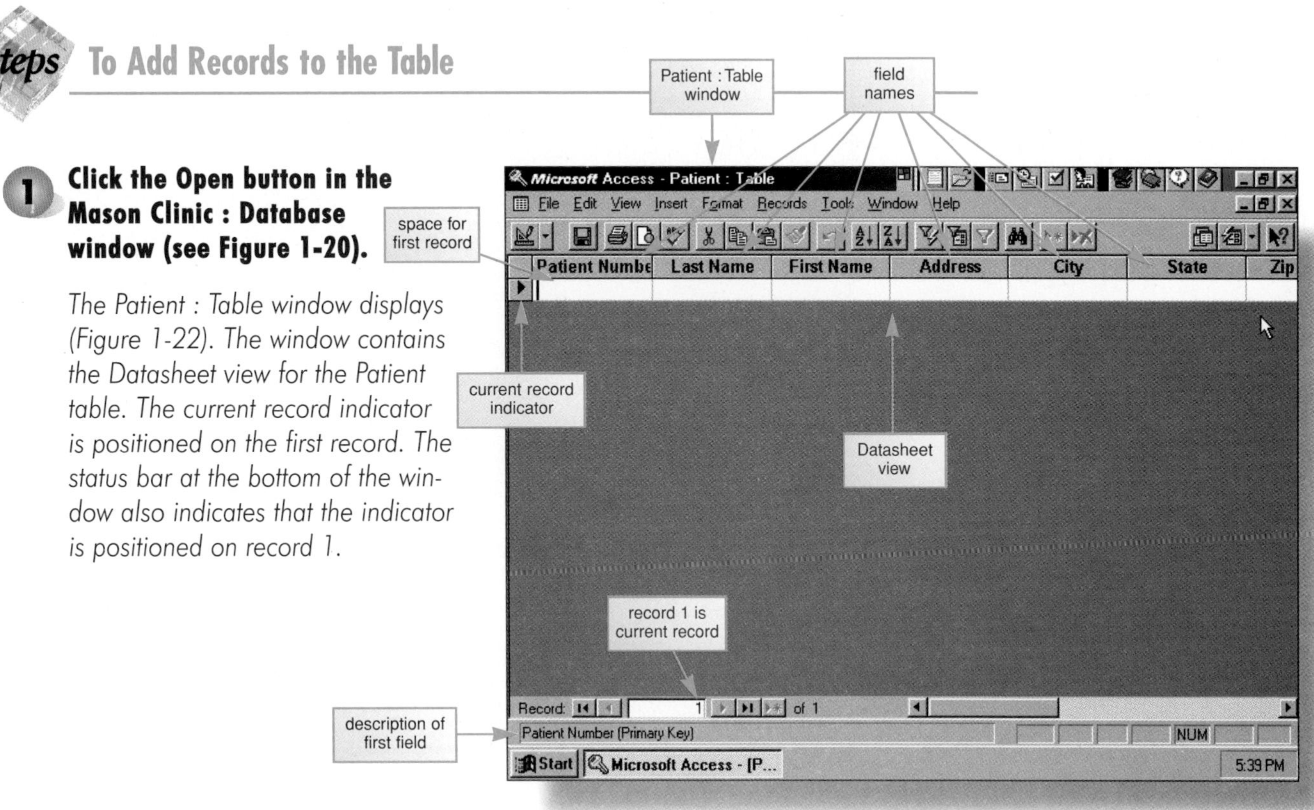

FIGURE 1-22

2 If your window is not already maximized, click the Maximize button to maximize the window containing the table. Type AL26 **as the first Patient Number, as shown in Figure 1-21. Be sure you type the letters in uppercase, because that is the way they are to be entered in the database.**

The Patient Number is entered, but the insertion point is still in the Patient Number field (Figure 1-23).

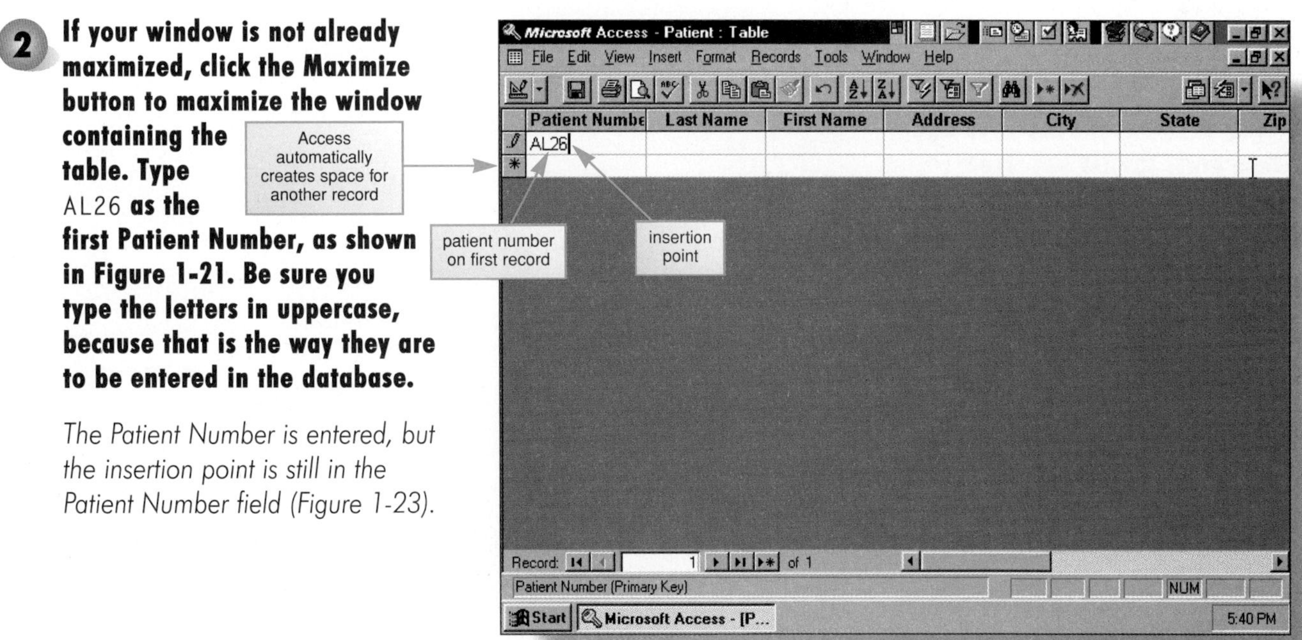

FIGURE 1-23

3 **Press the TAB key to complete the entry for the Patient Number field. Type** `Alardyce` **as the last name and then press the TAB key. Type** `Lisa` **as the first name and then press the TAB key. Type** `311 Birchwood` **as the address and then press the TAB key. Type** `Lamont` **as the city and then press the TAB key. Type** `MI` **as the State name.**

The Last Name, First Name, Address, and City fields are entered. The data for the State displays on the screen (Figure 1-24), but the entry is not complete because you have not yet pressed the TAB key.

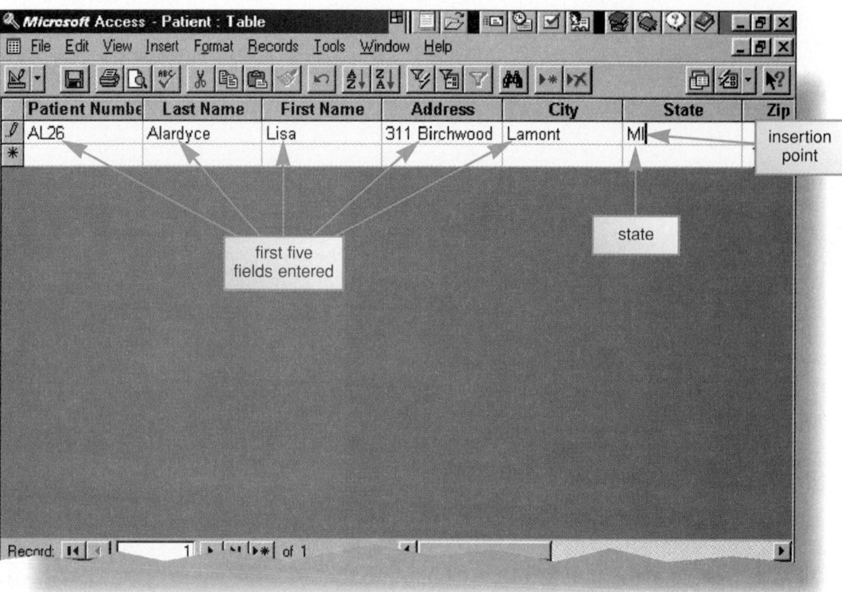

FIGURE 1-24

4 **Press the TAB key.**

The fields shift to the left (Figure 1-25). The Zip Code field displays.

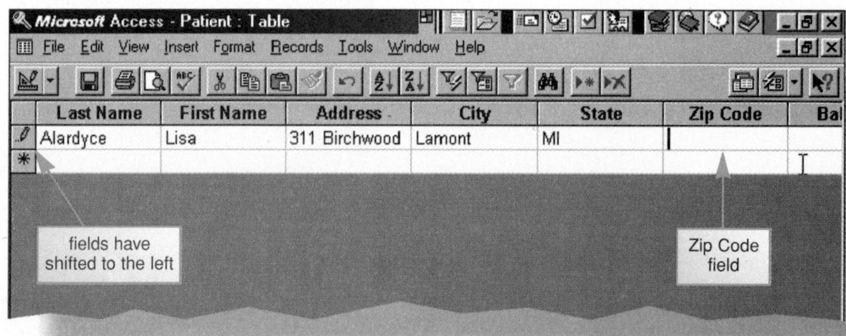

FIGURE 1-25

5 **Type** `49160` **as the Zip Code and then press the TAB key. Type** `196.62` **as the Balance and then press the TAB key. (You do not need to type dollar signs or commas. In addition, if the digits to the right of the decimal point were both zeros, you would not need to type the decimal point.) Type** `180` **as the Insurance amount and then press the TAB key. Type** `05` **as the Ther Number to complete the record.**

The fields have shifted to the left (Figure 1-26). The Balance and Insurance values display with dollar signs and decimal points. The value for the Ther Number has been entered, but the insertion point is still positioned on the field.

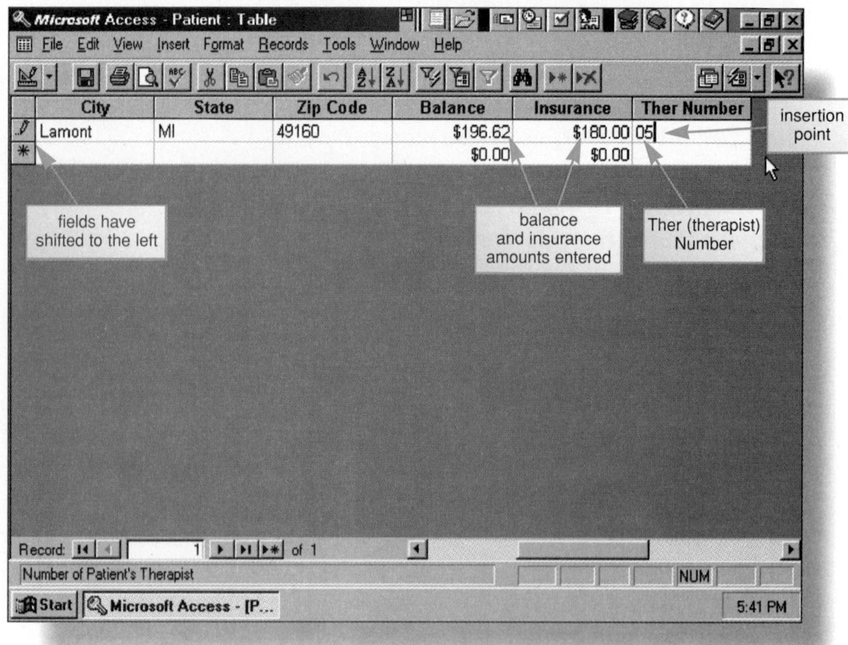

FIGURE 1-26

6 **Press the TAB key.**

The fields shift back to the right, the record is saved, and the insertion point moves to the Patient Number on the second row (Figure 1-27).

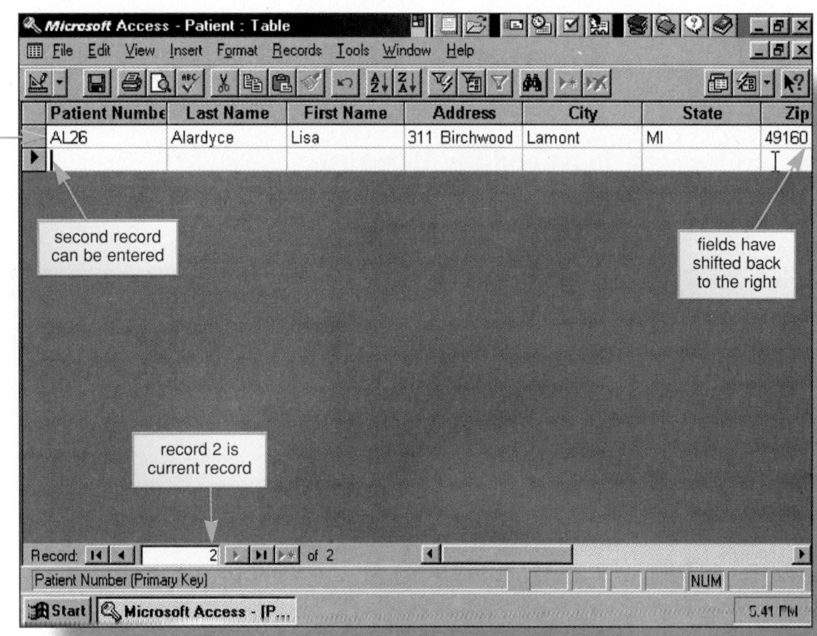

FIGURE 1-27

7 **Use the techniques shown in Steps 2 through 6 to add the data for the second record in Figure 1-21 on page A 1.20.**

The second record is added and the insertion point moves to the Patient Number on the third row (Figure 1-28).

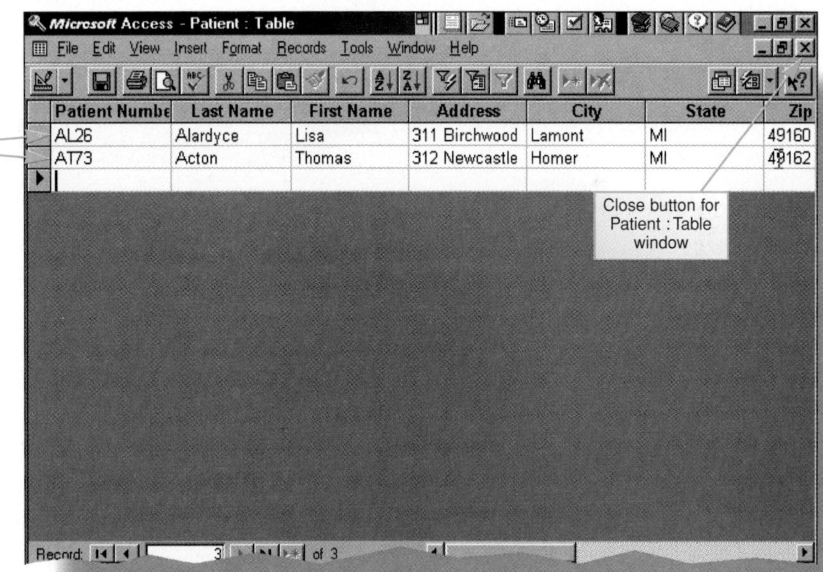

FIGURE 1-28

Closing a Table and a Database and Exiting Access

It is a good idea to close a table as soon as you have finished working with it. It keeps the screen from getting cluttered and also prevents you from making accidental changes to the data in the table. If you will no longer work with the database, you should close the database as well. With the creation of the Patient table complete, you can exit Access at this point.

Perform the following steps to close the table and the database and then exit Access.

To Close the Table and the Database

1. **Click the Close button for the Patient : Table window (see Figure 1-28 on page A 1.23).**

   The datasheet for the Patient table no longer displays (Figure 1-29).

2. **Click the Close button for the Mason Clinic : Database window (see Figure 1-29).**

   The Mason Clinic : Database window no longer displays.

3. **Click the Close button for the Microsoft Access window.**

   The Microsoft Access window no longer displays.

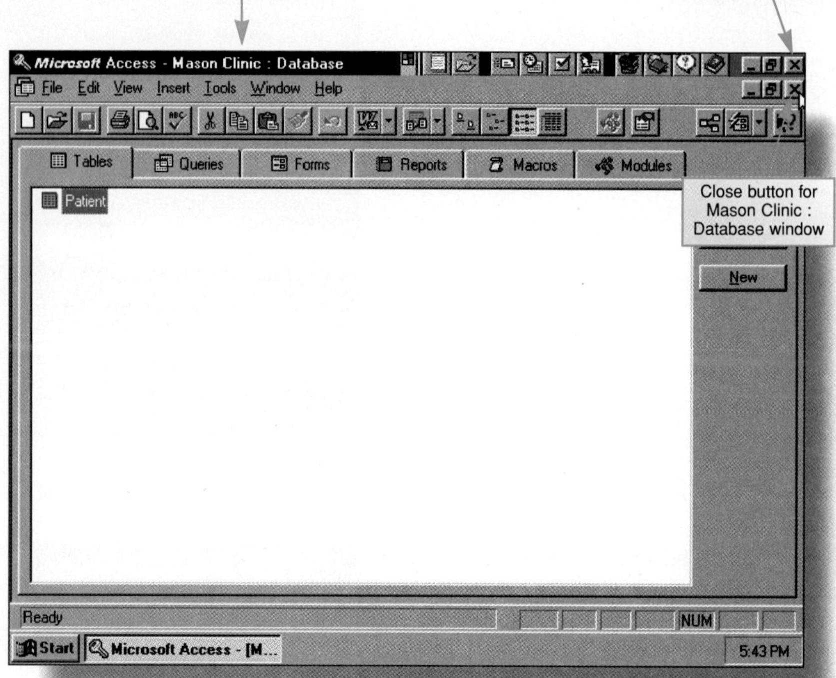

FIGURE 1-29

Other Ways

1. Double-click Control-menu icon on title bar for the window
2. On File menu click Close
3. Press CTRL+W or press CTRL+F4

Opening a Database

In order to work with any of the tables, reports, or forms in a database, the database must be open. To open a database from the Windows 95 desktop, click Open Office Document on the Start menu by performing the following steps. (The Other Ways box indicates ways to open a database from within Access.)

To Open a Database

1 **Click the Start button and then point to Open Office Document (Figure 1-30).**

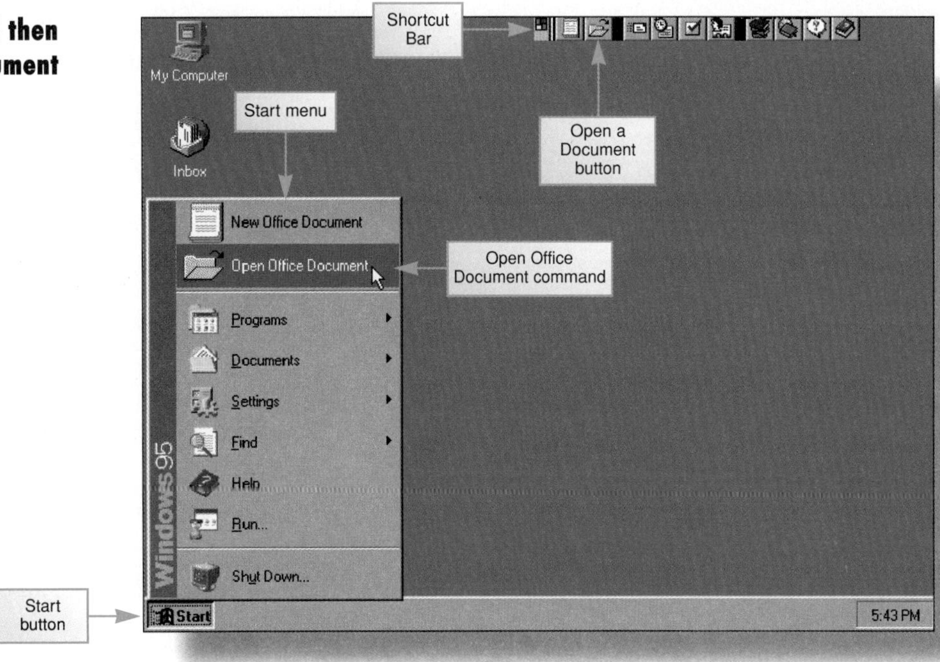

FIGURE 1-30

2 **Click Open Office Document. If necessary, click the Look in box arrow and then click 3½ Floppy [A:] in the Look in drop-down list box. If it is not already selected, click the Mason Clinic database name. Point to the Open button.**

The Open dialog box displays (Figure 1-31). The 3½ Floppy [A:] folder displays in the Look in box and the files on the floppy disk in drive A display. Your list may be different.

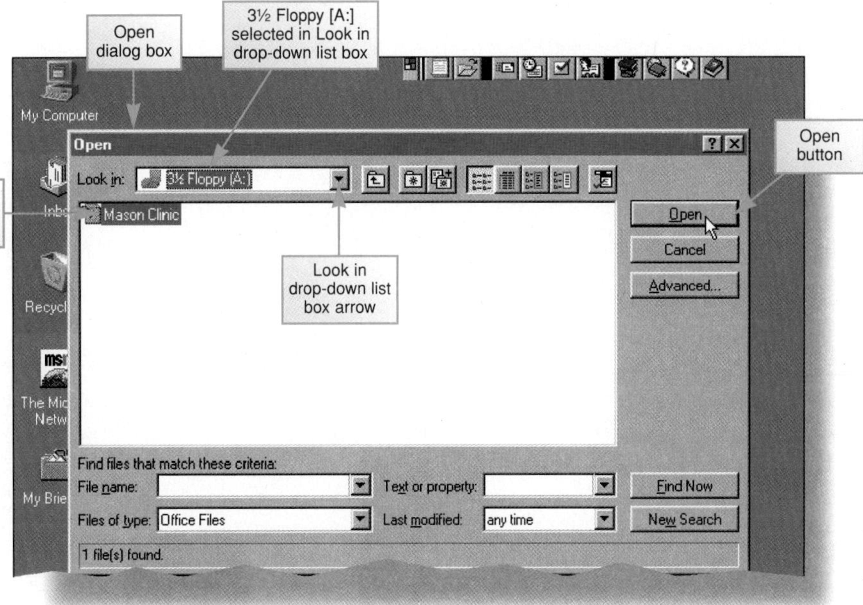

FIGURE 1-31

3 **Click the Open button.**

The database is open and the Mason Clinic : Database window displays.

OtherWays

1. Click Open Database button on toolbar
2. On File menu click Open Database
3. Press CTRL+O

Adding Additional Records

You can add records to a table that already contains data using a process almost identical to that used to add records to an empty table. The only difference is that you place the highlight after the last data record before you enter the additional data. To do so, use the **Navigation buttons** found near the lower left-hand corner of the screen. The purpose of each of the Navigation buttons is described in Table 1-1.

Table 1-1

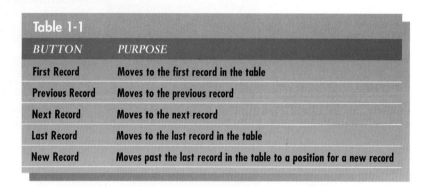

BUTTON	PURPOSE
First Record	Moves to the first record in the table
Previous Record	Moves to the previous record
Next Record	Moves to the next record
Last Record	Moves to the last record in the table
New Record	Moves past the last record in the table to a position for a new record

Complete the following steps to add the remaining records to the Patient table.

Steps To Add Additional Records to the Table

1. **With the Patient table selected in the Mason Clinic : Database window, click the Open button.**

2. **When the Patient table displays, maximize the window by clicking the Maximize button. Point to the New Record button.**

The datasheet displays (Figure 1-32).

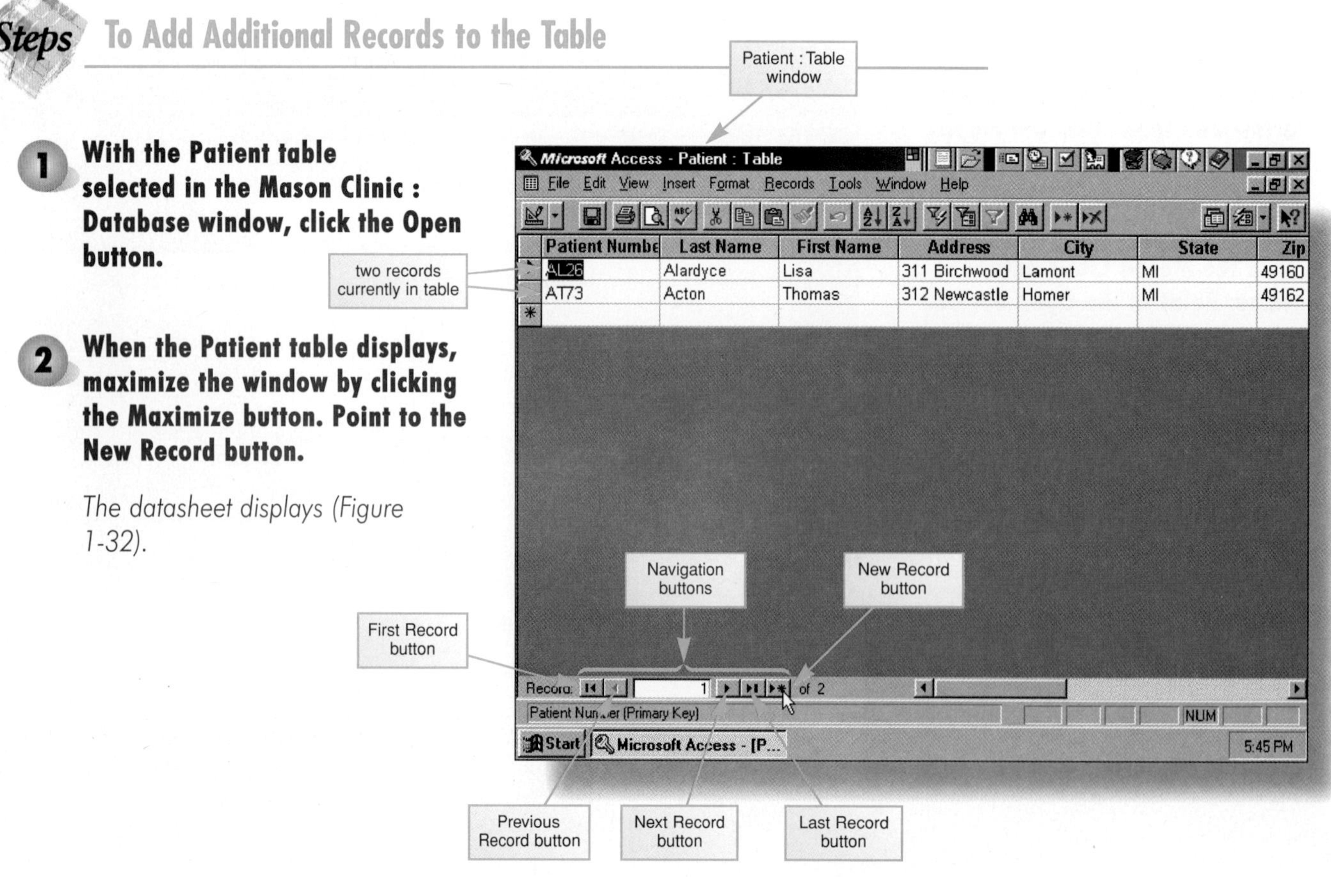

FIGURE 1-32

3 **Click the New Record button.**

Access places the insertion point in position to enter a new record (Figure 1-33).

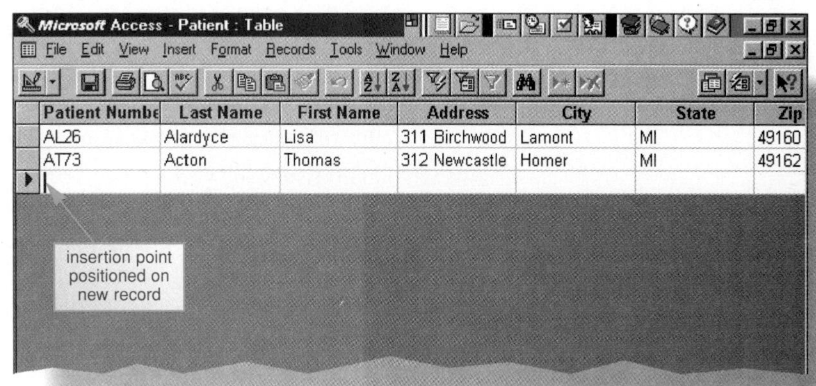

FIGURE 1-33

4 **Add the remaining records from Figure 1-34 using the same techniques you used to add the first two records.**

The additional records are added (Figure 1-35).

Patient Table (last 8 records)

PATIENT NUMBER	LAST NAME	FIRST NAME	ADDRESS	CITY	STATE	ZIP CODE	BALANCE	INSURANCE	THER NUMBER
BR31	Bryce	Roger	617 College	Lamont	MI	49160	$96.00	$0.00	08
DI32	Dalton	Irene	41 Lafayette	Madison	IN	42909	$875.00	$600.00	14
GC92	Gutierez	Carlos	476 Fulton	Jackson	OH	49401	$273.00	$150.00	05
GT43	Grant	Thomas	247 Fuller	Lamont	MI	49160	$276.00	$0.00	08
JG22	Jenkins	Glen	201 Plymouth	Madison	IN	42909	$0.00	$0.00	08
LI66	Lawrence	Irving	912 Devonshire	Beulah	MI	45621	$346.50	$175.00	05
PE33	Pezato	Eduardo	346 Vernor	Homer	MI	49162	$467.12	$500.00	14
PE76	Perez	Enzo	216 Four Mile	Perry	MI	47211	$216.00	$0.00	08

FIGURE 1-34

5 **Close the table by clicking its Close button.**

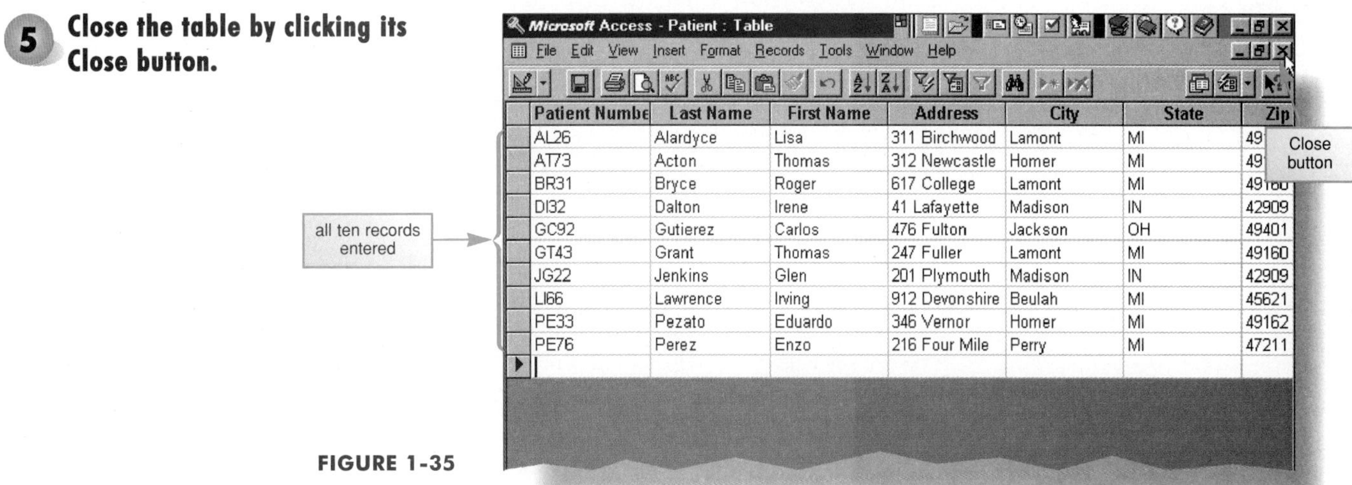

FIGURE 1-35

Correcting Errors in the Data

Just as when you created the table, check the entries carefully to ensure they are correct. If you make a mistake and discover it before you press the TAB key, correct it by pressing the BACKSPACE key until the incorrect characters are removed and then typing the correct characters.

If you discover an incorrect entry later, correct the error by clicking the incorrect entry, and then making the appropriate correction. If the record you must correct is not on the screen, use the Navigation buttons (Next Record, Previous Record, and so on) to move to it. If the field you want to correct is not visible on the screen, use the horizontal scroll bar along the bottom of the screen to shift all the fields until the one you want displays. Then make the correction.

If you accidentally add an extra record, select the record by pointing to the box that immediately precedes the record and clicking the left mouse button. Then, press the DELETE key. This will remove the record from the table. If you forget a record, add it using the same procedure as for all the other records. Access will automatically place it in the correct location in the table.

If you cannot determine how to correct the data, you have a problem. Access will neither allow you to move to any other record until you have made the correction, nor will it allow you to close the table. You are, in effect, stuck on the record. If you should ever find yourself in this situation, simply press the ESC key. This will remove the record you are trying to add from the screen. You can then move to any other record, close the table, or take any other action you desire.

Previewing and Printing the Contents of a Table

More *About* Printing the Contents of a Table

Using the Page sheet in the Page Setup dialog box, you can change the paper size, paper source, or the printer that will be used to print the report. To change either of these, click the appropriate down arrow and select the desired size.

When working with a database, you often will need to **print** a copy of the table contents. Figure 1-36 shows a printed copy of the contents of the Patient table. (Yours may look slightly different, depending on your printer.) Because the Patient table is substantially wider than the screen, it also will be wider than the normal printed page in portrait orientation. **Portrait orientation** means the printout is across the width of the page. **Landscape orientation** means the printout is across the length of the page. Thus, to print the wide database table, use landscape orientation. If you are printing the contents of a table that fits on the screen, you will not need landscape orientation. A convenient way to change to landscape orientation is to **preview** what the printed copy will look like by using Print Preview. This allows you to determine whether landscape orientation is necessary and, if it is, to easily change the orientation to landscape. In addition, you also can use Print Preview to determine whether any adjustments are necessary to the page margins.

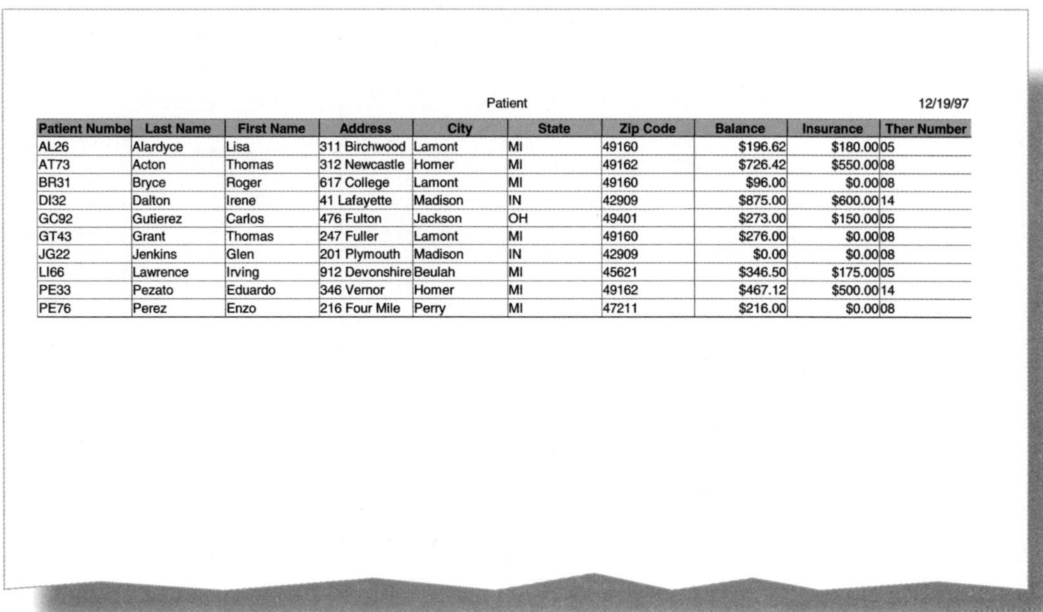

Patient 12/19/97

Patient Numbe	Last Name	First Name	Address	City	State	Zip Code	Balance	Insurance	Ther Number
AL26	Alardyce	Lisa	311 Birchwood	Lamont	MI	49160	$196.62	$180.00	05
AT73	Acton	Thomas	312 Newcastle	Homer	MI	49162	$726.42	$550.00	08
BR31	Bryce	Roger	617 College	Lamont	MI	49160	$96.00	$0.00	08
DI32	Dalton	Irene	41 Lafayette	Madison	IN	42909	$875.00	$600.00	14
GC92	Gutierez	Carlos	476 Fulton	Jackson	OH	49401	$273.00	$150.00	05
GT43	Grant	Thomas	247 Fuller	Lamont	MI	49160	$276.00	$0.00	08
JG22	Jenkins	Glen	201 Plymouth	Madison	IN	42909	$0.00	$0.00	08
LI66	Lawrence	Irving	912 Devonshire	Beulah	MI	45621	$346.50	$175.00	05
PE33	Pezato	Eduardo	346 Vernor	Homer	MI	49162	$467.12	$500.00	14
PE76	Perez	Enzo	216 Four Mile	Perry	MI	47211	$216.00	$0.00	08

FIGURE 1-36

Perform the following steps to use Print Preview to preview and then print the Patient table.

Steps To Preview and Print the Contents of the Table

1. **Make sure the Patient table is selected, and then point to the Print Preview button on the toolbar (Figure 1-37).**

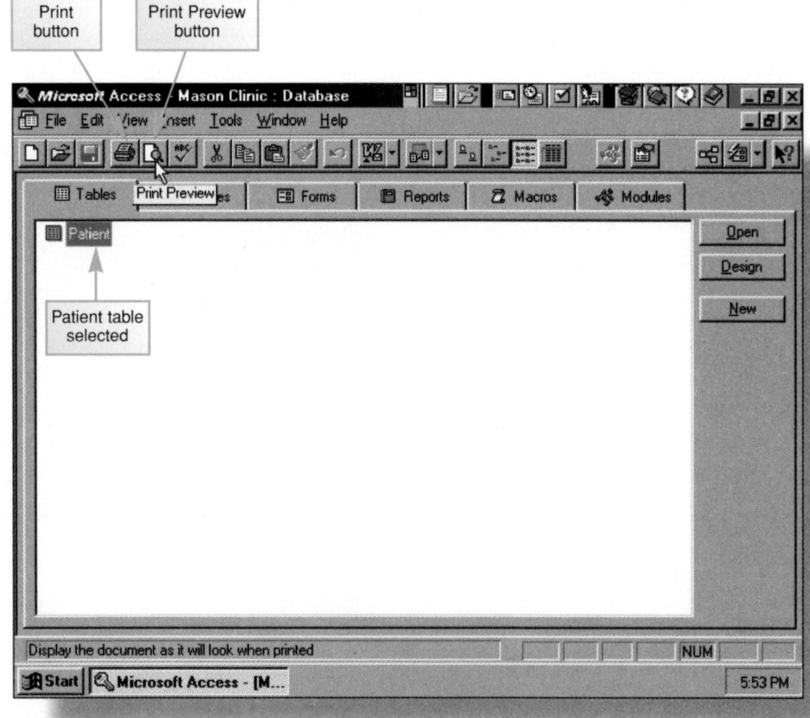

FIGURE 1-37

2 Click the Print Preview button, click File on the menu bar, and then point to Page Setup.

The preview of the report displays (Figure 1-38). In the figure, the report displays in portrait orientation, which will not display all fields on a page. The File menu displays.

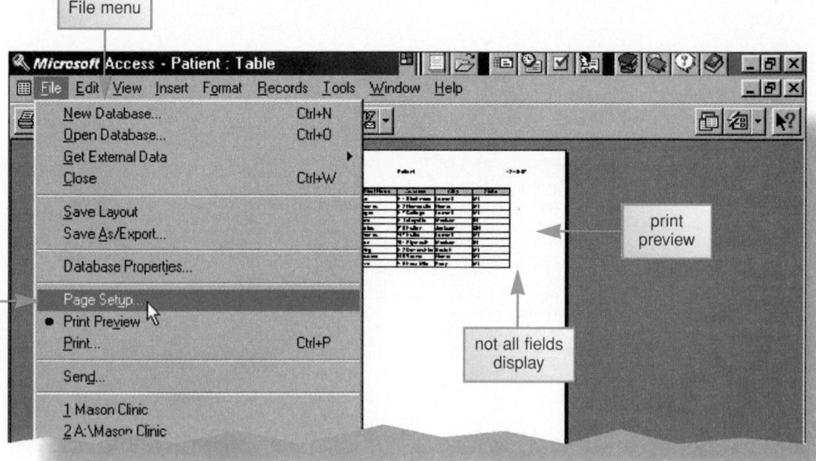

FIGURE 1-38

3 Click Page Setup, and then point to the Page tab.

The Page Setup dialog box displays (Figure 1-39).

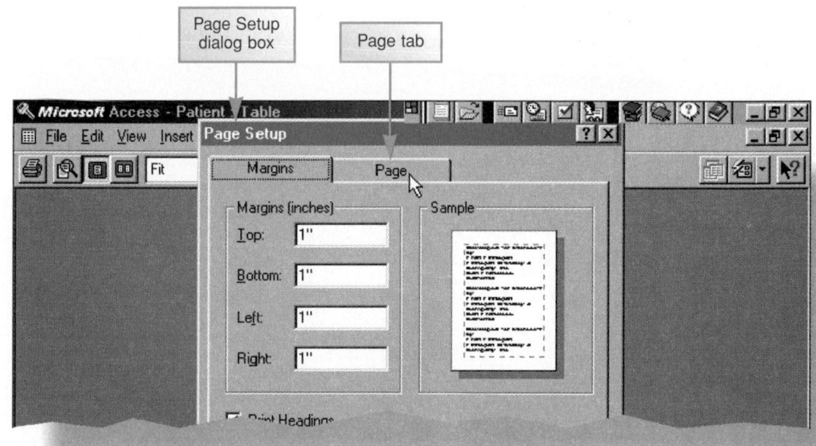

FIGURE 1-39

4 Click the Page tab.

The Page options display (Figure 1-40). The Portrait option button currently is selected.

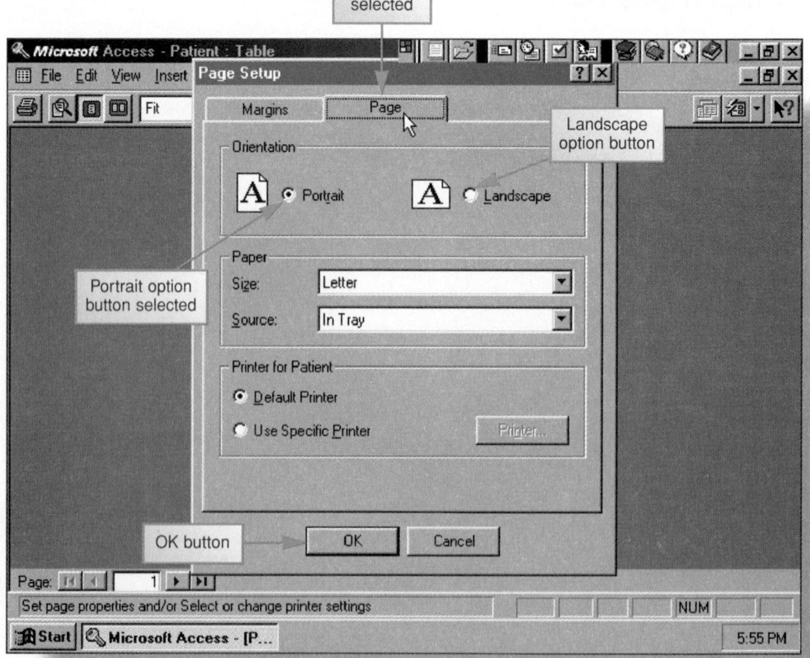

FIGURE 1-40

5 **Click Landscape and then click the OK button.**

The orientation is changed to landscape as shown by the report that displays on the screen (Figure 1-41). The characters in the report are so small that it is difficult to determine whether all fields currently display. To zoom in on a portion of the report, click the desired portion of the report.

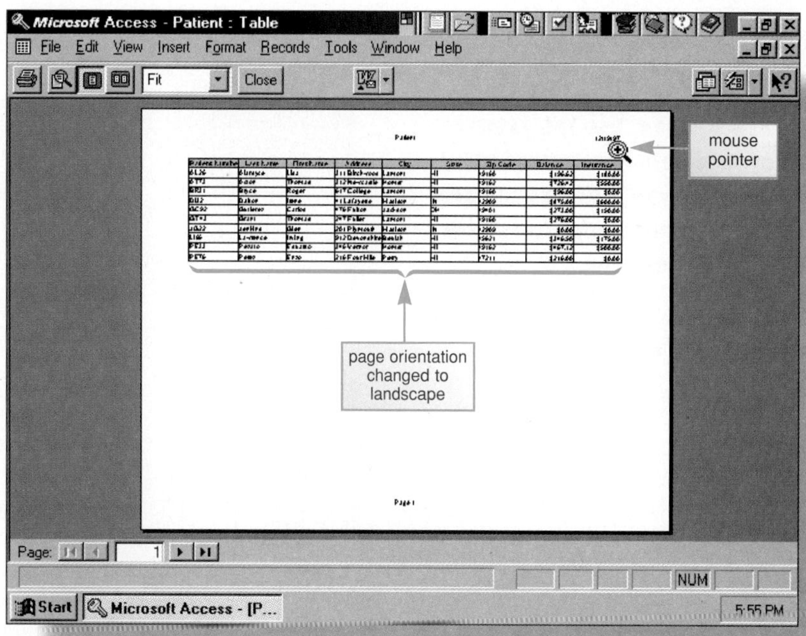

FIGURE 1-41

6 **With the mouse pointer, which displays as a magnifying glass, in the position shown in Figure 1-41, click the left mouse button.**

The portion surrounding the mouse pointer is magnified (Figure 1-42). The last field that displays is the Insurance field. The Ther Number field does not display. To make it display, decrease the ***left*** *and* ***right margins****, the amount of space left by Access on the left and right edges of the report. (You may need to experiment with the left and right margins to find appropriate numbers.)*

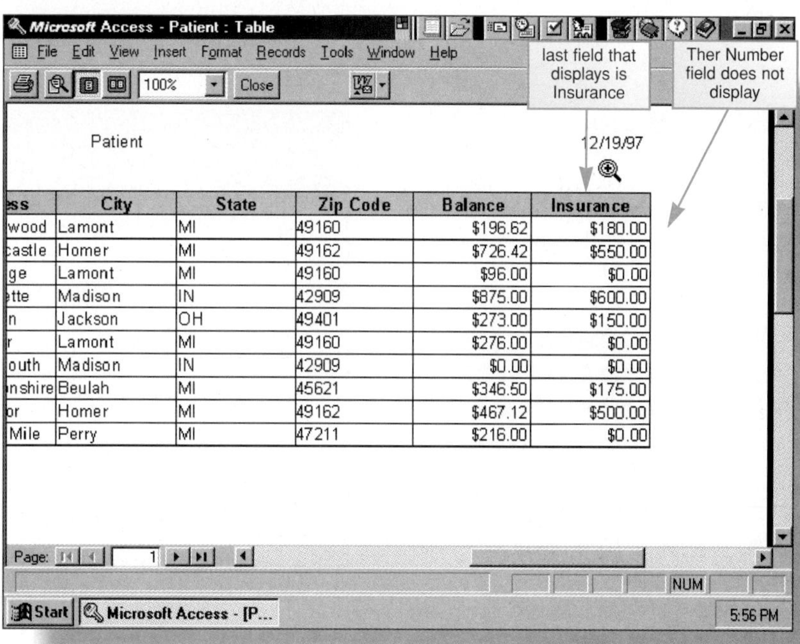

FIGURE 1-42

7 **Click File on the menu bar and then click Page Setup. Click the Left text box in the Margins (inches) area, use the BACKSPACE key to delete the current entry, and then type .333 as the new entry. Repeat the process with the Right text box.**

The Page Setup dialog box displays (Figure 1-43). The Left and Right margins have been changed to .333".

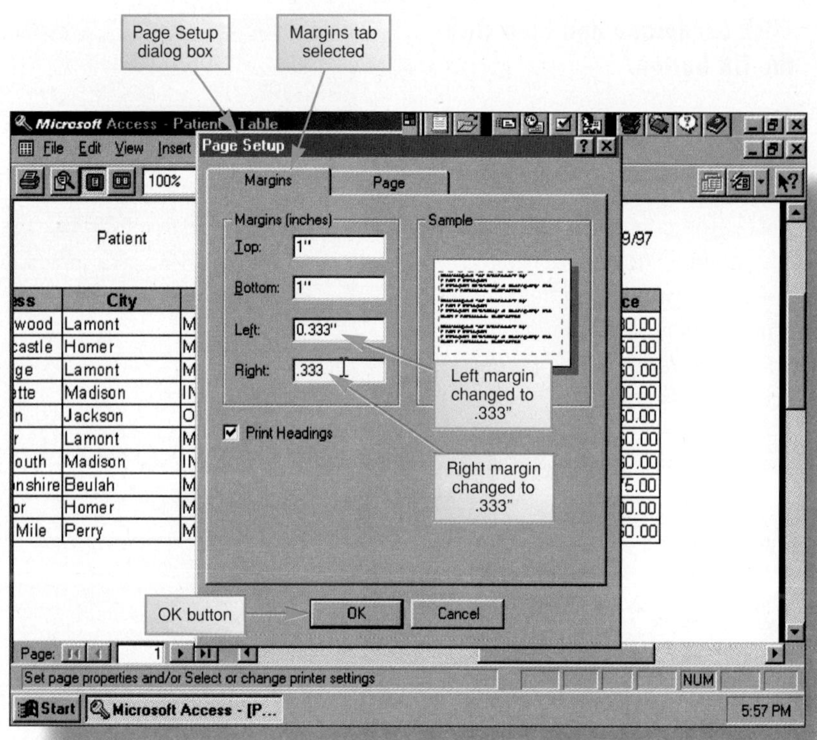

FIGURE 1-43

8 **Click the OK button.**

All fields now display in the report (Figure 1-44).

9 **Click the Print button to print the report. Click the Close button when the report has been printed to close the Preview window.**

The Preview window no longer displays.

Print button

Ther Number field displays

Close button

Patient 12/19/97

State	Zip Code	Balance	Insurance	Ther Number
MI	49160	$196.62	$180.00	05
MI	49162	$726.42	$550.00	08
MI	49160	$96.00	$0.00	08
IN	42909	$875.00	$600.00	14
OH	49401	$273.00	$150.00	05
MI	49160	$276.00	$0.00	08
IN	42909	$0.00	$0.00	08
MI	45621	$346.50	$175.00	05
MI	49162	$467.12	$500.00	14
MI	47211	$216.00	$0.00	08

FIGURE 1-44

Other Ways

1. On File menu click Print Preview to preview; on File menu click Print to print
2. Press CTRL+P to print

Creating Additional Tables

A database typically consists of more than one table. The sample database contains two, the Patient table and the Therapist table. You need to repeat the process of creating a table and adding records for each table in the database. In the sample database, you need to create and add records to the Therapist table. The structure and data for the table are given in Figure 1-45. The steps to create the table follow.

Structure of Therapist Table

FIELD NAME	DATA TYPE	FIELD SIZE	PRIMARY KEY?	DESCRIPTION
Ther Number	Text	2	Yes	Therapist Number (Primary Key)
Last Name	Text	10		Last Name of Therapist
First Name	Text	8		First Name of Therapist
Address	Text	15		Street Address
City	Text	15		City
State	Text	2		State (Two-Character Abbreviation)
Zip Code	Text	5		Zip Code (Five-Character Version)
Billing	Currency			Total Billing Amount of Therapist
Paid	Currency			Amount Already Paid by Patient or Insurance Company

Data for Therapist Table

THER NUMBER	LAST NAME	FIRST NAME	ADDRESS	CITY	STATE	ZIP CODE	BILLING	PAID
05	Hughes	Mary	4613 Essex	Burnips	MI	49277	$62,277.00	$46,245.25
08	Foster	Richard	6621 Eastern	Stockton	IN	47962	$71,245.00	$65,121.33
14	Galvez	Juanita	684 Valley	Leland	MI	47205	$34,252.50	$22,645.90

FIGURE 1-45

To Create an Additional Table

1. **Make sure the Mason Clinic database is open. Point to the New button.**

The Mason Clinic : Database window displays (Figure 1-46). If you recently maximized another window, this window also will be maximized as shown in the figure. If not, it will appear in its normal size.

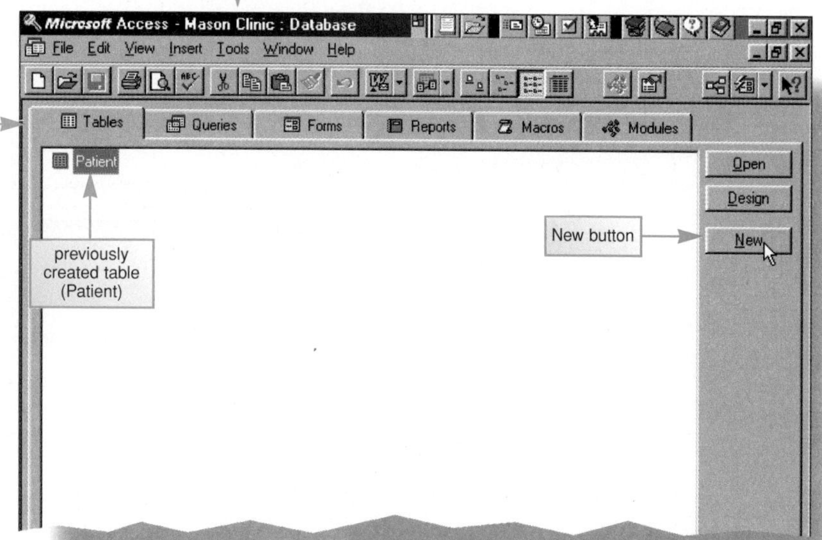

FIGURE 1-46

2 Click the New button, click Design View in the New Table dialog box, click the OK button, and then enter the data for the fields for the Therapist table from Figure 1-45 on page A 1.33. Be sure to click the Primary Key button when you enter the Ther Number field. Point to the Save button on the toolbar.

The entries display (Figure 1-47).

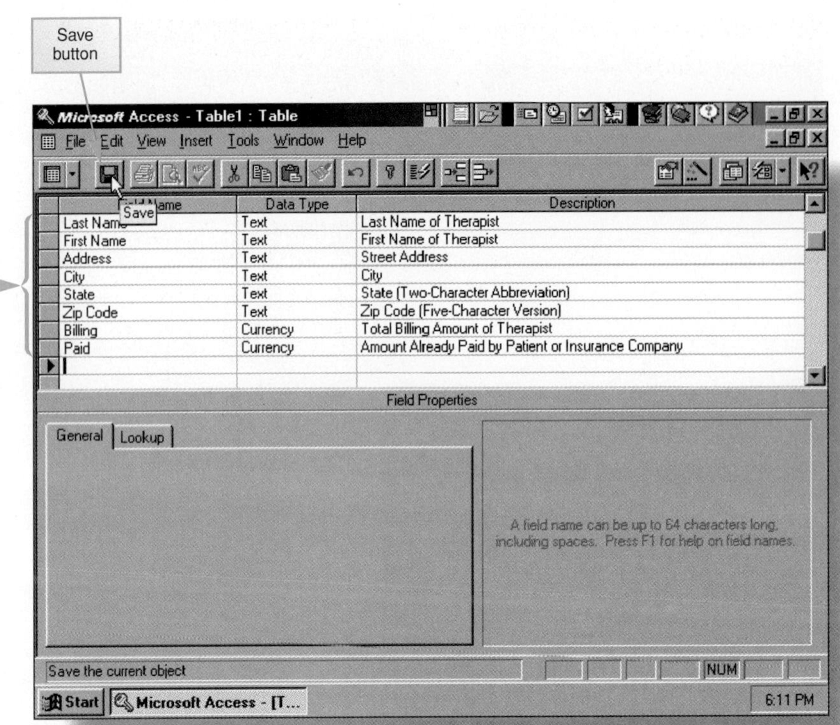

FIGURE 1-47

3 Click the Save button, type `Therapist` **as the name of the table, and click the OK button.**

4 Click the Close button to close the Table window.

The table is saved in the Mason Clinic database. The Table window no longer displays.

Adding Records to the Therapist Table

Now that you have created the Therapist table, use the following steps to add records to it.

To Add Records to the Additional Table

1 Click the Therapist table in the Database window.

The Therapist table is selected (Figure 1-48).

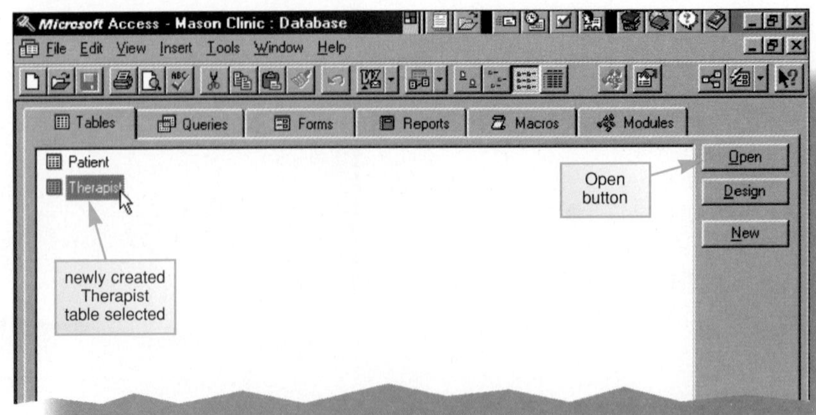

FIGURE 1-48

2 **Click the Open button and then enter the Therapist data from Figure 1-45 into the Therapist table.**

The datasheet displays with three records entered (Figure 1-49).

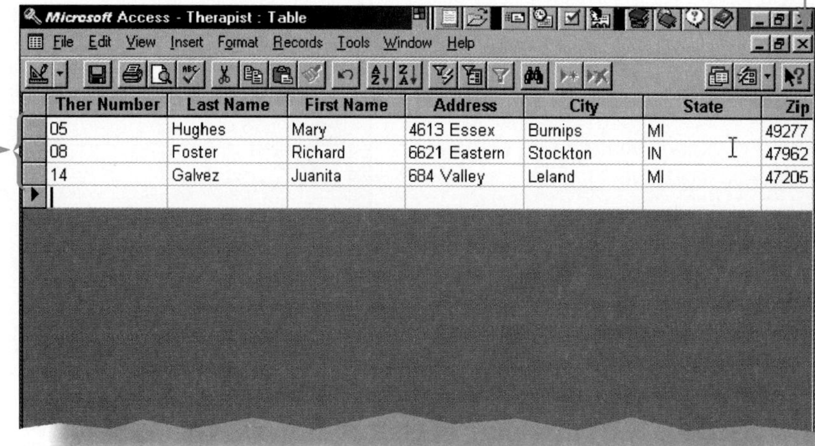

FIGURE 1-49

3 **Click the Close button for the Therapist : Table window to close the table.**

Access closes the table and removes the datasheet from the screen.

Using a Form to View Data

In creating tables, you have used Datasheet view; that is, the data on the screen displayed as a table. You also can use **Form view**, in which you see a single record at a time.

The advantage with Datasheet view is you can see multiple records at once. It has the disadvantage that, unless you have few fields in the table, you cannot see all the fields at the same time. With Form view you see only a single record, but you can see all the fields in the record. The view you click is a matter of personal preference.

To use Form view, you first must **create a form**. The simplest way to create a form is to use the New Object button on the toolbar. To do so, first select the table for which the form is to be created in the Database window, and then click the New Object button. A list of available objects displays. Select AutoForm from the list by clicking it in the list.

Perform the following steps using the New Object button to create a form for the Patient table.

More About Forms

Forms are very powerful tools in database management systems. Forms can incorporate data from multiple tables in the same form. They also can include special types of data such as pictures and sounds.

Steps To Use the New Object Button to Create the Form

1 **Make sure the Mason Clinic database is open, the Database window displays, and the Patient table is selected. Point to the New Object button down arrow on the toolbar (Figure 1-50).**

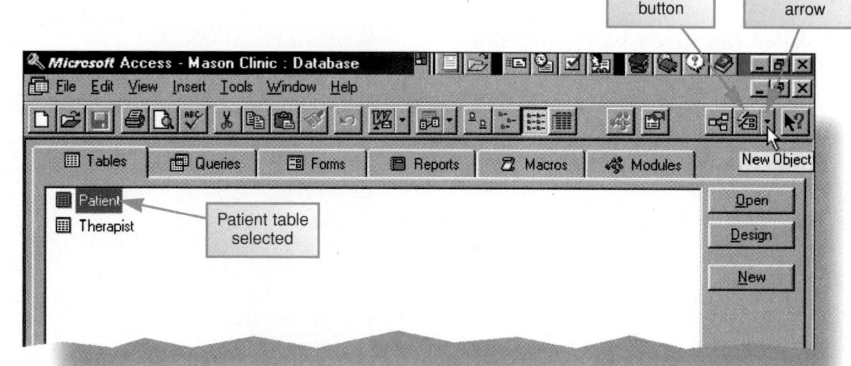

FIGURE 1-50

2 **Click the New Object button down arrow and then point to AutoForm.**

A list of objects that can be created displays (Figure 1-51).

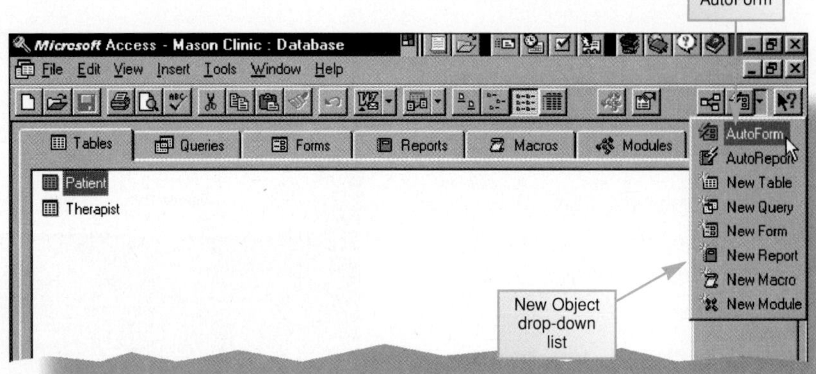

FIGURE 1-51

3 **Click AutoForm in the New Object drop-down list.**

The form displays (Figure 1-52).

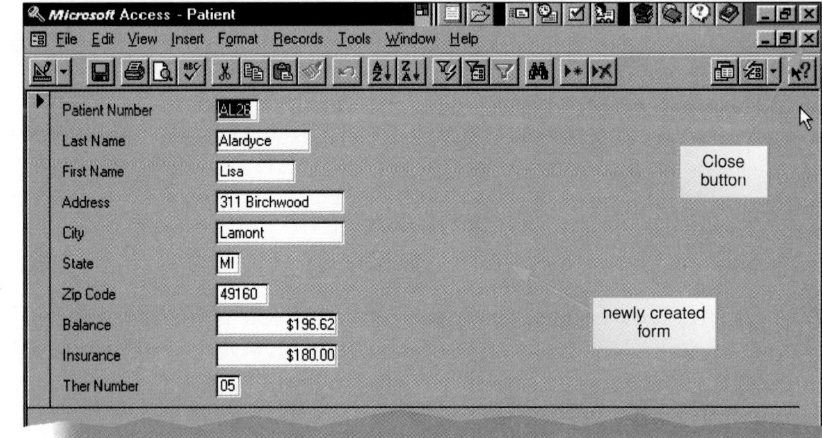

FIGURE 1-52

Closing and Saving the Form

Closing a form is similar to closing a table. The only difference is that you will be asked if you want to **save the form** unless you have previously saved it. Perform the following steps to close the form and save it as Patient form.

To Close and Save the Form

1 **Click the Close button for the Patient window (see Figure 1-52).**

The Microsoft Access dialog box displays (Figure 1-53).

FIGURE 1-53

2 **Click the Yes button and then point to the OK button.**

The Save As dialog box displays (Figure 1-54). The name of the table (Patient) has been automatically entered as the name of the form. If you wished, you could replace it with another name.

3 **Click the OK button in the Save As dialog box.**

The form is saved as part of the database and is removed from the screen. The Mason Clinic : Database window again displays.

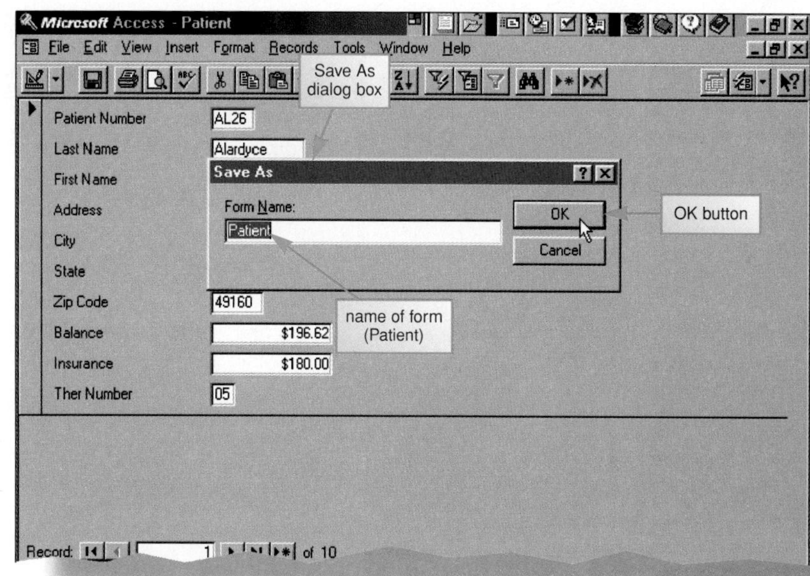

FIGURE 1-54

OtherWays

1. Double-click Control-menu icon on title bar for window
2. On File menu click Close
3. Press CTRL+W or press CTRL+F4

Opening the Saved Form

Once you have saved a form, you can use it at any time in the future by opening it. **Opening a form** is similar to opening a table; that is, make sure the form to be opened is selected and then click the Open button. Before opening the form, however, the Forms tab, rather than the Tables tab, must be selected.

Perform the following steps to open the Patient form.

Steps To Open the Form

1 **With the Mason Clinic database open and the Database window on the screen, point to the Forms tab (Figure 1-55).**

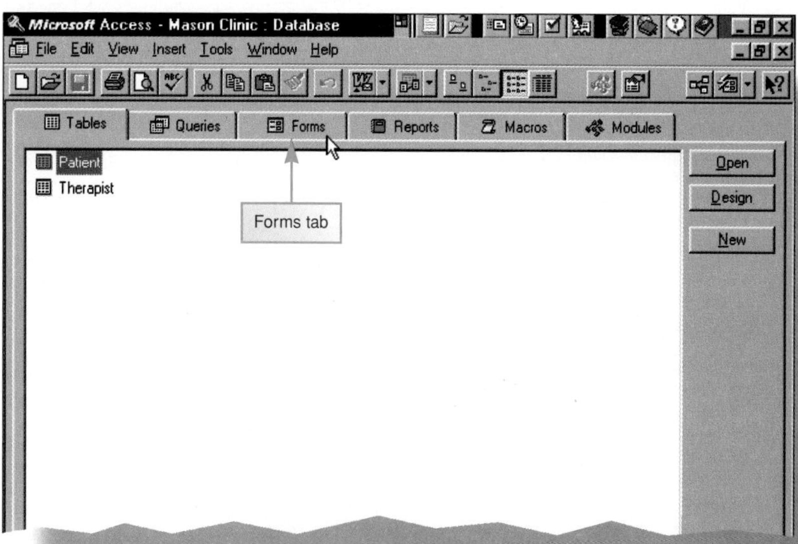

FIGURE 1-55

2 **Click the Forms tab.**

The Forms tab is selected and the list of available forms displays (Figure 1-56). Currently, the Patient form is the only form.

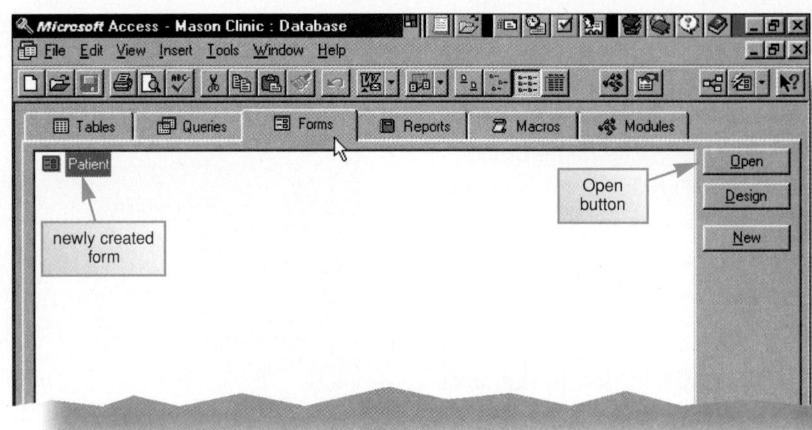

FIGURE 1-56

3 **Click the Open button.**

The Patient form displays (Figure 1-57).

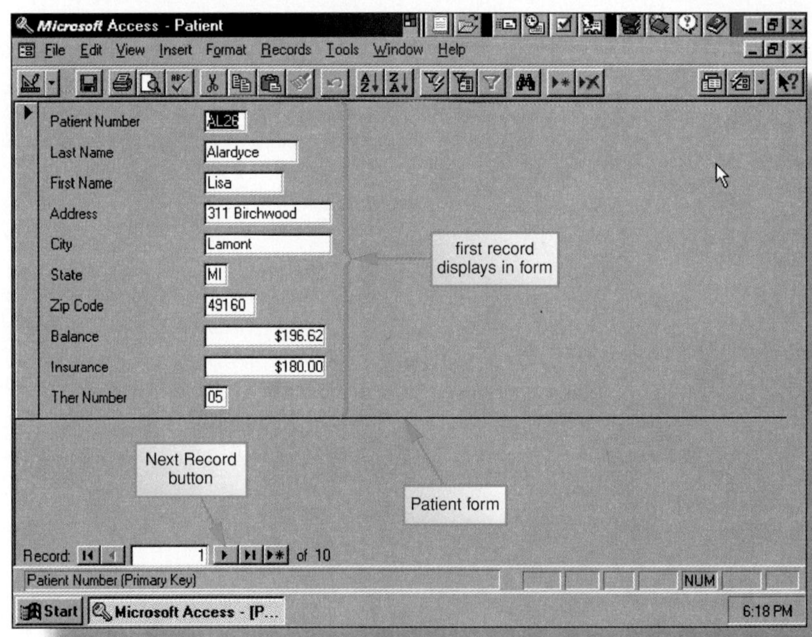

FIGURE 1-57

Other Ways

1. Click Forms tab, double-click desired form
2. On context-sensitive menu click Open
3. Press ALT+O

Using the Form

You can **use the form** just as you used Datasheet view. You use the Navigation buttons to move between records. You can add new records or change existing ones. Press the DELETE key to delete the record displayed on the screen after selecting the record by clicking its row selector. In other words, you can perform database operations using either Form view or Datasheet view.

Because you can see only one record at a time in Form view, to see a different record, such as the fifth record, use the Navigation buttons to move to it. To move from record to record in Form view, perform the following step.

To Use the Form

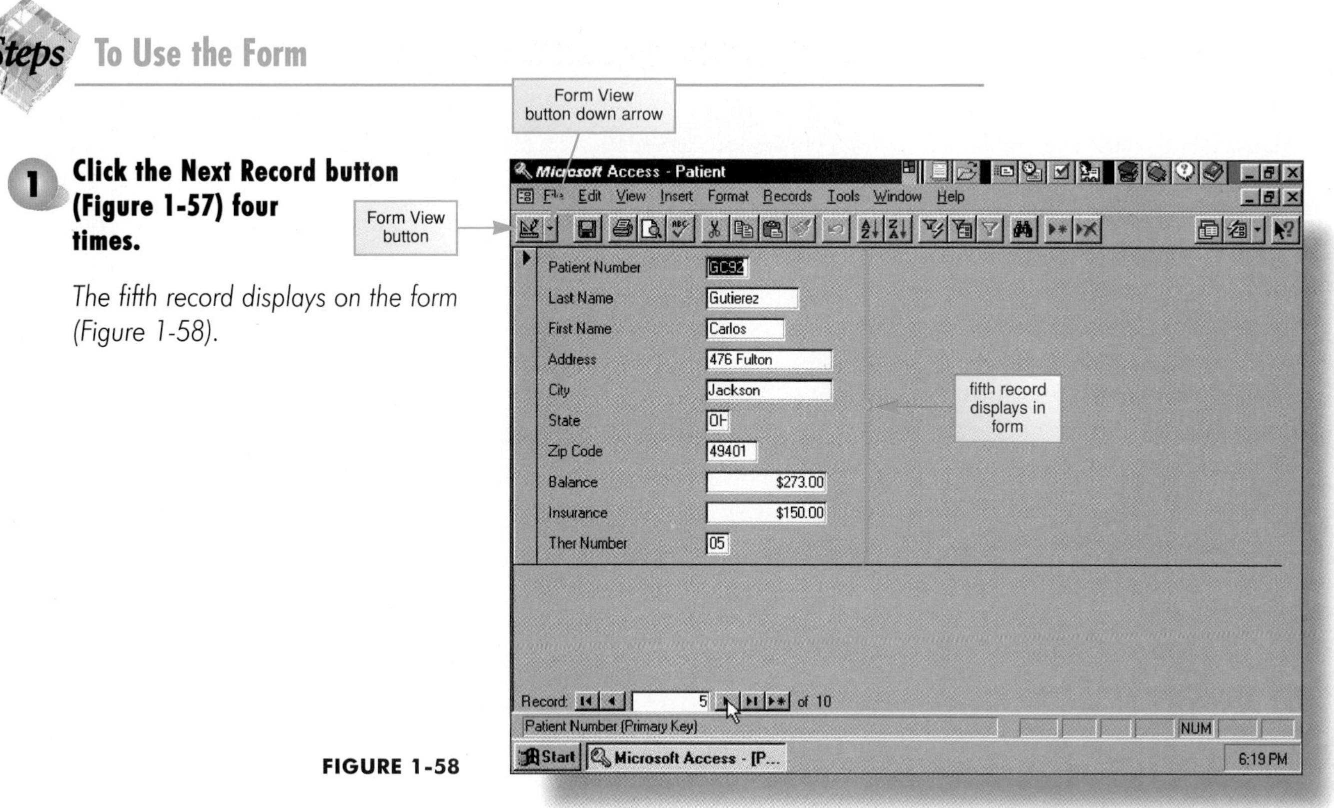

1 **Click the Next Record button (Figure 1-57) four times.**

The fifth record displays on the form (Figure 1-58).

FIGURE 1-58

Switching Between Form View and Datasheet View

In some cases, once you have seen a record in Form view, you will want to move to Datasheet view to once again see a collection of records. To do so, click the Form View button down arrow on the toolbar and then click Datasheet View in the drop-down list that displays.

Perform the following steps to transfer from Form view to Datasheet view.

More About Reports

The capability to create sophisticated custom reports is one of the major benefits of a database management system. Reports can incorporate data from multiple tables. They also can be formatted in a wide variety of ways.

To Switch from Form View to Datasheet View

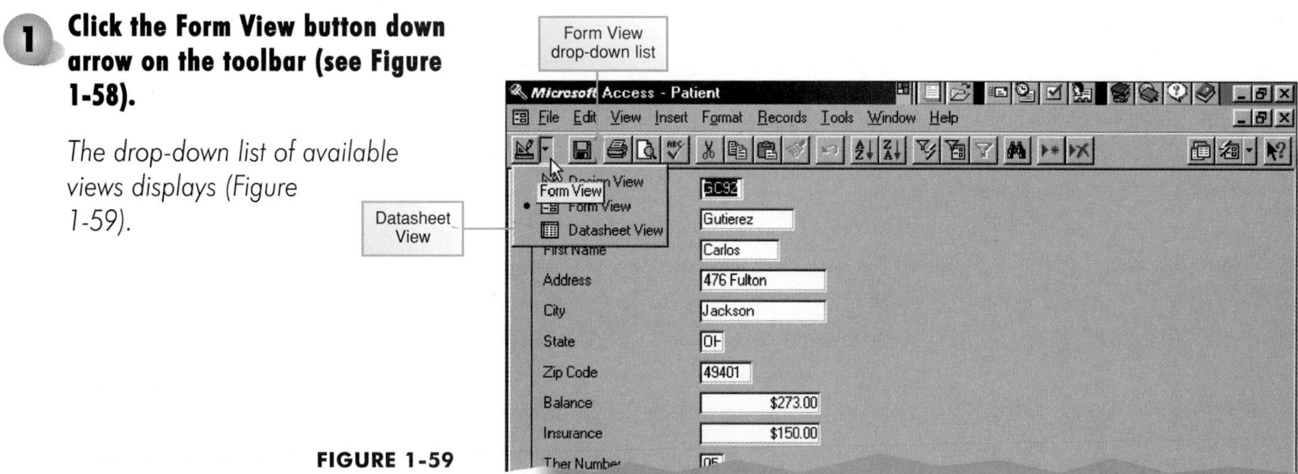

1 **Click the Form View button down arrow on the toolbar (see Figure 1-58).**

The drop-down list of available views displays (Figure 1-59).

FIGURE 1-59

2 Click Datasheet View.

The table displays in Datasheet view (Figure 1-60). The highlight is positioned on the fifth record.

3 Close the Patient window by clicking its Close button.

The datasheet no longer displays.

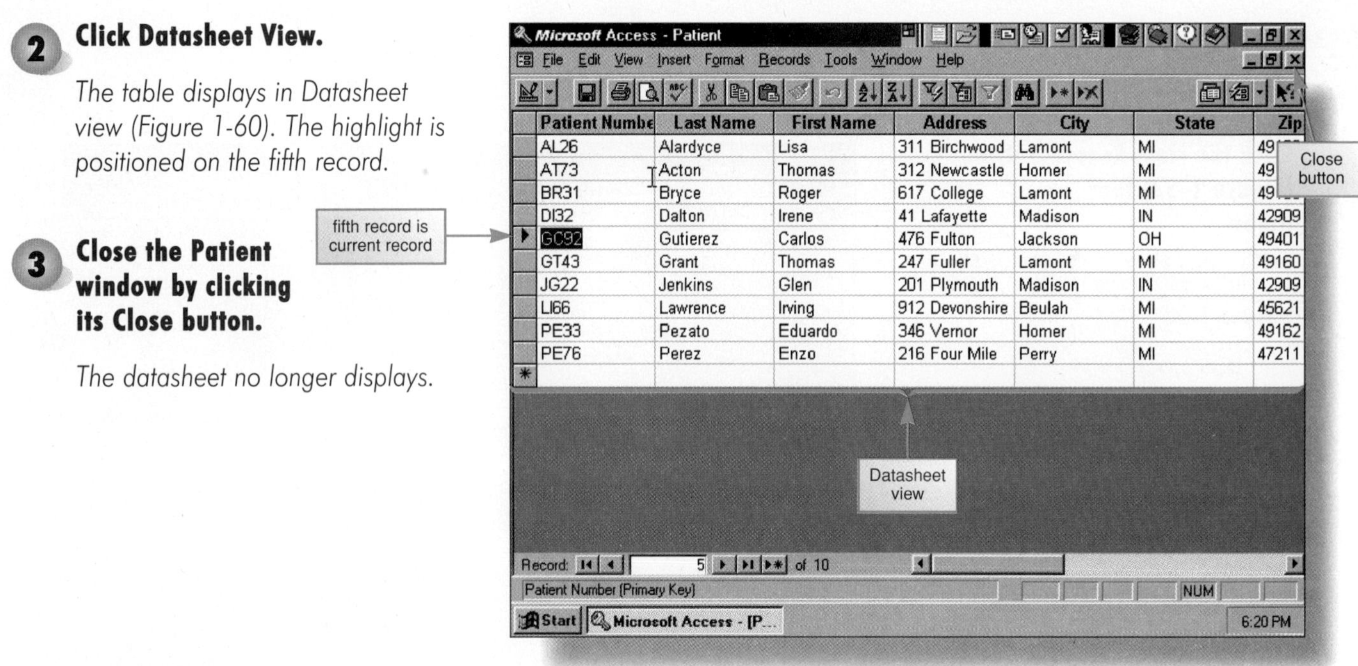

FIGURE 1-60

OtherWays

1. On View menu click Datasheet

Creating a Report

Earlier in this project, you printed a table using the Print button. The report you produced was shown in Figure 1-36 on page A 1.29. While this type of report presented the data in an organized manner, it was not very flexible. It included all fields, in precisely the same order in which they occurred in the table. A way to change the title was not presented. It was simply Patient, whether or not you wanted that title.

In this section, you will **create the report** shown in Figure 1-61. This report features significant differences from the one in Figure 1-36. The portion at the top of the report in Figure 1-61, called a **page header**, contains a custom title. The contents of this page header appear at the top of each page. The **detail lines**, the lines that are printed for each record, contain only those fields you specify.

Financial Report

Patient Number	*First Name*	*Last Name*	*Balance*	*Insurance*
AL26	Lisa	Alardyce	$196.62	$180.00
AT73	Thomas	Acton	$726.42	$550.00
BR31	Roger	Bryce	$96.00	$0.00
DI32	Irene	Dalton	$875.00	$600.00
GC92	Carlos	Gutierez	$273.00	$150.00
GT43	Thomas	Grant	$276.00	$0.00
JG22	Glen	Jenkins	$0.00	$0.00
LI66	Irving	Lawrence	$346.50	$175.00
PE33	Eduardo	Pezato	$467.12	$500.00
PE76	Enzo	Perez	$216.00	$0.00

FIGURE 1-61

Perform the following steps to create the report in Figure 1-61.

To Create the Report

1. **Click the Tables tab. Make sure the Patient table is selected. Click the New Object button down arrow on the toolbar.**

The drop-down list of available objects displays (Figure 1-62).

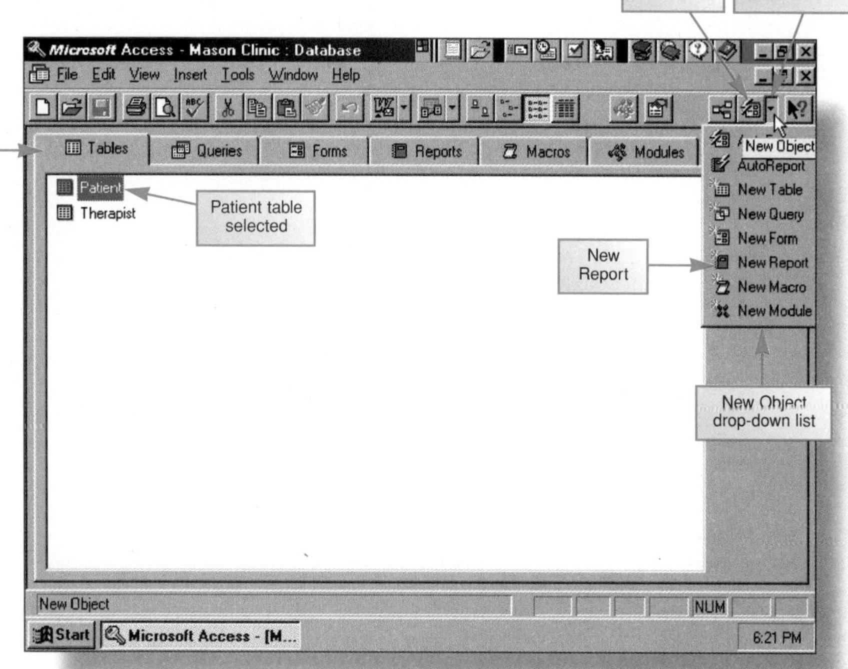

FIGURE 1-62

2. **Click New Report and then point to Report Wizard.**

The New Report dialog box displays (Figure 1-63).

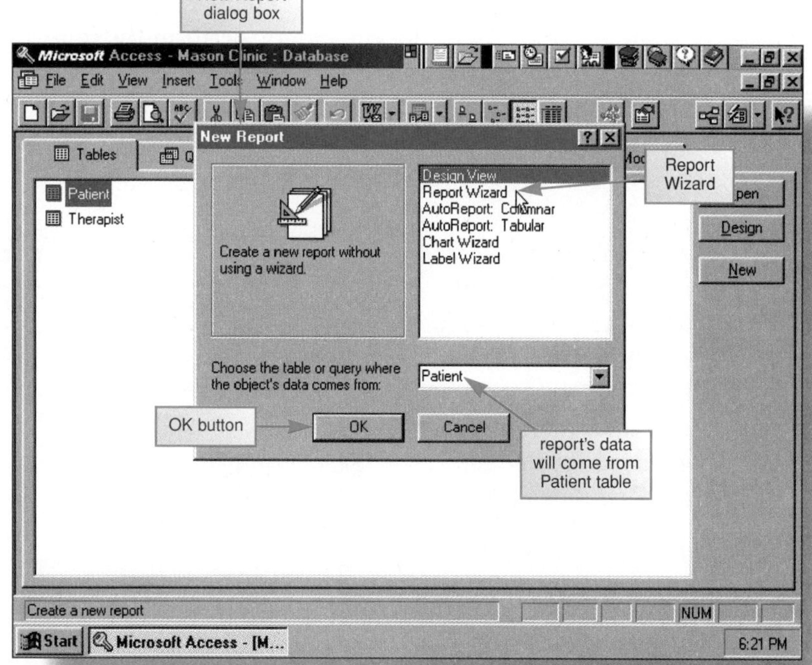

FIGURE 1-63

3 **Click Report Wizard and then click the OK button. Point to the Add Field button.**

The Report Wizard dialog box displays (Figure 1-64).

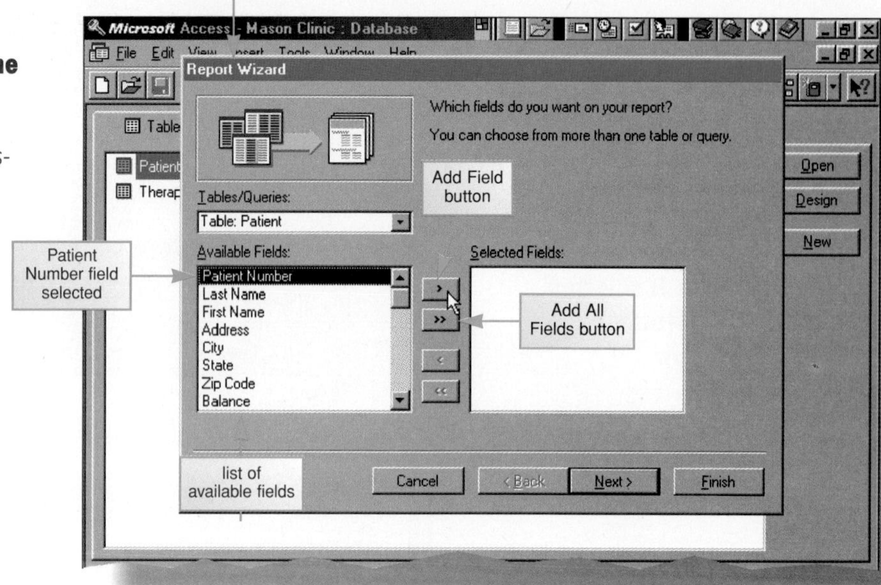

FIGURE 1-64

OtherWays

1. On Insert menu click Report

Selecting the Fields for the Report

To **select a field** for the report; that is, to indicate the field that is to be included in the report, click the field in the Available Fields list box. Next, click the Add Field button. This will move the field from the Available Fields list box to the Selected Fields list box, thus including the field in the report. If you wanted to select all fields, a shortcut is available by simply clicking the Add All Fields button.

To select the Patient Number, First Name, Last Name, Balance, and Insurance fields for the report, perform the following steps.

Steps To Select the Fields for the Report

1 **Click the Add Field button to add the Patient Number field. Add the First Name field by clicking it, and then clicking the Add Field button. Add the Last Name, Balance, and Insurance fields just as you added the Patient Number and First Name fields.**

The fields for the report display in the Selected Fields list box (Figure 1-65).

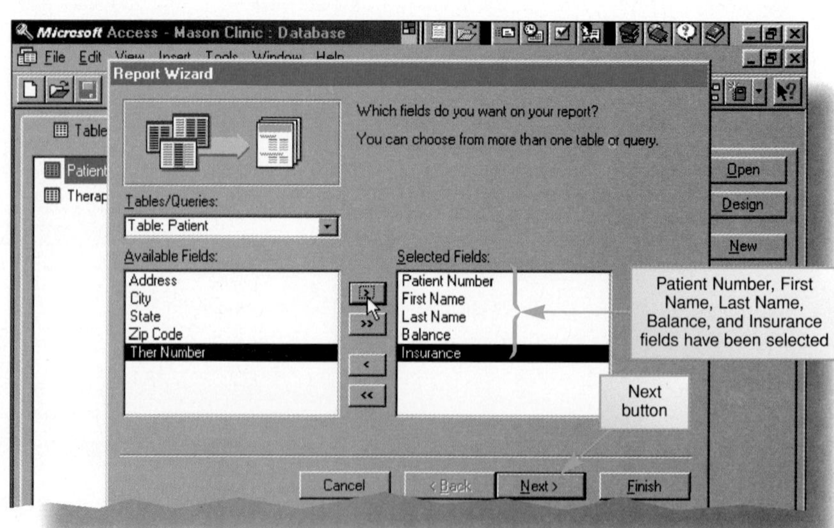

FIGURE 1-65

2 **Click the Next button.**

The Report Wizard dialog box displays (Figure 1-66).

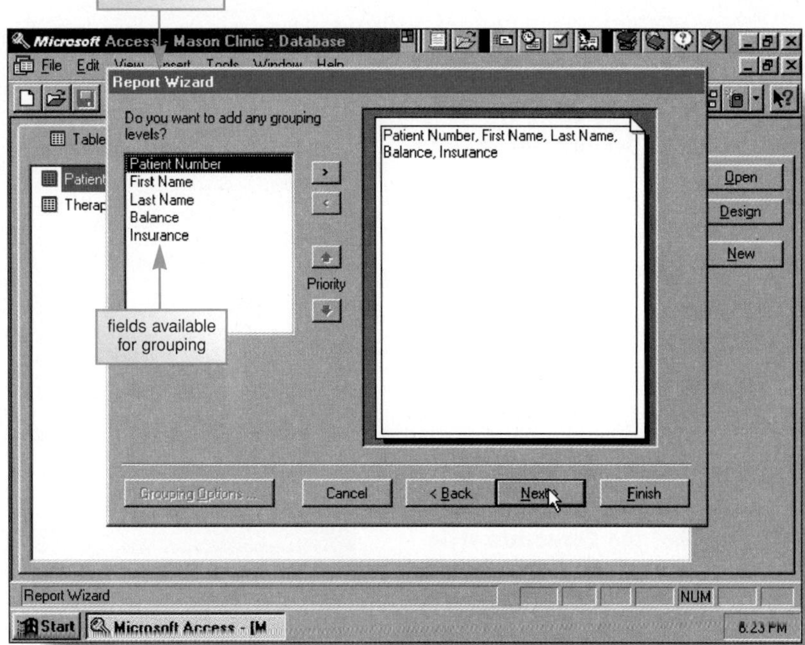

FIGURE 1-66

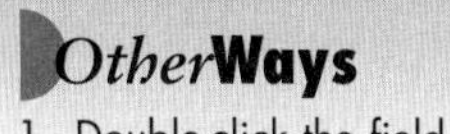

OtherWays

1. Double-click the field

Completing the Report

Several additional steps are involved in **completing the report.** With the exception of changing the title, the selections Access has already made in these other steps are acceptable, so you will simply click the Next button.

Perform the following steps to complete the report.

To Complete the Report

1 **Because you will not specify any grouping, click the Next button in the Report Wizard dialog box (see Figure 1-66). Click the Next button a second time because you will not need to make changes on the screen that follows.**

The Report Wizard dialog box displays (Figure 1-67). Use this dialog box to change the layout or orientation of the report.

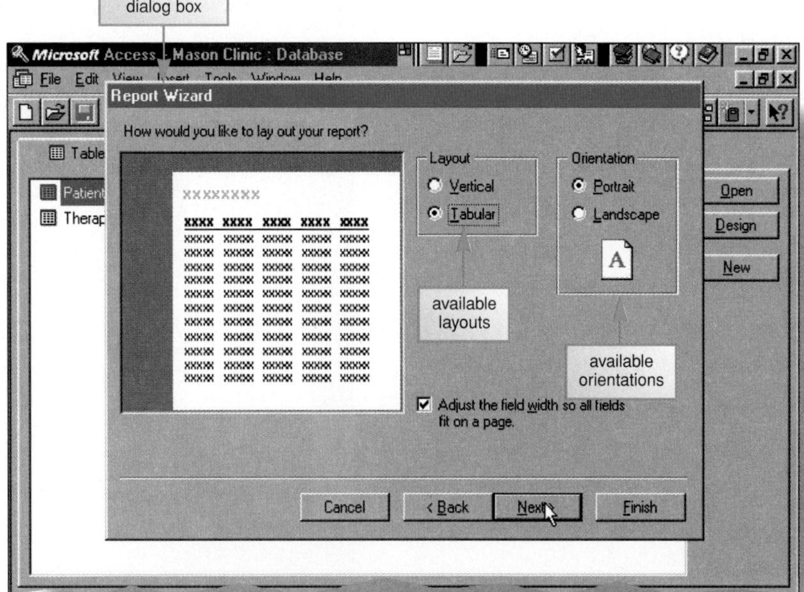

FIGURE 1-67

2 **Because the options currently selected in the dialog box in Figure 1-67 on page A 1.43 are acceptable, click the Next button.**

The Report Wizard dialog box displays (Figure 1-68). Use this dialog box to select a style for the report.

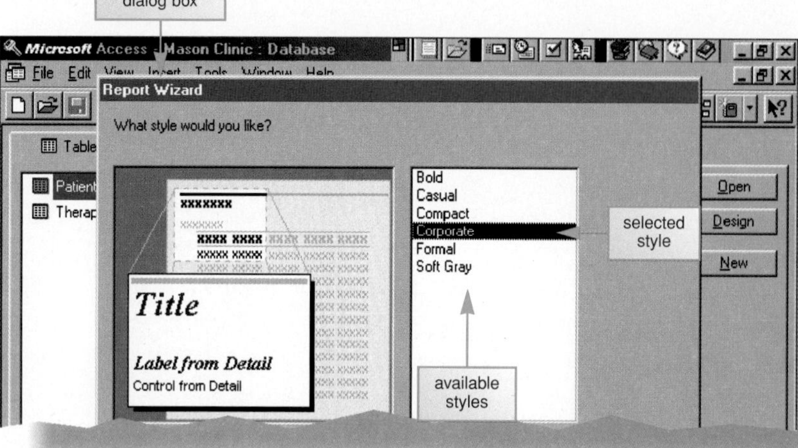

FIGURE 1-68

3 **Be sure that the Corporate style is selected and then click the Next button.**

The Report Wizard dialog box displays (Figure 1-69). Use this dialog box to specify a title for the report.

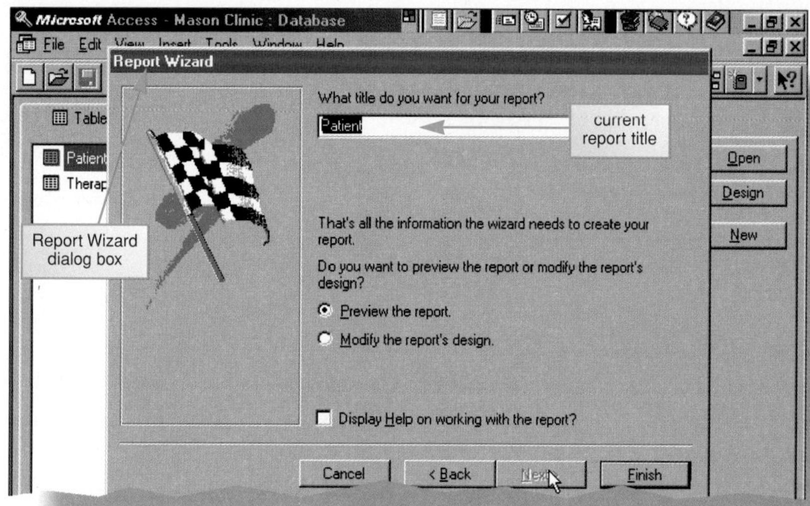

FIGURE 1-69

4 **Type** `Financial Report` **as the new title, and then click the Finish button.**

A preview of the report displays (Figure 1-70). Yours may look slightly different, depending on your printer.

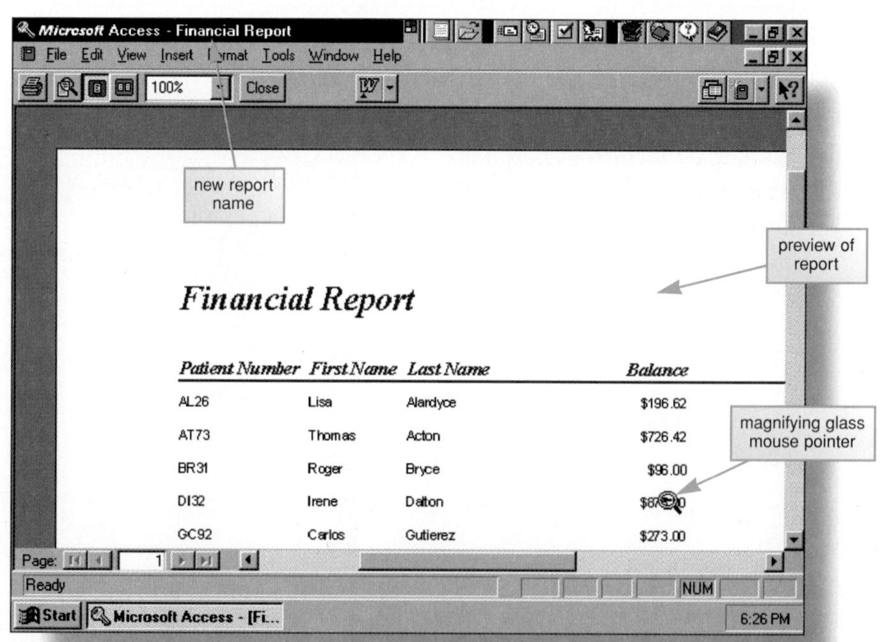

FIGURE 1-70

5 **To see the entire report, click the magnifying glass mouse pointer somewhere within the report.**

The entire report displays (Figure 1-71).

6 **Close the report by clicking the Close button for the Financial Report window.**

The report no longer displays. It has been saved automatically using the name Financial Report.

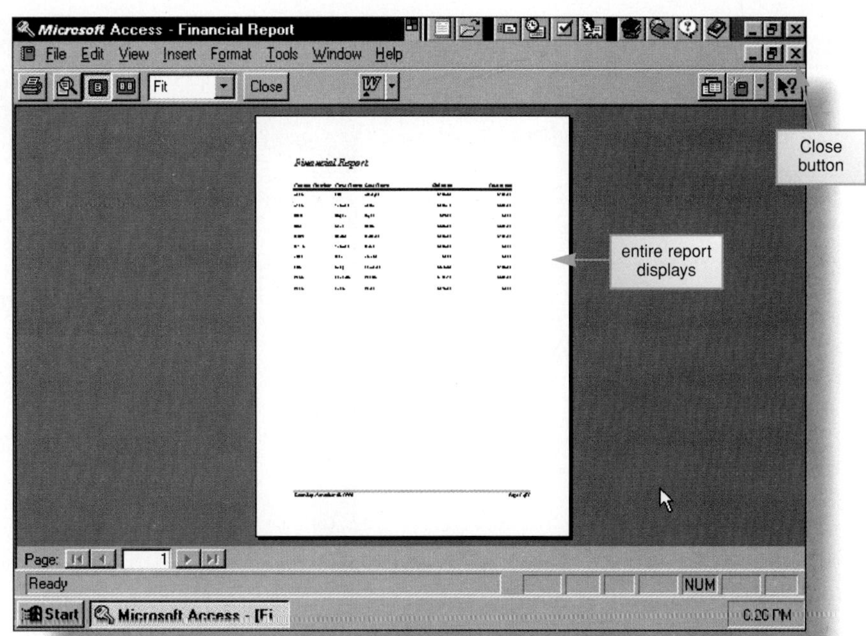

FIGURE 1-71

Printing the Report

To **print a report** from the Database window, first make sure that the reports display. If they do not, click the Reports tab. Next, make sure the report you want to print is selected, and then click the Preview button. After the preview displays and you have verified it is the correct report, click the Print button on the toolbar just as you did earlier.

Perform the following steps to print the report.

To Print the Report

1 **Click the Reports tab in the Database window.**

The list of reports displays (Figure 1-72). Currently, the only report is the Financial Report.

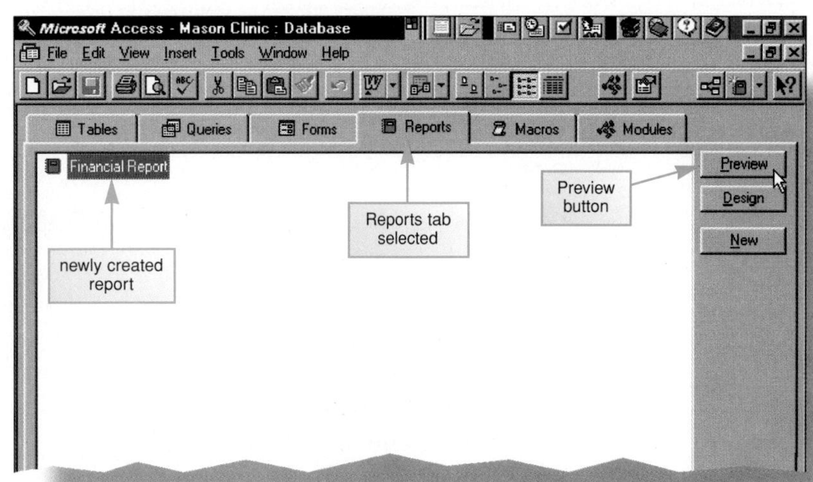

FIGURE 1-72

2 **Because the desired report is already selected, click the Preview button. Point to the Print button on the toolbar.**

A preview of the report displays (Figure 1-73).

3 **Click the Print button on the toolbar.**

The report prints. It looks similar to the one in Figure 1-61 on page A 1.40.

4 **Close the report by clicking the Close button for the Financial Report window.**

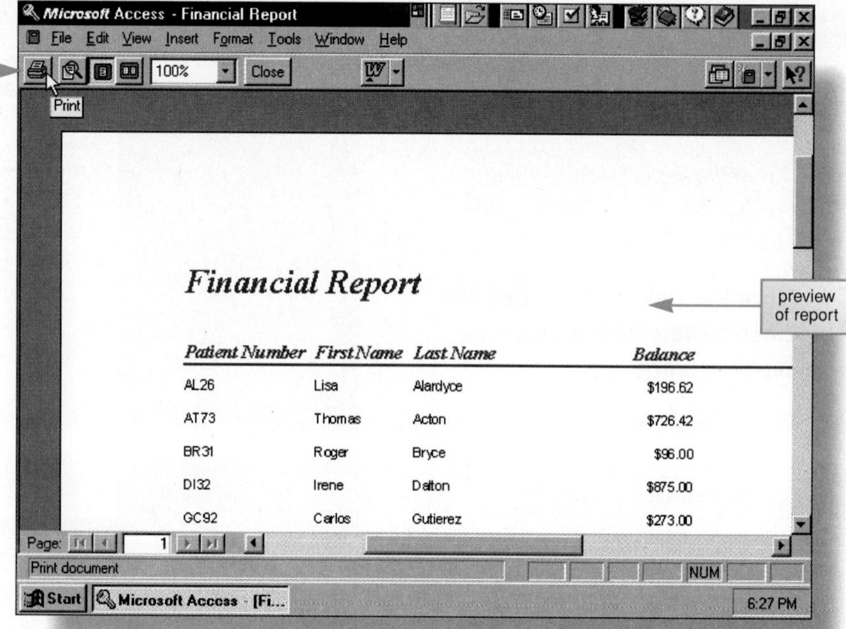

FIGURE 1-73

OtherWays

1. On File menu click Print Preview to preview; on File menu click Print to print
2. Press CTRL+P to print

Closing the Database

Once you have finished working with a database, you should close it. The following step closes the database by closing its Database window.

TO CLOSE A DATABASE

Step 1: Click the Close button for the Mason Clinic : Database window.

Access Online Help

At any time while you are using Access, you can answer your Access questions by using **online Help**. Used properly, this form of online assistance can increase your productivity and reduce your frustrations by minimizing the time you spend learning how to use Access.

Using the Contents Sheet to Obtain Help

The **Contents sheet** in the Help Topics dialog box offers you assistance when you know the general category of the topic in question, but not the specifics. Use the Contents sheet in the same manner you would use a table of contents at the front of a textbook.

The following steps show how to use the Contents sheet tab to obtain information on adding or editing data.

To Obtain Help Using the Contents Sheet

1 **Double-click the Help button on the toolbar (the button containing an arrowhead and question mark).**

The Help Topics: Microsoft Access for Windows 95 dialog box displays (Figure 1-74).

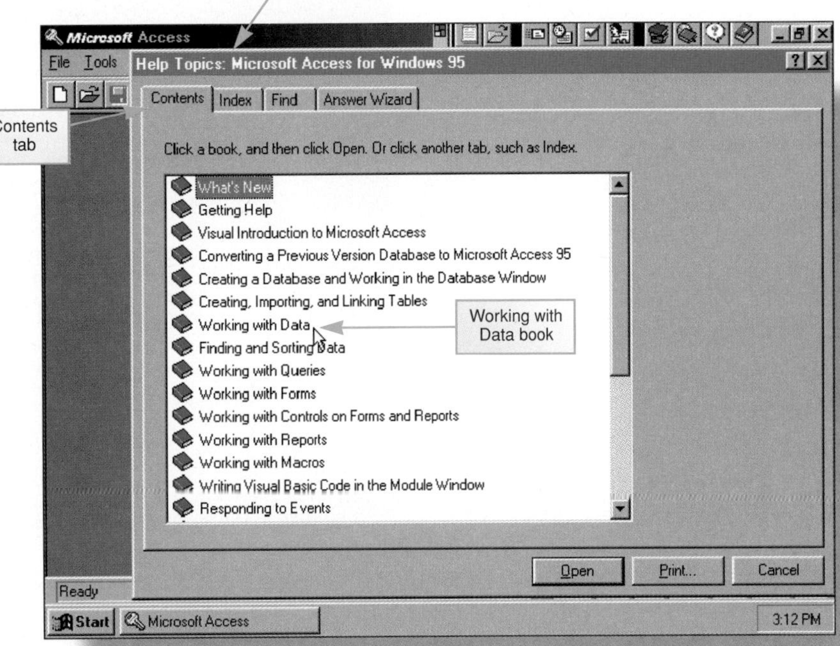

FIGURE 1-74

2 **If necessary, click the Contents tab to make the Contents sheet active. In the list box, double-click the Working with Data book.**

Each topic on the Contents sheet is preceded by a book or question mark icon. A ***book icon*** *means there are subtopics. A* ***question mark icon*** *means information will display on the topic if the title is double-clicked. Notice how the book icon opens when the book (or its title) is double-clicked (Figure 1-75).*

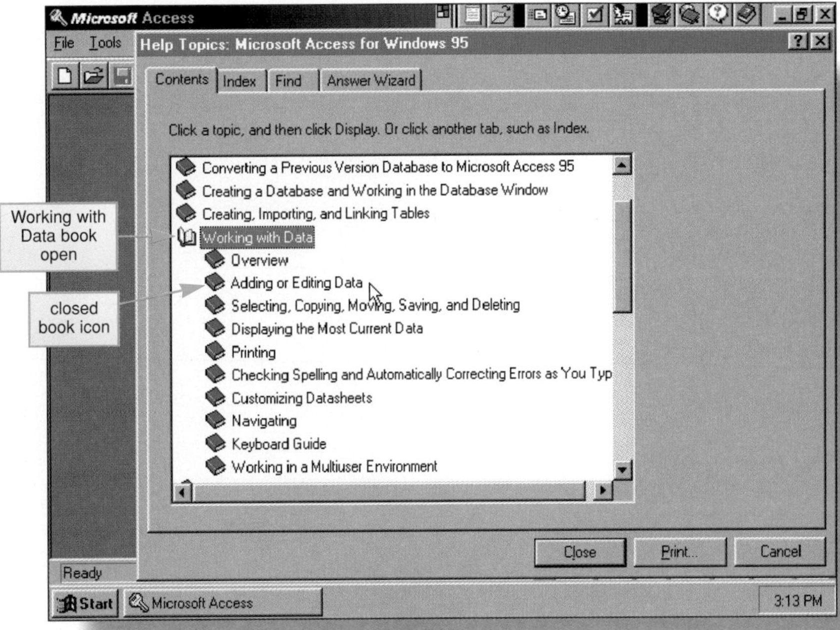

FIGURE 1-75

3 **Double-click the book Adding or Editing Data listed below the open book Working with Data.**

The Adding or Editing Data book is open with a list of topics (Figure 1-76).

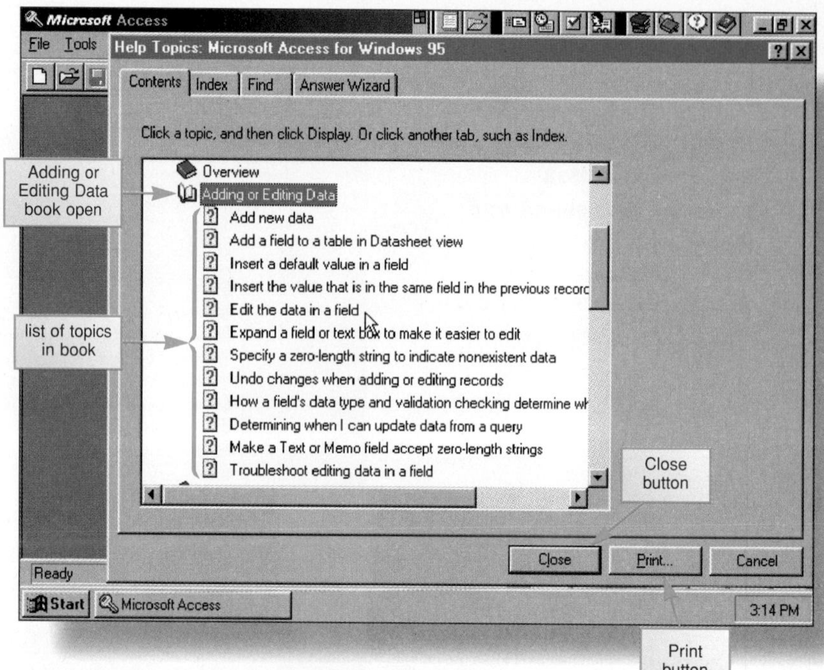

FIGURE 1-76

4 **Double-click the topic, Edit the data in a field, listed below the open book Adding or Editing Data.**

A Microsoft Access for Win Help window displays describing the steps for editing the data in a field (Figure 1-77).

5 **After reading the information, click the Close button in the Microsoft Access for Win Help window.**

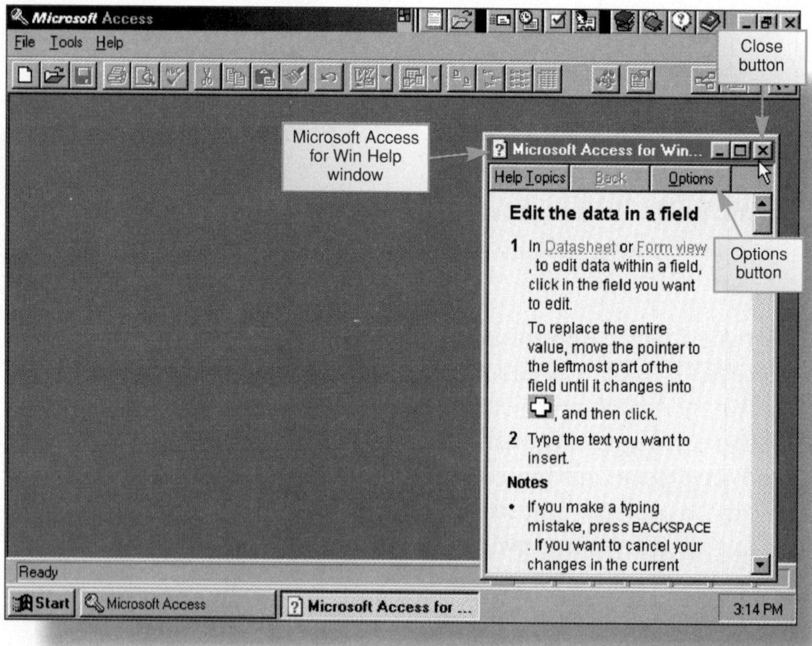

FIGURE 1-77

*Other*Ways

1. On Help menu, click either Microsoft Access Help Topics or Answer Wizard
2. Press F1

Rather than double-clicking a topic in the list box, you can click it and then use the buttons at the bottom of the Help Topics dialog box to open a book, display information on a topic, or print information on a topic (Figure 1-76).

You also can print the information in the Help window by right-clicking in the window (Figure 1-77) or clicking the Options button and then clicking Print Topic. To close the Help window, click its Close button to return to Access or click the Help Topics button to return to the Contents sheet.

Using the Index Sheet to Obtain Help

The next sheet in the Help Topics: Microsoft Access for Windows 95 dialog box is the Index sheet. Use the **Index sheet** when you know the term you are after or at least the first few letters of the term. Use the Index sheet in the same manner you would an index at the back of a textbook.

The following steps show how to obtain information on primary keys by using the Index sheet and entering the letters, pri, the first three letters of primary.

To Obtain Help Using the Index Sheet

1 Double-click the Help button on the toolbar.

The Help Topics: Microsoft Access for Windows 95 dialog box displays.

2 If necessary, click the Index tab. Type `pri` in the top box labeled 1.

The term primary keys displays in the lower box labeled 2 (Figure 1-78). Several index entries relating to primary keys are in the list.

FIGURE 1-78

3 Double-click the index entry, setting, under primary keys. Double-click Set or change the primary key in the Topics Found dialog box.

Information on setting, or changing the primary key displays in the Microsoft Access for Win Help window (Figure 1-79).

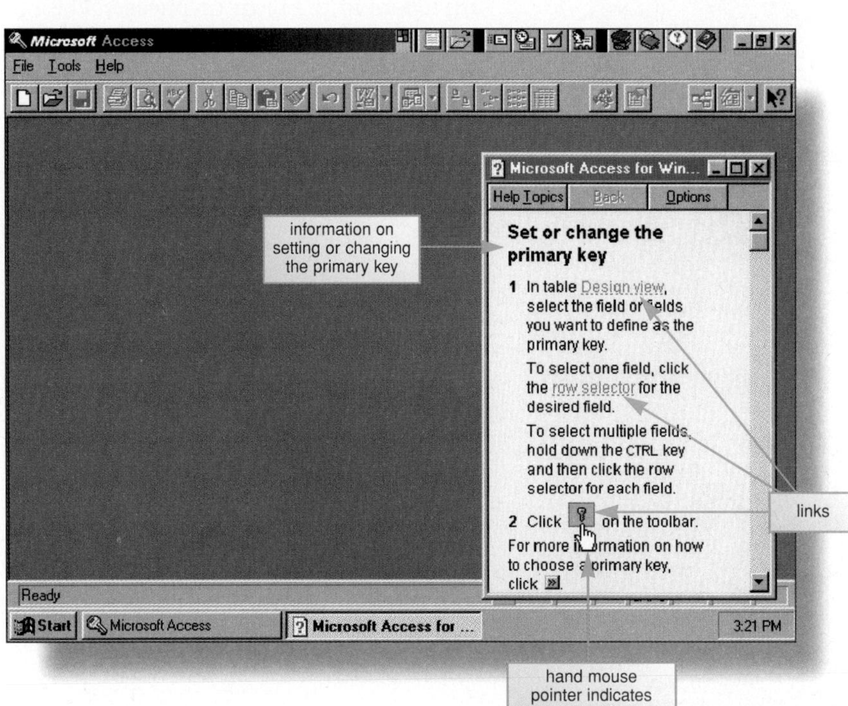

FIGURE 1-79

4 **Point to the Primary Key button link. Click the mouse pointer when it changes to a hand.**

The information on the Primary Key button displays above the Primary Key button link (Figure 1-80). When you click a ***link****, a picture, or phrase, Access displays further Help information.*

5 **Click anywhere in the Primary Key button information box to close it, and then click the Close button in the upper right corner of the Microsoft Access for Win Help window to close it.**

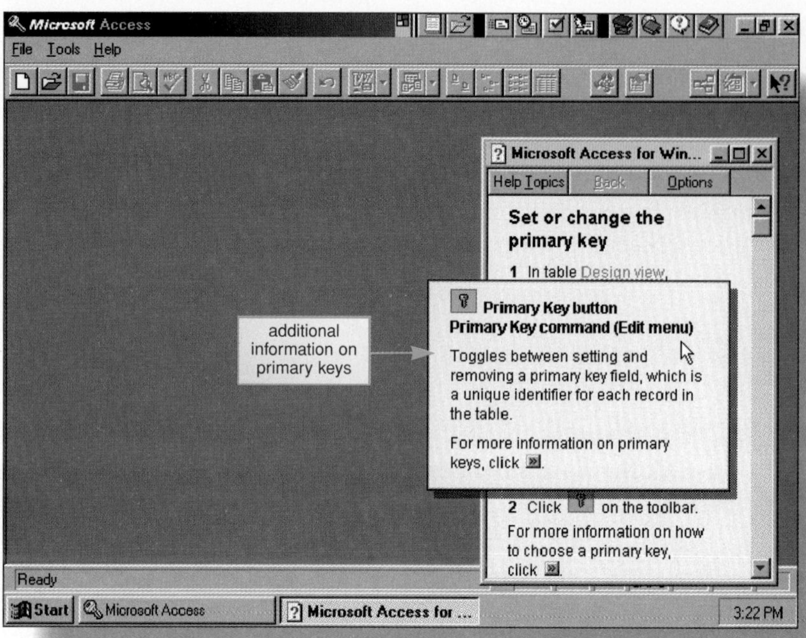

FIGURE 1-80

OtherWays

1. On Help menu, click either Microsoft Access Help Topics or Answer Wizard
2. Press F1

Not all information you look up through online Help is printable. Generally speaking if the Help window contains an Options button, then you can print the information.

Using the Find Sheet to Obtain Help

The third sheet in the Help Topics: Microsoft Access for Windows 95 dialog box is the Find sheet. Use the **Find sheet** when you know a word that is located *anywhere* in the term or phrase. The Find sheet will return a list of all topics pertaining to the word. You then can further select words to narrow your search.

The following steps show how to obtain information on adding a field to a table structure.

To Obtain Help Using the Find Sheet

1 **Double-click the Help button on the toolbar.**

The Help Topics: Microsoft Access for Windows 95 dialog box displays.

2 **If necessary, click the Find tab. Type** add **in the top box labeled 1.**

Matching words display in the middle box labeled 2, and 714 topics relating to the term add are accessible in the lower box labeled 3 (Figure 1-81). Your computer may contain fewer or more topics found.

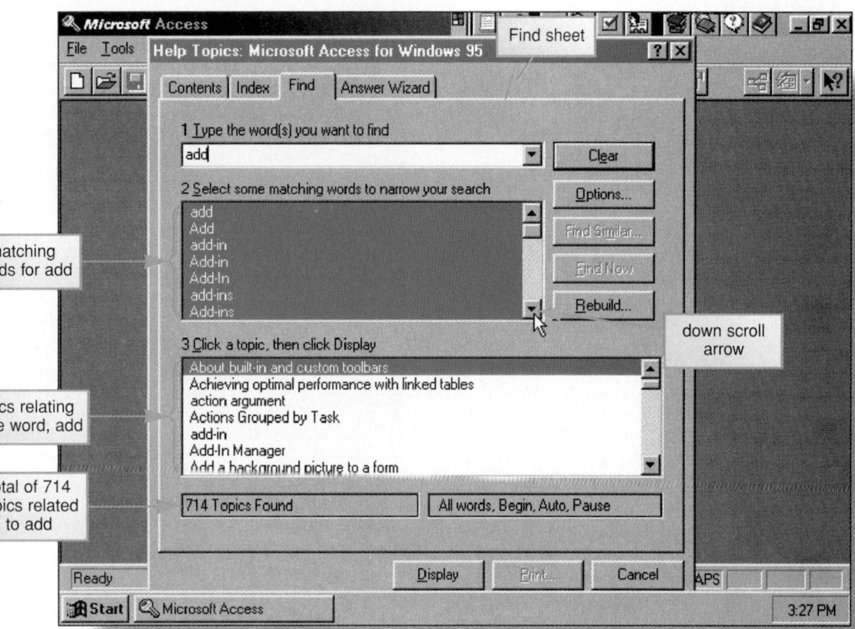

FIGURE 1-81

3 **Click the down scroll arrow to display the word, adding. Click the word, adding, in the middle box labeled 2.**

The number of topics found changes from 714 to 74 in the lower box labeled 3 (Figure 1-82). The number may be different on your computer.

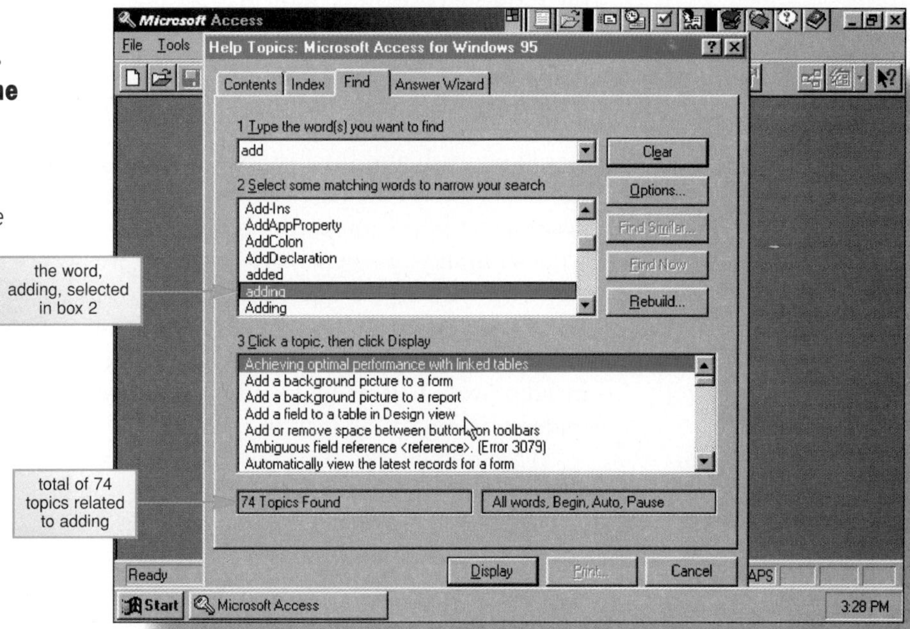

FIGURE 1-82

4 **Double-click the topic, Add a field to a table in Design view, in the lower box labeled 3 on the Find sheet.**

The information regarding adding a field to a table in Design view displays as shown in Figure 1-83. To display more information click the Insert Row button link.

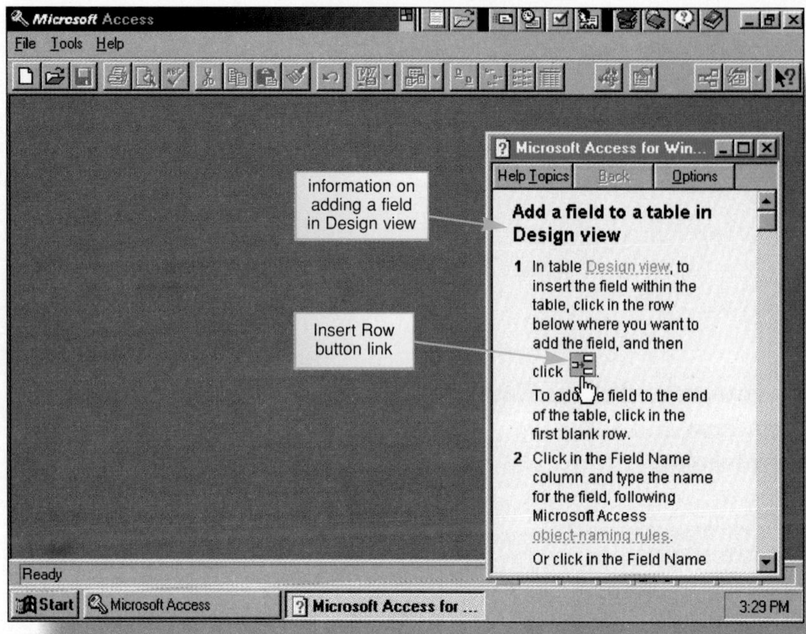

FIGURE 1-83

OtherWays

1. On Help menu, click either Microsoft Access Help Topics or Answer Wizard
2. Press F1

You can see from the previous steps that the Find sheet allows you to enter a word similar to the Index sheet, but instead of displaying an alphabetical listing, the Find sheet lists all the words or phrases that include the word you entered. You then can click the appropriate words or phrases to narrow your search.

Using the Answer Wizard to Obtain Help

The fourth and final sheet in the Help Topics: Microsoft Access for Windows 95 dialog box is the Answer Wizard sheet. Use the **Answer Wizard** sheet when you know what you want to do, but have no idea what the task is called. Simply type a question in your own words and the Answer Wizard will assist you. For example, when you type a question such as, "How do I create a table?" on the Answer Wizard sheet, it responds by displaying two categories of topics - *How Do I* and *Tell Me About*. The *How Do I* topics show how to complete a task, listing a step-by-step procedure or by example. The *Tell Me About* topics give you a better understanding of the task in question.

The following steps show how to obtain information on creating a table by entering the question, "How do I create a table?"

Steps To Obtain Help Using the Answer Wizard

1. **Double-click the Help button on the toolbar.**

   The Help Topics: Microsoft Access for Windows 95 dialog box displays.

2. **If necessary, click the Answer Wizard tab. Type** `how do i create a table` **in the box labeled 1. Click the Search button.**

   The Answer Wizard responds by displaying two categories (How Do I and Tell Me About) of topics in the lower box labeled 2 (Figure 1-84).

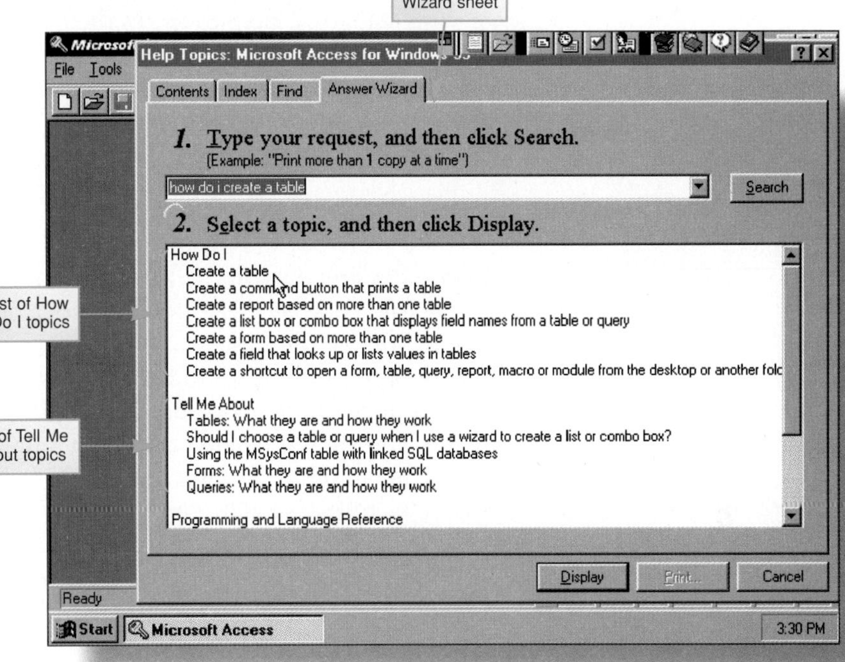

FIGURE 1-84

3. **Double-click the topic Create a table in the lower box labeled 2.**

   A Microsoft Access for Windows 95 Help window displays describing the various ways you can create a table (Figure 1-85).

4. **After reviewing the information, click the Close button in the upper right corner of the Help window to close it.**

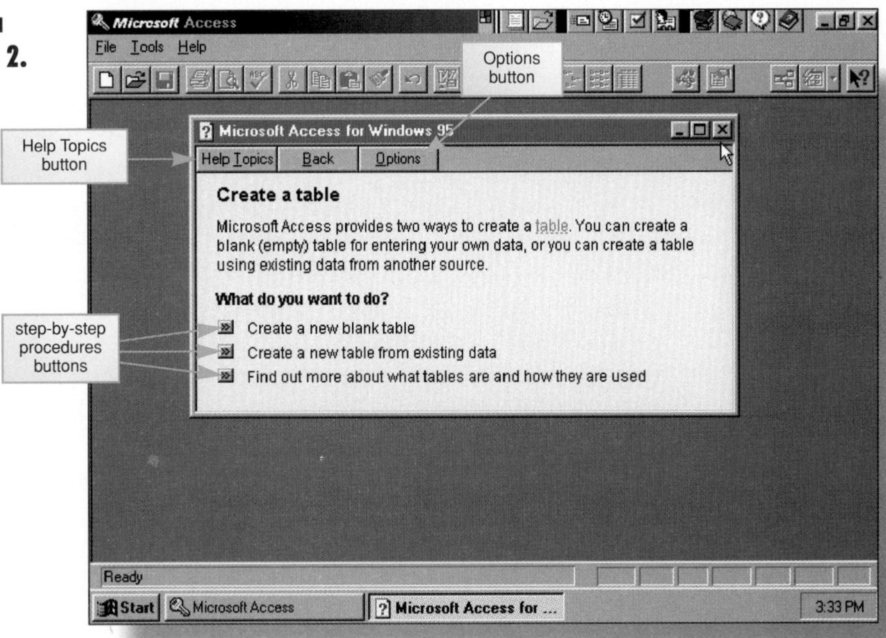

FIGURE 1-85

OtherWays

1. On Help menu, click either Microsoft Access Help Topics or Answer Wizard
2. Press F1

Here again, you can print the information in Figure 1-85 by right-clicking in the Help window or by clicking the Options button. Instead of quitting online Help by clicking the Close button in Step 4, you can click the Help Topics button (Figure 1-85) to return to the Answer Wizard sheet shown in Figure 1-84.

The four online Help features (Contents, Index, Find, and Answer Wizard) of Access presented thus far are powerful and easy to use. The best way to familiarize yourself with these Help tools is to use them. Also to give you more experience with using the Help tools, in the Student Assignments at the end of each project is a section titled Use Help. It is recommended that you step through these Help exercises to gain a better understanding of Access online Help.

More *About* Database Design

When database designs become more complex, a special technique called normalization identifies and eliminates redundancy. For a description of this and other database design techniques, refer to one of the more advanced textbooks available on concepts of database management.

Designing a Database

Database design refers to the arrangement of data into tables and fields. In the example in this project, the design is specified, but in many cases, you will have to determine the design based on what you want the system to accomplish.

With large, complex databases, the database design process can be extensive. Major sections of advanced database textbooks are devoted to this topic. Often, however, you should be able to design a database effectively by keeping one simple principle in mind: *Design to remove redundancy.* **Redundancy** means storing the same fact in more than one place.

To illustrate, you need to maintain the following information shown in Figure 1-86. In the figure, all the data is contained in a single table. Notice that the data for a given therapist (number, name, address, and so on) occurs on more than one record.

Patient Table

PATIENT NUMBER	LAST NAME	FIRST NAME	ADDRESS	CITY	STATE	ZIP CODE	BALANCE	INSURANCE	THER NUMBER	LAST NAME	FIRST NAME	ADDRESS	CITY	STATE	ZIP CODE	BILLING	PAID
AL26	Alardyce	Lisa	311 Birchwood	Lamont	MI	49160	$196.62	$180.00	05	Hughes	Mary	4613 Essex	Burnips	MI	49277	$62,277.00	$46,245.25
AT73	Acton	Thomas	312 Newcastle	Homer	MI	49162	$726.42	$550.00	08	Foster	Richard	6621 Eastern	Stockton	IN	47962	$71,245.00	$65,121.33
BR31	Bryce	Roger	617 College	Lamont	MI	49160	$96.00	$5,000.00	08	Foster	Richard	6621 Eastern	Stockton	IN	47962	$71,245.00	$65,121.33
DI32	Dalton	Irene	41 Lafayette	Madison	IN	42909	$875.00	$600.00	14	Galvez	Maria	684 Valley	Leland	MI	47205	$34,252.50	$22,645.90
GC92	Gutierez	Carlos	476 Fulton	Jackson	OH	49401	$273.00	$150.00	05	Hughes	Mary	4613 Essex	Burnips	MI	49277	$62,277.00	$46,245.25
GT43	Grant	Thomas	247 Fuller	Lamont	MI	49160	$276.00	$0.00	08	Foster	Richard	6621 Eastern	Stockton	IN	47962	$71,245.00	$65,121.33
JG22	Jenkins	Glen	201 Plymouth	Madison	IN	42909	$0.00	$0.00	08	Foster	Richard	6621 Eastern	Stockton	IN	47962	$71,245.00	$65,121.33
LI66	Lawrence	Irving	912 Devonshire	Beulah	MI	45621	$346.50	$175.00	05	Hughes	Mary	4613 Essex	Burnips	MI	49277	$62,277.00	$46,245.25
PE33	Pezato	Eduardo	346 Vernor	Homer	MI	49162	$467.12	$500.00	14	Galvez	Maria	684 Valley	Leland	MI	47205	$34,252.50	$22,645.90
PE76	Perez	Enzo	216 Four Mile	Perry	MI	47211	$216.00	$0.00	08	Foster	Richard	6621 Eastern	Stockton	IN	47962	$71,245.00	$65,121.33

duplicate therapist names

FIGURE 1-86

Storing this data on multiple records is an example of redundancy, which causes several problems:

1. Redundancy wastes space on the disk. The address of therapist 05 (Mary Hughes), for example, should be stored only once. Storing this fact several times is wasteful.
2. Redundancy makes updating the database more difficult. If, for example, Mary Hughes moves, her address would need to be changed in several different places.
3. A possibility of inconsistent data exists. Suppose, for example, that you change the address of Mary Hughes on patient GC92's record to 146 Valley, but do not change it on patient AL26's record. In both cases, the Ther Number is 05, but the addresses are different. In other words, the data is *inconsistent*.

The solution to the problem is to place the redundant data in a separate table, one in which the data will no longer be redundant. If, for example, you place the data for therapists in a separate table (Figure 1-87), the data for each therapist will appear only once.

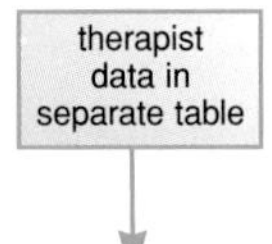

Therapist Table

THER NUMBER	LAST NAME	FIRST NAME	ADDRESS	CITY	STATE	ZIP CODE	BILLING	PAID
05	Hughes	Mary	4613 Essex	Burnips	MI	49277	$62,277.00	$46,245.25
08	Foster	Richard	6621 Eastern	Stockton	IN	47962	$71,245.00	$65,121.33
14	Galvez	Juanita	684 Valley	Leland	MI	47205	$34,252.50	$22,645.90

Patient Table

PATIENT NUMBER	LAST NAME	FIRST NAME	ADDRESS	CITY	STATE	ZIP CODE	BALANCE	INSURANCE	THER NUMBER
AL26	Alardyce	Lisa	311 Birchwood	Lamont	MI	49160	$196.62	$180.00	05
AT73	Acton	Thomas	312 Newcastle	Homer	MI	49162	$726.42	$550.00	08
BR31	Bryce	Roger	617 College	Lamont	MI	49160	$96.00	$0.00	08
DI32	Dalton	Irene	41 Lafayette	Madison	IN	42909	$875.00	$600.00	14
GC92	Gutierez	Carlos	476 Fulton	Jackson	OH	49401	$273.00	$150.00	05
GT43	Grant	Thomas	247 Fuller	Lamont	MI	49160	$276.00	$0.00	08
JG22	Jenkins	Glen	201 Plymouth	Madison	IN	42909	$0.00	$0.00	08
LI66	Lawrence	Irving	912 Devonshire	Beulah	MI	45621	$346.50	$175.00	05
PE33	Pezato	Eduardo	346 Vernor	Homer	MI	49162	$467.12	$500.00	14
PE76	Perez	Enzo	216 Four Mile	Perry	MI	47211	$216.00	$0.00	08

FIGURE 1-87

Notice that you need to have the Ther Number in both tables. Without it, there would be no way to tell which therapist was associated with which patient. All the other therapist data, however, was removed from the Patient table and placed in the Therapist table. This new arrangement corrects the problems:

1. Because the data for each therapist is stored only once, space is not wasted.
2. Changing the address of a therapist is easy. You have only to change one row in the Therapist table.
3. Because the data for a therapist is stored only once, inconsistent data cannot occur.

Designing to omit redundancy will help you to produce good and valid database designs.

Project Summary

Project 1 introduced you to starting Access and creating a database. You created the database that will be used by Mason Clinic. Within the Mason Clinic database, you created the Patient and Therapist tables by defining the fields within them. You then added records to these tables. Once you created the tables, you printed the contents of the tables. You also used a form to view the data in the table. Finally, you used the Report Wizard to create a report containing the patient number, first name, last name, balance, and insurance amount fields for each patient of Mason Clinic.

What You Should Know

Having completed this project, you should now be able to perform the following tasks:

- Add Additional Records to the Table *(A 1.26)*
- Add Records to the Additional Table *(A 1.34)*
- Add Records to the Table *(A 1.21)*
- Begin Creating the Table *(A 1.15)*
- Create a New Database *(A 1.10)*
- Create an Additional Table *(A 1.33)*
- Create the Report *(A 1.41)*
- Close and Save the Form *(A 1.36)*
- Close the Table and the Database *(A 1.24)*
- Complete the Report *(A 1.43)*
- Define the Fields in the Table *(A 1.16)*
- Exit Access *(A 1.23)*
- Obtain Help Using the Answer Wizard *(A 1.53)*
- Obtain Help Using the Contents Sheet *(A 1.47)*
- Obtain Help Using the Find Sheet *(A 1.51)*
- Obtain Help Using the Index Sheet *(A 1.49)*
- Open a Database *(A 1.25)*
- Open the Form *(A 1.37)*
- Preview and Print the Contents of the Table *(A 1.29)*
- Print the Report *(A 1.45)*
- Save the Table *(A 1.19)*
- Select the Fields for the Report *(A 1.42)*
- Start Access *(A 1.10)*
- Switch from Form View to Datasheet View *(A 1.39)*
- Use the Form *(A 1.39)*
- Use the New Object Button to Create the Form *(A 1.35)*

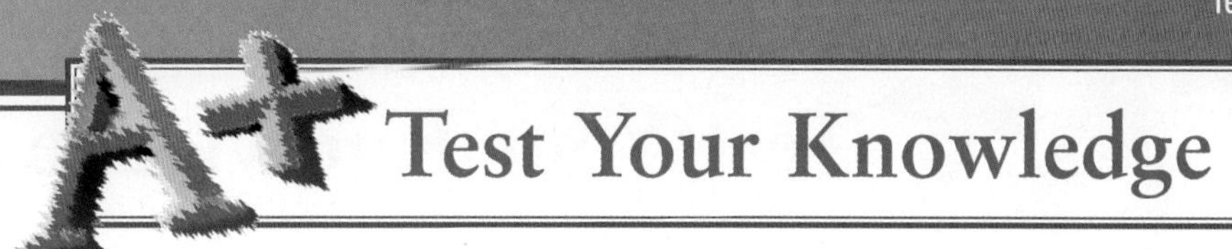

Test Your Knowledge

1 True/False

Instructions: Circle T if the statement is true or F if the statement is false.

T F 1. The term database describes a collection of data organized in a manner that allows access, retrieval, and use of that data.
T F 2. Table names can be from one to 64 characters in length and can include blank spaces.
T F 3. If you do not assign a width to a text field, Access assumes the width is 50.
T F 4. You can use the TAB key to move to the next field in a record in Datasheet view.
T F 5. Field names can be no more than 64 characters in length and cannot include numeric digits.
T F 6. The only field type available for fields that must be used in arithmetic operations is Number.
T F 7. If you enter 10000 in a field that has been defined as a currency field type, then the value will display as $10,000.00.
T F 8. To delete a record from a table, select the record and then press CTRL+DELETE.
T F 9. To add a field to a table structure, select the field that will follow the field you wish to add, click Edit on the menu bar, and then click Insert Row.
T F 10. Controlling redundancy results in an increase in consistency.

2 Multiple Choice

Instructions: Circle the correct response.

1. A database is __________.
   a. the same as a file
   b. a software product
   c. a collection of data organized in a manner that allows access, retrieval, and use of that data
   d. none of the above
2. Which of the following is not a benefit of controlling redundancy?
   a. greater consistency is maintained
   b. less space is occupied
   c. update is easier
   d. all of the above are benefits
3. A field that uniquely identifies a particular record in a table is called a __________.
   a. foreign key
   b. secondary key
   c. primary key
   d. principal key
4. Access is a(n) __________.
   a. applications software package
   b. DBMS
   c. database
   d. both a and b

(continued)

Test Your Knowledge

Multiple Choice *(continued)*

5. To change to landscape orientation to print a table, click __________ on the File menu.
   a. Print Settings
   b. Page Setup
   c. Print Preview
   d. Print
6. A record in Access is composed of a __________.
   a. series of databases
   b. series of files
   c. series of records
   d. series of fields
7. To make a field the primary key for a table, select the field and then click the __________ button on the toolbar.
   a. Unique Key
   b. Single Key
   c. First Key
   d. Primary Key
8. To remove a field from a table structure, select the field and then press the __________ key(s).
   a. DELETE
   b. CTRL+D
   c. CTRL+DELETE
   d. CTRL+Y
9. To create a form for a table, highlight the table and click the __________ button down arrow on the toolbar, and then click AutoForm on the drop-down list.
   a. New Form
   b. New Object
   c. Create Form
   d. Create Object
10. To move from the upper pane, the one where you define fields, in the Table window to the lower pane, the one where you define field properties, press the __________ key.
    a. F3
    b. F4
    c. F6
    d. F7

3 Understanding Access Windows

Instructions: In Figure 1-88, arrows point to the major components of an Access window. Identify the various parts of the window in the spaces provided.

Test Your Knowledge

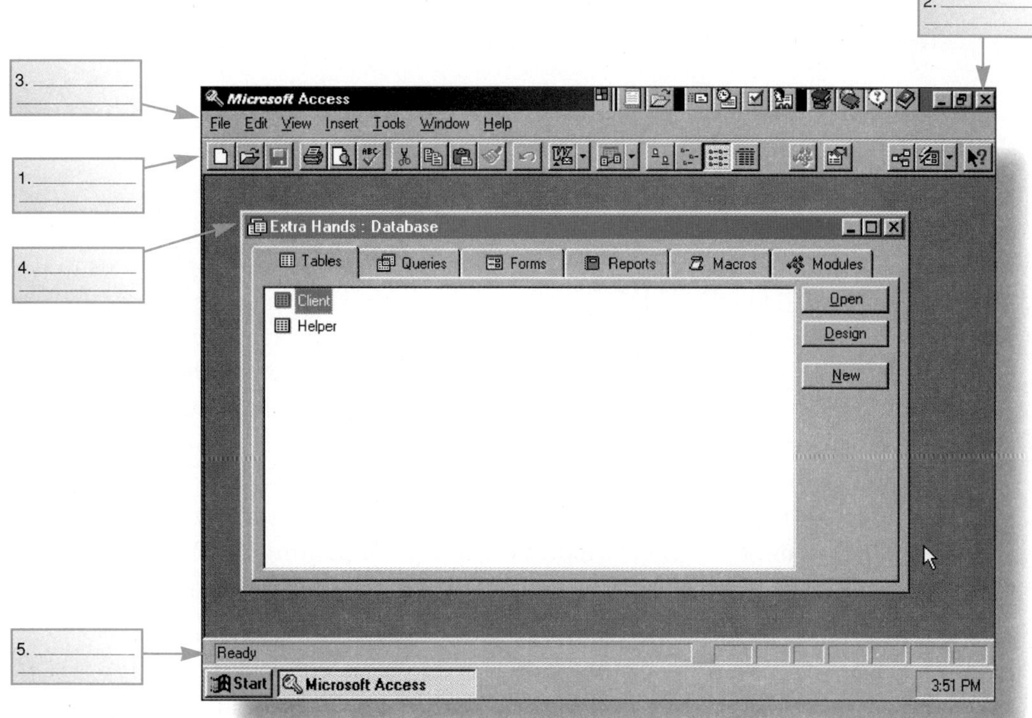

FIGURE 1-88

4 Understanding the Table Window in Form View

Instructions: On the form in Figure 1-89, arrows point to several of the buttons on the toolbar and status bar. In the spaces provided, identify each button.

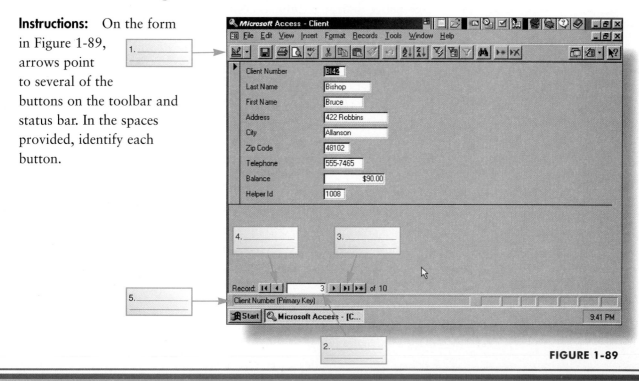

FIGURE 1-89

Use Help

1 Reviewing Project Activities

Instructions: Perform the following tasks using a computer.

1. Start Access.
2. Double-click the Help button on the toolbar to display the Help Topics: Microsoft Access for Windows 95 dialog box.
3. Click the Index tab. Type `Datasheet` in box 1, and then double-click editing records under Datasheet view in box 2. Double-click Delete a record in Datasheet or Form view in the Topics Found dialog box. When the Help information displays, read it. Next, right-click within the window, and then click Print Topic. Hand in the printout to your instructor. Click the Help Topics button to return to the Help Topics: Microsoft Access for Windows 95 dialog box.
4. Click the Find tab. Type `preview` in box 1. Click Previewing in box 2. Double-click Preview a report in box 3. When the Microsoft Access for Windows 95 Help window displays, read it, ready the printer, right-click in the window, and click Print Topic. Click the Preview all the data in the report page by page button in the Help window. Print the Help information. Hand in the printouts to your instructor. Click the Help Topics button to return to the Help Topics: Microsoft Access for Windows 95 dialog box.
5. Click the Answer Wizard tab. Type `how do i use data types` in box 1. Click the Search button. Double-click What data type should I use for a field in my table? in box 2 under Tell Me About. Read and print the Help information. Hand in the printout to your instructor.

2 Expanding on the Basics

Instructions: Use Access online Help to better understand the topics listed below. Begin each of the following by double-clicking the Help button on the toolbar. If you are unable to print the Help information, then answer the question on your own paper.

1. Using the Working with Data book on the Contents sheet in the Help Topics: Microsoft Access for Windows 95 dialog box, answer the following questions:
   a. When does Access save the data in a record?
   b. How can you save the data in a record while you are editing it?
2. Using the key term, *shortcut keys*, and the Index tab in the Help Topics: Microsoft Access for Windows 95 dialog box, display and print the shortcut keys to use in Datasheet view and Form view. Then, answer the following questions:
   a. Which key or combination keys add a new record?
   b. Which key or combination keys delete a record?
   c. Which key or combination keys save changes to the current record?
   d. Which key or combination keys undo changes in the current field?
   e. Which key or combination keys check spelling?
3. Use the Find sheet in the Help Topics: Microsoft Access for Windows 95 dialog box to display and print information about correcting two capital letters in a row automatically.
4. Use the Answer Wizard in the Help Topics: Microsoft Access for Windows 95 dialog box to display and print information about backing up a database.

Apply Your Knowledge

CAUTION: It is recommended that you create a backup copy of the Student Floppy Disk that accompanies this book and then remove unneeded folders on the backup floppy disk to free up space. Do the following: (1) insert the Student Floppy Disk in drive A; (2) start Explorer; (3) right-click the 3½ Floppy [A:] folder in the All Folders side of the window; (4) click Copy Disk; (5) click Start and OK as required; (6) insert the backup floppy disk when requested; (7) delete folders on the backup floppy disk except the Access folder.

1 Changing Data and Creating Reports

Instructions: Read the Caution box. Start Access and open the Extra Hands document from the Access folder on the Student Floppy Disk that accompanies this book. Extra Hands is a local company that provides various services to individuals in the community. Helpers run errands, clean houses, drive people to appointments, and assist with other chores. Extra Hands has a database that keeps track of their clients and their helpers. The database has two tables. The Client table contains data on the clients who use the Extra Hands service. The Helper table contains data on individuals employed by Extra Hands. The data and structure are shown for the Client table in Figure 1-90 and for the Helper table in Figure 1-91 on the next page.

Structure of Client Table

FIELD NAME	DATA TYPE	FIELD SIZE	PRIMARY KEY?	DESCRIPTION
Client Number	Text	4	Yes	Client Number (Primary Key)
Last Name	Text	10		Last Name of Client
First Name	Text	8		First Name of Client
Address	Text	15		Street Address
City	Text	15		City
Zip Code	Text	5		Zip Code (Five-Character Version)
Telephone	Text	8		Telephone Number (999-9999 Version)
Balance	Currency			Amount Owed by Client
Helper Id	Text	4		Id of Client's Helper

Data for Client Table

CLIENT NUMBER	LAST NAME	FIRST NAME	ADDRESS	CITY	ZIP CODE	TELEPHONE	BALANCE	HELPER ID
AR86	Arends	Carolyn	268 Getty	Allanson	48102	555-9523	$35.00	1001
AT24	Atwater	Shelly	542 Dune	Allanson	48103	555-1354	$0.00	1008
BI42	Bishop	Bruce	422 Robbins	Allanson	48102	555-7465	$90.00	1008
CH26	Chiang	Doi	62 Stryker	Oakdale	48101	555-2018	$0.00	1012
CH66	Chown	Douglas	266 Norton	Oakdale	48101	555-4890	$55.00	1001
JO12	Johns	Patricia	420 Robbins	Allanson	48102	555-9182	$24.00	1008
KI15	Kirk	Robert	12 Hellerman	Oakdale	48101	555-8273	$65.00	1008
MA21	Martinez	Marie	215 Glen	Allanson	48102	555-1234	$0.00	1001
MO31	Morton	Julie	557 Dune	Allanson	48103	555-5361	$78.00	1012
RO92	Robertson	Mary	345 Magee	Oakdale	48101	555-2056	$43.00	1008

FIGURE 1-90

(continued)

Apply Your Knowledge

Changing Data and Creating Reports *(continued)*

Structure of Helper Table

FIELD NAME	DATA TYPE	FIELD SIZE	PRIMARY KEY?	DESCRIPTION
Helper Id	Text	4	Yes	Helper Identification Number (Primary Key)
Last Name	Text	10		Last Name of Helper
First Name	Text	8		First Name of Helper
Address	Text	15		Street Address
City	Text	15		City
Zip Code	Text	5		Zip Code (Five-Character Version)
Telephone	Text	8		Telephone Number (999-9999 Version)
Pay Rate	Currency			Hourly Pay Rate

Data for Helper Table

HELPER ID	LAST NAME	FIRST NAME	ADDRESS	CITY	ZIP CODE	TELEPHONE	PAY RATE
1001	Carson	Helen	872 Devon	Allanson	48102	555-7980	$7.25
1008	Ortez	Julia	96 Pierce	Oakdale	48101	555-2395	$6.95
1012	Zwieback	Robert	35 Henry	Allanson	48103	555-2040	$6.35

FIGURE 1-91

Perform the following tasks:

1. Open the Helper table in Datasheet view and add the following record to the table:

1010	Rassler	John	12 Seminole	Oakdale	48101	555-4112	$6.75

   To add the record, move past the first three records and then type the data for the new record. Close the Helper table.
2. Open the Helper table again. Notice that the record you just added has been moved. It is no longer at the end of the table. The records are in order by the primary key, Helper Id.
3. Print the Helper table.
4. Open the Client table.
5. Change the Helper Id for client KI15 to 1010.
6. Print the Client table.
7. Create the report shown in Figure 1-92 for the Client table.

Apply Your Knowledge

Balance Due Report

Client Number	First Name	Last Name	Balance
AR86	Carolyn	Arends	$35.00
AT24	Shelly	Atwater	$0.00
BI42	Bruce	Bishop	$90.00
CH26	Doi	Chiang	$0.00
CH66	Douglas	Chown	$55.00
JO12	Patricia	Johns	$24.00
KI15	Robert	Kirk	$65.00
MA21	Marie	Martinez	$0.00
MO31	Julie	Morton	$78.00
RO92	Mary	Robertson	$43.00

Friday, December 19, 1997

FIGURE 1-92

8. Print the report.

In the Lab

1 Creating the Symphony Shop Database

Problem: The local symphony raises money by selling musical novelties during concerts. Volunteers purchase novelty items from distributors that specialize in musical products. The president of the symphony board has asked you to create and update a database that volunteers can use. The database consists of two tables. The Novelty table contains information on items available for sale. The Distributor table contains information on the distributors.

Instructions: Perform the following tasks:

1. Create a new database in which to store all the objects related to the musical novelty data. Call the database Symphony Shop.
2. Create the Novelty table using the structure shown in Figure 1-93. Use the name Novelty for the table.

Structure of Novelty Table

FIELD NAME	DATA TYPE	FIELD SIZE	PRIMARY KEY?	DESCRIPTION
Novelty Id	Text	3	Yes	Novelty Id Number (Primary Key)
Description	Text	15		Description of Novelty Item
Units On Hand	Number	Long Integer		Number of Units On Hand
Cost	Currency			Unit Cost of Novelty Item
Selling Price	Currency			Selling Price of Novelty Item
Dist Code	Text	2		Code of Distributor of Novelty Item

Data for Novelty Table

NOVELTY ID	DESCRIPTION	UNITS ON HAND	COST	SELLING PRICE	DIST CODE
E01	Erasers	35	$0.15	$0.25	MM
G05	Gloves	10	$2.95	$4.00	CC
K03	Key Chains	25	$0.95	$1.20	AD
N01	Note Pads	20	$1.00	$1.50	AD
P02	Pencils	70	$0.10	$0.25	MM
P03	Pens	50	$0.75	$1.00	MM
S10	Scarves	5	$4.95	$6.50	CC
S12	Socks	15	$1.95	$3.00	CC
S25	Stationery	8	$3.95	$5.00	AD
U10	Umbrellas	12	$6.95	$8.00	CC

FIGURE 1-93

In the Lab

3. Add the data shown in Figure 1-93 to the Novelty table.
4. Print the Novelty table.
5. Create the Distributor table using the structure shown in Figure 1-94. Use the name Distributor for the table.
6. Add the data shown in Figure 1-94 to the Distributor table.

Structure of Distributor Table

FIELD NAME	DATA TYPE	FIELD SIZE	PRIMARY KEY?	DESCRIPTION
Dist Code	Text	2	Yes	Distributor Code (Primary Key)
Name	Text	18		Name of Distributor
Address	Text	15		Street Address
City	Text	15		City
State	Text	2		State (Two-Character Abbreviation)
Zip Code	Text	5		Zip Code (Five-Character Version)
Telephone	Text	12		Telephone Number (999-999-9999 Version)

Data for Distributor Table

DIST CODE	NAME	ADDRESS	CITY	STATE	ZIP CODE	TELEPHONE
AD	AAA Distributor	9661 King	Nova	MI	49401	517-555-3953
CC	Cook's Catalog	1625 Brook	Adelaide	MI	49441	616-555-8292
MM	Music Makers	145 Oak	Grand Fork	IL	49302	317-555-4477

FIGURE 1-94

7. Print the Distributor table.
8. Create a form for the Novelty table. Use the name Novelty for the form.
9. Create the report shown in Figure 1-95 on the next page for the Novelty table.

(continued)

Creating the Symphony Shop Database *(continued)*

Inventory Report

Novelty Id	*Description*	*Units On Hand*	*Cost*
E01	Erasers	35	$0.15
G05	Gloves	10	$2.95
K03	Key Chains	25	$0.95
N01	Note Pads	20	$1.00
P02	Pencils	70	$0.10
P03	Pens	50	$0.75
S10	Scarves	5	$4.95
S12	Socks	15	$1.95
S25	Stationery	8	$3.95
U10	Umbrellas	12	$6.95

FIGURE 1-95

2 Creating the College Telephone System Database

Problem: The Telecommunications group at your school operates the school telephone system. Each user is billed separately for monthly charges and all the bills for a department are sent to the department chair. The telephone manager has asked you to create and update a database that the school can use as a telephone tracking system. The database consists of two tables. The User table contains information on the individuals with telephone accounts. The Department table contains information on the department to which the individual is assigned.

Instructions: Perform the following tasks:

1. Create a new database in which to store all the objects related to the telephone system data. Call the database College Telephone System.
2. Create the User table using the structure shown in Figure 1-96. Use the name User for the table.
3. Add the data shown in Figure 1-96 to the User table.

In the Lab

Structure of User Table

FIELD NAME	DATA TYPE	FIELD SIZE	PRIMARY KEY?	DESCRIPTION
User Id	Text	5	Yes	User Id Number (Primary Key)
Last Name	Text	14		Last Name of User
First Name	Text	10		First Name of User
Phone Ext	Text	4		Telephone Extension (9999 Version)
Office	Text	6		Office Location (Room Number and Building Code)
Basic Charge	Currency			Basic Service Charge (per Month)
Extra Charges	Currency			Extra Charges for Special Services and Long Distance Calls (per Month)
Dept Code	Text	3		Code of User's Department

Data for User Table

USER ID	LAST NAME	FIRST NAME	PHONE EXT	OFFICE	BASIC CHARGE	EXTRA CHARGES	DEPT CODE
T1290	Chou	Tanya	2383	112ABH	$15.00	$27.00	ACC
T2389	Cookson	Christin	2495	120EMH	$18.00	$34.95	BIO
T3487	Hoveman	Benjamin	3267	223SHH	$15.00	$12.75	ENG
T4521	Janson	Catherine	2156	244ABH	$22.00	$57.85	MTH
T5364	Keatty	Richard	2578	116ABH	$18.00	$23.75	ACC
T6457	Medlar	Michelle	3445	212SHH	$26.00	$7.75	ENG
T7579	Nadzia	Rodean	2068	268SHH	$15.00	$18.55	HIS
T7890	Richardson	Maria	2418	122EMH	$22.00	$78.95	BIO
T8521	Sanchez	Javier	2134	248ABH	$16.00	$11.25	MTH
T8883	TenHoopen	Adrian	2414	134EMH	$15.00	$42.45	BIO

FIGURE 1-96

4. Print the User table.
5. Create the Department table using the structure shown in Figure 1-97. Use the name Department for the table.
6. Add the data shown in Figure 1-97 on the next page to the Department table.

(continued)

In the Lab

Creating the College Telephone System Database *(continued)*

Structure of Department Table

FIELD NAME	DATA TYPE	FIELD SIZE	PRIMARY KEY?	DESCRIPTION
Dept Code	Text	3	Yes	Department Code (Primary Key)
Name	Text	14		Name of Department
Location	Text	6		Location of Departmental Office (Room Number and Building Code)
First Name	Text	8		First Name of Department Chair
Last Name	Text	12		Last Name of Department Chair

Data for Department Table

DEPT CODE	NAME	LOCATION	FIRST NAME	LAST NAME
ACC	Accounting	100ABH	Leslie	Anderson
BIO	Biology	110EMH	Donald	Kleinfelter
ENG	English	200SHH	Louisa	Fernandez
HIS	History	260SHH	Peter	Chou
MTH	Mathematics	210ABH	Phyllis	Patterson

FIGURE 1-97

7. Print the Department table.
8. Create a form for the User table. Use the name User for the form.
9. Use the form you created to add the following two new faculty members to the User table.

T6503	Myrich	Bruce	2038	132ABH	$15.00	$0.00	ACC
T7654	Rabon	Claudia	2239	268ABH	$18.00	$0.00	MTH

10. Create the report shown in Figure 1-98 for the User table. When the Report Wizard asks What Sort Order do you want for your records, click the Last Name field.

In the Lab

Telephone List

Last Name	*First Name*	*Phone Ext*	*Office*	*Dept Code*
Chou	Tanya	2383	112ABH	ACC
Cookson	Christin	2495	120EM	BIO
Hoveman	Benjamin	3267	223SHH	ENG
Janson	Catherine	2156	244ABH	MTH
Keatty	Richard	2578	116ABH	ACC
Medlar	Michelle	3445	212SHH	ENG
Myrich	Bruce	2038	132ABH	ACC
Nadzia	Rodean	2068	268SHH	HIS
Rabon	Claudia	[illegible]	268ABH	MTH
Richardson	Maria	2418	122EM	BIO
Sanchez	Javier	2134	248ABH	MTH
TenHoopen	Adrian	2414	134EM	BIO

FIGURE 1-98

3 Creating the WWWW Radio Station Database

Problem: The WWWW Radio Station relies on advertising to help finance its operations. Local firms buy advertising from account representatives that work for the radio station. Account representatives are paid a base salary and receive a commission based on the advertising revenues that they generate. The manager of the radio station has asked you to create and update a database that will keep track of the advertising accounts and account representatives. The database consists of two tables. The Accounts table contains information on the organizations that advertise on the radio station. The Account Reps table contains information on the representative assigned to the account.

Instructions: Perform the following tasks:

1. Create a new database in which to store all the objects related to the advertising data. Call the database WWWW Radio Station.
2. Create the Accounts table using the structure shown in Figure 1-99. Use the name Accounts for the table.
3. Add the data shown in Figure 1-99 on the next page to the Accounts table.

(continued)

In the Lab

Creating the WWWW Radio Station Database *(continued)*

Structure of Accounts Table

FIELD NAME	DATA TYPE	FIELD SIZE	PRIMARY KEY?	DESCRIPTION
Account Number	Text	4	Yes	Account Number (Primary Key)
Name	Text	20		Name of Account
Address	Text	15		Street Address
City	Text	15		City
State	Text	2		State (Two-Character Abbreviation)
Zip Code	Text	5		Zip Code (Five-Character Version)
Balance	Currency			Amount Currently Owed
Amount Paid	Currency			Amount Paid Year-to-Date
Acc Rep Number	Text	2		Number of Account Representative

Data for Accounts Table

ACCOUNT NUMBER	NAME	ADDRESS	CITY	STATE	ZIP CODE	BALANCE	AMOUNT PAID	ACC REP NUMBER
A125	Allen Cleaners	24 Ryan	Kensington	PA	19117	$50.00	$525.00	15
B099	Bea's Bakery	234 Tyson	Mayfair	PA	19111	$0.00	$785.00	18
B133	Bob the Barber	12 Adams	Lawndale	NJ	18923	$145.00	$335.00	18
C046	Carter Shoes	65 Reisling	Mayfair	PA	19111	$90.00	$1,025.00	21
D205	Dennis & Son	457 Oakley	Roxborough	NJ	18919	$250.00	$475.00	15
F304	Fred's Pet Shop	34 Passmore	Kensington	PA	19117	$0.00	$1,275.00	18
G075	Geo's Tires	569 Brea	Kensington	PA	19117	$175.00	$950.00	18
H001	Howard Toys	78 Leland	Roxborough	NJ	18919	$25.00	$650.00	15
M012	Mary's Marina	97 Ada	Lawndale	NJ	18923	$425.00	$1,100.00	21
R111	Ruth's Diner	102 Main	Mayfair	PA	19111	$75.00	$575.00	15

FIGURE 1-99

4. Print the Accounts table.
5. Create the Account Reps table using the structure shown in Figure 1-100. Use the name Account Reps for the table. Be sure to change the field size for the Comm Rate field to Double.
6. Add the data shown in Figure 1-100 to the Account Reps table.

In the Lab

Structure of Account Reps Table

FIELD NAME	DATA TYPE	FIELD SIZE	PRIMARY KEY?	DESCRIPTION
Acc Rep Number	Text	2	Yes	Account Rep Number (Primary Key)
Last Name	Text	10		Last Name of Account Representative
First Name	Text	8		First Name of Account Representative
Address	Text	15		Street Address
City	Text	15		City
State	Text	2		State (Two-Character Abbreviation)
Zip Code	Text	5		Zip Code (Five-Character Version)
Salary	Currency			Base Salary
Comm Rate	Number	Double		Commission Rate on Advertising Sales

Data for Account Reps Table

ACC REP NUMBER	LAST NAME	FIRST NAME	ADDRESS	CITY	STATE	ZIP CODE	SALARY	COMM RATE
15	Glynn	Nancy	26 Barton	Mayfair	PA	19111	$12,000.00	0.08
18	Helko	Brian	12 Shaw	Lawndale	NJ	18923	$11,500.00	0.07
21	Rogers	Helen	34 Manly	Kensington	PA	19117	$13,000.00	0.08

FIGURE 1-100

7. Print the Account Reps table.
8. Create a form for the Accounts table. Use the name Accounts for the form.
9. Open the form you created and change the address for Account Number G075 to 569 Breame.
10. Change to Datasheet view and delete the record for Account Number F304.
11. Print the Accounts table.
12. Create the report shown in Figure 1-101 on the next page for the Accounts table.

(continued)

Creating the WWWW Radio Station Database *(continued)*

Status Report

Account Number	Name	Balance	Amount Paid
A125	Allen Cleaners	$50.00	$525.00
B099	Bea's Bakery	$0.00	$785.00
B133	Bob the Barber	$145.00	$335.00
C046	Carter Shoes	$90.00	$1,025.00
D205	Dennis & Son	$250.00	$475.00
G075	Geo's Tires	$175.00	$950.00
H001	Howard Toys	$25.00	$650.00
M012	Mary's Marina	$425.00	$1,100.00
R111	Ruth's Diner	$75.00	$575.00

Friday, December 19, 1997 Pa

FIGURE 1-101

Cases and Places

The difficulty of these case studies varies:

◗ Case studies preceded by a single half moon are the least difficult. You are asked to create the required database based on information that has already been placed in an organized form.
◗◗ Case studies preceded by two half moons are more difficult. You must organize the information presented before using it to create the desired database.
◗◗◗ Case studies preceded by three half moons are the most difficult. You must choose a specific topic, and then obtain and organize the necessary information before using it to create the required database.

1 ◗ You often consult the telephone directory for the numbers of local restaurants to make reservations and to order food for carry out and delivery. You have decided to create a database to store these numbers, along with other pertinent data about the establishment such as address, hours of operation, type of food, and days when specials are offered. You gather the information shown in Figure 1-102.

Create a database to store the file related to the restaurants. Then create a table, enter the data from Figure 1-102, and print the table.

NAME	PHONE	ADDRESS	OPEN	CLOSE	FOOD TYPE	SPECIALS	CARRYOUT	DELIVERY
Pablo's Tacos	(714) 555-2339	223 N. Jackson	11:00 a.m.	11:00 p.m.	Mexican	Wednesday	Yes	No
Italian Villages	(714) 555-5444	3294 E. Devon	4:00 p.m.	10:00 p.m.	Italian	Monday	Yes	Yes
Madras Ovens	(714) 555-8001	1632 W. Clark	3:00 p.m.	1:00 a.m.	Indian	Friday	No	No
Parthenon	(714) 555-2470	3140 W. Halsted	11:00 a.m.	4:00 a.m.	Greek	Thursday	Yes	No
New Orient	(714) 555-9337	1805 W. Broadway	3:30 p.m.	10:00 p.m.	Chinese	Monday	Yes	No
Pizza Mia	(714) 555-1673	2200 E. Lawrence	4:30 p.m.	1:00 a.m.	Italian	Thursday	Yes	Yes
Hat Dancers	(714) 555-8632	13 N. Devon	11:30 a.m.	2:00 a.m.	Mexican	Wednesday	Yes	No
Bukhara Bar	(714) 555-3377	1027 E. Wells	5:00 p.m.	2:00 a.m.	Indian	Thursday	Yes	No
Taranio's	(714) 555-6168	787 N. Monroe	10:30 a.m.	3:00 a.m.	Italian	Tuesday	Yes	Yes
Mr. Ming's	(714) 555-7373	1939 W. Michigan	11:00 a.m.	11:00 p.m.	Chinese	Wednesday	Yes	No

FIGURE 1-102

Cases and Places

2 ◗ Book prices increase every semester, so you want to devise a system to curb these expenses. You organize a system whereby students can locate other students who have used a particular book in a previous semester and want to sell it to another student. You advertise your plan in the campus newspaper and receive the responses shown in Figure 1-103

Create a database to store the file related to the textbooks. Then create a table, enter the data from Figure 1-103, and print the table.

BOOK TITLE	AUTHOR	COURSE USED	PRICE	SELLER'S NAME	SELLER'S PHONE NUMBER	CONDITION (E=Excellent, G=Good, P=Poor)
Psychology Today	Murrow	Psy 101	$15	Joe Tran	555-7632	G
Rhetoric for Writers	Swan & Stuart	Eng 101	$19	Mary Nord	555-9421	E
Reach for the Stars	Alvarez	Ast 210	$24	John Mote	555-9981	E
Rhetoric for Writers	Swan & Stuart	Eng 101	$16	Peter Rodgers	555-9156	E
History for Today's Society	Garrison & Pierce	Hst 310	$20	Sandi Radleman	555-7636	P
Psychology Today	Murrow	Psy 101	$18	Daniel Lewis	555-0873	E
Understanding Sociology	Navarre	Soc 101	$23	Karen Sim	555-9802	P
Electronic Circuitry	Carlson	Egr 255	$37	Karen Sim	555-9802	G
Nutrition for Our Souls	Francis	Nrs 320	$18	Dave Corsi	555-2384	E
Pediatric Nursing	Dyer	Nrs 253	$36	Margaret Healy	555-9932	E

FIGURE 1-103

3 ◗◗ Heart disease is one of the leading killers of adults in this country. With this knowledge the meat industry has aggressively tried to deliver products that are low in fat and yet high in nutrients. The American Heart Association states that lean meat can be part of a healthy diet, as long as the meat is served in moderation. Three cooked ounces of lean cuts of beef have various nutritional contents. Eye of round has 140 calories, top round steak has 150 calories, tip round roast has 160 calories, sirloin steak has 170 calories, and top loin and tenderloin steaks both have 180 calories. Regarding fat content, eye of round and top round steak have four fat grams in three ounces, tip round roast and sirloin both have six grams, top loin steak has eight grams, and tenderloin steak has the most with nine grams. Cholesterol also varies, with eye of round the lowest at 60 milligrams in three ounces, top loin with 65 mg, top round, tip round, and tenderloin with 70 mg, and sirloin the highest with 75 mg. Create a database to store the file related to the nutritional content of meat. Then create a table, enter the data, and print the table.

Cases and Places

4 ▶▶ You have a variety of classic movies on videocassette, and you want to make an inventory of your favorite films in the collection. One rainy afternoon you sort through your boxes and list each movie's name, leading actors, year produced, original running time, and your rating system of one to four stars. You create the following list: *The Little Princess*, starring Shirley Temple and Richard Greene, 1939, 94 minutes, three stars; *North by Northwest*, Cary Grant and Eva Marie Saint, 1959, 136 minutes, four stars; *Of Mice and Men*, Burgess Meredith and Lon Chaney Jr., 1939, 107 minutes, four stars; *The Quiet Man*, John Wayne and Maureen O'Hara, 1952, 129 minutes, four stars; *On the Waterfront*, Marlon Brando and Eva Marie Saint, 1954, 108 minutes, four stars; *Pardon My Sarong*, Bud Abbott and Lou Costello, 1942, 84 minutes, three stars; *Ride 'em Cowboy*, Bud Abbott and Lou Costello, 1942, 82 minutes, two stars; *You Can't Take It With You*, Jean Arthur and Lionel Barrymore, 1938, 127 minutes, three stars; *The Undefeated*, John Wayne and Rock Hudson, 1969, 119 minutes, two stars; and *Operation Pacific*, John Wayne and Patricia Neal, 1951, 109 minutes, three stars. Using this information, create a database to store the file related to these movies. Then create a table, enter the data, and print the table.

5 ▶▶▶ You do not participate in a retirement plan at work, so your tax preparer advises you to open an Individual Retirement Account (IRA). You analyze your financial situation and estimate you could afford to invest $1,000 now to open the account. Visit or call a total of five local banks, credit unions, or savings and loan associations. Make a list of the current interest rates for an IRA opened with $1,000, minimum investment amount, total amount earned by the time you turn age 65, annual fees, and amount you would be penalized if you withdrew the money in two years. Using this information, create a database and enter the data showing the types of financial institutions (bank, savings and loan, or credit union), names of the financial institutions, their addresses and telephone numbers, interest rates, annual fees, total values of the IRAs by age 65, amount of interest earned in this time, and amount you would be penalized if you withdrew the money in two years. Print this table, and then create and print a bar graph indicating the amount of interest you would earn and the total value of your IRA at age 65 for each financial institution.

6 ▶▶▶ You often have difficulty finding your campus directory to get the telephone numbers of campus personnel and offices. When you do locate the book, usually you cannot find the information you need. Consequently, you have decided to create your own database containing this pertinent information. Obtain important names, phone numbers, and office room numbers of campus offices that you frequent. Start by organizing the data in the categories of faculty, administration, and services. In the faculty category, list your adviser and your instructors from this semester. In the administration category, list the registrar, the dean of your area, and the financial aid director. In the services category, list the bookstore, campus police station, baby-sitting services, and library reference desk. Add other pertinent data to any of the categories. Then create a table, enter the data you obtained, and print the table.

Cases and Places

7 ▶▶▶ Food and drug store prices can vary dramatically from one store to another. Make a list of five specific items you purchase frequently from area stores in the four categories of dairy (for example, milk, yogurt, butter, sour cream, cottage cheese), snacks (for example, pretzels, soda, granola bars, raisins, rice cakes), cosmetics/toiletries (for example, deodorant, bath soap, toothpaste, shampoo, contact lens solution), and kitchen supplies (for example, paper towels, dish washing detergent, scouring pads, trash bags, sandwich bags). List the size or weight of each item. Then, visit a local convenience store, grocery store, and discount store to compare prices. Be certain you obtain prices on identical products. Then create a table, enter the data you obtained in each category, and print the table.

Microsoft Access 7

Windows 95

Querying a Database Using the Select Query Window

Objectives:

You will have mastered the material in this project when you can:

- State the purpose of queries
- Create a new query
- Use a query to display all records and all fields
- Run a query
- Print the answer to a query
- Close a query
- Clear a query
- Use a query to display selected fields
- Use character data in criteria in a query
- Use wildcards in criteria
- Use numeric data in criteria
- Use comparison operators
- Use compound criteria involving AND
- Use compound criteria involving OR
- Sort the answer to a query
- Join tables in a query
- Restrict the records in a join
- Use computed fields in a query
- Calculate statistics in a query
- Use grouping with statistics
- Save a query
- Use a saved query

Kick Up Your Feet and Go Grocery Shopping

Grocery shopping is a chore 60 percent of us dislike. From hunting for a parking space to waiting in long checkout lines, the entire experience, which on average requires 66 minutes, often is tiring and frustrating.

But this task does not have to be so taxing. In fact, it can be quick and efficient by using a computer. Microsoft Chairman Bill Gates predicts one-third of all grocery shopping will be done with interactive devices such as computers and televisions by the year 2005. Consumers in Chicago and San Francisco already are shopping online with a service called Peapod.

Here's how Peapod works. A shopper uses custom software to select from more than 25,000 items, ranging from apples to zinnias, available in a local grocery or drug store. The customer can shop by product category (e.g., produce, deli, meat/poultry), aisle (e.g., cereal and breakfast, ethnic foods), or specific item (e.g, reduced fat chocolate chip cookies).

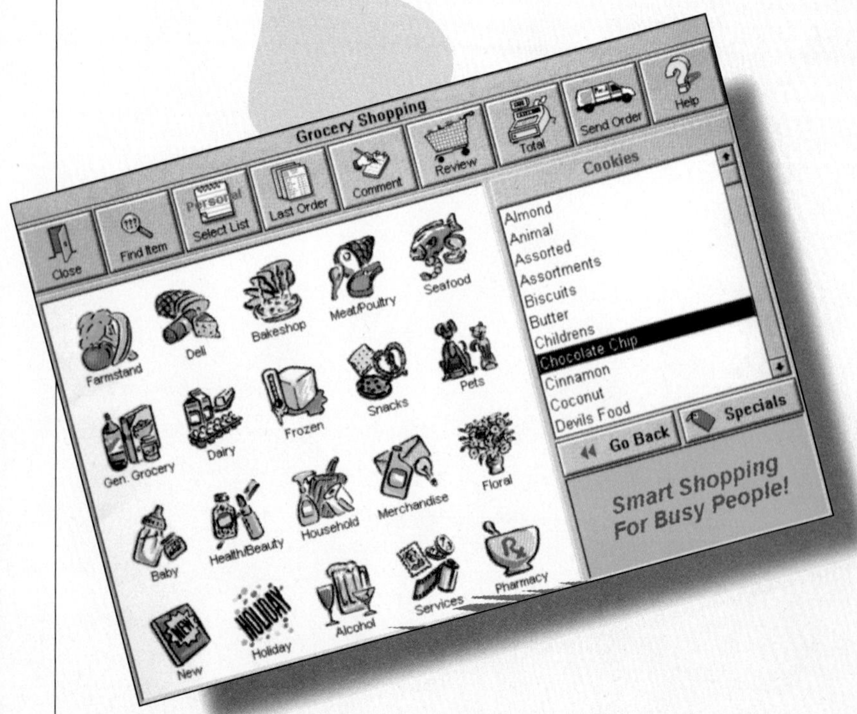

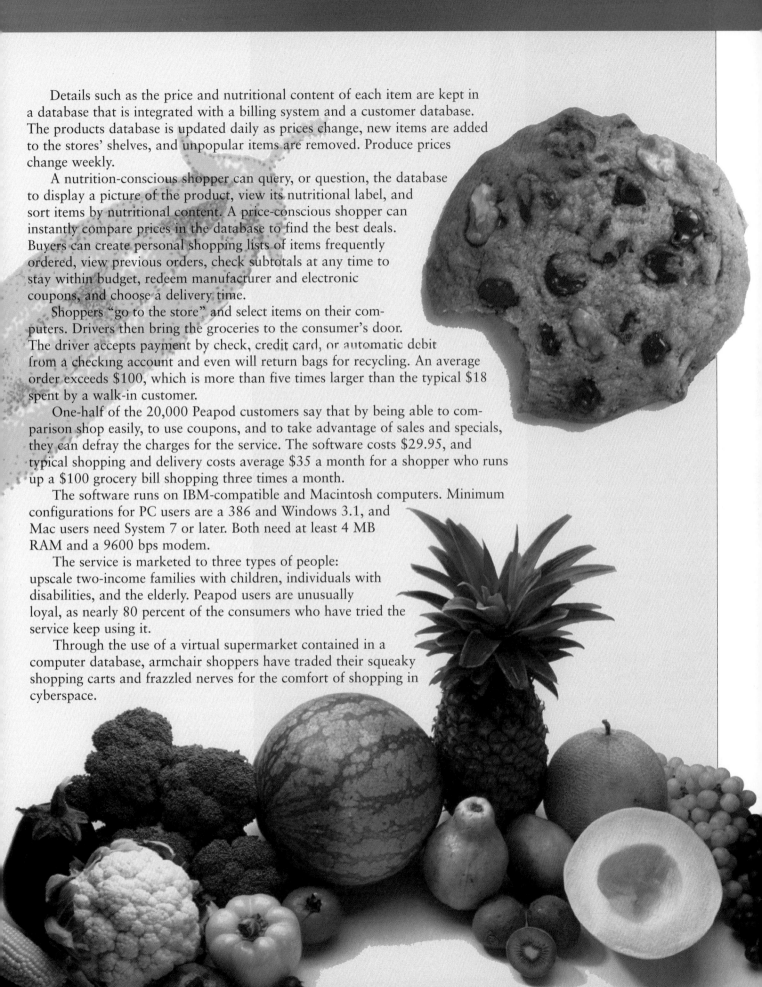

Details such as the price and nutritional content of each item are kept in a database that is integrated with a billing system and a customer database. The products database is updated daily as prices change, new items are added to the stores' shelves, and unpopular items are removed. Produce prices change weekly.

A nutrition-conscious shopper can query, or question, the database to display a picture of the product, view its nutritional label, and sort items by nutritional content. A price-conscious shopper can instantly compare prices in the database to find the best deals. Buyers can create personal shopping lists of items frequently ordered, view previous orders, check subtotals at any time to stay within budget, redeem manufacturer and electronic coupons, and choose a delivery time.

Shoppers "go to the store" and select items on their computers. Drivers then bring the groceries to the consumer's door. The driver accepts payment by check, credit card, or automatic debit from a checking account and even will return bags for recycling. An average order exceeds $100, which is more than five times larger than the typical $18 spent by a walk-in customer.

One-half of the 20,000 Peapod customers say that by being able to comparison shop easily, to use coupons, and to take advantage of sales and specials, they can defray the charges for the service. The software costs $29.95, and typical shopping and delivery costs average $35 a month for a shopper who runs up a $100 grocery bill shopping three times a month.

The software runs on IBM-compatible and Macintosh computers. Minimum configurations for PC users are a 386 and Windows 3.1, and Mac users need System 7 or later. Both need at least 4 MB RAM and a 9600 bps modem.

The service is marketed to three types of people: upscale two-income families with children, individuals with disabilities, and the elderly. Peapod users are unusually loyal, as nearly 80 percent of the consumers who have tried the service keep using it.

Through the use of a virtual supermarket contained in a computer database, armchair shoppers have traded their squeaky shopping carts and frazzled nerves for the comfort of shopping in cyberspace.

Microsoft
Access 7
Windows 95

Querying a Database Using the Select Query Window

Case Perspective

Now that Mason Clinic has created a database with patient and therapist data, the management and staff of the clinic hope to gain the benefits they expected when they set up the database. One of the more important benefits is the capability to easily ask questions concerning the data in the database and rapidly obtain the answers. Among the questions they want answered are the following:

1. What is the balance of patient DI32?
2. Which patients' last names begin with the letters, Pe?
3. Which patients are located in Lamont?
4. What is the patient portion of the amount each patient owes (the balance minus the expected insurance payment)?
5. Which patients of therapist 08 currently do not have any money due to be paid by their insurance companies?

Introduction

A database management system like Access offers many useful features, among them the capability to answer questions such as those posed by the management of Mason Clinic (Figure 2-1). The answers to these questions, and many more, are found in the database, and Access can quickly find the answers. When you pose a question to Access, or any other database management system, the question is called a query. A **query** is simply a question represented in a way that Access can understand.

Thus, to find the answer to a question, you first create a corresponding query using the techniques illustrated in this project. Once you have created the query, you instruct Access to **run the query**; that is, to perform the steps necessary to obtain the answer. When finished, Access will display the answer to your question in the format shown at the bottom of Figure 2-1.

Project Two – Mason Clinic

You must obtain answers to the questions posed by the management of Mason Clinic. These include the questions shown in Figure 2-1, as well as any other questions management deems important.

Queries

What is the balance of patient D132?

Which patients' last names begin with letters, Pe?

Which patients live in Lamont?

What is the patient amount (balance - insurance) of each patient?

Which patients of therapist 08 have a $0.00 insurance amount?

Patient Table

PATIENT NUMBER	LAST NAME	FIRST NAME	ADDRESS	CITY	STATE	ZIP CODE	BALANCE	INSURANCE	THER NUMBER
AL26	Alardyce	Lisa	311 Birchwood	Lamont	MI	49160	$196.62	$180.00	05
AT73	Acton	Thomas	312 Newcastle	Homer	MI	49162	$726.42	$550.00	08
BR31	Bryce	Roger	617 College	Lamont	MI	49160	$96.00	$0.00	08
DI32	Dalton	Irene	41 Lafayette	Madison	IN	42909	$875.00	$600.00	14
GC92	Gutierez	Carlos	476 Fulton	Jackson	OH	49401	$273.00	$150.00	05
GT43	Grant	Thomas	247 Fuller	Lamont	MI	49160	$276.00	$0.00	08
JG22	Jenkins	Glen	201 Plymouth	Madison	IN	42909	$0.00	$0.00	08
LI66	Lawrence	Irving	912 Devonshire	Beulah	MI	45621	$346.50	$175.00	05
PE33	Pezato	Eduardo	346 Vernor	Homer	MI	49162	$467.12	$500.00	14
PE76	Perez	Enzo	216 Four Mile	Perry	MI	47211	$216.00	$0.00	08

Results

PATIENT NUMBER	BALANCE
DI32	$875.00

PATIENT NUMBER	LAST NAME
PE33	Pezato
PE76	Perez

PATIENT NUMBER	LAST NAME	FIRST NAME
BR31	Bryce	Roger
GT43	Grant	Thomas
JG22	Jenkins	Glen
PE76	Perez	Enzo

PATIENT NUMBER	LAST NAME	FIRST NAME	ADDRESS
AL26	Alardyce	Lisa	311 Birchwood
BR31	Bryce	Roger	617 College
GT43	Grant	Thomas	247 Fuller

PATIENT NUMBER	LAST NAME	FIRST NAME	PATIENT AMOUNT
AL26	Alardyce	Lisa	$16.62
AT73	Acton	Thomas	$176.42
BR31	Bryce	Roger	$96.00
DI32	Dalton	Irene	$275.00
GC92	Gutierez	Carlos	$123.00
GT43	Grant	Thomas	$276.00
JG22	Jenkins	Glen	$0.00
LI66	Lawrence	Irving	$171.50
PE33	Pezato	Eduardo	($32.88)
PE76	Perez	Enzo	$216.00

FIGURE 2-1

Overview of Project Steps

The project steps give you an overview of how the Mason Clinic database will be queried in this project. The following tasks will be completed in this project.

1. Start Access and open the Mason Clinic database.
2. Create a new query
3. Create and run a query to display all records and all fields.
4. Print the results of a query; that is, print the answer to the question.
5. Create and run a query to display the patient number, last name, first name, and balance of patient DI32.
6. Create and run a query to display only selected fields.
7. Create and run a query to display the number, name, and address of those patients whose names begin with the letters, Pe.
8. Create and run a query to display the number, last name, first name, and address for patients living in Lamont.
9. Create and run a query to display all patients whose insurance amount is $0.00.
10. Create and run a query to display all patients whose balance is more than $500.
11. Create and run a query to display all patients whose insurance amount is $0.00 and whose therapist is therapist 08.
12. Create and run a query to display all patients whose balance is more than $500 or whose therapist is therapist 08.
13. Create and run a query to display the cities in which the patients reside in alphabetical order.
14. Create and run a query to display the number, name, therapist number, and insurance amount for all patients sorted by insurance amount within therapist number.
15. Create and run a query to display the patient number, last name, first name, therapist number, therapist's last name, and therapist's first name for all patients.
16. Create and run a query to display the patient number, last name, first name, therapist number, therapist's last name, and therapist's first name for all patients whose balance is more than $200.
17. Create and run a query to display the number, name, and patient amount (balance minus insurance) for all patients.
18. Create and run a query to calculate the average balance for all patients.
19. Create and run a query to calculate the average balance for patients of therapist 08.
20. Create and run a query to calculate the average balance for patients of each therapist.
21. Create and save a query that will display, for each therapist, the therapist's number and last name as well as the number, last name, and first name of each of the therapist's patients.

The following pages contain a detailed explanation of each of these steps.

Opening the Database

Before creating queries, first you must open the database. Perform the following steps to complete this task.

TO OPEN A DATABASE

Step 1: Click the Start button.
Step 2: Click Open Office Document, and then click 3½ Floppy [A:] in the Look in text box. Make sure the database called Mason Clinic is selected.
Step 3: Click the Open button. If the Tables tab is not already selected, click the Tables tab.

The database is open and the Mason Clinic : Database window displays.

Creating a New Query

You **create a query** by making entries in a special window called a **Select Query window**. Once the database is open, the first step in creating a query is to select the table for which you are creating a query in the Database window. Next, click the New Object button down arrow, click New Query, and select Design View. The Select Query window will then display. It is typically easier to work with the Select Query window if it is maximized. Thus, as a standard practice, maximize the Select Query window as soon as you have created it.

Perform the following steps to begin the creation of a query.

More About Queries: Query Languages

Query languages, which are languages that made it easy to obtain answers to questions concerning data in a database, first appeared in the early 1970s. Prior to that time, obtaining such answers required having someone write lengthy (several hundred line) programs in languages such as COBOL.

To Create a Query

1 **With the Mason Clinic database open, the Tables tab selected, and the Patient table selected, click the New Object button down arrow on the toolbar.**

The list of available objects displays (Figure 2-2).

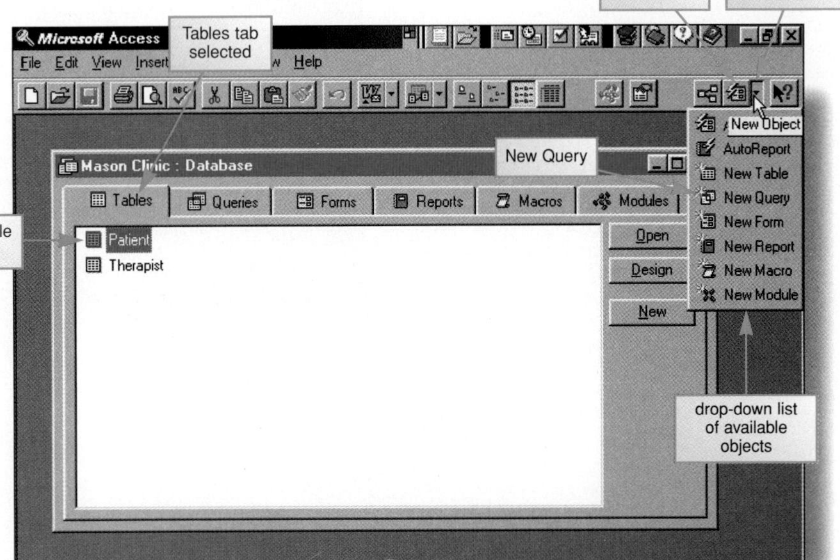

FIGURE 2-2

2 **Click New Query.**

The New Query dialog box displays (Figure 2-3).

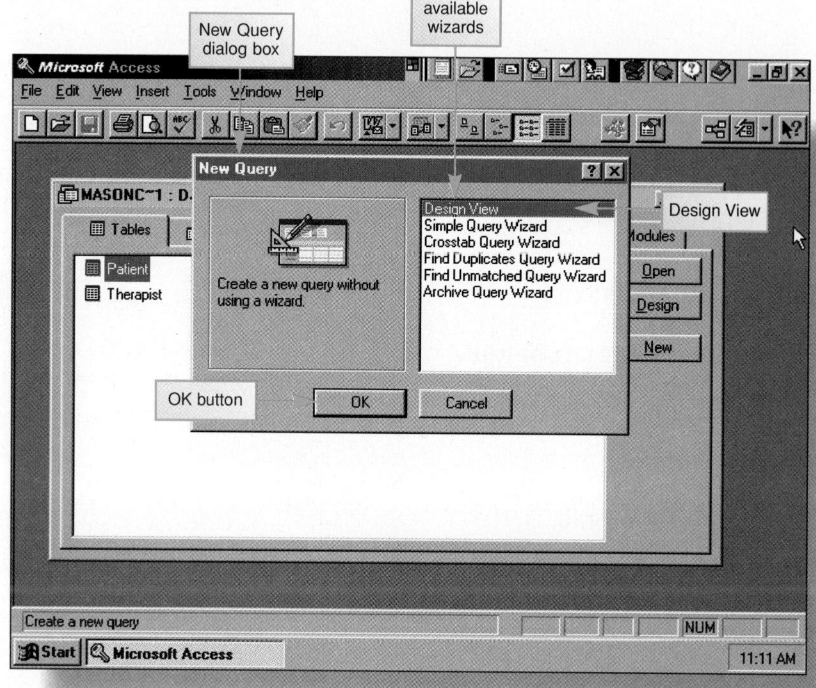

FIGURE 2-3

3 **With Design View highlighted, click the OK button.**

The Query1 : Select Query window displays (Figure 2-4).

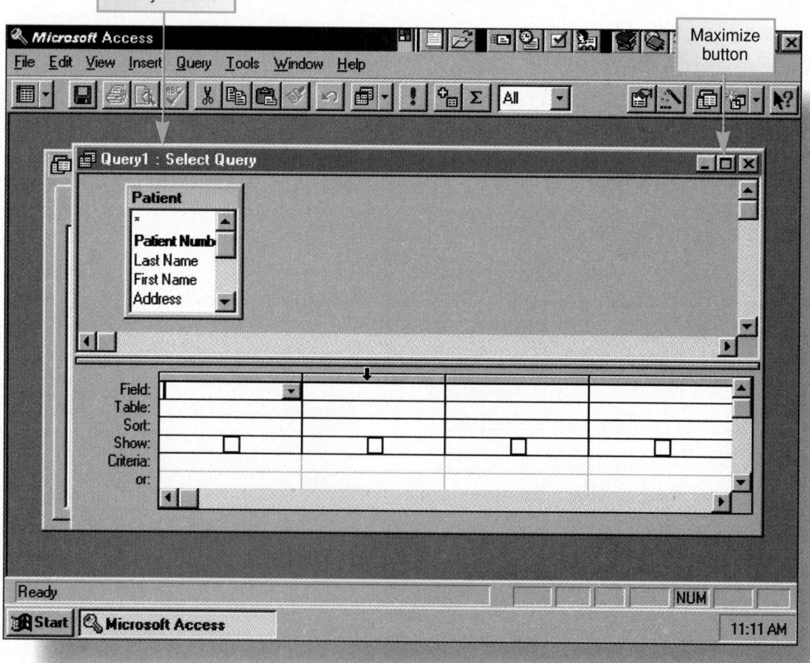

FIGURE 2-4

4 **Maximize the Query1 : Select Query window by clicking its Maximize button, and then point to the line that separates the upper and lower panes of the window. The mouse pointer will change shape to a double-headed arrow with a horizontal bar.**

The Select Query window is maximized (Figure 2-5). The upper pane of the window contains a field list for the Patient table. The lower pane contains the ***design grid****, the area where you specify fields to be included, sort order, and the criteria the records you are looking for must satisfy.*

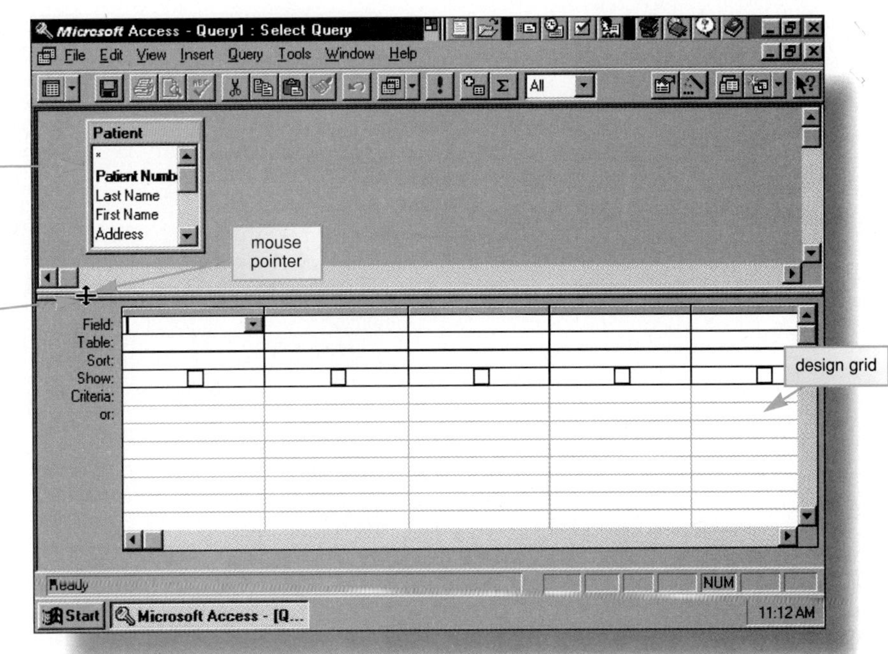

FIGURE 2-5

5 **Drag the line down to the approximate position shown in Figure 2-6 and then move the mouse pointer to the lower edge of the field list box so it changes shape to a double-headed arrow as shown in the figure.**

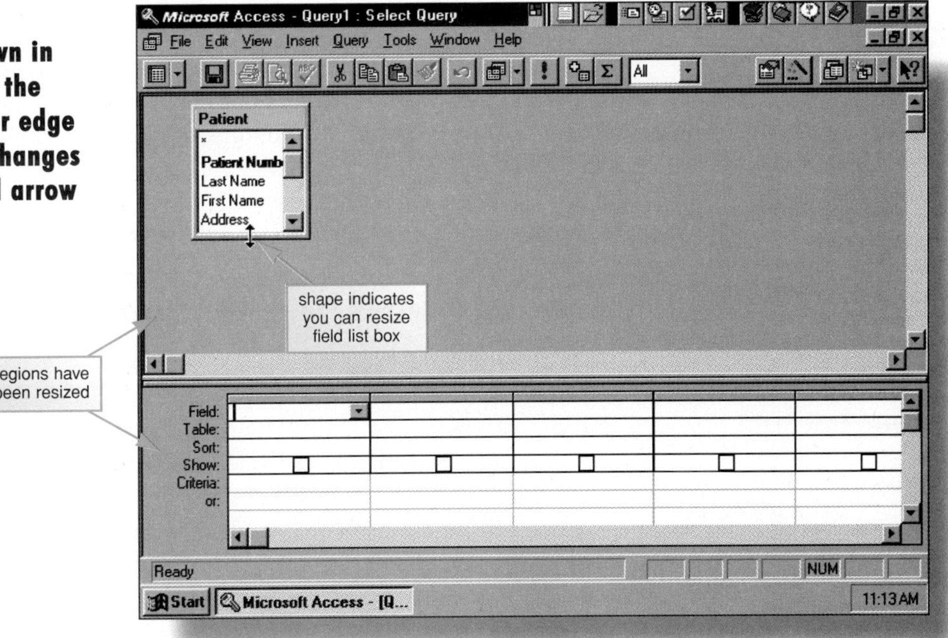

FIGURE 2-6

6 Drag the lower edge of the box down far enough so that all fields in the Patient table are visible.

All fields in the Patient table display (Figure 2-7).

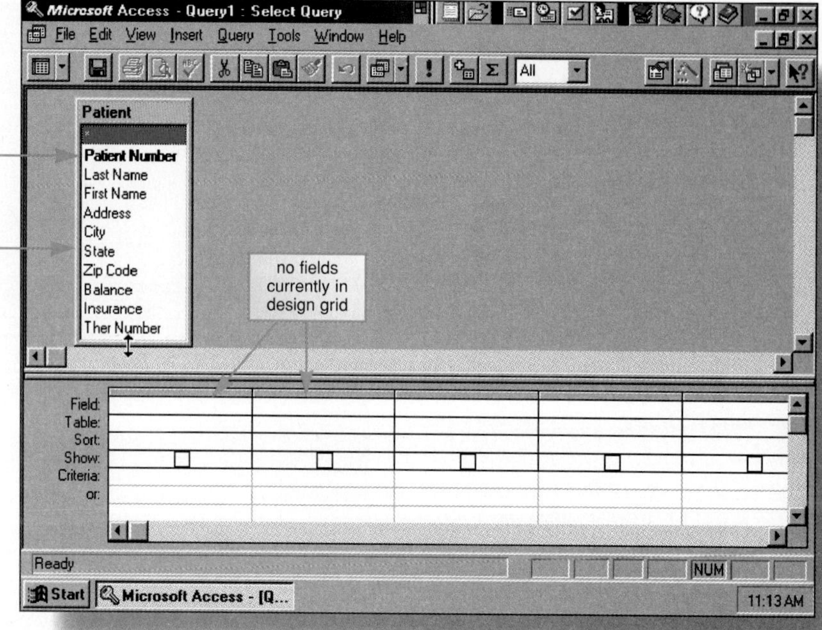

FIGURE 2-7

Other Ways

1. Click Queries tab, click New
2. On Insert menu click Query

Using the Select Query Window

Once you have created a new Select Query window, you are ready to create the actual query by making entries in the design grid that appears in the lower portion of the window. You enter the names of the fields you want included in the Field row in the grid. You also can enter criteria, such as the patient number must be DI32, in the Criteria row of the grid. When you do so, only the record or records that match the criterion will be included in the answer.

More About Queries: Query-by-Example

One of the early approaches to querying a database was called Query-by-Example, often referred to as QBE. In this approach, users asked questions by filling in a table on the screen. The approach taken in Access, as well as several other database management systems, is based on Query-by-Example.

Displaying Selected Fields in a Query

Only the fields that appear in the design grid will be included in the results of the query. Thus, to display only certain fields, place only these fields in the grid, and no others. If you inadvertently place the wrong field in the grid, click Edit on the menu bar and then click Delete to remove it. Alternatively, you could click Clear Grid to clear the entire design grid and then start over.

The following steps create a query to show the patient number, last name, first name, and therapist number for all patients by including only those fields in the design grid.

Steps To Include Fields in the Design Grid

1. **Make sure you have a maximized Select Query window containing a field list for the Patient table in the upper pane of the window and an empty design grid in the lower pane (see Figure 2-7).**

2. **Double-click the Patient Number field to include the Patient Number field in the query.**

   The Patient Number is included as the first field in the design grid (Figure 2-8).

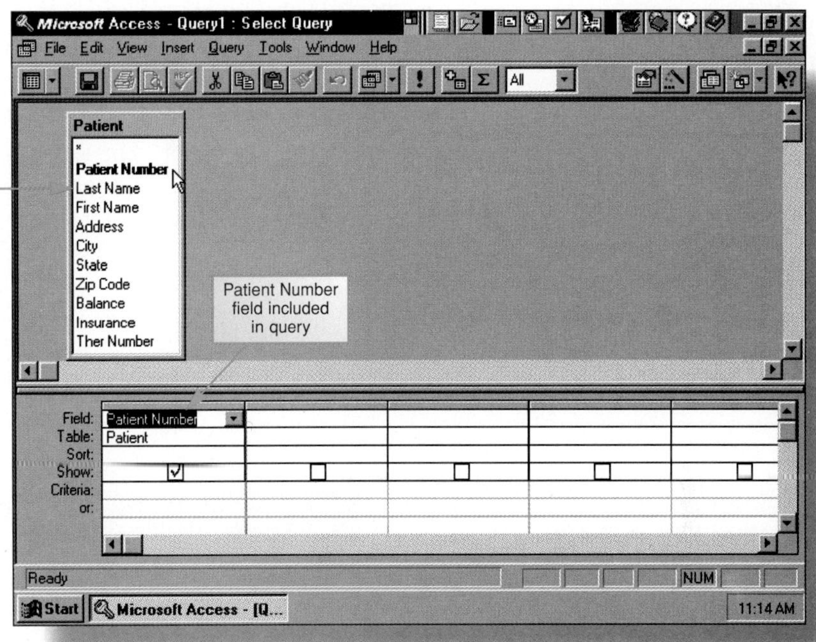

FIGURE 2-8

3. **Double-click the Last Name field to include it in the query. Include both the First Name and Ther Number fields using the same technique.**

   The Patient Number, Last Name, First Name, and Ther Number fields are included in the query (Figure 2-9).

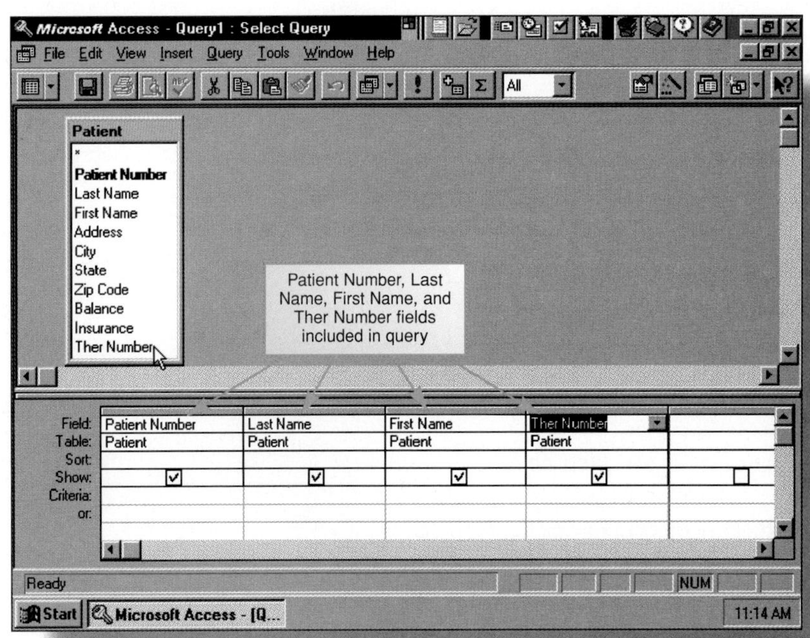

FIGURE 2-9

More About Queries: SQL

Another major approach to querying a database is a language called SQL. In SQL, users type commands such as SELECT BALANCE FROM PATIENT WHERE CITY = "LAMONT" to find the balances of all patients who live in Lamont. Many database management systems, including Access, offer SQL as one option for querying databases.

Running a Query

Once you have created the query, you need to **run the query** to produce the results. To do so, click the Run button. Access will then perform the steps necessary to obtain and display the answer. The set of records that make up the answer will be displayed in Datasheet view. Although it looks like a table that is stored on your disk, it really is not. The records are constructed from data in the existing Patient table. If you were to change the data in the Patient table and then rerun this same query, the results would reflect the changes.

Steps To Run the Query

1. **Point to the Run button on the toolbar (Figure 2-10).**

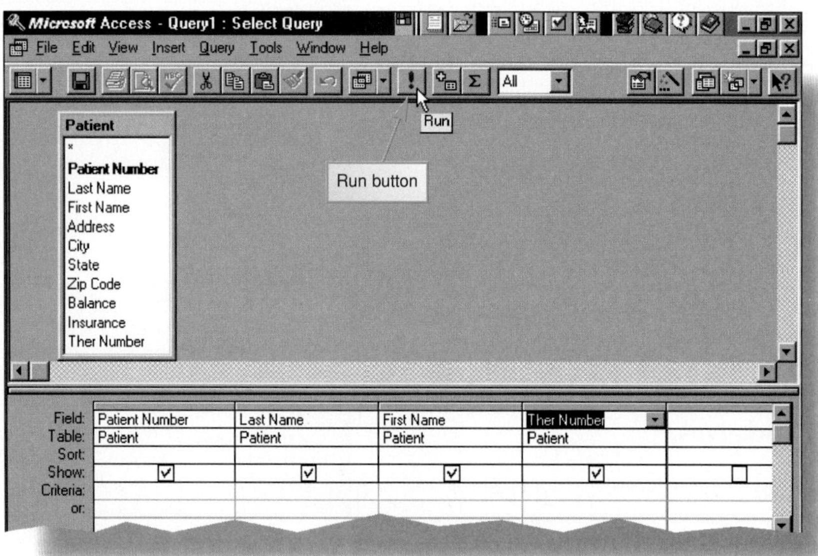

FIGURE 2-10

2. **Click the Run button.**

The query is executed and the results display (Figure 2-11). If the mouse pointer points to the Filter by Selection button, the description of the button may obscure a portion of the first record.

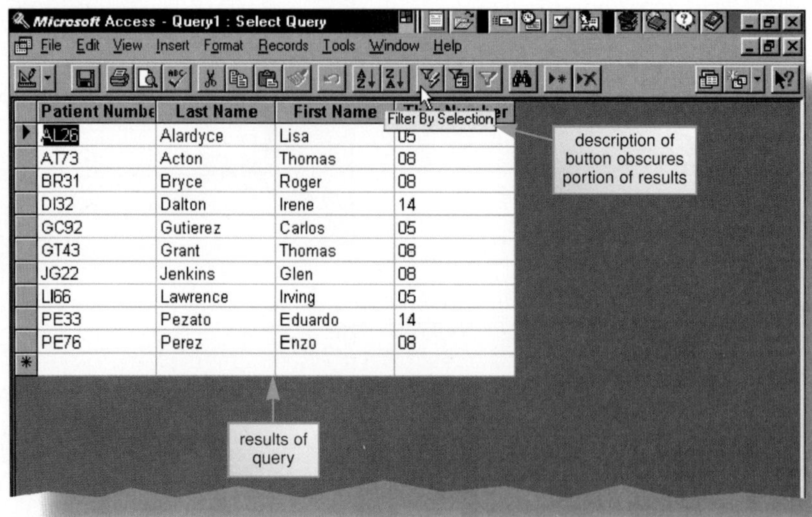

FIGURE 2-11

3 Move the mouse pointer to a position that is outside of the data and is not on the toolbar.

The data displays without obstruction (Figure 2-12). Notice that an extra blank row, marking the end of the table, displays at the end of the results. This will always be the case.

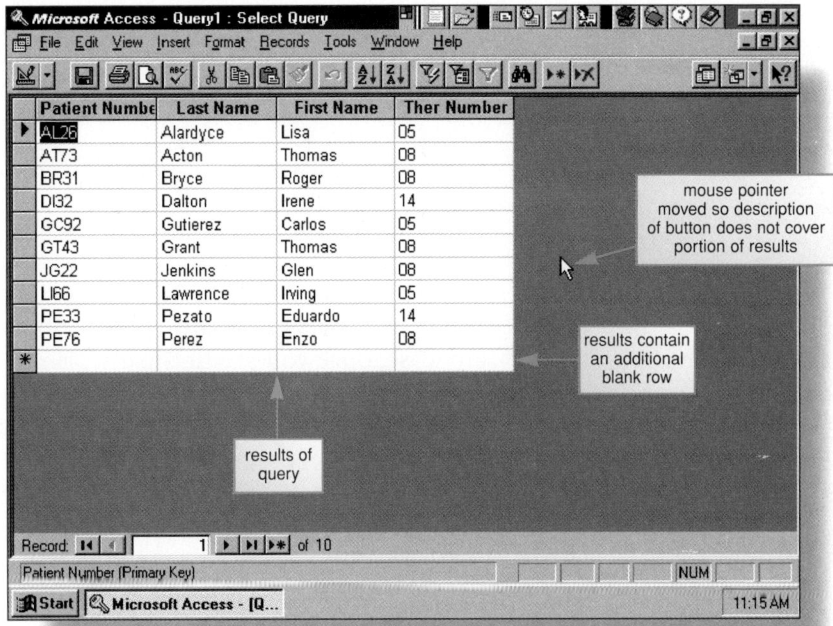

FIGURE 2-12

1. On Query menu click Run

In all future examples, after running a query, move the mouse pointer so the table displays without obstruction.

Printing the Results of a Query

To print the results of a query, use the same techniques you learned in Project 1 to print the data in the table. Complete the following step to print the query results that currently display on the screen.

To Print the Results of a Query

1 Click the Print button on the toolbar (Figure 2-13).

The results print.

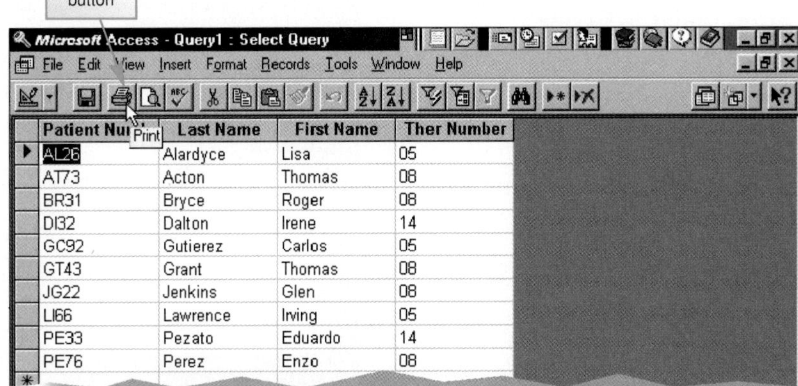

FIGURE 2-13

If the results of a query require landscape orientation, switch to landscape orientation before you click the Print button as indicated in Project 1 on page A1.31.

Returning to the Select Query Window

You can examine the results of a query on your screen to see the answer to your question. You can scroll through the records, if necessary, just as you scroll through the records of any other table. You also can print a copy of the table. In any case, once you are finished working with the results, you can return to the Select Query window to ask another question. To do so, click the Query View button down arrow as shown in the following steps.

To Return to the Select Query Window

1 Point to the Query View button down arrow on the toolbar (Figure 2-14).

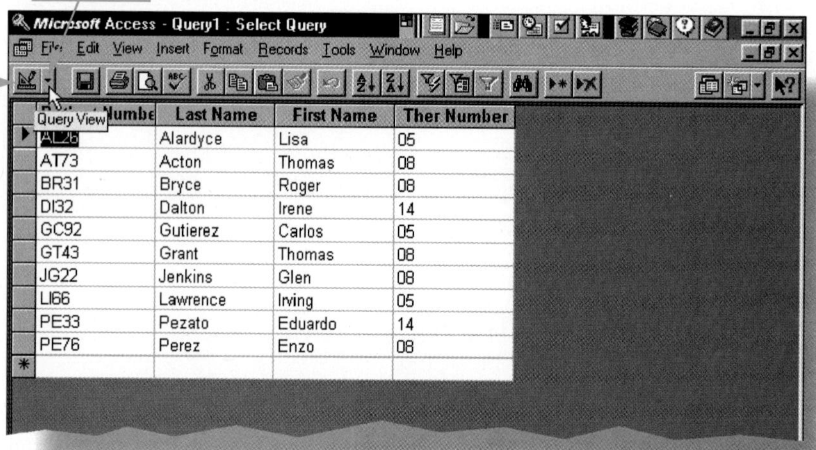

FIGURE 2-14

2 Click the Query View button down arrow. Point to Design View.

The Query View drop-down list displays (Figure 2-15).

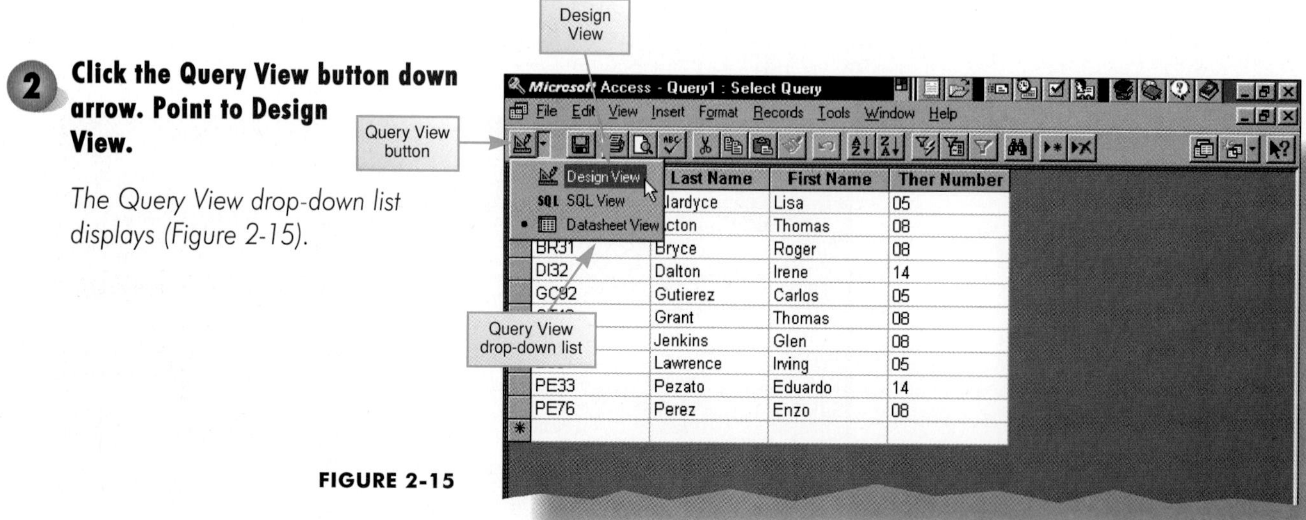

FIGURE 2-15

3 **Click Design View.**

The Select Query window displays once again (Figure 2-16).

FIGURE 2-16

OtherWays

1. On View menu click Query Design

Closing a Query

To **close a query**, close the Select Query window. When you do so, Access asks if you want to save your query for future use. If you expect you will need to create the same exact query often, you should save the query. For now, you will not save any queries. You will see how to save them later in the project. The following steps close a query without saving it.

Steps To Close the Query

1 **Click the Close button for the Select Query window (see Figure 2-16).**

The Microsoft Access dialog box displays (Figure 2-17). Click the Yes button to save the query or click the No button to close the query without saving.

2 **Click the No button in the Microsoft Access dialog box.**

The Select Query window is removed from the desktop.

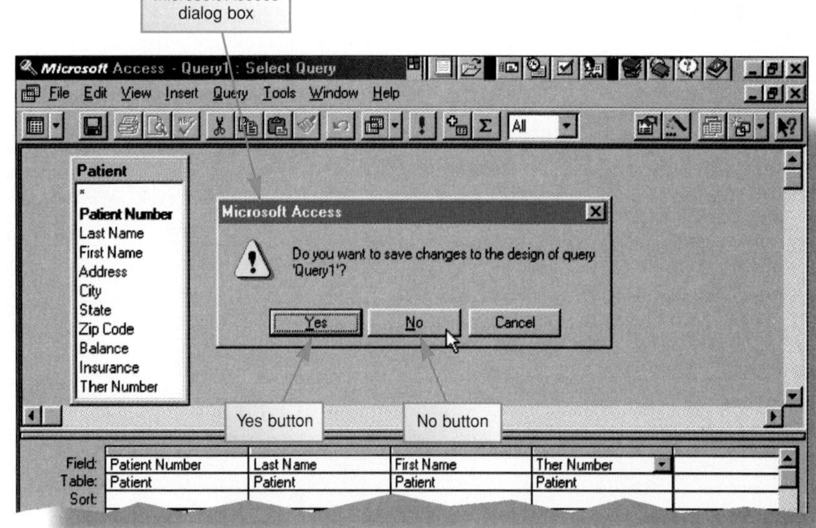

FIGURE 2-17

OtherWays

1. Double-click Control-menu icon
2. On File menu click Close
3. Press CTRL+W

Including All Fields in a Query

If you want to **include all fields** in a query, you could select each field individually. There is a simpler way, however. By selecting the asterisk (*) that appears in the field list, you are indicating that all fields are to be included. Complete the following steps to use the asterisk to include all fields.

Steps To Include All Fields in a Query

1 Be sure you have a maximized Select Query window containing a field list for the Patient table in the upper pane of the window and an empty design grid in the lower pane. (See Steps 1 through 6 on pages A 2.7 through A 2.10.) Point to the asterisk at the top of the field list box.

A maximized Select Query window displays (Figure 2-18). The two panes of the window have been resized.

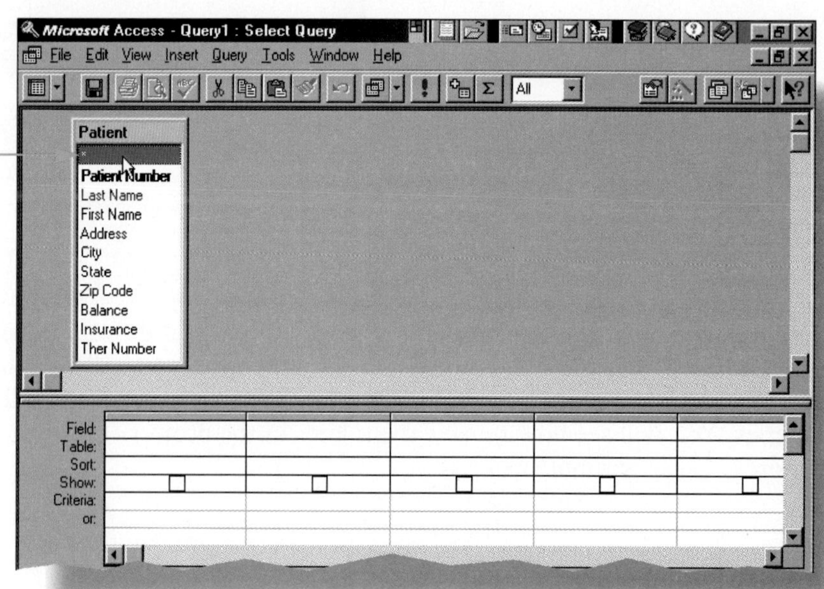

FIGURE 2-18

2 Double-click the asterisk in the field list box (see Figure 2-18) and then point to the Run button on the toolbar.

The table name, Patient, followed by an asterisk is added to the design grid (Figure 2-19), indicating all fields are included.

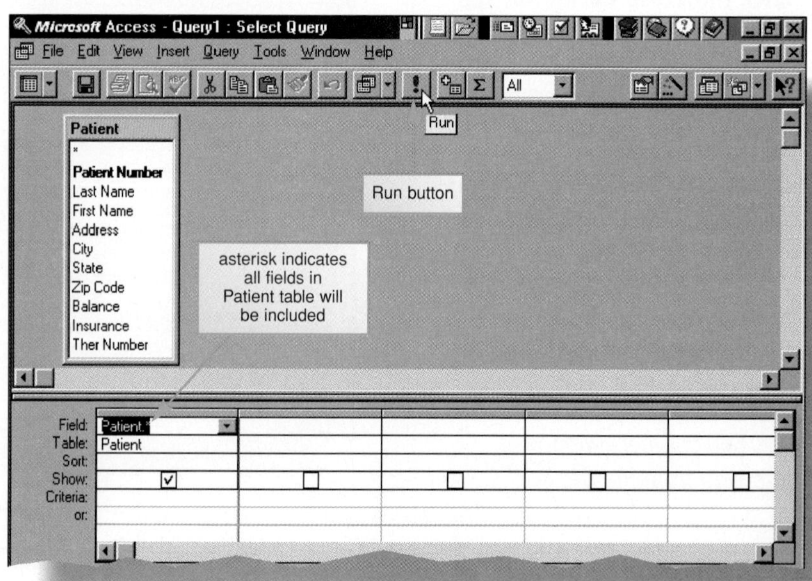

FIGURE 2-19

3 **Click the Run button.**

The results display and all fields in the Patient table are included (Figure 2-20).

4 **Click the Query View button down arrow on the toolbar to return to the Select Query window. Click Design View.**

The datasheet is replaced by the Select Query window.

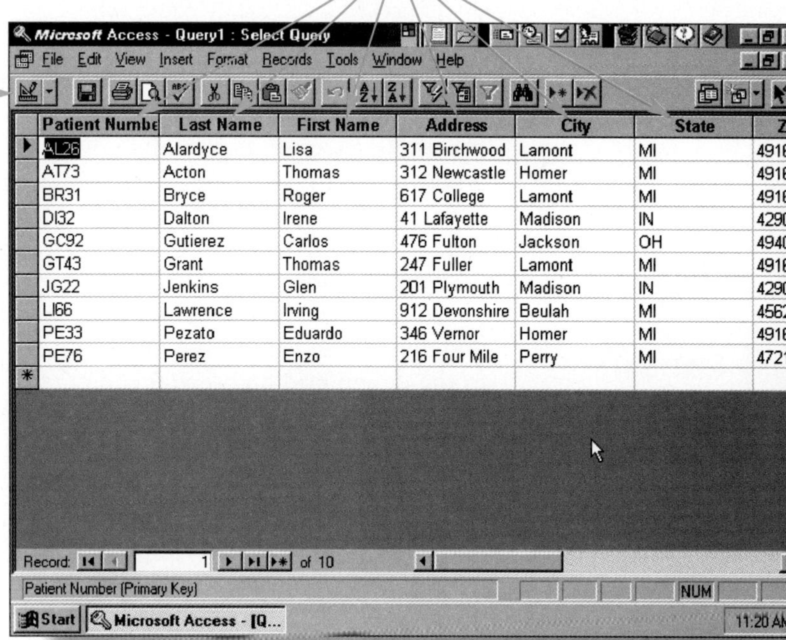

FIGURE 2-20

OtherWays

1. Drag asterisk from list box to grid
2. Click column in grid, click arrow, click asterisk

Clearing the Design Grid

If you make mistakes as you are creating a query, you can fix them individually. Alternatively, you simply may want to **clear the query**; that is, clear out the entries in the design grid and start over. One way to clear out the entries is to close the Select Query window and then start a new query just as you did earlier. A simpler approach, however, is to click Clear Grid on the Edit menu.

Steps To Clear a Query

1 **Click Edit on the menu bar.**

The Edit menu displays (Figure 2-21).

2 **Click Clear Grid.**

Access clears the design grid so you can enter your next query.

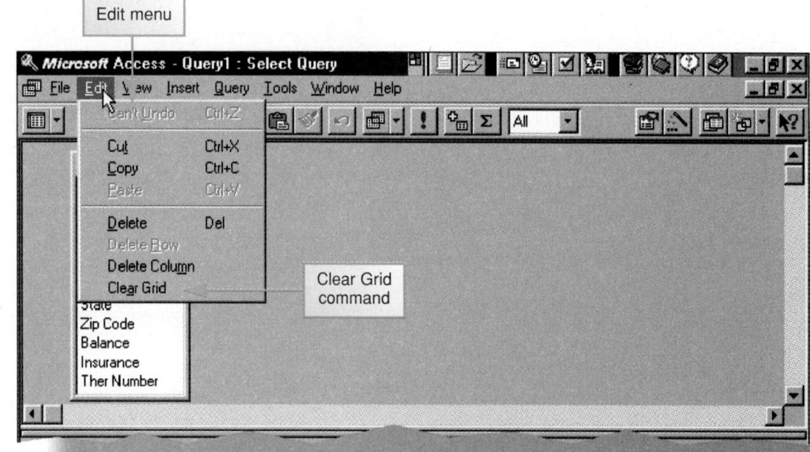

FIGURE 2-21

Entering Criteria

When you use queries, usually you are looking for those records that satisfy some criterion. You might want the name of the patient whose number is DI32, for example, or the numbers, names, and addresses of those patients whose names start with the letters, Pe. To enter criteria, enter them on the Criteria row in the design grid underneath the field name to which the criterion applies. For example, to indicate that the patient number must be DI32, type DI32 in the Criteria row underneath the Patient Number field. You first must add the Patient Number field to the design grid before you can enter the criterion.

The next examples illustrate the types of criteria that are available.

More *About* **Using Text Data in Criteria**

In many database management systems, text data must be enclosed in quotation marks. For example, to find customers in Michigan, "MI" would be entered as the criterion for the State field. In Access this is not necessary, since Access will insert the quotation marks automatically.

Using Text Data in Criteria

To use **text data** (data in a field whose type is text) in criteria, simply type the text in the Criteria row below the corresponding field name. The following steps query the Patient table and display the patient number, last name, first name, and balance of patient DI32.

Steps To Use Text Data in a Criterion

1. **One-by-one, double-click the Patient Number, Last Name, First Name, and Balance fields to add them to the query. Then point to the Criteria entry for the first field in the design grid.**

The Patient Number, Last Name, First Name, and Balance fields are added to the design grid (Figure 2-22). The mouse pointer on the Criteria entry for the first field (Patient Number) has changed shape to an I-beam.

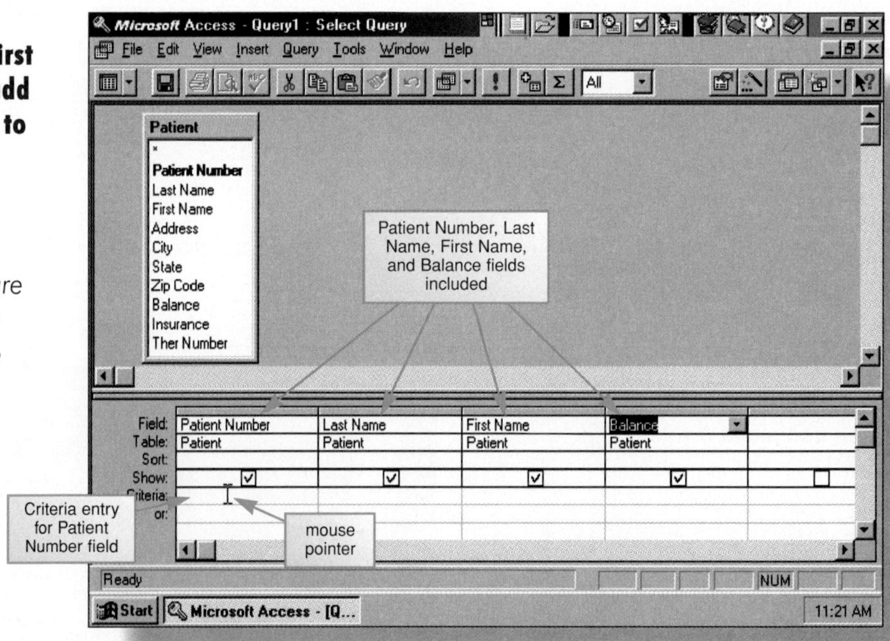

FIGURE 2-22

2 **Click the criteria entry, type** `DI32` **as the criteria for the Patient Number field, and then point to the Run button on the toolbar. (Be sure you type the letter I and not the number 1.)**

The criteria is entered (Figure 2-23).

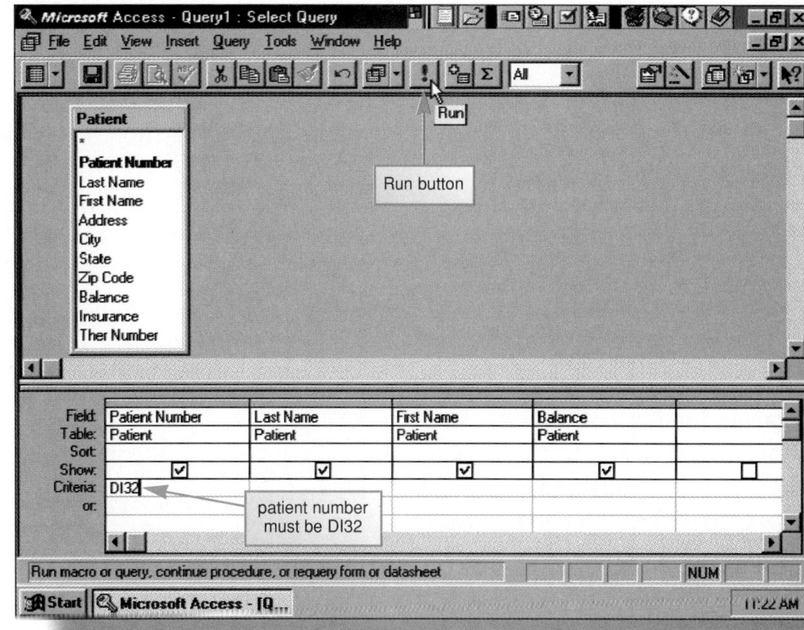

FIGURE 2-23

3 **Run the query by clicking the Run button.**

The results display (Figure 2-24). Only patient DI32 is included. (The extra blank row contains $0.00 in the Balance field. Unlike text fields, which are left blank, number and currency fields in the extra row contain 0. Because Balance is a currency field, the value displays as $0.00.)

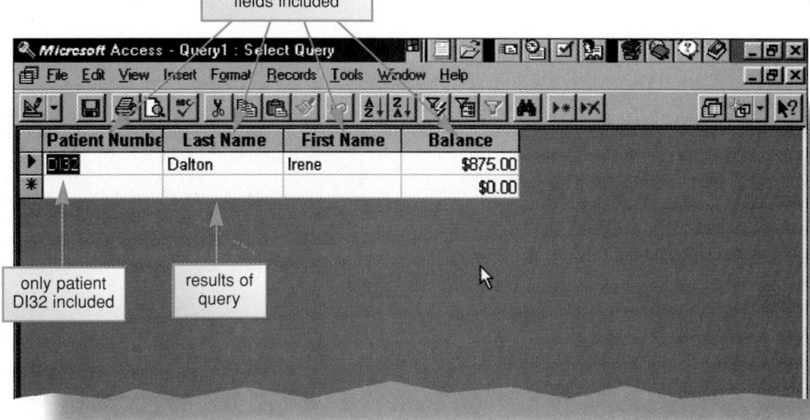

FIGURE 2-24

Using Wildcards

Two special **wildcards** are available in Microsoft Access. Wildcards are symbols that represent any character or combination of characters.

The first of the two wildcards, the asterisk (*), represents any collection of characters. Thus pe* represents the letters, Pe, followed by any collection of characters. The other wildcard symbol is the question mark (?), which represents any individual character. Thus t?m represents the letter, T, followed by any single character followed by the letter, m, such as Tim or Tom.

The steps on the next page use a wildcard to find the number, name, and address of those patients whose names begin with Pe. Because you do not know how many characters will follow the Pe, the asterisk is appropriate.

Steps To Use a Wildcard

1. **Use the Query View button on the toolbar to return to the Select Query window. On the Edit menu, click Clear Grid.**

   Access clears the design grid so you can enter the next query.

2. **Include the Patient Number, Last Name, First Name, and Address fields in the query and then click the Criteria entry for the second field. Type** `LIKE PE*` **as the entry.**

   The fields are selected and LIKE PE is entered as the criterion (Figure 2-25).*

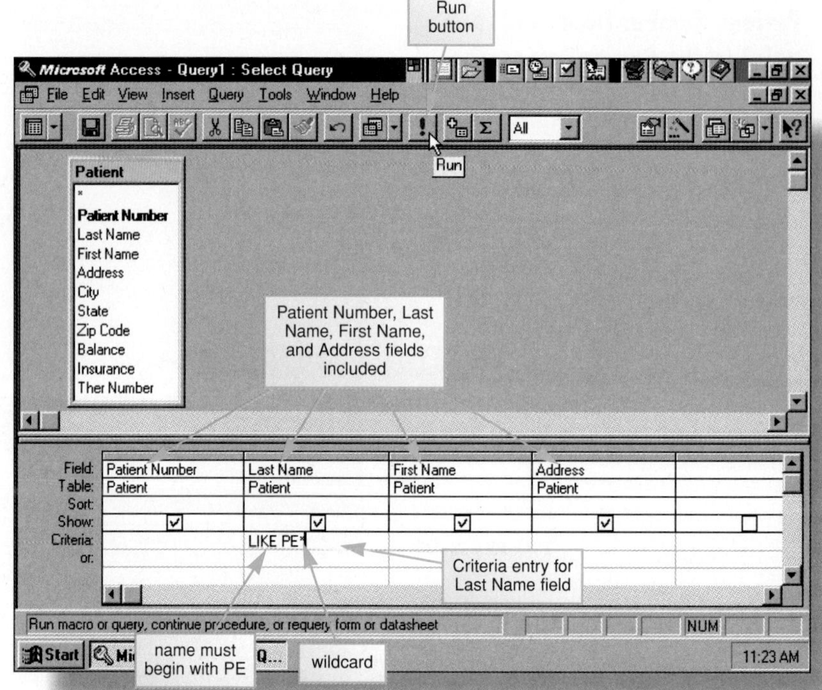

FIGURE 2-25

3. **Click the Run button on the toolbar.**

   The results display (Figure 2-26). Only the patients whose names start with "Pe" are included.

Patient Numbe	Last Name	First Name	Address
PE33	Pezato	Eduardo	346 Vernor
PE76	Perez	Enzo	216 Four Mile

results of query

names in Patient table that begin with PE

FIGURE 2-26

Criteria for a Field Not in the Result

In some cases, you may have criteria for a particular field that should not appear in the results of the query. For example, you may wish to see the patient number, last name, first name, and address for all patients who live in Lamont. The criteria involves the City field, which is not one of the fields to be included in the results.

To enter a criterion for the City field, it must be included in the design grid. Normally, this also would mean it would appear in the results. To prevent this from happening, remove the check mark from its **Show check box**, the box in the Show row of the grid. The following steps illustrate the process by displaying the patient number, last name, first name, and address for patients living in Lamont.

Steps To Use Criteria for a Field Not Included in the Results

1 **Use the Query View button on the toolbar to return to the Select Query window. On the Edit menu, click Clear Grid.**

Access clears the design grid so you can enter next query.

2 **Include the Patient Number, Last Name, First Name, Address, and City fields in the query. Type** `Lamont` **as the criteria for the City field and then point to the City field's Show check box.**

The fields are included in the grid, and the criteria for the City field is entered (Figure 2-27). The gap between the left scroll arrow and the scroll box indicates that fields are off the leftmost edge of the grid. In this case, the first field, Patient Number, currently does not display. Clicking the left scroll arrow will move the scroll box to the left, shift the fields currently in the grid to the right, and cause the Patient Number field to display.

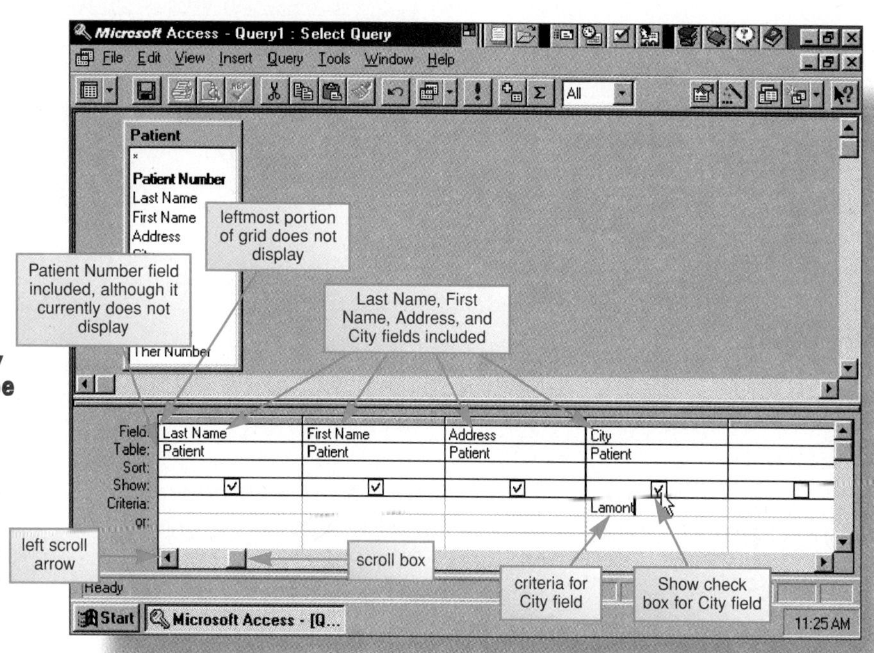

FIGURE 2-27

3 **Click the Show check box to remove the check mark (✓).**

The check mark is removed from the Show check box for the City field (Figure 2-28), indicating it will not show in the result. Access has automatically added quotation marks before and after Lamont.

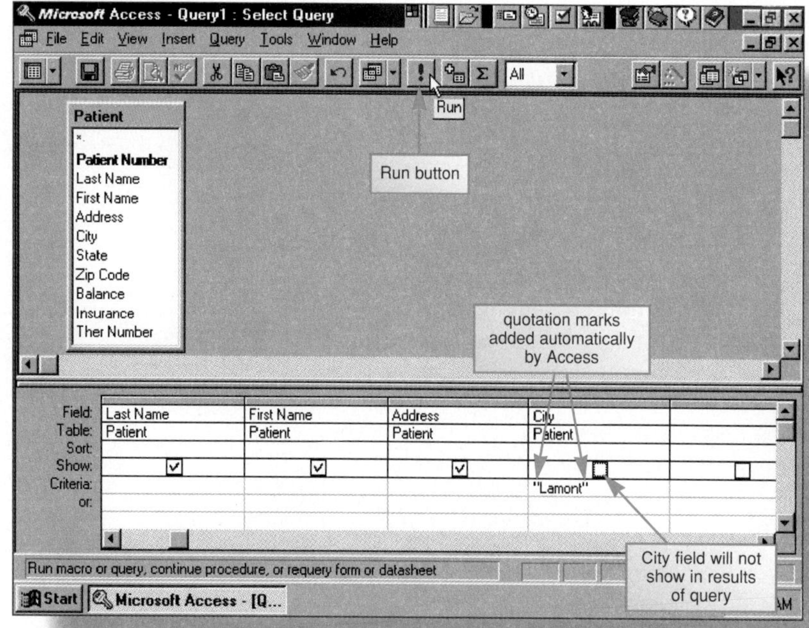

FIGURE 2-28

4 **Click the Run button on the toolbar.**

The results display (Figure 2-29). The City field does not appear. The only patients included are those who live in Lamont.

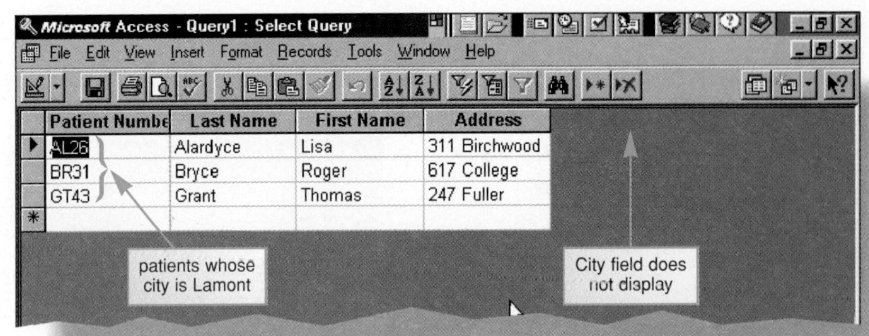

FIGURE 2-29

Using Numeric Data in Criteria

To enter a number in a criterion, type the number without any dollar signs or commas. Complete the following steps to display all patients whose insurance amount is $0.00 To do so, you will need to type 0 as criteria for the Insurance field.

To Use a Number in a Criterion

1 **Use the Query View button on the toolbar to return to the Select Query window. On the Edit menu, click Clear Grid. Click the left scroll arrow so no space exists between the scroll arrow and the scroll box.**

Access clears the design grid so you can enter the next query.

2 **Include the Patient Number, Last Name, First Name, Balance, and Insurance fields, in the query. Type** 0 **as the criterion for the Insurance field. You need not enter a dollar sign or decimal point in the criterion.**

The fields are selected and the criterion is entered (Figure 2-30).

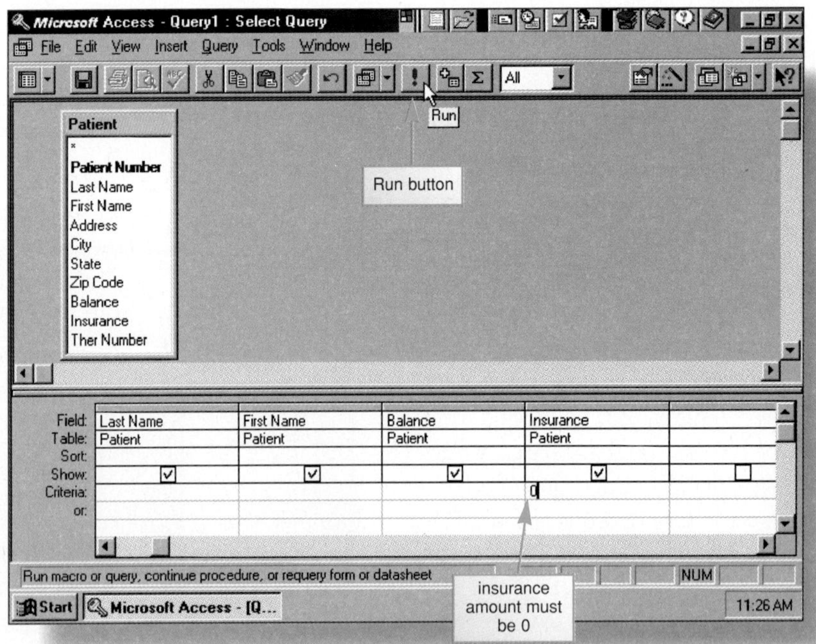

FIGURE 2-30

3 **Click the Run button on the toolbar.**

The results display (Figure 2-31). Only those patients who have an insurance amount of $0.00 are included.

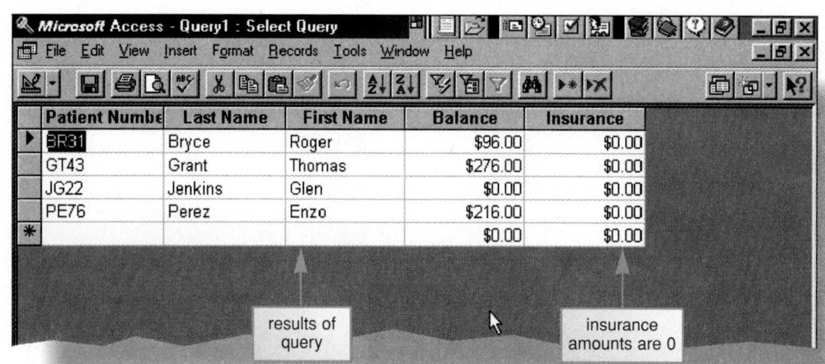

FIGURE 2-31

Using Comparison Operators

Unless you specify otherwise, Access assumes that the criteria you enter involve equality (exact matches). In the last query, for example, you were requesting those patients whose insurance amount is *equal to* 0. If you want something other than an exact match, you must enter the appropriate **comparison operator**. The comparison operators are > (greater than), < (less than), >= (greater than or equal to), <= (less than or equal to), and NOT (not equal to).

Perform the following steps to use the > operator to find all patients whose balance is more than $500.

Steps To Use a Comparison Operator in a Criterion

1 **Use the Query View button on the toolbar to return to the Select Query window. On the Edit menu, click Clear Grid. Click the left scroll arrow so no space exists between the scroll arrow and the scroll box.**

Access clears the design grid so you can enter the next query.

2 **Include the Patient Number, Last Name, First Name, Balance, and Insurance fields in the query. Type >500 as the criterion for the Balance field.**

The fields are selected and the criterion is entered (Figure 2-32).

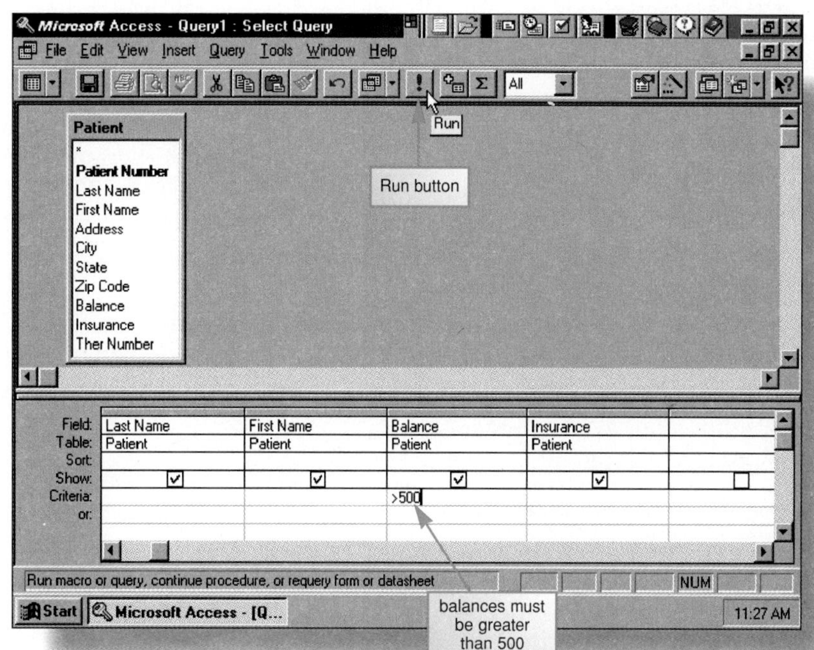

FIGURE 2-32

3 **Click the Run button on the toolbar.**

The results display (Figure 2-33). Only those patients who have a balance more than $500 are included.

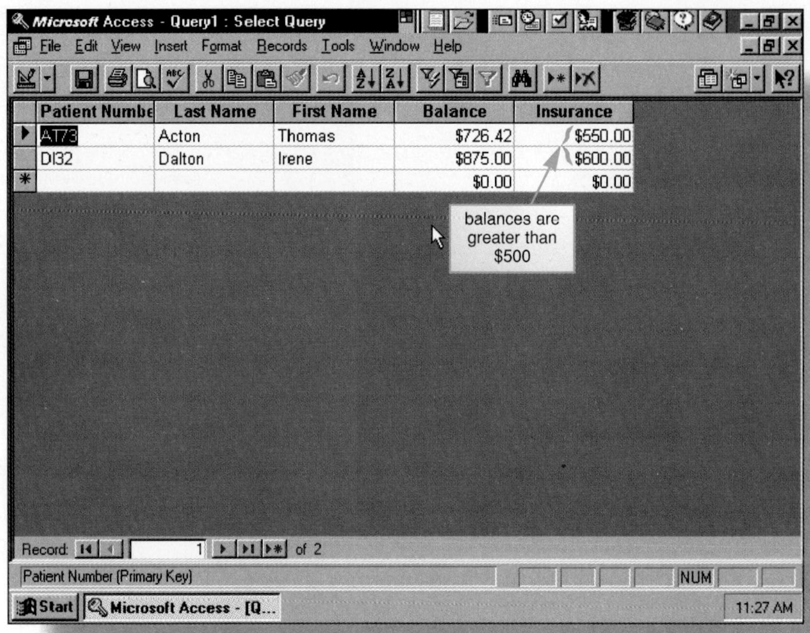

FIGURE 2-33

More ***About*** **Compound Criteria**

The approach taken by Access to compound criteria is precisely the approach that was proposed for Query-by-Example. (Placing criteria on the same lines indicates they are connected by the word AND. Placing them on separate lines indicates they are connected by the word OR.)

Using Compound Criteria

Often you will have more than one criterion that the data for which you are searching must satisfy. This type of criterion is called a **compound criterion**. There are two types of compound criteria.

In **AND criterion**, each individual criterion must be true in order for the compound criterion to be true. For example, an AND criterion would allow you to find those patients who have an insurance amount of $0.00 *and* whose therapist is therapist 08.

OR criterion, on the other hand, are true provided either individual criterion is true. An OR criterion would allow you to find those patients who have a balance greater than $500 *or* whose therapist is therapist 08. In this case, any patient whose balance is greater than $500 would be included in the answer whether or not the patient's therapist is therapist 08. Likewise, any patient whose therapist is therapist 08 would be included whether or not the patient had a balance more than $500.

To combine criteria with AND, place the criteria on the same line. Perform the following steps to use an AND criterion to find those patients whose insurance amount is $0.00 and whose therapist is therapist 08.

Steps To Use a Compound Criterion Involving AND

1 **Use the Query View button on the toolbar to return to the Select Query window. On the Edit menu, click Clear Grid.**

Access clears the design grid so you can enter the next query.

2 **Include the Patient Number, Last Name, First Name, Balance, Insurance, and Ther Number fields in the query.**

3 **Click the Criteria entry for the Insurance field, and then type** 0 **as a criterion for the Insurance field. Click the Criteria entry for the Ther Number field and then type** 08 **as the criterion for the Ther Number field.**

The fields shift to the left (Figure 2-34). Criteria have been entered for the Insurance and Ther Number fields.

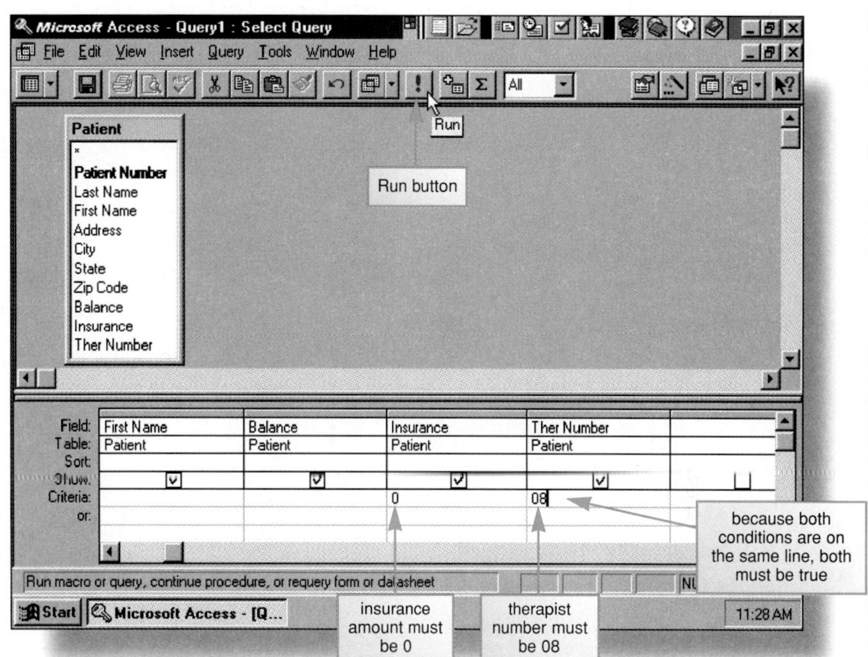

FIGURE 2-34

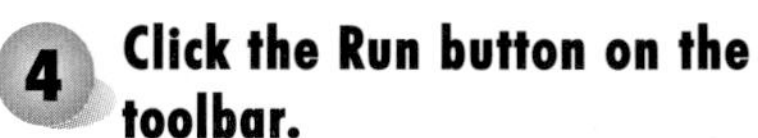

4 **Click the Run button on the toolbar.**

The results display (Figure 2-35). Only those patients whose insurance is $0.00 and whose therapist number is 08 are included.

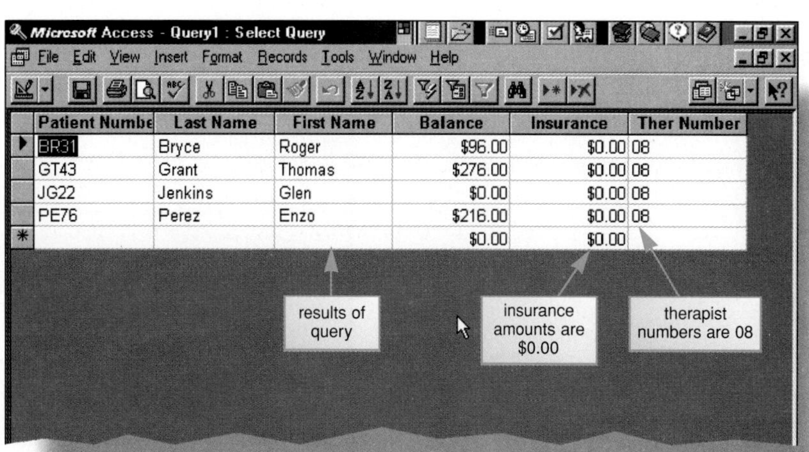

Patient Number	Last Name	First Name	Balance	Insurance	Ther Number
BR31	Bryce	Roger	$96.00	$0.00	08
GT43	Grant	Thomas	$276.00	$0.00	08
JG22	Jenkins	Glen	$0.00	$0.00	08
PE76	Perez	Enzo	$216.00	$0.00	08
*			$0.00	$0.00	

FIGURE 2-35

To combine criteria with OR, the criteria must go on separate lines in the Criteria area of the grid. The steps on the next page use an OR criterion to find those patients whose balance is more than $500 or whose therapist is therapist 08 (or both).

Steps To Use a Compound Criterion Involving OR

1. **Use the Query View button on the toolbar to return to the Select Query window.**

2. **Click the Criteria entry for the Insurance field. Use the BACKSPACE key to delete the entry (0). Click the Criteria entry for the Balance field. Type** >500 **as the criterion. Click the Criteria entry for the Ther Number field. Use the BACKSPACE key to delete the entry (*"08"*).**

3. **Click the or entry (the second line of Criteria) for the Ther Number field and then type** 08 **as the entry.**

   The criteria are entered for the Insurance and Ther Number fields on different lines (Figure 2-36).

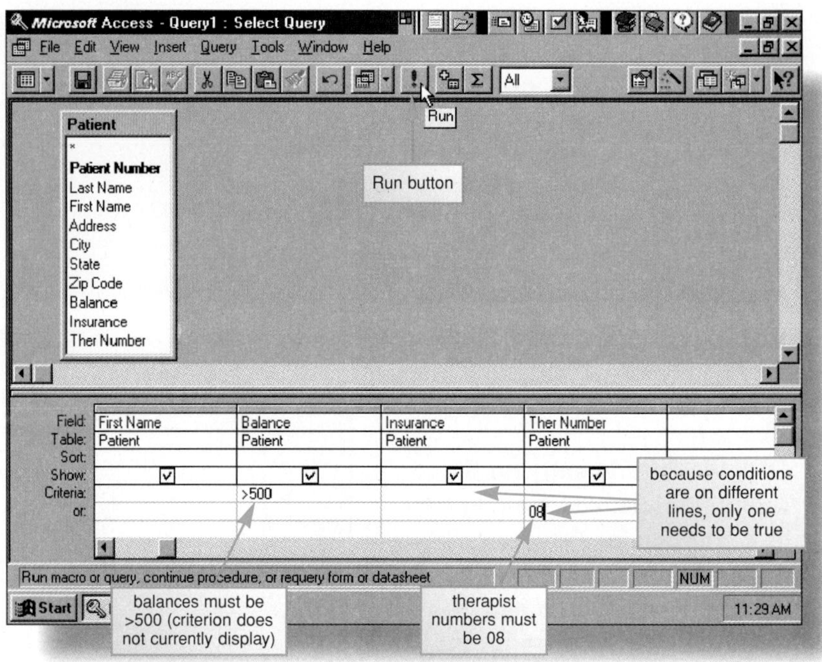

FIGURE 2-36

4. **Click the Run button on the toolbar.**

   The results display (Figure 2-37). Only those patients whose balance is more than $500 or whose therapist number is 08 are included.

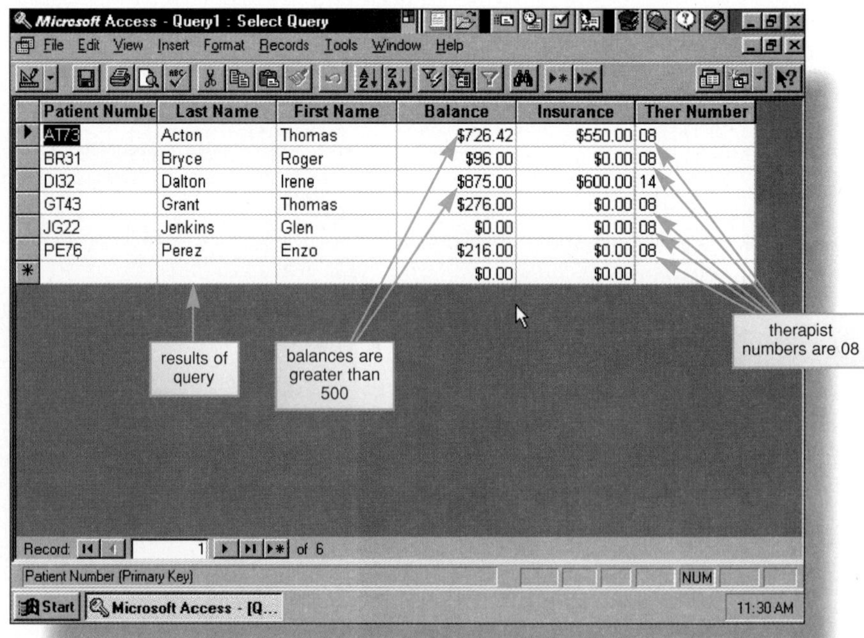

FIGURE 2-37

Sorting Data in a Query

In some queries, the order in which the records are displayed really does not matter. All you need be concerned about are the records that appear in the results. It does not matter which one is first or which one is last.

In other queries, however, the order can be very important. You may want to see the cities in which patients are located and would like them arranged alphabetically. Perhaps you want to see the patients listed by therapist number. Further, within all the patients of any given therapist, you would like them to be listed by insurance amount.

To order the records in the answer to a query in a particular way, you **sort** the records. The field or fields on which the records are sorted is called the **sort key**. If you are sorting on more than one field (such as sorting by insurance amount within therapist number), the more important field (Ther Number) is called the **major key** and the less important field (Insurance) is called the **minor key**.

To sort in Microsoft Access, specify the sort order in the Sort line of the design grid underneath the field that is the sort key. If you specify more than one sort key, the sort key on the left will be the major sort key and the one on the right will be the minor key.

The following steps sort the cities in the Patient table.

More *About* Sorting Data in a Query

When a query involves sorting, the records in the underlying tables (the tables on which the query is based) are not actually rearranged. Instead, Access will determine the most efficient method of simply displaying the records in the requested order. The records in the underlying tables remain in their original order.

Steps To Sort Data in a Query

1 **Use the Query View button on the toolbar to return to the Select Query window. On the Edit menu, click Clear Grid. Click the left scroll arrow so no space exists between the scroll arrow and the scroll box.**

2 **Include the City field in the design grid. Click the Sort entry under the City field, and then click the down arrow that appears.**

The City field is included (Figure 2-38). A list of available sort orders displays.

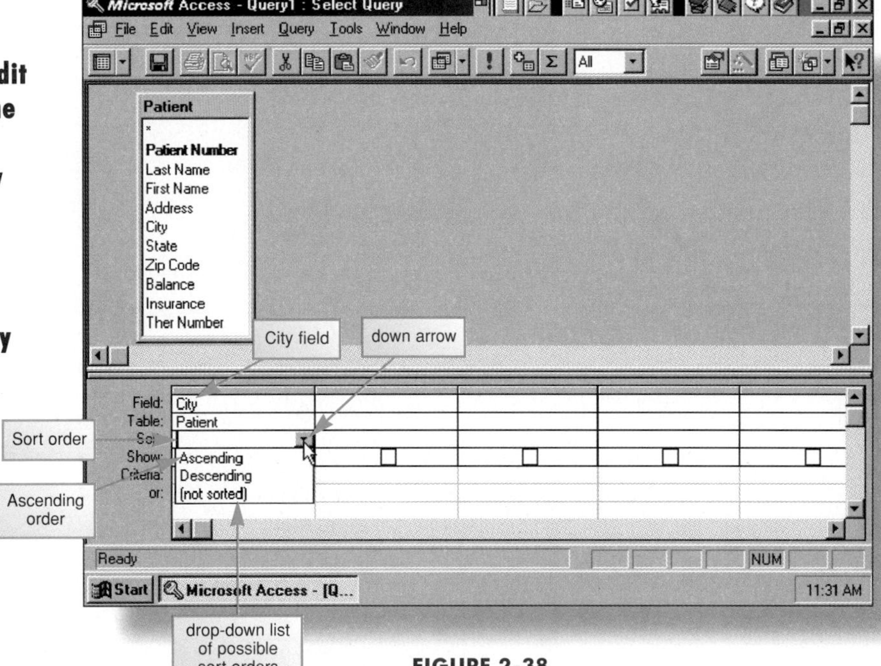

FIGURE 2-38

3 **Click Ascending.**

Ascending is selected as the order (Figure 2-39).

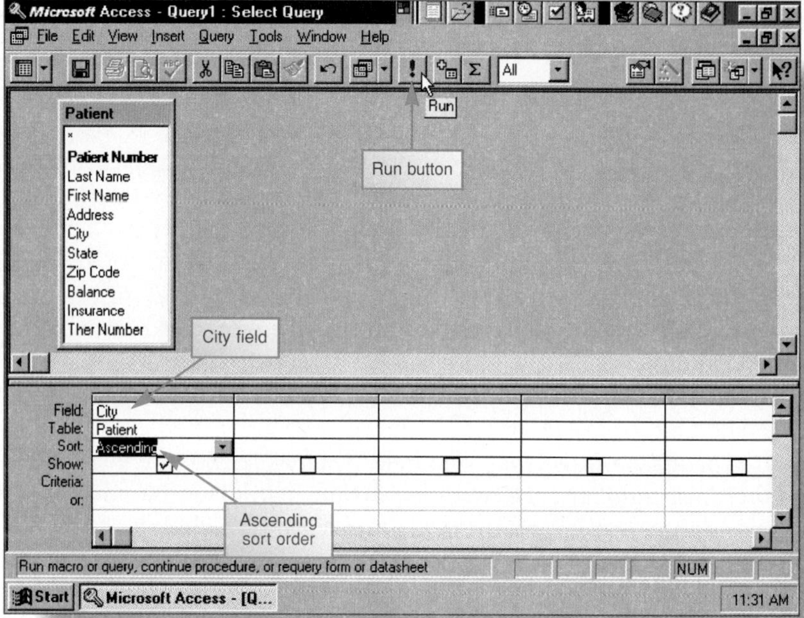

FIGURE 2-39

4 **Run the query by clicking the Run button on the toolbar.**

The results contain the cities from the Patient table (Figure 2-40). The cities display in alphabetical order. ***Duplicates****, that is, identical rows, are included.*

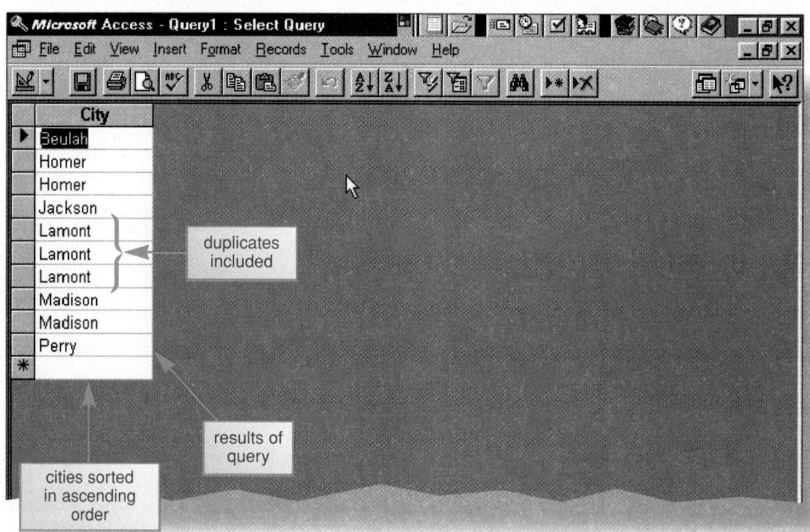

FIGURE 2-40

Sorting on Multiple Keys

The next example lists the number, name, therapist number, and insurance amount for all patients. The data is to be sorted by descending insurance amount *within* therapist number, which means that the Ther Number field is the major key and the Insurance field is the minor key. It also means that the Insurance field should be sorted in descending order.

The following steps accomplish this sorting by specifying the Ther Number and Insurance fields as sort keys and by selecting Descending as the sort order for the Insurance field.

To Sort on Multiple Keys

1 **Use the Query View button on the toolbar to return to the Select Query window. On the Edit menu, click Clear Grid.**

2 **Include the Patient Number, Last Name, First Name, Ther Number, and Insurance fields in the query *in this order*. Select Ascending as the sort order for the Ther Number field and Descending as the sort order for the Insurance field (Figure 2-41).**

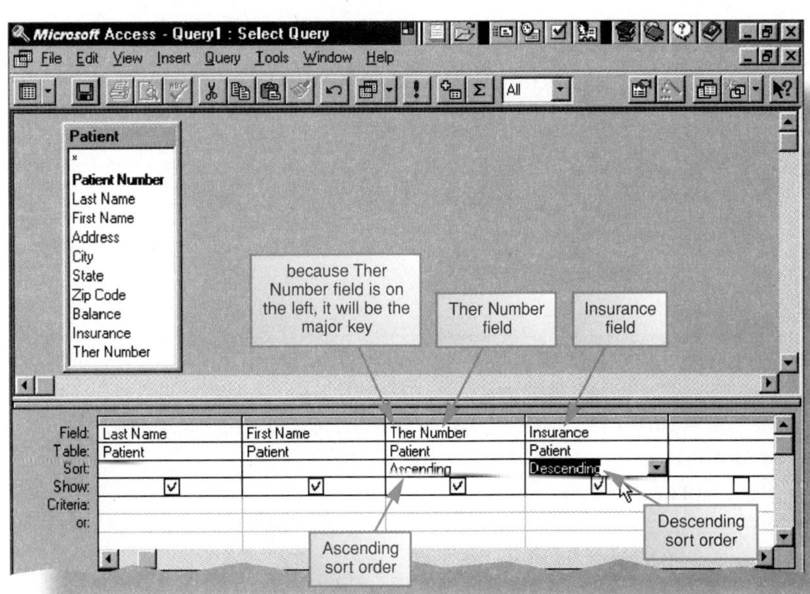

FIGURE 2-41

3 **Run the query.**

The results display (Figure 2-42). The patients are sorted by therapist number. Within the collection of patients having the same therapist, the patients are sorted by descending insurance amount.

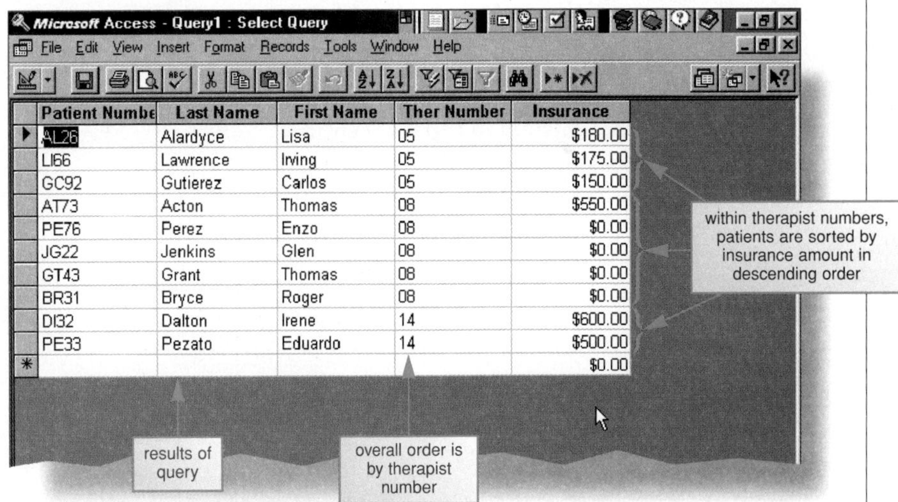

FIGURE 2-42

It is important to remember that the major sort key must appear to the left of the minor sort key in the design grid. If you attempted to sort the patient data by insurance amount within therapist number, for example, but placed the Insurance field to the left of the Ther Number field, your results would be incorrect.

Omitting Duplicates

As you saw earlier, when you sort data, duplicates are included. In Figure 2-40 on page A 2.28, for example, Homer appeared two times, Lamont appeared three times, and Madison appeared twice. If you do not want duplicates included, use the Query Properties command and specify Unique Values Only. Perform the following steps to produce a sorted list of the cities in the Patient table in which each city is listed only once.

To Omit Duplicates

1. **Use the Query View button on the toolbar to return to the Select Query window. On the Edit menu, click Clear Grid. Click the left scroll arrow so no space exists between the scroll arrow and the scroll box.**

2. **Include the City field, click Ascending as the sort order, and click the *second* field in the design grid (the empty field following City). Then right-click.**

   The shortcut menu displays (Figure 2-43).

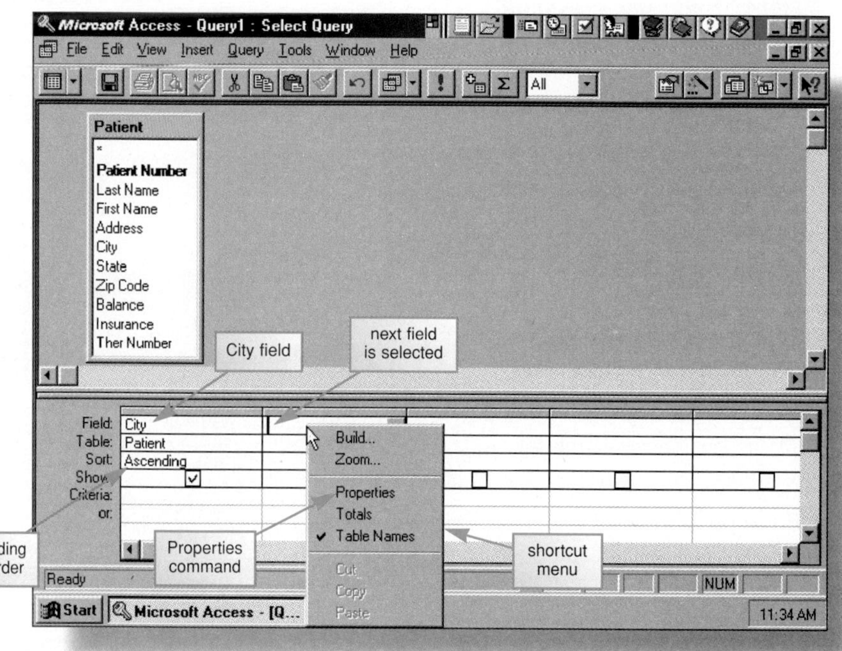

FIGURE 2-43

3. **Click Properties.**

   The Query Properties dialog box displays (Figure 2-44).

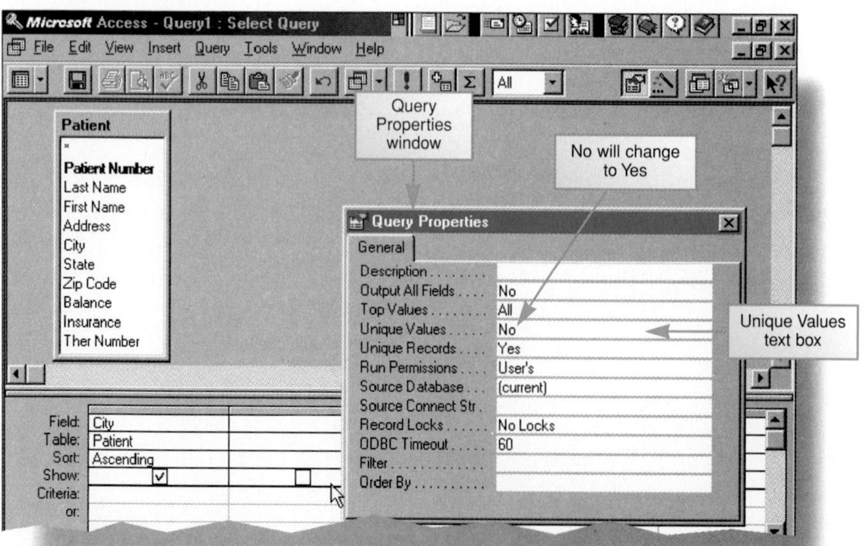

FIGURE 2-44

4 **Click the Unique Values text box, and then click the down arrow that displays to produce a list of available choices for Unique Values (Figure 2-45).**

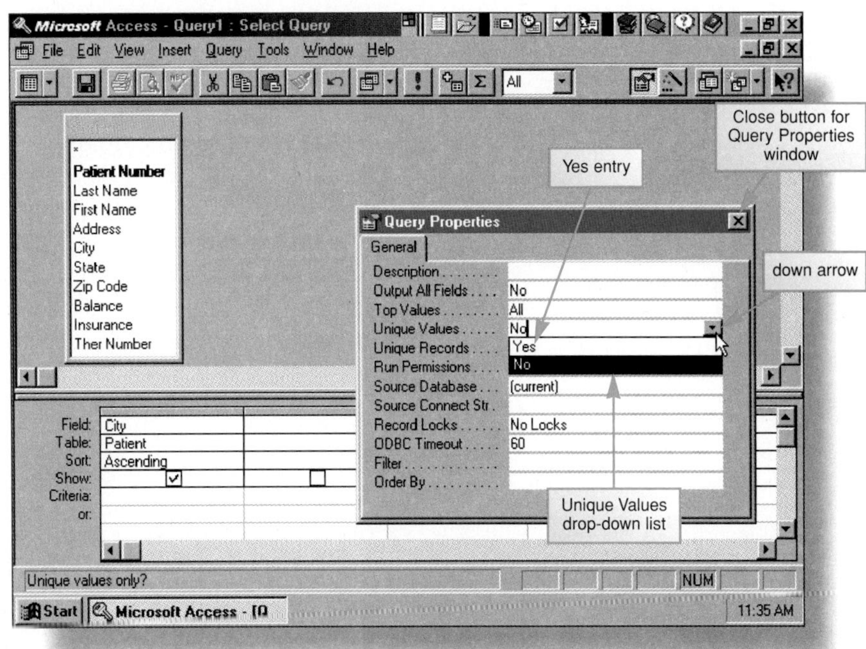

FIGURE 2-45

5 **Click Yes, and then click the Close button for the Query Properties dialog box to close the dialog box. Run the query by clicking the Run button on the toolbar.**

The results display (Figure 2-46). The cities are sorted alphabetically. Each city is included only once.

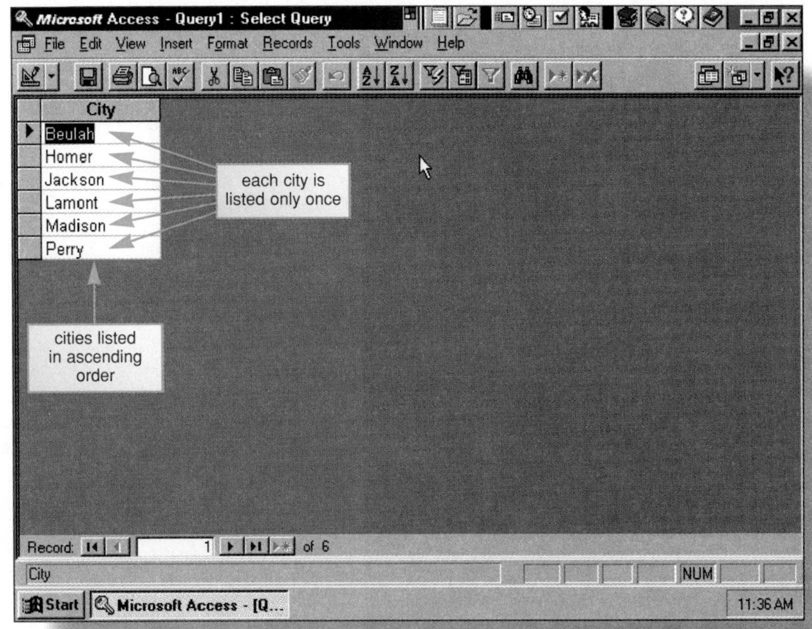

FIGURE 2-46

*Other*Ways

1. Right click, in upper pane of window, click Properties on shortcut menu
2. Click Properties button on toolbar
3. On View menu click Properties

More About Joining Tables

The ability to join tables, that is, to create queries that draw data from multiple tables is a key feature that has always distinguished database management systems from file systems. Several types of joins are available. The most common type, the one illustrated in the text, is formally called the natural join.

Joining Tables

Mason Clinic needs to list the number and name of each patient along with the number and name of the patient's therapist. The patient's name is in the Patient table, whereas the therapist's name is in the Therapist table. Thus, this query cannot be satisfied using a single table. You need to **join** the tables; that is, to find records in the two tables that have identical values in matching fields (Figure 2-47). In this example, you need to find records in the Patient table and the Therapist table that have the same value in the Ther Number fields.

give the number and name of each patient along with the number and name of the patient's therapist

Patient Table

PATIENT NAME	LAST NAME	FIRST NAME	. . .	THER NUMBER
AL26	Alardyce	Lisa	. . .	05
AT73	Acton	Thomas	. . .	08
BR31	Bryce	Roger	. . .	08
DI32	Dalton	Irene	. . .	14
GC92	Gutierez	Carlos	. . .	05
GT43	Grant	Thomas	. . .	08
JG22	Jenkins	Glen	. . .	08
LI66	Lawrence	Irving	. . .	05
PE33	Pezato	Eduardo	. . .	14
PE76	Perez	Enzo	. . .	08

Therapist Table

THER NUMBER	LAST NAME	FIRST NAME	. . .
05	Hughes	Mary	. . .
08	Foster	Richard	. . .
14	Galvez	Maria	. . .

PATIENT NUMBER	LAST NAME	FIRST NAME	THER NUMBER	LAST NAME	FIRST NAME
AL26	Alardyce	Lisa	05	Hughes	Mary
AT73	Acton	Thomas	08	Foster	Richard
BR31	Bryce	Roger	08	Foster	Richard
DI32	Dalton	Irene	14	Galvez	Maria
GC92	Gutierez	Carlos	05	Hughes	Mary
GT43	Grant	Thomas	08	Foster	Richard
JG22	Jenkins	Glen	08	Foster	Richard
LI66	Lawrence	Irving	05	Hughes	Mary
PE33	Pezato	Eduardo	14	Galvez	Maria
PE76	Perez	Enzo	08	Foster	Richard

FIGURE 2-47

To join tables in Access, first you bring field lists for both tables to the upper pane of the Select Query window. Access will draw a line between matching fields in the two tables indicating that the tables are related. You then can select fields from either table. Access will join the tables automatically.

The first step is to add an additional table to the query as illustrated in the following steps, which add the Therapist table.

To Join Tables

1 **Use the Query View button on the toolbar to return to the Select Query window. On the Edit menu, click Clear Grid.**

2 **Right-click any open area in the upper pane of the Select Query window.**

The shortcut menu displays (Figure 2-48).

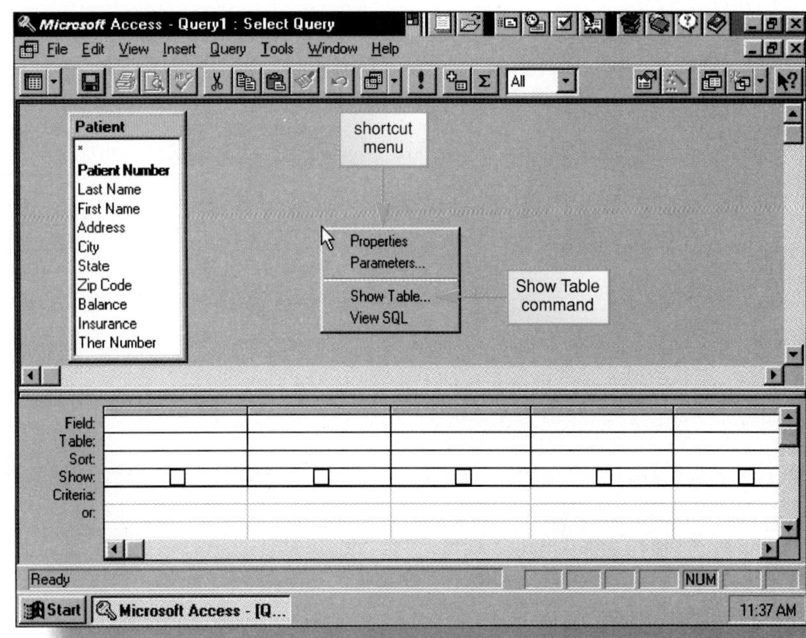

FIGURE 2-48

3 **Click Show Table on the shortcut menu.**

The Show Table dialog box displays (Figure 2-49).

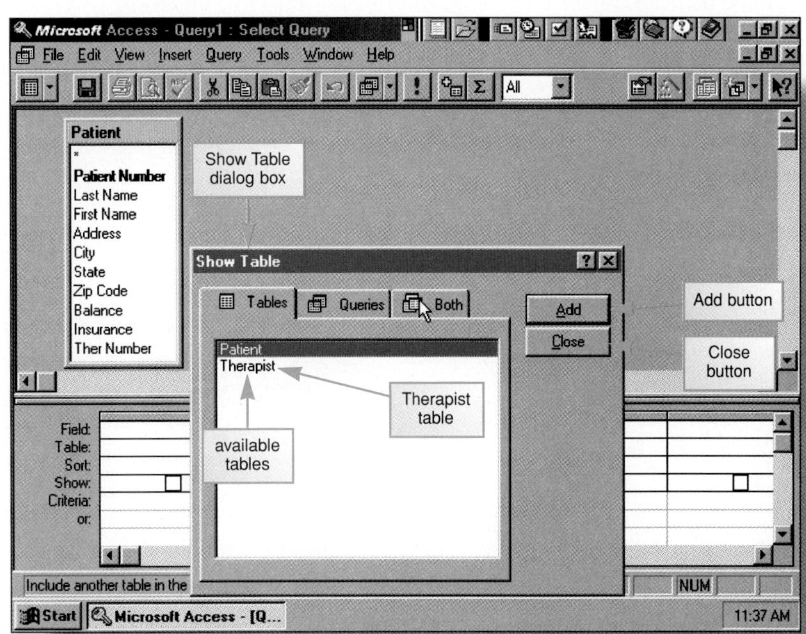

FIGURE 2-49

4 **Click Therapist to select the Therapist table, and then click the Add button. Close the Show Table dialog box by clicking its Close button. Expand the size of the field list so all the fields in the Therapist table display.**

A field list for the Therapist table displays (Figure 2-50). It has been enlarged so all the Therapist fields are visible. A line appears joining the Ther Number fields in the two field lists. This line indicates how the tables are related; that is, linked through the matching fields. (If you did not give the matching fields the same name, Access will not insert the line. You can insert it manually by clicking one of the two matching fields and dragging the mouse pointer to the other matching field.)

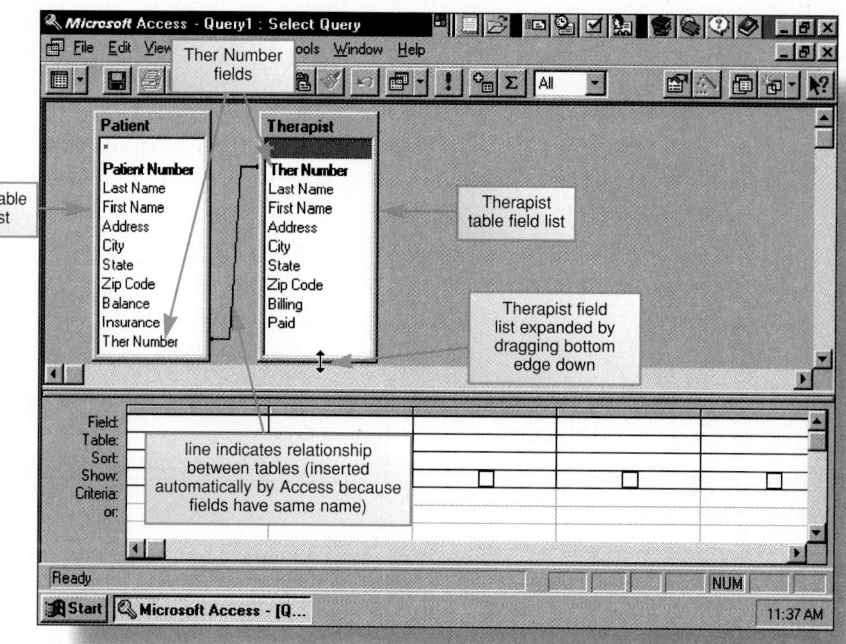

FIGURE 2-50

5 **Include the Patient Number, Last Name, First Name, and Ther Number fields from the Patient table and the Last Name and First Name fields in the Therapist table.**

The fields from both tables are selected (Figure 2-51). Notice that you do not have to click the Ther Number from both tables for the join to work.

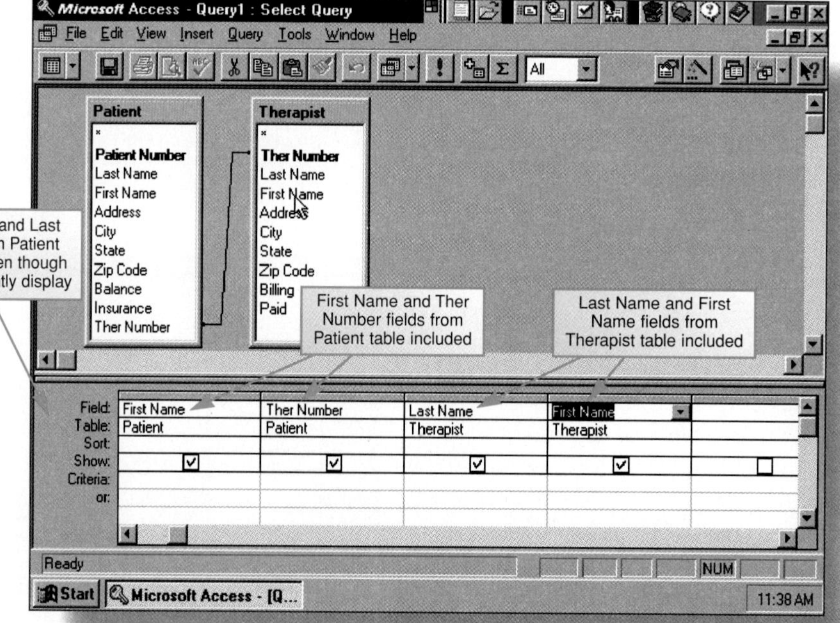

FIGURE 2-51

6 **Run the query.**

The results display (Figure 2-52). They contain data from the Patient table as well as data from the Therapist table.

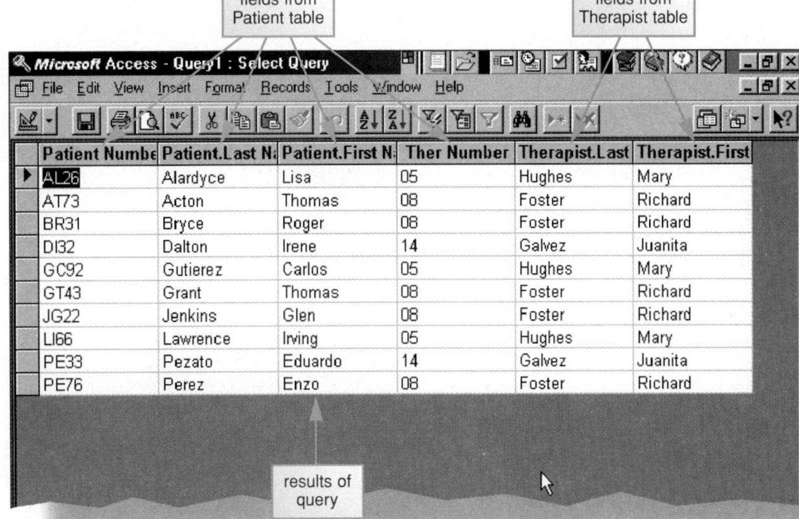

FIGURE 2-52

*Other*Ways

1. Click Show Table button on toolbar
2. On Query menu click Show Table

Restricting Records in a Join

Sometimes you will want to join tables, but you will not want to include all possible records. In such cases, you will relate the tables and include fields just as you did before. You also will include criteria. For example, to include the same fields as in the previous query, but only those patients whose balance is more than $200, you will make the same entries as before and then also type the number >200 as a criterion for the Balance field.

The following steps modify the query from the previous example to restrict the records that will be included in the join.

Steps To Restrict the Records in a Join

1 **Use the Query View button on the toolbar to return to the Select Query window. Add the Balance field to the query. Type** >200 **as the criterion for the Balance field and then click the Show check box for the Balance field to remove the check mark.**

The Balance field displays in the design grid (Figure 2-53). A criterion is entered for the Balance field and the Show check box is empty, indicating that the field will not display in the results of the query.

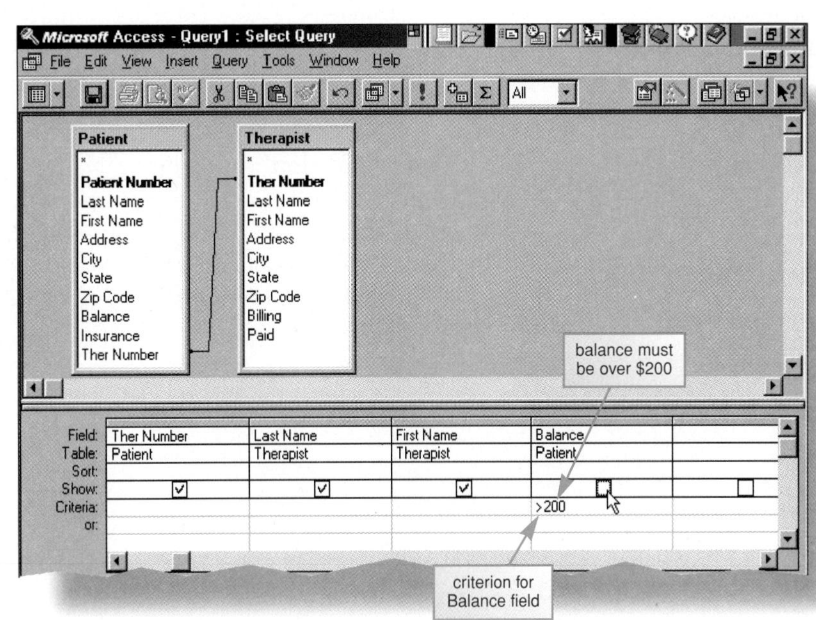

FIGURE 2-53

Run the query.

The results display (Figure 2-54). Only those patients with a balance more than $200 appear in the result. The Balance field does not display.

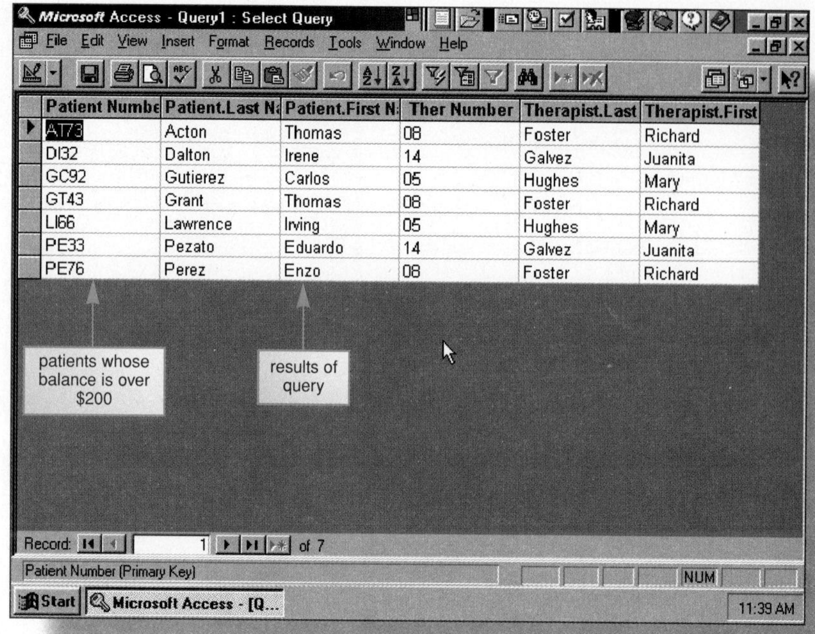

FIGURE 2-54

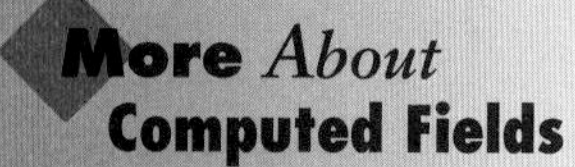

More About Computed Fields

Computed fields, also called calculated fields, play an important role in database management. Because it is easy to calculate values in a query, there is no need to store them in a database. There is no need, for example, to store the patient amount (Balance - Insurance), since it can be calculated whenever it is required.

Using Computed Fields in a Query

It is important to the Mason Clinic to know the amount expected to be paid by each patient; that is, the amount owed by the patient minus the amount expected to be paid by the patient's insurance. This poses a problem because there is no such field in the Patient table. You can compute it, however, because the expected amount is equal to the balance minus the insurance amount. Such a field is called a **computed field**.

To include computed fields in queries, you enter a name for the computed field, a colon, and then the expression in one of the columns in the Field row. For the patient amount, for example, you will type Patient Amount:[Balance]-[Insurance]. You can type this directly into the Field row. You will not be able to see the entire entry, however, because not enough room is available for it. A better way is to select the column in the Field row, right-click to display the shortcut menu, and then click Zoom. The Zoom dialog box will display. You then can type the expression in the dialog box.

You are not restricted to subtraction in computations. You can use addition (+), multiplication (*), or division (/). Also, you can include parentheses in your computations to indicate which computations should be done first.

Perform the following steps to use a computed field to display the number, name, and patient amount of all patients.

Steps To Use a Computed Field in a Query

1 Use the Query View button on the toolbar to return to the Select Query window. Right-click any field in the list of fields in the Therapist table.

The shortcut menu displays (Figure 2-55).

2 Click Remove Table to remove the Therapist table from the Select Query window. On the Edit menu, click Clear Grid. Click the left scroll arrow so no space exists between the scroll arrow and the scroll box.

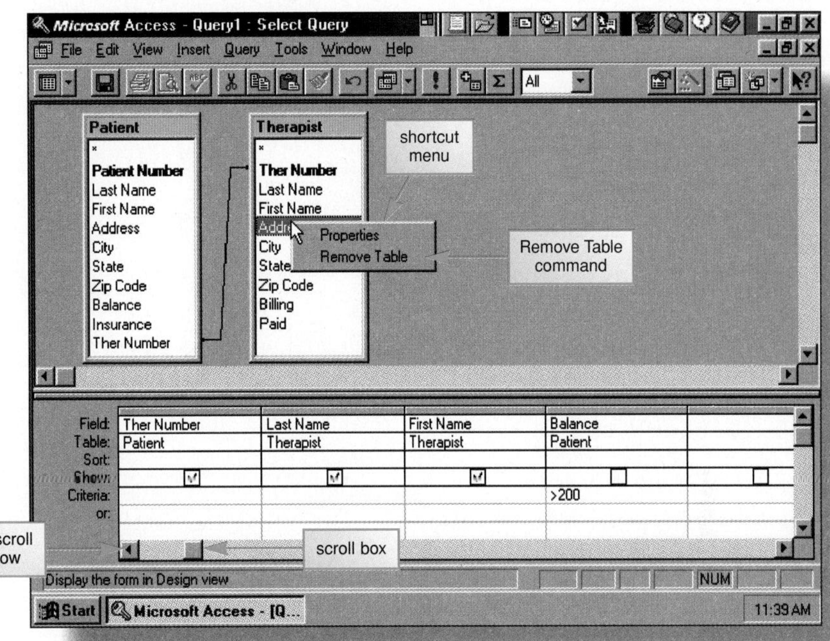

FIGURE 2-55

3 Include the Patient Number, Last Name, and First Name fields. Click the Field entry in the fourth column in the design grid to select the field. Right-click and then click Zoom on the shortcut menu. Type `Patient Amount:[Balance]-[Insurance]` **in the Zoom dialog box that displays.**

The Zoom dialog box displays (Figure 2-56). The expression you typed displays within the dialog box.

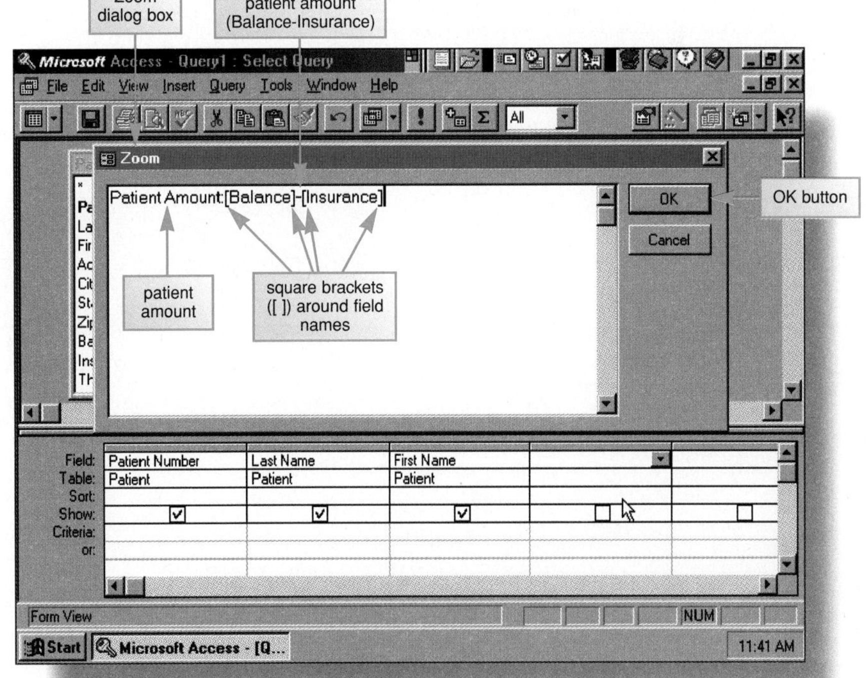

FIGURE 2-56

4 **Click the OK button.**

The Zoom dialog box no longer displays (Figure 2-57). A portion of the expression you entered displays in the fourth field within the design grid.

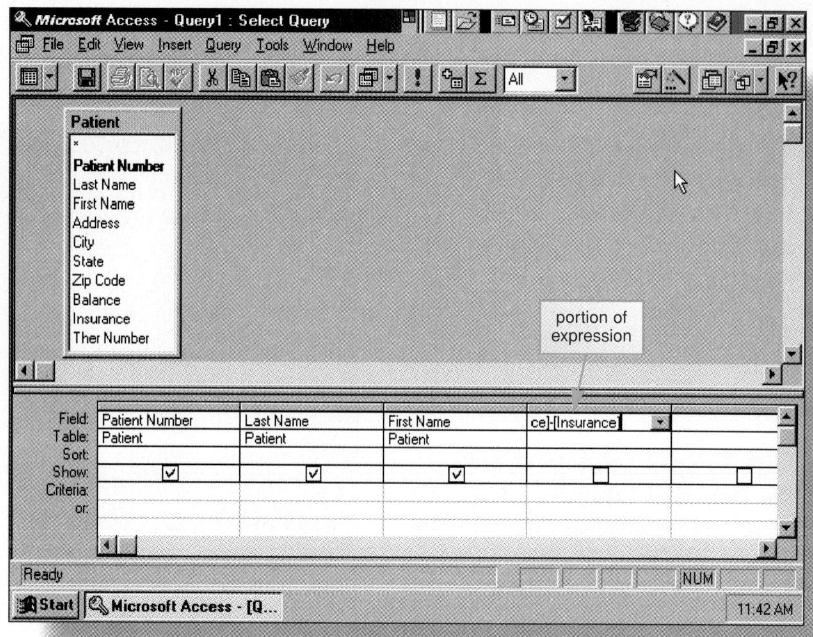

FIGURE 2-57

5 **Run the query.**

The results display (Figure 2-58). Microsoft Access has calculated and displayed the patient amounts. The parentheses around the $32.88 indicate it is a negative number; that is, the patient evidently has already paid more than the patient portion.

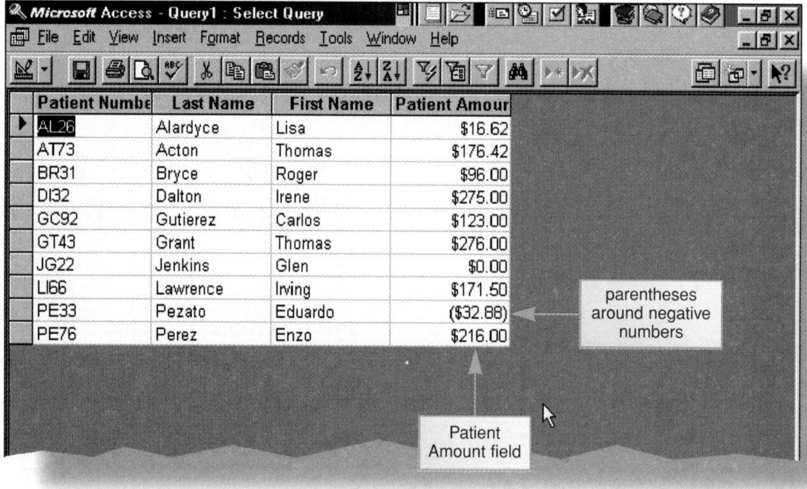

FIGURE 2-58

Other Ways

1. Press SHIFT+F2

More About Calculating Statistics

Virtually all database management systems support the basic set of statistical calculations: sum, average, count, maximum, and minimum as part of their query feature. Some systems, including Access, add several more, such as standard deviation, variance, first, and last.

Calculating Statistics

Microsoft Access supports the built-in **statistics**: COUNT, SUM, AVG (average), MAX (largest value), MIN (smallest value), STD (standard deviation), VAR (variance), FIRST, and LAST. To use any of these in a query, you include it in the Total row in the design grid. The Total row routinely does not appear in the grid. To include it, right-click the grid, and then click Totals on the shortcut menu.

The following example illustrates how you use these functions by calculating the average balance for all patients.

To Calculate Statistics

1 **Use the Query View button on the toolbar to return to the Select Query window. On the Edit menu, click Clear Grid.**

2 **Right-click the grid.**

The shortcut menu displays (see Figure 2-59).

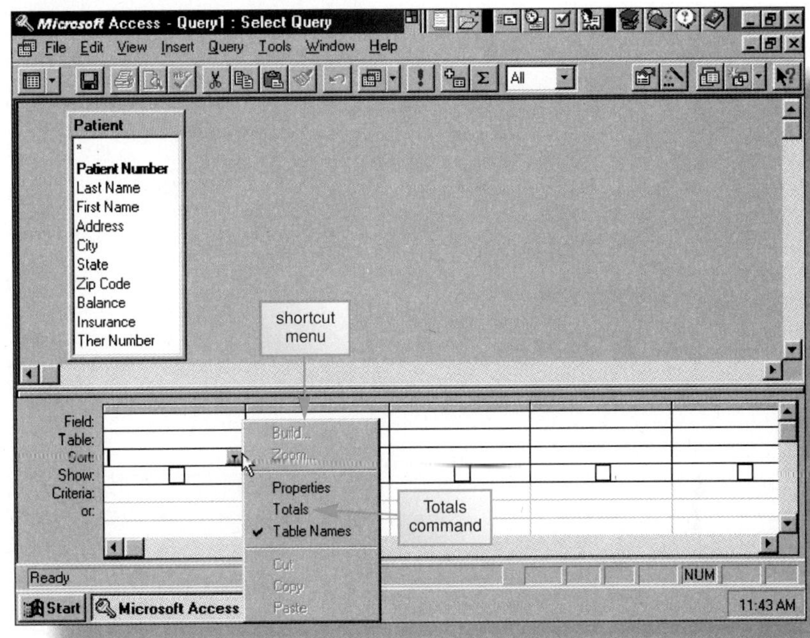

FIGURE 2-59

3 **Click Totals on the shortcut menu and then include the Balance field. Point to the Totals line for the Balance field.**

The Total row is now included in the design grid (Figure 2-60). The Balance field is included, and the entry in the Total row is Group By. The mouse pointer, which has changed shape to an I-beam, is positioned on the Total row under the Balance field.

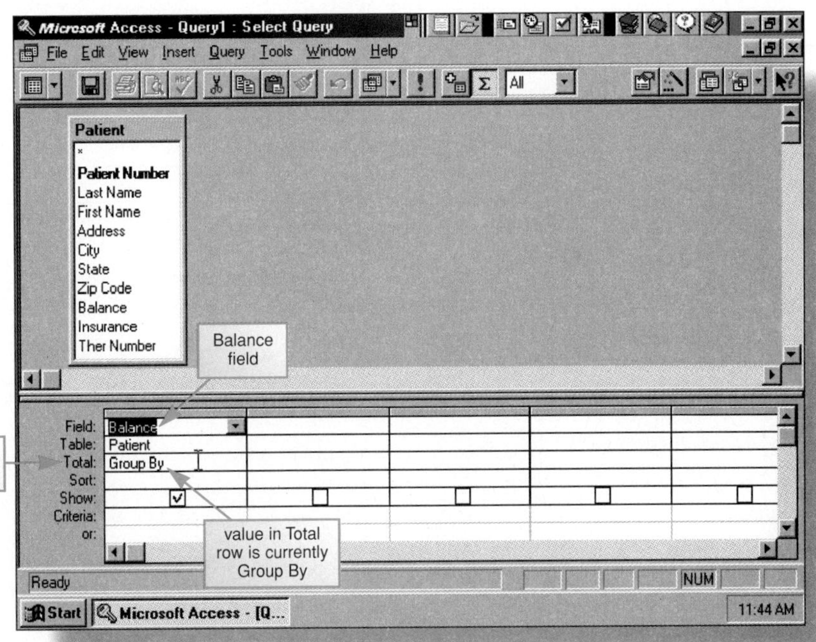

FIGURE 2-60

4 **Click the Total row under the Balance field, and then click the arrow that appears.**

The list of available selections displays (Figure 2-61).

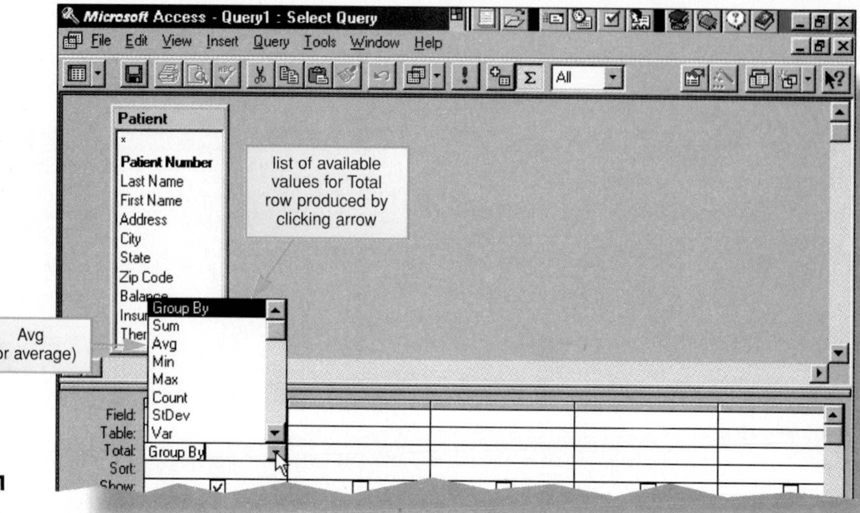

FIGURE 2-61

5 **Click Avg.**

Avg is selected (Figure 2-62).

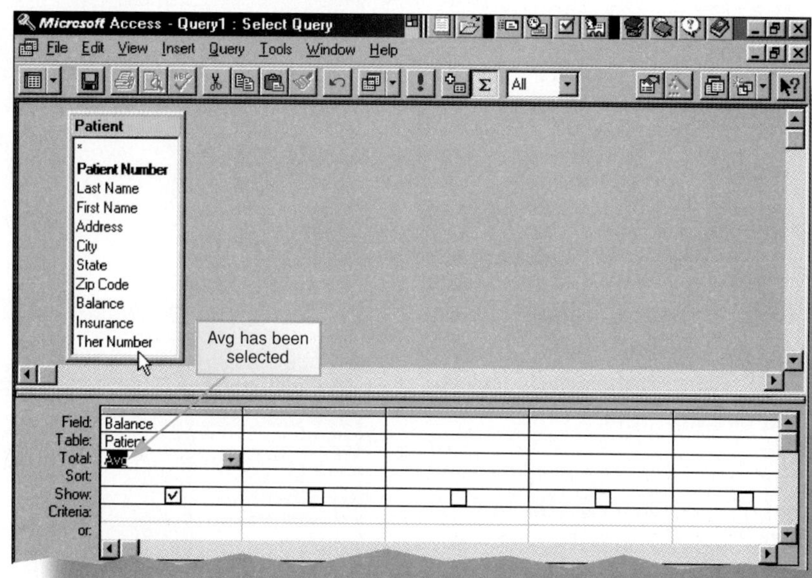

FIGURE 2-62

6 **Run the query.**

The result displays (Figure 2-63), showing the average balance for all patients.

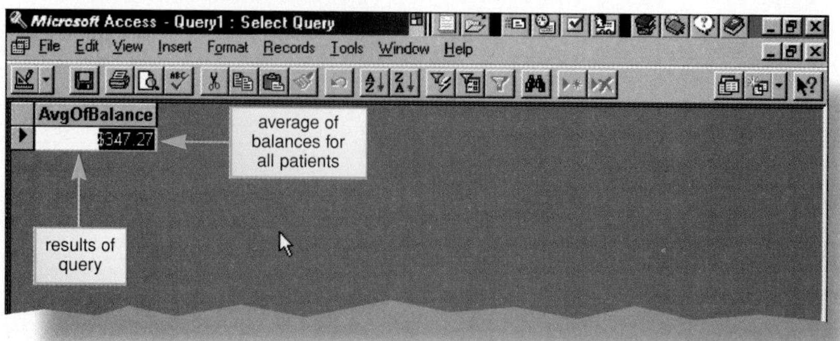

FIGURE 2-63

Other Ways

1. Click Totals button on toolbar
2. On View menu click Totals

Using Criteria in Calculating Statistics

Sometimes calculating statistics for all the records in the table is appropriate. In other cases, however, you will need to calculate the statistics for only those records that satisfy certain criteria. To enter a criterion in a field, first you select Where as the entry in the Total row for the field and then enter the criterion in the Criteria row. The following steps use this technique to calculate the average balance for patients of therapist 08.

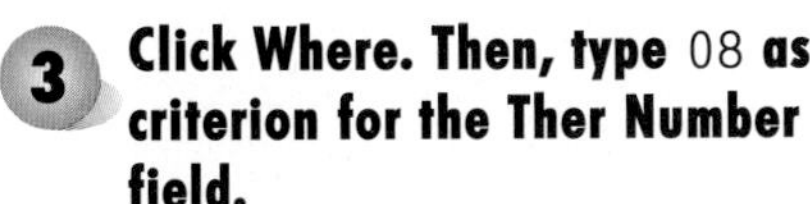

Steps To Use Criteria in Calculating Statistics

1. **Use the Query View button on the toolbar to return to the Select Query window.**

2. **Be sure totals are included in the query just as you did in the previous example. (If they are not, click the Totals button.) Include the Ther Number field in the second column of the Total row on the design grid. Next, produce the list of available options for the Total entry just as you did when you selected Avg for the Balance field. Use the vertical scroll bar to move through the options until the word, Where, displays.**

   The list of available selections displays (Figure 2-64).

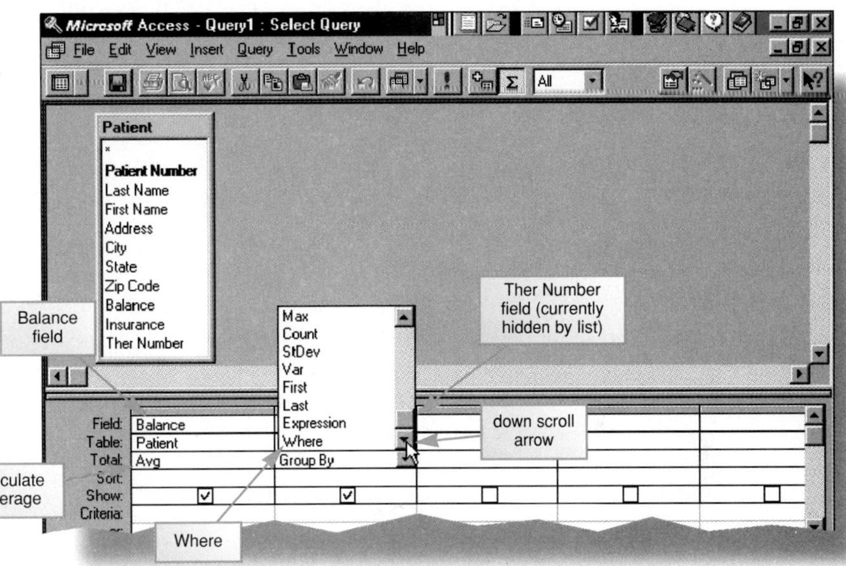

FIGURE 2-64

3. **Click Where. Then, type** 08 **as criterion for the Ther Number field.**

   Where is selected as the entry in the Total row for the Ther Number field (Figure 2-65) and 08 is entered as the Criteria.

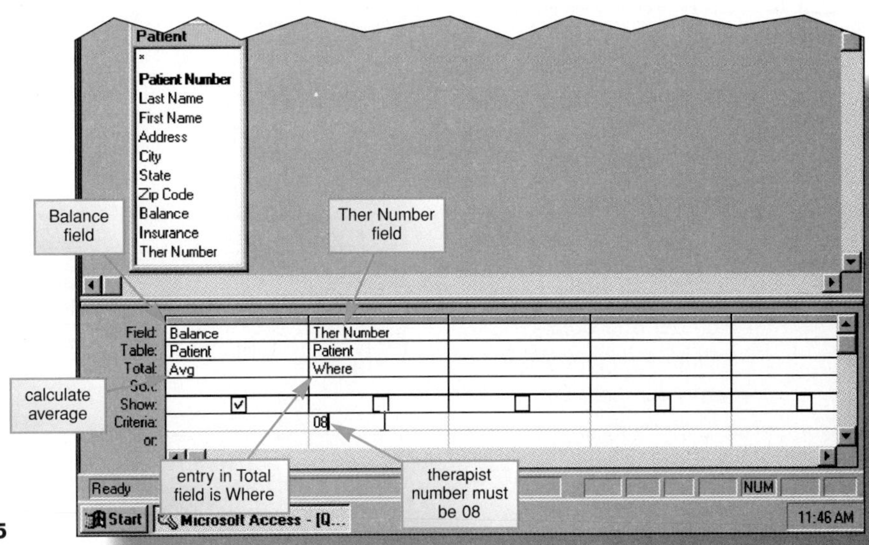

FIGURE 2-65

4 Run the query.

The result displays (Figure 2-66), giving the average balance for patients of therapist 08.

FIGURE 2-66

Grouping

Another way statistics are often used is in combination with grouping. The statistics are then calculated for groups of records. You may, for example, need to calculate the average balance for the patients of each therapist. You will want the average for the patients of therapist 05, the average for patients of therapist 08, and so on.

This type of calculation involves **grouping**, which simply means creating groups of records that share some common characteristic. In grouping by Ther Number, the patients of therapist 05 would form one group, the patients of therapist 08 would be a second, and the patients of therapist 14 form a third. The calculations are then made for each group. To indicate grouping in Access, select Group By as the entry in the Total row for the field to be used for grouping.

Perform the following steps to calculate the average balance for patients of each therapist.

Steps To Use Grouping

1 Use the Query View button on the toolbar to return to the Select Query window. On the Edit menu, click Clear Grid.

2 Include the Ther Number field. Include the Balance field, and then click Avg as the calculation.

The Ther Number and Balance fields are included (Figure 2-67). The Totals entry for the Ther Number field currently is Group By, which is correct, so it did not need to be changed.

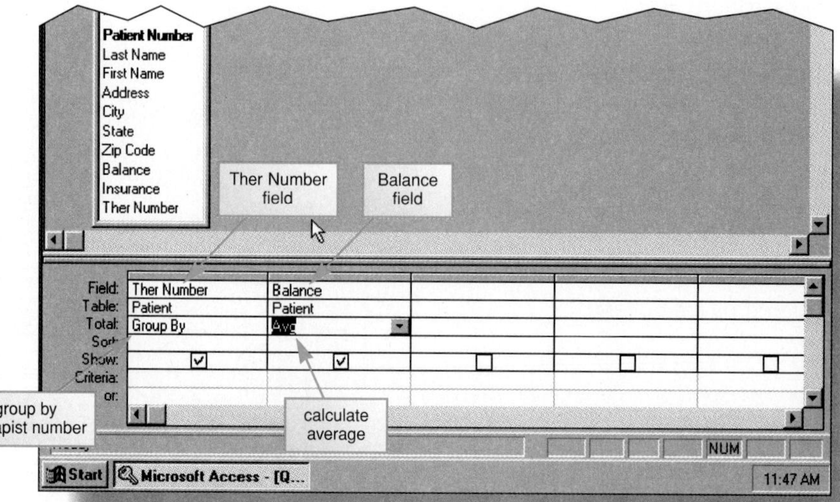

FIGURE 2-67

3 **Run the query.**

The result displays (Figure 2-68), showing each therapist's number along with the average balance of the patients of that therapist.

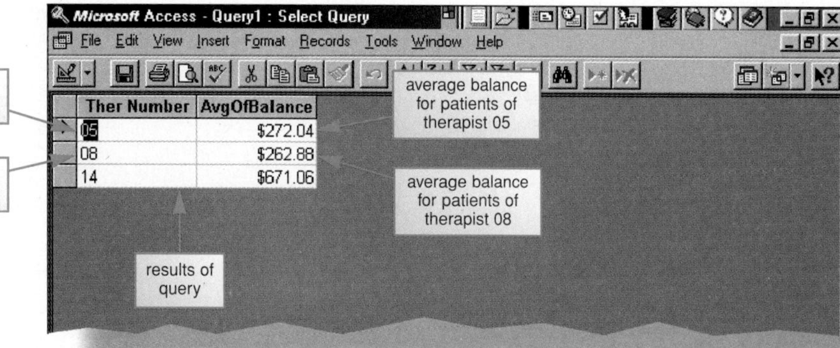

FIGURE 2-68

Saving a Query

In some cases, you will construct a query that you think you will want to use again. You can avoid having to repeat all your entries by **saving the query**. To do so, click the Save button on the toolbar after you have created the query and then assign a name to the query. The following steps illustrate the process by creating and saving a query and calling it Therapists and Patients.

More *About* Saved Queries

Saved queries can be used in forms and reports just as tables are used. To create a report or form for the query, click the Query tab, select the query, click the New Object button, and then click the appropriate command (New Report or New Form).

Steps To Save a Query

1 **Return to the Select Query screen and clear the grid. Right-click the design grid.**

The shortcut menu displays (Figure 2-69).

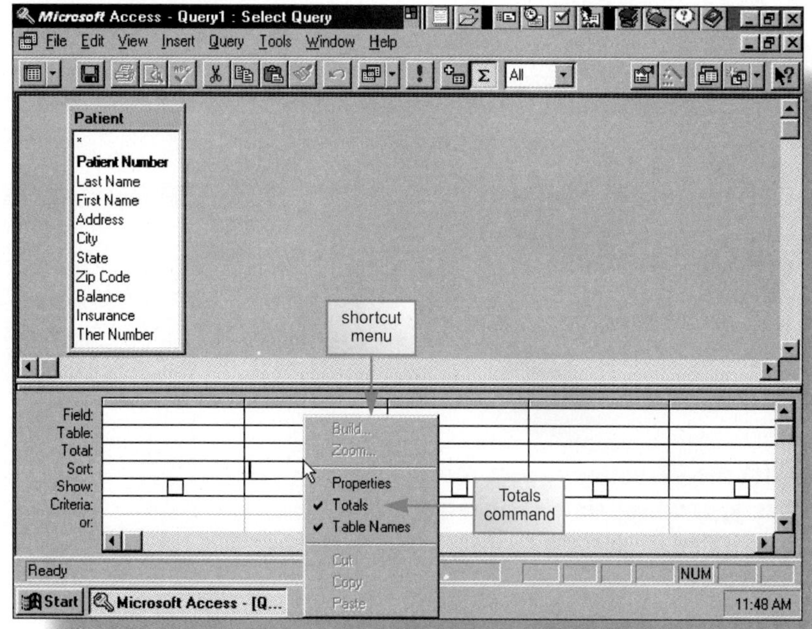

FIGURE 2-69

2 **Click Totals on the shortcut menu to remove the Total row. (It is not used in this query.) Right-click the upper pane of the Select Query window.**

The shortcut menu displays (Figure 2-70).

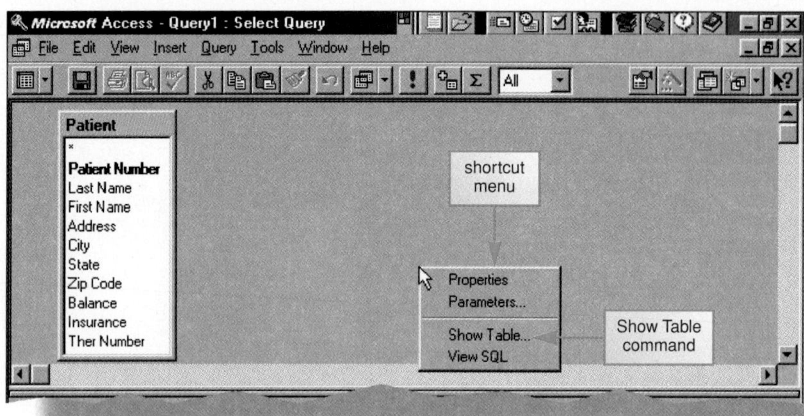

FIGURE 2-70

3 **Click Show Table on the shortcut menu. Click Therapist in the Show Table dialog box, and then click the Add button. Close the dialog box. Expand the Therapist field list so all fields display. To the query, add the Ther Number field and the Last Name field from the Therapist table; and add the Patient Number field, the Last Name field, the First Name field, and the Balance field from the Patient table. Point to the Save button on the toolbar.**

The query design is complete (Figure 2-71).

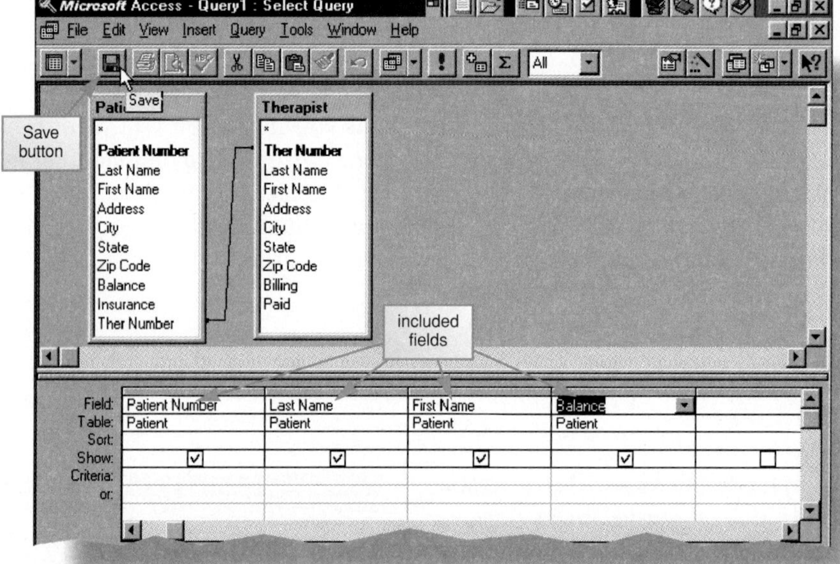

FIGURE 2-71

4 **Click the Save button and then type** `Therapists and Patients` **as the name of the query.**

The Save As dialog box displays (Figure 2-72). The name of the query has been entered.

5 **Click the OK button to save the query, and then close the query by clicking its window's Close button.**

Access saves the query and closes the Select Query window.

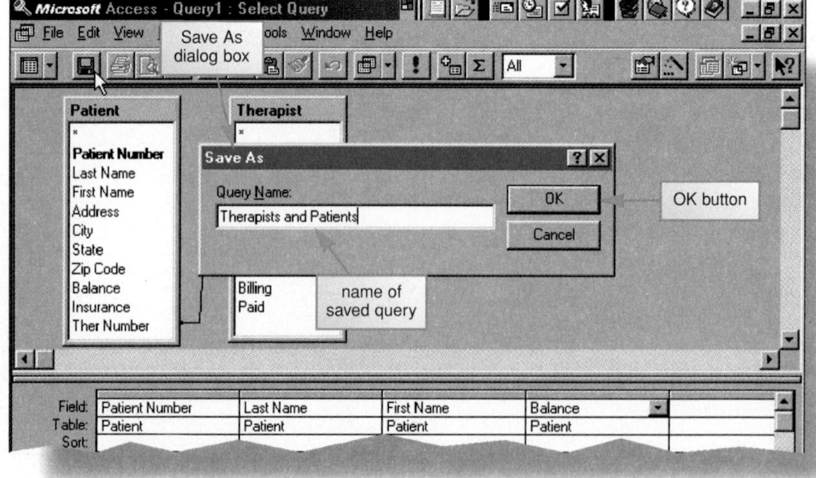

FIGURE 2-72

*Other*Ways

1. On File menu click Save As
2. Press CTRL+S

Once you have saved a query, you can use it at any time in the future by *opening* it. To open a saved query, click the Queries tab in the Database window, right-click the query, and then click Open.

The query is run against the current database. Thus, if changes have been made to the data since the last time you ran it, the results of the query may be different.

Closing the Database

The following step closes the database by closing its Database window.

TO CLOSE A DATABASE

Step 1: Click the Close button for the Mason Clinic : Database window.

Project Summary

Project 2 introduced you to querying a database using Access. You created and ran queries for Mason Clinic. You used various types of criteria in these queries. You joined tables in some of the queries. Some Mason Clinic queries used calculated fields and statistics. Finally, you saved one of the queries for future use.

What You Should Know

Having completed this project, you should now be able to perform the following tasks:

- Calculate Statistics (*A 2.39*)
- Clear a Query (*A 2.17*)
- Close a Database (*A 2.45*)
- Close the Query (*A 2.15*)
- Create a Query (*A 2.7*)
- Include All Fields in a Query (*A 2.16*)
- Include Fields in the Design Grid (*A 2.11*)
- Join Tables (*A 2.33*)
- Omit Duplicates (*A 2.30*)
- Open a Database (*A 2.7*)
- Print the Results of a Query (*A 2.13*)
- Restrict the Records in a Join (*A 2.35*)
- Return to the Select Query Window (*A 2.14*)
- Run the Query (*A 2.12*)
- Save a Query (*A 2.43*)
- Sort Data in a Query (*A 2.27*)
- Sort on Multiple Keys (*A 2.29*)
- Use a Comparison Operator in a Criterion (*A 2.23*)
- Use a Compound Criterion Involving AND (*A 2.25*)
- Use a Compound Criterion Involving OR (*A 2.26*)
- Use a Computed Field in a Query (*A 2.37*)
- Use a Number in a Criterion (*A 2.22*)
- Use a Wildcard (*A 2.20*)
- Use Criteria for a Field Not Included in the Results (*A 2.21*)
- Use Criteria in Calculating Statistics (*A 2.41*)
- Use Grouping (*A 2.42*)
- Use Text Data in a Criterion (*A 2.18*)

1 True/False

Instructions: Circle T if the statement is true or F if the statement is false.

T F 1. To include all the fields in a record in a query, click the asterisk (*) that appears in the field list.

T F 2. To create a compound criterion using OR, type the word, UNION, before the second criterion.

T F 3. To create a compound criterion using AND, enter all criteria on the same line.

T F 4. To create a criterion involving Equals, you must type the equal sign (=).

T F 5. When you enter a criteria for a particular field, that field must appear in the results of the query.

T F 6. To find all Patients whose balance is $100 or less, type <=$100.00 as the criterion for the Balance field.

T F 7. To clear all the entries in a design grid, from the Query menu, click Clear Grid.

T F 8. When you sort a query on more than one key, the major sort key must appear to the left of the minor sort key.

T F 9. To omit duplicates from a query, use the Query Properties command and specify Unique Values Only.

T F 10. The wildcard symbols available for use in a query are * and &.

2 Multiple Choice

Instructions: Circle the correct response.

1. To list only certain records in a table use a ________.
   a. list
   b. query
   c. question
   d. answer
2. To find all Patients whose balance is $100 or less, type ________ as the criteria for the Balance field.
   a. <= $100.00
   b. <=100
   c. =<$100.00
   d. =<100
3. To clear all the entries in a design grid, from the ________ menu, click Clear Grid.
   a. File
   b. Edit
   c. View
   d. Query

Test Your Knowledge

4. The wildcard symbols available for use in a query are the ________ and the ________.
   a. double period (..), asterisk (*)
   b. question mark (?), ampersand (&)
   c. double period (..), at symbol (@)
   d. question mark (?), asterisk (*)
5. Equal to (=), less than (<), and greater than (>) are examples of ________.
   a. criteria
   b. comparison operators
   c. values
   d. compound criteria
6. When two or more criteria are connected with AND or OR, the result is called a ________.
   a. compound criterion
   b. simple criterion
   c. character criterion
   d. pattern criterion
7. To add an additional table to a query, click _____ on the shortcut menu for the Select Query window.
   a. Show Table
   b. Join Table
   c. Include Table
   d. Add Table
8. Use a query to ________ tables; that is, find records in two tables that have identical values in matching fields.
   a. merge
   b. match
   c. join
   d. combine
9. To remove a table from a query, right-click any field in the field list for the table and click ________ on the shortcut menu.
   a. Delete Table
   b. Remove Table
   c. Erase Table
   d. Clear Table
10. To add a Total row to a design grid, click ________ on the shortcut menu for the Select Query window.
    a. Statistics
    b. Totals
    c. Aggregates
    d. Functions

Test Your Knowledge

3 Understanding the Select Query Window

Instructions: In Figure 2-73, arrows point to the major components of the Select Query window. Identify the various parts of the Query window in the spaces provided.

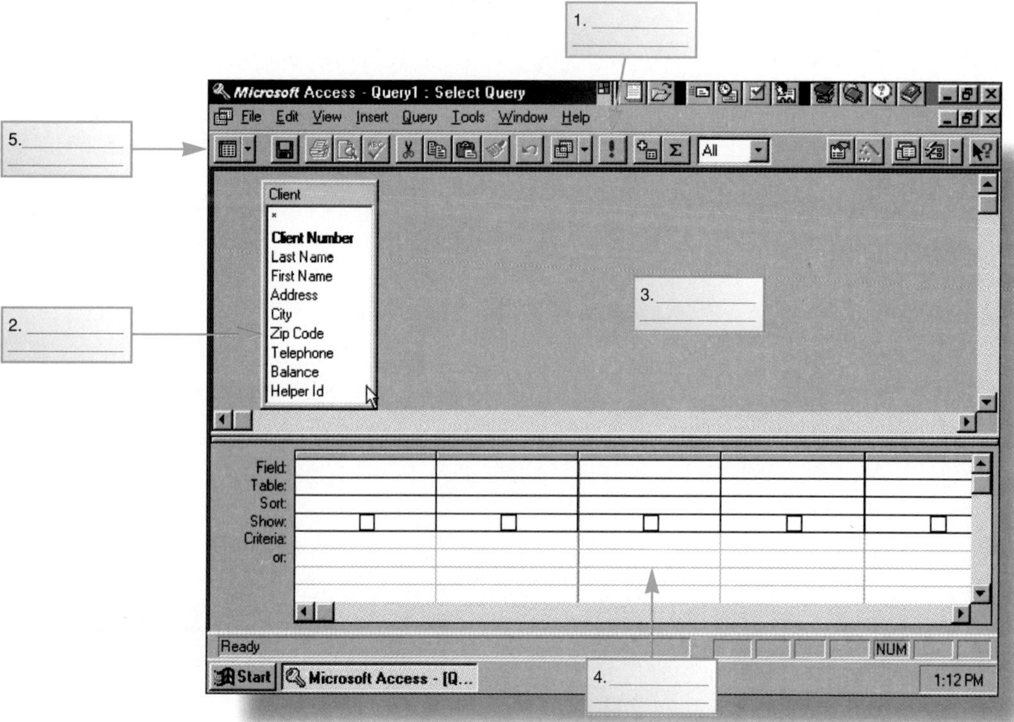

FIGURE 2-73

4 Understanding Statistics

Instructions: Figure 2-74 shows a created query using statistics for the Client table and Figure 2-75 lists the contents of the Client table. List the answer to this query in the spaces provided.

Test Your Knowledge

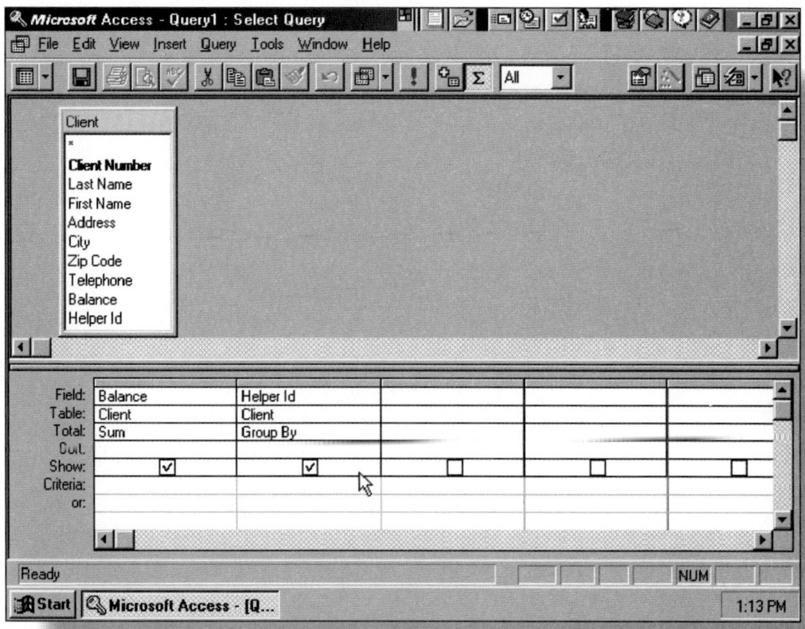

FIGURE 2-74

Data for Client Table

CLIENT NUMBER	LAST NAME	FIRST NAME	ADDRESS	CITY	ZIP CODE	TELEPHONE	BALANCE	HELPER ID
AR86	Arends	Carolyn	268 Getty	Allanson	48102	555-9523	$35.00	1001
AT24	Atwater	Shelly	542 Dune	Allanson	48103	555-1354	$0.00	1008
BI42	Bishop	Bruce	422 Robbins	Allanson	48102	555-7465	$90.00	1008
CH26	Chiang	Doi	62 Stryker	Oakdale	48101	555-2018	$0.00	1012
CH66	Chown	Douglas	266 Norton	Oakdale	48101	555-4890	$55.00	1001
JO12	Johns	Patricia	420 Robbins	Allanson	48102	555-9182	$24.00	1008
KI15	Kirk	Robert	12 Hellerman	Oakdale	48101	555-8273	$65.00	1010
MA21	Martinez	Marie	215 Glen	Allanson	48102	555-1234	$0.00	1001
MO31	Morton	Julie	557 Dune	Allanson	48103	555-5361	$78.00	1012
RO92	Robertson	Mary	345 Magee	Oakdale	48101	555-2056	$43.00	1008

FIGURE 2-75

Use Help

1 Reviewing Project Activities

Instructions: Perform the following tasks using a computer.

1. Start Access.
2. Double-click the Help button on the toolbar to display the Help Topics: Microsoft Access for Windows 95 dialog box.
3. Click the Contents tab. Double-click the Working with Queries book. Double-click the Creating a Query book. Double-click Queries: What they are and how they work.
4. Read the Help information. Use the Next button in the lower right corner of the screen to move to the next Help windows. A total of three Help windows will display. When you finish reading the Help information, click the Close button in the lower right corner of the third Help window.
5. Double-click the Help button on the toolbar to display the Help Topics: Microsoft Access for Windows 95 dialog box. Click the Index tab. Type `sort` in box 1, and then double-click sorting records in queries in box 2. When the Help information displays, read it. Next, right-click within the box, and then click Print Topic. Hand in the printout to your instructor. Click the Help Topics button to return to the Help Topics: Microsoft Access for Windows 95 dialog box.
6. Click the Find tab. Type `wildcard` in box 1. Double-click Criteria expressions that use wildcard characters in box 3. When the Help information displays, read it, ready the printer, right-click, and click Print Topic. Hand in the printout to your instructor. Click the Help Topics button to return to the Help Topics: Microsoft Access for Windows 95 dialog box.
7. Click the Answer Wizard tab. Type `how do i add calculated fields to a query` in box 1. Click the Search button. Double-click Create a calculated field for custom calculations in a query in box 2 under How Do I. Read and print the Help information. Hand in the printout to your instructor.

Use Help

2 Expanding on the Basics

Instructions: Use Access online Help to better understand the topics listed below. Begin each of the following by double-clicking the Help button on the toolbar. If you cannot print the Help information, then answer the question on your own paper.

1. Using the Working with Queries book on the Contents sheet in the Help Topics: Microsoft Access for Windows 95 dialog box, answer the following questions:
   a. How do you insert a field between other fields in the design grid of a query?
   b. How do you remove a field from the design grid?
   c. How do you change a field name in a query?
   d. When you use the asterisk (*) to select all fields, how do you specify criteria for fields?
   e. How do you insert a Criteria row in the design grid?
2. Using the key term *format* and the Index tab in the Help Topics: Microsoft Access for Windows 95 dialog box, display and print information on formatting data in a query's results. Then, answer the following questions:
   a. How can you display a field's property sheet using the menu bar?
   b. How do the Regional Settings on the Windows Control Panel affect the formats in a query?
3. Use the Find tab in the Help Topics: Microsoft Access for Windows 95 dialog box to display and then print information about using criteria to retrieve certain records. Then answer the following questions:
   a. How do you enter criteria to OR two values in one field?
   b. How do you enter criteria to AND two values in one field?
   c. How do you enter criteria to OR and AND in three fields?
4. Use the Answer Wizard in the Help Topics: Microsoft Access for Windows 95 dialog box to display and print information on searching for a range of values.

Apply Your Knowledge

1 Querying the Extra Hands Database

Instructions: Start Access. Open the Extra Hands database from the Access folder on the Student Floppy Disk that accompanies this book. Perform the following tasks:

1. Create a new query for the Client table.
2. Add the Client Number, Last Name, First Name, and Balance fields to the design grid as shown in Figure 2-76.
3. Restrict retrieval to only those records where the balance is greater than $50.00.
4. Run the query and print the results.
5. Return to the Select Query window and clear the grid.
6. Add the Client Number, Last Name, First Name, City, Balance, and Helper Id fields to the design grid.
7. Restrict retrieval to only those records where the Helper Id is either 1010 or 1012.
8. Sort the records in order by Balance (descending) within City (ascending).
9. Run the query and print the results.
10. Return to the Select Query window and clear the grid.
11. Join the Client and Helper tables. Add the Client Number, Last Name, First Name, and Helper Id fields from the Client table and the Last Name field from the Helper table.
12. Sort the records in ascending order by Helper Id.
13. Run the query and print the results.

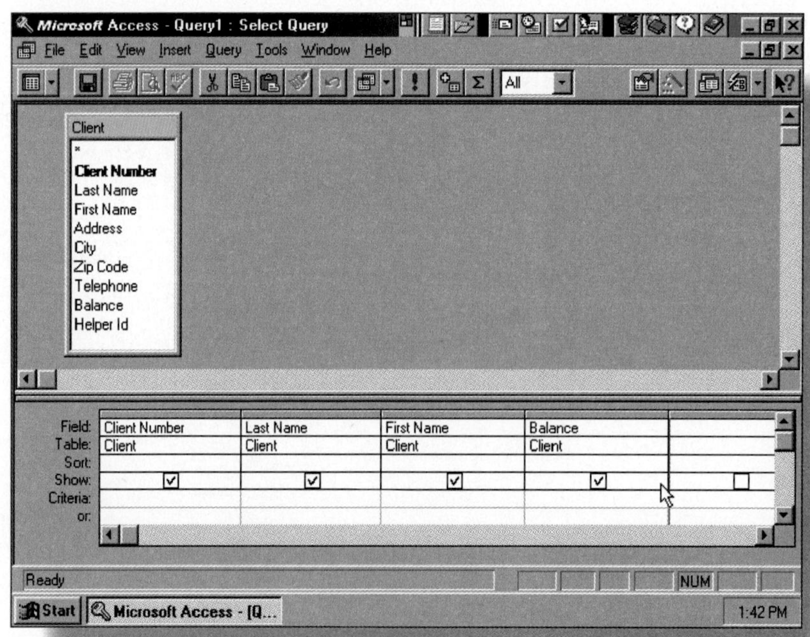

FIGURE 2-76

In the Lab

1 Querying the Symphony Shop Database

Problem: The Symphony Shop volunteers have determined a number of questions they want the database management system to answer. You must obtain answers to the questions posed by the volunteers.

Instructions: Use the database created in the In the Lab 1 of Project 1 for this assignment. Perform the following tasks:

1. Open the Symphony Shop database and create a new query for the Novelty table.
2. Display and print the Novelty Id, Description, and Selling Price for all records in the table as shown in Figure 2-77 on the next page.
3. Display all fields and print all the records in the table.
4. Display and print the Novelty Id, Description, Cost and Dist Code for all novelties where the Dist Code is MM
5. Display and print the Novelty Id and Description for all novelties where the Description begins with the letters, Pe.
6. Display and print the Novelty Id, Description, and Dist Code for all novelties that cost more than $3.00.
7. Display and print the Novelty Id and Description for all novelties that have a Selling Price of $1.00 or less.
8. Display and print all fields for those novelties that cost more than $3.00 and where the number of units on hand is less than 10.
9. Display and print all fields for those novelties that have a Dist Code of AD or have a Selling Price greater than $4.00.
10. Join the Novelty table and the Distributor table. Display the Novelty Id, Description, Cost, Name, and Telephone fields. Run the query and print the results.
11. Restrict the records retrieved in task 10 above to only those novelties where the number of units on hand is less than 10. Display and print the results.
12. Remove the Distributor table and clear the design grid.
13. Include the Novelty Id and Description in the design grid. Compute the on-hand value (units on hand * cost) for all records in the table. Display and print the results.
14. Display and print the average selling price of all novelties.
15. Display and print the average selling price of novelties grouped by Dist Code.
16. Join the Novelty and Distributor tables. Include the Dist Code and Name fields from the Distributor table. Include the Novelty Id, Description, Cost, and Units On Hand fields from the Novelty table. Save the query as Distributors and Novelties.

(continued)

Querying the Symphony Shop Database *(continued)*

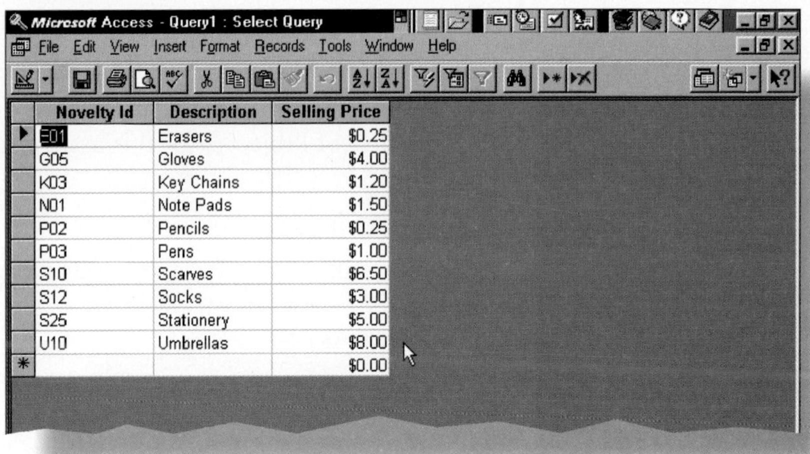

FIGURE 2-77

2 Querying the College Telephone System Database

Problem: The telephone manager has determined a number of questions that she wants the database management system to answer. You must obtain answers to the questions posed by the telephone manager.

Instructions: Use the database created in the In the Lab 2 of Project 1 for this assignment. Perform the following tasks:

1. Open the College Telephone System database and create a new query for the User table.
2. Display and print the User Id, Last Name, First Name, Phone Ext, and Office for all the records in the table as shown in Figure 2-78.
3. Display all fields and print all the records in the table.
4. Display and print the User Id, First Name, Last Name, Basic Charge, and Extra Charges for all users in the department with the code of MTH.
5. Display and print the User Id, First Name, Last Name, and Office of all users whose office is located in the ABH building.
6. Display and print the User Id, First Name, Last Name, and Phone Ext for all users whose basic charge is $15.00 per month.
7. Display and print the User Id, First Name, Last Name, and Extra Charges for all users in the department with a code BIO who have Extra Charges greater than $40.00. List the records in descending order by Extra Charges.
8. Display and print the User Id, First Name, Last Name, and Extra Charges for all users who have extra charges greater than $50.00 and are in either the Mathematics (MTH) or Biology (BIO) department. (Hint: Use information from Use Help Exercise 2 to solve this problem.)

9. Display and print the Basic Charge in ascending order. List each Basic Charge only once.
10. Join the User table and the Department table. Display and print the User Id, Last Name, First Name, Basic Charge, Extra Charges, Name of the department, and Location of the department.
11. Restrict the records retrieved in task 10 above to only those users who have extra charges greater than $20.00.
12. Remove the Department table and clear the design grid.
13. Include the User Id, First Name, Last Name, Basic Charge, and Extra Charges in the design grid. Compute the total bill for each user (Basic Charge + Extra Charges). Display and print the results.
14. Display and print the average extra charges.
15. Display and print the highest extra charge.
16. Display and print the average extra charges for each department.
17. Join the User and Department tables. Include the department Name, Location, User Id, Last Name, First Name, Phone Ext, Basic Charge, and Extra Charges. Save the query as Departments and Users.

Microsoft Access - Query1 : Select Query

File Edit View Insert Format Records Tools Window Help

User Id	Last Name	First Name	Phone Ext	Office
T1290	Chou	Tanya	2383	112ABH
T2389	Cookson	Christin	2495	120EMH
T3487	Hoveman	Benjamin	3267	223SHH
T4521	Janson	Catherine	2156	244ABH
T5364	Keatty	Richard	2578	116ABH
T6457	Medlar	Michelle	3445	212SHH
T6503	Myrich	Bruce	2038	132ABH
T7579	Nadzia	Rodean	2068	268SHH
T7654	Rabon	Claudia	2239	268ABH
T7890	Richardson	Maria	2418	122EMH
T8521	Sanchez	Javier	2134	248ABH
T8883	TenHoopen	Adrian	2414	134EMH

FIGURE 2-78

3 Querying the WWWW Radio Station Database

Problem: The manager of the radio station has determined a number of questions that he wants the database management system to answer. You must obtain answers to the questions posed by the radio station manager.

Instructions: Use the database created in the In the Lab 3 of Project 1 for this assignment. Perform the following tasks:

1. Open the WWWW Radio Station database and create a new query for the Accounts table.
2. Display and print the Account Number, Name, Balance, and Amount Paid for all the records in the table as shown in Figure 2-79 on the next page.

(continued)

Querying the WWWW Radio Station Database *(continued)*

3. Display and print the Account Number, Name, and Balance for all accounts where the Acc Rep Number is 18.
4. Display and print the Account Number, Name, and Balance for all accounts where the balance is greater than $100.00.
5. Display and print the Account Number, Name, and Amount Paid for all accounts where the Acc Rep Number is 15 and the Amount Paid is greater than $500.00.
6. Display and print the Account Number and Name of all accounts where the Name begins with B.
7. Display and print the Account Number, Name and Balance for all accounts where the Acc Rep Number is 18 or the Balance is less than $100.00.
8. Include the Account Number, Name, City, and State in the design grid. Sort the records in ascending order by City within State. Display and print the results. The City field should display in the result to the left of the State field. (Hint: Use information from Use Help Exercise 1.)
9. Display and print the cities in ascending order. Each city should display only once.
10. Join the Accounts table and the Account Reps table. Display and print the Account Number, Name, Balance, and Amount Paid from the Accounts table and the First Name, Last Name, and Comm Rate from the Account Reps table.
11. Restrict the records retrieved in task 10 above to only those accounts that are in NJ. Display and print the results.
12. Clear the design grid and add the Last Name, First Name, and Comm Rate from the Account Reps table to the grid. Add Amount Paid from the Accounts table. Compute the Commission (Amount Paid * Comm Rate) for the Account Rep. Sort the records in ascending order by Last Name and format Commission as currency. (Hint: Use information from Use Help Exercise 2 to solve this problem.)
13. Remove the Account Reps table and clear the design grid.
14. Display and print the total of all balances and amounts paid.
15. Display and print the total of all balances for Acc Rep Number 15.
16. Display and print the average amount paid by Acc Rep Number.
17. Join the Accounts and Account Reps tables. Display and print the Acc Rep Number, Last Name, Account Number, Name, Balance, and Amount Paid. Save the query as Account Reps and Accounts.

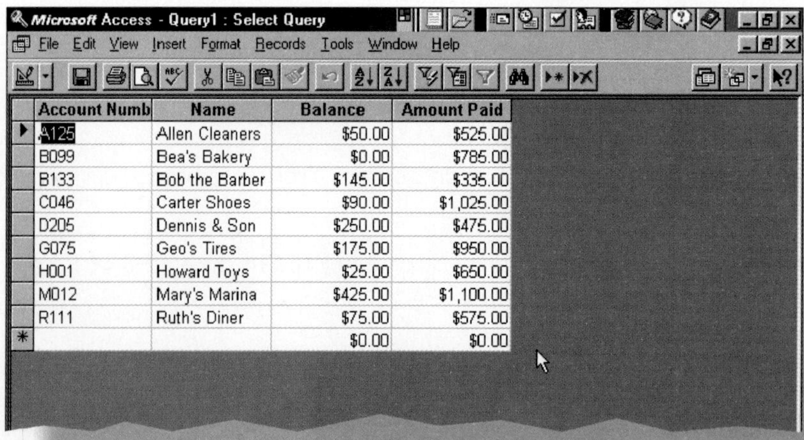

Account Numb	Name	Balance	Amount Paid
A125	Allen Cleaners	$50.00	$525.00
B099	Bea's Bakery	$0.00	$785.00
B133	Bob the Barber	$145.00	$335.00
C046	Carter Shoes	$90.00	$1,025.00
D205	Dennis & Son	$250.00	$475.00
G075	Geo's Tires	$175.00	$950.00
H001	Howard Toys	$25.00	$650.00
M012	Mary's Marina	$425.00	$1,100.00
R111	Ruth's Diner	$75.00	$575.00
*		$0.00	$0.00

FIGURE 2-79

Cases and Places

The difficulty of these case studies varies:

◗ Case studies preceded by a single half moon are the least difficult. You are asked to create the required database based on information that has already been placed in an organized form.
◗◗ Case studies preceded by two half moons are more difficult. You must organize the information presented before using it to create the desired database.
◗◗◗ Case studies preceded by three half moons are the most difficult. You must choose a specific topic, and then obtain and organize the necessary information before using it to create the required database.

1 ◗ Use the restaurant database created in Case Study 1 of Project 1 for this assignment. Perform the following: (a) It is 10:30 p.m. and you have a craving for a pizza. Display and print the names and phone numbers of all Italian restaurants open that will deliver your order. (b) You are cramming for an exam at 2:00 a.m. and would settle for any type of food. Display and print the names, phone numbers, addresses, and closing times of all restaurants that are open. (c) Your last class on Wednesday ends at 3:50 p.m., and you want to pick up some food to take home to eat before you leave for work. Display and print the names, addresses, and opening times of all restaurants that open before 5:00 p.m. (d) Payday is Friday and you are short on cash at midweek. Display and print the names, addresses, phone numbers, and food types of all restaurants that have specials on Wednesday or Thursday. (e) You and a friend decide to meet for lunch. Display and print the names, addresses, phone numbers, and opening times of all restaurants that open before noon.

2 ◗ Use the textbook database created in Case Study 2 of Project 1 for this assignment. Perform the following: (a) You receive a call asking if anyone is selling a book for Eng 101. Display and print the sellers' names and phone numbers and their asking prices for books available for that course. (b) Karen Sim asks you which books she has submitted. Display and print the titles, authors, and courses of her books. (c) Several nursing students call to ask which textbooks from that department are available. Display and print the titles, authors, and courses of the nursing books. (d) Display and print the titles, authors, and prices of books listed for less than $20. (e) Display and print the titles and course numbers for books in excellent condition.

3 ◗◗ The American Heart Association recommends a maximum of two, three-ounce cooked servings of lean meat, or six ounces total daily. A three-ounce serving is the size of a woman's palm. Use the nutritional content database created in Case Study 3 of Project 1 for this assignment. Perform the following: (a) Display and print the cuts of beef with less than 70 milligrams of cholesterol in one, three-ounce serving. (b) Display and print the cuts of beef with more than 160 calories in a three-ounce serving. (c) Your nutritionist has told you to consume less than 20 grams of fat daily. During the day you have eaten food with a total fat gram content of 15. Display and print the cuts of beef that would be within the nutritionist's advice.

Cases and Places

4 ▶▶ Use the movie collection database created in Case Study 4 of Project 1 for this assignment. Perform the following: (a) Display and print the movie titles in ascending order, along with the two actors and year produced. (b) You have less than two hours to watch a movie tonight. Display and print the movie titles and running times that would fit this time constraint. (c) Display and print the movie titles starring John Wayne. (d) Display and print the movie titles starring Eva Marie Saint. (e) You are in the mood for a comedy. Display and print the movies starring Abbott and Costello. (f) Display and print the movie titles and leading actors of films rated more than two stars. (g) Display and print the movies produced before you were born.

5 ▶▶▶ Use the financial institutions database created in Case Study 5 of Project 1 for this assignment. Display and print the following: (a) The names of the financial institutions and total values of the IRAs at age 65 in descending order. (b) The names and phone numbers of the financial institutions and total amounts of interest earned at age 65 in descending order. (c) The average value of the IRAs at age 65. (d) The average interest rates for the banks, savings and loans, and credit unions. (e) The name, address, and interest rate of the financial institution with the highest interest rate. (f) The name, phone number, and interest rate of the financial institution with the lowest interest rate. (g) The names of the financial institutions and penalties for early withdrawal in two years in ascending order. (h) The names of the financial institutions and annual fees in descending order.

6 ▶▶▶ Use the campus directory database created in Case Study 6 of Project 1 for this assignment. Display and print the following: (a) The names of your instructors in ascending order, along with their phone numbers and room numbers. (b) The names of the administrators in ascending order, along with their phone numbers and room numbers. (c) The services in ascending order, including phone numbers and room numbers.

7 ▶▶▶ Use the product comparison database created in Case Study 7 of Project 1 for this assignment. Display and print the following: (a) The five specific items in ascending order, along with sizes and prices for the dairy items at the convenience, grocery, and discount stores. (b) The five specific items in ascending order, along with sizes and prices for the snack items at the convenience, grocery, and discount stores. (c) The five specific items in ascending order, along with sizes and prices for the cosmetics/toiletries items at the convenience, grocery, and discount stores. (d) The five specific items in ascending order, along with sizes and prices for the kitchen supplies items at the convenience, grocery, and discount stores.

Microsoft *Access 7*

Windows 95

Maintaining a Database Using the Design and Update Features of Access

Objectives:

You will have mastered the material in this project when you can:

- Add records to a table
- Locate records
- Change the contents of records in a table
- Delete records from a table
- Restructure a table
- Change field characteristics
- Add a field
- Save the changes to the structure
- Update the contents of a single field
- Make changes to groups of records
- Delete groups of records
- Specify a required field
- Specify a range
- Specify a default value
- Specify legal values
- Specify a format
- Update a table with validation rules
- Specify referential integrity
- Order records
- Create single-field and multiple-field indexes

Computer-Aided Dispatch System Makes Responding to EMERGENCIES a Real Gas

In its pure state, natural gas is odorless, colorless, and tasteless. To help keep their customers safe, natural gas utility companies add a distinctive odor that alerts customers to the presence of this gas. If this smell is present around a gas furnace, water heater, or other natural gas appliance, it is important to call the local gas utility company right away for help.

That is where Northern Illinois Gas's computer-aided dispatching system comes in.

No matter where the resident is calling from in the utility's 17,000 square mile territory, the call is received by a centralized customer service center. A customer service representative at the center queries a database containing hundreds of pieces of data for each of the 1.8 million residential, commercial, and industrial customers. The representative can locate this customer information by entering the customer's name, address, account number, or gas meter number on a computer.

MOTOROLA MOBILE WORKSTATION 9100-38

The representative then asks the customer what work needs to be done, enters this information in a field on the screen, and transmits the updated record back to the database. If the customer service representative makes a service request, it is forwarded to the computer-aided dispatching system. The service request record generated by the system contains data such as trouble codes (for example, the customer smells gas or needs a meter changed), times when the customer plans to be home, and whether the customer has a dog, as well as information about the type of service required.

In a non-emergency situation, the service request is saved in the database and assigned to a mechanic at a later time. In an emergency, however, the call immediately is assigned to a dispatcher. The dispatcher can ask the system to analyze the address of the emergency and identify which mechanics are in the area. At all times, the system knows where each mechanic is working, the type of work being done, and when the job was started. This information is obtained from radio signals transmitted to and from the dispatch center and small computer terminals mounted in more than 260 mechanics' and supervisors' vehicles. The terminals include a small screen, a full keyboard, and 10 megabytes of memory.

The system recommends up to eight mechanics who can be assigned to the order. The dispatcher chooses one of the recommended people and transmits the work order to that mechanic's truck. There, the screen displays a message stating an emergency has been assigned to that worker. The worker pushes a button on the terminal to transmit a signal back to the dispatching center to acknowledge receiving the emergency service request.

The system monitors the status of the order and continually updates, or maintains, the database. If the dispatcher does not assign the work order in a designated amount of time, a warning is displayed. If the mechanic assigned the order does not respond to the request, the dispatcher is notified and may reassign the job. The system records when the mechanic is en route to, working on, and finished with the job. Thus, the customer's record contains a complete picture of the job from start to finish.

Northern Illinois Gas's computer-aided dispatch system eliminates an estimated 700,000 pieces of paper per year, with each sheet representing one customer order. If it fails, however, the computer instantaneously switches to the former paper system, using 5-by-8-inch work order sheets and dispatchers giving orders using two-way radios.

When you smell gas at three o' clock in the morning, it is comforting to know that a utility company has developed a system to respond to your emergency in record time.

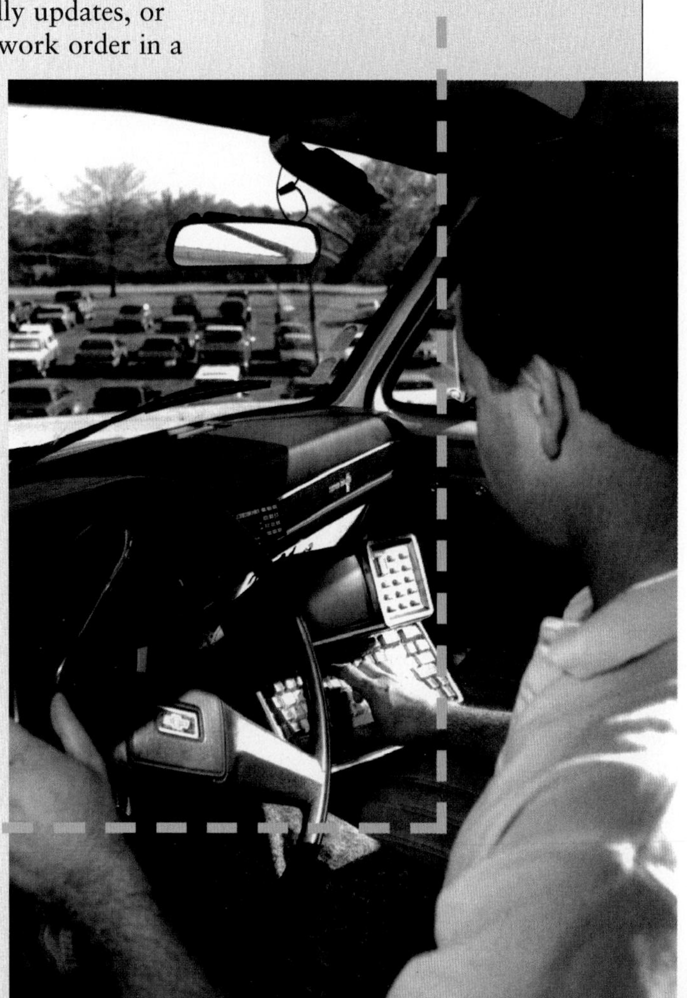

Microsoft
Access 7
Windows 95

Maintaining a Database Using the Design and Update Features of Access

Case Perspective

Mason Clinic has created a database and loaded it with patient and therapist data. The management and staff have received many benefits from the database, including the capability to ask a variety of questions concerning the data in the database. They now face the task of keeping the database up to date. They must add new records as they take on new patients and therapists. They must make changes to existing records to reflect additional charges, payments, change of addresses, and so on. Mason Clinic management also found that they needed to change the structure of the database in two specific ways. The clinic decided the database needed to include the type of insurance carrier that each patient has. They found the Last Name field was too short to contain the name of one of the patients. They also determined that they needed to improve the efficiency of certain types of database processing and found that to do so, they needed to create indexes, which are similar to indexes found in the back of books.

Introduction

Once a database has been created and loaded with data, it must be maintained. **Maintaining the database** means modifying the data to keep it up to date, such as adding new records, changing the data for existing records, and deleting records. **Updating** can include mass updates or deletions; that is, updates to, or deletions of, many records at the same time.

In addition to adding, changing, and deleting records, maintenance of a database can periodically involve the need to **restructure** the database; that is, to change the database structure. This can include adding new fields to a table, changing the characteristics of existing fields, and removing existing fields. It can also involve the creation of **indexes**, which are similar to indexes found in the back of books and which are used to improve the efficiency of certain operations.

Figure 3-1 summarizes some of the various types of activities involved in maintaining a database.

Project Three – Mason Clinic

You are to make the changes to the data in the Mason Clinic database as requested by the management of Mason Clinic. You must also restructure the database to meet the current needs of the clinic. This includes adding an additional field as well as increasing the width of one of the existing fields. You must also modify the structure of the database in a way that prevents users from entering invalid data. Finally, management is concerned that some operations, for example, those involving sorting the data, seem to be taking a little longer than they would like. You are to create indexes to attempt to address this problem.

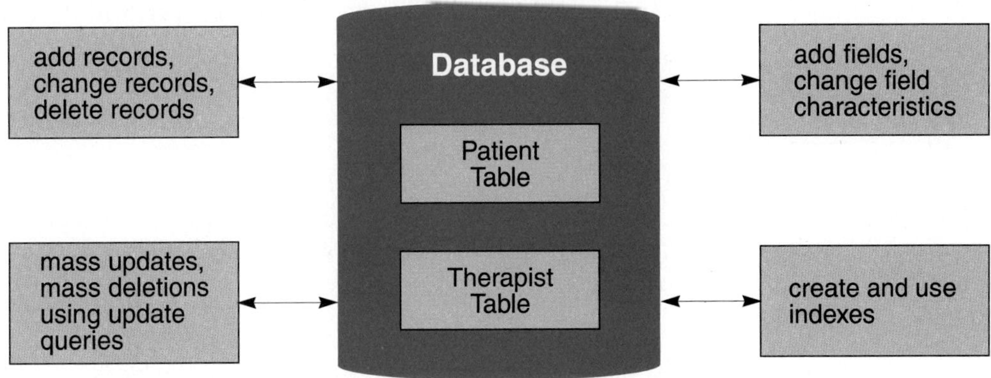

FIGURE 3-1

Overview of Project Steps

These steps give you an overview of how the Mason Clinic database will be maintained in this project. The following tasks will be completed in this project.

1. Start Access and open the Mason Clinic database.
2. Use a form to add a new record to the Patient table.
3. Locate the record for patient PE33 and then change the last name of the patient.
4. Delete the record for patient JG22.
5. Increase the width of the Last Name field to accommodate a patient name that will not fit in the current structure.
6. Add a field for insurance carrier (called Ins Carrier) to the Patient table.
7. Change the name of patient DI32 (the one that previously would not fit).
8. Resize the columns in Datasheet view.
9. Use an update query to initially set all the values in the Ins Carrier field to ORG, the most common carrier type.

10. Use a delete query to delete all patients in Zip Code 45621.
11. Create a validation rule to make the Last Name field a required field.
12. Create a validation rule to ensure that only values between $0.00 and $2,000.00 may be entered in the Balance field.
13. Specify that ORG is to be the default value for the Ins Carrier field.
14. Create a validation rule to ensure that only the values of ORG, GVT, or PRS may be entered in the Ins Carrier field.
15. Specify that any letters entered in the Patient Number field are to be converted automatically to uppercase.
16. Specify referential integrity between the Patient and Therapist tables.
17. Use the Sort buttons to sort records in the database.
18. Create and use indexes to improve performance.

Opening the Database

Before creating queries, first you must open the database. To do so, perform the following steps.

TO OPEN A DATABASE

Step 1: Click the Start button.
Step 2: Click Open Office Document, and then click 3½ Floppy [A:] in the Look in drop-down list box. If it is not already selected, click the Mason Clinic database name.
Step 3: Click the Open button.

The database is open and the Mason Clinic : Database window displays.

Adding, Changing, and Deleting

Keeping the data in a database up to date requires three tasks: adding new records, changing the data in existing records, and deleting existing records.

Adding Records

In Project 1, you added records to a database using Datasheet view; that is, as you were adding records, the records were displayed on the screen in the form of a datasheet, or table. When you need to add additional records, you can use the same techniques.

In Project 1, you used a form to view records. This is called **Form view**. You can also use Form view to update the data in a table. You can add new records, change existing records, or delete records. To do so, use the same techniques you used in Datasheet view. To add a record to the Patient table with a form, for example, use the following steps. These steps use the Patient form you created in Project 1.

Steps To Use a Form to Add Records

1 **With the Mason Clinic database open, point to the Forms tab (Figure 3-2).**

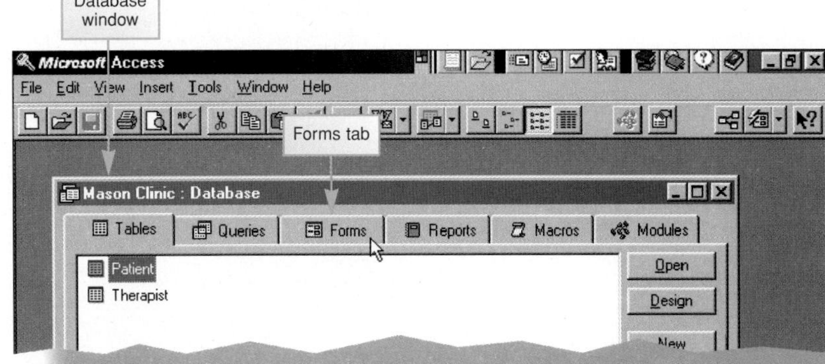

FIGURE 3-2

2 **Click the Forms tab. Right-click Patient.**

The shortcut menu displays (Figure 3-3).

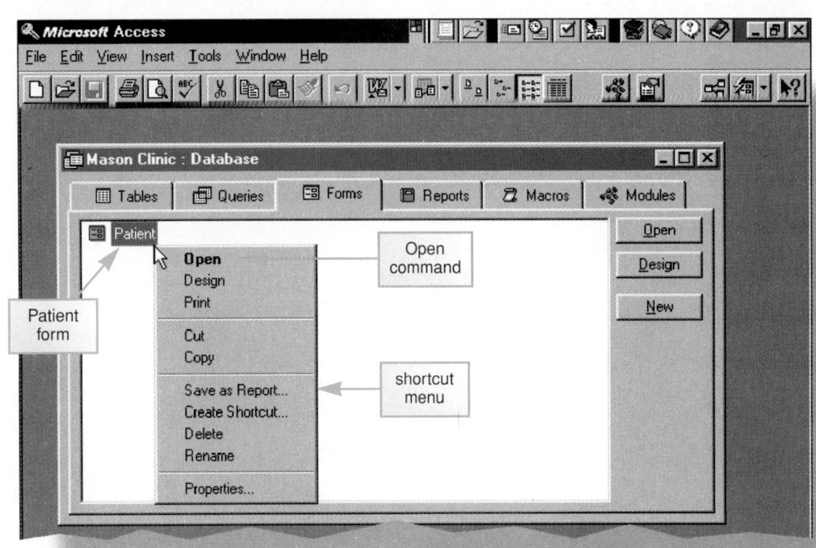

FIGURE 3-3

3 **Click Open.**

The form for the Patient table displays (Figure 3-4).

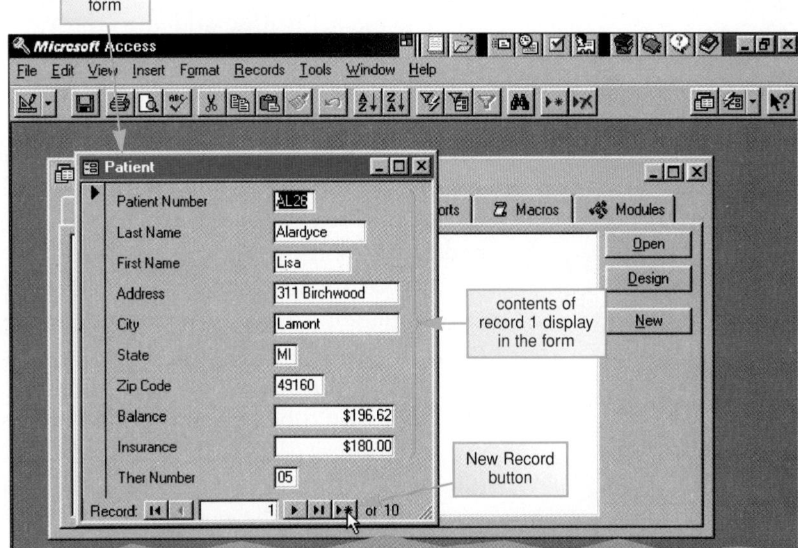

FIGURE 3-4

4 **Click the New Record button.**

The contents of the form are erased in preparation for a new record (Figure 3-5).

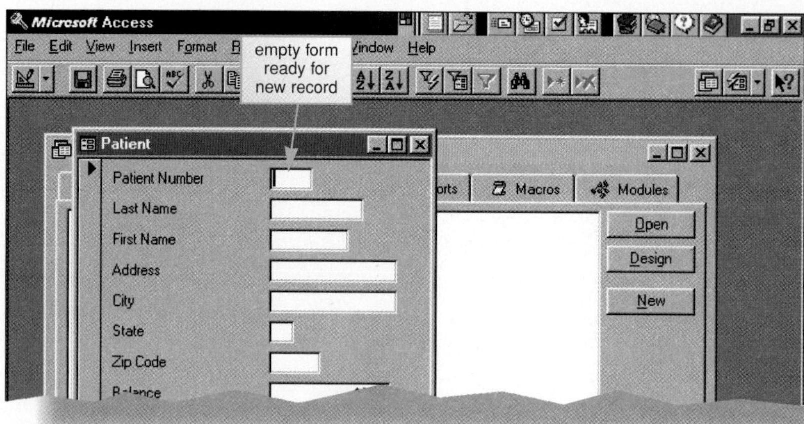

FIGURE 3-5

5 **Type the data for the new record as shown in Figure 3-6. Press the TAB key after typing the data in each field. Once you press the TAB key after typing the final field (Ther Number), the record will be added and the contents of the form erased.**

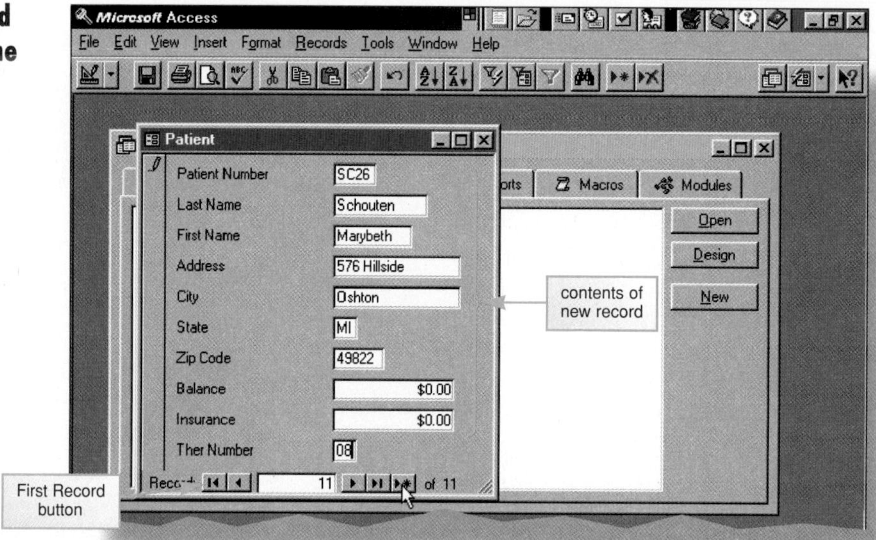

FIGURE 3-6

OtherWays

1. Click Forms tab, click form object, click Open button
2. Click Forms tab, double-click form object

The record is now added to the Patient table.

More About Searching for a Record

In searching for a record, clicking the Find First button will change the position to the first record that satisfies the condition, regardless of the current position in the table. Clicking the Find Next button will start the search at the current position.

Searching for a Record

In the database environment, **searching** means looking for records that satisfy some criteria. Looking for all the patients whose therapist number is 05 is an example of searching. The queries in Project 2 were examples of searching. Access had to locate those records that satisfied the criteria.

A need for searching also exists when using Form view or Datasheet view. To update patient PE33, for example, first you need to find the patient. In a small table, repeatedly pressing the Next Record button until patient PE33 is on the screen may not be particularly difficult. In a large table with many records, however, this would be extremely cumbersome. You need a way to be able to go directly to a record just by giving the value in some field. This is the function of the Find button. Prior to clicking the Find button, select the field for the search.

Perform the following steps to move to the first record in the file, select the Patient Number field, and then use the Find button to search for the patient whose number is PE33.

Steps To Search for a Record

1 Make sure the Patient table is open and the form (Patient form) for the Patient table is on the screen. Click the First Record button (see Figure 3-6) to display the first record. If the Patient Number field is not currently selected (highlighted), select it by clicking the field name. Point to the Find button on the toolbar.

The first record displays in the form (Figure 3-7)

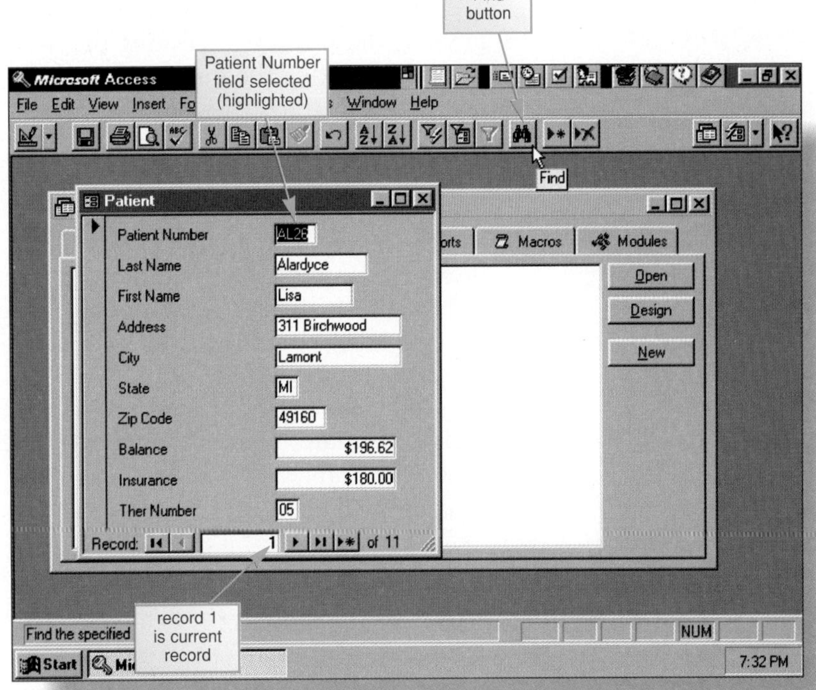

FIGURE 3-7

2 Click the Find button. Type PE33 **in the Find What text box.**

The Find in field: 'Patient Numbe' dialog box displays (Figure 3-8). The Find What text box contains the entry, PE33.

3 Click the Find Next button and then click the Close button.

Access locates the record for patient PE33.

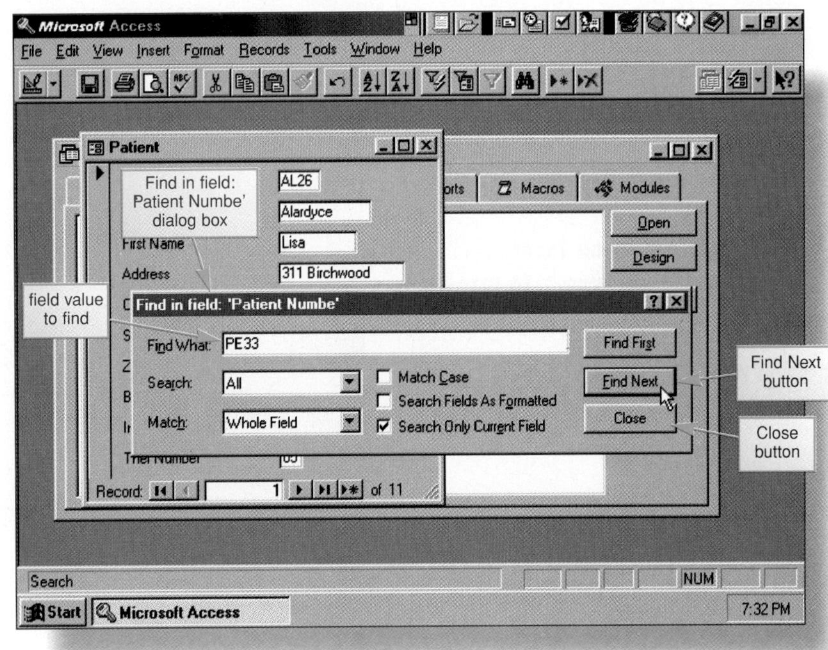

FIGURE 3-8

OtherWays

1. On Edit menu click Find
2. Press CTRL+F

After locating a record that satisfies a criterion, to find the next record that satisfies the same criterion, repeat the same process. (You will not need to retype the value.)

More About Changing the Contents of a Record

In changing a field, clicking within the field will produce an insertion point. Clicking the name of the field will select the entire field. The new entry typed then will completely replace the previous entry.

Changing the Contents of a Record

After locating the record to be changed, select the field to be changed by pressing the TAB key or clicking the field name. Then make the appropriate changes. Clicking the field name automatically produces an insertion point in the field name text box. If you press the TAB key, press F2 to produce an insertion point.

Normally, Access is in Insert mode, so the characters typed will be inserted at the appropriate position. To change to Overtype mode, press the INSERT key. The letters, OVR, will appear near the bottom right edge of the status bar. To return to Insert mode, press the INSERT key. In Insert mode, if the data in the field completely fills the field, no additional characters can be inserted. In this case, increase the size of the field before inserting the characters. You will see how to do this later in the project.

Complete the following steps to use Form view to change the name of patient PE33 to Pezzato by inserting an extra z. Sufficient room exists in the field to make this change.

To Update the Contents of a Field

1. **Position the mouse pointer in the First Name field text box for patient PE33 where the extra letter is to be inserted (that is, immediately after the z (Figure 3-9)).**

   The mouse pointer appears as an I-beam.

2. **Click to produce an insertion point, and then type z to insert the letter.**

   The name is now Pezzato.

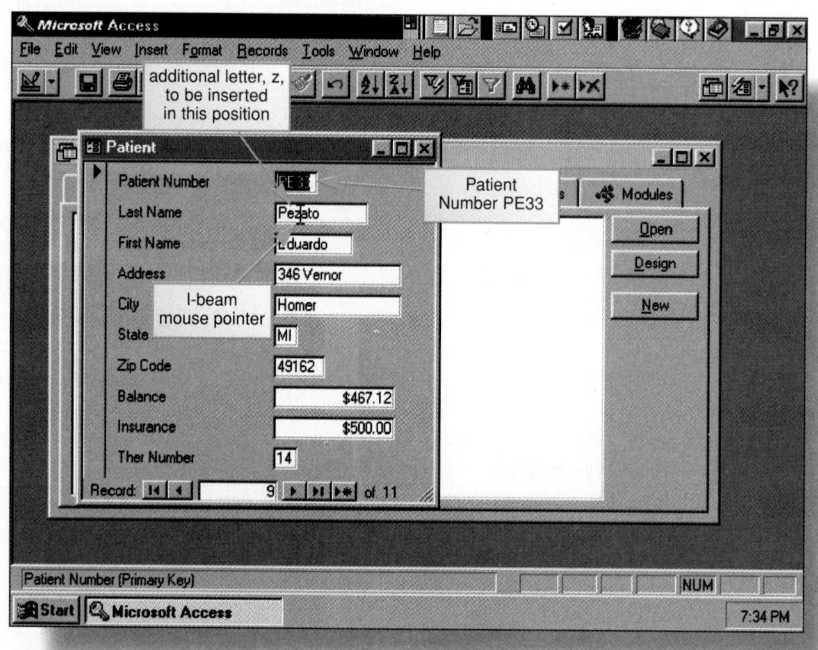

FIGURE 3-9

More About Using the Form View Button

Repeatedly clicking the Form View button will transfer back and forth between Form view and the design of the form, called Design view. To move to Datasheet view, you *must* click the down arrow, and then click Datasheet View in the drop-down list that displays.

Switching Between Views

Sometimes, after working in Form view where you can see all fields, but only one record, it would be helpful to see several records at a time. To do so, switch to Datasheet view by clicking the Form View button down arrow and then clicking Datasheet View. Perform the following steps to switch from Form view to Datasheet view.

Steps To Switch from Form View to Datasheet View

1 Point to the Form View button down arrow on the toolbar (Figure 3-10).

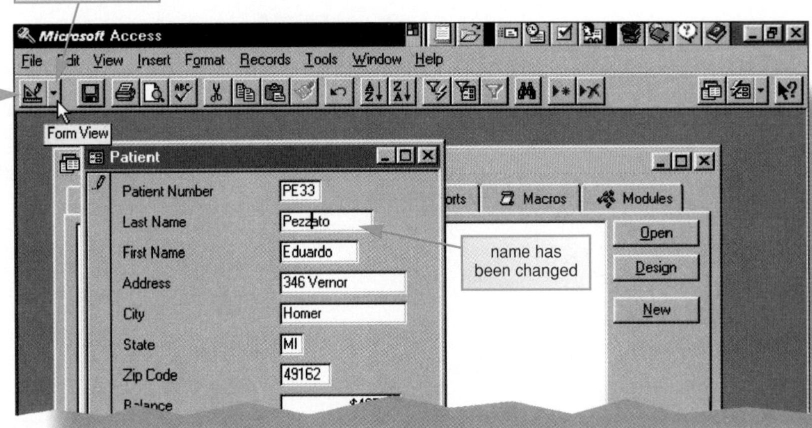

FIGURE 3-10

2 Click the Form View button down arrow. Point to Datasheet View.

The Form View drop-down list displays (Figure 3-11).

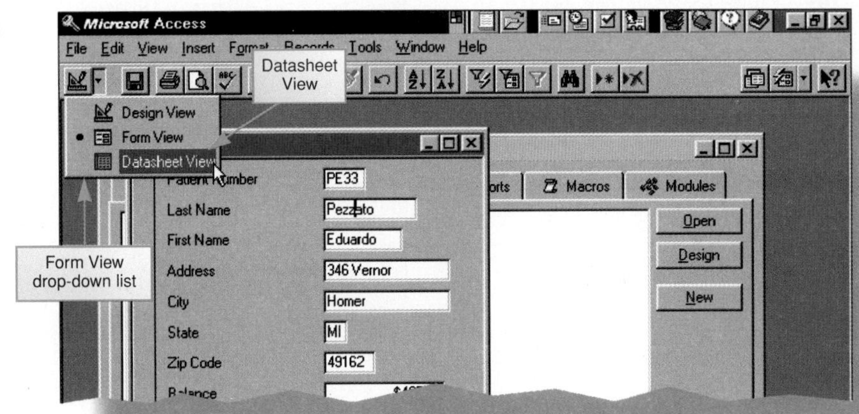

FIGURE 3-11

3 Click Datasheet View, and then maximize the window containing the datasheet.

The datasheet displays (Figure 3-12). The position in the table is maintained. The current record indicator points to patient PE33, the patient that displayed on the screen in Form view. The Last Name field, the field in which the insertion point displayed, is highlighted.

Microsoft Access - Patient

Patient Numbe	Last Name	First Name	Address	City	State	Zip
AL26	Alardyce	Lisa	311 Birchwood	Lamont	MI	49160
AT73	Acton	Thomas	312 Newcastle	Homer	MI	49162
BR31	Bryce	Roger	617 College	Lamont	MI	49160
DI32	Dalton	Irene	41 Lafayette	Madison	IN	42909
GC92	Gutierez	Carlos	476 Fulton	Jackson	OH	49401
GT43	Grant	Thomas	247 Fuller	Lamont	MI	49160
JG22	Jenkins	Glen	201 Plymouth	Madison	IN	42909
LI66	Lawrence	Irving	912 Devonshire	Beulah	MI	45621
PE33	Pezzato	Eduardo	346 Vernor	Homer	MI	49162
PE76	Perez	Enzo	216 Four Mile	Perry	MI	47211
SC26	Schouten	Marybeth	576 Hillside	Oshton	MI	49822

table displays in Datasheet view

Last Name field for customer PE33 is still selected (highlighted)

FIGURE 3-12

OtherWays

1. On View menu click Datasheet

If you wanted to return to Form view, you would use the same process. The only difference is that you would click Form View rather than Datasheet View.

Deleting Records

When records are no longer needed, **delete the records** (remove them) from the table. If, for example, patient JG22 has moved and will no longer be coming in for therapy, that patient's record should be deleted. To delete a record, first locate it and then press the DELETE key. Complete the following steps to delete patient JG22.

To Delete a Record

1 **With the datasheet for the Patient table on the screen, position the mouse pointer on the row selector of the record in which the patient number is JG22 (Figure 3-13).**

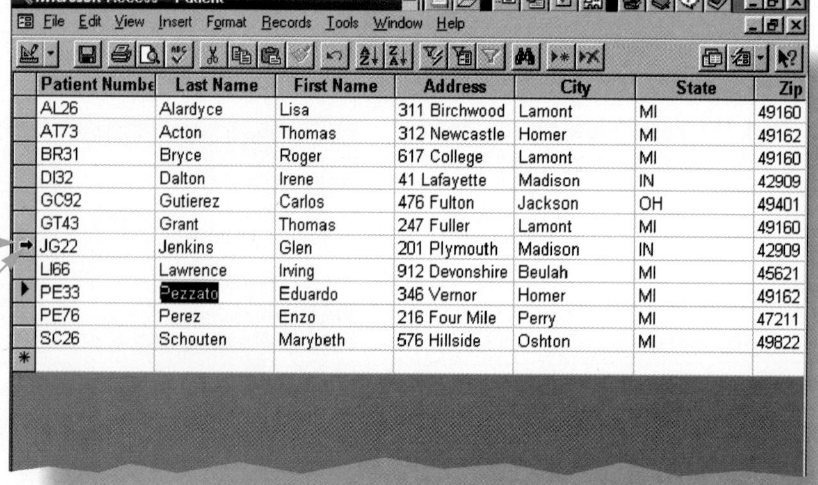

FIGURE 3-13

2 **Click the row selector to select the record, and then press the DELETE key to delete the record.**

The Microsoft Access dialog box displays (Figure 3-14). The message indicates that one record will be deleted.

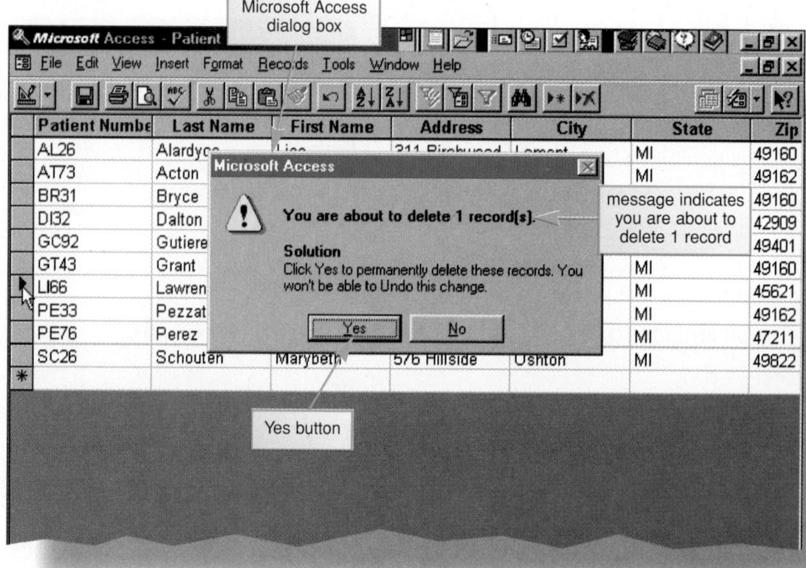

FIGURE 3-14

3 **Click the Yes button to complete the deletion.**

The record is deleted (Figure 3-15).

4 **Close the window containing the table by clicking its Close button.**

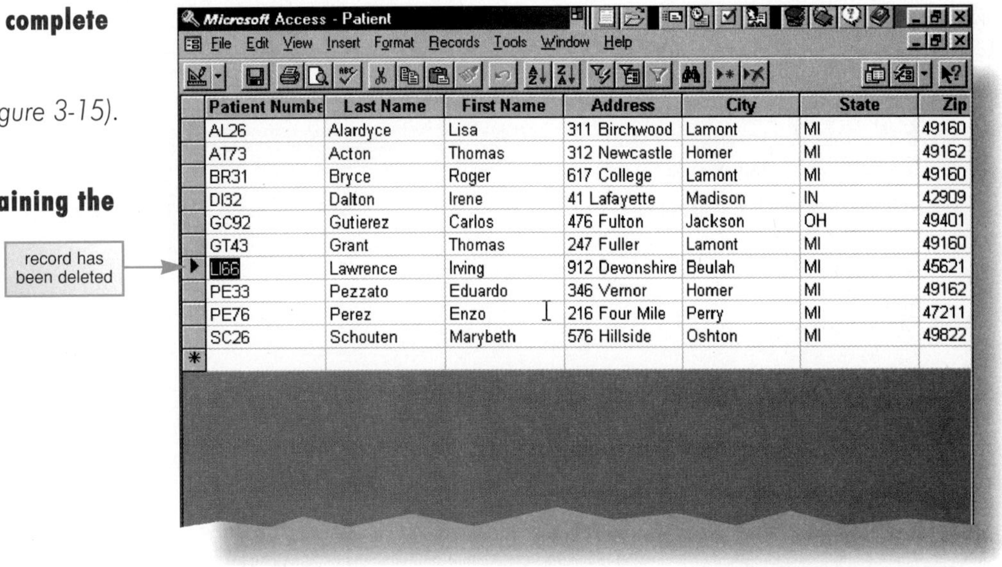

record has been deleted

Patient Numbe	Last Name	First Name	Address	City	State	Zip
AL26	Alardyce	Lisa	311 Birchwood	Lamont	MI	49160
AT73	Acton	Thomas	312 Newcastle	Homer	MI	49162
BR31	Bryce	Roger	617 College	Lamont	MI	49160
DI32	Dalton	Irene	41 Lafayette	Madison	IN	42909
GC92	Gutierez	Carlos	476 Fulton	Jackson	OH	49401
GT43	Grant	Thomas	247 Fuller	Lamont	MI	49160
LI66	Lawrence	Irving	912 Devonshire	Beulah	MI	45621
PE33	Pezzato	Eduardo	346 Vernor	Homer	MI	49162
PE76	Perez	Enzo	216 Four Mile	Perry	MI	47211
SC26	Schouten	Marybeth	576 Hillside	Oshton	MI	49822

FIGURE 3-15

OtherWays

1. Click record to delete, click Delete Record button on toolbar
2. Click record to delete, on Edit menu click Delete Record

Changing the Structure

When you initially create a database, you define its **structure**; that is, you indicate the names, types, and sizes of all the fields. In many cases, the structure you first defined will not continue to be appropriate as you use the database. A variety of reasons exist why the structure of a table might need to change. Changes in the needs of users of the database may require additional fields to be added. In the Patient table, for example, if it is important to store a code indicating the insurance carrier of a patient, you need to add such a field.

Characteristics of a given field might need to change. For example, the patient Irene Dalton's name is stored incorrectly in the database. It should be Irene Dalton-Manters. The Last Name field is not large enough, however, to hold the correct name. To accommodate this change, increase the width of the Last Name field.

It may be that a field currently in the table is no longer necessary. If no one ever uses a particular field, there is no point in having it in the table. Because it is occupying space and serving no useful purpose, it should be removed from the table. You would also need to delete the field from any forms, reports, or queries that include it.

To make any of these changes, click the Design button in the Database window.

More About Changing the Structure

The ease with which the structure of a table can be changed is a real advantage of using a database management system like Access. In a nondatabase environment, changes to the structure can be very cumbersome, requiring difficult and time-consuming changes to many programs.

Changing the Size of a Field

The steps on the next page change the size of the Last Name field from 10 to 14 to accommodate the change of name from Dalton to Dalton-Manters.

Steps To Change the Size of a Field

1 With the Database window on the screen, click the Tables tab, and then right-click Patient.

The shortcut menu displays (Figure 3-16).

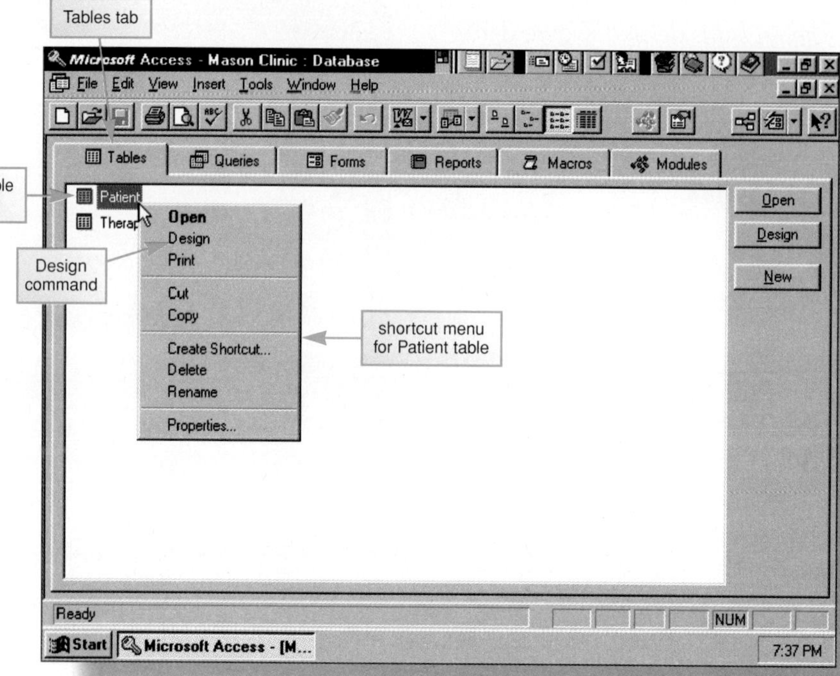

FIGURE 3-16

2 Click Design, and then point to the row selector for the Last Name field.

The Patient : Table window displays (Figure 3-17).

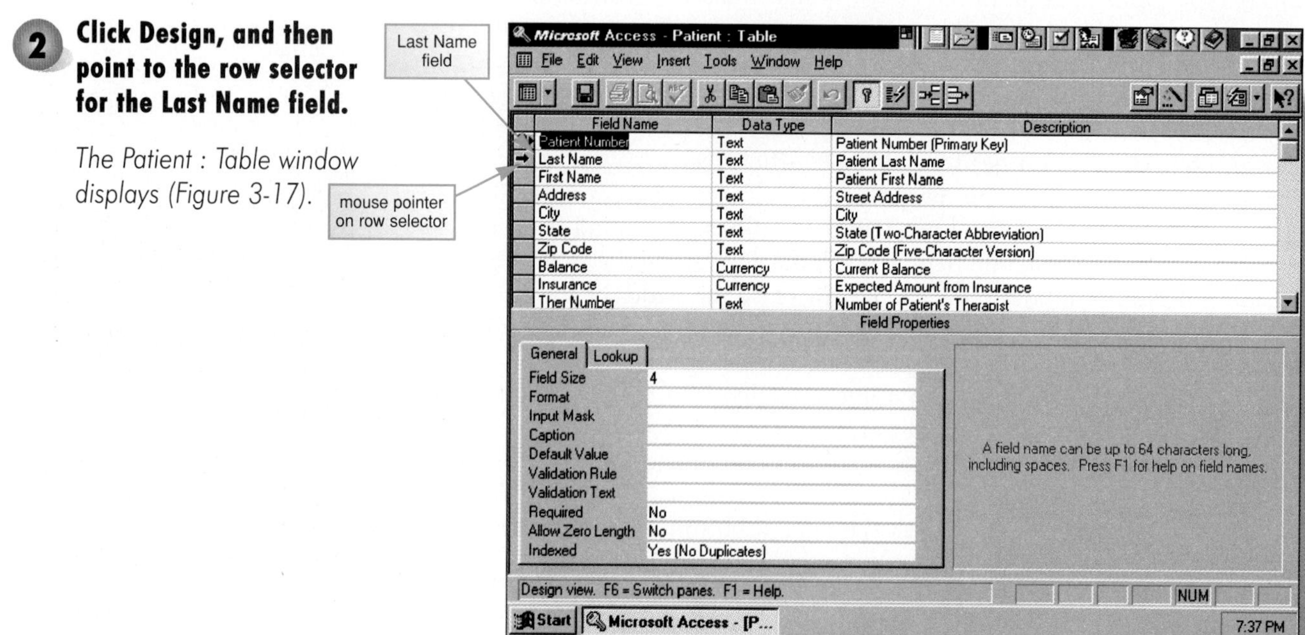

FIGURE 3-17

3 **Click the row selector for the Last Name field.**

The Last Name field is selected (Figure 3-18).

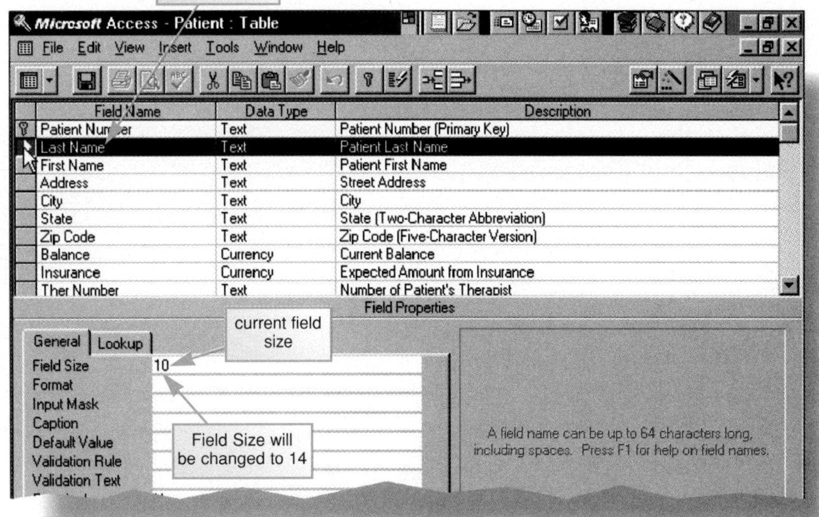

FIGURE 3-18

4 **Press F6 to highlight the field size, type 14 as the new size, and press F6 again.**

The size is changed (Figure 3-19).

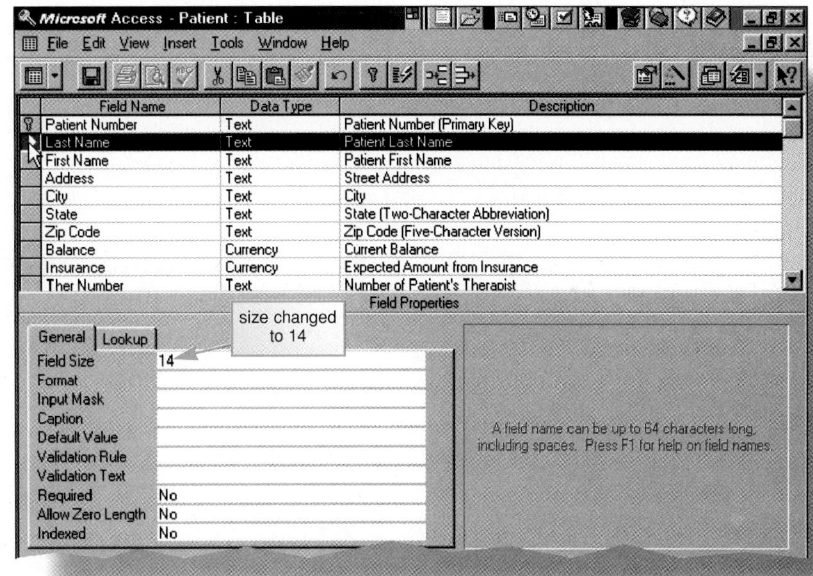

FIGURE 3-19

Adding a New Field

The following steps add a new field, called Ins Carrier, to the table. This field is used to indicate the type insurance coverage the patient has. The possible entries in this field are ORG (covered by insurance through an organization where the patient works), GVT (covered by government insurance), and PRS (covered by personal insurance). The new field will follow the Zip Code in the list of fields; that is, it will be the *seventh* field in the restructured table. The current seventh field (Balance) will become the eighth field, Insurance will become the ninth field, and so on. Complete the steps on the next page to add the field.

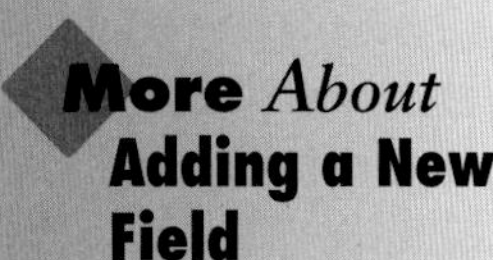

More About Adding a New Field

A variety of reasons exists why new fields are added to tables. Users needs can change. The field may have been omitted by mistake when the table was first created. Government regulations may change in such a way that an organization needs to maintain additional information.

To Add a Field to a Table

1 **Point to the row selector for the Balance field (Figure 3-20).**

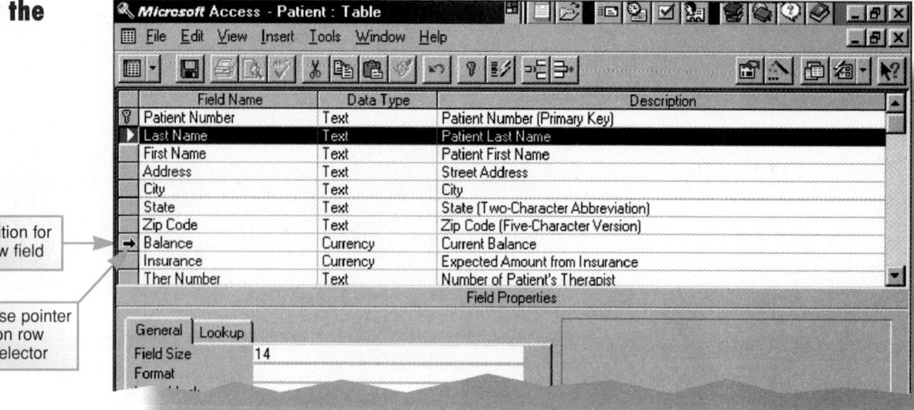

FIGURE 3-20

2 **Click the row selector for the Balance field and then press the INSERT key to insert a blank row.**

A blank row displays in the position for the new field (Figure 3-21).

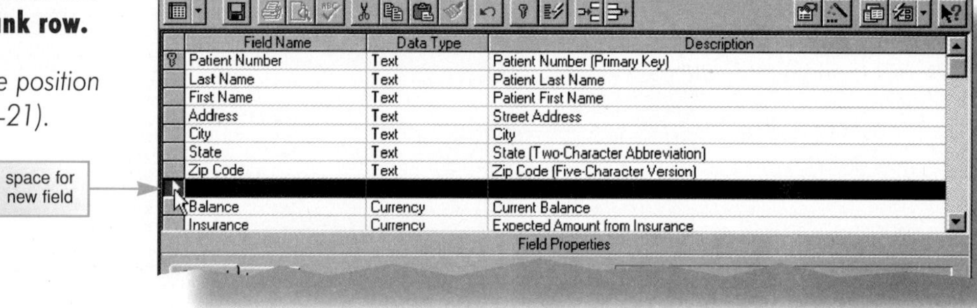

FIGURE 3-21

3 **Click the Field Name column for the new field. Type** `Ins Carrier` **(field name) and then press the TAB key. Select the Text data type by pressing the TAB key. Type** `Insurance Carrier (ORG, GVT, or PRS)` **as the description. Press F6 to move to the Field Size text box, type** `3` **(the size of the Ins Carrier field), and press F6 again.**

The entries for the new field are complete (Figure 3-22).

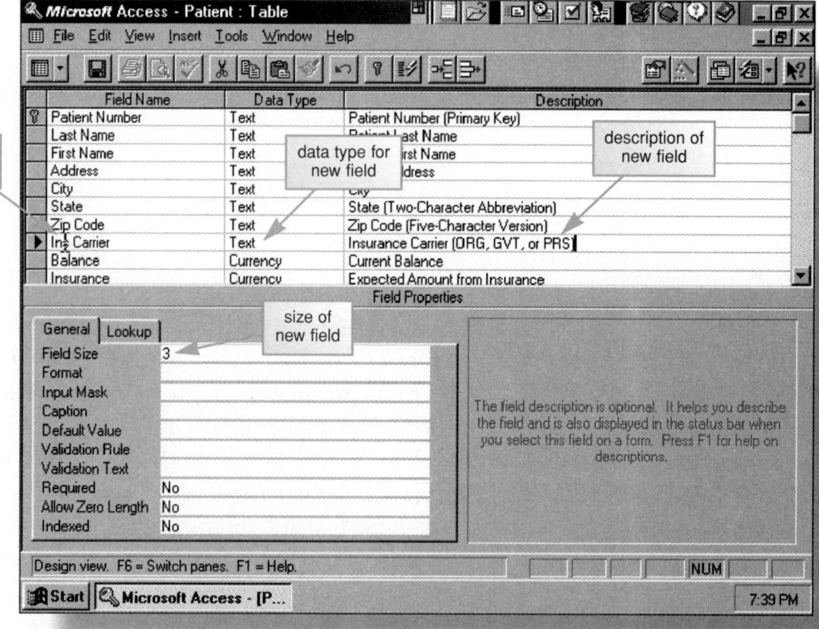

FIGURE 3-22

4 **Close the Patient : Table window by clicking its Close button.**

The Microsoft Access dialog box displays (Figure 3-23).

5 **Click the Yes button to save the changes.**

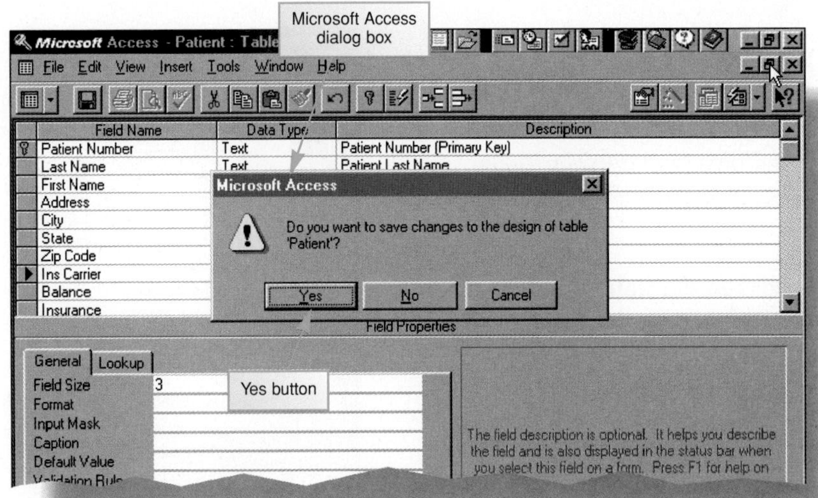

FIGURE 3-23

*Other*Ways

1. Click row selector below where new field is to be added, click Insert Row button on toolbar
2. Click row selector below where new field is to be added, on Insert menu click Field

Updating the Restructured Database

Changes to the structure are available immediately. The Last Name field is longer, although it does not appear that way on the screen, and the new Ins Carrier field is included.

To make a change to a single field, such as changing the name from Dalton to Dalton-Manters, click the field to be changed, and then type the new value. If the record to be changed is not on the screen, use the Navigation buttons (Next Record, Previous Record) to move to it. If the field to be corrected simply is not visible on the screen, use the horizontal scroll bar along the bottom of the screen to shift all the fields until the correct one displays. Then make the change.

Perform the following steps to change the name of Dalton to Dalton-Manters, and at the same time increase the column width so the entire name is visible.

To Update the Contents of a Field

1 **Right-click Patient.**

The shortcut menu displays (Figure 3-24).

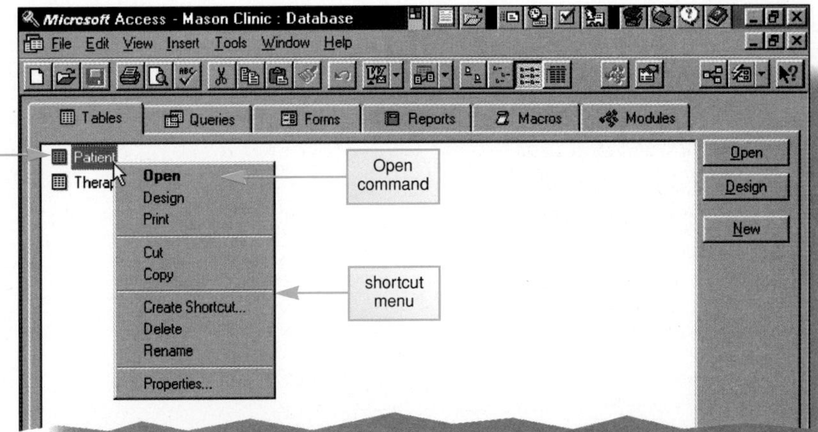

FIGURE 3-24

2 **Click Open. Position the I-Beam mouse pointer to the right of the n of Dalton (customer DI32).**

The datasheet displays (Figure 3-25).

3 **Click in the field, and then type** `-Manters` **as the addition to the name.**

The name is changed from Dalton to Dalton-Manters.

Microsoft Access - Patient : Table

I-beam mouse pointer

name to be changed

Patient Numbe	Last Name	First Name	Address	City	State	Zip
AL26	Alardyce	Lisa	311 Birchwood	Lamont	MI	49160
AT73	Acton	Thomas	312 Newcastle	Homer	MI	49162
BR31	Bryce	Roger	617 College	Lamont	MI	49160
DI32	Dalton	Irene	41 Lafayette	Madison	IN	42909
GC92	Gutierez	Carlos	476 Fulton	Jackson	OH	49401
GT43	Grant	Thomas	247 Fuller	Lamont	MI	49160
LI66	Lawrence	Irving	912 Devonshire	Beulah	MI	45621
PE	ezzato	Eduardo	346 Vernor	Homer	MI	49162
PE	erez	Enzo	216 Four Mile	Perry	MI	47211
SC26	Schouten	Marybeth	576 Hillside	Oshton	MI	49822

Record: 1 of 10

Patient Number (Primary Key)

NUM

Start | Microsoft Access - [P... | 7:42 PM

FIGURE 3-25

More *About* **Updating a Restructured Database**

In a nondatabase environment, after changing a structure, it can take several hours before the new structure is available for use. Computer jobs to change the structure often would run overnight or even over a weekend. Having the changes available immediately is a major benefit to using a system like Access.

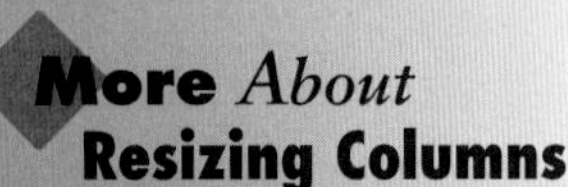

More *About* **Resizing Columns**

Changes to the size of a field are not reflected automatically on the forms you have created. If you used the AutoForm command, you can change the field sizes by simply recreating the form. To do so, right-click the form, click Delete, and create the form as you did in Project 1.

Resizing Columns

After changing the size of a field, you will often need to **resize the column** (change its size) for the field in the datasheet. In this case, because the larger name, Dalton-Manters, still displays, it is not necessary. In other cases, however, the expanded name might not completely display. To correct this problem, you would expand the size of the column.

In some instances, you may want to reduce the size of a column. The City field, for example, is short enough that it does not require all the space on the screen that is allotted to it.

Both types of changes are made the same way. Position the mouse pointer on the line in the column heading immediately to the right of the column to be resized. The mouse pointer will change to a double-headed arrow with a vertical bar. You then can drag the line to resize the column. Also, you can double-click in the column heading immediately to the right of the column to be resized. Access then determines the best size for the column.

The following steps illustrate the process for resizing the City column to the best size.

To Resize a Column

1 Point to the line in the column heading immediately to the right of the column heading for the City field (Figure 3-26).

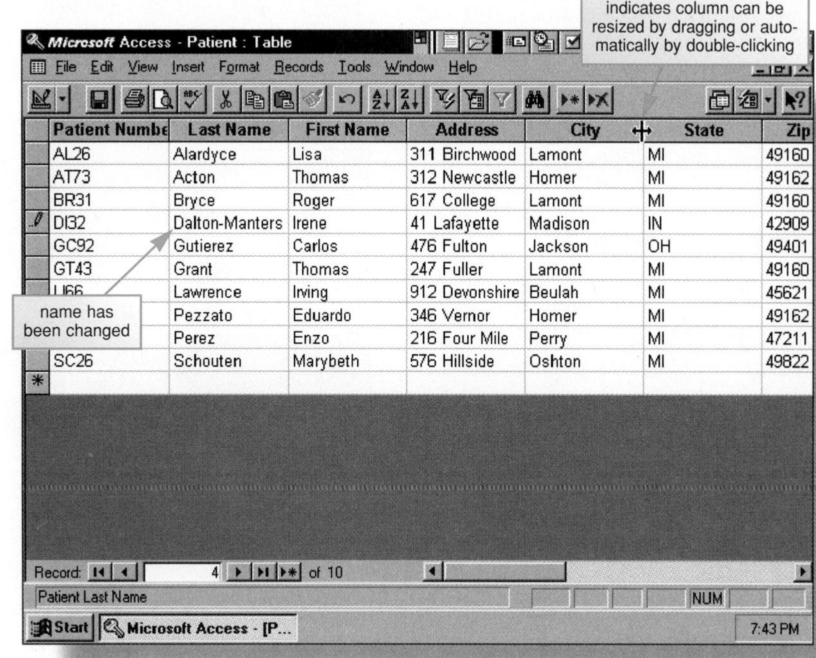
mouse pointer shape indicates column can be resized by dragging or automatically by double-clicking
name has been changed

FIGURE 3-26

2 Double-click the line in the column heading.

The City column has been resized to the best size to fit the data (Figure 3-27).

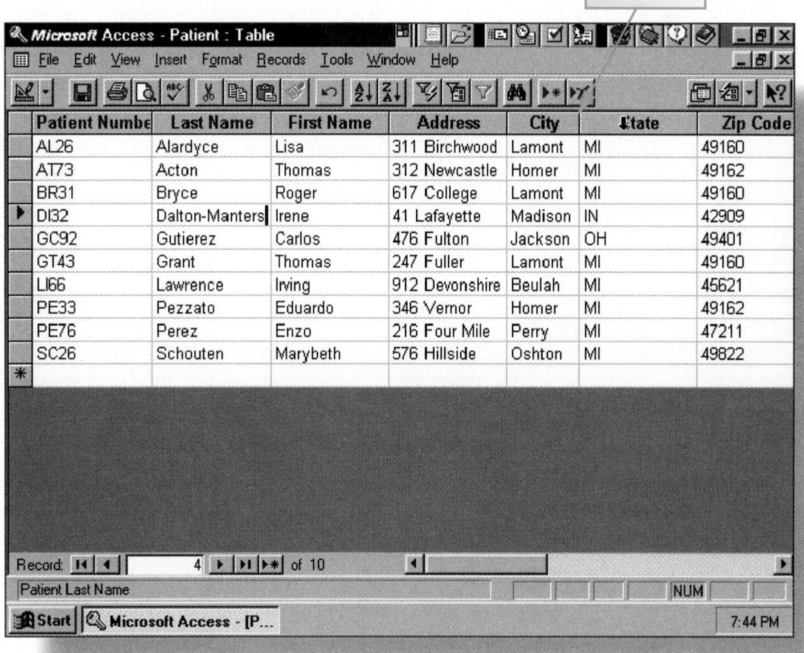
column has been resized

FIGURE 3-27

3 **Close the Patient : Table window by clicking its Close button.**

The Microsoft Access dialog box displays (Figure 3-28). If you wanted to save this change to the width of the City column, you would click the Yes button.

4 **Click the No button.**

The change is not saved. The next time the datasheet displays, the City column will have its original width.

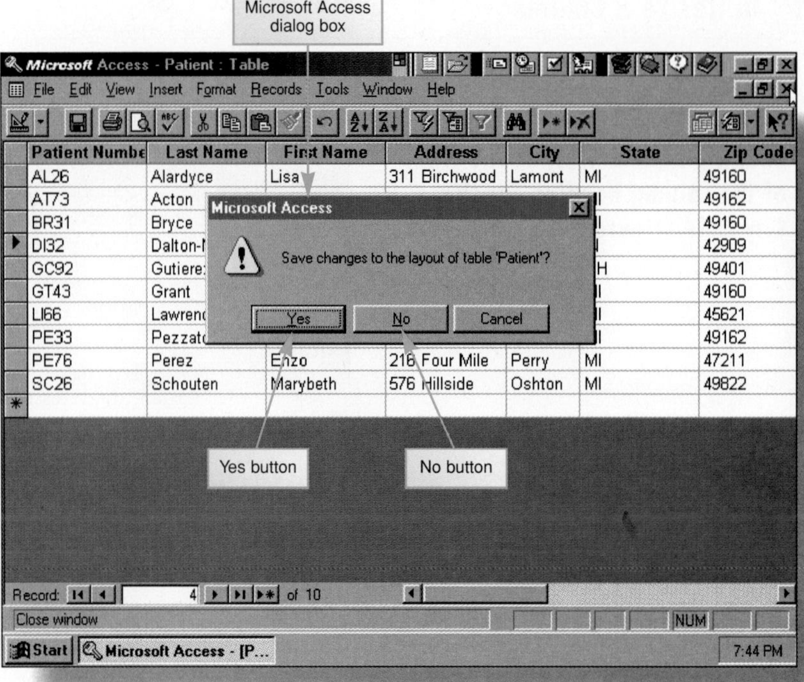

FIGURE 3-28

OtherWays

1. On Format menu click Column Width, click Best Fit

More About Update Queries

Each database management system offers some mechanism for updating multiple records at a time, that is, for making the same change to all the records that satisfy some criterion. Some systems, including Access, accomplish this through the query tool by providing a special type of query for this purpose.

Using an Update Query

The Ins Carrier field is blank on every record. One approach to entering the information for the field would be to step through the entire table, changing the value on each record to what it should be. If most of the patients have the same type, a simpler approach is available.

Suppose, for example, that more patients are type ORG (organization). Initially, you can set all the values to ORG. To quickly and easily accomplish this, you use a special type of query called an **update query**. Later, you can change the type for the patients covered by personal or by government insurance individually.

The process for creating an update query begins the same as the process for creating the queries in Project 2. After selecting the table for the query, click the Query Type button and then click Update on the menu that displays. An extra row, Update To:, displays in the design grid. Use this additional row to indicate the way the data will be updated. If a criterion is entered, then only those records that satisfy the criterion will be updated.

Perform the following steps to change the value in the Ins Carrier field to ORG for all the records. Because all records are to be updated, no criteria will be entered.

To Use an Update Query to Update All Records

1 **With the Patient table selected click the New Object button down arrow on the toolbar.**

The New Object drop-down list displays (Figure 3-29).

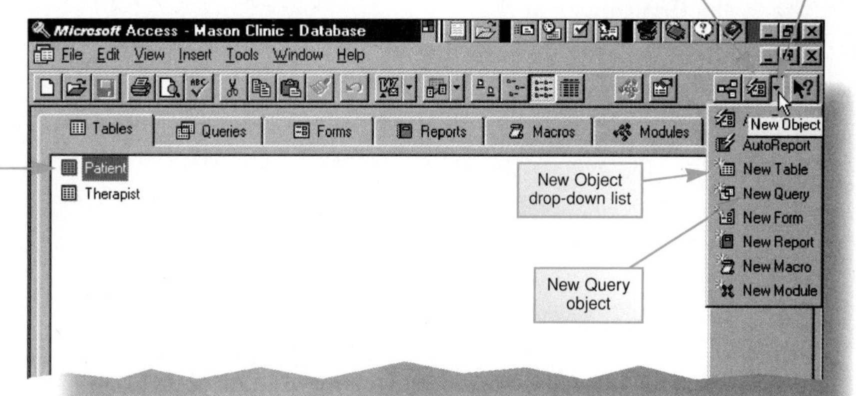

FIGURE 3-29

2 **Click New Query.**

The New Query dialog box displays (Figure 3-30). Design View is selected (highlighted).

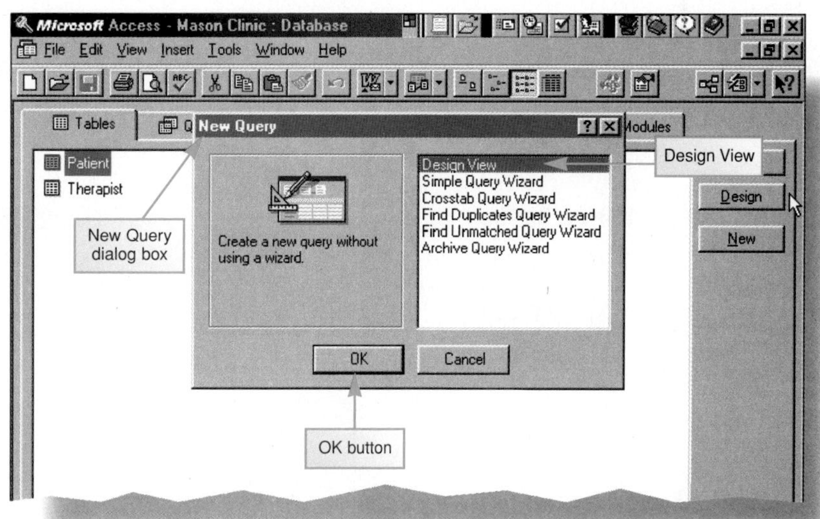

FIGURE 3-30

3 **Click the OK button, and be sure the Query1 : Select Query window is maximized. Resize the upper and lower panes of the screen as well as the Patient field list so all fields in the Patient table display (see pages A 2.7 through A 2.10 in Project 2). Click the Query Type button down arrow on the toolbar.**

The Query Type drop-down list displays (Figure 3-31).

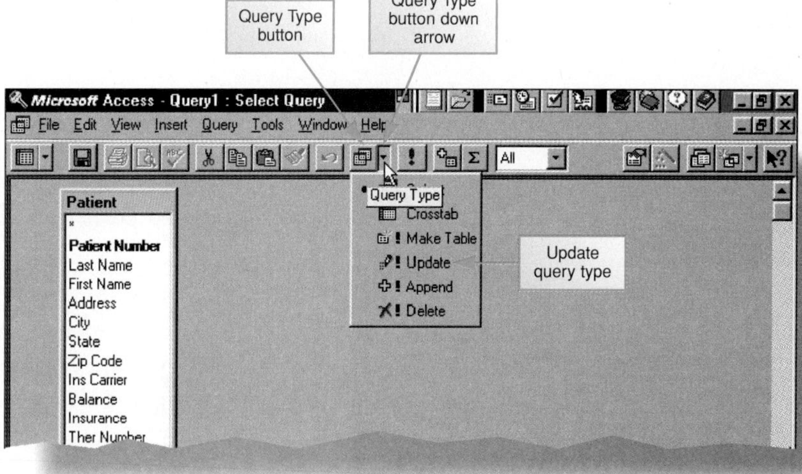

FIGURE 3-31

4 **Click Update, double-click the Ins Carrier field to select the field, click the Update To text box in the first column of the design grid, and type** `ORG` **as the new value.**

The Ins Carrier field is selected (Figure 3-32). The value to which the field is to be changed is entered as ORG. Because no criteria are entered, the Ins Carrier value on every row will be changed to ORG.

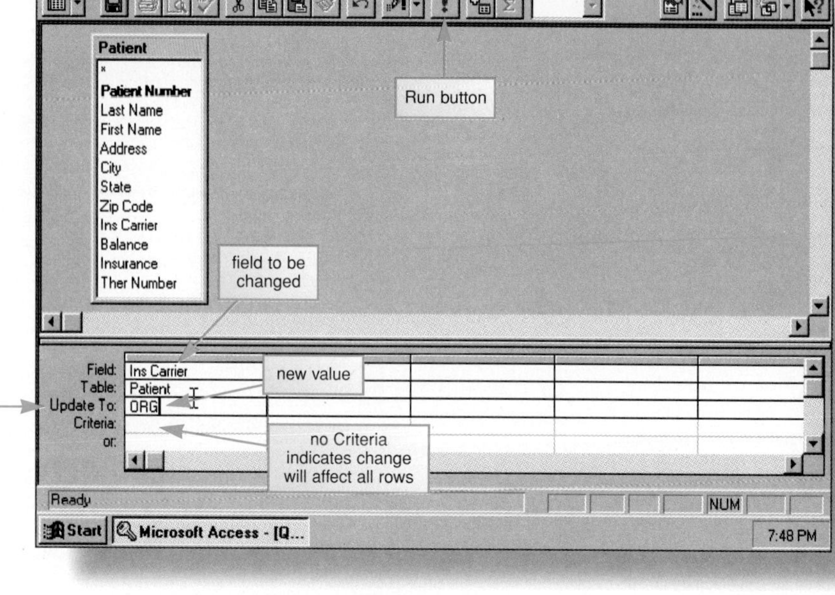

FIGURE 3-32

5 **Click the Run button on the toolbar.**

The Microsoft Access dialog box displays (Figure 3-33). The message indicates that 10 rows will be updated by the query.

6 **Click the Yes button.**

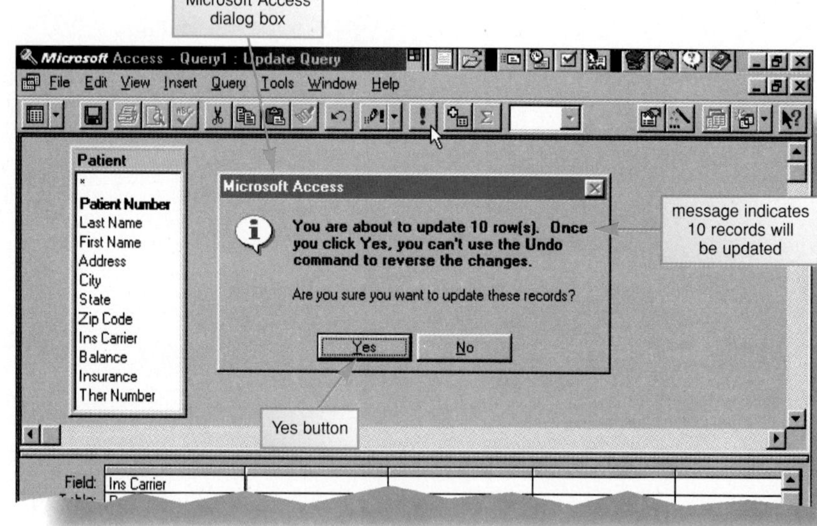

FIGURE 3-33

OtherWays

1. On Query menu click Update

Using a Delete Query to Delete a Group of Records

In some cases, several records are deleted at a time. If, for example, another neighboring clinic will be serving all patients in a particular Zip Code, all the patients who have this Zip Code can be deleted from the Mason Clinic database. Rather than deleting these patients individually, which would be very cumbersome, delete them in one operation by using a delete query.

Perform the following steps to use a delete query to delete all patients whose Zip Code is 45621.

To Use a Delete Query to Delete a Group of Records

1 **Clear the grid by clicking Edit on the menu bar and then clicking Clear Grid. Click the Query Type button down arrow on the toolbar.**

The Query Type drop-down list displays (Figure 3-34).

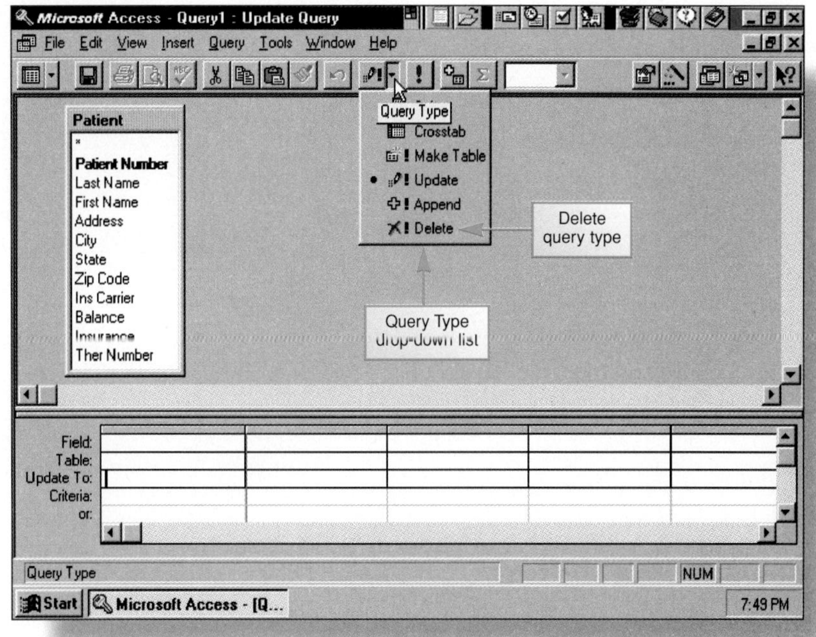

FIGURE 3-34

2 **Click Delete, double-click the Zip Code field to select the field, and click the Criteria box. Type** `45621` **as the criteria.**

The criteria is entered in the Zip Code column (Figure 3-35).

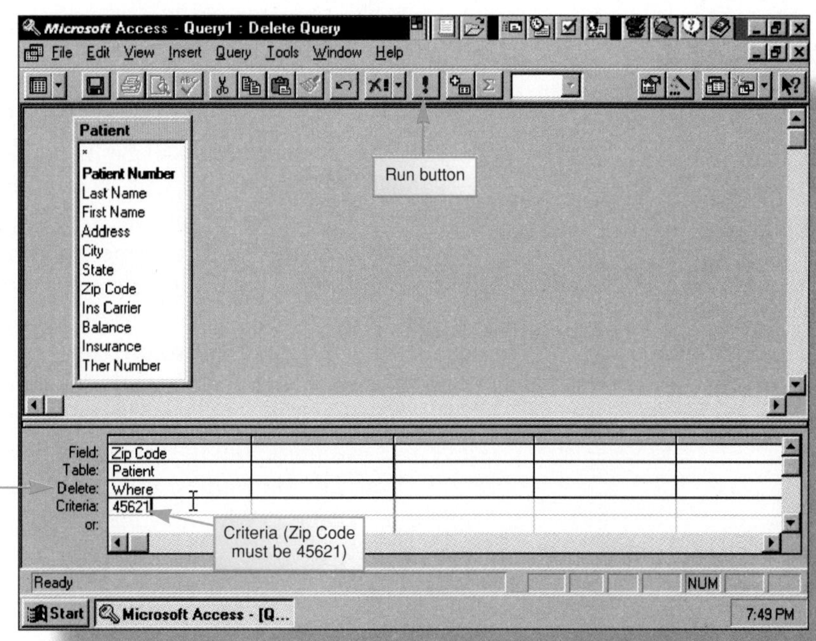

FIGURE 3-35

3 Run the query.

The Microsoft Access dialog box displays (Figure 3-36). The message indicates the query will delete 1 row (record).

4 Click the Yes button. Close the Query window. Do not save the query.

One patient (LI66) has been removed from the table.

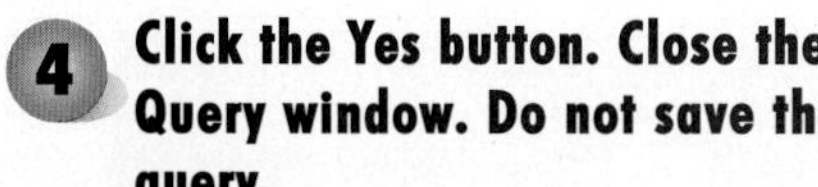

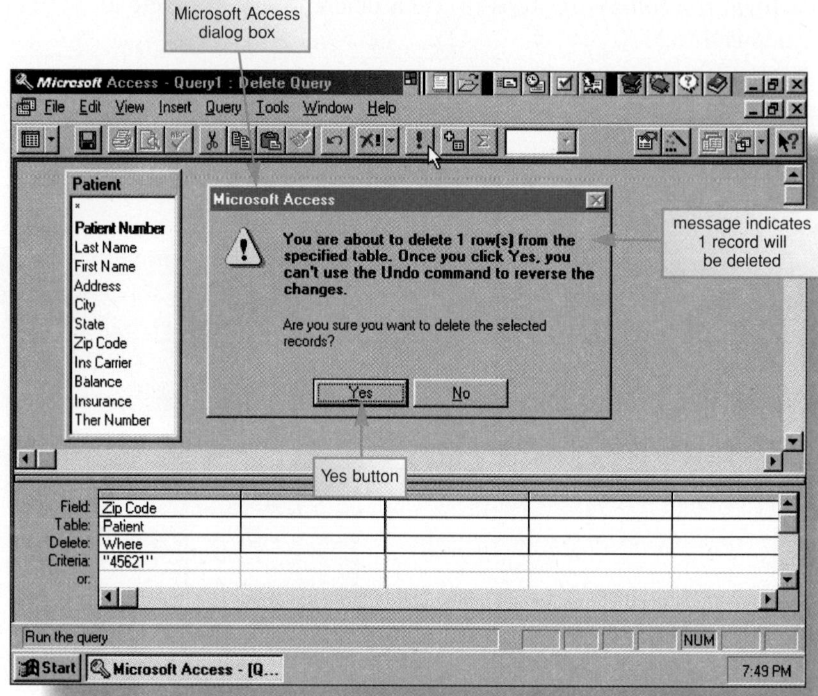

FIGURE 3-36

OtherWays

1. On Query menu click Delete

Creating Validation Rules

More About Delete Queries

Each database management system offers some mechanism for deleting multiple records at a time, that is, for deleting all the records that satisfy some criterion. Some systems, including Access, accomplish this through the query tool by providing a special type of query for this purpose.

Up to this point in this book, you have created, loaded, queried, and updated a database. Nothing done so far, however, ensures that users enter only valid data. This section explains how to create **validation rules**; that is, rules that the data entered by a user must follow. As you will see, Access will prevent users from entering data that does not follow the rules. The steps also specify **validation text**, which is the message that will be displayed if a user violates the validation rule.

Validation rules can indicate a **required field**, a field in which the user must actually enter data. For example, by making the Last Name field a required field, a user must actually enter a name (that is, the user cannot leave it blank). Validation rules can make sure a user's entry lies within a certain **range of values**; for example, that the values in the Balance field are between $0.00 and $2,000.00. They can specify a **default value**; that is, a value that Access will display on the screen in a particular field before the user begins adding a record. To make data entry of patient numbers more convenient, you can also have lowercase letters converted automatically to uppercase. Finally, validation rules can specify a collection of acceptable values; for example, that the only legitimate entries for Ins Carrier are ORG, GVT, and PRS.

Specifying a Required Field

To specify that the Last Name field is to be a required field, perform the following steps.

To Specify a Required Field

1 **With the Database window on the screen and the Tables tab selected, right-click Patient.**

The shortcut menu displays (Figure 3-37).

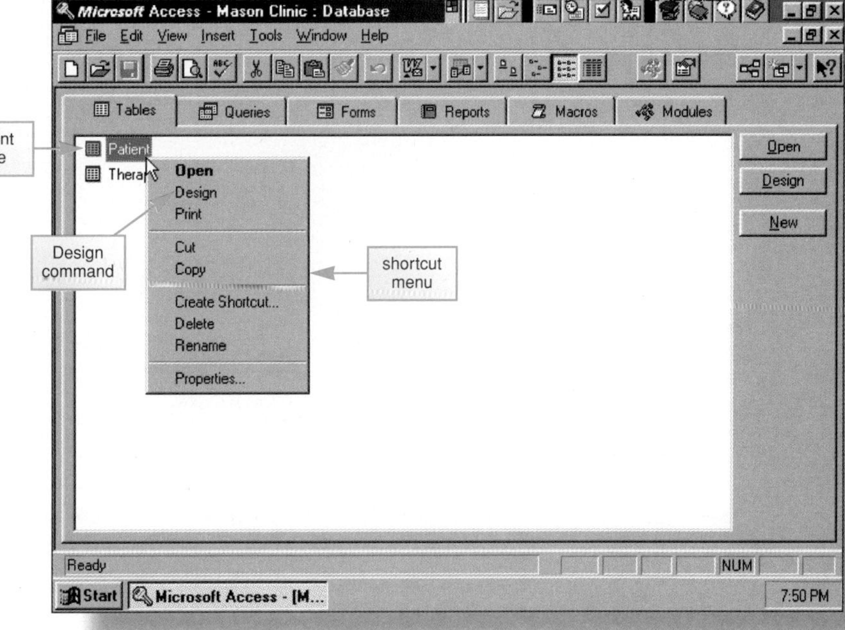

FIGURE 3-37

2 **Click Design, select the Last Name field by clicking its row selector. Point to the Required text box.**

The Patient : Table window displays (Figure 3-38). The Last Name field is selected.

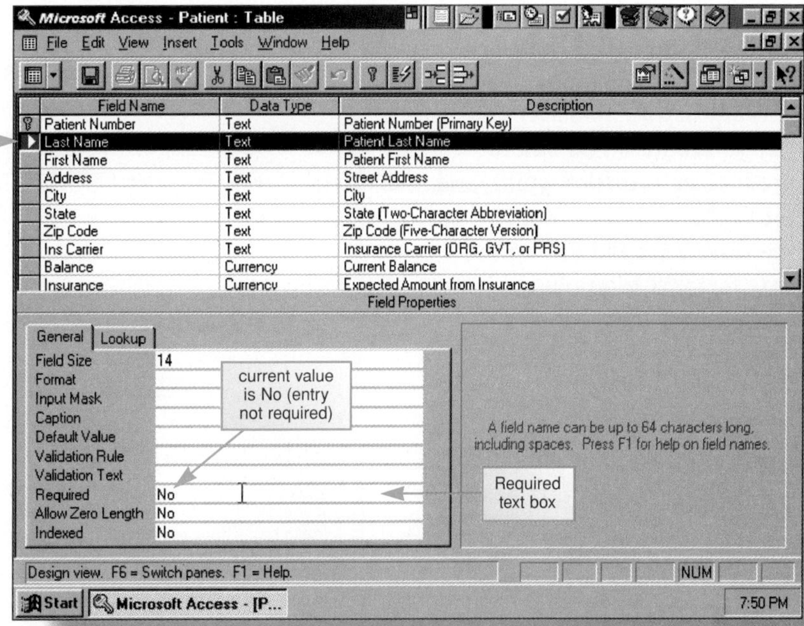

FIGURE 3-38

3 **Click the Required text box in the Field Properties area, and then click the down arrow that displays. Click Yes in the drop-down list.**

The value in the Required text box changes to Yes (Figure 3-39). It is now required that the user enter data into the Last Name field when adding a record.

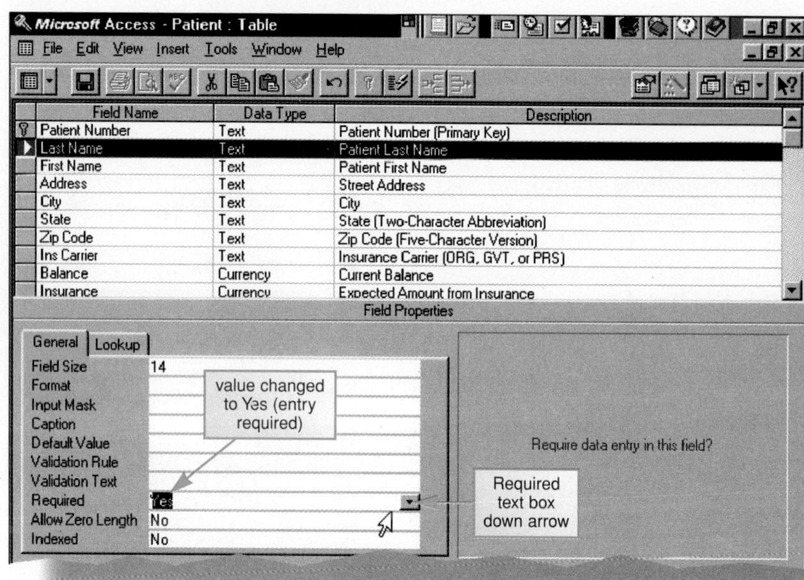

FIGURE 3-39

Specifying a Range

The following steps specify that entries in the Balance field must be between $0.00 and $2,000.00. To indicate this range, you will enter a condition that specifies that the balance must be both >= 0 (greater than or equal to zero) and <= 2000 (less than or equal to 2,000).

To Specify a Range

1 **Select the Balance field by clicking its row selector. Click the Validation Rule text box to produce an insertion point, and then type** `>=0 and <=2000` **as the rule. Click the Validation Text text box to produce an insertion point, and then type** `Must be between $0.00 and $2,000.00` **as the text. You must type all the text, including the dollar signs in this text box.**

The validation rule and text are entered (Figure 3-40).

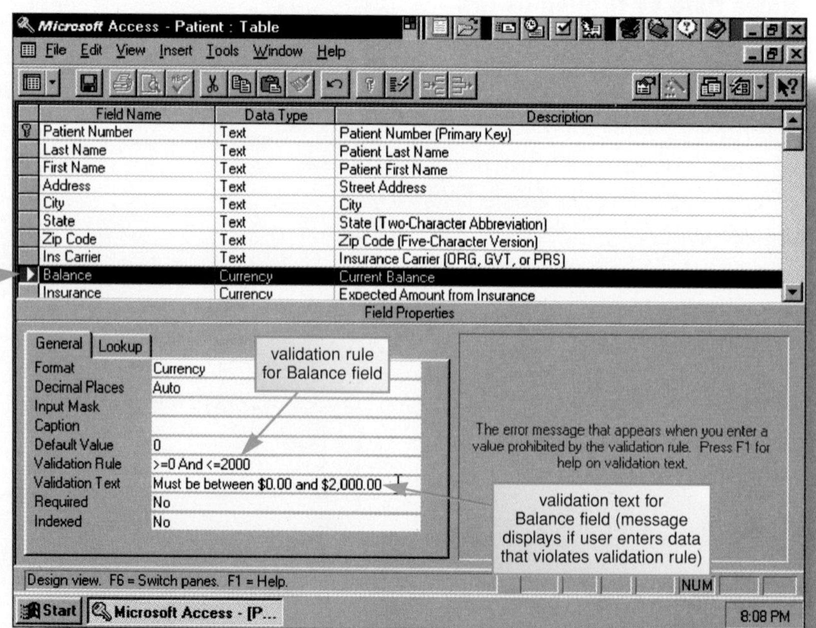

FIGURE 3-40

Users will now be prohibited from entering a balance that is either less than $0.00 or greater than $2,000.00 when they add records or change the value in the Balance field.

Specifying a Default Value

To specify a default value of ORG for the Ins Carrier field, complete the following step. By specifying this value, it simply means that if users do not enter an insurance carrier, the insurance carrier will be ORG.

To Specify a Default Value

1 **Select the Ins Carrier field. Click the Default Value text box and then type =ORG as the value.**

The Ins Carrier field is selected. The default value is entered in the Default Value text box (Figure 3-41).

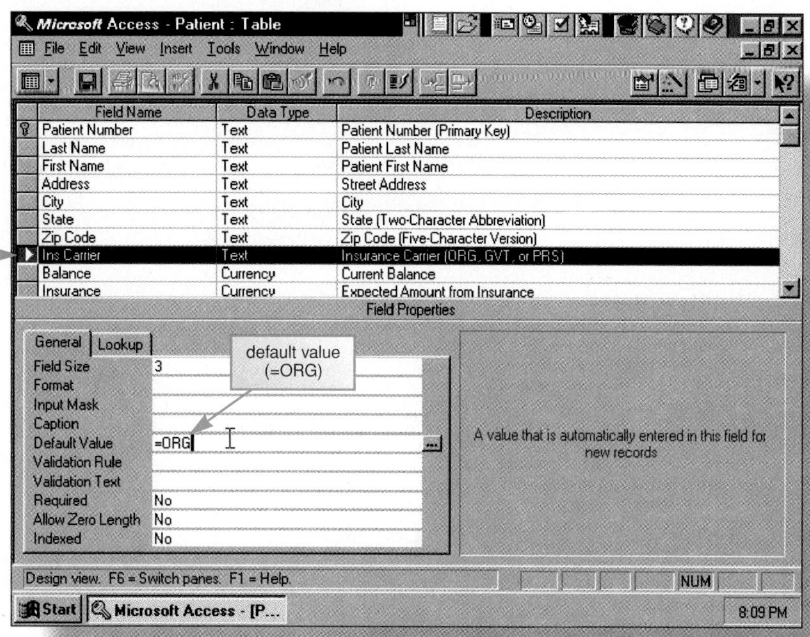

FIGURE 3-41

From this point on, if users do not make an entry in the Ins Carrier field when adding records, Access will set the value to ORG.

Specifying a Collection of Legal Values

The only legal values for the Ins Carrier field are ORG, GVT, and PRS. An appropriate validation rule for this field can direct Access to reject any entry other than these three possibilities. In other words, these three are the only **legal values.** Perform the step on the next page to specify the legal values for the Ins Carrier field.

To Specify a Collection of Legal Values

1 **Make sure the Ins Carrier field is selected. Click the Validation Rule text box and then type** `=ORG or =GVT or =PRS` **as the collection of values. Click the Validation Text text box and then type** `Must be ORG, GVT, or PRS` **as the collection of values.**

The Ins Carrier field is selected. The validation rule and text have been entered (Figure 3-42). In the Validation Rule text box, Access automatically inserted quotation marks around the ORG, GVT, and PRS values and changed the lowercase letter, o, to uppercase in the word, or.

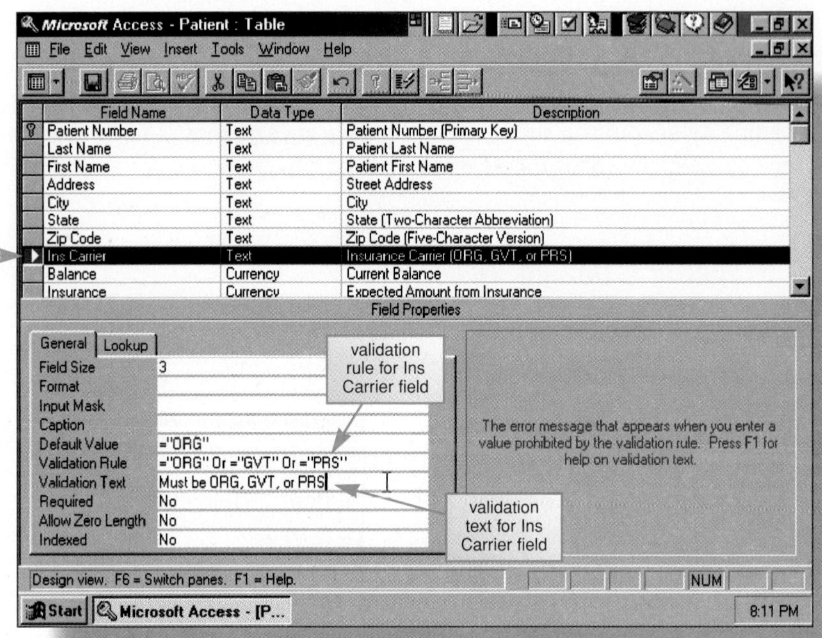

FIGURE 3-42

Users now will be allowed to enter only ORG, GVT, or PRS in the Ins Carrier field when they add records or make changes to this field.

Using a Format

To affect the way data is entered in a field, you can use a **format**. To do so, you enter a special symbol, called a **format symbol**, in the field's Format text box. The following step specifies a format for the Patient Number field in the Patient table. The format symbol used in the example is >, which causes Access to automatically convert lowercase letters to uppercase. The format symbol < causes Access to automatically convert uppercase letters to lowercase.

To Specify a Format

1 **Select the Patient Number field. Click the Format text box and then type > (Figure 3-43).**

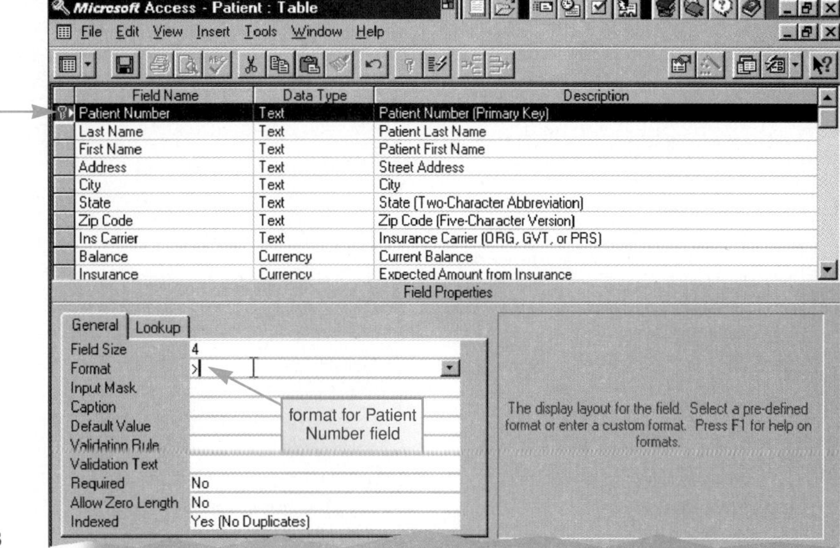

FIGURE 3-43

From this point on, any lowercase letters will be converted automatically to uppercase when users add records or change the value in the Patient Number field.

Saving Rules, Values, and Formats

To save the validation rules, default values, and formats, perform the following steps.

To Save the Validation Rules, Default Values, and Formats

1 **Click the Close button for the Patient : Table window to close the window.**
The Microsoft Access dialog box displays asking if you want to save your changes (Figure 3-44).

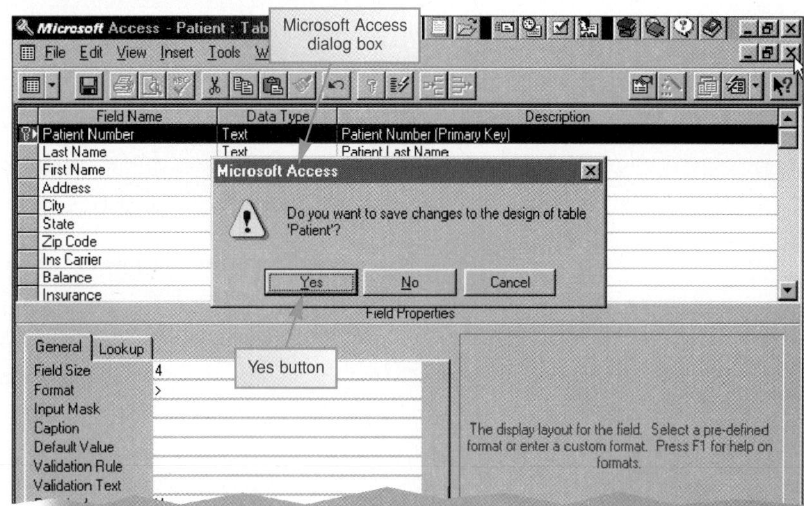

FIGURE 3-44

Click the Yes button to save the changes.

The Microsoft Access dialog box displays (Figure 3-45). This message asks if you want the new rules applied to current records. If this were a database used to run a business or to solve some other critical need, you would click Yes. You would not want to take the chance that some of the data already in the database violates the rules.

Click the No button.

The rules are not violated by the data in the Patient table. The changes are made.

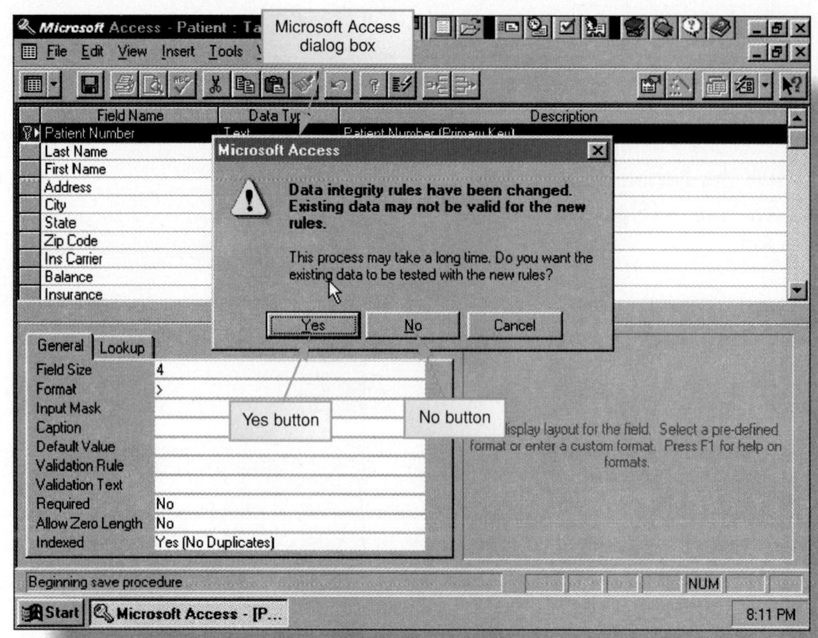

FIGURE 3-45

Updating a Table that Contains Validation Rules

When updating a table that contains validation rules, Access provides plenty of assistance in making sure the data entered is valid. It helps in making sure that data is formatted correctly. Access also will not accept invalid data. Entering a number that is out of the required range, for example, or entering a value that is not one of the possible choices, will produce an error message in the form of a dialog box. The database will not be updated until the error is corrected.

If the patient number entered contains lowercase letters, such as ab24 (Figure 3-46), Access will automatically convert the data to AB24 (Figure 3-47).

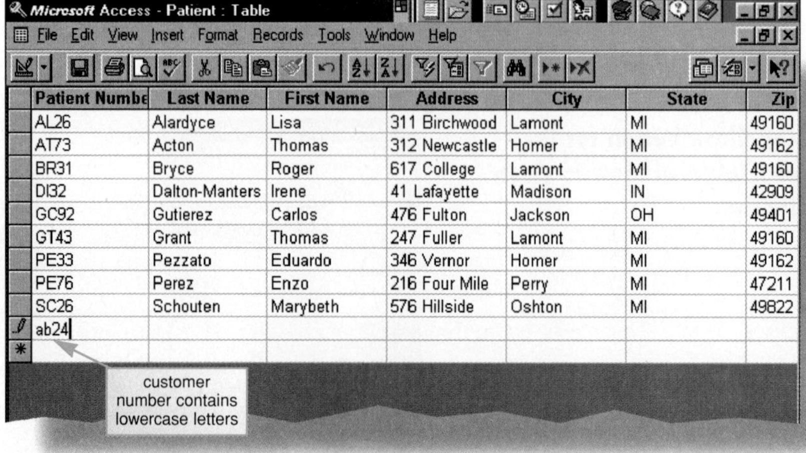

FIGURE 3-46

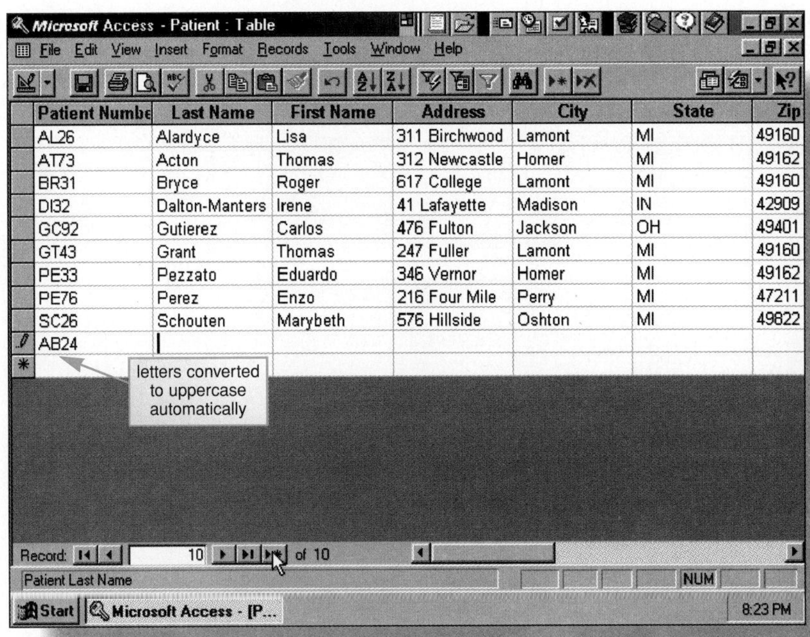

FIGURE 3-47

Instead of the Ins Carrier field initially being blank, it now contains the value ORG (Figure 3-48), because ORG is the default value. Thus, for any patient whose insurance carrier is ORG, it is not necessary to enter the value. By pressing the TAB key, the value ORG is accepted.

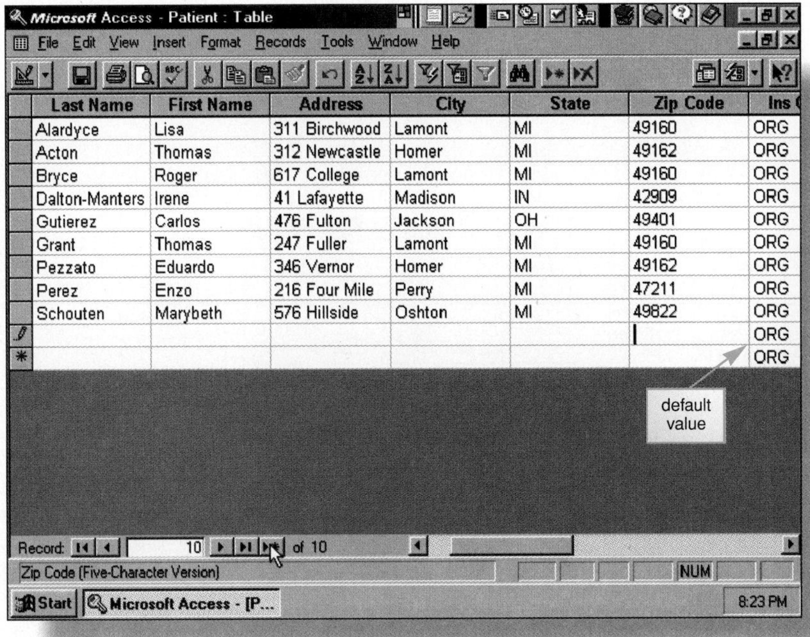

FIGURE 3-48

If the insurance carrier is not valid, such as xxx, Access will display the text message you specified (Figure 3-49) and not allow the data to enter the database.

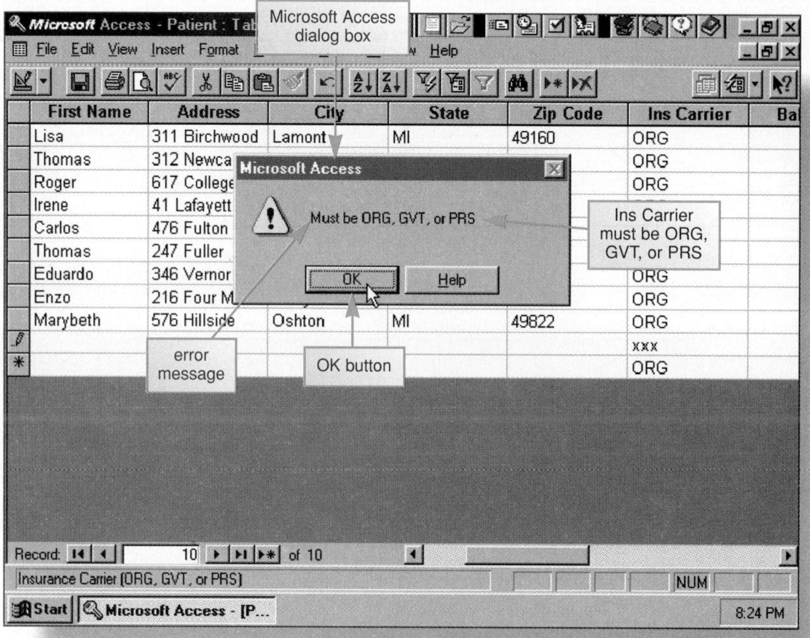

FIGURE 3-49

If the balance is not valid, such as 2200, Access also displays the appropriate message (Figure 3-50) and refuses to accept the data.

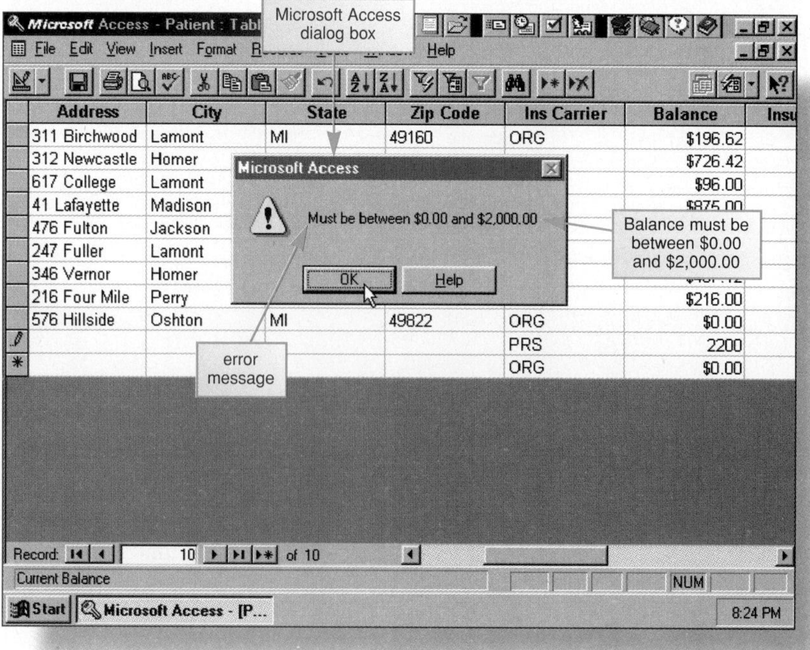

FIGURE 3-50

If a required field contains no data, Access indicates this by displaying an error message as soon as you attempt to leave the record (Figure 3-51). This field *must* be filled in before Access will move to a different record.

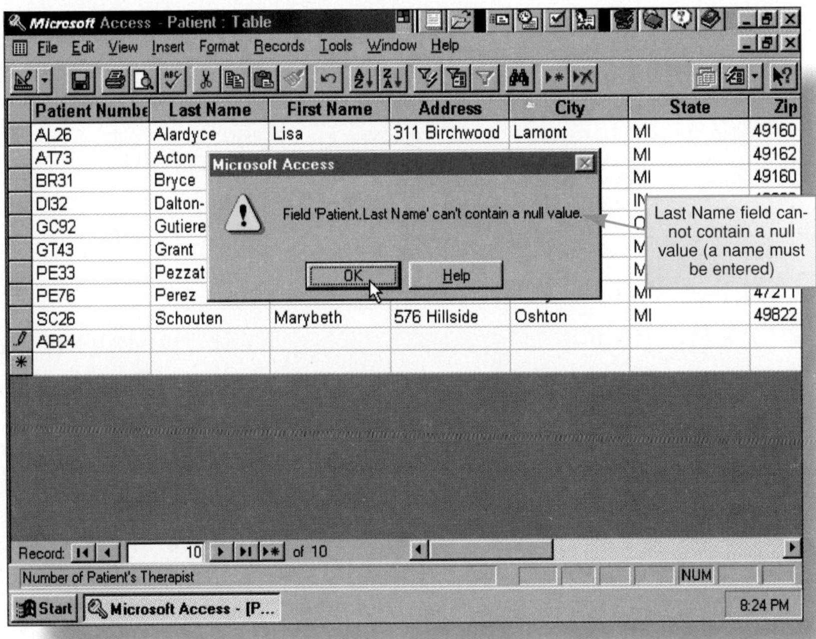

FIGURE 3-51

Take care when creating validation rules as you may come to an impasse where you can neither leave the field nor close the table because you have entered data into a field that violates the validation rule. It may be that you cannot remember the validation rule you created or it was created incorrectly.

First try to type an acceptable entry. If this does not work, repeatedly press the BACKSPACE key to erase the contents of the field and then try to leave the field. If, for some reason, this does not work, press the ESC key until the record is removed from the screen. The record will not be added to the database.

If you ever have to take such drastic action, you probably have a faulty validation rule. Use the techniques of the previous sections to correct the existing validation rules for the field.

Making Individual Changes to a Field

Earlier, you changed all the entries in the Ins Carrier field to ORG. You now have created a rule that will ensure that only legitimate values (ORG, GVT, or PRS) can be entered in the field. To make a change, click the field to be changed to produce an insertion point, use the BACKSPACE or DELETE key to delete the current entry, and then type the new entry.

Complete the steps on the next page to change the Ins Carrier value on the second and fourth records to PRS and on the fifth record to GVT.

To Make Individual Changes

1 **Make sure the Patient table displays in Datasheet view. Click the right scroll arrow twice.**

The Patient table displays in Datasheet view (Figure 3-52).

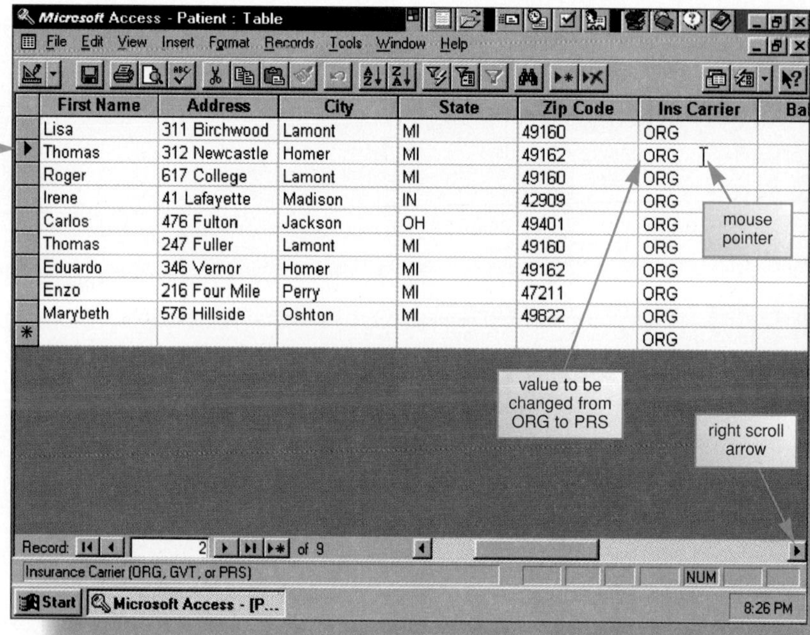

FIGURE 3-52

2 **Click to the right of the ORG entry in the Ins Carrier field on the second record to produce an insertion point. Press the BACKSPACE key three times to delete ORG and then type** PRS **as the new value. In a similar fashion, change the ORG on the fourth record by typing** PRS **and the fifth record by typing** GVT **(Figure 3-53).**

3 **Close the Patient : Table window by clicking its Close button.**

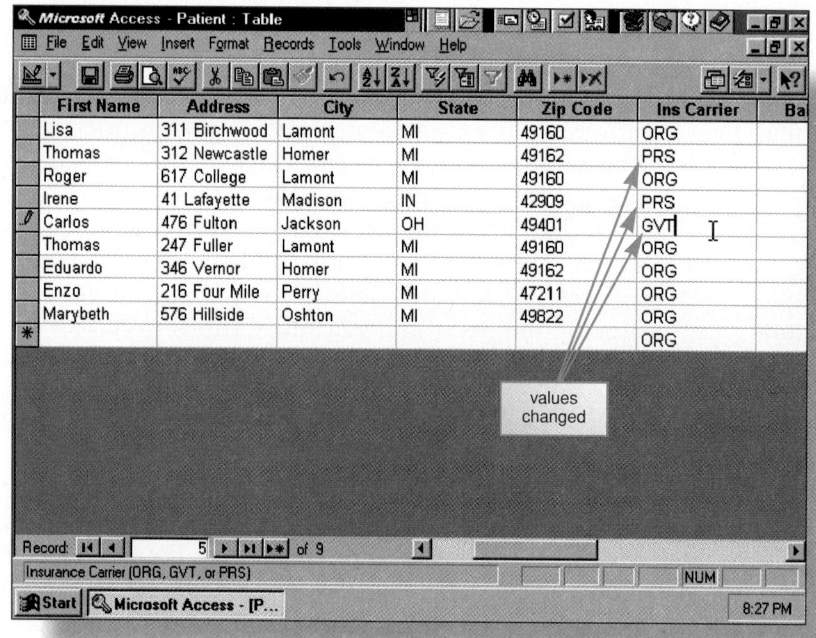

FIGURE 3-53

The Ins Carrier field changes are now complete.

Specifying Referential Integrity

A **foreign key** is a field in one table whose values are required to match the **primary key** of another table. For example, the therapist number in the Patient table must match the primary key of the Therapist table. In other words, the therapist number for any patient must be that of a *real* therapist; that is, a therapist currently in the Therapist table. A patient whose therapist number is 02, for example, should not be stored if therapist 02 does not exist. The property that affirms the value in a foreign key must match that of another table's primary key is called **referential integrity**.

In Access, to specify referential integrity, define a relationship between the tables by using the Relationships command. Access then prohibits any updates to the database that would violate the referential integrity. Access will not allow you to store a patient with a therapist number that does not match a therapist currently in the Therapist table. Access also will prevent you from deleting a therapist who currently has patients. Therapist 08, for example, currently has several patients in the Patient table. If you deleted therapist 08, these patients' therapist numbers would no longer match anyone in the Therapist table.

The type of relationship between two tables specified by the Relationships command is referred to as a **one-to-many relationship**. This means that one record in the first table is related to (matches) many records in the second table, but each record in the second table is related to only one record in the first. In the sample database, for example, a one-to-many relationship exists between the Therapist table and the Patient table. One therapist is associated with many patients but each patient is associated with a single therapist. In general, the table containing the foreign key will be the *many* part of the relationship.

The following steps use the Relationships command to specify referential integrity by specifying a relationship between the Therapist and Patient tables.

More *About* Referential Integrity

Enforcing referential integrity efficiently proved to be one of the most difficult tasks facing the developers of relational database management systems. Although the problem was worked on throughout the 1970s, it was not until the late 1980s that relational systems were able to satisfactorily enforce referential integrity.

To Specify Referential Integrity

1. **Close any open datasheet on the screen by clicking its Close button. Then, point to the Relationships button on the toolbar (Figure 3-54).**

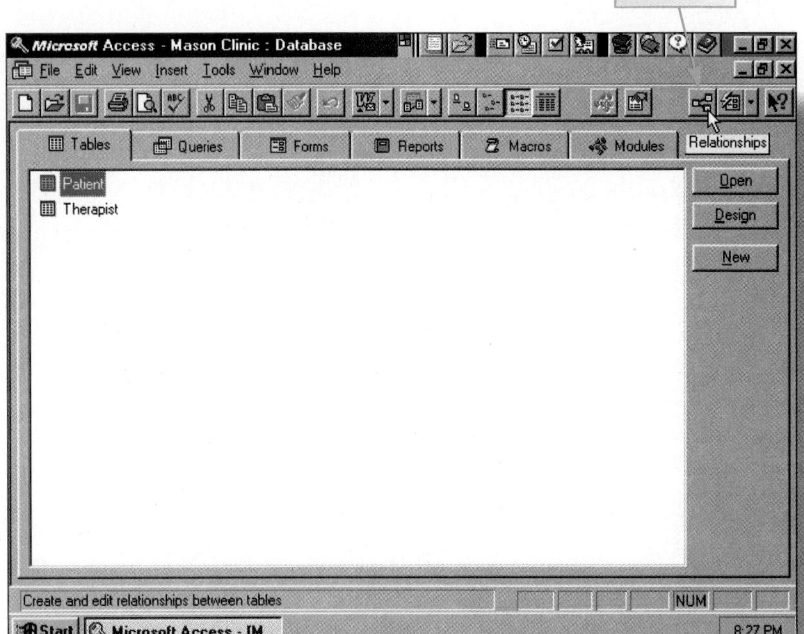

FIGURE 3-54

2 **Click the Relationships button and then click the Therapist table. Point to the Add button.**

The Show Table dialog box displays (Figure 3-55). The Therapist table is selected.

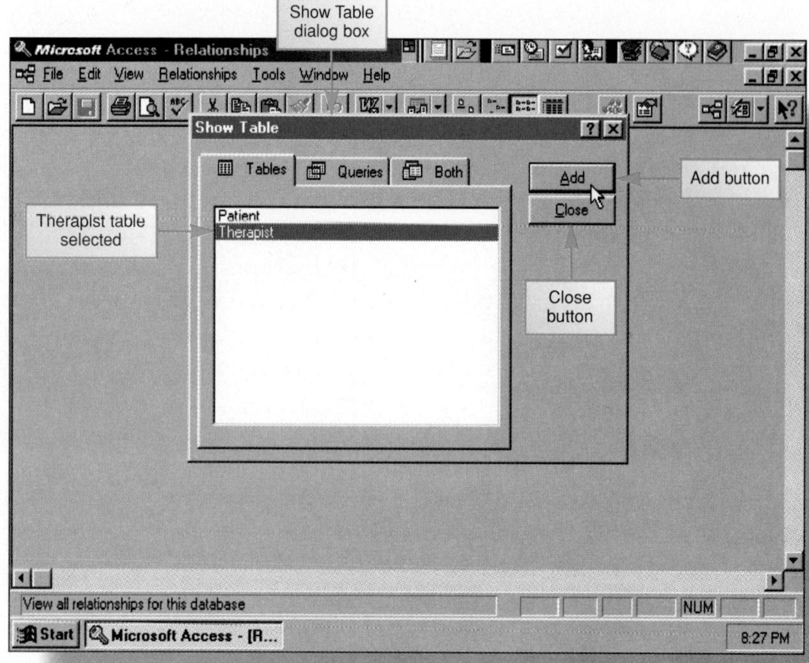

FIGURE 3-55

3 **Click the Add button, click the Patient table, click the Add button again, and then click the Close button. Resize the field list boxes that display so all fields are visible. Point to the Ther Number field in the Therapist table.**

Field list boxes for the Therapist and Patient tables display (Figure 3-56). The boxes have been resized so all fields are visible.

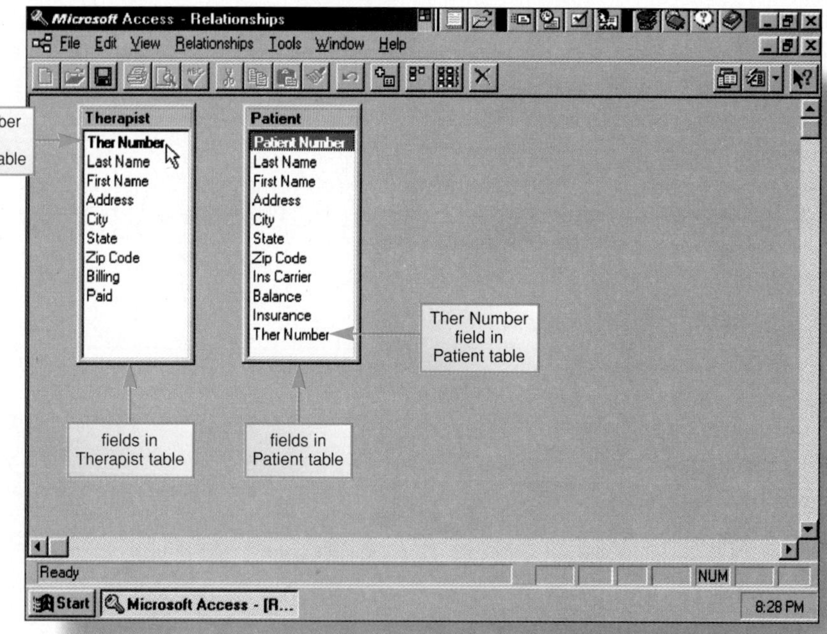

FIGURE 3-56

4 **Drag the Ther Number field in the Therapist table field list box to the Ther Number field in the Patient table field list box. Point to the Enforce Referential Integrity check box.**

The Relationships dialog box displays (Figure 3-57). The correct fields (the Ther Number fields) have been identified as the matching fields.

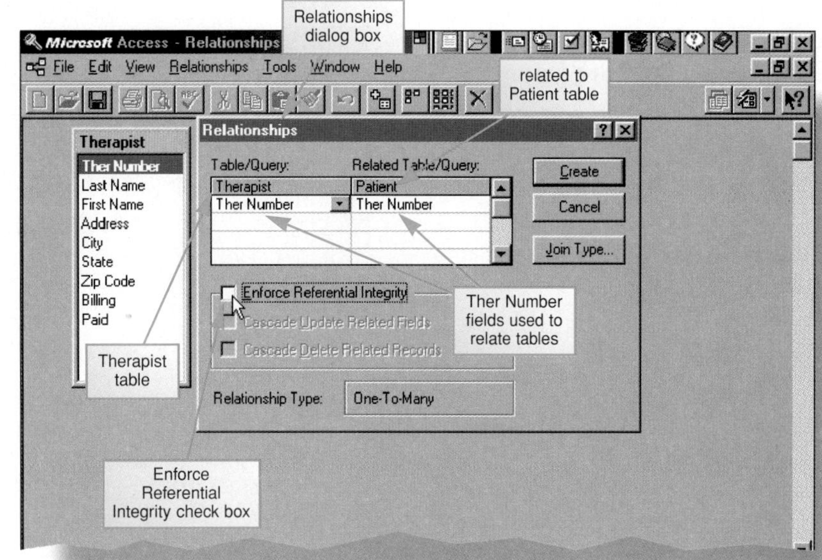

FIGURE 3-57

5 **Click Enforce Referential Integrity.**

Enforce Referential Integrity is selected (Figure 3-58). This will cause Access to reject any update that would violate referential integrity.

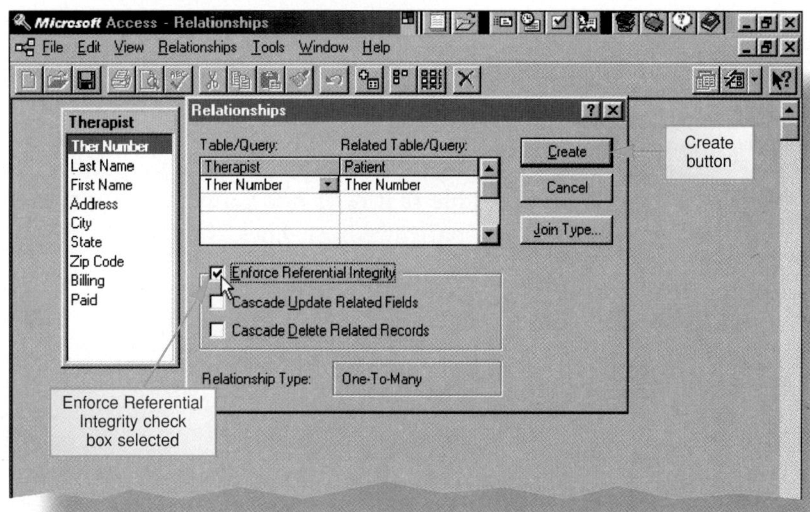

FIGURE 3-58

6 **Click the Create button.**

Access creates the relationship and displays it visually with the ***relationship line*** *joining the two Ther Number fields (Figure 3-59). The number 1 by the Ther Number field in the Therapist table indicates that the Therapist table is the one part of the relationship. The ∞ symbol at the other end of the line indicates that the Patient table is the many part of the relationship.*

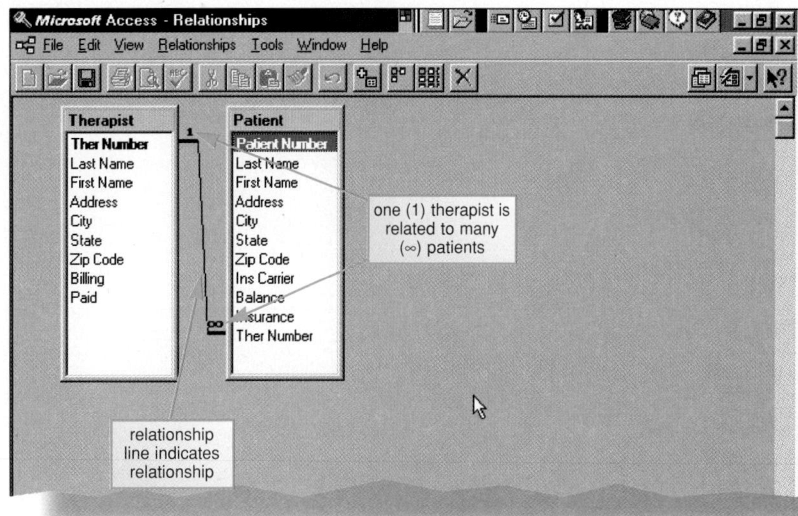

FIGURE 3-59

7 **Close the Relationships window by clicking its Close button.**

The Microsoft Access dialog box displays (Figure 3-60).

8 **Click the Yes button to save your work.**

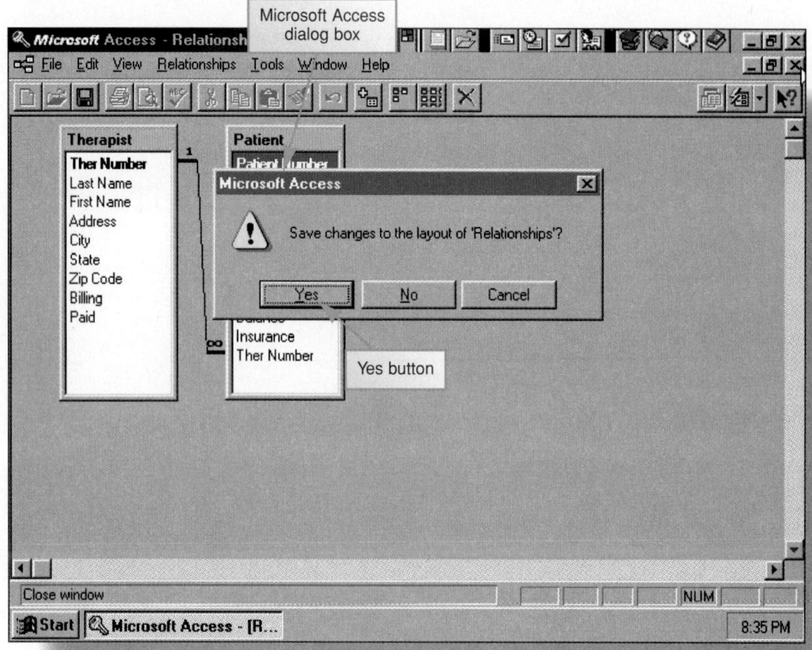

FIGURE 3-60

OtherWays

1. On Tools menu click Relationships

Access will now reject any number in the Ther Number field in the Patient table that does not match a therapist number in the Therapist table. Trying to add a patient whose Ther Number does not match would result in the error message shown in Figure 3-61.

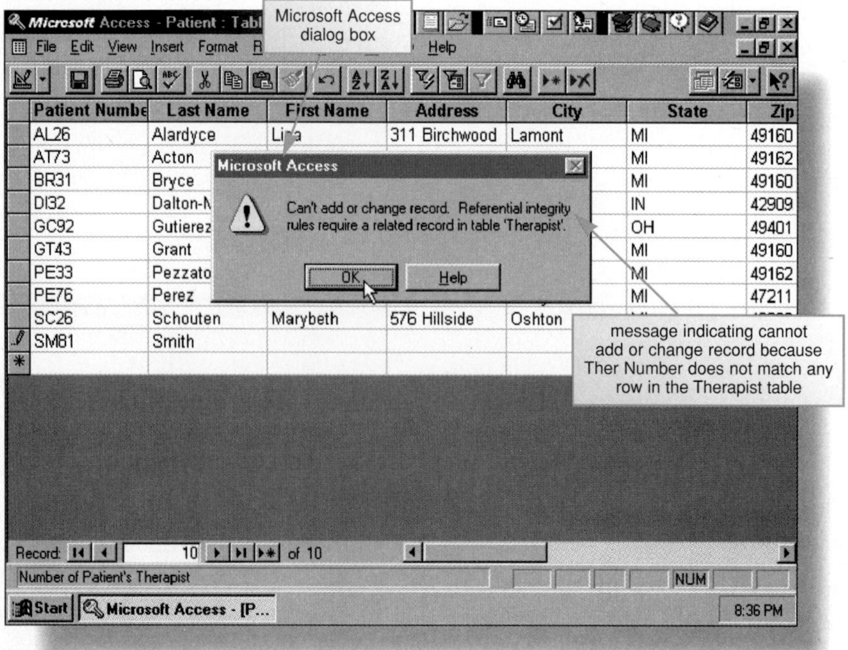

FIGURE 3-61

Deleting a therapist for whom there are related patients would also cause a problem. These patients would have a therapist number that does not match any therapist in the Therapist table. Deleting therapist 05 from the Therapist table, for example, would cause a problem for all records in the Patient table on which the therapist number is 05. To prevent this problem, Access will prohibit such a deletion. Instead of deleting the record, Access will display the message shown in Figure 3-62.

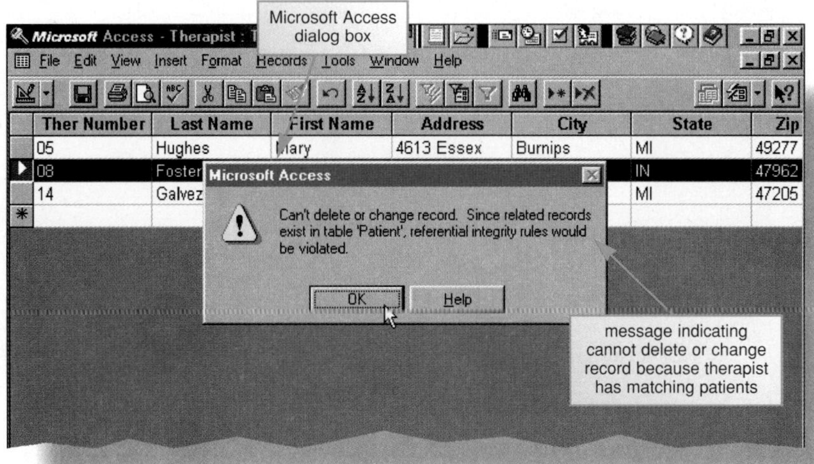

FIGURE 3-62

Ordering Records

Recall from previous discussions that Access sequences the records by patient number whenever listing them because patient number is the primary key. To change the order in which records appear, click the Sort Ascending or Sort Descending buttons on the toolbar. Either button reorders the records based on the field in which the cursor is located.

Perform the following steps to order the records by patient name using the Sort Ascending button.

Steps To Use the Sort Ascending Button to Order Records

1 Open the Patient table in Datasheet view, and then click the Last Name field on the first record (any other record would do as well). Point to the Sort Ascending button on the toolbar (Figure 3-63).

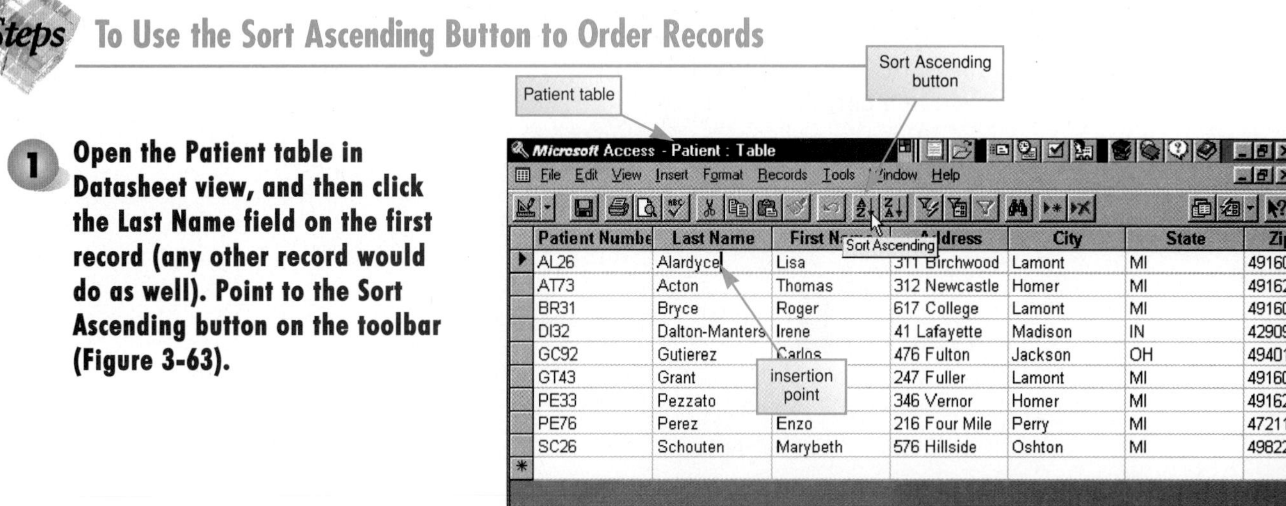

FIGURE 3-63

Click the Sort Ascending button.

The rows are now ordered by last name (Figure 3-64).

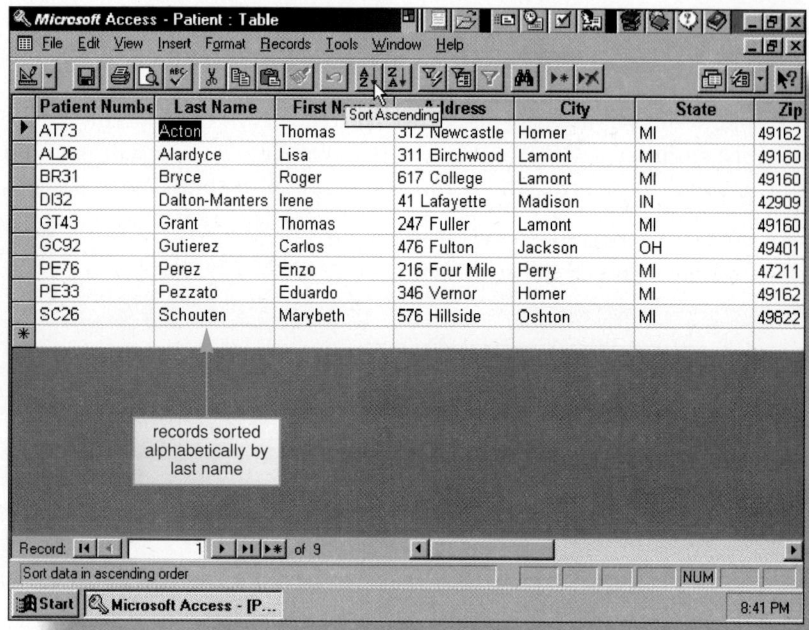

FIGURE 3-64

OtherWays

1. On Records menu click Sort, click Ascending or Descending

If you wanted to sort the data in reverse order, click the Sort Descending button instead of the Sort Ascending button.

Ordering Rows on Multiple Fields

Just as you can sort the answer to a query on multiple fields, you can also sort the data that displays in a datasheet on multiple fields. To do so, the major key and minor key must be next to each other in the datasheet with the major key on the left. (If this is not the case, you can drag the columns into the correct position. Instead of dragging, however, usually it will be easier to use a query that has the data sorted in the desired order.)

Provided the major and minor keys are in the correct position, select both fields and then click the Sort Ascending button on the toolbar. To select the fields, click the field selector for the first field (the major key). Next hold down the SHIFT key and then click the field selector for the second field (the minor key). A **field selector** is the small bar at the top of the column that you click to select an entire field in a datasheet.

Order records on the combination of insurance carrier and balance using the Sort Ascending button by completing the following steps.

Steps To Use the Sort Ascending Button to Order Records on Multiple Fields

1 **Scroll the table to bring the rightmost fields into view. Click the field selector at the top of the Ins Carrier column to select the entire column. Hold down the SHIFT key and then click the field selector for the Balance column.**

The Ins Carrier and Balance fields are selected (Figure 3-65).

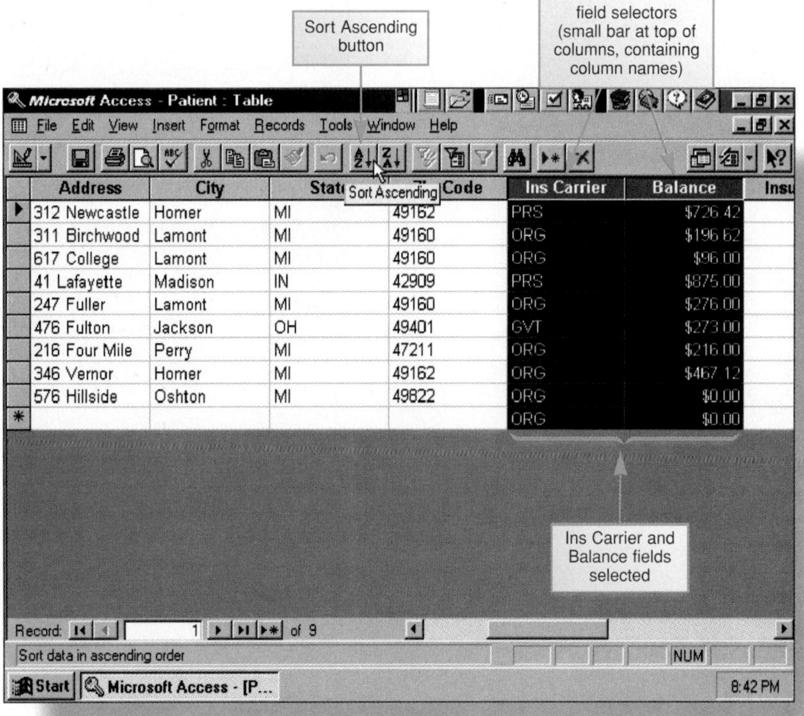

FIGURE 3-65

2 **Click the Sort Ascending button on the toolbar.**

The rows are ordered by insurance carrier (Figure 3-66). Within each group of Patients having the same carrier, the rows are ordered by balance.

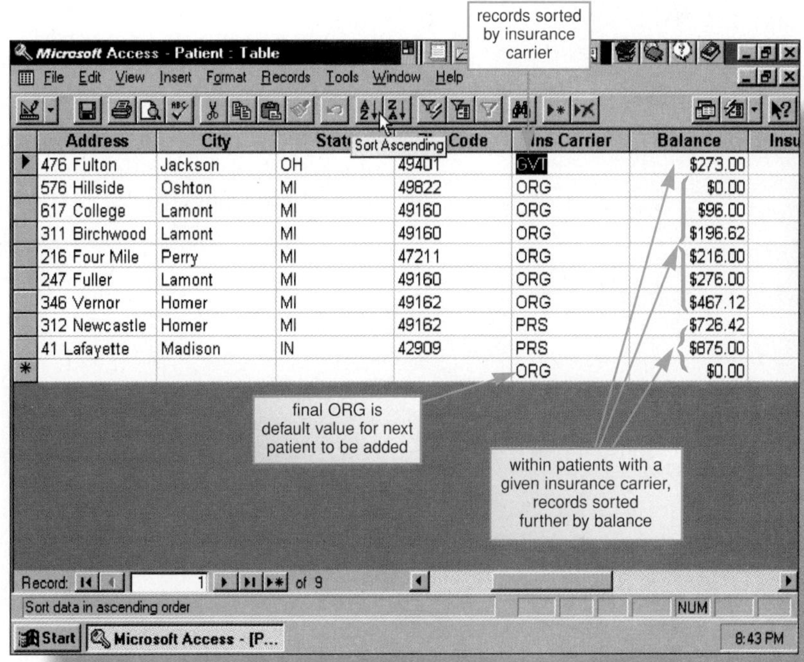

FIGURE 3-66

3 **Close the Patient : Table window by clicking its Close button.**

The Microsoft Access dialog box displays (Figure 3-67) asking if you want to save the changes to the design; that is, do you want to save the order in which the records currently display?

Click the No button to abandon changes.

The next time the table is open, the records will display in their original order.

FIGURE 3-67

Creating and Using Indexes

What Is an Index?

You are already familiar with the concept of an index. The index in the back of a book contains important words or phrases together with a list of pages on which the given words or phrases can be found. An **index** for a table is similar. Figure 3-68, for example, shows the Patient table along with an index built on last names. In this case, the items of interest are last names rather than key words or phrases as is the case in the back of this book. The field or fields on which the index is built is called the **index key**. Thus, in Figure 3-68, the Last Name field is the index key.

Each last name occurs in the index along with the number of the record on which the corresponding patient is located. Further, the names appear in the index in alphabetical order. If Access were to use this index to find the record on which the last name is Grant, for example, it could rapidly scan

FIGURE 3-68

Index on Last Name Field

LAST NAME	RECORD NUMBER
Acton	2
Alardyce	1
Bryce	3
Dalton-Manters	4
Grant	6
Gutierez	5
Perez	8
Pezzato	7
Schouten	9

Patient Table

RECORD NUMBER	PATIENT NUMBER	LAST NAME	FIRST NAME	STREET	CITY	STATE	ZIP CODE	...
1	AL26	Alardyce	Lisa	311 Birchwood	Lamont	MI	49160	...
2	AT73	Acton	Thomas	312 Newcastle	Homer	MI	49162	...
3	BR31	Bryce	Roger	617 College	Lamont	MI	49160	...
4	DI32	Dalton-Manters	Irene	41 Lafayette	Madison	IN	42909	...
5	GC92	Gutierez	Carlos	476 Fulton	Jackson	OH	49401	...
6	GT43	Grant	Thomas	247 Fuller	Lamont	MI	49160	...
7	PE33	Pezzato	Eduardo	346 Vernor	Homer	MI	49162	...
8	PE76	Perez	Enzo	216 Four Mile	Perry	MI	47211	...
9	SC26	Schouten	Marybeth	576 Hillside	Oshton	MI	49822	...

Patient Table

RECORD NUMBER	PATIENT NUMBER	LAST NAME	FIRST NAME	STREET	CITY	STATE	ZIP CODE	...
1	AL26	Alardyce	Lisa	311 Birchwood	Lamont	MI	49160	...
2	AT73	Acton	Thomas	312 Newcastle	Homer	MI	49162	...
3	BR31	Bryce	Roger	617 College	Lamont	MI	49160	...
4	DI32	Dalton-Manters	Irene	41 Lafayette	Madison	IN	42909	...
5	GC92	Gutierez	Carlos	476 Fulton	Jackson	OH	49401	...
6	GT43	Grant	Thomas	247 Fuller	Lamont	MI	49160	...
7	PE33	Pezzato	Eduardo	346 Vernor	Homer	MI	49162	...
8	PE76	Perez	Enzo	216 Four Mile	Perry	MI	47211	...
9	SC26	Schouten	Marybeth	576 Hillside	Oshton	MI	49822	...

the names in the index to find Grant. Once it did, it would determine the corresponding record number (5) and then go immediately to record 5 in the Patient table, thus finding this Patient much more rapidly than if it had to look through the entire Patient table one record at a time. Indexes make the process of retrieving records very fast and efficient.

Because no two patients happen to have the same last name, the Record Number column contains only single values. This may not always be the case. Consider the index on the Zip Code field shown in Figure 3-69. In this index, the Record Number column contains several values, namely all the records on which the corresponding Zip Code appears. The first row, for example, indicates that Zip Code 42909 is found only on record 4; whereas, the third row indicates that Zip Code 49160 is found on records 1, 3, and 6. If Access were to use this index to find all patients in Zip Code 49160, it could rapidly scan the Zip Codes in the index to find 49160. Once it did, it would determine the corresponding record numbers (1, 3, and 6) and then go immediately to these records. It would not have to examine any other records in the Patient table.

Index on Zip Code Field

ZIP CODE	RECORD NUMBER
42909	4
47211	8
49160	1, 3, 6
49162	2, 7
49401	5
49822	9

FIGURE 3-69

Another benefit to indexes is that they provide an efficient alternative to sorting. That is, if the records are to appear in a certain order, Access can use an index rather than having to physically rearrange the records in the database file. Physically rearranging the records in a different order, which is called **sorting**, can be a very time-consuming process.

To see how indexes can be used for alphabetizing records, look at the record numbers in the index (Figure 3-68) and suppose you used these to list all patients. That is, simply follow down the Record Number column, listing the corresponding patients. In this example, first you would list the patient on record 2 (Acton), then the patient on record 1 (Alardyce), then the patient on record 3 (Bryce), and so on. The patients would be listed alphabetically by last name without actually sorting the table.

To gain the benefits from an index, you must first create one. Access automatically creates an index on the primary key as well as some other special fields. If, as is the case with both the Patient and Therapist tables, a table contains a field called Zip Code, for example, Access will create an index for it automatically. You must create any other indexes you feel you need, indicating the field or fields on which the index is to be built.

More *About* **Indexes**

Indexes in Access, and in many other database management systems, are stored in a very special structure called a B-tree. This is a highly efficient structure that supports very rapid access to records in the database as well as a rapid alternative to sorting records.

Although the index key will usually be a single field, it can be a combination of fields. For example, you might want to sort records by balance within therapist number. In other words, the records are ordered by a combination of fields: Ther Number and Balance. An index can be used for this purpose by using a combination of fields for the index key. In this case, you must assign a name to the index. It is a good idea to assign a name that represents the combination of fields. For example, an index whose key is the combination of Ther Number and Balance, might be called Therbal.

How Does Access Use an Index?

Access creates an index whenever you request that it do so. It takes care of all the work in setting up and maintaining the index. In addition, it will use the index automatically.

If you request that data be sorted in a particular order and Access determines that an index is available it can use to make the process efficient, it will do so. If no index is available, it will still sort the data in the order you requested; it will just take longer.

Similarly, if you request that Access locate a particular record that has a certain value in a particular field, Access will use an index if an appropriate one exists. If not, it will have to examine each record until it finds the one you want.

In both cases, the added efficiency provided by an index will not be readily apparent in tables that have only a few records. Once your tables have more records in them, the difference can be dramatic. Even with only fifty to one hundred records, you will notice a difference. You can imagine how dramatic the difference would be in a table with fifty thousand records.

When Should You Create an Index?

An index improves efficiency for sorting and finding records. On the contrary, indexes occupy space on your disk. They also require Access to do extra work. Access must maintain all the indexes that have been created up to date. Thus, there are both advantages and disadvantages to indexes. Consequently, the decision as to which indexes to create is an important one. The following guidelines should help you in this process.

Create an index on a field (or combination of fields) if one or more of the following conditions are present:

1. The field is the primary key of the table (Access will create this index automatically)
2. The field is the foreign key in a relationship you have created (Access also will create this index automatically when you specify the relationship)
3. You will frequently need your data to be sorted on the field
4. You will frequently need to locate a record based on a value in this field

Because Access handles 1 and 2 automatically, you need only to concern yourself about 3 and 4. If you think you will need to see patient data arranged in order of patient balances, for example, you should create an index on the Balance field. If you think you will need to see the data arranged by balance within therapist number, you should create an index on the combination of the Ther Number field and the Balance field. Similarly, if you think you will need to find a patient given the patient's last name, you should create an index on the Last Name field.

Creating Single-Field Indexes

A **single-field index** is an index whose key is a single field. In this case, the index key is to be the Last Name field. In creating an index, you need to indicate whether to allow duplicates in the index key; that is, two records that have the same value. For example, in the index for the Last Name field, if duplicates are not allowed, Access would not allow the addition of a patient whose last name is the same as the last name of a patient already in the database. In the index for the Last Name field, duplicates will be allowed. Perform the following steps to create a single-field index.

Steps To Create a Single-Field Index

1 **Right-click Patient.**

The shortcut menu displays (Figure 3-70).

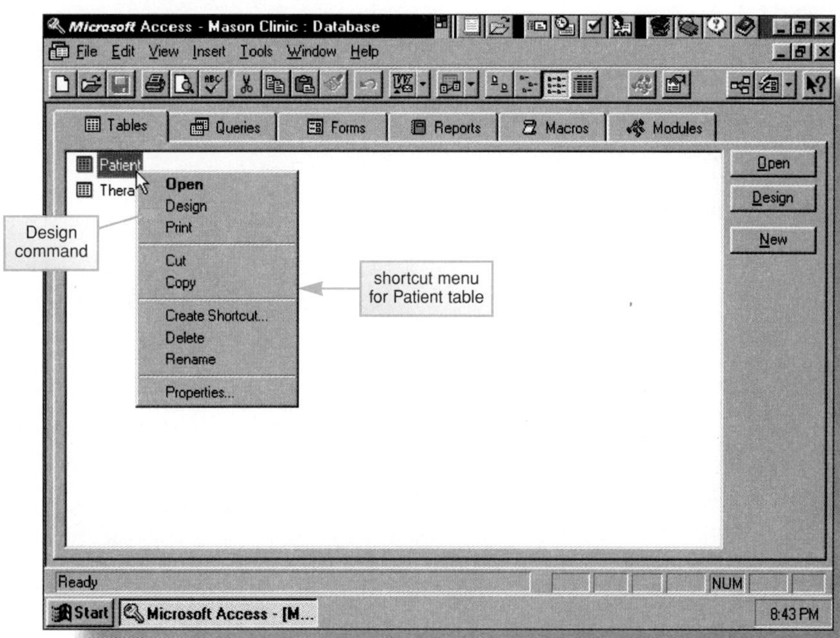

FIGURE 3-70

2 **Click Design and then maximize the Patient : Table window if necessary. Click the row selector to select the Last Name field. Point to the Indexed text box.**

A maximized Patient : Table window displays (Figure 3-71). The Last Name field is selected.

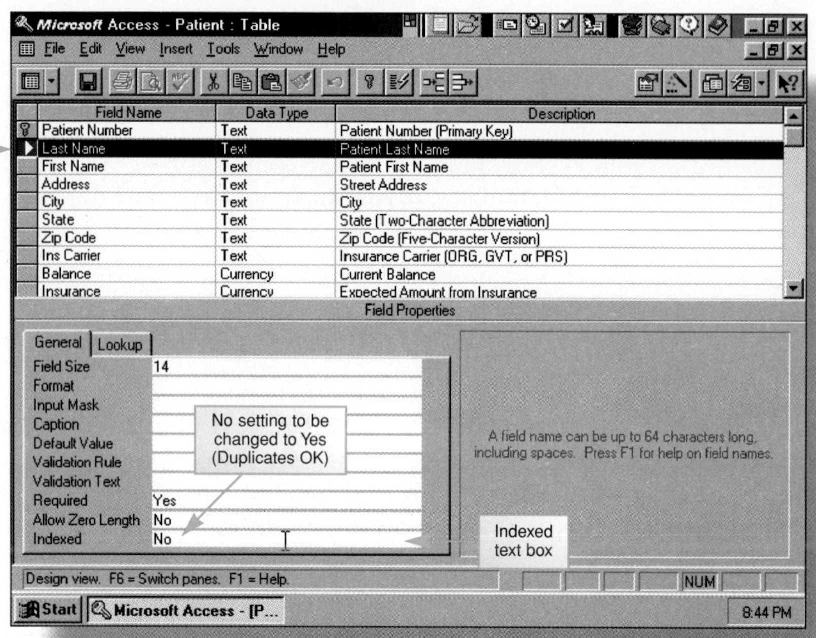

FIGURE 3-71

3 **Click the Indexed text box in the Field Properties pane. Click the down arrow that displays.**

The Indexed drop-down list displays (Figure 3-72). The settings are No (no index), Yes (Duplicates OK) (create an index and allow duplicates), and Yes (No Duplicates) (create an index but reject (do not allow) duplicates).

4 **Click Yes (Duplicates OK).**

The indexes on the Last Name field now will be created and are ready for use as soon as you save your work.

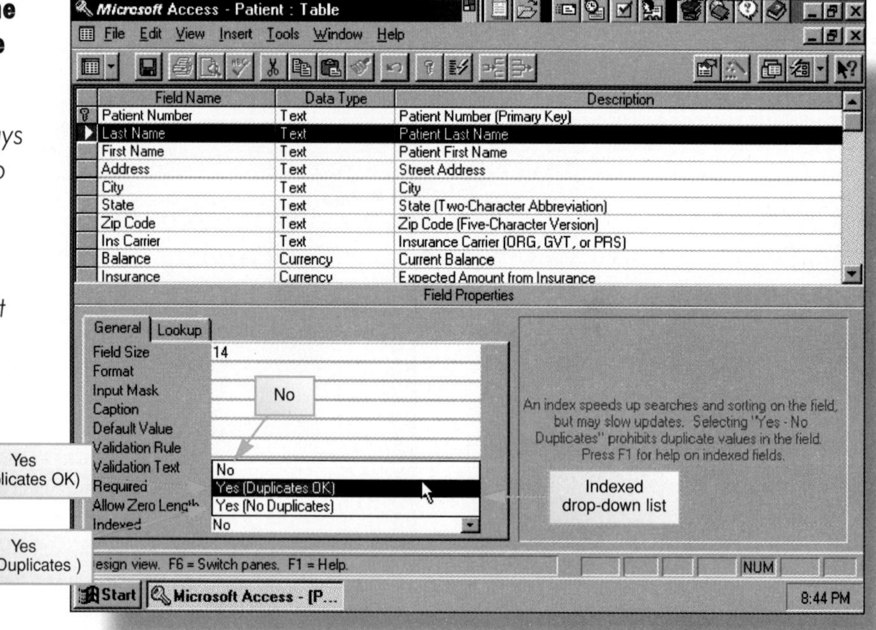

FIGURE 3-72

Creating Multiple-Field Indexes

Creating **multiple-field indexes**, that is indexes whose key is a combination of fields, involves a different process from creating single-field indexes. Click the Indexes button on the toolbar, enter a name for the index, and then enter the combination of fields that make up the index key. The following steps create a multiple-field index with the name Therbal. The key will be the combination of the Ther Number field and the Balance field.

To Create a Multiple-Field Index

1 **Point to the Indexes button on the toolbar (Figure 3-73).**

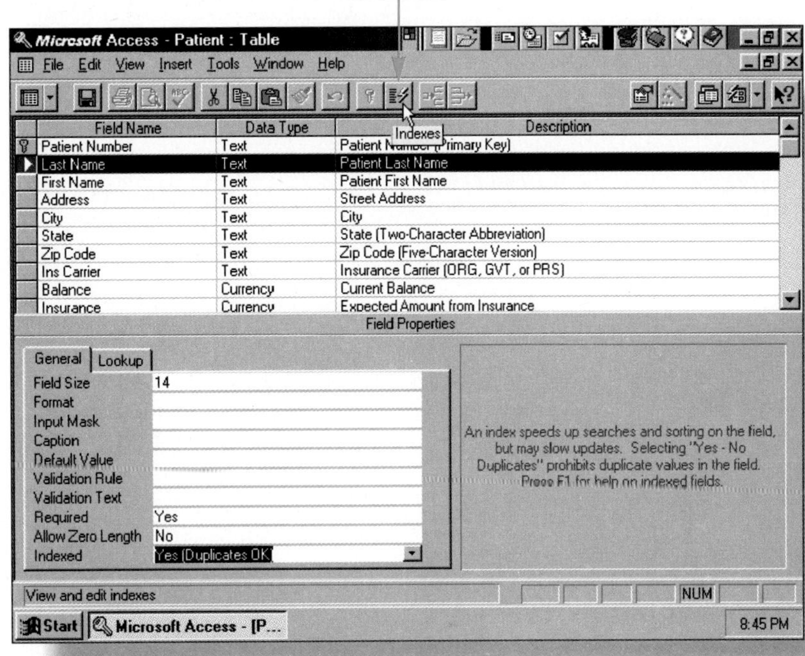

FIGURE 3-73

2 **Click the Indexes button.**

The Indexes: Patient dialog box displays (Figure 3-74). The index on Patient Number is the primary index and was created automatically by Access. The index on Last Name is the one just created. Access created an index automatically on the Zip Code field. Use this dialog box to create additional indexes.

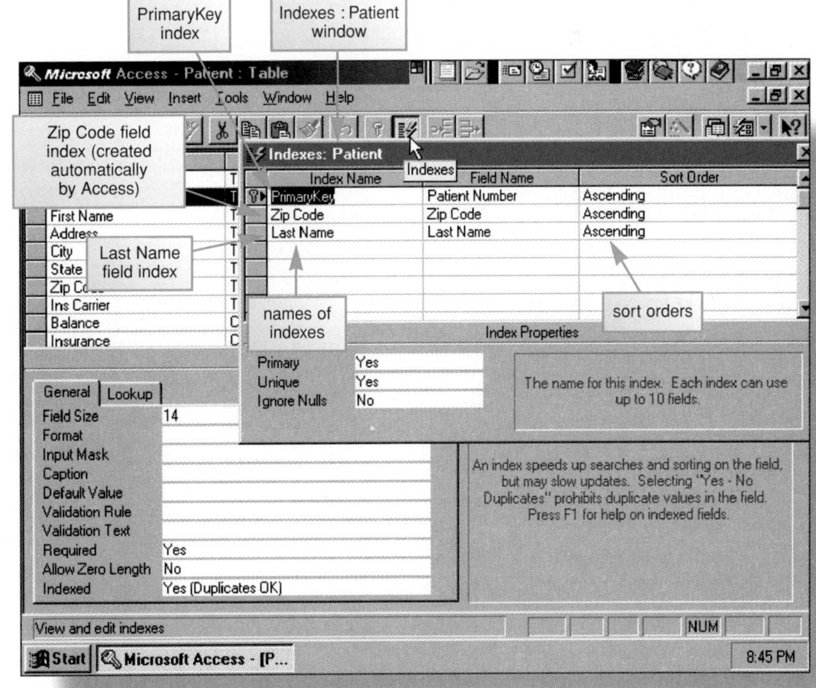

FIGURE 3-74

3 **Click the Index Name entry on the row following Last Name. Type** `Therbal` **as the index name, and then press the TAB key. Point to the down arrow.**

The index name has been entered as Therbal (Figure 3-75). An insertion point displays in the Field Name column.

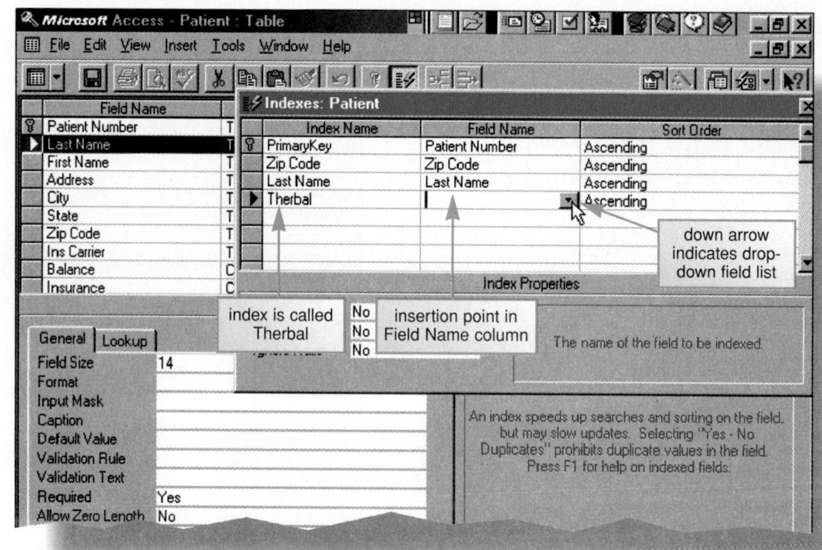

FIGURE 3-75

4 **Click the down arrow in the Field Name column to produce a list of fields in the Patient table, scroll down the list, and select Ther Number. Press the TAB key three times to move to the Field Name entry on the following row. Select the Balance field in the same manner as the Ther Number field.**

Ther Number and Balance are selected as the two fields for the Therbal index (Figure 3-76). The absence of an index name on the row containing the Balance field indicates that it is part of the previous index, Therbal.

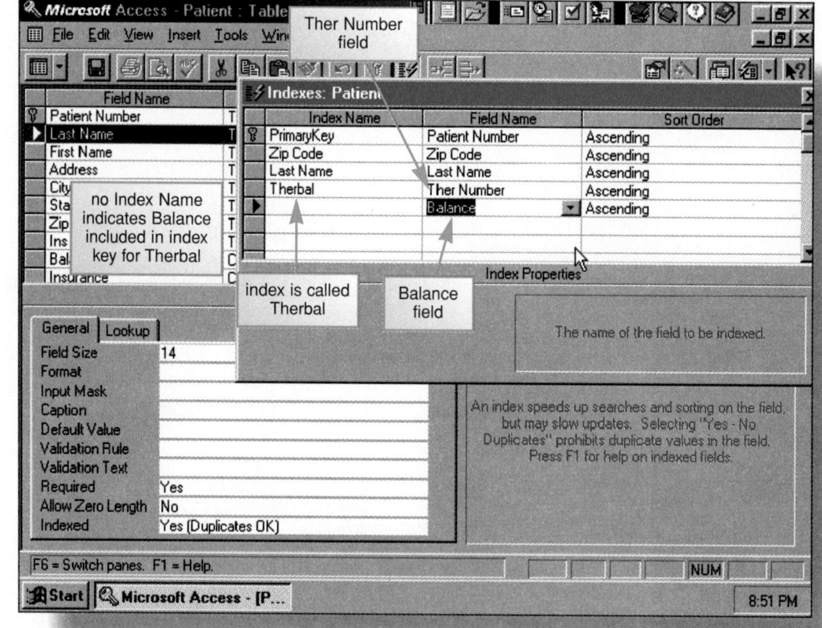

FIGURE 3-76

5 **Close the Indexes: Patient dialog box by clicking its Close button.**

6 **Close the Patient : Table window by clicking its Close button. When asked if you want to save your changes, click the Yes button.**

The indexes are created and the Database window displays.

OtherWays

1. On View menu click Indexes

Closing the Database

The following step closes the database by closing its Database window.

TO CLOSE A DATABASE

Step 1: Click the Close button for the Mason Clinic : Database window.

The indexes now have been created. Access will use them automatically whenever possible to improve efficiency of ordering or finding records. Access will also maintain them automatically. That is, whenever the data in the Patient table is changed, Access will automatically make appropriate changes in the indexes.

Project Summary

Project 3 covered the issues involved in maintaining a database. You used Form view to add a record to the Mason Clinic database and also searched for a record satisfying a criterion. You changed and deleted records. You changed the structure of the Patient table in the Mason Clinic database, created validation rules, and specified referential integrity between the Patient and the Therapist tables by creating relationships. You made mass changes to the Patient table. Finally, you created indexes to improve performance.

What You Should Know

Having completed this project, you should now be able to perform the following tasks:

- Add a Field to a Table *(A 3.16)*
- Change the Size of a Field *(A 3.14)*
- Close a Database *(A 3.49)*
- Create a Multiple-Field Index *(A 3.47)*
- Create a Single-Field Index *(A 3.45)*
- Delete a Record *(A 3.12)*
- Make Individual Changes *(A 3.34)*
- Open a Database *(A 3.6)*
- Resize a Column *(A 3.19)*
- Save the Validation Rules, Default Values, and Formats *(A 3.29)*
- Search for a Record *(A 3.9)*
- Specify a Collection of Legal Values *(A 3.28)*
- Specify a Default Value *(A 3.27)*
- Specify a Format *(A 3.29)*
- Specify a Range *(A 3.26)*
- Specify a Required Field *(A 3.25)*
- Specify Referential Integrity *(A 3.35)*
- Switch from Form View to Datasheet View *(A 3.11)*
- Update the Contents of a Field *(A 3.10, A 3.17)*
- Use a Delete Query to Delete a Group of Records *(A 3.23)*
- Use a Form to Add Records *(A 3.7)*
- Use an Update Query to Update All Records *(A 3.21)*
- Use the Sort Ascending Button to Order Records *(A 3.39)*
- Use the Sort Ascending Button to Order Records on Multiple Fields *(A 3.41)*

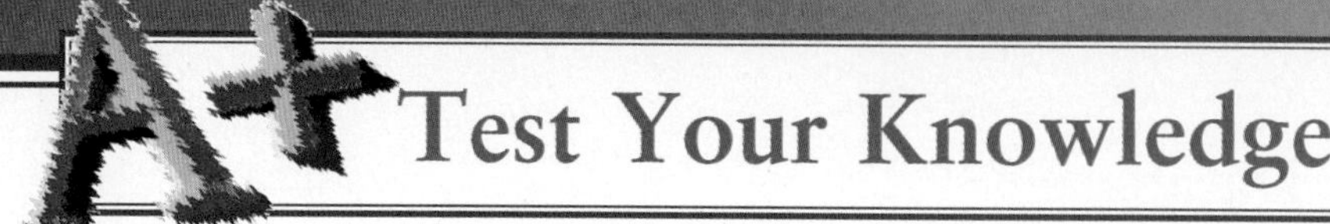

Test Your Knowledge

1 True/False

Instructions: Circle T if the statement is true or F if the statement is false.

T F 1. Access sorts records automatically by the primary index.
T F 2. Indexes provide an efficient alternative to sorting.
T F 3. To force all letters in a field to display as uppercase, use the > symbol in the Format text box.
T F 4. You can add and change records using Form view, but you can only delete records using Datasheet view.
T F 5. To change the order in which records appear in a table, click the Sort Ascending or Sort Descending button on the toolbar.
T F 6. To delete a record from a table, click the row selector for the record, and then press CTRL+D.
T F 7. To delete a group of records that satisfy a criteria, use a query.
T F 8. A foreign key is a field in one table whose values are required to match a primary key of another table.
T F 9. The property that the value in a foreign key must match that of another table's primary key is called entity integrity.
T F 10. To specify referential integrity, click the Referential Integrity button on the toolbar.

2 Multiple Choice

Instructions: Circle the correct response.

1. Indexes __________.
   a. provide an efficient alternative to sorting
   b. allow rapid retrieval of records
   c. allow rapid retrieval of tables
   d. both a and b
2. To create a multiple-field index, click the __________ button in the Table Design window.
   a. Secondary Index
   b. Define Secondary Indexes
   c. Indexes
   d. Define Indexes
3. __________ are rules that the data entered by a user must follow.
   a. Data rules
   b. Edit rules
   c. Integrity rules
   d. Validation rules

Test Your Knowledge

4. To search for a specific record in a table, select the field to search and click the __________ button.
   a. Search
   b. Locate
   c. Find
   d. Locator
5. To force all letters in a field to display as uppercase, use the __________ symbol in the Format text box.
   a. ?
   b. >
   c. @
   d. &
6. A(n) __________ is a field in one table whose values are required to match a primary key of another table.
   a. secondary key
   b. auxiliary key
   c. foreign key
   d. matching key
7. The property that the value in a foreign key must match that of another table's primary key is called __________ integrity.
   a. entity
   b. referential
   c. relationship
   d. inter-relation
8. To delete a record from a table, click the row selector for the record, and then press __________.
   a. CTRL+U
   b. CTRL+D
   c. DELETE
   d. CTRL+DELETE
9. To specify referential integrity, click the __________ button.
   a. Referential Integrity
   b. Integrity
   c. Relationships
   d. Primary Key
10. To add a field to a table structure, select the field below where you would like the new field inserted and then press __________.
    a. CTRL+N
    b. CTRL+INSERT
    c. INSERT
    d. ALT+INSERT

Test Your Knowledge

3 Adding, Changing, and Deleting Records

Instructions: Figure 3-77 shows the first record in the Client table in Form view. Use this figure to help explain how to perform the following tasks in Form view. Write your answers on your own paper.

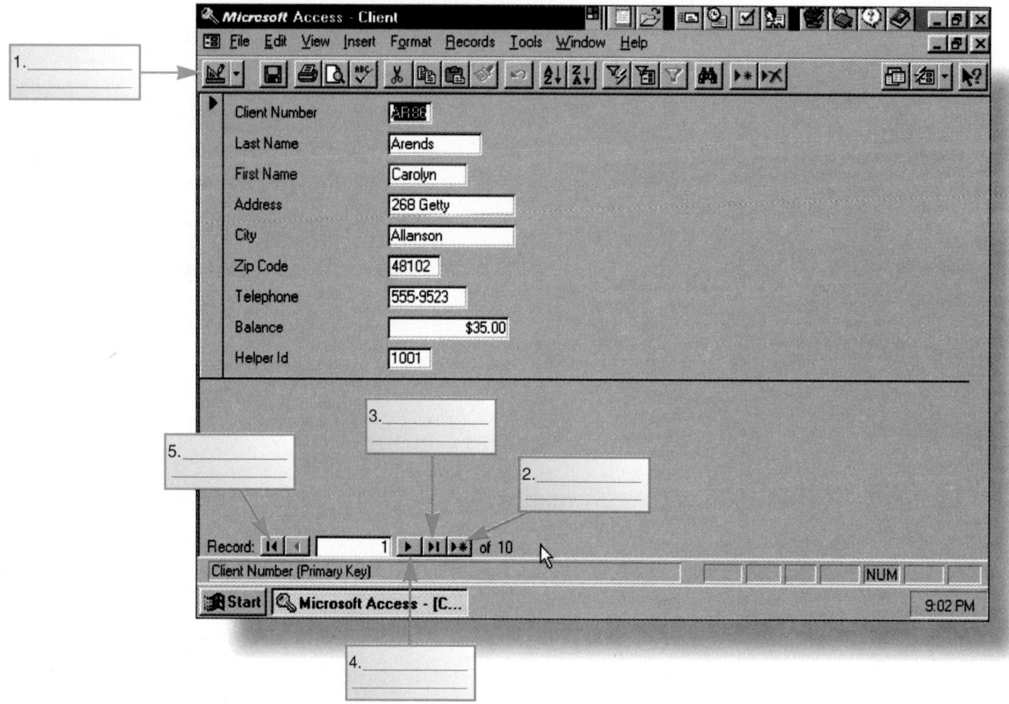

FIGURE 3-77

1. Change the Last Name from Arends to Arendsen.
2. Add a new record to the Client table.
3. Locate the record that contains the value MA21 in the Client Number field.
4. Switch to Datasheet view.
5. In Datasheet view, delete the record where the Client Number is MA21.

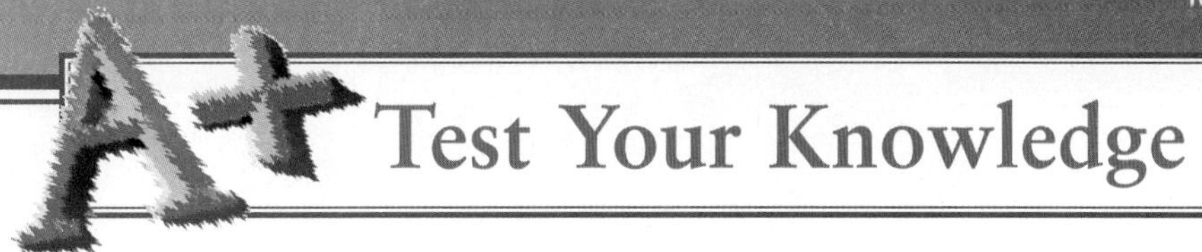

Test Your Knowledge

4 Understanding Validation Rules and Indexes

Instructions: Figure 3-78 shows the Helper table in Design view. Use this figure to help explain how to create the following validation rules and indexes. For each question, assume that the proper field already has been selected. Write your answers on your own paper.

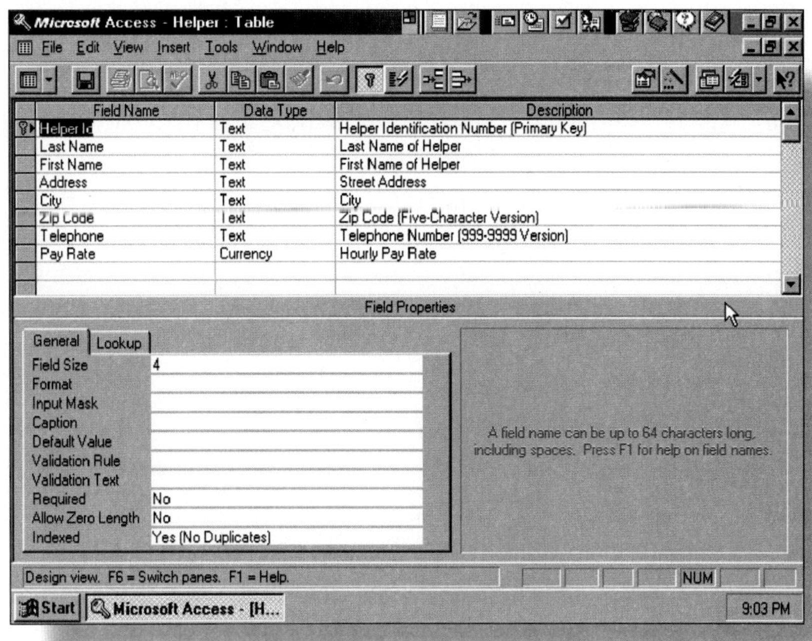

FIGURE 3-78

1. Make the Last Name field a required field.
2. Specify a default value of $5.00 for the Pay Rate field.
3. Specify that any value entered in the Pay Rate field must be greater than or equal to $5.00 and less than or equal to $10.00.
4. Create an index on the Last Name field that allows duplicates.

1 Reviewing Project Activities

Instructions: Perform the following tasks using a computer.

1. Start Access.
2. Double-click the Help button on the toolbar to display the Help Topics: Microsoft Access for Windows 95 dialog box.
3. Click the Contents tab. Double-click the Finding and Sorting Data book. Double-click the Finding Records or Data book. Double-click Find specific occurrences of a value in a field.
4. Read the Help information. Next, right-click within the box, and then click Print Topic. Hand in the printout to your instructor. Click the Help Topics button to return to the Help Topics: Microsoft Access for Windows 95 dialog box.
5. Click the Index tab. Type `sort` in box 1 and then double-click sorting records in tables in box 2. Double-click Working in table Datasheet view in the Topics Found dialog box. Click the Sort, filter, or find records link and then read the Help information. Click the remaining four links and read their Help information. Click the Close button.
6. Double-click the Help button on the toolbar. Click the Find tab. Type `validation` in box 1. Click Validation in box 2. Double-click Define validation rules to control what values can be entered into a field in box 3. When the Help information displays, read it, ready the printer, right-click, and click Print Topic. Hand in the printout to your instructor. Click the Help Topics button to return to the Help Topics: Microsoft Access for Windows 95 dialog box.
7. Click the Answer Wizard tab. Type `how do i create indexes` in box 1. Click the Search button. Double-click Decide if and when to use an index in box 2 under How Do I. Read and print the Help information. Hand in the printout to your instructor.

Use Help

2 Expanding the Basics

Instructions: Use Access online Help to better understand the topics listed below. Begin each of the following by double-clicking the Help button on the toolbar. If you are unable to print the Help information, then answer the question on your own paper.

1. Using the Creating, Importing, and Linking Tables book on the Contents sheet on the Help Topics: Microsoft Access for Windows 95 dialog box, answer the following questions:
   a. How do you delete an index?
   b. You cannot create indexes on fields of certain data types. What are these data types?
   c. What is the maximum number of fields in a multiple-field index?
   d. How can you create a primary key that includes more than one field?
2. Using the key term *update* and the Index tab in the Help Topics: Microsoft Access for Windows 95 dialog box, display and print information on update queries. Then, answer the following questions:
   a. How can you see a list of records that will be updated?
   b. How can you stop a query after you start it?
3. Use the Find tab in the Help Topics: Microsoft Access for Windows 95 dialog box to display and then print information about replacing specific occurrences of a value in a field. Then answer the following questions:
   a. What are the advantages of using the Replace command instead of an update query?
   b. What is a null value?
4. Use the Answer Wizard in the Help Topics: Microsoft Access for Windows 95 dialog box to display and print information on defining a custom data display format for a field.

Apply Your Knowledge

1 Maintaining the Extra Hands Database

Instructions: Start Access. Open the Extra Hands database from the Access folder on the Student Floppy Disk that accompanies this book. Perform the following tasks:

1. Open the Client table in Design view as shown in Figure 3-79.
2. Increase the size of the Last Name field to 15.
3. Format the Client Number field so any lowercase letters display in uppercase.
4. Make the Last Name field a required field.
5. Specify that balance amounts must be greater than or equal to $0.00 and less than or equal to $150.00. Include validation text.
6. Create an index that allows duplicates for the Last Name field.
7. Save the changes to the structure.
8. Open the Client table in Datasheet view.
9. Change the last name of Client Number JO12 to *Johns-Rivers*.
10. Print the table.
11. Delete the record of Client Number MA21.
12. Print the table.
13. Sort the data in ascending order by Zip Code within City.
14. Print the table. Close the table. If you are asked to save changes to the design of the table, click the No button.
15. Establish referential integrity between the Helper table (the *one* table) and the Client table (the *many* table).

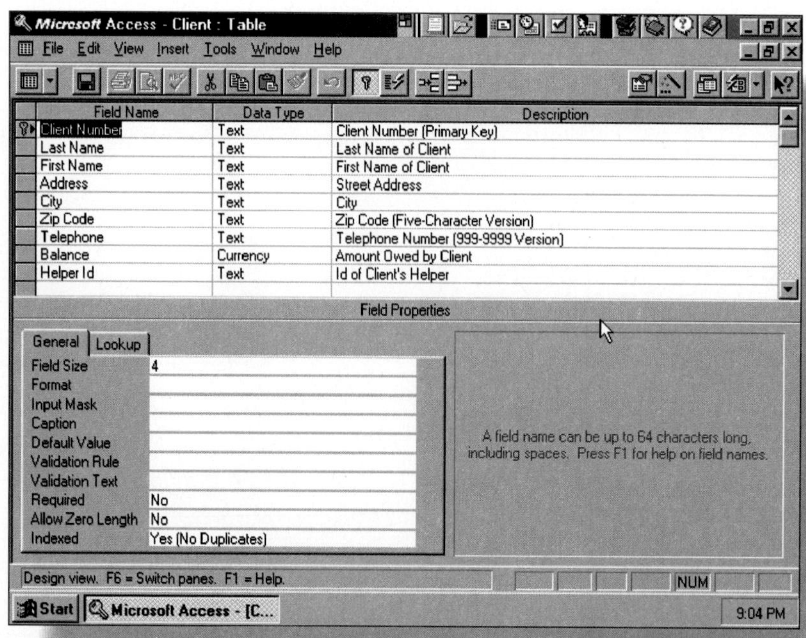

FIGURE 3-79

In the Lab

1 Maintaining the Symphony Shop Database

Problem: The Symphony Shop volunteers have determined that they would like to make some changes to the database structure. They need to increase the size of the Description field and add an additional index. Because several different individuals update the data, the volunteers also would like to add some validation rules to the database. Finally, there are some novelty items that must be added to the database.

Instructions: Use the database created in the In the Lab 1 of Project 1 for this assignment. Perform the following tasks:

1. Open the Symphony Shop database and open the Novelty table in Design view as shown in Figure 3-80 on the next page.
2. Create an index for the Description field. Be sure to allow duplicates.
3. Create and save the following validation rules for the Novelty table. List the steps involved on your own paper.
   a. Make the Description field a required field.
   b. Ensure that any lowercase letters entered in the Novelty Id field are converted to uppercase.
   c. Ensure that any lowercase letters entered in the Dist Code field are converted to uppercase.
   d. Specify that Units On Hand must be between 0 and 100. Include validation text.
4. Save the changes.
5. Open the Novelty form you created in Project 1, and then add the following record to the Novelty table:

P04	Pencil Cases	20	$.95	$1.50	MM

6. Switch to Datasheet view and sort the records in ascending order by Description.
7. Print the table. Close the table. If you are asked to save changes to the design of the table, click the No button.
8. Create a new query for the Novelty table.
9. Using a query, delete all records in the Novelty table where the Description starts with the letter K. (Hint: Use information from Use Help Exercise 2 to solve this problem.) Close the query without saving it.
10. Print the Novelty table.
11. Open the Distributor table in Design view, change the field width of the Name field to 22, and save the change.
12. Open the Distributor table in Datasheet view, and then change the name on the first record to *AAA Arts Distributor*. Resize the column so the complete name displays.
13. Print the table. Save the change to the layout of the table.
14. Specify referential integrity between the Distributor table (the *one* table) and the Novelty table (the *many* table). List the steps involved on your own paper.

(continued)

Maintaining the Symphony Shop Database *(continued)*

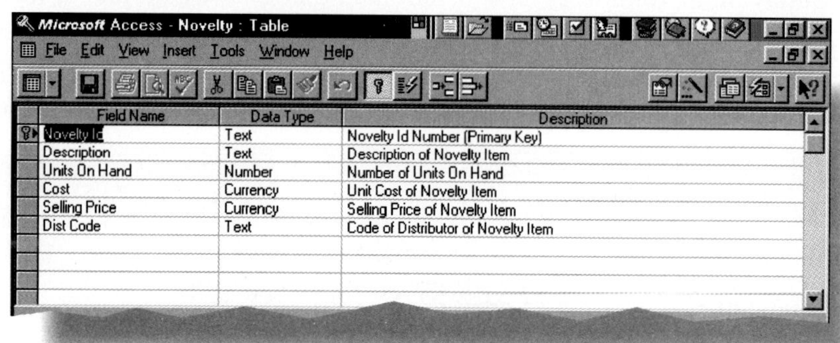

Field Name	Data Type	Description
Novelty Id	Text	Novelty Id Number (Primary Key)
Description	Text	Description of Novelty Item
Units On Hand	Number	Number of Units On Hand
Cost	Currency	Unit Cost of Novelty Item
Selling Price	Currency	Selling Price of Novelty Item
Dist Code	Text	Code of Distributor of Novelty Item

FIGURE 3-80

2 Maintaining the College Telephone System Database

Problem: The manager of the College Telephone System has determined that she would like to make some changes to the database structure. Another field must be added to the database, and the size of the Last Name field must be increased. Because several different individuals update the data, the manager also would like to add some validation rules to the database. Finally, there are some additions and deletions to the database.

Instructions: Use the database created in the In the Lab 2 of Project 1 for this assignment. Perform the following tasks:

1. Open the College Telephone System database and open the User table in Design view as shown in Figure 3-81.
2. Create an index for the Last Name field. Be sure to allow duplicates.
3. Create an index on the combination of the Dept Code and Last Name fields. Name the index Deptname.
4. Change the field width of the First Name field to 14.
5. Save these changes and display the User table in Datasheet view.
6. Change the first name for User Id T4521 to *Catherine Anne*.
7. Print the table.
8. Sort the records in ascending order by Dept Code.
9. Print the table. Close the table. If you are asked to save changes to the design of the table, click the No button.
10. Open the User table in Design view, and then add the Staff Code field to the User table. Define the field as Text with a width of 3. Insert the Staff Code field after the Extra Charges field. This field will contain data on whether the user is faculty (FAC), professional (PRO), or Administrative (ADM). Save the changes to the User table.
11. Create a new query for the User table.

In the Lab

12. Using this query, change all the entries in the Staff Code column to FAC. This will be the status of most users. Do not save the query.
13. Print the table.
14. Open the User table in Design view and create the following validation rules for the User table. List the steps involved on your own paper.
    a. Make First Name and Last Name required fields.
    b. Specify the legal values, FAC, PRO, and ADM for the Staff Code field. Include validation text.
    c. Ensure that any letters entered in the User Id, Office, and Dept Code fields are converted to uppercase.
    d. Specify a default value of $15.00 for the Basic Charge field.
15. Save the changes.
16. You can use either Form view or Datasheet view to add records to a table. To use Form view, you must replace the form you created in Project 1 with a form that includes the new field, Staff Code. With the User table selected, click the New Object button down arrow on the toolbar. Click AutoForm. Use this form that contains staff code to add the following record:

T8967	Schleer	Lois	3578	225SSH	$15.00	$0.00	ADM	ENG

17. Close the form. Click the Yes button when asked if you want to save the form. Save the form as *User*. Click the Yes button when asked if you want to replace the User form you created in Project 1.
18. Open the User form and then locate the users with User Ids T2389 and T8521. Change the Staff Code for each record to PRO.
19. Change to Datasheet view and print the table in order by last name. Close the table. If you are asked to save changes to the design of the table, click the No button.
20. Create a new query for the User table.
21. Using a query, delete all records in the User table where the Dept Code is HIS.
22. Close the query without saving it.
23. Print the User table.
24. Specify referential integrity between the Department table (the *one* table) and the User table (the *many* table). List the steps involved on your own paper.

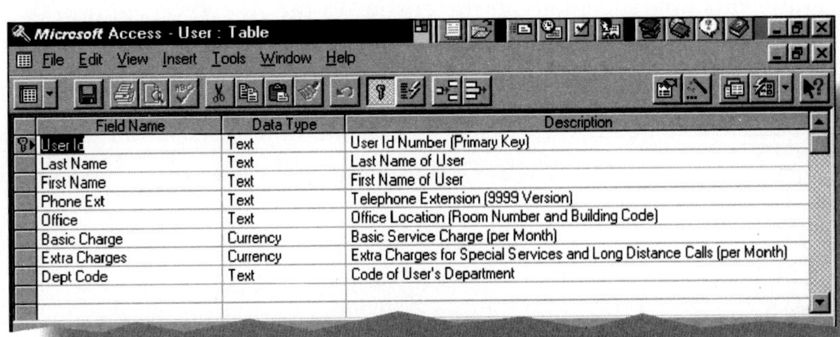

FIGURE 3-81

3 Maintaining the WWWW Radio Station Database

Problem: The radio station manager has determined that some changes must be made to the database structure. Another field must be added and the size of the Name field must be increased. Because several different individuals update the data, the manager also would like to add some validation rules to the database. Finally, there are some additions and deletions to the database.

Instructions: Use the database created in the In the Lab 3 of Project 1 for this assignment. Perform the following tasks:

1. Open the WWWW Radio Station database and open the Accounts table in Design view as shown in Figure 3-82.
2. Create an index for the Name field. Be sure to allow duplicates.
3. Create an index on the combination of the State and Zip Code fields. Name the index Statezip.
4. Save these changes and display the Accounts table in Datasheet view.
5. Order the records in the Accounts table by Zip Code within State.
6. Print the table. Close the table. If you are asked to save changes to the design of the table, click the No button.
7. Open the Accounts table in Design view, and then change the field width of the Name field to 25.
8. Add the field Acc Type to the Accounts table. Define the field as Text with a width of 3. Insert the Acc Type field after the Zip Code field. This field will contain data on the type of account. Accounts are classified as retail (RET), service (SRV), and industry (IND).
9. Save these changes and display the Accounts table in Datasheet view.
10. Change the name of account G075 to *Geo's Tires & Balancing*. Change the name of account C046 to *Boan-Carter Shoes*.
11. Resize the Name column to fit the changed entries. Decrease the width of the State, Zip Code, and Acc Type columns.
12. Print the table. If necessary, change the margins so the table prints on one page in landscape orientation. Close the table. Save the layout changes to the table.
13. Create a new query for the Accounts table.
14. Using this query, change all the entries in the Acc Type column to RET. This will be the type of most accounts. Do not save the query.
15. Open the Accounts table and order the records by name. Print the table. Close the table. If you are asked to save changes to the design of the table, click the No button.
16. Open the Accounts table in Design view, and then create the following validation rules. List the steps involved on your own paper.
    a. Make Name a required field.
    b. Specify the legal values RET, SRV, and IND for the Acc Type field. Include validation text.
    c. Ensure that any letters entered in the Account Number and State fields are converted to uppercase.
    d. Specify that balance must be between $0.00 and $500.00. Include validation text.

In the Lab

17. Save the changes to the Accounts table.
18. You can use either Form view or Datasheet view to add records to a table. To use Form view, you must replace the form you created in Project 1 with a form that includes the new field, Acc Type. With the Accounts table selected, click the New Object button down arrow on the toolbar. Click AutoForm. Use this form that contains Acc Type to add the following record:

S001	Stand Electric	12 Benson	Germantown	PA	19113	IND	$0.00	$0.00	21

19. Close the form. Click the Yes button when asked if you want to save the form. Save the form as *Accounts*. Click the Yes button when asked if you want to replace the Accounts form you created in Project 1.
20. Open the Accounts form and locate the accounts with Account Numbers B133, M012, and R111 and then change the Acc Type for each record to SRV.
21. Change to Datasheet view and print the table.
22. Create a new query for the Accounts table.
23. Using the query screen, delete all records in the table where the account has the Acc Type of IND.
24. Close the query without saving it.
25. Print the Accounts table.
26. Specify referential integrity between the Account Reps table (the *one* table) and the Accounts table (the *many* table). List the steps involved on your own paper.

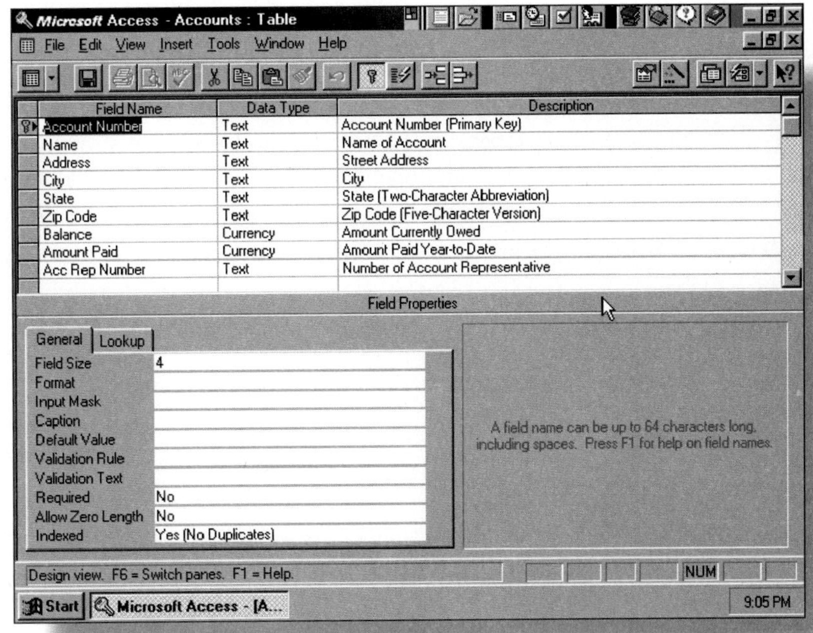

FIGURE 3-82

Cases and Places

The difficulty of these case studies varies:

◗ Case studies preceded by a single half moon are the least difficult. You are asked to create the required database based on information that has already been placed in an organized form.
◗◗ Case studies preceded by two half moons are more difficult. You must organize the information presented before using it to create the desired database.
◗◗◗ Case studies preceded by three half moons are the most difficult. You must choose a specific topic, and then obtain and organize the necessary information before using it to create the required database.

1 ◗ Use the restaurant database created in Case Study 1 of Project 1 for this assignment. Execute each of these tasks and then print the results: (a) Del Licious now occupies the storefront formerly occupied by Hat Dancers, which has gone out of business. Del Licious serves American cuisine, is open from 6:00 a.m. to 11:00 p.m., and has carryout but no delivery service. Its phone number is (714) 555-3628. You are fond of the all-you-can-eat special on Tuesdays. (b) Pablo's Tacos and Mr. Ming's now offer delivery service. (c) New Orient now opens at 11:00 a.m. and closes at 11:00 p.m. (d) Taranio's has moved to 532 S. Madison. (e) Parthenon and Taranio's have changed their specials from Tuesday to Monday. (f) Madras Ovens now offers carryout service.

2 ◗ Use the textbook database created in Case Study 2 of Project 1 for this assignment. Execute each of these tasks and then print the results: (a) Margaret Healy has dropped the price of her textbook from $36 to $30. (b) Mary Nord has sold her book, so you can delete her record from your database. (c) John Mote informs you he gave you the wrong course number for his textbook. It is used in Ast 120 instead of Ast 210. (d) You decide to sell your computer book you are using in this class for $35. It is in good condition. (e) The Psychology department has changed textbooks in the introductory course for the upcoming semester. Delete the books listed for Psy 101. (f) Dave Corsi's book is in poor condition. (g) Sandi Radleman has changed her phone number to 555-1782.

Cases and Places

3 ▶▶ Use the nutritional content database created in Case Study 3 of Project 1 for this assignment. Execute each of these tasks and then print the results: (a) Other meat also can be considered lean. For example, pork tenderloin has the same calories and fat as eye of round and has 65 mg of cholesterol. Top pork loin chop and center chop both have 170 calories, 7 grams of fat, and 70 mg of cholesterol. Boneless ham is one of the most nutritional meats, with 125 calories, 4 grams of fat, and 45 mg of cholesterol. Lamb loin chop has 180 calories, 8 grams of fat, and 80 mg of cholesterol, and whole leg of lamb has 160 calories, 7 grams of fat, and 75 mg of cholesterol. Add these cuts of meat to the database. (b) Display and print the cuts of meat with less than 70 milligrams of cholesterol in a three-ounce serving. (c) Display and print the cuts of meat with more than 160 calories in a three-ounce serving. (d) Your nutritionist has told you to consume less than 20 grams of fat daily. During the day, you have eaten food with a total fat gram content of 15. Display and print the cuts of meat that would be within the nutritionist's advice.

4 ▶▶ Use the movie collection database created in Case Study 4 of Project 1 for this assignment. Add five of your favorite movie titles to the table. Print the entire table sorted by movie title in ascending order.

5 ▶▶▶ Many national brokers offer IRAs. Call three of these brokerage companies and obtain the same information for investing $1,000 that you needed to complete Case Study 5 of Project 1 in the financial institutions database. Add these records to the table. Then display and print the following: (a) The names of all the financial institutions in the table and total values of the IRAs at age 65 in descending order. (b) The names and phone numbers of the financial institutions and total amounts of interest earned at age 65 in descending order. (c) The average value of the IRAs at age 65. (d) The average interest rates for the banks, savings and loans, credit unions, and brokerage companies. (e) The name, address, and interest rate of the financial institution with the highest interest rate. (f) The name, phone number, and interest rate of the financial institution with the lowest interest rate. (g) The names of the financial institutions and penalties for early withdrawal in two years in ascending order. (h) The names of the financial institutions and annual fees in ascending order. (i) A bar graph indicating the amount of interest you would earn and the total value of your IRA at age 65 for each financial institution.

Cases and Places

6 ▶▶▶ You have found the campus directory database you created in Case Study 6 of Project 1 to be invaluable. You have been handwriting additional names and numbers and making changes to the printout, and now you want to update the table. Add a new category called secretaries, and add the names, phone numbers, and room numbers of secretaries you call. In the faculty category, list your favorite instructors from previous semesters. Add your current instructors' office hours to the table. In the administration category, add data for the president and vice president of the school. In the services category, add the library circulation desk, athletic office, and theatre box office data. Print the entire table. Then print the instructors' names in ascending order, along with their phone numbers, office hours, and office room numbers. Create a similar printout for the administrators and for the secretaries. Finally, print the services in ascending order, including phone numbers and room numbers.

7 ▶▶▶ Use the product comparison database you created in Case Study 7 of Project 1 for this assignment. Often generic items are available for products on your shopping list. During your next shopping trip, locate any generic items that you could substitute for the 20 items in the table. Create a new field in the table and add the generic prices. Then, print the five items in each of the four categories in ascending order, along with the sizes and prices.

Integrating Excel Worksheet Data into an Access Database

Case Perspective

Eastern Office Supply has been using Excel to automate a variety of tasks for several years. Employees at Eastern have created several useful worksheets that have simplified their work tremendously. Along with the worksheets, they have created attractive charts for visual representation of the data.

When Eastern decided it needed to maintain customer data, the familiarity with Excel led to the decision to maintain the data as an Excel worksheet. For a while, this seemed to work fine. As time passed, however, they began to question whether Excel was the best choice. Their counterparts at other companies indicated that they were using Access to maintain customer data. Access had worked well for them. As the structure of their data became more complex, Access adapted easily to the increased complexity. They appreciated the power of the query and reporting features in Access. Finally, officials at Eastern decided that they should follow the lead of the other companies. They decided to convert their data from Excel to Access.

Introduction

It is not uncommon for people to use an application for some specific purpose, only to find later that another application may be better suited. For example, a company such as Eastern Office Supply might initially keep data in an Excel worksheet, only to discover later that the data would be better maintained in an Access database. Some common reasons for using a database instead of a worksheet are:

1. The worksheet contains a great deal of redundant data. As discussed in Project 1 on pages A 1.54 through A 1.56, databases can be designed to eliminate redundant data.
2. The worksheet would need to be larger than Excel can handle. Excel has a limit of 16,384 rows; whereas in Access, no such limit exists.
3. The data to be maintained consists of multiple interrelated items. For example, at Mason Clinic, they need to maintain data on two items, Patients and Therapists, and these items are interrelated. A patient has a single therapist and each therapist treats several patients. The Mason Clinic database is a very simple one. Databases can easily contain thirty or more interrelated items.
4. You want to use the extremely powerful query and report capabilities of Microsoft Access.

More *About* Converting Data: Worksheets

In Microsoft Excel, you can convert a single worksheet within a multiple-worksheet workbook to an Access table. This is not true with other spreadsheet packages, in which you must first save the worksheet as an individual file and then convert the individual file.

Regardless of the reasons for making the change from a worksheet to a database, it is important to be able to make the change easily. In the not-too-distant past, converting data from one tool to another often could be a very difficult, time-consuming task. Fortunately, an easy way of converting data from Excel to Access is available.

Figure 1 illustrates the conversion process. The type of worksheet that can be converted is one in which the data is stored as a **list**, that is, a labeled series of rows in which each row contains the same type of data. For example, in the worksheet at the top of Figure 1, the first row contains the labels, which are entries indicating the type of data found in the column. The entry in the first column, for example, is Customer Number, indicating that all the other values in the column are customer numbers. The entry in the second column is Name, indicating that all the other values in the column are names. Other than the first row, which contains the labels, all the rows contain precisely the same type of data: a customer number in the first column, a name in the second column, an address in the third column, and so on.

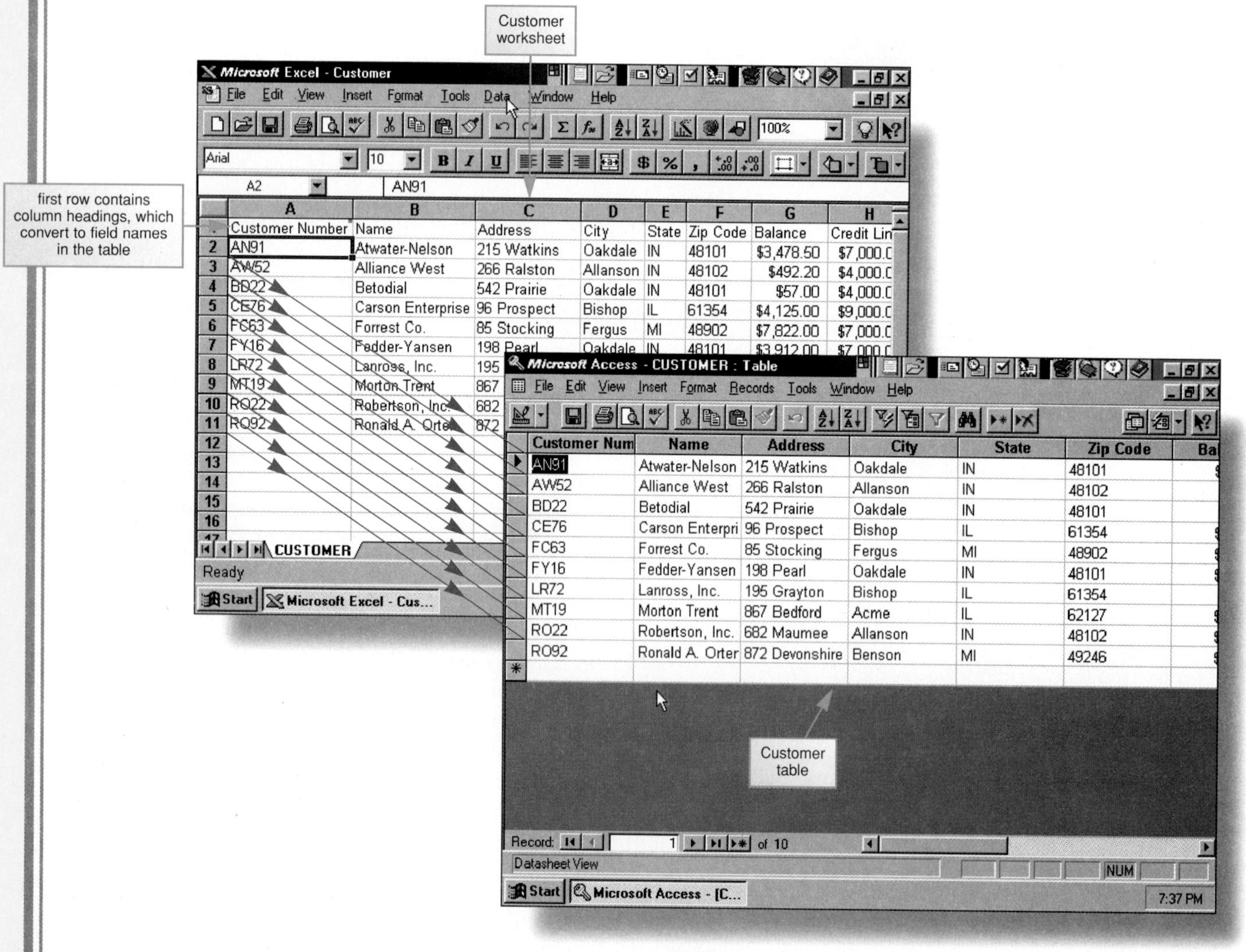

Customer worksheet

first row contains column headings, which convert to field names in the table

Customer table

FIGURE 1

As Figure 1 illustrates, the worksheet, shown at the upper left of the figure, is converted to a database table, shown at the lower right. The columns in the worksheet become the fields. The column headings in the first row of the worksheet become the field names. The rows of the worksheet, other than the first row, which contains the labels, become the records in the table. In the process, each field will be assigned the data type that seems the most reasonable, given the data currently in the worksheet.

The conversion process, which uses the Import Spreadsheet Wizard, can begin from either Excel or Access. The steps are very similar in both cases. The wizard takes you through some basic steps, asking a few simple questions. Once you have answered the questions, the wizard will perform the conversion.

Once the data has been converted, you can use a wizard to analyze the table data in case you are not sure your design is appropriate. The wizard then will attempt to find redundancy; that is, duplication, in the data (see Project 1, pages A 1.54 through A 1.56 for a discussion of redundancy in a database). If the wizard finds redundancy, it will suggest a way of splitting your table to remove the redundancy. If, for example, you were to create a worksheet containing the data as shown in Figure 1-86 on page A 1.54, the resulting table would contain all the problems with redundancy that were discussed in that section. To correct these problems, the wizard will recommend the splitting shown in Figure 1-87 on page A 1.55. If you accept the wizard's recommendation, it will split the tables for you automatically.

More About Converting Data: Databases

In addition to converting data from a worksheet to a database, you can also convert data from one database management system to another. Access, for example, provides tools for easily converting data from such database systems as dBASE III, dBASE IV, and Paradox.

More About Converting Data: Other Formats

Data can be converted to a database from a variety of formats, such as delimited and fixed-width text files. If you cannot convert directly from another worksheet or database to Access, often you can convert to one of these special formats and then convert the resulting file to Access.

Opening an Excel Workbook

Before converting the data, open the workbook in Excel by performing the following steps.

TO OPEN AN EXCEL WORKBOOK

Step 1: Click the Start button.
Step 2: Click Open Office Document, select 3½ Floppy [A:] in the Look in drop-down list box, and select the Access folder. Make sure the Customer workbook is selected.
Step 3: Click the Open button.

The Excel worksheet displays (Figure 2).

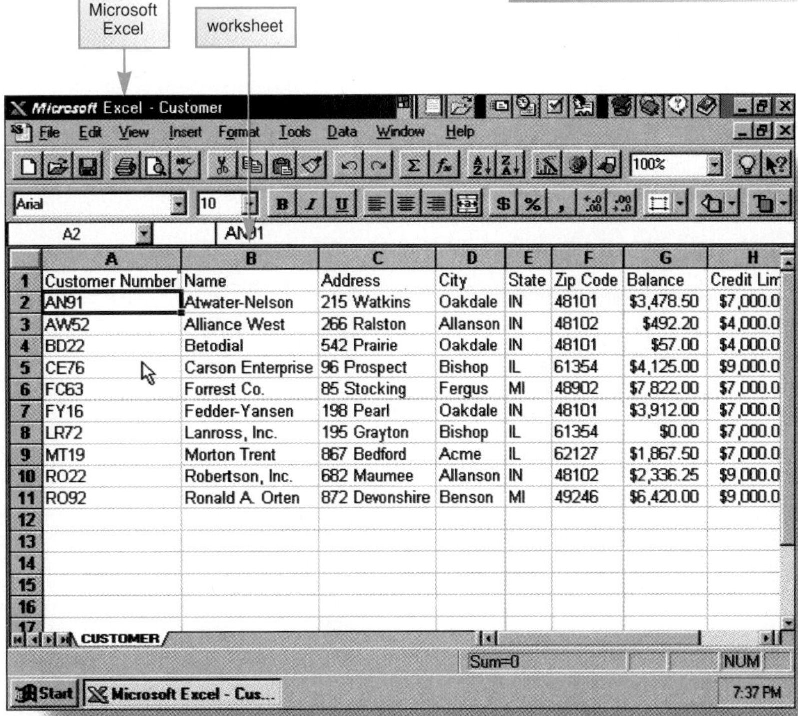

	A	B	C	D	E	F	G	H
1	Customer Number	Name	Address	City	State	Zip Code	Balance	Credit Lim
2	AN91	Atwater-Nelson	215 Watkins	Oakdale	IN	48101	$3,478.50	$7,000.0
3	AW52	Alliance West	266 Ralston	Allanson	IN	48102	$492.20	$4,000.0
4	BD22	Betodial	542 Prairie	Oakdale	IN	48101	$57.00	$4,000.0
5	CE76	Carson Enterprise	96 Prospect	Bishop	IL	61354	$4,125.00	$9,000.0
6	FC63	Forrest Co.	85 Stocking	Fergus	MI	48902	$7,822.00	$7,000.0
7	FY16	Fedder-Yansen	198 Pearl	Oakdale	IN	48101	$3,912.00	$7,000.0
8	LR72	Lanross, Inc.	195 Grayton	Bishop	IL	61354	$0.00	$7,000.0
9	MT19	Morton Trent	867 Bedford	Acme	IL	62127	$1,867.50	$7,000.0
10	RO22	Robertson, Inc.	682 Maumee	Allanson	IN	48102	$2,336.25	$9,000.0
11	RO92	Ronald A. Orten	872 Devonshire	Benson	MI	49246	$6,420.00	$9,000.0
12								
13								
14								
15								
16								
17								

FIGURE 2

Converting an Excel Worksheet to an Access Database

To convert the data, you will use the Import Spreadsheet Wizard. In the process, you will indicate that the first row contains the column headings. These column headings will then become the field names in the Access table. In addition, you will indicate the primary key for the table. As part of the process, you can, if you desire, choose not to include all the fields from the worksheet in the resulting table. Some of the steps may take a significant amount of time for Access to execute.

Steps To Convert an Excel Worksheet to an Access Database

1 Click any cell in the worksheet, click Data on the menu bar, and then click Convert to Access.

The Convert to Microsoft Access dialog box displays (Figure 3). Use this dialog box to indicate whether the table that is created is to be placed in a new database or an existing database.

FIGURE 3

2 Make sure the New database option button is selected and then click the OK button.

The Import Spreadsheet Wizard dialog box displays (Figure 4). It displays a portion of the worksheet that is being converted. In this dialog box you indicate that the first row of the worksheet contains the column headings. The wizard uses these values as the field names in the Access table.

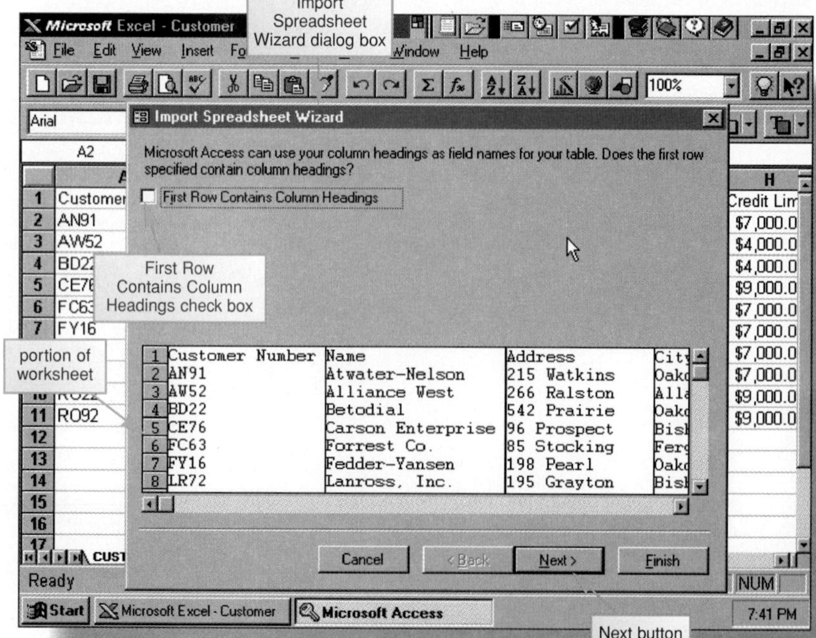

FIGURE 4

3 **Click First Row Contains Column Headings and then click the Next button.**

The Import Spreadsheet Wizard dialog box displays giving you the opportunity to specify field options (Figure 5). You can specify that indexes are to be created for certain fields. You also can specify that certain fields should not be included in the Access table.

FIGURE 5

4 **Click the Next button.**

The Import Spreadsheet Wizard dialog box displays (Figure 6). Use this dialog box to indicate the primary key of the Access table. You can allow Access to add a special field to serve as the primary key as illustrated in the figure. You can choose an existing field to serve as the primary key. You also can indicate no primary key. Most of the time, one of the existing fields will serve as the primary key. In this worksheet, for example, the Customer Number serves as the primary key.

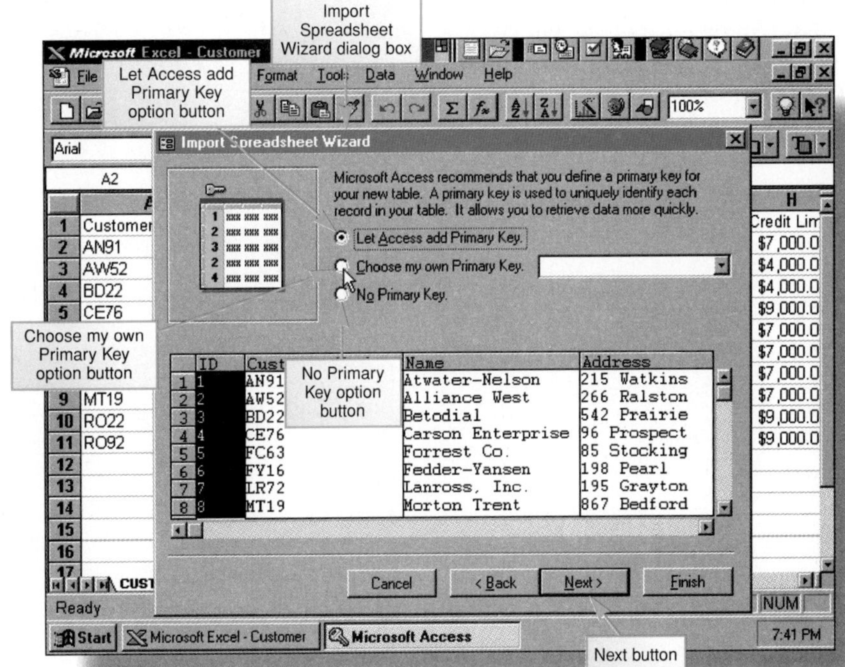

FIGURE 6

5 **Click Choose my own Primary Key.**

The Customer Number field will be the primary key (Figure 7).

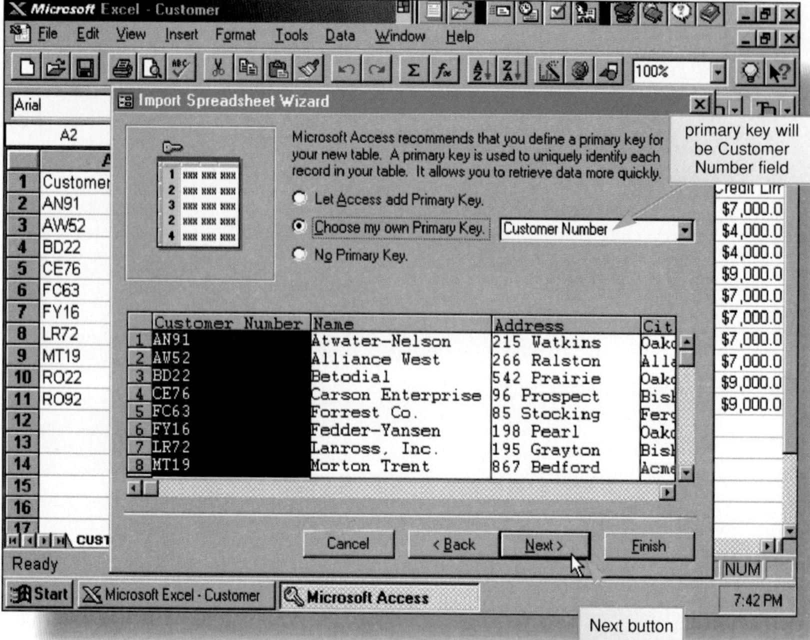

FIGURE 7

6 **Click the Next button. Be sure CUSTOMER displays in the Import to Table text box and the button requesting a wizard to analyze the table is not checked.**

The Import Spreadsheet Wizard dialog box displays (Figure 8). The name of the table will be CUSTOMER.

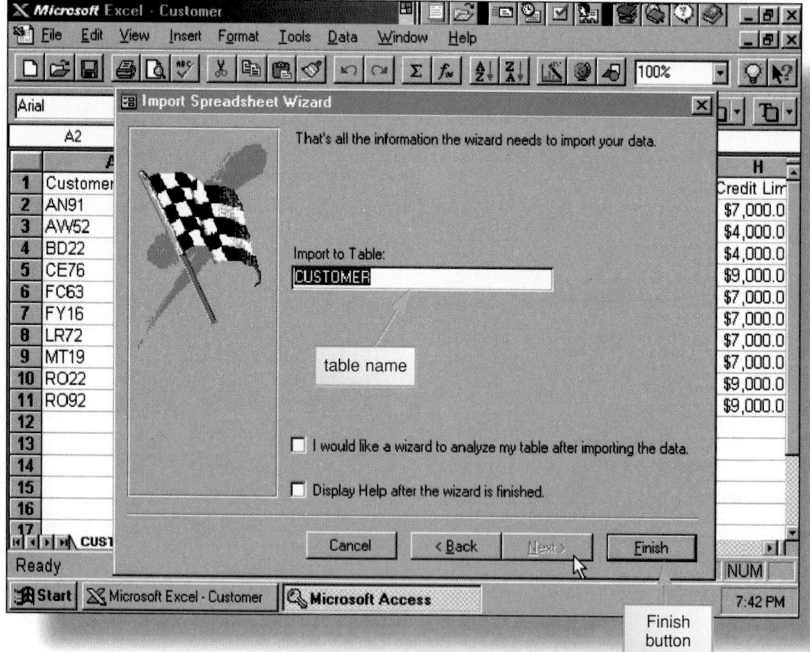

FIGURE 8

7 **Click the Finish button.**

The worksheet will be converted into an Access table. When the process is completed the Import Spreadsheet Wizard dialog box will display (Figure 9).

8 **Click the OK button.**

The table has now been created (see Figure 1 on page AI 1.2).

9 **Close Access, and then close Excel. Do not save the worksheet.**

The customer table has been created in a database also called Customer.

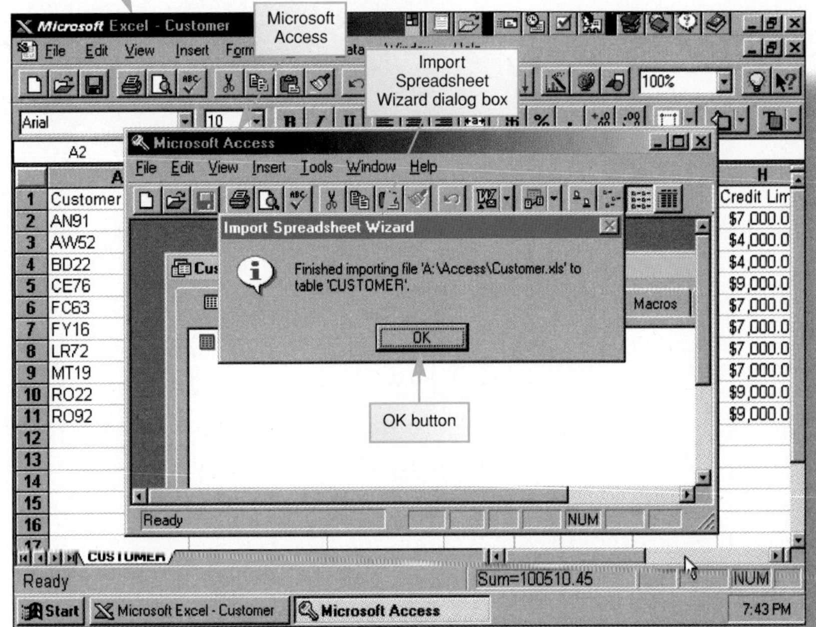

FIGURE 9

Using the Access Table

Once the Access version of the table has been created, you can treat it as you would any other table. After first opening the database containing the table, you can open the table in Datasheet view (Figure 1 on page AI 1.2). You can make changes to the data. You can create queries that use the data in the table.

By clicking Design on the table's shortcut menu, you can view the table's structure and make any necessary changes to the structure. The changes may include changing field sizes and types, creating indexes, or adding additional fields. To accomplish any of these tasks, use the same steps you used in Project 3.

Summary

The Integration Feature covered the process of integrating an Excel worksheet into an Access database. To convert a worksheet to an Access table, you learned to use the Import Spreadsheet Wizard. Working with the wizard, you identified the first row of the worksheet as the row containing the column headings and you indicated the primary key. The wizard then created the table for you and placed it in a new database.

What You Should Know

Having completed this Integration Feature, you should be able to perform the following tasks:

- Convert an Excel Worksheet to an Access Database *(AI 1.4)*
- Open an Excel Workbook *(AI 1.3)*

In the Lab

1 Using Help

Instructions: Perform the following tasks using a computer.

1. Start Access.
2. Double-click the Help button on the toolbar to display the Help Topics: Microsoft Access for Windows 95 dialog box. Click the Index tab. Type `import` in box 1 and then double-click spreadsheets under importing data in box 2. Double-click Import or link a spreadsheet in the Topics Found dialog box. When the Help information displays, read it. Next, right-click within the box, and then click Print Topic. Hand in the printout to your instructor. Click the Help Topics button to return to the Help Topics: Microsoft Access for Windows 95 dialog box.
3. Click the Answer Wizard tab. Type `how do i use the table analyzer wizard` in box 1. Click the Search button. Double-click Normalize a table using the Table Analyzer Wizard in box 2 under How Do I. Read and print the Help information. Hand in the printout to your instructor.

2 Converting the Software Worksheet

Problem: Great Lakes Educational Software has been using Excel to keep track of its inventory. Employees at Great Lakes use several worksheets to re-order software, keep track of carrying costs, and graph trends in software buying. The company is expanding rapidly and branching out into other educational products. They now need to maintain additional data and would like to produce more sophisticated reports and queries. The company management has asked you to convert its inventory data to an Access database.

Instructions: Perform the following tasks.

1. Open the Software worksheet (Figure 10) in the Access folder on the Student Floppy Disk that accompanies this book.
2. Convert the Software worksheet to an Access table. Use Software as the name of the Access table and Software Number as the primary key.
3. Open and print the table in Access.

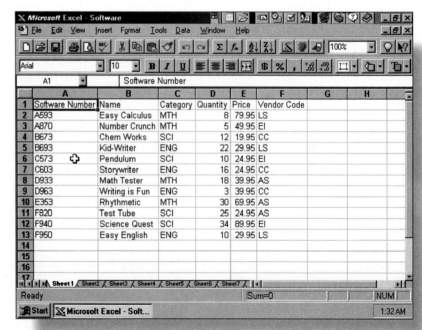

Microsoft Excel - Software

	A	B	C	D	E	F
1	Software Number	Name	Category	Quantity	Price	Vendor Code
2	A593	Easy Calculus	MTH	8	79.95	LS
3	A870	Number Crunch	MTH	5	49.95	EI
4	B673	Chem Works	SCI	12	19.95	CC
5	B693	Kid-Writer	ENG	22	29.95	LS
6	C573	Pendulum	SCI	10	24.95	EI
7	C603	Storywriter	ENG	16	24.95	CC
8	D933	Math Tester	MTH	18	39.95	AS
9	D963	Writing is Fun	ENG	3	39.95	CC
10	E353	Rhythmetic	MTH	30	69.95	AS
11	F820	Test Tube	SCI	25	24.95	AS
12	F940	Science Quest	SCI	34	89.95	EI
13	F950	Easy English	ENG	10	29.95	LS

FIGURE 10

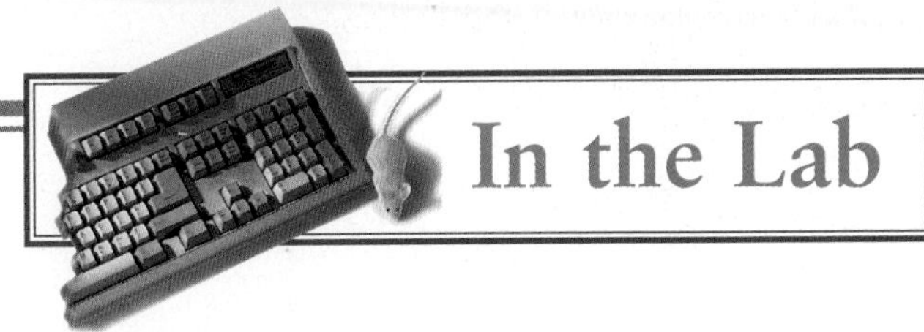

3 Converting the Employee Worksheet

Problem: The Great Outdoors Catalog Company has been using Excel to keep track of its inventory and do limited tracking of its employees. Employees at Great Outdoors Catalog Company use several worksheets to re-order products, keep track of carrying costs, and maintain employee records. The company realizes that employee data would be better handled in Access. The company management has asked you to convert its employee data to an Access database.

Instructions: Perform the following tasks.

1. Create a new database in which to store all the objects related to the employee data. Call the database Great Outdoors.
2. Import the Employee worksheet shown in Figure 11 into Access. Open the Employee worksheet in the Access folder on the Student Floppy Disk that accompanies this book. (Hint: Using Help on the previous page can help you solve this problem.)
3. Use Employee as the name of the Access table and SS Number as the primary key.
4. Open and print the Employee table.

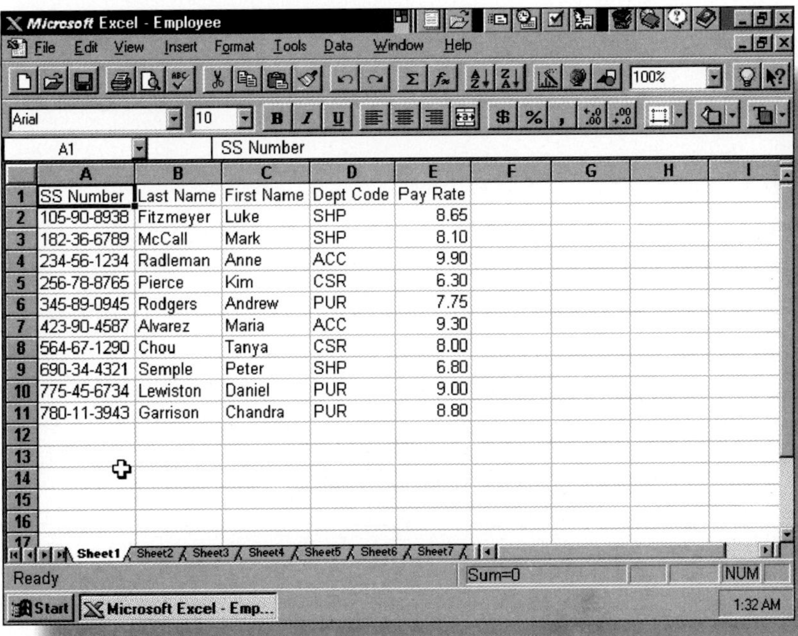

SS Number	Last Name	First Name	Dept Code	Pay Rate
105-90-8938	Fitzmeyer	Luke	SHP	8.65
182-36-6789	McCall	Mark	SHP	8.10
234-56-1234	Radleman	Anne	ACC	9.90
256-78-8765	Pierce	Kim	CSR	6.30
345-89-0945	Rodgers	Andrew	PUR	7.75
423-90-4587	Alvarez	Maria	ACC	9.30
564-67-1290	Chou	Tanya	CSR	8.00
690-34-4321	Semple	Peter	SHP	6.80
775-45-6734	Lewiston	Daniel	PUR	9.00
780-11-3943	Garrison	Chandra	PUR	8.80

FIGURE 11

PROJECT ONE

Using a Design Template and Style Checker to Create a Presentation

PROJECT TWO

Using Outline View and Clip Art to Create an Electronic Slide Show

INTEGRATION FEATURE

Linking an Excel Chart to a PowerPoint Presentation

Microsoft PowerPoint 7

Windows 95

Using A Design Template And Style Checker To Create A Presentation

Objectives:

You will have mastered the material in this project when you can:

- Start a new PowerPoint document
- Describe the PowerPoint window
- Select a Design Template
- Create a title slide
- Change the font size of selected text
- Italicize selected text
- Save a presentation
- Add a new slide
- Demote a bulleted paragraph
- Promote a bulleted paragraph
- View a presentation in Slide Show view
- Close PowerPoint
- Open a presentation
- Use Style Checker to identify spelling, visual clarity, case, and end punctuation inconsistencies
- Edit a presentation
- Change line spacing on the Slide Master
- Display a presentation in black and white
- Print a presentation in black and white
- Use online help

Picture This!

A Story without Words

A modern movie without dialogue? The 1981 movie, *Quest for Fire*, contained no dialogue yet told a clear, compelling story about prehistoric humans who had no language to speak. Since the dawn of mankind, humans have relied on graphic images to communicate, even after the advent of spoken language. In today's global village, images play a vital role in promoting understanding between peoples of different languages.

People have long used pictures, or graphics, as guides for building structures involving complex spatial relationships. Imagine trying to build the Pharaoh's pyramids without a plan drawn out on papyrus or a Boeing 767 without engineering drawings.

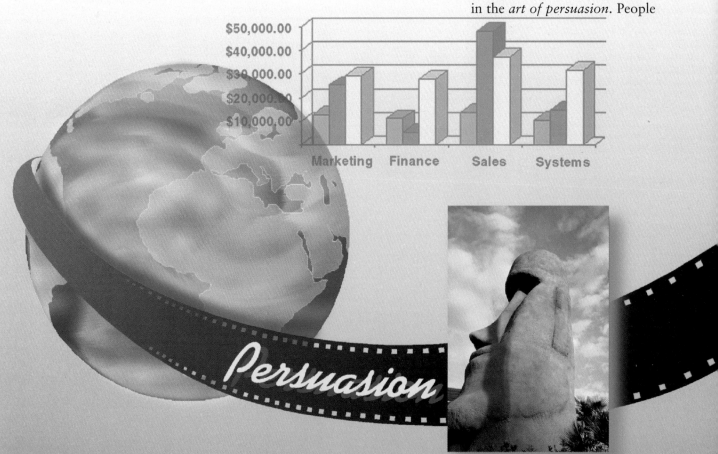

Yet, in recent years, graphics have assumed an even greater role in the *art of persuasion*. People understand arguments far more easily when pictures are used; pictures help establish credibility, which is the first step in persuasion. From sales presentations to the perennial debate over the U.S. federal budget to Presidential addresses, people turn to images to persuade others to adopt their points of view. Human beings grasp information more quickly and remember it longer when images augment words.

It has not always been so easy to create winning graphics. In the past, teams of artists often required days, even weeks, using special equipment many times more expensive than personal computers to lay out slide presentations. Corrections or changes were costly and time-consuming, whereas now, changes can be made inexpensively, in seconds.

Microsoft PowerPoint is an outstanding example of the marriage of pictures and text to help people present persuasive arguments or simply to inform or entertain. Bar graphs, pie charts, scatter diagrams, Gantt charts, and other visuals can be created quickly and easily within PowerPoint or imported from other applications such as Microsoft Excel or Microsoft Works.

For people who need help, Wizards simplify the job of getting started. Wizards provide more than 100 predesigned *looks* and can guide the user through a series of steps to create a unique presentation within one of several popular formats. And it is easy to modify the style, color, and content of all images created with PowerPoint.

PowerPoint can be a boon to students by helping to organize and format papers, prepare overhead slides, and lay out storyboards. Especially where numbers are involved, papers can be enhanced by the inclusion of a graphic from PowerPoint.

In a world increasingly dependent on images as well as language to communicate and persuade, the capability to create those images becomes essential. Who knows what improvements in gradepoint averages may result — with the right graphics presented to the right professor?

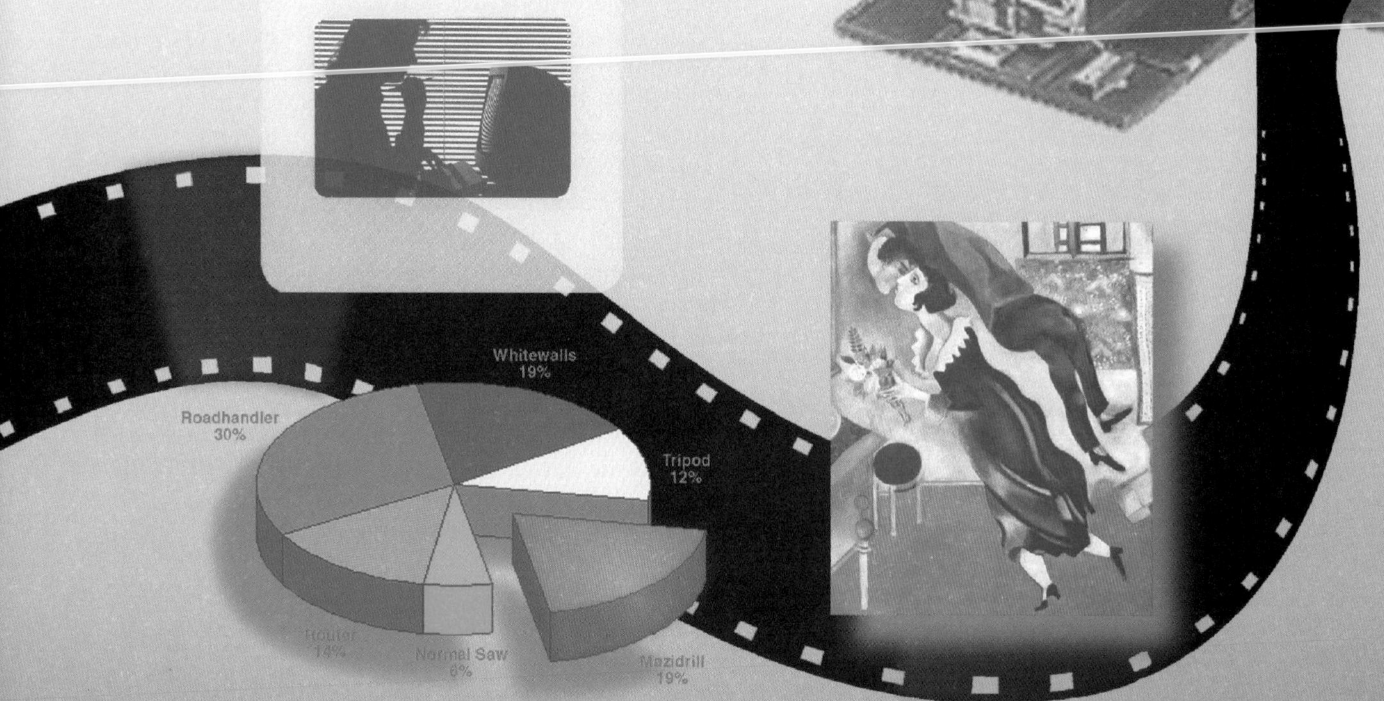

Microsoft
PowerPoint 7
Windows 95

Using a Design Template and Style Checker to Create a Presentation

Case Perspective

Each summer, Hammond University conducts an orientation seminar for all students new to the campus. As a new part of the orientation process, the Office of Student Services is conducting a short presentation on how to survive on campus. Ms. Margaret Ray, Director of Student Services, provides you with data and assigns you the task of designing the presentation. Because the location of the orientation session is uncertain, you also must create overhead transparencies.

The data is an accumulation of responses collected each spring from student surveys. The survey focuses on three areas of campus life: dormitory, classroom, and social. Students completing the survey suggest survival tips for each of these three areas. Ms. Ray analyzes the survey responses and identifies the four tips most frequently submitted in each category.

You and Ms. Ray decide the presentation will consist of a title slide and three bulleted list slides.

What is PowerPoint?

Microsoft PowerPoint is a complete presentation graphics program that allows you to produce professional-looking presentations. PowerPoint gives you the flexibility to make informal presentations using overhead transparencies (top of Figure 1-1), make electronic presentations using a projection device attached to a personal computer (middle of Figure 1-1), or make formal presentations using 35mm slides (bottom of Figure 1-1). Additionally, PowerPoint can create paper printouts, outlines, speaker notes and audience handouts.

PowerPoint contains several features to simplify creating a presentation. For example, you can instruct PowerPoint to create a predesigned presentation, and then you can modify the presentation to fulfill your requirements. You quickly can format a presentation using one of the professionally designed presentation Design Templates. To make your presentation more impressive, you can add tables, graphs, pictures, video, and sound; and you can be certain your presentation meets specific design criteria by using Style Checker to locate inconsistencies in spelling, visual clarity, uppercase and lowercase usage, and end punctuation. For example,

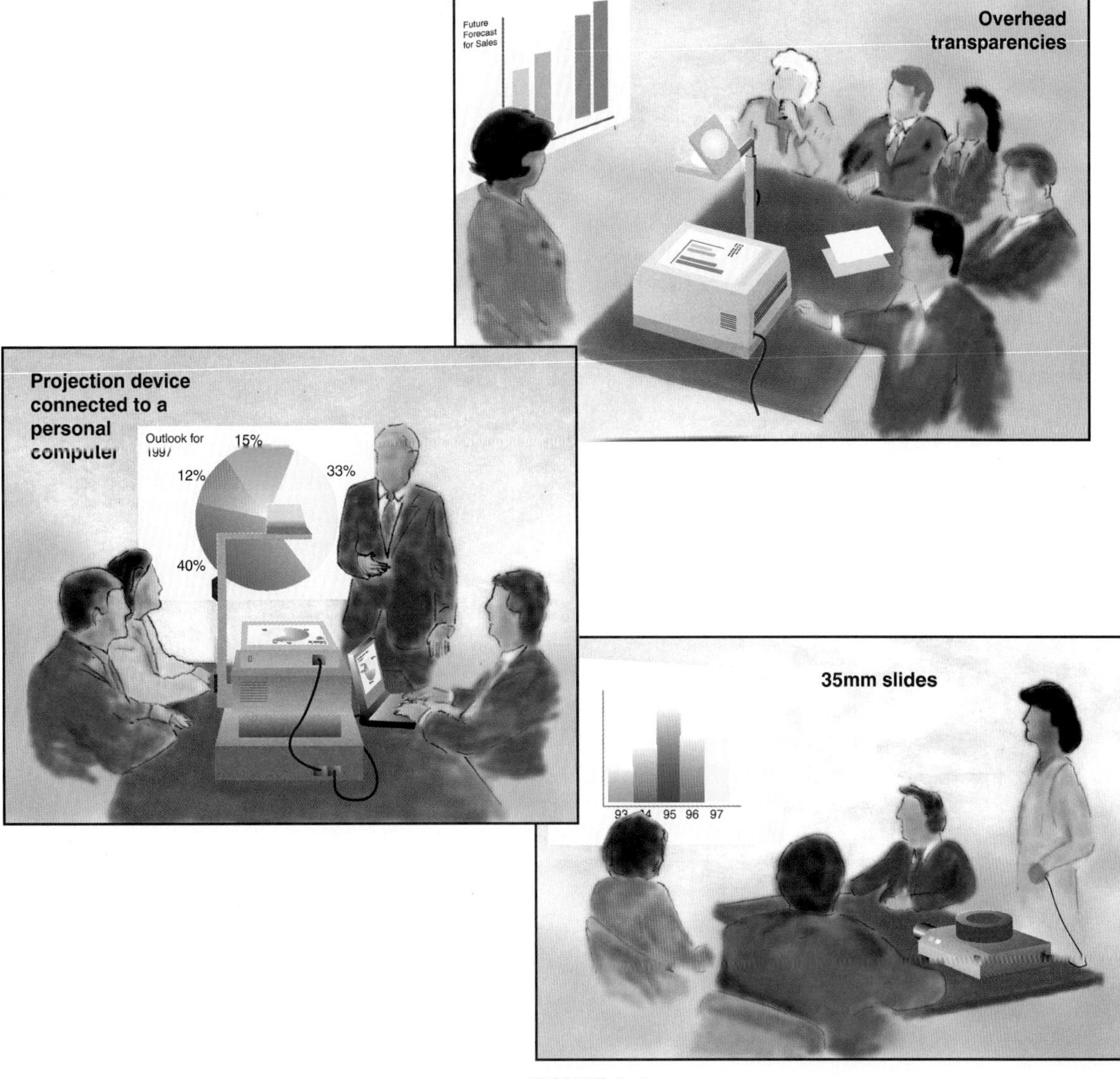

FIGURE 1-1

you can instruct PowerPoint to restrict the number of bulleted items on a slide or limit the number of words in each paragraph. Additional PowerPoint features include the following:

- **Word Processing** — **Word Processing** allows you to create bulleted lists, combine words and images, find and replace text, and use multiple fonts and type sizes. Using its IntelliSense features, PowerPoint can perform tasks such as checking spelling and formatting text – *all while you are typing.*
- **Outlining** — **Outlining** allows you quickly to create your presentation using an outline format. You also can import outlines from Microsoft Word or other word processors.
- **Graphing** — **Graphing** allows you to create and insert charts into your presentations. Graph formats include two-dimensional (2D) graphs: area, bar, column, combination, line, pie, xy (scatter); and three-dimensional (3D) graphs: area, bar, column, line, and pie.

More *About* **Overhead Transparencies**

Overhead transparencies are best when you want audience interaction in a lighted room, for groups less than 40 people, or when other equipment is not available.

More *About*
Electronic Presentations

Use an electronic presentation for any size audience. The choice of projection device depends on the number of people in the audience. Be certain you test the system before you deliver the presentation.

More *About*
35mm Slides

35mm slides are best for formal presentations made to any size audience and are highly recommended when audience size exceeds 50 people. 35mm slide presentations are best-suited for a non-interactive presentation because the room is dark.

More *About*
Presentation Graphics

Presentation graphics help people see what they hear. People remember:
10% of what they *read*
20% of what they *hear*
30% of what they *see*
70% of what they *see* and *hear*

More *About*
Presentation Design

Identify the purpose of the presentation. Is it to sell an idea or product, report results of a study, or educate the audience? Whatever the purpose, your goal is to capture the attention of the audience and to explain the data or concept in a manner that is easy to understand.

- **Drawing — Drawing** allows you to create diagrams using shapes such as arcs, arrows, cubes, rectangles, stars, and triangles. Drawing also allows you to modify shapes without redrawing.
- **Clip Art — ClipArt** allows you to insert artwork into your presentation without creating it yourself. You can find hundreds of graphic images in the Microsoft ClipArt Gallery, or you can import art from other applications. With the **AutoClipArt feature**, PowerPoint can suggest a clip art image appropriate for your presentation.
- **Multimedia Effects** — To add interest and keep your audience attentive, **multimedia effects**, such as sound and video, can be added to your presentations.
- **Presentation Management — Presentation management** allows you to control the design and arrangement of your presentation, as well as add special presentation effects, such as flying bullets.
- **Wizards** — A **wizard** is a tutorial approach for quickly and efficiently creating a presentation. PowerPoint wizards make it easy to create quality presentations by prompting you for specific content criteria. For example, the **AutoContent Wizard** asks you what are you going to talk about and the type of presentation you are going to give, such as recommending a strategy or selling a product. The **Answer Wizard** allows you to ask questions in your own words and then displays step-by-step instructions and visual examples showing how to complete the task. When giving a presentation away from the computer on which you created your presentation, it is important you take all the necessary files. The **Pack And Go Wizard** helps you bundle everything you need, including any objects associated with that presentation.

Project One – College Survival

This book presents a series of projects using PowerPoint to produce slides similar to those you would develop in an academic or business environment. Project 1 uses PowerPoint to create the presentation shown in Figure 1-2. The objective is to produce a presentation, called College Survival, to be presented using an overhead projector. As an introduction to PowerPoint, this project steps you through the most common type of presentation, a bulleted list. A **bulleted list** is a list of paragraphs, each preceded by a bullet. A **bullet** is a symbol (usually a heavy dot (•)) that precedes text when the text warrants special emphasis. The first of the four slides is called the title slide. The **title slide** introduces the presentation to the audience.

Mouse Usage

In this book, the mouse is used as the primary way to communicate with Microsoft PowerPoint. You can perform seven operations with a mouse: point, click, right-click, double-click, triple-click, drag, and right-drag.

Point means you move the mouse across a flat surface until the mouse pointer rests on the item of choice on the screen. As you move the mouse, the mouse pointer moves across the screen in the same direction.

Click means you press and release the left mouse button. The terminology used in this book to direct you to point to a particular item and then click is, Click the particular item. For example, Click the Bold button, means point to the Bold button and then click.

Right-click means you press and release the right mouse button. As with the left mouse button, you normally will point to an item on the screen before right-clicking.

Double-click means you quickly press and release the left mouse button twice without moving the mouse. In most cases, you must point to an item before double-clicking. In this book, **triple-clicking** in a text object selects the entire paragraph.

Drag means you point to an item, hold down the left mouse button, move the item to the desired location on the screen, and then release the left mouse button. **Right-drag** means you point to an item, hold down the right mouse button, move the item to the desired location, and then release the right mouse button.

The use of the mouse is an important skill when working with PowerPoint 7 for Windows 95.

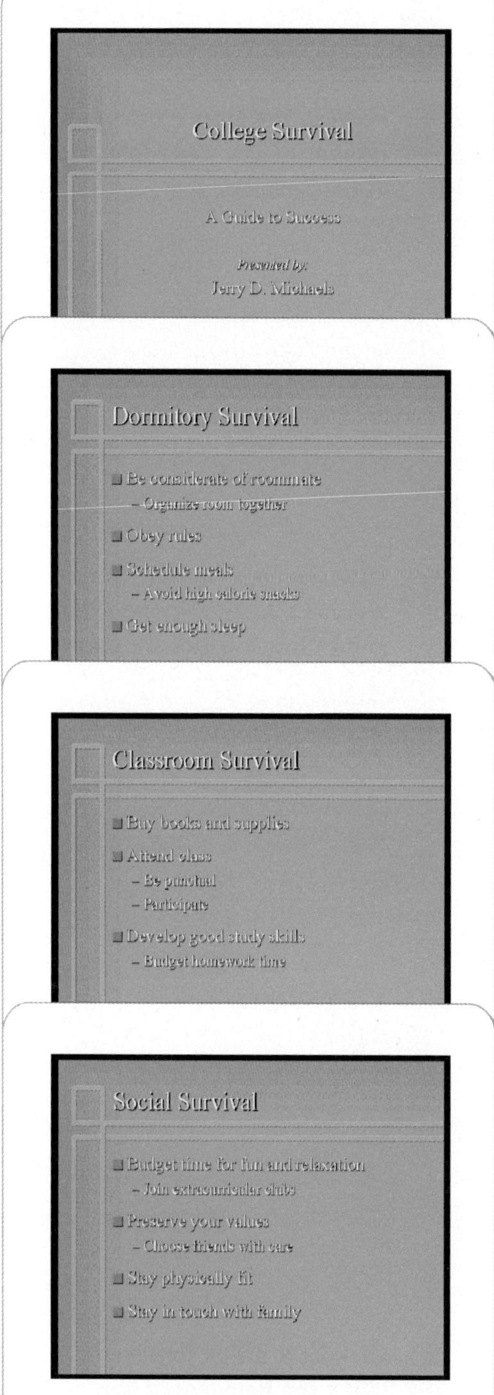

FIGURE 1-2

Slide Preparation Steps

The preparation steps summarize how the slide presentation shown in Figure 1-2 will be developed in Project 1. The following tasks will be completed in this project:

1. Start a new Office document.
2. Select a Design Template.
3. Create a title slide.
4. Save the presentation on a floppy disk.
5. Create three multi-level bulleted lists.
6. Save the presentation again.
7. Close PowerPoint.
8. Open the presentation as a Microsoft Office document.
9. Style check the presentation.
10. Edit the presentation.
11. Print the presentation.
12. Close PowerPoint.

The following pages contain a detailed explanation of these tasks.

Starting a Presentation as a New Office Document

A PowerPoint document is called a **presentation**. The quickest way to begin a new presentation is to use the **Start button** on the **taskbar** at the bottom of your screen. When you click the Start button, the **Start menu** displays several commands for simplifying tasks in Windows 95. When Microsoft Office 95 is installed, the Start menu displays two commands: New Office Document and Open Office Document. You use the **New Office Document** command to designate the type of Office document you are creating. Then, you specify the Design Template or wizard on which you wish to base your document. A **Design Template** provides consistency in design and color throughout the entire presentation. The Design Template determines the color scheme, font face and size, and layout of your presentation. Then PowerPoint starts and the specified template or wizard displays. The Open Office Document command is discussed later in this project. Perform the steps on the following pages to start a new presentation, or ask your instructor how to start PowerPoint on your system.

To Start a New Presentation

1 Point to the Start button on the taskbar at the lower left corner of the desktop.

When you position the mouse pointer on the Start button, a ToolTip displays, Click here to begin (Figure 1-3). Your computer system displays the time on the clock at the right end of the taskbar.

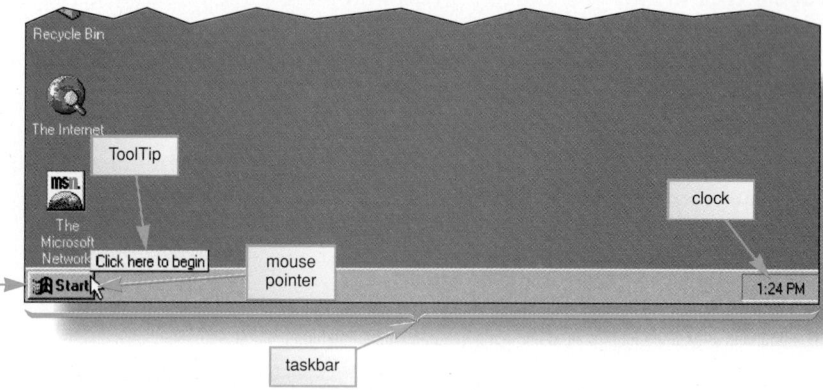

FIGURE 1-3

2 Click the Start button. When the Windows 95 Start menu displays, point to New Office Document.

The Windows 95 Start menu displays the names of several programs. The mouse pointer points to New Office Document (Figure 1-4). When the mouse pointer points to a name on the menu, the name is highlighted.

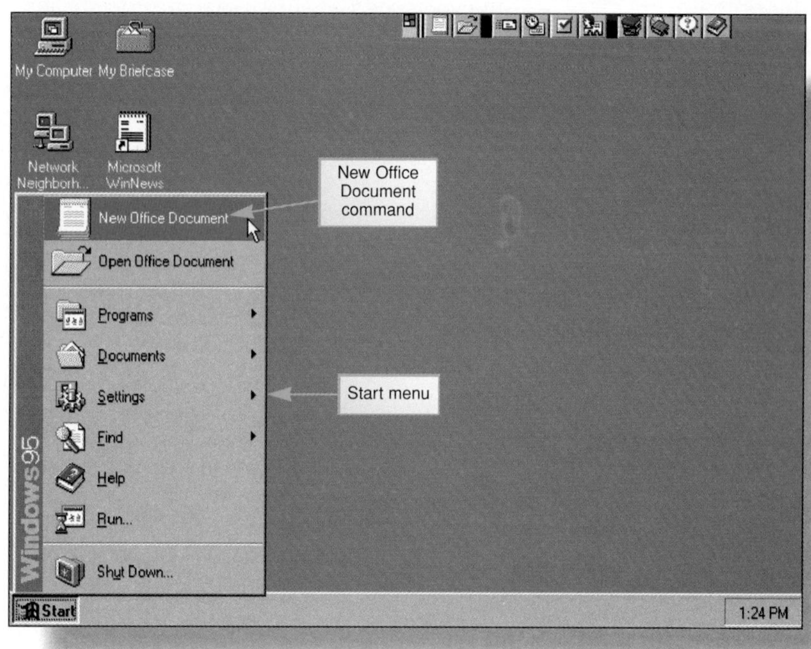

FIGURE 1-4

3 Click New Office Document. When the New dialog box displays, point to the Presentation Designs tab.

The New dialog box displays on the desktop and the mouse pointer points to the Presentation Designs tab (Figure 1-5). Depending on your installation, your computer may display a Design tab.

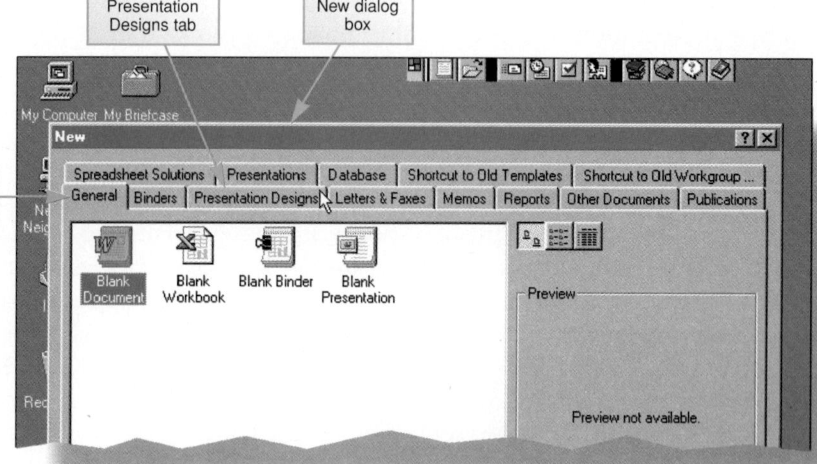

FIGURE 1-5

4 **Click the Presentation Designs tab. When the Presentation Designs sheet displays, point to Embossed.**

The Presentation Designs sheet displays (Figure 1-6). The Presentation Designs sheet displays the names and icons for several Design Templates. The Preview box displays a message about how to see a preview of a presentation Design Template. The OK button currently is dimmed, which means it is not available, because a Design Template icon has not been selected. The Cancel button is available, however, as indicated by the black text on the button. The Cancel button is used to close the New dialog box and return to the desktop or return to the window from which you started.

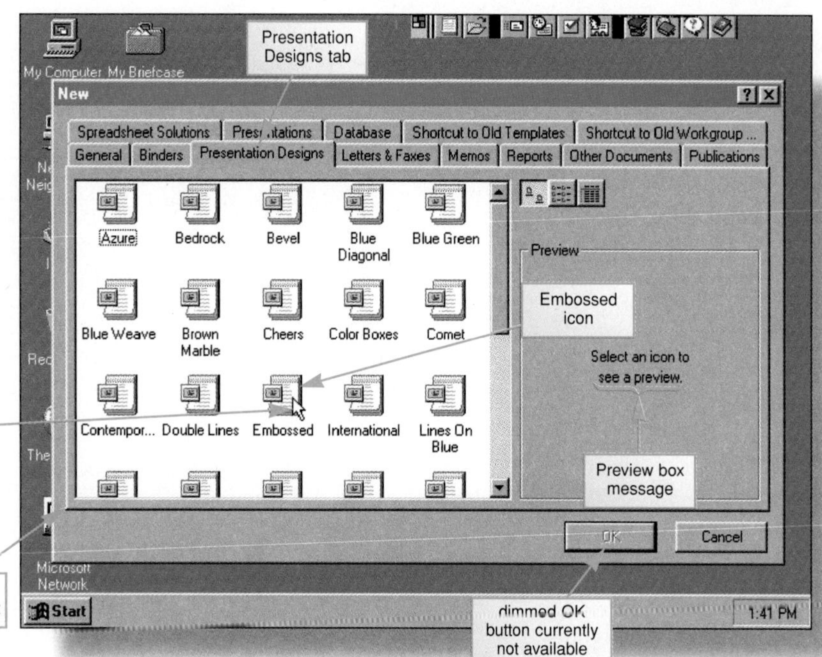

FIGURE 1-6

5 **Click Embossed.**

The Embossed Design Template icon is highlighted and a thumbnail view of the Design Template displays in the Preview box (Figure 1-7). The OK button now is available as indicated by the black text on the button.

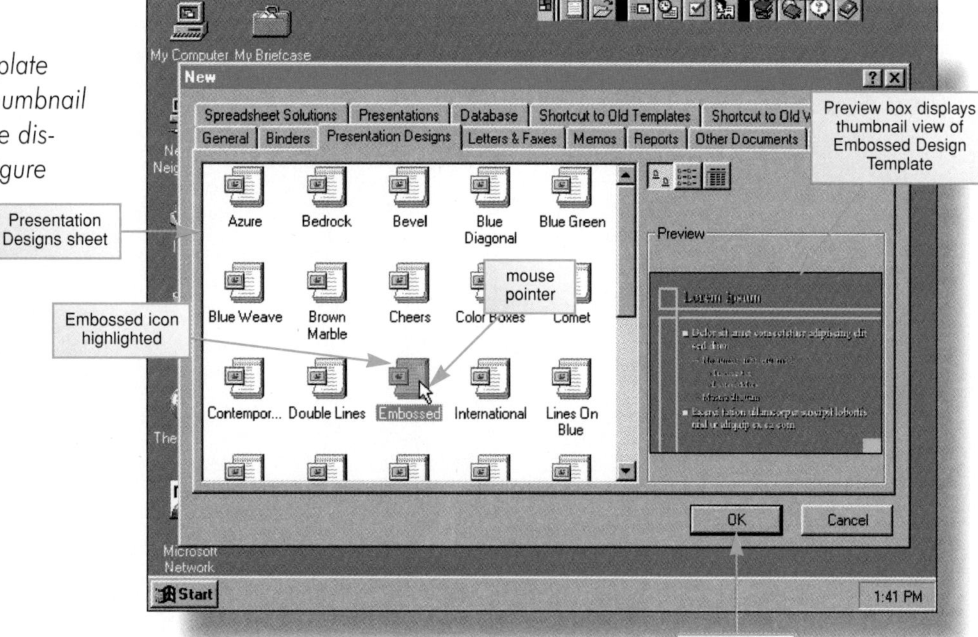

FIGURE 1-7

6 **Select the Embossed Design Template by double-clicking Embossed. When the New Slide dialog box displays, point to the OK button.**

Double-clicking the Embossed Design Template icon indicates that you are using a PowerPoint template. As a result, PowerPoint starts and the New Slide dialog box displays (Figure 1-8). In the New Slide dialog box, a frame displays around the Title Slide AutoLayout to indicate it is selected. At the bottom of the screen, Microsoft PowerPoint displays as a button on the taskbar.

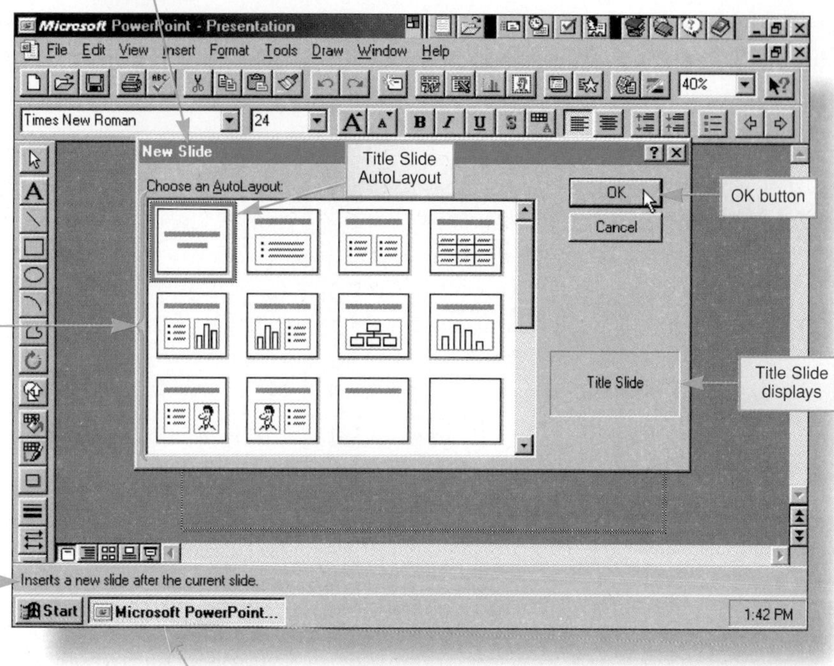

FIGURE 1-8

7 **Click the OK button. Maximize the screen if it does not display maximized.**

PowerPoint displays the maximized Title Slide AutoLayout and the Embossed Design Template on Slide 1 (Figure 1-9). The title bar identifies this as a Microsoft PowerPoint presentation currently titled Presentation. The status bar displays information about the current slide, such as the slide number and the current Design Template.

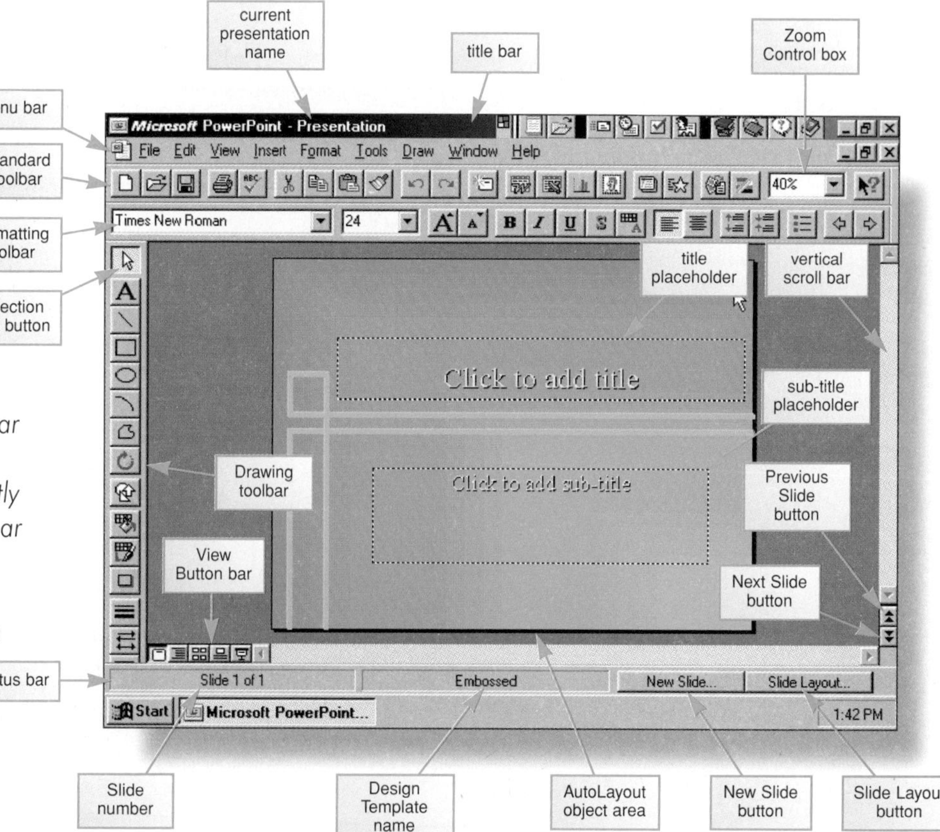

FIGURE 1-9

As an alternative to double-clicking the Embossed Design Template in Step 6, you can click the OK button to apply the selected Design Template.

The PowerPoint Window

The basic unit of a PowerPoint presentation is a **slide**. **Objects** are the building blocks for a PowerPoint slide. A slide contains one or many objects, such as a title, text, graphics, tables, charts, and drawings. In PowerPoint, you have the option of using the PowerPoint default settings or establishing your own. A **default setting** is a particular value for a variable that is assigned initially by PowerPoint and remains in effect unless canceled or overridden by the user. These settings control the placement of objects, the color scheme, the transition between slides, and other slide attributes. **Attributes** are the properties or characteristics of an object. For example, if you underline the title of a slide, the title is the object and the underline is the attribute. When you start PowerPoint, the default **slide layout** is **landscape orientation**, in which the slide width is greater than its height. In landscape orientation, the slide size is preset to 10 inches wide and 7.5 inches high. The slide layout can be changed to **portrait orientation,** so that the slide height is greater than its width, by clicking Slide Setup on the File menu. In portrait orientation, the slide height is 10 inches and its width is 7.5 inches.

More *About* Design Templates

When deciding on a Design Template, choose one designed to display light colored text on a medium to dark background. Light text on a dark background provides a stronger contrast than light text on a light background.

PowerPoint Views

PowerPoint has five views: Slide view, Outline view, Slide Sorter view, Notes Pages view, and Slide Show view. A **view** is the mode in which the presentation displays on the screen. You may use any or all views when creating your presentation, but you can use only one at a time. Change views by clicking one of the view buttons found on the **View Button bar** at the bottom of the PowerPoint screen (see Figure 1-9). The PowerPoint window display is dependent on the view. Some views are graphical while others are textual.

Table 1-1 identifies the view buttons and provides an explanation of each view.

Table 1-1

VIEW BUTTON	*VIEW*	*EXPLANATION*
	Slide view	Displays a single slide as it appears in your presentation. Use Slide view to create or edit a presentation. Slide view also is used to incorporate text and graphic objects and to create line-by-line progressive disclosure, called build effects.
	Outline view	Displays a presentation in an outline format showing slide titles and text. It is best used for organizing and developing the content of your presentation.
	Slide Sorter view	Displays miniatures of the slides in your presentation. You can then copy, cut, paste, or otherwise change slide position to modify your presentation. Slide Sorter view also is used to add slide transitions.
	Notes Pages view	Displays the current notes page. Notes Pages view allows you to create speaker's notes to use when you give your presentation. Each notes page corresponds to a slide and includes a reduced slide image.
	Slide Show view	Displays your slides as an electronic presentation on the full screen of your computer's monitor. Looking much like a slide projector display, you can see the effect of transitions, build effects, and slide timings.

PowerPoint Window in Slide View

The PowerPoint window in Slide view contains the title bar; the menu bar; the status bar; the toolbars: Standard, Formatting, and Drawing; the AutoLayout object area; the mouse pointer; the scroll bars; and the view buttons.

More *About* **Presentation Design**

The audience determines the level of detail you place on one slide. Before you create your presentation, determine who is likely to attend. Design your presentation around the amount of detail the audience wants to see. Remember, you want to keep their attention, not bore them with details.

TITLE BAR The **title bar** (see Figure 1-9 on page PP 1.12) displays the name of the current PowerPoint document. Until you save your presentation, PowerPoint assigns the default name Presentation.

MENU BAR The **menu bar** (see Figure 1-9) displays the PowerPoint menu names. Each menu name represents a list of commands that allows you to retrieve, store, print, and change objects in your presentation. To display a menu, such as the File menu, click the name File on the menu bar.

STATUS BAR Located at the bottom of the PowerPoint window, the **status bar** consists of a message area, a presentation Design Template identifier, and two buttons: the New Slide button and the Slide Layout button (see Figure 1-9). Most of the time, the current slide number and the total number of slides in the presentation display in the message area. For example, in Figure 1-9, the message area displays Slide 1 of 1. Slide 1 is the current slide, and of 1 indicates there is only one slide in the presentation. When you point to a command or a button, however, the status bar provides a short message about that command or button.

NEW SLIDE BUTTON Clicking the **New Slide button** (see Figure 1-9) inserts a new slide into a presentation after the current slide.

SLIDE LAYOUT BUTTON Clicking the **Slide Layout button** (see Figure 1-9) displays the Slide Layout dialog box. Selecting a slide layout from the options in a dialog box allows you to change the existing layout.

SCROLL BARS The **vertical scroll bar** (see Figure 1-9), located on the right side of the PowerPoint window, allows you to move forward or backward through your presentation. Clicking the **Next Slide button** (see Figure 1-9), located on the vertical scroll bar, advances to the next slide in the presentation. Clicking the **Previous Slide button** (see Figure 1-9), located on the vertical scroll bar, backs up to the slide preceding the current slide.

The **horizontal scroll bar** (see Figure 1-9), located on the bottom of the PowerPoint window, allows you to display a portion of the window when the entire window does not fit on the screen.

It should be noted that in Slide view, both the vertical and horizontal scroll bar actions are dependent upon **Zoom Control**. You control how large or small a document appears on the PowerPoint window with Zoom Control. If you are in Slide view and Zoom Control is set such that the entire slide is not visible in the Slide window, clicking the up arrow on the vertical scroll bar displays the next portion of your slide, not the previous slide. Recall that to go to the previous slide, click the Previous Slide button. To go to the next slide, click the Next Slide button.

AUTOLAYOUT OBJECT AREA The **AutoLayout object area** (see Figure 1-9) is a collection of placeholders for the title, text, clip art, graphs, tables, and media clips (video and sound). These placeholders display when you create a new slide. You can change the AutoLayout any time during the creation of your presentation by clicking the Slide Layout button on the status bar and then selecting a different slide layout.

PLACEHOLDERS Surrounded by a dashed line, **placeholders** are the empty objects on a new slide. Depending on the AutoLayout selected, placeholders will display for the title, text, graphs, tables, organization charts, media clips, and clip art. Once you place contents in a placeholder, the placeholder becomes an object. For example, text typed in a placeholder becomes a text object.

TITLE PLACEHOLDER Surrounded by a dashed line, the **title placeholder** is the empty title object on a new slide (see Figure 1-9 on page PP 1.12). Text typed in the title placeholder becomes the **title object.**

SUB-TITLE PLACEHOLDER Surrounded by a dashed line, the **sub-title placeholder** is the empty sub-title object that displays below the title placeholder on a title slide (see Figure 1-9).

MOUSE POINTER The **mouse pointer** can become one of several different shapes depending on the task you are performing in PowerPoint and the pointer's location on the screen. The different shapes are discussed when they display in subsequent projects. The mouse pointer in Figure 1-9 has the shape of a left-pointing block arrow.

TOOLBARS PowerPoint **toolbars** consist of buttons that allow you to perform tasks more quickly than when using the menu bar. For example, to save, click the Save button on the Standard toolbar. Each button face has a graphical representation that helps you remember its function. Figure 1-10 below, and Figures 1-11 and 1-12 on the next page illustrate the buttons on each of the three toolbars that display when you start PowerPoint and display a slide in Slide view. They are the Standard toolbar, the Formatting toolbar, and the Drawing toolbar. Each button is explained in detail when it is used.

PowerPoint has several additional toolbars you can display by clicking View on the menu bar. You also can display a toolbar by pointing to a toolbar and right-clicking to display a shortcut menu, which lists the available toolbars. A **shortcut menu** contains a list of commands or items that relate to the item to which you are pointing when you right-click.

PowerPoint allows you to customize all toolbars and to add the toolbar buttons you use most often. In the same manner, you can remove those toolbar buttons you do not use. To customize a toolbar, click Tools on the menu bar, and then click Customize to modify the toolbar to meet your requirements.

More *About* Presentation Design

Pace your information over several slides. The purpose of a slide is to identify ideas or concepts. Do not create a slide filled with text. As the presenter, it is your responsibility to introduce the topic and then explain the details.

STANDARD TOOLBAR The **Standard toolbar** (Figure 1-10) contains the tools to execute the most common commands found on the menu bar, such as Open, Print, Save, Copy, Cut, Paste, and many more. The Standard toolbar contains a button for setting Zoom Control. Recall that you control how large or small a document appears in the PowerPoint window with Zoom Control.

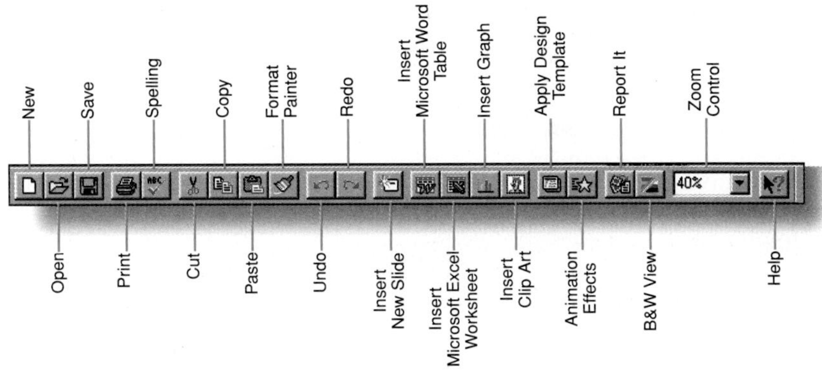

FIGURE 1-10

FORMATTING TOOLBAR The **Formatting toolbar** (Figure 1-11) contains the tools for changing text attributes. The Formatting toolbar allows you to quickly change font, font size, and alignment. It also contains tools to bold, italicize, underline, shadow, color, and bullet text. The five **attribute buttons**, **Bold**, **Italic**, **Underline**, **Text Shadow**, and **Bullet On/Off**, are on/off switches, or toggles. Click the button once to turn the attribute on; then click it again to turn the attribute off.

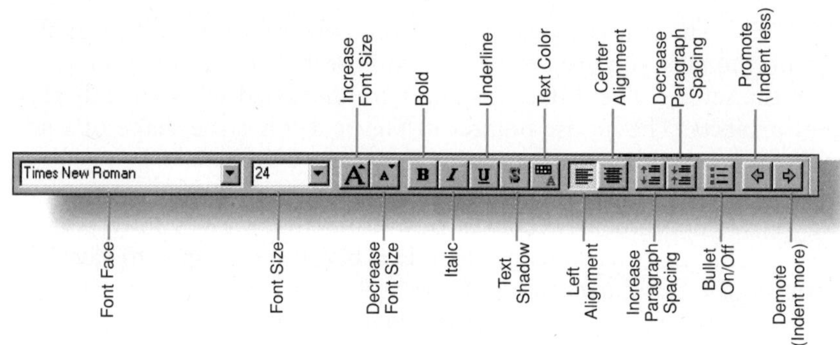

FIGURE 1-11

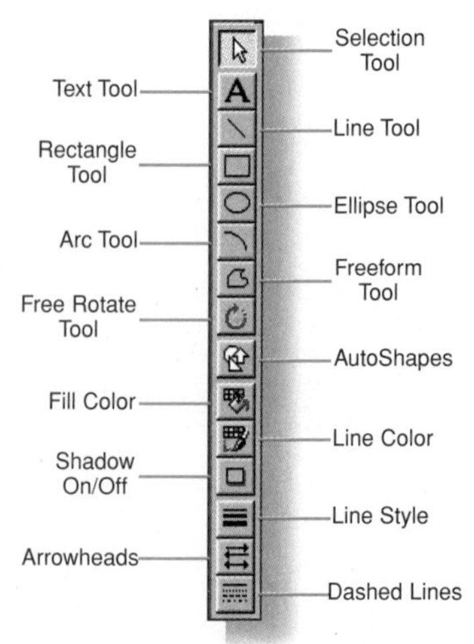

FIGURE 1-12

DRAWING TOOLBAR The **Drawing toolbar** (Figure 1-12) is a collection of tools for drawing objects such as lines, circles, and boxes. The Drawing toolbar also contains tools to edit the objects once you have drawn them. For example, you can add text to an object by clicking the **Text Tool button**, change the color of an object with the **Fill Color button**, or rotate an object by clicking the **Free Rotate Tool** button.

Creating a Title Slide

The purpose of a title slide is to introduce the presentation to the audience. PowerPoint assumes the first slide in a new presentation is the title slide. With the exception of a blank slide, PowerPoint also assumes every new slide has a title. To make creating your presentation easier, any text you type after a new slide displays becomes the title object. In other words, you do not have to first select the title placeholder before typing the title text. The AutoLayout for the title slide has a title placeholder near the middle of the window and a sub-title placeholder directly below the title placeholder (see Figure 1-13).

Entering the Presentation Title

The presentation title for Project 1 is College Survival. Type the presentation title in the title placeholder on the title slide. Perform the following step to create the title slide for this project.

More *About* Title Slides

To identify a new section in a long presentation, insert a title slide with the name of the new section.

Steps To Enter the Presentation Title

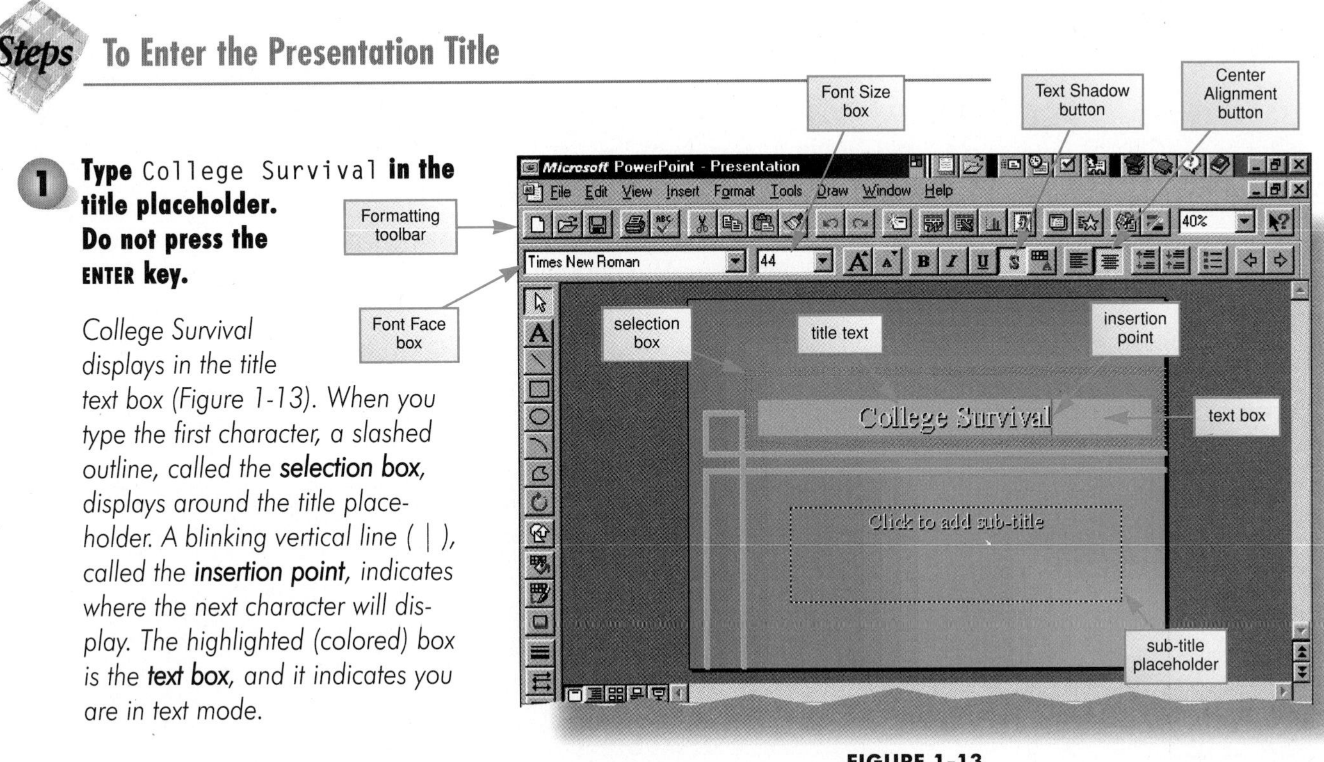

1 **Type** `College Survival` **in the title placeholder. Do not press the ENTER key.**

College Survival displays in the title text box (Figure 1-13). When you type the first character, a slashed outline, called the ***selection box****, displays around the title placeholder. A blinking vertical line (|), called the* ***insertion point****, indicates where the next character will display. The highlighted (colored) box is the* ***text box****, and it indicates you are in text mode.*

FIGURE 1-13

Notice that you do not press the ENTER key after the word Survival. If you press the ENTER key after typing the title, PowerPoint creates a new paragraph. A **paragraph** is a segment of text with the same format that begins when you press the ENTER key and ends when you press the ENTER key again. Pressing the ENTER key creates a new line in a new paragraph. Therefore, do not press the ENTER key unless you want to create a two-paragraph title. Additionally, PowerPoint **line wraps** text that exceeds the width of the placeholder. For example, if the title were College Survival, the Freshman Experience, it would exceed the width of the title placeholder and display on two lines.

The title is centered in the window because the Embossed Design Template alignment attribute is centered. The Center Alignment button is recessed on the Formatting toolbar in Figure 1-13.

More About Presentation Design

Uppercase letters are less distinct, therefore, more difficult to read than lowercase letters. For emphasis, it is acceptable to use all uppercase letters in short titles. Capitalize only the first letter in all words in long titles, except for short articles, unless the article is the first word in the title.

Correcting a Mistake When Typing

If you type the wrong letter and notice the error before pressing the ENTER key, press the BACKSPACE key to erase all the characters back to and including the one that is incorrect. If you mistakenly press the ENTER key after entering the title and the cursor is on the new line, simply press the BACKSPACE key to return the insertion point to the right of the letter l in the word Survival.

When you first install PowerPoint, the default setting allows you to reverse up to the last twenty changes by clicking the Undo button on the Standard toolbar, or by clicking the Undo Typing command on the Edit menu. The number of times you can click the Undo button to reverse changes can be modified. To increase or decrease the number of undos, click Tools on the menu bar, click Options, and then click the Advanced tab. Use the up and down arrows in the Maximum Number of Undos box to change the number of undos. The maximum number of undos is 150; the minimum number is 3.

You can reapply a change that you reversed with the Undo button by clicking the Redo button on the Standard toolbar. Clicking the **Redo button** reverses the last undo action.

Entering the Presentation Subtitle

The next step in creating the title slide is to enter the subtitle text into the sub-title placeholder. Complete the steps below to enter the presentation subtitle.

Steps To Enter the Presentation Subtitle

1 Click the label, Click to add sub-title, located inside the sub-title placeholder.

The insertion point is in the sub-title text box (Figure 1-14). The mouse pointer changes to an I-beam. The I-beam mouse pointer indicates the mouse is within a text placeholder. The selection box indicates the sub-title placeholder is selected.

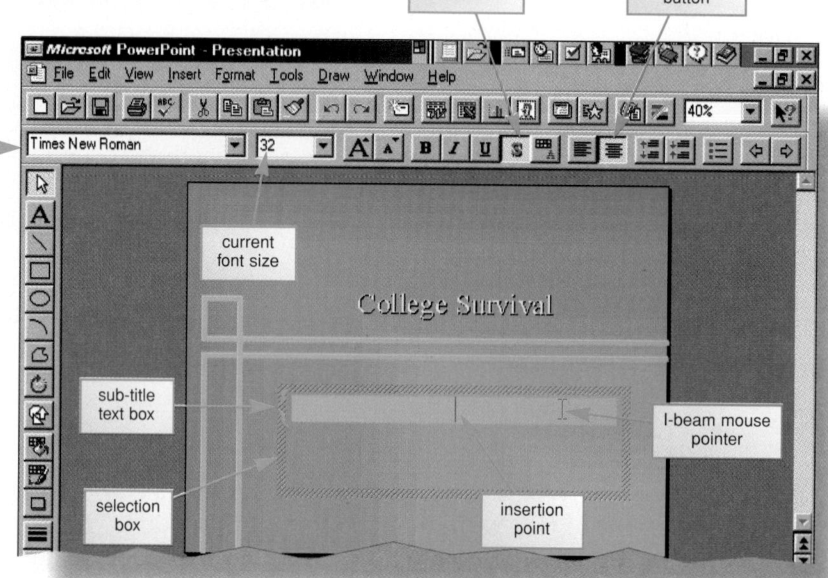

FIGURE 1-14

2 Type `A Guide to Success` **and press the ENTER key two times. Type** `Presented by:` **and press the ENTER key. Type** `J. D. Michaels` **but do not press the ENTER key.**

The text displays in the sub-title object as shown in Figure 1-15. The insertion point displays after the letter s in Michaels.

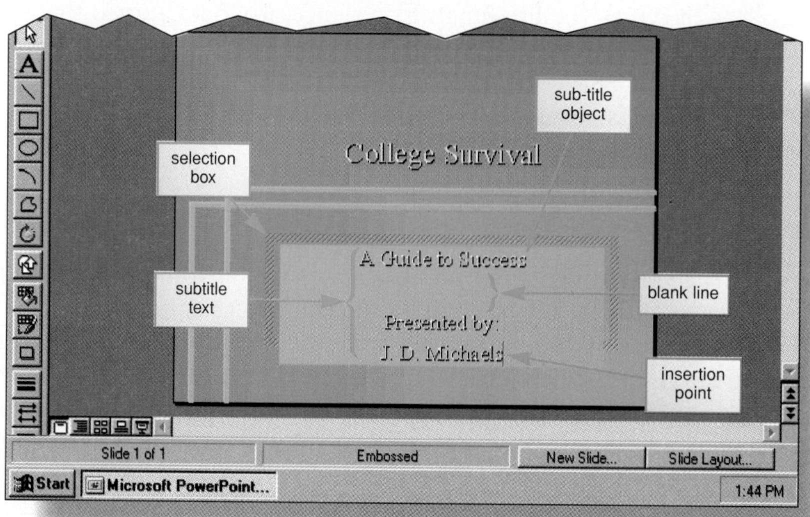

FIGURE 1-15

The previous section created a title slide using an AutoLayout for the title slide. PowerPoint displayed the title slide layout because you created a new presentation. You entered text in the title placeholder without selecting the title placeholder because PowerPoint assumes every slide has a title. You could, however, click the title placeholder to select it and then type your title. In general, to type text in any text placeholder, click the text placeholder and begin typing. You also added a subtitle that identifies the presenter. While this is not required, it is often useful information for the audience.

Text Attributes

This presentation is using the Embossed Design Template that you selected from the Presentation Designs sheet. Each Design Template has its own text attributes. A **text attribute** is a characteristic of the text, such as font face, font size, font style, or text color. You can adjust text attributes any time before, during, or after you type the text. Recall that a Design Template determines the color scheme, font face and size, and layout of your presentation. Most of the time, you use the Design Template's text attributes and color scheme. There are times when you wish to change the way your presentation looks, however, and still keep a particular Design Template. PowerPoint gives you that flexibility. You can use the Design Template you wish and change the text color, text size, text font face, and text style. Table 1-2 explains the different text attributes available in PowerPoint.

More About Text Attributes

Be consistent with color and text attributes. Use bold and italics sparingly for emphasis. Use no more than three type fonts and styles.

Table 1-2

ATTRIBUTE	DESCRIPTION
Font face	Defines the appearance and shape of letters, numbers, and special characters.
Text color	Defines the color of the text. Displaying text in color requires a color monitor. Printing text in color requires a color printer or plotter.
Font size	Specifies the size of the characters on the screen. Character size is gauged by a measurement system called points. A single *point* is about 1/72 of an inch in height. Thus, a character with a point size of eighteen is about 18/72 (or 1/4) of an inch in height.
Text style	Defines text characteristics. Text styles include plain, italic, bold, shadowed, and underlined. Text may have one or more styles at a time.
Subscript	Defines the placement of a character in relationship to another. A subscript character displays or prints slightly below and immediately to one side of another character.
Superscript	Defines the placement of a character in relationship to another. A superscript character displays or prints above and immediately to one side of another character.

The next two sections explain how to change the font size and text style attributes.

Changing the Font Size

The Embossed Design Template default font size is 32 points for body text and 44 points for title text. A point is 1/72 of an inch in height. Thus, a character with a point size of 44 is about 44/72 (or 11/18) of an inch in height. Slide 1 requires you to decrease the font size for the paragraph, Presented by:. Perform the steps on the next pages to change font size.

Steps To Decrease Font Size

Triple-click the paragraph, Presented by:, in the sub-title object.

The paragraph, Presented by:, is highlighted (Figure 1-16).

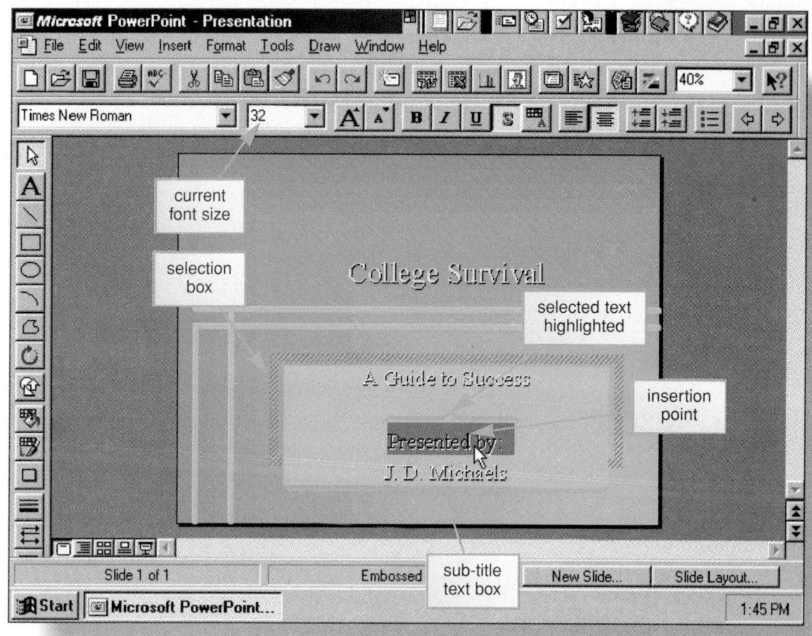

FIGURE 1-16

With Presented by: highlighted, point to the Decrease Font Size button on the Formatting toolbar.

When you point to a button on a toolbar, PowerPoint displays a ToolTip. A ***ToolTip*** *contains the name of the tool to which you are pointing. When pointing to the* ***Decrease Font Size button****, the ToolTip displays the words, Decrease Font Size (Figure 1-17).*

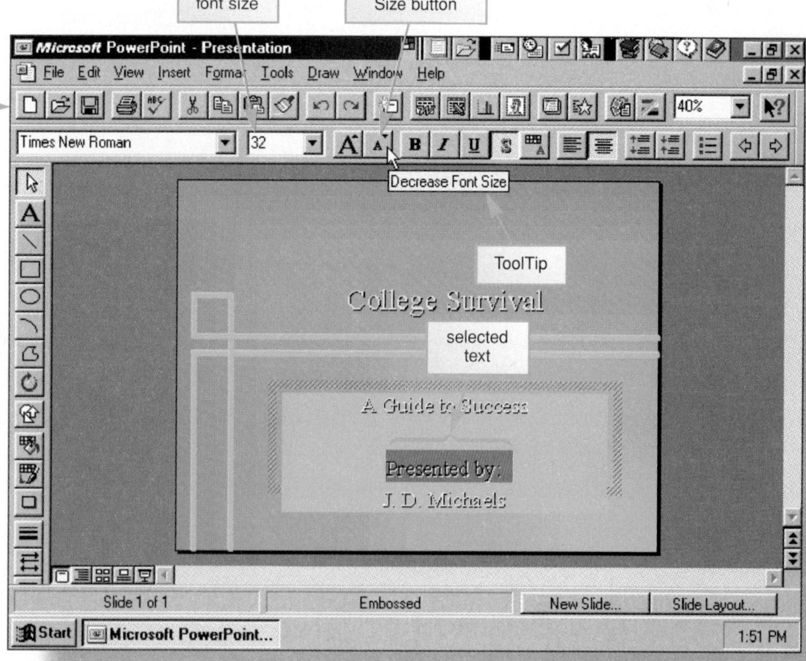

FIGURE 1-17

3 **Click the Decrease Font Size button twice so that 24 displays in the Font Size box on the Formatting toolbar.**

The paragraph, Presented by:, reduces to 24 points (Figure 1-18). The **Font Size box** *displays the new font size as 24.*

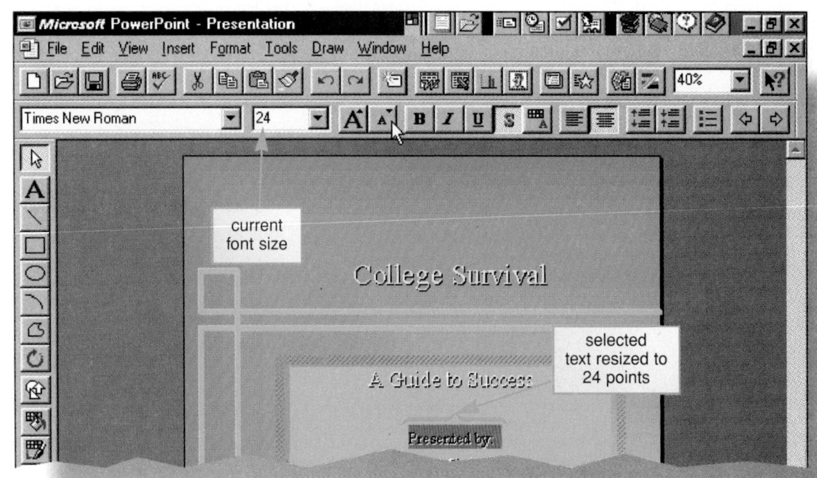

FIGURE 1-18

OtherWays

1. Right-click selected text, click Font on shortcut menu, click new font size in Size list box
2. Click Font Size arrow on Formatting toolbar, click one of listed font sizes, or click Font Size box on Formatting toolbar, type font size between 1 and 4000
3. On Format menu click Font, click new font size in Size list box

If you need to increase the font size, click the **Increase Font size button**, located immediately to the left of the Decrease Font Size button on the Formatting toolbar.

Changing the Style of Text to Italic

Text styles include plain, italic, bold, shadowed, and underlined. PowerPoint allows you to use one or more text styles in your presentation. Perform the following steps to add emphasis to the title slide by changing plain text to italic text.

Steps To Change the Text Style to Italic

1 **With the paragraph, Presented by:, highlighted, click the Italic button on the Formatting toolbar.**

The text is italicized and the **Italic button** *is recessed (Figure 1-19).*

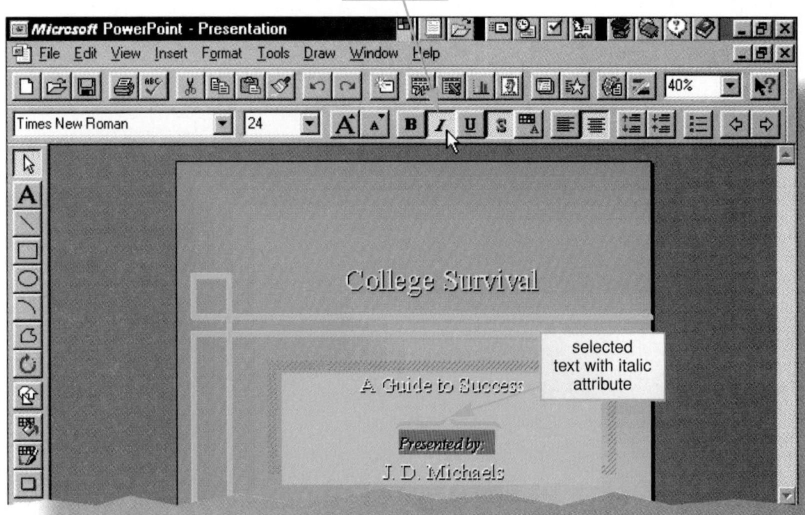

FIGURE 1-19

OtherWays

1. Right-click selected text, click Font on shortcut menu, click Italic in Font Style list box
2. On Format menu click Font, click Italic in Font Style list box
3. Press CTRL+I

More About Saving

Before you make extreme changes to your presentation, save a copy of it with a different filename using the Save As command on the File menu. This way, if you decide you do not like the new version, you will still have a copy of the original presentation.

To remove italics from text, select the italicized text and then click the Italic button. As a result, the Italic button is not recessed and the text does not have the italic font style.

Saving a Presentation to a Floppy Disk

While you are building your presentation, the computer stores it in main memory. It is important to save your presentation frequently because, if the computer is turned off or you lose electrical power, the presentation is lost. Another reason to save your work is that if you run out of lab time before completing your project, you may finish the project later without having to start over. Therefore, you must save any presentation you will use later. Before you continue with Project 1, save the work completed thus far. Perform the following steps to save a presentation to a floppy disk in drive A using the Save button on the Standard toolbar.

Steps To Save a Presentation to a Floppy Disk

1 Insert a formatted floppy disk in drive A. Then click the Save button on the Standard toolbar.

The File Save dialog displays (Figure 1-20). The insertion point displays in the File name drop-down list box. The default folder, My Documents, displays in the Save in drop-down list box. Presentations displays in the Save as type drop-down list box. The Save button is dimmed (not available) because you have not yet entered a name in the File name drop-down list box. The Cancel button is available, as indicated by the black text on the button. Clicking the Cancel button closes the File Save dialog box and returns to the PowerPoint window.

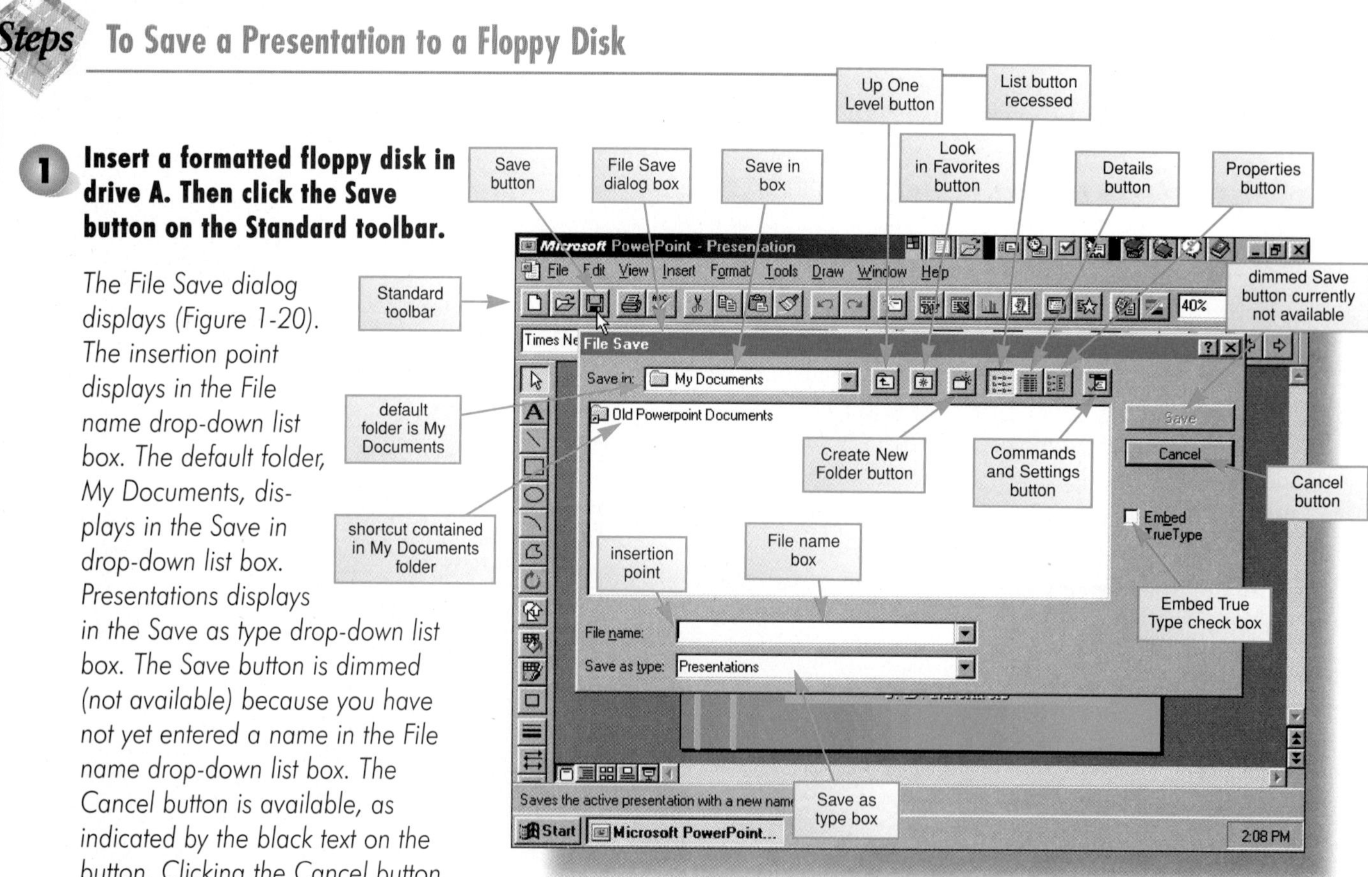

FIGURE 1-20

2 **Type** `College Survival` **in the File name box. Do not press the ENTER key after typing the filename. Click the Save in box arrow.**

The name, College Survival, displays in the File name drop-down list box. The Save in drop-down list box displays a list of locations to which you can save your presentation (Figure 1-21). Your list may look different depending on the configuration of your system. The black text on the Save button indicates it is available.

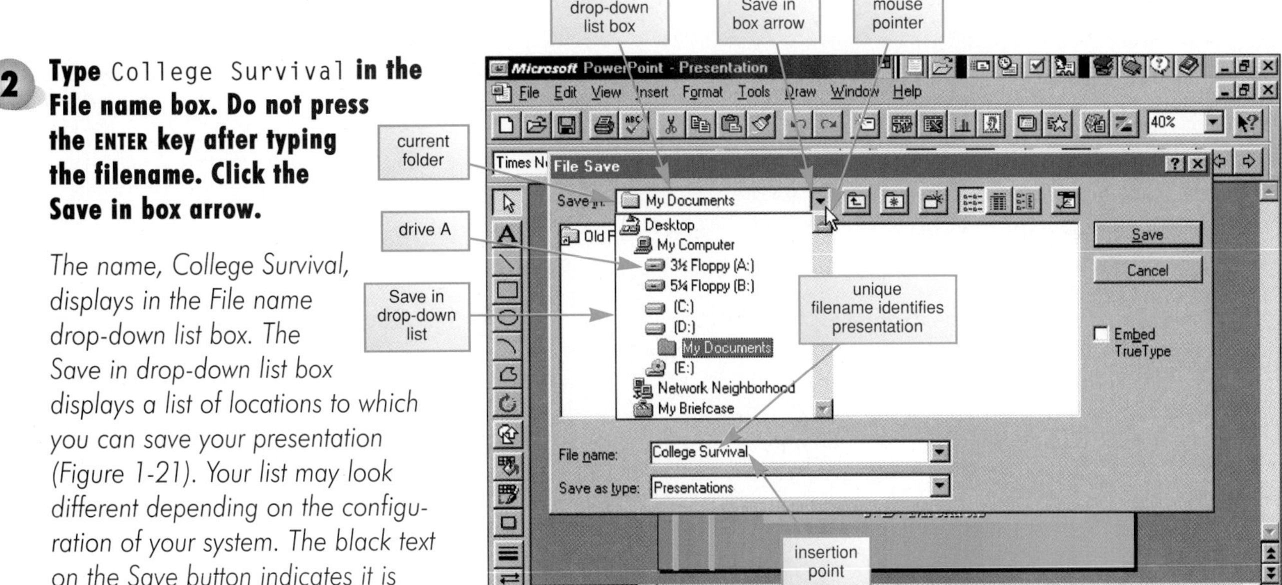

FIGURE 1-21

3 **Point to 3½ Floppy [A:] in the Save in drop-down list.**

3½ Floppy [A:] is highlighted (Figure 1-22).

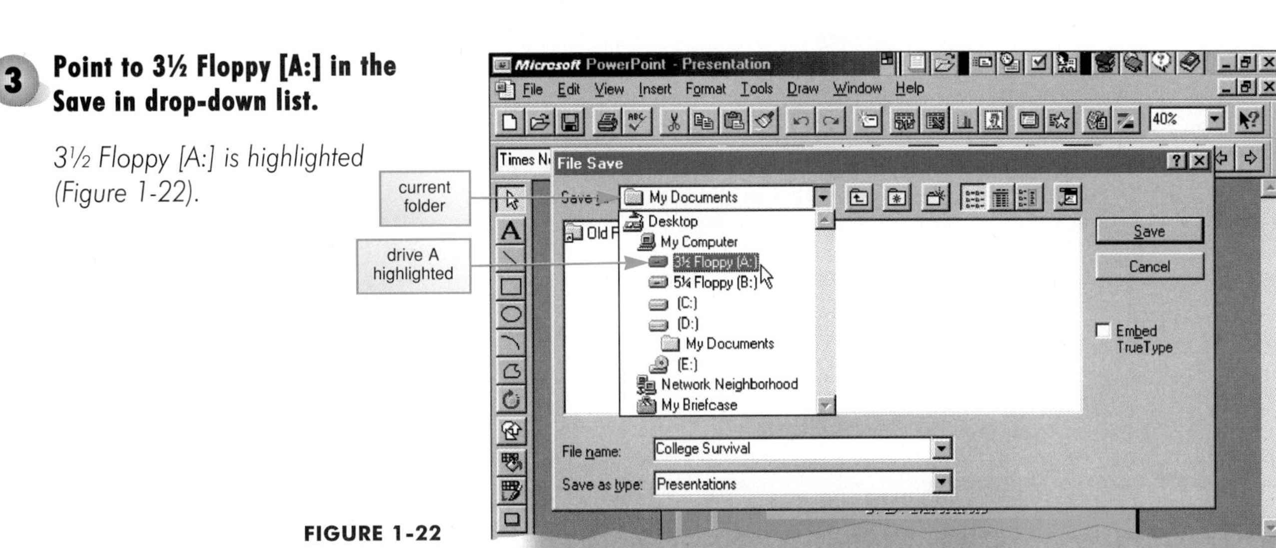

FIGURE 1-22

4 **Click 3½ Floppy [A:]. Then point to the Save button.**

Drive A becomes the current drive (Figure 1-23).

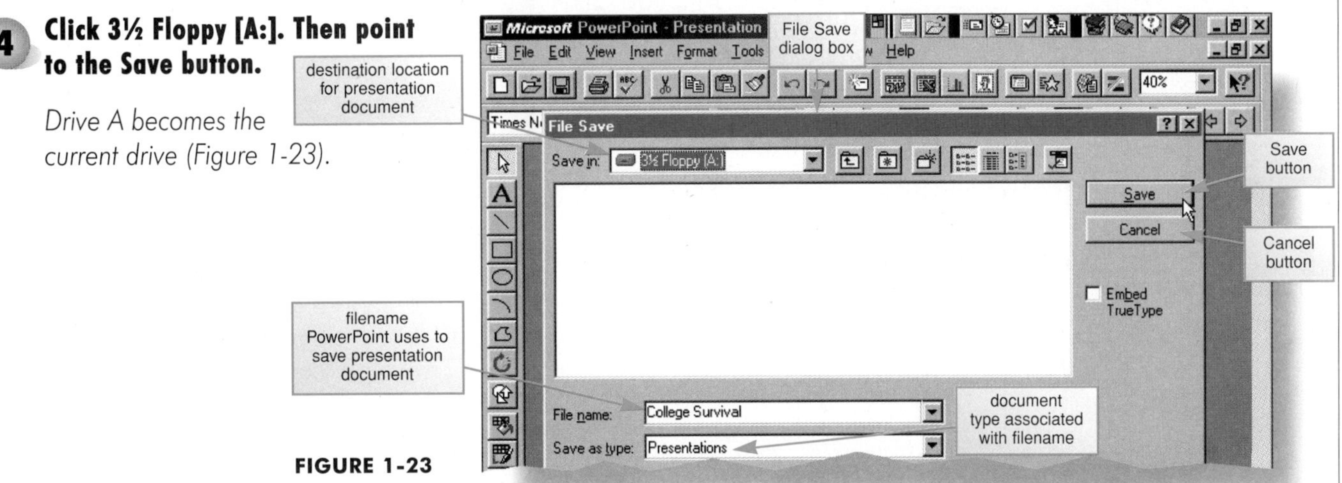

FIGURE 1-23

filename displays in title bar

5 Click the Save button.

PowerPoint saves the presentation to your data floppy disk in drive A. Slide 1 displays in Slide view. The title bar displays College Survival, the filename used to save the presentation (Figure 1-24).

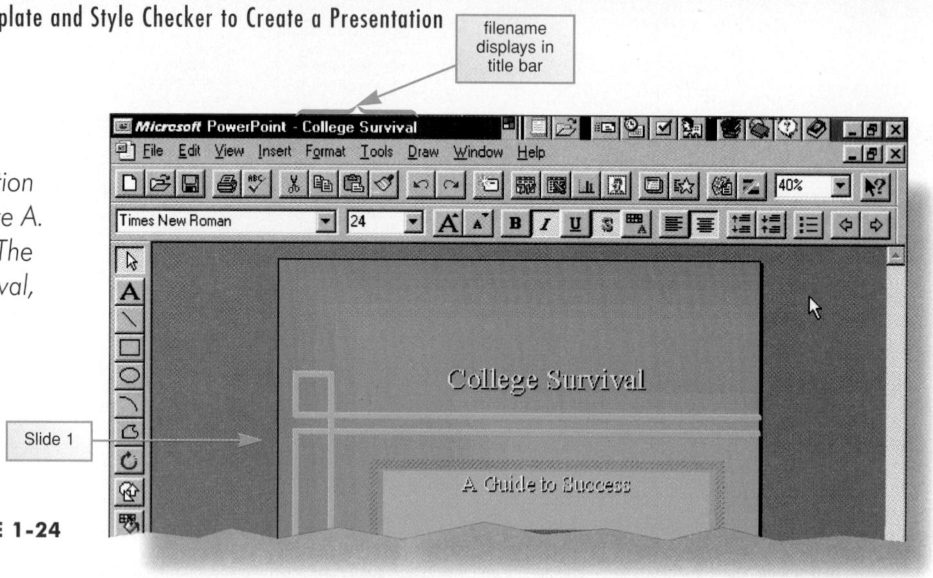

Slide 1

FIGURE 1-24

OtherWays

1. On File menu click Save
2. Press CTRL+S or press SHIFT+F12

PowerPoint automatically appends to the filename, College Survival, the extension **.ppt**, which stands for **P**ower**P**oint. Although the presentation, College Survival, is saved on a floppy disk, it also remains in main memory and displays on the screen.

It is a good practice to save periodically while you are working on a project. By doing so, you protect yourself from losing all the work you have done since the last time you saved.

Adding a New Slide to a Presentation

The title slide for your presentation is created. The next step is to add the first bulleted list slide in Project 1. Clicking the New Slide button on the status bar adds a slide into the presentation immediately after the current slide. Usually when you create your presentation, you are adding slides with text, graphics, or charts. When you add a new slide, PowerPoint displays a dialog box for you to choose one of the AutoLayouts. These AutoLayouts have placeholders for various objects, such as a title, text, graphics, graphs, and charts. Some placeholders provide access to other PowerPoint objects by allowing you to double-click the placeholder. Figure 1-25 displays the twenty-four different AutoLayouts available in PowerPoint. More information about using AutoLayout placeholders to add graphics follows in subsequent projects. Perform the following steps to add a new slide using the Bulleted List AutoLayout.

Bulleted List AutoLayout

twenty-four different AutoLayouts

Title Slide, Bulleted List, 2 Column Text, Table, Text & Graph, Graph & Text, Organization Chart, Graph, Text & Clip Art, Clip Art & Text, Title Only, Blank, Text & Object, Object & Text, Large Object, Object, Text & Media Clip, Media Clip & Text, Object over Text, Text over Object, Text & 2 Objects, 2 Objects & Text, 2 Objects over Text, 4 Objects

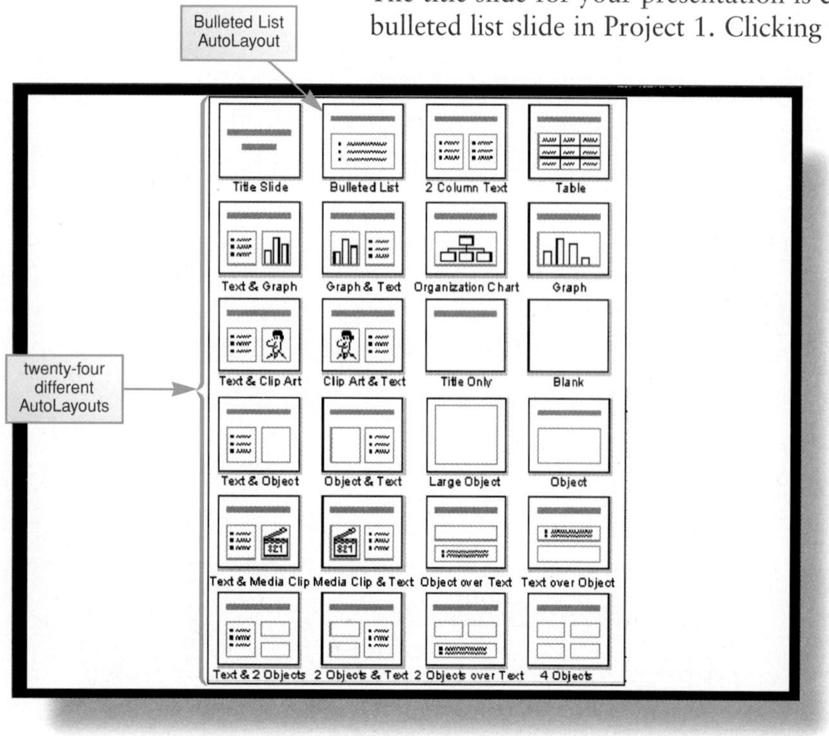

FIGURE 1-25

To Add a New Slide Using the Bulleted List AutoLayout

1 **Point to the New Slide button on the status bar (Figure 1-26).**

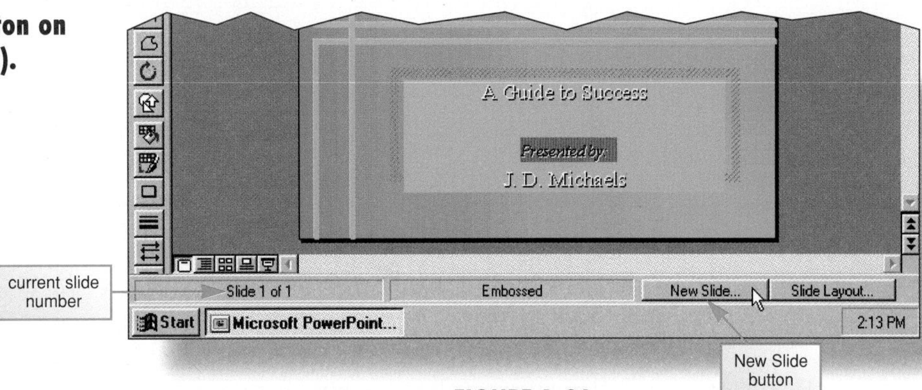

FIGURE 1-26

2 **Click the New Slide button. When the New Slide dialog box displays, point to the OK button.**

The New Slide dialog box displays (Figure 1-27). The Bulleted List AutoLayout is selected and the AutoLayout title, Bulleted List, displays at the bottom right corner of the New Slide dialog box.

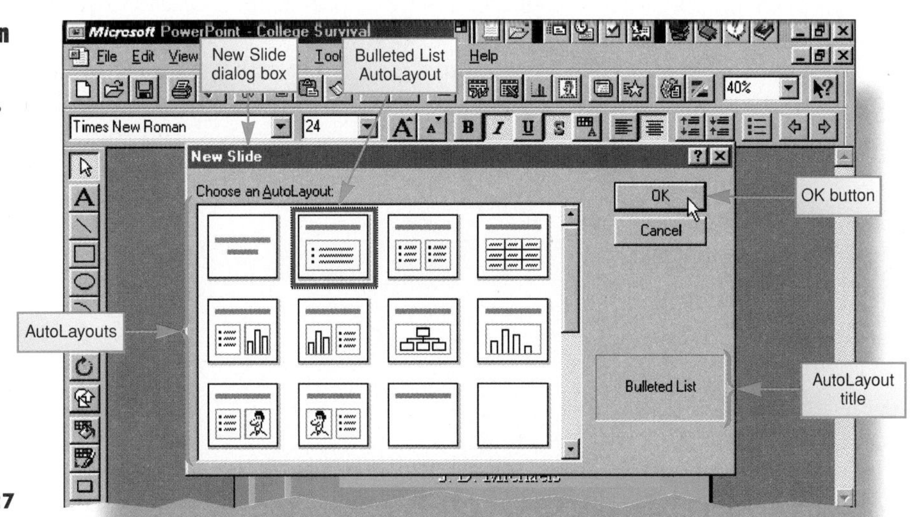

FIGURE 1-27

3 **Click the OK button.**

Slide 2 displays, keeping the attributes of the Embossed Design Template (Figure 1-28). Slide 2 of 2 displays on the status bar.

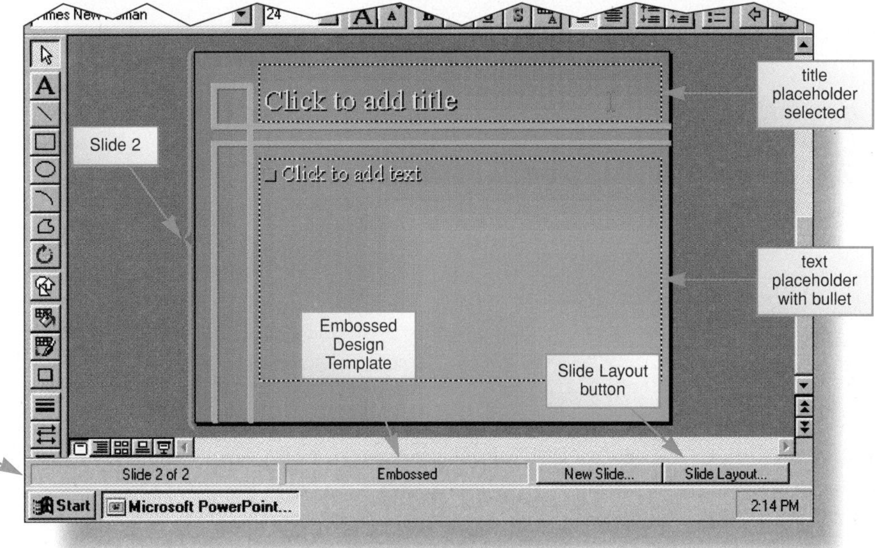

FIGURE 1-28

OtherWays

1. Click Insert New Slide button on Standard toolbar
2. On Insert menu click New Slide
3. Press CTRL+ENTER or press CTRL+M

Because you selected the Bulleted List AutoLayout, PowerPoint displays Slide 2 with a title placeholder and a text placeholder with a bullet. You can change the layout for a slide at any time during the creation of your presentation by clicking the Layout button on the status bar and then double-clicking the AutoLayout of your choice.

More *About* **Bulleted Lists**

Short lines of text are easier to read than long lines.

Creating a Bulleted List Slide

The bulleted list slides in Figure 1-2 on page PP 1.9, contain more than one level of bulleted text. A slide with more than one level of bulleted text is called a **multi-level bulleted list slide**. A **level** is a position within a structure, such as an outline, that indicates a magnitude of importance. PowerPoint allows for five paragraph levels. Each paragraph level has an associated bullet. The bullet font is dependent on the Design Template. Figure 1-29 identifies the five paragraph levels and the bullet fonts for the Embossed Design Template. Beginning with the Second Level, each paragraph indents .5 inch to the right of the preceding level. For example, the Level Two paragraph indents .5 inch to the right of the Level One paragraph. The Level Three paragraph indents .5 inch to the right of the Level Two paragraph or 1 inch to the right of the Level One paragraph.

An indented paragraph is said to be **demoted**, or pushed down to a lower level. For example, if you demote a First Level paragraph, it becomes a Second Level paragraph. This lower level paragraph is a subset of the higher level paragraph. It usually contains information that supports the topic in the paragraph immediately above it. You demote a paragraph by clicking the **Demote (Indent more) button** on the Formatting toolbar.

When you want to raise a paragraph from a lower level to a higher level, you **promote** the paragraph by clicking the **Promote (Indent less) button** on the Formatting toolbar.

Creating a multi-level bulleted list slide requires several steps. Initially, you enter a slide title. Next, you select a text placeholder. Then you type the text for the multi-level bulleted list, demoting and promoting paragraphs as needed. The next several sections explain how to add a multi-level bulleted list slide.

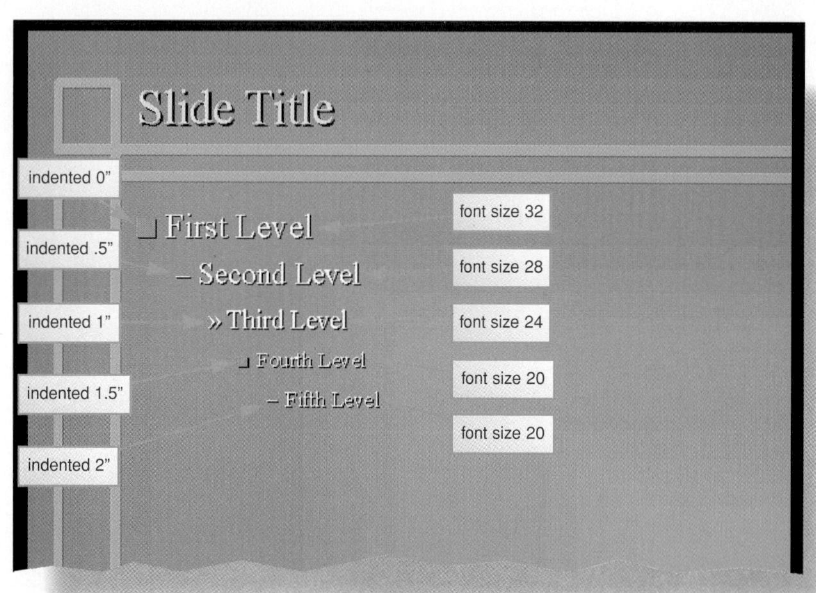

FIGURE 1-29

Entering a Slide Title

PowerPoint assumes every new slide has a title. Therefore, any text you type after a new slide displays becomes the title object. The title for Slide 2 is Dormitory Survival. Perform the following step to enter this title.

Steps To Enter a Slide Title

1 Type `Dormitory Survival` **in the title placeholder. Do not press the ENTER key.**

The title, Dormitory Survival, displays in the title object (Figure 1-30). The insertion point displays after the l in Survival.

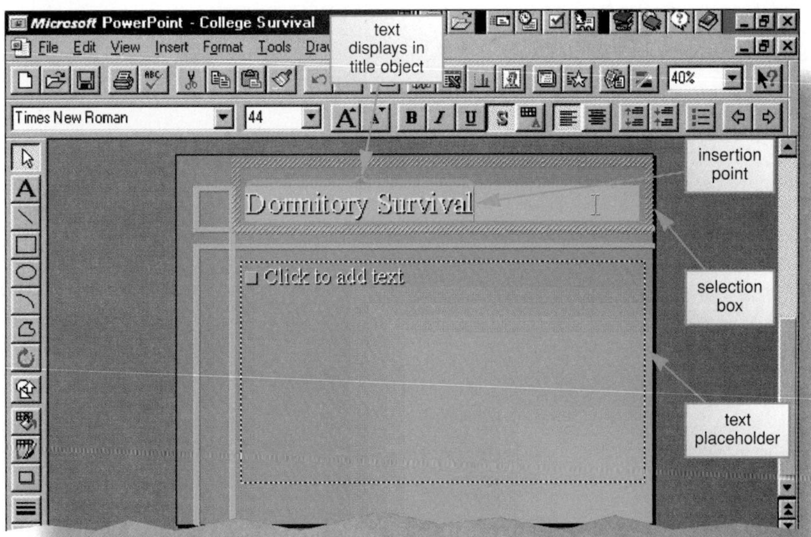

FIGURE 1-30

Selecting a Text Placeholder

Before you can type text into the text placeholder, you must first select it. Perform the following step to select the text placeholder on Slide 2.

Steps To Select A Text Placeholder

1 Click the bulleted paragraph labeled, Click to add text.

The insertion point displays immediately after the bullet on Slide 2 (Figure 1-31). The Bullet On/Off button is recessed.

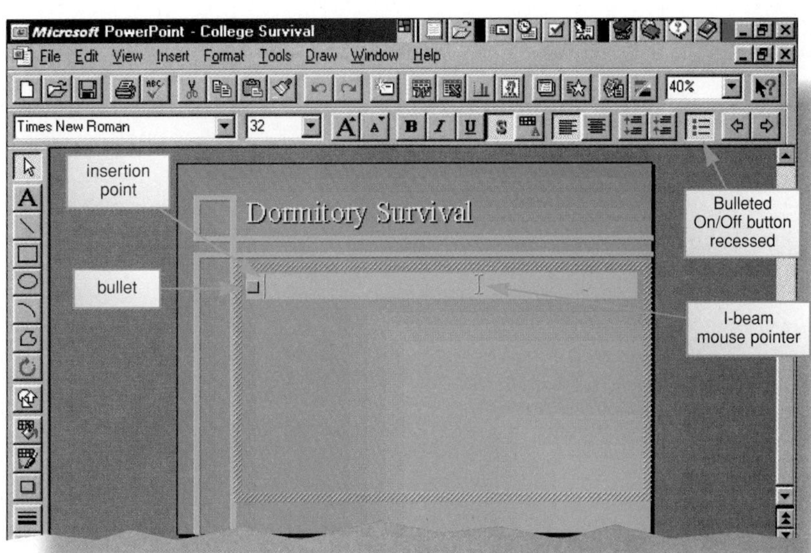

FIGURE 1-31

OtherWays

1. Press CTRL+ENTER

Typing a Multi-level Bulleted List

Recall that a bulleted list is a list of paragraphs, each of which is preceded by a bullet. Also recall that a paragraph is a segment of text ended by pressing the ENTER key. The next step is to type the multi-level bulleted list, which consists of the six entries shown in Figure 1-2 on page PP 1.9. Perform the following steps to type a multi-level bulleted list.

To Type a Multi-level Bulleted List

1 **Type** `Be considerate of roommate` **and press the ENTER key.**

The paragraph, Be considerate of roommate, displays. The font size is 32. The insertion point displays after the second bullet (Figure 1-32). When you press the ENTER key, the word processing feature of PowerPoint marks the end of one paragraph and begins a new paragraph. Because you are using the Bulleted List AutoLayout, PowerPoint places a bullet in front of the new paragraph.

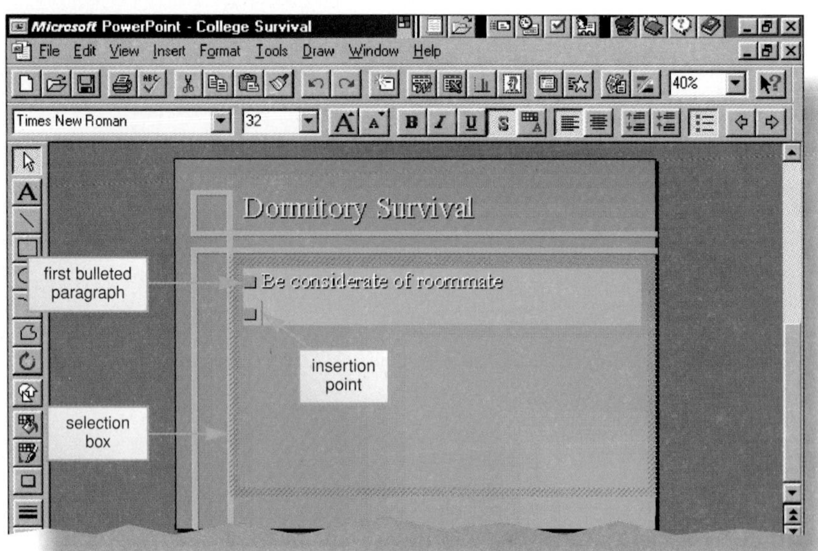

FIGURE 1-32

2 **Point to the Demote (Indent more) button on the Formatting toolbar (Figure 1-33).**

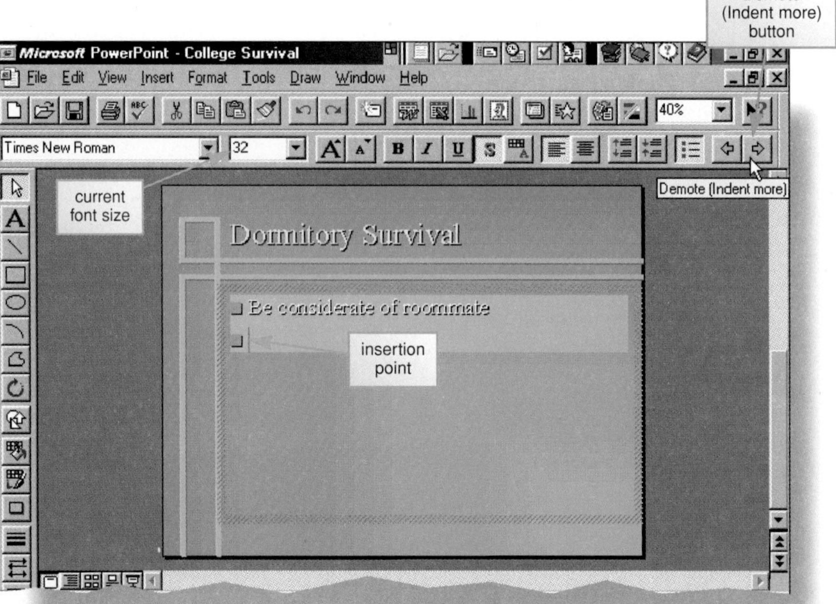

FIGURE 1-33

3 **Click the Demote (Indent more) button.**

The second paragraph indents under the first and becomes a Second Level paragraph (Figure 1-34). Notice the bullet in front of the second paragraph changes from a block to a dash and the font size for the demoted paragraph is now 28. The insertion point displays after the dash.

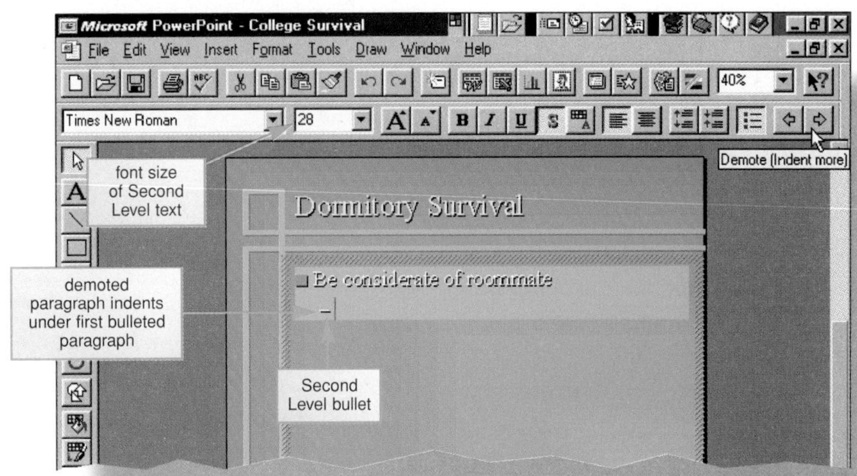

FIGURE 1-34

4 **Type** `Organize room together` **and press the ENTER key.**

A new Second Level paragraph displays with a dash bullet (Figure 1-35). When you press the ENTER key, PowerPoint adds a new paragraph at the same level as the previous paragraph.

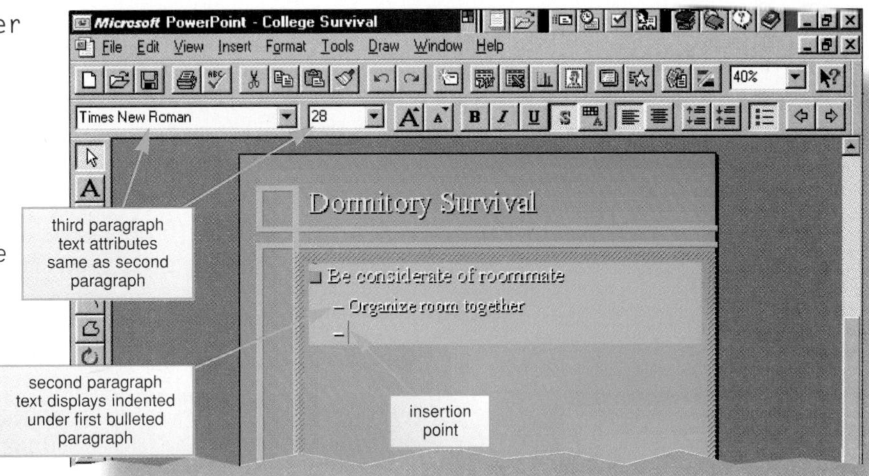

FIGURE 1-35

5 **Point to the Promote (Indent less) button on the Formatting toolbar (Figure 1-36).**

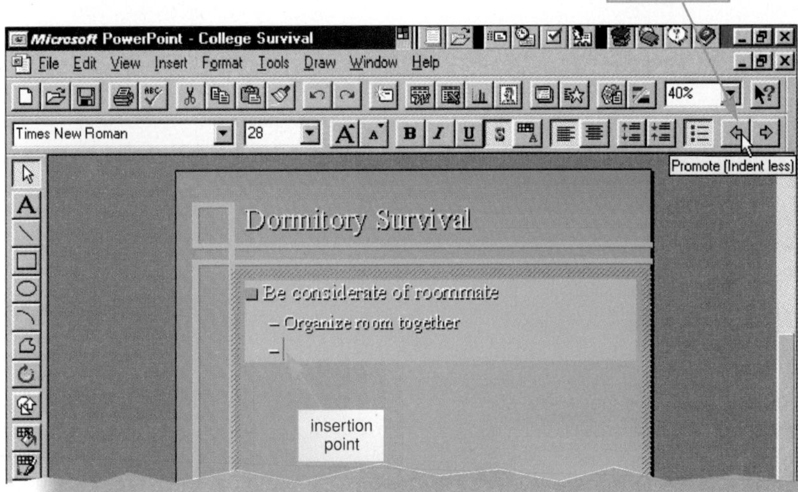

FIGURE 1-36

6 Click the Promote (Indent less) button.

The Second Level paragraph becomes a First Level paragraph (Figure 1-37). Notice the bullet in front of the new paragraph changes from a dash to a block and the font size for the promoted paragraph is 32. The insertion point displays after the block bullet.

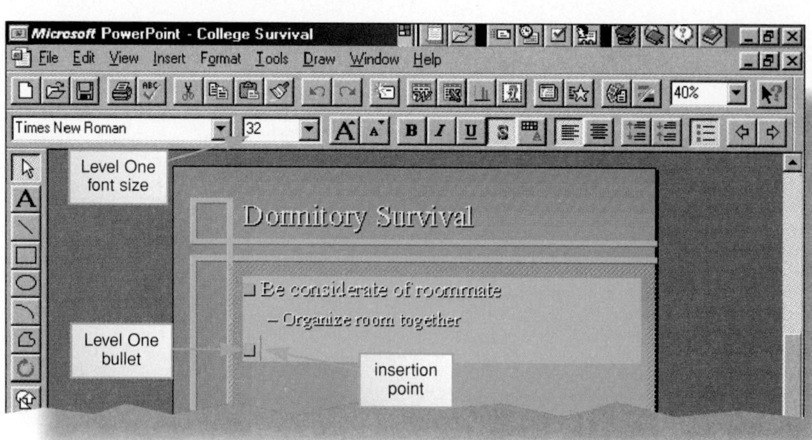

FIGURE 1-37

Perform the following steps to complete the text for Slide 2.

TO TYPE THE REMAINING TEXT FOR SLIDE 2

Step 1: Type `Obey rules` and press the ENTER key.
Step 2: Type `Schedule meals` and press the ENTER key.
Step 3: Click the Demote (Indent more) button.
Step 4: Type `Avoid high calorie snacks` and press the ENTER key.
Step 5: Click the Promote (Indent less) button.
Step 6: Type `Get enough sleep` but do not press the ENTER key.

The insertion point displays after the p in sleep (Figure 1-38).

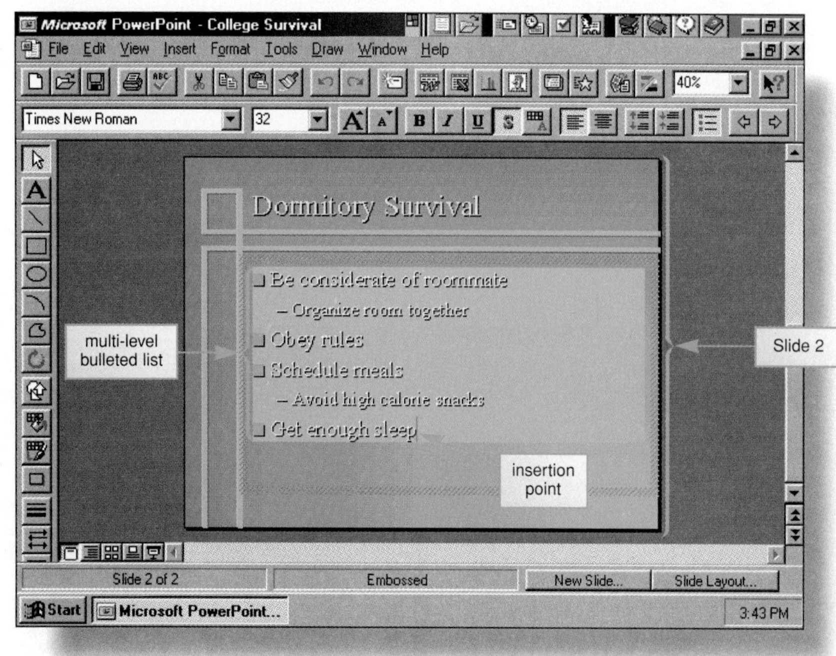

FIGURE 1-38

Notice that you did not press the ENTER key after typing the last paragraph in Step 6. If you press the ENTER key, a new bullet displays after the last entry on this slide. To remove an extra bullet, press the BACKSPACE key.

Adding a New Slide with the Same AutoLayout

When you add a new slide to a presentation and want to keep the same AutoLayout used on the previous slide, PowerPoint gives you a shortcut. Instead of clicking the New Slide button and clicking an AutoLayout in the New Slide dialog box, you can press and hold down the SHIFT key and click the New Slide button. Perform the following step to add a new slide (Slide 3) and keep the Bulleted List AutoLayout used on the previous slide.

To Add a New Slide with the Same AutoLayout

1 Press and hold down the SHIFT key. Click the New Slide button on the status bar. Then release the SHIFT key.

Slide 3 displays with the Bulleted List AutoLayout (Figure 1-39). Slide 3 of 3 displays on the status bar.

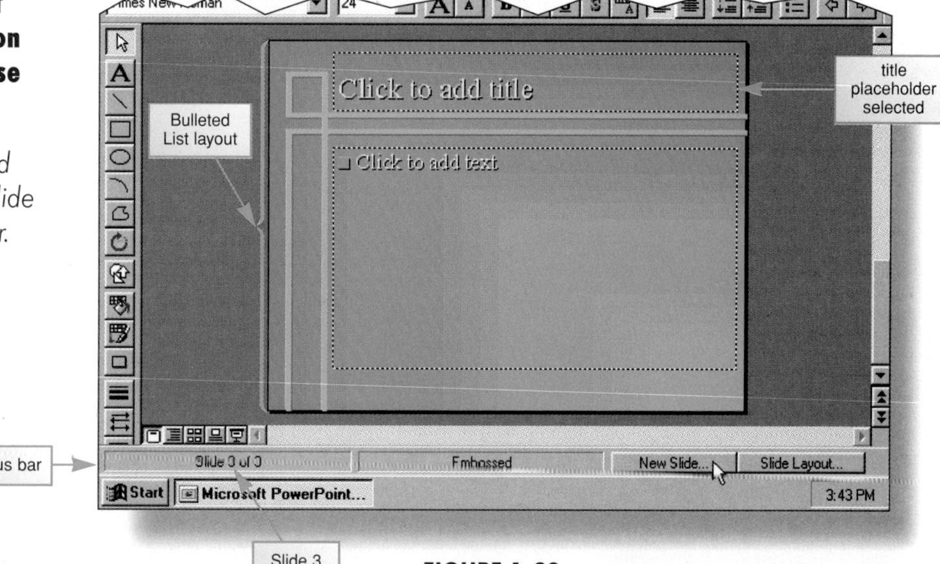

FIGURE 1-39

OtherWays

1. Press SHIFT+CTRL+M

Slide 3 is added to the presentation. Perform the following steps to add text to Slide 3 and create a multi-level bulleted list.

TO CREATE SLIDE 3

Step 1: Type `Classroom Survival` in the title placeholder.
Step 2: Click the text placeholder.
Step 3: Type `Learn your way around campus` and press the ENTER key.
Step 4: Type `Buy books and supplies` and press the ENTER key.
Step 5: Type `Attend class` and press the ENTER key.
Step 6: Click the Demote (Indent more) button. Then type `Be punctual` and press the ENTER key.
Step 7: Type `Participate` and press the ENTER key.
Step 8: Click the Promote (Indent less) button. Then type `Develop good study skills` and press the ENTER key.
Step 9: Click the Demote (Indent more) button. Then type `Budget homework time` but do not press the ENTER key.

Slide 3 displays as shown in Figure 1-40.

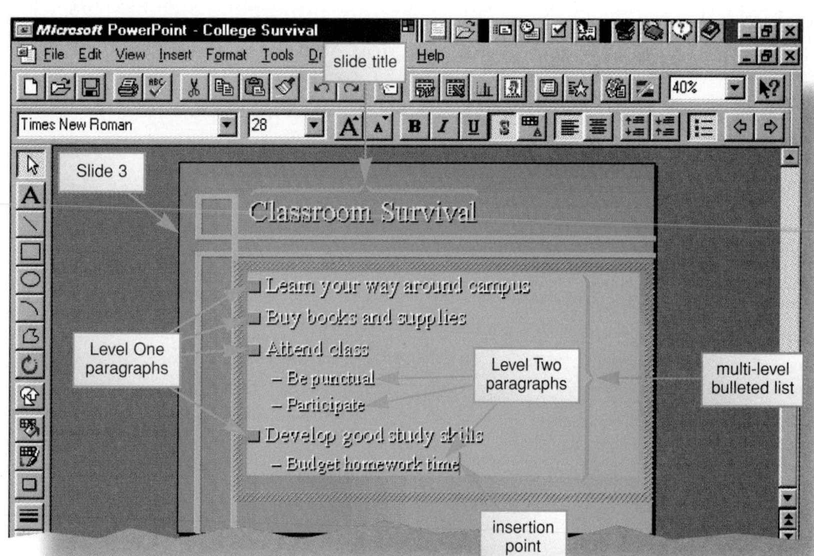

FIGURE 1-40

Slide 4 is the last slide in this presentation. It, too, is a multi-level bulleted list. Perform the steps on the next page to create Slide 4.

TO CREATE SLIDE 4

Step 1: Press and hold down the SHIFT key and click the New Slide button on the status bar. Release the SHIFT key.
Step 2: Type `Social Survival` in the title placeholder.
Step 3: Click the text placeholder.
Step 4: Type `Budget time for fun and relaxation` and press the ENTER key.
Step 5: Click the Demote (Indent more) button. Then type `Join extracurricular clubs` and press the ENTER key.
Step 6: Click the Promote (Indent less) button. Then type `Preserve your values` and press the ENTER key.
Step 7: Click the Demote (Indent more) button. Then type `Choose friends with care` and press the ENTER key.
Step 8: Click the Promote (Indent less) button. Then type `Stay physically fit` and press the ENTER key.
Step 9: Type `Stay in touch with family` but do not press the ENTER key.

The slide title and text object display as shown in Figure 1-41.

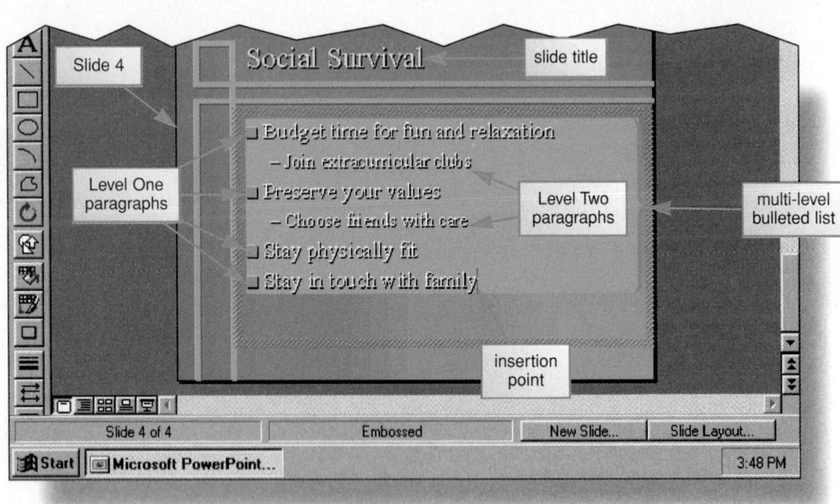

FIGURE 1-41

All slides for the College Survival presentation are created. This presentation consists of a title slide and three multi-level bulleted list slides.

Saving a Presentation with the Same Filename

Saving frequently never can be overemphasized. When you first saved the presentation, you clicked the Save button on the Standard toolbar and the File Save dialog box displayed. When you want to save the changes made to the presentation after your last save, you again click the Save button. This time, however, the File Save dialog box does not display because PowerPoint updates the document called College Survival.ppt on your data floppy disk. Perform the following steps to save the presentation again.

TO SAVE A PRESENTATION WITH THE SAME FILENAME

Step 1: Be sure your data floppy disk is in drive A.
Step 2: Click the Save button on the Standard toolbar.

PowerPoint overwrites the old College Survival.ppt document on the data floppy disk in drive A with the revised presentation document, College Survival.ppt. Slide 4 displays in the PowerPoint window.

Moving to Another Slide in Slide View

When creating or editing a presentation in Slide view, you often want to display a slide other than the current one. Dragging the vertical scroll bar box up or down moves you through your presentation. The box on the vertical scroll bar is called the **elevator** and is shown in Figure 1-42. When you drag the elevator, the **slide indicator** displays the number and the title of the slide you are about to display. Releasing the mouse button displays the slide.

Using the Vertical Scroll Bar to Move to Another Slide

Before continuing with Project 1, you want to display the title slide. Perform the following steps to move from Slide 4 to the Slide 1 using the vertical scroll bar.

OtherWays

1. Click Next Slide button on vertical scroll bar to move forward one slide, or click Previous Slide button on the vertical scroll bar to move back one slide
2. Press PAGE DOWN to move forward one slide, or press PAGE UP to move back one slide

Steps To Use the Vertical Scroll Bar to Move to Another Slide

1 **Position the mouse pointer on the elevator. Press and hold down the left mouse button.**

Slide: 4, Social Survival, displays in the slide indicator (Figure 1-42).

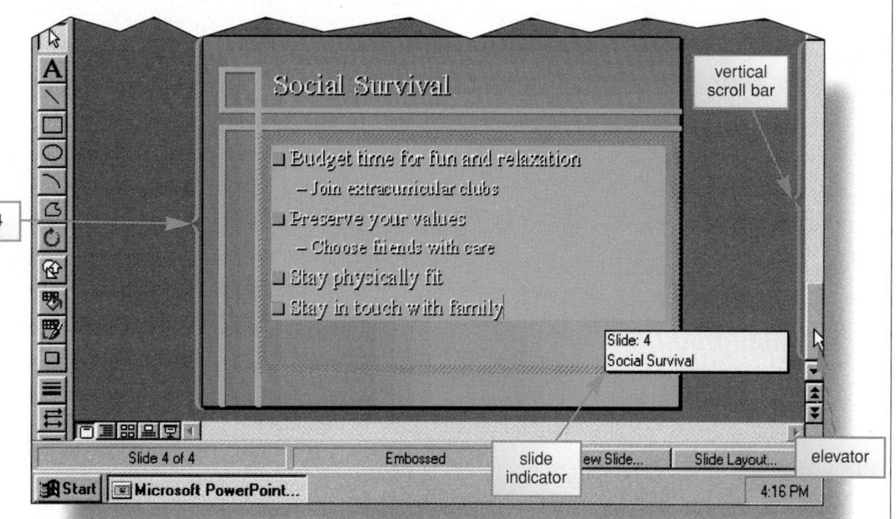

FIGURE 1-42

2 **Drag the elevator up the vertical scroll bar until Slide: 1 College Survival displays in the slide indicator.**

Slide: 1, College Survival, displays in the slide indicator. Slide 4 still displays in the PowerPoint window (Figure 1-43).

3 **Release the left mouse button.**

Slide 1, titled College Survival, displays in the PowerPoint window.

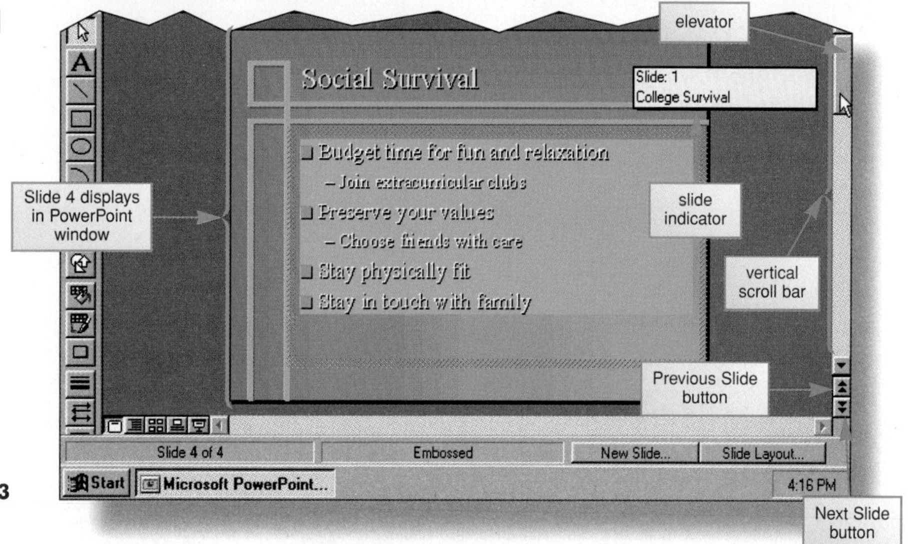

FIGURE 1-43

Viewing the Presentation Using Slide Show

The **Slide Show button**, located at the bottom left of the PowerPoint window, allows you to display your presentation electronically using a computer. The computer acts like a slide projector, displaying each slide on a full screen. The full screen slide hides the toolbars, menus, and other PowerPoint window elements.

Starting Slide Show View

Slide Show view begins when you click the Slide Show button. PowerPoint then displays the current slide on the full screen without any of the PowerPoint window objects, such as the menu bar or toolbars. Perform the following steps to start Slide Show view.

Steps To Start Slide Show View

1. **Point to the Slide Show button on the View Button bar.**

   The Slide View button is recessed because you are still in Slide view (Figure 1-44).

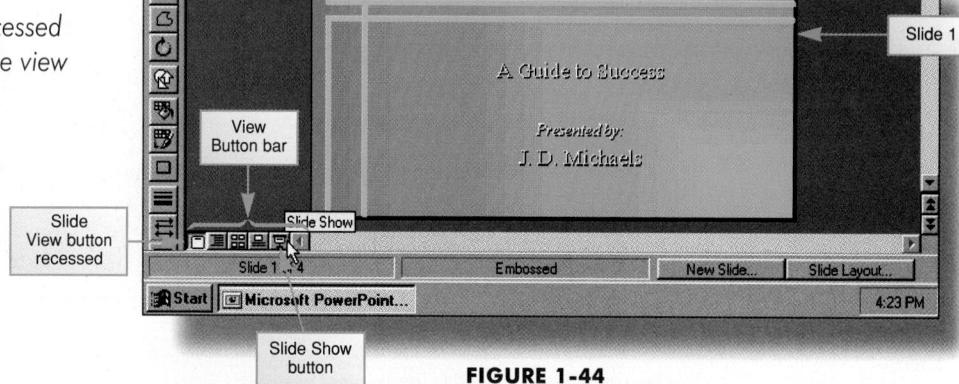

FIGURE 1-44

2. **Click the Slide Show button.**

   The title slide fills the screen (Figure 1-45). The PowerPoint window is hidden.

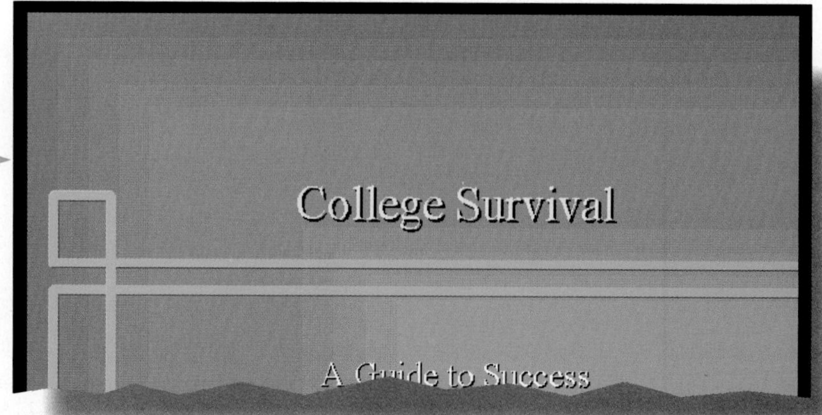

FIGURE 1-45

OtherWays

1. On View menu click Slide Show

Advancing through a Slide Show Manually

After you begin Slide Show view, you can move forward or backward through your slides. PowerPoint allows you to advance through your slides manually or automatically. Automatic advancing is discussed in a later project. Perform the step below to manually move through your slides.

Steps To Manually Move Through Slides in a Slide Show

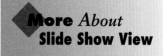

1 Click each slide until the last slide of the presentation, Slide 4, Social Survival, displays.

Each slide in your presentation displays on the screen, one slide at a time. Each time you click the mouse button, the next slide displays (Figure 1-46).

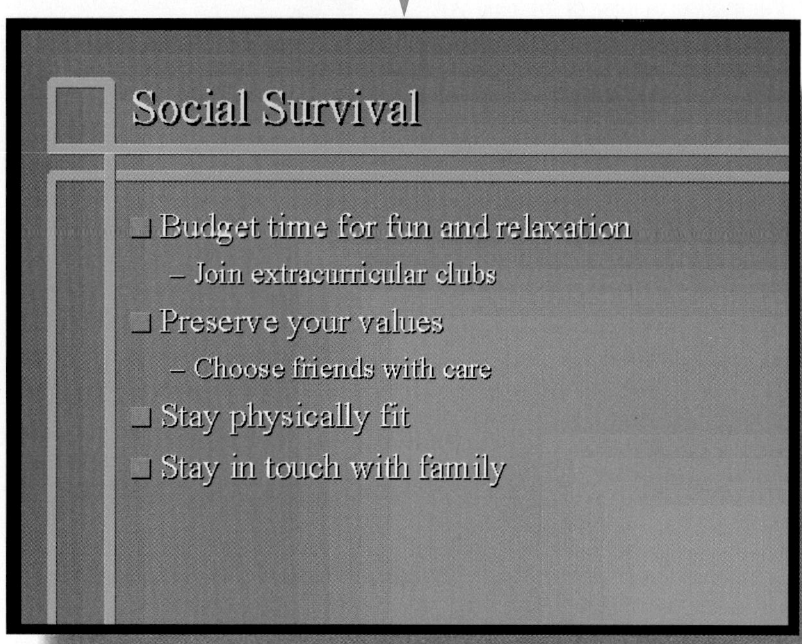

FIGURE 1-46

OtherWays

1. Press PAGE DOWN to advance one slide at a time, or press PAGE UP to go backward one slide at a time

Displaying the Popup Menu in Slide Show View

Slide Show view has a shortcut menu, called **Popup Menu**, that displays when you right-click a slide in Slide Show view. The Popup Menu contains commands to assist you during a slide show. For example, clicking the **Next command** moves you to the next slide. Clicking the **Previous command** moves you to the previous slide. You can jump to any slide in your presentation by clicking the **Go To command**, which displays the Slide Navigator dialog box. The Slide Navigator dialog box contains a list of the slides in your presentation. Jump to the requested slide by double-clicking the name of that slide.

Additional Popup Menu commands allow you to create a list of action items during a slide show, change the mouse pointer from an arrow to a pen, blacken the screen, and end the slide show. Popup Menu commands are discussed in subsequent projects. Perform the step on the next page to display the Slide Show View Popup Menu.

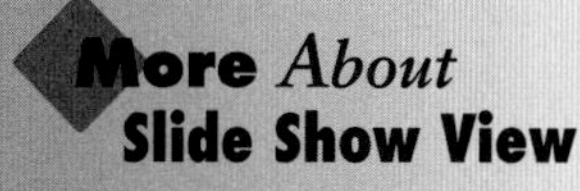

More About Slide Show View

The Pen command on the Popup Menu turns the mouse pointer into a pen that you can use to mark on the slides. The effect is similar to the electronic white board used by television sports announcers as they explain a play. The markings are not saved with the presentation.

To Display the Slide Show View Popup Menu

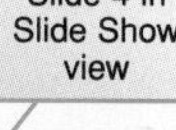

1 With Slide 4 displaying in Slide Show view, right-click the slide.

The Popup menu displays on Slide 4 (Figure 1-47). Your screen may look different because the Popup menu displays near the location of the mouse pointer at the time you right-click.

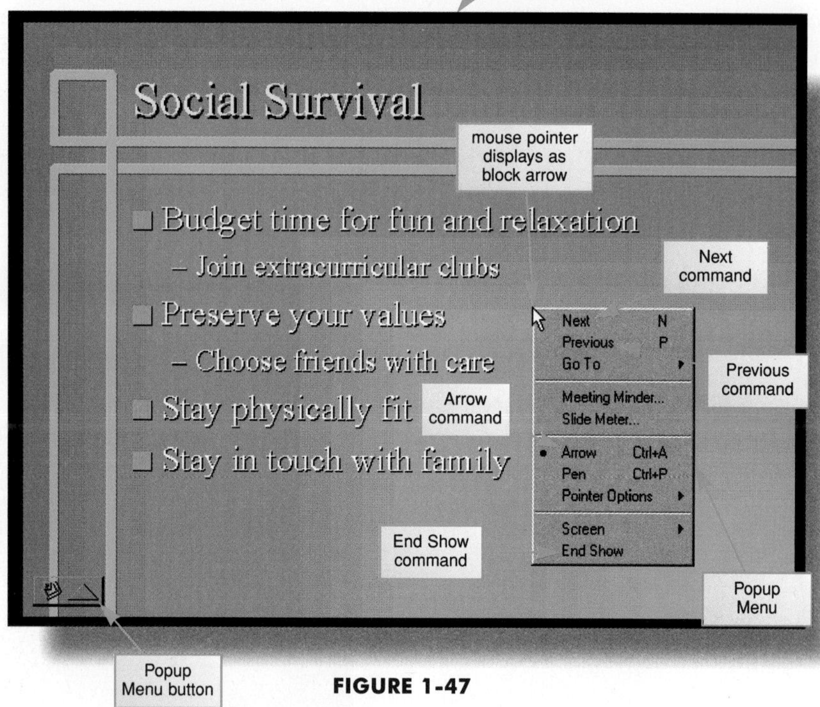

FIGURE 1-47

OtherWays

1. Move mouse pointer during slide show to display the Popup Menu button, then click Popup Menu button

Some presenters prefer to right-click to move backward through a slide show. Because you can display the Slide Show view Popup menu by clicking the Slide Show view Popup Menu button, you can turn off an option setting that displays the Slide Navigator when you right-click. To turn off the Popup Menu on the Right Mouse Click, on the Tools menu, click Options, click the View tab to display the View sheet, click Popup Menu on Right Mouse Click, and then click the OK button. After turning off the Popup Menu on the Right Mouse Click option setting, you can right-click to move backward, one slide at a time, in Slide Show view.

Using the Popup Menu to End a Slide Show

The **End Show command** on the Popup Menu exits Slide Show view and returns to the view you were in when you clicked the Slide Show button. Perform the following step to end Slide Show view.

To Use the Popup Menu to End a Slide Show

1 Click End Show on the Popup Menu.

PowerPoint exits Slide Show view and displays the slide last displayed in Slide Show view, which in this instance, is Slide 4 (Figure 1-48).

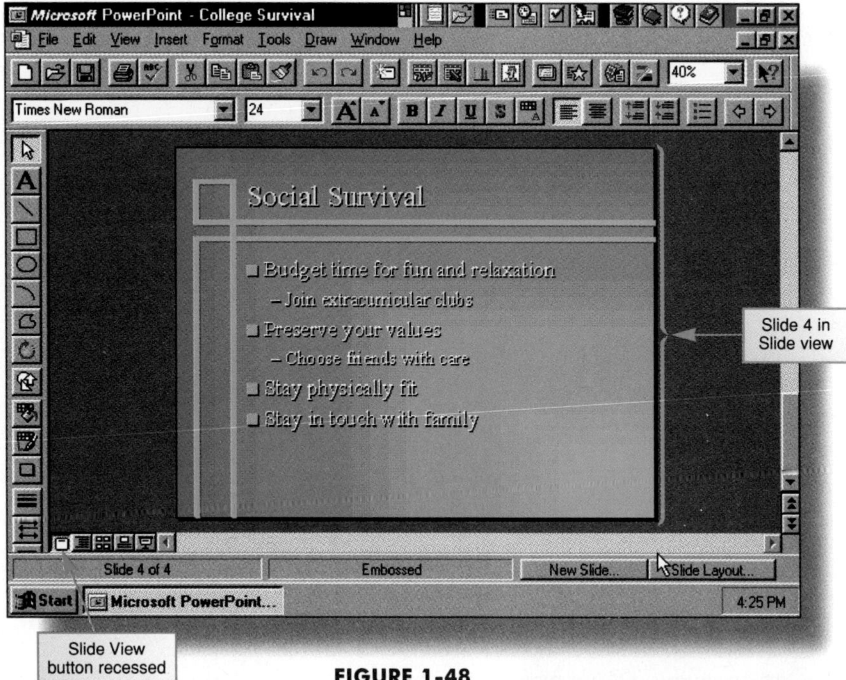

FIGURE 1-48

OtherWays

1. Click the last slide in presentation to return to the slide at which you began Slide Show view
2. Press ESC to display slide last viewed in Slide Show view

Slide Show view is excellent for rehearsing a presentation. You can start Slide Show view from any view: Slide view, Outline view, Slide Sorter view, or Notes Pages view.

Closing PowerPoint

The College Survival presentation now is complete. When you close PowerPoint, PowerPoint prompts you to save any changes made to the presentation since the last save, closes all PowerPoint windows, and then quits PowerPoint. Closing PowerPoint returns control to the desktop. Perform the steps on the next page to close PowerPoint.

Steps To Close PowerPoint

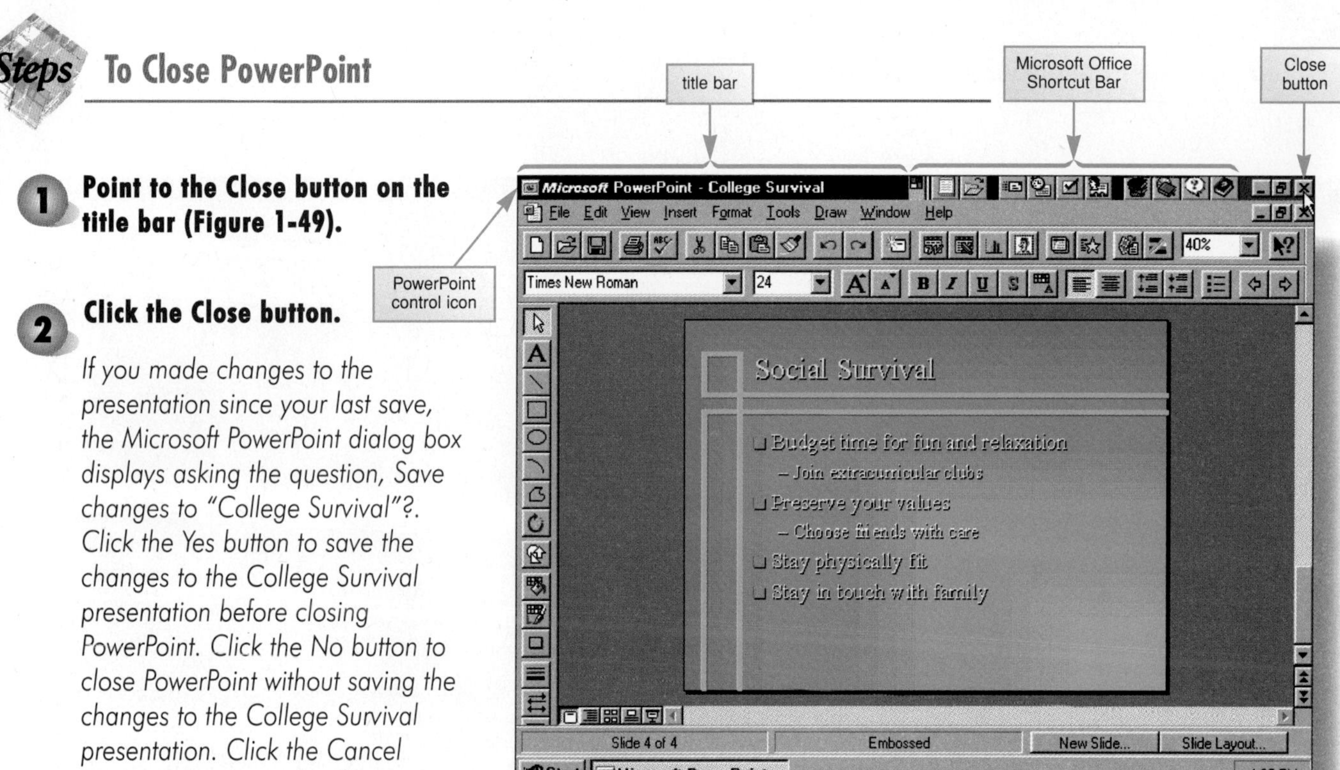

FIGURE 1-49

1. **Point to the Close button on the title bar (Figure 1-49).**

2. **Click the Close button.**

   If you made changes to the presentation since your last save, the Microsoft PowerPoint dialog box displays asking the question, Save changes to "College Survival"?. Click the Yes button to save the changes to the College Survival presentation before closing PowerPoint. Click the No button to close PowerPoint without saving the changes to the College Survival presentation. Click the Cancel button to terminate the Close command and return to the presentation. If you did not make changes to your presentation since your last save, this dialog box does not display.

Other Ways

1. On title bar double-click PowerPoint control icon; or on title bar, click PowerPoint control icon click Close
2. On File menu click Exit
3. Press CTRL+Q, or press ALT+F4

Opening a Presentation

Earlier, you saved the presentation on a floppy disk using the filename, College Survival.ppt. Once you create and save a presentation, you may need to retrieve it from the floppy disk to make changes. For example, you may want to replace the Design Template or modify some text. Recall that a presentation is a PowerPoint document. Use the **Open Office Document command** to open an existing presentation.

Opening an Existing Presentation

Ensure that the data floppy disk used to save College Survival.ppt is in drive A. Then perform the following steps to open the College Survival presentation using the Open Office Document command on the Start menu.

To Open an Existing Presentation

1 **Click the Start button on the taskbar and point to Open Office Document.**

The Windows 95 Start menu displays (Figure 1-50). Open Office Document is highlighted.

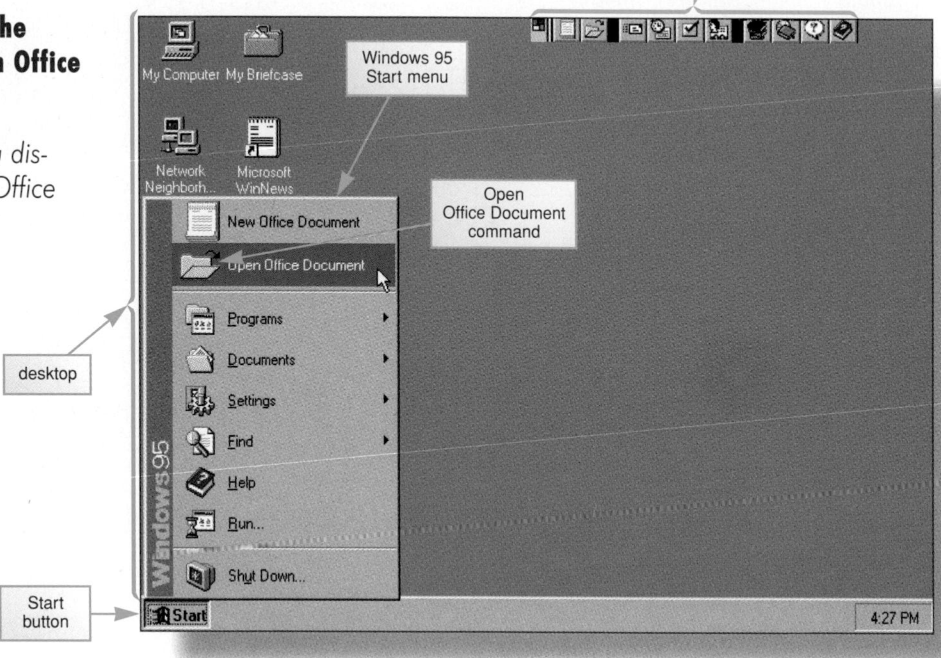

FIGURE 1-50

2 **Click Open Office Document. When the Open dialog box displays, click the Look in box arrow and then click 3½ Floppy [A:] (see Figures 1-21 and 1-22 on page PP 1.23 to review this process).**

The Open dialog box displays (Figure 1-51). A list of existing files on drive A displays because your data floppy disk is in drive A. Notice that Office Files displays in the Files of type drop-down list box. The file, College Survival, is highlighted. Your list of existing files may be different depending on the files saved on your data floppy disk.

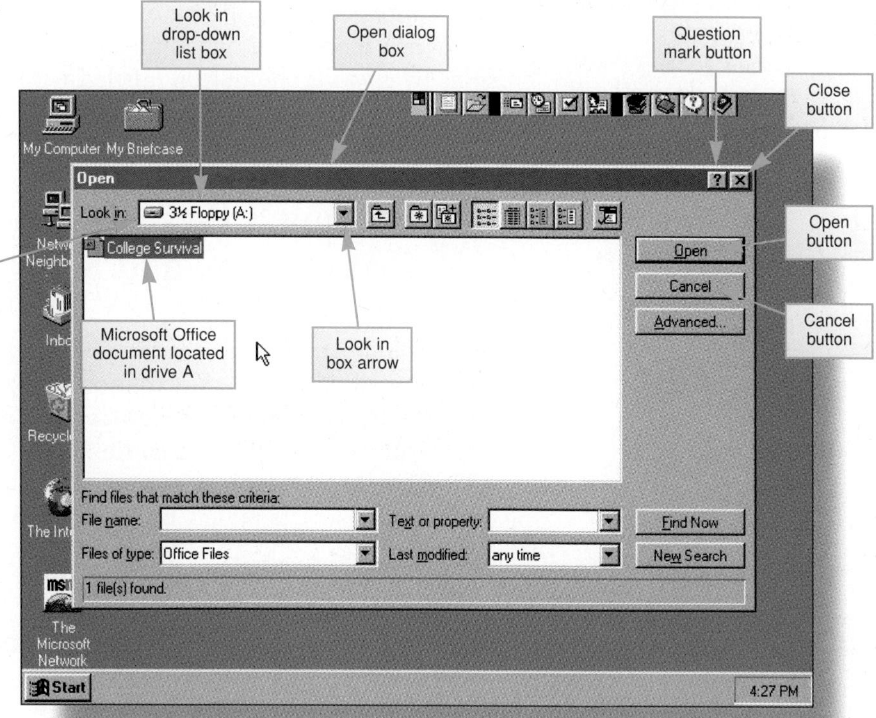

FIGURE 1-51

3 Double-click College Survival.

PowerPoint starts and opens College Survival.ppt from drive A into main memory and displays the first slide on the screen (Figure 1-52). The presentation displays in Slide view because PowerPoint opens presentations in the same view in which they were saved.

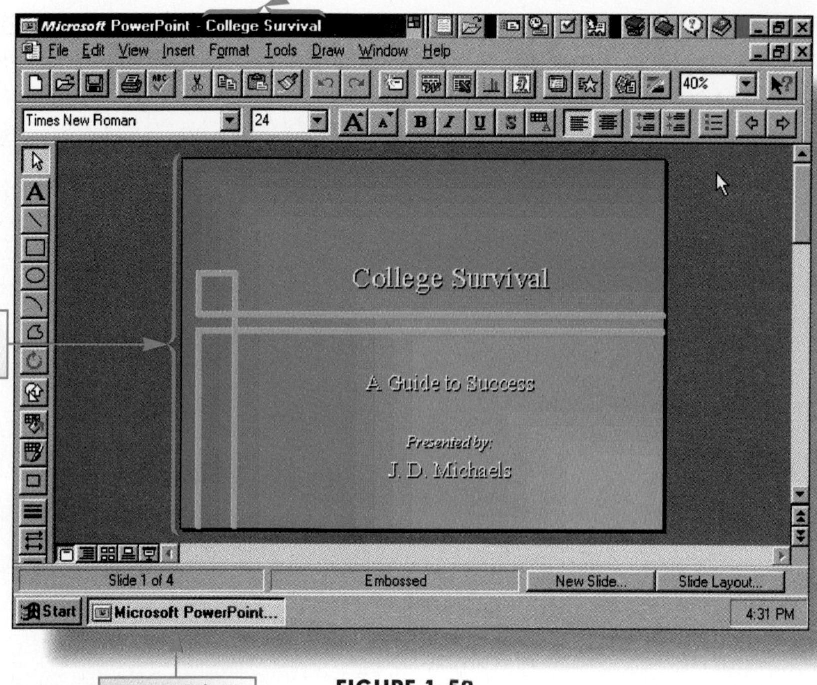

FIGURE 1-52

Other Ways

1. Click Open a Document button on Microsoft Office Shortcut Bar, click folder or drive name in Look in drop-down list box, double-click document name
2. On Start menu click Documents, click document name

When an application is open, its name displays on a button on the taskbar. The **active application** is the one displaying in the foreground of the desktop. That application's corresponding button on the taskbar appears recessed.

When more than one application is open, you can switch between applications by clicking the button labeled with the name of the application to which you want to switch.

Checking a Presentation for Visual Clarity, Consistency, and Style

After you create a presentation, you should proofread it for errors. Typical errors include spelling errors, punctuation errors, and design errors. PowerPoint has a tool, called **Style Checker**, that helps you identify errors in your presentation. When you start Style Checker, the Style Checker dialog box displays three check boxes: Spelling, Visual Clarity, and Case and End Punctuation. A check mark in a check box instructs Style Checker to look for that particular type of inconsistency. For example, a check mark in the Spelling check box causes Style Checker to check the presentation for spelling errors. Table 1-3 identifies the purpose of each check box in the Style Checker dialog box.

Table 1-3

CHECK BOX	PURPOSE
Spelling	Checks the presentation for spelling errors.
Visual Clarity	Checks the presentation for design and style errors, such as fonts too small for the audience to read, too many bullets on a slide, or too many words per paragraph.
Case and End Punctuation	Checks the presentation for consistent usage of capitalization and end punctuation.

PowerPoint checks your presentation for spelling errors using a standard dictionary contained in the Microsoft Office group. This dictionary is shared with the other Microsoft Office applications such as Word and Excel. A **custom dictionary** is available if you want to add special words such as proper names, cities, and acronyms. When checking a presentation for spelling errors, PowerPoint opens the standard dictionary and the custom dictionary file, if one exists. If a word is not found in either dictionary, PowerPoint displays a dialog box. When a word appears in the Spelling dialog box, you have several options which are explained in Table 1-4.

Table 1-4

OPTION	DESCRIPTION
Manually correct the word	Retype the word with the proper spelling and click Change. PowerPoint continues checking the rest of the presentation.
Ignore the word	Click Ignore when the word is spelled correctly but not found in the dictionaries. PowerPoint continues checking the rest of the presentation.
Ignore all occurrences of the word	Click Ignore All when the word is spelled correctly but not found in the dictionaries. PowerPoint ignores all occurrences of the word and continues checking the rest of the presentation.
Select a different spelling	Click the proper spelling of the word from the list in the Suggestions box. Click Change. PowerPoint corrects the word and continues checking the rest of the presentation.
Change all occurrences of the misspelling to a different spelling	Click the proper spelling of the word on the list in the Suggestions box. Click Change All. PowerPoint changes all occurrences of the misspelled word and continues checking the rest of the presentation.
Add a word to the custom dictionary	Click Add. PowerPoint opens the custom dictionary, adds the word, and continues checking the rest of the presentation.
Suggest alternative spellings	Click Suggest. PowerPoint lists suggested spellings. Click the correct word from the Suggestions box or type the proper spelling. Then Click Change. PowerPoint continues checking the rest of the presentation.

The standard dictionary contains commonly used English words. It does not, however, contain proper names, abbreviations, technical terms, poetic contractions, or antiquated terms. PowerPoint treats words not found in the dictionaries as misspellings.

Starting Style Checker

Start Style Checker by clicking the Style Checker command on the Tools menu. Perform the steps on the next pages to start Style Checker.

More *About* Presentation Design

Keep to one concept per slide. Highlight the subject rather than presenting a page of text. Limit your slide to five to seven words per line and five to seven lines per slide. Do not clutter; use empty space effectively.

To Start Style Checker

1 Click Tools on the menu bar. Then point to Style Checker (Figure 1-53).

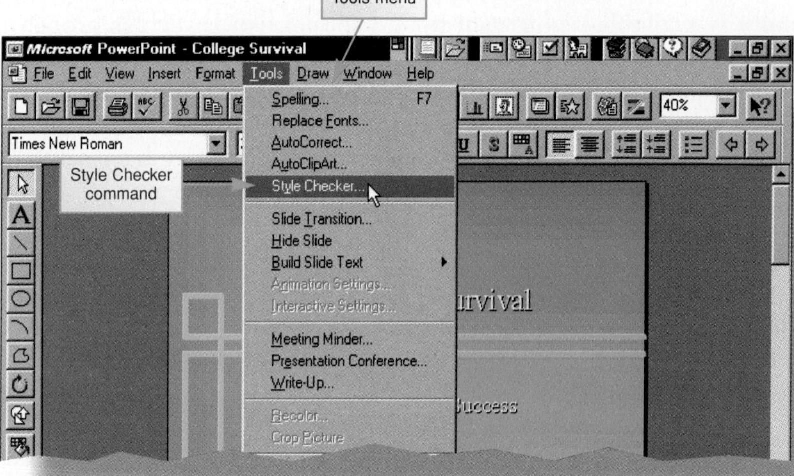

FIGURE 1-53

2 Click Style Checker. When the Style Checker dialog box displays, point to the Start button.

The Style Checker dialog box displays (Figure 1-54). A check mark displays in each of the three check boxes in the Check For box. The mouse pointer points to the Start button.

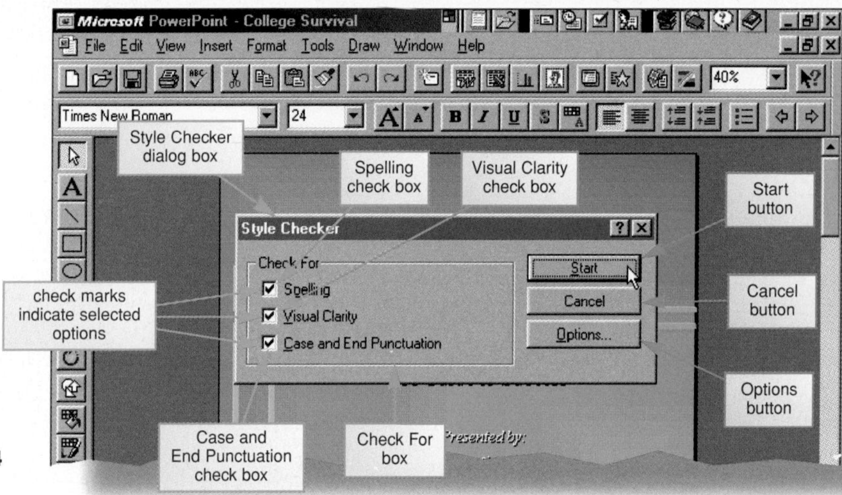

FIGURE 1-54

3 Click the Start button.

PowerPoint launches the spelling feature and displays the Spelling dialog box (Figure 1-55). Michaels displays in the Not in Dictionary box. Because it is a common proper name, two suggested spellings display in the Suggestions box. PowerPoint suggests that Michaels should be the possessive form, Michael's, and displays the suggested spelling in the Change To box.

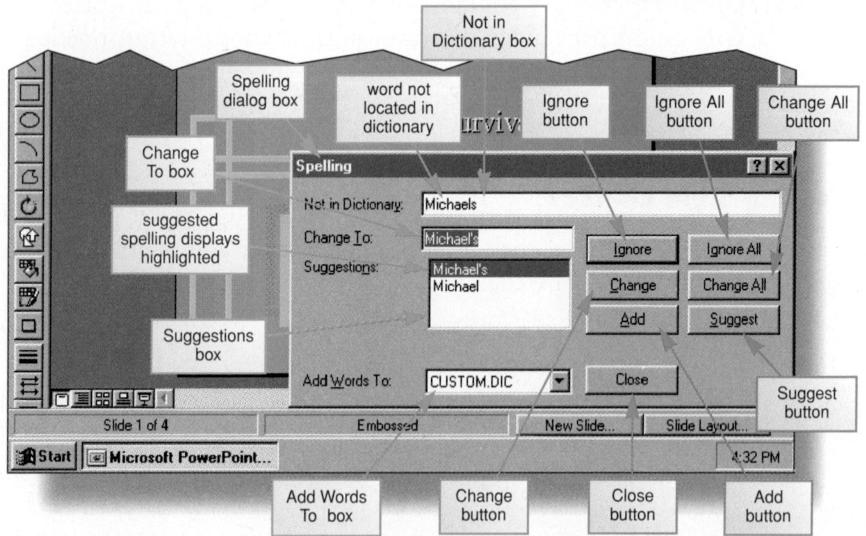

FIGURE 1-55

4 **Click the Ignore button.**

PowerPoint ignores the word Michaels and continues searching for additional misspelled words. PowerPoint may stop on additional words depending on your typing accuracy. When PowerPoint has checked all slides for misspellings, it begins checking for style errors and displays the Style Checker dialog box (Figure 1-56). The Style Checker dialog box displays a message indicating the slide number currently being checked and displays punctuation errors. If you have punctuation errors, you can click one of the buttons to ignore or change them. If you want to stop Style Checker and return to the current slide, click the Cancel button.

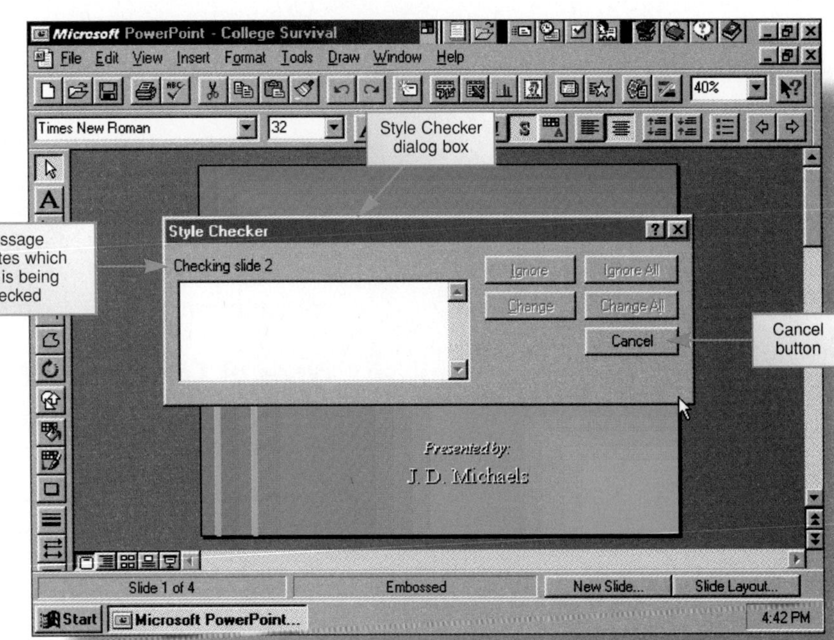

FIGURE 1-56

5 **If the Style Checker lists visual clarity inconsistencies in the Style Checker Summary dialog box, write the slide number and the message on a sheet of paper (Figure 1-57).**

6 **Click the OK button.**

PowerPoint closes Style Checker and returns to the current slide, Slide 1, or to the slide where a misspelled word occurred.

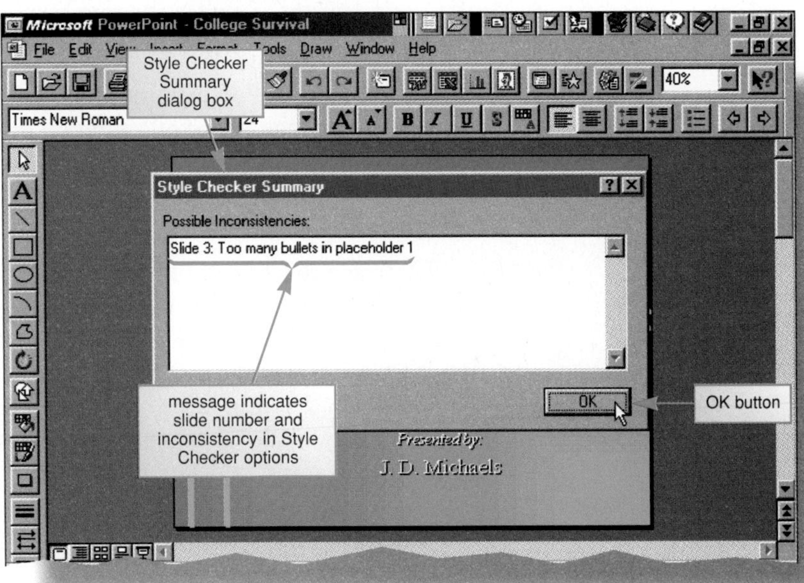

FIGURE 1-57

The Style Checker dialog box contains an **Options button** (see Figure 1-54), which when clicked, displays the Style Checker Options dialog box. The Style Checker Options dialog box has two tabbed sheets: Case and End Punctuation, and Visual Clarity. Each tabbed sheet has several options that can be changed to suit your design specifications. Table 1-5 on the next page identifies each option available in Style Checker and each default setting.

Table 1-5

OPTION	SETTING
CASE	
Slide Title Style	Title Case
Body Text Style	Sentence Case
END PUNCTUATION	
Slide Title Periods	Remove
Body Text Periods	Remove
VISUAL CLARITY	
Number of Fonts Should Not Exceed	3
Title	36 points
Body Text Size Should Be at Least	24 points
Number of Bullets Should Be at Least	6
Number of Lines per Title Should Be at Least	2
Number of Lines per Bullet Should Be at Least	2
Check for Title and Placeholder Text Off Slide	On

Correcting Errors

After creating a presentation and running Style Checker, you may find that you must make changes. Changes may be required because a slide contains an error, the scope of the presentation shifts, or Style Checker found a style inconsistency. This section explains the types of errors that commonly occur when creating a presentation.

Types of Corrections Made to Presentations

There usually are three types of corrections to text in a presentation: additions, deletions, and replacements.

- **Additions** — Additions are necessary when you omit text from a slide and need to add it later. You may need to insert text in the form of a sentence, word, or single character. For example, you may want to add the rest of the presenter's first name on your title slide.
- **Deletions** — Deletions are required when text on a slide is incorrect or is no longer relevant to the presentation. For example, Style Checker identified too many bullets on Slide 3. Therefore, you may want to remove one of the bulleted paragraphs.
- **Replacements** — Replacements are needed when you want to revise the text in your presentation. For example, you may want to substitute the word their for the word there.

Editing text in PowerPoint is basically the same as editing text in a word processing package. The following sections illustrate the most common changes made to text in a presentation.

Deleting Text

There are three methods for deleting text. One is to use the BACKSPACE key to remove text just typed. The second is to position the insertion point to the left of the text you wish to delete and then press the DELETE key. The third method is to drag through the text you wish to delete and press the DELETE key. (Use the third method when deleting large sections of text.)

Previously, Style Checker identified that Slide 3 has too many bullets. Perform the following steps to delete one of the bulleted paragraphs.

TO DELETE A PARAGRAPH

Step 1: Drag the elevator to display Slide 3.
Step 2: Click the bullet in front of the first paragraph, Learn your way around campus.
Step 3: Press the DELETE key.

The selected paragraph is deleted from Slide 3. The remaining 6 bulleted paragraphs move up one paragraph in the text object to take the place of the deleted paragraph. Slide 3 now satisfies the Style Checker design rule, not to exceed 6 bullets per slide.

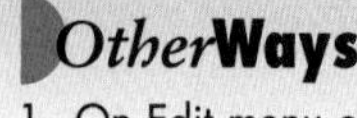

1. On Edit menu click Clear

Recall from the beginning of this project that if you make a mistake (such as deleting text), you can click the Undo button on the Standard toolbar to reverse your mistake.

Replacing Text into an Existing Slide

When you need to correct a word or phrase, you can replace the text by selecting the text to be replaced and then typing the new text. As soon as you press any key on the keyboard, the highlighted text is deleted and the new text displays.

PowerPoint inserts text to the left of the insertion point. The text to the right of the insertion point moves to the right (and shifts downward if necessary) to accommodate the added text. Perform the following steps to replace the period after the letter J with the rest of J. D. Michaels' first name, Jerry.

TO REPLACE TEXT

Step 1: Drag the elevator to display Slide 1. Select the period between the J and the D in J. D. Michaels by dragging the I-beam mouse pointer.

Step 2: Type `erry` to replace the period and insert the rest of the first name, Jerry.

The title slide now displays Jerry D. Michaels first name, as shown in Figure 1-2 on page PP 1.9, instead of his initials.

Changing Line Spacing

The bulleted lists on Slides 2, 3, and 4 look crowded; yet, there is ample blank space that could be used to separate the paragraphs. You can adjust the spacing on each slide, but when several slides need to be changed, you should change the Slide Master. Each PowerPoint component (slides, audience handouts, and notes pages) has a **master**, which controls its appearance. Slides have two masters, Title Master and Slide Master. The **Title Master** controls the appearance of the title slide. The **Slide Master** controls the appearance of the other slides in your presentation.

Each Design Template has a specially designed Slide Master; so if you select a Design Template, but want to change one of its components, you can override that component by changing the Slide Master. Any change to the Slide Master results in changing every slide in the presentation, except the title slide. For example, if you change the line spacing to .5 inches before each paragraph on the Slide Master, each slide (except the title slide) changes line spacing after each paragraph to .5 inches. The Slide Master components most frequently changed are listed in Table 1-6.

Table 1-6

COMPONENT	DESCRIPTION
Font face	Defines the appearance and shape of letters, numbers, and special characters.
Font size	Specifies the size of the characters on the screen. Character size is gauged by a measurement system called points. A single point is about 1/72 of an inch in height. Thus, a character with a point size of eighteen is about 18/72 (or 1/4) of an inch in height.
Text style	Text styles include plain, italic, bold, shadowed, and underlined. Text may have more than one style at a time.
Text position	Positions of text in a paragraph left aligned, right aligned, centered, or justified. Justified text is proportionally spaced across the object.
Color scheme	A coordinated set of eight colors designed to complement each other. Color schemes consist of background color, line and text color, shadow color, title text color, object fill color, and three different accent colors.
Background items	Any object other than the title object or text object. Typical items include borders, graphics–such as a company logo, page number, date, and time.
Slide number	Inserts the special symbol used to print the slide number.
Date	Inserts the special symbol used to print the date the presentation was printed.
Time	Inserts the special symbol used to print the time the presentation was printed.

Additionally, each view has its own master. You can access the master by holding down the SHIFT key while clicking the appropriate view button. For example, holding down the SHIFT key and clicking the Slide view button displays the Slide Master. To exit a master, click the view button to which you wish to return. To return to Slide view, for example, click the Slide View button.

Displaying the Slide Master

Before you can change line spacing on the Slide Master, you first must display it. Perform the following steps to display the Slide Master.

To Display the Slide Master

1 **Drag the elevator to display Slide 2. Press and hold down the SHIFT key and then point to the Slide View button.**

When you hold down the SHIFT key, the ToolTip box displays Slide Master (Figure 1-58).

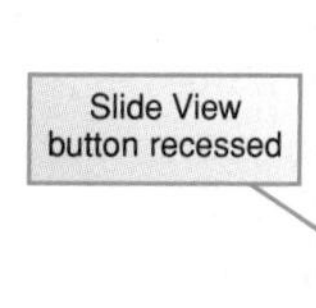

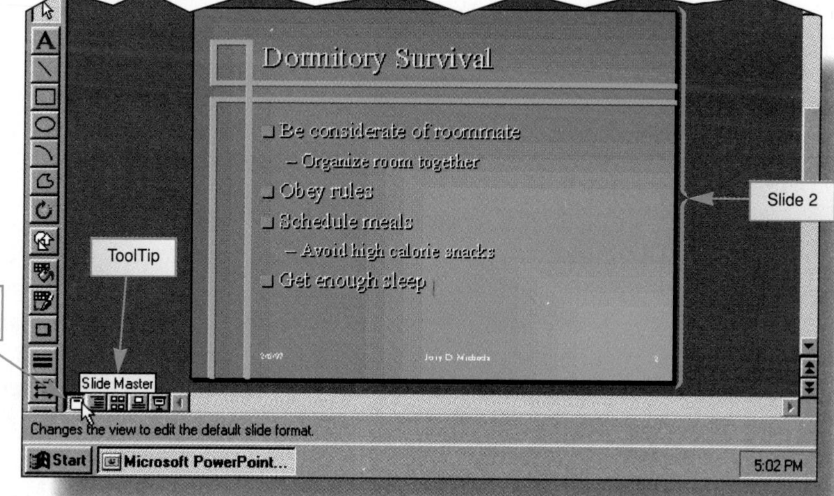

FIGURE 1-58

2 **While holding down the SHIFT key, click the Slide View button. Then release the SHIFT key.**

The Slide Master displays (Figure 1-59).

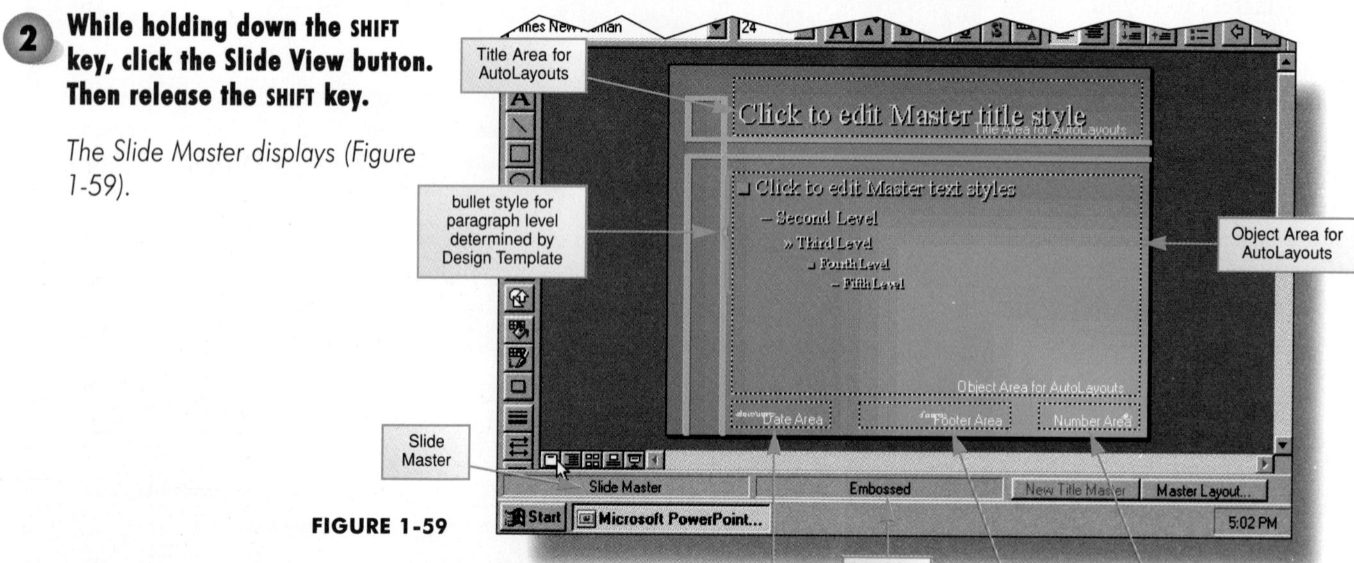

FIGURE 1-59

***Other*Ways**

1. On View menu click Master, click Slide Master

Changing Line Spacing on the Slide Master

Change line spacing by clicking the Line Spacing command on the Format menu. When you click the **Line Spacing command**, the Line Spacing dialog box displays. The Line Spacing dialog box contains three boxes, Line Spacing, Before Paragraph, and After Paragraph, which allow you to adjust line spacing within a paragraph, before a paragraph, and after a paragraph, respectively.

In this project, you change the number in the amount of space box to increase the amount of space that displays before every paragraph, except the first paragraph, on every slide. For example, increasing the amount of space box to 0.5 lines increases the amount of space that displays before each paragraph. The first paragraph on every slide, however, does not change. Perform the following steps to change the line spacing.

To Change Line Spacing on the Slide Master

1. **Click the bulleted paragraph labeled, Click to edit Master text styles.**

   The insertion point displays at the point you clicked (Figure 1-60). The text object area is selected.

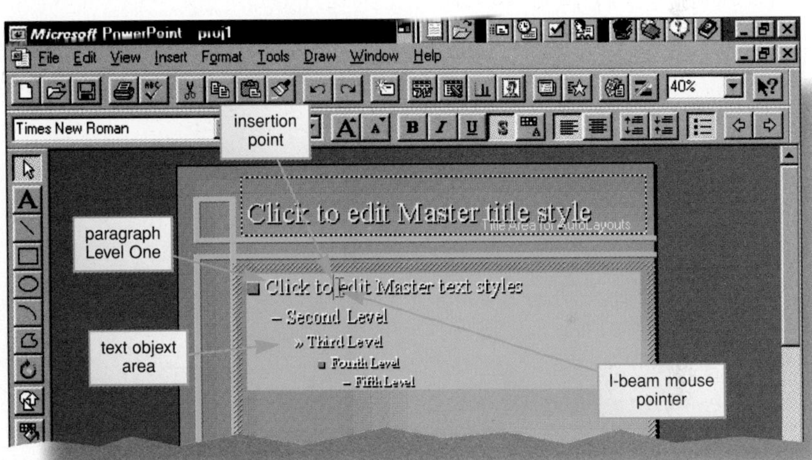

FIGURE 1-60

2. **Click Format on the menu bar and then point to Line Spacing (Figure 1-61).**

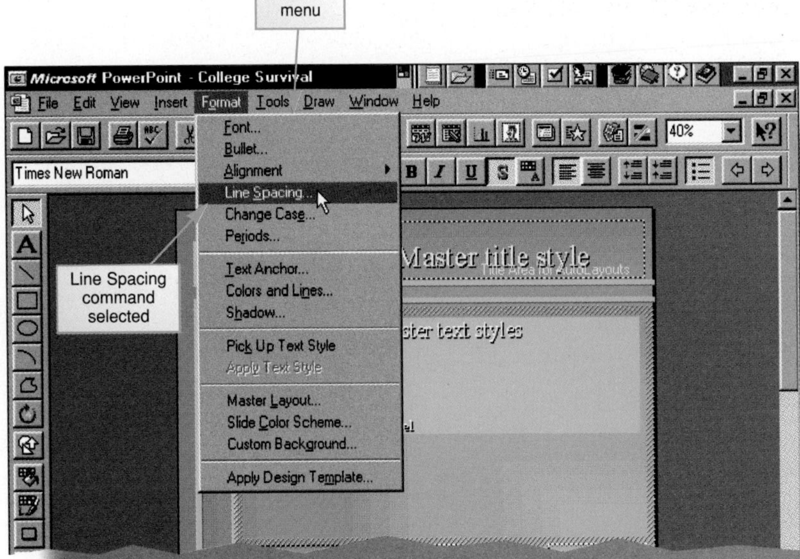

FIGURE 1-61

3 Click Line Spacing. Point to the up arrow in the amount of space box in the Before Paragraph box.

PowerPoint displays the Line Spacing dialog box (Figure 1-62).

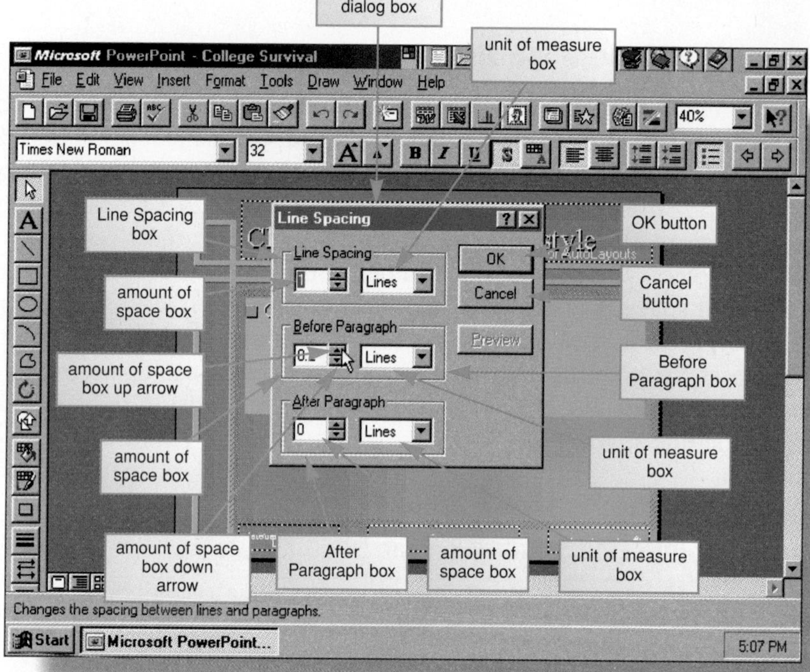

FIGURE 1-62

4 Click the amount of space box up arrow six times so that 0.5 displays.

The amount of space box displays 0.5 (Figure 1-63). The Preview button is available after a change is made in the Line Spacing dialog box.

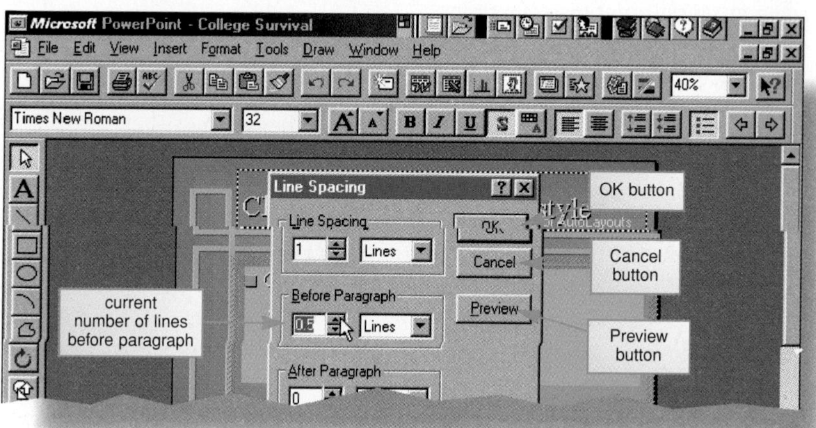

FIGURE 1-63

5 Click the OK button.

The Slide Master text placeholder displays the new Before Paragraph line spacing (Figure 1-64). Depending on the video drivers installed, the spacing on your screen may appear slightly different than this figure.

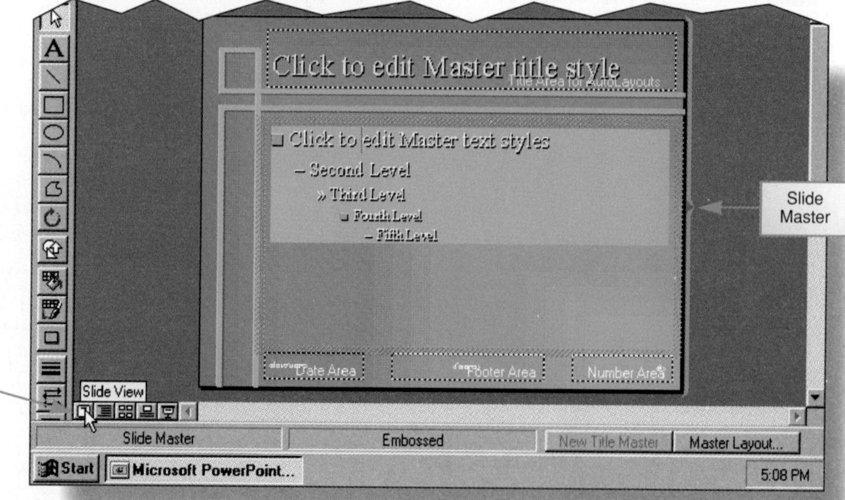

FIGURE 1-64

6 Click the Slide View button to return to Slide view.

Slide 2 displays with the Before Paragraph line spacing set to 0.5 lines (Figure 1-65).

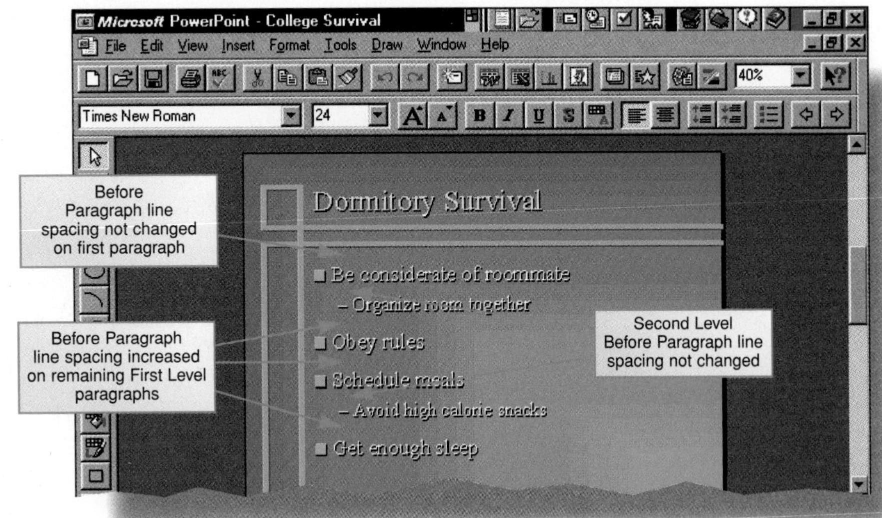

FIGURE 1-65

To display your line spacing changes without making them permanent, click the Preview button. If you want to close the Line Spacing dialog box without applying the changes, click the Cancel button.

Before Paragraph line spacing is controlled by setting the number of units before a paragraph. Units are either lines or points; lines are the default unit. Points may be selected by clicking the down arrow next to the Before Paragraph drop-down list box (see Figure 1-62). Recall from page PP 1.19 that a single point is about 1/72 of an inch in height.

The Line Spacing box and the After Paragraph box each contain an amount of space box and a unit of measure box. To change the amount of space displaying between paragraphs, click the amount of space box up arrow or down arrow in the Line Spacing box. To change the amount of space displaying after a paragraph, click the amount of space box up arrow or down arrow in the After Paragraph box. To change the unit of measure from Lines to Points in either the Line Spacing box or the After Paragraph box, click the down arrow next to the unit of measure drop-down list box and then click Points.

The placeholder at the top of the Slide Master (Figure 1-64) is used to edit the Master title style. The large placeholder under the Master title placeholder is used to edit the Master text styles. Here you make changes to the various bullet levels. Changes can be made to line spacing, bullet font, text and line color, alignment, and text shadow. It is also the object area for AutoLayouts.

More *About* Line Spacing

Resist the temptation to regard blank space on a slide as wasted space. Blank space added for the purpose of directing the attention of the audience to specific text or graphics is called **white space**. White space is a powerful design tool. Used effectively, white space improves audience attention.

Displaying a Presentation in Black and White

This project explains how to print a presentation for the purpose of making transparencies. PowerPoint's **B&W View button** allows you to display the presentation in black and white before you print it. Table 1-7 identifies how PowerPoint objects display in black and white.

Table 1-7

OBJECT	*APPEARANCE IN BLACK AND WHITE VIEW*
Text	Black
Text shadows	Hidden
Embossing	Hidden
Fills	Grayscale
Frame	1 point frame
Pattern fills	Grayscale
Lines	Black
Object shadows	Gray
Bitmaps/Pictures	Grayscale
Slide backgrounds	White

Perform the following steps to display the presentation in black and white.

To Display a Presentation in Black and White

1 Point to the B&W View button on the Standard toolbar (Figure 1-66).

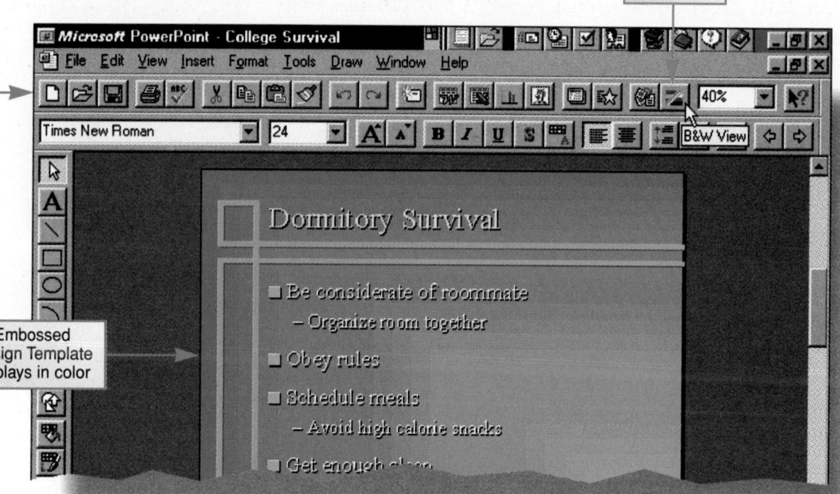

FIGURE 1-66

2 Click the B&W View button.

The presentation displays in black and white (Figure 1-67). The B&W View button is recessed. The Color View box displays a miniature of the current slide in color.

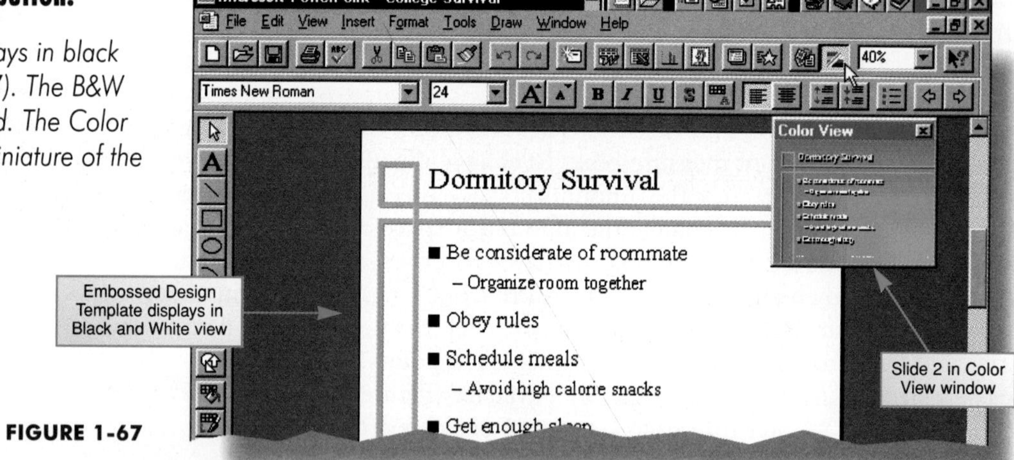

FIGURE 1-67

OtherWays

1. On View menu click Black and White

To return to the color view of the presentation, click the B&W View button again.

Printing a Presentation

After you create a presentation, you often want to print it. A printed version of the presentation is called a **hard copy**, or **printout**. The first printing of the presentation is called a **rough draft**. The rough draft allows you to proofread the presentation to check for errors and readability. After correcting errors, you print the final copy of your presentation.

Saving Before Printing

Prior to printing your presentation, you should save your work in the event you experience difficulties with the printer. You occasionally may encounter system problems that can be resolved only by restarting the computer. In such an instance, you will need to reopen your presentation. As a precaution, always save your presentation before you print. Perform the following steps to save the presentation before printing.

TO SAVE A PRESENTATION BEFORE PRINTING

Step 1: Verify that your data floppy disk is in drive A.
Step 2: Click the Save button on the Standard toolbar.

All changes made after your last save are now saved on a floppy disk.

Printing the Presentation

After saving the presentation, you are ready to print. Because you are in Slide view, clicking the **Print button** on the Standard toolbar causes PowerPoint to print all slides in the presentation. Additionally, because you are currently viewing the presentation in black and white, the slides print in black and white, even if you have a color printer. Perform the following steps to print the presentation slides.

To Print a Presentation

1 **Ready the printer according to the printer instructions. Then, click the Print button on the Standard toolbar.**

The mouse pointer momentarily changes to an hourglass. PowerPoint then displays a message on the status bar indicating it is preparing to print the presentation in the background. An animated printer icon displays on the status bar identifying which slide is being prepared. After several moments, the presentation begins printing on the printer. The printer icon, next to the clock on the taskbar, indicates there is a print job processing (Figure 1-68). When the presentation is finished printing, the printer icon on the taskbar disappears.

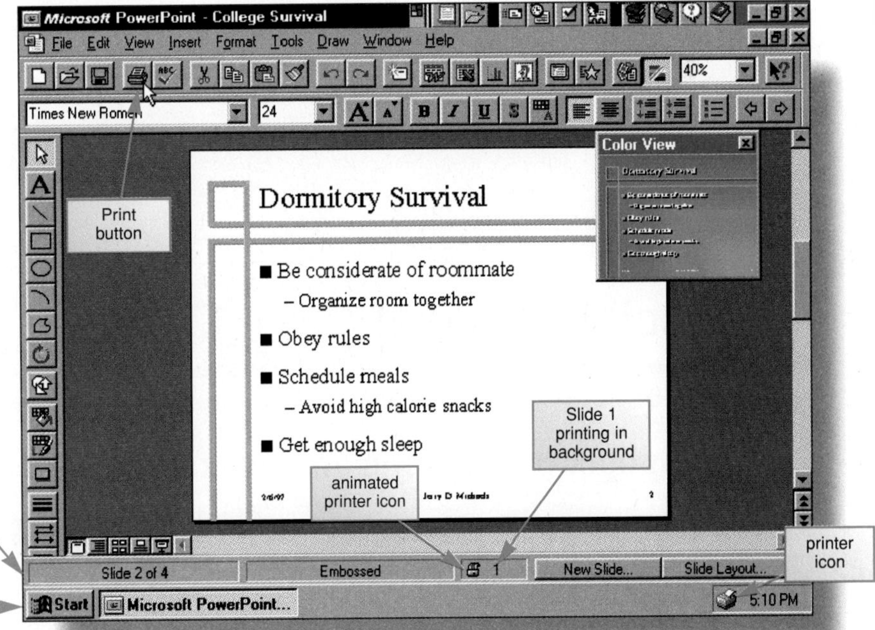

FIGURE 1-68

2 When the printer stops, retrieve the printouts of the slides.

The presentation, College Survival, prints on four pages (Figure 1-69).

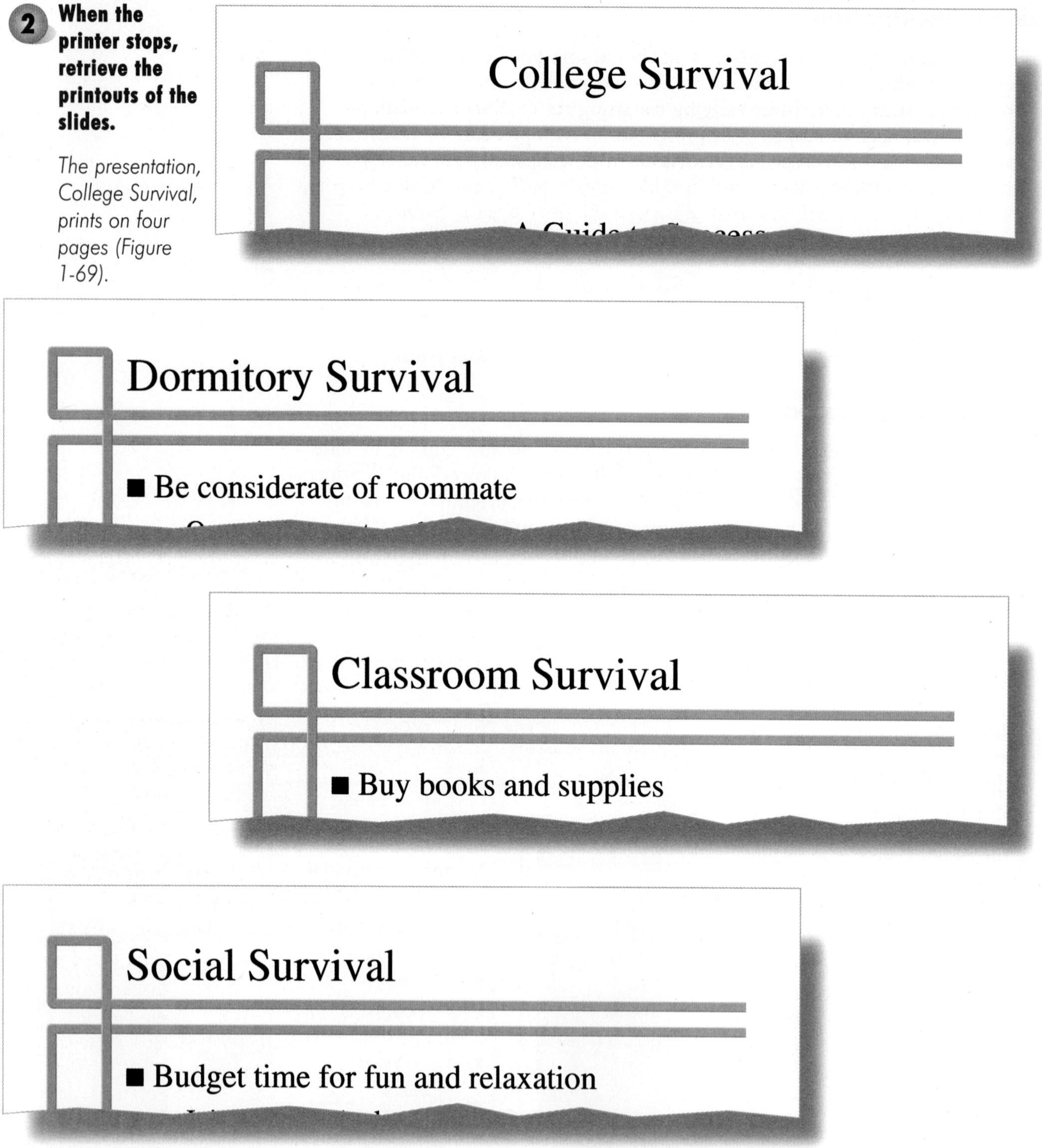

College Survival

Dormitory Survival

■ Be considerate of roommate

Classroom Survival

■ Buy books and supplies

Social Survival

■ Budget time for fun and relaxation

FIGURE 1-69

Other Ways

1. On File menu click Print
2. Press CTRL+P, or press CTRL+SHIFT+F12

Double-clicking the animated printer icon on the status bar cancels the printing process.

Making a Transparency

This project requires you to make overhead transparencies. You make transparencies using one of several devices. One device is a printer attached to your computer, such as an ink jet printer or a laser printer. Transparencies produced on a printer may be in black and white or color, depending on the printer. Another device is a photocopier. A third device is a thermal copier. A thermal copier transfers a carbonaceous substance, like toner from a photocopier, from a paper master to an acetate film. Because each of the three devices requires a special transparency film, check the user's manual for the film requirement of your specific device, or ask your instructor.

More *About* Presentation Design

Every slide must pass the Floor Test. Place the slide on the floor and read it while you are standing. If you can read the slide, it passes; if not, it fails. Text too small to read during the Floor Test is too small to read when projected on a screen.

PowerPoint Help

You can get assistance anytime while you are working in PowerPoint using **online help**. When used effectively, online help can increase your productivity and reduce the amount of time you spend learning how to use PowerPoint. Table 1-8 summarizes the six categories of online help.

The following sections show examples of each category of online help described in Table 1-8.

Table 1-8

HELP CATEGORY	SUMMARY	HOW TO START
Answer Wizard sheet	Allows you to enter, in your own words, an English-type question. For example, How do I change bullet fonts?	Double-click the Help button on the Standard toolbar; or on the Help menu, click Microsoft PowerPoint Help Topics, and then click the Answer Wizard tab.
Contents sheet	Groups help topics by general categories. Use when you know, in general, what you want.	Double-click the Help button on the Standard toolbar; or on the Help menu, click Microsoft PowerPoint Help Topics, and then click the Contents tab.
Find sheet	Searches the index for all phrases that include the term you specify. For example, bullets.	Double-click the Help button on the Standard toolbar; or on the Help menu, click Microsoft PowerPoint Help Topics, and then click the Find tab.
Help button	Provides an explanation of objects on the screen.	Click the Help button on the Standard toolbar and then click an object on the screen.
Index sheet	Lists help topics alphabetically. Similar to an index in a book. Use when you know exactly what you want. For example, adding footers.	Double-click the Help button on the Standard toolbar; or on the Help menu, click Microsoft PowerPoint Help Topics, and then click the Index tab.
Question mark button	Provides an explanation of objects on the screen.	In a dialog box, click the Question mark button and then click a dialog box object.

Using the Contents Sheet to Obtain Help

The **Contents sheet** in the Help Topics dialog box assists you in finding help about a specific subject. Use the Contents sheet in the same manner you use the table of contents in a book. Perform the steps on the next page to use the Contents sheet to obtain help on using the Slide Master to change the appearance of your presentation.

To Obtain Help Using the Contents Sheet

1 **Double-click the Help button on the Standard toolbar.**

The Help Topics: Microsoft PowerPoint dialog box displays.

2 **If necessary, click the Contents tab to activate the Contents sheet. In the list box, double-click the book icon labeled Changing the Appearance of Your Presentation.**

An icon precedes each entry in the list box. A **Book icon** *indicates there are subtopics. A* **Question mark icon** *indicates information will display when the title is double-clicked (Figure 1-70).*

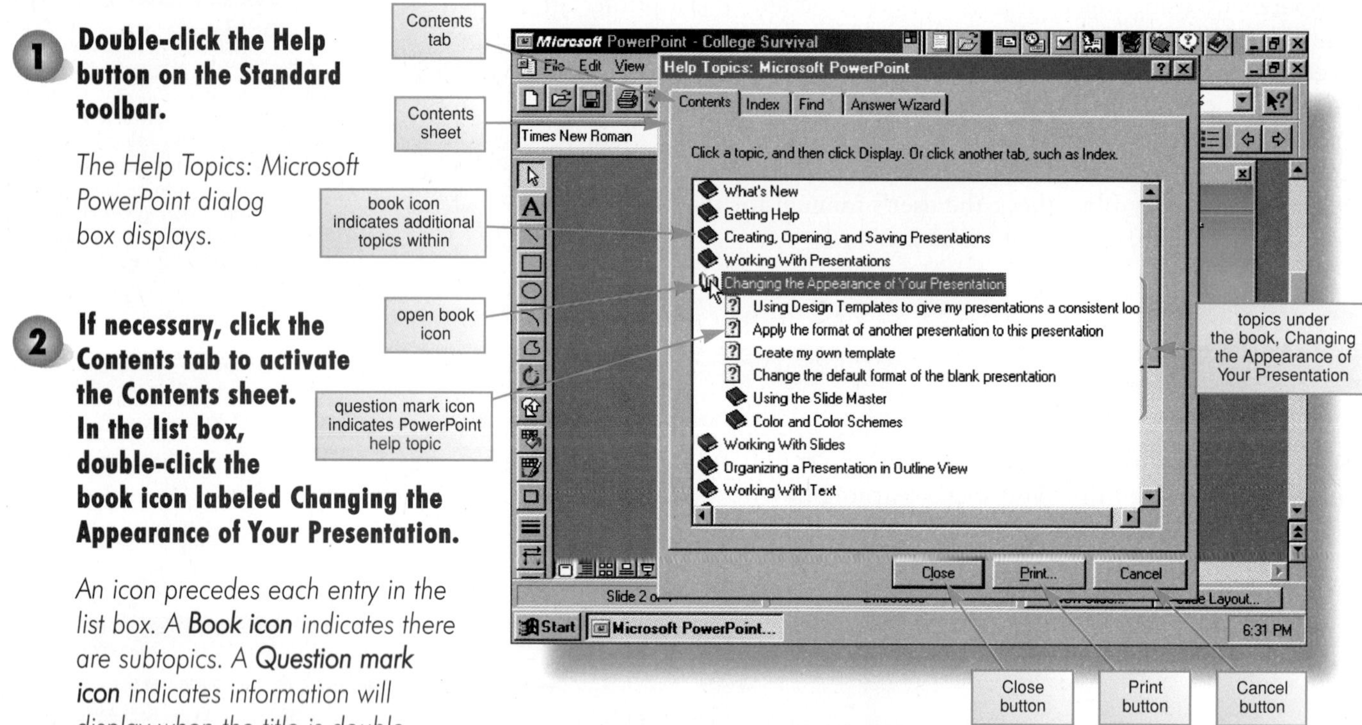

FIGURE 1-70

3 **Double-click the topic labeled Using Design Templates to give my presentations a consistent look.**

A Microsoft PowerPoint window displays information about using Design Templates to give a presentation a consistent look (Figure 1-71).

4 **After reading the information, click the Close button in the Microsoft PowerPoint window.**

The Microsoft PowerPoint window closes.

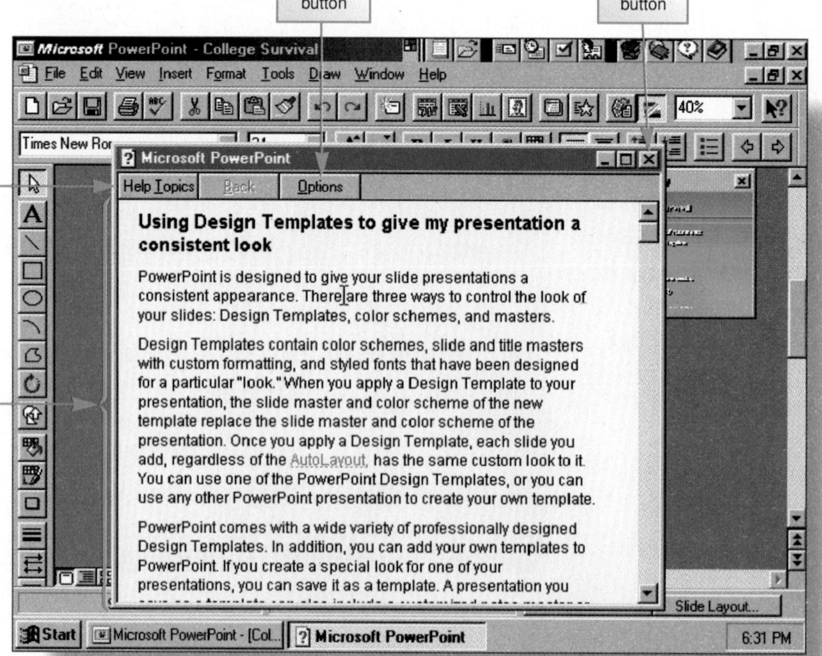

FIGURE 1-71

Other Ways

1. On Help menu click Microsoft PowerPoint Help Topics, click Contents tab
2. Press F1

As an alternative to double-clicking the topic name in the list box, you can click it and then use the buttons at the bottom of the Microsoft PowerPoint window to display information on a topic or print information on a topic (Figure 1-70). Additionally, you can print information on a topic by pointing to the help window, right-clicking, and then clicking Print Topic; or by clicking the Options button at the top of the Microsoft PowerPoint window, and then clicking Print Topic (Figure 1-71). To close or cancel the Microsoft PowerPoint window, click the Close button to return to PowerPoint, or click the **Help Topics button** to return to the Contents sheet.

Using the Index Sheet to Obtain Help

Use the **Index sheet** in the Help Topics: Microsoft PowerPoint dialog box when you know the term about which you are seeking help. You can locate the term you are looking for by typing part or all of the word, or you can scroll through the alphabetical list and click the term. You use the Index sheet in the same manner you use an index at the back of a book.

Many of the online help topics provide you with a demonstration of how to accomplish a task. For example, if you want to find out how to add footers to the Slide Master, PowerPoint shows you by pointing to the View menu and then pointing to the Header and Footer command. Perform the following steps to obtain information about adding footers to the Slide Master by typing foo, the first three letters of the word footer.

Steps To Obtain Help Using the Index Sheet

1 Double-click the Help button on the Standard toolbar.

The Help Topics: Microsoft PowerPoint dialog box displays.

2 If necessary, click the Index tab to display the Index sheet. Type `foo` **in the box labeled 1.**

The term footers is highlighted in the box labeled 2 (Figure 1-72).

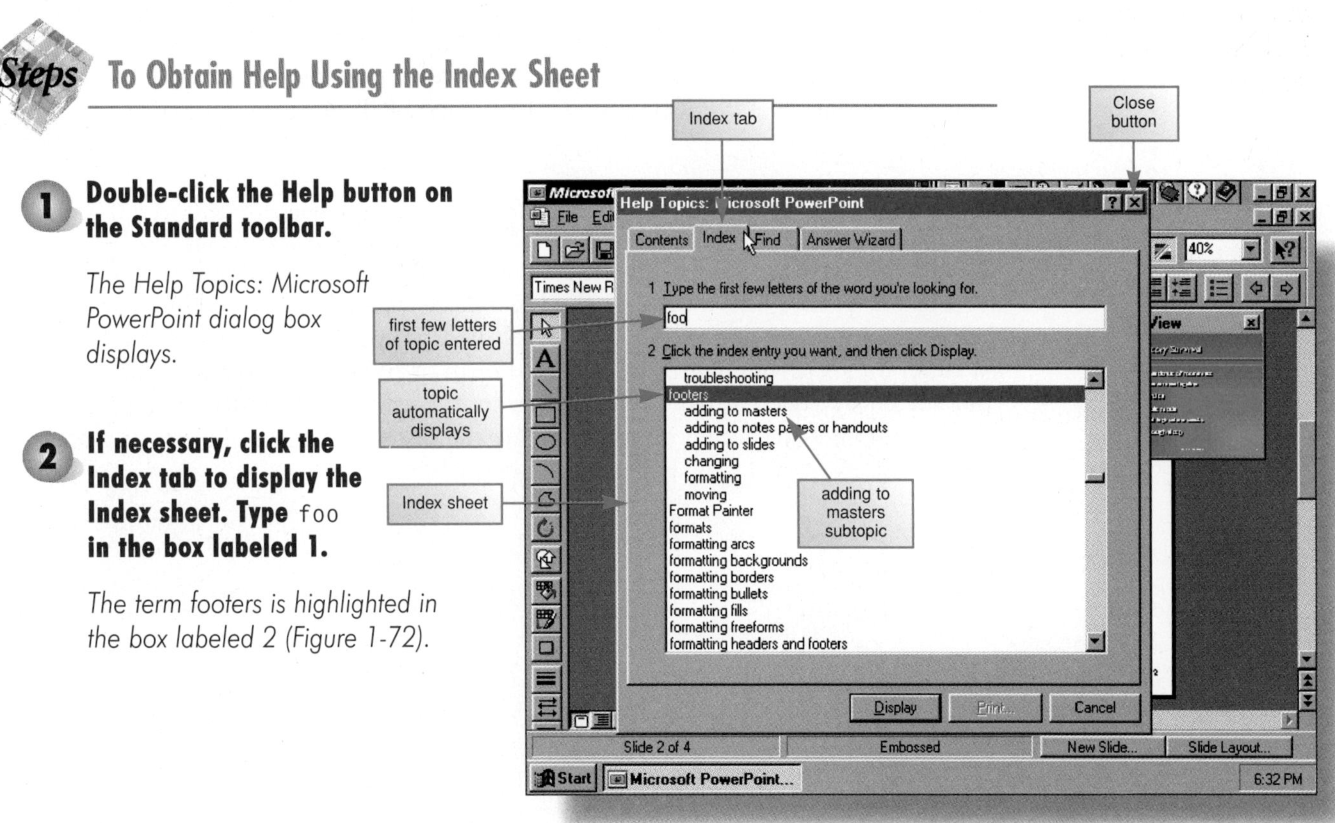

FIGURE 1-72

3 Double-click the subtopic labeled adding to masters (see Figure 1-72 on the previous page).

PowerPoint demonstrates how to add footers to the Slide Master. After which, PowerPoint displays a ScreenTip about the Slide Master (Figure 1-73).

4 After reading the information, click anywhere outside the ScreenTip to close it.

The ScreenTip closes.

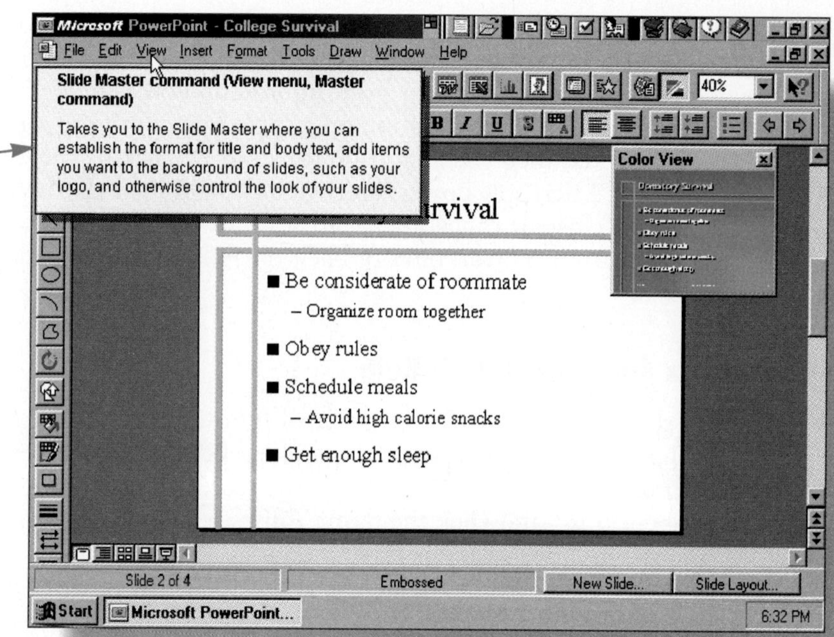

FIGURE 1-73

OtherWays

1. On Help menu click Microsoft PowerPoint Help Topics, click Index tab
2. Press F1

Not all online help information is printable. For example, the Slide Master ScreenTip (Figure 1-73) is not printable. Generally speaking, if the window contains an Options button (Figure 1-71 on page PP 1.54), you can print the information.

More About Presentation Design

Two acronyms pertain directly to presentation design:
— K.I.S. (Keep It Simple)
— C.C.C. (Clutter Creates Confusion)

Using the Find Sheet to Obtain Help

The **Find sheet** in the Help Topics: Microsoft PowerPoint dialog box locates the word or phrase you want. Use the Find sheet when you wish to find information about a term or a word contained within a phrase. The Find sheet displays a list of all topics pertaining to the specified term or phrase. You then can narrow your search by selecting words or phrases from the list. Perform the following steps to obtain information about changing the distance between bullets and text.

Steps To Obtain Help Using the Find Sheet

1 Double-click the Help button on the Standard toolbar.

The Help Topics: Microsoft PowerPoint dialog box displays.

2 If necessary, click the Find tab. Type `bulleted` **in the box labeled 1. Then point to the topic in the box labeled 3, change the distance between bullets and text.**

Three topics display in the box labeled 3 that contain the word bulleted. The topic, Add, change, or remove a bullet, is highlighted (Figure 1-74).

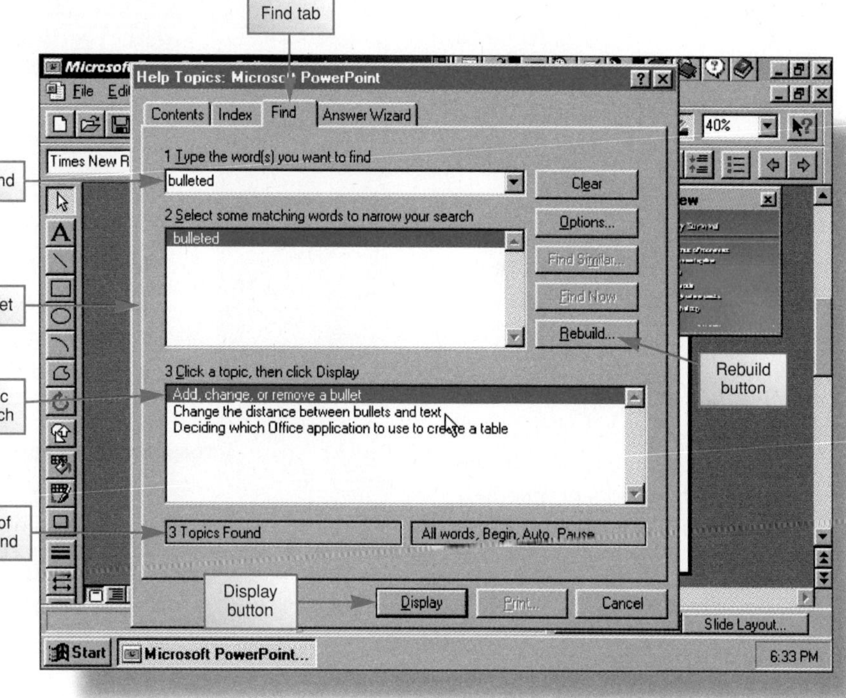

FIGURE 1-74

3 Double-click the topic, Change the distance between bullets and text, in the box labeled 3 on the Find sheet. When the Microsoft PowerPoint window displays the information about changing the distance between bullets and text, point to the green underlined words, slide master, located in the Note at the bottom of the Microsoft PowerPoint window.

A Microsoft PowerPoint window displays information about changing the distance between bullets and text. The green underlined text at the bottom of the Microsoft PowerPoint window identifies a jump to additional information (Figure 1-75a).

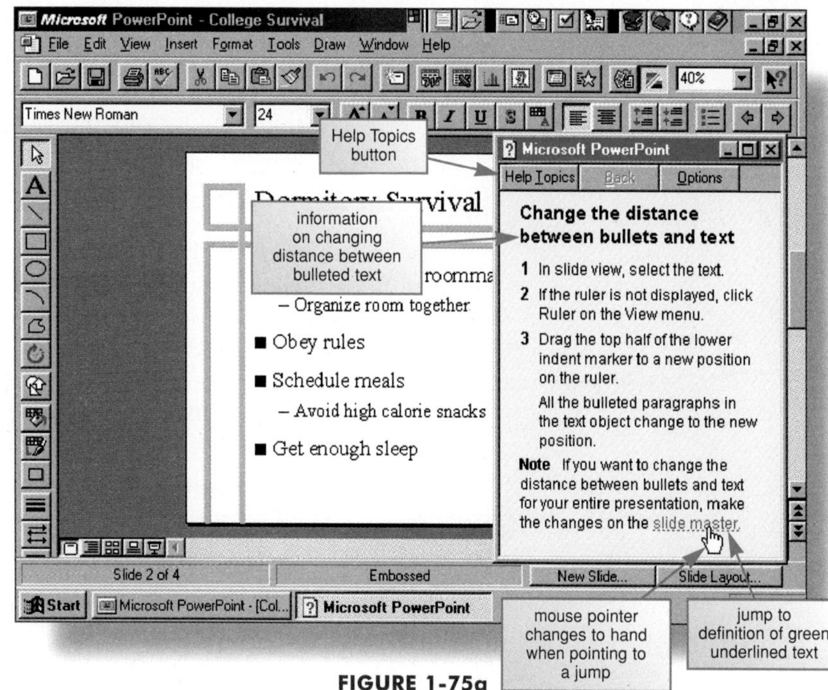

FIGURE 1-75a

4 **Click slide master.**

Clicking the green underlined text displays a ScreenTip (Figure 1-75b). The ScreenTip provides additional information about the word (often a definition).

5 **Read the ScreenTip, and then click the Close button on the Microsoft PowerPoint window two times.**

Clicking the Close button once closes the ScreenTip. Clicking the Close button a second time closes the Microsoft PowerPoint window and returns to PowerPoint.

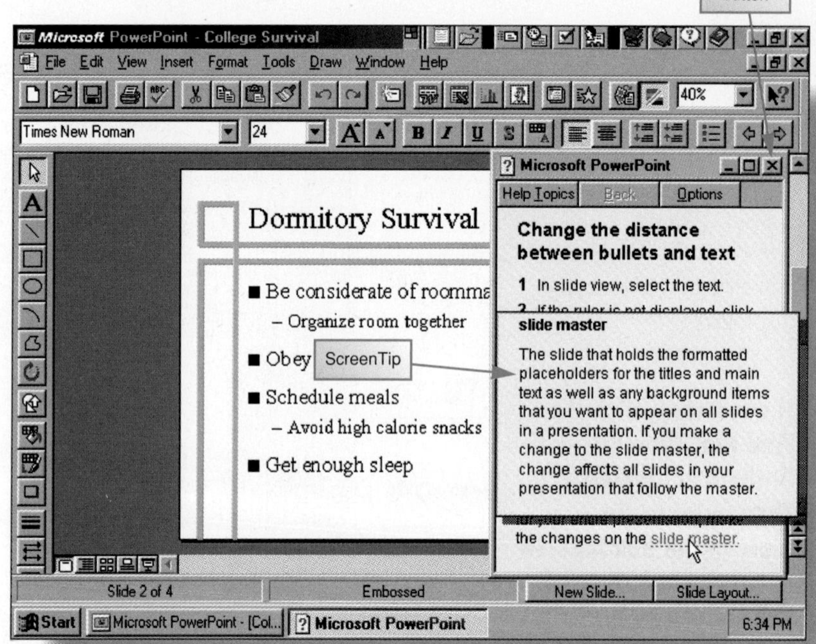

FIGURE 1-75b

OtherWays

1. On Help menu click Microsoft PowerPoint Help Topics, click Find tab
2. Press F1

You may specify more than one word in the box labeled 1 (Figure 1-74 on the previous page) if you separate the words with a space. If you specify words in uppercase letters, then only uppercase occurrences of the words (within the Help Topics) are found. If you specify words in lowercase letters, however, both uppercase and lowercase occurrences of the words are found. Search options can be changed by clicking the Options button on the Find sheet.

Using the Answer Wizard Sheet to Obtain Help

The last sheet in the Help Topics: Microsoft PowerPoint dialog box is the Answer Wizard sheet. Use the **Answer Wizard sheet** when you know what you want to do but do not know what the task is called. Recall that the Answer Wizard allows you to ask a question in your own words. The Answer Wizard then finds topics that contain the words in your question. For example, when you type a question such as, What is new? (to find the new features in PowerPoint 95) on the Answer Wizard sheet, it displays two sections: How Do I and Tell Me About. The **How Do I topics** provide you with easy-to-follow instructions. Some step-by-step visual answers take you to the command or option you need to complete the task. The **Tell Me About topics** give you background information about the selected topic.

Perform the following steps to obtain information on the new features in PowerPoint 95 by typing the question, What is new?

Steps To Obtain Help Using the Answer Wizard

1. **Double-click the Help button on the Standard toolbar.**

   The Help Topics: Microsoft PowerPoint dialog box displays.

2. **If necessary, click the Answer Wizard tab. Type** `What is new?` **in the box labeled 1. Click the Search button. Then, in the box labeled 2, in the Tell Me About section, point to the topic, What's new in Microsoft PowerPoint 95.**

   The Answer Wizard displays two sections in the box labeled 2: How Do I and Tell Me About (Figure 1-76).

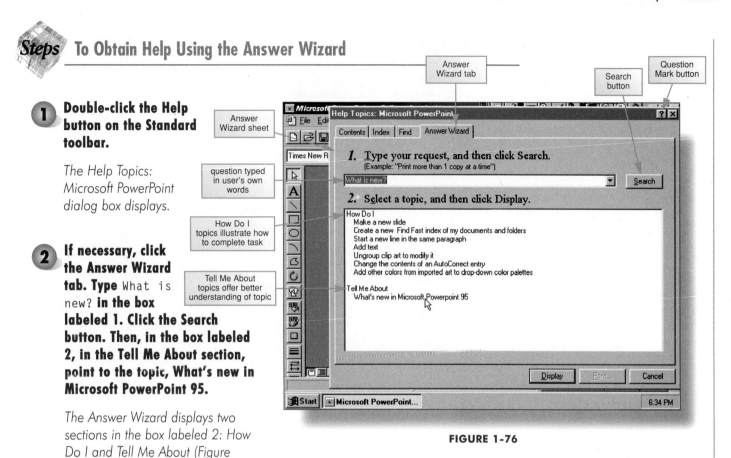

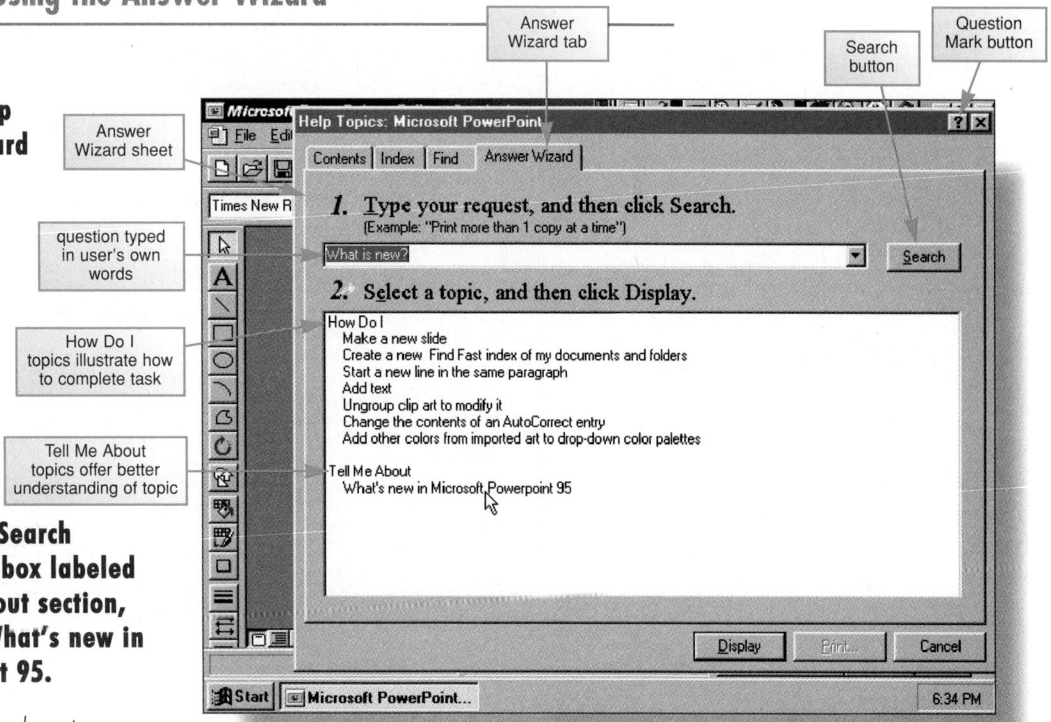

FIGURE 1-76

3. **Double-click What's new in Microsoft PowerPoint 95. Then point to the button in front of AutoCorrect in the Microsoft PowerPoint for Windows 95 window.**

   The Microsoft PowerPoint for Windows 95 window displays a list of features new to PowerPoint 95. A button displays in front of each topic. When you point to a topic, the mouse pointer changes to a hand (Figure 1-77).

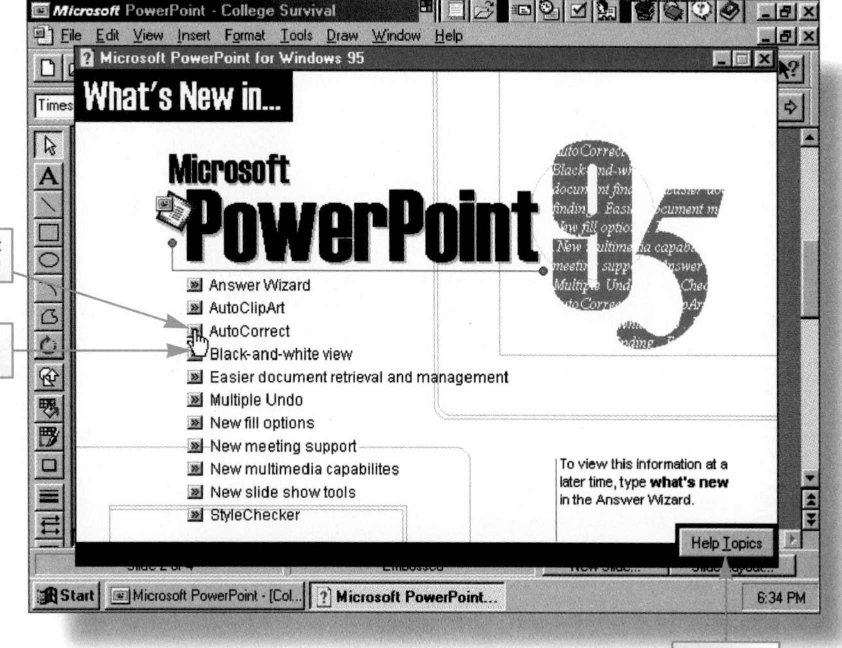

FIGURE 1-77

4 **Click the button in front of AutoCorrect. Click the box labeled Easier to be effective.**

PowerPoint displays a Microsoft PowerPoint for Windows 95 window containing jump boxes that point to specific items on a slide. When you click the jump box labeled Easier to be effective, a ScreenTip displays containing information about AutoCorrect (Figure 1-78).

5 **Read the ScreenTip. Then click the Close button in the Microsoft PowerPoint for Windows 95 window to return to PowerPoint.**

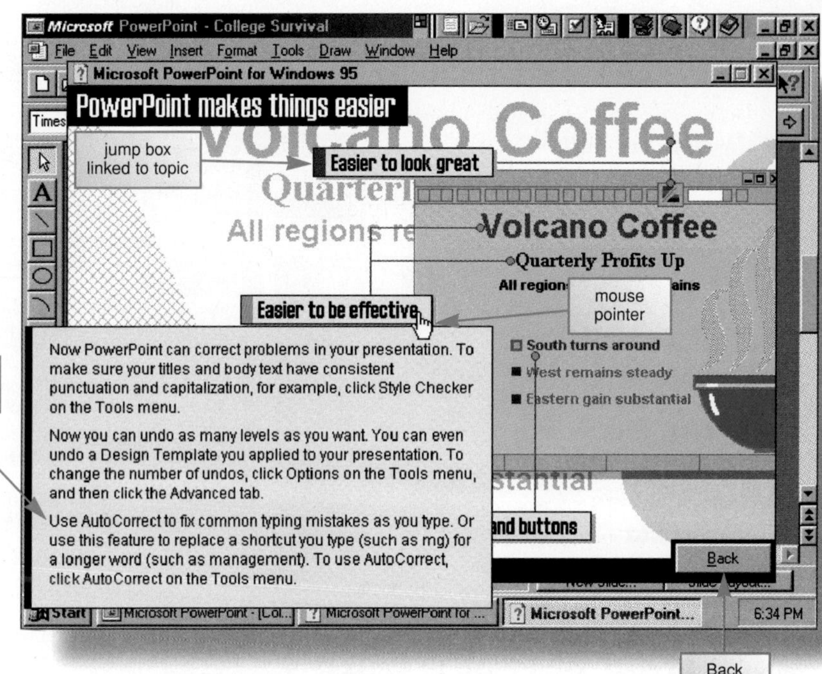

FIGURE 1-78

*Other*Ways

1. From Help menu click Microsoft PowerPoint Help Topics or Answer Wizard
2. Press F1

As an alternative to clicking the Close button in Step 5, you can click the **Back button** to return to the previous dialog box shown in Figure 1-77 on the previous page.

The four online help features of PowerPoint (Contents, Index, Find, and Answer Wizard) are easy to use, yet powerful. The best way to familiarize yourself with these help tools is to use them. In the Student Assignments at the end of each project is a section titled Use Help. It is recommended that you step through these exercises to gain a better understanding of how PowerPoint online help works.

Using the Help button

When you are not certain about what an object is in the PowerPoint window, use the **Help button**. When you click the Help button, the mouse pointer changes to an arrow with a question mark. Then, when you click an object in the PowerPoint window, a ScreenTip displays. Once you click the Help button, you can move the arrow and question mark pointer to any menu name, button, or object, and click to display a ScreenTip. For example, clicking the Help button, and then clicking the Spelling button on the Standard toolbar results in the ScreenTip shown in Figure 1-79. Click anywhere on the PowerPoint window to close the ScreenTip.

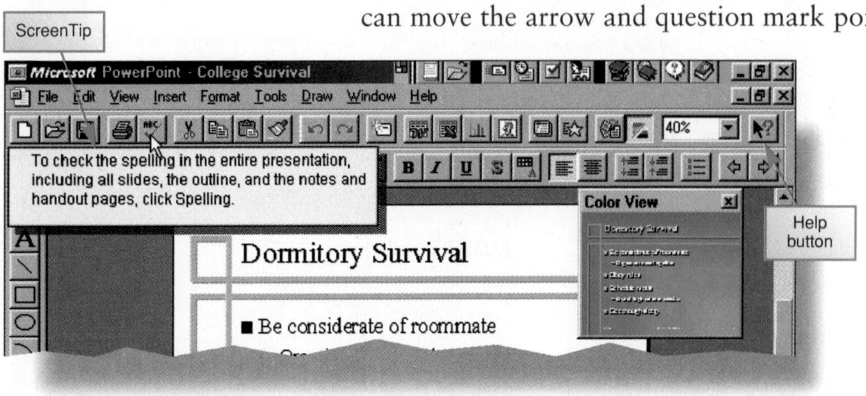

FIGURE 1-79

Using the Question Mark button

The **Question mark button** (see Figure 1-76 on page PP 1.59) is similar to the Help button. Use the Question mark button when you are not certain about the purpose of an object in a dialog box. When you click the Question mark button, the mouse pointer changes to an arrow with a question mark. Then, when you click an object in a dialog box, a ScreenTip displays.

Closing PowerPoint

Project 1 is complete. The final task is to close the presentation and PowerPoint. Perform the following steps to close PowerPoint.

TO CLOSE POWERPOINT

Step 1: Click the Close button on the title bar.
Step 2: Click the Yes button in the Microsoft PowerPoint dialog box.

The Microsoft PowerPoint dialog box displays when you close PowerPoint without first saving any changes (Figure 1-80).

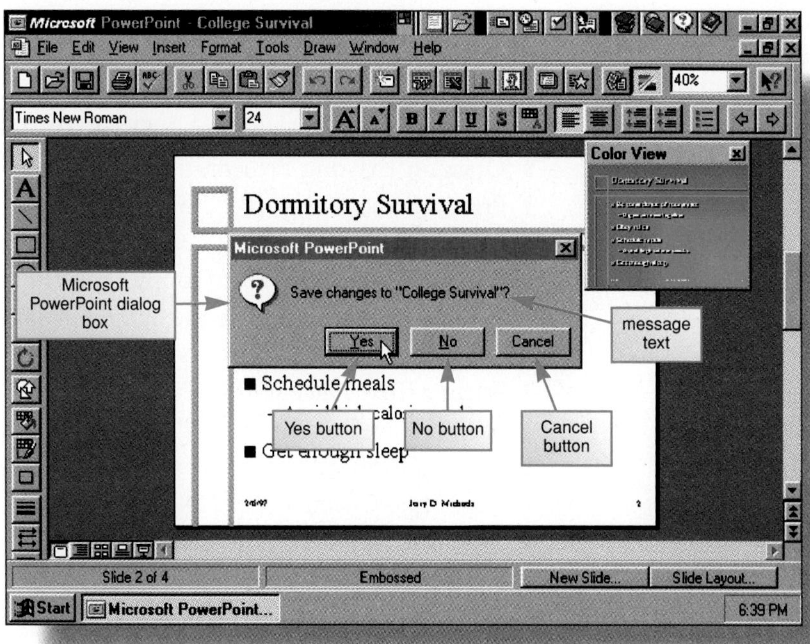

FIGURE 1-80

Clicking the No button in the Microsoft PowerPoint dialog box closes the presentation and PowerPoint without saving the changes made after your last save. Clicking the Cancel button, returns to PowerPoint and the current presentation.

Project Summary

Project 1 introduced you to starting PowerPoint and creating a multi-level bulleted list presentation. You learned about PowerPoint Design Templates, objects, and attributes. Project 1 illustrated how to change the text style to italic and decrease font size on the title slide. Completing these tasks, you saved your presentation. Then, you created three multi-level bulleted list slides. Next, you learned how to view the presentation in Slide Show view. After which, you learned how to close PowerPoint and how to open an existing presentation. Using Style Checker, you learned how to look for spelling errors and identify inconsistencies in design specifications. After running Style Checker, you edited the presentation to correct the design errors and insert text. Using the Slide Master, you adjusted the Before Paragraph line spacing to make better use of white space. You learned how to display the presentation in black and white before printing it; and then, you learned how to print hard copies of your slides. Finally, you learned how to use PowerPoint online help.

What You Should Know

Having completed this project, you now should be able to perform the following tasks:

- Add a New Slide with the Bulleted List AutoLayout *(PP 1.25)*
- Add a New Slide with the Same AutoLayout *(PP 1.30)*
- Change Line Spacing on the Slide Master *(PP 1.47)*
- Change the Style Text to Italic *(PP 1.21)*
- Close PowerPoint *(PP 1.38, PP 1.61)*
- Decrease Font Size *(PP 1.20)*
- Delete a Paragraph *(PP 1.44)*
- Display a Presentation in Black and White *(PP 1.50)*
- Display the Slide Master *(PP 1.46)*
- Display the Slide Show View Popup Menu *(PP 1.36)*
- Enter the Presentation Subtitle *(PP 1.18)*
- Enter the Presentation Title *(PP 1.17)*
- Enter a Slide Title *(PP 1.27)*
- Manually Move through Slides in a Slide Show *(PP 1.35)*
- Obtain Help Using the Answer Wizard *(PP 1.59)*
- Obtain Help Using the Contents Sheet *(PP 1.54)*
- Obtain Help Using the Find Sheet *(PP 1.57)*
- Obtain Help Using the Index Sheet *(PP 1.55)*
- Open an Existing Presentation *(PP 1.38)*
- Print a Presentation *(PP 1.51)*
- Replace Text *(PP 1.45)*
- Save a Presentation to a Floppy Disk *(PP 1.22)*
- Save a Presentation with the Same Filename *(PP 1.32, PP 1.51)*
- Select a Text Placeholder *(PP 1.27)*
- Start a New Presentation *(PP 1.10)*
- Start Slide Show View *(PP 1.34)*
- Start Style Checker *(PP 1.42)*
- Type a Multi-level Bulleted List *(PP 1.28)*
- Use the Popup Menu to End a Slide Show *(PP 1.37)*
- Use the Vertical Scroll Bar to Move to Another Slide *(PP 1.33)*

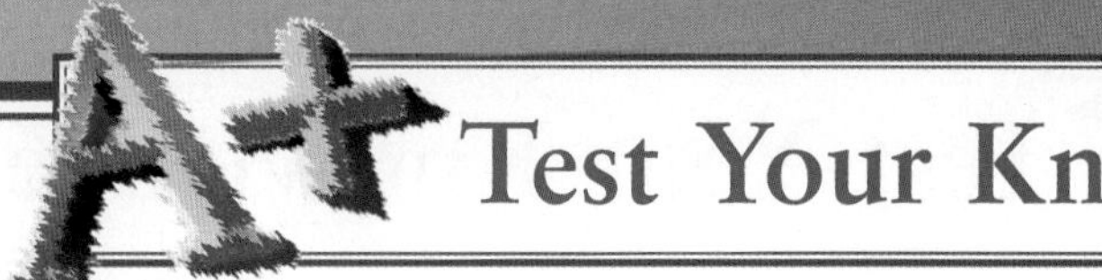

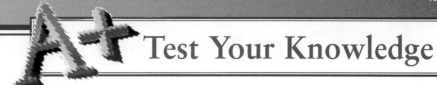

Test Your Knowledge

1 True/False

Instructions: Circle T if the statement is true or F if the statement is false.

T F 1. A PowerPoint document is called a presentation.
T F 2. The basic unit of a PowerPoint presentation is a slide.
T F 3. The menu bar displays the name of the current PowerPoint file.
T F 4. Toolbars consist of buttons that access commonly used PowerPoint tools.
T F 5. Objects are the building blocks for a PowerPoint slide.
T F 6. In PowerPoint, the Formatting toolbar contains tools for changing text attributes.
T F 7. Every time you add a slide to an open presentation, PowerPoint prompts you to choose an AutoLayout.
T F 8. PowerPoint assumes the first slide in a presentation is the Slide Master.
T F 9. The function of the Undo button is limited to reversing the last action.
T F 10. The slide indicator shows the slide number and slide title.

2 Multiple Choice

Instructions: Circle the correct response.

1. When the mouse pointer is pointing to a menu, it has the shape of a(n) __________.
   a. hand
   b. hourglass
   c. I-beam
   d. left-pointing block arrow
2. To close a presentation and PowerPoint, click the __________ button.
   a. Save
   b. Save As
   c. Close
   d. Exit
3. __________ displays a single slide in the PowerPoint window as it appears in your presentation.
   a. Slide view
   b. Outline view
   c. Notes Pages view
   d. Slide Sorter view
4. To display online help information by asking a question in your own words, use the __________.
   a. Content sheet
   b. Index sheet
   c. Find sheet
   d. Answer Wizard sheet

(continued)

Test Your Knowledge

Multiple Choice *(continued)*

5. The Design Template controls the layout and attributes of the __________.
   a. title object
   b. title text
   c. body object
   d. all of the above
6. Before you italicize a paragraph, you must first __________.
   a. highlight the first word in the paragraph to be formatted
   b. highlight the paragraph to be formatted
   c. position the mouse pointer beside the first character in the paragraph to be formatted
   d. underscore the paragraph to be formatted
7. If you add objects to the Slide Master, they display on __________.
   a. the Slide Master
   b. every slide
   c. every slide except the title slide
   d. both a and c
8. To erase a character to the left of the insertion point, press the __________ key.
   a. DELETE
   b. INSERT
   c. BACKSPACE
   d. both a and c
9. When you close PowerPoint, __________.
   a. control is returned to the desktop
   b. the presentation is erased from a floppy disk
   c. the presentation is removed from the screen
   d. both a and c
10. PowerPoint automatically appends the extension __________ to a filename when you save a presentation.
    a. .DOC
    b. .PPT
    c. .TXT
    d. .XLS

Test Your Knowledge

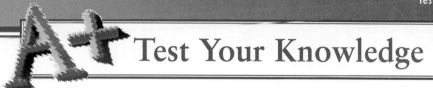

3 Understanding the PowerPoint Window

Instructions: In Figure 1-81, arrows point to the major components of the PowerPoint window. Identify the various parts of the window in the space provided.

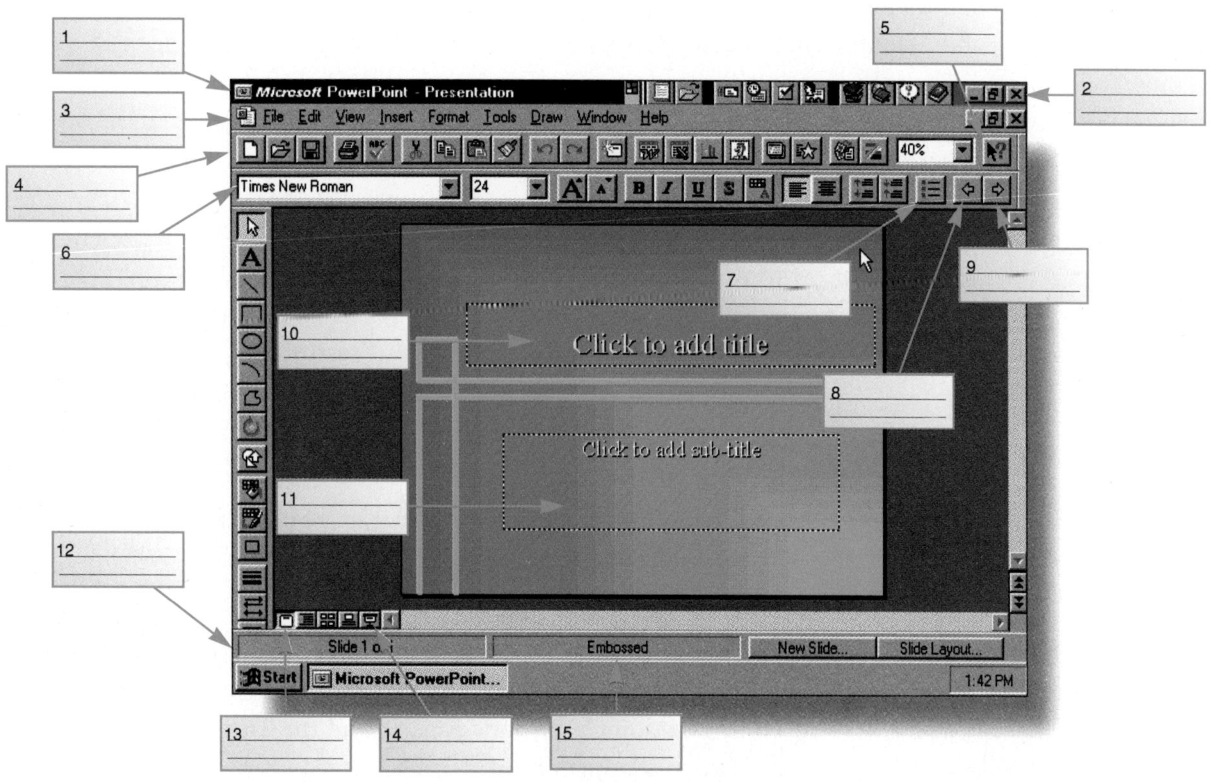

FIGURE 1-81

4 Understanding the PowerPoint Toolbars

Instructions: In Figure 1-82, arrows point to several buttons on the Standard and Formatting toolbars. Identify the buttons in the space provided.

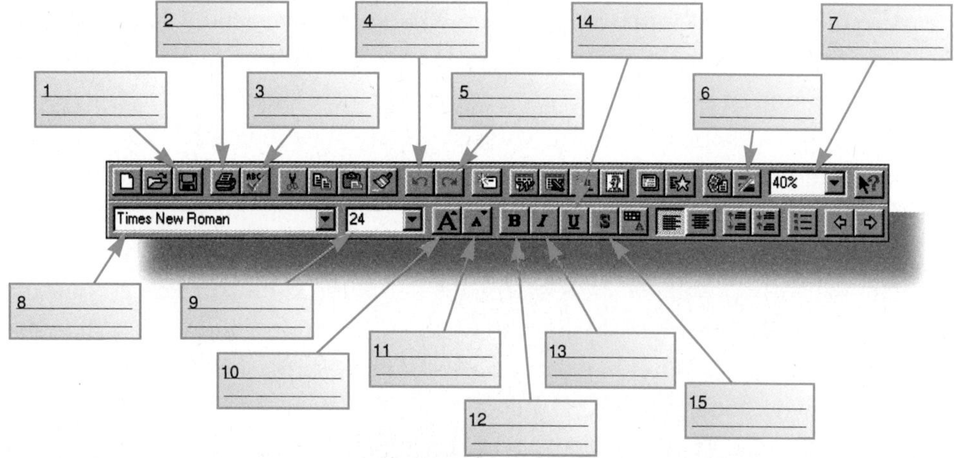

FIGURE 1-82

Use Help

1 Reviewing Project Activities

Instructions: Perform the following tasks using a computer.

1. Start PowerPoint. Double-click the Help button on the Standard toolbar to display the Help Topics: Microsoft PowerPoint dialog box.
2. Click the Contents tab. Double-click the Working With Presentations book icon. Double-click What PowerPoint creates. Click the Overhead transparencies link and read the help information. Click the remaining four links and read their help information. Click the Help Topics button in the lower right corner of the Microsoft PowerPoint for Windows 95 dialog box to return to the Help Topics: Microsoft PowerPoint dialog box.
3. Click the Find tab. Type `print` in box 1. Click printed in box 2. Double-click Printing a presentation in box 3. When the Microsoft PowerPoint window displays, read the information, right-click the window, and click Print Topic. When the Print dialog box displays, click the OK button. Click the Close button to return to PowerPoint. Submit the printout to your instructor.

2 Expanding on the Basics

Instructions: Use PowerPoint online help to better understand the topics listed below. Begin each of the following by double-clicking the Help button on the Standard toolbar. If you cannot print the help information, answer the question on a separate piece of paper.

1. Using the Changing the Appearance of Your Presentation book icon on the Contents sheet in the Help Topics: Microsoft PowerPoint dialog box, answer the following questions. (a) How do you display the Slide Master? (b) What is the function of the Slide Master and the Title Master? and (c) How do you display an object on all slides in a presentation?
2. Using the key term, line spacing, and the Index sheet in the Help Topics: Microsoft PowerPoint dialog box, display and print the answers for the following questions. (a) How do you change the After Paragraph line spacing? (b) How do you change the amount of space within a paragraph? and (c) How do you change the alignment of all text in a text placeholder?
3. Use the Find sheet in the Help Topics: Microsoft PowerPoint dialog box to display and then print information about the function keys. Then answer the following questions: (a) Which key, or combination of keys, do you press to create a new slide? (b) Which key, or combination of keys, do you press to create a new slide without a New Slide dialog box? (c) Which key, or combination of keys, do you press to move up one paragraph? (d) Which key, or combination of keys, do you press to open a new presentation? and (e) Which key, or combination of keys, do you press to save a presentation with a different name?
4. Use the Answer Wizard sheet on the Help Topics: Microsoft PowerPoint dialog box to display and then print the information about masters. (a) How do you create a slide that is different from the Slide Master? (b) What happens to a slide when its master changes? and (c) What is master text and how do you apply it to a slide?

Apply Your Knowledge

CAUTION: It is recommended that you create a backup copy of the Student Floppy Disk that accompanies this book and then remove unneeded folders on the backup floppy disk to free up space. Do the following: (1) insert the Student Floppy Disk in drive A; (2) start Explorer; (3) right-click the 3½ Floppy [A:] folder in the All Folders side of the window; (4) click Copy Disk; (5) click Start and OK as required; (6) insert the backup floppy disk when requested; (7) delete folders on the backup floppy disk except the PowerPoint folder.

1 Formatting a Slide

Instructions: Read the CAUTION box. Start PowerPoint. Open the presentation, Insurance Plan, from the PowerPoint folder on the Student Floppy Disk that accompanies this book. This slide lists the features of a new student insurance plan. Perform the following tasks to change the slide so it looks like the one in Figure 1-83.

1. Press and hold down the SHIFT key, and then click the Slide View button to display the Slide Master. Click the paragraph, Click to edit Master text styles. Click Format on the menu bar and then click Line Spacing. Increase the Before Paragraph line spacing to 0.75 lines. Click the OK button. Then click the Slide View button to return to Slide view.
2. Select the title text. Click the Bold button on the Formatting toolbar.
3. Select the No deductible paragraph. Click the Underline button on the Formatting toolbar.
4. Click the paragraph, No out-of-pocket expense, and then click the Demote (Indent more) button on the Formatting toolbar. Then, demote the paragraphs, Preventative care and Annual check-up.
5. Click File on the menu bar and then click Save As. Type `Student Insurance` in the File name box. If drive A is not already displaying in the Save in box, click the Save in down arrow and click drive A. Then, click the Save button.
6. Click the B&W View button on the Standard toolbar to display the presentation in black and white.
7. Click the Print button on the Standard toolbar.
8. Close PowerPoint.
9. Submit the printout to your instructor.

Student Health Benefits

- No deductible
  - No out-of-pocket expense
- Choose your physician
- Health maintenance
  - Preventative care
  - Annual check-up

FIGURE 1-83

1 Designing and Creating a Presentation

Problem: You are the Assistant Director for the Career Development and Placement Center at San Baarbo University. An emergency arises and you have been asked to substitute for an instructor this afternoon. The instructor suggests you discuss strategies for interviewing. To prepare for the class, you quickly create the presentation shown in Figure 1-84.

Instructions: Perform the following tasks.

1. Create a new presentation using the Bedrock Design Template.
2. Using the typewritten notes illustrated in Figure 1-85, create the title slide shown in Figure 1-84 using your name in place of Dana Fox. Decrease the font size of the paragraphs, Presented by:, Assistant Director, and Career Development Center, to 24. Increase the font size of your name to 36.
3. Using the typewritten notes in Figure 1-85, create the three multi-level bulleted list slides shown in Figure 1-84.

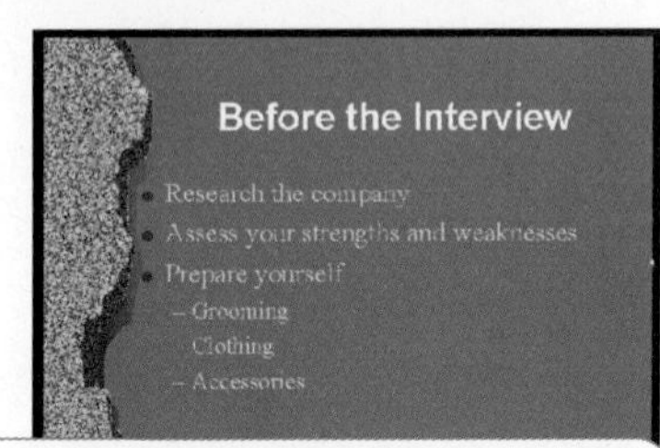

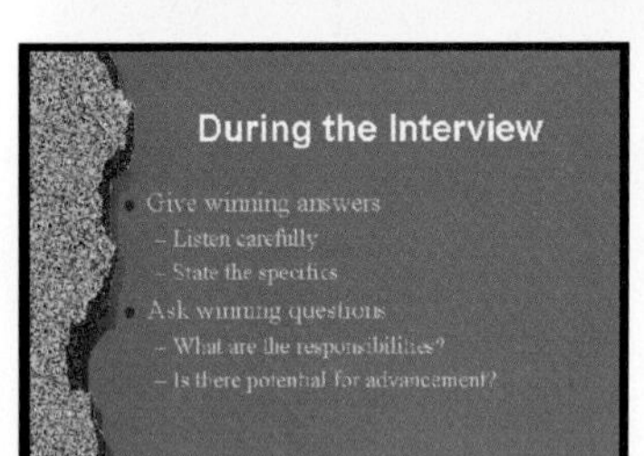

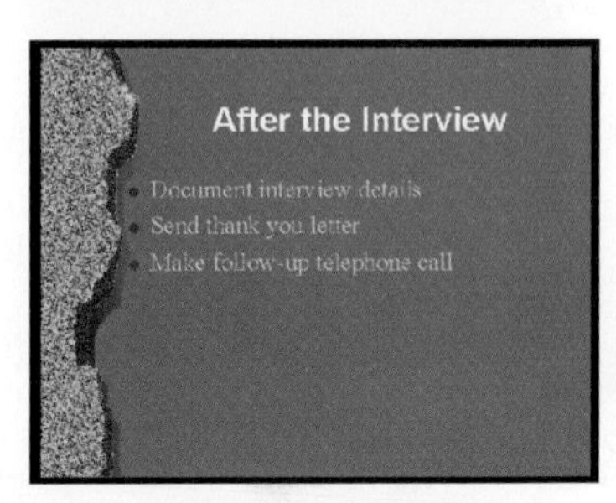

FIGURE 1-84

1) **The Successful First Interview**
Presented by: Dana Fox
Assistant Director
Career Development Center

2) **Before the Interview**
· Research the company
· Assess your strengths and weaknesses
· Prepare yourself
 * Grooming
 * Clothing
 * Accessories

3) **During the Interview**
· Give winning answers
 * Listen carefully
 * State the specifics
· Ask winning questions
 * What are the responsibilities?
 * Is there potential for advancement?

4) **After the Interview**
· Document interview details
· Send thank you letter
· Make follow-up telephone call

FIGURE 1-85

In the Lab

4. Run Style Checker to check spelling, visual clarity, and case and end punctuation. Correct your errors.
5. Save the presentation on your data floppy disk using the filename First Interview.
6. Display the presentation in black and white.
7. Print the black and white presentation.
8. Close PowerPoint.

2 Using Masters to Modify a Design Template

Problem: You are the Health & Safety Director for your company. This week's health and safety topic is Repetitive Strain Injuries. You select a Design Template but want to modify it. ***Hint:*** Use Help to solve this problem.

Instructions: Perform the following tasks.

1. Create a new presentation using the Blue Weave Design Template.
2. Using the notes in Figure 1-86, create the title slide shown in Figure 1-87 on the next page using your name in place of John Albrey. Decrease the font size of the paragraphs, Presented by:, and Health & Safety Director, to 24. Increase the font size of your name to 36.
3. Using the notes in Figure 1-86, create the multi-level bulleted list slides shown in Figure 1-87.
4. Display the Slide Master. Click the paragraph, Click to edit Master title style, and then click the Text Shadow button on the Formatting toolbar. Click the paragraph, Click to edit Master text styles. On the Format menu, click Line Spacing, and then increase the Before Paragraph line spacing to 0.75 lines. Drag the mouse pointer to select the paragraphs, Second level and Third level. On the Format menu, click Line Spacing, and then increase the After Paragraph spacing to 0.2 lines.

```
1)    Repetitive Strain Injuries
          Presented by:
          John Albrey
          Health & Safety Director

2)    What Is Repetitive Strain Injury (RSI)?
      .   Injury to the hands and/or wrists
          *   Tendons or muscles are strained or torn
          *   Blood circulation is impaired
          *   Tissues deprived of nutrients
          *   Toxins allowed to build

3)    Who Gets RSI?
      .   People with jobs that require repetitive hand or wrist motion
      .   Examples:
          *   Computer users
          *   Typists
          *   Assembly-line workers
          *   Meat cutters

4)    How Do You Prevent RSI?
      .   Before Work
          *   Perform wrist and hand warm-up exercises
      .   During Work
          *   Relax and keep hands warm
          *   Maintain good posture
          *   Keep wrists and forearms parallel to floor
```

FIGURE 1-86

(continued)

Using Masters to Modify a Design Template *(continued)*

5. Drag the elevator to display the Title Master. Click the paragraph, Click to edit Master title style, and then click the Text Shadow button on the Formatting toolbar. On the View menu, click Header and Footer. Then add the current date, slide number, and your name to the footer. Display the footer on all slides. Return to Slide view.
6. Run Style Checker to check spelling, visual larity, and case and end punctuation. Correct your errors.
7. Drag the elevator to display Slide 1. Click the Slide Show button to start Slide Show view. Then click to display each slide.
8. Save the presentation on your data floppy disk using the filename, Repetitive Strain Injuries.
9. Display and print the presentation in black and white.
10. Close PowerPoint.

FIGURE 1-87

3 Creating a Training Presentation

Problem: You are a financial planner conducting a personal finance seminar. Over the years, you have accumulated many proven methods for saving money and spending less.

Instructions: Using the list in Figure 1-88, design and create a presentation. The presentation is to include a title slide and five bulleted list slides. Modify the list to conform to Style Checker defaults. Perform the following tasks:

1. Create a new presentation using the Blue Green Design Template.
2. Create a title slide titled Money. Include Are You Saving or Slaving? as the subtitle.
3. Using Figure 1-88, create five multi-level bulleted list slides. Modify the list illustrated in Figure 1-88 to conform to Style Checker defaults (see Table 1-5 on PP 1.44).

In the Lab

4. Adjust Before Paragraph and After Paragraph line spacing to utilize the available white space.
5. Save the presentation to your data floppy disk with the filename Money.
6. View the presentation in Slide Show view to look for errors. Correct any errors.
7. Print the presentation in black and white.
8. Close PowerPoint.

Money
Are You Saving or Slaving?

- I. **Saving Savvy**
  - A. Save consistently
    - 1. Deposit a little money every week
      - a) Saving $10 a week easier than $40 a month
    - 2. Use payroll deductions
      - a) Savings bonds
      - b) 401K plan
      - c) Thrift plan
    - 3. Make savings part of your budget
      - a) Deposit cash saved from discounts
  - B. Open specialty savings accounts
    - 1. Vacation club
    - 2. College fund
    - 3. Christmas club
- II. **Reduce Finance Charges**
  - A. Pay cash
    - 1. Don't create additional debt
    - 2. Save until you can pay cash for an item
  - B. Eliminate high interest debt
    - 1. Make larger payments
      - a) Pay more then minimum amount due
      - b) Make more frequent payments
        - (1) Make bimonthly payments
        - (2) Make weekly payments
    - 2. Consolidate bills
      - a) Eliminate several bills into one
      - b) Refinance at lower interest rate
- III. **Food Savings**
  - A. Brown-bag your lunch
    - 1. Plan meals for entire week
    - 2. Use restaurant "doggie-bag" leftovers for next day's lunch
  - B. Grocery shop from a list
    - 1. Resist impulse buying
      - a) Don't shop when hungry
    - 2. Read cost-per-unit labels
    - 3. Use coupons for what you normally buy
      - a) Don't buy an item because you have a coupon
    - 4. Buy in bulk
      - a) Only if you'll use before it spoils
- IV. **Car Savings**
  - A. Insurance
    - 1. Insure all cars with same company
      - a) Look for 15 to 20 percent discount
    - 2. Reduce coverage on old cars
      - a) Consider eliminating collision coverage
  - B. Maintenance
    - 1. Read warranty carefully
      - a) Dealer might be required to fix
    - 2. Buy supplies at discount stores
    - 3. Do minor repairs yourself
  - C. Driving
    - 1. Get ready before you start engine
      - a) Adjust mirrors and seat
      - b) Fasten seatbelt
    - 2. Gradually increase and decrease speed
- V. **Bill Paying Strategy**
  - A. Organize bills
  - B. Write check when bill arrives
    - 1. Mail just before due date
  - C. Don't skip payments
    - 1. Send small amounts to every creditor
    - 2. Call creditor if you must pay late

FIGURE 1-88

Cases and Places

The difficulty of these case studies varies:

◗ Case studies preceded by a single half moon are the least difficult. You are asked to create the required presentation based on information that has already been placed in an organized form.

◗◗ Case studies preceded by two half moons are more difficult. You must organize the information given before using it to create the required presentation.

◗◗◗ Case studies preceded by three half moons are the most difficult. You must decide on a specific topic, and then obtain and organize the necessary information before using it to create the required presentation.

1 ◗ Pauline Gauguin, an art instructor from the Synthétiste School, is giving a presentation at the next parent-teachers meeting. She has written out a recipe for finger paint (Figure 1-89).

With this recipe, Ms. Gauguin has asked you to prepare four slides that can be used on an overhead projector. Use the concepts and techniques introduced in this project to create the presentation.

Homemade Finger Paint

Ingredients

- ✔ *1/3 cup cornstarch*
- ✔ *3 cups sugar*
- ✔ *2 cups cold water*
- ✔ *food color*

Preparation

- ✔ *Mix cornstarch, sugar, and water*
  Use 1-quart saucepan
- ✔ *Cover and stir over medium heat*
  About 5 minutes or until thickened
- ✔ *Remove from heat*

Adding Color

- ✔ *Divide mixture into separate cups*
- ✔ *Tint each cup with a different food color*
  Stir several times until cool
- ✔ *Store in airtight container*
  Paint works best if used the same day

FIGURE 1-89

Cases and Places

2 ◗ Bill Henry, managing director for the Skoon County Fair, has prepared some notes for a presentation that will be given to the local chamber of commerce (Figure 1-90).

With these notes, the fair director has asked you to prepare four slides that can be used on an overhead projector. Use the concepts and techniques introduced in this project to create the presentation.

25th Annual Skoon County Fair

P.B. Pillbottom's Midway
- *Over 50 rides and attractions*
  World's largest carousel
- *Games of skill and chance*
- *The Kiddie Corral*
  Activities for children under 8

Popular Exhibits
- *Arts and crafts*
  Prizes in 32 separate categories
- *Domesticated animals*
  Prizes in 26 classes
- *Commercial demonstrations*

Family Entertainment
- *The Neighborhood Bigtop*
  Bring a camera to film the kids
- *Western Rodeo Jamboree*
- *Music and shows*
  The Bronco Brothers
  "Thank God I'm a Country Boy"

FIGURE 1-90

3 ◗◗ As part of a symposium on the history of American education, you are giving a presentation on the Curriculum of General Schools, as proposed in a letter by Thomas Jefferson to Peter Carr. Jefferson divides the general school curriculum into three departments—language, mathematics, and philosophy. The language department is composed of languages and history (both may be attained by the same course of reading), grammar, belles lettres (poetry, composition, and criticism), and rhetoric and oratory. The department of mathematics includes: mathematics pure, physico-mathematics (physical subjects aided by mathematical calculation), natural history (mineralogy, botany, zoology, and anatomy), and the theory of medicine. The philosophical department encompasses ideology, ethics, law of nature and nations, and government (political economy). In addition to a title slide, you plan to develop three other slides that can be used with an overhead projector. Use the concepts and techniques introduced in this project to create the presentation.

Cases and Places

4 ▶▶ You are a consultant in the field of ergonomics (an applied science devoted to making the equipment people use and the surrounding work area safer and more efficient). You have been hired by a large company to give a presentation on Computer User Health Guidelines, and you have been asked to cover three topics—a well-designed work area, equipment in the workplace, and ways to reduce physical and mental fatigue. A well-designed work area contains a desk approximately 30 inches high; a chair with adjustable backrest, seat, and height and 5 legs for stability; and adequate lighting using nonglare bulbs. Equipment in the workplace should consist of a keyboard at a height apropos to the height of the operator; a monitor at a viewing distance between 18 and 28 inches (a viewing angle of 20° to center of screen); a monitor designed to minimize electromagnetic radiation (EMR); and a document holder placed at the same height and distance as screen. Ways to reduce physical and mental fatigue are to alternate work activities (change the order of work to provide variety); minimize surrounding noise; take frequent breaks (look away from the screen every 15 minutes, get out of the chair at least once each hour, and take a 15 minute break every two hours); and incorporate stretching exercises into breaks. In addition to a title slide, you plan to develop three other slides that can be used with an overhead projector. Use the concepts and techniques introduced in this project to create the presentation.

5 ▶▶▶ Appreciation of local landmarks—historical sites, museums, or natural wonders—often can be increased by a preliminary presentation. Go to an area landmark and gather information on its significance, history, popularity, etc. Using this information, together with the concepts and techniques introduced in this project, prepare a presentation to familiarize visitors with the landmark. Create a title slide and at least three other slides that can be used with an overhead projector to enhance the presentation.

6 ▶▶▶ Some instructors use the first class meeting to provide a broad orientation for their students. At this time, students may learn about course requirements, grading policies, academic deadlines, necessary supplies, or the instructor's office hours. Choose a class you are currently taking and outline the information you feel should be offered to students on the first day of class. Using this information, together with the concepts and techniques introduced in this project, prepare a presentation to orient students on opening day. Create a title slide and at least three other slides that can be used with an overhead projector to enhance the presentation.

7 ▶▶▶ Schools often purchase computer equipment on the basis of a sales representative's presentation. Visit a computer vendor and select the system you feel is most appropriate for an elementary school. Determine the features that would make this system attractive to a grade school, such as ease of use, suitability of software, processing power, and available peripheral devices. Using this information, together with the concepts and techniques introduced in this project, prepare a presentation to sell the system to an elementary school's staff. Create a title slide and at least three other slides that can be used with an overhead projector to enhance the presentation.

Microsoft *PowerPoint 7*

Using Outline View and Clip Art to Create an Electronic Slide Show

Objectives:

You will have mastered the material in this project when you can:

- Create a presentation in Outline view
- Describe the PowerPoint window in Outline view
- Insert a blank line in a bulleted list
- Change the slide layout
- Move text between objects
- Insert clip art from the ClipArt Gallery
- Change the clip art size
- Add a header and a footer to outline pages
- Add slide transition effects
- Add text build effects
- Print a presentation outline
- Change printing options
- Change the slide order
- Copy a slide

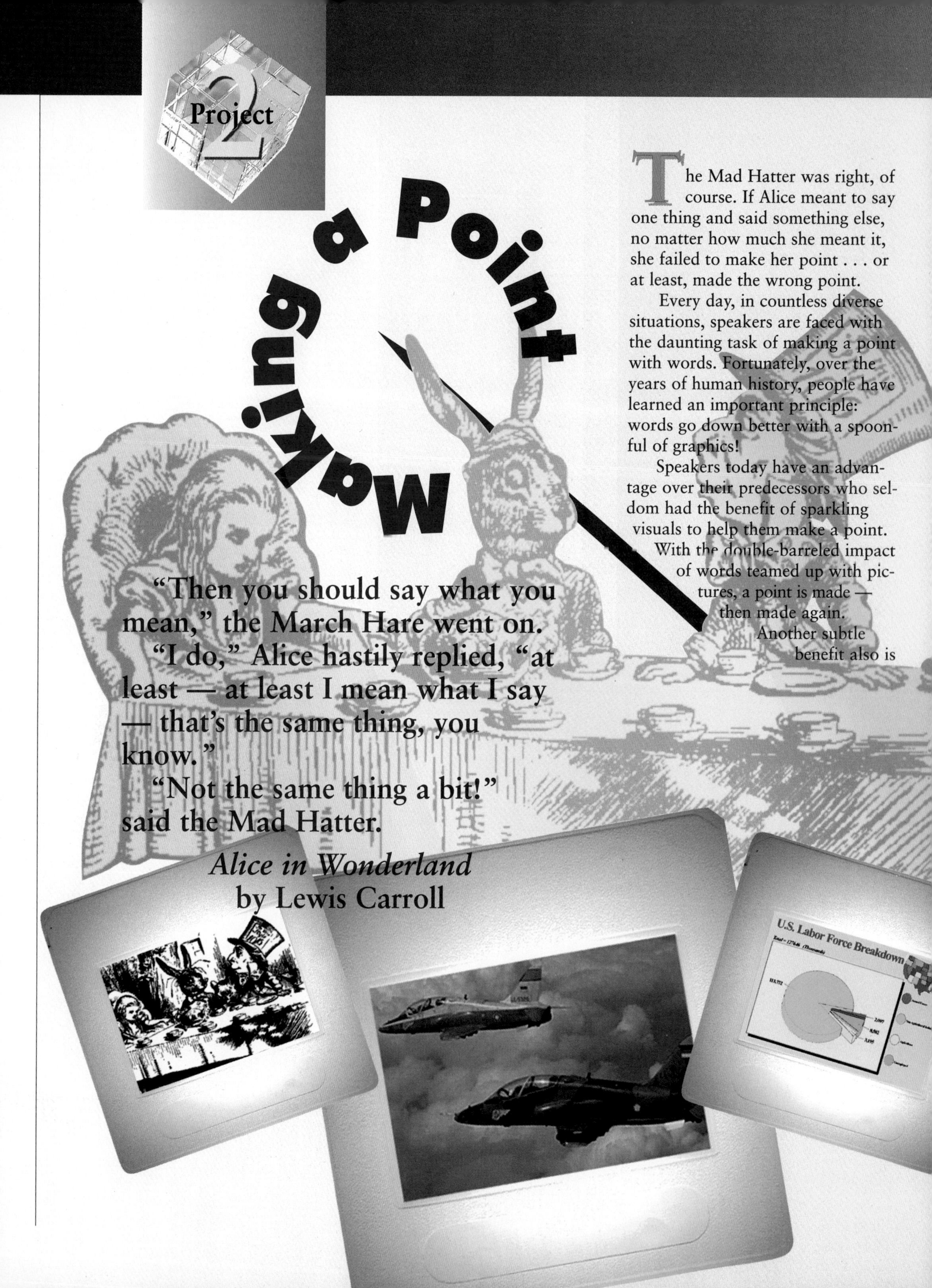

Project 2

Making a Point

"Then you should say what you mean," the March Hare went on.

"I do," Alice hastily replied, "at least — at least I mean what I say — that's the same thing, you know."

"Not the same thing a bit!" said the Mad Hatter.

Alice in Wonderland
by Lewis Carroll

The Mad Hatter was right, of course. If Alice meant to say one thing and said something else, no matter how much she meant it, she failed to make her point . . . or at least, made the wrong point.

Every day, in countless diverse situations, speakers are faced with the daunting task of making a point with words. Fortunately, over the years of human history, people have learned an important principle: words go down better with a spoonful of graphics!

Speakers today have an advantage over their predecessors who seldom had the benefit of sparkling visuals to help them make a point. With the double-barreled impact of words teamed up with pictures, a point is made — then made again.

Another subtle benefit also is

present: good graphics can help a speaker stay on track and on target. Practically everyone, from political candidate to college student to general to salesperson, has the means to create dynamic, attractive slide presentations to reinforce verbal remarks.

Armed with presentation graphics software, a user can generate a complete slide presentation often in less time than it takes to write a speech. Visuals may become the thematic focal points of a paper or oral presentation, around which one or more ideas can be built with written text or speech. By clearly establishing the expectations of the reader or listener, a picture can be the "point guard" for the ideas that follow.

General Norman Schwarzkopf, Marcia Clark, Ross Perot, and every U.S. president from Lyndon Johnson to Bill Clinton are just a few of the famous people who have used computer-generated graphics to emphasize or clarify their remarks.

College students not only are able to make a point, but are able to make *grade* points, as well, using computer-generated graphics in virtually any kind of course, whether for inclusion in a paper or an oral presentation. Every day, sales people deliver countless stand-up presentations using graphic slides to underscore each of their points, known as features and benefits. Aircraft engineers use graphics to point out the characteristics of supersonic aircraft.

In a competitive world, Microsoft PowerPoint and every other available tool should be used to make an argument more persuasive. Then, upon yielding the floor, to hear someone say, "A point well-taken... ," that is the ultimate reward.

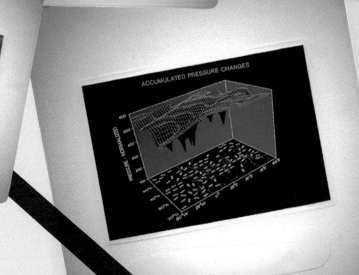

Microsoft
PowerPoint 7
Windows 95

Using Outline View and Clip Art to Create an Electronic Slide Show

Case Perspective

Web Island Resort is promoting Web Island to college students as *the* place for spring break vacations. While developing a presentation to promote two new spring break vacation packages to Web Island, your boss, Mr. Hayes, receives a telephone call. During the call, Western University invites Web Island Resort to make a presentation at their Spring Break Vacation Fair. For some unspecified reason, another resort is canceling, thereby giving Web Island Resort an opportunity to present. The Vacation Fair is tomorrow. In order for Mr. Hayes to finalize his travel arrangements, he asks you to put together a short six slide presentation. The purpose of the presentation is to entice students to buy one of the spring break vacation packages.

Web Island Resort's Marketing Department supplies you with an outline to use to create the presentation. The outline contains promotional information about the new spring break vacation packages.

To persuade students to buy a Web Island Resort spring break vacation package, you choose a design template with a tropical theme. You also include pictures to intensify the text.

Creating a Presentation from an Outline

At some time during either your academic or business life, you probably will make a presentation. Most academic presentations are informative—providing detailed information about some topic. Business presentations, however, are usually sales presentations, such as selling a proposal or a product to a client, convincing management to approve a new project, or persuading the board of directors to accept the fiscal budget. As an alternative to creating your presentation in Slide view, as you did in Project 1, PowerPoint provides an outlining feature to help you organize your thoughts. When the outline is complete, it becomes the foundation for your presentation.

You create a presentation outline in Outline view. When you create an outline, you type all of your text at one time, as if you were typing an outline on a sheet of paper. This is different than Slide view where you type text as you create each individual slide.

The first step in creating a presentation in Outline view is to type a title for the outline. The outline title is the subject of the presentation and later becomes the presentation title slide. Then you type the remainder of the outline, indenting appropriately to establish a structure or hierarchy. Once the outline is complete, you make your presentation more persuasive by adding graphics. This project uses outlining to create the presentation and clip art graphics to visually support the text.

FIGURES 2-1a

Project Two – Spring Break Specials

Project 2 uses PowerPoint to create the six slide Web Island Resort Spring Break Specials presentation shown in Figure 2-1. You create the presentation from the outline in Figure 2-2 on the next page.

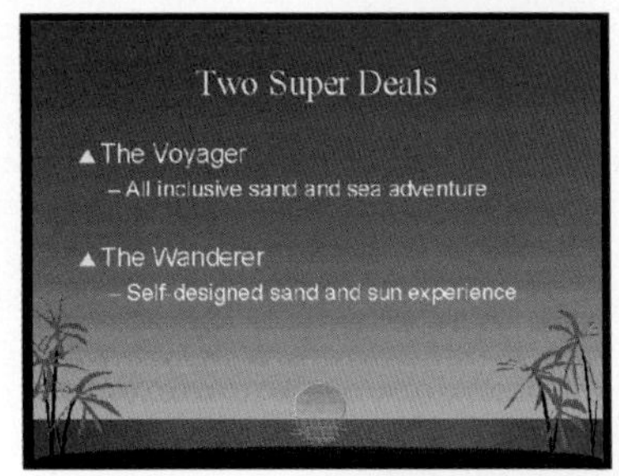

FIGURES 2-1b

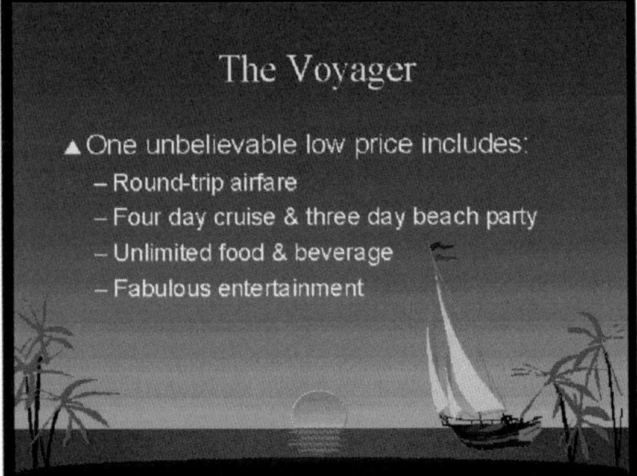

FIGURES 2-1c

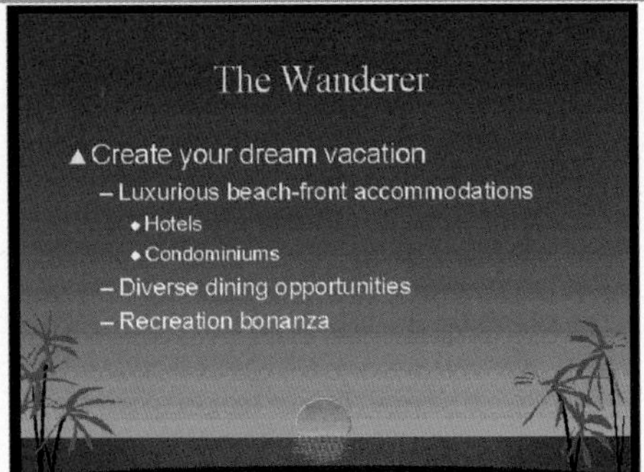

FIGURES 2-1d

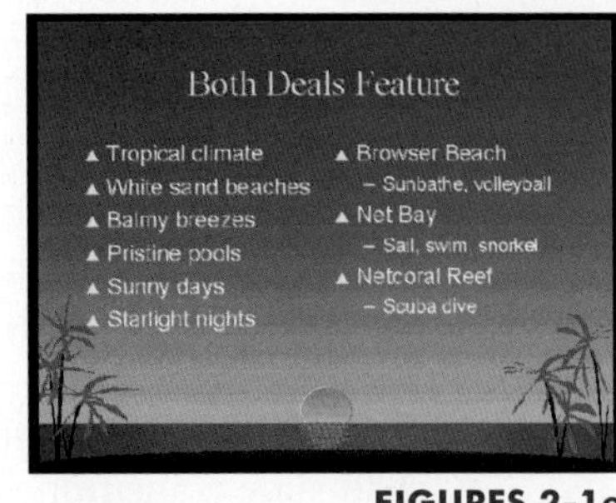

FIGURES 2-1e

FIGURES 2-1f

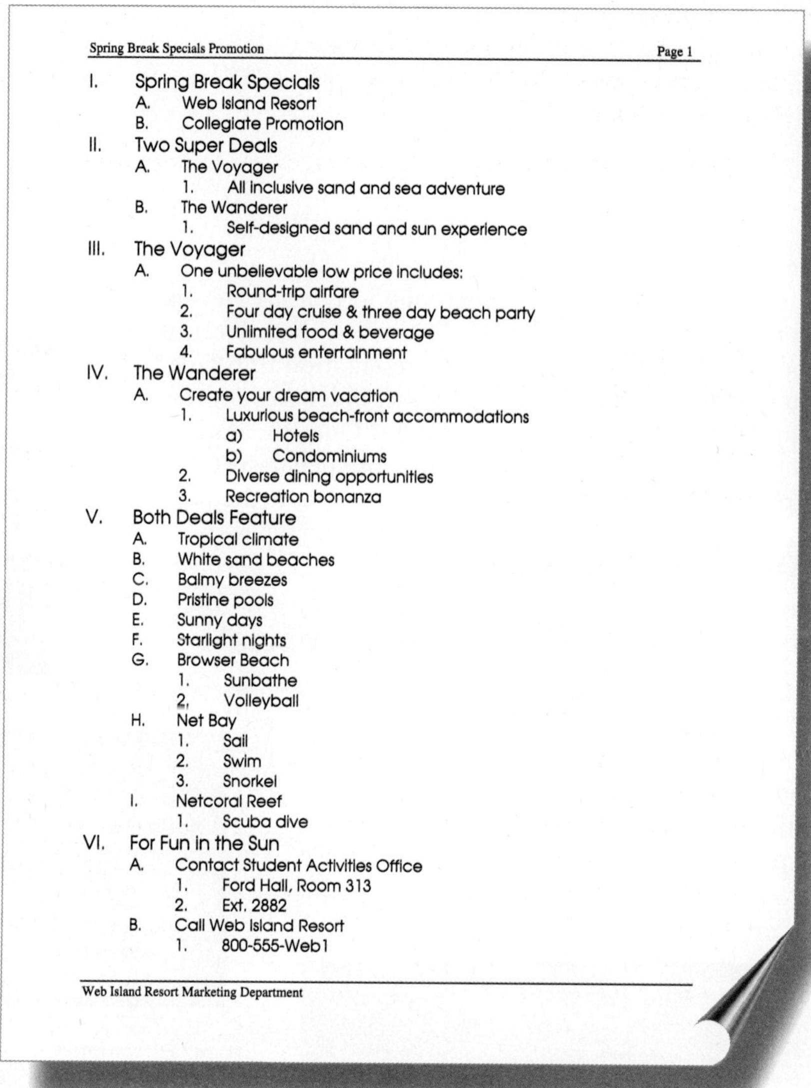

Spring Break Specials Promotion — Page 1

I. Spring Break Specials
   A. Web Island Resort
   B. Collegiate Promotion
II. Two Super Deals
   A. The Voyager
      1. All inclusive sand and sea adventure
   B. The Wanderer
      1. Self-designed sand and sun experience
III. The Voyager
   A. One unbelievable low price includes:
      1. Round-trip airfare
      2. Four day cruise & three day beach party
      3. Unlimited food & beverage
      4. Fabulous entertainment
IV. The Wanderer
   A. Create your dream vacation
      1. Luxurious beach-front accommodations
         a) Hotels
         b) Condominiums
      2. Diverse dining opportunities
      3. Recreation bonanza
V. Both Deals Feature
   A. Tropical climate
   B. White sand beaches
   C. Balmy breezes
   D. Pristine pools
   E. Sunny days
   F. Starlight nights
   G. Browser Beach
      1. Sunbathe
      2. Volleyball
   H. Net Bay
      1. Sail
      2. Swim
      3. Snorkel
   I. Netcoral Reef
      1. Scuba dive
VI. For Fun in the Sun
   A. Contact Student Activities Office
      1. Ford Hall, Room 313
      2. Ext. 2882
   B. Call Web Island Resort
      1. 800-555-Web1

Web Island Resort Marketing Department

FIGURE 2-2

Presentation Preparation Steps

The preparation steps summarize how the slide presentation shown in Figure 2-1 on page PP 2.5 will be developed in Project 2. The following tasks will be completed in this project.

1. Start a new document and apply a Design Template.
2. Create a presentation in Outline view.
3. Save the presentation.
4. Insert a blank line on Slide 2.
5. Change the Slide 5 layout to 2 Column Text and move text from the left column to the right column.
6. Change the Slide 6 layout to Clip Art and Text and insert a clip art picture into a clip art placeholder.
7. Insert clip art in Slide 3. Move and reduce the size of the clip art picture.
8. Add header and footer text to the outline pages.
9. Add slide transition effects and text build effects.

10. Save the presentation.
11. Print the presentation outline and slides.
12. Edit the presentation in Outline view and in Slide Sorter view.
13. Close PowerPoint.

The following pages contain a detailed explanation of these tasks.

Starting a New Presentation

Project 1 introduced you to starting a presentation document and applying a Design Template. The following steps summarize how to start a new presentation, apply a Design Template, and choose an AutoLayout. For a more detailed explanation, see pages PP 1.9 through PP 1.12. Perform the following steps to start a new presentation.

TO START A NEW PRESENTATION

Step 1: Click the Start button on the taskbar.
Step 2: Click New Office Document.
Step 3: Click the Presentation Designs tab. When the Presentation Designs sheet displays, scroll down the list of Design Templates until Tropical displays.
Step 4: Double-click Tropical.
Step 5: When the New Slide dialog box displays, click the OK button.

PowerPoint displays the Title Slide AutoLayout and the Tropical Design Template on Slide 1 in Slide View (Figure 2-3).

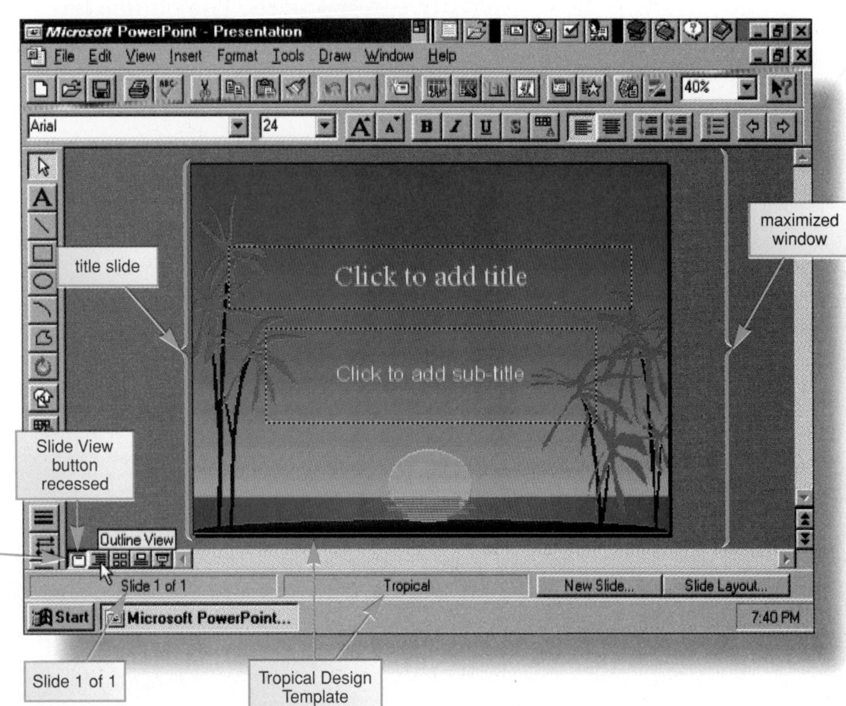

FIGURE 2-3

Using Outline View

Outline view provides a quick, easy way to create a presentation. Outlining allows you to organize your thoughts in a structured format. An outline uses indentation to establish a hierarchy, which denotes levels of importance to the main topic. An **outline** is a summary of thoughts, presented as headings and subheadings, often used as a preliminary draft when you create a presentation.

More *About* Design Templates

You can build a presentation with the default Design Template and later select a different one. When you change Design Templates, PowerPoint automatically updates color scheme, font attributes, and location of slide objects on every slide in the presentation.

More *About* **Presentation Design**

The key to a successful presentation is organization. Begin by jotting down your ideas. Next, look over your list and decide on three or four major topics. Then group the remaining ideas around the major topics, selecting ideas that support the major topics and leaving out those that do not.

In Outline view, title text displays at the left side of the window along with a slide icon and a slide number. Body text is indented under the title text. Graphic objects, such as pictures, graphs, or tables, do not display in Outline view. When a slide contains a graphic object, the slide icon next to the slide title displays with a small graphic on it. The slide icon is blank when a slide does not contain graphics. The attributes for text in Outline view are the same as in Slide view except for color and paragraph style.

PowerPoint limits the number of outline levels to six. The first outline level is the slide title. The remaining five outline levels are the same as the five indent levels in Slide view. Recall from Project 1 that PowerPoint allows for five indent levels and that each indent level has an associated bullet.

The outline begins with a title on **outline level one**. The title is the main topic of the slide. Text supporting the main topic begins on **outline level two** and indents under outline level one. **Outline level three** indents under outline level two and contains text to support outline level two. **Outline level four**, **outline level five**, and **outline level six** indent under outline level three, outline level four, and outline level five, respectively. Use outline levels four, five, and six as required. They are generally used for scientific and engineering presentations requiring vast amounts of detail. Business and sales presentations usually focus on summary information and use outline level one, outline level two, and outline level three.

PowerPoint initially displays in Slide view when you start a new presentation. Change from Slide view to Outline view by clicking the Outline View button on the View Button bar. Perform the following steps to change the view from Slide view to Outline view.

Steps To Change the View to Outline View

1 Point to the Outline View button located on the View Button bar at the lower-left of the PowerPoint window (Figure 2-4).

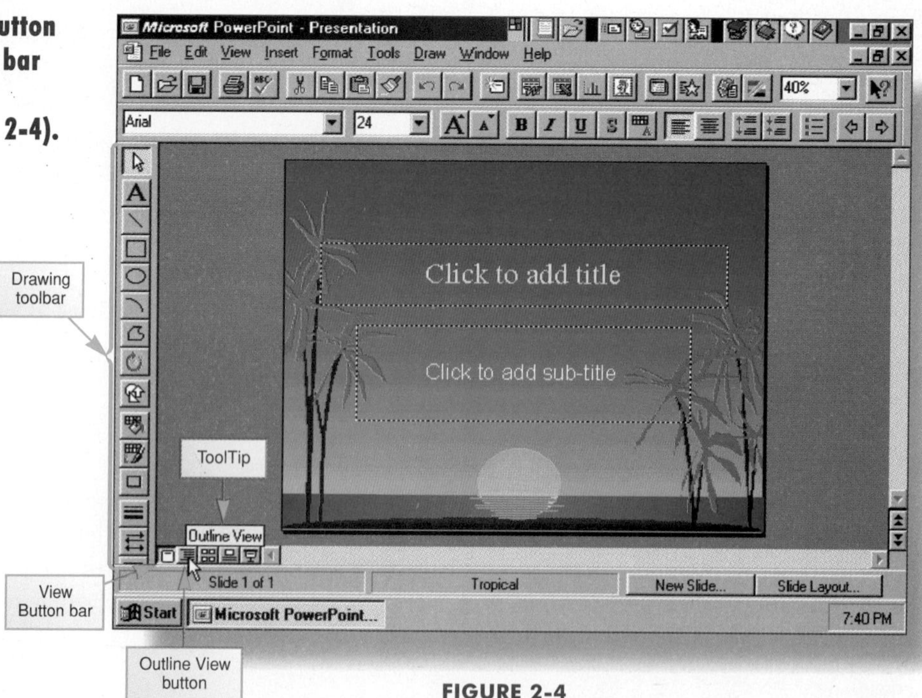

FIGURE 2-4

2 **Click the Outline View button.**

PowerPoint displays the Outline View window (Figure 2-5).

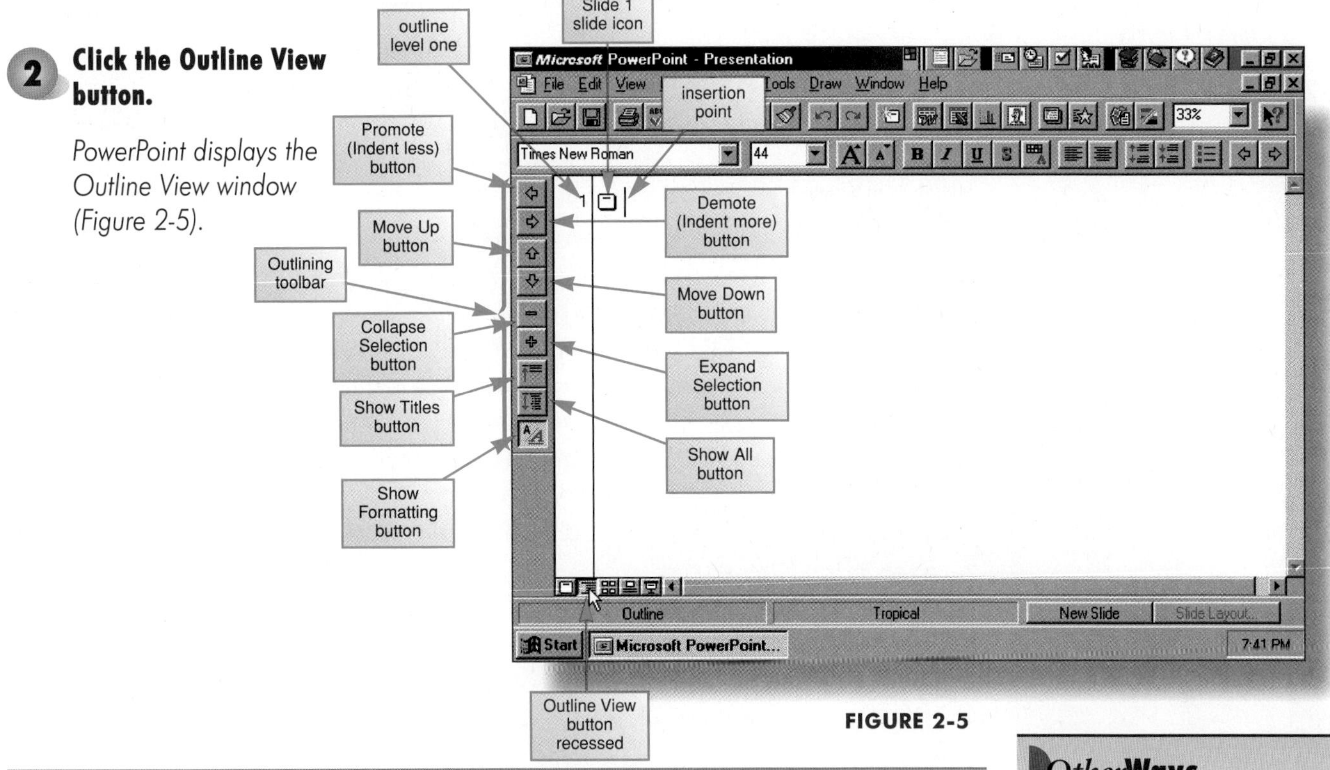

FIGURE 2-5

***Other*Ways**

1. On menu bar click View, click Outline
2. Press ALT+V, press O

You can create and edit your presentation in Outline view. Outline view also makes it easy to sequence slides and to relocate title text and body text from one slide to another. In addition to typing text to create a new presentation in Outline view, PowerPoint can produce slides from an outline created in Microsoft Word or another word processor, if you save the outline as an RTF file or as a plain text file. The file extension **RTF** stands for **R**ich **T**ext **F**ormat.

The PowerPoint Window in Outline View

The PowerPoint window in Outline view differs from the window in Slide view because the Outlining toolbar displays and the Drawing toolbar does not display (see Figures 2-4 and 2-5). Table 2-1 on the next page describes the buttons on the Outlining toolbar.

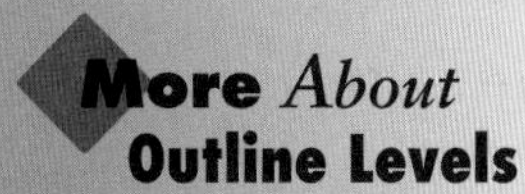

More *About* Outline Levels

A topic needing more than six outline levels has too much detail and may overwhelm the audience. Decompose large topics into two or more subtopics. Then, create a new slide for each group of subtopics.

Table 2-1

BUTTON	BUTTON NAME	DESCRIPTION
	Promote button	The Promote (Indent less) button moves the selected paragraph up one level in the outline hierarchy each time you click the button. Promoting a paragraph moves it to the left until you reach outline level one.
	Demote button	The Demote (Indent more) button moves the selected paragraph down, or to the right, one level in the outline hierarchy each time you click the button. You can only demote to the sixth outline level.
	Move Up button	The Move Up button moves selected text up one paragraph at a time while maintaining its hierarchical outline level and text style. The selected text exchanges position with the paragraph located above it.
	Move Down button	The Move Down button moves selected text down one paragraph at time while maintaining its hierarchical outline level and text style. The selected text exchanges position with the paragraph located below it.
	Collapse Selection button	The Collapse Selection button hides all outline levels except the slide title of the selected slide. This button is useful when you want to collapse one slide in your outline.
	Expand Selection button	The Expand Selection button displays all outline levels for the selected slide. This button is useful when you want to expand one slide in your outline.
	Show Titles button	The Show Titles button collapses all outline levels to show only the slide titles. This button is useful when you are looking at the organization of your presentation and do not care to see all the details.
	Show All button	The Show All button expands all outline levels to display the title and text for all slides.
	Show Formatting button	The Show Formatting button is a toggle that displays or hides the text attributes in Outline view. This is useful when you want to work with plain text as opposed to working with bolded, italicized, or underlined text. When printing your outline, plain text often speeds up the printing process.

Creating a Presentation in Outline View

Outline view enables you to view title and body text, add and delete slides, **drag and drop** slide text, drag and drop slides to change slide order, promote and demote text, save a presentation, print an outline, print slides, copy and paste slides or text to and from other presentations, apply a Design Template, and import an outline.

Developing a presentation in Outline view is quick because you type the text for all slides on one screen. Once you type the outline, the presentation is fundamentally complete. If you choose, you can then go to Slide view to enhance your presentation with graphics.

Creating a Title Slide in Outline View

Recall from Project 1 that the title slide introduces the presentation to the audience. Additionally, Project 2 uses the title slide to capture the attention of the audience by using a Design Template with a tropical theme. The Tropical Design Template enhances the presentation title with tropical plants and a setting sun. Remember, Web Island Resort is trying to sell vacation packages. They want students to focus on a warm, tropical climate. Perform the following steps to create a title slide in Outline view.

To Create a Title Slide in Outline View

1 Type `Spring Break Specials` **and press the ENTER key.**

Spring Break Specials displays as the title for Slide 1 and is called outline level one. A slide icon displays to the left of each slide title. The font for outline level one is Times New Roman and the font size is 44 points. In Outline view, the Zoom Control default setting is 33% of the actual slide size. Pressing the ENTER key moves the insertion point to the next line and maintains the same outline level. The insertion point, therefore, is in position for typing the title for Slide 2 (Figure 2-6).

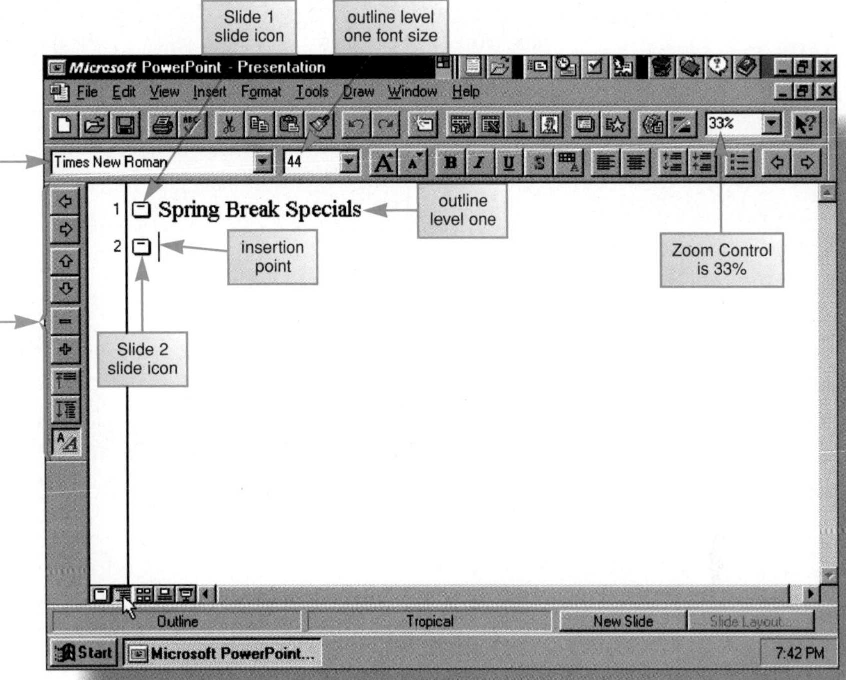

FIGURE 2-6

2 Point to the Demote (Indent more) button on the Outlining toolbar.

The Demote (Indent more) ToolTip displays (Figure 2-7).

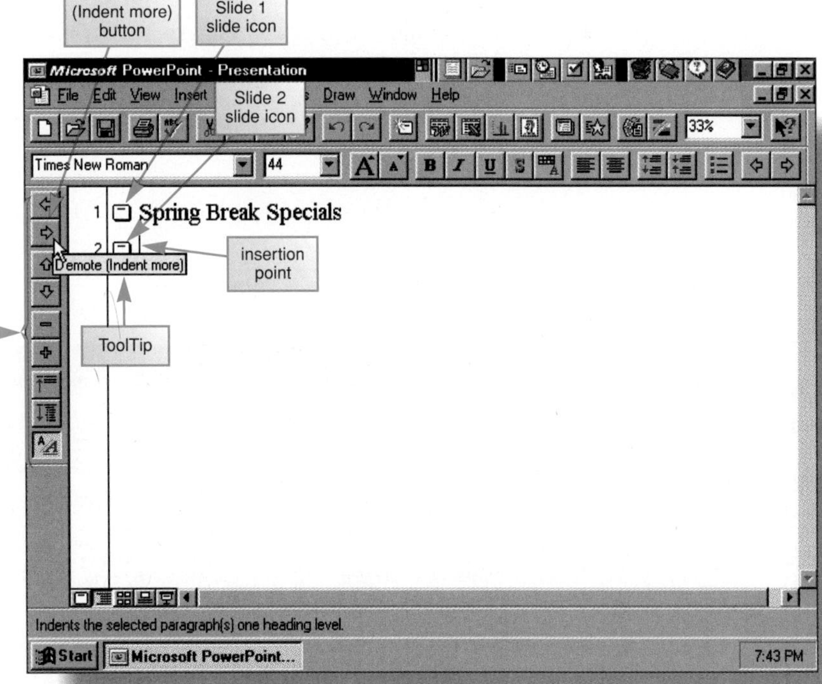

FIGURE 2-7

3 **Click the Demote (Indent more) button. Type** `Web Island Resort` **and press the ENTER key. Type** `Collegiate Promotion` **and press the ENTER key.**

The Slide 2 slide icon does not display (Figure 2-8). The lines, Web Island Resort and Collegiate Promotion, are subtitles on the title slide (Slide 1) and demote to outline level two. Outline level two is indented to the right under outline level one. The outline level two font is Arial and the outline level two font size is 32 points.

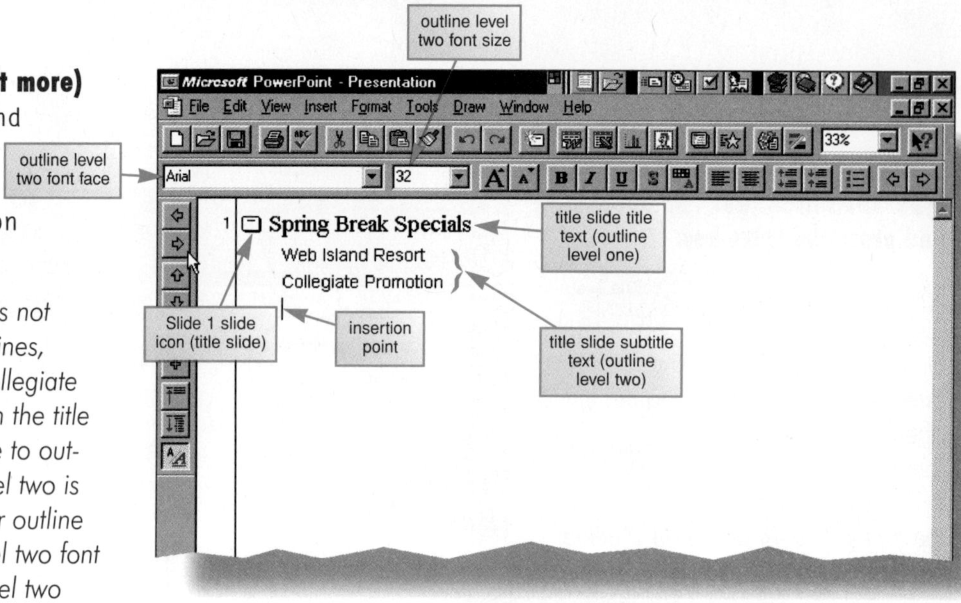

FIGURE 2-8

The title slide for the Spring Break Specials presentation is complete. The next section explains how to add a slide in Outline view.

Adding a Slide in Outline View

Recall from Project 1 that when you add a new slide, PowerPoint defaults to the Bulleted List slide layout. This is true in Outline view as well. One way to add a new slide in Outline view is to promote a paragraph to outline level one. You do this by clicking the Promote (Indent less) button until the insertion point is at outline level one. A slide icon displays when you reach outline level one. Perform the following steps to add a slide in Outline view.

To Add a Slide in Outline View

1 **Point to the Promote (Indent less) button on the Outlining toolbar.**

The insertion point is still positioned at outline level two (Figure 2-9).

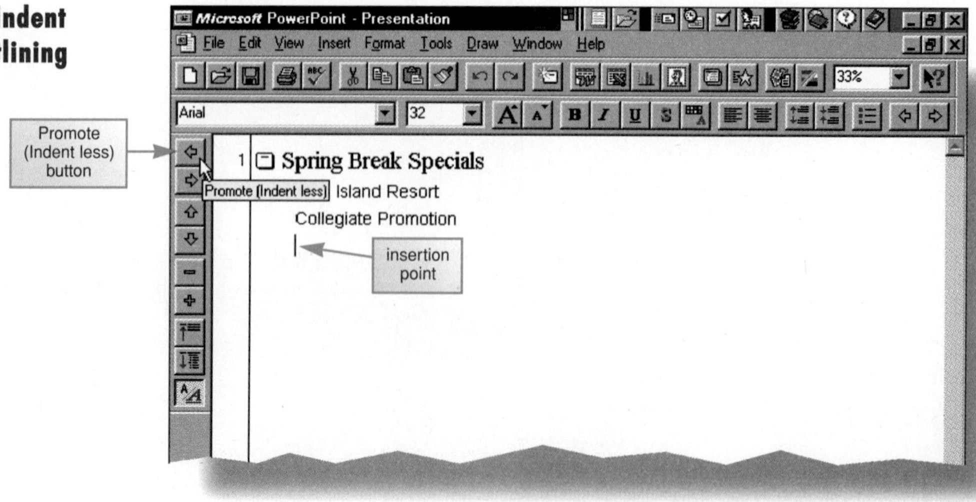

FIGURE 2-9

2 **Click the Promote (Indent less) button.**

The Slide 2 slide icon displays indicating a new slide is added to the presentation (Figure 2-10). The insertion point is in position to type the title for Slide 2 at outline level one.

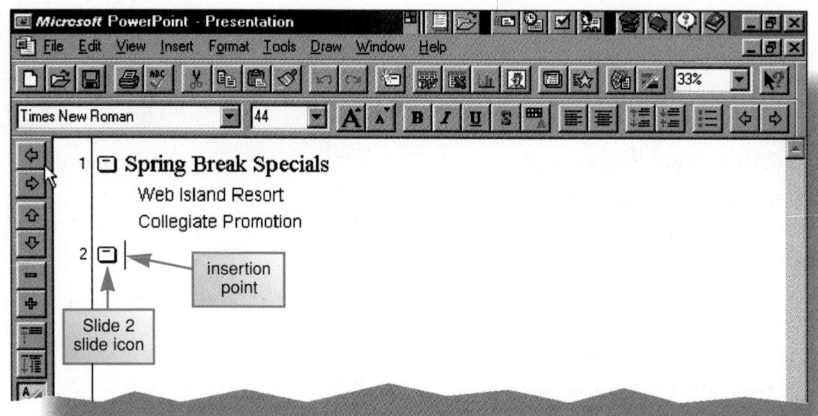

FIGURE 2-10

OtherWays

1. On Standard toolbar click Insert New Slide button
2. On status bar click New Slide button
3. Press CTRL+M

After you add a slide, you are ready to type the slide text. The next section explains how to create a multi-level bulleted list slide in Outline view.

Creating Multi-level Bulleted List Slides in Outline View

To create a multi-level bulleted list slide, you demote or promote the insertion point to the appropriate outline level and then type the paragraph text. Recall from Project 1, when you demote a paragraph, PowerPoint adds a bullet to the left of each outline level. Each outline level has a different bullet font. Also recall that the Design Template determines font attributes, including the bullet font.

Slide 2 is the first informational slide for Project 2. Slide 2 introduces the main topic — two new spring break vacation packages offered by Web Island Resort. Each vacation package displays as outline level two, and each supportive paragraph displays as outline level three. The following steps explain how to create a multi-level bulleted list slide in Outline view.

Steps To Create a Multi-level Slide in Outline View

1 **Type** `Two Super Deals` **and press the ENTER key. Then click the Demote (Indent more) button to demote to outline level two.**

The title for Slide 2, Two Super Deals, displays and the insertion point is in position to type the first bulleted paragraph (Figure 2-11). A triangle shaped bullet displays to the left of the insertion point.

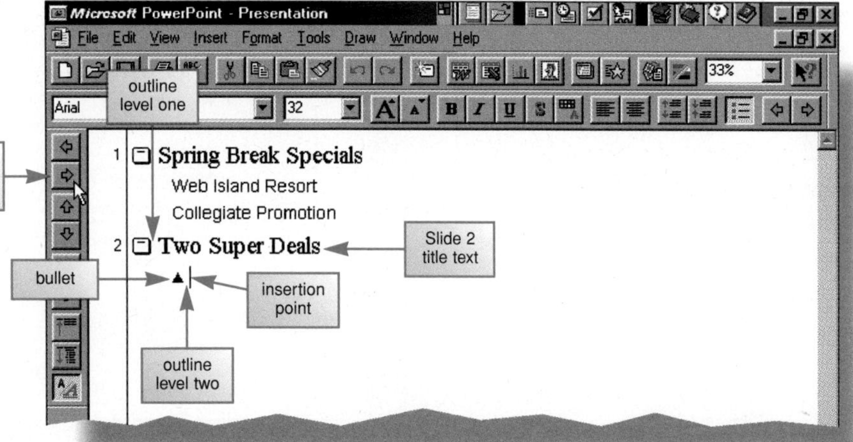

FIGURE 2-11

2 **Type** `The Voyager` **and press the ENTER key. Then click the Demote (Indent more) button to demote to outline level three.**

Slide 2 displays three outline levels: the title, Two Super Deals, on outline level one, the bulleted paragraph, The Voyager, on outline level two, and the insertion point on outline level three (Figure 2-12). The bullet for outline level two is a triangle. The bullet for outline level three is a dash.

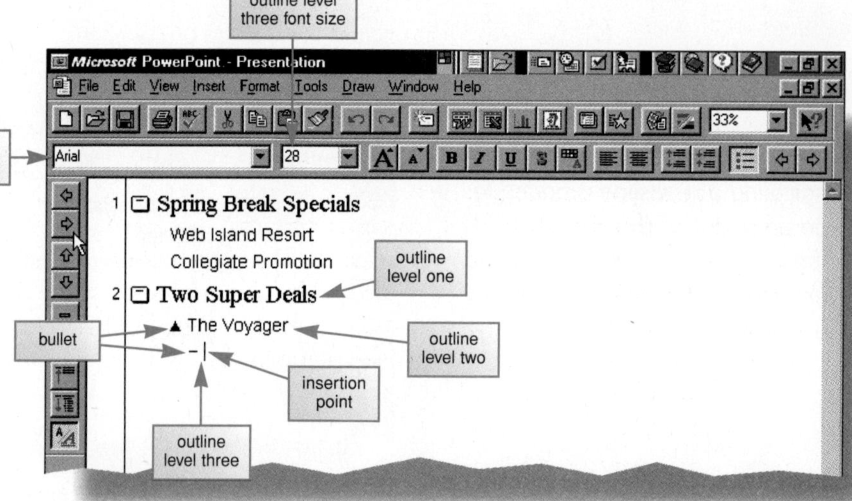

FIGURE 2-12

3 **Type** `All inclusive sand and sea adventure` **and press the ENTER key. Then click the Promote (Indent less) button.**

Pressing the ENTER key begins a new paragraph at the same outline level as the previous paragraph. Clicking the Promote (Indent less) button moves the insertion point left and elevates the paragraph from outline level three to outline level two (Figure 2-13).

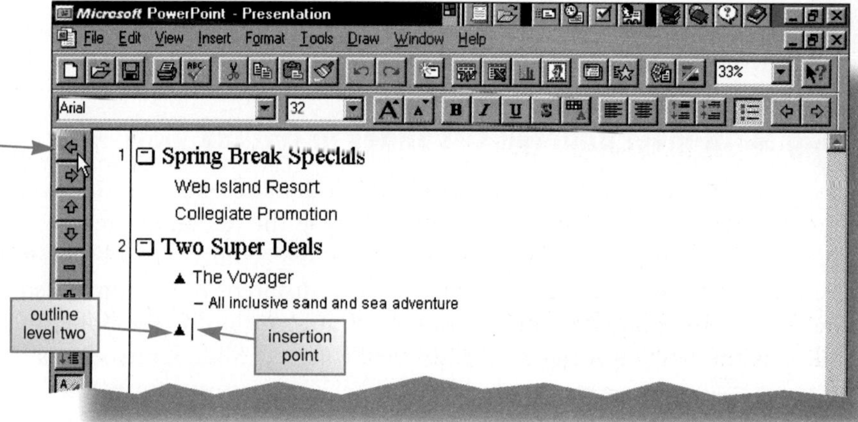

FIGURE 2-13

4 **Type** `The Wanderer` **and press the ENTER key. Click the Demote (Indent more) button. Type** `Self-designed sand and sun experience` **and press the ENTER key (Figure 2-14).**

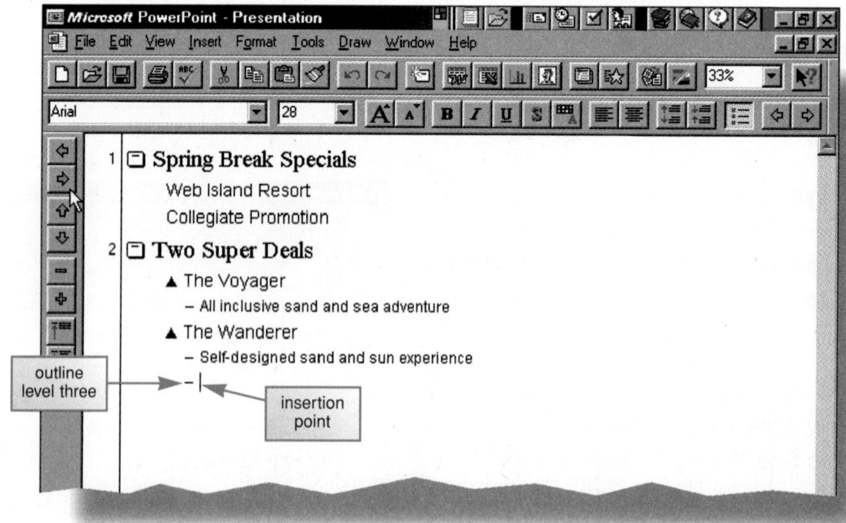

FIGURE 2-14

Other Ways

1. Press TAB to Demote
2. Press ALT+SHIFT+RIGHT ARROW to Demote

Other Ways

1. Press SHIFT+TAB to Promote
2. Press ALT+SHIFT+LEFT ARROW to Promote

Creating a Subordinate Slide

When developing your presentation, begin with a main topic and follow with subsequent slides to support the main topic. Placing all your information on one slide may overwhelm your audience. Decompose your presentation, therefore, into several slides with three to six bullets per slide or per object. The following steps explain how to create a subordinate slide that further explains the spring break package, The Voyager, introduced on Slide 2. This new slide, Slide 3, provides additional information that supports the first outline level two on Slide 2. Later in this project, you will create another subordinate slide to support the second outline level two on Slide 2, The Wanderer.

TO CREATE A SUBORDINATE SLIDE

Step 1: Click the Promote (Indent less) button two times so that Slide 3 is added to the end of the presentation.
Step 2: Type `The Voyager` and press the ENTER key.
Step 3: Click the Demote (Indent more) button to demote to outline level two.
Step 4: Type `One unbelievable low price includes:` and press the ENTER key.
Step 5: Click the Demote (Indent more) button to demote to outline level three.
Step 6: Type `Round-trip airfare` and press the ENTER key.
Step 7: Type `Four day cruise & three day beach party` and press the ENTER key.
Step 8: Type `Unlimited food & beverage` and press the ENTER key.
Step 9: Type `Fabulous entertainment` and press the ENTER key.

The screen displays as shown in Figure 2-15.

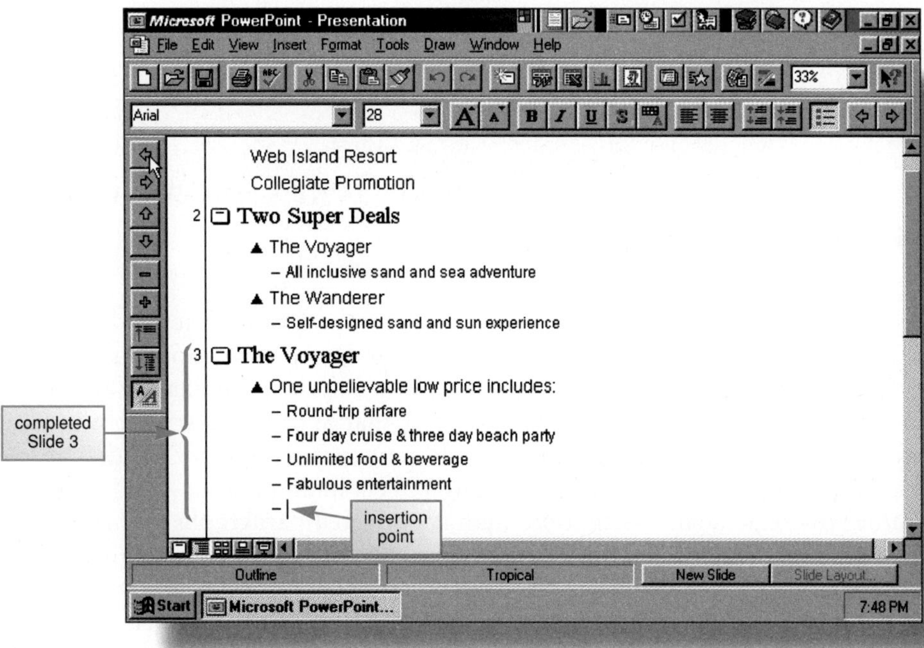

FIGURE 2-15

Creating a Second Subordinate Slide

The next step is to create the slide that supports The Wanderer, which is the second outline level two on Slide 2. Perform the following steps to create this subordinate slide.

TO CREATE A SECOND SUBORDINATE SLIDE

Step 1: Click the Promote (Indent less) button two times so that Slide 4 is added to the end of the presentation. Type `The Wanderer` and press the ENTER key.

Step 2: Click the Demote (Indent more) button to demote to outline level two. Type `Create your dream vacation` and press the ENTER key.

Step 3: Click the Demote (Indent more) button to demote to outline level three. Type `Luxurious beach-front accommodations` and press the ENTER key.

Step 4: Click the Demote (Indent more) button to demote to outline level four. Type `Hotels` and press the ENTER key. Type `Condominiums` and press the ENTER key.

Step 5: Click the Promote (Indent less) button to promote to outline level three. Type `Diverse dining opportunities` and press the ENTER key. Type `Recreation bonanza` and press the ENTER key.

The screen displays as shown in Figure 2-16.

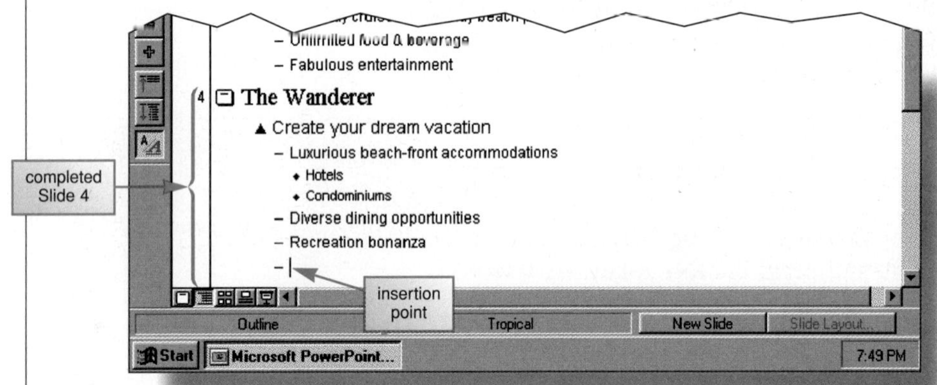

FIGURE 2-16

Creating a Slide with Multiple Text Objects in Outline View

All of the slides you have created to this point consist of a title object and one text object. Occasionally, you need to provide the audience with a long list of items. If you use the Bulleted List slide layout, Style Checker will identify the slide as having too many bullets. Recall from Project 1 that Style Checker checks a presentation for spelling, visual clarity, and end punctuation. One of the design standards Style Checker looks for is too many bullets in an object.

In order to create a slide with more than six bulleted paragraphs and still comply with design standards, break the list into two or more objects. When you divide the text into multiple objects, each object complies with PowerPoint's default settings for visual clarity in Style Checker, as long as the number of bullets per object is less than or equal to six. Six is the default setting for the number of bullets per object.

Because you are creating the presentation in Outline view, type the text for this slide as a bulleted list. Later in this project, you convert the bulleted list slide into a multiple object slide by changing views, changing slide layout, and moving some of the text from the bulleted list to another object. Perform the steps below to create a slide with multiple text objects in Outline view.

TO CREATE A SLIDE WITH MULTIPLE TEXT OBJECTS IN OUTLINE VIEW

Step 1: Click the Promote (Indent less) button two times so that Slide 5 is added to the end of the presentation. Type `Both Deals Feature` as the slide title and press the ENTER key.

Step 2: Click the Demote (Indent more) button to demote to outline level two. Type `Tropical climate` and press the ENTER key. Type `White sand beaches` and press the ENTER key. Type `Balmy breezes` and press the ENTER key. Type `Pristine pools` and press the ENTER key. Type `Sunny days` and press the ENTER key. Type `Starlight nights` and press the ENTER key. Type `Browser Beach` and press the ENTER key.

Step 3: Click the Demote (Indent more) button to demote to outline level three. Type `Sunbathe, volleyball` and press the ENTER key.

Step 4: Click the Promote (Indent less) button to promote to outline level two. Type `Net Bay` and press the ENTER key.

Step 5: Click the Demote (Indent more) button to demote to outline level three. Type `Sail, swim, snorkel` and press the ENTER key

Step 6: Click the Promote (Indent less) button to promote to outline level two. Type `Net Coral Reef` and press the ENTER key.

Step 7: Click the Demote (Indent more) button to demote to outline level three. Type `Scuba dive` and press the ENTER key.

The screen displays as shown in Figure 2-17.

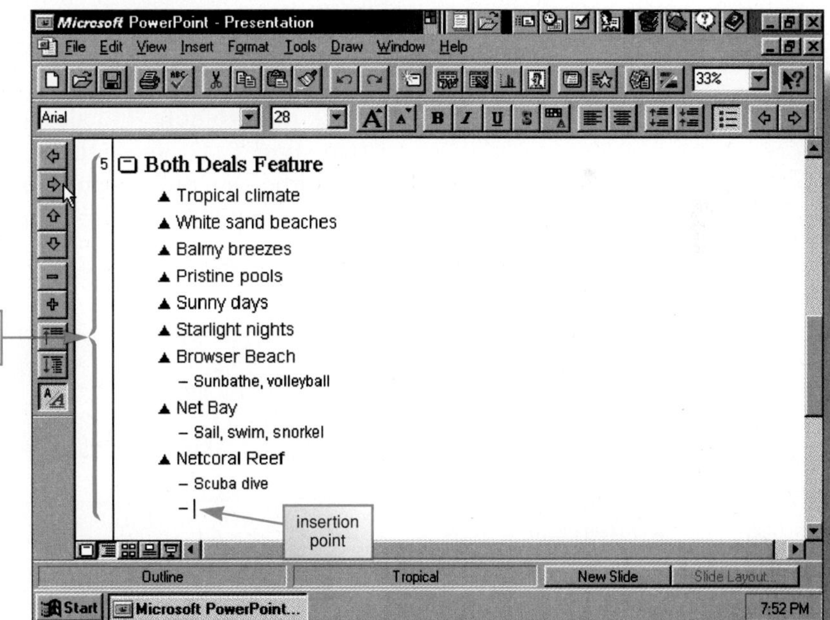

FIGURE 2-17

Creating a Closing Slide in Outline View

The last slide in your presentation is the **closing slide**. A closing slide gracefully ends a presentation. Often used during a question and answer session, the closing slide usually remains on the screen to reinforce the message delivered during the presentation. Professional speakers design the closing slide with one or more of the methods on the next page.

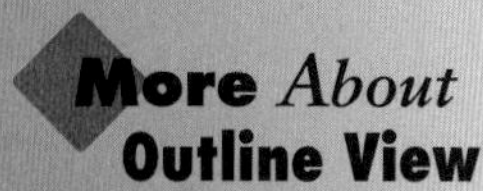

When working in Outline view, many people prefer to use keyboard keys instead of toolbar buttons. This way their hands never leave the keyboard and their typing is finished more quickly. For example, instead of clicking the Demote button to demote text, press the TAB key.

1. List important information. Tell the audience what to do next.
2. Provide a memorable illustration or example to make a point.
3. Appeal to emotions. Remind the audience to take action or accept responsibility.
4. Summarize the main points of the presentation.
5. Cite a quotation that directly relates to the main points of the presentation. This is most effective if the presentation started with a quotation.

The closing slide in this project combines listing important information and providing an illustration. Because Web Island Resort wants students to buy one of the tropical island vacations, they combine telling students what to do next with providing a list of telephone numbers on the Tropical Design Template. In this presentation, the design template serves as a recurrent illustration. Perform the following steps to create this closing slide.

TO CREATE A CLOSING SLIDE IN OUTLINE VIEW

Step 1: Click the Promote (Indent less) button two times so that Slide 6 is added to the end of the presentation. Type `For Fun in the Sun` as the slide title and press the ENTER key.
Step 2: Click the Demote (Indent more) button to demote to outline level two. Type `Contact Student Activities Office` and press the ENTER key.
Step 3: Click the Demote (Indent more) button to demote to outline level three. Type `Ford Hall, Room 313` and press the ENTER key. Type `Ext. 2882` and press the ENTER key.
Step 4: Click the Promote (Indent less) button to promote to outline level two. Type `Call Web Island Resort` and press the ENTER key.
Step 5: Click the Demote (Indent more) button to demote to outline level three. Type `800-555-Web1` but do not press the ENTER key.

Slide 6 displays as shown in Figure 2-18.

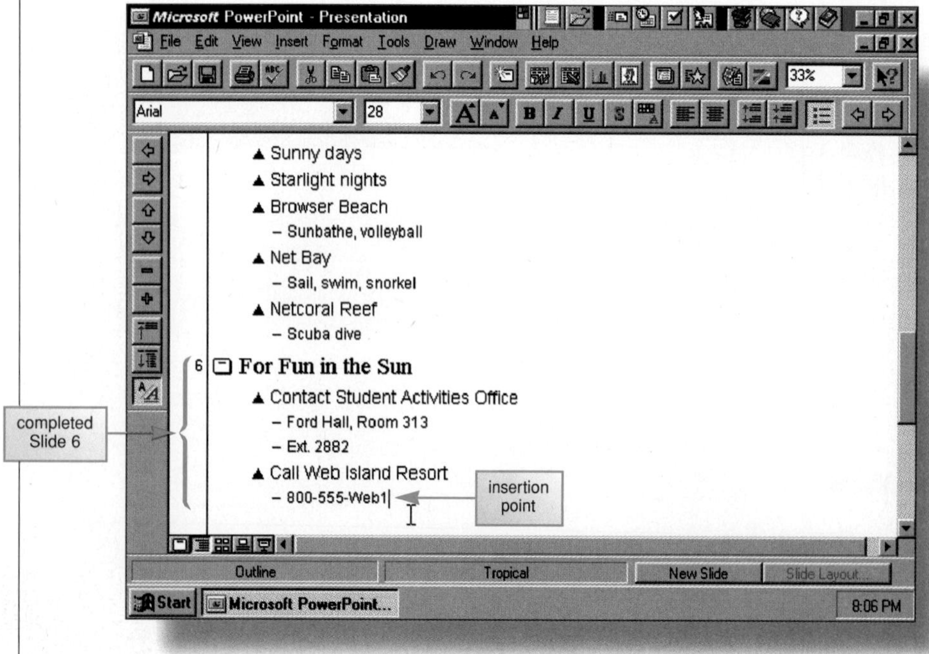

FIGURE 2-18

The outline is now complete and the presentation should be saved. The next section explains how to save the presentation.

Saving the Presentation

Recall from Project 1 that it is wise to frequently save your presentation on disk. Because you have created all the text for your presentation, you should save your presentation now. For a detailed explanation of the steps summarized on the next page, refer to pages PP 1.22 through PP 1.24 in Project 1.

TO SAVE A PRESENTATION

Step 1: Insert a formatted floppy disk in drive A. Then click the Save button on the Standard toolbar.
Step 2: Type `Spring Break Specials` in the File Name box. Do not press the ENTER key.
Step 3: Click the Save in down arrow. Click 3½ Floppy [A:] in the Save in drop-down list.
Step 4: Click the Save button.

The presentation is saved to drive A under the name Spring Break Specials.

Reviewing a Presentation in Slide Sorter View

When you create a presentation in Outline view, only the text is visible. You cannot see how the text looks on the slide nor how the design template affects the text objects. You must, therefore, see how the text looks on the slides to evaluate necessary changes. Changing to Slide Sorter view allows you to display your presentation slides in miniature so that you can quickly review the slides for content, organization, and overall appearance.

In Project 1, you displayed slides in Slide Show view to look at individual slides. Slide Show view limits you to looking at one slide at a time. Slide Sorter view, however, allows you to look at several slides at one time, which is helpful when you review your presentation for slide order. You will learn how to change slide order in Slide Sorter view later in this project. Perform the following steps to change from Outline view to Slide Sorter view.

Steps To Change the View to Slide Sorter View

1 **Point to the Slide Sorter View button on the View Button bar at the bottom of the PowerPoint window (Figure 2-19).**

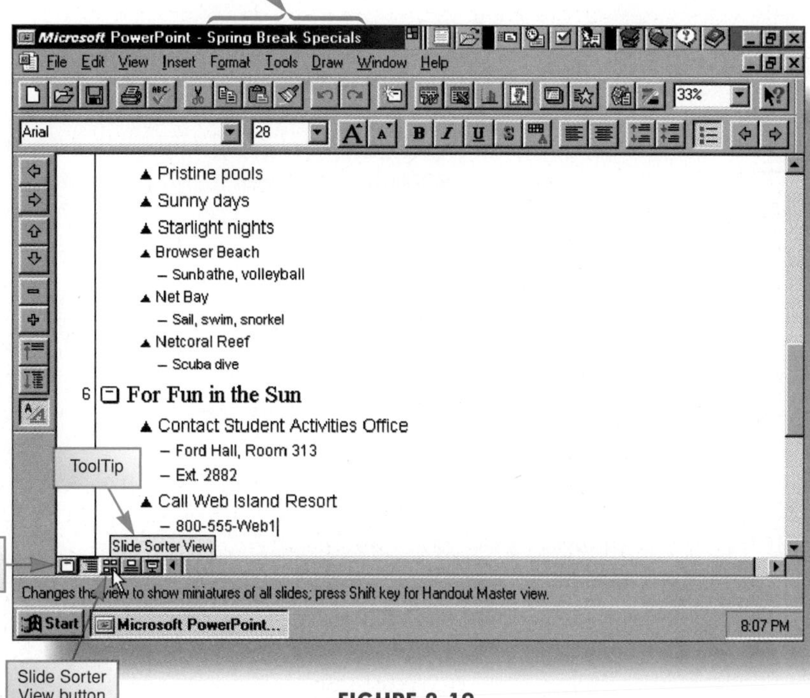

FIGURE 2-19

2 Click the Slide Sorter View button.

PowerPoint displays the presentation in Slide Sorter view (Figure 2-20). Slide 6 is selected because it was the current slide in Outline view.

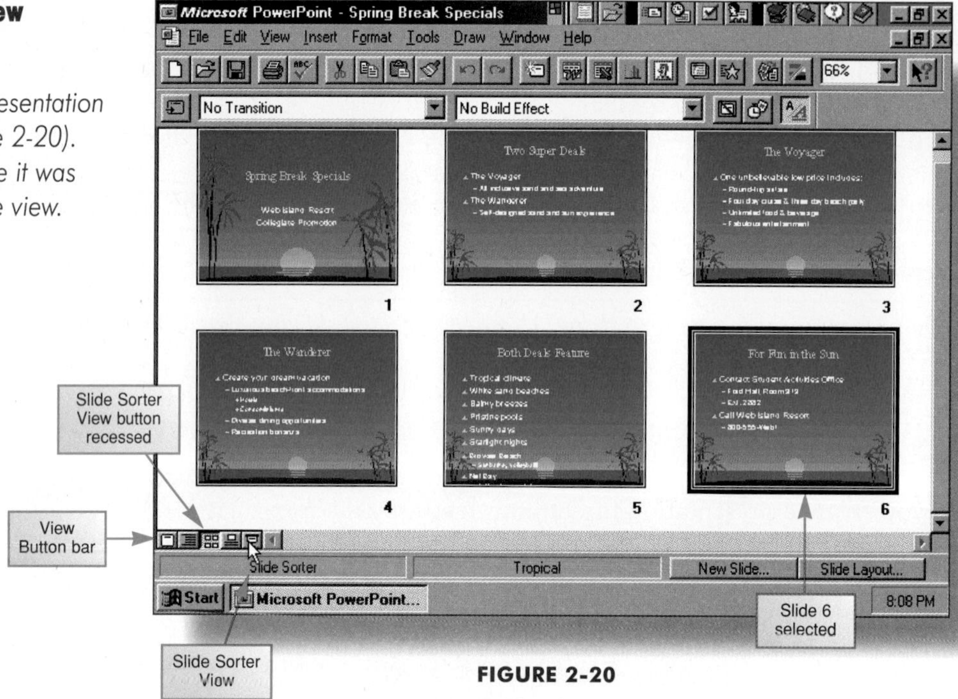

FIGURE 2-20

OtherWays

1. On menu bar click View, click Slide Sorter
2. Press ALT+V, press D

Because there are only six slides in this presentation and Zoom Control is 66%, you can review all slides at this time. Notice that Slide 2, Slide 3, and Slide 6 appear to need changes in line spacing. Slide 5 has text running off the bottom of the slide. Additionally, the presentation lacks pizzazz. To make the presentation more exciting, you may wish to add clip art. The next several sections explain how to improve the presentation by adding a blank line, changing slide layouts, and adding clip art.

Adding a Blank Line

The first improvement to this presentation is adding a blank line to Slide 2. In order to increase white space between paragraphs, add a blank line after the outline level three paragraph, All inclusive sand and sea adventure. Recall that a paragraph begins when you press the ENTER key and ends when you again press the ENTER key. Also recall that in a bulleted list, PowerPoint adds a bullet in front of each new paragraph. Thus, to create a blank line, you must also remove the bullet.

You can change text in both Slide view and Outline view. Recall that if you return to Outline view to add the blank line, you cannot see how the Design Template affects the text object. It is best, therefore, to change the view to Slide view so that you can see the result of editing the text object. Perform the following steps to change the view to Slide view.

To Change the View to Slide View

1 **Point to the slide miniature of Slide 2 (Figure 2-21)**

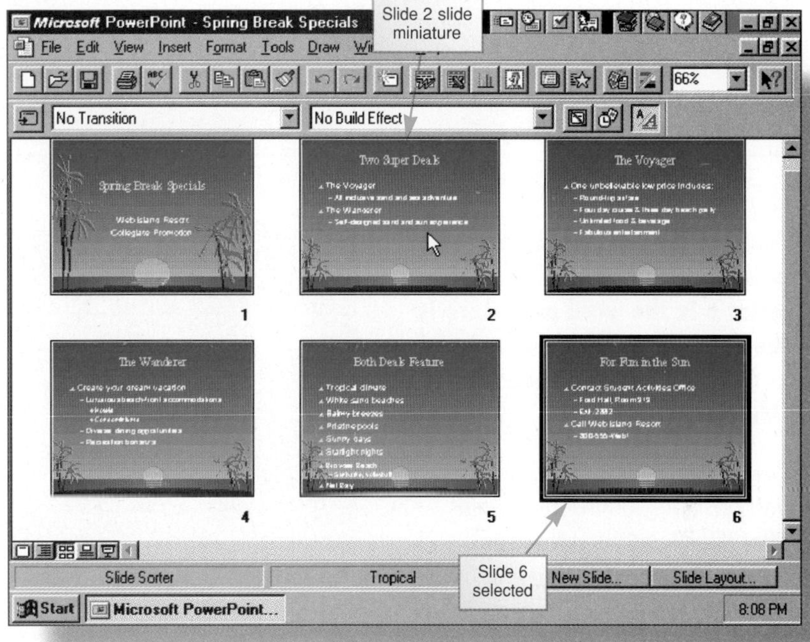

FIGURE 2-21

2 **Double-click the Slide 2 slide miniature.**

Slide 2 displays in Slide view (Figure 2-22). The Slide View button is recessed on the View Button bar.

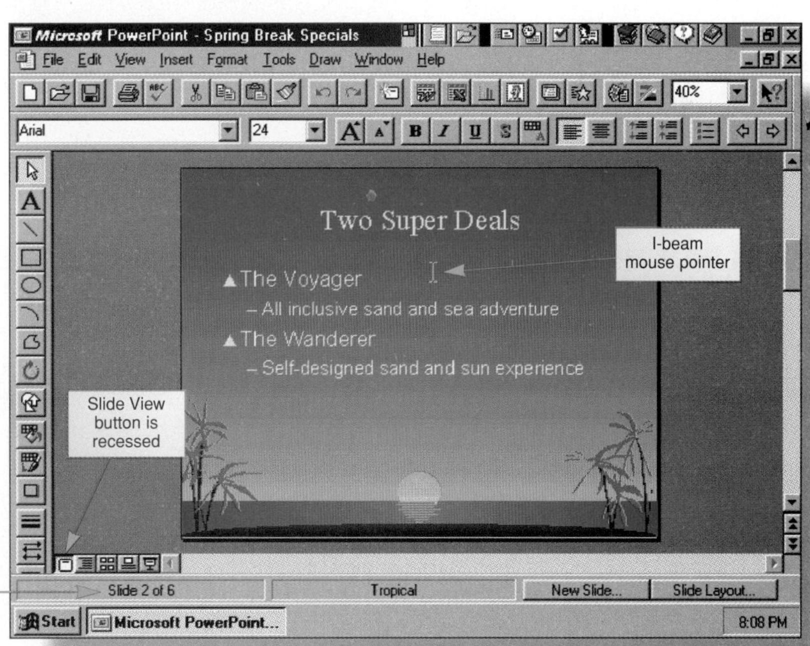

FIGURE 2-22

The next section explains how to add a blank line to Slide 2.

Other Ways

1. On View Button bar click Slide View button
2. On menu bar click View, click Slides
3. Press ALT+V, press S

Adding a Blank Line to Slide 2

Now that Slide 2 displays in Slide view, you are ready to add a blank line after the paragraph, All inclusive sand and sea adventure. Perform the following steps to add a blank line.

Steps To Add a Blank Line

1. **Position the I-beam mouse pointer to the right of the second letter e in the word adventure in the paragraph All inclusive sand and sea adventure. Then click the left mouse button.**

PowerPoint selects the text object and positions the insertion point after the second e in the word, adventure (Figure 2-23). The mouse pointer displays as an I-beam when located in a text object.

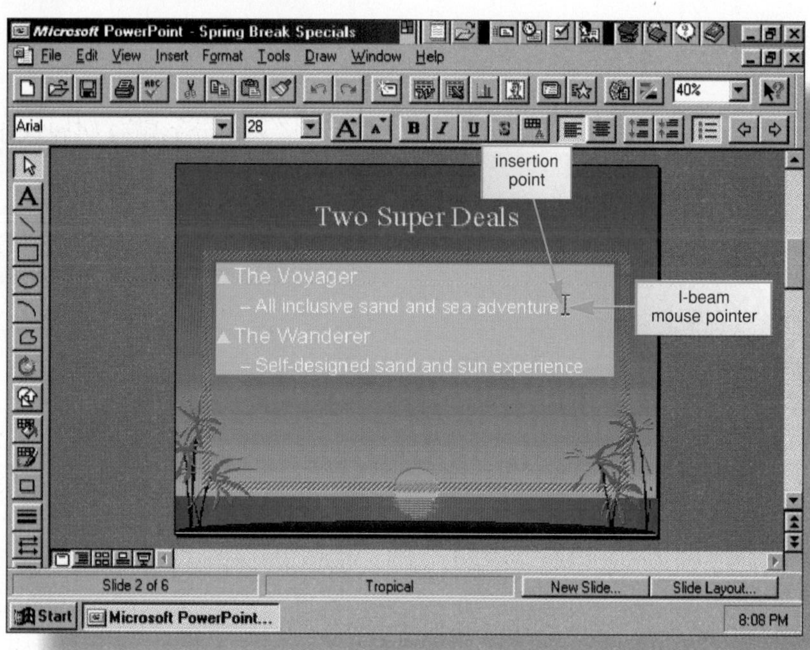

FIGURE 2-23

2. **Press the ENTER key.**

PowerPoint inserts a new paragraph (Figure 2-24). The new paragraph has the same attributes as the previous paragraph. The Bullet On/Off button is recessed on the Formatting toolbar.

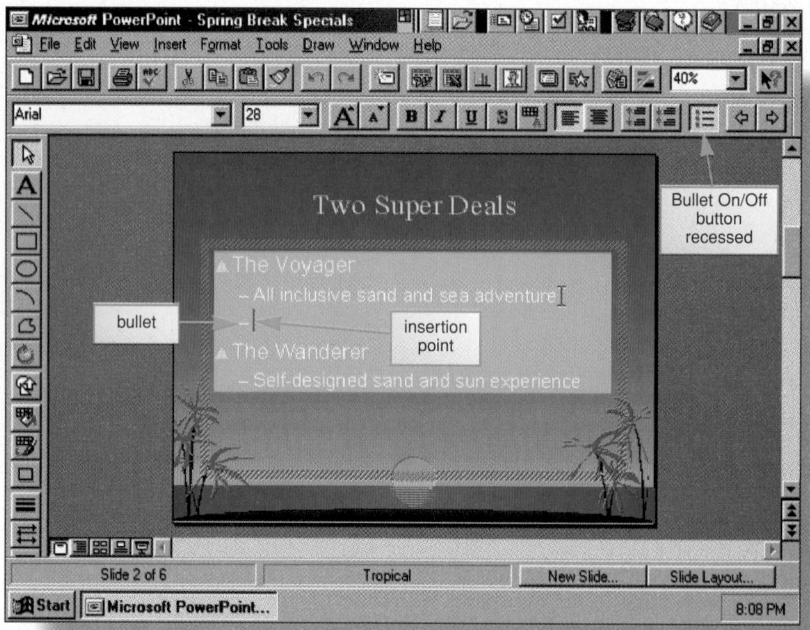

FIGURE 2-24

3 Click the Bullet On/Off button to remove the bullet.

The line displays blank because the bullet does not display (Figure 2-25). The Bullet On/Off button is not recessed.

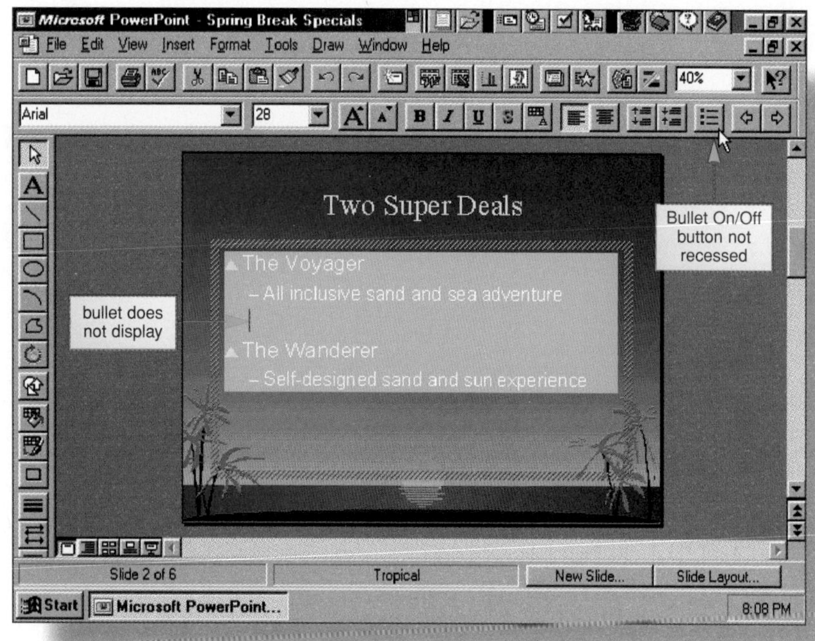

FIGURE 2-25

OtherWays

1. Press and hold down SHIFT, then press ENTER

To display a bullet on a selected paragraph, click the Bullet On/Off button on the Formatting toolbar.

Changing Slide Layout

Recall from Project 1 that when you add a new slide, PowerPoint displays the New Slide dialog box from which you choose one of the slide AutoLayouts. After creating a slide, you can change its layout by clicking the **Slide Layout button** on the status bar. The Slide Layout dialog box then displays. Like the AutoLayout dialog box, the Slide Layout dialog box allows you to choose one of the twenty-four different slide layouts.

When you change the layout of a slide, PowerPoint retains the text and graphics and repositions them into the appropriate placeholders. Using slide layouts eliminates the need to resize objects because PowerPoint automatically sizes the object to fit the placeholder.

To keep your presentation interesting, PowerPoint includes several slide layouts to combine text with nontext objects, such as clip art. The placement of the text, in relationship to the nontext object, depends on the slide layout. The nontext object placeholder may be to the right or left of the text, above the text, or below the text. Additionally, some slide layouts are constructed with two nontext object placeholders. Refer to Project 1 for a list of the available slide layouts (Figure 1-25 on PP 1.24). The instructions on the next page explain how to change the slide layout from a bulleted list to two columns of text.

More About Slide Layout

Vary your slide layouts to keep a presentation from becoming monotonous. Choose layouts designed for one text object, multiple text objects, graphs, tables, and clip art. While varying slide layouts increases audience attention, be careful to maintain a common theme throughout the presentation by using a Design Template or color scheme.

To Change Slide Layout

1 **Drag the elevator to display Slide 5 (Figure 2-26).**

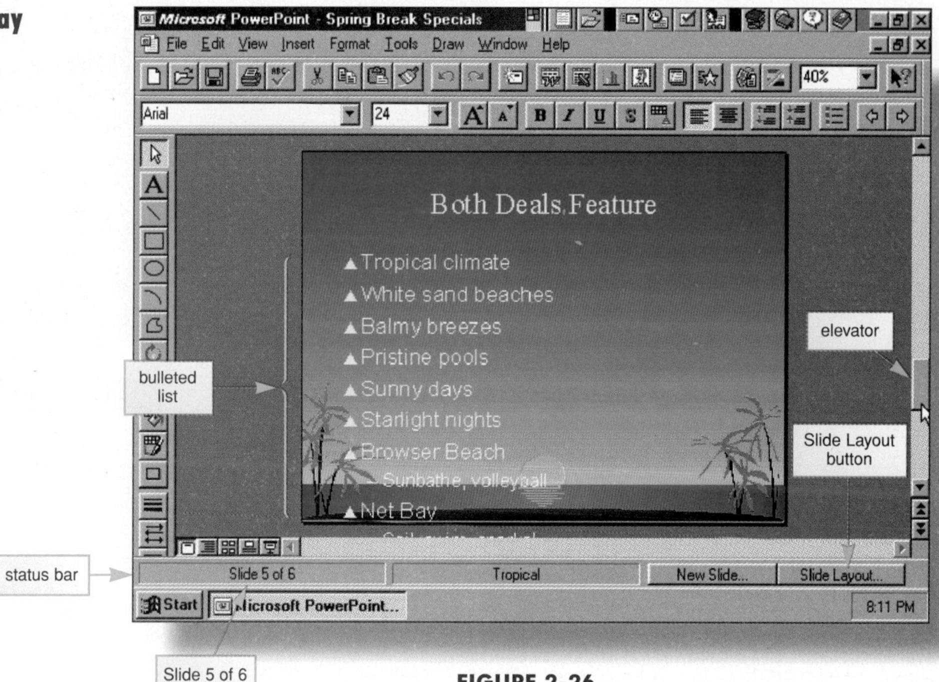

FIGURE 2-26

2 **Click the Slide Layout button on the status bar. When the Slide Layout dialog box displays, click the 2 Column Text slide layout located in the row one, column three.**

The Slide Layout dialog box displays (Figure 2-27). The 2 Column Text slide layout is selected. When you click a slide layout, its name displays in the box at the lower right of the Slide Layout dialog box.

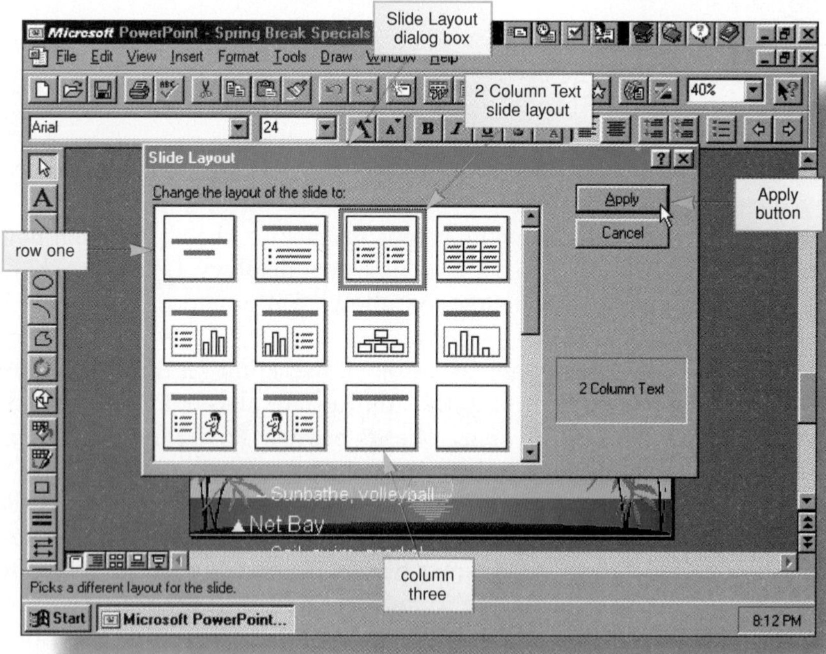

FIGURE 2-27

3 **Click the Apply button.**

Slide 5 displays the bulleted list in the left column text object (Figure 2-28). The right column text placeholder displays the message, Click to add text.

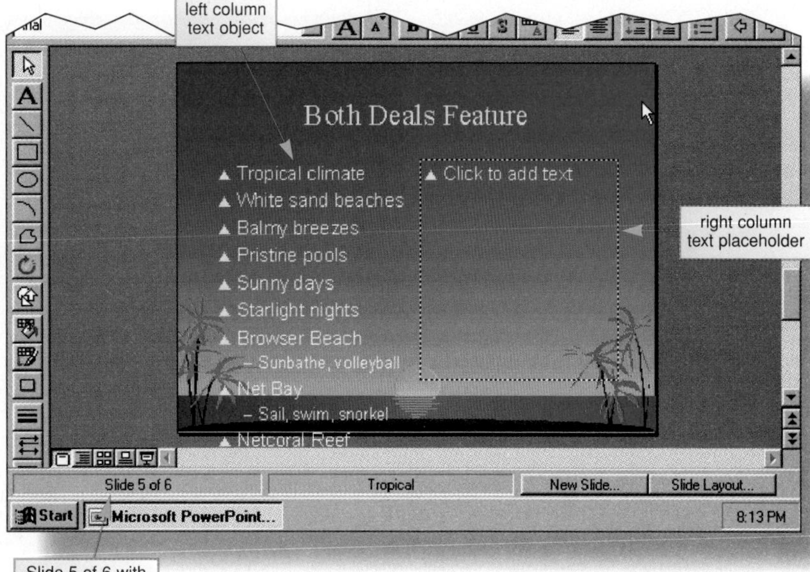

FIGURE 2-28

***Other*Ways**

1. Right-click slide anywhere except an object or object placeholder, click Slide Layout
2. On menu bar click Format, click Slide Layout
3. Press ALT+O, press L

The text in the left column of Slide 5 is too lengthy to fit into the text object. The next section explains how to move the text at the bottom of the left column to the top of the right column text placeholder.

Moving Text

Because the bulleted list on Slide 5 contains more paragraphs than will fit in the left column text object, select a portion of the list and move it to the right column text placeholder. Perform the following steps to select a portion of the text in the left column and then move it to the right column.

To Move Text

1 **Position the I-beam mouse pointer immediately to the left of the B in Browser. Drag to the right and down so that the last six bulleted paragraphs are selected.**

The six bulleted paragraphs, Browser Beach, Sunbathe, volleyball; Net Bay, Sail, swim, snorkel; Netcoral Reef, and Scuba dive, are selected (Figure 2-29).

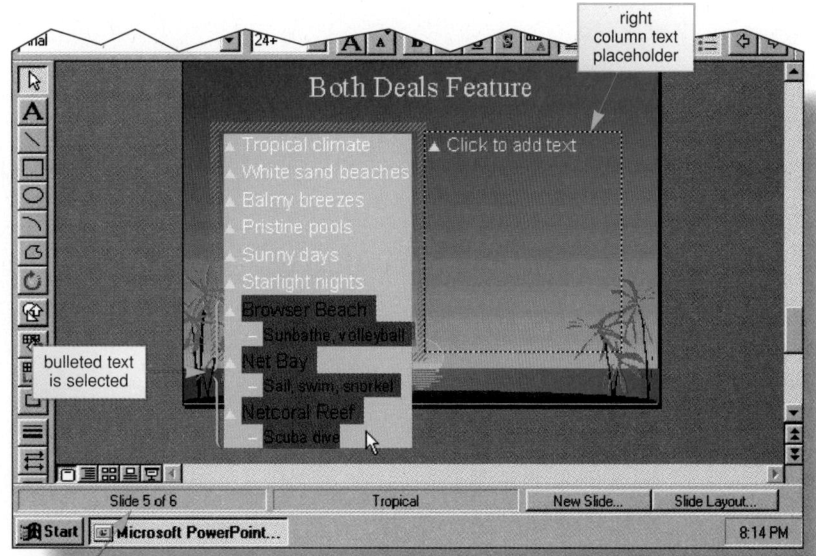

FIGURE 2-29

2 **Point to the selected text. If the mouse pointer displays as a four-headed arrow, move the mouse pointer to the right of the bullets so that it is positioned over the text. Then drag the selected text to the right column text placeholder.**

As you drag the text, the mouse pointer displays as a block arrow with a small dotted box around the arrow shaft. The six selected paragraphs are moved to the right column text placeholder (Figure 2-30). When you insert text into a text placeholder, it becomes a text object.

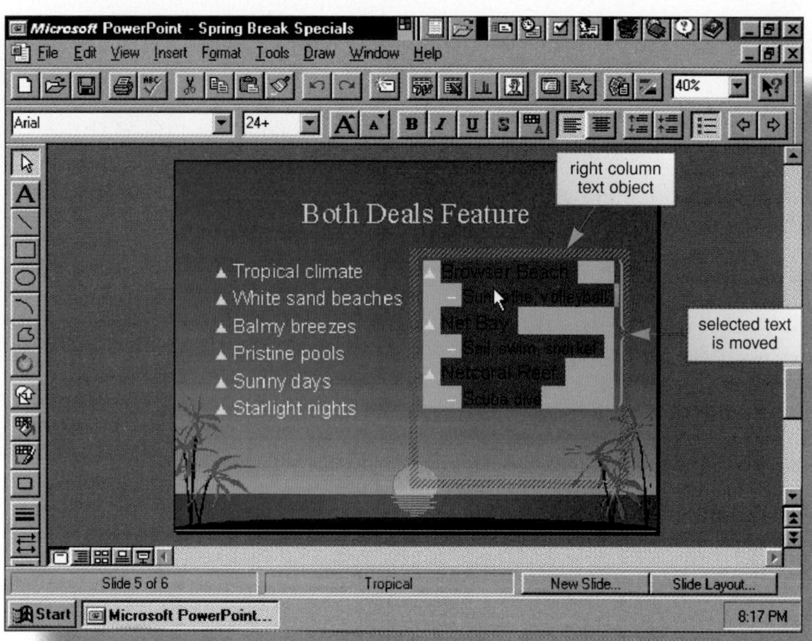

FIGURE 2-30

OtherWays

1. Right-click selected text, click Cut, position mouse pointer at new text location, right-click, click Paste
2. On menu bar click Edit, click Cut, position insertion point at new text location, on menu bar click Edit, click Paste

Recall from Project 1 that you must select an object before you can modify it.

Adding Clip Art to a Slide

Clip art offers a quick way to add professional-looking graphic images to your presentation without creating the images yourself. **Microsoft ClipArt Gallery 2.0** contains a wide variety of graphic images and is shared with other Microsoft Office applications. Microsoft ClipArt Gallery 2.0 combines topic-related clip art images into categories. Insert clip art to your presentation by selecting a clip art image from Microsoft ClipArt Gallery 2.0.

Table 2-2 gives you an idea of the organization of Microsoft ClipArt Gallery 2.0 that accompanies PowerPoint. The table contains four of the categories from Microsoft ClipArt Gallery 2.0 and a description of the clip art contained therein. Clip art image descriptions are nouns and verbs that associate an image with various entities, activities, labels, and emotions. In most instances, the description does not contain the name of the physical object. For example, an image of a magnifying glass in the Academic category

Table 2-2

CATEGORY	DESCRIPTION
Academic	Seven images: Professor Leadership Information text Communication, Meeting Communication Information, Figures Discord, Information, Focus Identify Small, Focus Investigate Identify Small, and Reward Accomplishment.
Cartoons	Ninety-three cartoon and stick people images; e.g., Reward, Worried, Problem Priority, Happy Joy Laugh, Target, Surprise, Idea Brainstorm, Planning Busy Human, Travel Human, and Fast Human.
Household	Eight images: Security Unlock, Security Unlock Solution, Cutback Scissors, Solution Band-Aid, Timeline Schedule Clock, Patience Timeline, Security Unlock Lock and Keys, and Direction.
Transportation	Seven images: Performance Fast Sports Car, Performance Ship, War Battle Powerful Battleship, Performance Fast Plane, Performance Fast War Battle Plane, Performance Fast Plane, and Priority Traffic Light.

has a description of Focus Investigate Identify Small. As a result, you may find it necessary to scroll through several categories to find an appropriate picture.

In this project you use clip art images from the Popular.pcs clip art file. Contact your instructor if you are missing clip art when you perform the following steps. A full installation of PowerPoint is required before all clip art images are available.

Using AutoLayouts to Add Clip Art

PowerPoint simplifies adding clip art to a slide by providing numerous AutoLayouts designed specifically for clip art. Recall from Project 1 that an AutoLayout is a collection of placeholders for the title, text, clip art, graphs, tables, and media clips. When you use an AutoLayout placeholder, PowerPoint automatically sizes clip art to fit the placeholder. If the clip art is in landscape orientation, PowerPoint sizes it to the width of the placeholder. If the clip art is in portrait orientation, PowerPoint sizes it to the height of the placeholder.

Adding clip art to Slide 6 requires two steps. First, you change the slide layout to Clip Art & Text. Then you insert clip art into the clip art placeholder. The next two sections explain how to add clip art into an AutoLayout placeholder.

More *About* **Clip Art**

Humor and interest are just two of several reasons to add clip art to your presentation. People have limited attention spans. A carefully placed humorous clip art image can spark attention and interest. When interest is high, it greatly increases the chance that your concept or idea will be remembered.

Changing Slide Layout to Clip Art & Text

Before you insert clip art into an AutoLayout placeholder, you must first select one of the slide layouts that includes a clip art placeholder. The clip art placeholder on the left side of Slide 6 will hold clip art. Perform the following steps to change the slide layout to Clip Art & Text.

Steps To Change the Slide Layout to Clip Art & Text

1 **Drag the elevator to display Slide 6 (Figure 2-31).**

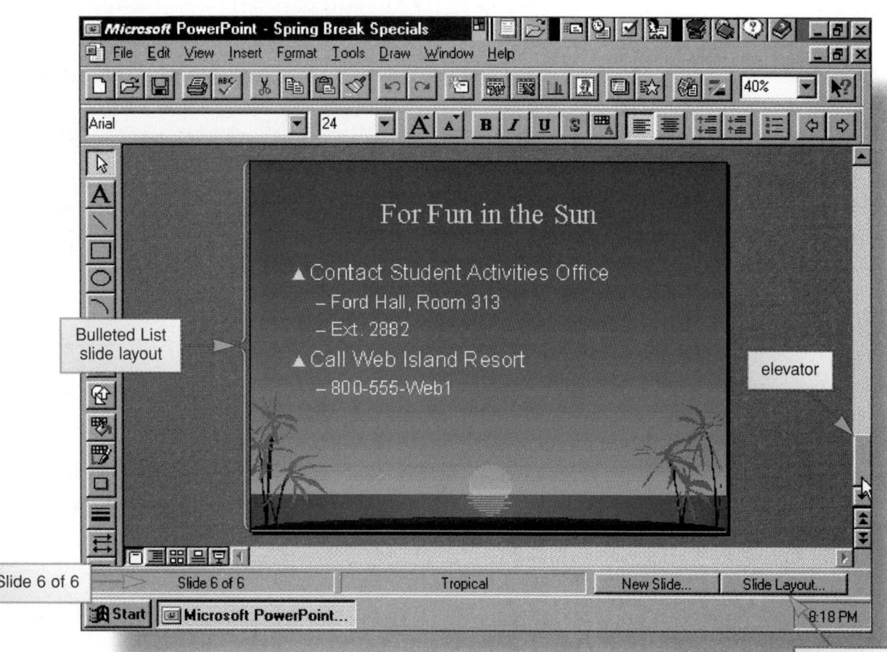

FIGURE 2-31

2 **Click the Slide Layout button. When the Slide Layout dialog box displays, click the Clip Art & Text slide layout located in row three, column two. Then point to the Apply button.**

The Clip Art & Text slide layout is selected in the Slide Layout dialog box (Figure 2-32).

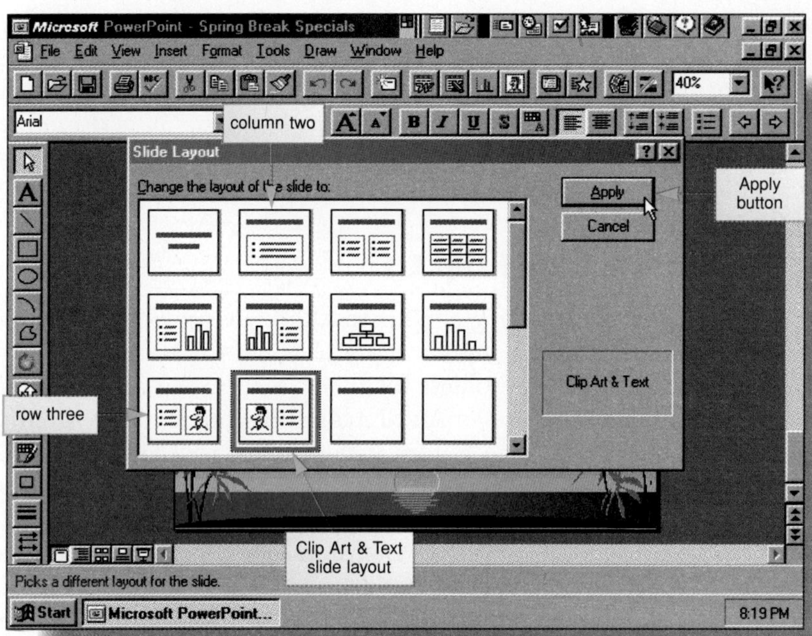

FIGURE 2-32

3 **Click the Apply button.**

Slide 6 displays the Clip Art & Text slide layout (Figure 2-33). PowerPoint moves the text object and automatically resizes the text to fit the object.

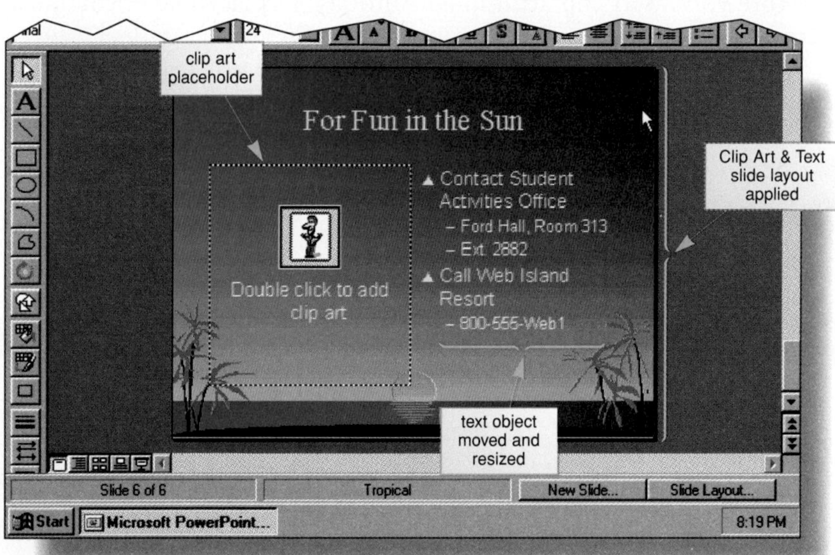

FIGURE 2-33

***Other*Ways**

1. Right-click anywhere on slide except placeholders, click Slide Layout
2. On menu bar click Format, click Slide Layout
3. Press ALT+O, press L

You can use an AutoLayout placeholder to insert clip art even if the AutoLayout doesn't have a clip art placeholder. For example, to insert clip art into the object placeholder of the Object AutoLayout, click the placeholder to select it, click the Insert Clip Art button, and then select a clip art picture.

Inserting Clip Art into a Clip Art Placeholder

Now that the Clip Art & Text placeholder is applied to Slide 6, you must insert clip art into the clip art placeholder. Perform the following steps to insert clip art to the clip art placeholder on Slide 6.

Steps To Insert Clip Art into a Clip Art Placeholder

1 **Position the mouse pointer anywhere within the clip art placeholder.**

The mouse pointer is positioned inside the clip art placeholder (Figure 2-34). It is not necessary to point to the picture inside the placeholder.

FIGURE 2-34

2 **Double-click the clip art placeholder on the left side of Slide 6.**

PowerPoint displays the Microsoft ClipArt Gallery 2.0 dialog box (Figure 2-35). When you open Microsoft ClipArt Gallery 2.0, All Categories is the selected category in the Categories box. The Pictures box displays clip art images by category. The selected image is a bear. Your selected image may be different depending on the clip art installed on your computer. If this is the first time you access clip art after an installation, the Microsoft ClipArt Gallery dialog box displays a message asking if you want to add clip art from PowerPoint now. Click the Yes or Add button. PowerPoint then displays the Microsoft ClipArt Gallery 2.0 dialog box.

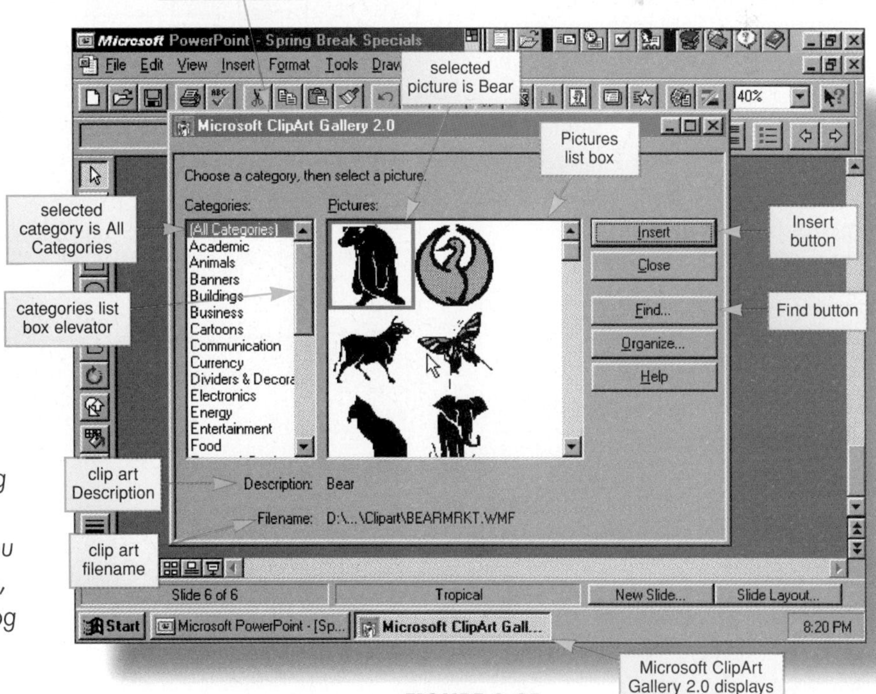

FIGURE 2-35

3 **Click the Find button.**

The Find ClipArt dialog box displays three boxes in which you enter clip art search criteria (Figure 2-36). The Description box is selected and contains the description, All Descriptions. Use the Description box to find clip art when you know a word from the image's description. Use the Filename containing box when you know the name of the file containing the desired clip art image. Use the Picture type box when you want to find clip art saved in a specific format.

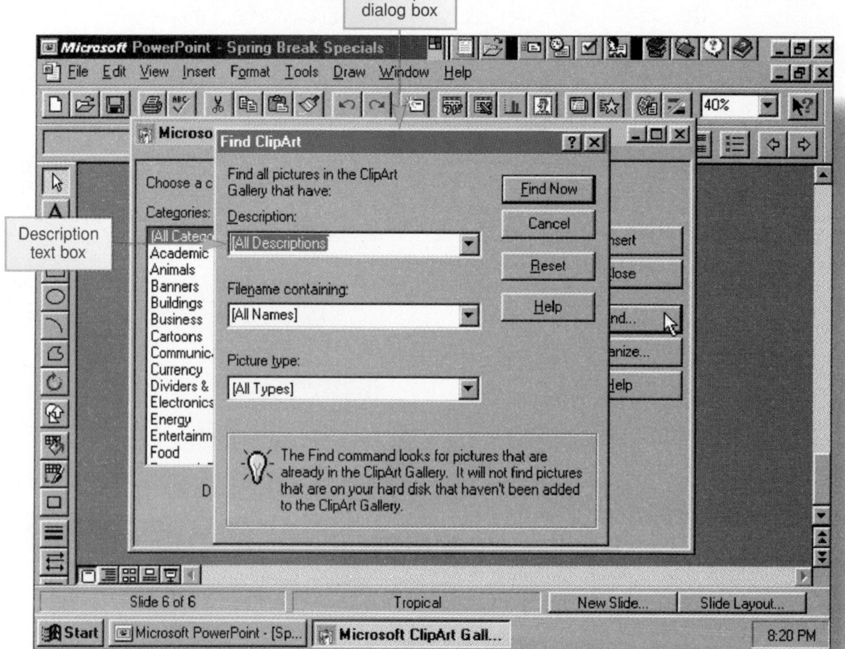

FIGURE 2-36

4 **Type** `disappoint` **in the Description box and point to the Find Now button.**

The Description box contains disappoint, which is a portion of the description, disappointment (Figure 2-37). You do not need to type the full description because the Find feature of Microsoft ClipArt Gallery 2.0 searches for all pictures containing the consecutive letters typed in the Description box. The Find Now button initiates the clip art search. The Reset button resets the Description, Filename containing, and Picture type boxes. Click the Reset button when you wish to begin a new search.

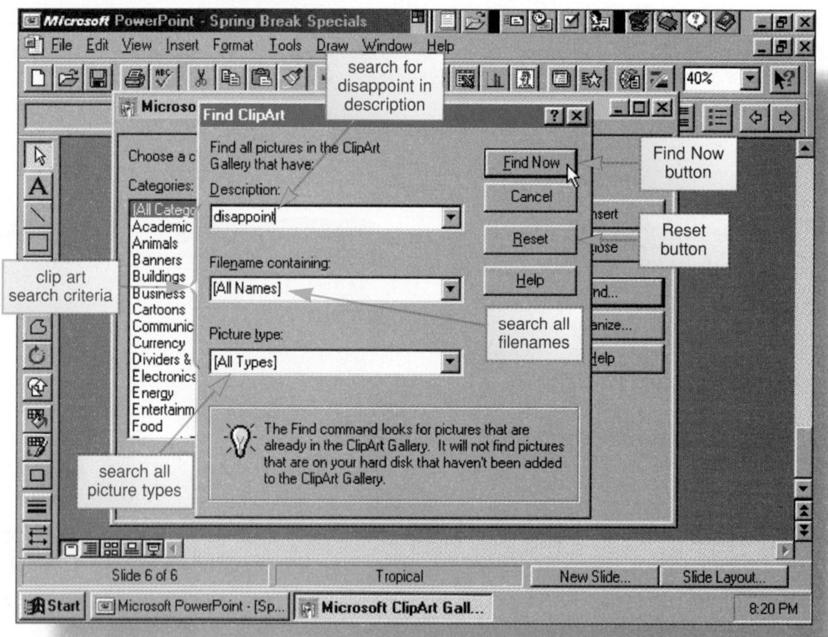

FIGURE 2-37

More *About* Clip Art

Clip art serves a purpose in a presentation – it conveys a message. Clip art should contribute to the understandability of the slide. It should not be used decoratively. Before adding clip art to a presentation, ask yourself: "Does the clip art convey or support the slide topic?" If the answer is yes, put the clip art on the slide.

5 Click the Find Now button.

The Microsoft ClipArt Gallery searches for all pictures that contain disappoint in the description. All pictures that match the description display in the Pictures box (Figure 2-38). The picture of a person sitting at a desk holding a telephone receiver is selected. The selected category changes to Results of Last F(ind). Disappointment displays as the description of the selected picture at the bottom of the Microsoft ClipArt Gallery 2.0 dialog box. Your selected picture may be different depending on the clip art installed on your computer.

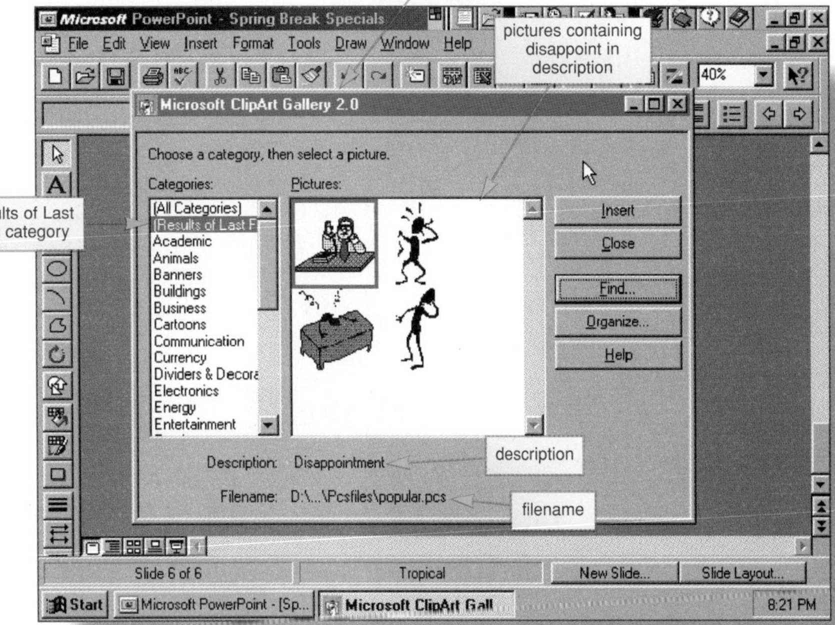

FIGURE 2-38

6 Click the Insert button.

The selected picture is inserted into the clip art placeholder on Slide 6 (2-39). PowerPoint automatically sizes the picture to a size that best fits the placeholder. In this instance, the picture is wider it is than tall (landscape orientation), so PowerPoint sizes the picture to fit the width of the placeholder. When a picture is in portrait orientation, PowerPoint sizes the picture to fit the height of the placeholder.

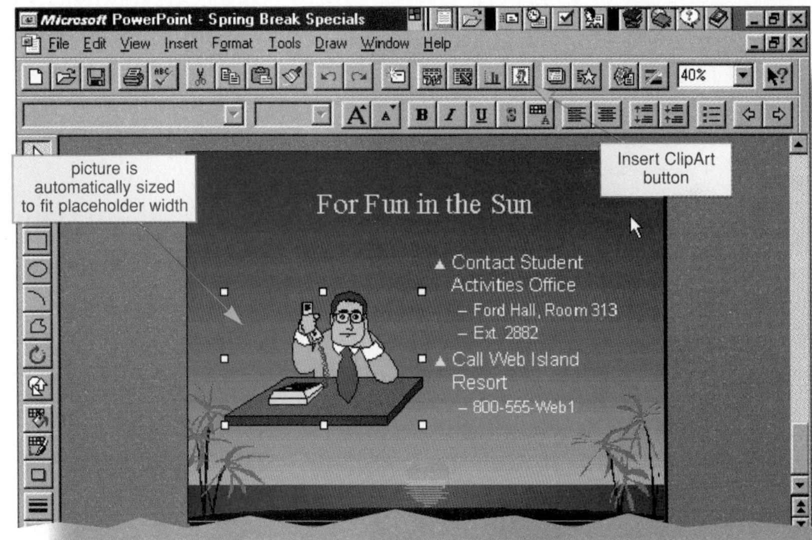

FIGURE 2-39

Other Ways

1. Right-click clip art placeholder, click Edit Placeholder Object
2. Click clip art placeholder, on Standard toolbar click Insert Clip Art button
3. Click clip art placeholder, on menu bar click Insert, click Clip Art
4. Click clip art placeholder, press ALT+I, press C

Occasionally, you find a clip art image that enhances your presentation but has a description that does not match your topic. The description is not the factor by which you select your clip art. The effectiveness of the picture determines if you add it to your presentation, not its description.

In addition to the graphic images in Microsoft ClipArt Gallery 2.0, there are other sources for clip art such as retailers specializing in computer software, the Internet, bulletin board systems, and online information systems. Some popular online information systems are Microsoft Network, America Online, CompuServe, and Prodigy. A **bulletin board system** is a computer system that allows users to communicate with each other and share files.

Table 2-3

FORMAT	FILE EXTENSION
AutoCAD Format 2-D	*.dxf
CompuServe GIF	*.gif
Computer Graphics Metafile	*.cgm
CorelDRAW!	*.cdr
DrawPerfect Graphics	*.wpg
Encapsulated PostScript	*.eps
HP Graphics Language	*.hgl
JPEG Filter	*.jpg
Kodak Photo CD	*.pcd
Lotus 1-2-3 Graphics	*.pic
Macintosh PICT	*.pct
Micrografx Designer/Draw	*.drw
PC Paintbrush	*.pcx
Tagged Image File Format	*.tif
Targa	*.tga
Windows Bitmaps	*.dib, *.bmp
Windows Metafile	*.wmf
WordPerfect Graphics	*.wpg

Additionally, you can include pictures into your presentation. These may include scanned photographs, line art, and artwork from compact discs. To insert a picture into a presentation, the picture must be saved in a format that PowerPoint can recognize. Table 2-3 identifies the formats PowerPoint recognizes.

PowerPoint converts pictures saved in the formats listed in Table 2-3 by using filters. These filters are shipped with the PowerPoint installation software and must be installed before PowerPoint can properly convert files.

Inserting Clip Art on a Slide without a Clip Art Placeholder

PowerPoint does not require you to use an AutoLayout containing a clip art placeholder to add clip art to a slide. You can insert clip art on any slide regardless of its slide layout. On Slide 3, you are adding a picture of a sailboat to illustrate the type of sailing vessel used in the Voyager vacation package. Recall that the slide layout on Slide 3 is a Bulleted List. Because the Bulleted List AutoLayout does not contain a clip art placeholder, you click the Insert Clip Art button on the Standard toolbar to start Microsoft ClipArt Gallery 2.0. The picture for which you are searching is a sailing ship. Its description is Performance Ship. Perform the following steps to insert the picture of a ship on a slide that does not have a clip art placeholder.

OtherWays

1. On menu bar click Insert, click Clip Art
2. Press ALT+I, press C

TO INSERT CLIP ART ON A SLIDE WITHOUT A CLIP ART PLACEHOLDER

Step 1: Drag the elevator to display Slide 3, titled The Voyager.
Step 2: Click the Insert ClipArt button on the Standard toolbar (see Figure 2-39 on page PP 2.31).
Step 3: Click the Find button. When the Find ClipArt dialog box displays, type `ship` in the Description box. Click the Find Now button.
Step 4: When the Pictures box in the Microsoft ClipArt Gallery 2.0 dialog box displays the results, click the down arrow on the Pictures box scroll bar until the sailboat displays. If the sailboat is not installed on your computer, see your instructor for an appropriate replacement picture.
Step 5: Click the picture of the sailboat.
Step 6: Click the Insert button.

The sailboat displays on Slide 3 (Figure 2-40). A selection box indicates the clip art is selected.

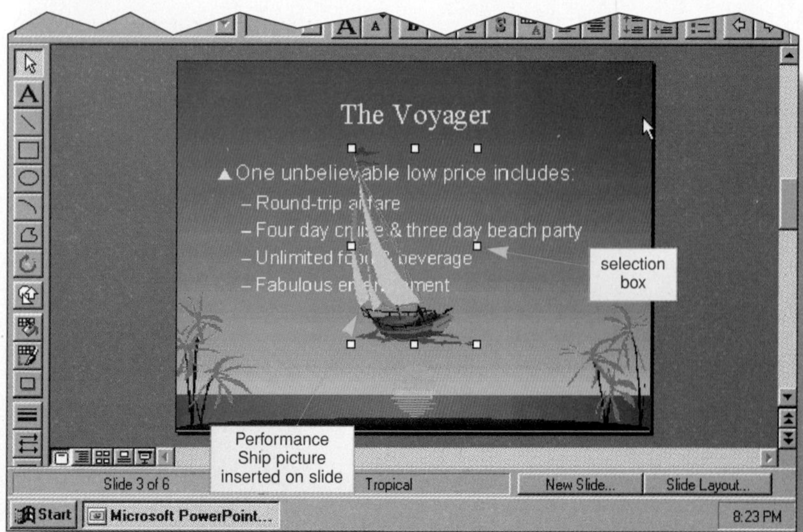

FIGURE 2-40

Moving Clip Art

After you insert clip art on a slide, you may want to reposition it. The picture of the sailboat overlays the bulleted list on Slide 3. Moving the picture to the lower right corner of the slide places the sailboat onto the water and away from the text. Perform the steps below to move the sailboat to the lower-right portion of the slide.

More About Clip Art

When used appropriately, clip art reduces misconceptions. If a presentation consists of words alone, the audience creates its own mental picture. The mental picture created may be different than the concept you are trying to convey. The audience better understands the concept when clip art is included.

To Move Clip Art

1. **If the picture of the sailboat is not already selected, use the mouse pointer to point to the sailboat and click.**

2. **Press and hold down the left mouse button. Drag the picture of the sailboat down to the bottom of the slide and then to the right until the left edge of the dotted box aligns below the b in beach. Release the left mouse button.**

When you drag an object, a dotted box displays. The dotted box indicates the new position of the object. When you release the left mouse button, the picture of the sailboat displays in the new location (Figure 2-41). Resize handles appear at the corners and along the edges of the selection box.

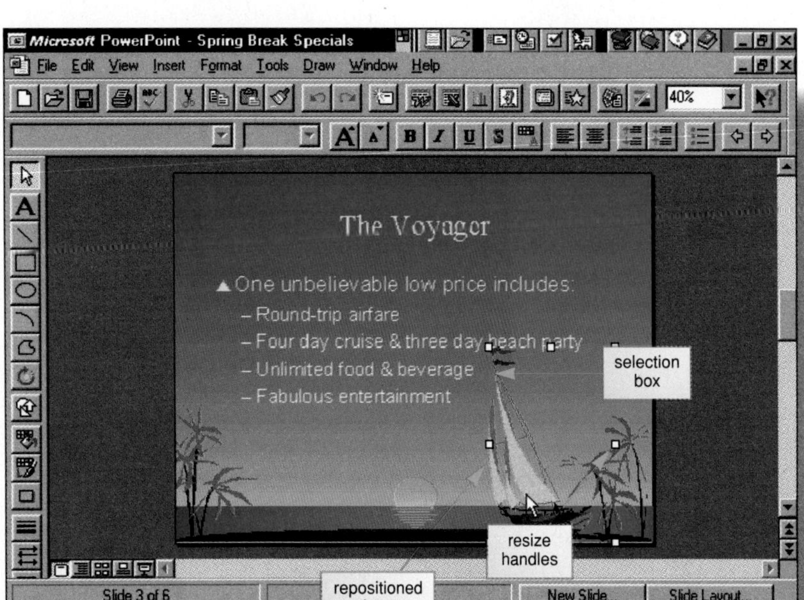

FIGURE 2-41

OtherWays

1. On status bar click Slide Layout button, click slide layout containing clip art or media clip placeholder
2. Select clip art object, press arrow keys

Changing the Size of Clip Art Using the Scale Command

You may sometimes find it necessary to change the size of clip art. For example, on Slide 3, the mast on the sailboat slightly overlaps the bulleted text. To improve legibility, reduce the size of the picture. To change the size of a clip art picture by an exact percentage, use the Scale command. The advantage of using the Scale command is the ability to maintain the aspect ratio when you resize the picture. The **aspect ratio** is the relationship between the height and width of an object. Additionally, because the Scale dialog box contains a Preview button, you can make changes and see how the picture looks on the slide without permanently changing its size. When you are satisfied with the size of the picture, click the OK button to apply the settings in the Scale dialog box. Perform the steps on the next pages to reduce the size of the sailboat.

Steps To Change the Size of Clip Art Using the Scale Command

1 **With the picture of the sailboat selected, click Draw on the menu bar. Then point to Scale (Figure 2-42).**

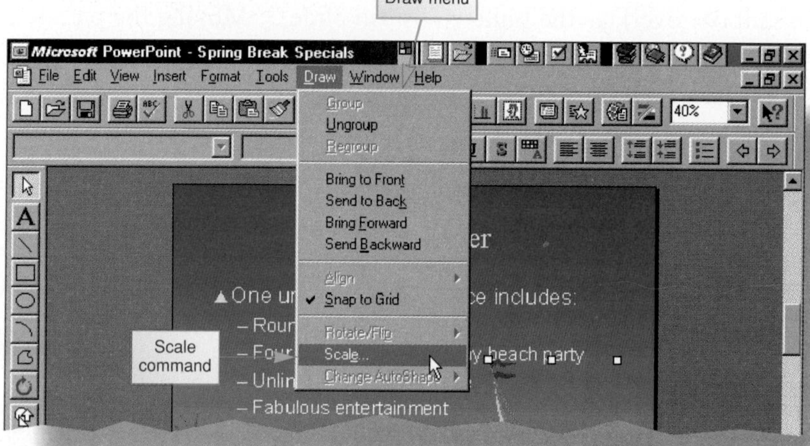

FIGURE 2-42

2 **Click Scale.**

The Scale dialog box displays (Figure 2-43). The Scale To box displays the current percentage of the sailboat picture, 99.6. A check mark in the Relative to Original Picture Size box instructs PowerPoint to maintain the aspect ratio of the picture.

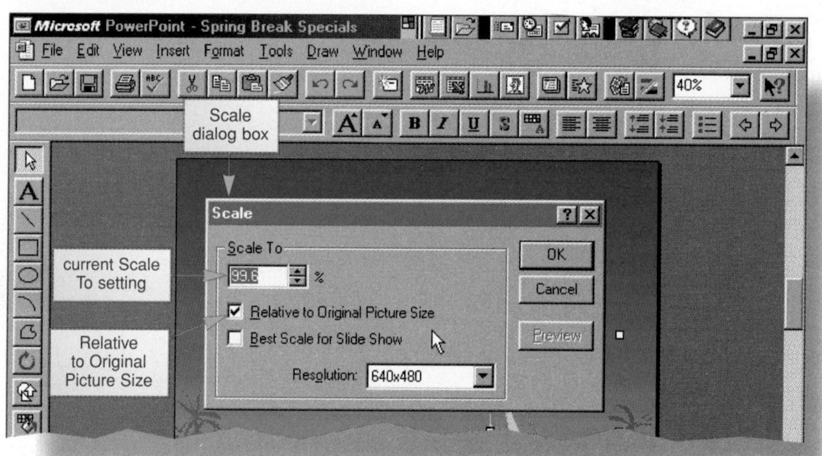

FIGURE 2-43

3 **Point to the Scale dialog box title bar and drag it to the upper left corner of the slide window.**

The sailboat is fully visible (Figure 2-44).

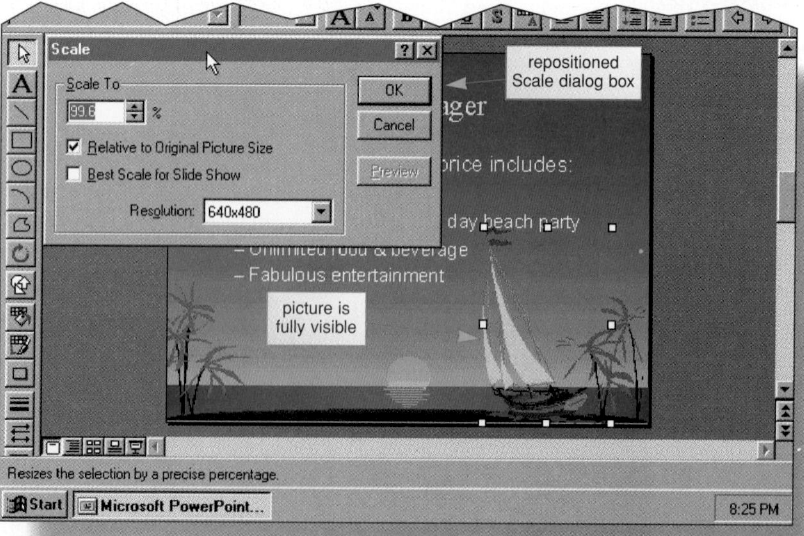

FIGURE 2-44

4 Type 85 **and click the Preview button.**

PowerPoint temporarily resizes the sailboat to 85 percent of its original size and displays it on Slide 3 (Figure 2-45). The Preview button is dimmed, or not available at this time. If the sailboat picture were still covering part of the text, you would want to try another scaling percentage to make it smaller. When you type a number in the Scale To box, the Preview button becomes available again. The OK button is used when you are satisfied with the scaling results.

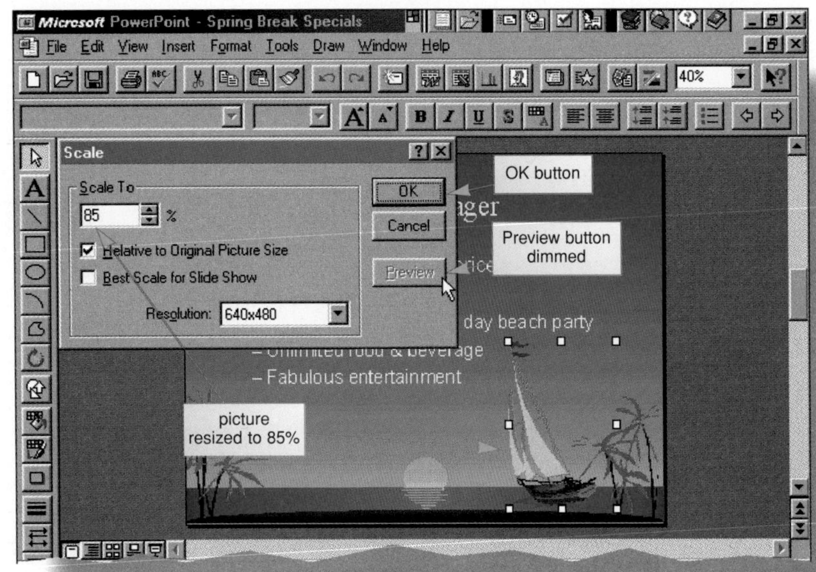

FIGURE 2-45

5 Click the OK button.

PowerPoint displays the reduced sailboat picture and closes the Scale dialog box (Figure 2-46).

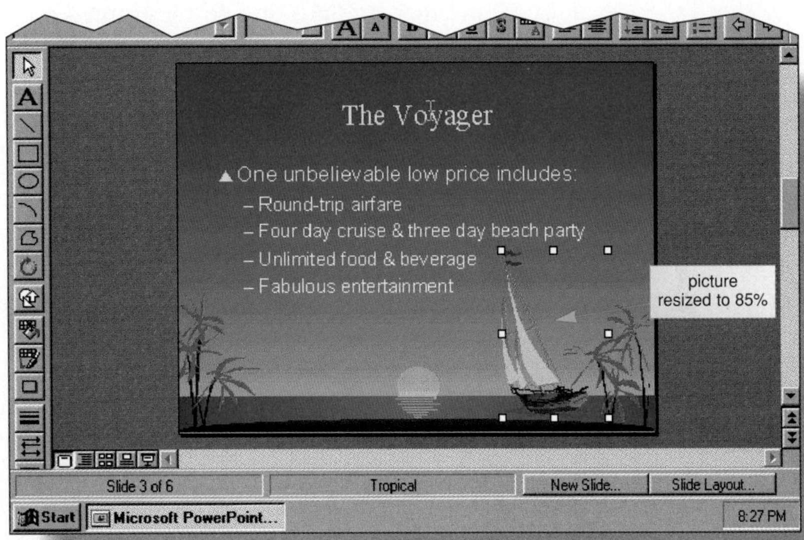

FIGURE 2-46

OtherWays

1. Select clip art object, drag a resize handle
2. Select clip art object, press ALT+D, press E

The Scale command is available only when a selected object displays in Slide view or Notes Pages view.

When you use the Scale command to change the size of a clip art image, the image increases or decreases proportionately to the percentage specified in the Scale To box. For example, if you wish to decrease the size of a picture to one-half its original size, type 50 in the Scale To box. If you wish to double the size of a picture (two times its original size), type 200 in the Scale To box.

Saving the Presentation

To preserve the work completed this far, save the presentation again by clicking the Save button on the Standard toolbar.

More *About* **Headers and Footers**

Consider placing footers on slides that are used for making overhead transparencies. A slide number and presentation name help keep the presentation organized. The slide number can be a great time saver in the event you drop your transparencies.

Adding a Header and a Footer to Outline Pages

A printout of the presentation outline often is used as an audience handout. Distributing a copy of the outline provides the audience with paper upon which to write notes or comments. Another benefit of distributing a copy of the outline is to help the audience see the text on the slides when lighting is poor or the room is too large. To help identify the source of the printed outline, add a descriptive header and footer.

Using the Notes and Handouts Sheet to Add Headers and Footers

Add headers and footers to outline pages by clicking the Notes and Handouts sheet in the Header and Footer dialog box and entering the information you wish to print. Perform the following steps to add the current date, a header, the page number, and a footer to the printed outline.

Steps To Use the Notes and Handouts Sheet to Add Headers and Footers

1. **Click View on the menu bar. Point to Header and Footer (Figure 2-47).**

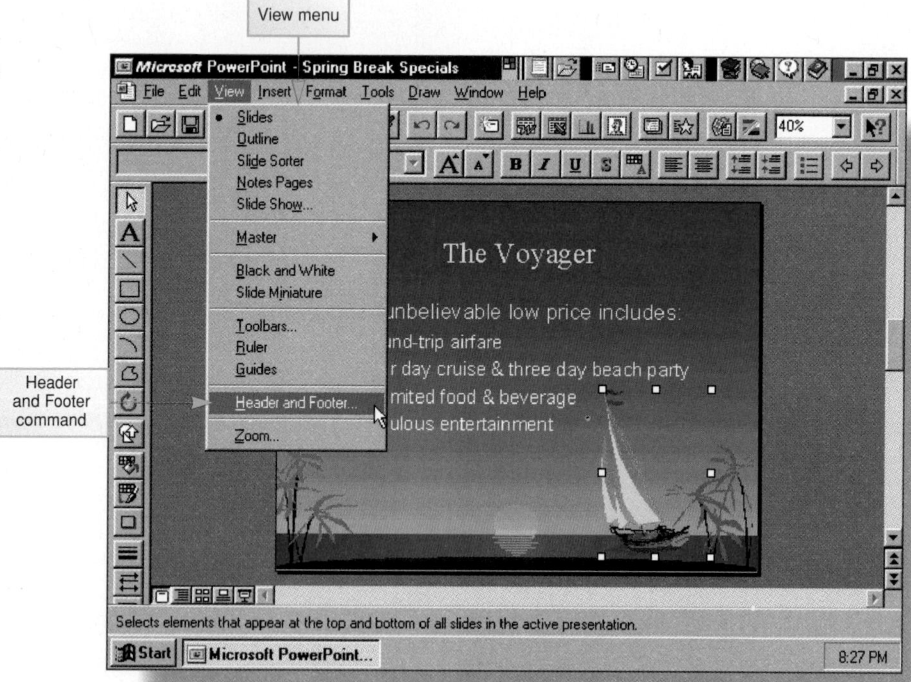

FIGURE 2-47

2 Click Header and Footer.

The Header and Footer dialog box displays (Figure 2-48). The Slide sheet displays.

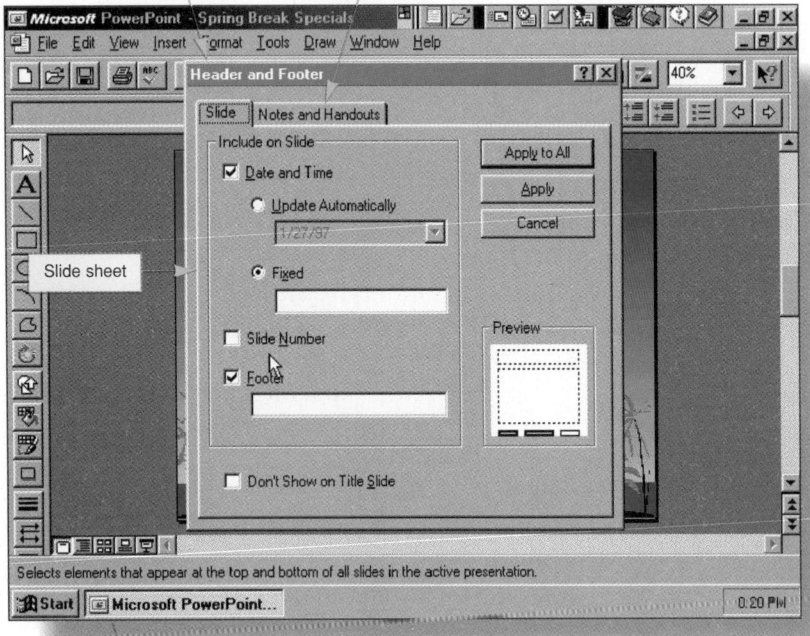

FIGURE 2-48

3 Click the Notes and Handouts tab.

The Notes and Handouts sheet displays (Figure 2-49). Check marks display in the Date and Time, Header, Page Number, and Footer check boxes. The Fixed option button is selected.

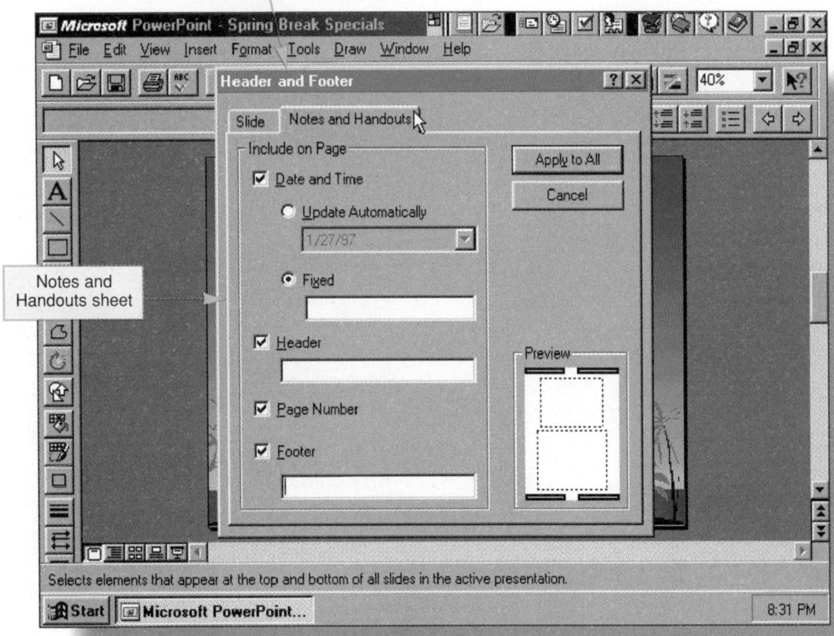

FIGURE 2-49

4 **Click the Update Automatically option button. Type** `Spring Break Specials` **in the Header text box. Type** `Web Island Resort` **in the Footer text box. Then point to the Apply to All button (Figure 2-50).**

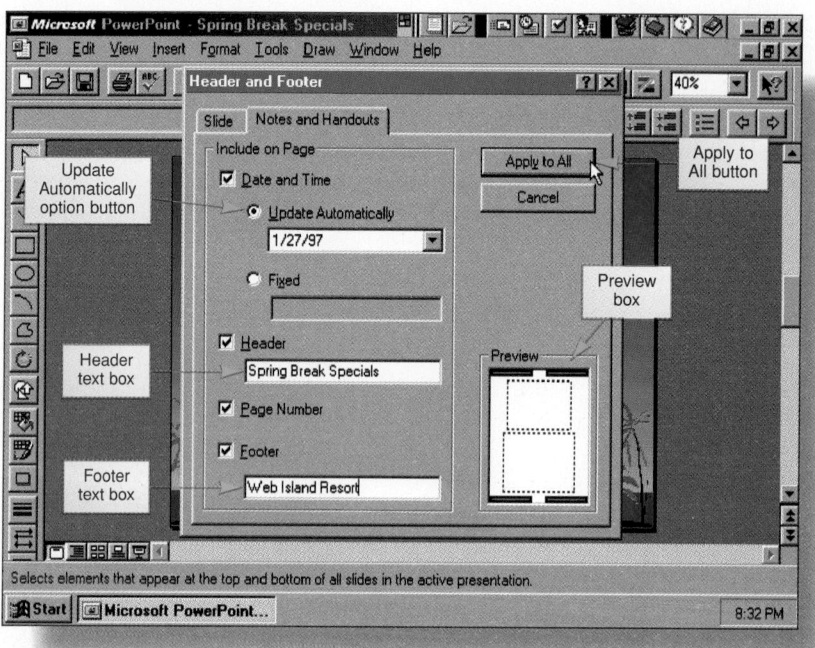

FIGURE 2-50

5 **Click the Apply to All button.**

PowerPoint applies the header and footer text to the outline, closes the Header and Footer dialog box, and displays Slide 3 (Figure 2-51). You cannot see header and footer text until you print the outline.

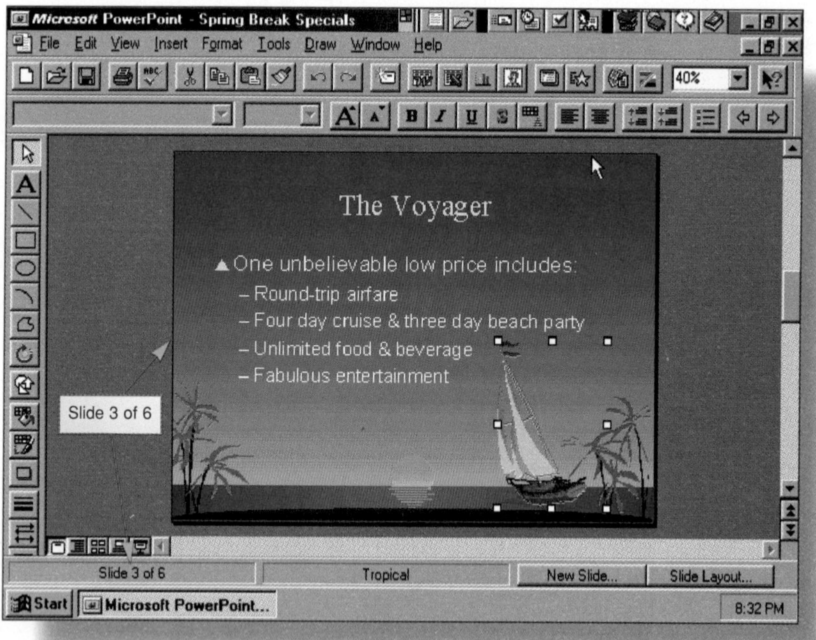

FIGURE 2-51

Checking the Presentation for Spelling and Style Errors

Now that the individual slide changes have been made, you should run Style Checker to identify errors in your presentation. Recall from Project 1 that Style Checker identifies possible errors in spelling, visual clarity, case, and end punctuation. Perform the following steps to run Style Checker.

TO RUN STYLE CHECKER

Step 1: Click Tools on the menu bar.
Step 2: Click Style Checker.
Step 3: When the Style Checker dialog box displays, click the Start button.
Step 4: Correct spelling errors and ignore correct spellings of words not located in the standard dictionary.
Step 5: If Style Checker lists visual clarity inconsistencies in the Style Checker Summary dialog box, write the slide number and the message on a sheet of paper.
Step 6: When the Style Checker Status dialog box displays, press the OK button.

PowerPoint closes Style Checker and displays the slide containing the last word not in the dictionaries, Slide 6 (Figure 2-52). This presentation contains no visual clarity inconsistencies. If Style Checker identifies any visual clarity inconsistencies, review the steps for creating the identified slide and make the appropriate corrections.

FIGURE 2-52

For more information about Style Checker, see page PP 1.40 in Project 1.

Adding Animation Effects

PowerPoint provides many animation effects to make your slide show presentation look professional. Two of these animation effects are slide transition and text build. **Slide transition effects** control how a slide displays on and exits the screen. **Text build effects** control how the objects on a slide display. The following pages discuss each of these animation effects in detail.

More *About* **Slide Transition**

Resist the temptation to use several slide transition effects within a presentation. Too many different slide transition effects will cause the audience to focus on the visual effects and not on your topic. A general presentation design rule is to limit the number of slide transition effects to two.

Adding Slide Transitions to a Slide Show

PowerPoint allows you to control the way you advance from one slide to the next by adding slide transitions to an on-screen slide show. Slide transitions are visual effects that display when you move one slide off the screen and bring the next one on. PowerPoint has forty-six different slide transitions. The name of the slide transition characterizes the visual effect that displays. For example, the slide transition effect, Split Vertical In, displays the next slide by covering the previous slide with two vertical boxes moving toward the center of the screen until the two boxes meet. The effect is similar to closing draw drapes over a window.

PowerPoint requires you to select a slide before applying slide transition effects. In this presentation, you apply slide transition effects to all slides except the title slide. Because Slide 6 is already selected, you must select Slides 2 through 5. The technique used to select more than one slide is the **SHIFT+click technique.** To perform the SHIFT+click technique, hold down the SHIFT key as you click each slide. After you click the slides to which you want to add text build effects, release the SHIFT key.

In the Spring Break Specials presentation, you wish to display the Box Out slide transition effect between slides. That is, all slides begin stacked on top of one another, like a deck of cards. As you click the mouse to view the next slide, the new slide enters the screen by starting at the center of the slide and exploding out toward the edges of the slide while maintaining a box shape. Perform the following steps to apply the Box Out slide transition effect to the Spring Break Specials presentation.

To Add Slide Transitions to a Slide Show

1 Click the Slide Sorter View button at the bottom of the PowerPoint screen.

PowerPoint displays the presentation in Slide Sorter view (Figure 2-53). Slide 6 is selected. Slide 6 currently does not have a slide transition effect as noted in the Slide Transition Effects box on the Slide Sorter toolbar.

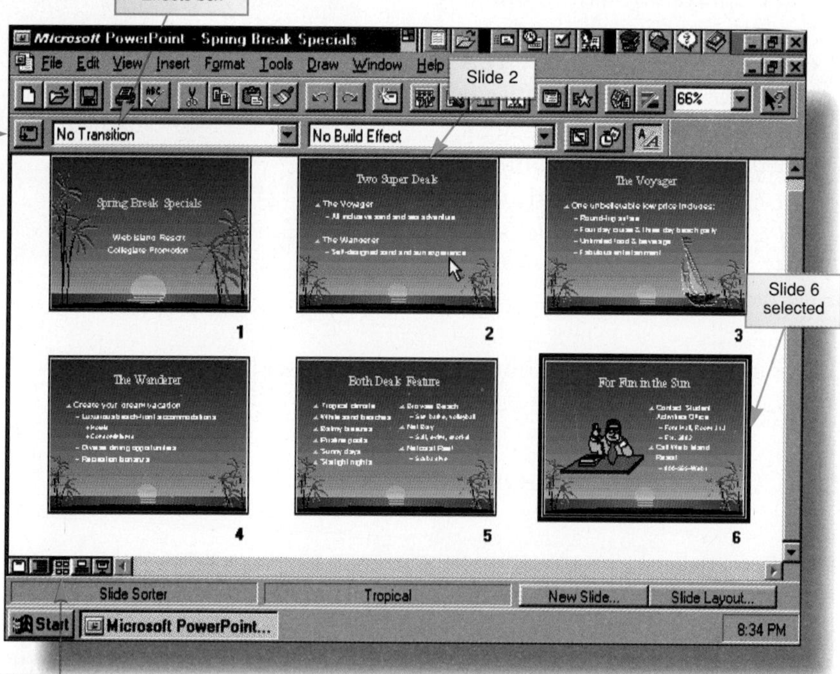

FIGURE 2-53

2 **Press and hold down the SHIFT key and click Slide 2, Slide 3, Slide 4, and Slide 5. Release the SHIFT key.**

Slides 2 through 6 are selected, as indicated by the heavy border around each slide (Figure 2-54).

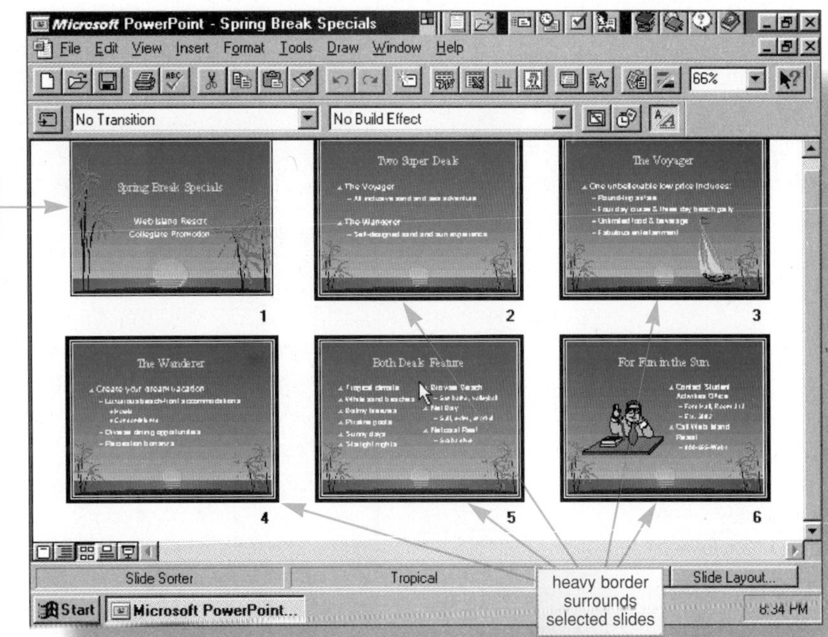

FIGURE 2-54

3 **Point to Slide 5 and right-click. When a shortcut menu displays, point to Slide Transition (Figure 2-55).**

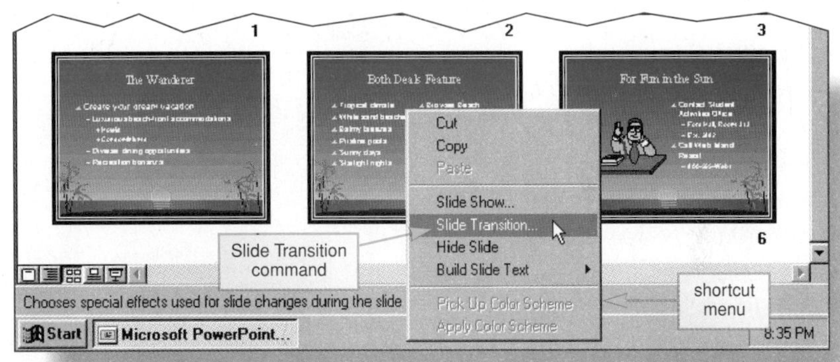

FIGURE 2-55

4 **Click Slide Transition. When the Slide Transition dialog box displays, click the Effect box arrow and point to Box Out.**

The Slide Transition dialog box displays (Figure 2-56). The Effect drop-down list displays available slide transition effects.

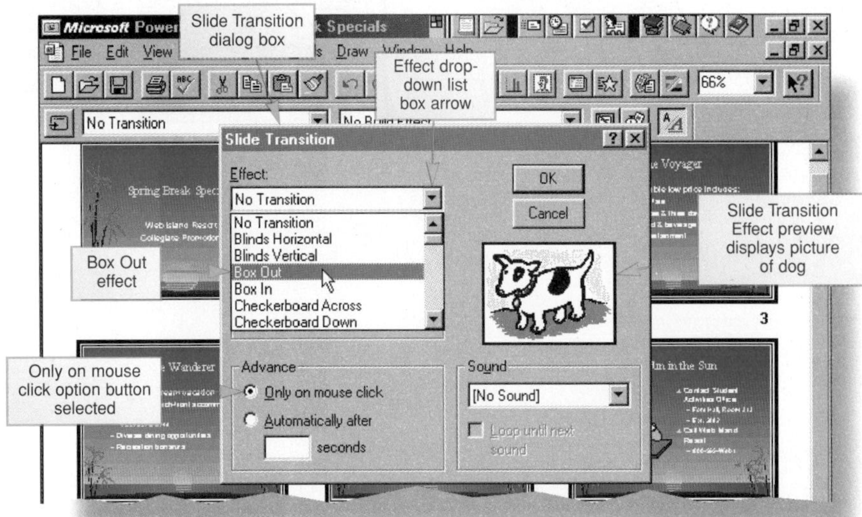

FIGURE 2-56

5 Click Box Out.

The Slide Transition Effect preview demonstrates the Box Out effect (Figure 2-57). To see the demonstration again, click the picture in the Slide Transition Effect preview.

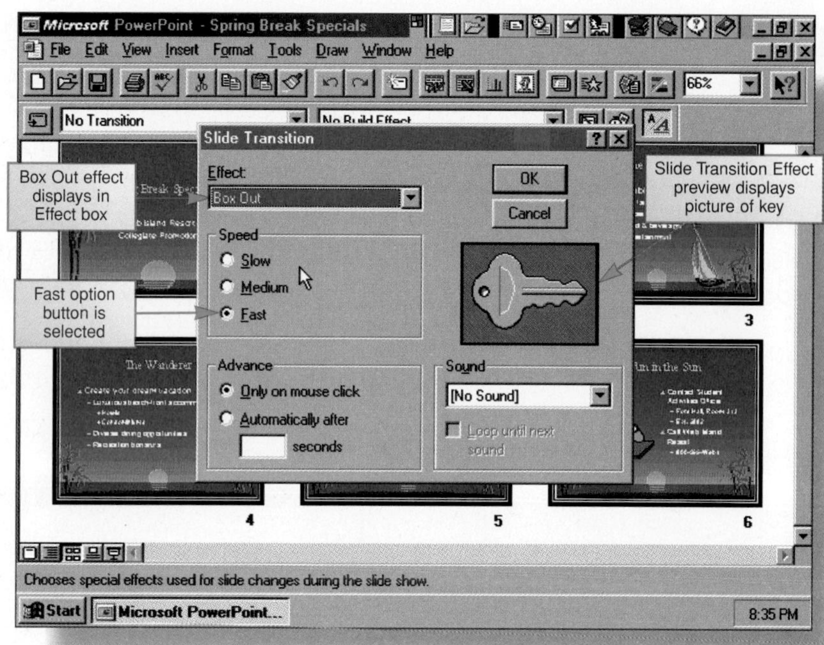

FIGURE 2-57

6 Click the OK button.

PowerPoint displays the presentation in Slide Sorter view (Figure 2-58). A slide transition icon displays under each selected slide, which indicates that slide transition effects have been added to those slides. The current slide transition effect, Box Out, displays in the Slide Transition Effects box.

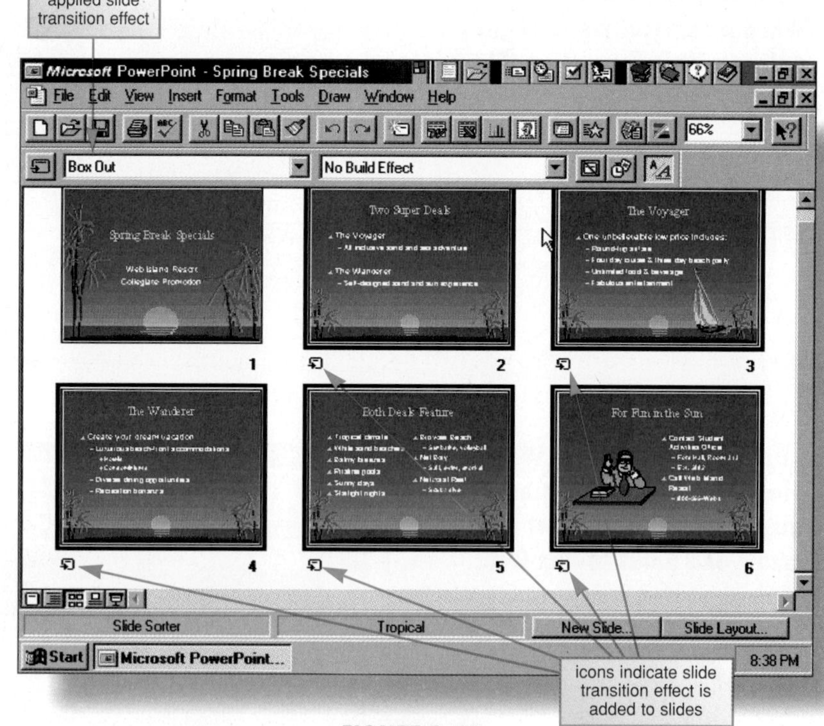

FIGURE 2-58

Other Ways

1. On Slide Sorter toolbar click Slide Transition button
2. On menu bar click Tools, click Slide Transition
3. Press ALT+T, press T

Slide Sorter Toolbar

PowerPoint provides you with multiple methods for accomplishing most tasks. Generally, the fastest method is to right-click to display a shortcut menu. Another frequently used method is to click a toolbar button. For example, you can apply slide transition effects by clicking the Slide Transition Effects box on the Slide Sorter toolbar.

The Slide Sorter toolbar displays only when you are in Slide Sorter view. It displays beneath the Standard toolbar, in place of the Formatting toolbar. The Slide Sorter toolbar contains tools to help you quickly add animation effects to your slide show. Table 2-4 explains the function of the buttons and boxes on the Slide Sorter toolbar.

TABLE 2-4

ICON	NAME	FUNCTION
	Slide Transition button	Displays the Slide Transition dialog box, which lists special effects used for slide changes during a slide show.
Box Out	Slide Transition Effects box	Displays a list of slide transition effects. Selecting a slide transition effect from the list applies it to the selected slide(s) and demonstrates it in the preview box.
Fly From Bottom-Left	Text Build Effects box	Displays a list of text build effects.
	Hide Slide button	Excludes a slide from the presentation without deleting it.
	Rehearse Timings button	Records the amount of time spent on each slide during a presentation rehearsal.
	Show Formatting button	Displays or hides character formatting attributes.

A slide transition effect has been applied to the presentation. The next step in creating this slide show is to add animation effects to individual slides.

Applying Text Build Effects to Bulleted Slides

Text build effects are animation effects that are applied to bulleted paragraphs. This special effect instructs PowerPoint to progressively disclose each bulleted paragraph, one at a time, during the running of a slide show. PowerPoint has thirty-eight text build effects and the capability to dim the bulleted paragraphs already on the slide when a new paragraph is displayed.

The next step is to apply the Fly From Bottom-Left build text effect to Slides 2, 3, 4, 5, and 6 in the Spring Break Specials presentation. Perform the steps on the next pages to apply text build effects to the bulleted slides in this presentation.

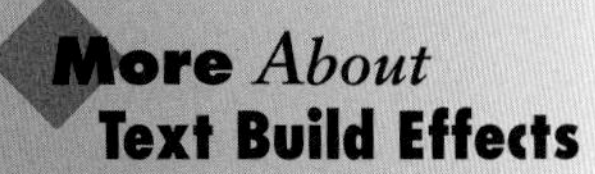

Clicking the Dim Previous Points check box in the Build dialog box changes the color of the current bulleted paragraph as the next one displays. The default dim color displays in the Dim Previous Points color drop-down list box. To choose a different dim color, click the Dim Previous Points down arrow.

To Apply Text Build Effects to Bulleted Slides

1. **If Slides 2 through 6 are not selected, use the SHIFT+click method to select them.**

2. **Right-click Slide 2. When a shortcut menu displays, point to Build Slide Text.**

   When Build Slide Text is highlighted, a submenu displays (Figure 2-59). A right-pointing arrow after a menu command indicates a submenu exists. The bullet in front of the Off command in the submenu identifies the current setting.

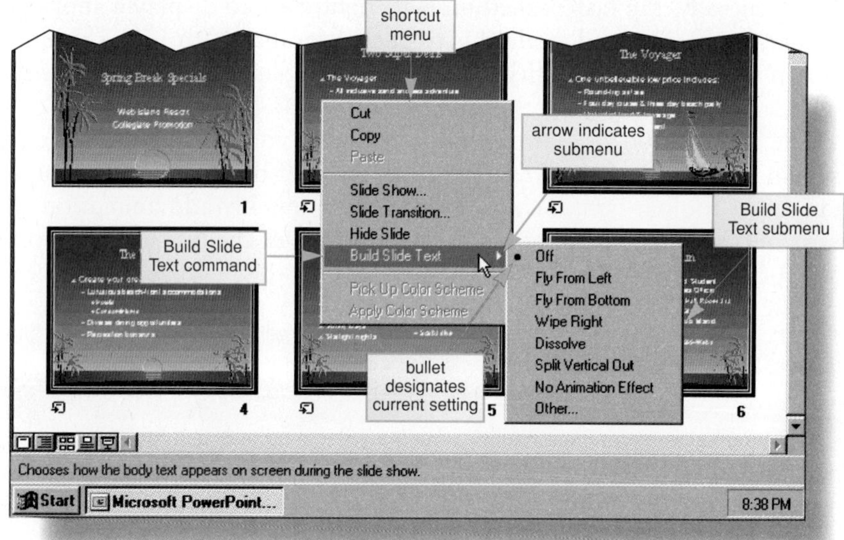

FIGURE 2-59

3. **Point to Other in the Build Slide Text submenu (Figure 2-60).**

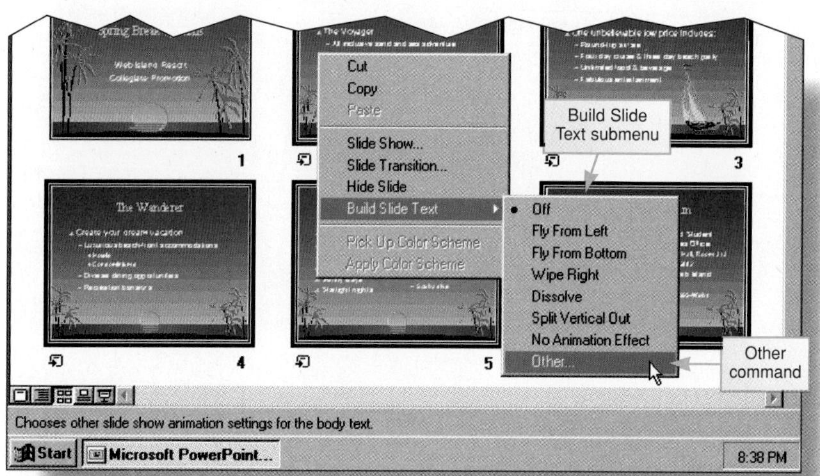

FIGURE 2-60

4. **Click Other. When the Animation Settings dialog box displays, click the Build Options box down arrow. Then point to By 3rd Level Paragraphs.**

   The Build Options drop-down list displays various build options for slide text (Figure 2-61). The current build option is Don't Build as indicated in the Build Options box.

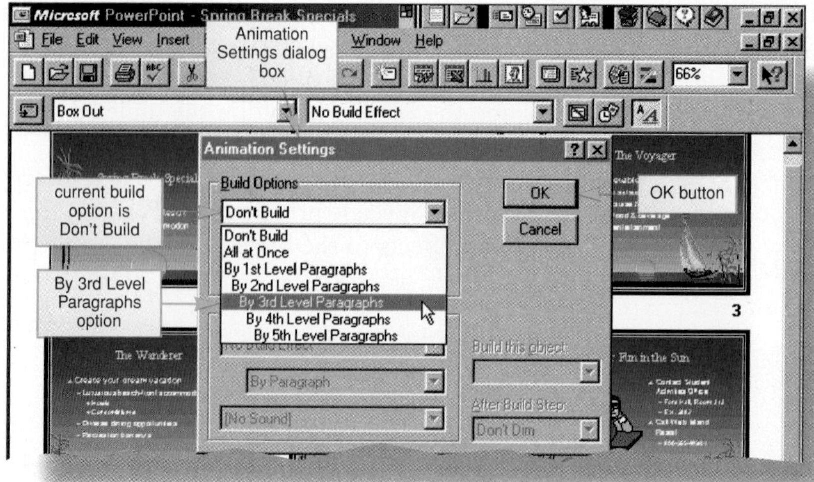

FIGURE 2-61

5 **Click By 3rd Level Paragraphs. Click the Effects box arrow. Then point to Fly From Bottom-Left (Figure 2-62).**

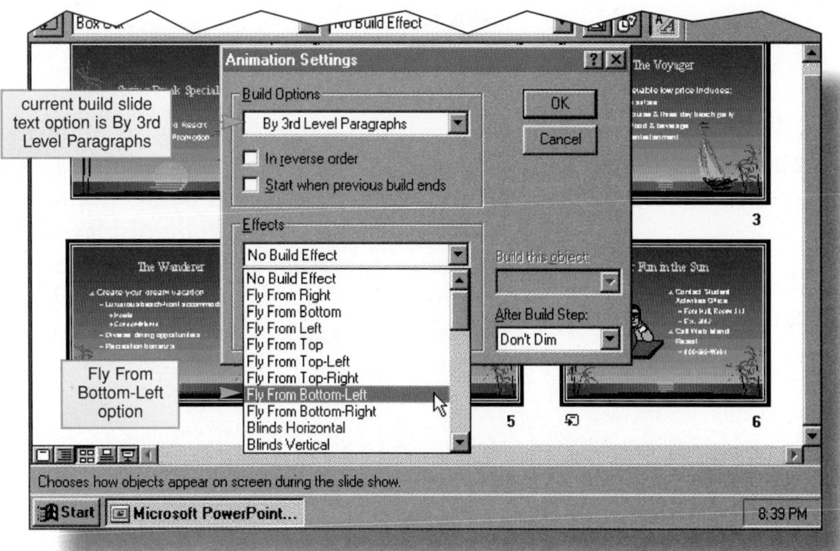

FIGURE 2-62

6 **Click Fly From Bottom-Left. Then click the OK button.**

PowerPoint applies the Fly From Bottom-Left text build effect to the selected slides (Figure 2-63). Fly From Bottom-Left displays in the Text Build Effects box. Icons below each selected slide indicate text build effects are applied to the slides.

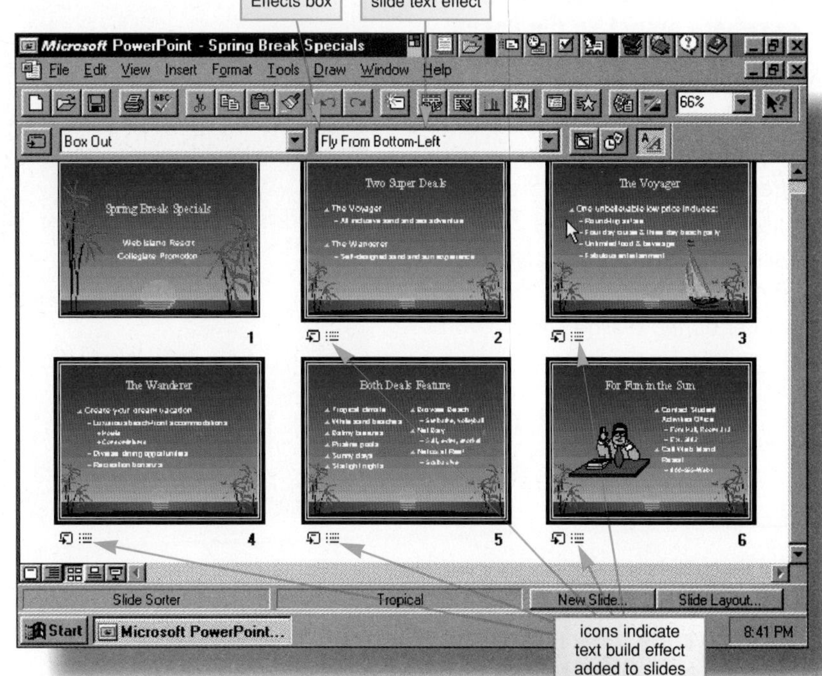

FIGURE 2-63

OtherWays

1. On Slide Sorter toolbar click Text Build Effects box
2. In Slide view, click Tools on menu bar, click Animation Settings
3. In Slide view, press ALT+T, press B, press letter of text build effect

Slide transition and text build effects complete this presentation. You are now ready to run the presentation in Slide Show view.

Saving the Presentation Again

Because several changes have been made since your last save, you should save the presentation again by clicking the Save button on the Standard toolbar.

Running a Slide Show with Animation Effects

Project 1 introduced you to using Slide Show view to look at your presentation one slide at a time. This project introduces you to running a slide show with slide transition effects and text build effects. When you run a slide show with slide transition effects, PowerPoint displays the slide transition effect when you click the mouse to advance to the next slide. When a slide has text build effects, each paragraph level displays as determined by the animation settings. Perform the following steps to run the Spring Break Specials slide show with animation effects.

Steps To Run a Slide Show with Animation Effects

1 **Click Slide 1. Click the Slide Show button on the View Button bar. When Slide 1 displays in Slide Show view, click the slide anywhere except on the Popup Menu button.**

PowerPoint first displays the Box Out slide transition effect and then displays Slide 2 with only the slide title (Figure 2-64). Recall the Popup Menu button displays when you move the mouse pointer during a slide show.

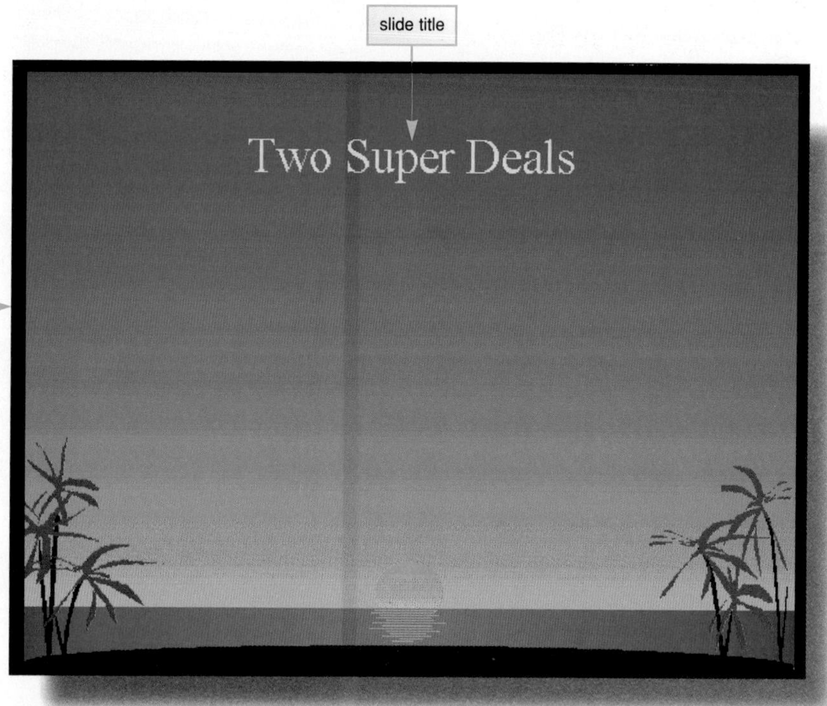

FIGURE 2-64

2 **Click the slide anywhere except on the Popup Menu button.**

PowerPoint displays the first Level One bulleted paragraph using the Fly From Bottom-Left text build effect (Figure 2-65).

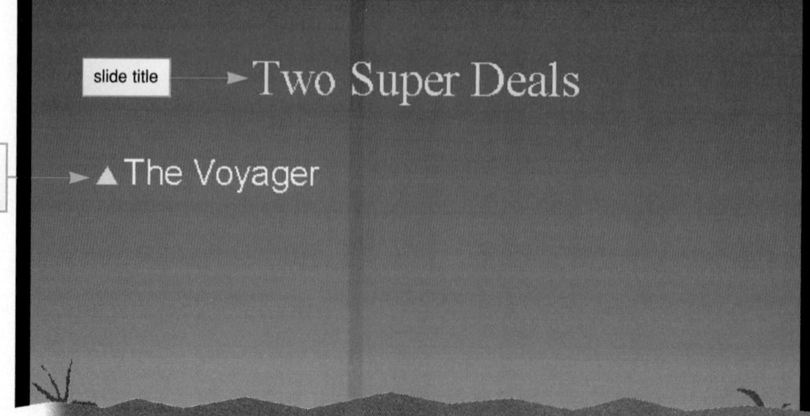

FIGURE 2-65

3 **Click the slide anywhere except on the Popup Menu button.**

PowerPoint displays the first Level Two bulleted paragraph beneath the Level One bulleted paragraph. PowerPoint again uses the Fly From Bottom-Left text build effect (Figure 2-66).

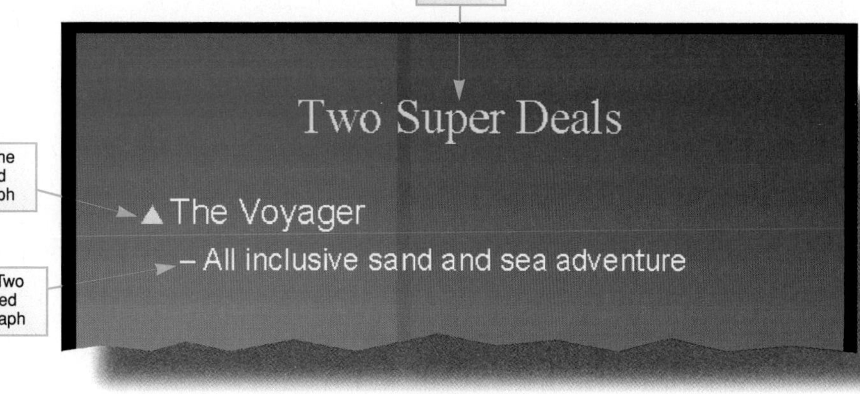

FIGURE 2-66

4 **Click the slide two times anywhere except on the Popup Menu button.**

PowerPoint displays the blank line and the second Level One bulleted list (Figure 2-67). The first click displays the blank line. The second click displays the second Level One bulleted paragraph.

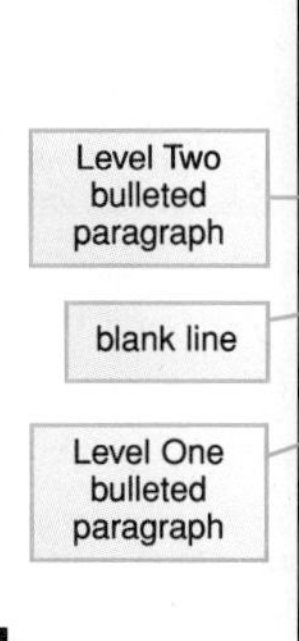

FIGURE 2-67

5 **Continue clicking to finish running the slide show and return to Slide Sorter View.**

PowerPoint builds each slide based on the animation settings. When you click the slide after the last paragraph displays, PowerPoint exits Slide Show and returns to Slide Sorter View.

Printing in Outline View

PowerPoint allows you to print a hard copy of the current view using the Print button on the Standard toolbar. Recall from Project 1 that, while in Slide view, you click the Print button to print hard copies of the presentation slides. PowerPoint also allows you print a hard copy of views other than the current view using the Print command in the File menu. The next two sections explain how to use the Print button to print the presentation outline and how to use the Print command to print the presentation slides.

Printing an Outline

During the development of a lengthy presentation, it is often easier to review your outline in print rather than on-screen. Printing your outline also is useful for audience handouts or when your supervisor or instructor wants to review your subject matter before you fully develop your presentation.

When you display a presentation in Slide view, clicking the Print button causes PowerPoint to print all slides in the presentation. Similarly, when you display a presentation in Outline view, clicking the Print button causes PowerPoint to print the outline. The outline, however, prints as last viewed in Outline view. This means that you must select the Zoom Control setting to display the outline text as you wish to print it. If you are uncertain of the Zoom Control setting, you should review it prior to printing. Perform the following steps to print an outline in Outline view.

To Print an Outline

1 Click the Outline View button on the View Button bar.

2 Ready the printer according to the printer instructions. Then click the Print button on the Standard toolbar.

The mouse pointer momentarily changes to an hourglass shape, and then PowerPoint briefly displays a message on the status bar indicating it is preparing to print the outline in the background. An animated printer icon displays on the status bar, identifying which page is being prepared to print. After several moments, the outline begins printing on the printer. The printer icon next to the clock on the taskbar indicates a print job is processing (Figure 2-68). When the outline is finished printing, the printer icon on the taskbar disappears.

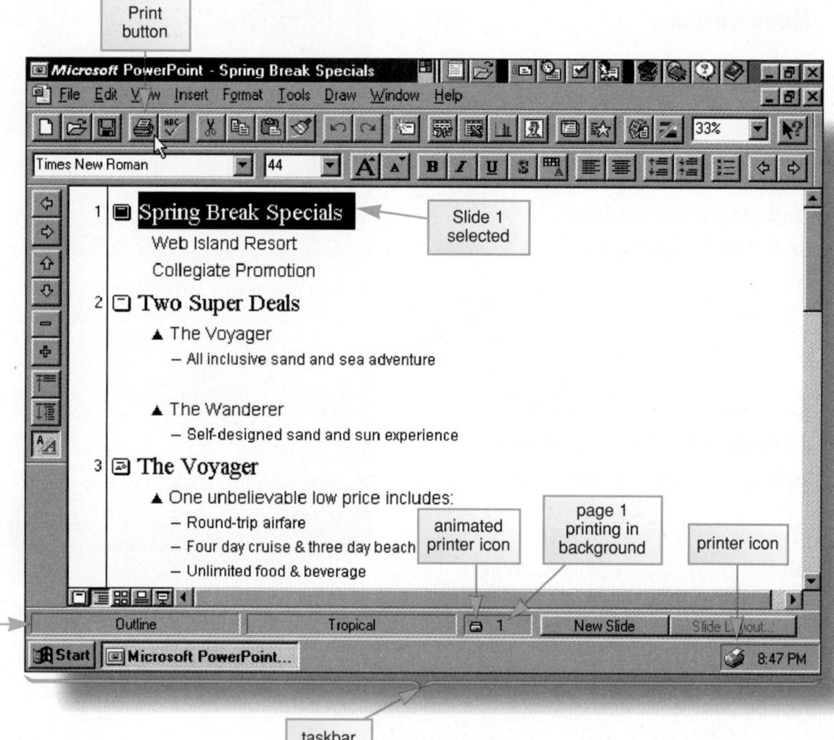

FIGURE 2-68

3 **When the printer stops, retrieve the printout of the outline (Figure 2-69).**

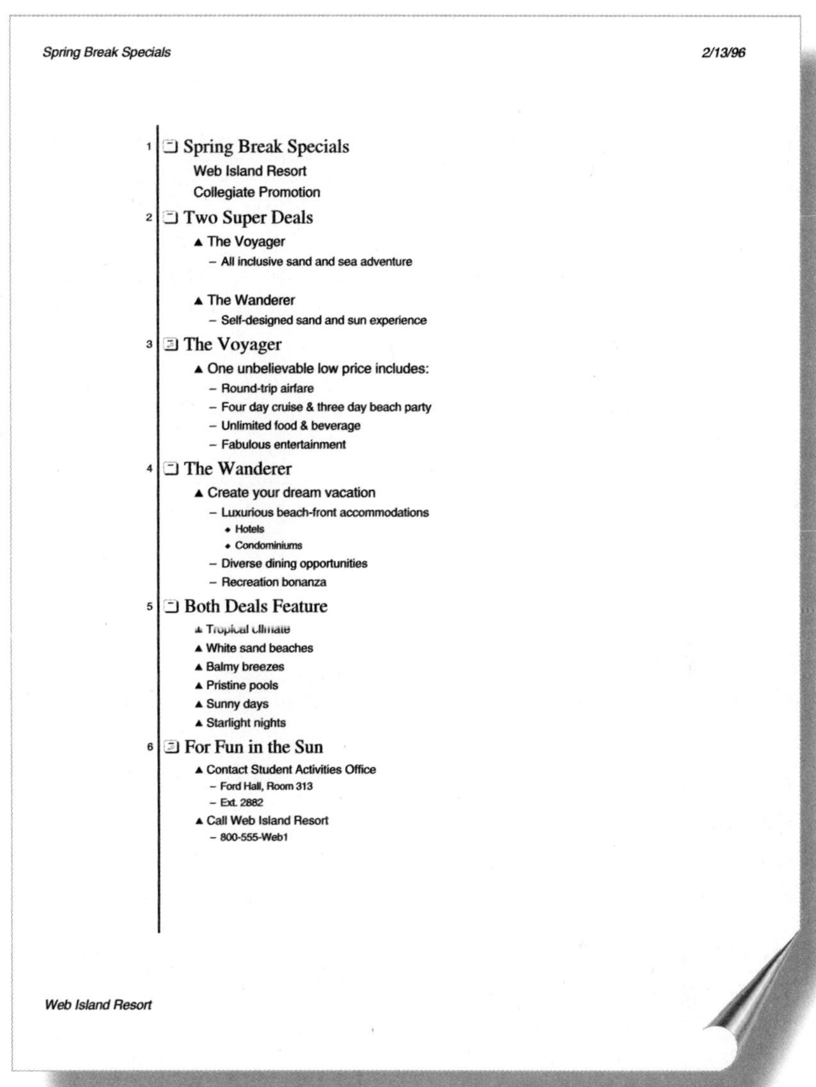

FIGURE 2-69

OtherWays

1. On menu bar click File, click Print, click Outline View in Print what box
2. Press CTRL+P, click Outline View in Print what box

Printing Presentation Slides in Outline View

After correcting errors, you will want to print a final copy of your presentation. If you made any changes to your presentation since your last save, be sure to save your presentation before you print.

Perform the steps on the next pages to print the presentation slides while in Outline view.

To Print Presentation Slides

1. **Ready the printer according to the printer instructions.**

2. **Click File on the menu bar. Then point to Print (Figure 2-70).**

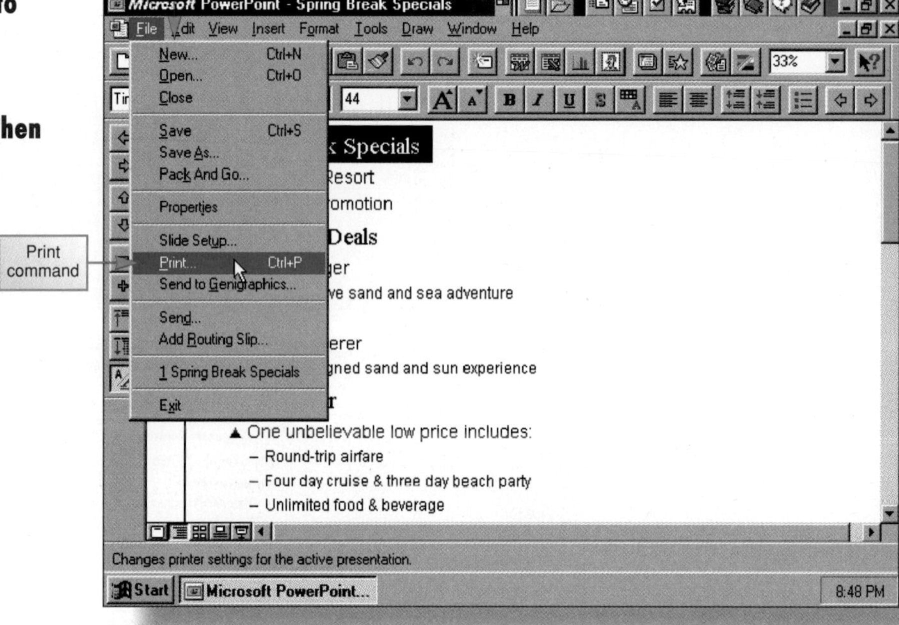

FIGURE 2-70

3. **Click Print. When the Print dialog box displays, click the Print what box arrow.**

The Print dialog box displays (Figure 2-71). The Print what drop-down list box displays hard copy options. Outline View is selected because it is the current view.

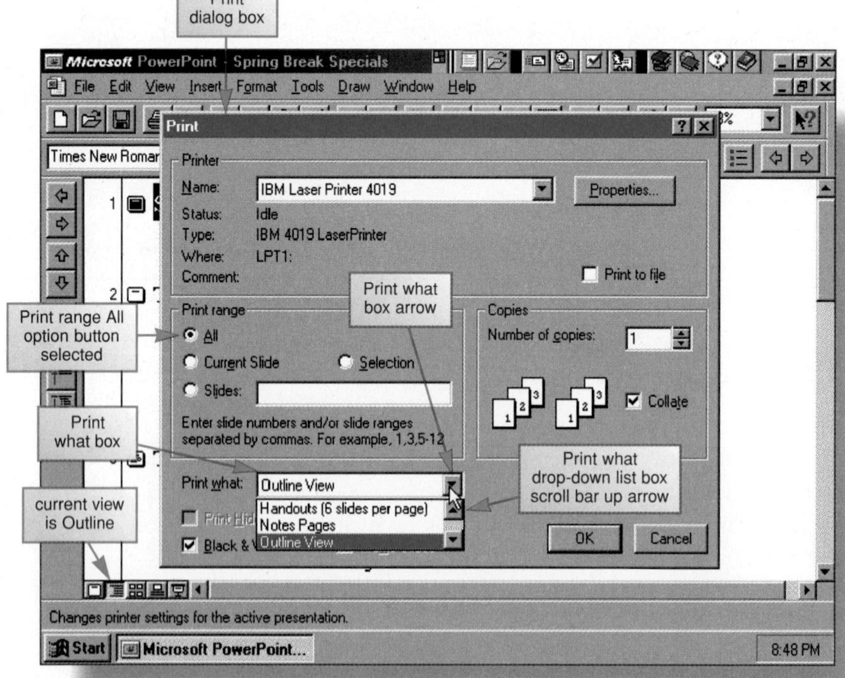

FIGURE 2-71

4 **Click the Print what drop-down list scroll bar up arrow until Slides (without Builds) displays. Then point to Slides (without Builds) (Figure 2-72).**

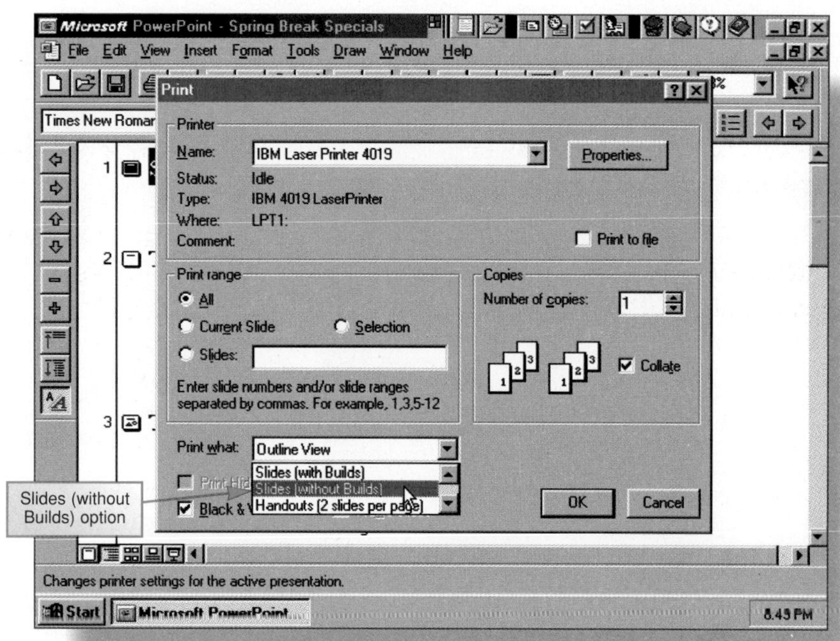

FIGURE 2-72

5 **Click Slides (without Builds) (Figure 2-73).**

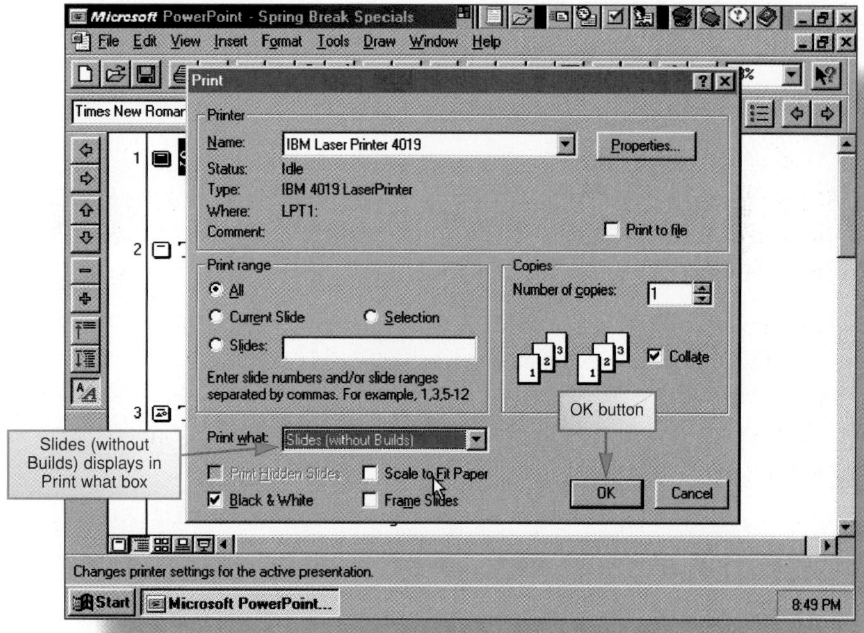

FIGURE 2-73

6 **Click the OK button in the Print dialog box. When the printer stops, retrieve the printouts.**

The printouts should look like the slides in Figure 2-74.

FIGURE 2-74a

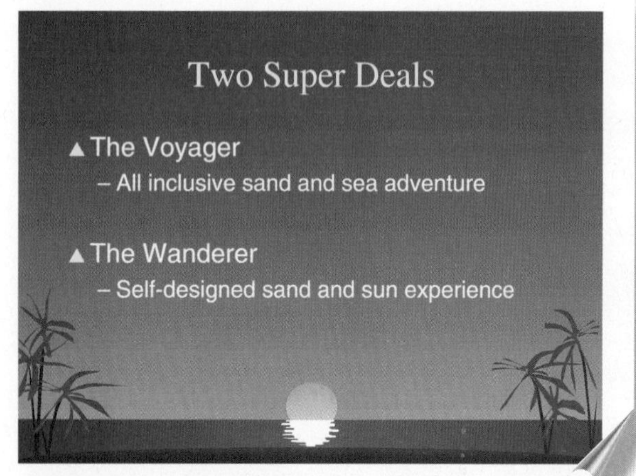

FIGURE 2-74b

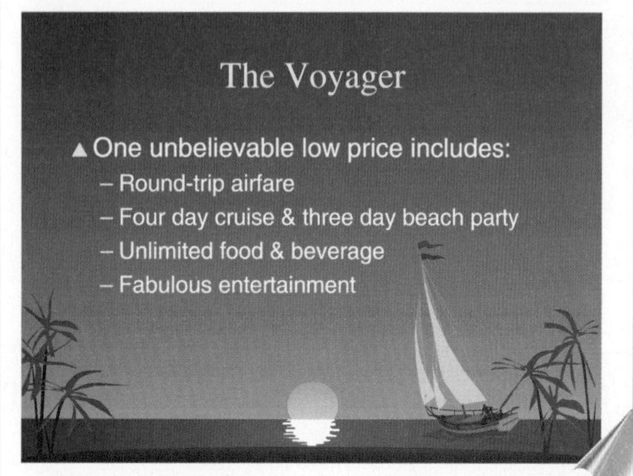

FIGURE 2-74c

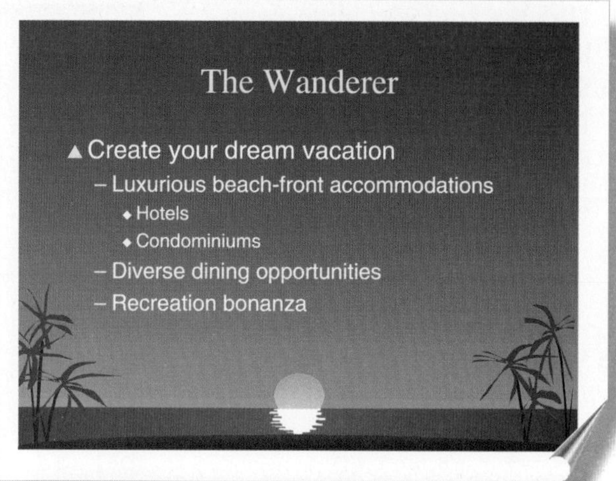

FIGURE 2-74d

FIGURE 2-74e

FIGURE 2-74f

*Other*Ways

1. On View Button bar click Slide View button, click Print button
2. Press CTRL+P, click Slides in Print what box

The Print what drop-down list in the Print dialog box contains options for printing two, three, or six slide images per page. These options are labeled as Handouts [2 slides per page], Handouts [3 slides per page], and Handouts [6 slides per page]. Printing handouts is useful for reviewing a presentation because you print several slides on one page. Additionally, many businesses distribute handouts of the slide show before a presentation so the attendees have a hard copy to which to refer.

Editing a Presentation

Now that the Spring Break Specials presentation is complete, you want to review it for content and presentation flow. If you find that your slides need to be in a different sequence, you can easily change the slide order by dragging the slide to its new position. You can change slide order in either Outline view or Slide Sorter view. The following sections explain several editing features of PowerPoint. First, you will change slide order in Outline view and then in Slide Sorter view. You will also copy a slide and paste it into the presentation. Finally, you will use the Undo button to reverse the last edit action.

Displaying Slide Titles in Outline View

When moving slides in Outline view, it is easier to display only the slide titles. Displaying just the slide titles makes a large presentation more manageable by allowing you to work with one line of text per slide. The nontitle text displays as a gray line under the slide title. Showing only slide titles also prevents you from combining slides by moving one slide into the bulleted text of another. Perform the following steps to display only the slide titles in Outline view.

To Display Slide Titles in Outline View

1 Point to the Show Titles button on the Outlining toolbar (Figure 2-75).

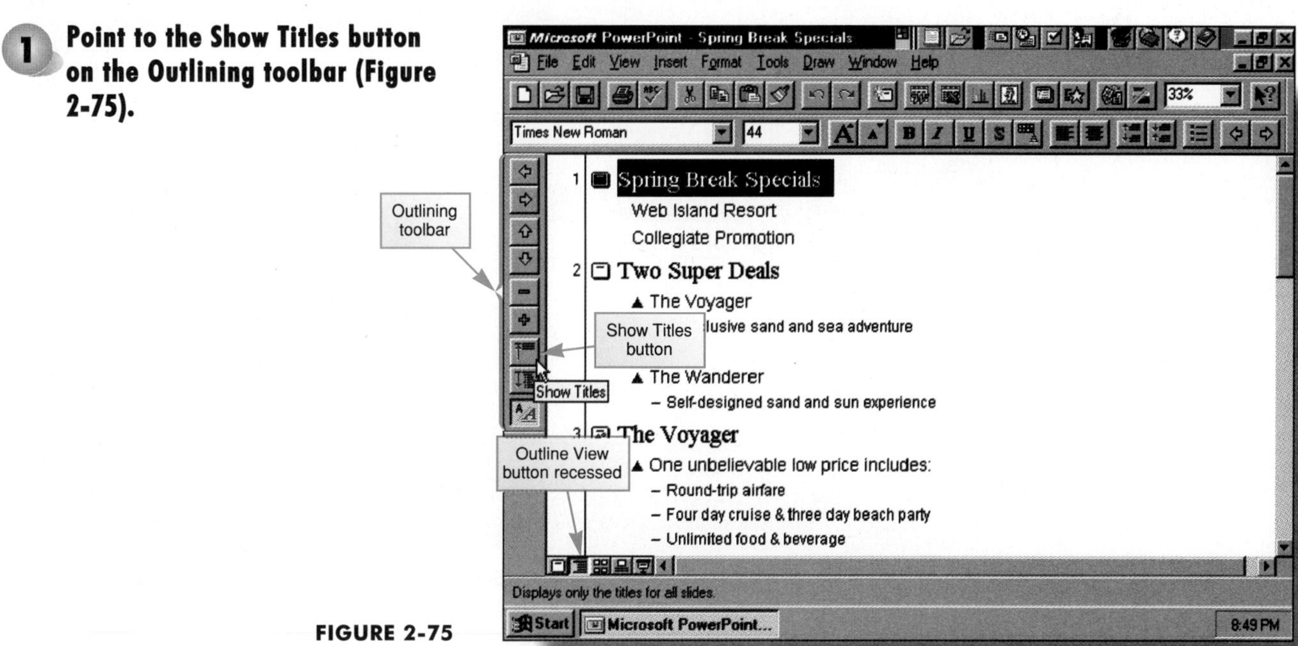

FIGURE 2-75

2 Click the Show Titles button.

PowerPoint compresses the slides so that only the six slide titles display in the Outline view window (Figure 2-76). Slide 1 is highlighted because it is the current slide. Nontitle text is indicated by a gray line under the title. Slides containing graphics display with graphic symbols in the slide icon.

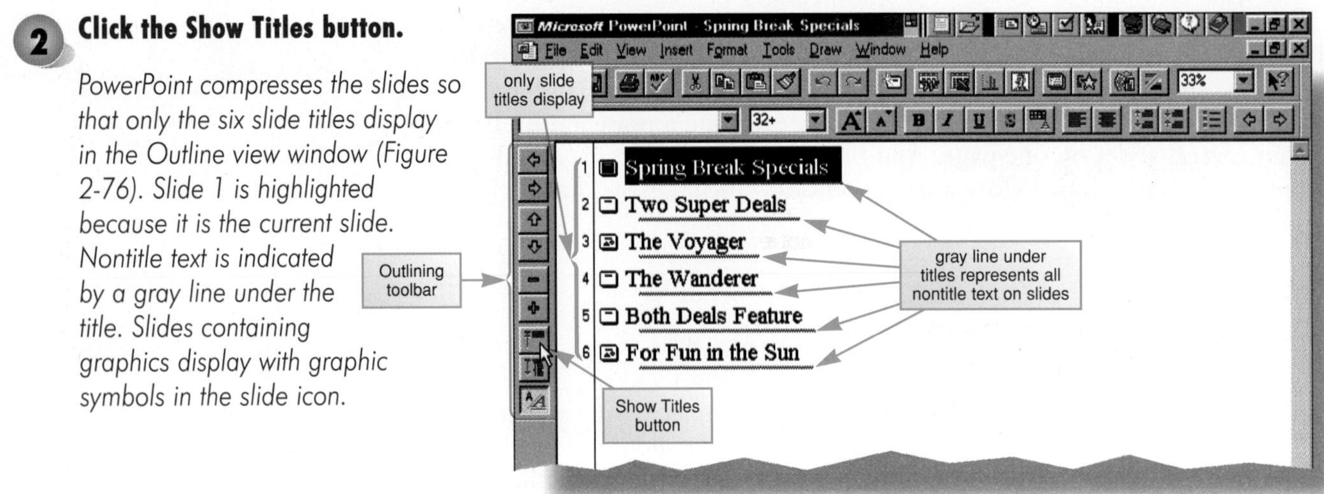

FIGURE 2-76

Changing Slide Order in Outline View

You move a slide to a new location, in Outline view, by dragging the slide icon until the horizontal placement indicator displays at the location where you want to position the slide. Perform the following steps to change slide order in Outline view.

To Change Slide Order in Outline View

1 Position the mouse pointer over the slide icon for Slide 5. Click the Slide 5 slide icon.

Slide 5 is selected (Figure 2-77). The mouse pointer becomes a four-headed arrow when positioned over the slide icon.

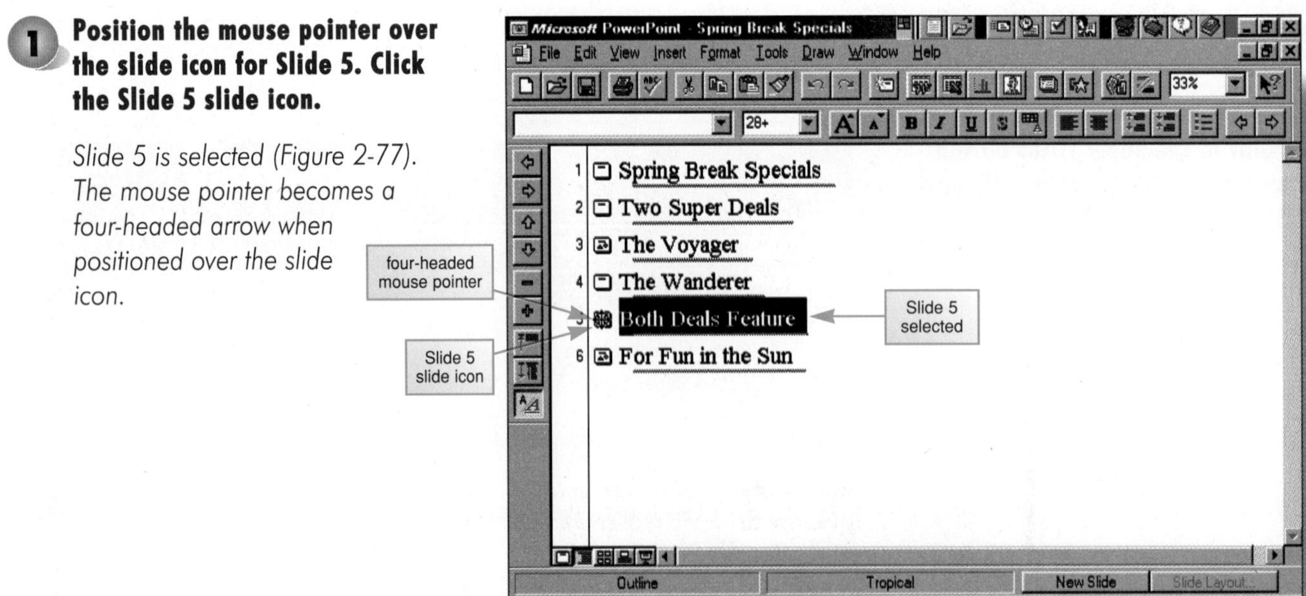

FIGURE 2-77

2 **Press and hold down the left mouse button. Drag the Slide 5 slide icon up until the horizontal placement indicator displays below Slide 2, Two Super Deals, and above Slide 3, The Voyager.**

The horizontal placement indicator displays below Slide 2 and above Slide 3 (Figure 2-78). The mouse pointer displays as a two-headed arrow.

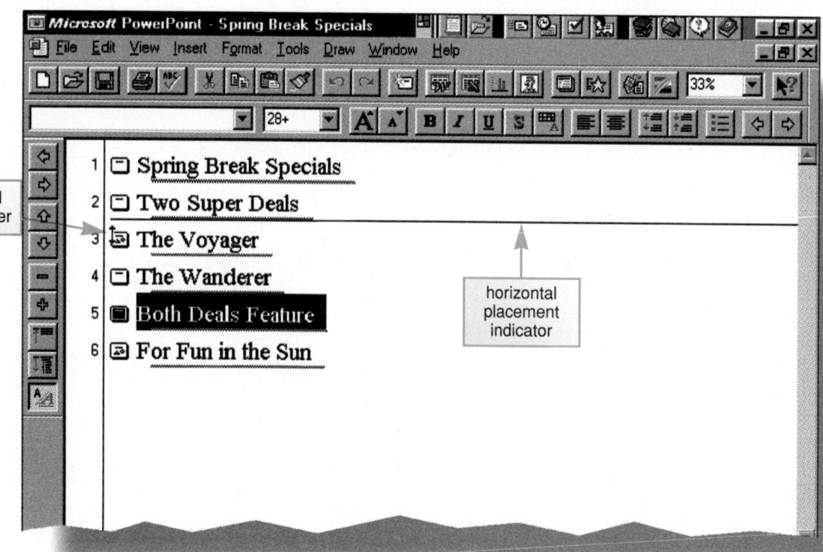

FIGURE 2-78

3 **Release the left mouse button.**

The slide titled Both Deals Feature becomes Slide 3 (Figure 2-79). PowerPoint automatically renumbers the slides. The mouse pointer displays as a four-headed arrow.

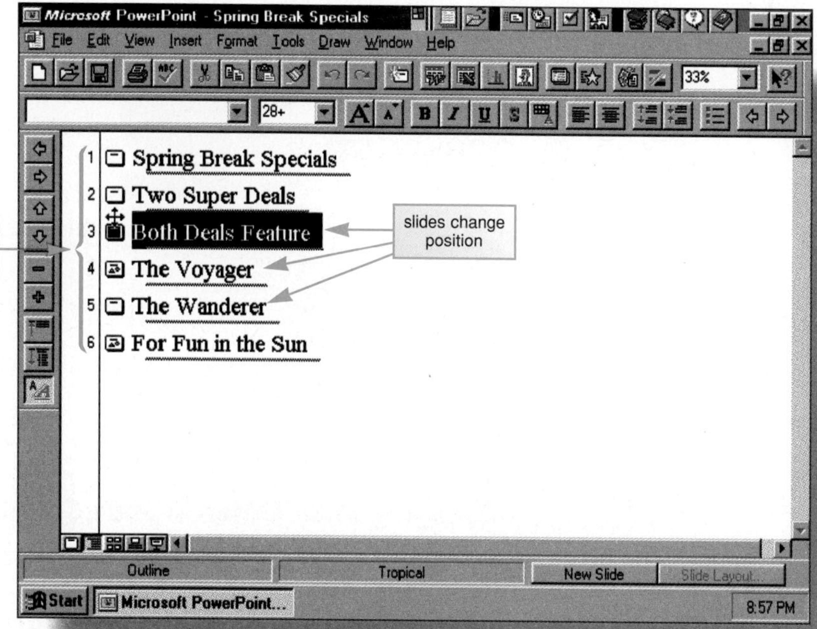

FIGURE 2-79

As you drag the slide icon, a horizontal placement indicator displays as soon as you move off the slide. The horizontal placement indicator is useful for identifying the exact location to drop the slide when changing slide order in Outline view.

Displaying All Text in Outline View

After moving slides, it is advisable to review the presentation again. Before you review the presentation, display the entire outline. Perform the following step to display all outline text.

To Display All Text in Outline View

1 Click the Show All button on the Outlining toolbar (see Figure 2-5 on page PP 2.9).

PowerPoint expands the outline text (Figure 2-80). Slide 3 is the current slide.

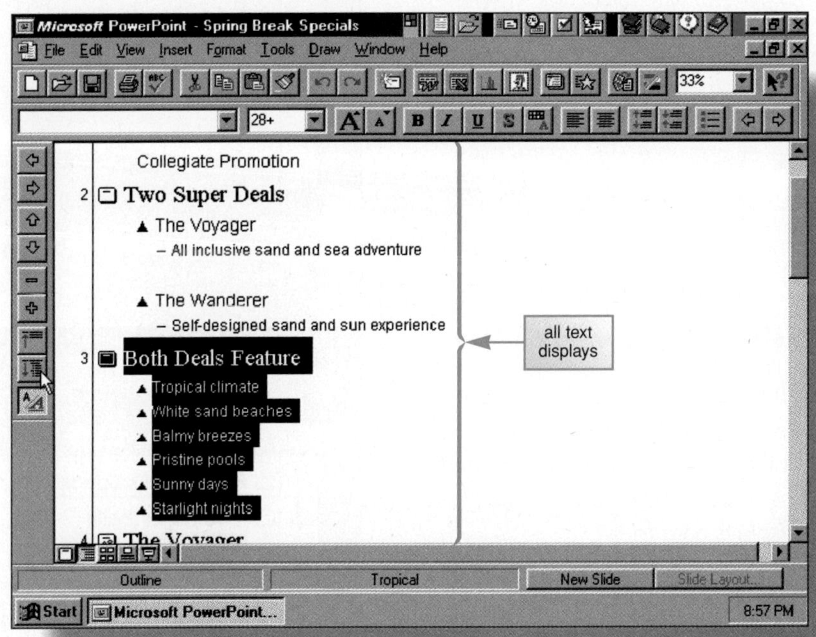

FIGURE 2-80

Changing Slide Order in Slide Sorter View

As previously stated, changing slide order in Slide Sorter view is as simple as dragging and dropping the slide into its new position. When you drag a slide to a new location in Slide Sorter view, a placement indicator displays to identify the slide's new position. The placement indicator is a dotted line. As you drag a slide, the mouse pointer displays as an arrow with a box around the arrow shaft. You move the slide to its new location by dragging the mouse pointer until the placement indicator displays at the location where you want to insert the slide. Because you cannot drop one slide on top of another slide in Slide Sorter view, the placement indicator appears to jump in front of a slide or after a slide as the mouse pointer moves around the window. Perform the following steps to change slide order in Slide Sorter view.

To Change Slide Order in Slide Sorter View

1 **Click the Slide Sorter View button on the View Button bar.**

The presentation displays in Slide Sorter view (Figure 2-81). Slide 3 is selected because it was the current slide in Outline view. PowerPoint assigns a number to each slide.

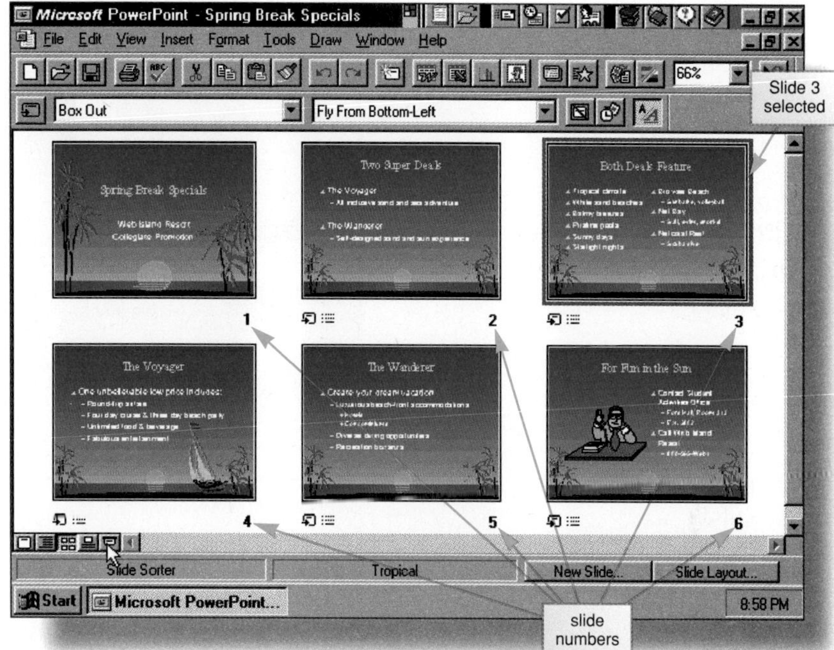

FIGURE 2-81

2 **Point to Slide 3, and then press and hold down the left mouse button. Drag Slide 3 down and to the left until the placement indicator displays after Slide 5 (Figure 2-82).**

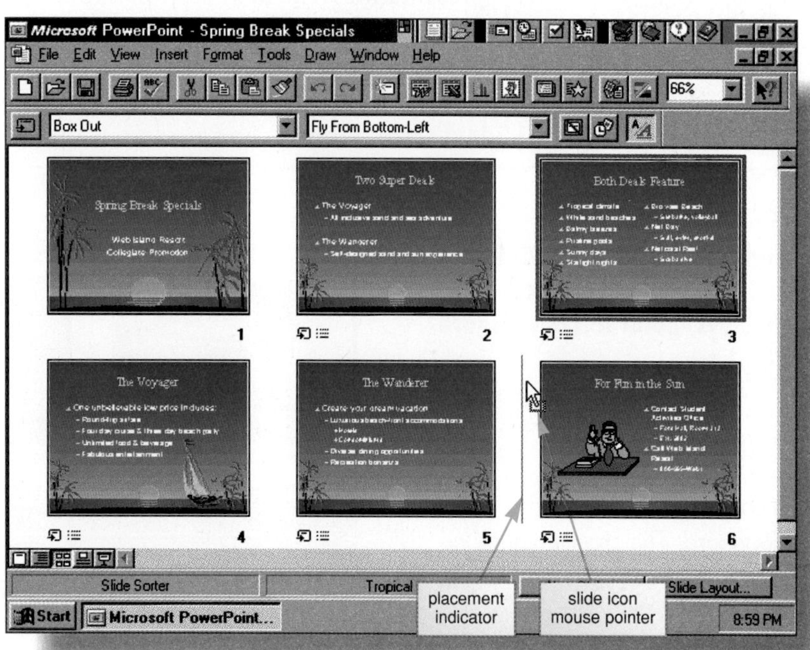

FIGURE 2-82

3 Release the left mouse button to drop Slide 3 after Slide 5.

Slide 3, titled, Both Deals Feature, becomes Slide 5 (Figure 2-83). PowerPoint automatically renumbers the slides.

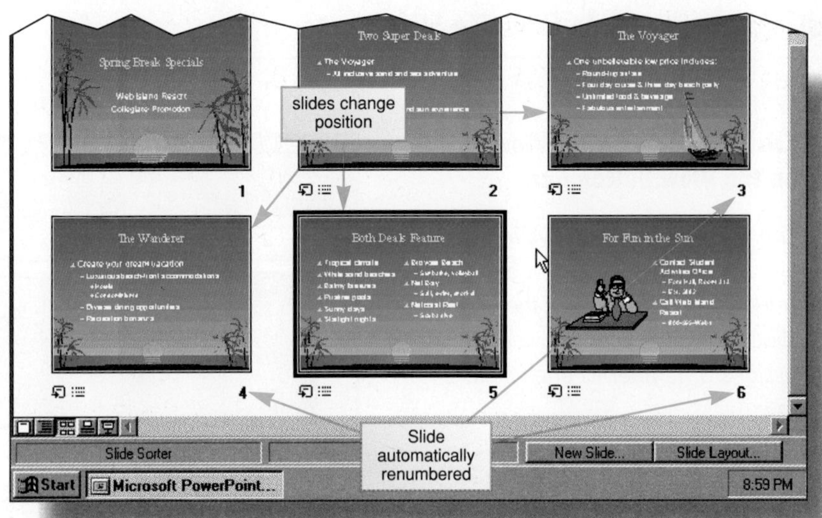

FIGURE 2-83

Copying a Slide

Occasionally you will want to copy a slide and then make changes to it. PowerPoint has a copy command that allows you to quickly duplicate a slide or any object on a slide. After you make a copy, you paste it elsewhere in your presentation. The next section explains how to copy and paste a slide in Slide Sorter view.

Steps To Copy a Slide in Slide Sorter View

1 Right-click Slide 5, Both Deals Feature. When a shortcut menu displays, point to Copy (Figure 2-84).

2 Click Copy.

A copy of Slide 5 is placed on the Clipboard. The shortcut menu no longer displays.

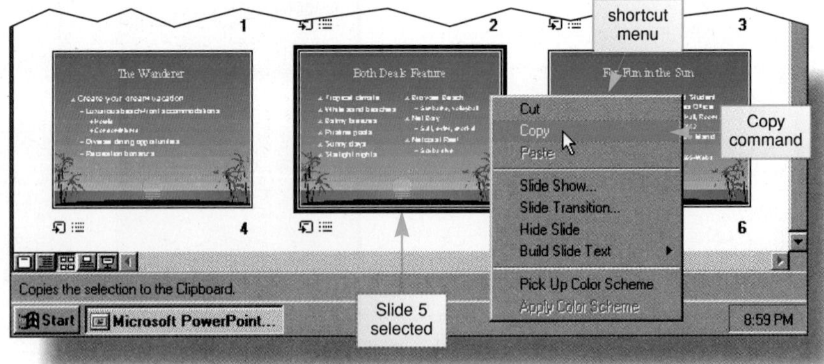

FIGURE 2-84

Other Ways

1. On Standard toolbar click Copy button
2. On menu bar click Edit, click Copy
3. Press CTRL+C

The Clipboard stores one copy at a time. If you copy another slide to the Clipboard, it replaces the first. To prevent the accidental loss of the contents of the Clipboard, immediately follow the Copy command with the Paste command. The next section explains how to paste the contents of the Clipboard into a presentation.

Pasting a Slide into a Presentation

Because a copy of Slide 5 is on the Clipboard, paste that copy into the presentation between Slide 2 and Slide 3. Perform the following steps to paste the contents of the Clipboard to the presentation.

More About Pasting Slides

When you paste a slide, PowerPoint automatically applies the Design Template of the presentation being pasted to. For example, if you paste a slide that has the Bedrock Design Template to a presentation that has the Cheers Design Template, PowerPoint applies the Cheers Design Template to the slide being pasted.

To Paste a Slide into a Presentation

1 Position the mouse pointer between Slide 2 and Slide 3 and right-click. When a shortcut menu displays, point to Paste.

The insertion point displays after Slide 2 and in front of Slide 3 (Figure 2-85). A shortcut menu displays. To reduce the possibility that you may accidentally replace the contents of the Clipboard, only the Paste and Slide Show commands are available.

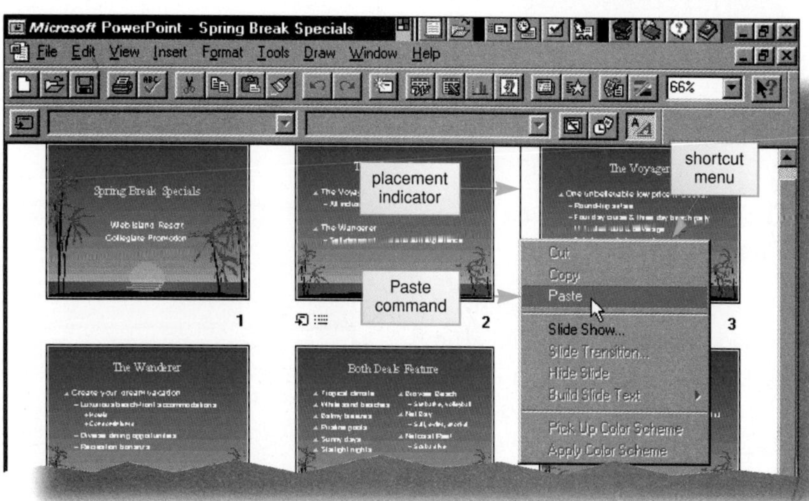

FIGURE 2-85

2 Click Paste on the shortcut menu.

A copy of Slide 5, titled Both Deals Feature, is inserted after Slide 2 (Figure 2-86). PowerPoint renumbers the slides. Both Slide 3 and Slide 6 are titled Both Deals Feature. The presence of the elevator in the scroll bar indicates more slides are in the presentation than can display in the Slide Sorter view window. The presentation now has seven slides because you added another slide to the presentation when you pasted a copy of the slide titled Both Deals Feature.

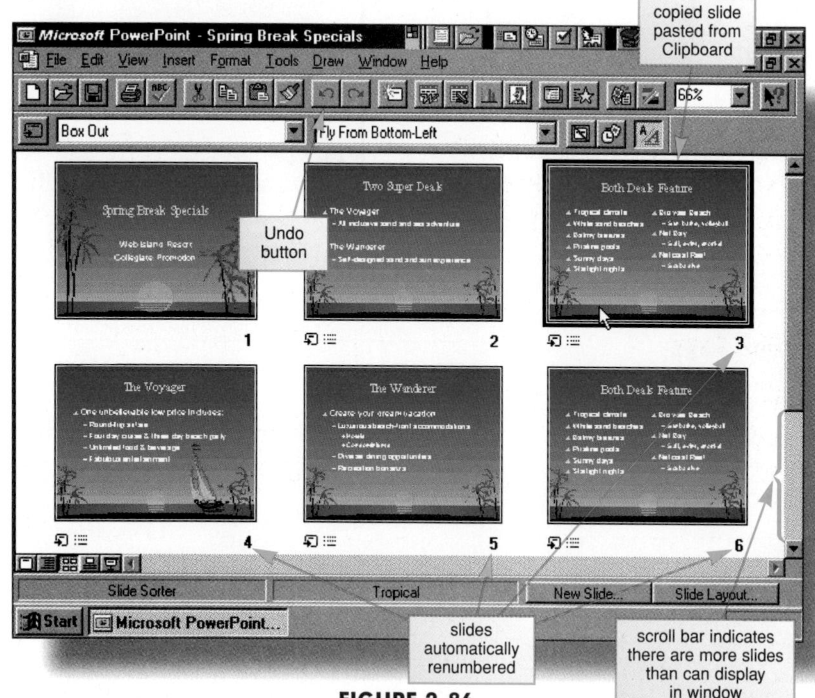

FIGURE 2-86

OtherWays

1. On Standard toolbar click Paste button
2. On menu bar click Edit, click Paste
3. Press CTRL+V

Using the Undo Button to Reverse the Last Edit

PowerPoint has an Undo button to reverse the last edit task. For example, if you delete an object, but realize you still want it to display, click the Undo button and the object again displays. By default, PowerPoint stores twenty edits in a buffer. A **buffer** is an area used temporarily to store data. As soon as you perform another edit task, the new task is stored in the Undo buffer. You can change the number of edits stored by PowerPoint by clicking Tools on the menu bar, clicking Options, clicking the Advanced tab in the Options dialog box, and changing the number in the Maximum Number of Undos box.

Follow the step below to use the Undo button to reverse the pasting of the copy of Slide 5 performed in the previous step.

Steps To Use the Undo Button to Reverse the Last Edit

1 Click the Undo button on the Standard toolbar.

The copy of Slide 5, previously pasted between Slide 2 and Slide 3, no longer displays (Figure 2-87). The insertion point displays where the slide previously displayed. PowerPoint renumbers the slides.

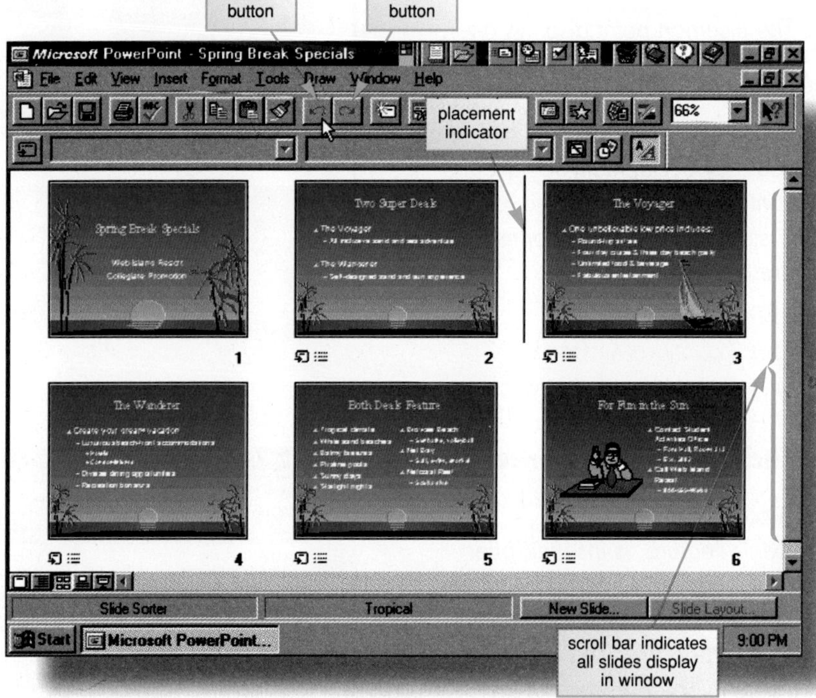

FIGURE 2-87

OtherWays

1. On menu bar click Edit, click Undo (command statement reflects most recent edit)
2. Press CTRL+Z

Located to the right of the Undo button is the Redo button. Clicking the Redo button returns the presentation to the state it was in prior to clicking the Undo button.

Saving and Closing PowerPoint

If you made any changes to your presentation since your last save, you should save it again by clicking the Save button. Close the presentation and PowerPoint by clicking the Close button on the title bar. For more details on closing PowerPoint, refer to page PP 1.37.

Project Summary

Project 2 introduced you to Outline view and clip art. You created a slide presentation in Outline view where you entered all the text in the form of an outline. You arranged the text using the Promote (Indent less) and Demote (Indent more) buttons. Once your outline was complete, you changed slide layouts and added clip art. You added slide transition effects and text build effects. Then you ran the slide show to demonstrate the animation effects, slide transition and text build. You learned how to print the presentation outline and slides in Outline view. Finally, you edited a presentation by rearranging slide order, copying and pasting, and reversing the last edit using the Undo button.

What You Should Know

Having completed this project, you now should be able to perform the following tasks:

- Add a Blank Line *(PP 2.20)*
- Add a Slide in Outline View *(PP 2.12)*
- Add Slide Transitions to a Slide Show *(PP 2.39)*
- Apply Text Build Effects to Bulleted Slides *(PP 2.43)*
- Change Slide Layout *(PP 2.23)*
- Change Slide Layout to Clip Art & Text *(PP 2.27)*
- Change Slide Order in Outline View *(PP 2.54)*
- Change Slide Order in Slide Sorter View *(PP 2.56)*
- Change the Size of Clip Art Using the Scale Command *(PP 2.33)*
- Change View to Outline View *(PP 2.8)*
- Change View to Slide Sorter View *(PP 2.19)*
- Copy a Slide in Slide Sorter View *(PP 2.58)*
- Create a Multi-level Slide in Outline View *(PP 2.13)*
- Create a Title Slide in Outline View *(PP 2.10)*
- Display All Text in Outline View *(PP 2.56)*
- Display Slide Titles in Outline View *(PP 2.53)*
- Insert Clip Art into a Clip Art Placeholder *(PP 2.28)*
- Insert Clip Art on a Slide without a Clip Art Placeholder *(PP 2.32)*
- Move Clip Art *(PP 2.33)*
- Paste a Slide into a Presentation *(PP 2.59)*
- Print an Outline *(PP 2.48)*
- Print Presentation Slides *(PP 2.50)*
- Run a Slide Show with Animation Effects *(PP 2.46)*
- Use the Notes and Handouts Sheet to Add Headers and Footers *(PP 2.36)*
- Use the Undo Button to Reverse the Last Edit *(PP 2.60)*

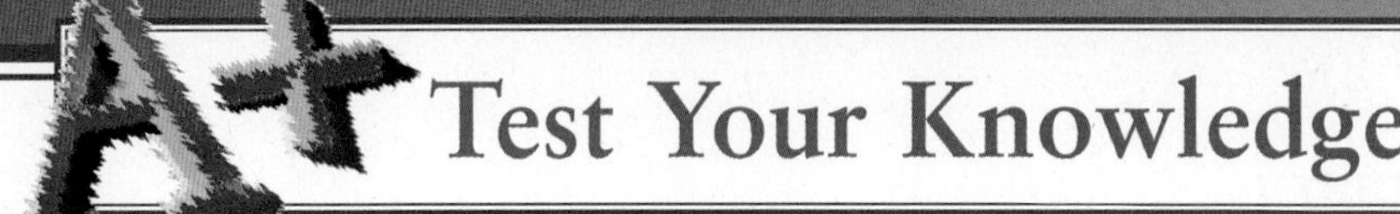

Test Your Knowledge

1 True/False

Instructions: Circle T if the statement is true or F if the statement is false.

T F 1. An outline is a summary of thoughts presented as headings and subheadings.
T F 2. Graphic objects, such as pictures, graphs, and tables, display in Outline view.
T F 3. In Outline view, the subtitle on the title slide displays on outline level one.
T F 4. The Demote (Indent more) button moves the selected paragraph up one level in the outline hierarchy each time you click the button.
T F 5. Clip art provides a quick way to add professional-looking graphic images to your presentation without creating the images yourself.
T F 6. The Scale command resizes clip art while maintaining its aspect ratio.
T F 7. PowerPoint automatically sizes clip art to fit a clip art placeholder.
T F 8. Slide view Zoom Control affects the size of text when printing an outline.
T F 9. Double-clicking a slide miniature in Slide Sorter view displays that slide in Outline view.
T F 10. Print slides from Outline view by clicking the Print button on the Standard toolbar.

2 Multiple Choice

Instructions: Circle the correct response.

1. Outline view provides a quick, easy way to ________________.
   a. insert clip art
   b. change slide layout
   c. display slide miniatures
   d. create a presentation
2. To add a new slide to a presentation in Outline view, ________________.
   a. click the New Slide button on the status bar
   b. click the Promote (Indent less) button until the insertion point displays at outline level one
   c. press CTRL+M
   d. all of the above
3. A presentation outline begins with a title on ________________.
   a. outline level zero
   b. outline level two
   c. outline level one
   d. none of the above
4. Move a slide in Outline view by dragging the ________________ to its new position.
   a. paragraph
   b. slide icon
   c. bullet
   d. none of the above

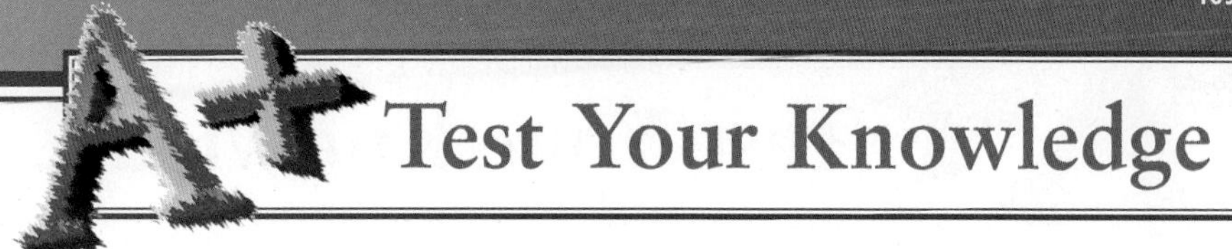

Test Your Knowledge

5. PowerPoint provides a(n) _______________ button to reverse the latest edit task.
   a. Paste
   b. Undo
   c. Edit
   d. Copy
6. The presentation outline may be printed by selecting the Print command from the File menu when in _______________.
   a. Notes Pages view
   b. Slide view
   c. Slide Sorter view
   d. all of the above
7. The animation effect that instructs PowerPoint to progressively disclose each bulleted paragraph during the running of a slide show is called _______________.
   a. Slide Show
   b. Slide Transition
   c. Build Slide Transition
   d. Build Slide Text
8. The Scale command _______________.
   a. is available in Outline view
   b. changes the size of a clip art image by a specific percentage
   c. changes the aspect ratio of the clip art image
   d. all of the above
9. Insert clip art on a slide that has a(n) _______________.
   a. object placeholder
   b. clip art placeholder
   c. text placeholder
   d. all of the above
10. The horizontal placement indicator is useful for identifying the exact location to drop a slide when changing slide order in _______________.
    a. Outline view
    b. Slide view
    c. Slide Sorter view
    d. all of the above

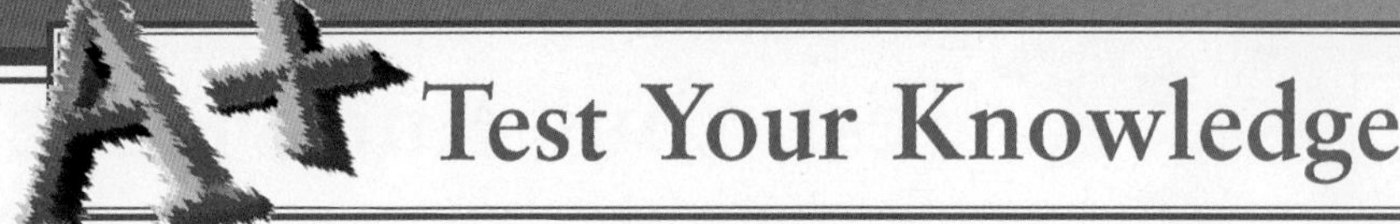

Test Your Knowledge

3 Understanding the Outlining View Window

Instructions: Arrows in Figure 2-88 point to the major components of a PowerPoint window in Outline view. Identify the various parts of the window in the space provided.

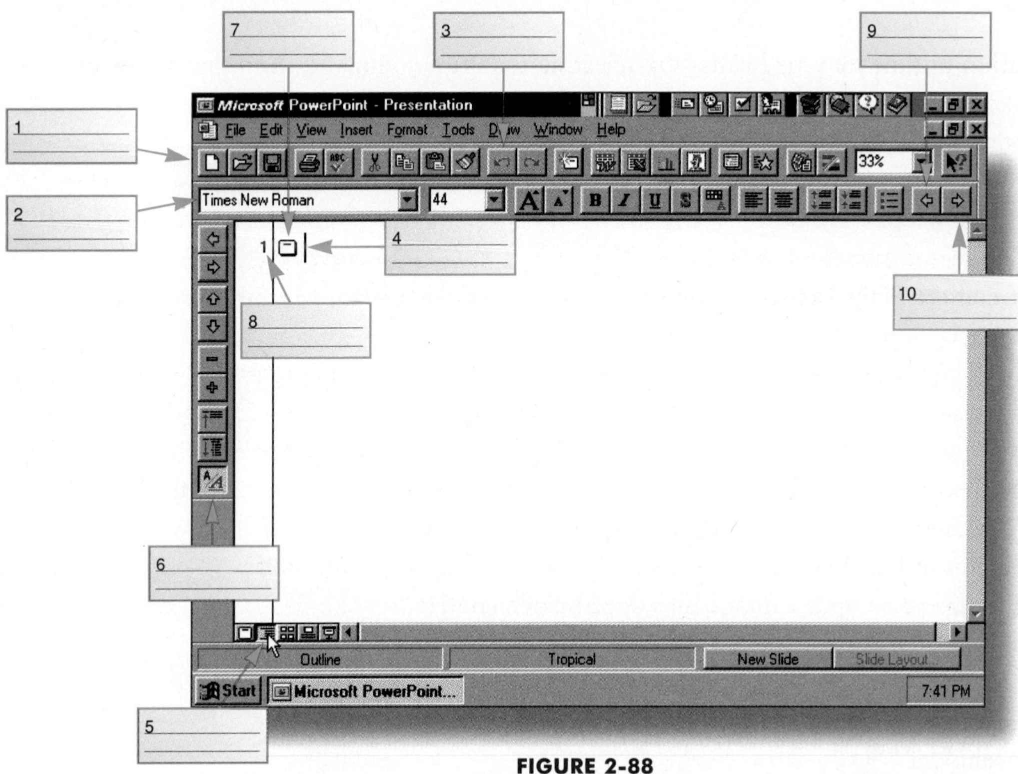

FIGURE 2-88

4 Understanding the Outlining Toolbar

Instructions: In Figure 2-89 below, arrows point to several of the buttons on the Outlining toolbar. In the space provided, briefly explain the purpose of each button.

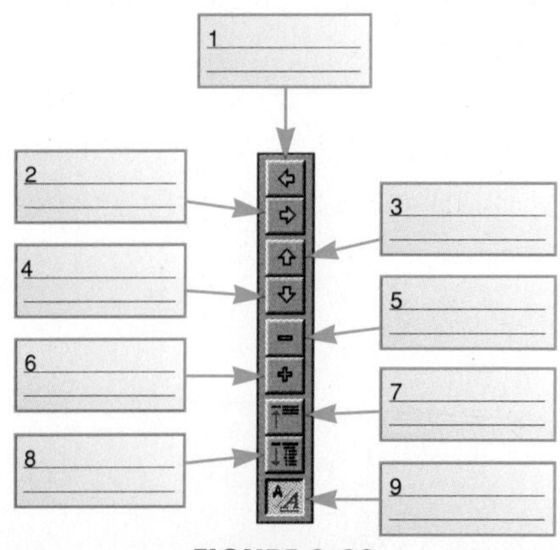

FIGURE 2-89

Use Help

1 Learning More about PowerPoint

Instructions: Perform the following tasks using a computer.

1. If PowerPoint is not already started, start a new PowerPoint presentation and select any AutoLayout.
2. Double-click the Help button on the Standard toolbar to display the Help Topics: Microsoft PowerPoint dialog box.
3. Click the Index tab. Type `templates` in box 1 and then double-click templates in box 2. When the Topics Found dialog box displays, double-click Using Design Templates to give my presentation a consistent look. When the Microsoft PowerPoint window displays, read the information, right-click within the dialog box, and click Print Topic. When the Print dialog box displays, click the OK button. Click the Help Topics button to return to the Help Topics: Microsoft PowerPoint dialog box.
4. Type `bullets` in box 1 and then press the ENTER key. When the Topics Found dialog box displays, double-click Add, change, or remove a bullet. When the Microsoft PowerPoint window displays, read and print the information. Click Change the distance between the bullet and the text. When the Microsoft PowerPoint window displays, read and print the information. Click the Help Topics button to return to the Help Topics: Microsoft PowerPoint dialog box.
5. Type `trouble` in box 1 and then double-click troubleshooting bullets in box 2. When the Microsoft PowerPoint window displays, read and print the I can't select a bullet information. Click the Close button to exit Help. Submit the printouts to your instructor.

2 Expanding on the Basics

Instructions: Use PowerPoint online help to better understand the topics listed below. Begin each of the following by double-clicking the Help button on the Standard toolbar. If you can't print the help information, answer the question on a separate piece of paper.

1. When in Outline view, how do you change the color of a bullet for all slides in a presentation?
2. How do you prevent a bullet from displaying?
3. How do you change the bullet character from a dot to an open file folder?
4. How do you change the size of a bullet?
5. How do you add a period to the end of every paragraph in a list?
6. How do you replace one clip art picture in a slide with another picture?
7. How do you build a slide with a clip art image that appears to fly onto the slide?

Apply Your Knowledge

1 Intensifying a Presentation by Applying a Design Template, Changing Slide Layout, and Adding Clip Art.

Instructions: Start PowerPoint. Open the presentation Triathlon from the PowerPoint folder on the Student Floppy Disk that accompanies this book. Perform the following tasks to change the presentation to look like Figure 2-90. ***Hint:*** Use Help to solve this problem.

1. Apply the Soaring Design Template. Add the current date, slide number, and your name to the footer. Display the footer on all slides.
2. Change the Slide Master line spacing for the First Level bullet to 0.5-lines before each paragraph.
3. On Slide 1, insert one blank paragraph after the August 16, 1997 paragraph. Insert the runner clip art image shown in Figure 2-90 that has the description, Victory Performance. Drag the runner clip art image to align the left side of the dotted box under the letter l in the word Triathlon and to display the image of the runner in the middle of the light blue pathway as shown in Figure 2-90. Decrease font size of Sponsored by: to 24 points.
4. Go to Slide 3. Change the slide layout to 2 Column Text. Move the six female categories to the right column placeholder.
5. Go to Slide 4. Change the slide layout to Text & Clip Art. Insert the trophy clip art image shown in Figure 2-90 that has the description, Goal Success. Scale the trophy clip art image to 90%.
6. Go to Slide 5. Change the slide layout to Clip Art & Text. Insert the hourglass clip art image shown in Figure 2-90 that has the description, Patience Timeline. Scale the hourglass clip art image to 95%. Change the line spacing for the First Level bullets to 1 line before each paragraph.
7. Check the presentation for spelling errors.
8. Add the Strips Down-Right slide transition effect to all slides except the title slide.
9. Save the presentation on your data floppy disk using the filename, Two-State Triathlon.
10. Print the presentation in black and white.
11. Close PowerPoint.

Apply Your Knowledge

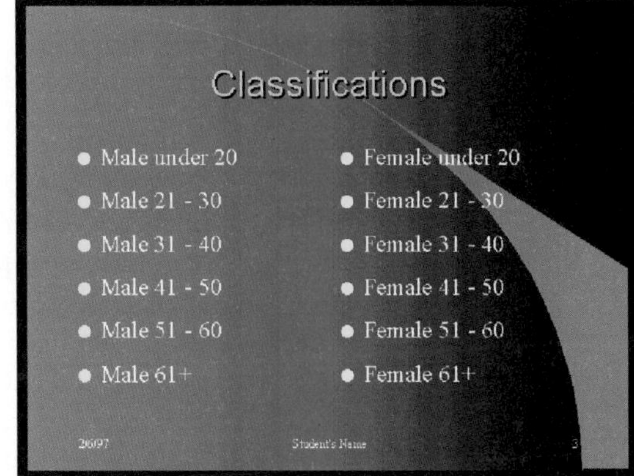

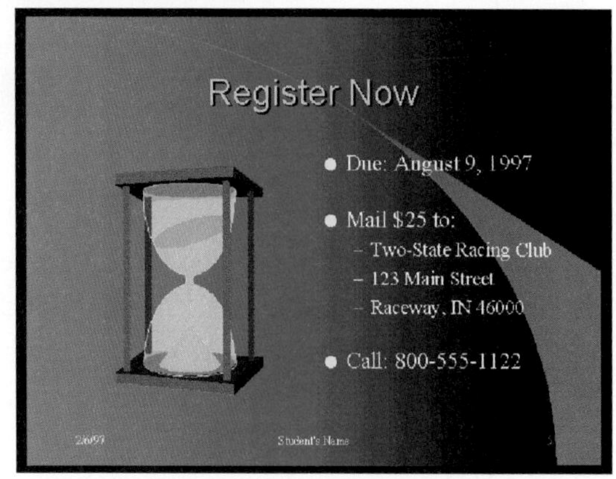

FIGURE 2-90

In the Lab

1 Adding Clip Art and Animation Effects to a Presentation Created in Outline View

Problem: You are a student in Psych 101. Your psychology professor assigns a research paper and requires you to present your findings during a five minute presentation. Your topic is having a positive attitude. To prepare for the presentation, you create the outline shown in Figure 2-91. You then use the outline to create the slide show shown in Figure 2-92. Because of your research findings, you create a unique closing slide. *Hint:* Use Help to solve this problem.

Instructions: Perform the following tasks:

1. Create a new presentation using the Cheers Design Template.
2. Using the outline shown in Figure 2-91, create the title slide shown in Figure 2-92. Use your name instead of the name Adam East. Increase the font size of your name to 36 points.
3. Using the outline in Figure 2-91, create the three bulleted list slides shown in Figure 2-92.
4. Change the slide layout on Slide 2 to Clip Art & Text. Using the clip art placeholder, insert the clip art shown in Figure 2-92 that has the description, Happy Joy Laugh. Increase the bulleted list font size to 36 points.
5. Change the slide layout on Slide 3 to Text & Clip Art. Using the clip art placeholder, insert the clip art shown in Figure 2-92 that has the description, Consensus. Increase the bulleted list line spacing to 0.3-lines before each paragraph.
6. Drag the slide title on Slide 4 to the text placeholder. Change the case of Possible, Positive, and Attitude to lowercase letters. Increase the text font size to 66 points.
7. Add the slide number and your name to the slide footer. Display the footer on all slides except the title slide. Add your name to the outline header and your school's name to the outline footer.
8. Apply the Dissolve slide transition effect to all slides. Apply the Wipe Right text build effect to all First Level paragraphs on Slide 2 and Slide 3.

I. Improving Your Attitude
   Adam East
   Psychology 101
II. Positive Attitude Characteristics
   A. Cheerful
   B. Friendly
   C. Neat
   D. Courteous
   E. Thoughtful
   F. Considerate
III. How to Improve Your Attitude
   A. Associate with positive people
   B. Speak well of others
   C. Isolate negative thoughts
   D. Treat others with respect
   E. Forgive and forge on
IV. Anything is Possible with a Positive Attitude

FIGURE 2-91

9. Run Style Checker to check spelling, visual clarity, case, and end punctuation. Ignore the Visual Clarity Error on Slide 4 in order to create this special effect. Correct any other errors identified by Style Checker.
10. Save the presentation on your data floppy disk using the filename, Improving Your Attitude.
11. Print the presentation outline.
12. Print the black and white presentation.
13. Close PowerPoint.

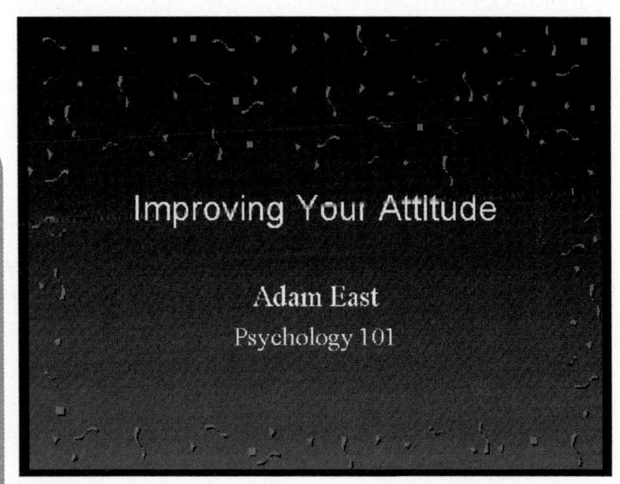

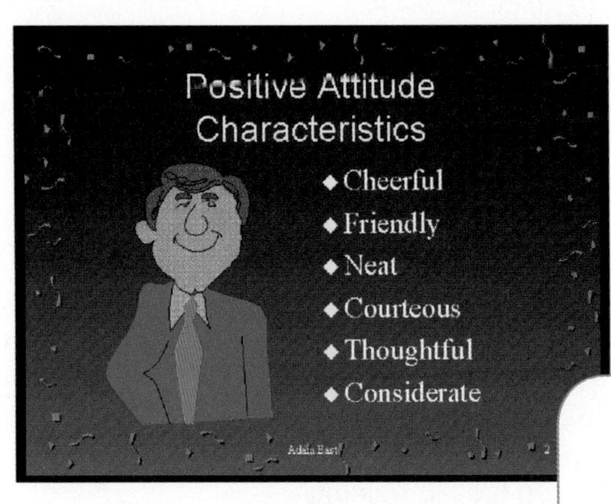

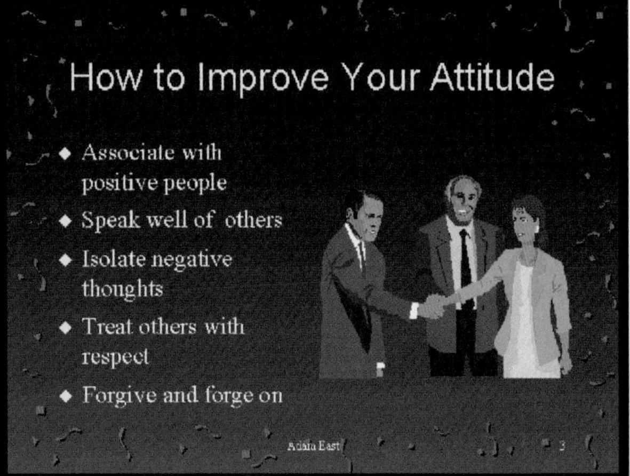

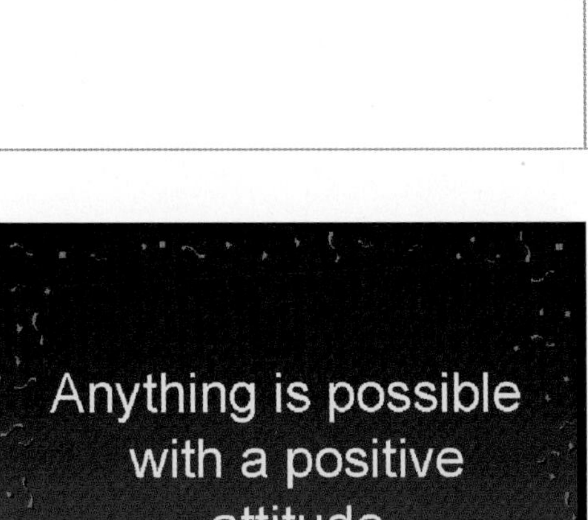

FIGURE 2-92

2 Using Clip Art, Slide Transition Effects, and Text Build Effects to Refine a Presentation

Problem: You are the Director of Career Development and Placement at Green Valley University. A local middle school principal has asked you to speak to his eighth grade students about career opportunities. You create the presentation using the outline shown in Figure 2-93. You then refine the presentation using clip art, slide transitions, and text build effects to create the slide show shown in Figure 2-94.

Instructions: Perform the following tasks.

1. Create a new presentation using the Splatter Design Template and the outline in Figure 2-93.
2. On the title slide, use your name instead of the name Ms. Janet Jakoby. Decrease the font size of the paragraphs, Presented by: and Green Valley University, to 24 points.
3. Change the slide layout on Slides 2, 3, and 4 to Clip Art & Text.
4. Use Figure 2-94 as a reference. On Slide 2, insert the clip art that has the description, Future Forecast. On Slide 3, insert the clip art that has the description, Surprise. On Slide 4, insert the clip art that has the description, Confusion Dilemma.
5. Add the slide number and your name to the slide footer. Display the footer on all slides except the title slide. Add your name to the outline header, and the name of the school, Green Valley University, to the outline footer.

I. The Future Is Yours
What to Consider
Presented by:
Ms. Janet Jakoby
Green Valley University
II. What Is In Your Future?
- **A. Education**
  - **1. College**
  - **2. Technical School**
  - **3. Apprenticeship**
- **B. Work**
  - **1. On the job training**

III. Possible Career Choices
- **A. Chef**
- **B. Engineer**
- **C. Entertainer**
- **D. Flight attendant**
- **E. Machinist**
- **F. Nurse**
- **G. Teacher**
- **H. Veterinarian**

IV. How Do You Choose?
- **A. Consider likes and dislikes**
  - **1. Working with your hands**
  - **2. Reading and writing**
  - **3. Working with people**
  - **4. Working with computers**
  - **5. Working with animals**

FIGURE 2-93

In the Lab

6. Check the presentation for spelling errors.
7. Apply the Uncover Right-Down slide transition effect to all slides. Apply the Split Vertical Out text build effect by 2nd level paragraphs to Slides 2 through 4.
8. Save the presentation on your data floppy disk using the filename, The Future is Yours.
9. Run the electronic slide show.
10. Print the presentation outline. Print the presentation slides without builds in black and white.
11. Close PowerPoint.

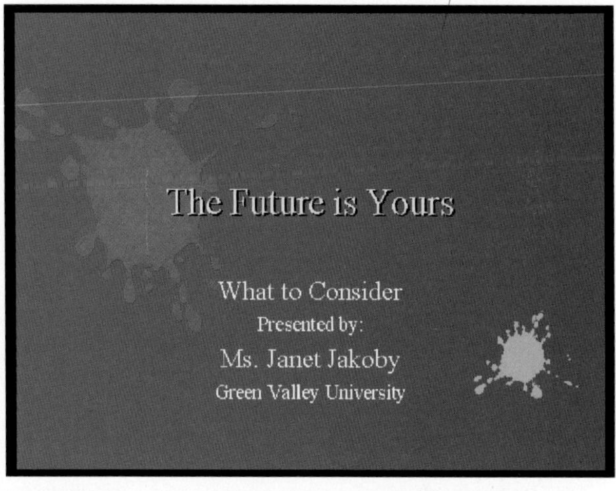

FIGURE 2-94

3 Animating a Slide Show

Problem: You are the sales director for Olympic Pharmaceuticals, a manufacturer of vitamins and other nutritional supplements. Experience tells you that sales are directly related to the quality of the sales presentation. Sales quotas are higher than last year and you want to make sure your sales staff understands the importance of practicing the delivery of a presentation. After much research, you prepare the outline shown in Figure 2-95. When you practice your presentation, you decide to add animation effects to the slide show. The completed slide show is shown in Figure 2-96 on pages PP 2.73 and PP 2.74.

Instructions: Perform the following tasks.

1. Create a new presentation using the Blue Green Design Template and the outline shown in Figure 2-95.
2. On the title slide, use your name instead of the name Les Deal. Decrease the font size of Presented by: to 20 points. Decrease the font size of Sales Director and Olympic Pharmaceuticals to 24 points.
3. On Slide 2, increase the font size of the Level One bullets to 36 points and Level Two bullets to 32 points. Increase the line spacing for Level Two bullets to 0.75-lines before each paragraph. Using Figure 2-96 as a reference, insert the clip art that has the description, Target. Scale the clip art to 120% and drag it to the lower-right corner of the slide.
4. On Slide 3, insert the clip art shown in Figure 2-96 that has the description, Happy Joy Laugh. Drag the clip art to the right side of the slide.

I. Polishing Your Presentation
    Presented by:
    Les Deal
    Sales Director
    Olympic Pharmaceuticals
II. Practice Makes Perfect
    A. Three key factors for a successful presentation
        1. Practice
        2. Practice
        3. Practice
III. Why Practice?
    A. Increase confidence
    B. Develop rhythm
        1. Pause for emphasis
    C. Improve articulation
        1. Vary pitch and inflection
    D. Establish timings
    E. Identify problems
IV. How To Practice
    A. Speak out loud
        1. Make a recording
            a) Video
            b) Audio
        2. Look into a mirror
        3. Find a live audience
            a) Friend or co-worker
            b) Group or team
    B. Go to delivery site
        1. Inspect equipment
            a) Audio-visual
            b) Lectern
        2. Check environment
            a) Noise
            b) Lighting
            c) Room temperature
V. Practice Makes Perfect

FIGURE 2-95

In the Lab

5. On Slide 4, change the slide layout to 2 Column Text. Drag the text into the right column placeholder so that your slide looks like Slide 4 in Figure 2-96. Increase the line spacing to 0.4-lines before each paragraph.
6. On Slide 5, change the slide layout to Object. Insert the clip art that has the description, Target.
7. Add the current date, slide number, and your name to the slide footer. Display the footer on all slides except the title slide. Include the current date and your name on the outline header. Include Olympic Pharmaceuticals and the page number on the outline footer.
8. Apply the Strips Up-Right slide transition effect to all slides. Apply the Fly From Bottom text build effect to Slides 2 through 4.
9. Animate the clip art on Slide 2 using the Fly From Left text build effect so it displays immediately after the slide title when you run the slide show.
10. Save the presentation on your data floppy disk using the filename, Polishing Your Presentation.
11. Print the presentation outline. Print the presentation slides without builds in black and white.
12. Close PowerPoint.

FIGURE 2-96a

FIGURE 2-96b

(continued)

Animating a Slide Show *(continued)*

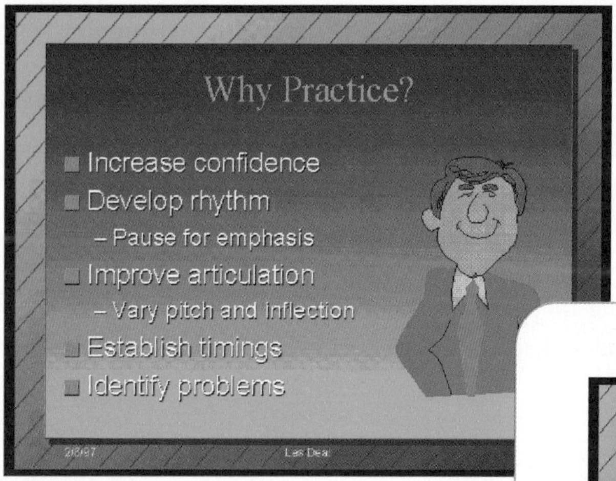

Why Practice?

- Increase confidence
- Develop rhythm
  - Pause for emphasis
- Improve articulation
  - Vary pitch and inflection
- Establish timings
- Identify problems

Les Deal

FIGURE 2-96c

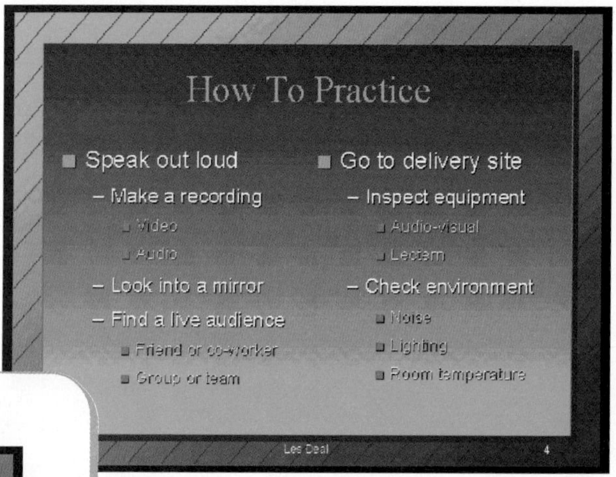

How To Practice

- Speak out loud
  - Make a recording
    - Video
    - Audio
  - Look into a mirror
  - Find a live audience
    - Friend or co-worker
    - Group or team
- Go to delivery site
  - Inspect equipment
    - Audio-visual
    - Lectern
  - Check environment
    - Noise
    - Lighting
    - Room temperature

Les Deal 4

FIGURE 2-96d

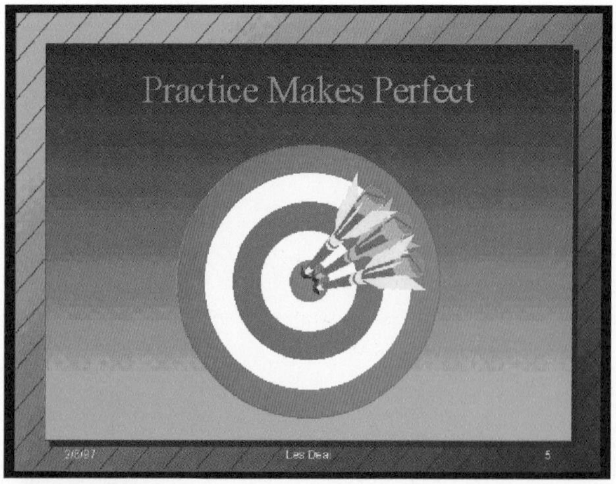

Practice Makes Perfect

Les Deal 5

FIGURE 2-96e

Cases and Places

The difficulty of these case studies varies:

◗ Case studies preceded by a single half moon are the least difficult. You are asked to create the required document based on information that has already been placed in an organized form.
◗◗ Case studies preceded by two half moons are more difficult. You must organize the information presented before using it to create the required document.
◗◗◗ Case studies preceded by three half moons are the most difficult. You must decide on a specific topic, then obtain and organize the necessary information before using it to create the required document.

1 ◗ Easy Rider Limousine Service plans to show programs in local high schools to promote their prom night packages. The owner of the limousine service has outlined the presentation.

With this outline, the owner has asked you to develop slides for the presentation, using clip art and special effects to add interest. The owner also would like a printed outline that can be distributed to students at the presentation's conclusion. Use the concepts and techniques introduced in this project to create the presentation.

I. Easy Rider Limousine Service
    A. A special ride on your special night
    B. Safe transportation to and from the prom
II. Three Great Packages
    A. The Dance
        1. Secure transport at reasonable rates
    B. The Promenade
        1. Conveyance with an extra flair
    C. The Cotillion
        1. A once-in-a-lifetime adventure
III. The Dance
    A. Our basic package provides:
        1. Terra Nova minivan
        2. Courteous, licensed driver
IV. The Promenade
    A. Our most popular package offers:
        1. Jackson World Town Car
        2. Courteous, licensed driver in chauffer's cap
        3. Refreshments
            a. Soft drinks and hors d'oeuvres
        4. Eight-speaker CD sound system
V. The Cotillion
    A. Our aristocratic package presents:
        1. La'Hambra Classic Limousine
        2. Courteous, licensed driver in top hat and tails
        3. Refreshments
            a. Soft drinks and hors d'oeuvres
            b. Lobster salad or prime rib sandwiches
        4. Live music
            a. Concert violinist performs a selection of songs
VI. To experience a prom trip remembered forever
    A. Call Easy Rider Limousine
        1. 555-EASY
    B. Talk to Your High School Guidance Office

FIGURE 2-97

Cases and Places

2 ◗ Phrank Ishua, director of the Ishua Institute, has outlined a presentation plugging the institute that will be given at various adult education classes and club meetings.

With this outline, Professor Ishua has asked you to develop slides for the presentation, using clip art and special effects to add interest. The owner also would like a printed outline that can be distributed to attendees at the presentation's conclusion. Use the concepts and techniques introduced in this project to create the presentation.

I. The Ishua Institute
   A. Expand physical and intellectual horizons
   B. Revelations for people of all ages
II. The Institute's Programs
   A. Training the body
      1. Practices that promote health and wellness
   B. Educating the mind
      1. Activities that enhance spiritual awareness
III. Training the Body
   A. Reach new levels of fitness through:
      1. Aerobic exercise sessions
      2. Interpretive dance
      3. Non-competitive games
      4. Rigorous isometric exercise
IV. Educating the Mind
   A. Learn to think in new ways with:
      1. Consciousness-raising workshops
      2. Alternative thought classes
         a. Extraterrestrial metaphysics
         b. Dynamics of contemplation
         c. Animated introspection
      3. Incidental meditation

V. Each Stay at the Ishua Institue Includes:
   A. Modest solitary accomodations
   B. Three nourishing meals daily
      1. Nutritionally complete fare
      2. Organically grown vegetables
      3. Salubrious confections and desserts
   C. Nightly self-examination
   D. Evening enrichment
   E. Use of extraordinary facilities
      1. Antediluvian mud baths
      2. Primeval hot springs
   F. Tours of Reflection Lake
   G. Lectures by guest instructors
VI. For a week, month, or year of rejuvenation
   A. Call Phrank Ishua
      1. 800-555-0609
   B. Write the Ishua Institute
      1. Mountbatten, WY 43721

FIGURE 2-98

Cases and Places

3 ▸▸ This summer you are working at Our Four Footed Friends, the largest pet shop in the community. The shop deals in all aspects of animal care: selling pets, providing supplies, and offering services. In addition to traditional pets, such as dogs and cats, the store peddles more unusual quadrupeds—raccoons, mongooses, wart hogs, etc. The shop stocks food, medicine, collars, grooming aids, and clothing for almost every type of pet. The store also makes pets presentable (clipping both fur and nails), supplies basic veterinary maintenance, and gives obedience classes. The workers are knowledgeable, helpful, and caring. The shop is open from 9:00 a.m. to 9:00 p.m. Monday through Saturday, and customers can call 555-PETS for information or appointments. As a break from cleaning cages, you have offered to develop a presentation marketing Our Four Footed Friends that will be exhibited at the county fair. Use the concepts and techniques introduced in this project to create the presentation. Enhance the presentation with clip art and special effects. Print an outline of the presentation that can be distributed to fair visitors.

4 ▸▸ As a well-known historian, you have been asked to develop a presentation for the International Association of Aliment Preservationists (IAAP) on the origin of canned food. You've decided to focus on two early 19th century innovators—Nicholas Appert, a wine bottler and cook, and Bryan Donkin, a one-time wallpaper manufacturer. Appert invented the canning process by placing foods in champagne bottles, corking the bottles, and then preserving the foods by boiling the bottles for varying lengths of time. The food, found to be in perfect condition after eight months, soon provisioned Napoleon's armies. Appert's methods were published in a book entitled L'art de conserver pendant plusieurs années toutes les substances animales or végétales. When Donkin's wallpaper business failed, he purchased the canning process patent and turned his idle machines to the manufacture of canned goods. Because of England's metal working industry, Donkin used tin cans (about twice the size of today's average can) instead of glass bottles. Although the canned food was lauded by the royal family and utilized on Arctic explorations, it was unpopular with the general public. The cans were expensive, in limited supply, and required a hammer and chisel to open. The trade was further crippled when some cans were found to have spoiled food. In the early 19th century the work of Louis Pasteur led to proper sterilization of food and the rebirth of the canning industry. Using this information, together with the concepts and techniques introduced in this project, create your presentation on the birth of the canned food. Enhance the presentation with clip art and special effects. Print an outline of the presentation that can be distributed to members of the IAAP.

5 ▸▸▸ While at one time most American businesses manufactured a some type of product, today an increasing number of companies instead offer a service. To be successful, service-oriented businesses must be able to clearly and convincingly explain how they can benefit prospective clients. Visit a business that provides a service and learn all you can about the service and the people to whom it is being offered. Using this information, together with the concepts and techniques introduced in this project, prepare a presentation promoting the company's services. Enhance the presentation with clip art and special effects and print an outline of the presentation.

Cases and Places

6 ▸▸▸ Visuals not only add interest to a class, they also make the class more memorable. Studies show that people recall only about ½ of what they hear, but more than ¾ of what they see and hear. Think of a lecture you have heard recently that could be improved with the addition of graphic materials. Outline the lecture's content. Use your outline, together with the concepts and techniques introduced in this project, to prepare a presentation that would augment the lecture. Enhance the presentation with clip art and special effects and print the outline of the presentation. Make an appointment with the instructor who delivered the lecture, show your presentation, and solicit comments or suggestions. Using the instructor's critique, rework the presentation. Give a copy of the presentation to the instructor.

7 ▸▸▸ In addition to Microsoft PowerPoint, other presentation graphics software packages include Aldus Persuasion, Lotus Freelance Graphics, and SPC Harvard Graphics. Visit a software vendor and try one of these, or another presentation graphics package. Use current computer magazines or other resources to learn more about the package you tested. Based on what you have discovered, together with the concepts and techniques introduced in this project, prepare a presentation comparing the package you tested to Microsoft PowerPoint. Contrast the capabilities, strengths, weaknesses, ease of use, and cost of each package. End by noting which package you prefer and why. Enhance the presentation with clip art and special effects and print the outline of the presentation.

Linking an Excel Chart to a PowerPoint Presentation

Case Perspective

Because of the success of the spring break promotion, Mr. Hayes, your boss at Web Island Resort, decides to run the promotion every year. You suggest that he include the results of the annual guest satisfaction survey to emphasize the quality of the resort. Mr. Hayes agrees and asks you to add a slide with a chart that illustrates the high percentage of guest satisfaction into the Spring Break Specials presentation. You contact the Marketing Department for the previous year's survey results. They e-mail you a file containing an Excel worksheet and a pie chart that summarizes the results of the 1996 guest satisfaction survey. Because you know Mr. Hayes is going to use this presentation every year and the chart will change each time the survey results change, you decide to link the pie chart to the presentation. Linking the chart ensures that you always present the most current survey results.

Introduction

This Integration Feature uses the Object Linking and Embedding (OLE) feature of Microsoft Office to insert an Excel chart into a PowerPoint slide. OLE allows you to incorporate parts of documents or entire documents from one application into another. In this section, you will open the Spring Break Specials presentation created in Project 2, insert a new slide, and link the pie chart shown in Figure 1 on the next page to a new slide shown in Figure 2 on the next page. The pie chart in Excel is called the **source document** and the Spring Break Specials presentation is the **container document.**

The three most common methods of copying objects between applications are copy and paste, copy and embed, and copy and link. This Integration Feature introduces a fourth method called insert object. Use the **insert object** method when you want to insert an entire file. The insert object method allows you to insert the source file without opening the source document. In this section, you use the insert object method to link the guest satisfaction survey file to the presentation.

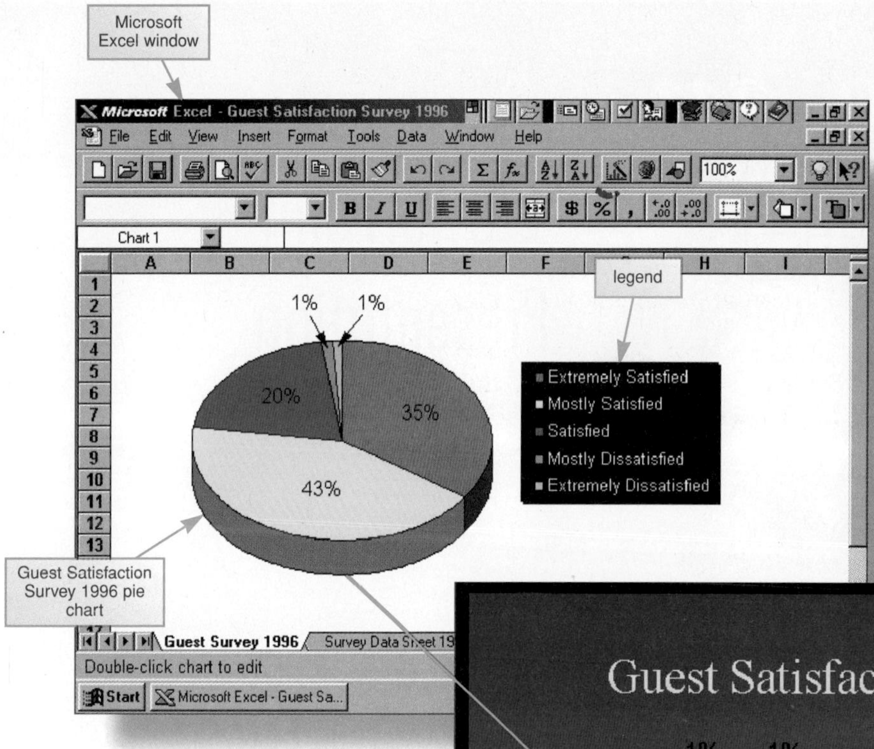

Microsoft Excel window

legend

Guest Satisfaction Survey 1996 pie chart

FIGURE 1

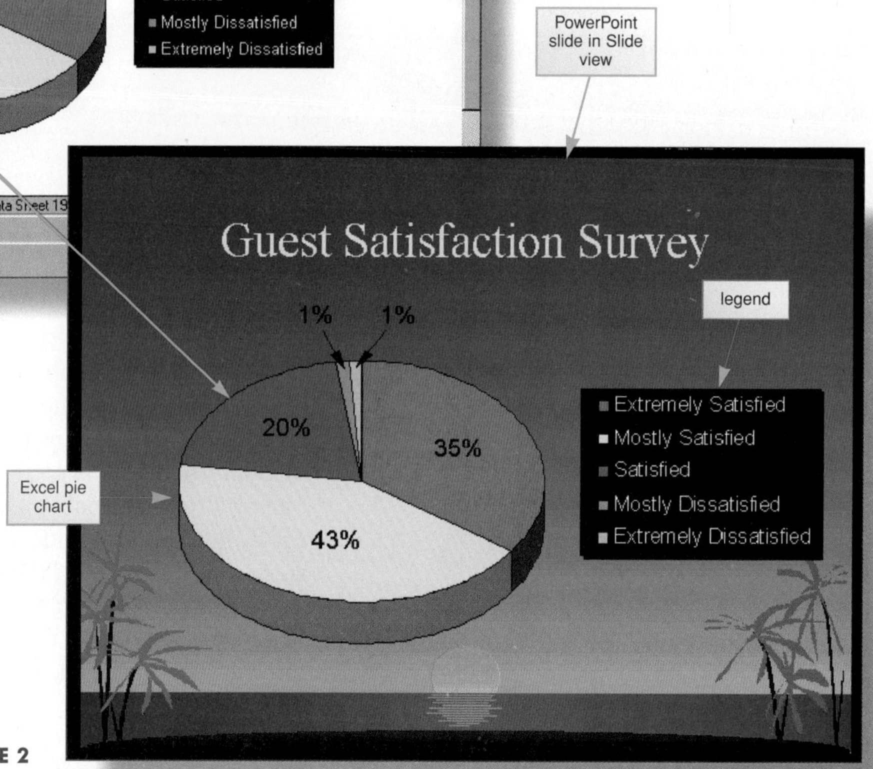

PowerPoint slide in Slide view

legend

Excel pie chart

FIGURE 2

Opening an Existing Presentation and Saving It with a New Filename

To add a chart to the Spring Break Specials presentation created in Project 2, the first step is to open the presentation. To keep the original Spring Break Specials presentation intact, you save the presentation with a new name, Spring Break Specials Chart. You then add a new slide to the Spring Break Specials Chart presentation and link the chart to the guest satisfaction survey.

Before adding a new slide, first you must open the presentation. Perform the following steps to open the Spring Break Specials presentation.

TO OPEN AN EXISTING PRESENTATION

Step 1: Insert your data floppy disk that contains the Spring Break Specials presentation created in Project 2 into drive A.
Step 2: Click the Start button on the taskbar. Click Open Office Document. Click 3½ Floppy [A:] in the Look in drop-down list box.
Step 3: Double-click the presentation Spring Break Specials.

PowerPoint opens and displays the presentation in the view it was in when last saved. Project 2 last saved the presentation in Slide Sorter view.

To preserve the original Spring Break Specials presentation, you save the open presentation with a new filename. Then, you make the changes to the new presentation. Essentially you are making a duplicate copy of a file. Perform the following steps to save the Spring Break Specials presentation with a new filename using the Save As command.

TO SAVE A PRESENTATION WITH A NEW FILENAME

Step 1: Click File on the menu bar. Click Save As.
Step 2: Type `Spring Break Specials Chart` in the File name box.
Step 3: Click the Save button.

The Spring Break Specials presentation is saved with the filename Spring Break Specials Chart. The new filename displays in the title bar.

Creating a Chart Slide

Several steps are necessary to create a slide containing a linked Excel chart. You must insert a new slide with the Object AutoLayout between Slides 5 and 6. Next, you type the slide title. Finally, you link the Excel chart. The steps on the following pages explain how to create a slide containing a linked Excel chart.

Inserting a New Slide Between Two Slides

The slide containing the Excel chart displays after Slide 5, Both Deals Feature. Perform the following steps to insert a new slide with the Object AutoLayout.

TO INSERT A NEW SLIDE

Step 1: Click between Slide 5 and Slide 6.
Step 2: Click the New Slide button on the status bar.
Step 3: When the New Slide dialog box displays, scroll down to display the Object AutoLayout. Double-click the Object AutoLayout.

PowerPoint inserts a slide after Slide 5, numbers the new slide as Slide 6 and renumbers the original Slide 6 as Slide 7 (Figure 3 on the next page). Slide 7 is not visible in Figure 3.

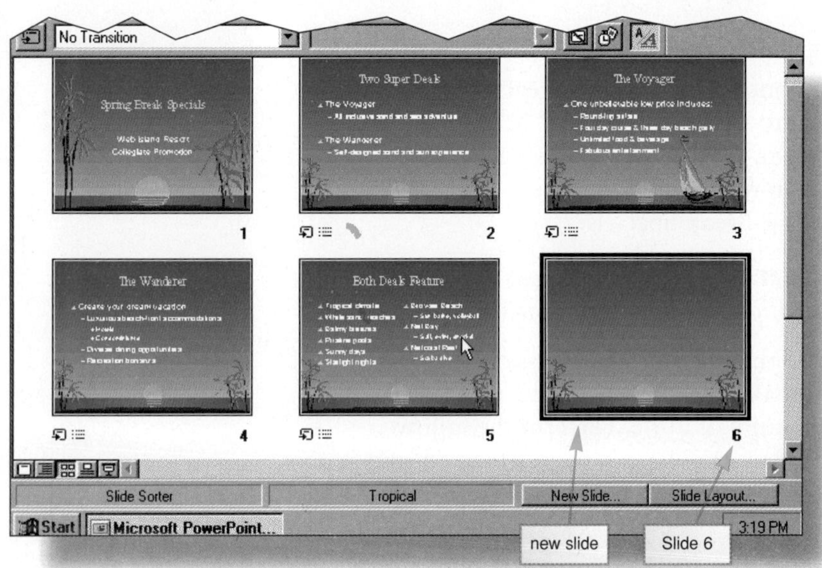

FIGURE 3

Typing a Slide Title

The next step is to type the slide title. The chart represents the results of the guest satisfaction survey. The slide title, therefore, is Guest Satisfaction Survey. Before typing, you must change views. Perform the following steps to type the slide title.

TO TYPE A SLIDE TITLE

Step 1: Double-click Slide 6 to display the slide in Slide view.
Step 2: Type `Guest Satisfaction Survey` in the title placeholder.

The slide title for Slide 6 displays.

More *About* **Linked Objects**

When the name or location of a source document changes, you must reconnect the link. Click the linked object and then click Links on the Edit menu. In the Links box, click the source document, click the Change Source button, and select the renamed or moved source document. Click the Update Now button.

Linking an Excel Chart to a Presentation

The Web Island Resort Marketing Department created the chart from the results of the 1996 Guest Satisfaction Survey. You link the existing chart to Slide 6 so the chart always reflects the current survey results. The Student Floppy Disk contains the chart, Guest Satisfaction Survey 1996, in the PowerPoint folder. Perform the following steps to link the Excel chart to Slide 6 in the Spring Break Specials Chart presentation.

Steps To Link the Excel Chart to Slide 6

1 Remove your data floppy disk from drive A. Insert the Student Floppy Disk that accompanies this book into drive A. Double-click the Object placeholder on Slide 6.

The Insert Object dialog box displays (Figure 4). Create New is the default. AutoSketch is selected as the default object type. The default object type on your computer may be different depending on options selected during the installation of Microsoft Office 95.

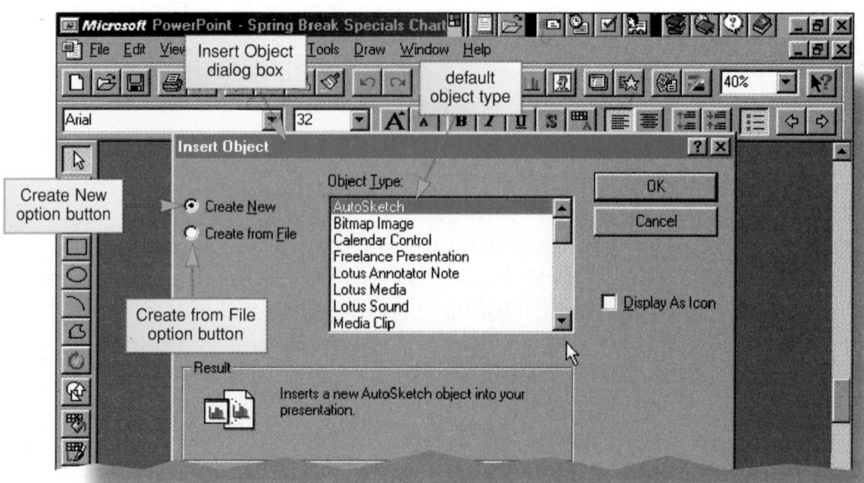

FIGURE 4

2 **Click Create from File. Point to the Browse button (Figure 5).**

3 **Click the Browse button. When the Browse dialog box displays, double-click the PowerPoint folder. Click Guest Satisfaction Survey.**

The Guest Satisfaction Survey file is highlighted in the Name box.

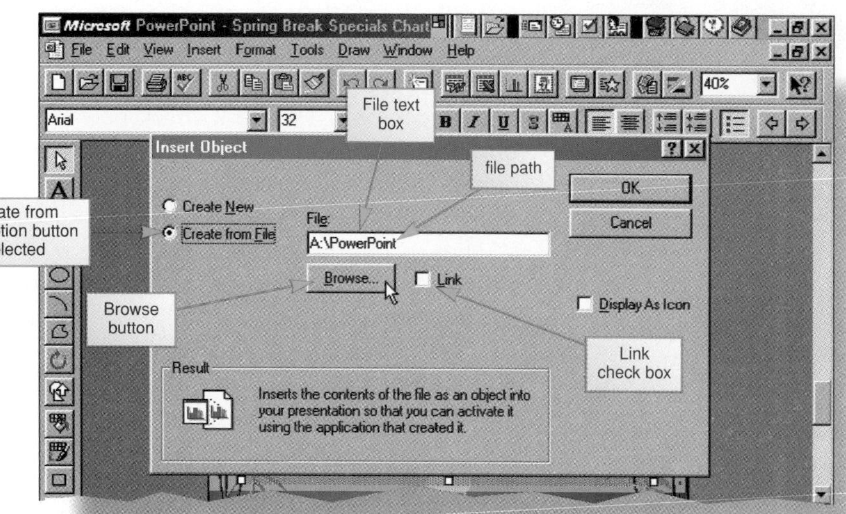

FIGURE 5

4 **Click the OK button. When the Insert Object dialog box displays, click Link.**

The File text box displays the path, or location, of the Excel chart (Figure 6). The check mark in the Link check box indicates the file listed in the File text box will be linked to the presentation.

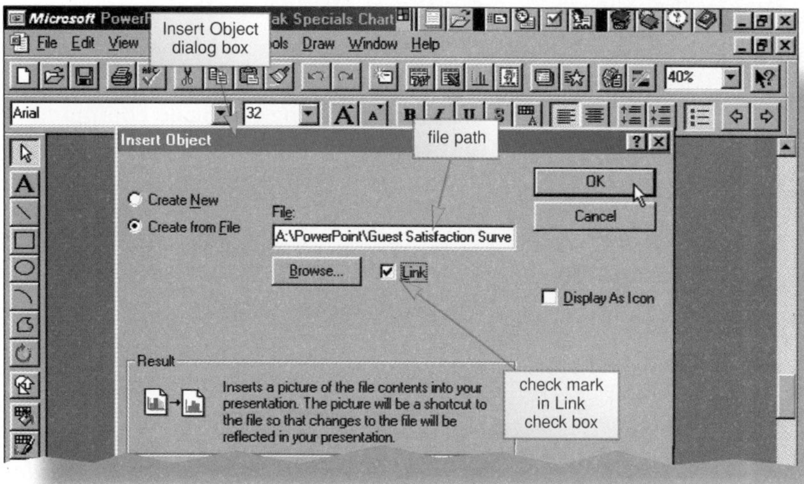

FIGURE 6

5 **Click the OK button.**

PowerPoint automatically sizes and displays the chart to fit the Object placeholder on Slide 6 (Figure 7). PowerPoint links the Customer Satisfaction Survey 1996 file, located on the Student Floppy Disk in drive A, to the presentation.

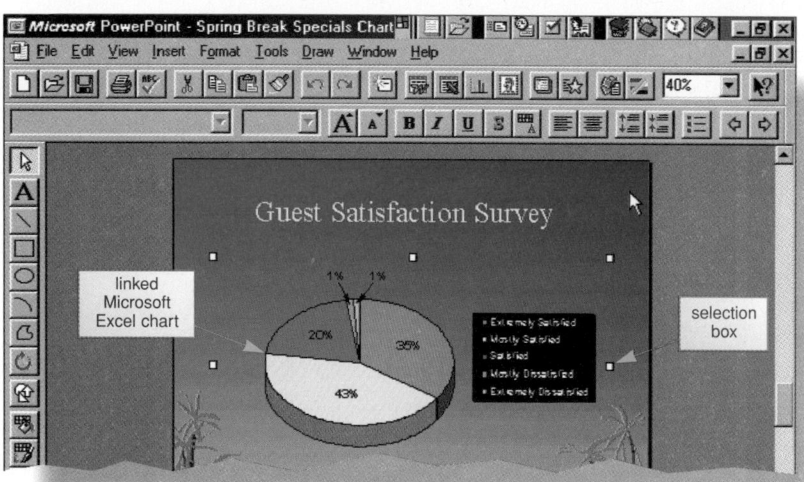

FIGURE 7

More *About* **Linking Objects**

If you deliver a presentation containing linked objects on a computer other than the one on which it was created, be certain to include a copy of the source files. The source files must be stored in the location as originally specified when you linked them to the presentation.

More *About* **Linking Charts**

To edit a linked chart, right-click the chart and then click Edit Worksheet Link. With the help of OLE, PowerPoint displays the chart without running Excel. When you finish your edits, select the worksheet to link to PowerPoint and then save the workbook. PowerPoint displays the top worksheet in the linked object.

When you click Create from File in the Insert Object dialog box, the dialog box changes (Figure 5 on page PPI 1.5). The Object Type list box no longer displays and is replaced by the File text box. Another change to the dialog box is the Link check box. The **Link** check box inserts the object as a linked object. A **linked object** maintains a connection to its source. If the original object changes, the linked object on the slide also changes. The linked object itself is stored in the source file where it was created, not in the presentation.

For example, the Excel chart you inserted into the slide is stored in the Guest Satisfaction Survey file on the Student Floppy Disk. Because you linked the Guest Satisfaction Survey file to the presentation, the Guest Satisfaction Survey file changes to display automatically on the chart on Slide 6. The PowerPoint presentation stores a representation of the original Guest Satisfaction Survey file and information about its location. Later, if you move or delete the source file, the link is broken and the object is not available.

Now that the linked pie chart displays on Slide 6, you want to improve the readability of the chart by increasing its size. The next section explains how to increase the size of the chart to best fit the slide.

Scaling a Linked Object

Increasing the size of the pie chart on Slide 6 improves the readability of the chart and improves the overall appearance of the slide. You increase the size of the pie chart using the Scale command on the Draw menu. Recall from Project 2 that the Scale command maintains the aspect ratio of the object. Perform the following steps to increase the size of the pie chart.

TO SCALE A LINKED OBJECT

Step 1: If not already selected, click the pie chart.
Step 2: Click Draw on the menu bar. Click Scale.
Step 3: Type `200` and then press the ENTER key. Click the OK button.

PowerPoint resizes the chart. PowerPoint limits the scaling percentage to the maximum height or width of a slide. The chart, therefore, is limited to 187.1 percent instead of 200 percent because of the width of the slide.

The changes to Slide 6 are complete. The next section explains how to save and print the linked presentation.

Saving and Printing a Linked Presentation

Perform the following steps to save and then print the Spring Break Specials Chart presentation.

TO SAVE AND PRINT A LINKED PRESENTATION

Step 1: Click the Save button on the Standard toolbar.
Step 2: Click the Print button on the Standard toolbar.

Summary

This Integration Feature introduced you to linking an object to a presentation. First, you opened an existing presentation, saved it with a new filename, and inserted a new slide onto which the chart from Excel was linked. Then, you performed the linking process. When you open a linked presentation, the object linking and embedding function of Microsoft Office 95 opens the presentation and updates the link to the chart file, providing the most current version of the chart. Next, you scaled the linked object to improve the readability. Finally, you saved and printed the linked presentation.

What You Should Know

Having completed this Integration Feature, you should be able to perform the following tasks:

- Insert a New Slide *(PPI 1.3)*
- Link the Excel Chart to Slide 6 *(PPI 1.4)*
- Open an Existing Presentation *(PPI 1.3)*
- Save a Presentation with a New Filename *(PPI 1.3)*
- Save and Print a Linked Presentation *(PPI 1.6)*
- Scale a Linked Object *(PPI 1.6)*
- Type a Slide Title *(PPI 1.4)*

1 Using Help

Instructions: Perform the following tasks using a computer.

1. Start PowerPoint. Double-click the Help button on the Standard toolbar to display the Help Topics: Microsoft PowerPoint dialog box.
2. Click the Answer Wizard tab. Type `ole` in box 1 and then click the Search button. In the Tell Me About section in box 2, double-click Exchanging information with other applications. Read the Help information about Sharing information, Linking information, and Embedding objects. Click the Help Topics button.
3. Click the Search button in the Help Topics: Microsoft PowerPoint dialog box. In the Tell Me About section, double-click Updating a link. Read and print the Help information. Click the Help Topics button.
4. Type `linked objects` in box 1 and then click the Search button. In the How Do I section, double-click Update a link manually. Read and print the Help information. Click the Help Topics button.
5. Click the Search button. In the How Do I section, double-click Reconnect links to renamed or moved documents. Read and print the Help information. Click the Close button.
6. Label each printout with your name. Submit the printouts to your instructor.

In the Lab

2 Linking a 3-D Bar Chart to a Slide

Problem: You are the general manager of Vacation Vistas travel agency applying for a short-term loan to cover operating expenses. The bank requests that you present an analysis of your first-quarter expenses, both budgeted and actual. Wanting to appear professional, you create a PowerPoint slide show. Knowing the bank will request this analysis again, you link the chart to the presentation.

Instructions: Perform the following tasks.

1. Open the document, Vacation Vistas, from the PowerPoint folder on the Student Floppy Disk that accompanies this book.
2. On Slide 2, link the file, Expense Comparison 1st Quarter 1997, located in the PowerPoint folder on the Student Floppy Disk. Scale the chart to 150%. Center the chart on the slide.
3. Add your name in the footer on all slides.
4. Save the presentation as Vacation Vistas Budget on your data floppy disk. Print the presentation in black and white. Close PowerPoint.

3 Linking Two-Column Charts to a Presentation

Problem: Your manager at Mega-Money Management, Mr. Richard Rich, conducts weekly investment seminars at which he displays Excel charts to illustrate his topic. He recently learned that you could create a PowerPoint presentation and link his Excel charts. He asks you to create a PowerPoint presentation and link two Excel charts to illustrate this week's topic, Risky Money.

Instructions: Perform the following tasks.

1. Open the document, Risk, from the PowerPoint folder on the Student Floppy Disk that accompanies this book.
2. Use the Large Object AutoLayout and insert a new slide after Slide 2. Link the file, Secured Fund, located in the PowerPoint folder on the Student Floppy Disk. Scale the chart to 170%. Center the chart on the slide.
3. Use the Large Object AutoLayout and insert a new slide after Slide 3. Link the file, Index 500 Stock, located in the PowerPoint folder on the Student Floppy Disk. Scale the chart to 170%. Center the chart on the slide.
4. Add your name in the footer on all slides.
5. Save the presentation as Risky Money on your data floppy disk. Print the presentation in black and white. Close PowerPoint.

▶ PROJECT ONE

Personal Information Management Using Schedule+

Objectives:

You will have mastered the material in this project when you can:

- Describe and define a personal information management system
- Understand the parts of the Schedule+ window
- Start and log on to Schedule+
- Create a schedule
- Enter appointments
- Set recurring appointments
- Save a schedule and exit Schedule+
- Open a schedule
- Edit and delete appointments
- Move appointments to new times
- Move appointments to new dates
- Schedule an event
- View the schedule in Daily, Weekly, and Monthly views
- Create a To Do List
- Print a schedule
- Print a To Do List
- Create a Contacts List
- Print a Contacts List

People to See, Places to Go, Things to Do!

Time and its derivatives have become buzzwords of the business world. You would not need to eavesdrop long in any corporate lounge to hear some of them: quality *time*, flex*time*, real *time*, *time*-share, *time* management, ad nauseam. The lament, "I just don't have time!" has become so common as to be a cliché. These words have become an anthem of this decade. Life in the 90s has become a race against the clock. With 60- and even 70-hour work weeks the norm among the executive set, scheduling time prudently is a necessity.

Personal information management systems, or PIMS, such as Microsoft Schedule+, have become standard equipment for many business people. Using Schedule+ is the easiest way for individuals and networked teams to manage and share calendars, tasks, and contacts for improved personal and team productivity.

Schedule+ even offers the Timex Data Link Watch option, which costs about $100. A far

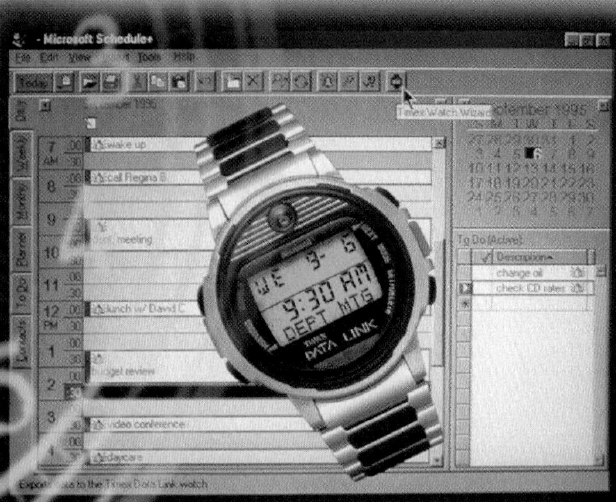

Time is Money

cry from the archaic wristwatch of the past, this watch enables busy workers to download appointments from their Schedule+ programs to their wristwatches. Timex's wireless technology and Microsoft's Schedule+ allow a user to receive scheduling information simply by pointing the Timex Data Link Watch at the personal computer monitor. Thus loaded, the wristwatch displays appointment information and issues reminders. What used to be solely a timepiece, a silent reminder of time's passing, or in some cases mere ornamentation, has taken on near-secretarial aspects.

Benjamin Franklin's succinct advice that, "Time is money," probably is even truer today than when it was first uttered. Stories abound regarding the wise use of time and how with hard work, little sleep, and no play at all, ordinary people not only prospered, but virtually built empires. Laurence J. Peter, a famous Canadian educator, once said, "If you don't know where you are going, you will probably end up somewhere else." This could translate to the following: know your appointments and keep them; maintain a good contact list; and make sure all the items on your To Do List are checked off at the end of the day.

While it cannot be denied that hard work and being organized usually are behind a successful venture, sometimes being too busy to objectively view a situation prevents greatness from occurring. It is difficult for creativity to flourish if every moment of the day has already been claimed, scheduled, or earmarked for other tasks. You are not likely to find great ideas or bold actions allocated a time slot in an appointment book. Success often happens, however, precisely because people decide to step back from their plans, think it through, and then act. The wise use of time – figuratively stepping back and rethinking your goals – is what determines success.

Using time wisely always has been and always will be important. Over scheduling, however, can be just as damaging as wasting time. Having tunnel vision about any project or task, no matter how worthy, can cause a person to fail to see the implications of the bigger picture.

Time Management

Real Time

Microsoft

Schedule+

Windows 95

Personal Information Management Using Schedule+

Case Perspective

Brittany Lang is a freshman student at Wilshire University, a residential campus in Illinois with approximately 2,000 students. Brittany is eager to make new friends and learn about the campus. In addition to being registered for a full schedule of classes, she has joined the Spanish Club and plans to attend several social functions on campus.

As a resident with housing on campus, one of the belongings Brittany has brought to her new dorm is her personal computer. One of the programs contained on her computer is Microsoft Office 95. Upon discovering the Schedule+ program, Brittany has decided to use the few days before classes begin to create her personal schedule for the entire first semester. Her social calendar, schedule of classes, and various club obligations must be entered into her schedule.

Introduction

A **personal information management** system, or **PIM**, is a tool designed to help you organize your daily activities. In days past, personal organizers were made of paper, with appointments and events penciled in at the appropriate times. If several people were required to attend the same meeting, numerous phone calls were placed in order to determine the attendees' availability. Changing a meeting time or location involved erasing the old entry and penciling in the new. These activities are all fading into obsolescence as computerized PIMs, such as Schedule+, become more popular and widely used.

Schedule+

Schedule+, an application contained in Microsoft Office 95, is a powerful time-management tool that assists in keeping track of your daily activities. Primarily designed for a business environment, it is equally useful in a home or academic setting.

Schedule+ can keep track of Daily, Weekly, and Monthly schedules, similar to those displayed in Figure 1-1. With just a few clicks of the mouse, you can check dates or schedule events that are weeks or even months in the future. A handy To Do List can be created to help track projects or to remind you of tasks that must be accomplished on a specific date. The Contacts List, much like an electronic address book, provides quick access to frequently used telephone numbers and addresses. Entries in the Contacts List can be grouped into meaningful segments, such as business or personal contacts, or people associated with a particular project or task.

In this project, you will use Schedule+ to create Daily, Weekly, and Monthly schedules, a To Do List, and a Contacts List as shown in Figure 1-1 on the next page.

Overview of Project Steps

The preparation steps below summarize how the Schedule+ tasks shown in Figure 1-1 will be developed in Project 1.

1. Start the Schedule+ program.
2. Enter the schedule name (my appointment book).
3. Create a schedule using both recurring and non-recurring appointments.
4. Delete all appointments on September 1 (Labor Day).
5. Use the Event Scheduler to schedule an event on September 25.
6. Create a To Do List.
7. Print the schedule in daily, weekly, and monthly format.
8. Print the To Do List.
9. Create and print a Contacts List.
10. Save the schedule on a floppy disk and exit Schedule+.

The following pages contain a detailed explanation of these tasks.

Mouse Usage

In this book, the mouse is the primary way to communicate with Schedule+. You can perform six operations with a mouse: point, click, right-click, double-click, drag, and right-drag.

Point means you can move the mouse across a flat surface until the mouse pointer rests on the item of choice on the screen. As you move the mouse, the mouse pointer moves across the screen in the same direction. **Click** means you press and release the left mouse button. The terminology used in this book to direct you to point to a particular item and then click is, click the particular item. For example, *Click the Paste button* means point to the Paste button and click.

Right-click means you press and release the right mouse button. As with the left mouse button, you normally will point to an item on the screen prior to right-clicking.

Double-click means you quickly press and release the left mouse button twice without moving the mouse. In most cases, you must point to an item before double-clicking. **Drag** means you point to an item, hold down the left mouse button. **Right-drag** means you point to an item, hold down the right mouse button, move the item to the desired location, and then release the right mouse button.

The use of the mouse is an important skill when working with Schedule+.

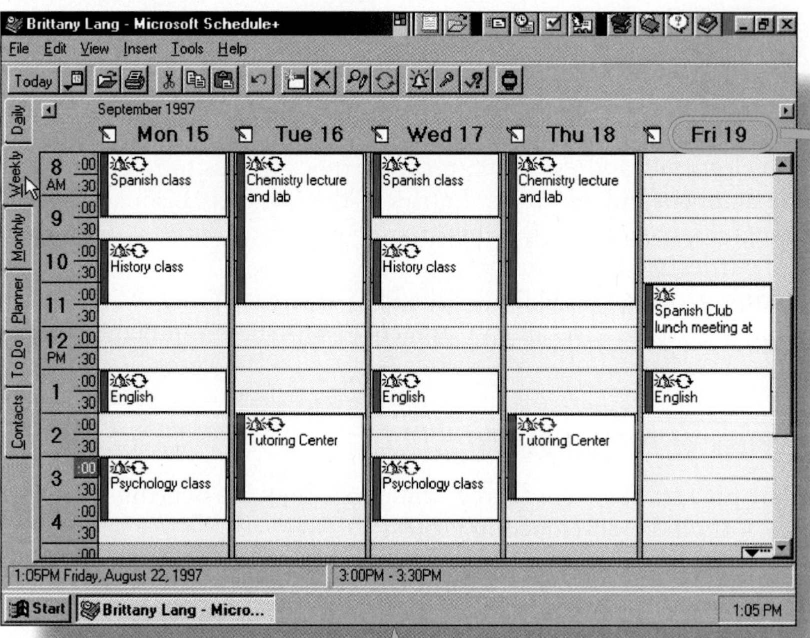

(b) Weekly Schedule

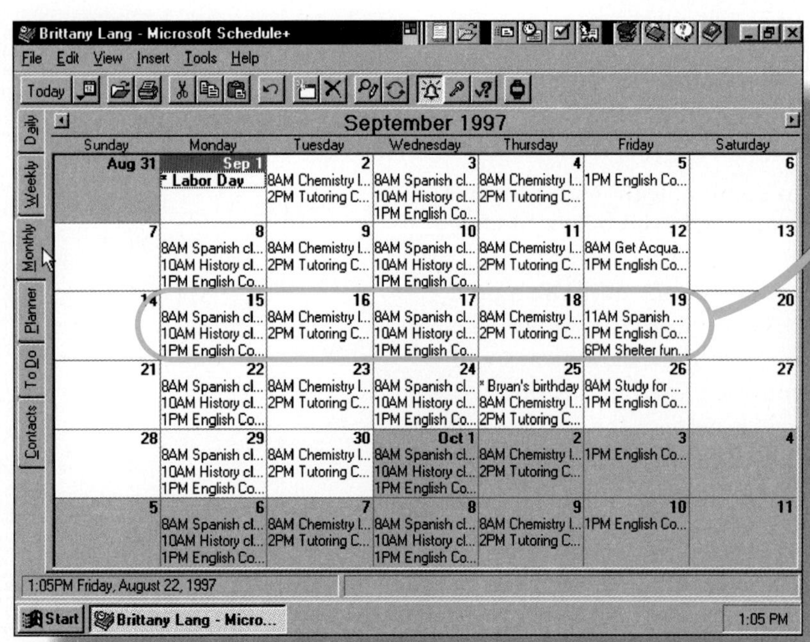

(a) Monthly Schedule

FIGURE 1-1

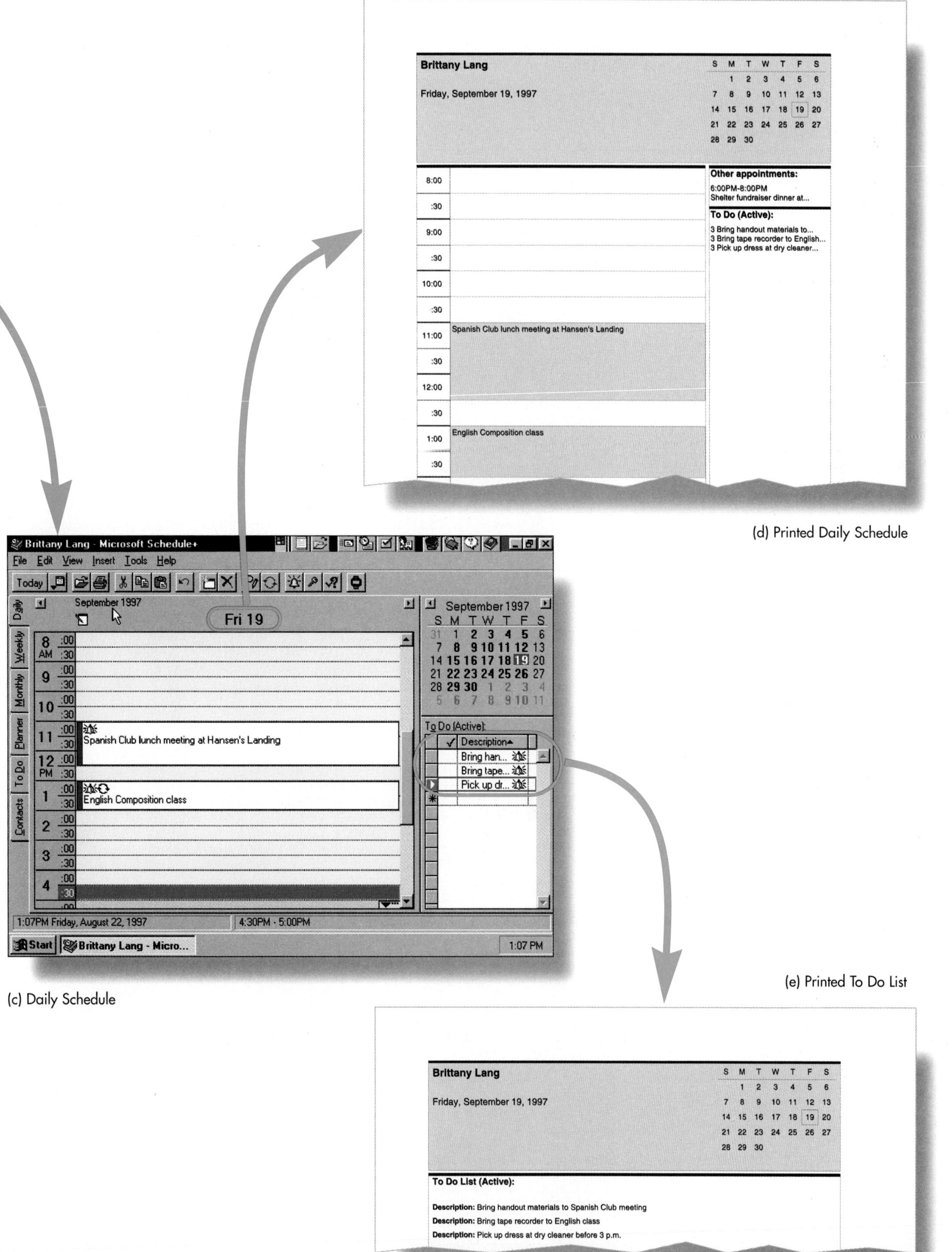

(d) Printed Daily Schedule

(c) Daily Schedule

(e) Printed To Do List

To start Schedule+, Windows 95 must be running. Perform the following steps to start Schedule+.

Steps To Start Schedule+

1 Click the Start button. Point to Programs, then click Schedule+ on the Programs submenu.

The Schedule+ Logon box displays (Figure 1-2). Depending on how Schedule+ was set up, it may bypass the Logon box and go directly into Schedule+. If you or someone else previously used Schedule+ to create a schedule, a name might already be displayed in the User name text box.

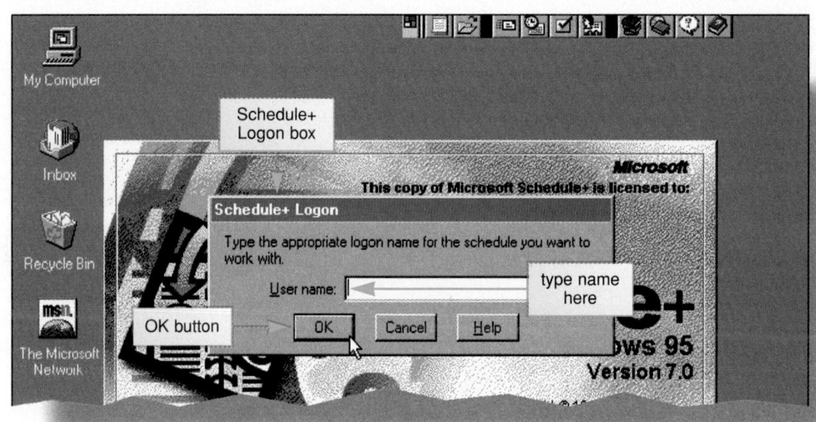

FIGURE 1-2

2 Type `Brittany Lang` **in the User name text box, and then click the OK button.**

The Microsoft Schedule+ Welcome box displays (Figure 1-3). This box displays the first time you create a schedule.

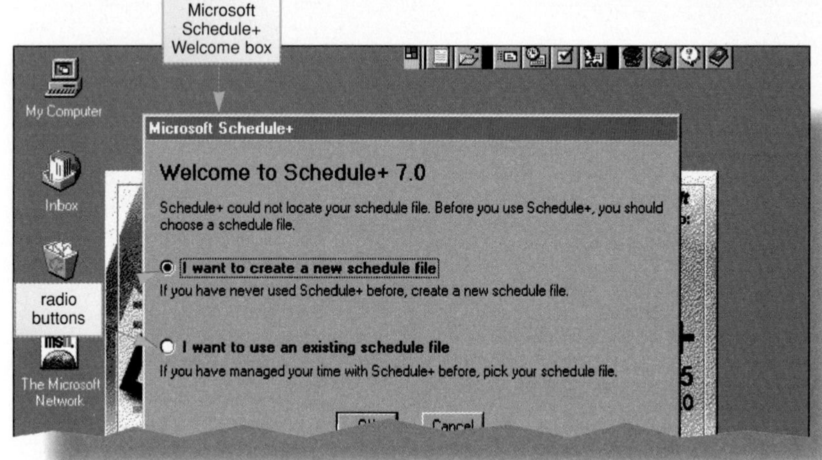

FIGURE 1-3

3 With the I want to create a new schedule file radio button selected, click the OK button.

The Select Local Schedule dialog box displays (Figure 1-4).

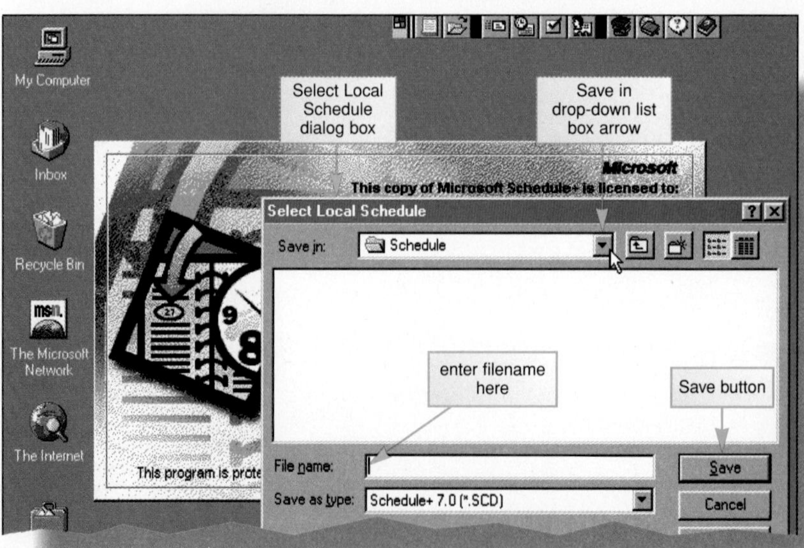

FIGURE 1-4

4 **Type** `my appointment book` **in the File name box. Click the Save in drop-down list box arrow. Click 3½ Floppy (A:) in the drop-down list box to ensure that the schedule you create is saved to the floppy disk in drive A.**

The Select Local Schedule dialog box displays as shown in Figure 1-5.

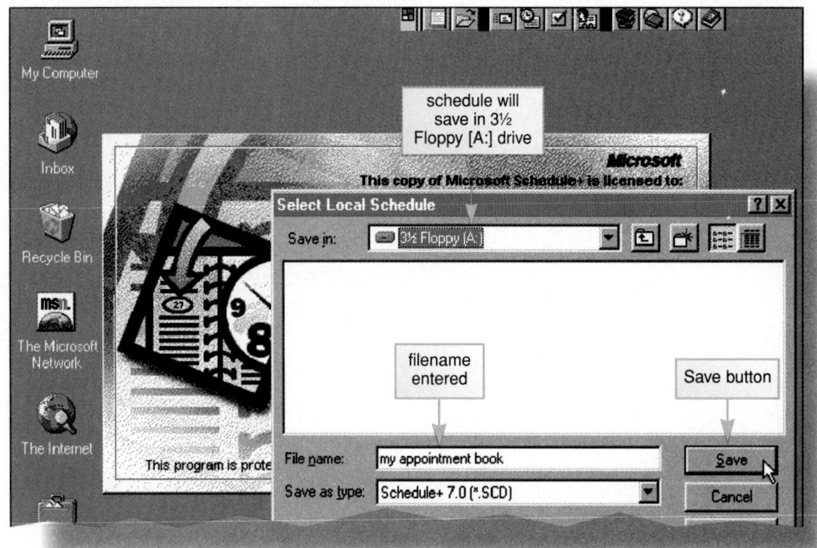

FIGURE 1-5

5 **Click the Save button. If necessary click the Maximize button to maximize the Schedule+ window.**

Schedule+ creates a new schedule called my appointment book on your floppy disk and displays a blank daily schedule (Figure 1-6).

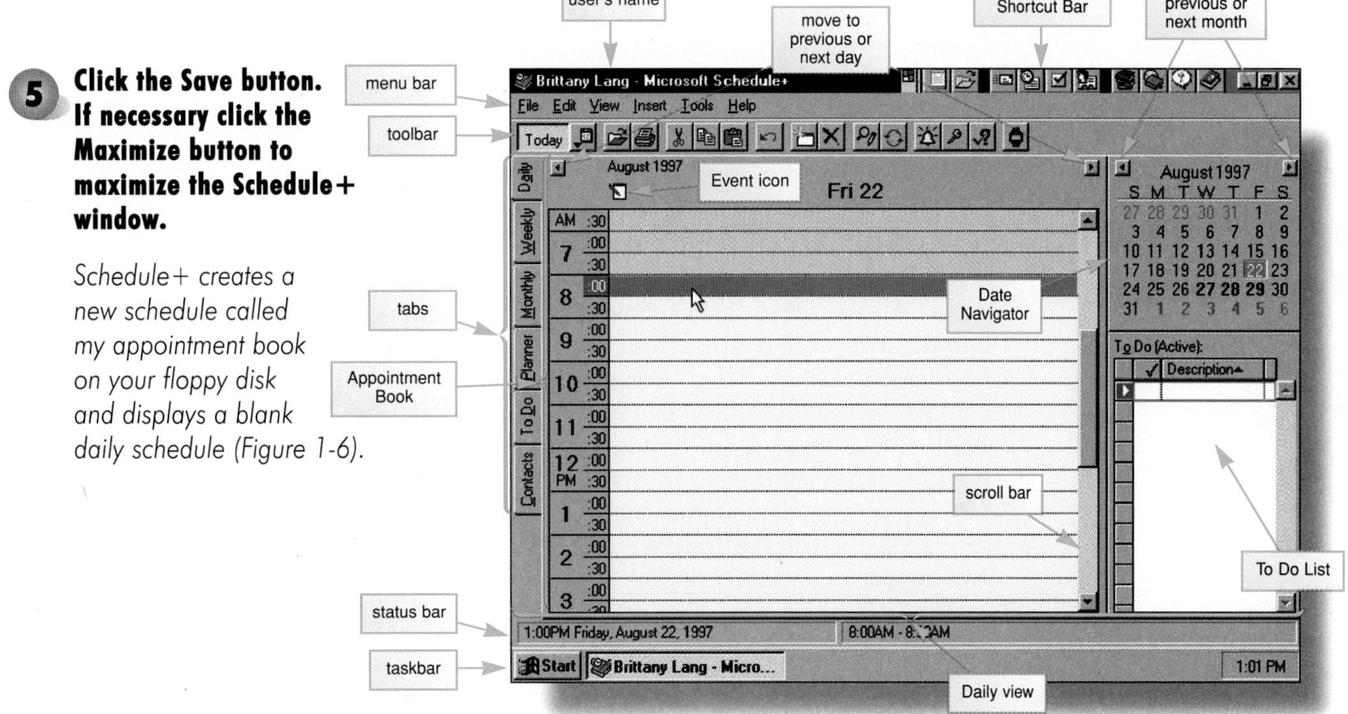

FIGURE 1-6

*Other*Ways

1. On the Microsoft Office Shortcut bar, click Make an Appointment button
2. On the Microsoft Office Shortcut bar, click Add a Task button
3. On the Microsoft Office Shortcut bar, click Add a Contact button

If you are completing this project on a computer and you want your dates to exactly match those in the figures, you must double-click the Tray status area on the taskbar and set the date to August 22, 1997. Be certain you set it back to today's date before shutting down Windows 95.

Schedule+ Window

The Schedule+ window in Figure 1-6 on the previous page contains several elements in addition to the toolbar, Microsoft Office Shortcut Bar, menu bar, and status bar that you should understand in order to use Schedule+ more efficiently. By default, the **Daily view** is displayed when Schedule+ first opens. This is so you can see the day's planned activities and obligations at a glance.

More *About* the Tabs

You can add or remove tabs by right-clicking any of the tabs, and then clicking Tab Gallery on the Shortcut menu. You can also accomplish this through the View menu.

Tabs

Along the left side of the window are six tabs that allow you to view your schedule in different ways. The **Daily tab** displays the schedule in Daily view, with lines for each appointment time. The **Weekly tab** displays the schedule by the week, or five consecutive days. The **Monthly tab** displays the schedule by month and has an appearance similar to that of a calendar.The **Planner tab** shows the schedule with black boxes indicating busy times and white spaces indicating free times. If you are on a network and have access to schedules other than your own, the Planner allows you to quickly verify free times when scheduling a meeting. The **To Do tab** allows you to keep track of projects and duties associated with your schedule. The **Contacts tab** allows you to create a list of people you frequently contact. These contacts can be personal friends, business associates, family members, classmates, or any number of other groups. The Contacts List is actually a database you can use to access telephone numbers, addresses, company names, business telephone numbers, or several other items of information.

More *About* the Appointment Book

You can resize the Appointment Book by dragging the right edge of it until it has reached the desired size.

Appointment Book

The **Appointment Book**, which comprises the largest part of Daily view, looks much like a sheet of lined yellow paper, with times displayed along the left edge and the current date at the top. The time slots, by default, are broken into half-hour increments, and it is here that appointments, meetings, and other items are entered into the schedule. The two small arrows at the top of the Appointment Book allow you to scroll forward or backward one day at a time. If you press and hold down the left mouse button, you quickly page through days.

The commonly accepted business hours of 8:00 A.M. through 5:00 P.M. are displayed in a brighter yellow color. Time slots prior to 8:00 A.M. and after 5:00 P.M. appear in a slightly darker yellow color.

Date Navigator

To the right of the Appointment Book is the Date Navigator. The **Date Navigator**, which looks like a calendar, allows you to quickly change the date displayed in the Appointment Book. Click any date in the Date Navigator to display the appointments for that date. The two small arrows to the left and right of the date are used much like the arrows in the Appointment Book. Click the left arrow to display the previous month, and click the right arrow to display the next month. The blue highlight in the Date Navigator indicates the date currently displayed in the Appointment Book, which is Friday, August 22, 1997. The date that appears boxed, or recessed, is the current date. In the case of Figure 1-6 on the previous page, the date displayed and the current date are the same.

To Do List

The To Do List displays beneath the Date Navigator. The **To Do List** allows you to enter a list of tasks to be completed for or by the date displayed in Daily view.

Toolbar

Figure 1-7 shows the Schedule+ toolbar and each button's function. Each button on the toolbar can be clicked to perform a frequently used task, such as deleting, printing, and undoing.

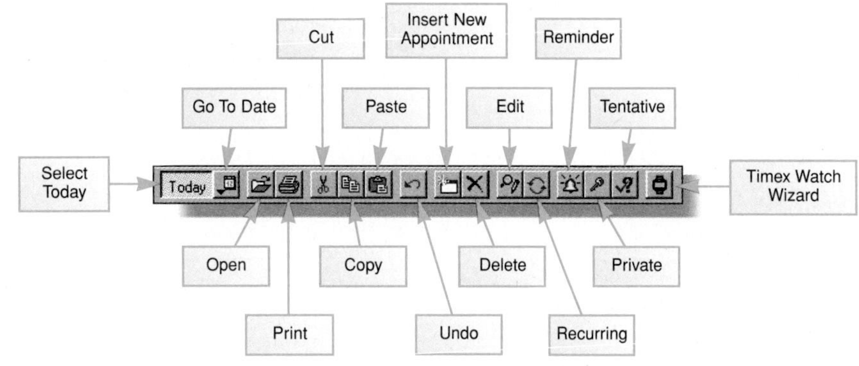

FIGURE 1-7

Creating a Schedule

Now that you understand the different parts of Daily view, you can begin entering items into the schedule. Any item you enter into a time slot is called an **appointment**. If you need to enter an appointment into a time slot that is not visible in the Appointment Book, use the vertical scroll bar to bring the time slot into view.

The next section describes how to enter Brittany Long's appointments in Table 1-1 into the Appointment Book beginning on August 25, 1997. Once an appointment is entered, you can perform ordinary editing actions, such as moving, deleting, or copying.

More *About* the the Toolbar

You can hide or display the toolbar (or the status bar) by right-clicking the toolbar. You can also accomplish this by clicking Toolbar on the View menu.

Table 1-1

TIME	*APPOINTMENT*	*RECURRING ON*
8:00 A.M. – 9:30 A.M.	Spanish class	Monday, Wednesday
10:00 A.M. – 11:30 A.M.	History class	Monday, Wednesday
1:00 P.M. – 2:00 P.M.	English Composition class	Monday, Wednesday, Friday
8:00 A.M. – 11:30 A.M.	Chemistry lecture and lab	Tuesday, Thursday
2:00 P.M. – 4:00 P.M.	Tutoring Center	Tuesday, Thursday
3:00 P.M. – 4:30 P.M.	Psychology class	Monday, Wednesday

The steps on the next page describe how to enter appointments in the Appointment Book.

To Enter Appointments in the Appointment Book

1 **Click August 25 on the Date navigator to display the first day that classes will meet. Drag through the 8:00 A.M. – 9:30 A.M. time slot.**

The 8:00 A.M. - 9:30 A.M. time slot is highlighted. While the left mouse button is pressed, the selected time displays in a box to the left of the time slot (Figure 1-8).

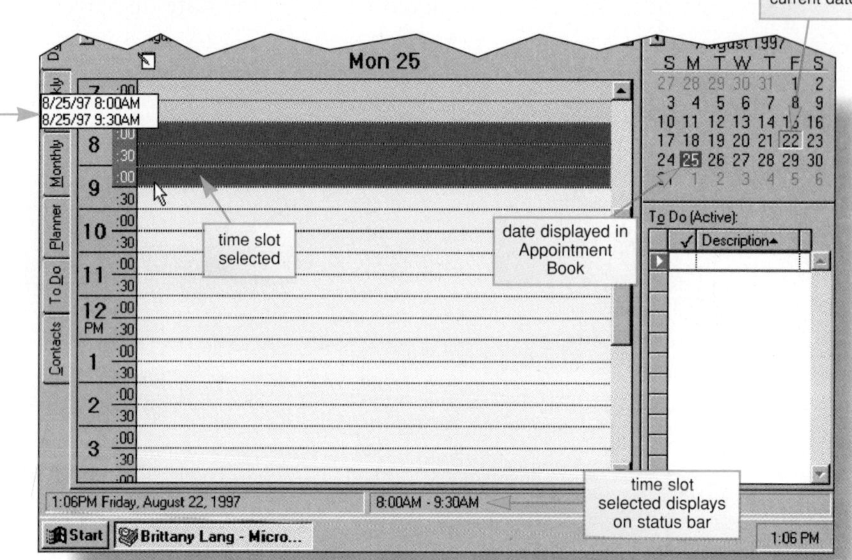

FIGURE 1-8

2 **Type** `Spanish class` **to enter the first appointment, and then click anywhere outside the selection.**

The first appointment is entered into the Appointment Book (Figure 1-9). By default, a **Reminder icon** *is assigned to each appointment. This means the computer will beep 15 minutes before the appointment is to begin.*

3 **Drag through the 10:00 A.M. – 11:30 A.M. time slot, and then type** `History class` **to enter the second appointment.**

The second appointment in Table 1-1 is entered into the Appointment Book.

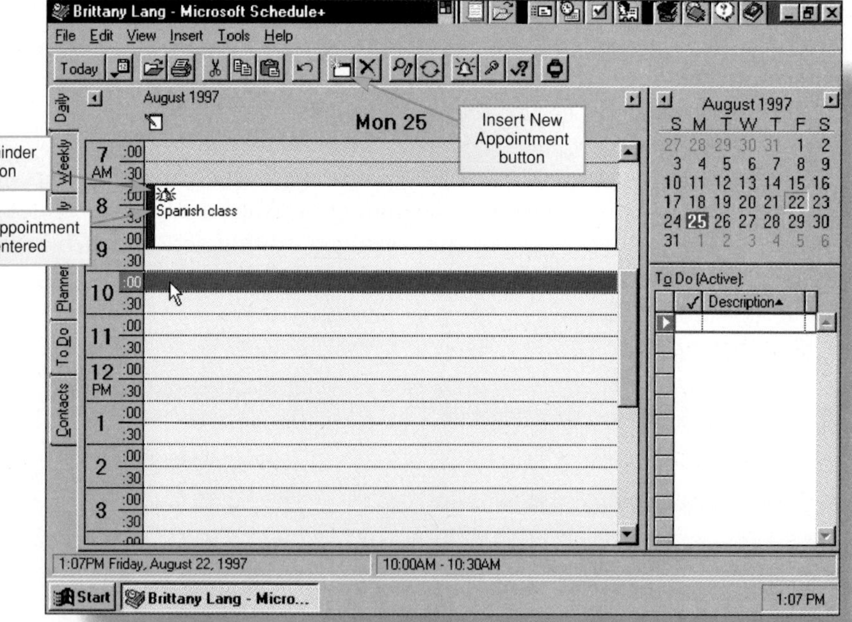

FIGURE 1-9

Entering Appointments with the Appointment Dialog Box

Appointments can be either directly typed into the Appointment Book as shown in the previous section, or they can be entered by using the Appointment dialog box. The Appointment dialog box is a slightly more involved process, but you can combine several steps into one when you use it.

The following steps describe how to enter appointments using the Appointment dialog box.

Steps To Enter Appointments using the Appointment Dialog Box

1 **Drag through the 1:00 P.M. – 2:00 P.M. time slot, and then click the Insert New Appointment button on the toolbar. Click the General tab.**

The Appointment dialog box displays. The insertion point is positioned in the Description text box.

2 **Type** `English Composition class` **to enter the appointment description, and then point to the OK button.**

The description is entered in the Description text box (Figure 1-10). More information can be entered through this dialog box.

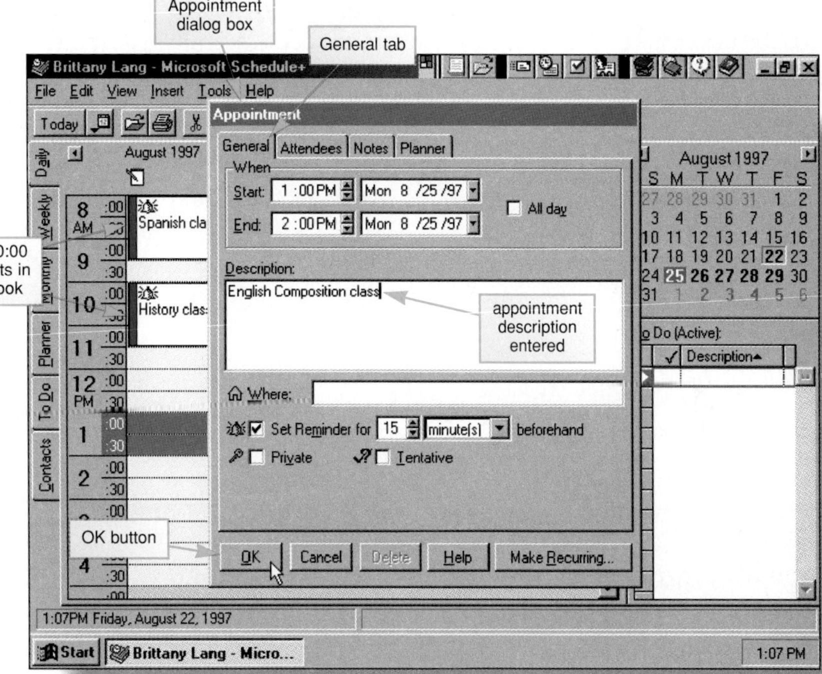

FIGURE 1-10

3 **Click the OK button to enter the appointment into the Appointment Book.**

4 **As described in Steps 1 through 3, drag through the 3:00 P.M. – 4:30 P.M. time slot and type** `Psychology class` **as the next appointment.**

The completed Appointment Book for Monday, August 25 appears as shown in Figure 1-11.

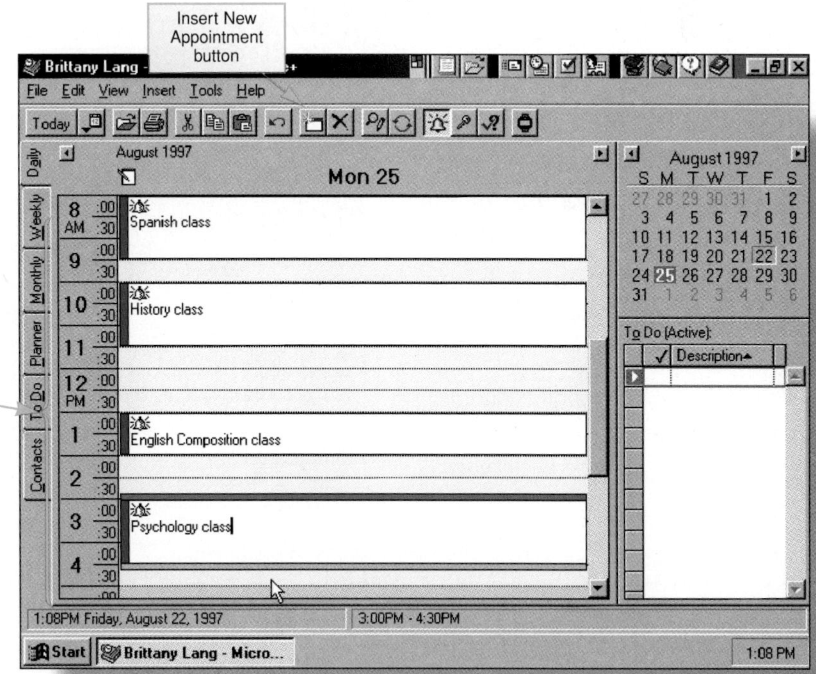

FIGURE 1-11

OtherWays

1. Double-click the time slot
2. On Microsoft Office Shortcut bar, click Make an Appointment button

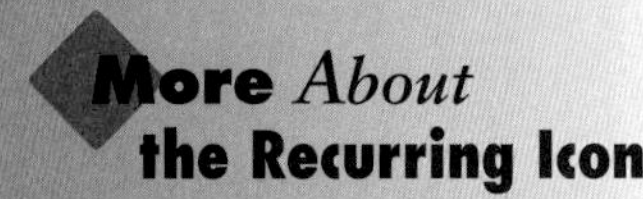

More About the Recurring Icon

You can use the Recurring icon on tasks in the To Do List. If a task must be performed on a regular basis, click the task in the To Do List, then click the Recurring icon. The task will automatically be placed on the To Do List on the appropriate days, according to the time interval you specify.

The Reminder icon is automatically assigned to each appointment. Because it is the default, it will be used throughout this project. You can, however, turn it off by clicking anywhere in the appointment, and then clicking the Reminder button on the toolbar. You also can turn off the Reminder symbol in the Appointment dialog box.

Recurring Appointments

Many appointments are **recurring**, or occur at regular intervals. For example, a company may hold its department meetings from 1:00 P.M. through 3:00 P.M. every Friday afternoon. In the example in this project, the student's classes meet at regular intervals. Typing them in time slots on each day they meet for the entire semester would be extremely time-consuming. By designating an appointment as recurring, you need to type the appointment entry only once, and then specify the days on which it recurs.

The following steps illustrate how to set recurring appointments.

Steps To Set Recurring Appointments

1 Click inside the first appointment that is to be changed to recurring, the 8:00 A.M. – 9:30 A.M. time slot, and then point to the Recurring button on the toolbar, as shown in Figure 1-12.

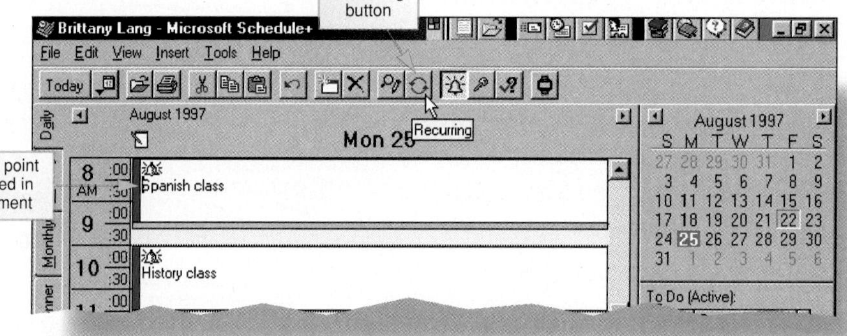

FIGURE 1-12

2 Click the Recurring button on the toolbar.

The Appointment Series dialog box displays (Figure 1-13). If necessary, click the When tab. Pertinent information about the appointment displays, including start and end times, the date, and the next occurrence.

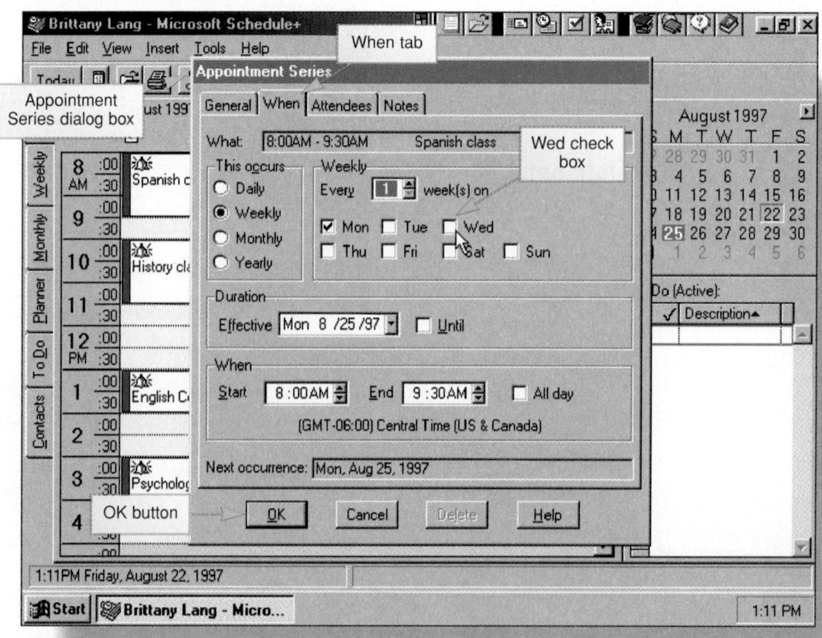

FIGURE 1-13

3 **Click the Wed check box to include Wednesday as a day this appointment will recur, and then click the OK button.**

A Recurring icon displays in the time slot (Figure 1-14). The Recurring button is pressed on the toolbar.

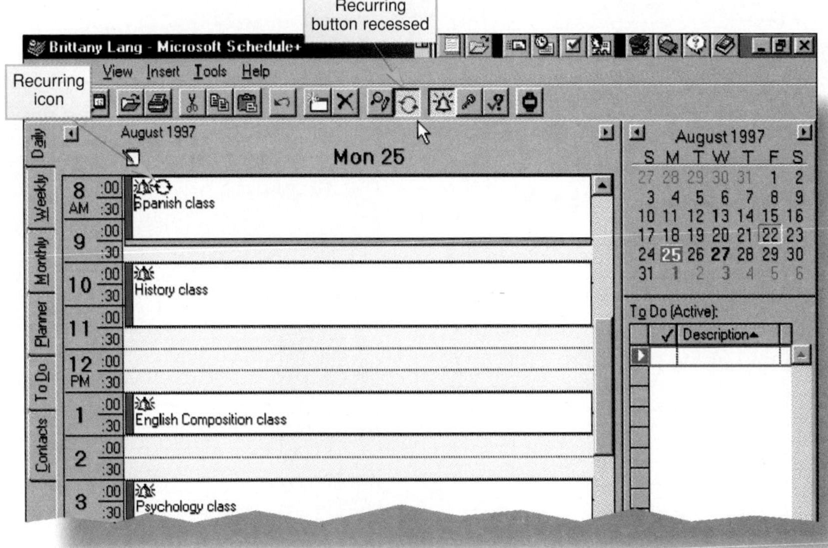

FIGURE 1-14

4 **Repeat Steps 1 through 3 to make the recurring appointments as described in Table 1-1 on page S 1.12.**

The completed Monday schedule should look like Figure 1-15. Each recurring appointment will have both the Recurring icon and the Reminder icon, which was assigned by default, above the appointment description.

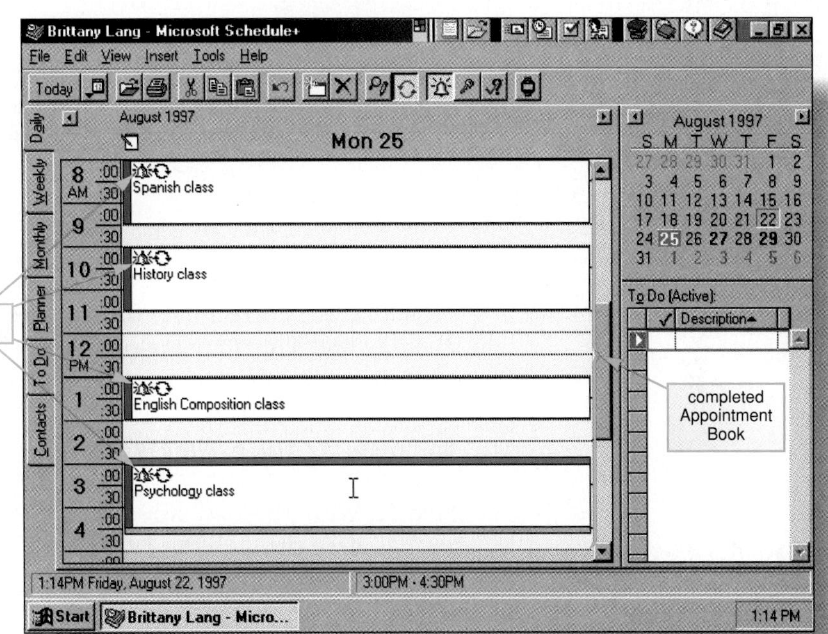

FIGURE 1-15

OtherWays

1. On Insert menu click Appointment, then click Make Recurring button
2. On Microsoft Office Shortcut Bar, click Make an Appointment button
3. Right-click appointment, click Make Recurring
4. Press CTRL+N, tab to Make Recurring, type R

Moving to the Next Day in the Appointment Book

The Monday, Wednesday, and Friday schedule is now complete. The next step is to enter appointments in the time slots for Tuesday and Thursday. In order to do so, Tuesday must be displayed in the Appointment Book. The following step illustrates how to move to the next day.

Steps To Display the Next Day in the Appointment Book

Click the right arrow at the top of the Appointment Book.

Tuesday, August 26 displays in the Appointment Book (Figure 1-16). The last selected time slot is highlighted in the new date.

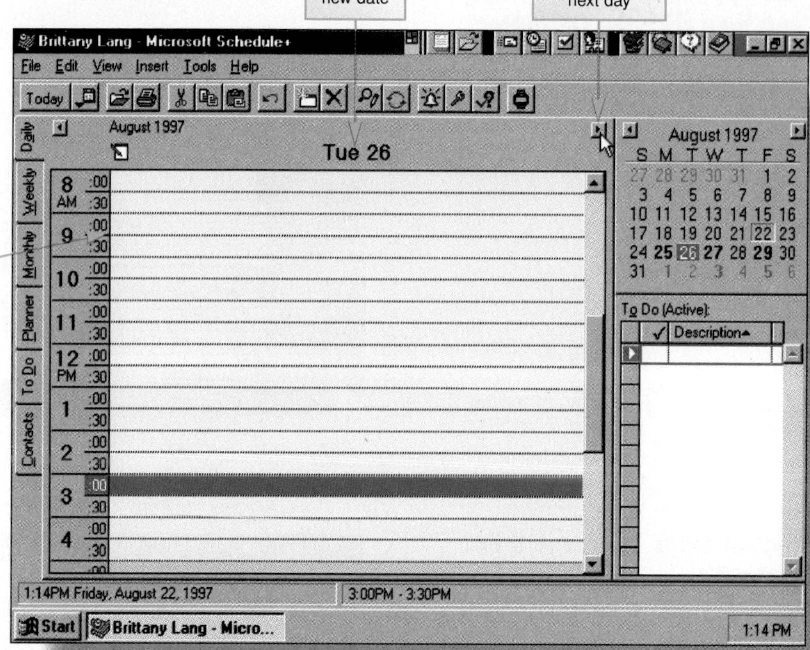

FIGURE 1-16

OtherWays

1. Click the desired date on the Date Navigator
2. Click the Go To Date button.

Now that the correct date displays in the Appointment Book, you can enter the Tuesday and Thursday appointments. The following steps describe how to complete the schedule.

TO COMPLETE THE RECURRING APPOINTMENTS

Step 1: With Tuesday, August 26, 1997 displayed in the Appointment Book, drag through the 8:00 A.M. - 11:30 A.M. time slot, and then type `Chemistry lecture and lab` to enter the appointment description. Click the Recurring button, click the Thu check box, and then click the OK button.

Step 2: Drag through the 2:00 P.M. - 4:00 P.M. time slot, and then type `Tutoring Center` to enter the appointment description. Click the Recurring button, click the Thu check box, and then click the OK button.

The completed schedule for Tuesday, August 26 should look like Figure 1-17.

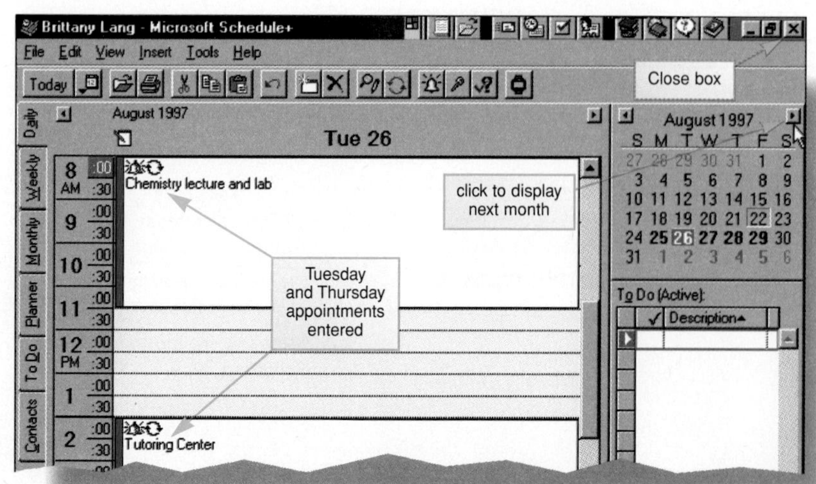

FIGURE 1-17

TO COMPLETE THE SCHEDULE

Step 1: Click the small right arrow at the top of the Date Navigator to move to the month of September, and then click September 12 on the Date Navigator to display the Appointment Book for that date. Drag through the 8:00 A.M. – 10:00 A.M. time slot, and then type `Get Acquainted Breakfast, Student Lounge` to enter the appointment description.

Step 2: Click September 19 on the Date Navigator, drag through the 11:00 A.M. – 12:30 P.M. time slot, and then type `Spanish Club meeting, Hansen's Landing` to enter the appointment description.

Step 3: With the September 19 Appointment Book still displayed, drag through the 6:00 P.M. – 8:00 P.M. time slot, and then type `Shelter fundraiser, Roundtable Restaurant` to enter the appointment description.

Step 4: Drag through September 26 on the Date Navigator, drag through the 8:00 A.M. – 10:00 A.M. time slot, and type `Study for History test` to enter the appointment description.

Because the appointments entered are not recurring, it is not necessary to use the Recurring button.

More *About* **the Apointment Book**

You can search for specific text in the Appointment Book through the Edit menu. You can specify either a forward or backward search, and as the search progresses, the percentage of the schedule searched displays in the Schedule+ window. When the search text is found, the date on which it appears displays in the Appointment Book with the search text highlighted.

Saving the Schedule and Exiting Schedule+

Once the schedule is complete, it should be saved on a floppy disk. When you exit Schedule+, your schedule is automatically saved to the drive you specified in the Select Local Schedule dialog box that displayed during the logon procedure. The file is saved under the name you assigned at that time, as well. At the beginning of this project, you specified drive A in the Save in box, and assigned the filename, my appointment book. Therefore, when you exit Schedule+, the file you created automatically will be saved on drive A under the filename my appointment book.

The following step describes how to save the schedule and exit Schedule+.

TO SAVE THE SCHEDULE AND EXIT SCHEDULE+

Step 1: Click the Close box on the right side of the title bar.

Schedule+ closes and the schedule is automatically saved on the floppy disk in drive A. The Windows 95 desktop displays.

More *About* **Saving**

Because Schedule+ automatically saves the schedule when you exit, it's a good idea to create an archive file before exiting. An archive file preserves the old version of a schedule, and it can serve as a valuable reference if you need to check outdated information or any past appointments. Archive files are easily created by choosing Archive from the File menu.

Opening a Schedule

Once a schedule has been created and saved on a floppy disk, it can be opened and then viewed, edited, or printed. The steps on the next page describe how to open an existing schedule.

More About Opening Schedules

If you have access permission, you can open another user's schedule and make appointments, check free times, schedule meeting, check or copy contacts, or just about anything you could do with your own personal schedule. This feature is particularly useful if you are required to schedule meetings or events that hinge upon other people's schedules.

TO OPEN AN EXISTING SCHEDULE

Step 1: Make sure the floppy disk containing your schedule is in drive A, and then click the Start button. Point to Programs, and then click Microsoft Schedule+ on the Programs submenu.
Step 2: The Schedule+ Logon box displays. Depending on how Schedule+ was set up, it may bypass the Logon box and go directly into Schedule+. Your name should display in the User name box, and Schedule+ automatically looks in the last location specified, in this case drive A. If your name does not display, enter it in the User name box. If the Welcome screen displays, click the I want to use an existing schedule file radio button, and then click the OK button.
Step 3: Click the OK button.

The schedule displays the current date in the Appointment Book.

More About Editing

You can drag any task from the To Do List to a time slot in the Appointment Book, thereby making the task an appointment.

Editing Appointments

Schedules often need to be rearranged and juggled. Schedule+ provides several different ways of editing appointments. Typing errors can be corrected by pressing the BACKSPACE or DELETE keys, and then retyping the entry, as described in previous projects. Appointments also can be deleted, moved, or copied. You can edit the appointment by clicking inside the appointment to be edited, and then clicking the Edit Appointment button on the toolbar.

Deleting Appointments

Appointments often are cancelled and must be deleted from the schedule. The schedule created thus far in this project contains appointments on September 1, 1997. Because September 1 is Labor Day, no classes will meet. The following steps describe how to delete an appointment from the schedule.

Steps To Delete an Appointment

1. **Click September 1 in the Date Navigator to display the Appointment Book. Click anywhere within the first appointment to be deleted, the 8:00 A.M. – 9:30 A.M. Spanish class, and then point to the Delete button on the toolbar, as shown in Figure 1-18.**

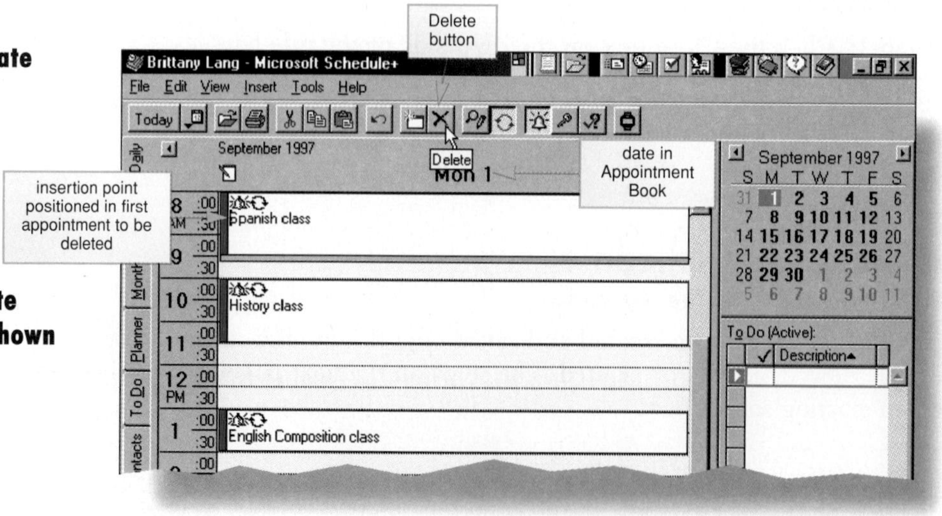

FIGURE 1-18

2 **Click the Delete button on the toolbar.**

Because the appointment you are attempting to delete is a recurring appointment, a dialog box displays, asking if you want to delete all instances of the item (Figure 1-19).

3 **Click the No button.**

The appointment is deleted.

4 **Repeat Steps 1 through 3 to delete the remaining three appointments scheduled for September 1.**

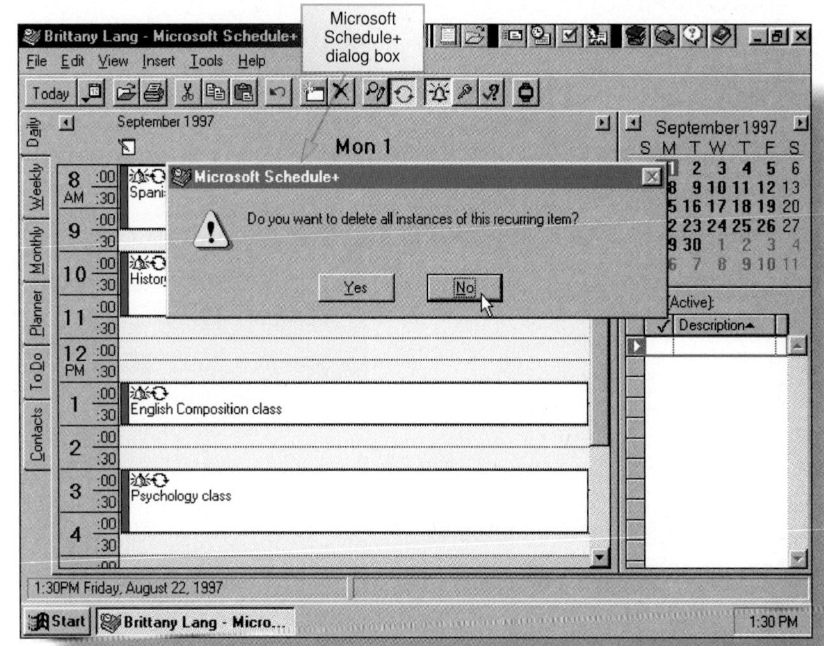

FIGURE 1-19

OtherWays

1. Right-click the appointment to be deleted, click Delete Item

Merely using the BACKSPACE key or DELETE key to delete individual characters of the appointment does not entirely remove the entry. The time slot remains active and the icons remain in place.

Moving Appointments to a New Time

Schedule+ provides several easy ways of moving appointments. Suppose, for instance, that the Shelter fundraiser on September 19 was changed from 6:00 P.M. to 7:30 P.M. Instead of deleting and then retyping the appointment in the new time slot, you can simply drag it there. The following steps describe how to move an appointment to a new time slot.

Steps To Move an Appointment to a New Time

1 **Click September 19 on the Date Navigator, and then click anywhere in the 6:00 P.M. – 8:00 P.M. time slot. Position the mouse pointer on the top border of the time slot.**

The mouse pointer changes to a four-pointed arrow, as shown in Figure 1-20.

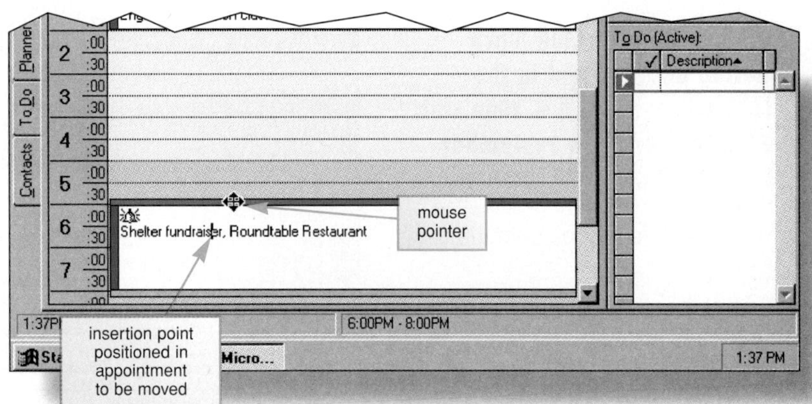

FIGURE 1-20

2 Drag the appointment to the 7:30 P.M. time slot.

The display of the boxed date and times for the new time slot becomes visible as the mouse pointer moves into position (Figure 1-21).

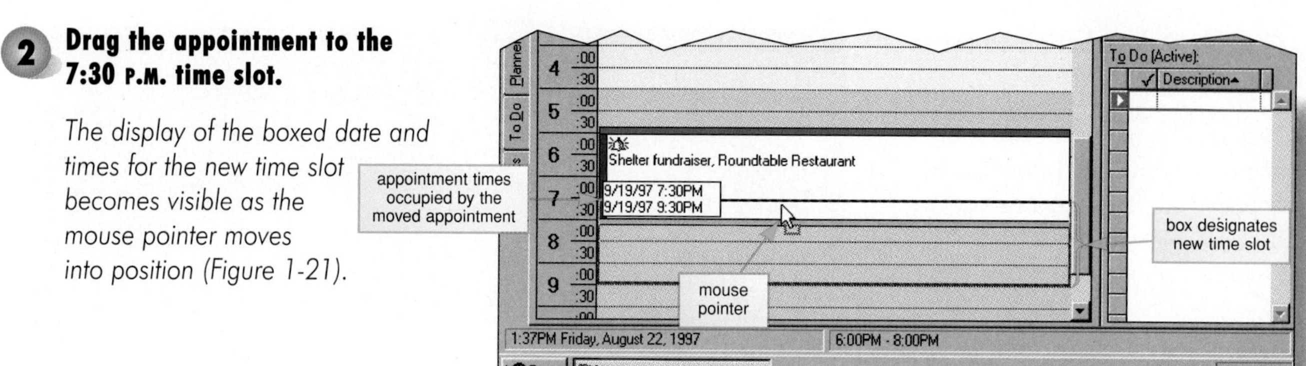

FIGURE 1-21

3 Release the left mouse button to drop the appointment in the new time slot.

The appointment is placed in the 7:30 P.M. time slot (Figure 1-22). Adequate time is automatically allowed so the same amount of time — in this case two hours — is occupied by the moved appointment.

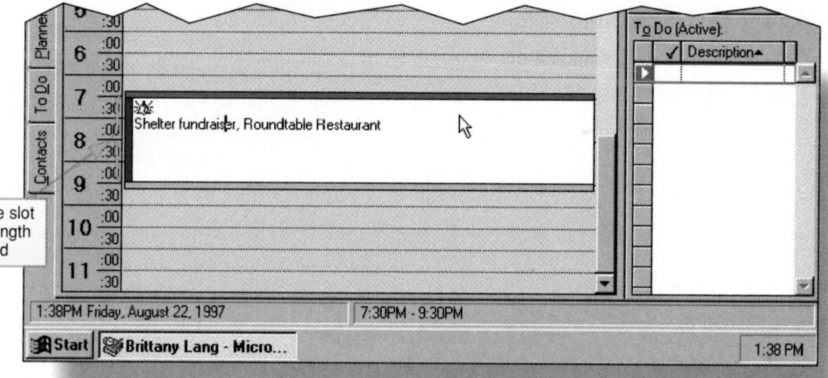

FIGURE 1-22

*Other*Ways

1. Click anywhere in appointment, click Edit menu, click Cut, reposition mouse pointer, click Edit menu, click Paste
2. Click anywhere in appointment, right-click, click Move Appt

Moving Appointments to a New Date

If an appointment is being moved to a new date but keeping the same time slot, you can use the Date Navigator. This method quickly and easily moves an appointment to a new date, as shown in the following steps.

Steps To Move an Appointment to a New Date

1 Drag the Spanish Club lunch meeting appointment in the 11:00 A.M. – 12:30 P.M. time slot on September 19 to September 26 on the Date Navigator.

The Appointment Book appears as shown in Figure 1-23.

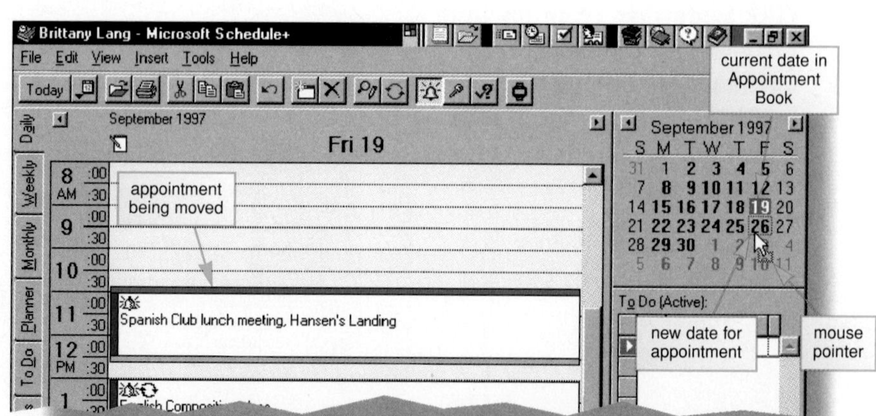

FIGURE 1-23

2 **Release the left mouse button to drop the appointment at the new date in the Date Navigator.**

The appointment is moved from September 19 to September 26 (Figure 1-24). The new date displays in the Appointment Book.

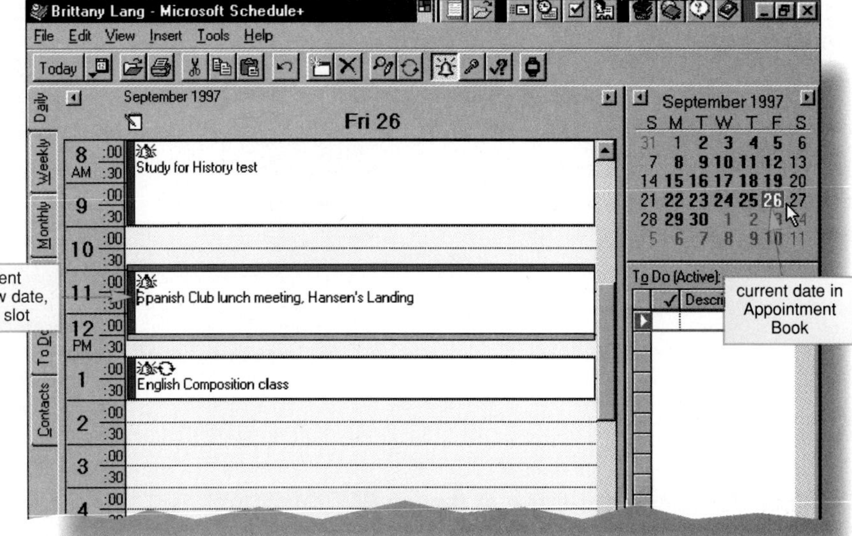

FIGURE 1-24

Moving an Appointment to a New Month

If a date is being moved to a month other than the month currently displayed in the Date Navigator, a different approach must be taken. Because you cannot drag an appointment to a date that isn't displayed, the cut and paste method is the most efficient method to use. The following steps describe how to move an appointment using the cut and paste method.

To Move an Appointment to a New Month

1 **If necessary, click anywhere within the Spanish Club lunch meeting appointment you just moved, now scheduled from 11:00 A.M. – 12:30 P.M. on September 26. Point to the Cut button on the toolbar (Figure 1-25).**

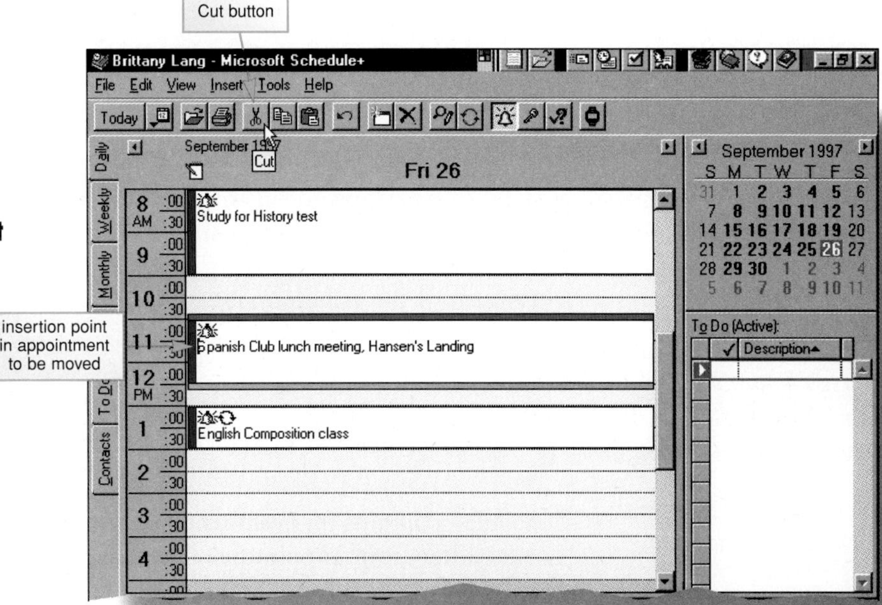

FIGURE 1-25

2 **Click the Cut button on the toolbar.**

The appointment disappears from the time slot (Figure 1-26). The appointment is placed on the Clipboard until the new location is specified.

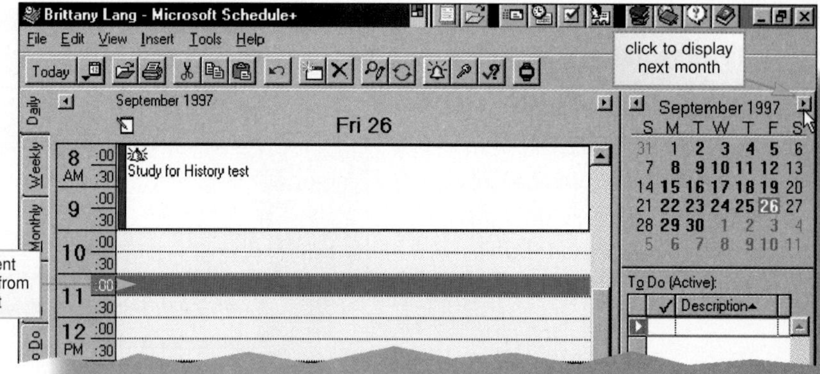

FIGURE 1-26

3 **Click the small right arrow at the top of the Date Navigator to display the month of October, and then click 17 to display the Appointment Book for October 17.**

4 **The 11:00 A.M. time slot already should be highlighted, but if not, click anywhere within it. Click the Paste button on the toolbar.**

The appointment is inserted (pasted) in the 11:00 A.M. – 12:30 P.M. time slot on October 17 (Figure 1-27).

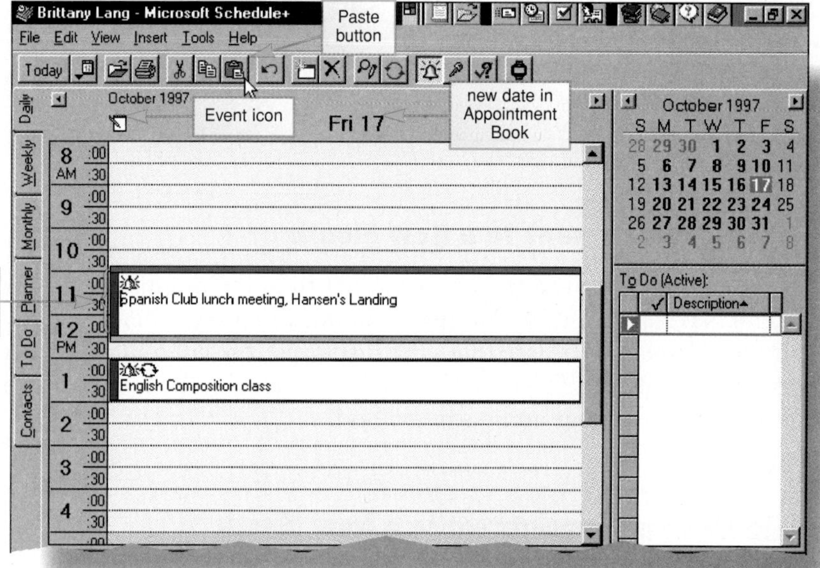

FIGURE 1-27

More About the Event Scheduler

You can see in list form all the events or annual events you have scheduled by using the Edit menu. Once displayed, you can check the list to see upcoming events or to edit or delete any event listed. To view the list of events, click the Edit List of command in the Edit menu. When the submenu displays, click either Events or Annual Events, depending upon which type of event you want to list. The events will display in a dialog box, which allows you to view, edit, delete, or add events.

It is important to understand when each method of moving should be used. In general, if an appointment is being moved on the same day, use the drag and drop method directly in the Appointment Book. If the appointment is being moved within the same month, drag the appointment to the desired date on the Date Navigator. If the appointment is being moved to another month, use the cut and paste method.

Using the Event Scheduler

Schedule+ contains an **Event scheduler** to help you keep track of important events. Events differ from appointments in that they do not affect individual time slots in the Appointment Book. Examples of events include holidays, friends' or family members' birthdays, conferences, weddings, vacations, and so forth. When you schedule an event, its description displays at the top of the Appointment Book. The date also displays bold in the Date Navigator.

You have the choice of scheduling an event or an annual event. An **event** might occur on a different day every week, month, or year. Examples of events could be final exam week, last day of the semester, spring vacation, or the first day of summer school classes. An **annual event** occurs on the same date every year, such as a birthday or anniversary. If you schedule an annual event, it will automatically be carried over to the same date of the next year in Schedule+.

The following steps describe how to insert an annual event.

To Insert an Annual Event

1. **Display the date September 25 in the Appointment Book, and then click the Event icon at the top of the Appointment Book.**

   The Insert Event drop-down list displays.

2. **Click Insert annual event.**

   The Annual Event dialog box displays (Figure 1-28). The current date already is assigned in the Annual event on text box.

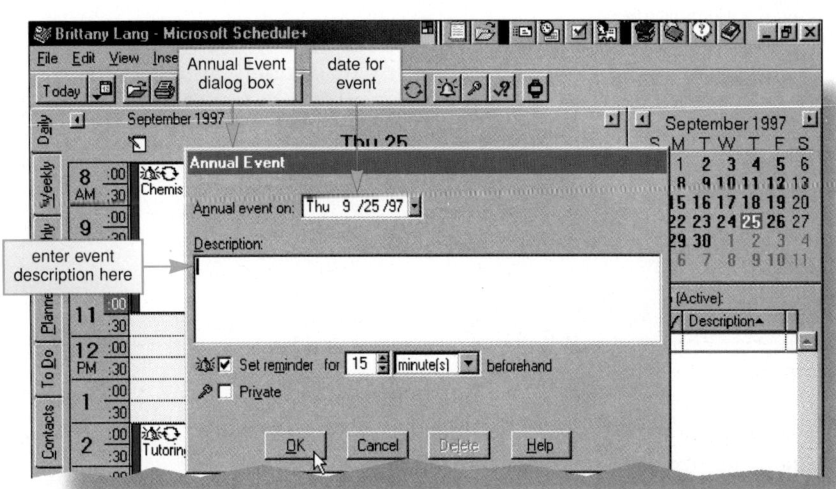

FIGURE 1-28

3. **In the Description text box, type** `Bryan's birthday` **and then click the OK button.**

   The event description displays above the first time slot in the Appointment Book (Figure 1-29). The Event icon appears to contain writing to remind you that an event is scheduled for the date currently displayed.

event displays above first time slot in Appointment Book

Event icon contains writing

FIGURE 1-29

OtherWays

1. On Insert menu click Annual Event

To correct or edit an event, click the Event icon, and then click the event's description that displays in the drop-down list box. When the Annual Event dialog box displays, edit the description text or edit the check boxes until the desired results are obtained, and then click the OK button.

More About Opening Schedules

You can have several schedules open at any one time during a Schedule+ session. If you have access to other users' schedules, you can open their Appointment Books, Contact Lists, or any part of their schedule. You can also open an archived copy of your schedule while a current copy is open. Click the Open button on the toolbar to open additional schedules, or use the File menu.

Using Weekly and Monthly Views to Display the Schedule

Now that the schedule is complete, you can see what it looks like displayed in Weekly or Monthly view. Although the screen appears quite differently in Weekly and Monthly views, you can perform the same tasks that are available in Daily view. Events can be scheduled, appointments can be added or edited, reminders set and removed, and so forth.

Weekly View

The advantage of displaying a schedule in **Weekly view** is that you can see how heavily or sparsely scheduled any given week is. The Weekly view displays appointments quite differently than the Daily view does. The default is to display a five-day week (Monday through Friday), although you can change to a seven-day week by choosing Number of Days from the View menu. The following step describes how to display the schedule in Weekly view.

Steps To Change to Weekly View

1 Display the September 15 date in the Appointment Book, and then click the Weekly tab.

The schedule displays in Weekly view (Figure 1-30).

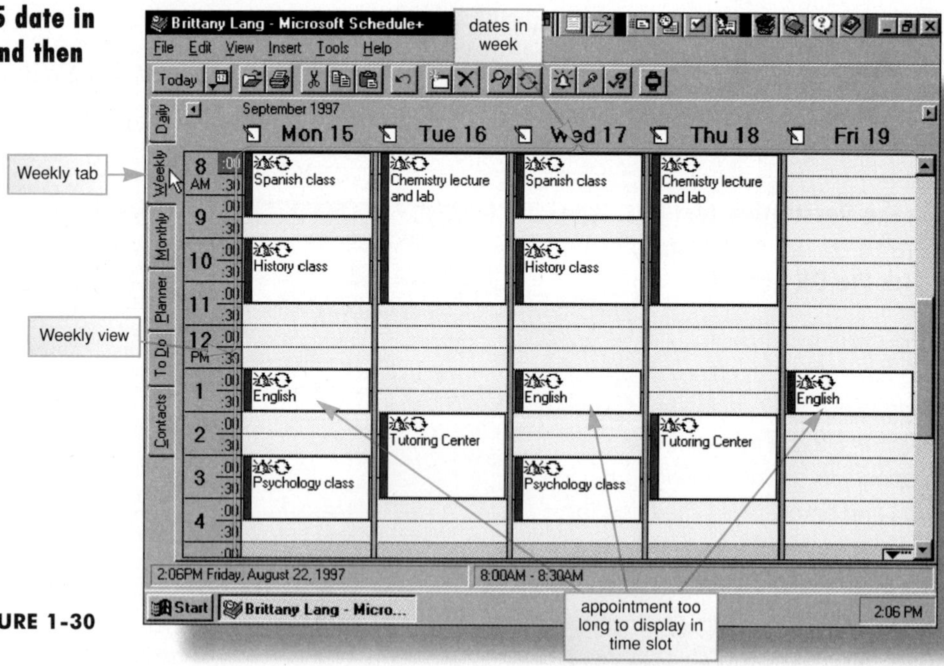

FIGURE 1-30

Other Ways

1. Press ALT+W

Some appointments may be too long to display in their entirety in Weekly view. The vertical scroll bar at the right side of the screen allows you to scroll through the time slots. The small left and right arrow buttons at the top of the screen allow you to move quickly backward or forward a week at a time, much like the arrows in Daily view. Each weekday has its own Event icon directly to the left of the date.

Monthly View

The **Monthly view** looks similar to a standard calendar page and displays your schedule for an entire month. Times and appointments are listed in each date box in the calendar.

The following step shows how to use Monthly view to display your schedule.

To Change to Monthly View

1 **Click the Monthly tab.**

The schedule displays in Monthly view (Figure 1-31). Dates that contain more appointments than can be displayed in the allotted space will display a scroll bar when clicked. You can use the scroll bar to scroll through the appointments for each date on the calendar.

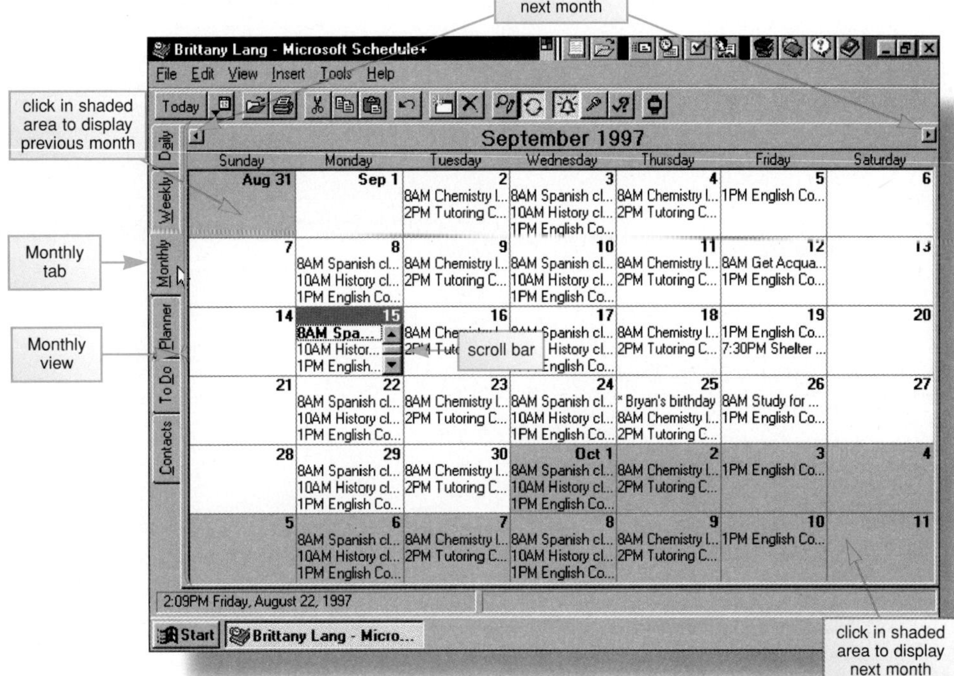

FIGURE 1-31

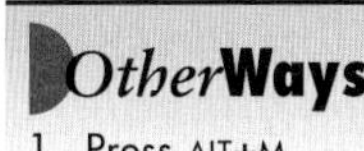

Other Ways

1. Press ALT+M

As with Daily and Weekly views, you can edit or add new appointments while in Monthly view. However, because the appointments are even more abbreviated in Monthly view, it is easier to switch back to Daily view in order to edit. The small left and right arrow buttons at the top of the screen allow you to move quickly backward or forward a month at a time. You also can move forward or backward a month at a time by clicking in the shaded dates of the calendar. Clicking in any shaded date prior to the first of the month displays the previous month's schedule, and clicking in any shaded date following the last day of the month displays the next month's schedule.

Creating a To Do List

The **To Do List** enables you to keep track of tasks that should be carried out by specific dates. The list can be as simple as a shopping list, or as complex as parts of a major project to be completed over an extended period of time.

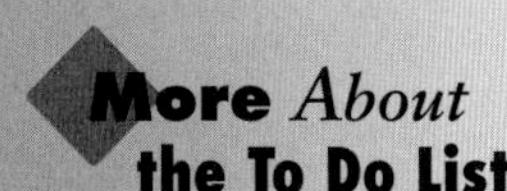

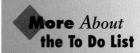

More About the To Do List

You can easily customize the appearance and layout of the To Do List by using the Columns command in the View menu. This command enables you to change the column headings, column widths, and grid lines.

Table 1-2

Table 1-2
Bring tape recorder to English class
Pick up dress at dry cleaners by 3 P.M.
Bring handout materials to fundraiser

When you create a To Do List, you are, in effect, creating a database to track specific tasks. Because Schedule+ treats it as a database, the To Do List can be manipulated in sophisticated ways. Tasks can be grouped, sorted, and prioritized. Start and end dates can be specified, and a percentage of completion statistics can be calculated for any given project.

In this project, a simple To Do List (Table 1-2) will be created for a date in the Appointment Book, as shown in the following steps.

Steps To Create a To Do List

1. **Click the Daily tab, and then display September 19 in the Appointment Book.**

2. **Click the To Do tab.**

   *The To Do List displays (Figure 1-32). The format is similar to an Excel worksheet, with similar terminology. The headings (Description, Priority, Ends, etc.) that run across the table are called **columns** or **fields**. Each line going up and down the page is called a **row** or **record**. Each intersection point of a column and row is called a **cell**.*

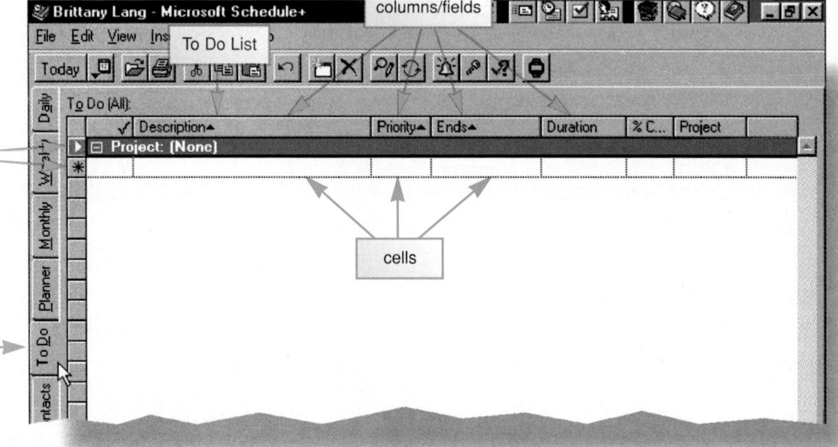

FIGURE 1-32

3. **Click the first empty cell in the Description column, and then type** `Bring tape recorder to English class` **to enter the first task.**

4. **Click the next empty cell in the Description column, and then type** `Pick up dress at dry cleaners by 3 P.M.` **to enter the next task.**

5. **Click the next empty cell in the Description column, and then type** `Bring handout materials to fundraiser` **to enter the last task in the To Do List.**

   When complete, the To Do List appears as shown in Figure 1-33.

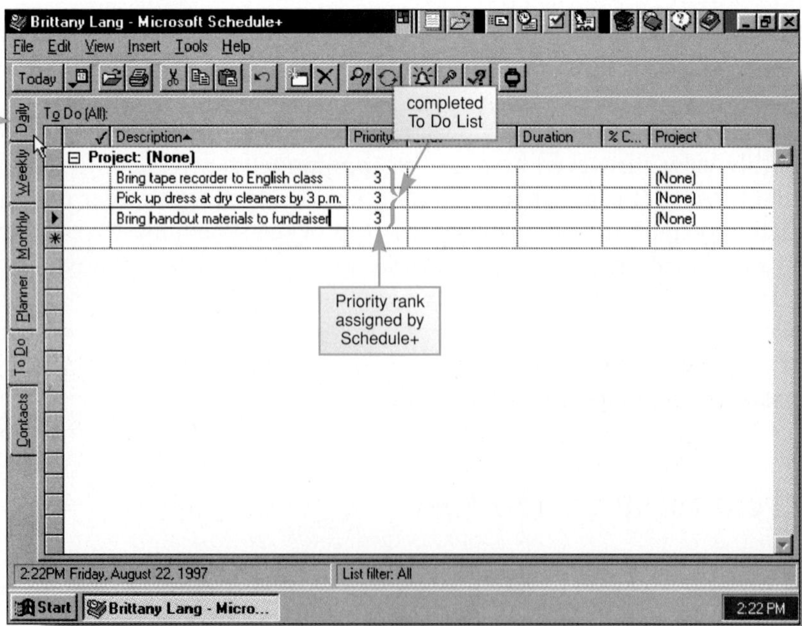

FIGURE 1-33

6 Click the Daily tab.

The completed To Do List displays in Daily view (Figure 1-34). The tasks are automatically alphabetized by the first character of the description.

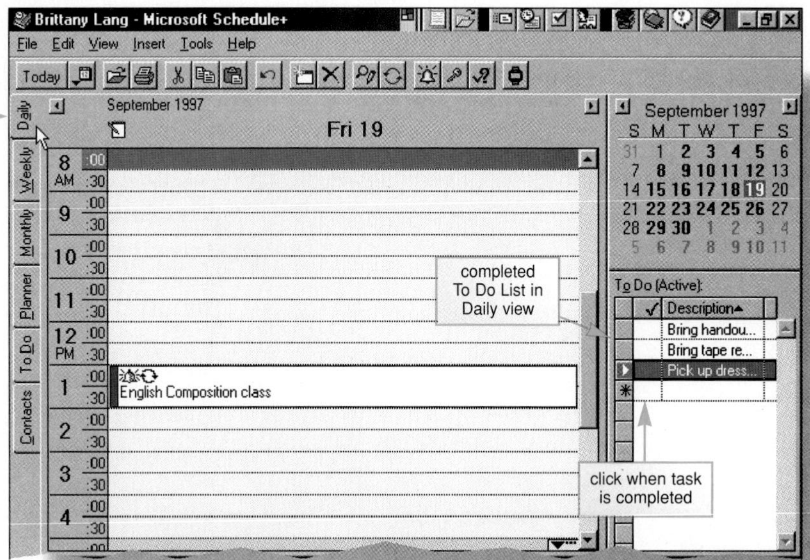

FIGURE 1-34

OtherWays

1. Click the To Do tab, click Insert New Task button on toolbar
2. Double-click row selection button in front of task in To Do List
3. On Microsoft Office Shortcut bar, click Add a Task
4. On Insert menu click Task
5. Press ALT+D

You can click the To Do tab and then double-click each task in the To Do List as it is completed. Each time you double-click a task, the Task dialog box appears. Click the Cancel button to continue. A check mark will display in the box to the left of the task's description, and a line will be placed through the task indicating it has been completed or *crossed out*.

To edit the To Do List, click the To Do tab and edit the entries in the same way you would edit an appointment.

Printing a Schedule

You can print any part of the schedule you want in any number of different layouts. The following pages describe how to print the different sections of the schedule you created using attractive, easy-to-read layouts.

Steps To Print the Daily Schedule

1 Ready the printer according to instructions. Display September 8 in Daily view, and then point to the Print button on the toolbar (Figure 1-35).

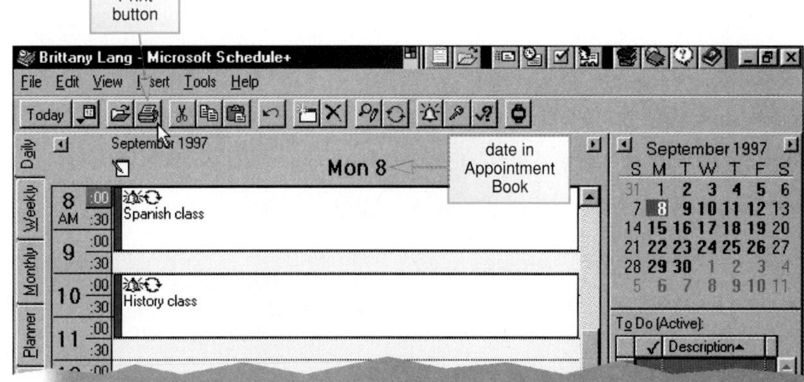

FIGURE 1-35

Click the Print button.

The Print dialog box displays. The different layout options available while printing display in the Print layout list box (Figure 1-36).

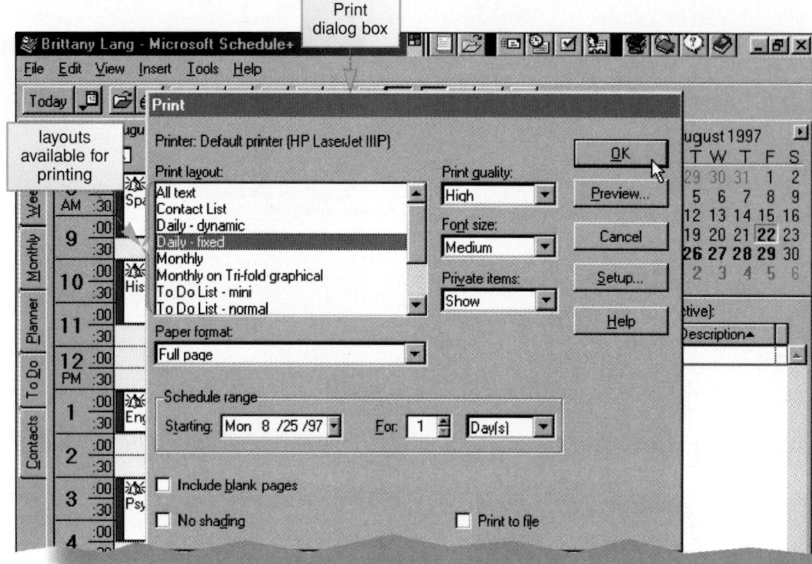

FIGURE 1-36

3 Click Daily - fixed in the Print layout list box, and then click the OK button.

The daily schedule of appointments prints on the printer. The printout should appear as shown in Figure 1-37.

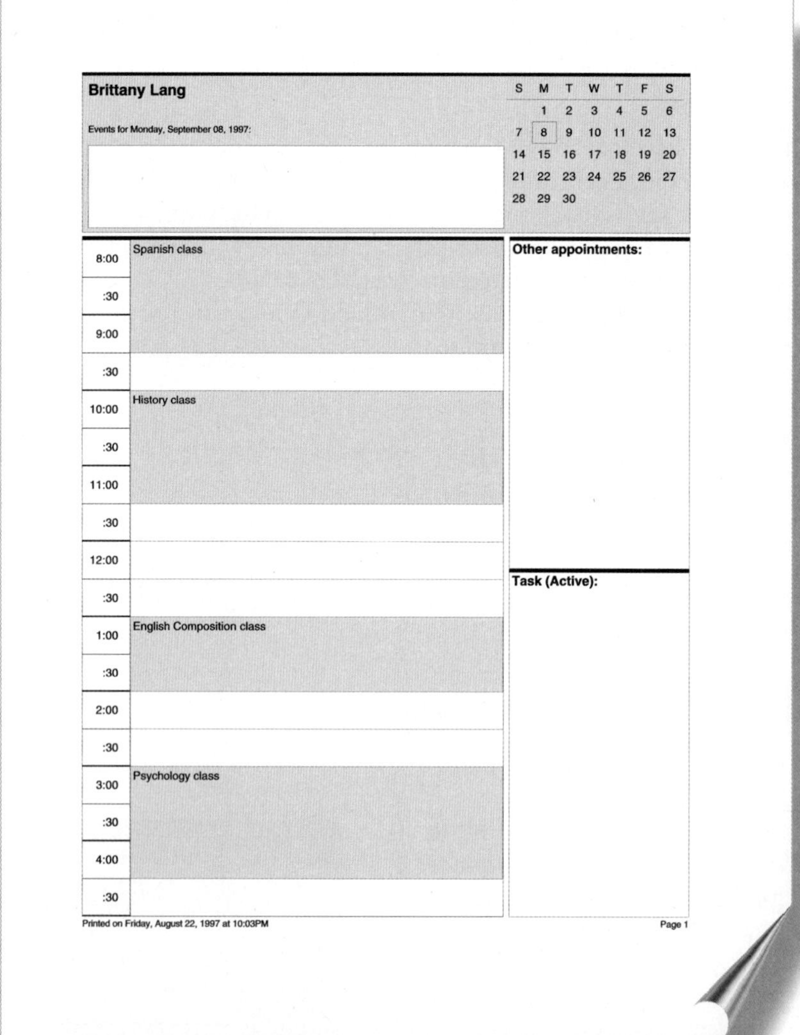

Brittany Lang

Events for Monday, September 08, 1997:

S	M	T	W	T	F	S
	1	2	3	4	5	6
7	8	9	10	11	12	13
14	15	16	17	18	19	20
21	22	23	24	25	26	27
28	29	30				

8:00	Spanish class
:30	
9:00	
:30	
10:00	History class
:30	
11:00	
:30	
12:00	
:30	
1:00	English Composition class
:30	
2:00	
:30	
3:00	Psychology class
:30	
4:00	
:30	

Other appointments:

Task (Active):

Printed on Friday, August 22, 1997 at 10:03PM

Page 1

FIGURE 1-37

OtherWays

1. On File menu click Print
2. Press CTRL+P

To Print the Weekly Schedule

1 **With September 8 still displayed, click the Print button on the toolbar.**

2 **Click Weekly – 5 day in the Print layout list box, and then click the OK button.**

The weekly schedule prints on the printer (Figure 1-38). If the Weekly - 7 day option had been chosen, a seven-day schedule (including the weekend days, Saturday and Sunday) would have printed.

Brittany Lang

Monday, September 08, 1997

	Monday	Tuesday	Wednesday	Thursday	Friday
8:00	Spanish class	Chemistry lecture and lab	Spanish class	Chemistry lecture and lab	Get Acquainted Breakfast, Student Lounge
:30					
9:00					
:30					
10:00	History class		History class		
:30					
11:00					
.00					
12:00					
:30					
1:00	English Composition class		English Composition class		English Composition class
:30					
2:00		Tutoring Center		Tutoring Center	
:30					
3:00	Psychology class		Psychology class		
:30					
4:00					
:30					
Other:					

Printed on Friday, August 22, 1997 at 10:06PM — Page 1

FIGURE 1-38

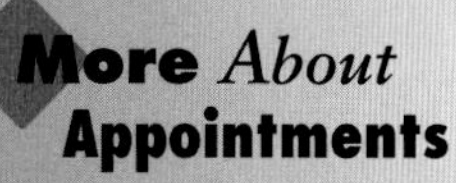

More *About*
Appointments

You can mark text as private, thereby preventing it from being seen by other users who have access to your schedule. Use either the Private button on the toolbar, or the Hide Private Text command in the View menu in order to mark text as private. Once marked as private, a key symbol displays next to the text, indicating the information is private, or "locked." This feature can be applied to appointments, tasks, meetings, or contacts.

To Print the Monthly Schedule

1 **With September 8 still displayed, click the Print button on the toolbar.**

2 **Click Monthly in the Print layout list box, and then click the OK button.**

The monthly schedule prints on the printer (Figure 1-39). If you had chosen the Monthly on Tri-fold graphical option, a different format would print. This format prints the Daily and Monthly schedules, as well as the To Do List(s) on one page.

August 1997

S	M	T	W	T	F	S
					1	2
3	4	5	6	7	8	9
10	11	12	13	14	15	16
17	18	19	20	21	22	23
24	25	26	27	28	29	30
31						

Brittany Lang

September 1997

October 1997

S	M	T	W	T	F	S
			1	2	3	4
5	6	7	8	9	10	11
12	13	14	15	16	17	18
19	20	21	22	23	24	25
26	27	28	29	30	31	

Sun	Mon	Tue	Wed	Thu	Fri	Sat
	1	2 8:00AM-11:30AM Chemistry lecture... 2:00PM-4:00PM Tutoring Center	3 8:00AM-9:30AM Spanish class 10:00AM-11:30AM History class 1:00PM-2:00PM English... 3:00PM-4:30PM Psychology class	4 8:00AM-11:30AM Chemistry lecture... 2:00PM-4:00PM Tutoring Center	5 1:00PM-2:00PM English...	6
7	8 8:00AM-9:30AM Spanish class 10:00AM-11:30AM History class 1:00PM-2:00PM English... 3:00PM-4:30PM Psychology class	9 8:00AM-11:30AM Chemistry lecture... 2:00PM-4:00PM Tutoring Center	10 8:00AM-9:30AM Spanish class 10:00AM-11:30AM History class 1:00PM-2:00PM English... 3:00PM-4:30PM Psychology class	11 8:00AM-11:30AM Chemistry lecture... 2:00PM-4:00PM Tutoring Center	12 8:00AM-10:00AM Get Acquainted... 1:00PM-2:00PM English...	13
14	15 8:00AM-9:30AM Spanish class 10:00AM-11:30AM History class 1:00PM-2:00PM English... 3:00PM-4:30PM Psychology class	16 8:00AM-11:30AM Chemistry lecture... 2:00PM-4:00PM Tutoring Center	17 8:00AM-9:30AM Spanish class 10:00AM-11:30AM History class 1:00PM-2:00PM English... 3:00PM-4:30PM Psychology class	18 8:00AM-11:30AM Chemistry lecture... 2:00PM-4:00PM Tutoring Center	19 11:00AM-12:30PM Spanish Club lunch... 1:00PM-2:00PM English... 6:00PM-8:00PM Shelter fundraiser...	20
21	22 8:00AM-9:30AM Spanish class 10:00AM-11:30AM History class 1:00PM-2:00PM English... 3:00PM-4:30PM Psychology class	23 8:00AM-11:30AM Chemistry lecture... 2:00PM-4:00PM Tutoring Center	24 8:00AM-9:30AM Spanish class 10:00AM-11:30AM History class 1:00PM-2:00PM English... 3:00PM-4:30PM Psychology class	25 *Bryan's birthday* 8:00AM-11:30AM Chemistry lecture... 2:00PM-4:00PM Tutoring Center	26 8:00AM-10:00AM Study for History test 1:00PM-2:00PM English...	27
28	29 8:00AM-9:30AM Spanish class 10:00AM-11:30AM History class 1:00PM-2:00PM English... 3:00PM-4:30PM Psychology class	30 8:00AM-11:30AM Chemistry lecture... 2:00PM-4:00PM Tutoring Center				

Printed on Friday, August 22, 1997 at 10:15PM — Page 1

FIGURE 1-39

More *About* **Printing**

You can use the Print Setup dialog box to change the margins, orientation, or paper size of the paper on which your schedule prints.

Steps To Print the To Do List

1 Display September 19 in the Appointment Book, and then click the Print button on the toolbar. When the Print dialog box displays, click To Do List – text, and in the Print layout list box, and then click the OK button.

The To Do List prints on the printer (Figure 1-40). The To Do List – mini option prints the tasks associated with a specific date. The To Do List – normal options prints the To Do List in its entirety, including priority, end date, completion percentage, and so forth.

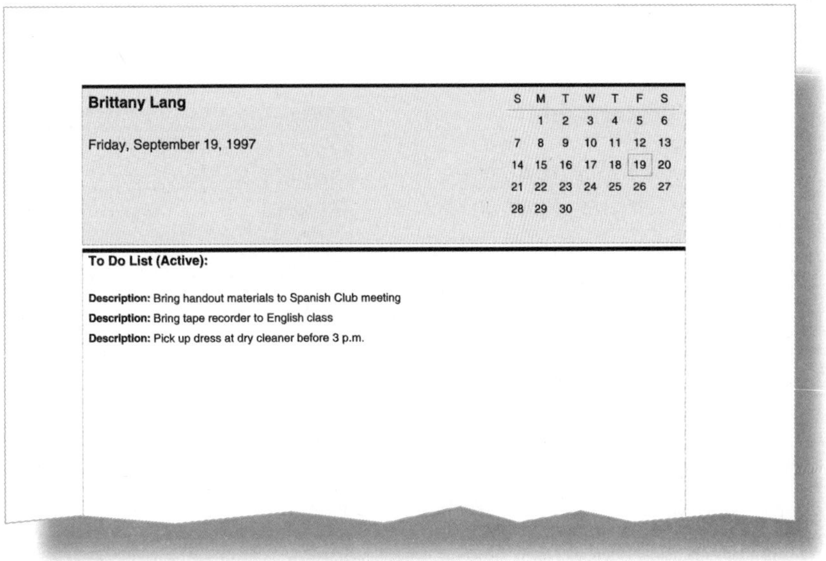

Brittany Lang

Friday, September 19, 1997

S	M	T	W	T	F	S
	1	2	3	4	5	6
7	8	9	10	11	12	13
14	15	16	17	18	19	20
21	22	23	24	25	26	27
28	29	30				

To Do List (Active):

Description: Bring handout materials to Spanish Club meeting
Description: Bring tape recorder to English class
Description: Pick up dress at dry cleaner before 3 p.m.

FIGURE 1-40

Contacts List

The **Contacts List** is like an electronic address book. You enter the names, addresses, and other information about the people you frequently contact. Once the information has been entered, you can retrieve, sort, edit, organize, or print it. Like the To Do List, the Contacts List is treated like an Excel worksheet. Information is entered into columns/fields, and each completed contact entry becomes a record in a row.

More *About* the Contacts List

You can import other Contacts Lists through the Import menu. The Schedule+ Interchange command allows you to copy information that exists in other applications to Schedule+. The information can be imported from other applications, including compatible scheduling software.

Creating a Contacts List

The Contacts List provides five different tabs to enter different types of information about each contact: Business, Phone, Address, Personal, and Notes. In this project, only the Address tab is used for each contact. If you wanted to enter information on other tabs, simply click the desired tab and fill in the information.

Because the Contacts List is not attached to any specific date, any date can be displayed in the Appointment Book when you create the list.The next section describes how to create a Contacts List for the contacts shown in Table 1-3.

Table 1-3

NAME	ADDRESS	TELEPHONE NUMBER
Denise Markens	84 West 150th Ct. Chicago, IL 60105	(312) 555-1600
Sara Vincent	2312 Jefferson Avenue Lombard, IL 60148	(708) 555-9061
Nick Gold	7886 Chestnut Lane Lombard, IL 60148	(708) 555-0982
Don Lee	934 - 68th Avenue Chicago, IL 60602	(312) 555-6707

The following steps describe how to create a Contacts List.

Steps To Create a Contacts List

Click the Contacts tab.

The Contacts List displays (Figure 1-41). The left side of the window contains the Contacts area, or a blank Contacts List, where names of contacts display after being entered. The right side of the window contains the Name area. The Name area is displayed in a card format, and it is where information about each contact will be entered.

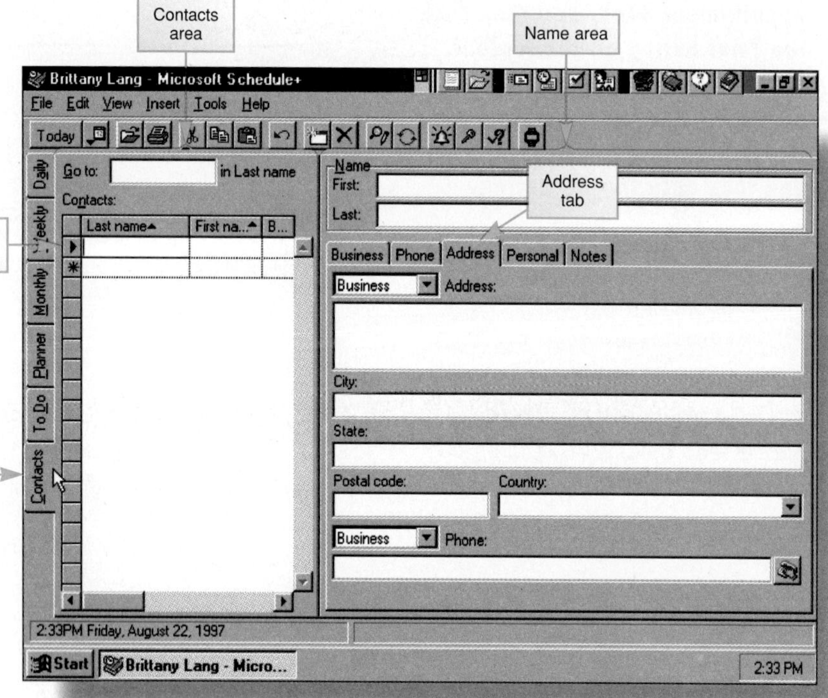

FIGURE 1-41

2 **If necessary, click the Address tab in the Name area, and then click the First text box. Type** `Denise` **to enter the first name of the first contact. Click the Last text box, and then type** `Markens` **to enter the first contact's last name.**

The first and last name of the first contact are entered (Figure 1-42).

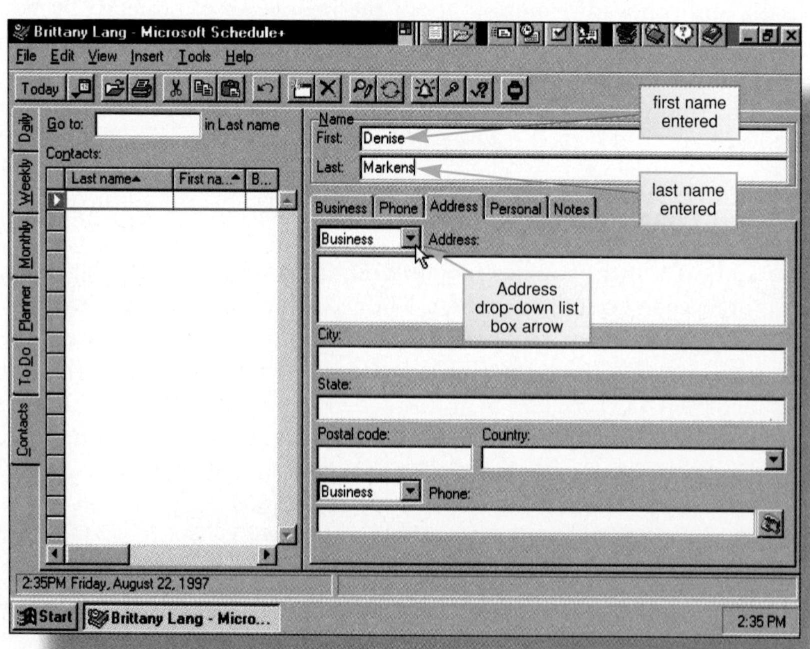

FIGURE 1-42

3 **Click the Address drop-down list box arrow, and then click Home, so that the field name accurately reflects its contents. Click in the Address box below, and then type** `84 West 150th Ct.` **to enter the street address. Enter the remaining information for the first contact in Table 1-3 on page S 1.31. Click the Phone drop-down list box arrow and then click Home to change the field to home telephone number. When the information has been entered, click the row selection button in the first empty row in the Contacts list.**

The first contact's information is entered in the Name area and now displays in the Contacts area (Figure 1-43).

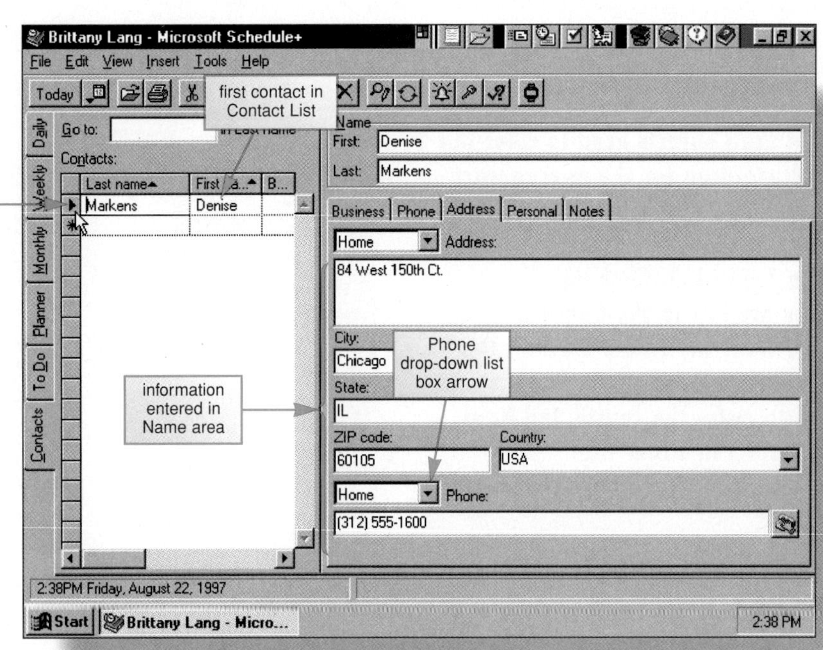

FIGURE 1-43

4 **Click an empty row in the Contacts area.**

The Name area clears so a new contact can be entered (Figure 1-44).

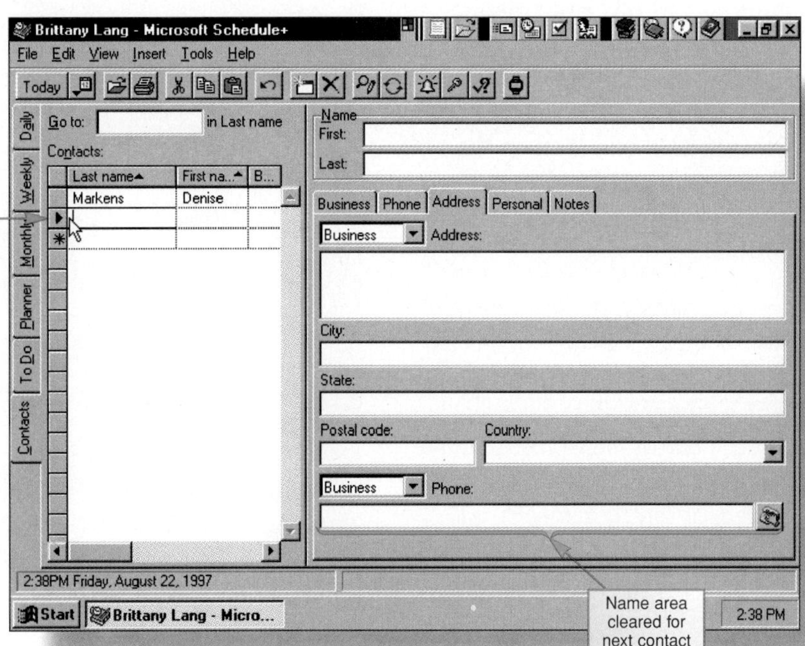

FIGURE 1-44

5 **Repeat Steps 2 and 3 to enter the next contact in Table 1-3 on page S 1.31. Click an empty row in the Contacts area to clear the Name area for the next contact. Repeat Steps 2 and 3 to enter the third contact in Table 1-3. Click an empty row in the Contacts area to clear the Name area for the next contact. Repeat Steps 2 and 3 to enter the fourth and final contact in Table 1-3.**

When complete, the Contacts List should look like Figure 1-45. Schedule+ automatically lists the contacts in alphabetical order.

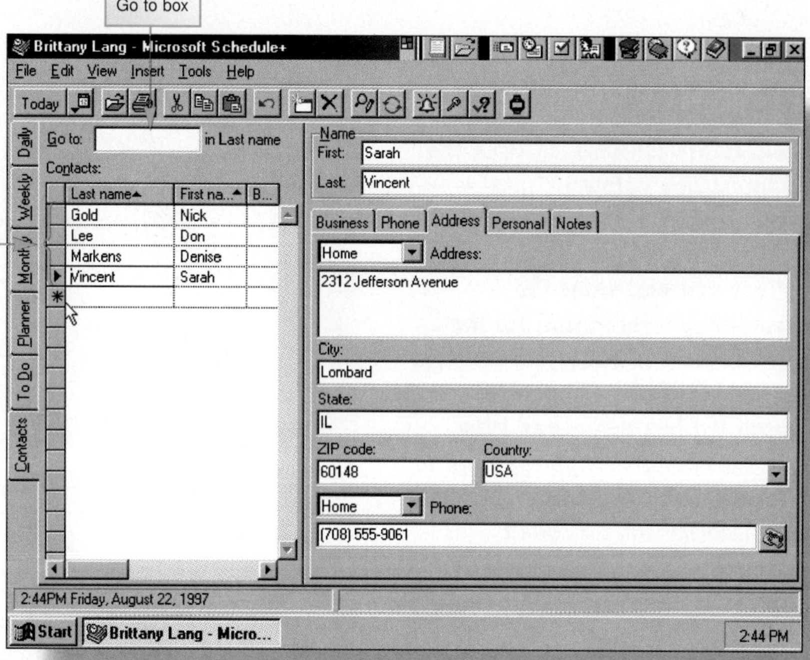

FIGURE 1-45

6 **Because the default setting prints the Contacts List with only the first and last name fields, you must include additional fields if you want them to print on the list. If necessary, click the Contacts tab, and then on the View menu, point to Columns. From the Columns submenu, click Custom.**

The Columns dialog box displays (Figure 1-46). Your list may include additional fields. The Available fields list box contains fields that you can add to the Contacts List so that when the Contacts List is printed, all the chosen fields will print instead of just the first and last names.

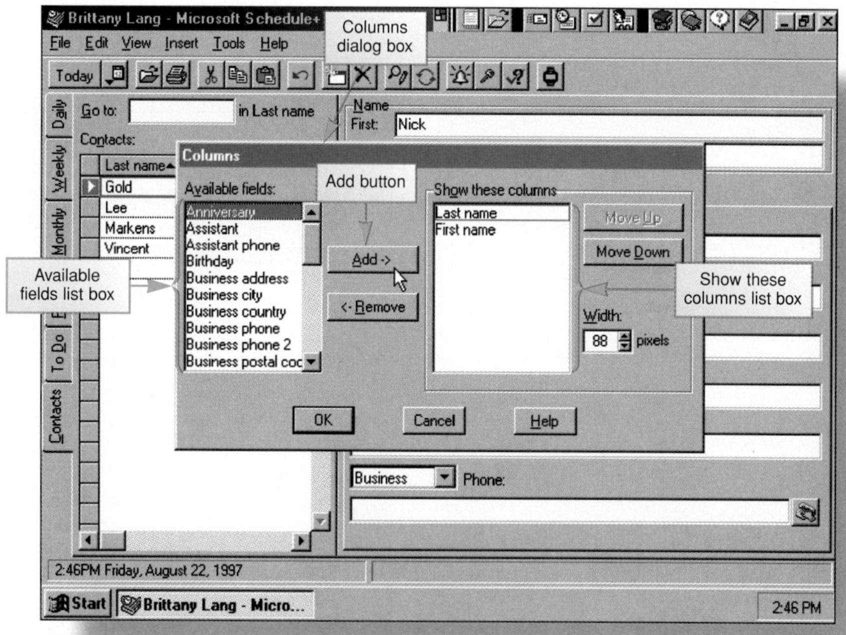

FIGURE 1-46

7 **Use the scroll arrows on the Available fields list box, if necessary, until the Home address field displays. Click Home address, and then click the Add button.**

Home address is added to the Show these columns list (Figure 1-47).

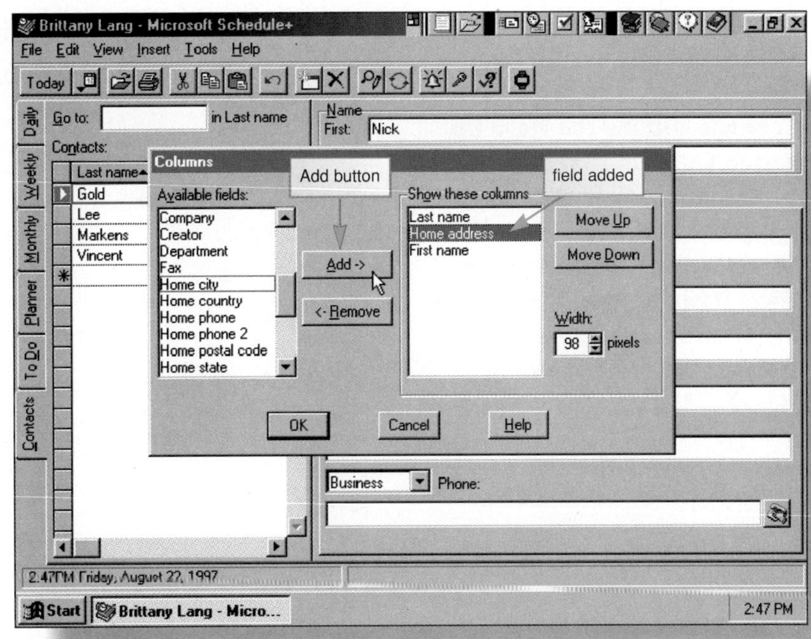

FIGURE 1-47

8 **Repeat Step 7 above to add the Home city, Home state, Home postal code, and Home phone fields to the Show these columns list.**

The Show these columns list should appear as shown in Figure 1-48. Step 9 will place the fields in their proper order.

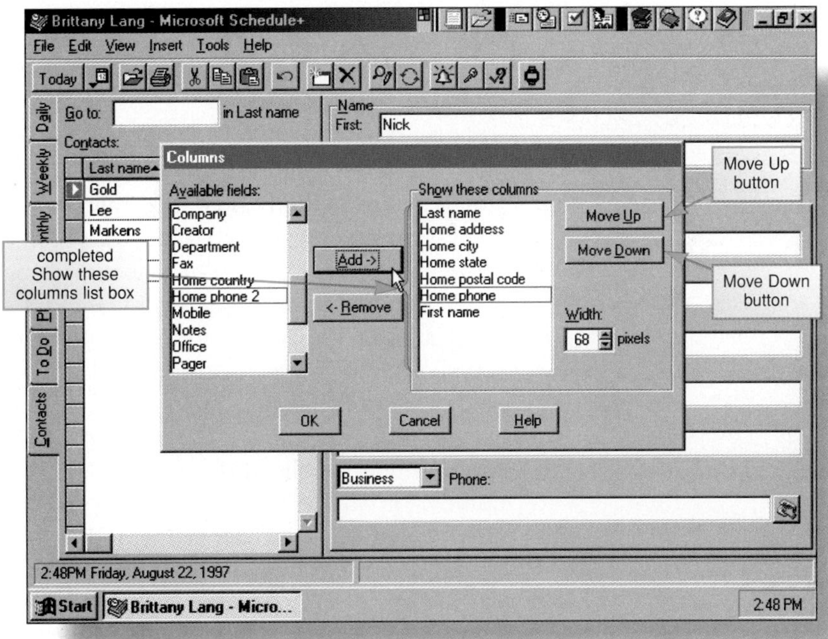

FIGURE 1-48

9 **Click the First name field in the Show these columns list, and then click the Move Up button. Continue clicking the Move Up button until the First name field is placed second in the list, under the Last name field. If necessary, use the Move Up or Move Down buttons to rearrange the Show these columns list so it matches the order shown in Figure 1-49.**

The First name field moves up in the list. The fields should be ordered as shown in Figure 1-49.

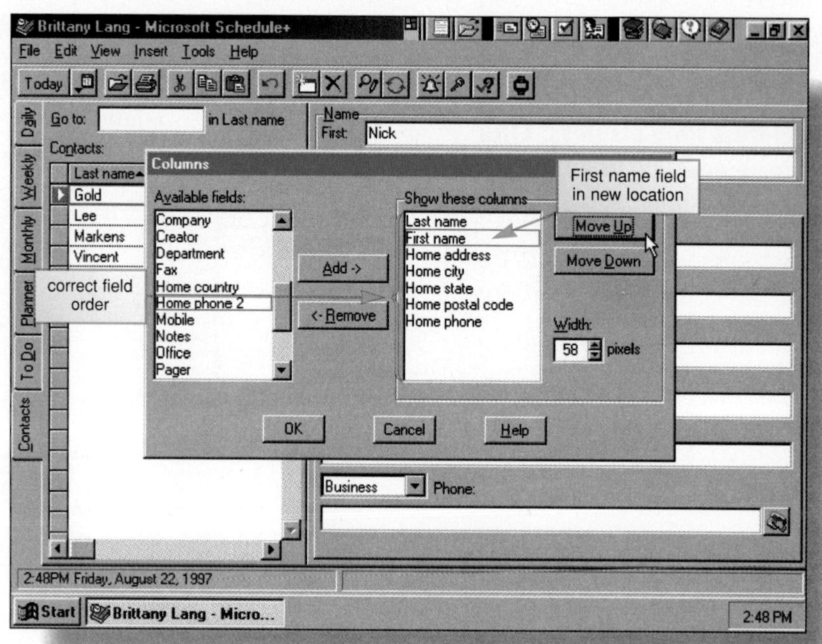

FIGURE 1-49

10 **Click the OK button in the Columns dialog box.**

The Contacts List is complete and the Contacts view displays.

More *About* the Contacts List

Each tab in the Contacts List contains a Phone Dialer button. If you have a modem, you can click the Phone Dialer button to call any contact in your Contacts List for whom a number is listed. When you click the button, the number displayed in the Phone list box is automatically dialed.

Once the Contacts List is complete, it can be viewed, edited, or updated at any time. To display information on each contact, click the desired name in the Contacts area. The related information will display in the Name area. You can display any record to be edited, and then edit it as you would an Appointment Book entry. You can add or delete information or fill in other tabs.

The example in this project created a simple Contacts List, but because it is an organized list, information it contains can be manipulated in sophisticated ways. You can keep track of personal information, such as a spouse's name, birthday, anniversary, and so forth. If you wish, you can schedule these days as events in the Contacts List and they automatically will appear as events in your Appointment Book on the appropriate date. You can sort the Contacts List in any number of ways. For example, you can group employees of the same company, members of the same department, people on the same project, in the same class, or just about any way you might choose.

Because this Contacts List is very short, all the names display in the Contacts area on the Schedule+ window. In longer lists, however, you can quickly locate a specific contact by using the Go to box at the top of the Contacts area. Click in the Go to box, and then type any information about the contact, such as name, company, or address. The name immediately displays in the Contacts area, and the related information displays in the Name area.

Printing the Contacts List

Printing the Contacts List is an easy way to obtain a listing of people you frequently contact. The printed list can be used for business mailings, social gatherings, or even a Christmas card list. Because you added fields to the Contacts List in the previous section, the contact's last name, first name, home address, city, state, postal code, and telephone number will print on the printout. The following steps describe how to print the Contacts List. Because the Contacts List is not attached to any particular date in the schedule, any view can be displayed when you print the Contacts List.

Steps To Print the Contacts List

1. **With any view of the schedule displayed, click the Print button on the toolbar.**

2. **When the Print dialog box displays, click Contacts List in the Print layout list box, and then click the Ok button.**

   The printed Contacts List should look like Figure 1-50.

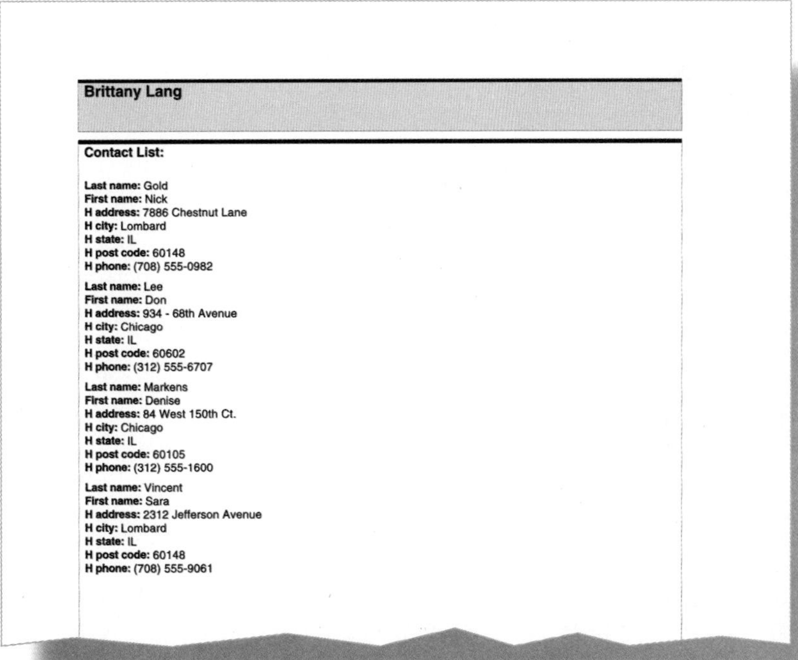

Brittany Lang

Contact List:

Last name: Gold
First name: Nick
H address: 7886 Chestnut Lane
H city: Lombard
H state: IL
H post code: 60148
H phone: (708) 555-0982

Last name: Lee
First name: Don
H address: 934 - 68th Avenue
H city: Chicago
H state: IL
H post code: 60602
H phone: (312) 555-6707

Last name: Markens
First name: Denise
H address: 84 West 150th Ct.
H city: Chicago
H state: IL
H post code: 60105
H phone: (312) 555-1600

Last name: Vincent
First name: Sara
H address: 2312 Jefferson Avenue
H city: Lombard
H state: IL
H post code: 60148
H phone: (708) 555-9061

FIGURE 1-50

Exiting Schedule+

The project is now complete. The last step required is to exit Schedule+ and end the session. Because you have made changes to the schedule since the last time you saved it, the old version will be replaced with the new version of the schedule. The step on the next page summarizes how to save the schedule and exit Schedule+.

More About Appointments

Schedule+ allows you to quickly change time zones if you travel to a location in a different time zone. You can also specify two different time zones, the primary and secondary zones, so that your appointment time slots are not affected if you travel. You also are provided with the option of allowing Schedule+ to automatically adjust your appointments to reflect Daylight Savings Time. The Time Zone tab is contained under Options in the Tools menu.

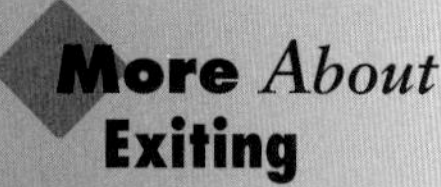

More About Exiting

If you have more than one schedule open, be certain you close each one by clicking the Close button, or by clicking Exit on the File menu.

TO SAVE THE SCHEDULE AND EXIT SCHEDULE+

Step 1: Click the Close button on the right side of the title bar.

The schedule is saved on the floppy disk in drive A under the name you assigned the first time it was saved. The Windows 95 desktop displays.

If you changed the date at the beginning of this project, change it back to today's date before shutting down Windows 95.

Project Summary

Brittany Lang's class schedule is entered for the entire semester, and her current social engagements through September also are entered in her Appointment Book. In this project, you learned about personal information management systems by using Schedule+ to create a personal schedule. You learned to enter appointments, create recurring appointments, move appointments to new dates, schedule events, and see your schedule in its daily, weekly, and monthly form. You created a To Do List to serve as a reminder of tasks to be completed on a specific date. Finally, you created and printed a Contacts List.

What You Should Know

Having completed this project, you should be able to perform the following tasks:

- Change to Monthly View *(S 1.25)*
- Change to Weekly View *(S 1.24)*
- Complete the Recurring Appointments (*(S 1.16)*
- Complete the Schedule *(S 1.17)*
- Create a Contacts List *(S 1.32)*
- Create a To Do List *(S 1.26)*
- Delete an Appointment *(S 1.18)*
- Display the Next Day in the Appointment Book *(S 1.16)*
- Enter Appointments in the Appointment Book *(S 1.12)*
- Enter Appointments Using the Appointment Dialog Box *(S 1.13)*
- Insert an Annual Event *(S 1.23)*
- Move an Appointment to a New Date *(S 1.20)*
- Move an Appointment to a New Month *(S 1.21)*
- Move an Appointment to a New Time *(S 1.19)*
- Open an Existing Schedule *(S 1.18)*
- Print the Contacts List *(S 1.37)*
- Print the Daily Schedule *(S 1.27)*
- Print the Monthly Schedule *(S 1.30)*
- Print the Weekly Schedule *(S 1.29)*
- Print the To Do List *(S 1.31)*
- Save the Schedule and Exit Schedule+ *(S 1.17, S 1.38)*
- Set Recurring Appointments *(S 1.14)*
- Start Schedule+ *(S 1.8)*

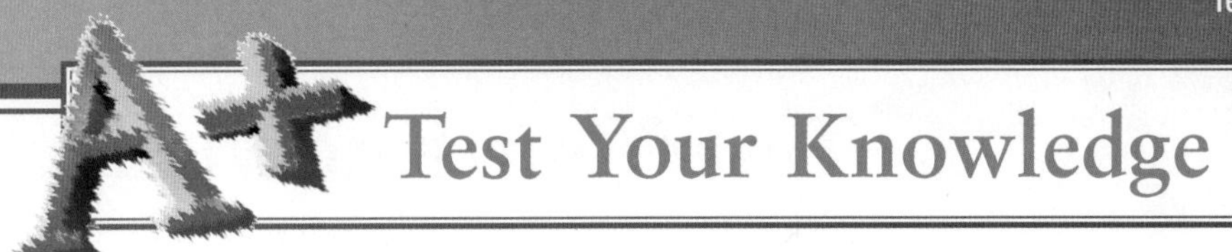

Test Your Knowledge

1 True/False

Instructions: Circle T if the statement is true or F if the statement is false.

T F 1. Events display in the status bar in Daily view.
T F 2. The To Do List is accessed by clicking the To Do tab.
T F 3. The Contacts List is treated like a database with each entry being a record.
T F 4. You cannot include both business and home telephone numbers in the Contacts List.
T F 5. A Reminder icon is assigned by default to all appointments entered in the Appointment Book.
T F 6. The Welcome dialog box displays every time you start Schedule+.
T F 7. To move an appointment to a different month, you can drag and drop it.
T F 8. The Date Navigator is part of Daily view.
T F 9. Appointment times display on Monthly view.
T F 10. A quick way to move ahead one day in Daily view is to click the right arrow at the top of the Appointment Book.

2 Multiple Choice

Instructions: Circle the correct response.

1. To change from Daily view to Monthly view, you would __________.
   a. click the Weekly tab first, and then the Monthly tab
   b. click the Monthly tab
   c. click the Monthly icon on the toolbar
   d. click the shaded area of Daily view
2. To edit an appointment already typed in the Appointment Book, you would __________.
   a. click in the appointment to be edited, then make corrections to the entry
   b. delete the appointment character by character, and then click the New Appointment button on the toolbar
   c. click the Edit button
   d. all of the above
3. The To Do List __________.
   a. keeps track of tasks that must be accomplished by or on a specific date
   b. is treated like a database
   c. is accessed by clicking the To Do tab
   d. all of the above
4. In the Contacts List, __________.
   a. entries are treated as records in a database
   b. you can enter many different types of information about each contact
   c. only the business telephone can be entered
   d. both a and b

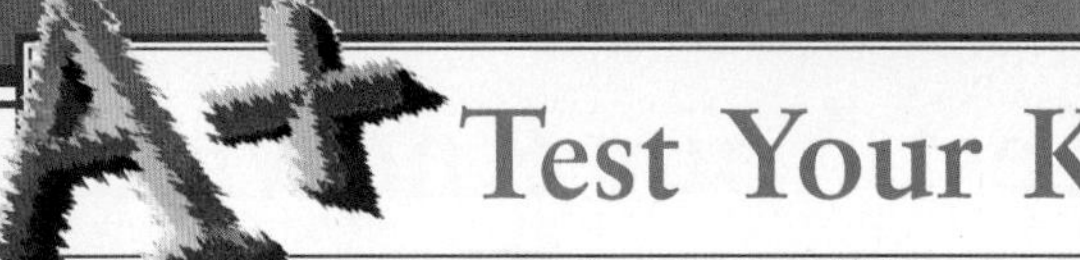

Test Your Knowledge

5. By default, a(n) __________ is assigned to each appointment typed in the Appointment Book.
   a. Appointment icon
   b. Recurring icon
   c. Reminder icon
   d. default filename
6. You can quickly locate a contact in the Contacts List by __________.
   a. using the scroll bar to manually scan each entry
   b. typing a name in the Go to box
   c. clicking the Find Contact button on the toolbar
   d. clicking the Reminder icon
7. The best way of moving an appointment to the same time on a new date within the same month is to __________.
   a. drag the appointment to the new date on the Date Navigator
   b. cut the appointment and paste it in the new location
   c. click the Move Appointment button on the toolbar
   d. none of the above
8. The best way to move an appointment to a time slot in a new month is to __________.
   a. click the New Month button on the toolbar
   b. drag the appointment to the new date using the Date Navigator
   c. cut the appointment and paste it in the new location
   d. none of the above
9. The part of Daily view that looks like a sheet of yellow lined paper is the __________.
   a. Appointment Book
   b. To Do List
   c. Date Navigator
   d. Event scheduler
10. An event displays in Daily view __________.
   a. above the first entry on the Appointment book
   b. as a blinking bell symbol
   c. in large characters above the date
   d. none of the above; events do not display in Daily view

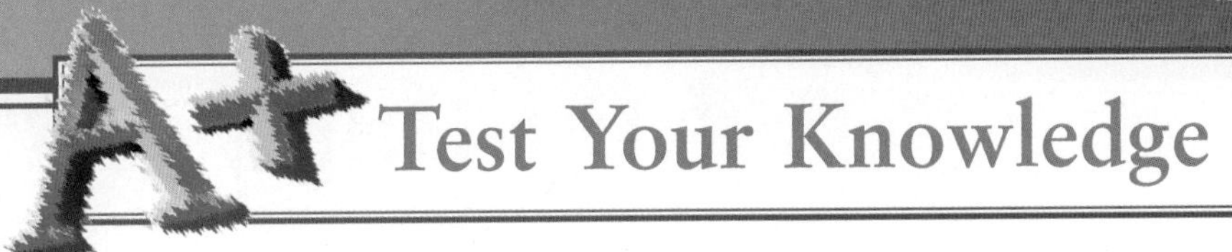

Test Your Knowledge

3 Understanding the Schedule+ Window

Instructions: In Figure 1-51, arrows point to several items in the Schedule+ window. Identify the items in the spaces provided.

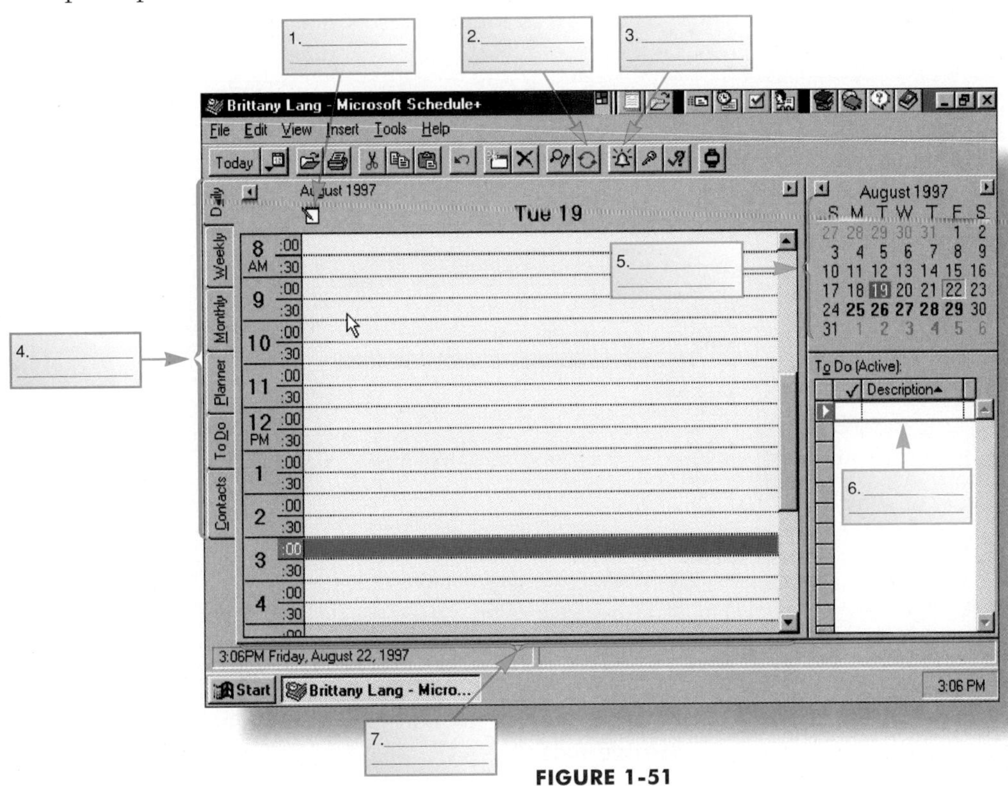

FIGURE 1-51

4 Adding an Event

Instructions: Figure 1-52 shows the Daily view of a calendar date. Describe the steps necessary to schedule this date as an event.

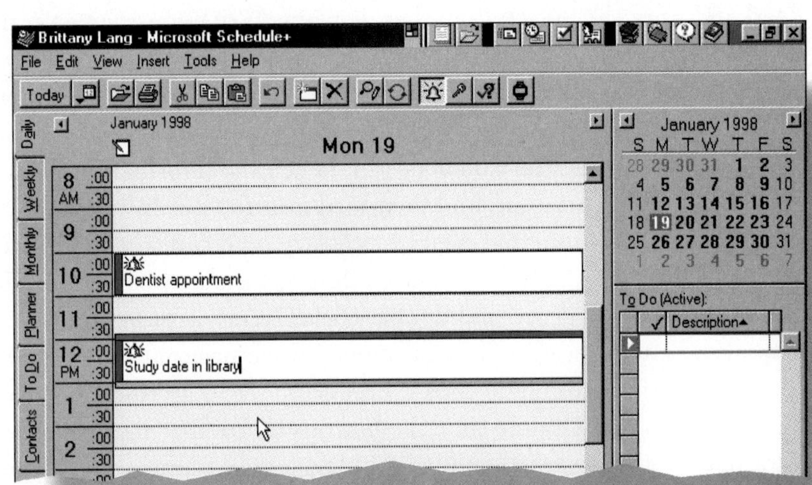

FIGURE 1-52

Use Help

1 Reviewing Project Activities

Instructions: Use Schedule+ Help and a computer to perform the following tasks.

1. Start Schedule+. With any view of the schedule displayed, click Help on the menu bar. Click Microsoft Schedule+ Help Topics. Click the Index tab. Type `events` in the number 1 box. Click the annual, adding topic in the number 2 box, as shown in Figure 1-53. Click the Display button.

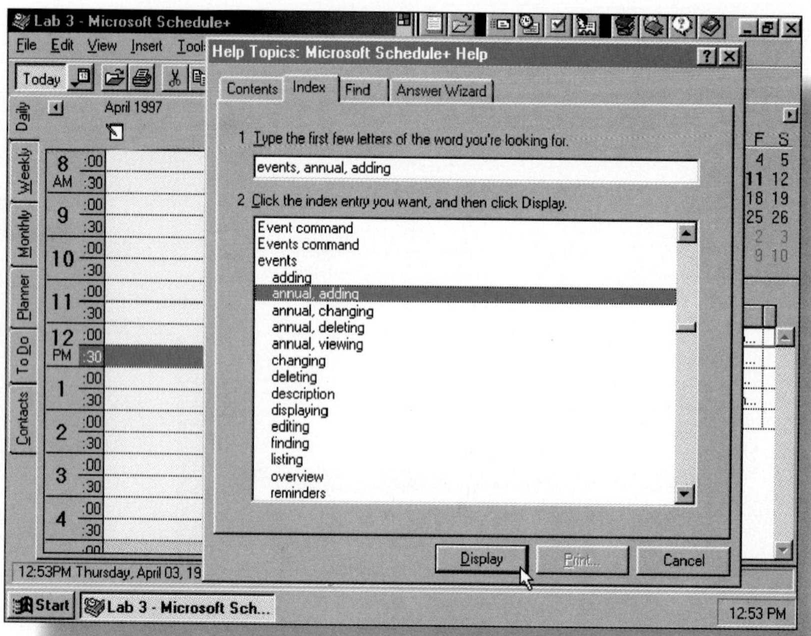

FIGURE 1-53

2. When the Topics Found dialog box displays, double-click the Add Events and Annual Events topic.
3. Read and print the information that displays. Write your name on the printout, and then turn it in to your instructor.
4. Click the Index button, type `contacts` in the number 1 text box, and then double-click the contacts, adding topic in the number 2 box. When the Topics Found dialog box displays, double-click Add a Contact Using the Contacts Tab. When the information displays, read and print it, write your name on the printout, and then turn it in to your instructor.
5. Click the Index button, and then if necessary type `contacts` in the number 1 box. Double-click the overview topic listed under contacts, adding in the number 2 box. When the Topics Found dialog box displays, scroll down and double-click Overview of Schedule+ topic. When the information displays, read and print it, write your name on the printout, and turn it in to your instructor.
6. Click the Index button, and then if necessary, scroll up to display the buttons on toolbar topic in the number 2 box. Double-click the buttons on toolbar topic in the number 2 box. When the information displays, read and print it, write your name on the printout, and turn it in to your instructor.

In the Lab

1 Creating a Schedule

Problem: You are a sophomore student at a university. In addition to carrying a full class load this semester, you are on a committee to organize the spring dance and a member of Student Government. You also hold a part-time job in the campus bookstore. Using Schedule+, you are to create a schedule for your spring semester, which begins January 20, 1997.

Instructions: Perform the following tasks:

1. Create the schedule shown in Figure 1-54 on the next page using the class information in Table 1-4. All classes are recurring.
2. Add Tuesday from 10:30 A.M. – 1:00 P.M. and Friday from 5:00 P.M. – 7:00 P.M. as the hours you work in the bookstore.
3. The Spring Dance Committee meeting is on Wednesday, January 29 from 3:00 P.M. – 5:00 P.M.
4. A Student Government meeting is to be held on Thursday, January 30 from 6:00 P.M. – 7:30 P.M.
5. Your Information Systems class for Thursday, January 30 has been cancelled. Only the single occurrence should be deleted, not all recurring instances.
6. Print the completed Weekly schedule for the week of January 27, 1997 (Figure 1-54).

Table 1-3

CLASS	DAYS	TIME
Information Systems lecture	Tuesday, Thursday	1:30 P.M. – 3:00 P.M.
Information Systems lab	Tuesday	8:00 A.M. – 10:00 A.M.
Calculus	Monday, Wednesday, Friday	9:00 A.M. – 10:00 A.M.
Accounting	Monday, Wednesday, Friday	10:00 A.M. – 11:00 A.M.
Political Issues	Tuesday, Thursday	3:30 P.M. – 5:00 P.M.
Marketing	Monday, Wednesday, Friday	1:00 P.M. – 2:00 P.M.

2 Creating a Contacts List

Problem: You have been elected the new chairperson of the Neighborhood Watch Committee. Your predecessor lived in the neighborhood for many years and knew most of the neighbors personally. Having recently moved to the neighborhood, you are not nearly as familiar with the people around you. You would like to have the block captains' names, addresses, and telephone numbers readily available in the event of an emergency.

Instructions: Create a Contacts List for the people listed in Table 1-5. Print the Contacts List. It should look like Figure 1-55 on page S 1.46.

Table 1-5

NAME	ADDRESS	TELEPHONE
Sherman Green	1823 Sandy Lane	(812) 555-0085
Diana Kolbert	8743 Dune Drive	(812) 555-1012
Chris Ihman	8765 Driftwood Court	(812) 555-1219
Dan Davis	9021 Sunset Blvd.	(812) 555-0227
Marshall Farmer	2308 Hilltop Drive	Unlisted
Marion Jackson	1901 Gull Lane	(812) 555-7445
Ron Nicholas	1775 Winding Trail	(812) 555-8861

Lab 1

Monday, January 27, 1997

	Monday	Tuesday	Wednesday	Thursday	Friday
8:00		Information Systems lab			
:30					
9:00	Calculus		Calculus		Calculus
:30					
10:00	Accounting		Accounting		Accounting
:30		Work in Bookstore			
11:00					
:30					
12:00					
:30					
1:00	Marketing		Marketing		Marketing
:30		Information Systems lecture			
2:00					
:30					
3:00			Spring Dance Committee meeting		
:30		Political Issues		Political Issues	
4:00					
:30					
Other:				6:00PM-7:30PM Student...	5:00PM-7:00PM Work in Bookstore

Printed on Wednesday, January 22, 1997 at 11:30PM

Page 1

FIGURE 1-54

3 Creating a Schedule and a To Do List

Problem: You are the owner of a landscaping company. Your company has experienced rapid growth the last several months, and with spring approaching, appointments are being heavily scheduled. Because you perform much of the physical work yourself, you must have access to the day's appointments in order to know what type of job is scheduled next. Because you are the owner, you have administrative duties to perform as well, such as meetings, interviews, and business telephone calls. You need to create a schedule of appointments as well as a list to keep track of your various tasks and responsi-bilities each day.

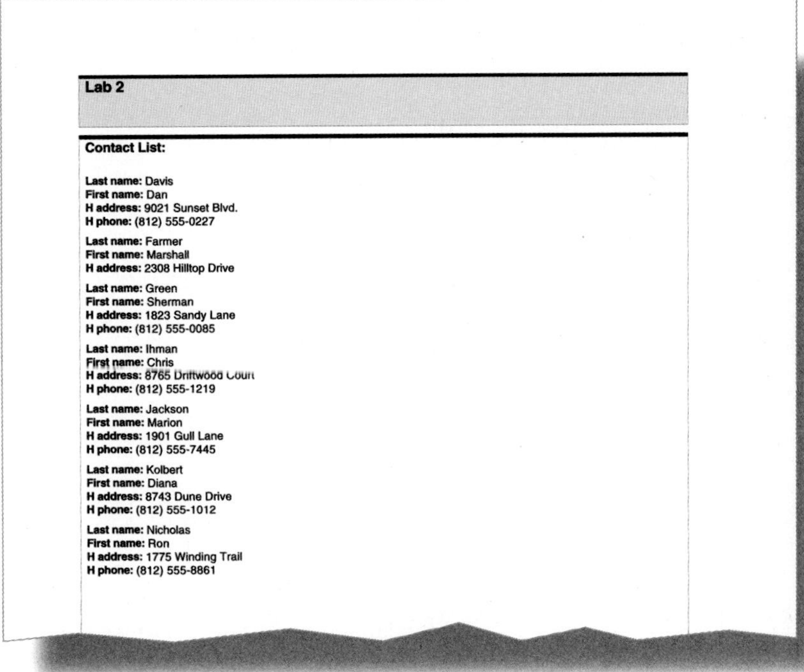

Lab 2

Contact List:

Last name: Davis
First name: Dan
H address: 9021 Sunset Blvd.
H phone: (812) 555-0227

Last name: Farmer
First name: Marshall
H address: 2308 Hilltop Drive

Last name: Green
First name: Sherman
H address: 1823 Sandy Lane
H phone: (812) 555-0085

Last name: Ihman
First name: Chris
H address: 8765 Driftwood Court
H phone: (812) 555-1219

Last name: Jackson
First name: Marion
H address: 1901 Gull Lane
H phone: (812) 555-7445

Last name: Kolbert
First name: Diana
H address: 8743 Dune Drive
H phone: (812) 555-1012

Last name: Nicholas
First name: Ron
H address: 1775 Winding Trail
H phone: (812) 555-8861

FIGURE 1-55

Instructions: Perform the following tasks:

1. Create a schedule complete with a To Do List as shown in Figure 1-56 (a) on the next page.
2. Enter the information for the dates and times shown in Table 1-6 into the Appointment Book.
3. Create a To Do List to contain the following tasks:
   - Call Davis to reschedule bark delivery
   - Bring plans for Spohn
   - Call nursery re: sod availability
   - Pick up edging for Stevens
4. Print the Weekly schedule and the To Do List for the week of April 7, 1997. They should appear as shown in Figure 1-56 (b).

Table 1-6

DESCRIPTION	DATE	TIME
Spohn's, plant three large and two small trees	April 7	7:00 A.M. – 11:30 A.M.
Mendelson's, repair utility easement damage	April 8	8:00 A.M. – 11:00 A.M.
Stevens', edging on sidewalks, trees, driveway	April 9	8:00 A.M. – 1:00 P.M.
Patrick's, deliver dirt, half truck	April 8	1:00 P.M. – 2:00 P.M.
Tudor's, deliver bark, full truck	April 7	2:00 P.M. – 3:00 P.M.
Canteras', river rock around trees	April 9	3:00 P.M. – 4:00 P.M.
Anger's, new bark around house perimeter	April 10	8:00 A.M. – 2:00 P.M.
Chin's, lay sod, 15K square feet	April 11	8:00 A.M. – 3:00 P.M.

Lab 3

Monday, April 07, 1997

	Monday	Tuesday	Wednesday	Thursday	Friday
8:00	7:00AM - 11:30AM Spohn's, plant three large and two small trees	Mendelson's, repair utility easement damage	Stevens', edging on sidewalks, trees, driveway	Anger's, new bark around house perimeter	Chin's, lay sod, 15K square feet
:30					
9:00					
:30					
10:00					
:30					
11:00					
:30					
12:00					
:30					
1:00		Patrick's, deliver dirt, half truck			
:30					
2:00	Tudor's, deliver bark, full truck				
:30					
3:00			Canteras', river rock around trees		
:30					
4:00					
:30					
Other:	7:00AM-11:30AM Spohn's, plant...				

Printed on Thursday, April 03, 1997 at 10:58PM Page 1

FIGURE 1-56(a)

Lab 3

Tuesday, April 08, 1997

S	M	T	W	T	F	S
		1	2	3	4	5
6	7	8	9	10	11	12
13	14	15	16	17	18	19
20	21	22	23	24	25	26
27	28	29	30			

To Do List (Active):

Description: Bring plans for Spohn's
Description: Call Davis' to reschedule bark delivery
Description: Call nursery re: sod availability
Description: Pick up edging for Stevens'

FIGURE 1-56(b)

200 MHz

Cases and Places

The difficulty of these case studies varies:

◗ Case studies preceded by a single half moon are the least difficult. You are asked to create the required worksheet based on information that has already been placed in an organized form.

◗◗ Case studies preceded by two half moons are more difficult. You must organize the information presented before using it to create the desired worksheet.

◗◗◗ Case studies preceded by three half moons are the most difficult. You must choose a specific topic, and then obtain and organize the necessary information before using it to create the required worksheet.

1 ◗ You are the secretary for a university academic office. Part of your job is to let students know when advising hours are during registration periods. You are responsible for posting advising hours for the five professors in your department. Professor Abrams keeps hours on Monday, Wednesday, and Friday from 12:00 P.M. – 3:30 P.M.. Professor Brent is in from 8:00 A.M. – 10:00 A.M. on Monday, Tuesday, and Wednesday. Professor Collier is in on Tuesday and Thursday from 12:00 P.M. – 4:00 P.M. Professor Diaz is in on Tuesday and Thursday from 8:00 A.M. – 11:30 A.M. Professor Ezral is available every Monday and Tuesday from 5:00 P.M. – 8:00 P.M. Registration starts in two weeks, and students have begun requesting advising hours for the professors. Create a schedule showing when each professor has advising hours.

2 ◗ You have secured a part-time position in the Tutoring Center. As part of your duties, you are in charge of scheduling hours for open tutoring. Three tutors are available for four hours each day, and two other tutors are available for three hours twice each week. Create a schedule showing the hours available for open tutoring.

3 ◗◗ Create your own schedule for this semester. Include a To Do List. If you are a part-time student, or not a student at all, create a schedule showing your social or business obligations for the next four months.

4 ◗◗ You are the manager of Java Joe's, a small coffee shop. As manager, you are responsible for scheduling the employees' work hours. The coffee shop is open from 6:00 A.M. – 6:00 P.M. on Monday through Saturday, and from 7:00 A.M. – 4:00 P.M. on Sundays. In addition to yourself and two full-time workers, you have seven part-time employees. Each employee has been guaranteed at least twelve, but not more than twenty, hours of work each week. Choose fictional names and create a schedule showing the hours for each employee. Use a seven-day week.

200 MHz

Cases and Places

5 ▸▸ Create a Contacts List containing your own friends, family, classmates, co-workers, or business contacts. Be certain you include at the very least, the name, home address and telephone number. If you use business contacts, you also should include a business address and telephone number. For friends, use the Personal tab to list their birthdates and spouses' names, if any.

6 ▸▸ You are a volunteer at the county library. Part of your job includes keeping a posted schedule of the large Community Conference Room, which is used by various local groups. Three groups meet before 12:00 P.M.: the Preschoolers' Craft Fair, Toddler Hour, and Children's Story Time. From 3:30 P.M. – 5:00 P.M. each weekday, the After School Club meets. In the evening, from 7:00 P.M. – 9:00 P.M., the Neighborhood Watch Committee meets twice each week, and the Good Reads book discussion group and the Friends of the Library meet once each week. Based on this information, create a schedule showing the reservations for the conference room.

7 ▸▸▸ You have secured a job with the county. The fair is coming to town for three days, Friday, Saturday, and Sunday. Your responsibilities concerning the fair are to schedule events for the arena, one during the morning hours and one during the evening hours on each day of the fair. Create a schedule for the arena, based on the following information: The Monster Mash truck show must occur during the daytime before the Demolition Derby; the Demolition Derby must be at night before the Livestock Competition; the Livestock Competition must be the last event held the last night of the fair; the Agriculture Booths must be displayed during the day before the Livestock Competition; the Craft show must be during the day before the Livestock Competition; and the Clown Rodeo must be at night before the Livestock Competition.

▶ PROJECT ONE

Introduction to Integrating Office 95 Applications

Objectives:

You will have mastered the material in this project when you can:

- Create and edit an embedded chart in an Excel workbook
- Insert clip art and use WordArt to create a letterhead
- Link Excel worksheet and chart data to a Word document
- Query an Access table
- Insert merge fields in a Word document to create a Mail Merge main document
- Merge a Word main document with an Access query data source to create form letters and labels
- Create and print a report based on an Access query
- Create a Word template
- Create and insert AutoText
- Create and update a Schedule+ Contacts List
- Merge name and address data from a Schedule+ Contacts List with a Word document to create letters and envelopes
- Add events to a Schedule+ calendar
- Print a monthly Schedule+ calendar
- Copy a Word document to a PowerPoint slide
- Link Excel worksheet and chart data to a PowerPoint slide
- Apply a presentation Design Template to a PowerPoint slide presentation
- Add graphics to the Title and Slide Masters for a PowerPoint presentation
- Add text build and slide transition effects in a PowerPoint presentation
- Print slides
- Create a Binder

Adding a Personal Touch to Your BU$INE$$ Dealings

Integrating the Microsoft Office Applications

Shopping for car and homeowners insurance often amounts to a frustrating attempt to compare quotes scribbled on scraps of paper from various companies. Insurance agents can simplify this process by writing a personalized letter describing the vehicle or property and including a table with figures showing exact coverage, deductibles, and premiums. Producing this letter and many others can be simple activities if the agent uses software combining a word processor, database, and spreadsheet.

Several of these integrated programs are available in the insurance industry, including The Agency Manager® (TAM) developed by Applied Systems. Utilizing the latest version of TAM, the agent starts the development of a quote using a Workflow Wizard.

If the client already has a policy with the agent or has made a previous inquiry, the agent can retrieve this information from the database.

If the client is a first-time caller, the agent creates a new record in the database. TAM then switches to Microsoft Word and generates a survey to guide the agent in gathering required data, such as children's names and ages and whether a burglar alarm is installed on the vehicle or property. This data is stored in the client's database record.

Using a digital camera, the agent photographs the property and stores the image. The camera also has the capability to scan a client's correspondence so the agent can attempt to eliminate paper files in the office. In addition, by switching to Microsoft Excel, the agent is able to prepare charts and worksheets to integrate into the quote.

Finally, Word extracts the client's data from the database and from the Excel worksheet, inserts these components into the document, and prints the completed personalized proposal.

Five major versions of TAM have been developed since the company's inception in 1980. The first was created by Applied Systems' chairman, Robert Eustance, who at the time owned an insurance agency and had an idea for automating his office. The latest version integrates Windows 95 software and other packages, including e-mail, personnel, and accounting.

More than 9,000 independent insurance agents are using TAM in the United States, Canada, England, Hong Kong, Jamaica, and the Virgin Islands in offices with as many as 300 computers. These agents use the integrated software for a variety of purposes, such as preparing standard insurance forms, cancellation letters, checks, insurance identification cards, and billing. For example, two months before the customer's policy expires, the database interfaces with Microsoft Word to generate an invoice.

Personnel at Applied Systems also use TAM's integrated features to track sales prospects, generate invoices, and market upgrades to current users. Technical support personnel use the software's interface with an automated call director to help route service calls to the proper technician. The company promotes TAM as "designed by its users, delivered by Applied Systems."

By using this customized, integrated software combining the database manager with a word processor and worksheet, insurance agents make their contacts with clients more personalized and friendly.

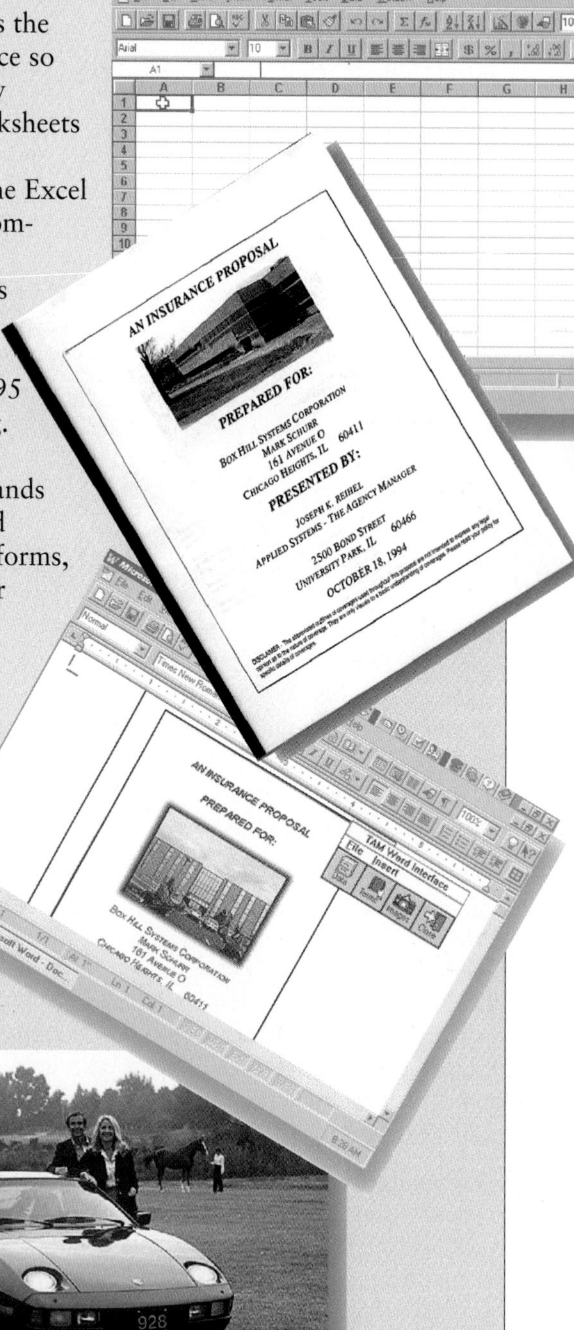

Office 95
Integration

Introduction to Integrating Office 95 Applications

Case Perspective

Community Youth Programs is a nonprofit organization that provides athletic and educational programs for children and teenagers in the community. Operating funds for Community Youth Programs are generated from contributions made by families with children who participate in the programs, business contributors, and other interested community sponsors.

Director Robert Younger needs to send letters soliciting contributions from selected family participants. He also wants to send letters of invitation for the Annual Fund-Raising Gala to selected corporate and community sponsors. These solicitation and invitation letters must contain both data and a chart highlighting the next year's operating budget.

Mr. Younger has requested that you prepare a report listing the name, title, organization, work telephone number, and pledge data for all business contributors. This report will be used for telephone solicitations. A monthly calendar of activities for Community Youth Programs must be printed. Finally, as part of the Annual Fund-Raising Gala program, Mr. Younger is to present a slide show outlining next year's budget.

Introduction

In previous projects, you used Word to create and print documents, Excel to analyze numbers, Access to manage and report data, and PowerPoint to create slide show presentations. You often can increase your productivity by using these software programs together to produce letters, reports, and presentations. In this project, you will integrate Excel and Word by linking Excel worksheet data and a chart to a Word form letter document. You will then merge data from an Access database with the Word form letter document to create multiple letters.

You will maintain names and addresses in the Schedule+ Contacts List and then merge them into a custom form letter template created in Word. Next, you will create a monthly calendar of events and maintain it in Schedule+. Integrating Word, Excel, and PowerPoint is demonstrated by copying a Word document into a PowerPoint slide and then linking Excel worksheet data and a chart to slides in a PowerPoint presentation.

Integration Project – Community Youth Programs Fund-Raising System

From your meeting with Mr. Younger, you have determined the following sources of data, the graph requirements, and the output to be produced for the fund-raising system.

Source of Data: Mr. Younger has a relatively new personal computer and is running Microsoft Windows 95 and Microsoft Office 95. The data required for this fund-raising system is on Mr. Younger's personal computer and is described below:

1. The budget information is maintained in the Excel Budget workbook (Figure 1-1a on the next page).
2. The contributors' names and addresses are in an Access database (Figure 1-1b on the next page).
3. The solicitation letter to family contributors (Figure 1-1c on the next page) and the invitation letter (Figure 1-2b on page I 1.8 and Figure 1-2c on page I 1.9) are Word documents.
4. The Contacts List is a Schedule+ file (Figure 1-2a on page I 1.8).

Graph Requirements: An embedded 3-D Pie chart must be created in the Excel Budget workbook using selected data in the workbook so it appears as shown in Figure 1-1a.

Output: The fund-raising system must produce the following:

1. An Access report that shows the names of business contributors, their company, their telephone number, the amount pledged, and the date the pledge was paid (Figure 1-1d on the next page).
2. Solicitation letters (Figure 1-1e on page I 1.7) that are automatically addressed to the family contributors in the Access database table of contributors. Mail labels are required for the envelopes.
3. Invitation letters (Figure 1-2c) that are automatically addressed to those in the Schedule+ Contacts List (Figure 1-2a).
4. A PowerPoint presentation (Figure 1-3 on page I 1.8) with links to the Excel worksheet and embedded 3-D Pie chart (Figure 1-1a).
5. A monthly calendar (Figure 1-4 on page I 1.9) of the events related to the Community Youth Programs fund-raiser.

Creating an Embedded Excel Chart

This project integrates Word, Excel, Access, PowerPoint, and Schedule+ documents. The first document you will work with is an Excel worksheet, into which you will embed an Excel chart. The next section on page I 1.10 provides an overview of the steps necessary to embed an Excel chart into an Excel worksheet.

EXCEL WORKBOOK – BUDGET

Community Youth Programs
1998-1999 Operating Budget

	Qtr1	Qtr2	Qtr3	Qtr4	Total
Operating Funds					
Family Contributions	$26,200	$ 31,500	$ 32,000	$ 29,500	$119,200
Business & Organization Contributions	22,000	30,000	40,000	35,000	127,000
Talent Shows	1,500	750	1,000	1,200	4,450
Garage Sales	8,000	7,500	9,500	10,000	35,000
Team Sponsorships	30,000	25,000	32,000	19,000	106,000
Celebrity Golf Tournaments	10,000	12,000	15,000	8,000	45,000
Total Operating Funds	$97,700	$106,750	$129,500	$102,700	$436,650
Operating Expenses					
Programs	$77,000	$ 87,000	$110,000	$ 82,000	$356,000
Administrative	20,000	20,000	20,000	20,000	80,000
Total Operating Expenses	$97,000	$107,000	$130,000	$102,000	$436,000
Surplus (Deficit)	$ 700	$ (250)	$ (500)	$ 700	$ 650

LINK

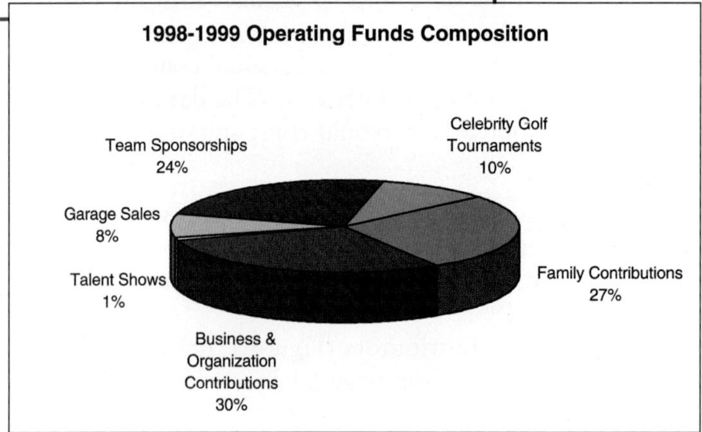

LINK

FIGURE 1-1a

ACCESS DATABASE TABLE – CONTRIBUTORS

Prefix	First Name	Initial	Last Name	Title	Company	Address	City	State	Zip	W Phone	Status	Pledge	Pledge Date	Paid Date
Mr.	John	J.	Deidrick			3807 Brier Gardens	Houston	TX	77056	(713) 555-5525	Family	$300.00	7/1/97	7/15/97
Mr.	James	R.	Gaby	President	Gaby Engineering	6110 N. Trafalger Ct.	Houston	TX	77023	(713) 555-5754	Business	$1,000.00	5/15/97	5/25/97
Ms.	Janet	L.	Horstmann			14063 Homestead Park	Houston	TX	77095	(713) 555-9186	Family	$250.00	1/30/97	2/11/97
Ms.	Ruby	J.	Towns	President	Towns Services	3723 Westhamton Square	Houston	TX	77035	(713) 555-0820	Business	$1,000.00	5/1/97	5/5/97
Mr.	Javier	G.	Gomez			1514 Bunkerhill	Houston	TX	77024	(713) 555-0023	Family	$500.00	11/15/96	12/1/96
Ms.	Nancy	V.	Wong			7326 Eagle Drive	Houston	TX	77019	(713) 555-6061	Family	$250.00	3/1/97	3/25/97
Mr.	Nash	A.	Jackson	Sr. Vice President	IDX Communications, Inc.	13210 Richmond	Houston	TX	77057	(713) 555-1675	Business	$1,500.00	4/1/97	5/15/97
Ms.	Helen	B.	Stapleton	Director	WGI Resources	7327 Woodoak	Houston	TX	77047	(713) 555-7578	Business	$2,000.00	1/20/97	1/30/97
Ms.	Laura	L.	Cox			12410 Kitty	Houston	TX	77096	(713) 555-9222	Family	$250.00	2/10/97	3/1/97
Mr.	Troy	E.	Thomas			5822 Pershing	Houston	TX	77042	(713) 555-1407	Family	$150.00	1/25/97	3/10/97

FIGURE 1-1b

completed business contributors' phone list report

ACCESS REPORT – BUSINESS CONTRIBUTORS

QUERY

Business Contributors' Phone List

Last Name	First Name	Title	Company	W Phone	Pledge	Paid Date
Gaby	James	President	Gaby Engineering	(713) 555-5754	$1,000.00	5/25/97
Jackson	Nash	Sr. Vice President	IDX Communications, Inc.	(713) 555-1675	$1,500.00	5/15/97
Stapleton	Helen	Director	WGI Resources	(713) 555-7578	$2,000.00	1/30/97
Towns	Ruby	President	Towns Services	(713) 555-0820	$1,000.00	5/5/97

FIGURE 1-1d

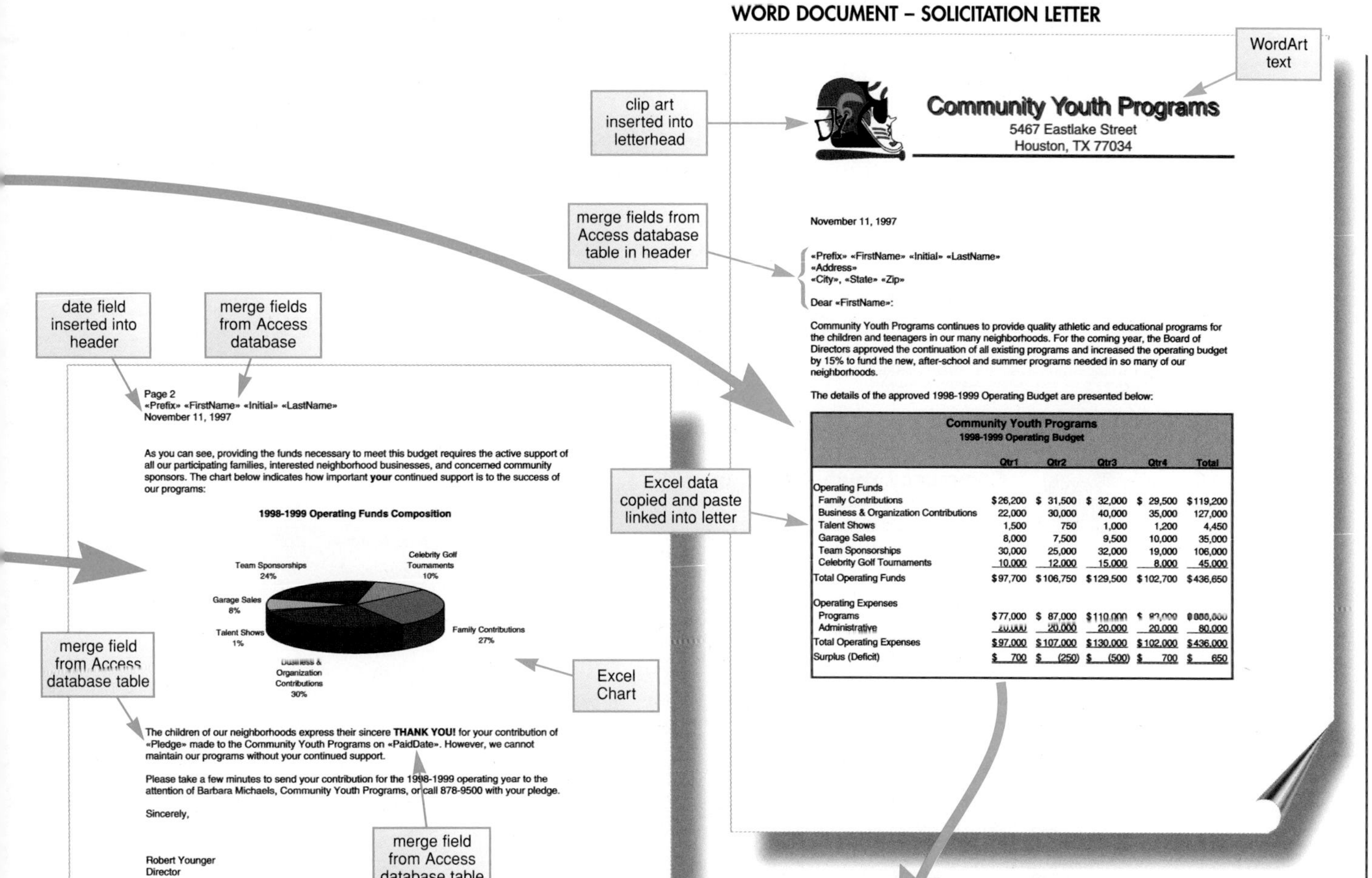

WORD DOCUMENT – SOLICITATION LETTER

Community Youth Programs
5467 Eastlake Street
Houston, TX 77034

November 11, 1997

«Prefix» «FirstName» «Initial» «LastName»
«Address»
«City», «State» «Zip»

Dear «FirstName»:

Community Youth Programs continues to provide quality athletic and educational programs for the children and teenagers in our many neighborhoods. For the coming year, the Board of Directors approved the continuation of all existing programs and increased the operating budget by 15% to fund the new, after-school and summer programs needed in so many of our neighborhoods.

The details of the approved 1998-1999 Operating Budget are presented below:

Community Youth Programs 1998-1999 Operating Budget	Qtr1	Qtr2	Qtr3	Qtr4	Total
Operating Funds					
Family Contributions	$26,200	$ 31,500	$ 32,000	$ 29,500	$119,200
Business & Organization Contributions	22,000	30,000	40,000	35,000	127,000
Talent Shows	1,500	750	1,000	1,200	4,450
Garage Sales	8,000	7,500	9,500	10,000	35,000
Team Sponsorships	30,000	25,000	32,000	19,000	106,000
Celebrity Golf Tournaments	10,000	12,000	15,000	8,000	45,000
Total Operating Funds	$97,700	$106,750	$129,500	$102,700	$436,650
Operating Expenses					
Programs	$77,000	$ 87,000	$110,000	[illegible]	[illegible]
Administrative	20,000	20,000	20,000	20,000	80,000
Total Operating Expenses	$97,000	$107,000	$130,000	$102,000	$436,000
Surplus (Deficit)	$ 700	$ (250)	$ (500)	$ 700	$ 650

Page 2
«Prefix» «FirstName» «Initial» «LastName»
November 11, 1997

As you can see, providing the funds necessary to meet this budget requires the active support of all our participating families, interested neighborhood businesses, and concerned community sponsors. The chart below indicates how important **your** continued support is to the success of our programs:

1998-1999 Operating Funds Composition

The children of our neighborhoods express their sincere **THANK YOU!** for your contribution of «Pledge» made to the Community Youth Programs on «PaidDate». However, we cannot maintain our programs without your continued support.

Please take a few minutes to send your contribution for the 1998-1999 operating year to the attention of Barbara Michaels, Community Youth Programs, or call 878-9500 with your pledge.

Sincerely,

Robert Younger
Director

FIGURE 1-1c

MAIL MERGE

SOLICITATION LETTER

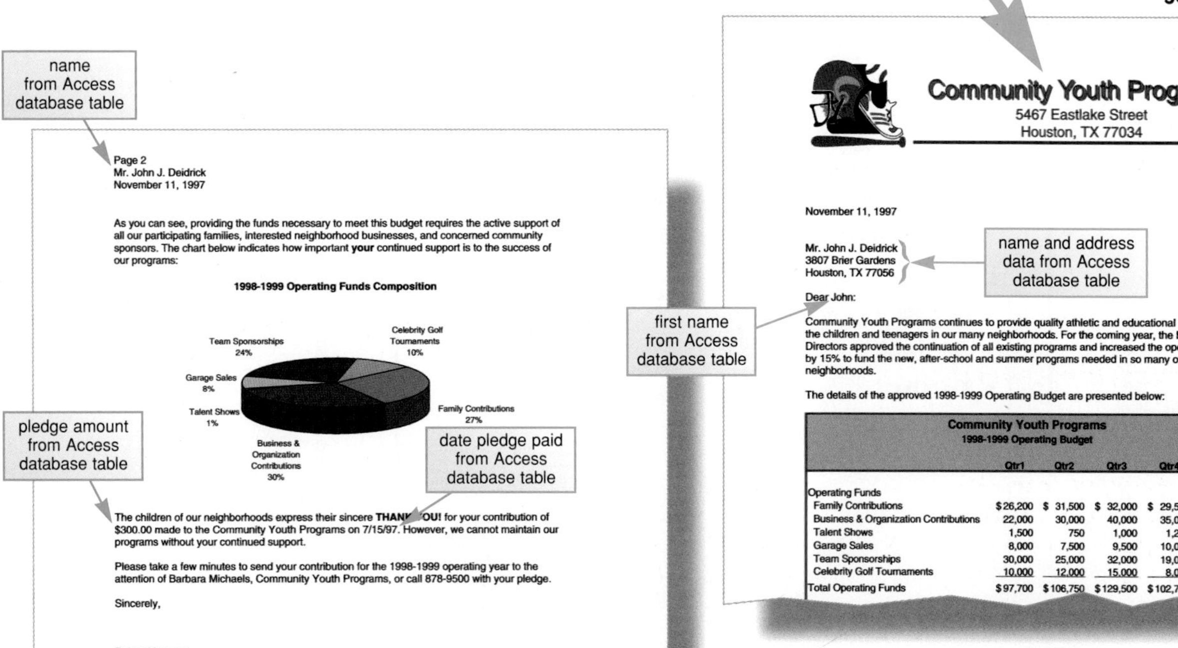

Community Youth Programs
5467 Eastlake Street
Houston, TX 77034

November 11, 1997

Mr. John J. Deidrick
3807 Brier Gardens
Houston, TX 77056

Dear John:

Community Youth Programs continues to provide quality athletic and educational programs for the children and teenagers in our many neighborhoods. For the coming year, the Board of Directors approved the continuation of all existing programs and increased the operating budget by 15% to fund the new, after-school and summer programs needed in so many of our neighborhoods.

The details of the approved 1998-1999 Operating Budget are presented below:

Community Youth Programs 1998-1999 Operating Budget	Qtr1	Qtr2	Qtr3	Qtr4	Total
Operating Funds					
Family Contributions	$26,200	$ 31,500	$ 32,000	$ 29,500	$119,200
Business & Organization Contributions	22,000	30,000	40,000	35,000	127,000
Talent Shows	1,500	750	1,000	1,200	4,450
Garage Sales	8,000	7,500	9,500	10,000	35,000
Team Sponsorships	30,000	25,000	32,000	19,000	106,000
Celebrity Golf Tournaments	10,000	12,000	15,000	8,000	45,000
Total Operating Funds	$97,700	$106,750	$129,500	$102,700	$436,650

Page 2
Mr. John J. Deidrick
November 11, 1997

As you can see, providing the funds necessary to meet this budget requires the active support of all our participating families, interested neighborhood businesses, and concerned community sponsors. The chart below indicates how important **your** continued support is to the success of our programs:

1998-1999 Operating Funds Composition

The children of our neighborhoods express their sincere **THANK YOU!** for your contribution of $300.00 made to the Community Youth Programs on 7/15/97. However, we cannot maintain our programs without your continued support.

Please take a few minutes to send your contribution for the 1998-1999 operating year to the attention of Barbara Michaels, Community Youth Programs, or call 878-9500 with your pledge.

Sincerely,

Robert Younger
Director

FIGURE 1-1e

SCHEDULE+ CONTACTS LIST

Student Schedule - Microsoft Schedule+

File Edit View Insert Tools Help

Today

Daily Weekly Monthly Planner To Do Contacts

Go to: in Last name

Contacts:

Last name	First na...	B...
Dozier	Ralph	(7...
Kirklin	Lucy	(7...
McIntyre	Robert	(7...

Name
First: Robert
Last: McIntyre

Business Phone

Title: President

Company: Hightower Engine

Department:

Office:

Assistant:

Business

(713) 555-9976

1:14PM Tuesday, November 11, 1997

Start | Microsoft Word | Student Schedu

Contacts List

FIGURE 1-2a

WORD DOCUMENT – INVITATION LETTER

Page 2
November 11, 1997

As you can see, providing the funds necessary to meet this budget requires the active support of all our participating families, interested neighborhood businesses, and concerned community sponsors. The chart below indicates how important **your** continued support is to the success of our programs:

The children of our … the outstanding pro… maintain our progra…

We cordially invite … entertainment at ou… Everton Hotel. The…

Call Barbara Micha…

Sincerely,

Robert Younger
Director

Community Youth Programs
5467 Eastlake Street
Houston, TX 77034

November 11, 1997 ← date field

«Prefix» «FirstName» «Initial» «LastName»
«Address»
«City», «State» «Zip»

Dear «FirstName»:

Community Youth Programs continues to provide quality athletic and educational programs for the children and teenagers in our many neighborhoods. For the coming year, the Board of Directors approved the continuation of all existing programs and increased the operating budget by 15% to fund the new, after-school and summer programs needed in so many of our neighborhoods.

The details of the approved 1998-1999 Operating Budget are presented below:

Community Youth Programs
1998-1999 Operating Budget

	Qtr1	Qtr2	Qtr3	Qtr4	Total
Operating Funds					
Family Contributions	$26,200	$ 31,500	$ 32,000	$ 29,500	$119,200
Business & Organization Contributions	22,000	30,000	40,000	35,000	127,000
Talent Shows	1,500	750	1,000	1,200	4,450
Garage Sales	8,000	7,500	9,500	10,000	35,000
Team Sponsorships	30,000	25,000	32,000	19,000	106,000
Celebrity Golf Tournaments	10,000	12,000	15,000	8,000	45,000
Total Operating Funds	$97,700	$106,750	$129,500	$102,700	$436,650

FIGURE 1-2b

MAIL MERGE

POWERPOINT PRESENTATION – BULLETED LIST SLIDE

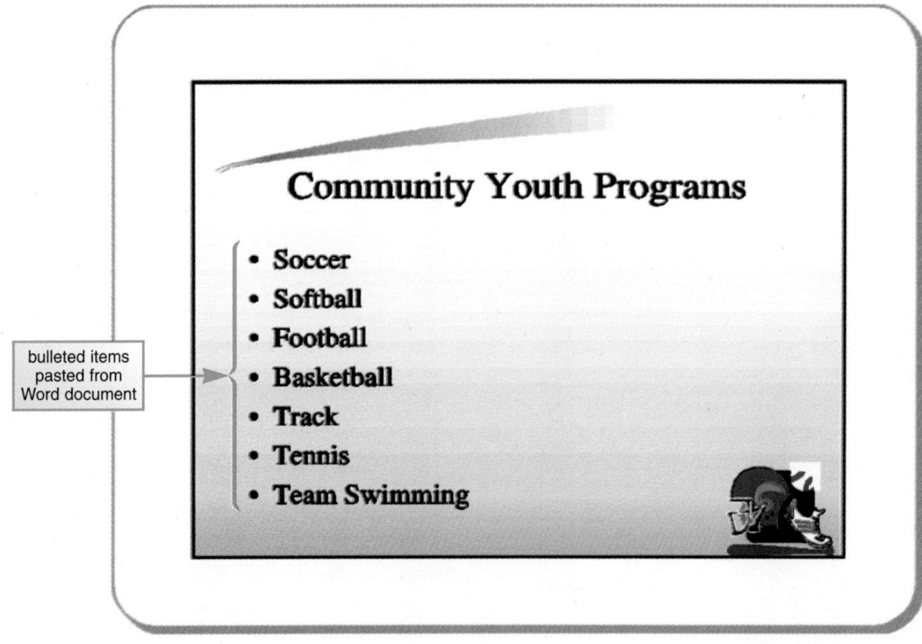

FIGURE 1-3

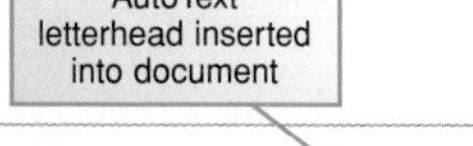

INVITATION LETTER

Community Youth Programs
5467 Eastlake Street
Houston, TX 77034

name and address data merged from Schedule+ Contacts List

November 11, 1997

Ralph Dozier
President
Landsdowne Company
2250 Bering Drive
Houston, TX 77057

Dear Ralph:

Community Youth Programs continues to provide quality athletic and educational programs for the children and teenagers in our many neighborhoods. For the coming year, the Board of Directors approved the continuation of all existing programs and increased the operating budget by 15% to fund the new, after-school and summer programs needed in so many of our neighborhoods.

The details of the approved 1998-1999 Operating Budget are presented below:

Community Youth Programs
1998-1999 Operating Budget

	Qtr1	Qtr2	Qtr3	Qtr4	Total
Operating Funds					
Family Contributions	$26,200	$ 31,500	$ 32,000	$ 29,500	$119,200
Business & Organization Contributions	22,000	30,000	40,000	35,000	127,000
Talent Shows	1,500	750	1,000	1,200	4,450
Garage Sales	8,000	7,500	9,500	10,000	35,000
Team Sponsorships	30,000	25,000	32,000	19,000	106,000
Celebrity Golf Tournaments	10,000	12,000	15,000	8,000	45,000
Total Operating Funds	$97,700	$106,750	$129,500	$102,700	$436,650
Operating Expenses					
Programs	$77,000	$ 87,000	$110,000	$ 82,000	$356,000
Administrative	20,000	20,000	20,000	20,000	80,000
Total Operating Expenses	$97,000	$107,000	$130,000	$102,000	$436,000
Surplus (Deficit)	$ 700	$ (250)	$ (500)	$ 700	$ 650

Page 2
November 11, 1997

As you can see, providing the funds necessary to meet this budget requires the active support of all our participating families, interested neighborhood businesses, and concerned community sponsors. The chart below indicates how important **your** continued support is to the success of our programs:

1998-1999 Operating Funds Composition

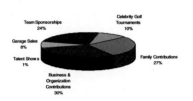

Team Sponsorships 24%
Celebrity Golf Tournaments 10%
Garage Sales 8%
Family Contributions 27%
Talent Shows 1%
Business & Organization Contributions 30%

The children of our neighborhoods express their sincere **THANK YOU!** for your past support of the outstanding programs provided by Community Youth Programs. However, we cannot maintain our programs without your continued support.

We cordially invite you and your guests to attend an exciting evening of dinner, dancing, and entertainment at our Annual Fund-Raising Gala on Saturday, January 27, in the Ballroom at the Everton Hotel. The festivities will begin at 7:30 p.m.

Call Barbara Michaels, Community Youth Services, at 878-9500 to reserve your table now!

Sincerely,

Robert Younger
Director

FIGURE 1-2c

SCHEDULE+ MONTHLY CALENDAR – EVENTS

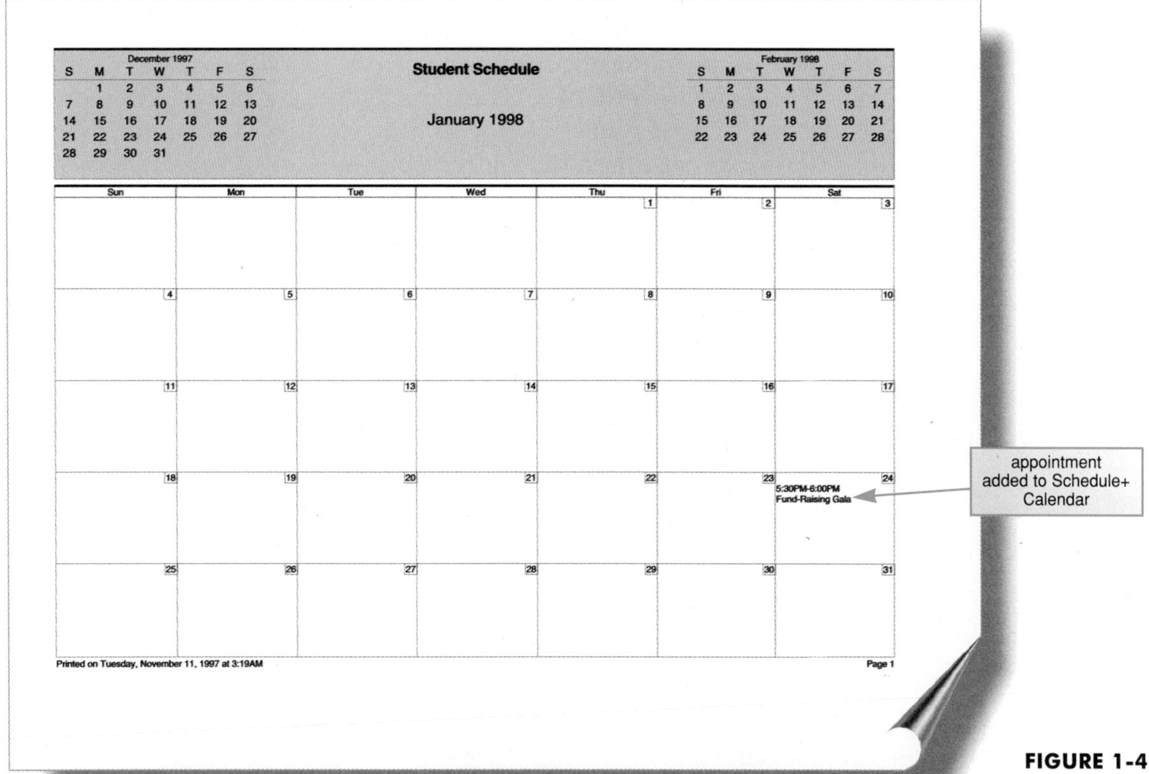

FIGURE 1-4

More About Embedding

Embedding is the process of inserting an object into a document. An object can be a table, graphic, chart, equation, or any other information. The application used to initially create the object is called the source application. The document containing the embedded object is called the container file.

Overview of Steps to Create an Embedded Excel Chart

You can create a three-dimensional embedded Pie chart with data labels to illustrate the relationship of budgeted operating funds for each fund-raising activity to the total budgeted operating funds. This data is in the Excel Budget workbook on the Budget worksheet. You will perform the following tasks in this section of the project.

1. Start Excel.
2. Open the Budget file.
3. Select the data ranges to be charted.
4. Use the ChartWizard to position the chart, specify the Pie chart type, select the chart format that includes data labels, and add the chart title.
5. Size the selected embedded chart.
6. Activate and edit the embedded chart.
7. Deactivate and deselect the embedded chart.
8. Save the workbook.

The following pages contain a detailed explanation of these tasks. It is recommended that you create a copy of the files required for this project on a floppy disk separate from the Student Floppy Disk that accompanies this book so you will have space to store the files you create during this project. To copy the files required for this project, complete the following steps: (1) insert your Student Floppy Disk in drive A; (2) start Explorer from the My Computer icon; (3) click the 3½ Floppy [A:] icon in the All Folders area of the window; (4) right-drag the Integration folder from the Contents window of Explorer to the desktop, and click Copy Here on the context-sensitive menu; (5) insert the floppy disk on which you want to store the files for this project in drive A; (6)right-drag the Integration folder from the desktop to the 3½ Floppy [A:] icon in the All Folders area of Explorer, and click Move Here on the context-sensitive menu.

Starting Excel and Opening a Workbook

First, you must start Excel and then open the Budget workbook file on the floppy disk you made before you can create the embedded chart for this project. The Budget workbook contains the Budget worksheet. The worksheet contains data that is used to create the embedded chart. Perform the following steps to start Excel and open the Budget worksheet.

TO START EXCEL AND OPEN AN EXISTING WORKBOOK

Step 1: Insert your floppy disk into drive A. Click the Start button on the taskbar and then click Open Office Document on the Start menu.
Step 2: Click the Look in box arrow and then click 3½ Floppy [A:].
Step 3: Double-click the Integration folder icon.
Step 4: Click the Budget file icon in the Integration folder window.

Excel starts and then the Budget workbook opens. The Budget worksheet is active (Figure 1-5).

Now that the worksheet is open, you are ready to create the Pie chart shown in Figure 1-1a on page I 1.6. The next section explains how to create the 3-D Pie chart.

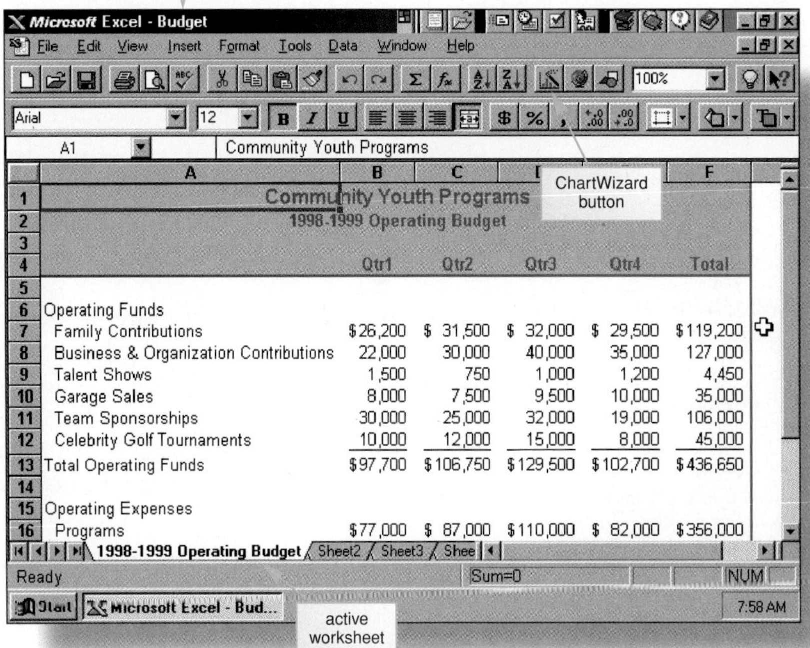

Budget workbook in Excel
Microsoft Excel - Budget
File Edit View Insert Format Tools Data Window Help
Community Youth Programs
ChartWizard button
Community Youth Programs
1998-1999 Operating Budget
Qtr1 Qtr2 Qtr3 Qtr4 Total
Operating Funds
Family Contributions $26,200 $ 31,500 $ 32,000 $ 29,500 $119,200
Business & Organization Contributions 22,000 30,000 40,000 35,000 127,000
Talent Shows 1,500 750 1,000 1,200 4,450
Garage Sales 8,000 7,500 9,500 10,000 35,000
Team Sponsorships 30,000 25,000 32,000 19,000 106,000
Celebrity Golf Tournaments 10,000 12,000 15,000 8,000 45,000
Total Operating Funds $97,700 $106,750 $129,500 $102,700 $436,650
Operating Expenses
Programs $77,000 $ 87,000 $110,000 $ 82,000 $356,000
1998-1999 Operating Budget
Ready
Sum=0
active worksheet

FIGURE 1-5

Using the ChartWizard to Create an Embedded Chart

The ChartWizard in Excel can assist you in creating a chart. Before you create a chart, first you must select the data to include in the chart. Perform the following steps to select cells and then use the ChartWizard to create a 3-D Pie chart.

TO SELECT A DATA RANGE FOR AN EMBEDDED CHART

Step 1: Select the nonadjacent ranges A7:A12 and F7:F12.

Step 2: Click the ChartWizard button on the Standard toolbar and then move the mouse pointer to cell A24.

Step 3: Drag to select the range A24:F35 below the worksheet data to position the embedded chart. Release the left mouse button.

Step 4: When the ChartWizard – Step 1 of 5 dialog box displays, verify that the data ranges selected are $A$7:$A$12,$F$7:$F$12 in the Range text box and then click the Next button. If not, make the appropriate changes.

Step 5: When the ChartWizard – Step 2 of 5 dialog box displays, click 3-D Pie and then click the Next button.

Step 6: When the ChartWizard – Step 3 of 5 dialog box displays, verify Format 7 is selected and then click the Next button. If it is not, click the Format 7 box.

Step 7: When the ChartWizard – Step 4 of 5 dialog box displays, verify that the Data Series is in Columns, that Column 1 identifies the Pie Slice Labels, and that Row 0 identifies the Chart Title. If any of these is not correct, select the proper entries. Click the Next button.

Step 8: When the ChartWizard – Step 5 of 5 dialog box displays, click the Chart Title text box and then type `1998-1999 Operating Funds Composition` in the text box.

Step 9: Click the Finish button to complete the chart.

The 3-D Pie chart displays below the worksheet data (Figure 1-6).

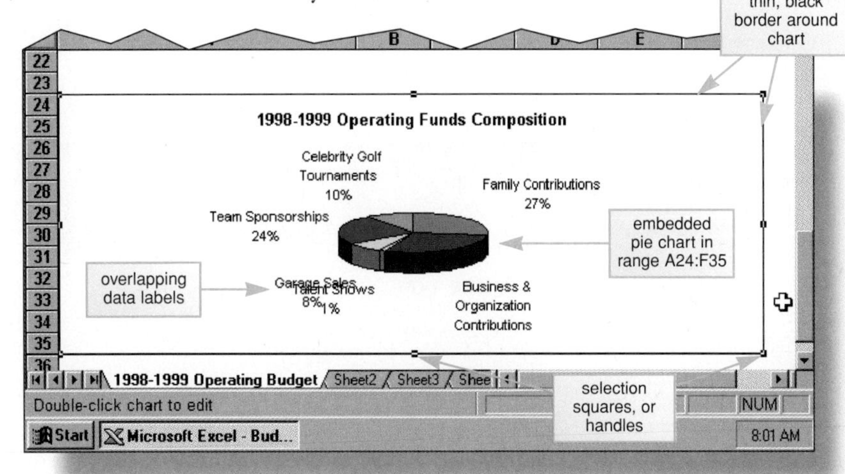

FIGURE 1-6

Notice several items in Figure 1-6 on the previous page. The embedded Pie chart object displays below the worksheet data. The chart is selected. The data labels for the Garage Sales and Talent Shows pie slices overlap slightly because of the default layout of the pie wedges. Also, the percentage value for Business and Organization Contributions does not display.

The next section explains how to improve the appearance of the Pie chart.

Resizing an Embedded Chart and Removing Borders

> **More About Charts**
>
> Each type of chart has a specific function. A pie chart is used to show how 100% of an amount is divided. A column chart is similar to a pie chart; the difference is the chart stacks the percentages vertically in a column. A line chart is used to show changes in data over time. A bar chart shows trends and comparisons.

To make the Pie chart more attractive and easier to read you can enlarge it, rotate the pie slices, and remove the outside border. The mouse pointer becomes a two-headed arrow when placed on a selection handle. You can use the two-headed arrow to drag a selection handle to resize an embedded chart. You also can remove the outside border when the chart is selected. Perform the following steps to resize the Pie chart and remove its border.

TO RESIZE AN EMBEDDED CHART AND REMOVE THE BORDER

Step 1: Point to the bottom center selection handle and then drag downward until the chart range is extended to row 40.
Step 2: Right-click the embedded chart object.
Step 3: Click Format Object on the shortcut menu. Click the Patterns tab, if necessary, when the Format Object dialog box first opens.
Step 4: Click None in the Border group and then click the OK button.

The border no longer displays (Figure 1-7).

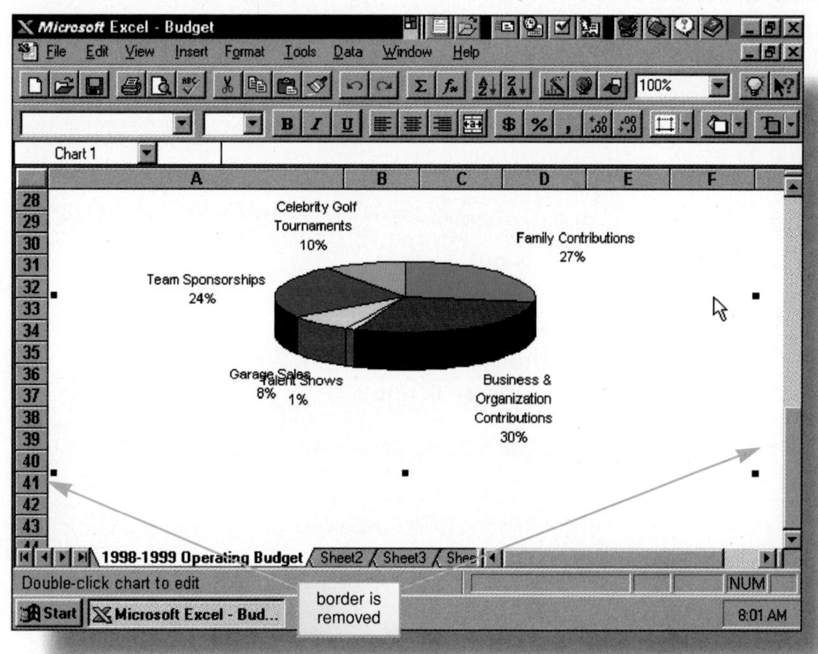

FIGURE 1-7

The selected embedded chart object is enlarged and the border is removed. The next section explains how to change the Pie chart to make it easier to read.

Rotating Pie Slices in an Embedded Chart

Notice in Figure 1-7, the Garage Sales and Talent Shows data labels overlap. You can rotate the pie slices to remove the overlap between the data labels. When you rotate the pie slices 50 degrees, the overlap is corrected. To rotate the pie slices, first you must activate the chart as explained in the following steps.

To Rotate Pie Slices in an Embedded Chart

1 Double-click the embedded chart object.

The embedded chart is activated and placed in an editing window titled [Budget.xls]1998-1999 Operating Budget Chart 1 (Figure 1-8). You can now edit the chart with menu commands.

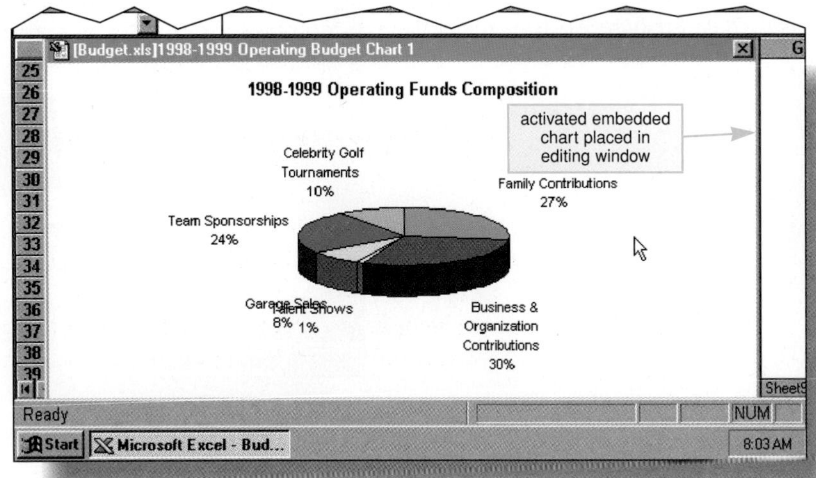

FIGURE 1-8

2 Right-click the activated chart and then click Format 3-D Pie Group on the shortcut menu. Click the Options tab if necessary when the Format 3-D Pie Group dialog box first opens.

The Options sheet in the Format 3-D Pie Group dialog box displays (Figure 1-9). You change the angle of the pie slices in this dialog box.

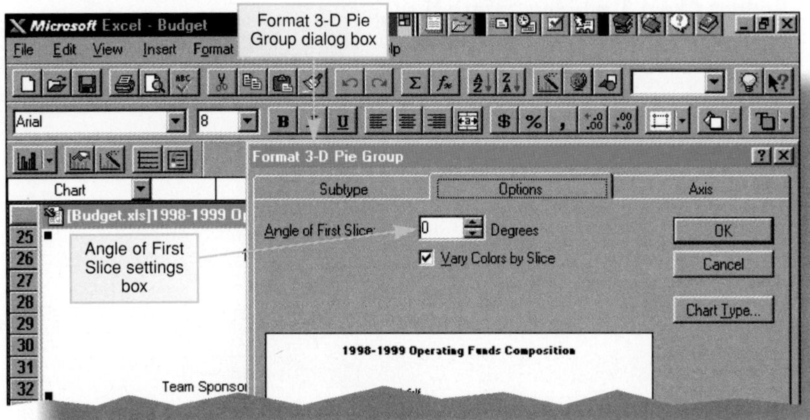

FIGURE 1-9

3 Click the Angle of First Slice settings box up arrow until the first pie slice is rotated 50 degrees.

You can view the change in the angle of the pie slices in the Preview window (Figure 1-10).

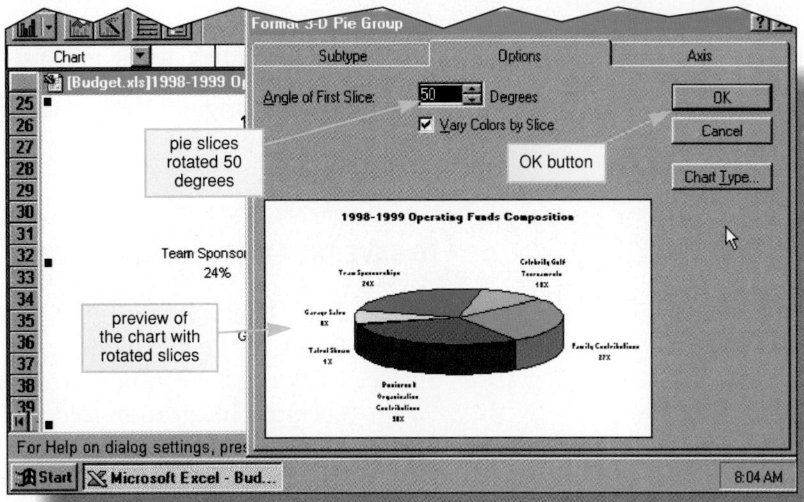

FIGURE 1-10

4 Click the OK button.

The Format 3-D Pie Group dialog box closes and the embedded chart is modified (Figure 1-11).

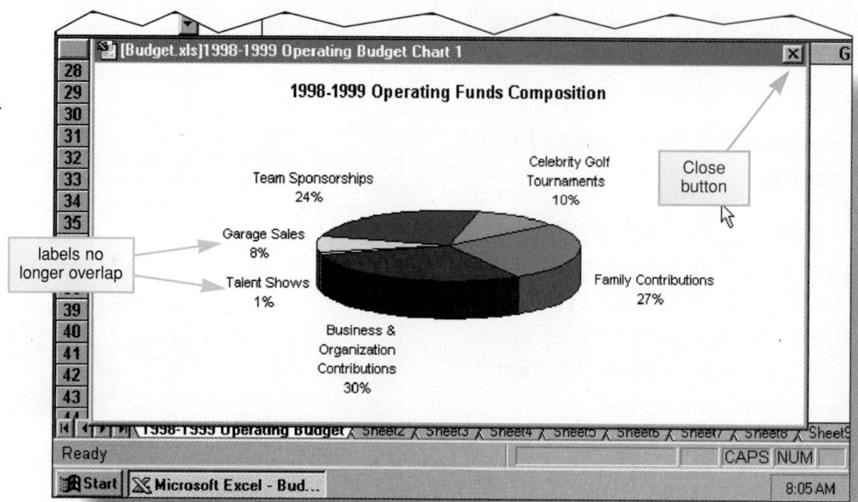

FIGURE 1-11

5 Click the Close button in the [Budget.xls]1998-1999 Operating Budget Chart 1 window, press the ESC key, and then scroll to view the embedded chart.

The embedded chart is deactivated and deselected (Figure 1-12).

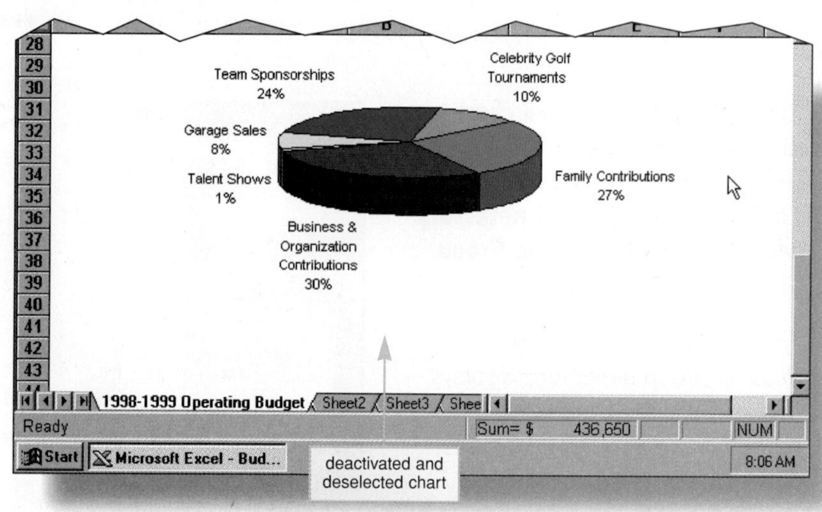

FIGURE 1-12

Other Ways

1. Click Format on menu bar, click 3-D Pie Group
2. Press ALT+O keys, press 1

Saving the Workbook with a New Name and Closing Excel

To preserve the original Budget workbook, you should save the workbook with the embedded chart using a new name and then close Excel as explained in the following steps.

TO SAVE THE EXCEL WORKBOOK WITH A NEW NAME AND CLOSE EXCEL

Step 1: Click File on the menu bar and then click Save As. Type `Budget With Chart` in the File name text box.
Step 2: Click the Save in box arrow, click 3½ Floppy [A:], and then double-click the Integration folder icon, if necessary.
Step 3: Click the Save button.
Step 4: Click the Close button on the Excel title bar.

The workbook is now saved on the floppy disk with the name Budget With Chart, and Excel is closed.

Creating a Mail Merge Document

The next step in this project is to create the mail merge main document that contains the data and chart from the Budget With Chart workbook. You can create a form letter soliciting contributions from family contributors using the basic text from last year's letter; however, first you must create a new letterhead for the letter.

Overview of Steps to Create a Letterhead Using Clip Art and WordArt

The letterhead text contains the name and address of Community Youth Programs. Clip art is also added to the letterhead (see Figure 1-1c on page I 1.7 in the first couple of pages). You create the Community Youth Programs text with WordArt. The WordArt text is formatted with the 24-point Arial font, blue shading, and a red shadow. The address, in 14-point Arial font, is added below the WordArt text. The WordArt text and address are centered. A border is added to the last paragraph of the address text. The address and border are formatted with the blue color. Blank lines and a date field are added below the letterhead text. The complete letterhead including text, clip art, blank lines, and date field is saved as AutoText. You will perform the following tasks in this section of the project.

1. Start Word.
2. Open the Basic Solicitation Letter document.
3. Position the insertion point and then open WordArt.
4. Create and format the letterhead text.
5. Close WordArt and then insert the letterhead text into the document.
6. Add and format any additional Word letterhead text.
7. Center the letterhead text.
8. Add a border.
9. Insert clip art into the document and position it as part of the letterhead.
10. Add blank lines and a date field.
11. Select the letterhead text, clip art, blank lines, and date field.
12. Create an AutoText entry.
13. Save the letterhead document.

The following pages contain a detailed explanation of these tasks.

More *About* **Form Letters**

The basic contents of a group of form letters are similar; however, items such as name and address change from one letter to the next. Thus, the form letters are personalized to the addressee. An individual is more likely to open and read a personalized letter than a standard Dear Sir or Dear Madam letter.

Starting Word and Opening an Existing Document

The first step in creating a new Community Youth Programs letterhead is to open Word and the Basic Solicitation Letter document. After the Basic Solicitation Letter document is open, you can modify the document to create a new letterhead. Perform the following steps to start Word and then open the Basic Solicitation Letter document.

TO START WORD AND OPEN AN EXISTING DOCUMENT

Step 1: Click the Start button on the taskbar and then click Open Office Document.

Step 2: Click the Look in box arrow, click 3½ Floppy [A:], and double-click the Integration folder icon.

More *About* **WordArt**

Microsoft Word includes three applications (WordArt, Equation Editor, and Graph) that allow you to create an object and then embed that object into a Word document. With WordArt, the Word document is called the container file because it contains the embedded object from WordArt, the source application.

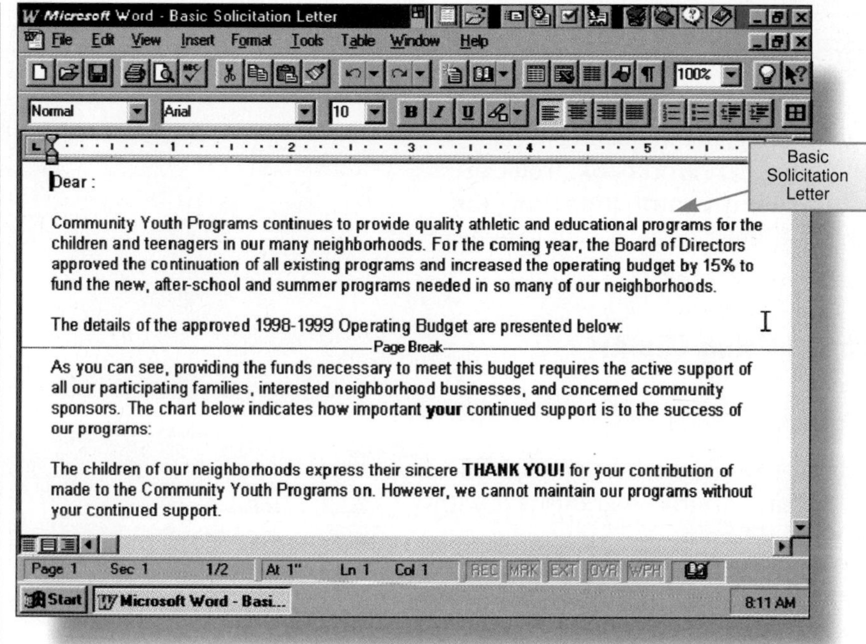

FIGURE 1-13

Step 3: Double-click Basic Solicitation Letter.

The Basic Solicitation Letter displays in the Word window (Figure 1-13).

Using WordArt to Create Special Text Effects

Now that the Basic Solicitation Letter is open, you can create the letterhead shown in Figure 1-1c on page I 1.7. WordArt is a supplementary software program you can use to add special effects to text. Perform the following steps to create the letterhead text using WordArt.

Steps To Use WordArt to Create Letterhead Text

1 Verify that the insertion point is at the top of the document. Press the ENTER key four times to add four blank lines at the top of the document, and then move the insertion point to the first blank line. If not already recessed, click the Show/Hide ¶ button on the Standard toolbar.

The four paragraph marks (¶) indicate four blank lines. The insertion point is positioned at the beginning of the first blank line (Figure 1-14).

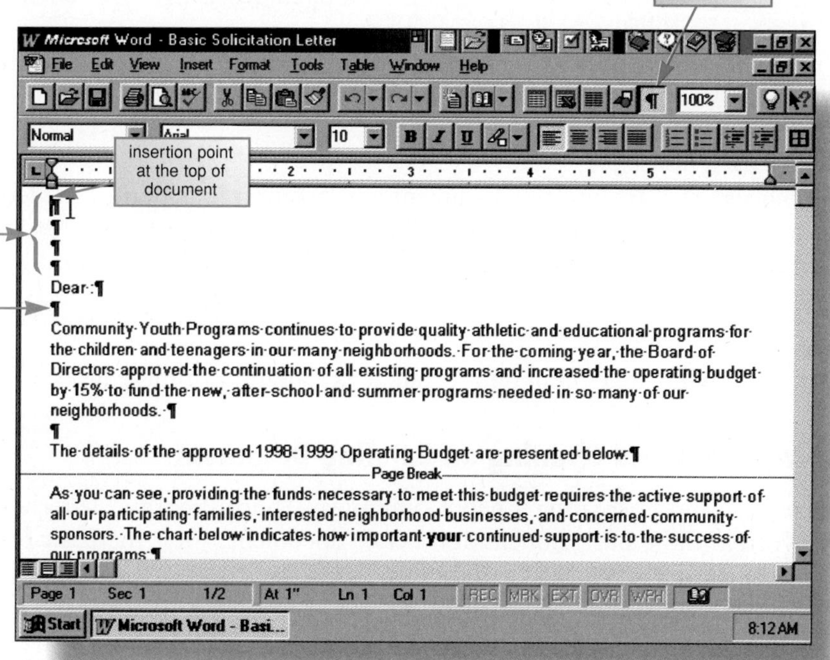

FIGURE 1-14

2 **Click Insert on the menu bar and then click Object on the Insert menu. Click the Create New tab, if necessary, when the Object dialog box first opens. If necessary, scroll through the Object Type list to view Microsoft WordArt 2.0. If WordArt 2.0 has not been installed on your computer, discuss alternatives with your instructor.**

The Create New sheet in the Object dialog box displays (Figure 1-15).

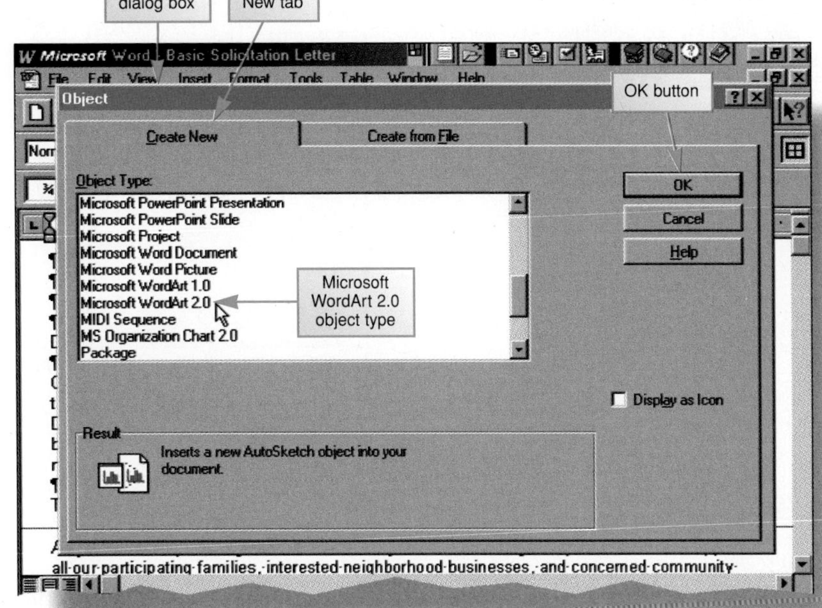

FIGURE 1-15

3 **Click Microsoft WordArt 2.0 and then click the OK button.**

In a few seconds, WordArt opens. The WordArt toolbar, menu bar, and Enter Your Text Here window display (Figure 1-16). Notice that the Word menu bar and toolbars have been replaced with a WordArt menu bar and toolbar.

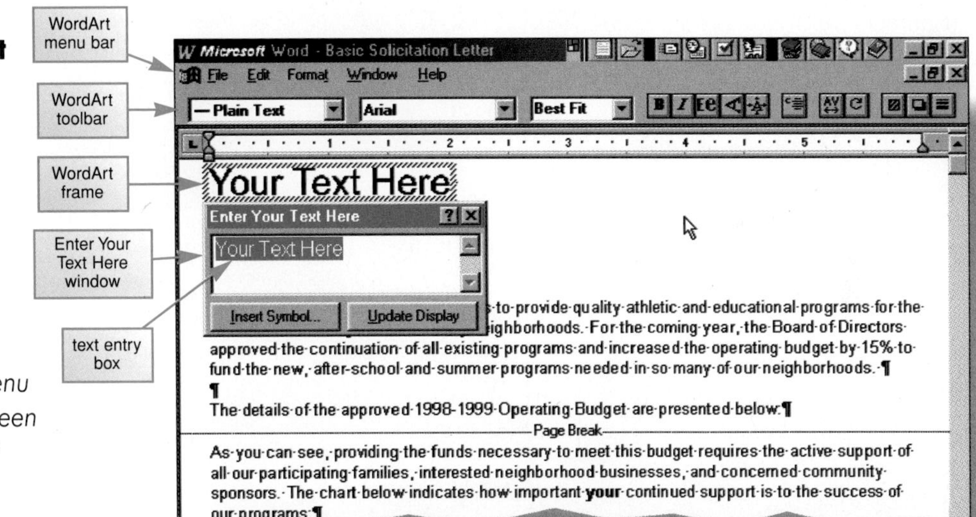

FIGURE 1-16

4 **Type** `Community Youth Programs` **in the text entry box and then click the Update Display button.**

The text displays in the text entry box and in the WordArt frame (Figure 1-17).

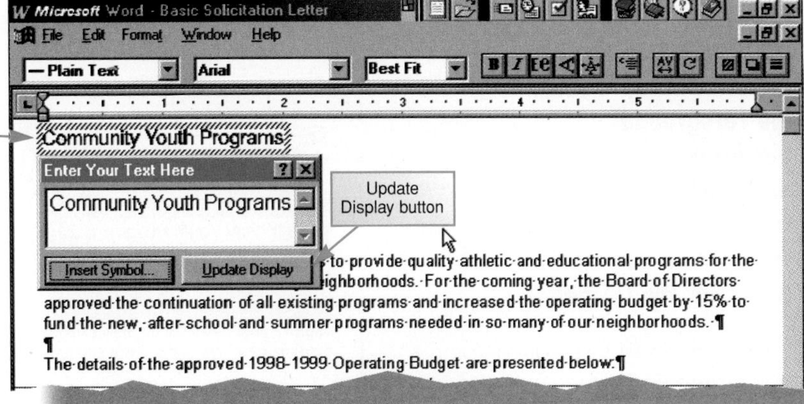

FIGURE 1-17

5 Click the Font Size box arrow on the toolbar and then click 24.

The font size of the WordArt text changes to 24 point (Figure 1-18).

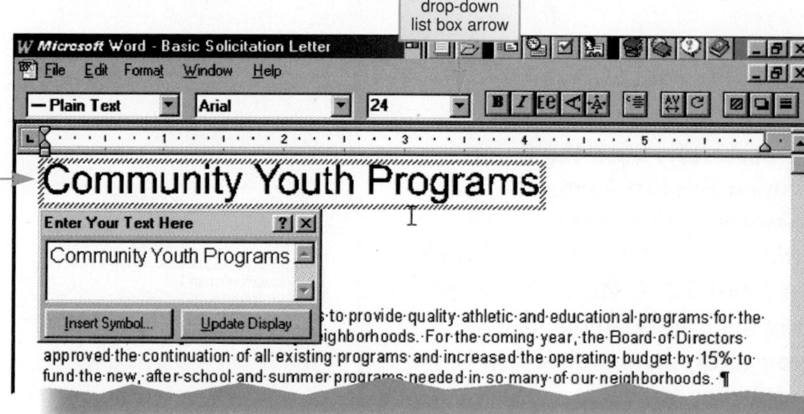

FIGURE 1-18

6 Click the Shading button on the WordArt toolbar.

The Shading dialog box displays (Figure 1-19). You select the shading style for the Foreground and Background of the WordArt text in this dialog box.

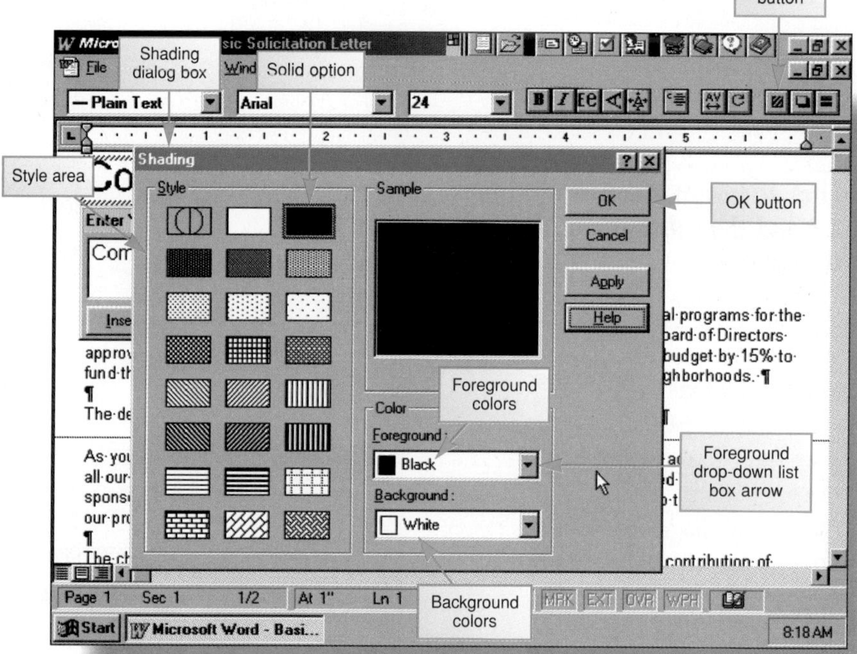

FIGURE 1-19

7 Verify the Solid option (the third option on the first line in the Style area) is selected. Click the Foreground box arrow and then click the color Blue. Verify the color in the Background box is White and then click the OK button.

The WordArt text foreground color is blue and the text background color remains white (Figure 1-20).

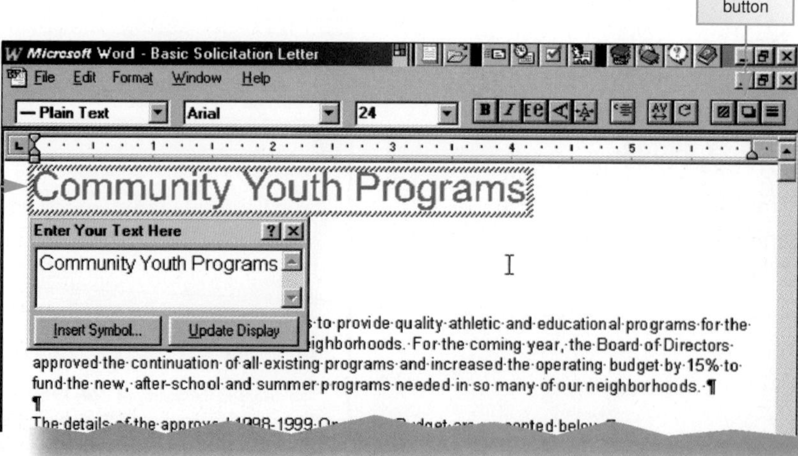

FIGURE 1-20

8 **Click the Shadow button on the WordArt toolbar. If the Shadow grid displays, click More to display the Shadow dialog box. Click the third shadow option in the list, click the Shadow Color box arrow and then scroll to view the color Red. Click Red.**

The Shadow dialog box displays and the WordArt text now has a red shadow image (Figure 1-21).

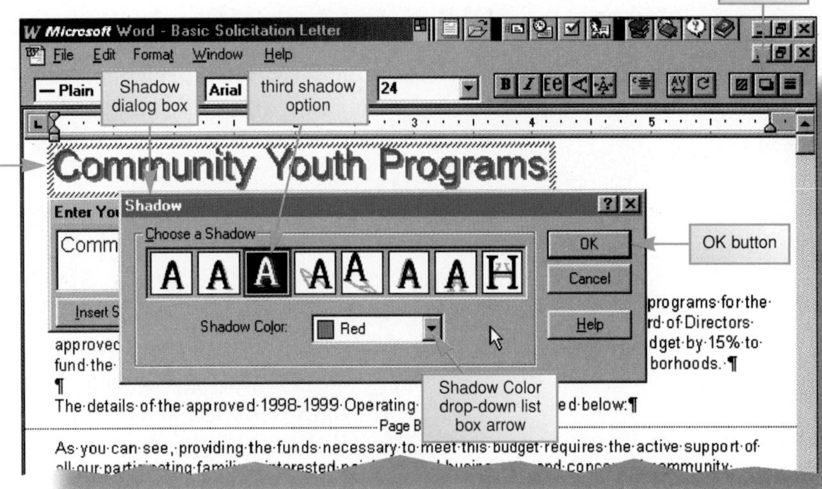

FIGURE 1-21

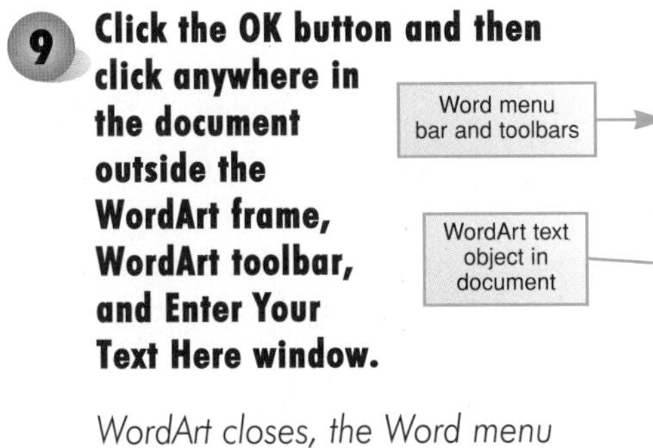

9 **Click the OK button and then click anywhere in the document outside the WordArt frame, WordArt toolbar, and Enter Your Text Here window.**

WordArt closes, the Word menu bar and toolbars display, and the WordArt text object is inserted into the form letter document in the Word window (Figure 1-22). Notice the sizing handles on the object boundary indicating the WordArt text object is selected.

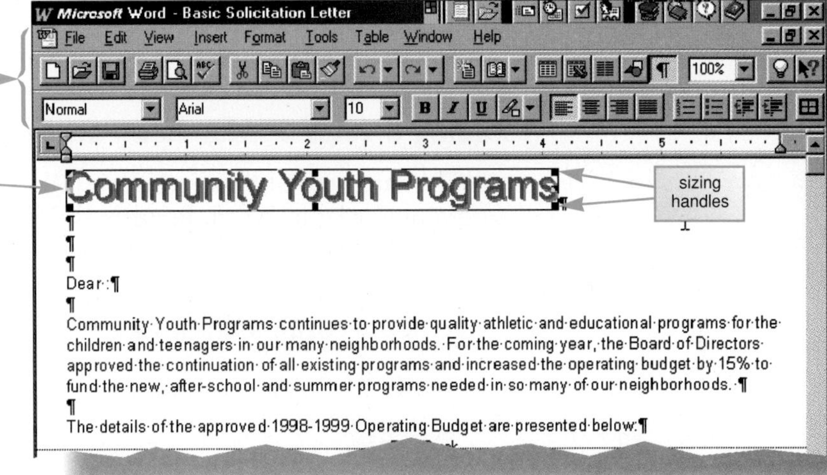

FIGURE 1-22

10 **Click the Center button on the Formatting toolbar and then click the blank line below the WordArt text.**

The WordArt text is deselected, centered between the left and right margins, and the insertion point is moved to line 2 (Figure 1-23).

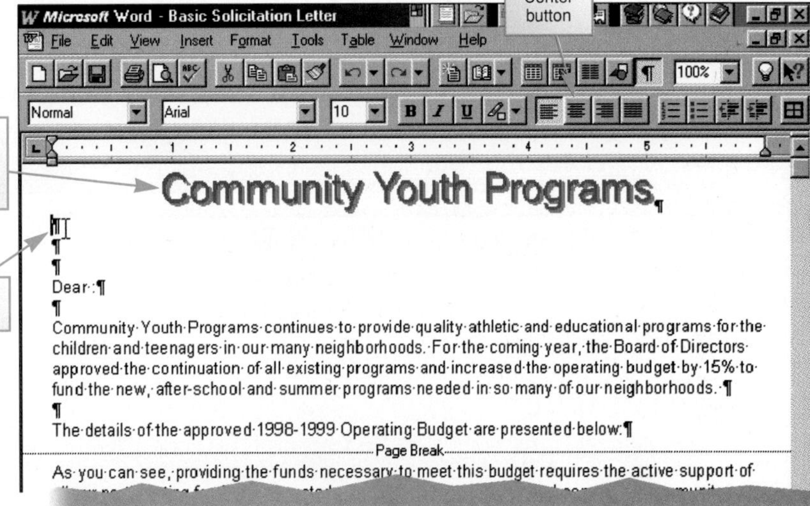

FIGURE 1-23

Adding and Formatting Letterhead Text

To complete the letterhead, you must add the address text. After the text is entered, you can format it. Perform the following steps to complete the letterhead text and then format it.

TO ADD AND FORMAT LETTERHEAD TEXT

Step 1: Type `5467 Eastlake Street` and then press the ENTER key.
Step 2: Type `Houston, TX 77034` and then press the ENTER key.
Step 3: Select the two lines of the address and then click the Center button on the Formatting toolbar.
Step 4: Right-click the selected text and then click Font on the shortcut menu.
Step 5: Click the Font tab, if necessary, when the Font dialog box first opens.
Step 6: Click Arial in the Font box, if necessary, and then click 14 in the Size box.
Step 7: Click the Color box arrow and then click the color Blue.
Step 8: Click the OK button.
Step 9: Deselect the two lines of the address.

The letterhead address lines are entered and formatted (Figure 1-24 below).

Adding a Color Border to a Paragraph

The letterhead shown in Figure 1-1c on page I 1.7 displays a blue line, called a bottom border in Word. Perform the following steps to add a blue bottom border to the last paragraph of the letterhead.

TO ADD A COLOR BORDER TO A PARAGRAPH

Step 1: Move the insertion point to the last line of the address (line 3 in the document).
Step 2: Click Format on the menu bar and then click Borders and Shading.
Step 3: Click the Borders tab, if necessary, when the Borders and Shading dialog box first opens.
Step 4: Click 3 pt in the Style box and then click the bottom line of the Border sample in the Border area.
Step 5: Click the Color box arrow and then click Blue.
Step 6: Click the OK button.

A blue border displays below the last paragraph in the letterhead (Figure 1-24).

FIGURE 1-24

Adding Clip Art

The next step in creating the Community Youth Programs letterhead is to add clip art that suggests the nature of the Community Youth Programs activities. Perform the following steps to insert clip art into the letterhead.

To Add a Clip Art Object to a Letterhead

1. **Move the insertion point to the top of the document. Click Insert on the menu bar and then click Picture. Be sure the Clipart folder displays in the Look in box. If not recessed, click the Preview button. Scroll through the Name box to display Sports.wmf and then click it.**

   The Insert Picture dialog box displays the Sports.wmf clip art file (Figure 1-25). You can preview clip art files and select clip art files to insert into a document in this dialog box.

FIGURE 1-25

2. **Click the OK button.**

   The Sports.wmf clip art file is inserted as an object at the top of the document (Figure 1-26).

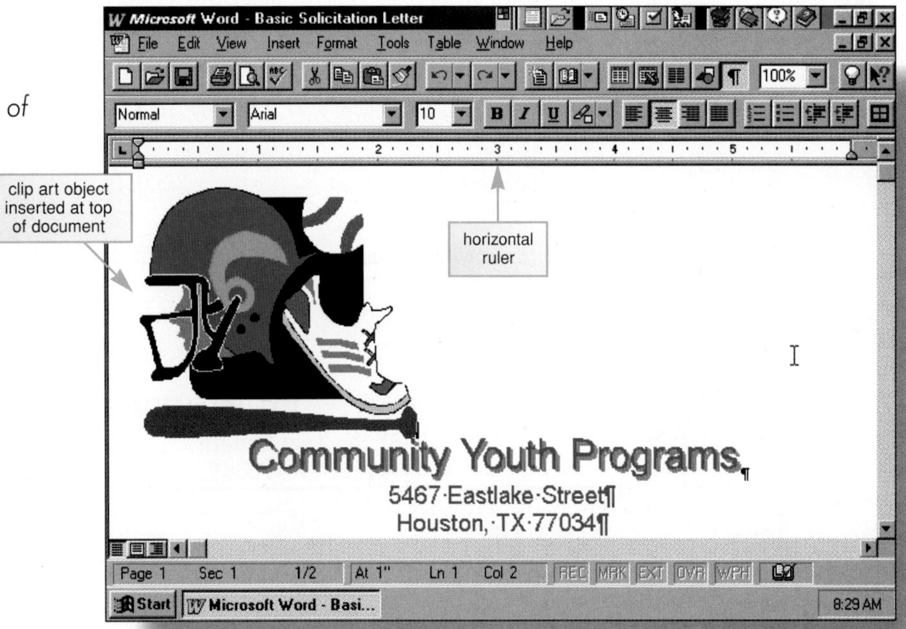

FIGURE 1-26

Other Ways

1. Press ALT+I keys, press P key

More About Windows Metafiles

Word for Windows 95 includes a series of predefined graphics, called clip art files or Windows metafiles. You insert, or import, these graphics into a Word document through the Picture command on the Insert menu. Windows metafiles have an extension of .wmf and are, by default, located in the Clipart folder on your system.

Sizing a Clip Art Object

Before you change the size of a clip art object, first you must select it. You select a clip art object by clicking it. You size a clip art object by dragging a sizing handle. Perform the following steps to select and size a clip art object.

TO SIZE A CLIP ART OBJECT

Step 1: Click the clip art object to select it.
Step 2: Move the mouse pointer to the top left sizing handle and then drag downward and to the right until the clip art object is approximately one inch square. Use the horizontal ruler at the top of the window to help size the clip art.

The Sports clip art object is smaller and remains selected.

More About Frames

Both text and graphics can be framed. A frame displays on the screen as a crosshatched border surrounding the object. When you position the mouse on the frame to move or resize it, the mouse pointer changes to a positioning pointer, a left pointing block arrow with a four-headed arrow attached to it.

Framing and Moving Clip Art

Inserting a **frame** around the selected clip art object helps you position the object in a document. You move a clip art object into a text object by inserting a frame around the object and then formatting the frame position, or by dragging the frame to the desired location within the document. Perform the following steps to insert a frame around clip art and then move the object to a new position in the document.

TO INSERT A FRAME AROUND A CLIP ART OBJECT AND MOVE A CLIP ART OBJECT

Step 1: Right-click the clip art object, click Frame Picture on the shortcut menu, and then click the Yes button in the Microsoft Word dialog box.
Step 2: Move the mouse pointer to the bottom border of the frame.
Step 3: Drag the frame upward until the baseball bat in the picture is level with the blue border under the last address line.

The clip art object displays to the left of the text in the letterhead (Figure 1-27). The frame displays around the clip art. Sizing handles display within the frame.

FIGURE 1-27

Adding Blank Lines and a Date Field

You complete the letterhead by adding blank lines and a date field that automatically updates whenever the document is opened. Perform the following steps to add blank lines and a date field to the letterhead.

TO ADD BLANK LINES AND A DATE FIELD

Step 1: Click the blank line above the salutation (line 6) to deselect the frame and position the insertion point on line 6.
Step 2: Press the ENTER key three times to insert three blank lines.
Step 3: Click Insert on the menu bar and then click Date and Time. Click the fourth option, which is the current date in month-day-year format.
Step 4: Click Update Automatically (Insert as Field), if necessary, to insert the date as a field.
Step 5: Click the OK button.
Step 6: Press the ENTER key three times to insert three blank lines.

Word displays the current date in the document, but inserts a date field that updates the current date each time the form letter document opens. Five blank lines display under the bottom border. The date line displays. Then three additional blank lines display. The insertion point is positioned on the blank line directly above the salutation.

More About Fields

A field is a set of codes that instructs Word to insert information into a document. Field contents change depending on the status of Word and the system. If a field displays incorrect information, it may need to be updated. Word updates a field when you print the document, or click the field and then press F9.

Saving an AutoText Entry

When you have a portion of a document that you use repeatedly, save it as an AutoText entry. In this project, you use the letterhead in other documents. Because all of the text and clip art for the new letterhead is created, save the letterhead as an AutoText entry so the complete letterhead can be inserted into other documents. Recall that AutoText is a Microsoft Word feature that allows you to create an object, save it with a name, and then use that name as a shortcut for embedding the entire object.

Perform the following steps to save the Community Youth Programs letterhead as AutoText so you can use it again later without having to create it.

TO SAVE AN AUTOTEXT ENTRY

Step 1: Click the Normal View button. Press and hold down the SHIFT key, and then select all the lines of the letterhead from the clip art object at the top left of the document through the three blank lines following the date.
Step 2: Click Edit on the menu bar and then click AutoText on the Edit menu.
Step 3: Type `letterhead` in the Name text box and then click the Add button.
Step 4: Deselect the letterhead.

The letterhead is saved as an AutoText entry with the name of letterhead. To insert the letterhead into a Word document, type the word, letterhead, and then press the F3 key.

Saving a Word Document with a New Filename

To preserve the original fund-raising document, Basic Solicitation Letter, on disk, you should save the current document using a new name. Perform the steps on the next page to save the document with the new filename, Solicitation Letter.

TO SAVE A WORD DOCUMENT WITH A NEW NAME

Step 1: Click File on the menu bar and then click Save As. Click the Save in box arrow, click 3½ Floppy [A:], and double-click the Integration folder icon, if necessary.
Step 2: Type `Solicitation Letter` in the File name text box.
Step 3: Click the Save button.

Word saves the document with the filename, Solicitation Letter.

More *About* **Linking**

Linking is the process of copying information from a source file and then pasting it into a destination file. When you update the information in the source file, it is also updated in the destination file. The linked information is actually stored in the source file, and the destination file contains a pointer to the location of the source file.

Linking Excel Data to a Word Document

This section of the Community Youth Programs project explains how to link an Excel worksheet and chart to a Word document. Because you want the Solicitation Letter to contain the most current version of the Budget worksheet, you should link the worksheet to the letter. Then, every time you open the Solicitation Letter, Word displays the latest Excel Budget worksheet as part of the letter.

Overview of Steps to Link Excel Data to a Word Document

To link the Excel Budget, Budget worksheet data and chart to the Word Solicitation Letter document, you will perform the following tasks in this section of the project.

1. Start Excel.
2. Open the Budget With Chart workbook.
3. Select the Budget With Chart worksheet data and copy it to the Clipboard.
4. Switch to the Word form letter document.
5. Position the insertion point and paste link the worksheet data into the form letter.
6. Switch to the Excel workbook.
7. Select the embedded chart and copy it to the Clipboard.
8. Switch to the Word form letter document.
9. Position the insertion point and paste link the chart into the form letter.
10. Save the form letter.
11. Close Word.
12. Close Excel.

The following pages contain a detailed explanation of these tasks.

Starting Excel and Opening a Workbook

Before you can link the Excel data and chart to the Word document, you must start Excel and open the Budget With Chart workbook. Perform the following steps to start Excel and then open the Budget With Chart workbook.

TO START EXCEL AND OPEN AN EXISTING WORKBOOK

Step 1: Click the Start button on the taskbar and then click Open Office Document.
Step 2: Click the Look in box arrow, double-click 3½ Floppy [A:], and double-click the Integration folder icon, if necessary.
Step 3: Double-click Budget With Chart.

Excel starts and the Budget With Chart workbook opens. The Budget With Chart worksheet is active.

Using the Copy and Paste Special Commands to Link Excel Worksheet Data to a Word Document

Next, you must select worksheet data, copy it to the Clipboard, and then paste link the data into the Solicitation Letter document. The Paste Link option of the Paste Special command establishes a reference to the Excel worksheet so each time the Word document opens, the most current version of the worksheet data displays. The worksheet is not saved with the Word document. Only the reference to the Excel chart is saved with the Word document. Perform the following steps to paste link Excel data to the Solicitation Letter document.

TO COPY AND PASTE LINK EXCEL WORKSHEET DATA TO A WORD DOCUMENT

Step 1: Select the range A1:F20, right-click the selected range, and then click Copy on the shortcut menu.
Step 2: Click the Microsoft Word button on the taskbar to switch to Word and the Solicitation Letter document.
Step 3: Move the insertion point to the end of the line above the page break on the first page and then press the ENTER key twice to insert two blank lines.
Step 4: Click Edit on the menu bar and then click Paste Special.
Step 5: When the Paste Special dialog box displays, click Paste Link, click Microsoft Excel Worksheet Object, and then click the OK button.

The worksheet displays in the Solicitation Letter document (Figure 1-28). Word is the active window as indicated by the taskbar.

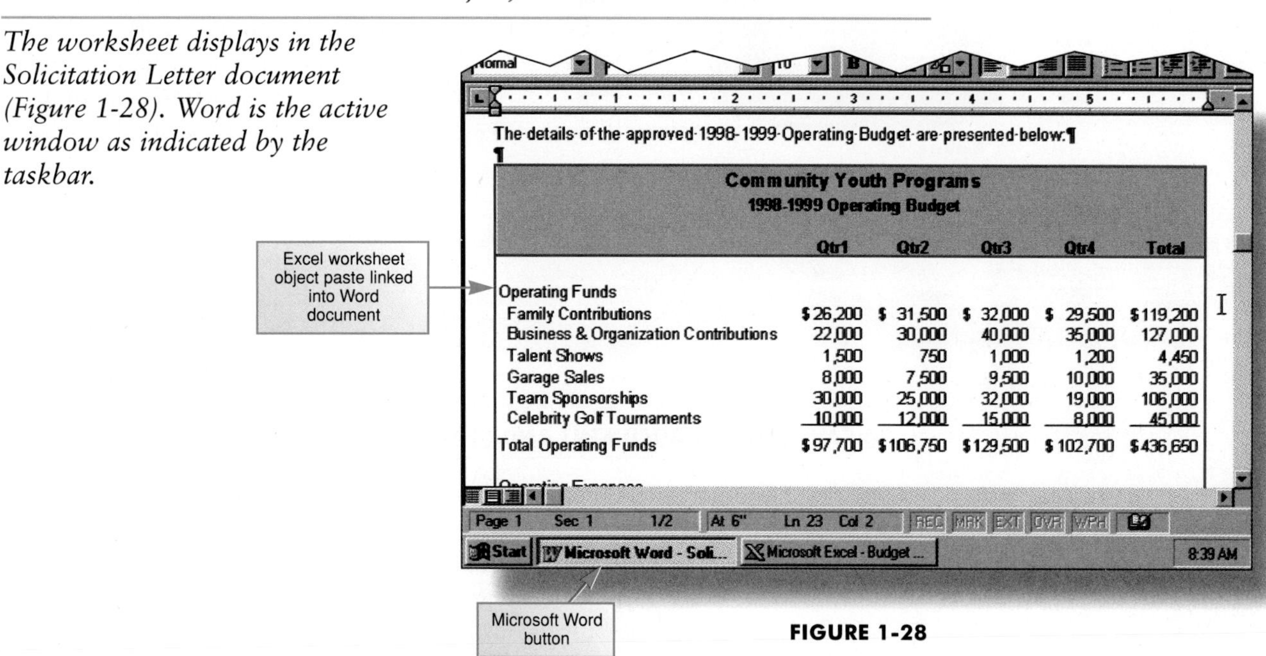

FIGURE 1-28

The Excel worksheet data is inserted into the Solicitation Letter document as a linked object. To select the linked worksheet object, click it. To return to Excel and the workbook to edit the object, double-click the linked worksheet object in the Word document. Any changes made to the worksheet data will automatically update the linked object in the Word document.

Next, select the embedded Pie chart, copy it to the Clipboard, and then paste link the chart to the Solicitation Letter document as described in the following steps.

TO COPY AND PASTE LINK AN EXCEL CHART TO A WORD DOCUMENT

Step 1: Click the Microsoft Excel button on the taskbar to switch back to Excel and the Budget With Chart workbook. Scroll to view the embedded chart.
Step 2: Right-click the embedded chart and then click Copy on the shortcut menu.
Step 3: Click the Microsoft Word button on the taskbar to switch to Word and the Solicitation Letter document.
Step 4: Move the insertion point to the end of the first paragraph on the second page.
Step 5: Press the ENTER key to insert a blank line.
Step 6: Click Edit on the menu bar, click Paste Special, click Paste Link, and then click the OK button.

FIGURE 1-29

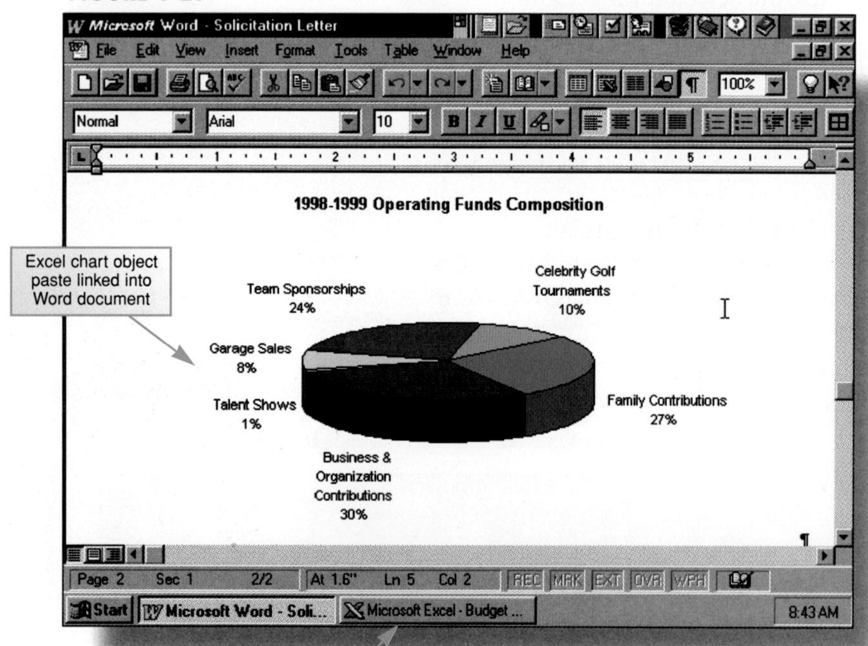

The Pie chart displays on page 2 of the Solicitation Letter document (Figure 1-29).

Saving a Word Document and Closing Excel and Word

The Solicitation Letter now contains links to the the data and chart from the workbook. Before you begin the process of merging the Word document with an Access query, you must save the document and close Excel. Perform the following steps to save the Solicitation Letter document and then close both Word and Excel.

TO SAVE A WORD DOCUMENT AND CLOSE EXCEL AND WORD

Step 1: Click the Save button on the Standard toolbar to save the Solicitation Letter document.
Step 2: Right-click the Microsoft Excel button on the taskbar and then click Close on the shortcut menu.
Step 3: Click the Close button on the Word title bar.

The Solicitation Letter document is saved. Excel and Word are closed.

Querying an Access Table

Before you merge an Access table data source with a Word main document, you may need to create a query to select the appropriate records to be included in the merge process. In this project, you want to select only family contributors' records for the Solicitation Letter document merge process. The following section provides an overview of the steps necessary to query an Access table.

More About Data Sources

A data source contains the changing, or variable, data for each form letter. One form letter prints for each record, or row, in the data source. A data source can be any table or query defined in an Access database. When Word retrieves the records from the data source, it always retrieves the current information in the records.

Overview of Steps to Query an Access Table

You perform the following tasks in this section of the project.

1. Start Access.
2. Open the Contributors database.
3. Create a new query.
4. Select the appropriate table to be queried.
5. Add the desired fields from the table to the query grid.
6. Enter the query criteria.
7. Save and name the query.
8. Display the query in Datasheet view.
9. Close the query.
10. Close Access.

The following pages contain a detailed explanation of these tasks.

Starting Access and Opening an Existing Database

Before you can query a database, you must start Access and then open a database. In this project, you are using data contained in the Contributors database. Perform the following steps to start Access and open the Contributors database.

More About Databases

A database file is a collection of tables. Each table contains rows and columns. Rows are often referred to as records, and columns are often called fields. Each field or column, must have a field name that uniquely identifies its contents, e.g., FirstName. Access databases have an extension of .mdb.

TO START ACCESS AND OPEN AN EXISTING DATABASE

Step 1: Click the Start button on the taskbar and then click Open Office Document.
Step 2: Click the Look in box arrow, click 3½ Floppy [A:], and double-click the Integration folder icon, if necessary.
Step 3: Double-click Contributors.

Access starts and the Contributors database containing the Mailing List table opens.

Creating an Access Query

The Mailing List table includes data for both family and business contributors. You must query the table to list only selected data for family contributors. The data in this query is then merged with the Word Solicitation Letter document.

TO CREATE AN ACCESS QUERY

Step 1: Click the Queries tab and then click the New button.
Step 2: Verify that Design view is selected and then click the OK button.

Step 3: Select the Mailing List table, if necessary, click the Add button, and then click the Close button.
Step 4: Click the Mailing List ID field in the Mailing List field list box above the design grid. Select all the remaining fields except the Title, Company, Hphone, and Wphone fields.
Step 5: Point to the list of selected fields in the Mailing List field list box above the design grid and then drag the selected fields to the first Field location in the design grid.
Step 6: Click the vertical scroll box to scroll to the right to view the Status field in the design grid. Then click the Criteria box in the Status field column.
Step 7: Type `=Family` in the Status field.
Step 8: Click the Save button on the toolbar.
Step 9: Type `Family List` in the Query Name box and then click the OK button.

Access creates a new query based on the selected fields and on the Family criteria specified in the Status field. The query is saved with the name Family List.

Closing an Access Query

To remove the Query window from the desktop, you must close it. Perform the following step to close an Access query.

TO CLOSE AN ACCESS QUERY

Step 1: Click the Close button on the Family List : Select Query title bar.

Access closes the Family List : Select Query window. Access remains open.

More *About* **Merging**

Creating form letters requires merging a main document (the form letter) with a data source. The main document contains the constant, or unchanging, text, punctuation, spaces, and graphics. It also contains field names that indicate the data to be merged, or blended, from the data source.

Merging an Access Query with a Word Document

When you need to send the same letter to many people, it is more efficient to create a form letter. A form letter is a fill-in-the-blank document in which you substitute data for the blanks. When you have data organized in a database table, you use the table field names instead of blanks. Community Youth Programs uses an Access database table to organize membership information. When they send a letter to some of their members, they query the table for the appropriate members and then use Word to create a form letter. Finally, they combine the form letter and the table information to create a merged document. The following section provides an overview of the steps required to merge an Access query with a Word document.

Overview of Steps to Merge an Access Query with a Word Document

The next step is to merge the Family List Access query with the Word Solicitation Letter document. You will perform the following tasks in this section of the project.

1. Use the OfficeLinks feature in Access to open Word and the Solicitation Letter document.
2. Insert the required merge fields into the Word document.

3. Save the Word document.
4. Preview the merge and make any necessary corrections or revisions.
5. Create and print the merged letters.

The following pages contain a detailed explanation of these tasks.

To Merge an Access Query with a Word Document in Access

1 Verify that the Queries tab is selected and that the Family List query is selected. Click the OfficeLinks button on the toolbar.

After a few moments, the Microsoft Word Mail Merge Wizard dialog box displays (Figure 1-30). In this dialog box, you can open Word with an existing document or a new blank document.

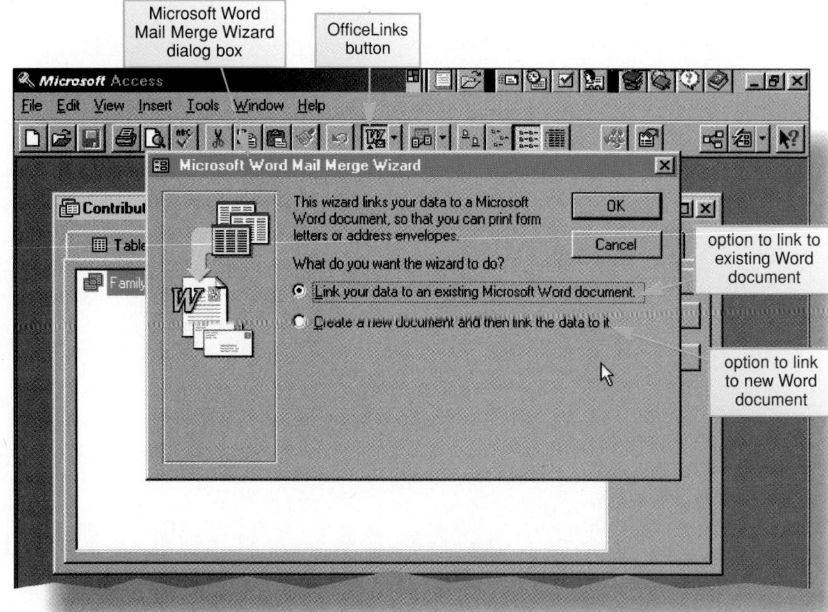

FIGURE 1-30

2 Verify that Link your data to an existing Microsoft Word document is selected and then click the OK button.

The Select Microsoft Word Document dialog box displays (Figure 1-31).

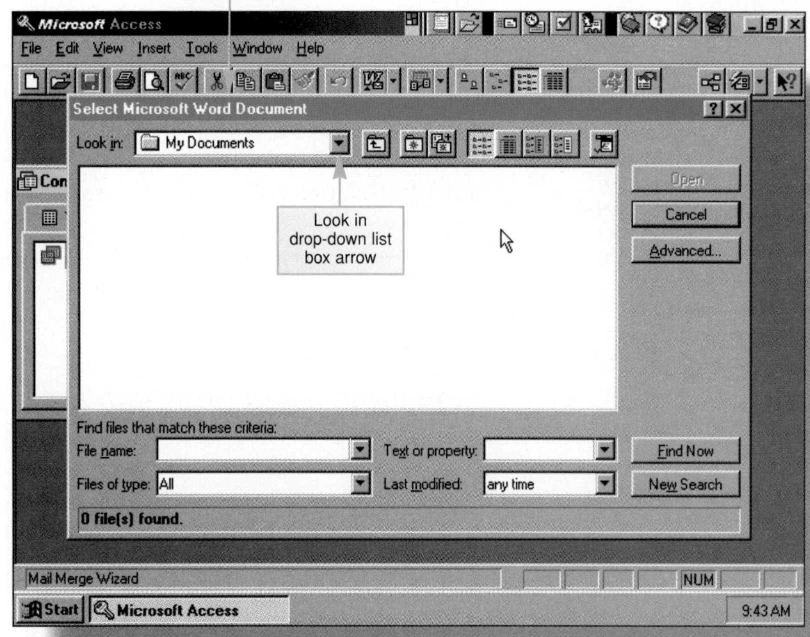

FIGURE 1-31

3 **If necessary, click the Look in box arrow, click 3½ Floppy [A:], double-click the Integration folder icon, and then double-click Solicitation Letter.**

After a few moments, Word and the Solicitation Letter document open. The length of time it takes to open Word and the Solicitation Letter document depends on your computer resources. Notice that the Mail Merge toolbar displays below the Borders toolbar. You can now insert the appropriate merge fields into the Solicitation Letter document (Figure 1-32).

FIGURE 1-32

OtherWays

1. Click Tools on menu bar, click OfficeLinks, click Merge It
2. Press ALT+T keys, press L key, press M key

More About Field Codes

If, when you print form letters, field codes print rather than the data source records, you must turn off field codes. To do this, click Tools on the menu bar, click Options, click the Print tab, click Field Codes to turn off the check box, and then click the OK button. To show or hide field codes in the document window, press ALT+F9.

Inserting Merge Fields into a Word Document

A merge field in a Word document is a placeholder for data contained in another file, such as a database table. In this project, you must click the Insert Merge Field button on the Mail Merge toolbar to display a list of fields located in the Contributors database Mailing List table. You insert fields in the document in place of actual details. For example, in this form letter, you will insert the FirstName field, press the SPACEBAR to separate the names, insert the LastName field, and then press the ENTER key to end the name line. The FirstName field, when merged with database table fields, is replaced with the first name of the first row in the database table that complies with the table row selection criterion. The LastName field is replaced with the last name of the same row of the database table. In this project, the Family List query created earlier selects rows from the table.

As you insert merge fields into a document, you must include any necessary spacing and punctuation. Perform the following steps to insert merge fields into the Solicitation Letter document.

TO INSERT MERGE FIELDS INTO A WORD DOCUMENT

Step 1: Maximize the Word window, if necessary, and then move the insertion point to the blank line above the salutation.

Step 2: Click the Insert Merge Field button on the Mail Merge toolbar, click Prefix in the Merge Field list, and then press the SPACEBAR.

Step 3: Click the Insert Merge Field button on the Mail Merge toolbar, click FirstName in the Merge Field list, and then press the SPACEBAR.

Step 4: Insert the Initial and LastName fields in the same manner. Press the ENTER key. Insert the Address field and then press the ENTER key. Insert the City field, press the COMMA key, and then press the SPACEBAR. Insert the State and Zip fields to complete the inside address. Press the ENTER key after the Zip merge field is inserted. Remember to insert the appropriate spaces, punctuation, and new lines as necessary for an inside address.
Step 5: Click in front of the colon in the salutation, press the SPACEBAR, and then insert the FirstName field.
Step 6: Scroll to view the paragraph below the chart object on page 2.
Step 7: Move the insertion point to the end of the first line of the paragraph.
Step 8: Insert the Pledge merge field and then press the SPACEBAR.
Step 9: Move the insertion point to the left of the period at the end of the sentence.
Step 10: Press the SPACEBAR and then insert the PaidDate merge field.

The required merge fields are inserted in the Solicitation Letter document. The merge fields inserted into the body of the letter are shown in Figure 1-33.

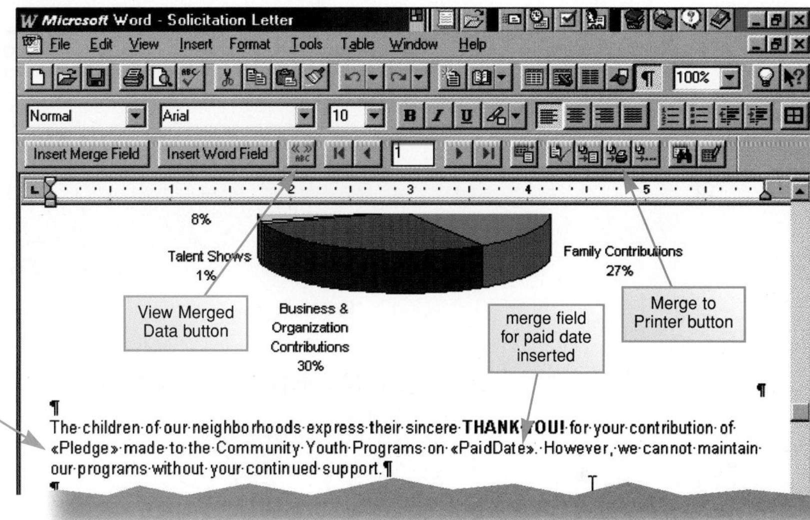

FIGURE 1-33

Creating a Header in a Word Document

The next step in this merge document is to create a second page header that includes the page number, Title, FirstName and LastName merge fields, and a date field as described in the following steps.

TO CREATE A HEADER IN A WORD DOCUMENT

Step 1: Click View on the menu bar and then click Header and Footer.
Step 2: Type `Page` and then press the SPACEBAR.
Step 3: Click the Page Numbers button on the Header and Footer toolbar and then press the ENTER key.
Step 4: Insert the Prefix, FirstName, Initial, and LastName merge fields and then press the ENTER key. Remember to insert the appropriate spaces between the merge fields.
Step 5: Click Insert on the menu bar and then click Date and Time. Click the fourth option in the Date and Time dialog box, which displays the month-day-year format.
Step 6: Verify a Date field will be inserted and then click the OK button.
Step 7: Select the three lines of the header.
Step 8: Click the Font box arrow on the Formatting toolbar and then click Arial.
Step 9: Deselect the header lines.
Step 10: Click the Page Setup button on the Header and Footer toolbar.
Step 11: Click Different First Page, if necessary, and then click the OK button.
Step 12: Click the Close button on the Header and Footer toolbar.

Step 13: Move the insertion point to the top of page 2. Click the Page Layout View button.

Step 14: Press the ENTER key twice to add two blank lines between the header and the text.

The header for page 2 of the Solicitation Letter document contains the merge fields for the addressee's name, and the two blank lines below display (Figure 1-34).

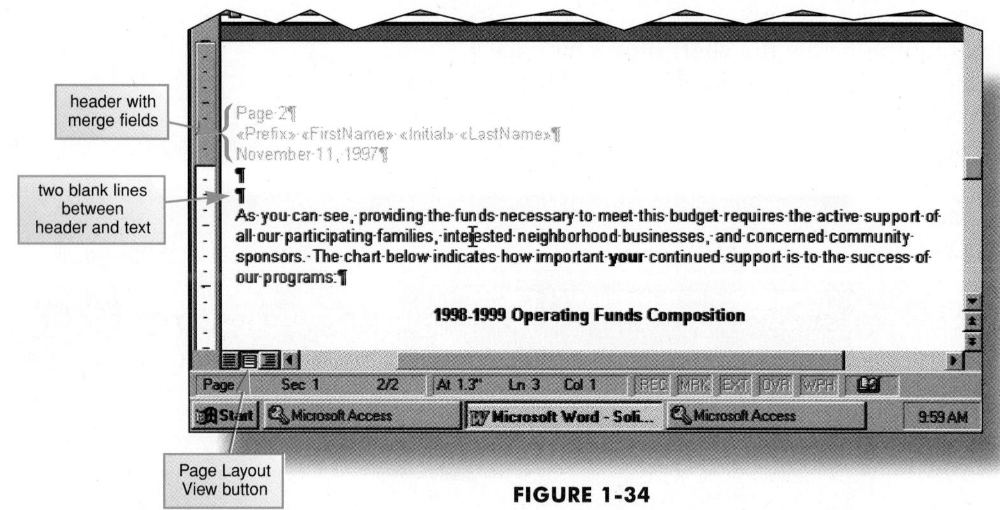

FIGURE 1-34

Saving a Word Document on Disk

You are now ready to complete the merge process. First, you should save the Solicitation Letter document to update the copy on disk with the added merge fields and header as described in the following step.

TO UPDATE A WORD DOCUMENT ON DISK

Step 1: Click the Save button on the Standard toolbar.

Word updates the existing Solicitation Letter document.

Previewing and Printing Mail Merge Letters

Next, you should preview the merge document to verify the database records are correct and to proofread the document. When you are satisfied the document is correct, merge the Solicitation Letter document and the Access query directly to a printer. Perform the following steps to preview and print the mail merge letters.

TO PREVIEW AND PRINT MAIL MERGE LETTERS

Step 1: Move the insertion point to the top of the document and then click the View Merged Data button on the Mail Merge toolbar.

Step 2: Scroll to view the inside address and the salutation for record number 1.

Step 3: Scroll to view the merged data below the embedded chart on page 2.

Step 4: Click the View Merged Data button on the Mail Merge toolbar to turn off the preview and return to the Solicitation Letter main document.

Step 5: Click the Merge to Printer button on the Mail Merge toolbar and then click the OK button to print one copy of each of the six two-page merge letters.

After a few moments, the merged documents print on the printer as shown by the example in Figure 1-35.

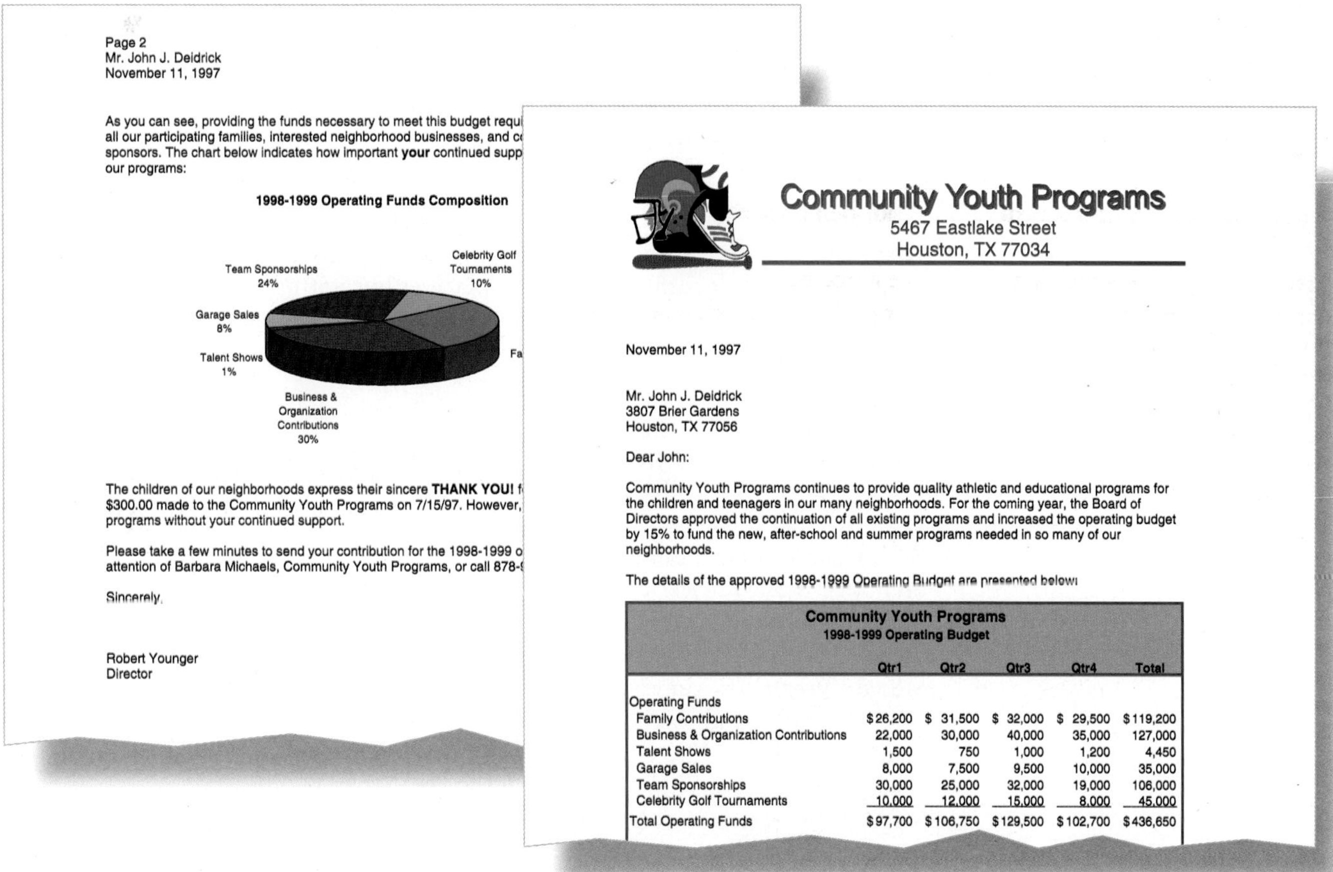

Page 2
Mr. John J. Deidrick
November 11, 1997

As you can see, providing the funds necessary to meet this budget requi
all our participating families, interested neighborhood businesses, and c
sponsors. The chart below indicates how important **your** continued supp
our programs:

The children of our neighborhoods express their sincere **THANK YOU!** f
$300.00 made to the Community Youth Programs on 7/15/97. However,
programs without your continued support.

Please take a few minutes to send your contribution for the 1998-1999 o
attention of Barbara Michaels, Community Youth Programs, or call 878-

Sincerely,

Robert Younger
Director

Community Youth Programs
5467 Eastlake Street
Houston, TX 77034

November 11, 1997

Mr. John J. Deidrick
3807 Brier Gardens
Houston, TX 77056

Dear John:

Community Youth Programs continues to provide quality athletic and educational programs for the children and teenagers in our many neighborhoods. For the coming year, the Board of Directors approved the continuation of all existing programs and increased the operating budget by 15% to fund the new, after-school and summer programs needed in so many of our neighborhoods.

The details of the approved 1998-1999 Operating Budget are presented below:

Community Youth Programs 1998-1999 Operating Budget					
	Qtr1	Qtr2	Qtr3	Qtr4	Total
Operating Funds					
Family Contributions	$26,200	$ 31,500	$ 32,000	$ 29,500	$119,200
Business & Organization Contributions	22,000	30,000	40,000	35,000	127,000
Talent Shows	1,500	750	1,000	1,200	4,450
Garage Sales	8,000	7,500	9,500	10,000	35,000
Team Sponsorships	30,000	25,000	32,000	19,000	106,000
Celebrity Golf Tournaments	10,000	12,000	15,000	8,000	45,000
Total Operating Funds	$97,700	$106,750	$129,500	$102,700	$436,650

FIGURE 1-35

If you find an error when you preview the merge documents, determine if the error is caused by the selection of records from the table. If this is the cause, carefully review the selection criterion used in the design grid in Access. If the cause for the error is in Word, however, make the correction, and then preview the merge documents again.

Saving and Closing a Word Mail Merge Main Document and Closing Word and Access

The merge process is complete for the Solicitation form letters. You should save and close the Solicitation Letter mail merge main document before you create mailing labels for the form letters. You can also close Word and Access, as described in these steps.

TO SAVE AND CLOSE A WORD MAIL MERGE MAIN DOCUMENT AND CLOSE WORD AND ACCESS

Step 1: Click the Close button on the Word title bar.
Step 2: Click Yes to save changes.
Step 3: Right-click the Microsoft Access button on the taskbar and then click Close.

Word saves changes to the mail merge main document and then closes it. Word closes and then Access closes.

More *About* **Envelopes**

If your printer can print graphics, you can insert a postal bar code used by the United States Postal Service into your envelopes or mailing labels. The bar code can be inserted either as a POSTNET delivery-point bar code or as a Facing Identification Mark (FIM). Using a bar code speeds up the delivery service.

Merging an Access Query with a Word Document to Create Mailing Labels

Many times, labels are needed for mailing letters. In this project, labels must be prepared for the letters just merged. You can create labels by merging the Family List Access query with a new label document. Merging data from an Access database table to a Word document may take place either within Access using the Access OfficeLinks feature, or within Word using the Word Mail Merge feature. To you create the labels in Word, complete the following steps.

TO MERGE AN ACCESS QUERY WITH A NEW WORD DOCUMENT TO CREATE MAILING LABELS

Step 1: Click the Start button on the taskbar and then click New Office Document on the Start menu.
Step 2: Double-click thc Blank Document icon.
Step 3: Click the Normal View button, if necessary.
Step 4: Click Tools on the menu bar and then click Mail Merge.
Step 5: When the Mail Merge Helper dialog box displays, click the Create button and then click Mailing Labels.
Step 6: When the Microsoft Word dialog box displays, click the Active Window button.
Step 7: When the Mail Merge Helper dialog box displays, click the Get Data button and then click Open Data Source.
Step 8: When the Open Data Source dialog box displays, click the Look in box arrow and then click 3½ Floppy [A:], if necessary.
Step 9: Click the Files of type box arrow and then click MS Access Databases.
Step 10: Double-click Contributors.

Word uses the Mail Merge Helper dialog box to identify the database table. A Microsoft Access dialog box displays.

Selecting a Query for a Mail Merge Document

You can select either an Access table or an Access query as your data source. In the next steps, you will select an Access query because you created the letters based on the Family List query. Perform the following steps to select the query to use for the mailing label merge document.

To Select a Query for a Mail Merge Document

1 **Click the Queries tab in the Microsoft Access dialog box.**

The Queries sheet in the Microsoft Access dialog box displays (Figure 1-36).

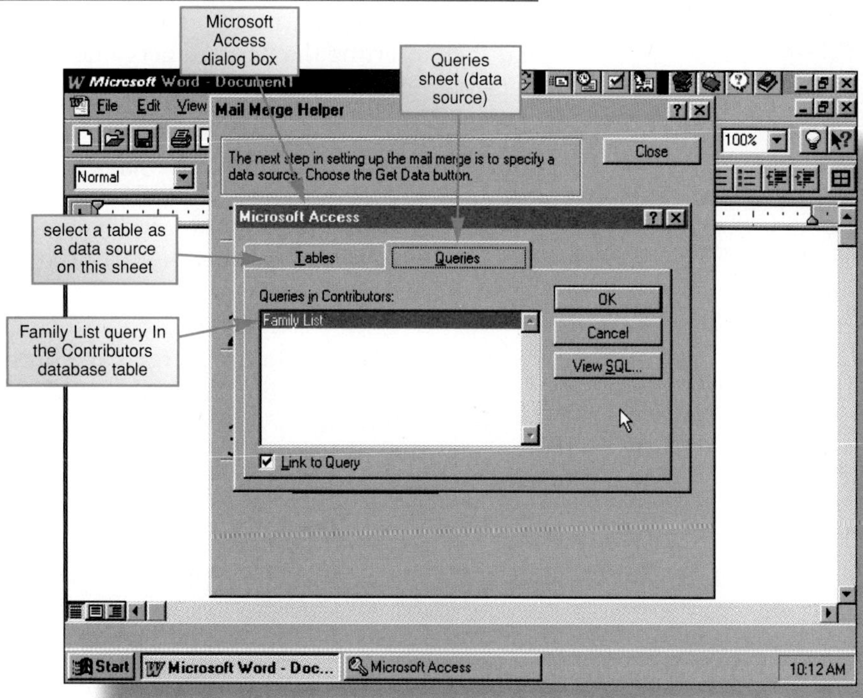

FIGURE 1-36

2 **Click Family List in the Queries in Computers list, if necessary, and then click the OK button.**

After a few moments, Access and the Family List query in the Contributors database are available for the merge process (Figure 1-37). You can now set up the label main document.

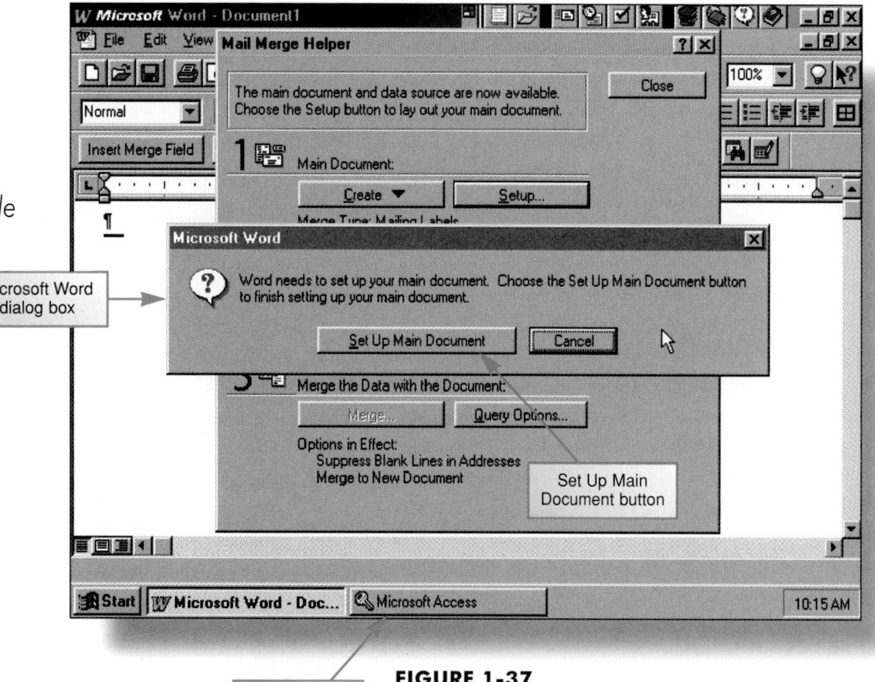

FIGURE 1-37

More About Labels

Word uses product numbers for Avery mailing labels. The product number list of mailing labels lists all possible Avery mailing label sheets compatible with your printer. Look on your mailing label box for the product number and then locate it in the list.

Setting Up a Label Main Document

The next step is to set up the main label document by specifying the label size and then inserting the desired merge fields into the document as described in the steps on the next page.

TO SET UP A LABEL MAIN DOCUMENT

Step 1: Click the Set Up Main Document button.
Step 2: Click the Product Number box down scroll arrow and scroll to view 5160 – Address.
Step 3: Click 5160 – Address and then click the OK button.
Step 4: Click the Insert Merge Field button in the Create Labels dialog box and then click Prefix in the Merge Field list.
Step 5: Press the SPACEBAR and then click the Insert Merge Field button.
Step 6: Click FirstName in the Merge Field list.
Step 7: Press the SPACEBAR and then continue inserting the Initial and LastName fields. Press the ENTER key and then insert the Address field. Press the ENTER key. Insert the City field, type a comma, press the SPACEBAR, insert the State field, press the SPACEBAR and insert the Zip field.
Step 8: Click the OK button and then click the Close button in the Mail Merge Helper dialog box.

The label main document displays (Figure 1-38). The 5160 – Address label is designed to print three labels across each row.

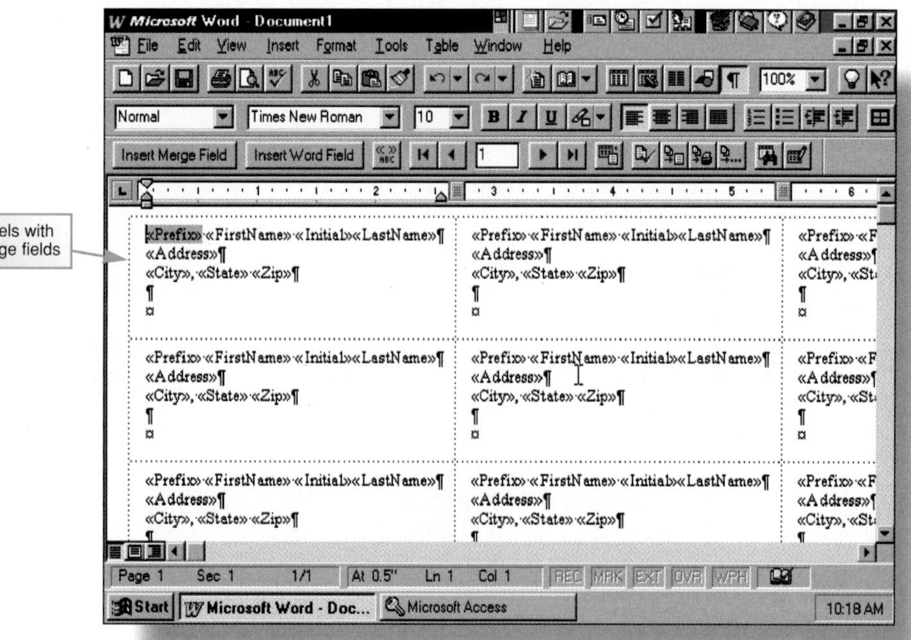

FIGURE 1-38

Previewing and Printing a Merge Document

You can now preview the label merge, correct any errors, and then print the labels as described in the following steps.

TO PREVIEW AND PRINT A MERGE DOCUMENT

Step 1: Click the View Merged Data button on the Mail Merge toolbar.
Step 2: Verify the data and label format are correct.
Step 3: Click the View Merged Data button on the Mail Merge toolbar to return to the label main document.
Step 4: Click the Merge to Printer button on the Mail Merge toolbar, and then click the OK button in the Print dialog box.

After a few moments, the merged labels print on the printer as shown in Figure 1-39.

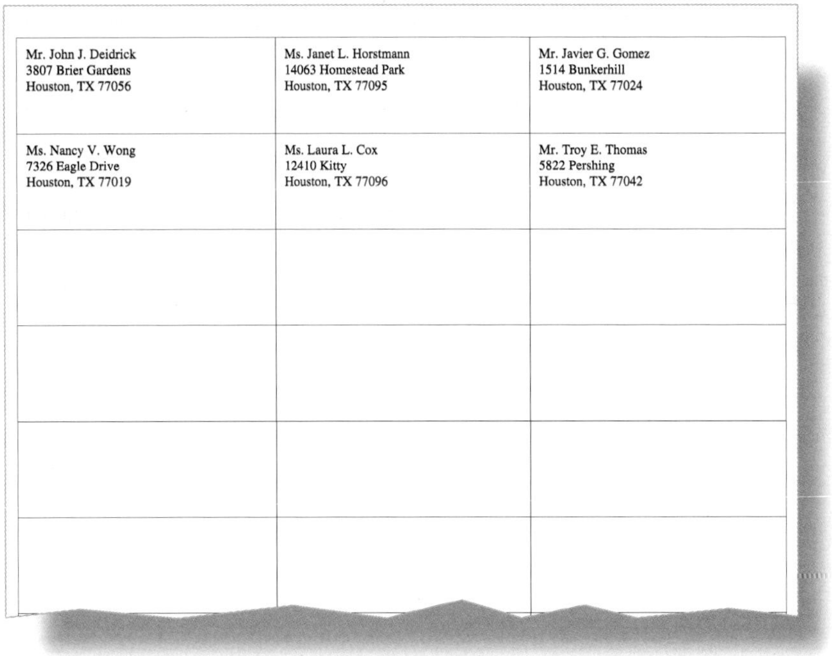

Mr. John J. Deidrick 3807 Brier Gardens Houston, TX 77056	Ms. Janet L. Horstmann 14063 Homestead Park Houston, TX 77095	Mr. Javier G. Gomez 1514 Bunkerhill Houston, TX 77024
Ms. Nancy V. Wong 7326 Eagle Drive Houston, TX 77019	Ms. Laura L. Cox 12410 Kitty Houston, TX 77096	Mr. Troy E. Thomas 5822 Pershing Houston, TX 77042

FIGURE 1-39

If you find an error when you preview the merge document, determine if the error is caused by the selection of records from the table. If this is the cause, carefully review the selection criterion used in the design grid in Access. If the cause for the error is in the Word document, however, make the correction and then preview the merge document again.

Saving and Closing a Document and Word

After you print the labels, you should save and close the label main document and Word as described in the following steps.

TO SAVE AND CLOSE THE DOCUMENT AND WORD

Step 1: Click File on the menu bar and then click Save As.
Step 2: Type `Solicitation Labels` in the File name box.
Step 3: Click the Save in box arrow, click 3½ Floppy [A:], and double-click the Integration folder icon, if necessary.
Step 4: Click the Save button.
Step 5: Click the Close button on the Word title bar.

Word saves and then closes the Solicitation Labels document. Word closes.

Creating an Access Report

The next step is to prepare a report from an Access database table that can be used to contact all business contributors to Community Youth Programs. The section on the next page gives an overview of the steps to create an Access report.

Overview of Steps to Create an Access Report

You want to list all business contributors in the Mailing List table of the Access Contributors database. The report should be a tabular report listing only the name, company, title, work phone number, pledge date, and pledge amount data from each business contributor. The records should be sorted alphabetically by the last name. The following tasks will be completed in this section of the project.

1. Start Access.
2. Open the appropriate database.
3. Create a new query.
4. Create a new report based on the query by using the Tabular Report Wizard.
5. Save the report.
6. Print the report.
7. Close the report and Access.

The following pages contain a detailed explanation of these tasks.

Starting Access and Opening an Existing Database

Before you generate an Access report, you need to start Access and open a database. In this project, use the Contributors database for the report data. Perform the following steps to start Access and open an existing database.

TO START ACCESS AND OPEN AN EXISTING DATABASE

Step 1: Click the Start button on the taskbar and then click Open Office Document.
Step 2: Click the Look in box arrow, click 3½ Floppy [A:], and double-click the Integration folder icon, if necessary.
Step 3: Double-click Contributors.

Access and the Contributors database open.

Creating an Access Query

The Mailing List table in the Contributors database includes data for both family and business contributors. In this section, you query the table to list only selected data for business contributors. The data in this query is later used in an Access report.

TO CREATE AN ACCESS QUERY

Step 1: Click the Queries tab, if necessary, and then click the New button.
Step 2: Verify that Design View is selected and then click the OK button.
Step 3: Maximize the Access window. Select the Mailing List table, if necessary, click the Add button, and then click the Close button.
Step 4: Click the FirstName field in the Mailing List field list box above the design grid. Select the LastName, Title, Company, Wphone, Status, Pledge, and PaidDate fields.
Step 5: Drag the selected fields in the Mailing List field list box to the first Field location in the design grid.

Step 6: Using the horizontal scroll bar in the design grid, scroll right until the Status field column is fully visible. Click the Show check box to remove the check mark in the Status field column. Then, click the Criteria box in the Status field column.
Step 7: Type `=Business` in the status field.
Step 8: Click the Save button on the toolbar.
Step 9: Type `Business Contributors` in the Query Name box and then click the OK button.
Step 10: Click the Close button on the Business Contributors : Select Query title bar.

The Business Contributors query is complete. The Contributor's : Database window displays.

Creating an Access Report Using the Report Wizard

Next, you must create a report based on the Business Contributors query. Access has a **Report Wizard** that quickly generates a report based on the fields chosen from a query or a database table. Perform the following steps to create an Access report using the Report Wizard.

To Create an Access Report Using the Report Wizard

1. **Click the Reports tab in the Contributor's : Database dialog box and then click the New button.**

   The New Report dialog box displays (Figure 1-40). You select a table or query as the basis for the report in this dialog box. You can use the Wizards or AutoReports to assist in creating the report, or you can create a report manually in Design view.

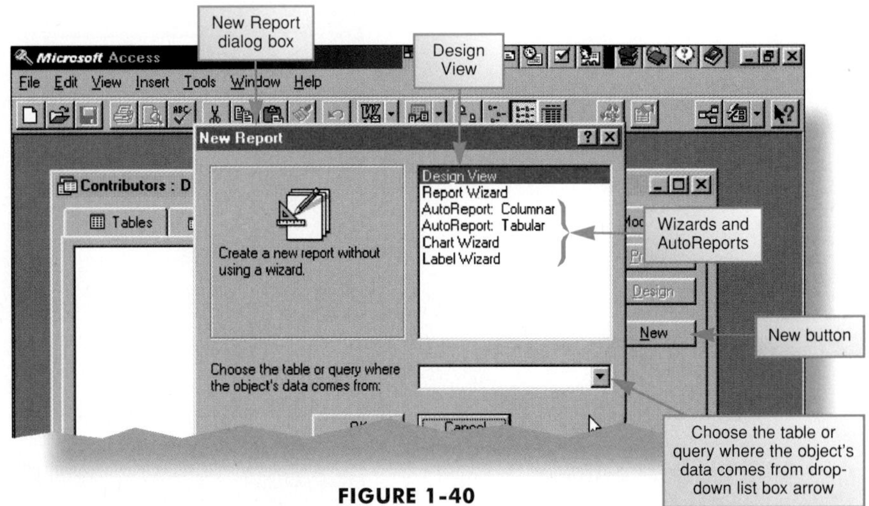

FIGURE 1-40

2. **Click Report Wizard, click the Choose the table or query where the object's data comes from box arrow, and then click Business Contributors.**

   The Business Contributors query's name displays and the file contains the data for the report (Figure 1-41).

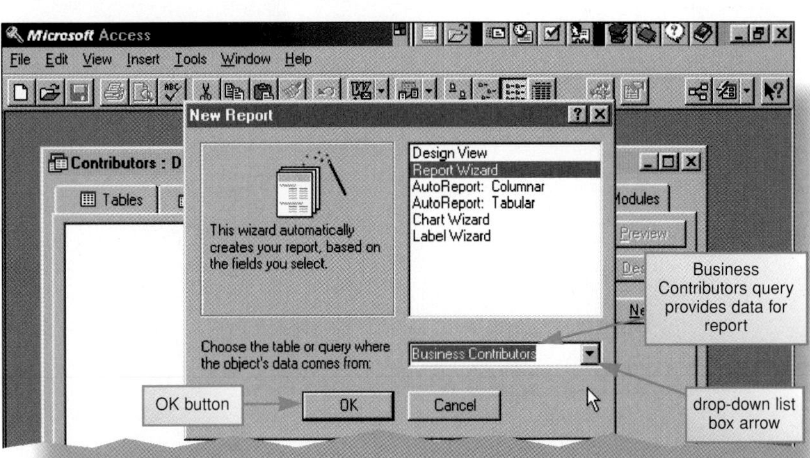

FIGURE 1-41

3 **Click the OK button.**

The first Report Wizard dialog box displays (Figure 1-42). You specify the fields to be included in the report from this Report Wizard dialog box.

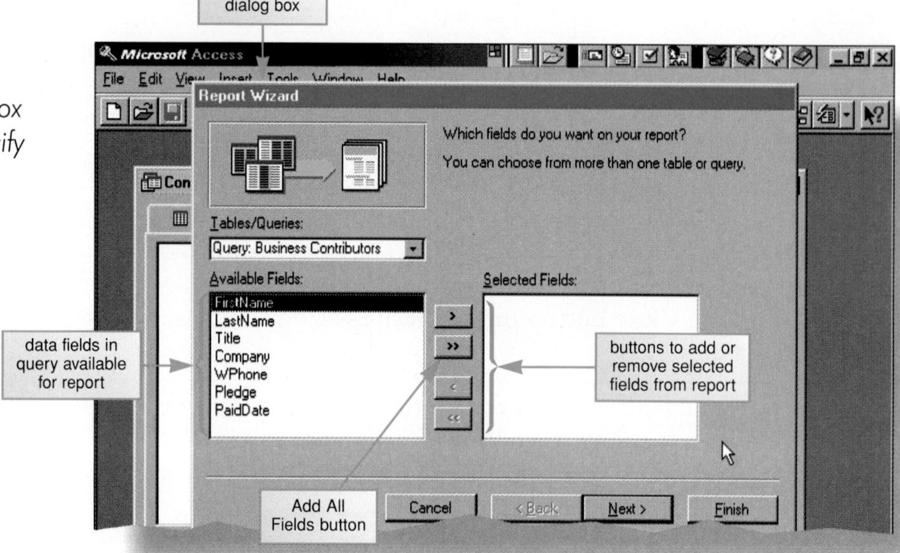

FIGURE 1-42

4 **Click the Add All Fields button to add all the fields to the report, and then point to the Next button.**

All fields display in the Selected Fields list box (Figure 1-43).

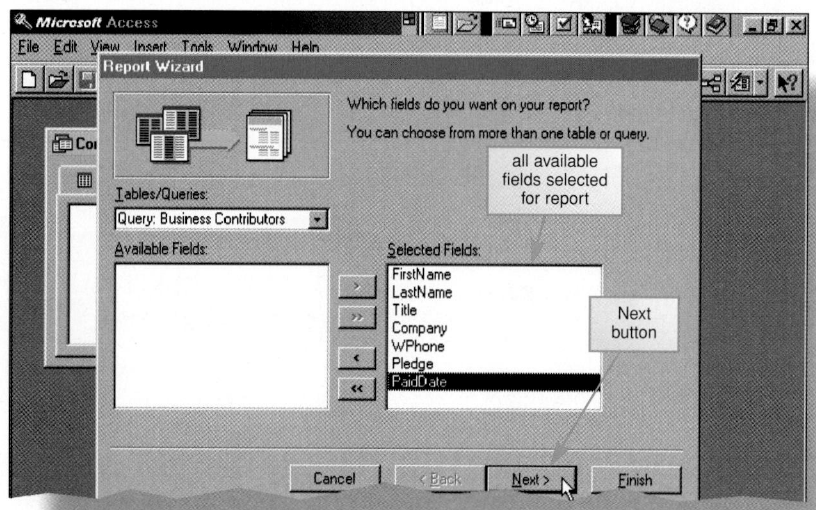

FIGURE 1-43

5 **Click the Next button.**

The next Report Wizard dialog box displays (Figure 1-44).

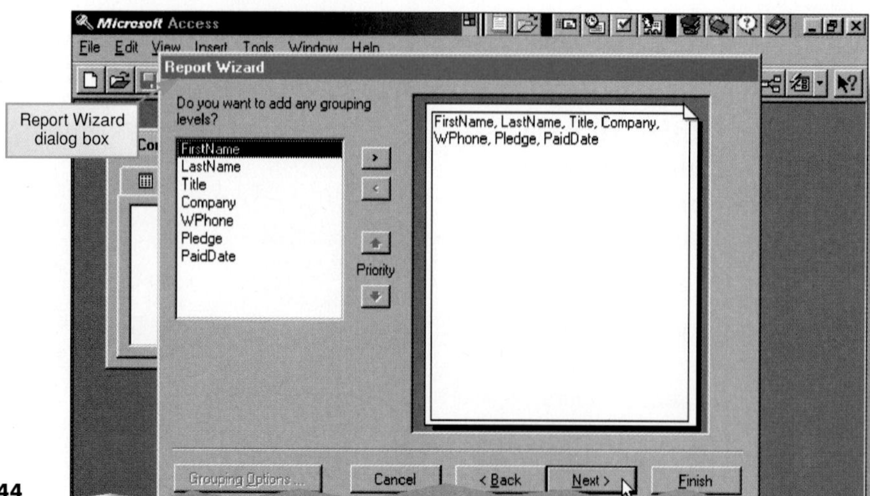

FIGURE 1-44

6 Click the Next button.

The next Report Wizard dialog box displays (Figure 1-45). You specify the sorting order of the records in this dialog box. In this report, you wish to sort the records alphabetically by last name.

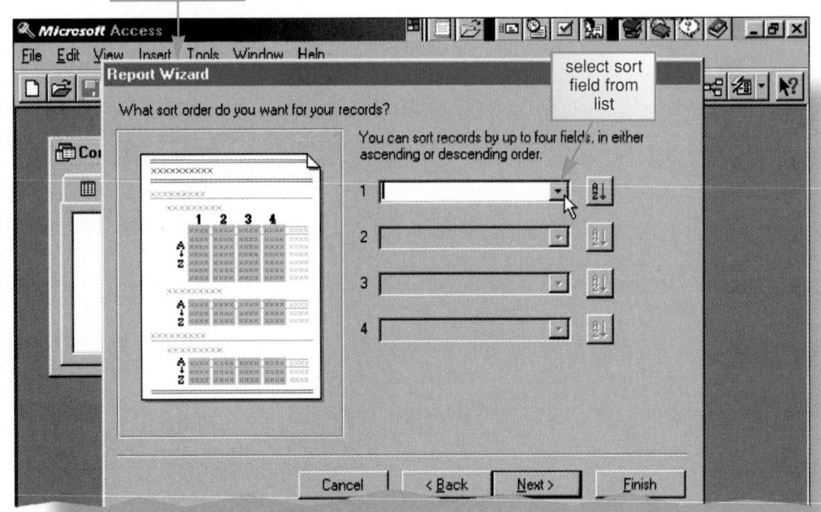

FIGURE 1-45

7 Click the box 1 arrow, click LastName, and then click the Next button.

The next Report Wizard dialog box displays (Figure 1-46). You specify the report layout in this dialog box. You want a Tabular report so that the report displays in columns, Landscape orientation so the report prints across the length of the paper, and field widths adjusted so that all fields fit on one page.

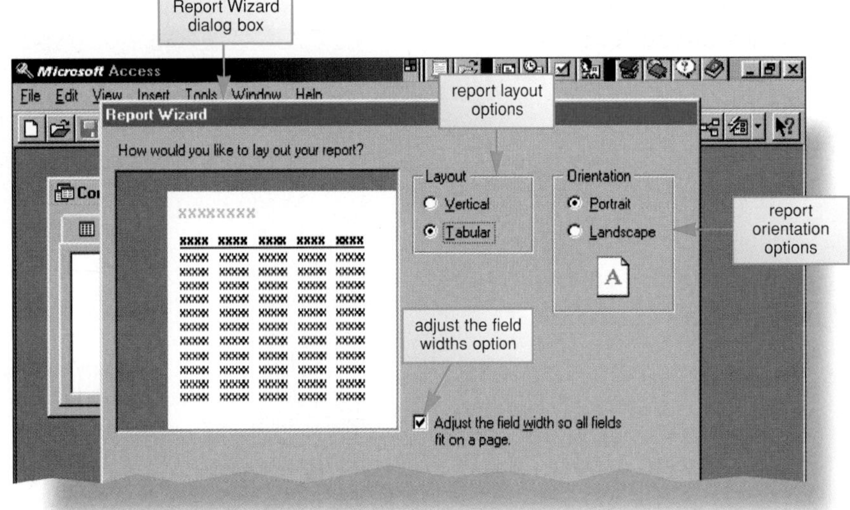

FIGURE 1-46

8 Click Tabular and then click Landscape. Click Adjust the field width so all fields fit on a page. Then, click the Next button.

The next Report Wizard dialog box displays (Figure 1-47). You select a style for your report in this dialog box.

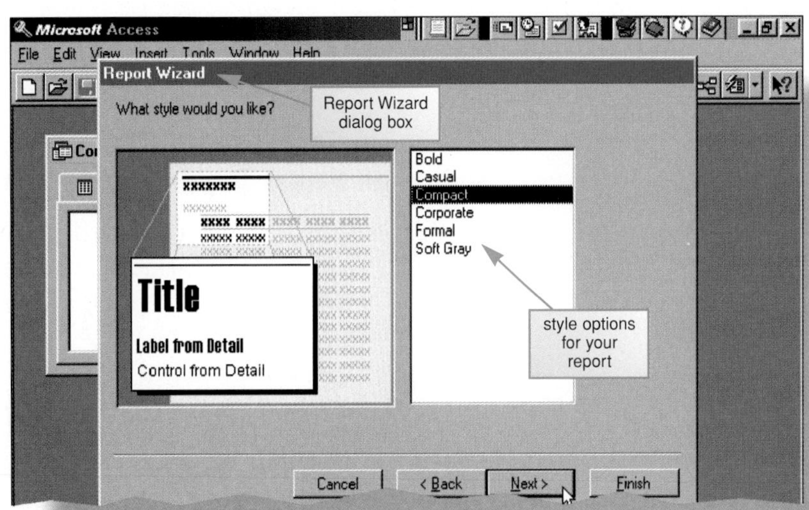

FIGURE 1-47

9 **If not already selected, click Compact. Then, click the Next button.**

The final Report Wizard dialog box displays (Figure 1-48). You give your report a title and then preview it.

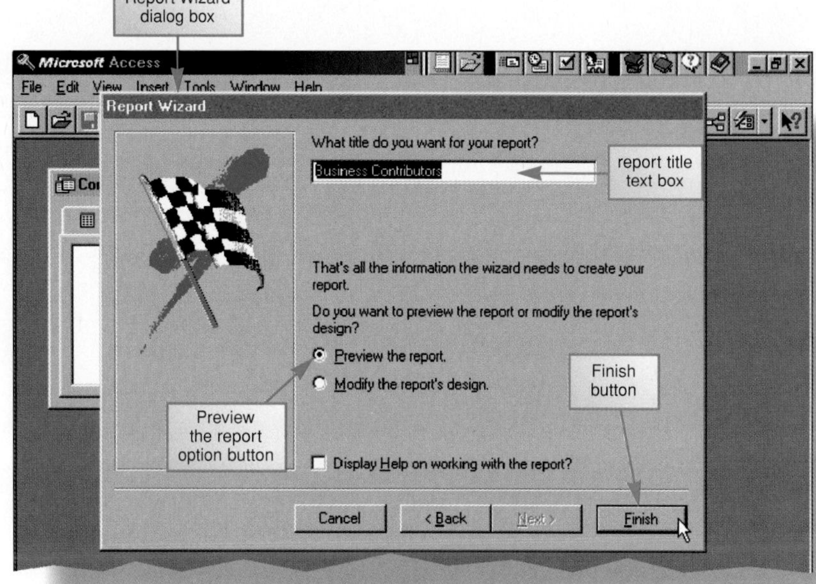

FIGURE 1-48

10 **When the next Report Wizard dialog box displays, type** `Business Contributors' Phone List` **in the What title do you want for your report? text box. Click Preview the report, if necessary. Then, click the Finish button.**

After a few moments, the top left corner of the report is displayed in Report view (Figure 1-49). You can scroll the report to view it.

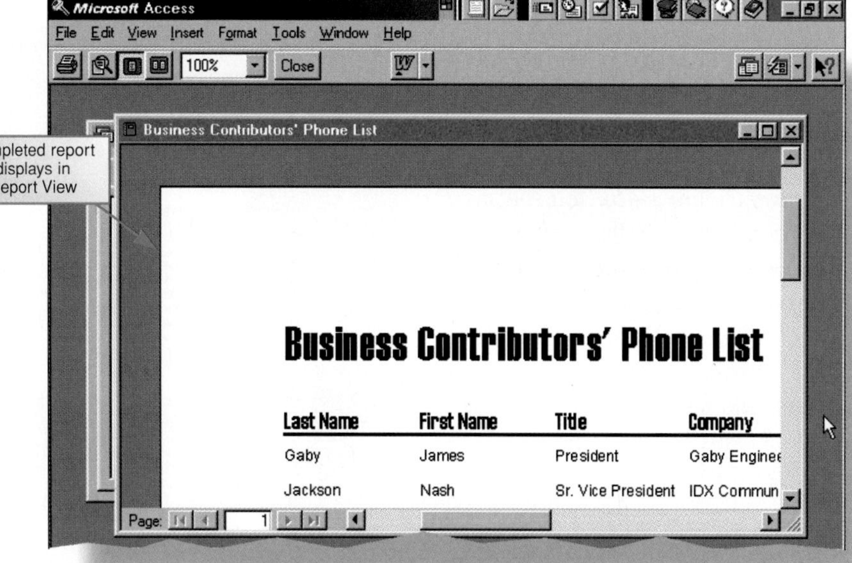

FIGURE 1-49

OtherWays

1. Click Insert on menu bar, click Report, click Report Wizard, click Choose the table or query where the objects data comes from down arrow, select table or query, click OK button
2. Press ALT+I keys, press R keys, press DOWN ARROW key to highlight Report Wizard, press TAB key, press DOWN ARROW to display table or query, press ENTER key.

Saving an Access Report and Closing Access

Because you may want to use the report again, you should save the report before you print it. After printing, you want to close the report and then close Access. The next three sections explain how to save and close a report, print a report, and then close Access.

TO SAVE AND CLOSE AN ACCESS REPORT

Step 1: Click File on the menu bar and then click Save As/Export.

Step 2: Click Within the current database as New Name, if necessary.
Step 3: Verify that Business Contributors' Phone List is in the New name box and then click the OK button.
Step 4: Click the Close button on the Business Contributors' Phone List preview window title bar.

Access saves the report with the filename, Business Contributors' Phone List, and then closes it.

The next section explains how to print an Access report.

Printing an Access Report in Word

Access reports can be printed from Access by clicking the Print command on the File menu or by clicking the Print button on the Standard toolbar. You can also export the report to Word as an RTF, or Rich Text Format, file. The RTF document then can be modified, printed, and saved as a Word document. You can use the Access OfficeLinks feature to export the report to Word. After you export the report to Word, you can format the report to your individual or company standards. The next two sections explain how to export an Access report to Word and how to format, save, and print the report.

Exporting an Access Report to Word

The first step in printing an Access report in Word is to export the report to a file format that Word can recognize. In this project, you export the Access report to a Rich Text Format (RTF) file. Perform the following steps to export an Access report to Word as an RTF file.

To Export an Access Report to Word

1. **Click the OfficeLinks button arrow on the toolbar.**

   The OfficeLinks list displays (Figure 1-50).

FIGURE 1-50

2 **Click Publish It with MS Word.**

After a few moments, Access saves the report as an RTF file, and Word opens and displays the Business Contributors' Phone List.RTF document (Figure 1-51).

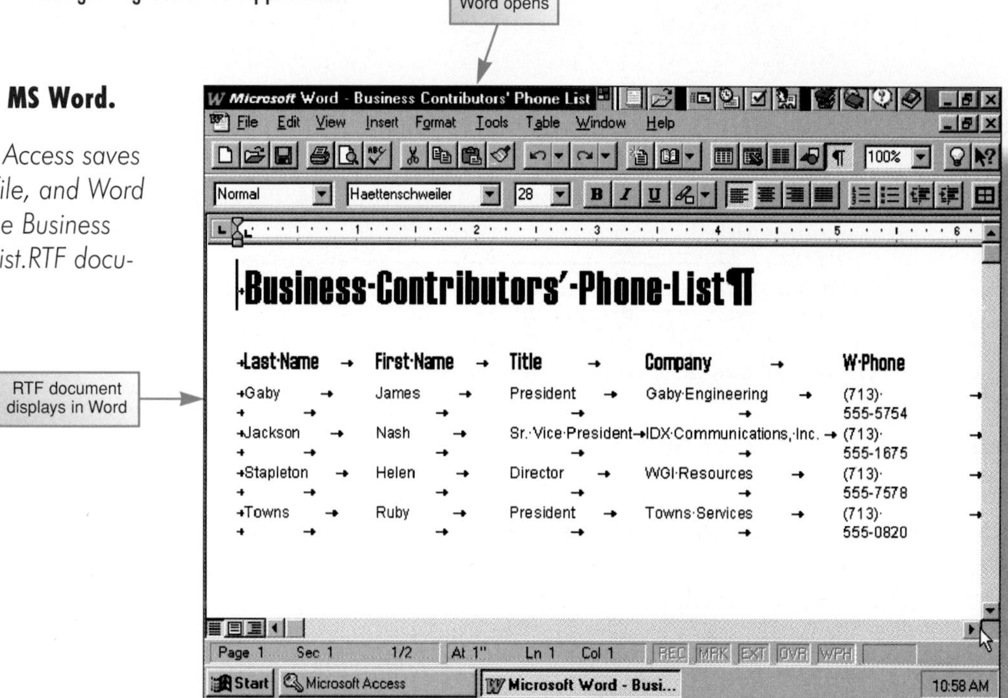

FIGURE 1-51

OtherWays

1. Click Tools on menu bar, point to OfficeLinks, click Publish It With MS Word
2. Press ALT+T keys, press L key, press P key

You can now format, print, and save the Business Contributors' Phone List document using Word's editing features.

Formatting, Saving, Printing, and Closing a Rich Text Format Document in Word

To make the report easier to read, you want to change the right margin of the Pledge column. After you make the column change, save the document and then print it. When you finish printing the document, close Word. Perform the following steps to format, save, print, and then close an RTF document in Word.

TO FORMAT, SAVE, PRINT, AND CLOSE A RICH TEXT FORMAT DOCUMENT IN WORD

Step 1: Select all the lines of text beginning with the column heading line.
Step 2: Scroll to view the far right side of the horizontal ruler.
Step 3: Drag the right-aligned tab stop on the horizontal ruler for the Pledge column to the left approximately ½ inch. Reposition other tab stops as desired and deselect the text.
Step 4: Click File on the menu bar, click Save As on the File menu, click the Save in box arrow, click 3½ Floppy [A:], and double-click the Integration folder icon. Verify that the filename is Business Contributors' Phone List.
Step 5: Click the Save as type box arrow, click Word Document, and then click the Save button.
Step 6: Click the Print button on the Standard toolbar.
Step 7: Click the Close button on the menu bar.

Word saves and prints the Business Contributors' Phone List (Figure 1-52). The Word document is closed, but Word and Access remain open.

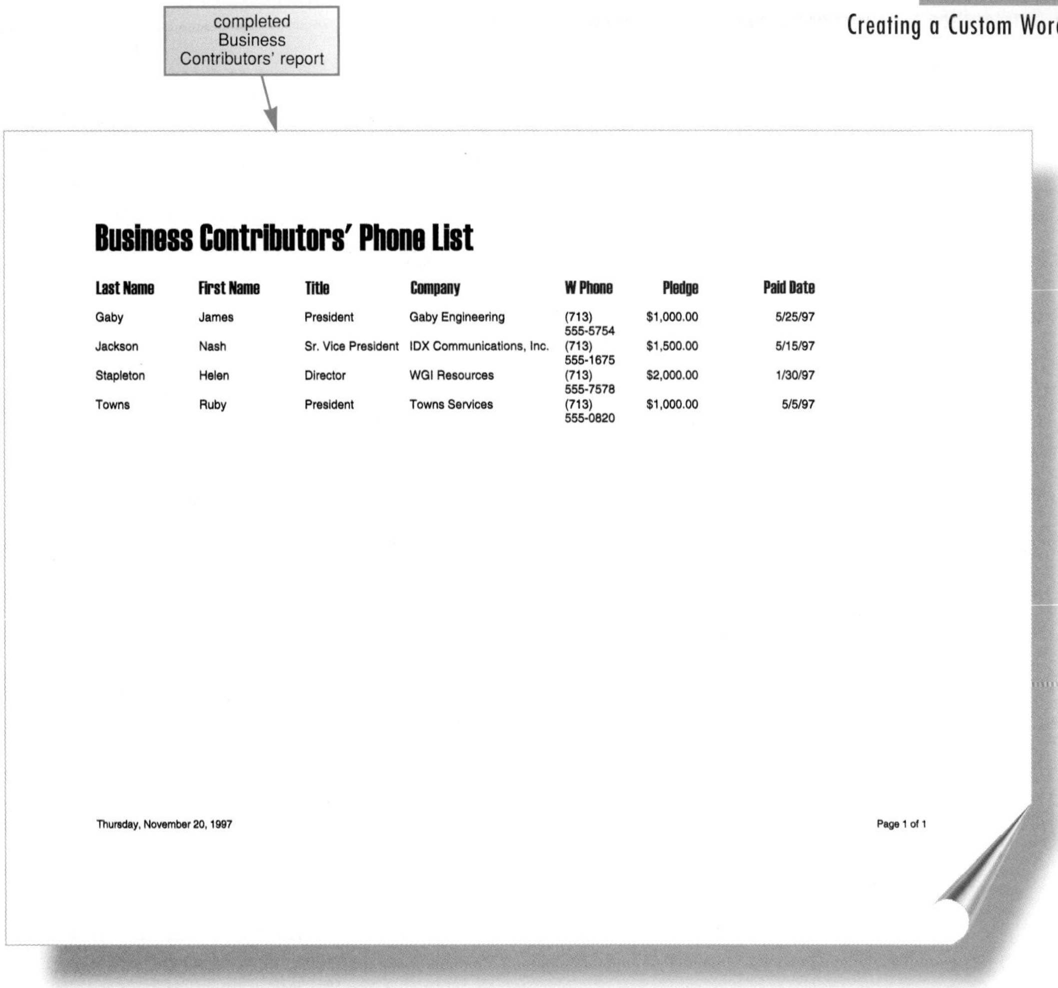

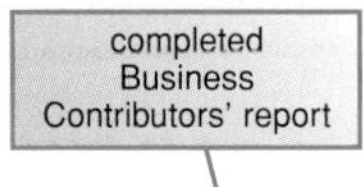

Business Contributors' Phone List

Last Name	First Name	Title	Company	W Phone	Pledge	Paid Date
Gaby	James	President	Gaby Engineering	(713) 555-5754	$1,000.00	5/25/97
Jackson	Nash	Sr. Vice President	IDX Communications, Inc.	(713) 555-1675	$1,500.00	5/15/97
Stapleton	Helen	Director	WGI Resources	(713) 555-7578	$2,000.00	1/30/97
Towns	Ruby	President	Towns Services	(713) 555-0820	$1,000.00	5/5/97

Thursday, November 20, 1997 Page 1 of 1

FIGURE 1-52

Closing Access and an Access Report

The Business Contributors' Phone List report is complete. The next step is to close the report and Access before you create the invitation letters. Perform the following step to close Access.

TO CLOSE ACCESS AND AN ACCESS REPORT

Step 1: Right-click the Access button on the taskbar and then click Close.

After a few moments, Access closes the Business Contributors' Phone List. Then, Access closes.

More *About* **Templates**

Templates save you time in document preparation, especially if you have several documents that contain similar information. A template is like a blueprint; that is, Word prepares the document according to the predefined text and/or formatting in the template. You then use the template to create your document.

Creating a Custom Word Template

It is not uncommon to use an existing document as a template for a new document, because it is usually quicker to modify an old document than to create a new one. Word allows you to create a custom template and then save it with the other Word templates. After you create a custom template, you can select it from the list of templates that display when you start a new Office document.

This section of the project prepares letters of invitation to the 1998-1999 Fund-Raising Gala for sponsors of Community Youth Programs. The section on the next page provides an overview of the steps necessary to create a custom Word template.

Overview of Steps to Create a Custom Word Template

The basic shell of the template contains the same information as the Solicitation Letter. You use the Template Shell document on the backup floppy disk to create a template by example. You complete the following tasks in this section of the project.

1. Verify that Word is open.
2. Open an existing document.
3. Modify the document to remove any variable information and/or change the text as necessary.
4. Save the document as a template.
5. Close the template document.

The following pages contain a detailed explanation of these tasks.

Opening an Existing Word Document

You want to create a custom template using the Template Shell document. First, you must open the Template Shell document before you can modify it to create your template. Perform the following steps to open the Template Shell document.

TO OPEN AN EXISTING WORD DOCUMENT

Step 1: Verify that Word is open.
Step 2: Click the Open button on the Standard toolbar. If not already selected, click 3½ Floppy [A:] and then double-click the Integration folder icon.
Step 3: Double-click Template Shell.

Word displays the Template Shell document.

Inserting AutoText

The next step is to modify the Template Shell by inserting the AutoText letterhead and then saving the Template Shell as a new custom template as described in the following steps.

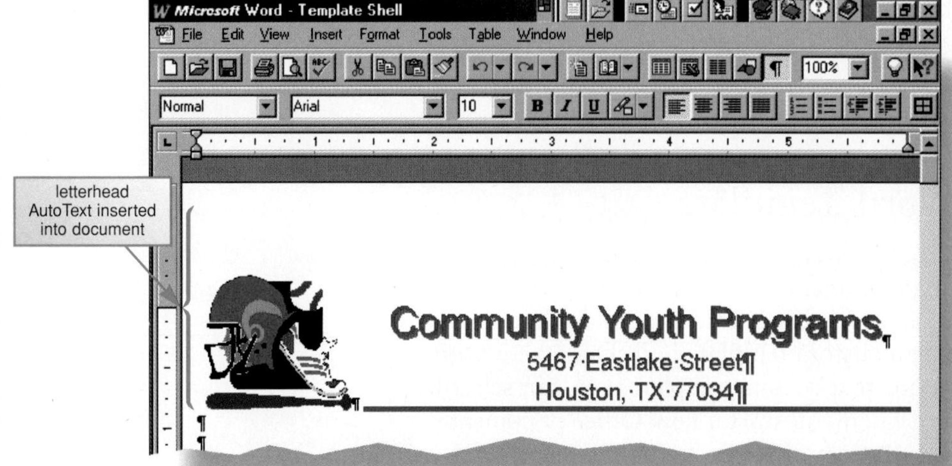

FIGURE 1-53

TO INSERT AUTOTEXT

Step 1: Move the insertion point to the top of the document, if necessary.
Step 2: Type `letterhead` and then press the F3 key to insert the AutoText entry.
Step 3: Click the Page Layout View button and then scroll to view the letterhead.

Word inserts the letterhead AutoText (Figure 1-53).

Saving a Word Document as a Template

If you want this document to become a template, you must save it as a Word template document. Then, to reduce clutter on your desktop, you want to close the template document and minimize Word.

TO SAVE A WORD DOCUMENT AS A TEMPLATE

Step 1: Click File on the menu bar and then click Save As.
Step 2: Type `Invitation Letter` in the File name box.
Step 3: Click the Save File as type box arrow and then click Document Template.
Step 4: Double-click the Letters & Faxes folder.
Step 5: Click the Save button.
Step 6: Click the Close button on the menu bar.
Step 7: Click the Minimize button on the Word title bar.

The new custom template, Invitation Letter, is saved in the Letters & Faxes folder.

You save the Invitation Letter template in the Letters & Faxes folder so that when you start a new Word document, the template is available. Furthermore, an Invitation Letter icon displays on the Letters & Faxes sheet.

The next section explains how to create a Contacts Lists that later will be merged with the Invitation Letter template to create letters.

Creating a Schedule+ Contacts List

You are now ready to use the Invitation Letter template to create invitation letters. First, you must create a Schedule+ Contacts List with the names and addresses of community sponsors. The following section provides an overview of steps necessary to create a Schedule+ Contacts List.

Overview of Steps to Create a Schedule+ Contacts List

The names and addresses of community sponsors are maintained in the Schedule+ Contacts List. You create the Schedule+ Contacts List and then update it with the name, title, company or organization name, and address for each new sponsor. You will complete the following tasks in this section of the project.

1. Open Schedule+.
2. Create a new file.
3. Enter the data for each sponsor.
4. Close Schedule+.

The following pages contain a detailed explanation of each of these steps.

Starting Schedule+ and Creating a New Schedule File

Before you can create a new schedule file, first you must open Schedule+. Then, you save the new schedule file with the filename Community Youth Programs to your floppy disk in drive A as described in the steps on the next page.

TO START SCHEDULE+ AND CREATE A NEW SCHEDULE FILE

Step 1: Click the Start button on the taskbar, point to Programs on the Start menu, and then click Microsoft Schedule+.
Step 2: Type `Student Schedule` in the User name box and then click the OK button.
Step 3: Click I want to create a new schedule file, and then click the OK button.
Step 4: Type `Community Youth Programs` in the File name box.
Step 5: Click the Save in box arrow, click 3½ Floppy [A:], and double-click the Integration folder icon.
Step 6: Click the Save button.
Step 7: Click the Maximize button on the Student Schedule - Microsoft Schedule+ title bar, if necessary.

The Student Schedule – Microsoft Schedule+ window displays (Figure 1-54).

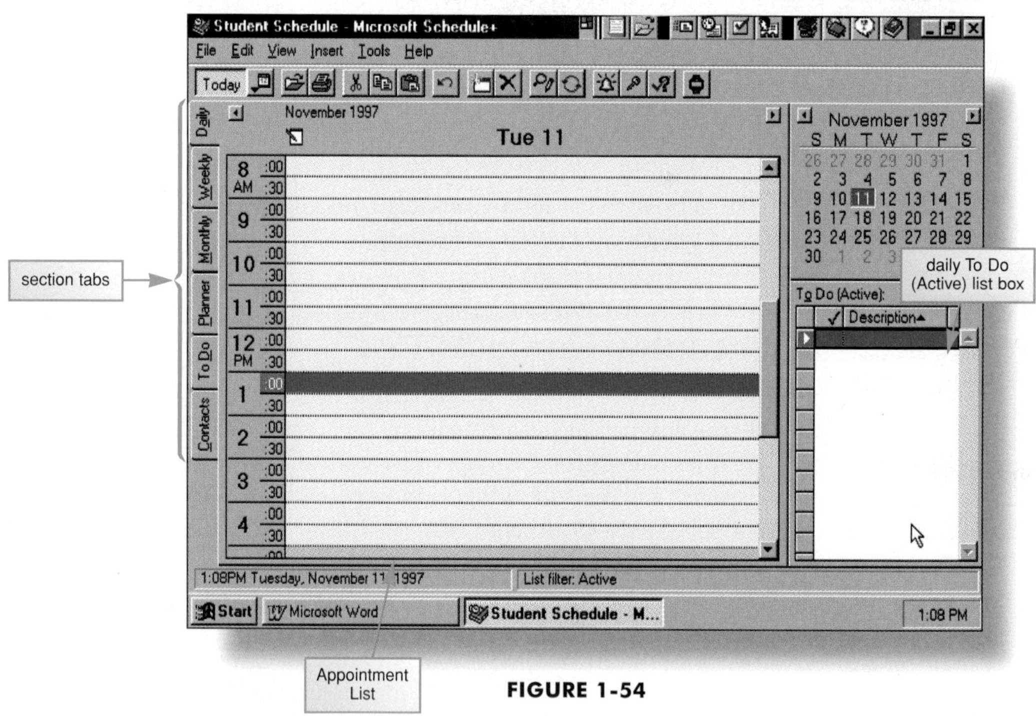

FIGURE 1-54

The next section explains how to update the Contacts List.

Updating a Schedule+ Contacts List

A Contacts List changes from time to time. The Community Youth Programs Contacts List was increased by three. Perform the following steps to add three sponsor contacts to the Schedule+ Contacts List.

More *About* Maintenance

Updating is a global term referring to the process of adding, changing, or deleting. Adding involves adding a record, such as a customer. Changing involves correcting data within an existing record, such as an address. Deleting involves removing an existing record. These three activities are also referred to as maintaining data.

TO UPDATE THE SCHEDULE+ CONTACTS LIST

Step 1: Click the Contacts tab and then click the Insert New Contact button on the toolbar. Click the Business tab, if necessary.
Step 2: In the Name area, type `Ralph` in the First box and then press the TAB key.
Step 3: Type `Dozier` in the Last box and then press the TAB key.

Step 4: Type `2250 Bering Drive` in the Address box and then press the TAB key. (Depending on the installation, your display may be different. If necessary, click the Address tab to enter the address).
Step 5: Type `Houston` in the City box and then press the TAB key.
Step 6: Type `TX` in the State box and then press the TAB key.
Step 7: Type `77057` in the Postal Code box and then press the TAB key twice.
Step 8: Type `President` in the Title box and then press the TAB key.
Step 9: Type `Landsdowne Company` in the Company box and then press the TAB key until the insertion point is in the Phone number box.
Step 10: Type `(713) 555-3214` in the Phone number Business text box and then click the OK button.
Step 11: Repeat Steps 1 through 10 to add the following new sponsor data:

Lucy Kirklin	Robert McIntyre
Vice President	President
Kirklin Enterprises	Hightower Engineering
6960 Bellaire Blvd.	14500 W. Southwind Avenue
Bellaire, TX 77074	Houston, TX 77097
(713) 555-1816	(713) 555-9976

The new contacts are added to the Contacts List (Figure 1-55). The current contact displays highlighted in the Contacts box.

Closing Schedule+

The updates to the Contacts List are complete and you no longer need to keep Schedule+ open. Perform the following step to close Schedule+.

TO CLOSE SCHEDULE+

Step 1: Click the Close button on the Student Schedule – Microsoft Schedule+ title bar.

Schedule+ closes.

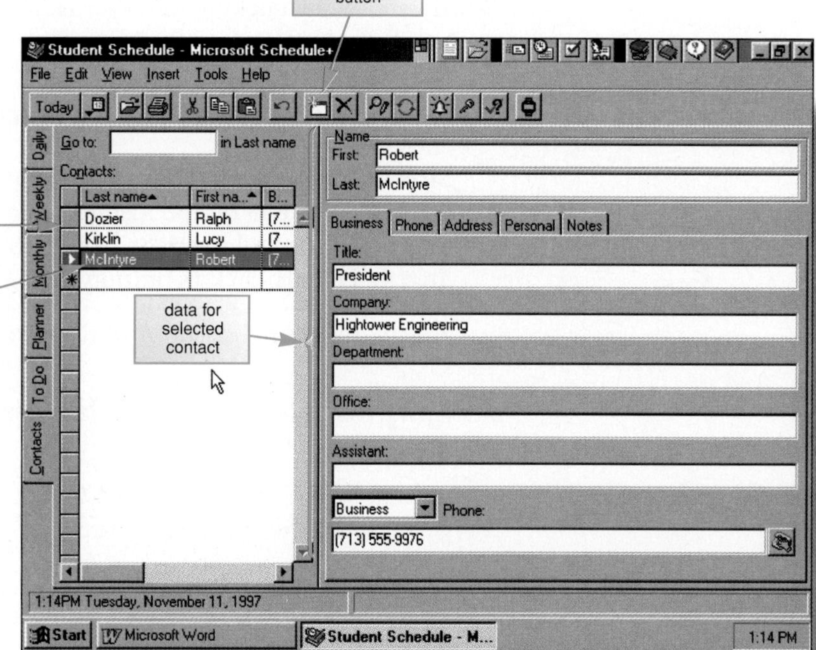

FIGURE 1-55

Creating a Document Based on a Custom Template and a Schedule+ Contacts List

The next step is to merge the names and addresses from the Schedule+ Contacts List into letters created from the Invitation Letter template. The section on the next page provides an overview of the steps necessary to create invitation letters by merging the Contacts List with a template document.

Overview of Steps to Create a Document Based on a Custom Template and the Schedule+ Contacts List

Invitation letters and envelopes must be prepared for the three sponsors in the Schedule+ Contacts List. You complete the following tasks in this section of the project.

1. Display the New dialog box.
2. Select the type of template document.
3. Select the appropriate template and create a new document based on the template.
4. Merge the data from the Schedule+ Contacts List.
5. Save the merge document.
6. Print the merged letters.

The following pages contain a detailed explanation of these tasks.

Creating a Document Based on a Custom Word Template

Recall that you created a custom template earlier in this project. You use this template to create the invitation letters for the three new sponsors in the Schedule+ Contacts List. Because Word is open, but minimized, you maximize the Word window by clicking the Microsoft Word button on the taskbar as explained in the following steps.

TO CREATE A DOCUMENT BASED ON A CUSTOM WORD TEMPLATE

Step 1: Click the Microsoft Word button on the taskbar.
Step 2: Click File on the menu bar and then click New.
Step 3: Click the Letters & Faxes tab.
Step 4: Double-click Invitation Letter.

A new document based on the Invitation Letter template displays.

Merging Data from a Schedule+ Contacts List into a Word Document

The next step in creating the invitation letters is to merge the name and address data from the Schedule+ Contacts List. Perform the following steps to merge data into the Invitation Letter.

TO MERGE DATA FROM THE SCHEDULE+ CONTACTS LIST INTO A WORD DOCUMENT

Step 1: Move the insertion point to the blank line above the salutation.
Step 2: Click Tools on the menu bar and then click Mail Merge.
Step 3: Click the Create button and then click Form Letters.
Step 4: Click the Active Window button.
Step 5: Click the Get Data button and then click Use Address Book.
Step 6: Click Schedule+ Contact List, if necessary, and then click the OK button.
Step 7: Verify Student Schedule is in the User name box and then click the OK button.
Step 8: Click the Edit Main Document button.
Step 9: Click the Insert Merge Field button on the Merge toolbar, click First_Name in the Merge Field list, and then press the SPACEBAR.

Step 10: Click the Insert Merge Field button, click Last_Name in the Merge Field list, and then press the ENTER key.
Step 11: Continue inserting the Job_Title, Company, Business_Address, Business_City, Business_State, and Business_ZipCode fields to complete the inside address. Press the ENTER key after the Business_ZipCode merge field is inserted. Remember to insert the appropriate spaces, punctuation, and new lines as necessary for an inside address.
Step 12: Click before the colon in the salutation and then insert the First_Name field.
Step 13: Click File on the menu bar, click Save As, click the Save in box arrow, click 3½ Floppy [A:], and double-click the Integration folder icon, if necessary.
Step 14: Type `Sponsor Letter` in the File name box and then click the Save button.

Fields from the Contacts List display in the Sponsor Letter document (Figure 1-56).

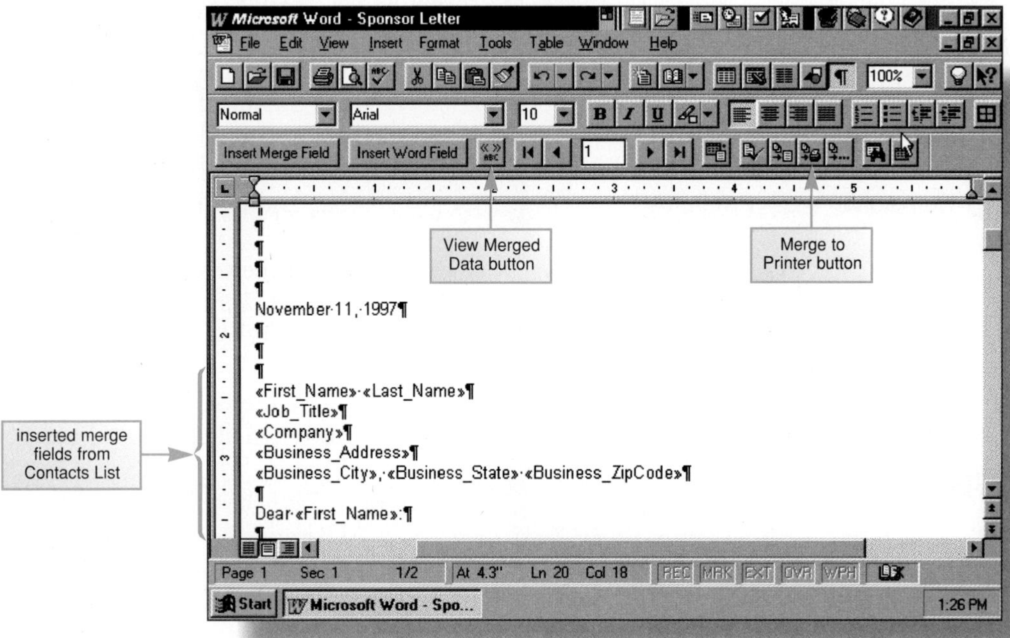

FIGURE 1-56

Previewing and Printing Mail Merge Letters

The Sponsor Letter document is ready to preview with the merge fields displaying data from the Contacts List. When you are satisfied with the merged document, print the letters. Perform the following steps to preview and then print the merged Sponsor Letter.

TO PREVIEW AND PRINT MAIL MERGE LETTERS

Step 1: Click the View Merged Data button on the Mail Merge toolbar.
Step 2: Click the View Merged Data button on the Mail Merge toolbar to turn off the preview and return to the Sponsor Letter main document.
Step 3: Click the Merge to Printer button on the Mail Merge toolbar and then click the OK button to print one copy of each of the merged letters.

Step 4: Click the Close button on the menu bar to close the Sponsor Letter main document.

Step 5: Click Yes to save any changes to the Sponsor Letter main document, if necessary.

Word prints the merged letters and then closes the Sponsor Letter main document. The first of the three letters is shown in Figure 1-57. If you made changes to the document after the last save, Word prompts you to save the document before closing it, as explained in Step 5.

Creating Envelopes from a Schedule+ Contacts List

You can create envelopes for letters by merging an envelope document with the Schedule+ Contacts List. Perform the following steps to merge the Schedule+ Contacts List data to create envelopes.

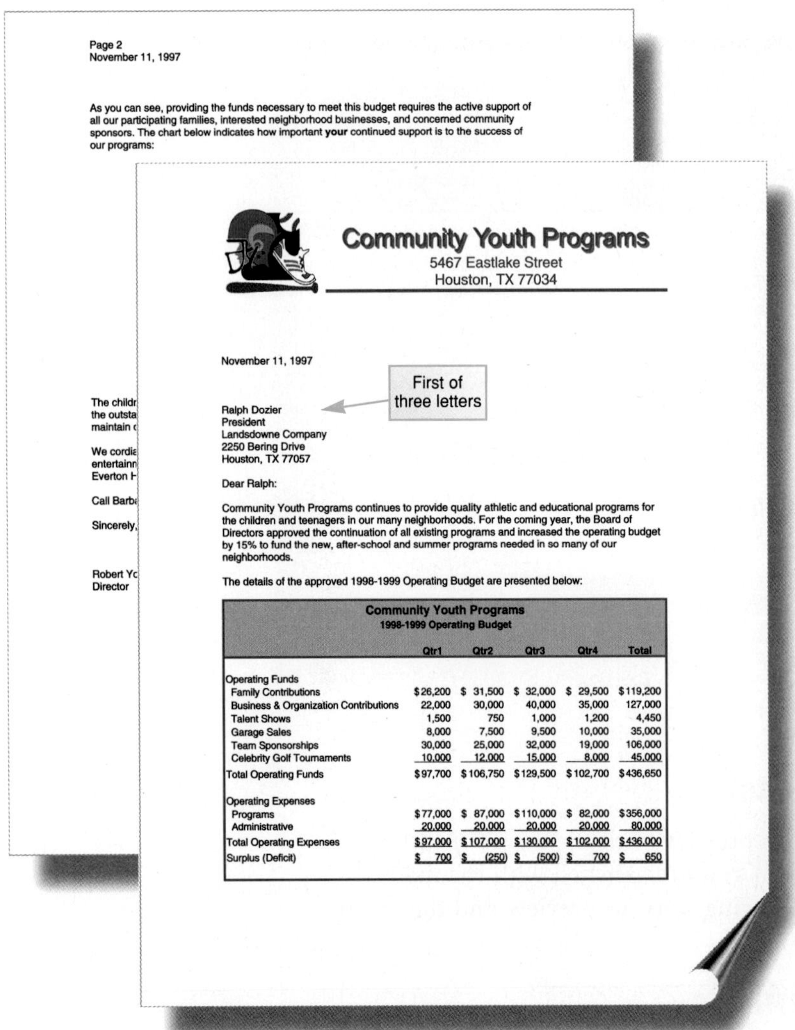

Page 2
November 11, 1997

As you can see, providing the funds necessary to meet this budget requires the active support of all our participating families, interested neighborhood businesses, and concerned community sponsors. The chart below indicates how important **your** continued support is to the success of our programs:

Community Youth Programs
5467 Eastlake Street
Houston, TX 77034

November 11, 1997

Ralph Dozier
President
Landsdowne Company
2250 Bering Drive
Houston, TX 77057

Dear Ralph:

Community Youth Programs continues to provide quality athletic and educational programs for the children and teenagers in our many neighborhoods. For the coming year, the Board of Directors approved the continuation of all existing programs and increased the operating budget by 15% to fund the new, after-school and summer programs needed in so many of our neighborhoods.

The details of the approved 1998-1999 Operating Budget are presented below:

Community Youth Programs
1998-1999 Operating Budget

	Qtr1	Qtr2	Qtr3	Qtr4	Total
Operating Funds					
Family Contributions	$26,200	$ 31,500	$ 32,000	$ 29,500	$119,200
Business & Organization Contributions	22,000	30,000	40,000	35,000	127,000
Talent Shows	1,500	750	1,000	1,200	4,450
Garage Sales	8,000	7,500	9,500	10,000	35,000
Team Sponsorships	30,000	25,000	32,000	19,000	106,000
Celebrity Golf Tournaments	10,000	12,000	15,000	8,000	45,000
Total Operating Funds	$97,700	$106,750	$129,500	$102,700	$436,650
Operating Expenses					
Programs	$77,000	$ 87,000	$110,000	$ 82,000	$356,000
Administrative	20,000	20,000	20,000	20,000	80,000
Total Operating Expenses	$97,000	$107,000	$130,000	$102,000	$436,000
Surplus (Deficit)	$ 700	$ (250)	$ (500)	$ 700	$ 650

FIGURE 1-57

TO CREATE ENVELOPES FROM A SCHEDULE+ CONTACTS LIST

Step 1: Click the New button on the Standard toolbar to create a new, blank document.

Step 2: Click Tools on the menu bar and then click Mail Merge.

Step 3: Click the Create button and then click Envelopes.

Step 4: Click the Active Window button.

Step 5: Click the Get Data button and then click Use Address Book.

Step 6: Click Schedule+ Contacts List and then click the OK button.

Step 7: Verify that Student Schedule is in the User name box and then click the OK button.

Step 8: If necessary, open the existing Community Youth Programs Schedule+ file.

The Mail Merge Helper dialog box displays.

Setting Up an Envelope Main Document

You set up the main envelope document by specifying the envelope size and then inserting the desired merge fields into the document as described in the following steps.

TO SET UP AN ENVELOPE MAIN DOCUMENT

Step 1: Click the Set Up Main Document button.
Step 2: Click the Envelope Size arrow, click Size 10, which is a standard 4 1/8 x 9 1/2-inch envelope, and then click the OK button.
Step 3: Click the Insert Merge Field button, click First_Name in the Merge Field list, and then press the SPACEBAR.
Step 4: Click the Insert Merge Field button, click Last_Name in the Merge Field list, and then press the ENTER key.
Step 5: Continue inserting the Job_Title, Company, Business_Address, Business_City, Business_State, and Business_ZipCode fields to complete the inside address. Press the ENTER key after the Business_ZipCode merge field is inserted. Remember to insert the appropriate spaces, punctuation, and new lines as necessary for a mailing address.
Step 6: Click the OK button.
Step 7: Click the Close button.

The envelope main document displays (Figure 1-58).

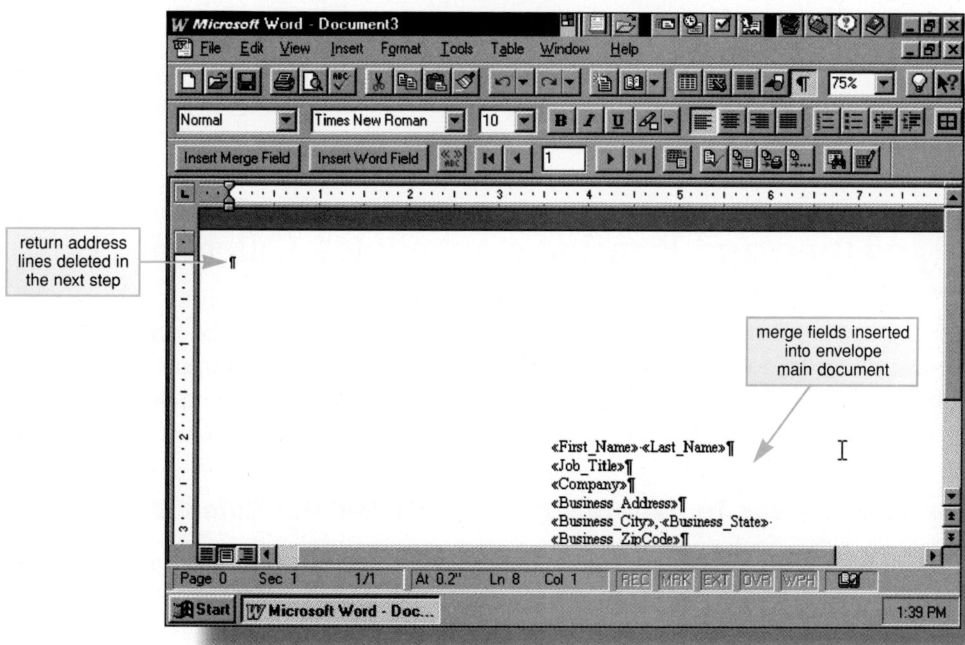

FIGURE 1-58

Previewing, Editing, and Printing a Merge Document

You can now preview the envelope merge, correct any errors, and then print the envelopes as described in the following steps.

TO PREVIEW, EDIT, AND PRINT A MERGE DOCUMENT

Step 1: Click the View Merged Data button on the Merge toolbar.

Step 2: Verify that the data and the envelope format are correct. Notice the return address. You are using envelopes that have a preprinted return address; therefore, you delete the return address on the envelope main document.
Step 3: Click the View Merged Data button on the Merge toolbar to return to the label main document.
Step 4: Select the lines of the return address and then press the DELETE key.
Step 5: Click the Merge to Printer button on the Merge toolbar and then click the OK button in the Print dialog box.

Word prints the envelopes merging data from the Contacts List.

Saving and Closing a Document

After you print the envelopes, you should save and close the envelope main document and minimize Word. Perform the following steps to save and close the envelope document.

TO SAVE AND CLOSE A DOCUMENT

Step 1: Click File on the menu bar, click Save As, click the Save in box arrow, click 3½ Floppy [A:], and double-click the Integration folder icon, if necessary.
Step 2: Type `Sponsor Envelopes` in the File name box.
Step 3: Click the Save button and then click the Close button on the menu bar.
Step 4: Click the Minimize button on the Word title bar.

Word saves the envelope document with the filename, Sponsor Envelopes. The Word window is minimized.

Updating and Printing a Schedule+ Calendar

After the Invitation Letters are printed, you are ready to update the Schedule+ calendar of events to include the Annual Fund-Raising Gala on January 24, 1998 beginning at 7:30PM. You then print the January calendar. The next section provides a list of steps necessary to update and print a Schedule+ calendar.

Overview of Steps to Update and Print a Schedule+ Calendar

To maintain the Schedule+ calendar, you should add or remove events and appointments. You will complete the following tasks in this section of the project.

1. Open Schedule+.
2. Select the schedule file to be updated.
3. Enter or delete the event from the calendar.
4. Close Schedule+.

The following pages contain a detailed explanation of these tasks.

Updating a Schedule+ Calendar

A **schedule** is an organizational tool used to keep track of appointments and tasks. Microsoft Office has a scheduling application called Schedule+. In order to maximize the potential of Schedule+, you must routinely make changes to your schedule. This includes adding new appointments, changing existing appointments, and deleting old or cancelled appointments. Perform the following steps to update a Schedule+ calendar to include the Fund-Raising Gala.

TO UPDATE A SCHEDULE+ CALENDAR

Step 1: Click the Start button on the taskbar, point to Programs on the Start menu, and then click Microsoft Schedule+.
Step 2: Verify that Student Schedule is in the User name box and then click the OK button.
Step 3: Maximize the Schedule+ window, click the right selection arrow in the top right corner of the calendar until the January calendar displays, and then click the 24th day in the body of the calendar.
Step 4: Scroll the Appointment List to view the 7:30 PM time slot and then click 7:30 PM.
Step 5: Type `Fund-Raising Gala` in the Appointment List in the 7:30 PM time slot and then, if necessary, click the Reminder button on the toolbar to turn off the reminder bell.

The Fund-Raising Gala is scheduled. You turned off the reminder bell to prevent it from sounding. The ***reminder bell*** *functions like an alarm clock to remind you of appointments.*

Printing a Schedule+ Calendar

Recall from the beginning of this project, Mr. Younger wants to review the January calendar. Schedule+ allows you to print a calendar for a day, a week, or a month. When you print a calendar in Schedule+, it prints all scheduled appointments for the designated time period. For example, if you print a monthly calendar, then all appointments for the month display on the date for which they were scheduled. Perform the following steps to print the calendar for January.

To Print a Schedule+ Calendar

1 Click File on the menu bar and then click Print.

The Print dialog box displays (Figure 1-59). You specify the layout, quality, font, page format, setup, and date range for the calendar in this dialog box.

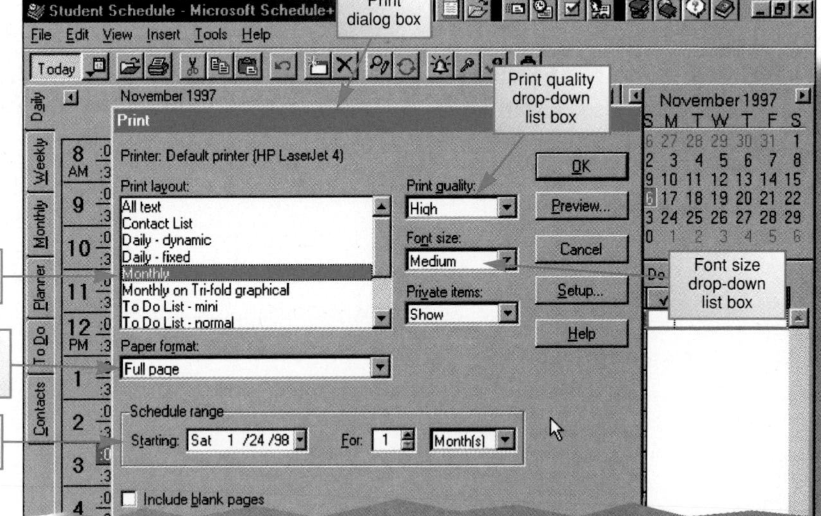

FIGURE 1-59

2 **Click Monthly in the Print layout list box, if necessary. Verify that the Paper format is Full page, the Print quality is High, the Font size is Medium, and Show displays in the Private items list box. Click 24 in the Starting box to select it, type 1 and then verify that 1 and Month(s) appear in the For text boxes (Figure 1-60).**

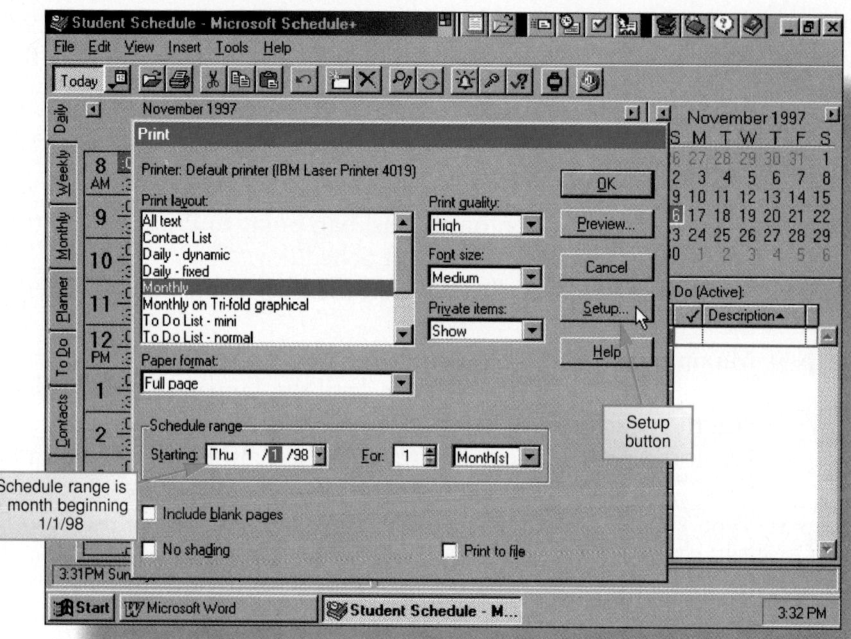

FIGURE 1-60

3 **Click the Setup button.**

The Print Setup dialog box displays (Figure 1-61). You specify the printer, paper size, margins, and paper orientation in this dialog box.

4 **Click the Printer box arrow and then select the appropriate printer. Verify that Letter 8½ x 11 is in the Form box. Click Landscape, change the top, bottom, left, and right margins to .5 inch, if necessary, and click the OK button. Click the OK button in the Print dialog box. Click the Close button on the Schedule+ title bar.**

Schedule+ prints the January calendar and then closes.

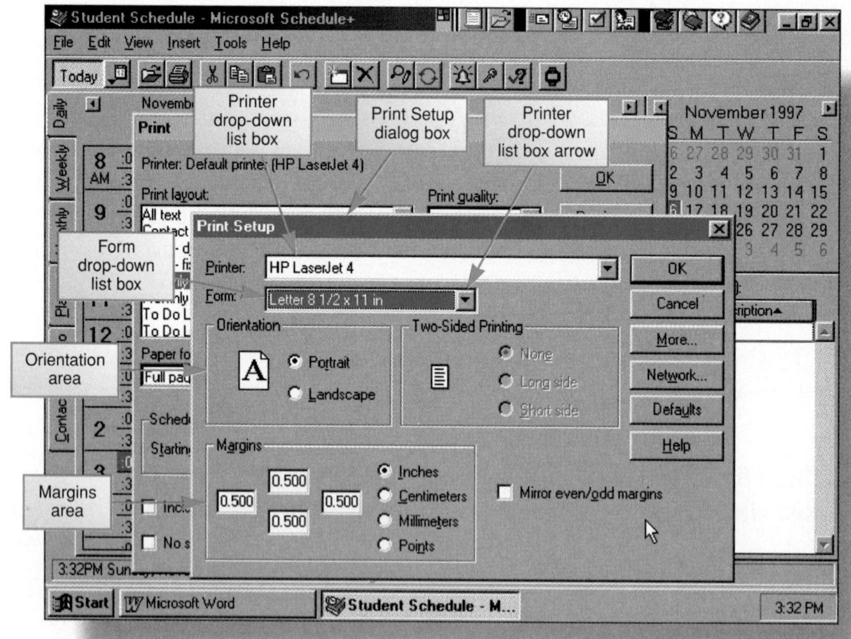

FIGURE 1-61

OtherWays

1. Click Print button on Standard toolbar
2. Press ALT+F keys, press P key
3. Press CTRL+P keys

Figure 1-4 on page I 1.9 illustrates a printed Schedule+ calendar.

Creating a Slide Show Presentation

The solicitation letters and labels, the Business Contributors' Phone List report, the Fund-Raising Gala invitation letters and envelopes, and the updated calendar for January are prepared. Next, you complete the project by creating a slide show presentation to be given by Mr. Younger at the Fund-Raising Gala. The next section provides a list of steps necessary to create a slide show presentation.

Overview of Steps to Create a Slide Show Presentation

You create the slide show presentation using PowerPoint. The presentation includes a title slide, a bulleted list slide identifying different athletic programs, a slide containing data from the Excel Budget With Chart workbook, a slide displaying the Pie chart from the Excel Budget With Chart workbook, a slide with an organization chart, and a blank slide at the end of the presentation for a graceful closing. You apply a Design Template to the presentation and add clip art to the Slide Master and Title Master. Finally, you add text build effects and slide transition effects to enhance the presentation. You complete the following tasks in this section of the project.

1. Start PowerPoint.
2. Create a new blank presentation.
3. Create the desired slides using the AutoLayout formats.
4. Copy and paste data from Word and Excel onto appropriate slides.
5. Apply a Design Template to the presentation.
6. Modify the Slide Master and Title Master.
7. Add text build and slide transition effects to the appropriate slides.
8. Modify the Handout Master.
9. Display the slides in Slide Show view.
10. Save the presentation.
11. Print slides.
12. Close PowerPoint.

The following pages contain a detailed explanation of each of these steps.

Starting PowerPoint and Creating a Blank Presentation

This presentation uses the default Blank Presentation template to create the slide show. Perform the following steps to start PowerPoint and create a blank presentation.

TO START POWERPOINT AND CREATE A BLANK PRESENTATION

Step 1: Click the Start button on the taskbar and then click New Office Document on the Start menu.

Step 2: Click the General tab, if necessary, and then double-click Blank Presentation.

PowerPoint applies the Blank Presentation template and then displays the New Slides dialog box.

Creating a Title Slide

Next, you create the individual slides in the presentation. The first slide you create is the title slide. PowerPoint assumes that every presentation has a title slide and automatically selects the Title Slide AutoLayout in the AutoLayout dialog box.

PowerPoint also assumes every slide has a title and, therefore, automatically selects the title object placeholder when a new slide displays. As a result, you can type the slide title without first selecting the title object. Perform the following steps to create a title slide.

TO CREATE A TITLE SLIDE

Step 1: Click the Title Slide AutoLayout, if necessary, and then click the OK button.
Step 2: Type `Community Youth Programs` as the title.
Step 3: Click the sub-title placeholder and then type `1998-1999 Operating Year` as the subtitle.

The title slide is complete (Figure 1-62).

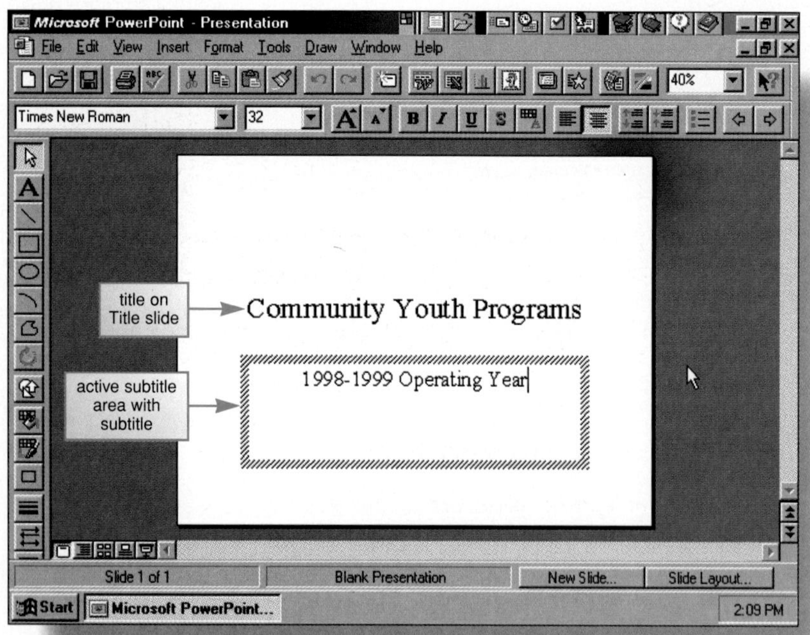

FIGURE 1-62

Creating a Bulleted List Slide

The next step is to create a bulleted list slide. You create this slide by copying text in a Word document and then pasting the text onto a PowerPoint slide. Creating the bulleted list slide for this project requires several steps. This section describes creating the bulleted list slide by adding a new slide, typing a slide title, opening a Word document, and then copying the Word document text. The next section describes how to paste the copied text onto the PowerPoint slide. Perform the following steps to create a bulleted list slide using text copied in a Word document.

TO CREATE A BULLETED LIST SLIDE

Step 1: Click the New Slide button on the status bar. When the New Slide dialog box displays, double-click Bulleted List.
Step 2: Type `Community Youth Programs` as the slide title.
Step 3: Click the bulleted list placeholder.
Step 4: Click the Microsoft Word button on the taskbar and then click the Open button on the Standard toolbar.
Step 5: Click the Look in box arrow, click 3½ Floppy [A:], and double-click the Integration folder icon, if necessary.
Step 6: Double-click Presentation List.

Step 7: Select the entire document, right-click the selection, and then click Copy on the shortcut menu.
Step 8: Click the Microsoft PowerPoint button on the taskbar and then click the Paste button on the Standard toolbar.
Step 9: Press the BACKSPACE key, if necessary, to remove the extra bullet.

The text copied from the Word document is pasted onto the slide and displays in the text object (Figure 1-63). After you paste text from another document, you sometimes see an extra bullet without text on the slide. This happens when you copy a paragraph mark from the original document. Pressing the BACKSPACE *key removes the extra bullet.*

Closing Word

You no longer need Word or any Word documents. Perform the following step to close Word.

TO CLOSE WORD

Step 1: Right-click the Microsoft Word button on the taskbar and then click Close.

Word closes and the PowerPoint window displays.

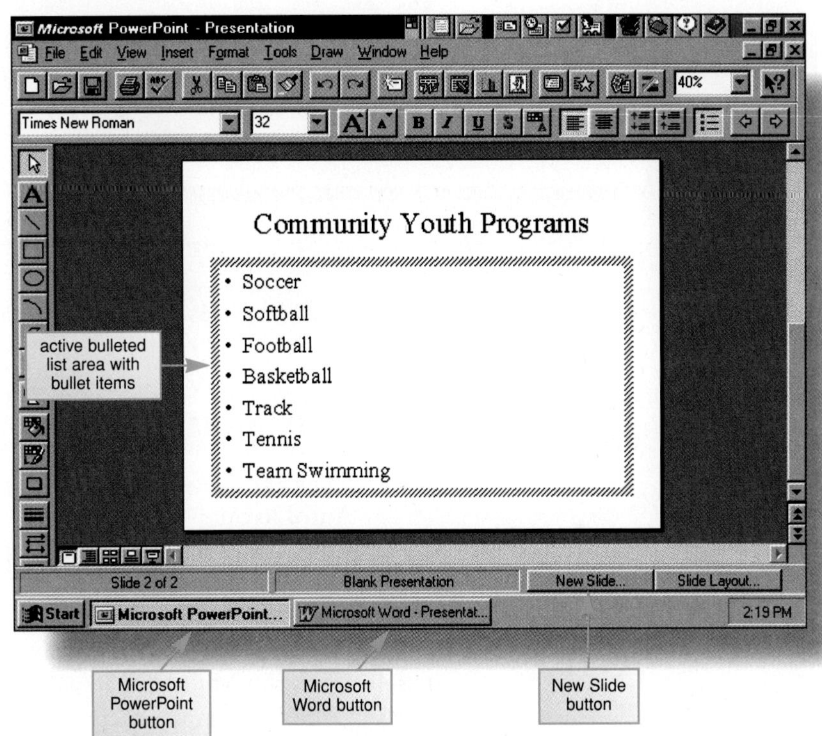

FIGURE 1-63

Linking Excel Data to a Slide

The next step is to copy and paste link the data and chart from the Excel Budget With Chart workbook to the next two slides. Because you want more than one object from the same workbook, you use the Paste Link function of the Paste Special command to link the objects instead of using the PowerPoint Object AutoLayout. Perform the following steps to paste link Excel worksheet data and a Pie chart to PowerPoint slides.

TO PASTE LINK EXCEL DATA TO A SLIDE

Step 1: Click the New Slide button and then double-click Blank AutoLayout.
Step 2: Click the Start button on the taskbar and then click Open Office Document on the Start menu.
Step 3: Click the Look in box arrow, click 3½ Floppy [A:], and double-click the Integration folder icon, if necessary.
Step 4: Double-click Budget With Chart.
Step 5: Select the cells in the range A1:F20, right-click the range, and then click Copy on the shortcut menu.
Step 6: Click the Microsoft PowerPoint button on the taskbar.
Step 7: Click Edit on the menu bar and then click Paste Special.
Step 8: Click Paste Link and then click the OK button.

Step 9: Press and hold down the CTRL key and then drag the resize handles until the Excel worksheet object is enlarged and positioned attractively on the slide. Release the CTRL key.

The Budget worksheet displays on Slide 3 (Figure 1-64).

FIGURE 1-64

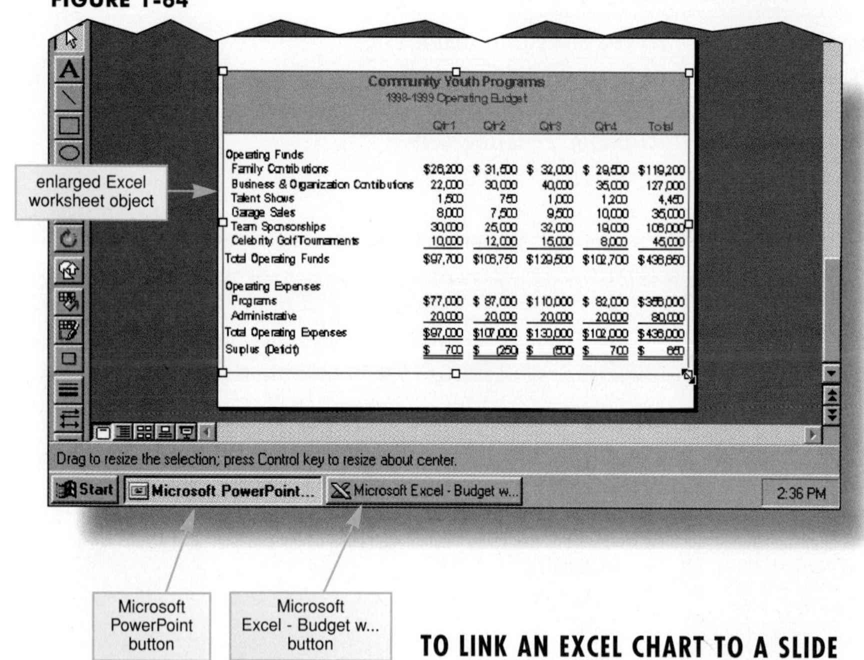

When you hold down the CTRL key and drag a resize handle, as in Step 9, you constrain, or restrict, the object so all resizing occurs about its center point. This is called **resizing about center.**

Linking an Excel Chart to a Slide

Slide 4 of the Community Youth Programs slide show contains the embedded Pie chart in the Budget worksheet. You again use the paste link function to link the pie chart to the slide as described in the following steps.

TO LINK AN EXCEL CHART TO A SLIDE

Step 1: Click the New Slide button, and then double-click the Blank AutoLayout.
Step 2: Click the Microsoft Excel button on the taskbar and then scroll to view the embedded chart.
Step 3: Right-click the embedded chart and then click Copy on the shortcut menu.
Step 4: Click the Microsoft PowerPoint button on the taskbar.
Step 5: Click Edit on the menu bar and then click Paste Special.
Step 6: Click Paste Link and then click the OK button.
Step 7: Press and hold down the CTRL key and then drag the upper right resize handle until the chart is enlarged and attractively positioned on the slide.
Step 8: Right-click the Microsoft Excel button on the taskbar and then click Close on the shortcut menu.

The Pie chart displays on Slide 4 (Figure 1-65). Excel closes.

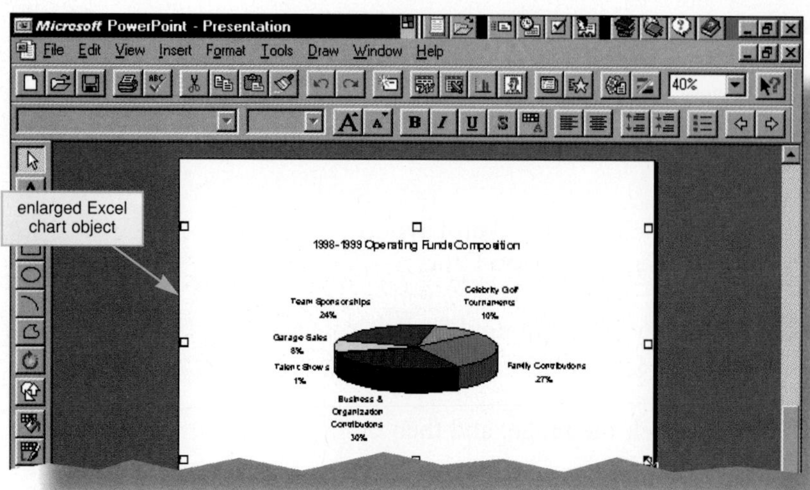

FIGURE 1-65

Creating an Organization Chart Slide

The next step is to create an Organization Chart slide that highlights the Administrative Staff of Community Youth Programs. Perform the following steps to create a slide containing an organization chart.

TO CREATE AN ORGANIZATION CHART SLIDE

Step 1: Click the New Slide button, and then double-click the Organization Chart AutoLayout.
Step 2: Type `Administrative Staff` for the title.
Step 3: Double-click the add org chart placeholder.
Step 4: When the Microsoft Organization Chart – [Object in Presentation] window displays, type `Robert Younger` in the first level box and then press the ENTER key.
Step 5: Type `Director` as the title text.
Step 6: Click the left box on the second level, type `Dorothy Blevins`, and then press the ENTER key.
Step 7: Type `Athletic Director` as the title text.
Step 8: Repeat Steps 6 and 7 to complete the remaining boxes on the second level using the following information:
James Bradley, Finance Director
Lena Garcia, Membership Director
Step 9: Click the Subordinate button on the toolbar and click the first level box for Robert Younger.
Step 10: Type `Barbara Michaels` and then press the ENTER key.
Step 11: Type `Administrative Assistant` as the title text.
Step 12: Click the Organization Chart background to deselect the boxes.

The organization chart displays in the Microsoft Organization Chart window (Figure 1-66).

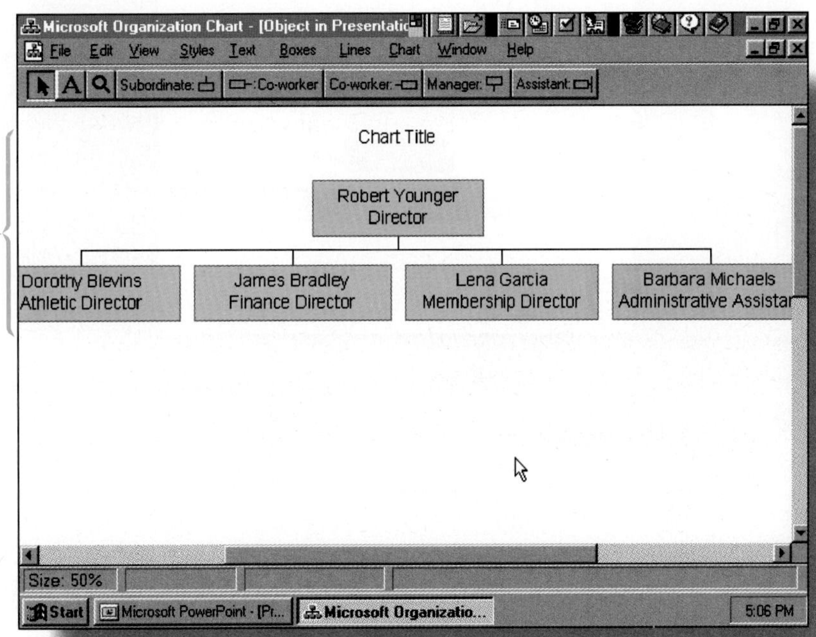

FIGURE 1-66

The next section explains how to format the organization chart.

Formatting an Organization Chart

To make the completed organization chart more attractive and easier to read, format the box borders for style and color, and then change the color inside the boxes. Perform the steps on the next page to format an organization chart.

TO FORMAT AN ORGANIZATION CHART

Step 1: Click Edit on the menu bar, point to Select, and then click All on the submenu.
Step 2: Click Boxes on the menu bar, point to Border Style, and then click the third style box in the first column.
Step 3: Click Boxes on the menu bar, click Border Color, click black, and then click the OK button.
Step 4: Click Boxes on the menu bar, click Color, click medium blue (row 2, column 4), and then click the OK button.
Step 5: Click Text on the menu bar, click Color, click white, and then click the OK button.
Step 6: Click File on the menu bar and then click Exit and Return to Presentation.
Step 7: Click Yes in the Microsoft Organization Chart dialog box.
Step 8: Press and hold down the CTRL key, and then drag the upper right resize handle to enlarge the organization chart and position it attractively on the slide.

The organization chart displays on Slide 5 (Figure 1-67).

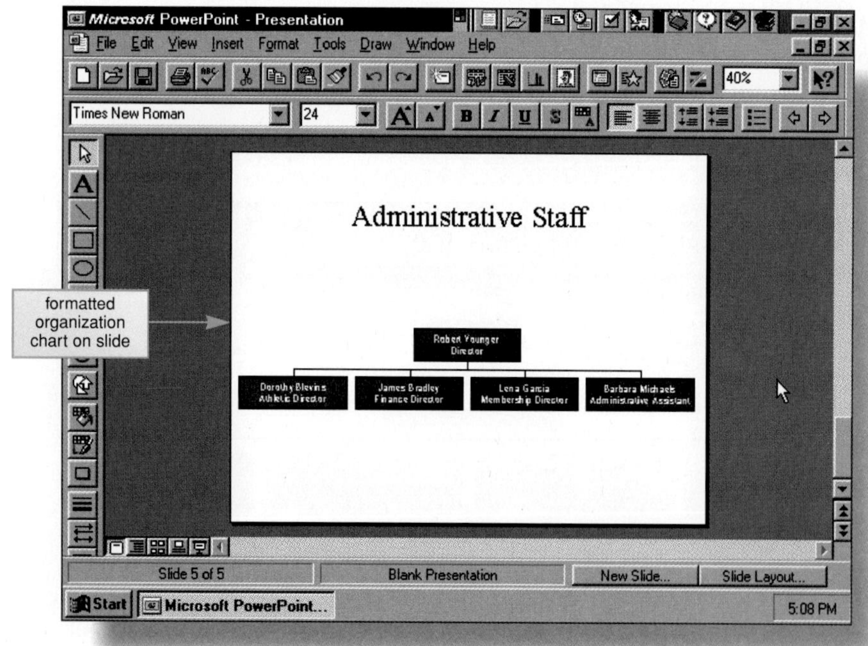

FIGURE 1-67

Adding a Blank Closing Slide

To complete the slide show and create a graceful ending to the presentation, add a blank slide to the end of the presentation. Perform the following steps to add a blank closing slide.

TO ADD A BLANK CLOSING SLIDE

Step 1: Click the New Slide button and then click the Blank AutoLayout.
Step 2: Click the OK button.

Slide 6 displays without objects.

Applying a Design Template and Modifying the Color Scheme

Applying a Design Template to the presentation makes it more interesting. Another way to make a presentation interesting is to edit the Slide Master to add clip art, dates, and other objects so they appear on all the slides. Additionally, you can edit the Title Master to add objects to the title slide. In this project, you apply a Design Template, modify the slide color scheme, and add a clip art object to the Slide and Title Masters. The next section explains how to apply and then modify a Design Template. Later in this project, you add clip art to the masters. Perform the following steps to apply a Design Template and then modify its color scheme.

TO APPLY A DESIGN TEMPLATE AND MODIFY THE COLOR SCHEME

Step 1: Drag the elevator on the vertical scroll bar to display Slide 1.
Step 2: Double-click Blank Presentation on the status bar.
Step 3: When the Apply Design Template dialog box displays, double-click Comet in the Name list box.
Step 4: Right-click anywhere on the slide except on an object. Click Slide Color Scheme on the shortcut menu.
Step 5: Click the Standard tab, if necessary. In the Color Schemes area of the Standard sheet, click the color scheme with the medium blue background color (row 2, column 2).
Step 6: Click the Apply to All button.

Slide 1 displays the Comet Design Template. PowerPoint applies the Comet Design Template to all slides in the presentation. The new color scheme replaces the default color scheme of the Comet Design Template.

Editing the Title Master and Slide Master

Changes made to the Title Master display only on the title slide. Changes made to the Slide Master display on every slide except the title slide. When you want an object to display on every slide, including the title slide, you must add it to both masters. To both masters, add the same clip art picture you added to the letterhead in the Solicitation Letter document. Perform the following steps to add clip art to every slide by editing the Title Master and Slide Master.

TO EDIT THE TITLE MASTER AND SLIDE MASTER

Step 1: Press and hold down the SHIFT key and then click the Slide View button to display the Title Master. Release the SHIFT key.
Step 2: Click the Insert Clip Art button on the Standard toolbar.
Step 3: Scroll the Category list box to display Sports & Leisure. Click Sports & Leisure in the Categories list and then click the Sports.wmf picture in the Pictures list.
Step 4: Click the Insert button to insert the clip art onto the Title Master.
Step 5: Click Draw on the menu bar, click Scale, type 50 in the Scale To box, and then click the OK button.
Step 6: Drag the clip art object to the bottom right corner of the Title Master.
Step 7: Right-click the clip art and then click Copy on the shortcut menu.
Step 8: Drag the elevator on the vertical scroll bar to display the Slide Master.
Step 9: Right-click the Slide Master anywhere except on a placeholder and then click Paste on the shortcut menu.
Step 10: Click the Slide View button to observe the Title slide with the clip art picture in the bottom right corner of the slide.
Step 11: Drag the elevator to scroll the slides to view the Comet Design Template, color scheme, and clip art object. Make adjustments to the size of the clip art object, if desired, by redisplaying the appropriate master and scaling the object.

The Sports clip art displays on each slide in the slide show as shown in Figure 1-68 on the next page.

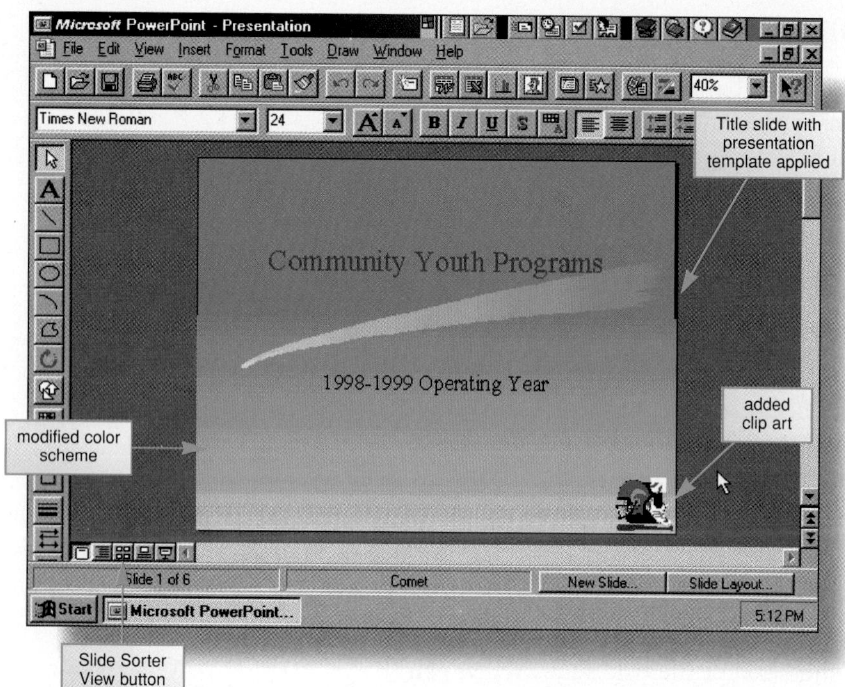

FIGURE 1-68

Adding Text Build Effects, Slide Transition Effects, and Viewing a Slide Show

Adding text build effects and slide transition effects make a slide show presentation more interesting. In this project, you add text build effects to the bulleted list slide and slide transition effects to all the slides. You then view the slide presentation on your computer screen. Perform the following steps to add the text build effects, slide transition effects, and then view the slide show.

TO ADD TEXT BUILD EFFECTS, SLIDE TRANSITION EFFECTS, AND VIEW A SLIDE SHOW

Step 1: Click the Slide Sorter View button.
Step 2: Click Slide 2.
Step 3: Click the Text Build Effects box arrow and then click Fly From Left.
Step 4: Click Edit on the menu bar and then click Select All.
Step 5: Click the Slide Transition Effects box arrow and then click Blinds Horizontal.
Step 6: Click the Slide Show button to view the presentation. Click to move through the text builds on the bulleted list slide and to advance from one slide to the next.
Step 7: When the slide show is finished, click the Slide View button.

The slide show is complete. Slide 1 displays in Slide view.

Saving, Spell Checking, and Printing Presentation Slides

To finalize the presentation, save it, spell check it, and then print the slides.

TO SAVE, SPELL CHECK, AND PRINT PRESENTATION SLIDES

Step 1: Click the Save button on the Standard toolbar.
Step 2: Type `Community Youth Presentation` in the File name box.
Step 3: Click the Save in box arrow, click 3½ Floppy [A:], and double-click the Integration folder icon, if necessary.
Step 4: Click the Save button.
Step 5: Click the Spelling button on the Standard toolbar. Make any necessary corrections and save the presentation again, if necessary.

Step 6: Click the Print button on the Standard toolbar to print the slides.
Step 7: Click the Close button on the PowerPoint title bar.

PowerPoint saves the presentation, checks for spelling errors, and prints the presentation slides as shown in Slide 2 in Figure 1-69.

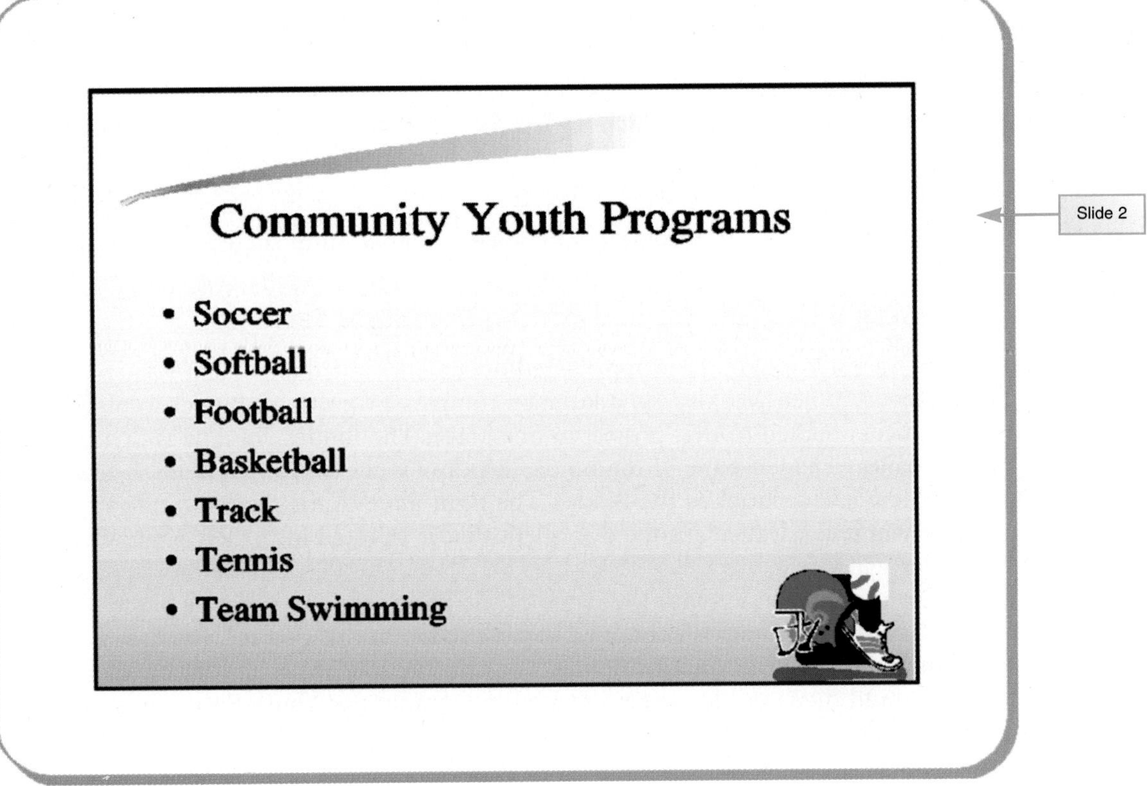

FIGURE 1-69

Creating a Binder

Now that all the tasks related to the fund-raising activities are complete, it might be helpful for future use to have some of the fund-raising documents placed together in a Binder. When you open a Binder, all of the documents are available for editing or printing. You place the fund-raising documents for Community Youth Programs in a new Binder. The section on the next page provides an overview of the steps necessary to create a new Binder.

More About Binders

Think of a binder as a project notebook. You may purchase a 3-ring binder to hold all documents for a college class. Likewise, a binder contains all information relative to a particular project. Working with the binder as a unit makes the project much more manageable and efficient.

Overview of Steps for Creating a Binder

Each document you store in a Binder becomes a separate section of the Binder. You can edit and print individual sections of a Binder. You also can control the appearance of printed pages in a Binder by changing Page Setup. You complete the following tasks in this section of the project.

1. Create a new Binder.
2. Add documents to a Binder.
3. Save a Binder.
4. Close a Binder.
5. Open an existing Binder.
6. Select and edit a document in a Binder section.
7. Select and print Binder sections.

The following pages contain a detailed explanation of these tasks.

Creating a New Binder and Adding Document Sections

Binder allows you to group related documents together to help you stay organized. When working on a large or complex project, use Binder to place all documents related to that project in one place. The Binder window is divided into two panes. The left pane of the Binder window is the **section list pane.** It lists the document sections in the Binder. The right pane of the Binder window is the **document pane.** It displays the document that is selected in the left pane of the Binder window.

You save a Binder with the name of the project or a descriptive name that identifies the documents contained in the Binder. In this project, you create a Community Youth Programs Binder. Perform the following steps to create a new Binder and then add documents related to Community Youth Programs to the new Binder.

Steps To Create a New Binder and Add Document Sections

1 Click the Start button on the taskbar, point to Programs, and then click Microsoft Binder on the Programs menu. Click the Maximize button on the Microsoft Office Binder – Binder1 title bar, if necessary.

The Microsoft Office Binder – Binder1 window displays (Figure 1-70). You will add the Community Youth Programs fund-raising documents to this Binder.

FIGURE 1-70

2 **Click Section on the menu bar and then click Add from File.**

The Add from File dialog box displays (Figure 1-71). You select the document file to be added to the Binder in this dialog box.

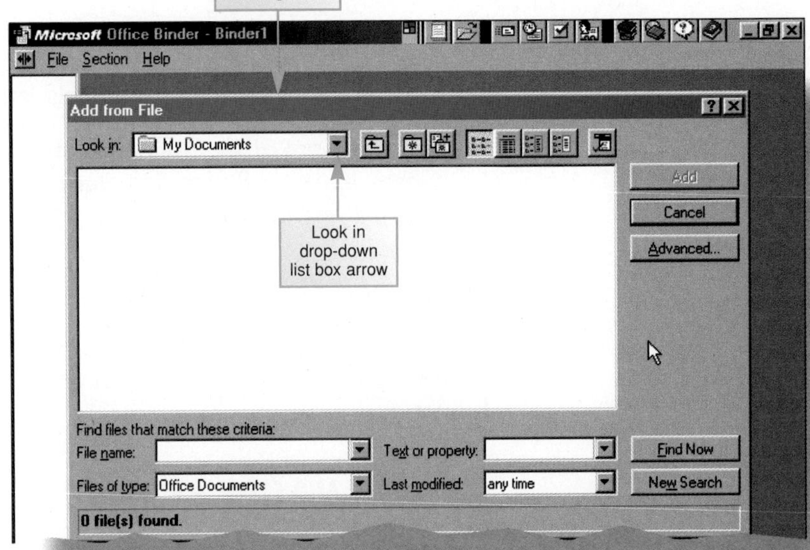

FIGURE 1-71

3 **Click the Look in box arrow, click 3½ Floppy [A:], double-click the Integration folder icon, and double-click Budget With Chart.**

After a few moments, the Budget With Chart Excel workbook is added as a section to the Binder (Figure 1-72). You can display the entire document for editing by clicking the Binder button that is located to the left of the File menu name on the menu bar.

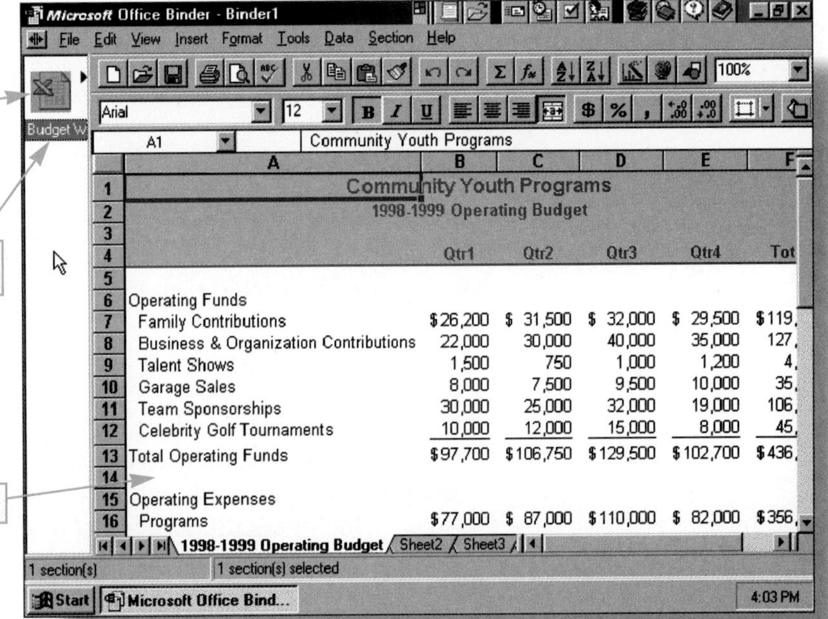

FIGURE 1-72

OtherWays

1. Press CTRL+N keys
2. Press ALT+F keys, press N key

You now can add the remaining fund-raising documents to the Binder. Perform the following steps to finish adding the Community Youth Programs fund-raising documents to the Binder.

TO ADD DOCUMENTS TO A BINDER

Step 1: Click Section on the menu bar and then click Add from File.
Step 2: Click the Look in box arrow and then click 3½ Floppy [A:], if necessary.

Step 3: Double-click Sponsor Letter.
Step 4: Repeat Steps 1 through 3 for the following documents: Solicitation Letter, Solicitation Labels, and Community Youth Presentation.

The left pane of the Binder window lists five document sections: Budget With Chart, Sponsor Letter, Solicitation Letter, Solicitation Labels, and Community Youth Presentation.

Saving and Closing a Binder

To preserve the new Binder, save it using the name of the project. Perform the following steps to save the Binder for Community Youth Programs and then close Binder.

TO SAVE AND CLOSE A BINDER

Step 1: Click File on the menu bar, click Save Binder As, click the Save in box arrow, click 3½ Floppy [A:], and double-click the Integration folder icon, if necessary.
Step 2: Type `Community Youth Programs` in the File name box and then click the Save button.
Step 3: Click the Close button on the Binder title bar.

Binder saves the Community Youth Programs Binder and then closes.

Opening a Binder

When you want to make changes to a document in a Binder, first you must start Binder and then open the Binder you want to edit. Perform the following steps to start Binder and then open the Community Youth Programs Binder.

TO OPEN A BINDER

Step 1: Click the Start button on the taskbar, and then click Open Office Document on the Start menu.
Step 2: Click the Look in box arrow, click 3½ Floppy [A:], and double-click the Integration folder icon, if necessary.
Step 3: Double-click Community Youth Programs.

The Community Youth Programs Binder opens.

Selecting and Editing a Binder Section

You now can select a document section, edit the document section, select multiple document sections, and print document sections. Perform the following steps to select and print a Binder section.

Steps To Select and Edit a Binder Section

1 Click Sponsor Letter in the Section list.

The Sponsor Letter section is selected (Figure 1-73). You can now edit the text in the document.

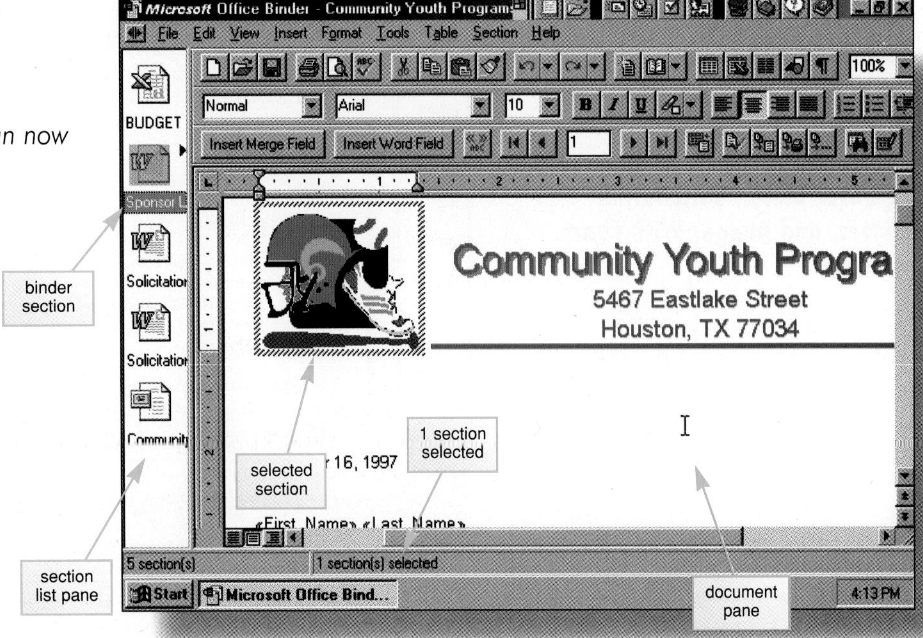

FIGURE 1-73

2 Click the Binder button to hide the section list pane and enlarge the document pane containing the Sponsor Letter document. Scroll to view the first paragraph in the body of the letter.

The document pane is enlarged to display the Sponsor Letter document (Figure 1-74). The section list pane of the Binder window is hidden.

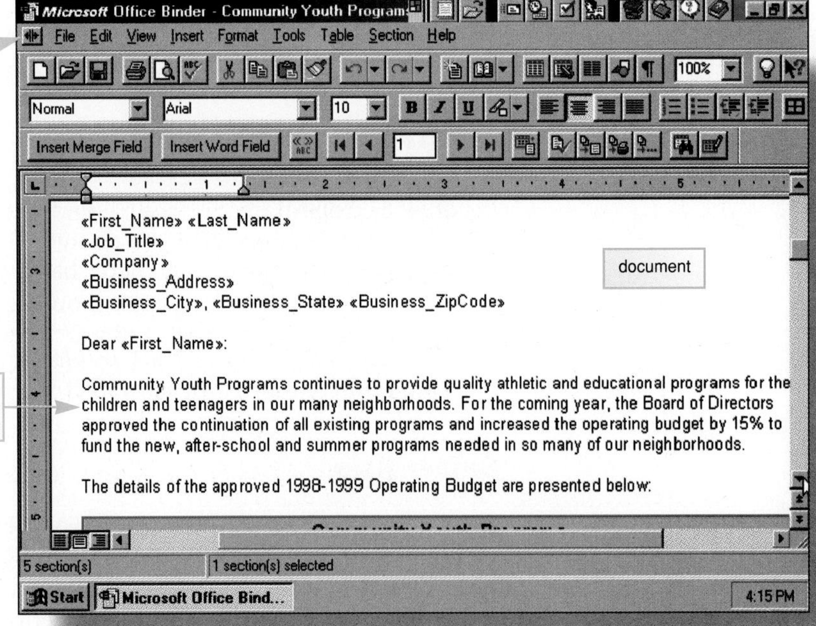

FIGURE 1-74

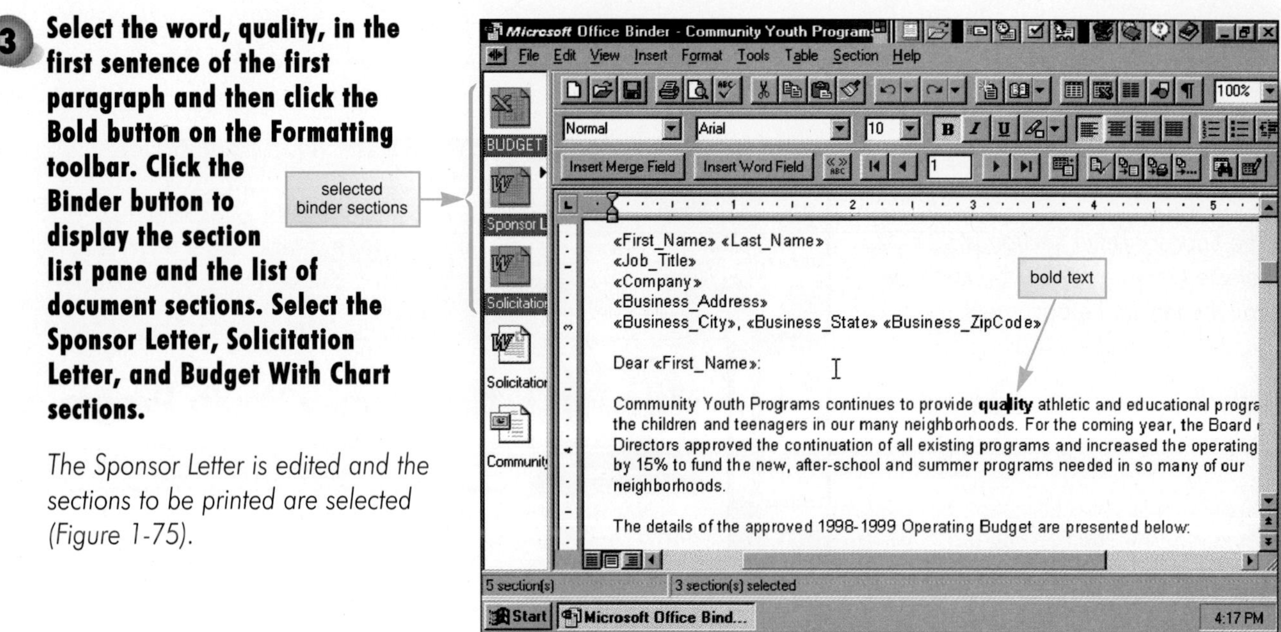

FIGURE 1-75

Printing, Saving, and Closing a Binder

The selected Binder sections are ready to print. After you print the document sections, you save the Binder to save the edits made to the Sponsor Letter document section. Perform the following steps to print, save, and then close a Binder.

TO PRINT, SAVE, AND CLOSE A BINDER

Step 1: Click File on the menu bar, click Print Binder, click Selected Sections, and then click the OK button.
Step 2: Click File on the menu bar and then click Save Binder.
Step 3: Click the Close button on the Binder title bar.

The selected sections of the Binder are printed. The Community Youth Programs Binder is saved, and Binder is closed.

Binder Help

As in all Microsoft Office applications, Binder has online Help; but when you display a document section in the document pane, you can access online Help for both Binder and the application in which the document was created. For example, when the Sponsor Letter document section displays in the document pane of the Binder window and you click Help on the menu bar, a submenu displays Binder Help and Word Help. You then can click the submenu to select the type of online Help you want.

Project Summary

Integrating Office 95 programs increases your productivity by combining documents to produce letters, reports, and presentations. In this Integration project, you created documents with Word, merged Word documents with data maintained in an Access database table and with data in your Schedule+ Contacts List, and linked data and charts created in Excel to your Word documents. You also created an interesting and dynamic slide show presentation by copying text created in Word, and then pasting the text to a slide. You also linked data and charts created in Excel to slides in your presentation. You then stored all your related documents together in a Binder so you can open, edit, print, and save them together.

What You Should Know

Having completed this project, you should be able to perform the following tasks:

- Add a Blank Closing Slide *(I 1.62)*
- Add a Clip Art Object to a Letterhead *(I 1.21)*
- Add a Color Border to a Paragraph *(I 1.20)*
- Add and Format Letterhead Text *(I 1.20)*
- Add Blank Lines and a Date Field *(I 1.23)*
- Add Documents to a Binder *(I 1.67)*
- Add Text Build Effects, Slide Transition Effects, and View a Slide Show *(I 1.64)*
- Apply a Design Template and Modify the Color Scheme *(I 1.63)*
- Copy and Paste Link an Excel Chart to a Word Document *(I 1.26)*
- Copy and Paste Link Excel Worksheet Data to a Word Document *(I 1.25)*
- Create a Bulleted List Slide *(I 1.58)*
- Create a Document Based on a Custom Word Template *(I 1.50)*
- Create a New Binder and Add Document Sections *(I 1.66)*
- Create a Title Slide *(I 1.58)*
- Create an Access Query *(I 1.27, 1.38)*
- Create an Access Report Using Report Wizard *(I 1.39)*
- Create an Organization Chart Slide *(I 1.61)*
- Create Envelopes from a Schedule+ Contacts List *(I 1.52)*
- Edit the Title Master and Slide Master *(I 1.63)*
- Export an Access Report to Word *(I 1.43)*
- Format, Save, Print, and Close a Rich Text Format Document in Word *(I 1.44)*
- Insert a Frame Around a Clip Art Object and Move a Clip Art Object *(I 1.22)*
- Insert AutoText *(I 1.46)*
- Insert Merge Fields into a Word Document *(I 1.30)*
- Link an Excel Chart to a Slide *(I 1.60)*
- Merge an Access Query with a New Word Document to Create Mailing Labels *(I 1.34)*
- Merge an Access Query with a Word Document in Access *(I 1.29)*
- Merge Data from the Schedule+ Contacts List into a Word Document *(I 1.50)*
- Paste Link Excel Data to a Slide *(I 1.59)*
- Preview and Print Mail Merge Letters *(I 1.32, 1.51)*
- Preview, Edit, and Print a Merge Document *(I 1.53)*
- Print a Schedule+ Calendar *(I 1.55)*
- Resize an Embedded Chart and Remove the Border *(I 1.12)*
- Rotate Pie Slices in an Embedded Chart *(I 1.13)*
- Save a Word Document as a Template *(I 1.47)*
- Save an AutoText Entry *(I 1.23)*
- Save, Spell Check, and Print Presentation Slides *(I 1.64)*
- Select a Data Range for an Embedded Chart *(I 1.11)*
- Select a Query for a Mail Merge Document *(I 1.35)*
- Select and Edit a Binder Section *(I 1.69)*
- Set Up a Label Main Document *(I 1.36)*
- Set Up an Envelope Main Document *(I 1.53)*
- Size a Clip Art Object *(I 1.22)*
- Start Schedule+ and Create a New Schedule File *(I 1.48)*
- Update a Schedule+ Calendar *(I 1.55)*
- Update the Schedule+ Contacts List *(I 1.48)*
- Use WordArt to Create Letterhead Text *(I 1.16)*

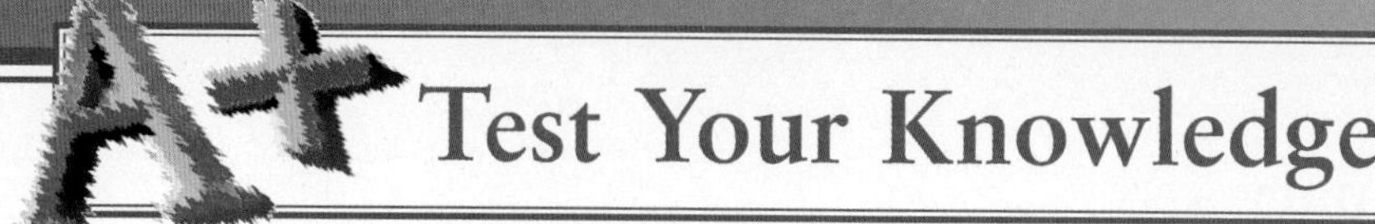

Test Your Knowledge

1 True/False

Instructions: Circle T if the statement is true or F if the statement is false.

T F 1. To move a clip art object in Word, drag a sizing handle.

T F 2. Placing a frame on a clip art object in Word allows you to position the clip art into the text of the document.

T F 3. To save AutoText in Word, click Edit on the menu bar and then click AutoText.

T F 4. The OfficeLinks feature in Access merges an Access query with a Word document.

T F 5. To insert an AutoText entry into a document, type the AutoText entry name and then press the F8 key.

T F 6. Word has a Report Wizard that quickly generates a report based on the fields chosen from a query.

T F 7. You can use Access database table fields only to merge data to a Word document.

T F 8. In PowerPoint, placing clip art on the Slide Master causes it to display on every slide in the presentation.

T F 9. The right, or document, pane of the Binder window lists the documents in the Binder.

T F 10. To print a selected Binder document section, click the Print button on the Standard toolbar.

2 Multiple Choice

Instructions: Circle the correct response.

1 Merging data from an Access database table to a Word document may take place either within Access using the Access __________ feature, or within Word using the Word __________ feature.
   a. Query, OfficeLinks
   b. Insert Merge Field, Query
   c. Mail Merge, OfficeLinks
   d. OfficeLinks, Mail Merge

2. To link Access table fields to a Word document, click __________ on the menu bar and then click Mail Merge to start the mail merge.
   a. Insert
   b. Format
   c. Tools
   d. Edit

3. You can use the Access __________ feature to export an Access report to Word.
   a. Analyze
   b. Report
   c. OfficeLinks
   d. Forms

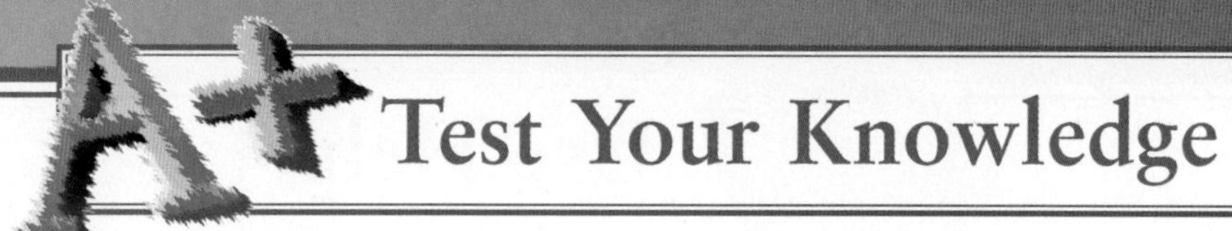

Test Your Knowledge

4. To insert an AutoText entry into a Word document, type the AutoText entry name and then press the __________ key.
   a. F1
   b. F2
   c. F3
   d. F4
5. To view data in a merge document before printing, click the __________ button.
   a. Merge to Printer
   b. Insert Merge Field
   c. View Merged Data
   d. Insert Word Field
6. Schedule+ prints appointment calendars for __________.
   a. a day, a week, a month, or a year
   b. a day, a week, or a year
   c. a day, a week, or a month
   d. all of the above
7. The __________ command on the PowerPoint Edit menu links an Excel chart to a PowerPoint slide.
   a. Paste
   b. Paste Special
   c. Paste Link
   d. all of the above
8. During the running of a PowerPoint slide show, the effect that removes one slide from the screen and then displays the next is called __________.
   a. Slide Show
   b. Slide Transition
   c. Build Slide Transition
   d. Build Slide Text
9. The left pane of the Binder window displays __________.
   a. toolbars for the selected document section
   b. a list of document sections
   c. the selected document
   d. all of the above
10. When a PowerPoint presentation section is open in Binder and you click Help on the menu bar, you can get online Help for __________.
    a. Binder
    b. PowerPoint
    c. both a and b
    d. none of the above

? Use Help

1 Learning More about Microsoft Office Binder

Instructions: Perform the following tasks using a computer.

1. Start Office Binder. Click Help on the menu bar and then click Office Binder Help Topics to display the Help Topics: Binder dialog box.
2. Click the Contents tab. Double-click Creating, Opening, and Saving Binders. Double-click Templates included with Office Binder. Read and print the information in the Binder Help window.
3. Click the link at the bottom of the Binder Help window. Read and print the Create a binder template information.
4. Click the Help Topics button to return to the Help Topics: Binder dialog box. Double-click Modify a binder template. Read and print the Modify a binder template information. Click the sections jump. Then read and print the binder section ScreenTip.
5. Close the binder section ScreenTip. Close the Binder Help window and then close Binder. Submit the printouts to your instructor.

2 Expanding on the Basics

Instructions: Use online Help in the appropriate Microsoft Office application to better understand the topics listed below. Answer the questions on a separate piece of paper.

1. When using Microsoft Binder, how do you:
   a. Control the appearance of printed pages?
   b. Print headers and footers for a binder?
   c. Check the spelling of documents in a binder?
2. When using Microsoft Schedule+, how do you:
   a. Automatically schedule an event to occur the fourth Sunday in March every year?
   b. Display two time zones on your daily schedule?
   c. Set a reminder for a task in your To Do List?
3. When using Microsoft Word, how do you:
   a. Reconnect a link when the source file moves or is renamed?
   b. Use AutoText to create an automatic signature for e-mail messages?
   c. Edit an AutoText entry?

1 Integrating Access, Word, and Excel to Create Mail Merge Documents

Problem: Every year, HomeTown High School tests sophomore students for English, Math, and Science proficiency. The State Board of Education calculates the test results and then generates a printed report that consists of student information and test scores. Because HomeTown High School recently switched to Microsoft Office, you have been requested to create a student database that contains the student data and test scores and then use that data to generate a mail merge letter to report test results to each student tested. Also included in the letter is a graph reporting regional averages. *Hint:* Use Help to solve this problem.

Instructions: Perform the following tasks:

1. Use Access and the table in Figure 1-76 on the next page to create the student database. Save the database with the filename, Student Test Results.
2. Create an Excel worksheet and column chart for the average scores from the information in Figure 1-77 on the next page. Save the worksheet with the filename, 1997 Test Averages.
3. Create and print form letters to be sent to each student using the format shown in Figure 1-78 on the next page. Insert the student's test scores and advisor information from the Student Test Results database. Insert the bar chart from the Test Result Averages worksheet. Save the letter on a floppy disk using the filename, Test Result Letter.
4. Save the letterhead as AutoText using the filename, HomeTown.
5. Print a mailing label for each student using the Avery Standard 5160 Address label. Save the labels on a floppy disk using the filename, Test Result Letter Label.
6. Use the Student Test Results database to create a query of the top 25% of student test scores. Extract the students with the top 25% of all scores by specifying MAX on the Total line in the design grid for English, Math, and Science. Sort English, Math, and Science in descending order. Enter 25% in the Top Values box on the Query Design toolbar.
7. Create and print form letters to be sent to each student scoring in the top 25% of all test scores as shown in Figure 1-79 on page I 1.77. Use the HomeTown AutoText created in Step 4 above. Save the letter on a floppy disk using the filename, Top 25 Percent Letter.
8. Print a mailing label for each letter using the Avery Standard 5160 Address label. Save the labels on a floppy disk using the filename, Top 25 Percent Label.

Student ID	First Name	M.I.	Last Name	Address	City	State	Zip	English	Math	Science	Test Date	Advisor
790	Mary	A.	Jones	642 N. Barry	HomeTown	IN	46300-	780	750	775	3/19/97	Mr. Black
995	James	D.	Walker	17 Lakeside Terrace	HomeTown	IN	46300-	590	675	654	3/19/97	Mrs. Lane
1040	Ira	R.	Smith	15 April Lane	HomeTown	IN	46300-	590	610	640	3/19/97	Mrs. Lane
1234	Mark	L.	Adams	890 S. Oak St.	HomeTown	IN	46300-	774	651	770	3/19/97	Mr. Black
1244	Jane	A.	Ball	1233 Maple St.	HomeTown	IN	46300-	652	675	650	3/19/97	Ms. Jackson
2001	Hal	B.	David	21 Monolithic Lane	HomeTown	IN	46300-	678	725	710	3/19/97	Ms. Jackson

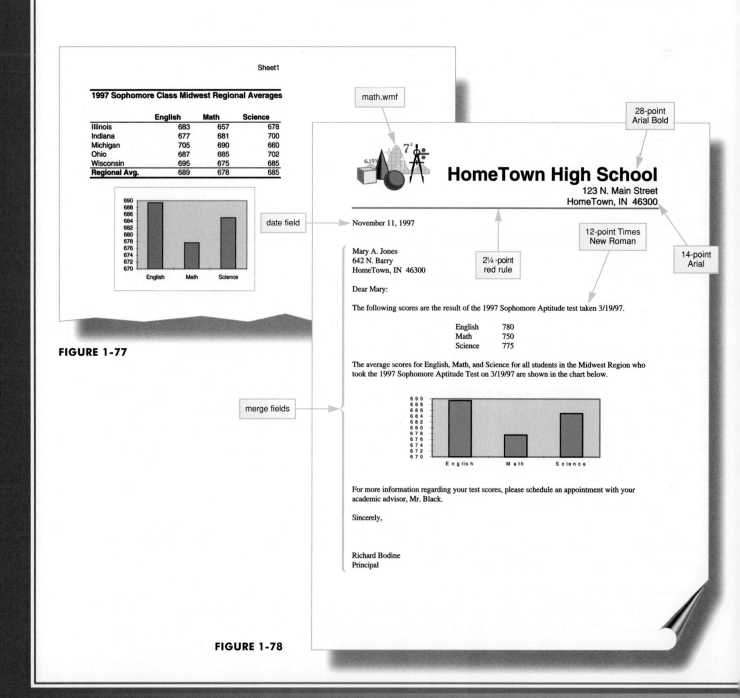

FIGURE 1-76

Sheet1

1997 Sophomore Class Midwest Regional Averages

	English	Math	Science
Illinois	683	657	678
Indiana	677	681	700
Michigan	705	690	660
Ohio	687	685	702
Wisconsin	695	675	685
Regional Avg.	689	678	685

FIGURE 1-77

HomeTown High School
123 N. Main Street
HomeTown, IN 46300

November 11, 1997

Mary A. Jones
642 N. Barry
HomeTown, IN 46300

Dear Mary:

The following scores are the result of the 1997 Sophomore Aptitude test taken 3/19/97.

English	780
Math	750
Science	775

The average scores for English, Math, and Science for all students in the Midwest Region who took the 1997 Sophomore Aptitude Test on 3/19/97 are shown in the chart below.

For more information regarding your test scores, please schedule an appointment with your academic advisor, Mr. Black.

Sincerely,

Richard Bodine
Principal

FIGURE 1-78

In the Lab

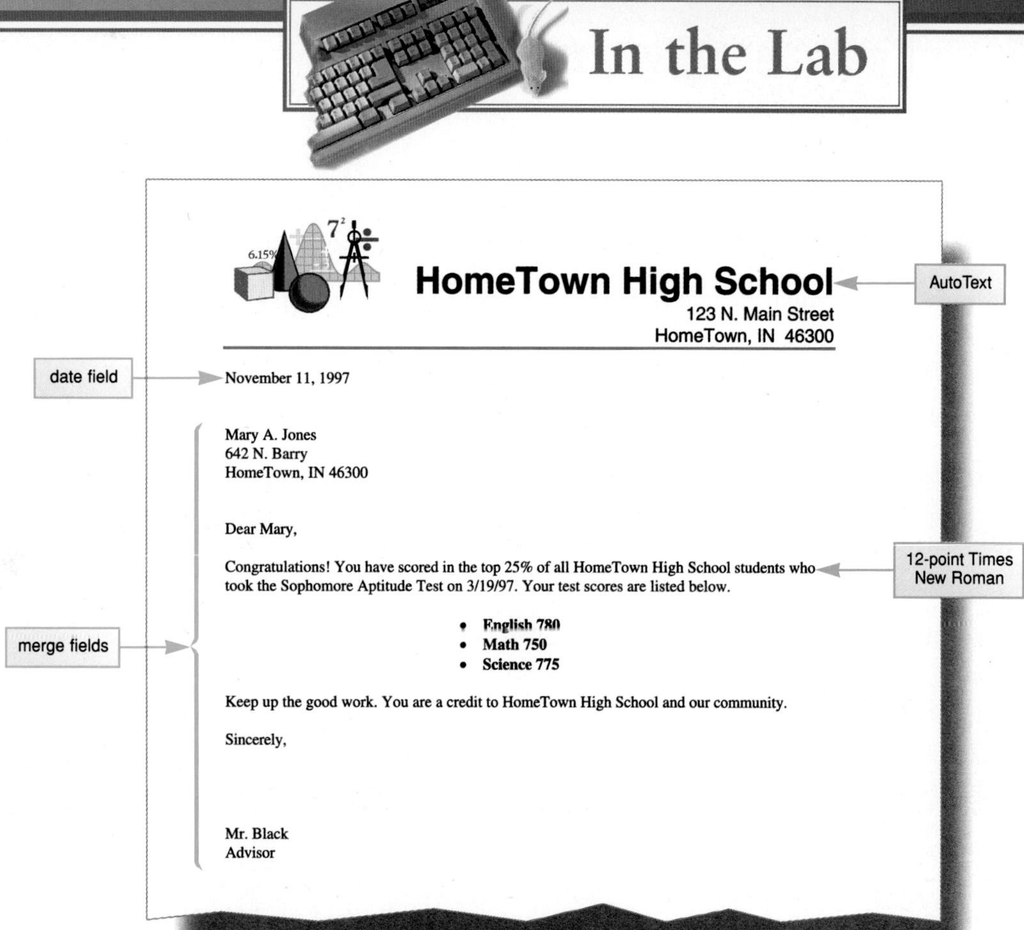

FIGURE 1-79

2 Linking Access, Word, Excel, and PowerPoint Documents

Problem: Channel 13 is a television station on the Public Broadcast Service (PBS). Continuous fund-raising is required to support the station's operating expenses. Once each year, Channel 13 runs a membership drive. Membership pledges are solicited on the air, through solicitation letters, and by way of telephone calls. Because follow-up is critical to collecting membership pledges, Channel 13 has decided to create a pledge database. They want to track pledges and membership payments so they can improve the percentage of pledge money collected. As the summer intern, it is your responsibility to create the pledge database. You are to generate letters to thank people for pledging membership to Channel 13. To substantiate that membership funds are primarily used toward the production of public television programs, you generate a worksheet explaining how each contributed dollar is spent. Next week, the program director is making a presentation to a group of business leaders to solicit corporate memberships. He instructs you to create a short PowerPoint presentation emphasizing contributions and operating expenses. *Hint:* Use Help to solve this problem.

Instructions: Perform the following tasks:

1. Copy the Contributors database on the backup floppy disk, paste it to the Integrated Project folder, and rename it Pledges. Open the Pledges database. Add the data shown in Figure 1-80 on page I 1.79 to the Mailing List table.

(continued)

Linking Access, Word, Excel, and PowerPoint Documents *(continued)*

2. Generate a query for all unpaid pledges. Save the query to your backup Floppy Disk with the filename, Unpaid Pledges.
3. Use the data in Table 1-1 to create an Excel worksheet and a Pie chart for the total operating expenses as shown in Figure 1-81. Save the worksheet with the filename, Operating Expenses.

Table 1-1 Channel 13 Operating Expenses

	1ST QUARTER	2ND QUARTER	3RD QUARTER	4TH QUARTER
Program Rent	$ 54,755	$ 52,600	$ 51,200	$ 58,650
Utilities	$ 22,675	$ 20,000	$ 21,250	$ 19,980
Maintenance	$ 12,760	$ 16,295	$ 13,350	$ 12,650
Supplies	$ 12,450	$ 11,895	$ 10,055	$ 13,975
Salaries	$113,775	$108,536	$105,465	$115,322
Taxes & Insurance	$ 12,110	$ 12,250	$ 11,985	$ 12,409

4. Create and print form letters to send to all contributors with unpaid pledges. Follow the format shown in Figure 1-82. Insert and size the clip art file, Cityscpe.wmf, as shown in Figure 1-82. Link the chart from the Operating Expenses worksheet. Save the letter on a floppy disk using the filename, Pledge Reminder Letter.
5. Print a mailing label for each letter using the Avery Standard 5160 Address label. Save the labels on a floppy disk using the filename, Pledge Reminder Letter Labels.
6. Use the television address to print a mailing label for the return envelope. Use the Avery Standard 5160 Address label. Save the labels on a floppy disk using the filename, Channel 13 Labels.
7. Use the Blank Presentation template to create a new presentation titled The Price of Quality Public Television. Insert the Cityscpe.wmf clip art file in the lower right corner of every slide. Scale the clip art to 60%. Change the color scheme of all slides to the color scheme with a light yellow background, located in row 1 column 3 of the Standard sheet in the Color Scheme dialog box. Create a bulleted list slide for Slide 2. Title it Channel 13 Funding. Use the following items for the bulleted list: Public Broadcasting Service, Corporation for Public Broadcasting, Texas Public Telecommunications Council, Texas Program Services Grant, Auction, Membership. Link the Operating Expenses worksheet on Slide 3. Link the Operating Expenses chart on Slide 4. Add a blank slide at the end of the presentation. Animate the presentation by applying text build effects and slide transition effects. Save the presentation with the filename, Channel 13.
8. Create a binder. Add the following documents to the binder in sequence: Operating Expenses worksheet and chart, the Pledge Reminder Letter the Pledge Reminder Letter Labels, and the Channel 13 presentation. Save the binder with the filename, Channel 13.
9. Print all the documents in the Channel 13 Binder.

Prefix	First Name	Initial	Last Name	Title	Company	Address	City	State	Zip	H Phone	W Phone	Status	Pledge	Pledge Date	Paid Date
Mr.	Marvin	M.	Botkin	President	Botkin & Bokin, Inc.	4343 S. Pipeline Drive	Houston	TX	77096	(713) 555-1000	(713) 555-2200	Business	$5,000.00	3/2/97	
Mr.	Bob	J.	West	Director	West & Associates	22 Wall Street	Houston	TX	77041	(713) 555-2800	(713) 555-0025	Business	$3,000.00	3/22/97	
Ms.	Vicki	L.	Austin			40 S. Indiana Street	Houston	TX	77023	(713) 555-1724	(713) 555-5587	Family	$75.00	5/22/97	
Mrs.	Sandy	L.	North			6240 Rhode Island Drive	Houston	TX	77024	(713) 555-1312	(713) 555-9255	Family	$50.00	4/30/97	
Mr.	Roy	A.	Victor	President	Victor Records	2225 S. Wabash St.	Houston	TX	77041	(713) 555-3705	(713) 555-2225	Business	$2,500.00	4/15/97	

FIGURE 1-80

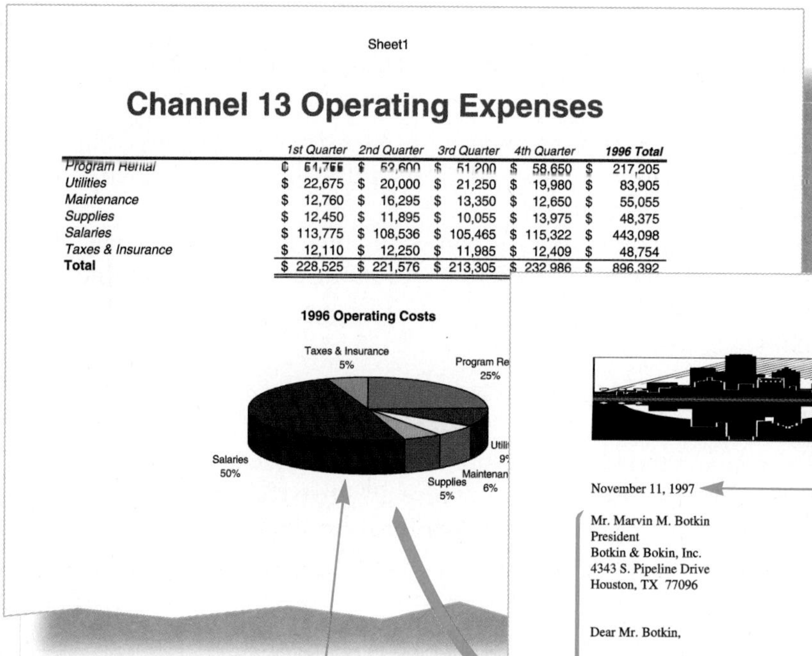

Sheet1

Channel 13 Operating Expenses

	1st Quarter	2nd Quarter	3rd Quarter	4th Quarter	1996 Total
Program Rental	$ 54,755	$ 52,600	$ 51,200	$ 58,650	$ 217,205
Utilities	$ 22,675	$ 20,000	$ 21,250	$ 19,980	$ 83,905
Maintenance	$ 12,760	$ 16,295	$ 13,350	$ 12,650	$ 55,055
Supplies	$ 12,450	$ 11,895	$ 10,055	$ 13,975	$ 48,375
Salaries	$ 113,775	$ 108,536	$ 105,465	$ 115,322	$ 443,098
Taxes & Insurance	$ 12,110	$ 12,250	$ 11,985	$ 12,409	$ 48,754
Total	$ 228,525	$ 221,576	$ 213,305	$ 232,986	$ 896,392

1996 Operating Costs

Taxes & Insurance 5%
Program Re 25%
Salaries 50%
Supplies 5%
Maintenan 6%
Utili 9

FIGURE 1-81

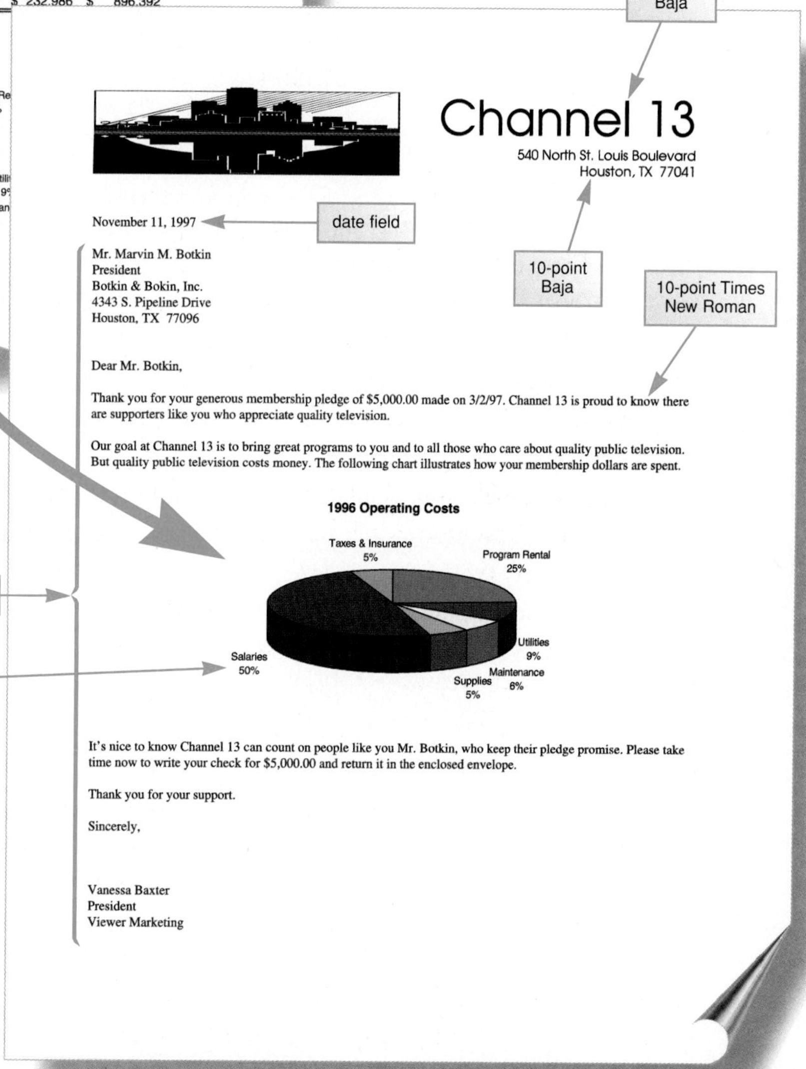

Channel 13
540 North St. Louis Boulevard
Houston, TX 77041

November 11, 1997

Mr. Marvin M. Botkin
President
Botkin & Bokin, Inc.
4343 S. Pipeline Drive
Houston, TX 77096

Dear Mr. Botkin,

Thank you for your generous membership pledge of $5,000.00 made on 3/2/97. Channel 13 is proud to know there are supporters like you who appreciate quality television.

Our goal at Channel 13 is to bring great programs to you and to all those who care about quality public television. But quality public television costs money. The following chart illustrates how your membership dollars are spent.

1996 Operating Costs

Taxes & Insurance 5%
Program Rental 25%
Utilities 9%
Maintenance 6%
Supplies 5%
Salaries 50%

It's nice to know Channel 13 can count on people like you Mr. Botkin, who keep their pledge promise. Please take time now to write your check for $5,000.00 and return it in the enclosed envelope.

Thank you for your support.

Sincerely,

Vanessa Baxter
President
Viewer Marketing

36-point Baja
10-point Baja
10-point Times New Roman
date field
merge fields
Operating Expenses chart

FIGURE 1-82

Cases and Places

The difficulty of these case studies varies:

◗ Case studies preceded by a single half moon are the least difficult. You are asked to created the required document based on the information that has already been placed in an organized form.
◗◗ Case studies preceded by two half moons are more difficult. You must organize the information presented before using it to create the required document.
◗◗◗ Case studies preceded by three half moons are the most difficult. You must decide on a specific topic, then obtain and organize the necessary information before using it to create the required document.

1 ◗ Each spring, Wagit's Veterinarian Clinic sends a letter to owners of older dogs, reminding them of the dangers of heartworms. The director of the clinic has prepared a rough draft of this year's letter and a list of the owners of older animals cared for by the clinic.

With this information, develop a database containing the pet owner's name, address, pet name, and pet type. Then, create a mail merge letter to dog owners. Use WordArt to fabricate a letterhead. Include the date, inside address, and appropriate database fields in each letter. Address envelopes. Print the envelopes and letters for each dog owner.

2 ◗◗ Leukemia, or cancer of the blood, is a characterized by overproduction of atypical white blood cells. These cells are produced in the bone marrow, and one of the more effective treatments for leukemia is a bone marrow transplant. Because marrow can only be transplanted when there is an exact tissue match between donor and patient, the National Marrow Donor Program emphasizes the importance of having as many potential donors on file as possible. To be placed in the national registry, volunteers must be between the ages of 18 and 55, in good health, and willing to sign a donor card. Donors are screened with a blood test. You have offered to contact students and faculty at your school in an effort to expand the file of prospective donors. Blood tests will be held next Friday in room 225 in the Student Union. Create mail merge document urging five students and five faculty members to participate in the project. Use Schedule+ to schedule the blood drive and print the monthly calendar.

3 ◗◗◗ Entrepreneurs have discovered that offering reasonable access fees to the Internet can be a lucrative business opportunity. National online services, such as the Microsoft Network (MSN). CompuServe, America Online (AOL), now find they are competing with local companies to provide Internet access. Research access providers in your community. Create an Excel worksheet listing each provider's name, monthly fees, number of minutes per month, and any special features. Contrast each provider's services to those offered by MSN, CompuServe, and America Online. Create a bar chart to graphically compare the costs of the providers. Develop a PowerPoint presentation on Internet access providers to show at your monthly computer club meeting. Link Internet providers. Use a Design Template, slide transition effects, and text build effects in your presentation.

Index